S0-ACX-749

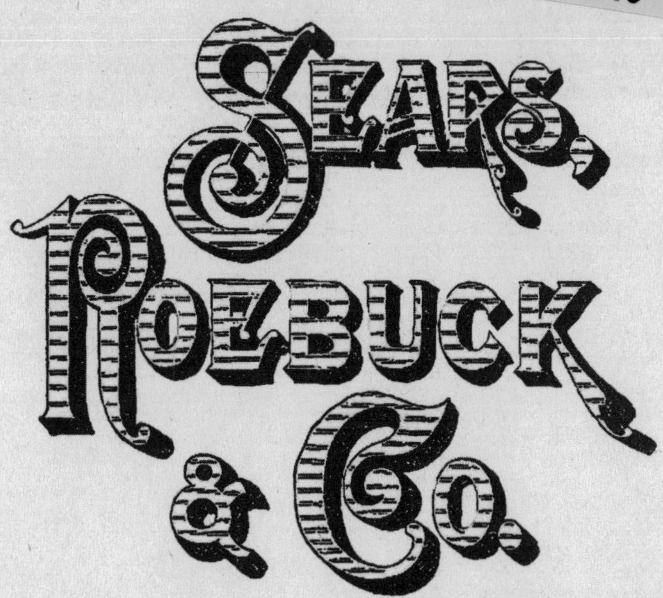
SEARS, ROEBUCK & CO.

Edited by Leslie Parr,
Andrea Hicks, and Marie Stareck

Foreword by Nick Lyons

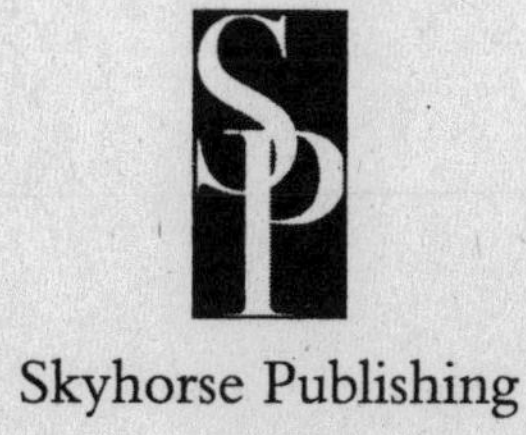

Skyhorse Publishing

Skyhorse Publishing books may be purchased in bulk at special discounts for sales promotion, corporate gifts, fund-raising, or educational purposes. Special editions can also be created to specifications. For details, contact the Special Sales Department, Skyhorse Publishing, 307 West 36th Street, 11th Floor, New York, NY 10018 or info@skyhorsepublishing.com.

www.skyhorsepublishing.com

10 9 8 7 6 5 4 3 2 1

Library of Congress Cataloging-in-Publication Data is available on file.

ISBN: 978-1-61608-180-5

Printed in Canada

FOREWORD

by Nick Lyons

Unlike a number of facsimile reprints of the famous Sears, Roebuck & Co. catalog for various specific years, this volume is a compendium of especially intriguing items from five consecutive years, 1905 to 1910, a full hundred years ago. The focus in this collection is directed to "collectibles," many of which are eagerly sought today. As such, this book is more than a nostalgic trip to an earlier time, when prices (by today's standards) were deliciously low and the variety of goods offered cut across all categories; it is as exciting as any historical book and it is an invaluable resource for any investigation into the early years of scores of items that still regularly grace estate sales, country auctions, and attics and basements everywhere.

For the Sears catalogs sought out the farthest corners of America and even went into Canada and broadly overseas. The late nineteenth and early twentieth centuries were days long before shopping malls, discount and "company" stores, cyber sales of all kinds, when much of what Sears offered went to folks who lived far from shops that afforded direct access to their products. The first Montgomery Ward catalog, a one-page list of some hundred-odd items for sale, was issued in 1872, the year the company was founded. By 1895 their catalog was nearly two inches thick and more than 625 pages; but by 1888, Ward had a first blast from a formidable competitor in Sears, which issued its first specialized catalog, of watches and jewelry, that year; a general merchandise catalog would follow in 1894. A few years later, the Sears catalog had itself grown to more than 500 pages and by 1906, one of the years covered herein, their huge new Sears Merchandise Building Tower in Chicago became the hub of all of its catalog sales.

This particular compendium offers a unique look not at one year's offerings but those over a representative five-year period. The products and prices are perfectly fascinating: corncob pipes (for 2 cents), "German Porcelain Pipes" (83 cents), and Meerschaums (for up to $5.29). Clocks, always a much sought-after collectible today, ranged from an "Imported Alarm Clock (49 cents) to "The Lexington Eight-Day Mantel Clock" ($4.55) to the "Highest Quality Imported Quail and Cuckoo Clock" ($14.95, reduced from $16.88). "Imported"—the very word resonated in the minds of rural Americans at the turn of the century; it was a golden selling designation. Not only physical imports but the world beyond American borders was exotic, compelling, and was brought to the hinterlands in books like *Pictorial History of the World* (three volumes, "only $1.98 per set, $2.75 for the Deluxe Edition), and *The Illustrated Home Book of the World's Greatest Nations*

(98 cents); some of these books must have been unalloyed imperialist propaganda, like *The History and Conquest of the Phillippines and Our Other Island Possessions*, but closer to home, Sears sold the *Story of Abraham Lincoln* (58 cents), *Life of Washington* (38 cents), and a batch of titles on the bigger than life Theodore Roosevelt, who always made good copy.

The first widely distributed and now highly collectible cameras were marketed by Sears during this period: a "No. 2 Conley View Camera" ($9.95) and all of the Conley plates, "inside kits," and other paraphernalia, including a *Complete Instructions in Photography* book (with twenty-two chapters) offered free with every Conley Camera.

One always enjoys, in such old catalogs, to hear of items new in nature, like "The Latest 1907 Model No. 3A Harvard Disc Talking Machine" (for only $14.90) or what was called the "Monarch Columbia Cylinder Graphophone" ($45). These similar products were surely the forerunners of record players, tape recorders, tapes, and CDs of course, while some of the medicines (though not all of them) happily vanished forever, like the "Twenty-Minute Cold Cure—It Never Fails" (15 cents) or the "Secret de Ninon—The Great Freckle Lotion" (25 cents). Some of the early laxatives and liniments and "effervescent salts" sound promising and surely better than snake oil, and you could buy whole stocked medical cabinets for as little as $4.50, some medicines from which might actually have worked. Mixed in, to our delight, is an item or two that is as effective today as it was then, such as Bromo Seltzer.

Musical instruments like banjos and zithers were popular and also autoharps; people without television or radio might well be expected to provide more of their own entertainment, and they did. There was a "Beckwith Special Concert Grand Piano" for those who could pay $195, but violins were available from $1.95 to $22.45, with a "Conservatory Violin" at $3.95 and an instrument surely named by a forefather of the most inventive Madison Avenue "mad" men, a "Stradivarius Model" violin (only $1.95).

The Sears catalogs of those days, especially with competition from the fuller Montgomery Ward catalogs, had to be all things to all people, and included in these selected pages you will find novelties of all kinds, toys of many stripes, a dozen varieties of stoves, a plethora of pocket knives (still a staple at country yard and tag sales), some pistols (a little too readily available, I fear) for a couple of bucks and up, shotguns for up to twenty dollars, those marvelous old wall telephones, and "stereoscopes" with hilarious comic views of such delicacies as the "French Bicycle Girls" series with images like "Barbed-Wire Fence Bars the Path" and a "Fun with Pretty Girls" series offering one called "Here's to Your Health, Old Man" that this old man would like to have seen.

Nostalgic, informative, uniquely valuable for collectors, at times hilarious or even sexy, and always offering a shrewd glimpse into cunning marketing that is all too modern, *Sears, Roebuck & Co.: The Best of 1905–1910 Collectibles* is a memorable treat. It is sure to be read with the eager anticipation felt by those who read these pages a hundred years ago.

THE COLLECTIBLES

Cameras and Photographic Equipment
Gramophones, Talking Machines and Records
Pipes and Smoking Articles
Watches and Watch Fobs
Clocks
Dolls and Toys
Sewing Machines
Musical Instruments
Trunks and Suitcases
Drugs and Cosmetics
Lamps and Chandeliers
Telephones
Guns and Pistols
Books, Stationery and Typewriters
Stoves and Ranges
Pocket Knives

CAMERAS

CAMERAS AND PHOTO SUPPLIES

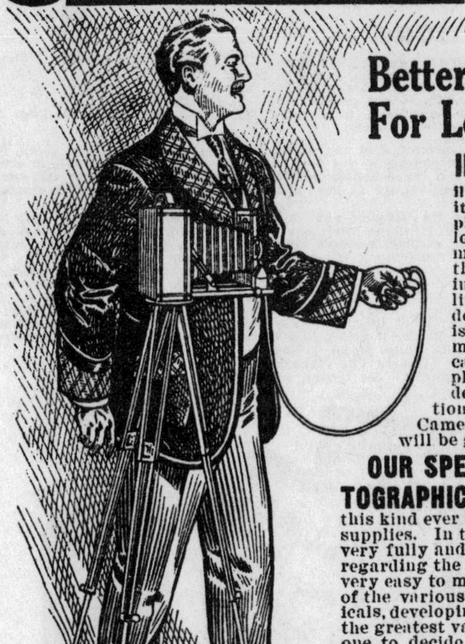

Better Cameras Than Others Sell For Less Money Than Others Ask

IN THE FOLLOWING PAGES of our big General Catalog we illustrate and describe only the more important items in our line of cameras and photographic supplies. The space available in this big General Catalog compels us to shorten descriptions, reduce or in many cases omit illustrations; still we give you, in the following pages, sufficient information regarding the most important items in our photographic line so that you can conveniently make up your order direct from these pages. We guarantee to satisfy you with anything you order or return your money. But if you want to see our entire line of cameras and photographic goods with more complete descriptions, large illustrations showing all the details, and wish to take advantage of the instructions and valuable information contained in our special Camera Catalog, by all means write for it at once. We will be glad to send it to you.

OUR SPECIAL CATALOG OF CAMERAS AND PHOTOGRAPHIC SUPPLIES is the most complete, the most interesting and the most valuable book of this kind ever sent out by any dealer in photographic supplies. In this special catalog all of the goods are very fully and completely described and information regarding the uses of each article is given so that it is very easy to make proper selections. In the descriptions of the various lenses, dry plates, sensitized papers, chemicals, developing tanks, ray filters, etc., there is information of the greatest value to all photographers, information that enables one to decide what is best for his requirements. There is no other photographic supply catalog published which describes goods so fully and which describes so complete a line of photographic merchandise.

THIS SPECIAL CATALOG QUOTES THE LOWEST PRICES ever known for high grade cameras, lenses and photographic accessories of all kinds, including sensitized papers, dry plates, card mounts and chemicals. Even if you do not buy from us, you ought to have this catalog so that you can check up the prices which you pay to other dealers, and for the information which it gives you regarding actual values in photographic merchandise. If you own a camera or if you ever expect to purchase a camera and take up the fascinating work of photography, you should by all means have a copy of our special Camera Catalog. If you are already using a camera, it will give you new ideas regarding the things you can do. It will double your pleasure and in this way actually increase the value of your own camera. If you have not yet purchased a camera this special Camera Catalog will give you valuable and practical information regarding the selection of an outfit.

PROMPT SHIPMENTS AND CLEAN FRESH GOODS

Our photographic supply business is so great that we can carry a very large stock at all times, thus insuring prompt shipments. Practically every order received in our Photographic Department is shipped the same day that it is received. We have the goods on hand all the time. Our sales of dry plates and sensitized papers are so large that we can get in shipments fresh from the factory every day in the year, **thus insuring fresh goods** to our customers at all times. This is an exceedingly important matter. The ordinary photographic supply house constantly accumulates supplies of papers and plates which are too old to be good. They cannot afford to throw away such goods and, as a general rule, they are shipped out to their customers. The enormous business which we do in these goods together with our perfect system of stock keeping and our daily shipments from the factories, enables us to absolutely guarantee fresh papers, fresh plates and fresh chemicals on every order that we fill.

WE CAN SAVE YOU MONEY on all photographic goods and we can give you better service and better goods than most dealers in photographic supplies. On this basis we solicit your business.

If you are interested in photographic goods, we will be very glad to send you our special Photographic Supply Catalog upon receipt of a postal card from you stating that you desire it.

Our Special 72-page Catalog of CAMERAS AND PHOTOGRAPHIC SUPPLIES

Mailed Free and Postpaid on Request

WHY WE CAN GIVE YOU BETTER SERVICE AT LOWER PRICES THAN OTHER DEALERS IN PHOTOGRAPHIC GOODS

Our special connection with the Conley Camera Company enables us to offer "better cameras than others sell, for less money than others ask." Our prices for the Conley Cameras are based on actual factory costs. The Conley Camera Company is not compelled to add a large percentage to the cost of its cameras for advertising, traveling salesmen and other overhead expenses. The Conley Camera Company has no expenses of this kind and the result is **a lower cost of production than is possible in any other camera factory.** It is this economical production, this saving of overhead expenses which enables us to give you in the Conley Cameras **"better cameras than others sell, for less money than others ask."**

OUR THIRTY DAYS' TRIAL OFFER. **Send us your order for any camera described in this catalog,** enclosing our price as quoted, and we will ship the camera, guaranteeing that it will reach you in perfect order and with the understanding and agreement that you can try it for thirty days. During these thirty days you can put it to any test, you can compare it with other cameras costing two or three times the price we ask, and if you do not find it all that we claim for it in every way, equal to cameras regularly sold at double our price, you can send it back to us by express, at our expense, and we will return to you the amount which you paid us for the camera, together with any money you may have paid for transportation charges.

"COMPLETE INSTRUCTIONS IN PHOTOGRAPHY"
FREE WITH EVERY CONLEY CAMERA

"COMPLETE INSTRUCTIONS IN PHOTOGRAPHY" is an instruction book that is different from all other instruction books. It was written expressly for the beginner in photography. It explains everything fully, clearly and in detail, and it does not assume any previous knowledge on the part of the reader. It explains all those little points which the writers of other instruction books assume the beginner to know in advance and which he is thereby forced to find out for himself, often at the expense of much valuable time and costly materials. "Complete Instructions in Photography" starts at the very beginning. It tells you everything that you need to know about cameras, all about the various apparatus and accessories used in photography. It tells you all about the various materials, including plates, sensitized papers, chemicals, etc. It tells you everything that you need to know, and tells it in a clear, simple and easily understood manner, which enables you to make good pictures right from the start.

BESIDES THE VALUABLE INFORMATION FOR BEGINNERS, it also contains information of the greatest possible value to the most experienced photographers, becoming a valuable reference book both for the expert amateur and the professional photographer.

TWENTY-TWO CHAPTERS. "Complete Instructions in Photography" contains twenty-two chapters so arranged and divided into paragraphs that any desired subject may be found with the least possible trouble, making it an easy matter to refer instantly to any of the various questions on which you may happen to desire information.

HOW TO GET THIS BOOK FREE.

FIRST WAY: With every camera that we sell, every camera shown in this catalog, we include without any extra charge whatever a copy of "Complete Instructions in Photography." We do this because we want everyone who purchases a camera from us to be successful in using it, and "Complete Instructions in Photography" will enable anyone to be successful without even the slightest previous experience. If you order a camera from us you will get the book free with the camera.

SECOND WAY: If you will send us an order, amounting to $3.00 or more, for photographic materials of any kind, accessories, dry plates, papers, card mounts, chemicals, anything that you may need in the photographic line, we will include free of charge a copy of "Complete Instructions in Photography," provided you state in your order that you desire it. We make this special offer in order that you may obtain possession of this book, even though you are not in the market for a camera. You can always find use for at least $3.00 worth of photographic goods, especially at the astonishingly low prices which we quote on all kinds of photographic merchandise, and if you will just make up an order for photographic goods amounting to $3.00 or more we will be very glad to include a copy of "Complete Instructions in Photography" in your shipment without any cost to you. Be sure to state that you want it.

4x5 MODEL I CONLEY CAMERA $1.78

$1.78 FOR THE CAMERA ALONE, $2.98 FOR THE CAMERA AND COMPLETE OUTFIT

SPECIFICATIONS.

Size of Picture—4x5 inches.
Lens—Genuine meniscus achromatic, universal focus, speed F.16.
Shutter—Conley time and instantaneous.
View Finders—Two, ground glass type.
Tripod Sockets—Two, adapting camera to either horizontal or vertical use.
Covering—Seal grain keratol.
Metal Parts—Steel, oxidized finish.
Plate Holder—Conley flexible valve.
Capacity—Three double plate holders (six plates).
Dimensions—5½ inches wide, 7⅛ inches high, 8⅛ inches long.
Weight—35 ounces.

YOU WILL BE SURPRISED to see how easy it is to take pictures with the Model I Conley Camera, and you will be equally surprised to see what good pictures it will take. Cameras of this size and style of construction are by far the most popular cameras made for amateur use, and the enormous number of these cameras that we sell every year has enabled us to reduce the manufacturing cost so that we can sell this camera at less than one-half the price ordinarily charged for cameras of this style and quality.

EASY TO OPERATE. **The Model I Conley Camera is one of the simplest and easiest cameras in the world to use;** no previous experience is necessary; everything is simple and easy to understand, and the big book of instructions which comes free with every one of these cameras tells you in plain and simple language all that you need know in order to make good pictures. The shutter is entirely automatic in action, being operated for either time or instantaneous exposures simply by pressing the lever at the side of the camera. It is always set and always ready for immediate action. Its construction is exceedingly simple and there are no complicated parts to get out of order, making it a most effective and reliable instrument. Two view finders are provided, one for use when making pictures the long way of the plate, and the other when making pictures the short way of the plate, so that the shape and style of the picture may be adapted to the subject. This camera is also provided with two tripod sockets, so that in case a tripod is used, the pictures may still be made either way of the plate. The Conley Improved Flexible Valve Plate Holder which is furnished with these cameras is exactly the same style and quality of holder that we furnish with our very finest cameras.

COMPLETE INSTRUCTIONS IN PHOTOGRAPHY. **With every Model I Conley Camera we include, without extra charge, our big manual, "Complete Instructions in Photography,"** the largest, the simplest and the most complete guide to photography ever published. This book makes everything plain, clear, simple and easy to understand, and not only insures success to the beginner in picture making, but contains a fund of valuable information for the experienced photographer. See page 749 for description of this book.

The big Developing, Finishing and Material Outfit which we furnish with the Model I Conley Camera at the price quoted below, contains everything necessary for developing, printing, toning and mounting the pictures complete. Every item that goes into this outfit is good. The plates and paper are guaranteed to be fresh and perfect, the chemicals full strength and of the highest degree of purity, and all the other items strictly high class, well made and serviceable.

UNDERSTAND, **we furnish the camera alone (with one double plate holder and "Complete Instructions in Photography") for $1.78,** but we especially urge that you order the camera and outfit all complete, at our special price of $2.98, so that you can commence making pictures as soon as you receive it.

The complete outfit at $2.98 contains the following items:

1 4x5 Model I Conley Camera.
1 4x5 Conley Double Plate Holder.
1 Metal Dark Room Lamp.
1 4x5 Tray for Developing Plates.
1 4x5 Tray for Fixing Plates.
1 4x5 Tray for Toning Prints.
1 Print Roller for smoothing down the mounted prints.
½ dozen 4x5 Dry Plates.
1 Paste Brush.
1 dozen 4x5 Card Mounts with fancy embossed borders.
1 Graduated Glass for measuring liquids.
1 package Concentrated Dry Developer (makes 8 ounces of solution).
1 package Concentrated Dry Toner (makes 8 ounces of solution).
1 dozen 4x5 sheets DuVoll's Paper.
1 4x5 Printing Frame.
1 package Hypo for fixing negatives and prints.
1 tube of fine Photo Mounting Paste.
1 copy of "Complete Instructions in Photography."

No. 20T270 Model I Conley Camera, with one plate holder and "Complete Instructions in Photography." Shipping weight, 4 pounds. Price....$1.78
No. 20T271 Model I Conley Camera, with one plate holder and complete Series A Outfit. Shipping weight, 10¼ pounds. Price....$2.98
No. 20T561 Extra Plate Holders. (See page 764.) Price, each.... .38

THE SERIES A DEVELOPING OUTFIT.

The Model I Conley Camera and this Big Developing, Finishing and Material Outfit, all complete, for $2.98. See No. 20T271.

4x5 MODEL II CONLEY CAMERA $2.65

$2.65 for the Camera Alone. $3.85 for the Camera and Complete Outfit

SPECIFICATIONS.

Size of Picture—4x5 inches.
Lens—High grade, universal focus, achromatic, speed F.16.
Shutter—Conley special time and instantaneous (with bulb release if desired).
View Finders—Two, of ground glass and mirror type.
Tripod Sockets—Two, so that pictures may be taken either the long or short way of the plate.
Covering—Genuine walrus grain leather.
Metal Parts—Brass, fully nickel plated.
Plate Holder—Conley flexible valve.
Capacity—Three double plate holders (six plates).
Dimensions—5½ inches wide; 7⅛ inches high; 8⅛ inches long.
Weight—36 ounces.

THIS NEW MODEL II CONLEY CAMERA **was designed and built by the Conley Camera Company to meet the requirements of those who are willing to pay 87 cents more for the sake of a camera made a little better,** finished a little more finely and a little more convenient to handle than the Model I Conley Camera. This camera is covered with genuine walrus grain leather; all metal parts are of brass, nickel plated and highly polished, and it is equipped with the Conley bulb release shutter, built on exactly the same principles as the shutter that we put on the Conley Magazine Camera. This shutter is so constructed that it can be operated by either bulb release or finger release, and the bulb may be instantly detached when it is not required. As the bulb and tube are not absolutely essential, we quote our price on the camera without bulb and tube, furnishing this as an extra part to those who desire it. While the bulb is not an actual necessity, it is a very great convenience and insures a better average quality in the pictures, as there is no danger of jarring the camera when the shutter is operated by the bulb, and it is an especially desirable feature when making time exposures.

WITH COMPLETE DEVELOPING, FINISHING AND MATERIAL OUTFIT. As with the Model I Conley Camera described above, we furnish this camera either with or without complete outfit, our price for the camera alone, including one Conley Plate Holder and "Complete Instructions in Photography," being $2.65, and for the camera with complete developing, finishing and material outfit $3.85. The outfit which we furnish with this camera is exactly the same as the one furnished with the Model I Conley Camera, which is fully illustrated and described above, and we recommend by all means that you purchase the complete outfit at $3.85, so that you will be able to commence actual work with the camera as soon as it reaches you.

No. 20T276 Model II Conley Camera (bulb and tube not included), with one plate holder and "Complete Instructions in Photography." Shipping weight, 4¼ pounds. Price....$2.65
No. 20T277 Model II Conley Camera (bulb and tube not included), with one plate holder and complete Series A Outfit. Shipping weight, 10½ pounds. Price....$3.85
No. 20T885 Bulb and Tube, with special connector for Model II Conley Camera. (Cannot be used with Model I Camera.) Price....15c
If mail shipment, postage extra, 3 cents.
Note—If bulb and tube is not ordered, the shutter may be operated by finger release.
No. 20T561 Extra Plate Holders. (See page 764.) Price, each..38c

4x5 MODEL III CONLEY MAGAZINE CAMERA $3.95

TWELVE PICTURES WITH ONE LOADING

SPECIFICATIONS.

Size of Picture—4x5 inches.
Lens—High grade achromatic, of universal focus, speed F.16.
Shutter—Conley special, metal base, time and instantaneous with bulb release.
View Finders—Two, of brilliant type.
Tripod Sockets—Two.
Covering—Genuine leather, seal grain.
Metal Parts—Brass, fully nickel plated.
Plate Changing Device—Conley patent, absolutely positive in action.
Register—Automatic, indicating number of plates exposed.
Capacity—One dozen plates (twelve pictures with one loading).
Dimensions—6⅝ inches wide; 7⅛ inches high; 8 inches long.
Weight—64 ounces.

THE SPECIAL ADVANTAGE **of a magazine camera lies in the fact that it dispenses entirely with the use of extra plate holders,** the construction being such that twelve plates can be placed directly in the camera and it is then ready for the making of twelve exposures without the necessity of returning to the dark room to reload and without carrying any separate or extra plate holders.

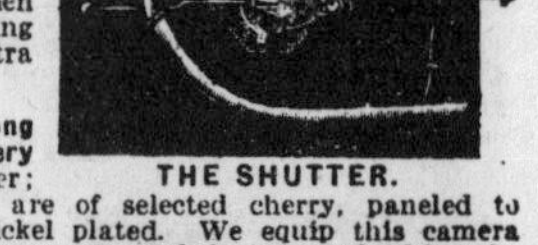

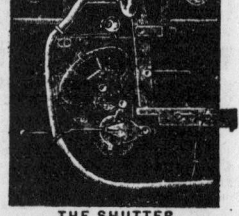

THE SHUTTER.

THE GENERAL CONSTRUCTION **of this camera is strong and substantial in every way.** It is covered with the best quality of genuine seal grain leather; the wood is carefully selected, air seasoned and kiln dried; the doors are of selected cherry, paneled to prevent shrinking or swelling, and all exposed metal parts are heavily nickel plated. We equip this camera with an entirely new shutter which is entirely automatic in action, always set, and is operated either by pressing a button, or by bulb and tube.

THE PLATE DROPPING DEVICE **is the result of years of experience in building cameras of this type.** It is absolutely positive in action and so constructed that difference in the thickness of plates does not interfere with its operation. It is impossible to drop more than one plate at a time, a fault which is quite common to other magazine cameras, and at the same time it is absolutely certain to drop one plate every time the operating lever is moved. The plates are inserted at the back of the camera, and as each one is exposed it is dropped forward and to the bottom of the camera and the next one brought into position, simply by a turn of the small lever on the side of the camera. The plates are inserted through a hinged door at the back of the camera and after exposure are removed through another hinged door in the bottom of the camera. Any number of exposed plates may be removed at any time without disturbing the unexposed ones still remaining. An automatic tally shows at all times the number of plates that have been exposed.

No. 20T285 Model III Conley Magazine Camera, with "Complete Instructions in Photography." Shipping weight, 5½ pounds. Price....$3.95
No. 20T286 Model III Conley Magazine Camera, with Series A Outfit. (See description above.) Shipping weight, 12 pounds. Price....$5.15
weight, 24 pounds. Price....$6.43
No. 20T287 Model III Conley Magazine Camera, with Series C Outfit. (See page 765.) Shipping
No. 20T288 Portrait Device. For use only with the Conley Magazine Camera. A simple device which enables the camera to be used closer to the subject in portrait work, thus increasing the size of the face. Price....(If mail shipment, postage extra, 4 cents)....12c
No. 20T289 3¼x4¼ Kits. These kits permit the use of 3¼x4¼ plates instead of 4x5 if desired, thus reducing the expense. Put up in sets of twelve. Price, per set....60c
No. 20T290 Keratol Carrying Case for Conley Magazine Camera. Price....85c
No. 20T291 Leather Carrying Case for Conley Magazine Camera. Shipping weight, 3 pounds. Price....$3.35

$6.95 SEROCO COMPACT FOLDING CAMERA $6.95

FOR 4X5 PICTURES.

SPECIFICATIONS.

WOODWORK. Solid mahogany, dovetailed corners, piano finish.
METAL PARTS. Brass, heavily nickel plated and highly polished.
COVERING. Genuine seal grain leather.
BELLOWS. Best red Russia leather.
FRONT. All metal, with rising and falling adjustment.
FRONT CLAMP. New Conley Automatic.
FINDER. Brilliant, reversible, brass bound.
PIANO HINGE. Extra quality
SHUTTER. Wollensak Senior automatic pneumatic release.
LENS. Fine double rectilinear
PLATE HOLDER. Seroco Improved Flexible Valve.
Dimension of Camera closed 5½ x 6¼ x 2 in. focal capacity 7¾ in.

IMPROVED 1907 MODEL.
Uses either Plates or Films.

Seroco Compact Folding Camera, Closed.

MADE IN 4x5 SIZE ONLY.

$6.95 IS A PRICE NEVER BEFORE MADE on so complete and so high class a camera as the Seroco Compact. Made of solid mahogany all the way through covered with genuine seal grain leather, all metal parts of brass, nickel plated and highly polished, and best red Russia leather bellows, lined with lightproof gossamer cloth. The materials and workmanship in the Seroco Compact Camera are as good as it is possible to put into any camera; exactly the same high grade of mahogany, exactly the same high grade morocco leather covering, the metal parts just as heavily nickel plated, just as highly polished and just as carefully adjusted the bellows made of the same high grade leather, the entire camera just as carefully tested and just as thoroughly made as cameras ordinarily sold at three and four times the price we ask for the Seroco Compact.

SPECIAL FEATURES. We equip this camera with features which have heretofore been offered only in high priced cameras. This is the first camera ever sold at so low a price equipped with the Conley Automatic Patented Front Clamp, the most convenient and most satisfactory front clamp ever devised. This is the first camera ever sold at so low a price having the new all metal front, with rising and falling adjustment. This camera is equipped with brilliant, reversible brass bound finder, with extra quality nickel plated piano hinge, with ornamental nickel plated side arms, with strong leather handle, with spring actuated ground glass focusing screen and mahogany back panel.

THE HIGH GRADE DOUBLE RECTILINEAR LENS furnished with this camera possesses great depth of focus and is guaranteed to cover the plate sharply to the extreme corners. This lens is equipped with the latest pneumatic release, Wollensak Senior Automatic Shutter, arranged for instantaneous exposures or bulb and time exposures, of any desired length.

No. 20G1291 Seroco Compact Folding Camera. for 4x5 pictures. Price... **$6.95**
This price includes the camera complete, ready for use, with lens and shutter and one double plate holder, but does not include carrying case, which is unnecessary with compact cameras of this type, as the camera is virtually self contained. This camera uses the Seroco Improved Flexible Valve Plate Holders.
For complete description see No. 20G1800.

AS A DAYLIGHT LOADING FILM CAMERA. The Seroco Compact Folding Camera is so constructed that it takes the Premo film pack, the most convenient and satisfactory form in which films have ever been furnished. With the film pack, this camera becomes a daylight loading film camera, thus combining all the advantages of both plates and films.

Seroco Compact Folding Camera, Extended.

THE FILM PACK consists of twelve flat films, enclosed in a compact, lightproof case. In order to use the film pack, a film pack adapter must be purchased. This adapter is a device for holding the film pack, and is similar in form and size to an ordinary plate holder. It may be removed from the camera between exposures the same as an ordinary plate holder so that each exposure, if desired, may be sharply focused on the ground glass the same as when using dry plates.

"Complete Instructions in Photography" free with this camera, see page 955.

FILM PACKS AND FILM PACK ADAPTERS.

No. 20G1821 Film Pack Adapter, for 4x5 camera. Price....................$1.50
If by mail postage extra, 7 cents.
No. 20G1831 Film Pack, 4x5 (12 exposures). Price.................... .90
If by mail, postage extra, 8 cents.

SEROCO A FOLDING CAMERA

IMPROVED 1907 MODEL. Uses either Plates or Films.

SPECIFICATIONS.

WOODWORK. Solid mahogany, dovetailed corners, piano finish.
METAL PARTS. Brass, nickel plated and highly polished.
COVERING. Genuine seal grain leather.
BELLOWS. Best red Russia leather.
BACK. Non-reversible.
FRONT. All metal, with rising and falling adjustment.
FRONT CLAMP. New Conley Automatic.
FINDER. Ground glass, reversible.
PIANO HINGE. Nickel plated.
SHUTTER. Wollensak Regular, double valve, pneumatic release.
LENS. Double rectilinear.
PLATE HOLDER. Seroco Improved Flexible Valve.
CARRYING CASE. Solid sole leather.

SPECIAL FEATURES. This camera is equipped with the new Conley Automatic Front Clamp, the very best front clamp ever invented, the new all metal front, with rising and falling adjustment, spring actuated ground glass focusing screen, with mahogany back panel, accurately adjusted focusing scale, two tripod sockets, and high grade ground glass finder. The carrying case is made from the best grade black sole leather, made without corner seams, stiffened and strengthened by an interlining of heavy strawboard, and lined with black cloth.

THE LENS is a high grade double rapid rectilinear, made especially for us by the Wollensak Optical Co., being a lens that we can guarantee to cover the plate sharply to the extreme corners, and fitted with the latest type of the Wollensak Optical Co's Regular double valve shutter, the same shutter that we use on many of our highest priced cameras.

WE MAKE THE SEROCO A FOLDING CAMERA just as good as we know how. We put into it the very best materials that we can buy, genuine Honduras mahogany, thoroughly seasoned and kiln dried, with the finest French polish or piano finish; heavily nickel plated metal parts, best grade genuine leather covering and fine quality red leather bellows lined with lightproof gossamer cloth. Every part of the camera made by the same workmen who build our very highest priced instruments.

DIMENSIONS.

	Focal Capacity, inches	Camera Closed, inches	Carrying Case, inches	Capacity of Carrying Case
4 x 5	6¾	2½x5¼x6¼	3 x6¾x11	Camera and Four Holders
5 x 7	8	2¾x6⅝x8½	3¼x8⅞x13½	Camera and Five Holders

Carrying Case for Seroco A Camera.

No. 20G1302 New Model Seroco A Folding Camera, 4x5.
Price, including "Complete Instructions in Photography"........$ 9.30
No. 20G1303 New Model Seroco A Folding Camera, 5x7.
Price, including "Complete Instructions in Photography"..........12.50
These prices include the camera complete. Just as described and shown on this page, with one Seroco Double Plate Holder and Sole Leather Carrying Case.

AS A DAYLIGHT LOADING FILM CAMERA. The Improved Seroco A Camera is so constructed that it takes the Premo film pack, the most convenient and satisfactory form in which films have ever been furnished. With the film pack, this camera becomes a daylight loading film camera, thus combining all the advantages of both plates and films.

THE FILM PACK consists of twelve flat films, enclosed in a compact, lightproof case. In order to use the film pack, a film pack adapter must be purchased. This adapter is a device for holding the film pack, and is similar in form and size to an ordinary plate holder. It may be removed from the camera between exposures, the same as an ordinary plate holder, so that each exposure, if desired, may be sharply focused on the ground glass the same as when using dry plates.

USES EITHER PLATES OR FILMS.

FILM PACKS AND FILM PACK ADAPTERS.

No. 20G1821 Film Pack Adapter, for 4x5 camera. Price....................$1.50
If by mail, postage extra, 7 cents.
No. 20G1822 Film Pack Adapter, for 5x7 camera. Price....................2.50
If by mail, postage extra, 10 cents.
No. 20G1831 Film Pack, 4x5 (12 exposures). Price.................... .90
If by mail, postage extra, 8 cents.
No. 20G1832 Film Pack, 5x7 (12 exposures). Price.................... 1.60
If by mail, postage extra 11 cents

This TARGET RIFLE is FREE For only $25.00 in PROFIT SHARING CERTIFICATES.

IF YOUR PURCHASES IN OUR CAMERA DEPARTMENT or in any other department aggregate $25.00, within a year, you are entitled to this Target Rifle FREE as your share of our profits, if you want it. This is a first class rifle in every particular, and any boy would be proud to own it. The liberality of our revised Profit Sharing Plan is illustrated by the case with which you can obtain this splendid Target Rifle ABSOLUTELY FREE OF CHARGE. Every time you send us an order for $1.00 or more we send you a Profit Sharing Certificate for the full amount of your order, and when you have accumulated only $25.00 in Profit Sharing Certificates you are entitled to choose from a great variety of articles which are described in our Profit Sharing Catalogue, free, in exchange for $25.00 in Profit Sharing Certificates. Many articles which we gave last year for $50.00 in Profit Sharing Certificates are now given for only $25.00 in Profit Sharing Certificates. Other $100.00 articles are given FREE for $50.00 in Profit Sharing Certificates, so you see that the value of every Profit Sharing Certificate has been largely increased and in many cases more than doubled. You will find the last edition of our Customers' Profit Sharing Catalogue full of delightful surprises in the wonderful variety and the high value of the articles it brings within your reach, ABSOLUTELY WITHOUT ONE CENT OF COST. Send today for the Big FREE Profit Sharing Book.

MODEL XII
CONLEY FOLDING CAMERA $12.65

For Pictures 3¼x5½. Post Card Size.

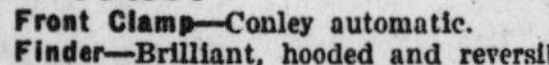

SPECIFICATIONS:

Woodwork—Solid African mahogany, with hand rubbed piano finish, corners dovetailed and rounded.
Metal Parts—Brass, nickel plated and highly polished.
Covering—High grade leather, with handsome bear grain.
Bellows—Best red Russia leather, gossamer lined, extra long; capacity, 10⅜ inches.
Back—Non-reversible, with spring actuated ground glass focusing screen and piano hinge leather covered back panel.
Focus Movement—Rack and pinion.
Front—New Conley metal with wood front board.
Front Clamp—Conley automatic.
Finder—Brilliant, hooded and reversible.
Bed—Conley all metal, three-section (double extension) with piano hinge.
Level—Double, conveniently located on bed of camera.
Shutter—Conley Automatic, with pneumatic and finger release.
Lens—Special Rapid rectilinear, speed F.8 (U. S. 4).
Plate Holder—Conley flexible valve.
Dimensions—Closed, 3x4¼x6⅞ inches.
Carrying Case—Solid sole leather with space for camera and five plate holders.

THIS POST CARD CAMERA will meet with approval from the most exacting photographer. It is made with the Conley all metal double extension bed, exactly the same construction as our famous Double Extension Camera, and the bellows is extra long, having ample capacity for all ordinary requirements. The finish, materials and workmanship throughout are extra high class, carefully selected mahogany, extra heavy leather with fine grain effects, all metal parts nickel plated and highly polished; a camera that is as pleasing in appearance as it is efficient in operation.

THIS CAMERA OPENS HORIZONTALLY, a special advantage, as most pictures are taken in this position. This style of construction in cameras of this size is possible only with the double extension bed. The front is made with side shift movement, an adjustment that is frequently desirable with pictures of this shape when the camera is used horizontally, and when the camera is turned to take pictures vertically this side shift movement becomes a rising and falling adjustment.

THE LENS with which we equip this camera is very rapid, working at F.8, and the bellows capacity is sufficient to permit the use of the rear combination alone, provided the front combination is removed and the rear combination screwed into the front of the shutter.

No. 20T333 Model XII Conley Folding Camera, complete with lens and shutter, as described, one plate holder and "Complete Instructions in Photography." (Without carrying case.) Shipping weight, 3¾ lbs. Price **$12.65**

No. 20T334 Model XII Conley Folding Camera, complete with No. 2 Series V Conley Anastigmat Lens and Conley Safety Shutter. Price **$31.25**

No. 20T335 Leather Carrying Case for Model XII Camera, containing space for camera and five plate holders. Shipping weight, 3½ pounds. Price **$2.20**
Shipping weight of camera and carrying case together, 7 pounds.

MODEL XIV
4¼x6½ CONLEY FOLDING CAMERA $12.50

SPECIFICATIONS:

Woodwork—Solid African mahogany, with hand rubbed piano finish, dovetailed and rounded corners.
Metal Parts—Brass, nickel plated and highly polished.
Covering—High grade leather, with handsome bear grain.
Bellows—Best red Russia leather, gossamer lined, capacity, 11½ inches.
Back—Non-reversible, with spring actuated ground glass focusing screen, leather covered mahogany back panel and vertical swing.
Focus Movement—Rack and pinion.
Front—Mahogany with both vertical and horizontal adjustment and removable lens board.
Front Clamp—Conley automatic.
Finder—Ground glass and mirror type, reversible.
Level—Double spirit.
Shutter—Conley Safety, with pneumatic and finger release.
Lens—High grade double rapid rectilinear, speed F.11 (U. S. 8).
Plate Holder—Conley flexible valve.
Dimensions—Closed, 3½x6x8 inches.
Carrying Case—Sole leather, with space for camera and five plate holders.

WE HAVE HAD MANY INQUIRIES for a camera to make pictures of this very artistic and desirable size, 4¼x6½, and in designing this Model XIV Camera we have endeavored to make a camera which will meet the requirements of the majority of photographers. We have equipped it with the most essential and most desirable adjustments, including vertical swing, rack and pinion focus movement, rising and falling front with side shift and removable lens board, automatic front clamp, and reversible finder. We have equipped it with a high grade F.11 rapid rectilinear lens that we can guarantee to cover the plate fully to the extreme corners and our Conley Safety Shutter.

IN DESIGNING THIS CAMERA it has been our aim to produce a thoroughly efficient, dependable and finely finished instrument at a moderate and reasonable price, and for general all around work, including landscapes, architectural subjects, interiors, full figure portraits, groups, etc., it will fill all requirements.

No. 20T360 Model XIV Conley Camera, complete with lens and shutter as described, one plate holder and "Complete Instructions in Photography." (Without carrying case.) Shipping weight, 5½ pounds. Price **$12.50**

No. 20T361 Keratol Carrying Case for Model XIV Camera. Contains space for camera and five plate holders. Shipping weight, 4½ pounds. Price **85c**

No. 20T362 Leather Carrying Case for Model XIV Camera. Same size as No. 20T361. Shipping weight, 4½ pounds. Price **$2.50**
Shipping weight of camera and carrying case together, 10 pounds.

WONDER AUTOMATIC CANNON PHOTO BUTTON MACHINE $15.00

This remarkable Cannon Camera takes, develops and finishes a button photograph in less than one minute and if sold at 5 cents each the net profit on each button is 400 per cent.

THE NOVEL AND STRIKING APPEARANCE of this machine quickly attracts attention, and at picnics, fairs, celebrations, frequented street corners, or any place where crowds of people gather, it is a quick and easy money maker.

EASY TO OPERATE. This machine is exceedingly simple and easy to operate and may be successfully used by anyone of average intelligence, even though without the slightest knowledge of photography. The exposure is made simply by pressing the bulb, after which a lever is pressed which drops the button into the lower part of the machine where it is automatically developed and fixed and **in just a few seconds it can be delivered to your customer ready to wear.** Most operators charge 5 cents for the buttons, at which price they yield a profit of 400 per cent on the investment, but nearly everyone will also want one of the handsome gilt frames shown below, which readily bring 10 cents each, thus greatly increasing the profit.

THIS MACHINE is manufactured of metal throughout, and is the simplest and most attractive machine on the market. It is entirely free from complications and can be taken apart and put together in a few minutes. The developing cup, which contains the developing jar, is made of fine polished aluminum. The lens is specially ground and polished and is peculiarly adapted for this kind of work on account of its speed and sharp brilliant definition. The plates are packed in lightproof tin tubes and can be loaded into the machine in broad daylight in a few seconds. No darkroom is required.

COMPLETE OUTFIT, $24.40

While we quote prices on this machine and each of the various supplies separately we advise the purchase of this complete outfit at $24.40, because it contains everything necessary for immediate results and enables the purchaser to start work at once. Additional supplies may be ordered with the outfit if desired, and if you live some distance from Chicago it might be well to include some extra plates, frames and developing powders with your order to avoid delay after getting to work. The complete outfit contains the following items: 1 Cannon Photo Button Machine, as shown in illustration; 1 tripod, 300 plates, 288 gilt frames, 2 packages of developing powders, 1 ammonia tester. Shipping wt., 7 lbs.

No. 20T499 Complete Photo Button Outfit. Price **$24.40**

SUPPOSE YOU PURCHASE THE COMPLETE OUTFIT AT $24.40. Let us figure the possible profit. There are plates enough in the outfit to make 300 buttons, which, at 5 cents each, sell for $15.00. There are two gross of frames, which, at 10 cents each, will sell for $28.80, making the total sales $43.80, leaving a profit of $19.40 in actual money, besides the outfit itself. Now, on future business, 1,000 plates will cost you $10.00, and the necessary developer for same about $1.50; the finished buttons sell for $50.00. Five gross (720) of frames, at $1.75 per gross, will cost you $8.75 and sell for $72.00. Total cost, $20.25; total sales, $122.00; net profit, $101.75. This is figuring on the basis that less than three-fourths of the people will order frames, but the percentage is usually higher. It looks good, doesn't it?

No. 20T501 The Wonder Cannon Photo Button Machine, complete, as shown in illustration. Price.. **$15.00**

No. 20T503 Tripod for Wonder Cannon Photo Button Machine. Price **1.90**

No. 20T505 Sensitized Plates fpr Wonder Cannon Photo Button Machine. These plates are of the exact size for photo buttons, measuring 1 inch in diameter. Put up in light tight tin tubes, ready to load into the camera; 100 plates in each tube. Price, per 1,000 (10 tubes) **10.00**

No. 20T507 Gilt Frames for photo buttons. Illustration shows exact size. Price, per gross **1.25**

No. 20T508 Gilt Frames for photo buttons. Better and heavier than No. 20T507. Price, per gross.... **1.75**

No. 20T509 Developing Powders. For use they are simply dissolved in water and a little ammonia added, making a solution which **automatically develops and finishes the button picture in one operation.** Price, per package .... **.25**

No. 20T510 Ammonia Tester. You can buy the ammonia for the developer at any drug store, but it should be tested to be sure of the quality. Price .... **.40**

This illustration shows the finished button, exact size.

Gilt Frame No. 20T507

$1.70 THE CONLEY JUNIOR BOX CAMERA

WITH GENUINE CONLEY FLEXIBLE VALVE PLATE HOLDER.

MADE IN OUR OWN FACTORY AT ROCHESTER AND SOLD TO YOU AT MANUFACTURER'S PRICE, ONE-HALF THE PRICE ASKED BY OTHERS FOR CAMERAS OF EQUAL MERIT.

For Pictures $3\frac{1}{2}$x$3\frac{1}{2}$

USES DRY PLATES ONLY

THE LENS AND SHUTTER in this camera are of exactly the same high standard of excellence as those used in the 4x5 Conley Senior Box Camera, a high grade, specially ground, single achromatic meniscus lens of fixed focus, and our own unequaled automatic time and instantaneous shutter. Remember, the lens is always in focus, the shutter is always set and thus the camera is always ready for instant use.

CONLEY IMPROVED FLEXIBLE VALVE PLATE HOLDER. With this Conley Junior Box Camera, as with all our own Conley Cameras, we include one Conley Improved Plate Holder, made with the famous Drake Lightproof Flexible Valve, a plate holder that never leaks light and never spoils a plate.

SIZE AND FINISH. The 3½x3½ Conley Junior Box Camera is 5 inches wide, 5⅝ inches high and 7½ inches long. It weighs 26 ounces. There is room enough in the back to carry three double plate holders, each containing two dry plates. The inside woodwork is stained black, the covering is fine black seal grain keratol and all metal parts are oxidized. An accurately adjusted view finder makes it easy to quickly center and locate the picture, and a tripod socket is provided so that the camera may be used on a tripod if desired.

"COMPLETE INSTRUCTIONS IN PHOTOGRAPHY," our own big 112-page manual, is included FREE of charge with this camera and will enable anyone without the slightest previous experience or knowledge of photography to start right in and make good pictures from the very beginning.

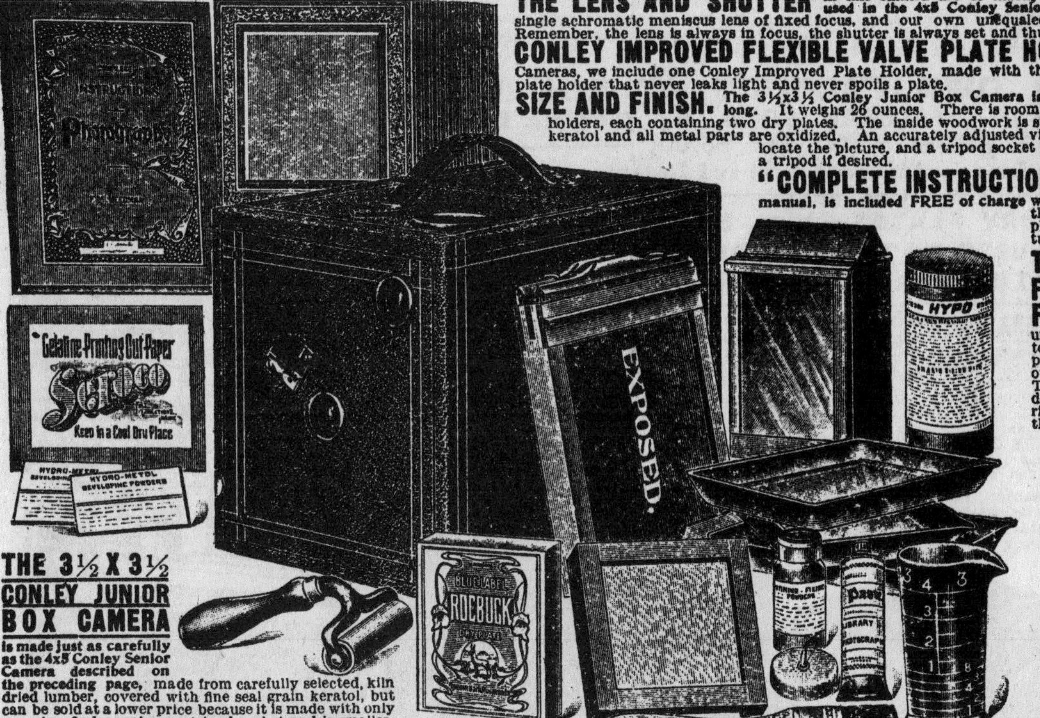

THE COMPLETE DEVELOPING, FINISHING AND MATERIAL OUTFIT. Although we sell this camera alone (with one plate holder) for $1.70, we especially urge you, particularly if you are a beginner in photography, to buy the entire outfit, the camera, plate holder, developing, finishing and material outfit, all complete, for which the price is $2.75. Then you will have everything necessary for developing, printing and finishing your pictures right at the start. The complete outfit, for which the price is $2.75, contains the following items:

- 1 3½x3½ Conley Junior Box Camera
- 1 3½x3½ Conley Improved Flexible Valve Plate Holder
- 1 Metal Dark Room Lamp
- 1 Tray for developing plates
- 1 Tray for fixing plates
- 1 Tray for toning prints
- 1 Printing Frame
- 1 Measuring Glass
- 1 Print Roller for smoothing down the prints when mounted
- 1 Paste Brush for mounting
- ½ doz. Dry Plates for making negatives
- 1 doz. Sheets Sensitized Paper
- 1 doz. Embossed Border Cards for mounting the pictures
- 1 Package Dry Developer (makes 8 ounces of solution)
- 1 Package Dry Toner (makes 8 oz. of solution)
- 1 Package Hypo, for fixing negatives and prints
- 1 Tube Prepared and Scented Mounting Paste
- 1 Copy "Complete Instructions in Photography"

THE 3½ X 3½ CONLEY JUNIOR BOX CAMERA is made just as carefully as the 4x5 Conley Senior Camera described on the preceding page, made from carefully selected, kiln dried lumber, covered with fine seal grain keratol, but can be sold at a lower price because it is made with only one view finder, only one tripod socket and is smaller. In quality and workmanship this camera is just as good as the 4x5 Conley Senior Box Camera, but it takes a smaller picture, which from a standpoint of economy is an advantage, as dry plates, sensitized papers and all other supplies used with the camera will be proportionately cheaper. This camera makes pictures 3½x3½ inches, perfectly square pictures, which makes only one view finder and one tripod socket necessary (as the camera is always used in the same position) and thus reduces the cost of manufacture.

NOTHING TO GET OUT OF ORDER. The construction of the 3½x3½ Conley Junior Box Camera is so simple and so substantial that there is practically nothing about it to get out of order. There are no unnecessary springs, catches or adjustments to go wrong and annoy the owner or create a source of expense. It is a universal focus camera, always in adjustment, requiring no focusing or other work before taking the picture.

No. 20H50 The 3½x3½ Conley Junior Box Camera with one Conley Improved Flexible Valve Plate Holder, and complete Developing, Finishing and Material Outfit, exactly as described and illustrated on this page. Price........................ **$2.75**
Shipping weight, 8¼ pounds.

No. 20H51 The 3½x3½ Conley Junior Box Camera with one Conley Improved Flexible Valve Double Plate Holder, but without Developing, Finishing and Material Outfit. Price........................ **$1.70**
Shipping weight, 3½ pounds.

No. 20H650 Extra Plate Holders, for 3½x3½ Conley Junior Box Camera, genuine Conley Improved Flexible Valve Plate Holders. Each holder will carry two dry plates. Price, each........................ **33c**
If by mail, postage extra, 5 cents.

$3.95 IMPROVED CONLEY MAGAZINE CAMERA

FOR PICTURES 4x5

12 PLATES WITH ONE LOADING

12 EXPOSURES IN 12 SECONDS

TWO LARGE, BRILLIANT VIEW FINDERS; GENUINE LEATHER COVERING; TWO TRIPOD SOCKETS; IMPROVED PLATE DROPPING DEVICE; METAL BASE AUTOMATIC SHUTTER; HIGH GRADE ACHROMATIC LENS.

GENERAL CONSTRUCTION. The Improved Conley Magazine Camera is the culmination of years of practical experience in building cameras of this type. The construction throughout is strong and substantial. The lumber is carefully selected and kiln dried. The doors are selected cherry, paneled to prevent shrinking or swelling, and all inside woodwork is stained to a dead black color. All exposed metal parts are heavily nickel plated and the entire camera is covered with the best quality of seal grain black morocco leather, making it not only strong and substantial, but at the same time, handsome and ornamental in its appearance.

THE PLATE DROPPING DEVICE is absolutely positive in action, and so constructed that any difference in the thickness of the plates will not interfere with its successful operation. It is so assembled that a slight swelling or shrinking of the woodwork in the camera will not put it out of order, and by a most ingenious arrangement which we have fully protected by patents—it is impossible to drop more than one plate at a time—a fault which is quite common to many other magazine cameras—and at the same time it is absolutely certain to drop one plate every time the operating lever is moved.

LENS. This Camera is equipped with the best single Achromatic Universal Focus lens that we can procure, made from the finest imported optical glass, and every lens is individually focused in each camera, insuring sharp images. This lens possesses unusual depth of focus for lenses of this class, and covers the plate to the extreme corners.

SHUTTER. We equip the Conley Improved Magazine Camera with an entirely new shutter which overcomes all of the difficulties formerly experienced with box camera shutters. It is assembled entirely on a metal base, the working parts having no connection with the woodwork at any point. This insures perfect operation of the shutter at all times, as any slight shrinking or swelling of the wood, due to exceedingly dry or exceedingly moist weather, has no effect on the working parts. This shutter is entirely automatic in action, always set, and is operated either by pressing a button, or by bulb and tube. The bulb and tube are detachable and may be dispensed with if preferred.

LOADING AND UNLOADING. The plates are inserted at the back of the camera, and after exposure are removed through a hinged door at the bottom of the camera. Any number of exposed plates may be removed from the camera at any time without disturbing the unexposed plates still remaining. An automatic tally shows at all times the number of unexposed plates still remaining in the camera.

SPECIAL ADVANTAGES. The Improved Conley Magazine Camera is equal to a film camera in compactness and simplicity of operation, the use of plate holders being entirely dispensed with. Twelve plates are placed directly in the camera, and the instrument is then ready for the making of twelve exposures without recourse to the dark room, and without carrying detached or extra plate holders. It possesses all the advantages of a film camera, so far as compactness and ability to carry a large number of exposures are concerned, yet it uses glass dry plates instead of films, the same plates that professional photographers, who may be presumed to have studied the matter very carefully, always use. A further advantage possessed by dry plates over film is the relative cost, a dozen dry plates costing one half as much as an equal quantity of film.

No. 20H70 The 4x5 Improved Conley Magazine Camera, with one copy "Complete Instructions in Photography." Price........................ **$3.95**
Shipping weight, 5½ pounds.

THE 4 x 5 CONLEY SENIOR BOX CAMERA WITH GENUINE CONLEY FLEXIBLE VALVE PLATE HOLDER $1.95

MADE IN OUR OWN FACTORY AT ROCHESTER.

BETTER THAN BOX CAMERAS SOLD BY OTHER DEALERS AT FROM $4.00 TO $5.00.

Genuine Meniscus Achromatic Lens. Automatic Time and Instantaneous Shutter. Conley Flexible Valve Plate Holder.

THIS CAMERA USES DRY PLATES ONLY, EXACTLY THE SAME KIND OF PLATES USED BY THE BEST PROFESSIONAL PHOTOGRAPHERS.

THE CONLEY SENIOR BOX CAMERA represents by far the most popular size and style of camera made for amateur use, a statement which will be more fully appreciated when we take into consideration the fact that more than half of all the amateur cameras sold are cameras of this size and style. While this camera takes a full size 4x5 picture (practically cabinet size) the camera itself measures only 5½ inches wide by 7 inches high by 8¼ inches long and weighs only 34 ounces. There is sufficient space in the back of the camera to accommodate three double plate holders, thus giving the camera a capacity of six plates, and in addition, as many extra plate holders as desired (each containing two plates) may be carried. **THE CONLEY SENIOR BOX CAMERA presents a most handsome appearance**, being covered with the finest quality of black seal grain keratol leather, and all metal parts are made with fine oxidized finish.

EASY TO OPERATE. The Conley Senior Box Camera is the simplest and easiest kind of a camera to use. No previous experience is necessary, everything is simple and easy to understand, and the big book of instructions, which comes free with the camera, tells you in plain and simple language all that you need to know in order to make GOOD PICTURES.

YOU WILL BE SURPRISED to see how easy it is to take GOOD PICTURES with the Conley Senior Box Camera, and you will derive the greatest pleasure from the beautiful pictures you can make of your friends and relatives, brothers and sisters; your dogs, cats and horses; the home, both inside and out; pretty landscapes, buildings and places of interest seen while traveling; and especially pictures of the baby in all its cute and amusing positions. It will not be fully realized, until after years, what treasures have been secured in the way of pictures of friends and places or things of interest.

THE LENS is a fine single achromatic, of the Meniscus style of construction, specially ground from the finest imported Mantois optical glass, the best universal or fixed focus lens that can be made. This lens possesses great depth of focus, giving perfectly sharp detail both to objects at a distance and to those which are nearby, and is guaranteed to cover the plate fully to the extreme corners.

THE SHUTTER is entirely automatic in action, being operated for either time or instantaneous exposures simply by pressing the lever at the side of the camera. This shutter is always set and ready for immediate action, its construction is exceedingly simple, there are no complicated parts to get out of order and of all shutters heretofore designed for use with box cameras this one is the simplest, the most effective and the most reliable.

TWO VIEW FINDERS are provided, one for use when making pictures the long way of the plate (4 inches high and 5 inches wide), and the other for use when making pictures the short way of the plate (5 inches high and 4 inches wide), thus enabling the operator to accommodate the shape and style of picture to the subject. These view finders are most carefully and accurately made and perfectly adjusted.

TWO TRIPOD SOCKETS. The Conley Senior Box Camera is made with two tripod sockets, one on the side, the other on the bottom of the camera, so that pictures may be made either the long or the short way of the plate when using a tripod.

UNDERSTAND, HOWEVER, THIS CAMERA MAY BE USED EITHER WITH OR WITHOUT A TRIPOD,

just as the user prefers. A tripod is a convenience, especially when making time exposures, but is not by any means a necessity, and the finest kind of pictures may be made without a tripod.

REMEMBER HOW SIMPLE THE CONLEY SENIOR BOX CAMERA is, the shutter is always set, you don't have to turn any buttons or push any levers before making an exposure, operations which are very apt to be forgotten or wrongly executed in the excitement of the moment; and **you don't have to focus each time a picture is made**, as the lens is of universal focus, **always ready**. With other cameras many a fine picture is lost because of the delay in setting the shutter, focusing, etc. In the meantime the subject is gone or the scene is changed, **but the Conley Senior Box Camera is always ready for instant action.**

CONLEY IMPROVED FLEXIBLE VALVE PLATE HOLDER. With every Conley Senior Box Camera we furnish the genuine Conley Improved Flexible Valve Double Plate Holder, made with the famous Drake Light Proof Flexible Valve, the very best plate holder on the market. It is the custom of practically all camera manufacturers to furnish cheap, poorly made plate holders with box cameras, and three-fourths of all the failures in picture making are due to faulty plate holders. As a matter of fact, the plate holder is the most important part of a camera, because good pictures cannot be made with the best camera in the world unless the holders are absolutely light tight and perfect in construction. That is why we furnish with the Conley Senior Box Camera the genuine Conley Improved Flexible Valve Plate Holder, the exact same style and quality of holder that we furnish with our very highest priced folding cameras.

"Complete Instructions in Photography" FREE.

WITH EVERY CONLEY SENIOR BOX CAMERA we include, without extra charge, our big 112-page manual, "Complete Instructions in Photography," the largest, the simplest and the most complete guide to photography ever published. This book makes everything plain, clear, simple and easy to understand, and not only insures success to the beginner in picture making but contains a fund of valuable information for the experienced photographer.

COMPLETE DEVELOPING, FINISHING AND MATERIAL OUTFIT.

The Big Outfit which we furnish with the Conley Senior Box Camera, at the prices quoted below, contains everything necessary for developing, printing, toning and mounting pictures complete. Every item that goes into this outfit is good, the plates and paper are guaranteed fresh and perfect, the chemicals full strength and of the highest purity, and all the other items strictly high class, well made and serviceable. **Understand,** we furnish the camera alone (with one double plate holder) for **$1.95**, but we especially urge that you order the **Camera and Outfit**, all complete, ready for use, at our special price of **$3.15**.

The Complete Outfit at **$3.15** contains the following items:

- 1 4x5 Conley Senior Box Camera
- 1 4x5 Conley Improved Flexible Valve Plate Holder
- 1 Metal Dark Room Lamp
- 1 Tray for Developing Plates
- 1 Tray for Fixing Plates
- 1 Tray for Toning Prints
- 1 Print Roller for smoothing down the mounted prints
- ½ Dozen Dry Plates
- 1 Paste Brush
- 1 Graduated Glass for Measuring Liquids
- 1 Dozen Card Mounts, with fancy embossed borders
- 1 Package Concentrated Dry Developer (makes 8 ounces of solution)
- 1 Copy of "Complete Instructions in Photography"
- 1 Package Concentrated Dry Toner (makes 8 ounces of solution)
- 1 Dozen Sheets Sensitized Paper
- 1 Printing Frame
- 1 Package Hypo for fixing Negatives and Prints
- 1 Tube of fine Scented Photo Mounting Paste

No. 20H60 The 4x5 Conley Senior Box Camera, with one Conley Improved Flexible Valve Double Plate Holder, and Complete Developing, Finishing and Material Outfit, exactly as described and illustrated on this page. Price......(Shipping weight, 10¼ pounds)....... **$3.15**

No. 20H61 The 4x5 Conley Senior Box Camera, with one Conley Improved Flexible Valve Double Plate Holder, but **without** Developing, Finishing and Material Outfit. Price......(Shipping weight, 4 pounds)....... **$1.95**

No. 20H656 Extra Plate Holders, for 4x5 Conley Senior Box Camera, Genuine Conley Improved Flexible Valve Plate Holders, each holder will carry two dry plates. Price, 5 for **$1.85**; each (If by mail, postage extra, each, 6 cents)...... **38c**

$4.95 CONLEY STEREO BOX CAMERA

STEREOSCOPIC PHOTOGRAPHY is intensely interesting, and there is nothing more beautiful than a stereoscopic photograph, but many photographers have a mistaken idea that stereoscopic pictures are difficult to make, while as an actual matter of fact, they are just as easy to make as any other photograph, provided one is equipped with the proper apparatus. Any one who can operate a camera of any kind can operate a stereoscopic camera and can make high class stereoscopic pictures.

A STEREOSCOPIC VIEW seen through the stereoscope brings the original scene before us in a way that seems almost like magic, so wonderful is the effect of distance, depth, relief and solidity. The marvelously true to life appearance, everything seemingly full, natural life size; the wonderful detail, the perspective, the figures springing up in the foreground as distinct and real as if alive, makes the stereoscopic view a most delightful entertainer. Seen for the first time, the effect is most startling, and yet the making of these marvelously wonderful pictures is very simple.

OUR CONLEY STEREO BOX CAMERA AT $4.95, a mere fraction of the price at which stereoscopic cameras have heretofore been offered, is perfectly designed, well made and capable of making the most perfect stereoscopic views. This camera uses 4¼x6½ plates and makes full regular size stereoscopic views, the exact same style, size and quality of views that you, no doubt, have often seen offered for sale by canvassers at $2.00 or more per dozen. With this simple and inexpensive stereoscopic camera, you can make stereoscopic views of your own home, your friends, your family and objects of interest of all kinds.

THE LENSES AND SHUTTER. This camera is fitted with two perfectly matched, single achromatic, fixed focus lenses, made especially for stereoscopic work, each pair carefully and accurately matched. The shutter is the Conley Special Automatic Stereo Shutter, a shutter that is very easy to operate, very effective and reliable, and of the simplest possible construction. The shutter is always set, always ready for an exposure, and is operated simply by pressing the small lever at the side of the camera. With the indicator set to I, a single pressure of the lever makes an instantaneous exposure, simultaneously opening and closing both lenses. With the indicator set to T the shutter is ready for time exposures, the first pressure opening the shutter, which remains open until the lever is again pressed.

$4.95 IS AN UNHEARD OF PRICE for a stereoscopic camera, and yet at this price we offer in the Conley Stereo Box Camera, an instrument that we can absolutely guarantee to make high class stereoscopic pictures. It is substantially made from thoroughly seasoned and kiln dried lumber, covered with best quality of seal grain black keratol with nickel plated trimmings. It measures 5½x5¾x8 inches, and weighs, complete, including plate holder, 33 ounces.

COMPLETE INSTRUCTIONS for making stereoscopic pictures are sent free of charge with every stereoscopic camera that we sell, and anyone with the help of these simple instructions, can easily make the most interesting and beautiful stereoscopic pictures.

No. 20L135 Conley Stereo Box Camera, exactly as illustrated and described above, with one Conley Improved Flexible Valve Plate Holder, 4¼x6½. Shipping weight, 3½ pounds. Price.................. **$4.95**

Extra plate holders are 45 cents each. See page 264.

CONLEY SPECIAL STEREOSCOPIC CAMERA

$14.90

THE CONLEY SPECIAL STEREOSCOPIC CAMERA is designed for those who want something more complete and elaborate than the box camera, and yet at a moderate price. Only the best materials are used in the construction of this camera, selected mahogany for the woodwork, genuine leather for the covering, every part made with the utmost care and the entire camera assembled and put together in the most accurate manner.

THE LENS AND SHUTTER. We equip this camera with a pair of rapid rectilinear lenses, very carefully and accurately matched for stereoscopic work, and these lenses are mounted in the Wollensak Senior Automatic Shutter.

SPECIFICATIONS.

WOODWORK—All solid mahogany, dovetailed corners, piano finish.
METAL PARTS—Brass, heavily nickel plated, highly polished.
COVERING—Genuine seal grain leather.
BELLOWS—Best red Russia leather, gossamer lined.
FOCUS MOVEMENT—Rack and pinion.
LENS BOARD—Detachable.
FRONT—Mahogany with rising and falling movement.
FRONT CLAMP—Conley Automatic.
FINDER—Ground glass, brass bound.
SHUTTER—Wollensak Senior Automatic.
LENS—High grade rapid rectilinear.
PLATE HOLDER—Conley Improved Flexible Valve.
CARRYING CASE—Keratol covered, with space for camera and five plate holders.
DIMENSIONS—3¾x6⅜x8½ inches, closed.

No. 20L138 Conley Special Stereoscopic Camera, complete with lens and shutter as illustrated and described above, with keratol covered carrying case and one 5x7 Conley Improved Flexible Valve Plate Holder. Price...... **$14.90**

CONLEY PROFESSIONAL STEREOSCOPIC CAMERA

$28.50

THE CONLEY PROFESSIONAL STEREOSCOPIC CAMERA is our highest grade stereoscopic camera, a camera that is absolutely complete in every detail, possessing every adjustment and every improvement that has in any way been found useful in stereoscopic photography. This stereoscopic camera is made with the latest improved automatic spring roller septum, which rolls up or unrolls automatically as the camera is opened or closed, double shifting front with both rising and falling movement and side shift, detachable lens board, rack and pinion focus movement, reversible back, brilliant hooded finder, ground glass focusing screen protected by hinged, leather covered, mahogany panel, genuine leather covering, nickel plated metal parts, and genuine leather bellows.

SPECIFICATIONS.

WOODWORK—All solid mahogany, dovetailed corners, piano finish.
METAL PARTS—Brass, heavily nickel plated and highly polished.
COVERING—Best seal grain leather.
BELLOWS—Best red Russia leather, gossamer lined.
BACK—Reversible, with single button release and improved swing.
FOCUS MOVEMENT—Rack and pinion.
LENS BOARD—Detachable, instantly removed or replaced.
FRONT—Mahogany, double shifting with both vertical and horizontal movements.
FRONT CLAMP—New Conley Automatic.
FINDER—Brilliant, hooded.
PIANO HINGE—Nickel plated.
SHUTTER—Wollensak Regular, double valve stereoscopic.
LENSES—High grade, stereoscopic, double symmetrical.
SEPTUM—Improved spring roller curtain.
PLATE HOLDER—Conley Improved Flexible Valve.
CARRYING CASE—Heavy sole leather, with space for camera and six plate holders.
DIMENSIONS—Camera closed, 3¾x8½x8¾ inches; focal capacity, 16 inches; carrying case, 4¼x9x15¼ inches.

A COMBINATION CAMERA. At $28.50 we furnish this camera equipped only for stereoscopic work, but by adding the 5x7 lens and shutter with extra front board, which we furnish for $6.30 extra, the camera may be used for either full size single 5x7 pictures or for stereoscopic views. As a 5x7 camera it possesses all of the adjustments and good qualities that are necessary for the highest grade of work, corresponding practically in its various details and adjustments to our 5x7 Long Focus Camera.

THE LENS AND SHUTTER. We equip the Conley Professional Stereoscopic Camera with a pair of extra high grade, double symmetrical lenses, especially ground for stereoscopic work and accurately matched. These lenses are mounted in the Wollensak Double Valve Regular Shutter arranged for automatic instantaneous exposures of various lengths from one second to one hundredth part of a second, and time or bulb exposures of any desired length.

No. 20L140 Conley Professional Stereoscopic Camera, complete, with double symmetrical stereoscopic lenses, Wollensak Regular Stereoscopic Shutter, one 5x7 Conley Improved Flexible Valve Plate Holder, and sole leather carrying case. Shipping weight, 16 pounds.
Price.................. **$28.50**

No. 20L142 Double Symmetrical Lens, for single 5x7 pictures, with Conley Safety Shutter and extra front board to fit the Conley Professional Stereoscopic Camera. If by mail postage extra 8 cents.
Price, complete with shutter, front board, bulb and tube.................. **$6.30**

THE EXPO WATCH CAMERA

A True Vest Pocket Detective Camera. The Expo Camera is the smallest practical camera ever made, and, although it is so small that it can readily be carried in the vest pocket, it is at the same time a strictly high class practical instrument in every way. The Expo Camera is a daylight loading camera using film, and can be loaded for twenty-five exposures at a time. This camera looks exactly like a fair size watch and pictures can be taken with it anywhere without anyone suspecting that a camera is being used. The pictures taken with the Expo Camera are ⅞ of an inch long by ⅝ of an inch wide, the exact size shown in our illustration. This camera can be used for either time or instantaneous exposures and is suitable for landscapes, street scenes, groups, portraits, etc., in fact, just exactly the same kind of work which is accomplished by larger and more expensive cameras. The Expo Camera is carefully constructed from metal throughout, nickel plated, fitted with a fine achromatic lens and is guaranteed in every respect. So perfect are the negatives made with this little vest pocket camera that the pictures can be enlarged without sacrificing the detail or other good qualities.

Expo Picture, Exact Size

No. 20L375 The Expo Watch Camera Price complete, without film.............. **$2.25**
If by mail, postage extra, 10 cents.

No. 20L376 View Finder, for Expo Watch Camera. Price.................. **45c**
If by mail, postage extra, 5 cents.

No. 20L377 Daylight Loading Film for Expo Camera, twenty-five exposures to the roll. Price, per roll.................. **18c**
If by mail, postage extra, 1 cent.

OUR SPECIAL PORTRAIT OUTFIT

No. 20L500 THIS OUTFIT CONSISTS OF AN 8x10 CAMERA, Camera Stand and Reversible Cabinet attachment.

CAMERA IS MADE FROM BEST HARDWOOD finely finished. All adjustments are automatic and self locking. Has 30-inch bed, best India rubber bellows.

STAND IS THE WIZARD No. 7, fitted with automatic balancing device, raises and lowers with the lightest touch, can be locked in any position by lever at side. Firm and rigid, made of hardwood, finely finished. Top measures 17x32¾ inches.

THE NELSON AUTOMATIC HOLDER is included, the best studio plate holder made. Plates are put in or removed without turning a button, the back does not require to be opened, no spring to press on back of plate. Takes any size of plate from 8x10 to 5x8.

THE REVERSIBLE CABINET ATTACHMENT has spring actuated ground glass, and uses modern double plate holders.

THE FOLDING RACK is made of hardwood, holds twelve double plate holders, and is attached to side of stand.

Price, complete.................. **$36.75**
No lens or shutter is included.

We recommend our No. 20L1125 Lens and the No. 20L850 Silent Shutter for use with this outfit.

OUR BEST PENNY PICTURE CAMERA.

No. 20L510 This Camera is made from carefully selected hardwood and handsomely finished. It can be used for any regular portrait work in the studio, up to and including 5x7; also for copying. As a multiplying or penny picture camera, it makes 1, 4, 9, 12, 16, 20, 30, or 42 pictures on one 5x7 plate. Only one lens required. The mechanism is exceedingly simple, very easy to operate. Made with rising front and self locking focus lever. This camera has a 30-inch bed, rubber bellows and uses double plate holders of modern style.

Price, with one double plate holder.................. **$16.90**
Extra plate holders, each.................. **45c**

We especially recommend our Portrait Lens No. 20L1125 for use with this camera.

No. 20L511 Camera Stand suitable for the above Penny Picture Camera. This is the well known No. 00 stand made with patent stop for holding adjustable central support at any height, and semi-automatic tilting attachment. Answers all ordinary requirements.
Price.................. **$3.15**

No. 1 CONLEY VIEW CAMERA

NEW MODELS FOR 1909 AT $16.10 FOR THE 6½x8½ SIZE $18.25 FOR THE 8x10 SIZE $14.65 FOR THE 5x7 SIZE

THESE PRICES INCLUDE ONE CONLEY FLEXIBLE VALVE PLATE HOLDER, COMBINATION TRIPOD, AND LONG CARRYING CASE.

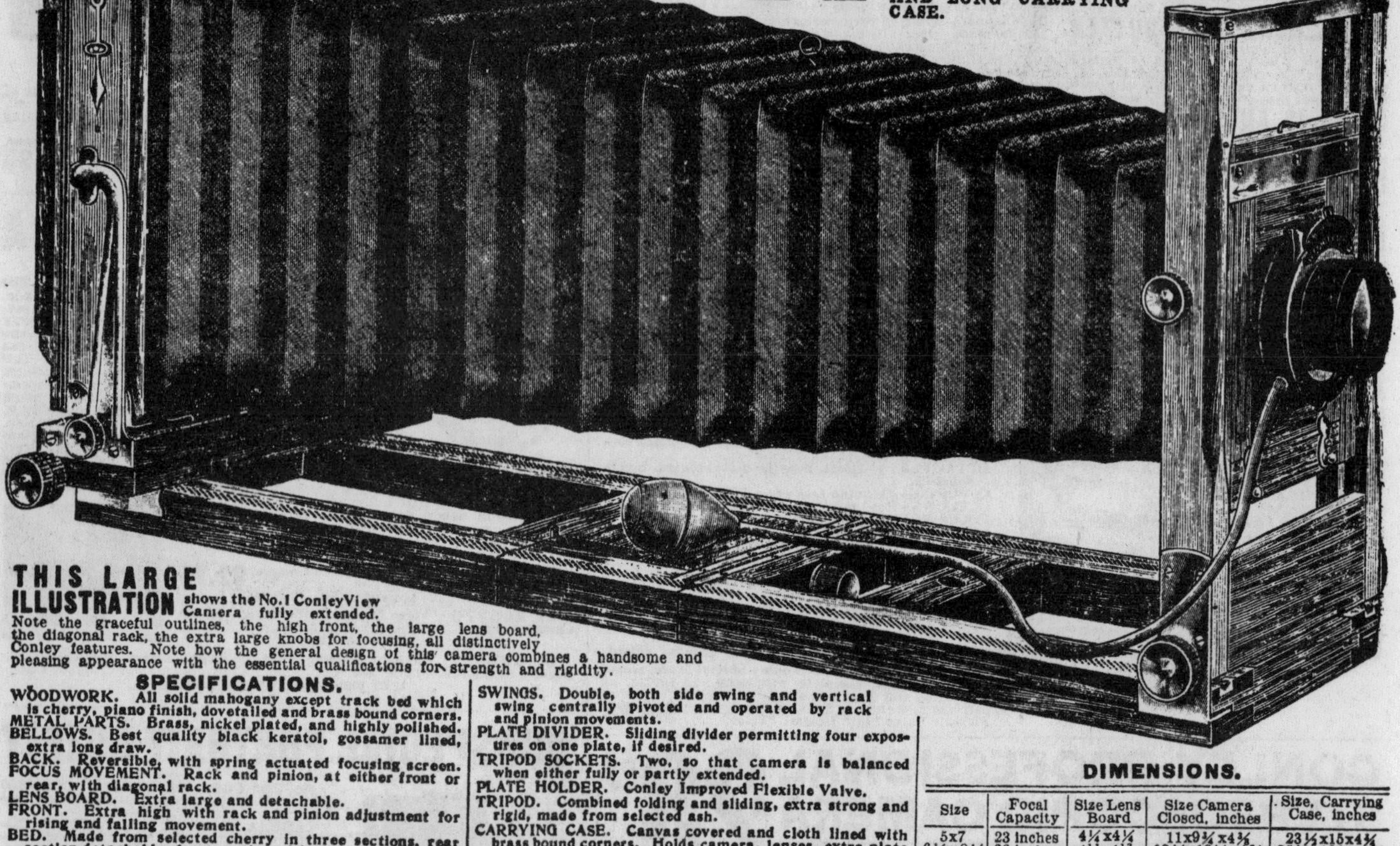

THIS LARGE ILLUSTRATION shows the No. 1 Conley View Camera fully extended. Note the graceful outlines, the high front, the large lens board, the diagonal rack, the extra large knobs for focusing, all distinctively Conley features. Note how the general design of this camera combines a handsome and pleasing appearance with the essential qualifications for strength and rigidity.

SPECIFICATIONS.

WOODWORK. All solid mahogany except track bed which is cherry, piano finish, dovetailed and brass bound corners.
METAL PARTS. Brass, nickel plated, and highly polished.
BELLOWS. Best quality black keratol, gossamer lined, extra long draw.
BACK. Reversible, with spring actuated focusing screen.
FOCUS MOVEMENT. Rack and pinion, at either front or rear, with diagonal rack.
LENS BOARD. Extra large and detachable.
FRONT. Extra high with rack and pinion adjustment for rising and falling movement.
BED. Made from selected cherry in three sections, rear section detachable, front section with piano hinge.
SWINGS. Double, both side swing and vertical swing centrally pivoted and operated by rack and pinion movements.
PLATE DIVIDER. Sliding divider permitting four exposures on one plate, if desired.
TRIPOD SOCKETS. Two, so that camera is balanced when either fully or partly extended.
PLATE HOLDER. Conley Improved Flexible Valve.
TRIPOD. Combined folding and sliding, extra strong and rigid, made from selected ash.
CARRYING CASE. Canvas covered and cloth lined with brass bound corners. Holds camera, lenses, extra plate holders and tripod.

DIMENSIONS.

Size	Focal Capacity	Size Lens Board	Size Camera Closed, inches	Size, Carrying Case, inches
5x7	23 inches	4¼x4¼	11x9¾x4⅜	23½x15x4¾
6½x8½	26 inches	4 11/16x4 13/16	12½x10⅛x4⅞	25¼x16¾x4⅞
8x10	30 inches	5⅜x5⅝	14⅛x12x5	28½x19x5¼

THE No. 1 CONLEY VIEW CAMERA is a business like camera for real photographers who are seriously interested in their work and who want an outfit that is, above all other considerations, thoroughly practical in every detail. We cannot too strongly recommend the No. 1 Conley View Camera to both amateur and professional for general photographic work. It combines ease of operation, completeness of adjustment, strength and durability to a degree not reached in other styles of cameras. The bellows is made amply long, the swings possess great latitude, the front has a wide range of movement, all adjustments are easy to get at and therefore convenient to manipulate. The style of construction permits the use of extreme wide angle lenses, or any kind of rapid rectilinear or anastigmat lenses, even the largest sizes, and the ample size and strength of the front even permit the use of the smaller types of portrait lenses. Nothing that will add to its convenience of operation, its accuracy and ease of adjustment, in short, to its effectiveness as a picture taking machine, is sacrificed for mere elegance of appearance or compactness.

This illustration shows the use of the vertical swing and the rising front adjustments, which in most view cameras are so limited in range of movement that certain pictures cannot be successfully made. Note that although the camera is very much tilted, the back remains perfectly vertical, and note also the extreme height to which the front may be raised.

STRONG AND DURABLE. The No. 1 Conley View Camera is suited to the hardest kind of practical service, strong, rigid and substantial throughout. There is plenty of material in it, heavy metal work and plenty of wood. Good workmanship combined with good materials makes it a camera that is not only extremely convenient to manipulate, but a handy camera to use in every way, and at the same time a camera that is durable, a camera that does not get out of order, a camera that can be depended upon year after year, even though subjected to the severest requirements.

SPECIAL FEATURES.

WHILE THE GENERAL CONSTRUCTION, good materials and fine workmanship make the No. 1 Conley View Camera equal in every way to view cameras sold by other makers at nearly double our prices, there are besides certain special features in our camera which make it not only equal in every detail to the cameras of manufacturers who are competing with us, but which put this camera in a class by itself as a more effective camera with a wider range of usefulness than is possessed by other view cameras, among which should be mentioned particularly the diagonal rack for the focus movement, the extra large front, the unusual range of movement in the front and the sliding plate device.

This illustration shows the No. 1 View Camera with both front and rear racked forward for extremely wide angle work. This construction of the camera permits the use of the shortest focus lenses made, without using any extra attachments or devices of any kind.

THE DIAGONAL RACK is a great improvement over the old style rack still used by other camera makers. This style of rack was first employed in the focus movement of fine microscopes where it is essential that absolutely all lost motion be eliminated, and we have applied this same principle to the No. 1 Conley View Camera, resulting in a smoothness of action and an absence of lost motion that is not found in any other view camera.

THE EXTRA LARGE FRONT is a feature of the No. 1 Conley View Camera that distinguishes it from other view cameras. Even in the 5x7 size the front board is 4¼x4¼ inches, permitting the use of the largest anastigmat lens made or even the smaller sizes of portrait lenses, making this camera in every sense of the word a universal camera, as any desired lens equipment is easily installed.

THE SPECIAL CONSTRUCTION OF THE FRONT permits a range of movement which is unusually great, a feature which is appreciated in the photographing of buildings and other architectural work, the 8x10 size having a movement up and down of 5½ inches, permitting the lens to be raised 2¾ inches above center or lowered the same distance below center. In the 6½x8½ size the range of the rising and falling front is 4⅜ inches, and in the 5x7 it is 3⅜ inches. In many view cameras the range of movement is less than half these figures.

THE SLIDING PLATE DIVIDER is a very desirable feature, permitting the operator to make four exposures on one plate. For this divider we use a special semi-flexible fiber material, possessing the advantage that it may be instantly removed or replaced, so that the change from using the entire plate to that of using one-fourth the plate is made instantly and without any trouble.

No. 1 Conley View Camera, folded.

ADJUSTMENTS.

WHILE KEEPING FOREMOST IN OUR MINDS at all times the fact that a view camera must be suited to the hardest kind of service, must be strong, rigid and substantial, we have at the same time incorporated into this camera all those conveniences, all those adjustments, and all those improvements that help to make the camera easy to use, and that make it possible to do things that cannot be accomplished with less fully equipped instruments.

Nos. 7 and 8 SEROCO FOCUSING FILM CAMERAS.

Daylight Loading.

FACTORY PRICES, according to size,

$12.80 and $13.75

THE Nos. 7 and 8 SEROCO FOCUSING FILM CAMERAS represent a new departure in the line of film cameras, being so constructed that a regulation full size ground glass focusing screen in the rear of the camera may be used the same as in a glass plate camera.

Open.

THESE CAMERAS are made with Rack and Pinion Focusing Movement, Brilliant Reversible Finders, Extension Bed and Extra Long Bellows. They are made throughout of solid mahogany with piano finish. The covering is the best grade of pebbled morocco leather. All metal parts are nickel plated and both material and workmanship throughout are the best that can be obtained.

THE SHUTTER is the latest improved style of Bausch & Lomb's Famous Automatic with retarding device, the highest grade shutter made. The Lens is an Extra Rapid Long Focus Symmetrical, of great depth of focus and covering power.

Closed.

No. 20C2277 No. 7 Seroco Focusing Film Camera for 3¼x4¼ pictures. Our special factory to user price, $12.80

No. 20C2278 No. 8 Seroco Focusing Film Camera for 4x5 pictures. Our special factory to user price $13.75

No. 20C2279 Sole Leather Carrying Case for No. 7, $1.60; for No. 8, 1.90

OUR SPECIAL PORTRAIT OUTFIT.

No. 20C2300 This outfit consists of an 8x10 Camera, Camera Stand and Reversible Cabinet Attachment.

CAMERA is made from best hard wood, finely finished. All adjustments are automatic and self locking. Has 30-inch bed, best india rubber bellows.

STAND IS THE WIZARD No. 7, fitted with automatic balancing device, raises and lowers with the lightest touch, can be locked in any position by lever at side. Firm and rigid, made of hardwood, finely finished. Top measures 17x32½ inches.

THE NELSON AUTOMATIC HOLDER is included, the best studio plate holder made. Plates are put in or removed without turning a button, the back does not require to be opened, no spring to press on back of plate. Takes any size of plate from 8x10 to 2x2.

THE REVERSIBLE CABINET ATTACHMENT has spring actuated ground glass, and uses modern double plate holders.

THE FOLDING RACK is made of hardwood, holds twelve double plate holders, and is attached to side of stand.

KITS FOR 6½X8½, 4¼x6½ AND 3¼x 4¼ PLATES are furnished so that the outfit is complete for any size work from 8x10 down.

Price, complete, **$34.75**

No lens or shutter is included. Make selection from pages 348 and 349 to suit your requirements.

Portrait Camera.

No. 20C2305 This Camera is made from hardwood, finely finished, and has all the advantages of higher priced cameras at a very low price.

AUTOMATIC SELF LOCKING LEVER SWINGS, patent focus lever, india rubber bellows, fitted with regulation curtain slide holder.

Size	Length of Bed	Price
6½x8½	24 inches	$14.60
8 x10	30 inches	17.50
10 x12	34 inches	21.00
11 x14	36 inches	25.75
14 x17	40 inches	30.40
17 x20	43 inches	39.00

IN MAKING UP YOUR ORDER FOR SUPPLIES
REMEMBER THAT
COMPLETE INSTRUCTIONS IN PHOTOGRAPHY IS FURNISHED FREE
IF YOU ASK FOR IT, WITH EVERY $2.50 ORDER.

Studio Camera.

No. 20C2310 This Camera is made from finely finished hardwood, has india rubber bellows, swinging ground glass, double swing and automatic self locking focus lever. Fitted with reversible cabinet attachment, with one 5x7 double plate holder for same, also regular curtain slide holder. Length of bed, 24 inches, made in 8x10 size only. Price, complete with cabinet attachment $19.90

Price, without cabinet attachment $13.20

Price of extra holders for cabinet attachment, 98c each.

Improved Victoria Camera for Ferrotype Work.

No. 20C2315 Made from selected hardwood, provided with all the latest adjustments, and finely finished. This camera is made for 5x7 plates, but is also fitted with diaphragms for making 4¼x5½ and 3¼x 4¼ pictures with one lens. With four Gem lenses this camera makes either four or eight pictures on a 5x7 plate.

Price, complete with four quarter-size Gem lenses $18.90

Price, without lenses 9.50

Our Best Penny Picture Camera.

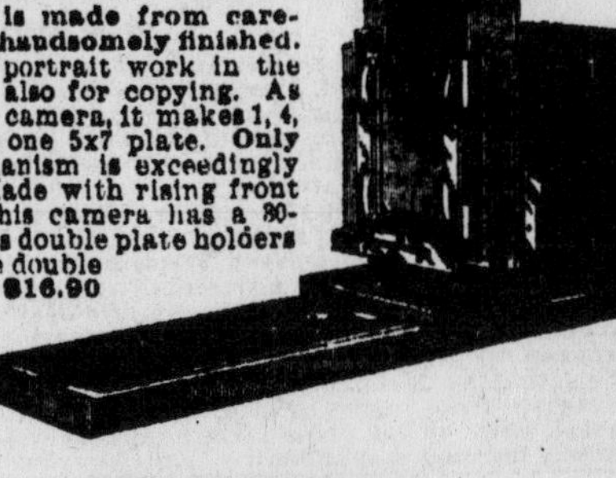

No. 20C2320 This Camera is made from carefully selected hardwood and handsomely finished. It can be used for any regular portrait work in the studio, up to and including 5x7; also for copying. As a multiplying or penny picture camera, it makes 1, 4, 9, 12, 16, 20, 30 or 42 pictures on one 5x7 plate. Only one lens required. The mechanism is exceedingly simple, very easy to operate. Made with rising front and self locking focus lever. This camera has a 30-inch bed, rubber bellows and uses double plate holders of modern style. Price, with one double plate holder $16.90

Extra plate holders, each 65c

We especially recommend our Portrait Lens No. 20C2432 for use with this camera.

Special Penny Picture Camera.

No. 20C2325 This Camera is adapted for regular portrait work as well as penny pictures, and makes an excellent all around studio camera. Made from hardwood, well finished, has india rubber bellows, and a sliding back, which makes it unnecessary to remove the holders between exposures. Made in two sizes, 4x5 and 5x7. The 4x5 camera makes 1, 4, 9 or 12 pictures on one 4x5 plate. The 5x7 camera makes 1, 4, 9, 12 or 24 pictures on one 5x7 plate. Uses modern double plate holders. Only one lens is required. Price, 4x5 camera, with one double plate holder $9.85

Price, 5x7 camera, with one double plate holder 12.25

Extra plate holders for 4x5 cameras, each .... .60

Extra plate holders for 5x7 cameras, each .... .65

See No. 20C2432 for prices on lenses suitable for this camera.

Camera Stands.

No. 20C2350 Camera Stand No. 0. Made of hardwood, with tilting top and automatic lock, by which top is raised or lowered. Top measures 11x19 inches. Can be taken apart or set up without tools. Price $2.80

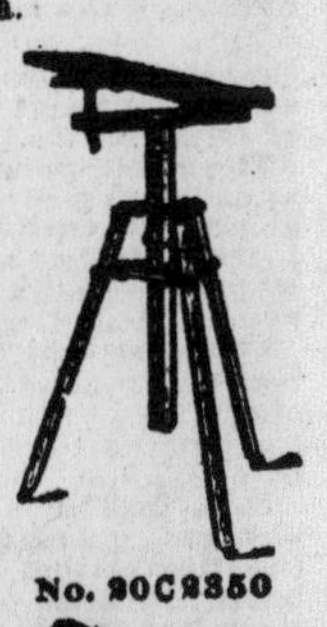

No. 20C2350

No. 20C2354

No. 20C2354 The Wizard Stand No. 7, a very solidly built stand, made of finely finished hardwood. Has automatic balancing device, which can be regulated to balance any camera from 10x12 down. Raises and lowers with the lightest touch, and is firmly locked in any position by lever at side. Very firm and rigid; our best stand. Size of top, 17x32½ inches; for cameras 10x12 or smaller.

Price $13.40

POSING CHAIR, $3.50.

No. 20C2370 Our Special Posing Chair, a neat and well made chair, seat and back of oak, pedestal of steel wire with antique copper finish. Seat can be raised and lowered, or placed in any position and held firmly by tightening knob under seat. Price $3.50

No. 20C2370

The Monarch Wide Angle Lens.

No. 20C2415 The Monarch Wide Angle Lens embraces an angle of 90 degrees, making it especially adapted to photographing the interiors of buildings, out of door views in confined situations; in fact, any work where it is difficult or impossible to get far enough away from the subject in order to get it all on the plate with an ordinary lens. **Our Monarch Wide Angle Lenses** are handsomely mounted in lacquered brass with a set of revolving diaphragms. Made expressly for us by the Bausch & Lomb Optical Company, and represents the latest advances in the making of lenses of this type. **The speed of this lens is F. 16.**

Size of View, Inches	Equivalent Focus, Inches	Back Focus, Inches	Diameter of Lenses, Inches	Diameter Across Hood, Inches	Price
4 x 5	3½	3¼	¾	1 9/32	$5.70
5 x 7	5¼	4⅜	¾	1 9/32	6.80
5 x 8	5½	5⅛	¾	1 9/32	7.10
6½ x 8½	6½	6 3/16	⅞	1 9/32	9.90
8 x 10	8	7½	1⅛	1 9/32	12.80

Seroco Rapid Rectilinear Lens.

No. 20C2421 The Seroco Rapid Rectilinear Lens, a double lens of the rapid rectilinear type, very handsomely mounted in lacquered brass with Waterhouse diaphragms. **This lens is perfectly rectilinear,** rendering the straight lines of buildings, or other subjects, absolutely without distortion, possesses a remarkable depth of focus and flatness of field, giving the most brilliant definition and detail. **This lens is unsurpassed for landscape work,** views of buildings, and other architectural subjects, flash lights, groups and instantaneous work. **Represents better value than any other lens on the market, and is superior in every respect to many lenses** sold at double the prices. In sizes 4x5 to 8x10 inches, inclusive, we furnish the Seroco Rapid Rectilinear Lens either with or without the Unicum Shutter. **The speed of this lens is F. 8.**

The Seroco Rapid Rectilinear Lens.

The Unicum Shutter.

The Unicum Shutter gives automatic exposures of 1 second, ½ second, ¼ second, 1/25 second or 1/100 second, with one pressure of the bulb. With indicator set to "B" a pressure of the bulb opens the shutter, which remains open until the pressure is released. With indicator set to "T" the first pressure of the bulb opens the shutter, which remains open until the bulb is again pressed. Back of the shutter blades is a perfect **Iris Diaphragm,** the opening being instantly adjustable to any desired size by the index lever at lower margin of shutter. **Accuracy and entire freedom from jarring are secured by a pneumatic retarding device,** and the actuating mechanism of the shutter is fully protected from injury or dust. Made from bronze metal, with nickel plated trimmings, very handsomely finished throughout.

The Seroco Rapid Rectilinear Lens with Unicum Shutter.

Size of View, Inches	Equivalent Focus, Inches	Back Focus Inches	Diameter Image Circle, Inches	Diameter of Lenses, Inches	Diameter Across Hood, Inches	Price of Lens Alone With Waterhouse Stops	Price of Lens Complete With Unicum Shutter
4 x 5	6¾	6	9	1	1½	$ 5.70	$ 8.50
5 x 7	8¾	7½	10½	1⅜	2 1/16	6.80	9.50
5 x 8	9¼	8	11	1⅜	2 1/16	7.10	11.25
6½ x 8½	12	10¼	13¼	1⅝	2 11/32	9.90	14.75
8 x 10	14¾	13	16	2	3	12.80	16.75
10 x 12	17	15	19½	2¼	3 9/16	17.50	Not Made
11 x 14	18½	16½	22½	2 9/16	4 1/16	26.32	Not Made
14 x 17	22½	20	26	2⅞	4 9/16	36.00	Not Made

The Seroco Extra Rapid Symmetrical Lens.

SPEED F. 6. THE QUICKEST RECTILINEAR LENS MADE.

No. 20C2430 The Seroco Extra Rapid Symmetrical Lens is particularly well suited to the most rapid instantaneous work and for use on dark, cloudy or misty days, where an ordinary lens would utterly fail. **Requires only one-half the exposure** that must be given with the ordinary rectilinear lens. **For all around work, including landscapes, general viewing, high speed instantaneous work, etc., the Seroco Extra Rapid Symmetrical lens offers advantages over any other existing type of lens on the market today.**

The Seroco Extra Rapid Symmetrical Lens with Iris diaphragm.

This lens is **perfectly rectilinear,** rendering the straight lines of buildings or other subjects absolutely without distortion, possesses **great depth of focus,** flatness of field **and brilliant definition.**

The great speed of this lens, almost equal to that of an ordinary portrait lens, makes it particularly desirable **for portrait work,** and for those who do not care to invest in both a rectilinear lens and a portrait lens, we can especially recommend the Seroco Extra Rapid Symmetrical Lens, **which will answer both requirements.**

Construction: This lens is composed of two systems, both the front and back systems each being composed of two lenses cemented together. Both front and rear combinations are perfectly corrected and either may be used alone when a greater focal length is desired.

It is provided with a finely adjusted Iris Diaphragm, operated by a small lever, as shown in the illustration, beautifully mounted in lacquered brass. In sizes 4x5 to 8x10 inclusive, we furnish these lenses either with or without the new Bausch & Lomb Automatic Shutter.

Seroco Extra Rapid Symmetrical Lens with Automatic Shutter.

Size of View, Inches	Equivalent Focus, Inches	Back Focus, Inches	Diameter Image Circle, Inches	Diameter of Lenses, Inches	Diameter Across Hood, Inches	Price of Lens Alone with Iris Diaphragm	Price of Lens Complete with Automatic Shutter
4 x 5	6⅜	5 9/16	8¾	1⅛	1 9/16	$15.68	$20.55
5 x 7	8	7	10¾	1½	1 13/32	20.10	24.75
6½ x 8½	9 7/16	8¼	12¾	1¾	1 21/32	25.12	29.62
8 x 10	11¼	9 13/16	15½	2⅛	2 11/32	32.40	36.60
10 x 12	14¼	12 7/16	19	2⅝	2⅞	41.92	Not Made
11 x 14	17½	15¼	24	3 5/16	3⅝	56.00	Not Made
14 x 17	22¾	19⅜	25¾	3¾	4⅛	72.52	Not Made

The 5x7 lens will cover a 5x8 plate sharply to extreme corners.

The new Bausch & Lomb Automatic Shutter, in general appearance and principles of operation closely resembles the Unicum, which we fully describe under No. 20C2421, but **it requires no setting,** as the mechanism is so constructed that it automatically resets itself after each exposure.

The Seroco Extra Rapid Portrait Lens.

SPEED, F. 4. THE QUICKEST LENS MADE.

No. 20C2440 At $48.00 we offer the 6½x8½ Seroco Extra Rapid Portrait Lens as the equal in every way of portrait lenses heretofore sold at several times our price. In quality of glass, perfection of finish, careful adjustment and fine workmanship; in softness, delicacy and depth of focus; in speed, flatness of field, and brilliancy of illumination; **the Seroco Extra Rapid Portrait Lens** is not equaled by any other portrait lens on the market, regardless of price or maker. **The Seroco Extra Rapid Portrait Lens** represents the very latest advances in scientific lens grinding, possessing all those peculiar optical qualities and special brilliancy of definition so necessary in high grade portrait work. **The Seroco Extra Rapid Portrait Lens** preserves that softness and roundness so essential in portrait making, even when stopped down, a quality possessed by no other portrait lens made, as all other lenses become distinctly wiry when a small diaphragm is employed. **We particularly invite comparison of the Seroco Extra Rapid Portrait Lens with any other portrait lens on the market regardless of price or maker,** as we know that in all these special points, whereby a portrait lens is judged, **the Seroco Extra Rapid Portrait Lens** is the best that money can buy.

CONSTRUCTION: The Seroco Extra Rapid Portrait Lens is composed of two systems, the elementary lenses of the front system being cemented together, while the elementary lenses of the back system are separated. The back system is mounted in an adjustable mounting, enabling the operator to vary the distance between these lenses, thus varying the depth of focus and quality of definition. Any desired degree of softness, roundness or distribution of focus can be obtained by thus varying the distance between the elementary lenses of the back system. A perfect Iris Diaphragm is provided with this lens, thus doing away entirely with loose stops to mislay or lose.

Number	Size of Plate Covered, inches	Diameter of Lenses, inches	Back Focus, inches	Diameter Across Hood, inches	Price
1	5 x 8	3 5/16	8½	4 9/16	$33.75
2	6½ x 8½	4 1/16	11½	5 9/16	48.00
3	8 x 10	4¼	13½	5 9/16	90.00

Distance required between subject and lens to make a standing figure 6 inches high of a person 6 feet tall is as follows: With the 5x8 size, 12 feet; with the 6½x8½ size, 17¼ feet; with the 8x10 size, 19 feet.

OUR TEN DAYS' FREE TRIAL OFFER.

WE SEND OUT

ANY OF OUR LENSES

with the understanding and agreement that you can keep the lens for ten days, during which time you can put it to any test. You can compare it with other lenses of the most celebrated makes, lenses costing two and three times the amount we ask you for our lens, and, if our lens does not prove equal to any lens with which it may be compared in depth of focus, covering power, definition in short, in all those qualities by which lenses are judged, you may send it back to us and we will refund your money, including the express charges both ways.

THE SEROCO PORTRAIT LENS.

SPEED F. 6.

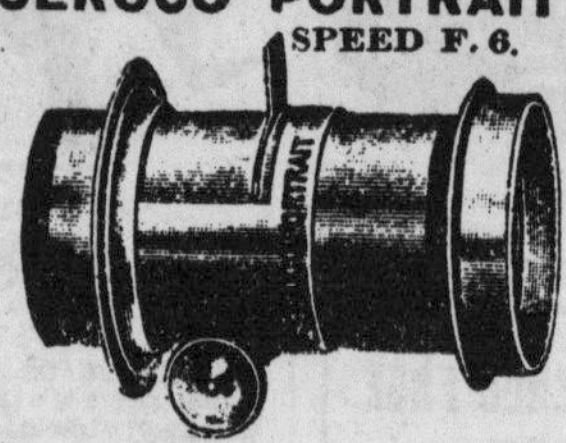

No. 20C2432 This lens possesses those peculiar optical qualities necessary in portrait work, working very rapidly and yielding soft, brilliant negatives. **The ¼-size is particularly suitable for penny picture work** and for small portraits. Many photographers purchase ordinary rectilinear lenses for penny picture work on account of the comparatively low price of such lenses as compared with regular portrait lenses, but in this lens we offer you an opportunity to equip your outfit with a lens designed and made expressly for portrait work, at a price even lower than the cost of a rectilinear lens. **The ½-size and 4-4 size are both designed for regular cabinet work** and of the two the 4-4 size is the most popular, as it can also be used for small groups and full figures.

CONSTRUCTION: The Seroco Portrait Lens is a double combination, the front system composed of two lenses cemented together, the rear system of two separated lenses, which is the true portrait method of construction. The lens tube is nickel plated and highly polished, the hood, flange and barrel of lacquered brass, and **a fine rack and pinion movement** is provided for accurate focusing, also a set of Waterhouse diaphragms in morocco case.

Size	Plate covered inches	Diameter lenses, inches	Back Focus, inches	Price
¼	3¼x4¼	1⅜	4½	$ 7.75
½	4¼x6½	2⅜	7	13.70
4-4	6½x8½	3¼	11	24.00

THE SEROCO VIEW CAMERA.

5 x 7 Outfit....	$23.00
6½x8½ Outfit...	28.95
8 x 10 Outfit....	32.25

MADE IN OUR FACTORY AT ROCHESTER.

Our special prices are actual factory cost, with only our one small profit added, less than corresponding trust cameras cost the largest dealers.

SPECIFICATIONS: SOLID MAHOGANY, PIANO FINISH; NICKEL PLATED METAL WORK; KERATOL BELLOWS; REVERSIBLE BACK; RACK AND PINION SLIDING FRONT, RACK AND PINION FOCUS MOVEMENT; RACK AND PINION DOUBLE SWING, CENTRALLY PIVOTED; BOTH FRONT AND BACK FOCUS; EXTRA LONG DRAW; THREE SECTION, DOUBLE GROOVED BED.

THE SEROCO VIEW CAMERA is the highest grade view camera made, combining convenience, strength, rigidity, compactness and adaptability for the widest possible range of work to a degree never before attained. We honestly believe the Seroco View Camera to be the best view camera made, regardless of price.

THE SEROCO VIEW CAMERA meets all requirements for the very best amateur or professional work. It is a camera that is elegant in appearance, a camera that will give you perfect results and a camera that you will enjoy using.

THE WOODWORK of the Seroco View Camera is solid mahogany throughout, thoroughly seasoned and highly polished.

THE METAL PARTS are all of nickel plated brass, highly finished, carefully and accurately adjusted.

FOCUSING may be accomplished by moving either the front or the back, both being operated by fine rack and pinion adjustment.

The Seroco View Camera with rear section of bed detached.

THE BACK is reversible and may be instantly changed to either upright or horizontal work.

THE DOUBLE SWING, which is pivoted at the center, is easily and quickly adjusted to any desired angle, both vertical and side swings being operated by fine rack and pinion movement

THE FRONT is adjustable, permitting a wide range of movement either above or below the center, operated by rack and pinion, and is securely clamped at any height by simply tightening a milled head screw.

THE BELLOWS is made from the best grade of keratol, lined with a special light proof gossamer cloth; elegant in appearance, absolutely light tight; strong and durable; the best bellows possible to make.

FOR WIDE ANGLE WORK the back may be racked close up to the front, thus permitting the use of the shortest focus lenses made, leaving no part of the bed in range of the lens.

THE BED is made in three sections, the front section hinged and arranged to fold back against the camera. The rear section is detachable, being necessary only when the extreme length of draw is used.

The Seroco View Camera Folded.

STRONG, RIGID, SUBSTANTIAL AND AT THE SAME TIME LIGHT AND COMPACT.

THE FOCAL CAPACITY of the Seroco View Camera constitutes a most important feature, the 5x7 size having a bellows length of 24 inches, the 6½x8½ size, 27 inches and the 8x10 size, 30½ inches.

The Seroco View Camera and Combination Tripod.

THE TRIPOD. We furnish with the Seroco View Camera a high grade Combination Tripod, a combined sliding and folding tripod with detachable head, made from selected ash, strong, substantial, absolutely rigid, the best tripod that can be made. This tripod is easily and quickly set up, readily adjusted to any desired height, and folds up so compactly that it can be put into the carrying case with the camera.

THE LENS AND SHUTTER. We equip the Seroco View Camera with either our Seroco Rapid Rectilinear Lens and Unicum Shutter (for prices see No. 20E2208 below), or with our Seroco Extra Rapid Symmetrical Lens and Automatic Shutter (for prices see No. 20E2209 below.) For illustrations and complete descriptions of these lenses and shutters we refer you to page 333.

THE CARRYING CASE. We put the Seroco View Camera in a fine carrying case, with compartments for containing the camera, the tripod, the lens and shutter and six extra plate holders. Compare the convenience of this outfit in which everything is contained in one easily carried case, with other outfits in which the case contains only the camera and about two holders, making it necessary to carry the lens and shutter, the tripod and the extra plate holders in separate packages.

The Carrying Case, with compartments for Camera, Lens and Shutter, Tripod and six Double Plate Holders.

FOR PRICES On these Cameras with ANASTIGMAT LENSES See Page 334.

COMPLETE DEVELOPING, FINISHING AND MATERIAL OUTFITS.

For the convenience of those who desire everything necessary for making, developing and finishing pictures, we put up special outfits suitable for use with the Seroco View Camera. These outfits contain the following complete list of apparatus and materials:

1 High Grade Metal Ruby Lamp with Oil Burner.
1 Compressed Fibre Tray for developing.
1 Compressed Fibre Tray for fixing.
1 Compressed Fibre Tray for toning.
1 Folding Negative Rack to hold 24 plates.
1 8-Ounce Cone Shaped Graduate.
1 Print Roller.
1 Heavy Printing Frame.
1 Paste Brush.
1 Fine Gossamer Focus Cloth.
1 Dozen Extra Rapid Roebuck Dry Plates.
1 Dozen Seroco Sensitized Paper.
25 Card Mounts.
1 Package Hydro-Metol Developing Powders (makes 24 ounces developer).
1 Package Toning and Fixing Powders (makes 24 ounces of Toner).
1 Pound Hypo-Sulphite of Soda.
1 Jar Photo Paste.
1 Copy "Complete Instructions in Photography."

FOR PRICES OF OUTFITS SEE No. 20E2211.

Order by Number.

PRICES:

No. 20E2208 The Seroco View Camera, complete with Seroco Rapid Rectilinear Lens, Unicum Shutter, Combination Tripod, one Double Plate Holder and Carrying Case.

Size, 5 x 7.	Price........... $23.00
Size, 6½ x 8½.	Price........... 28.95
Size, 8 x 10.	Price........... 32.25

No. 20E2209 The Seroco View Camera, complete with Seroco Extra Rapid Symmetrical Lens, Automatic Shutter, Combination Tripod, one Double Plate Holder and Carrying Case.

Size, 5 x 7.	Price........... $38.25
Size, 6½ x 8½.	Price........... 43.80
Size, 8 x 10.	Price........... 52.10

No. 20E2210 The Seroco View Camera, with Combination Tripod, one Double Plate Holder and Carrying Case, but **without Lens or Shutter.**

Size, 5 x 7.	Price........... $13.50
Size, 6½ x 8½.	Price........... 14.20
Size, 8 x 10.	Price........... 15.50

Extra Holders, 5x7, 60c each; 6½x8½, 79c each; 8x10, $1.10 each. See No. 20E2510

No. 20E2211 Developing, Finishing and Material Outfits, complete, just as described above and shown in the illustration on this page.

Outfit for 5 x 7 Camera....	$3.34
Outfit for 6½ x 8½ Camera....	3.86
Outfit for 8 x 10 Camera....	4.02

FILM CAMERAS.

No. 2 Buster Brown Film Camera, $1.65.

FOR PICTURES, 2¼x3¼.

No. 20E2236 THE No. 2 BUSTER BROWN CAMERA is a thoroughly reliable and practicable camera, although sold almost at the price of a toy. **This camera takes pictures 2¼ inches wide by 3¼ inches long,** and is suitable for making pictures of buildings, residences, street scenes, landscapes, pictures of animals, groups, portraits, interior views, etc. In fact it can be used for general all around work, just the same as higher priced cameras.

THE LENS is a first quality single achromatic, guaranteed to make good sharp pictures The shutter is of very simple construction, not liable to get out of order, and arranged for both time and instantaneous exposures.

THE No. 2 BUSTER BROWN CAMERA is made from thoroughly kiln dried wood, covered with imitation leather, carefully and accurately constructed, all metal parts nickel plated and finely finished.

THIS CAMERA USES FILM ONLY and the film comes in rolls of six exposures each.

Price..$1.65

If by mail, postage extra, 25 cents.

See No. 20E2970 for prices on films for Buster Brown cameras.

"COMPLETE INSTRUCTIONS IN PHOTOGRAPHY" FREE with the Buster Brown cameras. See page 325.

No. 20E2237 THE No. 1 BUSTER BROWN CAMERA, same style as the No. 2 described above, but smaller size. Takes pictures 2¼x2¼ inches

Price..85c

If by mail, postage extra, 20 cents.

No. 1 Ansco Film Camera, $4.10.

FOR PICTURES 3½x3½.

No. 20E2240 No. 1 ANSCO FILM CAMERA. This is a small, compact camera, thoroughly well made throughout, guaranteed to make perfect pictures and exceedingly simple of operation. It is covered with the best grade of seal grain morocco leather, fitted with first quality single achromatic lens of universal focus, with three diaphragms and automatic shutter, arranged for three speeds of instantaneous exposures or time exposures of any length.

THE CAMERA IS COMPLETE in itself, there are no loose parts to become broken or lost. Fitted with one brilliant finder and tripod socket, all metal parts nickel plated and polished. Price............$4.10

No. 20E2242 No. 2 ANSCO FILM CAMERA. Same style of construction as the No. 1, but of larger size, making **pictures 3¼x4¼ inches,** and fitted with two view finders and two tripod sockets, adapting the camera to either horizontal or vertical pictures. Weight of camera, 25 ounces. Size, 6⅞x4⅞x4⅜ inches. Price, complete............$4.95

No. 20E2243 No. 3 ANSCO FILM CAMERA. Same as No. 2 described above, but larger size, making **pictures 4x5 inches.** Price............$5.85

"COMPLETE INSTRUCTIONS IN PHOTOGRAPHY" FREE with the Ansco cameras. See page 325.

Nos. 6 and 7 Folding Pocket Ansco Film Cameras.

DAYLIGHT LOADING.

3¼x4¼, $13.25 **4x5, $16.25**

Nos. 6 AND 7 FOLDING POCKET ANSCO FILM CAMERAS. Perfect and complete film cameras in every respect, fitted with all the latest adjustments, highest grade workmanship throughout. These cameras are fitted with high grade double rapid rectilinear lenses, carefully selected and tested, and equipped with the new improved Wollensak automatic shutters with Iris diaphragms, making instantaneous exposures of various speeds, bulb exposures and time exposures.

THE Nos. 6 AND 7 FOLDING POCKET ANSCO FILM CAMERAS are made throughout from the finest selected mahogany; all metal parts, except the shutter, are nickel plated and highly polished, and the covering is the best grade of black seal grain morocco leather, genuine leather double extension bellows, fine rack and pinion focus movement, brilliant reversible finder, two tripod sockets, in short, all the latest improvements.

No. 20E2283 No. 6 Folding Pocket Ansco Film Camera, for 3¼x4¼ pictures. Price............$13.25

No. 20E2284 No. 7 Folding Pocket Ansco Film Camera, for 4x5 pictures. Price............$16.25

"COMPLETE INSTRUCTIONS IN PHOTOGRAPHY" FREE WITH THESE ANSCO CAMERAS. SEE PAGE 325.

THE REFLEX CAMERA.

LATEST 1906 MODEL.

WITH FOCAL PLANE SHUTTER FOR HIGH SPEED INSTANTANEOUS WORK.

REFLEX CAMERA OPEN FOR USE.

THE REFLEX CAMERA is the greatest camera in the world for high speed instantaneous work. It is made especially for

Photographing Race Horses at Full Speed, Athletic Work, Yacht Races, Birds and Animals, Football and Baseball Games, Street Scenes, Newspaper Work, etc.

THE REFLEX CAMERA IS USED BY NEWSPAPER MEN in getting **pictures for their papers, because it is the only camera that fully meets the exacting requirements in this line of work.** Newspaper men must make pictures when and where they are wanted, irrespective of light and weather conditions, irrespective of the time of day or night, and without regard to rapid movement on the part of the subject. **They must be able to make pictures under the most difficult conditions,** with poor light, with rapidly moving and changing scenes, hampered by the presence of big crowds, etc., and **the Reflex Camera is the only camera that fulfills all the conditions for this difficult class of work.**

THE REFLEX CAMERA is not only adapted to the difficult lines of work mentioned above, but at the same time is suitable for the every day needs of the amateur photographer, being capable of doing not only all work any ordinary camera does, but in addition it does the high speed, exacting work referred to above.

IN APPEARANCE the Reflex Camera is not unlike the ordinary box camera, and it is made throughout from the finest carefully selected kiln dried mahogany, covered with the very best grade of heavy morocco leather, and all metal work is finished in dead black, with nickel plated trimmings.

PRINCIPLE OF CONSTRUCTION. The great difference between the Reflex Camera and cameras of the ordinary style lies in the fact that a very fine optically perfect mirror is placed between the lens and the plate at such an angle that the image is reflected to **the ground glass which is located in the top of the camera. THIS ARRANGEMENT PERMITS THE OPERATOR TO SEE THE IMAGE ON THE GROUND GLASS RIGHT SIDE UP UNTIL THE VERY INSTANT OF EXPOSURE.** Focusing is accomplished by a milled screw conveniently located on the left hand side of the camera, **and the picture can be focused right up to the very instant of exposure.**

REFLEX CAMERA CLOSED.

THE ADVANTAGES of being able to focus and of seeing the image on the ground glass, right side up, until the very instant of exposure, will be readily appreciated by anyone who has ever tried to photograph rapidly moving objects. Remember, that the slide can be drawn from the plate holder before the camera is focused; you can insert the plate holder in the back of the camera, draw the slide, and then, **while actually looking at the picture on the ground glass,** you can move around with the camera, follow your moving object, watch it closely all the time on the ground glass, **changing the focus** as the distance between the camera and the subject is changed, until, when everything is just exactly right, the subject in just exactly the position you wish it, and the picture focused perfectly sharp, the button is pressed and **the picture is made just exactly as you saw it on the ground glass right up to the instant of exposure.**

THE SHUTTER with which the Reflex Camera is equipped is an extra high grade focal plane shutter, that is, a curtain shutter working at the back of the camera, directly across the face of the plate. This shutter makes instantaneous exposures of any desired length from ⅕ of a second up to the 1/1000 part of a second. **The speed** of this shutter is varied by changing the width of the slit in the curtain, and by changing the tension of the spring, both of which adjustments are made without opening the camera. **The shutter is set** from the outside by means of a large milled head screw, and the width of the slit in the shutter curtain is also adjusted by means of this same screw. The speed of the shutter is adjusted by means of a small lever, also located on the outside of the camera. **The focal plane shutter,** with which the Reflex Camera is equipped, is, without any exception, the simplest focal plane shutter made, the least liable to get out of order and the easiest to operate.

THE BACK OF THE REFLEX CAMERA is reversible and instantly detachable, making the camera available for either upright or horizontal pictures, and the plate holder can be inserted from either the right or left hand side of the camera, as desired

WE FURNISH THIS CAMERA WITHOUT LENS, or with any of our regular styles of lenses, as described in this catalogue. We recommend, however, that, in order to take full advantage of the special features of this camera, a lens of large aperture; that is, a very rapid working lens, be selected. We particularly recommend for use with this camera our Series II Busch Anastigmat Lens, which works at a speed of F 5.5, which will be found in practice amply sufficient for high speed work. Under favorable conditions as to light, for example, on a sunny day in the summer, exposures of 1/1000 part of a second, made with the Reflex Camera and the Series II Busch Anastigmat Lens, will give fully timed negatives. For athletic events, running races, pole vaulting, football games, etc., exposures varying from 1/300 to 1/800 of a second are usually found sufficiently short to produce a sharp picture.

REMEMBER that the Reflex Camera is always ready for instant action. With the ordinary camera it is necessary first to focus, then to set the shutter, insert the plate holder and draw the slide, and during the time elapsing while all this is being done the picture may change entirely, but with the Reflex Camera the plate holder is in place, the slide is drawn, the shutter is set, and **the operator sees the image on the ground glass and can focus right up to the very instant of pressing the button** to make the exposure. No time whatever elapses between the moment when the picture is seen on the ground glass and the exposure itself.

NO FOCUS CLOTH IS NECESSARY, as the ground glass is located in the top of the camera and entirely protected by a fine leather focusing hood. This hood is collapsible and folds compactly into the camera when not in use.

WHEN YOU ARE TAKING PICTURES with the Reflex Camera "there is nothing to watch but the ground glass."

REMEMBER that the prices we quote on the Reflex Camera are for the latest 1906 style, embodying all of the improvements which several years of practical experience have brought to the makers of this wonderful camera, making this camera not only the simplest but at the same time the most effective camera in the world.

YOU SHARE IN OUR PROFITS, as explained on the last pages.

PRICES ON THE 1906 MODEL REFLEX CAMERA.

No. 20E2225

EQUIPMENT	Size, 4x5	Size, 5x7	Size, 6½x8½
Camera with Focal Plane Shutter, but without Lens	$52.00	$60.00	$72.00
Camera complete, with Focal Plane Shutter and Seroco Rapid Rectilinear Lens, F 8.	57.60	66.65	81.75
Camera complete, with Focal Plane Shutter and Seroco Extra Rapid Symmetrical Lens, F 6	66.90	79.10	95.85
Camera complete, with Focal Plane Shutter and Busch Series II Anastigmat Lens, F 5.5	73.20	86.45	114.00
Camera complete, with Focal Plane Shutter and Busch Series III Anastigmat Lens, F 7.7	66.00	75.75	103.50
Camera complete, with Focal Plane Shutter and Seroco-Goerz Series II Anastigmat Lens, F 6.8	68.65	82.00	106.90

All above prices include one Double Plate Holder.

"COMPLETE INSTRUCTIONS IN PHOTOGRAPHY" FREE with the Reflex Camera. See page 325.

No. 20E2226 Extra Plate Holders for Reflex Camera. Price, each, 4x5, 75c; 5x7, 94c; 6½x8½, $1.20

WRITE FOR FREE SAMPLE BOOK No. 89, MEN'S READY MADE CLOTHING. OVER 100 SAMPLES.

MODEL VI CONLEY FOLDING CAMERA $6.95

A REMARKABLY GOOD CAMERA AT A VERY LOW PRICE

SPECIFICATIONS.

Woodwork—Solid mahogany, corners dovetailed and rounded, with fine hand rubbed piano finish.
Metal Parts—Brass, nickel plated and highly polished.
Covering—Genuine leather with walrus grain.
Bellows—Red Russia leather, gossamer lined. Capacity, 8¾ inches.
Back — Non - reversible, with spring actuated ground glass focusing screen and hinged leather covered wooden back panel.
Focus Movement — Rack and pinion.
Front—All metal, nickel plated, with rising and falling adjustment.
Front Clamp—Conley automatic.
Finder—Brilliant, reversible.
Shutter—Wollensak Senior, with both bulb and finger release, automatic.
Lens — Rapid rectilinear (double), speed F.11 (U. S. 8); focal length, 6¼ inches.
Plate Holder—Conley flexible valve.
Carrying Case—Optional, keratol covered, solid sole leather, or none at all, according to price.
Dimensions—Closed, 5⅞x6¼x2 inches.

IN MANUFACTURING this camera the Conley Company use only the very highest grade materials, the exact same style and quality of materials that are employed in their very highest grade cameras. The best quality of carefully selected, thoroughly seasoned, kiln dried mahogany is used for all of the woodwork, and the covering is a fine quality of genuine leather. The bellows is made from the best red Russia leather, lined with lightproof black gossamer cloth. All metal parts are brass, nickel plated and highly polished. The workmanship is in every way high class, these cameras being put up by the same workmen who put up our highest priced instruments.

ADJUSTMENTS AND SPECIAL FEATURES. This camera is made with rack and pinion focus movement and the Conley automatic front clamp, the most satisfactory and convenient front clamp ever devised. The front is constructed entirely of brass, nickel plated and highly polished, and is made with rising and falling adjustment for regulating the relative amounts of sky and foreground. It is equipped with an extra quality reversible brilliant view finder, nickel plated piano hinge, ornamental side arms, strong leather handle and spring actuated ground glass focusing screen protected by leather covered mahogany back panel. It is equipped with a double rapid rectilinear lens guaranteed to cover the entire plate to the extreme corners and produces an unusually clear cut and snappy negative. The Wollensak Senior Automatic Shutter is a very durable form of shutter, arranged for instantaneous exposures and bulb or time exposures of any desired length, a shutter that is easy of adjustment, smooth working parts and entirely automatic.

No. 20T310 Model VI Conley Folding Camera, complete with lens and shutter as described, one plate holder and "Complete Instructions in Photography." (Without carrying case.) Shipping weight, 3½ pounds. Price....................**$6.95**

No. 20T311 Keratol Carrying Case for Model VI Conley Folding Camera. Contains space for camera and four plate holders. Shipping weight, 2½ pounds. Price....................**57c**

No. 20T312 Leather Carrying Case for Model VI Conley Folding Camera. Contains space for camera and four holders. Shipping weight, 2½ pounds. Price....................**$1.60**
Shipping weight, camera and carrying case together, 4¾ pounds.

MODEL VIII CONLEY FOLDING CAMERA $8.00

$8.00 FOR THE 4x5 SIZE.
$9.55 FOR THE 5x7 SIZE.

SPECIFICATIONS.

Woodwork—Solid mahogany, rounded and dovetailed corners, hand rubbed piano finish.
Metal Parts—Brass, nickel plated and highly polished.
Covering—Genuine seal grain leather.
Bellows—Best red Russia leather, gossamer lined.
Back—Non-reversible, with spring actuated ground glass and hinged back panel.
Front—All metal, with rising and falling adjustment.
Front Clamp—Conley automatic.
Finder—Ground glass and mirror type, reversible.
Shutter—Conley Junior Automatic, pneumatic release.
Lens—Double rectilinear, working at F.11 (U. S. 8).
Plate Holder—Conley improved flexible valve.
Carrying Case—Solid sole leather, with space for camera and extra holders.
Dimensions—4x5 size, focal capacity, 6¾ inches; camera closed, 2½x5¼x6¼ inches; carrying case, 3x6¾x11 inches; capacity of carrying case, camera and four holders, 5x7 size, focal capacity, 8 inches; camera closed, 2¾x6⅞x8½ inches; carrying case, 3¼x8⅞x13½ inches; capacity of carrying case, camera and five holders.

THE MODEL VIII CONLEY CAMERA is cheap in price only. It is made just as good as the manufacturers know how. They put good materials into it all the way through, good mahogany, good leather and good workmanship. The parts of the Model VIII Conley Folding Camera are made by the same mechanics who make the parts for our highest priced cameras. They are assembled, put together and finished by exactly the same workmen that are employed on our highest grade long focus and double extension cameras, and throughout the factory these cameras receive exactly the same painstaking care, the same rigid inspection and the same strict attention to the smallest details of construction.

LENS AND SHUTTER. This camera is equipped with a double rapid rectilinear lens working at F.11, which is ample speed for making instantaneous exposures except under very unfavorable conditions. This lens covers the plate sharply to the extreme corners, even with full aperture, and yields a sharp, clear cut and snappy negative. The shutter is the new Conley Junior Automatic with pump and valve completely enclosed within the case.

ADJUSTMENTS. This camera is made with rising and falling front, Conley automatic front clamp, spring actuated ground glass focusing screen protected by leather covered, hinged, mahogany back panel, reversible view finder, an accurately adjusted focus scale and two tripod sockets.

No. 20T350 Model VIII Conley Camera, complete with lens and shutter as described, one plate holder and "Complete Instructions in Photography." (Carrying case not included.) **State size wanted.**
Size, 4x5. Shipping weight, 2¾ pounds. Price....................**$8.00**
Size, 5x7. Shipping weight, 4¾ pounds. Price....................**9.55**

No. 20T351 Keratol Carrying Cases for Model VIII Conley Cameras. The 4x5 size takes the camera and four plate holders, the 5x7 size the camera and five plate holders. **State size wanted.**
Size, 4x5. Price..........**60c** Size, 5x7. Price..........**85c**

No. 20T352 Leather Carrying Cases for Model VIII Conley Cameras. Same sizes as the keratol cases quoted above. **Mention size.**
Size, 4x5. Price..........**$1.60** Size, 5x7. Price..........**$2.45**
Shipping weights of cameras and carrying case together: 4x5 size, 5½ pounds; 5x7 size, 8 pounds.

STEREOSCOPIC PHOTOGRAPHY

STEREOSCOPIC PHOTOGRAPHY is intensely interesting, as no picture is more fascinating than a stereoscopic photograph, but many photographers have a mistaken idea that stereoscopic pictures are difficult to make. As an actual matter of fact, they are just as easy to make as any other photograph, provided one is equipped with the proper apparatus. Anyone who can operate a camera of any kind can operate a stereoscopic camera and can make high class stereoscopic pictures.

A STEREOSCOPIC VIEW seen through the stereoscope brings the original scene before us in a way that seems like magic, so wonderful is the effect of distance, depth, relief and solidity. The marvelously true to life appearance, everything seemingly full life size; the wonderful detail, the perspective, the figures springing up in the foreground as distinct and real as if actually living, make the stereoscopic view a most delightful entertainer. Seen for the first time, the effect is almost startling, and yet the making of these wonderfully lifelike pictures is just as simple as the making of ordinary single photographs.

AS A MONEY MAKING PROPOSITION a stereoscopic camera presents special advantages, as there are people everywhere who would like stereo views of their own home and surroundings and who will pay good prices for such pictures. The opportunity to do this profitable work is open to every photographer, both professional and amateur, and a good stereoscopic camera is almost certain to prove a profitable investment, as well as a source of great pleasure.

MODEL XVII CONLEY STEREOSCOPIC CAMERA AND STEREOSCOPE $4.95

SPECIFICATIONS.

Lenses—Perfectly matched, single achromatic, universal focus.
Shutter—Conley special, automatic, finger release, time and instantaneous.
View Finder—Ground glass and mirror type.
Covering—Seal grain keratol.
Metal Parts—Brass, nickel plated.
Plate Holder—Conley flexible valve, 4¼x6½.
Dimensions—5½x5⅞x8 in.
Weight—33 ounces.

THE MODEL XVII CONLEY STEREO CAMERA AT $4.95, a mere fraction of the price at which stereoscopic cameras have heretofore been sold, is perfectly designed, well made and capable of making perfect stereoscopic views. This camera uses 4¼x6½ plates, thus making full size stereoscopic views, the exact same style, size and quality of views that you see offered for sale by canvassers at $2.00 or more per dozen.

No. 20T410 Model XVII Conley Stereo Camera, complete with one 4¼x6½ plate holder, hardwood stereoscope and "Complete Instructions in Photography." Shipping weight, 3½ pounds. Price....................**$4.95**

MODEL XVIII CONLEY STEREOSCOPIC CAMERA WITH ALUMINUM HOOD STEREOSCOPE $18.00

SPECIFICATIONS.

Woodwork—All solid mahogany, dovetailed corners, piano finish.
Metal Parts—Brass, heavily nickel plated.
Covering—Genuine leather, walrus grain.
Bellows—Best red Russia leather, gossamer lined.
Focus Movement—Rack and pinion.
Lens Board—Detachable.
Front—Mahogany, with rising and falling movement.
Front Clamp—Conley automatic.
Finder—Ground glass, brass bound.
Shutter—Wollensak Senior, automatic.
Lenses—High grade rapid rectilinear, F.11.
Septum—Folding and removable.
Plate Holder—Conley flexible valve, 5x7.
Carrying Case—Keratol covered, with space for camera and five plate holders.
Dimensions—Camera, closed, 3¾x6⅝x8½ inches. Carrying case, 4½x9x13½ inches.

IN THIS CAMERA we use only the best materials, selected mahogany for the woodwork, genuine leather for the covering, every part made with the utmost care, and the entire camera assembled and put together in the most accurate manner. It is made with rack and pinion focus movement, Conley automatic front clamp, rising and falling front, detachable lens board and special folding septum.

Prices quoted for this camera include one 5x7 plate holder, keratol case with space for camera holder and five plate holders, and aluminum hood stereoscope.

No. 20T415 Model XVIII Conley Stereoscopic Camera, without lenses or shutter. Shipping weight, 7 pounds. Price....................**$9.55**

No. 20T416 Model XVIII Conley Stereoscopic Camera, complete with regular equipment as described above, Rapid Rectilinear F.11 Stereoscopic Lenses and Wollensak Senior Stereoscopic Shutter. Shipping weight, 7½ pounds. Price....................**$18.00**

No. 20T417 5x7 F.11 Rapid Rectilinear Lens and Conley Safety Shutter. We furnish this 5x7 lens and shutter complete mounted on lens board for the Model XVIII Camera, making it interchangeable with the regular stereoscopic lenses. Price....................**$4.15**
If mail shipment, postage extra, 10 cents.

MODEL XIX CONLEY STEREOSCOPIC CAMERA AND ALUMINUM HOOD STEREOSCOPE $29.60

SPECIFICATIONS.

Woodwork—All solid mahogany, dovetailed corners, piano finish.
Metal Parts—Brass, heavily nickel plated and highly polished.
Covering—Extra quality genuine leather.
Bellows—Genuine leather, gossamer lined.
Back—Reversible, with single button release and improved swing.
Focus Movement—Rack and pinion.
Lens Board—Detachable, instantly removed or replaced.
Front—Mahogany, with both vertical and horizontal movements.
Front Clamp—Conley automatic.
Finder—Brilliant, hooded.
Auxiliary Bed—All metal, nickel plated, for using wide angle lens.
Shutter—Wollensak Regular, double valve stereoscopic.
Lenses—High grade, stereoscopic, double symmetrical.
Septum—Improved spring roller curtain.
Plate Holder—Conley 5x7 flexible valve. for camera and six plate holders.
Dimensions — Camera closed, 4⅛x8¾x8¾ inches; focal capacity, 16 inches; carrying case, 4½x9x16¼ inches.

COMPLETE IN EVERY DETAIL. The Model XIX Conley Stereoscopic Camera is absolutely complete in every detail, equipped with every adjustment and every improvement that has in any way been found useful in stereoscopic photography. This camera is made with the latest improved automatic spring roller septum, which rolls up or unrolls automatically as the camera front is extended, mahogany front with both rising and falling adjustment and side shift, detachable lens board, rack and pinion focus movement, reversible back and brilliant hooded finder. The woodwork throughout is solid mahogany, beautifully finished; the covering is extra quality genuine leather; all metal parts are of brass, nickel plated and highly polished.

No. 20T422 Model XIX Conley Stereoscopic Camera, without lenses or shutter. Shipping weight, 15 pounds. Price....................**$15.10**

No. 20T423 Model XIX Conley Stereoscopic Camera, complete with regular equipment as described above, Double Symmetrical F.8 Stereoscopic Lenses and Wollensak Regular Stereoscopic Shutter. Shipping weight, 16 pounds. Price....................**$29.60**

No. 20T424 Model XIX Conley Stereoscopic Camera, complete with special equipment, Series V Anastigmat Lenses of 5-inch focus and Wollensak Regular Stereoscopic Shutter. Price....................**$61.95**

Prices quoted for the Model XIX Conley Stereoscopic Camera include one 5x7 plate holder, leather carrying case with space for camera and six holders and fine aluminum hood stereoscope.

No. 20T425 Conley Rapid Orthographic F.8 Lens for 5x7 pictures. We furnish this lens complete with Conley Safety Shutter, mounted on front board to fit the Model XIX Conley Stereoscopic Camera, and interchangeable with the stereoscopic lenses. Price.....**$5.20**
If mail shipment, postage extra, 12 cents.

ALL OF OUR CAMERAS are more fully and completely described in our special CAMERA CATALOG which we will be glad to send you free of any charge. In this special catalog we show large illustrations of every camera, both open and closed and in various positions to show the adjustments and all the special features of construction.

The illustrations in this special Camera Catalog are exact halftone reproductions of original photographs of the cameras, and will give you as clear an idea of the Conley Cameras as could be gained by an actual examination of the cameras themselves.

INDEX, PINK PAGES 552 TO 559, TO FIND WHAT YOU WANT.

POST CARD MAGIC LANTERN OUTFIT $2.98

WITH 50 COLORED POST CARDS

OUR NEW POST CARD MAGIC LANTERN is the most marvelously ingenious and at the same time the simplest and most entertaining magic lantern ever made. It is something entirely new in magic lanterns, and you can delight and amuse your friends for hours at a time with this wonderful machine. Unlike the ordinary magic lantern, it does not require glass slides or prepared pictures of any kind, but will reproduce upon the screen, enlarged to three or four feet in size and showing all of the beautiful, natural colors, any post card, photograph, stereoscopic view, newspaper or magazine clipping; in fact, almost any kind of picture that you want to use.

POST CARDS HAVE BECOME SO POPULAR and there have been so many beautiful and interesting styles designed that we have made up several special assortments of colored post cards, all of which have been carefully selected for use with the post card magic lantern, and we include 50 of these post cards with every outfit. Many of your friends have post cards which they will be glad to loan you, or you can use photographs of any kind or illustrations clipped from magazines or newspapers. You can astonish your friends by showing their own photographs on the screen, enlarged to many times its actual size. You can show a watch on the screen, with the case open, and can easily see every movement of the works, while it is enlarged to a wonderful size. By placing your face at the picture opening, you can startle your friends by reproducing your own picture on the screen, laughing and talking in a most natural and amusing manner while you appear before them enlarged to an enormous size. There is hardly any limit to the surprising things that can be done with this wonderful and marvelous machine.

COLORED POST CARDS FOR MAGIC LANTERN.

No. 20L2920 50 Comic Post Cards, all in colors. Price, per set of 50..........20c

No. 20L2921 50 Travel Post Cards, all in colors, including pictures from every part of the world; also many beautiful landscape views. Price, per set of 50..........20c

No. 20L2922 50 Miscellaneous Post Cards, all in colors; a variety of beautiful scenes, including many reproductions of famous paintings. Price, per set of 50..........20c

If by mail, postage extra, on 50 post cards, 10 cents.

NOTE—See page 277 for description of our complete line of high grade post cards. Don't fail to read over the big list before ordering.

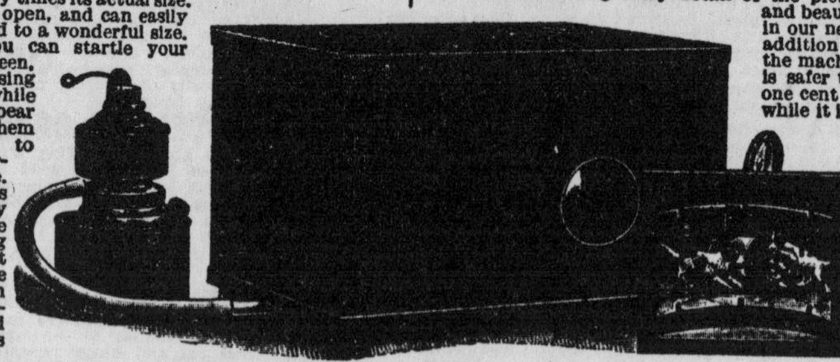

and magnificent coloring. These views have full descriptions printed on the back, so that you can make up a regular lecture on any of the interesting subjects. With the "Around the World" set, you can take your friends for a trip all around the world, showing them the historical and interesting sights of every country. Or with the "San Francisco Earthquake" views, you can visit the scene of this great disaster and spend hours among the hot and smoking ruins. The "Holy Land" set, the "St. Louis World's Fair," "Comic," and others of these big sets offer wonderful opportunities for anyone to make up a most interesting and delightful evening entertainment with the aid of this marvelous machine.

WE CAN FURNISH THIS MACHINE with the acetylene gas making outfit or we can fit the machine with regular Welsbach gas burners for use with city gas. The acetylene gas will give a powerful white light upon the screen, showing every detail of the picture and bringing out the colors with a brilliancy and beauty that is absolutely astonishing. The gas is made in our new safety carbide generator which requires only the addition of a few spoonfuls of carbide and a little water and the machine is instantly ready for use. The acetylene gas is safer to use than kerosene or coal oil and costs less than one cent for a full evening's entertainment. The city gas, while it is a little more convenient to use, does not give any brighter or more powerful light than the acetylene gas, and its only advantage is that you do not have to make your own gas. By city gas, we mean the gas which is made at a big city gas plant and piped underneath the street to the houses where it passes through a meter and is used in regular gas light fixtures. If you have these gas fixtures in your house and use gas for lighting or cooking purposes, we can fit the Post Card Magic Lantern with regular gas burners and Welsbach mantles, so that you can attach the machine to any gas jet with the rubber tubing and use the city gas in your machine.

EACH MACHINE has two burners, whether for acetylene gas or for city gas, so as to give the greatest amount of illumination, and this is still further increased by the extra large, highly polished reflectors. The machine is well made throughout; simple in design and substantial in construction, so as to fulfill every requirement of the home. It is so simple that it cannot get out of adjustment, and so easy to use that any boy or girl can operate it. Many interesting entertainments can be given with this wonderful machine, and the money made will more than repay the cost of the complete outfit, while the fun of advertising the show, selling the tickets and giving the exhibition will be worth many times the cost of the whole investment.

STEREOSCOPIC VIEWS CAN BE SHOWN in this magic lantern. We furnish a complete line of beautifully colored stereoscopic views (all of which are fully described on pages 282 to 286 of this catalogue) which can be shown upon the screen in all their wonderful beauty

No. 20L2915 Post Card Magic Lantern, complete with acetylene gas making outfit, two full size burners and extra large, highly polished reflectors, including 50 beautiful colored post cards. Shipping weight, 15 pounds. Price..........$3.98

NOTE—We do not furnish carbide for use in the acetylene generator. You will have to buy this carbide in your own city. It can usually be obtained at any store at a cost of a very few cents a pound. A pound package will last for many entertainments and should always be kept in tight cans.

No. 20L2916 Post Card Magic Lantern, complete with two extra large burners, Welsbach gas mantles and polished reflectors for use with city gas, including 50 beautiful colored post cards. Shipping weight, 15 pounds. Price..........$2.98

$4.65 BUYS THIS FULL SIZE BUCKEYE STEREOPTICON

USES REGULAR PROFESSIONAL SIZE LANTERN SLIDES, 3¼x4 INCHES.

THE BUCKEYE STEREOPTICON is a thoroughly efficient and practical stereopticon, using regular professional size lantern slides, 3¼x4 inches, and can be used for giving home entertainments and also for public exhibitions in small theaters, lodge halls, churches, school houses, etc. It is the only practical stereopticon ever made, which uses the regular size lantern slide, 3¼x4 inches, and which is sold at such an extremely low price as to place it within the reach of everyone. It will enlarge the picture on the screen up to 6 feet in size, with every detail as clear and sharp as other stereopticons costing many times as much.

WE FURNISH COMPLETE LECTURE SETS, containing twelve transparent lantern slides, regular professional size, 3¼x4 inches, with descriptive reading, printed and bound in book form, which can be read or recited while the pictures are shown on the screen, thus making a most interesting and delightful entertainment. These lecture sets are fully described on the lower part of this page.

YOU CAN GIVE PUBLIC ENTERTAINMENTS with the Buckeye Stereopticon, and make the entire cost of your outfit back in the profits of your exhibitions. For use in the school room this stereopticon fills every requirement. For the church and Sunday school it will give the very best of satisfaction. For lodges it will make the degree work and initiation ceremonies more interesting and impressive than ever. For those who make their own lantern slides this stereopticon offers every possible advantage and at a price less than one-fifth that charged for other stereopticons.

ELECTRIC, CITY GAS OR COAL OIL LIGHT. We can equip the Buckeye Stereopticon for use with either electric light, city gas, or ordinary coal oil or kerosene. If there is an electric light plant in your city, and the wires are run to the place where you want to use the stereopticon, you can order the stereopticon equipped for electric light, and we will fit it with an incandescent lamp, wire and socket, so that you can attach the machine right to the electric light fixtures in the room. If there is a gas plant in your city, and your house is piped for using the gas and has gas fixtures already put up in the room, then you can order the machine equipped for use with city gas, and we will fit it with a gas burner, Welsbach mantle and rubber tubing, so that you can attach the machine right to the gas jet. If there is no electric light and no gas plant in your city then you will have to use the coal oil or kerosene light, and we will fit your machine with a good two-wick oil lamp with extra large powerful reflector, so that you will have plenty of light for your work.

No. 20L2925 Buckeye Stereopticon Outfit with one dozen colored stereopticon slides, 3¼x4 inches, fitted with 50-candle power incandescent electric bulb, connecting wire and attachment plug. Price..........$4.65

NOTE—In ordering the electric light equipment be sure to state plainly the voltage of the current in your city. The voltage is usually 110 or 220, and you can easily find this out by asking the local electrician. Be sure to state this in your letter as we always send lamp for 110 volts unless otherwise ordered.

No. 20L2926 Buckeye Stereopticon Outfit with one dozen colored stereopticon slides, 3¼x4 inches, fitted with city gas burner, Welsbach mantle and rubber tubing for connecting to regular gas jet. Price..........$4.65

No. 20L2927 Buckeye Stereopticon Outfit with one dozen colored stereopticon slides, 3¼x4 inches, fitted with two-wick oil lamp for using coal oil or ordinary kerosene. Shipping weight of any Buckeye Stereopticon Outfit, 12 pounds. Price..........$4.65

THE HOME MAGIC LANTERN OUTFIT 48c

The Complete Home Magic Lantern Outfit contains handsome black enameled metal lantern, beautifully decorated in gilt and mounted on wood base board, twenty-five large advertising posters, twenty-five admission tickets and also six or twelve colored slides, according to price of outfit selected, with three to four pictures on each slide. The lenses are of good quality, clear optical glass and the lamp is made to burn either ordinary kerosene or coal oil. A good lantern for home entertainments.

No. 20L2805 Home Magic Lantern Outfit No. 1, complete as above described, with six colored slides, 1 3-16 inches wide, magnifying pictures to one foot in diameter. Price..........48c If by mail, postage extra, 24 cents.

No. 20L2808 Home Magic Lantern Outfit No. 2, same as No. 20L2805, but with twelve colored slides, 1 9-16 inches wide magnifying pictures to two feet in diameter. Price, complete........(If by mail, postage extra, 52 cents.)..........$1.25

No. 20L2811 Home Magic Lantern Outfit No. 3, same as No. 20L2805, but with twelve colored slides, 2 inches wide, magnifying pictures to three feet diameter. Shipping weight, 4½ pounds. Price, complete..........$1.89

No. 20L2865 Extra Chimney to fit any size Home Magic Lantern. Price, each, 10c

No. 20L2866 Extra Wicks to fit any size Home Magic Lantern. Price, 6 for 5c

NOTE—When ordering chimneys or wicks, be sure to state which size lantern they are to fit.

EXTRA SLIDES FOR HOME LANTERN.

No. 20L2841 Highly colored slides put up in packages containing one dozen assorted comic and scenic views. Each slide has three to four pictures. We cannot sell less than one dozen slides, and are unable to furnish special subjects.

Width, inches	Price, per pkg. of 1 dozen	If by mail, postage extra	Width, inches	Price, per pkg. of 1 dozen	If by mail, postage extra
1 3-16	20c	9c	2	$0.64	23c
1⅜	30c	12c	2⅜	.85	31c
1 9-16	36c	18c	2¾	1.11	38c
1¾	51c	21c			

PHOTOGRAPHIC SLIDES FOR HOME LANTERN.

No. 20L2848 Real photographic slides with four genuine photographs on each slide. Each set contains twelve slides or forty-eight views. We include printed lecture with every set, which fully describes each view. We cannot sell less than complete sets.

Spanish-American War, 48 views.
Russian-Japanese War, 48 views.
St. Louis Exposition, 48 views.
San Francisco Earthquake, 48 views.
Bible Pictures, 48 views.

Width, inches	Price, per set, with lecture	If by mail, postage extra
1 9-16	$1.13	20c
2	1.35	26c
2⅜	2.48	38c
2¾	2.93	44c

COLORED SLIDES FOR BUCKEYE STEREOPTICON.

These slides are brilliantly colored and all full professional size, 3¼X4 inches, and each set comes complete with printed lecture fully describing each view.

No. 20L2930 Lion Hunter Set, 12 slides with lecture.
No. 20L2931 Indian Warfare Set, 12 slides with lecture.
No. 20L2932 Robinson Crusoe Set, 12 slides with lecture.
No. 20L2933 Paul and Virginia, 12 slides with lecture.
No. 20L2934 American History, 12 slides with lecture.

Price of any of the above sets, Nos. 20L2930 to 20L2934, inclusive..(If by mail, postage extra, per set, 22 cents.)..79c

PHOTOGRAPHIC SLIDES FOR BUCKEYE STEREOPTICON.

These genuine photographic slides are the highest grade lantern slides made. They are the regular professional size, 3¼x4 inches, uncolored, and are exactly the same size, style and quality used by professional exhibitors. With each set we include a printed lecture in book form.

No. 20L2940 Japan Set, 12 slides with lecture.
No. 20L2941 India Set, 12 slides with lecture.
No. 20L2942 Germany Set, 12 slides with lecture.
No. 20L2943 Yellowstone Park Set, 12 slides with lecture.
No. 20L2944 Niagara Falls Set, 12 slides with lecture.

Price, per set, Nos. 20L2940 to 20L2944, inclusive ..(Postage extra, per set, 25c.)... $2.35

STEREOSCOPIC VIEW DEPARTMENT

A TALK WITH OUR BUYER ABOUT QUALITY

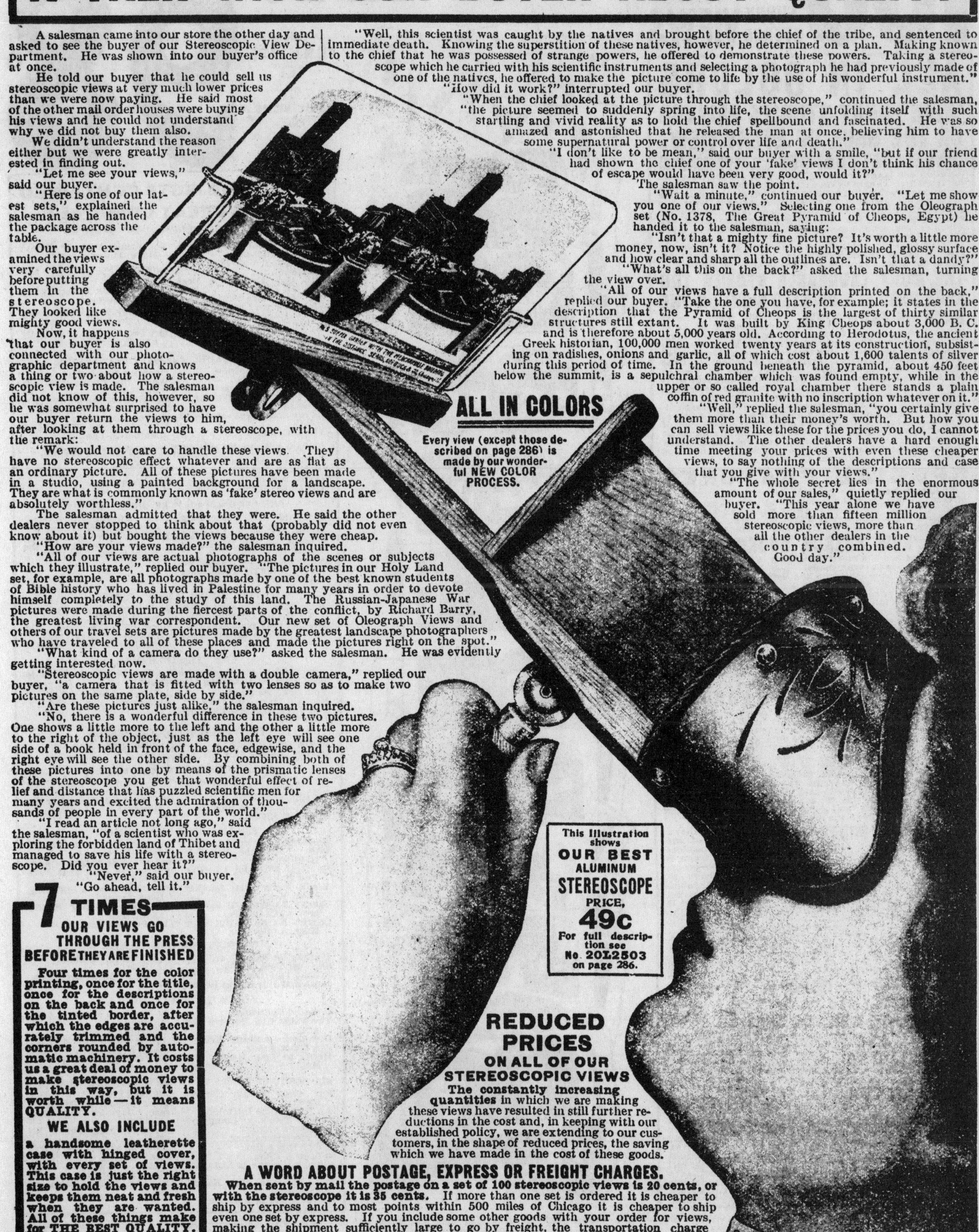

A salesman came into our store the other day and asked to see the buyer of our Stereoscopic View Department. He was shown into our buyer's office at once.

He told our buyer that he could sell us stereoscopic views at very much lower prices than we were now paying. He said most of the other mail order houses were buying his views and he could not understand why we did not buy them also.

We didn't understand the reason either but we were greatly interested in finding out.

"Let me see your views," said our buyer.

"Here is one of our latest sets," explained the salesman as he handed the package across the table.

Our buyer examined the views very carefully before putting them in the stereoscope. They looked like mighty good views.

Now, it happens that our buyer is also connected with our photographic department and knows a thing or two about how a stereoscopic view is made. The salesman did not know of this, however, so he was somewhat surprised to have our buyer return the views to him, after looking at them through a stereoscope, with the remark:

"We would not care to handle these views. They have no stereoscopic effect whatever and are as flat as an ordinary picture. All of these pictures have been made in a studio, using a painted background for a landscape. They are what is commonly known as 'fake' stereo views and are absolutely worthless."

The salesman admitted that they were. He said the other dealers never stopped to think about that (probably did not even know about it) but bought the views because they were cheap.

"How are your views made?" the salesman inquired.

"All of our views are actual photographs of the scenes or subjects which they illustrate," replied our buyer. "The pictures in our Holy Land set, for example, are all photographs made by one of the best known students of Bible history who has lived in Palestine for many years in order to devote himself completely to the study of this land. The Russian-Japanese War pictures were made during the fiercest parts of the conflict, by Richard Barry, the greatest living war correspondent. Our new set of Oleograph Views and others of our travel sets are pictures made by the greatest landscape photographers who have traveled to all of these places and made the pictures right on the spot."

"What kind of a camera do they use?" asked the salesman. He was evidently getting interested now.

"Stereoscopic views are made with a double camera," replied our buyer, "a camera that is fitted with two lenses so as to make two pictures on the same plate, side by side."

"Are these pictures just alike," the salesman inquired.

"No, there is a wonderful difference in these two pictures. One shows a little more to the left and the other a little more to the right of the object, just as the left eye will see one side of a book held in front of the face, edgewise, and the right eye will see the other side. By combining both of these pictures into one by means of the prismatic lenses of the stereoscope you get that wonderful effect of relief and distance that has puzzled scientific men for many years and excited the admiration of thousands of people in every part of the world."

"I read an article not long ago," said the salesman, "of a scientist who was exploring the forbidden land of Thibet and managed to save his life with a stereoscope. Did you ever hear it?"

"Never," said our buyer. "Go ahead, tell it."

"Well, this scientist was caught by the natives and brought before the chief of the tribe, and sentenced to immediate death. Knowing the superstition of these natives, however, he determined on a plan. Making known to the chief that he was possessed of strange powers, he offered to demonstrate these powers. Taking a stereoscope which he carried with his scientific instruments and selecting a photograph he had previously made of one of the natives, he offered to make the picture come to life by the use of his wonderful instrument."

"How did it work?" interrupted our buyer.

"When the chief looked at the picture through the stereoscope," continued the salesman, "the picture seemed to suddenly spring into life, the scene unfolding itself with such startling and vivid reality as to hold the chief spellbound and fascinated. He was so amazed and astonished that he released the man at once, believing him to have some supernatural power or control over life and death."

"I don't like to be mean," said our buyer with a smile, "but if our friend had shown the chief one of your 'fake' views I don't think his chance of escape would have been very good, would it?"

The salesman saw the point.

"Wait a minute," continued our buyer. "Let me show you one of our views." Selecting one from the Oleograph set (No. 1378, The Great Pyramid of Cheops, Egypt) he handed it to the salesman, saying:

"Isn't that a mighty fine picture? It's worth a little more money, now, isn't it? Notice the highly polished, glossy surface and how clear and sharp all the outlines are. Isn't that a dandy?"

"What's all this on the back?" asked the salesman, turning the view over.

"All of our views have a full description printed on the back," replied our buyer. "Take the one you have, for example; it states in the description that the Pyramid of Cheops is the largest of thirty similar structures still extant. It was built by King Cheops about 3,000 B. C. and is therefore about 5,000 years old. According to Herodotus, the ancient Greek historian, 100,000 men worked twenty years at its construction, subsisting on radishes, onions and garlic, all of which cost about 1,600 talents of silver during this period of time. In the ground beneath the pyramid, about 450 feet below the summit, is a sepulchral chamber which was found empty, while in the upper or so called royal chamber there stands a plain coffin of red granite with no inscription whatever on it."

"Well," replied the salesman, "you certainly give them more than their money's worth. But how you can sell views like these for the prices you do, I cannot understand. The other dealers have a hard enough time meeting your prices with even these cheaper views, to say nothing of the descriptions and case that you give with your views."

"The whole secret lies in the enormous amount of our sales," quietly replied our buyer. "This year alone we have sold more than fifteen million stereoscopic views, more than all the other dealers in the country combined. Good day."

ALL IN COLORS

Every view (except those described on page 286) is made by our wonderful NEW COLOR PROCESS.

This Illustration shows **OUR BEST ALUMINUM STEREOSCOPE** PRICE, **49c** For full description see No. 20L2503 on page 286.

7 TIMES OUR VIEWS GO THROUGH THE PRESS BEFORE THEY ARE FINISHED

Four times for the color printing, once for the title, once for the descriptions on the back and once for the tinted border, after which the edges are accurately trimmed and the corners rounded by automatic machinery. It costs us a great deal of money to make stereoscopic views in this way, but it is worth while—it means QUALITY.

WE ALSO INCLUDE

a handsome leatherette case with hinged cover, with every set of views. This case is just the right size to hold the views and keeps them neat and fresh when they are wanted. All of these things make for THE BEST QUALITY.

REDUCED PRICES ON ALL OF OUR STEREOSCOPIC VIEWS

The constantly increasing quantities in which we are making these views have resulted in still further reductions in the cost and, in keeping with our established policy, we are extending to our customers, in the shape of reduced prices, the saving which we have made in the cost of these goods.

A WORD ABOUT POSTAGE, EXPRESS OR FREIGHT CHARGES.

When sent by mail the postage on a set of 100 stereoscopic views is 20 cents, or with the stereoscope it is 35 cents. If more than one set is ordered it is cheaper to ship by express and to most points within 500 miles of Chicago it is cheaper to ship even one set by express. If you include some other goods with your order for views, making the shipment sufficiently large to go by freight, the transportation charge on the views will be so small that it is not worth considering.

100 GREAT COMIC VIEWS

FUNNY STEREO VIEWS

REDUCED TO

THE FUNNIEST SET OF COMIC VIEWS YOU EVER SAW

ALL IN COLORS

WITH FUNNY STORIES PRINTED ON THE BACK OF EVERY VIEW.

THIS BIG SET CONTAINS the newest and most original subjects, the amusing and laugh provoking pictures of the prettiest and daintiest girls caught by the artist in the most embarrassing situations, the funniest hugging and kissing scenes, ludicrous bathing scenes and improprieties of every conceivable sort, the funniest kind of funny things that go to make up the humorous and comical side of life. The list of titles printed on this page will give you some idea of what this big set really is. Read this list over carefully—and then read it all over again. But to really appreciate this set, to understand why this is the greatest set of Comic Stereoscopic Views ever offered for sale at any price, you must see these pictures for yourself.

THE MOST LAUGHABLE STORIES YOU EVER READ ARE PRINTED RIGHT ON THE BACK OF EACH VIEW. The 100 funny stories printed on the backs of these pictures are the funniest stories that you ever read. They are all brand new stories. They are stories that you have never heard before; stories that have never been printed in any book or newspaper. If you want stories to read to the children, order our famous "Children's Story Set," which contains the finest stories for children that were ever written; but if you want some good stories for yourself, stories to make you laugh, stories that you can tell to your friends, order this big comic set. Every one of these 100 stories sparkles with wit and humor, an avalanche of mirth and a barrel of smiles. These 100 stories are a most happy combination of wit and humor, melody and pathos, written by a humorist who sees the humor of everything and who has a happy faculty of relating these laughter provoking absurdities in a manner that is original and entertaining.

SPECIAL FEATURES

To help make this the greatest set of comic views ever offered, we include in this wonderful assortment five of the greatest "series" of comic views ever made. Each series is a complete story in itself, a story told in pictures and the pictures themselves a triumph in the art of stereoscopic photography.

THE "NEW FRENCH COOK" SERIES. The wittiest and the most beautifully executed series of stereoscopic views ever made. You have missed something if you have not seen the dainty little French cook through the scope, and when you see her you will not wonder that Mr. Newlywed lost his head and became a little indiscreet. She certainly did look tempting as he found her there in the kitchen. You will certainly laugh at the unfortunate and absurdly ridiculous oversight that put Mrs. Newlywed wise to his sins, and you will watch with interest and sympathy, in the succeeding pictures, his efforts at reconciliation; and, perhaps with sorrow, you will note the departure of the dear little French cook. Everything comes out all right in the end, however, just as it ought to, and you will laugh again when you see the new cook that Mrs. Newlywed installs in place of the bewitching little French beauty.

THE "COURTSHIP AND WEDDING" SERIES. Twelve of the greatest stereoscopic pictures you ever saw, telling the story of the courtship, the wedding and subsequent marital troubles from "Popping the Question" until the unlucky day, when hubby, forgetting for a moment his newly acquired responsibility as a married man, falls under the spell of a new charmer and is surprised by the arrival of his loyal little wife. Of course, tears, explanations and promises of good behavior in the future follow, but, was ever man more unlucky? The last picture shows mother-in-law "butting into the game." This ends the series, but we can easily imagine that ever after, under her stern and relentless eye, our unfortunate friend keeps carefully in the straight and narrow path.

THE "DYING MINER" SERIES. The pathetic story of the dying miner and the efforts of his loyal "pard" to comfort him and minister to his wants during his last hours is eloquently told by this series of unsurpassed stereoscopic pictures. The first of these splendid pictures shows so realistically the miner's friends at the door of the cabin, anxiously waiting for the doctor, that one cannot help sharing their anxiety, and when, in the next picture, the doctor is seen in the cabin at the miner's bedside, one can feel the alternate hope and fear of his "pards" as they wait for the doctor's verdict. In the succeeding pictures we see "Jack," his faithful "pard," writing a farewell letter home for him, then singing his favorite songs, in an effort to cheer his last moments, and as we come to the final pictures of the series, "Good Bye, Old Pard, I'm Hitting the Long Trail," and "Gone Over the Big Divide," it is hard to repress the tears.

"AN AFFAIR OF HONOR;" THE DUELING SERIES. A feminine battle with swords is surely a novelty, as dueling is usually thought of as a peculiarly masculine prerogative; but in this exciting series of stereoscopic views the principals are two fair Parisian girls, who come to this beautiful and secluded spot in the environs of Paris to seek satisfaction for their wounded honor in mortal combat. We have been unusually fortunate in securing this splendid set of pictures to form a part of our great Comic Set, as every scene, from "Facing the Adversary" to "The Vanquished," is full of real interest and every one is a triumph in the art of Stereoscopic Photography.

THE "FRENCH BICYCLE GIRLS" SERIES. Two pretty French maidens, out for a spin through the country on their bicycles, furnished the opportunity for our artist to make this unique series of beautiful stereoscopic pictures. While, of course, the fair bicyclists themselves, who meet with various mild adventures, including a barbed wire fence to be climbed and a brook to be waded, are the real objects of interest, one cannot help exclaiming over the beauty of the scenes amid which the artist caught them, the delicate coloring and pretty effects of light and shadow giving these pictures the appearance of exquisite water color paintings.

LIST OF SUBJECTS CONTAINED IN THIS GREAT COMIC SET.

THE "NEW FRENCH COOK" SERIES.

The Queen of Mrs. Newlywed's Kitchen.
How Soon Will Dinner Be Served?
My! But You Are a Dear Little Cook.
Oh! How Dare You, Sir?
Sh—, Madam Comes.
Whose Hands? What Can She Mean?
You Can't Deny It. Oh! She Shall Go This Minute.
No, Donald, I Never Would Have Thought It of You.
Forgive Me, Dearie, and Let's Go to the Opera.
And the New Wench Cook Reigns Supreme.
Mr. Newlywed Just Looks Into the Kitchen Again.
But There Is No Dear Little French Cook In Sight.

THE "COURTSHIP AND WEDDING" SERIES.

Popping the Question.
Guess Who He Is.
Love Reigns Supreme.
The Bride in Her Boudoir.
Dressing the Bride.
I Pronounce You Man and Wife.
The Blessing.
Honoring Her Quests.
When the Lights Are Dim and Low.
One Heart's Enough For Me.
All Aboard for Dreamland.
Heavens! My Wife.
What Is Home Without a Mother-in-Law?

"AN AFFAIR OF HONOR," THE DUELING SERIES.

Facing the Adversary.
On Guard, Ready!
Thrust and Parry.
The Home Thrust.
Revenged.
Reconciliation.
The Vanquished.

THE "FRENCH BICYCLE GIRLS" SERIES.

A Horrid Wire Fence Bars the Path.
The Path Is Shady and They Want to See Where It Goes to.
A Stream and No Bridge, So They Take Off Their Shoes and Stockings.
They Wade Bravely Through, Carrying Their Wheels.
But They Have to Climb the Same Old Fence On the Way Back.

THE "DYING MINER" SERIES.

Bill's Pards Anxiously Await the Doctor's Arrival.
Has Bill Any Show, Doc?
Jack Writes a Letter Home For His Pard.
Jack Sings Bill's Favorite Songs to Him.
Good Bye, Old Pard, I'm Hitting the Long Trail.
Gone Over the Big Divide.

THE "TIRED" SERIES.

In which a young man learns that he shouldn't go to sleep while he is holding his best girl.

You Make Me Tired.
Now I'll Make You Tired.
Too Tired to Know the Difference.
A Different Kind of Tired Feeling.

THE "FRENCH TOILET" SERIES.

Is Anyone Around?
Getting Along Nicely.
Cool and Refreshing.

THE "JOHN AND MARIA" SERIES.

What Makes You So Slow?
Last In Bed Puts Out the Light.
It's Up to You to Blow It.
A Nip On the Sly.
Well, John! Did You Think I Was Asleep?
Oh! What a Difference in the Morning!

AMUSING TWO-VIEW SERIES.

Be Careful, Let Me Help You.
Well! I Like the Way You Help Me.
Be Real Nice and I'll Give You One.
You'll Never Get Another From Me.
Caught Napping—Willie Improves His Chance.
Caught Napping—But Very Much Awake Now.
Oh, Yes, My Dear, I'll Be Home Early.
And He Rolls In Quite Early.
B'lieve I've Seen That Face Before.
Must 'Ave Had a Smashing Good Time.
The Model—Getting Ready for the Pose.
The Model—Posing.

COMICAL BATHING SCENES.

Waiting for Bath Hour.
She Just Took a Peep.
Caught This Time.
Jacks and Jills On the Beach.
Drying Off in the Shade.
The Diver.
A Frolic at Rockaway Beach, N. Y.

FUN WITH PRETTY GIRLS.

Cool and Contented.
The Ballet Girl Between the Acts.
Dreaming—A Shady Nook—A Quiet Brook.
Here's to Your Health, Old Man.
The Mandolin Player. A La Oriental.
Undergoing Repairs.
Keeping Pretty Comfortable.
A Good Supporter.
I Don't Care for Signs.

ALL SORTS OF FUNNY ONES, EACH GOOD FOR A LAUGH.

Far Away From Curious Eyes.
An Unwelcome Intrusion.
When Two's a Company, Three's a Crowd.
Oh! Keep Her Going.
Biddy Sees a Rat.
Off For a Ride.
Cupid's Message to Listening Ears.
Old Bill and His Happy Family.
Warm Meals at All Hours.
A Hungry Crowd.
Taking Toll at the Bridge.
Wash Day for the New Woman.
You Mean Thing! That's No Fair.
Like a Can of Sardines. (Thirteen in Bed, Count 'Em.)
Mamie, Won't You Kiss Your Honey Boy?
And She Didn't Seem to Mind.

No. 20L2575 New Comic Set, 100 Colored Stereoscopic Views, just as illustrated and described on this page with leatherette case for views. Price, without stereoscope ....(If by mail, postage extra, 20 cents.)........................ $0.98

Price of this set with our best hardwood stereoscope ....(If by mail, postage extra, 35 cents.)........................ 1.15

A TRIP THROUGH SEARS ROEBUCK & CO'S BIG STORE

WOULD YOU LIKE TO SEE how our enormous amount of business is handled every day by the nine thousand employes of our great institution? The fifty stereoscopic views we have prepared for this set of views, and which you will find fully described on this page, are a wonderful revelation of the marvelous methods by which we are able to promptly and accurately handle the orders we receive from nearly six million customers each year. These pictures tell the full story, and you can follow the order right through our house and know just exactly how it is handled by all of the clerks, order fillers, recheckers, packers, etc. Every view has a complete description printed on the back which fully de scribes just what the hundreds of employes shown in these pictures are doing, tells the reason why they do it, and fully explains the manner in which it is done. Be sure to read this big list of subjects.

No. 1. Mr. R. W. Sears seated at his desk.
No. 2. General View of Our Great Buildings.
No. 3. Main entrance, Merchandise Building.
No. 4. Merchandise Building, Largest in the World.
No. 5. Sunken Garden, Merchandise Building in distance.
No. 6. Railroad Yards, showing hundreds of cars.
No. 7. Automatic Weighing Machines in Grocery Department.
No. 8. Watchmaking in Jewelry Department.
No. 9. Cutting Suits of Clothes by Electricity.
No. 10. An Aisle in Talking Machine Department.
No. 11. How Goods are Packed for Shipment.
No. 12. A Corner in our Mail Packing Section.
No. 13. Loading Freight Trains in Glass Covered Train Shed.
No. 14. Our Long Distance Telephone Switchboard.
No. 15. Marvelous Automatic Telephone Switchboard.
No. 16. Portion of Pneumatic Tube Station.
No. 17. The Great Tunnel, a Mile Long.
No. 18. Noon Time on the Street.
No. 19. Magnificent Administration Building.
No. 20. Another View of the Administration Building.
No. 21. Grand Marble Entrance, Administration Building.
No. 22. Handling Money by the Armfuls.
No. 23. Preparing Records of our Customers' Orders.
No. 24. How We Route our Shipments to Customers.
No. 25. Writing Letters to Customers.
No. 26. Typewriting Ten Thousand Letters per Day.

SOME VISITORS from foreign countries made a trip through our store the other day. They were shown through all of our great buildings. They saw how our orders were handled on a regular schedule so that nearly every order is shipped within twenty-four hours after it is received. They saw the printing of the great catalogue, where twenty large printing presses, like those used in producing the great magazines of the country, run day and night to supply the millions of catalogues that we send out each year. They saw the immense power house, with a capacity of twelve thousand horse power, with its gigantic dynamos, air compressors, pumps, etc. They saw our beautiful grounds with the Sunken Garden and Greek Pagoia, and at last, when they were leaving, they said: "It's simply wonderful. There is nothing like it in our country, and we never dreamed that such an immense institution as this existed in any part of the world. It is typical of everything American." These views will show you just exactly why they said that.

No. 27. Keeping a Record of our Orders.
No. 28. Where the Money is Counted.
No. 29. Street Scene at Closing Hour.
No. 30. Setting Type for the Great Catalogue.
No. 31. Marvelous Type-Setting Machines.
No. 32. Making Printing Plates by Electricity.
No. 33. Sending 437,000 Miles of Paper through the Press.
No. 34. Busy Corner in the Press Room.
No. 35. A Machine that is almost Human.
No. 36. How the Big Catalogue is put together.
No. 37. Trimming 2,500 Sheets of Paper at One Stroke.
No. 38. Cleanest Boiler Room in the World.
No. 39. The Million Dollar Engine Room.
No. 40. Largest Switchboard in the World.
No. 41. One of our five Great Restaurants.
No. 42. Girls at Lunch in Cafeteria.
No. 43. Preparing Food for 9,000 Meals.
No. 44. Inside the Great Refrigerator.
No. 45. The Beautiful Sunken Garden in Summer.
No. 46. A Walk through the Garden.
No. 47. Grecian Pergola amid the Flowers.
No. 48. School where we Teach New Employes.
No. 49. Exciting Drill of our Fire Department.
No. 50. A Corner in our own Hospital.

No. 20L2519 50 Views, as above described, in leatherette case. Price.... **30c**
If by mail, postage extra, 12 cents.

No. 20L2518 50 Views, same as above, but with our best, hardwood stereoscope. Price.......................**45c**
If by mail, postage extra, 27 cents.

GENUINE PHOTOGRAPHIC VIEWS

32c PER DOZEN FOR THESE PHOTOGRAPHIC VIEWS. These are genuine photographic views printed from negatives upon regular photographic paper, mounted on good cards and burnished, the exact same quality sold by canvassers at $1.00 per dozen.

No. 20L2750 New Comic Views. The funniest, most original and laugh provoking collection of stereoscopic pictures ever made.
No. 20L2751 Great Cities of America. Showing the beautiful parks, public buildings, and magnificent structures.
No. 20L2752 Picturesque America. Presenting the most interesting and beautiful portions of our great American Continent.
No. 20L2753 Yellowstone National Park, the wonderland of the world. Showing the boiling springs and the wonderful rock formations of this picturesque region.
No. 20L2754 Sportsman Adventures. Actual photographs of hunting and fishing scenes. These views bring back pleasant memories of the past and anticipate the delightful days to come.
No. 20L2755 Holy Land; through ancient Palestine. Showing the sacred localities of this land of Bible history.
No. 20L2756 Tours of Europe. The picturesque scenery of France, Germany and Holland; a wonderful collection of views.
No. 20L2757 Sweden. Showing the rugged landscape, beautiful fjords, and strange old cities of this far northland.
No. 20L2758 British Isles. Showing the romantic beauties and historical localities of England, Ireland and Scotland.
No. 20L2759 Switzerland. Untrodden Alpine Peaks and quaint little villages among the mountain valleys.
No. 20L2760 Spain. The land of the castanet and its romantic beauty and wonderful scenery.
No. 20L2761 Italy. Showing the sunny land of the Eternal City in all its artistic beauty.
No. 20L2762 Egypt. That fascinating land of mystery along the banks of the River Nile.
No. 20L2763 Turkey. The land of the Koran, with its sacred mosques and strange old cities.
No. 20L2764 Oriental Lands. Views in China and Japan, showing the magnificent splendor of the Orient in all its glory.

Price on above views Nos. 20L2750 to 20L2764 inclusive, per dozen, all different..**$0.32**
Per 100 assorted views..**2.55**

48c EXTRA HIGH GRADE VIEWS, 48c PER DOZEN. The best photographic stereo views that can be made, the exact same style sold everywhere by canvassers at $2.00 per dozen. Every one of these views is made from an original retouched negative, printed on the finest quality of photographic paper, highly polished, and mounted on the best quality extra heavy cards.

No. 20L2770 High Grade Comic Views. A superb collection of the most laugh provoking and comical scenes, all photographed direct from life.
No. 20L2771 Glimpses of American Cities. Showing the public buildings, beautiful parks and magnificent palaces.
No. 20L2772 Picturesque Scenery of America. Illustrating the most beautiful and interesting portions of the United States.
No. 20L2773 Yellowstone National Park, the world's wonderland. Views of spouting geysers, boiling springs, and the strangest rock formations in the world.
No. 20L2774 Yosemite Valley. Showing the giant red wood trees, the Yosemite Falls, the Sentinels, and other natural beauties of this region.
No. 20L2775 Sportsman Series. Actual photographs of hunting and fishing adventures. They bring to mind pleasant days spent in the woods and revive the memories of long dead campfires.
No. 20L2776 Palestine. Showing the ancient cities and the sacred localities of the Holy Land.
No. 20L2777 Sweden and Norway. The picturesque beauty of this northland where the sun illuminates the landscape at the midnight hour.
No. 20L2778 Travels across Europe. Showing the wonderful mountain scenery and picturesque landscape of the old world countries.
No. 20L2779 Ancient Egypt, Greece and Rome. Ruins of colossal statues, temples and monuments built centuries ago.
No. 20L2780 Oriental Realms. China and Japan in the wealth and splendor of their oriental glory.
No. 20L2781 Jap-Russian War Views. Taken during the terrible conflict between the little brown men and the Russians.
No. 20L2782 Miscellaneous Views. A superb assortment of stereoscopic views, including pictures of Presidents McKinley and Roosevelt; also views of Mexico and many other lands. 100 different subjects.

Price on above views Nos. 20L2770 to 20L2782 inclusive, per dozen, all different..**$0.48**
Per 100 assorted views..**3.80**

STANDARD HARDWOOD STEREOSCOPE.

24c A GOOD STEREOSCOPE—EXTRA LARGE LENSES.

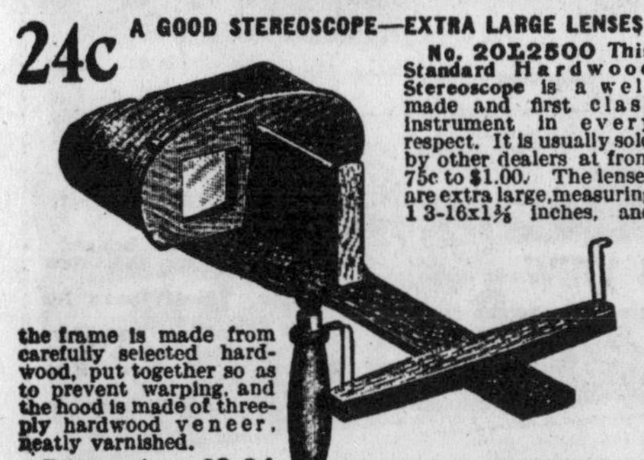

No. 20L2500 This Standard Hardwood Stereoscope is a well made and first class instrument in every respect. It is usually sold by other dealers at from 75c to $1.00. The lenses are extra large, measuring 1 3-16x1⅛ inches, and the frame is made from carefully selected hardwood, put together so as to prevent warping, and the hood is made of threeply hardwood veneer, neatly varnished.

Price, each....**$0.24**
Per dozen.....**2.75**
If by mail, postage extra, each, 19 cents.

A surprisingly good instrument for those who desire an inexpensive stereoscope.

SPECIAL ALUMINUM STEREOSCOPE.

36c A BARGAIN IN ALUMINUM STEREOSCOPES.

No. 20L2502 This big value Aluminum Stereoscope is a thoroughly high grade instrument and a universal favorite with canvassers. The very low price which we quote on this stereoscope is made possible only by the fact that we have contracted for an immense quantity of these goods, thus enabling the manufacturer to reduce his cost to the lowest possible figure. The lenses are of the clearest optical glass, made extra large, and carefully fitted to the frame. The hood is made of aluminum, bound with dark red velvet. The frame is made of carefully selected hardwood and fitted with patent folding handle. Price, per dozen, $4.25; each............**36c**
If by mail, postage extra, each, 19 cents.

IMPROVED ALUMINUM STEREOSCOPE.

49c ALUMINUM LENS LOCKS—ENGRAVED HOOD.

No. 20L2503 This Elegant Frosted Aluminum Hood Stereoscope is the finest stereoscope that can be produced. The beautiful frosted aluminum hood is richly engraved and bound with dark red velvet. The frame is made of cherry wood, varnished by hand, and provided with patent folding handle. The lenses are made from the finest quality of clear optical glass and are firmly held in place by the patent aluminum lens lock, which makes it impossible for them to ever get out of adjustment at any time.

Price, each..**$0.49**
Per dozen...**5.64**
If by mail, postage extra, each, 19 cents.

YOUR MONEY WILL BE IMMEDIATELY RETURNED TO YOU FOR ANY GOODS NOT PERFECTLY SATISFACTORY.

The brilliant coloring in these pictures is so marvelous, the stereoscopic effect so surprising and extraordinary, and the pictures themselves so beautiful as to make this set the most wonderful collection of colored stereoscopic views ever made by any process. Our new color process enables us to reproduce the pictures in from ten to twenty separate tints, giving them a highly polished, glossy finish and mounting them on extra heavy special cardboard.

No. 20L2520 200 Oleograph Colored Views, with printed descriptions on the back, handsome leatherette case and hardwood stereoscope. Price reduced to..........**$2.14**
Shipping weight, 5½ pounds. Unmailable on account of weight.

No. 20L2521 Same as No. 20L2520, but without scope. Price reduced to..**$1.98**
Shipping weight, 4½ pounds. Unmailable on account of weight.

100 COLORED VIEWS AROUND THE WORLD REDUCED TO 82c

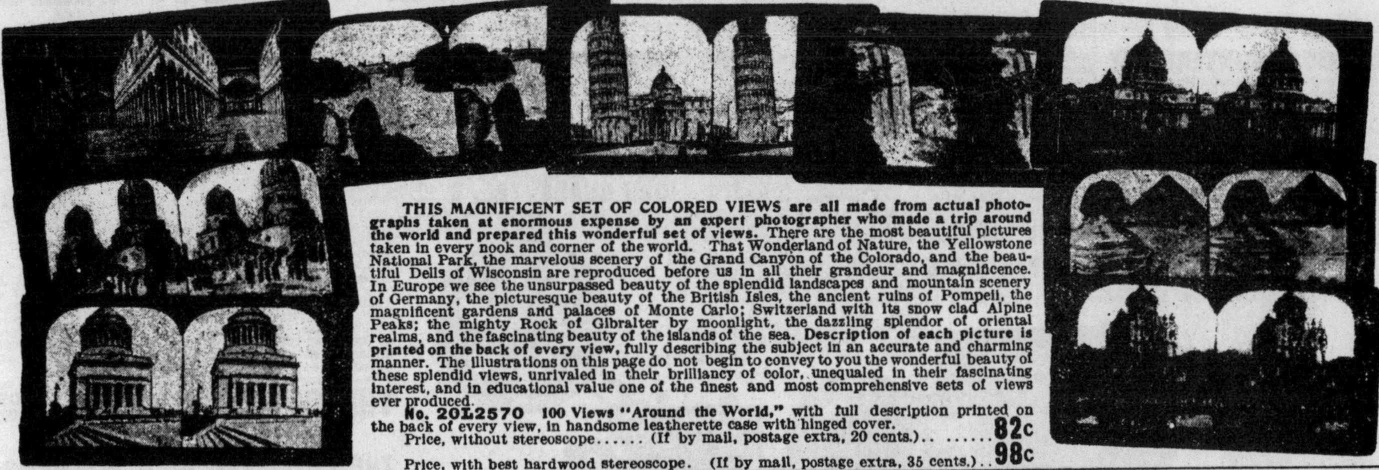

THIS MAGNIFICENT SET OF COLORED VIEWS are all made from actual photographs taken at enormous expense by an expert photographer who made a trip around the world and prepared this wonderful set of views. There are the most beautiful pictures taken in every nook and corner of the world. That Wonderland of Nature, the Yellowstone National Park, the marvelous scenery of the Grand Canyon of the Colorado, and the beautiful Dells of Wisconsin are reproduced before us in all their grandeur and magnificence. In Europe we see the unsurpassed beauty of the splendid landscapes and mountain scenery of Germany, the picturesque beauty of the British Isles, the ancient ruins of Pompeii, the magnificent gardens and palaces of Monte Carlo; Switzerland with its snow clad Alpine Peaks; the mighty Rock of Gibralter by moonlight, the dazzling splendor of oriental realms, and the fascinating beauty of the islands of the sea. Description of each picture is printed on the back of every view, fully describing the subject in an accurate and charming manner. The illustrations on this page do not begin to convey to you the wonderful beauty of these splendid views, unrivaled in their brilliancy of color, unequaled in their fascinating interest, and in educational value one of the finest and most comprehensive sets of views ever produced.

No. 20L2570 100 Views "Around the World," with full description printed on the back of every view, in handsome leatherette case with hinged cover.
Price, without stereoscope...... (If by mail, postage extra, 20 cents.)...... 82c
Price, with best hardwood stereoscope. (If by mail, postage extra, 35 cents.).. 98c

100 COLORED VIEWS AMERICA REDUCED TO 79c

No. 20L2565 America. Views of the Cliff Dwellers of New Mexico, the beautiful Dells of Wisconsin, our Yellowstone National Park, the giant redwood trees and colored scenery of the Yosemite Valley, the Grand Canyon of the Colorado, the beautiful Niagara Falls, Alaska with its Indian totem poles, and many other features. Printed description on the back of every view.

100 Colored Views, America, with printed description on the back of every view, in handsome leatherette case with hinged cover.
Price, without stereoscope..... 79c Price, with hardwood stereoscope........ 95c

100 COLORED VIEWS EUROPE REDUCED TO 82c

No. 20L2530 Europe. Beautiful colored views of ancient mountain castles in Switzerland, wonderful art galleries of Germany, the artistic beauties of France, picturesque landscapes of Norway, the ancient ruins of Greece, silent monuments and pyramids of Egypt, beautiful palaces and gardens of Monte Carlo, the magnificent splendor of oriental realms. Full description is printed on the back of every view.

100 Colored European Views, with full description on the back of each view, in handsome leatherette case with hinged cover.
Price, without stereoscope..... 82c Price, with hardwood stereoscope........ 98c

100 COLORED VIEWS SPORTSMAN NOW ONLY 82c

No. 20L2545 Sportsman Views. Pictures of hunting adventures in the woods, of struggles with the gamey black bass and wary trout in some secluded nook, of Indian warriors in full dress, etc. Pictures that will bring back memories of the days spent in the woods, along some shady stream and revive the long forgotten memories of dead camp fires. Accurate information on hunting, fishing, camping and Indian life printed on the back of every view.

100 Colored Views, with full descriptions, in handsome leatherette case. Price, without stereoscope........... 82c
Price, with best hardwood stereoscope................ 98c

60 COLORED VIEWS SAN FRANCISCO REDUCED TO 75c

No. 20L2560 San Francisco Earthquake. The utter desolation of this once beautiful city, the torn and twisted streets, the yawning chasms, the hot and smoking ruins of palaces, give us some idea of the appalling magnitude of this calamity. No other pictures will ever be made of this awful disaster. Send for this set at once.

60 Colored Views, with historic descriptions printed on the backs, in handsome leatherette case.
Price, without stereoscope, (Postage extra, 13 cents.) 75c
Price, with hardwood stereoscope. (Postage extra, 35c.). 90c

100 COLORED VIEWS WORLD'S FAIR NOW ONLY 78c

No. 20L2550 St. Louis World's Fair. The wonderful Cascades and Sunken Gardens, the great Floral Clock, the immense Machinery Hall, the myriad of attractions on the "Pike," the Tyrolean Alps with their pretty girls and quaint old taverns, the Ancient Streets of Cairo, Scenes in the Philippine Village, etc., etc. The most realistic views of this most stupendous exposition.

100 Colored Views, with full descriptions, in handsome leatherette case. Price, without stereoscope...... 78c
Price, with best hardwood stereoscope................ 94c

100 COLORED VIEWS PORT ARTHUR REDUCED TO 83c

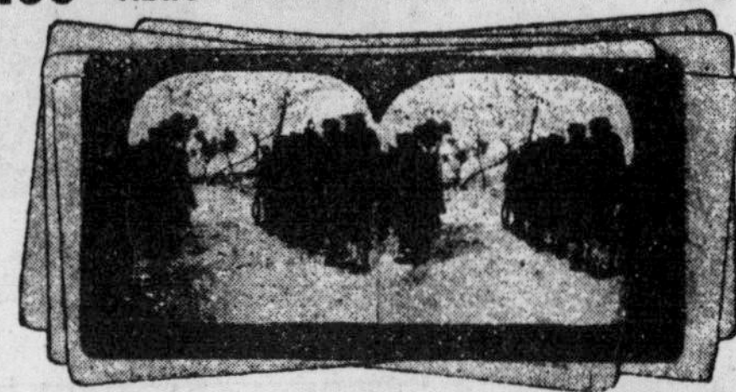

No. 20L2555 Siege of Port Arthur. A thrilling set of stereoscopic views, reproducing the fierce and desperate conflicts in the trenches, the bombardments with the gigantic cannon together with the most interesting scenes and incidents of camp life in the Japanese army. All made direct from photographs taken by Richard Barry, the greatest living war correspondent of the age, and show the vivid details of this most terrible siege.

100 Colored Views, with description printed on the back of every view, in handsome leatherette case with hinged cover. Price, without stereoscope.................. 83c
Price, with best hardwood stereoscope................ 99c

100 COLORED VIEWS JAPAN REDUCED TO 78c

No. 20L2525 Japan. No where is there such a wealth of glorious color as in this Island Empire. The pretty Geisha girls, the ancient Treasure Houses, the Temple of a Thousand Lanterns, busy days in the rice field, street scenes in Yokohama, festival gaiety in Tokio, and views of that sacred volcano Fujiyama, rising twelve thousand feet above the sea, are included in the wonderful pictures of this set. Complete description is printed on the back of every view.

100 Colored Views, with full descriptions, in handsome leatherette case. Price, without stereoscope.......... 78c
Price, with best hardwood stereoscope.............. 94c

"HOLY LAND" 100 COLORED VIEWS NOW REDUCED TO 83c

THESE BEAUTIFUL PICTURES OF THE HOLY LAND were made by an expert photographer, who has taken up his residence in the land of Palestine and devoted his life to the study of Bible history. There are views of Jerusalem, showing the great temple, the Via Dolorosa, and the mosque of Omar; of Nazareth nestling among the beautiful green hills of Canaan; of Gethsemane with its ancient olive trees; of the sacred valley of the River Jordan; of the desolate shores of the Dead Sea; and the great plain of Sharon; the city of Damascus, Joppa on the sea coast, etc. The largest, most complete series of Holy Land pictures ever produced.

No. 20L2535 100 Holy Land Colored Views, with Bible story and description on the back of every view, in leatherette case with hinged cover. 83c
Price, without stereoscope..................
Price, with hardwood stereoscope............... 99c

100 CHILDREN'S STORY VIEWS 98c FASCINATING PICTURES FOR THE LITTLE ONES

A WONDERFUL SET OF COLORED VIEWS for the children. They will find countless hours of the most delightful fun and amusement, as with bright eyes and eager faces they gaze at these wonderful pictures and read the fascinating stories printed on the back of every view. These stories sparkle with the choicest gems of childish wit and humor, and are by far the most charming children's stories ever written. An evening spent at home with the children and this wonderful set of views will repay a thousand times the small expenditure of money we ask for this great set of children's story views.

No. 20L2540 100 Children's Story Views, with printed story on the back of every view, in handsome leatherette case with hinged cover.
Price, without stereoscope.................. 98c
Price, with hardwood stereoscope............ $1.14

NOTE—POSTAGE, IF SENT BY MAIL, ON ANY SET OF 100 VIEWS, 20 CENTS; ON ANY SET OF 100 VIEWS AND STEREOSCOPE, 35 CENTS.

DEPARTMENT OF MOTION PICTURE MACHINES

Magic Lanterns, Double Stereopticons, Gas Making Outfits, Lantern Slides and Films, Complete Line of Optical Projection Apparatus and Supplies.

IF YOU ARE INTERESTED in Projection Instruments of any kind, Magic Lanterns, Stereopticons or Motion Picture Machines for public exhibition work, street advertising, educational purposes, religious and reform work, lodges and secret societies or home amusement, send for our BIG FREE CATALOGUE OF MOTION PICTURE MACHINES AND MAGIC LANTERNS.

A PROFITABLE BUSINESS may be done in almost any locality with a well selected and well managed Stereopticon and Motion Picture Outfit. Since the introduction of motion pictures the business of exhibiting has grown better and better, and it never was so good as at the present time. There is an opening in almost any locality for a profitable business exhibiting in public halls, churches, schoolhouses, theaters, etc. This class of exhibiting may be done within a small radius of home, going over and over the same ground say once or twice a year with a new program, or it may be extended to any part of the country. Shows in store rooms or in tents, giving thirty minute entertainments at an admission of five to ten cents, are paying large returns on the investment. These may be permanently located or may be moved from time to time to other nearby towns.

FOR MORE COMPLETE DESCRIPTIONS of these machines, with larger illustrations and complete descriptions of all other instruments, accessories and supplies in the way of optical projection apparatus which we handle, we refer you to our Special Catalogue of Motion Picture Machines and Magic Lanterns, which we will be glad to send to any address free. In this catalogue we show the most complete line of everything used for public exhibition work, advertising, educational work, church work, lectures of all kinds, and outfits suitable for home entertainment. We show the most complete line of Magic Lantern Slides, Moving Picture Films, supplies and accessories of all kinds, all priced at the lowest prices ever known for strictly high class, thoroughly dependable goods.

OUR GUARANTEE. Everything that we sell in the way of Optical Projection Apparatus, Moving Picture Machines, Magic Lanterns, Stereopticons, Slides, Films, complete outfits of all kinds, is sent out under our positive binding guarantee, under the terms of which any of the goods not proving entirely satisfactory in every way, no matter for what reason, may be returned to us at our expense, and the amount which you paid for the goods will be refunded to you in full, including the money you have paid out for transportation charges. We are the only house selling Optical Projection Apparatus of all kinds upon these terms, and you will readily understand that this policy upon our part is in itself an assurance that you will get the very best that the market affords as we could not send out inferior or defective goods under our policy of returning the money in full on any purchases not entirely satisfactory.

STREET ADVERTISING pays good returns. In this class of work stereopticon views and motion pictures are shown alternately with the advertisements of local merchants, patent medicine, tobacco, cigar and other concerns, who recognize this as one of the best methods of bringing their ads to the attention of the public.

WE ILLUSTRATE AND DESCRIBE on this page the new No. 4 Optigraph, the Oxylithe Gas Making Outfit, and two of our Magic Lanterns, simply to give you an idea of the style and quality of goods that we handle in our Department of Moving Picture Machines and Magic Lanterns.

THE OPTIGRAPH No. 4, MODEL 1907

THE LATEST AND THE MOST PERFECT MOTION PICTURE MACHINE.

THE OPTIGRAPH No. 4 has the only perfect framing device, the vise grip sliding attachment, the compound rewind reel head, a geared detachable take up, interchangeable spring catch handle, and fireproof magazines. It excels in quality of workmanship, quality of material, durability, portability, convenience, artistic design, and for results on the screen it has no equal. There are more than forty reasons why the new Optigraph No. 4, 1907 model is the best picture machine, and these forty reasons are fully explained in our Special Catalogue of Motion Picture Machines and Magic Lanterns.

No. 21F2000 Optigraph No. 4, mechanism with 8-inch reel, lens, round base, belt, plain reel head and detachable crank. Price......$39.00

No. 21F2050 Takeup attachment with plain reel head, 8-inch rewinding wheel. Price......$8.00

No. 21F2075 Sliding attachment, without bracket, arm or screw ring. Price......$4.00

No. 21F2080 COMPLETE MACHINE ON SEPARABLE OAK BASE with Optigraph No. 4. Sliding adjustable lamp house, condensing lenses, burner support, sliding attachment, bracket, arm, screw ring, ½-size stereopticon lens, 8-inch reel, plain reel head, arc lamp, rheostat (52 to 110 volts), knife switch and 30 feet of insulated wire. Price......$68.50

No. 21F2090 Complete machine, with high grade calcium jet and 8 feet of rubber tubing instead of arc lamp, rheostat, switch, wire, etc. Price......$65.50

NOTE:—If takeup device is desired with any of the above machines, add to the above prices......$8.00

OPTIGRAPH No. 4, THE NEW 1907 — MODEL —

And Vise Grip Sliding Attachment in Combination with the Enterprise Double Dissolving Stereopticon.

A highly successful and economic arrangement for showing Motion Pictures and Lantern Views. With this combination stereopticon views may be dissolved at will, and but a moment is required to change to motion pictures. With the Single Lantern in combination with the Motion Picture Machine, lantern views may be quickly and artistically changed by the use of the rapid slide changer, which accompanies the lantern.

No. 21F2100 Optigraph No 4, with sliding attachment, single Enterprise Lantern, extension legs for lantern lenses and slide carrier. Price......$68.50

No. 21F2110 Optigraph No. 4, with sliding attachment, double dissolving stereopticon, extension legs on lower lantern, lenses and two slide carriers. Price......$93.50

The above prices do not include jets, dissolving key, etc. For more description of Optigraph and Lanterns see our Special Catalogue of Motion Picture Machines and Magic Lanterns.

OUR MODEL "A" SINGLE STEREOPTICON, $15.00

(FOR ILLUSTRATION SEE OUR SPECIAL CATALOGUE).

Adapted to the requirements of ministers in church work, teachers in classroom work, public exhibitors, lodges, etc. Has large Russia iron lamp house, extension front, folding bellows, telescopic nickel plated adjustment rods, a good quality of condensing lenses and achromatic objective lense. Material and workmanship throughout is the best and it is equipped with all attachments requisite for successful projection work. Our Model "A" Stereopticon may be used with calcium light, electric light, sun rival vapor light or any system of lighting at present employed by public exhibitors, but, at our special price of $15.00 as listed below the light is not included.

No. 21F2200 Model "A" Stereopticon, complete as described above. Price......$15.00

If ready made oxygen or hydrogen gases are purchased in steel tanks no additional apparatus will be required, except six feet of small rubber tubing (at 10 cents per foot) to connect tank to lantern, and a can of limes (costing 95 cents).

$30.00

THE ENTERPRISE Stereopticon has all necessary adjustments known in high class stereopticon work, is equipped with all the latest improvements, and is the neatest design as well as the most compact and convenient stereopticon made. It is made of metal throughout and beautifully nickel plated, has dark red bellows, steel lamp house and polished and nickel plated lens mountings.

THE DISSOLVING EFFECT which constitutes the highest art in stereopticon or magic lantern projection can be accomplished by adding the top section, which makes it a regular double dissolving stereopticon.

The Sliding Optigraph Attachment may be added to either the single or the double stereopticon at any time and is attached by means of machine screws which are furnished with the sliding attachment.

THE OBJECTIVE LENSES are Achromatic Rectilinear of high grade and fully guaranteed. Unless otherwise ordered we furnish what is known as the Short Focus Lens, which projects ten-foot picture at about thirty feet from the screen. The Objective Lens is attached to the stereopticon by a hinged door, which enables the operator to get at the rear combination instantly, and especially adapts it to use in connection with the Optigraph Motion Picture Machine and Sliding Attachment, as the Stereopticon Objective Lens can be instantly swung out of position and the Motion Picture Machine and Lens at the same time swung into its place, it being unnecessary to change the adjustments. The Lamp House is made of a fine grade of planished steel, is extra large so as to accommodate burners for vapor, gas, oxy-hydrogen, calcium, electric, acetylene or other illumination and is fully enclosed (except for ventilation).

No. 21F2150 The Enterprise Single Stereopticon, full nickel plated with high grade Achromatic Rectilinear Objective Lens, one pair 4½-inch grade Condensing Lenses, dark red bellows, planished dark steel fully enclosed lamp house, all complete. Price......$30.00

No. 21F2180 Enterprise Double Stereopticon, complete, with carrying case. Price......60.00

Don't fail to send for our Big FREE Catalogue of

MOTION PICTURE MACHINES AND STEREOPTICONS

Showing our complete line of public exhibition apparatus, everything in the way of Magic Lanterns, Slides, Films and Supplies. We can save you money on your outfit.

See page 695 for Juvenile Magic Lantern Outfits.

OXYLITHE GAS MAKING OUTFIT $39.50

THE OXYLITHE Gas Making Apparatus represents the greatest advance made in magic lantern apparatus since the original invention of the lantern. This new apparatus, which enables the operator to instantly and easily produce a supply of absolutely pure oxygen gas at any time, will, we confidently predict, revolutionize the exhibition business. It is a well known fact to exhibitors that outside of the electric light, which is available only in the larger cities, the only practicable light for public exhibition work, either for stationary or moving pictures, is the calcium light, and until the invention of this wonderful new oxygen gas making outfit which we now place upon the market for the first time, the only means of producing the calcium light was by an expensive, heavy, cumbersome gas making outfit, very difficult to operate, actually dangerous owing to frequent explosions and successful only in the hands of expert and experienced chemists. The Oxylithe Gas Making Outfit does away with all the danger, with all the trouble and with practically all of the expense attached to the operation of these old style gas making outfits. Our illustration engraved direct from a photograph of the apparatus, shows how simple, compact and portable it is. It can be packed into a small carrying case, measuring only about 10 inches square by 30 inches long, and weighs complete only about 30 pounds. The only chemical required in operating this new oxygen gas making outfit is oxylithe, and a small package of this oxylithe, weighing only a few ounces, is sufficient for an evening's entertainment. The operation of this outfit is simplicity itself. There is no possible chance for mistakes, no possible chance for failure and absolutely no danger. A small quantity of the oxylithe is placed in the tank, which contains a little water, and the generation of oxygen gas commences at once, and is conveyed from the gas making outfit by means of a small rubber tube directly to the burner of the lantern.

No. 21F2300 The Oxylithe Gas Making Apparatus complete. Price......$39.50

No. 21F2305 Oxylithe, for use with the Oxylithe Gas Outfit. Price, per box......$1.35

COMPLETE HOME ENTERTAINMENT OUTFITS

YOU CAN MAKE LOTS OF MONEY BY GIVING EVENING ENTERTAINMENTS RIGHT IN YOUR OWN NEIGHBORHOOD

OUR PREMIER MOVING PICTURE OUTFIT

$8.95 BUYS THE COMPLETE OUTFIT

OUR NEW PREMIER MODEL MOVING PICTURE MACHINE is a thoroughly high grade and up to date machine that has been designed especially for use in giving home entertainments. These machines are built on exactly the same principles as the big moving picture machines which are used in the regular theaters. With this machine you can entertain your friends as they never have been entertained before, you can delight your neighbors when they call and can easily become the most popular young man or woman in the neighborhood, while the money that you can make by giving entertainments, the pleasure you will derive in advertising the show, selling the tickets and all of the other various details connected with the management of an exhibition of this kind will afford you the greatest enjoyment and you will find no difficulty in paying for the cost of your entire outfit out of the profits of your entertainments.

THE MOVING PICTURE MACHINE IS THE GREATEST INVENTION OF THE AGE. Imagine sitting right in your own home and seeing a great railroad train dash by on the screen at a tremendous rate of speed, pulling its long string of swaying Pullmans as it flashes past. You can almost hear the roar of the giant wheels as the monster thunders by and vanishes in the distance, leaving a cloud of smoke and dust behind. You can see the exciting automobile races, with the great crowds of people surging back and forth on the road and then pressing back against the sides as the huge cars sweep past with a flash. Ocean steamships coming into port with clouds of black smoke pouring from their funnels, the adventures of the pretty housemaid while flirting with the Irish policeman, big crowds of people moving along the street just as natural as life, boys diving from springboards, and the funniest kind of comic and laugh provoking scenes, all of these can be seen on the screen just as real and lifelike as if you were there looking right at the actual scene itself.

THE ILLUSTRATION on this page will give you some idea of the handsome appearance of our new Premier Model Moving Picture Machine. The moving picture mechanism is a most ingenious device and consists of a special gear arrangement and trigger movement with balance wheel and crank handle, all made from the best quality steel and reinforced wherever necessary to insure the greatest strength and durability. The lamp house is made of extra heavy, genuine Russia sheet metal, finely finished and mounted on hardwood baseboard. The lenses are specially ground from the clearest optical glass, and enlarge the picture on the screen up to two or three feet in size, with every detail plain and clear.

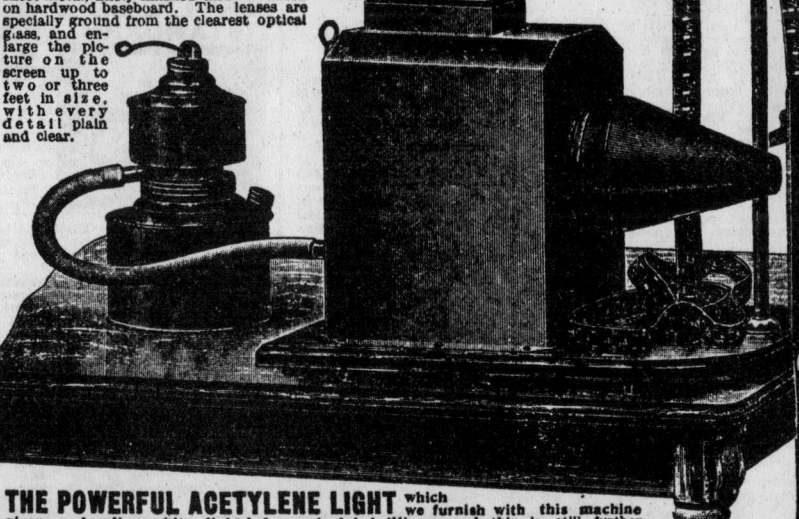

LIST OF MOVING PICTURE FILMS

No. 20L2910 Films for use with our Premier Moving Picture Machine, or any other machine using films of the size and style of perforation, as shown in the illustration.

	Length	Price
Automobile Race	10 ft.	$0.90
Train Scene	10 ft.	.90
Governor Hughes	20 ft.	1.80
Egg Trick	30 ft.	2.70
Sunset Lake	20 ft.	1.80
New York Harbor	10 ft.	.90
City Hall Park, New York, from World Building Dome	10 ft.	.90
Central Park, New York	10 ft.	.90
Ocean Steamer (Lusitania)	20 ft	1.80
Love without Interruption	10 ft.	.90
Good Appetite	10 ft.	.90
Firemen's Parade	30 ft.	2.70
Fire Alarm	10 ft.	.90
Making Sausage	20 ft.	1.80
Too Much Whisky	10 ft.	.90
Poker Game	10 ft.	.90
Barnyard Scene	20 ft.	1.80
New York Street Scene	10 ft.	.90
Crap Game	10 ft.	.90
Tenement House	10 ft.	.90
Shooting the Chutes	10 ft.	.90
Aerial Swing	10 ft.	.90
Scenic Railway	20 ft.	1.80
Shooting the Chutes — from inside boat	20 ft.	1.80
Air Ships	20 ft.	1.80
Loop the Loop	10 ft.	.90
Panoramic View of Coney Island	10 ft.	.90
Bathing at Coney Island	10 ft.	.90
Bowery Scene at Coney Island	10 ft.	.90
The Twister	10 ft.	.90
Heavy Surf	10 ft.	.90

If by mail, postage extra on any of the above films, 2 cents.

GO INTO THE SHOW BUSINESS FOR YOURSELF.

THE POWERFUL ACETYLENE LIGHT which we furnish with this machine gives a dazzling white light of wonderful brilliancy and this is still further increased by the extra large highly polished reflector which is placed behind the burner. The gas is made in our new safety carbide generator and requires only the addition of a few spoonfuls of carbide and a little water and the machine is instantly ready for operation. This is the same kind of generator that is used for bicycle or automobile lights and is so simple and easy to operate that anyone can use it with perfect safety by following the simple directions that come with each machine. This powerful light costs less than one cent for a full evening's entertainment. There is no danger whatever; it is safer to use than the kerosene or coal oil lamp and is so bright and powerful that it makes every detail of the picture plain and distinct upon the screen.

FOR ELECTRIC LIGHT. This machine can also be fitted for attaching to any regular electric light fixture. If you have these fixtures in your house, connected by the city light wires to the electric light plant, you can order the machine with electric light equipment. Understand, however, we do not furnish any apparatus for making the electricity, and the machine cannot be operated by batteries. If you do not have electric fixtures in your home, you will have to use the acetylene gas light. Be the first in your neighborhood to get one of these moving picture machine outfits and you will not only have more fun and amusement than you ever had before but you will be in great demand at parties, socials and entertainments of all kinds and can easily make back in profit the entire cost of your outfit, after which all the money you take in will be clear profit.

No. 20L2900 Premier Moving Picture Machine Outfit, just as illustrated and described on this page, including the complete moving picture machine with safety carbide generator, extra large burner with polished reflector and 10 feet of moving picture film. Shipping weight, 18 pounds. Price.......... **$8.95**

No. 20L2905 Premier Moving Picture Machine Outfit, for electric light, with 50-candle power incandescent bulb, connecting wire, plug and 10 feet of moving picture film. Shipping weight, 18 pounds. Price.......... **9.95**

NOTE: We do not furnish the carbide for use in the acetylene gas generator. You will have to buy this carbide in your own city but it can usually be obtained at any store and costs only a few cents for a pound package.

MOTION PICTURE FILMS

No. 20T2910 **Films for Motion Picture Machines.** Genuine photographic films which fit any of the Biopticons described on the preceding page, also the Premier Motion Picture Machine which we sold last season, or any other machine using films of this size. These films are extra high grade, all made direct from original negatives, of very fine photographic quality, the exact same style and quality used by professional exhibitors except that they are narrower, the width being 11-16 of an inch. They have single perforations, and contain twenty-four pictures to the foot, resulting in very smooth and lifelike motion.

All films are liable to vary slightly from lengths stated, because of difficulty in producing exact lengths by photographic process.

No. 20T2911 **Film Cement,** for mending broken films. Price, per bottle......**12c**
If mail shipment, postage extra, 10 cents.

No. 20T2912 **Film Spacer,** a little device to insure accurate spacing when mending broken films. Price....................**24c**
If mail shipment, postage extra, 2 cents.

COMIC.

No. 1. The Funny Story—Very humorous facial expressions of a Southern darky. Length, 15 feet. Price..........**$1.35**

No. 9. Lung Test—A practical joke. Length, 20 feet. Price..........**$1.80**

No. 10. Breaking Up Housekeeping—A drunkard comes home, smashes dishes, furniture, etc. Length, 25 feet. Price.....**$2.25**

No. 11. Professor Killem—Showing an amateur knocking out a professional prize fighter. Length, 30 feet. Price....**$2.70**

No. 12. Reading a Letter—Showing a colored gentleman reading news of the death of his mother-in-law. Length, 20 feet. Price..........**$1.80**

No. 16. Darktown Cafe—What happens to a swell coon who cannot pay his bill. Length, 35 feet. Price..........**$3.15**

No. 18. Coon Kiss—Two darky lovers, disciples of the Soul Kiss, in practice. Length, 15 feet. Price..........**$1.35**

No. 20. The Cakewalk—The real thing. Length, 15 feet. Price.....**$1.35**

No. 24. The Policeman and the Cook—Mishaps of a cop in the kitchen. Length, 30 feet. Price..........**$2.70**

No. 29. Clown's Head—Grimaces of Marceline, the famous clown. Length, 15 feet. Price........**$1.35**

No. 30. Conversation of Two Circus Clowns—Very funny. Length, 20 feet. Price..........**$1.80**

No. 31. Making Up—An old maid puts on her war paint. Length, 40 feet. Price..........**$3.60**

No. 33. The Watch Dog—A dog, a burglar and a policeman. Length, 15 feet. Price.**$1.35**

No. 38. Two Old Cronies—Sly old chaps reading a comic paper. Length, 20 feet. Price..........**$1.80**

No. 47. The Washerwomen—The dangers of flirting with a pretty laundress. Length, 25 feet. Price..........**$2.25**

No. 56. The Soul Kiss—The longest kiss on record; count the seconds. Length, 5 feet. Price..........**45c**

No. 61. The Clown.—A funny fellow. Length, 5 feet. Price..........**45c**

No. 62. Two Clowns—In animated conversation. Length, 10 feet. Price.......**90c**

No. 78. The Tramp's Bath—A young lady mistakes a tramp for her sweetheart, who suddenly comes on the scene and the tramp's dream ends. Length, 40 feet. Price..**$3.60**

No. 87. Fire in Coontown—A fire breaks out in a house in coon town. Length, 65 feet. Price..........**$5.85**

No. 88. Who Said Watermelon?—A crowd of newsboys attack an old negro, carrying a watermelon, occasioning a mixup. Length, 25 feet. Price..........**$2.25**

No. 89. The Tramp and the Dog—A tramp enters a yard and steals some pies. A bulldog appears on the scene and then things happen. Length, 75 feet. Price.......**$6.75**

No. 92. The Dull Razor—A man tries shaving himself with a dull razor. See the consequences. Length, 45 feet. Price....**$4.05**

No. 105. Wanted, A Dog—A young widow who advertises for a dog receives so many visits from insistent dog owners that she is forced to run, the crowd at her heels. She finally takes refuge in an insane asylum. Length, 95 feet. Price..........**$8.35**

No. 107. Foxy Tramps—Three members of the Hobos' Society refused charity at a farmhouse, get all that's coming to them. Length, 70 feet. Price..........**$6.30**

No. 115. Papa's Stove Pipe Hat—Papa shows off his new folding opera hat. Baby tries to fold up papa's stove pipe hat and makes a beautiful wreck of it. Length, 25 feet. Price..........**$2.25**

No. 116. Lightning Hair Restorer—A bald man grows a thick crop of hair in a very short time. Length, 20 feet. Price..**$1.80**

No. 117. Lover's Parting—Two lovers spooning, when the girl's father comes up with a club and bestows a parental "blessing." Length, 30 feet. Price........**$2.70**

MAGIC.

No. 32. The Disappearing Tramp—Shows a tramp being pursued by a policeman. He hides in a basket but vanishes like air. Length, 10 feet. Price..........**90c**

No. 34. The Cop's Fourth—A sleepy policeman, a boy, some firecrackers, Bang! Poor cop! Length, 15 feet. Price.......**$1.35**

No. 46. Magic Hoop—A mystifying occurrence with a hoop. Length, 15 feet. Price..........**$1.35**

No. 50. The Magic Head—An egg is changed into the head of a girl. Length, 25 feet. Price..........**$2.25**

No. 72. The Magic Face—The magic changes of a face. Length, 10 feet. Price..... **90c**

SENSATIONAL.

No. 0. The Nelson-Gans Fight—Part of the famous fight at Colma, Cal., Sept. 9, 1908, is reproduced on this film. In the last round the knockout and utter collapse of Gans is plainly seen. Length, 50 feet. Price..........**$4.50**

No. 3. The Dude and the Mine Explosion—The mishaps of a dude in a mine. Length, 35 feet. Price..........**$3.15**

No. 15. The Human Trolley—At Steeplechase Park, Coney Island. Length, 15 feet. Price..........**$1.35**

No. 42. The Stolen Bicycle—A tramp runs off with a bicycle, has very exciting experiences and is followed by an ever increasing crowd. Length, 85 feet. Price......**$7.65**

No. 44. The Burglary—A policeman surprises a burglar at work and chases him over hill and dale, finally capturing him swimming in a river. Length, 85 feet. Price..........**$7.65**

No. 58. Roller Coaster—At White City, Chicago. Length, 5 feet. Price........**45c**

No. 70. The Kidnaping—A young mother is choked unconscious and her child stolen. She tries to drown herself, but is rescued, and finally the child is restored to her. Length, 100 feet. Price..........**$9.00**

No. 76. Lassoing on "101" Ranch—Oklahoma cowboys lasso a drove of steers. Length, 20 feet. Price..........**$1.80**

No. 77. Pickups on "101" Ranch—Showing expertness of cowboy riders. Length, 20 feet. Price..........**$1.80**

No. 80. Riding the Steer on "101" Ranch—A daring cowboy rides a vicious steer around the corral. Length, 10 feet. Price..........**90c**

No. 81. The Cock Fight—Two game cocks are engaged in mortal combat. Length, 15 feet. Price..........**$1.35**

No. 90. The Little Nest Robbers—A crowd of boys rob a nest, and a farmer discovers it and chases them over hill and dale, until they finally take refuge in the pond near by. Length, 75 feet. Price..........**$6.75**

No. 93. Dieppe Circuit—Scene in a famous French auto race, where autos round a dangerous curve on two wheels at high rate of speed. Length, 10 feet. Price........**90c**

No. 94. Vanderbilt Cup Race—Several views of this famous automobile race. Length, 100 feet. Price..........**$9.00**

No. 99. Drama in Midair—A balloon is struck by lightning, and the aeronauts are plunged into the water and finally rescued by a boat sent from a passing steamer. Length, 25 feet. Price..........**$2.25**

No. 104. Mother's Little Helper—A four-year old child takes the place of her sick mother as manager of the farm. She milks the cows, goes to market, chides the shiftless servants, etc. Length, 100 feet. Price.**$9.00**

No. 108. Wild Goose Chase—A ferocious goose chases a man over fences, through sewers and rivers, and finally catches him under a sheet, then the feathers fly. A scream from beginning to end. Length, 100 feet. Price..........**$9.00**

No. 114. The Snake Charmer—A big rattlesnake twines about a man's neck and wriggles back and forth. Length, 5 feet. Price..**45c**

No. 119. Stage Coach Robbery—Bandits hold up a stage coach; after robbing the passengers, ride off with their booty. Length, 55 feet. Price..........**$4.95**

No. 120. Cowboy Life—Shows feats of lassoing, wrestling and broncho busting and a bar scene where the cowboys make an unfortunate tenderfoot dance to the tune of bullets. Length, 60 feet. Price......**$5.40**

SCENIC AND TRAVEL.

No. 2. Skating—A vivid reproduction of this popular winter sport. Length, 20 feet. Price..........**$1.80**

No. 7. Shooting the Chutes—At Coney Island. Length, 15 feet. Price.....**$1.35**

No. 13. Herald Square—A busy corner at the intersection of Broadway, 6th Avenue and 34th Street, New York. Length, 20 feet. Price..........**$1.80**

No. 17. Washington Flyer—Shows a ponderous train thundering past at great speed. Length, 20 feet. Price..........**$1.80**

No. 22. Fifth Avenue and 42d Street, New York—The busiest corner in New York. Length, 15 feet. Price..........**$1.35**

No. 25. Scenic Railway—At White City, Chicago. Length, 25 feet. Price....**$2.25**

No. 26. Miniature Railway—The smallest train in the world. Length, 10 feet. Price..........**90c**

No. 27. The Waterfall—In the Catskill Mountains. Length, 10 feet. Price.....**90c**

No. 28. Coast Scene—A view of the beach near Dover, England. Length, 25 feet. Price..........**$2.25**

No. 36. The Panorama of a Railroad—A scene from the rear of a fast train. Length, 15 feet. Price..........**$1.35**

No. 37. Board Walk, Atlantic City—A daily scene on this famous thoroughfare. Length, 15 feet. Price..........**$1.35**

No. 45. Sailing Sheepshead Bay, N. Y.—Sailboats, launches, etc., on this popular bay. Length, 30 feet. Price..........**$2.70**

No. 49. North River Panorama—Steamers, ferryboats, etc., are shown moving on this great waterway. Length, 35 feet. Price..........**$3.15**

No. 53. The Lake in Winter—A group of boys skating. Length, 10 feet. Price..**90c**

No. 54. Down the Chutes—Shooting the Chutes at Coney Island. Length, 5 feet. Price..........**45c**

No. 57. The Busy Crossing—5th Avenue and 42d Street, New York. Length, 10 feet. Price..........**90c**

No. 59. The Cascade—A beautiful waterfall. Length, 5 feet. Price.........**45c**

No. 60. The Breakers—Shows great waves dashing over the pier. Very beautiful. Length, 10 feet. Price..........**90c**

No. 64. Railroad Panorama—Taken from rear of swiftly moving train. Length, 10 feet. Price..........**90c**

No. 65. The Board Walk—Atlantic City's famous promenade. Length, 10 feet. Price..........**90c**

No. 82. Niagara Falls—A beautiful picture, showing four views of the Falls and Rapids in motion. Length, 25 feet. Price....**$2.25**

No. 83. Twentieth Century Limited—Showing one of the fastest trains in the world passing a local train at a tremendous speed. Length, 15 feet. Price..........**$1.35**

No. 95. American Falls—A view of the most beautiful part of Niagara in motion. Length, 5 feet. Price..........**45c**

No. 97. Trip Through Colorado—Showing glimpses of the beautiful Colorado scenery. Length, 80 feet. Price..........**$7.20**

No. 98. Trip Through Canada—Showing scenery along the St. Lawrence river. Length, 60 feet. Price..........**$5.40**

No. 100. Japanese Children—Showing child life in Japan. Length, 15 feet. Price.**$1.35**

No. 101. Off For the War—Japanese soldiers no their way to Mukden. Length, 40 feet. Price..........**$3.60**

No. 103. Bay of Biscay—A pretty view of this stormy bay. Length, 45 feet. Price..........**$4.05**

No. 106. Rocky Mountain Scenery—A particularly beautiful picture of the rugged scenes in the Rockies. Length, 45 feet. Price..........**$4.05**

No. 109. Mount Vesuvius in Eruption—Two views of this stupendous phenomenon; one at the brink of the crater, and the other showing a great river of molten lava in motion. Length, 55 feet. Price..........**$4.95**

No. 110. Scenes in Florida—Shows various beautiful scenes in this state, and also a herd of alligators. Length, 50 feet. Price..........**$4.50**

No. 111. Inaugural Ceremonies at Washington—Beautiful views of the inauguration of President Taft on March 4, 1909. Length, 100 feet. Price..........**$9.00**

MISCELLANEOUS.

No. 4. Lady Acrobats—Full of life and action. Length, 25 feet. Price......**$2.25**

No. 6. Trick Elephant—A famous baby elephant performs some wonderful tricks. Length, 15 feet. Price..........**$1.35**

No. 8. French Dancing Girls—Showing a famous French dance. Length, 20 feet. Price..........**$1.80**

No. 19. Barnum & Bailey Circus—Parade of animals, chariots, acrobats, etc., at the greatest show on earth. Length, 70 feet. Price..........**$6.30**

No. 21. Street Circus Parade—A very clear outdoor picture of this always most interesting parade. Length, 30 feet. Price..**$2.70**

No. 23. Baby's Bath—"Oh! Isn't he a darling" exactly describes this beautiful film. Length, 40 feet. Price..........**$3.60**

No. 35. Boys Swimming—Lifelike scene, very amusing when reversed. Length, 15 feet. Price..........**$1.35**

No. 39. Ring Around A-Rosie—Beautiful picture of child life. Length, 10 feet. Price..........**90c**

No. 40. Feeding Chickens—Very rural picture. Length, 10 feet. Price..........**90c**

No. 41. The Divers—Expert diving from a springboard. Length, 20 feet. Price...**$1.80**

No. 43. The Clay Modeler—Remarkable reproduction of a famous artist at work. Length, 40 feet. Price..........**$3.60**

No. 48. The Ostrich Farm—These gigantic birds are shown to good advantage in this film. Length, 20 feet. Price........**$1.80**

No. 51. "101" Ranch—Miller Bros.' ranch at Bliss, Okla., showing parade of cowboys, Indians, etc. Length, 50 feet. Price..**$4.50**

No. 52. On Parade—A regiment of soldiers marching down Broad Street, Philadelphia. Length, 25 feet. Price..........**$2.25**

No. 55. Dancing Acrobats—A very strenuous dance. Length, 10 feet. Price.....**90c**

No. 63. Boys Diving—From a lofty pier into a deep bay. Length, 5 feet. Price..**45c**

No. 66. Ring Around—Children at play. Length, 5 feet. Price..........**45c**

No. 67. The Barnyard—A farmer's wife feeding the chickens. Length, 5 feet. Price..........**45c**

No. 68. The Springboard—Showing fancy diving. Length, 5 feet. Price.......**45c**

No. 69. The Ostriches—On a California ostrich farm. Length, 10 feet. Price..**90c**

No. 71. Teddy Bears at Play—Two bears frolicking in their cages. Length, 15 feet. Price..........**$1.35**

No. 73. Houchee Couchee Dance—Good reproduction of this famous dance. Length, 20 feet. Price..........**$1.80**

No. 74. Roly-Poly—Women, children and dogs rolling down hill, unaware of the presence of the camera man. Length, 10 feet. Price..........**90c**

No. 75. The Chinaman and the Tramp—In a dexterous juggling feat. Length, 20 feet. Price..........**$1.80**

No. 79. Leap Frog—A pastime of bathers on the beach. Length, 15 feet. Price..**$1.35**

No. 84. Fire Boat in Action—Throwing powerful streams of water to a great height. Length, 20 feet. Price..........**$1.80**

No. 85. Fire Engines at Work—A good view of this always interesting sight. Length, 35 feet. Price..........**$3.15**

No. 86. Going to the Fire—Fire apparatus dashing down a crowded street. Length, 35 feet. Price..........**$3.15**

No. 91. Babies and Kittens—A cunning picture. Length, 20 feet. Price.......**$1.80**

No. 96. The Punctured Tire—Scenes in an auto race, when a tire gets punctured. Shows quick action. Length, 70 feet. Price..**$6.30**

RELIGIOUS.

No. 121. Birth of Christ and the Three Wise Men—Length, 60 feet. Price...**$5.40**

No. 122. Christ in Jerusalem—Length, 60 feet. Price..........**$5.40**

No. 123. Mary Magdalene—Length, 60 feet. Price..........**$5.40**

No. 124. Christ Before Pilate—Length, 50 feet. Price..........**$4.50**

No. 125. Christ in Wilderness—Length, 30 feet. Price..........**$2.70**

No. 126. Judas Betrays Christ—Length, 40 feet. Price..........**$3.60**

No. 127. Christ Bearing Cross—Length, 85 feet. Price..........**$7.65**

No. 128. Crucifixion of Christ—Length, 50 feet. Price..........**$4.50**

No. 129. Ascension of Christ—Length, 15 feet. Price..........**$1.35**

No. 130. The Last Supper—Length, 25 feet. Price..........**$2.25**

STANDARD SIZE PHOTOGRAPHIC SLIDES.

No. 20T2945 **The following Lantern Slides are all genuine photographic slides** made from original negatives and are suitable for use with the No. 3 Biopticon, the Buckeye Magic Lantern or any other magic lantern or stereopticon that uses standard size slides. These slides measure 3¼x4 inches, exactly the same size and exactly the same style used by public exhibitors and lecturers. These slides are all put up in sets of twelve, and we do not sell less than a set. We furnish them plain (uncolored) or beautifully colored by hand.

Order No. 20T2945 and state name of set wanted.

Price, per set, plain..........**$2.16**
Price, per set, colored..........**3.12**

Washington, D. C.—Twelve accurate pictures of the government buildings, street scenes, monuments and historical points in our national capitol.

New York City—Twelve interesting pictures of prominent buildings, streets, harbor scenes, etc., in this largest of American cities.

Western Scenes—A set of twelve fine views illustrating the most interesting things on the Pacific Coast.

Chicago—This set includes twelve pictures made in this busy city, street scenes, pictures of skyscraper buildings, views in the parks, etc. A very interesting set.

Yellowstone National Park, No. 1—Twelve splendid pictures, illustrating the most interesting of the natural phenomena in this wonderland.

Yellowstone National Park, No. 2—The remarkable features of the Yellowstone Park are so numerous that we have prepared a second set of twelve pictures, all entirely different from the pictures of set No. 1, so if you order both sets you will have twenty-four different pictures of this wonderful land of geysers, boiling springs, beautiful rock formations, wild mountain scenery, waterfalls, etc.

Yosemite Valley—This set of twelve slides contains some of the most beautiful views we sell, as the marvelous scenery of this valley is probably unequaled in any other part of the world.

Niagara Falls—Included in this set of twelve pictures are views made both in summer and in winter, illustrating in a wonderfully realistic manner the beauties of this famous waterfall.

Philippine Islands—Twelve very interesting views, illustrating the manners and customs of the people in this new possession of the United States.

Egypt—This set of twelve slides includes some particularly fine views made in this intensely interesting country.

Italy—Twelve beautiful views made in sunny and picturesque Italy, including very interesting views of the noted buildings in Rome.

Paris—Twelve splendid views of the most interesting points in the gayest city of the world.

Germany—Twelve wonderfully realistic pictures of places that people travel thousands of miles to see.

England—About half of the twelve pictures in this set were made in the city of London, the others in various interesting parts of England.

England, Ireland and Scotland—This set of twelve slides includes views from each of these countries, and none of the views that are included in the English set are duplicated, so both sets may be purchased without fear of obtaining duplicate pictures.

Switzerland—Twelve magnificent pictures of the grandest and most rugged mountain scenery in the world, including beautiful mountains, lakes, glaciers, etc.

India—Twelve carefully selected pictures illustrating in a striking manner the most interesting things in this land of mystery.

Holy Land—This set of twelve slides includes some of the finest pictures made in Palestine, illustrating places and objects of interest in connection with Bible history.

Animals—This set of twelve pictures will please the young people, as they are actual photographs from life of such animals as the lion, elephant, camel, zebra, etc.

Comic—No collection of magic lantern views is complete without at least one set of comic views, and the twelve pictures included in this set are sure to please both young and old.

MOTION PICTURE FILMS

No. 20R2910 Films for Motion Picture Machines. Genuine photographic films which fit any of the Biopticons described on the preceding page, also the Premier Motion Picture Machine which we sold last season, or any other machine using films of this size. These films are extra high grade, all made direct from original negatives, of very fine photographic quality, the exact same style and quality used by professional exhibitors except that they are narrower, the width being 11-16 of an inch. They have single perforations, and contain twenty-four pictures to the foot, resulting in very smooth and lifelike motion.

No.	Title	Length, feet	Price
1	The Funny Story	15	$1.35
2	Skating	20	1.80
3	The Dude and the Mine Explosion	35	3.15
4	Lady Acrobats	25	2.25
6	Trick Elephant	15	1.35
7	Shooting the Chutes	15	1.35
8	French Dancing Girls	20	1.80
9	The Lung Test	20	1.80
10	Breaking Up House-keeping	25	2.25
11	Professor Killem	30	2.70
12	Reading a Letter	20	1.80
13	Herald Square	20	1.80
15	The Human Trolley	15	1.35
16	Darktown Cafe	35	3.15
17	Washington Flyer	20	1.80
18	Coon Kiss	15	1.35
20	Cake Walk	15	1.35
21	Street Circus Parade	30	2.70
23	Baby's Bath	40	3.60
24	A Policeman and the Cook	30	2.70
25	Scenic Railway	25	2.25
26	Miniature Railway	10	.90
27	Waterfall	10	.90
28	Coast Scene	25	2.25
29	Clown's Head	15	1.35
30	Conversation of Two Circus Clowns	20	1.80
31	Making Up	40	3.60
32	Disappearing Tramp	10	.90
33	The Watch Dog	15	1.35
34	The Cop's Fourth	15	1.35
35	Boys Swimming	15	1.35
36	Panorama of Railroad	15	1.35
38	Two Old Cronies	20	1.80
40	Feeding Chickens	10	.90
41	The Divers	20	1.80
42	Stolen Bicycle	85	7.65
43	The Clay Molder	40	3.60
44	The Burglar	85	7.65
45	Sailing Sheepshead Bay, N. Y.	30	2.70
46	Magic Hoop	15	1.35
47	Washerwoman	25	2.25
50	The Magic Head	25	2.25
51	"101" Ranch	50	4.50
52	On Parade	25	2.25
53	The Lake in Winter	10	$0.90
54	Down the Chute	5	.45
55	Dancing Acrobats	10	.90
56	The Soul Kiss	5	.45
57	The Busy Crossing	10	.90
58	Roller Coaster	5	.45
59	The Cascade	5	.45
60	The Breakers	10	.90
61	The Clown	5	.45
62	Two Clowns	10	.90
63	Boys Diving	5	.45
64	Railroad Panorama	10	.90
65	Board Walk	10	.90
66	Ring-a-Round	5	.45
67	Barnyard	5	.45
68	The Springboard	5	.45
69	Ostriches	10	.90
71	Teddy Bears at Play	15	1.35
72	The Magic Face	10	.90
76	Lassoingon 101 Ranch	20	1.80
78	The Tramp's Bath	40	3.60
79	Leap Frog	15	1.35
81	Cock Fight	15	1.35
82	Niagara Falls	25	2.25
83	Twentieth Century Limited	15	1.35
84	Fireboat in Action	20	1.80
85	Fire Engine at Work	35	3.15
88	WhoSaidWatermelon	25	2.25
91	Babies and Kittens	20	1.80
92	The Dull Razor. Very funny	45	4.05
93	Dieppe Circuit. Auto race	10	.90
94	Vanderbilt Cup Race	100	9.00
95	Niagara Falls. American side	5	.45
96	The Punctured Tire. How a professional chauffeur can work when he wants to	70	6.30
99	Tragedy in Mid-Air. Showing balloon struck by lightning	25	2.25
100	Japanese Children. School parade	15	1.35
101	Off for the War. Japanese soldiers	40	3.60

All films are liable to vary slightly from lengths stated, because of difficulty in producing exact lengths by photographic process.

No. 20R2911 Film Cement, for mending broken films. Price, per bottle......**12c**
If mail shipment, postage extra, 10 cents.

No. 20R2912 Film Spacer, a little device to insure accurate spacing when mending broken films. Price **24c**
If mail shipment, postage extra, 2 cents.

TOY MAGIC LANTERNS AT 48c TO $1.89

These complete Home Magic Lantern Outfits each contain a handsome black enameled metal lantern, decorated in gilt and mounted on wood baseboard, twenty-five large advertising posters, twenty-five admission tickets and also six or twelve colored slides, according to price of outfit selected, with three to four pictures on each slide. The lenses are of good quality, clear optical glass and the lamp is made to burn ordinary kerosene or coal oil.

No. 20R2805 Home Magic Lantern Outfit

Slide used in Home Lantern

No. 1, complete as above described, with six colored slides, 1⅛ inches wide, magnifying pictures to one foot in diameter.
Price..........(If mail shipment, postage extra, 24 cents.).............**48c**

No. 20R2806 Extra slides, colored, for lantern No. 20R2805. Price, per package (12 slides).....(If mail shipment, postage extra, 9 cents.)....**20c**

No. 20R2808 Home Magic Lantern Outfit No. 2, same as No. 20R2805, but with twelve colored slides, 1⅜ inches wide, magnifying pictures to two feet in diameter. Price, complete **$1.25**
If mail shipment, postage extra, 52 cents.

No. 20R2809 Extra Slides, colored, for lantern No. 20R2808. Price, per package (12 slides)....(If mail shipment, postage extra, 18 cents.).....**36c**

No. 20R2811 Home Magic Lantern Outfit No. 3, same as No. 20R2805, but with 12 colored slides, 2 inches wide, magnifying pictures to three feet diameter. Shipping wt., 4½ lbs. Price, complete **$1.89**

No. 20R2812 Extra Slides, colored, for lantern No. 20R2811. Price, per package (12 slides) ......(If mail shipment, postage extra, 23 cents.) **64c**

No. 20R2865 Extra Chimney to fit any size Home Magic Lantern. Price, each..**10c**

No. 20R2866 Extra Wicks to fit any size Home Magic Lantern. Price, 6 for..**5c**

NOTE—When ordering chimneys or wicks, be sure to state which size lantern they are to fit.

GENUINE PHOTOGRAPHIC SLIDES.

No. 20R2848 These slides are real photographs, made by exactly the same process as the slides used by professional exhibitors and are much superior to the slides ordinarily furnished with lanterns for home amusement. These photographic slides are put up in sets of twelve slides, and there are four views on each slide so each set contains forty-eight pictures. With each set we furnish a printed lecture which gives full information about each picture. We furnish these photographic slides in five different sets, as follows: **Spanish-American War, Russian-Japanese War, St. Louis Exposition, San Francisco Earthquake, Bible Views.**

Size	Price per set	If mail shipment, postage extra,
1⅛ in. wide	$1.13	20c
2 in. wide	1.35	26c
2⅜ in. wide	2.48	38c
2¾ in. wide	2.93	44c

When ordering be sure to state which set you want, and size. These slides can be used in any of the lanterns shown on this page except the No. 20R2805.

THE GLORIA MAGIC LANTERN OUTFITS $5.30 TO $7.40

GENUINE GLORIA MAGIC LANTERNS

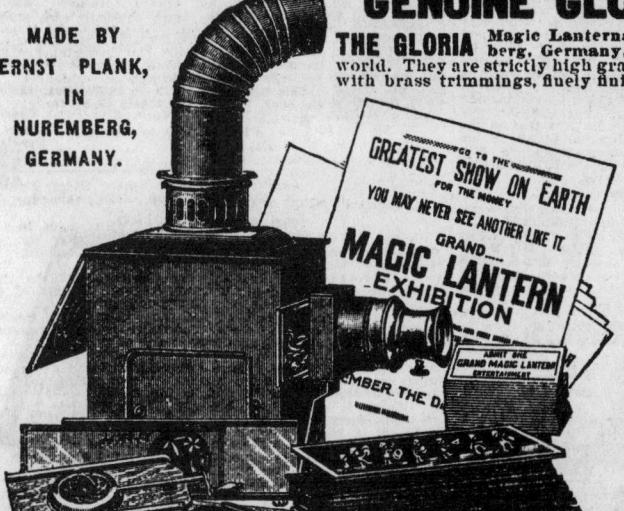

MADE BY ERNST PLANK, IN NUREMBERG, GERMANY.

THE GLORIA Magic Lanterns come from the famous factory of Ernst Plank, Nuremberg, Germany, noted as the maker of the finest magic lanterns in the world. They are strictly high grade lanterns, made of genuine Russia sheet iron lacquered, with brass trimmings, finely finished all the way through; handsome and fine appearing, thoroughly practical, strong and durable lanterns.

THE LENSES and other special features. The Gloria Lanterns are provided with two large size condensing lenses, and a fine, specially ground projection lens which is focused by rack and pinion movement. This perfect optical construction, together with the powerful duplex lamp, results in producing on the screen a sharp, clean cut picture of unusual brilliancy and clearness. The lamp with which the Gloria Lantern is equipped is made with double or duplex burner, giving an exceptionally white and powerful light, and perfect ventilation is secured by the ample air spaces at the bottom of the lantern and the tall Russia iron chimney. This lantern burns ordinary kerosene (coal oil) and is an exceptionally fine instrument for parlor exhibitions.

Each Gloria Magic Lantern Outfit Contains One Gloria Magic Lantern,
Twelve Colored Slides with four pictures on each slide, making forty-eight different pictures.
One Comic Slip Slide producing most amusing effects.
One Movable Scenery Slide always an interesting feature to the youngsters.
One Brilliant Chromotrope or artificial fire works slide.
Fifty Advertising Posters large size, sure to bring out a big audience.
Fifty Admission Tickets regular full size tickets.

PACKED IN WOODEN CASE The Gloria Lantern, together with all the slides, the colored slide, the slip slide, the movable scenery slide, the chromotrope, and one extra glass chimney, comes packed in a well made hinged cover wooden case, and will certainly delight and please any boy or girl who is fortunate enough to get one.

PLEASURE AND PROFIT. The young people not only derive great pleasure from giving MAGIC LANTERN EXHIBITIONS, but the business training which they gain in all the various details connected with the management, putting up advertising posters, selling tickets, etc., gives them ideas of the rudiments of money making which starts them on the highway to business success. REMEMBER that each outfit contains a fine Magic Lantern, a splendid assortment of Colored Views, a large supply of Posters and plenty of Tickets. Interesting, instructive and profitable. You will easily make the original cost of the outfit in your first exhibition; after that it is all profit.

No. 20R2831 Gloria Magic Lantern Outfit, size No. 1. Exactly as illustrated and described above, using slides 2 inches wide, producing pictures on the screen from 3 to 4 feet in diameter. Shipping wt., 11 lbs.
Price for the complete outfit **$5.30**

No. 20R2832 Extra Slides, colored, for lantern No. 20R2831.
Price, per package (12 slides)..**64c**

No. 20R2833 Gloria Magic Lantern Outfit, size No. 2. Exactly the same as outfit No. 20R2831, but larger size, using slides 2⅜ inches wide, and producing pictures 4 to 5 feet in diameter. Shipping wt., 12 lbs.
Price for the complete outfit..**$6.50**

No. 20R2834 Extra Slides, colored, for lantern No. 20R2833.
Price, per package (12 slides)..**85c**

No. 20R2835 Gloria Magic Lantern Outfit, size No. 3. Exactly the same as outfit No. 20R2831, but still larger, using slides 2¾ inches wide, and producing pictures from 5 to 6 feet in diameter. Shipping wt., 14½ lbs.
Price for the complete outfit **$7.40**

No. 20R2836 Extra Slides, colored, for lantern No. 20R2835.
Price, per package (12 slides)..**$1.12**

No. 20R2837 Extra Chimneys, for any style Gloria Lanterns. State which lantern chimney is to fit.
Price, each..**10c**

PRINTS AT NIGHT

The Finest of Developing Papers.

All Darko papers may be printed either by lamplight or by daylight. Underexposed prints may be brought out fully by simply leaving them in the developer a little longer, and overexposed prints may be saved by removal from the developer a little sooner. In development the picture does not flash up almost instantaneously as it does with other

PRINTS ON DARKO PAPER may be made at any time, on dark, cloudy days, or at night, and any kind of light may be used, a kerosene lamp, a gas jet, an electric light, or diffused sunlight. Printing is, of course, accomplished more rapidly with a brilliant light than a weak one. For example, the paper will print more rapidly with an electric arc lamp than it will with a kerosene lamp, but prints made with a kerosene lamp are just as good, in fact, are exactly the same as prints made by any other light, the only difference being the time required for printing. The length of time required for printing Darko paper depends upon the brilliancy of the light and the density of the negative. With a very thing negative and a very bright light, just a few seconds may be sufficient while several minutes may be required with a denser negative or a weaker light; but with an average negative and a bright kerosene lamp, for example, the time required is from one to two minutes.

THE BEAUTIFUL RESULTS which can be secured with the various styles of Darko paper commend it to both the amateur and the professional photographer. It is an ideal paper for the amateur who finds his time too much occupied during the day for photographic work, because the prints may be made and finished in the evening, and it is an ideal paper for the professional photographer, because it makes him independent of the weather. It enables him to deliver his pictures when they are promised whether the sun shines or not.

CARBON AND PLATINUM EFFECTS. Prints made on the various styles of Darko paper combine the artistic qualities of both the carbon and platinum processes. There is a richness of tone in the shadows, a clearness in the whites, and a sharpness of outline that is unequaled by other developing papers. The prints are remarkable for their softness without loss of detail; the high lights are distinct and well defined without harshness, and the shadows are full of detail which passes by imperceptible gradations into the high lights.

IT IS VERY EASY TO MAKE AND FINISH PRINTS on any of the various styles of Darko papers. Only a few moments are required for printing; developing is accomplished in just a few seconds, after which the prints are fixed and washed in the usual manner and the pictures are complete. In simplicity and ease of operation, beautiful results, and as a time saver, Darko papers are unrivaled.

AS COMPARED WITH OTHER DEVELOPING PAPERS, Darko possesses certain special points of superiority, among which is its great latitude in development. Slight errors of underexposure or overexposure are readily corrected in the developer. developing papers, but comes up slowly and evenly, the entire period of development occupying from five to ten seconds, which permits the operator to watch the progress of development and avoid over or under development.

No. 20R1703 Carbon Matte Darko. This style of Darko is made with a fine matte surface, a surface that may perhaps be better described as a dull finish. It is not a rough surface, and yet it is not a glossy surface. It is suited to almost any kind of a picture and gives particularly pleasing effects for landscapes. Carbon Matte Darko is best suited to soft negatives. For prices, see list below.

No. 20R1704 Rough Darko. The surface of this style of Darko is quite rough, a finish that is rapidly becoming more popular than ever, because of its unusually artistic effects. It is especially suited to landscape views and large portraits, and is adapted to practically any kind of a negative. For prices, see list below.

No. 20R1705 Glossy Darko. This style of Darko is made with a highly polished or glossy surface, similar to the surface of a gelatine printing-out paper. Prints made on this paper should be squeegeed or mounted upon cards and burnished in order to bring out the full extent of polish or glossiness. It is suited to negatives of almost any kind, and the prints show a greater amount of detail than the dull finish or rough styles. For prices, see list below.

No. 20R1706 Smooth Portrait Darko. The surface of this paper is the same as the Carbon Matte Darko, but the emulsion is particularly suited to negative that show a great deal of contrast. Of the four styles of Darko here described, the Smooth Portrait is perhaps the best style for general all around work. It is an excellent paper for landscape views, gives fine results with architectural subjects, and is a very good paper for groups.

CARBON MATTE, ROUGH, GLOSSY AND SMOOTH PORTRAIT

Four Standard Varieties of Darko.

Prices on Carbon Matte, Rough, Glossy and Smooth Portrait Darko.

Order by catalog number as shown above.

Size	Dozen	Half Gross	Gross	Size	Dozen	Half Gross	Gross
3½x3½	8c	46c	$0.87	3⅞x5½ (cab.)	11c	63c	$1.19
3¼x4¼	9c	52c	.98	4 x6	13c	74c	1.41
3¼x5½	10c	58c	1.12	4¼x6½	15c	80c	1.55
4 x5	10c	57c	1.08	5 x7	16c	91c	1.73

Size	Dozen	Half Gross	Gross	Size	Dozen	Half Gross	Gross
5 x 8	19c	$1.09	$2.06	7 x 9	33c	$1.80	$3.45
6 x 8	26c	1.44	2.85	7½x 9½	36c	1.95	3.75
6½x 8½	29c	1.66	3.14	8 x10	40c	2.28	4.32
3½x 6 (Die cut, with arched tops, for stereoscopic pictures), made in glossy only	14c	.68	1.30				

Order by the gross; all Darko papers keep good for months. For working formulas see special Camera Catalog or instructions which are enclosed with each package.

Silvered Darko, A Novelty

Silvered Darko is distinguished from all other sensitized papers by its beautiful, burnished, silvery surface. There is a thin metallic coating under the emulsion itself which gives to the pictures a beautiful silvery sheen. Prints made on this paper are striking in appearance and entirely different from any other kind of print.

Silvered Darko is particularly suitable for marine and winter scenes, producing effects which are not obtainable with any other paper, and very pleasing results are obtained in landscape work. Silvered Darko is worked just the same as all the other styles of Darko, printed by artificial light, and just as easy and simple to manipulate as any of the other styles.

No. 20R1735 Silvered Darke Paper.

Size	Doz.	½ Gro.	Size	Doz.	½ Gro.
3½x3½	13c	$0.72	5 x7	32c	1.70
3¼x4¼	14c	.75	5 x8	36c	2.00
4 x5	22c	1.05	6½x8½	54c	2.95
3⅞x5½	23c	1.10	8 x10	72c	4.15

This paper keeps good indefinitely.

You can order by the gross without fear of its spoiling on your hands.

Monox Bromide Paper.

Monox is a thoroughly reliable and uniform Bromide paper. It is noted for its soft, beautiful blacks, deep, rich, transparent shadows, and in its class is unequaled for detail. Monox Bromide Paper is very rapid, gives a sharp image, and has a brilliant and subtle individuality that distinguishes it from all other bromide papers. There are no cold blue tones in Monox paper, no chalky whites, no intense blacks. It is an ideal paper for enlargements, and has been brought to so high a degree of perfection that it is also perfectly satisfactory for contact printing.

No. 20R1750 Monox Bromide Paper.

Size	Price, Per Dozen	Price, Per Half Gross	Price, Per Gross
5 x 7	$0.22	$ 1.27	$ 2.44
6½x 8½	.41	2.18	4.12
8 x10	.53	3.10	6.00
10 x12	.82	4.80	9.00
11 x14	1.05	6.00	11.55
14 x17	1.61	9.38	18.00
16 x20	2.10	12.00	23.62
20 x24	3.15	18.75	36.00

To those who prefer to purchase "ready to use" preparations we recommend our Darko Developing powder; (for this Bromide powder see page 775), dissolving each tube in 6 ounces of water, instead of 4 ounces as directed for Darko papers.

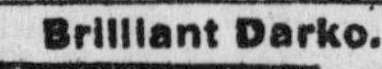

Brilliant Darko.

Prints made on Brilliant Darko have the characteristic surface, finish and general effect of prints made on collodion matte surface papers. It is an ideal paper for the professional photographer, as the prints possess all the peculiarly characteristic effects of tone, surface and detail of the best collodion matte surface papers, and yet it may be printed by artificial light, making the photographer entirely independent of the weather. Brilliant Darko is coated on the same high grade of imported stock that we use for all of the other varieties of Darko paper, the prints are absolutely permanent and there is a wealth of detail in the halftones that is not equaled by any other developing paper.

No. 20R1725 Brilliant Darko Paper.

Size	Doz.	½ Gro.	Gross	Size	Doz.	½ Gro.	Gross
3½x3½	9c	$0.49	$0.93	4 x6	16c	$0.80	$1.52
3¼x4¼	10c	.52	.99	5 x7	18c	.98	1.86
4 x5	12c	.62	1.18	6½x8½	33c	1.80	3.42
3⅞x5½	13c	.65	1.24	8 x10	45c	2.45	4.65

10-foot rolls, 26 inches wide, each 1.65

10-yard rolls, 26 inches wide, each 4.10

Cardboard Darko.

This style of Darko is coated upon a stiff cardboard about the thickness and weight of an ordinary postal card, and the prints do not need to be mounted. The surface and emulsion are just the same as the Smooth Portrait Darko, the prints have exactly the same finish and it is suitable for the same classes of work. Very pleasing results are produced by printing with a mask, thus leaving a white margin all around the picture.

If you like to leave your prints unmounted, Cardboard Darko is an ideal paper to use.

No. 20R1730 Cardboard Darko Paper.

Size	Doz.	½ Gro.	Size	Doz.	½ Gro.
3½x3½	9c	$0.49	5 x7	19c	$0.98
3¼x4¼	10c	.50	5 x8	22c	1.10
4 x5	12c	.60	6½x8½	33c	1.80
3⅞x5½	14c	.65	8 x10	45c	2.45

Cardboard Darko keeps for months, so you can order in quantity and thus reduce cost of transportation.

Azuro Blue Print Paper.

Blue Print Paper affords the simplest process known for producing a photographic print, as it requires no chemicals of any kind. It is simply printed by sunlight in the ordinary manner and then washed in clear water, which completes the process of making a finished blue print photograph. The prints are a brilliant blue and white color, and the extreme simplicity, low cost and beautiful results make this paper well worthy of the popularity it has always possessed. Azuro Blue Print Paper is an unusually high grade paper, coated on the very best quality of imported stock, and the prints possess a brilliancy, depth and clearness that is unequaled by other blue print papers.

This paper is put up in hermetically sealed tin cans, twenty-four sheets to a can.

No. 20R1755 Azuro Blue Print Paper.

Size	Price, Per Can	Size	Price, Per Can
3½x3½	12c	5 x7	25c
3¼x4¼	12c	6½x8½	35c
4 x5	15c	8 x10	60c

No chemicals of any kind are required in using this paper.

India-Tint Darko.

India-Tint Darko is an entirely new idea in sensitized paper and of an artistic quality which adds greatly to the possibilities in real pictorial photography. The paper upon which India-Tint Darko is coated is a rough surface paper of a soft India tint color, so the high lights in the picture are of a delicate sepia or light buff tone.

India-Tint Darko is manipulated just the same as the other varieties of Darko, printed, developed, fixed and washed just the same as any developing paper, and is very easy to work. The India tint of the paper itself, contrasted with the rich blacks of the picture, gives an effect that is unique and beautiful.

The Darko Sepia Toner gives particularly pleasing effects with India-Tint Darko, the delicate cream tint of the paper itself harmonizing delightfully with the warm sepia tones and imparting to the print the soft delicacy of an old etching.

No. 20R1728 India-Tint Darko Paper.

Each package contains twenty-four sheets.

Size	Price, Per Package	Size	Price, Per Package
3½x3½	20c	5 x7	40c
3¼x4¼	22c	6½x8½	70c
4 x5	26c	8 x10	95c
3⅞x5½	28c		

There are twenty-four sheets to a package.

DU VOLL'S GELATINE PRINTING-OUT PAPER.

10 CENTS PER DOZEN FOR THE 4X5 SIZE, OTHER SIZES IN PROPORTION.

PRINTS BY SUNLIGHT

DU VOLL'S PAPER IS VERY EASY TO WORK.

It is printed by sunlight and may be toned in an ordinary gold toning solution that anyone can make up without the slightest trouble. After toning the prints are fixed in a plain hypo bath, a simple solution made by dissolving hypo in water, and after fixing they are washed in clear water. It may also be worked by the combined toning and fixing process in which the prints are toned and fixed in one solution, this being a still simpler and easier method of working. The entire process of printing, toning, fixing and washing is very simple and very easy. No dark room is required, and good results, even in the hands of a beginner, are practically certain.

ANY DESIRED TONE

Prints made on Du Voll's Gelatine Printing-Out Paper may be toned to any desired shade from a very warm sepia to a deep purple, or by using a platinum toning bath they may be toned to a rich black. The surface is glossy, and if the prints are squeegeed they have an exceptionally brilliant luster. Gelatine printing-out papers are especially desirable where it is necessary to preserve absolutely all the detail that exists in the negative. No other paper preserves detail so perfectly as a gelatine printing-out paper.

IMPORTED STOCK. **Du Voll's paper is coated on the very best grade of imported stock.** Only the very finest quality of imported gelatine, together with chemicals of the highest degree of purity, are employed in preparing the emulsion for it. The emulsion is very rich in silver, the most important ingredient of sensitized papers, as the brilliancy, richness and detail of the finished prints depend largely upon the purity and quantity of silver in the emulsion.

INSPECTED AND SORTED. **Du Voll's paper is very carefully sorted and thoroughly examined before it is packed.** Every sheet is subjected to the most rigid scrutiny for blemishes or imperfections of any kind, and we absolutely guarantee every sheet of this paper to be perfect. Every gross will yield 144 perfect prints.

PRICES:

No. 20R1702 Du Voll's Printing-Out Paper.

Size		Price, Per Dozen	Price, Per Gross
2½x 2½		$0.07	$ 0.68
3½x 3½		.09	.90
3¼x 4¼		.09	.90
4 x 5		.10	.97
3¼x 5½		.10	.85
3⅞x 5½	(Cabinet)	.11	.98
3½x 6	(Stereo, die cut with arch tops)	.12	.95
4 x 6		.15	1.25
4¼x 6½		.19	1.90
5 x 7		$0.23	$2.12
5 x 8		.24	2.35
6 x 8		.30	2.90
6½x 8½		.33	3.10
7 x 9		.38	3.85
7½x 9½		.42	4.25
8 x10		.44	4.75
4 x 5	Seconds	....	.73
Cabinet	Seconds	....	.80

For larger sizes and rolls see special Camera Catalog. **Less than one gross is sold at dozen rates only.** For example, one-half gross of 4x5 (which is 6 dozen) would cost 60 cents; (6 dozen at 10 cents per dozen), and not one-half of 97 cents. **We cannot violate this rule under any circumstances.**

Sensitized Post Cards.

Sensitized Post Cards enable you to make delightful souvenir postals from your own negatives. For the amateur they offer a means of making post cards that will be far more interesting to those who receive them than would cards which might be purchased ready made. For the professional they are big money makers, as cards made with local views meet with ready sale everywhere at prices which allow a handsome margin of profit. All of our Sensitized Post Cards are of the same size and style as the regular Government postals, 3½x5½ inches, sensitized on one side and divided into spaces for correspondence and address on the other side, as shown in the illustration.

To print post cards from negatives 4x5 or smaller, use a 4¼x6½, or a 5x7 printing frame with glass. To print from negatives 3¼x5½ use a 3⅝x6 frame with glass. To print from negatives 5x7 or larger use a frame of the same size as the negative, without glass.

Post Card Albums. Make post card prints from your favorite negatives and keep them in a Post Card Album. A handsome Post Card Album, filled with the pictures in which you and your friends are most interested makes a delightful souvenir. We show a fine line of new and attractive Post Card Albums on page 777, albums of unusually high quality and all quoted at astonishingly low prices. These albums are handsome in appearance and convenient to use, as the cards are put in without pasting and can be easily removed and rearranged to make room for new ones.

Carbon Matte Darko Post Cards.

No. 20R1740 Our Carbon Matte Darko Post Cards are made with a fine matte surface, just the same as our regular Carbon Matte Darko Paper, and the emulsion is best suited to rather soft negatives. Price, per dozen........**$0.15**
Price, per ½ gross........**.75**
Price, per 1,000........**6.50**

Glossy Darko Post Cards.

No. 20R1741 The Glossy Darko Post Cards are coated on a special pure white stock with a highly glossy surface. They make brilliant prints distinguished by the wealth of detail that is possible only with glossy papers. To bring out the full degree of glossiness they should be squeegeed.
Price, per dozen........**$0.15**
Price, per ½ gross........**.75**
Price, per 1,000........**6.50**

Velvet Darko Post Cards.

No. 20R1742 The surface of the Velvet Darko Post Cards is a semi-matte, a happy medium between that of the Carbon Matte and the Glossy styles. They yield prints which are particularly rich and velvety, with excellent detail.
Price, per dozen........**$0.15**
Price, per ½ gross........**.75**
Price, per 1,000........**6.50**

Du Voll's Printing-Out Post Cards.

No. 20R1745 Du Voll's Printing-Out Post Cards yield glossy prints of the finest delicacy and gradation. The shadows are richly transparent, deep and brilliant and there is a minuteness of detail which is possible only with glossy printing-out papers. These cards are printed by sunlight and toned and fixed just the same as our regular gelatine printing-out paper. Price, per gross, **$1.35**; per dozen. **15c**

Blue Print Post Cards.

No. 20R1748 Blue Print Post Cards afford a very economical and simple method of making souvenir post cards from your own negatives. They are printed by sunlight and finished by washing in water, just the same as any other style of blue paper. No chemicals of any kind are required. Put up in hermetically sealed tin cans, each can containing twelve cards. Price, per can........**13c**

Hammer's Extra Fast Plates.

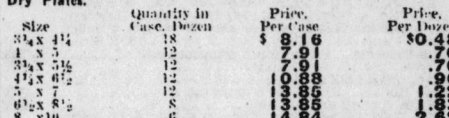

Of the various styles and grades of plates made by the Hammer Dry Plate Company, the Extra Fast is the most popular, being designed especially to meet the requirements for general all around photography. For outdoor work of any kind, instantaneous views, interiors, home portraiture, studio use, architectural subjects, etc. they are unsurpassed, possessing the speed, uniformity and brilliancy so essential in all these classes of work.

No. 20R1760 Hammer's Extra Fast Dry Plates.

Size	Quantity in Case, Dozen	Price, Per Case	Price, Per Dozen
3½x 3½	30	$ 7.57	$0.27
3¼x 4¼	30	8.51	.32
4 x 5	30	12.30	.44
3¼x 5½	30	12.30	.44
4¼x 6½	30	17.02	.61
5 x 7	20	13.87	.75
5 x 8	20	15.76	.85
6½x 8½	12	12.48	1.11
8 x10	12	18.16	1.63

For larger sizes of Hammer's Plates in all styles see our Special Camera Catalog.

Hammer's Special Extra Fast Plates.

Hammer's Special Extra Fast Plates are the most rapid plates made. They are especially adapted to the making of large portraits and large groups in the studio where small stops are necessary. They are fine for flash light work, laughing babies, difficult groups of children and high speed instantaneous work.

No. 20R1761 Hammer's Special Extra Fast Dry Plates.

Size	Quantity in Case, Dozen	Price, Per Case	Price, Per Dozen
3½x 3½	30	$ 8.73	$0.31
3¼x 4¼	30	9.82	.35
4 x 5	30	14.19	.50
5 x 7	20	16.00	.85
6½x 8½	12	14.40	1.28
8 x10	12	20.95	1.86

Hammer's Orthochromatic Extra Fast Plates.

Hammer's Orthochromatic Extra Fast Plates are of the same speed as the regular Extra Fast Plates and are made especially sensitive to orange, yellow, green and the ordinary reds. The color sensitiveness of these plates makes them especially suitable for landscape work, portrait work and all subjects in which color values are particularly important, especially such subjects as flowers and paintings. Landscapes made with these Orthochromatic plates possess a brilliancy that cannot be obtained with ordinary plates. Flowers, paintings and other highly colored subjects can not be successfully photographed without the use of Orthochromatic plates.

No. 20R1764 Hammer's Orthochromatic Extra Fast Dry plates.

Size	Quantity in Case, Dozen	Price, Per Case	Price, Per Dozen
3½x 3½	18	$ 5.59	$0.33
3¼x 4¼	18	6.29	.37
4 x 5	12	6.05	.54
5 x 7	12	10.24	.91
6½x 8½	8	10.24	1.36
8 x10	6	11.17	1.98

The Blue Label Roebuck Plates.

The Blue Label Roebuck Dry Plates are coated on the finest grade of imported glass, carefully sorted, and guaranteed to be free from bubbles, scratches or other imperfections. The emulsion is rich in silver, yielding strong, vigorous negatives, with a wealth of detail and no tendency whatever toward fog. Negatives made with Roebuck Plates are of perfect printing quality, equally suited to either developing papers or printing-out papers, clear, clean, brilliant negatives that will please the most exacting operator.

Roebuck Dry Plates are designed especially to meet the requirements for general all around photography and we recommend them for landscapes, architectural subjects, general instantaneous work, portraits in the studio or in the home, groups and general commercial work. They are absolutely reliable, uniform in speed and quality, and adapted to the widest possible range of work.

Roebuck Plates are easy to work, because they permit unusual latitude in exposure, thus greatly decreasing the possibility of failure by reason of over or under timing. While possessing ample speed for all ordinary requirements, including quick instantaneous exposures under comparatively unfavorable conditions, they are not of **extreme rapidity.**

The Roebuck Plate is fast, but it is not of extreme rapidity. With an ordinary rectilinear lens, an exposure of 1-100 of a second is sufficient, under normal conditions, to make a fully timed negative. With a faster lens, or unusually favorable conditions of light or subject, exposures as short as 1-300 of a second or even less, will produce fully timed negatives with the Roebuck Dry Plate.

Advantages of the Roebuck Dry Plate: First, they produce strong, vigorous negatives of the finest possible printing quality, and are absolutely uniform, both in speed and quality. Second, there is great latitude in exposure and freedom from fog, which makes them easy to work and insures a larger percentage of perfect negatives than is possible with most plates. Third, we sell them at a lower price than is made by any dealer for any other dry plate of equal quality.

No. 20R1775 Blue Label Roebuck Dry Plates.

Size	Quantity in Case, Dozen	Price, Per Case	Price, Per Dozen
2 x 2	50	$ 6.18	$0.13
2½x 2½	50	7.60	.16
2½x 4	50	9.03	.19
3½x 3½	36	7.52	.22
3¼x 4¼	36	8.55	.25
4¼x 4¼	30	9.40	.33
4 x 5	30	10.26	.36
3¼x 5½	30	10.55	.37
4¼x 5½	24	9.35	.41
4¼x 6½	24	11.17	.49
5 x 7	24	13.68	.60
5 x 8	24	15.51	.68
6½x 8½	12	10.26	.90
8 x10	12	14.82	1.30

Hammer's Aurora Double Coated Non-Halation Plates.

These plates are coated first with a slow emulsion which is allowed to dry as usual, after which the plates are again coated, the second coating being the regular Extra Fast emulsion, and the result is a plate possessing great advantages for subjects with great contrast. With these plates interior views may be made directly toward bright windows or open doors without the slightest trace of halation. They preserve perfect detail in tree tops outlined against a bright sky, add wonderfully to the brilliancy of white draperies and are indispensable for snow scenes.

No. 20R1766 Hammer's Aurora Double Coated Non-Halation Dry Plates.

Size	Quantity in Case, Dozen	Price, Per Case	Price, Per Dozen
3¼x 4¼	18	$ 7.68	$0.45
4 x 5	12	7.45	.66
5 x 7	12	13.04	1.15
6½x 8½	8	13.04	1.73
8 x10	6	13.97	2.47

Hammer's Orthochromatic Double Coated Plates.

These plates combine the good qualities of the Aurora Non-Halation Plates and the regular Orthochromatic Plates, possessing the same color sensitiveness as the Orthochromatic plate and the same freedom from halation as the Aurora Non-Halation Plate. The under coating is a Slow Orthochromatic emulsion and the top coating is the Extra Fast Orthochromatic emulsion. For interiors, portrait work, landscapes, cloud effects, flowers, paintings, etc., there is no plate made that surpasses Hammer's Orthochromatic Double Coated Plate.

No. 20R1769 Hammer's Orthochromatic Double Coated Dry Plates.

Size	Quantity in Case, Dozen	Price, Per Case	Price, Per Dozen
3¼x 4¼	18	$ 8.16	$0.48
4 x 5	12	7.91	.70
3¼x 5½	12	7.91	.70
4¼x 6½	12	10.88	.96
5 x 7	12	13.85	1.22
6½x 8½	8	13.85	1.83
8 x10	6	14.84	2.62

Hammer's Lantern Slide Plates.

No. 20R1794 Hammer's Lantern Slide Plates. Extra high grade plates for lantern slide making. Standard size, 3¼x4 inches.

Price, per case (30 dozen), **$12.37**; per dozen........**44c**

Hammer's Dry Plates.

MADE BY HAMMER DRY PLATE CO.
NOT IN THE TRUST.

No. 20L1780 Hammer's Dry Plates, another of the well known standard brands; is considered by professional photographers to be one of the best plates made. We furnish this plate in one speed only—the extra fast—suitable for studio work or general all around photography.

Size	Quantity in Case	Price, per Case	Price, per Doz.
3½x 3½	30 doz.	$ 7.57	$0.28
3¼x 4¼	30 doz.	8.52	.31
4 x 5	30 doz.	12.30	.44
4¼x 6½	30 doz.	17.03	.62
5 x 7	20 doz.	13.90	.75
5 x 8	20 doz.	15.77	.85
6½x 8½	12 doz.	12.48	1.12
8 x10	12 doz.	18.16	1.63
10 x12	4 doz.	10.60	2.86
11 x14	4 doz.	15.14	4.08
14 x17	3 doz.	17.03	6.12

Seed's Dry Plates.

No. 20L1782 Seed's Plates have been on the market so long and are so widely known as **good plates** that comment upon their merits is almost unnecessary. The No. 27 is extremely rapid, but the No. 26X is fast enough for all ordinary work, even including instantaneous exposures.

Size	Quantity in Case	No. 26X Price, per Case	No. 26X Price, per Doz.	No. 27 Price, per Case	No. 27 Price, per Doz.
3½x 3½	30 doz.	$ 8.15	$0.29	$ 8.73	$0.31
3¼x 4¼	30 doz.	9.17	.33	9.82	.35
4 x 5	30 doz.	13.25	.47	14.19	.51
4¼x 6½	30 doz.	18.34	.66	19.65	.70
5 x 7	20 doz.	14.94	.80	16.01	.86
5 x 8	20 doz.	16.98	.91	18.20	.97
6½x 8½	12 doz.	13.45	1.20	14.41	1.28
8 x10	10 doz.	16.30	1.75	17.46	1.87
10 x12	4 doz.	11.41	3.06	12.23	3.26
11 x14	4 doz.	16.30	4.37	17.46	4.66
14 x17	3 doz.	18.34	6.55	19.65	6.99

ANSCO FILM.

Daylight Loading, Non-Curling, and Orthoohromadio.

For use in any Kodak, Buckeye, Ansco, Hawkeye or Seroco Film Camera.

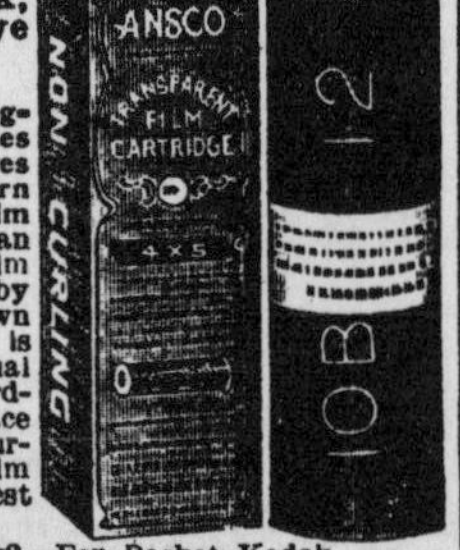

Ansco film is put up in regular daylight loading cartridges of either six or twelve exposures and is adapted to any modern make of daylight loading film camera, including the Eastman Kodaks and the Seroco Film Cameras. This film is made by one of the largest and best known film makers in the world and is guaranteed by them to be equal to any film on the market regardless of price. We will replace with new film or refund the purchase price of any Ansco film found defective to the slightest extent.

No. 20L1825 Size, 1½x2—For Pocket Kodak. Price, per 12 exposure roll $0.21

No. 20L1826 Size, 2¼x2¼—For No. 1 Brownie or No. 1 Buster Brown Camera.
Price per 6 exposure roll .... .12

No. 20L1827 Size, 2¼x3¼—For No. 2 Brownie, No. 2 Buster Brown, No. 3 Buster Brown and No. 1 Folding Buster Brown. Price, per 6 exposure roll .... .17

No. 20L1828 Size, 1⅝x2½—For No. 0 Folding Pocket Kodak. Price, per 6 exposure roll .... .12
Price, per 12 exposure roll .... .21

No. 20L1829 Size, 2¼x3¼—For No. 1 Folding Pocket Kodak. Price, per 6 exposure roll .... .17
Price, per 12 exposure roll .... .34

No. 20L1830 Size, 2½x4¼—For No. 1A Folding Pocket Kodak and Ansco Jr. Price, per 6 exposure roll, .21
Price, per 12 exposure roll .... .42

No. 20L1831 Size, 3¼x4¼—For No. 3 Folding Pocket Kodak, No. 3 Weno Hawkeye, Stereo Weno Hawkeye, No. 3 Buckeye, Nos. 2, 4 and 6 Ansco and Nos. 3, 5, 7 and Stereoscopic Seroco Film Cameras.
Price, per 6 exposure roll .... .30
Price, per 12 exposure roll .... .58

No. 20L1832 Size, 3½x3½—For No. 2 Folding Pocket Kodak, No. 2 Flexo, No. 2 Bullseye, No. 2 Bullet, No. 2 Stereo Kodak, No. 4 Panorama Kodak, Tourist Buckeye No. 2 Weno Hawkeye, No. 3B Al Vista, No. 1 Ansco and No. 1 Seroco Film Camera.
Price, per 6 exposure roll .... .25
Price, per 12 exposure roll .... .50

No. 20L1833 Size, 3¼x5½, For No. 3A Folding Pocket Kodak and Nos. 9 and 10 Ansco.
Price, per 6 exposure roll .... .34
Price, per 10 exposure roll .... .58

No. 20L1834 Size, 4x5—For Nos. 3, 5 and 7 Ansco, No. 4 Folding Buckeye, No. 4 Weno Hawkeye, No. 4 Folding Hawkeye, No. 4 Bullseye, No. 4 Bullet, Nos. 4B and 4G Al Vista, Nos. 2, 4, 6 and 8 Seroco Film Cameras. Price, per 6 exposure roll .... .38
Price, per 12 exposure roll .... .75

No. 20L1835 Size, 4¼x3¼—For No. 3 Cartridge Kodak. Price, per 6 exposure roll .... .30
Price, per 12 exposure roll .... .58

No. 20L1836 Size, 5x4—For No. 4 Cartridge Kodak and Nos. 5B, 5D, 5F and 5C Al Vistas. Price, per 6 exposure roll .... .38
Price, per 12 exposure roll .... .75

No. 20L1837 Size, 7x5—For No. 5 Cartridge Kodak and Nos. 7D, 7E and 7F Al Vistas. Price per 6 exposure roll .... .67
Price, per 12 exposure roll 1.34

THE "BLUE LABEL" ROEBUCK DRY PLATES.

NOT MADE BY THE TRUST.

4X5 **36c**

5X7 **60c**

No. 20L1775 We offer the new "Blue Label" Roebuck Dry Plate as the equal of any dry plate made, a plate that can be depended upon under any conditions, a plate that is suitable for any kind of work.

THE ROEBUCK DRY PLATES are coated on the finest quality of imported Belgian glass, carefully sorted and free from bubbles, scratches or other imperfections.

THE EMULSION IS RICH IN SILVER, yielding strong, vigorous negatives with a wealth of detail and no tendency whatever toward fogging. The factory in which the "Blue Label" Roebuck plates are made is one of the most perfectly equipped dry plate factories ever built, furnished with the very latest and most approved styles of coating machines, and a most complete system of ventilation and refrigeration, giving perfect control of both temperature and hygroscopic conditions. **It is this perfect equipment** combined with long experience in dry plate making and the most perfect materials, which enables us to produce perfect plates **and offer them at prices heretofore considered impossible.**

THE "BLUE LABEL" ROEBUCK PLATES ARE EXCEEDINGLY RAPID giving the finest possible results in the studio where short exposures are so desirable. For landscapes, portraiture, interiors, flashlight work, instantaneous exposures, in fact, any work requiring a uniformly rapid and reliable plate, the Roebuck plate is unsurpassed. In brilliancy, detail, uniformity and speed, this plate will satisfy the most exacting operator.

Size	Quantity in Case, Dozen	Price, per Case	Price, per Dozen	Size	Quantity in Case, Dozen	Price, per Case	Price, per Dozen
2 x 2	50	$6.18	$0.13	4¼x 6½	24	$11.17	$0.49
2½x 2½	50	7.60	.16	5 x 7	24	13.68	.60
2½x 4	50	9.03	.19	5 x 8	24	15.51	.68
3½x 3½	36	7.52	.22	6½x 8½	12	10.26	.90
3¼x 4¼	36	8.55	.25	8 x10	12	14.82	1.30
4¼x 4¼	30	9.40	.33	10 x12	4	8.63	2.27
4 x 5	30	10.26	.36	11 x14	3	9.24	3.24
4¼x 5½	24	9.35	.41	14 x17	3	13.85	4.86

LUMIERE'S DRY PLATES.

For a great many years the Lumiere Plates have been known as the best and highest grade of dry plates manufactured in Europe.

THE LUMIERE COMPANY is the largest manufacturer of sensitized products in Europe, and this famous company has now opened a factory in the United States, in which they are making their complete line of extra high class dry plates.

WE CAN CONSCIENTIOUSLY RECOMMEND the Lumiere plates to our customers as plates representing in every respect the highest degree of perfection. We carry in stock the Sigma, the Blue Label, the Panchromatic C and the Non-Halation Simplex brands of the Lumiere plates, affording a wide range of special qualities.

Lumiere's Sigma Plates.

No. 20L1785 The Sigma brand of Lumiere dry plate is a plate of extreme rapidity, twice as fast as any other plate on the market. The Sigma plate produces negatives that are exceptionally fine grained and absolutely free from chemical fog. These plates are especially adapted to studio work on dark days, to flashlight work, instantaneous pictures on gloomy days, and for all classes of work where an extremely rapid plate is desirable. For general use with folding hand cameras, where most of the exposures are instantaneous, and where many of the pictures are taken under adverse conditions, these plates are unexcelled. For high speed instantaneous work such as focal plane shutter exposures with the Reflex camera, the Sigma plate stands without an equal. See prices below.

Lumiere's Blue Label Plates.

No. 20L1787 The Blue Label brand of the Lumiere plate is exactly the same kind of a plate as the Sigma, possessing all the good qualities of the Sigma plate, but is not quite so rapid, requiring exposures about 50 per cent longer than the Sigma. The Blue Label Lumiere plate is adapted to general all around work, especially for portrait work in the studio. Although not possessing as great rapidity as the Sigma plate, it is at the same time sufficiently rapid for all ordinary requirements, including quick, instantaneous exposures. The Blue Label plate allows a little more latitude in exposure than the Sigma, owing to the fact that it is a little slower, and for this reason is perhaps a somewhat easier plate to use, and is preferred by most workers for general purposes.

Size	Quantity in Case	No. 20L1787 Blue Label Price, per Case	No. 20L1787 Blue Label Price, per Doz.	No. 20L1785 Sigma Price, per Case	No. 20L1785 Sigma Price, per Doz.
3½x 3½	30 doz.	$ 6.84	$0.24	$ 8.90	$0.31
3¼x 4¼	30 doz.	7.70	.27	10.00	.35
4 x 5	30 doz.	11.12	.39	14.45	.51
5 x 7	20 doz.	12.54	.66	16.30	.86
5 x 8	20 doz.	14.25	.75	18.53	.97
6½x 8½	12 doz.	11.30	.99	14.67	1.28
8 x10	10 doz.	13.68	1.44	17.79	1.87
10 x12	4 doz.	9.58	2.52	12.45	3.26
11 x14	4 doz.	13.68	3.60	17.79	4.66
14 x17	3 doz.	15.39	5.40	20.00	6.99

Lantern Slide Plates.

No. 20L1793 Lumiere's Lantern Slide Plates. An extra high grade lantern slide plate, 3¼x4 inches.
Price, per case (thirty dozen), **$9.60**; per dozen 34c

Special Lumiere Chemicals.

Lumiere plates can be worked with any of the standard developers and other chemicals in common use, but the special Lumiere chemicals are exceptionally good and we recommend them not only for the Lumiere plates, but for all other plates as well.

No. 20L1795 Dianol, a new developing agent requiring no alkali. Put up in tubes ready for use.
Price, per box of five tubes 30c
If by mail, postage extra, 5 cents.

No. 20L1797 Formosulphite, a new product, used as a substitute for both preservative and alkali (sulphite of soda and carbonates) in developers. Used with pyro, hydrochinon and other developers it produces greater density and brilliancy. Other advantages are greater economy, good keeping qualities and hardening effect on the film.
Price, per pound, **45c**; per 4-ounce bottle 18c

No. 20L1799 Lumiere's Fixing Salt, makes one quart of fixing solution for plates; very fine. Price, per package .. 10c

Lumiere's Panchromatic C Plates.

No. 20L1789 Lumiere's Panchromatic C Dry Plates are true orthochromatic plates, made especially sensitive to green, yellow and red, making them particularly adapted to landscape work and general outdoor photography.

The Panchromatic C Plates are particularly desirable for photographing landscapes, flowers, paintings, portrait work, etc., as they give true color values—that is, they show a difference between certain shades or colors, which would all appear alike if photographed with an ordinary plate.

With ordinary plates we have reds that take too black, blues that take too white, and yellow or orange that takes the same as red, black or green. These Panchromatic C plates discriminate in these and other colors, making negatives in which the true values of these colors are shown.

Landscapes made with the Panchromatic C plates possess a brilliancy not to be obtained with any ordinary plate. Flowers, paintings, and other highly colored subjects cannot be successfully photographed without the use of these color sensitive plates. Portraits made with these plates are far superior to portraits made with ordinary plates.

The speed of this plate is the same as the Lumiere Blue Label. See prices below.

Lumiere's Non-Halation Simplex Plates.

NO EXTRA MANIPULATION, USED JUST LIKE AN ORDINARY PLATE.

No. 20L1792 Lumiere's Non-Halation Simplex Plate is a combination orthochromatic and non-halation plate of the very highest quality.

Interior views can be made with these plates directly toward bright windows or open doors. They preserve perfect detail in tree tops outlined against a bright sky, they add wonderfully to the brilliancy of white draperies in portraiture, they are indispensable for photographing snow scenes. The combined non-halation and orthochromatic properties of this plate make it an ideal plate for landscape work, yielding brilliant negatives, absolutely free from halation, and with true color values.

Halation is avoided in this plate by an entirely new process, the plate being coated, before the emulsion is put on, with a dark brown dye, which absorbs all light rays penetrating the emulsion, absolutely preventing reflection from the glass and in this way overcoming all halation.

There is no extra manipulation of any kind in using these new plates as the brown dye all comes out in the fixing bath.

The speed of this Non-Halation Simplex Plate is the same as Lumiere's Blue Label Plate, making it suitable for general photography, including very quick, instantaneous work.

Size	Quantity in Case	No. 20L1789 Panchromatic C Price, per Case	No. 20L1789 Panchromatic C Price, per Doz.	No. 20L1792 Non-Halation Simplex Price, per Case	No. 20L1792 Non-Halation Simplex Price, per Doz.
3½x 3½	18 doz.	$ 5.75	$0.34	$ 5.75	$0.34
3¼x 4¼	18 doz.	6.46	.38	6.46	.38
4 x 5	12 doz.	6.22	.55	6.22	.55
5 x 7	12 doz.	10.53	.92	10.53	.92
6½x 8½	8 doz.	10.53	1.39	10.53	1.39
8 x10	6 doz.	11.49	2.02	11.49	2.02
10 x12	2 doz.	6.70	3.53	6.70	3.53
11 x14	2 doz.	9.58	5.04	9.58	5.04
14 x17	2 doz.	14.36	7.56	14.36	7.56

COMPLETE DEVELOPING AND FINISHING OUTFITS

SERIES "C" DEVELOPING OUTFITS
$2.48 to $4.95, According to Size.

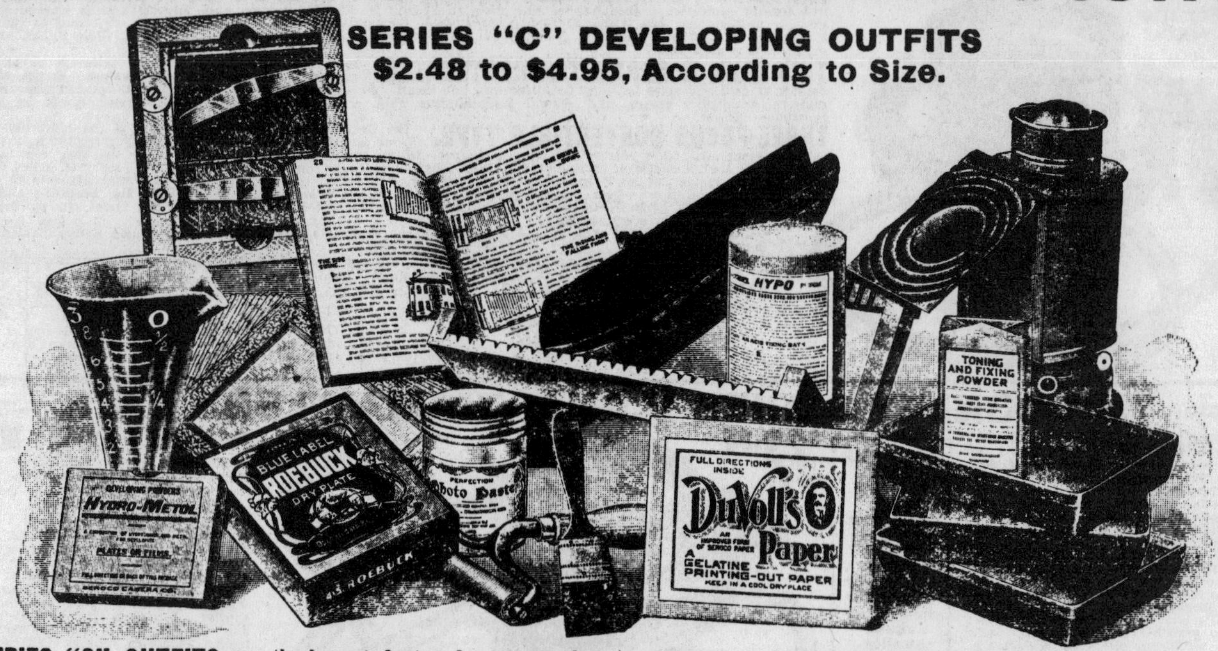

OUR SERIES "C" OUTFITS are the largest, best and most complete outfits of this kind ever put up. They are suitable for use with any plate camera that we sell, or for any film camera. While our Series "A" Outfits, as described on this page, contain everything necessary for finishing up your first pictures, we strongly advise everyone who purchases a camera to buy one of these bigger, larger and more complete Series "C" Outfits in preference to the smaller outfit, thus securing this big assortment of necessary supplies and apparatus for less than one-half the money the same goods would cost if purchased separately from the regular dealers in photographic supplies.

Every item contained in these big outfits is extra high grade, the best the market affords, and suitable for use with the very best cameras. Not an unnecessary item is included, and you will find use for everything contained in these outfits when you commence making pictures.

Each Series "C" Outfit contains the following items:

- 1 High Grade Oil Ruby Lamp.
- 1 Fine Professional Printing Frame.
- 1 Composition Tray for developing.
- 1 Composition Tray for fixing.
- 1 Composition Tray for toning.
- 1 Folding Negative Rack.
- 1 8-Ounce Cone-Shaped Graduate.
- 1 Bristle Paste Brush.
- 1 Rubber Covered Print Roller.
- 25 Fine Quality Card Mounts.
- 1 Jar Photo Paste.
- 1 Dozen Roebuck Extra Rapid Dry Plates.
- 1 Dozen DuVoll's Sensitized Paper.
- 1 Package Toning and Fixing Powders (makes 24 ounces of toner).
- 1 Package Hydro-Metol Developing Powders (makes 24 ounces of developer).
- 1 Package Hyposulphite of Soda.
- 1 Fine Gossamer Focus Cloth.
- 1 Copy "Complete Instructions in Photography."

No.		Shipping weight	Price
No. 20T825	Series "C" Outfit for 4 x5 Plate Camera.	18 pounds.	$2.48
No. 20T826	Series "C" Outfit for 3¼x5½ Plate Camera.	18 pounds.	2.55
No. 20T827	Series "C" Outfit for 4¼x6½ Plate Camera.	24 pounds.	3.25
No. 20T828	Series "C" Outfit for 5 x7 Plate Camera.	26 pounds.	3.45
No. 20T829	Series "C" Outfit for 6½x8½ Plate Camera.	31 pounds.	3.98
No. 20T830	Series "C" Outfit for 8 x10 Plate Camera.	42 pounds.	4.95

There is no camera included with any of these outfits.

SERIES, "A" DEVELOPING OUTFITS
98c TO $1.20 According to Size.

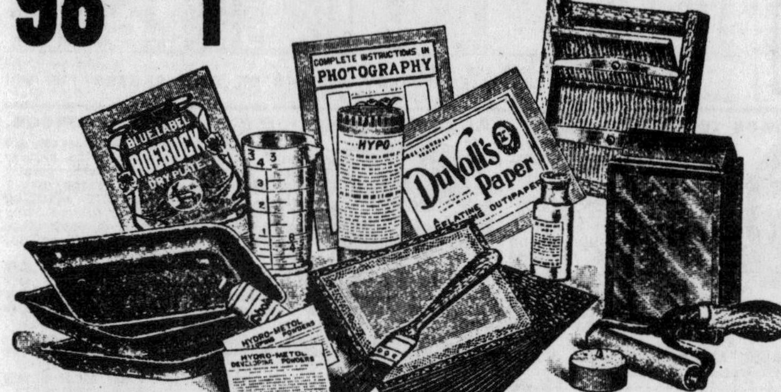

OUR SERIES "A" DEVELOPING OUTFITS contain everything necessary for developing and finishing pictures, and we urge everyone who orders a camera from us to include in the order a complete developing outfit, either this Series "A" style, or the still larger and more complete Series "C" Outfit. By ordering one of these outfits you secure, right at the start and at the lowest possible cost, everything necessary to commence work. Everything that we put into these outfits is good; the plates and papers are guaranteed to be fresh and perfect; the chemicals are guaranteed to be full weight and full strength, and each of the various other items is guaranteed to be strictly high grade, well made and serviceable. These Series "A" Outfits are suitable for use with any camera of corresponding size that we sell.

Each Series "A" Outfit contains the following items:

- 1 Package Toning Powder (makes 8 ounces of toning solution).
- 1 Package Developing Powders (makes 8 ounces of developer).
- 1 Package of Hypo (makes 32 ounces of fixing solution).
- ½ Dozen Roebuck Dry Plates.
- 1 Dozen Du Voll's Sensitized Paper.
- 1 Tray for developing plates.
- 1 Tray for fixing plates.
- 1 Tray for toning prints.
- 1 Candle Ruby Lamp.
- 1 Amateur Printing Frame.
- 1 4-Inch Print Roller.
- 1 Paste Brush.
- 1 4-Ounce Measuring Glass.
- 1 Tube of Mounting Paste.
- 1 Dozen Embossed Border Card Mounts.
- 1 Copy "Complete Instructions in Photography."

No.		Price
No. 20T801	Series "A" Outfit for 2½x2½ Plate Camera.	$0.98
No. 20T803	Series "A" Outfit for 3½x3½ Plate Camera.	1.05
No. 20T804	Series "A" Outfit for 3¼x4¼ Plate Camera.	1.12
No. 20T805	Series "A" Outfit for 4x5 Plate Camera.	1.20

There is no camera included with these outfits. Shipping weight of any Series "A" Outfit for plate camera, 11 pounds.

INGENTO DAYLIGHT ENLARGER.
No. 1.

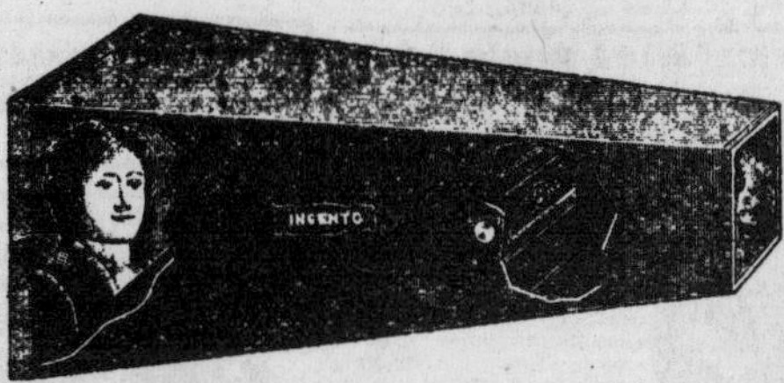

No. 20T525 This is a very simple form of a Daylight Enlarging Camera. It requires no adjustment whatever, as it is a fixed focus camera. To make an enlargement the negative and a piece of bromide paper are simply placed in the camera, the operation being practically as easy as making a print with an ordinary printing frame. With this enlarging camera 8x10 prints may be made from 4x5 negatives. It is nicely made of hardwood and fitted with a high grade achromatic lens and sliding shutter. Shipping weight, 15 pounds. Price $5.25

INGENTO DAYLIGHT ENLARGER.
No. 2.

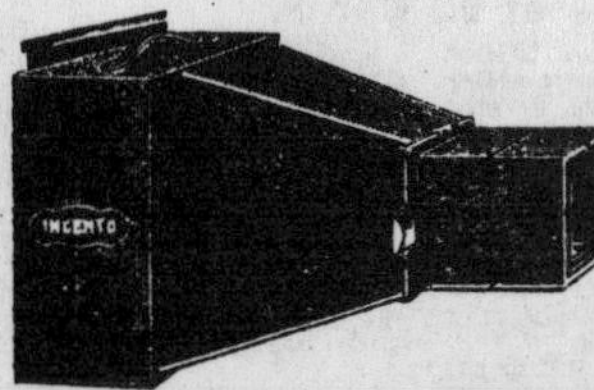

No. 20T526 This Enlarging Camera works on the same plan as the No. 1, but is so constructed that it may be folded up into a compact space when not in use. It is also more convenient for loading, as it is supplied with a plate holder, so that it is unnecessary to take the camera into the dark room in order to put the bromide paper in place. This camera can also be used to make enlarged negatives or positives on glass, the plates for this purpose being placed in the plate holder. 8x10 enlargements may be made with this camera from either 3¼x4¼ or 4x5 plates. It is made of polished hardwood of fine workmanship, and fitted with a first quality achromatic lens and sliding shutter. Shipping weight, 15 pounds. Price....................$6.50

CONLEY F.8 THREE-FOCUS RAPID RECTILINEAR LENS

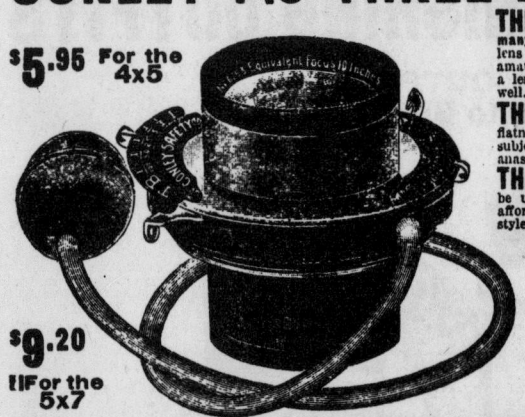

$5.95 For the 4x5

$9.20 For the 5x7

THE CONLEY RAPID RECTILINEAR LENS is as good a rectilinear lens as can be manufactured and is fully equal in every way to rapid rectilinear lenses sold by many photographic supply dealers under high sounding names at two and three times the price we ask. This is a good lens for the professional photographer who does all around work, both indoors and outdoors. It is a good lens for the amateur photographer who wants an instrument suitable for landscape work, buildings, groups, etc., and at the same time a lens that is capable of making a good portrait. The Conley Rapid Rectilinear Lens will do all these things, and do them well. It is a good lens.

THIS LENS IS PERFECTLY RECTILINEAR, rendering the straight lines of buildings or other subjects absolutely true and without curvature. It possesses unusual flatness of field and gives brilliant definition and fine detail. For landscape work, views of buildings and other architectural subjects, flashlights, groups, and general instantaneous work, this lens is absolutely unsurpassed except by the genuine anastigmat lenses.

THREE-FOCUS CONVERTIBLE TYPE. The Conley Rapid Rectilinear Lens is of the convertible type, both front and rear combinations being fully corrected so that they may be used alone, the front combination having a focal length about 40 per cent greater than the rear combination, thus affording the user a choice of three different focal lengths, which is equivalent to owning three separate lenses of the older styles. These lenses are made especially for us in one of the best equipped lens grinding establishments in the United States, and the greatest possible care is exercised in the grinding, polishing, cementing, centering and mounting. Every one is carefully inspected and tested before it leaves the factory and goes out under our positive guarantee to be perfect in every respect.

No. 20T1102 The Conley F.8 Three-Focus Rapid Rectilinear Lens, with Conley Safety Shutter, including bulb and tube.

Lens No.	Plate Covered at F.8	Equivalent Focus	Focus Rear Combination	Focus Front Combination	Diameter Image Circle	Diameter Across Hood	Price
1	4x5	6¼ in.	10½ in.	14½ in.	8¼ in.	1¼ in.	$ 5.95
2	5x7	8 in.	14 in.	18 in.	9¼ in.	1⅝ in.	9.20
4	6½x8½	10½ in.	17½ in.	23½ in.	13 in.	1 25/32 in.	14.50
5	8x10	12½ in.	20 in.	28½ in.	15 in.	2¼ in.	18.35
7	11x14	18½ in.	31 in.	43 in.	19 in.	2⅝ in.	27.50

THE CONLEY SERIES V ANASTIGMAT LENS F.6.8

A UNIVERSAL LENS. The Conley Series V Anastigmat Lens is in every sense of the word a universal lens, being suitable for any kind of photographic work, landscapes, architectural subjects, portraits, groups, studio use and high speed instantaneous work. It is a double anastigmat of the most perfect type, symmetrical in construction, and the designers and makers have succeeded in absolutely eliminating all traces of astigmatism, and at the same time the lens is absolutely free from both chromatic and spherical aberration. Technically speaking, this lens is of the double anastigmat, symmetrical type, composed of two systems or combinations, each combination made up of four elementary lenses cemented together in pairs. Both the front combination and the rear combination are fully corrected and may be used alone, each having a focal length of about twice that of the complete lens. This lens being of the symmetrical type, both the front and rear combinations are of the same focal length. In the making of these lenses nothing is neglected, from the original grinding and polishing of the glass to the cementing, centering and final mounting, that will in any way contribute to the absolute perfection of both its mechanical and optical qualities. With all extremely high grade lenses absolute accuracy of adjustment is necessary, and the final mounting and adjusting of these lenses is entrusted only to the most expert workmen of long experience. Each lens is treated individually and carefully studied and tested before it is shipped.

COMPARE OUR PRICES on Anastigmat Lenses with the prices quoted by others for lenses of equal quality. WE SAVE YOU 50 PER CENT

$23.55 For the 4x5

$31.20 For the 5x7

SPEED. The Conley Series V Anastigmat Lens works at a speed of F.6.8, which is amply sufficient for instantaneous work, even under adverse conditions of light and which, under favorable conditions, permits exposures with the focal plane shutter as short as the 1-1000 part of a second. As compared with even the best rapid rectilinear lenses, this lens possesses greater speed, better definition, a flatter field and greater covering power.

FOR HOME PORTRAIT WORK this lens is a perfect instrument that will enable you to make good portraits in your own home. For successful portrait work under the ordinary conditions existing in the home, a fast lens is necessary, and the Conley Series V Anastigmat Lens has speed. It is fast enough to permit exposures as short as 1-25 of a second in an ordinarily well lighted living room. It is fast enough to make snap shots of the baby in your parlor at home, provided good judgment is used in posing the baby where full advantage is taken of all the light possible. Pictures made at home with natural and accustomed surroundings are better than the pictures you would get amid the distracting conditions of the professional photographer's studio. Portrait work is the most interesting branch of photography and requires some skill and a knowledge of lighting. This skill and knowledge of lighting, however, is of no avail unless backed up with a good lens, and the Conley Series V Anastigmat Lens is a good lens, not only for portrait work, but for all kinds of photography.

THE CONLEY SAFETY SHUTTER is a double pump shutter with all working parts enclosed within the case. It makes time or bulb exposures of any desired length and automatically controlled exposures of 1-100, 1-50, 1-25, 1-5, ½ and 1 second. It is one of the most satisfactory shutters for all around work that can be secured and is made especially for the Conley cameras by the Wollensak Optical Company.

THE KOILOS is a remarkably efficient and beautifully made shutter. It makes time or bulb exposures of any desired length and automatically controlled exposures ranging from 1-300 to one full second. The case is made of aluminum, finely finished, and all interior parts are of hardened steel, precluding any possibility of wear, and of great durability. The shutter blades are of the three-leaf type, admitting an unusually full and even volume of light, and it is claimed by the French manufacturer that this style of construction admits at least 33⅓ per cent greater illumination than is possible with the usual system of shutter blades.

THE OPTIMO IS A NEW HIGH SPEED SHUTTER made by the Wollensak Optical Co., and in our opinion possesses advantages over any between the lens shutter now on the market. There are five shutter leaves which revolve in making the exposure, the end of each leaf passing from the opening and the other end taking its place, which makes high speed possible in opening and closing. The aperture is star shaped, the points of the star reaching to the edges of the opening, thus giving the greatest possible illumination to the plate. The Optimo makes time and bulb exposures in the ordinary manner, and automatically controlled exposures of 1-300, 1-200, 1-100, 1-50, 1-25, 1-5, ½ and 1 second. Even when working at the unusual speed of 1-300 of a second it sets and releases very easily and operates without the slightest jar or recoil. All working parts are entirely enclosed within the case, making it perfectly dustproof.

No. 20T1110 The Series V, F.6.8, Conley Anastigmat Lens. Prices as follows:

Lens No.	Size of Plate Covered at Full Aperture	Diameter of Image Circle, inches	Equivalent Focus, inches	Focal Length Single Combinations, inches	Diameter Measured Across Hood, inches	Price, with Conley Safety Shutter	Price, with Koilos Shutter	Price, with Optimo Shutter
1	3¼ x 4¼	6½	5	10	1¼	$21.70	$28.85	$28.95
2	4 x 5	8½	6	12	1 5-16	23.55	30.70	32.20
3	5 x 7	11	7	14	1⅜	31.20	41.30	38.05
4	6½ x 8½	14	10	20	1 13-16	41.85	51.95	50.20
5	8 x 10	17	13	26	2 7-16	55.50	66.35	63.00
6	10 x 12	20	15	30	2⅞	68.80	not made	not made
7	11 x 14	24	16½	33	3 1-16	88.00	not made	not made

These prices include bulb and tube.

THIS LENS CAN BE FITTED TO ANY FOLDING OR VIEW CAMERA. We will mount the lens on your front board without extra charge.

Monarch Symmetrical Wide Angle Lens.

No. 20T1120 The Monarch Symmetrical Wide Angle Lens is a finely made instrument, especially adapted to the photographing of interiors and is also used for out of door views in confined situations. It is handsomely mounted in lacquered brass with a fine iris diaphragm, and is a strictly high grade lens that will be found entirely satisfactory for all work requiring a short focus or wide angle lens.

Lens No.	Size Plate Covered	Equivalent Focus	Diameter Across Hood	Price
1	4 x 5	3½ inches	1¼ inches	$ 5.70
2	5 x 7	5¼ inches	1¼ inches	6.80
3	6½ x 8½	6½ inches	1⅜ inches	9.90
4	8 x 10	8 inches	2 3/32 inches	12.80

PORTRAIT LENSES are shown in our special Camera Catalog. Sent free upon request.

Ray Filters at 60 Cents.

No. 20T1140 A Ray Filter absorbs the violet and ultra-violet rays of light and produces a picture in which the color values are correct. Clouds in a photograph improve the artistic value of the picture wonderfully, and you can get them with a ray filter. Landscapes photographed with the ray filter possess a brilliancy and contrast which it is impossible to obtain otherwise; and in the photographing of flowers, paintings or any brightly colored subjects, the ray filter is practically indispensable.

No. 1 for lenses 1 5-16 inches in diameter............$0.60
No. 2 for fixed focus or box cameras..................60
No. 3 for lenses 1 7-16 inches in diameter..............60
No. 5 for lenses 1¾ inches in diameter.................90
No. 6 for lenses 2 inches in diameter..................90
No. 7 for lenses 2¼ inches in diameter...............1.05

Postage extra, on Nos. 1 to 6, 4 cents; No. 7, 6 cents.

This Ray Filter cannot be used with the Magazine Camera. For other sizes see special Camera Catalog.

Any of the above sizes are suitable for lenses ¼ inch less in diameter than size mentioned.

State outside diameter of lens when ordering.

Wide Angle Lenses to Fit Shutters.

This wide angle lens is furnished without barrel or shutter, the front and rear combinations being mounted in cells to fit the shutters ordinarily used with folding hand cameras. To use these lenses the front and rear combinations of your regular lens are simply unscrewed from the shutter, and these wide angle lens combinations screwed into their place.

No. 20T1121 Wide Angle Lenses in cells to fit the Wollensak Regular or the Wollensak Automatic Shutters.

Size, 4x5. Price....................$2.90
Size, 5x7. Price....................3.70
Size, 6½x8½. Price..................5.95
Size, 8x10. Price...................7.80

No. 20T1122 Wide Angle Lenses in cells to fit the Conley Safety or the Conley Automatic Shutters.

Size, 4x5. Price....................$2.90
Size, 5x7. Price....................3.70
Size, 6½x8½. Price..................5.95
Size, 8x10. Price...................7.80

If you have a camera fitted with Wollensak Regular or Automatic Shutter, the Wide Angle Lens No. 20T1121 will fit your shutter.

If you already have or if you are just ordering one of the latest model Conley Cameras with Conley Safety or Conley Automatic Shutter, then the wide angle lens that is listed under No. 20T1122 will fit your shutter.

Any Size Duplicator for 17 Cents.

No. 20T1148 Duplicator. A device enabling one to photograph a person in two positions on the same plate. Very humorous and interesting pictures can be made in this way. Can be used with any folding camera. **Cannot be used with box cameras. State outside diameter of lens. Be sure to state size.**

Price, each, any size.........17c

If mail shipment, postage extra, 3 to 5 cents.

Auxiliary Enlarging and Copying Lenses.

No. 20T1155 These lenses are used in connection with the regular lens of any folding camera, greatly increasing its power. By the use of these lenses copying and enlarging may be done with short focus folding cameras, enabling one to copy other pictures or photograph small articles to their full size or even larger.

No. 1 for 4x5 camera with lens 1 5-16 inches in diam.$0.90
No. 2 for 5x7 camera with lens 1 5-16 inches in diam. .90
No. 8 any size camera with lens 1¾ inches in diam. 1.35
No. 9 any size camera with lens 2 inches in diam. 1.50

Postage extra, on Nos. 1 and 2, 3 cents; Nos. 8 and 9, 6 cents.

In measuring your lens, take the outside diameter, remembering that the enlarging lens slips over your regular lens same as a cap.

Any of the above sizes are suitable for lenses ¼ inch less in diameter than size mentioned.

For other sizes of Ray Filters and Auxiliary Lenses, send for special Camera Catalog.

Auxiliary Portrait Lenses.

No. 20T1158 In making portraits with the ordinary short focus folding hand camera, the great difficulty heretofore has been the small size of the faces. This portrait lens, however, entirely overcomes this difficulty and enables anyone with any kind of a folding camera to make portraits in which the faces are large and distinct. Constructed in the same style and used in same manner as the enlarging lens No. 20T1155.

No. 1 for 4x5 camera with lens 1 5-16 inches in diam.$0.90
No. 2 for 5x7 camera with lens 1 5-16 inches in diam. .90
No. 8 any size camera with lens 1¾ inches in diam. 1.35
No. 9 any size camera with lens 2 inches in diam. 1.50

Postage extra, on Nos. 1 and 2, 3 cents; Nos. 8 and 9, 6 cents.

For other sizes see special Camera Catalog.

In measuring lens, take the outside diameter, remembering that the portrait lens slips over your regular lens same as a cap.

Any of the above sizes may be used on lenses ¼ inch less in diameter than size given.

For complete sets of Auxiliary Lenses see next page.

For complete sets of Auxiliary Lenses see next page.

COMPLETE DEVELOPING, FINISHING AND MATERIAL OUTFITS

AT 98c TO $1.35 ACCORDING TO SIZE

WE FURNISH THESE SERIES "A" OUTFITS FOR EITHER PLATE CAMERAS OR FILM CAMERAS

THESE SERIES "A" Developing, Finishing and Material Outfits contain everything that is necessary for developing, printing and finishing pictures. We urge everyone who orders a camera from us to include, with the camera, one of the fine outfits and thus secure, right at the start, at the lowest possible cost, everything necessary to commence work. Everything that we put into these outfits is good; plates and papers guaranteed fresh and perfect; chemicals guaranteed full weight and full strength; accessories guaranteed strictly high class, well made and serviceable. The Series "A" Outfits are put up in seven sizes and are suitable for use with any cameras of corresponding size that we sell.

Arranged for plate cameras, each outfit contains the following items:

1 Package Concentrated Dry Toner (makes 8 ounces of solution).
1 Tray for Developing Plates.
1 Tray for Fixing Plates.
1 Package Concentrated Dry Developer (makes 8 ounces solution).
1 Metal Dark Room Lamp.
1 Tray for toning prints.
1 Print Roller for smoothing down the mounted prints.
½ Dozen Dry Plates.
1 Dozen Sheets Du Voll's Sensitized Paper.
1 Printing Frame.
1 Package Hypo for fixing Negatives and Prints.
1 Paste Brush.
1 Graduated Glass for Measuring Liquids.
1 Dozen Card Mounts, with fancy embossed borders.
1 Tube of fine scented Photo Mounting Paste.
1 Copy of "Complete Instructions in Photography."

ARRANGED FOR FILM CAMERAS.

As put up for film cameras these outfits contain the same list of items as shown above except that we put in one roll of film (six exposures) instead of the package of dry plates, and the printing frame is fitted with a glass.

No. 20L610 Series "A" Outfit for 2¼x3¼ film cameras. Price..........$1.00
No. 20L611 Series "A" Outfit for 2¼x4¼ film cameras. Price..........1.05
No. 20L612 Series "A" Outfit for 3¼x3¼ film cameras. Price..........1.10
No. 20L613 Series "A" Outfit for 3¼x4¼ film cameras. Price..........1.15
No. 20L614 Series "A" Outfit for 4 x 5 film cameras. Price..........1.30
No. 20L615 Series "A" Outfit for 3¼x5½ film cameras. Price..........1.35
There is no Camera included with these Outfits.

ARRANGED FOR PLATE CAMERAS.

No. 20L601 Series "A" Outfit for 2½x2½ plate camera. Price..........$0.98
No. 20L602 Series "A" Outfit for 3½x3½ plate camera. Price..........1.05
No. 20L603 Series "A" Outfit for 3¼x4¼ plate camera. Price..........1.12
No. 20L604 Series "A" Outfit for 4 x 5 plate camera. Price..........1.20
There is no Camera included with these Outfits.

$2.48 FOR THE 4X5 SIZE — OUR SERIES "C" DEVELOPING OUTFITS.

BIG OUTFITS OF HIGH GRADE SUPPLIES AND ACCESSORIES SUITABLE FOR EITHER PROFESSIONAL OR AMATEUR

OUR SERIES "C" OUTFITS ARE the largest, the best and the most complete outfits ever offered. They are suitable for use with every 4x5, 5x7, 6½x8½ and 8x10 camera which we sell and we strongly advise everyone who buys a 4x5 or larger camera to order one of these outfits and thus secure this big assortment of necessary supplies and apparatus for less than one-half the money these same goods would cost if purchased separately from the regular dealers in photographic supplies. Every item contained in our big Series "C" Outfits is extra high grade, the best the market affords, suitable for use with our very best cameras. Not an unnecessary item is included. You will need everything contained in these outfits when you commence making pictures. Arranged for plate cameras, each outfit contains the following items:

1 High Grade Metal Ruby Lamp with Oil Burner.
25 Fine Quality Card Mounts.
1 Special Composition Tray for developing.
1 Special Composition Tray for fixing.
1 Special Composition Tray for toning.
1 Folding Negative Rack to hold 24 plates.
1 8-ounce Cone Shaped Graduate.
1 Professional Printing Frame.
1 Bristle Paste Brush.
1 Fine Gossamer Focus Cloth.
1 Dozen Extra Rapid Roebuck Dry Plates.
1 Package Toning and Fixing Powders (makes 24 ounces of toner).
1 Package Hydro-Metol Developing Powders (makes 24 ounces developer).
1 Package Hyposulphite of Soda.
1 Print Roller.
1 Dozen Sheets Du Voll's Sensitized Paper.
1 Jar Photo Paste.
1 Copy of "Complete Instructions in Photography."

ARRANGED FOR FILM PLATE CAMERAS.

We also put up these Series "C" Outfits arranged for film cameras, the list of items being the same as included in the outfits for plate cameras, except that we put in one roll or film (12 exposures) in place of the dry plates, a box of push pins in place of the negative rack; the focus cloth is omitted and a printing frame is provided with a glass.

No. 20L642 Series "C" Outfit for 3¼x3¼ film camera. Price..........$2.25
No. 20L643 Series "C" Outfit for 3¼x4¼ film camera. Price..........2.35
No. 20L644 Series "C" Outfit for 4x5 film camera. Price..........2.65
There is no Camera included with these Outfits.

With both the 3¼x3¼ and 3¼x4¼ outfits for film cameras we furnish 4x5 trays and printing frame, as this size is more convenient to work with.

ARRANGED FOR PLATE CAMERAS.

No. 20L634 Series "C" Outfit for 4x5 plate camera. Price..........$2.48
No. 20L635 Series "C" Outfit for 5x7 plate camera. Price..........3.45
No. 20L636 Series "C" Outfit for 6½x8½ plate camera. Price..........3.98
No. 20L637 Series "C" Outfit for 8x10 plate camera. Price..........4.95
There is no Camera included in these Outfits.

Sliding Tripod, 45 Cents.

No. 20L701. Sliding Tripod for 4x5 cameras. A light, well made, handsomely finished tripod, made from selected spruce, folding compactly, and adapted to any 4x5 hand camera or folding hand camera, such as the Seroco Sr. Box or other light cameras. Price, 45c

Combination Tripod, $1.20.

No. 20L704 Combination Tripod for 4x5 cameras. A light, well made, combined sliding and folding tripod, with detachable head; suitable for use with any 4x5 camera, and even for 5x7, provided the camera is not very heavy. Price..........$1.20

No. 20L701 — No. 20L704

Ebony Combination Tripod, $1.50

No. 20L706 Ebony Combination Tripod, same as No. 20L704, but with dead black ebony finish and nickel plated metal parts. A very handsome and high grade tripod. Price, $1.50

Sliding Tripods, $1.40 to $2.10.

Our Best Grade Sliding Tripod is without a doubt the most perfect sliding tripod made. Constructed of best selected spruce, **top of three-piece wood to prevent warping** and covered with felt. A special brass binding plate, operated by set screw, clamps the legs securely at any desired height. **Suitable for hand cameras, folding hand cameras or regular view cameras.** Be sure to state size wanted.

No. 20L710 Sliding Tripod. For cameras from 4x5 to 6½x8½.
Price..........$1.40

No. 20L711 Sliding Tripod. For cameras from 5x8 to 8x10.
Price..........$1.75

No. 20L712 Sliding Tripod. For cameras from 8x10 to 11x14.
Price..........$2.10

Combination Tripods, $2.10 to $3.15.

Combination Tripod. A combined sliding and folding tripod, one of the most convenient forms yet devised. Made in three sections with detachable head; the lower section slides into the second, while the upper section folds back upon it, thus making a very compact tripod. Made from specially selected, straight grained, thoroughly seasoned ash. Be sure to state size wanted.

THE BEST TRIPOD MADE.

No. 20L717 Combination Tripod. For cameras from 4x5 to 6½x8½.
Price..........$2.10

No. 20L718 Combination Tripod. For cameras from 6½x8½ to 10x12.
Price..........$2.45

No. 20L719 Combination Tripod. For cameras from 10x12 to 14x17. Price..........$3.15

NOTE. **We believe it pays to use good, strong, heavy, rigid tripods.** Tripods corresponding in weight, strength and rigidity to our No. 20L717 combination are recommended by most dealers and manufacturers for 6½x8½ cameras. In our opinion a tripod of this weight is best suited to a 5x7 or 4x5 camera. Most dealers recommend a tripod corresponding to our No. 20L718 combination for 11x14 and 14x17 cameras. In our opinion a tripod of this weight is best suited to an 8x10 camera. Compared with other tripods of the same weight, strength and serviceability, our prices are lower than the prices of any dealer with whom we have compared.

Telescopic Metal Tripods.

These New Telescopic Metal Tripods are the lightest and most compact tripods on the market. They are very convenient to use under all conditions and especially desirable when traveling. They are very substantially constructed, very carefully made and finely finished throughout. Each joint telescopes, or slides into the joint above it, a spring catch holding the legs of the tripod firmly when they are fully extended.

No. 20L725 Telescopic Tripod. Three sections, adapted to light 4x5 or smaller cameras. Price..........$1.50

No. 20L727 Telescopic Tripod. Four sections, heavier tubing than No. 20L725 adapted to ordinary 4x5 cameras.
Price..........$1.95

No. 20L729 Telescopic Tripod. Five sections and heavier and stronger tubing, adapted to heavy 4x5 and light 5x7 cameras.
Price..........$2.65

No. 20L731 Telescopic Tripod. Seven sections, extra high grade, made of heavier tubing giving additional strength and greater compactness, as the seven sections, when folded, fit together very compactly. Suitable for any style of 4x5 or 5x7 camera.
Price..........$3.00

Combination Tripod.

No. 20C2569 Combination Tripod, a combined sliding and folding tripod, one of the most convenient forms yet devised. Quickly set up for use, readily adjusted to any desired height and perfectly rigid. Made in three sections with detachable head, the lower section slides into the second, while the upper section folds back upon it, thus making a very compact tripod. The best tripod made.

Size No. 1, for 4x5 or 5x7 cameras. Price.....$1.60
Size No. 2, for 6½x8½ cameras. Price.....$1.90
Size No. 3, for 8x10 cameras. Price.....$2.25
Size No. 4, for 10x12 or 11x14 cameras. Price.....$2.45

The New Silent Shutter.

No. 20C2574 The Silent Shutter, a new device absolutely noiseless in opening. The photographer who has experienced repeated failures by reason of a child subject or a member of a group looking toward the lens at the critical moment because he heard the "click" of the shutter will appreciate this new shutter, which opens with absolute silence. The cups at the sides form air cushions which arrest the wings as they open, thus avoiding all sound. Bulb and 6 foot of rubber hose furnished with each shutter.

This shutter is placed back of lens or inside of front board.

Size of Opening, inches	2	2½	3	3½	
Size of Shutter, inches	3⅝x4½	4⅜x5	5x5½	5⅝x6	
Price	$4.50	$4.50	$4.50	$4.50	
Size of Opening, ins.	4	4½	5	5½	6
Size of Shutter, ins.	6x6½	6½x7	7x7½	7½x8	8x8½
Price	$4.50	$5.40	$6.30	$7.20	$8.10

Camera Level.

No. 20C2576 This Little Level is intended to be attached to the bed of the camera, enabling the operator to quickly and easily place the camera perfectly level. It is nicely made from brass, finely finished and accurately adjusted.
Price.....99c

Camera Bulbs.

No. 20C2577 Bulb and Tube for Camera. Made from the very best quality of red rubber, very elastic; tube is 2 feet long and can be fitted to any shutter. Rubber always becomes hard, brittle or rotten after a certain length of time, and if the bulb and tube you now have has become useless you can easily fit one of these to your shutter.
Price.......(If by mail, postage extra, 3c).....18c

Light Printing Frames.

No. 20C2580 Light Weight Printing Frame. The best light weight frame made and a great improvement over the ordinary style. A special point of advantage is the piano hinge, heretofore fitted only to the highest priced frames, giving strength and durability. The finish throughout is good.

Size, inches	2½x2½	3¼x3¼	3¼x4¼	4¼x4¼	4x5	5x7
Price	9c	9c	9c	9c	10c	13c

Not made in larger sizes.

Heavy Weight Printing Frames.

No. 20C2583 Heavy Weight Printing Frames. The finest printing frame manufactured, strongly and substantially constructed throughout, heavy brass springs sliding under brass plates instead of grooves in the wood, thus preventing all wear, mortised corners, back in three pieces to prevent warping, high grade piano hinge, finished throughout in the best possible manner. It pays to get good printing frames, and these frames are the best made.

Size	Price, per dozen	Price, each	Size	Price, per dozen	Price, each
3¼x 4¼	$2.22	$0.19	6½x 8½	$3.70	$0.32
4 x 5	2.45	.21	8 x10	4.30	.37
4¼x6½	2.68	.23	10 x12	5.59	.48
5 x7	2.78	.24	11 x14	11.06	.95
5 x8	2.90	.25	14 x17	13.97	1.20

Masks.

Every package contains a large assortment of fancy and novel designs.

A NECESSARY ADDITION TO ANY PHOTOGRAPHIC OUTFIT.

No. 20C2587 Made from tough opaque paper, and designed to be placed between negative and sensitized paper while printing, thus producing oval, circular or various fancy shaped prints from any negative. The illustration shows only one of the many sizes of styles. Made for the following negatives: 2¼x3¼, 3¼x3¼, 3¼x4¼, 4¼x4¼, 4x5 and 5x7.

Assortment No. 1 contains one oval, one circle, one rectangle, one round corner rectangle, the balance being a variety of ornamental designs. Assortment No. 2 is composed entirely of ornamental designs, all different from Assortment No. 1.

Price, per package, any size.....18c

If by mail, postage extra, on small sizes, 2 cents; on size 4x5, 3 cents; size 5x7, 4 cents.

State which assortment you want and size of negative.

Our Special Trays.

No. 20C2588 Our Special Trays. These are the best trays on the market for general purposes, developing negatives, toning, washing prints, etc. They are manufactured expressly for us from a peculiar composition material known as compressed fibre. These trays are jet black, perfectly smooth, without seam or joint, and perfect in shape. We guarantee them to stand all photographic chemicals without deterioration and to be acid and alkali proof. In shape, finish and durability they are superior to all other composition trays.

For Plates, inches	2½x2½	3¼x3¼	3¼x4¼	4x5	
Price	5c	7c	7c	9c	
For Plates, inches	5x7	5x8	6½x8½	8x10	10x12
Price	16c	17c	25c	38c	83c

Japanned Metal Trays.

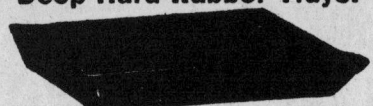

No. 20C2590 An entirely new style of japanned metal tray and superior to all others. These trays are stamped from one solid piece of metal without joints or seams, and coated with an enamel which is a special japan and rubber preparation, rendering them entirely chemical proof.

For Plates, inches	4x5	5x7	5x8	6½x8½
Price	6c	13c	16c	24c

Deep Hard Rubber Trays.

No. 20C2592 Hard Rubber Trays are generally considered the best trays manufactured, and the quality we handle is the best we can buy, genuine hard rubber (not composition), made extra deep and with lip at corner for pouring.

For Plates, inches	4x5	5x7	5x8	6½x8½
Price	34c	43c	52c	68c
For Plates, inches	8x10	10x12	12x16	15x19
Price	$0.85	$1.40	$1.95	$3.90

Porcelain Trays.

No. 20C2593 Porcelain Trays, the best grade of imported white porcelain, extra deep. These trays are very easy to keep clean, are absolutely chemical proof, and are generally considered the finest trays made for toning and other work.

For Plates, inches	5x7	5½x8½	7x9	8x10	
Price	49c	60c	65c	80c	
For Plates, in.	10x12	11x14	14x17	15x19	19x24
Price	$1.32	$2.11	$4.80	$6.00	$10.00

Measuring Glasses.

No. 20C2600 Tumbler Shaped Measuring Glasses. For liquids; graduated with ounces and drams; not quite as convenient as the regular cone shaped graduate, but preferred by many on account of the extremely low price.

Price, 2 ounce.....4c
Price, 4 ounce.....6c
Price, 8 ounce.....9c

Not mailable.

Pressed Line Graduates.

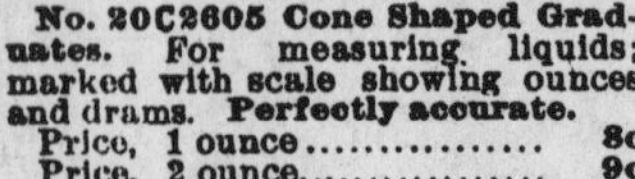

No. 20C2605 Cone Shaped Graduates. For measuring liquids; marked with scale showing ounces and drams. **Perfectly accurate.**

Price, 1 ounce.....8c
Price, 2 ounce.....9c
Price, 4 ounce.....12c
Price, 8 ounce.....18c
Price, 16 ounce.....27c

Engraved Graduates.

No. 20C2606 Cone Shaped Graduates, all lines and figures engraved by hand, the most carefully made and accurate graduate on the market.

Price, 1 ounce.....12c
Price, 2 ounce.....13c
Price, 4 ounce.....20c
Price, 8 ounce.....32c
Price, 16 ounce.....50c
Price, 32 ounce.....88c

Fixing Baths.

No. 20C2610 These Fixing Baths are made of metal, thoroughly coated with a preparation which renders them impervious to the action of hypo. They are a very great convenience at a very low price. The use of these baths for fixing avoids the danger of spots and stains, which is the frequent result of fixing in the ordinary tray. They hold six plates each. These baths are provided with a rising bottom, so that the plates are readily raised above the top—a great convenience in removing them from the box and avoiding the danger of scratching.

No. 0, for plates 3¼x3¼. Price.....38c
No. 1, for plates 3¼x4¼. Price.....38c
No. 2, for plates 4 x5. Price.....38c
No. 3, for plates 5x7 or 5x8. Price.....55c

If by mail, postage extra, 10, 16 and 22 cents.

Zinc Washing Box.

No. 20C2615 Zinc Washing Box, a perfect device for washing plates, and should form a part of every photographic outfit. Constructed throughout of zinc and cannot rust. The water enters through the inlet tube, is circulated through the whole area of the box and passes off through the outlet tube. The patent lifting bottom is a valuable feature of this box, as the plates can be lifted out with no danger whatever of scratching. If running water is not at hand, the box is simply filled and emptied several times, in this way thoroughly washing the plates. Once used you will never be without again.

No. 1, for plates 3¼x3¼. Price.....$0.86
No. 2, for plates 4x5 or 5x7. Price.....93
No. 3, for plates 3¼x4¼, 4¼x4¼ or 4¼x6½. Price.....93
No. 4, for plates 5x7 or 6½x8½. Price.....1.29
No. 5, for plates 6½x8½ or 8x10. Price.....1.47

Too heavy to send by mail.

Glass Funnels.

No. 20C2630 Glass Funnels, plain, for filtering, bottling solutions, etc.

½ pint. Price.....7c
1 pint. Price.....9c
1 quart. Price.....17c
2 quart. Price.....22c

Fluted Glass Funnels.

No. 20C2631 Glass Funnels, fluted, for filtering. More desirable than plain funnels, because filtering is much more rapid.

½ pint. Price.....13c
1 pint. Price.....17c
1 quart. Price.....23c
2 quart. Price.....34c

Too heavy to send by mail.

New Style Photo Scale for 32 Cents.

No. 20C2656 The best scale yet devised at a low price; answers all the requirements in making up solutions, etc. Simple, nothing to get out of order, accurate and convenient. Weighs up to 12 drams. Pan is made of glass and easily cleaned.
Price.....32c

If by mail, postage extra, 10 cents.

Extra Glass Pans for No. 20C2656 Scale. Price.10c

An Imported Scale for $1.00.

No. 20C2658 Our Imported Balance Scale, made in Germany, has 2¼-inch brass pans, brass pillar, 6-inch beam, and stands 12 inches high when set up for use. The entire scale packs away in the box on which it is set up, has complete set of weights from ½ grain to 1 ounce and comes complete in oak box.

Price, complete.....$1.00
If by mail, postage extra, 20 cents.

FOR COMPLETE INDEX REFER TO PINK PAGES IN MIDDLE OF BOOK.

Print Trimmers.

No. 20C2700 Prints always have to be trimmed before mounting, and while this can of course be done fairly well with scissors or knife, at the same time the advantages of a regular trimmer as here illustrated will be readily apparent. **It trims the prints quickly, easily and squarely.** The blade is made of finest tempered steel, the board of polished hardwood, has graduated measure which also serves as guide for the paper. Our illustration shows way in which this trimmer is used. Trims any size from 4x5 down. Price..........45c

No. 20C2701 Trimming Board, same as No. 20C2700, but larger, suitable for prints up to 5x7. Price..........85c

No. 20C2702 Trimming Board, same as No. 20C2700, but with 10½-inch blade, suitable for any size up to and including 8x10. Price..........59c

Our Best Grade Trimmer.

No. 20C2710 The blade is made from the same steel used in the best paper cutting machines, finely tempered and ground to a perfect edge. **The board** is made of hardwood, polished, and so constructed that it cannot warp. **The spring joint,** by which the blade is attached, allows a slight lateral motion, so that the two cutting edges are in perfect contact at every point, insuring perfect, clean cut edges to either cards or paper. The illustration shows method of trimming a print.

Length of blade, inches	6½	8½	10½	12½
Price	90c	$1.25	$1.90	$2.30

Our Best Photo Scale.

No. 20C2659 All metal parts are nickel plated; it has large nickel plated pan, 3½ in. in diameter; it is very sensitive, finely finished, accurately adjusted and durable. **Two complete sets** of weights are included, one set of **avoirdupois,** $\frac{1}{16}$ of an ounce to 2 ounces, and one set of **dram, scruple and grain** weights. Price, complete..........$1.85

If by mail, postage extra, 40 cents.

WRITE THE CATALOGUE NUMBER IN FULL ALWAYS.

Flash Light Cartridges.

No. 20C2669 For making flash light pictures without a lamp. Each cartridge contains sufficient powder for one exposure, and for use the cartridge is simply placed on a stove shovel or other article which will not be injured and the fuse lighted. A blinding flash of white light follows and the picture is made instantaneously. Made in three sizes and put up in packages of ½ dozen each. Price per pkg.

Size No. 1, ½ dozen 20-grain cartridges..........10c
Size No. 2, ½ dozen 40-grain cartridges..........20c
Size No. 3, ½ dozen 60-grain cartridges..........25c
(Unmailable.)

Folding Negative Racks.

No. 20C2675 The Folding Negative Rack is a very convenient and necessary accessory for the support of negatives while drying and **prevents them from being scratched;** will hold 12 negatives. For plates, 4x5 or smaller. Price..........8c

No. 20C2676 Folding Negative Rack. Same as above, but larger, holds 24 negatives, suitable for any size up to and including 8x10. Price..........9c

Ruby Lamps.

No. 20C2680 Candle Ruby Lamp, constructed of metal, has deep ruby glass, burns candle. A very convenient and satisfactory lamp at a low price. Price..........14c

Extra Candles.

No. 20C2681 Candles to fit this lamp, small flat paraffine candles in pasteboard cups, burn two hours. Made especially for dark room lamps.

Price, per dozen 17c

Oil Ruby Lamp.

No. 20C2683 Oil Ruby Lamp. A strictly first class metal lamp, fitted with both orange and ruby glass, which gives the safest and best light. Has adjustable screen for shielding the eyes, ventilation is perfect, reservoir can be filled from outside and light be turned up or down without opening the lamp. A regular $1.00 lamp. Price..........40c

No. 20C2685 Ruby Oil Lamp, same as No. 20C2683. Regular $1.50 size. Price..........80c

Print Rollers.

Indispensable for smoothing down prints after mounting and for squeegeeing prints on ferrotype plates.

No. 20C2695 4-inch Print Roller, rubber covered, large wood handle, as shown in illustration. Price..........10c

No. 20C2697 6-inch Print Roller, rubber covered, large wood handle, as shown in illustration. Price..........18c

BACKGROUNDS.

Our backgrounds are all painted in oil on fine muslin, perfectly waterproof, and will not crack, practically indestructible. **Do not compare** our grounds with water color grounds or distemper, which are ruined if touched by water and can hardly be handled without cracking. **A secret process** known only to the painter who makes our backgrounds, enables him to get a perfect dull or dead finished surface in oil, making an ideal background, crack proof, waterproof and photographically correct.

CLOUDED HEADGROUNDS.

No. 20C2721 The following grounds, in clouded designs, No. 40 and No. 41, are especially suitable for bust pictures, although the larger sizes, 5x7 and 6x8 are extensively used for full figure work and small groups. Very artistic, up to date grounds, giving the soft shadowy effects so desirable in portrait work. Painted in oil on the best muslin. No better headgrounds are made at any price.

State whether you want design No. 40 or 41. These grounds are suitable for either right or left light, and several different effects can be obtained by using the ground in different positions.

Price, size, 4x4 feet..........$0.70
Price, size, 5x6 feet..........84
Price, size, 5x7 feet..........1.05
Price, size, 6x8 feet..........1.50

Clouded Design No. 40.

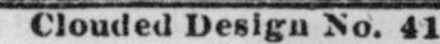

Clouded Design No. 41.

SCENIC BACKGROUNDS.

Scenic Design No. 1.

Scenic Design No. 2.

Scenic Design No. 3.

Scenic Design No. 4.

Scenic Design No. 5.

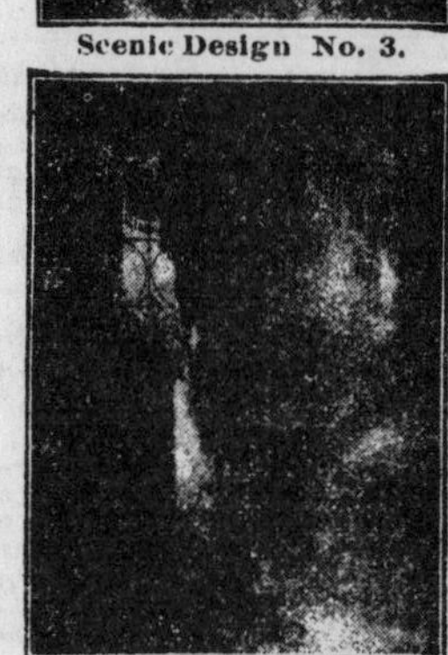

Scenic Design No. 6.

Scenic Design No. 7.

Scenic Design No. 8.

No. 20C2722 The above illustrations show our line of scenic backgrounds, painted expressly for us, the very latest and most artistic designs, painted in oil, on the best grade of muslin, guaranteed to be waterproof, will not crack, and will stand more rough handling than any other grounds made.

Size, 6x 8 feet. Price..........$3.50
Size, 8x 8 feet. Price..........4.30
Size, 8x10 feet. Price..........5.40
Size, 8x12 feet. Price..........7.39
Size, 6x15 feet. With Floor Extension. Price..........5.90
Size, 8x15 feet. With Floor Extension. Price..........6.15
Size, 10x15 feet. With Floor Extension. Price..........7.48
Size, 12x15 feet. With Floor Extension. Price..........8.60

State size, design, and which side light falls on, when ordering. If light falls on right side of sitter, when sitter is in position, it is **"right light."** Right light falls on left side of operator when operator faces sitter. **Do not judge these backgrounds by the prices we ask for them. There are no better grounds painted at any price.**

Ruby and Orange Glass.

No. 20L1216 **Deep ruby glass for dark room use**, replacing ruby glass in ruby lamps, etc. Carefully selected for non-actinic qualities.

Size, inches.		Price
3¼x 4¼	Fits our candle lamp........	7c
3⅝x 4⅝	Fits our medium oil lamp........	8c
4 x 5		8c
4⅝x 5⅝	Fits our large oil lamp	10c
5 x 7	....	12c
6½x 8½	....	16c
8 x10	....	20c
10 x12	....	30c
11 x14	....	45c
16 x20	....	85c

No. 20L1217 Orange glass, used in combination with ruby glass for dark room lights, also very fine for working developing papers by. Sizes and prices same as quoted above for ruby glass.

Ruby Fabric, 15 Cents.

No. 20L1219 Ruby Fabric. A good substitute for ruby glass, and not liable to breakage. Size, 15x18 inches. Price, per sheet in mailing tube........ 15c
If by mail, postage extra, per sheet, 5 cents.

One Dozen Postoffice Papers, 12 Cents.

No. 20L1220 Postoffice Paper. A yellow paper for dark room use, making ruby light, etc.
Size, 18x22 inches. Price, per dozen sheets........ 12c
If by mail, postage extra, 15 cents.

Ground Glass.

No. 20L1230 Ground Glass for replacing broken screens in cameras, making transparencies, etc., finest quality, mud ground. State size wanted.

Size	Price	Size	Price
3¼x4¼........	6c	6½x8½........	15c
4 x5........	8c	8x10........	20c
4¼x6½........	10c	10x12........	32c
5 x7........	11c	11x14........	42c
5 x8........	13c		

Measuring Glasses, 4 Cents.

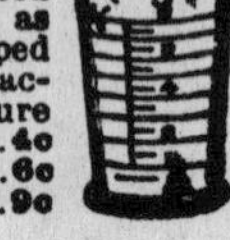

No. 20L1240 Tumbler Shaped Measuring Glasses. For liquids; graduated with ounces and drams; not quite as convenient as the regular cone shaped graduate, but preferred by many on account of the extremely low price. Be sure to state size wanted. Price, 2 ounce.... 4c
Price, 4 ounce........ 6c
Price, 8 ounce........ 9c
Not mailable.

Pressed Line Graduates.

No. 20L1242 Cone Shaped Graduates. For measuring liquids; marked with scale showing ounces and drams. **Perfectly accurate. State size wanted.** Price, 1 ounce........ 8c
Price, 2 ounce........ 9c
Price, 4 ounce........ 13c
Price, 8 ounce........ 19c
Price, 16 ounce........ 27c

Engraved Graduates.

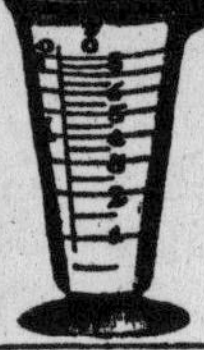

No. 20L1244 Cone Shaped Graduates, all lines and figures engraved by hand, the most carefully made and accurate graduate on the market. Be sure to state size wanted.

Price, 1 ounce........ 12c
Price, 2 ounce........ 13c
Price, 4 ounce........ 20c
Price, 8 ounce........ 32c
Price, 16 ounce........ 50c
Price, 32 ounce........ 88c

Hydrometers, 16 Cents.

No. 20L1248 For making up solutions by hydrometer test instead of using scales and weights; very convenient. Complete, with glass jar, in wooden box.
Price........ 16c
If by mail, postage extra, 9 cents.

Fluted Glass Funnels, 13 Cents.

No. 20L1255 Glass Funnels, fluted, for filtering. More desirable than plain funnels, because filtering is much more rapid. Be sure to state size wanted.

Size	Price	Size	Price
½ pint........	13c	1 quart........	20c
1 pint........	16c	2 quart........	34c

Too heavy to send by mail.

Filter Paper, 6 Cents.

No. 20L1258 Filter Paper. Round, in packages of 10 sheets. Be sure to state size wanted.

Price, 18 inches in diameter, per package........ 16c
Price, 13 inches in diameter, per package........ 9c
Price, 10 inches in diameter, per package........ 7c
Price, 8 inches in diameter, per package........ 6c

New Style Photo Scale for 35 Cents

No. 20L1265 The best scale yet devised at a low price; answers all the requirements in making up solutions, etc. **Simple,** nothing to get out of order, **accurate and convenient, no loose weights.** Weighs up to 12 drams. Pan is made of glass and easily cleaned. Price........ 35c
If by mail, postage extra, 6 cents.

No. 20L1267 Extra Glass Pans for No. 20L1265 Scale.
Price........ 10c

An Imported Scale for $1.20

$1.20

No. 20L1268 Our Imported Balance Scale, made in Germany, has 2¼-inch brass pans, brass pillar, 6-inch beam, and stands 12 inches high when set up for use. The entire scale packs away in the box on which it is set up, has complete set of weights from ⅛ grain to 2 drams and comes complete in oak box.
Price, complete........ $1.20
If by mail, postage extra, 13 cents.

This Scale Reduced to $1.98.

$1.98

No. 20L1274 All metal parts are nickel plated; it has large nickel plated pan, 3½ in. in diameter; it is very sensitive, finely finished, accurately adjusted and durable. Two complete sets of weights are included, one set of avoirdupois, 1/16 of an ounce to 2 ounces, and one set of dram, scruple and grain weights.
Price, complete........ $1.98
If by mail, postage extra, 22 cents.

Professional Photographer's Scale, $2.65.

This is a thoroughly practical, durable and accurate scale, very much superior to any moderate priced photographer's scale now on the market. It is very finely adjusted and guaranteed to be sensitive to one-half grain. The pans are large and interchangeable. By means of the adjusting screws, a perfect balance is sure at all times. All the metal work on this scale, including the weights, is nickel plated and polished. The base is of quarter sawed oak, making it a very handsome article. A very complete set of weights is included with this scale, running from two ounces down to one-half grain.
No. 20L1275 Professional Photographer's Scale. Price........ $2.65
If by mail, postage extra, 30 cents.

Special Composition Trays.

No. 20L1280 These new trays are jet black, perfectly smooth, without seam or joint and perfect in shape. We guarantee them to stand all photographic chemicals without deterioration and to be acid and alkali proof. In shape, finish and durability they are superior to all other composition trays. They are the best moderate priced trays on the market for general purposes, developing negatives, toning, washing prints, etc.

For plates 3¼x3¼ or 3¼x4¼ in. Price, each........ 10c
For plates 4x5 inches. Price, each........ 11c
For plates 5x7 inches. Price, each........ 21c
For plates 5x8 inches. Price, each........ 23c
For plates 6½x8½ inches. Price, each........ 32c
For plates 8x10 inches. Price, each........ 47c

You can save time in the dark room by using large trays. For example, you can develop two 4x5 plates at once in a 5x8 tray, and two 5x7 or four 4x5 plates in an 8x10 tray.

Best Grade Elite Enameled Steel Trays.

No. 20L1287 Genuine Imported Elite Steel Ware Trays for photographic use; guaranteed to be absolutely chemical proof. These trays are superior to all enameled steel trays for general all around purposes. They are equally well adapted to developing and fixing plates, toning prints and washing. They are as easily cleaned as a porcelain tray. They are absolutely proof against the action of all chemicals, including the most powerful acids. They are made in one solid piece, without joints or seams, and are practically unbreakable. The Elite steel trays are undergiazed and quadruple coated and guaranteed to be the very finest tray that can be produced. Be sure to state size wanted.

For plates, inches	4x5	5x7	6½x8½	8x10
Price........	21c	44c	65c	96c
For plates, inches	10x12	11x14	12x16	14x17
Price........	$1.44	$1.92	$2.25	$3.25
For plates, inches........			16x20	18x22
Price........			$3.85	$5.45

The large sizes are fine for toning.

Porcelain Trays.

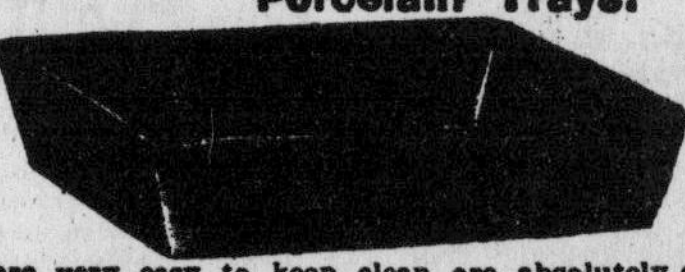

No. 20L1288 Porcelain Trays, the best grade of imported white porcelain, extra deep. These trays are very easy to keep clean, are absolutely chemical proof, and are generally considered the finest trays made for toning and other work. Be sure to state size wanted.

For plates, inches	4x5	5x7	5x8	6½x8½	8x10
Price........	40c	52c	63c	68c	85c

Developing Tank for Films, 88 Cents.

No. 20L1295 Developing Tank for developing roll films. This device consists of a tank 7 inches long by 4 inches wide, with a nickel plated metal rod extended lengthwise of the tank in such a manner that the end of a strip of film can be slipped under the roller and the film drawn up and down through the developing solution contained in the tank. This tank not only makes the developing of roll film in strips very easy and insures good results, but at the same time it is very economical, as the amount of developing solution required in a tank of this design is much less than would be used with an ordinary tray. Strongly and substantially made throughout of metal, and nickel plated.
Price........ 88c

Rubber Finger Tips, 9 Cents.

No. 20L1309 Rubber Finger Tips, made of pure rubber, put up in sets of three; prevents staining the fingers when developing, etc. Price, per set........ 9c
If by mail, postage extra, 1 cent.

Rubber Aprons, 39 Cents.

No. 20L1312 Rubber Aprons. Made especially for photographers; protect the clothing from chemical stains and dirt of all kinds. Length, 40 inches. Price... 39c

Fixing Baths.

25c

These Fixing Baths are made of metal, thoroughly coated with a preparation which renders them impervious to the action of hypo. They are a very great convenience at a very low price. The use of these baths for fixing **avoids the danger of spots and stains,** which is the frequent result of fixing in the ordinary tray. They hold six plates each. **These baths are provided with a rising bottom,** so that the plates are readily raised above the top—a great convenience in removing them from the box and avoiding the danger of scratching

No. 20L1316	For plates 3¼x3¼.	Price.... 25c
No. 20L1317	For plates 3¼x4¼.	Price.... 27c
No. 20L1318	For plates 4x5.	Price.... 30c
No. 20L1319	For plates 5x7 or 5x8.	Price.... 42c

If by mail, postage extra, 9, 9, 10 and 17 cents.

Zinc Washing Box.

This washer is perfect in its construction. The water enters through the inlet tube and is carried to the bottom, and is circulated over the whole area of the box, thus **insuring uniform washing of the plates.** It is carried off through the outlet tube. The water can be carried to the box by attaching a rubber hose from the faucet to the inlet tube, or the box can be placed under the faucet and the water allowed to run into the funnel. We guarantee that you can **wash twenty 4x5 negatives in fifteen minutes** in our washer.

The corrugations are extra deep and extend from the top downward, as will be seen in the illustration. One of the many good qualities and one that has greatly been the means of making our washer celebrated is our **patent lifting bottom;** by means of the rod in the center, the perforated bottom can be lifted up as high as the bottom of the corrugations, which brings the plates above the top of the box so that they can be held by the edge, thus **removing all danger of scratching the films.**

Where running water cannot be procured, this is still the **"Ideal Washer."** It will be seen that the inlet tube enters from the top, which allows the box to remain full of water, so that by filling and emptying the box a few times and allowing several minutes between each operation, plates can be thoroughly washed.

This washer is **constructed of heavy zinc throughout.** The lifting bottom can be taken out if necessary.

No. 20L1344	For plates 3¼x3½ or 3¼x3¼. Price	$0.78
No. 20L1345	For plates 4x5 and 5x7. Price	.83
No. 20L1346	For plates 3¼x4¼, 4¼x4¼ or 4¼ x 6½. Price	.85
No. 20L1347	For plates 5x7 and 6½x8½. Price	1.18
No. 20L1348	For plates 6½x8½ and 8x10. Price	1.35
No. 20L1349	Rubber Hose, suitable for attaching these boxes to hydrant. Price, per foot....	.08

Print Washers.

This Print Washer is so constructed that prints are kept thoroughly separated and constantly in motion without requiring any attention whatever during the entire process of washing. The eccentric motion that is imparted to the water within the washer has the peculiar faculty of keeping the prints separate from each other all the time and keeping them in constant motion and always in contact with fresh water. This Print Washer not only saves a great deal of work, as the process of washing by the old methods is a long, tiresome and tedious one, but at the same time it insures better results.

No. 20L1360 For prints 4x5 or smaller, 9 inches in diameter. Price........$1.12
No. 20L1362 For prints 5x7 or smaller, 12 inches in diameter. Price........1.55
No. 20L1363 For prints 6½x8½ or smaller, 16 inches in diameter. Price........2.70
No. 20L1364 For prints 8x10 or smaller, 20 inches in diameter. Price........3.85

Folding Negative Rack, 13 Cents.

13c

No. 20L1365 This Negative Drying Rack is strongly and neatly made, folds up compactly and is by far the best low priced rack made. It will hold 24 negatives and is suitable for any size up to 8x10. Made of hard wood, oil finished.
Price.......13c

Developing Tanks.

For Automatic Development of Glass Plate Negatives. The process of the tank development is rapidly superceding the older method of development in trays and is not only simpler and more convenient in every way, but the results obtained are as good, if not better than can be obtained by the old process of developing in a tray in a dark room. The exposed plates are transferred from the plate holder to the developing tank in the dark room or in a changing bag, after which the tank can be carried out into ordinary light, developer poured in through the funnel, and at the end of fifteen or twenty minutes the plates will be fully developed and can then be fixed and washed in the ordinary manner.

Zinc Tanks for Development Only.

These Zinc Tanks can be used only for developing, as zinc will not stand the action of hypo.

No. 20L1371 Zinc Tank for plates, 3¼x4¼ inches or lantern slides. Price........$0.80
No. 20L1372 Zinc Tank for plates, 4x5. Price.. .85
No. 20L1373 Zinc Tank for plates, 5x7. Price.. 1.17
No. 20L1374 Zinc Tank for plates, 6½x8½. Price, 1.50
No. 20L1375 Zinc Tank for plates, 8x10. Price.. 1.68

Nickel Plated Brass Tanks for Development and Fixing.

$1.73

These tanks are constructed from brass throughout and heavily nickel plated, so that they stand the action of hypo and may therefore be used for both developing and fixing. This tank used in connection with the changing bag listed above makes it possible to perform the entire process of developing and fixing a glass plate negative by daylight. With an equipment consisting of this Automatic Daylight Developing Tank and the Changing Bag listed above, negatives can be made at any time and in any place without using a dark room at all. Any developer can be used, but it is customary to make it a little weaker by adding more water than when developing in the ordinary manner in a tray. Full instructions are sent with each outfit.

No. 20L1376 Brass Tank for plates, 3¼x4¼ inches or lantern slides. Price........$1.73
No. 20L1377 Brass Tank for plates, 4x5. Price.. 1.80
No. 20L1378 Brass Tank for plates, 5x7. Price.. 2.63
No. 20L1379 Brass Tank for plates, 6½x8½. Price 2.98
No. 20L1380 Brass Tank for plates, 8x10. Price.. 3.95

Reversible Developing Tank.

This is the latest and the most perfect form of developing tank yet devised. It comprises two tanks, an inner and outer, and the outer tank is fitted with a removable plate rack, and the cover is held on firmly with strong latches. The exposed plates are inserted in the inner tank, the cover fastened on, and the tank can then be brought into daylight and lowered into the outer tank containing the developing solution. When the plates are half developed, the inner tank may be removed and turned over or reversed which insures perfect uniformity in development.

The tanks are made of brass throughout, heavily nickel plated and finely finished. They may be used for both developing and fixing, and also for the final washing. After the plates are washed, the removable plate rack holding the finished negatives is lifted out of the tank, and used as a drying rack, if desired.

No. 20L1391 Reversible Tank, for 4x5 plates. Price........$3.15
No. 20L1394 Reversible Tank, for 5x7 plates. Price........4.05
No. 20L1395 Reversible Tank, for 6½x8½ plates. Price........5.85
No. 20L1396 Reversible Tank, for 8x10 plates. Price........6.75

Developing Powder.

FOR AUTOMATIC TANK DEVELOPMENT, 20 CENTS.

No. 20L1381 Tank Developing Powder put up in packages of six powders, each powder sufficient to make eighteen ounces of developer, or a total for the package of one hundred and eight ounces. Price, per package (six powders sufficient for one hundred and eight ounces of developer.. 20c
If by mail, postage extra, 3 cents.

Changing Bag.

$1.10

This is an exceedingly well made, perfectly light tight and easily handled Changing Bag. It is made from a fine quality of black sateen lined with the best black rubber cloth, making an absolutely light tight bag. By means of this bag plate holders can be loaded at any time in daylight, the bag being opened at the bottom, the box of plates and the plate holders placed inside, and the bag then closed up. The hands are then placed through the arm holes, and the plates can be easily removed from the box and put into the plate holders without the slightest danger of injury by light. Equipped with one of these Changing Bags and the Automatic Brass Developing Tank described below, the holders can be loaded and the plates developed without the use of a dark room at all. Price

No. 20L1385 Suitable for plates 4x5 or smaller $1.10
No. 20L1386 Suitable for plates 5x7 or smaller.... 1.40
No. 20L1387 Suitable for plates 6½x8½ or smaller.. 1.50
No. 20L1388 Suitable for plates 8x10 or smaller.... 2.10

Amateur Printing Frames.

Light Weight Printing Frame. The best light weight frame made and a great improvement over the ordinary style. A special point of advantage is the piano hinge, heretofore fitted only to the highest priced frames, giving strength and durability. The finish throughout is good. Be sure to state size wanted.

No. 20L1410 Amateur Printing Frames, without glass.

Size, inches	2½x2½	3½x3½	3¼x4¼
Price	10c	11c	12c
Size, inches	4x5	3⅝x6	5x7
Price	13c	14c	17c

The 3⅝x6 frame is used for printing post cards from negatives 3¼x5½ inches or smaller.

No. 20L1411 Amateur Printing Frames, with glass.

Size, inches	2½x2½	3½x3½	3¼x4¼
Price	12c	13c	14c
Size, inches	4x5	3⅝x6	5x7
Price	16c	18c	22c

Glass in a printing frame is necessary when printing from glass negatives smaller than the frame, and in all cases when printing from film negatives. We furnish only the best imported glass.

Professional Printing Frames.

24c

Heavy Weight Printing Frames. The finest printing frame manufactured; strongly and substantially constructed throughout, heavy brass springs sliding under brass plates instead of grooves in the wood, thus preventing all wear; mortised corners; back in three pieces to prevent warping; finished throughout in the best possible manner. **It pays to get good printing frames, and these frames are the best made.**

No. 20L1415 Professional Printing Frames, without glass.

Size, inches	3¼x4¼	4x5	4¼x6½	5x7	5x8
Price	24c	25c	28c	33c	35c
Size, inches	6½x8½	8x10	10x12	11x14	14x17
Price	40c	50c	83c	$1.20	$1.50

No. 20L1416 Professional Printing Frames, with glass.

Size, inches	3¼x4¼	4x5	4¼x6½	5x7
Price	26c	28c	32c	38c
Size, inches		5x8	6½x8½	8x10
Price		41c	48c	61c

Glass in printing frame is necessary when printing from film negatives, also when using glass negatives that are smaller than the frame. Our frames are fitted with the finest imported glass, guaranteed absolutely free from blemishes of any kind.

Masks, 19 Cents.

Every package contains a large assortment of fancy and novel designs.

A NECESSARY ADDITION TO ANY PHOTOGRAPHIC OUTFIT.

Made from tough opaque paper, and designed to be placed between negative and sensitized paper while printing, thus producing oval, circular or various fancy shaped prints from any negative. The illustration shows only one of the many sizes of styles. Made for the following negatives: 2¼x3¼, 3½x3½, 3¼x4¼, 3¼x5½, (for post cards) 4x5 and 5x7.

No. 20L1425 Masks. Assortment No. 1 contains one oval, one circle, one rectangle, one round corner rectangle, the balance being a variety of ornamental designs.
Price, per package, any size........19c

No. 20L1426 Masks. Assortment No. 2 composed entirely of ornamental designs, all different from Assortment No. 1.. Price, per package, any size........19c
If by mail, postage extra, any size, 2 cents.
Be sure to state size wanted.

Print Trimmers, 14 and 16 Cents.

No. 20L1435 Straight Trimmers, for trimming prints; the cutting knife is a small wheel which revolves and leaves very clean edge.
Price.....(If by mail, postage extra, 3 cents).......14c
No. 20L1436 Extra wheels........8c

No. 20L1438 Swivel Trimmers, Same as No. 20L1435, but cutting wheel is swivel mounted and can follow curved surface. Price........16c
If by mail, postage extra, 3 cents.
No. 20L1439 Extra wheels, each........8c

NOTE—Prints must be laid on a sheet of metal or piece of glass when using above trimmers or the rotary trimmer described below.

Professional Revolving Trimmer.

80c

No. 20L1440 This is a High Grade Trimmer, made to withstand long and hard use. The cutting wheel is turned from carbon steel and so well made and tempered that it will out-last a dozen wheels of the ordinary grade. The bearings are highly finished and accurate, eliminating all possible friction.
Price....(If by mail, postage extra, 5 cents.).......80c

Trimming Forms, 14 Cents.

No. 20 1455 Perfectly made steel trimming forms, with copper oxidized finish. Be sure to state size wanted.

	Size		Size
No. 0. Oval...	1⅜x2	A. Oval...	1 7/16x2 7/16 inches
No. 1. Oval...	2x2¾, ¼ Cab.	B. Oval...	1⅜x3⅛ inches
No. 2. Oval...	3x4 1/16, ⅜ Cab.	C. Oval...	2 3/16x5 1/16 inches
No. 3. Oval...	3 7/16x4, 11/16 Cab.	D. Oval...	1⅜x2 11/16 inches
No. 4. Oval...	2 5/16x3 7/16	E. Oval...	2¼x4 inches
No. 5. Oval...	3¾x5¾	F. Oval...	2⅜x5 1/16 inches
No. 6. Oval...	4¼x6	G. Oval...	2⅛x5⅝ inches
No. 9. Circle...	2¾ inches	H. Oval...	1 13/16x3 9/16 inches
No. 10. Circle...	3 inches	J. Oval...	2¾x5 3/16 inches
No. 11. Circle...	3¼ inches	K. Oval...	3 1/16x6⅜ inches
		L. Oval...	1⅞x2 11/16 inches
		M. Oval...	2½x3½, ½ Cab.

Price, each, any size........14c
Be sure to state size wanted.

Trimming Boards, 36 Cents.

36c

No. 20L1465 Prints always have to be trimmed before mounting, and while this can, of course, be done fairly well with scissors or knife, at the same time the advantages of a regular trimmer as here illustrated will be readily apparent. It trims the prints quickly, easily and squarely. The blade is made of finest tempered steel, the board of polished hardwood, has graduated measure which also serves as guide for the paper. Our illustration shows way in which this trimmer is used. Trims any size up to and including 4x5. Price........36c

No. 20L1466 Trimming Board, same as No. 20L1465, but larger, suitable for prints up to 5x7. Price........54c
No. 20L1467 Trimming Board, same as No. 20L1465, but with 10½-inch blade, suitable for any size up to and including 8x10. Price........98c

Our Best Trimming Boards.

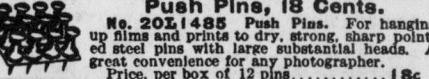

No. 20L1472 The blade is made from the same steel used in the best paper cutting machines finely tempered and ground to a perfect edge. The board is made of hardwood, polished, and so constructed that it cannot warp. The spring joint, by which the blade is attached, allows a slight lateral motion, so that the two cutting edges are in perfect contact at every point, insuring perfect, clean cut edges to either cards or paper. The illustration shows method of trimming a print.

Length of blade, inches. ...	6½	8½	10½	12½
Price	95c	$1.30	$1.55	$2.10

Centering Square, 22 Cents.

No. 20L1480 Centering Square. A novel device by means of which photographic prints can be instantly and accurately centered on the card mount. Everyone knows how difficult it is to put the pictures square on the card sometimes, and this little device overcomes all this trouble resulting in much better looking pictures. Made of brass, nickel plated; full instructions with each one.
Price........22c

Push Pins, 18 Cents.

No. 20L1485 Push Pins. For hanging up films and prints to dry, strong, sharp pointed steel pins with large substantial heads. A great convenience for any photographer.
Price, per box of 12 pins........18c

Print Rollers, 12 and 16 Cents.

Indispensable for smoothing down prints after mounting and for squeegeeing prints on ferrotype plates.

No. 20L1490 4-inch Print Roller, rubber covered, large wood handle, as shown in illustration. Price........12c
No. 20L1491 6-inch Print Roller, rubber covered, large wood handle, as shown in illustration. Price........16c

Dry Plate Attachments for Ansco Film Cameras.

The Ansco Dry Plate Attachment consists of an interchangeable back by means of which dry plates can be used with the Nos. 4, 5, 6, 7, 9, and 10 Ansco Film Cameras, thus converting these cameras into combination film and plate cameras.

No. 20H350 Ansco Dry Plate Attachment, 3¼x4¼, for Nos. 4 or 6 Ansco Cameras, complete with one double plate holder. Price........ $3.15

No. 20H351 Ansco Dry Plate Attachment, 4x5, for Nos. 5 or 7 Ansco Cameras, complete with one double plate holder. Price........ $3.15

No. 20H352 Ansco Dry Plate Attachment, 3¼x5½, for Nos. 9 and 10 Ansco Cameras, complete with one double plate holder. Price........ $3.15

No. 20H355 Extra Plate Holders, double, for Ansco Dry Plate Attachments.
3¼x4¼. Price, each........ $1.10
4x5. Price, each........ 1.10
3¼x5½. Price, each........ 1.10

The Expo Watch Camera.

A True Vest Pocket Detective Camera. The Expo Camera is the smallest practical camera ever made, and, although it is so small that it can readily be carried in the vest pocket, it is at the same time a strictly high class practical instrument in every way. The Expo Camera is a daylight loading camera using film, and can be loaded for twenty-five exposures at a time. This camera looks exactly like a fair sized watch and pictures can be taken with it anywhere without anyone suspecting that a camera is being used. The pictures taken with the Expo Camera are ⅞ of an inch long by ⅝ of an inch wide, the exact size shown in our illustration. This camera can be used for either time or instantaneous exposures and is suitable for landscapes, street scenes, groups, portraits, etc., in fact, just exactly the same kind of work which is accomplished by larger and more expensive cameras. The Expo Camera is carefully constructed from metal throughout, nickel plated, fitted with a fine achromatic lens and is guaranteed in every respect. So perfect are the negatives made with this little vest pocket camera that the pictures can be enlarged without sacrificing the detail or other good qualities.

Expo Picture, Exact Size.

No. 20H375 The Expo Watch Camera. Price, complete, without film....(Postage extra, 10 cents)...... $2.25

No. 20H376 View Finder, for Expo Watch Camera. Price........ 45c
If by mail, postage extra, 5 cents.

No. 20H377 Daylight Loading Film for Expo Camera, twenty-five exposures to the roll. Price, per roll....... 18c
If by mail, postage extra, 1 cent.

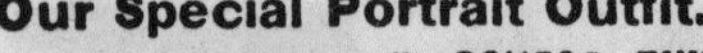

Our Special Portrait Outfit.

No. 20H500 THIS OUTFIT CONSISTS OF AN 8x10 CAMERA, Camera Stand and Reversible Cabinet attachment.

CAMERA IS MADE FROM BEST HARDWOOD finely finished. All adjustments are automatic and self locking. Has 30-inch bed, best India rubber bellows.

STAND IS THE WIZARD No. 7, fitted with automatic balancing device, raises and lowers with the lightest touch, can be locked in any position by lever at side. Firm and rigid, made of hardwood, finely finished. Top measures 17x32⅛ inches.

THE NELSON AUTOMATIC HOLDER is included, the best studio plate holder made. Plates are put in or removed without turning a button, the back does not require to be opened, no spring to press on back of plate. Takes any size of plate from 8x10 to 2x2.

THE REVERSIBLE CABINET ATTACHMENT has spring actuated ground glass, and uses modern double plate holders.

THE FOLDING RACK is made of hardwood, holds twelve double plate holders, and is attached to side of stand.

Price, complete........ $34.75

No lens or shutter is included.

We recommend our No. 20H1125 Lens and the No. 20H850 Silent Shutter for use with this outfit.

Our Best Penny Picture Camera.

No. 20H510 This Camera is made from carefully selected hardwood and handsomely finished. It can be used for any regular portrait work in the studio, up to and including 5x7; also for copying. As a multiplying or penny picture camera, it makes 1, 4, 9, 12, 16, 20, 30 or 42 pictures on one 5x7 plate. **Only one lens required.** The mechanism is exceedingly simple, very easy to operate. Made with rising front and self locking focus lever. This camera has a 30-inch bed, rubber bellows and uses double plate holders of modern style.

Price, with one double plate holder..... $16.90
Extra plate holders, each........ .65

We especially recommend our Portrait Lens No 20H1125 for use with this camera.

No. 20H511 Camera Stand, suitable for the above Penny Picture Camera. This is the well known No. 00 stand, made with patent stop for holding adjustable central support at any height, and semi-automatic tilting attachment. Answers all ordinary requirements.

Price........ $3.15

COMPLETE INSTRUCTIONS IN PHOTOGRAPHY

OUR NEW 112-PAGE MANUAL FREE WITH EVERY CAMERA WE SELL.

A SPECIAL FEATURE of our photographic outfits is the book, "Complete Instructions in Photography," a 112-page manual, which is included free of charge with every camera or complete outfit.

THIS BOOK WAS WRITTEN EXPRESSLY FOR US by one of the most expert photographers in the United States; a man who has spent fifteen years in making photographs, teaching photography, and selling photographic merchandise to both amateur and professional photographers. The experience thus gained, not only in the actual processes of photography, but in contact with other photographers—with amateurs and with beginners—enables him to appreciate and to understand, better than anyone else, the difficulties met with and the errors made by beginners. This experience enables him to understand just what the beginner wants to know, enables him to make it plain and simple, and the success which is attending the efforts of those who are already using "Complete Instructions in Photography" is the best proof we can offer as to its value.

COMPLETE INSTRUCTIONS IN PHOTOGRAPHY answers all your questions, solves all your difficulties, anticipates all your troubles and makes photography easy. Indispensable to the beginner, invaluable to the advanced photographer. "Complete Instructions in Photography" tells secrets of the trade never before published; gives valuable information heretofore possessed only by a few professional photographers; GIVES DOZENS OF VALUABLE FORMULAS OR RECIPES; tells you how to make your own developers, your own solutions of all kinds; tells you how to determine the correct amount of exposure, how to save plates which are wrongly exposed, how to make good portraits, how to make blue paper, how to dry a negative in five minutes, HOW TO MAKE MONEY IN PHOTOGRAPHY, how to avoid all the troubles sometimes met with by beginners, how to select a camera; tells all about a hundred other things which we haven't space to mention here.

REMEMBER, There is no other book like it. It was written expressly for us. It is published only by us, and can be secured only from us.

IT COSTS YOU NOTHING.

WE INCLUDE IT FREE OF CHARGE with every camera which we sell. If you already have an outfit and desire a copy of the book, we will include it free of charge with an order for photographic supplies amounting to $2.50 or more (provided you state in your order that you desire it). We do not sell this book. We had it written and publish it exclusively for the benefit of our customers, but in order to protect ourselves against actual loss, we are obliged to give it only to those who send us an order for at least $2.50 worth of photographic goods, and state in their order that a copy of "Complete Instructions in Photography" is desired.

SERIES "A" DEVELOPING, FINISHING AND MATERIAL OUTFITS FOR EITHER PLATE CAMERAS OR FILM CAMERAS

98c to $1.35

ACCORDING TO SIZE.

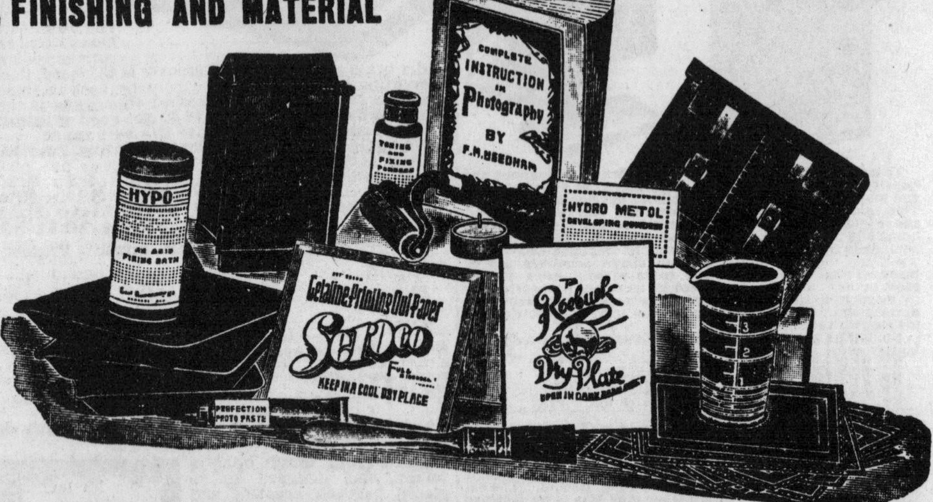

THESE SERIES "A" Developing, Finishing and Material Outfits contain everything necessary for developing, printing and finishing pictures. We urge everyone who orders a camera from us to include, with the camera, one of these fine outfits and thus secure, right at the start, at the lowest possible cost, everything necessary to commence work. Everything that we put into these outfits is good; plates and papers guaranteed fresh and perfect; chemicals guaranteed full weight and full strength; accessories guaranteed strictly high class, well made and serviceable. The Series "A" Outfits are put up in seven sizes and are suitable for use with any cameras of corresponding sizes that we sell.

Arranged for plate cameras, each outfit contains the following items:

- 1 Package Concentrated Dry Toner (makes 8 ounces of solution).
- 1 Tray for Developing Plates.
- 1 Tray for Fixing Plates.
- 1 Package Concentrated Dry Developer (makes 8 ounces of solution.)
- 1 Metal Dark Room Lamp.
- 1 Tray for Toning Prints.
- 1 Print Roller for smoothing down the mounted prints.
- ½ Dozen Dry Plates.
- 1 Dozen Sheets Sensitized Paper.
- 1 Printing Frame.
- 1 Package Hypo for fixing Negatives and Prints.
- 1 Paste Brush.
- 1 Graduated Glass for Measuring Liquids.
- 1 Dozen Card Mounts, with fancy embossed borders.
- 1 Tube of Fine Scented Photo Mounting Paste.
- 1 Copy of "Complete Instructions in Photography."

Outfits for Plate Camera.

No. 20H601	Series "A" Outfit for 2½x2½ plate camera.	Price.. $0.98
No. 20H602	Series "A" Outfit for 3½x3½ plate camera.	Price.. 1.05
No. 20H603	Series "A" Outfit for 3¼x4¼ plate camera.	Price... 1.12
No. 20H604	Series "A" Outfit for 4x5 plate camera.	Price... 1.20

There is no Camera included with these Outfits.

Outfits for Film Cameras.

We also put up these outfits arranged especially for film cameras, the list of items being the same as included in the outfits for plate cameras, except that we put in one roll of film (six exposures) instead of the package of dry plates, and the printing frame is fitted with a glass.

No. 20H610	Series "A" Outfit for 2¼x3¼ film cameras.	Price, $1.00
No. 20H611	Series "A" Outfit for 2½x4¼ film cameras.	Price, 1.05
No. 20H612	Series "A" Outfit for 3½x3½ film cameras.	Price, 1.10
No. 20H613	Series "A" Outfit for 3¼x4¼ film cameras.	Price, 1.15
No. 20H614	Series "A" Outfit for 4x5 film cameras.	Price, 1.30
No. 20H615	Series "A" Outfit for 3¼x5½ film cameras.	Price, 1.35

There is no Camera included with these Outfits.

DEVELOPING OUTFITS CONTINUED ON NEXT PAGE.

Monarch Symmetrical Wide Angle Lens.

The Monarch Symmetrical Wide Angle Lens is a finely made instrument, especially adapted to the photographing of interiors and is also used for out of door views in confined situations. Wide angle lenses are absolutely necessary in all cases where it is difficult or impossible to get far enough away from the subject in order to get it all on the plate with an ordinary lens. The Monarch Wide Angle Lens is handsomely mounted in lacquered brass with a fine iris diaphragm, and is a strictly high grade lens that will be found entirely satisfactory for all work requiring a short focus or wide angle lens. This lens is of the symmetrical type of construction, both front and rear combinations of the same focal length. It works at a speed of F. 16, is guaranteed to cover the plate for which it is listed sharply to the extreme corners, and its construction throughout is based upon the most modern principles of high grade lens construction.

No. 20L1120 The Monarch Symmetrical Wide Angle Lens, in barrel with iris diaphragm, as illustrated.

Lens No.	Size Plate Covered	Equivalent Focus	Diameter Across Hood	Price
1	4 x 5	3½ inches	1¼ inches	$ 5.70
2	5 x 7	5¼ inches	1¼ inches	6.80
3	6½ x 8½	6½ inches	1 5/32 inches	9.90
4	8 x 10	8 inches	2 13/32 inches	12.80

Wide Angle Lenses in Cells to Fit Shutters.

This wide angle lens is furnished without barrel or shutter, the front and rear combinations being mounted in cells as shown in the illustration. These cells fit the shutters ordinarily used with folding hand cameras, such as the Conley Long Focus, or the Conley Double Extension and other cameras of this kind. To use these lenses, the front and rear combinations of your regular lens are simply unscrewed from the shutter, and these wide angle lens combinations screwed into their place. These lenses are strictly high grade instruments, made throughout in the best possible manner; in fact, they are ground and finished with exactly the same care as is given to our Monarch Symmetrical Wide Angle Lens listed above.

No. 20L1121 Wide Angle Lenses in cells to fit the Wollensak Regular or the Wollensak Automatic Shutters.

Size	Price
4x5	$2.90
5x7	3.70
6½x8½	5.95
8x10	7.80

No. 20L1122 Wide Angle Lenses in cells to fit the Conley Safety or the Conley Automatic Shutters.

Size	Price
4x5	$2.90
5x7	3.70
6½x8½	5.95
8x10	7.80

Example: If you have a 5x7 Seroco or Conley Long Focus Camera fitted with Wollensak Regular Shutter, the 5x7 Wide Angle Lens No. 20L1121 will fit your shutter.

If you already have or if you are just ordering one of the latest model Conley Cameras with Conley Safety or Conley Automatic Shutter, then the wide angle lens that is listed under No. 20L1122 will fit your shutter.

Conley Series II Portrait Lens, F5.

The Series II Conley Portrait Lens is a true portrait lens of the most approved type of portrait lens construction. These lenses are ground from the best imported optical glass, composed of two systems of two glasses each, the front system cemented and the rear system made with an air space between the two glasses. The special formula by which these lenses are ground, combined with their large diameter, gives them a high working speed, producing brilliant negatives with plenty of detail with the shortest possible exposures.

We recommend the Series II Conley Portrait Lens as the very best moderate priced portrait lens ever placed on the market, and for general all around work in the studio these lenses cannot be surpassed. These lenses are beautifully finished in lacquered brass with black trimmings, and mounted with the same care and accuracy that is given to our highest priced portrait lenses.

We furnish this lens in sizes above No. 2, either with or without the Wollensak Studio Shutter. When sold without the shutter the lens is equipped with a fine iris diaphragm. See following number for description of this studio shutter.

No. 20L1126 The Conley Series II Portrait Lens.

Lens No.	Size of Plate Covered, inches	Diameter of Lens, inches	Equivalent Focus, in.	Distance for Standing Cabinet, feet	Price with Iris Diaphragm	Price with Studio Shutter
1	3¼ x4¼	1⅝	6	..	$ 7.95	Not furnished
2	4 x5	1⅞	7	about 8	11.65	Not furnished
3	5 x7	2¼	10	about 10½	13.50	$16.50
4	6½x8½	2½	12	about 13	18.75	22.50
5	8 x10	3	14	about 15	30.00	34.50

The Nos. 1 and 2 Lenses make fine lenses for penny picture work, also for home portrait work, and can be used with the Conley View Camera.

COMPLETE INSTRUCTIONS IN PHOTOGRAPHY

IS A MIGHTY GOOD BOOK FOR ANY PHOTOGRAPHER TO OWN. IF YOUR ORDER FOR PHOTOGRAPHIC GOODS AMOUNTS TO $2.50, WE WILL INCLUDE A COPY OF THIS BOOK WITHOUT CHARGE.

The Conley Series III Extra Rapid Portrait Lens, F3.8.

At the wonderfully low prices quoted below, we offer the series III Conley Extra Rapid Portrait Lens as the equal in every way of portrait lenses heretofore sold at from $75.00 to $150.00 according to size. It is as good a portrait lens as money will buy, and combines the very finest optical qualities with a perfection of mechanical detail that places it in the very front ranks of high grade portrait lenses.

HIGH SPEED—**This lens works at the extremely high speed of F3.8 and may be used at full aperture for portrait work in heads and busts, and by using a smaller diaphragm it is a fine lens for groups.**

In softness, delicacy and depth, in speed, flatness of field and brilliancy of illumination, the Series III Conley Portrait Lens is not excelled by any other portrait lens on the market, regardless of price or maker. It represents the very latest advances in scientific lens grinding, possessing all of those peculiar optical qualities and that special brilliancy of definition so much sought after by the most famous portrait photographers. Even when stopped down this lens preserves that softness and roundness so essential in portrait making, a rare quality in lenses, as nearly all other lenses become distinctly wiry when used with a small diaphragm.

CONSTRUCTION—**This lens is composed of two systems of two glasses each,** the front system cemented together, and the rear glasses mounted without cementing and in such a manner that the degree of separation may be varied, by moving the front lens of the rear combination for diffusing effect and is operated by a rack and pinion movement so that any desired degree of diffusion may be obtained without interfering with the optical properties of the lens. The diffusion is controlled by the large pinion knob which is engraved with a scale so that the exact degree of separation of the rear combination is always shown.

No expense is spared in mounting these lenses, and they represent the highest degree of mechanical perfection, beautifully finished in lacquered brass with engraved diaphragm scales and black trimmings. **Shutter.** Our illustration shows the Conley Series III Portrait Lens equipped with the Wollensak Studio Shutter, and while we also furnish the lens in barrel with iris diaphragm, as quoted below, the Wollensak Studio Shutter is such a good shutter, so convenient, so compact, and so satisfactory in every way that we strongly advise the purchase of the lens complete with shutter. This shutter is made with rubber cushions at all points of contact, making it practically noiseless, is constructed on the iris diaphragm principle, and is so compact that it does not appreciably increase the size of the outfit, as will be seen by the illustration which shows the lens complete with shutter. This shutter itself acts as an iris diaphragm and may be set at any desired opening or full aperture for focusing purposes. It opens with a single pressure of the bulb and closes when the pressure is released. By means of the small lever on the side of the lens, the shutter may be opened for long time exposures and closed in the same manner.

No. 20L1130 The Series III Conley Extra Rapid Portrait Lens, F3.8. Prices as follows:

Lens No.	Size of Plate Covered, inches	Diameter of Lens, inches	Equivalent Focus, in.	Distance Lens to Sitter for 2-inch head, feet	Outside Diameter of Flange, in.	Price with Shutter	Price without Shutter
1	5 x8	3	10	about 6	5⅜	$49.50	$45.00
2	6½x8½	3 9-16	13	about 7½	6½	65.25	60.00
3	8 x10	4 3-16	16	about 9½	7⅜	81.00	75.00

When furnished without shutter the lens is equipped with fine iris diaphragm.

Ray Filters at 60 Cents.

No. 20L1140 A Ray Filter absorbs the violet and ultra-violet rays of light and produces a picture in which the color values are correct. Clouds in a photograph improve the artistic value of the picture wonderfully, and you can get them with a ray filter. **Landscapes** photographed with the ray filter possess a brilliancy and contrast which it is impossible to obtain otherwise; and in the photographing of flowers, paintings or any brightly colored subjects, the ray filter is practically indispensable.

No. 1 for lenses 1 5/16 inches in diameter $0.60
No. 2 for fixed focus or box cameras.......... .60
No. 3 for lenses 1 7/16 inches in diameter .... .60
No. 4 for lenses 1½ inches in diameter .... .75
No. 5 for lenses 1¾ inches in diameter .... .90
No. 6 for lenses 2 inches in diameter .... .90
No. 7 for lenses 2¼ inches in diameter 1.05
No. 8 for lenses 2½ inches in diametor 1.20
No. 9 for lenses 2¾ inches in diameter 1.35

If by mail, postage extra, on Nos. 1 to 6, 4 cents; Nos. 7 to 10, 6 cents.

Any of the above sizes are suitable for lenses ⅛ inch less in diameter than size mentioned.

State exact diameter of lens when ordering.

Any Size Duplicator for 17 Cents.

No. 20L1148 Duplicator. A device enabling one to photograph a person in two positions on the same plate. Very humorous and interesting pictures can be made in this way. Can be used with any folding camera. Made in sizes Nos. 1 to 9, inclusive, corresponding to our auxiliary lenses.

Cannot be used with box cameras. State diameter of lens. Be careful to state size wanted.

Price, each, any size........................ 17c

If by mail, postage extra, 3 to 5 cents.

Bargains in Anastigmat and Portrait Lenses.

We have on hand a number of unlisted lenses, all brand new goods, in perfect order which we will close out at the wonderfully low prices quoted below.

THESE PRICES ARE LESS THAN THE ACTUAL COST of the goods and give you an exceptional opportunity to secure a high class lens at a marvelously low price. The Busch Anastigmat Lenses shown in the following list are exceptionally desirable lenses, genuine anastigmats of the highest degree of excellence. The Seroco-Goerz Anastigmat Lenses are also wonderful bargains, made expressly for us by the C. P. Goerz Optical Company. Opportunities to purchase high grade lenses at these prices are rare and are made possible only because of change in certain trade conditions over which we have no control, and because we have been compelled to give up the exclusive American agency for the Busch lenses.

No. 20L1132 SPECIAL CLOSE OUT PRICES on **genuine Anastigmat and Portrait Lenses.** Be sure to state size and style wanted. All orders are accepted subject to previous sale, as our total stock consists of less than two hundred lenses, and we urge you to take advantage of these special prices at the earliest possible moment. It may be too late if your order is not received promptly.

Series III F7.7 Busch Anastigmat Lens, 4x5, with Wollensak Automatic Shutter. Price.............................$13.95
Series III F7.7 Busch Anastigmat Lens, 6½x8½, with Wollensack Automatic Shutter. Price............$27.00
Series III F7.7 Busch Anastigmat Lens, 8x10, with Woll-ensak Automatic Shutter. Price....................$38.90
Series III F7.7 Busch Anastigmat Lens, 4x5, with Volute Shutter. Price.....................................$23.00
Series III F7.7 Busch Anastigmat Lens, 6½x8½, with Volute Shutter. Price.............................$32.75
Series III F7.7 Busch Anastigmat Lens, 8x10, with Volute Shutter. Price.....................................$45.00
Series II F5.5 Busch Anastigmat Lens, 4x5, with Wollensak Automatic Shutter. Price.........................$17.95
Series II F5.5 Busch Anastigmat Lens, 5x7, with Wollensak Automatic Shutter. Price.........................$24.00
Series II F5.5 Busch Anastigmat Lens, 6½x8½, with Wollensak Automatic Shutter. Price............$29.90
Series II F5.5 Busch Anastigmat Lens, 4x5, with Volute Shutter. Price.....................................$23.85
Series II F5.5 Busch Anastigmat Lens, 5x7, with Volute Shutter. Price.....................................$28.00
Series II F5.5 Busch Anastigmat Lens, 6½x8½, with Volute Shutter. Price.............................$39.00
Series II F5.5 Busch Anastigmat Lens, 8x10, with Volute Shutter. Price.............................$59.00
F6.8 Seroco-Goerz Anastigmat Lens, 6½x8½, with Wollensak Automatic Shutter. Price $26.30
F6.8 Seroco-Goerz Anastigmat Lens, 8 x 10 with Wollensak Automatic Shutter. Price..........$34.50
F6.8 Seroco-Goerz Anastigmat Lens, 4x5, with Volute Shutter. Price $21.60
F6.8 Seroco-Goerz Anastigmat Lens, 6½x8½, with Volute Shutter. Price $33.80
F6.8 Seroco-Goerz Anastigmat Lens, 8x10, with Volute Shutter. Price $42.20

We have on hand a few very fine portrait lenses made especially for us by the Bausch & Lomb Optical Company, speed F4, with iris diaphragm and diffusing attachment, strictly high class instruments. which we will close out at the following phenomenally low prices.

No. 1. Covers plate 5x8, back focus 8½ inches. Price..$29.00
No. 2. Covers plate 6½x8½, back focus 11½ inches. Price.................................. 43.80
No. 3. Covers plate 8x10, back focus 13½ inches. Price.. 67.90

We have also a few special portrait lenses that work at F5, made for us by the Bausch & Lomb Optical Company, mounted with rack and pinion focus movement and iris diaphragm, which we offer at the following astonishing prices.

No. 1. ¼ size, back focus 4½ inches. Fine for penny pictures. Price ....$ 5.95
No. 2. ½ size, back focus 7 inches. Price.... 8.90
No. 3. 4-4 size, back focus 11 inches. Price... 19.40

Even if you do not need a lens just now, you may at some future date, and we advise you by all means to take advantage of this opportunity to secure a high class lens at less than cost to the largest dealers. Remember, every one of these lenses is new, not second hand junk, not old lenses that have been found unsatisfactory by their owners and disposed of to be polished up, relacquered and offered as bargains by so called second hand dealers. Every one is brand new, absolutely perfect, and your order is accepted with the understanding and agreement that the lens may be returned to us if not found entirely satisfactory, and your money will be refunded.

Auxiliary Enlarging and Copying Lenses.

No. 20L1155 These lenses are used in connection with the regular lens of any folding camera, greatly increasing its power. By the use of these lenses copying and enlarging may be done with any folding camera, enabling one to copy other pictures or photograph small articles to their full size or even larger. A 4x5 photograph copied with an ordinary camera will make a picture about the size of a postage stamp, but when copied with the aid of this lens can be made full size or larger. Many uses for this valuable discovery will readily suggest themselves to the user.

No. 1 for 4x5 camera with lens 1 5/16 in. in diam. $0.90
No. 2 for 5x7 camera with lens 1 5/16 in. in diam. .90
No. 3 for fixed focus or box cameras............ .90
No. 4 for 4x5 camera with lens 1 7/16 in. in diam. .90
No. 5 for 5x7 camera with lens 1 7/16 in. in diam. .90
No. 6 for 4x5 camera with lens 1½ in. in diam. 1.20
No. 7 for 5x7 camera with lens 1½ in. in diam. 1.20
No. 8 any size camera with lens 1¾ in. in diam. 1.35
No. 9 any size camera with lens 2 in. in diam. 1.50
No. 10 any size camera with lens 2¼ in. in diam. 1.65
No. 11 any size camera with lens 2½ in. in diam. 1.80
No. 12 any size camera with lens 2¾ in. in diam. 1.95
No. 13 any size camera with lens 3 in. in diam. 2.10

If by mail, postage extra, on Nos. 1 to 7, **3 cents; Nos. 8 to 10, 6 cents;** Nos. 11 to 13, **10 cents.**

In measuring your lens, take the outside diameter, remembering that the enlarging lens slips over your regular lens same as a cap.

Any of the above sizes are suitable for lenses ⅛ inch less in diameter than size mentioned.

FREE. **If your order for photographic goods amounts to $2.50 we will include without charge a copy of Complete Instructions in Photography, as described on page 252.**

Auxiliary Portrait Lenses.

No. 20L1153 In making portraits with the ordinary folding hand camera, the great difficulty heretofore has been the small size of the faces. This portrait lens, however, entirely overcomes this difficulty and enables anyone with any kind of a folding camera to make portraits in which the faces are large and distinct. Constructed in the same style and used in same manner as the enlarging lens No. 20L1155.

No. 1 for 4x5 camera with lens 1⅛ in. in diam... $0.90
No. 2 for 5x7 camera with lens 1⅛ in. in diam... .90
No. 3 for fixed focus or box cameras... .90
No. 4 for 4x5 camera with lens 1⅜ in. in diam... .90
No. 5 for 5x7 camera with lens 1⅜ in. in diam... .90
No. 6 for 4x5 camera with lens 1½ in. in diam... 1.20
No. 7 for 5x7 camera with lens 1½ in. in diam... 1.20
No. 8 any size camera with lens 1¾ in. in diam... 1.35
No. 9 any size camera with lens 2 in. in diam... 1.50
No. 10 any size camera with lens 2¼ in. in diam... 1.65
No. 11 any size camera with lens 2½ in. in diam... 1.80

If by mail, postage extra, on Nos. 1 to 7, 3 cents; Nos. 8 to 10, 6 cents; No. 11, 10 cents.

In measuring your lens, take the outside diameter, remember that the portrait lens slips over your regular lens same as a cap.

Any of the above sizes may be used on lenses ¼ inch less in diameter than size given.

Auxiliary Lens Sets, $2.55.

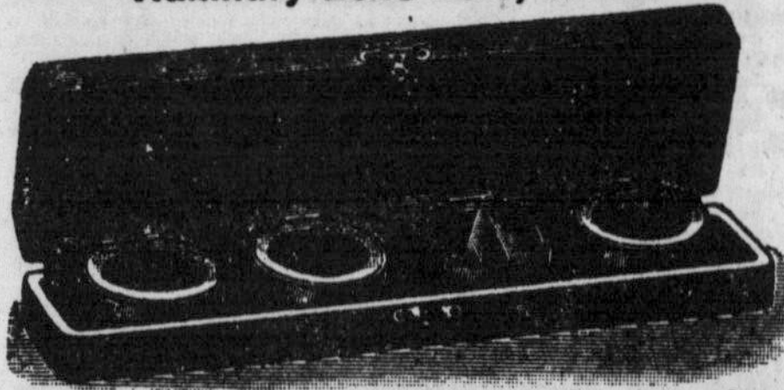

No. 20L1162 These sets contain one copying and enlarging lens, one portrait lens, one ray filter and one duplicator, all contained in a beautiful plush lined leather case. Be careful to mention size wanted.

Put up only in the following sizes:
Set No. 1 for 4x5 camera with lens 1⅛ in. diam.. $2.55
Set No. 2 for 5x7 camera with lens 1⅛ in. diam... 2.55
Set No. 3 for 4x5 camera with lens 1⅞ in. diam... 2.55
Set No. 4 for 5x7 camera with lens 1⅞ in. diam... 2.55

Postage extra on any size, if sent by mail, 10 cents.
Larger sizes are not put up in cases.

Photo Beacon Exposure Card, 15 Cents.

No. 20L775 A Little Book of Tables which gives you the exact exposure at any hour of the day, and any day of the year, with any brand of plates, or any speed of lens. Simple and absolutely correct. No more over exposed or under exposed plates. Price..(If by mail, postage extra, 1c).. 15c

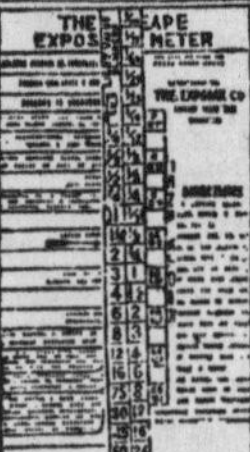

Exposure Meter.

No. 20L778 Cheape Exposure Meter. A simple and easily used device by means of which the correct exposure for any kind of picture, either indoors or outdoors, under any kind of weather conditions, may be instantly and accurately determined. The Cheape Exposure Meter is very nicely made from white celluloid, with letters and figures in blue and red. It is one of the easiest to use and the most satisfactory exposure meters on the market. Full directions with each one.

Price... 25c
If by mail, postage extra, 1 cent.

Exposure Meter.

No. 20L780 The Bee Exposure Meter. A thoroughly reliable, practical and easily used exposure meter, made same size and shape as a small watch, diameter only 1¾ inches. The use of this little exposure meter does away entirely with the annoying calculations as to the time of day and weather conditions, which are a part of the process of using exposure meters of other types. With this meter a little strip of sensitized paper is exposed through a slot in the face of the instrument until its tint matches the printed tint beside the slot, and, with the length of time required for matching this tint as a factor, the correct exposure under any conditions of light or weather, at any time of the day or year, indoors or outdoors, with any brand of plates, is instantly determined.

Price, complete, with a supply of sensitized paper, full instructions and speed card... $1.10
If by mail, postage extra, 4 cents.

The Conley Silent Shutter.

No. 20L850 The Silent Shutter, a new device absolutely noiseless in opening. The photographer who has experienced repeated failures by reason of a child subject, or a member of a group looking toward the lens at the critical moment, because he heard the "click" of the shutter will appreciate this new shutter, which opens with absolute silence. The cups at the sides form air cushions which arrest the wings as they open, thus avoiding all sound. Rubber hose and 6 feet of rubber hose furnished with each shutter

This shutter is placed back of lens or inside of front board. Be sure to state size wanted.

Size of opening, inches	2	2½	3	3½
Size of shutter, inches	3¾x4¾	4⅝x5	5x5¾	5⅝x6
Price	$4.50	$4.50	$4.50	$4.50
Size of opening, ins.	4	4½	5	5½	6
Size of shutter, ins.	6x6½	6½x7	7x7½	7½x8	8x8½
Price	$4.50	$5.40	$6.30	$7.20	$8.10

The Morrison Vignetter.

No. 20L860 The Morrison Vignetter is a very ingenious device, which can be attached to any ordinary folding camera of any size and is used in portrait work for shading off the picture gradually toward the edges, just the same as is done by professional photographers. Our illustration shows the manner in which this vignetter is used, and it is substantially constructed from spring brass, nickel plated, is quickly and easily attached to the camera and should form a part of every photographic outfit. There are two vignetting cards, each with different colors on each side, making four colors in all: black, dark gray, light gray and white, so that the color of any background can be exactly matched. Price, 42c

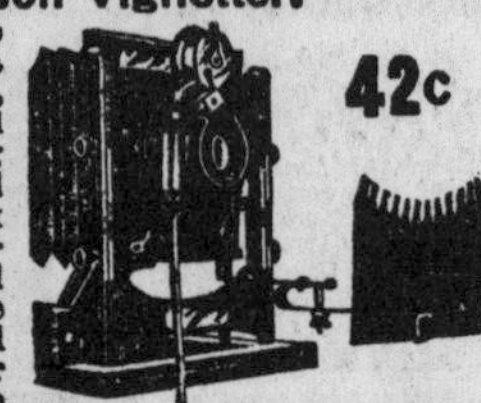

42c

If by mail, postage extra, 4 cents.

Camera Level, 31 Cents.

No. 20L870 This Little Level is intended to be attached to the bed of the camera, enabling the operator to quickly and easily place the camera perfectly level. It is nicely made from brass, finely finished and accurately adjusted.

Price... 31c
If by mail, postage extra, 2 cents.

Camera Bulbs, 15 and 18 Cents.

No. 20L882 Bulb and Tube for Camera. Made from the very best quality of red rubber, very elastic; tube is 14 in. long and can be fitted to any shutter. Rubber always becomes hard, brittle or rotten after a certain length of time, and if the bulb and tube you now have has become useless you can easily fit one of these to your shutter.

Price........(If by mail, postage extra, 3c.).... 18c

No. 20L883 Bulb and Tube. Same as above, but small size for compact folding film cameras; short tube. Price... 15c
If by mail, postage extra, 3 cents.

Rubber Tubing.

No. 20L884 Rubber Tubing, for camera bulbs, best grade red rubber, diameter, $\frac{3}{16}$ inch. Price, per foot... 4c
If by mail, postage extra, for five feet or less, 2 cents; five to twelve feet, 3 cents.

Focus Cloth, 25 Cents.

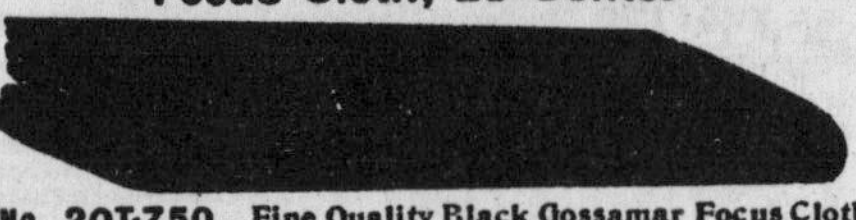

No. 20L750 Fine Quality Black Gossamar Focus Cloth 36x36 inches. Price... 25c
If by mail, postage extra, 9 cents.

No. 20L751 Focus Cloth. Same as above, but double size. 36x72 inches. Price... 50c
If by mail, postage extra, 17 cents.

Negative Preservers.

No. 20L760 Envelopes for preserving Negatives, made of strong manila, the proper size for negatives, open at the end and have notched cut for admitting thumb and finger in removing; printed on the face with lines for numbers, description, etc.; put up in packages of 50 each. Be sure to state size wanted.

Size	Per pkg.	Size	Per pkg.
3¼x3¼	7c	5 x 8	16c
3¼x4¼	8c	6½x 8½	18c
4¼x5½	11c	8 x10	23c
5 x7	14c		

The Complete Photographer, $3.15.

No. 20L969 "The Complete Photographer" by R. Child Bayley, is a splendid book, containing 397 pages, 59 halftone illustrations and 40 line cuts. This book includes an authoritative history of photography, its development and progress from its earliest beginnings to the present day; an exhaustive modern demonstration of every phase of photography—landscape, portraiture, pictorial, architectural, scientific; a perfect guide to the correct application of formulae to photography, which makes it a thoroughly practical working manual for the beginner and the professional; a model exposition of the camera, with valuable hints as to its handling; of the lens in principle, the lens in use, with advice on the selection of a lens; a lucid and valuable discussion on the comparative merits of plates and films, their rapidity, halation and its causes, etc. The book contains also an illuminating chapter on each of the following subjects: Exposure, development, intensification and reduction, the print, platinum printing, the drawing of a photograph, the carbon process, bromide papers, dodging and "faking," the dark room, the hand camera, pinhole photography, orthochromatic and three-color photography, enlarging, reducing, slide making, exhibitions and societies, photography and the printing press. Every camera enthusiast will find The Complete Photographer indispensable. Even those who do not develop or print their own pictures will want to have it for its practical field suggestions. The book will be treasured, too, for the superb series of illustrations which represents the crowning efforts of photography in every field, from the subtlest portraiture to the most ideal landscape. Our price... $3.15

If by mail, postage extra, 17 cents.

Photographic Instruction Book.

281 PAGES. FULLY ILLUSTRATED. BOUND IN CLOTH BY TOWNSEND D. STITH.

Publisher's price, $1.00; our price.. 40c

No. 20L965 A systematic course and working guide in all the processes which ordinarily take up the attention of camera workers. This is absolutely the best book on the subject published. It tells how to choose a camera, all about developing, all about printing and the different methods of toning. Tells all about the different kinds of plates and sensitized papers, how to use each and their special advantages. Explains in detail the best way to make interiors, flashlights, portrait groups, landscapes. Hints on retouching, copying, making lantern slides and enlargements, and thousands of other subjects of interest for all who would know and understand the camera. Size, 5x7 inches. 281 pages. Publisher's price, $1.00; our price.....(If by mail, postage extra, 8 cents.)..... 40c

The Book of Photography, $2.48.

744 PAGES, 1,000 ILLUSTRATIONS, 48 FULL PAGE PLATES.

No. 20L967 "The Book of Photography," by Paul N. Hasluck, is the most comprehensive description of the art yet published. A complete photographic library in one big, handsome volume, 7x10 inches, substantially bound in cloth. Contains a vast amount of information, put in a simple and direct way. No other book approaches this in the fulness and up to date character of its information. Formulae and working methods accompany the processes with illustrations. The index, covering 24 pages, gives instantaneous reference to the contents of the work in detail. Our price... $2.48
If by mail, postage extra, 32 cents.

Candle Ruby Lamp, 14 Cents.

No. 20L1206 Candle Ruby Lamp, constructed of metal, has deep ruby glass, burns candle. A very convenient and satisfactory lamp at a low price. Price... 14c
Not mailable.

Extra Candles.

No. 20L1207 Candles to fit above lamp, small flat paraffine candles in pasteboard cups, burn two hours. Made especially for dark room lamps.
Price, per dozen... 17c
If by mail, postage extra, per doz., 13c.

Large Oil Ruby Lamp, 65 Cents.

65c

No. 20L1210 This is an extra large high class oil burning dark room lamp, made on improved and scientific plans. It is provided with a new patent burner, giving a volume of light never before secured with lamps of this style, and the general construction is such as to insure perfect combustion without smoke or odor. It is made with hinged metal front, which can be placed at any angle to regulate the volume of light and is fitted with both orange and deep ruby glass, insuring a perfectly safe or non-actinic light. The reservoir can be filled from the outside and the light can be turned up or down without opening the lamp. The height of this lamp is 10⅜ inches; size of glasses, 4⅝x5¾ inches.
Price...(Not mailable.)... 65c

Medium Size Oil Ruby Lamp, 40 Cents.

No. 20L1211 This lamp is made exactly the same as the large lamp described above, but is smaller, measuring 8⅛ inches high, with ruby and orange glasses 3⅝x4⅝ inches.
Price... 40c
Not mailable.

Electric Dark Room Lamp.

No. 20L1212 This lamp is designed for the use of those having connection with a regular electric lighting current. It is constructed of metal, is of cylindrical shape, has an opening at the top, and fits over the ordinary incandescent electric lamp. If a lamp is hung directly over the developing table, this device affords a very clean and convenient method of dark room illumination. The bottom is provided with a deep ruby glass, and the body of the lamp is provided with openings, so arranged that by turning the body of the lamp, a white light or a yellow light may be obtained.
Price... 90c
This price does not include the electric bulb.
If by mail, postage extra, 20 cents.

Savigny's Transparent Water Colors.

Extra high grade transparent moist colors, put up in collapsible tin tubes, the most permanent, purest and finest transparent water colors made. Savigny's transparent water colors are made especially for coloring photographs or lantern slides, but at the same time are also suitable for engravings, halftone pictures, etc. No previous experience or skill is required in using these colors, and you can add very greatly to the beautiful appearance of your photographs by coloring them with these permanent, easily applied colors.

No. 20L1900 Size No. 0. Eight different colors, in pasteboard box. Price **75c**
If by mail, postage extra, 8 cents.

No. 20L1901 Size No. 1. Twelve different colors, in polished cherry box. Price **$1.40**
If by mail, postage extra, 12 cents.

No. 20L1902 Size No. 2. Sixteen different colors, in polished cherry box. Price **$1.87**
If by mail, postage extra, 14 cents.

Litmus Paper.

No. 20L1912 Litmus Paper, for testing solutions to ascertain whether alkaline or acid; very useful in making toning baths. Put up in bottles containing 100 sheets. State whether red or blue is desired. Price, per bottle **8c**
If by mail, postage extra, 3 cents.

Opaque.

No. 20L1916 It is frequently desirable to block out or render opaque certain parts of a negative, and this can easily be done with this preparation, which is simply applied to the negative with a small camel's hair brush. Price, per box .. **20c**
If by mail, postage extra, 3 cents.

Polish for Ferro Plates.

No. 20L1920 Ferrotype Plate Polish. A small quantity of this preparation rubbed over the ferrotype plate before squeegeeing makes it impossible for the print to stick to the plate. Price, per box **10c**
If by mail, postage extra, 2 cents.

Martin's Specialties.

A line of special photographic preparations, radically different from anything on the market and of great merit.

No. 20L1925 Soline, a liquid for sensitizing cloth, paper, postal cards or other materials. Prints made on cloth can be washed without injury; very useful in making sofa pillows, banners, tidies, book marks, etc. Price **30c**

No. 20L1926 Intensine, an intensifier in dry form for glass or film negatives or lantern slides. An extra good intensifier. Price **15c**

No. 20L1927 Platyn, a single platinum toner that gives fine platinum tones on any kind of printing-out paper, or on cloth prints made with Soline. Price, per ½-ounce bottle, sufficient for 80 ounces toning bath **32c**

Blue Print Powder.

No. 20L1933 Blue Print Powder. A special chemical preparation for sensitizing paper, cloth, cards or other materials for making blue prints. The powder is simply dissolved in water and the solution applied to the paper or cloth, or whatever it is desired to make the picture upon, with a camel's hair brush. By using this special blue print sensitizing preparation you can make beautiful blue prints on writing paper, on cloth, on cardboard, or on almost any material that you may desire. Full directions with each package.

Price, per 1-ounce bottle, **13c**; per tube **9c**
If by mail, postage extra per ounce, 3c, per tube 2c.

Hydro-Metol Developer.

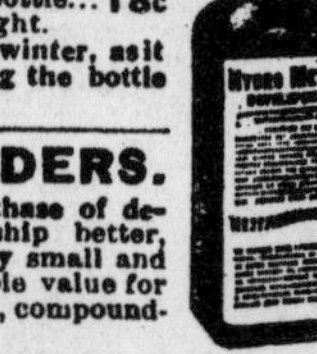

No. 20L1945 We consider this the best liquid developer, being a combination of the well known hydrochinon and metol; works very rapidly, never fogs the plate, brings out all the details and gives a very brilliant negative. Price, per 8-oz. bottle ... **18c**
Unmailable on account of weight.

Do not order liquid developer in the winter, as it may freeze on the way to you, breaking the bottle and damaging other goods.

DEVELOPING POWDERS.

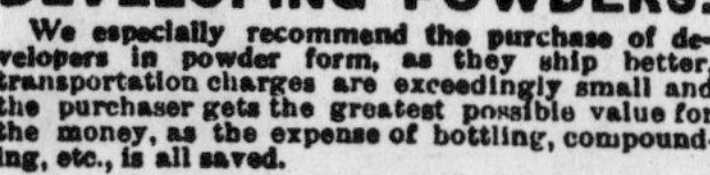

We especially recommend the purchase of developers in powder form, as they ship better, transportation charges are exceedingly small and the purchaser gets the greatest possible value for the money, as the expense of bottling, compounding, etc., is all saved.

Eikonogen Developing Powder.

No. 20L1950 These Powders afford a very convenient means for preparing the liquid Eikonogen developer; avoids the risk of breakage in transportation, and always insures a fresh and strong developer. Each package contains six sets of powders, which is sufficient to prepare 24 ounces of concentrated developer.
Price, per package **15c**
If by mail, postage extra, 3 cents.

Hydro-Metol Developing Powders.

No. 20L1952 Our Hydro-Metol Developing Powders, a combination of hydrochinon and metol, are made from the purest chemicals, put up in the most careful and exact manner, and will be found a perfect developer in every way. Our Hydro-Metol Developing Powders work very rapidly, do not fog or stain the plate, and produce brilliant, sparkling negatives, full of detail and of the most perfect printing quality. The best developing powder made.

Price, per package containing six powders, sufficient to make 24 ounces of developer. Price **16c**
If by mail, postage extra, 3 cents.

Eiko-Hydro Developing Powders.

No. 20L1954 A combination of Eikonogen and Hydrochinon, making a developer equally well suited to time exposures or instantaneous work, and one of our most popular productions. This developer works rapidly, is clean and stainless and produces a bright, snappy negative.

Price, per package of six powders, sufficient for 24 ounces of developer **15c**
If by mail, postage extra, 3 cents.

Toning and Fixing Bath, 16 Cents.

No. 20L1960 Combined Toning and Fixing Solution, a high grade toning and fixing bath in one solution. For toning DuVoll's paper or any kind of gelatin printing-out paper. Our Combined Toning and Fixing Solution yields a variety of tones, and as it is rich in gold it may be used repeatedly. Price, per 16-ounce bottle, **29c**; per 8-ounce bottle **16c**
Unmailable on account of weight.

Gold Toning Solution, 27 Cents.

No. 20L1962 Many photographers prefer to work their paper in separate baths, that is, the toning and fixing being done in two separate baths; and this is certainly the most correct method, as prints made in a combined toning and fixing bath are very apt to fade or discolor in time. This gold toning solution requires only to be diluted with water, and after toning the prints are fixed in a plain solution of hypo. Concentrated. Price, per 8-ounce bottle **27c**
Unmailable on account of weight.

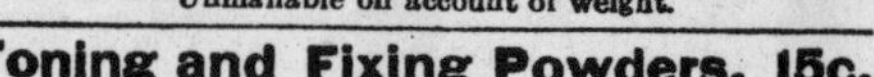

Toning and Fixing Powders, 15c.

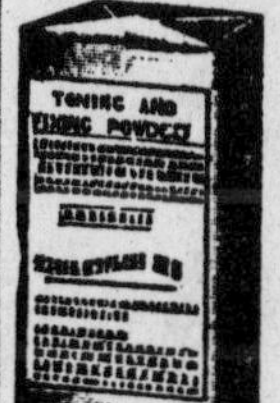

No. 20L1964 Toning and Fixing Powders, for preparing the combined toning and fixing bath. The toning bath made from these powders possesses all the good points of our regular liquid toner, and for use is simply dissolved in water. **These Toning and Fixing Powders** are radically different from any other preparation of the kind on the market, and are the only thoroughly reliable and perfect toner and fixer in dry form ever made. Made especially for DuVoll's paper, but yield splendid results with any gelatin printing-out paper. Price, per package, sufficient for 36 ounces solution. **15c**
If by mail, postage extra, 7 cents.

Platinum Toning Solution, 39c.

No. 20L1966 Platinum Toning Solution, for producing black tones on any gelatin printing-out paper, such as DuVoll's. The platinum finish is very popular and this toning bath affords an easy method of obtaining fine black platinum tones at small expense; also produces fine results with Autotone paper.
Price, per 8-ounce bottle, concentrated **39c**
Unmailable on account of weight.

Intensifying Powders, 16 Cents.

No. 20L1970 Intensifying Powders, for strengthening weak negatives. Require only to be dissolved in water to make ready for use. One package makes 24 ounces of solution.
Price, per package **16c**
Unmailable.

Reducing Powders, 15 Cents.

No. 20L1972 Reducing Powders for thinning negatives which are too dense. When dissolved in water this powder forms a reducing solution ready for use. Each package makes 24 ounces of solution. Price, per package **15c**
If by mail, postage extra, 2 cents.

Neg-Dry, 17 Cents.

No. 20L1980 Neg-Dry is a hardener for either plates or paper and is a most remarkable preparation. One of the most annoying things in photography is the long time required for a negative to dry after washing. **When treated with this preparation the negative can be dried in five minutes by artificial heat,** and the film becomes so hard that it can scarcely be scratched or marred in any way. Used with Darko paper, the finished prints can be dried within a few minutes after development. **Can be used over and over again.** Price, per 4-ounce bottle **17c**
Unmailable on account of weight.

Acid Hypo, 6 Cents.

No. 20L1985 Acid Hypo is a preparation in dry form for making the acid fixing bath. Requires only the addition of water to make it ready for use. The acid fixing bath is of great advantage, both for plates and films, and for developing papers, having a clearing effect and preventing fog.

Price, per ¼-pound box. Makes 16 oz. solution **6c**
If by mail, postage extra, 5 cents.
Price, per ½-pound box. Makes 32 oz. solution **10c**
If by mail, postage extra, 10 cents.
Price, per 1-pound box. Makes 64 oz. solution **18c**
If by mail, postage extra, 20 cents.

Photographic Chemicals.

We absolutely guarantee the purity of our photographic chemicals.

No. 20L2001 Pyrogallic Acid, the old reliable developer. Our Pyro is a pure, resublimed pyrogallic acid, of the very finest quality, guaranteed equal to any pyro on the market, regardless of price. Put up in tins.

Price, per pound	**$2.30**	Price, per ¼-pound	**65c**
Price, per ½-pound	**1.25**	Price, per ounce	**20c**

No. 20L2003 Schering's Pyro, a standard make of pyro, still preferred by many photographers.

Price, per pound	**$2.30**	Price, per ¼-pound	**65c**
Price, per ½-pound	**1.25**	Price, per ounce	**20c**

No. 20L2005 Hydrochinon, strictly chemically pure, perfectly white, the best hydrochinon we can buy.

Price, per pound	**$1.92**	Price, per ¼-pound	**50c**
Price, per ½-pound	**.98**	Price, per ounce	**16c**

No. 20L2007 Eikonogen, best grade, imported from Germany. Put up in tins.

Price, per pound	**$3.35**	Price, per ¼-pound	**$1.02**
Price, per ½-pound	**1.79**	Price, per ounce	**.30**

No. 20L2008 Metol, in original packages.

Price, per pound	**$8.00**	Price, per ¼-pound	**$2.42**
Price, per ½-pound	**4.46**	Price, per ounce	**.65**

No. 20L2009 Glycin, in original packages.

Price, per pound	**$8.00**	Price, per ¼-pound	**$2.42**
Price, per ½-pound	**4.46**	Price, per ounce	**.65**

No. 20L2010 Amidol, in original packages.

Price, per pound	**$8.00**	Price, per ¼-pound	**$2.42**
Price, per ½-pound	**4.46**	Price, per ounce	**.65**

Defendol.

A New Developing Agent for either Plates or Paper.

No. 20L2015 Defendol, the new developing agent, offers advantages over any developer yet produced and is suitable for any paper, such as Darko, Luster, etc., or for dry plates. **Defendol is not poisonous,** it does not stain the fingers; plates can be left in it for hours and still remain clear; it is cheaper than other developers; it keeps indefinitely in dry form; it remains clear in solution longer than other developers. Defendol retains its working qualities to the last drop, being practically inexhaustible; it can be used over and over again, and it is the best developer known for bromide papers. **No sulphite of soda is necessary in making up Defendol developer, no other chemical except dry carbonate of soda being required.**

	Price
½-oz. package makes about 30 ozs. developer	$0.21
1-oz. package makes about 60 ozs. developer	.40
4-oz. package makes about 7½ qts. developer	1.50
8-oz. package makes about 7½ gals. developer	2.80
16-oz. package makes about 15 gals. developer	5.20

No. 20L2020 Acetic acid, No. 8, 1-oz. bottle, **5c**; 1-lb. bottle .... **.20**
No. 20L2022 Citric acid, crystals, 1-oz. bottle .... **.10**
No. 20L2024 Muriatic acid (known also as hydrochloric acid), 2-oz. bottle, **18c**; 1-lb. bottle .... **.44**
No. 20L2026 Nitric acid, 1-oz. bottle, **12c**; 1-lb. bottle .... **.36**
No. 20L2028 Oxalic acid, crystals, 2-oz. bottle, **15c**; 1-lb. bottle .... **.30**
No. 20L2030 Sulphuric acid, C. P., 1-oz. bottle, **12c**; 1-lb. bottle .... **.33**
No. 20L2035 Alcohol, pure, for photographic uses, ½-pint bottle .... **.35**
No. 20L2043 Alum, pulverized, 1-lb. package .... **.15**
No. 20L2045 Alum, chrome, 1-lb. box .... **.15**
No. 20L2047 Ammonia, liquid conc., U. S. P., 1-lb. bottle .... **.26**
No. 20L2053 Ammonium bromide, 1-oz. bottle .... **.12**
No. 20L2055 Ammonium bichromate, 1-oz. bottle, **15c**; 1-lb. bottle **1.12**
No. 20L2057 Ammonium carbonate, 1-lb. bottle .... **.40**
No. 20L2059 Ammonium chloride, 1-oz. bottle, **10c**; 1-lb. bottle .... **.35**
No. 20L2061 Ammonium sulphocyanide, 1-oz. bot. **.15**
No. 20L2065 Formalin, put up in 4-oz. bottles. Per bottle .... **.18**
No. 20L2068 Glycerin, very pure, 1-oz. bottle .... **.08**

Gold Chloride at 40 Cents.

Guaranteed Full Weight.

No. 20L2075 Gold chloride, pure, 15-gr. bottle, per dozen, **$4.72**; each **40c**
No. 20L2076 Gold and sodium, chloride, 15-gr. bot. **35c**
No. 20L2079 Iodine, resublimed 1-oz. bottle **33c**
No. 20L2082 Iron protosulphate, 1-lb. package **6c**
No. 20L2084 Iron and ammonia, citrate, 1-oz. bot. **12c**
No. 20L2087 Lead nitrate, 1-oz. bottle **12c**
No. 20L2089 Lead acetate (sugar of lead), 1-oz. bot. **12c**
No. 20L2095 Mercury bichloride (corrosive sublimate), 1-oz. bottle **15c**
No. 20L2105 Potassium bromide, 1-oz. bottle **10c**
No. 20L2107 Potassium carbonate, 1-lb. package **25c**
No. 20L2109 Potassium cyanide, 4-oz. can, **20c**; 1-lb. can **60c**
No. 20L2111 Potassium ferrocyanide (yellow prussiate of potash), 1-oz. package **12c**
No. 20L2113 Potassium ferricyanide (red prussiate of potash), 1-oz package **15c**
No. 20L2115 Potassium iodide, 1-oz. package **30c**
No. 20L2117 Potassium oxalate, neutral, 1-lb. pkg. **25c**
No. 20L2120 Platinum chloride, 15-gr. bottle **70c**
No. 20L2125 Silver nitrate, 1-oz. bottle **55c**
No. 20L2130 Sodium acetate, 1-oz. bottle **8c**
No. 20L2132 Sodium bicarbonate, 1-oz. package. **5c**
No. 20L2134 Sodium bisulphite (acid sulphite), pure, 1-oz. bottle **12c**
No. 20L2136 Sodium carbonate (sal soda), crystals, pure, 1-lb. package **9c**
No. 20L2138 Carbonate of soda, dry, a very high grade carbonate (sal soda), guaranteed absolutely chemically pure, 1-lb. bottle **22c**
No. 20L2140 Sodium citrate, 1-oz. bottle **14c**
No. 20L2142 Sodium sulphite, crystals, pure, 1-lb. tin **10c**
No. 20L2144 Sulphite of soda, dry, a very high grade sulphite, guaranteed absolutely chemically pure, 1-lb. bottle **32c**

10 Pounds of Hypo for 35 Cents.

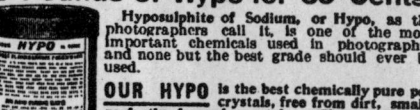

Hyposulphite of Sodium, or Hypo, as the photographers call it, is one of the most important chemicals used in photography, and none but the best grade should ever be used.

OUR HYPO is the best chemically pure pea crystals, free from dirt, small, perfectly formed crystals. Clean and dry. No caking, no waste.

No. 20L2150 Pea Crystal Hypo, in 1-lb. sealed cartons. Price, per lb. **$0.04**
If by mail, postage extra, 21 cents.

No. 20L2152 Pea Crystal Hypo, in 10-lb. sealed package. Price, per package (10 lbs.) .... **.35**

No. 20L2155 Pea Crystal Hypo, in original keg. Price, per keg (100 lbs.) **2.00**

Our Hypo is all sold in sealed packages, clean and pure.

Collins' Plain Bevel Edge Melton Cards.

No. 20L2203 A perfectly plain, fine quality, round cornered, bevel edged melton surface card, suitable for almost any kind of a picture.

Colors, Scotch gray or carbon black.

Size of Card	For Photos	Price, per 100	Price, per 25
4¼x4¼	3½x3½	$0.40	11c
4¼x5¼	3¼x4¼	.45	12c
5¼x6¼	4 x5	.68	18c
5¼x7½	3¼x5½	.80	22c
7 x9	5 x7	1.28	35c

Be sure to state size and color wanted.

Collins' "Mantello" Cards.

No. 20L2207 This is a good quality card, with fancy embossed border of very handsome design, wide margin, square corners and straight edges.

Colors, sage green, ash gray or enameled white.

Size of Card	For Photos	Price, per 100	Price, per 25
2⅞x3⅜	1½x2	$0.24	7c
3½x3½	2½x2½	.32	9c
4 x5	2¼x3¼	.47	12c
5 x5	3½x3½	.56	15c
4¾x5¾	3¼x4¼	.58	16c
4¼x6	2½x4¼	.60	17c
5½x6½	4 x5	.72	19c
5 x7¼	3¼x5½	.74	20c
7 x9	5 x7	1.40	38c

Be sure to state size and color wanted.

Collins' "Magnifico" Cards.

No. 20L2213 A remarkably attractive card at an exceedingly low price. Square corners, plain beveled edges, white center and ash gray border with delicate ornamental design in white (not embossed). The white center gives a masked effect to the mounted print.

Color, border, ash gray; center and design, white.

Size of Card	For Photos	Price, per 100	Price, per 25
5 x5	3½x3½	$0.70	18c
4¾x5¾	3¼x4¼	.72	19c
5½x6½	4 x5	.92	25c
7 x9	5 x7	1.48	39c

Be sure to state size wanted.

Collins' "Grando" Cards.

No. 20L2214 A card intended especially for landscape photographs. Color and design exactly the same as the "Magnifico" cards, but made with straight edges and somewhat lighter stock.

Color, border, ash gray; center and design, white.

Size of Card	For Photos	Price, per 100	Price, per 25
7x 9	5 x7	$1.15	30c
9x11	6½x8½	1.60	42c
10x12	8 x10	2.08	55c

Be sure to state size wanted.

"The Harvard Special" Cards.

No. 20L2218 An unusually handsome card, made especially for us by the A. M. Collins Manufacturing Co. Made from a fine quality of cardboard with extra wide border, beautifully embossed with an entirely new and very attractive design. Plain straight edges and square corners.

Colors, Scotch gray or carbon black.

Size of Card	For Photos	Price, per 100	Price, per 25
4¼x6	2½x4¼	$0.68	18c
5¼x5¼	3½x3½	.75	20c
5 x6	3¼x4¼	.80	22c
5¼x7½	3¼x5½	.93	25c
6 x7	4 x5	.95	26c
7 x9	5 x7	1.04	40c

Be sure to state size and color wanted.

Collins' "958" Embossed Cards.

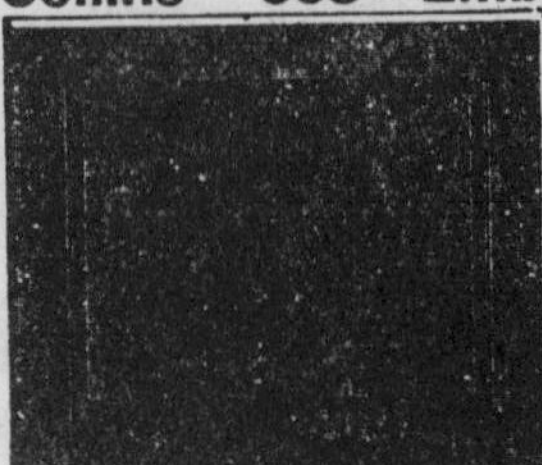

No. 20L2223 A quietly elegant and unobtrusive card, with narrow design around center, embossed in color which adds to the appearance of the mount and assists greatly in bringing out the full value of the mounted photograph. The ash gray card is very effective for prints on Darko paper.

Colors, ash gray or carbon black.

Size of Card	For Photos	Price, per 100	Price, per 25
5¼x5¼	3½x3½	$0.82	22c
5 x6	3¼x4¼	.90	24c
5¼x7½	3¼x5½	1.00	27c
6 x7	4 x5	1.04	28c

Be sure to state size and color wanted.

Collins' Enameled "Mantello" Cards.

No. 20L2227 This is a very pretty mount, made from fine enameled cardboard with white center and queen's gray border. The border, which is wide, is embossed in a very pleasing design. Square corners and plain edges.

Color, center, white; border, queen's gray.

Size of Card.	For Photos.	Price, per 100	Price, per 25
5 x5	3½x3½	$0.90	24c
4¾x5¾	3¼x4¼	.94	25c
5½x6½	4 x5	1.05	27c
7 x9	5 x7	2.15	55c

Be sure to state size wanted.

Collins' "1776" Embossed Cards.

No. 20L2232 This is probably the most artistic mount at a reasonable price that has ever been offered. It is made from extra heavy, thick stock of fine quality and embossed in color with very handsome design. Made with square corners and plain beveled edges.

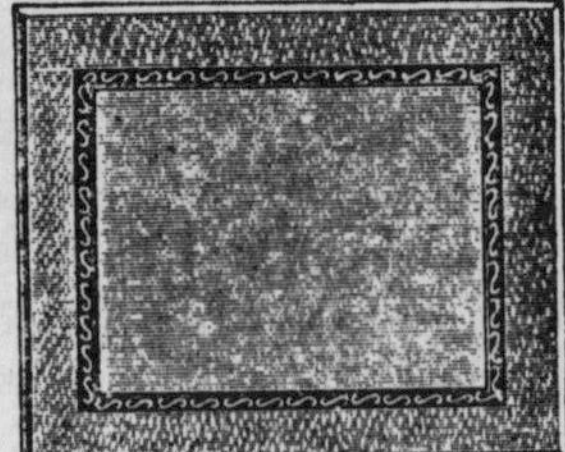

Colors, white or ash gray.

Size of Card	For Photos	Price, per 100	Price, per 25
6 x7	4 x5	$1.22	32c
5¼x7½	3¼x5½	1.30	34c
7 x9½	4¼x6½	1.80	47c
7 x9	5 x7	1.90	50c

Be sure to state size and color wanted.

Collins' "Semper Paratus" Slip Cards.

No. 20L2242 These cards require no pasting, the prints being slipped into place through the opening at the back of the card. The print is held firmly in place, but may be easily removed if desired. Made from fine quality of stock with square corners and plain beveled edges.

Color, carbon black.

Size of Card	For Photos	Shape of Opening	Price, per 100	Price, per 25
5 x5	3½x3½	square	$1.26	32c
4⅝x5⅝	3¼x4¼	square	1.18	30c
5½x6½	4 x5	square	1.52	39c
4⅞x7⅛	3¼x5½	square	1.68	43c
7 x9	5 x7	square	2.38	60c
5 x5	3½x3½	oval	1.30	33c
4⅝x5⅝	3¼x4¼	oval	1.22	31c
5½x6½	4 x5	oval	1.58	40c

Be sure to state size wanted.

Plain White Cardboard.

No. 20L2252 Plain White Cardboard of fairly good quality, with square corners and straight edges. Enameled on one side. Put up in packages of 50.

Size of Card	Price, per 1,000	Price, per 50
4½x 5½	$ 1.56	8c
5 x 7	2.33	12c
5 x 8	2.51	14c
6½x 8½	4.46	23c
8 x10	6.60	34c
10 x12	9.70	50c
11 x14	11.64	60c

Be sure to state size wanted.

Collins' Standard Mounting Board.

We furnish this high grade melton cardboard, the standard Collins' board, in three weights, 10-ply, 12-ply and 16-ply, the thickness being shown by the following lines:

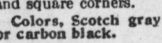

10-ply.

12-ply.

16-ply.

This board is noted for its absolutely smooth surface and freedom from imperfections. It takes the print better than any other cardboard made and is used by the best photographers everywhere.

Colors, carbon black or Burmese brown.

Note—Carbon black is not a dead black, and it harmonizes with almost any kind of a print. The Burmese brown cards harmonize very nicely with prints on developing papers.

Size of Card	No. 20L2257 10-ply		No. 20L2258 12-ply		No. 20L2259 16-ply	
	Price, per 100	Price, per 25	Price, per 100	Price, per 25	Price, per 100	Price, per 25
7 x 9	$0.60	16c	$0.80	21c	$1.20	$0.32
8 x 10	.72	19c	.92	24c	1.40	.37
10 x 12	1.00	27c	1.28	34c	2.00	.53
11 x 14	1.24	33c	1.60	43c	2.48	.65
14 x 17	2.48	65c	3.20	85c	4.96	1.28

Be sure to state size and color wanted.

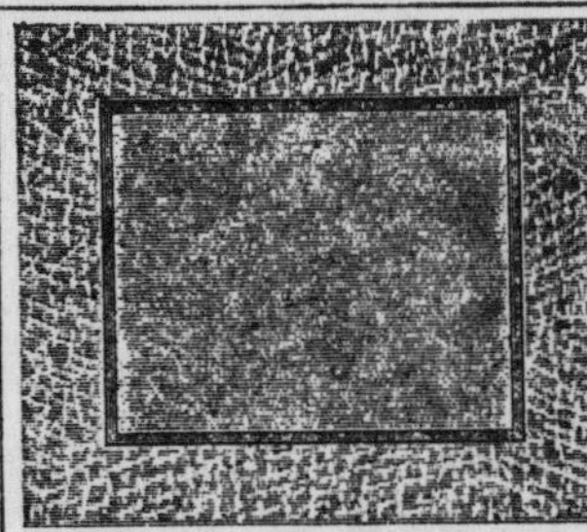

Collins' "Mantello" Mounts.

No. 20L2262 Fine quality embossed cards, made from good solid 14-ply stock, square corners and plain straight edges.

Colors, carbon black or Scotch gray.

Size of Card.	For Photos	Price, per 100	Price, per 25
7 x 9	3⅞ x 5½	$1.40	36c
8 x 10	5 x 7	1.87	48c
10 x 12	6½ x 8½	2.72	70c
11 x 14	8 x 10	2.98	77c

Be sure to state size and color wanted.

Collins' Penny Picture Cards.

No. 20L2267 Good quality cards, for penny pictures, with handsome embossed border. Size of card, 2⅝x2¾, for photos 1¼x1½.

Colors, queen's gray, sage green or white enamel.

Price, per 1,000.... **$1.40**; per package of 250... **38c**

Be sure to state color wanted.

Collins' "Novella" Portrait Cards.

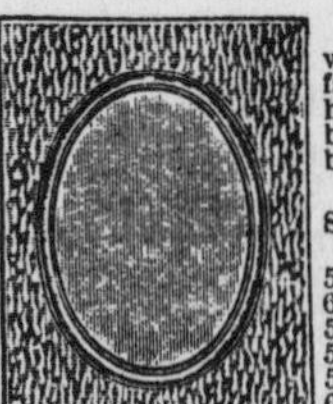

No.20L2272 A surprisingly good card at a very low price. In beauty of design and finish this strong and substantial card stands at the head of moderate priced mounts, heavy stock, square corners and plain beveled edges.

Colors, white, Burmese brown or ebony black.

Size of Card	For Oval Photos	Price, per 100	Price, per 25
4¼x6	2 x2¼	$0.75	20c
5 x7	2⅝x3⅝	1.00	26c
5¼x7¼	3 x4⅛	1.02	27c
6 x8	3½x5	1.24	32c
5 x8½	2¾x5¼	1.25	33c

Be sure to state size and color wanted.

Collins' "Alexandra" Portrait Cards.

No. 20L2277 A fine portrait card, beautifully embossed in color. The embossed design harmonizes in color with the shade of the mount, is richly ornamental, but not in the least obtrusive—one of the best dark border cards made.

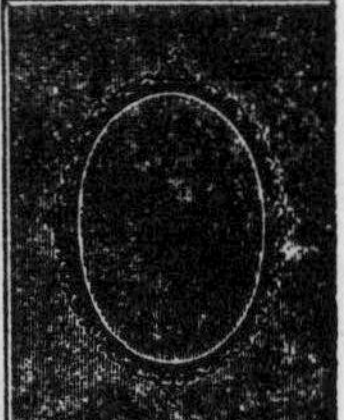

Colors, Burmese brown or ash gray.

Size of Card	For Oval Photos	Price, per 100	Price, per 25
4¼x6½	2 x2¾	$0.89	23c
5 x6½	2⅝x3⅝	1.04	27c
5¼x7¼	3 x4⅛	1.08	28c
6 x8	3½x5	1.27	33c
4¼x7⅛	1⅞x3⅝	1.00	26c
5 x8½	2¾x5¼	1.28	34c

Be sure to state size and color wanted.

Collins' "Imperator" Portrait Cards.

No. 20L2286 A staple mount with a wonderfully effective rough surface and wide, massive roll design, good heavy stock, square corners and plain bevel edges. Has every appearance of being a much more expensive mount.

Colors, white or ash gray.

Size of Card	For Photo	Shape of Opening	Price, per 100	Price, per 25
5¼x7¼	2¾x3⅞	square	$1.21	32c
6 x8	3⅞x5½	square	1.59	41c
5½x9	3 x5½	square	1.68	44c
5¼x7¼	2⅝x3⅝	oval	1.25	33c
5¼x7¼	3 x4⅛	oval	1.25	33c
6 x8	3½x5	oval	1.59	41c

Be sure to state size and color wanted.

Collins' "Liberty" Folder.

No. 20L2295 A most effective holder at a very low price. The cover is the best quality of heavy paper, the tissue a beautiful moire embossed pattern, and the enclosed mount is of fine heavy stock with handsome embossed design, square corners and plain beveled edges.

Colors, Cornwall gray and sable brown.

Size of Folder	For Photos	Shape of Opening	Price, per 100	Price, per 25
5⅜x7½	2⅝x3⅝	oval	$2.47	65c
6¼x9¼	3½x5	oval	3.19	83c
6¼x9¼	2¾x5½	oval	3.19	83c
5⅜x7½	2¾x3⅞	square	2.47	65c
6¼x9¼	3⅞x5½	square	3.19	83c
6¼x9¼	3 x5½	square	3.19	83c

Be sure to state size and color wanted.

SAVE MONEY ON YOUR FREIGHT OR EXPRESS CHARGES and thus make the saving in buying your merchandise from us just that much greater. Railroad companies carry 100 pounds of freight for the same charges as a shipment of less weight. Before sending an order that you know will not amount to 100 pounds in weight, think of the needs of your household, office or farm and look through this catalogue and add as many items as possible. The freight charges on each item in your shipment will amount to practically nothing. You can even add several items to almost any express shipment without increasing the express charges.

FLEXIBLE LEAF ALBUMS FOR PHOTOGRAPHS.

Flexible Leaf Album. Style No. 2 Binding.

THESE NEW AND UP TO DATE FLEXIBLE LEAF ALBUMS are made in various handsome and attractive styles of binding, and the leaves are an extra quality of chemically pure paper in the new Egyptian black tint, harmonizing with almost any kind of print, and making the albums suitable either for mat surface prints on developing paper or for glossy squeegeed prints on printing out papers. In mounting on these thin flexible leaves it is only necessary to put a little paste on each corner or along one edge of the print.

FIVE DIFFERENT STYLES OF BINDING. We furnish these albums in five styles of binding which, for convenience in ordering, we designate as Style 1, Style 2, etc.

Style No. 1 is a fine quality of black English book cloth. Style No. 2 is an imitation leather in a beautiful pearl gray color with heavy alligator grain. It is so perfect an imitation of leather as to deceive almost anyone and the color and grain is remarkably handsome. Style No. 3 is genuine leather black, with heavy seal grain. Style No. 4 is genuine leather, black, with horn back alligator grain. Style No. 5 is extra quality genuine leather, brown in color, beautifully shaded with handsome horn back alligator grain.

Catalogue Number	Size of Leaf, inches	Number of Leaves	Binding Style	Price, Each	Catalogue Number	Size of Leaf, inches	Number of leaves	Binding Style	Price, Each
20L2350	4½x 5½	25	1	$0.17	20L2367	7 x10	50	2	$0.56
20L2351	4½x 5½	25	2	.23	20L2368	7 x10	50	3	.88
20L2352	4½x 5½	50	1	.22	20L2369	7 x10	50	4	.92
20L2353	4½x 5½	50	2	.34	20L2370	7 x10	50	5	1.50
20L2354	4½x 5½	50	3	.46	20L2371	10 x12	25	1	.60
20L2355	4½x 5½	50	4	.48	20L2372	10 x12	50	1	.67
20L2356	4½x 5½	50	5	.73	20L2373	10 x12	50	2	.88
20L2357	5½x 7	25	1	.20	20L2374	10 x12	50	3	1.45
20L2358	5½x 7	25	2	.30	20L2375	10 x12	50	4	1.55
20L2359	5½x 7	50	1	.30	20L2376	10 x12	50	5	2.65
20L2360	5½x 7	50	2	.40	20L2377	11 x14	25	1	.67
20L2361	5½x 7	50	3	.57	20L2378	11 x14	50	1	.90
20L2362	5½x 7	50	4	.60	20L2379	11 x14	50	2	1.10
20L2363	5½x 7	50	5	1.06	20L2380	11 x14	50	3	1.90
20L2364	7 x10	25	1	.30	20L2381	11 x14	50	4	2.10
20L2365	7 x10	25	2	.47	20L2382	11 x14	50	5	3.35
20L2366	7 x10	50	1	.44					

THE LITTLE GEM ALBUMS.

You frequently have a few pictures which are especially interesting and which if mounted on cards are apt to get soiled or misplaced; but this neat little booklet will exactly fill your requirements, bring out the beauty of your photographs and please your friends. Made in two sizes only, one for 5x7 pictures, the other for pictures 4x5 or smaller. Has six flexible leaves, thus holding 12 pictures each.

No. 20L2401 The Little Gem Album, for pictures 4x5 or smaller. Price................8c

No. 20L2402 The Little Gem Album, for pictures 5x7. Price................12c

Order several, they are cheaper than card mounts.

POST CARD ALBUMS.

BOARD COVER ALBUMS AT 15 AND 20 CENTS.

No. 20L2440 Post Card Album, stiff pasteboard covers with ornamental design in gilt. Black leaves, holding three cards to a page; capacity, 100 cards.

Price, 15c

No. 20L2441 Post Card Album, same as No. 20L2440, but with capacity of 150 cards. Price................20c

Imperial Post Card Album.

No. 20L2479 Imperial Post Card Album, size, 9¼x12¼ inches. Contains 26 leaves. Imitation cloth cover, elaborately stamped and embossed in assorted designs in brilliant color and gold. The largest, most effective and most beautiful postal card album ever offered for the money. Holds either 3 or 4 cards to a page.

Price..(Postage extra, 26 cents.).45c

THE LEXINGTON POST CARD ALBUMS.

The Lexington Albums for souvenir postal cards, as shown under Nos. 20L2442 to 20L2468 inclusive, are unusually well made books. They are so designed that they keep their shape perfectly, even when filled with cards to their full capacity. These albums are all made with fine quality black leaves, with narrow die cut openings 1-16 inch wide (not mere slits) for the corners of the cards, so that cards may be inserted or removed with the greatest ease.

No. 20L2457

No. 20L2467

Catalogue Number	Capacity, Cards	No. of Cards to a Page	Binding	Price, Each
20L2442	100	1	black cloth	$0.38
20L2443	100	1	imit'ion leather	.43
20L4444	100	1	genuine leather	.59
20L2446	200	2	black cloth	.65
20L2447	300	2	black cloth	.74
20L2449	200	2	imit'ion leather	.73
20L2450	300	2	imit'ion leather	.88
20L2452	200	2	genuine leather	1.15
20L2453	300	2	genuine leather	1.25
20L2454	200	3	black cloth	.88
20L2455	300	3	black cloth	1.03
20L2456	500	3	black cloth	1.31
20L2457	200	3	imit'ion leather	.99
20L2458	300	3	imit'ion leather	1.67
20L2459	500	3	imit'ion leather	1.46
20L2460	200	3	genuine leather	1.34
20L2461	300	3	genuine leather	1.65
20L2462	500	3	genuine leather	2.10
20L2463	500	4	black cloth	1.47
20L2464	800	4	black cloth	2.29
20L2465	500	4	imit'ion leather	1.56
20L2466	800	4	imit'ion leather	2.63
20L2467	500	4	genuine leather	2.65
20L2468	800	4	genuine leather	3.20

No. 20L2444

No. 20L2449

Loose Leaf Post Card Album, $1.10.

No. 20L2469 This Album is so made that new leaves may be inserted or old ones removed at any time. The binding is a fine quality of black imitation horn back alligator leather. The leaves are black and hold two cards to a page. Capacity, 200 cards.
Price................$1.10

No. 20L2470 Extra Leaves for Album No. 20L2469 put up in sections of 12 leaves. Price, per section. 7c

No. 20L2471 Loose Leaf Post Card Album, same as No. 20L2469, but larger, holding 300 cards, three to a page. Price................$1.45

No. 20L2472 Extra Leaves, for Album No. 20L2471, put up in sections of 12 leaves.
Price, per section......9c

Padded Cover Post Card Albums, $1.35

No. 20L2473 This is a very stylish and well made album with thick, padded covers, bound in imitation Spanish leather, of dark brown tint. It has fine quality black leaves, and holds two cards on a page. It remains perfectly flat even when filled completely, and has a capacity of 200 cards.
Price..........$1.35

No. 20L2474 Padded Cover Post Card Album, same as No. 20L2473, but larger with a capacity of 300 cards, three on a page.
Price............$2.40

Genuine Spanish Leather Indian Head Album, $2.75.

No. 20L2475 This is our very finest Post Card Album, and ordinarily sells at $5.00 in the big city stores. It is made with thick padded covers, bound in genuine Spanish leather of fine quality, alligator grain, with an Indian head embossed on the front. This album remains perfectly flat when completely filled; is exceptionally well made in every detail, and presents a most handsome and stylish appearance. The leaves are black, holding two cards on a page; capacity, 200 cards.
Price................$2.75

No. 20L2476 Genuine Spanish Leather Indian Head Album, same as No. 20L2475, but larger; capacity, 300 cards, three on a page. Price......$3.90

SOUVENIR POST CARDS.

No. 20L2160 Series A. Leather Post Cards, first quality leather, comic and sentimental designs, hand colored, printed in brown, having the effect of burnt leather. Very fine for making sofa pillows and hand bags. 24 cards are just enough for one sofa pillow. Regular retail price, 10 cents each.
Price, per package of 12, all different. 50c
Price, per package of 24, all different, 95c

No. 20L2161 Series B. Leather Post Cards, designs heavily embossed, bringing them out in strong relief. Floral, humorous and sentimental subjects, hand colored.
Price, per set of 12, all different....$0.60
Price, per set of 24, all different.... 1.12

No. 20L2162 Series C. American Cities. Famous buildings, street scenes, park views, public institutions, etc., a very interesting series, all in colors. Extra quality stock.
Price, per set of 50, all different....$0.65
Price, per set of 100, all different... 1.25

No. 20L2163 Series D. Capitols of United States. State capitol buildings in the United States, including the capitol at Washington, and a number of national flag designs.
Price, per set of 50, all different......69c

No. 20L2164 Series E. Comic Post Cards. Clever and laughable subjects printed in colors on high grade of post card stock.
Price, per set of 100, all different.....48c

No. 20L2165 Series F. Humorous and sentimental subjects. High grade cards, some with glossy surface and some with embossed designs.
Price per set of 50, all different.......60c

No. 20L2166 Series G. Comic Subjects, posed from life, printed in black and white in imitation of photographs, with glossy surface. Some very humorous titles.
Price, per set of 25, all different........20c

No. 20L2167 Series H. Ping Pong Post Cards, with cut out oval openings for inserting penny size photographs. Very handsome embossed designs in colors, with glittering tinseled greetings, each card in a transparent envelope. The designs in this series are unusually beautiful.
Price, per set of 12, all different....$0.55
Price, per set of 25, all different.... 1.15

No. 20L2168 Series J. Silk Embroidered Post Cards. The silk embroidery may be removed from the card and used in decorating pillow tops, center pieces, table spreads, watch fobs, pin cushions, hand bags, etc. The designs consist of stars, anchors, emblematic figures, athletic series initial letters, etc. Each card has appropriate verse or motto. Sold everywhere at 10 cents.
Price, per set of 10, all different....$0.58
Price, per set of 20, all different.... 1.12
Price, per set of 35, all different.... 1.75
Price, per set of 50, all different.... 2.69

No. 20L2169 Series K. Holiday Post Cards. Christmas, New Year's, Valentine and Easter subjects in beautiful gold and embossed designs with appropriate greetings for each season. These cards make delightful souvenirs when mailed to your friends and beautiful additions to your own collection.
Price, per set of 50, all different....$0.60
Price, per set of 100, all different... 1.15

No. 20L2170 Series L. Miscellaneous Subjects, including landscapes, birds, animals, flowers, fruit, puzzle scenes, birthday subjects, mottoes, etc., a very popular series, nearly all printed in colors. A very fine series for use in the post card magic lanterns.
Price, per set of 50, all different......48c
Price, per set of 100, all different......95c

No. 20L2171 Series M. Embossed Silk and Silk Plush Floral Designs, exquisitely beautiful cards. The flowers themselves are made of silk or silk plush, heavily embossed and mounted on a fine quality of post card stock with gold backgrounds. All hand colored. Regular retail price, 25 cents each.
Our price, per set of 6, all different, with silk embossed designs..................65c
Our price, per set of 6, all different, with silk plush embossed designs..........75c

No. 20L2172 Series N. Embossed Hand Colored Cards in imitation of the silk and plush designs listed above, flowers, fruit, birds, etc., hand colored.
Price, per set of 20, all different......50c
Price, per set of 35, all different......68c

No. 20L2173 Series P. Novelty Cards. Cards with miniature novelties of all sorts attached, small sunbonnets, neckties, ribbon bows, leather novelties, balls and bats, etc., all with humorous messages appropriate to the article. Price, per set of 25, all different. 85c

LOCAL VIEW POST CARDS MADE TO ORDER.

YOU CAN MAKE BIG MONEY, selling local souvenir post cards in your own town. The cards which we furnish you at $5.30 per thousand can be sold at the rate of two for 5 cents ($25.00 for the entire lot), which gives you a profit of more than 350 per cent.

Send us a photograph of any scene that you want reproduced on a postal card, and we will make you fine quality souvenir post cards from it at the prices shown below. Any size of photograph will do, but the better the photograph is the better will be the cards that we can make from it.

Don't overlook this opportunity to make some easy money. Everybody buys souvenir post cards, and everybody wants local views. It's up to you to supply this demand and make the profit.

Black and White Post Cards.

No. 20L2200 Send us a photograph of the scene you want reproduced, and we will make fine quality souvenir post cards by the halftone process, printed in black and white, at the following prices.

1,000 Post Cards, all from the same subject. Price................$5.30
500 Post Cards, all from the same subject. Price................$4.50
250 Post Cards, all from the same subject. Price................$4.25

German Color Process Post Cards.

No. 20L2201 From any photograph which you may send to us we will make beautiful colored post cards by the well known German color process, reproducing the scene in all its original colors, at the following prices. State colors of the principal objects in the scene. See note below.

1,000 Post Cards from one subject. Price................$9.90

Hand Colored Post Cards.

No. 20L2203 From any photograph that you may send to us we will make beautiful hand colored souvenir post cards at the following prices. Many of our customers sell these hand colored cards at 5 cents straight instead of two for 5 cents, but when sold at the rate of two for 5 cents they net you a profit of 150 per cent. If sold at 5 cents each they make a profit of more than 400 per cent.

1,000 Post Cards, all from the same subject. Price................$10.30
500 Post Cards, all from the same subject. Price................$8.00
250 Post Cards, all from the same subject. Price................$7.30

When Ordering Colored Post Cards, be sure to state the colors of the principal objects in the scene so that we can color the cards correctly. For example, if there is a brick building, tell us whether it is red, buff, or yellow brick. Write the information regarding the colors on the back of the photograph itself.

IMPORTANT READ THIS BEFORE ORDERING. When you send us a photograph from which to make post cards, mark the package very plainly: Sears, Roebuck & Co., Chicago, Illinois, Souvenir Post Card Division, Dept. 20.

Write your name and address plainly on the outside of the package, and also write it on the back of the photograph itself, so there will be no possible chance of getting your pictures mixed up with those belonging to some one else.

Enclose your order and the money to pay for the post cards in the same package with the photograph, and put letter postage on the package at the rate of two cents for one-half ounce or fraction thereof.

Time Required. It takes from two to four weeks to make new post cards to order, and you must allow us time to finish them up and ship them to you.

GRAMOPHONES AND RECORDS

THIS NEW FLEXIBLE ARM OXFORD CYLINDER
TALKING MACHINE
EQUAL IN TONE QUALITY AND VOLUME OF SOUND TO ANY $30.00 MACHINE EVER SOLD
The biggest Talking Machine Bargain that we have ever offered. Less than one-half the price at which machines of this type have ever before been sold.
$14.95
THIS NEW OXFORD TALKING MACHINE is made with the latest improved flexible arm and extra large, perfectly constructed flower horn. These improvements, this new flexible arm, and the big flower horn, result in a tone quality, a genuine musical quality heretofore possessed only by the highest priced machines. Not until you have heard this machine can you appreciate the wonderful power, the softness, the sweetness, and full round volume of sound, the marvelously exact reproduction of the human voice and instrumental music of all kinds, including even the largest choruses, bands, and orchestras.
THE IMPROVED FLEXIBLE ARM represents the very highest development of sound-reproducing mechanisms. This hollow and flexible arm, combined with the large flower horn, gives to the reproduction a beauty and naturalness of tone, a mellowness and genuine musical quality that is unequaled by talking machines of the older types. This combination of hollow flexible arm and flower horn results in special acoustic properties that enable this machine to bring out more fully than has ever before been accomplished with cylinder talking machines, the full and exact tone quality of the original music. This flower horn is so attached to the machine that it can be swung around and pointed in any direction without moving the machine itself, a great convenience when using the machine where a number of people are listening to the music.
THE LARGE FLOWER HORN is of an entirely new shape, this design being the result of a series of experiments to determine the exact shape that would produce the most natural and beautiful tone. It is made upon true acoustic principles, resulting in a volume of sound and fullness and richness of tone that is surprising. The body of this horn is made from the best sheet steel with fine black enamel finish, and resembles in shape a huge morning glory.
THE NEW SPRING CONTACT REPRODUCER, with button shaped sapphire, enables this machine to bring out tones heretofore entirely indistinguishable. The shape of the sapphire button and the fact that it is held closely in contact with the surface of the record at all times, greatly increases the volume of sound and enriches the quality. This reproducer is the exact same style now furnished with the expensive $30.00 and $40.00 machines, the best reproducer that can be made.
THE MOTOR with which this new Oxford Talking Machine is equipped is powerful, absolutely smooth running, noiseless and made with the latest type of speed regulator and governing device. It is made throughout from the best tool steel and brass, carefully and accurately assembled, made with machine cut gears, latest style of start and stop arrangement, and is thoroughly enclosed in the handsome oak cabinet as a protection from dust or injury. The motor can be wound while playing, a feature found only in high priced machines.
No. 20L5002
THE CABINET is made from solid quarter sawed oak, finely finished, all corners dovetailed, giving strength and durability, and is provided with a handsome bent oak cover, as shown in the illustration, to protect the machine from injury when not in use.
YOU CAN PAY A HIGHER PRICE for a graphophone if you prefer and you may get a machine that is finished a little finer than this one, a machine that may be a little more elaborately ornamented and that may perhaps look like a finer and handsomer piece of "furniture," but no matter what price you pay you cannot get any kind of a cylinder record talking machine that will produce any better music than this new Oxford machine. You cannot get a machine at any price that will have more real musical quality, that will reproduce the human voice with more perfect fidelity or that will render instrumental music with any greater degree of perfection.
IT TALKS, IT SINGS, IT LAUGHS, IT PLAYS, and all so naturally that it seems impossible that it can be a mere machine. As an entertainer nothing in the world equals a good talking machine as it brings to your home the same musicians, the same entertainers, the great bands and orchestras that amuse delight and entertain great audiences in our most famous theaters. You can sing to its accompaniment, you can dance to its music, you can play to its songs.
COMPLETE OUTFIT, FLEXIBLE ARM OXFORD CYLINDER GRAPHOPHONE AND TWO DOZEN GENUINE COLUMBIA P RECORDS $18.95
At $18.95 we offer this new Flexible Arm Oxford Cylinder Talking Machine, complete with two dozen standard size genuine Columbia P Records. Your own selection of subjects.
YOU CAN SELECT YOUR OWN RECORDS. The 24 records included with this wonderful Oxford Talking Machine Outfit are the famous Columbia P Records, standard size wax cylinder records and you can make your own selection of titles from the big list given on pages 302 and 303. You can pick out any selections you want, vocal solos, quartettes, bands, orchestras, instrumental solos, vaudeville and talking selections, exactly the kinds and titles that you like best and the only condition we make is that you make your selection from the Columbia P Records, from the lists given on pages 302 and 303.
IF YOU PREFER TO LEAVE THE SELECTION TO US we will give you the very finest assortment offered by our stock of more than 1,000,000 records, and by leaving it to us you may get an even more desirable collection than you would by selecting each title yourself, as we are thoroughly familiar with all the best titles and often have in stock selections of particular merit that may not be shown in our regular list.
No. 20L5002 Flexible Arm Oxford Cylinder Talking Machine, complete, just as illustrated and described, with large flower horn, spring contact reproducer, etc. Price, without records.......... $14.95
Shipping weight, 35 pounds.
No. 20L5003 Complete Outfit, consisting of Flexible Arm Oxford Cylinder Talking Machine and 24 Columbia P Records. Price.......(Shipping weight, 40 pounds.).. $18.95

SEE INDEX, PINK PAGES 552 TO 559, TO FIND WHAT YOU WANT.

$20.00 TALKING MACHINE OUTFIT FOR.... $9.90

GENUINE $7.50 HARVARD JUNIOR TALKING MACHINE 50 REGULAR 25-CENT COLUMBIA P RECORDS

You Would Pay Others $10.00 for 40 Records Only and No Machine.

We give you 50 Records and a $7.50 Harvard Jr. Machine for Only $9.90.

Your Own Selection of Records from Big List on Pages 302 and 303.

ORDER AT ONCE = DO NOT DELAY

WE HAVE ONLY A FEW THOUSAND of these machines and when they are gone we can secure no more. When our present stock of these machines is sold there will be no more; your last opportunity to buy a good machine and a big supply of records at less than wholesale cost will be lost.

REMEMBER, never again will this opportunity come to you, never again can you own such an outfit at this price. ORDER TODAY.

OUR GUARANTEE. We send out every one of these big talking machine outfits under our positive binding guarantee. If the machine and the records are not found equal in every way to other machines and records with which they may be compared, if the outfit is not found entirely satisfactory in every respect, the biggest value you ever saw or heard of, you can return the entire outfit to us at our expense and we will refund your money without question, including all transportation charges.

THIS NEW HARVARD JR. TALKING MACHINE is a strictly high class talking machine, a machine using any standard wax cylinder record. It is a thoroughly well made machine, a machine that cannot be compared in any way with the cheap talking machines which have been so extensively advertised lately. It is a high class machine, made in America, made by expert and experienced workmen in one of the largest and most successful talking machine factories in the world. It is made of good materials throughout, fitted with a high class spring motor, with machine cut gears; everything about it strong and substantial.

AUTOMATIC FEED DEVICE. The Harvard Jr. Talking Machine is made with automatic feed device which holds the reproducer firmly in place as it travels along over the surface of the records. There are cheap talking machines made without feed device, machines in which the reproducer is supposed to follow the groove in the record without being automatically held in place —and in such machines the reproducer slips and slides off the surface of the record, resulting in a very poor reproduction and in a short time damaging the record to such an extent as to render it useless. This trouble is prevented entirely in the Harvard Jr. Talking Machine as the reproducer is held firmly in place and guided in its course over the record by this new patent feed device, exactly the same as in the highest priced talking machines.

The Harvard Jr. Talking Machine is made with heavy, solid and substantial iron base, finished in black enamel and decorated with gold stripes. It is made with the standard size tapered mandrel and will use any standard size wax cylinder record, Columbia, Edison or any other standard make.

THE REPRODUCTION OF THE HUMAN VOICE OR INSTRUMENTAL MUSIC as rendered by the Harvard Jr. Talking Machine is just exactly as good as with machines costing ten and fifteen times the price we ask for these machines. It is made with a high grade aluminum style D1 reproducer, with mica diaphragm and Brazilian sapphire reproducing point. This machine is fitted with a fine black and gold horn, with large, extra wide bell, the body of the horn is made from the best sheet steel with fine black enamel finish, the bell is made of solid brass, highly polished, giving the machine a most handsome and ornamental appearance. The tone qualities of this large black and gold horn are unexcelled, adding greatly to the volume of sound and naturalness and sweetness of tone.

UNDERSTAND, THE HARVARD JR. TALKING MACHINE IS NOT A TOY; it is a high class talking machine, a machine that cannot be purchased in the ordinary market at less than two or three times our price. It is made of good materials all the way through; it is strong and substantial and easy to operate; made with fine spring motor, automatic feed device and extra large black and gold horn.

ONE MILLION RECORDS. We purchased from one of the largest manufacturer of records in the world expressly for these outfits, one million high class standard size wax cylinder records—genuine Columbia P records, the exact same records that were sold for years at 50 cents each and which today cannot be purchased in any market for less than 25 cents. By contracting for this enormous quantity of one million records (more than fifty carloads —the largest order ever placed for talking machine records by any dealer in the world), we have succeeded in reducing the cost to just the merest fraction over the actual cost of labor and materials, the lowest cost at which high class graphophone records have ever been purchased by any dealer, and in making up these big outfits we are giving you the benefit of the saving which we effected by this tremendous purchase.

EVERY RECORD GUARANTEED. We send out these genuine high class Columbia P records, your own selection of subjects, with the understanding and agreement that you can compare them with other records, test them under any conditions that you may desire and if you do not find them entirely satisfactory and in every way the equal in volume of sound, naturalness and tone quality, and in all those points whereby a record is judged; if you do not find them equal in all respects to any wax cylinder record (regardless of price) with which you may compare them, you can return the outfit at our expense, and we will promptly refund your money in full, including all transportation charges.

YOU CAN MAKE YOUR OWN SELECTION of subjects for either of these two big outfits from the list of titles shown on pages 302 and 303. We want you to get the exact titles and selections that you prefer when you order either of these big outfits. Make your own selection from pages 302 and 303.

YOU CAN LEAVE THE SELECTION OF TITLES TO US if you prefer, thus getting the benefit of our experience and personal knowledge of every record in the big list, and if you leave the selection to us we can assure you that you will receive the finest possible assortment as we can, when we are allowed to make the selection, give you the very cream of the best titles from our enormous stock of more than one million records.

50 OUTFIT No. 1. RECORDS AND TALKING MACHINE $9.90

No. 20L5006 The Harvard Jr. Talking Machine and fifty genuine Columbia P Records, your own selection of titles, just as shown in the illustration and described above, all complete. Price $9.90

100 OUTFIT No. 2. RECORDS AND TALKING MACHINE $15.95

No. 20L5007 The Harvard Jr. Talking Machine and 100 genuine Columbia P Records, your own selection of titles, just as shown in the illustration and described above, all complete. Price $15.95

YOUR MONEY WILL BE IMMEDIATELY RETURNED TO YOU FOR ANY GOODS NOT PERFECTLY SATISFACTORY.

$6.95 ONLY A FEW HUNDRED OF THESE HARVARD SENIOR MACHINES LEFT

AND WHILE THEY LAST WE WILL CLOSE THEM OUT AT $6.95

EVERY MACHINE COMES COMPLETE WITH D 1 REPRODUCER, BEAUTIFUL FLOWER HORN, FOLDING HORN STAND AND OAK COVER FOR MACHINE

THE HARVARD SENIOR TALKING MACHINE is an exceedingly handsome machine, thoroughly well made in every respect and perfectly finished. The operating power is furnished by a powerful spring motor, guaranteed not to get out of order. The gears and pinions are all machine cut, thus insuring perfect accuracy of action. The governor and tension screws effectively maintain the speed at an absolutely uniform rate. Large size reproducer, extra loud, made from aluminum, with sapphire reproducing point and latest improved mica diaphragm.

THE TALKING MACHINE is substantially mounted on a handsome oak base with highly finished bent oak cover with handle, thus forming in itself a convenient and effective carrying case for the machine.

THE BIG HANDSOME FLOWER HORN with which the Harvard Senior Machine is equipped adds immensely to the beauty and appearance of this outfit, and gives to the reproduction a tone quality, a genuine musical quality heretofore possessed only by the highest priced machines. Not until you have heard this outfit can you appreciate the wonderful power, the softness, the sweetness and the volume of sound, the marvelously exact reproduction of the human voice and the instrumental music of all kinds, even the largest bands and orchestras. It sings, it talks, it plays, it laughs, and all so naturally that it seems impossible that it can be a mere machine.

A REGULAR $20.00 OUTFIT FOR LESS THAN MANUFACTURER'S COST.

USES STANDARD SIZE CYLINDER RECORDS.

Greatest Entertainer in the World.

Nothing equals the talking machine as an entertainer. It brings to your home the same musicians, the same entertainers, the same great bands and orchestras that amuse, delight and entertain great audiences in our most famous theaters. You can sing to its accompaniment, you can dance to its music, you can play to its songs.

No. 20L5035 Harvard Senior Talking Machine, complete, just as described and illustrated above, with genuine D 1 reproducer, extra large flower horn, folding horn stand and handsome oak cover. Shipping weight, 40 pounds. Price (without records) **$6.95**

See pages 303 and 304 for list of Columbia X P and P Records, the best records made for use with this machine.

3A HARVARD DISC TALKING MACHINE

REDUCED TO $12.95

THE 3A HARVARD Disc Talking Machine is made with large substantial and ornamental oak cabinet, powerful clockwork spring motor and fine black and gold horn. There is no talking machine made which will reproduce records any better than the 3A Harvard Machine, although of course there are machines which are worth more money because of large size and more elaborate ornamentation.

THE CABINET with which we equip the No. 3A Harvard Disc Talking Machine is made from solid quarter sawed oak, hard oil hand rubbed finish throughout, workmanship and material guaranteed in every way. In design this cabinet is very handsome, making the machine an ornamental addition to any parlor.

USES ANY STYLE OR MAKE OF DISC RECORDS.

THE POWERFUL SPRING MOTOR with which we equip the No. 3A Harvard Machine is the highest grade spring motor made for talking machines. It is made with machine cut gears, the latest type of governor and the most approved style of speed regulating device. It is a motor that we can absolutely guarantee to give satisfaction under any conditions.

THE SOUND BOX or reproducer is of the very latest type, designed expressly for the Harvard Talking Machines, made with extra heavy mica diaphragm, a sound box that is equal in volume, sweetness and perfect reproduction to any sound box with which it may be compared. This reproducer is made with the latest automatic needle clamp, by which needles are inserted or removed simply by pressing a little lever, doing away entirely with the annoyance of the old style thumb screw arrangement.

THE BLACK AND GOLD HORN is the same high grade horn that we use on all of the Harvard Machines, made of the best sheet steel, with solid brass bell, finished in black and gold, of large size, 21 inches long.

No. 20L5036 No. 3A Harvard Disc Talking Machine, all complete with 21-inch black and gold horn, improved sound box and 100 needles. Price **$12.95**
Shipping weight 40 pounds.

No. 4 HARVARD DISC TALKING MACHINE

An instrument that is in every way equal to other makes sold at $30.00 to $40.00.

REDUCED TO AN EVEN $16.00

IN APPEARANCE, size and beauty of design, elegance of finish, and in all of those points which mean quality and satisfaction in a talking machine the No. 4 Harvard Machine is in every way equal and in most respects superior to disc talking machines sold by other dealers at more than double our price.

USES ANY STYLE OR MAKE OF DISC RECORDS

THE CABINET OF THE No. 4 HARVARD DISC TALKING MACHINE is in every way a beautiful piece of work, made from solid quarter sawed oak especially selected, thoroughly kiln dried and put together by high class experienced workmen. It is made with a five-ply built up top, hand turned decorations and lock cornered mitered moulding. The finish is the highest grade dead oil hand rubbed finish, a finish that is not only pleasing in appearance but at the same time durable.

THE MOTOR is an extra powerful tandem spring clockwork of the very latest type, made with machine cut gears, latest improved governor and patented speed regulating device.

THE HORN is the same high grade black and gold horn with which we equip all of the Harvard Machines and is the largest size which we use on this line of machines, measuring 30 inches in length with bell 12 inches in diameter. This horn is made with solid sheet steel body, oxidized in black, with solid brass bell highly burnished.

THE SOUND BOX is our highest grade mica diaphragm Harvard reproducer, unsurpassed by any reproducer or sound box on the market in volume, naturalness of tone and freedom from scratch. This reproducer is made with the latest automatic needle clamp, by which needles are inserted or removed simply by pressing a little lever, doing away entirely with the annoyance of the old style thumbscrew arrangement.

No. 20L5037 No. 4 Harvard Disc Talking Machine, all complete, with solid oak highly ornamental cabinet, extra large 30-inch black and gold horn, improved Harvard sound box and 100 needles. Shipping weight, 60 pounds. Price.... **$16.00**

THE COLUMBIA JEWEL — CYLINDER GRAPHOPHONE

$20.00

THE COLUMBIA JEWEL GRAPHOPHONE, Type BK, is equipped with the new improved Lyric Reproducer, the finest and most perfect high grade reproducer ever made. This reproducer is entirely different from any other style, is constructed upon the most improved principles and is fitted with a genuine sapphire point, held in place by a new and ingenious spiral spring arrangement which keeps the sapphire point pressed against the record at exactly the same tension all the time.

THE POWERFUL DOUBLE SPRING motor is made with extra strong steel spring and the best grade of machine cut gears. It is assembled by the most expert workmen and fitted with the latest style of speed controlling governor, which insures perfect reproduction of the record. The motor is furnished with an instantaneous start and stop device and also a speed regulator for playing the records rapidly or slowly as desired.

FOR THE HOME this machine is an ideal entertainer. The handsome quarter sawed oak cabinet is made in a beautiful, ornamental design, finely finished and provided with a strong bent oak cover, as shown in the illustration.

No. 20L5050 Columbia Jewel Graphophone, Type BK, with Lyric Reproducer, 14-inch brass horn and bent oak cover, for cylinder records.
Price $20.00
Shipping weight, 45 pounds.

NEW MONARCH COLUMBIA — CYLINDER GRAPHOPHONE

$45.00

THE NEW MONARCH COLUMBIA GRAPHOPHONE, Type BO, represents the very latest development of the cylinder talking machine. The wonderful aluminum tone arm is a feature which has heretofore been found only in the high priced disc graphophones. In the new Monarch Graphophone, however, we offer for the first time a standard Columbia Cylinder Graphophone with the new flexible aluminum tone arm which reproduces cylinder records with all of the richness and volume of tone it is possible to secure.

EVERY MACHINE is equipped with the improved Lyric Tone Reproducer, the most perfect reproducer ever made. It has a genuine sapphire point which is held against the record by an unique spring tension device which prevents any slipping or jumping of the reproducer.

THE LARGE enameled flower horn is of a beautiful floral design and is highly polished. The motor has three large, extra powerful springs, machine cut gears and is suspended in the cabinet in such a way as to insure smooth and easy running. Cabinet is made of solid quarter sawed oak and is beautifully polished by hand.

No. 20L5061 Monarch Cylinder Graphophone Type BO, with flexible aluminum tone arm, lyric reproducer and large enameled horn, just as described and illustrated.
Price $45.00
Shipping weight, 50 pounds.

THE KING

$25.00

THE NEW COLUMBIA DISC TONE ARM GRAPHOPHONE

THE NEW COLUMBIA DISC GRAPHOPHONE, Type BN, is the biggest surprise ever offered in high grade aluminum tone arm disc talking machines. In beauty of appearance and in tone qualities this machine is equal and superior to many of the graphophones that are sold by other dealers at from two to three times our price. The wonderful sound carrying properties of the new aluminum tone arm, the large swinging flower horn made upon the most improved acoustic principles, the extra sensitive sound analyzing reproducer, with built up mica diaphragm, all unite in making this talking machine one that cannot be excelled in tone quality and sound reproducing ability.

A ROYAL TREAT and one that will be enjoyed by everyone in the family. This graphophone plays all of the latest musical productions, sings the most popular songs, tells the funniest stories, laughs, whistles, shouts, and does it all so naturally as to be almost beyond belief. For a home entertainment the graphophone has no equal. You can dance to its lively music, sing to its accompaniment, entertain a social gathering and have more real fun, pleasure and enjoyment from this machine than from any other purchase you could possibly make.

THE MARVELOUS TONE QUALITIES of the new King Graphophone, the rich mellow tones and round full volume of the music it produces are features never before attained in talking machine construction. It plays any size disc records and plays them so as to bring out the full musical qualities in the most perfect manner possible. Every machine is fully guaranteed, so that you may order this machine, place it in your home and give it a thorough trial and if you don't find it to be equal in every way to graphophones that are sold at much higher prices, and if you are not in every way more than satisfied with this new King Tone Arm Disc Graphophone, you may return it to us at once and your money will be promptly refunded.

No. 20L5065 Columbia King Tone Arm Disc Graphophone, Type BN, complete as illustrated and described above.
Price.........(Shipping weight, 50 pounds.).........$25.00

THE POINTS OF EXCELLENCE

1. SWINGING FLOWER HORN. Made in the shape of a huge morning glory, beautifully enameled and handsomely decorated with gold stripes. Is 17¾ inches long and 19 inches across the bell. Can be swung clear around and turned in any direction without moving machine.

2. SOUND ANALYZING REPRODUCER. The most vital part of a graphophone is the reproducer. Our new sound analyzing reproducer is made with extra sensitive mica diaphragm and equipped with the most improved automatic needle clamp. The highest grade and most accurate reproducer ever made.

3. ALUMINUM TONE ARM. Aluminum has the remarkable property when used as a sound conveyor of eliminating all scratch and harshness from the sound, reproducing the record with all of the natural sweetness and soft full tones of the original music itself.

4. INSIDE THE CABINET. The motor is equipped with an extra strong steel spring, made with the best grade machine cut gears and is suspended from the top of the cabinet so as to avoid all vibrations and insure smooth and noiseless running at all times. The speed can be regulated as desired. Motor can be started or stopped instantly and can be wound while playing a feature found only in the very best graphophones. The cabinet measures 12½ inches by 12½ inches by 8 inches, and is made from solid quarter sawed oak of simple but elegant design. Furnished with 10-inch turntable and extra long crank for winding motor.

NEW IMPERIAL COLUMBIA TONE ARM CYLINDER GRAPHOPHONE

$30.00

THIS NEW COLUMBIA, Type BQ, Graphophone is one of the most popular cylinder talking machines ever placed on the market. It is made with flexible aluminum tone arm, which gives it all of the advantages in tone quality that were heretofore only possessed by the high priced disc machines. The large horn on this machine is made in the shape of a beautiful morning glory and enameled in handsome colors, strikingly decorated by gold stripes.

A LYRIC TONE REPRODUCER is included with every machine. This reproducer is the most perfect device for the reproduction of sound that has ever been invented. It is fitted with a genuine sapphire reproducing point which is held in contact with the record by an unique spring tension device, which prevents the point from slipping or jumping at any time.

THE MOTOR consists of two extra strong springs, and a mechanism of machine cut gears controlled by an automatic governor device that insures smooth and easy running of the motor. Can be regulated to any speed desired and seldom if ever has to be repaired.

THE CABINET is made from the best quality, quarter sawed oak, beautifully polished and of very ornamental design. For a cylinder machine that will produce the records with all the volume and fullness of tone of the original itself, this graphophone is unexcelled.

No. 20L5056 Imperial Columbia Graphophone, Type BQ, with flexible aluminum tone arm, lyric reproducer and enameled flower horn, complete as above described and illustrated. Price................(Shipping weight, 45 pounds.)..................$30.00

THE STERLING COLUMBIA DISC GRAPHOPHONE

$45.00

THE COLUMBIA STERLING GRAPHOPHONE is a thoroughly high grade disc talking machine, made with the new aluminum tone arm and latest style of sound analyzing reproducer which is fitted with the improved automatic needle clamp thus doing away with the old style thumbscrew arrangement. The heavy and substantial construction of the working parts of this machine, combined with the elegant and rich appearance of the whole, make it one of the most thoroughly high grade and up to date graphophones on the market.

THE LARGE FLOWER HORN is made in the shape of an immense morning glory, richly nickel plated and beautifully polished. The graceful curves of this horn not only add beauty to the appearance of the machine but greatly increase the fullness and volume of the sound.

THE ALUMINUM TONE ARM is one of the most important features of this machine. Aluminum has a peculiar property in conveying sound that does away with the disagreeable scratching sound and brings out the tone qualities of any record with a fullness and softness that is almost incredible.

THE CABINET is made in a rich, massive design, built of solid quarter sawed oak and highly polished and given the very best grade of piano hardwood finish. The motor has an extra large double spring and worm gear, insuring smooth running and noiseless operation. Altogether this is a machine which equals in appearance and construction many of the machines which are offered by other dealers at more than double our prices.

No. 20L5070 Columbia Sterling Graphophone, Type BI, complete as above described and illustrated. Price.......................................$45.00
Shipping weight, 50 pounds.

$8.75
$8.75 BUYS THE No. 1 HARVARD DISC TALKING MACHINE
THIS TALKING MACHINE uses the wonderful disc records, the most marvelously realistic reproductions of sound ever made. This machine is strictly high grade in every respect, made from the very best materials, constructed in the most careful, accurate and substantial manner, exactly the same machine that is being sold today by other dealers for $15.00, and never before sold for less than $15.00. THIS DISC TALKING MACHINE is made with extra powerful clockwork spring motor, made with machine cut bevels and gears, and an improved form of governor, insuring an absolutely uniform rate of speed. THE MECHANISM is entirely enclosed within the case in such a way that it is perfectly protected from dust or injury and will require practically no attention whatever.
THE CABINET is strongly and substantially constructed from solid oak, made in a very handsome design and finely finished.
THE SOUND BOX, also known as the reproducer, is of an improved type, made with the latest mica diaphragm, producing a volume of sound combined with a fullness and roundness of tone which is a revelation to those accustomed to the ordinary wax cylinder talking machines. This talking machine uses THE NEW PROCESS DISC RECORDS, THE GREATEST IMPROVEMENT IN RECORD MAKING SINCE THE INVENTION OF TALKING MACHINES.
THE DISC RECORDS ARE LOUDER AND CLEARER, and the reproduction is more perfect and more absolutely true to the original sound than has ever before been produced by any process. Those who have been accustomed to hearing the ordinary talking machine and the ordinary wax cylinder records will be astounded when listening for the first time to the latest new process disc records as used by this and our other disc machines.
FOR PUBLIC EXHIBITION WORK the disc machine is the only machine that should ever be used, as it is the only talking machine which reproduces the human voice, bands, orchestras and other instrumental music with sufficient volume, musical quality and absolutely perfect fidelity. THIS TALKING MACHINE WITH THE NEW PROCESS HARVARD OR COLUMBIA DISC RECORDS MUST BE HEARD TO BE APPRECIATED. It is impossible for anyone not having heard these wonderful machines to appreciate in any way the marvelous results which they give.
No. 21F207 No. 1 Harvard Disc Talking Machine, complete, as shown in illustration, with 16-inch japanned horn, improved sound box and 100 needles. Shipping weight, 28 pounds. Price.............. $8.75
THE HARVARD TALKING MACHINES USE EITHER SIZE OF HARVARD RECORDS, COLUMBIA RECORDS, OXFORD RECORDS, OR ANY OTHER MAKE OF 7-INCH OR 10-INCH DISC RECORDS.
HARVARD
LATEST 1907 MODEL No. 3A HARVARD DISC TALKING MACHINE, $14.90
Don't Miss Our Big Sale of Genuine Harvard 7-inch and 10-inch Disc Records at 28c and 52c each.
For complete list of selections see pages 648 to 650. This Harvard Graphophone uses the Harvard Records, the Columbia Records, either 7-inch or 10-inch, or any other style of flat disc records.
THE No. 3A HARVARD DISC TALKING MACHINE
is similar in principle to our No 1 Harvard, but is a larger and finer machine, made with a larger horn, a larger, more substantial and more ornamental cabinet and a larger and more powerful clockwork spring motor. We have designed this machine especially to meet the ideas of those who desire a somewhat better, larger and handsomer machine than the No. 1 Harvard Machine, and we have been able, in spite of the increased cost and the improvements made in this machine, to keep the price down to a figure within the reach of almost anyone.
THE POWERFUL SPRING MOTOR with which we equip the No. 3A Harvard Machine is the highest grade spring motor made for talking machines. It is made with machine cut gears, the latest type of governor and the most approved style of speed regulating device. It is a motor that we can absolutely guarantee to give satisfaction under any conditions.
THE SOUND BOX OR REPRODUCER is of the very latest type, designed expressly for the Harvard Talking Machines, made with extra heavy mica diaphragm, a sound box that is equal in volume sweetness and perfect reproduction to any sound box with which it may be compared This reproducer is made with the latest automatic needle clamp, by which needles are inserted or removed simply by pressing a little lever, doing away entirely with the annoyance of the old style thumb screw arrangement.
THE CABINET with which we equip the No. 3A Harvard Disc Talking Machine is made from solid quarter sawed oak, hard oil hand rubbed finish throughout, workmanship and material guaranteed in every way. In design this cabinet is very handsome, making the machine an ornamental addition to any parlor.
THE BLACK AND GOLD HORN is the same high grade horn that we use on all of the Harvard Machines, made of the best sheet steel, with solid brass bell, finished in black and gold, of large size, 21 inches long.
No. 21F282 No. 3A Harvard Disc Talking Machine, all complete, with 21-inch black and gold horn, improved sound box and 100 needles.
Price..$14.90
Shipping weight, 40 pounds.
HARVARD
HARVARD
LATEST 1907 MODEL No. 4 HARVARD DISC TALKING MACHINE, $17.40
THIS IS THE HIGHEST GRADE HARVARD DISC TALKING MACHINE that we make, a machine that is equal in every way to disc talking machines sold by other dealers at from $30.00 to $40.00.
THE CABINET OF THE No. 4 HARVARD DISC TALKING MACHINE is in every way a beautiful piece of work, made from solid quarter sawed oak especially selected, thoroughly kiln dried and put together by high class experienced workmen. It is made with a five-ply, built up top, hand turned decorations and lock cornered mitred moulding. The finish is the highest grade dead oil hand rubbed finish, a finish that is not only pleasing in appearance, but at the same time durable.
THE MOTOR is an extra powerful tandem spring clockwork of the very latest type, made with machine cut gears, latest improved governor and patented speed regulating device.
THE SOUND BOX is our highest grade mica diaphragm Harvard reproducer, unsurpassed by any reproducer or sound box on the market in volume, naturalness of tone and freedom from scratch. This reproducer is made with the latest automatic needle clamp, by which needles are inserted or removed simply by pressing a little lever, doing away entirely with the annoyance of the old style thumb screw arrangement.
THE HORN is the same high grade black and gold horn with which we equip all of the Harvard Machines and is the largest size which we use on this line of machines, measuring 30 inches in length with bell 12 inches in diameter. This horn is made with solid sheet steel body, oxidized in black, with solid brass bell highly burnished.
IN APPEARANCE, SIZE, BEAUTY OF DESIGN, elegance of finish, and in all those points which mean quality and satisfaction in a talking machine, the No. 4 Harvard Machine is in every way equal and in most respects superior to disc talking machines sold by other dealers at more than double our price.
No. 21F284 No. 4 Harvard Disc Talking Machine, all complete, with solid oak highly ornamental cabinet, extra large 30-inch black and gold horn, improved Harvard sound box and 100 needles. Shipping weight 60 pounds. Price..... $17.40
HARVARD
HARVARD
REMEMBER,
This No. 4 Harvard Machine
USES OUR FAMOUS
28-CENT HARVARD RECORDS.
For complete list of selections, see page 648.
This machine runs five 7-inch records or three 10-inch records with one winding.
Besides the Harvard Records, this machine, and all other Harvard machines described on this page, use any style, any size or any make of flat disc records.

YOUR MONEY WILL BE IMMEDIATELY RETURNED TO YOU FOR ANY GOODS NOT PERFECTLY SATISFACTORY.

THE OXFORD DISC TALKING MACHINE

A THOROUGHLY GOOD RELIABLE DISC TALKING MACHINE AT A VERY LOW PRICE

SOLID OAK CABINET.

BLACK AND GOLD HORN WITH LARGE BELL.

LATEST SOUND ANALYZING REPRODUCER.

THE NEW OXFORD DISC TALKING MACHINE will use any size, any make or any style of disc records. Although sold at the exceedingly low price of $9.75 it is a thoroughly well made machine, and while not so highly ornamented nor so finely finished as some of the high priced machines, it will reproduce the record with exactly the same fulness and richness of tone, the same volume and real musical quality that is characteristic of the most high priced machines. In designing this machine we have aimed to produce a machine that could be sold at a low price and which would be equal in sound reproducing qualities to the best machines on the market. Every item of expense that went only to enhance the appearance, every cent of expense that went simply to more elaborate ornamentation or higher finish has been eliminated. We have put the cost of this machine entirely into the essential features, including a smooth running motor, the best type of reproducer, a horn of the proper design and material, and good workmanship throughout.

THE NEW SOUND ANALYZING REPRODUCER with which **the Oxford machine is equipped is made with the bar pivoted on delicate points,** practically eliminating all friction, and enabling this reproducer to reveal tones that are not brought out at all with the older styles. This reproducer is made with extra heavy mica diaphragm, all metal parts are of the best tool steel; everything about it is strongly and substantially made. It is equipped with automatic needle holder, the needle being inserted or removed simply by pressing a small lever.

THE SPRING MOTOR **is made with the latest tension screw speed regulator,** improved start and stop mechanism and an improved governor, resulting in perfectly even and uniform speed, thus insuring smooth and perfect reproduction. All gears and pinions are machine cut, made from brass and high grade steel, the frame is of cast iron, and the entire motor is carefully and accurately assembled by skilled mechanics.

CABINET AND HORN. **The Oxford Talking Machine is put up in a plain but well made and substantial solid oak cabinet,** made with removable top to afford access to the motor for any necessary cleaning, oiling or repairs. The fine black and gold horn is of the size and design found by experience to yield the purest musical tones; the body constructed of sheet steel with fine black enamel finish, the bell of solid brass with transparent lacquer finish.

THE CABINET MEASURES **11 inches square by 5 inches high,** the horn is 16 inches long and 9¼ inches in diameter at the bell, the turntable is 10 inches in diameter and the machine complete weighs 12½ pounds.

No. 20H5045 Oxford Disc Talking Machine, complete, with black and gold horn, sound analyzing reproducer and 100 needles, just as illustrated and described above. Shipping weight, 25 pounds. Price........................ **$9.75**

THE TYPE F H HARVARD DISC TALKING MACHINE

$15 90

The Large Flower Horn with which this machine is equipped, possesses, to an unusual degree, the magnificent accoustic or tone qualities which are peculiar to the latest type of flower horns. The unusual musical qualities of the flower horn, its ability to reproduce sound more absolutely true to the original music, is due to the peculiar curves and the extra wide flaring bell, which avoids the usual retardation of the sound waves, thereby giving a deep, clear and natural tone to every note.

THIS HORN **is made with fine baked on enamel finish,** ornamented with gold stripes, and besides the great improvement which it makes in the musical quality of the machine, also contributes greatly to the beautiful appearance of the outfit.

THE MELLOWNESS OF TONE AND REAL MUSICAL QUALITY of the reproduction, as rendered by the Type F H Harvard Talking Machine, is due partly to the new sound analyzing reproducer with which it is equipped and partly to the special acoustic properties of the flower horn, or rather to the combination of these two features. This reproducer is the latest product of the largest talking machine manufacturer in the world and represents the result of years of constant experiment and improvement. It is called the "sound analyzing" reproducer because of its ability to bring out every tone clearly and with the exact tone quality of the original music. It not only increases the volume of sound, but enriches the quality and reveals tones which with the earlier and less perfect types of reproducers were lost entirely. It is equipped with the automatic needle holder by which the needle is clamped into place and held securely by a spring lever; a slight pressure upon this lever instantly releases the needle, thus avoiding the use of the annoying set screw arrangement used in other reproducers.

GENERAL CONSTRUCTION. **The Type F H Harvard Disc Talking Machine is made with golden oak cabinet of plain but elegant design,** substantially made, all corners dovetailed and with removable top to afford access to the motor for oiling or occasional cleaning. The swinging arm and bracket, supporting the horn and reproducer, are beautifully designed and made from aluminum, highly ornamental and non-tarnishable. The turntable, of a special composition metal, is 10 inches in diameter, the cabinet measures 11¼ inches square by 5¼ inches high, the horn is 19 inches long with bell 17 inches in diameter. This machine is equipped with a powerful spring clock work motor, made throughout from brass and the best quality of steel, all gears and pinions machine cut to insure absolutely even and smooth running qualities. Perfectly uniform speed, essential to perfect reproduction, is obtained by the improved automatic governor and worm gear, perfect control of the speed is obtained by the new tension screw speed regulator, and the motor is stopped or started simply by pressing in or pulling out a small knobbed rod.

USES ANY KIND OF DISC RECORD. **This machine is adapted to any style, any size or any make of flat disc record.** We list, on the following pages of this catalogue, a complete line of Oxford 7-inch disc records at 21 cents each, 10-inch Columbia records at 60 cents each and the new Velvet Tone Marconi records at 75 cents each, and any of these records are suitable for use with the Type F H Harvard machine. Just think of the great variety of selections available for use with this machine and the wonderful possibilities for entertainment which it affords.

No. 20H5048 The Type F H Harvard Disc Talking Machine, with golden oak cabinet, large flower horn, sound analyzing reproducer, exactly as illustrated and described above. Shipping weight, 35 pounds. Price........................ **$15.90**

COLUMBIA CYLINDER RECORD GRAPHOPHONES

COLUMBIA JEWEL LYRIC REPRODUCER GRAPHOPHONE

$20.00

THE COLUMBIA JEWEL GRAPHOPHONE TYPE BK is equipped with the improved Lyric Tone Reproducer, exactly the same reproducer described and shown in the illustration on this page, made with genuine sapphire reproducing point. This high grade Columbia Jewel Graphophone is an ideal machine for home entertainment, a genuine Columbia Graphophone of the very latest type constructed with a view to strength and durability, and at the same time with a view to beauty and elegance of design.

AN EXTRA POWERFUL TANDEM SPRING MOTOR furnishes the power for operating this Columbia Jewel Graphophone, and this motor is made with the latest type of governor and speed regulator, insuring perfect and natural reproduction, made with machine cut gears, finely adjusted and guaranteed in every respect.

THE CABINET is made from quarter sawed oak, finely finished, with the best workmanship throughout and provided with a handsome bent oak top or cover, as shown in our illustration.

No. 20H5050 Columbia Jewel Graphophone, type B K, complete, with Lyric Tone Reproducer, 14-inch brass horn and bent oak cover. Plays Columbia, XP, P or Edison Cylinder records. Price.......... $20.00

Shipping weight, 45 pounds.

COLUMBIA LEADER LYRIC REPRODUCER GRAPHOPHONE

$30.00

THE COLUMBIA LEADER GRAPHOPHONE, TYPE B E, for cylinder records, is equipped with the new Lyric Tone Reproducer, the very highest grade and the most perfect reproducer made, exactly as described and shown in the illustration on this page. This reproducer works perfectly with any style or make of wax cylinder record, reproducing all records with greater volume of sound, greater clearness and with more natural tone than any other reproducer made.

THE MOTOR in the Columbia Leader Graphophone is an extra powerful triple spring clock work motor, guaranteed to run four records with one winding and made with the latest style of speed regulating device and governor. This motor has extra long winding crank, special machine cut gears, in short everything that will contribute to uniformity of speed, smoothness of operation and freedom from liability to get out of order.

THE CABINET is extra large and ornamental, of very handsome design, made from solid quarter sawed oak, beautifully finished, with fine bent oak cover, just as shown in our illustration. An extra sensitive recorder, made of the same style and upon the same principle as the new Lyric Tone Reproducer, is furnished with this machine, enabling the user to make his own records and greatly increasing the pleasure to be derived from a talking machine.

No. 20H5055 The Columbia Leader Lyric Reproducer Graphophone, type B E, complete, just as shown in our illustration, with Lyric Tone Reproducer, extra sensitive recorder, handsome bent oak cover and 14-inch solid brass horn. Plays Columbia, XP, P or Edison cylinder records. Price.......... $30.00

Shipping weight, 40 pounds.

COLUMBIA PEERLESS LYRIC REPRODUCER GRAPHOPHONE

$40.00

THE COLUMBIA PEERLESS GRAPHOPHONE, TYPE B F, like the Jewel and the Leader, is equipped with the new Lyric Tone Reproducer, with genuine sapphire reproducing point, but is a larger, more ornamental and more powerful machine. The cabinet is made of solid quarter sawed oak, of very elaborate and handsome design, beautifully finished, highly polished, making the machine an ornament to any parlor. The powerful quadruple spring motor is suspended from the top of the cabinet in such a way as to completely avoid all vibration, and is so constructed that it can be wound while playing. Provided with four powerful springs, this motor will play eight or more of the ordinary cylinder records with one winding. It is provided with extra long winding crank, accurately cut gears, the most approved style of speed regulating and governing devices, provided with easily accessible oil cups, in short, a motor that will give good results all the time with the least possible danger of becoming out of order.

AN EXTRA SENSITIVE RECORDER with genuine sapphire recording point is furnished with this graphophone, enabling the owner of this Peerless machine to make records as well as to reproduce those which may be purchased.

No. 20H5060 Columbia Peerless Lyric Tone Reproducer, type B F, Graphophone complete, with Lyric Tone Reproducer, extra sensitive recorder, bent oak cover and 14-inch brass horn. Plays Columbia, XP, P, BC or Edison cylinder records. Price.......... $40.00

Shipping weight, 50 pounds.

COLUMBIA DISC RECORD GRAPHOPHONES

THE NEW COLUMBIA B M GRAPHOPHONE

$25.00

THE TONE ARM TALKING MACHINE represents the very highest development of machines for the reproduction of sound. The hollow tone arm, combined with the wide bellflower horn, gives to the reproduction a beauty and naturalness of tone, a mellowness and genuine musical quality absolutely unequaled by talking machines of other types.

MUSICAL RECORDS are reproduced by this new machine more perfectly and more true to the original music than has ever been possible with machines of the older styles. The volume of sound, the fullness and roundness of tone resulting from this combined use of the new tone arm principle and the improved design flower horn is a revelation to those accustomed to talking machines of the ordinary style.

LATEST SOUND ANALYZING REPRODUCER. This talking machine is equipped with the new sound analyzing reproducer or sound box, made with extra heavy mica diaphragm, and equipped with the Automatic Needle Clamp, by which needles are inserted or removed simply by pressing a small lever, a great improvement over the old style thumbscrew arrangement.

THE COLUMBIA B M TONE ARM TALKING MACHINE is equipped with a powerful spring motor, strongly and accurately constructed; made with fine machine cut gears, the latest governing device and the most approved style of speed regulating mechanism, a motor that is absolutely guaranteed in every respect. THE CABINET is made from solid quarter sawed oak, of plain but elegant design, strong, substantial and of handsome appearance. The cabinet measures 12½ inches by 12½ inches by 8 inches. The turn table is 10 inches in diameter, and the large flower horn beautifully finished in black japan with gold stripes, is 17¾ inches long and the diameter is 19 inches.

No. 20H5065 The Columbia B M Tone Arm Disc Talking Machine, complete just as illustrated and described above. Price (without records).......... $25.00

Shipping weight, 50 pounds.

COLUMBIA STERLING TALKING MACHINE

$45.00

THE COLUMBIA STERLING GRAPHOPHONE is a still larger, finer and more complete talking machine of the new aluminum tone arm construction, made with extra powerful double spring motor, with worm gear, insuring the most perfect operation, absolute noiselessness, every part fitted with the same care that is used in making a watch.

THE CABINET is very substantially made of solid quarter sawed oak, of very handsome and ornamental design, with piano finish.

THE SOUND ANALYZING REPRODUCER with automatic needle clamp, doing away entirely with the old style thumb screw, the most perfect reproducer made, is included with the Sterling Graphophone. Plays any make of 7 or 10-inch disc records.

THE HORN IS OF A BEAUTIFUL FLORAL DESIGN, resembling in shape a great morning glory, nickel plated and highly polished throughout, 17½ inches long, with 21¼-inch bell, contributing greatly to the perfection of sound reproduction, and adding greatly to the ornamental appearance of the machine.

THE NEW ALUMINUM TONE ARM constitutes the greatest improvement made in talking machines for many years. This type of construction gives the greatest possible volume of sound, the clearest and most natural reproduction, the finest and most perfect musical quality, and does away with the disagreeable scratching sound heretofore noticed in machines of the ordinary style of construction.

No. 20H5070 Columbia Sterling Type B I Graphophone, complete, with aluminum tone arm, sound analyzing reproducer, and nickel plated floral horn, just as described above and shown in our illustration. Price, without records.......... $45.00

Shipping weight, 50 pounds.

SEE INDEX, PINK PAGES 598 TO 607, TO FIND WHAT YOU WANT.

24 GENUINE COLUMBIA P RECORDS AND THE OXFORD JR. TALKING MACHINE ALL COMPLETE

$8.75

YOUR OWN SELECTION OF SUBJECTS.

THE NEW OXFORD JR. TALKING MACHINE IS A STRICTLY HIGH CLASS TALKING MACHINE FOR REPRODUCING STANDARD SIZE WAX CYLINDER RECORDS. IT IS A THOROUGHLY WELL MADE MACHINE AND NOT TO BE COMPARED IN ANY WAY WITH THE CHEAP MACHINES THAT HAVE BEEN SO EXTENSIVELY ADVERTISED RECENTLY.

IT IS A HIGH CLASS MACHINE, MADE IN AMERICA, made by expert and experienced workmen in one of the largest and most successful talking machine factories in the world. It is made of good materials throughout, fitted with a high class spring motor, with machine cut gears, everything about it strong and substantial. It is made with patent feed device which holds the reproducer firmly in place as it travels along over the surface of the record There are cheap talking machines made without feed device, and with such machines the reproducer slips and slides off the surface of the record, but this trouble is entirely prevented in the Oxford Jr. Talking Machine, as the reproducer is held firmly and guided in its course over the surface of the record by the patent feed device, exactly the same as the highest priced machines. This machine is made with heavy, solid and substantial iron base, finished in black enamel, with gold stripe decorations. It is made with standard size tapered mandrel, and will use any standard size of wax cylinder record, Columbia, Edison or any other standard make.

THE REPRODUCTION of the human voice or of instrumental music, as rendered by the Oxford Jr. Talking Machine, is just exactly as good as with machines costing ten and fifteen times the price which we ask for this machine. It is made with a high grade, aluminum style D 1 reproducer, with mica diaphragm and Brazilian sapphire reproducing point It is equipped with black and gold horn with large extra wide bell, the body of the horn made of the best sheet steel, with fine black enamel finish; the bell made of solid brass, highly polished, giving the machine a most handsome and ornamental appearance. The tone qualities of this large black and gold horn are unexcelled, adding greatly to the volume of sound and naturalness and sweetness of tone.

THE OXFORD JR. TALKING MACHINE is not a toy It is a high class machine, a machine that cannot be purchased in the ordinary market at less than double our price. Made of good materials all the way through, strong and substantial, easy to operate, made with fine clock work motor, automatic feed device and extra large black and gold horn.

FIFTY THOUSAND RECORDS PER MONTH. Under our new contracts with the largest manufacturer of records in the world they are to furnish us for these outfits 50,000 high class standard size wax cylinder records per month, genuine Columbia P Records, the exact same records that have for years been sold at 50 cents, and today cannot be purchased in any other market for less than 25 cents each. By contracting for this enormous quantity of one million records (more than fifty car loads), the largest order ever placed for talking machine records by any dealer anywhere in the world, we have succeeded in reducing the cost to us just the merest fraction over the actual cost of labor and materials, the lowest cost at which high class graphophone records have ever been purchased by any dealer and in making up these outfits, consisting of the OXFORD JR. TALKING MACHINE AND TWENTY-FOUR OF THESE HIGH CLASS STANDARD SIZE RECORDS AT $8.75, we are giving you the benefit of the saving which we effect by means of our tremendous purchasing power.

UNDERSTAND, OUR SPECIAL PRICE $8.75 includes the 24 Columbia P Records, the Oxford Jr. Talking Machine complete with clock work motor, style D 1 aluminum reproducer, large black and gold horn, an outfit that a few months ago could not have been purchased for less than $15.00.

No. 20H5010 Oxford Jr. Talking Machine and 24 Columbia P Records, complete outfit, just as illustrated and described above. Shipping weight, 20 pounds. Price.....$ 8.75
No. 20H5011 Oxford Jr. Talking Machine Outfit, consisting of Oxford Jr. machine as illustrated and described above and 48 Genuine Columbia P Records. Price...... 12.95
Shipping weight 30 pounds. Make your selection of Records from the list on pages 789 and 790, the list of genuine Columbia P Records.

SPECIAL REDUCTION. HARVARD DISC RECORDS AT LESS THAN 14 1-2 Cts. EACH

THE LOWEST PRICE EVER MADE ON DISC RECORDS.

BECAUSE OF CERTAIN AGREEMENTS with manufacturers and owners of patents, we are compelled to discontinue the manufacture of the Harvard Disc Record, the record that we have advertised and sold in enormous quantities during the past two years, and in order to dispose of our large stock of these records without further advertising or the expense of filling orders for special selections, we have decided to put them up in lots of 15, 25 and 50, our own selection of titles, and close them out at less than cost, at less than one-half the price at which they were made to sell.

WE ARE SELLING THESE RECORDS AT A LOSS, and in order to make this loss as small as possible, in order to make the expense of handling and filling the orders for these records at this special below cost price of less than 14½ cents each, just as low as possible, we have taken our entire big stock of Harvard records and packed them up in lots of 15, 25 and 50.

IN ORDER to box these records in advance and thus reduce the cost of handling and boxing to the very lowest figure, and in order to save entirely the cost of filling orders for special subjects, we must ask you to accept the subjects we have selected, as they are all packed and boxed ready for shipment and no change can now be made.

SPLENDID ASSORTMENTS in these 15, 25 and 50 lots. In putting up these special collections to sell at less than cost we have so arranged the division that every 12, 25 or 50 lot will contain a great variety of subjects, the finest possible assortment of band and orchestra selections, vocal and instrumental solos, duets and quartettes, special talking and novelty records, vaudeville and descriptive selections, a variety and class of subjects that is certain to please the most particular buyer.

FIVE NEW PURPLE LABEL OXFORD RECORDS FREE. As a special inducement for you to take advantage of our very best offer, our big 50 lot collection of Harvard disc records at $7.95 we will include, ABSOLUTELY FREE OF CHARGE, five of the new Purple Label Oxford disc records with every lot of 50 Harvard records at this special value below cost price of $7.95.

UNDERSTAND YOU GET THE HARVARD RECORDS AT LESS THAN COST AND YOU GET THE 5 PURPLE LABEL OXFORD RECORDS FREE

IF YOU DO NOT OWN A TALKING MACHINE we will, to enable you to take advantage of this special offer, furnish you with a strictly high class, serviceable disc talking machine, a genuine Oxford machine, for only $6.90. Understand, we offer this machine for $6.90 only to those sending us an order for the Harvard Records at these special close out prices.

WE CANNOT ACCEPT AN ORDER FOR THE MACHINE ALONE AT $6.90 We offer the machine at this unheard of price simply as an accommodation to those who do not already own a machine, and who might, therefore, be unable to take advantage of this wonderful record offer unless we also furnished a machine upon the same liberal terms.

No. 20H5013 50 Harvard Disc Records, and 5 New Purple Label Oxford Records, exactly as above described. 55 records in all. Our special close out price........$7 95
At this price the records cost you less than 14½ cents each. Shipping weight, 20 pounds.
No. 20H5014 25 Harvard Disc Records, exactly as described above. Special close out price..................(Shipping weight, 10 pounds)..................$3 90
No. 20H5015 15 Harvard Disc Records, exactly as described above. Special close out price..................(Shipping weight, 6 pounds)..................2 45
No. 20H5016 Special Oxford Disc Talking Machine, made with oak cabinet, Japanned horn, spring motor, improved reproducer and 10-inch turn table, a thoroughly good machine. Our special price..................(Shipping weight 30 pounds)..................$6 90

Understand, we offer this machine at this price only as accommodation to those wishing to take advantage of our wonderful bargain lot prices on Harvard Records, and we cannot agree to furnish the machine at this price, except with order for Harvard Records

THE NEW OXFORD DISC TALKING MACHINE OUTFIT

THE IMPROVED OXFORD DISC TALKING MACHINE

A REGULAR $15.00 MACHINE.

36 IMPROVED OXFORD RECORDS

The New Purple Label Oxfords.

REGULAR 35-CENT RECORDS.

OUR SPECIAL PRICE, $16.80

YOU CAN MAKE YOUR OWN SELECTION OF RECORDS from the small list given on this page, or, better still, pick them from the complete list of new Purple Label Oxford Records, on pages 793 and 794.

SOME OF THE TITLES YOU CAN SELECT. FOR FULL LIST SEE PAGES 793 AND 794.

719 Husking Bee Dance. Talking
721 The Arkansaw Traveler. Talking
722 I'm Old, but I'm Awfully Tough. Rube laughing song
723 Schultz on Kissing. Dutch dialect series
733 Dese Bones Shall Rise Again. Minstrels
734 Stump Speech on Love. Talking
735 A Negro Sermon. Talking
744 Home, Sweet Home. Baritone solo
755 In the House of Too Much Trouble. Tenor solo
757 Good Bye, Sweet Dreams, Good Bye. Tenor solo
768 Uncle Josh in a Department Store. Laughing story
771 Uncle Josh at a Baseball Game. Laughing story
772 Uncle Josh on a Bicycle. Laughing story
774 Uncle Josh and the Lightning Rod Agent. Laughing story
776 Uncle Josh's Troubles in a Hotel. Laughing story
777 Fare Thee Well, Molly Darling. Baritone solo
779 The Mosquito Parade ("A Jersey Review")—Whitney. Band
782 Tell Me, Pretty Maiden (from "Florodora")—Stuart. Band
786 Just Because She Made Dem Goo Goo Eyes (coon song). Tenor solo
798 Intermezzo (from "Cavalleria Rusticana.") Clarionet solo
7105 And Then I Laughed (Rube song). Laughing song
7106 On a Sunday Afternoon. Baritone solo
7108 Die Wacht am Rhein. Vocal solo in German
7111 Who Threw the Overalls in Mistress Murphy's Chowder? Tenor solo
7113 Good Bye, Dolly Gray. Tenor solo
7129 He Laid Away a Suit of Gray to Wear the Union Blue. Orchestra
7146 Calvary. Baritone solo
7151 Brown October Ale (from "Robin Hood"). Baritone solo
7157 Asleep in the Deep. Bass solo
7160 Lincoln's Speech at Gettysburg. Talking
7175 Sally in Our Alley. Tenor solo
7185 Bridal March from "Lohengrin"—Wagner. Band
7190 Love's Old Sweet Song. Baritone solo
7194 Wearing of the Green. Baritone solo
7195 I Heard the Voice of Jesus Say. Baritone solo
7199 Where is My Wandering Boy Tonight? Tenor solo
7210 Negro Laughing Song (an old standard). Laughing song
7211 The Whistling Coon (the old favorite). Song with whistling chorus
7212 Schubert's Serenade. Violin solo
7221 Absence Makes the Heart Grow Fonder. Tenor solo
7230 Hello! Central, Give Me Heaven. Tenor solo
7240 Wedding March—Mendelssohn. Band
7242 Jolly Coppersmith (descriptive, with anvil effect and vocal chorus). Orchestra
7243 Night Alarm. Orchestra
7247 The Forge in the Forest (descriptive, with cock crow, anvil, etc.). Orchestra
7259 'Mid the Green Fields of Virginia. Baritone and tenor duet
7261 While the Leaves Came Drifting Down. Baritone and tenor duet
7262 Just as the Sun Went Down. Baritone and tenor duet
7263 Echoes of the Forest (descriptive, with bird effects). Orchestra
7285 America. Band
7292 Coon Songs. Banjo solo
7320 My Old Kentucky Home. Tenor solo
7325 Dancing in the Dark (song and dance with clogs). Band
7326 He Laid Away a Suit of Gray to Wear the Union Blue. Tenor solo
7330 Creole Bells (with violin) —J. B. Lampe. Orchestra
7337 Go 'Way Back and Sit Down. Orchestra
7354 Die Wacht am Rhein. Band
7356 Killarney. Tenor solo
7361 Dixie. Band
7377 Go 'Way Back and Sit Down (comic). Baritone solo
7381 Good Morning, Carrie. Baritone solo
7389 Evening Chimes in the Mountains. Band
7403 Where the Sweet Magnolias Bloom. Baritone solo
7406 At a Georgia Camp Meeting. Band
7420 High School Cadets March. Sousa Band
7422 Selections from "Il Trovatore." Band
7428 Medley of Irish Airs. Band
7432 Kathleen Mavourneen. Bass solo
7436 The Jolly Cadet (march characteristic). Band
7447 The Holy City (with voice and organ). Chimes
7450 The Sleigh Ride Party. Vocal quartette, male voices
7451 Dixie Land. Vocal quartette, male voices
7456 Coon Wedding in Southern Georgia. Vocal quartette, male voices
7458 Night Trip to Buffalo. Vocal quartette, male voices
7461 A Coon Band Contest. Banjo solo
7465 Creole Bells. Banjo solo
7478 Liberty Bell March (with bell effect) —Sousa. Band
7498 A Rag Time Skedaddle. Piccolo solo
7507 Marching Through Georgia. Band
7511 Carry Me Back to Old Virginia. Vocal quartette, male voices
7512 My Old Kentucky Home. Vocal quartette, male voices
7514 Tenting Tonight on the Old Camp Ground. Vocal quartette, male voices
7521 The Old Oaken Bucket. Vocal quartette, male voices
7555 Star Spangled Banner. Band
7558 When You Were Sweet Sixteen. Baritone solo
7564 Till We Meet Again Waltz. Band
7586 Sleep, Baby, Sleep (Yodle song). Tenor
7591 Hi! Le! Hi! Lo! (Yodle song). Tenor
7600 Darkey Tickle (plantation medley). Orchestra
7602 Down on the Suwanee River. Orchestra
7608 Happy Days in Dixie (plantation medley). Orchestra
7629 Stars and Stripes Forever March—Sousa. Orchestra
7640 Bugle Calls of the United States Army. Bugle Calls
7642 Hear Dem Bells. Minstrels
7644 The Laughing Song. Minstrels
7645 The Old Log Cabin. Minstrels
7649 Camp Meeting. Vocal trio, male voices
7664 The Twenty-third Psalm and the Lord's Prayer. Talking
7674 The Turkish Patrol. Band
7689 Break the News to Mother. Baritone solo
7701 Come Back to Erin. Baritone solo
7716 Annie Laurie. Vocal quartette, male voices
7726 I'll Come Back When the Hawthorn Blooms Again. Baritone solo
7759 Ticklish Reuben (Rube song). Laughing song
7798 I've a Longing in My Heart for You, Louise. Minstrels
7818 Suwanee River. Vocal quartette male voices
7851 Dissertation on Love. Talking
7894 Tales from the Vienna Woods Waltz. Vienna Orchestra
7940 In the Good Old Summer Time. Baritone solo (orchestra accompaniment)
7970 Under the Bamboo Tree. Baritone and tenor duet
71057 Down Where the Wurzburger Flows. Baritone solo
71111 Spring Blossoms (caprice gavotte) Orchestra
71155 Hiawatha (a summer idyl). Orchestra
71184 Oh, That We Two Were Maying. Contralto and baritone duet
71199 The Last Rose of Summer. Cornet solo
71372 Selections from "Cavalleria Rusticana." Band
71408 Uncle Josh at a Camp Meeting. Laughing story
71525 When I Hold Your Hand in Mine—Chattaway. Tenor solo
71574 Up in the Cocoanut Tree. Baritone solo
71579 Hiawatha. Baritone solo
71600 You're as Welcome as the Flowers in May. Baritone solo
71616 Parody on Hiawatha. Baritone and tenor duet
71821 Pretty as a Butterfly. Orchestra bells
71868 Uncle Josh and the Insurance Company. Laughing story
71897 Noisy Bill (characteristic march). Band
73023 Jesus, Lover of My Soul (organ accompaniment). Tenor solo
73029 The Vacant Chair (orchestra accompaniment). Baritone solo
73033 By the Watermelon Vine (piano accompaniment). Baritone solo
73037 I've Got a Feeling for You (piano accompaniment). Baritone solo
73074 By the Old Oak Tree (piano accompaniment). Tenor solo

THE IMPROVED OXFORD DISC TALKING MACHINE is a high class, serviceable machine that we can guarantee to give satisfaction. It is made from the best materials throughout, assembled in the most careful, accurate and substantial manner, and with ordinary care will last for years, as there is nothing about it to wear out or get out of order.

THE POWERFUL SPRING MOTOR is made with all pinions and gears machine cut, insuring perfect accuracy of action. It is provided with improved governor, resulting in absolutely even and uniform reproduction; it has the latest tension screw speed regulator and improved stop and start device.

THE NEW SOUND ANALYZING REPRODUCER is made with the bar pivoted on delicate points, practically eliminating all friction and this form of construction results in the full reproduction of tones heretofore entirely inaudible as rendered by the earlier styles of machines. This reproducer is made with the new automatic needle holder by which the needle is inserted or removed simply by pressing a small lever, a great improvement over the old style with the troublesome set screw arrangement.

CABINET AND HORN. We put up the Oxford Disc Talking Machine in a finely finished and substantial golden oak cabinet with removable top, to afford access to the motor for oiling, cleaning or repairs. The horn is the best black and gold horn we can obtain, the body made from a high grade of sheet steel with black enamel finish, the bell from solid brass with transparent lacquer finish to prevent tarnishing.

THIS MACHINE BRINGS THE SINGER, the musician, the band or the orchestra into the audible presence of the listener in a manner that is truly marvelous. To those unfamiliar with the perfection of modern talking machines, to those who are unaware of the marvels accomplished by modern sound reproducing mechanisms, the absolute naturalness, the full volume, and the tone quality of the Oxford machine and the wonderful new Purple Label Oxford Records, will seem almost beyond belief. The sound is so real, so resonant and so vibrant and of such wondrous beauty of tone and melody that it never fails to charm all who hear it.

36 NEW PURPLE LABEL OXFORD RECORDS are included in this outfit, three dozen of these wonderful new 7-inch disc records, your own selection of subjects, vocal solos quartettes, bands, orchestras, instrumental solos, talking and vaudeville selections, anything that your taste may dictate, classical or popular music, sacred or secular, humorous or pathetic subjects, all are to be found in the big list on pages 793 and 794.

OUR SPECIAL OFFER. Pick out the 36 records that you like best, making your selection from the small list shown on this page, or, better still, from the complete list of new Purple Label Oxford Records on pages 793 and 794, send us your order with $16.80 inclosed and we will forward the big outfit complete, the 36 new Purple Label Oxford Records that you select, and the Oxford Talking Machine, exactly as illustrated and described on this page. We will ship the outfit with the understanding and agreement that you can take it to your home, play every one of the 36 records, compare it with any other talking machine outfit that you have ever seen, and if you do not feel perfectly satisfied with it, if you do not feel that you have secured the biggest talking machine bargain that you ever saw or heard of, you can pack it up again, ship it back to us, and we will refund the entire amount paid, including all freight charges.

No. 20H5025 The Oxford Disc Talking Machine Outfit, consisting of 36 new Purple Label Oxford Records and the Oxford Disc Talking Machine exactly as illustrated and described on this page. Shipping weight, 38 pounds. Price **$16.80**

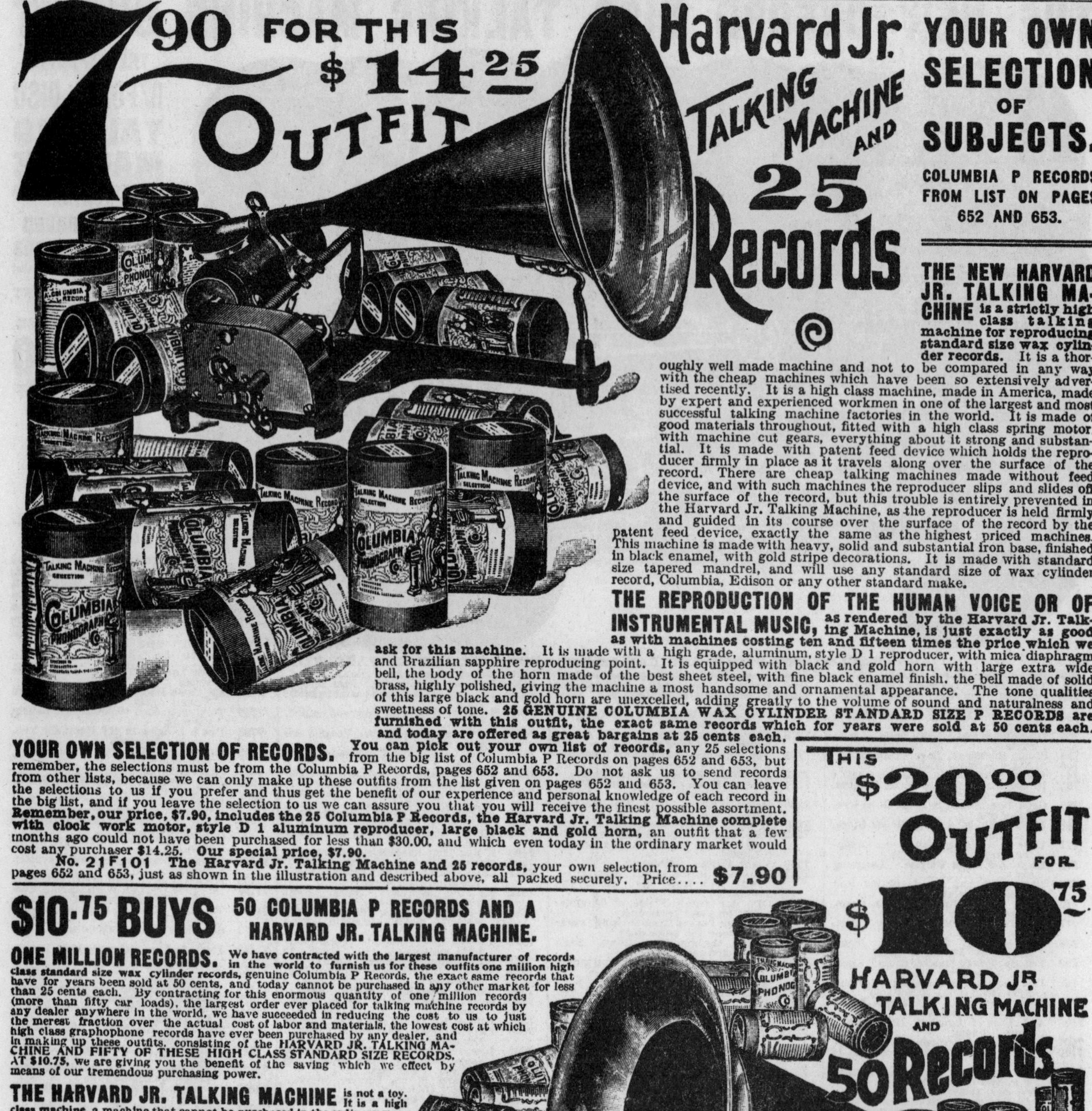

$7.90 FOR THIS $14.25 OUTFIT Harvard Jr. Talking Machine and 25 Records

YOUR OWN SELECTION OF SUBJECTS.

COLUMBIA P RECORDS FROM LIST ON PAGES 652 AND 653.

THE NEW HARVARD JR. TALKING MACHINE is a strictly high class talking machine for reproducing standard size wax cylinder records. It is a thoroughly well made machine and not to be compared in any way with the cheap machines which have been so extensively advertised recently. It is a high class machine, made in America, made by expert and experienced workmen in one of the largest and most successful talking machine factories in the world. It is made of good materials throughout, fitted with a high class spring motor, with machine cut gears, everything about it strong and substantial. It is made with patent feed device which holds the reproducer firmly in place as it travels along over the surface of the record. There are cheap talking machines made without feed device, and with such machines the reproducer slips and slides off the surface of the record, but this trouble is entirely prevented in the Harvard Jr. Talking Machine, as the reproducer is held firmly and guided in its course over the surface of the record by the patent feed device, exactly the same as the highest priced machines. This machine is made with heavy, solid and substantial iron base, finished in black enamel, with gold stripe decorations. It is made with standard size tapered mandrel, and will use any standard size of wax cylinder record, Columbia, Edison or any other standard make.

THE REPRODUCTION OF THE HUMAN VOICE OR OF INSTRUMENTAL MUSIC, as rendered by the Harvard Jr. Talking Machine, is just exactly as good as with machines costing ten and fifteen times the price which we ask for this machine. It is made with a high grade, aluminum, style D 1 reproducer, with mica diaphragm and Brazilian sapphire reproducing point. It is equipped with black and gold horn with large extra wide bell, the body of the horn made of the best sheet steel, with fine black enamel finish, the bell made of solid brass, highly polished, giving the machine a most handsome and ornamental appearance. The tone qualities of this large black and gold horn are unexcelled, adding greatly to the volume of sound and naturalness and sweetness of tone. **25 GENUINE COLUMBIA WAX CYLINDER STANDARD SIZE P RECORDS are furnished with this outfit, the exact same records which for years were sold at 50 cents each, and today are offered as great bargains at 25 cents each.**

YOUR OWN SELECTION OF RECORDS. You can pick out your own list of records, any 25 selections from the big list of Columbia P Records on pages 652 and 653, but remember, the selections must be from the Columbia P Records, pages 652 and 653. Do not ask us to send records from other lists, because we can only make up these outfits from the list given on pages 652 and 653. You can leave the selections to us if you prefer and thus get the benefit of our experience and personal knowledge of each record in the big list, and if you leave the selection to us we can assure you that you will receive the finest possible assortment. **Remember, our price, $7.90, includes the 25 Columbia P Records, the Harvard Jr. Talking Machine complete with clock work motor, style D 1 aluminum reproducer, large black and gold horn,** an outfit that a few months ago could not have been purchased for less than $30.00, and which even today in the ordinary market would cost any purchaser $14.25. **Our special price, $7.90.**

No. 21F101 **The Harvard Jr. Talking Machine and 25 records,** your own selection, from pages 652 and 653, just as shown in the illustration and described above, all packed securely. Price.... **$7.90**

THIS $20.00 OUTFIT FOR $10.75 HARVARD JR. TALKING MACHINE AND 50 Records

$10.75 BUYS 50 COLUMBIA P RECORDS AND A HARVARD JR. TALKING MACHINE.

ONE MILLION RECORDS. We have contracted with the largest manufacturer of records in the world to furnish us for these outfits one million high class standard size wax cylinder records, genuine Columbia P Records, the exact same records that have for years been sold at 50 cents, and today cannot be purchased in any other market for less than 25 cents each. By contracting for this enormous quantity of one million records (more than fifty car loads), the largest order ever placed for talking machine records by any dealer anywhere in the world, we have succeeded in reducing the cost to us to just the merest fraction over the actual cost of labor and materials, the lowest cost at which high class graphophone records have ever been purchased by any dealer, and in making up these outfits, consisting of the HARVARD JR. TALKING MACHINE AND FIFTY OF THESE HIGH CLASS STANDARD SIZE RECORDS, AT $10.75, we are giving you the benefit of the saving which we effect by means of our tremendous purchasing power.

THE HARVARD JR. TALKING MACHINE is not a toy. It is a high class machine, a machine that cannot be purchased in the ordinary market at less than double our price. Made of good materials all the way through, strong and substantial, easy to operate, made with fine clock work motor, automatic feed device and extra large black and gold horn.

YOU CAN SELECT YOUR OWN RECORDS for this big outfit. We want you to get the exact titles and selections that you prefer when you order this big outfit, and on pages 652 and 653 you will find a complete list of the records which we include with these outfits. **Make your selection from these two pages.** Remember, we do not furnish any of the records shown on other pages with these outfits. You must make your selection from pages 652 and 653, the genuine Columbia standard size wax cylinder P records.

WE ALLOW YOU TO SELECT ANY RECORDS YOU DESIRE in this outfit, provided the selection is made from pages 652 and 653. Understand, if the records for these outfits are selected from any other list or any other page we will be compelled to put up the outfit with our own selection of records. If you leave the selection to us we will give you the very cream of the best titles from our enormous stock of 1,000,000 high class records.

No. 21F102 **The Harvard Jr. Talking Machine Outfit,** complete with 50 genuine Columbia standard size wax cylinder P records, your own selection of subjects from pages 652 and 653. Price, complete..... **$10.75**

COLUMBIA TYPE A K DISC GRAPHOPHONE, $15.00

THIS MACHINE is one of the Columbia Phonograph Co.'s VERY LATEST PRODUCTIONS, embodying all of the features of the highest grade talking machines and yet sold at a moderate price. It is made with powerful clockwork spring motor and contained in a fine oak cabinet of handsome design. The sound box or reproducer is the latest type concert style with improved knife edge bearings, heavy mica diaphragm, the highest grade sound box furnished with any talking machine, regardless of price. The ornamental horn supporting arms, which are detachable, are of very handsome design and made of aluminum, this metal being most perfectly adapted for this purpose.

THE BLACK AND GOLD HORN is the highest grade horn made for Disc Talking Machines, the body of this horn being made from fine sheet steel with black oxidized finish and the bell of polished brass, giving it a very ornamental appearance.

Uses any kind of disc records, of any size or make.

No. 21E230 Columbia Type A K Disc Graphophone, complete with 16-inch black and gold horn and 100 needles. Price, **$15.00**
Shipping weight, 28 pounds.

COLUMBIA TYPE A J DISC GRAPHOPHONE, $22.50

THE TYPE A J DISC GRAPHOPHONE is made with hinged cabinet top, thus giving easy access to the motor for the purpose of oiling or cleaning. The clockwork spring motor is extra powerful, made with the latest improved governor and most perfect speed regulator. It runs two 10-inch or three 7-inch records with one winding. We particularly recommend this A J disc machine either for home entertainment or for public exhibition work, as it has proven the most popular talking machine we have ever handled. This disc graphophone, similar to the type A K described opposite, is a somewhat larger machine with a larger, heavier and more handsomely designed cabinet made from solid quarter sawed oak.

THE SOUND BOX OR REPRODUCER is the latest knife edge style, extra large size, made with mica diaphragm, and is the very highest grade sound box furnished with any talking machine, regardless of price.

Uses any kind of disc records, of any size or make.

No. 21E241 Columbia Type A J Disc Graphophone, complete with 16-inch horn and 100 needles. Price **$22.50**
Shipping weight, 30 pounds.

COLUMBIA TYPE A H DISC GRAPHOPHONE, $30.00

THE TYPE A H DISC GRAPHOPHONE is one of the highest grade automatic talking machines made by the Columbia Phonograph Co., and represents a very high degree of perfection in the making of talking machines. The cabinet is extra large and heavy of a very handsome and ornamental design, made from solid quarter sawed oak, and very finely finished throughout.

THE SOUND BOX is the very latest improved knife edge pattern, extra large, with heavy mica diaphragm, the most perfect reproducer yet constructed.

THE POWERFUL DOUBLE SPRING MOTOR with special governor and improved speed regulator is easily accessible for cleaning and oiling, and runs three 10-inch records, or five 7-inch records with one winding.

THE MOTOR IS ABSOLUTELY NOISELESS. THE ONLY DISC MACHINE MOTOR MADE WHICH OPERATES ENTIRELY WITHOUT SOUND.

Read about our WONDERFUL PROFIT SHARING PLAN on the last pages of this book. We guarantee to save you money on every purchase, to furnish better goods for less money than you can get elsewhere, and at the same time we allow our customers to share in the profits of this business. Don't forget that you will get a **Profit Sharing Certificate** for every purchase.

REMEMBER, that this graphophone, and all the other graphophones described on this page, use our **FAMOUS 28-CENT HARVARD DISC RECORDS.**

For list of selections, see page 367.

DON'T MISS THIS OPPORTUNITY to put in a good supply of high class, absolutely guaranteed disc records at only **28 cents each, or $3.25 per dozen.**

THIS GRAPHOPHONE RUNS EITHER THE 7 OR 10-INCH COLUMBIA RECORDS, OR THE HARVARD DISC RECORDS,

A complete list of which you will find on pages 367, 368, 372 and 373.

IF YOU WANT A TALKING MACHINE which will create a sensation in your locality, a machine which people will come miles to hear, order this **A H MACHINE and a selection of 10-inch records.**

THE FINE BLACK AND GOLD HORN is of extra large size, being 22 inches long, with 11½-inch bell, the body of this horn being constructed from the finest quality sheet steel, oxidized in black, and the bell is made of extra heavy polished brass. This type of horn greatly improves the quality and sweetness of tone.

No. 21E250 Columbia Type A H Graphophone, complete with 22-inch black and gold horn and 100 needles.
Price **$30.00**
Shipping weight, 65 pounds.

NEW COLUMBIA ALUMINUM TONE ARM GRAPHOPHONES CHAMPION, $30.00. STERLING, 45.00.

COLUMBIA CHAMPION DISC GRAPHOPHONE.

THE NEW ALUMINUM TONE ARM GRAPHOPHONES represent the latest and highest development in disc talking machines. In these machines the sound is transmitted directly from the reproducer, through the hollow aluminum tone arm, to the horn, securing in this way the **greatest possible volume of sound, the greatest beauty and naturalness of tone, and preventing, to a very large extent, the scratching sound** sometimes noticed with machines of other styles of construction.

THE MOTOR is noiseless in operation, made with the most perfect speed regulator and governor, fine machine cut gears, made to run noiselessly, uniformly, and so simple in construction that repairs of any kind are very seldom necessary, and **can be wound while playing.**

THE CABINET is made from solid quarter sawed oak, with dark finish, highly polished, handsome and ornamental design. It is fitted with a 10-inch turntable, making the machine suitable for disc records of any size.

THE REPRODUCER is the latest Columbia, knife edge, sound analyzing style, made with automatic needle clamp, by means of which the needle is inserted or removed simply by pressing a lever.

THE BEAUTIFUL FLORAL HORN adds greatly to the beauty of this instrument. This horn is made of steel, with black enamel satin finish, and gold bands, and is 17¾ inches long with 19-inch bell.

No. 21E261 Columbia Champion Type B H Graphophone, complete with aluminum tone arm, sound analyzing reproducer, and black satin finish floral horn, just as described above and shown in our illustration. Price, complete **$30.00**
Shipping weight, 30 pounds.

COLUMBIA STERLING TALKING MACHINE.

THE COLUMBIA STERLING GRAPHOPHONE is a still larger, finer and more complete talking machine of the new aluminum tone arm construction, made with **extra powerful double spring motor, with worm gear, insuring the most perfect operation, absolute noiselessness, every part fitted with the same care that is used in making a watch.**

THE CABINET is very substantially made of solid quarter sawed oak, of very handsome and ornamental design, with piano finish.

THE SOUND ANALYZING REPRODUCER with automatic needle clamp, doing away entirely with the old style thumb screw, the most perfect reproducer made, is included with the Sterling graphophone.

THE HORN IS OF A BEAUTIFUL FLORAL DESIGN, resembling in shape a great morning glory, nickel plated and highly polished throughout, 17½ inches long, with 21¼-inch bell, contributing greatly to the perfection of sound reproduction, and adding greatly to the ornamental appearance of the machine.

THE NEW ALUMINUM TONE ARM constitutes the greatest improvement made in talking machines for many years. This type of construction gives the greatest possible volume of sound, the clearest and most natural reproduction, the finest and most perfect musical quality, and **does away with the disagreeable scratching sound heretofore noticed in machines of the ordinary style of construction.**

No. 21E263 Columbia Sterling Type B I Graphophone, complete with aluminum tone arm, sound analyzing reproducer, and nickel plated floral horn, just as described above and shown in our illustration. Price, complete **$45.00**
Shipping weight, 45 pounds.

LATEST 1906 MODEL No. 3A HARVARD TALKING MACHINE.

No. 3A HARVARD DISC TALKING MACHINE, $14.90

Don't Miss Our Big Sale of

Genuine Harvard 7-inch and 10-inch Disc Records at 28c and 52c each.

For complete list of selections see pages 367 and 368. This Harvard Graphophone uses the Harvard Records, the Columbia Records, either 7-inch or 10-inch, or any other style of flat disc records.

THE No. 3A HARVARD DISC TALKING MACHINE is similar in principle to our No 1 Harvard, but is a larger and finer machine, made with a larger horn, a larger, more substantial and more ornamental cabinet and a larger and more powerful clockwork spring motor. We have designed this machine especially to meet the ideas of those who desire a somewhat better, larger and handsomer machine than the No. 1 Harvard Machine, and we have been able, in spite of the increased cost and the improvements made in this machine, to keep the price down to a figure within the reach of almost anyone.

THE POWERFUL SPRING MOTOR with which we equip the No. 3A Harvard Machine is the highest grade spring motor made for talking machines. It is made with machine cut gears, the latest type of governor and the most approved style of speed regulating device. It is a motor that we can absolutely guarantee to give satisfaction under any conditions.

THE SOUND BOX OR REPRODUCER is of the very latest type, designed expressly for the Harvard Talking Machines, made with extra heavy mica diaphragm, a sound box that is equal in volume, sweetness and perfect reproduction to any sound box with which it may be compared. This reproducer is made with the **latest automatic needle clamp,** by which needles are inserted or removed simply by pressing a little lever, doing away entirely with the annoyance of the old style thumb screw arrangement.

THE CABINET with which we equip the No. 3A Harvard Disc Talking Machine is made from solid quarter sawed oak, hard oil hand rubbed finish throughout, workmanship and material guaranteed in every way. In design this cabinet is very handsome, making the machine an ornamental addition to any parlor.

THE BLACK AND GOLD HORN is the same high grade horn that we use on all of the Harvard Machines, made of the best sheet steel, with solid brass bell, finished in black and gold, of large size, 21 inches long.

No. 21E282 No. 3A Harvard Disc Talking Machine, all complete, with 21-inch black and gold horn, improved sound box and 100 needles. Price........ **$14.90**
Shipping weight, 40 pounds.

LATEST 1906 MODEL No. 4 HARVARD DISC TALKING MACHINE, $17.40

THIS IS THE HIGHEST GRADE HARVARD DISC TALKING MACHINE that we make, a machine that is equal in every way to disc talking machines sold by other dealers at from $30.00 to $40.00.

THE CABINET OF THE No. 4 HARVARD DISC TALKING MACHINE is in every way a beautiful piece of work, made from solid quarter sawed oak, especially selected, thoroughly kiln dried and put together by high class experienced workmen. It is made with a five-ply, built up top, hand turned decorations and lock cornered mitred moulding. The finish is the highest grade dead oil, hand rubbed finish, a finish that is not only pleasing in appearance, but at the same time durable.

THE MOTOR is an extra powerful tandem spring clockwork of the very latest type, made with machine cut gears, latest improved governor and patented speed regulating device.

THE SOUND BOX is our highest grade mica diaphragm Harvard reproducer, unsurpassed by any reproducer or sound box on the market in volume, naturalness of tone and freedom from scratch. This reproducer is made with the **latest automatic needle clamp,** by which needles are inserted or removed simply by pressing a little lever, doing away entirely with the annoyance of the old style thumb screw arrangement.

THE HORN is the same high grade black and gold horn with which we equip all of the Harvard Machines and is the largest size which we use on this line of machines, measuring 30 inches in length with bell 12 inches in diameter. This horn is made with solid sheet steel body, oxidized in black, with solid brass bell highly burnished.

REMEMBER,

This No. 4 Harvard Machine.

uses our famous 28-cent Harvard Records. For complete list of selections, see page 367. This machine runs five 7-inch records or three 10-inch records with one winding.

Besides the Harvard Records, this machine, and all other Harvard machines described on this page, use any style, any size or any make of flat disc records.

CONSIDER OUR PROFIT SHARING PLAN.

Your PROFIT SHARING CERTIFICATE will go a long way toward getting you something handsome and valuable, shown on the last pages of this catalogue.

IN APPEARANCE, SIZE, BEAUTY OF DESIGN, elegance of finish, and in all those points which mean quality and satisfaction in a talking machine, the No. 4 Harvard Machine is in every way equal and in most respects superior to disc talking machines sold by other dealers at more than double our price.

No. 21E284 No. 4 Harvard Disc Talking Machine, all complete, with solid oak highly ornamental cabinet, extra large 30-inch black and gold horn, improved Harvard sound box and 100 needles. Shipping weight, 60 pounds. Price........ **$17.40**

Miscellaneous.

No. 21E585 Recorder, for Q, QC, QQ, or our special Home Graphophone. Price........ **$2.50**

No. 21E590 Recorder, for BX, AT, AO, or Gem Graphophone........ **$5.00**

No. 21E595 Reproducer, for Q, QC, QQ, or our special Home Graphophone. Price........ **$2.50**

No. 21E599 Reproducer, Style D, for any wax cylinder graphophone **except** Q, QC, QQ and our special Home, Latest improved style, extra large, with built up mica diaphragm. Price........ **$5.00**

SPECIAL OFFER: Send us your old reproducer and $3.00 in cash and we will send you this latest model improved "D" Reproducer.

No. 21E625 Diaphragm Glasses, best French glass. Price, per dozen, 30c; each........ **4c**

No. 21E628 Mica Diaphragms, for "D" reproducers only, best quality, built up. Price, each ..**19c**

No. 21E632 Mica Diaphragms, for sound boxes of any style Disc Graphophone. Price, each **10c**

No. 21E640 Rubber Gaskets, for reproducers or recorders. Price, per set of three, ordinary size...**5c**
Per set of two, for large "D" reproducer........**4c**

No. 21E650 Reproducer Ball, made of Brazilian pebble, but sold by many dealers as sapphire.
Price, each........ **20c**

No. 21E651 Reproducer Ball, made of genuine sapphire, highest grade. Price, each........**75c**

No. 21E653 Governor Springs, for types Q, QC, QQ, BX, AB and our Special Home Graphophones. Price........**10c**

No. 21E654 Governor Springs, for types AT, AO, AZ, AK, AJ, AH, AR and our $8.75 Disc Graphophones. Price........**15c**

No. 21E660 Recorder Points, made of Brazilian pebble, but often sold as sapphire.
Price, each, in setting, flat edge........**52c**
Price, each, in setting, cupped edge........**60c**

No. 21E661 Recorder Points, genuine sapphire, highest grade made.
Price, each, in setting, flat edge........**$1.10**
Price, each, in setting, cupped edge........**1.80**

No. 21E670 Main Spring, single, for Q, QC, QQ, BX, AB and our special Home Graphophones.
Price, each........**18c**

State kind of Graphophone for which spring is wanted.

No. 21E672 Main Spring, single, for AT, AK, AJ, AH and our $8.75 Disc Graphophones.
Price, each........**45c**

No. 21E800 Speaking Tube, for use in record making, mohair covered, with spiral spring, lining and hard rubber mouthpiece; 22 inches long. Price **75c**

No. 21E830 Camel's Hair Brushes, 1½ inches wide, for dusting records. Price, each........**15c**

No. 21E850 Needle Box, two parts, for used and unused needles. Price, each........**15c**

No. 21E875 Blank Cylinders, for record making. Standard size, same as P or XP records.
Price, each........**15c**

Needles at 4 Cents per 100.

No. 21E900 These Needles, for disc talking machines of any make, are made from cold drawn, oil tempered steel wire, and guaranteed to be the finest needles manufactured. Put up in envelopes of 100 each. Price, per 100........**4c**
If by mail, postage extra, 2 cents.
Put up in boxes. Price, per 1,000........**35c**
If by mail, postage extra, 8 cents.

No. 21E920 Rubber Hose, large size, for connecting large horns to any style talking machine.
Price, per foot........**16c**

OXFORD TAPERING ARM DISC TALKING MACHINE

$9.45

1909 MODEL—TYPE L. E.

SPECIFICATIONS.

CABINET — Genuine oak, 10⅜ inches square at base; 8¾ inches square at top; height, 4⅞ inches, with fine hand rubbed finish.

HORN—Ornamental flower shaped, scientifically designed to secure the best acoustic properties; diameter of bell, 14 inches; length, 12½ inches. Finish, dark red enamel with gold stripes.

TURN TABLE—8 inches in diameter, felt covered; takes either 7 or 10-inch record.

MOTOR—Noiseless, all parts interchangeable, with improved automatic governor and extra long worm gear, resulting in absolutely uniform speed. Combination start and stop lever and speed regulator on side of cabinet. Single spring, runs one 10-inch or two 7-inch records with one winding, and can be wound while running.

TAPERING ARM—Nickel plated, of the most improved design, fully protected by patents, affording unobstructed passage for sound waves from the reproducer to the horn.

REPRODUCER — Oxford Special, heavy mica diaphragm, positive screw clamp for needle, the exact same style used on machines selling at from $50.00 to $75.00.

WEIGHT—11½ pounds.

This Tapering Arm Oxford Talking Machine will surprise you with its wonderful naturalness of tone. Its mellowness and real musical quality, marvelous volume, full rich tones and absolute fidelity to the original music, is the combined result of the **tapering arm, the acoustically correct horn, the perfect reproducer, and the uniform motor speed.** It is a machine that is made right in every detail of workmanship, the best materials all through, perfect in action, strong, durable and simple, a machine that will give you no trouble and will afford a never failing source of pleasure to you and your friends for many years.

No. 20T5071 Oxford Disc Talking Machine, Type L. E. Price.............. **$9.45**

Shipping weight, 35 pounds.

OXFORD TAPERING ARM DISC TALKING MACHINE

1909 MODEL—TYPE O. D.

$11.60

SPECIFICATIONS.

CABINET—Solid oak, 11⅛ inches by 10⅛ inches at base; 10⅛ inches by 9⅜ inches at top; 5⅛ inches high. Fine hand rubbed finish.

HORN—Flower shaped, very ornamental, and possessing the best acoustic properties obtainable in a horn of this size. Diameter of bell, 14 inches; length, 12½ inches. Finish, dark red enamel with gold stripes.

TURN TABLE—8 inches in diameter, covered with green felt. Takes either 7 or 10-inch records.

MOTOR—Single spring, finely made throughout, practically the same as the motor of our type L. E. machine, but with start and stop lever and speed regulator both on top of cabinet. Noiseless in operation, absolutely uniform in speed, insuring perfect reproduction. May be wound while running.

TAPERING ARM—Nickel plated, the same up to date construction used on types L. E., J. F., and R. W., the feature which distinguishes the new 1909 Oxford machines from all others.

REPRODUCER — Oxford Special design, made with heavy mica diaphragm and positive screw clamp for needle. Cannot rattle, buzz or blast, the same reproducer we furnish with all the 1909 Oxford machines shown on this page.

WEIGHT—13 pounds.

An ideal musical instrument for home use, a perpetual entertainer and ever ready source of pleasure and amusement. Machines of this style, quality and size have heretofore been sold at $25.00 by dealers everywhere. Think of the value we give you in pricing this machine, this new up to date 1909 Type O. D. Oxford Tapering Arm Machine, exactly as illustrated and described at only $11.60, less than half the regular price; a little better than type L. E.; not quite so good as the type J. F., and a wonderful bargain at our special price. If $11.60 fits your pocketbook, you will make no mistake in ordering the type O. D. machine.

No. 20T5073 Oxford Disc Talking Machine, Type O. D. Price...................... **$11.60**

Shipping weight, 40 pounds.

OXFORD TAPERING ARM DISC TALKING MACHINES

1909 MODELS

NOT MERE "TALKING MACHINES" BUT MUSICAL INSTRUMENTS OF THE HIGHEST ORDER

THE FIRST TALKING MACHINES AND RECORDS, crude in design and workmanship, were simply curiosities, scientific novelties that interested and amused merely by reason of their novelty. The mere fact that they reproduced sounds at all with sufficient clearness and accuracy so that they could be recognized, even though with difficulty, was in itself so remarkable, so truly a miracle of modern science that deficiencies and imperfections of all kinds were overlooked and excused.

BUT TODAY, the talking machine is no longer a curiosity; it is not even a novelty. It has made for itself a place in almost every home, and it is the most popular entertainer in the world. Why? Because, while the world was still marveling that a mere machine could actually talk and sing (even though it squeaked and scratched and wheezed), great scientists, resourceful inventors, and skilled designers who foresaw its possibilities were busily engaged in perfecting it. They perfected not only the machine itself, but they discovered and worked out new and better ways of making the records, and from the first crude "phonograph" has been evolved that modern musical instrument, the tapering arm disc talking machine, and that perfect example of sound recording, the modern disc record.

THE TALKING MACHINE OF TODAY IS A MUSICAL INSTRUMENT and better than any other musical instrument because it combines them all, a whole band or orchestra, if you choose, besides rendering vocal selections, solos or choruses, with such remarkable fidelity that only by an effort do we realize that the singers are not actually present. It brings to your own home the same musicians, the same great singers, the same entertainers, the same bands and orchestras that delight great audiences in our most famous theaters.

TODAY, THE WALDORF-ASTORIA, New York City's most famous hotel, the mecca of wealth and fashion, entertains its guests at luncheon with a tapering arm disc talking machine. Today the Bellevue-Stratford, Philadelphia's most magnificent hotel, where expense is reckoned neither by host nor guest, where the only question is **quality**, the tapering arm disc talking machine takes the place of an orchestra in the great dining room. Would these great hotels, whose guests demand the best of everything, attempt to delight and entertain them with a talking machine if it was not a **real musical instrument**—in fact, the greatest of all musical instruments?

LET US SEND YOU an Oxford Tapering Arm Disc Talking Machine, any of the new 1909 styles shown on this page, and a nice assortment of Oxford disc records, either the 7-inch, 10-inch or 12-inch (if you think you do not care for talking machines, remember, you have not heard the 1909 Oxford), and if you are not immensely pleased with it, if you do not find it a most delightful entertainer and the best investment you ever made, if you do not find the Oxford machine and records better than you can buy elsewhere for twice our price, just pack up the outfit and send it back to us. We will return all the money you paid us for it and any money you have paid for freight or express charges.

OXFORD TAPERING ARM DISC TALKING MACHINE

$14.90

1909 MODEL, TYPE J. F.

SPECIFICATIONS.

CABINET—Solid quarter sawed oak. Base 13 inches square; top, 11 inches square; height, 5⅞ inches. Extra fine hand rubbed finish.

HORN—Large and ornamental, of splendid acoustic properties and handsome flower shape. Diameter of bell, 18 inches; length, 14½ inches. Finish, dark red enamel with gold stripes.

TURN TABLE—10 inches in diameter, covered with green felt. Takes any record, either 7, 10 or 12-inch.

MOTOR—Same style and quality throughout as the motor of the type R. W. machine, but made with a single instead of double spring. Runs one 10-inch or two 7-inch records with one winding, and may be wound while running. Noiseless, smooth running and absolutely uniform in speed.

TAPERING ARM—Exactly the same style with which we equip all the Oxford Disc Talking Machines, the feature which, in connection with the perfect reproducer, gives to these machines their wonderful musical quality.

REPRODUCER—Oxford Special, exactly the same style with which we equip all 1909 Oxford Disc Talking Machines. Made with heavy mica diaphragm and positive screw needle clamp, the best reproducer made.

WEIGHT—17 pounds.

The Type J. F. Oxford Disc Talking Machine is almost as good as our highest priced model. The horn is a little shorter, and the machine requires winding a little oftener than the type R. W., but so far as the reproduction is concerned, it is hard to see any difference. Of course, it is not quite so large and not quite so handsome in appearance, but it reproduces the record just as perfectly as any machine, regardless of price, and it is exactly the same style, grade and quality of machine that retail dealers sell at $30.00; yet we ask you only $14.90.

No. 20T5075 Oxford Disc Talking Machine, Type J. F. Price.... **$14.90**

Shipping weight, 45 pounds.

OXFORD TAPERING ARM DISC TALKING MACHINE

1909 MODEL—TYPE R. W.

SPECIFICATIONS.

CABINET—Genuine quarter sawed oak; base, 12¾ inches square; top, 11½ inches square; height, 6½ inches, with extra fine hand-rubbed finish.

HORN—Latest flower shape, very ornamental, and of wonderful acoustic properties. Diameter of bell, 18 inches. Length, 16 inches. Finish, dark blue enamel with gold stripes.

TURN TABLE—10 inches in diameter, covered with green felt. Takes any size of record, either 7, 10, or 12-inch.

MOTOR—Finest possible workmanship throughout, suspended from top to avoid all vibration, absolutely noiseless, runs with perfect uniformity and steadiness, automatic governor, extra long worm gear. Start and stop lever and improved speed regulating device both on top of cabinet. Double spring, runs five 7-inch or three 10-inch records with one winding, and can be wound while running.

TAPERING ARM—Nickel plated and scientifically designed, so that it affords a passage for the sound waves from the reproducer to the horn entirely without obstruction, resulting in greater volume and better tone quality.

REPRODUCER — Oxford Special design, made with heavy mica diaphragm and positive screw clamp for needle. Accuracy and clearness of reproduction depend almost entirely upon the reproducer, and there is no reproducer made that excels the Oxford Special.

WEIGHT—21 pounds.

This splendid tapering arm talking machine, our very highest grade Oxford machine, is all that a talking machine ought to be. It is mechanically perfect, pleasing in appearance, and is an ideal musical instrument. As compared with other Oxford machines, types L. E., O. D. or J. F., this instrument is larger, plays longer with one winding, and because of the larger horn, the volume of sound is somewhat greater, and the tone is a little more full and round. The machine, as a whole, presents an even more handsome and ornamental appearance than any of the lower priced models.

No. 20T5076 Oxford Disc Talking Machine, Type R. W. Price.... **$18.85**

Shipping weight, 50 pounds.

$18.85

THE HARVARD JUNIOR TALKING MACHINE $4.40

Uses Either Columbia or Edison Standard Size Wax Cylinder Records.

1907 MODEL $4.40

THE NEW HARVARD JR. TALKING MACHINE is a strictly high class talking machine for reproducing standard size wax cylinder records. It is a thoroughly well made machine and not to be compared in any way with the cheap machines which have been so extensively advertised recently. It is a high class machine, made in America, made by expert and experienced workmen in one of the largest and most successful talking machine factories in the world. It is made of good materials throughout, fitted with a high class spring motor, with machine cut gears, everything about it strong and substantial.

PATENT FEED DEVICE. This machine is made with patent feed device which holds the reproducer firmly in place as it travels along over the surface of the record. There are cheap talking machines made without feed device, and with such machines the reproducer slips and slides off the surface of the record, but this trouble is entirely prevented in the Harvard Jr. Talking Machine, as the reproducer is held firmly and guided in its course over the surface of the record by the patent feed device, exactly the same as the highest priced machines. This machine is made with heavy, solid and substantial iron base, finished in black enamel, with gold stripe decorations. It is made with standard size tapered mandrel, and will use any standard size of wax cylinder record, Columbia, Edison, or any other standard make.

THE REPRODUCTION OF THE HUMAN VOICE or of instrumental music, as rendered by the Harvard Jr. Talking Machine, is just exactly as good as with machines costing ten and fifteen times the price which we ask for this machine. It is made with a high grade, aluminum, style D 1 reproducer, with mica diaphragm and Brazilian sapphire reproducing point. It is equipped with black and gold horn with large extra wide bell, the body of the horn made of the best sheet steel, with fine black enamel finish, the bell made of solid brass, highly polished, giving the machine a most handsome and ornamental appearance. The tone qualities of this large black and gold horn are unexcelled, adding greatly to the volume of sound and naturalness and sweetness of tone.

UNDERSTAND, the Harvard Jr. Talking Machine is not a toy, it is a high class machine. A machine that cannot be purchased in the ordinary market at less than double our price. Made of good materials all the way through, strong and substantial, easy to operate, made with fine clock work motor, automatic feed device and extra large black and gold horn.

No. 21G103 The Harvard Jr. Talking Machine, complete, just as illustrated and described above, with large mica diaphragm, D 1 reproducer, and special large size black and gold horn. Shipping weight, 18 pounds. Price (without records)............**$4.40**

For records suitable for this machine see the list of genuine Columbia XP and P Records on pages 29 and 30.

THE No. 9 HARVARD SPECIAL TONE ARM DISC TALKING MACHINE $18.50

This machine uses any size or any make of standard disc records, including the Harvards and Columbias, complete lists of which are shown on pages 26 and 29.

THE TONE ARM TALKING MACHINE represents the very highest development of for the reproduction of sound. The hollow tone arm, combined with the wide bell flower horn, gives to the reproduction a beauty and naturalness of tone, a mellowness and genuine musical quality absolutely unequaled by talking machines of other types.

MUSICAL RECORDS are reproduced by this new machine more perfectly and more true to the original music than has ever been possible with machines of the older styles. The volume of sound, the fullness and roundness of tone resulting from this combined use of the new tone arm principle and the improved design flower horn is a revelation to those accustomed to talking machines of the ordinary style.

LATEST SOUND ANALYZING REPRODUCER. This talking machine is equipped with the new sound analyzing reproducer or sound box, made with extra heavy mica diaphragm, and equipped with the Automatic Needle Clamp, by which needles are inserted or removed simply by pressing a small lever, a great improvement over the old style thumb screw arrangement.

THE No. 9 HARVARD SPECIAL TONE ARM TALKING MACHINE is equipped with a powerful spring motor, strongly and accurately constructed; made with fine machine cut gears, the latest governing device and the most approved style of speed regulating mechanism, a motor that is absolutely guaranteed in every respect. THE CABINET is made from solid quarter sawed oak, of plain but elegant design, strong, substantial and of handsome appearance. The cabinet measures 12½ inches by 12½ inches by 8 inches. The turn table is 10 inches in diameter, and the large flower horn beautifully finished in black japan with gold stripes, is 17¾ inches long and the diameter is 19 inches. Shipping weight, 50 pounds.

No. 21G290 The No. 9 Harvard Special Tone Arm Disc Talking Machine, complete just as illustrated and described above. Price (without records)...............**$18.50**

IMPROVED 1907 MODEL

THE HARVARD SENIOR TALKING MACHINE

A REGULAR $20.00 OUTFIT FOR 12.30

With Extra Large Flower Horn and Folding Horn Stand.

THE HARVARD SENIOR TALKING MACHINE is an exceedingly handsome machine, thoroughly well made in every respect and perfectly finished. The operating power is furnished by a powerful spring motor guaranteed not to get out of order. The gears and pinions are all machine cut, thus insuring perfect accuracy of action. The governor and tension screws effectively maintain the speed at an absolutely uniform rate. Large size reproducer, extra loud, made from aluminum, with sapphire reproducing point and latest improved mica diaphragm.

THIS TALKING MACHINE is substantially mounted on a handsome oak base with highly finished bent oak cover with handle, thus forming in itself a convenient and effective carrying case for the machine.

THE BIG HANDSOME FLOWER HORN with which the Harvard Senior Machine is equipped, adds immensely to the beauty and appearance of this outfit, and gives to the reproduction a tone quality, a genuine musical quality, heretofore possessed only by the highest priced machines. Not until you have heard this outfit can you appreciate the wonderful power, the softness, the sweetness and the volume of sound, the marvelously exact reproduction of the human voice and instrumental music of all kinds, even the largest bands and orchestras. It sings, it talks, it plays, it laughs, and all so naturally that it seems impossible that it can be a mere machine.

The GRAPHOPHONE

Greatest Entertainer in the World.

Nothing equals the talking machine as an entertainer. It brings to your home the same musicians, the same entertainers, the same great bands and orchestras that amuse, delight and entertain great audiences in our most famous theaters. You can sing to its accompaniment, you can dance to its music, you can play to its songs.

No. 21G109 Harvard Senior Talking Machine, complete just as described and illustrated above, with genuine D 1 reproducer, extra large flower horn, folding horn stand and handsome oak cover. Shipping weight, 40 pounds. Price (without records)............**$12.30**

See pages 29 and 30 for list of Columbia XP and P Records, the best records made for use with this machine.

FOR THE No. 5 HARVARD DISC TALKING MACHINE

THE No. 5 HARVARD DISC TALKING MACHINE IS A GOOD, RELIABLE MACHINE AT A VERY LOW PRICE. IT IS EQUIPPED WITH A LARGE BLACK AND GOLD WIDE BELL HORN. THE BODY OF THE HORN IS MADE FROM THE BEST SHEET STEEL, FINISHED IN BLACK JAPAN, AND THE BELL IS MADE FROM SOLID BRASS, HIGHLY POLISHED.

THE SOUND BOX **is the latest style of sound analyzing reproducer,** made with extra heavy mica diaphragm and automatic needle clamp, by means of which the needles are inserted or removed simply by pressing a small lever.

THE SWINGING ARM **and the stationary arm or bracket are made from aluminum,** in a beautiful and highly ornamental design.

THE CABINET **is made throughout from solid oak with dovetailed corners,** strongly and substantially made. This machine is operated by a powerful spring motor, made from brass and steel, all gears machine cut, equipped with automatic governor, the latest stop and start device and speed regulating screw, and is entirely enclosed within the cabinet in such a way that it is protected from dust or injury of any kind.

The cabinet measures 10 inches by 10 inches by 8 inches. The horn is 21 inches long, and the diameter of the bell is 12 inches. The turn table is 10 inches in diameter.

This machine uses any size or any make of standard disc records, including the Oxfords and the Columbias, complete lists of which will be found on pages 26 and 29.

No. 21G280 No. 5 Harvard Disc Talking Machine, complete with black and gold horn, sound analyzing reproducer, etc., just as illustrated and described above. Price.................................... **$9.90**
Shipping weight, 28 pounds.

IN DESIGNING THE No. 6 HARVARD

Disc Talking Machine, we have had in mind only the production of a thoroughly dependable, reliable and efficient talking machine AT THE LOWEST POSSIBLE COST, and this machine at $14.00 will give just as good satisfaction, will last just as long and prove just as thoroughly dependable in every way as machines ordinarily sold at from $25.00 to $30.00.

No. 21G283
Price, $14.00

This machine uses any of the standard makes of disc records in any size, including the Harvards and the Columbias. See pages 26 to 29 for complete list of these records.

BUYS THE No. 6 HARVARD DISC TALKING MACHINE

THE MOTOR **with which the No. 6 Harvard Disc Talking Machine is equipped, is an extra powerful clock work motor,** made throughout from brass and the best quality of steel, carefully and accurately constructed, strong and powerful, made with machine cut gears, automatic governor, the latest style of stop and start arrangement, the best speed regulator and is fully guaranteed.

THE LARGE FLOWER HORN **with which this machine is equipped, possesses, to an unusual degree, the magnificent accoustic or tone qualities which are peculiar to the latest type of flower horns.** The unusual musical qualities of the flower horn, its ability to reproduce sound more absolutely true to the original music, is due to the peculiar curves and the extra wide flaring bell, which avoids the usual retardation of the sound waves, thereby giving a deep, clear and natural tone to every note.

THE CABINET **is made from solid quarter sawed oak, of plain but elegant design,** with dovetailed corners, a strong, substantial cabinet in every way. **The swinging arm** and the stationary arm or bracket are handsomely designed and made from aluminum. **The sound box** is the latest type of sound analyzing reproducer, the same sound box that we use on all of our Harvard Disc Talking Machines, the best sound box that can be made. **The turn table** is 10 inches in diameter, and the flower horn is 17 inches long and 19 inches in diameter.

No. 21G283 No. 6 Harvard Disc Talking Machine, complete with 17x19-inch flower horn, beautifully finished in maroon enamel with gold stripes, and sound analyzing reproducer, just as described and illustrated above. Shipping weight, 30 pounds. Price.................... **$14.00**

COLUMBIA TYPE Q SPECIAL GRAPHOPHONE

This beautifully finished and thoroughly practical home entertainment graphophone is the regular genuine Columbia Phonograph Company's Type Q Special, made with large, heavy, substantial nickel plated and highly ornamental metal base, which not only adds to the attractive appearance of the machine, but gives it greater weight and stability, contributing to steadiness and thereby increasing the efficiency of the machine.

A fine aluminum horn, 14 inches in length, with 7-inch bell, increases the volume of sound and very greatly improves the tone.

LATEST STYLE D ALUMINUM REPRODUCER **made extra large, fitted with indestructible mica diaphragm and Brazilian pebble reproducing point,** exactly the same as furnished with wax cylinder machines costing two or three times the price we ask for this outfit, enables this machine to reproduce all styles of wax cylinder records just as well as the higher priced machines.

No. 21G176 Columbia Type Q Special Graphophone, complete, with nickel plated ornamental base, 14-inch aluminum horn and style D aluminum reproducer, just as shown in the illustration. Shipping weight, 16 pounds. Price.................................... **$8.40**

REMEMBER, **when you have bought $25.00 worth of goods or more from us, you get your choice of many valuable articles free, as shown in our new Profit Sharing Book.**

200 WONDERFUL COLORED STEREOSCOPIC VIEWS AND STEREOSCOPE FREE

Here is an opportunity for any customer of ours any where to secure a fine big set of 200 Colored Stereoscopic Views and a high grade hard wood Stereoscope free, and thus secure many hours' enjoyment and a liberal education. This big set of Colored Stereoscopic Views and Scope is given free by us to any customer in exchange for only $25.00 in Profit Sharing Certificates. We do not know of any more liberal method by which we can show our appreciation of the patronage our customers send us than that of our newly revised and enlarged Profit Sharing Plan, by which we share the profits of this business with our customers. Every customer of ours is practically a partner in this business, for the reason that every time a customer sends us an order, the day his order reaches us we send him a Profit Sharing Certificate for the full amount of money sent us, and when he has saved Profit Sharing Certificates amounting to a total of $25.00 or more he then can have his choice from a vast variety of rich, valuable Profit Sharing Articles, which we give our customers free in exchange for them.

When you receive this big set of Colored Stereoscopic Views and Scope which we give free in exchange for only $25.00 in Profit Sharing Certificates, you will be more than delighted with them, you will say that we have been wonderfully liberal in sharing our profits with you, and certainly you will feel as thousands of our customers have felt, that under the terms of this liberal Profit Sharing Plan you can well afford to send to us for practically everything you need. If you will always consult the pages of this Big Catalogue, you will be astonished to learn how much we can save you in the course of the year, and you will be surprised to learn, if you send to us for the goods you need, how quickly you will be enabled to secure Profit Sharing Certificates sufficient in volume to entitle you not only to this big set of 200 Colored Stereoscopic Views, but your choice of many others of the hundreds of rich, valuable Profit Sharing Articles, which we give free in exchange for Profit Sharing Certificates, as explained in the pages of our Big Free Profit Sharing Book.

GRAPHOPHONE DEPARTMENT.

OUR $5.00 GRAPHOPHONE TALKING MACHINE.

THIS IS A GENUINE TYPE A Q COLUMBIA GRAPHOPHONE, made by the Columbia Phonograph Co., of New York and London, and uses the regular Columbia Phonograph Co.'s standard size wax cylinder records.

THIS GRAPHOPHONE, as shown in the illustration, is one of the latest 1905 styles, made with clockwork spring motor enclosed in a dustproof metal barrel. It is provided with a speed regulator and leveling screw and has a high grade governor for maintaining a

UNIFORM SPEED,

just the same as furnished with the highest grade talking machines.

A NEW AND IMPROVED FEED SCREW DEVICE carries the reproducer along over the surface of the record, holding it firmly in place and preventing it from slipping or injuring the record.

THE LARGE SIZE ALUMINUM REPRODUCER, made with mica diaphragm, is securely attached to the 10-inch japanned amplifying horn, and will reproduce standard size wax cylinder records with the most wonderful clearness and fidelity. Uses any standard size wax cylinder records.

No. 21C102 Price, complete, without records........ $5.00

AQ GRAPHOPHONE AND SIX COLUMBIA RECORDS $5.90

No. 21C103 When sorting out our enormous stock of standard size genuine Columbia records to make up into collections of twelve, twenty-five and fifty, as explained on page 382, we made up a large quantity into collections of six, little assortments of extra nice records, and we now offer the A Q Graphophone, as shown above, together with one of these extra good collections of six records, for only $5.90, thus presenting an exceptional opportunity for you to get a complete outfit for very little money.

Remember, the outfit is complete, the A Q Graphophone and six genuine Columbia records, all different. Price........ $5.90

THE COLUMBIA TYPE Q GRAPHOPHONE AT $7.50.

THIS IS THE COLUMBIA PHONOGRAPH CO.'S GENUINE TYPE Q MACHINE, one of the most perfectly constructed talking machines ever placed on the market for so low a price.

$7.50

THIS MACHINE will run the regular standard size wax cylinder records just as perfectly as the higher priced machines and it is especially well suited for home entertainment purposes.

THE CAREFULLY CONSTRUCTED SPRING MOTOR which operates this graphophone is encased in a dustproof barrel, and the high grade governor, with latest style speed regulator, insures perfect uniformity of speed.

THE REPRODUCER, made with best mica diaphragm and sapphire reproducing point, is detachable and reproduces the musical and talking records as perfectly as many machines costing two and three times as much. We particularly recommend this graphophone to anyone desiring a strictly high grade instrument for home amusement at a very moderate price. We call your special attention to the possibility of making up a very moderate priced graphophone outfit by purchasing this little machine and an assortment of twelve, twenty-five or fifty of the Columbia Phonograph Co.'s records, which we are now selling in lots of 50 at 15 cents each, as explained on page 382.

No. 21C110 Type Q Graphophone, complete with 10-inch japanned horn and high grade aluminum reproducer, but without records. Price........ $7.50

RECORDS MUST BE PURCHASED EXTRA, and this machine will use either the XP records, illustrated and described on pages 380 and 381, or the Columbia records, which we are now offering, while they last, in lots of 50 at 15 cents each, as explained on page 382.

A LARGE AMPLIFYING HORN makes a wonderful difference in the effect produced with a graphophone. By attaching a large amplifying horn to a graphophone, you increase its efficiency 50 per cent. If you buy either the $7.50, $8.60 or $20.00 graphophone, we would suggest in addition that you order an amplifying horn, of which we give a selection on page 378. You can hardly appreciate what a difference in the volume of sound an amplifying horn produces until you have made the trial. It is the cheapest way of making a high grade graphophone out of a cheap machine.

RECORDS AT 15 CENTS.

At 15 cents each, in lots of 50, we sell Genuine Columbia Standard Size Wax Cylinder Records suitable for use with any graphophone described on this page. For full information regarding this

GREAT RECORD SALE SEE PAGE 382.

$8.60 BUYS OUR SPECIAL HOME TALKING MACHINE.

THIS BEAUTIFULLY FINISHED and thoroughly practicable home entertainment graphophone is made expressly for us by the Columbia Phonograph Co., of New York and London, and we offer it to our customers as a talking machine which is more brilliant in its reproduction and in every way better than any other low priced machine on the market today.

$8.60

CAREFULLY MADE THROUGHOUT, with powerful clockwork spring motor, perfectly adjusted governor for maintaining an absolutely uniform speed of reproduction, and high grade aluminum reproducer with French diaphragm glass.

THE HEAVILY NICKEL PLATED and highly ornamental base and the large 14-inch aluminum amplifying horn, finished in the natural silvery color of aluminum, make this machine in every respect a little beauty, a machine that will brighten the home, entertain yourself, your family and your friends and keep you in touch with the best and latest music of the finest bands and orchestras and the most celebrated public singers. Uses standard size wax cylinder records.

No. 21C115 The Home Graphophone, complete with nickel plated ornamental metal base, 14-inch aluminum amplifying horn and reproducer, just as shown in our illustration, but without records. $8.60

As a machine for home amusement or parlor entertainment, where a low priced graphophone is desired, there is no talking machine that will answer the purpose better or give better satisfaction than this, our special $8.60 Home Talking Machine. In the first place, it is a strictly high grade machine, well made, perfectly constructed, with all improvements, and with the 14-inch aluminum amplifying horn which is included, gives a wonderful volume of sound. In the second place, it is a very handsome machine, and will prove an ornament as well as a source of entertainment in any home.

When you consider that you can buy 50 different records and selections, the very best musical and talking records, for only $7.50, 15 cents each in lots of 50, and when you can get a full sized, substantial, perfectly operating graphophone from $5.00 up, there seems to be no reason why everyone should not take advantage of these offerings.

See page 382 for our wonderful offer on the regular Columbia records.

THE TYPE AT COLUMBIA GRAPHOPHONE FOR $20.00

RUNS STANDARD SIZE WAX CYLINDER RECORDS.

THIS HIGH GRADE COLUMBIA GRAPHOPHONE is an ideal machine for home entertainment, made with all the latest improvements, constructed with a view to strength and durability, and at the same time with a view to beauty and elegance of design, which makes it an ornament to any parlor.

THE REPRODUCER furnished with this A T Graphophone is the Columbia Phonograph Co.'s latest production, the D reproducer, with indestructible diaphragm, made of built-up mica, 1¼ inches in diameter, furnished with highest grade genuine sapphire reproducing point. In volume, sweetness and naturalness of tone, this machine exceeds any wax cylinder talking machine made.

An extra powerful tandem motor is furnished with this machine, made with the most perfect governor and speed regulating device, insuring perfect reproduction, and it runs five records with one winding. The cabinet is constructed from solid quarter sawed oak, of elegant design and beautifully finished.

YOU CAN MAKE YOUR OWN RECORDS with this machine, as we furnish with each one the latest improved recorder, and half the pleasure in owning a graphophone is derived from record making. Successful record making cannot be accomplished without a machine that is as perfect in its operation as a watch, and this graphophone fulfills all requirements.

With this A T Columbia Graphophone you have an additional opportunity for entertainment and instruction, for the reason that you can make your own records. You can put on a blank record and have any one sing or talk into the machine, and then keep this record indefinitely and reproduce it as often as you care to. Just think of preserving the voices of each and every one in the family, and what a pleasure it would be to listen to these voices and reproduce these records in after years.

If you are willing to invest as much as $20.00 in a graphophone, we especially recommend the purchase of this machine. It is a strictly high grade graphophone, beautifully built in a handsome, solid quarter sawed oak cabinet, with a beautiful bent oak cover to protect it from dust and dirt when the machine is not in use. All of the operating parts are thoroughly protected, the machine throughout is built extra strong and durable and runs five records with one winding. With each machine we include a D reproducer, the latest improved recorder for making records, and a 14-inch aluminum horn, exactly as illustrated.

No. 21C120 Columbia A T Graphophone, complete with D reproducer, recorder and 14-inch aluminum horn, but without records. Price........ $20.00

For list of XP records suitable for this machine see pages 380 and 381.
For price of blank records see No. 21C875, page 378.

$8.75 BUYS THE HARVARD DISC TALKING MACHINE.

THIS TALKING MACHINE uses the wonderful disc records, the most marvelously realistic reproductions of sound ever made. This machine is strictly high grade in every respect, made from the very best materials, constructed in the most careful, accurate and substantial manner, exactly the same machine that is being sold today by other dealers for $15.00, and never before sold for less than $15.00. THIS DISC TALKING MACHINE is made with extra powerful clockwork spring motor, made with machine cut bevels and gears, and an improved form of governor, insuring an absolutely uniform rate of speed. THE MECHANISM is entirely enclosed within the case in such a way that it is perfectly protected from dust or injury and will require practically no attention whatever. THE CABINET is strongly and substantially constructed from solid oak made in a very handsome design and finely finished.

THE SOUND BOX, also known as the reproducer, is of an improved type, made with the latest mica diaphragm, producing a volume of sound combined with a fullness and roundness of tone which is a revelation to those accustomed to the ordinary wax cylinder talking machines. This talking machine uses THE NEW PROCESS DISC RECORDS, THE GREATEST IMPROVEMENT IN RECORD MAKING SINCE THE INVENTION OF TALKING MACHINES.

THE DISC RECORDS ARE LOUDER AND CLEARER, and the reproduction is more perfect and more absolutely true to the original sound than has ever before been produced by any process. Those who have been accustomed to hearing the ordinary talking machine and the ordinary wax cylinder records will be astounded when listening for the first time to the latest new process disc records as used by this and our other disc machine.

FOR PUBLIC EXHIBITION WORK the disc machine is the only machine that should ever be used, as it is the only talking machine which reproduces the human voice, bands, orchestras and other instrumental music with sufficient volume, musical quality and absolutely perfect fidelity. THIS TALKING MACHINE WITH THE NEW PROCESS HARVARD OR COLUMBIA DISC RECORDS MUST BE HEARD TO BE APPRECIATED. It is impossible for anyone not having heard these wonderful machines to appreciate in any way the marvelous results which they give.

No. 21C207 Harvard Disc Talking Machine, complete, as shown in illustration, with 16-inch japanned horn, improved sound box and 100 needles. Price.............. **$8.75**

THE HARVARD TALKING MACHINE USES THE 7-INCH HARVARD RECORDS, 7-INCH OR 10-INCH COLUMBIA RECORDS, OR ANY OTHER MAKE OF 7-INCH OR 10-INCH DISC RECORDS.

COMPLETE PUBLIC EXHIBITION OUTFIT FOR $18.25.

REALIZING THE SUPERIORITY of the disc machine over all other types of talking machines and realizing also that the disc machine is the only talking machine suitable for public exhibition work, no other machine being sufficiently loud, clear and perfect in its reproduction of musical sounds, we recommend that for public exhibition work a disc machine be used in all cases. At $18.25 we furnish a complete public exhibition outfit, an outfit which we know from practical experience in this line of work will meet all requirements for the public exhibitor and prove a profitable business investment.

THIS COMPLETE PUBLIC EXHIBITION TALKING MACHINE OUTFIT AT $18.25 includes everything necessary for public exhibition work, and consists of the following items: One improved Harvard Disc Talking Machine, the same as shown in the above illustration and described under No. 21C207; Twenty-four Genuine Harvard Improved 7-inch Disc Records, your own selection, see page 379. Five Hundred Posters, large size; One Thousand Admission Tickets; One Fine Rubber Printing Outfit with movable type, for filling in dates, etc.

No. 21C208 Complete Disc Talking Machine Exhibition Outfit. Price........ .... **$18.25**

YOU CAN MAKE BIG MONEY with one of these outfits, giving entertainments in churches, school houses, concert halls, etc. It is so loud and clear that it is also suitable for outdoor use and will prove a profitable venture at picnics and other out of door gatherings.

A $12.00 GRAPHOPHONE FOR $8.40.

THIS IS A REGULAR COLUMBIA PHONOGRAPH CO.'S HIGH GRADE $12.00 GRAPHOPHONE NEVER BEFORE SOLD BY ANY DEALER IN THE WORLD FOR LESS THAN $12.00. OUR PRICE, $8.40

THIS GRAPHOPHONE IS THE REGULAR TYPE B X, exactly the same as furnished by the Columbia Phonograph Co., and by all dealers in talking machines at $12.00, except that instead of the little 10-inch horn which all other dealers furnish with this machine at $12.00 we furnish a LARGE CONCERT SIZE, 26-inch Japanned Amplifying Horn with 12-inch bell and folding japanned horn stand, this horn and stand alone being sold by other dealers at from $1.00 to $2.00.

THIS COLUMBIA PHONOGRAPH CO.'S BX GRAPHOPHONE is an exceedingly handsome machine, thoroughly well made in every respect and perfectly finished. The operating power is furnished by a powerful spring motor guaranteed not to get out of order. THE GEARS AND PINIONS are all machine cut, thus insuring perfect accuracy of action. THE GOVERNOR AND TENSION SCREW effectively maintain the speed at an absolutely uniform rate. LARGE SIZE REPRODUCER extra loud, made from aluminum, with sapphire reproducing point and latest improved mica diaphragm.

THIS GRAPHOPHONE is substantially mounted on a handsome oak base with highly finished bent oak cover with handle, thus forming in itself a convenient and effective carrying case for the machine.

THIS B X GRAPHOPHONE AND 50 RECORDS **$14.95**

NO BETTER, HANDSOMER OR MORE DURABLE talking machine was ever before offered by any dealer for less than $12.00, and our special price of $8.40 represents the very lowest price at which a strictly high grade first quality reliable talking machine has ever been sold.

No. 21C216 Columbia Phonograph Co.'s B X Graphophone, complete with aluminum reproducer, mammoth 26-inch amplifying horn and folding horn stand. Price...... **$8.40**

No. 21C217 COMPLETE B X GRAPHOPHONE OUTFIT, consisting of Columbia B X Graphophone with 26-inch Amplifying Horn, japanned stand, large aluminum reproducer, just as shown in illustration and 50 genuine Columbia standard size wax cylinder records, as illustrated and described on page 382. Shipping weight, 48 pounds.
Price for the entire outfit, all complete........................ **$14.95**

GRAPHOPHONES THAT USE STANDARD SIZE WAX CYLINDER RECORDS.

$7.50 COLUMBIA Type Q GRAPHOPHONE

No. 21E110 This is the genuine Type Q Graphophone, made by the Columbia Phonograph Company, one of the most perfectly constructed talking machines ever placed on the market at so low a price. This machine runs the regular standard size wax cylinder records just as perfectly as the higher priced machines, and is especially well suited for home entertainment purposes.

THE STRONGLY MADE SPRING MOTOR which operates the Q Graphophone, is enclosed in a dustproof barrel. Is made with a high grade governor, latest style speed regulator and is guaranteed to work perfectly. The reproducer is the latest style D, large sized aluminum reproducer, made with mica diaphragm and Brazilian pebble reproducing point.

THIS MACHINE REPRODUCES the standard size wax cylinder records just as perfectly as any talking machines costing three or four times as much.

Uses our 16-cent records, also the regular 25-cent Columbia XP records or any other make of standard size wax cylinder records.

No. 21E110 Price complete, with 10-inch japanned horn, and style D mica diaphragm aluminum reproducer. Shipping weight, 10 pounds.............. **$7.50**

COLUMBIA Type Q Special GRAPHOPHONE.

No. 21E116 Columbia Q Special Graphophone. This beautifully finished and thoroughly practical home entertainment graphophone is the regular genuine Columbia Phonograph Company's Type Q Special, made with large, heavy, substantial nickel plated and highly ornamental metal base, which not only adds to the attractive appearance of the machine, but gives it greater weight and stability, contributing to steadiness and thereby increasing the efficiency of the machine.

A fine aluminum horn 14 inches in length, with 7-inch bell, increases the volume of sound and very greatly improves the tone.

$8.40

LATEST STYLE D ALUMINUM REPRODUCER, made extra large, fitted with indestructible mica diaphragm and Brazilian pebble reproducing point, exactly the same as furnished with wax cylinder machines costing two or three times the price we ask for this outfit, enables this machine to reproduce all styles of wax cylinder records just as well as the higher priced machines.

No. 21E116 Our special price for the Type Q Special Graphophone complete, with nickel plated ornamental base, 14-inch aluminum horn and style D aluminum reproducer, just as shown in the illustration. Shipping weight, 16 pounds. Price.. **$8.40**

COLUMBIA Type AT GRAPHOPHONE,

Runs our 16-cent Records, also the Columbia XP 25-cent Records, or any other style or make of standard size wax cylinder records.

$20.00

This high grade Columbia Graphophone is an ideal machine for home entertainment, a genuine Columbia machine, made by the Columbia Phonograph Company, made with all the latest improvements, constructed with a view to strength and durability and at the same time with a view to beauty and elegance of design, making it an ornament to any parlor.

THE REPRODUCER furnished with the AT graphophone is the latest extra large style D aluminum reproducer, with indestructible built up mica diaphragm and genuine sapphire reproducing point.

An extra powerful triple spring motor is furnished with the AT machine, made with the most perfect governor and the latest speed regulator device, insuring perfect and natural reproduction, and this extra powerful motor enables the machine to run five records with one winding.

The cabinet is constructed from quarter sawed oak of elegant design, just as shown in our illustration, beautifully finished, first class workmanship throughout.

YOU CAN MAKE YOUR OWN RECORDS with this machine, as each machine comes complete with the latest improved recorder, and half the pleasure in owning a graphophone is derived from record making.

No. 21E120 Columbia AT Graphophone, complete with style D reproducer, 14-inch aluminum horn, handsome bent oak top (not shown in illustration) and latest style recorder. Shipping weight, 45 pounds. Price........................ **$20.00**

REMEMBER THAT ANY OF THESE MACHINES WILL USE OUR **16c RECORDS**

See pages 369 and 370 for particulars regarding Our Great Record Sale.

COLUMBIA Type AZ GRAPHOPHONE.

$25.00

Runs our 16-cent Records, also the Columbia XP 25-cent Records, or any other style of standard size wax cylinder records.

This new type of genuine Columbia Graphophone is similar to the type AT previously described, made with solid quarter sawed oak cabinet, with special hard oil rubbed finish, a most handsome and ornamental machine in every respect, furnished with fine solid oak bent top (not illustrated), completely protecting the machine from dust, dirt or injury of any kind; made with extra powerful double spring motor, running eight records with one winding. Workmanship and finish throughout the very best.

THE NEW LYRE SHAPED REPRODUCER is the special feature which distinguishes this machine from all other wax cylinder talking machines on the market. This new lyre shaped reproducer is the latest product of the Columbia Phonograph Company, a reproducer that is simply marvelous from a mechanical point of view and which reproduces any kind of standard size wax cylinder records without the slightest scratching or harsh metallic sound. This reproducer represents the acme of perfection in sound reproducing devices, works as smooth as velvet, producing a sweet, resonant and delightful tone.

REMEMBER, this machine, so far as the cabinet, the motor, the workmanship and general construction is concerned, is in quality exactly the same as the AT machine previously described, and its superiority over the AT machine lies simply in the new lyre shaped reproducer.

No. 21E125 Columbia Type AZ Graphophone, complete with lyre shaped reproducer, 14-inch aluminum horn, fine oak top (not shown in illustration). Price... **$25.00**

NOTE—No recorder is included with this machine. Shipping weight, 50 lbs.

COLUMBIA Type BE GRAPHOPHONE

$30.00

Runs our 16-cent Records, also the Columbia XP 25-cent Records, or any other style or make of standard size wax cylinder records.

This is the very latest and most improved style of genuine Columbia wax cylinder talking machine, embodying all the very latest improvements, including the **NEW STYLE FLOATING WEIGHT REPRODUCER.** This is the best reproducer ever made, being so constructed that the lever raises only the reproducer point from the record instead of the entire reproducer, thus making it impossible to harm the record in any way. This new style floating weight reproducer is extra loud, reproducing the record with greater volume of sound and greater clearness than any other reproducer made. The triple spring motor, extra powerful, runs eight records with one winding, and is made with the latest style of speed regulating device and governor. Made with extra long winding crank, special machine cut gears, in short, everything that will contribute to uniformity of speed, smoothness in operation, and freedom from liability to get out of order. Oil cups are located in the rear of the machine, through which every gear and bearing in the machine can be oiled without trouble.

THE CABINET is extra large and ornamental, of very handsome design, made from solid quarter sawed oak, beautifully finished, exactly as shown in our illustration, and in addition it is provided with a fine quarter sawed oak top or cover (not shown in the illustration.)

No. 21E131 COLUMBIA TYPE BE GRAPHOPHONE, complete with new floating weight reproducer, highest grade recorder, 14-inch brass horn, and ornamental quarter sawed oak cover (not shown in illustration, but is very handsome.) Shipping weight, 40 pounds. Price.................... **$30.00**

AMPLIFYING HORNS SOLID BRASS OR BLACK AND GOLD.

For other Horns, see page 364.

A large amplifying horn adds wonderfully to the volume of sound, improves the tone quality greatly and in every way increases the efficiency of any style of talking machine.

Our black and gold horns are made with sheet steel bodies, oxidized in black, and burnished brass bells, giving them an exceedingly handsome appearance, and the use of steel for the body enables us to sell them cheaper than the solid brass horns.

Our solid brass horns are made from brass throughout, the very finest horns it is possible to produce. In our opinion there is very little, if any, difference in the quality of reproduction or tone of the black and gold and solid brass horns, although many users consider the tone of the brass horn superior to the black and gold. **The volume of sound, purity and fullness of tone** is very largely influenced by the size of the bell, the very finest effects being produced by horns having the widest bells.

Regular Width Horns.

No. 21E350 These horns have bells of the ordinary width. The quality and workmanship are the very best.

Length, inches	Width of Bell, inches	Price, Solid Brass	Price, Black and Gold
18	7⅝	$0.63	$0.60
30	13¾	1.54	1.26
36	16⅛	2.73	2.38
42	16¾	3.50	3.15
48	20⅛	5.46	4.90
56	20⅛	6.44	5.60

Wide Horns.

No. 21E365 These wide bell horns have bells which are wider in proportion to the length than the preceding style and give a corresponding increase in volume and fullness of tone.

Length, inches	Width of Bell, inches	Price, Solid Brass	Price, Black and Gold
24	13¾	$1.40	$1.23
30	16⅛	2.10	1.75
36	20⅛	4.41	3.99
42	20⅛	4.90	4.55
56	23¾	9.10	8.04

THE A K DISC GRAPHOPHONE

THIS MACHINE IS ONE OF THE COLUMBIA PHONOGRAPH CO.'S

VERY LATEST PRODUCTIONS

$15.00

EMBODYING ALL OF THE FEATURES OF THE HIGHEST GRADE TALKING MACHINES AND YET SOLD AT A MODERATE PRICE.

IT IS MADE with extra powerful clockwork spring motor and contained in a fine oak cabinet of very handsome design.

THE SOUND BOX OR REPRODUCER is the very latest type concert style with improved knife edge bearings, heavy mica diaphragm, and is absolutely the highest grade sound box furnished with any talking machine, regardless of price.

THE ORNAMENTAL HORN SUPPORTING ARMS, which are detachable, are of very handsome design and made of aluminum, this metal being most perfectly adapted for this purpose.

THE BLACK AND GOLD HORN is the highest grade horn made for Disc Talking Machines, the body of this horn being made from fine sheet steel with black oxidized finish and the bell of polished brass, giving it a very ornamental appearance.

EITHER THE 7-INCH OR 10-INCH RECORDS MAY BE USED WITH THIS MACHINE, AND ON PAGES 383 AND 384 WE GIVE A VERY COMPLETE LIST OF SELECTIONS WHICH WE CAN FURNISH IN THESE MARVELOUS DISC RECORDS.

No. 21C230 The Columbia Phonograph Co.'s Type A K Disc Graphophone, complete with latest improved knife edge reproducer, 16-inch black and gold horn and 100 needles........ **$15.00**

No. 21C231 Type A K Columbia Disc Graphophone, equipped with 22-inch black and gold horn, otherwise same as described above. Price..... ...... **18.50**

THE A J DISC GRAPHOPHONE

AT **$20.00**

THE TYPE **A J DISC GRAPHOPHONE** IS MADE WITH DETACHABLE CABINET TOP, THUS GIVING EASY ACCESS TO THE MOTOR FOR THE PURPOSE OF OILING OR CLEANING. : : :

THE CLOCKWORK Spring Motor is extra powerful, made with the latest improved governor and most perfect speed regulator. It runs two 10-inch or three 7-inch records with one winding. We particularly recommend this A J Disc Machine either for home entertainment or for public exhibition work, as it has proven the most popular talking machine we have ever handled.

THIS DISC GRAPHOPHONE similar to the type A K described opposite, is a somewhat larger machine with a larger, heavier and more handsomely designed cabinet made from solid quarter sawed oak.

THE SOUND BOX OR REPRODUCER is the latest knife edge style, extra large size, made with mica diaphragm, and is the very highest grade sound box furnished with any talking machine, regardless of price.

The Wonderful Disc Records, the records which have created a sensation wherever heard, and made it possible to say that the talking machine has at last been perfected, are used with this machine.

SEE PAGES 383 AND 384 FOR SELECTIONS.
EITHER 7-INCH OR 10-INCH CAN BE USED.

No. 21C240 The Columbia Phonograph Co.'s Type A J Disc Graphophone, complete with knife edge reproducer, 16-in black and gold horn with polished brass bell and 100 needles. **$20.00**

No. 21C241 Type A J Columbia Disc Graphophone, same as described above, except that cabinet is more elaborate and more highly finished, making the machine very ornamental. Price.................. **$22.50**

No. 21C242 Type A J Columbia Disc Graphophone, same as described under No. 21C241, but equipped with large 22-inch black and gold horn. Price.................. **25.00**

THE A H DISC GRAPHOPHONE FOR $30.00

THE TYPE A H DISC GRAPHOPHONE IS THE VERY HIGHEST GRADE AUTOMATIC TALKING MACHINE MADE BY THE COLUMBIA PHONOGRAPH CO., and represents the highest degree of perfection yet attained in the making of talking machines.

THE CABINET IS EXTRA LARGE AND HEAVY OF A VERY HANDSOME AND ORNAMENTAL DESIGN, made from solid quarter sawed oak, and very finely finished throughout.

THE SOUND BOX IS THE VERY LATEST IMPROVED KNIFE EDGE PATTERN, extra large, with heavy mica diaphragm, the most perfect reproducer yet constructed.

THIS GRAPHOPHONE RUNS EITHER THE **7 OR 10-INCH DISC RECORDS,** A COMPLETE LIST OF WHICH YOU WILL FIND ON PAGES 383 AND 384.

THE POWERFUL DOUBLE SPRING MOTOR WITH SPECIAL GOVERNOR AND IMPROVED SPEED REGULATOR IS EASILY ACCESSIBLE FOR CLEANING AND OILING, AND RUNS THREE 10-INCH RECORDS, OR FIVE 7-INCH RECORDS WITH ONE WINDING.

The motor is absolutely noiseless. The only disc machine motor made which operates entirely without sound.

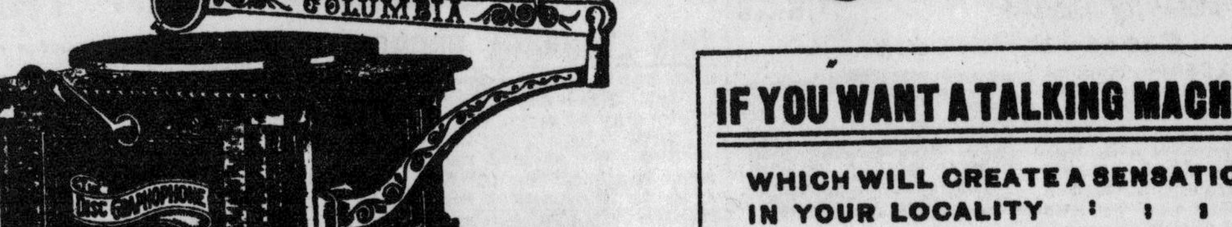

IF YOU WANT A TALKING MACHINE WHICH WILL CREATE A SENSATION IN YOUR LOCALITY : : : :

A Machine Which People Will Come Miles to Hear. Order This A H Machine and a Selection of 10-inch Records. . . . .

THE FINE BLACK AND GOLD HORN is of extra large size, being 22 inches long, with 11½-inch bell, the body of this horn being constructed from the finest quality sheet steel, oxidized in black, and the bell is made of extra heavy polished brass. This type of horn greatly improves the quality and sweetness of tone.

No. 21C250 The Columbia Phonograph Co.'s Type A H Graphophone, complete with the latest improved knife edge sound box, 22-inch black and gold horn and 100 needles. Price.................. **$30.00**

No. 21C251 Type A H Columbia Disc Graphophone, same as described above, but with extra large black and gold horn, 30 inches long, with 16½ inch bell. Price.................. **40.00**

No. 21C252 Type A H Columbia Disc Graphophone, same as described above, but with extra large 36-inch aluminum horn. Price.................. **45.00**

AMPLIFYING HORNS.
SOLID BRASS OR BLACK AND GOLD.

A large amplifying horn adds wonderfully to the volume of sound, improves the tone quality greatly and in every way increases the efficiency of any style of talking machine.

Our black and gold horns are made with sheet steel bodies, oxidized in black, and burnished brass bells, giving them an exceedingly handsome appearance, and the use of steel for the body enables us to sell them cheaper than the solid brass horns.

Our solid brass horns are made from brass throughout, the very finest horns it is possible to produce. In our opinion there is very little, if any, difference in the quality of reproduction or tone of the black and gold and solid brass horns, although many users consider the tone of the brass horn superior to the black and gold. The volume of sound, purity and fullness of tone is very largely influenced by the size of the bell, the very finest effects being produced by horns having the widest bells.

Regular Width Horns.

No. 21C350 These horns have bells of the ordinary width. The quality and workmanship are the very best.

Length, inches	Width of Bell, inches	Price, Solid Brass	Price, Black and Gold
18	7⅝	$0.63	$0.60
30	13¾	1.54	1.26
36	16½	2.73	2.38
42	16¾	3.50	3.15
48	20½	5.46	4.90
56	20½	6.44	5.60

Wide Horns.

No. 21C365 These wide bell horns have bells which are wider in proportion to the length than the preceding style, and give a corresponding increase in volume and fullness of tone.

Length, inches	Width of Bell, inches	Price, Solid Brass	Price, Black and Gold
24	13¾	$1.40	$1.23
30	16½	2.10	1.75
36	20½	4.41	3.99
42	20½	4.90	4.55
56	23¾	9.10	8.04

Extra Wide Flaring Horns.

No. 21C380 These extra wide flaring horns are the largest and finest horns made, regardless of price. In volume of sound and fullness of tone they are not equaled by any other horns made.

Length inches	Width of Bell inches	Price, Solid Brass	Price, Black and Gold
30	20½	$ 4.20	$ 3.85
42	23¾	8.54	7.35
56	28	13.30	12.25

Any of our horns can be used with either wax cylinder or disc machines of any make. A horn stand, as described below, is necessary with any of the above horns.

Folding Horn Stands.

No. 21C540 Horn Stand, black japanned, folds into small space, suitable for 30-inch and smaller horns. Price.......... 35c

No. 21C542 Imperial Horn Stand, a handsome and efficient folding stand, finely made throughout and nickel plated; adapted to any size horn up to 42-inch. Price.......... 82c

No. 21C544 No. 1 Horn Stand, our best stand, extra strong and heavy; adapted to any size horn, including the largest 48-inch and 56-inch; nickel plated; folds very compactly. Price.......... $1.40

Cases for Records.

No. 21C560 Record Boxes, for standard size wax cylinder records. Made of strong pasteboard, covered with imitation leather, affording a convenient means of keeping the records safe and easily accessible.

No. 1 size, holds 12 records. Price.......... 23c
No. 2 size, holds 24 records. Price.......... 40c

No. 21C565 Carrying Cases for Standard Size Wax Cylinder Records, black seal grain covering, with improved pegs for records, full nickeled trimmings, two snap locks and lock and key. Best record cases made.

No. 1, holds 24 standard size records. Price.. $2.00
No. 2, holds 36 standard size records. Price.. 2.25
No. 3, holds 72 standard size records. Price.. 3.40

Disc Record Cases.

No. 21C570 Disc Record Cases, strongly and substantially made from wood, covered with black seal grain imitation leather, nickel plated trimmings, two snap catches, lock and key and leather handle. Provided with numbered separators and numbered blank on inside of cover for list of selections, so any desired record may be instantly found.

No. 1, holds 50 7-inch disc records. Price.......... $1.35
No. 2, holds 50 10-inch disc records. Price.... 1.55

Miscellaneous.

No. 21C585 Recorder, for Q, QC, QQ, or our special Home Graphophone. Price.......... $2.50

No. 21C590 Recorder, for BX, AT, AO, or Gem Graphophone.......... $5.00

No. 21C595 Reproducer, for Q, QC, QQ, or our special Home Graphophone. Price.......... $2.50

No. 21C599 Reproducer, Style D, for any wax cylinder graphophone except Q, QC, QQ and our special Home, latest improved style, extra large, with built up mica diaphragm. Price.......... $5.00

SPECIAL OFFER: Send us your old reproducer and $3.00 in cash and we will send you this latest model improved "D" Reproducer.

No. 21C625 Diaphragm Glasses, best French glass. Price, per dozen, 30c; each.......... 4c

No. 21C628 Mica Diaphragms, for "D" reproducers only, best quality, built up. Price, each.. 19c

No. 21C632 Mica Diaphragms, for sound boxes of any style Disc Graphophone. Price, each.......... 10c

No. 21C640 Rubber Gaskets, for reproducers or recorders. Price, per set of three, ordinary size.. 5c
Per set of two, for large "D" reproducer.......... 4c

No. 21C650 Reproducer Ball, made of Brazilian pebble, but sold by many dealers as sapphire. Price, each.......... 20c

No. 21C651 Reproducer Ball, made of genuine sapphire, highest grade. Price, each.......... 75c

MISCELLANEOUS—Continued.

No. 21C660 Recorder Points, made of Brazilian pebble, but often sold as sapphire.
Price, each, in setting, flat edge.......... 52c
Price, each, in setting, cupped edge.......... 60c

No. 21C661 Recorder Points genuine sapphire, highest grade made.
Price, each, in setting, flat edge.......... $1.10
Price, each, in setting, cupped edge.......... 1.80

No. 21C670 Main Spring, single, for Q, QC, QQ, BX, AB and our special Home Graphophones. Price, each.......... 21c

State kind of Graphophone for which spring is wanted.

No. 21C672 Main Spring, single, for AT, AK, AJ and our $8.75 Disc Graphophones. Price, each.......... 55c

No. 21C674 Main Spring, single, for AH Graphophones. Price, each.......... 60c

No. 21C800 Speaking Tube, for use in record making, mohair covered, with spiral spring, lining and hard rubber mouthpiece; 22 inches long. Price 75c

No. 21C830 Camel's Hair Brushes, 1½ inches wide, for dusting records. Price, each.......... 15c

No. 21C850 Needle Box, two parts, for used and unused needles. Price, each.......... 15c

No. 21C875 Blank Cylinders, for record making. Standard size, same as P or XP records. Price, each.......... 15c

Needles at 4 Cents per 100.

No. 21C900 These Needles, for disc talking machines of any make, are made from cold drawn, oil tempered steel wire, and guaranteed to be the finest needles manufactured. Put up in envelopes of 100 each. Price, per 100.......... 4c

If by mail, postage extra, 2 cents.

Per 1,000.......... 37c

If by mail, postage extra, 8 cents.

No. 21C920 Rubber Hose, large size, for connecting large horns to any style talking machine. Price, per foot.......... 16c

No. 21C930 Rubber Hose, small size, for hearing tubes, etc. Price, per foot.......... 3c

NEW RECORDS EXCHANGED FOR OLD ONES

7-INCH COLUMBIA DISC RECORDS AT 25 CENTS (IN EXCHANGE)

10-INCH COLUMBIA DISC RECORDS AT 50 CENTS (IN EXCHANGE)

OUR NEW RECORD EXCHANGE PROPOSITION

ENABLES YOU TO KEEP UP YOUR ASSORTMENT OF RECORDS AT

ONE-HALF REGULAR COST

How to Get Genuine Columbia, Latest Improved, Brand New, 7-Inch Disc Records for 25 Cents Each.

For each new 7-inch Columbia record that you desire, send us one old or worn 7-inch record of either Columbia or Victor make and 25 cents in cash. In exchange for your old record and 25 cents we will send you one new 7-inch Columbia disc record, your own selection.

Remember, one old record and 25 cents cash buys one new record. Twelve old records and $3.00 cash buys twelve new records, and so on in the same way for any desired quantity, large or small.

How to Get Genuine Columbia, Latest Improved, Brand New, 10-Inch Disc Records for 50 Cents Each.

For each new 10-inch Columbia record that you desire, send us one old or worn 10-inch record of either Columbia or Victor make, and 50 cents in cash. In exchange for your old record, and 50 cents, we will send you one new 10-inch Columbia disc record, your own selection.

Remember, one old record and 50 cents cash buys one new record. Two old records and $1.00 in cash, buys two new records. Twelve old records and $6.00 cash, buys twelve new records, and so on in the same way for any desired quantity, large or small.

CONDITIONS OF THIS OFFER.

THIS EXCHANGE PROPOSITION makes it possible for you to keep up your supply with the latest, up to date, improved disc records, at just one-half the regular cost, but each and every exchange must be subject to the following rules and regulations:

1st. Each exchange must be complete in itself, and the worn records must reach us in good order. (They may be worn, but they must not be broken.)

2nd. The old records must be sent to us, CHARGES PREPAID.

3rd. We cannot receive any old records to be credited against future purchases, but the exchange must be complete and the transaction closed at the time the records are sent.

4th. We cannot make a cash allowance for old records under any circumstances. We accept old records only in accordance with the above proposition as part payment for an equal number of new records.

AS AN EXAMPLE: Suppose you have on hand twenty-four 10-inch disc records, either Columbia or Victor make, which have been used until they are no longer clear and satisfactory, send us these twenty-four old, worn records and $12.00 in cash (50 cents for each record), and we will send you in exchange twenty-four new Columbia 10-inch records, your own selection of subjects.

WHEN SENDING YOUR RECORDS TO US FOR EXCHANGE, be sure to pack them very securely, because we cannot allow credit for any records received broken. Be sure to put your name and address on the outside of the package (don't forget this) and mark the package, "Old records for exchange." If you send the old records to us by express, you can enclose your letter (telling us what records you want in exchange) with the package of records. But if you send your old records to us by mail, do not put your letter in the package; send your letter separately; just put your own name and address on the outside of the package. Don't fail to prepay all charges (express or postage) on records returned to us.

Be sure to put your name and address on the package and prepay the charges.

This proposition does not apply to the Harvard disc records. We cannot make any exchange proposition on Harvard disc records, owing to the exceedingly low price at which we sell them.

REMEMBER, we accept only Columbia disc or Victor records in part payment for new records as explained above.

ON XP OR OTHER WAX CYLINDER RECORDS WE DO NOT MAKE ANY EXCHANGE PROPOSITION. We cannot allow any credit whatever for wax cylinder records of any kind.

THE NEW LYRIC REPRODUCER

THE REPRODUCER is the most important part of a talking machine. The tone, the volume of sound, the clearness of reproduction, all depend upon the reproducer. No matter how perfect the machine may be in other respects, it cannot reproduce the record in the best possible way unless it is equipped with the very best reproducer.

THE IMPROVED LYRIC TONE REPRODUCER is the very latest and most perfect reproducer yet invented. It is made upon an entirely new scientific idea in the reproduction of sound, and results in greatly improved reproduction. If you have not heard the "New Lyric Tone" you have no idea how perfectly it is possible for a cylinder record graphophone to reproduce the human voice or instrumental music.

THIS ILLUSTRATION will give you some idea of the appearance of the new Lyric Tone Reproducer, which in its general construction is entirely different from all reproducers in use heretofore. It is made with the very highest grade genuine sapphire reproducing point, which by a most ingenious arrangement is kept pressed against the surface of the record at exactly the same tension all the time. All of the cylinder record graphophones described on this page, the Jewel at $20.00, the Leader at $30.00, and the Peerless at $40.00, are equipped with this magnificent new Lyric Tone Reproducer.

WE DO NOT SELL THIS REPRODUCER SEPARATELY, because it cannot be used on any of the ordinary types of machines, but is suitable only for use with the Jewel, the Leader and the Peerless machines; and these machines all come equipped with this reproducer.

UNDERSTAND, if you buy any one of the Cylinder Record Graphophones described on this page, the Jewel, the Leader or the Peerless, you get a machine equipped with the New Lyric Tone Reproducer.

COLUMBIA JEWEL LYRIC REPRODUCER GRAPHOPHONE

$20.00

THE COLUMBIA JEWEL GRAPHOPHONE TYPE BK is equipped with the Improved Lyric Tone Reproducer, exactly the same reproducer described and shown in the illustration on this page, made with genuine sapphire reproducing point. This high grade Columbia Jewel Graphophone is an ideal machine for home entertainment, a genuine Columbia Graphophone of the very latest type constructed with a view to strength and durability, and at the same time with a view to beauty and elegance of design.

AN EXTRA POWERFUL TANDEM SPRING MOTOR furnishes the power for operating this Columbia Jewel Graphophone, and this motor is made with the latest type of governor and speed regulator, insuring perfect and natural reproduction, made with machine cut gears, finely adjusted and guaranteed in every respect.

THE CABINET is made from quarter sawed oak, finely finished, with the best workmanship throughout and provided with a handsome bent oak top or cover, as shown in our illustration.

No. 21G121 Columbia Jewel Graphophone, type B K, complete, with Lyric Tone Reproducer, 14-inch brass horn and bent oak cover. Plays Columbia, XP, P or Edison Cylinder records. Price ....(Shipping weight, 45 pounds.)............$20.00

COLUMBIA LEADER LYRIC REPRODUCER GRAPHOPHONE

$30.00

THE COLUMBIA LEADER GRAPHOPHONE, TYPE B E, for cylinder records, is equipped with the new Lyric Tone Reproducer, the very highest grade and the most perfect reproducer made, exactly as described and shown in the illustration on this page. This reproducer works perfectly with any style or make of wax cylinder record, reproducing all records with greater volume of sound, greater clearness and with more natural tone than any other reproducer made.

THE MOTOR in the Columbia Leader Graphophone is an extra powerful triple spring clock work motor, guaranteed to run four records with one winding and made with the latest style of speed regulating device and governor. This motor has extra long winding crank, special machine cut gears, in short everything that will contribute to uniformity of speed, smoothness of operation and freedom from liability to get out of order.

THE CABINET is extra large and ornamental, of very handsome design, made from solid quarter sawed oak, beautifully finished, with fine bent oak cover, just as shown in our illustration. An extra sensitive recorder, made of the same style and upon the same principle as the new Lyric Tone Reproducer, is furnished with this machine, enabling the user to make his own records and greatly increasing the pleasure to be derived from a talking machine.

No. 21G126 The Columbia Leader Lyric Reproducer Graphophone, type B E, complete, just as shown in our illustration, with Lyric Tone Reproducer, extra sensitive recorder, handsome bent oak cover and 14-inch solid brass horn. Plays Columbia, XP, P or Edison cylinder records. Price..........$30.00
Shipping weight, 40 pounds.

COLUMBIA PEERLESS LYRIC REPRODUCER GRAPHOPHONE

$40.00

THE COLUMBIA PEERLESS GRAPHOPHONE, TYPE B F, like the Jewel and the Leader, is equipped with the new Lyric Tone Reproducer, with genuine sapphire reproducing point, but is a larger, more ornamental and more powerful machine. The cabinet is made of solid quarter sawed oak, of very elaborate and handsome design, beautifully finished, highly polished, making the machine an ornament to any parlor. The powerful quadruple spring motor is suspended from the top of the cabinet in such a way as to completely avoid all vibration, and is so constructed that it can be wound while playing. Provided with four powerful springs, this motor will play eight or more of the ordinary cylinder records with one winding. It is provided with extra long winding crank, accurately cut gears, the most approved style of speed regulating and governing devices, provided with easily accessible oil cups, in short, a motor that will give good results all the time with the least possible danger of becoming out of order.

AN EXTRA SENSITIVE RECORDER with genuine sapphire recording point is furnished with this graphophone, enabling the owner of this Peerless machine to make records as well as to reproduce those which may be purchased.

No. 21G128 Columbia Peerless Lyric Tone Reproducer, type B F, Graphophone complete, with Lyric Tone Reproducer, extra sensitive recorder, bent oak cover and 14-inch brass horn. Plays Columbia, XP, P, BC or Edison cylinder records. Price ...$40.00
Shipping weight, 50 pounds.

NEW COLUMBIA ALUMINUM TONE ARM GRAPHOPHONES CHAMPION, $30.00 STERLING, 45.00

COLUMBIA CHAMPION DISC GRAPHOPHONE.

THE NEW ALUMINUM TONE ARM GRAPHOPHONES represent the latest and highest development in disc talking machines. In these machines the sound is transmitted directly from the reproducer, through the hollow aluminum tone arm, to the horn, securing in this way the greatest possible volume of sound, the greatest beauty and naturalness of tone, and preventing, to a very large extent, the scratching sound sometimes noticed with machines of other styles of construction.

THE MOTOR is noiseless in operation, made with the most perfect speed regulator and governor, fine machine cut gears, made to run noiselessly, uniformly, and so simple in construction that repairs of any kind are very seldom necessary, and can be wound while playing.

THE CABINET is made from solid quarter sawed oak, with dark finish, highly polished, handsome and ornamental design. It is fitted with a 10-inch turntable, making the machine suitable for disc records of any size.

THE REPRODUCER is the latest Columbia, knife edge, sound analyzing style, made with automatic needle clamp, by means of which the needle is inserted or removed simply by pressing a lever. Plays any make of 7 or 10-inch disc records.

THE BEAUTIFUL FLORAL HORN adds greatly to the beauty of this instrument. This horn is made of steel, with black enamel satin finish, and gold stripes, and is 17¾ inches long with 19-inch bell.

No. 21G261 Columbia Champion Type B H Graphophone, complete with aluminum tone arm, sound analyzing reproducer and black satin finish floral horn, just as described above and shown in our illustration. Price, complete.......... $30.00
Shipping weight, 40 pounds.

COLUMBIA STERLING TALKING MACHINE.

THE COLUMBIA STERLING GRAPHOPHONE is a still larger, finer and more complete talking machine of the new aluminum tone arm construction, made with extra powerful double spring motor, with worm gear, insuring the most perfect operation, absolute noiselessness, every part fitted with the same care that is used in making a watch.

THE CABINET is very substantially made of solid quarter sawed oak, of very handsome and ornamental design, with piano finish.

THE SOUND ANALYZING REPRODUCER with automatic needle clamp, doing away entirely with the old style thumb screw, the most perfect reproducer made, is included with the Sterling Graphophone. Plays any make of 7 or 10-inch disc records.

THE HORN IS OF A BEAUTIFUL FLORAL DESIGN, resembling in shape a great morning glory, nickel plated and highly polished throughout, 17½ inches long, with 21¼-inch bell, contributing greatly to the perfection of sound reproduction, and adding greatly to the ornamental appearance of the machine.

THE NEW ALUMINUM TONE ARM constitutes the greatest improvement made in talking machines for many years. This type of construction gives the greatest possible volume of sound, the clearest and most natural reproduction, the finest and most perfect musical quality, and does away with the disagreeable scratching sound heretofore noticed in machines of the ordinary style of construction.

No. 21G263 Columbia Sterling Type B I Graphophone, complete, with aluminum tone arm, sound analyzing reproducer, and nickel plated floral horn, just as described above and shown in our illustration. Price, complete $45.00
Shipping weight, 50 pounds.

GENUINE COLUMBIA P RECORDS, 19 Cents Each, $2.25 Per Dozen.

THESE ARE THE RECORDS INCLUDED WITH THE SPECIAL HARVARD JR. OUTFIT, 50 RECORDS AND TALKING MACHINE FOR $10.75.

STANDARD SIZE WAX CYLINDER RECORDS THAT CAN BE USED ON ANY GRAPHOPHONE, PHONOGRAPH OR OTHER STYLE OF TALKING MACHINE USING THE REGULAR STANDARD SIZE WAX CYLINDER RECORDS.

EVERY RECORD GUARANTEED. **We send out these genuine high class Columbia P Records, at 19 cents each, or $2.25 per dozen,** your own selection of subjects, with the distinct understanding and agreement that they can be carefully compared with other records, tested on any kind of a wax cylinder graphophone, phonograph or other style of talking machine, and if not found entirely satisfactory in every way, the equal in volume of sound, naturalness of tone, musical quality, and all other points whereby a record is judged; if they are not equal in all respects to any wax cylinder record, regardless of price, with which they may be compared, they can be returned to us at our expense, including transportation charges, and your money in full will be refunded. **Bear in mind that these records,** although sold at the lowest price ever known for standard size wax cylinder records, your own selection of subjects, are strictly high grade, first quality records, records that will compare with records sold by other dealers at 25 cents, 35 cents and 50 cents each.

SELECT YOUR OWN SUBJECTS from the following complete list. Pick out the exact selections you like best. Our stock of subjects contained in the following list is very complete, and you can order with full assurance that you will get exactly what you send for, records that you will like, records that are sure to please you, and at less than one-half the price you pay for records of corresponding quality elsewhere.

No. 21G1090 Columbia P Records. Price, per dozen, **$2.25**; each........ **19c**

BAND RECORDS.

51544 Admiral's Favorite March
51514 America
532311 Anona (intermezzo two-step) by Mabel McKinley
532362 Any Rags (schottische)
531867 Arkansaw Husking Bee, An
532389 Bedelia, medley march (introducing "He was a Sailor")
51505 "Bohemian Girl," Selections from
5533 Bride Elect March, The
531530 Bunch of Blackberries (cake walk)
531486 Colored Major, The (ragtime march)
51550 Columbia Phonograph Co. March
5538 Coon Band Contest
5529 Dancing in the Dark (song and dance with clogs)
51518 Die Wacht Am Rhein
5518 Directorate March
51516 Dixie
51508 El Miserere, from "Il Trovatore"
5501 High School Cadets March
5526 Honeymoon March
51642 International Cake Walk
532297 Jack Tar March (Sousa's latest, introducing sailor's hornpipe, eight bells, boatswain's whistle)
5507 Jolly Coppersmith (descriptive)
5506 King Cotton March
531625 Love's Dreamland Waltz
5537 Man Behind the Gun March
5519 Manhattan Beach March
51638 Marching Through Georgia
51522 Nearer, My God, to Thee (with cornet solo)
51539 Rock of Ages
5516 Say Au Revoir, But Not Good-Bye
531526 Sousa's Band's Coming (descriptive patrol)
51512 Star Spangled Banner
5532 Stars and Stripes Forever March
51588 Till We Meet Again Waltz
5520 Washington Post March

CORNET RECORDS.

52807 Home, Sweet Home, duet
532491 Marriage Bells, (with chimes effect), solo
52814 Mid' the Green Fields of Virginia, duet
52813 My Old Kentucky Home, duet
52812 Nearer, My God, to Thee, duet
52815 She Was Bred in Old Kentucky, duet
532030 Sweet Sixteen Waltz, solo

ORCHESTRA RECORDS.

515132 Angels' Serenade (piccolo and cornet duet)
515194 Battle of Manila (descriptive)
515162 Blue Danube Waltz
515206 Bugler's Dream, The (descriptive—introducing "Just Before the Battle, Mother," Bugle Calls, etc., and ending with "Nearer, My God, to Thee")
515191 Capture of Santiago (descriptive—The Bugle Call, Fall In, March, Opening of the Battle, In the Thick of the Fight, Caring for the Wounded, Cease Firing, The Battle Won, Patriotic Music)
53'488 Creole Belle
515010 Dancing in the Kitchen (song and dance with clogs)
515145 Darky's Dream (with clogs)
515159 Darky Tickle (plantation medley, with clogs, shouts, etc.)
515229 Dewey's Return (descriptive, with steamboat whistles, cheers, etc. Music, "See The Conquering Hero Comes")
532191 Dixieland March, introducing "Dixie" and "Old Black Joe"
515064 Down on the Suwanee River (descriptive—pulling in the gang plank, steamboat bells, whistle, dance on board, with negro shouts and clogs)
515114 Flora Waltz (cornet solo, with full orchestra accompaniment)
515202 Georgia Camp Meeting, At a (march and two-step)
532460 Gondolier (intermezzo two-step, the latest popular success)
515007 Happy Days in Dixie (plantation medley, with clogs, shouts, etc.)
515142 Husking Bee (descriptive, introducing rural characters and scenes, with country dance and call in dialect)
532283 Laughing Water
515121 Let Her Rip (quadrille, with figures called)
515139 Limited Express, The (descriptive)
515063 Night Alarm (with all the familiar descriptive effects, representing a fire alarm at night—fire bells, cries, horses' hoofs, winding of hose reel, whistle of engine, ending with firemen's chorus)
515195 Roosevelt's Rough Riders, Charge of
515044 Rose from the South Waltz
515220 Smoky Mokes March
515059 Virginia Skedaddle (plantation medley, with clogs, shouts, etc.)
515203 Whistling Rufus

DRUM, FIFE AND BUGLE CORPS.

512801 Marching Thro' Georgia, and Dixie
512800 The Girl I Left Behind Me and Auld Lang Syne

RECORDS BY VIENNA ORCHESTRA.

The Violin Effects of a String Orchestra Are Here Shown to Their Best Advantage.

531681 Life in Vienna Waltz
531847 Night in Venice Waltz, A

BUGLE CALLS.

53769 Rough Riders in Their Charge Up San Juan Hill, Bugle Calls of the
53768 United States Army, Bugle Calls of the

ORCHESTRA BELLS.

512516 Chiming Bells

VIOLIN SOLOS.

531492 Holy City
527006 Imitation of Bagpipes and Scotch Airs, special arrangement.
527013 El Miserere from "Il Trovatore"

CLARIONET SOLO.

53409 My Old Kentucky Home (with variations)

BANJO SOLOS.

53861 Bunch of Rags
531412 Coon Band Contest, A
53816 Darky's Dream
53825 El Capitan March
53856 Eli Green's Cake Walk
53860 Old Folks at Home (with variations)
53830 Rag Time Medley (introducing "All Coons Look Alike to Me," and "Oh, Mr. Johnson")
53859 Whistling Rufus
531780 Whoa, Bill!

XYLOPHONE SOLOS.

512020 Dancing in the Sunlight
512009 Mocking Bird, The

PICCOLO SOLOS.

523505 Hornpipe Polka

WHISTLING SOLOS.

512604 Home, Sweet Home
57701 Mocking Bird, The (with bird imitations running throughout the record)

MINSTRELS.

These records each embrace overture, new jokes, laughter and applause, and end with song given in title, with orchestra and vocal quartette.

532045A Introductory Overture by the entire company
532045D End Man Song, "I'm a Nigger That's Living High," by Billy Golden
532045E Jokes between Interlocutor and End Man
532045F I'm Wearing My Heart Away for You. Tenor solo by George J. Gaskin, with chorus by the entire company.
532045G Jokes between Interlocutor and End Man
532045L Banjo Solo, "Yankee Doodle," by Vess L. Ossman, with orchestra accompaniment
531609 Coon, Coon, Coon
513000 Dese Bones Shall Rise Again
531608 Good-Bye, Dolly Gray
513005 Hear Dem Bells
531691 I'd Leave My Happy Home for You

VOCAL SEXTETTES—Mixed Voices.

531604 Tell Me, Pretty Maiden (from "Florodora")

MENDELSSOHN QUARTETTE—Mixed Voices.

532074 Good Night, Good Night, Beloved
532332 Home, Sweet Home, by John Howard Payne
532238 The Lord's Prayer and Gloria Patria

VOCAL QUARTETTES—Male Voices.

These songs are finely rendered, and the effect is so natural that no stretch of the imagination is required to bring the singers so strongly forward in spirit that their actual presence seems to be achieved.

59014 Annie Laurie
59071 Blue and The Gray, The
59067 Camp Meeting Jubilee (negro shout)
59068 Carry Me Back to Old Virginia (coon song)
59039 Church Scene from "The Old Homestead" (with church bell effect)
59046 Coon Songs, Medley of
532242 Coon Wedding in Southern Georgia, A
59037 Farmyard Medley (imitation of fowls, cattle, etc.)
59049 Fireman's Duty, The (descriptive—bells, horses' hoofs, gallant rescue, etc.)
531654 Hymns and Prayer from the Funeral Service over President McKinley
59070 I'd Leave My Happy Home for You (coon song)
59010 I'se Gwine Back to Dixie (coon song)
531693 Laughing Quartette, The
531668 Lead, Kindly Light
59015 Little Alabama Coon (with baby cry and clog)
59033 Massa's in the Cold, Cold Ground (coon song, with banjo imitation)
59008 Moonlight on the Lake
59019 My Old Kentucky Home
59045 My Old New Hampshire Home
59050 Old Black Joe (coon song)
59030 Old Folks at Home, The
59018 Old Oaken Bucket, The
532241 Plantation Songs. Medley of (introducing "In the Evening by the Moonlight," "Down in the Cornfield," "Carry Me Back to Old Virginia" and "My Old Cabin Home")
59011 Rocked in the Cradle of the Deep
59064 Rock of Ages.
59040 Sleigh Ride Party, The (descriptive)
531548 Soldier's Farewell, The
59041 Steamboat Medley (descriptive)
532236 St. Patrick's Day at Clancy's ("Loike Ould Times in Kilkenny, begorra")
59048 Tenting on the Old Camp Ground
59038 Trip to the County Fair (imitation of railway, fakirs and Rubes)
59029 Way Down Yonder in the Cornfield (coon song)
59061 Where is My Wandering Boy Tonight?
59069 Where the Sweet Magnolias Bloom

VOCAL TRIOS.

57707 Camp Meeting (opening with chorus by trio, followed by a negro sermon and ending with song by trio)
57705 Mocking Bird Medley, The (tenor solo, whistling, chorus by trio)

VOCAL DUETS.

58416 Almost Persuaded. Baritone and tenor.
58404 Bye and Bye You Will Forget Me. Baritone and tenor
531343 I Loved You Better than You Knew. Baritone and tenor
532209 It's a Lovely Day for a Walk (serio-comic). Contralto and baritone
531878 Jerry Murphy is a Friend of Mine. Baritone and tenor
531703 McManus and the Parrot (comic Irish song). Baritone and tenor
531611 Reuben and Cynthia (a duet interspersed with humorous dialogue between male and female characters. One of Hoyt's great successes). Soprano and baritone
58420 Shadow of the Pines, In the. Baritone and tenor
532409 Under the Anheuser Bush. Baritone and tenor
531910 Under the Bamboo Tree (as sung by Miss Marie Cahill in the musical comedy "Sally in Our Alley") Baritone and tenor
58421 While the Leaves Came Drifting Down. Baritone and tenor
531684 Whoa, Bill! (a trombone extravaganza). Baritone and tenor

VOCAL DUETS WITH ORCHESTRA ACCOMPANIMENT.

532551 Down on the Brandywine (with chime effects). Very tuneful and catchy. Baritone and tenor
532531 Listen to the Mocking Bird (with bird imitations). Contralto and baritone.

VOCAL SOLOS WITH CHURCH ORGAN ACCOMPANIMENT.

532496 I Need Thee Every Hour. Tenor
531364 Jesus, Lover of My Soul. Baritone
531356 Nearer, My God, to Thee. Baritone
531358 Rock of Ages. Baritone
531367 There is a Fountain. Baritone
531357 Where is My Wandering Boy Tonight? Baritone

VOCAL SOLOS WITH BANJO ACCOMPANIMENT.

57200-c Hot Time in the Old Town Tonight.
57200-h Little Old Log Cabin in the Lane. Baritone

VOCAL SOLOS WITH PIANO ACCOMPANIMENT.

531549 Absence Makes the Heart Grow Fonder. Tenor
531677 Ain't Dat a Shame (coon song). Baritone
56318 And the Parrot Said (comic). Tenor
531786 Bill Bailey, Won't You Come Home? (coon song). Baritone
54586 Break the News to Mother. Baritone
532089 C-h-i-c-k-e-n; That's the Way to Spell Chicken. Baritone
531338 Columbia, the Gem of the Ocean. Baritone
531603 Coon, Coon, Coon (coon song). Baritone
54615 Darling Nellie Gray. Baritone
532323 Down on the Farm (ballad). Baritone
55851 Fatal Rose of Red, The. Baritone
57181 Girl I Loved in Sunny Tennessee, The. Baritone
531311 Good-Bye, Dolly Gray. Baritone
531649 Go 'Way Back and Sit Down. Tenor
531671 He Laid Away a Suit of Gray to Wear the Union Blue. Tenor
531628 Hello, Central; Give Me Heaven (sentimental). Baritone
55801 Holy City, The. Baritone
56309 I Couldn't (comic). Tenor
531706 If Time Was Money, I'd Be a Millionaire (coon song). Baritone

REMEMBER

WHEN YOU HAVE BOUGHT $25.00 WORTH OF GOODS OR MORE FROM US YOU GET YOUR CHOICE OF MANY VALUABLE ARTICLES FREE, AS SHOWN IN OUR FREE PROFIT SHARING BOOK

No. 21G1090 Columbia P Records. Price, per dozen, **$2.25**; each........ **19c**

LIST OF COLUMBIA P RECORDS CONTINUED ON NEXT PAGE.

YOUR MONEY WILL BE IMMEDIATELY RETURNED TO YOU FOR ANY GOODS NOT PERFECTLY SATISFACTORY.

10 INCH OXFORD DISC RECORDS

30 CENTS EACH — $3.50 PER DOZEN

Oxford
DiscRecord
ORCHESTRA
MERRY WIDOW WALTZ
857

WHY PAY 60 CENTS EACH OR $7.20 PER DOZ. for other disc records when we furnish the new Purple Label 10-inch Oxford Records at 30 cents each or $3.50 per dozen, and absolutely guarantee them equal in musical quality, durability and appearance to any record ever made at any price? **THE MAKING** of good records requires the services of high class musicians, help of the highest degree of skill in the recording laboratory, and last, but by no means least, a high grade and expensive material, and these conditions are complied with to the limit in the manufacture of the Oxford disc records. You will be surprised at their marvelous tone, their freedom from scratch and their wearing quality.

YOUR MONEY BACK and no questions asked if you don't like them. We accept orders for Oxford Disc Records with the understanding and agreement that you can compare them with other records costing twice the price we ask, or judge them by the highest standards of musical and technical excellence, and if you do not find them equal in every way to the best records on the market and superior to most records; if you are not entirely satisfied with them and immensely pleased, you can send them back to us and we will return your money in full, including all freight or express charges you may have paid.

SELECTIONS FROM THE MERRY WIDOW.

1003 **Cavalier**—Duet, from Act II. Alice C. Stevenson and Frank C. Stanley.
1005 **Girls at Maxim's**—Song with chorus, solo by Alice C. Stevenson.
1002 **I Love You So**—Waltz duet. Alice C. Stevenson and Frank C. Stanley.
1001 **Maxim's Song.** Frank C. Stanley.
971 **Merry Widow March**—Concert Band.
857 **Merry Widow Waltz**—Orchestra.
1006 **Women**—March septet, from Act. II. Peerless quartette and chorus.

BAND SELECTIONS.

62 **Artful Artie**—March and two-step.
76 **America**—Our national anthem.
369 **Anvil Chorus from "Il Trovatore."**
476 **Baby Parade**—Two-step patrol.
176 **Banner March**—A bright, catchy record.
501 **Blue and the Gray**—Patrol.
201 **Blue Danube Waltz**—Popular waltz.
811 **Boston Commandery March**—(Onward Christian Soldiers).
976 **Bugle Call Polka**—A unique dance.
503 **Cheyenne Medley**—March and two-step—Introducing "Cheyenne," "Won't You Try," and "The Little Chauffeur."
271 **Chicken Charlie**—Rag-time cake walk.
205 **Chirpers**—With whistling solo.
228 **Cocoanut Dance**—Characteristic piece.
477 **Colleen Bawn**—Two-step—medley march.
*1099 **Cubs on Parade**—Baseball march.
*1038 **Cotton**—A Southern breakdown.
895 **Cowboy's Patrol**—Characteristic number.
1127 **Dancing in the Barn**—Schottische.
*1163 **Dixie.**
812 **Does You Love Your Baby, Honey**—Cakewalk.
901 **Dream on the Ocean**—Waltz.
748 **Dreams of Childhood Waltz.**
814 **1863 Medley**—A rousing march medley, "Annie Laurie," "Dixie," "Arkansas Traveler," "The Girl I Left Behind" (Fife and Drum), "Auld Lang Syne," "Marching Thro' Georgia," and "Yankee Doodle."
402 **Everybody Works But Father**—Humoresque musical burlesque.
101 **Famous 22nd Regiment March**—A great military march by the famous Gilmore.
178 **Fantasie on My Old Kentucky Home.**
301 **First Brigade Illinois N. G. March**—with a fife and drum corps.
478 **Free Lance March**—On to victory.
1020 **Gathering of the Clans**—Scotch dance medley.
*1100 **Genee Waltzes**—Containing favorite melodies from the "Soul Kiss."
754 **Gen. Mixup U. S. A.**—A "mixup" of favorite national airs.
1137 **German Patrol.**
978 **Girl I Left Behind Me**—Humoresque—Variations and solos for all instruments.
603 **Glorious America March**—Lively martial two-step.
249 **Happy Heinie**—Characteristic march introducing "Du, Du," "Wacht am Rhein," etc.
653 **Highland Echoes**—Bright, snappy march, of Scottish airs.
401 **High School Cadets March.**
604 **His Honor The Mayor**—Selections from.
902 **Hoosier Slide**—Two-step—Unique and characteristic.
836 **I'd Like to Know Your Address and Your Name**—Medley waltz—from "The Parisian Model."
837 **I'd Rather Two-Step Than Waltz, Bill**—Medley two-step.
677 **Jig Medley**—Lively jig with excellent clogs.
154 **Jolly Blacksmiths**—Anvil introduced.
226 **Kaiser Friederich March**—A bass solo is very effectively introduced.
31 **Laces and Graces**—Very pretty number.
352 **La Graziosa**—Spanish dance.
76 **La Marseillaise**—French National air.
376 **La Mexicana**—Mexican waltzes.
57 **Larboard Watch**—With cornet and trombone duet.
451 **Liberty Bell March.**
838 **Marching Home Thro' Dixie Land.**
453 **Marching Through Georgia.**
377 **Mit Schwert und Lanze March**—A favorite German military march.
381 **Mountain Echoes**—A bright little mazurka with cornet solo.
490 **Moving Day**—Medley march—Played in dance tempo.
355 **My Maryland March**—A military march introducing "Maryland."
479 **Old Settlers on Parade**—March Comique, introducing "Reuben, Reuben, I've Been Thinking," "Turkey in the Straw," "Old Black Joe," "Tramp, Tramp, Tramp, the Boys are Marching," etc.
190 **Our Navy Boys**—March and two-step.
726 **Popular Songs**—Medley two-step.
629 **Preacher and the Bear**—Grotesque ragtime two-step.
929 **Radium March**—"Lights and shades" of the musical world.

STAR (*) SELECTIONS. Realizing the difficulty of selecting records merely by name, especially those which may be unknown to you, and considering the fact that in every large list of records certain selections are better than others, we have marked with a star (*) those selections which are extra good and which are most frequently purchased by customers who have an opportunity to hear the records before buying. If you are in doubt, just include plenty of these star (*) numbers in your order, even though you never heard of them, and you will be surprised to find how good they are.

EVERY OXFORD RECORD IS GOOD, because no selection is included in our list until it has been critically tried, considered and pronounced "high class" and you can pick them out at random, or leave the selection entirely to us, and be sure of an assortment that will please, but the star (*) numbers are the extra good numbers, the cream of the entire big list.

WHEN ORDERING 10-Inch Oxford Disc Records, mention Catalogue No. 20N5117, and give the selection number of each record you want. Do not order 7 or 12-inch records from the following list, as these numbers are made in 10-inch size only. For 7 and 12-inch selections, see pages 313 and 314.
See note on page 313 regarding machines these records will fit.

*1040 **Red Wing**—Indian intermezzo.
529 **Roosevelt March (G. O. P.).**
778 **Salome**—Intermezzo, Oriental number.
8 **Schubert's Serenade**—Trumpet solo, band accompaniment.
428 **Scotch, Irish and English Airs**—Grand fantasie.
1064 **Shannon**—Irish novelty march, introducing "Kathleen Mavourneen," "Killarney," "Wearing of the Green," and "Come Back to Erin."
378 **Star Spangled Banner.**
854 **Sunbeam Dance**—Schottische.
305 **Sundown at West Point.**
454 **Tally-Ho Galop**—Descriptive.
4 **Tannhauser March.**
330 **Tell Me, Pretty Maiden**—"Florodora."
879 **Time, The Place and The Girl, The**—Medley march.
429 **Tone Pictures of the 71st Regiment Leaving for Cuba.**
481 **Trip Through Dixie**—A bright ragtime march.
274 **Under the Double Eagle March.**
326 **Under the Flag of Victory March.**
580 **Washington Post March.**
1167 **Wee Macgreegor, The**—Highland patrol.
331 **What a Friend We Have in Jesus.**
332 **Whistler and His Dog**—Caprice.
756 **Won't You Come Over to My House?**—Medley waltz.
206 **Yankee Patrol.**
1129 **Yankee Prince.**—Two Step.

ORCHESTRA SELECTIONS.

880 **Au Revoir Waltz.**
306 **Bells of St. Paul**—Christmas record.
657 **Bull Frog's Dance**—An excellent schottische.
658 **Camp Meeting Time**—Medley two-step.
59 **Chimes of Normandy.**
1009 **Chiquita**—Serenade—A dreamy Mexican number.
406 **College Songs**—**Medley**—Introduces "Bingo," "Spanish Cavalier," "Jingle Bells," etc.
456 **Darkies' Tickle.**
434 **Dolly Dollars**—Waltzes.
636 **Dream of the Rarebit Fiend.**
335 **Earl and The Girl**—Medley two-step.
633 **Eileen Asthore**—Selections—Contains "Eileen Asthore," "Wearers of the Green," and "Day Dreams."
842 **Gibson Girl**—Waltz.
*1170 **Girls of Gottenberg**—Waltz—A tuneful waltz which introduces the following melodies: "The Only Girl," "Dance from Act 2," "I Love My Love with an A," "The Titsy-Bitsy Girl" and "Do You Know Mr. Schneider?" from "The Girls of Gottenberg."
559 **Hearts and Flowers.**
1114 **Home, Sweet Home Medley**—"Good Night" waltz.
458 **Hunting Scene**—Descriptive.
683 **Ida-Ho**—March and two-step.
432 **In the Clock Store.**
278 **In the Shade of the Old Apple Tree**—Medley waltz—Introducing "Down in the Subway."
82 **Isle of Spice**—Medley.
882 **It's Great to Be a Soldier Man**—Medley two-step.
728 **Jamestown Rag**—Patriotic march and two-step.
433 **Jolly Coppersmith**—The anvil, singing and whistling are excellent.
279 **Keep a Little Cosy Corner in Your Heart For Me**—Medley two-step.
907 **Kentucky**—March and two-step.
1041 **Luna Waltz**—Dainty dance selection.
1171 **Made in Germany**—A medley of favorite German songs.
483 **Medley of Reels.**
133 **Moonlight**—Serenade Intermezzo.
161 **Moon Winks**—Three-step. A new dance.
83 **My Kickapoo**—Indian characteristic march.
*1044 **Original Reels.**
760 **Parisian Model**—Medley two-step, composed of the hits of Anna Held's latest success.
407 **Passion**—Intermezzo.
759 **Peaches and Cream**—A delectable rag.
*1172 **Popular Chorus Medley No. 3**—Two-step. A brilliant, lively two-step for dancing.
1151 **Popular Waltz Chorus Medley.**
*1070 **Prosit**—A Rathskeller Intermezzo.
782 **Pretzel Pete**—A German ragtime.
661 **Red Mill**—**Selections**—Contains "For Every Day is Ladies' Day for Me," "In the Isle of Our Dreams," Dance from "Whistle It," (Xylophone solo), "Good-A-Bye, John," and "Because You're You."
36 **Royal Chef**—Medley—Introducing "A Way They Have in Chicago," "Mother Goose," etc.
338 **Silver Heels**—March and two-step.
*1011 **Skip**—**Schottische**—A rollicking number which defies the listener to keep from dancing.
531 **Southern Dream Patrol**—Containing "Sailor's Hornpipe," "Massa's in the Cold, Cold Ground," "Swanee River," "Old Black Joe," and "Turkey in the Straw."
460 **Spring Blossoms**—Caprice gavotte—Played as a clarionet and flute duet.
184 **Tammany**—Medley—Introducing "Tammany," "Nellie Dean," "Delia," "The Prettiest Gal in Borneo," etc.
859 **Tattooed Man**—Waltz—Contains: "The Floral Wedding," "Boys Will Be Boys and Girls Will Be Girls," "Omar Khayyam" (Bell solo), "The Land of Dreams," and "Nobody Loves Me."
12 **Teasing**—Medley March—Introducing orchestra bells and singing in the chorus.
731 **Teddy Bears' Picnic** — Characteristic novelty.
408 **Two Little Girls Loved One Little Boy.** Medley waltz—Fine for dancing.
781 **U. S. A. Patrol**—With trumpet and drum calls and favorite old-time American melodies.
1046 **Virginia**—Introducing "Star Spangled Banner," "Yankee Doodle," "Dixie," with clogs and fife and drums.
307 **Wait Till the Sun Shines, Nellie**—Overture—Containing "Wait Till the Sun Shines, Nellie," and "What You Going to Do When the Rent Comes Round."
339 **Whistlers**—Intermezzo—From German comic opera. "Fruhlingsluft."
310 **Winona**—A wigwam wooing—Splendid violin tones.
860 **Yankee Tourist**—Two-step—"The Glad Hand Girl" (Bell solo), "Wouldn't You Like to Have Me For a Sweetheart?" "Irish Lads," "Come and Have a Smile With Me," make this a charming record.

ACCORDION SOLOS.

*861 **Cakewalk**—Beautiful rendered.
783 **Irish Jigs and Reels Medley**—Spirited and snappy.
843 **Straight Jigs**—Medley—Old-time clog and sand dance.
234 **Yankee Doodle Dandy**—Fine reproduction.

BANJO SOLOS.

With Orchestra Accompaniment.

*585 **Bay State Quickstep**—Played in perfect time.
762 **Donnybrook Fair**—Marvelous for its precision and fullness of tone.
14 **Hoosier Frolics**—Real banjo quality.
637 **Popularity**—March and two-step.
213 **Razzle Dazzle**—Characteristic cakewalk.
1092 **Sunflower Dance.**
233 **Yankee Girl**—With fife and drum effect.
162 **Yankee Land March**—Characteristic.

BELL SOLOS.

With Orchestra Accompaniment.

586 **Dancing Sunrays**—A bright and cheerful schottische.
784 **In Moonland** — Intermezzo — Charming solo.
*981 **Sweet the Angelus Was Ringing**—Sweet, clear, melodious tones.

CHIMES.

311 **Adeste Fideles**—O Come, All Ye Faithful.
312 **Hark, the Herald Angels Sing.**
510 **Trinity**—Sacred intermezzo—Band acc.

CLARINET SOLOS.

185 **Bluebells of Scotland**—With variations. Very clear and the execution brilliant.
283 **Huguenots**—**Cavatina**—A very soft and effective record.
844 **Little Nell**—A bright, dainty song and dance.

CORNET SOLOS.

55 **Centennial Polka**—Introducing a variation of "Auld Lang Syne."
29 **Fantasie Characteristic.** Jules Levy
6 **Fantasie on Irish Airs**—Contains many favorite Irish Airs.
89 **Oh, How Delightful**—Good tone quality.
111 **Sing, Smile, Slumber** — Exceptionally fine record.

FLUTE SOLOS.

232 **Durand Concert Waltz**—Arrangement particularly fine.
34 **Endearing Young Charms**—The violins of accompaniment are very good.
757 **Merry Lark**—Very interesting number, flute and clarinet duet.
363 **Sleep Well, Thou Sweet Angel**—The flute tone is very soft and sweet.

VIOLIN SOLOS.

511 **Cavalleria Rusticana**—Intermezzo—Deserves special mention.
535 **Melody in "F"**—Very pure, natural violin tone.
972 **Serenade**—Noticeable for its great pathos and coloring.
804 **Swan**—Melody—Classic solo.

XYLOPHONE SOLOS.

135 **Celia Polka Mazurka**—Very bright and snappy.
254 **Galop Bravoura**—A marvelous record.
*686 **Mr. Black Man**—Cakewalk.

WHISTLING SOLOS.

313 **Birds and the Brook**—With bird imitations.
*1094 **Birds Festival Waltz**—Very effective and natural bird imitations.
982 **Dance of the Song Birds**—One of the best.
463 **Independentia March**—Excellent reproduction.
285 **Over the Waves Waltz**—For dancing.
935 **Snow Bird**—Excellent imitation of the tones of the Snow Bird.
956 **Whistle**—Intermezzo two-step.

VOCAL SOLOS.

With Orchestra Accompaniment.

With every vocal selection we give the singer's initials, as shown below. For example, "No. 188, Ben Bolt," is followed by the initials "S. B.," signifying that his record was made by the famous contralto, Miss Suzanne Baker. By these initial letters, you can easily pick out selections by your favorite singers, an advantage quickly appreciated by all talking machine enthusiasts.

Alexander, George,	Baritone.	G. A.
Baker, Miss Suzanne,	Contralto.	S. B.
Belmont, Joe,	Whistler.	J. B.
Burr, Henry,	Tenor.	H. B.
Clifford, A.,	Baritone.	A. Cl.
Collins, Arthur,	Baritone.	A. C.
Denny Will,	Tenor.	W. D.
Favor, Ed. M.,	Tenor.	E. F.
Fisher, J. J.,	Baritone.	J. F.
Gaskin, Geo. J.,	Tenor.	G. G.
Glanville, Miss Roberta,	Soprano.	R. G.
Golden, Billy,	Negro Shouts.	B. G.
Harlan, Byron G.,	Tenor.	B. H.
Harrison, J. F.,	Baritone.	J. H.
Heins, Billy,	Baritone.	B. He.
Hickman, Miss Mina,	Soprano.	M. H.
Howard, Frank,	Tenor.	F. H.
Johnson, Geo. W.,	"Coon" songs.	G. J.
Jones, Miss Ada,	Soprano.	A. J.
La Mar, Pete,	Yodler.	P. L.
Lambert, Fred,	Baritone.	F. L.
Morgan, Miss Corinne,	Contralto.	C. M.
Murray, Billy,	Tenor.	B. M.
Myers, J. W.,	Baritone.	J. M.
Natus, Joe H.,	Tenor.	J. N.
Potter, F. H.,	Tenor.	F. P.
Quinn, Dan W.,	Baritone.	D. Q.
Reed, James,	Tenor.	J. R.
Roberts, Bob,	Baritone.	B. R.
Stanley, Frank C.,	Baritone.	F. S.
Stevenson, Miss Alice C.,	Soprano.	A. S.
Stewart, Cal,	Baritone.	C. S.
Spencer, Len,	Baritone.	L. S.
Tally, Harry,	Tenor.	H. T.
Turner, Alan,	Baritone.	A. T.
Watson, Geo. P.,	Yodle tenor.	G. W.

LIST OF 10-INCH OXFORD DISC RECORDS CONTINUED ON NEXT PAGE.

10-INCH OXFORD DISC RECORDS.—Continued.

VOCAL SOLOS—Continued.

614 Ain't You Coming Back to Old New Hampshire, Molly? F. S.
687 All in, Down and Out. A. C.
1095 All the Girls Look Good to Me. W. D.
*1153 Any Old Port in a Storm—A splendid solo, exhibiting Mr. Stanley's powerful voice and wide range to great advantage. F. S.
863 Ballooning—From "Fascinating Flora." H. T.
410 Battle Hymn of the Republic. F. S.
188 Ben Bolt—The best contralto record ever made. S. B.
637 Bird on Nellie's Hat. F. L.
938 Brother Noah Gave Out Checks for Rain—Clever coon song. A. C.
958 Bye, Bye, Dearie. B. H.
236 Bye, Bye, Ma Honey—Comic negro shout. B. G.
286 Can't You See I'm Lonely. B. M.
565 Cheyenne—Breezy song of love in Wyoming long ago. B. M.
566 Columbia, the Gem of the Ocean. G. A.
974 Creole Love Song. R. G.
514 Dearie. F. P.
665 Dixie's Land. F. S.
125 Down Deep Within the Cellar—Favorite German drinking song. F. S.
287 Down Where the Silvery Mohawk Flows. F. S.
190 Down Where the Swanee River Flows. F. H.
258 Everybody Works but Father. B. R.
164 Every Dollar Carries Trouble of its Own. B. R.
466 Everyone is in Slumberland but You and Me. B. M.
96 For All Eternity—With violin obligato. A. S.
941 Gee Whiz, Ain't It Tough to Be Poor. B. M.
438 Ghost of the Banjo Coon. A. C.
139 Girl Who Cares for Me—Pretty waltz song. F. S.
140 Give My Regards to Broadway. B. M.
288 Good-Bye, Sweet Old Manhattan Isle. H. T.
539 Good Old U. S. A. B. H.
343 Have You Seen My Henry Brown?—Coon song. A. J.
449 Heart Bowed Down. A. T.
786 He Goes to Church on Sunday. B. M.
394 He's Nobody's Friend, Not Even His Own—Coon song. A. C.
518 He Walked Right In, Turned Around and Walked Right Out Again. B. R.
317 Holy City. J. H.
42 Home, Sweet Home. C. M.
344 How'd You Like to Spoon With Me?—From "The Earl and The Girl." B. M.
986 How Firm a Foundation—Sacred. With organ accompaniment. F. S.
540 I Don't Know Where I'm Goin', but I'm on My Way—Coon song. A. C.
825 I'd Rather Two-Step Than Waltz, Bill—Bright novelty song. B. M.
913 If I'm Going to Die, I'm Going to Have Some Fun—Comic coon song. A. C.
*1118 If It's Good Enough for Washington, It's Good Enough for Me. F. S.
787 If With All Your Hearts Ye Truly Seek Me—From the Oratorio "Elijah." H. B.
1049 I Just Can't Keep My Feet Still, When the Band Begins to Play. A. C.
942 I'll Be Waiting, Dearie, When You Come Back Home—March song. F. S.
411 I'll Be Waiting in the Gloaming, Sweet Genevieve. A. T.
*1050 I Love and the World is Mine—Featured in "A Waltz Dream." H. B.
*1030 I'm Afraid to Come Home in the Dark. B. M.
116 I'm Longing for My Old Kentucky Home. J. H.
1051 I'm Looking for the Man that Wrote "The Merry Widow" Waltz. B. M.
141 I'm Trying So Hard to Forget You. F. H.
*866 I'm Tying the Leaves So They Won't Come Down—Sentimental child song. B. H.
17 I'm Wearing My Heart Away For You. J. R.
289 In Dear Old Georgia. H. T.
345 In Old Madrid. J. H.
73 In the Shade of the Old Apple Tree—Pretty sentimental song. F. H.
541 It's All Right in the Summer Time—As sung by Vesta Victoria. A. J.
117 I've Got My Fingers Crossed, You Can't Touch Me. B. H.
733 I've Told His Missus All About Him—Sequel to "Waitin' at the Church." A. J.
1073 I Want to Be a Merry, Merry Widow. A. J.
*1131 I Was a Hero, Too—A comic song from the Broadway success "Nearly a Hero," containing a humorous definition of the word "Hero." B. M.
*1120 I Was Roaming Along—An amusing song of the luck experienced by "Bill," a care-free individual, while "roaming along." The chorus has an exceedingly pleasing, melodious swing. A. C.
395 I Would Like to Marry You—From "The Earl and the Girl." B. M.
868 Jack and Jill—From "Fifty Miles From Boston." A. J.
19 Jerusalem. J. H.
143 Just Across the Bridge of Gold. B. H.
915 Just As I am—Sacred. Organ accompaniment. F. S.
396 Just Before the Battle, Mother. J. M.
245 Keep a Little Cosy Corner in Your Heart for Me—Good novelty song. B. H.
1157 Killarney; My Home O'er the Sea. F.H.
*1074 Lanky Yankee Boys in Blue—A stirring military march song with fife and drum solo between the verses. B. M.
799 Last Rose of Summer is the Sweetest Song of All—Sentimental ballad. F.S.
71 Laughing Song—By the originator of this song. G. J.
99 Little Boy Called Taps—Popular march song. B. H.
145 Longing For You—Pretty love song of a little boy and girl. F. H.
946 Love's Old Sweet Song—Dignified and finished rendition. A. T.
167 Love's Sorrow—A beautiful record of this standard selection. J. H.
46 Make a Fuss Over Me—Coon song written by Theo. Morse. B. R.
830 Mammy's Little Curly Head—Pleasing little lullaby. A. J.
918 Medley of Yodles. G. W.
444 Mother, Pin a Rose on Me. B. M.
961 Much Obliged to You—Clever coon song. A. C.
219 My Irish Molly O—From "Sergeant Brue." B. M.
*1181 My Dream of the U. S. A. F. S.
369 My Name is Morgan, but it Ain't J. P.—Coon song. B. R.
296 Nobody. B. R.
546 Not Because Your Hair is Curly. B. M.
*1076 Nothin' Ever Worries Me—Humorous darky song. A. C.
348 Nothin' From Nothin' Leaves You—Coon song. B. R.
742 No Wedding Bells for Me. B. M.
50 Old Folks at Home. C. M.
320 On an Automobile Honeymoon. H. T.
474 One Called Mother and the Other Home Sweet Home—A beautiful ballad. B. H.
241 Pal of Mine. F. S.
1110 Party That Wrote Home Sweet Home Never Was a Married Man, The. F. L.
1106 Parson Jones' Three Reasons. A. C.
889 Playing Hide and Seek—A descriptive child ballad. B. H.
21 Please Come and Play in My Yard—Loud and clear record. H. B.
120 Preacher and the Bear. A. C.
322 Rocked in the Cradle of the Deep—A clear, distinct record. J. M.
1079 Roll Around. H. T.
*900 School Days (When We Were a Couple of Kids). B. H.
420 Since Father Went to Work—Another "Father" song. F. L.
197 Sleep, Baby, Sleep. F. L.
1108 Smarty—Popular juvenile song. B. H.
989 So Long, Bill—Clever "rube" song from "The Yankee Tourist." B. M.
1132 Somebody That I Know and You Know Too. A. C.
350 Somebody's Sweetheart I Want to Be. B. H.
475 Songs My Mammy Sang to Me—Introducing choruses of several Irish ditties. A. J.
1109 Stupid Mr. Cupid. A. J.
873 Take Me Back to New York Town. H. T.
*1185 Take Me Out to the Ball Game. F. L.
832 Take Me Where There's a Big Brass Band. B. M.
24 Teasing—Great record of this popular song. H. B.
172 Tell Me, Pretty Girl, Did You Smile on Me—Pretty waltz song. F. H.
199 Tell Me With Your Eyes. F. H.
523 There's No One Like the Old Folks After All—Beautiful ballad. F. S.
922 Thursday is My Jonah Day—From "The Time, The Place, and The Girl." B. M.
*1147 Tipperary—A rollicking Irish love march song. B. M.
*1134 True Heart—A march ballad. F. H.
174 Turkey in the Straw—An excellent record of this old favorite. B. G.
924 Two Blue Eyes—A simple pathetic march song. B. H.
422 Uncle's Quit Work, Too. B. H.
*1058 Under Any Old Flag at All. B. M.
499 Waiting at the Church—English character song. A. J.
269 Wait 'Till the Sun Shines, Nellie. B. H.
500 Waltz Me Around Again, Willie—Waltz song. B. M.
*1060 Warrior Bold. F. S.
124 Watermelon is Good Enough for Me. B. R.
324 We'll Be Together When the Clouds Roll By—A waltz ballad. F. H.
450 We Parted as the Sun Went Down—A sentimental ballad. F. S.
647 What's the Use of Loving, If You Can't Love All the Time? A. C.
298 What You Going to Do When the Rent Comes 'Round? A. C.
*1111 When It's Moonlight, Mary Darling, 'Neath the Old Grape Arbor Shade. H. B.
594 When Daddy Sings the Little Ones to Sleep—Tuneful selection. A. J.
1161 When Highland Mary Did the Highland Fling—Very funny. B. M.
596 When Tommy Atkins Marries Dolly Gray. B. M.
725 When You Know You're Not Forgotten by the Girl You Can't Forget. F. H.
268 Whole Damm Family. B. R.
525 Won't You Be My Girlie—Tuneful waltz song. F. S.
325 Yankee Boodle. B. R.
75 Yankee Doodle Boy—A good, spirited march song. B. M.
1136 Yankee Doodle's Come to Town. B. M.
675 You Can Have Broadway—From "The Governor's Son." B. M.
399 You Can Sail in My Boat—Ballad from "Edmund Burke." F. H.
*1148 You Have Always Been the Same Old Pal. H. B.
425 You're a Grand Old Rag. B. M.
51 You're the Flower of My Heart, Sweet Adeline—Popular ballad. F. H.

No. 20N5117 Ten-Inch Oxford Disc Records. Price, per dozen, **$3.50**; each (If sent by mail, postage extra, per record, 23 cents) **30c**
Shipping weight of one dozen, 8 pounds.
Do not order 7-inch or 12-inch records from this list, because the numbers shown in this list are made in 10-inch size only.

VOCAL DUETS—With Orchestra Accompaniment. By Collins and Harlan.

616 Arrah Wanna—An Irish-Indian matrimonial venture.
664 Bake Dat Chicken Pie—Melodious and humorous.
315 Bye-Bye, Ma Eva, Bye-Bye—A bright coon song.
340 Central, Give Me Back My Dime.
114 Coax Me—Popular ballad.
189 Come Along, Little Girl, Come Along.
1014 Come On and Kiss Your Baby—A joyous darky love song.
*1175 Don't Go Away—An excellent duet of this catchy love song.
*1143 Down in Jungle Town.
846 Ev'ry Little Bit Added to What You've Got Makes Just a Little Bit More.
115 Farmer and the Dude—Some good repartee is introduced.
237 Hey, Mr. Joshua—Story of two rubes who visit the city.
468 Honey, Won't You Love Me Like You Used To.
1104 Honey Won't You Please Come Down.
770 If You Want to Pick a Fuss, Wait 'Til the Sun Shines—Bright and tuneful.
412 I'm a Dreaming of You—A pleasing duet.
290 In My Merry Oldsmobile.
262 Jasper, Don't You Hear Me Calling You.
443 L-A-Z-Y Spells Lazy.
775 Lovin' Time.
194 Meet Me Down at Luna, Lena—A trip through Luna Park, Coney Island.
*1121 Mother Hasn't Spoke to Father Since.
418 My Lovin' Henry.
446 Niggah Love His Possum—Coon song.
398 On the Banks of the Rhine With a Stein—Bright waltz song.
807 Since Arrah Wanna Married Barney Carney—Companion song to "Arrah Wanna."
798 That Welcome on the Mat Ain't Meant for Me—A late coon song.
424 When Mose With His Nose Leads the Band—A new "Hebrew" march song.
1085 Who Do You Love.
809 Won't You Let Me Put My Arms Around You?—A lively number.
650 Won't You Throw a Kiss to Me?
597 Would You Leave Your Happy Home for Me?—Clever selection.
625 Yimminy Yee, I Yumped My Yob for You—Humorous Swedish dialect.

VOCAL DUETS—With Orchestra Accompaniment. By Ada Jones and William Murray.

736 Don't You Think It's Time to Marry?—From the "Blue Moon."
792 I'd Like to Know Your Address and Your Name—Clever flirtation duet.
713 I'd Like to See a Little More of You—(The Peek-a-Boo Sextette)—from "A Parisian Model."
669 I'm Sorry—From "About Town."
898 In Monkey Land.
943 It's Nice to Have a Sweetheart.
*1130 I've Taken Quite a Fancy to You—A clever flirtation song.
715 Kiss, Kiss, Kiss—Musical dialogue from "The Parisian Model."
899 Let's Take an Old-Fashioned Walk—Selection from "Honeymooners."
987 Make Believe—A dainty and melodious love number.
964 Smile, Smile, Smile—Bright duet from "The Rogers Brothers in Panama."
*1154 The Boy Who Stuttered and the Girl Who Lisped—An amusing flirtation song.
1135 When We Are M-A-Double R-I-E-D.
1084 When You Steal a Kiss or Two.
674 Wouldn't You Like to Flirt With Me—A harmless flirtation, cleverly carried on.
925 Wouldn't You Like to Have Me for a Sweetheart?—Duet from "A Yankee Tourist."
767 You Can't Give Your Heart to Somebody Else and Still Hold Hands With Me.

VOCAL DUETS—With Orchestra Accompaniment. By Ada Jones and Len Spencer.

513 Bashful Henry and His Lovin' Lucy—Talking and singing selection.
773 Becky and Izzy—A ludicrous "Hebrew" specialty descriptive of a "Yiddish Courtship."
937 Broncho Bob—An episode of the western plains.
489 Coming Home From Coney Island—Describing the trip home on the last car from Coney Isle.
617 Down on the Farm—Descriptive selection.
341 Fair Fisher Maid and Her Catch—Clever imitation of society belle at seashore.
516 Fritz and Louisa—Amusing German sketch of wit and humor.
732 Giving Mat the Mitten—A down-east courtship.
342 Golden Wedding—Portraying a celebration after fifty years of married life.
619 Good-a-Bye, John—Italian dialect selection from "The Red Mill."
316 Hand of Fate—A burlesque Melodrama.
366 Heinie—A German vaudeville sketch.
272 Henry—Coon vaudeville sketch.
865 Herman and Minnie—Clever German sketch.
*1144 House Cleaning Time—A domestic episode of a serio humorous character.
*1052 Jimmie and Maggie at "The Merry Widow"—Descriptive. Funny and melodious.
826 Jimmie and Maggie in Nickel Land—A characteristic description.
473 Mandy and Her Man—A laughable dialogue.
917 Mariutch at Coney Island—An Italian sketch.
717 Meet Me Down at the Corner—Irish comedy sketch.
968 You've Got to Love Me a Lot—A negro courtship.

VOCAL DUETS—With Orchestra Accompaniment. By Stanley and Burr.

936 Asleep in Jesus—Sacred selection.
*763 Calvary—Sacred. Organ accompaniment.
690 Larboard Watch—Popular nautical duet.
*1105 More Love to Thee—Sacred.
849 Rescue the Perishing—Organ accompaniment.
949 She's the Fairest Little Flower Dear Old Dixie Ever Grew—Late ballad.
808 When Johnny Comes Marching Home. A reminiscence of the days of '61.
967 When Summer Tells Autumn Good-Bye—Sentimental love ballad.
810 Why Do You Wait?—Beautiful and touching hymn.
893 Yankee Doodle—One of our national airs.

VOCAL DUETS—With Orchestra Accompaniment. By Corinne Morgan and J. F. Harrison.

318 I Will Magnify Thee, O Lord—Sacred.
144 Just My Style—Selection from "Fantana."
173 There's Nothing New to Say.

MISCELLANEOUS DUETS.

92 Almost Persuaded—Favorite sacred selection. Harlan and Stanley.
138 Farwell, Mr. Abner Hemingway. Murray and Roberts.
716 Linger Longer Girl—Broadway success. Alice C. Stevenson and F. C. Stanley.
549 Whistling Mike. Mr. Quinn sings the verses, Miss Trix whistles the chorus.

TRIOS.

1097 Dreaming.
916 Knocking, Knocking—Favorite hymn—Unaccompanied.
888 My Faith Looks Up to Thee—Sacred—Unaccompanied.
962 Nothing but Leaves—Will appeal to all lovers of saced music—Unaccompanied.
1055 Praise Ye the Lord—Sacred.
1017 Stars of the Summer Night—Unaccompanied.
875 Yield Not to Temptation—Old-time hymn—Unaccompanied.
744 Whistle It—Humorous trio from "The Red Mill."

MIXED QUARTETTE.

992 An Evening in an Hungarian Restaurant—A scence in "Little Hungary," the famous New York restaurant.
314 Birthday of a King—Organ accompaniment.
912 Christian, the Morn Breaks Sweet O'er Thee—Organ accompaniment.
828 Holy, Holy, Holy—Organ acc.
743 Jesus, Lover of My Soul—Sung to the tune "Refuge." Organ accompaniment.
950 Softly Now the Light of Day—Organ accompaniment.
522 Sweet and Low—Unaccompanied.
1133 Tale of the Turtle Dove.
833 Where Are You Going, My Pretty Maid?—Unaccompanied.

MALE QUARTETTE.

390 Barbecue in Old Kentucky—Descriptive of negro life "In Old Kentucky"—Unaccompanied.
364 Barnyard Medley—Life down on the farm—Unaccompanied.
1013 Black Jim.
1096 Call to Arms—Realistic descriptive selection portraying a scene in camp during war time.
939 Carry Me Back to Old Virginny—Orchestra accompaniment.
391 Characteristic Negro Medley—Medley of coon songs—Unaccompanied.
688 Church Scene from "The Old Homestead."
567 Every Day Will Be Sunday Bye-and-Bye—Humorous selection—Unaccompanied.
831 Glory Song (Oh, That Will Be Glory)—Sacred—Organ accompaniment.
897 Honey Boy—A popular march song—Orchestra accompaniment.
867 Irish Section Gang — Descriptive — Bright and humorous—Unaccompanied.
543 Lead, Kindly Light—Unaccompanied.
794 Life Boat Crew—Descriptive selection—Unaccompanied.
544 Little Darling, Dream of Me—Unaccompanied.
1053 Maggie Murphy's Lawn Party.
1158 Medley of Popular Choruses—"When It's Moonlight, Mary Darling," "I'm Afraid to Come Home in the Dark," "There Never Was a Girl Like You" and "Sweetheart Days."
692 Meeting of the Hen Roost Club—Humorous—Unaccompanied.
823 Moonlight on the Lake—Unaccompanied.
*520 Nearer, My God, to Thee—Unaccompanied.
*20 Old Black Joe—Unaccompanied.
696 Old Oaken Bucket—Unaccompanied.
718 Onward, Christian Soldiers—Unaccompanied.
1077 Owl and the Pussy Cat.
*1124 Price of the Prairie—A little love episode of the western prairie.
547 Rock of Ages—Unaccompanied.
521 Rosary—Very well rendered—Orchestra accompaniment.
373 Sleigh-Ride Party—A jolly party out for a good time—Unaccompanied.
919 Southern Girl—A tribute to the "Southern Girl"—Orchestra accompaniment.
72 Soldier's Farewell—Blending of voices is fine.
*1082 Tell Mother I'll Be There.
1098 Tennessee Tessie.
892 Tenting On the Old Camp Ground—Orchestra accompaniment.
700 Vacant Chair—World famous selection—Unaccompanied.
673 Where is My Wandering Boy Tonight?—Artistically rendered—Unaccompanied.
991 Winter Song—A well known and popular selection—Orchestra accompaniment.

DESCRIPTIVE VOCAL SELECTIONS.

1174 Alderman Dolan's Campaign Speech—Extremely amusing. Steve Porter
985 Flanagan at the Barber's—A selection of rapid fire wit and humor. Porter
1016 Flanagan in a Broadway Car. Porter
515 Flanagan's Night Off—Humorous selection. Spencer and Porter
464 Flogging scene from "Uncle Tom's Cabin"—Dialogue between "Simon Legree" and "Uncle Tom," with orchestra accompaniment.
494 Jokesmiths—A rapid fire broadside of wit and humor. Spencer and Por-

LIST OF 10-INCH OXFORD DISC RECORDS CONTINUED ON NEXT PAGE.

10-INCH OXFORD DISC RECORDS.—Continued.

347 Musical Yankee—A bright record full of jokes. Spencer
592 Old Mother Hubbard—Presents several well known "Mother Goose" rhymes. Spencer and Holt
370 Our National Airs—A patriotic poem. With the closing line of each verse the orchestra takes up the air. The melodies introduced are "Marching Through Georgia," "America," "Dixie" and "The Star Spangled Banner." Spencer
372 Scene at a Dog Fight—Most realistic record imaginable. Spencer and Holt
389 Transformation Scene from "Dr. Jekyll and Mr. Hyde." Spencer

UNCLE JOSH WEATHERBY'S YANKEE DIALECT STORIES.

The quaint humor, original witticisms and infectious laugh of our genial friend, Mr. Cal Stewart, are a sure cure for "the blues."

722 Sunday School Picnic at Pumpkin Centre—Mr. and Mrs. Cal Stewart and male quartette.
821 Uncle Josh and Nancy Go to Housekeeping—Mr. and Mrs. Cal Stewart and male quartette.
990 Uncle Josh and the Insurance Company Our genial friend in his usual happy mood.
698 Uncle Josh at the Chinese Laundry—He relates his experience while trying to get his wash.
723 Uncle Josh in a Department Store.
699 Uncle Josh in a Roller Skating Rink.
768 Uncle Josh's Trip to Coney Island—Very amusing.
745 Uncle Josh's Visit to New York—He is somewhat awed by the sights.

MINSTRELS.

Carnivals of mirth and melody, introducing overtures, dialogues, jokes and songs.

720 Rambler Minstrels No. 1—Opens with "In the Good Old United States," by the entire company, followed by bright jokes, concluding with the song "San Antonio."
741 Rambler Minstrels No. 2—Opens with a chorus of "Wait Till the Sun Shines, Nellie," followed by a number of humorous jokes, and concluding with a verse of the song, "You'll Have to Wait Till My Ship Comes In."
789 Rambler Minstrels No. 3—Opens with Good-Bye, New York Town," by entire company, followed by clever jokes, concluding with a verse of "My Creole Sadie," quartette joining in chorus.
790 Rambler Minstrels No. 4 — Opening chorus, "College Life," by entire company, followed by clever jokes, concluding with "My Kickapoo Queen."
871 Rambler Minstrels No. 5—Opens with the chorus of "It's Always the Same in Dixie," by the entire company, followed by witty jokes, concluding with a verse of the song, "I Know Dat I'll Be Happy Till I Die."
963 Rambler Minstrels No. 6 — Opening chorus, "Bye Bye, My Sailor Boy, Jack Tar," by entire company, followed by bright jokes, concluding with a verse of "Good-Bye, Honey, Good-Bye."
988 Rambler Minstrels No. 7 — Opening chorus, "Bye, Bye, My Caroline," by entire company, followed by jokes, concluding with "At the Meeting House Tonight."
1056 Rambler Minstrels No. 8 — Opening chorus, "Make a Lot of Noise;" closing song, "Ev'ry Day She Wanted Something Else," interspersed with clever jokes and laughter.
1078 Rambler Minstrels No. 9—Opens with the chorus of "Broncho Buster," by entire company, concludes with song "I'm Happy When the Band Plays Dixie." Clever jokes, laughter and applause are interspersed.
1146 Rambler Minstrels No. 10 — Another lively and entertaining minstrel show, introducing as an opening chorus, "My Dream of the U. S. A.," and after the usual wit and comedy it concludes with the chorus of "Moon Beams"
*1184 Rambler Minstrels No. 11—Opening chorus, "Dixie and the Girl I Love," clever jokes and witty repartee; closing chorus, "Some Day, Melinda."

No. 20N5117 Ten-Inch Oxford Disc Records. Shipping weight of one dozen, 8 pounds. Price, per dozen, **$3.50**; each.....(By mail, postage extra, per record, 23c.)....**30c**
Do not order 7-inch or 12-inch records from this list, because the numbers shown in this list are made in 10-inch size only.

7-INCH OXFORD DISC RECORDS

17 Cents Each. $1.98 Per Dozen

OUR 7-INCH OXFORD DISC RECORDS ARE MIGHTY GOOD RECORDS.

IN MUSICAL QUALITY, smoothness and freedom from scratch, volume and sweetness of tone, they are equal to any records made regardless of size or price.

REMEMBER, these 7-Inch Oxford Disc Records sound just the same as the 10-inch records, because they are made by exactly the same process, the same high grade material is used, the same high class musicians are employed, but they do not play as long as the 10-inch, because they are smaller. That's the only difference. The 7-inch record is a shorter piece of music. The quality is there in the 7-inch Oxford record just the same as in the 10-inch size, and they are sold under the same guarantee, your money, including freight or express charges, returned to you without question or argument if you don't like them.

When ordering 7-inch Oxford Disc Records, mention "Catalogue No. 20N5116" and give the selection number of each record you want. Do not order 10-inch or 12-inch records from this list, as these numbers are made in 7-inch size only. For 10 and 12-inch selections see pages 311 and 312. See note below regarding machines these records will fit.

BAND SELECTIONS.

5027 American Eagle March.
5028 American Marines—March.
5800 American Patrol.
5922 Arkansas Huskin' Bee.
5063 Battle of Manila—Descriptive.
5066 Blue and the Gray Patrol.
5065 Blue Grass Beauties.
5014 Bohemian Girl—Selection.
5015 Carmen Selection. Bizet.
5824 Cavalleria Rusticana Intermezzo.
5071 Coming Through the Rye—With piccolo solo.
5810 Cottonfield Capers—Descriptive.
5812 Darkies' Dream—Descriptive.
5016 Daughter of the Regiment—Selection.
5755 Dixie Girl March.
5034 El Capitan March.
5023 Faust Waltz.
5037 Floredora March.
5114 Florodora, Tell Me, Pretty Maiden.
5084 Gloria 12th Mass. Mozart.
5003 Hallelujah Chorus, Messiah.
5040 Hands Across the Sea March.
5085 Hearts and Flowers.
5597 Hiawatha—From the Runaways
5086 Home, Sweet Home.
5632 Jack Tar March.
5020 King Dodo—Selection.
5093 La Marseillaise.
5646 Marriage Bells—Cornet solo.
5007 Merry Wives of Windsor.
5626 Midnight Flyer.
5101 Nearer My God to Thee.
5050 New England's Finest March.
5102 Old Church Organ.
5051 Peace Forever March.
5008 Poet and Peasant—Overture.
6013 Romany Rye Intermezzo.
5108 Salome Intermezzo.
5868 Sea Shell Waltz—Trombone solo with band accompaniment.
5109 Smoky Mokes.
5110 Spring Song. Mendelssohn.
5055 Stars and Stripes Forever—March.
5111 Star Spangled Banner.
5002 Tannhauser—Grand March.
5011 Tannhauser Pilgrim's Chorus.
5116 Tone Pictures of the 71st Regiment Leaving for Cuba.
5000 Trovatore Anvil Chorus. Verdi.
5056 Twenty-Third Regiment—March.
5048 Wedding March.
5947 Winona.

ORCHESTRA SELECTIONS.

5811 Dancing on the Housetops—Descriptive.
5162 Dandy Sandy.
5161 Darkies' Jubilee.
5813 Darkie Tickle—Descriptive.
5579 Dixie Land—Two Step.
5957 Dreamland Medley.
5843 Gondolier.
5964 Handsome Harry.
5164 Happy Hooligan.
5165 Hunting Scene—Descriptive.
5865 In a Nutshell.
5827 In Zanzibar.
5168 In the Clock Store—Descriptive.
5170 Jolly Coppersmith—Descriptive.
5933 Jovial Joe.
5172 La Paloma.
5633 Laughing Water.
5174 Limited Express.
5175 Lion Tamer Galop.
5180 Midnight Alarm—Descriptive.
5179 Mill in the Forest—Descriptive
5181 Mississippi Bubble.
5834 Navajo.
5186 Nightingale and the Frog—With piccolo solo.
6009 Over the Waves.
5187 Plantation Pastimes.
5188 Pretty Mollie Shannon Waltz.
5148 Ragtime Skedaddle.
5584 Rose, My Rose, Waltz.
5586 Scarecrow Dance.
5195 Sentimental Tommy.
5863 Simple Simon.
5941 Soko—A Moorish intermezzo.
5196 Southern Roses Waltz.
5197 Stein Song.
5581 Sun Dance.
5649 Sunburst.
5977 Three Jolly Cobblers—Descriptive.
5200 Titi's Serenade.
5850 Uncle Sammy.
5981 Unter den Linden.
5208 Virginia Reel.
5210 We're All Good Fellows.
5760 Winona.
5211 Yale Boola.
5212 Zallah—Egyptian intermezzo.

BRASS QUARTETTE.

5809 Come Where My Love Lies Dreaming.
5816 Down on the Farm.
5938 Nearer My God to Thee.
5912 Sweet and Low.

ACCORDION SOLOS.

5996 Bedelia—With variations.
6006 Irish Jigs and Reels—Medley.

BANJO SOLOS.

5231 Blaze Away.
5232 California Dance.
5233 Colored Major.
5234 Coon Band Contest.
5235 Donkey Laugh.
5236 Harmony Mose.
5237 Hot Corn Jubilee.
5238 Marriage Bells.
5239 Medley—Introducing "Josephine, My Joe."
5240 Mosquito Parade.
5241 Pearl of the Harem.
5242 Raggy Ragians.
5243 Tell Me, Pretty Maiden.
5244 Whoa Bill.
5245 Yankee Doodle.

CLARIONET SOLOS.

5259 How Can I Leave Thee.
5260 Little Nell.
5261 Long, Long Ago.
5262 Sanctus. Gounod.

CORNET SOLOS.

5219 Be My Own.
5220 Carnival of Venice.
5769 Cary Waltz.
5815 Don't Be Cross.
5222 Down Deep Within the Cellar.
5777 King Carnival.
5842 Sweet Sixteen.

CORNET AND TROMBONE DUETS.

5226 Alice Where Art Thou.
5228 The Palms.
5229 Tyroleans.
5230 Utility Polka.

FLUTE SOLOS.

5246 Ave Maria.
5247 Carnival of Venice.
5248 Sleep Well, Thou Sweet Angel
5786 Sweet Longing Romance.

VIOLIN SOLOS.

5825 Cavalleria Rusticana—Intermezzo.
5832 Mocking Bird.

XYLOPHONE SOLOS.

5263 Brilliant Galop.
5264 Carnival of Venice.
5265 Dancing in the Sunlight.
5652 Dinah Jones.
5266 Du Du—With variations.
5267 Fire Fly Galop.
5269 Medley of Popular Airs.
5271 My Old Kentucky Home.
5273 Scotch Airs.

FLUTE AND SAXOPHONE DUETS.

5860 Call Me Thine Own—Romance.
5858 Caprice Juanita.
5859 Happy Days.

FIFE AND DRUM CORPS SELECTIONS.

5214 An Election District Parade in New York City.
5215 Recollections of 1861.
5216 Red, White and Blue.
5217 Spirit of '76.

PICCOLO SOLOS.

5249 Dance of the Hoboes.
5251 Humming Bird Polka.
5252 Medley Jig.
5253 Nigger Fever.
5255 Ragtime Skedaddle.
5256 Spring Warbling Polka.

WHISTLING SOLOS.

5437 Independentia March.
5438 Over the Waves.

VOCAL SOLOS.

Piano accompaniment unless otherwise specified. Initial letters for singers' names are same as specified on preceding pages for 10-inch records.

5891 Ain't It Funny What a Difference Just a Few Hours Make. D. Q.
5921 All Aboard for Dreamland. W. D.
5798 Always in the Way. G. A.
5277 And Then I Laughed. C. S.
5278 Anna Let Me Hear From You. W. D.
5992 Annie Laurie—With orchestra accompaniment. J. H.
5634 Anona. G. A.
5653 Answer—With orchestra accompaniment. G. A.
5279 Any Old Place I Hang My Hat is Home Sweet Home to Me. W. D.
5635 Any Rags—With orchestra accompaniment. A. C.
5950 Back Among the Clover and the Corn. J. H.
5715 Banjo Evangelist. L. S.
5716 Banquet in Misery Hall. A. C.
5995 Because. J. H.
5636 Bedelia—With orchestra accompaniment. A. C.
5607 Beer That Made Milwaukee Famous. D. Q.
5589 Believe. G. A.
5806 Blue Bell. H. B.
5767 Bye, Bye, Ma Honey. B. G.
5768 By the Sycamore Tree. B. R.
5290 Carving the Duck. G. J.
5877 Come Back to Erin. G. G.
5293 Come Down Ma Evening Star A. C.
5659 Congo Love Song—From "Nancy Brown." A. C.
5296 Creole Belles. A. C.
5999 Dat Minstrel Man of Mine—With banjo accompaniment by Parke Hunter. L. S.
5298 Dat's the Way to Spell Chicken. A. C.
5925 Dear Old Girl. J. N.
5954 Dis-pos-zes Means Move. B. He.
5665 Dixie Land. G. G.
5666 Doing His Duty Ooty. E. F.
5667 Down in Mobile Long Ago. A. C.
5955 Down on the Brandywine. B. He.
5927 Down on the Farm. J. N.
5956 Dreaming, Dreaming. J. H.
5670 Drinking Song—From Martha. G. A.
5301 Emmet's Lullaby. P. L.
5302 Emmet's Yodle. P. L.
5672 Everybody's Awfully Good to Me. E. F.
5928 Every Day is Sunshine When the Heart Beats True. J. N.
5614 Every Morn I Bring Her Chicken. A. C.
5303 Everything at Reilly's Must Be Done in Irish Style. E. F.
5594 Father Wants the Cradle Back. D. Q.
5930 Follow the Merry Crowd. W. D.
5615 For All Eternity. G. A.
5931 For Sale—A Baby. J. N.
5717 Girl You Love. From "Three Little Maids." A. C.
5900 Gondolier—With orchestra accompaniment. A. C.
5674 Good-Bye. G. A.
5960 Good-Bye, Little Girl, Good-Bye. H. T.
5820 Good-Bye Liza Jane—With orchestra accompaniment. B. R.
5983 Good-Bye, Ma Lady Love. H. B.
5756 Happy Days—With orchestra accompaniment. G. A.
5675 He Didn't Know Exactly What to Do. E. F.
5822 He May Get Over It, But He'll Never Look the Same. B. R.
5575 Hiawatha—From the "Runaways." D. Q.
5757 Holy City. G. A.
5680 Home, Sweet Home—With orchestra accompaniment. G. A.
5965 Hooray for a Holiday. B. He.
5316 If Time Was Money, I'd Be a Millionaire. A. C.
5876 I Got Company and You Can't Come In. B. R.
5321 I'm Old, but I'm Awfully Tough. C. S.
5685 I Love Only One Girl in This Wide, Wide World—From "The Wizard of Oz." H. B.
5616 I'm a Jonah Man—Williams and Walker. A. C.
5871 I'm on the Water Wagon Now. D. Q.
5617 I'm Thinking of You All the While. A.C.
5327 I Need the Money. E. F.
5966 In the Ladies' Home Journal. B. R.
5690 In the Land of Make Believe. A. C.
5333 I Once Did Love a Pretty Yaller Girl. A. C.
5893 Irish, the Irish. D. Q.
5692 It Was the Dutch. E. F.
5899 I've Got a Feeling for You—With orchestra accompaniment. B. R.
5336 I Want Someone to Care for Me. W. D.
5339 I Was Certainly Dreaming. W. D.
5897 I Wonder What Makes It Snow—With orchestra accompaniment. B. R.
5887 Just Remember I Love You. J. N.
5697 Laughing Coon. G. J.
5631 Laughing Song. G. J.
5778 Laughing Water—From "Mother Goose." M. H.
5348 Lazy Little Mazy Jones. A. C.
5886 Like a Star That Falls From Heaven. J. N.
5969 Lost Chord. J. H.
5600 Maybe. G. A.
5357 Medley of Emmet's Yodles. P. L.
5934 Meet Me in St. Louis, Louis. W. D.
5831 Message of the Violet. G. A.
5935 Mississippi Mamie. J. N.
5703 Moon, Moon—From "The Toreador." E. F.
5576 Must You—From "The Wizard of Oz." D. Q.
5704 My Baby's Kiss. E. F.
5705 My Little Coney Isle. E. F.
5754 Nancy Brown. E. F.
5836 Navajo—With orch. accomp. G. G.
5974 Nigger That's Living High. B. G.
5619 Nobody's Looking but the Owl and the Moon. A. C.
5377 Oh, Didn't He Ramble. A. C.
5975 Oh, Lord, Be Thou My Light. A. Cl.
5883 On a Good Old Trolley Ride. J. N.
5838 One Sweetly Solemn Thought. A. Cl.
5386 Please Let Me Sleep. A. C.
5782 Rabbit Hash. B. G.
5989 Rare Old Bird. A. C.
5389 Roll on Silver Moon. P. L.
5784 Roll on the Ground. B. G.
5609 Rosary. G. A.
5604 Sally in Our Alley. G. G.
5394 Schneider Does Your Mother Know You're Out? P. L.
6014 Seminole. H. T.
5624 Since I First Met You—From "The Sultan of Sulu." G. A.
5625 Sleep, Baby, Sleep. P. L.
5397 Stay in Your Own Backyard. A. C.
5942 Sweetest Girl in Dixie. J. H.
5874 'Tain't no Disgrace to Run When You are Skeered. B. R.
5606 That's Where She Sits All Day—From "The Wizard of Oz." D. Q.
5577 Then I'd Be Satisfied With Life—From "The Silver Slipper." D. Q.
5846 There is a Little Street in Heaven That They Call Broadway." E. F.
5574 There's a Lot of Things You Never Learned at School—From "The Wizard of Oz." D. Q.
5406 Ticklish Reuben. C. S.
5979 Tippecanoe. B. R.
5410 Turkey and the Turk. W. D.
5789 Turkey in the Straw. B. G.
6017 Two Eyes of Brown. J. H.
5411 Uncle Jefferson. A. C.
5847 Under the Anheuser Bush—With orchestra accompaniment. B. R.
5412 Under the Bamboo Tree. A. C.
5873 Under the Mistletoe Bough. D. Q.
5728 Under the Rose. G. A.
5729 Upper Broadway After Dark. E. F.
5890 Valley by the Sea. E. F.
5851 Violets. G. A.
5943 We've Got to Move Today. H. T.

REGARDING MACHINES THE OXFORD DISC RECORDS WILL FIT. Oxford Disc Records, either 7-inch, 10-inch or 12-inch, fit any disc talking machine that we have ever sold, including the Harvard machines, the Oxford machines and the Columbia Graphophones. They fit any Victor talking machine, any Zonophone, any Star talking machine or any other make or style of disc talking machine that takes a record having a hole in the center ¼ inch in diameter. The only machines that the disc records will not fit are the Aretino, the Standard and the Harmony. These machines are so constructed that they require a special record; for example, the Aretino requires a record having a hole in the center about 3 inches in diameter.

LIST OF 7-INCH OXFORD DISC RECORDS CONTINUED ON NEXT PAGE.

7-INCH OXFORD DISC RECORDS.—Continued.

VOCAL SOLOS—Continued.

5613 What's the Matter With the Moon Tonight—From "The Mocking Bird." G. A.
5425 When It's All Going Out and Nothing Coming In. A. C.
5426 When I Was a Dear Little Baby. P. L.
5944 When the Coons Have a Dreamland of Their Own. B. R.
5429 When the Mists Have Rolled Away. J. F.
5733 When You Love, Love, Love—From "The Wizard of Oz." H. B.
5431 Whippoorwill Whistling.
5432 Whistling Coon. G. J.
5852 Whistling Girl. G. J.
5853 Whistling Riley. E. F.
5434 Will You Always Love Me Darling? J. F.
5854 Winsome Winnie. G. A.
5628 Witch Behind the Moon—From "The Wizard of Oz." G. A.
5795 Woodchuck Song. B. R.
5796 Wouldn't It Make You Hungry? B. R.
5630 You Can't Fool All the People All the Time. A. C.
5734 You'd Better Ask Me. G. A.
5894 You're Always Behind Like an Old Cow's Tail. A. C.
5946 You're as Welcome as the Flowers in May. J. H.
5884 You're the Sweetest Flower That Grows in Tennessee. J. N.

VOCAL DUETS BY COLLINS AND HARLAN.

5440 Closing Time in a Country Grocery.
5914 Come Down From the Big Fig Tree.
6000 Does You Love Me as You Used to, Miss Jane?
5442 First Rehearsal of the Husking Bee.
6092 Have You Seen Maggy Riley?
5736 Hiawatha Parody.
5598 Hurrah for Baffin's Bay—From "The Wizard of Oz."
5443 I'm Unlucky.
5737 It Was the Dutch.
5444 Jerry Murphy Is a Friend of Mine.
5599 Marriage Is Sublime.
5837 Never Bank on a Travel Man.
5446 Nursery Rhymes.
5447 On Broadway to Dahomey Bye and Bye.
5450 They Were All Doing the Same.
5449 Troubles of the Reuben and the Maid.
5451 Two Rubes in a Tavern.

MALE QUARTETTE.

5583 Barbecue in Old Kentucky.
5738 Camp Meeting Jubilee.
5590 Characteristic Negro Medley.
5592 Coon Wedding in Southern Georgia.
5456 Farmyard Medley.
5608 Hoozier Hollow Quilting Party.
5457 I'se Gwine Back to Dixie.
5458 Kathleen Mavourneen.
5459 Laughing Medley.
5460 Little Darling, Dream of Me.
5461 Massa's in the Cold, Cold Ground.
5462 My Old Kentucky Home.
5455 Night Trip to Buffalo.
5463 Old Folks at Home.
5603 On Board the Battleship Oregon.
5465 Sleighride Party.
5466 Steamboat Medley.
5605 St. Patrick's Day at Clancy's.
5468 Trip to the County Fair.
5587 Virginia Christening.

MINSTRELS.

5470 Dese Bones Shall Rise Again.
5471 Hear Dem Bells.
5473 Laughing Song.
5476 Upon the Golden Shore.

VAUDEVILLE SELECTIONS.

5494 Arkansas Traveler—With violin.
5489 Auction Sale of Household Goods.
5804 Auction Sale of Musical Instruments—By Len Spencer and Parke Hunter.
5911 Difference Between a German and Irish Picnic—By Cal. Stewart and John Kaiser.
5775 Having Fun with the Orchestra—By Len Spencer and orchestra.
5910 Jim Jackson's Racetrack Story—By Spencer and Holt.
5830 Levee Scene—By Spencer and orchestra.
5780 Musical Act "Ebony Emperors of Melody"—Len Spencer, quartette and orchestra.
5781 Prize Waltz Contest—Len Spencer and orchestra.
5839 Reuben Haskin's Trip Around the World in His Airship "Luna"—Len Spencer and Parke Hunter.
5909 Whistling Newsboy—Spencer and Holt.

RECITATIONS.

5739 Carolina Jim.
5740 Independence Bell.
5741 Leap for Life.
5743 Newsboy's Christmas.
5742 Ole Laughlin.
5488 Wedding of the Frog and the Mouse—A story for little folks.
5758 Yaller Dog's Love for a Nigger.

UNCLE JOSH WEATHERBY'S YANKEE DIALECT LAUGHING STORIES—By Cal Stewart.

5493 Husking Bee—With violin.
5744 Jim Lawson's Hogs.
5495 Jim Lawson's Horse Trade.
5496 Last Day of School at Pumpkin Center.
5745 Si Pittingell's Brooms.
5787 Thrashing Time at Pumpkin Center.
5746 Three Little Owls and the Naughty Little Mice.
5747 Uncle Josh and Aunt Nancy Smith on a Visit to New York.
5902 Uncle Josh's Arrival in New York City.
5497 Uncle Josh at a Camp Meeting.
5908 Uncle Josh at a Circus.
5903 Uncle Josh at Delmonico's.
5498 Uncle Josh in a Chinese Laundry.
5499 Uncle Josh in a Department Store.
5906 Uncle Josh's Invitation to His Farm.
5907 Uncle Josh on a Bicycle.
5901 Uncle Josh on a Fifth Ave. Bus.
5905 Uncle Josh on a Street Car.
5748 Uncle Josh on an Automobile.
5848 Uncle Josh Playing Baseball.
5500 Uncle Josh Playing Golf.
5501 Uncle Josh's Trip to Boston.
5904 Uncle Josh's Troubles in a Hotel.
5849 Uncle Josh's Visit to Coney Island

FUNNY STORIES.

5492 Piccolo Player's Reward.
5491 Pietro and the Polar Bear.
5840 Rube Haskin's Ride on a Cyclone Auto.

No. 20N5116 Seven-Inch Oxford Disc Records. Price, per dozen, $1.98; each..................(If sent by mail, postage extra, per record, 23 cents)..........17c
Shipping weight of one dozen, packed for express or freight shipment, 8 pounds.

Do not order 10-inch records from this list. The selections shown in this list are not made in 10-inch size. See preceding pages for 10-inch records.

58c EACH — 12-INCH OXFORD DISC RECORDS — $6.85 PER DOZEN

THE BIG 12-INCH OXFORD DISC RECORD represents the highest degree of perfection in record making. Not only do they play much longer than smaller records, but they are actually better in musical and wearing qualities. The large disc allows recording at a greater speed, making longer and less abrupt curves in the record grooves, resulting in better reproduction of original sounds and increases the wearing quality of the record, as the needle in following these longer curves avoids breaking down the walls of the record groove so quickly as in following shorter curves.

THE GREAT EXPENSE of producing the original masters for these large 12-inch records makes it impossible to put up as large a list of selections as are shown in the 7-inch and 10-inch records, but very special care has been exercised in selecting the titles for this list, and every selection is a record of unusual merit. You can safely order any record in this list, even though the selection is unknown to you, with the assurance that you will be more than pleased, and your friends and neighbors will envy you whenever they hear them. They are marvelous examples of the perfection which has been reached in the recording and reproducing of sound.

When ordering 12-inch records mention No. 20N5118 and give the selection number of each record wanted.
Do not order 7-inch or 10-inch records from this list, as the numbers shown in this list are made in 12-inch size only.
See note on page 313 regarding machines these records will fit.

CONCERT BAND.

7037 Beautiful Galatea—Overture—A striking melodious overture, by the well known composer, F. von Suppe.
7041 Coronation March—From "Le Prophet" A superb record of Meyerbeer's stately, majestic march.
7001 Der Tambour der Garde—Overture—With excellent solo parts for wood, wind, brass and drums.
7042 Doctrinen Waltz—This waltz is only another example of the magnetic style of the "Waltz King," Strauss.
7002 Forget-Me-Not — Intermezzo — Dainty number in concert style.
7043 Gardes du Corps March.
7003 G. A. R. Patrol—The fife and drum, the trumpet and drum parts cannot be surpassed.
7038 Hallelujah Chorus—From the Oratorio "The Messiah"—An excellent record.
7004 Linger Longer—Novelty Two-Step—Something new—a solo clog dance.
7005 Morning Journal's Waltz—An old time favorite by the great "Waltz King," Johann Strauss.
7039 Old Church Organ—Serenade.
7045 Pas des Fleurs—An exquisite, dainty waltz intermezzo from ballet "Naila," by Delibes.
7044 Robert Le Diable Selection—Meyerbeer—A well rendered selection from this famous opera.
7046 Triumph of Old Glory—Our President's March—By Arthur Pryor.
7040 Uncle Sam—March—Composed of four of our most beloved and popular patriotic songs, "Star Spangled Banner," "America," "Glory, Glory, Hallelujah" and "Rally 'Round the Flag."
7006 Wayside Chapel—Reverie.
7047 Wedding March—From "Midsummer Night's Dream," by Mendelssohn.

ORCHESTRA.

7007 Freut Euch des Lebens—Waltz—(Life Let Us Cherish)—A delightful Strauss waltz.
7048 Hearts and Flowers—An especially attractive part is that in which the strains of the violin predominate.
7049 Malaguena—From the Opera "Boabdil" (Moszkowski).
7050 Ma Voisine—Polka—With melodious bell strains in the trio.
7008 Miss Dolly Dollars—Lanciers Figs. 1 and 2.
7009 Miss Dolly Dollars—Lanciers Figs. 3 and 4.
7010 Miss Dolly Dollars—Lanciers Figure 5. Thoroughly up to date brilliant lanciers.
7051 Pansy—Valse Intermezzo—Concert waltz.
7011 Sonora—Spanish Novelette.
7012 Southern Roses—Very entrancing waltz from the operetta, "A Merry War."
7052 Spring Morning Idyll—Attention is called to the natural toned pizzicato of the violins.
7053 Violets' Waltz—Pleasing melodious waltz in perfect tempo for dancing.
7054 Visions of an Easter Morning—With Chimes—The glad tidings of the resurrection are heralded forth by the following hymns: "He Is Risen" (Chimes), "Alleluia" (Brasses and Organ Imitation), "All Hail the Power of Jesus' Name" (Brass Quartette) and "Christ the Lord Is Risen Today" (Chimes).

ACCORDION SOLO BY J. J. KIMMEL.

7026 Marche de Concert—Brilliantly executed.

BELL SOLO BY ED. KING.

With Orchestra Accompaniment.

7013 Garden Matinee—Entr'acte—The double tones in the first strain are worthy of special mention.

CORNET DUET BY SENECA AND OZRA MYGRANT.

With Orchestra Accompaniment.

7055 I Would That My Love—Beautiful Duet of Mendelssohn's.

FLUTE AND SAXOPHONE DUET BY FRANK MAZZIOTTA AND STEPHEN PORPORA.

With Orchestra Accompaniment.

7027 Voice of Love—Plaintive and entreating.

PICCOLO SOLO BY FRANK MAZZIOTTA.

With Orchestra Accompaniment.

7014 Comin' Thro' the Rye—With variations, pleasingly executed.

VIOLIN AND FLUTE DUET BY HENRY HESS AND FRANK MAZZIOTTA.

7015 Susses Shenen (Sweet Longing)—Romance. Charming concert number.

VOCAL SELECTIONS.

With Orchestra Accompaniment.

7018 Bonnie Sweet Bessie—Beautiful old Scotch ballad. Henry Burr.
7057 Face to Face—Sacred. Frank C. Stanley.
7058 For He Shall Give His Angels Charge over Thee—Sacred aria. Frank C. Stanley.
7028 From the Depths—An impressive sacred song. Frank C. Stanley.
7029 Good Night Little Girl, Good Night—A refined sentimental ballad. Henry Burr.
7059 Home, Sweet Home—The theme of this old ballad is the expression of everyone's sentiment. Alice C. Stevenson.
7030 I'm Praying for You—(With organ accompaniment). An inspiring sacred song. Frank C. Stanley.
7049 In Time of Trouble He Shall Hide Me—"For in the time of trouble He shall Hide me in His pavilion. . . ." Psalm 27:5. Impressive and inspiring sacred selection. Frank C. Stanley.
7036 Last Rose of Summer. Roberta Glanville.
7061 My Dreams—A love ballad of the better class. Henry Burr.
7020 My Old Kentucky Home—Plantation melody of the Sunny South. Henry Burr.
7021 O, Dry Those Tears—Favorite ballad. Henry Burr.
7035 Shine On, Oh Stars—A tuneful romanza. Henry Burr.
7062 Sing Me to Sleep—A beautiful dreamy ballad. Henry Burr.
7022 Tale the Church Bell Tolled—Popular ballad of the better class. Frank C. Stanley.

DUETS.

With Orchestra Accompaniment.

7017 Crucifix—Superior reproduction of this sacred duet. Frank C. Stanley and Henry Burr.
7056 Excelsior. Frank C. Stanley and Henry Burr.
7031 My Faith Looks Up to Thee—Music arranged by William K. Bassford. Frank C. Stanley and Henry Burr.
7023 Take a Little Ride With Me—A conversation, with music, between an automobilist and a dairy maid. Composed by Theo. Morse. Alice C. Stevenson and Frank C. Stanley.
7064 Though Your Sins Be As Scarlet—An old favorite hymn. Frank C. Stanley and Henry Burr.

DESCRIPTIVE SELECTION BY ADA JONES AND LEN SPENCER.

With Orchestra Accompaniment.

7033 Rudolph and Rosie at the Skating Rink—Our Teutonic friends pay a visit the rink.

PEERLESS QUARTETTE.

7016 Come Where My Love Lies Dreaming—Blending of voices is extremely pleasing.
7060 Hymns of the Old Church Choir—A semi-religious piece.
7063 Lead, Kindly Light—Grand old hymn.
7032 New Parson at the Darktown Church—(Descriptive)—A melodious and humorous selection.
7034 Sally in Our Alley—This song is still very popular.

MENDELSSOHN MIXED QUARTETTE.

Organ Accompaniment.

7065 Saviour, When Night Involves the Skies—A sacred selection.

UNCLE JOSH WEATHERBY'S YANKEE DIALECT STORIES BY MR. CAL STEWART.

7024 Uncle Josh and the Labor Union—Amusing and ludicrous description of our jovial friend's experience with "Union" farm hands.
7025 Uncle Josh at the Post Office—Uncle Josh receives a letter from "hum," which he reads for the entertainment of his friends.

No. 20N5118 Twelve-Inch Oxford Disc Records. Price, per dozen, $6.85; each................(If sent by mail, postage extra, per record, 35 cents)..........58c
Shipping weight of one dozen, 14 pounds.

Harvard Disc Talking Machine Reduced to $6.95

SPECIFICATIONS.

Cabinet—Golden Oak, with shellac finish. Dovetailed corners, size, 11½x11½ inches at base, 10¾x10¾ inches at top, 5½ inches high.
Horn—Made of sheet steel, with black enamel finish 13½ inches long, with 8½-inch bell.
Sound Box—Latest sound analysing, with automatic spring, needle holder, and heavy mica diaphragm.
Motor—Single spring, with two ball governor and friction disc speed regulator. Runs one 10-inch or two 7-inch records with one winding.
Turntable—10-inch, takes any size disc record, 7, 10, or 12-inch.
Weight—14 pounds.

These machines were made to retail for $15.00. We have only a few hundred of them left, and having closed extensive contracts for the Oxford Tapering Arm Machines, shown on a preceding page, we have decided to close out these Harvard machines, regardless of cost. They are good machines, and you will make no mistake in taking advantage of this special price.

$6.95

No. 20N5038 Harvard Disc Talking Machine, complete, as illustrated and specified. Shipping weight, 28 pounds.
Special close out price..............................$6.95

Harvard Flower Horn Cylinder Talking Machine, 1909 Model, Type P. D. $7.95

Base—Oak, nicely finished, 11¾ inches long, 7 inches wide.
Top—Bent oak, with handle, affording perfect protection to the mechanism and forming a convenient and effective carrying case.
Horn—Latest flower shape, enameled in color, with gold stripes. Handsome in appearance and of finest acoustic properties.
Motor—Single spring, clock work motor, with accurately cut gear and pinions, improved governor and special speed regulator.
Reproducer—Extra large size. Style D1, made from aluminum with special built up mica diaphragm and genuine sapphire reproducing point.
Weight—8 pounds.

This new type P. D. Harvard Cylinder Talking Machine is the best cylinder machine we have ever been able to sell at so low a price. It is well made throughout, strong and durable, and so simple in construction that it is almost impossible for it to get out of order. Look at the big list of Oxford cylinder records available for use with this machine and see how cheaply you can make up a big complete outfit, embracing all the latest selections, besides all the good old time favorites, too.

$7.95

No. 20N5036 Harvard Flower Horn Cylinder Talking Machine, Type P. D. Shipping weight, 25 pounds. Price..............................$7.95

ORD TONE ARM CYLINDER TALKING HINE, 1909 MODEL, TYPE G. H. $13.75

Cabinet—Solid oak, with dovetailed corners, measuring $7\frac{1}{4}$x$10\frac{1}{4}$ inches at the base and $6\frac{3}{8}$x10 inches at the top. Affords to the motor complete protection from dust or injury of any kind.

Cover—Handsome bent oak cover or top for protection to the upper mechanism and constituting at the same time a convenient carrying case. Total height with cover, $8\frac{3}{8}$ inches.

Horn—Handsome flower shape, of perfect acoustic properties. Diameter of bell, $16\frac{3}{8}$ inches; length, $16\frac{1}{2}$ inches. Finish, baked on black enamel, with gold stripes.

Motor—Powerful, noiseless and smooth running, with latest type of speed regulator and governor, insuring absolutely uniform speed. Can be wound while running.

Tone Arm—Flexible and affording unobstructed passage for sound waves from reproducer to horn.

Reproducer—New, spring contact, with button shaped sapphire point.

Weight—13 pounds.

Never until we placed this type G. H. machine on the market had a Tone Arm cylinder talking machine been sold for less than $30.00, yet we have this season reduced our price for this machine to $13.75, the lowest price ever known for a cylinder talking machine with flexible tone arm, spring contact reproducer and large flower horn, the latest improvements in machines of this kind.

No. 20N5002 Oxford Tone Arm Cylinder Talking Machine, Type G. H. Price....................$13.75
Shipping weight, 35 pounds.

OXFORD TONE ARM CYLINDER TALKING MACHINE, 1909 MODEL, TYPE W. M. $18.75

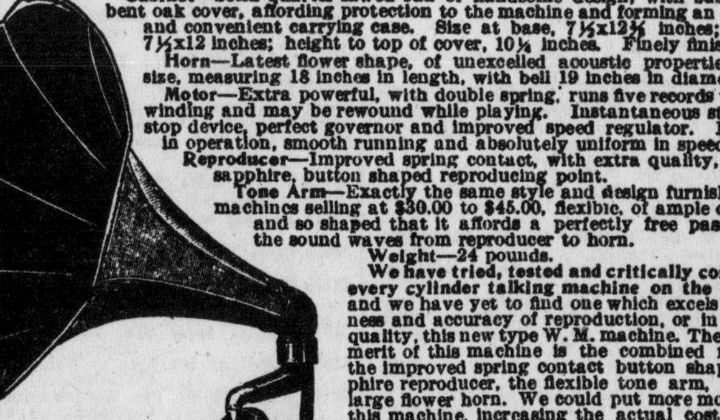

Cabinet—Solid quarter sawed oak of handsome design, with substantial bent oak cover, affording protection to the machine and forming an effective and convenient carrying case. Size at base, $7\frac{1}{2}$x$12\frac{3}{8}$ inches; at top, $7\frac{1}{2}$x12 inches; height to top of cover, $10\frac{1}{8}$ inches. Finely finished.

Horn—Latest flower shape, of unexcelled acoustic properties, large size, measuring 18 inches in length, with bell 19 inches in diameter.

Motor—Extra powerful, with double spring; runs five records with one winding and may be rewound while playing. Instantaneous start and stop device, perfect governor and improved speed regulator. Noiseless in operation, smooth running and absolutely uniform in speed.

Reproducer—Improved spring contact, with extra quality, genuine sapphire, button shaped reproducing point.

Tone Arm—Exactly the same style and design furnished with machines selling at $30.00 to $45.00, flexible, of ample diameter and so shaped that it affords a perfectly free passage for the sound waves from reproducer to horn.

Weight—24 pounds.

We have tried, tested and critically considered every cylinder talking machine on the market, and we have yet to find one which excels in clearness and accuracy of reproduction, or in musical quality, this new type W. M. machine. The unusual merit of this machine is the combined result of the improved spring contact button shaped sapphire reproducer, the flexible tone arm, and the large flower horn. We could put more money into this machine, increasing the actual cost of production, but we could not increase the efficiency of the essential parts. Any increase in the cost of building this talking machine would necessarily be limited to making it more ornamental, perhaps giving it a big hand carved cabinet, or gold plating the metal parts, but no additional money put into its construction would improve the tone or the accuracy of reproduction.

No. 20N5007 Oxford Tone Arm Cylinder Talking Machine, Type W. M. Price....$18.75
Shipping weight, 50 pounds.

18 CENTS EACH — OXFORD CYLINDER RECORDS — $2.15 PER DOZEN

THE OXFORD CYLINDER RECORDS

are standard size wax records of the highest degree of excellence. They are made by the very latest and most approved method, moulded in gold lined metallic moulds, and in clearness of reproduction, accuracy and musical quality, are unsurpassed by any wax cylinder records made.

THESE RECORDS FIT ANY MACHINE

using standard size wax cylinder records; they fit any cylinder record machine that we have ever sold; they fit any cylinder talking machine or Graphophone made or sold by the Columbia Phonograph Company; they fit any Phonograph or Edison talking machine; they fit any of the small low priced imported talking machines, such as the "Lyra" or the "Little Princess," or any of the various machines of this type which have been extensively sold and given as premiums.

They do not fit the "Busy Bee," because this machine is made with a mandrel that is larger than standard size. These Oxford cylinder records are exactly 4 inches long; the outside diameter is exactly 2 3-16 inches and the inside diameter varies from $1\frac{3}{4}$ inches at one end to $1\frac{7}{8}$ inches at the other end. They are exactly the same size as the Columbia Phonograph Company's XP records or the Edison records.

We accept all orders for these new Oxford cylinder records with the understanding and agreement that you can try them on your machine, compare them with other records costing twice the price we ask you, and if you do not find them entirely satisfactory, as good, if not better, than any cylinder record you ever heard, you can return them to us at our expense, and we will cheerfully, without question or argument, refund your money in full, including any transportation charges you may have paid.

In ordering Oxford Cylinder Records mention catalogue No. 20N5103 and also state selection number of each one wanted.

BAND SELECTIONS.

31529 American Students' Waltz.
33068 Banner March, The.
32413 By the Sycamore Tree Medley.
32579 Capture of Forts at Port Arthur.
31957 Chariot Race March—(With whistling solo.)
32650 "Coax Me" Medley.
31933 Crown Diamonds Overture. Auber.
40502 Crystal Wave Waltz. Onda Cristalina.
33007 Destruction of San Francisco—Descriptive.
32982 Dixie Queen March.
33101 Dream of the Rarebit Fiend.
514 El Capitan March.
31891 "Faust"—Ballet music.
1603 God Save the King.
33102 Golden West March.
40504 Gondolier's Waltz—El Gondolero.
32832 Happy Heinie—March and two-step.
501 High School Cadets' March.
55031 Hipp, Hipp, Hurrah.
32735 Hobo Band.
33095 Honor and Glory March.
31775 In a Cosy Corner.
33067 In the Lead—March and two-step.
32107 Invitation to the Waltz. Weber.
200984 Jersey Carnival March.
31559 Jolly Cadet, The—March characteristic.
31931 Jolly Robbers Overture—Von Suppe.
1526 La Marseillaise.
32702 Lewis and Clarke Centennial March.
500 Liberty Bell March—Bell effect.
33026 Lord Baltimore March.
32110 Love's Dream After the Ball—Czibulka.
33096 Mascot of the Troop March.
32816 Me and Me Banjo.
32902 Men of Harlech—Quick step.
1583 Merry War March.
40503 Mexican Love Waltz—Amor Mexicano.
40340 Military School March.
32802 My Irish Molly O—Medley.
1509 My Pretty Peggy—With cornet solo.
32905 Nightingale Polka—With piccolo solo.
32600 Noisy Bill—Characteristic march.
32971 On to Victory March—From "The Free Lance."
1537 O, Promise Me—From "Robin Hood," with cornet solo.
32313 Princess of Kensington—Selections from.
31543 Queen's Trumpeters—Cornet duet.
1601 Robin Hood—Selections from.
32749 Roosevelt's Inaugural Parade.
33044 Rosebud Medley.
40547 Sailing With the Wind March.
32649 Sho-Gun, The—Selections from.
33185 Shoulder Straps—March and two-step.
32845 Silver Heels March and Two-Step.
32983 Slidihg Jim—Trombone extravaganza.
32599 Soldier's Dream—With cornet solo.
32598 Stadium March.
31912 Stradella Overture—Flowtow.
201582 Tearin' o' the Green, The
32607 Teasing Medley.
33027 Under Arms March.
1564 Under the Double Eagle March.
32883 Wait Till the Sun Shines, Nelly—Medley
32815 Whistler and His Dog—Caprice.
31670 With Sword and Lance March.

ORCHESTRA SELECTIONS.

15194 Battle of Manilla—Descriptive.
32121 Broadway Hits—Medley march.
32855 Church Parade March.
15141 Circus Galop—Descriptive.
32304 Departure of a Hamburg-American Liner—Descriptive.
32857 Happyland, Selections from.
32912 Irish-American March and Two-Step.
32770 Jolly Blacksmith—With anvil and bell effects.
15039 Jolly Coppersmith—Descriptive, with anvil effect and vocal chorus.
40313 La Paloma—The Dove.
32321 Lucky Duck, A.
32506 Obeja—March and two-step.
692 Polly Prim—March and two-step.
:045 Red Mill Selections From The.
:195 Roosevelt's Rough Riders, Charge of.
32950 Seeing New York, or a Trip on the Rubberneck Coach—Descriptive.
15220 Smoky Mokes March.
32843 St. Louis Tickle.
32929 Trip to the Races.
32387 Winona—Two-step.
32769 Yankee Grit, March and Two-Step—With bell solo.

INSTRUMENTAL SELECTIONS—MISCELLANEOUS.

32612 American Patrol—Orchestra Accompaniment. Xylophone.
31324 Arbucklenian Polka. Cornet.
3768 Bugle Calls of United States Army. Bugle.
27001 Cavalleria Rusticana—Intermezzo from Violin.
33103 Dance California—Orchestra Accompaniment Piccolo.
32590 Dance of the Lightning Bugs—Orchestra accompaniment. Orchestra Bells.
33134 Dixie Blossoms—Orchestra accompaniment. Xylophone.
33030 Donnybrook Fair—Two-step, orchestra accompaniment. Xylophone.
33147 Florida Rag—Orchestra accompaniment. Banjo.
32879 Happy Heinie March and Two-Step—Orchestra accompaniment. Xylophone.
31389 Hawthorne Club Two-Step. Mandolin.
32863 Honeymoon Waltz—Band accompaniment. Trombone.
32699 Hurrah Boys Two-Step. Banjo Trio.
32034 Il Trovatore—El Miserere. Cornet and Trombone Duet.
23503 Irish Reel. Piccolo.
33069 Jigs and Reels Medley—Orchestra accompaniment. Violin.
32984 Koontown, Koffee Klatsch—March and two-step. Banjo, Mandolin and Harpguitar Trio.
33148 Love's Menu—Intermezzo, orchestra accompaniment. Orchestra Bells.
33133 Maple Leaf Rag—Orchestra accompaniment. Banjo.
32985 Mayor of Tokio, The—Selections from. Banjo, Mandolin and Harpguitar Trio.
33084 Motor March—Orchestra accompaniment. Banjo.
33046 Popularity—Orchestra accompaniment. Banjo.
32728 Pretty Peggy—Song and dance, orchestra accompaniment. Orchestra Bells.
32576 St. Louis Rag—Orchestra accompaniment. Banjo.
33016 Sunflower Dance—Orchestra accompaniment. Banjo.
33086 Sweet Birdie Polka—Orchestra accompaniment. Piccolo.
33085 Tannhauser—To the Evening Star—Orchestra accompaniment. Violincello.
32888 Teach Me How to Win a Beau—Orchestra accompaniment. Orchestra Bells.
32771 True Soldier, March and Two-Step—Orchestra accompaniment. Xylophone.
32033 Utility Polka. Cornet and Trombone Duet.
31766 Vienna Beauties Waltz. Vienna String Orchestra.

BARITONE SOLOS WITH ORCHESTRA ACCOMPANIMENT.

32615 Abraham—Coon song.
32563 Alexander.
32637 America.
32820 And the World Goes On.
32564 Back, Back to Baltimore.
32588 Because. Guy d'Hardelot.
32925 By the Light of the Honeymoon.
32591 By the Watermelon Vine.
32589 Come Take a Trip in My Airship.
33165 Everloving Spoony Sam—Coon Song.
32830 Everybody Works But Father.
32725 Ev'ry Little Bit Helps.
33037 Fare Thee Well My Old Kentucky Home.
32974 Gee! But This Is a Lonesome Town—From the "Earl and the Girl."
32788 Gimme Hush Money or I'll Tell on You.
32811 Girl Who Cares For Me.
31750 Good Bye, Dolly Gray.
32571 Goo Goo Man, The.
32841 Have You Seen My Henry Brown?
33077 He Handed Me a Lemon—Comic song.
32457 Here's My Friend.
33020 He Walked Right In, Turned Around, and He Walked Right Out Again.
32854 Home Sweet Home.
33005 I Don't Know Where I'm Goin', But I'm On My Way—A coon song oddity.
33193 If I'm Going to Die, I'm Going to Have Some Fun.
33089 If That Place Called Heaven Was Mine.
33194 I Get Dippy When I Do That Two-Step Dance.
33058 I Love the Last One Best of All.
32570 I May Be Crazy, But I Ain't No Fool.
32805 In Dear Old Georgia.
32793 In Sweet Loveland.
33054 In the Gleaming.
32891 Is Everybody Happy?
32924 It's the Same Old Girl.
33091 I've Got a Vacant Room for You.
32747 I Wants a Graphone—Coon song.
32895 I Wish They'd Do It Now.
32917 Jessamine.
32433 Just Before the Battle, Mother.
32646 Listen to the Big Brass Band.
32790 Little Girl, You'll Do.
32866 Load That Father Carried, The.
32660 Maryland! My Maryland!
32453 Message, The.
32991 Minstrel Boy, The.
32755 Mormon Coon.
32958 My Dusky Rose—Coon song.
33123 My Irish Rosie.
32874 My Name is Morgan, But It Ain't J. P.
32865 My Old Kentucky Home.
32617 Nothing But a Rose.
32819 Nothing From Nothing Leaves You.
33139 No Wedding Bells for Me—Comic.
32959 Parson and the Turkey, The—Coon song.
32960 Poor Old Man, The—Comic.
32720 Preacher and the Bear.
32665 Ramblin' Sam.
32710 Shame on You!—Coon song.
201452 Square Peg in a Round Hole, A.
32622 There's a Dark Man Coming with a Bundle.
32963 There's No One Like the Old Folks After All.
32975 Twenty-Three—That Means Skidoo.
32923 Uncle Quit Work, Too.
32756 Under the Banana Tree.
32882 Wait Till the Sun Shines, Nelly.
33057 We'll Be Sweethearts to the End.
32869 What's the Use of Knocking When a Man is Down.
32614 What the Brass Band Played.
32799 What You Goin' to Do When De Rent Comes 'Round—Rufus Rastus Johnson Brown.
33012 When a Poor Relation Comes to Town.
32846 When the Evening Breeze is Sighing Home Sweet Home.
32889 When the Mocking Birds Are Singing in the Wildwood.
33078 When the Snow Birds Cross the Valley.
33166 Where the Silv'ry Colorado Wends It's Way.
32994 Won't You Be My Girlie?
32900 Yankee Boodle.
32939 You Look Awfully Good to Father.
32605 You Must Think I'm Santa Claus.
32976 You're Just the Girl I'm Looking For—From "The Social Whirl."
32961 You Will Have to Read the Answer in the Stars—Comic.

TENOR SOLOS WITH ORCHESTRA ACCOMPANIMENT.

32533 A Bit o' Blarney.

LIST OF OXFORD CYLINDER RECORDS CONTINUED ON NEXT PAGE.

OXFORD CYLINDER RECORDS.—Continued.

33179 Always Leave Them Laughing When You Say Good-Bye.
32945 Anxious.
33140 Ask Me Not—Comic.
32641 Bunker Hill.
32476 By the Old Oak Tree.
32946 Can't You See I'm Lonely.
33127 Captain Baby Bunting.
33023 Cheer Up, Mary.
32887 December and May—Will you love me in December as you do in May?
33178 Dreaming—Serenade.
32732 Farewell, Soldier Boy.
32844 Girl of the U. S. A.
32812 Good-Bye, Sweet Old Manhattan Isle.
32875 Good Night, Little Girl, Good Night.
32997 Good Old U. S. A., The.
32806 I'll Be Waiting in the Gloaming, Sweet Genevieve.
32582 I'm Longing for You, Sweetheart, Day by Day.
33061 In My Merry Oldsmobile.
32664 In the Shade of the Old Apple Tree.
32943 Is There Any Room in Heaven for a Little Girl Like Me?
32658 It Makes Me Think of Home, Sweet Home.
32726 Just Across the Bridge of Gold.
32860 Just a Little Rocking Chair and You.
32798 Keep a Little Cozy Corner in Your Heart for Me.
32942 Keep on the Sunny Side.
33080 Lemon in the Garden of Love, A.
32908 Let Me Write What I Never Dared to Tell.
32566 Little Boy Called "Taps," A.
33168 Little Suit of Blue.
32719 Longing for You.
32618 Mamma's Boy—Marching song.
32909 "Mayor of Tokio, The," I Like You.
32465 My Cosy Corner Girl.
32778 My Irish Molly O.
33015 Not Because Your Hair Is Curly.
32919 Nothing Like That in Our Family.
32773 On a Summer Night.
32969 One Called "Mother" and the Other "Home, Sweet Home."
32877 Only Forty-Five Minutes From Broadway.
32774 Picnic for Two.
32859 Robinson Crusoe's Isle.
32427 Runaway Motor Car, The.
33128 School Days.
32852 Somebody's Sweetheart I Want to Be.
33062 Streets of New York, The.
32513 Sweetest Girl in Dixie.
32828 Sweethearts in Every Town.
33196 Take Me Back to New York Town.
32560 Teasing.
33205 Two Blue Eyes.
32941 We Parted as the Sun Went Down.
32881 What Has the Night Time to Do With the Girl?
33060 When the Flowers Bloom in the Springtime, Molly Dear.
32458 When the Sunset Turns the Ocean's Blue to Gold.
32470 When the Trees Are White with Blossoms, I'll Return.
32967 When the Whip-poor-will Sings, Marguerite.
32814 Where the Morning Glories Twine Around the Door.
32619 Why Don't They Play with Me?
32970 With the Robins I'll Return.
32910 "Wizard of Oz, The"—Football.
32373 "Wizard of Oz, The"—Sammy.
32489 "Yankee Consul, The"—Ain't It Funny What a Difference Just a Few Hours Make?
32625 Yankee Doodle Boy.
32853 You Don't Seem Like the Girl I Used to Know.
33157 You'll Have to Get Off and Walk.
32920 You're a Grand Old Rag.

SOPRANO SOLOS WITH ORCHESTRA ACCOMPANIMENT.

33082 Everyone Is in Slumberland But You and Me.
33063 Fancy Little Nancy.
33083 If the Man in the Moon Were a Coon.
33097 I Just Can't Make My Eyes Behave.
33004 It's All Right in the Summer Time, or the Artist's Model.
32911 So Long, Mary—From "Forty-Five Minutes From Broadway."
32746 You Ain't the Man I Thought You Was.
33160 You Splash Me and I'll Splash You.
32972 Waiting at the Church—My Wife Won't Let Me.

VOCAL SOLOS IN GERMAN.

32158 Am Rhein und Beim Wein.
32157 Das Edelweiss.
31855 Dein Gedenk'ich Margaretha.
32105 Gut Nacht, Fahr Wohl.
32097 Staendchen von Schubert.
32063 Uebers Jahr.

BARITONE AND TENOR DUETS—ORCHESTRA ACCOMPANIMENT.

33150 And a Little Bit More.
33050 Arrah Wanna—An Irish Indian song.
33105 Bake Dat Chicken Pie.
32894 Central Give Me Back My Dime.
32621 Coax Me.
32777 Come Along Little Girl, Come Along.
33009 Come, Take a Skate With Me.
32485 Dixie.
32611 Down Where the Sweet Potatoes Grow.
33173 Ev'ry Little Bit, Added to What You've Got, Makes Just a Little Bit More.
32724 Farewell, Mister Abner Hemingway.
33051 Good-a-Bye, John.
32914 Gretchen.
32601 Heinie—Comic German dialect song.
32988 Honey Won't You Love Me Like You Used To.
33073 Iola—An Indian love song.
32871 I'm a Dreaming of You.
33202 I'm a Running After Nancy.
33087 I'm Keeping My Love Lamp Burning for You.
33071 I'm Thinking 'Bout You Honey All the Time.
32954 It's Up to You to Move.
32935 I Was Just Supposing.
32843 Jasper, Don't You Hear Me Calling You?
33174 Just Help Yourself.
33120 Lovin' Time.
32484 Marching Through Georgia.
32893 My Loving Henry.
32848 Nigger Loves His Possum.
32642 Oh, Oh, Sallie.
32872 Out in an Automobile.
33121 Owatonna.
32751 Peter Piper.
33163 Red Wing—An Indian Fable.
33203 Some Day You'll Come Back to Me.
32776 Take a Car.
32399 What Would the Neighbors Say?
32934 When Mose With His Nose Leads the Band.
33175 When Summer Tells Autumn Good-Bye.
33072 Won't You Throw a Kiss to Me.
33018 Would You Leave Your Happy Home for Me.

DUETS — ORCHESTRA ACCOMPANIMENT—MIXED VOICES.

33098 Because You're You. Soprano and baritone.
32973 Cross Your Heart—From "The Umpire." Contralto and baritone.
33122 I'd Like to See a Little More of You; or the Game of Peek-a-Boo. Soprano and tenor.
33074 Linger Longer Girl, The. Soprano and baritone.
32955 Moon has His Eyes on You, The. Contralto and baritone.
32119 Oh, That We Two Were Maying. Contralto and baritone.
32765 Sweet Maid Divine. Contralto and baritone.
32956 Tale of a Stroll, The. Contralto and baritone.
33164 Won't You Be My Honey. Soprano and tenor.
33088 You Can't Give Your Heart to Somebody Else and Still Hold Hands With Me. Soprano and tenor.

MALE QUARTETTES.

33048 Ain't You Coming Back to Old New Hampshire, Molly?
33049 Alice, Where Art Thou Going?—Orchestra accompaniment.
33201 Black Jim—Orchestra accompaniment.
32931 Call to Arms, A—Descriptive.
33033 Christmas Morning at Flannigan's—Descriptive.
32836 Darling Nellie Gray—Solo and chorus.
32907 Down in Chinkapin Lane—Orchestra accompaniment.
9037 Farmyard Medley—Imitation of fowls, cattle, etc.
32690 Good-Bye, Sis—Solo and chorus—Orchestra accompaniment.
33188 Honey Boy.
32237 Hoosier Hollow Quilting Party—Stewart.
32764 In the Shade of the Old Apple Tree—Orchestra accompaniment.
32722 In the Sweet Bye and Bye.
9045 My Old New Hampshire Home.
9042 Nationality Medley—With bag pipes, banjo imitations, shouts, etc.
32704 Nellie Was a Lady.
9030 Old Folks at Home, The.
9044 Oregon Before Santiago, On Board the—Descriptive.
32782 Rescue by the Life Boat Crew.
9011 Rocked in the Cradle of the Deep.
32703 Tell Me With Your Eyes—Solo and chorus—Orchestra accompaniment.
9029 Way Down Yonder in the Cornfield—Coon song.
33070 When Daddy Sings the Little Ones to Sleep—Orchestra accompaniment.
32653 When the Bees Are in the Hive—Orchestra accompaniment.
32989 While the Old Mill Wheel Is Turning—Orchestra accompaniment.
32584 You're the Flower of My Heart, Sweet Adeline.

VOCAL QUINTETTES — MALE VOICES.

32635 Around the Camp Fire in the Philippines.
32654 Camp of the Hoboes.
32705 Parson Pinkney Discourses on Adam and Eve.

MINSTRELS.

Carnivals of mirth and melody, each record embracing overture, jokes, laughter and applause, ending with song given in title with orchestra accompaniment.

31609 Coon, Coon, Coon.
13000 Dese Bones Shall Rise Again.
32986 Dixie Dear.
32952 Good-Bye, Mr. Greenback.
13001 High Old Time, A.
31691 I'd Leave My Happy Home for You.
33161 I Know That I'll Be Happy 'Till I Die.
13004 Laughing Song, The.
33031 Moses Andrew Jackson, Good-bye.
13002 Old Log Cabin, The.
33104 San Antonio.

VAUDEVILLE SELECTIONS.

Full of fun and Catchy Music.

32795 Anthony and Cleopatra—Shakespearian Travesty—Orchestra accompaniment.
33182 At the Village Postoffice—Comic Rube Sketch.
33000 Barnyard Serenade, A—Descriptive.
11024 "Blazing Ray" Concert Hall, The.
33206 Bronco Bob and His Little Cheyenne—Orchestra accompaniment.
32981 Coming Home From Coney Island—Orchestra accompaniment.
32980 Darktown Courtship, A—Orchestra acc.
32628 Down the Pike at the St. Louis Exposition—Orchestra accompaniment.
32730 Ev'ry Little Bit Helps—Orchestra acc.
33170 Flanagan at the Barber's—Orch. acc.
33198 Flanagan at the Doctor's—Orch. acc.
33183 Flanagan at the Vocal Teacher's—Orchestra accompaniment.
33129 Flanagan on a Broadway Car—Orchestra accompaniment.
33144 Flanagan on a Farm—Irish character sketch—Orchestra accompaniment.
32868 Fritz and Louisa—Orchestra acc.
32738 Heinie—German dialect—Orchestra accompaniment.
33169 Herman and Minnie—Introducing the song "Herman"—Orchestra acc.
32892 I'm Old But I'm Awfully Tough—Laughing Song—Orchestra acc.
33064 Jealous—Orchestra accompaniment.
32947 Maggie Clancy's New Piano.
33143 Meet Me Down at the Corner—Irish character sketch—Orchestra acc.
32998 Monkey on a String, A—Orch. acc.
32766 Mr. and Mrs. 'Awkins—Orch. acc.
32780 Mr. and Mrs. Murphy—Orch. acc.
33014 Mrs. Hiram Offen Discharges Bridget O'Sullivan.
32948 Mrs. Hiram Offen Engaging Bridget O'Sullivan.
33002 Mrs. Reilly's Troubles With the Dumb Waiter—Comic—Descriptive.
32700 Musical Congress of Nations.
32901 Original Cohens, The—Orchestra acc.
32999 Peaches and Cream—Orchestra acc.
33115 Pedro, the Hand Organ Man—Descriptive.
32585 Pompernickel's Silver Wedding—Orchestra accompaniment.
32667 Professor and the Musical Tramp, The—Orchestra accompaniment.
33114 Rudolph and Rosie at the Roller Rink—Orchestra accompaniment.
33065 Turkey in the Straw—Orchestra accompaniment. Negro Shout. A fine new record of this old favorite.
33207 Vagabonds, The, Roger and I—Descriptive.
32627 When the Circus Comes Around. Laughing Song.

MISCELLANEOUS TALKING SELECTIONS.

33043 An Evening at Mrs. Clancy's Boarding House.
11102 Backyard Conversation Between Two Jealous Irish Washerwomen.
32604 "Dr. Jekyll and Mr. Hyde"—Transformation scene from, incidental orchestra music.
32949 Flanagan's Night Off.
32623 Hand of Fate, The—Incidental orchestra music.
32655 Krausmeyer and His Dog Schneider.
32603 Night Before Christmas, The.
33001 Punch and Judy—Descriptive.
32249 Reuben Haskins' Ride on a Cyclone Auto.
32569 Rheumatism Cure in Jayville Center.

UNCLE JOSH WEATHERBY'S FAMOUS LAUGHING STORIES.

33003 The Eclipse of the Sun at Pumpkin Center.
14018 Uncle Josh and the Fire Department.
33130 Uncle Josh at the Dentist's.
14016 Uncle Josh at a Camp Meeting.
32580 Uncle Josh and the Insurance C[o.]
32633 Wedding of Uncle Josh and Aun[t] Smith.
32606 Uncle Josh's Courtship.
32831 Christmas Time at Pumpkin Cente[r]
32709 Uncle Josh and Aunt Nancy Smith [in] the Subway.
32729 Uncle Josh Weatherby at the White House.
32864 Uncle Josh's New Year Pledge.
32926 Sunday School Picnic at Pumpkin Center.
32896 Ground Hog Day at Pumpkin Center.
32781 Uncle Josh and Aunt Nancy Go to Housekeeping.
33024 Uncle Josh at a Roller Skating Rink.
33116 Uncle Josh Weatherby's Visit to New York.

SACRED SELECTIONS.

33019 Abide With Me—Orchestra accompaniment. Baritone solo.
32913 All Hail the Power of Jesus' Name. Male quartette.
33108 From Greenland's Icy Mountains—Orchestra accompaniment. Baritone solo.
32697 Hosanna—Orchestra accompaniment. Baritone solo.
33039 I Love to Tell the Story—Organ accompaniment. Baritone solo.
33036 In the Sweet Bye and Bye—With bell tolling effect—Orchestra accompaniment. Baritone solo.
32689 Just As I Am—Organ accompaniment. Tenor solo.
1522 Nearer My God to Thee—With cornet solo. Brass band.
32701 One More Day's Work for Jesus—Organ accompaniment. Tenor solo.
33035 Over the Line—Orchestra accompaniment. Baritone and Tenor duet.
32497 Rock of Ages—Organ accompaniment. Tenor solo.
32469 Safe in the Arms of Jesus—Organ accompaniment. Tenor solo.
33056 Saviour, Thy Dying Love—Organ accompaniment. Baritone solo.
32964 Sun of My Soul—Organ accompaniment. Tenor solo.
31357 Where Is My Wandering Boy Tonight? Organ accompaniment. Baritone solo.

No. 20N5103 Oxford Cylinder Records. Your own selection of titles from the list shown on this and the preceding page. Price, per dozen, **$2.15**; each............**18c**

If sent by mail, postage extra, per record, 9 cents. Shipping weight of one dozen packed for express or freight shipment, 7 pounds.

STANDARD NEEDLES.

1,000 for 5 Cents.

No. 20N5350 These needles for disc talking machines of any make are made from cold drawn, oil tempered steel wire, and guaranteed to be the finest needles manufactured.

Price, per 100 (put up in envelopes of 100 each)..........**4c**

If by mail, postage extra, 2c.

Price, per 1,000 (put up in boxes of 1,000 each)..........**35c**

If by mail, postage extra, 8 cents.

SOFT TONE NEEDLES.

500 for 25 Cents.

No. 20N5355 These Soft Tone Needles are noted for the soft, sweet and natural tone which they produce, making them particularly suitable for use in small rooms, where the standard needle reproduces the record too loudly. Put up only in packages of 500.

Price, per package (500 needles)..........**25c**

If by mail, postage extra, 4c.

SPEAR POINT OR DOUBLE TONE NEEDLES.

250 for 25 Cents.

No. 20N5360 These new Spear Point Needles are particularly desirable, as the tone and volume of sound can be varied at will, giving either a soft or loud reproduction. With this needle the high notes are brought out with a sweet melody not obtainable with any other needle. Put up only in packages of 250.

Price, per package......**25c**

If by mail, postage extra, 3 cents.

DISC RECORD CASES.

No. 20N5205 Disc Record Cases, strongly and substantially made from wood, covered with black seal grain imitation leather, nickel plated trimmings, two snap catches, lock and key and leather handle. Provided with numbered separators and numbered blank on inside of cover for list of selections, so any desired record may be instantly found. No. 1 holds 50 7-inch disc records. Price........**$1.35**

No. 2 holds 50 10-inch disc records. Price..........**$1.55**

DISC RECORD RACKS.

No. 20N5206 Disc Record Rack, a very convenient means for keeping your collection of disc records, so that any selection is instantly accessible. Putting four records in each space, the rack will accommodate 100 records, and takes either 7, 10 or 12-inch records. Strongly and substantially made of oak, nicely finished, measuring 20¾ inches long by 14¾ inches high. Price........**65c**

No. 20N5207 Disc Record Rack, practically the same as rack No. 20N5206, but made with table top on which the machine can be placed. This makes a very convenient arrangement, the rack offering a firm and solid support for the machine, the records being conveniently arranged, takes any size of disc record, and will accommodate 100 records. Price..........**85c**

CYLINDER RECORD CASES.

Carrying Cases, suit case style, for Standard Size Wax Cylinder Records, black seal grain covering, with improved pegs for records, full nickeled trimmings, two snap locks and lock and key. Best record cases made.

No. 20N5201 Case, No. 2, holds 36 standard size records. Size, 16¾ in. long, 16⅜ in. wide, 5 in. high. Price....**$2.25**

No. 20N5202 Case No. 3, holds 72 standard size records. Size, 16¾ in. long, 16⅜ in. wide, 9½ in. high. Price....**$3.96**

REPAIR PARTS.

No. 20N5254 Reproducer, for Q, QC, QQ, Q Special, or our Special Home Graphophone. Price..........**$2.50**

No. 20N5260 Diaphragm Glasses, best French glass, for recorders and old style reproducers, 1 5-16 inches diameter. Price, per dozen, **30c**; each..........**4c**

No. 20N5262 Mica Diaphragms, for D reproducers only, best quality, built up. Price, each..........**19c**

No. 20N5264 Mica Diaphragms, for sound boxes of any style Disc Graphophone. Price, each..........**10c**

No. 20N5266 Rubber Gaskets, for reproducers or recorders. Price, per set of three, ordinary size..........**5c**

Per set of two, for large D reproducer....**4c**

No. 20N5270 Reproducer Ball, made of Brazilian pebble, but sold by many dealers as sapphire. Price, each..........**20c**

No. 20N5272 Reproducer Ball, made of genuine sapphire, highest grade. Price, ea.**75**

No. 20N5275 Governor Springs, for types Q, QC, QQ, BX, AB, Q Special Harvard Jr. and Sr. and our Special Home Graphophones. Price, each..........**5c**

No. 20N5278 Governor Springs, for types AK, AJ, AH, AR, AY, BH, BI, BD and Harvard Disc Talking Machines. Price, each..........**6c**

No. 20N5280 Governor Springs, for types AT, AO, AZ, AW, BK, BE, BF, BG. Price, each..........**6c**

No. 20N5282 Governor Spring, with ball attached for Oxford Cylinder Talking Machine. Price..........**25c**

No. 20N5290 Main Spring, single, for Q, QC, QQ, BX, AB or Harvard Jr., Oxford Jr., Harvard Sr. Graphophones. Price, ea.**18c**

No. 20N5292 Main Spring, for Oxford Disc, Harvard No. 5 Disc Graphophones. Price, each..........**48c**

No. 20N5294 Main Spring, single, for Columbia machines, AT, AK, AJ, AH, BH, BI, BE, BK, BF. This spring is made with hole in each end for attaching. Price....**45c**

No. 20N5296 Main Spring, for latest style Columbia machine, FH, BN and BI, this spring has no hole in either end, but fastens with short loops to spring shaft and spring barrel. Price..........**6**

No. 20N5298 Main Spring, for Oxford Cylinder Talking Machine. Price..........**2**

No. 20N5300 10-inch Turn Tables, fit any Columbia Disc Machine. Price, **$1.**

PIPES AND SMOKING ARTICLES

PIPES AND SMOKERS' ARTICLES

SMOKERS! IT WILL PAY YOU TO INVESTIGATE THE OFFERS WHICH WE MAKE ON PIPES. WE CAN SAVE YOU ONE-THIRD OR MORE IN PRICE AND ABSOLUTELY GUARANTEE OUR GOODS TO BE OF THE HIGHEST GRADES AND FINEST QUALITIES.

TAKE PARTICULAR NOTICE OF OUR CUT PRICES ON STRICTLY FIRST QUALITY GENUINE MEERSCHAUMS.

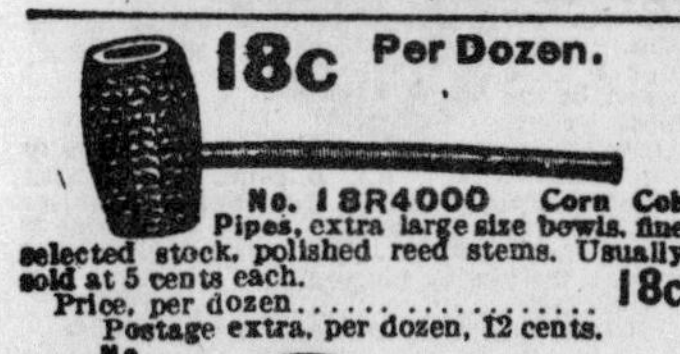

18c Per Dozen.

No. 18R4000 Corn Cob Pipes, extra large size bowls, fine selected stock, polished reed stems. Usually sold at 5 cents each.
Price, per dozen.................... 18c
Postage extra, per dozen, 12 cents.

No. 18R4004 Our Special Value Genuine Briar Pipe with 2½-inch hard rubber stem, and nickeled band. Entire length of pipe, 5 inches. A pipe that is always sold at 25 cents. 17c
Our price.................................. 17c
If mail shipment, postage extra, 4 cents.

No. 18R4016 Self Cleaning Pipe, genuine French briar bulldog bowl trimmed with nickel band and fitted with 2⅛-inch imitation amber mouthpiece with bone attachment for collecting the nicotine, etc. Pipe can be cleaned by simply unscrewing the stem. Length of pipe, 5½ inches. SELF CLEANER.
Price....(Postage extra, 3 cents.)... 22c

No. 18R4020 Special Value Pipe, for farmers, mechanics and others who smoke while working, curved egg shape bowl made of genuine French briar with 2¼-inch horn bit. Has heavy nickeled band and patented cover. Entire length of pipe, 5 inches. Price...(Postage extra, 5c.).. 25c

No. 18R4024 Genuine French Briar Pipe with egg shape bowl. Extra long briar stem to which is fitted 2-inch imitation amber mouthpiece. Entire length of pipe is 7 inches. This is an exceptionally good pipe for those who like large shapes, being especially adapted for knockabout use. Well worth 50 cents. A Fine Smoker. 30c
Our price..(Postage extra, 7 cents.)... 30c

Auto Pipe.

No. 18R4028 The New Auto Pipe, made of genuine French briar with solid vulcanized rubber mouthpiece. This is a very popular style on account of its oval shaped bowl and mouthpiece which can be reversed so that pipe will very easily fit into the vest pocket. Length of pipe, 4½ inches. Regular 50-cent value. Our price.................. 33c
If mail shipment, postage extra, 5 cents.

The Windsor Pipe.

No. 18R4032 Windsor Briar Pipe. A pipe that is made in four parts consisting of best quality briar bowl, fitted with gilt and nickel trimmed cover, long vulcanized rubber mouthpiece, with rubber under bowl and nicotine absorber. Pipe is easily taken apart and cleaned. Entire length of pipe 7 inches. Usually retails for 75 cents. 33c
Our price..................... 33c
Postage extra, 7 cents.

No. 18R4036 Fancy Egg Shape Genuine French Briar Pipe, with curved horn bit and screw at bottom of bowl for removing saliva, nicotine, etc. Nickel band on stem and bottom of bowl, fancy gilt patented cover. A pipe that is desirable on account of being easy to clean, and a cool smoker. Entire length of pipe, 6½ inches. 38c
Price....(Postage extra, 6 cents.)... 38c

A New Shape Double Draught.

No. 18R4048 M. D. French Briar Pipe, with imitation meerschaum set in screw bowl. Has push rubber bit with double draft, that is, has two separate borings, which insure a free and easy draught and a cool smoke. We cannot recommend this pipe too highly. A very popular shape. Entire length, 6 inches. A wonderful value. Price (Postage extra, 7 cents.) 44c

Special Value Eagle Claw Pipe.

No. 18R4060 Straight Stem Eagle Claw Briar Pipe, with 2½-inch heavy horn bit. Made of good quality genuine French briar in the very popular hand carved eagle claw design. Nicely finished and polished. Entire length of pipe, 5¾ inches. Never sold at less than 50 cents. 39c
Our price.................................. 39c
If mail shipment, postage extra, 6 cents

Our Five Days' Free Trial Offer
Smoke either a No-Nic, Marlborough or Wellington pipe for five days and if you are not satisfied that it is the best smoking, cleanest pipe ever offered at the price, return it at our expense and we will refund your money.

THE CELEBRATED NO-NIC PIPE
Genuine $1.00 Value, Our Introductory Price, 50 Cents.

This pipe is so constructed that you cannot draw the nicotine from the tobacco into your mouth. The illustration tells the story. Made of genuine briar root with hard rubber detachable stem. Has wide nickel band.
No. 18R4061 Straight No-Nic Pipe. Price, 6-inch........................ 50c
No. 18R4063 Curved No-Nic Pipe. Price, 5½-inch..................... 50c
If mail shipment, postage extra, 4 cents.

THE POPULAR MARLBOROUGH STYLE.

No. 18R4065 Clever invention which eliminates the nicotine and cools the smoke. The broken draft does the work. (See illustration.) Bowl of genuine high quality briar root with fine solid rubber mouthpiece and nickel band. Bent shape only. Full length, 4½ inches. 38c
Our price.................................. 38c
If mail shipment, postage extra, 4 cents.

RELIABLE WELLINGTON PIPES.

No. 18R4052 Wellington Reservoir Well Pipe. With this pipe anyone can enjoy a cool and comfortable smoke. The well of this pipe collects the saliva which in ordinary pipes runs down into the bowl and moistens the tobacco. The solid vulcanized rubber mouthpiece is made with the boring through the upper part, and its special distinctive shape allows the tongue to rest underneath the boring, so that the smoke will pass over the tongue and will not irritate the mouth. This pipe is patterned after the famous "Peterson Make" and the best quality briar only is used, fitted with heavy nickel band. Regular 50-cent size. Length, 6¼ inches. 39c SEE THE WELL
Our price.................................. 39c
If mail shipment, postage extra, 5 cents.

No. 18R4056 Wellington Reservoir Well Pipe made of same quality materials as above, but smaller. Length, 5 inches. 35-cent size. Price.................................. 23c
If mail shipment, postage extra, 4 cents.

Fancy Chip Meerschaum Pipe.

No. 18R4068 Large size, best quality, Vienna Chip Meerschaum Pipe. Large egg shape bowl fitted with cherry stem and 1¼-inch imitation amber mouthpiece, decorated with silk cord and tassel. A very popular and handsome pipe. Regular 75-cent value. Length of pipe, 8¼ inches. 38c
Our price.................................. 38c
If mail shipment, postage extra, 6 cents.

Chip Meerschaum Pipe in Case.

No. 18R4076 Vienna Chip Meerschaum Pipe. A high grade bulldog shape, chip meerschaum bowl fitted with 2¼-inch imitation amber stem and ornamented with fancy chased band. Has plush lined leatherette case. A high grade article finished with wax which should not be confused with the cheaper imitation meerschaum. Length of pipe, 5½ inches. Price.................. 88c
If mail shipment, postage extra, 5 cents.

Best Quality Chip Meerschaum Pipe, Amber Stem and Case, $1.75.

No. 18R4080 Best Quality Vienna Chip Meerschaum Pipe, with 2½-inch genuine amber mouthpiece. This pipe is made of the chips of meerschaum moulded together and will with proper handling color the same as genuine block meerschaum. They are very finely finished and waxed. This is such a perfect imitation that only experts can tell it from the genuine block quality. We can recommend this article very highly. Put up in imitation leather plush lined case. Entire length of pipe, 5 inches. Price. $1.75
If mail shipment, postage extra, 6 cents.

A Turkish Water Pipe at 48c.

No. 18R4086 Heretofore this class of pipe has never been sold for less than $2.00. Regardless of the tobacco used, we guarantee a cool clean smoke. The pipe is made of a water bottle, 6 inches in height, into which is fitted a good quality corn cob bowl to which is fastened a 30-inch rubber stem with bone mouthpiece. Entire height of pipe, 8 inches. Shipping wt., 1 lb. Price, each.................. 48c

German Porcelain Pipe.

No. 18R4088 A regular $2.00 Horn Stem German Porcelain Pipe for $1.33. This pipe is certainly a favorite with the person who will always enjoy a clean, cool smoke. The horn stem, measuring 12 inches, is made in eight parts which can be unscrewed and cleaned separately, is fitted with flexible top with fancy horn mouthpiece. The highly decorated porcelain bowl with patented cover sets into horn reservoir fitted with detachable nicotine receiver, in all a very handsome pipe. Trimmed with long silk cord and tassels. Entire length of pipe, 15 inches. Weight, 1¾ pounds. Price........ $1.33

Genuine French Briar Pipes With Real Amber Stems.

No. 18R4092 Genuine French Briar Bulldog Shape Pipe. Bowl fitted with 1¾-inch genuine amber straight stem, highly polished and well finished. Length of pipe, 5 inches. Regular 75-cent value. Our price........ 55c
If mail shipment, postage extra, 7 cents.

No. 18R4096 One of the most handsome and serviceable pipes made. Bowl and stem of highly polished rosewood fitted with removable chip meerschaum set in bowl. Has genuine amber bit. Length of pipe, 5½ inches. Put up in leather covered, plush lined case. Price.................. 75c
If mail shipment, postage extra, 4 cents.

CIGARS? SEE OUR GROCERY PAGES of OUR BIG CATALOG

No. 18R4100 Highest quality Genuine French Briar Pipe. Highly polished and finely finished egg shaped bowl with 2¼-inch genuine amber square stem mounted with sterling silver band. A neat appearing medium sized pipe, measuring in length 5½ inches. 93c
Price.................................. 93c
If mail shipment, postage extra, 5 cents.

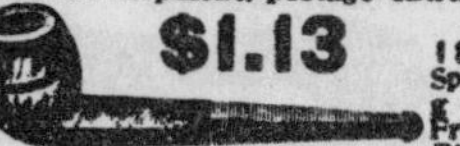

No. 18R4104 Special value Genuine French Briar Pipe. Bulldog shape bowl, highly polished with dark finish, fitted with 3-inch genuine amber straight square stem. Entire length of pipe, 6¾ inches. Easily worth $1.75.
Our price.................................. $1.13
If mail shipment, postage extra, 5 cents.

Straight Stem Briar Pipes in Cases.

No. 18R4108 Genuine French Briar Bulldog Shape Pipe. Highly polished and nicely finished, fitted with 2-inch genuine amber mouthpiece. Leather covered plush lined case. A medium sized, neat appearing pipe. Price........ $1.25
If mail shipment, postage extra, 5 cents.

No. 18R4112 Genuine French Briar Pipe. Bulldog shape bowl. Top of bowl and stem ornamented with heavy chased gold plated bands, highly polished, fitted with 2-inch genuine amber stem. Fitted in leather covered plush lined case. Excellent value at $2.50. Our price........ $1.69
If mail shipment, postage extra, 6 cents.

No. 18R4116 Large size imported French Briar Pipe. Bulldog shape bowl, finely polished and finished throughout with heavy 3-inch genuine amber stem, and trimmed with beautifully engraved heavy gold plated top band with band around stem to match. Entire length of pipe, 6¾ inches. Fitted in leather covered silk plush lined case. Price.................. $2.25
If mail shipment, postage extra, 5 cents.

No. 18R4120 Our best quality straight Bulldog Shape French Briar Pipe. Made of selected stock briar root, highly polished, fitted with extra heavy 3½-inch genuine amber stem, ornamented with gold plated top band with stem band to match. Entire length of pipe, 7 inches. Fitted in best quality leather covered silk plush lined case. Easily worth $4.00. $2.98
Our price.................................. $2.98
If mail shipment, postage extra, 5 cents.

No. 18R4124 Genuine Curved French Briar Pipe. An exceptional value, fitted with 1¾-inch genuine amber curved bit, trimmed with chased gold plated band. Regular $1.50 value. Length of pipe, 4½ inches.
Our price.................................. $1.05
If mail shipment, postage extra, 6 cents.

Briar Pipe With Curved Amber Stem in Case.

No. 18R4128 College Shape Genuine French Briar Pipe. Bulldog shape bowl, fitted with 1½-inch genuine amber mouthpiece, trimmed with engraved gold plated band. Length of pipe, 4½ inches. In leather covered silk plush lined case. A pipe that is easily worth $2.00, and a popular shape. $1.35
Our price.................................. $1.35
If mail shipment, postage extra, 5 cents.

HIGHEST QUALITY MEERSCHAUM PIPES AT REAL WHOLESALE PRICES.

Neat Bulldog Shape.

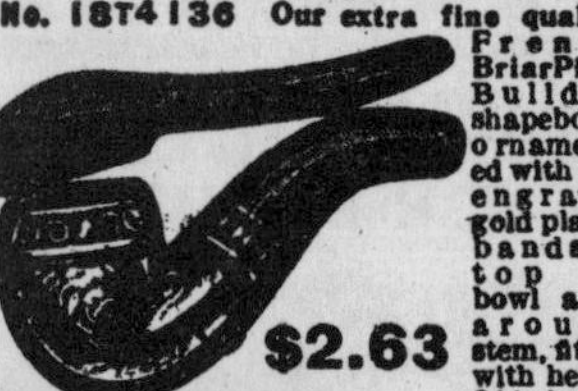

No. 18T4136 Our extra fine quality French Briar Pipe. Bulldog shape bowl, ornamented with fine engraved gold plated bands on top of bowl and around stem, fitted with heavy 2¼-inch genuine amber curved mouthpiece. Entire length of pipe, 5¼ inches. Fitted in extra quality silk plush lined case. Easily worth $3.50. Our price........ **$2.63**
If mail shipment, postage extra, 5c.

Best Quality Extra Heavy Amber Stem.

No. 18T4140 Our best quality extra value French Briar Pipe. Oil boiled, extra finished bulldog shape bowl. The bowl and stem are ornamented with very heavy gold plated bands, with raised silver ornaments in a very neat and attractive design. Pipe is fitted with extra heavy 3-inch genuine amber curved mouthpiece. Entire length of pipe, 6 inches. Pipe is fitted in best quality chamois covered silk plush lined case. $5.00 value. Our price........ **$3.95**
If mail shipment, postage extra, 5c.

Best Quality Meerschaum Bowls.

No. 18T4184 Genuine Meerschaum Bowls. Made from the finest quality block meerschaum. This style of bowl will color the quickest and is very popular for the reason that the case remains on the pipe while smoking, so that the fingers will not touch the meerschaum. These bowls, used with our No. 18T4192 genuine Weichsel stems, will make as fine a pipe as can be obtained at any price. Fitted in plush lined chamois leather case. Come in four sizes, as follows:

No. 5 bowl. Price........	$3.48
No. 6 bowl. Price........	3.66
No. 7 bowl. Price........	4.89
No. 8 bowl. Price........	5.69

If mail shipment, postage extra, 4 cents.

Special Value Genuine Meerschaum Pipe.

No. 18T4160 Our Special Genuine Block Meerschaum Egg Shape, Curved Stem Pipe. Made of the best quality meerschaum and fitted with curved genuine amber mouthpiece. In chamois covered silk plush lined case. Entire length of pipe, 5 inches. Well worth $4.50. Our price........ **$3.19**
If mail shipment, postage extra, 6 cents.

Our Most Popular Meerschaum Style.

$5.29

No. 18T4156 Our best quality and most popular genuine Meerschaum Straight Stem Pipe. Made of absolutely the best quality genuine block meerschaum by expert workmen. No. 7 bowl, fitted with 3-inch genuine amber square mouthpiece, heavy chased gold plated band on stem and bowl. Fitted in finest quality chamois covered silk plush lined case. No better straight stem meerschaum pipe at any price. A bargain at any store at $8.00. Our price........ **$5.29**
If mail shipment, postage extra, 6 cents.

Two Genuine Meerschaum Pipes in Fine Case for $5.68.

No. 18T4200 Smoker's Companion, containing two genuine first quality meerschaum pipes; one is a straight medium sized bulldog shape, 4½ inches long, fitted with 2¼-inch amber mouthpiece; the other is a bent bulldog shape, 4 inches long, fitted with 2¼-inch curved amber mouthpiece. Both pipes ornamented with plain gold plated bands and fitted into best quality chamois covered silk plush lined case. It is well known that by using two or more pipes better results can be obtained as regards coloring, etc., therefore, we advise the smoker to purchase this set. Price........ **$5.68**
If mail shipment, postage extra, 15 cents.

$6.75

Finest Quality Imported Genuine Black Amber Pipe.

No. 18T4182 Nothing finer made than this beautiful imported article. An elegant house pipe. Made of genuine black amber with a screw in top bowl of first quality meerschaum. Has 2½-inch yellow amber stem. Entire length of pipe, 5½ inches. Fitted with plush lined chamois covered case. We guarantee this pipe to be a big $10.00 value in any store. Our price........ **$6.75**
If mail shipment, postage extra, 10 cents.

Our Finest Meerschaum Pipe.

No. 18T4180 Our Finest Meerschaum Pipe. Made of the highest grade genuine meerschaum, cut from the largest blocks of meerschaum obtainable, with fancy shape square design bowl, fitted with extra heavy square cut genuine amber stem 2¾ inches in length, so shaped that the pipe may be easily held by the stem instead of the bowl, trimmed with heavy solid gold plated band ornamented with French gray silver trimming. Fitted in genuine Russia leather covered silk plush lined case. An exceptional value. This pipe will be found in stores throughout the country at from $10.00 to $12.00. Our price.....(Postage extra, 10c).... **$7.38**

$3.95

No. 18T4152 Genuine Block Meerschaum Pipe, London egg shape bowl, finest quality meerschaum, with 2¾-inch round amber mouthpiece and No. 6 bowl. Total length of pipe, 5 inches. Pipe is ornamented with fancy gold band around stem. Inlaid in chamois covered silk plush lined case; very high grade. Price........ **$3.95**
If mail shipment, postage extra, 5c.

No. 18T4196 Chip Meerschaum Coloring Bowls in two styles, style A is suitable for large pipes and style B for small pipes. By using one of these bowls the pipe itself will not burn but will color beautifully. **Be sure to state which style you desire.** Price........ **18c**
Style A. Style B.
If mail shipment, postage extra, 2 cents.

$4.48

No. 18T4168 Neat pattern, highest grade Genuine Block Meerschaum Pipe. No. 6 egg shape bowl, trimmed at top and stem with plain gold plated bands, has genuine amber mouthpiece, 2¾ inches in length; in all a very neat and rich looking pipe. Fitted in genuine morocco leather covered plush lined case. An excellent value and sure to please. Price........ **$4.48**
If mail shipment, postage extra, 8 cents.

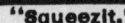

Weichsel Pipe Stems.

No. 18T4188 Extra Pipe Stems. 6½-inch Weichsel Pipe Stems for use with pipe No. 18T4068, and bowl No. 18T4184; fitted with hard rubber bits. Price........ **13c**
If mail shipment, postage extra, 3 cents.

No. 18T4192 Genuine Weichsel Stem, fitted with real amber mouthpiece; length, 6 inches. Price........ **52c**
If mail shipment, postage extra, 2 cents.

A $7.50 Pipe for $4.67.

No. 18T4172 Eagle Claw, first quality Meerschaum Pipe. Fitted in silk plush lined chamois covered case. This pipe is hand carved by the most expert Austrian workmen, finished very carefully and artistically. No. 6 bowl, fitted with genuine amber curved mouthpiece. Entire length of pipe, 5½ inches. This same pipe is usually sold at $7.50. We import them and make a big saving for you. Our price........ **$4.67**
If mail shipment, postage extra, 8 cents.

Bulldog Shape, Gold Mounted.

$5.99

No. 18T4176 Our best Bulldog Shape Genuine Block Meerschaum Pipe. Made with the finest quality No. 7 meerschaum bowl, fitted with extra heavy 3-inch genuine amber mouthpiece, handsomely ornamented at top and on stem with extra heavy chased gold plated bands. Fitted in chamois covered, best silk plush lined case. Price.....(Postage extra, 6c).... **$5.99**

Straight Plain Style.

$3.19

No. 18T4144 Genuine Meerschaum Bulldog Shape Pipes. Guaranteed to be the best quality block meerschaum, fitted with genuine amber mouthpiece. These pipes are absolutely free of any flaws. The amber mouthpieces vary in thickness and length according to the size of the bowl and length of pipe. Each pipe in chamois covered silk plush lined case. Your choice of three sizes.

Size of Bowl	Length of Pipe	Price
5	4½	$3.19
7	5½	4.29
8	6	4.78

If mail shipment, postage extra, 5 cents.

Fancy Carved Designs.
A Really Great Bargain.

$2.83

No. 18T4148 Genuine Block Meerschaum Pipe. A special value, handsomely carved bowl. Can furnish assorted designs, such as lions, dogs, horses, etc. Fitted with genuine amber mouthpiece. Length of pipe, 5 inches. In silk plush lined chamois covered case. A special value and a great favorite. Price....(Postage extra, 6 cents.)... **$2.83**

Fine Imported Cigar Holders.

No. 18T4204 Genuine Meerschaum Cigar Holder, fancy carved, with real amber bit, each in leather plush lined case. Price........ **59c**
If mail shipment, postage extra, 3 cents.

No. 18T4208 Genuine Meerschaum Cigar Holder, made of first quality heavy block meerschaum with genuine amber mouthpiece of select grade, set in a neat silk plush lined chamois case. Length, 3 inches. Price........ **98c**
If mail shipment, postage extra, 4 cents.

No. 18T4212 Genuine Meerschaum Cigar Holder with real amber mouthpiece in pretty assorted carved designs. Length, 4 inches, in leather covered silk plush lined case. Price........ **$1.15**
If mail shipment, postage extra, 4 cents.

No. 18T4216 Finest Quality Genuine Amber Cigar Holder. Very popular shape. We can furnish these cigar holders either with or without chamois covered, plush lined case.
2-in., with case, $1.10 | 3-in., with case, $1.50
Without case.. .88 | Without case.. 1.25
If mail shipment, postage extra, 2 cents.

"Squeezit."

No. 18T4219 "Squeezit," an attachment to be used with tobacco bags, saves all pulling of strings and saves much tobacco. Once adjusted, your sack is always ready for use. Our price.....(Postage extra, 2c)..... **7c**

Self Closing Rubber Pouch.

No. 18T4220 Raleigh Velvet Rubber Tobacco Pouch. Self closing, tan color. Diameter, 3⅜ inches. Keeps tobacco moist, clean and sweet. 25-cent value. Price........ **18c**
If mail shipment, postage extra, 3 cents.

Leather Tobacco Pouch.

No. 18T4224 Malster's Tobacco Pouch. Made of one piece of genuine leather, fastened by means of heavy drawstrings and additional glove catch. Also used for coin. Price........ **23c**
If mail shipment, postage extra, 3 cents.

Plain Nickel Finished Match Safe.

No. 18T4228 Combination Match Safe and Cigar Cutter. Nickel finish leather covering. Price........ **19c**
Postage extra, 2 cents.

German Silver Match Safe.

No. 18T4232 This pretty Match Safe is made of German silver, with handsome embossed design of bright silver finish. Very neat and tasty design. 75-cent value. Our price........ **48c**
Postage extra, 2 cents.

Trick Match Box.

No. 18T4231 A very clever little article for holding matches. Made in such a manner that matches will appear or disappear, as desired. It is useful as well as having this clever trick feature. Made of heavy metal, nickel plated. Size, 2½x1¼ inches. Price........ **15c**
If mail shipment, postage extra, 2 cents.

Trick Cigarette Box.

No. 18T4233 Made in such a manner that you can offer your friend a cigarette, and when he reaches for it the box will appear empty. Made of heavy metal, nickel plated, with the word "Cigarettes" embossed upon one side. Size, 3½x2¼ inches. Price, each........ **21c**
If mail shipment, postage extra, 4 cents.

Pipe Cleaners.

No. 18T4198 Cotton Covered Wire Pipe Cleaners. One dozen in package. Our price, two packages for........ **5c**
If mail shipment, postage extra for two packages, 2 cents.

Leather Cigar Cases.

No. 18T4236 Telescope style and molded into shape, fine polished tan sole leather case, stitched French edges, front embossed in English heraldic design, large size. Size, 1x3¼x5¼ inches. 50-cent value. Our price........ **29c**
Postage extra, 5c.

No. 18T4241 Cigar Case, made of a very good imitation of walrus leather on riveted frame, with good clasp. Sateen lined. Very well made throughout. Size when closed, 5½ x 3½ inches. Price........ **49c**
Postage, 5 cents.

No. 18T4245 Genuine Leather Cigar Case, alligator finish. Well made on riveted frame, with extra good clasp. Moire lined. Size, when closed, 5½ x 3¼ inches. $1.25 value. Our price........ **88c**
Postage extra, 5 cents.

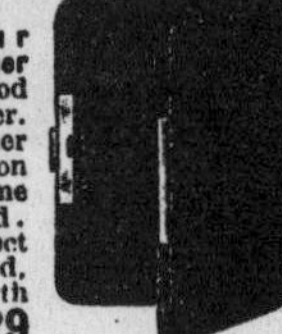

No. 18T4249 Our Best All Genuine Leather Cigar Case, made of a good quality seal grain leather. Leather lined with leather match compartment on inside. Heavy nickel frame is also leather covered. Heavily padded to protect cigars. Size when closed, 5½x4 inches. Well worth $2.00. Our Price........ **$1.29**
Postage, 5 cents.

PIPES AND SMOKER'S ARTICLES

The quality and worth of a good pipe is determined largely by the brier root or meerschaum used in the bowl and by the weight and size of the amber used in the stem. Our pipes represent the highest art in pipe making, our prices are much lower than any other dealer will quote, quality considered. We cannot show the quality of these goods in the illustrations, but we guarantee satisfaction on every purchase and a saving of 25 to 50 per cent.

No. 18G1586 Fine Selected Corncob Pipe, extra large size bowl, finely polished reed stems, a regular 5-cent article. Price, per dozen........18c
If by mail, postage extra, per dozen, 12 cents.

14c

No. 18G1590 Very Elegant Brier Pipe, medium size, 5½ inches long, with polished hard rubber stem and nickel band.
Price, 3 for 40c; each........14c
If by mail, postage extra, each, 3 cents.

19c

No. 18G1598 Imitation Meerschaum Pipe, medium size, handsomely nickel mounted. Imitation amber mouthpiece, good sized bowl.
Price, 3 for 54c; each........19c
If by mail, postage extra, each, 3 cents.

20c

No. 18G1656 French Brier Pipe, Morgan shape, with best vulcanized rubber shove bit. A fine nickel band on stem, holding inside an absorbent paper cartridge, which effectually absorbs the nicotine. Length of pipe, 5 inches.
Price, 3 for 57c; each........20c
If by mail, postage extra, each, 6 cents.

No. 18G1658 Extra Cartridges to replace used cartridges in above pipe.
10 in a box. Price, for 3 boxes........10c
If by mail, postage extra, each, 3 cents.

22c

No. 18G1660 Fine Brier Pipe, bull dog shape, with imitation amber shove bit, plain nickel band, a very handsome pipe which we recommend very highly. Price, 3 for 62c; each........22c
If by mail, postage extra, each, 4 cents.

24 Cents for a Self Cleaner.

No. 18G1662 A Genuine French Brier English Bulldog Pipe. Handsome imitation amber mouthpiece. Length, 5½ inches, long self cleaner handsome nickel band, finely made and finished. Price, 3 for 69c; each........24c
If by mail, postage extra, each, 3 cents.

No. 18G1664 Fine French Brier Pipe, bulldog shape bowl, with long stem and 3½-inch celluloid bit. Entire length of pipe, 6 inches. Price, 3 for 72c; each..25c
If by mail, postage extra, each, 5 cents.

30c

No. 18G1666 French Brier Pipe, highly polished brier; heavy bulldog pattern bowl; has 3½-inch horn mouthpiece with fancy nickel band; total length of pipe, 6¼ inches; a substantial and sightly pipe.
Price, 3 for 85c; each........30c
If by mail, postage extra, each, 5 cents.

The New Ring Pipe.

For a cool smoke and to prevent the nicotine from passing into the mouth.

No. 18G1668 Genuine Brier Bowl, with imitation amber mouthpiece, and having the latest invented ring attachment. Tobacco in pipe is always kept dry, insuring a sweet, cool smoke. Easily cleaned. A boon for smokers. Price, 3 for $1.27; each........44c
If by mail, postage extra, each, 5 cents.

Pipes with Curved Bits.

No. 18G1673 Curved Egg Shape Genuine French Brier, with 2¾-inch horn bit, heavy nickel cover and band. **25c** A specially good pipe for farmers and those who smoke in barns or in the fields or anywhere out of doors. Whole length, 5 inches.
Price, 3 for 72c; each........25c
If by mail, postage extra, each, 5 cents.

Genuine French Brier.

No. 18G1675 Genuine French Brier Pipe, egg shape bowl with 2-inch curved celluloid bit, square stem. Entire length of pipe, 5 inches.
Price, 3 for 78c; each........27c
If by mail, postage extra, each, 5 cents.

The New Reservoir Well Pipe.

44c

No. 18G1679 The Pipe with a Well, for a cool smoke. Easily cleaned. The reservoir pipe offers two important advantages. The well of the bowl collects the saliva and thereby leaves the tobacco dry to the last. The peculiar shaped mouthpiece permits the tongue to rest easily underneath the curve and the upper boring of the draft hole compels the smoke to pass over the tongue and does not irritate the mouth. Made by skilled workmen. Patterned after the famous Peterson, made of the best selected French brier, and the mouthpiece of finest quality hard rubber, has heavy nickel band around stem. Large size. Length, 6½ inches.
Price, 3 for $1.27; each........44c
If by mail, postage extra, each, 5 cents.

No. 18G1681 The New Reservoir Well Pipe. Made of fine quality genuine French brier with hard rubber bit and heavy nickel band. Regular 50c size. Length of pipe, 5 inches. Price, each........29c
3 for........84c
If by mail, postage extra, each, 5 cents.

An Old Favorite.

29c

No. 18G1683 Handsomely Carved Brier Bowl, cherry stem, 6 inches long with rubber mouthpiece; entire length of pipe, 7 inches. A pipe that is easily cleaned and kept in order and always gives satisfaction.
Price, each........29c
3 for........84c
If by mail, postage extra, each, 6 cents.

Fancy Brier Pipes.

No. 18G1685 The Always Clean Brier Bowl, long rubber stem, nicotine absorber, handsomely decorated cover; a pipe that can be taken apart in four pieces and usually retails for $1.00.
Price, each..30c
3 for........87c
If by mail, postage extra, each, 7 cents.

30c

No. 18G1686 Fancy Shaped Genuine Brier Pipe, with curved horn bit and horn screw to let the saliva out. Nickel band on stem and bottom of bowl, fancy tower cover. This is a very desirable pipe. Length of pipe, 6½ inches.
Price, 3 for $1.09; each........38c
If by mail, postage extra, each, 6 cents.

No. 18G1687 Fine Eagle Claw French Brier Pipe, with fancy curved horn mouthpiece. A large size egg shape bowl. Length of pipe, 6 inches. Price, 3 for $1.37; each, 48c
If by mail, postage extra, each, 6 cents.

48c

38c

No. 18G1689 Large Sized Fine Vienna Chip Meerschaum Pipe, large egg shaped bowl and handsome cherry stem, with silk cord and tassel and imitation amber mouthpiece. An exceptionally handsome article.
Price, each..$0.38
3 for........1.09
If by mail, postage extra, each, 6 cents.

No. 18G1691 Fancy Shape Vienna Chip Meerschaum Pipe, artistically carved design lady's head. Pipe is boiled in wax and colored like genuine meerschaum, has 4-inch cherry stem, with curved celluloid bit. Length of pipe, 8½ inches. Price, 3 for $1.69; each, 59c
If by mail, postage extra, each, 6 cents.

No. 18G1688 6½-inch Weichsel Pipe Stem, with curved rubber mouthpiece.
Price, 3 for 37c; each........13c

No. 18G1690 7-inch Cherry Pipe Stem, with curved rubber mouthpiece. Price, 3 for 25c; each........9c
If by mail, postage extra, each, 3 cents.

German Favorite

83c

German Porcelain Pipes.

No. 18G1695 German Porcelain Pipe, handsomely decorated; just the thing for a good old fashioned smoke. This is an exceptionally fine and handsome German porcelain pipe. Made with very fine long stem, fitted with flexible top and extra fine hard rubber mouthpiece. Long, genuine porcelain bowl artistically and handsomely decorated. The bowl can readily be taken apart for cleaning, thus assuring a clean, cool smoke. Shipping weight, each, 1½ pounds.
Price, 3 for $2.39; each, 83c

High Grade German Porcelain Pipe, $1.22.

No. 18G1697 German Porcelain Pipe. This is an exceptionally high grade German pipe with a large elaborately decorated bowl, with nicotine receiver on bottom which can be unscrewed, long fancy carved horn stem, fitted with flexible top and fine hard rubber mouthpiece. Finished with long silk cord and tassels. All the different parts can be separated, so that you can easily clean. Shipping weight, each, 1¾ pounds. Price each, $1.22
3 for........3.52

Genuine French Brier Pipes.

59c

No. 18G1699 Genuine French Brier Pipe, Genuine Amber, highly polished, dark finish, bulldog shape, with 1½-inch genuine amber straight stem. Length of pipe, 5 inches. 75-cent value. Price, each...$0.59
3 for........1.69
If by mail, postage extra, each, 7 cents.

99c Genuine Amber.

No. 18G1703 Excellent Quality Highly Finished Genuine French Brier; egg shape bowl with square 2¼-inch genuine amber stem. Has plain, sterling silver band, giving pipe a very pretty appearance. Whole length of pipe, 5 inches. Price, each..$0.99
3 for........2.89
If by mail, postage extra, each, 6 cents.

No. 18G1705 Curved Genuine French Brier Pipe. Egg shape bowl, with 1⅞-inch genuine amber bit and chased gold band. This is an excellent quality, but inexpensive pipe. Whole length, 4½ inches.
Price, 3 for $3.07; each........$1.05
If by mail, postage extra, each, 6 cents.

$1.05

79c

No. 18G1709 This is certainly one of the very handsomest pipes made. It is made from highly polished rosewood with removable set in bowl of chip meerschaum, which can be unscrewed and easily cleaned. Genuine amber mouthpiece. Length of pipe, 5½ inches. Put up in handsome leather covered satin lined case.
Price, 3 for $2.29; each........79c
If by mail, postage extra, each, 4 cents.

No. 18G1711 Selected French Brier Pipe, bulldog shape bowl with 2-inch genuine amber mouthpiece. A large size pipe in leather covered velvet lined case. Entire length of pipe is 5½ inches.
Price, 3 for $3.25; each........$1.12
If by mail, postage extra, each, 2 cents.

No. 18G1717 High Grade French Brier Pipe, with heavy bulldog shape bowl and 2-inch amber stem. The pipe is trimmed with a heavy chased gold band on bowl and stem. Length of pipe, 5¾ inches. In leather covered velvet lined case.
Price, 3 for $4.95; each........$1.69
If by mail, postage extra, each 6 cents.

No. 18G1721 Fine Imported French Brier Pipe, with heavy bulldog shape bowl fitted with heavy 3-inch amber stem. The bowl is trimmed with heavily engraved top and the stem with band to match. Entire length of pipe, 6¾ inches. In leather covered silk plush lined case.
Price, 3 for $6.83; each........$2.33
If by mail, postage extra, each, 5 cents.

French Brier Pipes.

No. 18G1723 High Grade French Brier Pipe with highly polished large bulldog shape bowl. Has extra heavy 3½-inch amber stem. The bowl is mounted with 14kt. gold plated band with raised French gray silver ornaments. The same design on band of stem. Entire length of pipe 7 inches. In chamois covered silk plush lined case.
Price, 3 for $9.43; each........$3.19
If by mail, postage extra, each 5 cents.

No. 18G1725 Genuine French Brier Pipe, bulldog shape bowl with 1¾-inch genuine amber bit, has engraved gold band around stem. Length of pipe, 4½ inches. In leather covered silk plush lined case. Price, 3 for $3.97; each, $1.35
If by mail, postage extra, each, 5 cents.

No. 18G1727 Large Bulldog Genuine French Brier Pipe with 2-inch genuine amber bent mouthpiece. Has chased gold band around stem. Length of pipe, 4¾ inches. In leather covered silk plush lined case. Price, 3 for $5.11; ea., $1.75
If by mail, postage extra, each, 5 cents.

No. 18G1729 Very Fine Quality French Brier Pipe, bulldog shape bowl, has a 2½-inch genuine amber curved mouthpiece. The bowl is mounted with beautifully engraved gold band, the stem is also ornamented with gold band, same design. Length of pipe, 5¼ inches. In leather covered silk plush lined case.
Price, 3 for $7.95; each........$2.69
If by mail, postage extra, each, 5 cents.

No. 18G1731 Extra Quality French Brier Pipe, with heavy bull-bitch shape bowl. Has an extra heavy 3-inch curved genuine amber mouthpiece. The bowl and stem are ornamented with very heavy 14kt. gold plated band with raised silver ornaments, a new and attractive design. Length of pipe, 6 inches. In fine chamois covered silk plush lined case.
Price, 3 for $11.69; each........$3.95
If by mail, postage extra, each, 5 cents.

Genuine Meerschaum Pipes.

$3.19

No. 18G1733 Genuine Meerschaum Pipes. High grade quality meerschaum, with best amber mouthpieces. In silk plush lined chamois case. The bowl is of the bulldog pattern and is of the best selected meerschaum. The amber mouthpieces vary in thickness according to size of bowl. State size wanted. Your choice in four sizes, as follows:

Size of bowl, No.	Length of amber, inches	Price, 3 for	Price, each
5	2½	$ 9.45	$3.19
6	2¾	10.93	3.69
7	3	12.71	4.29
8	3¼	14.81	4.99

If by mail, postage extra, each, 8 cents.

No. 18G1735 Genuine Block Meerschaum Pipe, handsomely carved bowl, assorted designs, such as lions; dogs, deer, etc., amber mouthpiece, 2½ inches long, with a No. 5 bowl in a satin lined case. State design wanted. Price, 3 for $7.83; ea., $2.65
If by mail, postage extra, each, 6 cents.

No. 18G1737 Genuine Meerschaum Pipe, London egg shape bowl, finest quality meerschaum, with 2¾-inch round amber mouthpiece and No. 6 bowl. Total length of pipe, 5 in. Pipe is ornamented with fancy gold band around stem. Inlaid in chamois covered silk plush lined case; very high grade.
Price, 3 for $11.83; each........$3.99
If by mail, postage extra, each, 5 cents.

Our $5.29 Meerschaum Pipe.

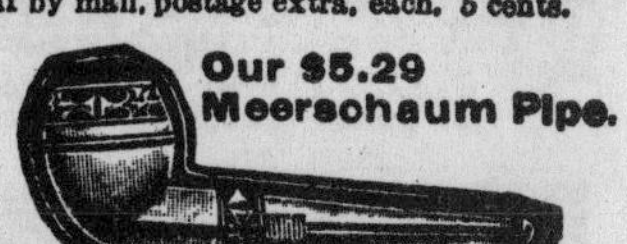

No. 18G1739 Genuine Meerschaum Pipe, straight bulldog shape, with 3-inch genuine amber mouthpiece and No. 7 bowl, heavy chased gold band on stem and bowl; inlaid in finest plush lined chamois covered case. No better pipe at any price.
Price, 3 for $15.69; each........$5.29
If by mail, postage extra, each, 6 cents.

No. 18G1743 High Grade Genuine Meerschaum Pipe with large egg shape, size 6, bowl. Has a curved, square, genuine amber mouthpiece, 2¾ inches in length. The pipe is trimmed with plain gold band on top of bowl and stem, making a very rich and swell looking pipe. Entire length of pipe, 4½ inches. Fitted in morocco leather covered, plush lined case. None better made.
Price, 3 for $14.65; each.....$4.93
If by mail, postage extra, each 8 cents.

No. 18G1747 Eagle Claw Meerschaum Pipe, in silk plush lined chamois case. This genuine meerschaum pipe is very high grade, having 3-inch bent amber mouthpiece and number 7 bowl. Total length of pipe is 5½ inches. The workmanship is of the very finest, being carved carefully with artistic skill. The same pipes are retailed at some exclusive stores for $7.50. Price, 3 for $13.89; each, $4.67
If by mail, postage extra, each, 8 cents.

Gold Mounted Meerschaum Pipe, $5.99.

No. 18G1749 Square Stem, Curved Meerschaum Pipe. A very high grade pipe, with 3-inch square genuine amber mouthpiece and number 7 bowl. Pipe is handsomely mounted with gold bands on top of bowl and around stem of pipe. Inlaid in fine chamois, plush lined case.
Price, 3 for $17.79; each.....$5.99
If by mail, postage extra, each, 6 cents.

No. 18G1751 High Grade Genuine Meerschaum Pipe made of very heavy solid piece of block meerschaum in a fancy shape square design bowl. The mouthpiece is cut square out of a very heavy block of finest quality genuine amber and is so shaped that the pipe may be held by the stem instead of bowl. The stem is trimmed with a heavy solid gold band with French gray silver ornaments. Length of stem 2¾ inches. Entire length of pipe, 4½ inches. In a beautiful Russian leather covered, silk plush lined case.
Price, 3 for $22.29; each.....$7.50
If by mail, postage extra, each, 8 cents.

First Quality Genuine Meerschaum Bowls in Chamois Lined Cases.

No. 18G1753 Genuine Meerschaum Bowl, finest quality block meerschaum. This style of meerschaum colors quickest, and is the best style for use with the popular Weichsel stem; comes in fine plush lined chamois leather case; the finest grade of meerschaums on the market. Compare our prices. Come in four sizes, as follows:

	Price for 3	Price, each
No. 5 bowl	$10.29	$3.48
No. 6 bowl	11.83	3.99
No. 7 bowl	14.51	4.89
No. 8 bowl	16.95	5.69

If by mail, postage extra, each, 4 cents.

No. 18G1755 Genuine Weichsel Stem with real amber mouthpiece. Length, 6 inches. This stem is used in connection with the meerschaum bowl under preceding No. 18G1753.
Price 3 for $1.49; each.....52c
If by mail, postage extra, each, 3 cents.

No. 18G1759 Smoker's Set, consisting of two high grade French brier pipes, one bulldog shape and one egg shape, the pipes being 5 inches in length with a 2-inch genuine amber mouthpiece. Has also a 1¾-inch genuine amber cigar holder. All three pieces are trimmed with heavy engraved gold bands, in beautiful chamois covered, silk plush lined case.
Price, 3 sets for $12.71; per set..$4.29
If by mail, postage extra, per set, 12 cents.

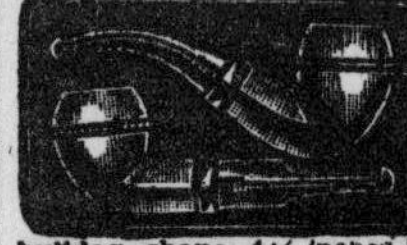

No. 18G1761 Smoker's Companion, containing two genuine first quality meerschaum pipes. One is straight, medium size, bulldog shape, 4½ inches long with a genuine 2¼-inch amber bit and the other is a bent bulldog shape, 4 inches long with 2¾-inch curved amber bit. Both have plain gold bands. This case is of unique shape, made of chamois leather, silk plush lined.
Price, 3 sets for $16.92; per set..$5.68
If by mail, postage extra, per set, 15 cents.

No. 18G1769 Genuine Meerschaum Cigar Holder with celluloid mouthpiece. Length, 2½ inches, in plush lined case. Price, 3 for 95c; each.....33c
If by mail, postage extra, each, 2 cents.

No. 18G1771 Genuine Meerschaum Cigar Holder, fancy carved with real amber bit, each in leather plush lined case. Order by number.
Price, 3 for $1.73; each.....59c
If by mail, postage extra, each, 3 cents.

No. 18G1773 Genuine Meerschaum Cigar Holder with real amber mouthpiece in pretty assorted carved designs. Length, 4 inches, in leather covered, silk plush lined case. Price, 3 for $2.89; each.....99c
If by mail, postage extra, each, 4 cents.

Solid Amber Cigar Holder.

No. 18G1775 Finest Quality Real Amber Cigar Holder, chamois covered and plush lined case, a very fine article. Comes in four sizes, as follows.

	Price for 3	Price, each
1½-inch length	$2.63	$0.90
2 -inch length	2.92	1.00
2½-inch length	3.66	1.25
3 -inch length	4.39	1.50

If by mail, postage extra, each, 2 cents.

Self Closing Rubber Pouch.

No. 18G1779 Raleigh Velvet Rubber Tobacco Pouch. Self closing, tan color. Diameter, 3½ inches. Keeps tobacco moist, clean and sweet.
Price, 3 for 50c; each.....18c
If by mail, postage extra, each, 3 cents.

Plain Nickel Finished Match Safe.

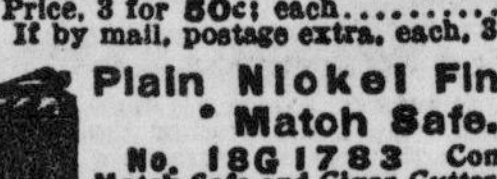

No. 18G1783 Combination Match Safe and Cigar Cutter. Nickel finish, leather covering.
Price, 3 for 56c; each.....20c
If by mail postage extra, each, 2c.

No. 18G1785 This pretty Match Safe is made of German silver, with handsome embossed design of bright silver finish. Very neat and tasty design.
Price, 3 for $1.33; each..46c
If by mail, postage extra, each, 2c.

Cigar Cases.

No. 18G1787 Cigar Case, telescope style and moulded into shape, fine polished tan sole leather case, stitched French edges, front embossed in English heraldic design, large size. Size, 1x3½x5¼ inches.
Price, 3 for 71c; each..25c
If by mail, postage extra, each, 5 cents.

No. 18G1789 Cigar Case made of morocco, grained in black with riveted nickel frame. Silk embroidered inner pocket. Size, 5¼x3½ inches.
Price, each.....$0.50
3 for.....1.44
If by mail, postage extra, each, 5 cents.

No. 18G1791 Fancy Marbleized Leather Cigar Case with embossed medallion design fitted with good nickel riveted frame. The inner pockets are made of good material, has small scissors, cigar cutter and match scratcher. Size 5¼x3½ inches.
Price, each.....$0.89
3 for.....2.59
If by mail, postage extra, each, 5 cents.

No. 18G1793 Alligator Leather Cigar Case, lined with leather, has fine imported leather covered frame with best nickel spring catch. Size, 5¼x3½ inches.
Price, each.....$1.20
3 for.....3.49
If by mail, postage extra, 5 cents.

REMEMBER

WHEN YOU HAVE BOUGHT $25.00 WORTH OF GOODS OR MORE FROM US YOU GET YOUR CHOICE OF MANY VALUABLE ARTICLES FREE AS SHOWN IN OUR FREE PROFIT SHARING BOOK.

HAIR ORNAMENTS.

Everything that is new and pretty for the Hair Moderately priced. You save big money on this line.

Great Bargain in Pin Cabinets, 13 Cents.

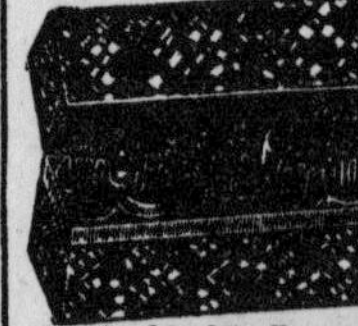

No. 18G1802 Contains 200 hairpins in all sizes from the smallest invisibles to the full size 3-inch pin, both straight and crimped. Has an assortment of 37 assorted colored, round headed toilet pins including 12, 2-inch shawl or belt pins in black, all mounted in a velvet pincushion. Also contains two rolls of adamantine pins. 40 black and 40 white. The box is finished in plaid paper and gilt edged.
Price, 3 for 37c; each.....13c
If by mail, postage extra, each, 8 cents.

No. 18G1807 Real Kid Hair Crimpers, 12 in a package

Length, ins.	3½	4	4½	5	6
Price for 2 pkgs.	4c	5c	6c	7c	8c

Postage extra, per 2 packages, 4 cents.

Aluminum Hair Pins.

No. 18G1816 Aluminum Hair Pins; extra heavy, fancy twist, our best number. Length, 3½ inches; worth double.
Price, 2 dozen for.....13c
If by mail, postage extra, per 2 dozen, 4 cents.

No. 18G1839 Imitation Tortoise Shell Hair Pin, round shape. Length, 4½ inches.
Price, 3 for.....10c
If by mail, postage extra, for 3, 3 cents.

No. 18G1844 Fine Polished Hair Pin. Imitation tortoise shell, an excellent style and shape. Length, 4½ inches.
Price, 3 for.....12c
If by mail, postage extra, for 3, 3 cents.

No. 18G1848 Hair Pin. Imitation tortoise shell, new improved pattern, a very popular shape. Length, 4¾ inches.
Price, 3 for.....12c
If by mail, postage extra, for 3, 3 cents.

No. 18G1816 No. 18G1839 No. 18G1844 No. 18G1848

No. 18G1861 Imitation Tortoise Shell Horn Hair Pin, put up one dozen in a box, in either straight or crimped. Length, 3¼ inches Just half value; our special leader
Price, 3 dozen for 28c; per dozen.....10c
If by mail, postage extra, per dozen, 2 cents.

No. 18G1864 Prima Horn Hair Pins. Elegant quality imitation shell hair pins, loop tops straight or crimped, very highly polished. 12 pins in a box. Length, 3 inches. Also in amber color. State choice.
Price 3 dozen for 59c per dozen.....21c
If by mail, postage extra, per dozen, 2 cents.

No. 18G1867 Parisienne Celluloid Hair Pin, made in imitation of tortoise shell. This is a 3-inch crimped hair pin, very highly polished and the right thickness.
Price, 2 dozen for 54c; per dozen.....19c
If by mail postage extra, per dozen, 2 cents.

No. 18G1868 Ladies' Jeweled Pompadour Comb. Imitation tortoise shell, set with forty-two brilliant rhinestones. Very closely set, durable as well as handsome. This same quality comb is retailed at 50 cents. Very high grade. Price, each.....29c
3 for.....83c
If by mail, postage extra, each, 5 cents

REMEMBER

Adjustable Puff Comb.

No. 18G1869 Adjustable Puff Comb. With this comb you can dress your hair pompadour style without the use of the hair rats. Made in imitation tortoise shell. 8½ inches long and 1¾ inches wide. Has the adjustable hinge, so that the hair can be worn on top or forward; will also give when the hat is put on.
Price, 3 for 50c; each.....18c
If by mail, postage extra, each, 3 cents.

No. 18G1871 The Olive Barette, for confining the stray hairs at the back. This barette, when used with the new spike comb, No. 18G1894 gives a very pleasing effect. Length 3 inches.
Price 3 for 50c; each.....18c
If by mail, postage extra, each, 2 cents.

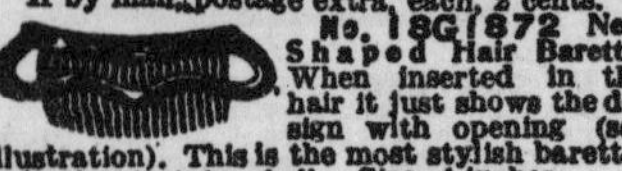

No. 18G1872 New Shaped Hair Barette. When inserted in the hair it just shows the design with opening (see illustration). This is the most stylish barette; imitation tortoise shell. Size, 4 inches.
Price, 3 for 49c; each.....17c
If by mail, postage extra, each, 2 cents.

Side Combs.

No. 18G1874 Side Combs, made of imitation tortoise shell, highly polished. Length, 4 inches. Has a very pretty scalloped top, as shown. Price per pair.....11c
3 pairs for..(Postage extra, per pr.. 2c.)..29c

No. 18G1875 Ladies' Side Combs. Very highly polished. Heavy top. Imitation of tortoise shell. A good heavy comb. Length, 4¼ inches. 35-cent value.
Price, 3 pairs for 44c; per pair.....16c
If by mail, postage extra, per pair, 3 cents.

No. 18G1877 Ladies' Side Combs Immitation of tortoise shell, very highly polished, heavy and fine finished teeth. Extra heavy top. The new curved shape. Looks as well as the real shell. Can also be ordered in amber. State choice. Retailed by dealers at 50 cents. Length, 4¾ inches
Price, 3 pairs for 73c; per pair.....26c
If by mail, postage extra, per pair, 4 cents

No. 18G1878 New Style Ball Design Side Combs, made of imitation tortoise shell, well finished and highly polished. Very pretty with back comb No. 18G1894. Length, 3½ inches.
Price, 3 pairs for 74c; per pair.....26c
If by mail postage extra, per pair, 5 cents.

No. 18G1890 Imitation Tortoise Shell Side Combs. Highly polished and finished; length, 4 inches. The top is ornamented with a strip of gold trimming in a Grecian design; set with 3 beautiful fancy colored jewel stones. Price, 3 pairs for 65c; per pair 23c
If by mail, postage extra, per pair, 3 cents.

No. 18G1893 Imitation Tortoise Shell Side Combs. Size, 3¾ inches. The top is ornamented with a strip of silver trimming set with rhinestones. The comb is well finished and has an extra heavy top. Price per pair.....29c
3 pairs for.....83c
If by mail, postage extra, per pair, 3 cents.

Ladies' Back Combs.

No. 18G1894 One of the season's successes, the new and popular Spike Back Comb. Made of fine quality, highly polished imitation tortoise shell. Length of comb, 4½ inches. Regular 50 cent value. Price, each. 24c
3 for..(Postage extra each 3 cents.) 68c

No. 18G1895 Imitation Tortoise Shell Heavy Top Neck or Back Comb. Has nicely rounded teeth and a grooved top which gives it a very splendid appearance. Length, 3½ inches; teeth, 1¾ inches long.
Price, 3 for 50c; each.....18c
If by mail, postage extra, each, 3 cents.

No. 18G1897 Imitation Tortoise Shell Back Comb, set with a silver strip and twenty-four brilliant rhinestones; has finely finished teeth and a reinforced top. Length of comb, 4 inches.
Price, 3 for 77c; each.....27c
If by mail, postage extra, each, 3 cents.

No. 18G1898 Imitation Tortoise Shell Back Comb, highly polished and finished comb, with beautiful design gold ornament, back set with handsome jewel stones. Regular 50-cent value. Length of comb, 4¾ inches. Price, 3 for $1.06; each.....37c
If by mail, postage extra, each 5 cents.

No. 18G1900 Imitation Tortoise Shell Back Comb Length, 4¼ inches. Has the new design high top and is ornamented with a very striking design in gilt set with two large jewel stones. Price, each. $0.48
3 for..(Postage extra, each. 5 cents.) 1 39

No. 18G1904 Fine Quality Imitation Tortoise Shell Back Comb, beautifully finished teeth. Mounted with a double row of 52 brilliant rhinestones. Length of comb, 5 inches. A rich looking article.
Price, 3 for $1.59; each.....55c
If by mail, postage extra, each 5 cents

No. 18G1907 Imitation Tortoise Shell Back Comb, 4½ inches long. Has nicely finished, well rounded teeth. Mounted in gilt in a beautiful, lily pattern, set with 6 pearl stones. Regular 75-cent value.
Price, 3 for $1.70; each.....59c
If by mail, postage extra, each, 5 cents.

Fancy Brier Pipes.

No. 18H11685 The Always Clean Brier Bowl, long rubber stem, nicotine absorber, handsomely decorated cover; a pipe that can be taken apart in four pieces and usually retails for $1.00.
Our price..33c
If by mail, postage extra, 7 cents.

33c

38c

No. 18H11686 Fancy Shaped Genuine Brier Pipe, with curved horn bit and horn screw to let the saliva out. Nickel band on stem and bottom of bowl, fancy tower cover. This is a very desirable pipe. Length of pipe, 6½ inches. Price......38c
If by mail, postage extra, 6 cents.

No. 18H11687 Fine Eagle Claw French Brier Pipe, with fancy curved horn mouthpiece. A large size egg shape bowl. Length of pipe, 6 inches.
Price......48c
If by mail, postage extra, 6 cents.

48c

38c

No. 18H11689 Large Sized Fine Vienna Chip Meerschaum Pipe, large egg shaped bowl and handsome cherry stem, with silk cord and tassel and imitation amber mouthpiece. An exceptionally handsome article. Price....38c
If by mail, postage extra, 6 cents.

No. 18H11691 Fancy Shape Vienna Chip Meerschaum Pipe, artistically carved design lady's head. Pipe is boiled in wax and will color like genuine meerschaum, has 4-inch cherry stem, with curved celluloid bit. Length of pipe, 8½ inches. Price.........68c
If by mail, postage extra, 6 cents.

68c

No. 18H11688 6½-inch Weichsel Pipe Stem, with curved rubber mouthpiece.
Price.........13c

No. 18H11690 7-inch Cherry Pipe Stem, with curved rubber mouthpiece. Price...9c
If by mail, postage extra, each, 3 cents.

German Favorite

83c

German Porcelain Pipes.

No. 18H11695 German Porcelain Pipe, handsomely decorated; just the thing for a good old fashioned smoke. This is an exceptionally fine and handsome German porcelain pipe. Made with very fine long stem, fitted with flexible top and extra fine hard rubber mouthpiece. Long genuine porcelain bowl, artistically and handsomely decorated. The bowl can readily be taken apart for cleaning, thus assuring a clean, cool smoke. Shipping weight, 1¾ pounds. Price..83c

Regular $2.00 German Porcelain Pipe, $1.38.

No. 18H11697 German Porcelain Pipe. This is an exceptionally high grade German pipe with a large elaborately decorated bowl, with nicotine receiver on bottom which can be unscrewed, long fancy carved horn stem, fitted with flexible top and fine hard rubber mouthpiece. Trimmed with long silk cord and tassels. All the different parts can be separated, so that you can easily clean. Shipping weight, 1¾ pounds. Price.........$1.38

Genuine French Brier Pipes, 59c.

No. 18H11699 Genuine French Brier Pipe, Genuine Amber, highly polished, dark finish, bulldog shape, with 1¾-inch genuine amber straight stem. Length of pipe, 5 inches. 75-cent value. Our price......59c
If by mail, postage extra, 7 cents.

No. 18H11700 This is certainly one of the very handsomest pipes made. It is made from highly polished rosewood with removable set in bowl of chip meerschaum, which can be unscrewed and easily cleaned. Genuine amber mouthpiece. Length of pipe, 5½ inches. Put up in handsome leather covered satin lined case. Price..........79c
If by mail, postage extra, 4 cents.

79c

Genuine French Brier.

No. 18H11703 Excellent Quality Highly Finished Genuine French Brier; egg shape bowl with square 2¼-inch genuine amber stem. Has plain sterling silver band, giving pipe a very pretty appearance. Whole length of pipe, 5 inches. Price.........99c
If by mail, postage extra, 6 cents.

99c Genuine Amber.

$1.19

Extra Value. Genuine Amber.

No. 18H11706 Genuine French Brier Pipe, Genuine Amber, highly polished, dark finish, with 3-inch genuine amber straight stem. This is the bulldog shape. Length of pipe, 6¼ inches. Worth $1.75, only..$1.19
If by mail, postage extra, 7 cents.

With Case $1.12

No. 18H11711 Selected French Brier Pipe, bulldog shape bowl with 2-inch genuine amber mouthpiece. Leather covered velvet lined case. Entire length of pipe is 5½ inches. Price.....$1.12
If by mail, postage extra, 2 cents.

No. 18H11717 High Grade French Brier Pipe, with heavy bulldog shape bowl and 2-inch amber stem. The pipe is trimmed with a heavy chased gold band on bowl and stem. Length of pipe, 5¾ inches. In leather covered velvet lined case. Price.....$1.69
If by mail, postage extra, 6 cents.

With Case $1.69

With Case $2.33

No. 18H11721 Fine Imported French Brier Pipe, with heavy bulldog shape bowl fitted with heavy 3-inch amber stem. The bowl is trimmed with heavily engraved top and the stem with band to match. Entire length of pipe, 6¾ inches. In leather covered silk plush lined case. Price.......$2.33
If by mail, postage extra, 5 cents.

No. 18H11723 High Grade French Brier Pipe with highly polished large bulldog shape bowl. Has extra heavy 3½-inch amber stem. The bowl is mounted with 14kt. gold plated top, with band to match. Entire length of pipe, 7 inches. In chamois covered silk plush lined case. Price.......$3.19
If by mail, postage extra, 5 cents.

$4.50 Value, $3.19

No. 18H11724 Curved Genuine French Brier Pipe. Egg shape bowl, with 1½-inch genuine amber bit and chased gold band. This is an excellent quality pipe. Whole length, 4½ inches. Price..........$1.05
If by mail, postage extra, 6 cents.

$1.05

No. 18H11725 Genuine French Brier Pipe, bulldog shape bowl with 1¾-inch genuine amber bit, has engraved gold band around stem. Length of pipe, 4½ inches. In leather covered silk plush lined case. Price.........$1.35
If by mail, postage extra, 5 cents.

College Style

No. 18H11727 Large Bulldog Genuine French Brier Pipe with 2-inch genuine amber bent mouthpiece. Has chased gold band around stem. Length of pipe, 4¾ inches. In leather covered silk plush lined case. Price.........$1.75
If by mail, postage extra, 5 cents.

$1.75

No. 18H11729 Very Fine Quality French Brier pipe, bulldog shape bowl, has a 2½-inch genuine amber curved mouthpiece. The bowl and stem are mounted with beautifully engraved gold bands, same design. Length of pipe, 5¼ inches. In leather covered silk plush lined case. Price.......$2.69
If by mail, postage extra, 5 cents.

Gold Mounted $2.69

No. 18H11731 Extra Quality French Brier Pipe, with heavy bull-bitch shape bowl. Has an extra heavy 3-inch curved genuine amber mouthpiece. The bowl and stem are ornamented with very heavy 14kt. gold plated band with raised silver ornaments, a new and attractive design. Length of pipe, 6 inches. In fine chamois covered silk plush lined case.
Price.........$3.95
If by mail, postage extra, 5 cents.

$3.95

Genuine Meerschaum Pipes.

$3.19

No. 18H11733 Genuine Meerschaum Pipes. High grade quality meerschaum, with best amber mouthpiece. In silk plush lined chamois case. The bowl is of the bulldog pattern and is of the best selected meerschaum. The amber mouthpieces vary in thickness according to size of bowl. State size wanted. Your choice in four sizes, as follows:

Size of bowl, No.	Length of amber, inches	Length of pipe	Price
5		4½ inches	$3.19
6		5½ inches	3.69
7	3	5½ inches	4.29
8	3¼	6 inches	4.99

If by mail, postage extra, each, 8 cents.

No. 18H11735 Genuine Block Meerschaum Pipe, handsomely carved bowl, assorted designs, such as lions, dogs, deer, etc., with genuine amber mouthpiece. Length of pipe, about 5 inches, with a No. 5 bowl in a satin lined case. State design wanted.
Price.........$2.88
If by mail, postage extra, 6 cents.

$2.88

No. 18H11737 Genuine Meerschaum Pipe, London egg shape bowl, finest quality meerschaum, with 2¾-inch round amber mouthpiece and No. 6 bowl. Total length of pipe, 5 in. Pipe is ornamented with fancy gold band around stem. Inlaid in chamois covered silk plush lined case; very high grade. Price.........$3.99
If by mail, postage extra, 5 cents.

Our $5.29 Meerschaum Pipe.

No. 18H11739 Genuine Meerschaum Pipe, straight bulldog shape, with 3-inch genuine amber mouthpiece and No. 7 bowl, heavy chased gold band on stem and bowl; inlaid in finest plush lined chamois covered case. No better pipe at any price. $8.00 value.
Our price..........$5.29
If by mail, postage extra, 6 cents.

No. 18H11741 Genuine Meerschaum Pipe with egg shape bowl and curved genuine amber mouthpiece, in chamois covered silk plush lined case. Length of pipe, 5 inches. Price.........$2.88
If by mail, postage extra, 8 cents.

$2.88

No. 18H11742 Fine Imported Meerschaum Pipe, in silk plush lined chamois case. The pipe is made of the highest grade meerschaum and first quality genuine amber mouthpiece. The model is the new Vienna pattern, egg shaped bowl with neat scroll design on the stem. Length of pipe, 5 inches. This pipe is an exceptional value, easily worth $5.50.
Our price..........$3.98
If by mail, postage extra, 7 cents.

$3.98

No. 18H11745 Best Quality Meerschaum Pipe, in silk plush lined chamois case with a curved genuine amber mouthpiece. The bowl is new and exclusive in shape and ornamented with a pretty Grecian design. For those wishing a high grade pipe, one that will color and insure a cool, pleasant smoke, we recommend the above pipe to embrace these qualities. Length of pipe, 5½ inches. Regular $6.00 value. Our price..........$4.15
If by mail, postage extra, 7 cents.

$4.15

High Grade Meerschaum.

Finest Quality

No. 18H11746 High Grade Genuine Meerschaum Pipe with large egg shape, size 6, bowl. Has a curved, square, genuine amber mouthpiece, 2¾ inches in length. The pipe is trimmed with plain gold band on top of bowl and stem, making a very rich and neat looking pipe. Entire length of pipe, 4½ inches. Fitted in morocco leather covered, plush lined case. None better made.
Price..........$4.48
If by mail, postage extra, 8 cents.

$4.48

No. 18H11747 Eagle Claw Meerschaum Pipe, in silk plush lined chamois case. This genuine meerschaum pipe is very high grade, having curved genuine amber mouthpiece and number 6 bowl. Total length of pipe is 5½ inches. The workmanship is of the very finest, being carved carefully and artistically by the most skilled workmen. The same pipes are retailed at exclusive pipe stores for $7.50.
Our price..........$4.67
If by mail, postage extra, 8 cents.

$4.67

Gold Mounted Meerschaum Pipe, $5.99.

No. 18H11749 Square Stem, Curved Meerschaum Pipe. A very high grade pipe, with 3-inch square genuine amber mouthpiece and number 7 bowl. Pipe is handsomely mounted with gold bands on top of bowl and around stem of pipe. Inlaid in fine chamois, plush lined case. Price..........$5.99
If by mail, postage extra, 6 cents.

Our Finest Meerschaum.

$10.00 Value $7.50

No. 18H11751 High Grade Genuine Meerschaum Pipe, made of very heavy solid piece of block meerschaum in a fancy shape square design bowl. The mouthpiece is cut square out of a very heavy block of finest quality genuine amber and is so shaped that the pipe may be held by the stem instead of bowl. The stem is trimmed with a heavy solid gold band with French gray silver ornaments. Length of stem, 2¾ inches. Entire length of pipe, 4¼ inches. In a beautiful Russian leather covered, silk plush lined case.
Our price..........$7.50
If by mail, postage extra, 8 cents.

First Quality Genuine Meerschaum Bowls in Chamois Lined Cases.

No. 18H11753 Genuine Meerschaum Bowl, finest quality block meerschaum. This style of meerschaum colors quickest, and is the best style for use with the popular Weichsel stem; the finest grade of meerschaums on the market; comes in fine plush lined chamois leather case. Compare our prices. Come in four sizes, as follows:

	Price
No. 5 bowl	$3.48
No. 6 bowl	3.99
No. 7 bowl	4.69
No. 8 bowl	5.69

If by mail, postage extra, 4 cents.

Genuine Weichsel Stem, 52c.

No. 18H11755 Genuine Weichsel Stem with real amber mouthpiece. Length, 6 inches. This stem is used in connection with the meerschaum bowl under preceding No. 18H11753.
Price..........52c
If by mail, postage extra, 2 cents.

Our $4.29 Smoker's Set.

No. 18H11759 Smoker's Set, consisting of two high grade French brier pipes, one bulldog shape and one egg shape, the pipes being 5 inches in length with a 2-inch genuine amber mouthpiece. Has also a 1¾-inch genuine amber cigar holder. All three pieces are trimmed with heavy engraved gold bands, in beautiful chamois covered, silk plush lined case.
Price, per set..........$4.29
If by mail, postage extra, per set, 12 cents.

Smoker's Companion.

No. 18H11761 Smoker's Companion, containing two genuine first quality meerschaum pipes. One is straight, medium size, bulldog shape, 4½ inches long with a genuine 2¼-inch amber bit, and the other is a bent bulldog shape, 4 inches long with 2¾-inch curved amber bit. Both have plain gold bands. This case is of unique shape, made of chamois leather, silk plush lined.
Price, per set..........$5.68
If by mail, postage extra, per set, 15 cents.

No. 18F1691 Fancy Shape Vienna Chip Meerschaum Pipe, artistically carved design lady's head. Pipe is boiled in wax and colored like genuine meerschaum, has 4-inch cherry stem, with curved celluloid bit. Length of pipe, 8¼ inches. Price.................59c
If by mail, postage extra, 6 cents.

No. 18F1688 6½-inch Weichsel Pipe Stem, with curved rubber mouthpiece. Price.................13c

No. 18F1690 7-inch Cherry Pipe Stem, with curved rubber mouthpiece. Price.........9c
If by mail, postage extra, 3 cents.

No. 18F1693 German Porcelain Pipe, with real weichsel wood stem with flexible top and horn mouthpiece, finished with cord and tassel. Porcelain bowl with nickel cover. The bowl is highly decorated with scenic design. Length of pipe, 20 inches. Price.................57c
Shipping weight, 1¼ pounds.

German Favorite

83c

German Porcelain Pipes.

No. 18F1695 German Porcelain Pipe, handsomely decorated; just the thing for a good old fashioned smoke. This is an exceptionally fine and handsome German porcelain pipe. Made with very fine long stem, fitted with flexible top and extra fine hard rubber mouthpiece. Long, genuine porcelain bowl artistically and handsomely decorated. The bowl can readily be taken apart for cleaning, thus assuring a clean, cool smoke. Shipping weight, 1¾ pounds.
Price.................83c

High Grade German Porcelain Pipe, $1.22.

No. 18F1697 German Porcelain Pipe. This is an exceptionally high grade German pipe with a large elaborately decorated bowl, with nicotine receiver on bottom which can be unscrewed, long fancy carved horn stem, fitted with flexible top and fine hard rubber mouthpiece. Finished with long silk cord and tassels. All the different parts can be separated, so that you can easily clean. Shipping weight, 1¾ pounds.
Price.................$1.22

Genuine French Brier Pipes.

59c

No. 18F1699 Genuine French Brier Pipe, Genuine Amber, highly polished, dark finish, bulldog shape, with 1¾-inch genuine amber straight stem. Length of pipe, 5 inches. 75-cent value. Price,.................59c
If by mail, postage extra, 7 cents.

Extra Value

No. 18F1701 Genuine French Brier Pipe, Genuine Amber, highly polished, dark finish with 3-inch genuine amber straight stem. This is the bulldog shape. Length of pipe, 6¼ inches. Worth $1.56. Price,.....$1.19
If by mail, postage extra, 7 cents.

99c Genuine Amber.

No. 18F1703 Excellent Quality Highly Finished Genuine French Brier; egg shape bowl with square 2¼-inch genuine amber stem. Has plain, sterling silver band, giving pipe a very pretty appearance. Whole length of pipe, 5 inches. Price.........99c
If by mail, postage extra, 6 cents.

No. 18F1705 Curved Genuine French Brier Pipe. Egg shape bowl, with 1½-inch genuine amber bit and chased gold band. This is an excellent quality, but inexpensive pipe. Whole length, 4½ inches.
Price.................$1.05
If by mail, postage extra, 6 cents.

$1.05

Pipes in Leather Covered Cases.

75c

No. 18F1707 Genuine French Brier Pipe, English bulldog shape. Length, 5 in. Handsome celluloid mouthpiece. Each one of these pipes is put up in a handsome leather covered case, with silk and velvet lining.
Price.................75c
If by mail, postage extra, 5 cents.

79c

No. 18F1709 This is certainly one of the very handsomest pipes made. It is made from highly polished rosewood with removable set in bowl of chip meerschaum, which can be unscrewed and easily cleaned. Genuine amber mouthpiece. Length of pipe, 5½ inches. Put up in handsome leather covered satin lined case. Price.................79c
If by mail, postage extra, 4 cents.

No. 18F1711 Selected French Brier Pipe bulldog shape bowl with 2-inch genuine amber mouthpiece. A large size pipe in leather covered velvet lined case. Entire length of pipe is 5½ inches.
Price.................$1.12
If by mail, postage extra, 2 cents.

No. 18F1713 Fine Quality French Brier Pipe, highly polished bulldog shape bowl, inlaid with heavy gold wire, has 1¼ inch genuine amber mouthpiece trimmed with plain gold band. Entire length of pipe, 5 inches. In leather covered velvet lined case. Price.................$1.05
If by mail, postage extra, 5 cents.

$1.59

No. 18F1715 French Brier Pipe, bulldog shape, with 2¼-inch genuine amber mouthpiece and trimmed with a sterling silver band, between stem and pipe. Entire length of pipe, 5¼ inches. Large size, highly polished bowl. Inlaid in fine plush lined leather case.
Price.................$1.59
If by mail, postage extra, 5 cents.

No. 18F1717 High Grade French Brier Pipe, with heavy bulldog shape bowl and 2-inch amber stem. The pipe is trimmed with a heavy chased gold band on bowl and stem. Length of pipe, 5¾ inches. In leather covered velvet lined case. Price.....$1.69
If by mail, postage extra, 6 cents.

No. 18F1719 Selected French Brier Pipe, with Hungarian straight shape bowl, broad, flat stem fitted with heavy 2-inch genuine amber mouthpiece, stem ornamented with heavily engraved gold band. Length of pipe, 6 inches. In chamois covered silk plush lined case. Price.................$1.83
If by mail, postage extra, 5 cents.

No. 18F1721 Fine Imported French Brier Pipe, with heavy bulldog shape bowl fitted with heavy 3-inch amber stem. The bowl is trimmed with heavily engraved top and the stem with band to match. Entire length of pipe, 6¾ inches. In leather covered silk plush lined case. Price.....$2.33
If by mail, postage extra, 5 cents.

No. 18F1723 High Grade French Brier Pipe with highly polished large bulldog shape bowl. Has extra heavy 3½-inch amber stem. The bowl is mounted with 14kt. gold plated band with raised French gray silver ornaments. The same design on band of stem. Entire length of pipe, 7 inches. In chamois covered silk plush lined case.
Price.................$3.19
If by mail, postage extra, 5 cents.

No. 18F1725 Genuine French Brier Pipe, bulldog shape bowl with 1¾-inch genuine amber bit, has engraved gold band around stem. Length of pipe, 4½ inches. In leather covered silk plush lined case. Price.................$1.35
If by mail, postage extra, 5 cents.

No. 18F1727 Large Bulldog Genuine French Brier Pipe with 2-inch genuine amber bent mouthpiece. Has chased gold band around stem. Length of pipe, 4¾ inches. In leather covered silk plush lined case. Price.................$1.75
If by mail, postage extra, 5 cents.

No. 18F1729 Very Fine Quality French Brier Pipe, bulldog shape bowl, has a 2½-inch genuine amber curved mouthpiece. The bowl is mounted with beautifully engraved gold band, the stem is also ornamented with gold band, same design. Length of pipe, 5½ inches. In leather covered silk plush lined case.
Price.................$2.69
If by mail, postage extra, 5 cents.

No. 18F1731 Extra Quality French Brier Pipe, with heavy bullbitch shape bowl. Has an extra heavy 3-inch curved genuine amber mouthpiece. The bowl and stem are ornamented with very heavy 14kt. gold plated band with raised silver ornaments, a new and attractive design. Length of pipe, 6 inches. In fine chamois covered silk plush lined case. Price.................$3.95
If by mail, postage extra, 5 cents.

Genuine Meerschaum Pipes.

No. 18F1733 Genuine Meerschaum Pipes. High grade quality meerschaum, with best amber mouthpieces. The bowl is of the bulldog pattern and is of the best selected meerschaum. The amber mouthpieces vary in thickness according to size of bowl. State size wanted. Your choice in four sizes, as follows:

Size of bowl, No.	Length of amber, inches	Price	Size of bowl, No.	Length of amber, inches	Price
5	2¼	$3.19	7	3	$4.29
6	2¾	3.69	8	3¼	4.99

If by mail, postage extra, 8 cents.

No. 18F1735 Genuine Block Meerschaum Pipe, handsomely carved bowl, assorted designs, such as lions, dogs, deer, etc., amber mouthpiece, 2½ inches long, with a No. 5 bowl in a satin lined case. State design wanted. Price.................$2.65
If by mail, postage extra, 6 cents.

No. 18F1737 Genuine Meerschaum Pipe, London egg shape bowl, finest quality meerschaum, with 2¾-inch round amber mouthpiece and No. 6 bowl. Total length of pipe, 5 in. Pipe is ornamented with fancy gold band around stem. Inlaid in chamois covered silk plush lined case; very high grade. Price.................$3.99
If by mail, postage extra, 5 cents.

Our $5.29 Meerschaum Pipe.

No. 18F1739 Genuine Meerschaum Pipe, straight bulldog shape, with 3-inch genuine amber mouthpiece and No. 7 bowl, heavy chased gold band on stem and bowl; inlaid in finest plush lined chamois covered case. No better pipe at any price. Price...$5.29
If by mail, postage extra, 6 cents.

No. 18F1741 Genuine Meerschaum Pipe with egg shape bowl and 2½-inch curved genuine amber mouthpiece, in chamois covered silk plush lined case. Length of pipe, 5 inches. Price,.................$2.88
If by mail, postage extra, 8 cents.

No. 18F1743 High Grade Genuine Meerschaum Pipe with large egg shape, size 6, bowl. Has a curved, square, genuine amber mouthpiece, 2¾ inches in length. The pipe is trimmed with plain gold band on top of bowl and stem, making a very rich and swell looking pipe. Entire length of pipe, 4½ inches. Fitted in morocco leather covered, plush lined case. None better made.
Price.................$4.93
If by mail, postage extra, 8 cents.

No. 18F1747 Eagle Claw Meerschaum Pipe. This genuine meerschaum pipe is very high grade, having 3-inch bent amber mouthpiece and number 7 bowl. Total length of pipe is 5½ inches. The workmanship is of the very finest, being carved carefully with artistic skill. The same pipes are retailed at some exclusive stores for $7.50. Price,.................$4.67
If by mail, postage extra, 8 cents.

Gold Mounted Meerschaum Pipe $5.99.

No. 18F1749 Square Stem, Curved Meerschaum Pipe. A very high grade pipe, with 3-inch square genuine amber mouthpiece and number 7 bowl. Pipe is handsomely mounted with gold bands on top of bowl and around stem of pipe. Inlaid in fine chamois, plush lined case. Price.................$5.99
If by mail, postage extra, 6 cents.

No. 18F1751 High Grade Genuine Meerschaum Pipe made of very heavy solid piece of block meerschaum in a fancy shape square design bowl. The mouthpiece is cut square out of a very heavy block of finest quality genuine amber and is so shaped that the pipe may be held by the stem instead of bowl. The stem is trimmed with a heavy solid gold band with French gray silver ornaments. Length of stem 2¾ inches. Entire length of pipe, 4½ inches. In a beautiful Russian leather covered, silk plush lined case.
Price.................$7.50
If by mail, postage extra, 8 cents.

First Quality Genuine Meerschaum Bowls in Chamois Lined Cases.

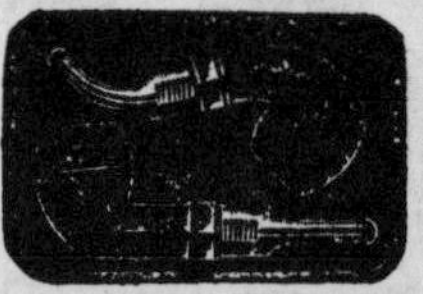

No. 18F1753 Genuine Meerschaum Bowl, finest quality block meerschaum. This style of meerschaum colors quickest, and the only quality and shape that will not break if you drop it; comes in fine plush lined chamois leather case; the finest grade of meerschaums on the market. Compare our prices. Come in four sizes, as follows:

No. 5 bowl. Price.................$3.48
No. 6 bowl. Price.................3.99
No. 7 bowl. Price.................4.89
No. 8 bowl. Price.................5.69
If by mail, postage extra, each, 4 cents.

No. 18F1755 Genuine Weichsel Stem with real amber mouthpiece. Length, 6 inches. This stem is used in connection with the meerschaum bowl under preceding No. 18F1753. Price, 52c
If by mail, postage extra, 3 cents.

No. 18F1757 Smoker's Companion, consisting of two pipes, one straight and one bent French brier, bulldog shape, with 2-inch genuine amber mouthpiece, solid gold band around stem, both pipes inlaid in a beautiful chamois covered and silk plush lined case.
Price, per set.................$3.39
If by mail, postage extra, 10 cents.

No. 18F1759 Smoker's Set, consisting of two high grade French brier pipes, one bulldog shape and one egg shape, the pipes being 5 inches in length with a 2-inch genuine amber mouthpiece. Has also a 1¾-inch genuine amber cigar holder. All three pieces are trimmed with heavy engraved gold bands, in beautiful chamois covered, silk plush lined case.
Price, per set.................$4.29
If by mail, postage extra, 12 cents.

No. 18F1761 Smoker's Companion, containing two genuine first quality meerschaum pipes. One is straight, medium size, bulldog shape, 4½ inches long with a genuine 2½-inch amber bit and the other is a bent bulldog shape, 4 inches long with 2½-inch curved amber bit. Both have plain gold bands. This case is of unique shape, made of chamois leather, plush lined.
Price, per set.................$5.68
If by mail, postage extra, 15 cents.

Turkish Water Pipes.

No. 18F1763 A Genuine Turkish Water Pipe. The bowl is made of fine colored glass, prettily decorated and has a long flexible stem, with small amber mouthpiece connected to pipe. In the center of head is a thin glass tube through which the smoke passes. The cup which holds the tobacco is made of Vienna meerschaum, which can be replaced if desired by the Vienna meerschaum cigar holder, which comes with the set. Entire height of pipe is about 10 inches. Shipping weight, 1 pound.
Price.................$1.94

No. 18F1765 Turkish Water Pipe. Same as above, but having two flexible stems from which two persons can smoke at the same time. The bowl is more elaborately decorated than the above and a little larger. The entire height about 10½ inches. Shipping weight, 1 pound. Price.........$2.75

No. 18F1766 Turkish Water Pipe. Has a very highly decorated bottle with German silver connections with three flexible tubes which are about 30 inches long and have amber mouthpieces. Inner meerschaum bowl fitted to each pipe. Total height, 11½ inches. Shipping weight, 1½ pounds. Price, $4.25

No. 18N4124 Genuine curved French Briar Pipe. An exceptional value, fitted with 1½-inch genuine amber curved bit, trimmed with chased gold plated band. Regular $1.50 value. Length of pipe, 4½ inches. **$1.05**
Our price........ **$1.05**
If by mail, postage extra, 6 cents.

Briar Pipes With Curved Amber Stems in Cases.

No. 18N4128 College Shape Genuine French Briar Pipe. Bulldog shape bowl, fitted with 1¾-inch genuine amber mouthpiece, trimmed with engraved gold plated band. Length of pipe, 4½ inches. In leather covered silk plush lined case. A pipe that is easily worth $2.00, and a popular shape. **$1.35**
Our price........ **$1.35**
If by mail, postage extra, 5 cents.

No. 18N4132 Special value Bulldog Shape Genuine French Briar Pipe. Fitted with 2-inch genuine amber bent mouthpiece, has an extra heavy chased gold plated band on stem. A neat appearing and very stylish shape. Length of pipe, 4¾ inches. Fitted in leather covered silk plush lined case. **$1.69**
Price...(Postage extra, 5 cents.).. **$1.69**

No. 18N4136 Our extra fine quality French Briar Pipe. Bulldog shape bowl, ornamented with fine engraved gold plated bands on top of bowl and around stem, fitted with heavy 2½-inch genuine amber curved mouthpiece. Entire length of pipe, 5¼ inches. Fitted in extra quality silk plush lined case. Easily worth $3.50. Our price........ **$2.63**
If by mail, postage extra, 5 cents.

Best Quality Extra Heavy Amber Stem.

No. 18N4140 Our best quality extra value French Briar Pipe. Oil boiled, extra finished bulldog shape bowl. The bowl and stem are ornamented with very heavy gold plated bands, with raised silver ornaments in a very neat and attractive design. Pipe is fitted with extra heavy 3-inch genuine amber curved mouthpiece. Entire length of pipe, 6 inches. Pipe is fitted in best quality chamois covered silk plush lined case. $5.00 value. Our price........ **$3.95**
If by mail, postage extra, 5 cents.

GENUINE MEERSCHAUM PIPES AT VERY LOW PRICES.

$3.19

No. 18N4144 Genuine Meerschaum Bulldog Shape Pipes. Guaranteed to be the best quality block meerschaum, fitted with genuine amber mouthpiece. These pipes are absolutely free of any flaws. The amber mouthpieces vary in thickness and length according to the size of the bowl and length of pipe. Each pipe in chamois covered silk plush lined case. Your choice of three sizes.

Size of Bowl	Length of Pipe	Price
5	4½	$3.19
7	5½	4.29
8	6	4.75

If by mail, postage extra, 5 cents.

No. 18N4148 Genuine Block Meerschaum Pipe. A special value, handsomely carved bowl. Can furnish assorted designs, such as lions, dogs, horses, etc. Fitted with genuine amber mouthpiece. Length of pipe, 5 inches. In silk plush lined chamois covered case. A special value and a great favorite. **$2.83**
Price..(Postage extra, 6 cents.).. **$2.83**

$3.95

No. 18N4152 Genuine Block Meerschaum Pipe, London egg shape bowl, finest quality meerschaum, with 2¾-inch round amber mouthpiece and No. 6 bowl. Total length of pipe, 5 inches. Pipe is ornamented with fancy gold band around stem. Inlaid in chamois covered silk plush lined case; very high grade. Price........ **$3.95**
If by mail, postage extra, 5 cents.

Our Popular Style.

$5.29

No. 18N4156 Our best quality and most popular Genuine Meerschaum Straight Stem Pipe. Made of absolutely the best quality genuine block meerschaum by expert workmen. No. 7 bowl, fitted with 3-inch genuine amber square mouthpiece, heavy chased gold plated band on stem and bowl. Fitted in finest quality chamois covered silk plush lined case. No better straight stem meerschaum pipe at any price. A bargain at any store at $8.00. Our price........ **$5.29**
If by mail, postage extra, 6 cents.

No. 18N4160 Our Special Genuine Block Meerschaum Egg Shape, Curved Stem Pipe. Made of the best quality meerschaum, and fitted with curved genuine amber mouthpiece. In chamois covered silk plush lined case. Entire length of pipe, 5 inches. Well worth $4.00. Our price........ **$3.19**
If by mail, postage extra, 6 cents.

No. 18N4164 Genuine Meerschaum Pipe, Calabash Shape. Made of first quality block meerschaum, extra thick with 3-inch bent amber mouthpiece in plush lined chamois covered case. A pipe that because of its unique shape will certainly please. Entire length of pipe, 5¼ inches. Well worth $5.00. Our price........ **$3.98**
If by mail, postage extra, 7 cents.

No. 18N4168 Neat pattern, highest grade Genuine Block Meerschaum Pipe. No. 6 egg shape bowl, trimmed at top and stem with plain gold plated bands, has genuine amber mouthpiece, 2¾ inches in length; in all a very neat and rich looking pipe. Fitted in genuine morocco leather covered, plush lined case. An excellent value and sure to please. Price........ **$4.48**
If by mail, postage extra, 8 cents.

A $7.50 Pipe for $4.67.

No. 18N4172 Eagle Claw, first quality Meerschaum Pipe. Fitted in silk plush lined chamois covered case. This pipe is hand carved by the most expert Austrian workmen, finished very carefully and artistically. No. 6 bowl, fitted with genuine amber curved mouthpiece. Entire length of pipe, 5½ inches. This same pipe is usually sold at $7.50. We import them and make a big saving for you. **$4.67**
Our price........ **$4.67**
If by mail, postage extra, 8 cents.

$5.99

No. 18N4176 Our best Bulldog Shape Genuine Block Meerschaum Pipe. Made with the finest quality No. 7 meerschaum bowl, fitted with extra heavy 3-inch genuine amber mouthpiece, handsomely ornamented at top and on stem with extra heavy chased gold plated bands. Fitted in chamois covered, best silk plush lined case.
Price.....(Postage extra, 6c).... **$5.99**

Our Finest Meerschaum Pipe.

$7.50

No. 18N4180 Our Finest Meerschaum Pipe. Made of the highest grade genuine meerschaum, cut from the largest blocks of meerschaum obtainable, with fancy shape square design bowl, fitted with extra heavy square cut genuine amber stem, 2¾ inches in length, so shaped that the pipe may be easily held by the stem instead of the bowl, trimmed with heavy solid gold plated band ornamented with French gray silver trimming. Fitted in genuine Russia leather covered, silk plush lined case. An exceptional value. This pipe will be found in stores throughout the country at from $10.00 to $12.00
Our price........ **$7.50**
If by mail, postage extra, 10 cents.

Best Quality Meerschaum Bowls.

No. 18N4184 Genuine Meerschaum Bowls. Made from the finest quality block meerschaum. This style of bowl will color the quickest and is very popular for the reason that the case remains on the pipe while smoking, so that the fingers will not touch the meerschaum. These bowls, used with our No. 18N4192 genuine Weichsel stems, will make as fine a pipe as can be obtained at any price. Fitted in plush lined chamois leather case. Come in four sizes, as follows:
No. 5 bowl. Price........ $3.48
No. 6 bowl. Price........ 3.66
No. 7 bowl. Price........ 4.89
No. 8 bowl. Price........ 5.69
If by mail, postage extra, 4 cents.

No. 18N4188 Extra Pipe Stems. 6½-inch Weichsel Pipe Stems for use with pipes No. 18N4068, and No. 18N4072 and bowl No. 18N4184; fitted with hard rubber bits.
Price........ **13c**
If by mail, postage extra, 3 cents.

No. 18N4192 Genuine Weichsel Stem, fitted with real amber mouthpiece; length, 6 inches; to be used in connection with meerschaum bowl, listed under No. 18N4184 and pipes No. 18N4068 and No. 18N4072.
Price........ **52c**
If by mail, postage extra, 2 cents.

No. 18N4196 Chip Meerschaum Coloring Bowl, for use with our genuine meerschaum pipes. By using this bowl the pipe itself will not burn but will color beautifully. Fitted with cork bottom so that it will fit securely in bowl. When ordering, give us inside diameter of your pipe bowl.
Price........ **18c**
If by mail, postage extra, 2 cents.

Two Genuine Meerschaum Pipes for $5.68.

No. 18N4200 Smoker's Companion, containing two genuine first quality meerschaum pipes; one is a straight medium sized bulldog shape, 4½ inches long, fitted with 2¼-inch amber mouthpiece; the other is a bent bulldog shape, 4 inches long, fitted with 2¼-inch curved amber mouthpiece. Both pipes ornamented with plain gold plated bands and fitted into best quality chamois covered, silk plush lined case. It is well known that by using two or more pipes better results can be obtained as regards coloring, etc., therefore, we advise the smoker to purchase this set. Price........ **$5.68**
If by mail, postage extra, 15 cents.

Meerschaum Cigar Holders.

No. 18N4204 Genuine Meerschaum Cigar Holder, fancy carved with real amber bit, each in leather plush lined case.
Price........ **59c**
If by mail, postage extra, 3 cents.

No. 18N4208 Genuine Meerschaum Cigar Holder, made of first quality heavy block meerschaum with genuine amber mouthpiece of select grade, set in a neat silk plush lined chamois case. This is an exceptionally high grade article, one that will color beautifully and give that satisfaction which only the best goods can. Length, 3 inches.
Price........ **98c**
If by mail, postage extra, 4 cents.

No. 18N4212 Genuine Meerschaum Cigar Holder with real amber mouthpiece in pretty assorted carved designs. Length, 4 inches, in leather covered, silk plush lined case.
Price........ **$1.15**
If by mail, postage extra, 4 cents.

Amber Cigar Holders.

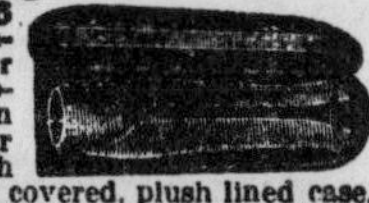

No. 18N4216 Finest Quality Genuine Amber Cigar Holder. Very popular shape. We can furnish these cigar holders either with or without chamois covered, plush lined case.
2-in., with case, $1.10 | 3-in., with case, $1.50
Without case... .88 | Without case... 1.25
If by mail, postage extra, 2 cents.

Simplex Cigarette Maker.

No. 18N4217 Simplex Cigarette Maker. A very simple device for rolling perfect cigarettes. Can be used in strong wind without the loss of tobacco. Full instructions with each outfit. Anyone can operate it.
Price....(Postage extra, 2 cents).... **19c**

No. 18N4219 "Squeezeit," an attachment to be used with tobacco bags, saves all pulling of strings and saves much tobacco. Once adjusted, your sack is always ready for use. This should also be used in connection with our Simplex Cigarette Maker.
Our price.....(Postage extra, 2c).... **7c**

Self Closing Rubber Pouch.

No. 18N4220 Raleigh Velvet Rubber Tobacco Pouch. Self closing, tan color. Diameter, 3⅝ inches. Keeps tobacco moist, clean and sweet. 25-cent value. Price........ **18c**
If by mail, postage extra, 3 cents.

Leather Tobacco or Coin Pouch.

No. 18N4224 Maister's Tobacco or Coin Pouch. Made of one piece of genuine leather with inside cloth pocket, fastened by means of heavy draw strings with metal knob ends and additional glove catch. This pouch can be used for either tobacco or coin.
Our price...(Postage extra, 3 cents.).. **23c**

Plain Nickel Finished Match Safe.

No. 18N4228 Combination Match Safe and Cigar Cutter. Nickel finish leather covering.
Price........ **19c**
If by mail, postage extra, 2 cents.

German Silver Match Safe.

No. 18N4232 This pretty Match Safe is made of German silver, or silver plated, with handsome embossed design of bright silver finish. Very neat and tasty design. 75-cent value.
Our price........ **48c**
If by mail, postage extra, 2 cents.

Cigar Cases.

No. 18N4236 Cigar Case, telescope style and moulded into shape, fine polished tan sole leather case, stitched French edges, front embossed in English heraldic design, large size. Size, 1x3¼x5¼ inches. 50-cent value. Our price.. **29c**
If by mail, postage extra, 5c.

No. 18N4240 Cigar Case, made of morocco grained imitation leather, in black with riveted nickel frame, floral design. Silk embroidered inner pocket. Size, 5¼x3¼ inches.
Price........ **49c**
By mail, postage extra, 5c.

No. 18N4244 Fancy Marbleized Leather Cigar Case with embossed medallion design, fitted with good nickel riveted frame. The inner pockets are made of good material, has small scissors, cigar cutter and match scratcher. Size, 5⅛x3½ inches. Price........ **89c**
If by mail, postage extra, 5c.

Alligator Leather Cigar Case.

No. 18N4248 Alligator Leather Cigar Case, has fine imported alligator leather covered frame with best nickel spring catch, leather lined throughout. Our best and most serviceable cigar case; makes a most acceptable gift. Regular $2.00 value. Size, 5⅛x3½ inches.
Our price........ **$1.20**
If by mail, postage extra, 5c.

No. 18R4132 Special value Bulldog Shape Genuine French Briar Pipe. Fitted with 2-inch genuine amber bent mouthpiece, has an extra heavy chased gold plated band on stem. A neat appearing and very stylish shape. Length of pipe, 4¾ inches. Fitted in leather covered silk plush lined case. $1.69
Price..(Postage extra, 5 cents.).. $1.69

No. 18R4136 Our extra fine quality French Briar Pipe. Bulldog shape bowl, ornamented with fine engraved gold plated bands on top of bowl and around stem, fitted with heavy 2½-inch genuine amber curved mouthpiece. Entire length of pipe, 5¼ inches. Fitted in extra quality silk plush lined case. Easily worth $3.50. Our price $2.63
If mail shipment, postage extra, 5c. $2.63

Best Quality Extra Heavy Amber Stem.

No. 18R4140 Our best quality extra value French Briar Pipe. Oil boiled, extra finished bulldog shape bowl. The bowl and stem are ornamented with very heavy gold plated bands, with raised silver ornaments in a very neat and attractive design. Pipe is fitted with extra heavy 3-inch genuine amber curved mouthpiece. Entire length of pipe, 6 inches. Pipe is fitted in best quality chamois covered silk plush lined case. $5.00 value. Our price $3.95
If mail shipment, postage extra, 5c. $3.95

GENUINE MEERSCHAUM PIPES AT VERY LOW PRICES.

$3.19

No. 18R4144 Genuine Meerschaum Bulldog Shape Pipes. Guaranteed to be the best quality block meerschaum, fitted with genuine amber mouthpiece. These pipes are absolutely free of any flaws. The amber mouthpieces vary in thickness and length according to the size of the bowl and length of pipe. Each pipe in chamois covered silk plush lined case. Your choice of three sizes.

Size of Bowl	Length of Pipe	Price
5	4½	$3.19
7	5½	4.29
8	6	4.75

If mail shipment, postage extra, 5 cents.

No. 18R4148 Genuine Block Meerschaum Pipe. A special value, handsomely carved bowl. Can furnish assorted designs, such as lions, dogs, horses, etc. Fitted with genuine amber mouthpiece. Length of pipe, 5 inches. In silk plush lined chamois covered case. A special value and a great favorite. $2.83
Price..(Postage extra, 6 cents.).. $2.83

$3.95

No. 18R4152 Genuine Block Meerschaum Pipe, London egg shape bowl, finest quality meerschaum, with 2¼-inch round amber mouthpiece and No. 6 bowl. Total length of pipe, 5 inches. Pipe is ornamented with fancy gold band around stem. Inlaid in chamois covered silk plush lined case; very high grade. Price $3.95
If mail shipment, postage extra, 5c.

No. 18R4160 Our Special Genuine Block Meerschaum Egg Shape, Curved Stem Pipe. Made of the best quality meerschaum and fitted with curved genuine amber mouthpiece. In chamois covered silk plush lined case. Entire length of pipe, 5 inches. Well worth $4.00. Our price $3.19
If mail shipment, postage extra, 6 cents.

No. 18R4164 Genuine Meerschaum Pipe, Calabash Shape. Made of first quality block meerschaum, extra thick, with 3-inch bent amber mouthpiece in plush lined chamois covered case. A pipe that because of its unique shape will certainly please. Entire length of pipe, 5¼ inches. Well worth $5.00. Our price $3.98
If mail shipment, postage extra, 7 cents.

No. 18R4168 Neat pattern, high-est grade Genuine Block Meerschaum Pipe. No. 6 egg shape bowl, trimmed at top and stem with plain gold plated bands, has genuine amber mouthpiece, 2¾ inches in length; in all a very neat and rich looking pipe. Fitted in genuine morocco leather covered plush lined case. An excellent value and sure to please. Price $4.48
If mail shipment, postage extra, 8 cents.

A $7.50 Pipe for $4.67.

No. 18R4172 Eagle Claw, first quality Meerschaum Pipe. Fitted in silk plush lined chamois covered case. This pipe is hand carved by the most expert Austrian workmen, finished very carefully and artistically. No. 6 bowl, fitted with genuine amber curved mouthpiece. Entire length of pipe, 5½ inches. This same pipe is usually sold at $7.50. We import them and make a big saving for you. Our price $4.67
If mail shipment, postage extra, 8 cents.

$5.99

No. 18R4176 Our best Bulldog Shape Genuine Block Meerschaum Pipe. Made with the finest quality No. 7 meerschaum bowl, fitted with extra heavy 3-inch genuine amber mouthpiece, handsomely ornamented at top and on stem with extra heavy chased gold plated bands. Fitted in chamois covered, best silk plush lined case. $5.99
Price....(Postage extra, 6c)... $5.99

Our Finest Meerschaum Pipe.

No. 18R4180 Our Finest Meerschaum Pipe. Made of the highest grade genuine meerschaum, cut from the largest blocks of meerschaum obtainable, with fancy shape square design bowl, fitted with extra heavy square cut genuine amber stem 2¾ inches in length, so shaped that the pipe may be easily held by the stem instead of the bowl, trimmed with heavy solid gold plated band ornamented with French gray silver trimming. Fitted in genuine Russia leather covered silk plush lined case. An exceptional value. This pipe will be found in stores throughout the country at from $10.00 to $12.00 $7.38
Our price..(Postage extra, 10c).. $7.38

Genuine Black Amber Pipe.

No. 18R4182 Nothing finer made than this beautiful imported article. An elegant house pipe. Made of genuine black amber with a screw in top bowl of first quality meerschaum. Has 2½-inch yellow amber stem. Entire length of pipe, 5½ inches. Fitted with plush lined chamois covered case. We guarantee this pipe to be a big $10.00 value in any store. $6.75
Our price $6.75
If mail shipment, postage extra, 10 cents.

Best Quality Meerschaum Bowls.

No. 18R4184 Genuine Meerschaum Bowls. Made from the finest quality block meerschaum. This style of bowl will color the quickest and is very popular for the reason that the case remains on the pipe while smoking, so that the fingers will not touch the meerschaum. These bowls, used with our No. 18R4192 genuine Weichsel stems, will make as fine a pipe as can be obtained at any price. Fitted in plush lined chamois leather case. Come in four sizes, as follows:

No. 5 bowl. Price	$3.48
No. 6 bowl. Price	3.86
No. 7 bowl. Price	4.29
No. 8 bowl. Price	5.69

If mail shipment, postage extra, 4 cents.

Weichsel Pipe Stems.

No. 18R4188 Extra Pipe Stems. 6½-inch Weichsel Pipe Stems for use with pipes No. 18R4068, and No. 18R4072 and bowl No. 18R4184; fitted with hard rubber bits. 13c
Price 13c
If mail shipment, postage extra, 3 cents.

No. 18R4192 Genuine Weichsel Stem, fitted with real amber mouthpiece; length, 6 inches; to be used in connection with meerschaum bowl, listed under No. 18R4184 and pipes No. 18R4068 and No. 18R4072. 52c
Price 52c
If mail shipment, postage extra, 2 cents.

Coloring Bowl.

No. 18R4196 Chip Meerschaum Coloring Bowl, for use with our genuine meerschaum pipes. By using this bowl the pipe itself will not burn but will color beautifully. Fitted with cork bottom so that it will fit securely in bowl. When ordering, give us inside diameter of your pipe bowl. 18c
Price 18c
If mail shipment, postage extra, 2 cents.

Two Genuine Meerschaum Pipes for $5.68.

No. 18R4200 Smoker's Companion, containing two genuine first quality meerschaum pipes; one is a straight medium sized bulldog shape, 4½ inches long, fitted with 2¼-inch amber mouthpiece; the other is a bent bulldog shape, 4 inches long, fitted with 2¼-inch curved amber mouthpiece. Both pipes ornamented with plain gold plated bands and fitted into best quality chamois covered silk plush lined case. It is well known that by using two or more pipes better results can be obtained as regards coloring, etc., therefore, we advise the smoker to purchase this set. Price $5.68
If mail shipment, postage extra, 15 cents.

Meerschaum Cigar Holders.

No. 18R4204 Genuine Meerschaum Cigar Holder, fancy carved, with real amber bit, each in leather plush lined case. 59c
Price 59c
If mail shipment, postage extra, 3 cents.

No. 18R4208 Genuine Meerschaum Cigar Holder, made of first quality heavy block meerschaum with genuine amber mouthpiece of select grade, set in a neat silk plush lined chamois case. This is an exceptionally high grade article, one that will color beautifully and give that satisfaction which only the best goods can. Length, 3 inches. 98c
Price 98c
If mail shipment, postage extra, 4 cents.

No. 18R4212 Genuine Meerschaum Cigar Holder with real amber mouthpiece in pretty assorted carved designs. Length, 4 inches, in leather covered, silk plush lined case. $1.15
Price $1.15
If mail shipment, postage extra, 4 cents.

Amber Cigar Holders.

No. 18R4216 Finest Quality Genuine Amber Cigar Holder. Very popular shape. We can furnish these cigar holders either with or without chamois covered, plush lined case.

2-in., with case,	$1.10	3-in., with case,	$1.50
Without case..	.88	Without case..	1.25

If mail shipment, postage extra, 2 cents.

No. 18R4219 "Squeezeit," an attachment to be used with tobacco bags, saves all pulling of strings and saves much tobacco. Once adjusted, your sack is always ready for use. This should also be used in connection with our Simplex Cigarette Maker.
Our price.....(Postage extra, 2c)..... 7c

Self Closing Rubber Pouch.

No. 18R4220 Raleigh Velvet Rubber Tobacco Pouch. Self closing, tan color. Diameter, 3½ inches. Keeps tobacco moist, clean and sweet. 25-cent value. Price 18c
If mail shipment, postage extra, 3 cents.

Leather Tobacco Pouch.

No. 18R4224 Maister's Tobacco Pouch. Made of one piece of genuine leather, fastened by means of heavy draw strings with metal knob ends and additional glove catch. 23c
Our price 23c
If mail shipment, postage extra, 3 cents.

Plain Nickel Finished Match Safe.

No. 18R4228 Combination Match Safe and Cigar Cutter. Nickel finish leather covering. 19c
Price 19c
Postage extra, 2 cents.

German Silver Match Safe.

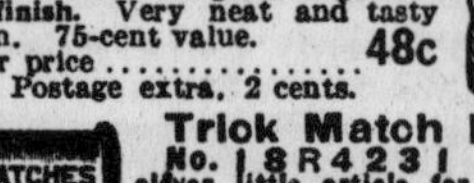

No. 18R4232 This pretty Match Safe is made of German silver, or silver plated, with handsome embossed design of bright silver finish. Very neat and tasty design. 75-cent value. 48c
Our price 48c
Postage extra, 2 cents.

Trick Match Box.

MATCHES

No. 18R4231 A very clever little article for holding matches. Made in such a manner that matches will appear or disappear, as desired. It is useful as well as having this trick feature, made for either patent or ordinary matches. Made of heavy metal, nickel plated. Size, 2½x1¼ inches. 15c
Price, each 15c
If mail shipment, postage extra, 2 cents.

Trick Cigarette Box.

No. 18R4233 Made in such a manner that you can offer your friend a cigarette, and when he reaches for it the box will appear empty. Made of heavy metal, nickel plated, with the word "Cigarettes" embossed upon one side. Size, 3½x2¼ inches. 21c
Price, each..(Postage extra, 4 cents).. 21c

Cigar Cases.

No. 18R4236 Cigar Case, telescope style and molded into shape, fine polished tan sole leather case, stitched French edges, front embossed in English heraldic design, large size. Size, 1x3¼x5½ inches. 50-cent value. Our price.. 29c
Postage extra, 5c.

No. 18R4241 Cigar Case, made of a very good imitation of walrus leather on riveted frame, with good clasp. Sateen lined. Very well made throughout. Size when closed, 5½ x 3½ inches. 49c
Price 49c
Postage, 5 cents.

No. 18R4245 Genuine Leather Cigar Case, alligator finish. Well made on riveted frame, with extra good clasp. Moire lined. Size, when closed, 5½ x 3½ inches. $1.25 value. 88c
Our price 88c
Postage extra, 5 cents.

No. 18R4249 Our Best All Genuine Leather Cigar Case, made of a good quality seal grain leather. Leather lined with leather match compartment on inside. Heavy nickel frame is also leather covered. Heavily padded to protect cigars. Size when closed, 5¼x4 inches. Well worth $2.00. Our price.. $1.29
Postage, 5 cents.

Our Popular Style.

$5.29

No. 18R4156 Our best quality and most popular genuine Meerschaum Straight Stem Pipe. Made of absolutely the best quality genuine block meerschaum by expert workmen. No. 7 bowl, fitted with 3-inch genuine amber square mouthpiece, heavy chased gold plated band on stem and bowl. Fitted in finest quality chamois covered silk plush lined case. No better straight stem meerschaum pipe at any price. A bargain at any store at $8.00.
Our price $5.29
If mail shipment, postage extra, 6 cents.

22 Cents for a Self Cleaner.

No. 18C5470 Genuine French Brier English Bulldog Pipe. Handsome Vienna amber mouthpiece. Length, 5¼ inches, long self cleaner, handsome nickel band, finely made and finished. Price, each....$0.22
Per dozen.... 2.25
If by mail, postage extra, each, 3c.

The New Ring Pipe.

For a Cool Smoke and to Prevent the Nicotine from Passing into the Mouth.

No. 18C5474 Genuine Brier Bowl, with imitation amber mouthpiece, and having the latest invention ring attachment. Tobacco in pipe is always kept dry, insuring a sweet, cool smoke. Easily cleaned. A boon for smokers. Price, per dozen, $4.25; each....38c
If by mail, postage extra, each, 5c.

Dublin Shape.

19c

No. 18C5490 French Brier Pipe, straight stem, Dublin shape bowl, 2-inch imitation amber mouthpiece. For a good smoke in a good pipe, buy this. Price, each....$0.19
Per dozen....2.15
If by mail, postage extra, each, 5c.

Handsome Brier Pipe, Bulldog Shape.

20c

No. 18C5494 Fine Brier Pipe, bulldog shape, with Chinese amber shove bit, plain nickel band, a very handsome pipe which we recommend very highly. Price, each....$0.20
Per dozen....2.25
If by mail, postage extra, each, 4c.

French Brier, 25 Cents.

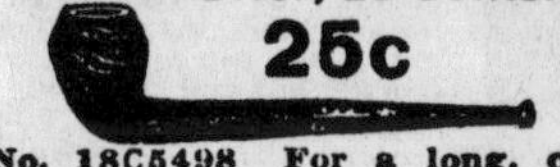

25c

No. 18C5498 For a long, cool smoke, we recommend this French Brier Pipe, made of highly stained dark polished French brier, with long, slender stem, amberite mouthpiece and bulldog shaped bowl. Total length of pipe, 6 inches. Price, each....$0.25
Per dozen....2.75
If by mail, postage extra, each, 4c.

Bent Brier, 25 Cents.

No. 18C5510 Large Size Bent Brier Pipe, with rubber stem; fine covered nickel top; for a fine, lasting smoke this pipe cannot be excelled. Price, each....$0.25
Per dozen....2.85
If by mail, postage extra, each, 3c.

25c

Straight French Brier.

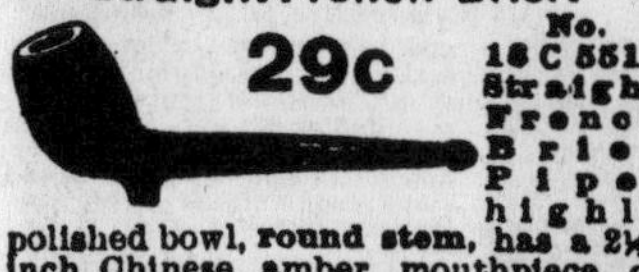

29c

No. 18C5514 Straight French Brier Pipe, highly polished bowl, round stem, has a 2¼-inch Chinese amber mouthpiece or stem, and a pipe that we can highly recommend. Price, each....$0.29
Per dozen....3.25
If by mail, postage extra, each, 5c.

Our 30-Cent Leader.

30c

No. 18C5518 French Brier Pipe, highly polished dark brier, heavy bulldog pattern bowl, has 3¼-inch horn mouthpiece with fancy nickel band; total length of pipe, 6¾ inches; a substantial and sightly pipe. Price, per dozen, $3.40; each....30c
If by mail, postage extra, each, 5c.

An Old Favorite.

24c

No. 18C5522 Handsomely Carved Brier Bowl, cherry stem, 3 inches long, and rubber mouthpiece; entire length of pipe 7 inches. A pipe that is easily cleaned and kept in order and always gives satisfaction.
Price, per dozen, $2.70; each..24c
If by mail, postage extra, each, 9c

Fancy Brier Pipes.

Easily Cleaned.

No. 18C5526 The Always Clean Brier Bowl, long rubber stem, nicotine absorber, handsomely decorated cover; a pipe that can be taken apart in four pieces, and usually retails for $1.00.

26c

Price, per dozen, $3.00; each....26c
If by mail, postage extra, each, 7c.

Yale Student Shape.

39c

No. 18C5530 Yale Student Pipe, is a heavy brier pipe with bent Chinese amber bit, heavy bull bitch shape. A fit companion for the millionaire, but at a price within reach of all.
Price, per dozen, $4.25; each..39c
If by mail, postage extra, each, 4c.

French Brier.

No. 18C5534 This splendid smoker is a French Brier, Bulldog Shape Bowl, with amberoid mouthpiece; the stem between bowl and mouthpiece is genuine Weichsel wood, and will not burn your tongue; worth 75 cents in the regular pipe stores.

25c

Price, per dozen, $2.75; each....25c
If by mail, postage extra, each, 5c.

Genuine French Brier Pipes.

48c

No. 18C5545 Genuine French Brier Pipe, highly polished, dark finish, bulldog shape, with 1¾-inch genuine amber straight stem. Length of pipe 5 inches. 75-cent value.
Price, per dozen, $5.50; each....48c
If by mail, postage extra, each, 7c.

Extra Value.

No. 18C5547 Genuine French Brier Pipe, highly polished, dark finish with 3-inch genuine amber straight stem. This is the bulldog shape. Length of pipe, 6¼ inches. Worth $1.50.
Price, each....$0.95
Per dozen....11.00
Postage extra, each, 7c.

German Favorite.

German Porcelain Pipes.

No. 18C5549 German Porcelain Pipe, handsomely decorated; just the thing for a good old fashioned smoke. This is an exceptionally fine and handsome German Porcelain Pipe. Made with very fine long stem, fitted with flexible top and extra fine hard rubber mouthpiece. Long, genuine porcelain bowl artistically and handsomely decorated. The bowl can readily be taken apart for cleaning, thus insuring a clean, cool smoke. Shipping weight, 1¾ pounds.
Price, each....$0.79
Per dozen....9.00

79c

High Grade German Porcelain Pipe, $1.10.

No. 18C5551 German Porcelain Pipe. This is an exceptionally high grade German pipe with a large elaborately decorated bowl, with nicotine receiver on bottom which can be unscrewed, long fancy carved horn stem, fitted with flexible top and fine hard rubber mouthpiece. Finished with long silk cord and tassels. All the different parts can easily be separated, so that you can easily clean. Shipping weight, 1¾ lbs.
Price, each...$ 1.10
Per dozen.....12.00

50 Cents for this Chip Meerschaum Pipe.

50c

No. 18C5550 Large Sized Fine Vienna Chip Meerschaum Pipe, large egg shaped bowl and handsome cherry stem, with silk cord and tassel and Chinese amber mouthpiece. An exceptionally handsome article.
Price, per dozen, $5.75; each....50c
If by mail, postage extra, each, 6c.

Chip Meerschaum Pipe.

90c

No. 18C5552 Fine Quality Chip Meerschaum Pipe. This is a large bowl with gilt rim and cover. Has a 5-inch cherry stem, to which is fitted a curved, amberoid mouthpiece. A small, gilt chain connects bowl with stem. Entire length of pipe about 9½ inches. A very attractive and desirable pipe. Price....90c
If by mail, postage extra, 8 cents.

Turkish Water Pipes.

No. 18C5554 A Genuine Turkish Water Pipe; the bowl is made of fine colored glass, prettily decorated, and has a long flexible stem, with small amber mouthpiece connected to pipe. In the center of head is a thin glass tube through which the smoke passes. The cup which holds the tobacco is made of Vienna meerschaum, which can be replaced, if desired, by the Vienna meerschaum cigar holder, which comes with the set. Entire height of same is about 10 inches. Price....$1.94
Shipping weight, 1 pound.

No. 18C5559 Turkish Water Pipe. Has a very highly decorated bottle, with German silver connections for three flexible tubes, which are 30 inches long and have amber mouthpieces; inner meerschaum bowl fitted to each pipe. Total height, 11½ inches.
Price....$4.25
Shipping weight, 1¼ pounds.

Pipes in Leather Covered Cases.

73c

No. 18C5562 Genuine French Brier Pipe, English bulldog shape. Length, 5 inches. Handsome Vienna amber mouthpiece. Each one of these pipes is put up in a handsome leather covered case, with silk and velvet lining.
Price....73c
If by mail, postage extra, 5 cents.

79c

No. 18C5566 This is certainly one of the very handsomest pipes made. It is made from highly polished rosewood with removable set in bowl of genuine meerschaum, which can be unscrewed and easily cleaned. Genuine Chinese amber mouthpiece; length, 5¼ inches. Put up in handsome leather covered, satin lined case. Price..79c
If by mail, postage extra, 4 cents.

$1.50

No. 18C5572 Genuine French Brier Pipe, bulldog shape, with genuine 2-inch amber mouthpiece. Highly polished, dark finish. The top of bowl and stem are mounted with fancy engraved gold bands. Inlaid in silk plush lined leather case. Length of pipe, 5 inches. Worth $2.50.
Price, per doz., $17.00; each. $1.50
If by mail, postage extra, each, 8c.

$1.47

No. 18C5577 French Brier Pipe, bulldog shape, with 2¼-inch genuine amber mouthpiece and trimmed with a sterling silver band between stem and pipe. Entire length of pipe, 5¼ inches. Large size, highly polished bowl. Inlaid in fine plush lined leather case. Price, $1.47
If by mail, postage extra, 5 cents.

$2.25

No. 18C5582 Genuine French Brier Pipe, bulldog shape, genuine 3-inch amber with mouthpiece, highly polished, dark finish. The top of bowl and stem are mounted with a heavy, fine, fancy gold band. Inlaid in fine silk plush lined leather case. Length of pipe, 6 inches. Good $3.50 value. Price....$2.25

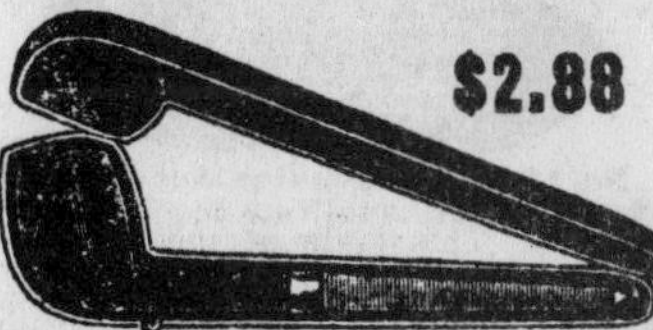

$2.88

No. 18C5587 This is a Fancy, Egg Shape, French Brier Pipe, with a round stem and ⅛-inch gold band and 4-inch amber mouthpiece. Entire length of pipe is 11 inches, making a delightful, cool smoke. Inlaid in fine plush lined chamois case. Price, $2.88
If by mail, postage extra, 8 cents.

$3.00

No. 18C5588 Genuine French Brier Pipe, bulldog shape, highly polished, dark finish, with a 3½-inch real amber mouthpiece. The bowl and stem are mounted with fine, heavy gold band. Inlaid in plush lined chamois case. Length of pipe, 6¼ inches. A $5.00 pipe. Price....(Postage extra, 8c), $3.00

No. 18C5594 Fine French Brier Pipe, ball shape. Highly polished bowl, with curved, square, genuine amber stem and trimmed with small gold band. Inlaid in plush lined leather case. A very desirable small pipe. Price....$1.85
If by mail, postage extra, 5 cents.

SEE INDEX, PINK PAGES 492 TO 499, TO FIND WHAT YOU WANT.

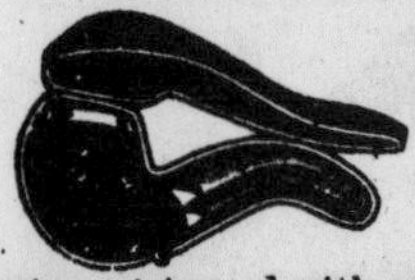

No. 18C5596 Highly Polished, Fine French Brier Pipe, bulldog shape, with curved 2½-inch genuine amber square stem; trimmed with gold band at top of the stem between the stem and bowl. A very handsome pipe. Inlaid in plush lined leather case. Price..... $2.75
If by mail, postage extra, 5 cents.

No. 18C5602 Fine French Brier Pipe, with a well shaped, large size egg bowl; trimmed with curved sterling silver band and 2¼-inch genuine amber, curved shove bit. Pipe inlaid in plush lined chamois leather case. Price.. $1.89
If by mail, postage extra, 4 cents.

No. 18C5605 Finest Quality French Brier Pipe, bull bitch shape. This handsome pipe has a thick, curved genuine amber stem, heavily mounted in real gold, such a pipe as you never expect to pay less than $7.50 for elsewhere. Price.. $3.72
If by mail, postage extra, 6 cents.

FINE MEERSCHAUM PIPES.

No. 18C5604 Chip Meerschaum Pipe, bulldog shape bowl, best English amber mouthpiece. We warrant this pipe to color; with satin lined leather covered case. **Do not unscrew stem from bowl.** Price.................97c
If by mail, postage extra, 5 cents.

Genuine Meerschaum Bowls.

No. 18C5606 Genuine Meerschaum Bowl, finest quality, block meerschaum. This style of meerschaum colors quickest, and the only quality and shape that will not break if you drop it; comes in fine plush lined chamois leather case; the finest grade of meerschaums on the market. Compare our prices for same high grade quality, as sold elsewhere, you will find a saving of one-half. Come in four sizes, as follows:

No. 5 bowl. Price.............. $3.29
No. 6 bowl. Price.............. 3.82
No. 7 bowl. Price.............. 4.49
No. 8 bowl. Price.............. 5.21
If by mail, postage extra, 4 cents.

No. 18C5610 Genuine Weichsel Stem with real amber mouthpiece. Length, 6 inches. This stem is used in connection with the meerschaum bowl under preceding No. 18C5606. Price, **52c**
If by mail, postage extra, 2 cents.

No. 18C5611 Genuine Meerschaum Pipes. High grade quality meerschaum, with best amber mouthpieces. We offer this line of pipes at prices far less than your local dealer can purchase them for from the jobbers. We buy them direct from the manufacturer and offer them with our small percentage of profit. The bowl is of the bulldog pattern and is of the best selected meerschaum and the amber mouthpieces are 2⅜ inches in length, but vary in thickness according to size of bowl. Every pipe we sell means a satisfied customer. We offer you your choice in four sizes, at prices as follows:

Size of bowl, No.	Length of amber, inches	Price	Size of bowl, No.	Length of amber, inches	Price
5	2⅜	$2.75	7	2⅜	$3.95
6	2⅜	3.48	8	2⅜	4.50

If by mail, postage extra, 8 cents.

No. 18C5613 Genuine Block Meerschaum Pipe, handsomely carved bowl, assorted designs, such as lions, dogs, deer, etc.; amber mouthpiece, 2¼ inches long; in a satin lined case. **Having received a large number of these pipes under particularly favorable circumstances we are able to offer unusual inducements.**
Price...(Postage extra, 6c)... $2.73

Our $4.95 Meerschaum Pipe.

No. 18C5615 Genuine Meerschaum Pipe, straight bulldog shape, with 3-inch genuine amber mouthpiece, heavy chased gold band onstem and bowl; inlaid in finest plush lined chamois covered case. No better pipe at any price. Price............. $4.95
If by mail, postage extra, 6 cents.

Genuine Meerschaum Pipe.

No. 18C5617 Genuine Meerschaum Pipe, London egg shape bowl, finest quality meerschaum, with 2⅜-inch round amber mouthpiece. Total length of pipe, 5 inches. Pipe is ornamented with fancy gold band around stem. Inlaid in chamois covered silk plush lined case; very high grade.
Price... (Postage extra, 6c.)... $3.88

No. 18C5620 High Grade Genuine Meerschaum Pipe with large egg-shape bowl. Has a curved, square, genuine amber mouthpiece 2⅜ inches in length. The pipe is trimmed with plain, gold band on top of bowl and stem, making a very rich and swell looking pipe. Entire length of pipe, 4½ inches. Fitted in leather covered, plush lined case. None better made.
Price ...(Postage extra, 8c). $4.60

Gold Mounted Meerschaum Pipe, $5.48.

No. 18C5621 Square Stem, Curved Meerschaum Pipe. A very high grade pipe, with 3-inch square genuine amber mouthpiece. Pipe is handsomely mounted with gold bands on top of bowl and around stem of pipe. Inlaid in fine chamois, plush lined case.
Price...(Postage extra, 6c) ... $5.48

No. 18C5623 Eagle Claw Meerschaum Pipe. This genuine meerschaum pipe is very high grade, having 3-inch bent amber mouthpiece. Total length of pipe is 5½ inches. The workmanship is of the very finest, being carved carefully with artistic skill. The same pipes are retailed at some exclusive stores for $7.50. Price.............. $4.25
If by mail, postage extra, 8 cents.

No. 18C5626 Fine Meerschaum Pipe with Weichsel stem in leather covered, silk plush lined case. Has a large, meerschaum bowl with brass cover. Fitted with Weichsel stem and genuine, amber mouthpiece, with brass chain connecting bowl and stem.
Price.......................... $2.75
Shipping weight, 10 ounces.

No. 18C5632 Smoker's Companion, consisting of two pipes, one straight French brier, bulldog shape, with 2-inch genuine amber mouthpiece, solid gold band, and one bent egg shape, highly polished French brier pipe with curved 2-inch genuine amber mouthpiece, solid gold band around stem, both pipes inlaid in a beautiful chamois covered and silk plush lined case.
Price, per set.................... $2.98
If by mail, postage extra, 10 cents.

SMOKERS' SUNDRIES.

No. 18C5640 French Brier Cigar Holder, with horn mouthpiece. Price................10c
If by mail, postage extra, 2 cents.

Twisted Rubber Cigar Holder.

No. 18C5642 Twisted Rubber Cigar Holder, something new, to give a nice cool smoke. Price..........................5c
Shipping weight, 3 ounces.

Solid Amber Cigar Holder.

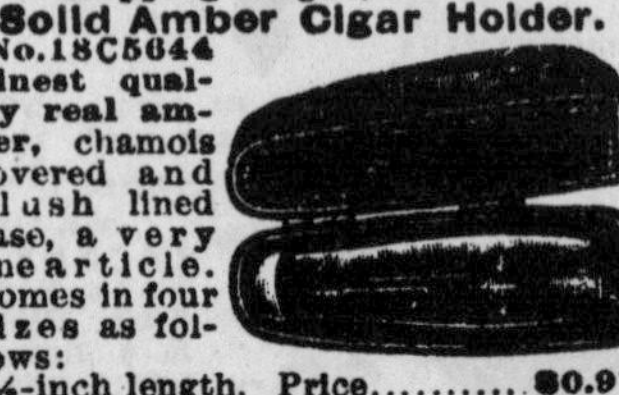

No. 18C5644 Finest quality real amber, chamois covered and plush lined case, a very fine article. Comes in four sizes as follows:

1½-inch length. Price.......... $0.97
2 -inch length. Price.......... 1.11
2½-inch length. Price.......... 1.34
3 -inch length. Price.......... 1.58
If by mail, postage extra, 2 cents.

Genuine Meerschaum Cigar Holders.

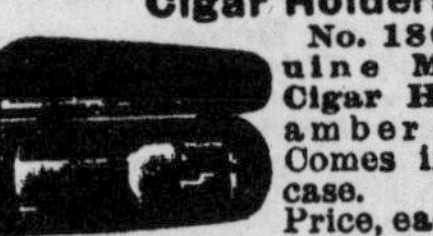

No. 18C5646 Genuine Meerschaum Cigar Holder, with amber mouthpiece. Comes in leather case.
Price, each.... $0.38
Per dozen.................... 4.00
If by mail, postage extra, each, 3c.

No. 18C5648 Genuine Meerschaum Cigar Holder, fancy carved, with real amber bit, each in leather case. **Order by number.** Price, each...... .... $0.50
Per dozen........................ 5.75
If by mail, postage extra, each, 3c.

No. 18C5650 Genuine Meerschaum Cigar Holder, similar to above, but finer, with fine amber mouthpiece. The meerschaum has carved designs, such as horse, dog, deer, etc.; inlaid in fine leather case, satin and plush lined. Length, 3¼ inches. Price, each... $0.89
Per dozen.......................... 9.50
If by mail, postage extra, each, 3c.

No. 18C5652 Genuine Meerschaum Cigar Holder, elegantly carved design; real amber mouthpiece. Total length of holder, 3½ inches. In finest plush lined case. Price, each........ $1.62
Per dozen.......................... 18.00
If by mail, postage extra, each, 3c.

French Brier Cigar Holder.

No. 18C5654 French Brier Cigar Holder, with 1½-inch genuine amber mouthpiece, ornamented with handsome design, gold trimmings. Total length of holder, 2½ inches. This is an extremely rich and handsome holder.
Price.....(Postage extra, 5 cents.)....$2.44

Rubber Mouthpieces.

No. 18C5656 2-inch Straight Rubber Mouthpiece. Price, per dozen, 20c; each, 2c
No. 18C5660 2½-inch Curved Rubber Mouthpiece. Price, per dozen, 40c; each, 4c
No. 18C5662 2-inch Square Rubber Mouthpiece. Price, per dozen, 42c; each, 4c
No. 18C5664 2½-inch Rubber Mouthpiece, with nickel ferrule.
Price, per dozen, 95c; each................9c
If by mail, postage extra, each, 2 cents.

Our 13-Cent Weichsel Pipe Stem.

No. 18C5666 6½-inch Weichsel Pipe Stem, with curved mouthpiece.
Price, per dozen, $1.30; each..........13c
No. 18C5668 7-inch Cherry Pipe Stem, with curved mouthpiece.
Price per dozen, $1.00; each..............9c
If by mail, postage extra, each, 3 cents.

Alcohol Pump Pipe Cleaner

No. 18C5670 Alcohol Pump Pipe Cleaner. The only way to remove all foul nicotine and keep your pipe sweet, is by pumping alcohol through it once a week. Half a cent's worth of alcohol pumped with force back and forth through the pipe does the work.
Price, per dozen, $2.00; each..19c
If by mail, postage extra, 4 cents.

Coin or Tobacco Pouch.

No. 18C5672 Prussian or Maltsters' Pouch. An excellent pouch for tobacco or coin. An inside pocket for gold. This pouch is manufactured from one solid piece of leather.
Price, per dozen, $1.30; each..12c
If by mail, postage extra, 3 cents.

Self Closing Rubber Pouch.

No. 18C5674 Raleigh Velvet Rubber Tobacco Pouch. Self closing, tan color. Diameter, 3⅜ inches. Keeps tobacco moist, clean and sweet.
Price, per dozen, $1.70; each..15c
If by mail, postage extra, 3 cents.

Nickeled Match Safe.

No. 18C5735 Nickeled Match Safe, smooth surface with stamped design, opens with a good spring.
Price, per dozen, 40c; each.......4c
If by mail, postage extra, 2 cents.

Plain Nickel Finished Match Safe.

No. 18C5737 A Plain Nickel Finished Metal Match Safe, splendid value at the price. Price, each, 9c
Per dozen.................95c
If by mail, postage extra, 2c.

Combination Match Safe and Cigar Cutter.

No. 18C5741 Combination Match Safe and Cigar Cutter. These have been used and highly recommended by thousands. Nickel finish, leather covering, metal top and bottom. Convenient and durable.
Price, each.............20c
Per dozen.................... $2.00
If by mail, postage extra, 2 cents.

Silver Finished Metal Safes.

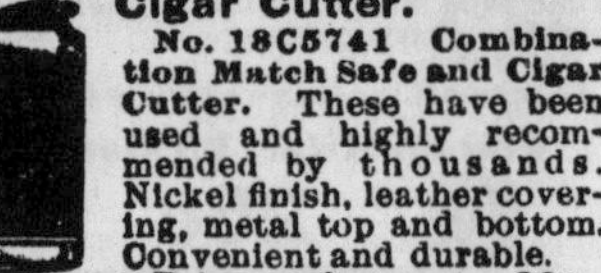

No. 18C5743 Silver Finished, Handsomely Embossed Match Safe, new and striking design.
Price, each........... $0.23
Per dozen............ 2.25
If by mail, postage extra, 2 cents.

No. 18C5745 This Pretty Match Safe is made of German silver, with handsome embossed design of bright silver finish. Very neat and tasty design.
Per doz., $5.00; each...46c
If by mail, postage extra, 2 cents.

Cigar Cases

No. 18C5749 Cigar Case, telescope style and moulded into shape, fine polished orange leather case, stitched French edges, front embossed in English heraldic design, large size. Size, 1x3¼x5¼ inches.
Price....................25c
If by mail, postage extra, 5c.

No. 18C5751 Cigar Case, telescope style and moulded into shape, made of genuine seal, mounted on the side with beautiful genuine sterling silver ornament; elegantly hand sewed and French finished edges. Size, 1x3¼x5¼ inches.
Price.................$1.00
If by mail, postage extra, 6c.

Our 75-Cent Cigar Case.

No. 18C5772 High Grade Seal Leather Cigar Case, with highly polished, strong nickeled frame, moire lining, a plain but very high grade case. Regular $1.00 value.
Price...................75c
If by mail, postage extra, 5c.

No. 18C5776 Fine Seal Leather Cigar Case, with best riveted frame, has a cigar cutter in pocket for same. Case is silk lined. An exceptionally high grade case. Worth $1.75.
Price.............$1.00
If by mail, postage extra, 5c.

Glove, Necktie and Handkerchief Boxes.

Leatherette Necktie Case. Leatherette covered complete. Heavy padded top. Tufted sateen lined throughout. A very acceptable and appropriate gift for any gentleman. Can also be used for glove or handkerchief box, if so desired. Fancy brass clasp and hinge cover. Size, 11x3x2¼ inches. Regular value, $1.25. Shipping weight, 12 ounces.
No. 8L1575 Our price..........77c

Our Special at 67 Cents.

Floral Design Glove and Handkerchief box. Top contains handsomely colored autumn scene with beautiful flowers in embossed gilt border. Tufted sateen lined throughout. Fancy metal clasp and hinge cover. Size, 12x3¾ x3 inches. Regular price, $100. Shipping weight, 14 ounces.
No. 8L1576 Our price..........67c

Floral Glove and Handkerchief Box. New desk shape, covered with floral design. Has full celluloid top handsomely embossed in gilt and bronze, with fancy brass clasp and hinge cover. Tufted satin lined throughout. Suitable as gift for either lady or gentleman. Exceptional value at the price. Size, 12½x4x3 inches. Regular price, $1.50 to $1.75. Shipping weight, 16 ozs.
No. 8L1577 Our price..........98c

Our Great Leader. Covered completely with beautiful holly design. Has full celluloid top with beautiful handsomely colored winter scene near each end. Tufted satin lined throughout. Fancy brass clasp and hinge cover. May be used for gloves, handkerchiefs, neckties, laces, and makes a gift suitable for either lady or gentleman. Size, 14x5x3 inches. Exceptional value, and a gift you may well be proud of. Ordinary values, $1.75 to $2.00.
Shipping weight, 20 ounces.
No. 8L1578 Our price..........$1.47

Wonderful Value. Three Best Quality Embossed Boxes for 98 Cents

Extraordinary Value Dresser Set, consisting of three boxes, one for gloves or neckties, another for handkerchiefs and the third for small articles or photographs. These boxes are made of taxiderme, the sides being embossed with raised floral designs and the tops being very handsomely decorated with embossed patterns of lilies in natural colors. It is only by a very large purchase that we are enabled to sell this set at the wonderfully low price of 98 cents. Suitable for either ladies' or gentlemen's use. The size of the handkerchief box is 6x7¼x2¼ inches; the glove box is 12¾x4x2¼ inches; the photo box is 10½x5½x2¼ inches. Shipping weight of set, 2¾ pounds.
No. 8L1579 Price for this set of three boxes, only..........98c

Cupid Glove and Handkerchief Set. Consists of two boxes, one for gloves and neckties, the other for handkerchiefs. Has cupid picture on cover, covered with celluloid, embossed in gilt and bronze. Brass clasp and hinges. Tufted sateen lined throughout. Suitable either for lady or gentleman. Size, glove box, 10x3x2¼ inches. Handkerchief box, 5½ inches square. Regular price, $1.50. Shipping weight, 2 pounds.
No. 8L1580 Our price, per set..99c

Genuine Walrus Grain Leather Glove and Handkerchief Boxes. $3.00 value at $1.52. An exceptionally fine high grade walrus grain set. Consists of a glove and necktie box and handkerchief box. Has padded top, fancy brass fasteners, lined throughout with good quality colored moire. An exceptionally fine value and a gift you may be well proud of. A very nice ornament for any dresser. Size of glove and necktie box, 12x4x3 inches. Handkerchief box, 7½ inches in diameter. Shipping weight, 2 pounds.
No. 8L1582 Our price, per set..$1.52

Our Celluloid Leader. An exceptionally fine set. Cover has beautiful design set in gilt embossed border. Remainder of box walrus grain covered. Lined throughout with the finest tufted satin; fancy brass clasp and hinges. Size, glove box, 13x3½x2½ inches. Handkerchief box, 6½ inches square. Ordinary value, $3.50. Shipping weight, 2 pounds.
No. 8L1584 Our price, per set..$2.47

Genuine Leather Necktie and Handkerchief Set. This is as fine as manufactured. Very latest design. Covered with the finest black leather; heavy padded top. Box lined throughout with finest tufted satin. Fancy brass clasp and silk hinge cover. Size, glove box, 11x4½x3 inches; handkerchief box, 7½x6½ inches. An exceptionally fine gift to give or receive. Ordinary value, $5.00. Shipping weight, 2 pounds.
No. 8L1585 Our price, per set $3.89

New Design Necktie, Glove, Cuff and Handkerchief Cases.

Manufactured of exceptionally fine soft grain leather and lined throughout with fine satin. These cases are of new design and much more suitable for traveling than the old design cases. Size of the necktie, glove and cuff case, 14x5 inches, and the handkerchief case, 7x7 inches. Made in brown, tan or black leather. Specify color.
No. 8L1588 Our price, necktie and glove case..........$1.83
If by mail, postage extra, 5 cents.
No. 8L1589 Our price, handkerchief case..........$1.29
If by mail, postage extra, 5 cents.

Smoking Sets.

Gent's Smoking Set. Composed of one fine imitation briar pipe with hard rubber mouthpiece and cigar and cigarette mouthpieces. Box is wood finish; tufted sateen lined throughout. Size, 6½x3½ x2 inches. Exceptional value.
No. 8L1600 Our price..........67c
If by mail, postage extra, 10 cents.

Genuine Rosewood Smoking Set. Handsome floral design box; top celluloid covered over beautifully colored scene. Tufted sateen lined throughout. Outfit comprises one fine rosewood pipe and mouthpiece, together with rosewood cigar and cigarette mouthpieces. Fancy brass clasp and hinge cover. Size, 6¾x4¾x2½ inches. Well worth $2.00.
No. 8L1602 Our price..........$1.29
If by mail, postage extra, 14 cents.

"Our Leader" Rosewood Smoking Set. An exceptionally fine outfit, composed of one genuine rosewood pipe with amber mouthpiece together with nickel plated match holder, rosewood cigar and cigarette mouthpieces. Top contains fine oxidized finish ash tray, 3¾x3¼ inches. Box fancy design, top celluloid covered, containing a large painted English hunting scene surrounded by fancy gilt embossing. Lined throughout with exceptionally fine tufted satin. Fancy brass clasp and hinge cover. Size, 8x5½x2¼ inches. An exceptionally fine gift and one you will be proud of. Ordinary values, $3.00 to $3.50.
No. 8L1604 Our price..........$2.27
If by mail, postage extra, 22 cents.

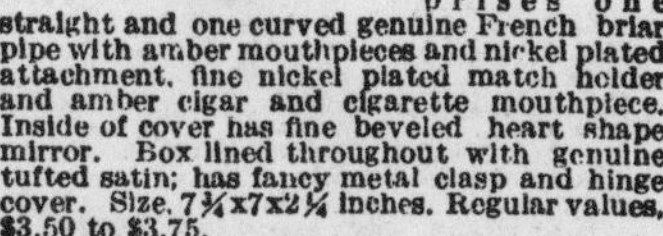

Genuine French Briar Smoking Set. This is one of the finest smoking outfits manufactured. Fancy floral design box, heart shape, covered with beautifully colored picture, set in gilt embossed heart. Set comprises one straight and one curved genuine French briar pipe with amber mouthpieces and nickel plated attachment, fine nickel plated match holder and amber cigar and cigarette mouthpiece. Inside of cover has fine beveled heart shape mirror. Box lined throughout with genuine tufted satin; fancy brass metal clasp and hinge cover. Size, 7¾x7x2¼ inches. Regular values, $3.50 to $3.75.
No. 8L1606 Our price..........$2.67
If by mail, postage extra, 22 cents.

Smoker's Companion

Our Two-Piece Smoker's Companion. Has cigar and match holders, top and bottom of which are beautifully polished and lacquered. Covered complete with wood imitation paper. Size, 7¼x5 inches. Ordinary $1.00 value.
No. 8L1610 Our price..........57c
If by mail, postage extra, 9 cents.

"Our Leader" Smoker's Companion. Has three containers, cigar, matches and ash tray. Bottom and top beautifully polished and lacquered. Covered complete with cigar band paper under transparent celluloid. Cigar container has head of beautiful woman on side in colors. Size, 6x9 inches. Ordinary $1.75 to $2.00 value. A beautiful gift for any gentleman.
No. 8L1612 Our price..........$1.25
If by mail, postage extra, 14 cents.

Smoker's Companion with Cigar Clipper and Holder. Comprises three containers, cigar, match and ash tray. Also contains cigar holder and cigar cutter. Made entirely of natural wood, beautifully polished. Has four brass knobs as base. An exceptionally fine gift. One you may well be proud of. 6½x9 inches. Ordinary value, $2.00.
No. 8L1614 Our price..........$1.47
If by mail, postage extra, 22 cents.

SHAVING OUTFITS.

German Silver Shaving Outfit. Has latest design soap box, German silver removable cover. Keeps soap clean and antiseptic. German silver handle hair shaving brush. Ordinary $1.00 value. Shipping weight, 1¾ pounds.
No. 8L1650 Our price..........69c

China Mug Shaving Outfit. Consists of natural color painted dog's head on china mug and good quality hair shaving brush to match. Packed in fancy white poplin cloth lined display box. Exceptional value at price quoted. Size box, 4½x6½x6½ inches. Ordinary $1.00 value. Shipping weight, 2 pounds.
No. 8L1652 Our price..........71c

Our Greatest Leader, Stag Shaving Outfit. Contains colored raised and embossed head of stag on each side of mug as well as on the handle of brush. Both made of cream tinted porcelain and will easily retail at $2.00 to $2.50. Also contains long rabbit's hair shaving brush with porcelain stag handle. Packed in fancy display blue lined poplin box. No description can do this outfit justice. Shipping weight, 2 pounds.
No. 8L1654 Our price..........$1.00

Silver Shaving Outfit. Consists of quadruple silver plated shaving mug gold lined, heavy German silver handle rabbit's hair brush, packed in fancy white satin grosgrain lined display box. Fancy hinge cover. An exceptionally fine gift. Size of box 6½x6½x4 inches. Ordinary price $2.50. Shipping wt., 2 lbs.
No. 8L1656 Our price..........$1.89

Celluloid Shaving Outfit. Fancy shaped shaving case, with colored head on cover under transparent celluloid set in embossed edge. Box lined throughout with fine colored sateen. On the inside of cover is a large mirror, size 8x6 inches. Decorated china cup and a good quality bone handle shaving brush and hard rubber dressing comb. Makes an exceptionally fine as well as durable shaving outfit. Size case, 9½x7½x4 inches. Ordinary value, $3.50. Shipping weight, 36 ounces.
No. 8L1660 Our price, complete, $1.79

Gent's Shaving Companion. Has new design glass soap box with heavy German silver removable cover, keeping soap clean and antiseptic. Has fine German silver handle shaving brush and two exceptionally fine sterling silver mounted, thirteen-row, long stiff white bristle military hair brushes. Well worth $3.00. You must see and handle this set to really appreciate its value. Packed in fancy blue satin lined box, hinge cover. Size, box, 11½x6½x2½ inches. Shipping weight, 2½ pounds.
No. 8L1658 Our price..........$2.10

Wonderful Value.

This beautiful imported fancy Straw Satin Lined Box has been a special favorite. Its many uses in the home as a photo container, fancy work or lace basket, handkerchief box, as well as a pleasing Christmas gift have made it very popular. Made of fancy colored imported straw, very tastefully decorated and braided, bordered with imported heavy broad reeds at top and bottom. Lined throughout with fine satin and inside of cover heavily padded under satin in diamond shape tuft, trimmed with silk cord and easily worth $1.75. We know you would buy this basket if you could only see it. A beauty and a great bargain. Size, 8x8x4½ inches.
No. 8L1795 Our price..........99c
If by mail, postage extra, 18 cents.

Sewing Boxes.

Child's Fancy Sewing and Work Box. This box is completely covered with holly design paper, and the top contains a fine 5x3-inch painted winter scene set in gilt embossed frame. Inside of cover has large mirror. Box lined with fancy tufted sateen and contains five useful sewing articles, with plenty of room for thread, needles, etc. Size, 6x4x2½ inches. Shipping weight, 1 pound. Ordinary value, 85 cents.
No. 8L1790 Our price..........59c

Teddy Bear Sewing and Work Box. Box contains a full transparent celluloid top of Teddy bear in colors set in gilt embossed frame. Sides of box beautifully colored embossed. Inside of cover contains a large 6x4½-inch mirror, and five very useful sewing articles. Lined throughout with fancy tufted sateen. Box well worth, $1.25. Size, 6½x5x3 inches. Shipping weight, 1½ pounds.
No. 8L1791 Our price..........79c

Holly Sewing and Work Box. Latest design beautiful holly covered celluloid top box. Inside of cover contains diamond shaped mirror. Lined throughout with fancy tufted sateen, and contains six very handy sewing articles. Plenty of room for other articles used by needle workers. A very pretty and useful gift. Size, 7½x5¾x3 inches. Shipping weight, 2 pounds. Regular value, $1.50.
No. 8L1792 Our price..........$1.12

Plush and Celluloid Sewing Box. This beautiful plush and celluloid combination work box is decorated with very pretty picture under transparent celluloid. Full modeled plush sides, flower design front with extension base. Inside of cover has large mirror. Box lined throughout with fancy tufted sateen and contains six useful sewing articles. Brass clasps and hinges. Size, 10x6½x4 inches. Shipping weight, 3½ pounds. Ordinary value $2.00.
No. 8L1793 Our price..........$1.47

Imported Palm Plants.

Fine Imported Palm Plants, extensively used for ornamenting parlors and halls. These plants are naturally prepared and very lasting. They come packed flat, without the pots. Are easily set up. Sizes and prices are as follows:

	No. 8L1796	No. 8L1797
Height, inches	36	40
Branches	4	5
Shipping wt., lbs.	6	8
Price, each	59c	73c

	No. 8L1798	No. 8L1799
Height, inches	45	60
Branches	7	10
Shipping wt., lbs.	8½	10
Price, each	88c	$2.19

The 10-branch palm comes in shape of a tree with removable branches to set in tin tubes, and branches much larger size than the 4, 5 and 7-inch plants.

WATCHES

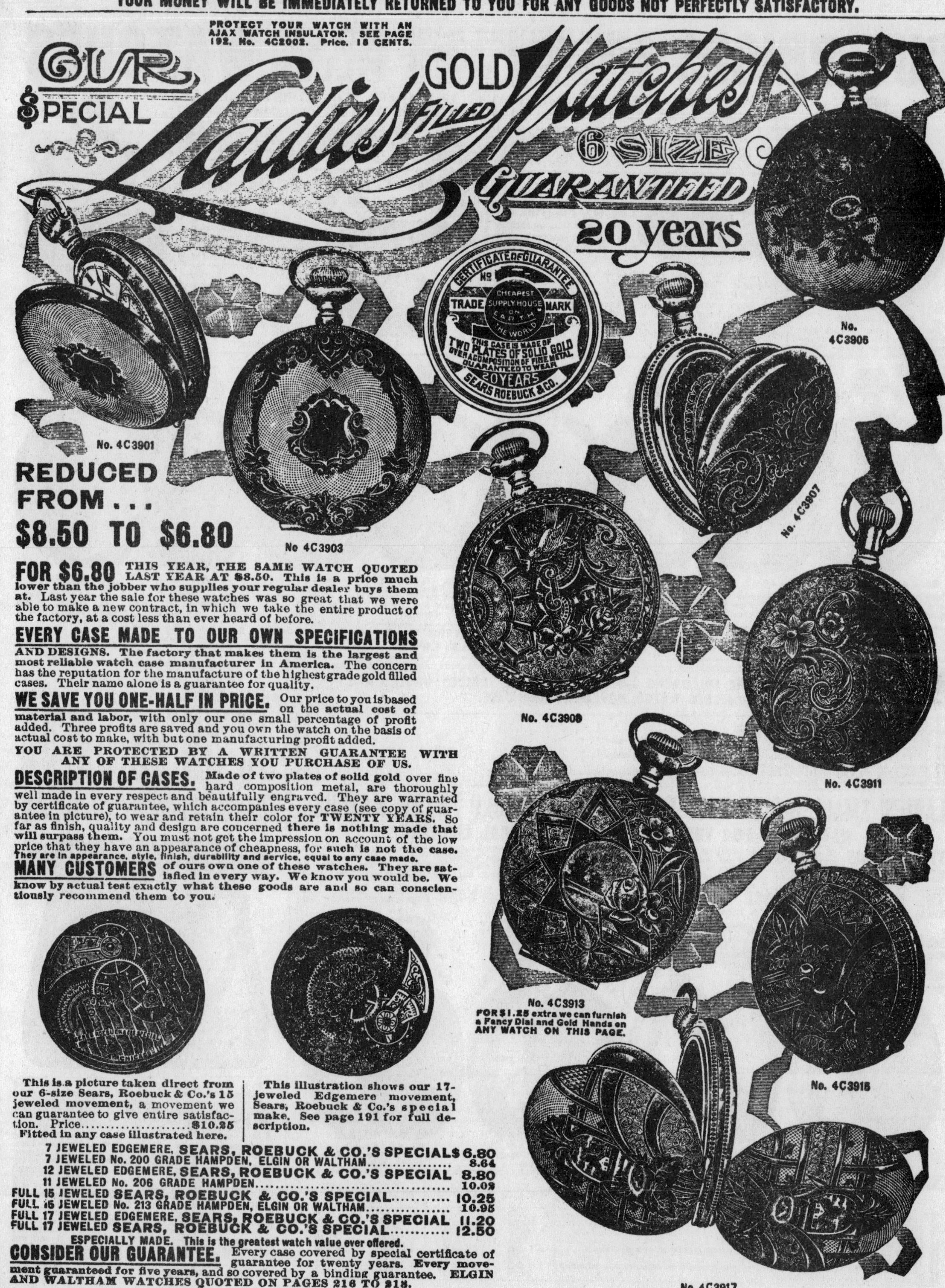
YOUR MONEY WILL BE IMMEDIATELY RETURNED TO YOU FOR ANY GOODS NOT PERFECTLY SATISFACTORY.
PROTECT YOUR WATCH WITH AN AJAX WATCH INSULATOR. SEE PAGE 192, No. 4C2002. Price, 18 CENTS.
OUR SPECIAL Ladies' GOLD FILLED Watches 6 SIZE GUARANTEED 20 years
CERTIFICATE OF GUARANTEE. No TRADE CHEAPEST SUPPLY HOUSE ON EARTH THE WORLD MARK
THIS CASE IS MADE OF TWO PLATES OF SOLID GOLD OVER A COMPOSITION OF FINE METAL GUARANTEED TO WEAR 20 YEARS SEARS ROEBUCK & CO.
No. 4C3901
No 4C3903
No. 4C3905
No. 4C3907
No. 4C3909
No. 4C3911
No. 4C3913
No. 4C3915
No. 4C3917
FOR $1.25 extra we can furnish a Fancy Dial and Gold Hands on ANY WATCH ON THIS PAGE.
REDUCED FROM ... $8.50 TO $6.80
FOR $6.80 THIS YEAR, THE SAME WATCH QUOTED LAST YEAR AT $8.50. This is a price much lower than the jobber who supplies your regular dealer buys them at. Last year the sale for these watches was so great that we were able to make a new contract, in which we take the entire product of the factory, at a cost less than ever heard of before.
EVERY CASE MADE TO OUR OWN SPECIFICATIONS AND DESIGNS. The factory that makes them is the largest and most reliable watch case manufacturer in America. The concern has the reputation for the manufacture of the highest grade gold filled cases. Their name alone is a guarantee for quality.
WE SAVE YOU ONE-HALF IN PRICE. Our price to you is based on the actual cost of material and labor, with only our one small percentage of profit added. Three profits are saved and you own the watch on the basis of actual cost to make, with but one manufacturing profit added.
YOU ARE PROTECTED BY A WRITTEN GUARANTEE WITH ANY OF THESE WATCHES YOU PURCHASE OF US.
DESCRIPTION OF CASES. Made of two plates of solid gold over fine hard composition metal, are thoroughly well made in every respect and beautifully engraved. They are warranted by certificate of guarantee, which accompanies every case (see copy of guarantee in picture), to wear and retain their color for TWENTY YEARS. So far as finish, quality and design are concerned there is nothing made that will surpass them. You must not get the impression on account of the low price that they have an appearance of cheapness, for such is not the case. They are in appearance, style, finish, durability and service, equal to any case made.
MANY CUSTOMERS of ours own one of these watches. They are satisfied in every way. We know you would be. We know by actual test exactly what these goods are and so can conscientiously recommend them to you.
This is a picture taken direct from our 6-size Sears, Roebuck & Co.'s 15 jeweled movement, a movement we can guarantee to give entire satisfaction. Price....................$10.25
Fitted in any case illustrated here.
This illustration shows our 17-jeweled Edgemere movement, Sears, Roebuck & Co.'s special make. See page 191 for full description.
7 JEWELED EDGEMERE, SEARS, ROEBUCK & CO.'S SPECIAL $6.80
7 JEWELED No. 200 GRADE HAMPDEN, ELGIN OR WALTHAM.................. 8.64
12 JEWELED EDGEMERE, SEARS, ROEBUCK & CO.'S SPECIAL 8.80
11 JEWELED No. 206 GRADE HAMPDEN.................................. 10.08
FULL 15 JEWELED SEARS, ROEBUCK & CO.'S SPECIAL.......... 10.25
FULL 16 JEWELED No. 213 GRADE HAMPDEN, ELGIN OR WALTHAM.................. 10.95
FULL 17 JEWELED EDGEMERE, SEARS, ROEBUCK & CO.'S SPECIAL 11.20
FULL 17 JEWELED SEARS, ROEBUCK & CO.'S SPECIAL.......... 12.50
ESPECIALLY MADE. This is the greatest watch value ever offered.
CONSIDER OUR GUARANTEE. Every case covered by special certificate of guarantee for twenty years. Every movement guaranteed for five years, and so covered by a binding guarantee. ELGIN AND WALTHAM WATCHES QUOTED ON PAGES 216 TO 218.

CUT PRICES IN LADIES' SMALL 0-SIZE 25-YEAR HUNTING STYLE AND PLYMOUTH GOLD FILLED CASES GUARANTEED FOR LIFE GOLD FILLED WATCHES

MANUFACTURED BY THE MOST REPRESENTATIVE GOLD FILLED CASE MANUFACTURERS IN THE WORLD. ILLUSTRATIONS SHOW EXACT SIZE.

WHAT WE MEAN BY THE PLYMOUTH LIFE GUARANTEED CASE. The Plymouth Life Guaranteed Case is a gold filled case of the very highest quality and the nearest approach to a solid gold case manufactured. The Plymouth Life Guaranteed Case means that should any one of these cases wear down to the inner composition metal any time within your natural life, whether you have owned the case five years, twenty years or fifty years, return it to us, and we will, on the receipt of the same, exchange it for a brand new case of same quality free of charge.

No. 4N14600

Set with genuine rose diamonds. Gold filled. Guaranteed for 25 years' wear. Made by the Illinois Watch Case Co

Fancy Dial.

We show here an illustration of the fancy dial and gold hands that we furnish on different watches quoted and illustrated on this page at 90 cents extra.

Fancy dials cannot be fitted on every watch in our catalogue. We caution you to order them only on such watches where it is clearly stated on page that we can furnish fancy dials. The illustration merely gives you an idea of how the fancy dials will look. They are not all exactly as this picture shows, as they vary in design. They come in various tints, with floral decorations and gold work, and all of them are beautiful.

This Fine Watch Box for 21 Cents.

No. 4N11000 This picture made from photograph shows one of our fine lined and leatherette covered watch boxes that we supply for only 21 cents extra with any watch purchased of us. In ordering, state what size watch the case is intended for.

Price......... 21c

If by mail, postage extra, 2 cents.

No. 4N14602

Set with genuine rose diamonds. Gold filled. Guaranteed for 25 years' wear. Made by the Illinois Watch Case Co.

$8.88 AND UP

LIFE GUARANTEE

LIFE GUARANTEE

$7.96 AND UP

No. 4N14620 Gold filled, guaranteed for life, Plymouth Watch Case.

No. 4N14622 Gold filled, guaranteed for life, Plymouth Watch Case.

No. 4N14624 Gold filled, guaranteed for life, Plymouth Watch Case.

No. 4N14604 Gold filled. Guaranteed for 25 years' wear. Made by the Illinois Watch Case Co.

No. 4N14608 Gold filled. Guaranteed for 25 years. Made by John C. Dueber.

No. 4N14610 Gold ornamented and genuine cut diamond set, gold filled, Guaranteed for 25 years' wear. Made by the Illinois Watch Case Co.

No. 4N14612 Same style and make as No. 4N14610, but set with genuine rose diamond.

No. 4N14614 Genuine diamond set, raised gold ornamented, gold filled. Guaranteed for 25 years' wear.

No. 4N14616 Gold filled. Guaranteed for 25 years. Plain polish. Made by the Illinois Watch Case Co.

No. 4N14618 Above make in Engine Turned.

TRY OUR PLYMOUTH MOVEMENT AND BE SATISFIED

25 CENTS WILL CARRY ANY WATCH TO ANY PART OF THE UNITED STATES BY EXPRESS

WE FIT THESE CASES WITH THE FOLLOWING 0-SIZE MOVEMENTS. PRICES QUOTED ARE FOR THE COMPLETE WATCH, MOVEMENT AND CASE.	Nos. 4N14604 4N14608 4N14616 4N14618	No. 4N14600	Nos. 4N14610 4N14614	No. 4N14612	Nos. 4N14620 4N14622 4N14624	No. 4N14602
7 Jeweled Swiss Lever	$ 7.96	$ 9.40	$14.00	$ 9.50	$ 8.88	$10.40
15 JEWELED EDGEMERE, special make	10.43	11.78	16.38	11.88	11.33	12.78
7 Jeweled Elgin or Waltham, nickel plates	10.63	11.98	16.58	12.08	11.53	12.98
15 Jeweled Elgin or Waltham, nickel plates	13.00	14.35	18.95	14.45	13.90	15.35
15 JEWELED PLYMOUTH WATCH CO., patent regulator, special make	12.75	14.10	18.70	14.20	13.65	15.10
16 Jeweled Lady Waltham, nickel plates	18.03	19.38	23.98	19.48	18.93	20.38
17 JEWELED PLYMOUTH WATCH CO., patent regulator, adjusted, special make	17.40	18.75	23.35	18.85	18.30	19.75
19 Jeweled No. 201 Grade Elgin	28.52	29.87	34.47	29.97	29.42	30.87

LADIES' SMALL 0-SIZE OPEN FACE PLYMOUTH GOLD FILLED WATCHES

WARRANTED FOR THE TERM OF YOUR NATURAL LIFETIME.

THIS IS ONE of our very latest additions in the Watch Department. The illustrations show the back and front of the watch, so that you can get a correct idea of exactly how this watch appears. These watches not alone carry our personal guarantee as to permanency of wear, but they likewise carry our written binding guarantee on the movement. You positively are insured on both the movement and the case on any watch you buy from us. We stand ready at any time within the period of the guarantee to make good every condition in it.

THE DIAMOND SET CASE illustrated on this page is a little beauty. It is bright polish, has a genuine rose diamond set in the back and, fitted with our 15 jeweled Edgemere movement, for $10.53, it is a value not to be purchased from others.

No. 4N14640 Plymouth Gold Filled. 20-Year Guarantee.

No. 4N14644 Diamond Set, Plymouth Gold Filled. Life Guarantee.

No. 4N14646 Plymouth Gold Filled. Life Guarantee.

No. 4N14648 Plymouth Gold Filled. Life Guarantee.

WE FIT THESE 0-SIZE OPEN FACE CASES WITH THE FOLLOWING 0-SIZE MOVEMENTS. PRICES QUOTED ARE FOR THE COMPLETE WATCH, MOVEMENT AND CASE.	No. 4N14640	No. 4N14646	No. 4N14648	No. 4N14644
7 Jeweled Swiss Lever	$ 6.35	$ 7.15	$ 7.65	$ 8.15
15 JEWELED EDGEMERE, special make	9.03	9.53	9.75	10.53
7 Jeweled Elgin or Waltham, nickel plates	9.23	9.73	9.95	10.73
15 Jeweled Elgin or Waltham, nickel plates	11.60	12.10	12.60	13.10
15 JEWELED PLYMOUTH WATCH CO., patent regulator, special make	11.35	11.85	12.05	12.85
16 Jeweled Lady Waltham, nickel plates	16.63	17.13	17.63	18.13
17 JEWELED PLYMOUTH WATCH CO., patent regulator, adjusted, special make	16.00	16.50	17.00	17.50
19 Jeweled No. 201 Grade Elgin	27.12	27.62	28.12	28.62

This is Our Selection of a Ladies' Gold Filled 0-Size Watch.

It is the highest grade possible in gold filled watches. The case is made of two plates of solid gold over an inner composition metal, beautifully finished, beautifully engraved and perfect in all details. We guarantee it for a term of your natural life. The movement is the highest grade 0-size 17 jeweled movement manufactured, made of nickel plates, has cut expansion balance, is stem wind and pendant set, contains all modern improvements; in fact, money cannot buy a better movement, and is guaranteed by us for a term of five years, against defective material and workmanship. Send us $18.30, together with the mail charges, 14 cents, total $18.44, and we will send you this, our selection of the highest grade gold filled watch manufactured in the United States. You are not taking any chances in ordering this watch from us. If it is not satisfactory in every way, you do not like our selection or our judgment does not prove good, you are at liberty to return it and get your money refunded, together with all transportation charges, or if you would rather, you may make another selection. Be sure to order by number.

No. 4N14650 **$18.30**

REDUCED PRICES IN LADIES' SMALL 0-SIZE HUNTING STYLE SOLID 14-KARAT GOLD WATCHES

$12.69 FOR THIS SOLID GOLD, 14-KARAT, OPEN FACE, EXTRA SMALL SIZE LADIES' CHATELAINE WATCH

No. 4N14700

Fitted with an Elgin or Waltham movement. Think of it! Who ever heard of its equal? The case is bright polished Bassene style, solid 14-karat gold. The movement is genuine Elgin or Waltham, whichever you desire. Is stem wind and pendant set. The very latest movement manufactured. Complete entire watch for $12.69.

Illustration shows both front and back view.
No. 4N14700 Price for complete watch.... $12.69

$10.95

Illustration shows both front and back view.
No. 4N14702 Three-quarter engraved.

$14.70

Illustration shows both front and back view.
No. 4N14704
Gold ornamentation.

$14.70

Illustration shows both front and back view.
No. 4N14706
Engine turned.

$15.15

Illustration shows both front and back view.
No. 4N14708
Genuine diamond set.

THE RAISED COLORED GOLD ORNAMENTATION IS ARTISTIC AND LENDS A BEAUTY TO THESE CASES UNEQUALED BY ANY OTHER METHOD OF EMBELLISHING WATCH CASES. YOU ARE PROTECTED IN EVERY WAY. IF GOODS ARE NOT SATISFACTORY, AND YOU DO NOT LIKE THEM WHEN YOU GET THEM, YOU CAN RETURN THEM AT ONCE AND HAVE YOUR MONEY REFUNDED TOGETHER WITH TRANSPORTATION CHARGES.

$17.45

Illustration shows both front and back view.
No. 4N14710
Three-quarter engraved and vermicelli work.

$17.45

Illustration shows both front and back view.
No. 4N14712
Full engraved.

$17.45

Illustration shows both front and back view.
No. 4N14714
Top and bottom engraved, engine turned center.

$16.40

Illustration shows both front and back view.
No. 4N14716
Plain polish Bassene style.
No. 4N14718
Same as above, but satin finish, Roman yellow color.

$18.65

Illustration shows both front and back view.
No. 4N14720
Three-quarter engraved, fine escalloped edge.

Our written binding guarantee accompanies every one; warranting them to be exactly as we describe them here.
25 CENTS WILL CARRY ANY WATCH TO ANY PART OF THE UNITED STATES BY EXPRESS.

$18.15

Illustration shows both front and back view.
No. 4N14722
Full engraved.

$18.15

Illustration shows both front and back view.
No. 4N14724
Escalloped edge and full engraved, fine vermicelli work.

$21.05

Illustration shows both front and back view.
No. 4N14726
Raised colored gold ornamentation.

$21.05

Illustration shows both front and back view. No. 4N14728
Bassene style, set with one genuine diamond, in bright polish or satin finish.

$21.05

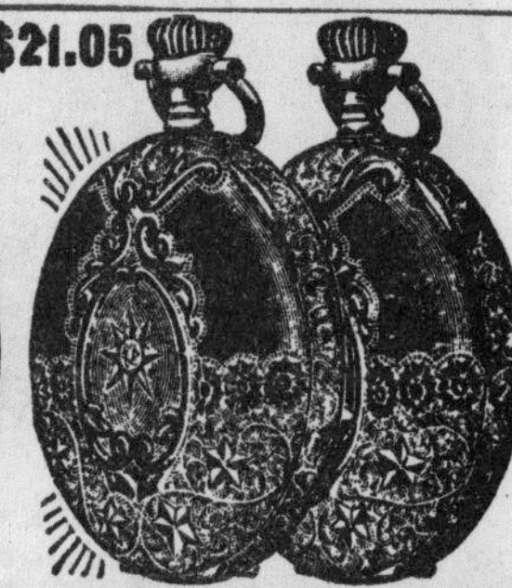

Illustration shows both front and back view.
No. 4N14730
Full fancy engraved and set with genuine diamond.

$21.05

Illustration shows both front and back view.
No. 4N14732
One-quarter engraved, genuine diamond set.

$22.95

Illustration shows both front and back view.
No. 4N14734
Bassene style, bright polished, set with genuine diamond, and raised gold ornamentation.

$22.95

Illustration shows both front and back view.
No. 4N14736
Full engraved, raised colored gold ornamentation, genuine diamond set.

$25.15

Illustration shows both front and back view.
No. 4N14738
Bassene style, plain polished, set with four genuine diamonds.

$24.65

No. 4N14740
This illustration shows case set with genuine diamonds and rubies, plain or satin finish, made with any name. This case is made to order and takes about 10 to 12 days. We can supply no other combination of stones than the ones mentioned.

Illustration shows both front and back view.
No. 4N14742
Same style as No. 4N14740, but without stone setting. Handsomely engraved name only.

WE FIT THESE CASES WITH THE FOLLOWING 0-SIZE MOVEMENTS. PRICES QUOTED ARE FOR THE COMPLETE WATCH, MOVEMENT AND CASE.	No. 4N14702	No. 4N14704 4N14706	No. 4N14708	No. 4N14716 4N14718	No. 4N14710 4N14712 4N14714	No. 4N14720	No. 4N14722 4N14724	4N14726 4N14728 4N14730 4N14732	No. 4N14734 4N14736	No. 4N14738	No. 4N14740	No. 4N14742
7 Jeweled Swiss Lever	$ 10.95	$ 14.70	$ 15.15	$ 16.40	$ 17.45	$ 18.65	$ 18.15	$ 21.05	$ 22.95	$ 25.15	$ 29.15	$ 24.65
15 JEWELED EDGEMERE, special make	13.53	17.08	17.53	18.78	19.83	21.03	20.53	23.43	25.33	27.53	28.99	27.03
7 Jeweled Elgin or Waltham, nickel plates	13.73	17.28	17.73	18.98	20.03	21.23	20.73	23.63	25.53	27.73	29.19	27.23
15 Jeweled Elgin or Waltham, nickel plates	16.10	19.65	20.10	21.35	22.40	23.60	22.10	26.00	27.90	30.10	31.89	29.60
15 Jeweled Plymouth Watch Co., patent regulator, special make	15.85	19.40	19.85	21.10	22.15	23.35	21.85	25.75	27.65	29.85	31.64	29.35
16 Jeweled Lady Waltham, nickel plates	21.13	24.68	25.13	26.38	27.43	28.63	28.13	31.03	32.93	35.13	36.49	34.63
17 Jeweled Plymouth Watch Co., patent regulator, adjusted, special make	20.50	24.05	24.05	25.75	26.80	28.00	27.50	30.40	32.30	34.50	38.50	34.00
19 Jeweled 201 Grade Elgin	31.62	35.17	35.62	36.87	37.92	39.12	38.62	41.52	43.42	45.62	46.49	45.12

YOUR MONEY WILL BE IMMEDIATELY RETURNED TO YOU FOR ANY GOODS NOT PERFECTLY SATISFACTORY.

THIN MODEL 16-SIZE OPEN FACE AND HUNTING, GUARANTEED FOR LIFE OR TWENTY-FIVE YEARS GOLD FILLED CASES.

For the best cheap watch in 16-size we recommend above all others our new 7 jeweled Edgemere; it is guaranteed; but for a watch that costs but a few dollars more, and gives better satisfaction for accuracy, we recommend our 15 jeweled Edgemere, our 15 jeweled Plymouth Watch Co., or our 17 jeweled Plymouth Watch Co., adjusted. All of the above carry our 5-year written binding guarantee. Above all others, as the highest possible perfection in watch movements for accurate timekeeping, we recommend the 21 jeweled, adjusted, Prince of Wales movement manufactured by the Plymouth Watch Co., quoted on this page and described and illustrated on page 37.

$7.60 AND UP
25 cents will carry any watch to any part of the United States by express.
PLYMOUTH
PLYMOUTH
ILLUSTRATIONS ON THIS PAGE SHOW EXACT SIZE.
PLYMOUTH
Protect your watch with an Ajax Watch Insulator. See page 38, No. 4G586 Price, 23c
PLYMOUTH
$8.60 AND UP

GOLD FILLED. GUARANTEED FOR 25 YEARS.

No. 4G2050 John C. Dueber, Open Face, Screw Bezel and Back.

No. 4G2051 Open Face, same make but engine turned.

No. 4G2052 Hunting Style.

No. 4G2053 Hunting Style, same make but engine turned.

GOLD FILLED. GUARANTEED FOR LIFE.

No. 4G2054 Plymouth, Open Face, Screw Back and Bezel.

No. 4G2055 Plymouth, Hunting Style.

GOLD FILLED. GUARANTEED FOR LIFE.

No. 4G2056 Plymouth, Open Face, Screw Back and Bezel.

No. 4G2057 Plymouth, Hunting Style.

GOLD FILLED, ENGINE TURNED. GUARANTEED FOR LIFE.

No. 4G2058 Plymouth, Open Face, Screw Back and Bezel.

No. 4G2059 Plymouth, Hunting Style.

GOLD FILLED. GUARANTEED FOR LIFE.

No. 4G2060 Plymouth, Open Face, Screw Back and Bezel.

No. 4G2061 Plymouth, Hunting Style.

GOLD FILLED. GUARANTEED FOR 25 YEARS.

No. 4G2066 Illinois Watch Case Co. Commander, Open Face, Screw Back and Bezel.

No. 4G2067 Illinois Watch Case Co. Commander, Hunting Style.

GOLD FILLED. GUARANTEED FOR 25 YEARS.

No. 4G2068 Wadsworth Watch Case Co., Open Face, Screw Back and Bezel.

No. 4G2069 Open Face, same make but engine turned.

No. 4G2070 Wadsworth Watch Case Co., Hunting Style.

No. 4G2071 Hunting Style, same make but engine turned.

FOR 90 CENTS EXTRA we can furnish a Fancy Dial and Gold Hands on any Watch on this page.

WE FIT THESE CASES WITH THE FOLLOWING 16-SIZE MOVEMENTS. PRICES QUOTED ARE FOR THE COMPLETE WATCH, MOVEMENT AND CASE.	Open Face 25-Year Warrant Nos. 4G2050 4G2051 4G2066 4G2068 4G2069	Hunting 25-Year Warrant Nos. 4G2052 4G2053 4G2067 4G2070 4G2071	Open Face Life Guarantee Nos. 4G2054 4G2056 4G2058 4G2060	Hunting Life Guarantee Nos. 4G2055 4G2057 4G2059 4G2061
7 JEWELED EDGEMERE, nickel plates, special make	$ 7.60	$ 9.60	$ 8.60	$ 11.10
7 Jeweled Elgin or Waltham, nickel plates	10.50	12.50	11.50	14.00
15 JEWELED EDGEMERE, patent regulator, nickel plates, special make	10.35	12.35	11.35	13.85
15 Jeweled Elgin or Waltham, nickel plates, patent regulator	12.60	14.60	13.60	16.10
15 JEWELED PLYMOUTH WATCH CO.	12.35	14.35	13.35	15.85
17 Jeweled Elgin or Waltham, not adjusted	14.70	16.70	15.70	18.20
17 Jeweled No. 241 Grade Elgin or 630 Grade Waltham, adjusted	17.33	19.33	18.33	20.83
17 JEWELED PLYMOUTH WATCH CO., nickel plates, patent regulator, adjusted	16.98	18.98	17.98	20.48
17 Jeweled Royal Waltham, adjusted, nickel plates	19.69	21.69	20.69	23.19
17 Jeweled No. 243 Grade Elgin, adjusted, nickel plates	28.35	30.35	29.35	31.85
21 JEWELED PRINCE OF WALES PLYMOUTH WATCH CO., full adjusted, patent regulator, nickel plates	22.25	24.25	23.25	25.75

REMEMBER

WHEN YOU HAVE BOUGHT $25.00 WORTH OF GOODS OR MORE FROM US YOU GET YOUR CHOICE OF MANY VALUABLE ARTICLES FREE, AS SHOWN IN OUR FREE PROFIT SHARING BOOK

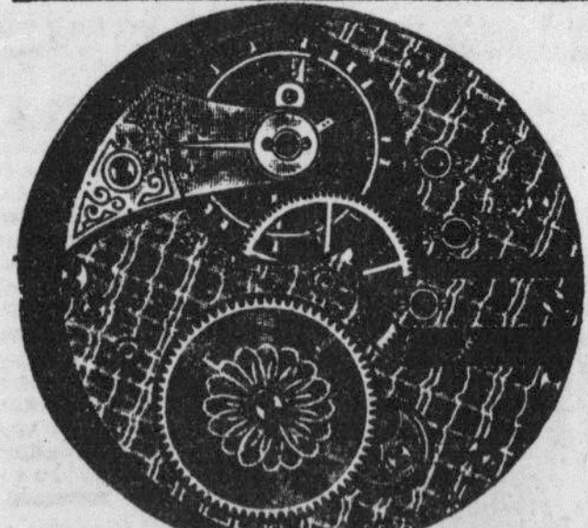

Gentlemen's 16-size, open face or hunting case, stem wind Plymouth Watch Co. movement in any of these cases, $12.35 to $16.98. This is positively the highest grade 15 jeweled 16-size movement made, each movement stamped "Plymouth Watch Co." It is full 15 jeweled, all jewels in screwed settings and it is accurately adjusted to positions; has cut expansion balance, overstrung Breguet hairspring, gotten out with a view of giving our customers in every respect a better 15 jeweled 16-size movement than is made or sold by any watch company in the country. This movement has the latest exposed winding wheel, every up to date feature found in any other 16-size movement, and still we furnish it at as low a price as any other 16-size movement made.

Gentlemen s 16-size, open face or hunting, 21 jeweled, nickel, patent regulator Prince of Wales movement, manufactured by the Plymouth Watch Company, in any of these cases, $22.25 to $25.75. This movement is a new addition to our exceptional value page and represents positively the highest grade watch in 21 jeweled manufactured. A new deal with a new company for an immense quantity enables us to sell this watch to you at less money than 17 jeweled named watches manufactured by others. This watch has full nickel plates, jewels all in settings, cut expansion balance, double sunk dial, in fact, all modern improvements, adjusted to temperature and positions, in fact, a watch such as cannot be compared with any other watch quoted or illustrated in our catalogue. If you purchase this watch you are making a saving of no less than $12.00 to $15.00 and are getting the best production of modern watch making.

YOUR CHOICE FOR $3.10.

$3.10

LADIES' O-SIZE OR GENTLEMEN'S EXTRA THIN 12-SIZE, BOTH OPEN FACE STYLE, SOLID GERMAN SILVER, ANTIQUE FINISH EMPIRE WATCH.

The exact copy of watches used in France when an Empire.

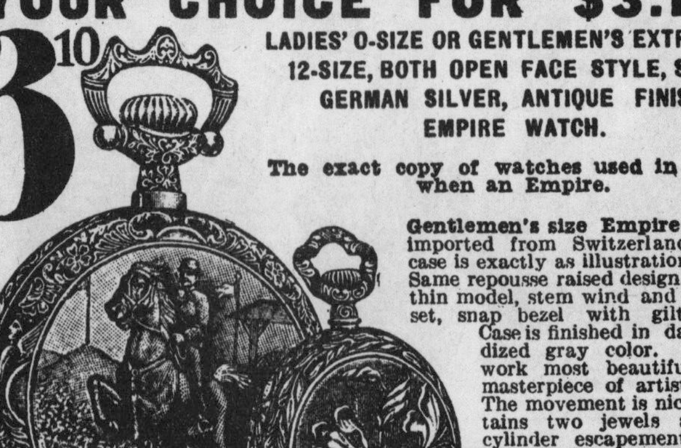

No. 4G1888 No. 4G1886

Gentlemen's size Empire watch, imported from Switzerland. The case is exactly as illustration shows. Same repousse raised design. Extra thin model, stem wind and pendant set, snap bezel with gilt crown. Case is finished in dark oxydized gray color. The die work most beautiful and a masterpiece of artistic skill. The movement is nickel, contains two jewels and has cylinder escapement. Each one timed and tested before leaving our establishment.

No. 4G1888
Price.........**$3.10**

No. 4G1886
Ladies' 0-size, as illustrated, dainty floral design.
Price.........**$3.10**

CUT PRICES IN LADIES' SMALL O-SIZE 25-YEAR HUNTING STYLE AND PLYMOUTH GOLD FILLED CASES GUARANTEED FOR LIFE GOLD FILLED WATCHES

MANUFACTURED BY THE MOST REPRESENTATIVE GOLD FILLED CASE MANUFACTURERS IN THE WORLD. ILLUSTRATIONS SHOW EXACT SIZE.

WHAT WE MEAN BY THE PLYMOUTH LIFE GUARANTEED CASE. The Plymouth Life Guaranteed Case is a gold filled case of the very highest quality and the nearest approach to a solid gold case manufactured. The Plymouth Life Guaranteed Case means that should any one of these cases wear down to the inner composition metal any time within your natural life, whether you have owned the case five years, twenty years or fifty years, return it to us, and we will on the receipt of the same, exchange it for a brand new case of same quality free of charge.

THIS ILLUSTRATION is a picture taken directly from a photograph of our 15 jeweled small 0-size Plymouth Watch Co. movement. This movement is the highest possible perfection in the 15 jeweled grade. We recommend it above all other makes. Quoted on this page with any kind of case you may select for

$12.75 to $18.70

$17.40 to $23.35

your choice of any case on this page fitted with the movement illustrated here directly from the photograph of the movement itself. We claim this, our 17 jeweled adjusted Plymouth Watch Co. movement, superior in timekeeping qualities to any ladies' watch manufactured in America, irrespective of the number of jewels it contains.

THIS FINE WATCH BOX FOR 21 CENTS.

No. 4L588 This picture made from photograph shows one of our fine lined and leatherette covered watch boxes that we supply for only 21 cents extra with any watch purchased of us. In ordering, state what size watch the case is intended for.
Price.. (Postage extra, 2 cents.) ..21c

LIFE GUARANTEE.

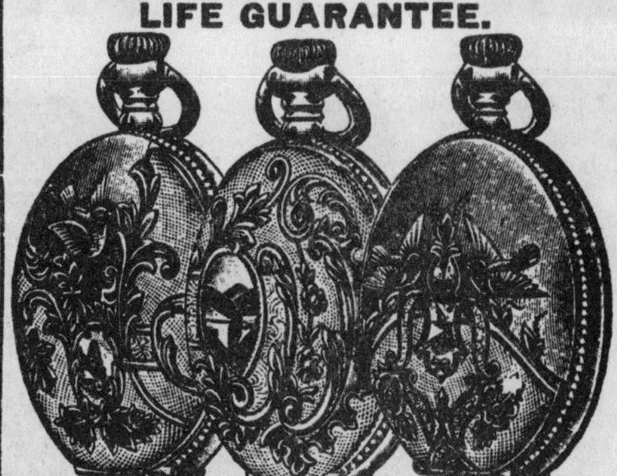

No. 4L3415 No. 4L3419 No. 4L3421
14-karat. Guaranteed for life. THE PLYMOUTH CASE.

No. 4L3455 14-karat. Guaranteed for 25 years' wear. Made by the Illinois Watch Case Co.

No. 4L3473 14-karat. Guaranteed for 25 years. Made by John C. Dueber.

No. 4L3456 Gold ornamented and genuine cut diamond set, 14-karat. Guaranteed for 25 years' wear. Made by the Illinois Watch Case Co.

No. 4L3457 Same style and make as No. 4L3456, but set with genuine rose diamond.

No. 4L3469 Genuine diamond set, raised gold ornamented, 14-karat. Guaranteed for 25 years' wear.

No. 4L3458 Set with genuine rose diamonds. 14-karat. Guaranteed for 25 years' wear. Made by the Illinois Watch Case Co.

No. 4L3478 14-karat. Guaranteed for 25 years. Plain polish. Made by the Illinois Watch Case Co.

No. 4L3479 Above make in Engine Turned.

No. 4L3460 Set with genuine rose diamonds, 14-karat. Guaranteed for 25 years' wear. Made by the Illinois Watch Case Co.

WE RECOMMEND SENDING WATCHES BY EXPRESS, AS THEY DO NOT RECEIVE THE HARD USAGE AS WHEN SENT BY MAIL.

TRY OUR EDGEMERE MOVEMENT AND BE SATISFIED.

25 CENTS WILL CARRY ANY WATCH TO ANY PART OF THE UNITED STATES BY EXPRESS.

WE FIT THESE CASES WITH THE FOLLOWING O-SIZE MOVEMENTS. PRICES QUOTED ARE FOR THE COMPLETE WATCH, MOVEMENT AND CASE.	Nos. 4L3455 4L3473 4L3478 4L3479	No. 4L3458	Nos. 4L3456 4L3469	No. 4L3457	Nos. 4L3415 4L3419 4L3421	No. 4L3460
7 Jeweled Swiss Lever	$ 7.96	$ 9.40	$14.00	$ 8.50	$ 8.88	$10.40
15 JEWELED EDGEMERE, special make	11.05	12.40	17.00	11.50	11.95	13.40
7 Jeweled Elgin or Waltham, nickel plates	10.63	11.98	16.58	11.08	11.53	12.98
15 Jeweled Elgin or Waltham, nickel plates	13.00	14.35	18.95	13.45	13.90	15.35
15 JEWELED PLYMOUTH WATCH CO., patent regulator, special make	12.75	14.10	18.70	13.20	13.65	15.10
16 Jeweled Lady Waltham, nickel plates	18.03	19.38	23.98	18.48	18.93	20.38
17 JEWELED PLYMOUTH WATCH CO., patent regulator, adjusted, special make	17.40	18.75	23.35	17.85	18.30	19.75
19 Jeweled No. 201 Grade Elgin	28.52	29.87	34.47	28.97	29.42	30.87

Fancy Dial.

We show here an illustration of the fancy dial and gold hands that we furnish on different watches quoted and illustrated on the following pages at 90 cents extra.

Fancy dials cannot be fitted on every watch in our catalogue. We caution you to order them only on such watches where it is clearly stated on page that we can furnish fancy dials. The illustration merely gives you an idea of how the fancy dials will look. They are not all exactly as this picture shows, as they vary in design. They come in various tints, with floral decorations and gold work, and all of them are beautiful.

The illustration is a dial made to fit 18-size watches. We furnish any size, 18, 16, 12, 6 or 0-size for American watches.

LADIES' SMALL O-SIZE OPEN FACE PLYMOUTH GOLD FILLED WATCHES

WARRANTED FOR THE TERM OF YOUR NATURAL LIFETIME.

THIS IS ONE of our very latest additions in the Watch Department. The illustrations show the back and front of the watch, so that you can get a correct idea of exactly how this watch appears. These watches not alone carry our personal guarantee as to permanency of wear, but they likewise carry our written binding guarantee on the movement. You positively are insured on both the movement and the case on any watch you buy from us. We stand ready at any time within the period of the guarantee to make good every condition in it.

THE DIAMOND SET CASE illustrated on this page is a little beauty. It is bright polish, has a genuine rose diamond set in the back and, fitted with our 15 jeweled Edgemere movement, for $11.15, it is a value not to be purchased from others.

No. 4L3655 Plymouth Gold Filled. 20-Year Guarantee.

No. 4L3659 Diamond Set, Plymouth Gold Filled. Life Guarantee.

No. 4L3661 Plymouth Gold Filled. Life Guarantee.

No. 4L3663 Plymouth Gold Filled. Life Guarantee.

WE FIT THESE O-SIZE OPEN FACE CASES WITH THE FOLLOWING O-SIZE MOVEMENTS. PRICES QUOTED ARE FOR THE COMPLETE WATCH, MOVEMENT AND CASE.	No. 4L3655	Nos. 4L3661 4L3663	No. 4L3659
7 Jeweled Swiss Lever	$ 6.35	$ 7.15	$ 8.15
15 JEWELED EDGEMERE, special make	9.65	10.15	11.15
7 Jeweled Elgin or Waltham, nickel plates	9.23	9.73	10.73
15 Jeweled Elgin or Waltham, nickel plates	11.60	12.10	13.10
15 JEWELED PLYMOUTH WATCH CO., patent regulator, special make	11.35	11.85	12.85
16 Jeweled Lady Waltham, nickel plates	16.63	17.13	18.13
17 JEWELED PLYMOUTH WATCH CO., patent regulator, adjusted, special make	16.00	16.50	17.50
19 Jeweled No. 201 Grade Elgin	27.12	27.62	28.62

CUT PRICES

LADIES' SOLID SILVER O-SIZE WATCHES.

An American made watch in this small size, made of silver, has been wanted by thousands of ladies. So as to make our catalogue complete, so as to positively quote all kinds and styles of watches, we show here the smallest silver American watch made. These cases are solid silver through and through, hand engraved; they have the antique bow; the entire case is perfectly finished in every respect. They are stem wind and pendant set. We guarantee the movement for a term of five years, and the case will last your natural lifetime. We can fit this case with any movement, both in open face or hunting style, at prices quoted below.

No. 4L3666 Open Face.
No. 4L3669 Hunting Style.

	Open Face No. 4L3666	Hunting Style No. 4L3669
7 Jeweled Swiss Lever	$ 5.58	$ 5.85
7 Jeweled Elgin or Waltham	7.25	8.40
15 Jeweled PLYMOUTH WATCH CO.	9.10	9.25
15 Jeweled Elgin or Waltham	10.95	11.10
17 Jeweled PLYMOUTH WATCH CO.	15.05	15.20

FOR COMPLETE INDEX REFER TO PINK PAGES IN MIDDLE OF BOOK.

GOLD FILLED 16-SIZE 20-YEAR GUARANTEED

EXTRA THIN MODEL WATCHES

OPEN FACE OR HUNTING STYLE.

$5 75 AND UP

Protect your watch with an Ajax Watch Insulator. See page 195 No. 4H586. Price 23c

Illustrations on this page show exact size.

5 75 AND UP

GOLD FILLED, HUNTING and OPEN FACE, SCREW BACK and BEZEL, DUST and DAMPPROOF CASES.

Dueber. Gold Filled. Guaranteed for 20 years.
No. 4H1974 Open face, screw back and bezel.
No. 4H1975 Hunting style.

Plymouth. Gold Filled. Engine Turned. Guaranteed for 20 years.
No. 4H1954 Open face, screw back and bezel.
No. 4H1955 Hunting style.

Plymouth. Gold Filled. Guaranteed for 20 years.
No. 4H1956 Plymouth, open face, screw back and bezel.
No. 4H1957 Plymouth, hunting style.

Plymouth. Gold Filled. Guaranteed for 20 years.
No. 4H1958 Plymouth, open face, screw back and bezel.
No. 4H1959 Plymouth, hunting style.

Illinois Watch Case Co. Giant. Gold Filled. Guaranteed for 20 years.
No. 4H1960 Open face, screw back and bezel.
No. 4H1961 Hunting style.

25 CENTS will carry any watch to any part of the United States by express. We recommend sending watches by express, as they do not receive the hard usage as when sent by mail. If sent by mail, postage extra, 6 cents. Watches amounting to $1.00 or over should be registered if sent by mail, which costs 8 cents extra, or a total of 14 cents for postage and registry.

$5 75 AND UP

WE POSITIVELY UNDERSELL EVERYONE ON WATCHES.

Plymouth. Gold filled, plain polished. Guaranteed for 20 years.
No. 4H1920 Open face, screw back and bezel.
No. 4H1925 Hunting style.

Dueber. Gold Filled. Guaranteed for 20 years.
No. 4H1962 Open face, screw back and bezel.
No. 4H1963 Hunting style, engraved.
No. 4H1964 Open face, same make, but engine turned.
No. 4H1965 Hunting style, same make, but engine turned.

Illinois Watch Case Co. Giant. Gold Filled. Guaranteed for 20 years.
No. 4H1970 Open face, screw back and bezel.
No. 4H1971 Open face, same make, but engine turned.
No. 4H1972 Hunting style, engraved.
No. 4H1973 Hunting, same make, but engine turned.

$3 33 AN ASTONISHING WATCH OFFER IN 16-SIZE LEVER ESCAPEMENT EXTRA THIN MODEL STYLE

No. 4H1983 Gunmetal.
No. 4H1984 Nickel Case.

We fit these cases with the following 16-size movements. Prices quoted are for the complete watch, movement and case.	Open Face	Hunting Style
7 JEWELED EDGEMERE, nickel plates, special make	$ 5.75	$ 7.60
7 Jeweled Elgin or Waltham, nickel plates	8.65	10.50
15 JEWELED EDGEMERE, patent regulator, nickel plates, special make	8.50	10.35
15 Jeweled Elgin or Waltham, nickel plates, patent regulator	10.75	12.60
17 Jeweled Elgin or Waltham, not adjusted	12.85	14.70
17 Jeweled No. 241 Grade Elgin, adjusted	15.48	17.33
17 JEWELED PLYMOUTH WATCH CO., nickel plates, patent regulator, adjusted	15.13	16.98
17 Jeweled No. 243 Grade Elgin, adjusted, nickel plates	26.50	28.35
21 JEWELED PRINCE OF WALES PLYMOUTH WATCH CO., full adjusted, patent regulator, nickel plates	20.40	22.25

The movements as shown by this illustration are the movements we recommend in preference to all other makes for accurate timekeeping and best value. The 17 jeweled Plymouth Watch Company adjusted movement and the 21 jeweled Prince of Wales full adjusted movement. These movements are 16-size, extra thin model, stem wind and pendant set. Plates are of solid nickel, richly damaskeened, full cut expansion balance, straight line lever escapement, Breguet hairspring, especially selected, double sunk, hard, white enameled dial, patent safety pinion, full protecting dust band, true timing screws; in fact, both of these movements, according to their grade, represents the highest degree of perfection in watch making art. Nothing finer made than the 17 jeweled grade, nothing better possible in the 21 jeweled grade. In selecting one of these movements you get more than twice the value for the money as compared with any other make or grade. Your choice of either hunting or open face case fitted with a 17 jeweled movement as illustrated for $15.13 or $16.98. But, if you desire spending a little more money and want absolutely the highest grade, best running, most accurate timekeeping watch in the United States, send us $20.40 if you desire an open face watch or $22.25 if you desire a hunting style, fitted with 17 jeweled Prince of Wales movement.

YOUR CHOICE, $3.33 for a 16-size, extra thin model, stem wind and pendant set movement, full nickel plates, 7 fine jewels, straight line lever escapement, true timing screws, fine hard, white enameled dial with plain Arabic numerals, fitted in an extra thin hinged back open face silver antique bow and crown gunmetal case, or $3.33 for this watch fitted in a solid nickel case. Watches at this price sold by others invariably are Swiss imported cylinder escapement movements and do not by any means represent watches known for accurate timekeeping and true running at these prices. Look at the illustration, which shows two views of the watch; the side view gives you an idea of the extreme thinness and the three-quarter view shows you the beautiful plain dial with the Arabic numerals. The watch is slightly smaller and slightly thinner than illustration shows; just the kind of a watch you want, one that will not weigh down or bulge out your pocket in an unsightly manner. The tendency of demand is for thinner and smaller watches. To meet this demand we have had made for us under special contract the watch we illustrate here by one of the largest watch factories in the world. If you select the gunmetal watch you will own one of the most attractive watches ever offered. But for those who prefer a silver-like appearing watch we have to offer at the same figure the same movement fitted in a solid nickel case. We sell this case for what it is, a solid nickel case, guaranteed to be nickel through and through, will not tarnish, always remains the same, not nickel plated as some watches offered by others. Please be sure to order by number.

No. 4H1983 7 jeweled, extra thin model gunmetal watch. Price..........$3.33

No. 4H1984 7 jeweled, extra thin model solid nickel watch. Price........ 3.33

Postage extra, by sealed registered mail, 14 cents.

GOLD FILLED THIN MODEL 16-SIZE OPEN FACE AND HUNTING, GUARANTEED FOR LIFE OR FOR TWENTY-FIVE YEARS, GOLD FILLED CASES

For the best cheap watch in 16-size we recommend above all others our new 7 jeweled Edgemere; it is guaranteed; but for a watch that costs but a few dollars more, and gives better satisfaction for accuracy, we recommend our 15 jeweled Edgemere. Our 17 jeweled Plymouth Watch Co., adjusted, is the best 17 Jeweled American made watch in the United States, and we know you would like it. All of the above carry our 5-year written binding guarantee. Above all others, as the highest possible perfection in watch movements for accurate time-keeping, we recommend the 21 jeweled, adjusted Prince of Wales movement manufactured by the Plymouth Watch Co., quoted, described and illustrated on this page.

$7.60 AND UP
25 cents will carry any watch to any part of the United States by express.
PLYMOUTH
For 90 cents extra we can furnish a fancy dial and gold hands on any watch on this page. For illustration, see page 194.
PLYMOUTH
ILLUSTRATIONS ON THIS PAGE SHOW EXACT SIZE.
PLYMOUTH
Protect your watch with an Ajax Watch Insulator. See page 195. No. 4H586 Price, 23c
$7.60 and up

GOLD FILLED. GUARANTEED FOR 25 YEARS.
No. 4H2050 John C. Dueber, Open Face, Screw Bezel and Back.
No. 4H2051 Open Face, same make but engine turned.
No. 4H2052 Hunting Style.
No. 4H2053 Hunting Style, same make but engine turned.

GOLD FILLED. GUARANTEED FOR LIFE.
No. 4H2054 Plymouth, Open Face, Screw Back and Bezel.
No. 4H2055 Plymouth, Hunting Style.

GOLD FILLED. GUARANTEED FOR LIFE.
No. 4H2056 Plymouth, Open Face, Screw Back and Bezel.
No. 4H2057 Plymouth, Hunting Style.

GOLD FILLED, ENGINE TURNED GUARANTEED FOR LIFE.
No. 4H2058 Plymouth, Open Face, Screw Back and Bezel.
No. 4H2059 Plymouth, Hunting Style.

GOLD FILLED. GUARANTEED FOR 25 YEARS.
No. 4H2066 Illinois Watch Case Co. Commander, Open Face, Screw Back and Bezel.
No. 4H2067 Illinois Watch Case Co. Commander, Hunting Style.

Your choice of either one of these two movements, fitted in any one of the above gold filled open face cases, at $16.98 or $22.25. Or, if you prefer the hunting style case, your choice for $18.98 or $25.75. These two movements positively represent the highest possible perfection in 17 and 21 jeweled American made watches, and we suggest selecting either one or the other in preference to any other American make if you are looking for the best value that your money can procure. The top movement, as illustration shows, is our 21 jeweled Prince of Wales Plymouth Watch Company movement, full nickel plates richly damaskeened, straight line lever escapement, cut expansion balance, overstrung Breguet hairspring, fine polished whiplash patent regulator with micrometer setting screw, patent safety pinion, plate jewels all with screw settings, stem wind and pendant set, fine selected double sunk, extra hard white enamel dial, full exposed high ornamented winding wheels. But if you wish to spend a little less money, select the

17 JEWELED PLYMOUTH WATCH COMPANY MOVEMENT,

as shown above. This movement represents the best finished, most accurately running 17 jeweled adjusted watch made in the United States. It will keep good time. It is perfectly finished and a most excellent watch.

FOR 90 CENTS EXTRA we can furnish a Fancy Dial and Gold Hands on any of the above Watches. See illustration on page 194.

WE FIT THESE CASES WITH THE FOLLOWING 16-SIZE MOVEMENTS. PRICES QUOTED ARE FOR THE COMPLETE WATCH, MOVEMENT AND CASE.	Open Face 25-Year Warrant Nos. 4H2050 4H2051 4H2066	Hunting 25-Year Warrant Nos. 4H2052 4H2053 4H2067	Open Face Life Guarantee Nos. 4H2054 4H2056 4H2058	Hunting Life Guarantee Nos. 4H2055 4H2057 4H2059
7 JEWELED EDGEMERE, nickel plates, special make	$ 7.60	$ 9.60	$ 8.60	$ 11.10
7 Jeweled Elgin or Waltham, nickel plates	10.50	12.50	11.50	14.00
15 JEWELED EDGEMERE, patent regulator, nickel plates, special make	10.35	12.35	11.35	13.85
15 Jeweled Elgin or Waltham, nickel plates, patent regulator	12.60	14.60	13.60	16.10
17 Jeweled Elgin or Waltham, not adjusted	14.70	16.70	15.70	18.20
17 Jeweled No. 241 Grade Elgin, adjusted	17.33	19.33	18.33	20.83
17 JEWELED PLYMOUTH WATCH CO., nickel plates, patent regulator, adjusted	16.98	18.98	17.98	20.48
17 Jeweled No. 243 Grade Elgin, adjusted, nickel plates	28.35	30.35	29.35	31.85
21 JEWELED PRINCE OF WALES PLYMOUTH WATCH CO., full adjusted, patent regulator, nickel plates	22.25	24.25	23.25	25.75

PLEASE TAKE NOTICE

In ordering any of these watches that the hunting style cases, that is, the double lidded ones, are quoted at different prices than the open face style. So there will be no mistake, very carefully read the table of prices and order by number. Some of our customers make mistakes in ordering an open face watch at the hunting price and inclose the price of the hunting watch, or order the hunting watch and inclose the price of the open face.

GENTLEMEN'S SOLID GOLD ORNAMENTED CASE

FITTED WITH A FINE 17 JEWELED OR 21 JEWELED AMERICAN MADE MOVEMENT FOR $22.00 OR $29.00. $28.00 OR $39.00 IF YOU SELECT THE SAME CASE FITTED WITH A BRANDED MOVEMENT MADE BY THE WALTHAM COMPANY.

THE CASE is manufactured by the Illinois Watch Case Co., of Elgin, Ill. It is 16 size, gold filled, guaranteed for 25 years' continual wear, ornamented with solid gold in various colors. One of the handsomest, most ornate cases ever placed on the market. Modern in every way, stem wind and pendant set. A watch that is the equal of solid gold in every way, but in intrinsic value. Solid gold ornamentation, floral sprays, in various gold colors, green, yellow and red being the prominent colors used, and all of it solid gold.

THE MOVEMENTS we advise you selecting because of their wonderful accuracy and the value you would be getting. Compare them with the prices asked for branded goods. This case fitted with 17 jeweled Plymouth Watch Company movement for $22.00, made by one of the best watchmakers in the United States, all plate jewels in fine screw settings, Breguet hairspring, cut expansion balance, true timing screws, patent safety pinion, fine selected double sunk white enamel dial, patent micrometer regulator and better than any other 17 jeweled, 16-size movement on the market, is adjusted to heat, cold and position. If you want absolute perfection and willing to spend a few more dollars, select the 21 jeweled Prince of Wales movement as the best value for the money, solid nickel plates, all plate jewels in screw settings, Breguet hairspring, cut expansion balance, true timing screws, patent safety pinion and better than any other 21 jeweled 16-size movement on the market, is adjusted to heat, cold, position and isochronism. The acme of perfection. Compare these two prices to what is asked by the manufacturer of branded goods.

After reading this very carefully you cannot help but note the wonderful saving if you select our own special brand of movements. In making your selection do not fail to order by number.

GOLD FILLED SOLID GOLD ORNAMENTED GUARANTEED FOR 25 YEARS, COMMANDER CASE.

No. 4H2070 Solid gold ornamented case filled with 17 jeweled Plymouth Watch Company movement.......$22.00
No. 4H2072 Fitted with 21 jeweled Prince of Wales movement.......29.00
No. 4H2074 Fitted with the Royal Waltham 17 jeweled movement.......28.00
No. 4H2076 Fitted with 21 jeweled Crescent St. Waltham movement.......39.00

YOUR CHOICE FOR $3.10.

$3.10

LADIES' O-SIZE OR GENTLEMEN'S EXTRA THIN 12-SIZE, BOTH OPEN FACE STYLE, SOLID GERMAN SILVER, ANTIQUE FINISH EMPIRE WATCH.

The exact copy of watches used in France when an Empire.

No. 4H2080 No. 4H2085

Gentlemen's size Empire watch, imported from Switzerland. The case is exactly as illustration shows. Same repousse raised design. Extra thin model, stem wind and pendant set, snap bezel with gilt crown. Case is finished in dark oxidized gray color. The die work most beautiful and a masterpiece of artistic skill. The movement is nickel, contains two jewels and has cylinder escapement. Each one timed and tested before leaving our establishment.

No. 4H2080
Gents' 12-size, as illustrated, repousse raised design.
Price..........$3.10

No. 4H2085
Ladies' 0-size, as illustrated, dainty floral design.
Price..........$3.10

12 AND 16-SIZE GENTLEMEN'S ELGIN AND WALTHAM WATCHES

Protect your Watch with an AJAX WATCH INSULATOR. See page 192. No. 4C2002 Price.. 18c

12 and 16-SIZE.

Open Face and Hunting Style.

REMEMBER, all of our Open Face Watches are screw bezel and screw back. This model of case is dust and damp proof, the best kind of a case to protect the movement. with. All employes of railroads, occupying responsible positions, use the Open Face Screw Back and Screw Bezel Dust and Damp Proof Cases. They know it is the best case made to protect valuable movements.

OUR GUARANTEE GOES WITH EVERY ONE SOLD. We will replace with a brand new case any Sears Gold Filled Case that shows the gold worn down to the composition metal within 20 years or any time in your entire lifetime, according to grade of case.

SILVER, SILVERODE AND GOLD FILLED.

20, 25 YEARS AND LIFE GUARANTEE.

WHAT WE MEAN BY THE SEARS LIFE GUARANTEE CASE. The Sears Life Guaranteed Case is a gold filled case of the very highest quality and the nearest approach to a solid gold case manufactured. The Sears Life Guaranteed Case means that should any one of these cases wear down to the inner composition metal any time within your natural life, whether you have owned the case five years, twenty years or fifty years, return it to us and we will upon the receipt of same exchange it for a brand new case of the same quality, free of charge.

The Sears Case comes in open face or hunting style, as desired. We always carry a complete line of them. Some people prefer the hunting style case.

LIFE GUARANTEE

Warranted for 20 and 25 years.

16-Size. Illinois Watch Case Co. Gold Filled.
No. 4C5063 Open Face, Screw Back and Bezel, 20-Year.
No. 4C5064 Hunting, 20-Year.
No. 4C5065 Open Face, Screw Back and Bezel, 25-Year.
No. 4C5066 Hunting, 25-Year.

16-SIZE. SEARS. GOLD FILLED.
No. 4C5067 Open Face, Screw Back and Bezel, 20-Year.
No. 4C5068 Hunting, 20-Year.
No. 4C5069 Open Face, Screw Back and Bezel, Life Guarantee.
No. 4C5070 Hunting, Life Guarantee.

16-SIZE. FAHYS. GOLD FILLED.
No. 4C5071 Open Face, Screw Back and Bezel, 20-Year.
No. 4C5072 Hunting, 20-Year.
No. 4C5073 Open Face, Screw Back and Bezel, 25-Year.
No. 4C5074 Hunting, 25-Year.

20-year Warranted, Gold Filled Open Face, 16-size Elgin or Waltham Watches........ **$7.99** | 20-year Warranted, Gold Filled Hunting, 16-size Elgin or Waltham Watches....... **$9.95**

PRICES QUOTED ARE FOR THE WATCHES COMPLETE.

WE FIT THE FOLLOWING MOVEMENTS IN ANY OF THESE 16-SIZE CASES, AS ILLUSTRATED.	4C5075 Open Face Silverode	4C5076 Hunting Silverode	No. 4C5077 Open Face Silver	No. 4C5078 Hunting Silver	Nos. 4C5063 4C5067	No. 4C5071	No. 4C5065	No. 4C5069	No. 4C5073	Nos. 4C5064 4C5068	No. 4C5072	No. 4C5066	No. 4C5070	No. 4C5074
7 Jeweled Grade Elgin or Waltham	$5.74	$6.09	$6.75	$7.25	$7.99	$9.15	$9.85	14.35	13.75	$9.95	11.75	11.55	15.50	$14.75
Full 15 Jeweled Grade Elgin or Waltham	Not Furnished.	Not Furnished.	10.40	10.90	11.60	12.80	13.50	18.00	17.40	13.65	15.40	15.15	19.15	18.40
Full 17 Jeweled Grade Elgin or Waltham			Not Furnished.	Not Furnished.	14.85	15.95	16.68	21.15	20.55	16.75	18.55	18.25	22.30	21.55
Full 17 Jeweled Royal Grade Waltham, Adjusted					17.15	18.35	19.03	23.55	22.95	19.05	20.95	20.55	24.70	23.95
Full 17 Jeweled No. 242 Grade Elgin, Adjusted					21.02	22.25	22.97	27.45	26.65	23.00	24.85	24.42	28.60	27.85
Full 17 Jeweled Riverside Grade Waltham, Adjusted					24.10	25.40	26.10	30.60	30.00	26.20	28.00	27.52	31.75	31.00
Full 17 Jeweled No. 243 Grade Elgin, Adjusted					25.80	27.00	27.70	32.20	31.60	27.80	29.60	29.06	33.35	32.60
Full 23 Jeweled Vanguard Grade Waltham, Adjusted					34.20	35.40	36.10	40.60	40.00	36.20	38.00	37.30	41.75	41.00
Full 21 Jeweled No. 156 Grade Elgin or Riverside Maximus Grade Waltham, Adjusted.					55.20	56.40	57.01	61.60	61.00	57.20	59.00	58.65	62.75	62.00

$5.74 AND UP.

16-SIZE. SOLID SILVER AND SILVERODE.
No. 4C5075 Open Face, Screw Back and Bezel Silverode.
No. 4C5076 Hunting, Silverode.
No. 4C5077 Open Face, Screw Back and Bezel, Solid Silver.
No. 4C5078 Hunting, Solid Silver.

20-year Warranted, Gold Filled Open Face, 12-size Elgin or Waltham Watches........ **$9.25** | 20-year Warranted Gold Filled Hunting, 12-size Elgin or Waltham Watches....... **$11.05**

PRICES QUOTED ARE FOR THE WATCHES COMPLETE.

WE FIT THE FOLLOWING MOVEMENTS TO ANY 12-SIZE CASE, AS ILLUSTRATED BELOW:	No. 4C5083	No. 4C5085	No. 4C5084	No. 4C5086	Nos. 4C5079 4C5087 4C5091	Nos. 4C5081 4C5093	Nos. 4C5080 4C5088 4C5092	Nos. 4C5082 4C5094	No. 4C5089	No. 4C5090
7 Jeweled Grade Elgin or Waltham	$10.30	$13.05	$12.80	$15.30	$9.25	$10.65	$11.05	$11.65	13.60	16.00
Full 15 Jeweled Grade Elgin or Waltham	13.20	15.95	15.70	18.20	12.15	13.58	13.94	14.58	16.50	18.90
Full 17 Jeweled No. 183 Grade Elgin or Royal Grade Waltham	18.15	20.90	20.65	23.15	17.35	18.75	19.15	19.75	21.45	23.85
Full 19 Jeweled Riverside Grade Waltham	25.25	28.00	27.75	30.25	24.20	25.60	26.00	26.60	28.55	30.95
Full 19 Jeweled No. 189 Grade Elgin	29.45	32.20	31.95	34.45	28.40	29.80	30.20	30.80	32.75	35.15
Full 21 Jeweled No. 236 Grade Elgin	44.15	46.90	46.65	49.15	43.10	44.50	44.90	45.50	47.45	49.85
Full 23 Jeweled No. 190 Grade Elgin	56.25	59.00	58.75	61.25	55.20	56.60	57.00	57.60	59.55	61.95

THE ENGRAVING. Regarding the engravings, we generally have the exact pattern; if not, we will send a very similar design.

FOR $1.25 EXTRA WE FURNISH FANCY DIAL AND GOLD HANDS ON ANY WATCH ON THIS PAGE.

25 CENTS will carry any Watch to any part of the United States by Express.

$9.25 TO $57.60

COMMANDER ELGIN

LIFE GUARANTEE

COMMANDER ELGIN

$9.25 TO $57.60

12-Size. Illinois Watch Case Co. Gold Filled.
No. 4C5079 Open Face, Screw Back and Bezel, 20-Year.
No. 4C5080 Hunting, 20-Year.
No. 4C5081 Open Face, Screw Back and Bezel, 25-Year.
No. 4C5082 Hunting, 25-Year.

12-SIZE. FAHYS. GOLD FILLED.
No. 4C5083 Open Face, Screw Back and Bezel, 20-Year.
No. 4C5084 Hunting, 20-Year.
No. 4C5085 Open Face, Screw Back and Bezel, 25-Year.
No. 4C5086 Hunting, 25-Year.

12-SIZE. SEARS. GOLD FILLED.
No. 4C5087 Open Face, Screw Back and Bezel, 20-Year.
No. 4C5088 Hunting, 20-Year.
No. 4C5089 Open Face, Screw Back and Bezel, Life Guarantee.
No. 4C5090 Hunting, Life Guarantee.

12-Size. Illinois Watch Case Co. Gold Filled
No. 4C5091 Open Face, Screw Back and Bezel, 20-Year.
No. 4C5092 Hunting 20-Year.
No. 4C5093 Open Face, Screw Back and Bezel, 25-Year.
No. 4C5094 Hunting, 25-Year.

FOR COMPLETE INDEX REFER TO PINK PAGES IN MIDDLE OF BOOK.

LADIES' 0-SIZE AND 6-SIZE GOLD FILLED, HUNTING STYLE ELGIN AND WALTHAM WATCHES FOR $9.25 AND UPWARDS.

GUARANTEED FOR 20 AND 25 YEARS AND FOR LIFE, ACCORDING TO GRADE OF CASE.

$10.52 AND UP

No charges for repairs on watches or clocks will be allowed unless our written consent is first secured in advance.

Illinois Watch Case Co.
GOLD FILLED—0-SIZE.
No. 4C5100 Warranted 20 yrs.
No. 4C5102 Warranted 25 yrs.

THE LATEST DESIGNS
IN CHASING AND ENGRAVING

Illinois Watch Case Co.
GOLD FILLED—0-SIZE.
No. 4C5104 Warranted 25 yrs.
Genuine Rose Diamond.

Sears.
GOLD FILLED—0-SIZE.
No. 4C5105 Warranted 20 yrs.
No. 4C5107 Warranted for life

If our goods are not exactly as represented and described, return them and we will cheerfully refund the money.

Fahys.
GOLD FILLED—0-SIZE.
No. 4C5110 Warranted 20 yrs.
No. 4C5112 Warranted 25 yrs.

FOR $1.25 Extra we can furnish fancy dial and gold hands on any watch on this page.

$10.52 AND UP

Dueber.
GOLD FILLED—0-SIZE.
No. 4C5114 Warranted 20 yrs.
No. 4C5116 Warranted 25 yrs.

$12.15 AND UP

Illinois Watch Case Co.
GOLD FILLED—0-SIZE.
No. 4C5118 Warranted 25 yrs.
Three Genuine Rose Diamonds.

ALL OF THE CASES SHOWN ON THIS PAGE ARE HUNTING STYLE ONLY.

THE SEARS GOLD FILLED CASE IS RECOMMENDED ABOVE ALL OTHERS.

Being made of two extra heavy plates of solid gold over a hard composition metal, will wear longer than any other gold filled case made, and is the handsomest, best finished and best fitting gold filled watch case made. If you select a Sears case you will have the best gold filled watch case ever made.

WE FIT THE FOLLOWING MOVEMENTS IN ANY OF THESE C-SIZE CASES. THE PRICES QUOTED ARE FOR THE WATCHES COMPLETE.	Nos. 4C5100 4C5105 4C5114 4C5120	No. 4C5110	Nos. 4C5102 4C5116 4C5122	No. 4C5107	No. 4C5112	No. 4C5104	No. 4C5118
7 Jeweled Grade Elgin or Waltham	$10.52	$11.50	$11.22	$13.65	$13.30	$11.82	$12.15
Full 15 Jeweled Grade Elgin or Waltham	14.20	15.50	14.90	17.35	17.00	15.50	15.75
Full 16 Jeweled Lady Waltham Grade Waltham	15.25	18.12	15.95	19.97	19.62	16.55	16.78
Full 17 Jeweled Riverside Waltham	25.22	26.55	25.92	28.40	28.05	26.52	26.57
Full 18 Jeweled No. 201 Grade Elgin	26.80	28.10	27.50	29.95	29.60	27.10	28.11
Full 19 Jeweled Riverside Maximus Grade Waltham	35.20	36.50	35.90	38.35	38.00	36.50	36.35

$10.52 AND UP

Illinois Watch Case Co.
GOLD FILLED—0-SIZE.
No. 4C5120 Warranted 20 yrs.
No. 4C5122 Warranted 25 yrs.

$9.25 AND UP

REGARDING THE ENGRAVINGS We generally have the exact pattern. If not, we send a very similar design.

Illinois Watch Case Co.
GOLD FILLED—6-SIZE.
No. 4C5125 Warranted 20 years.
No. 4C5127 Warranted 25 years.

For 20 cents we furnish a beautiful plush Presentation Case, to fit any watch. Order by number and give size of watch.
No. 4C2000 Price...20c

Illinois Watch Case Co.
GOLD FILLED—6-SIZE.
No. 4C5128 Warranted 25 years.
Set with Genuine Brilliant Cut Diamond. Raised Ornamentation.

Sears.
GOLD FILLED—6-SIZE.
No. 4C5129 Warranted 20 years.
No. 4C5131 Warranted for life.

25 cents will carry a ladies' watch to any point in the United States by express.

$10.75 AND UP

Fahys.
GOLD FILLED—6-SIZE.
No. 4C5134 Warranted 20 years.
No. 4C5136 Warranted 25 years.

$9.25 AND UP

Dueber.
GOLD FILLED—6-SIZE.
No. 4C5138 Warranted 20 years.
No. 4C5140 Warranted 25 years.

BUY THE BEST and you will select the SEARS case as the best gold filled case manufactured. The SEARS case being the latest gold filled case on the market, it has all the modern improvements. The designs are copied from the newest designs in solid gold cases by skilled engravers. The method of making the Sears case is up to date and only modern machinery is used. The amount of gold used on the Sears case is greater than on any other case made.

THE BEST CRITERION. We have sold thousands of SEARS cases and no doubt some friend or neighbor in your community owns one. Ask him or her what they think of the SEARS case. Judge from what is said. We are willing to accept the decree, we know it can mean nothing else but an order from you for a Sears case.

25 CENTS WILL CARRY ANY ONE OF THESE WATCHES TO ANY PART OF THE UNITED STATES BY EXPRESS.

WE FIT THE FOLLOWING MOVEMENTS IN ANY OF THESE 6-SIZE CASES. THE PRICES QUOTED ARE FOR THE WATCHES COMPLETE.	Nos. 4C5125 4C5129 4C5138 4C5143	No. 4C5134	Nos. 4C5127 4C5140 4C5145	No. 4C5131	No. 4C5136	No. 4C5128
7 Jeweled Grade Elgin or Waltham	$ 9.25	$10.75	$ 9.85	$12.75	$12.25	$15.11
15 Jeweled Grade Elgin or Waltham	11.10	12.62	11.70	14.62	14.12	16.91
Full 16 Jeweled Lady Waltham Grade Waltham	14.50	16.00	15.10	18.00	17.50	20.26

$9.25 AND UP

Illinois Watch Case Co.
GOLD FILLED—6-SIZE.
No. 4C5143 Warranted 20 years.
No. 4C5145 Warranted 25 years.

THE WORLD RENOWNED ALASKA SILVER 18-SIZE WATCHES AT PRICES NEVER HEARD OF BEFORE

$2.00 AND UP

This illustration shows our 18-Size Plymouth Watch Co. Special 17 Jeweled Movement. We recommend it as the greatest movement offer ever made for perfection of make and accuracy of time.

REMEMBER, WHEN YOU HAVE BOUGHT $25.00 WORTH OF GOODS OR MORE FROM US YOU GET YOUR CHOICE OF MANY VALUABLE ARTICLES FREE, AS SHOWN IN OUR NEW FREE PROFIT SHARING BOOK.

18 SIZE
No. 4G1100 Open Face, Jointed Case.
No. 4G1102 Open Face, 3-ounce Screw Back and Bezel.

18 SIZE
No. 4G1105 Hunting. Engraved Case.

No charges for repairs on watches or clocks will be allowed unless our written consent is first secured in advance.

For 90c extra, we can furnish a fancy dial and gold hands on any watch on this page.

18 SIZE
No. 4G1106 Screw Bezel and Solid Back. Dust and dampproof with patent nut and gold reflector.

PROTECT YOUR WATCH WITH AN AJAXWATCH INSULATOR. See page 38. No. 4G586. PRICE, 23c

18 SIZE
No. 4G1109 Hunting. Plain Case.

WE FIT THESE CASES WITH THE FOLLOWING 18-SIZE MOVEMENTS. PRICES QUOTED ARE FOR THE COMPLETE WATCH, MOVEMENT AND CASE.	4G1102	4G1100	4G1105 4G1106	4G1109	4G1110 4G1112
7 JEWELED EDGEMERE, nickel plates, special make	$ 2.00	$ 2.08	$ 2.45	$ 2.30	$ 2.50
7 Jeweled Elgin or Waltham, gilt plates	4.02	4.10	4.47	4.32	4.52
7 Jeweled Elgin or Walham, nickel plates	4.55	4.63	5.00	4.85	5.05
15 JEWELED PLYMOUTH WATCH CO., patent regulator, nickel plates, special make	5.40	5.48	5.85	5.70	5.90
15 Jeweled Waltham, gilt plates	5.08	5.16	5.53	5.38	5.58
15 Jeweled Elgin or Waltham, nickel plates	5.60	5.68	6.05	5.90	6.10
17 Jeweled Elgin or Waltham, not adjusted	6.65	6.73	7.10	6.95	7.15
17 JEWELED PLYMOUTH WATCH CO., patent regulator, adjusted, nickel plates, special make	8.35	8.43	8.80	8.65	8.85
17 Jeweled G. M. Wheeler Elgin or P. S. Bartlett Waltham, patent regulator, adjusted, nickel plates	8.75	8.83	9.20	9.05	9.25
21 JEWELED KING EDWARD PLYMOUTH WATCH CO., patent regulator, adjusted, nickel plates, special make	15.35	15.43	15.80	15.65	15.85
21 Jeweled John Hancock Hampden, patent regulator, adjusted, nickel plates	15.15	15.23	15.60	15.45	15.65
21 Jeweled Special Railway Hampden, patent regulator, adjusted, nickel plates	19.10	19.18	19.55	19.40	19.60
23 Jeweled Special Railway Hampden patent regulator, adjusted, nickel plates	26.60	26.68	27.05	26.90	27.10
TRAINMEN'S SPECIAL, stamped 23 jeweled adjusted, special make	2.70	2.78	3.15	3.00	3.20

$2.50

18 SIZE
No. 4G1110 Open Face, Screw Back and Bezel, Solid Gold Stag Onlaid.
No. 4G1112 Same style case as above, Solid Gold Engine Onlaid.

THE ONLY 4½-OUNCE ALASKA SILVER CASE MANUFACTURED IN THE WORLD. WE HAVE THEM. YOU CANNOT BUY THEM ELSEWHERE.

WE GUARANTEE this case to weigh 4½ ounces without the movement. An extra heavy watch is often called for by men who are engaged in heavy work, and to supply this demand we have had made this extra heavy 4½-ounce dust and dampproof Alaska silver case. This case is made to stand 800 pounds strain; in other words, your movement is safe in this case, no matter what might happen. The composition of this watch is of the best grade of Alaska silver composition metal, in every way excepting in intrinsic value the equal of coin silver. It is guaranteed to wear and retain its perfect coin silver color for a lifetime. This case is open face screw back and bezel, dust and dampproof. Our special price, **$2.30**, includes this case and a 7 jeweled stem wind and stem set quick train movement. **Weigh our cases. Compare them to any case advertised on the market as 5 or 5½ ounce. Nothing made in Alaska silver, silverine or nickel as heavy or heavier than this, our truly 4½-ounce Alaska silver case.**

AT $3.00 fitted with the 23 jeweled Trainmen's Special, exactly as illustrated and described.

TRAINMEN'S SPECIAL. American manufactured movement, 18-size, elaborately damaskeened nickel and gilt movement; ruby jewels in raised settings, train, straight line escapement, exposed pallets, compensation quick balance, stem wind and set, hard enameled dial, locomotive on movement and dial and movement stamped "23 jewels adjusted." Has the appearance of a $25.00 railroad movement.

ORDER ONE OF THESE WATCHES and if you don't find it in every way as described, return it and we will refund your money. We can fit in this case any movement you desire as quoted below. We fit these cases with the following 18-size movements. Prices quoted are for the complete watch, movement and case.

$2.30

No. 4G1114

7 JEWELED EDGEMERE, nickel plates, special make	$ 2.30
7 Jeweled Elgin or Waltham, gilt plates	4.32
7 Jeweled Elgin or Waltham, nickel plates	4.85
15 JEWELED PLYMOUTH WATCH CO., patent regulator, nickel plates, special make	5.70
15 Jeweled Waltham, gilt plates	5.38
15 Jeweled Elgin or Waltham, nickel plates	5.90
17 Jeweled Elgin or Waltham, not adjusted	6.95
17 JEWELED PLYMOUTH WATCH CO., patent regulator, adjusted, nickel plates, special make	8.80
17 Jeweled G. M. Wheeler Elgin or P. S. Bartlett Waltham, patent regulator, adjusted, nickel plates	9.05
21 JEWELED KING EDWARD PLYMOUTH WATCH CO., patent regulator, adjusted, nickel plates, special make	15.65
21 Jeweled John Hancock Hampden, patent regulator, adjusted, nickel plates	15.45
21 Jeweled Special Railway Hampden, patent regulator, adjusted, nickel plates	19.40
23 Jeweled Special Railway Hampden, patent regulator, adjusted, nickel plates	26.90
TRAINMEN'S SPECIAL, stamped 23 jeweled adjusted, special make	3.00

$1.79

No. 4G1115 Boys' cheap 16-size open face heavy metal Roskopf system lever watch. Stem wind and stem set. This watch is especially made for young boys. It is constructed under one of the oldest systems and gives the least trouble of any of the cheap watches manufactured. You cannot overwind this watch. When the limit of the mainspring has been reached a clicking sound is made showing the winder that the watch is wound up. The case is solid nickel. The back lid is hinged and the front bezel snaps on tightly The dial is solid porcelain with black numerals and fancy golden hands. Our guarantee does not accompany this watch, but we defy any competitor to show its equal for $2.00 and upward. Price.........$1.79

$2.68

No. 4G1116 Gentlemen's open face extra thin model 16-size bright polish gunmetal watch. This watch is one of the newest importations we have made this year from Switzerland; especially adapted for young men wishing an unpretentious yet handsome watch. The case has hinged back with snap bezel, full antique gold plated crown and bow. Is stem wind and pendant set. The dial is one of the latest Parisian effects; Roman yellow gold, perforated in circles so as to make the figures stand out prominently. The movement is of nickel, containing two jewels and cylinder escapement. Will run and keep fairly good time. We do not send with this watch our written binding guarantee, but with care there is no reason why this watch should not last for years.
Price, 6 for $15.28; each......$2.68

$14.98

A TREMENDOUS REDUCTION; WAS $17.85

WE HAVE GOTTEN A LOWER IMPORT COST AND OUR CUSTOMERS GET THE BENEFIT

IMPORTED

GENEVA WATCH

This illustration shows you where the solid gold sheets are placed on these cases. The sheets of solid gold are slightly pulled from the base metal, illustrating exactly how our Plymouth Life gold filled cases are made.

PLEASE READ THIS WONDERFUL WATCH OFFER

Do you want something most extraordinary in an especially fine ladies' or gentlemen's watch? Are you willing to pay as much as $14.98 for a very fine watch, something away out of the ordinary, a much better watch than you would be at all likely to find in any jewelry store in your section of the country? If you are willing to invest as much money as $14.98 in a watch, we offer you on this page an opportunity to get one of the finest and best watches made.

GENEVA, SWITZERLAND, EUROPE, turns out the very finest watch movements of the world. Go into the very finest jewelry store in Chicago, New York, or any other large American city and you will scarcely see an American made movement offered for sale. The movements they offer are all made in Geneva, Switzerland, but in such stores they get very fancy prices. Scarcely one Geneva watch is offered for less than $50.00 and from that figure they run at once up into the hundreds. All very fine watch movements, even one of the very special split second, repeaters, striking, chronograph, and especially fine made thin model movements, all the very finest watch movement work is done in, and therefore must come from Geneva, Switzerland, Europe.

WE ARE THE FIRST HOUSE in the world to bring the genuine high grade Geneva watch movements before the American public at anything like a low price, the first house to make a price low enough to bring such a fine watch within reach of all. No longer is it necessary to pay $50.00 to $100.00 to own a Geneva watch, for by a most wonderful and absorbing watch movement contract made by us, strange as it may seem, we are just now able to take the very highest grade life guaranteed, full engraved American gold filled watch case made and fit into this case a very fine genuine Geneva Swiss movement in your choice of two sizes for men, or one size for women, and, strange as it must seem to every one who reads this, and much as watch dealers will wonder, we can offer these marvelously fine watches for only $14.98.

FOR WONDERFUL TIME KEEPING QUALITIES and rare specimens of beauty, and for those who are willing to give a fine watch just reasonable care, only the reasonable care that such a fine piece of mechanism deserves, these fine Geneva watches are the only watches to buy.

BUY THIS GENEVA WATCH AT $14.98 in either gentlemen's or ladies' styles and no American watch even at $50.00 in price will compare with it. Let your friends see, examine and compare your Geneva watch with their watches and every judge will pronounce your $14.98 watch worth $50.00 to $100.00.

THE SIZES OF THESE GENEVA WATCHES

THE PICTURES HEREON show the exact size of these watches. The largest, 16-size gents' watch, just as illustrated, is 2 inches wide. The 12-size gents' watch, just as illustrated, is 1¾ inches wide. The ladies' 0-size, just as illustrated, is 1⅜ inches wide. All are made especially thin, neat and dainty, and all have unique antique bows. They are all smaller, thinner, lighter, neater and in every way handsomer and finer than what you can buy in American made watches; the 12 or 16-size, the ideal size, shape and style for the carrying timepiece of a real gentleman, and the 0-size is just the watch in size, thickness and weight for the most exacting, most fashionable lady to wear, and as for timekeeping dependability they are unequaled. The three illustrations on this page will give you just a little idea of the appearance of our Geneva watch and the several sizes in which it comes. The largest size, the 16-size for gentlemen, we offer for the first time in the history of the watch making industry in a genuine imported Geneva movement for only $14.98. One of the pictures in the group of three shows the front of the watch with its handsome Geneva special dial or face and gold hands. Another picture shows the back of the watch detailing the gold filled case with its beautiful engraving and elaborate finish. The third picture in the group shows the wonderful Geneva movement, and these three pictures are engraved by our artist direct from photographs and are exact in size and appearance.

DON'T BUY ONE of these fine watches then treat it as you would a dollar nickel watch. If you are at times engaged at dirty or heavy work; if your work takes you at times into dusty fields behind the harvester, or to the railroad section; if your work at times takes you otherwise into dirty or dusty places and when at work your watch is jammed and roughly used, on such occasions don't wear as fine a watch as this for the purpose. In such cases don't buy this watch at all, or buy this watch and also a cheap heavy watch for a dollar or so, using the cheap watch when at very dirty or rough work.

$14.98

No. 4N13510

16-Size, Open Face, Screw Back and Screw Bezel. Guaranteed for life. These illustrations of front and back view and movement are exact life size of gentlemen's 16-size watch.

No. 4N13505

12-Size, Open Face, Screw Back and Screw Bezel. Guaranteed for life. These illustrations are life size and show front, back and movement of the gentlemen's 12-size watch with genuine Geneva movement.

$14.98

PLYMOUTH.

These illustrations show front, back and open view of case, also movement of ladies 0-size watch fitted with genuine Geneva movement. The No. 4N13500 pictures are life size.

0-Size, Hunting Style. Guaranteed for life.

THESE GENEVA MOVEMENTS in all three sizes, 16, 12 and 0, are all alike, except for size, all made from very finest decarbonized nickel, all are full 17 jeweled, red hand turned ruby jewels in gold settings, jeweled both sides throughout, including centers, all adjusted to heat, cold, position isochronism; patent regulators, patent escapement, patent pinion, patent dust protector, quick train cut balance wheel, Breguet hairspring, compensating balance, Geneva compensating system, all hand and polished parts, all the movements the very best in every respect.

THE LIFE GUARANTEED gold filled cases in all three sizes, 16, 12 and 0-size, are all American made and the highest grade gold filled cases manufactured. Cases are made of heavy thick plates of fine solid gold over inner plates of hard composition metal and are guaranteed to wear and retain their pure gold color for a lifetime. They are most elaborately engraved, finished and decorated, wonderfully well finished, all fitted with genuine antique bows, all stem wind and patent pendant setting. The gentlemen's watches, the 16 and 12-sizes, are open face only, the 0-size ladies' watches are double or hunting case.

FANCY DIALS or faces. These Geneva watches all have very fancy dials (see illustrations), the most beautiful dials made, finished with gold and colored ornamentations and fancy gold hands.

BE SURE TO ORDER BY NUMBER.

No. 4N13500 Ladies' small size watch. Price $14.98
No. 4N13505 12-size gentlemen's watch. Price 14.98
No. 4N13510 16-size gentlemen's watch. Price 14.98

GENTLEMEN'S GUNMETAL WATCHES

$3.26 No. 4N13520 Gunmetal. No. 4N13522 Nickel Case.

AN ASTONISHING WATCH OFFER IN A 16-SIZE LEVER ESCAPEMENT EXTRA THIN MODEL STYLE.

YOUR CHOICE, $3.26 for a 16-size, extra thin model, stem wind and pendant set movement, full nickel plates, 7 fine jewels, straight line lever escapement, true timing screws, fine hard white enameled dial with plain Arabic numerals, fitted in an extra thin hinged back open face silver antique bow and crown gunmetal case, or $3.26 for this movement fitted in a solid nickel case. Look at the illustration which shows two views of the watch; the side view gives you an idea of the extreme thinness and the three-quarter view shows you the beautiful plain dial with the Arabic numerals. Just the kind of a watch you want, one that will not weigh down or bulge out your pocket in an unsightly manner. If you select the gunmetal watch you will own one of the most attractive watches ever offered. But for those who prefer a silverlike appearing watch we have to offer at the same figure the same movement fitted in a solid nickel case. We sell this case for what it is, a solid nickel case, guaranteed to be nickel through and through, will not tarnish, always remains the same, not nickel plated as some watches offered by others. Please be sure to order by number.

No. 4N13520 7 jeweled, extra thin model, gunmetal watch. Price $3.26
No. 4N13522 7 jeweled, extra thin model, solid nickel watch. Price 3.26
If by registered mail, postage extra, 14 cents.

EIGHT-DAY WATCHES

$7.80

IN NICKEL AND SOLID SILVER.

WATCHES WE ILLUSTRATE and describe here run for eight days with but one winding. $7.80 for this eight-day watch with solid nickel case. $9.25 for this eight-day watch with solid silver case. The principal and most important feature of this watch is the movement. See the illustration. It is stem wind and pendant set, made of solid nickel plates, has 15 fine jewels, Breguet hairspring, cut expansion balance with true timing screws, has straight line lever escapement, and runs eight days with but one winding. This watch is an accurate timekeeper and a fine running watch. We send our written binding 5-year movement guarantee with every one of them. The eight-day watch that we describe here is a marvel of mechanical ingenuity never before perfected, never before successfully made. For $9.25, we will send you this wonderful timekeeper fitted in a solid silver jointed open face, bright polished antique crown, bow and stem case.

FOR $7.80 we will send you the same movement fitted in the same type of case but made of solid high grade nickel that is guaranteed nickel through and through and not to tarnish or discolor, but to be like solid silver in appearance forever. This watch is imported from Switzerland, the home of high grade watch making and is manufactured by one of the largest and most representative concerns there.

No. 4N13524 Solid silver case, fitted with a 15 jeweled eight-day movement. Price $9.25
No. 4N13526 Solid nickel case, fitted with a 15 jeweled eight-day movement. Price $7.80

No 4N13524 New Model Antique Bow.

This guarantee accompanies each one of the cases illustrated on this page, and we mean every word it says.

PRICES REDUCED ON OUR KINGSTON BRAND CASES

THEY ARE GOLD FILLED, MADE FROM PLATES OF SOLID GOLD, HARD SOLDERED ON A COMPOSITION METAL

THESE PLATES are then worked up into the centers, lids, crowns, bows and stems. All visible parts are covered with a heavy sheet of gold so thick that we can give our own binding guarantee that warrants the case to retain its gold like appearance for a term of twenty years. After the lids have been formed and the centers made the ornamentation is put upon them. When this is finished the cases are stoned down, hinged and jointed, inside cap fitted, inside bezel that holds crystal fitted, and crown and bow put on.

FOR 90 CENTS EXTRA we can furnish a fancy dial and gold hands on any watch on this page. See page 457 for illustration. Protect your watch with an Ajax Watch Insulator. Price, 21 cents. See No. 4R11004 on page 457.

GENTLEMEN'S GOLD FILLED WATCHES

12-SIZE EXTRA THIN MODEL

This illustration shows you where the solid gold sheets are placed on these cases. The sheets of solid gold are slightly pulled from the base metal, illustrating exactly how our Kingston gold filled cases are made.

OUR FIVE-YEAR binding guarantee goes with the different movements listed on this page.

YOU ARE DOUBLY PROTECTED IN BUYING A WATCH FROM US

First, the manufacturer's guarantee is enclosed in each watch case and then OUR OWN WRITTEN BINDING GUARANTEE THAT COVERS THE CASE AND MOVEMENT.

$12.13 OR $13.93 for this movement fitted in either the open face or hunting style cases that you desire. This movement is our full 17 jeweled Plymouth Watch Company movement. It contains 17 fine ruby jewels, has full nickel damaskeened plates, patent regulator, patent safety pinion, cut expansion balance, straight line lever escapement, overstrung Breguet hairspring, is stem wind and pendant set, adjusted to heat, cold and position. If you are looking for a 17 jeweled watch and have about $12.00 or $14.00 to expend, buy this one.

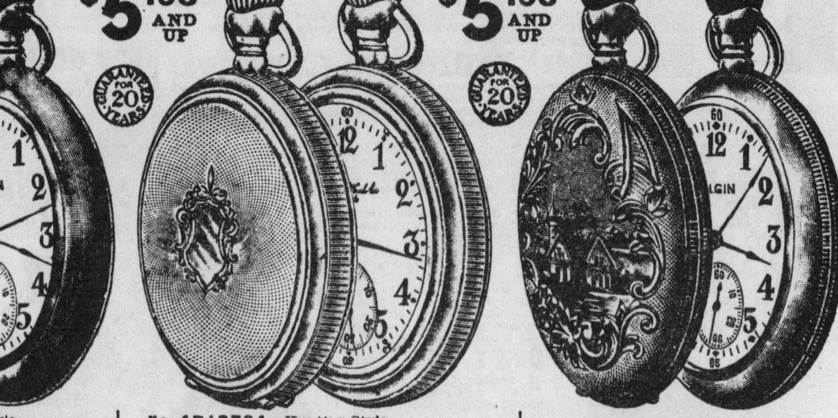

No. 4R13700 Hunting Style.
No. 4R13702 Open Face, screw back and screw bezel, dust and dampproof.

The above illustration shows you the full engraved style Bassene center and floral bird design with engine turning.

No. 4R13704 Hunting Style.
No. 4R13706 Open Face, screw back and screw bezel, dust and dampproof.

The above case illustrates a half Juergenson style with engine turning, a case that will not mar or scratch, showing the results of wear. It has been used for hundreds of years and is still one of the most popular styles used.

No. 4R13708 Hunting Style.

No. 4R13710 Open Face, screw back and screw bezel, dust and dampproof.

This case is half Bassene style, landscape with floral border and engine turned work.

We fit these cases with the following 12-size movements. Prices quoted are for the complete watch, movement and case.	No. 4R13702 No. 4R13706 No. 4R13710	No. 4R13700 No. 4R13704 No. 4R13708
7 Jeweled Swiss Lever, nickel plates	$ 5.98	$ 7.95
7 Jeweled Elgin or Waltham, nickel plates	8.15	9.95
15 Jeweled Elgin or Waltham, nickel plates, patent regulator	10.15	12.05
17 JEWELED PLYMOUTH WATCH CO., nickel plates patent regulator, special make.	**12.13**	**13.93**
17 Jeweled Elgin No. 344 Grade or Waltham No. 225 Grade, not adjusted	12.38	14.18
17 Jeweled No. 321 Grade Elgin	17.33	19.13
19 Jeweled No. 189 Grade Elgin	28.62	30.42

GENTLEMEN'S GOLD FILLED WATCHES, 16-SIZE EXTRA THIN MODEL

GUARANTEED FOR TWENTY YEARS

NEW 16-SIZE EXTRA THIN MODEL. The 16-size is one size smaller than the regulation 18-size. $5.50 for your choice of any one of these twenty-year guarantee, open face, gold filled cases, fitted with our 7 jeweled American made movement, means a record breaking price. This is our challenge offer, not equaled by any other merchant in the United States. Send us $5.50 and select one of these open face, gold filled cases, fitted with our American made movement, or if you desire the hunting style, send us $7.25 and we will send you that style, and if after you receive it and you do not find it one of the handsomest gold filled cases and one of the best looking, good timekeeping watches, considering the price, that you ever saw or heard of, return it and we will refund your money, together with the transportation charges. Here is a chance to convince yourself. When you get the watch you can examine it, compare it with any watch that any of your friends owns that they paid 30 to 50 per cent more for, compare it with watches offered by your local merchant at a much higher price and then if you find that it is not superior in every way, considering our price, return the watch to us and we will refund your money. Or, if after you receive the watch you do not find it exactly as we described it, detail for detail, size for size, make and finish, or if for any other reason you are dissatisfied, you can return it and upon its receipt we will at once refund your money, together with mail charges, without quibble or delay.

$5.50 AND UP

No. 4R13712 Hunting Style.
No. 4R13714 Open Face, screw back and screw bezel style.

The illustration shows both styles. The back of the open face is engraved the same as the hunting style watch shows.

Regarding the engraving: This is the full engraved Bassene engine turned type, copied after a solid gold design; the effect of the floral scrolls and birds, made prominent on account of the engine turned background, is a most unique innovation.

No. 4R13717 Hunting Style.
No. 4R13719 Open Face, screw back and screw bezel style.

The illustration shows both styles. The back of the open face watch is engraved the same as the hunting style watch shows.

Regarding the engraving: This is the Bassene style; it is very artistic and something new; will not show scratches or mars by continual wear.

No. 4R13721 Hunting Style.
No. 4R13723 Open Face, screw back and screw bezel style.

The illustration shows both styles. The back of the open face is engraved the same as the hunting style watch shows.

Regarding the engraving: This is our Bassene full engraved design.

PLEASE EXAMINE These two movements. They represent the highest perfection in watch making. The top one shows our 21 jeweled Prince of Wales movement, positively the highest grade 21 jewel adjusted movement made in the United States. It has 21 ruby jewels.

FOR THE BEST 17 jeweled watch, we recommend our 17 jeweled Plymouth, illustrated above. This movement represents the highest perfection in a 17 jeweled watch, and is an accurate timekeeper. No other 17 jeweled American watch can compare with it in finish, running ability or accuracy for timekeeping. Please read the description of these movements on page 456.

We fit these cases with the following 16-size movements. Prices quoted are for the complete watch, movement and case.	No. 4R13714 No. 4R13719 No. 4R13723	No. 4R13712 No. 4R13717 No. 4R13721
7 JEWELED AMERICAN MAKE	**$5.50**	**$ 7.25**
7 Jeweled Elgin, Hampden or Waltham, nickel plates	8.40	10.15
15 Jeweled Elgin, Hampden or Waltham, nickel plates, patent regulator	10.50	12.25
17 Jeweled Elgin, Hampden or Waltham, not adjusted	12.60	14.35

We fit these cases with the following 16-size movements. Prices quoted are for the complete watch, movement and case.	No. 4R13714 No. 4R13719 No. 4R13723	No. 4R13712 No. 4R13717 No. 4R13721
17 Jeweled No. 241 Grade Elgin, adjusted	$ 15.23	$ 16.98
17 JEWELED PLYMOUTH WATCH CO., nickel plates, patent regulator, adjusted	**14.88**	**16.63**
17 Jeweled No 243 Grade Elgin, adjusted, nickel plates	26.25	28.00
21 JEWELED PRINCE OF WALES PLYMOUTH WATCH CO., full adjusted, patent regulator, nickel plates	**16.15**	**17.90**

This illustration shows the 12-size extra thin model 17 jeweled Plymouth Watch Co. movement quoted at $12.43 to $18.73, according to your selection of case. For full description of movement, see page 456.

GENTLEMEN'S GOLD FILLED 12-SIZE OPEN FACE AND HUNTING STYLE WATCHES

GUARANTEED FOR 20 and 25 YEARS or the TERM OF YOUR NATURAL LIFETIME

When you buy a watch from us that is warranted, you are receiving a guarantee that is worth something. See the letter of the First National Bank of Chicago, whose capital and surplus is $14,000,000 in reference to us.

BY ALL MEANS SELECT THE LIFE GUARANTEE CASE

The Plymouth Life Guarantee Cases are Guaranteed to wear and retain their solid gold appearance for the term of your natural life.

THIS FINE WATCH BOX FOR 21 CENTS.

No. 4R11000 This illustration made from a photograph shows one of our fine lined and leatherette covered watch boxes that we supply for 21 cents extra with any watch purchased of us. In ordering, state what size watch the case is intended for. Price.....21c

If mail shipment, postage extra, 2 cents.

12-Size, Plymouth, Gold filled, 14-K. Guaranteed for Life. Engine Turned. No. 4R13800 Open face, screw back and bezel. No. 4R13802 Hunting style.

12-Size, Plymouth, Gold filled, 14-K. Guaranteed for Life. Half Engraved. No. 4R13804 Open face, screw back and bezel. No. 4R13806 Hunting style.

12-Size, Plymouth, Gold filled, 14-K. Guaranteed for Life. Full Engraved. No. 4R13808 Open face, screw back and bezel. No. 4R13810 Hunting style.

12-Size, Illinois Watch Case Co., Gold filled. Guaranteed 25 years. No. 4R13812 Open face, screw back and bezel. No. 4R13814 Hunting style.

12-Size, Dueber Watch Case Co., Gold filled. Plain polished. Guaranteed 25 years. No. 4R13816 Open face, screw back and bezel. No. 4R13818 Hunting style.

$10.40 AND UP

JUST LOOK at this beautiful solid gold ornamented gold filled case. We are proud of it. If you owned it, you would be owning one of the most artistic gold filled cases on the market. It is the proper size, has the latest antique crown, bow and stem. Comes in either open face or hunting style, as you desire. The solid gold onlaying in variegated colors of birds, flowers, etc., is what makes it artistic. It is copied after a solid gold watch that cost $65.00. You can own it for little money.

12-Size, Illinois Watch Case Co. Gold Filled. Solid Gold Ornamented. Guaranteed 25 years. No. 4R13820 Open face, screw back and bezel. No. 4R13822 Hunting style.

$10.40 —TO— $35.22 according to grade of movement.

$6.29 AND UP

25 Cents WILL CARRY ANY WATCH TO ANY PART OF THE UNITED STATES BY EXPRESS

$6.29 AND UP

12-Size, Plymouth Gold Filled Case. Guaranteed for 20 years. Engine Turned. No. 4R13840 Open face, screw back and bezel. No. 4R13842 Hunting style.

12-Size, Plymouth Gold Filled Case. Guaranteed for 20 years. Full Engraved. No. 4R13844 Open face, screw back and bezel. No. 4R13846 Hunting style.

12-Size, Dueber Watch Case Co. Gold Filled. Guaranteed for 20 years. No. 4R13848 Open face, screw back and bezel. No. 4R13850 Hunting style.

12-Size, Illinois Watch Case Co., Giant, Gold Filled. Guaranteed for 20 years. No. 4R13852 Open face, screw back and bezel. No. 4R13854 Hunting style.

This illustration shows the new up to date open face, solid back, screw back and screw bezel swing ring cup case. Comes in two grades, guaranteed for 20 and 25 years. For a neat appearing watch, one that is absolutely dust and damp-proof, by all means select this one. Be sure to order by number.

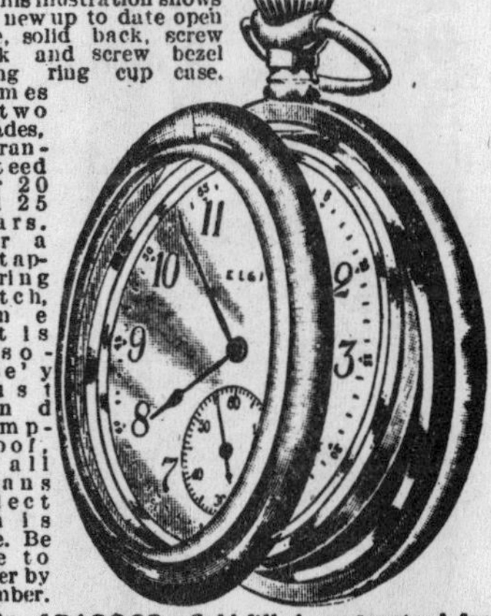

No. 4R13860 Gold filled, guaranteed for 20 years. Price, each.......... **$7.49 AND UP**

No. 4R13862 Gold filled, guaranteed for 25 years. Price, each.......... **$8.89 AND UP**

WE FIT THESE CASES WITH THE FOLLOWING 12-SIZE MOVEMENTS. PRICES QUOTED ARE FOR THE COMPLETE WATCH, MOVEMENT AND CASE.	20-Year Open Face No. 4R13840 4R13844 4R13848 4R13852	20-Year Hunting No. 4R13842 4R13846 4R13850 4R13854	25-Year Open Face No. 4R13812 4R13816	25-Year Hunting No. 4R13814 No. 4R13818	Life Guarantee Open Face No. 4R13800 4R13804 4R13808	Life Guarantee Hunting No. 4R13802 4R13806 4R13810	25-Year Open Face Gold Ornamented No. 4R13820	25-Year Hunting Gold Ornamented No. 4R13822	20-Year Swing Ring No. 4R13860	25-Year Swing Ring No. 4R13862
7 Jeweled Swiss Lever, nickel plates	$ 6.29	$ 8.55	$ 7.89	$ 9.25	$ 8.59	$10.00	$10.40	$12.75	$ 7.49	$ 8.89
7 Jeweled Elgin or Waltham, nickel plates..	8.45	10.55	10.15	11.25	10.75	12.00	12.40	14.75	9.65	11.15
15 Jeweled Elgin or Waltham, nickel plates, patent regulator	10.65	12.65	12.25	13.35	12.85	14.10	14.50	17.85	11.75	13.25
17 JEWELED PLYMOUTH WATCH CO., nickel plates, patent regulator, special make	12.43	14.53	14.13	15.23	14.73	15.98	16.38	18.73	13.63	15.13
17 Jeweled Elgin No. 344 Grade, or Waltham No. 225 Grade, not adjusted	12.68	14.78	14.38	15.48	14.98	16.23	16.63	18.98	13.88	15.38
17 Jeweled No. 321 Grade Elgin	17.63	19.73	19.33	20.43	19.93	21.18	21.58	23.93	18.83	20.33
19 Jeweled No. 189 Grade Elgin	28.92	31.02	30.62	31.72	31.22	32.47	32.87	35.22	30.12	31.62

SOLID GOLD ORNAMENTED GENTLEMEN'S SILVER WATCHES

$9.69 AND UP YOUR CHOICE of either one of these two most beautiful gentlemen's new 12-size or 16-size extra thin model, solid gold ornamented, solid silver cases with gold filled centers, crown, bow and stem, as shown in the illustration. By a system of dotted lines we show the solid gold inlaying, the location of the solid silver, we point out the gold filled center, gold filled crown and pendant and solid silver bow. A watch with solid silver sides and a gold filled center complete, in either size, the new 12-size or the new 16-size thin models, fitted with your own selection of movement. Can you appreciate the beauties of this watch? Can you picture in your mind's eye the novel contrast of the solid gold inlaying, beautiful floral scenes and landscapes on a pure white silver metal, contrasted with the gold filled guaranteed stem crown and centers?

OWN A WATCH THAT IS DIFFERENT FROM ANYONE ELSE'S. In this watch you will certainly have one of the most unique and best wearing high grade watches that money can buy. They are both hunting style; we cannot furnish the open face. They are stem wind and stem set; they both have the new up to date antique crown, bow and stem; each one has the inside protecting cap; each one is perfectly finished, no detail has been overlooked; each one surely represents a masterpiece in the watch case making line. We fit either one of these cases (be sure to give us the number of case you desire) with the following 12-size or 16-size movements:

7 Jeweled Elgin or Waltham	$ 9.69
15 Jeweled Elgin or Waltham movement, with patent regulator	12.25
17 Jeweled Elgin or Waltham	14.50
17 Jeweled Plymouth Watch Co., nickel plates, patent regulator, adjusted, the movement that we recommend, a watch that we guarantee, the highest grade 17 jeweled watch on the market, one that we know will give entire satisfaction	17.50

GUARANTEED SOLID SILVER

SOLID SILVER
GOLD FILLED
GOLD FILLED
SOLID SILVER
GOLD FILLED
SOLID GOLD INLAID

12-Size, Hunting. No. 4R13870

16-Size, Hunting. No. 4R13872

PLEASE ORDER BY NUMBER

GENTLEMEN'S 18-SIZE AND LADIES' 6-SIZE WATCHES

OPEN FACE AND HUNTING STYLE, MADE IN ELECTRO PLATE, GOLD FILLED AND SOLID SILVER

The movements quoted on this page are all of representative makes. They are all well known throughout the country. We warrant each one of them for a term of five years against defective material or workmanship.

$2 24 IN OPEN FACE OR HUNTING STYLE

Electro Plate, 18-Size.
No. 4F903 Open Face, Screw Back and Bezel.
No. 4F905 Hunting Style.

Above all others as the highest possible perfection in watch movements for accurate timekeeping, we recommend the 21 jeweled King Edward movement, manufactured by the Plymouth Watch Co., quoted on this page, described and illustrated on page 24.

These cases are often used by unscrupulous merchants and fake concerns and offered as "high grade gold filled and solid silver," but we tell you plainly just what they represent.

Gold Filled, 18-Size, Guaranteed for 2 Years.
No. 4F907 Open Face, Screw Back and Bezel.
No. 4F909 Hunting Style.

Gold Filled, 18-Size, Guaranteed for 5 years.
No. 4F911 Open Face, Screw Back and Bezel
No. 4F913 Hunting Style.

Gold Filled, 18-Size, Guaranteed for 10 years
No. 4F915 Open Face, Screw Back and Bezel.
No. 4F917 Hunting Style.

$4 40

Solid Silver, 18-Size.
No. 4F919 Hunting Style.

ELECTRO PLATED CASES.

These cases are made by the electro plating process. This is the cheapest known process of plating and we do not guarantee the wearing ability of them. They may wear for one month or six. We offer these electro plated cases for just what they are.

OUR SOLID SILVER CASES

We guarantee to be PURE COIN SILVER through and through, and give our written guarantee to that effect.

We can furnish a fine Leatherette Presentation Case to fit any watch. See page 25.

$4 05

For 90c extra we can furnish a fancy dial and gold hands on any watch on this page.

Solid Silver, 18-Size.
No. 4F921 Open Face, Screw Back and Bezel.

We fit these cases with the following 18-size movements. Prices quoted are for the complete watch, movement and case.	No. 4F903 4F905	No. 4F907	No. 4F909	No. 4F911	No. 4F913	No. 4F915	No. 4F917	No. 4F921	No. 4F919
7 JEWELED EDGEMERE, nickel plates, special make	$2.24	$3.15	$3.50	$3.55	$4.00	$3.85	$4.40	$4.05	$4.40
7 Jeweled Elgin or Waltham, gilt plates	4.26	5.17	5.52	5.57	6.02	5.87	6.42	6.07	6.42
7 Jeweled Elgin or Waltham, nickel plates	4.79	5.70	6.05	6.10	6.55	6.40	6.95	6.60	6.95
12 JEWELED EDGEMERE, nickel plates, special make	3.74	4.65	5.00	5.05	5.50	5.35	5.90	5.55	5.90
15 Jeweled Plymouth Watch Co., patent regulator, nickel plates, special make	5.24	6.15	6.50	6.55	7.00	6.85	7.40	7.05	7.40
15 Jeweled Waltham, gilt plates	5.32	6.23	6.58	6.63	7.08	6.93	7.48	7.13	7.48
15 Jewel Elgin or Waltham, nickel plates	5.84	6.75	7.10	7 15	7.60	7.45	8.00	7.65	8.00
17 JEWELED EDGEMERE, patent regulator, nickel plates, special make	5.14	6.05	6.40	6.45	6.90	6.75	7.30	6.95	7.30
17 Jeweled Elgin or Waltham, not adjusted	5.89	7.80	8.15	8.20	8.65	8.50	9.05	8.70	9.05
17 JEWELED PLYMOUTH WATCH CO., patent regulator, adjusted, nickel plates, special make	8.84	9 75	10.10	10.15	10.60	10.45	11.00	10.65	11.00
17 Jeweled G. M. Wheeler Elgin or P. S. Bartlett Waltham, patent regulator, adjusted, nickel plates	8.99	9.90	10.25	10.30	10.75	10.60	11.15	10.80	11.15
17 Jeweled Appleton, Tracy & Co. Waltham, patent regulator, adjusted, nickel plates	16.34	17.25	17.60	17.65	18.10	17.95	18.50	18.15	18.50
21 JEWELED KING EDWARD PLYMOUTH WATCH CO., patent regulator, adjusted, nickel plates, special make	15.59	16.50	16.85	16.90	17.35	17.20	17.75	17.40	17.75
21 Jeweled John Hancock Hampden, patent regulator, adjusted, nickel plates	15.39	16.30	16.65	16.70	17.15	17.00	17.55	17.20	17.55
21 Jeweled Special Railway Hampden, patent regulator, adjusted, nickel plates	19.34	20.25	20.60	20.65	21.10	20.95	21.50	21.15	21.50
23 Jeweled Special Railway Hampden, patent regulator, adjusted, nickel plates	26.84	27.75	28.10	28.15	28.60	28.45	29.00	28.65	29.00
TRAINMEN'S SPECIAL, STAMPED 23 jeweled, adjusted, special make	2.94	3.85	4.20	4.25	4.70	4.55	5.10	4.75	5.10

We fit these cases with the following 6-size movements. Prices quoted are for the complete watch, movement and case.	No. 4F923	No. 4F925	No. 4F927	No. 4F929	No. 4F931	No. 4F933
7 JEWELED EDGEMERE, special make	$3.20	$4.65	$4.95	$4.33	$4.55	$4.90
COUNTESS JANET, stamped 17 jeweled, adjusted	3.40	4.85	5.15	4.53	4.75	5.10
7 Jeweled Elgin or Waltham, gilt plates	4.75	6.20	6.50	5.88	6.10	6.45
7 Jeweled Elgin or Waltham, nickel plates	5.27	6.72	7.02	6.40	6.62	6.97
12 JEWELED EDGEMERE, nickel plates, special make	4.65	6.10	6.40	5.78	6.00	6.35
15 JEWELED PLYMOUTH WATCH CO., nickel plates, special make	6.15	7.60	7.90	6.98	7.50	7.85
15 Jeweled Elgin or Waltham, nickel plates	6.33	7.78	8.08	7.46	7.68	8.03
16 Jeweled Lady Waltham, nickel plates	8.95	10.40	10.70	10.08	10.30	10.65
17 JEWELED EDGEMERE, nickel plates, patent regulator, special make	5.75	7.20	7.50	6.88	7.10	7.45
17 JEWELED PLYMOUTH WATCH CO., nickel plates, patent regulator, special make	8.70	10.15	10.45	9.83	10.05	10.

$3 20

REGARDING the engraving we generally have the exact pattern, if not we will send very similar design.

Electro Plate, 6-Size.
No. 4F923 Hunting Style.

Solid Silver, 6-Size.
No. 4F925 Open Face.
No. 4F927 Hunting Style.

This is an exact picture of the 15 Jeweled Plymouth Watch Co. Movement.

At $6.15

This high grade 15 jeweled movement fitted in any one of these cases at $6.15 to $7.90, according to case.

WE give with each watch sold our own guarantee to substantiate and verify the manufacturer's.

Gold Filled, 6-Size.
Guaranteed for 2 years.
No. 4F929 Hunting Style.

Gold Filled, 6-Size.
Guaranteed for 5 years.
No. 4F931 Hunting Style.

$4 9-

Gold Filled, 6-Size.
Guaranteed for 10 ye
No 4F933 Hunting

$37.28 BUYS THESE 12 BEAUTIFUL WATCHES,

EXACTLY AS ILLUSTRATED.

SELL THEM IN ONE WEEK FOR $88.50

AND MAKE $51.22 NET PROFIT.

These twelve watches are all gents' 18-size, all stem wind and stem set, all high grade, all covered by our binding guarantee; they are watches that you can easily sell at from $2.00 to $15.00 or $20.00 each.

WATCH No. 1 is an 18-size, nickel plated, open face, an American made, stem wind and stem set watch, a watch you should sell readily for $2.00.

WATCH No. 2 is a gents' 18-size, nickel plated, open face American made watch, stem wind and stem set, a very reliable timepiece. You should be able to sell this watch easily for $2.50.

WATCH No. 3 is a gents' 18-size solid silver, open face, screw back and bezel case, fitted with a high grade 7 jeweled American movement. It's a stem wind watch you ought to be able to sell easily for $5.00.

WATCH No. 4 is a gents' 18-size, open face, screw back and bezel, stem wind and stem set, gold plated case, beautifully engraved, fitted with a 7 jeweled, high grade American movement, a watch you should be able to sell easily for $5.00.

WATCH No. 5 is a gents' 18-size hunting case, stem wind and stem set, gold plated, an elaborately engraved watch, fitted with a high grade 7 jeweled American movement, a watch you should be able to sell easily for $5.00.

WATCH No. 6 is a gents' 18-size, open face, a screw back and screw bezel, gold filled case, made of two plates of solid gold over an inner plate of hard composition metal, guaranteed for 10 years, elaborately engraved and decorated, fitted with a 7 jeweled American movement. You should be able to sell it easily for $10.00.

WATCH No. 7 is a gents' 18-size hunting case, stem wind and stem set, gold filled, guaranteed for 10 years. It is elaborately engraved and decorated, is fitted with a high grade 7 jeweled American movement, and you should be able to sell it easily for $10.00.

WATCH No. 8 is a gents' 18-size, screw back and screw bezel, gold filled watch, guaranteed for 5 years (will last a natural lifetime), elaborately engraved and decorated, stem wind and stem set, is fitted with a high grade 7 jeweled American movement. You should sell this watch easily for $7.00.

WATCH No. 9 is a gents' 18-size hunting case gold filled watch, guaranteed for 5 years, elaborately engraved, stem wind and stem set, fitted with a high grade 7 jeweled American movement. You should sell this watch easily for $7.00.

WATCH No. 10 is a gents' 18-size hunting gold filled case, guaranteed for 20 years, elaborately engraved and decorated, stem wind and stem set, fitted with an extra high grade 23 jeweled Locomotive Special Movement. This watch you should sell easily for $15.00.

WATCH No. 11 is a gents' 18-size open face, screw back and bezel gold filled case, guaranteed for 20 years, elaborately engraved, stem wind and stem set, fitted with a 23 jeweled Locomotive Special Movement. This watch you should sell easily for $15.00.

WATCH No. 12 is a 12-size gents' open face, snap front and snap back, oxidized white metal, an exact imitation of solid silver, fitted with a fine jeweled Swiss imported cylinder movement, stem wind and stem set. This watch you should sell easily for $5.00.

SEND US $37.28, mention Special Offer No. 4F950, we will send these watches to you by express, guaranteeing them to reach you in perfect order in just a few days. After you receive them you can give them a thorough test and if you are not perfectly satisfied with your purchase, if you are not satisfied you can sell these twelve watches at from $75.00 to $100.00 in a very short time and thus make from $50.00 to $75.00 net profit, you can return them to us at our expense, and we will immediately refund your money.

THE ILLUSTRATIONS AND ENGRAVINGS, taken direct from the watches by our artists, will give you a general idea of the appearance. They are all high grade, all new styles for this season. The movements shown hereon are the movements fitted in these watches, Trainmen's Locomotive Special, stamped 23 jewels, with patent regulator, and the other a high grade American movement. Among these watches are the highest grade 20-year, 10-year and 5-year gold filled cases made in the world. Cases made by the best makers in this country, made from two heavy plates of solid gold over inner plates of hard composition metal, and guaranteed to wear for five, ten and twenty years as stated, and with fair usage will last a natural lifetime. NEVER BEFORE WAS SUCH WATCH VALUE OFFERED

SEND $37.28 FOR THESE TWELVE WATCHES, trade one or two of the watches in even pay for a cow or a horse, trade them for horses, cattle, vehicles, accounts, due bills, sell them for cash, trade them in on lots and other property. You can realize the $37.28 you paid us three or four times over, for no such trading value was ever given in any lot of merchandise as we show in these twelve watches for only $37.28. AT OUR SPECIAL PRICE WE CANNOT BREAK THE LOT. Not less than twelve watches will be sold To get this heretofore unheard of price, to get a lot of watches that you can easily sell in a week's time at from $75.00 to $100.00 you must order the whole lot. Send us $37.28 and we will send the watches to you with the understanding and agreement that if they are not perfectly satisfactory you can return them to us at our expense and get your money back

YOUR MONEY BACK IN A DAY. It is more than likely if you send $37.28 for these twelve watches you will sell one or two of them the day you get the twelve for enough to pay for the entire lot of twelve watches. You will most likely sell the No. 10 or No. 11 or both 20-year gold filled cases with Locomotive Special Movements, you are likely to sell either of these watches for $37.28, you are likely to sell both of them for from $50.00 to $60.00 the day you get the outfit, thus getting your money back and leaving you ten watches over for your profit free of any cost to you. This is a great opportunity for dealers, for general stores, for traders of all kinds, for no such value ever before went out of any wholesale watch house or watch factory.

No. 4F950 TWELVE WATCHES AS DESCRIBED. Price..........$37.2

18-SIZE HUNTING STYLE AND OPEN FACE SCREW BACK AND SCREW BEZEL, 14-KARAT GOLD FILLED CASES, WARRANTED 25 YEARS.

WHAT WE MEAN BY THE SEARS LIFE GUARANTEED CASE.

The Sears Life Guaranteed Case is a gold filled case of the very highest quality and the nearest approach to a solid gold case manufactured. The Sears Life Guaranteed Case means that should any one of these cases wear down to the inner composition metal any time within your natural life, whether you have owned the case five years, twenty years or fifty years, return it to us, and we will, upon the receipt of same, exchange it for a brand new case of same quality, free of charge.

We recommend the SEARS LIFE GUARANTEED CASE.

For 90 cents extra we can furnish a fancy dial and gold hands on any watch on this page.

Illinois Watch Co. Warranted for 25 years.
No. 4E1802 Open Face, Screw Back and Bezel.
No. 4E1804 Hunting Style.

Description of Plymouth Watch Co.'s 17-Jeweled, 18-Size, Specially Made Movement.

Solid nickel through and through, 17 jewels, adjusted. Full plate, fancy solid gold damaskeened finish, lever escapement, five pair gold settings, full compensation double cut expansion balance wheel, adjusted to isochronism and position, patent micrometer regulator, genuine ruby jeweled pin, highly polished bevel edge screws, fully protecting dust band, safety pinion, double sunk, white enameled dial and sunk second hand dial. The superior construction of this movement adapts it to the most exacting service.

John C. Dueber Gold Filled. Warranted for 25 Years.
No. 4E1806 Open Face. Screw Back and Bezel.
No. 4E1808 Hunting Style.

Sears Gold Filled. Life Guarantee.
No. 4E1810 Open Face, Screw Back and Bezel.
No. 4E1812 Hunting Style.

$7.65 complete with the EDGEMERE MOVEMENT

For 20 cents we furnish a beautiful plush Presentation Case to fit any watch. See No. 4E588, page 27.

Sears Gold Filled. Life Guarantee.
No. 4E1814 Open Face, Screw Back and Bezel.
No. 4E1816 Hunting Style.

WE FIT THESE CASES WITH THE FOLLOWING 18-SIZE MOVEMENTS	Open Face. 25 yrs. 4E1802 4E1806 4E1819 4E1822 4E1830	Hunting. 25 yrs. 4E1804 4E1808 4E1821 4E1824 4E1832	Sears. Life. Open Face. 4E1810 4E1814 4E1826	Sears. Life. Hunting. 4E1812 4E1816 4E1828
7 Jeweled EDGEMERE, nickel plates.	$6.35	$8.30	$7.65	10.15
7 Jeweled Elgin or Waltham, gilt plates..	8.37	10.32	9.67	12.17
7 Jeweled Elgin or Waltham, nickel plates.	8.90	10.85	10.20	12.70
12 Jeweled EDGEMERE, nickel plates.	8.20	10.15	9.50	12.00
15 Jeweled PLYMOUTH WATCH CO., patent regulator, nickel plates.	9.80	11.75	11.10	13.60
15 Jeweled Waltham, gilt plates.	9.43	11.38	10.73	13.23
15 Jeweled Elgin or Waltham, nickel plates.	9.95	11.90	11.25	13.75
17 Jeweled EDGEMERE, patent regulator, nickel plates	9.30	11.25	10.60	13.10
17 Jeweled Elgin or Waltham, not adjusted.	11.00	12.95	12.30	14.80
17 Jeweled PLYMOUTH WATCH CO., patent regulator, adjusted, nickel plates	14.20	16.15	15.50	18.00
17 Jeweled G. M. Wheeler Elgin or P. S. Bartlett Waltham, patent regulator, adjusted, nickel plates......	15.20	17.15	16.50	19.00
17 Jeweled Appleton, Tracy & Co. Waltham, patent regulator, adjusted, nickel plates	20.45	22.40	21.75	24.25
21 Jeweled KING EDWARD, PLYMOUTH WATCH CO., patent regulator, adjusted, nickel plates........	19.45	21.40	20.75	23.25
21 Jeweled John Hancock, Hampden, patent regulator, adjusted, nickel plates.......	19.70	21.65	21.00	23.50
21 Jeweled Special Railway Hampden, patent regulator, adjusted, nickel plates	23.45	25.40	24.75	27.25
23 Jeweled Special Railway Hampden, patent regulator, adjusted, nickel plates	30.95	32.90	32.25	34.75
TRAINMEN'S SPECIAL, stamped 23 Jewels, adjusted..........	6.80	8.75	8.10	10.60

ABOVE ALL OTHERS, as the highest possible perfection in watch movements, for accurate time keeping, we recommend the 21 jeweled adjusted **KING EDWARD** movement, manufactured by the Plymouth Watch Company, quoted on this page and described and illustrated on page 25.

YOU CAN PICK ANY OF THESE DESIGNS AND HAVE THE BEST.

Protect your watch with an Ajax Watch Insulator. See page 27. No. 4E586 Price, 18c.

Wadsworth Gold Filled. Warranted 25 Years.
No. 4E1819 Open Face, Screw Back and Bezel.
No. 4E1821 Hunting Style.

IF NOT SATISFIED with Your Watch try a SEARS.

DEALERS AND TRADERS TAKE NOTE. Your choice of six 25-year gold filled watches, selected from this page, three open face and three hunting style, fitted with 7-jeweled Elgin or Waltham gilt movements for $63.82. When ordering this assortment, ask for assortment No. 4E14.

Ill. Watch Co. Gold Filled. Warranted for 25 Years.
No. 4E1822 Open Face, Screw Back and Bezel.
No. 4E1824 Hunting Style.

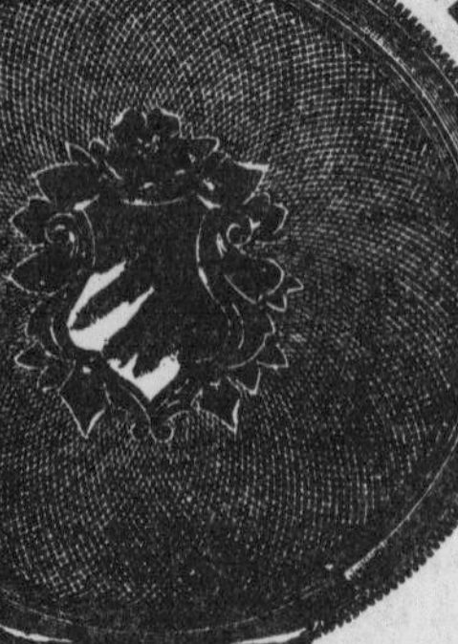

Sears Gold Filled. Life Guarantee.
No. 4E1826 Open Face, Screw Back and Bezel.
No. 4E1828 Hunting Style.

THIS IS THE PICTURE OF OUR PLYMOUTH WATCH CO.'S SPECIAL MOVEMENT.

IT IS A FULL 15 JEWELED,

Handsomely Damaskeened, patent regulator and escapement, safety pinion, jewels set in settings, guaranteed for five years and one of the best high grade movements on the market. We fit in any of these cases at $9.80 to $13.60.

FOR 90c extra we can furnish a fancy dial and gold hands on any watch on this page.

You can buy one watch from us cheaper than your local dealer does when he buys ten elsewhere.

Ill. Watch Co. Gold Filled. Warranted for 25 Years.
No. 4E1830 Open Face, Screw Back and Bezel.
No. 4E1832 Hunting Style.

16-SIZE GOLD FILLED EXTRA THIN MODEL WATCH CASES.

MANUFACTURED BY THE MOST CELEBRATED MAKERS.

Protect your Watch with an AJAX WATCH INSULATOR. See page 27. No. 4E586 Price.. 18c

GOLD FILLED, HUNTING AND OPEN FACE SCREW BACK AND BEZEL, DUST AND DAMP PROOF CASES.

For the best cheap watch in 16-size, we recommend above all others our new 7 jeweled Edgemere. It is guaranteed, but for a watch that costs but a few dollars more and gives better satisfaction, for accuracy, we recommend our 15 jeweled Plymouth Watch Co., or our 17 jeweled Plymouth Watch Co., Special adjusted.

All of the above carry our five-year written, binding guarantee.

The SEARS GOLD FILLED CASE is recommended above all others.

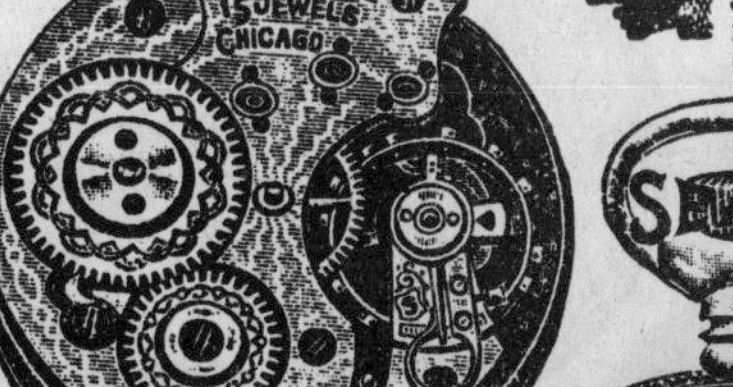

Picture of our 15 Jeweled EDGEMERE fitted in our SEARS CASE for $7.65.

$4.80 TO $27.50

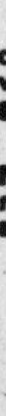

16-Size. Illinois Watch Case Co. Gold Filled.
No. 4E1900 Open Face, Screw Back and Bezel, 20-year.
No. 4E1901 Hunting, 20-year.

GUARANTEED FOR 20 YEARS.
No. 4E1902 Open Face, Screw Back and Bezel.
No. 4E1904 Hunting Style.

GUARANTEED FOR 20 YEARS.
No. 4E1911 Open Face, Screw Back and Bezel
No. 4E1913 Hunting Style.

$7.65 fitted with the 15-Jeweled Edgemere.

ABOVE ALL OTHERS, as the highest possible perfection in watch movements for accurate timekeeping, we recommend the 21 jeweled adjusted Prince of Wales movement, manufactured by the Plymouth Watch Co., quoted on this page and described and illustrated on page 25.

THE OPEN FACE CASES SHOWN ON THIS PAGE ARE ALL SCREW BEZEL AND SCREW BACK.

Illinois Watch Case Co. Gold Filled.
GUARANTEED FOR 20 YEARS.
No. 4E1906 Open Face, Screw Back and Bezel.
No. 4E1908 Hunting Style.

THE SEARS is the latest and best made

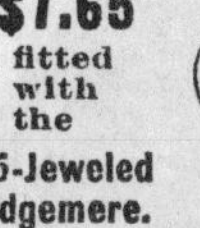

WE FIT THESE CASES WITH THE FOLLOWING 16-SIZE MOVEMENTS:	Open Face Screw Back and Bezel	Hunting Style
7 Jeweled EDGEMERE, NICKEL PLATES	$ 4.80	$ 6.55
7 Jeweled Elgin or Waltham	7.90	9.65
15 Jeweled EDGEMERE, NICKEL PLATES	7.65	9.40
15 Jeweled Elgin or Waltham	8.47	11.22
15 Jeweled Elgin or Waltham, patent regulator	10.00	11.75
15 Jeweled PLYMOUTH WATCH CO., SPECIAL MAKE	9.30	11.05
17 Jeweled Elgin or Waltham, not adjusted	12.10	13.85
17 Jeweled No. 241 grade Elgin or 630 grade Waltham, adjusted	14.72	16.47
17 Jeweled PLYMOUTH WATCH CO., SPECIAL MAKE, NICKEL PLATES, PATENT REGULATOR, ADJUSTED	13.15	14.90
17 Jeweled Royal Waltham, adjusted, nickel plates	17.08	18.83
17 Jeweled Riverside Waltham, adjusted, nickel plates	24.17	25.92
17 Jeweled No. 243 grade Elgin, adjusted, nickel plates	25.75	27.50
21 Jeweled PRINCE OF WALES, PLYMOUTH WATCH CO., FULL ADJUSTED, PATENT REGULATOR, NICKEL PLATES	19.65	21.40

GUARANTEED FOR 20 YEARS.
No. 4E1914 Open Face, Screw Back and Bezel.
No. 4E1916 Hunting Style.

14 CENTS Will carry any of these watches by registered mail to any part of the United States.

GUARANTEED FOR 20 YEARS.
No. 4E1919 Open Face, Screw Back and Bezel.
No. 4E1921 Hunting Style.

$4.80 TO $27.50

$19.65 fitted with our 21 Jeweled Adjusted Movement.

FOR 20 CENTS we furnish a beautiful plush Presentation Case to fit any watch. See No. 4E586 on page 27.

GUARANTEED FOR 20 YEARS.
No. 4E1926 Open Face, Screw Back and Bezel.
No. 4E1928 Hunting Style.

GUARANTEED FOR 20 YEARS.
No. 4E1930 Open Face, Screw Back and Bezel.
No. 4E1932 Hunting Style.

GUARANTEED FOR 20 YEARS.
No. 4E1923 Open Face, Screw Back and Bezel.
No. 4E1925 Hunting Style.

DEALERS AND TRADERS TAKE NOTE.
Your choice of any six watches on this page, three open face and three hunting style, fitted with 7 jeweled Edgemere movements, for $30.65, or if you prefer them fitted with the splendid Plymouth Watch Co. movements, we can supply the six watches for $54.95. When ordering this assortment, ask for assortment No. 4E16.

GUARANTEED FOR 20 YEARS.
No. 4E1934 Open Face, Screw Back and Bezel.
No. 4E1936 Hunting Style.

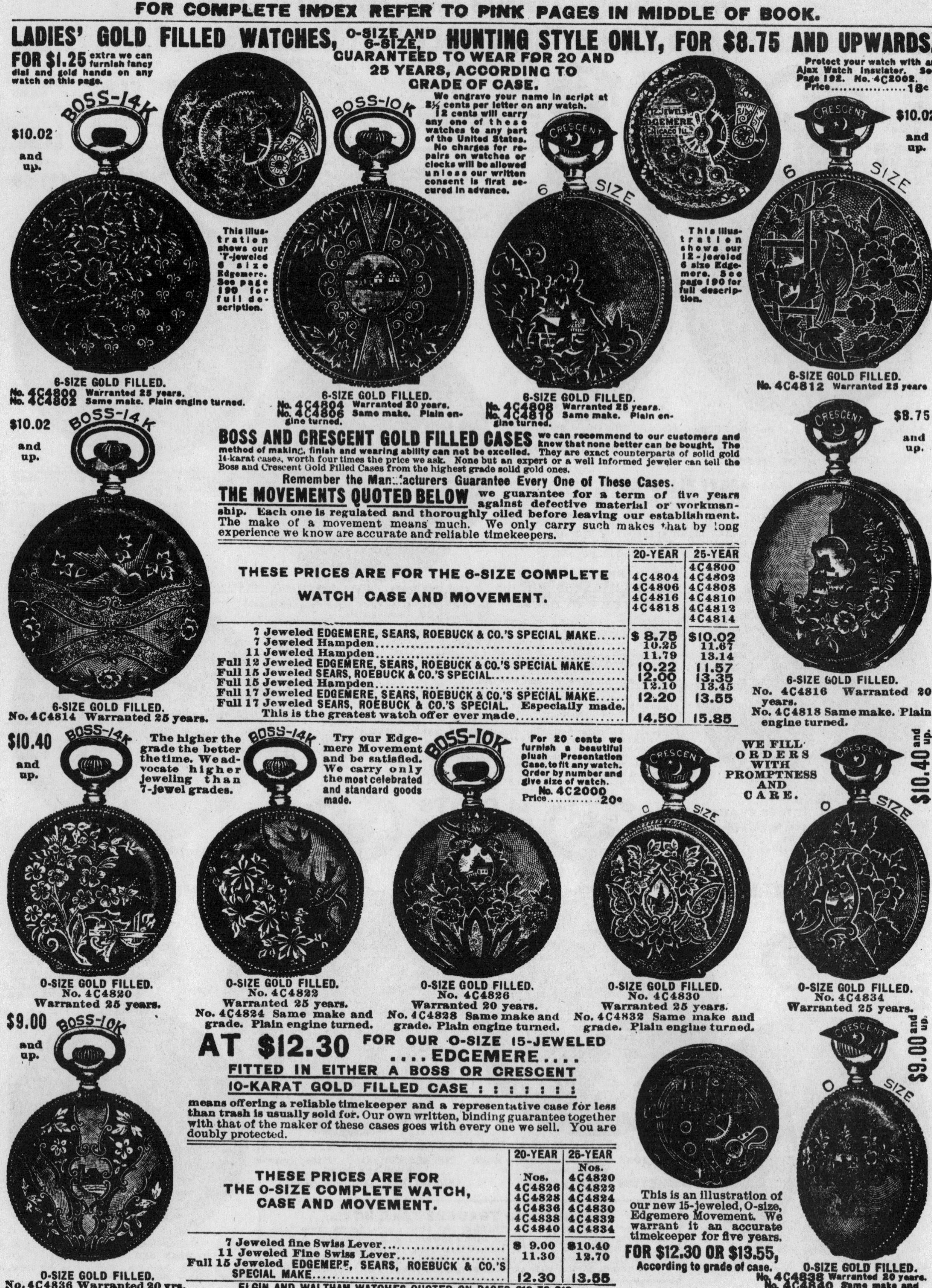

LADIES' GOLD FILLED WATCHES, 0-SIZE AND 6-SIZE, HUNTING STYLE ONLY, FOR $8.75 AND UPWARDS.

FOR $1.25 extra we can furnish fancy dial and gold hands on any watch on this page.

GUARANTEED TO WEAR FOR 20 AND 25 YEARS, ACCORDING TO GRADE OF CASE.

Protect your watch with an Ajax Watch Insulator. See Page 192. No. 4C2002. Price.................18c

We engrave your name in script at 2½ cents per letter on any watch.

12 cents will carry any one of these watches to any part of the United States.

No charges for repairs on watches or clocks will be allowed unless our written consent is first secured in advance.

BOSS-14K — $10.02 and up.

This illustration shows our 7-jeweled 6 size Edgemere. See page 190 for full description.

BOSS-10K

CRESCENT — 6 SIZE

This illustration shows our 12-jeweled 6 size Edgemere. See page 190 for full description.

CRESCENT — 6 SIZE — $10.02 and up.

6-SIZE GOLD FILLED.
No. 4C4800 Warranted 25 years.
No. 4C4802 Same make. Plain engine turned.

6-SIZE GOLD FILLED.
No. 4C4804 Warranted 20 years.
No. 4C4806 Same make. Plain engine turned.

6-SIZE GOLD FILLED.
No. 4C4808 Warranted 25 years.
No. 4C4810 Same make. Plain engine turned.

6-SIZE GOLD FILLED.
No. 4C4812 Warranted 25 years

BOSS-14K — $10.02 and up.

CRESCENT — $8.75 and up.

BOSS AND CRESCENT GOLD FILLED CASES

we can recommend to our customers and know that none better can be bought. The method of making, finish and wearing ability can not be excelled. They are exact counterparts of solid gold 14-karat cases, worth four times the price we ask. None but an expert or a well informed jeweler can tell the Boss and Crescent Gold Filled Cases from the highest grade solid gold ones.

Remember the Manufacturers Guarantee Every One of These Cases.

THE MOVEMENTS QUOTED BELOW we guarantee for a term of five years against defective material or workmanship. Each one is regulated and thoroughly oiled before leaving our establishment. The make of a movement means much. We only carry such makes that by long experience we know are accurate and reliable timekeepers.

THESE PRICES ARE FOR THE 6-SIZE COMPLETE WATCH CASE AND MOVEMENT.	20-YEAR 4C4804 4C4806 4C4816 4C4818	25-YEAR 4C4800 4C4802 4C4808 4C4810 4C4812 4C4814
7 Jeweled EDGEMERE, SEARS, ROEBUCK & CO.'S SPECIAL MAKE......	$ 8.75	$10.02
7 Jeweled Hampden..........	10.25	11.67
11 Jeweled Hampden..........	11.79	13.14
Full 12 Jeweled EDGEMERE, SEARS, ROEBUCK & CO.'S SPECIAL MAKE.......	10.22	11.57
Full 15 Jeweled SEARS, ROEBUCK & CO.'S SPECIAL..........	12.00	13.35
Full 15 Jeweled Hampden..........	12.10	13.45
Full 17 Jeweled EDGEMERE, SEARS, ROEBUCK & CO.'S SPECIAL MAKE......	12.20	13.55
Full 17 Jeweled SEARS, ROEBUCK & CO.'S SPECIAL. Especially made. This is the greatest watch offer ever made..........	14.50	15.85

6-SIZE GOLD FILLED.
No. 4C4814 Warranted 25 years.

6-SIZE GOLD FILLED.
No. 4C4816 Warranted 20 years.
No. 4C4818 Same make. Plain engine turned.

BOSS-14K — $10.40 and up.

The higher the grade the better the time. We advocate higher jeweling than 7-jewel grades.

BOSS-14K

Try our Edgemere Movement and be satisfied. We carry only the most celebrated and standard goods made.

BOSS-10K

For 20 cents we furnish a beautiful plush Presentation Case, to fit any watch. Order by number and give size of watch. No. 4C2000 Price..........20c

CRESCENT — 0 SIZE

WE FILL ORDERS WITH PROMPTNESS AND CARE.

CRESCENT — 0 SIZE — $10.40 and up.

0-SIZE GOLD FILLED.
No. 4C4820
Warranted 25 years.

0-SIZE GOLD FILLED.
No. 4C4822
Warranted 25 years.
No. 4C4824 Same make and grade. Plain engine turned.

0-SIZE GOLD FILLED.
No. 4C4826
Warranted 20 years.
No. 4C4828 Same make and grade. Plain engine turned.

0-SIZE GOLD FILLED.
No. 4C4830
Warranted 25 years.
No. 4C4832 Same make and grade. Plain engine turned.

0-SIZE GOLD FILLED.
No. 4C4834
Warranted 25 years.

BOSS-10K — $9.00 and up.

AT $12.30 FOR OUR 0-SIZE 15-JEWELED ....EDGEMERE.... FITTED IN EITHER A BOSS OR CRESCENT 10-KARAT GOLD FILLED CASE : : : : : : :

means offering a reliable timekeeper and a representative case for less than trash is usually sold for. Our own written, binding guarantee together with that of the maker of these cases goes with every one we sell. You are doubly protected.

THESE PRICES ARE FOR THE 0-SIZE COMPLETE WATCH, CASE AND MOVEMENT.	20-YEAR Nos. 4C4826 4C4828 4C4836 4C4838 4C4840	25-YEAR Nos. 4C4820 4C4822 4C4824 4C4830 4C4832 4C4834
7 Jeweled fine Swiss Lever..........	$ 9.00	$10.40
11 Jeweled Fine Swiss Lever..........	11.30	12.70
Full 15 Jeweled EDGEMERE, SEARS, ROEBUCK & CO.'S SPECIAL MAKE..........	12.30	13.55

ELGIN AND WALTHAM WATCHES QUOTED ON PAGES 216 TO 218.

0-SIZE GOLD FILLED.
No. 4C4836 Warranted 20 yrs.

This is an illustration of our new 15-jeweled, 0-size, Edgemere Movement. We warrant it an accurate timekeeper for five years.

FOR $12.30 OR $13.55, According to grade of case.

CRESCENT — 0 SIZE — $9.00 and up.

0-SIZE GOLD FILLED.
No. 4C4838 Warranted 20 years.
No. 4C4840 Same make and grade. Plain engine turned.

Gentlemen's Elgin and Waltham 18-Size Gold Filled, Solid Silver and Silverine Watches for $5.08 and Upwards

OPEN FACE AND HUNTING STYLE.

ALL OPEN FACE CASES SHOWN HERE ARE SCREW BACK AND SCREW BEZEL, DUST AND DAMP PROOF.

Protect your Watch with an Ajax Watch Insulator. See page 192. Price, 18c.

FOR 20 CENTS we furnish a beautiful plush PRESENTATION CASE to fit any watch. Order by number and give size of watch. No. 4C2000 Price, 20c

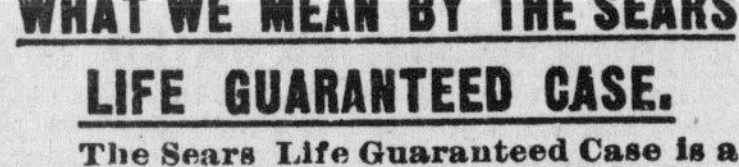

WHAT WE MEAN BY THE SEARS LIFE GUARANTEED CASE.

The Sears Life Guaranteed Case is a solid gold filled case of the very highest quality and the nearest approach to a solid gold case manufactured. The Sears Life Guaranteed Case means that should any one of these cases wear down to the inner composition metal any time within your natural life, whether you have owned the case five years, twenty years or fifty years, return it to us and we will upon the receipt of same exchange it for a brand new case of same quality, free of charge.

$7.48 AND UP.

SOLID SILVER.—3 and 4-ounce.
No. 4C4900 Open Face, Screw Back and Bezel, 3-ounce.
No. 4C4902 Hunting, 3-ounce.
No. 4C4904 Open Face, Screw Back and Bezel, 4-ounce.
No. 4C4906 Hunting, 4-ounce.
No. 4C4908 Open Face, Solid Back, Screw Front. Dust and damp proof.

SEARS. GOLD FILLED.
No. 4C4907 Open Face, Screw Back and Bezel, 20-year.
No. 4C4909 Hunting, 20-year.
No. 4C4911 Open Face, Screw Back and Bezel, Life Guarantee.
No. 4C4913 Hunting, Life Guarantee.

ILLINOIS WATCH CASE CO. GOLD FILLED.
No. 4C4919 Open Face, Screw Back and Bezel, 20-year.
No. 4C4921 Hunting, 20-year.
No. 4C4923 Open Face, Screw Back and Bezel, 25-year.
No. 4C4925 Hunting, 25-year.

WE FIT THESE CASES WITH THE FOLLOWING 18-SIZE MOVEMENTS:	Nos. 4C4900 4C4908 4C4907 4C4919 4C4926	No. 4C4934	No. 4C4902	Nos. 4C4946 4C4948	Nos. 4C4904 4C4906	Nos. 4C4909 4C4921 4C4928	No. 4C4936	Nos. 4C4923 4C4930	No. 4C4938	Nos. 4C4925 4C4932	No. 4C4940	No. 4C4911	No. 4C4913
7 Jeweled Grade Elgin or Waltham	$7.48	$9.17	$7.58	$7.88	$8.23	$9.53	11.47	$9.48	11.72	11.73	14.47	12.37	15.47
Full 15 Jeweled Grade Elgin or Waltham	9.05	10.75	9.15	9.55	9.78	11.10	13.05	11.05	13.30	13.30	16.05	13.95	17.05
Full 17 Jeweled Grade Elgin or Waltham	11.42	13.10	11.52	11.92	12.10	13.47	15.40	13.42	15.65	15.67	18.40	16.30	19.40
Full 17 Jeweled G. M. Wheeler, Elgin or P. S. Bartlett Waltham, adjusted	13.25	14.95	13.35	13.75	13.90	15.30	17.25	15.25	17.50	17.50	20.25	18.15	21.25
Full 17 Jeweled B. W. Raymond Elgin, or Appleton Tracy Premier Grade Waltham, adjusted........	22.17	23.87	22.27	22.67	22.92	24.22	26.17	24.22	26.42	26.42	29.15	27.07	30.15
Full 21 Jeweled "Father Time" Elgin or Crescent St. Waltham, adjusted..	26.37	28.07	26.47	26.87	Not fur-	28.42	30.37	28.37	30.62	30.62	33.37	31.27	34.37
Full 21 Jeweled Vanguard Waltham, adjusted..........	31.62	33.32	31.72	32.12	nished	33.67	35.62	33.62	35.87	35.87	38.62	36.52	39.62
Full 19 Jeweled B. W. Raymond Elgin, or Crescent St. Waltham. Made in Open Face Only.........	Not furnished	Not Made	Not Made	Not furnished	Not Made	Not Made	Not Made	25.75	28.00	Not Made	Not Made	28.65	Not Made
Full 19 Jeweled Vanguard Waltham......	29.00	30.70	29.10	29.50	Not furnished	31.05	33.01	31.00	33.26	33.25	36.00	33.91	37.00
Full 21 Jeweled Veritas Elgin, Made in Open Face Only..........	Not furnished	Not Made	Not Made	Not furnished	Not Made	Not Made	Not Made	33.62	35.87	Not Made	Not Made	36.52	Not Made
Full 23 Jeweled Veritas Elgin, Made in Open Face Only..........		Not Made	Not Made		Not Made	Not Made	Not Made	36.25	38.50	Not Made	Not Made	39.15	Not Made

$7.48 AND UP.

DUEBER. GOLD FILLED.
No. 4C4926 Open Face, Screw Back and Bezel, 20-year.
No. 4C4928 Hunting, 20-year.
No. 4C4930 Open Face, Screw Back and Bezel, 25-year.
No. 4C4932 Hunting, 25-year.

FOR $1.25 EXTRA WE CAN FURNISH FANCY DIAL AND GOLD HANDS ON ANY WATCH ON THIS PAGE.

$9.17 AND UP.

FAHYS. GOLD FILLED.
No. 4C4934 Open Face, Screw Back and Bezel, warranted 20 years.
No. 4C4936 Hunting, warranted 20 years.
No. 4C4938 Open Face, Screw Back and Bezel, warranted 25 years.
No. 4C4940 Hunting, warranted 25 years.

FOR $7.48 THE SEARS 20-year Open Face Gold Filled Case and an Elgin or Waltham movement or $9.53 for the same movement fitted in the SEARS HUNTING STYLE CASE means you can own the best for LITTLE MONEY

SILVERINE.
No. 4C4942 Open Face, Screw Back and Bezel. Fitted with 7-jeweled Elgin or Waltham movement. Price............ $5.08
Not furnished with any other movements.
No. 4C4944 Hunting. Fitted with 7-jeweled Elgin or Waltham movement. Price............ $5.43
Not furnished with any other Elgin or Waltham movements. SEE PAGE 195.

$7.88 AND UP.

SOLID SILVER. 3-ounce Solid Silver Open Face, Screw Back and Bezel, Gold Inlaid Subjects.
No. 4C4946 Engine Inlaid.
No. 4C4948 Stag Inlaid.

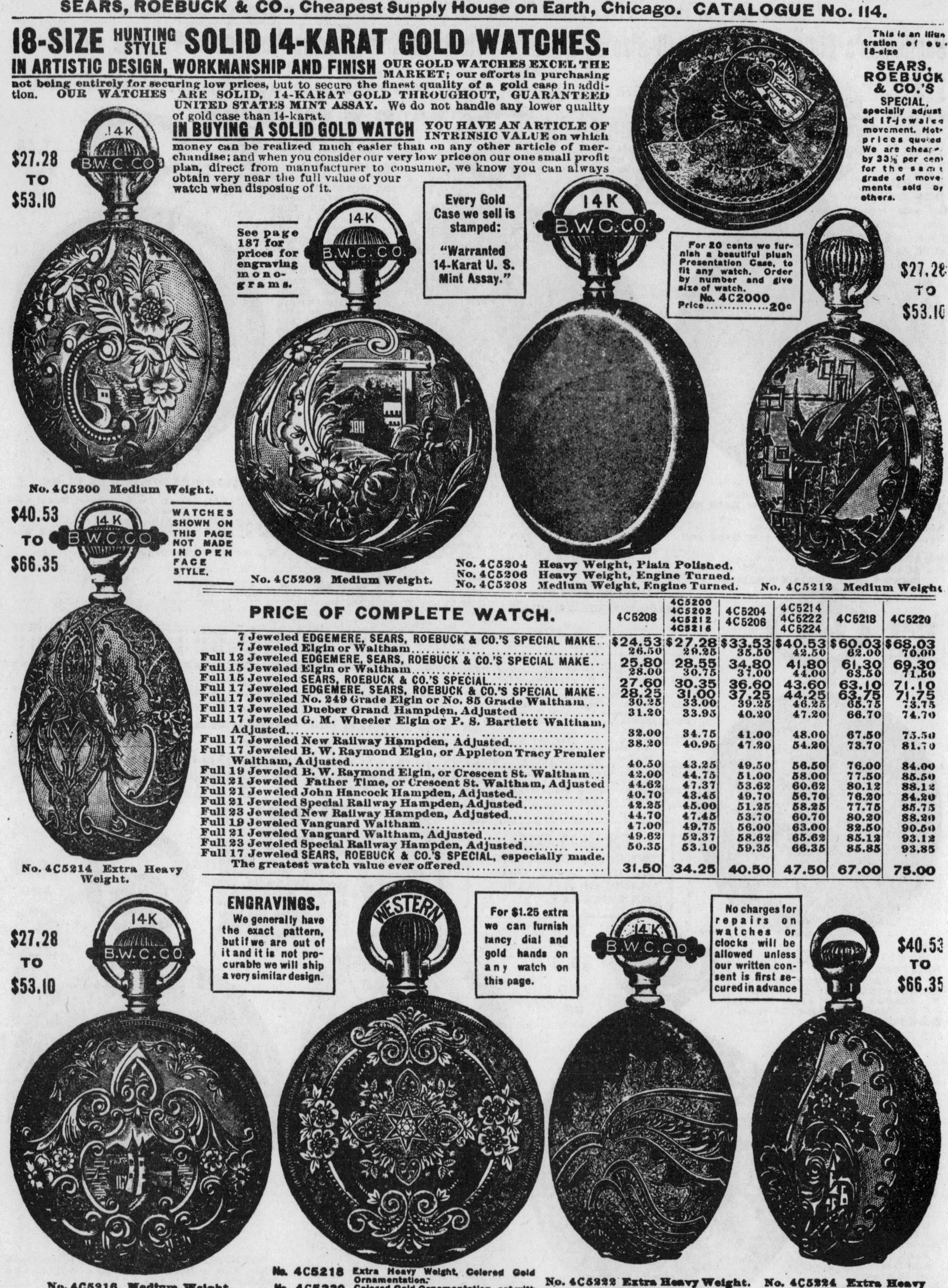

18-SIZE HUNTING STYLE SOLID 14-KARAT GOLD WATCHES.

IN ARTISTIC DESIGN, WORKMANSHIP AND FINISH OUR GOLD WATCHES EXCEL THE MARKET; our efforts in purchasing not being entirely for securing low prices, but to secure the finest quality of a gold case in addition. OUR WATCHES ARE SOLID, 14-KARAT GOLD THROUGHOUT, GUARANTEED UNITED STATES MINT ASSAY. We do not handle any lower quality of gold case than 14-karat.

IN BUYING A SOLID GOLD WATCH YOU HAVE AN ARTICLE OF INTRINSIC VALUE on which money can be realized much easier than on any other article of merchandise; and when you consider our very low price on our one small profit plan, direct from manufacturer to consumer, we know you can always obtain very near the full value of your watch when disposing of it.

This is an illustration of our 18-size SEARS, ROEBUCK & CO.'S SPECIAL, specially adjusted 17-jeweled movement. Hot-prices quoted. We are cheaper by 33⅓ per cent for the same grade of movements sold by others.

$27.28 TO $53.10

See page 187 for prices for engraving monograms.

Every Gold Case we sell is stamped: "Warranted 14-Karat U. S. Mint Assay."

For 20 cents we furnish a beautiful plush Presentation Case, to fit any watch. Order by number and give size of watch.
No. 4C2000
Price..............20c

$27.28 TO $53.10

No. 4C5200 Medium Weight.

$40.53 TO $66.35

WATCHES SHOWN ON THIS PAGE NOT MADE IN OPEN FACE STYLE.

No. 4C5202 Medium Weight.

No. 4C5204 Heavy Weight, Plain Polished.
No. 4C5206 Heavy Weight, Engine Turned.
No. 4C5208 Medium Weight, Engine Turned.

No. 4C5212 Medium Weight.

No. 4C5214 Extra Heavy Weight.

PRICE OF COMPLETE WATCH.

	4C5208	4C5200 4C5202 4C5212 4C5216	4C5204 4C5206	4C5214 4C5222 4C5224	4C5218	4C5220
7 Jeweled EDGEMERE, SEARS, ROEBUCK & CO.'S SPECIAL MAKE..	$24.53	$27.28	$33.53	$40.53	$60.03	$68.03
7 Jeweled Elgin or Waltham	26.50	29.25	35.50	42.50	62.00	70.00
Full 12 Jeweled EDGEMERE, SEARS, ROEBUCK & CO.'S SPECIAL MAKE..	25.80	28.55	34.80	41.80	61.30	69.30
Full 15 Jeweled Elgin or Waltham	28.00	30.75	37.00	44.00	63.50	71.50
Full 15 Jeweled SEARS, ROEBUCK & CO.'S SPECIAL	27.60	30.35	36.60	43.60	63.10	71.10
Full 17 Jeweled EDGEMERE, SEARS, ROEBUCK & CO.'S SPECIAL MAKE..	28.25	31.00	37.25	44.25	63.75	71.75
Full 17 Jeweled No. 249 Grade Elgin or No. 85 Grade Waltham	30.25	33.00	39.25	46.25	65.75	73.75
Full 17 Jeweled Dueber Grand Hampden, Adjusted	31.20	33.95	40.20	47.20	66.70	74.70
Full 17 Jeweled G. M. Wheeler Elgin or P. S. Bartlett Waltham, Adjusted	32.00	34.75	41.00	48.00	67.50	75.50
Full 17 Jeweled New Railway Hampden, Adjusted	38.20	40.95	47.20	54.20	73.70	81.70
Full 17 Jeweled B. W. Raymond Elgin, or Appleton Tracy Premier Waltham, Adjusted	40.50	43.25	49.50	56.50	76.00	84.00
Full 19 Jeweled B. W. Raymond Elgin, or Crescent St. Waltham	42.00	44.75	51.00	58.00	77.50	85.50
Full 21 Jeweled Father Time, or Crescent St. Waltham, Adjusted	44.62	47.37	53.62	60.62	80.12	88.12
Full 21 Jeweled John Hancock Hampden, Adjusted	40.70	43.45	49.70	56.70	76.20	84.20
Full 21 Jeweled Special Railway Hampden, Adjusted	42.25	45.00	51.25	58.25	77.75	85.75
Full 23 Jeweled New Railway Hampden, Adjusted	44.70	47.45	53.70	60.70	80.20	88.20
Full 19 Jeweled Vanguard Waltham	47.00	49.75	56.00	63.00	82.50	90.50
Full 21 Jeweled Vanguard Waltham, Adjusted	49.62	52.37	58.62	65.62	85.12	93.12
Full 23 Jeweled Special Railway Hampden, Adjusted	50.35	53.10	59.35	66.35	85.85	93.85
Full 17 Jeweled SEARS, ROEBUCK & CO.'S SPECIAL, especially made. The greatest watch value ever offered	31.50	34.25	40.50	47.50	67.00	75.00

$27.28 TO $53.10

ENGRAVINGS. We generally have the exact pattern, but if we are out of it and it is not procurable we will ship a very similar design.

For $1.25 extra we can furnish fancy dial and gold hands on any watch on this page.

No charges for repairs on watches or clocks will be allowed unless our written consent is first secured in advance.

$40.53 TO $66.35

No. 4C5216 Medium Weight.

No. 4C5218 Extra Heavy Weight, Colored Gold Ornamentation.
No. 4C5220 Colored Gold Ornamentation, set with Fine Large Diamond.

No. 4C5222 Extra Heavy Weight.

No. 4C5224 Extra Heavy Weight.

FOR COMPLETE INDEX REFER TO PINK PAGES IN MIDDLE OF BOOK.

12 AND 16-SIZE THIN MODEL SOLID GOLD 14-KARAT WATCHES

12-SIZE HUNTING AND OPEN FACE WATCHES.

12 Size.
No. 4C5300 Hunting Style.
No. 4C5302 Open Face.

12 Size.
No. 4C5304 Hunting Style.
No. 4C5306 Open Face.

12 Size.
Plain Polished.
No. 4C5308 Hunting Style.
No. 4C5310 Open Face.

AT $24.50 OR $25.75 OPEN FACE OR HUNTING STYLE. The latest 12-size solid gold 14-karat, warranted United States Assay. The case is fitted with a genuine Elgin or Waltham 7-jeweled grade movement; GUARANTEED AN ACCURATE TIMEKEEPER FOR A TERM OF 5 YEARS. The 12-Size WATCH IS THE LATEST SIZE MADE, and is the smallest gentlemen's size, a size larger than the largest ladies' size, the most popular size used in large cities.

THESE WATCHES have good weight cases, guaranteed to wear and GIVE ENTIRE SATISFACTION.

WARRANTED FINE 14-KARAT U. S. ASSAY.

The two Western Cases are extra heavy, the BEST Solid Gold Case manufactured, with no exception.

For $1.25 extra we can furnish fancy dial and gold hands on any watch on this page.

12 Size.
No. 4C5312 Hunting Style.
No. 4C5314 Open Face.

12 Size.
No. 4C5316 Hunting Style.
No. 4C5318 Open Face.

12 Size.
No. 4C5320 Hunting Style.
No. 4C5322 Open Face.

12 Size.
No. 4C5324 Hunting Style.
No. 4C5326 Open Face.

No. 4C5328 Hunting Style.
No. 4C5330 Open Face.

12 Size.

We Fit these Cases with the following 12-Size Movements. WARRANTED FOR 5 YEARS.	No. 4C5302 4C5310	No. 4C5314	No. 4C5300 4C5308	No. 4C5306	No. 4C5312	No. 4C5304 4C5326	No. 4C5318	No. 4C5324	No. 4C5322 4C5330	No. 4C5316	No. 4C5320 4C5328
7 Jeweled Grade Elgin or Waltham	$24.50	$26.25	$25.75	$26.75	$27.25	$29.75	$31.75	$32.75	$34.45	$36.25	$38.25
Full 10 Jeweled EDGEMERE, SEARS, ROEBUCK & CO.'S SPECIAL MAKE	24.30	26.05	25.55	26.55	27.05	29.50	31.55	32.55	34.25	36.05	38.05
Full 15 Jeweled Grade Elgin or Waltham	27.25	29.00	28.50	29.50	30.00	32.50	34.50	35.50	37.20	39.00	41.00
Full 17 Jeweled No. 275 Grade Elgin or Royal Grade Waltham	32.00	33.75	33.25	34.25	34.75	37.25	39.25	40.25	41.95	43.75	45.75
Full 19 Jeweled Riverside Grade Waltham	35.75	40.50	40.00	41.00	41.50	44.00	46.00	47.00	48.70	50.50	52.50
Full 19 Jeweled No. 189 Grade Elgin	42.75	44.50	44.00	45.00	45.50	48.00	50.00	51.00	52.70	54.50	56.50
Full 21 Jeweled No. 236 Grade Elgin	56.75	58.50	58.00	59.00	59.50	62.00	64.00	65.00	66.70	68.50	70.50
Full 23 Jeweled No. 190 Grade Elgin	68.25	70.00	69.50	70.50	71.00	73.50	75.50	76.50	78.20	80.00	82.00

16-Size Hunting Thin Model 14-Karat Solid Gold Case.

REMEMBER: We carry nothing but 14-karat quality in our solid gold cases.

$26.80 AND UPWARD

$36.30 TO **$81.50**

$36.30 AND UPWARD

This is Our New 16-Size Sears, Roebuck & Co.'s

Special 15-Jeweled Movement. See the description. It is full 15-jeweled, set in settings, solid gold plated, Roman color, beautifully finished, patent pinion and escapement, high grade finish throughout, guaranteed for five years.

16 Size.
No. 4C5331 Hunting Style. Plain or Engine Turned. Medium Weight.
No. 4C5332 Same as No. 4C5331. Heavy Weight.

16 Size.
No. 4C5336 Hunting Style. Medium Weight.

16 Size.
No. 4C5338 Hunting Style. Extra Heavy Weight.

16 Size.
No. 4C5340 Hunting Style. Heavy Weight.

WE FIT THESE CASES WITH THE FOLLOWING 16-SIZE MOVEMENTS.	No. 4C5336	No. 4C5331	4C5338 4C5340	No. 4C5332
7 Jeweled Grade Elgin or Waltham	$27.00	$29.00	$36.50	$32.50
Full 12 Jeweled EDGEMERE, SEARS, ROEBUCK & CO.'S SPECIAL MAKE	26.80	28.80	36.30	32.30
Full 15 Jeweled Grade Elgin or Waltham	30.50	32.50	40.00	36.00
Full 15 Jeweled SEARS, ROEBUCK & CO.'S SPECIAL, especially made	28.50	30.50	38.00	34.00
Full 17 Jeweled No. 241 Grade Elgin or No. 630 Grade Waltham	33.50	35.50	42.00	38.00
Full 17 Jeweled Royal Grade Waltham	35.75	37.75	45.25	41.25
Full 17 Jeweled No. 242 Grade Elgin	39.50	41.50	49.00	45.00
Full 17 Jeweled Riverside Grade Waltham	42.50	44.50	52.00	48.00
Full 17 Jeweled No. 243 Grade Elgin	44.00	46.00	53.50	49.50
Full 23 Jeweled Vanguard Grade Waltham	52.00	54.00	61.50	57.50
Full 21 Jeweled No. 156 Grade Elgin or Riverside Maximus Grade Waltham	72.00	74.00	81.50	77.50
Full 17 Jeweled SEARS, ROEBUCK & CO.'S SPECIAL, especially made. The greatest watch value ever offered	32.50	34.50	42.00	38.00

67c FOR THIS VERY GOOD RUNNING BOYS' AMERICAN MADE NICKEL PLATED WATCH.

It is stem wind and stem set, runs thirty hours with one winding. We guarantee it to reach destination in perfect going order. We have changed our source of supply, we buy them from a new maker.

No. 4R12102 Price..67c

BETTER THAN EVER OUR SAMPSON STRONG BOYS' WATCH FOR 85c

GUARANTEED FOR 1 YEAR.

Note the very handsome engraving on the back and the ornate attractive fancy dial, something new and tasty and sure to make any boy happy. It is stem wind and pendant set, 18-size, the proper size for any boy to own. We guarantee each one to reach destination in perfect going order. Understand, if you want the engraved boys' watch with a fancy dial, send us 85 cents. Be sure to order by number. 23 cents extra is a small sum of money, but for this amount extra ($1.08 in all) we will send you a gunmetal finished watch with fancy dial, beautifully engraved with an initial on the back. Be sure to mention the initial you want. We illustrate here the style of initial that we engrave. The movement is the same as in the Sampson Strong watch. This watch at $1.08 is the one we advise your selecting if you wish something a little bit better and more attractive than any cheap watch ever placed on the market. Be sure and order by number.

No. 4R12104 Engraved nickel plated fancy dial watch. Price..85c

No. 4R12106 Gunmetal finished watch with fancy dial, engraved with any initial. Price....$1.08

No. 4R12107 Same style as above, but in ladies' size, with any initial. Price........$1.60

$3.18 FOR THIS COMPLETE OUTFIT, INCLUDING WATCH, CHAIN AND CHARM.

No. 4R12415 Alaska Metal. 18 SIZE.

The watch is genuine Alaska metal, open face with tight fitting snap back and bezel, attractive corrugated design, stem wind and pendant set, and will last your natural lifetime. The movement is genuine American made, has 7 jewels, hard white enameled dial, substantial nickel plates, and is guaranteed for a term of five years against all defective material and workmanship. The chain is rolled gold plated, beautifully chased, soldered extra strong. The charm is rolled gold plated with compass in center.

GUARANTEED FOR 5 YEARS.

No. 4R12415 Price for complete outfit, watch, chain and charm..........$3.18

No. 4R12417 Same chain, charm and case, but fitted with a genuine 7 jeweled Elgin or Waltham movement...... 5.62

18-SIZE, THIN MODEL NICKEL OPEN FACE WATCH.

$1.59

A new watch manufactured by one of the most representative watch makers in the East for $1.59. This watch is guaranteed for a term of one year; we warrant it to run well and to run accurately for this time. It is stem wind and stem set, is jeweled, has fine porcelain dial, the case is nickel open face, is thin 18-size model, the exact same size as illustration shows. We likewise show the illustration of the movement. It is made of strong metal plates, the same watch under certain names brings at any retail store from $2.50 to $3.00. This astonishing offer is made by us and can be made by us only by reason of our omitting the manufacturer's name. Please don't ask it. You will observe we have carefully erased the manufacturer's name from the plate of the movement as well as from the dial. It runs from 30 to 36 hours with but one winding. We know that you will be more than pleased with it, as we know that you will be much surprised. Send us $1.59, together with 14 cents, the registry mail charges, a total of $1.73, and we will mail you this watch by registered mail. If you do not find it in every way satisfactory and in every way as described, you may return it and we will refund your money, together with all transportation charges you paid.

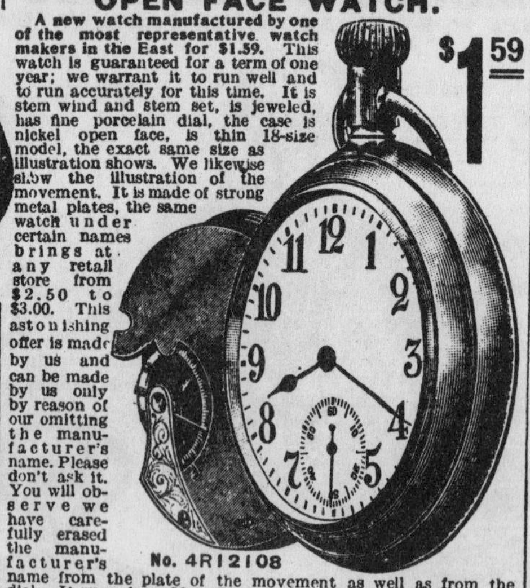

No. 4R12108

No. 4R12108 Price..........................$1.59

GENTLEMEN'S SMALL EXTRA THIN MODEL SOLID NICKEL WATCH.

$2.56

$2.56 is our bargain price. Never before has a watch in this small size thin model been offered at anything like these figures. The case is exactly as illustration shows; if anything, slightly smaller than what the artist has drawn it. It is of solid nickel, snap back and front, new antique crown, bow and stem, is stem wind and pendant set. The dial is very handsome and ornate, done in fancy colors; the hands are of the Louis XIV style, gilded duplicates of the very fine solid gold hands used on watches worth twenty times what we ask. The movement is imported from Switzerland (see the illustration), not a clock watch, but a regular fine cylinder escapement, full bridged model, warranted to run well and accurately. This watch is especially attractive to young men or those desiring a cheap but unpretentious yet modest watch, one that will last a lifetime if properly cared for.

Illustration shows partial view of the movement.

No. 4R12118

No. 4R12118 Price..........................$2.56

GUARANTEED FOR 5 YEARS.

Be sure to order by number, so as to avoid all mistakes and include with your order the mail charges, 14 cents if you order the ladies' watch or 16 cents if you order the gentlemen's watch, so as to defray the registry mail charges.

No. 4R12140 Gentlemen's open face watch with chain complete. Price..........$4.85

No. 4R12142 Gentlemen's hunting style watch with chain complete. Price..........4.85

No. 4R12144 Ladies' hunting style watch with chain complete. Price..........4.85

$2.15 $2.79

$2.15 OR $2.79 for this gold electro plated gentlemen's watch, 18-size, with either one of the two movements we illustrate here, just as you desire, and, furthermore, you can have them open face or hunting style, as the price is the same.

WE GUARANTEE these movements to be lever escapement, American made, to have 7 jewels, and guarantee them against all defective workmanship or material and to run well for a term of five years. The cases are splendid protections to the movements, but are not guaranteed for any period of time. They may wear for three months to a year like gold or they may not; it all depends on the care displayed in wearing them.

FOR $2.79, you will receive either an open face or a hunting style case according to your desire, fitted with the movement illustrated at the right, if you desire a flashy, conspicuous and beautiful appearing watch. This movement has the appearance, remember, only the appearance, of a 23 jeweled railway watch. As a matter of fact, this movement only contains 7 jewels, and is not adjusted. It is stem wind and stem set and runs for thirty to thirty-six hours with only one winding. Be sure to order by number.

No. 4R12120 Open face, 7 jeweled movement....$2.15

No. 4R12122 Hunting style, 7 jeweled movement. Price........................2.15

No. 4R12124 Open face, imitation 23 jeweled flashy movement. Price........................2.79

No. 4R12126 Hunting style, imitation 23 jeweled flashy movement. Price..............2.79

AMERICAN MADE THIN MODEL YOUNG MEN'S SIZE NICKEL OR GUNMETAL FINISHED OPEN FACE WATCHES.

$2.10 for your choice, either nickel or gunmetal finished, 12-size thin model genuine American made, stem wind and pendant set, guaranteed accurate running open face watches. The movement has nickel plates, 2 jewels, Duplex escapement, fine hard white enameled dial with plain numerals, blued steel hour, minute and second hands. The case, according to your choice, is thin model, nickel, snap back and snap bezel, tight fitting. The gunmetal watch is the same style as the nickel; both have the French antique crown bow and stem. Splendid values, readily retail for $3.00 to $3.50, especially adapted for those who desire a small, neat appearing, cheap non-bulky watch.

No. 4R12132 Nickel.
No. 4R12134 Gunmetal finish.

Be sure to order by number.

No. 4R12132 Nickel. Price..........................$2.10

No. 4R12134 Gunmetal finish. Price..................2.10

$4.85 IS THE PRICE FOR THESE GOLD FILLED WATCHES AND CHAINS, COMPLETE, EITHER LADIES' OR GENTLEMEN'S.

We show only a section of the chains; they both are regulation length. If you order the gentlemen's watch, you can have either open face or hunting style. All of these watches are stem wind and pendant set. The cases are engraved in various designs; the illustration gives you but an idea of them; they are all as beautiful, some even more so. All of them are new thin models.

The ladies' watch has the appearance of a 17 jeweled movement, and the gentlemen's has the appearance of a 23 jeweled movement, but in reality are only good 7 jeweled American made movements, the balance of the jewels that are screwed on the plates are imitation jewels, their purpose being to beautify the watch. Both of these movements have patent regulators, both of them are richly damaskeened, and good runners.

OUR GUARANTEE goes out with these watches for a term of five years, and you are protected should either the movement or case through faulty material or workmanship prove defective. The chains are rolled gold plate, soldered link, bright polish, strong and well made; the gentlemen's chain is 11 inches long, and the ladies' chain is 48 inches long, fitted with a very handsome slide.

LADIES' AND GENTLEMEN'S SPECIALLY PRICED WATCHES

For ladies or gentlemen who desire a modest priced watch, we have illustrated here watches that we can sell for $1.63 and upward in the ladies' sizes, $2.15 and upward in gentlemen's sizes.

THE WATCHES we offer on this page, while 20 to 50 per cent cheaper than offered by others, are not what we term high grade watches. They are modest priced goods and the biggest value ever offered for the money. They are in every way as illustrated and described. The movements quoted in the lists are all guaranteed for a term of five years against defective material and workmanship.

For 90 cents extra we can furnish a fancy dial and gold hands on any of these watches. See illustration on page 457.

OUR "TRAINMEN'S SPECIAL" MOVEMENT

has 7 jewels only, stamped "23 jewels," beautifully damaskeened and made in an ornate style so as to attract the eye and give the impression of being high grade. It is a genuine 7 jeweled American made movement, however, and guaranteed for a term of five years against defective material and workmanship.

Gold Electro Plate, 18-Size.
No. 4R12200 Open Face, Screw Back and Bezel.
No. 4R12202 Hunting Style.

Gold Filled, 18-Size, Guaranteed for 5 years.
No. 4R12204 Open Face, Screw Back and Bezel.
No. 4R12206 Hunting Style.

Gold Filled, 18-Size, Guaranteed for 10 years.
No. 4R12208 Open Face, Screw Back and Bezel.
No. 4R12210 Hunting Style.

Solid Silver, 18-Size, Full Engine Turned Pattern.
No. 4R12212 Hunting Style.

Solid Silver, 18-Size, Full Engine Turned Pattern.
No. 4R12214 Open Face, Screw Back and Bezel.

We fit these cases with the following 18-size movements. Prices quoted are for the complete watch, movement and case.	No. 4R12200 4R12202	No. 4R12204	No. 4R12208	No. 4R12206 4R12214	No. 4R12210 4R12212
7 JEWELED AMERICAN MAKE, nickel plates	$2.15	$3.42	$3.94	$3.94	$4.34
7 Jeweled Elgin or Waltham, gilt plates	4.26	5.57	6.07	6.24	6.59
7 Jeweled Elgin, Hampden or Waltham, nickel plates	4.79	6.10	6.60	6.80	7.15
15 Jeweled Waltham, gilt plates	5.32	6.63	7.13	7.65	7.70
15 Jeweled Elgin, Hampden or Waltham, nickel plates	5.84	7.15	7.65	7.90	8.25
17 Jeweled Elgin, Hampden or Waltham	6.89	8.20	8.70	9.00	9.35
17 Jeweled Dueber Grand, patent regulator, adjusted, Dueber-Hampden movement	9.00	10.30	10.80	10.80	10.25
TRAINMEN'S SPECIAL, stamped 23 jewels, adjusted, special make	2.79	4.10	4.60	4.60	4.95

LADIES' GOLD PLATED WATCH.

One size smaller than the ladies' 6-size. It is not guaranteed; will wear six months to a year if very carefully handled. It is a great watch to use for trading purposes. It is stem wind and stem set and the movement we fit in this watch is an imported 7 jeweled Swiss lever movement, and will give excellent satisfaction as a timekeeper. We warrant it being received in perfect going order.

No. 4R12216 Price for complete watch $3.36

Solid Silver, 6-Size, Full Engine Turned Pattern. No. 4R12220 Open Face.

Solid Silver, 6-Size, Full Engine Turned Pattern. No. 4R12222 Hunting Style.

Gold Electro Plate, 6-Size. No. 4R12224 Hunting Style.

Gold Filled, 6-Size. Guaranteed for 5 years. No. 4R12226 Hunting Style.

Gold Filled, 6-Size, Guaranteed for 10 years. No. 4R12228 Hunting Style.

SOMETHING NEW.

$3.10 AND UP

Solid Silver like Alaska Metal.
No. 4R12230 Open Face, Jointed Style.
No. 4R12232 Hunting Style.

Our 6-SIZE ALASKA METAL WATCHES in hunting and open face style. Alaska metal is one of the newly compounded metals. It looks like silver, wears like silver, has the same color and appearance as silver, but it is very much tougher and costs less.

We fit these cases with the following 6-size movements. Prices quoted are for the complete watch, movement and case.	No. 4R12224	No. 4R12220	No. 4R12222	No. 4R12226	No. 4R12228	No. 4R12230	No. 4R12232
7 JEWELED AMERICAN MAKE, nickel plates	$3.07	$4.72	$4.83	$4.41	$4.69	$3.10	$3.50
7 Jeweled Elgin or Waltham, gilt plates	4.75	6.61	6.70	6.10	5.95	4.85	5.25
7 Jeweled Elgin, Hampden or Waltham, nickel plates	5.27	7.15	7.24	6.62	6.47	5.40	5.80
15 Jeweled Elgin, Hampden or Waltham, nickel plates	6.33	8.29	8.38	7.68	7.53	6.50	6.90
16 Jeweled Lady Waltham, nickel plates	8.95	11.01	11.10	10.30	10.15	9.25	9.65

LADIES' NICKEL WATCH

REDUCED PRICE - - $1.63

Send us $1.63 and postage (8 cents) making a total of $1.71, and we will send you this very handsome small size thin model nickel American watch, exactly as the illustration shows. Each one comes in a handsome lined box.

The case is nickel. The movement, as illustration shows, is American made. The dial is porcelain, not paper. For a school girl, school teacher or a young person desiring a cheap, unpretentious watch that will give satisfaction, we advise this one; it is a good timekeeper; we guarantee it to run well and accurately for a year; with proper care it will wear five, ten and even fifteen years.

No. 4R12240 Price....$1.63

CUT PRICES.

$5.58 AND UP

No. 4R12242 Open Face.
No. 4R12244 Hunting Style.

LADIES' SOLID SILVER 0-SIZE WATCHES

An American made watch in this small size, made of silver, has been wanted by thousands of ladies. So as to make our catalog complete and to positively quote all kinds and styles of watches, we show here the smallest silver American watch made. These cases are solid silver through and through, hand engraved; they have the antique bow; the entire case is perfectly finished in every respect. They are stem wind and pendant set. We guarantee the movement for a term of five years, and the case will last your natural lifetime. We can fit this case with any movement, in either open face or hunting style, at prices quoted below.

	Open Face	Hunting Style
Catalog Nos.	4R12242	4R12244
7 Jeweled Swiss Lever	$ 5.58	$ 5.85
7 Jeweled Elgin or Waltham	7.25	8.40
15 Jeweled Elgin or Waltham	10.95	11.10

$15.15 IMPORTED GENEVA WATCH

A TREMENDOUS REDUCTION; WAS $17.85

WE HAVE GOTTEN A LOWER IMPORT COST AND OUR CUSTOMERS GET THE BENEFIT

PLEASE READ THIS WONDERFUL WATCH OFFER

Do you want something most extraordinary in an especially fine ladies' or gentlemen's watch? Are you willing to pa, as much as $15.15 for a very fine watch, something away out of the ordinary, a much better watch than you would be at all likely to find in any jewelry store in your section of the country? If you are willing to invest as much money as $15.15 in a watch, we offer you on this page an opportunity to get one of the finest and best watches made.

GENEVA, SWITZERLAND, EUROPE, turns out the very finest watch movements of the world. Go into the very finest jewelry store in Chicago, New York, or any other large American city and you will scarcely see an American made movement offered for sale. The movements they offer are all made in Geneva, Switzerland, but in such stores they get very fancy prices. Scarcely one Geneva watch is offered for less than $50.00 and from that figure they run at once up into the hundreds. All very fine watch movements, even one of the very special split second, repeaters, striking, chronograph, and especially fine made thin model movements, all the very finest watch movement work is done in, and therefore must come from Geneva, Switzerland, Europe.

WE ARE THE FIRST HOUSE in the world to bring the genuine high grade Geneva watch movements before the American public at anything like a low price. The first house to make a price low enough to bring such a fine watch with reach of all. No longer is it necessary to pay $50.00 to $100.00 to own a Geneva watch, for by a most wonderful and absorbing watch movement contract made by us, strange as it may seem, we are just now able to take the very highest grade life guaranteed, full engraved American gold filled watch case made and fit into this case a very fine genuine Geneva Swiss movement in your choice of two sizes for men, or one size for women, and, strange as it must seem to every one who reads this, and much as watch dealers will wonder, we can offer these marvelously fine watches for only $15.15.

DON'T BUY ONE of these fine watches then treat it as you would a dollar nickel watch. If you are at times engaged at dirty or heavy work; if your work takes you at times into dusty fields behind the harvester, or to the railroad section; if your work at times takes you otherwise into dirty or dusty places and when at work your watch is jammed and roughly used, on such occasions don't wear as fine a watch as this for the purpose. In such cases don't buy this watch at all, or buy this watch and also a cheap heavy watch for a dollar or so, using the cheap watch when at very dirty or rough work.

FOR WONDERFUL TIME KEEPING QUALITIES and rare specimens of beauty, and for those who are willing to give a fine watch just reasonable care, only the reasonable care that such a fine piece of mechanism deserves, these fine Geneva watches are the only watches to buy.

BUY THIS GENEVA WATCH AT $15.15 in either gentlemen's or ladies' styles and no American watch even at $50.00 in price will compare with it. Let your friends see, examine and compare your Geneva watch with their watches and every judge will pronounce your $15.15 watch worth $50.00 to $100.00.

THE SIZES OF THESE GENEVA WATCHES

THE PICTURES HEREON show the exact size of these watches. The largest, 16-size gents' watch, just as illustrated, is 2 inches wide. The 12-size gents' watch, just as illustrated, is 1⅞ inches wide. The ladies' 0-size, just as illustrated, is 1⅜ inches wide. All are made especially thin, neat and dainty, and all have unique antique bows. They are all smaller, thinner, lighter, neater and in every way handsomer and finer than what you can buy in American made watches; the 12 or 16-size, the ideal size, shape and style for the carrying timepiece of a real gentleman, and the 0-size is just the watch in size, thickness and weight for the most exacting, most fashionable lady to wear, and as for timekeeping dependability they are unequaled. The three illustrations on this page will give you just a little idea of the appearance of our Geneva watch and the several sizes in which it comes. The largest size, the 16-size for gentlemen, we offer for the first time in the history of the watch making industry in a genuine imported Geneva movement for only $15.15. One of the pictures in the group of three shows the front of the watch with its handsome Geneva special dial or face and gold hands. Another picture shows the back of the watch detailing the gold filled case with its beautiful engraving and elaborate finish. The third picture in the group shows the wonderful Geneva movement, and these three pictures are engraved by our artist direct from photographs and are exact in size and appearance

$15.15

No. 4L1905

16-Size, Open Face, Screw Back and Screw Bezel. These illustrations of front and back view and movement are exact life size of gentlemen's 16-size watch.

No. 4L1903

12-Size, Open Face, Screw Back and Screw Bezel. These illustrations are life size and show front, back and movement of the gentlemen's 12-size watch with genuine Geneva movement.

$15.15

These illustrations show front, back and open view of case, also movement of ladies' 0-size watch, fitted with genuine Geneva movement. The pictures are life size

No. 4L1901

0-Size, Hunting Style.

THESE GENEVA MOVEMENTS in all three sizes, 16, 12 and 0, are all alike, except for size, all made from very finest decarbonized nickel, all are full 17 jeweled, red hand turned ruby jewels in gold settings, jeweled both sides throughout, including centers, all adjusted to heat, cold, position isochronism; patent regulators, patent escapement, patent pinion, patent dust protector, quick train cut balance wheel, Brequet hairspring, compensating balance, Geneva compensating system, all hand and polished parts, all the movements the very best in every respect.

THE LIFE GUARANTEED gold filled cases in all three sizes, 16, 12 and 0-size, are all American made and the highest grade gold filled cases manufactured. Cases are made of heavy thick plates of fine solid gold over inner plates of hard composition metal and are guaranteed to wear and retain their pure gold color for a lifetime. They are most elaborately engraved, finished and decorated, wonderfully well finished, all fitted with genuine antique bows, all stem wind and patent pendant setting. The gentlemen's watches, the 16 and 12-sizes, are open face only, the 0-size ladies' watches are double or hunting case.

FANCY DIALS or faces. These Geneva watches all have very fancy dials (see illustrations), the most beautiful dials made, finished with gold and colored ornamentations and fancy gold hands.

BE SURE TO ORDER BY NUMBER.

No. 4L1901 Ladies' small size watch. Price $15.15
No. 4L1903 12-size gentlemen's watch. Price 15.15
No. 4L1905 16-size gentlemen's watch. Price 15.15

GENTLEMEN'S GUNMETAL WATCHES REDUCED PRICE

$3.26

No. 4L1941 Gunmetal.
No. 4L1943 Nickel Case.

AN ASTONISHING WATCH OFFER IN A 16-SIZE LEVER ESCAPEMENT EXTRA THIN MODEL STYLE.

YOUR CHOICE, $3.26 for a 16-size, extra thin model, stem wind and pendant set movement, full nickel plates, 7 fine jewels, straight line lever escapement, true timing screws, fine hard white enameled dial with plain Arabic numerals, fitted in an extra thin hinged back open face silver antique bow and crown gunmetal case, or $3.26 for this movement fitted in a solid nickel case. Look at the illustration which shows two views of the watch; the side view gives you an idea of the extreme thinness and the three-quarter view shows you the beautiful plain dial with the Arabic numerals. Just the kind of a watch you want, one that will not weigh down or bulge out your pocket in an unsightly manner. If you select the gunmetal watch you will own one of the most attractive watches ever offered. But for those who prefer a silverlike appearing watch we have to offer at the same figure the same movement fitted in a solid nickel case. We sell this case for what it is, a solid nickel case, guaranteed to be nickel through and through will not tarnish, always remains the same, not nickel plated as some watches offered by others. Please be sure to order by number.

No. 4L1941 7 jeweled, extra thin model, gunmetal watch. Price $3.26
No. 4L1943 7 jeweled, extra thin model, solid nickel watch. Price 3.26

If by registered mail, postage extra, 14 cents.

EIGHT-DAY WATCHES

IN NICKEL AND SOLID SILVER.

$7.80

WATCHES WE ILLUSTRATE and describe here, run for eight days with but one winding. $7.80 for this eight-day watch with solid nickel case. $9.25 for this eight-day watch with solid silver case. The principal and most important feature of this watch is the movement. See the illustration. It is stem wind and pendant set, made of solid nickel plates, has 15 fine jewels, Breguet hairspring, cut expansion balance with true timing screws, has straight line lever escapement, and runs eight days with but one winding. This watch is an accurate timekeeper and a fine running watch. We send our written binding 5-year movement guarantee with every one of them. The eight-day watch that we describe here is a marvel of mechanical ingenuity never before perfected, never before successfully made. For $9.25, we will send you this wonderful timekeeper fitted in a solid silver jointed open face, bright polished antique crown, bow and stem case.

FOR $7.80 we will send you the same movement fitted in the same type of case but made of solid high grade nickel that is guaranteed nickel through and through and not to tarnish or discolor, but to be like solid silver in appearance forever. This watch is imported from Switzerland, the home of high grade watch making and is manufactured by one of the largest and most representative concerns there.

No. 4L1945 Solid silver case, fitted with a 15 jeweled eight-day movement. Price $9.25
No. 4L1947 Solid nickel case, fitted with a 15 jeweled eight-day movement. Price $7.80

No. 4L1945

New Model Antique Bow.

12-SIZE OPEN FACE OR HUNTING STYLE DUEBER-HAMPDEN COMPLETE WATCHES AT $11.25 IN OPEN FACE OR $12.50 IN HUNTING STYLE.

SOLID GOLD AND GOLD FILLED CASES.

WE OFFER AT $11.25 the 12-size Hampden Watch Co.'s Complete Watch. The case is guaranteed 14-karat gold filled and warranted for a term of 25 years' wear. The movement is the Cantonian, 7 jeweled, exactly as described. Never before in the history of the watch business have such values been offered for the money.

THE MOVEMENTS. We can recommend any of the movements quoted as being an accurate timekeeper, perfectly finished in every detail, stem wind and lever set; all the latest modern improvements being employed. They positively are up to date in every respect.

$11.25 AND UP

$11.25 AND UP

No. 4F2350 Open Face Screw Back and Bezel, gold filled, warranted 25 years.
No. 4F2351 Hunting Style Case, same make and quality as above.
No. 4F2352 Hunting Style Case, solid gold, 14 karat, heavy weight.

No. 4F2353 Open Face, Screw Back and Bezel, gold filled, warranted 25 years.
No. 4F2354 Hunting Style Case, same make and quality as above.
No. 4F2355 Hunting Style Case, solid gold 14 karat, heavy weight.

No. 4F2356 Open Face, Screw Back and Bezel, gold filled, warranted 25 years.
No. 4F2357 Hunting Style Case, same make and quality as above.
No. 4F2358 Hunting Style Case, solid gold, 14 karat, heavy weight.

No. 4F2359 Open Face, Screw Back and Bezel, gold filled, warranted 25 years.
No. 4F2360 Hunting Style Case, same make and quality as above.
No. 4F2361 Hunting Style Case, solid gold, 14 karat, heavy weight.

No. 4F2362 Open Face, Screw Back and Bezel, gold filled, warranted 25 years.
No. 4F2363 Hunting Style Case, same make and quality as above.
No. 4F2364 Hunting Stylo Case, solid gold, 14 karat, heavy weight.

DESCRIPTION OF THE MOVEMENTS FITTED IN THE 12-SIZE COMPLETE DUEBER-HAMPDEN WATCHES.

THE CANTONIAN has 7 jewels, Arabic or Roman dial, solid nickel plates, Breguet hairspring, all pivot holes when not jeweled are bushed with antifriction metal. A very good movement.

THE GENERAL STARK has solid nickel plates, 15 ruby jewels in composition settings, Breguet hairspring, mean time screws, patent regulator, bright flat screws, plates are engraved and damaskeened, has Roman or Arabic dial with red marginal figures.

THE DUEBER GRAND has solid nickel plates, 17 ruby and sapphire jewels in composition settings, is adjusted, has Breguet hairspring, patent regulator, bright flat screws, beautifully engraved and damaskeened plates with gold letters, Arabic or Roman dial with red marginal figures.

THE JOHN HANCOCK has solid nickel plates, 21 fine ruby and sapphire jewels in gold settings, escapement is cap jeweled, has compensation balance, adjusted to temperature, isochronism and positions, has Breguet hairspring, new model micrometric regulator, bright bevel head screws, patent center pinion, finely polished steel work, double sunk enameled dial, beautifully finished nickel plates with gold letters. This is the finest finished movement of any of the 12-size Dueber-Hampden watches. It is very closely timed.

We fit these cases (Nos. 4F2350 to 4F2364) with the following 12-size movements. Prices quoted are for the complete watch, movement and case.	Open Face, Screw Back and Bezel	Hunting Style, Gold Filled	Hunting Style, Solid Gold
7 Jeweled Cantonian.....	$11.25	$12.50	$35.50
15 Jeweled General Stark..	13.25	14.50	37.50
17 Jeweled Dueber Grand..	16.25	17.50	40.50
21 Jeweled John Hancock..	29.75	31.50	55.00

$2.32 16-SIZE GUN-METAL

No. 4F2440 Gentlemen's 16-size, thin model, open face, plain polished, gun-metal watch. Has beautiful fancy dial as illustration shows. The movement is imported from Switzerland, has jeweled cylinder escapement and damaskeened nickel plates. It is recommended to all who desire a cheap and durable watch. Sold for twice what we ask for it by all the leading jewelers in the country. Price..............$2.32

6-SIZE ALASKA SILVER. SOMETHING NEW.

$3.13 TO $9.15

No. 4F2450

OUR 6-SIZE ALASKA SILVER WATCHES in hunting and open face style. Alaska silver is one of the newly compounded metals. It looks like silver, wears like silver, has the same color and appearance as silver, but is very much tougher and costs less. At $3.13 to $9.15 we are offering these Alaska silver ladies' watches.

THE MOVEMENTS are all representative makes, each one of them is guaranteed an accurate timekeeper and **WE FULLY WARRANT THEM FOR A TERM OF 5 YEARS** against defective material or workmanship.

No. 4F2450 Open Face Style.
No. 4F2452 Hunting Style.

We fit these cases with the following 6-size movements. Prices quoted are for the complete watch, movement and case.	No. 4F2450	No. 4F2452
7 JEWELED EDGEMERE, special make........	$3.13	$3.40
COUNTESS JANET, stamped 17 jeweled, adjusted	3.33	3.60
7 Jeweled Elgin or Waltham, gilt plates..........	4.68	4.95
7 Jeweled Elgin or Waltham, nickel plates........	5.20	5.47
12 JEWELED EDGEMERE, nickel plates, special make........	4.58	4.85
15 JEWELED PLYMOUTH WATCH CO., nickel plates, special make........	6.08	6.35
15 Jeweled Elgin or Waltham, nickel plates........	6.26	6.53
16 Jeweled Lady Waltham, nickel plates........	8.88	9.15
17 Jeweled Edgemere, nickel plates, patent regulator, special make........	5.68	5.95
17 JEWELED PLYMOUTH WATCH CO., nickel plates, patent regulator, special make........	8.63	8.90

AT $3.46 AND $3.98 WE OFFER A BOYS' SOLID SILVER WATCH.

$3.98 $3.46

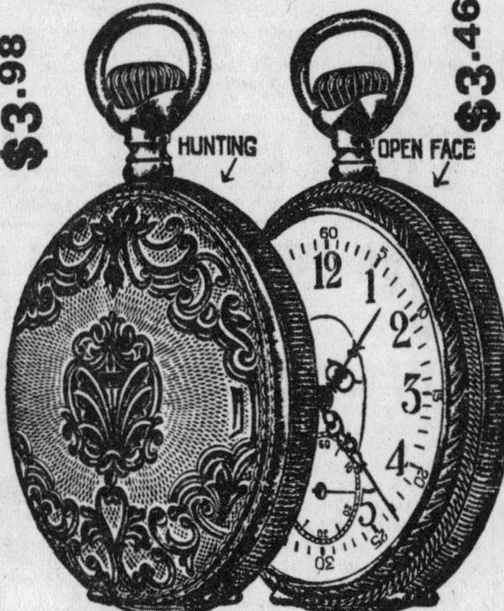

No. 4F2471 Hunting Style. **No. 4F2473** Open Face.

Either style, open face at $3.46 or Hunting at $3.98 each. These watches are the ideal size for a boy. The exact size as illustration. They are solid silver 925-1000 fine through and through, stem wind and stem set, beautifully hand engraved, perfect joints, close fitting lids, heavy and durable. Just the kind of watch your boy should have. **The movements of these watches are imported Swiss ones.** They have 7 jewels, the bridging beautifully damaskeened, perfectly finished throughout and will keep very good time. Never before has such a splendid watch been offered for anything like the price. **$3.46 in Open Face or $3.98 in Hunting. ORDER BY NUMBER.** Please your boy, order one and let him have a genuine Solid Silver Watch.

No. 4F2471 Hunting Style. Price..$3.98
No. 4F2473 Open Face. Price..... 3.46

12-SIZE SILVER AND ALASKA SILVER WATCHES.

$3.65 TO $27.72

DESCRIPTION OF THE EDGEMERE MOVEMENT 12-size open face or hunting; Alaska silver, bright polished, damaskeened plates; 10 fine ruby jewels, Breguet hairspring, cut balance, patent pinions, beveled screw heads, exposed winding arrangement, double sunk dial, moon hands and red marginal figures.

No. 4F2461 Alaska Silver, Open Face, Screw Back and Bezel.
No. 4F2463 Alaska Silver, Hunting Style.
No. 4F2465 Solid Silver, Open Face, Screw Back and Bezel.
No. 4F2467 Solid Silver, Hunting Style.
These watches are made of solid silver or Alaska silver through and through.

We fit these cases with the following 12-size movements. Prices quoted are for the complete watch, movement and case.	No. 4F2461	No. 4F2463	No. 4F2465	No. 4F2467
7 Jeweled Swiss Lever, nickel plates	$3.65	$4.05	$4.75	$5.25
7 Jeweled Elgin or Waltham, nickel plates...	5.65	6.05	6.75	7.25
10 JEWELED EDGEMERE, special make..	5.40	5.80	6.50	7.00
15 JEWELED PLYMOUTH WATCH CO., nickel plates, patent regulator, special make	7.40	7.80	8.50	9.00
15 Jeweled Elgin or Waltham, nickel plates, patent regulator......	7.75	8.15	8.85	9.35
17 JEWELED PLYMOUTH WATCH CO., nickel plates, patent regulator, special make	13.90	14.30	15.00	15.50
17 Jeweled No. 321 Grade Elgin or Royal Grade Waltham..........	14.83	15.23	15.93	16.43
19 Jeweled Riverside Waltham..........	21.92	22.32	23.02	23.52
19 Jeweled No. 189 Grade Elgin..........	26.12	26.52	27.22	27.72
21 JEWELED SWISS, nickel plates, patent regulator, adjusted....	20.05	20.45	21.15	21.65

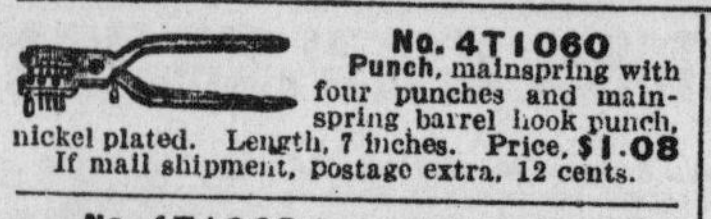

No. 4T1060 Punch, mainspring with four punches and mainspring barrel hook punch, nickel plated. Length, 7 inches. Price, $1.08
If mail shipment, postage extra, 12 cents.

No. 4T1062 Roller Remover, screw action. Price, each 52c

No. 4T1064 Ruby Pin Setter. Price, each...19c

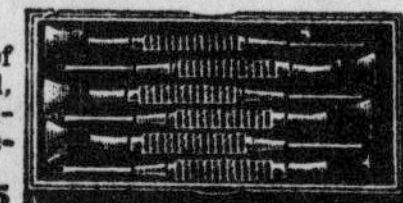

No. 4T1066 Screwdrivers, set of six, nickel plated, with colored celluloid heads; in pasteboard box. Set of six, $1.25

No. 4T1068 Metal Head Screwdriver, in small, medium or large size. **Be sure to state size wanted.** Price, each 8c

No. 4T1070 Screwdriver, adjustable, nickel plated, with four different sized blades. Price 19c

No. 4T1072 Stacking and Punching Set. 24 punches and hollow steel stake in boxwood box with cover. Price.....98c
Postage extra, 8 cents.

No. 4T1074 Drills. Set of forty-eight drills, assorted sizes, with drill stock in boxwood box. Price 94c

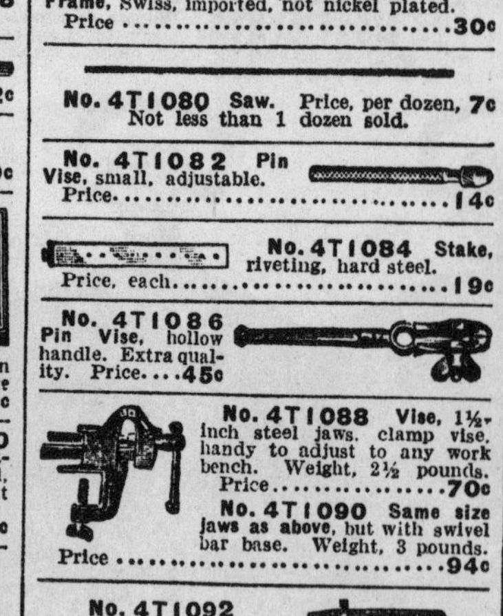

No. 4T1076 Saw Frame, nickel plated, extra quality. Price..58c

No. 4T1078 Saw Frame, Swiss, imported, not nickel plated. Price 30c

No. 4T1080 Saw. Price, per dozen, 7c
Not less than 1 dozen sold.

No. 4T1082 Pin Vise, small, adjustable. Price........14c

No. 4T1084 Stake, riveting, hard steel. Price, each........19c

No. 4T1086 Pin Vise, hollow handle. Extra quality. Price....45c

No. 4T1088 Vise, 1½-inch steel jaws, clamp vise, handy to adjust to any work bench. Weight, 2½ pounds. Price........70c

No. 4T1090 Same size jaws as above, but with swivel bar base. Weight, 3 pounds. Price 94c

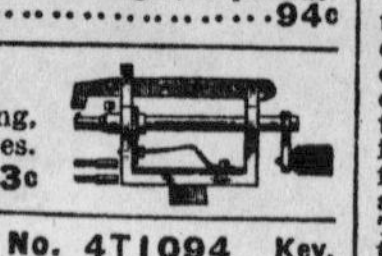

No. 4T1092 Winder, mainspring, Swiss. Length, 3½ inches. Price 33c

No. 4T1094 Key, Birch patent key; will wind any watch. Price, 9c

No. 4T1096 Jewelers' Cement. For cementing china, glass, ivory, beads, pearls, jewels, etc. Price, per bottle........23c

No. 4T1098 Granite Hold Fast Cement. Price, per bottle 14c

No. 4T1100 Gold Filled Bar, gents's size. Price........15c

No. 4T1102 Gold Filled Bar, ladies' size. Price........12c

No. 4T1104 Gold Filled Swivel, gents' size. Price......15c

No. 4T1106 Gold Filled Swivel, ladies' size. Price......12c

FANCY DIAL.

We show here an illustration of the fancy dial and gold hands that we furnish on different watches quoted and illustrated on the following pages at 90 cents extra. Fancy dials cannot be fitted on every watch in our catalog. We caution you only to order them on such watches where it is clearly stated on the page that we can furnish fancy dials. The illustration merely gives you an idea of how the fancy dial will look. They are not all exactly as this picture shows, as they vary in design. They come in various tints, with floral decorations and gold work, and all of them beautiful. We furnish any size, 18, 16, 12, 6 and 0-size for American watches.

CUT PRICE, 21 CENTS.

No. 4T1108 The Ajax Watch Insulator or Protector. Order by number. The maker guarantees that this insulator protects the watch case from wear and the movement from all ordinary magnetic influence. It fits all size watches, open face or hunting style of all makes. **When ordering don't fail to give size and make of case and whether open face or hunting style is wanted.** Price........21c
If mail shipment, postage extra, 2 cents.

Leather Watch Protector made so as to be able to read the time. Constructed of high grade leather, has silk gathering string on top, very transparent durable celluloid front stitched in. This watch protector is meant for open face watches only. We supply it in gentlemen's 18, 16 and 12-size only. **Be sure to give the size of bag wanted.** Order by number.
No. 4T1110 Price........15c

FINE WATCH BOX FOR 21c.

No. 4T1112 This illustration, made from a photograph, shows one of our fine lined and leatherette covered watch boxes that we supply for 21 cents extra with any watch purchased of us. **In ordering state what size watch the case is intended for.** Price........21c
If mail shipment, postage extra, 2 cents.

67c FOR THIS VERY GOOD RUNNING BOYS' AMERICAN MADE NICKEL PLATED WATCH.

It is stem wind and stem set, runs thirty hours with one winding. We guarantee it to reach destination in perfect going order. We have changed our source of supply, we buy them from a new maker.
No. 4T12102 Price 67c

BETTER THAN EVER, OUR SAMPSON STRONG BOYS' WATCH FOR 85c

Note the very handsome engraving on the back and the ornate attractive fancy dial, something new and tasty and sure to make any boy happy. It is stem wind and pendant set, 18-size, the proper size for any boy to own. We guarantee each one to reach destination in perfect going order. Understand, if you want the engraved boys' watch with a fancy dial, send us 85 cents. Be sure to order by number. 13 cents extra is a small sum of money, but for this amount extra (98c in all) we will send you a gunmetal finished watch with fancy dial, beautifully engraved with an initial on the back. Be sure to mention the initial you want. We illustrate here the style of initial that we engrave. The movement is the same as in the Sampson Strong watch. This watch at 98 cents is the one we advise your selecting if you wish something a little bit better and more attractive than any cheap watch ever placed on the market. Be sure and order by number.

No. 4T12104 Engraved nickel plated fancy dial watch. Price..85c

No. 4T12106 Gunmetal finished watch with fancy dial, engraved with any initial. Price........98c

No. 4T12107 Same style as above, but in ladies' size, with any initial. Price $1.60

$1.57 FOR $2.50 WATCHES LADIES' OR GENTS' SIZE.

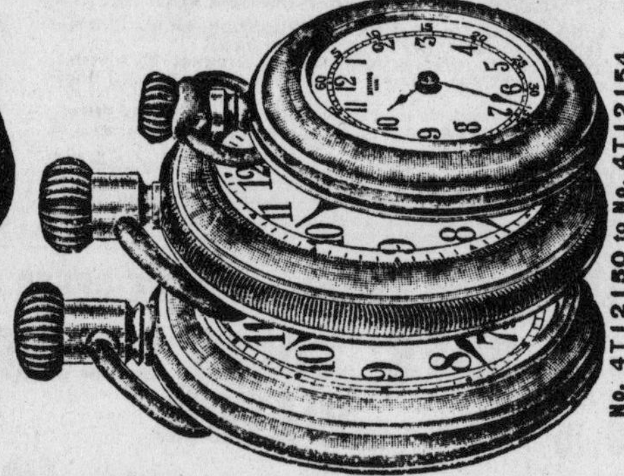

No. 4T12150 to No. 4T12154

These watches are sold the world over for $2.50 each. Your choice any size for $1.57, a gentlemen's regulation 16-size, gentlemen's regulation small 12-size or ladies' 6-size.

The movements are American made, stem wind and pendant set, all guaranteed for one year by the manufacturer; the manufacturer's guarantee accompanies each one. **The cases are nickel open face**, snap back and front. **Be sure to order by number.**

No. 4T12150 Gentlemen's 16-size. Price......$1.57
No. 4T12152 Gentlemen's 12-size. Price......1.57
No. 4T12154 Ladies' 6-size. Price......1.57
If mail shipment, postage extra, 4 cents.

$2.58 GENUINE SILVERODE 16-SIZE ALL AMERICAN WATCH.

$2.58 for this plain polished, extra thin model silverode, open face, dust and damp proof watch.

The movement is American made and guaranteed for five years, has 7 jewels, lever escapement, plates are solid nickel, beautifully damaskeened, fine blued steel hairspring and pretty tinted dial.

The case is solid genuine silverode through and through. Silverode is a composition metal, made to imitate silver. It is tougher than silver, of greater tensile strength. Will not rust or corrode, plain polished, Bassene style, with antique crown bow and stem, is open face, screw back and screw bezel, dust and damp proof. Complete case and movement for $2.58. We can fit this case with genuine 7-jewel Elgin movement for $6.28.

No. 4T12157
No. 4T12159

No. 4T12157 Solid Silverode Watch. Price $2.58

No. 4T12159 Solid Silverode Watch, with genuine 7-jewel Elgin movement. Price $6.28

18-SIZE THIN MODEL NICKEL OPEN FACE WATCH.

$1.59

A new watch manufactured by one of the most representative watch makers in the East for $1.59. This watch is guaranteed for a term of one year; we warrant it to run well and to run accurately for this time. It is stem wind and stem set, is jeweled, has fine porcelain dial, the case is nickel open face, is thin 18-size model, the exact same size as illustration shows. We likewise show the illustration of the movement. It is made of strong metal plates; the same watch under certain names brings at any retail store from $2.50 to $3.00. This astonishing offer is made by us and can be made by us only by reason of our omitting the manufacturer's name. Please don't ask it. You will observe we have carefully erased the manufacturer's name from the plate of the movement as well as from the dial. It runs from 30 to 36 hours with but one winding. We know that you will be more than pleased with it, as we know that you will be much surprised. Send us $1.59, together with 16 cents, the registry mail charges, a total of $1.75, and we will mail you this watch by registered mail. If you do not find it in every way satisfactory and in every way as described, you may return it and we will return your money, together with all transportation charges you paid.

No. 4T12160

No. 4T12160 Price........$1.59

GENTLEMEN'S SMALL EXTRA THIN MODEL SOLID NICKEL WATCH.

$2.56

$2.56 is our bargain price. Never before has a watch in this small size thin model been offered at anything like these figures. The case is exactly as illustration shows; if anything, slightly smaller than the artist has drawn it. It is of solid nickel, snap back and front, new antique crown, bow and stem, is stem wind and pendant set. The dial is very handsome and ornate, done in fancy colors; the hands are of the Louis XIV style, gilded duplicates of the very fine solid gold hands used on watches worth twenty times what we ask. The movement is imported from Switzerland (see the illustration), not a clock watch, but a regular fine cylinder escapement, full bridged model, warranted to run well and accurately. This watch is especially attractive to young men or those desiring a cheap but unpretentious yet modest watch, one that will last a lifetime if properly cared for.

Illustration shows partial view of the movement.

No. 4T12162

No. 4T12162 Price........$2

$2.98 FOR YOUR CHOICE OF THESE GOLD PLATED AMERICAN MADE WATCHES

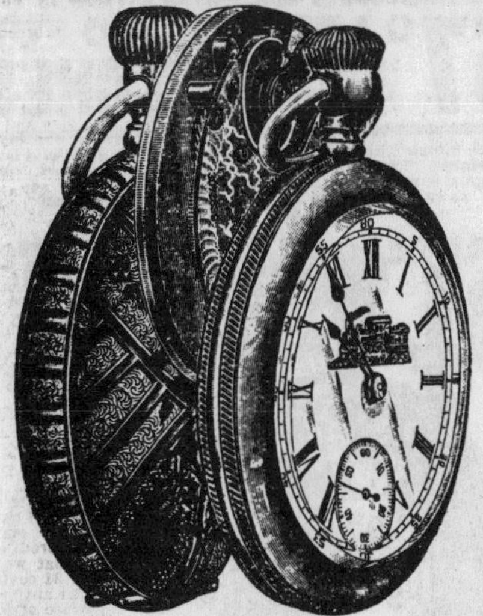

The cases come in hunting style or open face, according to your own selection; the price is the same. They are electro gold plated, have the appearance of gold filled; they are not warranted; they may wear for a few weeks or they may wear for six months, we do not know. They are used extensively by traders and auction men because they have the appearance of a high grade watch. They come in 18-size, as illustration shows, beautifully engraved, both stem wind and pendant set. The open face case is dust and damp proof, and makes a good protection to the movement. It is screw back and screw bezel, close jointed, and perfect in every detail. The hunting case has double lid with inside protecting cap, joints, seams and hinges splendidly finished. The movement fitted in either one of these two cases according to your choice for $2.98 is our celebrated nameless Trainmen movement. It has the appearance of a 23-jeweled high grade adjusted watch, but as a matter of fact, it is merely a 7-jeweled good running, fairly accurate timekeeper. It is made of nickel plates, beautifully damaskeened, has patent regulator, extra jewels screwed onto the back plate; these jewels are for appearance only, they have no utility. A beautiful engraving of a locomotive appears on the back plate, and, as illustration shows, on dial also. $2.98 is a world breaking price for this type of a watch. **Be sure to order by number.**

No. 4T12150 Open face style. Price............**$2.98**
No. 4T12152 Hunting style. Price............ **2.98**

$3.18 FOR THIS COMPLETE OUTFIT, INCLUDING WATCH, CHAIN AND CHARM

No. 4T12156 Alaska Metal. 18-SIZE.

The watch is genuine Alaska metal, open face with tight fitting snap back and bezel, attractive corrugated design, stem wind and pendant set, and will last your natural lifetime. The movement is genuine American made, has 7 jewels, hard white enameled dial, substantial nickel plates, and is guaranteed for a term of five years against all defective material and workmanship. The chain is rolled gold plated, beautifully chased, soldered extra strong. The charm is rolled gold plated with compass in center.

GUARANTEED FOR 5 YEARS.

No. 4T12156 Price for complete outfit, watch, chain and charm...........**$3.18**

No. 4T12158 Same chain, charm and case, but fitted with a genuine 7-jeweled Elgin or Waltham movement...... **5.62**

You cannot afford to buy anywhere else if you consider the money we save you, the reputation of the manufacturers of our movements and cases, and the perfect manner in which we handle, pack and ship watches, especially when you receive with your purchase our five-year guarantee.

$5.15 FOR YOUR CHOICE OF OPEN FACE OR HUNTING STYLE GOLD FILLED WATCHES

Fine Gold Filled Gentlemen's 18-Size Watch with chain as illustration shows. If you select the open face style, the one that we advise because it is dust and damp proof, you will receive the latest model gold filled, five-year guaranteed case. Has antique crown, bow and stem, beautifully engraved, all tight joints, fitted with a clear fine cut beveled edge crystal. A watch you can well be proud to carry. If you select the hunting style you will receive a beautifully engraved case guaranteed for a term of five years' continual wear. Has antique crown, bow and stem, double lid with inside protecting cap, tight joints, secure hinges, and a splendid protection to the movement. The chain that goes with either one of these two watches has soldered links, rolled gold plated; has fine swivel, bar and toggle for attaching a charm or locket. **Regulation length, 12 inches.** A chain that would bring anywhere from $2.00 to $2.50. The movement fitted in either one of these two cases is American made; has 7 jewels, very attractive in appearance, has locomotive on dial, the plates are beautifully engraved and damaskeened, has extra jewels screwed on them so as to further embellish and enhance their beauty. It is stamped "23 jewels adjusted," so as to have the appearance of a railway watch. We sell it for what it is, a good running 7-jeweled American made watch; it is stem wind and pendant set, has patent regulator; in fact, it makes a great trading watch; looks $30.00 value. **Be sure to order by number.**

No. 4T12160 Complete outfit, open face. Price, **$5.15**
No. 4T12162 Complete outfit, hunting style. Price, **5.15**

$4.72 FOR THIS HANDSOME COMPLETE GOLD FILLED LADIES' WATCH and CHAIN OUTFIT.

No. 4T12164

This is a gold filled proposition, the case is gold filled, and the beautiful soldered link ladies' watch guard is gold filled, 48 inches long with handsome stone set slide. The engraving, antique crown, bow and stem, tight joints, strong hinges and inside protecting cap make it the latest model. The movement is American made, stem wind and pendant set; a good, accurate timekeeping watch. Our guarantee for five years accompanies this watch. We guarantee both the case and movement for this term of years against all defective material and workmanship. The size is the appropriate size, just the size that any lady would want to have, not too large, nor too small, but just the size that makes it a good timepiece; technically called the 6-size, complete in beautiful leatherette covered, cloth lined presentation case. **Be sure to order by number.**

No. 4T12164 Price. **$4.72**

HORSE TIMER AT A CUT PRICE.

$3.92

New, up to date, solid nickel, Bassene style, stem wind, jeweled Horse Timer. This timer is operated from the crown by merely pressing down, the same mechanism as used in horse timers worth hundreds of dollars. It has start, stop and fly back arrangements; also, as illustration shows, has a minute register. The escapement is jeweled, increasing the accuracy of the timer. The case is of solid nickel, new Bassene style. Bright polish. The movement is imported from Switzerland, straight line cylinder escapement.

The lever movement, however, is the one we advise you to select. This principle, that is, the **lever escapement principle,** in watch making is accepted as the most accurate and most dependable. We always advise purchasing lever escapement movements.

No. 4T12170 Price........**$3.92**

No. 4T12172 Same style as No. 4T12170, but with fine jeweled lever escapement movement. Price, **$5.95**

No. 4T12170

GOLD FILLED OR SOLID SILVER SMALL O-SIZE LADIES' OPEN FACE WATCHES.

Your choice, $5.18 for a handsome plain polished open face, hinged back, stem wind and pendant set solid silver case, fitted with a very good 7-jeweled Swiss straight line lever movement; a good runner and an accurate timepiece, or the same movement fitted in a gold filled case, plain polish, jointed back and guaranteed for ten years' continual wear.

$7.55 for either one of these cases, solid silver or gold filled, fitted with a genuine Elgin or Waltham movement.

The cases are of perfect construction, small thin model, Bassene style, plain polish, each one fitted with a fine French crystal, antique crown, bow and stem. The Swiss movement quoted in either one of these cases at $5.18, considering the size and price, is a marvel of value. It has full nickeled plates, 7 fine jewels, cut expansion balance, straight line lever escapement.

The Elgin or Waltham movement, according to your choice, fitted in either one of these cases at $7.55, is the latest production of these companies; has all modern improvements; movements that will last your natural lifetime.

These watches are guaranteed to you. With each one we send our written binding guarantee for a term of five years that protects you against faulty material or workmanship.

See the illustration. The cases are perfectly plain, built over solid gold models. Illustration shows the front and back of the case. **Be sure to order by number.**

No. 4T12190 Silver Case, with Swiss movement. Price............**$5.18**
No. 4T12192 Gold Filled Case, with Swiss movement. Price............**$5.18**
No. 4T12194 Silver Case, with Elgin or Waltham movement. Price............**$7.55**
No. 4T12196 Gold Filled Case, with Elgin or Waltham movement. Price............**$7.55**

CUT PRICES.

Illustration shows slightly smaller size.

No. 4T12180

$3.89 for this stem wind and pendant set genuine French enameled open face chatelaine watch. The case is gold filled, enameled in various colors with beautiful intricate floral design. Your choice of any color to match your costume: ruby red, dark blue, light turquoise blue or emerald green. Don't think because of our low figure, $3.89, that it is not a high grade splendid little watch. Its equal is being sold the world over for twice what we ask. This case is up to date, antique stem, crown and bow with snap back and front. The movement is high grade, imported from Switzerland, with solid nickel damaskeened plates, exposed winding wheels and new process straight line cylinder escapement. Considering size of watch, it will keep good time. The illustration shows exact size of the watch. The double illustration gives a better idea of the watch, showing both front and back view. The entire outfit includes a very handsome plush covered, silk lined, shuttered presentation case, exactly as illustrated and a very handsome gold filled chatelette pin. **State color of enamel wanted.** Price............**$3.89**

CUT PRICES.

Illustration shows slightly smaller size.

No. 4T12198

Ladies' Imported non-breakable colored enamel open face chatelaine watch. $4.89 for the complete outfit, including watch, pin and velvet covered silk lined presentation case. The watch is gold filled with applied enamel front and back warranted not to warp, crack or peel off. Enameling done by a secret process. Miniature pictures of rustic scenes true to nature, done in enamel, a masterpiece of artistic skill. The movement is imported from Switzerland, full jeweled, gilt plates, straight line, new process cylinder escapement. Is stem wind and pendant set. Perfectly finished in every detail. The dial is fancy tinted and has solid gold hands. The pin is very handsome, plain polish and gold filled. For service, will last your natural lifetime and matches the watch. The case is the new shuttered style, silk velvet covered and silk lined. The illustration shows the exact picture of this watch. To better illustrate this watch picture shows both front and back view.

Price of outfit, complete including watch, case and chatelette pin............**$4.89**

REDUCED PRICE.

GENTLEMEN'S SMALL EXTRA THIN MODEL SOLID NICKEL WATCH.

$2.56 is our bargain price. Never before has a watch in this small size, thin model been offered at anything like these figures. The case is exactly as illustration shows, if anything, slightly smaller than what the artist has drawn it. It is of solid nickel, snap back and front, new antique crown, bow and stem, is stem wind and pendant set. The dial is very handsome and ornate, done in fancy colors; the illustration does not nor can it convey to you the beautiful effect of the fancy colors on the white dial. The hands are of the Louis XIV style, gilded duplicates of the very fine solid gold hands used on watches worth 20 times what we ask. The movement is imported from Switzerland, see the illustration, not a clock watch, but a regular fine cylinder escapement, full bridged model warranted to run well and accurately. This watch is especially attractive to young men or those desiring a cheap but unpretentious yet modest watch, one that will last a lifetime if properly cared for.

Illustration shows partial view of the movement.

No. 4L836

No. 4L836 Price..$2.56

THIS FINE WATCH BOX FOR 21 CENTS.

No. 4L588 This illustration made from a photograph, shows one of our fine lined and leatherette covered watch boxes that we supply for 21 cents extra with any watch purchased of us. In ordering, state what size watch the case is intended for.

Price........................21c

If by mail, postage extra, 2 cents.

CUT PRICE, 21 CENTS.

No. 4L586 The Ajax Watch Insulator or Protector protects your watch. It is made of a secret compounded metal, beautifully enameled and lined with velvet. Order by number. The maker guarantees that this insulator protects the watch case from wear and the movement from all ordinary magnetic influence. It fits all size watches, open face or hunting style of all makes. When ordering, don't fail to give size and make of case and whether open face or hunting style is wanted. Price..............21c

If by mail, postage extra, 2 cents.

FANCY DIAL.

We show here an illustration of the fancy dial and gold hands that we furnish on different watches quoted and illustrated on the following pages at 90 cents extra.

Fancy dials cannot be fitted on every watch in our catalogue. We caution you only to order them on such watches where it is clearly stated on the page that we can furnish fancy dials. The illustration merely gives you an idea of how the fancy dial will look. They are not all exactly as this picture shows, as they vary in design. They come in various tints, with floral decorations and gold work, and all of them beautiful.

The illustration is a dial made to fit 18-size watches. We furnish any size, 18, 16, 12, 6 and 0-size for American watches.

ALASKA METAL ALL AMERICAN OPEN FACE

WATCH AND CHAIN

No. 4L803

Snap back and snap bezel genuine Alaska metal all American thin model open face watch (the illustration shows both the front and back of watch), **complete with a good guaranteed rolled gold plate gentlemen's vest chain.** $2.49 for a good genuine American stem wind and pendant set nickeled movement fitted in a genuine Alaska metal open face snap back and bezel extra thin model case, together with a fine rolled gold plate, full 12-inch soldered link gentlemen's vest chain, guaranteed for six years, is a price unheard of before. With every watch sold, together with the guarantee on the chain, is sent our five-year written binding watch guarantee. This handsome case as illustrated is made of Alaska metal, a composition of several metals, giving the watch the appearance of solid coin silver. It has the appearance in every way of a very high grade solid silver watch, and in every way except in intrinsic value is its equal. It will wear and retain its solid silver color for a lifetime. The case is handsomely finished in the corrugated pattern with a heavy beaded edge. It is open face, full 18-size, stem wind and pendant set. It is fitted with a very heavy beveled edge French crystal. At $2.49 we furnish this complete outfit, case, movement and chain. The movement fitted in this watch is a genuine American made movement. It has 7 jewels, is stem wind and pendant set, made and sold exclusively by us, and is the output of one of the most representative and well known movement makers in the United States.

No. 4L803 Price, for complete outfit, including chain..$2.49

No. 4L805 The same case as No. 4L803, and chain, but fitted with a 7-jeweled Elgin or Waltham movement..$4.93

Leather Watch Protector made so as to be able to read the time. Constructed of high grade leather, has silk gathering string on top, very transparent durable celluloid front stitched in. This watch protector is meant for open face watches only. We supply it in gentlemen's 18, 16 and 12-size only. **Be sure and give the size of bag wanted.** Order by number.

No. 4L587 Price......15c

ANOTHER GREAT PRICE REDUCTION IN WATCHES THROUGHOUT OUR WATCH DIVISION.

57c AND UPWARD FOR American WATCHES

Nickel, Metal, Electro Plate, Silver, Gold Filled and Solid Gold Watches. Our prices are prices unknown to others. A great saving to buyers. Remember, we are always ready to refund your money if our goods are not found at all times as represented.

No. 4L790 No. 4L794

Your choice of American made watches for 57 cents or 87 cents, advertised and sold throughout the United States for $1.00 and $1.25. Different from the advertised dollar watch, our watch is stem wind and pendant set. No need to open the case to wind or set the hands. This watch for 57 cents is nickel plated, stem wind and pendant set, open face, patent lever movement, runs thirty to thirty-six hours with one winding. We guarantee it to reach destination in perfect going order.

No. 4L790 Price..57c

Our 87-cent watch, as illustrated, No. 4L794, is the watch we recommend. Better than any $1.25 watch sold. This watch is guaranteed American made, is stem wind and pendant set, small 16-size model, made thin and is up to date in every detail. The case is nickel plated, plain polished, open face, as illustration shows. The movement is a lever escapement and is guaranteed. Each one is accompanied by the manufacturer's guarantee for one year. We in turn give our unqualified guarantee backing his. You are doubly secured. Nothing would please your boy better than a watch, and you will be training him how to handle and how to carry a watch at very little cost.

No. 4L794 Price..87c

REDUCED PRICE.

18-SIZE, THIN MODEL, NICKEL OPEN FACE WATCH.

$1.62

A new watch manufactured by one of the most representative watch makers in the East for $1.62. Who ever heard of a really good watch being sold for anything like this money? Yet, we are able, on account of our vast purchasing ability, to procure it at a price which makes this price possible. This watch is guaranteed for a term of one year, we warrant it to run well and to run accurately for this time. Please understand while we give our guarantee for a period of only one year, there is no reason that we know of why this watch will not run well and accurately for five or ten years. It all depends on the care you give the watch. It is stem wind and stem set, is jeweled, has fine porcelain dial, the case is nickel open face, is thin 18-size model, the exact same size as illustration shows. We likewise show the illustration of the movement. It is made of strong metal plates, the same watch under certain names brings at any retail store from $2.50 to $3.00. This astonishing offer is made by us and can be made by us only by reason of our omitting the manufacturer's name. Please don't ask it. You will observe we have carefully erased the manufacturer's name from the plate of the movement as well as from the dial. It runs from 30 to 36 hours with but one winding, we know that you will be more than pleased with it, we know that you will be much surprised. Send us $1.62 together with 14 cents, the registry mail charges, a total of $1.76, and we will mail you this watch by registered mail. If you do not find it in every way satisfactory and in every way as described, you can return it and we will refund your money together with all transportation charges.

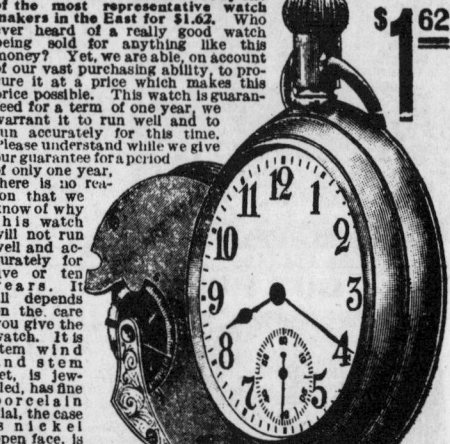

No. 4L829

No. 4L829 Price..$1.62

CASH WITH THE ORDER must be sent for all repair work. If you do not know what the cost will be, send what you think will more than cover it and we will refund the balance. If to be returned by mail, send 7 cents for each watch for postage and 8 cents extra for registry.

WATCH REPAIRS AT ONE-HALF THE PRICE ASKED BY OTHERS

REMEMBER **that a watch should not run longer than one and one-half years without having the oil cleaned off and fresh oil applied.** An engine or sewing machine will be oiled several times a day, but we have known people to carry a watch for ten years without having it cleaned or fresh oil applied. Usually a movement thus treated is of **no value, being entirely worn out.** Our charge for cleaning and oiling is **50 cents.** The regular price is $1.50. We give below a list of charges for repairs which will be subject to changes in some cases. For example: Old fusee watches, made some fifty or sixty years ago in England, the material of which is difficult to procure.

Balances, American Expansion	$1.50 to $2.75
Balances, American Steel or Nickel	.50
Balances, English, Steel or Composition	1.00
Balances, Swiss, Composition	.75
Balances, Swiss, with Screw	1.25
Balances, Swiss, Expansion, cut	3.00
Cleaning, ordinary Swiss, Duplex or American	.50
Cleaning, ordinary English	1.00
Demagnetizing Watch Movements	75c to 1.00
Dials, Swiss, without seconds	1.00
Dials, Swiss, with seconds	1.50
Hairsprings, ordinary flat	.75
Hairsprings, Breguet	1.50
Hands, common, each	.10
Hands, fine, each	.20
Jewels, American, Cock or Foot (with settings)	.50
Jewels, American, 3d, 4th or 'Scape	50c to .75
Jewels, Endstone, in setting	.50
Jewels, Cap, Swiss (with plate)	.25
Jewels, Swiss, 3d, 4th, 'Scape or Balance, set in plate	.50
Jewels, Swiss, 3d, 4th, 'Scape or Balance, Fine Ruby	1.50
Jewels, Swiss, Center, Fine Ruby in Gold Set	3.00
Jewels, Roller	.35
Jewels, Pallet, Set in Old Settings, American	.75
Mainsprings, Swiss	.50

Mainsprings, English, with hook	$0.75
Mainsprings, American	.50
Mainsprings, Repeaters, etc.	$1.00 to 1.50
Pallets, Fork and Arbor, complete, ordinary	3.00
Pallets, Fork and Arbor, complete, American	$1.25 to 2.50
Pinions, American, 3d, 4th or 'Scape	.75
Pinions, American Center	1.00
Pinions, American, Center, Patent, complete with Wheel	2.00
Pinions, Cannon	.50
Pinions, Swiss, 3d, 4th or 'Scape, ordinary	1.00
Pinions, Swiss, 3d, 4th or 'Scape, fine	$1.75 to 2.00
Pinions, Swiss, Center, ordinary	1.50
Pinions, Swiss, Center, fine	2.00
Pinions, Swiss, Cannon	.50
Ratchets, English, Swiss or American	.50
Staffs, Balance, American	75c to 1.25
Staffs, Balance, English, ordinary	1.25
Staffs, Balance, Swiss, ordinary	1.25
Staffs, Balance, Swiss, fine	2.50

CHANGING KEY WIND CASES TO STEM WIND.

Silver Cases	$1.50
Gold Cases	2.50

WHEN WATCHES **are sent with instructions to put them in good order we will do everything necessary to put them in good running condition,** but when the instructions are to repair a certain particular part of a watch, the repairs will be strictly confined to the part or parts specified and we cannot hold ourselves responsible for anything further than may be necessary to insure correct running of the watch. In sending any part of a watch, if your intention is to fit same yourself, do not instruct us to fit same, but kindly use the word "select." This prevents misunderstanding your wishes. If an idea of the cost cannot be obtained from this list, send the watch to us and on receipt of same we will examine it, quote cost of repairing and hold for instructions.

SHIPPING DIRECTIONS. **When shipping watches or jewelry for repairs or exchange, mark plainly as follows: "Sears, Roebuck & Co., Watch Repair Department, Chicago, Ill.,"** and in upper left hand corner put your own name and address, prefixing the word "From." Also enclose a card in the package with your own name and address and stating that the watch is for repairs. If you send a watch or small piece of jewelry by mail, be sure to put letter postage (2 cents an ounce) on it, because the writing on the card put inside the package makes it subject to first class mail charges. It is safer to send it as first class mail anyway, and it would be better to register it for 8 cents additional. The government guarantees safe delivery of registered mail. At the same time you send the package write us a separate letter, stating that you have sent a watch (by mail or express) for repairs, what repairs you want made, or that you wish us to quote cost of repairing.

GOLD ELECTRO PLATE, 18-SIZE OPEN FACE SCREW BACK AND BEZEL AND HUNTING STYLE

$2.15 $2.79

$2.15 OR $2.79 for this gold plated Gentlemen's Watch, 18-size, with either one of the two movements, we illustrate here, just as you desire and, furthermore you can have them open face or hunting style, the price is the same.

THESE ARE GUARANTEED WATCHES.

With every one, we send our five-year sweeping binding guarantee which applies ONLY on the movement. We guarantee these movements to be lever escapement, American made, to have seven jewels, and against all defective workmanship or material and to run well for a term of five years. The cases are splendid protections to the movements, but are not guaranteed for any period of time. They may wear for three months to a year like gold or they may not; it all depends on the care displayed in wearing it. The watch we send for $2.15; the case is 18-size, beautifully engraved, gold plated and has the appearance of a gold filled watch, advertised extensively in many periodicals and journals throughout the United States as a $3.75 to $5.00 value.

IF YOU WANT THE OPEN FACE CASE, you will receive a case made in the screw back and screw bezel pattern, it is dust and dampproof, and an excellent protection to the movement.

IF YOU ORDER THE HUNTING STYLE, you will receive a case made in the latest pattern, double lidded back and front with an inside protecting cap. The movement illustrated at the left, is the one you will receive fitted in this case for $2.15. This movement has 7 jewels, lever escapement, genuine American made and runs for 30 to 36 hours with one winding.

FOR $2.79, you will receive either an open face or a hunting style case according to your desire, fitted with the movement illustrated on the right. It is the movement, if you desire a flashy conspicuous and beautiful appearing watch, that we advise you to buy. This movement has the appearance, remember only the appearance, of a 23 jeweled railway watch, it is made with a view to supplying the demand for such a watch. Many individuals desire a movement that is flashy, many people desire a watch that has the appearance of the highest grade American timers at one-tenth the cost. This movement has this appearance. Large imitation jewels are fixed on the plates with screws, has a patent regulator, and an engraving of a locomotive running at full speed is outlined on the plates, likewise a photograph of a locomotive appears upon the dial. Each movement is stamped 23 jewels and the word "Adjusted." As a matter of fact, this movement only contains 7 jewels, is not adjusted, but it would take an expert, one well posted and well informed in watches to know that this was true. It is stem wind and stem set and runs for 30 to 36 hours with one winding. Be sure to order by number.

No. 4L860 Open face, 7 jeweled movement. Price, $2.15
No. 4L862 Hunting style, 7 jeweled movement. Price.......... 2.15
No 4L864 Open face, imitation 23 jeweled flashy movement. Price.......... 2.79
No. 4L866 Hunting style, imitation 23 jeweled flashy movement. Price.......... 2.79

16-SIZE GUNMETAL WATCH

$2.48

No. 4L870

REDUCED IN PRICE.

No. 4L870 Gentlemen's 16-size, thin model, open face, plain polished, gunmetal watch. Has beautiful fancy dial as illustration shows. The movement is imported from Switzerland, has jeweled cylinder escapement and damaskeened nickel plates. It is recommended to all who desire a cheap and durable watch. Price.......... $2.48

GENTLEMEN'S 16-SIZE OPEN FACE SOLID GOLD INLAID ON SOLID SILVER

$7.98

$7.98 for a solid gold inlaid solid silver case, 16-size extra thin model solid silver case, screw back and screw bezel, stem wind and stem set, the inlaying done in various colors of gold to represent different floral designs with a solid gold shield in the center in varicolored gold border.

THE GENUINE ARTICLE

Not a filled case, not a brass case, but a case that will wear your natural lifetime, being solid silver. $7.98 complete, this solid gold inlaid solid silver case fitted with a genuine 15 jeweled American model movement, a movement that we guarantee for five years, is one of our challenge offers. This movement is stem wind and pendant set, has 15 jewels in gold screw settings, Breguet hairspring, patent pinions, patent regulator, beautiful nickel damaskeened plates, in fact a high grade, up to date thin model movement, such as we know will give entire satisfaction. It carries our five-year written binding guarantee, protecting you against all breakages during the term of our guarantee when caused by faulty material or workmanship. Dustproof and dampproof. This is only possible in this style of case.

No. 4L868

No. 4L868 16-Size, Open Face, Screw Back and Screw Bezel.

THIS ILLUSTRATION SHOWS the handsome 15 jeweled, lever escapement, fine finished movement we fit in this case for **$7.98**

SEND US $7.98 and we will send you this watch and if you do not find it in every way exactly as described, return it to us and we will upon its receipt return your money, together with the transportation charges.

No. 4L868 Price.......... $7.98

6-SIZE SILVER LIKE ALASKA METAL COMPOUND CASES

$3.10 AND UP

Something New.

OUR 6-SIZE ALASKA METAL WATCHES in hunting and open face style. Alaska metal is one of the newly compounded metals. It looks like silver, wears like silver, has the same color and appearance as silver, but is very much tougher and costs less. At $3.10 to $9.65 we are offering these Alaska metal ladies' watches.

THE MOVEMENTS

are all representative makes, each one of them is guaranteed an accurate timekeeper and WE FULLY WARRANT THEM FOR A TERM OF 5 YEARS against defective material or workmanship.

No. 4L878 Open Face, Jointed Style. No. 4L880 Hunting Style.

$3.10 TO $9.65 for your choice of these cases, either the open face or the hunting style, fitted with your own selection. For a watch that will keep absolutely correct time and one that will be a pleasure to you forever, a movement that carries our 5-year written binding guarantee, we would suggest that you select either one of these cases fitted with the 17 jeweled Plymouth Watch Co. movement. See the quotations in the table below offering the watch at $9.00 or $9.40 according to style of case.

25 cents will carry any watch to any part of the United States by express.

We fit these cases with the following 6-size movements. Prices quoted are for the complete watch, movement and case.	No. 4L878 6-size Alaska Metal Open Face	No. 4L880 6-size Alaska Metal Hunting Style
7 JEWELED AMERICAN MAKE, nickel plates..........	$3.10	$3.50
COUNTESS JANET, stamped 17 jeweled, adjusted..........	3.30	3.70
7 Jeweled Elgin or Waltham, gilt plates..	4.85	5.25
7 Jeweled Elgin or Waltham, nickel plates	5.40	5.80
15 Jeweled Elgin or Waltham, nickel plates	6.50	6.90
16 Jeweled Lady Waltham, nickel plates..	9.25	9.65
17 JEWELED PLYMOUTH WATCH CO., nickel plates, patent regulator, special make..........	9.00	9.40

MOVING PICTURE WATCH REDUCED IN PRICE

No. 4L872 Panorama watch, 18-size, open face, extra thin model, solid back snap bezel, bright polished gunmetal novelty panorama watch. Something new and novel. Just brought over from Switzerland. It has a good jeweled Swiss cylinder movement and will keep fairly good time. The illustration shows the back view of the watch. This is a panorama watch. On the rear side, as illustration shows, a revolving disc, very ingeniously made, turns to view continually various French actresses. This panorama is protected by a crystal placed in a bright polished gold plated bezel, making a very pretty frame for each picture as it turns into place. The dial is one of the new illuminated fancy French dials done in colored enamel. It has a new, up to date pendant. The bow and crown are gold plated. While we do not guarantee this watch for any specified period of time we are conscientious in saying that it will give you entire satisfaction, and guarantee its being received in good going order.

$3.38 MOVING PICTURES.

No. 4L872

Price.......... $3.38

12-SIZE SOLID SILVER AND ALASKA METAL WATCHES

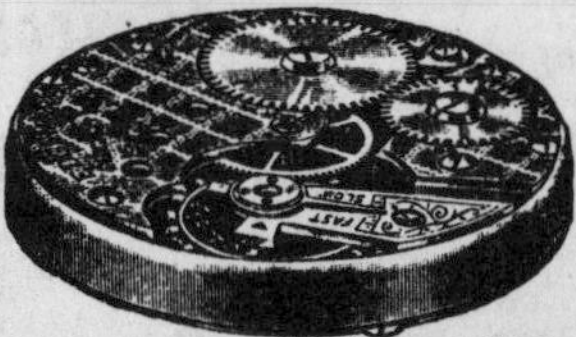

The above is an illustration of our 15 jewel 12-size Edgemere Movement, see page 21 for accurate description.

ALASKA METAL COMPOUND. This metal is the nearest approach in appearance to solid silver yet discovered. It looks like silver and will not tarnish. In fact, an ideal metal compound for the use of case making. We cannot tell you the ingredients. That part is secret, known only to the manufacturer. We can tell you only that a large percentage of pure nickel enters into its composition. Experts have been deceived in our Alaska metal compound, it so much resembles silver.

DESCRIPTION OF THE EDGEMERE MOVEMENT. 12-size, Open Face or Hunting; Alaska metal bright polished, damaskeened plates; 15 fine ruby jewels. Breguet hairspring, cut balance, patent pinions, beveled screw heads, exposed winding arrangement, double sunk dial, moon hands and red marginal figures.

No. 4L890 Alaska Metal, Open Face, Screw Back and Bezel.
No. 4L892 Alaska Metal, Hunting Style.
No. 4L894 Solid Silver, Open Face, Screw Back and Bezel.
No. 4L896 Solid Silver, Hunting Style.

These watches are made of solid silver or Alaska metal through and through.

$3.70 AND UP

The above illustration shows the open face, screw back and bezel and the hunting style, furnished in Alaska metal and solid silver.

We fit these cases with the following 12-size movements. Prices quoted are for the complete watch, movement and case.	No. 4L890 12-size Alaska Metal Open Face	No. 4L892 12-size Alaska Metal Hunting Style	No. 4L894 12-size Solid Silver Open Face	No. 4L896 12-size Solid Silver Hunting Style
7 Jeweled Edgemere, nickel plates..........	$ 3.70	$ 4.10	$ 5.25	$ 5.50
7 Jeweled Elgin or Waltham, nickel plates...	5.95	6.35	7.50	7.75
15 JEWELED EDGEMERE, special make..	5.75	6.10	7.25	7.50
15 Jeweled Elgin or Waltham, nickel plates, patent regulator..........	8.15	8.55	9.70	9.95
17 JEWELED PLYMOUTH WATCH CO., nickel plates, patent regulator, special make	9.35	9.60	15.22	15.62
17 Jeweled No. 321 Grade Elgin..........	15.57	15.97	17.12	17.37
19 Jeweled No. 189 Grade Elgin..........	27.90	28.30	28.95	29.20
21 JEWELED SWISS, nickel plates, patent regulator, adjusted....	20.10	20.50	21.65	21.90

GOLD FILLED WATCHES 16-SIZE, 12-SIZE, 6-SIZE AND 0-SIZE, ALL THIN MODELS REDUCED IN PRICE $4.40 AND UP

BOTH OPEN FACE AND HUNTING STYLE—Guaranteed for a Term of Ten Years

FOR 90 CENTS EXTRA we can furnish fancy dial and gold hands on any watch on this page. See Illustration on page 417.

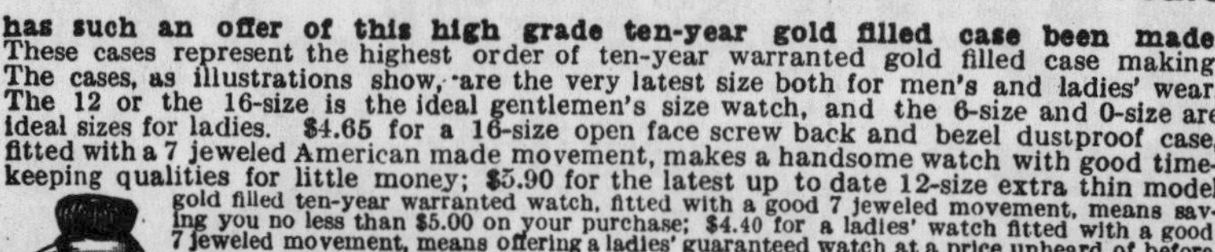

NEVER BEFORE has such an offer of this high grade ten-year gold filled case been made. These cases represent the highest order of ten-year warranted gold filled case making. The cases, as illustrations show, are the very latest size both for men's and ladies' wear. The 12 or the 16-size is the ideal gentlemen's size watch, and the 6-size and 0-size are ideal sizes for ladies. $4.65 for a 16-size open face screw back and bezel dustproof case, fitted with a 7 jeweled American made movement, makes a handsome watch with good timekeeping qualities for little money; $5.90 for the latest up to date 12-size extra thin model gold filled ten-year warranted watch, fitted with a good 7 jeweled movement, means saving you no less than $5.00 on your purchase; $4.40 for a ladies' watch fitted with a good 7 jeweled movement, means offering a ladies' guaranteed watch at a price unheard of before.

GUARANTEED FOR 10 YEARS

We fit these cases with the following 16-size movements. Prices quoted are for complete watch, movement and case.	No. 4T13202 16-Size Open Face	No. 4T13200 16-Size Hunting Style
7 Jeweled American Made Movement	$ 4.65	$ 4.95
7 Jeweled Elgin, Hampden or Waltham Movement	8.18	8.48
15 Jeweled Elgin, Hampden or Waltham Movement	10.65	10.95
17 Jeweled Elgin, Hampden or Waltham Movement	12.85	13.15

We fit these cases with the following 12-size movements. Prices quoted are for complete watch, movement and case.	No. 4T13206 12-Size Open Face	No. 4T13204 12-Size Hunting Style
7 Jeweled Swiss Movement	$ 5.90	$ 6.25
7 Jeweled Elgin or Waltham Movement	7.68	8.03
15 Jeweled Elgin or Waltham Movement	10.15	10.50
17 Jeweled Elgin or Waltham Movement	12.35	12.70

We fit the above cases with the following 6-size movements. Prices quoted are for complete watch, movement and case.	No. 4T13208 6-Size Hunting Style
7 Jeweled American Made Movement	$ 4.40
7 Jeweled Elgin, Hampden or Waltham Movement	6.30
15 Jeweled Elgin, Hampden or Waltham Movement	8.50
16 Jeweled Lady Waltham Movememt, adjusted grade	10.40

We fit above cases with the following 0-size movements. Prices quoted are for complete watch, movement and case.	No. 4T13210 0-Size Hunting Style
7 Jeweled Fine Swiss Movement	$ 6.30
7 Jeweled Elgin or Waltham Movement	8.40
15 Jeweled Elgin or Waltham Movement	11.70
16 Jeweled Lady Waltham Movement	14.80

GUARANTEED FOR 10 YEARS

16-SIZE No. 4T13200 Hunting Style. No. 4T13202 Open Face, Screw Back and Screw Bezel. 12-SIZE No. 4T13204 Hunting Style, No. 4T13206 Open Face, Screw Back and Screw Bezel. 6-SIZE No. 4T13208 Hunting Style only. 0-SIZE No. 4T13210 Hunting Style only.

GOLD FILLED GUARANTEED 12-SIZE WATCHES, EXTRA THIN MODEL OPEN FACE OR HUNTING STYLE

$4.98

$4.98 FOR YOUR CHOICE of either one of these gold filled gentlemen's extra thin model 12-size watches. The 12-size watch is one size smaller than the regulation 16-size; it is the smallest gentlemen's American watch manufactured. It does not weigh down or bulge out the pocket. For Sunday or holiday wear or when not occupied by heavy labor, it is the ideal size for a gentleman to carry.

OPEN FACE OR HUNTING STYLE, according to your own selection. The price is the same; they cost us the same, and we give you the advantage of the purchase.

THE CASES ARE GOLD FILLED, handsomely engraved, exactly as illustration shows. The open face case is screw back and screw bezel, dust and dampproof, and an excellent protection to the movement, a style that is very popular and most frequently purchased.

GUARANTEED FOR 5 YEARS

No. 4T13230 12-Size. Open Face. No. 4T13232 12-Size. Hunting Style.

THE HUNTING STYLE CASE is double lidded with inside protecting cap, engraved the same as the open face style.

THE MOVEMENT we fit in either one of these cases, open face or hunting style (be sure to give the number when ordering, so as to avoid all possible error), is a good 7 jeweled lever escapement movement, is stem wind and pendant set, has exposed winding wheels and nickeled plates, hard white enameled dial with fine blued spade steel hands.

No. 4T13230 Open Face Style. Price........................**$4.98**
No. 4T13232 Hunting Style. Price........................**4.98**

LOOK AT THIS ILLUSTRATION AND READ OUR CAREFUL DESCRIPTION OF THIS ASTONISHING GENTLEMEN'S GOLD FILLED WATCH VALUE

$4.28 CUT PRICE

YOUR CHOICE FOR $4.28 either one of these two watches, open face or hunting style, whichever you desire, gold filled guaranteed cases, manufactured by one of the most representative case makers in the United States. On account of this cut price we cannot mention the maker's name, but each one carries a five-year guarantee, together with our own written binding warrant, that insures and protects you for a term of five years. The movement, as illustrated and exactly as described, is manufactured by one of the largest watch movement factories in the world. If you select either one you are getting the very latest up to date, extra thin, 16-size model, stem wind and pendant set watch; modern in every way, perfectly finished in every detail and a marvel of value.

GUARANTEED FOR 5 YEARS

THE CASES (be sure to order by number) are made of two solid plates of gold overlaying an inner composition metal, and by the warrant and contract that we send they are guaranteed to wear for a term of five years. The engraving is artistic and attractive, varying somewhat from the illustration, although we aim always to have on hand the exact same design as illustration shows; if not, we send some very similar design with the understanding, of course, that the grade of the case is the same.

THE MOVEMENT used in these cases is stem wind and pendant set, high polished exposed winding wheels, full protecting dust bands, 7 fine ruby jewels, latest model straight line lever escapement, and unlike any other movement placed on the market and offered at double what we ask.

No. 4T13223 16-Size. Hunting Style. No. 4T13221 16-Size. Open Face, Screw Back and Bezel.

No. 4T13221 Open face, dust and dampproof, screw back and bezel case, gold filled and guaranteed for five years. Price........................**$4.28**

No. 4T13223 Hunting style, gold filled case, guaranteed for five years. Price........................**4.28**

Please do not fail to observe that you may have your choice, either the open face or hunting style watch, at precisely the same price, and that each one of them, open face or hunting style, carries with it our sweeping, binding guarantee for a term of five years, a protection not alone on the case, but also on the movement.

25c will carry any watch to any part of the United States by express. We recommend sending watches by express as they do not receive the hard usage as when sent by mail. If sent by mail, postage extra, including registry, 18 cents.

$6.66 FOR THIS SPLENDID TIMER.

A GENTLEMEN'S GOLD FILLED, GUARANTEED FOR TWENTY YEARS, 16-SIZE, EXTRA THIN MODEL ALL AMERICAN MADE WATCH.

GUARANTEED FOR 20 YEARS

The case is gold filled, plain polished, open face; illustration shows side view and three-quarter view of face, showing its extreme thinness and graceful outline. It is guaranteed for twenty years' continual wear, plainly stamped on the inside of back lid.

The movement is manufactured in the United States (see the illustration), it is made of nickel plates, has exposed winding wheels, straight line lever escapement, blued steel Breguet hairspring, polished escape wheel with true timing screws, is stem wind and pendant set. Our written binding guarantee goes with every one, which protects you against defective material and workmanship for five years. The dial is plain white hard enameled, beautiful in its simplicity. $6.66 means cutting the regular selling price no less than 25 per cent. **Be sure to order by number.**

No. 4T13244 Price, complete........................**$6.66**

$3.98 A MARVEL OF VALUE

GUARANTEED FOR 10 YEARS

GENTLEMEN'S GOLD FILLED THIN MODEL AMERICAN MADE 12-SIZE OPEN FACE WATCH.

$3.98 FOR THIS COMPLETE WATCH is an unheard of price for 12-size gold filled watches. See the illustration showing the front and full side view. The case is gold filled, new small 12-size, guaranteed for ten years, the maker's warrant is plainly stamped on inside of the back cap, it is plain polished, has the latest up to date French antique pendant. The dial, one of its handsomest features, is gold gilded with black numerals, has fancy engine turned center, something new and attractive. The movement is American made of nickel plates, duplex escapement, one of the simplest escapements known. Our five-year guarantee on the movement, protecting you against defective material and workmanship goes with each one.

No. 4T13240 Price........................**$3.98**

GOLD FILLED, 16-SIZE, 20-YEAR GUARANTEED OPEN FACE OR HUNTING STYLE. CUT PRICES IN EXTRA THIN MODEL WATCHES

$6.25 AND UP

For 90 cents extra we can furnish a fancy dial and gold hands on any of these watches.

Illustrations on this page show exact size.

Protect your watch with an Ajax Watch Insulator. See page 417. No. 4T1108 Price, 21 cents.

$6.25 AND UP

Plymouth. Gold Filled. Engine Turned. Guaranteed for 20 years.
No. 4T13300 Open face, screw back and bezel.
No. 4T13302 Hunting style.

Plymouth. Gold Filled. Guaranteed for 20 years.
No. 4T13303 Plymouth, open face, screw back and bezel.
No. 4T13305 Plymouth, hunting style.

Plymouth. Gold Filled. Guaranteed for 20 years.
No. 4T13307 Plymouth, open face, screw back and bezel.
No. 4T13309 Plymouth, hunting style.

Dueber. Gold Filled. Guaranteed for 20 years.
No. 4T13312 Open face, screw back and bezel.
No. 4T13314 Hunting style.

Illinois Watch Case Co. Giant. Gold Filled. Guaranteed for 20 years.
No. 4T13316 Open face, screw back and bezel.
No. 4T13318 Hunting style.

GUARANTEED FOR 20 YEARS

$6.25 AND UP

Plymouth. Gold filled, plain polished. Guaranteed for 20 years.
No. 4T13320 Open face, screw back and screw bezel.
No. 4T13322 Hunting style. Reduced price.

We fit these cases with the following 16-size movements. Prices quoted are for the complete watch, movement and case.	Nos. 4T13300 4T13303 4T13307 4T13312 4T13316 4T13320	Nos. 4T13302 4T13305 4T13309 4T13314 4T13318 4T13322
7 Jeweled American Made Movement	$ 6.25	$ 8.75
7 Jeweled Elgin, Hampden or Waltham Movement	9.78	12.28
15 Jeweled Elgin, Hampden or Waltham Movement	12.25	14.75
17 Jeweled Elgin, Hampden or Waltham Movement	14.45	16.95
17 Jeweled Elgin Movement, adjusted grade	17.20	19.70
17 Jeweled Royal Waltham Movement, adjusted grade	18.50	21.00
19 Jeweled Riverside Waltham Movement, adjusted grade	24.50	27.00
21 Jeweled Prince of Wales, Plymouth Watch Co., adjusted, patent regulator, nickel plates	18.40	20.25

Every movement quoted on this page is guaranteed against defective material and workmanship for a term of five years. Wherever this guarantee is mentioned in the catalog description we send it with the watch. Understand, this is a sweeping binding guarantee and protects you against defective material and workmanship.

MONEY REFUNDED, together with transportation charges, if you receive an unsatisfactory watch from us. When your watch arrives, examine it carefully, and if you do not find it in absolutely perfect condition, in every way exactly what you wanted, return it, and as soon as we receive it we will refund your money, together with all transportation charges, if you so desire.

GOLD FILLED, NEW THIN MODEL, DUEBER-HAMPDEN COMPLETE WATCHES

OPEN FACE AND HUNTING STYLE. 16-SIZE, 20-YEAR WARRANTED GOLD FILLED.

These cases are made by the Dueber Watch Co. They are the correct thing, the right size and shape, hand engraved and in every respect perfect. The movements are all new models manufactured by the Hampden Watch Co., each one guaranteed an accurate timepiece for five years. Note the prices and compare them with what others ask for the same watch.

Select the watch you want in gold filled open face or hunting style. The gold filled cases of the John C. Dueber factory are known to be exactly as represented, guaranteed for twenty and twenty-five years and so stamped on the inside lid, together with our own written binding guarantee. You are amply protected in selecting a John C. Dueber watch.

If you select the open face watch we will send you the new dust and damp proof, screw back and screw bezel case. Not jointed, but the latest idea in open face case making.

The hunting style cases are the Bassene type, close joined, no raw or unsightly edges.

GUARANTEED FOR 20 YEARS

$11.00 AND UP

No. 4T13341 Gold Filled. Open face, guaranteed for 20 years.
No. 4T13345 Hunting style, guaranteed for 20 years.

Prices quoted are for the complete watch, movement and case.	4T13341 Open Face, 20 years	4T13345 Hunting Style, 20 yrs.
Full 15 Jeweled Hampden Movement	$11.00	$13.50
Full 17 Jeweled General Stark Movement	13.00	15.50
Full 17 Jeweled William McKinley Movement	16.00	18.50
Full 21 Jeweled William McKinley Movement	26.50	29.00

$15.25 FOR A HIGH GRADE WATCH

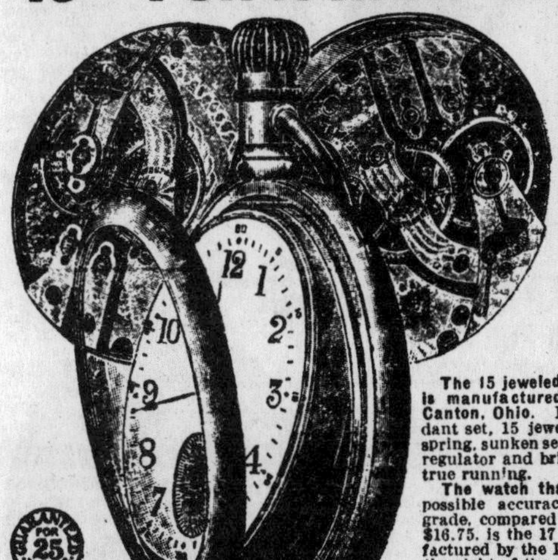

This gold filled absolutely dust and damp proof twenty-five year guaranteed watch for $15.25 if you select the 15 jeweled movement, or $16.75 if you select the 17 jeweled movement, means breaking all accepted prices. The case is gold filled, plain polished, manufactured by one of the most renowned watch case makers in the United States; their trade mark and warranty are stamped in the back of each case. Patent dust and damp proof solid back cup case means everything in an open face watch (see the illustration). The back is of solid metal, the front or bezel operates on a screw. The movement is fitted into a swinging ring which drops back into the cup or solid part of the case. By this device it is impossible for dust or damp to penetrate into the delicate mechanism of the movement. Together with this wonderful improvement, this case has the screw nut crown; dust or damp cannot filter into the works through this part of the watch.

The 15 jeweled movement quoted in this case for $15.25 is manufactured by the Dueber-Hampden Watch Co., of Canton, Ohio. It is made of nickel, stem wind and pendant set, 15 jewels in composition settings, Breguet hairspring, sunken second dial, patent safety pinion, micrometric regulator and bright flat screws, a marvel for accuracy and true running.

The watch that we recommend, however, for the highest possible accuracy, a watch that has no equal, grade for grade, compared with any other make and quoted here for $16.75, is the 17 jeweled Gen. Stark movement, also manufactured by the Dueber-Hampden Watch Co., illustrated on the right of the case. The jewels are genuine ruby set in composition settings, plates are bridge model of nickel, has Breguet hairspring, patent safety pinion, mean time screws, patent regulator, bright flat screws, plates are beautifully engraved and damaskeened in gold letter. We warrant these movements and send with every watch our five-year written binding guarantee protecting you against all defective material and workmanship.

We challenge investigation. Our claim is simply this, concerning the 15-jeweled grade Dueber-Hampden Watch Co. movement or their 17 jeweled grade. For true running and for accurate time there is no watch manufactured in the United States that can surpass them.

The John C. Dueber Watch Co. is one of the oldest manufacturers in the United States; the business has been handed down from father to son, and they are renowned from one end of the United States to the other for the perfection of their product, the care they exhibit in every detail and the personal pride they have in making every watch they turn out the best possible. **Order by number.**

No. 4T13370 Price, complete with the 15 jeweled movement......$15.25
No. 4T13372 Price, complete with the 17 jeweled movement......16.75

A BOSS GOLD FILLED, 16-SIZE, 17 JEWELED ADJUSTED WATCH

Your Choice, $14.42 for the Open Face or $16.90 for the Hunting Style.

GUARANTEED FOR 20 YEARS

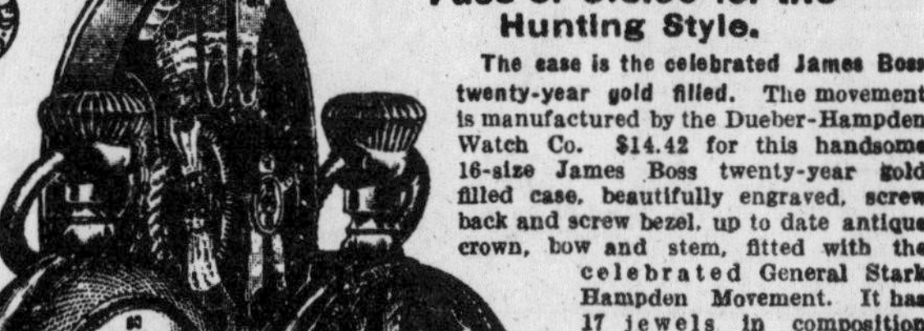

The case is the celebrated James Boss twenty-year gold filled. The movement is manufactured by the Dueber-Hampden Watch Co. $14.42 for this handsome 16-size James Boss twenty-year gold filled case, beautifully engraved, screw back and screw bezel, up to date antique crown, bow and stem, fitted with the celebrated General Stark Hampden Movement. It has 17 jewels in composition settings, patent center pinion, Breguet hairspring, mean time screws, patent regulator, bright flat screws; the plates are of nickel, engraved and damaskeened; has gold letter Arabic dial with red marginal figures; in fact, a movement that cannot be beaten for accurate and true running. $16.90 for hunting style, beautifully engraved twenty-year James Boss gold filled case with the same movement described above. **Order by number.**

No. 4T13380 Open face. Price........$14.42
No. 4T13382 Hunting style. Price........$16.90

FULL ENGRAVED SOLID SILVER, GOLD FILLED AND GUNMETAL MOON CALENDAR WATCHES FOR $4.85 AND UPWARD.

$4.85

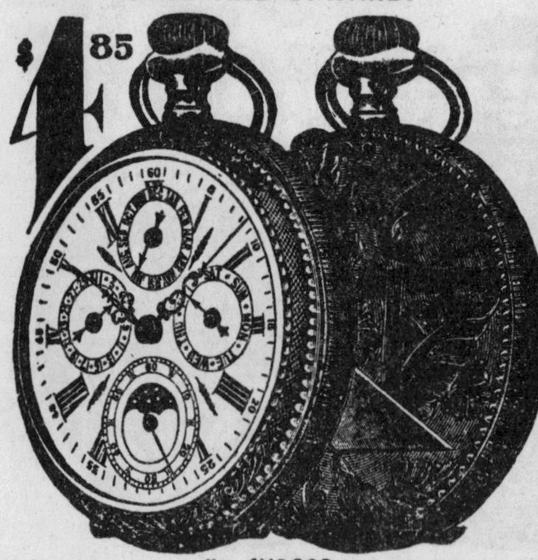

No. 4H2662

A mechanical wonder for $4.85. This watch not only tells the hours, minutes and seconds, but gives the days of the week, the dates of the days and the month. The most complicated, most wonderful mechanical piece of mechanism. Exact same size as illustration shows, exact thickness, exact counterpart in every way. It is not more easily broken, not more liable to get out of order, than any watch illustrated in this catalogue. The price is within reach of all. It is fully guaranteed to wear, the manufacturer in turn guarantees it to us. It comes in open face only, is stem wind and stem set, has antique stem and bow, beautifully engraved. Illustration shows both back and front of the watch. The movement is imported from Switzerland, is full 11 jeweled, finely polished exposed winding wheels, straight line lever escapement. In fact, such a watch that we recommend, and will send our five-year written binding guarantee with every one shipped. Remember, we can furnish this watch in open face only.

No. 4H2662 Price for solid oxidized gunmetal case, plain finish, with 11 jeweled movement .... $ 4.85

No. 4H2664 Price for solid silver case, fully engraved, with 11 jeweled movement 7.45

No. 4H2666 Price for gold filled case, handsomely engraved, guaranteed for 20 years, with 11 jeweled movement 13.70

OUR NEW IMPROVED CALENDAR WATCH.

$3.18

No. 4H2672

Own one of these watches and you can always tell the day of the month, the hour of the day or minute of the hour. $3.18 is what we ask for this unique watch. Simple in construction; not more liable to get out of order than any good watch. The case is made of solid nickel, has inside protecting glass cap, has jointed back and jointed front bezel, up to date antique bow and stem. The movement is a fine 5 jeweled cylinder movement, will keep very good time, has bright polish double exposed winding wheels, and the bridges are of the new graceful Swiss style. The dial, as illustration shows, is of fine white enamel. The outer margin shows the days of the month and the inner circle the figures of the hour of the day. You will note that the dial is equipped with four hands; the second hand the hour and the minute hand are made of fine goldine metal, fancy Louis XIV style; the calendar hand pointing out the day of the month is of fine blued steel of pleasing design. $3.18 is a very small amount of money to spend on a watch of such interesting parts. The calendar works automatically, always indicating accurately the day of the month. This watch is stem wind and stem set, exact same size as illustration shows, not too large not too thick, in fact a gentlemen's size watch. We guarantee to ship it in perfect going order. If you find after receiving this watch it is not in every way as described or fails to perform its duties perfectly, you can return it to us and we will, upon its receipt, at once refund your money.

No. 4H2672 Price $3.18

A MECHANICAL WONDER

$3.48

No. 4H2676

No. 4H2676 Panorama watch, 18-size, open face, extra thin model, solid back snap bezel, bright polished gunmetal novelty panorama watch. Something new and novel. Just brought over from Switzerland. It has a good jeweled Swiss cylinder movement and will keep fairly good time. The illustration shows the back view as well as the front of the watch. This is a panorama watch. On the rear side, as illustration shows, a revolving disc, very ingeniously made, turns to view continually various French actresses. This panorama is protected by a crystal placed in a bright polished gold plated bezel, making a very pretty frame for each picture as it turns into place. The dial is one of the new illuminated fancy French dials done in colored enamel. It has a new, up to date pendant. The bow and crown are gold plated. While we do not guarantee this watch for any specified period of time, we are conscientious in saying that it will give you entire satisfaction, and guarantee its being received in good going order.

Price $3.48

PRICES CUT ON WATCHES (8 DAY)

No. 4H2668 SILVER, $9.25
No. 4H2670 NICKEL, $7.80

$9.25 for an 8-day, 15 jeweled solid silver open face watch.

$7.80 for an 8-day, 15 jeweled solid nickel open face watch.

An Eight-Day Watch now perfected. Why be bothered winding your watch every night? Each one carries with it our written, binding, five-year guarantee; we warrant it to run accurately and give entire satisfaction for a term of five years. Remember, you need wind it but once every eight days. Never before, at anything like the price, has such a marvel of mechanical skill been offered; never before has an eight-day watch been successfully constructed. At $9.25 we have to offer a solid silver, eight-day, full 15 jeweled Swiss lever, stem wind and stem set watch, warranted for five years. The case is heavy solid silver, plain polished, open face, jointed front and back. The movement has 15 fine ruby jewels, finely gilded plates, has lever escapement, cut balance wheel, true timing screws, polished safety pinions, Breguet hairspring, and is manufactured by one of the largest and most reliable concerns in Switzerland.

No. 4H2668
New Model Antique Bow.

No. 4H2668 15 jeweled, solid silver, eight-day watch. Price $9.25

For $7.80 we offer a fine solid nickel case, open face, plain polished, stem wind and stem set, fitted with a fine eight-day, 15 jeweled, gilded movement, made in Switzerland. This movement has 15 fine ruby jewels, plates beautifully gilded, Breguet hairspring, true timing screws, polished safety pinions and is guaranteed for a term of five years.

No. 4H2670 15 jeweled solid, nickel, eight-day watch. Price $7.80

The above described watch actually runs for eight days. It is made remarkably small for such a wonderful time keeper, no larger than any regular 18-size watch, and still in this small compass is contained the mechanism that will run this watch for eight days after being fully wound. Own a watch of this description and be saved the annoyance which follows forgetting to wind a 36-hour watch.

$2.76

A WATCH YOU CAN LOOK THROUGH

No. 4H2674

No. 4H2674 $2.76 for this wonderful gentlemen' 18-size, thin model, solid nickel, stem wind and stem set, lever escapement exposed to view novelty watch. The case is made of solid nickel with crystal in front and back, snap joint, snap bezel back and front, gold plated antique crown and bow. The movement, as illustration shows, is so constructed that you can at all times see the entire workings of your watch. In fact, a watch that you can look through. Think of it! You can look through the watch and see a person on the other side by merely holding the watch close to your eye. All the mechanism, the minute wheel, the rapidly moving fork, the second wheel, the third wheel, the winding apparatus, the mainspring barrel, all the interesting mechanism plain to view. This watch is jeweled and beautifully finished in every respect and will wear as long as any other watch. We will not send our written binding guarantee with this watch at the price. However, we do guarantee it to reach you in perfect running order, and we know it will please you. Should you order one and do not find it in every way as we describe it you can return it to us and we will refund your money, together with all transportation charges. You assume no risk in ordering one of these watches from us.

Price $2.76

$3.98 BEAUTY

The very latest 16-size extra thin, oxidized polished gunmetal watch with illuminated dial. Send us $3.98 and 14 cents for mail charges, $4.12 in all, and we will at once ship you this newest gentlemen's watch by registered mail. The case is made with a solid back and snap front, and is absolutely dustproof. It is stem wind and stem set, is jeweled, has exposed balance wheel; illustration shows a new mechanical construction. This watch is imported by us from Switzerland, each one is guaranteed for a term of five years. At $3.98 we are selling this watch at 40 per cent less than similar but inferior watches are being sold for.

No. 4H2678
Price........$3.98

No. 4H2678

No. 4H2680 Same style as No. 4H2678, but case of solid silver, engine turned. Price.................. $5.45

No. 4H2682 Same style as No. 4H2678, but gold filled case, guaranteed 20 years. Price.............. $7.95

LOOK AT THIS OFFER.

SOLID GOLD INLAID ON SOLID SILVER FOR $8.00.

A watch with solid silver sides, gold filled center and solid gold inlaid work, complete, with a fine 7 jeweled lever Edgemere movement, a movement that is guaranteed for a term of five years against defective material or workmanship.

Price for complete watch, both case and movement $8.00

12-size, solid silver, gold ornamented, gold filled center, bow and crown, thin model hunting style gentlemen's watches. These cases are made to supply a certain demand for a watch a little different from the regulation old stereotyped style. The lids are of solid silver, richly ornamented with varicolored solid gold in beautiful floral designs. The center, or frame upon which the lids are fastened, is gold filled and guaranteed for a term of twenty years. The crown, bow and stem are likewise gold filled. This hunting style or double sided case is ornamented on both sides, each side being the same as the other with the exception of the shield of solid gold made to bear the owner's name or initials. This watch is stem wind and pendant set. Each movement, as quoted below at various prices according to the different grades, carries our written guarantee for a term of five years.

We Fit Case No. 4H2685 with the following 12-Size Movements. Prices quoted are for the complete watch, movement and case.	No. 4H2685 Hunting Style
7 Jeweled Edgmere, nickel	$ 8.00
7 Jeweled Elgin or Waltham, nickel plates	9.50
15 JEWELED EDGEMERE	9.25
15 Jeweled Elgin or Waltham, nickel plates	11.70
17 JEWELED PLYMOUTH WATCH CO., nickel plates	18.75
17 Jeweled No. 321 Grade Elgin	19.12
18 Jeweled No. 189 Grade Elgin	30.95
21 Jewéled Swiss, nickel plates	23.65

$8.00 AND UP

No. 4H2685
12-Size. Hunting Style

FOR $1.25 EXTRA we can furnish a fancy dial and gold hands on any watch on this page.

18 AND 16-SIZE BOSS AND CRESCENT GOLD FILLED WATCHES

IN 10 AND 14-KARAT QUALITY.
OPEN FACE OR HUNTING STYLE.

PROTECT YOUR WATCH WITH AN AJAX WATCH INSULATOR.

See page 192, No. 4C2002 Price **18** cents

$7.65 TO $39.15

18-SIZE. BOSS GOLD FILLED.

No. 4C4600 Open Face, Screw Back and Bezel, 20-Year. 10 karat.
No. 4C4602 Hunting, 20-Year. 10 karat.
No. 4C4604 Open Face, Screw Back and Bezel, 25-Year. 14 karat.
No. 4C4606 Hunting, 25-Year. 14 karat.

This illustration shows how our 17 Jeweled Edgemere looks. The greatest watch value ever offered for the money.

SEND 50 CENTS and we will send you any watch by express, C. O. D., the balance payable after watch is received and found satisfactory.

18 SIZE

18-SIZE. CRESCENT GOLD FILLED.

No. 4C4608 Open Face, Screw Back and Bezel, 20-Year. 10 karat.
No. 4C4610 Hunting, 20-Year. 10 karat.
No. 4C4612 Open Face, Screw Back and Bezel, 25-Year. 14 karat.
No. 4C4614 Hunting, 25-Year. 14 karat.

REGARDING THE ENGRAVINGS, we generally have the exact pattern as illustrated. If not, we send a very similar design.

$7.65 TO $39.15

18-SIZE. BOSS GOLD FILLED.

No. 4C4616 Open Face, Screw Back and Bezel, 20-Year. 10 karat.
No. 4C4618 Hunting, 20-Year. 10 karat.
No. 4C4620 Open Face, Screw Back and Bezel, 25-Year. 14 karat.
No. 4C4622 Hunting, 25-Year. 14 karat.

18-size, solid nickel, 17 jewels, straight line lever escapement, adjusted. Full plate, fancy solid gold damaskeened finish, five pairs gold settings, compensation full double cut expansion balance wheel, adjusted to isochronism and position, patent micrometer regulator, genuine ruby jeweled pin, highly polished beveled edged screws, fully protecting dust band, safety pinion, double sunk, white enameled dial and sunk second hand dial. The superior construction of this movement adapts it to the most exacting service.

THE SEARS GOLD FILLED CASE IS RECOMMENDED ABOVE ALL OTHERS,

being made of two extra heavy plates of solid gold over a hard composition metal. Will wear longer than any other gold filled case made, and is the handsomest, best finished and best fitting gold filled watch case made. If you select a Sears case you will have the best gold filled watch case ever made.

We fit these movements in any of the 18-size cases. Prices are for complete watches.	Nos. 4C4600 4C4608 4C4616	Nos. 4C4602 4C4610 4C4618	Nos. 4C4604 4C4612 4C4620	Nos. 4C4606 4C4614 4C4622
7 Jeweled Edgemere, SEARS, ROEBUCK & CO.'S special make	$ 7.65	$10.00	$10.55	$12.90
7 Jeweled Hampden	9.50	11.85	12.40	14.75
Trainmen's Special, Stamped, 17 Jewels, adjusted	8.45	10.80	11.35	13.70
11 Jeweled Hampden	10.23	12.58	13.13	15.48
Full 12 Jeweled EDGEMERE, especially made for SEARS, ROEBUCK & CO.	9.25	11.60	12.15	14.50
Full 15 Jeweled Hampden	11.20	13.55	14.10	16.45
Full 15 Jeweled SEARS, ROEBUCK & CO.'S especially made	11.00	13.35	13.90	16.25
Full 17 Jeweled Edgemere, SEARS, ROEBUCK & CO.'S special make	11.35	13.70	14.25	16.60
Full 17 Jeweled Dueber Grand Hampden	13.95	16.30	16.85	19.20
Full 17 Jeweled New Railway Hampden	22.90	25.25	25.80	28.15
Full 21 Jeweled John Hancock Hampden	24.70	27.05	28.00	30.35
Full 21 Jeweled Special Railway Hampden	26.30	28.65	29.20	31.25
Full 23 Jeweled New Railway Hampden	Not made	30.65	31.20	Not made
Full 23 Jeweled Special Railway Hampden	33.90	36.25	36.80	39.15
Full 17 Jeweled SEARS, ROEBUCK & CO.'S SPECIAL, especially made. The greatest watch bargain ever offered	15.50	17.85	18.40	20.75

16-size, solid nickel, fancy gold damaskeened finish. 17 genuine ruby jewels in solid gold settings, straight line lever escapement, exposed to view winding apparatus, the steel parts of which are highly polished and chamfered; patent micrometer regulator, five pairs of extra solid gold settings and gold train, genuine ruby pallette jewels visible to view, and ruby roller jewel, patent safety center pinion and barrel. Compensation double cut, full expansion balance wheel, adjusted in accordance to variations of the temperature, fully protecting dust band, double sunk, genuine hard French enamel dial. This movement will excel the highest grade movements on the market.

16-SIZE BOSS AND CRESCENT WATCHES.

$8.51 TO $21.00

16-SIZE. BOSS GOLD FILLED.

No. 4C4624 Open Face, Screw Back and Bezel, 20-Year. 10 karat.
No. 4C4626 Hunting, 20-Year. 10 karat.
No. 4C4628 Open Face, Screw Back and Bezel, 25-Year. 14 karat.
No. 4C4630 Hunting, 25-Year. 14 karat.

WE OFFER MOVEMENTS OF ESTABLISHED REPUTATION ONLY.

MOVEMENTS THAT HAVE STOOD THE TEST OF TIME and are known to be RELIABLE and ACCURATE. We have sold our watches in every locality, some of them can surely be found right in your own neighborhood. Ask your friend or neighbor what he thinks of the SEARS, ROEBUCK & CO.'S SPECIAL MOVEMENT, for we are willing to accept his judgment.

DON'T BUY A WATCH UNTIL YOU HAVE INVESTIGATED THE MOVEMENTS WE ILLUSTRATE ABOVE.

We fit the following movements in the 16-size cases at prices quoted. Prices are for the complete watch.	Nos. 4C4624 4C4632	Nos. 4C4626 4C4634	Nos. 4C4628 4C4636	Nos. 4C4630 4C4638
7 Jeweled Reliance	$ 8.51	$11.05	$11.61	$13.86
Full 12 Jeweled EDGEMERE, OUR SPECIAL MAKE	10.55	12.80	13.30	15.30
Full 15 Jeweled SEARS, ROEBUCK & CO.'S SPECIAL	12.25	14.50	15.00	17.00
Full 17 Jeweled SEARS, ROEBUCK & CO.'S SPECIAL, especially made, the greatest watch offer ever made	16.25	18.50	19.00	21.00

ELGIN AND WALTHAM WATCHES QUOTED ON PAGES 216 TO 218.

$8.51 TO $21.00

16 SIZE

16-SIZE. CRESCENT GOLD FILLED.

No. 4C4632 Open Face, Screw Back and Bezel, 20-Year. 10 karat.
No. 4C4634 Hunting, 20-Year. 10 karat.
No. 4C4636 Open Face, Screw Back and Bezel, 25-Year. 14 karat.
No. 4C4638 Hunting, 25-Year. 14 karat.

GENTLEMEN'S EXTRA THIN MODEL 12-SIZE SOLID GOLD AND GOLD FILLED

OPEN FACE OR HUNTING STYLE DUEBER-HAMPDEN COMPLETE WATCHES

PRICES MADE CHEAPER THAN EVER. A new method of handling this line makes it possible for us to reduce our selling price to a minimum. We give you advantage of every saving we can possibly make, we are satisfied with our regulation one small percentage of profit.

$11.25 for a 12-size Hampden Watch Co. complete watch; the case is guaranteed 14-karat gold filled and warranted by the celebrated Dueber-Hampden Watch Co. for a period of twenty-five years. The movement is the Cantonian, 7 jeweled. We illustrate and describe it here fully.

This illustration shows you the Dueber Grand, we fit in any one of these open face, gold filled cases for $16.25; in hunting style, $17.50; in solid gold, $40.50. It has solid nickel plates, 17 ruby and sapphire jewels in composition settings, is adjusted, has Breguet hairspring, patent regulator, bright flat screws, beautifully engraved and damaskeened plates with gold letters, Arabic or Roman dial with red marginal figures.

Plain, bright polish, Open Face or Hunting style.
No. 4L2751 Open face, screw back and screw bezel, gold filled, 25-year warrant.
No. 4L2753 Open face, screw back and screw bezel, solid 14-karat gold.
No. 4L2755 Hunting style, gold filled, 25-year warrant.
No. 4L2757 Hunting style, solid gold, 14-karat, heavy weight.

Diagonally engraved with Vermicelli work and bright polished top.
No. 4L2759 Open face, screw back and screw bezel, gold filled, 25-year guarantee.
No. 4L2761 Hunting style, gold filled, 25-year warrant.
No. 4L2763 Hunting style, solid gold, 14-karat, heavy weight.

Engine turned with shield center.
No. 4L2765 Open face, screw back and screw bezel, gold filled, 25-year guarantee.
No. 4L2767 Hunting style, gold filled, 25-year warrant.
No. 4L2769 Hunting style, solid gold, 14-karat, heavy weight.

Full engraved Bassene style.
No. 4L2771 Open face, screw back and screw bezel, gold filled, 25-year guarantee.
No. 4L2773 Hunting style, gold filled, 25-year warrant.
No. 4L2775 Hunting style, solid gold, 14-karat, heavy weight.

This illustration shows you the General Stark, 15 jeweled movement; it has solid nickel plates, 15 ruby jewels in composition settings, Breguet hairspring, mean time screws, patent regulator, bright flat screws, plates are engraved and damaskeened, has Roman or Arabic dial with red marginal figures.

This illustration shows you the John Hancock we fit in any one of these open face, gold filled cases for $29.75; in hunting style for $31.50; in solid gold for $55.00.

THE JOHN HANCOCK has solid nickel plates, 21 fine ruby and sapphire jewels in gold settings, escapement is cap jeweled, has compensation balance, adjusted to temperature, isochronism and positions, has Breguet hairspring, new model micrometric regulator, bright bevel headscrews, patent center pinion, finely polished steel work, double sunk enameled dial, beautifully finished nickel plates with gold letters. This is the finest finished movement of any of the 12-size Dueber-Hampden watches. It is very closely timed.

DESCRIPTION OF THE MOVEMENTS FITTED IN THE 12-SIZE COMPLETE DUEBER-HAMPDEN WATCHES.

THE CANTONIAN has 7 jewels, Arabic or Roman dial, solid nickel plates, Breguet hairspring, all pivot holes when not jeweled are bushed with anti-friction metal. A very good movement.

OUR $55.00 WATCH OFFER. If you select the $55.00 watch (the case is solid gold, heavy weight, hunting style, the movement is the 21 jeweled John Hancock), you would be buying as great a bargain and we would not be making one more percentage of profit than if you selected the $11.25 watch. The $55.00 watch is by far the superior watch, in fact, while in dollars and cents it is only represented as being about five times as good, in actual appearance, in actual wearing ability, in actual timekeeping, it is worth ten times as much.

FREE SAMPLE BOOKS OF CLOTHING, MEN'S OR BOYS'. SEE CLOTHING SECTION OF THIS CATALOGUE

We fit these cases (Nos. 4L2751 to 4L2775) with the following 12-size movements. Prices quoted are for the complete watch, movement and case.	No. 4L2751 No. 4L2759 No. 4L2765 No. 4L2771 Open Face, Screw Back and Bezel	No. 4L2755 No. 4L2761 No. 4L2767 No. 4L2773 Hunting Style, Gold Filled	No. 4L2757 No. 4L2763 No. 4L2769 No. 4L2775 Hunting Style, Solid Gold	No. 4L2753 Open Face, Screw Back and Bezel Solid Gold
7 Jeweled Cantonian	$11.25	$12.50	$35.50	$33.50
15 Jeweled General Stark	13.25	14.50	37.50	35.50
17 Jeweled Dueber Grand	16.25	17.50	40.50	38.50
21 Jeweled John Hancock	29.75	31.50	55.00	53.00

SOLID GOLD 14-KARAT 12-SIZE OPEN FACE AND HUNTING STYLE WATCHES

BIG REDUCTION IN PRICES

GENTLEMEN'S 12-SIZE, SOLID 14-KARAT GOLD WATCHES in open face or hunting style. Each one of these watches carries our written binding guarantee as to quality. We warrant them to be solid gold through and through of 14-karat quality, and all of them stem wind and pendant set. THE 12-SIZE WATCH IS THE LATEST GENTLEMEN'S WATCH SIZE. They are built on extra thin models, two sizes smaller than the regular 18-size, one size smaller than a 16-size. They fill a long felt want, because extra thin. They are ideal for carrying. Will not wear down or bulge out the pocket. Yet this size for mechanical requirements is perfect.

$21.80 and up

FOR 90 CENTS EXTRA WE CAN FURNISH A FANCY DIAL AND GOLD HANDS ON ANY WATCH ON THIS PAGE. See illustration on page 50.

The Antique Bow and the New French Bow Used Throughout these Cases.

25 cents will carry any watch to any part of the United States by express.

Nothing finer, nothing better made in solid gold watches in the United States.

$34.80 and up

12-size, solid gold, 14-karat, bright polish.
No. 4L2701 Hunting style, medium weight.
No. 4L2703 Hunting style, heavy weight.
No. 4L2705 Open face, jointed, medium weight.
No. 4L2707 Open face, jointed, heavy weight.

12-size, solid gold, 14-karat, engine turned.
No. 4L2709 Hunting style, medium weight.
No. 4L2711 Hunting style, heavy weight.
No. 4L2713 Open face, jointed, medium weight.
No. 4L2715 Open face, jointed, heavy weight.

12-size, solid gold, 14-karat, half engraved.
No. 4L2717 Hunting style only, medium weight.

Each case is stamped 14-karat, with the initial of the maker.

12-size, solid gold, 14-karat, full engraved, Bassene style.
No. 4L2719 Hunting style only, heavy weight.

12-size, solid gold, 14-karat, full engraved, new English antique bow, Bassene style.
No. 4L2721 Extra heavy weight. We recommend these watches in preference to all others.

We Fit These Solid Gold 12-Size Cases with the Following 12-Size Movements.	Nos. 4L2705 4L2713	No. 4L2709	Nos. 4L2703 4L2711 4L2707 4L2715 4L2719	Nos. 4L2701 4L2717	No. 4L2721
7 Jeweled Elgin or Waltham, nickel plates	$22.50	$21.50	$29.50	$24.50	$35.50
15 JEWELED EDGEMERE, special make	21 80	21.00	29.00	24.00	34.80
15 Jeweled Elgin or Waltham, nickel plates, patent regulator	24.70	23.70	31.70	26.70	37.70
17 JEWELED PLYMOUTH WATCH CO., nickel plates	25.45	23.95	29.95	26.45	35.95
17 Jeweled Elgin No. 344 Grade or Waltham No. 225 Grade, not adjusted	25.70	24.20	30.20	26.70	36.20
17 Jeweled No. 321 Grade Elgin	30.65	29.15	35.15	31.65	41.15
19 Jeweled No. 189 Grade Elgin	42.45	40.95	46.95	43.45	52.95
21 JEWELED SWISS, nickel plates, pat. reg., adjusted	35.00	33.50	39.50	36.00	45.50

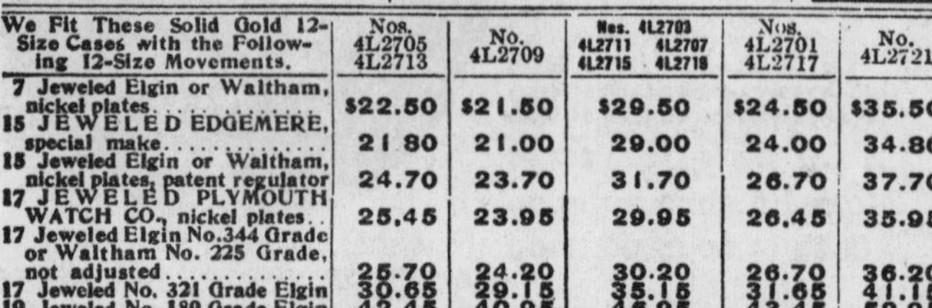

This is an illustration of our 21 jeweled 12-size imported Swiss movement. If you are willing to spend a little more money and want absolute perfection in a 12-size watch, by all means select this one. We import it for the purpose of furnishing our customers a watch high in grade, accurate in every way, at one-half the price of similar watches produced in this country. We fit this movement in any one of the cases that you select for from $33.50 to $45.50.

ORDER EITHER ONE OF THESE WATCHES if you are looking for a 17 jeweled movement or a 21 jeweled movement. They are the best value for the least money.

This illustration shows you our 12-size Plymouth Watch Company 17 jeweled, high grade nickel movement that we advise fitted in any one of these cases for $23.95 to $35.95. Think of it! Solid gold cases, 14 karats fine, with a high grade accurately running, American made watch, exactly as described on page 21, complete movement and case, for $23.95.

A LADIES' HUNTING STYLE GOLD FILLED $15.00 WATCH FOR $6.18

$6.18 FOR YOUR CHOICE OF ANY ONE OF THESE GOLD FILLED 20-YEAR GUARANTEED CASES ILLUSTRATED HERE, COMPLETE WITH A 7 JEWELED AMERICAN MADE MOVEMENT

WE ILLUSTRATE **only four cases of the most popular designs,** but they are four of the handsomest watches that can be procured, copied after solid gold patterns. In selecting one of these watches you will own a watch that has every appearance of being solid 14-karat gold. Each case has been selected with a view of putting in the hands of our customers a perfect article. Each case is perfectly finished in detail, special attention being given to the joints, no rough edges, no unsightly parts. The very latest, up to date antique bow, stem and crown. Finely finished, jointed inside protecting cap, perfectly finished inside bezel, well grooved, so that it holds the crystal of the watch securely.

$6.18 MAY SEEM A SMALL SUM OF MONEY **for a high grade gold filled watch,** but it is made possible only because of our immense purchasing power, together with the fact that these cases are made by one of the largest watch companies in the United States, branded with the name "Kingston," all useless expense being cut out. All of these advantages we are offering to you in this our $6.18 gold filled ladies' size watch offer.

$6.18 REDUCED IN PRICE

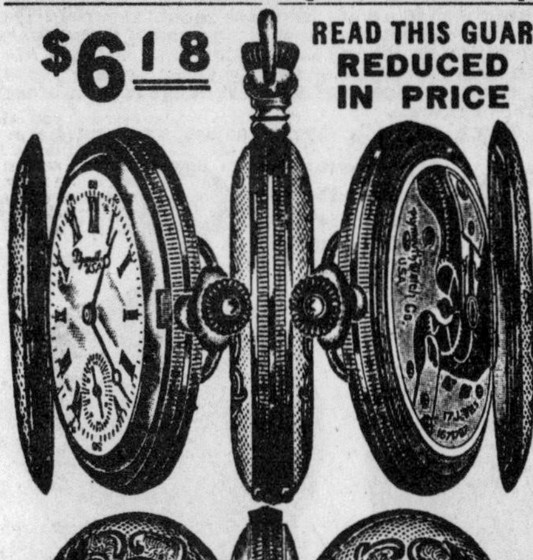

No. 4L2863 6-Size, Hunting Style.

This illustration shows our full engraved case and is engraved on perfectly bright, plain polished surfaces, ornamented with beautiful vermicelli work, floral sprays and landscapes, selected with a view to please those who desire full engraved cases.

READ THIS GUARANTEE. The illustration shows a facsimile of the guarantee that goes out with each case. Together with this case guarantee is our own written binding guarantee that we, as a firm, send out, which protects you for a term of twenty years.

OUR KINGSTON BRAND 6-SIZE CASES, guaranteed for twenty years, considering the price, leads them all. Made of plates of solid gold, rolled to the proper thickness, covering a composition metal, not cheap or shoddy, but the genuine article.

You have noted no doubt that there are but four varieties of cases illustrated on this page. Several of the illustrations merely show you the different views of the same watch so as to give a correct idea of how the watch will appear. Be sure to order by number and to plainly state the kind of movement wanted, inclosing with your order the correct amount of money, together with the mail charges. 12 cents will carry any one of these watches to any part of the United States by registered mail.

THE CASES shown on this page are copies of solid gold designs and the equal of any solid gold case in general appearance, engraving, finish, and, in fact, the equal of a solid gold case in everything except intrinsic value. None but an experienced jeweler would know but that they were solid gold.

25 cents will carry any watch to any part of the United States by express. We recommend sending watches by express as they do not receive the hard usage as when sent by mail. If sent by mail include 12 cents extra for postage and registry fee.

$6.18 For this movement fitted in the case you select. This our 7 jeweled American make movement, plates beautifully damaskeened, contains 7 jewels and is equal to any 7 jewel movement made. Worth two of the cheap movements being sold at 30 to 40 per cent more on the market now. Is stem wind and pendant set, has cut expansion balance, sunk second dial, improved in every way over cheap 7 jeweled watches quoted anywhere.

LOOK AT THIS!

$6.50 **For any one of these cases fitted with our Countess Janet movement.** Could any movement be made handsomer? Could any movement be made more attractive? It is stamped "17 jewels, adjusted," the plates are beautifully damaskeened, shows handsome jewel settings on the plate, yet we are able to sell you this watch complete with one of the four cases that you select and this movement for $6.50. As a matter of fact, though, the movement is merely 7 jeweled American made. Is stem wind and pendant set, a good timer, will give good satisfaction, as good satisfaction as any 7 jeweled movement.

$11.80 For this movement fitted in the watch case you select. In this watch you have the acme of perfection. This watch is stem wind and pendant set, has 17 fine ruby jewels, and if you are looking for a watch that is an accurate timekeeper, positively the best 17 jeweled watch possible to manufacture, by all means select this movement. It is worth twice what we ask and retail merchants would get $18.00 to $20.00 for this watch and consider that they are selling a bargain. Seventeen ruby jewels we guarantee this watch to contain, each jewel in screw setting. Has full protecting dust band, bridges beautifully damaskeened, cut expansion balance, overstrung Breguet hairspring, full polished screw heads, safety pinions, fine white select dial; in fact, we know no piece or part that has been overlooked.

$6.18 REDUCED IN PRICE

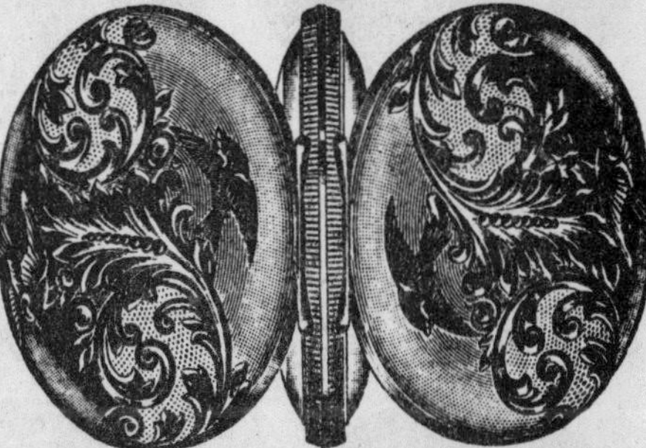

No. 4L2866 6-Size, Hunting Style.

This is our solid gold pattern bird design with ribbon engraved center effect, built after the Juergenson style. The center of the case is beaded. The top and bottom of the case are bright polished. Through the center runs a beautiful ribbon design with double bird engraving, making the design novel and unique.

For 90 cents extra we can furnish a fancy dial and gold hands on any watch on this page. See illustration on page 50.

REDUCED IN PRICE

No. 4L2869 6-Size, Hunting Style.

This case is one of the Bassene style. The lids are so constructed that when closed no space or edge is seen between the lid and the center, just the same as solid gold cases are made. Note the engraving. This style is patterned after solid gold designs, floral half engraved. The bottom shows beautiful vermicelli work, the top being bright polished.

We have listed here a complete line of movements that we can fit in any one of the four cases that you select at the prices quoted.

Should you, after reading the descriptions of the cases and the movements, decide to order one of these watches, remember to include 12 cents extra for the mail charges, as we will then send it to you by registered mail, and if after you have examined the watch and you do not find it in every way as we have described it, both movement and case, and if you do not find it is the value such as we claim for it, or for any other criticisms that you may have you do not desire it, you can return it to us and we will at once upon its receipt refund your money, together with the mail charges both ways. Such an offer as this absolutely must assure you how sincere we are in the value we offer. We do not ask you to take our word; use your own judgment. Compare the watch after you receive it, with any friend's watch or any watch shown by any jeweler and prove to yourself our statements are true.

We fit any case shown on this page with the following 6-size movements. Prices quoted are for the complete watch, movement and case.

7 JEWELED AMERICAN MAKE., nickel plates	$6.18
COUNTESS JANET, stamped 17 jeweled, adjusted	6.50
7 Jeweled Elgin or Waltham, gilt plates	7.85
7 Jeweled Elgin or Waltham, nickel plates	8.37
15 Jeweled Elgin or Waltham, nickel plates	10.43
16 Jeweled Lady Waltham, nickel plates	12.05
17 JEWELED PLYMOUTH WATCH CO., nickel plates, patent regulator, special make	11.80

REDUCED IN PRICE

For 21 cents we furnish a beautiful Leatherette Presentation Case to fit any watch. No. 4L588 on page 23.

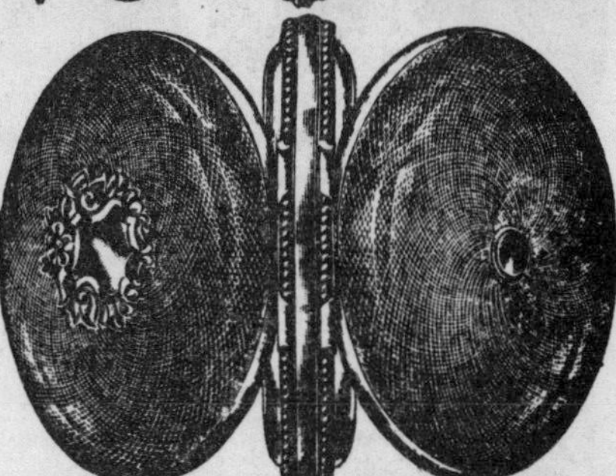

No. 4L2871 6-Size, Hunting Style.

This is our Juergenson engine turned, bright effect, solid gold pattern. Case selected with a view of pleasing those who wish a plain and simple case. This case never shows mars or scratches and can be worn a lifetime without obliterating. The design is as popular and up to date as it was 100 years ago, when it was brought out. It is considered one of the staple designs.

FOR COMPLETE INDEX REFER TO PINK PAGES IN MIDDLE OF BOOK.

LADIES' 0-SIZE 25-YEAR GOLD FILLED WATCHES

AND PLYMOUTH GOLD FILLED CASES GUARANTEED FOR LIFE.

This is a picture taken direct from our 15 jeweled EDGEMERE, the best 15 jeweled movement on the market.

We warrant it for five years.

DESCRIPTION OF OUR 0-SIZE 15 JEWELED EDGEMERE MOVEMENT. Solid nickel plates through and through, 15 finely polished ruby jewels, cut balance, lever escapement, patent pinion, perfect in finish and detail, and warranted for 5 years.

MANUFACTURED BY THE MOST REPRESENTATIVE GOLD FILLED CASE MANUFACTURERS IN THE WORLD.

THE GUARANTEE GIVEN: Each case is warranted by the maker, and we send, together with this, our own special binding guarantee.

WHAT WE MEAN BY THE PLYMOUTH LIFE GUARANTEED CASE

The Plymouth Life Guaranteed Case is a gold filled case of the very highest quality and the nearest approach to a solid gold case manufactured. The Plymouth Life Guaranteed Case means that should any one of these cases wear down to the inner composition metal any time within your natural life, whether you have owned the case five years, twenty years or fifty years, return it to us, and we will upon the receipt of same exchange it for a brand new case of same quality, free of charge.

REGARDING THE ENGRAVINGS, WE GENERALLY HAVE THE EXACT PATTERN; IF NOT, WE WILL SEND A VERY SIMILAR DESIGN.

$8.05 TO $28.52

FOR 90c EXTRA WE CAN FURNISH FANCY DIAL AND GOLD HANDS ON ANY WATCH ON THIS PAGE.

If sent by mail, include 12 cents extra for postage and registration fee.

25 cents will carry any watch to any part of the United States by express. We recommend sending watches by express, as they do not receive the hard usage as when sent by mail.

The higher the grade the better the time. We advocate higher jeweling than the 7 jeweled grades.

$9.40 AND UP

No. 4F3450 14-karat. Guaranteed for 25 years' wear. Made by the Illinois Watch Case Co.

No. 4F3452 14-karat. Guaranteed for 25 years' wear. Made by the Illinois Watch Case Co.

No. 4F3454 14-karat. Guaranteed for 25 years' wear. Made by the Wadsworth Watch Case Co.

No. 4F3456 Gold Ornamented and genuine cut diamond Set, 14-karat. Guaranteed for 25 years' wear. Made by the Illinois Watch Case Co.

No. 4F3458 Set with genuine rose diamonds. 14-karat. Guaranteed for 25 years' wear. Made by the Illinois Watch Case Co.

$10.40 AND UP

YOU GET A VALUABLE PROFIT SHARING CERTIFICATE AS WELL AS SAVING MONEY ON YOUR WATCH PURCHASE.

For 90c Extra We can furnish fancy dial and gold hands on any watch on this page.

No. 4F3457 Same style and make as No. 4F3456, but set with genuine rose diamond.

$14.00 AND UP

No. 4F3460 Set with genuine rose diamonds. 14-karat, Guaranteed for 25 years' wear. Made by the Illinois Watch Case Co.

No. 4F3462 14-karat. Guaranteed for life. THE PLYMOUTH CASE.

No. 4F3464 14-karat Guaranteed for 25 years' wear. Made by the Wadsworth Watch Case Co.

No. 4F3466 14-karat. Guaranteed for 25 years' wear. Made by John C. Dueber.
No. 4F3467 Above make. Plain Polished or Engine Turned.

No. 4F3469 Genuine diamond set, raised gold ornamented, 14-karat. Guaranteed for 25 years' wear.

TRY OUR EDGEMERE MOVEMENT AND BE SATISFIED.

The Plymouth cases we can recommend for elegant finish and durability.

For 23 cents we furnish a beautiful Leatherette Presentation Case to fit any watch. See No. 4F588 on page 25.

We carry only the most celebrated standard goods made.

No. 4F3470 14-karat. Guaranteed for life. THE PLYMOUTH CASE.

No. 4F3472 14-karat. Guaranteed for life. THE PLYMOUTH CASE.

No. 4F3474 14K. Guaranteed for 25 years. Made by the Illinois Watch Case Co.

No. 4F3476 14-karat. Guaranteed for life. THE PLYMOUTH CASE.

No. 4F3477 14K. Guaranteed for 25 years. Made by the Illinois Watch Case Co.

WE FIT THESE CASES WITH THE FOLLOWING 0-SIZE MOVEMENTS. PRICES QUOTED ARE FOR THE COMPLETE WATCH, MOVEMENT AND CASE.	Nos. 4F3450, 4F3466 Nos. 4F3454, 4F3467 Nos. 4F3452, 4F3474 Nos. 4F3464, 4F3477	No. 4F3458	Nos. 4F3456 4F3469	No. 4F3457	Nos. 4F3462 4F3472 4F3470 4F3476	No. 4F3460
7 Jeweled Swiss Lever	$ 8.05	$ 9.40	$14.00	$ 8.50	$ 8.95	$10.40
7 Jeweled Trenton	9.05	10.40	15.00	9.50	9.95	11.40
11 Jeweled Swiss Lever	9.25	10.60	15.20	9.70	10.15	11.60
15 JEWELED EDGEMERE, special make	11.05	12.40	17.00	11.50	11.95	13.40
7 Jeweled Elgin or Waltham, nickel plates	11.73	13.08	17.68	12.18	12.63	14.08
15 Jeweled Elgin or Waltham, nickel plates	15.40	16.75	21.35	15.85	16.30	17.75
15 JEWELED PLYMOUTH WATCH CO., patent regulator, special make	14.90	16.25	20.85	15.35	15.80	17.25
16 Jeweled Lady Waltham, nickel plates	18.03	19.38	23.98	18.48	18.93	20.38
17 Jeweled Riverside Waltham, nickel plates	24.32	25.67	30.27	24.77	25.22	26.67
17 JEWELED PLYMOUTH WATCH CO., patent regulator, adjusted, special make	17.40	18.75	23.35	17.85	18.30	19.75
19 Jeweled Riverside Maximus Waltham or No. 201 Grade Elgin	28.52	29.87	34.47	28.97	29.42	30.87

$9.90 Buys our 15 jeweled Edgemere, fitted in any of these high grade cases you may select.

LADIES' 0-SIZE HUNTING STYLE GOLD FILLED 20 YEAR GUARANTEED WATCHES

OUR NEW GOLD FILLED CASE LINE, $6.90 AND UP.

YOUR CHOICE of any of the following 12 patterns for $6.90. These cases are made especially for us at the Illinois Watch Case factory, one of the largest and most representative gold filled case manufacturers in the United States. They are made under a special contract. Unlike any other gold filled case, we know exactly the quantity of gold that goes into each one of these cases. They contain more gold and are better finished than brands advertised at twice what we ask. We call them our Challenge Case. Each one of these cases contains a circular case guarantee warranting each one of them to retain their solid gold like appearance for a term of 20 years. This guarantee is sent by the firm of Sears, Roebuck & Co. If any one of them does not give entire and absolute satisfaction in every particular, return it to us and we will exchange same for a new one of same grade and cost upon receipt. Together with this case guarantee our own regular binding guarantee covering the case together with the movement accompanies each watch. You are doubly protected

FOR $13.75 we will give you your choice of any one of these cases fitted with our new 15 jeweled Plymouth Watch Co. movement, which has Breguet hairspring, patent regulator, all up to date modern improvements such as no other 15 jeweled movement has. This price represents a saving over other 15 jeweled watches and you still are owning a better watch.

$16.25 FOR ANY ONE OF THESE CASES fitted with the 17 jeweled Plymouth Watch Co. Movement. Positively the highest grade and most accurate running 17 jeweled movements in the United States; jewels in gold settings, Breguet hairspring, patent safety pinion, pendant set and stem wind, beautifully damaskeened plates, in fact all improvements known to watch making. Yet we are able to offer it to you for $16.25, which represents a saving of no less than $8.00 to $10.00 on every watch you buy.

$6.90 AND UP

THE EDGEMERE IS OUR LATEST MOVEMENT BARGAIN.

ILLUSTRATIONS SHOW EXACT SIZE.

JEWELERS ASK 50 PER CENT MORE FOR WATCHES OF SAME GRADE.

25 CENTS WILL CARRY ANY WATCH TO ANY PART OF THE UNITED STATES BY EXPRESS.

We recommend sending watches by express as they do not receive the hard usage as when sent by mail. If sent by mail, postage extra including registry, 12 cents.

$6.90 AND UP

No. 4F3601  — No. 4F3603  — No. 4F3605  — No. 4F3607  — No. 4F3609  — No. 4F3613

For 23 cents we furnish a beautiful Leatherette Presentation Case to fit any watch. See No. 4F588 on page 25.

YOU HAVE YOUR CHOICE OF CASES.

YOU CAN MAKE MONEY SELLING THESE WATCHES.

$6.90 AND UP

OUR 0-SIZE EDGEMERE MOVEMENT HAS 15 FINE RUBY JEWELS.

No. 4F3615  — No. 4F3617  — No. 4F3619  — No. 4F3621  — No. 4F3623  — No. 4F3625

WE FIT ABOVE CASES WITH THE FOLLOWING 0-SIZE MOVEMENTS. PRICES QUOTED ARE FOR THE COMPLETE WATCH, MOVEMENT AND CASE.

PLEASE TAKE NOTE that we illustrate twelve separate and distinct patterns to select from, each one a masterpiece of the engraver's art, every one perfect in every detail, each one a counterpart of a solid gold pattern from which it was copied. The 0-size, a size smaller than the regular 6-size, an up to date size, a size that every lady desires in a watch.

12 cents will carry any one of these watches to any part of the United States by registered mail.

7 Jeweled Swiss Lever	$ 6.90
7 Jeweled Trenton	7.90
11 Jeweled Swiss Lever	8.10
15 JEWELED EDGEMERE, special make	9.90
7 Jeweled Elgin or Waltham, nickel plates	10.58
15 Jeweled Elgin or Waltham, nickel plates	11.85
15 JEWELED PLYMOUTH WATCH CO., patent regulator, special make	13.75
16 Jeweled Lady Waltham, nickel plates	16.88
17 Jeweled Riverside Waltham, nickel plates	23.17
17 JEWELED PLYMOUTH WATCH CO., patent regulator, adjusted, special make	16.25
19 Jeweled Riverside Maximus Waltham or 201 Grade Elgin	27.37

LADIES' SMALL 0-SIZE OPEN FACE PLYMOUTH GOLD FILLED WATCHES, WARRANTED FOR THE TERM OF YOUR NATURAL LIFETIME

THIS IS ONE of our very latest additions in the Watch Department. The illustrations show the back and front of the watch, so that you can get a correct idea of exactly how this watch appears, although no picture or engraving could possibly do justice to the fine effects and general get up of these watches. These watches not alone carry our personal guarantee as to permanency of wear, but they likewise carry our written binding guarantee on the movement. These two guarantees really mean an insurance, an insurance on the watch you buy, something you cannot procure elsewhere. You positively are insured on both the movement and the case on any watch you buy from us. We stand ready at any time within the period of the guarantee to make good every condition in it.

$6.65

No. 4F3655
Plymouth Gold Filled.
20 Year Guarantee.

No. 4F3657
Plymouth Gold Filled.
20 Year Guarantee.

No. 4F3659
Diamond Set, Plymouth Gold Filled. Life Guarantee.

No. 4F3661
Plymouth Gold Filled.
Life Guarantee.

No. 4F3663
Plymouth Gold Filled.
Life Guarantee.

THE DIAMOND SET CASE illustrated on this page is a little beauty. It is bright polished, has a genuine rose diamond set in the back and fitted with our 15 jeweled Edgemere movement, for $11.15 it is a value not to be purchased from others.

THIS PAGE IS OUR CHALLENGE PAGE.

There is not a watch that we quote or illustrate that is not a rare bargain and out ranks in value anything that has ever been offered by any jeweler, retailer or jobber in the world in small 0-size watches.

WE FIT THESE CASES WITH THE FOLLOWING 0-SIZE MOVEMENTS. PRICES QUOTED ARE FOR THE COMPLETE WATCH, MOVEMENT AND CASE.	Nos. 4F3655 4F3657	Nos. 4F3661 4F3663	No. 4F3659
7 Jeweled Swiss Lever	$ 6.65	$ 7.15	$ 8.15
7 Jeweled Trenton	7.65	8.15	9.15
11 Jeweled Swiss Lever	7.85	8.35	9.35
15 JEWELED EDGEMERE, special make	9.65	10.15	11.15
7 Jeweled Elgin or Waltham, nickel plates	10.33	10.83	11.83
15 Jeweled Elgin or Waltham, nickel plates	11.60	12.10	13.10
15 JEWELED PLYMOUTH WATCH CO., patent regulator, special make	13.50	14.00	15.00
16 Jeweled Lady Waltham, nickel plates	16.63	17.13	18.13
17 Jeweled Riverside Waltham, nickel plates	22.92	23.42	24.42
17 JEWELED PLYMOUTH WATCH CO., patent regulator, adjusted, special make	16.00	16.50	17.50
19 Jeweled Riverside Maximus Waltham or No. 201 Grade Elgin	27.12	27.62	28.62

GOLD FILLED EXTRA THIN 16-SIZE OPEN FACE OR HUNTING STYLE WATCHES. GUARANTEED FOR LIFE OR FOR 25 YEARS

25 cents will carry any Watch to any part of the United States by express.

Life Guarantee

PLYMOUTH

Life Guarantee

PLYMOUTH

Life Guarantee

PLYMOUTH

FOR 90 CENTS we can furnish a FANCY DIAL AND GOLD HANDS on any of these watches. See illustration on page 25.

Solid Gold Ornamented 16-Size Hunting Style.

GOLD FILLED. GUARANTEED FOR 25 YEARS.
No. 4N13402 John C. Dueber, Open Face, Screw Back and Bezel.
No. 4N13404 Open Face, same make but engine turned.
No. 4N13406 Hunting Style.
No. 4N13408 Hunting Style, same make but engine turned.

GOLD FILLED. GUARANTEED FOR 25 YEARS
No. 4N13410 Illinois Watch Case Co. Commander, Open Face, Screw Back and Bezel.
No. 4N13412 Illinois Watch Case Co. Commander, Hunting Style.

GOLD FILLED, DIAGONAL ENGRAVED GUARANTEED FOR LIFE.
No. 4N13414 Plymouth, Open Face, Screw Back and Bezel.
No. 4N13416 Plymouth, Hunting Style.

GOLD FILLED, ENGINE TURNED, GUARANTEED FOR LIFE.
No. 4N13418 Plymouth, Open Face, Screw Back and Bezel.
No. 4N13420 Plymouth, Hunting Style.

GOLD FILLED, FULL ENGRAVED, GUARANTEED FOR LIFE.
No. 4N13422 Plymouth, Open Face, Screw Back and Bezel.
No. 4N13424 Plymouth, Hunting Style.

No. 4N13426 GOLD FILLED SOLID GOLD ORNAMENTED, GUARANTEED FOR 25 YEARS, COMMANDER CASE.
Something truly magnificent, something out of the ordinary in a high grade gold filled watch, one that will last your lifetime.

These illustrations show the movements we recommend above all other makes in the 16-size. The top movement illustrates our 21 jeweled Prince of Wales movement the finest constructed and best 21 jeweled 16-size movement manufactured in the United States. The bottom movement illustrates our 17 jeweled Plymouth Watch Co. movement, the best 17 jeweled 16-size movement manufactured. If you are looking for a 21 jeweled movement or a 17 jeweled movement in this size of watch, these are the movements you should buy. For full description, see page 26.

WE FIT THESE CASES WITH THE FOLLOWING 16-SIZE MOVEMENTS. PRICES QUOTED ARE FOR THE COMPLETE WATCH, MOVEMENT AND CASE.	Open Face 25-Year Guarantee Nos. 4N13402 4N13404 4N13410	Hunting 25-Year Guarantee Nos. 4N13406 4N13408 4N13412	Open Face Life Guarantee Nos. 4N13414 4N13418 4N13422	Hunting Life Guarantee Nos. 4N13416 4N13420 4N13424	Hunting Style Gold Ornamented, No. 4N13426	Hunting Style Diamond Set Ornamented No. 4N13428
7 JEWELED EDGEMERE, nickel plates, special make	$7.49	$9.60	$8.60	$11.10	$14.35	$21.35
7 Jeweled Elgin or Waltham, nickel plates	10.50	12.50	11.50	14.00	17.50	24.50
15 JEWELED EDGEMERE, patent regulator, nickel plates, special make	10.35	12.35	11.35	13.85	17.10	24.10
15 Jeweled Elgin or Waltham, nickel plates, patent regulator	12.60	14.60	13.60	16.10	19.70	26.70
17 Jeweled Elgin or Waltham, not adjusted	14.70	16.70	15.70	18.20	21.90	28.90
17 Jeweled No. 241 Grade Elgin, adjusted	17.33	19.33	18.33	20.83	24.65	31.65
17 JEWELED PLYMOUTH WATCH CO., nickel plates, patent regulator, adjusted	16.98	18.98	17.98	20.48	24.30	31.30
17 Jeweled No. 243 Grade Elgin, adjusted, nickel plates	28.35	30.35	29.35	31.85	36.20	43.20
21 JEWELED PRINCE OF WALES PLYMOUTH WATCH CO., full adjusted, patent regulator, nickel plates	20.25	22.25	21.25	23.75	26.27	33.27

No. 4N13428 Hunting Style only. Genuine diamond set, solid gold, ornamented gold filled warranted for 25 years. $21.35 and upward for this genuine diamond set, solid gold, ornamented, 16-size case.

GENTLEMEN'S SOLID GOLD, 14-KARAT, 16-SIZE HUNTING STYLE WATCHES.

We take particular pride in offering this new line of solid gold 16-size watches. They have been selected with the greatest of care as being the best values money could possibly buy. The prices vary according to the weight of gold in the case and the amount of work on the engraving. However, even those cases we quote as being light weight are sufficiently heavy to give good satisfaction, and thick enough to properly protect the movement. Our written binding warrant goes out with each one, guaranteeing it to be exactly as shown and described.

16-size, solid gold, engine turned, Juergenson style, hunting case.
No. 4N13440 Medium weight.
No. 4N13442 Heavy weight.

16-size, solid gold, 14-karat, bright polish, Bassene style, hunting case.
No. 4N13444 Medium weight.
No. 4N13446 Heavy weight.

No. 4N3454 16-size, 14-karat, solid gold hunting style only, extra heavy weight, bright polish, set with fine large genuine regular cut diamond. The acme of beauty and perfection in solid gold case making. The diamond set in this case weighs about 3/16 karat.

16-size, solid gold, Bassene style, half engraved.
No. 4N13448 Hunting case.

16-size, solid gold, 14-karat, half Bassene, full engraved, heavy weight. Has raised colored gold ornamentation.
No. 4N13452 Hunting case.

$33.10

No. 4N13450 Hunting case. 16-size, solid gold, 14-karat, full engraved, extra heavy weight. Bassene style.

WE FIT THESE 16-SIZE SOLID GOLD CASES WITH THE FOLLOWING 16-SIZE MOVEMENTS.	Nos. 4N13440 4N13444	Nos. 4N13442 4N13446	No. 4N13448	No. 4N13450	No. 4N13452	No. 4N13454
7 Jeweled Elgin or Waltham, nickel plates	$24.50	$30.50	$27.50	$33.50	$28.50	$35.50
15 JEWELED EDGEMERE, patent regulator, nickel plates, special make	23.90	30.10	27.10	33.10	28.10	45.10
15 Jeweled Elgin or Waltham, nickel plates, patent regulator	26.70	32.70	29.70	35.70	30.70	47.70
17 Jeweled Elgin or Waltham, not adjusted	28.90	34.90	31.90	37.90	32.90	49.90
17 Jeweled No. 241 Grade Elgin, adjusted	30.15	35.15	31.65	38.15	33.15	50.15
17 JEWELED PLYMOUTH WATCH CO., nickel plates, patent regulator, adjusted	29.80	34.80	31.30	37.80	32.80	49.80
17 Jeweled No. 243 Grade Elgin, adjusted, nickel plates	41.70	46.70	43.20	49.70	44.70	61.70
21 JEWELED PRINCE OF WALES, Plymouth Watch Co., full adjusted, patent regulator, nickel plates	34.50	39.50	36.00	42.50	37.50	54.50

18-SIZE SOLID SILVER WATCHES.

For 90c extra we will furnish a fancy dial and gold hands on the silver watches on this page. For 23 cents we furnish a beautiful Leatherette Presentation Case to fit any watch. See No. 4G588 on page 36.

OPEN FACE, JOINTED FRONT AND BACK.

Same style as illustration shows.

No. 4G1312 3-ounce. Plain Polished Case

No. 4G1314 As above. Hand engraved.

No. 4G1316 4-ounce Plain Polished Case.

No. 4G1318 As above. Hand engraved.

PLAIN POLISHED, HAND ENGRAVED OR SOLID GOLD INLAID, OPEN FACE AND HUNTING STYLE IN ALL WEIGHTS.

Above all others, as the highest possible perfection in watch movements for accurate timekeeping, we recommend the 21 jeweled KING EDWARD movement, manufactured by the Plymouth Watch Co., quoted on this page and described and illustrated on page 37

See pages 37 and 38 for the descriptions and beautiful illustrations of Our Special Lines of Movements, Plymouth Watch Co. and Edgemere LINE OF WATCH MOVEMENTS.

$6.05 AND UP

REMEMBER when you have bought $25.00 worth or more of goods from us you get your choice of many valuable articles free, as shown in our new free Profit Sharing Book.

OPEN FACE, SCREW BACK AND BEZEL.

No. 4G1304 3-ounce Plain Polished Case.
No. 4G1306 As above. Hand engraved.
No. 4G1308 4-ounce Plain Polished Case.
No. 4G1310 As above. Hand engraved.

HUNTING STYLE OR OPEN FACE, JOINTED.

No. 4G1320 3-ounce Plain Polished Case.
No. 4G1322 As above. Hand engraved.
No. 4G1324 4-ounce Plain Polished Case.
No. 4G1326 As above. Hand engraved.
No. 4G1328 5-ounce Plain Polished Case.
No. 4G1330 5-ounce, as above, but hand engraved.

No. 4G1340 3-ounce Case, Open Face screw back and bezel, gold inlaid Stag
No. 4G1342 3-ounce Case, Open Face screw back and bezel, gold inlaid Engine.
No. 4G1344 4-ounce Case, Stag inlaid.
No. 4G1346 4-ounce Case. Engine inlaid.

Open Face, Screw Back and Bezel, hand engraved, box joints.
No. 4G1348 3-ounce. Engraved.
No. 4G1349 4-ounce. Engraved.

WE FIT THESE CASES WITH THE FOLLOWING 18-SIZE MOVEMENTS. Prices quoted are for the complete watch, movement and case.	No. 4G1304	No. 4G1306	No. 4G1332	No. 4G1308 4G1334 4G1312	No. 4G1320 4G1340 4G1342	No. 4G1310 4G1314	No. 4G1322	No. 4G1316	No. 4G1324 4G1344 4G1346	No. 4G1318 4G1326	No. 4G1336 4G1348	No. 4G1338	No. 4G1328	No. 4G1330 4G1349
7 JEWELED EDGEMERE, nickel plates, special mak	$ 4.00	$ 4.20	$ 4.30	$ 4.60	$ 4.65	$ 4.80	$ 5.05	$ 5.20	$ 5.35	$ 5.55	$ 6.05	$ 6.85	$ 7.10	$ 7.50
7 Jeweled Elgin or Waltham, gilt plates	6.02	6.22	6.32	6.62	6.67	6.82	7.07	7.22	7.37	7.57	8.07	8.87	9.12	9.52
7 Jeweled Elgin or Waltham, nickel plates	6.55	6.75	6.85	7.15	7.20	7.35	7.60	7.75	7.90	8.10	8.60	9.40	9.65	10 05
12 JEWELED EDGEMERE, nickel plates, special make	5.50	5.70	5.80	6.10	6.15	6.30	6.55	6.70	6.85	7.05	7.55	8.35	8.60	9.00
15 JEWELED PLYMOUTH WATCH CO., patent regulator, nickel plates, special make	7.40	7.60	7.70	8.00	8.05	8.20	8.45	8 60	8.75	8.95	9.45	10.25	10.50	10.90
15 Jeweled Waltham, gilt plates	7.08	7.28	7.38	7.68	7.73	7.88	8.13	8.28	8.43	8.63	9.13	9.93	10.18	10.58
15 Jeweled Elgin or Waltham, nickel plates	7.60	7.80	7.90	8.20	8.25	8.40	8.65	8.80	8.95	9.15	9.65	10.45	10.70	11.10
17 Jeweled Elgin or Waltham, not adjusted	8.65	8.85	8.95	9.25	9.30	9.45	9.70	9.85	10.00	10.20	10.70	11.50	11.75	12.15
17 JEWELED PLYMOUTH WHTCH CO., patent regulator, adjusted, nickel plates, special make	10.50	10.70	10.80	11.10	11.15	11.30	11.55	11.70	11.85	12.05	12.55	13.35	13.60	13.98
17 Jeweled G. M. Wheeler Elgin or P. S. Bartlett Waltham	10.75	10.95	11.05	11.35	11.40	11.55	11.80	11.95	12.10	12.30	12.80	13.60	13.85	14.25
21 JEWELED KING EDWARD PLYMOUTH WATCH CO., patent regulator, adjusted, nickel plates, special make	17.35	17.55	17.65	17.95	18.00	18.15	18.40	18.55	18.70	18.90	19.40	20.20	20.45	20.85
21 Jeweled John Hancock Hampden	17.15	17.35	17.45	17.75	17.80	17.95	18.20	18.35	18.50	18.70	19.20	20.00	20.25	20.65
21 Jeweled Special Railway Hampden	21.10	21.30	21.40	21.70	21.75	21.90	22.15	22.30	22.45	22.65	23.15	23.95	24.20	24.60
23 Jeweled Special Railway Hampden	28.60	28.80	28.90	29.20	29.25	29.40	29.65	29.80	29.95	30.15	30.65	31.45	31.70	32.10
TRAINMEN'S SPECIAL, stamped 23 jeweled, adjusted, special make	4.70	4.90	5.00	5.30	5.35	5.50	5.75	5.90	6.05	6.25	6.75	7.55	7.80	8.20

$11.55

$11.55 FOR A GOLD FILLED CENTER AND SOLID SILVER SIDED WATCH, 18-SIZE, STEM WIND AND PENDANT SET, HUNTING STYLE AND A 15 JEWELED MOVEMENT IS A REMARKABLE OFFER. This case represents the highest degree of artistic display in a silver watch, being made with a gold filled center, winding crown and pendant, and silver lids, solid gold in patterns. The gold filled portions are guaranteed for a period of twenty years' continual wear, the silver parts are of solid silver through and through. This case is hunting style. The movement that we fit in this watch for $11.55 has 15 genuine ruby jewels, stamped Plymouth Watch Co., on plate and dial. It has a patent regulator, safety pinion, solid nickel plates beautifully nickel and gilt damaskeened in various designs, has Breguet hairspring, jewels are all in screw settings, cut expansion balance, true timing screws, stem wind and pendant set, in fact, a movement that will give the best satisfaction. We guarantee it for a term of five years. Unlike any other watch on the market, although having gold filled center and gold filled pendant, has solid silver sides, which means that the gold filled portions are amply and properly protected, and although only guaranteed for 20 years, should wear a lifetime. This watch has all the beauties of a solid gold watch and just enough silver used in it to make up a very handsome contrast not found in any other combination of metals or in any other watch.

We can fit the following movements in the above case at the following prices:

No. 4G1377 Fitted with the 15 jeweled Plymouth Watch Co. movement; the finest 15 jeweled movement manufactured in the United States and made expressly for us, not procurable elsewhere. Price........$11.55

No. 4G1379 Fitted with the 15 jeweled Elgin or Waltham movement. Price........$11.75

No. 4G1381 Fitted with the 17 jeweled Plymouth Watch Co. move ment, which represents the highest perfection of any 17 jeweled movement is finer finished, more accurately running and has more modern improvements than any other 17 jeweled watch. Price.$14.65

No. 4G1383 Fitted with the G. M. Wheeler Elgin or P. S. Bartlett Waltham movement. Price........$14.90

No. 4G1385 Fitted with the 21 jeweled Plymouth Watch Co. movement, which represents the highest grade, most perfectly running 21 jeweled movement made in the United States, embodying the most modern improvements of any watch manufactured in the United States. Price........$21.50

$4.30 AND UP

No. 4G1332 2-ounce Plain Polished Case, dust and dampproof, screw bezel, solid back

No. 4G1334 As above, hand engraved.

No. 4G1336 3-ounce Heavy Plain Polished Screw Bezel and Solid Back Case, has gold reflector and dampproof crown with screw nut.

No. 4G1338 4-ounce, same style as No. 4G1336.

$9.55 FOR THIS WATCH COMPLETE WITH A 15 JEWELED AMERICAN MOVEMENT. A Duplex solid silver watch with a genuine 15 jeweled American made movement. The case is solid silver 18-size, Duplex model, an entirely new idea as applied to American watches. It embraces the good qualities of both the open face as well as the hunting style watch. You are able at all times to see the time without opening the case. See the illustration. When necessary the lid is opened as in any other hunting style watch by merely pressing down the crown. When closed you are able to see the time of day through the center small opening, which exposes part of the hour and minute hands. This small hole is covered by an extra heavy crystal. Around this crystal, enameled in dark blue, are the hour numerals and minute fractions. In fact, it is a watch with a double crystal and a double dial. The case is solid silver, 925-1000 fine, splendidly made, very tight jointed, finished and polished in all parts. This case fitted with a 15 jeweled American movement and is made for us under special contract; a regular 18 size solid nickel, beautifully nickel damaskeened and ornamented, patent regulator, upper plate full jeweled, all screws set in screw settings, cut expansion balance, true timing screws and Breguet hairspring. The watch is stem wind and stem set, runs thirty-six hours with one winding, just the same as any other high grade watch. Yet this novel, new, practical and serviceable watch we offer to sell you for $9.55. We guarantee it a splendid timepiece and warrant it to give entire satisfaction for a term of five years.

$9.55

No. 4G1389 Fitted with the 7 jeweled Elgin or Waltham, movemen gilt plates. Price........$8 17

No. 4G1391 Fitted with the 15 jeweled Plymouth Watch Co. pater regulator, nickel plates, special made movement, a movement that we guara tee to be the best 15 jeweled movement manufactured in the United Stat for........$9 55

No. 4G1393 Fitted with the 15 jeweled Elgin or Waltham movemen Price........$9.75

No. 4G1395 Fitted with the 17 jeweled Plymouth Watch Co., mov ment, which has a patent regulator, full nickel plates, and is adjusted, movement that we guarantee to be the best 17 jeweled movement manufa tured in the United States. Price........$12.75

No. 4G1396 Fitted with 21 jeweled King Edward movement, manufa tured by the Plymouth Watch Co., has patent regulator, is adjusted to ter perature, isochronism and position and positively without question one of t highest grade, and most accurate running 21 jeweled movements made in t United States, barring no make or kind. Price........$19.50

A LADIES' GOLD FILLED $15.00 WATCH FOR

$6.40 FOR YOUR CHOICE OF ANY ONE OF THESE GOLD FILLED 20-YEAR GUARANTEED CASES ILLUSTRATED HERE, COMPLETE WITH A 7 JEWELED AMERICAN MADE MOVEMENT

WE ILLUSTRATE only four cases of the most popular designs, but they are four of the handsomest watches that can be procured, copied after solid gold patterns. In selecting one of these watches you will own a watch that has every appearance of being solid 14-karat gold. Each case has been selected with a view of putting in the hands of our customers a perfect article. Each case is perfectly finished in detail, special attention given to the joints, no rough edges, no unsightly parts. The very latest, up to date antique bow, stem and crown. Finely finished, jointed inside protecting cap, perfectly finished inside bezel, well grooved, so that it holds the crystal of the watch securely.

OUR KINGSTON BRAND 6-SIZE CASES, guaranteed for twenty years, considering the price, leads them all. Made of plates of solid gold, rolled to the proper thickness, covering a composition metal, not cheap or shoddy, but the genuine article.

READ THIS GUARANTEE. **The illustration shows a facsimile of the guarantee that goes out with each case.** Together with this case guarantee is our own written binding guarantee that we, as a firm, send out, which protects you for a term of twenty years.

$6.40 MAY SEEM A SMALL SUM OF MONEY for a high grade gold filled watch, but it is made possible only because of our immense purchasing power, together with the fact that these cases are made by one of the largest watch companies in the United States, branded with the name "Kingston," all useless expense being cut out. All of these advantages we are offering to you in this our $6.40 gold filled ladies' size watch offer.

For 90 cents extra we can furnish a fancy dial and gold hands on any watch on this page. See illustration on page 194.

If sent by mail, include 12 cents extra for postage and registry fee.

For 23 cents we furnish a beautiful Leatherette Presentation Case to fit any watch. No. 4H588 on page 195.

25 cents will carry any watch to any part of the United States by express. We recommend sending watches by express as they do not receive the hard usage as when sent by mail.

No. 4H2801

This is our Juergenson engine turned, bright effect, solid gold pattern. Case selected with a view of pleasing those who wish a plain and simple case. This case never shows mars or scratches and can be worn a lifetime without obliterating. The design is as popular and up to date as it was 100 years ago, when it was brought out. It is considered one of the staple designs.

This illustration shows case No. 4H2801 with the front and back lids slightly open, exposing the face.

The cases shown on this page are copies of solid gold designs and the equal of any solid gold case in general appearance, engraving, finish and in fact, the equal of a solid gold case in everything except intrinsic value. None but an experienced jeweler would know but that they were solid gold.

No. 4H2804

This is our solid gold pattern bird design with ribbon engraved center effect, built after the Juergenson style. The center of the case is beaded. The top and bottom of the case are bright polished. Through the center runs a beautiful ribbon design with double bird engraving, making the design novel and unique. Only effects like these can be brought out in the highest grade cases. If you own this watch you are owning a watch just as good as solid gold in finish, design and beauty, the difference being only in intrinsic value.

No. 4H2805

This case is one of the Bassene style. The lids are so constructed that when closed no space or edge is seen between the lid and the center, just the same as solid gold cases are made. Note the engraving. This style is patterned after solid gold designs, floral half engraved. The bottom shows beautiful vermicelli work, the top being bright polished.

This illustration shows case No. 4H2805 fitted with the movement, with the front and back lids slightly open, exposing the movement to view.

You have noted no doubt that there are but four varieties of cases illustrated on this page. Several of the illustrations merely show you the different views of the same watch so as to give a correct idea of how the watch will appear. Be sure to order by number and to plainly state the kind of movement wanted, inclosing with your order the correct amount of money, together with the mail charges. 14 cents will carry any one of these watches to any part of the United States by registered mail.

No. 4H2813

This illustration shows our full engraved case and is engraved on perfectly bright plain polished surfaces, ornamented with beautiful vermicelli work, floral sprays and landscapes, selected with a view to please those who desire full engraved cases.

These illustrations show case No. 4H2813 with the lids closed, giving you an idea of the thickness of the watch, and likewise open, showing you how both lids look.

$6.40 for this movement fitted in the case you select. This our 7 jeweled Edgemere movement, plates beautifully damaskeened, contains 7 jewels and is equal to any 7 jewel movement made. Worth two of the cheap movements being sold at 30 to 40 per cent more on the market now. Is stem wind and pendant set, has cut expansion balance, sunk second dial, improved in every way over cheap 7 jeweled watches quoted anywhere.

Look at this. $6.60 for any one of these cases fitted with our Countess Janet movement. Could any movement be made handsomer? Could any movement be made more attractive? It is stamped "17 jewels, adjusted," the plates are beautifully damaskeened, shows handsome jewel settings on the plate, yet we are able to sell you this watch complete with one of the four cases that you select and this movement for $6.60. As a matter of fact, though, the movement is merely 7 jeweled American made. Is stem wind and pendant set, a good timer, will give good satisfaction, as good satisfaction as any 7 jeweled movement.

$11.90 for this movement fitted in the watch case you select. In this watch you have the acme of perfection. This watch is stem wind and pendant set, has 17 fine ruby jewels, and if you are looking for a watch that is an accurate timekeeper, positively the best 17 jeweled watch possible to manufacture, by all means select this movement. It is worth twice what we ask and retail merchants would get $18.00 to $20.00 for this watch and consider that they are selling a bargain. Seventeen ruby jewels we guarantee this watch to contain, each jewel in screw setting. Has full protecting dust band, bridges beautifully damaskeened, cut expansion balance, overstrung Breguet hairspring, full polished screw heads, safety pinions, fine white select dial; in fact, we know no piece or part that has been overlooked.

We have listed below a complete line of movements that we can fit in either one of the four cases that you select at the prices quoted.

Should you, after reading the descriptions of the cases and the movements, decide to order one of these watches, remember to include 12 cents extra for the mail charges, as we will then send it to you by registered mail, and if after you have examined the watch and you do not find it in every way as we have described it, both movement and case, and if you do not find it is the value such as we claim for it or for any other criticisms that you may have you do not desire it, you can return it to us and we will at once upon its receipt refund your money, together with the mail charges both ways. Such an offer as this absolutely must assure you how sincere we are in the value we offer. We do not ask you to take our word; use your own judgment. Compare the watch after you receive it, with any friend's watch or any watch shown by any jeweler and prove to yourself our statements are true.

We fit any case shown on this page with the following 6-size movements. Prices quoted are for the complete watch, movement and case.

7 JEWELED EDGEMERE, special make	$6.40
COUNTESS JANET, stamped 17 jeweled, adjusted	6.60
7 Jeweled Elgin or Waltham, gilt plates	7.95
7 Jeweled Elgin or Waltham, nickel plates	8.47
15 Jeweled Elgin or Waltham, nickel plates	10.53
16 Jeweled Lady Waltham, nickel plates	12.15
17 JEWELED PLYMOUTH WATCH CO., nickel plates, patent regulator, special make	11.90

LADIES' IMPORTED CHATELAINE WATCHES AND GENTLEMEN'S No. 4C4531 SPECIAL GUN METAL WATCH AT $2.25.

IN GUN METAL, SILVER INLAID, SOLID SILVER, GOLD FILLED, SOLID GOLD AND ENAMELED. The illustrations show exact size. Every one of our silver chatelaine watches is $\frac{935}{1000}$ fine, and guaranteed not to turn yellow. Some firms are offering silver watches only $\frac{800}{1000}$ fine, but we caution you that they will invariably turn in color. They cost to import less money by quite a percentage, but we do not desire to place on the market inferior goods.

Engraving can be done on any one of our plain polished cases. A monogram on the back on one of these watches increases its beauty materially. For 35 cents extra we can engrave a two or three letter monogram on any plain watch illustrated here.

$2.00

No. 4C4530 Ladies' gun metal open face stem wind and stem set chatelaine watch. Case is black, plain polished gun metal. The movement is Swiss imported, has 2 jewels. Will give very good satisfaction. A wonderful bargain for the price. Price, $2.00

No. 4C4531 Gentlemen's size. Price..........$2.25

No. 4C4532 Ladies' gun metal open face chatelaine watch. The case is plain polished, black gun metal. The movement is the celebrated full jeweled Leonore, manufactured in Switzerland. Has cut expansion balance, lever escapement and nickel plates, is stem wind and pendant set. Warranted for a term of five years. Price........$6.00

$6.00

$3.60

No. 4C4534 Ladies' solid silver open face stem wind and pendant set chatelaine watch. Case is solid silver, beautifully engraved. Illustration shows back and front of watch. The movement is Swiss imported, has cylinder escapement, 7 jewels. Price........$3.60

No. 4C4536 Ladies' solid silver open face stem wind and pendant set chatelaine watch. Case is solid silver, beautifully engraved. The illustration shows back and front of the watch. The movement is called the Lady Rose, imported from Switzerland, has cylinder escapement, damaskeened nickel plates, 10 fine ruby jewels, and is an excellent timekeeper. Price..........$4.90

$4.90

$6.75

No. 4C4538 Ladies' solid silver open face stem wind and pendant set chatelaine watch. The case is handsomely engraved. The illustration shows the back as well as the front of watch. The movement is the celebrated full jeweled Leonore, manufactured in Switzerland, has cut expansion balance, straight line escapement, with damaskeened nickel plates. This watch is warranted for five years. Price $6.75

Ladies' Solid Silver Watch, $4.20.

No. 4C4540 Ladies' solid silver hunting chatelaine watch, stem wind and stem set, with second hand. The case is handsomely engraved. The movement is imported from Switzerland, has 7 jewels, cylinder escapement and nickel plates. Price....$4.20

$4.20

$5.60

No. 4C4544 Ladies' silver inlaid open face stem wind and pendant set chatelaine watch. The case is gun metal with silver inlaid, called Niello. The movement is imported from Switzerland, has cylinder escapement, 7 jewels, plates of nickel. Price..........$4.00

$3.82

No. 4C4548 Ladies' enameled open face stem wind and stem set chatelaine watch. The case is beautifully enameled in colors with similar subjects, as illustration shows. The illustration shows both the back and front of the watch. The movement has 7 fine ruby jewels, gold plated lever escapement, and is a good timekeeper. Price. $4.65

$6.50

No. 4C4552 Ladies' gold filled open face plain polished screw back and bezel chatelaine watch. The case is warranted for twenty years wear. Is stem wind and pendant set, fitted with the celebrated full jeweled Leonore movement, manufactured in Switzerland. It has cut expansion balance, lever escapement and nickel plates. The movement is warranted for a term of five years. Price..............$8.50

No. 4C4542 Ladies' solid silver hunting style stem wind and stem set chatelaine watch. The case is beautifully engraved as illustration shows. The movement is Swiss imported, called Lady Rose, has cylinder escapement, damaskeened nickel plates and 10 fine ruby jewels and is an excellent timekeeper. Price..........$5.60

$4.00

No. 4C4546 Ladies' silver inlaid open face novelty chatelaine watch. The case is gun metal with silver inlaid, called Niello. Illustration shows the back and front of watch. The movement is a Swiss imported, has cylinder escapement and 7 jewels. Price..........$3.82

$4.65

We can supply Chatelette Pin and Box similar to No. 4C4556 at $1.00 extra.

No. 4C4550 Ladies' solid gold 10 karat plain polished stem wind and pendant set chatelaine watch. The movement has cylinder escapement, 7 jewels, beautiful damaskeening on nickel plates, fancy dial, as illustration shows. Price........$6.50

$8.50

$11.00

Ladies' Solid Gold Watch $11.00.

No. 4C4554 14 karat solid gold open face stem wind and stem set chatelaine watch. The case is plain polished. The movement is called the Rosalind, has 7 fine ruby jewels, cylinder escapement, with damaskeened nickel plates. Price..$11.00

No. 4C4556 Less money than before and better than ever. Genuine French Enameled Chatelaine Watch for $5.00. The case is gold filled, beautifully enameled in either blue, ruby red or green. The chatelaine matches the watch. The movement is an imported one, made in Switzerland, perfectly trued and adjusted; we guarantee it to give entire satisfaction. The picture is two-thirds size of watch. It is the exact size of watch No. 4C4548.

At $5.00 for the complete outfit, case, chatelaine and watch, you have a bargain at least 50 per cent cheaper than any local jeweler could possibly sell it. Price..............................$5.00

If by mail, postage extra, 16 cents.

Ladies' Solid Silver O-Size Watches.

OPEN FACE OR HUNTING STYLE AT THE SAME PRICE.

$5.25

AN AMERICAN MADE WATCH in this small size, made of silver, has been wanted by thousands of ladies. So as to make our catalogue complete, so as to positively quote all kinds and styles of watches, we show here **the smallest silver American watch made. These cases are solid sterling silver through and through,** hand engraved; they have the antique bow; the entire case is perfectly finished in every respect. They are stem wind and pendant set. **We guarantee the movement for a term of five years, and the case will last your natural lifetime.** We fit these cases with the following movements at prices quoted:

No. 4C4558 Open Face.
No. 4C4560 Hunting Style.

PRICES QUOTED HERE ARE FOR THE COMPLETE WATCH, OPEN FACE OR HUNTING STYLE.	4C4558 4C4560
7 Jeweled Swiss Lever	$5.25
7 Jeweled Elgin or Waltham	8.70
Full 15 Jeweled EDGEMERE, Sears, Roebuck & Co.'s Special	8.55

$8.98 AND UP REDUCED PRICES IN LADIES' SMALL 0-SIZE GOLD FILLED WATCHES $6.85 AND UP

HUNTING STYLE. GUARANTEED FOR TWENTY YEARS.

COMPETITION DEFIED on ladies' small size gold filled watches manufactured by representative watch makers. You can choose any make of case you desire, the product of the Plymouth Watch Case Co., the John C. Dueber or the Illinois Watch Case Co. All three of them positively represent the highest quality in case making.

No. 4L3300 Raised solid gold, ornamented in bird design, on gold filled stock, guaranteed for twenty years, manufactured by the Illinois Watch Case Co. This is one of the handsomest, most ornate twenty-year gold filled guaranteed cases on the market. See the prices quoted in table below.

YOU NEED NOT BE A MILLIONAIRE to afford a watch. Anybody in moderate circumstances can own or make a princely gift in the way of a watch when prices such as these are made.

$6.85 TO $29.62 means that you are getting watches today that a few years ago would have cost from $35.00 to $50.00. Do not be misled by the opinion that this small amount of money cannot buy a good watch. These watches are positively wonderful for the price.

A 15 JEWELED MOVEMENT WILL RUN BETTER AND THE TIME BE MORE ACCURATE THAN A WATCH CONSTRUCTED WITH A LESS NUMBER OF JEWELS

OUR 15 JEWELED EDGEMERE or the 15 jeweled Plymouth Watch Co. movement, quoted for $10.15 and $11.85, we know would please you. See the illustrations of these movements; you will then be able to form some idea of their general appearance. For full description see page 21 of this book. A little more money expended, if you so desire, would procure for you the 17 jeweled Plymouth Watch Co. movement fitted in any of these cases. This movement represents positively the highest order of ladies' watch movements manufactured in the United States.

No. 4L3300

$6.85 AND UP

25 cents will carry any watch to any part of the United States by express.

For 90 cents extra we will furnish a fancy dial and gold hands.

$6.85 AND UP

No. 4L3302 Guaranteed for 20 years. Plymouth Make.

No. 4L3305 Guaranteed for 20 years. Plymouth Make.

No. 4L3307 Guaranteed for 20 years. Plymouth Make.

No. 4L3308 Guaranteed for 20 years. Dueber Watch Case Co. Make.

No. 4L3310 Guaranteed for 20 years. Illinois Watch Case Co. make. **No. 4L3312** Same make, but Plain Engine Turned.

No. 4L3314 Guaranteed for 20 years. Dueber Watch Case Co. Make.

No. 4L3316 Guaranteed for 20 years. Illinois Watch Case Co. Make.

This is the picture of the 15 Jeweled Edgemere Movement. We advocate 15 jeweled movements. Try our 15 Jeweled Edgemere Movement. See page 21 for accurate description.

WE FIT THESE CASES WITH THE FOLLOWING 0-SIZE MOVEMENTS: PRICES QUOTED ARE FOR COMPLETE WATCH, MOVEMENT AND CASE.	PRICES FOR COMPLETE WATCH.				
	No. 4L3300	No. 4L3302 4L3305	No. 4L3307 4L3308	No. 4L3310 4L3312	No. 4L3314 4L3316
7 Jeweled Swiss	$ 8.98	$ 6.85	$ 6.85	$ 6.85	$ 6.85
15 JEWELED EDGEMERE SPECIAL MAKE	12.15	10.15	10.15	10.15	10.15
7 Jeweled Elgin or Waltham, nickel plates	11.73	9.73	9.73	9.73	9.73
15 Jeweled Elgin or Waltham, nickel plates	14.10	12.10	12.10	12.10	12.10
15 JEWELED PLYMOUTH WATCH CO., patent regulator, special make	13.85	11.85	11.85	11.85	11.85
16 Jeweled Lady Waltham, nickel plates	19.13	17.13	17.13	17.13	17.13
17 JEWELED PLYMOUTH WATCH CO., patent regulator, adjusted, special make	18.50	16.50	16.50	16.50	16.50
19 Jeweled 201 Grade Elgin	29.62	27.62	27.62	27.62	27.62

This is the picture of our 15 Jeweled 0-Size Plymouth Watch Co. Movement. See page 21 for accurate description.

LADIES' SOLID GOLD AND GOLD FILLED EXTRA SMALL SIZE AMERICAN MADE WATCHES $11.75 AND UP

REDUCED IN PRICE

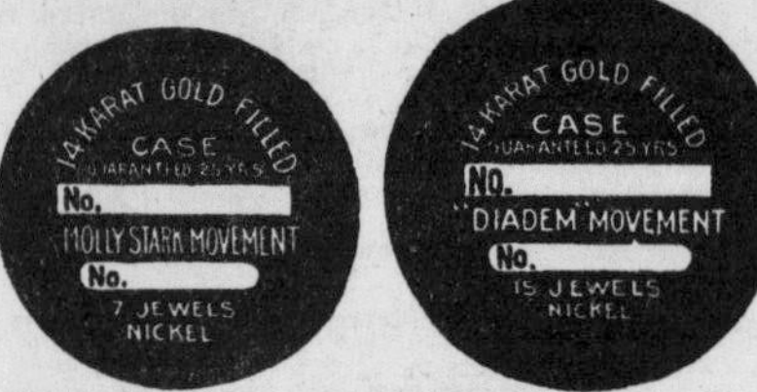

THIS IS AN ILLUSTRATION of the guarantee tag that goes out with the Dueber-Hampden Watch Co.'s watches that they themselves send out on each watch and is attached to the Molly Stark movement and the Diadem movement according to cases.

THE TRIPLE 0-SIZE called the 400-size, manufactured by the Dueber-Hampden Watch Co., of Canton, Ohio. Gold filled cases are made of gold filled stock, the outer sheet of gold being of such thickness as to give the watch a wearing quality equal to a solid gold case for a period of twenty-five years. The solid gold cases are made of 14-karat quality gold, they are gold through and through, each piece and particle of their makeup is of 14-karat gold.

THE 400-SIZE WATCH or the triple 0-size is the ideal ladies' size. John C. Dueber with the idea of filling a long felt want and supplying the ladies of the United States with the exact proper sized watch according to his ideas, has made this 400-size, as illustrated and described here.

WE WISH YOU TO FORM A CORRECT OPINION as to exactly how these watches appear; to be able to help you to decide and so as to give you every possible view of these watches, we have had each one photographed in various positions. Each watch is shown in such a way that you can see the back, front, the thickness and how it appears with the movement set in the case.

WE KNOW WHAT QUALITY the Dueber-Hampden Watch Co. offers and so as to doubly protect our customers, in addition to the guarantee of John C. Dueber Watch Co., we send our own written binding guarantee, covering all the salient points, giving you double assurance.

THESE TWO PICTURES SHOW the two movements we fit in these cases according to your own selection. The top movement is jeweled.

THE MOLLY STARK HAMPDEN MOVEMENT. This has 7 jewels, nickel plates fitted with bright screws, sunk second dial, spade hands and carries our five-year written binding guarantee. The bottom one is the 15 jeweled Diadem movement, has 15 jewels and raised gold setting, plates are made of solid nickel, the upper and lower center bearings bushed with anti-friction metal, Breguet hair spring blued steel hands, finely damaskeened plates and is beautifully finished throughout. We would advise you to select this movement if you want the most accurate timekeeper and one that will give splendid satisfaction.

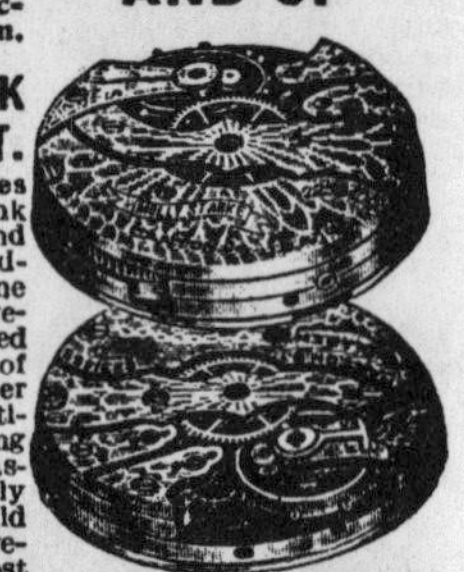

$11.75 AND UP

This group shows the gold filled diagonal engraved Bassene style case, back view and front view with the lid slightly open. Hunting style.

No. 4L3350 Gold filled case with the 7 Jeweled Molly Stark Movement. Price $11.75

No. 4L3352 Same case fitted with the 15 Jeweled Diadem Movement. Price $14.50

This group illustrates the gold filled and the 14-karat solid gold plain polished Bassene style hunting case, showing the thickness, back and front view with lid opened. Be sure to order by number. Hunting style.

No. 4L3354 Gold filled case fitted with the 7 Jeweled Molly Stark Movement. Price $11.75

No. 4L3356 Gold filled case fitted with the 15 Jeweled Diadem Movement. $14.50

No. 4L3358 Solid 14-karat gold case fitted with the 7 Jeweled Molly Stark Movement. Price $18.25

No. 4L3360 Solid 14-karat gold case fitted with the 15 Jeweled Diadem Movement. Price $21.00

This illustration shows you the gold filled, full engraved case, Bassene style, giving the side view, back view and front view. Hunting style.

No. 4L3362 Gold filled case fitted with the 7 Jeweled Molly Stark Movement. Price $11.75

No. 4L3364 Same case fitted with the 15 Jeweled Diadem Movement. Price $14.50

This group shows you the full engraved Bassene style 14-karat solid gold case, the most exquisite and daintiest little watch on the market. Hunting style.

No. 4L3366 Fitted with the 7 Jeweled Molly Stark Movement. Price $18.25

No. 4L3368 Fitted with the 15 Jeweled Diadem Movement. Price $21.00

GENTLEMEN'S 16-SIZE AND 12-SIZE THIN MODEL OPEN FACE AND HUNTING STYLE GOLD FILLED WATCHES.

OUR CHALLENGE CASE.

This, our Kingston case, is one of our challenge cases. We challenge any jeweler to equal this case for the money in quality, finish and wearing ability. These cases are made by the Illinois Watch Case Co. of Elgin, Ill. They carry a 20-year guarantee inside the case. Together with this warrant, is sent our own personal binding guarantee for a term of 20 years, signed by Sears, Roebuck & Co. This is the best cheap 16-size, guaranteed 20-year case on the market. When you select a watch case, select either a Kingston case or a Plymouth gold filled case, each one in its class representing the highest perfection in gold filled case making.

FOR THE BEST CHEAP WATCH in 16-size, we recommend above all others our new 7-jeweled Edgemere. It is guaranteed; but for a watch that costs but a few dollars more and gives better satisfaction, and for accuracy, we recommend our 15 jeweled Edgemere, our 15 jeweled Plymouth Watch Co. U. S. A. Special, or our 17 jeweled Plymouth Watch Co. U. S. A Special, adjusted. All of the above carry our five-year written, binding guarantee.

$5.60 AND UP

For 23 Cents we furnish a beautiful Leatherette Presentation CASE to fit any Watch. See No. 4G588 on Page 38.

FOR NEWEST STYLE WATCHES.

25 cents will carry any watch to any part of the United States by express. We recommend sending watches by express as they do not receive the hard usage as when sent by mail. If sent by mail postage extra including registry, 12c.

$5.60 AND UP

16-Size. Kingston Gold Filled.
No. 4G2273 Hunting Style.
No. 4G2275 Open Face Screw Back and Bezel.

16-Size. Kingston Gold Filled.
No. 4G2277 Hunting Style.
No. 4G2279 Open Face, Screw Back and Bezel.

16-Size. Kingston Gold Filled.
No. 4G2281 Hunting Style.
No. 4G2283 Open Face, Screw Back and Bezel.

We Fit these Cases with the following 16-Size Movements. Prices quoted are for the complete watch, movement and case	No. 4G2275 No. 4G2279 No. 4G2283	No. 4G2273 No. 4G2277 No. 4G2281
7 JEWELED EDGEMERE, nickel plates, special make	$ 5.60	$ 7.35
7 Jeweled Elgin or Waltham, nickel plates	8.50	10.25
15 JEWELED EDGEMERE, patent regulator nickel plates, special make	8.35	10.10
15 Jeweled Elgin or Waltham, nickel plates, patent regulator	10.60	12.35
15 JEWELED PLYMOUTH WATCH CO.	10.35	12.10
17 Jeweled Elgin or Waltham, not adjusted	12.70	14.45

We Fit there Cases with the following 16-Size Movements. Prices quoted are for the complete watch, movement and case.	No. 4G2275 No. 4G2279 No. 4G2283	No. 4G2273 No. 4G2277 No. 4G2281
17 Jeweled No. 241 Grade Elgin or 630 Grade Waltham, adjusted	$ 15.33	$ 17.08
17 JEWELED PLYMOUTH WATCH CO., nickel plates, patent regulator, adjusted	14.98	16.73
17 Jeweled Royal Waltham, adjusted, nickel plates	17.69	19.44
17 Jeweled No. 243 Grade Elgin, adjusted, nickel plates	26.35	28.10
21 JEWELED PRINCE OF WALES PLYMOUTH WATCH CO., full adjusted, patent regulator, nickel plates	20.25	22.00

Gentlemen's Thin Model Open Face and Hunting Style Filled Cases.

$6.25 AND UP

$8.00 and $9.80 For the COMPLETE WATCH fitted with the Edgemere Movement.

12-Size Extra Thin Model Open Face Style Gold. Guaranteed for 20 Years.

$3.98 BEAUTY

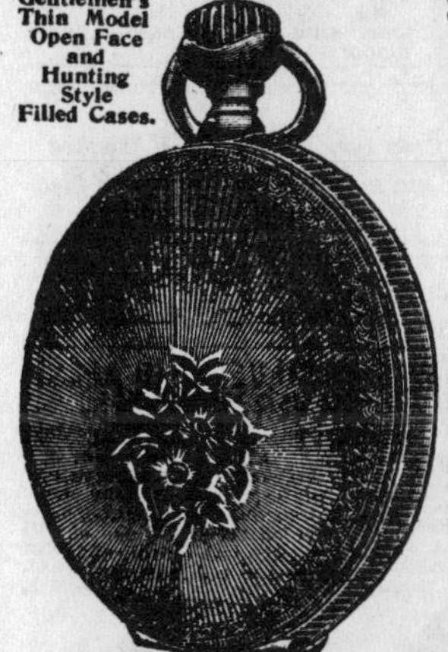

12-Size. Kingston Gold Filled
No. 4G2305 Hunting Style.
No. 4G2307 Open Face, Screw Back and Bezel.

12-Size. Kingston Gold Filled.
No. 4G2316 Hunting Style
No. 4G2318 Open Face, Screw Back and Bezel.

12-Size. Kingston Gold Filled.
No. 4G2320 Hunting Style.
No. 4G2322 Open Face Screw Back and Bezel.

12-Size. Kingston Gold Filled.
No. 4G2324 Hunting Style.
No. 4G2326 Open Face, Screw Back and Bezel.

No. 4G2340 The very latest 12-size extra thin, oxidized polished gunmetal watch with illuminated dial. Send us $3.98 and 14 cents for mail charges, $4.12 in all, and we will at once ship you this newest gentlemen's watch by registered mail. The case is made with a solid back and snap front, and is absolutely dustproof; it is stem wind and stem set, is full jeweled, has exposed balance wheel; illustration shows a new mechanical construction. This watch is imported by us from Switzerland; each one is guaranteed for a term of five years. At $3.98, we are selling this watch at 40 per cent less than similar but inferior watches are being sold for. Price.....$3.98

No. 4G2342 Same style as No. 4G2340, but case of solid silver, engine turned. Price.....$5.45

No. 4G2344 Same style as No. 4G2340, but gold filled case, guaranteed 20 years. Price.....$7.98

REMEMBER, when you have bought $25.00 worth of goods or more from us you get your choice of many valuable articles Free, as shown in our new free Profit Sharing Book.

For 90 Cents Extra we can furnish a fancy dial and gold hands on any watch on this page. Protect your watch with an Ajax Watch Insulator, 23c. See page 38, No. 4G586.

We Fit these Cases with the following 12-Size Movements Prices quoted are for the complete watch, movement and case.	No. 4G2307 No. 4G2318 No. 4G2322 No. 4G2326	No. 4G2305 No. 4G2316 No. 4G2320 No. 4G2324
7 Jeweled Swiss Lever, nickel plates	$ 6.25	$ 8.05
7 Jeweled Elgin or Waltham, nickel plates	8.25	10.05
10 JEWELED EDGEMERE, special make	8.00	9.80
15 JEWELED PLYMOUTH WATCH CO., nickel plates, patent regulator, special make	10.10	11.90
15 Jeweled Elgin or Waltham, nickel plates, patent regulator	10.35	12.15
17 JEWELED PLYMOUTH WATCH CO., nickel plates, patent regulator, special make	17.08	18.88
17 Jeweled No. 321 Grade Elgin or Royal Grade Waltham	17.43	19.23
19 Jeweled Riverside Waltham	24 52	26.32
19 Jeweled No. 189 Grade Elgin	28.72	30.52
21 JEWELED SWISS, nickel plates, patent regulator, adjusted	22.65	24.45

No. 4G2346 Open Face, Screw Back and Bezel.
No. 4G2347 Hunting Style.

12-size, solid silver, gold ornamented, gold filled center, bow and crown, thin model open face or hunting style gentlemen's watches. These cases are made to supply a certain demand for a watch a little different than the regulation old stereotyped style. The lids are of solid silver, richly ornamented with varicolored solid gold in beautiful floral designs. The center, or frame upon which the lids are fastened, is gold filled and guaranteed for a term of twenty years. The crown, bow and stem are likewise gold filled. The hunting style or double sided case is ornamented on both sides, each side being the same as the other with the exception of the shield of solid gold made to bear the owner's name or initials. The open face, screw back and bezel, dust and damp proof case is made throughout with the same care, with the same thoughtfulness for perfection as the hunting style. These watches are all stem wind and pendant set. Each movement as quoted below at various prices according to the different grades carries our written binding guarantee for a term of five years. If you are looking for a watch that is attractive, durable and strictly up to date, one that is different than is carried by others, and a watch that is dependable in every way, we certainly would suggest and recommend purchasing this watch.

We fit cases No. 4G2346 and No. 4G2347, with the following 12-size movements. Prices quoted are for the complete watch, movement and case.	No. 4G2346 Open Face Screw Back and Bezel	No. 4G2347 Hunting Style
7 Jeweled Swiss Lever, nickel	$ 6.75	$ 8.25
7 Jeweled Elgin or Waltham, nickel plates	8.75	10.25
10 JEWELED EDGEMERE	8.50	10.00
15 JEWELED PLYMOUTH WATCH CO., nickel plates	10.60	12.10
15 Jeweled Elgin or Waltham, nickel plates	10.85	12.35
17 JEWELED PLYMOUTH WATCH CO., nickel plates	17.58	19.08
17 Jeweled No. 321 Grade Elgin or Royal Grade Waltham	17.93	19.43
19 Jeweled Riverside Waltham	25.02	26.52
19 Jeweled No. 189 Grade Elgin	29.22	30.72
21 Jeweled Swiss, nickel plates	23.15	24.65

LADIES' GOLD PLATED WATCH.

$3.45

Special bargain in a ladies' 0-size gold plated trading watch. This watch is the exact counterpart of the finest grade gold filled watch manufactured. It is not guaranteed; will wear six months to a year if very carefully handled. It is a great watch to use for trading purposes. It is stem wind and stem set and the movement we fit in this watch is an imported 7-jeweled Swiss lever movement, and will give excellent satisfaction as a timekeeper. We warrant it being received in perfect going order. At $3.45 these watches are rare bargains. They are being offered by premium houses and newspaper advertisements at twice this amount and sold as gold filled. Remember, our price is but $3.45. Order by number.

No. 4G2348 Price for complete watch $3.45

12-SIZE OPEN FACE OR HUNTING STYLE DUEBER-HAMPDEN COMPLETE WATCHES AT $11.25 IN OPEN FACE OR $12.50 IN HUNTING STYLE.

SOLID GOLD AND GOLD FILLED CASES.

WE OFFER AT $11.25 the 12-size Hampden Watch Co.'s Complete Watch. The case is guaranteed 14-karat gold filled and warranted for a term of 25 years' wear. The movement is the Cantonian, 7 jeweled, exactly as described. Never before in the history of the watch business have such values been offered for the money.

THE MOVEMENTS. We can recommend any of the movements quoted as being an accurate timekeeper, perfectly finished in every detail, stem wind and lever set; all the latest modern improvements being employed. They positively are up to date in every respect.

No. 4G2350 Open Face Screw Back and Bezel, gold filled, warranted 25 years.
No. 4G2351 Hunting Style Case, same make and quality as above.
No. 4G2352 Hunting Style Case, solid gold 14-karat, heavy weight.

No. 4G2353 Open Face, Screw Back and Bezel, gold filled, warranted 25 years.
No. 4G2354 Hunting Style Case, same make and quality as above.
No. 4G2355 Hunting Style Case, solid gold 14-karat, heavy weight.

No. 4G2356 Open Face, Screw Back and Bezel, gold filled, warranted 25 years.
No. 4G2357 Hunting Style Case, same make and quality as above.
No. 4G2358 Hunting Style Case, solid gold, 14-karat, heavy weight.

No. 4G2359 Open Face, Screw Back and Bezel, gold filled, warranted 25 years.
No. 4G2360 Hunting Style Case, same make and quality as above.
No. 4G2361 Hunting Style Case, solid gold, 14-karat, heavy weight.

No. 4G2362 Open Face, Screw Back and Bezel, gold filled, warranted 25 years.
No. 4G2363 Hunting Style Case, same make and quality as above.
No. 4G2364 Hunting Style Case, solid gold, 14-karat heavy weight.

DESCRIPTION OF THE MOVEMENTS FITTED IN THE 12-SIZE COMPLETE DUEBER-HAMPDEN WATCHES.

THE CANTONIAN has 7 jewels, Arabic or Roman dial, solid nickel plates, Breguet hairspring, all pivot holes when not jeweled are bushed with antifriction metal. A very good movement.

THE GENERAL STARK has solid nickel plates, 15 ruby jewels in composition settings, Breguet hairspring, mean time screws, patent regulator, bright flat screws, plates are engraved and damaskeened, has Roman or Arabic dial with red marginal figures.

THE DUEBER GRAND has solid nickel plates, 17 ruby and sapphire jewels in composition settings, is adjusted, has Breguet hairspring, patent regulator, bright flat screws, beautifully engraved and damaskeened plates with gold letters, Arabic or Roman dial with red marginal figures.

THE JOHN HANCOCK has solid nickel plates, 21 fine ruby and sapphire jewels in gold settings, escapement is cap jeweled, has compensation balance, adjusted to temperature, isochronism and positions, has Breguet hairspring, new model micrometric regulator, bright bevel head screws, patent center pinion, finely polished steel work, double sunk enameled dial, beautifully finished nickel plates with gold letters. This is the finest finished movement of any of the 12-size Dueber-Hampden watches. It is very closely timed.

We fit these cases (Nos. 4G2350 to 4G2364) with the following 12-size movements. Prices quoted are for the complete watch, movement and case.	Open Face, Screw Back and Bezel	Hunting Style, Gold Filled	Hunting Style, Solid Gold
7 Jeweled Cantonian.....	$11 25	$12.50	$35.50
15 Jeweled General Stark..	13.25	14.50	37 50
17 Jeweled Dueber Grand..	16.25	17.50	40.50
21 Jeweled John Hancock..	29.75	31.50	55.00

16-SIZE GUN-METAL $2.32

No. 4G2440 Gentlemen's 16-size, thin model, open face, plain polished, gun-metal watch. Has beautiful fancy dial as illustration shows. The movement is imported from Switzerland, has jeweled cylinder escapement and damaskeened nickel plates. It is recommended to all who desire a cheap and durable watch. Sold for twice what we ask for it by all the leading jewelers in the country.
Price.....$2.32

6-SIZE ALASKA SILVER. SOMETHING NEW.

$3.13 TO $9.15

No. 4G2450

OUR 6-SIZE ALASKA SILVER WATCHES in hunting and open face style. Alaska silver is one of the newly compounded metals. It looks like silver, wears like silver, has the same color and appearance as silver, but is very much tougher and costs less. At $3.13 to $9.15 we are offering these Alaska silver ladies' watches.

THE MOVEMENTS are all representative makes, each one of them is guaranteed an accurate timekeeper and WE FULLY WARRANT THEM FOR A TERM OF 5 YEARS against defective material or workmanship.
No. 4G2450 Open Face Style.
No. 4G2452 Hunting Style.

We fit these cases with the following 6-size movements. Prices quoted are for the complete watch, movement and case.	No. 4G2450	No. 4G2452
7 JEWELED EDGEMERE, special make..........	$3.13	$3.40
COUNTESS JANET, stamped 17 jeweled, adjusted	3.33	3.60
7 Jeweled Elgin or Waltham, gilt plates..........	4.68	4.95
7 Jeweled Elgin or Waltham, nickel plates..........	5.20	5.47
12 JEWELED EDGEMERE, nickel plates, special make..........	6.08	6.35
15 Jeweled Elgin or Waltham, nickel plates........	6.26	6.53
16 Jeweled Lady Waltham, nickel plates..........	8.88	9.15
17 JEWELED PLYMOUTH WATCH CO. nickel plates, patent regulator, special make..........	8.63	8.90

FOR 23 CENTS we can furnish a fine leatherette covered, silk lined Presentation Box to fit any watch you order. Mention No. 4G588. Price, 23c

BOYS' SOLID SILVER 16-SIZE WATCHES.

$3.97 OPEN FACE — HUNTING $4.48

No. 4G2475 — No. 4G2477

EXACTLY AS ILLUSTRATION SHOWS, EXACTLY AS DESCRIBED.

For $3.97 and 14 cents for the mail charges we will send you one of the solid, highest grade silver 935/1000 fine watches. Open face, stem wind and pendant set, fine inside protecting cap, fully engraved, antique bow and crown. The movement is imported from Switzerland and has seven jewels, exposed winding wheels and cylinder escapement. Will keep good time and will wear for years.
No. 4G2475 Open Face Style.
Price.....$3.97

For $4.48 and 14 cents for the mail charges we will send the same movement but fitted in the Hunting style case, 16-size, exactly as illustration shows, handsomely engraved bow and stem, is stem wind and pendant set with inside protecting cap. No merchant in the watch world can offer such a watch, so high in quality, so splendid a timekeeper at double the amount we ask.
No. 4G2477 Hunting Style.
Price.....$4.48

Remember, when you have bought $25.00 worth of goods or more from us you get your choice of many valuable articles free, as shown in our new free Profit Sharing Book.

$3.65 TO $27.72

12-SIZE SILVER AND ALASKA SILVER WATCHES.

DESCRIPTION OF THE EDGEMERE MOVEMENT 12-size open face or hunting; Alaska silver, bright polished, damaskeened plates; 10 fine ruby jewels. Breguet hairspring, cut balance, patent pinions, beveled screw heads, exposed winding arrangement, double sunk dial, moon hands and red marginal figures.

No. 4G2461 Alaska Silver, Open Face, Screw Back and Bezel.
No. 4G2463 Alaska Silver, Hunting Style.
No. 4G2465 Solid Silver, Open Face, Screw Back and Bezel.
No. 4G2467 Solid Silver, Hunting Style.
These watches are made of solid silver or Alaska silver through and through.

We fit these cases with the following 12-size movements. Prices quoted are for the complete watch, movement and case.	No. 4G2461	No. 4G2463	No. 4G2465	No. 4G2467
7 Jeweled Swiss Lever, nickel plates	$ 3.65	$ 4.05	$ 4.75	$ 5.2[illegible]
7 Jeweled Elgin or Waltham, nickel plates...	5.65	6.05	6.75	7.25
10 JEWELED EDGEMERE, special make..	5.40	5.80	6.50	7.00
15 JEWELED PLYMOUTH WATCH CO., nickel plates, patent regulator, special make	7.55	7.95	8.65	9.15
15 Jeweled Elgin or Waltham, nickel plates, patent regulator.......	7.75	8.15	8.85	9.35
17 JEWELED PLYMOUTH WATCH CO., nickel plates, patent regulator, special make	13.90	14.30	15.00	15.5
17 Jeweled No. 321 Grade Elgin or Royal Grade Waltham..............	14.83	15.23	15.93	16.43
19 Jeweled Riverside Waltham..............	21.92	22.32	23.02	23.52
19 Jeweled No. 189 Grade Elgin..............	26.12	26.52	27.22	27.72
21 JEWELED SWISS, nickel plates, patent regulator, adjusted....	20.05	20.45	21.15	21.65

$10.40 Buys our 15 jeweled Edgemere, fitted in any of these high grade cases you may select.

ANOTHER CUT IN PRICES ON

LADIES' HIGHEST GRADE 0-SIZE HUNTING STYLE GOLD FILLED WATCHES

ONLY $7.10 for your choice of these beautifully engraved, high grade cases, as shown below, fitted with the genuine 7-jeweled SWISS LEVER MOVEMENT.

The Latest Styles. All Selected from Newest Designs. Never Before Shown. We Own the Exclusive Right to These Patterns. You Cannot See Them Elsewhere.

TWELVE DIFFERENT PATTERNS OF CASES to select from and all the latest designs. We earnestly believe that such a handsome, high grade, gold filled watch was never before offered for as little money as $7.10. It is a price that others would find impossible to duplicate, a price that is made possible only by reason of our immense outlet for high grade watches.

THESE LADIES', HANDSOME, 0-SIZE CASES, as illustrated below, are the best on the market. They are made by the most reputable watch case manufacturer in America, made by the highest grade method there is, on heavy plates of solid gold over an inner plate of hard composition metal, and are guaranteed by our special certificate to wear for twenty years. They come in the 0-size, one size smaller than the regular 6-size, the most popular, stylish and handsome size for ladies' wear made. They are beautifully engraved and decorated and the latest style antique bow and winding crown or stem wind and stem set hunting case style.

GUARANTEED FOR TWENTY YEARS.

OUR PROTECTIVE OFFER: IF, AFTER YOU EXAMINE THE WATCH YOU GET, you do not find it in EVERY WAY just as represented and warranted, return it to us, and we will REFUND YOU THE PURCHASE PRICE.

NO CHARGES FOR REPAIRS on watches or clocks will be allowed unless our written consent is first secured in advance.

$7.10 is the LOWEST price ever known on any case fitted with the 7-jeweled Swiss Lever movement.

THE EDGEMERE IS OUR LATEST MOVEMENT BARGAIN.

No. 4C4199 No. 4C4201

No. 4C4203 Special bargain in a ladies' 0-size gold plated trading watch. This watch is the exact counter part of the finest grade gold filled watch manufactured. It is not guaranteed; will wear six months to a year if very carefully handled. It is a great watch to use for trading purposes. It is stem wind and stem set and the movement we fit in this watch is an imported 7 jeweled Swiss lever movement, and will give excellent satisfaction as a timekeeper. We warrant it being received in a perfect going order. At $3.65 these watches are rare bargains. They are being offered by premium houses in newspaper advertisements at twice this amount and sold as gold filled. Remember our price is but $3.65. Order by number.

No. 4C4203 Price, for complete watch........................**$3.65**

YOU HAVE YOUR CHOICE OF CASES.

No. 4C4205 No. 4C4207

YOU CAN MAKE MONEY SELLING THESE WATCHES.

No. 4C4209 No. 4C4211

No. 4C4219 Our special 0-size solid silver case, with solid gold ornamentation. This case is one of the most beautiful productions this year in the watch market. The contrast between the different colored gold onlaid on the white silver surface makes an effect unequalled. This watch is stem wind and stem set, hunting style.

Fitted with the 7 jeweled Swiss lever movement. Price.....**$6.60**

Fitted with the 11 jeweled Swiss lever movement. Price.....**$7.35**

Fitted with the 7 jeweled Elgin or Waltham movement. Price, **$9.75**

Fitted with the celebrated 15 jeweled Edgemere, Sears, Roebuck & Co.'s special movement.

Price..........................**$8.85**

For 20 cents we furnish a beautiful Plush Presentation Case to fit any watch. See No. 4C2000, on page 192.

No. 4C4213 No. 4C4215

OUR 0-SIZE EDGEMERE MOVEMENT HAS 15 FINE RUBY JEWELS.

No. 4C4217 No. 4C4221

JEWELERS ASK 50 PER CENT MORE FOR WATCHES OF SAME GRADE.

No. 4C4223 No. 4C4225

WE CAN FIT THESE MOVEMENTS IN ANY OF THE ABOVE CASES.

7 Jeweled Swiss Lever Movement	$ 7.10
11 Jeweled Lever	9.40
7 Jeweled Elgin or Waltham	10.30
Full 15 Jeweled EDGEMERE, SEARS, ROEBUCK & CO.'S Special Make	$10.40
Full 15 Jeweled Elgin or Waltham	14.00

WE GUARANTEE ANY OF THE ABOVE MOVEMENTS FOR FIVE YEARS.

ELGIN AND WALTHAM WATCHES QUOTED ON PAGES 216 TO 218.

LADIES' 0-SIZE 25-YEAR GOLD FILLED WATCHES

AND SEARS GOLD FILLED CASES GUARANTEED FOR LIFE.

MANUFACTURED BY THE MOST REPRESENTATIVE GOLD FILLED CASE MANUFACTURERS IN THE WORLD.

THE QUALITY OF THESE CASES is the highest. They are 14-karat gold filled, guaranteed to wear for a term of 25 years. Nothing superior made. No case better in the market. They lead them all. The size is the very latest and best adapted for ladies' use. The designs are artistic copies of the highest grade solid gold patterns. The general finish is the same as in solid gold. They are hand engraved throughout. The antique bow and crown, lips and joints are perfect in every detail.

THE GUARANTEE GIVEN: Each case is warranted by the maker, and we send, together with this, our own special binding guarantee.

WHAT WE MEAN BY THE SEARS LIFE GUARANTEED CASE. The Sears Life Guaranteed Case is a gold filled case of the very highest quality and the nearest approach to a solid gold case manufactured. The Sears Life Guaranteed Case means that should any one of these cases wear down to the inner composition metal any time within your natural life, whether you have owned the case five years, twenty years or fifty years, return it to us, and we will upon the receipt of same exchange it for a brand new case of same quality, free of charge.

DESCRIPTION OF OUR 0-SIZE, 15-JEWELED EDGEMERE MOVEMENT. Solid nickel plates through and through, 15 finely polished ruby jewels, cut balance, lever escapement, patent pinion, perfect in finish and detail, and warranted for 5 years.

$8.30 TO $11.60

For $1.25 Extra WE CAN FURNISH FANCY DIAL AND GOLD HANDS ON ANY WATCH ON THIS PAGE.

No. 4C4132
14-karat. Guaranteed for 25 years' wear. Made by the Illinois Watch Case Co.

No. 4C4134
14-karat. Guaranteed for 25 years' wear. Made by the Illinois Watch Case Co.

REGARDING THE ENGRAVINGS, WE GENERALLY HAVE THE EXACT PATTERN; IF NOT, WE WILL SEND A VERY SIMILAR DESIGN.

This is a picture taken direct from our 15-jeweled Edgemere, the only and best 15 jeweled movement on the market. We warrant it for five years.

The higher the grade the better the time. We advocate higher jeweling than the 7-jewel grades.

No. 4C4136 Gold Ornamented.
14-karat. Guaranteed for 25 years' wear. Made by the Illinois Watch Case Co.

$14.75 TO $18.05

No. 4C4138 Gold Ornamented and Diamond Set.
14-karat. Guaranteed for 25 years' wear. Made by the Illinois Watch Case Co.

25 cents will carry a ladies' watch by express.

No. 4C4140
14-karat. Guaranteed for 25 years' wear.
No. 4C4142 Above make. Plain Engine Turned. Made by Joseph Fahys.

No. 4C4144
14-karat. Guaranteed for 25 years' wear.
Made by Joseph Fahys.

No. 4C4146
14-karat. Guaranteed for Life.
THE SEARS CASE.

For $1.25 Extra We can furnish fancy dial and gold hands on any watch on this page.

No. 4C4148
Set with 4 Genuine Diamonds.
14-karat. Guaranteed for 25 years' wear. Made by Joseph Fahys.

No. 4C4150
14-karat. Guaranteed for 25 years' wear.
No. 4C4152 Above make Plain Polished or Engine Turned. Made by John C. Dueber.

$8.30 TO $11.60

Try our Edgemere Movement and be satisfied.

No. 4C4154
14-karat. Guaranteed for 25 years' wear.
No. 4C4156 Plain Polished or Engine Turned. Same quality. Made by the Illinois Watch Case Co.

The Sears cases we can recommend for elegant finish and durability.

No. 4C4158
14-karat. Guaranteed for Life.
THE SEARS CASE.

For 20 cents we furnish a beautiful plush Presentation Case to fit any watch. See No. 4C2000 on page 192.

No. 4C4160
14-karat. Guaranteed for Life.
THE SEARS CASE.

We carry only the most celebrated standard goods made.

No. 4C4162
14-karat. Guaranteed for 25 years. Made by the Illinois Watch Case Co.

$9.15 TO $12.45

No. 4C4164
14-karat. Guaranteed for Life.
THE SEARS CASE.

WE FIT THESE CASES WITH THE FOLLOWING 0-SIZE MOVEMENTS AT $8.30 TO $18.05. WE RECOMMEND THE 15-JEWELED EDGEMERE MOVEMENT AND SEARS CASE AT $12.45.	No. 4C4140 No. 4C4142 No. 4C4144	No. 4C4132 No. 4C4134 No. 4C4150 No. 4C4152 No. 4C4154 No. 4C4156 No. 4C4162	No. 4C4136	No. 4C4138	No. 4C4148	No. 4C4146 No. 4C4158 No. 4C4160 No. 4C4164
7 jeweled Bijou Swiss Lever	$ 8.80	$ 8.30	$11.05	$14.75	$11.55	$ 9.15
11 jeweled Fine Swiss Lever	11.10	10.60	13.35	17.05	13.85	11.45
Full 15 jeweled EDGEMERE, SEARS, ROEBUCK & CO.'S SPECIAL MAKE	12.10	11.60	14.35	18.05	14.85	12.45

ELGIN AND WALTHAM WATCHES QUOTED ON PAGES 216 TO 218.

YOUR MONEY WILL BE IMMEDIATELY RETURNED TO YOU FOR ANY GOODS NOT PERFECTLY SATISFACTORY.

THIN MODEL 16-SIZE SEARS, DUEBER, ELGIN GIANT AND FAHYS GOLD FILLED, HUNTING AND OPEN FACE SCREW BACK and BEZEL, DUST and DAMP PROOF CASES.

$6.65 TO $16.95

THE SEARS GOLD FILLED CASE IS RECOMMENDED ABOVE ALL OTHERS.

PROTECT YOUR WATCH WITH AN AJAX WATCH INSULATOR. See page 192.
No. 4C2002 Price..18c

Picture of our 12-Jeweled EDGEMERE fitted in our SEARS CASE for $8.25.

$6.05 TO $16.50

GUARANTEED FOR 20 YEARS.
No. 4C3600 Open Face, Screw Back and Bezel, Engraved as Picture.
No. 4C3602 As above, Engine Turned or Plain Polished.
No. 4C3604 Hunting Style, Engraved as Picture.
No. 4C3606 As above, Engine Turned or Plain Polished.

GUARANTEED FOR 20 YEARS.
No. 4C3607 Open Face, Screw Back and Bezel.
No. 4C3608 Hunting Style.

GUARANTEED FOR 20 YEARS.
No. 4C3613 Open Face, Screw Back and Bezel.
No. 4C3615 Hunting Style.

$8.25 fitted with the 12-Jeweled Edgemere.

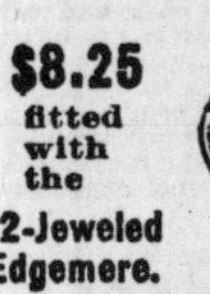

THE OPEN FACE CASES SHOWN ON THIS PAGE ARE ALL SCREW BEZEL AND SCREW BACK.

GUARANTEED FOR 20 YEARS.
No. 4C3609 Open Face, Screw Back Bezel.
No. 4C3611 Hunting Style.

THE SEARS is the latest and best made

WE FIT THESE CASES WITH THE FOLLOWING 16-SIZE MOVEMENTS:	No. 4C3607 4C3613 4C3616 4C3621 4C3624 4C3629 4C3633	No. 4C3600 4C3602 4C3609	No. 4C3608 4C3615 4C3618 4C3623 4C3626 4C3631 4C3635	No. 4C3604 4C3606 4C3611
7 Jeweled Reliance Movement	$ 6.05	$ 6.65	$ 8.60	$ 9.05
Full 12 Jeweled Edgemere, Sears, Roebuck & Co.'s Special make	8.25	8.85	10.80	11.25
Full 15 Jeweled Sears, Roebuck & Co.'s Special	9.95	10.55	12.50	12.95
Full 17 Jeweled Sears, Roebuck & Co.'s Special. Especially made. The Greatest Watch Value Ever Offered.	13.95	14.55	16.50	16.95

ELGIN AND WALTHAM WATCHES QUOTED ON PAGES 216 TO 218.

GUARANTEED FOR 20 YEARS.
No. 4C3616 Open Face, Screw Back and Bezel.
No. 4C3618 Hunting Style.

14 CENTS Will carry any of these watches by registered mail to any part of the United States.

GUARANTEED FOR 20 YEARS.
No. 4C3621 Open Face, Screw Back and Bezel.
No. 4C3623 Hunting Style.

FOR 20 CENTS we furnish a beautiful plush Presentation Case to fit any watch. See No. 4C2000 on page 192.

$13.95 fitted with our 17 Jeweled Adjusted Movement.

$6.05 TO $16.50

No. 4C3636

GUARANTEED FOR 20 YEARS.
No. 4C3629 Open Face, Screw Back and Bezel.
No. 4C3631 Hunting Style.

GUARANTEED FOR 20 YEARS.
No. 4C3633 Open Face, Screw Back and Bezel
No. 4C3635 Hunting Style.

GUARANTEED FOR 20 YEARS.
No. 4C3624 Open Face, Screw Back and Bezel.
No. 4C3626 Hunting Style.

An 18-Size Open Face Alarm Watch, the very latest invention out. You can set this watch to alarm any time you desire. The alarm is loud enough to awake the average sleeper. Full directions on a printed slip accompany every watch shipped. Price, $6.35. This watch is imported from Switzerland. It is stem wind and stem set, lever escapement, all important bearings are jeweled. It is guaranteed an accurate timekeeper. The case is gun metal, oxidized black. The illustration shows the exact size of the watch. Bear in mind this watch is not an intricate affair, but it is a simple practical device. It is a novelty wanted by many, but never until now has a practical one been placed on the market. We guarantee them to be perfect in every detail, and our five-year written guarantee goes with every one sold.

No. 4C3636 Price $6.35

STARTLING VALUES IN AMERICAN WATCHES

$3.16 A CUT PRICE IN GENUINE ALASKA METAL 16-SIZE SWING RING CUP CASE WATCH

Solid silver and Alaska metal, extra thin model, 16-size, swing ring dust and dampproof watches. Perfection has arrived at last; $3.16 for a watch with an absolutely dust and dampproof case means that you have a watch that will last a lifetime. Dampness and dust are the banes of watches. It is from these two causes that most tch troubles arise.

$3.16 and up

OUR $3.16 OFFER

Send us $3.16, together with the mail charges of 14 cents extra, and we will ship you, upon receipt, one of these solid Alaska metal watches, the nearest approach to solid silver yet discovered, fitted with a thin model, stem wind and pendant set 7 jeweled American made movement.

BUY THE SWING RING CASE. It is the best. Note the illustration, which shows the front bezel unscrewed and the swing ring slightly raised. When the watch is closed this swing ring falls back and the bezel is tightly screwed on. This makes the front and back of the watch absolutely dust and dampproof. The watch is protected from above by a new patent screw nut stem; the extra nut being used for filling the crevices on the inside of the watch between the crown and the stem makes it impossible for the dust and damp to filter through. No part has been overlooked to bring about this perfect dust and dampproof arrangement.

$4.95 FOR THE SAME WATCH IN SOLID SILVER. Think of it! $4.95 for this absolutely dust and dampproof solid silver watch. Competition defied when prices of such astonishing figures are being made. See the list of movements printed below. If you wish to own the best 17 jeweled movement manufactured in the United States, a movement that is stem wind and pendant set, containing 17 fine ruby jewels, with all modern improvements, a movement that will run accurately, one that can be guaranteed, a movement that you will be proud of, select the 17 jeweled Plymouth Watch Co. movement quoted at $13.15 and $14.90, according to case. In this case and in this movement you have the perfection of the watch world. For other movements, Elgin, Waltham, etc., see quotations listed below:

OPEN FACE SWING RING.

No. 4R13000 16-Size, Solid Silver, Open Face, Swing Ring.

No. 4R13002 16-Size, Alaska Metal, Open Face, Swing Ring.

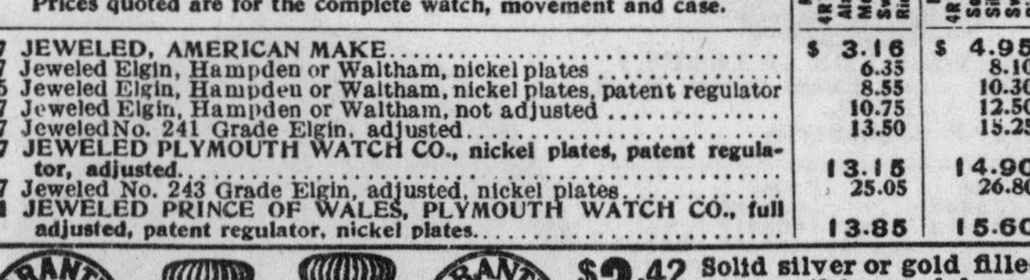

We fit these swing ring cases with the following 16-size movements. Prices quoted are for the complete watch, movement and case.	No. 4R13002 Alaska Metal Swing Ring	No. 4R13000 Solid Silver Swing Ring
7 JEWELED, AMERICAN MAKE	$ 3.16	$ 4.95
7 Jeweled Elgin, Hampden or Waltham, nickel plates	6.35	8.10
15 Jeweled Elgin, Hampden or Waltham, nickel plates, patent regulator	8.55	10.30
17 Jeweled Elgin, Hampden or Waltham, not adjusted	10.75	12.50
17 Jeweled No. 241 Grade Elgin, adjusted	13.50	15.25
17 JEWELED PLYMOUTH WATCH CO., nickel plates, patent regulator, adjusted	13.15	14.90
17 Jeweled No. 243 Grade Elgin, adjusted, nickel plates	25.05	26.80
21 JEWELED PRINCE OF WALES, PLYMOUTH WATCH CO., full adjusted, patent regulator, nickel plates	13.85	15.60

$3.42 Solid silver or gold filled 16-size thin model open face American watches.

Your choice, gold filled or solid silver. Be sure to order by number.

THE MOVEMENT we fit in either case is American made, has 7 jewels, lever escapement, is stem wind and pendant set, solid nickel plates, handsomely damaskeened, guaranteed against defective material or workmanship for a term of five years.

THE CASES are handsomely engraved, open face, screw back and screw bezel, dust and dampproof, substantially made throughout. The gold filled cases are guaranteed to retain their gold finish for a term of five years. The silver cases are solid silver, sterling quality, by that we mean, no less than 925/1000 fine. Your choice of either one, $3.42. If you desire, we can fit either of these cases with a genuine 7 jeweled Elgin movement for $6.85. Be sure to order by number.

No. 4R13030 Solid silver, with American made movement. Price..$3.42
No. 4R13032 Gold filled, with American made movement. Price.. 3.42
No. 4R13034 Solid silver, with genuine 7 jeweled Elgin movement.....6.85
No. 4R13036 Gold filled, with genuine 7 jeweled Elgin movement ..6.85

$4.08 Your choice, solid silver or gold filled hunting style 16-size extra thin model American watches

THE MOVEMENT is American made and guaranteed for a term of five years against defective material or workmanship, is stem wind and pendant set, lever escapement, beautifully damaskeened nickel plates, in every way well constructed, and a good runner. Your choice for $4.08, either gold filled or solid silver, hunting style.

THE CASES are handsomely engraved, beautifully finished in every detail. The gold filled cases are guaranteed by the manufacturer for a term of five years. The cases are solid silver and beautifully engraved. We can fit a genuine 7 jeweled Elgin movement in either of these cases for $7.20. Be sure to order by number.

No. 4R13040 Gold filled, with American made movement. Price $4.08
No. 4R13042 Solid silver, with American made movement. Price. 4.08
No. 4R13044 Gold filled, with 7 jeweled genuine Elgin movement. Price.......... 7.20
No. 4R13046 Solid silver, with 7 jeweled genuine Elgin movement. Price........... 7.20

CUT PRICE $2.76 OR $3.20 FOR A GENUINE ALASKA COMPOUND METAL, 16-SIZE, EXTRA THIN MODEL WATCH.

$2.76 for the open face, screw back and screw bezel, antique crown, stem and bow, or $3.20 for the hunting style case, inside protecting cap, especially made crystal bezel holder, either one representing values for which the competitor asks double our price. We want you to be the judge. Either of these watches quoted at $2.76 to $25.05, according to movement. Enclose with your remittance 14 cents extra to defray the registered mail charges. Upon receipt of your order we will make shipment of the watch at once. Examine it carefully, especially look at the movement that we send you, or offered by any other catalog firm, or compare it with the watch owned by your neighbor or friend, and if our watch, considering all factors, does not show you a saving of 20 to 33⅓ per cent, in other words, from $1.00 to $5.00 on the purchase, by all means return the watch to us and we will, upon receipt, refund your money, together with the transportation charges that have been incurred both ways.

$2.76 and up

SEE ILLUSTRATION. They are both bright polish. No. 4R13004 shows open face, screw back and screw bezel watch. No 4R13006 shows hunting style watch. Both extra thin models, the very latest up to date style, new antique crown, stem and bow. They are stem wind and pendant set, snappy, up to date watches in every respect.

No. 4R13004 16-Size, Alaska Metal Back and Screw Bezel. | No. 4R13006 16-Size, Alaska Metal, Hunting Style Case.

WHY WE ARE ABLE TO MAKE THIS OFFER. All price precedents have been swept aside and we own them at a figure just as though we own the factory. The factory absolutely produces these cases for us at cost. They do not make one cent of profit, and they supply them to us only because of our wonderful purchases of other goods from them and so as to give our customers a special bargain on a staple article, at the same time enabling them to keep their workmen busy in such seasons when the sale of watches is light, thereby keeping their organization together. This wonderful purchase of cases, together with the movement contract that we have, places us in such a safe position that we can sincerely and conscientiously make the offer.

We fit these 16-size Alaska metal cases with the following 16-size movements. Prices quoted are for complete watch, movement and case.	No. 4R13004 Open Face Alaska Metal	No. 4R13006 Hunting Style Alaska Metal
7 JEWELED EDGEMERE, nickel plates, special make	$ 2.76	$ 3.20
7 Jeweled Elgin, Hampden or Waltham, nickel plates	5.95	6.35
15 Jeweled Elgin, Hampden or Waltham, nickel plates, patent regulator	8.15	8.55
17 Jeweled Elgin, Hampden or Waltham, not adjusted	10.35	10.75
17 Jeweled No. 241 Grade Elgin, adjusted	13.05	13.50
17 JEWELED PLYMOUTH WATCH CO., nickel plates, patent regulator, adjusted	12.75	13.15
17 Jeweled No. 243 Grade Elgin adjusted, nickel plates	24.65	25.05
21 JEWELED PRINCE OF WALES, PLYMOUTH WATCH CO., full adjusted, patent regulator, nickel plates	13.45	13.65

GERMAN SILVER. $3.95

16-Size, Open Face, Screw Back and Bezel.

$3.95 for this solid German silver oxidized open face, screw back and screw bezel antique crown, bow and stem novelty watch. The case is made of genuine German silver through and through with raised floral work, oxidized dark to bring out the design; the illustration shows both front and back views. The movement is stem wind and pendant set, is 16-size, has 7 jewels, lever escapement, exposed winding wheels, cut expansion balance, patent regulator, nickel plates very prettily damaskeened; our five-year guarantee goes with each one. As a timekeeper this watch will give fine satisfaction, each one has been tried and tested. This case as a protection to the movement cannot be beat; German silver is a composition metal, it resembles solid silver; the process of making was first discovered in Germany, considered one of the best substitutes of solid silver known there.

No. 4R13014 With 7 jeweled movement. Price..............$3.95

POLISHED GUNMETAL GENTLEMEN'S WATCH.

$3.98 BEAUTY $3.98 for this mechanical wonder; it's a perfect beauty; the case is oxidized polished gunmetal, extra thin model; see the illustration. We show you a side and front view so that you can get a correct idea of its graceful lines. The movement is imported from Switzerland, straight line lever, is jeweled and a mechanical wonder because instead of showing the escapement balance, hairspring, etc., in the back of the watch, the mechanism has been reversed. You can see the watch operating when you look at the time, the action being visible from the dial as shown. $5.45 for the same movement fitted in a solid silver engine turned case.

No. 4R13018 Gunmetal. Price..........$3.98
No. 4R13020 Solid silver, engine turned design. Price.......... 5.45
No. 4R13022 Gold filled, guaranteed for twenty years. Price..............$7.56

$3.98 AND UP

No. 4R13018 Illustration shows dial and thickness of watch.

$7.98 AND UP LADIES' 6-SIZE GOLD FILLED REDUCED PRICES WATCHES $7.98 AND UP

GUARANTEED FOR 20 AND 25 YEARS AND FOR THE TERM OF YOUR NATURAL LIFE

WHEN YOU SELECT A WATCH, we advise you by all means to select the best. For a very little more money you can buy the Plymouth life guaranteed watch.

WHAT WE MEAN BY OUR LIFE GUARANTEE is simply this: Any watch case warranted and accompanied by our life guarantee can be returned to us at any time should the gold wear off exposing the inner composition metal, and we will immediately upon its receipt, exchange it for a brand new one, free of all charge and refund the transportation charges. This is in reality insuring your watch case for the term of your natural life.

IF YOU WISH TO EXPEND ONLY A SMALL SUM OF MONEY, then select the Plymouth twenty-year guaranteed case. We believe this the best value for your money as compared to any other twenty-year gold filled case on the market.

YOU WILL OBSERVE THAT WE SHOW AND DESCRIBE THE MOST REPRESENTATIVE MAKERS, JOHN C. DUEBER, THE ILLINOIS WATCH CASE CO., AND THE PLYMOUTH WATCH CASE CO. YOU CAN MAKE NO MISTAKE IN SELECTING ANY ONE OF THE THREE BRANDS.

$7.98 AND UP

For 21c we furnish a beautiful leatherette presentation case to fit any watch. See No. 4T1112 on page 417.

For 90 cents extra we can furnish fancy dial and gold hands on any watch on this page. For illustration, see page 417.

25 cents will carry any watch to any part of the United States by express.

Illustrations on this page show exact size.

$7.98 AND UP

PLYMOUTH. No. 4T14101 10-K. Gold Filled, 20 years guaranteed.

PLYMOUTH. No. 4T14103 10-K. Gold Filled, 20 years guaranteed.

PLYMOUTH. No. 4T14105 10-K. Gold Filled, 20 years guaranteed.

ILLINOIS WATCH CASE CO. No. 4T14106 10-K. Gold Filled, 20 years guaranteed.

DUEBER. No. 4T14108 10-K. Gold Filled, 20 years guaranteed.

ILLINOIS WATCH CASE CO. No. 4T14110 10-K. Gold Filled, 20 years guaranteed.

$9.75 AND UP

$9.75 AND UP

By all means buy the Plymouth.

No. 4T14112 PLYMOUTH. 14-Karat Gold Filled. Diagonal Engraving. Warranted for life. No. 4T14114 Same make, but engine turned. Complete with cloth lined case.

No. 4T14116 DUEBER. 14-Karat Gold Filled. Warranted 25 years. No. 4T14118 Same make. Plain engine turned.

No. 4T14120 Illinois Watch Case Co. 14-Karat Gold Filled. Warranted 25 years. No. 4T14122 Same make. Plain engine turned.

No. 4T14126 Illinois Watch Case Co. 14-Karat Gold Filled. Warranted 25 years. Set with genuine brilliant cut diamond. Raised ornamentation.

No. 4T14128 Illinois Watch Case Co. 14-Karat Gold Filled. Warranted 25 years. Plain polished. Set with five genuine rose diamonds.

No. 4T14130 PLYMOUTH. 14-Karat Gold Filled. Full engraved. Warranted for life.

WE FIT ABOVE CASES WITH THE FOLLOWING 6-SIZE MOVEMENTS. PRICES QUOTED ARE FOR THE COMPLETE WATCH, MOVEMENT AND CASE.	25-year Warrant. Nos. 4T14116 4T14118 4T14120 4T14122	Diamond Set, 25-year Warrant. No. 4T14128	Diamond Set, Ornamented, 25-year Warrant. No. 4T14126	Life Guarantee Nos. 4T14112 4T14114 4T14130 4T14132	Life Guarantee Diamond Set. No. 4T14134	20-year Warrant. Nos. 4T14101 4T14103 4T14105 4T14106 4T14108 4T14110
7 jeweled American Made Movement	$ 9.00	$10.50	$15.75	$ 9.75	$12.75	$ 7.98
7 jeweled Elgin, Hampden or Waltham Movement	10.90	12.40	17.65	11.65	14.65	9.90
15 jeweled Elgin, Hampden or Waltham Movement	13.10	14.60	19.85	13.85	16.85	12.10
16 jeweled Lady Waltham Movement, adjusted grade	15.00	16.50	21.75	15.75	18.75	14.00

No. 4T14132 PLYMOUTH. 14-Karat Gold Filled. Full Engraved. Warranted for life.

No. 4T14134 PLYMOUTH. 14-Karat Gold Filled. Warranted for life. Genuine diamond set. Plain polished.

$8.26 AND UP GENUINE DIAMOND SET, 20-YEAR GUARANTEED GOLD FILLED LADIES' HUNTING STYLE WATCH

GUARANTEED FOR 20 YEARS

The case as illustrated (showing back view with diamond) is guaranteed high grade 20-year gold filled, stem wind and pendant set, plain polished.

SET WITH A DIAMOND.

This case is set with a genuine diamond, brilliant and scintillating, in a very handsome raised solid gold star setting. The movement that we fit in this watch complete for $8.26, is a good 7 jeweled Swiss lever movement imported from Chaux de Fonds, Switzerland, the home of watch making. It is a good timekeeper, will give good satisfaction, and considering the price, a rare bargain.

This illustration shows how beautiful the diamond set watch No. 4T14140 appears in the silk lined leatherette presentation case, quoted for $8.26 complete in box.

No. 4T14140 0-SIZE HUNTING CASE. Genuine Diamond Set, Small 0-size, Gold Filled, Twenty-Year Guaranteed Watch.

STOP HERE AND CONSIDER. A genuine diamond set gold filled watch for $8.26, the like has never been heard of before. However, we advocate high grade watches, and we would suggest, considering the beauty and value of this case, that it be fitted with a higher grade movement. We therefore suggest the 15 jeweled Elgin Watch Co. movement quoted at $14.45. Observe the size of this watch; the very latest small 0-size, not a large, heavy, unsightly old style one, but the very latest model for ladies' use. Be sure to order by number, and write plainly the movement you desire fitted in the case.

WE FIT THIS CASE WITH THE FOLLOWING 0-SIZE MOVEMENTS. PRICES QUOTED ARE FOR COMPLETE WATCH, MOVEMENT AND CASE.

7 jeweled fine Swiss Movement	$ 8.26
7 jeweled Elgin or Waltham Movement	11.10
15 jeweled Elgin or Waltham Movement	14.45
16 jeweled Lady Waltham Movement	17.50
17 jeweled Elgin Movement, adjusted grade	19.35
19 jeweled Elgin Movement, adjusted grade	29.25
17 jeweled Plymouth Watch Co., adjusted, special make	16.75

FOR COMPLETE INDEX REFER TO PINK PAGES IN MIDDLE OF BOOK.

"THE FOUR HUNDRED"

SMALLEST AMERICAN WATCH MADE. HANDSOMEST LADIES' WATCH MADE. OPEN FACE OR HUNTING STYLE IN 14K SOLID GOLD AND 14K GOLD FILLED. GUARANTEED FOR 25 YEARS' WEAR. PRICES REDUCED AGAIN.

"MOLLY STARK" IS THE NAME OF THE 7-JEWELED HAMPDEN MOVEMENT. "DIADEM" IS THE NAME OF THE 15-JEWELED HAMPDEN MOVEMENT.

$16.48 AND $19.25 for 14-karat Solid Gold Cases, according to movement. **$10.65 TO $13.75** is our special offer, according to grade of movement for gold filled. **IN 14-KARAT SOLID GOLD** you have a watch second to none. They have just been put on the market and are meeting with great success.

WE WARRANT THESE GOODS BEING EXACTLY AS REPRESENTED.

THE DUEBER "400"-SIZE is the exact size as illustrated; all the rage in large cities; very dainty, very handsome and just as durable, just as accurate as the largest sizes. **THESE "400"-SIZE CASES** are stem wind and stem set hunting cases, elaborately engraved, decorated and ornamented as shown in illustrations, made with the latest style handsome antique bow.

No charges for repairs on watches or clocks will be allowed unless our written consent is first secured in advance.

ANY NAME ENGRAVED on THESE CASES AT THE RATE OF 2½ CTS. PER LETTER.

WE ADVOCATE THE 15 JEWELED GRADE MOVEMENT.

12 CENTS will carry one of these watches anywhere in the United States by registered mail.

No. 4C4400 14-K. Filled, Hunting.
No. 4C4402 As above, Open Face.
No. 4C4404 14-K. Solid Gold, Hunting.
No. 4C4406 As above, Open Face.

No. 4C4416 14-K. Filled, Hunting.
No. 4C4418 As above, Open Face.
No. 4C4420 14-K. Solid Gold, Hunting.
No. 4C4422 As above, Open Face.

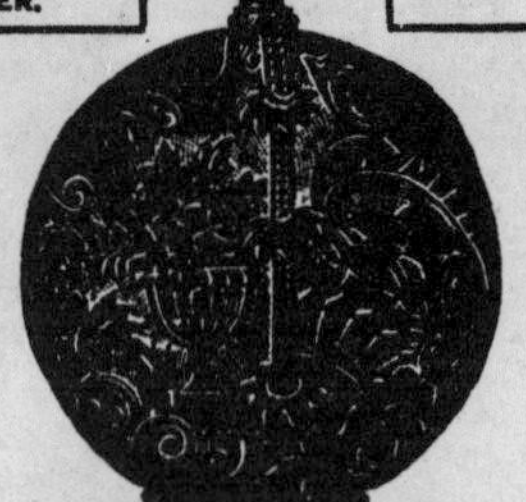

No. 4C4424 14-K. Filled, Hunting.
No. 4C4426 As above, Open Face.
No. 4C4428 14-K. Solid Gold, Hunting.
No. 4C4430 As above, Open Face.

No. 4C4432 14-K. Filled, Hunting.
No. 4C4434 As above, Open Face.
No. 4C4436 14-K. Solid Gold, Hunting.
No. 4C4438 As above, Open Face.

No. 4C4474 14-K. Filled, Hunting.
No. 4C4476 As above, Open Face.
No. 4C4478 14-K. Solid Gold, Hunting.
No. 4C4480 As above, Open Face.

HIGHEST GRADE GOLD FILLED MODEL. Made by the Great Dueber Watch Case Co., at Canton, Ohio, from extra heavy plates of 14-karat solid gold over an inner plate of hard composition metal, and is guaranteed to wear for 25 years. A written binding 25 years' certificate of guarantee signed by John C. Dueber accompanies each case, by the terms and conditions of which if the case wears through or changes color within 25 years it will be replaced with a new one FREE OF CHARGE.

WE FIT THESE CASES WITH THE FOLLOWING MOVEMENTS:	Hunting, Solid Gold	Open Face, Solid Gold	Hunting, Gold Filled	Open Face, Gold Filled
	Nos. 4C4404, 4C4428 4C4420, 4C4436 4C4478	Nos. 4C4406, 4C4430 4C4422, 4C4438 4C4480	Nos. 4C4400, 4C4424 4C4416, 4C4432 4C4474	Nos. 4C4402, 4C4426 4C4418, 4C4434 4C4476
Full 7-Jeweled Molly Stark Hampden.	$16.48	$16.48	$10.90	$10.65
Full 15-Jeweled Diadem Hampden....	19.25	19.25	13.75	13.50

ALL OF THE ABOVE MOVEMENTS WE GUARANTEE FOR A TERM OF FIVE YEARS.

16-SIZE, 12-SIZE AND 0-SIZE NAPOLEON GOLD FILLED CASES.

GUARANTEED FOR A TERM OF TEN YEARS.

Prices Cut to Less Than Wholesale.

$5.60 TO $7.90

$8.85 TO $11.15

ELGIN WATCHES QUOTED ON PAGES 216 TO 218.

$5.65 AND $8.24

NEVER BEFORE has a 10-year gold filled case been offered at the price we are asking. The very latest sizes shown here. 16-size, 12-size in Open Face or Hunting style and 0-size, the latest gentlemen's size, boys' size and ladies' size. The Napoleon Case is manufactured by the celebrated Illinois Watch Case Company, of Elgin, Ill., manufacturers of the Elgin Giant and Elgin Commander gold filled cases.

$5.90 for a gentlemen's 16-size gold filled watch, hunting style, fitted with the Reliance movement, is a price unheard of before. Our $5.65 price for this 0-size 10-karat 10-year gold filled case fitted with a fine 7-jeweled Swiss lever movement, means a saving to you of no less than 50 per cent

REMEMBER our liberal offer holds good with any of the watches you may select. If goods are not found as represented, return them and we will refund your money.

THE MOVEMENTS. We guarantee any of these movements for a term of five years against defect in material or workmanship.

No. 4C4483 16-Size Hunting Style.
No. 4C4485 16-Size Open Face, Screw Back and Bezel.

	4C4483	4C4485
With 7-Jeweled Reliance Movement	$5.90	$5.60
With 12-Jeweled Edgemere Movement,	7.90	7.60

No. 4C4486 12-Size Hunting Style.
No. 4C4488 12-Size Open Face, Screw Back and Screw Bezel.

	4C4486	4C4488
With 10-Jeweled Edgemere Movement	$9.15	$8.85
With 15-Jeweled Fine Swiss Lever Movement	11.15	10.85

No. 4C4490 0-Size.
With 7-Jeweled Fine Swiss Lever Movement.........$5.65
With 15-Jeweled Edgemere Movement........... 8.24

LADIES' SOLID GOLD EXTRA SMALL SIZE SWISS CHATELAINE WATCHES.

A NEW IMPORTATION WITH US. Many ladies want very small watches, and to fill this demand we have imported five extra small watches. The movements fitted in these cases are all fine jeweled cylinder movements, and while we cannot guarantee them to run accurately, that is to run to the minute, we do warrant them to give entire satisfaction. It is impossible for a watch of this very small size to run as accurately as the larger sizes, but for all practical uses will give satisfaction.

$10.75

The higher the grade the more accurate the time.

LATEST DESIGNS and PRETTIEST PATTERNS are the only ones we carry in stock.

REGARDING ENGRAVINGS. We generally have exact patterns, when not procurable we will send a very similar new design.

For 20c we furnish a beautiful plush Presentation Case, to fit any watch. Order by number and give size of watch. No. 4C2000 Price..20c

$12.50

No. 4C4491 Open Face Chatelaine. Yellow Roman color, satin finished solid gold case, stem wind and stem set, raised floral ornamentation.

Price for complete watch in beautiful plush case.................$10.75

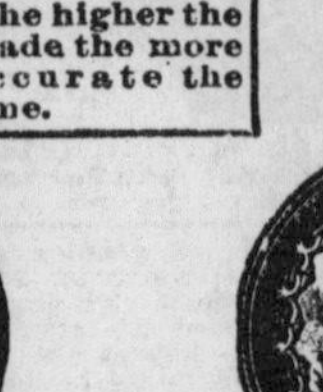

No. 4C4492 Open Face Chatelaine. Solid gold case, stem wind and stem set, fancy enameled subjects in appropriate colors, similar to illustration.

Price for complete watch in beautiful plush case...................$7.85

No. 4C4493 Open Face Chatelaine. Solid gold case, stem wind and stem set, fancy enameled subjects in appropriate colors, similar to illustration, with fancy enameled dial.

Price for complete watch in beautiful plush case.................$10.75

No. 4C4494 Open Face Chatelaine. Solid gold case, perfectly plain polished throughout, stem wind and stem set, with handsome fancy illuminated dial.

Price for complete watch in beautiful plush case.................$7.00

No. 4C4495 Open Face Chatelaine. Solid gold with beautiful solid gold Arabic dial. This is the smallest watch of the five shown here, and is fitted with the finest movement of them all.

Price for complete watch in beautiful plush case...........$12.50

$7.60 TO $12.75

LADIES' HUNTING STYLE 0-SIZE 10-KARAT GOLD FILLED WATCHES

GUARANTEED FOR 20 YEARS.

$7.60 TO $12.75

AT $7.60 TO $12.75 according to the prices listed below, we offer these handsome, beautifully engraved, guaranteed watches, made by the most responsible and representative manufacturers, at prices that are below any kind of competition. At $7.60 to $12.75, according to the movement selected, you can buy from us a ladies' 0-size, 10-karat case, 20-year guaranteed watch, the equal of what would cost you elsewhere 20 to 30 per cent more money.

EVERY MOVEMENT WE OFFER IS HIGH GRADE. Our Edgemere movement cannot be excelled. It is the very latest design and highest grade, and perfect in every way.

EVERY CASE IS A GEM OF THE ENGRAVER'S ART, and we call special attention to the handsome SEARS' CASE, as shown below. Every case represents a standard for quality. Whether you select a Dueber, Fahys, Sears or Giant case, you cannot make a mistake.

Edgemere Movement.

THE SEARS GOLD FILLED CASE is recommended above all others being made, of two extra heavy plates of solid gold over a hard composition metal. Will wear longer than any other gold filled case made, and is the handsomest, best finished and best fitting gold filled watch case made. IF YOU SELECT A SEARS CASE YOU WILL HAVE THE BEST GOLD FILLED WATCH CASE EVER MADE.

TRY OUR 15-JEWELED EDGEMERE Movement at $10.90 to $12.75, fitted in any one of these cases. ☞ This is the picture of the 15-Jeweled. We advocate 15-jeweled movements.

12 CENTS WILL CARRY ANY ONE OF THESE WATCHES TO ANY PART OF THE UNITED STATES BY MAIL. 25 CENTS BY EXPRESS.

$7.60 TO $10.90

We will treat you as we would like to be treated were we in your place.

Regarding the engravings. We generally have the exact pattern. If not, we will send a very similar design.

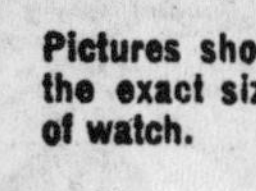

Pictures show the exact size of watch.

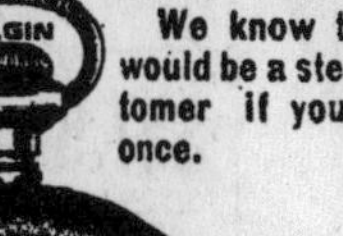

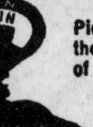

We know that you would be a steady customer if you bought once.

$7.60 TO $10.90

No. 4C4301
Guaranteed for 20 Years.
Illinois Watch Case Co. Make.

No. 4C4303
Guaranteed for 20 Years.
Illinois Watch Case Co. Make.

No. 4C4305
Guaranteed for 20 Years.
Illinois Watch Case Co. Make.

No. 4C4306 Colored Gold Ornamented.
Guaranteed for 20 Years.
Illinois Watch Case Co. Make

No. 4C4309
Guaranteed for 20 Years.
Sears' Make.

FOR PRICES SEE LIST AT BOTTOM OF PAGE.

$7.90 TO $11.20

THESE PICTURES SHOW THE EXACT SIZE OF THE WATCHES.

These cases come with assorted engravings, all the new designs.

$7.60 TO $10.90

No. 4C4311
Guaranteed for 20 Years.
Joseph Fahys' Make.

No. 4C4313 Engraved.
Guaranteed for 20 Years.
Joseph Fahys' Make.

No. 4C4317
Guaranteed for 20 Years.
Illinois Watch Case Co. Make.

No. 4C4318
Guaranteed for 20 Years.
Joseph Fahys' Make.

No. 4C4321
Guaranteed for 20 Years.
Sears' Make.

$7.60 TO $10.90

We fill orders with promptness and care.

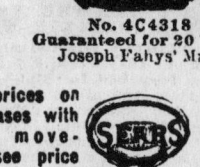

For prices on these cases with different movements, see price list below.

For 20 cents we furnish a beautiful plush Presentation Case, to fit any watch. See No. 4C2000 on page 192.

$7.90 TO $11.20

No. 4C4322
Guaranteed for 20 Years.
Illinois Watch Case Co. Make.
No. 4C4323 Same make, but Plain Engine Turned.

No. 4C4325
Guaranteed for 20 Years.
Illinois Watch Case Co. Make.

No. 4C4326
Guaranteed for 20 Years.
John C. Dueber's Make.

No. 4C4329
Guaranteed for 20 Years.
Sears' Make.

No. 4C4330
Guaranteed for 20 Years
Joseph Fahys' Make.

WE FIT THESE CASES WITH THE FOLLOWING 0-SIZE MOVEMENTS:

WE RECOMMEND 15 JEWELED MOVEMENTS.

	PRICES OF COMPLETE WATCH.		
	Nos. 4C4301, 4C4309, 4C4322, 4C4326; Nos. 4C4303, 4C4317, 4C4323; Nos. 4C4305, 4C4321, 4C4325, 4C4329	No. 4C4306	No. 4C4311, No. 4C4313, No. 4C4318, No. 4C4330
7 Jeweled Fine Swiss Lever	$ 7.60	$ 9.45	$ 7.90
11 Jeweled Fine Swiss Lever	9.90	11.75	10.20
FULL 15 JEWELED EDGEMERE, SEARS, ROEBUCK & CO.'S SPECIAL MAKE	10.90	12.75	11.20

HORSE TIMERS.

OUR.... **$4.20** Horse Timer

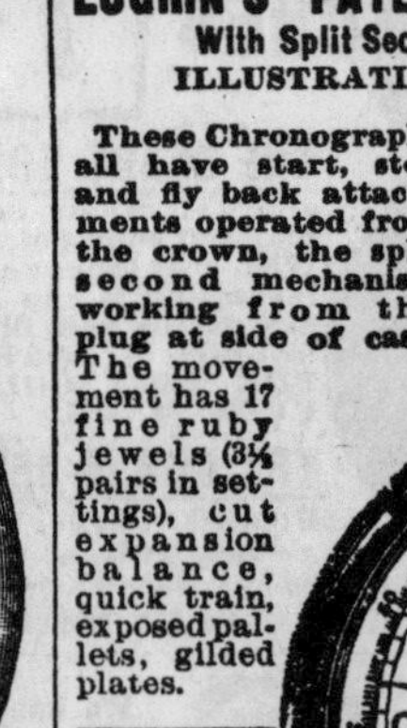

No. 4C2900

HORSE TIMER ONLY.

It has start, stop and fly back arrangement, operated from the crown. It is also provided with minute register. It has a metal case, heavily nickel plated, plain polished, and fitted with cylinder escapement, imported movement. Just the thing for those who do not care to invest much money in a timepiece for races of any kind.

No. 4C2900 Price..........$4.20

No. 4C2901 Same style as above but with fine jeweled lever escapement movement. Price, $5.95

LUGRIN'S PATENT OPEN FACE CHRONOGRAPHS

With Split Seconds, With or Without Minute Register.

ILLUSTRATION SHOWS MINUTE REGISTER.

These Chronographs all have start, stop and fly back attachments operated from the crown, the split second mechanism working from the plug at side of case. The movement has 17 fine ruby jewels (3½ pairs in settings), cut expansion balance, quick train, exposed pallets, gilded plates.

$27.50 TO $96.00

The Chronograph with minute register has the addition of three more jewels and the independent minute fly back register. We can recommend any one of these chronographs, as we know that they represent the very latest improvements, and are warranted to be accurate in every detail. You cannot get their equal anywhere for twice what we ask.

No. 4C2902 TO No. 4C2916

Chronograph with Split Seconds.

No. 4C2902	17 Jeweled, in Nickel Case	$27.50
No. 4C2904	17 Jeweled, in Silver Case	47.00
No. 4C2906	17 Jeweled, in 20-Year Gold Filled Case	57.00
No. 4C2908	17 Jeweled, in 14-Karat Solid Gold Case	91.00

Chronograph with Split Seconds and Minute Register.

No. 4C2910	20 Jeweled, in Nickel Case	$32.50
No. 4C2912	20 Jeweled, in Silver Case	52.00
No. 4C2914	20 Jeweled, in 20-Year Gold Filled Case	62.00
No. 4C2916	20 Jeweled, in 14-Karat Solid Gold Case	96.00

A WATCH WITHOUT HANDS.

No. 4C2919 **$8.15**

ORDER BY NUMBER

Our new solid silver small 18-size open face novelty watch. The center circle shows the hour and the oval the minute. It is wound and set the same as any other watch, but is less complicated and less liable to get out of order. You will never be bothered on account of the hands catching or dropping off, or finding that your watch does not keep accurate time on account of the hands being too loose. This watch comes in a size smaller than the regular 18-size. The case is solid silver, $\frac{925}{1000}$ fine, in other words, solid sterling silver, stem wind and stem set, comes in open face only. The dial is a beautiful silver dial with rich raised gold ornamentation, exactly as illustration shows. The movement is imported from Switzerland. It has 15 fine ruby jewels, straight line lever escapement, and is perfectly finished in every detail, a watch that we can recommend, being an accurate timekeeper.

No. 4C2919 Price..........$8.15

No. 4C2921 Same as No. 4C2919 but with black oxidized steel gun metal case. Price..........$6.90

20-YEAR GOLD FILLED **$9.43**

25-YEAR GOLD FILLED **$11.45**

No. 4C2926 Gold Filled. Guaranteed for 20 years. Plain polished or engine turned.

No. 4C2928 Gold Filled. Guaranteed for 25 years. Plain polished or engine turned.

$9.43 AND $11.45

18-SIZE, OPEN FACE, SOLID BACK, SWING RING, GOLD FILLED WATCHES.

Guaranteed for 20 and 25 years' continuous wear. The Illinois Watch Case Co., of Elgin, Ill., manufacturers of these cases, agree to replace with a brand new gold filled case of same style and grade, any one of their cases worn through to the base metal within 20 or 25 years.

The swing ring, a new improvement on gold filled cases, makes it possible to produce an absolutely dust and damp proof watch case. You can examine the movement in a swing ring case without difficulty. See illustration. The front or bezel screws off. The back is solid, made of one piece. The movement is fastened in the center ring which is securely joined to the case by a strong hinge. To examine the works, lift up the swing ring (illustration shows the ring partially lifted); to replace in case, let ring drop back in first position and screw on bezel.

$9.43 FOR THE COMPLETE WATCH.

This beautifully finished and new perfected case with our 12-jeweled Edgemere movement, exactly as described, for $9.43. To railway men, train starters and all others wanting a reliable timepiece, one that can be depended upon, we can recommend the 23-jeweled Special Railway, fitted in one of these new dust proof swing ring cases as an absolute protection against dust and damp.

No. 4C2930 Gold Filled. Guaranteed for 25 years. Hand engraved.

No. 4C2932 Gold Filled. Guaranteed for 20 years. Hand engraved.

THIS IS THE ILLUSTRATION OF OUR EDGEMERE full 17-jeweled movement, engraved by our artist direct from the movement. The Edgemere is solid nickel through and through. The top plate is beautifully damaskeened in gold and nickel.

IT HAS 17 RUBY JEWELS,

each jewel set in finely polished setting, fitted by screws. Bright polished patent regulator, double cut expansion balance wheel, genuine Breguet hairspring, safety barrel, patent safety pinions and goldine timing screws.

THE ENTIRE MOVEMENT IS PERFECTLY FINISHED IN EVERY DETAIL, TIMED AND REGULATED.

See the list of movements we offer. Each one at the price quoted is a bargain and represents a standard of excellence.	No. 4C2930 25 Year Engraved	No. 4C2926 20 Year	No. 4C2928 25 Year	No. 4C2932 20 Year Engraved
Full 12 jeweled Edgemere	$11.95	$ 9.43	$11.45	$ 9.93
Full 15 jeweled Sears, Roebuck & Co.'s Special	13.45	10.93	12.95	11.43
Full 17 jeweled Edgemere, S., R. & Co.'s Special make	14.32	11.80	13.82	12.30
Full 17 jeweled Sears, Roebuck & Co.'s Special	17.20	14.68	16.70	15.18
Full 21 jeweled Special Railway Hampden	27.95	25.43	27.45	25.93
Full 23 jeweled Special Railway Hampden	36.05	33.53	35.55	34.03

ANOTHER CUT. YOUR CHOICE, $4.85.

We give you the advantage of it. The manufacturer has again reduced the price to us. Last season we sold this watch for $5.25. Either Ladies' 0-size Hunting or Gents' 16-size hunting or open face, screw back and screw bezel. Order whichever you want, 5-year guaranteed gold filled hunting case in ladies' 0-size or gentlemen's 16-size hunting or open face, fitted with 7 jeweled movement.

No. 4C2936 No. 4C2938 **$4.85**

No. 4C2936 Gents' 16-size Hunting Style.

No. 4C2938 Gents' 16-size Open Face Style.

$4.85

No. 4C2935 Ladies' 0-size.

Description of the 16-size American made movement called "The Reliance," fitted in the gentlemen's size, 5-year guaranteed gold filled case. This movement has 7 ruby jewels, cut balance, patent safety pinion and barrel and double sunk second dial. **We give our written binding guarantee with every one sold, protecting you for a term of five years against defective material or workmanship.**

Description of Cases: These cases are manufactured by the celebrated Illinois Watch Case Co. Each case is accompanied by their personal guarantee. These cases are made of two plates of solid 10-karat gold, covering an inner composition of base metal, and are guaranteed to wear and retain their gold appearance for a term of five years. They are engraved and chased after the very latest gold designs. They have the antique bow; they both are stem wind and stem set; in fact, for $4.85 you have a watch that could not possibly be purchased by any retail jeweler for twice this amount.

You can sell them at $10.00 each and still offer a bargain.

Description of the movement used in the ladies' 0-size watch. This movement has 7 fine jewels, lever escapement, cut balance wheel, fine cut polished pinions. They are imported from Switzerland, the home of watches, and we give our 5-year guarantee with every one sold. We know they will give entire satisfaction. See the illustration of movement.

This is an illustration of the Ladies' 0-size movement.

This is an illustration of the movement we fit in the gents' case, complete watch, $4.85.

GENTLEMEN'S 16-SIZE AND 12-SIZE THIN MODEL OPEN FACE AND HUNTING STYLE GOLD FILLED WATCHES.

OUR CHALLENGE CASE.

This, our Kingston case, is one of our challenge cases. We challenge any jeweler to equal this case for the money in quality, finish and wearing ability. These cases are made by the Illinois Watch Case Co., of Elgin, Ill. They carry a 20-year guarantee inside the case. Together with this warrant, is sent our own personal binding guarantee for a term of 20 years, signed by Sears, Roebuck & Co. This is the best cheap 16-size, guaranteed 20-year case on the market. When you select a watch case, select either a Kingston case or a Plymouth gold filled case, each one in its class representing the highest perfection in gold filled case making.

FOR THE BEST CHEAP WATCH in 16-size, we recommend above all others our new 7-jeweled Edgemere. It is guaranteed; but for a watch that costs but a few dollars more and gives better satisfaction, and for accuracy, we recommend our 15 jeweled Edgemere, our 15 jeweled Plymouth Watch Co. U. S. A. Special, or our 17 jeweled Plymouth Watch Co. U. S. A. Special, adjusted. All of the above carry our five-year written, binding guarantee.

$5.60 AND UP — **FOR NEWEST STYLE WATCHES.** — **$5.60 AND UP**

16-Size. Kingston Gold Filled.
No. 4F2273 Hunting Style.
No. 4F2275 Open Face Screw Back and Bezel.

16-Size. Kingston Gold Filled.
No. 4F2277 Hunting Style.
No. 4F2279 Open Face, Screw Back and Bezel.

16-Size. Kingston Gold Filled.
No. 4F2281 Hunting Style.
No. 4F2283 Open Face, Screw Back and Bezel.

We Fit these Cases with the following 16-Size Movements. Prices quoted are for the complete watch, movement and case	No. 4F2275 No. 4F2279 No. 4F2283	No. 4F2273 No. 4F2277 No. 4F2281
7 JEWELED EDGEMERE, nickel plates, special make..	$ 5.60	$ 7.35
7 Jeweled Elgin or Waltham, nickel plates..............	8.50	10.25
15 JEWELED EDGEMERE, patent regulator nickel plates, special make'..	8.35	10.10
15 Jeweled Elgin or Waltham,nickel plates,patent regulator	10.60	12.35
15 JEWELED PLYMOUTH WATCH CO.	10.25	12.00
17 Jeweled Elgin or Waltham, not adjusted	12.70	14.45
17 Jeweled No.241 Grade Elgin or 630 Grade Waltham, adjusted	$ 15.33	$ 17.08
17 JEWELED PLYMOUTH WATCH CO., nickel plates, patent regulator, adjusted..	14.25	16.00
17 Jeweled Royal Waltham, adjusted, nickel plates	17.69	19.44
17 Jeweled No. 243 Grade Elgin, adjusted, nickel plates	26.35	28.10
21 JEWELED PRINCE OF WALES PLYMOUTH WATCH CO., full adjusted, patent regulator, nickel plates	20.25	22.00

Our 12-size 10 Jeweled EDGEMERE will give correct time.

GENTLEMEN'S THIN MODEL AND HUNTING FILLED CASES.

12-SIZE EXTRA OPEN FACE STYLE GOLD GUARANTEED FOR 20 YEARS.

This is the picture of our 10 Jeweled Edgemere movement, fitted in any of these 12-size cases at $8.00 for open face and $9.80 for hunting style. Prices quoted are for the complete watch.

12-Size. Kingston Gold Filled.
No. 4F2301 Hunting Style.
No. 4F2303 Open Face, Screw Back and Bezel.

12-Size. Kingston Gold Filled.
No. 4F2305 Hunting Style.
No. 4F2307 Open Face, Screw Back and Bezel.

12-Size. Kingston Gold Filled.
No. 4F2309 Hunting Style.
No. 4F2311 Open Face, Screw Back and Bezel.

No. 4F2340 The very latest 16-size extra thin, oxidized polished gunmetal watch with illuminated dial. Send us $3.98 and 14 cents for mail charges, $4.12 in all, and we will at once ship you this newest gentlemen's watch by registered mail. The case is made with a solid back and snap front, and is absolutely dustproof; it is stem wind and stem set, is full jeweled, has exposed balance wheel; illustration shows a new mechanical construction. This watch is imported by us from Switzerland; each one is guaranteed for a term of five years. At $3.98, we are selling this watch at 40 per cent less than similar but inferior watches are being sold for. Price........ $3.98

No. 4F2342 Same style as No. 4F2340, but case of solid silver, engine turned. Price $5.45

No. 4F2344 Same style as No. 4F2340, but gold filled case, guaranteed 20 years. Price $7.95

$6.25 AND UP

For 90 cents extra we can furnish a fancy dial and gold hands on any watch on this page. Protect your watch with an Ajax Watch Insulator, 23c See page 25, No. 4F586.

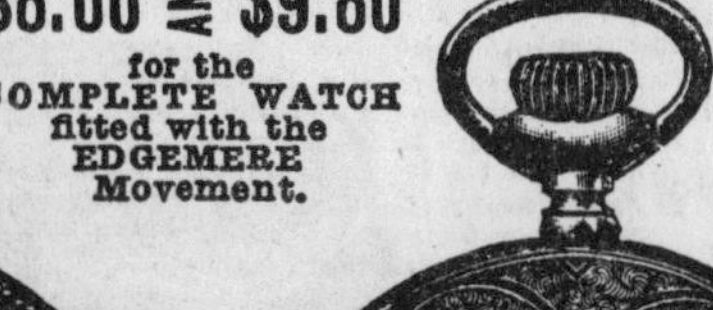

$8.00 AND $9.80 for the COMPLETE WATCH fitted with the EDGEMERE Movement.

$3.98 BEAUTY

12-Size. Kingston Gold Filled.
No. 4F2316 Hunting Style.
No. 4F2318 Open Face, Screw Back and Bezel.

12-Size. Kingston Gold Filled.
No. 4F2320 Hunting Style.
No. 4F2322 Open Face, Screw Back and Bezel.

12-Size. Kingston Gold Filled.
No. 4F2324 Hunting Style.
No. 4F2326 Open Face, Screw Back and Bezel.

We Fit these Cases with the Following 12-Size Movements. Prices quoted are for the complete watch, movement and case.	No. 4F2303 No. 4F2318 No. 4F2307 No. 4F2322 No. 4F2311 No. 4F2326	No. 4F2301 No. 4F2316 No. 4F2305 No. 4F2320 No. 4F2309 No. 4F2324
7 Jeweled Swiss Lever, nickel plates....................	$ 6.25	$ 8.05
7 Jeweled Elgin or Waltham, nickel plates..............	8.25	10.05
10 JEWELED EDGEMERE, special make	8.00	9.80
15 JEWELED PLYMOUTH WATCH CO., nickel plates, patent regulator, special make............................	10.10	11.90
15 Jeweled Elgin or Waltham,nickel plates, patent regulator	10.35	12.15
17 JEWELED PLYMOUTH WATCH CO., nickel plates, patent regulator, special make................................	$16.50	$18.30
17 Jeweled No. 321 Grade Elgin or Royal Grade Waltham .	17.43	19.23
19 Jeweled Riverside Waltham..............................	24 52	26.32
19 Jeweled No. 189 Grade Elgin	28.72	30.52
21 JEWELED SWISS, nickel plates, patent regulator, adjusted	22.65	24.45

DESCRIPTION OF WATCH MOVEMENTS WE RECOMMEND

ILLUSTRATED AND DESCRIBED HERE AND QUOTED THROUGHOUT THE FOLLOWING PAGES

THE MOVEMENTS WE RECOMMEND, listed throughout our watch department and priced complete in various cases, are made especially for us by watch companies known to be the largest and most reliable in America. Watch movements bearing the manufacturer's name are sold by the manufacturer at a fixed price, subject to certain fixed discounts. The quantity the wholesaler purchases, whether a dozen or a thousand at a time, does not alter this fixed price. The very smallest purchaser can buy as cheaply as the very largest, which means the manufacturer makes a very handsome profit; purchasing ability and outlet, which should enter into the proposition, does not; so, in order to equalize this and make it possible for our customers to reap all the benefits that our immense outlet and purchasing ability should bring about, we have had various movements (described and illustrated here) made without the stamp of the manufacturer's name, using instead a name that we ourselves selected. The manufacturers, therefore, agreed that on condition we would take a large per cent of the movements that they produce in their factories, and stamped with a name that we should select, and not their own, we could buy these movements at a cost approximately the same as if we owned the factories ourselves. We therefore are quoting and selling these movements, grade for grade compared with the manufacturer's own named movements, at about 33⅓ to 50 per cent less than the prices they put upon them. The manufacturer of our movements takes this position, in which he is quite correct, that if we were permitted to put the movements he manufactures under his own name and sell them, including the cases, at the price we do, it would ruin his business with every wholesale and retail watch dealer in America.

OUR 7 JEWELED EDGEMERE LINE THE BEST VALUE EVER OFFERED IN THE UNITED STATES.

NOTE THE ILLUSTRATIONS and descriptions of our 18-size, 16-size and 6-size Edgemere movements, and note especially the very low prices at which we furnish these movements fitted complete in the various cases as shown and quoted in the following pages, and bear in mind that in spite of the low price we guarantee this 7 jeweled Edgemere movement line the equal of any 7 jeweled movement made at 25 to 33⅓ per cent more than we ask, regardless of name, make or price. Above everything, don't compare this 7 jeweled Edgemere line of movements with the cheap 7 jeweled lines now on the market. We have discontinued the sale of the Trenton, Standard and Century 7 jeweled movements, since our contract enables us to offer you one of the highest grade 7 jeweled movements made at a lower price than other houses can sell even the cheap grade of the 7 jeweled movements. Our five-year binding guarantee goes out with the 7 jeweled Edgemere line. In running and lasting qualities these movements are worth more than double any of the cheap 7 jeweled movements. If you are looking for a watch at a very moderate price, order one of these movements, and if you are not satisfied and it is not worth double what others are asking for cheap 7 jeweled movements, you can return the watch and we will refund your money.

OUR PLYMOUTH WATCH COMPANY FULL ADJUSTED LINE.

POSITIVELY THE HIGHEST GRADE 17 and 21 jeweled American made movements made in the United States. Note the illustration and description. If you are looking for positively the highest order of watches, most accurate timekeeping, by all means order our Plymouth Watch Company brand. We recommend them above all other makes. Grade for grade, we are quoting them at one-half the price the manufacturer gets from the wholesaler for movements bearing the factory name. Our five-year binding guarantee goes with every one of these movements. If the watch does not prove exactly as described, exactly as illustrated, an accurate timekeeper, perfectly finished and timed in every way, you can return it to us and we will, upon its receipt, instantly refund your money without parley or waste of time.

OUR OTHER SPECIAL MOVEMENTS.

THE OTHER SPECIAL MOVEMENTS we offer in the different sizes and grades illustrated and described in these pages are movements that we own on the basis of actual cost of material and labor, and to which we add but one small percentage of profit; we therefore can furnish you any of these watches at about one-half the price that we can offer a watch of equal grade bearing the manufacturer's name.

OUR FIVE-YEAR GUARANTEE. Every one of these movements, the movements that we recommend, is covered by our binding five-year guarantee covering every piece and part that enters into its make, and if any part should fail to perform its duty within five years through defective material or workmanship it will be replaced or repaired by us free of charge.

Gents' 18-Size, Open Face or Hunting Case, Stem Wind, 17 Jeweled, Adjusted Plymouth Watch Co. Movement.

This movement is marked "Plymouth Watch Co.," is solid nickel, richly damaskeened and finished, has 17 ruby jewels, raised gold settings with screws, accurately and especially adjusted to heat, cold, isochronism and all positions, the most accurate and complete adjustment lines on any watch made; quick train, hand finished escape wheel, compensating balance, Breguet overstrung tempered hairspring, new improved patent micrometer regulator barrel arbor pivots, double sunk glass enamel dial with marginal figures. This 17 jeweled, full adjusted, full plate movement is gotten out for us with a view to furnishing a higher grade adjusted movement than is made and sold by any watch company in America. While we furnish it at a much lower price than you can buy a 17 jeweled adjusted movement bearing the manufacturer's name, if you order this movement and do not find, after giving it a thorough trial, that it gives better satisfaction than any other 17 jeweled movement made, you can return it to us at our expense and we will immediately refund your money

Gentlemen's 18-Size, Stem Wind, Lever Set, Open Face or Hunting Style, 21 Jeweled King Edward Movement, Manufactured by the Plymouth Watch Co.

This movement, procured by us under a new deal and in an immense quantity, represents the highest perfection in watchmaking. It has 21 fine ruby jewels in gold settings, cut expansion balance, Breguet hairspring, patent safety pinion, patent regulator, adjusted to temperature and the positions, the most accurate and most modern watch on the market today, quoted throughout our catalogue at less cost than the 17 jeweled adjusted movements bearing the makers' name. This watch we can recommend as being perfection in the watchmaking art, and is made with the idea not to equal any 21 jeweled watch on the market but to have something better than has been heretofore manufactured. By all means, if you want the best watch manufactured, we would advise either the Prince of Wales in the 16-size or the King Edward in the 18-size.

Gents' 18-Size, Open Face or Hunting Case, 7 Jeweled Edgemere Movement.

Gents' 18-size Edgemere, open face or hunting case, full nickel, 7 jeweled, neatly damaskeened, expansion balance, hairspring hardened and tempered, highly finished regulator, patent pinion, polished screws, marginal figures on dial, true timing screws, quick train, worth double any of the cheap 7 jeweled movements and guaranteed the equal of any 7 jeweled movement made.

NOTE—We sell this high grade 7 jeweled movement complete in any case for less than others sell the cheap grades of 7 jeweled movements.

TRAINMEN'S SPECIAL.

This is a Cheap Trading Watch, Made to Look Like the Most Expensive 23 Jeweled, Adjusted Railway Watch Made.

While it is in interior construction a plain 7 jeweled movement, to give to it all the appearance of the highest priced railway movement made, it is made of nickel, the upper plate is very showily gilt damaskeened, imitation of rich ruby jewels in imitation of solid gold screw settings have been set with the screws over the pinion places of the entire top of the plate, including all pinion spots, center first; second and third wheels and balance; has a patent regulator, it is stamped "23 jewels, adjusted;" it is also stamped with a locomotive on the plate and on the front or dial and is named "Trainmen's Special." It is essentially a trading watch. We have sold thousands of these movements to auctioneers, horse traders and other traders, peddlers, jewelers, publishers and scheme houses for premiums, etc., for while we sell it for just what it is, in interior construction a plain 7 jeweled American movement, it has all the appearance of a movement that you would pay $25.00 or more for. It is especially popular in our No. 4H1114 Alaska metal stem wind case, and all for $3.00, making an ideal trading watch or watch that really has the appearance of a $50.00 gold filled, 23 jeweled, adjusted watch, but you buy the complete watch for $3.00. Many of our customers among the traveling men carry them as a side line and sell them at from $5.00 to $20.00, adding from $5.00 to $25.00 a week to their net income. If you want a very showy watch for trading purposes there is nothing that will match this watch.

Gentlemen's 16-Size, Open Face or Hunting Style, 7 Jeweled, Nickel Edgemere Movement.

This movement is made for us under contract, and at our price, fitted with any 16-size case as shown on the following pages, will give you double the value that you can get in any 16-size 7 jeweled movement bearing the manufacturer's name on the market. This movement has nickel plates, richly damaskeened, exposed high polished winding wheels, non-magnetic balance and hairspring, full polished pinions, handsome double pressed dial with red marginal figures, is stem wind and pendant set and positively gives the best satisfaction of any 7 jeweled cheap watch on the market. Its equal cannot be procured for twice what we ask for it.

Gentlemen's 16-Size, Open Face or Hunting Style, 15 Jeweled, Patent Regulator Edgemere Movement.

This movement is made under our new arrangement, is highly finished and an accurate timekeeper, has full nickel plates, jewels in screw settings, high polished exposed winding apparatus, cut expansion balance, with Breguet hairspring, fine polished patent regulator, the equal of any 15 jeweled movement manufactured bearing the makers' name and, different from any other make, this movement is anti-magnetic, guaranteed by the maker. By reason of our new contract we are able to quote it in this catalogue on the various pages at less than we ask for 7 jeweled movements bearing the makers' name. If you want a good and accurate timekeeper, we would advise you to select this watch above all other 16-size movements with 7 jewels, stamped with the maker's name.

Gents' 16-Size, Open Face or Hunting Case, 17 Jeweled, Adjusted Plymouth Watch Co. Movement.

This is our gents' 17-jeweled adjusted 16-size movement, each movement stamped "Plymouth Watch Co." It is 17 jeweled, all jewels in screwed settings, accurately adjusted to heat, cold, position and isochronism; has the latest patent micrometer regulator, patent pinion and escapement, exposed winding wheel, has every new and up to date improvement, combines all the best in all the highest grade 17 jeweled 16-size movements made, and yet we offer it at a lower price than we can offer any other 17 jeweled movement.

Gentlemen's 16-Size, Open Face or Hunting, 21 Jeweled, Nickel, Patent Regulator Prince of Wales Movement, Manufactured by the Plymouth Watch Company.

This movement is a new addition to our exceptional value page and represents positively the highest grade watch in 21 jeweled manufactured. A new deal with a new company for an immense quantity enables us to sell this watch to you at less money than 17 jeweled named watches manufactured by others. This watch has full nickel plates, jewels all in settings, cut expansion balance, double sunk dial, patent regulator; in fact, all modern improvements, adjusted to temperature and positions, in fact, a watch such as cannot be compared with any other watch quoted or illustrated in our catalogue. If you purchase this watch you are making a saving of not less than $12.00 to $15.00 and are getting the best production of modern watchmaking.

Gentlemen's 12-Size, Open Face or Hunting Style, Solid Nickel, 7 Jewel, Stem Wind and Pendant Set Edgemere Movement.

This movement is made especially for us. It is stamped "7 Jewel Edgemere." Has straight line lever escapement, fine bright polished exposed winding wheels, bright polished screw heads, richly damaskeened nickel plates, fine selected white enamel dial with red marginal figures, and better than any other 7 jeweled movement, this our Edgemere movements are all fitted with anti-magnetic hairspring. The manufacturers claim they are absolutely impervious to magnetism, one of the greatest difficulties to overcome in accurate timekeeping. If you order this watch movement you are selecting the best 7 jeweled extra thin model, stem wind and pendant set watch on the market and at a price which means a saving of no less than from $2.50 to $3.50 to what regular named 7 jeweled watches bring on the market. We conscientiously recommend this watch above all other 12-size thin model 7 jeweled grades.

Gentlemen's 12-Size, Open Face or Hunting Style, 15 Jeweled, Stem Wind and Pendant Set Edgemere Movement.

This movement is stamped "Edgemere, 15 Jewels," has straight line lever escapement, fine damaskeened nickel plates, high polished exposed winding wheels, bright polished screw heads, all plate jewels in screw settings, fine selected white hard enamel dial, red marginal figures, and better than any other 15 jeweled, 12-size extra thin model movement on the market, this our Edgemere movement is fitted with a genuine anti-magnetic hairspring. The manufacturers claim this makes the movement impervious to magnetism. By this improvement one of the principal causes of watches running inaccurately has been overcome. If you are selecting the 15 jeweled, 12-size watch, by all means buy this one. We recommend it above all other makes of the same grade. If you order this watch, you not only will make a saving of from $2.00 to $5.00 on the price, but will be getting a more accurately running and more dependable watch.

Gentlemen's 12-Size, 17 Jeweled, Open Face or Hunting Style, Stem Wind and Pendant Set Plymouth Watch Co. Movement.

As positively the acme of perfection in 17 jeweled, 12-size movements, we offer this, our latest production from the factory. This movement is stamped "Plymouth Watch Co.," and represents the highest order in this grade above all other makes. This movement is adjusted, trued and timed before leaving the factory to the very closest possible degree. It has high polished exposed winding wheels, Breguet hairspring, true timing screws, patent safety pinion, handsomely damaskeened nickel plates and patent regulator, jewels in screw settings; in fact, every detail in watchmaking has been covered and perfected. While this movement stands pre-eminent for timekeeping and perfection of finish, still, by our new contract, in placing our immense order, we are able to sell it at less than watches stamped with the maker's name throughout these pages. We would advise, if you are looking for a small size extra thin gents' watch in a high jeweled grade, to positively select this one to the exclusion of all other grades and makes.

Gentlemen's 12-Size, 21 Jeweled, Adjusted Stem Wind and Pendant Set, Highest Grade Movement.

This movement is imported by us, for the express use of our customers who wish a high grade, accurate timekeeping, perfectly finished Swiss watch at a price much less than an American made watch of equal grade. This movement represents the highest possible perfection in the watchmaking art. It is extra thin model, has fine finished nickel plates, lever escapement, 21 fine ruby jewels in solid goldine composition metal, each plate setting fastened with screws, fine high polished exposed winding wheels, fine tapered regulator and regulator bar, cut expansion balance, true timing screws, genuine Breguet hairspring. The dial is of fine white enamel, with plain figures, fine blue tapered steel hands and red marginal figures. In fact, such a watch as cannot be duplicated in the United States in any factory, bearing the maker's name, for twice what we ask. Yet we are able, by importing these movements direct, to place in the hands of our customers a new, up to date, extra thin model, high grade, 12-size watch at not less than 50 per cent saving over the same grade made in the United States.

Remember, in selecting a watch, if you want the highest possible grade in the 12-size containing 21 jewels and adjusted, that nothing excels the Swiss production. The home of watchmaking, celebrated for the perfection and accurate timekeeping qualities of their watches. Our unqualified guarantee for a term of five years goes with this movement and we suggest and recommend this watch if you want a high grade gentlemen's size time watch.

Ladies' 6-Size, Hunting Case, Stem Wind and Pendant Set, 7 Jeweled Edgemere Movement.

Like the gents' 18-size movement, we guarantee this 7 jeweled movement the equal of any 7 jeweled 6-size movement made, and worth two of any of the cheap 7 jeweled movements on the market. It is the highest grade 7 jeweled movement made, and in selecting a ladies' watch, we would especially recommend that you select our 7 jeweled Edgemere; has gold damaskeening, cut expansion balance, sunk second enamel dial, a great improvement over any other 7 jeweled 6-size movement on the market.

Ladies' 6-Size, Hunting Style, Stem Wind and Pendant Set Countess Janet Movement, Stamped 17 Jewels.

This watch is made for a trading watch in ladies' size. Never before has a ladies' size watch been placed on the market for this purpose. It looks exactly like a high grade 17 jeweled or 19 jeweled watch; is richly nickeled; has 17 large imitation ruby jewels screwed on the plates, which, however, have no utility, but are made for show only. The movement itself is merely a good 7 jeweled American made movement, manufactured for our express use by one of the big watch companies. As a timekeeper will keep only fair time. It is richly damaskeened so as to make a beautiful appearance; is stem wind and pendant set. Our 18-size cheap trading watch for travelers has met with exceptionally fine sale. The profit from a watch of this sort cannot be estimated. Never before have they been placed on the market. They have the appearance of a watch being worth twenty times more than what we ask. This watch is particularly attractive for the purposes of watch trading, for peddlers' use, publishing houses, scheme houses, partial payment houses, in fact, any one wanting a watch having the appearance of the very highest grade for next to nothing in cost.

Ladies' 6-Size, Hunting Case, Stem Wind, 17 Jeweled Adjusted Movement.

These movements are marked "Plymouth Watch Co." They are positively the highest grade 17 jeweled 6-size movements made. Solid nickel, richly damaskeened in gold, full 17 jewels, finest ruby jewels in gold settings, settings set with screws, compensating cut balance, balance adjusted with true timing screws, finest overstrung patent Breguet hairspring, polished center wheel, quick train, patent pinion. Movement is accurately adjusted to heat, cold, position and isochronism, combining everything that you could get in any movement that you would pay three times the price for if sold by any manufacturer under the manufacturer's name and number; so in selecting the very finest thing in a ladies' 6-size watch we would especially recommend that you select this movement, and we will furnish it to you, quality for quality, at one-half the price you could buy any other make.

Ladies' 0-Size, 7 Jeweled, Stem Wind and Pendant Set Swiss Movement.

This movement is made for us under contract. It is full nickel, quick train, 7 jewels, patent pinion and patent lever escapement, and we guarantee it the highest grade 7 jeweled small 0-size movement made. You will find this movement will keep better time and last twice as long as any other 7 jeweled 0-size movement on the market, and yet, under our special arrangements with the manufacturer, we can furnish this in a much higher grade 7 jeweled movement than you could get elsewhere at less than the ordinary 7 jeweled movements are sold by others. In selecting a very small watch for a lady in an 0-size, unless you want to get our high grade 15-Jeweled Edgemere 0-size movement, we would especially advise that you select this in preference to any other 7 jeweled 0-size movement made.

Ladies' 0-Size, 15 Jeweled, Stem Wind and Pendant Set, Patent Regulator Edgemere Movement.

This small 0-size ladies movement is solid nickel, richly finished, full 15 jeweled, jewels in beautiful settings, full screwed. It is very elaborately finished, has the latest patent micrometer regulator, cut expansion balance, finest patent straight line lever escapement, quick train, patent pinion; in short, it is the highest grade 15 jeweled 0-size movement made and will outwear two of the ordinary 0-size 15 jeweled movements, and yet, under our special arrangements with the manufacturer, owning this movement as we do on the basis of the actual cost of material and labor, we can, after adding our one small percentage of profit, furnish it to you at a much lower price than we can furnish a 15 jeweled movement of other makes bearing the manufacturer's name and grade.

Ladies' 0-Size, 15 Jeweled, Patent Regulator Plymouth Watch Co. Movement.

Ladies' small 0-size 15 jeweled Plymouth Watch Co. movement. For the highest possible perfection in 15 jeweled small 0-size ladies' watch movements we recommend this, our specially made Plymouth Watch Co. movement, above all other makes. This movement is the latest production of one of the biggest factories in the United States. All latest improvements are embodied in it; all new devices and new ideas carried out to the fullest extent. The movement is made of solid nickel, plates beautifully damaskeened; has patent micrometer regulator; has full cut expansion balance with true timing screws; has the latest straight line patent lever escapement, highly polished and ornamented exposed winding wheels. The movement is stem wind and pendant set, and has 15 fine ruby and garnet jewels, each jewel in screw setting. The dial is selected, no blemish, no dust spots, as inferior watches sometimes show. In fact, it is the best 15 jeweled American made movement ever turned out, and if you want to buy a ladies' 0-size small watch, and want a 15 jeweled, high grade, fine running and accurate timekeeping movement, by all means select this movement above all other makes. We bar none made.

Ladies' 0-Size, 17 Jeweled, Stem Wind and Pendant Set Plymouth Watch Co. Movement.

Ladies' small 0-size 17 jeweled adjusted patent regulator movement, absolute perfection turned out at last by the watch company that makes our special movement. It is our especially made Plymouth Watch Co. movement, manufactured by one of the biggest makers in the United States, and we claim it to have more accurately running and timekeeping merit than any other 0-size movement, no matter the number of jewels, so far placed on the market. The movement is made of solid nickel with handsome moire antique damaskeening, high polished ornamented steel exposed winding wheels, fine, carefully adjusted micrometer regulator, full cut expansion balance with true timing screws, latest straight line full lever escapement. The movement contains 17 fine ruby and garnet jewels, the jewels firmly and securely set with screws. It is stem wind and pendant set. The dial is the first selection, no dust spots, no blemish, absolutely perfect. In fact, take this movement as a whole, dissect it, take it apart, examine it, compare it, and it will stand the most rigid inspection. It will be found perfect in every detail and positively give entire and absolute satisfaction. If you are looking for a ladies' watch that will be dependable, one that she can catch trains by and will not vary in time, one day running fast, the next day running slow, and the third day not running at all, by all means select this one. We recommend it and can sincerely say that it is the best 0-size 17 jeweled movement ever placed on the market.

Fancy Dial.

We show here an illustration of the fancy dial and gold hands that we furnish on different watches quoted and illustrated on the following pages at 90 cents extra.

Fancy dials cannot be fitted on every watch in our catalogue. We caution you only to order them on such watches where it is clearly stated on the page that we can furnish fancy dials. The illustration merely gives you an idea of how the fancy dial will look. They are not all exactly as this picture shows, as they vary in design. They come in various tints, with floral decorations and gold work, and all of them beautiful.

The illustration is a dial made to fit 18-size watches. We furnish any size, 18, 16, 12, 6 and 0-size for American watches.

Prices of Elgin and Waltham Movements Without Cases.

For the accommodation of our customers only, and so as to avoid inquiries for prices, we herewith quote our prices on Elgin and Waltham movements without cases. When ordering be sure to give the size and make of case, whether open face or hunting movement required; also keep in mind that only an open face movement will go in an open face case and the hunting style movement in the hunting case, and that we can furnish only stem wind movements. Stem wind movements cannot be fitted in key wind cases.

18-size, 7 jeweled Elgin or Waltham, gilded plates	$3.85
18-size, 7 jeweled Elgin or Waltham, nickel plates	4.40
18-size, 15 jeweled Elgin or Waltham, nickel plates	5.50
18-size, 17 jeweled Elgin or Waltham, nickel plates, not adjusted	6.60
18-size, 17 jeweled C. M. Wheeler or P. S. Bartlett, Waltham	8.80
16-size, 7 jeweled Elgin or Waltham, nickel plates	5.50
16-size, 15 jeweled Elgin or Waltham	7.70
16-size, 17 jeweled No. 241 Elgin	$12.65
12-size, 7 jeweled Elgin and Waltham, nickel plates	5.50
12-size, 15 jeweled Elgin or Waltham, nickel plates	7.70
12-size, 17 jeweled No. 275 grade Elgin	15.12
6-size, 7 jeweled Elgin or Waltham, nickel plates	4.95
6-size, 15 jeweled Elgin or Waltham, nickel plates	6.15
0-size, 7 jeweled Elgin or Waltham	7.15
0-size, 15 jeweled Elgin or Waltham	8.80
0-size, 17 jeweled Elgin	14.30

DO NOT OVERLOOK THE FACT that all of the watches illustrated and described on this and the previous page carry with them our written binding guarantee that amply secures and protects you for a term of five years. You positively take no chance, you run no risk when buying watches from us.

Gents' 18-Size, Open Face or Hunting Case, Stem Wind, 17-Jeweled, Adjusted Plymouth Watch Co. Movement.

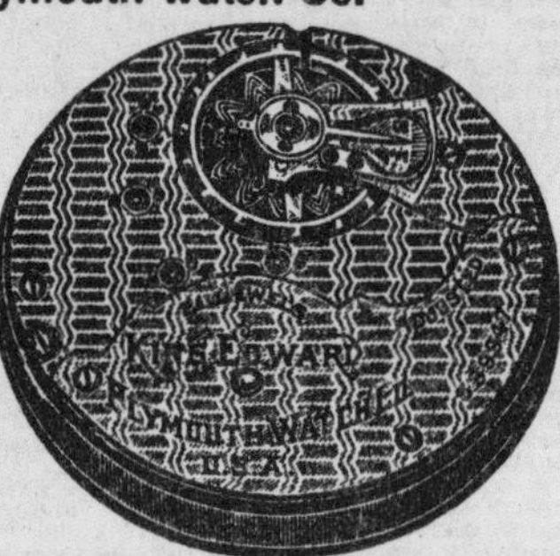

This movement is marked "Plymouth Watch Co.," is solid nickel, richly damaskeened and finished, has 17 ruby jewels, raised gold settings with screws, accurately and especially adjusted to heat, cold, isochronism and all positions, the most accurate and complete adjustment lines on any watch made; quick train, hand finished escape wheel, compensating balance, Breguet overstrung tempered hairspring, new improved patent micrometer regulator barrel arbor pivots, double sunk glass enamel dial with marginal figures. This 17-jeweled, full adjusted, full plate movement is gotten out for us with a view to furnishing a higher grade adjusted movement than is made and sold by any watch company in America. While we furnish it at a much lower price than you can buy a 17-jeweled adjusted movement bearing the manufacturer's name, if you order this movement and do not find, after giving it a thorough trial, that it gives better satisfaction than any other 17-jeweled movement made, you can return it to us at our expense and we will immediately refund your money.

REMEMBER

WHEN YOU HAVE BOUGHT [illegible] WORTH OF GOODS OR MORE FROM US YOU GET YOUR CHOICE OF MANY VALUABLE ARTICLES FREE AS SHOWN IN OUR FREE PROFIT SHARING BOOK.

Gentlemen's 18-Size, Stem Wind, Lever Set, Open Face or Hunting Style, 21-Jeweled King Edward Movement, Manufactured by the Plymouth Watch Co.

This movement procured by us under a new deal and in an immense quantity, represents the highest perfection in watchmaking. It has 21 fine ruby jewels in gold settings, cut expansion balance, Breguet hairspring, patent safety pinion, patent regulator, adjusted to temperature and the positions, the most accurate and most modern watch on the market to-day, quoted throughout our catalogue, at less cost than the 17-jeweled adjusted movements bearing the makers' name. This watch we can recommend as being perfection in the watchmaking art, and is made with the idea not to equal any 21-jeweled watch on the market but to have something better than has been heretofore manufactured. By all means, if you want the best watch manufactured, we would advise either the Prince of Wales in the 16-size or the King Edward in the 18-size.

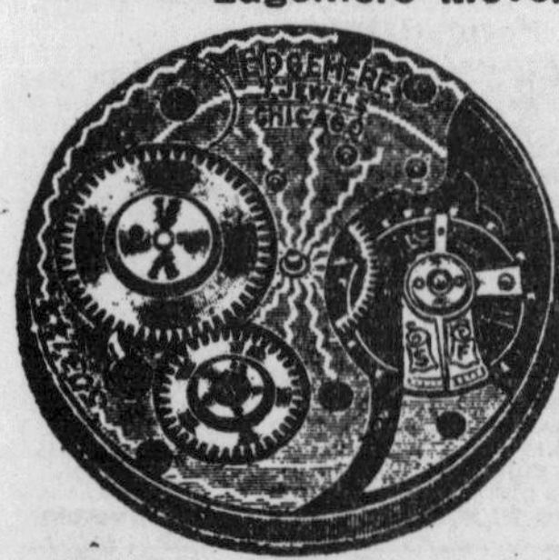

Gentlemen's 16-Size, Open Face or Hunting Style, 7-Jeweled Nickel Edgemere Movement.

This movement is made for us under contract, and at our price fitted with any 16-size case as shown on the following pages, will give you double the value that you can get in any 16-size 7-jeweled movement bearing the manufacturer's name on the market. This movement has nickel plates, richly damaskeened, exposed high polished winding wheels, non-magnetic balance and hairspring, full polished pinions, handsome double pressed dial with red marginal figures, is stem wind and pendant set and positively gives the best satisfaction of any 7-jeweled cheap watch on the market. Its equal cannot be procured for twice what we ask for it.

Gentlemen's 16-Size, Open Face or Hunting Style, 15-Jeweled Patent Regulator Edgemere Movement.

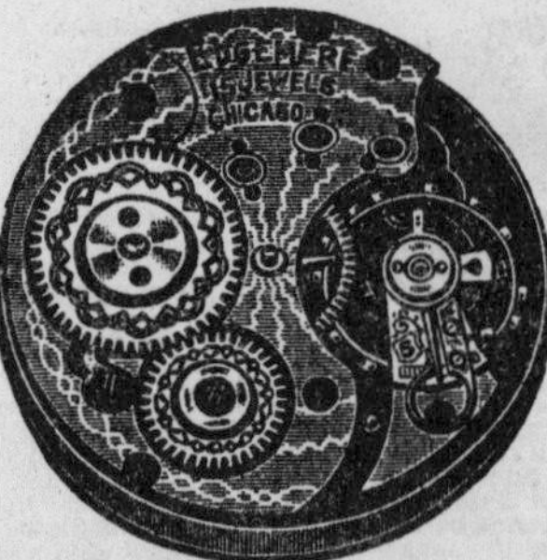

This movement is made under our new arrangement, is highly finished and an accurate timekeeper, has full nickel plates, jewels in screw settings, high polished exposed winding apparatus, cut expansion balance, with Breguet hairspring, fine polished patent regulator, the equal of any 15-jeweled movement manufactured bearing the makers' name. By reason of our new contract, we are able to quote it in this catalogue on the various pages at less than we ask for 7-jeweled movements bearing the makers' name. If you want a good and accurate timekeeper, we would advise you to select this watch above all other 16-size movements with 7 jewels, stamped with the makers' name.

Gents' 16-Size, Open Face or Hunting Case, Stem Wind Plymouth Watch Co. Movement.

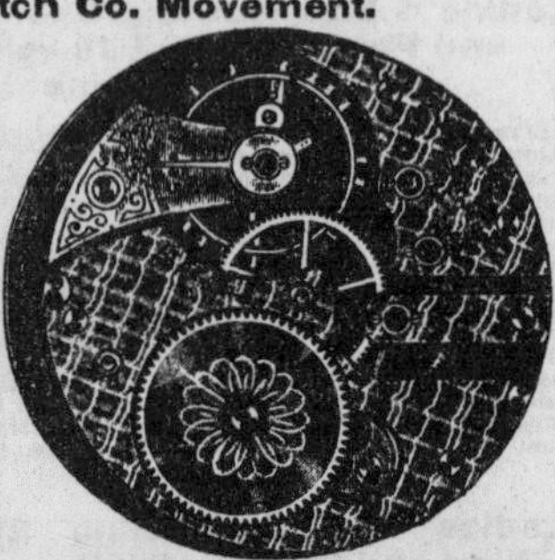

This is positively the highest grade 15-jeweled 16-size movement made, each movement stamped "Plymouth Watch Co." It is full 15-jeweled, all jewels in screwed settings and it is accurately adjusted to positions; has cut expansion balance, overstrung Breguet hairspring, gotten out with a view of giving our customers in every respect a better 15-jeweled 16-size movement than is made or sold by any watch company in the country. This movement has the latest exposed winding wheel, solid nickel plates, every up to date feature found in any other 16-size movement, and still we furnish it for a little less than any other named 16-size movement.

Gents' 16-Size, Open Face or Hunting Case, 17-Jeweled Adjusted Plymouth Watch Co. Movement.

This is our gents' 17-jeweled adjusted 16-size movement, each movement stamped "Plymouth Watch Co." It is 17-jeweled, all jewels in screwed settings, accurately adjusted to heat, cold, position and isochronism; has the latest patent micrometer regulator, patent pinion and escapement, exposed winding wheel, has every new and up to date improvement, combines all the best in all the highest grade 17-jeweled 16-size movements made, and yet we offer it at a lower price than we can offer any other 17-jeweled movement.

Gentlemen's 16-Size, Open Face or Hunting, 21-Jeweled, Nickel, Patent Regulator Prince of Wales Movement, Manufactured by the Plymouth Watch Company.

This movement is a new addition to our exceptional value page and represents positively the highest grade watch in 21-jeweled manufactured. A new deal with a new company for an immense quantity enables us to sell this watch to you at less money than 17-jeweled named watches manufactured by others. This watch has full nickel plates, jewels all in settings, cut expansion balance, double sunk dial, patent regulator, in fact, all modern improvements, adjusted to temperature and positions, in fact, a watch such as cannot be compared with any other watch quoted or illustrated in our catalogue. If you purchase this watch you are making a saving of no less than $12.00 to $15.00 and are getting the best production of modern watch making.

Gents' 12-Size, Open Face or Hunting Case, Solid Nickel, 10-Jeweled, Stem Wind and Stem Set Movement.

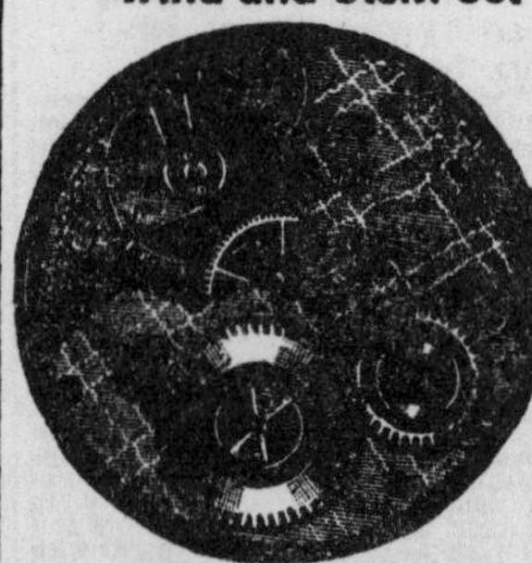

These movements are stamped "Edgemere." They are 10-jeweled, exposed winding wheel, cut expansion balance, Breguet hairspring, true timing screws. This is a movement made especially for us. It is extra high grade, and under our contract we can furnish it for less money than we can furnish 7-jeweled 12-size movements of other makes, and in buying a 12-size gents' watch, we especially recommend that you select this movement.

Gents' 12-Size, 15-Jeweled, Open Face or Hunting Style, Stem Wind and Stem Set, Plymouth Watch Co. Movement.

These movements are stamped "Plymouth Watch Co." They have fifteen fine ruby jewels, patent regulator, exposed polished winding wheels, Breguet hairspring, accurately trued and timed and positively the finest 15-jeweled 12-size movement manufactured. We control the prices on account of an immense contract and while this watch is positively the finest 15-jeweled 12-size movement on the market, still we are able to offer it at less money than any of the 12-size stamped movements offered by such factories as the Elgin, Waltham, Hampden and other makers. If you want the latest extra thin model 12-size watch in 15-jeweled grade, we recommend, above any other, this movement fitted in any of the cases illustrated and described in our catalogue.

Gentlemen's 12-Size, 17-Jeweled, Open Face or Hunting Style, Stem Wind and Pendant Set, Plymouth Watch Co. Movement.

As positively the acme of perfection in 17-jeweled, 12-size movements, we offer this, our latest production from the factory. This movement is stamped "Plymouth Watch Co.," and represents the highest order in this grade above all other makes. This movement is adjusted, trued and timed before leaving the factory to the very closest possible degree. It has high polished exposed winding wheels, Breguet hairspring, true timing screws, patent safety pinion, handsomely damaskeened nickel plates and patent regulator, jewels in screw settings; in fact, every detail in watchmaking has been covered and perfected. While this movement stands pre-eminent for timekeeping and perfection of finish, still, by our new contract in placing our immense order, we are able to sell it at less than watches stamped with the maker's name throughout these pages. We would advise, if you are looking for a small size extra thin gents' watch in a high jeweled grade, to positively select this one to the exclusion of all other grades and makes.

Imported Extra Thin Model 7-Jeweled Lever Escapement Watch Movement.

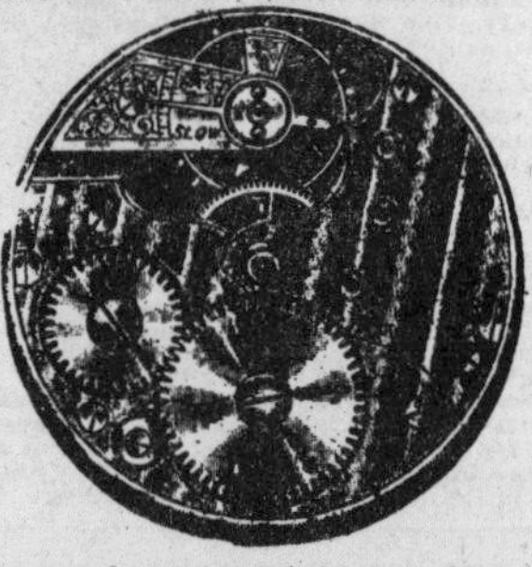

So as to offer a good running, accurate timekeeping thin model watch movement to our customers, thinner than is made in America, we imported direct from Switzerland, saving the expense of brokerage and importers' profits, this very excellent movement as illustrated. The plates are of solid nickel, damaskeened in modest but handsome lines, bevel edged throughout; full straight line lever escapement, fine polished exposed winding wheels, and different from many imported movements this, our 12-size extra thin model 7-jeweled movement, contains 7 garnet jewels. We guarantee them to be such. The dial is of extra fine white selected porcelain, such as is used in railway watches sold from $10.50 to $150.00 apiece. The running and timekeeping qualities of this watch are a special feature. We recommend them. If you want to own the best running, thinnest model, up to date 7-jeweled 12-size watch and save 50 per cent of your purchase price, by all means select this one. The same watch made in the United States, as handsomely finished and as accurately running, would cost twice what we ask. You will note that this movement is quoted throughout the 12-size pages of this catalogue. If this movement is not up to standard, in every way as described, you may return it to us and we will, upon its receipt, at once refund your money together with all transportation charges. This virtually means an insurance. We go on record in black type. You are absolutely protected.

Ladies' 6-Size, Hunting Case, Stem Wind and Stem Set, 7-Jeweled Edgemere Movement.

Like the gents' 18-size movement, we guarantee this 7-jeweled movement the equal of any 7-jeweled 6-size movement made, and worth two of any of the cheap 7-jeweled movements on the market. It is the highest grade 7-jeweled movement made, and in selecting a ladies' watch, we would especially recommend that you select our 7-jeweled Edgemere; has gold damaskeening, cut expansion balance, sunk second enamel dial, a great improvement over any other 7-jeweled 6-size movement on the market.

Ladies' Small 0-Size, Stem Wind and Pendant Set, 11-Jeweled Swiss Imported Movement.

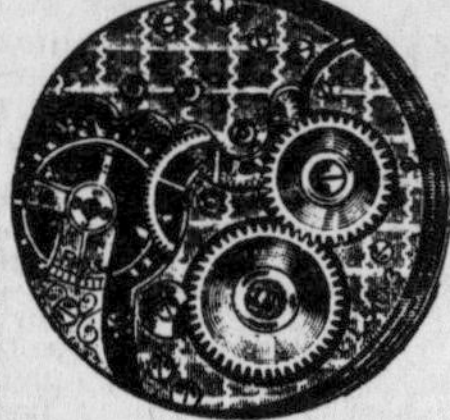

A special drive in 11-jeweled 0-size movements procured by us direct from the manufacturers in Chauxdefonds, Switzerland, made especially and in every way guaranteed to give entire satisfaction. The movement is made of solid nickel, handsomely damaskeened, full cut extension balance, with true timing screws, straight line up to date lever escapement, high polished exposed winding wheels, polished screw heads throughout, in fact such a movement made in America with the same perfections, the same care exercised in its construction would cost three times the price quoted throughout these pages. In importing this special drive in 11-jeweled movements we had but one object in mind, that was to procure the best running, most accurate timekeeping small 0-size 11-jeweled movement that our money could buy. We have it in this movement, and we can recommend it above all 11-jeweled movements offered on the market and made by others.

Ladies' 6-Size Hunting Style Countess Janet.

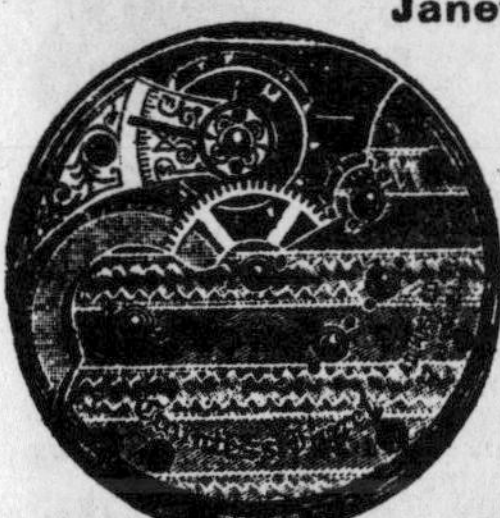

This watch is made for a trading watch in ladies' size. Never before has a ladies' size watch been placed on the market for this purpose. It looks exactly like a high grade 17-jeweled or 19-jeweled watch; is richly nickeled; has 17 large imitation ruby jewels screwed on the plates, which, however, have no utility, but are made for show only. The movement itself is merely a 7-jeweled American made movement, manufactured for our express use by one of the big watch companies. It is for a trading watch only but as a timekeeper will keep only fair time. It is richly damaskeened so as to make a beautiful appearance; is stem wind and stem set. Our 18-size cheap trading watch for travelers has met with exceptionally fine sale. The profit from a watch of this sort cannot be estimated. Never before have they been placed on the market. They have the appearance of a watch being worth twenty times more than what we ask. This watch is particularly attractive for the purposes of watch trading, for peddlers' use, publishing houses, scheme houses, partial payment houses, in fact, any one wanting a watch having the appearance of the very highest grade for next to nothing in cost.

Ladies' 6-Size, Hunting Case, Stem Wind and Stem Set, Solid Nickel, Ruby Jeweled Plymouth Watch Co.

These movements are especially made for us, and they are gotten out with a view of giving our customers a higher grade 15-jeweled 6-size movement than is made by any watch company in America. This movement is accurately adjusted to position, the 15 jewels are the highest grade rubies, perfect setting, set with screws, has the latest compensating cut balance, true timing screws, has the finest overstrung Breguet hairspring, is richly damaskeened in gold, has sunk second dial, patent pinion and escapement, quick train. Guaranteed the highest grade 6-size 15-jeweled movement on the market.

Ladies' 6-Size, Hunting Case, Stem Wind, 17-Jeweled Adjusted Movement.

These movements are marked "Plymouth Watch Co." They are positively the highest grade 17-jeweled 6-size movements made. Solid nickel, richly damaskeened in gold, full 17 jewels, finest ruby jewels in gold settings, settings set with screws, compensating cut balance, balance adjusted with true timing screws, finest overstrung patent Breguet hairspring, polished center wheel, quick train, patent pinion Movement is accurately adjusted to heat, cold, position and isochronism, combining everything that you could get in any movement that you would pay three times the price for if sold by any manufacturer under the manufacturer's name and number; so in selecting the very finest thing in a ladies' 6-size watch, we would especially recommend that you select this movement, and we will furnish it to you, quality for quality, at one-half the price you could buy any other make.

Ladies' 0-Size, 7-Jeweled, Stem Wind and Stem Set, Swiss Movement.

This movement is made for us under contract. It is full nickel, quick train, 7 jewels, patent pinion and patent lever escapement, and we guarantee it the highest grade 7-jewel, small 0-size movement made. You will find this movement will keep better time and last twice as long as any other 7-jeweled 0-size movement on the market, and yet, under our special arrangements with the manufacturer, we can furnish this in a much higher grade 7-jeweled movement than you could get elsewhere at less than the ordinary 7-jeweled movements are sold by others. In selecting a very small watch for a lady in an 0-size, unless you want to get our high grade Edgemere 0-size movement, we would especially advise that you select this in preference to any other 7-jeweled 0-size movement made.

THESE SPECIAL MOVEMENTS

AS ILLUSTRATED AND DESCRIBED ON THIS AND THE PRECEDING PAGES, **as before explained, we own under contract at the actual cost of material and labor with but our one small percentage of profit added.** As a result, they cost you very much less than any other movement we can offer, and if you will send us your order for any watch fitted with any one of our special movements it will go to you under our binding five years' guarantee, and with the understanding and agreement that if you do not find it, grade for grade, jeweling for jeweling, as good, if not better, than any movement made by any maker in America, regardless of name, make or price, you can return the watch (movement and case) to us at our expense and we will refund your money.

Ladies' 0-Size, 15-Jeweled, Patent Regulator Edgemere Movement.

This small 0-size ladies' movement is solid nickel, richly finished, full 15-jeweled, jewels in beautiful settings, full screwed. It is very elaborately finished, has the latest patent micrometer regulator, cut expansion balance, finest patent straight line lever escapement, quick train, patent pinion; in short, it is the highest grade 15-jeweled 0-size movement made and will outwear two of the ordinary 0-size 15-jeweled movements, and yet, under our special arrangements with the manufacturer, owning this movement as we do on the basis of the actual cost of material and labor, we can, after adding our one small percentage of profit, furnish it to you at a much lower price than we can furnish a 15-jeweled movement of other makes bearing the manufacturer's name and grade.

Ladies' 0-Size, 15-Jeweled, Patent Regulator Plymouth Watch Co. Movement.

Ladies' small 0-size 15-jeweled Plymouth Watch Co. movement. For the highest possible perfection in 15-jeweled small 0-size ladies' watch movements, we recommend this, our specially made Plymouth Watch Co. movement above all other makes. This movement is the latest production of one of the biggest factories in the United States. All latest improvements are embodied in it; all new devices and new ideas carried out to the fullest extent. The movement is made of solid nickel, plates beautifully damaskeened; has patent micrometer regulator; has full cut expansion balance with true timing screws; has the latest straight line patent lever escapement, highly polished and ornamented exposed winding wheels. The movement is stem wind and pendant set, and has 15 fine ruby and garnet jewels, each jewel in screw setting. The dial is selected, no blemish, no dust spot, as inferior watches sometimes show. In fact, it is the best, 15-jeweled American made movement ever turned out, and if you want to buy a ladies' 0-size small watch, and want a 15-jeweled high grade fine running and accurate timekeeping movement, by all means select this movement above all other makes. We bar none made.

Ladies' 0-Size, 17-Jeweled, Stem Wind and Pendant Set Plymouth Watch Co. Movement.

Ladies' small 0-size 17-jeweled adjusted patent regulator movement, absolute perfection turned out at last by the watch company that makes our special movement. It is our especially made Plymouth Watch Co. movement, manufactured by one of the biggest makers in the United States, and we claim it to have more accurately running and timekeeping merit than any other 0-size movement, no matter the number of jewels, so far placed on the market. The movement is made of solid nickel with handsome moire antique damaskeening, high polished ornamented steel exposed winding wheels, fine, carefully adjusted micrometer regulator, full cut expansion balance with true timing screws, latest straight line full lever escapement. The movement contains 17 fine ruby and garnet jewels, the jewels firmly and securely set with screws. It is stem wind and pendant set. The dial is the first selection, no dust spots, no blemish, absolutely perfect. In fact, take this movement as a whole, dissect it, take it apart, examine it, compare it, and it will stand the most rigid inspection. It will be found perfect in every detail and positively give entire and absolute satisfaction. If you are looking for a ladies' watch that will be dependable, one that she can catch trains by and will not vary in time, one day running fast, the next day running slow, and the third day not running at all, by all means select this one. We recommend it and can sincerely say that it is the best 0-size 17-jeweled movement ever placed on the market.

WATCH REPAIRS

AT ONE-HALF THE PRICE ASKED BY OTHERS.

REMEMBER, **that a watch should not run longer than one and one-half years without having the oil cleaned off and fresh oil applied.** An engine or sewing machine will be oiled several times a day, but we have known people to carry a watch for ten years without having it cleaned or fresh oil applied. Usually a movement thus treated is of **no value, being entirely worn out.** Our charge for cleaning and oiling is **50 cents.** The regular price is **$1.50.** We give below a list of charges for repairs which will be subject to changes in some cases. For example: Old fusee watches, made some fifty or sixty years ago in England, the material of which is difficult to procure.

Balances, American Expansion .... $1.50 to	$2.75
Balances, Am. Steel or Nickel...	.50
Balances, English, Steel or Composition..........	1.00
Balances, Swiss, Composition...	.75
Balances, Swiss, with screw.....	1.25
Balances, Swiss, Expansion, cut	3.00
Cleaning, ordinary Swiss, Duplex or American..............	.50
Cleaning, ordinary English... .	1.00
Demagnetizing Watch Movements, ordinary..............	.75
Demagnetizing Watch Movements, finer grades....$1.00 to	2.00
Dials, Swiss, without seconds...	1.00
Dials, Swiss, with seconds.......	1.50
Dust Bands, American...........	.25
Hairsprings, ordinary flat.......	.75
Hairsprings, Breguet...........	1.50
Hands, common......... .. .each	.10
Hands, fine............ each	.20
Jewels, American, Cock or Foot (with settings)..........	.50
Jewels, American, 3d, 4th or 'Scape.................50c to	.75
Jewels, Endstone, in setting....	.50
Jewels, Cap, Swiss (with plate)..	.25
Jewels, Swiss, 3d, 4th, 'Scape or Balance, set in plate..........	.50
Jewels, Swiss, 3d, 4th, 'Scape or Balance, Fine Ruby.....	1.50
Jewels, Swiss, Center, Fine Ruby in Gold Set.....................	3.00
Jewels, Roller	.35
Jewels, Pallet, Set in Old Settings, American......	.75

Mainsprings, Swiss................	$0.50
Mainsprings, English, with hook	.75
Mainsprings, American..........	.50
Mainsprings, Repeaters, etc..... ....$1.00 to	1.50
Pallets, Fork and Arbor, complete, ordinary.................	3.00
Pallets, Fork and Arbor, complete, American.......$1.25 to	2.50
Pinions, American, 3d, 4th or 'Scape..............................	.75
Pinions, American, Center......	1.00
Pinions, American, Center, Patent, complete with Wheel	2.00
Pinions, Cannon...................	.50
Pinions, Swiss, 3d, 4th or 'Scape, ordinary.........................	1.00
Pinions, Swiss, 3d, 4th or 'Scape, fine ....$1.75 to	2.00
Pinions, Swiss, Center, ordinary.	1.50
Pinions, Swiss, Center, fine......	2.00
Pinions, Swiss, Cannon...........	.50
Ratchets, English, Swiss or American...........................	.50
Staffs Balance, American, 75c to	1.25
Staffs Balance, Howard, etc.....	2.50
Staffs Balance, English, ordinary	1.25
Staffs Balance, English, fine.... ....$1.50 to	2.50
Staffs Balance, Swiss, ordinary	1.25
Staffs Balance, Swiss, fine....	2.50
Changing Key Wind Cases to Stem Wind.	
Silver Cases..........................	$1.50
Gold Cases............................	2.50

WHEN WATCHES are sent with instructions to put them in good order we will do everything necessary to put them in good running condition, but when the instructions are to repair a certain particular part of a watch, the repairs will be strictly confined only to the part or parts specified and we cannot hold ourselves responsible for anything further that may be necessary to insure correct running of the watch. In sending any part of a watch, if your intention is to fit same yourself, do not instruct us to fit same, but kindly use the word "select." This prevents misunderstanding your wishes.

If an idea of the cost of repairs cannot be obtained from this list, send the watch to us and on receipt of same we will examine it, quote cost of repairing and hold for instructions. SHIPPING DIRECTIONS—When shipping watches or jewelry for repairs or exchange, mark plainly as follows: Sears, Roebuck & Co., Watch Repair Dep't, Chicago, Ill., and in upper left hand corner put your own name and address, prefixing the word "From." Also enclose a card in the package with your name and address and state that the watch is for repairs. At the same time write us a letter stating that you have sent a watch (by mail or express) for repairs, what repairs you want made, or that you wish us to quote cost of repairing.

This Fine Watch Box for 23c.

No. 4G588 This picture, made from a photograph, shows one of our fine lined and leatherette covered watch boxes that we supply for 23 cents extra with any watch purchased of us. In ordering, state what size watch the case is intended for. Price, **23c**

If by mail, postage extra, 2 cents.

CUT PRICE, 23 CENTS.

No. 4G586 The Ajax Watch Insulator or protector protects your watch. It is made of a secret compounded metal, beautifully enameled and lined with velvet. **Order by number.** The maker guarantees that this insulator protects the watch case from wear and the movement from all ordinary magnetic influence. It fits all size watches, open face or hunting style of all makes. **When ordering don't fail to give size and make of case and whether open face or hunting style is wanted.** Price **23c**

If by mail, postage extra, 2 cents.

PACKING FOR SHIPMENT. Watches should be wrapped in some soft material (cotton batting is good), and packed in a strong box, about 2x3x3 inches. Do not try to ship more than one watch in a box of this size, as it requires considerable packing about each watch to insure safe shipment.

CASH WITH THE ORDER must be sent for all repair work. If you do not know what the cost will be, send what you think will more than cover it and we will refund the balance. If to be returned by mail, send 7 cents for each watch for postage and 8 cents extra for registry.

WE BUY OLD GOLD AND SILVER and pay the highest market price, namely 18-karat gold, 72c; 14-karat gold, 56c, and 10-karat gold, 40c per pennyweight. Silver fluctuates in value, but at the present time worth 60c per ounce. In all cases we hold old metal **until we are advised by customers that estimate of value is satisfactory.**

WE WANT JEWELERS, GENERAL MERCHANTS WHO HANDLE WATCHES, AND EVERYBODY TO SEND US THEIR WATCH REPAIRS.

IT WILL PAY THE JEWELER better to send his repairs to us and have the work properly done, with new material of the right kind, than to patch up the job with old material, soft solder or material which does not fit, as is the custom where there is not a large stock of well selected material and a good outfit of tools at hand. Our prices being from one-half to one-fourth the regular prices, there is a large profit left for the dealer or an equal saving to those who send their watches to us direct.

REMEMBER, that a watch should not run longer than one and one-half years without having the oil cleaned off and fresh oil applied. An engine or sewing machine will be oiled several times per day, but we have known people to carry a watch for ten years without having it cleaned or fresh oil applied. Usually, a movement thus treated is of no value, being entirely worn out. Our charge for cleaning and oiling is 50 cents. The regular retail price is $1.50. We give below a list of charges for repairs which will be subject to change in some cases. For example: Old fusee watches, made some fifty or sixty years ago in England, the material of which is difficult to procure.

Balances, American Expansion	$1.50 to $2.75
Balances, Am. Steel or Nickel	.50
Balances, English, Steel or Composition	1.00
Balances, Swiss, Composition	.75
Balances, Swiss, with screw	1.25
Balances, Swiss, Expansion, cut	3.00
Cleaning, ordinary Swiss, Duplex or American	.50
Cleaning, ordinary English	1.00
Demagnetizing Watch Movements, ordinary	1.50
Demagnetizing Watch Movements, finer grades	$2.00 to 4.00
Dials, Swiss, without seconds	1.00
Dials, Swiss, with seconds	1.50
Dust Bands, American	.25
Hairsprings, ordinary flat	.75
Hairsprings, Breguet	1.50
Hands, common, each	.10
Hands, fine, each	.20
Jewels, American, Cock or Foot (with settings)	.50
Jewels, American, 3d, 4th or 'Scape	50c to .75
Jewels, Endstone, in setting	.50
Jewels, Cap, Swiss (with plate)	.25
Jewels, Swiss, 3d, 4th, 'Scape or Balance, set in plate	.50
Jewels, Swiss, 3d, 4th, 'Scape or Balance, Fine Ruby	1.50
Jewels, Swiss, Center, Fine Ruby in Gold Set	3.00
Jewels, Roller	.35
Jewels, Pallet, Set in old Settings, American	.75
Mainsprings, Swiss	$0.50
Mainsprings, English, with hook	.75
Mainsprings, American	.50
Mainsprings, Repeaters, etc.	$1.00 to 1.50
Pallets, Fork and Arbor, complete, ordinary	3.00
Pallets, Fork and Arbor, complete, American	$1.25 to 2.50
Pinions, American, 3d, 4th or 'Scape	.75
Pinions, American, Center	1.00
Pinions, American, Center, Patent, complete with Wheel	2.00
Pinions, Cannon	.50
Pinions, Swiss, 3d, 4th or 'Scape, ordinary	1.00
Pinions, Swiss, 3d, 4th or 'Scape, fine	$1.75 to 2.00
Pinions, Swiss, Center, ordinary	1.50
Pinions, Swiss, Center, fine	2.00
Pinions, Swiss, Cannon	.50
Ratchets, English, Swiss or American	.50
Staffs Balance, American, 75c to	$1.25
Staffs Balance, Howard, etc.	2.50
Staffs Balance, English, ordinary	1.25
Staffs Balance, English, fine	$1.50 to 2.50
Staffs Balance, Swiss, ordinary	1.25
Staffs Balance, Swiss, fine	2.50
Changing Key Wind Cases to Stem Wind.	
Silver Cases	$1.50
Gold Cases	2.50

WHEN WATCHES are sent with instructions to put them in good order we will do everything necessary to put them in good running condition, but when the instructions are to repair a certain particular part of a watch, the repairs will be strictly confined only to the part or parts specified and we cannot hold ourselves responsible for anything further that may be necessary to insure correct running of the watch. In sending any part of a watch, if your intention is to fit same yourself, do not instruct us to fit same, but kindly use the word "select." This prevents misunderstanding your wishes.

If an idea of the cost of repairs cannot be obtained from the above list, send the watch to us and on receipt of same we will examine it, quote cost of repairing and hold for instructions. **SHIPPING DIRECTIONS**—When shipping watches or jewelry for repairs or exchange, mark plainly as follows: **SEARS, ROEBUCK & CO., Watch Repair Dep't, Fulton, Desplaines, Wayman and Jefferson Sts., Chicago, Ill.,** and in upper left hand corner put your own name and address, prefixing the word "From." Also inclose a card **in the package with your name and address** and state that the watch is for repairs. At the same time write us a letter stating that you have sent a watch (by mail or express) for repairs, what repairs you want made, or that you wish us to quote cost of repairing.

Our New Swiss Imported 12-Size Thin Model Jeweled Movement.

It has 17 fine ruby jewels, cut expansion balance wheel, patent high polished whip lash patent regulator, Brequet hairspring, plate jewels all in screw settings, has exposed winding wheels, full dust protecting side bands, is stem wind and pendant set. The dial has plain Arabic figures, with red marginal minute figures. Remember, this movement is not American make. However, it is offered and sold by many as a product of American manufacture. We sell them for what they are, a very fine Swiss imported movement, a movement that we can recommend and warrant to you for a term of five years. Each one carries our binding guarantee.

Prices in the various cases for the watch complete are as follows:

No. 4C1000 Fitted in Alaska silver open face case, screw back and bezel......$ 8.75

No. 4C1010 Fitted in solid silver Hunting case......11.00

No. 4C1020 Fitted in a 20-year gold filled case, open face, screw back and bezel, beautifully engraved......$11.27

No. 4C1030 Fitted in a 20-year gold filled case, Hunting style, beautifully engraved......$14.27

This Fine Watch Box for 20c.

No. 4C2000 This picture, made from a photograph, shows one of our fine silk plush lined and covered watch boxes that we supply for 20 cents extra with any watch purchased of us. In ordering, state what size watch the case is intended for.
Price......20c

CUT PRICE, 18 CENTS.

The Ajax Watch Insulator or Protector protects your watch. It is made of a secret compounded metal, beautifully enameled and lined with velvet. **Order by number.** The maker guarantees that this insulator protects the watch case from wear and the movement from all ordinary magnetic influence. It fits all size watches, open face or hunting style of all makes. **When ordering don't fail to give size and make of case and whether open face or hunting style is wanted.**
No. 4C2002 Price......18c

PACKING FOR SHIPMENT. **Watches should be wrapped in some soft material** (cotton batting is good), and packed in a strong box, about 2x3x3 inches. **Do not try and ship more than one watch in a box of this size,** as it requires considerable packing about each watch to insure safe shipment.

CASH WITH THE ORDER **must be sent for all repair work.** If you do not know what the cost will be, send what you think will more than cover it and we will refund the balance. If to be returned by mail, send 7 cents for each watch for postage and 8 cents extra for registry.

WE BUY OLD GOLD AND SILVER and pay the highest market price, namely, 18-karat gold, 72c; 14-karat gold, 56c, and 10-karat gold, 40c per pennyweight. Silver fluctuates in value, but at the present time is worth 50c per ounce. In all cases we hold old metal until we are advised by customers that estimate of value is satisfactory.

Watch Repairing.

By N. B. Sherwood.

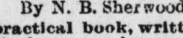

A practical book, written in a practical manner, by a practical man. Informs about the bench and its accessories, the vise and the oilstone, lathe appliances, the jacot lathe, depthing tool, expanding the web of a wheel, the spreading tool and its use, the rounding-up tool, stud remover, opening the regulator, roller remover, replacing broken teeth, graining, polishing blocks, polishing steel work, pivots, hardening, stamping, etc. Illustrated. Size, 5¼x7¾ inches.
No. 3C059330 Price......25c
If by mail, postage extra, 5 cents.

American Watchmaker and Jeweler.

By Henry G. Abbott.

Compiled from the best and most reliable sources. Contains complete directions for using all the latest tools, attachments and devices for watchmakers and jewelers; electroplating, bronzing and staining all metals; soldering and directions for making all kinds of hard and soft solder and fluxes; steel, its treatment in annealing, hardening, tempering, etc.; watch cleaning, repairing, etc.; a treatise on wheels and pinions and hundreds of miscellaneous recipes, formulas and hints on all kinds of work, of great value to every workman. 367 pages. Illustrated with 288 engravings. Size, 5¼x7½ inches. Retail price, $1.25.
No. 3C059312 Cloth. Our price......98c
If by mail, postage extra, 10 cents.

$15.23

$15.23

The engraving will be similar to the illustration.
No. 4C2450 25-year gold filled open face.
No. 4C2452 25-year gold filled hunting.
No. 4C2454 14-karat solid gold open face.
No. 4C2456 14-karat solid gold hunting.

NEW THIN MODEL OPEN FACE AND HUNTING STYLE

DUEBER-HAMPDEN

16-SIZE 25-YEAR WARRANTED GOLD FILLED AND 14-KARAT SOLID GOLD COMPLETE WATCHES

These cases are made by the Dueber Watch Company. They are the correct thing, the right size and shape, hand engraved and in every respect perfect. The movements are all new models manufactured by the Hampden Watch Company, each one guaranteed an accurate time piece for five years. Note the prices and compare them with what others ask for the same watch. We fit these movements into case as number shows.

	No. 4C2450	No. 4C2452	No. 4C2454	No. 4C2456
Full 17 jeweled General Stark movement	$15.23	$16.07	$30.00	$33.00
Full 17 jeweled William McKinley movement	16.93	17.77	31.70	34.70
Full 21 jeweled William McKinley movement	27.93	28.77	42.70	46.70

DEALERS AND ALL MERCHANTS WHO SELL WATCHES AND JEWELRY CAN MAKE MONEY by buying from us. We can furnish them any goods from our big Watch and Jewelry Department for much less than they can buy elsewhere. Our Watch and Jewelry Department offers a great opportunity for money making.

Gents' 18 Size, Open Face or Hunting Case, Stem Wind, 17-Jeweled, Adjusted S., R. & Co. Special Movement.

This movement is marked "Sears, Roebuck & Co. Special," is solid nickel, richly damaskeened and finished, has 17 ruby jewels, raised gold settings with screws, accurately and especially adjusted to heat, cold, isochronism and all positions, the most accurate and complete adjustment lines on any watch made; quick train, hand finished escape wheel, compensating balance, Breguet overstrung tempered hairspring, new improved patent micrometer regulator barrel arbor pivots, double sunk glass enamel dial, with marginal figures. This 17-jeweled, full adjusted, full plate movement is gotten out for us with a view to furnishing a higher grade adjusted movement than is made and sold by any watch company in America. While we furnish it at a much lower price than you can buy a 17-jeweled adjusted movement bearing the manufacturer's name, if you order this movement and do not find, after giving it a thorough trial, that it gives better satisfaction than any other 17-jeweled movement made, you can return it to us at our expense and we will immediately refund your money.

NOTE the difference between this 17-jeweled Sears, Roebuck & Co. Special and our 17-jeweled Edgemere. It is the very fine adjustment of this movement, the adjustment to all positions, temperature and isochronism, which accounts for the difference in cost to manufacture.

Gents' 16-Size, Open Face or Hunting Case, 12-Jeweled, Nickel, Patent Regulator Edgemere Movement.

This movement is made for us under contract, and at our price, fitted with any 16-size case as shown on the following pages, we can give you double the value in this movement that you can get in any 16-size movement bearing the manufacturer's name. It is a handsome movement, full 12-jeweled, has micrometer patent regulator, richly damaskeened and ornamented in gold. For accurate time keeping qualities and long service there is no movement made within several dollars of the price we name that will compare with this movement.

Gents' 16-Size, Open Face or Hunting Case, Stem Wind Movement.

This is positively the highest grade 15-jeweled 16 size movement made, each movement stamped "Sears, Roebuck & Co.'s Special." It is full 15-jeweled, all jewels in screwed settings and it is accurately adjusted to positions; has cut expansion balance, overstrung Breguet hairspring, gotten out with a view of giving our customers in every respect a better 15-jeweled 16-size movement than is made or sold by any watch company in the country. This movement has the latest exposed winding wheel, every up to date feature found in any other 16-size movement, and still we furnish it at as low a price as any other 16-size movement made.

Gents' 16-Size Open Face or Hunting Case, 17-Jeweled Adjusted Movement.

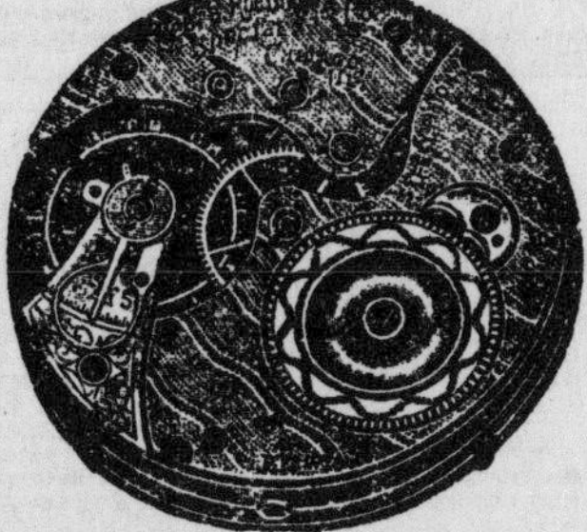

This is our gents' 17-jeweled adjusted 16-size movement, each movement stamped "Sears, Roebuck & Co.'s Special." It is 17-jeweled, all jewels in screwed settings, accurately adjusted to heat, cold, position and isochronism; has the latest patent micrometer regulator, patent pinion and escapement, exposed winding wheel, has every new and up to date improvement, combines all the best in all the highest grade 17-jeweled 16-size movements made, and yet we offer it at a lower price than we can offer any other 17-jeweled movement.

Gents' 12-Size, Open Face or Hunting Case, Solid Nickel, 10-Jeweled, Stem Wind and Stem Set Movement.

These movements are stamped "Edgemere, Sears, Roebuck & Co." They are 10-jeweled, exposed winding wheel, cut expansion balance, Breguet hairspring, true timing screws. This is a movement made especially for us. It is extra high grade, and under our contract we can furnish it for less money than we can furnish 7-jeweled 12-size movements of other makes, and in buying a 12-size gents' watch, we especially recommend that you select this movement.

Ladies' 6-Size, Hunting Case, Stem Wind and Stem Set, 7-Jeweled Edgemere Movement.

Like the gents' 18-size movement, we guarantee this 7-jeweled movement the equal of any 7-jeweled 6-size movement made, and worth two of any of the cheap 7-jeweled movements on the market. It is the highest grade 7-jeweled movement made, and in selecting a ladies' watch, we would especially recommend that you select our 7-jeweled Edgemere; has gold damaskeening, cut expansion balance, sunk second enamel dial, a great improvement over any other 7-jeweled 6-size movement on the market.

Ladies' 6-Size, Hunting Case, Stem Wind and Stem Set, Solid Nickel, 12-Jeweled Edgemere Movement.

This is the highest grade 12-jeweled 6-size movement made. All jewels are in screwed settings. It is richly damaskeened in gold, cut expansion balance, finest overstrung Breguet hairspring, patent pinion and escapement, quick train, fine enameled dial with marginal figures. While this movement is worth double that of any 7-jeweled movement on the market, with our special arrangements we furnish this movement as shown on the following pages at even less than the regular grade 7-jeweled movements.

Ladies' 6-Size, Stem Wind and Stem Set, Hunting Style, 17-Jeweled Edgemere Movement.

This movement is full 17-jeweled, all jewels in screwed settings, solid nickel, richly damaskeened and ornamented in gold, has cut expansion balance, true timing screws, finest overstrung Breguet hairspring, and yet, under our special arrangements, we can furnish this movement at about one-half the price charged by manufacturers for identically the same movement under their name. **Rather than buy a 7 or 15-jeweled movement of any other make we especially recommend that in selecting a ladies' 6-size watch you choose this, our 17-jeweled Edgemere.**

Ladies' 6-Size, Hunting Case, Stem Wind and Stem Set, Solid Nickel, Ruby Jeweled S., R. & Co.'s Special.

These movements are the Sears, Roebuck & Co Special, and they are gotten out with a view of giving our customers a higher grade 15-jeweled 6-size movement than is made by any watch company in America. This movement is accurately adjusted to position, the 15 jewels are the highest grade rubies, perfect settings, set with screws, has the latest compensating cut balance, true timing screws, has the finest overstrung Breguet hairspring, is richly damaskeened in gold, has sunk second dial, patent pinion and escapement, quick train, guaranteed the highest grade 6-size 15-jeweled movement on the market.

Ladies' 6-Size, Hunting Case, Stem Wind, 17-Jeweled, Adjusted Movement.

These movements are marked "Sears, Roebuck & Co.'s Special." They are positively the highest grade 17-jeweled 6-size movements made. Solid nickel, richly damaskeened in gold, full 17 jewels, finest ruby jewels in gold settings, settings set with screws, compensating cut balance, balance adjusted with true timing screws, finest overstrung patent Breguet hairspring, polished center wheel, quick train, patent pinion. Movement is accurately adjusted to heat, cold, position and isochronism, combining everything that you could get in any movement that you would pay three times the price for if sold by any manufacturer under the manufacturer's name and number, so in selecting the very finest thing in a ladies' 6-size watch, we would especially recommend that you select this movement, and we will furnish it to you, quality for quality, at one-half the price you could buy any other make.

Ladies' 0-Size, 7-Jeweled, Swiss Stem Wind and Stem Set Movement.

This movement is made for us under contract. It is full nickel, quick train, 7 jewels patent pinion and patent lever escapement, and we guarantee it the highest grade 7-jewel, small 0-size movement made. You will find this movement will keep better time and last twice as long as any other 7-jeweled 0-size movement on the market, and yet, under our special arrangements with the manufacturer, we can furnish this in a much higher grade 7-jeweled movement than you could get elsewhere at less than the ordinary 7-jeweled movements are sold by others. In selecting a very small watch for a lady in an 0-size, unless you want to get our high grade Edgemere 0-size movement, we would especially advise that you select this in preference to any other 7-jeweled 0-size movement made.

Ladies' 0-Size 15-Jeweled Patent Regulator Edgemere Movement.

This small 0-size ladies' movement is solid nickel, richly finished, full 15-jeweled, jewels in beautiful settings, full screwed. It is very elaborately finished, has the latest patent micrometer regulator, cut expansion balance, finest patent straight line lever escapement, quick train, patent pinion; in short, it is the highest grade 15-jeweled 0-size movement made and will outwear two of the ordinary 0-size 15-jeweled movements, and yet, under our special arrangements with the manufacturer, owning this movement as we do on the basis of the actual cost of material and labor, we can, after adding our one small percentage of profit, furnish it to you at a much lower price than we can furnish a 15-jeweled movement of other make bearing the manufacturer's name and grade.

If you want a small watch for a lady, select this, our highest grade 15-jeweled Edgemere movement, fit it in any 0-size case, and if, after giving it a fair trial, you are not convinced that it is the highest grade 15-jeweled 0-size movement made, you can return the watch to us at our expense and we will immediately refund your money.

ON THE DIFFERENT PAGES **in this catalogue in which the various watches are illustrated and described, together with the different cases we furnish in the various sizes, you will find listed various makes of movements and various styles of cases.** You will find the Elgin, Waltham and Hampden. You will also find listed and priced our various grades of special Edgemere and Sears, Roebuck & Co.'s Special Movements. You will observe, if you will follow these prices, that grade for grade, jeweling for jeweling, our Edgemere and Sears, Roebuck & Company movements are quoted at prices much lower than the Elgin, Waltham, Hampden and others. The reason for this marked difference in price is accounted for by the difference in cost to us.

THESE SPECIAL MOVEMENTS **as illustrated and described on this page, as before explained, we own under contract at the actual cost of material and labor, with but our one small percentage of profit added.** As a result they cost you very much less than any other movement we can offer, and if you will send us your order for any watch fitted with any one of our special movements it will go to you under our binding five years' guarantee, and with the understanding and agreement that if you do not find it, grade for grade, jeweling for jeweling, as good, if not better than any movement made by any maker in America, regardless of name, make or price, you can return the watch (movement and case) to us at our expense and we will refund your money.

THE WATCH MOVEMENTS WE RECOMMEND, AND WHY

THE CAREFUL READING OF THIS PAGE WILL SAVE YOU MONEY

The movements we recommend as particularly good value, watch movements that represent the highest degree of perfection, grade for grade, compared with any other movements manufactured, we illustrate and fully describe on this page.

Each one of the movements illustrated and described has been selected from an assortment comprising many hundreds, manufactured by various watch companies named and especially made for us. They have been thorougaly tested and tried, they have been matched grade for grade with all the other great makes and have proven even better grade for grade for perfection in construction, accuracy of timekeeping and reliability.

Guarantees accompany each one of the movements illustrated on this page. The guarantee that we sign and send you is to this effect: that should any of the movements illustrated and described on this page fail to run and run accurately for a term of five years, due to defective material or workmanship, you can return it and we will exchange it for a new one of same grade or repair it free of all cost to you, and at the same time refund to you the transportation charges both ways.

WHY WE RECOMMEND THESE MOVEMENTS.

Watch movements bearing the manufacturers' name are sold by the manufacturers at a fixed price, subject to certain discounts. The quantity the wholesaler purchases, whether a single one or a thousand at a time, does not alter this price. The smallest buyer can purchase as cheaply as the very largest, which means the manufacturer makes a very handsome profit, as it is much more profitable to produce them in large quantities than in small lots.

Purchasing ability, cash and the great outlet, which should enter into the proposition of buying merchandise, does not enter into the proposition at all with the branded and named watches sold by these large watch companies. To offset this and so as to give our customers all the advantages of our purchasing ability, outlet and cash money, we entered into a contract with two of the very largest watch companies in the United States, after we decided that their grades were positively the best when compared with others, to make for us the movements we illustrate on this page and brand them with a name such as we would select. They met us and accepted our agreement for the simple reason that by so doing they would not be competing against themselves, and at the same time have an outlet second to none in the United States.

They are quite right in the position they took, for if we were permitted to put the movements they manufactured on the market under their own names, and sell them, including the cases, at the price we do, it would ruin their business with every wholesale and retail watch dealer in America. The watches we recommend according to the size and grade are as follows:

In the gentlemen's 18-size, 21 jeweled adjusted King Edward or for a 17 jeweled, select the 18-size 17 jeweled adjusted Plymouth.

In the gentlemen's 16-size, the size smaller than the 18-size for gentlemen's use select the 21 jeweled adjusted Prince of Wales. For a 17 jeweled watch select the 17 jeweled adjusted Plymouth. For a 15 jeweled watch, select the 15 jeweled Edgemere.

If you want a still smaller size gentlemen's watch than either the 18 or 16-size, then select the 12-size (it is the latest extra thin model small gentlemen's size watch, a size smaller than the 16-size) the 21 jeweled Swiss imported movement.

For a 17 jeweled grade, select the 17 jeweled Plymouth Watch Co.

For a 15 jeweled watch, select the 15 jeweled Edgemere movement.

In ladies' watches, if you want the 6-size, select the 17 jeweled Plymouth watch.

The most popular size for ladies is the small 0-size. If you desire this size in the 17 jeweled grade, select the 17 jeweled Plymouth.

If a 15 jeweled movement is desired, select the 15 jeweled Plymouth or the 15 jeweled Edgemere. The 15 jeweled Plymouth will give better satisfaction though, we believe, in the long run.

PLYMOUTH WATCH CO. MOVEMENT.

GENTLEMEN'S 18-SIZE, 17 JEWELED OPEN FACE OR HUNTING STYLE.

This is the movement we recommend above all other movements if you are looking for an 18-size, 17 jeweled adjusted movement. It has 17 fine jewels, plate jewels in raised goldine settings, fitted with screws. It is especially adjusted to heat, cold, and regulated to positions, it has quick train, hand finished escape wheel, compensation balance, Breguet overstrung tempered hairspring, straight line lever escapement, new improved micrometer regulator, double sunk glass enamel dial with red marginal figures. Is a full plate movement. The open face is stem wind and pendant set, the hunting style comes stem wind and lever set. It is a 17 jeweled movement that is made a little stronger, a little better finished, a little closer adjusted, a little closer timed, and is a little better than any 17 jeweled adjusted movement on the market, and quoted throughout the following pages fitted in the various cases at less money.

Our five-year sweeping binding guarantee accompanies this movement.

KING EDWARD MOVEMENT.

GENTLEMEN'S 18-SIZE, 21 JEWELED ADJUSTED STEM WIND AND LEVER SET, OPEN FACE OR HUNTING STYLE.

If you are looking for a 21 jeweled, adjusted 18-size movement, then select this one. This movement we call the "King Edward;" it is full plate, has 21 jewels adjusted, fitted in goldine settings, straight line lever escapement, overstrung Breguet hairspring, fine micrometer regulator, true timing screws, beautifully damaskeened plates made in nickel, high polished screws, patent safety canyon pinion; the dial is double sunk with fine red marginal figures; in fact, a movement that we recommend above all other 21 jeweled movements illustrated and quoted in this catalogue. It is our object to save our customers money. In offering this watch at the prices quoted, fitted in the various cases, we are showing you a wonderful saving, and are offering you a watch for less money, that is a little better finished, a little finer adjusted, in fact, better in every way than the same size and same jeweled movements offered by anyone else. This watch is made for long service and accurate timekeeping, built on the latest modern principles. In it is contained the newest improvements, and yet by stamping it especially, omitting the manufacturer's name, we are able to save you from 25 to 40 per cent, if you select this watch.

Our five-year guarantee accompanies this movement.

EDGEMERE MOVEMENT.

GENTLEMEN'S 16-SIZE, 15 JEWELED OPEN FACE OR HUNTING STYLE.

This movement is a size smaller than the regulation 18-size. It is made especially for us. It has solid nickel handsomely damaskeened plates, straight line lever escapement, patent regulator, has 15 jewels in screw settings, is a little bit better than any 15 jeweled movement on the market, made with a view for long service and accurate running. It is stem wind and pendant set. By comparing the prices quoted in this catalogue for this movement, you will observe on account of the special arrangements we have made with the manufacturer, that we are offering these movements at even less than what branded movements of 7 jeweled grades are bringing.

Our five-year sweeping guarantee accompanies each one.

PLYMOUTH WATCH CO. MOVEMENT.

GENTLEMEN'S 16-SIZE, 17 JEWELED ADJUSTED OPEN FACE OR HUNTING STYLE.

If you are looking for a 17 jeweled movement in the 16-size, one size smaller than the regulation 18-size, and want an extra thin model watch, up to date in every way, then we can conscientiously recommend this watch. A little more care has been exercised in its construction, a little finer material has been used and it is a little closer adjusted than any competing grade in the United States. It has 17 fine jewels in goldine screw settings, patent high polished micrometer regulator, straight line lever escapement, patent canyon pinion, true timing screws, fine double sunk glass enamel dial, as illustration shows, is a full bridged movement with exposed winding wheels, made for accurate running and durability, is adjusted to heat, cold, and regulated to positions. We are offering it fitted in any case you may select illustrated and quoted throughout the following pages, at prices quoted which are less than the same size and same jeweled movements are made, as carefully as this one, at a very handsome saving in price. If this is the grade and size of watch you want, by all means select this one.

Our five-year sweeping binding guarantee accompanies this movement.

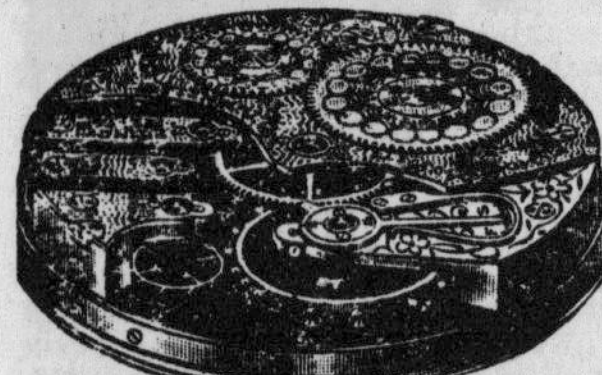

PRINCE OF WALES MOVEMENT.

GENTLEMEN'S 16-SIZE, 21 JEWELED OPEN FACE OR HUNTING STYLE.

If you are looking for the highest possible grade in a 16-size watch with 21 jewels, then buy this one. This movement is a full bridged movement, is adjusted to heat, cold, isochronism and positions, has 21 fine jewels in goldine screw settings, patent high polished micrometer regulator, straight line lever escapement, Breguet hairspring, true timing screws, high polished screw heads, high polished exposed winding wheels, plates beautifully damaskeened in design, patent canyon pinion, double sunk fine glass enamel dial with red marginal figures; in fact, we know of no point, no place where material or workmanship has been slighted in the production of this watch, made a little bit better for less money than any other 21 jeweled watch, bearing the manufacturer's name, on the market.

Our five-year guarantee goes with each one of these movements.

EDGEMERE MOVEMENT.

GENTLEMEN'S 12-SIZE, 15 JEWELED OPEN FACE OR HUNTING STYLE.

If you are looking for a 12-size movement in the 15 jeweled grade, select this one. The 12-size movement is a size smaller than the regulation 16-size. It is made under the new extra thin models, the plates are solid nickel, ¾ size, double exposed winding wheels, has 15 fine rubbed in jewels, and better than any 15 jeweled movement, is fitted with an anti-magnetic hairspring, which practically makes this watch anti-magnetic. We recommend it above all other makes, grade for grade. You are positively saving no less than 40 to 50 per cent, which means from $2.00 to $7.00 actual money, according to the case you select.

Our five-year binding guarantee accompanies this movement.

PLYMOUTH WATCH CO. MOVEMENT.

GENTLEMEN'S 12-SIZE, 17 JEWELED OPEN FACE OR HUNTING STYLE.

If you are looking for a 17 jeweled, 12-size gentlemen's watch, a size smaller than the regulation 16-size, then select this one. This watch is made of nickel, ¾ plate movement, beautifully damaskeened with high polished double exposed winding wheels, straight line lever escapement, has fine Breguet hairspring, high polished micrometer regulator, is adjusted to heat, cold, positions and isochronism, has true timing screws, the jewels are screw fitted, patent safety canyon pinion, fine double sunk glass enamel dial, is stem wind and pendant set; in fact, a 12-size watch that is a little better finished, a little higher grade material has been used, and a little closer adjusted than any 17 jeweled American made watch, bearing the manufacturer's name, on the market. In this watch you are getting the biggest value, the most accurate timer, and are saving money as compared with any other 17 jeweled movement illustrated and quoted in this catalogue.

Our five-year guarantee goes with each one.

GENTLEMEN'S 12-SIZE, 21 JEWELED ADJUSTED MOVEMENT.

If you are looking for a 12-size, extra thin model movement, that is, one size thinner and smaller than the regulation 16-size, then select this watch. This movement is imported from Switzerland. Our customers must positively have the best value that money can buy. This movement is made of nickel, very handsomely finished, ¾ plate style, has double high polished exposed winding wheels, straight line lever escapement, cut expansion balance, Breguet hairspring, true timing screws, 21 jewels, all plate jewels in fine screw goldine settings, and is adjusted to heat, cold, isochronism and positions. The dial is fine double sunk with red marginal figures, in fact, we know of no place, no part in assembling detail or material that this watch does not represent perfection considerably above any 21 jeweled movement on the market. We can conscientiously recommend this watch above all others as representing the highest 21 jeweled perfection with a wonderful saving of money at the same time.

Our five-year guarantee goes with this movement.

PLYMOUTH WATCH CO. MOVEMENT.

LADIES' 6-SIZE, 17 JEWELED.

This is the regulation ladies' size watch. Made of solid nickel, full bridged movement, has 17 fine jewels, each jewel in goldine screw settings, cut expansion balance, straight line lever escapement, has true timing screws, and regulated to positions; in fact, a watch that we can recommend. Ladies generally have considerable trouble in the running of their watches. We know that this watch will give the very best of satisfaction, dependable and accurate, and yet on account of stamping this watch with our own trade mark and not using the manufacturer's name, comparing quality for quality; grade for grade, we are selling it for about one-half the price that you could buy similar grades and not as accurate running of other makes.

Our five-year guarantee goes with each one of these movements.

EDGEMERE MOVEMENT.

LADIES' 0-SIZE, 15 JEWELED.

For those that desire a ladies' watch a size smaller than the regulation 6-size at a modest price, we recommend this one. It is stem wind and pendant set, has 15 jewels fitted in screw settings, patent micrometer regulator, cut expansion balance, Breguet hairspring, true timing screws, fine plain enamel dial; in fact, a watch that any lady could well be proud of; but being made especially for us and bought in immense quantities at a cash price, we are able to offer it at a wonderful saving as compared to 15 jeweled movements illustrated in this catalogue. If you are looking for a modest priced, good running ladies' watch, buy this one.

Our five-year written binding guarantee accompanies this movement.

PLYMOUTH WATCH CO. MOVEMENT.

LADIES' 0-SIZE, 15 JEWELED.

If you are looking for the highest grade 15 jeweled 0-size watch, a size smaller than the regulation 6-size, this is the watch we recommend. A little more time, a little more care, a little better material, a little closer adjustment has been exercised in the make of this watch. It is made of solid nickel, is straight line lever escapement, true timing screws, has 15 fine jewels in goldine screw settings, high polished exposed winding wheels, patent safety canyon pinion, patent high polished micrometer regulator, fine enamel dial with red marginal figures; in fact, a watch that will run well and accurately for a lifetime.

Our five-year guarantee goes with each one.

PLYMOUTH WATCH CO. MOVEMENT.

LADIES' 0-SIZE, 17 JEWELED.

This is the watch that we recommend above all other makes for ladies' use, if you are looking for an 0-size, 17 jeweled highest grade ladies' movement, a size smaller than the regulation 6-size. It is made of solid nickel, beautifully damaskeened plates, fine high polished exposed winding wheels, has 17 fine jewels fitted in screw goldine settings, high polished micrometer regulator, cut expansion balance, straight line lever escapement, true timing screws, patent safety pinion, fine double sunk dial with red marginal figures (built for durability and accuracy). It will run well and accurately for a lifetime.

Our five-year sweeping guarantee accompanies this movement.

Actual Sizes of Watches We Illustrate.

THIS ILLUSTRATION shows the relative sizes of gold filled watches. We placed the watches in a row, the larger ones overlapping, marked the sizes and photographed the group. Illustration shows actual sizes. This enables you to order the exact size you want. Watch illustrations throughout our catalog are from photographs of the watches and in every instance shows the exact size of the watch.

TARNISHED JEWELRY.

Jewelry like any metal to be kept bright must be washed and polished from time to time. Solid gold, gold filled and rolled plate jewelry will sometimes tarnish, especially when it is not continually worn, and allowed to lie unused in boxes or bureaus, etc. Coal gas, the contact of matches, sulphur, rubber and acids will cause tarnish or oxidization on gold and silver. All good jewelry can be made like new by the application of hot water, soap and a little ammonia in the water. Scrub the article with a brush, rinse off, submerge in alcohol, then dry in boxwood sawdust, polish by a rub up with a piece of chamois, a piece of Canton flannel or any soft cotton fabric. We can supply you with a box of boxwood sawdust for 10 cents; it will last for years. Order by number.

No. 4R500 Boxwood Sawdust. Price, per box... **10c**

WATCH REPAIRING.

We have a thoroughly equipped mechanical department, which is fitted with all the latest tools and appliances for the repairing of all kinds of watches. Our charges are about one-half what is usually charged and the work will be done in a very superior manner. We cannot give an accurate estimate of the cost of repairs without a thorough examination of the work. Our charges are merely enough to cover cost of material and labor. In sending a watch for repairing be sure to send it by registered mail, mark on the outside of the package your name and address, and write us at the same time that you have done so, giving full explanation regarding trouble with watch. **Do not fail when sending anything to us for repairs to plainly write your name and address on package.**

SHIPPING DIRECTIONS.

When shipping watches or jewelry for repairs or exchange, mark plainly as follows: "Sears, Roebuck & Co., Watch Repair Department, Chicago, Ill.," and in upper left hand corner put your own name and address, prefixing the word "From." Also enclose a card in the package with your own name and address and stating that the watch is for repairs. If you send a watch or small piece of jewelry by mail, be sure to put letter postage (2 cents an ounce) on it, because the writing on the card put inside the package makes it subject to first class mail charges. It is safer to send it as first class mail anyway, and it would be better to register it for 8 cents additional. The government guarantees safe delivery of registered mail. At the same time you send the package write us a separate letter, stating that you have sent a watch (by mail or express) for repairs, what repairs you want made, or that you wish us to quote cost of repairing.

PRICES OF ELGIN AND WALTHAM MOVEMENTS WITHOUT CASES.

For the accommodation of our customers only, we herewith quote our prices on Elgin and Waltham movements without cases. When ordering be sure to give the size and make of case, whether open face or hunting, movement required; also keep in mind that only an open face movement will go in an open face case and the hunting style movement in the hunting case, and that we can furnish only stem wind movements. Stem wind movements cannot be fitted in key wind cases. Do not fail to plainly write your name and address on package when sending a watch case to us for a new movement.

18-size, 7 jeweled Elgin or Waltham, nickel plates	$ 4.40
18-size, 15 jeweled Elgin or Waltham, nickel plates	5.50
18-size, 17 jeweled Elgin or Waltham, nickel plates, not adjusted	6.60
18-size, 17 jeweled C. M. Wheeler or P. S. Bartlett, Waltham	8.80
16-size, 7 jeweled Elgin or Waltham, nickel plates	5.50
16-size, 15 jeweled Elgin or Waltham	7.70
16-size, 17 jeweled No. 241 Elgin	12.65
12-size, 7 jeweled Elgin and Waltham, nickel plates	5.50
12-size, 15 jeweled Elgin or Waltham, nickel plates	7.70
12-size, 17 jeweled No. 275 grade Elgin	15.12
6-size, 7 jeweled Elgin or Waltham, nickel plates	4.95
6-size, 15 jeweled Elgin or Waltham, nickel plates	6.15
0-size, 7 jeweled Elgin or Waltham	6.05
0-size, 15 jeweled Elgin or Waltham	8.80
0-size, 17 jeweled Elgin	14.30

THERE IS NO QUESTION

regarding the quality, running ability and value of the watches that we quote and illustrate. We believe in offering **standard watches**, watches that are known throughout the watch world, Elgin, Waltham, Dueber, Hampden, Sears' Life, Kingston, Illinois and Boss gold filled cases. Nothing need to be said regarding a watch when you know it is of standard make. The names mentioned above, are in themselves sufficient guarantee as to their quality.

WE HAVE ENDEAVORED

to give the weights on the articles listed on this and the following page, or the exact postage required to mail each article. Where no postage or weight is given article can be mailed for 4 cents.

WATCH REPAIRS AT ONE-HALF THE PRICE ASKED BY OTHERS.

REMEMBER that a watch should not run longer than one and one-half years without having the oil cleaned off and fresh oil applied. An engine or sewing machine will be oiled several times a day, but we have known people to carry a watch for ten years without having it cleaned or fresh oil applied. Usually a movement thus treated **is of no value, being entirely worn out.** Our charge for cleaning and oiling is **50 cents.** The regular price is **$1.50.** We give below a list of charges for repairs which will be subject to changes in some cases; for example, old fusee watches, made some fifty or sixty years ago in England, the material of which is difficult to procure.

Balances, American Expansion	$1.50 to $2.75
Balances, American, Steel or Nickel	.50
Balances, English, Steel or Composition	1.00
Balances, Swiss, Composition	.75
Balances, Swiss, with Screw	1.25
Balances, Swiss Expansion, cut	3.00
Cleaning, ordinary Swiss, Duplex or American	.50
Cleaning, ordinary English	1.00
Demagnetizing Watch Movements	75c to 1.00
Dials, Swiss, without seconds	1.00
Dials, Swiss, with seconds	1.50
Hairsprings, ordinary flat	.75
Hairsprings, Breguet	1.50
Hands, common, each	.10
Hands, fine, each	.20
Jewels, American, Cock or Foot (with settings)	.50
Jewels, American, 3d, 4th or 'Scape	50c to .75
Jewels, Endstone, in setting	.50
Jewels, Cap, Swiss (with plate)	.25
Jewels, Swiss, 3d, 4th, 'Scape or Balance, set in plate	.50
Jewels, Swiss, 3d, 4th, 'Scape or Balance, Fine Ruby	1.50
Jewels, Swiss, Center, Fine Ruby in Gold Set	3.00
Jewels, Roller	.35
Jewels, Pallet, Set in Old Settings, American	$0.75
Mainsprings, Swiss	.50
Mainsprings, English, with hook	.75
Mainsprings, American	.50
Mainsprings, Repeaters, etc.	$1.00 to 1.50
Pallets, Fork and Arbor, complete, ordinary	3.00
Pallets, Fork and Arbor, complete, American	$1.25 to 2.50
Pinions, American, 3d, 4th or 'Scape	.75
Pinions, American Center	1.00
Pinions, American, Center, Patent, complete with Wheel	2.00
Pinions, Cannon	.50
Pinions, Swiss, 3d, 4th or 'Scape, ordinary	1.00
Pinions, Swiss, 3d, 4th or 'Scape, fine	$1.75 to 2.00
Pinions, Swiss, Center, ordinary	1.50
Pinions, Swiss, Center, fine	2.00
Pinions, Swiss, Cannon	.50
Ratchets, English, Swiss or American	.50
Staffs, Balance, American	75c to 1.25
Staffs, Balance, English, ordinary	1.25
Staffs, Balance, Swiss, ordinary	1.25
Staffs, Balance, Swiss, fine	2.50

CHANGING KEY WIND CASES TO STEM WIND.

Silver Cases	$1.50
Gold Cases	2.50

WHEN WATCHES

are sent with instructions to put them in good order we will do everything necessary to put them in good running condition, but when the instructions are to repair a certain particular part of a watch, the repairs will be strictly confined to the part or parts specified and we cannot hold ourselves responsible for anything further than may be necessary to insure correct running of the watch. In sending any part of a watch, if your intention is to fit same yourself, do not instruct us to fit same, but kindly use the word "select." This prevents misunderstanding your wishes. If an idea of the cost cannot be obtained from this list, send the watch to us and on receipt of same we will examine it, quote cost of repairing and hold for instructions.

FANCY DIAL.

We show here an illustration of the fancy dial and gold hands that we furnish on different watches quoted and illustrated on the following pages at 90 cents extra. Fancy dials cannot be fitted on every watch in our catalog. We caution you only to order them on such watches where it is clearly stated on the page that we can furnish fancy dials. The illustration merely gives you an idea of how the fancy dial will look. They are not all exactly as this picture shows, as they vary in design. They come in various tints, with floral decorations and gold work, and all of them beautiful. We furnish any size, 18, 16, 12, 6 and 0-size for American watches.

CUT PRICE, 21 CENTS.

No. 4R11004 The Ajax Watch Insulator or Protector protects your watch. It is made of a secret compounded metal, beautifully enameled, and lined with velvet. **Order by number.** The maker guarantees that this insulator protects the watch case from wear and the movement from all ordinary magnetic influence. It fits all size watches, open face or hunting style of all makes. **When ordering don't fail to give size and make of case and whether open face or hunting style is wanted.** Price......**21c**
If mail shipment, postage extra, 2 cents.

Leather Watch Protector made so as to be able to read the time. Constructed of high grade leather, has silk gathering string on top, very transparent durable celluloid front stitched in. This watch protector is meant for open face watches only. We supply it in gentlemen's 18, 16 and 12-size only. Be sure to give the size of bag wanted. Order by number.
No. 4R11008 Price......**15c**

No. 4R11010 Gold Filled Bar, gents's size. Price......**15c**
No. 4R11012 Gold Filled Bar, ladies' size. Price......**12c**

No. 4R11014 Gold Filled Swivel, gents' size. Price......**15c**
No. 4R11018 Gold Filled Swivel, ladies' size. Price......**12c**

THIS FINE WATCH BOX FOR 21 CENTS.

No. 4R11000 This illustration, made from a photograph, shows one of our fine lined and leatherette covered watch boxes that we supply for 21 cents extra with any watch purchased of us. In ordering state what size watch the case is intended for. Price......**21c**
If mail shipment, postage extra, 2 cents.

JEWELERS' COMPLETE TOOL SET FOR ONLY - - $7.12

47 Pieces in All.

Our mechanics here who do our watch work use our own tools, and the work done by us is excelled by none. This set for $7.12 consists of 47 separate and distinct pieces and text book. Any man of average mechanical skill can learn to rectify the majority of causes that make a watch stop. The set not alone includes tools necessary for watch repairing, but likewise includes a complete set of tools for silverware, jewelry and clock repairing. Shipping weight, 12 pounds.
No. 4N11278
Price for complete set, including text book............**$7.12**

WATCHMAKERS', JEWELERS' AND SILVERSMITHS' OUTFITS FOR $2.98

Our Special Drive in Tools. A Watchmakers', Jewelers' and Silversmiths' Outfit for $2.98, consisting of twenty-four distinct tools, each one being used to perform certain important work. A splendid set to practice with. You can always add from time to time necessary tools from our list of watchmakers' tools described on this page. This set consists of twenty-four separate and distinct tools and appliances, as follows: One jewelers' flat file with handle, 1 watchmakers' hammer with handle, 1 watchmakers' rubber magnifying eyeglass, 1 pair jewelers' cutting pliers, 1 pair calipers, 1 watchmakers' riveting stake, 1 small bench vise, 1 pair soldering tweezers, 1 pair watchmakers' tweezers, 1 pair of jewelers' flat pliers, 1 watchmakers' or jewelers' pin vise, 3 watchmakers' screwdrivers, each being a different size, 1 jewelers' soldering copper, 1 watchmakers' or clockmakers' brush, 4 needle files, very important for watchmakers and jewelers; 1 bundle pegwood, 3 pivot broaches. To this complete set of twenty-four distinct and separate tools is likewise added, 1 cube of refined jewelers' chalk, one bottle of watchmakers' oil, 1 bundle of watchmakers' pithwood, 1 bundle of brass wire, 1 text book. This book gives recipes, new methods, and much valuable information regarding watch repairing, stone setting and other valuable pointers. Weight, complete, about 6 pounds.
No. 4R11280 Price, complete, with all above mentioned additions..........**$2.98**

WIRE ARTISTS' OR WIRE WORKERS' COMPLETE TOOL SET FOR $1.12

SEND US $1.12 and we will ship you by express our entire Wire Workers' Outfit, exactly as illustrated. 1 pair snipe nose pliers, 1 pair round nose pliers, 1 pair side cutting pliers, 1 file with handle, 1 ounce gold plated wire (½ ounce round and ½ ounce square), ½ gross plated washers, assorted, 1 lot assorted shells, 1 drill, 2 sample names. Follow the principle used in making these names and you will know the entire art. Shipping wt., about 1¾ lbs. Order by number.
No. 4R11100 Price......**$1.12**
If mail shipment, postage extra, 18 cents.

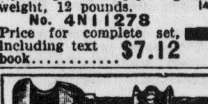

WE DO NOT carry any other watch and clock material for sale except that quoted and illustrated on this page. Should you desire balance staffs, hole jewels, mainsprings, etc., and you are not positive of the exact size of watch that you want them for, send a sample to us and state the name of the watch and the movement number and the size in inches and fractions of an inch, write us that you have sent the sample and enclose in the package your name and address so as to prevent possible loss and confusion. **REGARDING WATCH CRYSTALS.** We carry two kinds, the Geneva crystal used in hunting style cases and the mi-concave crystal or the thick beveled edge style for open face watches. These crystals vary in sizes and heights. The sizes vary 1-16 of a millimeter in diameter and the heights range from 4 to 8 millimeters. Therefore, it will be absolutely necessary, and we will not undertake to fill orders unless the exact sizes and heights are given. If you do not know these send us the bezel of the watch to be fitted with a crystal.

WATCHMAKERS', WIRE WORKERS' AND JEWELERS' TOOLS AND MATERIALS

Postage extra on articles where weight or postage not quoted in description, 4 cents.

No. 4R11102 Watch Glasses, hunting style. Price, per gross....$4.00

No. 4R11106 Watch Glasses, thick for open face. Price, per gross....$4.00

No. 4R11108 Hands, steel, for watches, hour and minute, for all sizes of American and imported watches. Price, per dozen pairs..........22c

No. 4R11112 Hands, for clocks, all lengths. Price, per dozen pairs..........20c

No. 4R11116 Hands, steel, seconds, for all sizes American and imported watches. Price, per dozen. 12c

No. 4R11120 Mainsprings, for watches, all styles and sizes. Price, per dozen...96c

No. 4R11124 Mainsprings, for clocks, 1-day. Price, each..........14c

No. 4R11128 Mainsprings, for clocks, 8-day. Price, each..........35c

No. 4R11130 Elgin Balance Staffs, all sizes. Price, per dozen..........94c

No. 4R11132 Waltham Balance Staffs, all sizes. Price, per dozen..........94c

No. 4R11136 Hampden, Springfield, Seth Thomas, Plymouth, New York Standard, Trenton or Rockford Balance Staffs, all sizes. Price, per dozen..........94c

No. 4R11140 Balance Hole Jewels, cock and foot, for Elgin, Waltham, Hampden, Springfield, Rockford, Plymouth, New York Standard, Trenton or Seth Thomas, for all sizes. Price, per dozen..........$1.18

No. 4R11144 Balance Cap or End Stones for Elgin, Waltham, Hampden, Springfield, Rockford, Plymouth, New York Standard, Trenton or Seth Thomas, all sizes. Doz..75c

No. 4R11148 Roller Jewels or Ruby Pins for Elgin, Waltham, Hampden, Springfield, Rockford, Plymouth, New York Standard, Trenton or Seth Thomas, all sizes. Price, per dozen..........60c

No. 4R11150 Alcohol Cup. Glass. Height, 1¾ inches. Diameter, 3 inches. Price..........18c Shipping wt., 11 oz.

No. 4R11262 Pegwood. Price, per bundle..........4c

No. 4R11264 Pithwood. Price, per bundle..........4c

No. 4R11154 Blow Pipe, with ball, 8 or 10 inches. Price..........14c

No. 4R11156 Blow Pipe, plain without ball, 8 or 10 inches. Price, each......8c

No. 4R11158 Watch Brush, 3-row. Price..........14c

No. 4R11160 4-row. Price..........23c

No. 4R11164 Calipers, 3½ inches long, plain brass. Price..........14c

No. 4R11168 Calipers, with bar, 3½ inches long. Plain brass. Price..........23c

No. 4R11274 Screw Plate, 36 holes. Price..........68c

No. 4R11276 Poising Tool, as illustrated, for poising and truing watch wheels. Price..........28c

No. 4R11266 Pliers, flat, Swiss make, 4-inch. Price..........19c

No. 4R11268 Pliers, or hand tongs. Price. 28c

No. 4R11270 Pliers, round, Swiss make, 4-inch. Price..........19c

No. 4R11178 Pliers, end cutting, Swiss make, 4-inch. Price..........42c

No. 4R11180 Pliers, side cutting, Swiss make, 4-inch. Price..........42c

No. 4R11166 Gauge, for watch mainsprings, with gauge for measuring thickness. Length, 5 inches. Price..........42c

No. 4R11172 Movement Holder. Adjustable for watch movements. Price..........28c

No. 4R11170 Oil Cup, boxwood, for watch oil. Price..........14c

No. 4R11174 Common All Glass Lamp. Price..........27c

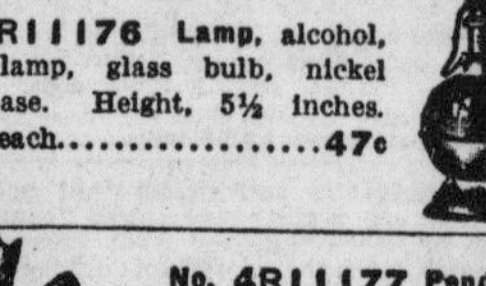

No. 4R11176 Lamp, alcohol, spheric lamp, glass bulb, nickel plated base. Height, 5½ inches. Price, each..........47c

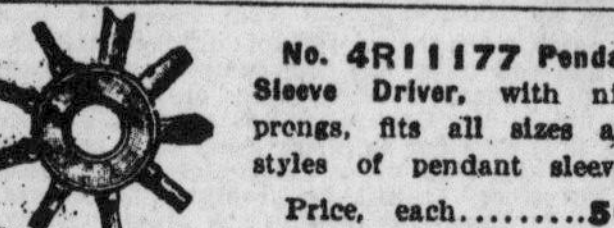

No. 4R11177 Pendant Sleeve Driver, with nine prongs, fits all sizes and styles of pendant sleeves. Price, each..........56c

Prices of Gold Plated Wire and Wire Workers' Material.

We cannot sell any of this material in smaller quantities than quoted.

No. 4R11182 1st quality round wire. Sizes, 16 to 21-gauge. Price, per ounce..........62c

No. 4R11184 2nd quality round wire. Sizes, 16 to 21-gauge. Price, per ounce..........43c

No. 4R11188 3rd quality round wire. Sizes, 16 to 21-gauge. Price, per ounce..........18c

No. 4R11190 1st quality square wire. Sizes, 18 to 22-gauge. Price, per ounce. 62c

No. 4R11194 2nd quality square wire. Sizes, 18 to 22-gauge. Price, per ounce..43c

No. 4R11198 3rd quality square wire. Sizes, 18 to 22-gauge. Price, per ounce..18c

No. 4R11200 Fine Eye Shells for Hat Pins. Price, per dozen..........28c

No. 4R11204 Jobbing Stones, assorted. Containing all colors and sizes in imitation of genuine. Per gross. 72c

No. 4R11208 Money Cowrie Shells for Cuff Buttons. Price, per 100.....34c

No. 4R11212 Shells. Assortment. In box. Price..........14c

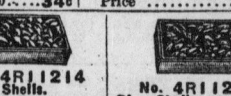

No. 4R11214 Coffee Shells. Price, per 100..........22c

No. 4R11218 Rice Shells. Price, per 100..16c

No. 4R11220 Panama Shells. Price, per 100..........$1.00

No. 4R11224 Large Brown Sea Beans. Price, per dozen. 18c

No. 4R11226 Large Red Sea Beans. Price, per 100..38c

No. 4R11230 Drills, 1 dozen, assorted sizes, Crown make. Price, per dozen..21c No less than 1 dozen sold.

No. 4R11232 Drill Stock. 10 inches long. Patent spiral with six drills extra, not shown in illustration. Price..22c

No. 4R11234 Drill Stock, patent geared with adjustable split chuck; top of drill unscrews and has receptacle for holding drills; 10½ inches long. Price..........(Postage, 16c)..........79c

No. 4R11236 Eye Glass, hard rubber with coil spring; 2 to 5-inch focus. Price..........34c

No. 4R11238 Eye Glass, plain, hard rubber, without spring; 2 to 5-inch focus. Price..........22c

No. 4R11240 Eye Glass, plain, without spring; 2 to 5-inch focus; aluminum frame. Price..........23c

No. 4R11242 Eye Glass, double lens. Very powerful, used for very accurate work. Price..........40c

No. 4R11246 Files, needle; any shape shown above. Length of file complete with handle, 4 inches. Price, set of six..........45c

No. 4R11248 Flat Files
3-inch cut 3. Price..........19c
4-inch cut 3. Price..........22c
5-inch cut 3. Price..........28c

No. 4R11250 Half Round Files.
3-inch cut 3. Price..........19c
4-inch cut 3. Price..........22c
5-inch cut 3. Price..........28c

No. 4R11254 Files, screw head, for filing slots in screw heads. Length, 3½ inches. Price..........18c

No. 11256 Hammers, Swiss.

2 inches. Each.	14c	2¾ inches. Each.	18c
2¼ inches. Each.	14c	3¼ inches. Each.	21c
2½ inches. Each.	14c	3¾ inches. Each.	23c

No. 4R11260 Handles, for hammers. Maple. Price..........4c

No. 4R11320 Soldering Copper, small, for jewelers. Price..........14c

No. 4R11322 Soldering Fluid. Price, per bottle......14c

No. 4R11324 Anti-Oxidizer, used for retaining the color on metal when hard soldering. Price, per bottle..........14c

No. 4R11326 Watch or Clock Oil. State kind wanted. Price, per bottle....14c

No. 4R11328 Watch Oil, nickel plated. Price..........8c

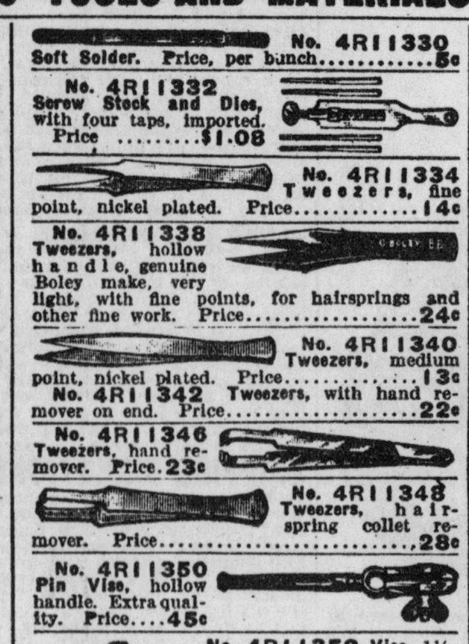

No. 4R11330 Soft Solder. Price, per bunch..........5c

No. 4R11332 Screw Stock and Dies, with four taps, imported. Price..........$1.08

No. 4R11334 Tweezers, fine point, nickel plated. Price..........14c

No. 4R11338 Tweezers, hollow handle, genuine Boley make, very light, with fine points, for hairsprings and other fine work. Price..........24c

No. 4R11340 Tweezers, medium point, nickel plated. Price..........13c

No. 4R11342 Tweezers, with hand remover on end. Price..........22c

No. 4R11346 Tweezers, hand remover. Price. 23c

No. 4R11348 Tweezers, hairspring collet remover. Price..........28c

No. 4R11350 Pin Vise, hollow handle. Extra quality. Price.....45c

No. 4R11358 Vise, 1½-inch steel jaws, clamp vise, handy to adjust to any work bench. Weight, 2½ pounds. Price..........70c

No. 4R11360 Same size jaws as above, but with swivel bar base. Weight, 3 pounds. Price..........94c

No. 4R11364 Winder, mainspring, Swiss. Length, 3½ inches. Price..........33c

No. 4R11282 Key. Birch patent key; will wind any watch. Price. 9c

No. 4R11286 Jewelers' Cement. For cementing china, glass, ivory, beads, pearls, jewels, etc. Price, per bottle..........23c

No. 4R11290 Granite Hold Fast Cement. Price, per bottle.......14c

No. 4R11292 Punch, mainspring with four punches and mainspring barrel hook punch, nickel plated. Length, 7 inches. Price. $1.08 If mail shipment, postage extra, 12 cents.

No. 4R11294 Roller Remover, screw action. Price, each...52c

No. 4R11296 Ruby Pin Setter. Price, each. 19c

No. 4R11298 Screwdrivers, set of six, nickel plated, with colored celluloid heads; in pasteboard box. Set of six. $1.25

No. 4R11300 Metal Head Screwdriver, in small, medium or large size. Be sure to state size wanted. Price, each..........8c

No. 4R11304 Screwdriver, adjustable, nickel plated, with four different sized blades. Price..........19c

No. 4R11306 Stacking and Punching Set. 24 punches and hollow steel stake in boxwood box with cover. Price..........98c Postage extra, 8 cents.

No. 4R11310 Drills. Set of forty-eight drills, assorted sizes with drill stock in boxwood box. Price..........94c

No. 4R11312 Saw Frame, nickel plated, extra quality. Price..........58c

No. 4R11314 Saw Frame, Swiss, imported, not nickel plated. Price..........30c

No. 4R11316 Saw. Price, per dozen. 7c Not less than 1 dozen sold.

No. 4R11354 Pin Vise, small, adjustable. Price..........14c

No. 4R11355 Stake, riveting, hard steel. Price, each..........19c

$1.57 FOR $2.50 WATCHES

LADIES' OR GENTS' SIZE

$1.57 EACH

These watches are sold the world over for $2.50 each. Your choice any size for $1.57, a gentlemen's regulation 16-size, gentlemen's regulation small 12-size or ladies' 6-size.

The movements are American made, stem wind and pendant set, all guaranteed for one year by the manufacturer; the manufacturer's guarantee accompanies each one.

The cases are nickel open face, snap back and front. Be sure to order by number.

No. 4R12150 Gentlemen's 16-size. Price..........$1.57

No. 4R12152 Gentlemen's 12-size. Price..........$1.57

No. 4R12154 Ladies' 6-size. Price..........$1.57

If mail shipment, postage extra, 4 cents.

No. 4R12150 to No. 4R12154

$2.28 GENUINE SILVERODE 16-SIZE ALL AMERICAN WATCH

$2.28 for this plain polished, extra thin model silverode, open face, dust and damp proof watch.

The movement is American made and guaranteed for 5 years, has 7 jewels, lever escapement, plates are solid nickel, beautifully damaskeened, fine blued steel hair spring, and pretty tinted dial.

The case is solid genuine silverode, through and through. Silverode is a composition metal, made to imitate silver. It is tougher than silver, of greater tensile strength. Will not rust or corrode, plain polished, Bassene style, with antique crown bow and stem, is open face, screw back and screw bezel, dust and damp proof. Complete case and movement for $2.28. We can fit this case with genuine 7-jewel Elgin movement for $5.95.

No. 4R12156 Solid Silverode Watch. Price..........$2.28

No. 4R12158 Solid Silverode Watch, with genuine 7-jewel Elgin movement. Price..........$5.95

No. 4R12156
No. 4R12158

ADIES' AND GENTLEMEN'S WATCH FOBS

The illustrations are all in reduced size with the exception of No. 4N15650, but we have in every instance given the true length and width of each one.

If by mail, postage on ladies' or gentlemen's fob, 3 cents; registered, 8 cents extra.

$3.98

No. 4N15650 Gentlemen's gold filled, patent hard soldered woven wire Safety Fob, with fancy lion's head stone set slide and signet charm, finished in bright polish or Roman yellow rose finish. Length, 4½ inches; width, 1 inch. This illustration gives you an idea of the appearance of a full sized fob, bringing out in detail the various engravings, scrollwork, stone sets and finish. Monogram cut in signet two or three letters, 20 cents extra. Price $3.98

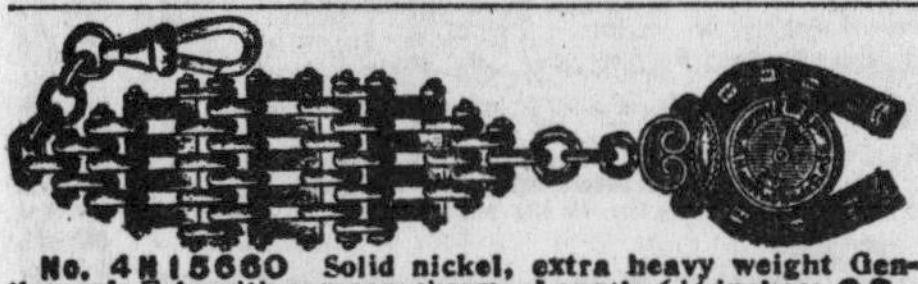

No. 4N15660 Solid nickel, extra heavy weight Gentlemen's Fob, with compass charm. Length, 6½ inches; width, 1 inch. Price 32c

No. 4N15662 Gentlemen's Silk Fob, rolled gold plate mountings, cameo set charm. Length, 7 inches; width, 1½ inches. Price 55c

No. 4N15664 Silk Fob, gold filled mountings, bright polish, fancy gold filled charm, Roman rose satin finish. Length, 7 inches; width, 1¾ inches. Price.. 87c

No. 4N15666 Ladies' Silk Ribbon Patent Safety Fob, with gold filled slide and gold filled signet charm. Length, 4¾ inches; width, ⅝ inch. Price $1.39
Monogram cut in signet, two or three letters, 15 cents extra.

No. 4N15668 Gentlemen's New Patent Safety Fob, fine ribbed silk ribbon with gold filled bright polish slide and charm set with fancy pink stone, something new and ornate. Length, 5¾ in.; width, 1 inch. Price $2.15

No. 4N15670 Gentlemen's Silk Fob, with bright polish gold filled slide and signet charm. Copied after a solid gold pattern. Length, 6½ in.; width, 1⅜ in. Price. $2.35
Monogram cut in signet, two or three letters, 20 cents extra.

No. 4N15672 Gentlemen's Silk Fob, with gold filled mounting and gold filled bright polish locket charm, holds two pictures. Length, 8½ in.; width, 1⅜ in. Price $2.60
Monogram cut on charm, two or three letters, 25 cents extra.

No. 4N15674 Solid gold charm and mountings, bright polish. Length, 6 inches; width, 1¼ inches. Price, complete $4.95
No. 4N15676 Same style and size as above, but in fine gold filled stock. Price, complete..... 1.80
Two or three-letter monogram engraved on either of the above, 40 cents extra.

No. 4N15678 Leather Fob with mother of pearl slide and hand carved ivory horse head charm. Bridle and bit in rolled gold plate. The leather is tanned with the natural hair still on; swivel, top bar and slides done in gold filled stock. Price..... $1.89

No. 4N15680 Ladies' Safety Fob, bright polish, gold filled, woven wire, has signet charm. Length, 4 inches; width, ½ inch. Price..... $1.60
Monogram cut in signet, two or three letters, 15 cents extra.

No. 4N15682 Gold filled, patent, ladies' hard soldered woven wire Safety Fob. Plain polish. Top and bottom ornaments hand chased, bright polished center slide. Length, 4¼ inches; width, ⅝ inch. Price, complete.. $1.72
Two-letter monogram, 20 cents extra.

No. 4N15684 Gold filled, patent, hard soldered woven wire Safety Fob. Bright polish. Top and bottom ornaments hand chased, bright polish center slide, signet charm. Length, 5 inches; width, ¾ inch. Price, complete... $1.79
Two-letter monogram, 20 cents extra.

No. 4N15686 Gold filled mountings, bright polish, gold filled, woven wire Watch Fob, signet charm made to be engraved Length, 5 inches; width, ⅞ inch. Price, complete..... $1.89
Two-letter monogram, 20 cents extra.

No. 4N15688 Ladies' gold filled, bright polish, soldered woven wire patent Safety Fob, with fancy red stone sets in slide and charm. Length, 3¾ inches; width, ½ inch. Price..... $1.90

No. 4N15690 Ladies' Safety Fob, bright polish, gold filled, woven wire, has signet charm. Length, 4 inches; width, ⅝ inch. Price, complete..... $2.10
Monogram cut in signet, two or three letters, 15 cents extra.

No. 4N15692 Gold filled, patent, hard soldered woven wire Safety Fob. Top and bottom ornaments hand chased, bright polish center slide, signet charm. Length of chain, 4½ inches; width, 1 inch. Price, complete..... $2.39
Two-letter monogram, 20 cents extra.

No. 4N15694 Gold filled, patent hard soldered woven wire Safety Fob with fancy slide and signet charm. Length, 5 inches; width, 1 inch. Price, complete..... $2.60
Monogram cut in signet, two or three letters, 20 cents extra.

No. 4N15696 Gold filled, patent hard soldered woven wire Safety Fob, top and bottom ornaments hand chased, bright polish center slide. Length, 4½ inches; width, 1 inch. Price, complete..... $2.65
Two-letter monogram, 20 cents extra.

No. 4N15714 Gentlemen's new patent Safety Fob, extra quality, gold filled, woven wire, bright polish, with fine flat signet charm. Length, 4¾ in.; width, 1 in. Price, $5.38

No. 4N15698 Gold filled, patent, hard soldered woven wire Safety Fob with fancy slide and signet charm. Length, 5 inches; width, 1 inch. Price, complete..... $2.90
Monogram cut in signet, 2 or 3 letters, 20c. extra.

No. 4N15700 Gold filled, patent hard soldered Safety Fob. Bright polish signet charm. Entire length, 5¼ inches; width, 1 inch. Price, complete..... $2.89
Two-letter monogram, 20 cents extra.

No. 4N15702 New Safety Fob, with patent fastener, gold filled mountings and one large fancy set in charm. Hand engraved buckle. Length, 5 in.; width, 1 inch. Price, complete..... $3.00

No. 4N15704 Gold filled, patent, hard soldered woven wire Safety Fob, bright polish signet charm. Entire length, 4½ inches; width, 1¼ inches. Price, complete, $3.14
Two-letter monogram, 20 cents extra.

No. 4N15706 Gold filled, patent, hard soldered woven wire Safety Fob, signet and charm. Bright polish. Entire length, 5 inches; width, 1¼ inches. Price, complete $3.26
Two-letter monogram, 20 cents extra.

No. 4N15708 Gold filled, patent, hard soldered woven wire Safty Fob. Top and bottom ornaments hand chased, bright polish center slide, fancy stone set charm. Length, 4½ inches; width, 1 inch. Price, complete.. $3.45
Two-letter monogram, 20 cents extra.

No. 4N15710 Gentlemen's new Safety Fob with patent fastener, gold filled woven wire, hard soldered ornaments, bright polish signet charm. Length, 5 inches; width, 1 inch. Price, complete..... $3.65
Monogram cut in signet, two or three letters, 20 cents extra.

No. 4N15712 Gentlemen's new gold filled, bright polish, patent Safety Fob with gold front hand engraved slide and signet charm. Fob built on the roller link principle, all jointed, all capped. L'gth, 4½ in.; width, 1 in. Price, $4.90
Monogram cut in signet, two or three letters, 20 cents extra.

LADIES' GUARD OR LORGNETTE CHAINS IN SILK, ROLLED GOLD PLATE, GOLD FILLED AND SOLID GOLD STOC

Postage on Ladies' Guard or Lorgnette Chains, each, 4 Cents. 8 Cents Extra for Registry.

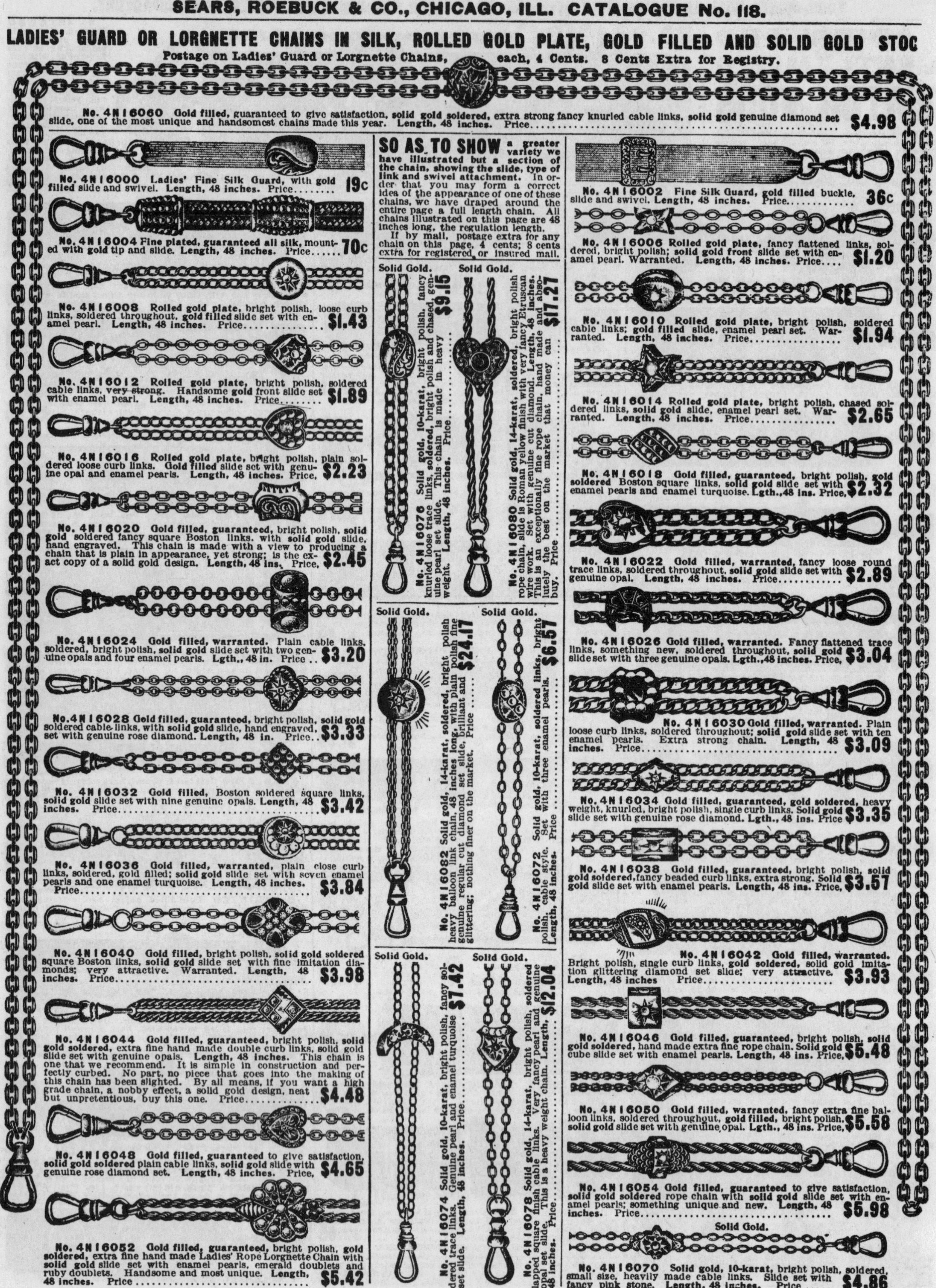

No. 4N16060 Gold filled, guaranteed to give satisfaction, solid gold soldered, extra strong fancy knurled cable links, solid gold genuine diamond set slide, one of the most unique and handsomest chains made this year. Length, 48 inches. Price........ **$4.98**

No. 4N16000 Ladies' Fine Silk Guard, with gold filled slide and swivel. Length, 48 inches. Price........ **19c**

No. 4N16004 Fine plated, guaranteed all silk, mounted with gold tip and slide. Length, 48 inches. Price...... **70c**

No. 4N16008 Rolled gold plate, bright polish, loose curb links, soldered throughout, gold filled slide set with enamel pearl. Length, 48 inches. Price.............. **$1.43**

No. 4N16012 Rolled gold plate, bright polish, soldered cable links, very strong. Handsome gold front slide set with enamel pearl. Length, 48 inches. Price........ **$1.89**

No. 4N16016 Rolled gold plate, bright polish, plain soldered loose curb links. Gold filled slide set with genuine opal and enamel pearls. Length, 48 inches. Price, **$2.23**

No. 4N16020 Gold filled, guaranteed, bright polish, solid gold soldered fancy square Boston links, with solid gold slide, hand engraved. This chain is made with a view to producing a chain that is plain in appearance, yet strong; is the exact copy of a solid gold design. Length, 48 ins. Price, **$2.45**

No. 4N16024 Gold filled, warranted. Plain cable links, soldered, bright polish, solid gold slide set with two genuine opals and four enamel pearls. Lgth., 48 in. Price.. **$3.20**

No. 4N16028 Gold filled, guaranteed, bright polish, solid gold soldered cable links, with solid gold slide, hand engraved, set with genuine rose diamond. Length, 48 in. Price.. **$3.33**

No. 4N16032 Gold filled, Boston soldered square links, solid gold slide set with nine genuine opals. Length, 48 inches. Price........ **$3.42**

No. 4N16036 Gold filled, warranted, plain close curb links, soldered, gold filled; solid gold slide set with seven enamel pearls and one enamel turquoise. Length, 48 inches. Price........ **$3.84**

No. 4N16040 Gold filled, bright polish, solid gold soldered square Boston links, solid gold slide set with fine imitation diamonds; very attractive. Warranted. Length, 48 inches. Price........ **$3.98**

No. 4N16044 Gold filled, guaranteed, bright polish, solid gold soldered, extra fine hand made double curb links, solid gold slide set with genuine opals. Length, 48 inches. This chain is one that we recommend. It is simple in construction and perfectly curbed. No part, no piece that goes into the making of this chain has been slighted. By all means, if you want a high grade chain, a nobby effect, a solid gold design, neat but unpretentious, buy this one. Price........ **$4.48**

No. 4N16048 Gold filled, guaranteed to give satisfaction, solid gold soldered plain cable links, solid gold slide with genuine rose diamond set. Length, 48 inches. Price, **$4.65**

No. 4N16052 Gold filled, guaranteed, bright polish, gold soldered, extra fine hand made Ladies' Rope Lorgnette Chain with solid gold slide set with enamel pearls, emerald doublets and ruby doublets. Handsome and most unique. Length, 48 inches. Price........ **$5.42**

SO AS TO SHOW a greater variety we have illustrated but a section of the chain, showing the slide, type of link and swivel attachment. In order that you may form a correct idea of the appearance of one of these chains, we have draped around the entire page a full length chain. All chains illustrated on this page are 48 inches long, the regulation length.

If by mail, postage extra for any chain on this page, 4 cents; 8 cents extra for registered or insured mail.

Solid Gold.

No. 4N16076 Solid gold, 10-karat, bright polish, fancy knurled loose trace links, soldered, bright polish and chased, genuine pearl set slide. This chain is made in heavy weight. Length, 48 inches. Price........ **$9.15**

Solid Gold.

No. 4N16080 Solid gold, 14-karat, soldered, bright polish rope chain, slide is Roman yellow finish with very fancy Etruscan wire work. Set with genuine cut diamond. Length, 48 inches. This is an exceptionally fine rope chain, hand made and absolutely the best on the market that money can buy. Price........ **$17.27**

Solid Gold.

No. 4N16082 Solid gold, 14-karat, soldered, bright polish heavy balloon link chain, 48 inches long, with plain polish fine genuine regular cut diamond set slide, brilliant and glittering; nothing finer on the market. Price **$24.17**

Solid Gold.

No. 4N16072 Solid gold, 10-karat, soldered links, bright polish, cable style. Set with three enamel pearls. Length, 48 inches. Price........ **$6.57**

Solid Gold.

No. 4N16074 Solid gold, 10-karat, bright polish, fancy soldered trace links. Genuine pearl and enamel turquoise set slide. Length, 48 inches. Price........ **$7.42**

Solid Gold.

No. 4N16078 Solid gold, 14-karat, bright polish, soldered lapped square finish cable links. Very fancy pearl and genuine opal set slide. This is a heavy weight chain. Length, 48 inches. Price........ **$12.04**

No. 4N16002 Fine Silk Guard, gold filled buckle, slide and swivel. Length, 48 inches. Price........ **36c**

No. 4N16006 Rolled gold plate, fancy flattened links, soldered, bright polish; solid gold front slide set with enamel pearl. Warranted. Length, 48 inches. Price.... **$1.20**

No. 4N16010 Rolled gold plate, bright polish, soldered cable links; gold filled slide, enamel pearl set. Warranted. Length, 48 inches. Price................ **$1.94**

No. 4N16014 Rolled gold plate, bright polish, chased soldered links, solid gold slide, enamel pearl set. Warranted. Length, 48 inches. Price........ **$2.65**

No. 4N16018 Gold filled, guaranteed, bright polish, gold soldered Boston square links, solid gold slide set with enamel pearls and enamel turquoise. Lgth., 48 ins. Price, **$2.32**

No. 4N16022 Gold filled, warranted, fancy loose round trace links, soldered throughout, solid gold slide set with genuine opal. Length, 48 inches. Price............ **$2.89**

No. 4N16026 Gold filled, warranted. Fancy flattened trace links, something new, soldered throughout, solid gold slide set with three genuine opals. Lgth., 48 inches. Price, **$3.04**

No. 4N16030 Gold filled, warranted. Plain loose curb links, soldered throughout; solid gold slide set with ten enamel pearls. Extra strong chain. Length, 48 inches. Price........ **$3.09**

No. 4N16034 Gold filled, guaranteed, gold soldered, heavy weight, knurled, bright polish, single curb links. Solid gold slide set with genuine rose diamond. Lgth., 48 ins. Price **$3.35**

No. 4N16038 Gold filled, guaranteed, bright polish, solid gold soldered, fancy beaded curb links, extra strong. Solid gold slide set with enamel pearls. Length, 48 ins. Price, **$3.57**

No. 4N16042 Gold filled, warranted. Bright polish, single curb links, gold soldered, solid gold imitation glittering diamond set slide; very attractive. Length, 48 inches Price........ **$3.93**

No. 4N16046 Gold filled, guaranteed, bright polish, solid gold soldered, hand made extra fine rope chain. Solid gold cube slide set with enamel pearls. Length, 48 ins. Price, **$5.48**

No. 4N16050 Gold filled, warranted, fancy extra fine balloon links, soldered throughout, gold filled, bright polish, solid gold slide set with genuine opal. Lgth., 48 ins. Price, **$5.58**

No. 4N16054 Gold filled, guaranteed to give satisfaction, solid gold soldered rope chain with solid gold slide set with enamel pearls; something unique and new. Length, 48 inches. Price........ **$5.98**

Solid Gold.

No. 4N16070 Solid gold, 10-karat, bright polish, soldered, small size, heavily made cable links. Slide set with fancy pink stone. Length, 48 inches. Price **$4.86**

GENTLEMEN'S ROYALTY CHAINS

$2.86

No. 4H0620 Gold filled, warranted 20 years, charm set with sardonyx. Illustration shows exact size. Price......$2.86

No. 4H0624 Gold filled, soldered, double rope, warranted 20 years, pearl set charm. Same style and length as No. 4H0620. Price.........................$3.57

No. 4H0622 Polished double links, gold filled, warranted 20 years, head engraved stone charm. Same style and length as No. 4H0620. Price..........................$3.09

No. 4H0654 Rolled gold plate pony vest chain, warranted 6 years, plain polish, sardonyx charm. Length, 8 inches. Price........96c

No. 4H0652 Gold filled pony vest chain, warranted 20 years, brown onyx set charm. Length, 8 inches. Price, $2.04

No. 4H0634 Fancy flattened loose trace links, rolled gold plate, bright polish, warranted 6 years. Fancy stone set charm. Same length as No. 4H0620. Price..$1.68

No. 4H0644 Sears' Life Guarantee chain, gold filled, bright polish, gold soldered loose curb links. Genuine stone set charm. Same length as No. 4H0620. Price..............$5.15

No. 4H0660 Ladies' Safety Fob Chain, gold filled, bright polish and engraved, with plain polish substantially made signet charm. Length, 3 inches. Price..................$4.00
Two or three-letter monogram, 25 cents extra.

BEST QUALITY ROLLED GOLD PLATE, GOLD FILLED AND SOLID GOLD MOUNTINGS, FOR GENTS' AND LADIES' HAIR AND SILK VEST CHAINS.

No. 4H0662 Gold filled, set with pearl and two garnets. Price, per set, including bar, toggle and swivel. Price..........................92c

No. 4H0664 Fine solid gold. Price, per set, including bar, toggle and swivel..............$4.75

HAIR CHAINS.

No. 4H0666 Hair Chain braided to order, like illustration. Price.....................$1.00
Requires about $1\frac{1}{2}$ ounces hair combings to braid a chain. Is made in two pieces, and together with mountings is $12\frac{1}{2}$ inches long. We do not do this braiding ourselves. We send it out; therefore we cannot guarantee same hair being used that is sent us: you must assume all risk. When you send in your hair to be braided be sure to write us when you do so and put your name and address on package. No extra charge for mounting the hair chain when the mountings are purchased from us.

No. 4H0661 Same as above; two strands. For mounting see No. 4H0667. Price..$1.50

No. 4H0784 Best quality gold filled fluted pattern, engraved. Price, per set, including, bar, toggle and swivel.......................76c

No. 4H0668 Fancy woven three-strand hair vest guard, $8\frac{1}{2}$ inches long with very fancy rolled gold plate tips, slide bar and swivel. Price, $1.19

We will not quote prices on this guard made to order, as the braiding is machine work.

No. 4H0673 Silk Vest Chain, gold filled mountings. Length, 12 inches. Price.........72c

No. 4H0667 Gold filled, hand engraved, made for double hair chain.

Price, per set, including bar, toggle and swivel..........................$1.10

No. 4H0670 Silk Vest Chain, three strands, gold filled mountings. Length, 9 inches. Price.......81c

No. 4H0672 Silk Vest Chain, gold filled mountings. Length, 11 inches. Price..........67c

No. 4H0674 Silk Vest Chain, fancy braided, gold filled mountings. Length, 7 inches. Price........82c

No. 4H0676 Silk Vest Chain, gold filled mountings. Length, 9 inches. Price......$1.20

NEW INITIAL SILK COMBINATION MONOGRAM FOB.

With New Patent Safety Chain. Any Combination of Three Letters, as You Desire, on Charm.

We are the first and only catalogue firm to come out with this latest idea in a gentleman's monogram, silk watch fob. Never before made, except in solid gold, selling for $12.00 to $25.00. This fob is manufactured by the P. J. Cummings Company, of Attleboro, Mass., and is patented. Chain, swivel and top bar being of rolled gold plate. The charm is gold front, bright polished. Fob is 7 inches long and ⅝ inch broad.

When ordering, be sure to give us catalogue number and state in your letter what three initials you want, being careful to print each letter plainly and distinctly. We cannot construct it with less than three letters.

We will be able to ship your order the same day we receive it. No delay in making same. This fob is meeting with gigantic success among schools and colleges as well as among individuals. If you are a college man and desire to have the three letters of the college fraternity used, we can do so.

No. 4H0677 Patent Safety Combination Monogram Fob, complete. Price..$1.96

No. 4H0678 Charm only, with three letters, can be used for watch charm or for ladies' neck pendant. Price, each..............................88c

GENTLEMEN'S ROLLED GOLD PLATE AND GOLD FILLED SOLID GOLD SOLDERED DOUBLE AND SINGLE ROYALTY CHAINS AND FOBS

IF BY MAIL, POSTAGE EXTRA, 3 CENTS; REGISTERED OR INSURED MAIL, 8 CENTS EXTRA.

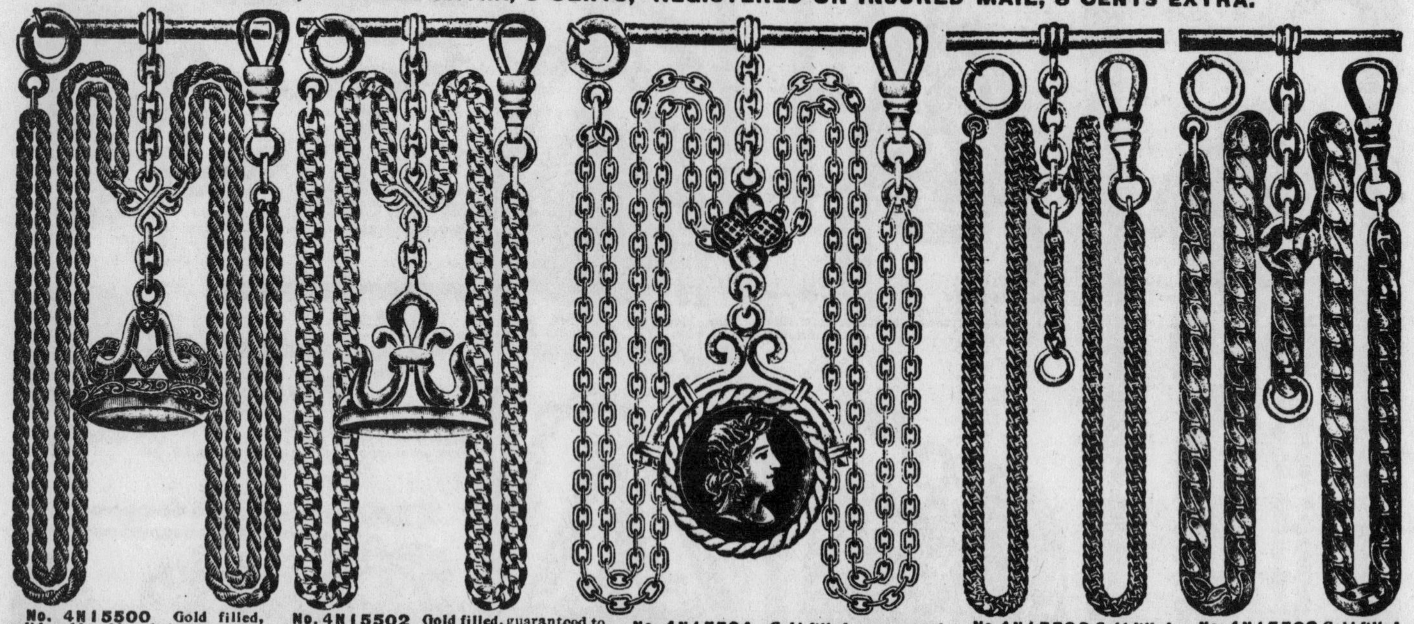

No. 4N15500 Gold filled, solid gold soldered, bright polish double rope chain. Length, 13 inches. Complete with gold filled, gold soldered, bright polish, chased, mother of pearl set charm. Price........ **$3.49**

No. 4N15502 Gold filled, guaranteed to give satisfaction; solid gold soldered, flattened double curb links. Length of chain from end to end, 14 inches. Fine gold filled signet charm. Price........... **$3.98**
Two or three-letter monogram cut in signet, 15 cents extra.

No. 4N15504 Gold filled, guaranteed, gold soldered, bright polish, plain strong cable links. Length of chain, 13 inches. Gold front, hand engraved center slide; gold filled, gold soldered, fancy cameo set charm. Price.............. **$2.63**

No. 4N15506 Gold filled, guaranteed to give satisfaction; solid gold soldered Royalty Chain, flattened double curb links. Length, 15 inches. Price........... **$2.85**

No. 4N15508 Gold filled guaranteed to give satisfaction; solid gold soldered, lapped squared curb links, extra strong. Length, 15½ inches. Price........... **$4.48**

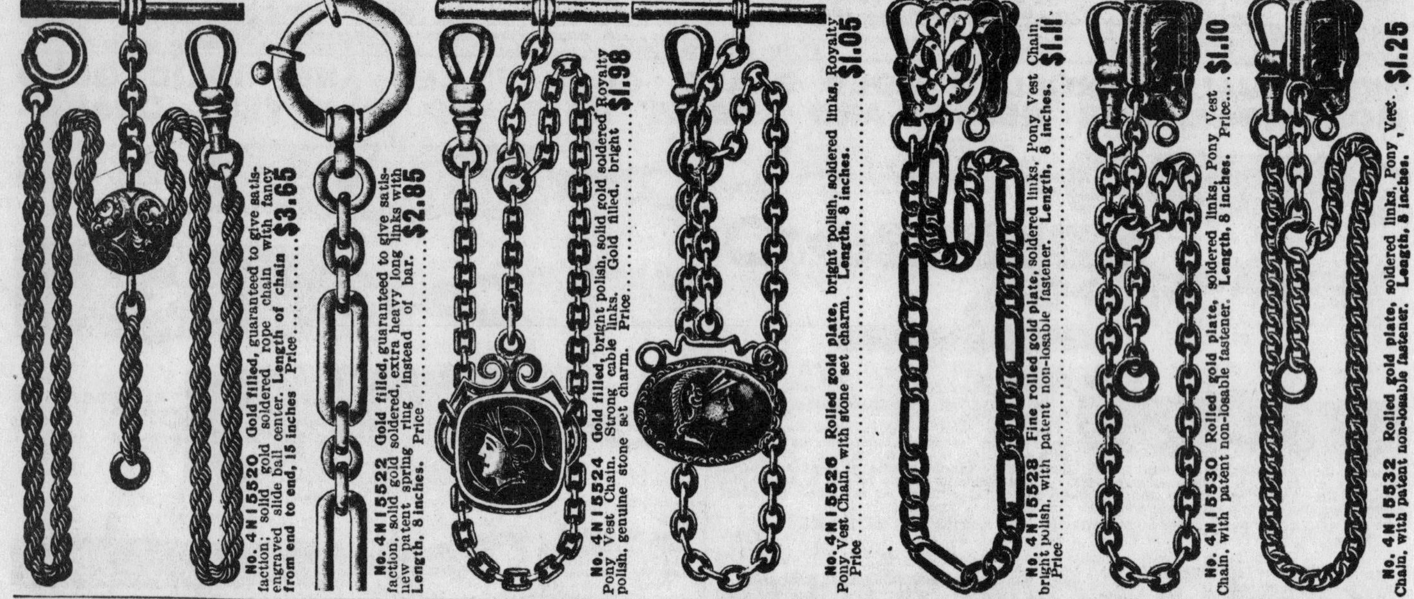

No. 4N15520 Gold filled, guaranteed to give satisfaction; solid gold soldered rope chain with fancy engraved slide ball center. Length of chain from end to end, 15 inches Price........... **$3.65**

No. 4N15522 Gold filled, guaranteed to give satisfaction, solid gold soldered, extra heavy long links with new patent spring ring instead of bar. Length, 8 inches. Price........... **$2.85**

No. 4N15524 Gold filled, bright polish, solid gold soldered Royalty Pony Vest Chain. Strong cable links. Gold filled, bright polish, genuine stone set charm. Price........... **$1.98**

No. 4N15526 Rolled gold plate, bright polish, soldered links, Royalty Pony Vest Chain, with stone set charm. Length, 8 inches. Price........... **$1.05**

No. 4N15528 Fine rolled gold plate, soldered links, Pony Vest Chain, bright polish, with patent non-losable fastener. Length, 8 inches. Price........... **$1.11**

No. 4N15530 Rolled gold plate, soldered links, Pony Vest Chain, with patent non-losable fastener. Length, 8 inches. Price.... **$1.10**

No. 4N15532 Rolled gold plate, soldered links, Pony Vest Chain, with patent non-losable fastener. Length, 8 inches. **$1.25**

No. 4N15534 Ladies' Gold Filled Patent Woven Wire Safety Fob, slide set with fancy stones. Length, 3¾ inches; width, ½ inch. Price **$2.25**

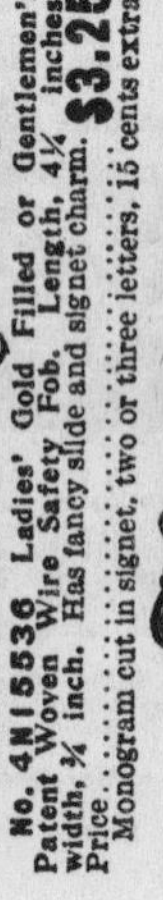

No. 4N15536 Ladies' Gold Filled or Gentlemen's Patent Woven Wire Safety Fob. Length, 4¼ inches; width, ¾ inch. Has fancy slide and signet charm. Price........... **$3.25**
Monogram cut in signet, two or three letters, 15 cents extra.

No. 4N15538 Gentlemen's Gold Filled Fancy Link Fob with patent safety fastener, signet charm. Length, 5 inches; width, ⅞ inch. Price...... **$3.98**
Monogram cut in signet, two or three letters, 15 cents extra.

No. 4N15540 Ladies' or Gentlemen's Gold Filled Woven Wire Patent Safety Fob, slide and signet charm. Length, 4½ inches; width, ⅝ inch. Price **$2.48**
Monogram cut in signet, two or three letters, 15 cents extra.

No. 4N15542 Gentlemen's Gold Filled Woven Wire Patent Safety Fob, tiger head slide set with fancy stones, signet charm. Length, 4½ inches; width, ¾ inch. Price........... **$3.48**
Monogram cut in signet, two or three letters, 15 cents extra.

$1.64

No. 4N15544 New Initial Silk Combination Monogram Fob with patent safety chain. Chain, swivel, and top bar are rolled gold plate, charm with letters is gold front. Length, 7 inches; width, 1⅜ inches. When ordering be sure to state distinctly the letters you want. No delay in making shipment; can supply either two or three-letter combination at the price quoted. Price........... **$1.64**

No. 4N15546 Black Leather Patent Safety Fob with chain attachment. Can supply any initials you may want, two or three letters; when ordering be sure to state distinctly the initials you want. Charm is gold front, bright polish. Length, 4⅞ inches; width, ½ inch. Price........... **$1.72**

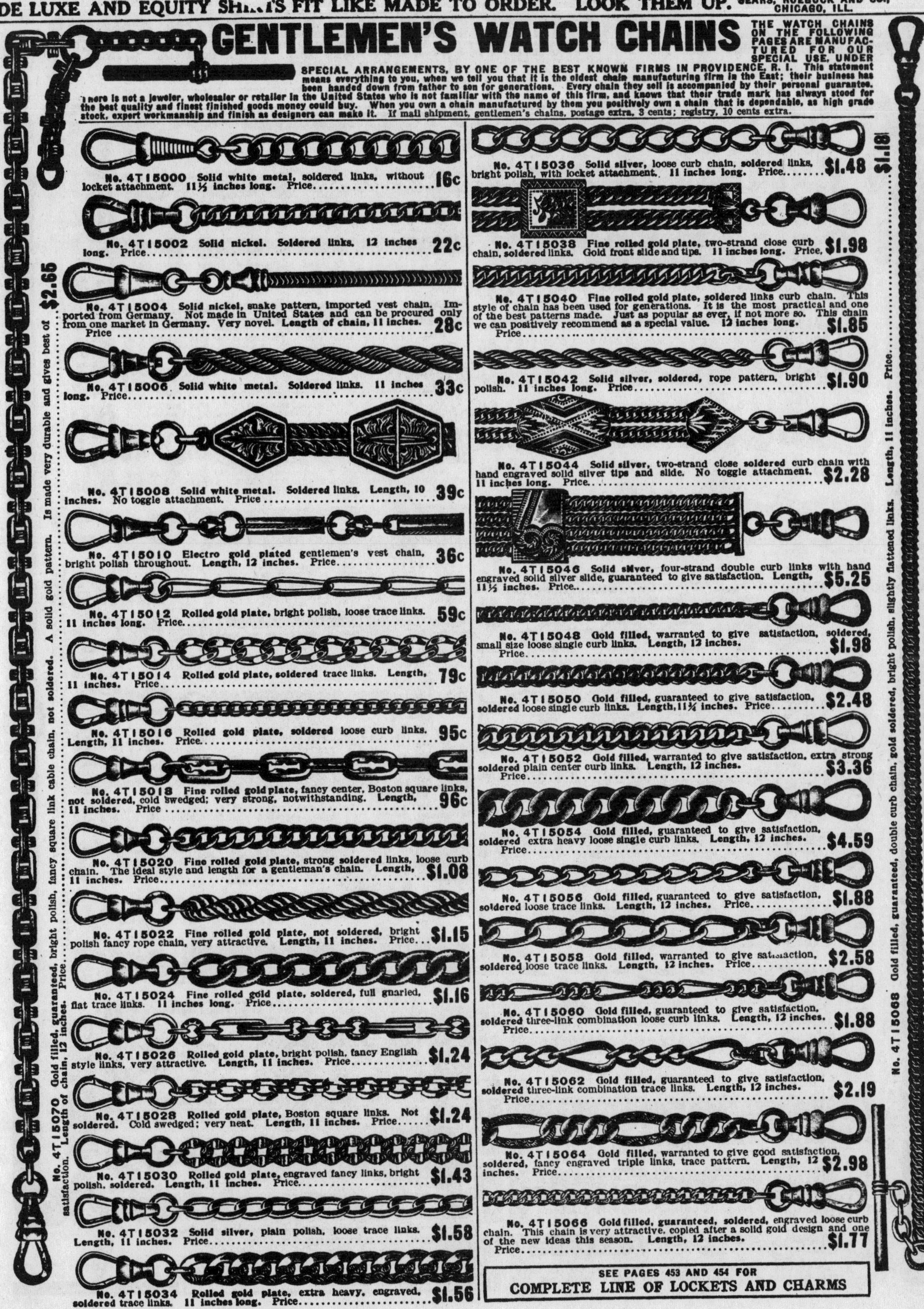

GENTLEMEN'S WATCH CHAINS

THE WATCH CHAINS ON THE FOLLOWING PAGES ARE MANUFACTURED FOR OUR SPECIAL USE, UNDER SPECIAL ARRANGEMENTS, BY ONE OF THE BEST KNOWN FIRMS IN PROVIDENCE, R. I. This statement means everything to you, when we tell you that it is the oldest chain manufacturing firm in the East; their business has been handed down from father to son for generations. Every chain they sell is accompanied by their personal guarantee. There is not a jeweler, wholesaler or retailer in the United States who is not familiar with the name of this firm, and knows that their trade mark has always stood for the best quality and finest finished goods money could buy. When you own a chain manufactured by them you positively own a chain that is dependable, as high grade stock, expert workmanship and finish as designers can make it. If mail shipment, gentlemen's chains, postage extra, 3 cents; registry, 10 cents extra.

No. 4T15070 Gold filled, guaranteed, bright polish, fancy square link cable chain, not soldered. A solid gold pattern. Is made very durable and gives best of satisfaction. Length of chain, 12 inches. Price........$2.65

No. 4T15000 Solid white metal, soldered links, without locket attachment. 11½ inches long. Price........16c

No. 4T15002 Solid nickel. Soldered links. 12 inches long. Price........22c

No. 4T15004 Solid nickel, snake pattern, imported vest chain. Imported from Germany. Not made in United States and can be procured only from one market in Germany. Very novel. Length of chain, 11 inches. Price........28c

No. 4T15006 Solid white metal. Soldered links. 11 inches long. Price........33c

No. 4T15008 Solid white metal. Soldered links. Length, 10 inches. No toggle attachment. Price........39c

No. 4T15010 Electro gold plated gentlemen's vest chain, bright polish throughout. Length, 12 inches. Price........36c

No. 4T15012 Rolled gold plate, bright polish, loose trace links. 11 inches long. Price........59c

No. 4T15014 Rolled gold plate, soldered trace links. Length, 11 inches. Price........79c

No. 4T15016 Rolled gold plate, soldered loose curb links. Length, 11 inches. Price........95c

No. 4T15018 Fine rolled gold plate, fancy center, Boston square links, not soldered, cold swedged; very strong, notwithstanding. Length, 11 inches. Price........96c

No. 4T15020 Fine rolled gold plate, strong soldered links, loose curb chain. The ideal style and length for a gentleman's chain. Length, 11 inches. Price........$1.08

No. 4T15022 Fine rolled gold plate, not soldered, bright polish fancy rope chain, very attractive. Length, 11 inches. Price........$1.15

No. 4T15024 Fine rolled gold plate, soldered, full gnarled, flat trace links. 11 inches long. Price........$1.16

No. 4T15026 Rolled gold plate, bright polish, fancy English style links, very attractive. Length, 11 inches. Price........$1.24

No. 4T15028 Rolled gold plate, Boston square links. Not soldered. Cold swedged; very neat. Length, 11 inches. Price........$1.24

No. 4T15030 Rolled gold plate, engraved fancy links, bright polish, soldered. Length, 11 inches. Price........$1.43

No. 4T15032 Solid silver, plain polish, loose trace links. Length, 11 inches. Price........$1.58

No. 4T15034 Rolled gold plate, extra heavy, engraved, soldered trace links. 11 inches long. Price........$1.56

No. 4T15036 Solid silver, loose curb chain, soldered links, bright polish, with locket attachment. 11 inches long. Price........$1.48

No. 4T15038 Fine rolled gold plate, two-strand close curb chain, soldered links. Gold front slide and tips. 11 inches long. Price........$1.98

No. 4T15040 Fine rolled gold plate, soldered links curb chain. This style of chain has been used for generations. It is the most practical and one of the best patterns made. Just as popular as ever, if not more so. This chain we can positively recommend as a special value. 12 inches long. Price........$1.85

No. 4T15042 Solid silver, soldered, rope pattern, bright polish. 11 inches long. Price........$1.90

No. 4T15044 Solid silver, two-strand close soldered curb chain with hand engraved solid silver tips and slide. No toggle attachment. 11 inches long. Price........$2.28

No. 4T15046 Solid silver, four-strand double curb links with hand engraved solid silver slide, guaranteed to give satisfaction. Length, 11½ inches. Price........$5.25

No. 4T15048 Gold filled, warranted to give satisfaction, soldered, small size loose single curb links. Length, 12 inches. Price........$1.98

No. 4T15050 Gold filled, guaranteed to give satisfaction, soldered loose single curb links. Length, 11¾ inches. Price........$2.48

No. 4T15052 Gold filled, warranted to give satisfaction, extra strong soldered plain center curb links. Length, 12 inches. Price........$3.36

No. 4T15054 Gold filled, guaranteed to give satisfaction, soldered extra heavy loose single curb links. Length, 12 inches. Price........$4.59

No. 4T15056 Gold filled, guaranteed to give satisfaction, soldered loose trace links. Length, 12 inches. Price........$1.88

No. 4T15058 Gold filled, warranted to give satisfaction, soldered loose trace links. Length, 12 inches. Price........$2.58

No. 4T15060 Gold filled, guaranteed to give satisfaction, soldered three-link combination loose curb links. Length, 12 inches. Price........$1.88

No. 4T15062 Gold filled, guaranteed to give satisfaction, soldered three-link combination trace links. Length, 12 inches. Price........$2.19

No. 4T15064 Gold filled, warranted to give good satisfaction, soldered, fancy engraved triple links, trace pattern. Length, 12 inches. Price........$2.98

No. 4T15066 Gold filled, guaranteed, soldered, engraved loose curb chain. This chain is very attractive, copied after a solid gold design and one of the new ideas this season. Length, 12 inches. Price........$1.77

No. 4T15068 Gold filled, guaranteed, double curb chain, gold soldered, bright polish, slightly flattened links. Length, 11 inches. Price........$1.18

SEE PAGES 453 AND 454 FOR COMPLETE LINE OF LOCKETS AND CHARMS

GENTLEMEN'S GOLD FILLED WATCH CHAINS

MADE LIKE HIGH GRADE GOLD FILLED WATCH CASES, THE SAME METHOD OF GOLD FILLING IS USED.

We guarantee any chain on this page to give entire satisfaction. You are at liberty to return any chain if it does not give entire satisfaction. They are in every way as illustrated and described. The two chains illustrated on each side of this page show the true lengths of the chains shown in the center. Each one comes complete with bar, swivel or catch and locket attachment called toggle.

Postage on gentlemen's watch chains, 3 cents; if by registered or insured mail, see page 14.

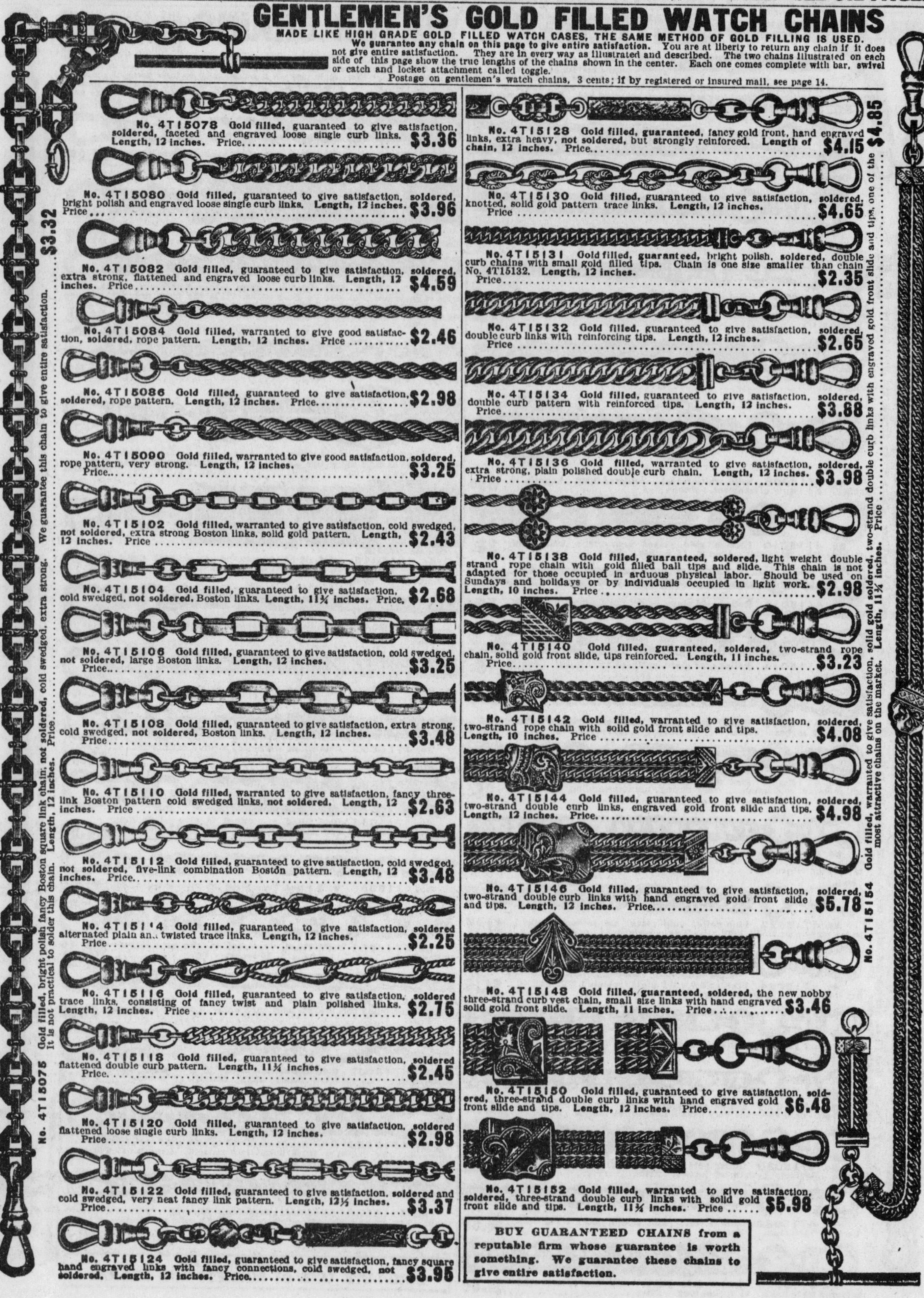

No. 4T15078 Gold filled, guaranteed to give satisfaction, soldered, faceted and engraved loose single curb links. Length, 12 inches. Price........ **$3.36**

No. 4T15080 Gold filled, guaranteed to give satisfaction, soldered, bright polish and engraved loose single curb links. Length, 12 inches. Price........ **$3.96**

No. 4T15082 Gold filled, guaranteed to give satisfaction, soldered, extra strong, flattened and engraved loose curb links. Length, 12 inches. Price........ **$4.59**

No. 4T15084 Gold filled, warranted to give good satisfaction, soldered, rope pattern. Length, 12 inches. Price........ **$2.46**

No. 4T15086 Gold filled, guaranteed to give satisfaction, soldered, rope pattern. Length, 12 inches. Price........ **$2.98**

No. 4T15090 Gold filled, warranted to give good satisfaction, soldered, rope pattern, very strong. Length, 12 inches. Price........ **$3.25**

No. 4T15102 Gold filled, warranted to give satisfaction, cold swedged, not soldered, extra strong Boston links, solid gold pattern. Length, 12 inches. Price........ **$2.43**

No. 4T15104 Gold filled, guaranteed to give satisfaction, cold swedged, not soldered, Boston links. Length, 11¾ inches. Price. **$2.68**

No. 4T15106 Gold filled, guaranteed to give satisfaction, cold swedged, not soldered, large Boston links. Length, 12 inches. Price........ **$3.25**

No. 4T15108 Gold filled, guaranteed to give satisfaction, extra strong, cold swedged, not soldered, Boston links. Length, 12 inches. Price........ **$3.48**

No. 4T15110 Gold filled, warranted to give satisfaction, fancy three-link Boston pattern cold swedged links, not soldered. Length, 12 inches. Price........ **$2.63**

No. 4T15112 Gold filled, guaranteed to give satisfaction, cold swedged, not soldered, five-link combination Boston pattern. Length, 12 inches. Price........ **$3.48**

No. 4T15114 Gold filled, guaranteed to give satisfaction, soldered alternated plain and twisted trace links. Length, 12 inches. Price........ **$2.25**

No. 4T15116 Gold filled, guaranteed to give satisfaction, soldered trace links, consisting of fancy twist and plain polished links. Length, 12 inches. Price........ **$2.75**

No. 4T15118 Gold filled, guaranteed to give satisfaction, soldered flattened double curb pattern. Length, 11¾ inches. Price........ **$2.45**

No. 4T15120 Gold filled, guaranteed to give satisfaction, soldered flattened loose single curb links. Length, 12 inches. Price........ **$2.98**

No. 4T15122 Gold filled, guaranteed to give satisfaction, soldered and cold swedged, very neat fancy link pattern. Length, 12½ inches. Price........ **$3.37**

No. 4T15124 Gold filled, guaranteed to give satisfaction, fancy square hand engraved links with fancy connections, cold swedged, not soldered. Length, 12 inches. Price........ **$3.95**

No. 4T15128 Gold filled, guaranteed, fancy gold front, hand engraved links, extra heavy, not soldered, but strongly reinforced. Length of chain, 12 inches. Price........ **$4.15**

No. 4T15130 Gold filled, guaranteed to give satisfaction, soldered, knotted, solid gold pattern trace links. Length, 12 inches. Price........ **$4.65**

No. 4T15131 Gold filled, guaranteed, bright polish, soldered, double curb chains with small gold filled tips. Chain is one size smaller than chain No. 4T15132. Length, 12 inches. Price........ **$2.35**

No. 4T15132 Gold filled, guaranteed to give satisfaction, soldered, double curb links with reinforcing tips. Length, 12 inches. Price........ **$2.65**

No. 4T15134 Gold filled, guaranteed to give satisfaction, soldered, double curb pattern with reinforced tips. Length, 12 inches. Price........ **$3.88**

No. 4T15136 Gold filled, warranted to give satisfaction, soldered, extra strong, plain polished double curb chain. Length, 12 inches. Price........ **$3.98**

No. 4T15138 Gold filled, guaranteed, soldered, light weight double strand rope chain with gold filled ball tips and slide. This chain is not adapted for those occupied in arduous physical labor. Should be used on Sundays and holidays or by individuals occupied in light work. Length, 10 inches. Price........ **$2.98**

No. 4T15140 Gold filled, guaranteed, soldered, two-strand rope chain, solid gold front slide, tips reinforced. Length, 11 inches. Price........ **$3.23**

No. 4T15142 Gold filled, warranted to give satisfaction, soldered, two-strand rope chain with solid gold front slide and tips. Length, 10 inches. Price........ **$4.08**

No. 4T15144 Gold filled, guaranteed to give satisfaction, soldered, two-strand double curb links, engraved gold front slide and tips. Length, 12 inches. Price........ **$4.98**

No. 4T15146 Gold filled, guaranteed to give satisfaction, soldered, two-strand double curb links with hand engraved gold front slide and tips. Length, 12 inches. Price........ **$5.78**

No. 4T15148 Gold filled, guaranteed, soldered, the new nobby three-strand curb vest chain, small size links with hand engraved solid gold front slide. Length, 11 inches. Price........ **$3.46**

No. 4T15150 Gold filled, guaranteed to give satisfaction, soldered, three-strand double curb links with hand engraved gold front slide and tips. Length, 12 inches. Price........ **$6.48**

No. 4T15152 Gold filled, warranted to give satisfaction, soldered, three-strand double curb links with solid gold front slide and tips. Length, 11¾ inches. Price........ **$5.98**

BUY GUARANTEED CHAINS from a reputable firm whose guarantee is worth something. We guarantee these chains to give entire satisfaction.

No. 4T15075 Gold filled, bright polish fancy Boston square link chain; not soldered, cold swedged, extra strong. We guarantee this chain to give entire satisfaction. It is not practical to solder this chain. Length, 12 inches. Price........ **$3.32**

No. 4T15154 Gold filled, warranted to give satisfaction, solid gold soldered, two-strand double curb links with engraved gold front slide and tips, one of the most attractive chains on the market. Length, 11¾ inches. Price........ **$4.85**

Gentlemen's FINEST QUALITY GOLD FILLED, ROLLED GOLD PLATE, GOLD ELECTRO PLATE, WHITE METAL, NICKEL AND SOLID SILVER Vest Chains

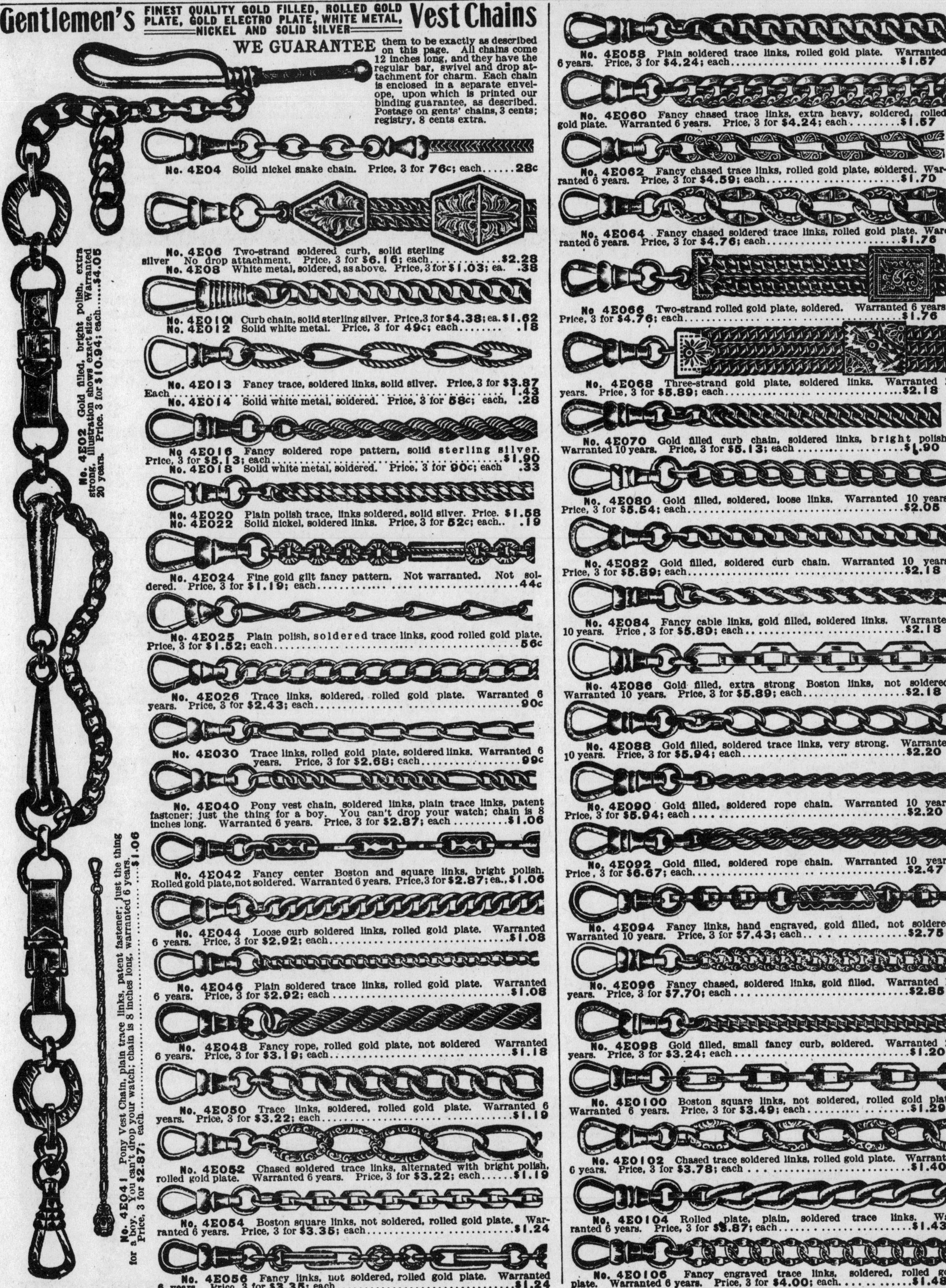

WE GUARANTEE them to be exactly as described on this page. All chains come 12 inches long, and they have the regular bar, swivel and drop attachment for charm. Each chain is enclosed in a separate envelope, upon which is printed our binding guarantee, as described. Postage on gents' chains, 3 cents; registry, 8 cents extra.

No. 4E02 Gold filled, bright polish, extra strong, illustration shows exact size. Warranted 20 years. Price, 3 for $10.94; each......$4.05

No. 4E041 Pony Vest Chain, plain trace links, patent fastener; just the thing for a boy. You can't drop your watch; chain is 8 inches long, warranted 6 years. Price, 3 for $2.87; each......$1.06

No. 4E04 Solid nickel snake chain. Price, 3 for 76c; each......28c

No. 4E06 Two-strand soldered curb, solid sterling silver. No drop attachment. Price, 3 for $6.16; each..........$2.28

No. 4E08 White metal, soldered, as above. Price, 3 for $1.03; ea. .38

No. 4E010 Curb chain, solid sterling silver. Price, 3 for $4.38; ea. $1.62

No. 4E012 Solid white metal. Price, 3 for 49c; each........ .18

No. 4E013 Fancy trace, soldered links, solid silver. Price, 3 for $3.87 Each.......... 1.43

No. 4E014 Solid white metal, soldered. Price, 3 for 58c; each. .28

No. 4E016 Fancy soldered rope pattern, solid sterling silver. Price, 3 for $5.13; each..........$1.90

No. 4E018 Solid white metal, soldered. Price, 3 for 90c; each .33

No. 4E020 Plain polish trace, links soldered, solid silver. Price. $1.58

No. 4E022 Solid nickel, soldered links. Price, 3 for 52c; each.. .19

No. 4E024 Fine gold gilt fancy pattern. Not warranted. Not soldered. Price, 3 for $1.19; each..........44c

No. 4E025 Plain polish, soldered trace links, good rolled gold plate. Price, 3 for $1.52; each..........56c

No. 4E026 Trace links, soldered, rolled gold plate. Warranted 6 years. Price, 3 for $2.43; each..........90c

No. 4E030 Trace links, rolled gold plate, soldered links. Warranted 6 years. Price, 3 for $2.68; each..........99c

No. 4E040 Pony vest chain, soldered links, plain trace links, patent fastener; just the thing for a boy. You can't drop your watch; chain is 8 inches long. Warranted 6 years. Price, 3 for $2.87; each..........$1.06

No. 4E042 Fancy center Boston and square links, bright polish. Rolled gold plate, not soldered. Warranted 6 years. Price, 3 for $2.87; ea., $1.06

No. 4E044 Loose curb soldered links, rolled gold plate. Warranted 6 years. Price, 3 for $2.92; each..........$1.08

No. 4E046 Plain soldered trace links, rolled gold plate. Warranted 6 years. Price, 3 for $2.92; each..........$1.08

No. 4E048 Fancy rope, rolled gold plate, not soldered Warranted 6 years. Price, 3 for $3.19; each..........$1.18

No. 4E050 Trace links, soldered, rolled gold plate. Warranted 6 years. Price, 3 for $3.22; each..........$1.19

No. 4E052 Chased soldered trace links, alternated with bright polish, rolled gold plate. Warranted 6 years. Price, 3 for $3.22; each......$1.19

No. 4E054 Boston square links, not soldered, rolled gold plate. Warranted 6 years. Price, 3 for $3.35; each..........$1.24

No. 4E056 Fancy links, not soldered, rolled gold plate. Warranted 6 years. Price, 3 for $3.35; each..........$1.24

No. 4E058 Plain soldered trace links, rolled gold plate. Warranted 6 years. Price, 3 for $4.24; each..........$1.57

No. 4E060 Fancy chased trace links, extra heavy, soldered, rolled gold plate. Warranted 6 years. Price, 3 for $4.24; each..........$1.57

No. 4E062 Fancy chased trace links, rolled gold plate, soldered. Warranted 6 years. Price, 3 for $4.59; each..........$1.70

No. 4E064 Fancy chased soldered trace links, rolled gold plate. Warranted 6 years. Price, 3 for $4.76; each..........$1.76

No 4E066 Two-strand rolled gold plate, soldered. Warranted 6 years. Price, 3 for $4.76; each..........$1.76

No. 4E068 Three-strand gold plate, soldered links. Warranted 3 years. Price, 3 for $5.89; each..........$2.18

No. 4E070 Gold filled curb chain, soldered links, bright polish. Warranted 10 years. Price, 3 for $5.13; each..........$1.90

No. 4E080 Gold filled, soldered, loose links. Warranted 10 years. Price, 3 for $5.54; each..........$2.05

No. 4E082 Gold filled, soldered curb chain. Warranted 10 years. Price, 3 for $5.89; each..........$2.18

No. 4E084 Fancy cable links, gold filled, soldered links. Warranted 10 years. Price, 3 for $5.89; each..........$2.18

No. 4E086 Gold filled, extra strong Boston links, not soldered. Warranted 10 years. Price, 3 for $5.89; each..........$2.18

No. 4E088 Gold filled, soldered trace links, very strong. Warranted 10 years. Price, 3 for $5.94; each..........$2.20

No. 4E090 Gold filled, soldered rope chain. Warranted 10 years. Price, 3 for $5.94; each..........$2.20

No. 4E092 Gold filled, soldered rope chain. Warranted 10 years. Price, 3 for $6.67; each..........$2.47

No. 4E094 Fancy links, hand engraved, gold filled, not soldered. Warranted 10 years. Price, 3 for $7.43; each..........$2.75

No. 4E096 Fancy chased, soldered links, gold filled. Warranted 10 years. Price, 3 for $7.70; each..........$2.85

No. 4E098 Gold filled, small fancy curb, soldered. Warranted 20 years. Price, 3 for $3.24; each..........$1.20

No. 4E0100 Boston square links, not soldered, rolled gold plate. Warranted 6 years. Price, 3 for $3.49; each..........$1.29

No. 4E0102 Chased trace soldered links, rolled gold plate. Warranted 6 years. Price, 3 for $3.78; each..........$1.40

No. 4E0104 Rolled plate, plain, soldered trace links. Warranted 6 years. Price, 3 for $3.87; each..........$1.43

No. 4E0106 Fancy engraved trace links, soldered, rolled gold plate. Warranted 6 years. Price, 3 for $4.00; each..........$1.48

CLOCKS

IN OUR CLOCK DEPARTMENT

THE BEST CLOCK MAKERS IN THE UNITED STATES ARE REPRESENTED. They are the oldest and most reliable makers. The Waterbury Clock Co., the Gilbert Clock Co., the New Haven Clock Co., and the Ansonia Clock Co., stand preeminent. Every clock we sell is guaranteed by the manufacturers, and we personally warrant every clock sold to give entire and absolute satisfaction; for the biggest value for the money, for clocks that we can and do give our written binding guarantee with every one sold, we would direct your attention to the following clocks. Each one is made under special contract for us. They are manufactured by one of the makers named, but on account of the very low price, we cannot print the maker's name. However, each one of these clocks carries our 5-year binding guarantee. For an alarm clock we recommend The Reliable Alarm, No. 5G2915, at 76 cents; our new Luminous Radium, No. 5G2907, at 85 cents; or our New Continuous Long Alarm, No. 5G2921, price, $1.89. For a cabinet clock, we would recommend our No. 5G3096, price, $2.20, or if this design does not suit you and you wish a calendar attachment together with a thermometer and barometer, we would direct your attention to our No. 5G3099, price, $2.64, or the Prophet, No. 5G3126, price, $3.24. If you want a mantel clock, something very fine, the greatest value for the money, you can surely make a selection from the following clocks: The movements are of the highest standard. It is only a question of design in the case. Conqueror at $4.70, No. 5G3290; our Prince Elias, No. 5G3302; our American Lady, No. 5G3917, price, $3.98; our Countess Janet, No. 5G3711, price, $3.62; or the Empress, No. 5G3901 price, $4.45.

BRONZE ORNAMENT.

75c

No. 5G2940 Very Artistic Bronze Figure of Horse, true to life, for a mantel or top of mantel clock; 8½ inches long base. Shipping wt., 5 pounds. Price, **75c**

No. 5G2938 Bronze Ornament, finely executed figure of Stag, 7¾ inches high; 5¾ inches wide at base. Shipping weight, 5 pounds. Price.... **70c**

No. 5G2946 Bronze Ornament. This figure represents a Roman warrior in battle, 8 inches high; 8 inches wide at base. Shipping weight, 5 pounds. Price **95c**

49 Cents or 68 Cents; Your Choice of Either One.

An Imported Alarm Clock manufactured in Germany. They give generally fair satisfaction. The only difficulty with the imported clock is the fact that when it gets out of order it is impossible to get the material to repair it properly. No. 5G2903 at 68 cents, is an American production, and considering the price is a marvel of value. We guarantee it for one year, but conscientiously believe that it should wear and give good satisfaction for many years if properly handled. Both of these clocks stand 6½ inches high. Both have 4-inch dials. The imported German clock has Roman numerals and the American made clock has Arabic numerals. Both alarm continuously for one-half minute. Weight of clock, packed ready for shipment, about 2 lbs.

No. 5G2901 No. 5G2903

No. 5G2901 Imported Alarm Clock. Price **49c**

No. 5G2903 American Made Alarm Clock. Price **68c**

Luminous Dial. Shows the Time in the Dark.

85c

Our New Luminous Radium Alarm Clock. You can see the time at night if you own one of these clocks. This clock has a 4-inch dial, being large enough to see the numerals from any part of the room. It is an improvement over all others. This clock carries with it our two-year guarantee. Directions enclosed with each clock, printed on back of guarantee.

No. 5G2907 Price, each **$0.85**
No. 5G2962 12 for **9.70**
If by mail, postage extra, each, 20 cents.

No. 5G2910 "Must Get Up" Nickel Alarm Clock. Height, 5⅝ inches; dial, 4⅛ inches; made by the Waterbury Clock Co. This clock has very large bell on the back of the clock; the alarm runs five minutes with one winding; can be made to run a short, medium, long, or extra long time, and can be stopped at pleasure.
Price **$1.16**
If by mail, postage extra, 29 cents.

$1.20

No. 5G2911 Our New Interval Alarm Clock. Height, 6 inches; dial, 4½ inches; bell on back of clock. It is one of our new clocks, being guaranteed for a term of two years. It rings at intervals for a duration of fifteen minutes. You cannot oversleep with one of these clocks. It is made for us under contract at a special price, with the idea of producing a better clock than any on the market. Our guarantee goes with every clock sold. Price **$1.20**
If by mail, postage extra, 28 cents.

The Fly Alarm Calendar Clock. Height, about 6½ inches; dial, 4 inches; one-day clock with calendar and alarm, manufactured by the New Haven Clock Company. Movement, very fine grade lever; a clock that we know will give entire satisfaction in every respect, has fine large nickel alarm bell on top, entire clock beautifully burnished, and thoroughly inspected before leaving our establishment. Has extra long alarm ring or can be regulated by winding apparatus for short ring.

No. 5G2914 Price, each **$0.85**
No. 5G2968 12 for **9.82**
If by mail, postage extra, each, 24 cents.

A $1.25 Alarm Clock for 76c.

No. 5G2915 Nickel Alarm Clock made especially for us by one of the largest clock companies in the United States, but on account of the low price at which we sell it we cannot give the maker's name. The movement is of the latest lever escapement, made of brass, and oil tempered steel parts. Each clock is thoroughly examined and tested for accurate timekeeping and running durability before leaving the factory. It is again examined in our house before shipping, which insures you an accurate timekeeper. Stands 6½ inches high. Dial is 4 inches in diameter.
Price, 12 for **$8.68**; each **76c**
If by mail, postage extra, 32 cents.

No. 5G2919 The Racket Strike Alarm Clock, made by the Ansonia Clock Co. Height, 6½ inches; width, 4½ inches; dial, 4½ inches. Remember this clock strikes the hours and half hours the same as a mantel clock. In addition it has an alarm attachment. A good timekeeper, guaranteed to give entire satisfaction.
Price **$1.36**
If by mail, postage extra, 36 cents.

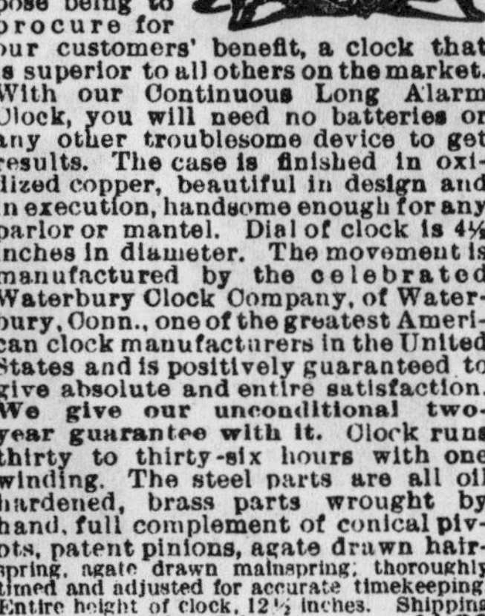

$1.89

No. 5G2921 Our New Continuous Long Alarm Clock. Rings from seven to ten minutes, but can be switched off when desired by throwing lever on the back of the clock. We have had this clock manufactured especially for us, our purpose being to procure for our customers' benefit, a clock that is superior to all others on the market. With our Continuous Long Alarm Clock, you will need no batteries or any other troublesome device to get results. The case is finished in oxidized copper, beautiful in design and in execution, handsome enough for any parlor or mantel. Dial of clock is 4½ inches in diameter. The movement is manufactured by the celebrated Waterbury Clock Company, of Waterbury, Conn., one of the greatest American clock manufacturers in the United States and is positively guaranteed to give absolute and entire satisfaction. **We give our unconditional two-year guarantee with it.** Clock runs thirty to thirty-six hours with one winding. The steel parts are all oil hardened, brass parts wrought by hand, full complement of conical pivots, patent pinions, agate drawn hairspring, agate drawn mainspring; thoroughly timed and adjusted for accurate timekeeping. Entire height of clock, 12½ inches. Shipping weight, 9 pounds. Price **$1.89**

92c

No. 5G2934 Our Dainty, Solid Gold Plated Small Boudoir Alarm Clock for 92c. Never before in the history of Boudoir clocks have dainty, handsome little clocks like here illustrated been offered at anything like this price. The immense quantity purchased is the only reason that makes this possible. Clock stands 8 inches high, 6¼ inches wide at base, with 2½-inch dial. Clock runs 30 hours with one winding, with regular alarm attachment, such as all other alarm clocks have, placed in rear of clock. Boxed ready for shipment, weight about 5 pounds. Price **92c**

No. 5G2932 Nickel Plated Glass Paneled High Grade Alarm Clock, manufactured with a view of producing a higher grade, more accurate and more dependable alarm clock than was on the market. This clock can be appropriately used on the mantel in your parlor, as well as in your bedroom. Nothing unsightly about it. Stands 6 inches high, 4¼ inches wide at base and 3 inches deep, has fine glass panels. You can observe the working of the movement through the sides. The dial is 2⅞ inches in diameter, has plain Roman numerals. This clock is beautified by gilt arabesque panel work in the front of the clock. The movement is straight line with nickel plated front and back plates, extra hardened brass wheels and oil tempered pinions and pivots. The back of the clock is so arranged that by opening a small door, swung on a strong hinge, you can regulate and wind same without difficulty. The movement is manufactured by the Waterbury Clock Co., one of the most reliable and best known clock makers in the United States. It runs thirty hours with one winding. The alarm attachment is invisible, being placed underneath the clock. This clock is not alone an alarm clock, but also strikes the hours and half hours on a bell. Weight, packed ready for shipment, about 4 pounds. Price... **$2.30**

$1.10

Our New Extra Heavy Iron One-Day Mantel Clock. This design is made for our exclusive use. One of the prettiest, one of the most dainty designs produced this year. Note the delicacy of the execution of this design, note the graceful pose, and yet by reason of our one small per cent of profit system, we are able to offer this very handsome one-day mantel clock for $1.10. It has the appearance of clocks worth from $6.00 to $8.00. The movement in this clock runs 30 hours with one winding, will keep good time and is thoroughly inspected and examined before leaving our institution. Clock stands 12 inches high, 10 inches wide at base; dial of clock is 2¾ inches in diameter. This clock comes in two finishes, whichever you desire, either ancient red bronze or bright yellow Roman gold finish. Clock packed ready for shipment weighs about 9 pounds.

No. 5G2936 Price, bronze finish, **$1.10**
No. 5G2937 Gold finish **1.19**

No. 5G2931 Wasp Alarm Clock, lever escapement, runs one day with one winding; stands 3½ inches high; dial 2 inches in diameter; is manufactured by the Waterbury Clock Company and is guaranteed to keep correct time. Price, **$1.06**
If by mail, postage extra, 10c.

No. 5G2933 Same as No. 5G2931, but without alarm; time only. Price **78c**

$2.48 for a Musical Alarm Clock.

One of the newest novelties on the market. We import them ourselves direct. This clock plays one tune for about ten minutes instead of ringing a bell. What is more beautiful than to be awakened from sleep by hearing a beautiful tune being played, instead of the harsh, clanging sound of an alarm bell. This clock stands 7 inches high, 5 inches wide with front arabesque ornamentation around dial, full nickel plated brass frame with glass sides so that the movement and its action is visible at all times. The movement is a very fine one imported from Germany. The musical attachment is ingeniously hidden at the bottom of this clock, and is so arranged that when the clock is set at a certain time, instead of the alarm from a bell being heard, a beautiful tune is played. The device is simple and strong in construction. The danger of it getting out of order is very remote. With care, that is, if the clock is not handled or played with, but merely wound and set, and placed on the mantel shelf or bureau, should last for many years and give entire satisfaction; construction is so simple, the parts are so well made that there should be no trouble in getting entire satisfaction, both for timekeeping and for music part combined. $2.48 is a remarkably low figure for such a unique piece of clock mechanism and this price is only possible on account of our one small percentage of profit system, and the fact that you are owning it exactly at what wholesalers would own this clock, as we import them ourselves direct, saving all the different handling expense. Weight of clock, packed ready for shipment, about 2½ pounds.

No. 5G3048 Musical Alarm Clock. Price **$2.48**

Gold Plated Clock for $1.10.

No. 5G3050 No. 5G3052

Bureau or Bedroom Clock. Runs 30 hours with one winding. This clock is made by the Waterbury Clock Co., stands 5 inches high, dial 2 inches. Frame is solid metal plated with pure gold and is a very handsome ornament as well as useful timepiece. Weight, 2 pounds.

No. 5G3050. Price **$1.10**
No. 5G3052 Price **1.10**

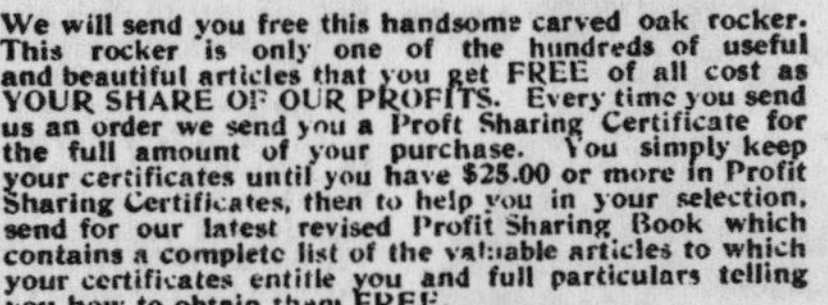

FREE IN EXCHANGE FOR $39.00 IN PROFIT SHARING CERTIFICATES.

We will send you free this handsome carved oak rocker. This rocker is only one of the hundreds of useful and beautiful articles that you get FREE of all cost as YOUR SHARE OF OUR PROFITS. Every time you send us an order we send you a Profit Sharing Certificate for the full amount of your purchase. You simply keep your certificates until you have $25.00 or more in Profit Sharing Certificates, then to help you in your selection, send for our latest revised Profit Sharing Book which contains a complete list of the valuable articles to which your certificates entitle you and full particulars telling you how to obtain them FREE.

You have a double object in dealing with us. First, our prices on everything you need are ALWAYS LOWEST. Second, we return you a liberal share of our profits by letting you choose from our amazing variety of household and personal articles, all of which are FREE, in exchange for the Profit Sharing Certificates which accompany every purchase you make.

Regular Eight-Day Clock with Perpetual Calendar Attachment for $6.40.

No. 5C3310 This clock is manufactured by the Waterbury Clock Company in either oak or walnut. Stands 28¼ inches high. It runs 8 days with one winding, strikes the hours and half hours on a cathedral gong. It has the calendar attachment, as shown on the lower dial, which is a perpetual one, marking even the leap years without having to be reset. The dials are 8 inches in diameter. This clock is particularly adapted for dining rooms, libraries and offices. We warrant it to be an accurate timekeeper. The parts are made of finely wrought brass and oil tempered steel, most accurate for timekeeping, and giving it great durability. **The case is beautifully hand engraved and embossed.** The glass in the door is decorated in black and gold. See our price, $6.40. **We absolutely guarantee it to give satisfaction.** Weight, boxed for shipment, about 25 pounds.

No. 5C3310 Price..$6.40

$2.94 Buys a Calendar Clock with Barometer and Thermometer.

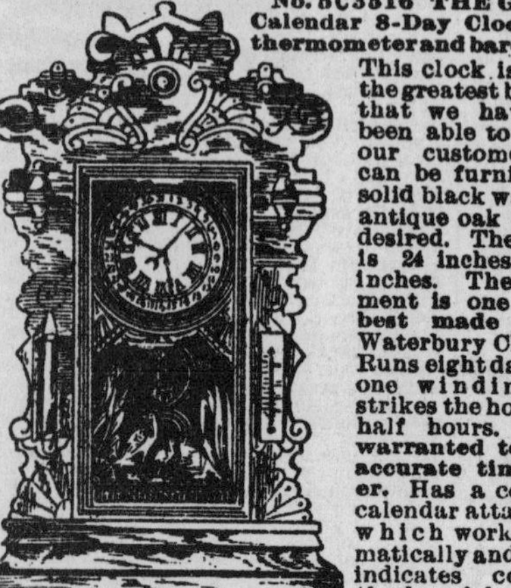

No. 5C3516 THE GIBSON Calendar 8-Day Clock with thermometer and barometer. This clock is one of the greatest bargains that we have ever been able to offer to our customers. It can be furnished in solid black walnut or antique oak case, as desired. The height is 24 inches, dial, 6 inches. The movement is one of the best made by the Waterbury Clock Co. Runs eight days with one winding and strikes the hours and half hours. It is warranted to be an accurate timekeeper. Has a complete calendar attachment which works automatically and always indicates correctly the day of the month. It has a perfect thermometer on one side and on the other a barometer. We cannot furnish it with alarm. Weight of clock, boxed ready for shipment, 17 pounds.

No. 5C3516 Price. $2.94

DROP OCTAGON. Has solid oak or fine veneered case. Made by the Waterbury Clock Company and is thoroughly reliable. Is designed for offices, schools or churches. Weight, boxed, 25 pounds.

No. 5C3518 Eight-day, 10-in dial, time only. Price..............$2.80

No. 5C3520 Eight-day, 10-in. dial; time only. with calendar. Price......$3.10

No. 5C3522 Eight-day, 10-in. dial; strikes hours and halves. Price........................$3.40

No. 5C3524 Eight-day, 12-in. dial; time only. Price....$3.10

No. 5C3526 Eight-day 12-in. dial; strikes hours and half hours. Price........................$3.50

No. 5C3528 Eight-day, 12-in. dial; time only, with calendar. Price........................$3.30

NOTE—The height of the clocks with 10-inch dial is 21 inches; 12-inch dial, 23½ inches.

No. 5C3555 CUCKOO CLOCK. Case is made of German oak or walnut, ornamented with inlaid ash, ebony and mahogany. Beautifully hand carved throughout, strikes the hours and half hours on a wire bell, the cuckoo appears and calls at the same time. Height of clock, 21 inches; width, 14 inches. The movement is made in the Black Forest, Germany, of the finest tempered steel and polished brass, finely finished and adjusted, guaranteed to be a good timekeeper. One of the most artistic ornaments for a parlor ever made. Weight, boxed, 25 pounds.

$4.78

No. 5C3555 Price..$4.78

German Cuckoo Clock, $6.75.

It strikes the hours and half hours on a wire bell, a cuckoo appears and calls at the same time.

$6.75

No. 5C3557 CUCKOO. Case made of German oak or walnut, hand carved bird top, hand carved oak leaves. The entire carving on this clock is done by hand by the natives of the Schwarzwald, Germany, and is especially fine and artistic. The figures are accurate and lifelike. The movement is made of the very finest tempered steel and highly wrought brass. It is finely finished and perfectly adjusted. Height, 18 inches; width, 14 inches. Weight, boxed, 20 lbs.

No. 5C3557 Price..........$6.75

Quail and Cuckoo Clock.

Price, $11.80.

No. 5C3561 The quail whistles the quarter hours and the cuckoo calls the full hours. The latest improved and genuine Black Forest masterpiece, imported especially for us from Germany. It is new, novel and practical. The case is hand carved German walnut or oak, as desired. Height of clock, 21 inches; width, 16 inches. The movement is of fine polished brass and steel. Each one is carefully examined and adjusted before shipment. It strikes the hours and quarter hours on a fine toned gong. The quail whistles the quarter hours and the cuckoo calls the full hours. Every detail in this clock is finished to perfection. Weight, boxed ready for shipment, about 25 pounds

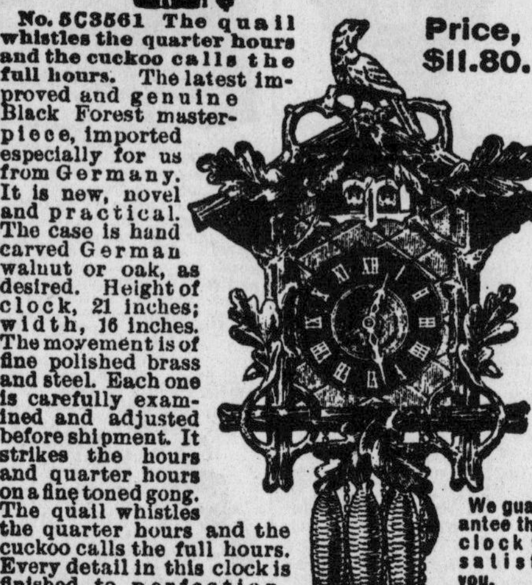

We guarantee this clock to satisfy you.

No. 5C3561 Price.... ....$11.80

Our $3.65 Eight-Day Clock.

No. 5C3706 The Dupont Mantel Clock runs eight days with one winding. It is manufactured by the celebrated Waterbury Clock Co., of Waterbury, Conn., and is guaranteed to give entire satisfaction. The case is 10¾ inches high, 13¾ inches wide, made of black hand polished wood with gilt engraving on base. It has gilt feet, side and front ornaments. The dial is 5½ inches in diameter. Strikes the hours on a gong and the half-hours on a cup bell. Weight of clock, boxed ready for shipment, 14 pounds.

Price..$3.65

$4.40 Buys an $8.00 Clock.

$4.40 $4.40

No. 5C3722 The Dawson. A polished wood, eight-day clock, strikes the hours on a gong and the half-hours on a cup bell. Clock stands 11 inches high; width, 16½ inches; dial, 5½ inches. The combination of two colors, black and marble, together with the gilt front, side ornaments and gilt feet, lends a beauty to this clock that cannot be described. You must see the clock to appreciate it. Remember, this clock is not made by a cheap manufacturer, but is the creation of the celebrated Waterbury Clock Co., Waterbury, Conn., and warranted in every respect. Weight, boxed ready for shipment, about 18 pounds.

Price,..$4.40

Beautiful Mantel Clock for $5.00.

$5.00

No. 5C3723 THE PATMOS. A very handsome mantel clock, a most excellent imitation of Mexican onyx, and unless it is examined very closely no one would believe that it was not a real onyx clock. **It holds a beautiful polish and with proper care will last a lifetime.** If the case gets soiled or dirty it can be wiped off with a damp cloth. Has fancy bronze feet in artistic design and side dragon head metal ornaments. The base is of the Corinthian style. Length of clock, 17 inches; height, 11½ inches. **Has an eight-day movement, made by Seth Thomas Clock Company. Strikes hours on a cathedral gong and half hours on a cup bell; regulated by patent regulator without touching the pendulum. Weight,** boxed, about 20 pounds.

Price..$5.00

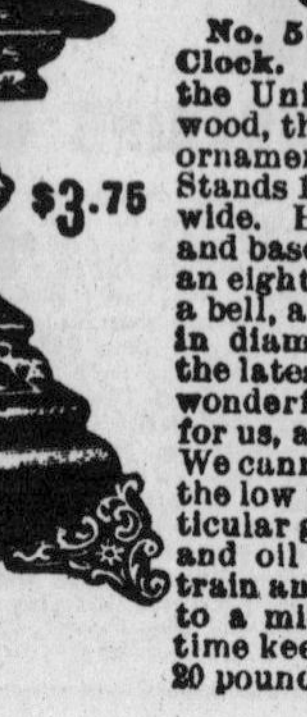

$3.75

Our $3.75 Mantel Clock.

No. 5C3711 OUR COUNTESS JANET Mantel Clock. The most wonderful bargain ever offered in the United States. This mantel clock is made of wood, then hard enameled in black with marbleized ornamentation, exactly as illustration shows. Stands 10¾ inches high, 7⅛ inches deep, 16½ inches wide. Has gilt metal feet, side ornaments and tops and bases of the two columns on front of clock. It has an eight-day movement, strikes the half-hours on a bell, and the hours on a gong. The dial is 5½ inches in diameter, with plain numerals; the dial sash is the latest Parisian pattern. This is one of the most wonderful values offered. It was made especially for us, and carries our five-year binding guarantee. We cannot divulge the maker's name on account of the low price quoted. The movement will give particular good satisfaction, it is of hard rolled brass and oil tempered steel parts. All friction in the train and delicate running parts has been reduced to a minimum, thereby giving it a life of accurate time keeping not possible in other clocks. Weight, 20 pounds. Price..$3.75

NO CHARGES FOR REPAIRS

on Watches and Clocks will be allowed unless our written consent is first secured in advance.

The Harvey Mantel Clock for $5.58.

$5.58

No. 5C3728 THE HARVEY, eight-day, enameled iron, made by the Waterbury Clock Co.; height, 10¾ inches; width, 16⅝ inches; dial, 5½ inches in diameter, fitted with the new rococo pattern sash and ornamented bezel. This clock strikes the hours on a gong and the half-hours on a cup bell. The ornamentation on this clock is exceptional, the gilt feet, front and side metal trimmings contrasting with the black enamel gives it a very rich appearance. You cannot wear this clock out, all the parts are of rolled brass and tempered steel, the case is of black iron heavily black enameled and then kiln baked. Weight of clock, boxed for shipment, 35 pounds. Price.....$5.58

Our Empress Mantel Clock, $4.60.

$4.60

No. 5C3901 OUR EMPRESS MANTEL CLOCK, exactly as illustration shows in every detail. It stands 10¾ inches high, 7 inches deep, 17½ inches wide. It has solid gilt bronze feet, gilt bronze side ornaments, gilt bronze caps and base of the six columns that ornament the front of the clock. Clock is made of wood, enameled in black, with marbleized trimmings. This enameling is guaranteed not to warp or chip off. A woolen cloth, slightly sprinkled with sweet oil, lightly rubbed over this clock, will keep it in perfect condition for practically a lifetime. The dial is plain, 5¾ inches in diameter. The sash which surrounds it is the very latest rococo design. The movement runs for eight days with one winding, strikes the half hours on a metal bell and the hours on a sweet toned gong. Each piece and part of this clock goes through a rigid inspection. It is manufactured by one of the most celebrated clock companies in the United States, but on account of the low price quoted here, we cannot print the maker's name. The movement in this clock, as in all of our own special clocks, we are particularly proud of, as it is made of hardened rolled brass and oil tempered steel parts. The bearings and all intricate and delicate parts, where friction reduces the wearing ability, are so constructed that it is reduced to a minimum, therefore we know our special line of clocks will outwear any on the market and give accurate time. **This clock is the most massive and most pretentious and biggest value for the money ever before offered.** Clocks sold by the makers of this clock, of similar design but not so massive or eleborate bring from the retail jewelers and from the jobbers from 25 to 30 per cent more than the price we ask. Seeing is believing. Don't buy this clock from us unless you find our statements are true. Just compare this clock with others, and we are satisfied that we will get your order. Weight, boxed for shipment, 22 pounds.
Price..$4.60

The Hollis. Rare Value for $4.68.

$4.68

No. 5C3905 THE HOLLIS. Beautiful adamantine finished clock, manufactured by the Seth Thomas Clock Co. The movement of this clock is a very fine handwrought brass movement, oil tempered steel parts, agate drawn hairspring and mainspring, conical pivots, patent pinions, **adamantine finish, which never dulls but is always beautiful as if newly polished, covers this case; it is guaranteed not to wear or chip off.** A beautiful head of a lion in solid bronze ornaments the sides. Handsome bronze feet. **Hand engraved scrolls of various designs ornament the front.** The dial is 5 inches, with Roman figures. This clock stands 11 inches high and 14 inches long, **goes eight days with one winding; strikes the hours and half hours upon a cathedral gong.** Warranted to keep accurate time, with care will last a natural lifetime. Weight of clock when boxed is about 20 pounds. Price.....................$4.68

A Beautiful Gilt Mantel, Desk or Bureau Clock, $1.06.

No. 5C3705 **Mantel, Desk or Bureau Clock. Runs 36 hours with one winding.** Has 2-inch dial, with fine French beveled glass. Clock stands 6 inches high, and is manufactured by the Waterbury Clock Co. We guarantee this clock to give entire satisfaction. Weight, boxed, ready for shipment, about 2¼ pounds.

No. 5C3705 Price..$1.06

The Beauty Mantel Clock for $5.95.

$5.95 as illustrated.

No. 5C3908 THE BEAUTY. **One of the finest and most artistic clocks ever manufactured.** We contracted with the factory to use an immense quantity at an unheard of price. We quote a selling price unheard of before for a clock of this high standard of make. Height, without ornament, 11 inches; base, 17 inches; with ornament, clock stands 19 inches high. **The movement is manufactured by the Seth Thomas Clock Company,** and is guaranteed to keep accurate time. It runs for eight days with one winding. The parts are made of fine wrought polished brass and oil tempered steel. It strikes the half hours on a cup bell and the hours on a cathedral gong that is toned with the church bells. **The case is adamantine finished and highly polished,** therefore can be cleaned without injury with a damp cloth. **Foot and side ornaments are of highly burnished bronze.** It is a clock such as you have never seen before for the price. Clock and ornament, boxed ready for shipment, weighs 25 pounds.

No. 5C3908 Price, complete with figure ...$5.95

No. 5C3910 Price, without figure............$4.95

No. 5C3912 Figure alone. Price..................$1.00

Our Edgemere Queen Mantel Clock at $5.15.

No. 5C3915 OUR EDGEMERE QUEEN MANTEL CLOCK. The latest and newest design in clocks. This is one of the Seth Thomas Clock Co.'s latest productions. The case is mahogany, covered with a transparent material called adamantine, guaranteed impervious to dust, damp and age. A damp cloth keeps it new and polished forever. It is always glossy, always new and one of the richest appearing clocks ever placed on the market. **Dimensions of clock**—Height, 11¾ inches; length, 16½ inches; depth, 6¼ inches. **The movement is one of the latest improved Seth Thomas clock movements.** It runs eight days with one winding, the parts are guaranteed fine wrought polished brass and oil tempered steel. It strikes the hours on a cathedral gong and half hours on a cup bell. **The case** is ornamented with two gilt lion heads, one on each end. The front is ornamented by four columns, topped and based with fine gilded metal ornaments. The entire clock rests upon four gilded feet, exactly as shown in illustration. **The dial is one of the latest Parisian patterns,** gilded and beautifully executed; the design is brought out most elaborately. Dial is 5¾ inches in diameter, making it possible for you to see the time from quite a distance. We consider this one of the most artistic, one of the most beautiful clocks on the market. It embodies the perfections of all and the faults of none. Weight, boxed for shipment, about 20 pounds.
Price..$5.15

Our American Lady Mantel Clock, $4.20.

$4.20

No. 5C3917 OUR AMERICAN LADY MANTEL CLOCK, manufactured by one of the biggest and most representative makers in the United States, but on account of the very low price quoted, we dare not print the maker's name. However, it carries our five-year written binding guarantee, and we know you will be entirely satisfied with it. This clock stands 10¾ inches high, 7 inches deep and 17 inches wide. It has solid gilt bronze feet and side ornaments, also metal top and base on the four columns, as illustration shows. The dial is 5¾ inches in diameter, the very latest pattern of fancy fret work, with a beautiful rococo sash. The case is of wood, black enameled, warranted not to peel, chip or crack off. A soft woolen cloth, sprinkled with sweet oil, will keep it as new, practically, for a lifetime. The movement runs eight days with one winding; strikes the half hours on a metal bell and the hours on a soft toned gong. **This, our American Lady mantel clock, is one of the special bargains we have referred you to in our description on page 270.** If this clock suits your taste, we refer to the design, we know that a better clock or a greater value for the money cannot be had for twice what we ask. We are particularly proud of the movement used in this clock, as it is made of solid hardened rolled brass and oil tempered steel parts. The bearings and other delicate parts are so constructed that the friction is reduced to a minimum, therefore the life of the clock is greater than any other. Weight, boxed for shipment, 20 pounds.
Price..$4.20

YOUR MONEY WILL BE IMMEDIATELY RETURNED TO YOU FOR ANY GOODS NOT PERFECTLY SATISFACTORY.

$6.35 FOR THIS GUARANTEED UP TO DATE CLOCK

RUNS EIGHT DAYS WITH ONE WINDING

STRIKES THE HOURS ON A BEAUTIFUL TONED GONG AND HALF HOURS ON A NICKEL CUP BELL.

THE CASE as illustration shows is something original and entirely new, imitating the facade and general outline of an ancient Greek temple, is made of wood, enameled to imitate black Italian marble and Mexican onyx. Beautiful metal ornaments embellish the bottoms and tops of columns, feet and top of facade of the case. The dial is new, being a rococo design, perforated, allowing the numerals to stand out prominent and clear from an ivory background. The hands are of the fleur de lis Louis XV style.

THE MOVEMENT, according to our opinion, is one of the most essential features of a clock. See the illustration. Different from any other concern. We want you to know exactly how the movement appears, and show you the running part of our clocks. This movement is made of solid brass and oil tempered steel, the mainsprings are agate drawn, the pivots and pinions have all been polished, each one thoroughly timed and adjusted, both in and out of the frame.

THE FINISH of this clock is remarkable. A piece of Canton flannel slightly moistened with oil and gently rubbed over the surface every once in a while, say about nine months or a year, will keep this clock as bright as when new. This clock surely would grace any parlor, ornamental as well as practical. Stands at highest point 12½ inches, 17¾ inches wide and 5½ inches deep, is different from most of the mantel clocks now being sold. You can adjust this clock from the front, you never need touch the back or tamper with the works.

OUR GUARANTEE. With this clock we send our written binding guarantee that protects and insures you against defective material and workmanship for a term of five years.

THIS CLOCK in its entirety is American manufactured, made here in the United States by one of the great five clock companies. We cannot divulge the maker's name on account of the ridiculously close price at which we are offering these goods. They sell the same goods to wholesale jewelers at a price that would astonish the retailer, as compared with what we sell it for. Clock, boxed ready for shipment, weighs about 25 pounds.

GUARANTEED FOR FIVE YEARS.

No. 5N3660 Eight-Day Mantel Clock. Price........ **$6.35**

$4.30 QUEEN MANTEL CLOCK AND FIGURE

Never before in the history of clock making has such a fine clock and figure been offered for the money. The case is made of fine wood, kiln dried. It is then enameled by a secret process to imitate black Italian marble with marbleized columns. The enamel is guaranteed never to crack or peel. A Canton flannel cloth sprinkled with sweet oil occasionally rubbed over the clock will make it look like new. A gilt rococo metal border ornaments the top edge of the clock. Gilt ornaments adorn the front underneath the dial, gilt bronze feet and side ornaments. Two massive marbleized columns on either side of dial. The clock is 11 inches high, 12½ inches wide at the base and 6 inches deep. The movement is made by one of the most representative clock makers in the United States; has the latest straight line verge escapement of hard wrought brass and oil tempered steel parts. Runs eight days with one winding, strikes the half hours on a brass bell and hours on a sweet toned cathedral gong. The dial is 5½ inches in diameter with gilt rococo design sash. The figure, 6¾ inches high, represents a figure true to life, is made of bronze and finished in gilt. Our written binding guarantee for five years goes with each clock. $4.30 represents the actual cost of material and manufacturing, with only one small percentage of profit added. Order the clock and upon examination if you do not find it to be exactly as illustrated and described, the best clock value ever offered, return it to us at our expense and we will cheerfully refund your money. Shipping weight, 22 pounds.

GUARANTEED FOR FIVE YEARS.

No. 5N3312 Queen Mantel Clock, including figure. Price **$4.30**

No. 5N3314 Figure alone. Price........ **.82**

$4.22 LADY ISABELLE EIGHT-DAY MANTEL CLOCK

OUR LADY ISABELLE EIGHT-DAY CLOCK FOR $4.22. THINK OF IT!

We will send you this specially made, rich appearing, eight-day striking mantel clock for one-half of what a similar clock would sell the world over.

The ornamentation on this clock is one of its most attractive features. It consists of two side ornaments, top and bottom capped columns, feet and front and bottom ornaments. The dial is simple, but rich in style. 5¾ inches in diameter. Dial sash fitted with heavy French crystal.

GUARANTEED FOR FIVE YEARS.

The movement fitted in the Lady Isabelle Clock is the best clock movement we know of and is made after our own ideas on the new anti-friction principle, friction being reduced to a minimum. It runs eight days with one winding. Strikes the hours on a beautifully toned cathedral wire gong and the half hours on a brass cup bell. All parts are oil tempered, pivots all highly polished. The newest French verge escapement, metal pendulum.

This clock is covered by our five-year guarantee. We enclose it with every one sold and it amply protects and insures you against defective material or workmanship in this clock for a term of five years. Shipping weight, 20 pounds.

No. 5N3602 Lady Isabelle Mantel Clock. Price........ **$4.22**

No. 5N3301 Handsome Bronze Figure, representing a cowboy on horseback, throwing a lariat. This figure placed on top of the Lady Isabelle Clock makes a most beautiful parlor ornament. Price, figure only........ **78c**

Our five-year guarantee against faulty material or workmanship goes with each one of them. You are insured and protected should this clock fail to perform its duties properly and by this contract you are at liberty to return it to us and have it repaired free of all cost at our expense of transportation charges. We are safe in doing this. We know that the clock will perform its duties properly and you will be entirely satisfied. The case is most attractive, but the illustration does not begin to show the coloring and brass so as to give a full idea of its beauty. Stands 11 inches high, 16¼ inches wide at base, 7 inches deep, of the Corinthian style, secretly treated wood covered by hard enamel, guaranteed not to warp, chip or scale off. Comes in black and variegated colors to imitate green onyx and Italian black marble.

$4.55 A STARTLING VALUE

THE LEXINGTON EIGHT-DAY MANTEL CLOCK.

GUARANTEED FOR FIVE YEARS.

$4.55 for this clock exactly as illustrated, exactly as described, means selling high grade clocks at unheard of prices. Don't compare this clock with clocks sold by others at $6.00, $7.00 and $8.00; compare with clocks offered at $9.00 and $10.00.

This mantel clock runs eight days with one winding. Strikes the half hours on a brass bell and the full hours on a beautifully toned wire cathedral gong.

The dimensions. Clock stands 11 inches high, 17 inches wide at base and 7½ inches deep. Large, massive and most attractive. The case is made of wood treated by a secret process to imitate black Italian marble and blue Mexican onyx. The feet, side ornaments, top and bottom of front columns are of hard metal heavily plated. The contrast of the gilt finish and the black marble is most pleasing.

The dial is elaborate and ornate, being a new perforated rococo design, 5¾ inches in diameter, the dial sash is fitted with a heavy French crystal glass. Hands of blue steel Louis XIV design, Arabic numerals, plain and distinct.

The movement is the most important feature of any clock. In this clock we have fitted our special anti-friction movement. All friction has been reduced to a minimum. All pivots are polished, fine metal pendulum, latest French verge escapement, accurately run and timed before being fitted into the case. The parts are made of roll tempered brass and oil tempered steel parts.

We insure this clock. With every one of these clocks we send our written binding five-year guarantee that protects you for this term of years against faulty material or workmanship. Never before has such an offer been made by any concern and it is only possible because we know the attractive contract we have for this our Lexington Mantel Clock. Weight of clock, boxed, about 20 pounds.

No. 5N3614 The Lexington Mantel Clock. Price........ **$4.55**

$5.90 CONSIDER THIS OFFER

QUEEN OF THE NIGHT 8-DAY PARLOR MANTEL CLOCK.

Designed especially for us by one of the greatest clock companies in the United States. We cannot give you the maker's name on account of special price. Never before has such a magnificent specimen of clock been sold for twice what we ask. The clock runs eight days with one winding. Strikes the hours on a cathedral gong and the half hours on a cup bell. We guarantee this clock. With each one we send our written binding guarantee, which insures and protects you for a term of five years against defective material or workmanship. We are able to do so only because we know how this clock has been constructed, and why it is superior to any that is on the market at anything near the price.

GUARANTEED FOR FIVE YEARS.

Five-year guarantee sent with this clock. The movement is made of solid brass, extra toughened oil tempered pivots, pinions and intricate steel parts. Different from all other clock movements. This movement is made after anti-friction models. All friction in these clocks has been reduced to a minimum and while we guarantee it to give good time for only a term of five years, it should last your natural lifetime if properly handled. The case is made of fine hardwood, finished by a secret enameling process representing black and pink Mexican onyx. It stands 13 inches high; width, 18 inches; depth, 6¾ inches. The front of the clock is ornamented by six imitation marble columns with gilt metal tops and bases. The sides have two conventionalized gilt metal floral design ornaments. The feet, as illustration shows, are artistic, massive and in splendid proportion, finished in gilt metal. The dial is gilt, perforated and ornamented in floral design, and is protected by a heavy French glass set in a rococo ornamented gilt sash. The numerals are Arabic style. This clock can be kept like new by applying a soft cloth or a piece of cotton flannel slightly dampened with sweet oil. This clock, boxed ready for shipment, weighs about 21 pounds.

No. 5N3934 Queen of the Night Mantel Clock. Price........ **$5.90**

CLOCK DEPARTMENT

THE BEST CLOCK MAKERS, the oldest and most reliable in the United States are here represented; namely, Waterbury Clock Co., Gilbert Clock Co., New Haven Clock Co., and Ansonia Clock Co. These manufacturers guarantee their clocks and we also warrant them to give absolute satisfaction. Our special five-year guaranteed clocks are made by one of the above named clock makers, but on account of low special prices we are not permitted to print the maker's name in the description or on the clocks themselves.

46c Cuckoo Clock.

No. 5R8502 Miniature Cuckoo Clock, facsimile of imported Black Forest cuckoo clocks in small size; does not cuckoo. Front is embossed to represent oak leaves and vine. Height, 7 inches; width, 5 inches; runs thirty hours by pulling up the weight. Will last for years and keep fairly good time. Shipping wt., 32 oz. Price..........46c

49c Your Choice of Either One. 65c

No. 5R8508 No. 5R8514

No. 5R8508 is, at 49 cents, an imported Alarm Clock manufactured in Germany. Gives generally fair satisfaction. No. 5R8514, at 65 cents, is an American production, and considering the price is a marvel of value. We guarantee it for one year. Both these clocks stand 6½ inches high and run 30 hours with one winding. Both have 4-inch dials. Both alarm continuously for one-half minute. Shipping wt., 27 oz.

No. 5R8508 Imported Alarm Clock. Price..........49c

No. 5R8514 American Made Alarm Clock. Price..........65c

Our Reliable Alarm. A SURE SLEEP BREAKER FOR 74c

No. 5R8520 Nickel Alarm Clock. Made especially for us by one of the largest clock companies in the United States, but on account of the low price at which we sell it we cannot give the maker's name. The movement is of the latest lever escapement, made of brass, and oil tempered steel parts. It runs thirty hours with one winding. Each clock is thoroughly examined and tested for accurate timekeeping and running durability before leaving the factory. It is again examined in our house before shipping, which insures you an accurate timekeeper. Stands 6½ inches high; dial is 4 inches in diameter. Shipping wt., 32 oz. Price..........74c

No. 5R8526 Wasp Alarm Clock, lever escapement. Runs one day with one winding; stands 3¼ inches high; dial, 2 inches in diameter, is manufactured by the Waterbury Clock Co., and is guaranteed to keep correct time. Shipping wt., 16 oz. Price..........$1.20

No. 5R8532 Same as No. 5R8526, but without alarm; time only. Price..........85c

No. 5R8538 Buzzer Repeating Alarm Clock. Runs for thirty hours with one winding, made by the Ansonia Clock Co. This clock has all the advantages of a repeating alarm clock that sells from $1.25 to $1.50. It alarms at intervals of five seconds; stands 6½ inches high; dial is 4 inches in diameter. Shipping wt., 32 oz. Price..........86c

No. 5R8550 Nickel Calendar Alarm Clock. Height, 6¼ inches; dial 4 inches, runs 30 hours with one winding, has a calendar attachment as well as alarm, is made by the New Haven Clock Co., and is guaranteed to give entire satisfaction. Has a large nickel bell on top. This clock automatically tells you the day of the month as well as being an alarm clock. Shipping wt., 31 oz. Price..........92c

96c Boudoir Alarm Clock.

No. 5R8556 Boudoir Alarm Clock. Our gold plated cupid design Boudoir Alarm Clock for 96 cents. Clock stands 10 inches high, 8½ inches wide at base; dial is 2¾ inches in diameter, fitted with a French crystal. The frame is made of metal. Different from all other boudoir clocks, this one has an alarm attachment. The movement runs thirty hours with one winding, is an excellent timekeeper, has an alarm attachment and rings the same as any alarm clock. Weight, boxed for shipment, 5 lbs. Price..........96c

No. 5R8562 Our New Interval Alarm Clock. $1.26 (GUARANTEED FOR 2 YEARS) Stands 6 inches high, has a 4-inch dial with Roman numerals, blue steel hands, and a 4-inch bell on the back. The best alarm clock on the market. With each clock we send our two-year guarantee. It runs for thirty hours with one winding. Made of hand wrought brass and oil tempered steel parts, polished pivots and pinions, which reduce friction to a minimum, thereby insuring accurate timekeeping. The 4-inch bell on the back of the clock rings for forty seconds, then is silent for twenty seconds and continues for fifteen minutes unless you shut it off. The 4-inch bell sounds like a fire gong when the alarm rings. You cannot oversleep if you have one of these clocks. Shipping wt., 35 oz. Price..........$1.26

$2.48 For a Musical Alarm Clock.

No. 5R8592 One of the newest novelties on the market. This clock plays one tune for about ten minutes instead of ringing a bell. This clock stands 7 inches high, 5 inches wide, with front arabesque ornamentation around dial, full nickel plated frame with glass sides so that the movement and its action are visible at all times. Runs thirty hours. The music attachment is ingeniously hidden at the bottom of the clock, and so arranged that when the clock is set at a certain time, instead of an alarm bell being heard, a beautiful tune is played. With care it should last for many years and give entire satisfaction. $2.48 is a remarkably low figure for such a unique piece of clock mechanism. Weight of clock, packed ready for shipment, about 3 pounds. Price..........$2.48

88c Luminous Dial Two-Year Guaranteed Alarm Clock.

(GUARANTEED FOR 2 YEARS)

No. 5R8544 This clock has a splendid movement. Runs thirty hours with one winding, and is guaranteed to run well and accurately for a term of two years. The diameter of the dial is 4 inches; height, 6¼ inches; has a beautiful brass nickeled case, strong glass protected dial, durably built and splendidly adjusted, a wonderful value at 88 cents. **Regarding the luminous effect:** The dial is covered with a substance of which the principal ingredient is phosphorus. When phosphorus is exposed to the light it absorbs more or less of the light, and at night for a certain period of time will give back the light it has absorbed. This illumination lasts from fifteen minutes to possibly two hours. We do not wish you to expect too much of this clock. Do not think that it will remain luminous all night long or that you can distinguish figures and hands. It is merely a novelty or a scientific curiosity that pleases everybody. However, it is the best luminous clock offered by any house. There is nothing better in this style of clocks made in the United States. Shipping wt., 31 oz. Price..........88c

$1.46

No. 5R8574 Strike Alarm Clock. Made by the Ansonia Clock Co., height, 6¼ inches; dial, 4½ inches, movement runs thirty hours with one winding. Different from any other alarm clock; this clock strikes the hours and half hours the same as a mantel clock. In addition it has an alarm attachment which alarms at any time set. The Ansonia Clock Co. is known for the excellent clocks which they manufacture and we guarantee this clock to be an excellent timekeeper and to give entire satisfaction. Shipping wt., 36 oz. Price..........$1.46

$1.96 Continuous Long Alarm Clock.

No. 5R8580 Continuous Long Alarm Clock. The case is metal, finished in bronze. The movement is made by one of the most representative clock companies in the United States, and is warranted to us by the manufacturer; we in turn, guarantee it to our customers. The alarm rings for 7 minutes, but can be turned off at will by moving the lever. Height, 12 inches; width at base, 8½ inches. Shipping weight, 11 pounds. Price..........$1.96

No. 5R8586 Nickel Plated Glass Paneled High Grade Alarm Clock. Stands 6 inches high, 4½ inches wide at base and 3 inches deep. The dial is 2¾ inches in diameter, has plain Roman numerals. This clock is beautified by gilt arabesque panel work in the front of the clock. The movement is manufactured by the Waterbury Clock Co. It runs thirty hours with one winding. The alarm attachment is invisible, being placed underneath the clock. This clock is not alone an alarm clock, but also strikes the hours and half hours on a bell. Weight, packed ready for shipment, about 4 pounds. Price..........$2.30

$1.39 For an Eight-Day Gold Plated Bureau or Bedroom Clock.

No. 5R8568 Eight-Day Clock. The clock stands 3¼ inches high, has a 2-inch dial with French bevel glass crystal. It is built on the order of a nickel plated alarm clock, but has no alarm, and runs eight days with one winding. Just the clock for your shelf, bureau, desk or library table. Shipping wt., 16 oz. Price..........$1.39

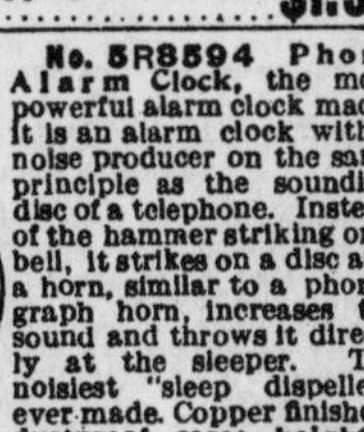

No. 5R8594 Phono Alarm Clock, the most powerful alarm clock made; it is an alarm clock with a noise producer on the same principle as the sounding disc of a telephone. Instead of the hammer striking on a bell, it strikes on a disc and a horn, similar to a phonograph horn, increases the sound and throws it directly at the sleeper. The noisiest "sleep dispeller" ever made. Copper finished, dustproof case; height 7 inches; Arabic dial, 4 inches in diameter. Shipping wt., 35 oz. Price..........$2.15

$3.29 For This Hanging Solid Oak Weathered Mission Eight-Day Clock.

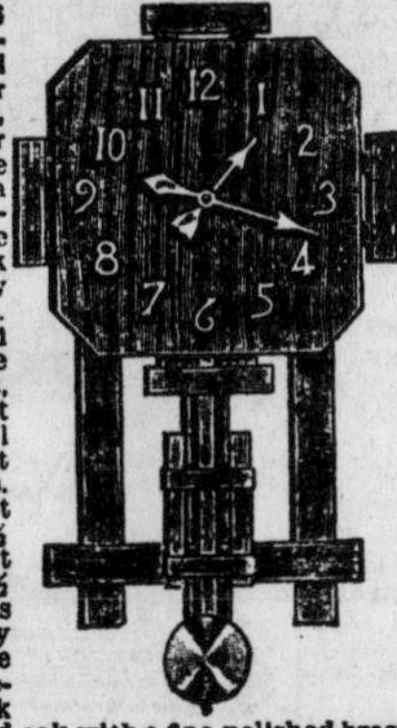

No. 5R9026 Nothing handsomer as a wall clock for your hall, dining room, den, bedroom or parlor. The movement is a fine runner, manufactured by the New Haven Clock Co., of New Haven, Conn. The dial is exposed exactly as the illustration shows, fitted with gilt solid metal numerals and gilt solid metal hands. The entire height of the clock is 27½ inches; width at widest point, 15½ inches. The dial is 15½ inches by 15½ inches. The pendulum is likewise solid dark colored weathered oak with a fine polished brass pendulum disc, and is adjustable. The movement runs for eight days, strikes the hours and half hours on a beautiful toned wire gong. Each one has been oiled and tested. This clock, boxed for shipment, weighs about 25 pounds. Price..........$3.29

THE ALDRICH. $1.85

Made by the Waterbury Clock Company, furnished in either oak or walnut as desired. Stands 22 inches high, 15 inches wide at base. Case is handsomely carved, perfectly fitted and jointed and is a marvel of value. Movement runs eight days with one winding, strikes the hours and half hours on a wire bell, has a 6-inch dial. Guaranteed to keep accurate time. Shipping weight, 16 pounds.

No. 5R9002 Strikes on a wire bell. Price..........$1.85

No. 5R9004 Strikes on a wire bell, with an alarm attachment. Price..........$2.30

No. 5R9008 Strikes on a gong bell, with an alarm attachment. Price..........$2.45

$2.38 CUT PRICE. Weathered Oak Mission Style Clock.

No. 5R9020 It stands at the highest point 20½ inches high; width at the base, 12 inches. The dial is plain and is also made of solid oak with bright metal numerals and bright metal hands. The movement runs for eight days with but one winding, and is manufactured by the renowned New Haven Clock Co. Strikes the hours and half hours on a sweet toned cathedral wire gong. We have contracted for an immense number; an immense quantity has made this astonishing price possible. We again offer you the advantage of the saving, adding only our own small per cent of profit to the original cost. This clock boxed, ready for shipment, weighs about 18 pounds. Price..........$2.38

$3.45

The Rochester Fancy Ornamental Cabinet Clock, made of solid black walnut, handsonely carved; height, 26¾ inches. Different from anyother cabinet clock, this clock has an 8-inch dial, 2-inch larger dial than anordinary cabinet clock, which makes it easy to see the time from any part of the room. It is fitted with an eight-day movement made by the Waterbury Clock Co., hard wrought brass and oil tempered steel parts, strikes the hours and half hours. In addition it has a calendar attachment which automatically registers the day of the month. Shipping weight, about 20 pounds.

No. 5R9032 Strikes on wire bell. Price..........$3.45

No. 5R9038 Strikes on cathedral gong. Price..........3.75

Combination Clock and Plate Rack. $2.48

No. 5R8596 $2.48 for this Combination Clock and Plate Rack, a new novelty in the clock line, a splendid ornament for any room, substantially and massively made of solid dark weathered oak, is 10½ inches high and 39½ inches long, made to hold six cups and six saucers or four fancy plates. The clock is a good running, accurate spring timer, runs for 24 hours. The dial is 5¾ inches in diameter, has solid brass numerals and brass hands, making a pretty contrast in colors, yellow brass and dark weathered oak. Boxed ready for shipment, about 18 pounds. Price..........$2.48

$2.18 TO $3.18 FOR CHOICE OF THESE FIVE-YEAR GUARANTEED CLOCKS

Made by the greatest clock makers in the United States.

PRICES REDUCED

$3.18 The Prophet.

Five-Year Written Guarantee Sent with this Clock.

No. 5R9066 Eight-Day Clock, shelf effect, with calendar, thermometer and barometer attached, called the Prophet. Our guarantee for a term of five years goes with every one sold. The manufacturer's name does not appear on it. It was made for us not with the idea of matching similar clocks on the market, but rather to improve on any heretofore manufactured, the idea being not how cheap a clock could be produced, but rather how fine a one for the price. Clock stands 27 inches high; width, 13 inches; has 6-inch dial. The case is handsomely carved oak. We do not supply it in walnut, nor can it be had with alarm attachment. This clock is especially adapted as a wall clock, having a shelf attachment. Runs eight days with one winding, and strikes the hours and half hours on a wire bell; likewise shows days of the month, temperature and changes of the weather, having calendar attachment and supplied with barometer and thermometer on either side of case, as illustration shows. The movement is of oil tempered, hard rolled steel and brass; pinions, pivots and all friction gear being well polished to avoid friction, thereby increasing its ability as a timekeeper. Weight, boxed ready for shipment, 16 pounds. Price $3.18

$2.59 The Netherlands.

Five-Year Written Guarantee Sent With This Clock.

No. 5R9062 THE NETHERLANDS. We cannot tell you the maker's name on account of the special cut price, but we can tell you that it is manufactured by one of the four big clock companies in the United States, and we guarantee it to give entire and absolute satisfaction. Our written binding guarantee goes with every clock sold. This clock is finished in oak only. The clock stands 22 inches high and is 15 inches wide. The movement runs eight days with one winding, strikes the hours and half hours, and has calendar attachment, showing the days of the month; likewise has barometer and thermometer, indicating at all times the temperature and enabling you to anticipate the changes in the weather. Dial, 6 inches in diameter. Our price for this specially made clock is $2.59. Don't think because we have named such a wonderfully low price on this clock that it is not the best on the market. Our $2.59 price is possible only for the reason that we maintain our one small per cent profit policy, and on account of a special arrangement with the factory for an immense quantity at a remarkably low price and, as always, we give you the benefit of this remarkable purchase. Weight of clock, boxed ready for shipment, 15 pounds. Price $2.59

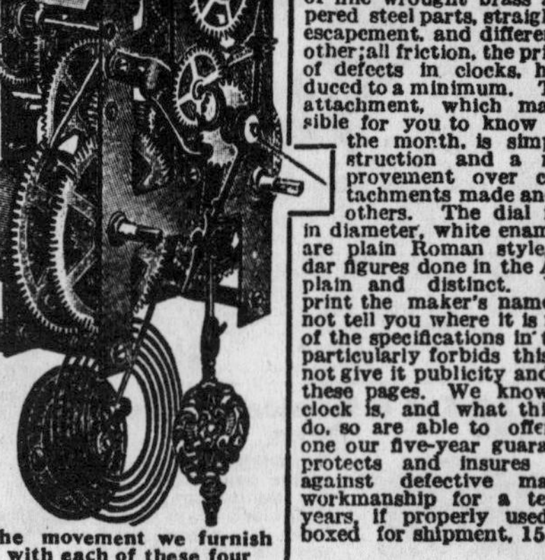

The movement we furnish with each of these four clocks.

$2.72 for a Five-Year Guaranteed Time and Calendar Clock.

No. 5R9058 THE LEOPOLD runs eight days with one winding, strikes the hours and half hours on a gong bell, likewise shows the days of the month. Stands 22 inches high; case is carved and embossed oak. The movement is made of fine wrought brass and oil tempered steel parts, straight line verge escapement, and different from any other; all friction, the principal cause of defects in clocks, has been reduced to a minimum. The calendar attachment, which makes it possible for you to know the day of the month, is simple in construction and a marked improvement over calendar attachments made and offered by others. The dial is 6 inches in diameter, white enameled figures are plain Roman style, the calendar figures done in the Arabic style, plain and distinct. We do not print the maker's name. We cannot tell you where it is made. One of the specifications in the contract particularly forbids this. We cannot give it publicity and print it on these pages. We know what this clock is, and what this clock can do, so are able to offer with each one our five-year guarantee, which protects and insures this clock against defective material and workmanship for a term of five years, if properly used. Weight, boxed for shipment, 15 pounds. Price $2.72

$2.18 Our Cabinet Clock.

Five-Year Written Guarantee Sent With This Clock.

THE AMSTERDAM Cabinet Clock. This clock stands 22 inches high and is 15 inches wide. Made exclusively for us by one of the four big clock manufacturers. The case is finished in oak only. The movement is manufactured by one of the most representative clock companies and carries with it our own special written binding guarantee for a term of five years. It runs eight days with one winding, strikes the hours and half hours. Dial, 6 inches in diameter. Weight of clock, boxed ready for shipment, about 15 pounds.

No. 5R9050 Price $2.18

No. 5R9054 Price, with alarm attachment, $2.40

Bronze Ornaments.

No. 5R3292 Finely executed bronze statue; beautiful clock or mantelpiece ornament. Height, 12 inches. Price 78c

Shipping weight, 6 lbs.

No. 5R2940 Very Artistic Bronze Figure of Horse, true to life, for a mantel or top of mantel clock; 8½ inches long base. Shipping weight, 5 pounds. Price 75c

$3.38 Our Challenge Clock.

For an Eight-Day Wall Clock. This clock is made by the Gilbert Clock Co., and is one of their latest productions. The case is made of golden oak, ornamented with carvings throughout. The movement is made of solid brass with oil tempered steel parts. The clock runs eight days with one winding, has long wooden pendulum with brass ball which can be lowered or raised so as to regulate the clock. This clock is sold regularly at $4.50 to $5.50, but on account of a special contract we are able to name the extremely low price of $3.38. The clock stands 37 inches high, is 15½ inches wide and has a 12-inch dial. Shipping weight, 28 pounds.

No. 5R9102 Time only. Price $3.38

No. 5R9104 Time and calendar. Price 3.88

No. 5R9106 Strikes half hours. Price 4.48

No. 5R9108 Strikes half hours, with calendar. Price $4.58

$6.75 Eight-Day Perpetual Calendar Clock.

Our Eight-Day Perpetual Calendar Clock, with 8-inch dial, manufactured especially for us by the Waterbury Clock Co., of Waterbury, Conn. The clock is made of oak, stands 28½ inches high. The case is beautifully embossed and carved throughout. Beautiful ornaments adorn the top and sides of this case. On either side are two massive oak columns which lend a richness to this clock that cannot be excelled. The case is made of extra heavy hardwood, kiln dried. All joints are perfectly fitted, protecting this movement from dust and dampness. The glass of door is decorated in black and gold. The movement is the latest straight line verge escapement, made of hard wrought brass and oil tempered steel pinions and pivots, no burred edges to interfere with the timekeeping qualities of the clock. Runs eight days with one winding. Strikes the hours and half hours on a sweet toned gong. The clock is guaranteed to us by the manufacturer and we in turn guarantee it to our customers, and with proper care it should last you your natural lifetime. Shipping weight, 25 pounds.

No. 5R9110 Price $6.75

$3.18 for an Eight-Day Drop Octagon Wall Clock.

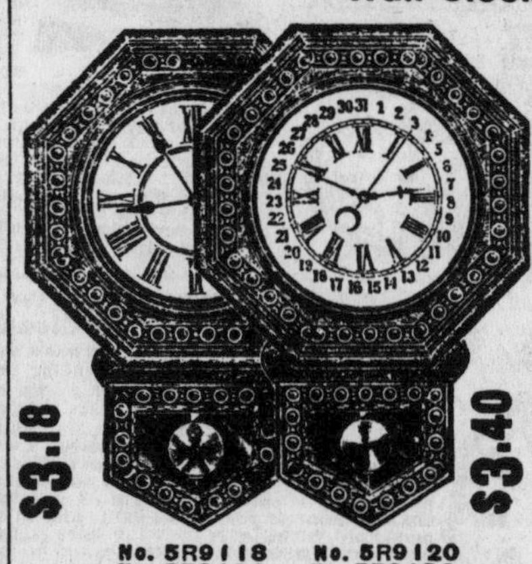

No. 5R9118 No. 5R9124 No. 5R9120 No. 5R9126

The case is made of oak, 24 inches high. The case is ornamented with beautifully carved molding which lends a richness to this clock seldom equaled. The dial is 10 inches in diameter, plain Roman numerals painted exceedingly large. The hands are made of blued steel in fleur de lis pattern. The dial is ornamented with a plain polished gilt sash. The movement is made by the Waterbury Clock Co., of hard wrought brass and oil tempered steel. Pinions and pivots are polished, assuring accurate timekeeping. The clock is guaranteed to us by the manufacturers and we in turn guarantee it to our customers. Shipping weight, 20 pounds.

No. 5R9118 10-inch dial, time only. Price $3.18
No. 5R9120 10-inch dial, time with calendar. Price 3.40
No. 5R9122 10-inch dial, time with strike. Price 3.50
No. 5R9124 12-inch dial, time only. Price 3.50
No. 5R9126 12-inch dial, time with calendar. Price 3.65
No. 5R9128 12-inch dial, time with strike. Price 3.78

Price, as illustrated, $4.70

The Conqueror.

$4.70 for a genuine Waterbury hard enameled eight-day bronze ornamented large size mantel clock with solid bronze figure.

This is our special offer, $4.70 for this grand clock, and we challenge any manufacturer, jobber or retailer to duplicate it.

We ask for comparison. We want you to investigate. Write for prices. Never before has such a value in a clock, marked with the name of one of the greatest clock manufacturers, been offered. The Conqueror, so named because it beats any clock on the market. Height, including figure, 23 inches; the width at base is 17½ inches; depth, 8 inches; height of clock alone, 11 inches. It is durably made of hard seasoned wood, guaranteed not to warp or crack, beautifully hard black enameled to imitate black marble, and trimmed in colors to imitate the lighter Mexican onyx.

A special feature of this clock is the secret process of enameling. It is guaranteed not to peel or chip off. A rag slightly moistened with oil and rubbed over the clock keeps it as new for a lifetime. This clock is magnificent in its bronze metal ornamentation, which includes the heavy one-inch border all around the clock just above the base, massive bronze feet and massive side bronze scroll ornaments. The dial is plain yet beautiful, with bright finished gilded sash.

The Waterbury Clock Co. guarantees the movement in this clock to give perfect satisfaction. It runs eight days with one winding, strikes the hours on a cathedral gong and the half hours on a cup bell. No clock but what is absolutely perfect in going and timekeeping is allowed to leave this splendidly organized factory. The manufacturer, by reason of a big contract, reduced his profits to a mere fraction compared to what he generally makes, and we, following out our accustomed rule and method, have added only our one small percentage of profit. Weight of clock, boxed ready for shipment, 20 pounds.

No. 5G3290 Price, including figure **$4.70**
No. 5G3292 Price of figure alone .... **.88**

$3.65 for Our Prince Elias.

OUR PRINCE ELIAS, the newest clock out of the factory, exactly in every particular as illustration shows, for **$3.65.** Don't think that you will not get or cannot buy from us a fine clock for this price. In fact, this price is no criterion. The clock is really worth twice as much. Your local dealer or the jobber he buys it from would pay 25 to 45 per cent more than we ask you for it. In other words, you would have to pay your local dealer for a clock as good as this and as handsome as this one, from $5.00 to $6.00. This clock is made expressly for us by the Waterbury Clock Co., of Waterbury, Conn. Each one of them is thoroughly guaranteed and we warrant them to give entire satisfaction.

DESCRIPTION OF CASE. The case is made of wood, covered with a secretly prepared enamel, imitating black marble. It is guaranteed not to chip or wear off, and always retains its deep black marblelike appearance. It has handsome gilt feet, marbleized gilt metal capped and gilt metal based columns, beautiful gilt scroll metal work at top and base. The sides are also ornamented by two gilt metal designs, exactly as the illustration shows. The dial is very pretentious, made of metal fancy work and is 5 inches in diameter.

DESCRIPTION OF MOVEMENT. The movement fitted in this case is one of the Waterbury guaranteed movements, runs eight days with one winding. It is made of the finest tempered steel and hand wrought brass; it strikes the hours on a cathedral gong and the half hours on a brass bell. You can always know the time without seeing the clock. The hands are very fine hand sawed blue steel of the fleur de lis pattern. Shipping weight, 16 pounds.

No. 5G3302 Price **$3.65**

Queen Mantel Clock and Figure for $4.18.

No. 5G3304 $4.18 for this handsome Polished Wood Clock with bronze figure does not represent the cost to manufacture. Never before in the history of clock making has such a fine clock and figure been offered for this money. The case is made of fine wood, kiln dried. It is then enameled by a secret process and polished to a high gloss. The enamel is guaranteed never to crack or peel. A canton flannel cloth sprinkled with sweet oil occasionally rubbed over the clock will make it look like new. A gilt rococo metal border ornaments the top edge of the clock. Gilt ornaments adorn the front underneath the dial, gilt bronze side ornaments. Two massive marbleized columns on either side of dial. The clock is 10½ inches high, is 12½ inches wide at the base and 6 inches deep. The movement is made by one of the most representative clock makers in the United States, has the latest straight line verge escapement of hand wrought brass and oil tempered steel parts. Runs eight days with one winding, strikes the half hours and hours on a sweet cathedral gong. The dial is 5½ inches in diameter, with gilt rococo design sash. The figure, 6¾ inches high, represents a figure true to life, is made of bronze and finished in gold gilt. Only by reason of purchasing these clocks in enormous quantities are we able to offer it at this remarkable price. $4.18 only represents the actual cost of material and manufacturing, with only our one small percentage of profit added. Order this clock and upon examination if you do not find it to be exactly as illustrated and described, the best clock value ever offered, return it to us at our expense and we will cheerfully refund your money. Shipping weight, 22 pounds. Price **$4.18**

$31.50 for Our Genuine Mahogany Grandfather's Eight-Day Clock.

$31.50

No. 5G3308 $31.50 for our Genuine Mahogany Grandfather's Eight-day Clock, exactly as illustrated, exactly as described below. The same clock costs the retail merchant, if he pays cash for his goods, $35.00 to $38.00. This very handsome clock is not an imported one, but is an American production, American case and American movement. We are able to make this price because we assemble the clocks ourselves; that is, we have had the case made under our specifications, and the movements we buy direct from the clock companies. We put the parts together and are able by this handling to save 25 to 30 per cent in the purchase. According to our customary rule, we give you the advantage of it, which means no less than $15.00 saving to you. The dimensions of the clock: Stands 7¼ feet high; 21½ inches wide at base; 13¼ inches deep; dial is 12 inches in diameter. The case is made of mahogany, beautifully finished and polished. No rough edges, no unfinished joints, in fact, a perfect masterpiece of the joiner's art. As illustration shows, the clock is beautifully ornamented by solid fancy turned top ornaments and side pillars. The crystals in this clock are all the finest beveled edge, firmly set in strong sashes hung on double hinges. The movement is a genuine American made movement, runs eight days with one winding; strikes the hours and half hours on a sweet toned cathedral gong; not a spring movement used in many cheap and shoddy clocks now on the market and advertised extensively in newspapers and periodicals as mission, grandfather's clocks, etc., but is a genuine weight clock; that is, the motive power which operates this timepiece is two fine brass weights. This mechanism when properly constructed is such that it insures the most accurate time possible, and is used by the big conservatories where accurate time without variation is required. Black numerals and fine blue steel hands on a silver dial lend a handsome effect to the clock. Inferior clocks sold as high grade have poorly penciled numerals and poor clock hands. The pendulum is 32 inches long, and is visible. The glass front makes it possible to see the swaying of the brass pendulum and the two weights hung on chains; one of the charms in a grandfather's clock. The movement is especially tested and tried before it leaves the factory and again before we make shipment of same. It is thoroughly oiled and regulated and we guarantee it to reach destination in perfect running order. Don't think because of this unheard of price for such a handsome grandfather's clock, $31.50, that this clock will not wear a lifetime. With proper care we guarantee it to be serviceable and to keep good and accurate time for the lifetime of any human being. In fact the facsimile of this clock purchased through any other channel in the regular way could not be procured for double what we ask. Weight, boxed and crated ready for shipment, about 180 pounds.

Price **$31.50**

Our Challenge Clock at $3.20.

For Church, School or Store Regulator. This clock is made by the Gilbert Clock Co., and is one of their latest productions. The case is made of golden oak, ornamented with hand carvings throughout. The movement is made of solid brass with oil tempered steel parts. The clock runs eight days with one winding, has long wooden pendulum with brass ball which can be lowered or raised so as to regulate the clock. The clock stands 37 inches high, is 15½ inches wide and has a 12-inch dial. Shipping weight, 28 lbs.

No. 5G3503 Time only. Price.... **$3.20**
No. 5G3505 Time and Calendar. Price.. **$3.30**
No. 5G3507 Strikes half hours. Price. **$3.80**
No. 5G3509 Strikes half hours, with Calendar. Price.......... **$3.90**

$2.75 for a $3.50 Drop Octagon Office Clock.

The case is made of solid oak, 24 inches high. The case is ornamented with a beautifully carved moulding which lends a richness to this clock seldom equaled. The dial is made of white enameled paper, plain Roman numerals painted exceedingly large. The hands are made of blued steel fleur de lis pattern. The dial is ornamented with a plain polished gilt sash. The movement is made by the Waterbury Clock Co., of hand wrought brass and oil tempered steel. Pinions and pivots are hand polished, assuring accurate timekeeping. The clock is guaranteed to us by the manufacturers and we in turn guarantee it to our customers. Shipping weight, 20 pounds.

No. 5G3519 10-inch dial, time only. Price **$2.75**
No. 5G3521 10-inch dial, time with calendar Price **$3.10**
No. 5G3523 10-inch dial, time with strike. Price **$3.18**
No. 5G3525 12-inch dial, time only. Price **$3.15**
No. 5G3527 12-inch dial, time with calendar. Price **$3.40**
No. 5G3529 12-inch dial, time with strike. Price **$3.55**

Eight-Day Regulator, $3.90.

No. 5G3547

$3.90 for this regulator, runs eight days with one winding, tells the days of the month, hours and minutes. Case stands 31 inches high and is manufactured of solid oak, very heavy, plain in style and very durable. All joints, all parts thoroughly finished and well made. The dial is 12 inches in diameter. The days of the month are shown by Arabic numerals and the hours by Roman figures distinctly painted, plain and conspicuous. The pendulum, differing from many regulators, is made of wood so as to overcome the variations of temperature, wood being a non-conductor of heat or cold. The movement is manufactured by one of the largest clock companies in the United States, is guaranteed to us an accurate timekeeper and warranted to give satisfaction. Runs eight days with one winding, is made of hard wrought brass and oil tempered steel parts, no burrs, no swedging, simple in construction and durable, specially adapted for school rooms, church lobbies, offices or places of public entertainment. Shipping weight, 28 pounds. Price **$3.90**

Second to None at the Price.

$4.05

No. 5G3555 CUCKOO CLOCK. Case is made of German oak or walnut ornamented with inlaid ash, ebony and mahogany. Beautifully hand carved throughout, strikes the hours and half hours on a wire bell, the cuckoo appears and calls at the same time. Height of clock, 21 inches; width, 14 inches. The movement is made in the Black Forest, Germany, of the finest tempered steel and polished brass, finely finished and adjusted, guaranteed to be a good timekeeper. One of the most artistic ornaments for a parlor ever made. Weight, boxed, 20 pounds.
Price......$4.05

Imported Cuckoo Clock.

$7.48

No. 5G3570 Hand Carved Solid Walnut Imported Cuckoo Clock for $7.48. This clock is manufactured in the Schwarzwald, Germany, the home of cuckoo clock making. Each leaf, the deer head, all parts as illustration shows, are guaranteed hand carved, true to life, and realistic. Positively nothing handsomer to ornament your parlor or dining room wall, nothing more attractive in the house, nothing will please the children more than to hear the cuckoo calling. Clock is 19 inches high, 14 inches wide, dial 5¼ inches in diameter, strikes the half hours on a beautifully toned wire bell. At the half hour and full hour the cuckoo appears, opening automatically the little door placed directly above the figure 12, and calls out the half hour and full hours. This clock is run by two weights. The weight system of operating clocks equalizes and distributes the motive power and is far superior to the spring movement for keeping accurate time. The movement, built under new plans, is made of solid brass with oil tempered steel parts, simple in design, simple in execution. Dial is very plain and distinct, and easily read from a distance, being 5¼ inches in diameter, fitted with applied figures and white bleached bone hands. Nothing to get out of order, nothing complicated, will give entire and perfect satisfaction. Full directions go with each clock, how to set it and to start it going. Weight, packed ready for shipment, about 24 pounds. Price......$7.48

Imported Quail and Cuckoo Clock.

$12.65

No. 5G3572 $12.65 for a Quail and Cuckoo Clock. No home, especially where children are, is complete without it. This clock is manufactured of solid walnut, not veneered, not pieced. Cannot warp, crack or chip as veneered and pieced cuckoo clocks do. It is imported from the Schwarzwald, Germany, the home of cuckoo clock making. As a masterpiece, an example for hand carving, this, our quail and cuckoo clock, is second to none. Please examine in detail the beautiful ornamentation. The case consists of overlapping and overlaying grape vines, grapes and grape leaves. Each grape and leaf, each section of vine hand carved. The pendulum consists of a wreath of grape vines, centered by grape leaves. The movement is made under the latest American principles of clock making, on square lines, straight line verge escapement, hand wrought hardened brass and oil tempered steel parts. Clock stands 21 inches high, 16 inches wide. Dial is 6⅝ inches in diameter, plain and distinct, easily seen from any part of the room, with white Roman numerals and white bleached bone hands. This clock runs by three weights, acorn style, handsomely bronzed, as illustration shows. For ages the weight system in clocks has been used with the best results. It equalizes and distributes the motive power throughout. The quail and cuckoo attachment is absolutely perfect. You have one bird appearing at quarter hour intervals. The two doors, as illustration shows, situated above the figure 12, open automatically. Out steps the quail or cuckoo, warbling or calling the quarter or full hour. Together with the calling of the birds, the quarter or full hours are struck on a beautifully toned bell. Nothing more complete in clock making, nothing more ingenious and nothing more interesting. Weight, packed ready for shipping, about 32 pounds. Price......$12.65

Highest Quality Imported Quail and Cuckoo Clock, $16.98.

No. 5G3574 $16.98 for absolute perfection in Quail and Cuckoo Clock. On account of the demand for something more perfect, something handsomer than has ever been offered for the money before, we have had imported for us this 22½-inch high Schwarzwald genuine hand carved solid walnut quail and cuckoo clock. The case is designed in solid walnut, representing sprays of German oak leaves artistically arranged by overlapping and drooping, knotted here and there by the conventional acorn. Surmounting this masterpiece stands an eagle. No pains, no expense, no care has been lacking to make this our special drive in large size cuckoo clocks the best value for the money. The case stands 22½ inches high, 18 inches wide, dial 6⅝ inches, not pieced, not veneered, but one solid massive piece of solid walnut, preventing the possibility of cracking, chipping or warping. The figures on dial are applied plain white, the hands hand sawed bleached white bone. This clock is run by three weights. The weight system of operating clocks equalizes and distributes the motive power throughout, insuring accurate timekeeping. The movement is made under American models at the Schwarzwald, of extra thick, extra toughened hand wrought brass, hand polished oil tempered steel parts and pinions, straight line verge escapement. Nothing intricate, nothing complicated, the liability of getting out of order has practically been removed. The quail and cuckoo attachment is the acme of perfection. Two birds with automatically adjusted wings and beaks appear through the automatically opened doors. At the quarter hours the quail bird appears and cherups the quarter hours. The cuckoo bird appears at the full hours and calls the hour. At the same time that the full hours are called they are likewise sounded on a beautifully toned wire gong. This clock, unlike many cuckoo clocks, has been perfected in every detail. No part has been overlooked, either in artistic design or manner of execution. Each one of these clocks is guaranteed to us and we in turn guarantee them to our customers. The pendulum is hand carved, with adjusting screw on the bottom the raising or lowering of same regulates the clock. Full instructions are sent with each one when shipped. No difficulty to place it on the wall. No hardship to handle. Weight, packed ready for shipment, about 32 pounds. Price..........$16.98

Eight-Day Perpetual Calendar Clock, $6.75.

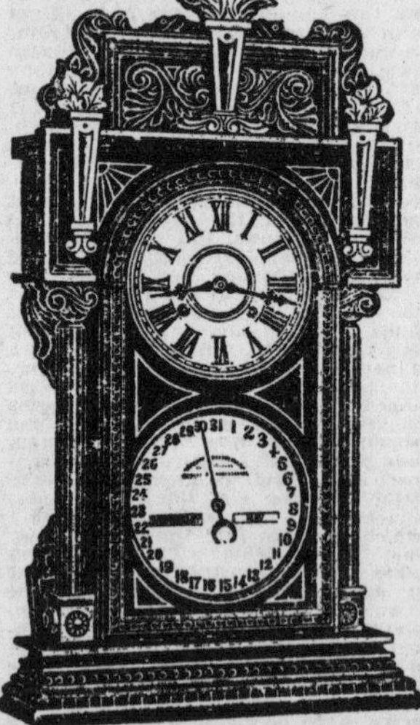

No. 5G3580 Our Eight-Day Perpetual Calendar Clock, with 8-inch dial, manufactured especially for us by the Waterbury Mfg. Co. of Waterbury, Conn. The clock is made of solid oak, stands 28½ inches high. The case is beautifully embossed and hand carved throughout. Beautiful ornaments adorn the top and sides of this case. On either side are two massive oak columns which lend a richness to this clock that cannot be excelled. The case is made of extra heavy hard wood kiln dried. All joints are perfectly fitted, protecting this movement from dust and dampness. The door of this clock is swung on brass hinges and has a patent safety catch. The glass of door is decorated in black and gold. The movement is the latest straight line verge escapement, made of hand wrought brass and oil tempered steel pinions and pivots, no burred edges to interfere with the timekeeping qualities of the clock. Runs eight days with one winding. Strikes the hours and half hours on a sweet toned gong. The clock is guaranteed to us by the manufacturer and in turn is guaranteed to our customers and with proper care should last you your natural life. Shipping weight, 25 pounds. Price..........$6.75

A Five-Year Guarantee with this Clock.

$3.62

No. 5G3711 OUR COUNTESS JANET Mantel Clock. The most wonderful bargain ever offered in the United States. This mantel clock is made of wood, then hard enameled in black with marbleized ornamentation, exactly as illustration shows. Stands 10¾ inches high, 7¼ inches deep, 16½ inches wide. Has gilt metal feet, side ornaments and tops and bases of the two columns on front of clock. It has an eight-day movement, strikes the half hours on a bell, and the hours on a gong. The dial is 5½ inches in diameter, with plain numerals; the dial sash is the latest Parisian pattern. This is one of the most wonderful values offered. It was made especially for us, and carries our five-year binding guarantee. We cannot divulge the maker's name on account of the low price quoted. The movement will give particularly good satisfaction, it is of hard rolled brass and oil tempered steel parts. All friction in the train and delicate running parts has been reduced to a minimum, thereby giving it a life of accurate timekeeping not possible in other clocks. Weight, 18 pounds. Price..........$3.62

No. 5G3301 Handsome Bronze Figure, representing a cowboy on horseback, throwing a lariat. This figure placed on top of the Countess Janet Clock makes a most beautiful parlor ornament. Price, figure only..........78c

Wonder Value at $4.45.

$4.45

A 5-Year Guarantee Given with this Clock.

No. 5G3901 OUR EMPRESS MANTEL CLOCK, exactly as illustration shows in every detail. It stands 10½ inches high, 7 inches deep, 17½ inches wide. It has solid gilt bronze feet, gilt bronze ornaments on the front of the clock. Clock is made of wood, enameled in black, with marbleized trimmings. This enameling is guaranteed not to warp or chip off. A woolen cloth, slightly sprinkled with sweet oil, lightly rubbed over this clock, will keep it in perfect condition for a lifetime. The dial is 5¾ inches in diameter. The sash which surrounds it is the very latest rococo design. The movement runs for eight days with one winding, strikes the half hours on a metal bell and the hours on a sweet toned gong. It is manufactured by one of the most celebrated clock companies in the United States. On account of the low price quoted here we cannot print the maker's name. The movement, as in all of our own special clocks, is made of hardened rolled brass and oil tempered steel parts. The bearings and all intricate and delicate parts, where friction reduces the wearing ability, are so constructed that it is reduced to a minimum, therefore we know our special line of clocks will outwear any on the market and give accurate time. **This clock is the most massive and most pretentious and biggest value for the money ever before offered.** Clocks sold by the makers of this clock, of similar design but not so massive or elaborate, bring from the retail jewelers and from the jobbers from 25 to 30 per cent more than the price we ask. Just compare this with others, and we are satisfied that we will get your order. Weight, boxed for shipment, 18 pounds. Price......$4.45

THIS HANDSOME FUR PIECE IS FREE

ANY CUSTOMER OF OURS ANYWHERE CAN HAVE THIS BEAUTIFUL FUR PIECE, made in the very latest style, one of the prettiest neck pieces shown this season, without paying one penny for it, by saving our Profit Sharing Certificates until they amount to only $25.00, then send them to us and we will give you this fur piece free. In addition to our wonderfully low prices, the lowest prices ever quoted, we share our profits with our customers, we give back a liberal percentage of every dollar sent us for merchandise, and under this liberal Profit Sharing Plan it is not only possible to secure this handsome fur piece free, but hundreds of other useful, beautiful and valuable Profit Sharing Articles, as fully described in our new, revised and enlarged free Profit Sharing Book.

At $4.50 We Defy Competition.

No. 5G3900 Our new eight-day, striking, black finished, six column Waterbury Clock for $4.50. The case is of hard, black enameled wood, not a joint, crack or crevice to be found in any part of it. It is warranted to give entire and absolute satisfaction. A woolen cloth slightly sprinkled with sweet oil lightly rubbed over this clock will keep it in its pristine beauty for many years. Six columns, made to imitate Mexican marble and ornamented with gilt tops and bases, ornament the sides. This is a new idea in clock ornamentation. The feet are of fine gilt metal with beautiful scroll work, which lends a fancy and charm to this clock rarely equaled. The sash which holds the dial is of fine gilt brass 5¼ inches in diameter. The dial is plain and distinctly marked with Roman numerals and fitted with fine fleur de lis hands. The clock stands 10¾ inches high; the base from foot to foot, 15½ inches wide; depth, 7 inches. The movement is manufactured by the Waterbury Clock Co., of Waterbury, Conn., and is trued and timed and guaranteed in every respect; runs eight days with one winding; strikes the half hours on a brass bell and the hours on a cathedral toned gong. It is made of fine hard wrought brass, oil tempered steel parts, and with care will wear and keep time for a lifetime. Weight, packed for shipment, about 20 pounds. Price $4.50

Our Leader. $14.46 for this $25.00 Clock.

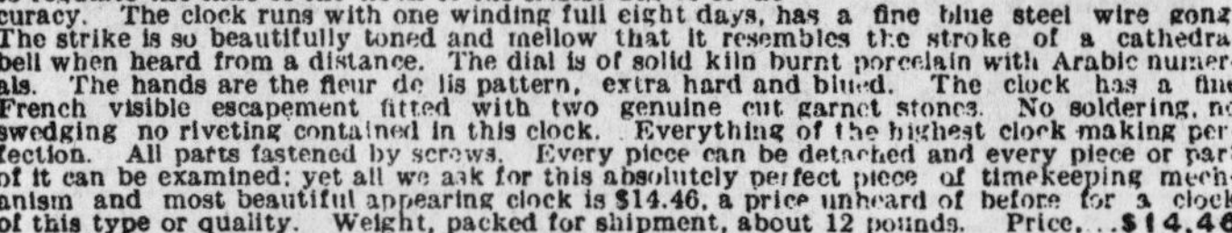

No. 5G3904 A genuine French pattern, American made, full polished, solid gold plated brass, eight-day crystal clock and the highest possible degree of perfection in clock making, for $14.46. A steady inquiry and a persistent demand for a high grade crystal sided clock, such as is here illustrated, impelled us to make under special contract this beautiful highly polished solid brass beveled crystal plate glass sided clock at a special price for a large quantity. The case is solid brass, heavily gold plated, has the rich California yellow pure gold finish. The case stands 10½ inches high, 4½ inches deep with a 6¾-inch base. The front, back and sides are paneled, as illustration shows, with the finest beveled edge crystal glass, free from any blemish, flaw or defect. The front of the clock opens, has a patent safety catch, swung on an extra strong pivoted steel hinge. By this arrangement the clock is practically dustproof. The movement is manufactured by the Waterbury Clock Co. The duplicate, made in France and imported to this country, would cost no less than $40.00 to $50.00. The steel parts, pivots, pinions and wheels are all made in the highest possible perfection. No part, no piece left unfinished or unpolished, even the screws used throughout are blued and screw tempered. The pendulum is of the attractive regulator style, being an imitation of the accurate going mercury pendulum, an exact imitation of a pendulum that would cost no less than $10.00 to $15.00. It can be adjusted so as to regulate the time of the clock to the closest degree of accuracy. The clock runs with one winding full eight days, has a fine blue steel wire gong. The strike is so beautifully toned and mellow that it resembles the stroke of a cathedral bell when heard from a distance. The dial is of solid kiln burnt porcelain with Arabic numerals. The hands are the fleur de lis pattern, extra hard and blued. The clock has a fine French visible escapement fitted with two genuine cut garnet stones. No soldering, no swedging no riveting contained in this clock. Everything of the highest clock making perfection. All parts fastened by screws. Every piece can be detached and every piece or part of it can be examined; yet all we ask for this absolutely perfect piece of timekeeping mechanism and most beautiful appearing clock is $14.46, a price unheard of before for a clock of this type or quality. Weight, packed for shipment, about 12 pounds. Price....$14.46

Only $3.98 for this Guaranteed Clock.

Five-Year Guarantee sent with this Clock.

No. 5G3917 OUR AMERICAN LADY MANTEL CLOCK, manufactured by one of the biggest and most representative makers in the United States, but on account of the very low price quoted, we dare not print the maker's name. However, it carries our five-year written binding guarantee, and we know you will be entirely satisfied with it. This clock stands 10¾ inches high, 7 inches deep and 17 inches wide. It has solid gilt bronze ornaments; also metal top and base on the four columns, as illustration shows. The dial is 5¾ inches in diameter, the very latest pattern of fancy fret work, with a beautiful rococo sash. The case is of wood, black enameled, warranted not to peel, chip or crack off. A soft woolen cloth, sprinkled with sweet oil, will keep it as new, practically, for a lifetime. The movement runs eight days with one winding; strikes the half hours on a metal bell and the hours on a soft toned gong. This, our American Lady Mantel Clock, is one of the special bargains we have referred you to in our description on page 134. If this clock suits your taste (we refer to the design), we know that a better clock or a greater value for the money cannot be had for twice what we ask. We are particularly proud of the movement used in this clock, as it is made of solid hardened rolled brass and oil tempered steel parts. The bearings and other delicate parts are so constructed that the friction is reduced to a minimum, therefore, the life of the clock is greater than any other. Weight, boxed, 18 pounds. Price....$3.98

WE GIVE YOU THIS STAND FREE

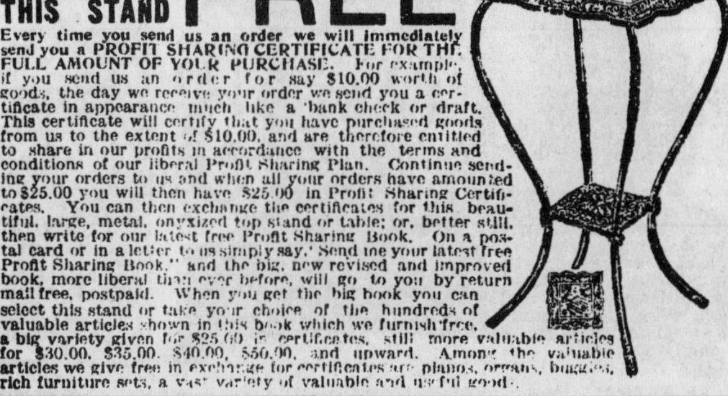

Every time you send us an order we will immediately send you a PROFIT SHARING CERTIFICATE FOR THE FULL AMOUNT OF YOUR PURCHASE. For example, if you send us an order for say $10.00 worth of goods, the day we receive your order we send you a certificate in appearance much like a bank check or draft. This certificate will certify that you have purchased goods from us to the extent of $10.00, and are therefore entitled to share in our profits in accordance with the terms and conditions of our liberal Profit Sharing Plan. Continue sending your orders to us and when all your orders have amounted to $25.00 you will then have $25.00 in Profit Sharing Certificates. You can then exchange the certificates for this beautiful, large, metal, onyxized top stand or table; or, better still, then write for our latest free Profit Sharing Book. On a postal card or in a letter to us simply say, "Send me your latest free Profit Sharing Book," and the big, new revised and improved book, more liberal than ever before, will go to you by return mail free, postpaid. When you get the big book you can select this stand or take your choice of the hundreds of valuable articles shown in this book which we furnish free, a big variety given for $25.00 in certificates, still more valuable articles for $30.00, $35.00, $40.00, $50.00, and upward. Among the valuable articles we give free in exchange for certificates are pianos, organs, buggies, rich furniture sets, a vast variety of valuable and useful goods.

Eight-Day Porcelain Clock, $5.28.

No. 5G3930 The Jack Rose, an eight day clock, manufactured by the Ansonia Clock Co., of Brooklyn, N. Y. The case is made of porcelain, richly tinted in fancy colors and ornamented by hand painted Jack roses and gilt floral work. Nothing handsomer, nothing more beautiful, nothing more serviceable in a mantel clock. You need look no farther for absolute perfection in clock making. The case is made of genuine Royal Bonn imported from Germany. The stamp of the pottery is plainly seen on the back. Stands 12 inches high, 10 inches wide at base and 4 inches thick. Absolute protection to the movement, being positively dust and dampproof. The movement is made at the factory of the Ansonia Clock Co., polished front and back plates, hand wrought brass parts, oil tempered steel and hand polished pinions and pivots. Runs eight days with one winding, strikes the hours and half hours on a beautifully toned gong. Each movement is thoroughly oiled, examined and inspected before it leaves the factory and in turn is re-examined before it leaves our establishment. The dial of this clock is particularly attractive, being finished in gold gilt, rococo ornamented edges, heavy crystal glass fitted to the sash by an inside ornamented gilt rim. The figures are plain and distinct, the hands are blued steel, carefully pointed and fitted with nut and screw. The hands cannot drop or advance as in cheaply constructed clocks where this improvement has not been made. No illustration, no description could possibly give you an adequate idea of all its beauties. $8.00 to $10.00 is what the average jeweler or retail merchant would ask for this clock, yet on account of our one small per cent of profit system and our immense purchasing ability we are able to quote the remarkably low figure of $5.28. Weight, packed ready for shipment, about 18 pounds. Price....$5.28

Value Unexcelled at $5.55.

No. 5G3932 $5.55 for this solid iron black enameled eight-day Parlor Clock. For wearing ability, for absolute protection to the movement, for a clock that has the appearance of being solid marble, the counterpart of which would cost from $25.00 to $30.00. The case is made of iron enameled by a patent process, is guaranteed not to mar, peel or chip. It would require an expert to know the difference between this patent enamel iron clock and the genuine black Italian marble imported from Italy. Clock stands 10½ inches high, 15½ inches wide at base, 7 inches deep. Solid gold plated front ornaments, solid gold plated lion head side ornaments, solid gold plated feet and dial sash lend a richness and artistic value to this clock unequaled by any other. The dial is its most handsome feature, having a solid gold plated rim richly ornamented by a fancy rococo chased border with genuine mother of pearl inlaid figures. The numerals are plain and distinct, easily seen and exactly as illustration shows. The dial is six inches in diameter. The hands are of the Henry VI style, well made of blue steel. The movement fitted in this case manufactured by the celebrated New Haven Clock Co., of New Haven, Conn., runs eight days with one winding, is made of fine hard wrought brass and oil tempered steel parts. Hand polished pinions and pivots make this clock in running ability second to none. The latest improved, straight line verge escapement friction reduced, non-burred wheels, simple in construction, perfectly finished and perfectly adjusted, insures this clock to run and give absolute satisfaction. Strikes the hours and half hours on a sweet toned gong. Different from any other clock by reason of its peculiar construction, the movement is absolutely dust and dampproof, being cased in a thoroughly lacquered, thoroughly jointed iron frame. The clock is warranted to us by the manufacturers and we in turn warrant it to you to give entire and absolute satisfaction. Weight, packed ready for shipment, about 35 pounds. Price, complete....$5.55

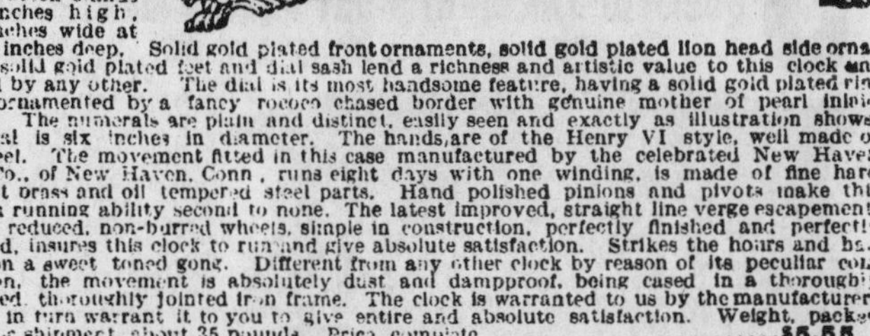

Beautiful Parlor Clock at $5.98.

Queen of the Night Parlor Mantel Clock.

Five-Year Guarantee sent with this Clock.

No. 5G3934 $5.98 for this eight-day strike metal ornamented Parlor Mantel Clock. A masterpiece of clock making. Of very latest creation. Designed especially for us by one of the greatest clock companies in the United States. We cannot give you the maker's name, on account of special price. Never before has such a magnificent specimen of clock been sold for twice what we ask. The clock runs eight days with one winding. Strikes the hours on a cathedral gong and the half hours on a cup bell. We guarantee this clock. With each one we send our written binding guarantee, which insures and protects you for a term of five years against defective material or workmanship. We are able to do so only because we know how this clock has been constructed, and why it is superior to any that is on the market at anything near the price.

The movement is made of solid brass, extra toughened oil tempered pivots, pinions and intricate steel parts. Different from all other clock movements. This movement is made after anti-friction models. Clocks giving poor time and wearing out soon are caused by excessive friction. All friction in these clocks has been reduced to a minimum and while we only guarantee it to give good time for a term of five years, it should last your natural lifetime if properly handled.

The case is made of fine hardwood, finished by a secret enameling process representing black and pink Mexican onyx. It stands 13 inches high, width 18 inches, depth 6¾ inches. The front of the clock is ornamented by six imitation marble columns with metal gold plated tops and bases. The sides have two conventionalized metal gold gilt floral designed ornaments. The feet, as illustrations show, are artistic, massive and in splendid proportion, finished in gold gilt metal. The dial is gold gilt, perforated and ornamented in floral design, and is protected by a heavy French glass set in a rococo ornamented gilt sash. The numerals are Arabic and plain and distinct, yet in keeping with the ornamental design. The hands are blue steel Henry VI style. This clock can be kept like new by applying a soft cloth or a piece of cotton flannel slightly dampened with sweet oil. $5.98 is the price arrived at after figuring exact cost of material in the case, exact cost of the movement and exact cost of making and handling with one small percentage of profit added. The clock company's profit, the jobber's profit and the retailer's profit have all been reduced and you are the gainer by no less than $4.00 to $5.00 by this method of figuring. This clock, boxed ready for shipment, weighs about 21 pounds. Price....$5.98

THE ROUGH RIDER CLOCK

$5.38 FOR THIS MASSIVE, HANDSOME 8-DAY MANTEL CLOCK, COMPLETE, AS ILLUSTRATION SHOWS.

THIS CLOCK is one of the latest productions of the Waterbury Clock Co., of Waterbury, Conn., and they guarantee it. We, in turn, warrant it. The reputation of the Waterbury Clock Company is second to none. When you buy a clock of their production you are owning a clock made as finely as skilled labor and high grade material will allow, considering the price. We call this clock our Rough Rider Clock because of the beautiful figure done in bronze of a western cowboy with lariat in hand, gracefully posed on a galloping broncho.

PLEASE OBSERVE the beautiful lines of this clock, take particular note of the handsome bronze metal side ornaments and metal feet. See the metal dial sash and frame done in Arabesque rococo work; the dial is white with Roman numerals 5¾ inches in diameter, plain and distinct, easily seen from any part of the room. The clock, including the figure, is 19½ inches high, width at base, 17½ inches; depth, 8 inches.

THE CASE is made of fine seasoned wood guaranteed not to warp, covered by a secret prepared enamel to imitate black marble and Mexican onyx; this preparation is guaranteed not to crack, peel or chip off. A cloth slightly moistened with sweet oil gently rubbed over this clock will keep it like new forever.

A MANTEL CLOCK is as good as the movement that is fitted into it; the movement that is fitted into this clock is as fine as can be made of wrought brass and tempered steel, runs eight days with one winding, strikes the hours on a cathedral gong and the half hours on a cup bell. Each one is timed and adjusted before being fitted in the case and again after fitted. The clock comes complete, boxed, ready to be set up, with full instructions plainly printed on the back of the clock, how to hang the pendulum, how to wind, how to set and various other important instructions.

No. 5L3291 Price, including figure $5.38
No. 5L3301 Price, figure alone .... .78
Weight, boxed ready for shipment, about 25 pounds.

$5.90 INVESTIGATE THIS OFFER

QUEEN OF THE NIGHT 8-DAY PARLOR MANTEL CLOCK

Designed especially for us by one of the greatest clock companies in the United States. We cannot give you the maker's name on account of special price. Never before has such a magnificent specimen of clock been sold for twice what we ask. The clock runs eight days with one winding. Strikes the hours on a cathedral gong and the half hours on a cup bell. We guarantee this clock. With each one we send our written binding guarantee, which insures and protects you for a term of five years against defective material or workmanship. We are able to do so only because we know how this clock has been constructed, and why it is superior to any that is on the market at anything near the price.

Different from any other concern, we show you the movement. Please note the illustration. The movement is made of solid brass, extra toughened oil tempered pivots, pinions and intricate steel parts. Different from all other clock movements. This movement is made after anti-friction models. All friction in these clocks has been reduced to a minimum and while we guarantee it to give good time for only a term of five years, it should last your natural lifetime if properly handled. The case is made of fine hardwood, finished by a secret enameling process representing black and pink Mexican onyx. It stands 13 inches high; width, 18 inches; depth, 6¾ inches. The front of the clock is ornamented by six imitation marble columns with gilt metal tops and bases. The sides have two conventionalized gilt metal floral design ornaments. The feet, as illustration shows, are artistic, massive and in splendid proportion, finished in gilt metal. The dial is gilt, perforated and ornamented in floral design, and is protected by a heavy French glass set in a rococo ornamented gilt sash. The numerals are Arabic style. This clock can be kept like new by applying a soft cloth or a piece of cotton flannel slightly dampened with sweet oil. This clock, boxed ready for shipment, weighs about 21 lbs.

No. 5L3934

Five-Year Guarantee sent with this Clock.

No. 5L3934 Price. $5.90

Weathered Oak Mission Style Clock.

No. 5L3158 It stands at the highest point 20½ inches high, width at the base 12 inches. The dial is plain and is also made of solid oak with bright metal numerals and bright metal hands. The movement runs for eight days with but one winding, and is manufactured by the renowned New Haven Clock Co. Strikes the hours and half hours on a sweet toned cathedral wire gong. We have contracted for an immense number; an immense quantity has made this astonishing price possible. We again offer you the advantage of the saving, adding only our own small per cent of profit to the original cost. This clock boxed, ready for shipment, weighs about 18 pounds.

Price $2.98

$3.18 for an Eight-Day Drop Octagon Office Clock.

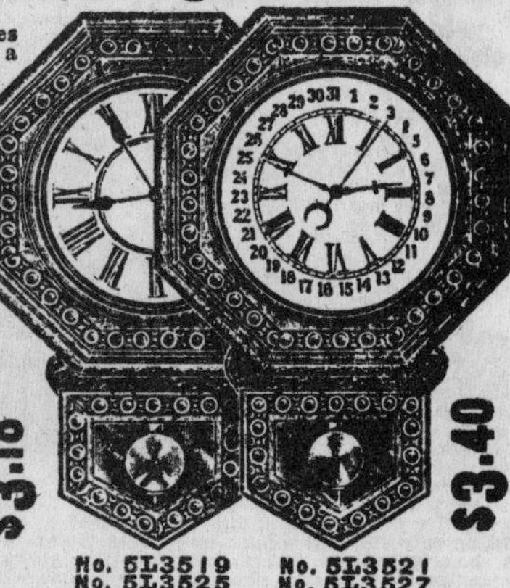

The case is made of oak, 24 inches high. The case is ornamented with a beautifully carved moulding which lends a richness to this clock seldom equaled. The dial is made of white enameled paper, plain Roman numerals painted exceedingly large. The hands are made of blued steel in fleur de lis pattern. The dial is ornamented with a plain polished gilt sash. The movement is made by the Waterbury Clock Co., of hard wrought brass and oil tempered steel. Pinions and pivots are hand polished, assuring accurate timekeeping. The clock is guaranteed to us by the manufacturers and we in turn guarantee it to our customers. Shipping weight, 20 pounds.

No. 5L3519 10-inch dial, time only. Price $3.18
No. 5L3521 10-inch dial, time with calendar. Price $3.40
No. 5L3523 10-inch dial, time with strike. Price $3.50
No. 5L3525 12-inch dial, time only. Price $3.50
No. 5L3527 12-inch dial, time with calendar. Price $3.65
No. 5L3529 12-inch dial, time with strike. Price $3.78

THIS IS AN EIGHT-DAY CLOCK

Others Cannot Meet This Price. $4.46

Our new eight-day, striking, black finished, six-column Waterbury Clock for $4.46. The case is of hard, black enameled wood, not a joint, crack or crevice to be found in any part of it. It is warranted to give entire and absolute satisfaction. A woolen cloth slightly sprinkled with sweet oil lightly rubbed over this clock will keep it in its original beauty for many years. Six columns, made to imitate Mexican marble and ornamented with gilt tops and bases ornament the sides. This is a new idea in clock ornamentation. The feet are of fine gilt metal with beautiful scroll work, which lends a richness and charm to this clock rarely equaled. The sash which holds the dial is of fine gilt brass, 5¾ inches in diameter. The dial is plain and distinctly marked with Roman numerals and fitted with fine fleur de lis hands. The clock stands 10¾ inches high; the base from foot to foot, 15½ inches wide; depth, 7 inches. The movement is trued and timed and guaranteed in every respect; runs eight days with one winding; strikes the half hours on a brass bell and the hours on a cathedral toned gong. It is made of fine hard wrought brass, oil tempered steel parts, and with care will wear and keep time for a lifetime. Weight, packed for shipment, about 20 pounds.

No. 5L3900 Price $4.46

$6.75 Eight-Day Perpetual Calendar Clock.

Our Eight-Day Perpetual Calendar Clock, with 8-inch dial, manufactured especially for us by the Waterbury Clock Co., of Waterbury, Conn. The clock is made of oak, stands 28½ inches high. The case is beautifully embossed and carved throughout. Beautiful ornaments adorn the top and sides of this case. On either side are two massive oak columns which lend a richness to this clock that cannot be excelled. The case is made of extra heavy hardwood, kiln dried. All joints are perfectly fitted, protecting this movement from dust and dampness. The glass of door is decorated in black and gold. The movement is the latest straight line verge escapement, made of hard wrought brass and oil tempered, steel pinions and pivots, no burred edges to interfere with the timekeeping qualities of the clock. Runs eight days with one winding. Strikes the hours and half hours on a sweet toned gong. The clock is guaranteed to us by the manufacturer and we in turn guarantee it to our customers, and with proper care it should last you your natural lifetime. Shipping weight, 25 pounds.

No. 5L3580 Price $6.75

Actually Priced at One-Half Value.

$5.50 for this solid iron black enameled Eight-Day Parlor Clock. Clock stands 10½ inches high, 15½ inches wide at base, 7 inches deep. Gilt front ornaments, gilt lion head side ornaments and gilt feet and dial sash lend a richness and artistic value to this clock unequaled by any other. The dial is its most handsome feature, having a gilt finished rim richly ornamented by a fancy rococo chased border with genuine mother of pearl inlaid figures. The dial is 6 inches in diameter. The hands are well made of blued steel. The movement fitted in this case manufactured by the celebrated New Haven Clock Co. runs eight days with one winding. Strikes the hours and half hours on a sweet toned gong. The clock is warranted to us by the manufacturers and we in turn warrant it to you to give entire and absolute satisfaction. Weight, packed ready for shipment, about 35 pounds.

No. 5L3932 Price $5.50

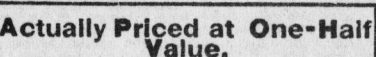

$2.62 Weathered Oak Mission Style Clock.

No. 5N3158 It stands at the highest point 20½ inches high; width at the base, 12 inches. The dial is plain and is also made of solid oak with bright metal numerals and bright metal hands. The movement runs for eight days with but one winding, and is manufactured by the renowned New Haven Clock Co. Strikes the hours and half hours on a sweet toned cathedral wire gong. We have contracted for an immense number; an immense quantity has made this astonishing price possible. We again offer you the advantage of the saving, adding only our own small per cent of profit to the original cost. This clock boxed, ready for shipment, weighs about 18 pounds. Price **$2.62**

$3.29 For This Hanging Solid Oak Weathered Mission Eight-Day Clock.

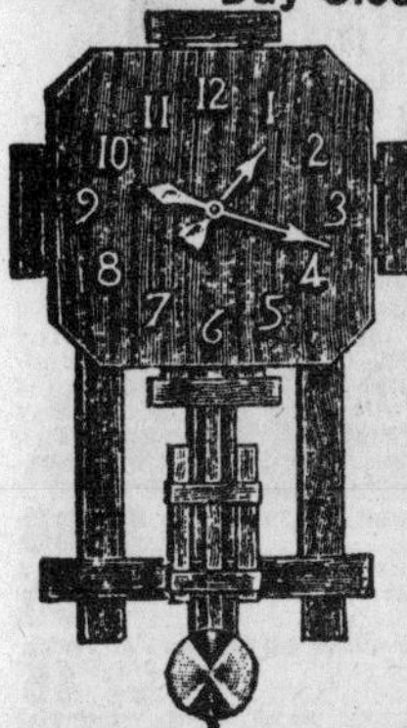

No. 5N3648 Nothing handsomer as a wall clock for your hall, dining room, den, bedroom or parlor. The movement is a fine runner, manufactured by the New Haven Clock Co., of New Haven, Conn. The dial is exposed exactly as the illustration shows, fitted with gilt solid metal numerals and gilt solid metal hands. The entire height of the clock is 27½ inches; width at widest point, 15½ inches. The dial is 15½ inches by 15½ inches. The pendulum is likewise solid dark colored weathered oak with a fine polished brass pendulum disc, and is adjustable. The movement runs for eight days, strikes the hours and half hours on a beautiful toned wire gong. Each one has been oiled and tested. This clock, boxed for shipment, weighs about 25 pounds. Price **$3.29**

96c Boudoir Alarm Clock.

No. 5N2941 Boudoir Alarm Clock. Our gold plated cupid design Boudoir Alarm Clock for 96 cents. Clock stands 10 inches high, 8½ inches wide at base; dial is 2¾ inches in diameter, fitted with a French crystal. The frame is made of metal. Different from all other boudoir clocks, this one has an alarm attachment. The movement runs thirty hours with one winding, is an excellent timekeeper, has an alarm attachment and rings the same as any alarm clock. Price **96c**

Weight, boxed ready for shipment, 5 pounds.

$2.48 For a Musical Alarm Clock.

No. 5N3048 One of the newest novelties on the market. This clock plays one tune for about ten minutes instead of ringing a bell. This clock stands 7 inches high, 5 inches wide, with front arabesque ornamentation around dial, full nickel plated frame with glass sides so that the movement and its action are visible at all times. Runs thirty hours. The music attachment is ingeniously hidden at the bottom of the clock, and so arranged that when the clock is set at a certain time, instead of an alarm bell being heard, a beautiful tune is played. With care it should last for many years and give entire satisfaction. $2.48 is a remarkably low figure for such a unique piece of clock mechanism. Weight of clock, packed ready for shipment, about 3 pounds. Price **$2.48**

FREE WALL PAPER SAMPLE BOOK. Write for it today. 3 cents and up per double roll of 16 yards. See wall paper section of our Big Catalogue.

$1.96 Continuous Long Alarm Clock.

No. 5N2951 Continuous Long Alarm Clock. The case is metal, finished in bronze. The movement is made by one of the most representative clock companies in the United States, and is warranted to us by the manufacturer; we in turn, guarantee it to our customers. The alarm rings for 7 minutes, but can be turned off at will by moving the lever. Height, 12 inches; width at base, 8½ inches. Shipping weight, 11 pounds. Price. **$1.96**

46c Cuckoo Clock.

No. 5N3552 Miniature Cuckoo Clock, facsimile of imported Black Forest cuckoo clocks in small size; does not cuckoo. Front is embossed to represent oak leaves and vine. Height, 7 inches; width, 5 inches; runs thirty hours by pulling up the weight. Will last for years and keep fairly good time. Price **46c**

If by mail, postage extra, 32 cents.

$1.39 For a Gold Plated Eight-Day Bureau or Bedroom Clock.

The clock stands 3½ inches high, has a 2-inch dial with French bevel glass crystal. It is built on the order of a nickel plated alarm clock, but has no alarm, and runs eight days with one winding. Just the clock for your shelf, bureau, desk or library table.

No. 5N2928 Price **$1.39**

If by mail, postage extra, 16 cents.

THE ALDRICH. $1.85

Made by the Waterbury Clock Company, furnished in either oak or walnut as desired. Stands 22 inches high, 15 inches wide at base. Case is handsomely carved, perfectly fitted and jointed and is a marvel of value. Movement runs eight days with one winding, strikes the hours and half hours on a wire bell, has a 6-inch dial. Guaranteed to keep accurate time. Shipping weight, 16 pounds.

No. 5N3102 Strikes on a wire bell. Price **$1.85**

No. 5N3104 Strikes on a wire bell, with an alarm attachment. Price **$2.30**

No. 5N3108 Strikes on a gong bell, with an alarm attachment. Price **$2.45**

$3.45 The Rochester Fancy Ornamental Cabinet Clock

made of solid black walnut, handsomely carved; height, 26¾ inches. Different from any other cabinet clock, this clock has an 8-inch dial, a 2-inch larger dial than an ordinary cabinet clock, which makes it easy to see the time from any part of the room. It is fitted with an eight-day movement made by the Waterbury Clock Co., hard wrought brass and oil tempered steel parts, strikes the hours and half hours. In addition it has a calendar attachment which automatically registers the day of the month. Shipping weight, about 20 pounds.

No. 5N3151 Strikes on wire bell. **$3.45**

No. 5N3153 Strikes on cathedral gong. Price. **3.75**

$3.94 FOR THIS VERY HANDSOME WOOD MANTEL CLOCK Stands 12⅞ Inches High, 17 Inches wide at Base.

THE MOVEMENT IS A GOOD ONE. Runs eight days with one winding, strikes the hours on a cathedral gong and half hours on a cup bell. It will last you for years. This clock is manufactured with the idea of producing something ornate, attractive and large for little money. Never has such a clock value been offered before. Note the ornamentation: Six beautiful columns ornament the front of the clock and handsome metal ornaments are fixed on its sides. It is equipped with fine metal feet. The clock is actually worth double what we ask; any store would ask from $6.00 to $10.00 for it.

No. 5N3902 Price **$3.94**

Weight, boxed ready for shipment, about 20 pounds.

ACTUALLY PRICED AT ONE-HALF ITS VALUE

$5.43 for this solid iron black enameled Eight-Day Parlor Clock. Clock stands 10½ inches high, 15½ inches wide at base, 7 inches deep. Gilt front ornaments, gilt lion head side ornaments and gilt feet and dial sash lend a richness and artistic value to this clock unequaled by any other. The dial is its most handsome feature, having a gilt finished rim richly ornamented by a fancy rococo chased border with genuine mother of pearl inlaid figures. The dial is 6 inches in diameter. The hands are well made of blued steel. The movement fitted in this case manufactured by the celebrated New Haven Clock Co. runs eight days with one winding. Strikes the hours and half hours on a sweet toned gong.

$5.43

Weight, packed ready for shipment, about 35 pounds.

No. 5N3932 Price **$5.43**

THIS IS AN EIGHT-DAY CLOCK

Others Cannot Meet This Price. $4.38

Our new eight-day, striking, black finished, six-column Waterbury Clock for $4.38. The case is of hard, black enameled wood, not a joint, crack or crevice to be found in any part of it. It is warranted to give entire and absolute satisfaction. A woolen cloth slightly sprinkled with sweet oil lightly rubbed over this clock will keep it in its original beauty for many years. Six columns, made to imitate Mexican marble and ornamented with gilt tops and bases ornament the sides. This is a new idea in clock ornamentation. The feet are of fine gilt metal with beautiful scroll work, which lends a richness and charm to this clock rarely equaled. The sash which holds the dial is of fine gilt brass, 5¾ inches in diameter. The dial is plain and distinctly marked with Roman numerals and fitted with fine fleur de lis hands. The clock stands 10¾ inches high; the base from foot to foot, 15½ inches wide; depth, 7 inches. The movement is trued and timed and guaranteed in every respect; runs eight days with one winding; strikes the half hours on a brass bell and the hours on a cathedral toned gong. It is made of fine hard wrought brass, oil tempered steel parts, and with care will wear and keep time for a lifetime. Weight, packed for shipment, about 20 pounds.

No. 5N3900 Price **$4.38**

$5.32 FOR THIS HANDSOME COMBINATION METAL AND WOOD MANTEL CLOCK. $5.32

No. 5N3903 It is a fine timer. Manufactured by the Gilbert Clock Co., runs for eight days with one winding and strikes the hours and half hours on a curfew bell. The curfew bell is exposed on the top of the clock. It is made of metal, beautifully plated, thus producing one of the handsomest clocks manufactured this year. The case, including the curfew bell, stands 17⅜ inches high; width at base, 16½ inches. With the exception of the curfew bell part, this clock is manufactured of the finest kiln dried wood, beautifully enameled to imitate black Italian marble and green onyx. Note the ornamentation, the beautiful gilded metal feet and the handsome rococo sash surrounding the dial, the delicate scroll work on the facade of the clock. The movement is one that we can highly recommend, manufactured by the Gilbert Clock Company. Every clock user should be familiar with this great clockmaker's name. The parts are of the finest brass and hardened steel, properly timed and adjusted before it leaves the factory. We warrant it to reach destination in perfect order. Weight of clock, boxed ready for shipment, about 20 pounds. Price **$5.32**

FOR COMPLETE INDEX REFER TO PINK PAGES IN MIDDLE OF BOOK.

PRICES REDUCED IN OUR CLOCK DEPARTMENT

49 Cents or 68 Cents; Your Choice of Either One.

An Imported Alarm Clock manufactured in Germany. They give generally fair satisfaction. The only difficulty with the imported clock is the fact that when it gets out of order it is difficult to get the material to repair it properly. No. 5L2903 at 68 cents, is an American production, and considering the price is a marvel of value. We guarantee it for one year, but conscientiously believe that it should wear and give good satisfaction for many years if properly handled. Both of these clocks stand 6½ inches high and run 30 hours with one winding. Both have 4-inch dials. The imported German clock has Roman numerals and the American made clock has Arabic numerals. Both alarm continuously for one-half minute.

No. 5L2901 No. 5L2903

No. 5L2901 Imported Alarm Clock. Price **49c**
No. 5L2903 American Made Alarm Clock. Price... (Postage 27c) **68c**

89c

No. 5L2907 Our New Luminous Radium Alarm Clock. By a secret process the dial is covered with a luminous substance which causes the dial to throw out a ray of light like a ball of fire when placed in the dark. This enables you to see the time from any part of the room. This clock is an excellent timekeeper and will give entire satisfaction. 6¼ inches high, has 4-inch dial. We know exactly how it is made, how it is adjusted and regulated, and therefore send our two-year guarantee with each clock. SEE THE MOVEMENT as illustrated. It is made of brass with oil tempered steel parts, is the latest model in this style of clock and built on anti-friction principles. Runs 30 hours with one winding, alarms 30 seconds on a clear nickel bell. Different from any other concern, we show you the movement, so that you know exactly what you are getting. Price.......... **89c**
If by mail, postage extra, 31 cents.

$1.26

No. 5L2911 Our New Interval Alarm Clock, made especially for us. This clock is made under our own specifications. Stands 6 inches high, has a 4-inch dial with Roman numerals, blue steel hands, and a 4-inch bell on the back. The best alarm clock on the market. With each clock we send our two-year guarantee. See the movement in this clock. We illustrate it here. It runs for 30 hours with one winding. Made of hand wrought brass and oil tempered steel parts, polished pivots and pinions which reduce friction to a minimum, thereby insuring accurate timekeeping. The 4-inch bell on the back of the clock rings for 40 seconds, then is silent for 20 seconds and continues for 15 minutes unless you shut it off. The 4-inch bell sounds like a fire gong when the alarm rings. You cannot oversleep if you have one of these clocks.
Price.....(Postage extra, 35c).... **$1.26**

92c

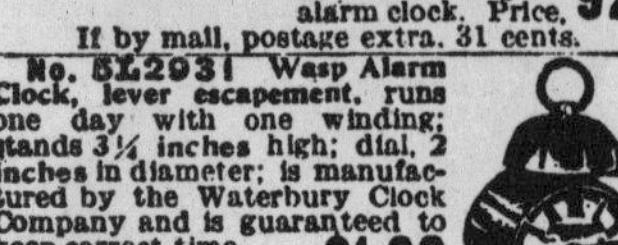

No. 5L2914 Nickel Calendar Alarm Clock, height, 6¼ inches; dial 4 inches, runs 30 hours with one winding, has a calendar attachment as well as alarm, is made by the New Haven Clock Company and is guaranteed to give entire satisfaction. Has a large nickel bell on top. This clock automatically tells you the day of the month as well as being an alarm clock. Price, **92c**
If by mail, postage extra, 31 cents.

No. 5L2931 Wasp Alarm Clock, lever escapement, runs one day with one winding; stands 3¼ inches high; dial, 2 inches in diameter; is manufactured by the Waterbury Clock Company and is guaranteed to keep correct time.
Price **$1.20**
If by mail, postage extra, 16c.
No. 5L2933 Same as No. 5L2931, but without alarm; time only.
Price.......... **85c**

THE BEST CLOCK MAKERS in the United States are here represented. They are the oldest and most reliable makers.

The Waterbury Clock Co., the Gilbert Clock Co., the New Haven Clock Co. and the Ansonia Clock Co., stand pre-eminent. Every clock we sell is guaranteed by the manufacturers, and we personally warrant every clock sold to give entire and absolute satisfaction but on account of low special prices, we cannot print the makers' names under our special clocks.

Reliable Alarm. A SURE SLEEP BREAKER FOR 74c

No. 5L2915 Nickel Alarm Clock made especially for us by one of the largest clock companies in the United States, but on account of the low price at which we sell it we cannot give the maker's name. The movement is of the latest lever escapement, made of brass, and oil tempered steel parts. Runs 30 hours with one winding. Each clock is thoroughly examined and tested for accurate timekeeping and running durability before leaving the factory. It is again examined in our house before shipping, which insures you an accurate timekeeper. Stands 6½ inches high, dial is 4 inches in diameter.
Price.............................. **74c**
If by mail, postage extra, 32 cents.

$1.52

No. 5L2925 Strike Alarm Clock, made by the Ansonia Clock Company, height, 6¼ inches; dial, 4½ inches, movement runs 30 hours with one winding, different from any other alarm clock. This clock strikes the hours and half hours the same as a mantel clock. In addition it has an alarm attachment which alarms at any time set. The Ansonia Clock Company is known for the excellent clocks which they manufacture and we guarantee this clock to be an excellent timekeeper and to give entire satisfaction.
Price.............. **$1.52**
If by mail, postage extra, 36 cents.

No. 5L2923 Buzzer Repeating Alarm Clock, runs for 30 hours with one winding, made by the Ansonia Clock Co. This clock has all the advantages of a repeating alarm clock that sells from $1.25 to $1.50. It alarms at intervals of 5 seconds, stands 6½ inches high, dial is 4 inches in diameter.
Price.......... **89c**
If by mail, postage extra, 32 cents.

No. 5L2932 Nickel Plated Glass Paneled High Grade Alarm Clock. Stands 6 inches high, 4¾ inches wide at base and 3 inches deep. The dial is 2⅜ inches in diameter, has plain Roman numerals. This clock is beautified by gilt arabesque panel work in the front of the clock. The movement is manufactured by the Waterbury Clock Co. It runs 30 hours with one winding. The alarm attachment is invisible, being placed underneath the clock. This clock is not alone an alarm clock, but also strikes the hours and half hours on a bell. Weight, packed ready for shipment, about 4 pounds.
Price.............. **$2.30**

96c Boudoir Alarm Clock.

No. 5L2941 Boudoir Alarm Clock. Our gold plated cupid design Boudoir Alarm Clocks for 96 cents. Clock stands 10 inches high, 8½ inches wide at base, dial is 2¾ inches in diameter, fitted with a French crystal. The frame is made of metal. Different from all other boudoir clocks, this one has an alarm attachment. The movement (see the illustration) runs 30 hours with one winding, is an excellent timekeeper, has an alarm attachment and rings the same as any alarm clock.
Price.............. **96c**
Weight, boxed ready for shipment, 5 pounds.

$2.48 For a Musical Alarm Clock.

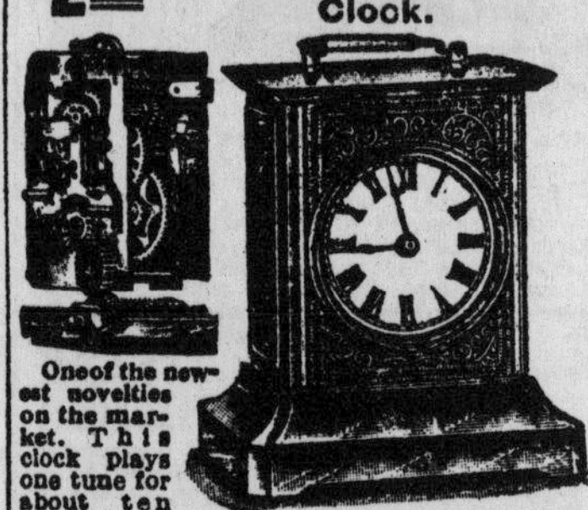

One of the newest novelties on the market. This clock plays one tune for about ten minutes instead of ringing a bell. This clock stands 7 inches high, 5 inches wide with front arabesque ornamentation around dial, full nickel plated frame with glass sides so that the movement and its action are visible at all times. Runs 30 hours. The illustration shows the movement as well as the music attachment which is ingeniously hidden at the bottom of the clock, and so arranged that when the clock is set at a certain time, instead of an alarm bell being heard, a beautiful tune is played. With care it should last for many years and give entire satisfaction. $2.48 is a remarkably low figure for such a unique piece of clock mechanism. Weight of clock, packed ready for shipment, about 3 pounds.
No. 5L3048 Musical Alarm Clock. Price.......... **$2.48**

No. 5L3552 Miniature Cuckoo Clock, facsimile of imported Black Forest cuckoo clocks in small size; does not cuckoo. Front is embossed to represent oak leaves and vine. Height, 7 inches; width 5 inches; runs 30 hours by pulling up the weight. Will last for years and keep good time.
Price............ **46c**
If by mail, postage extra, 32 cents.

$1.98 Your Choice, Either One of These Clocks for $1.98

Be sure to order by number.

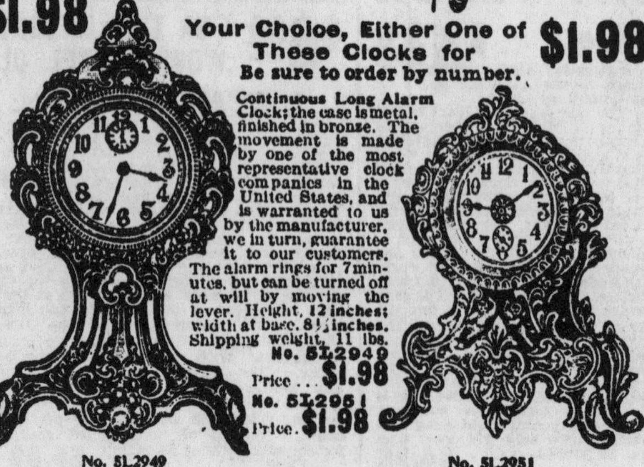

Continuous Long Alarm Clock; the case is metal, finished in bronze. The movement is made by one of the most representative clock companies in the United States, and is warranted to us by the manufacturer, we in turn, guarantee it to our customers. The alarm rings for 7 minutes, but can be turned off at will by moving the lever. Height, 12 inches; width at base, 8½ inches. Shipping weight, 11 lbs.
No. 5L2949 Price... **$1.98**
No. 5L2951 Price. **$1.98**

No. 5L2949 No. 5L2951

$3.65 NICKEL CHAFING DISHES

No. 5L2812 Chafing Dish, ebony trimmings, nickel finish; capacity, 3 pints; 9 inches in diameter. Shipping wt., about 10 pounds.
Price...... **$3.65**

$5.45

No. 5L2814 Chafing Dish, ebony trimmings, nickel, with fancy border. Improved lamp; capacity, 3 pints; 9 inches in diameter. Shipping weight, 10 pounds.
Price, complete **$5.45**

THE ALDRICH. $1.85

Made by the Waterbury Clock Company, furnished in either oak or walnut as desired. Stands 22 inches high, 15 inches wide at base. Case is handsomely carved, perfectly fitted and jointed and is a marvel of value. Movement runs eight days with one winding, strikes the hours and half hours on a wire bell, has a 6-inch dial. Guaranteed to keep accurate time. Shipping weight, 16 pounds.

No. 5L3102 Strikes on a wire bell. Price **$1.85**
No. 5L3104 Strikes on a wire bell, with an alarm attachment.
Price **$2.30**
No. 5L3108 Strikes on a gong bell, with an alarm attachment.
Price **$2.45**

$3.45

The Rochester Fancy Ornamental Cabinet Clock, made of solid black walnut, handsomely carved; height, 26¾ inches. Different from any other cabinet clock, this clock has an 8-inch dial, a 2-inch larger dial than an ordinary cabinet clock, which makes it easy to see the time from any part of the room. It is fitted with an eight-day movement made by the Waterbury Clock Co., hard wrought brass and oil tempered steel parts, strikes the hours and half hours. In addition it has a calendar attachment which automatically registers the day of the month. Shipping weight, about 20 pounds.
No. 5L3151 Strikes on wire bell. Price **$3.45**
No. 5L3153 Strikes on cathedral gong. Price **3.75**

$4.92 For This Elaborate Eight-Day Solid Oak Mantel or Shelf Clock.

The movement runs eight days with one winding, strikes the half hours and hours on a wire bell. The case is 24 inches high; width, 16½ inches. The ornamentation on this clock is its special feature. Two handsome gilded figures, one on each side resting on a pedestal, behind these figures are panels of mirror reflecting the figures, lending a charm difficult to describe. Hand carved top piece, heavy moulding and fine gilded bas relief top, conventionalized design base ornament in addition, perfect and finishes off the entire clock. Boxed ready for shipment; wt., about 22 lbs.
No. 5L3155 Price **$4.92**
No. 5L3157 Price with alarm attachment **$5.22**

$4.55 A STARTLING VALUE
THE LEXINGTON EIGHT-DAY MANTEL CLOCK.

$4.55 for this clock exactly as illustrated, exactly as described, means selling high grade clocks at unheard of prices. Don't compare this clock with clocks sold by others at $6.00, $7.00 and $8.00; compare with clocks offered at $9.00 and $10.00.

THIS MANTEL CLOCK runs eight days with one winding. Strikes the half hours on a brass bell and the full hours on a beautifully toned wire cathedral gong.

THE DIMENSIONS. Clock stands 11 inches high, 17 inches wide at base and 7½ inches deep. Large, massive and most attractive. The case is made of wood treated by a secret process to imitate black Italian marble and blue Mexican onyx. The feet, side ornaments, top and bottom of front columns are of hard metal heavily plated. The contrast of the gilt finish and the black marble is most pleasing.

THE DIAL, as illustration shows, is elaborate and ornate, being a new perforated rococo design, 5¼ inches in diameter, the dial sash is fitted with a heavy French crystal glass. Hands of blue steel Louis XIV design, Arabic numerals, plain and distinct.

THE MOVEMENT is the most important feature of any clock (see the illustration). In this clock we have fitted our special anti-friction movement. All friction has been reduced to a minimum. See the illustration showing the counter sinking. All pivots are polished, fine metal pendulum, latest French verge escapement, accurately run and timed before being fitted into the case. The parts are made of roll tempered brass and oil tempered steel parts.

WE INSURE THIS CLOCK. With every one of these clocks we send our written binding five-year guarantee that protects you for this term of years against faulty material or workmanship. Never before has such an offer been made by any concern and it is only possible because we know the attractive contract we have for this our Lexington Mantel Clock. Weight of clock, boxed, about 20 pounds.

No. 5L3614 The Lexington Mantel Clock. Price **$4.55**

$3.35 For This Hanging Solid Oak Weathered Mission 8-Day Clock.

Nothing handsomer as a wall clock for your hall, dining room, den, bedroom or parlor. The movement is a fine runner, manufactured by the New Haven Clock Co., of New Haven, Conn. The dial is exposed exactly as the illustration shows, fitted with gilt solid metal numerals and gilt solid metal hands. The entire height of the clock is 27½ inches, width at widest point, 15½ inches. The dial is 15½ inches by 15½ inches. The pendulum is likewise solid dark colored weathered oak with a fine polished brass pendulum disc, and is adjustable. The movement runs for eight days, strikes the hours and half hours on a beautiful toned wire gong. Each one has been oiled and tested. This clock, boxed for shipment, weighs about 25 pounds.

No. 5L3648 Price . $3.35

Our Challenge Clock at a Cut Price. $3.38

For Church, School or Store Regulator. This clock is made by the Gilbert Clock Co., and is one of their latest productions. The case is made of golden oak, ornamented with hand carvings throughout. The movement is made of solid brass with oil tempered steel parts. The clock runs eight days with one winding, has long wooden pendulum with brass ball which can be lowered or raised so as to regulate the clock. This clock is sold regularly at $4.50 to $5.50, but on account of a special contract we are able to name the extremely low price of $3.38. The clock stands 37 inches high, is 15½ inches wide and has a 12-inch dial. Shipping weight, 28 pounds.

No. 5L3503 Time only. Price $3.38
No. 5L3505 Time and calendar. Price $3.88
No. 5L3507 Strikes half hours. Price, $4.48
No. 5L3509 Strikes half hours, with calendar. Price $4.58

$4.44 Our Wonderful Clock Offer.

This Cuckoo Clock is manufactured in Schwarzwald, Germany. Comes in German oak or walnut finish, case is hand carved, of an oak leaf design with inlaid ash and mahogany as illustration shows. Stands 21 inches high, 14 inches wide. Diameter of dial, 5¼ inches. Movement is made in the Black Forest, Germany, of hard rolled brass and oil tempered steel parts, perfectly adjusted, perfectly fitted and timed, see the illustration. Runs 30 hours with one winding, strikes the hours on a wire bell and at the same time the cuckoo appears on the top and calls the hours. This clock runs by weights. The weight system of

The movement illustrated above is the one used u our Cuckoo Clocks.

operating clock equalizes and distributes the motive power and is far superior to the spring movement for keeping accurate time. Weight, boxed ready for shipment, 26 pounds.

No. 5L3555 Price...... $4.44
No. 5L3554 Same style as No. 5L3555, but inferior finish, made of inferior wood and not so good generally. We guarantee it to be received in going order. Price $3.95

$4.30 QUEEN MANTEL CLOCK AND FIGURE.

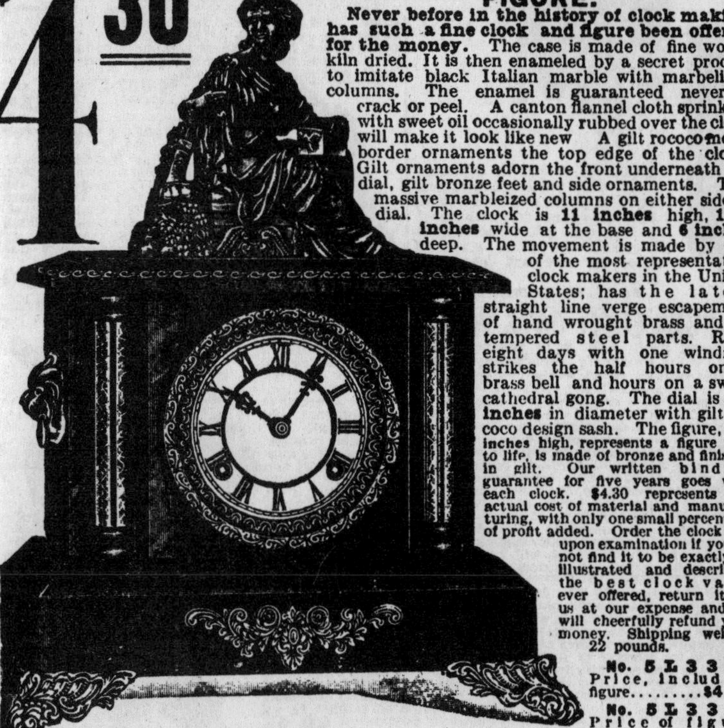

Never before in the history of clock making has such a fine clock and figure been offered for the money. The case is made of fine wood, kiln dried. It is then enameled by a secret process to imitate black Italian marble with marbelized columns. The enamel is guaranteed never to crack or peel. A canton flannel cloth sprinkled with sweet oil occasionally rubbed over the clock will make it look like new A gilt rococo metal border ornaments the top edge of the clock. Gilt ornaments adorn the front underneath the dial, gilt bronze feet and side ornaments. Two massive marbleized columns on either side of dial. The clock is **11 inches** high, **12½ inches** wide at the base and **6 inches** deep. The movement is made by one of the most representative clock makers in the United States; has the latest straight line verge escapement of hand wrought brass and oil tempered steel parts. Runs eight days with one winding, strikes the half hours on a brass bell and hours on a sweet cathedral gong. The dial is **5½ inches** in diameter with gilt rococo design sash. The figure, **6⅝ inches high**, represents a figure true to life, is made of bronze and finished in gilt. Our written binding guarantee for five years goes with each clock. $4.30 represents the actual cost of material and manufacturing, with only one small percentage of profit added. Order the clock and upon examination if you do not find it to be exactly as illustrated and described, the best clock value ever offered, return it to us at our expense and we will cheerfully refund your money. Shipping weight, 22 pounds.

No. 5L3312 Price, including figure......... $4.30
No. 5L3314 Price of figure alone........... 82c

Highest Quality Imported Quail and Cuckoo Clock. Reduced From $16.88 to $14.98.

$14.98 for absolute perfection in a Quail and Cuckoo Clock. On account of the demand for something more perfect, something handsomer than has ever been offered for the money before, we have had imported for us this **22½ inches** high Schwarzwald genuine hand carved German walnut finished quail and cuckoo clock. The case is designed in German walnut, representing sprays of German oak leaves artistically arranged by overlapping and drooping. Surmounting this masterpiece stands an eagle. The case stands **22½ inches** high, **18 inches** wide, dial, **6⅝ inches**. The figures on the dial are applied plain white, the hands hand sawed bleached white bone. This clock is run by three weights. The weight system of operating clocks equalizes and distributes the motive power throughout, insuring accurate timekeeping. The movement runs thirty hours, is made after American models at Schwarzwald, of extra thick, extra toughened hard wrought brass, hand polished oil tempered steel parts and pinions, straight line verge escapement. Nothing intricate, nothing complicated, the liability of getting out of order has practically been removed. The quail and cuckoo attached are the acme of perfection. Two birds with automatically adjusted wings and beaks appear through the automatically opened doors. At the quarter hours the quail bird appears and chirrups the quarter hours. The cuckoo bird appears at the full hours and calls the hour. At the same time that the full hours are called they are likewise sounded on a beautifully toned wire gong. This clock is guaranteed to us and we in turn guarantee it to our customers. The pendulum is hand carved, with adjusting screw on the bottom. Full instructions are sent with each one when shipped. No difficulty to place it on the wall. No hardship to handle. Weight, packed for shipment, 32 pounds.

No. 5L3574 Price **$14.98**

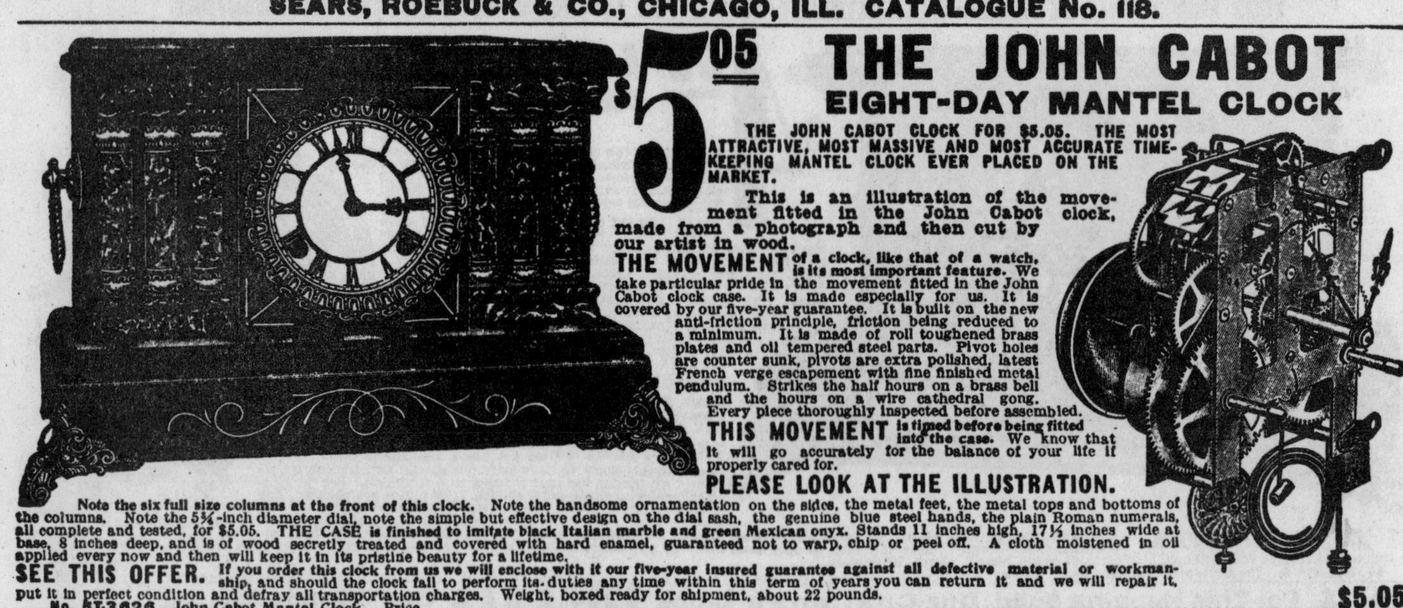

$5.05 THE JOHN CABOT EIGHT-DAY MANTEL CLOCK

THE JOHN CABOT CLOCK FOR $5.05. THE MOST ATTRACTIVE, MOST MASSIVE AND MOST ACCURATE TIME-KEEPING MANTEL CLOCK EVER PLACED ON THE MARKET.

This is an illustration of the movement fitted in the John Cabot clock, made from a photograph and then cut by our artist in wood.

THE MOVEMENT of a clock, like that of a watch, is its most important feature. We take particular pride in the movement fitted in the John Cabot clock case. It is made especially for us. It is covered by our five-year guarantee. It is built on the new anti-friction principle, friction being reduced to a minimum. It is made of roll toughened brass plates and oil tempered steel parts. Pivot holes are counter sunk, pivots are extra polished, latest French verge escapement with fine finished metal pendulum. Strikes the half hours on a brass bell and the hours on a wire cathedral gong. Every piece thoroughly inspected before assembled.

THIS MOVEMENT is timed before being fitted into the case. We know that it will go accurately for the balance of your life if properly cared for.

PLEASE LOOK AT THE ILLUSTRATION.

Note the six full size columns at the front of this clock. Note the handsome ornamentation on the sides, the metal feet, the metal tops and bottoms of the columns. Note the 5¾-inch diameter dial, note the simple but effective design on the dial sash, the genuine blue steel hands, the plain Roman numerals, all complete and tested, for $5.05. THE CASE is finished to imitate black Italian marble and green Mexican onyx. Stands 11 inches high, 17½ inches wide at base, 8 inches deep, and is of wood secretly treated and covered with hard enamel, guaranteed not to warp, chip or peel off. A cloth moistened in oil applied every now and then will keep it in its pristine beauty for a lifetime.

SEE THIS OFFER. If you order this clock from us we will enclose with it our five-year insured guarantee against all defective material or workmanship, and should the clock fail to perform its duties any time within this term of years you can return it and we will repair it, put it in perfect condition and defray all transportation charges. Weight, boxed ready for shipment, about 22 pounds.

No. 5L3626 John Cabot Mantel Clock. Price........ **$5.05**

$3.62 WORTH $7.50 EIGHT-DAY CLOCK

$3.62

OUR PRINCE ELIAS, the newest clock out of the factory, exactly in every particular as illustration shows, for $3.62. Don't think that you will not get or cannot buy from us a fine clock for this price. In fact, this price is no criterion. The clock is really worth twice as much. This clock is made expressly for us by the Waterbury Clock Co., of Waterbury, Conn. Each one of them is thoroughly guaranteed and we warrant them to give entire satisfaction.

DESCRIPTION OF CASE. The case is made of wood, covered with a secretly prepared enamel, imitating black marble; stands 12¾ inches high, 13 inches wide and 8 inches deep. It is guaranteed not to chip or wear off, and always retains its deep black marblelike appearance. It has handsome gilt feet, marbleized gilt metal capped and gilt metal based columns, beautiful gilt scroll metal work at top and base. The sides are also ornamented by two gilt metal designs, exactly as the illustration shows. The dial is very pretentious, made of metal fancy work and is 5 inches in diameter.

DESCRIPTION OF MOVEMENT. The movement fitted in this case is one of the Waterbury guaranteed movements, runs eight days with one winding. It is made of the finest tempered steel and hard wrought brass; it strikes the hours on a cathedral gong and the half hours on a brass bell. You can always know the time without seeing the clock. The hands are very fine hand sawed blue steel of the fleur de lis pattern. Shipping weight, 16 pounds.

No. 5L3202 Price........ **$3.62**

One-Day Imported Cuckoo Clock. $7.39

Hand Carved German Walnut Finished Imported Cuckoo Clock for $7.39. This clock is manufactured in the Schwarzwald, Germany, the home of cuckoo clock making. Each leaf, the deer head, all parts as illustration shows, are guaranteed hand carved; nothing will please the children more than to hear the cuckoo calling. Clock is 19 inches high, 14 inches wide, strikes the half hours on a beautifully toned wire bell. At the half hour and full hour the cuckoo appears, opening automatically the little door placed directly above the figure 12, and calls out the half hour and full hours. This clock is run by two weights. The weight system of operating clocks equalizes and distributes the motive power and is far superior to the spring movement for keeping accurate time. The movement runs thirty hours by pulling up the weight (see the illustration), built under new plans, is made of solid brass with oil tempered steel parts, simple in design, simple in execution.

Dial 5¼ inches in diameter, fitted with applied figures and white bleached bone hands. Full directions go with each clock, how to set it and to start it going. Weight, packed ready for shipment, about 24 pounds.

No. 5L3570 Price, **$7.39**

High Grade One-Day Imported Quail and Cuckoo Clock. $11.48

Comes to us direct from the Schwarzwald, Germany, the home of Cuckoo clock making. Height, 19½ inches; width, 15½ inches; dial is 5½ inches.

THE QUAIL AND CUCKOO CALL LENDS A UNIQUE CHARM TO THIS CLOCK, making it a most interesting and novel acquisition, pleasing to young and old.

THE QUAIL BIRD appears automatically and calls the quarter hours and the CUCKOO appears calling the full hours. You need not be in the room to know the time.

THE CASE is handsomely carved, same design as illustration shows. This clock is walnut finished, guaranteed not to warp, check or crack.

THE MOVEMENT is excellently constructed, timed and tested, and guaranteed to perform its duties well and accurately.

THE MOTIVE POWER is by weights, not a spring clock. It is a known fact that clocks run on this principle are more accurate and longer running than by any other system; runs 30 hours with one winding; to wind the clock pull up the weights. Boxed ready for shipment, weight about 32 pounds.

No. 5L3571 Quail and Cuckoo Clock. Price........ **$11.48**

Gold Plated Clock for $1.10.

Bureau or Bedroom Clock. Runs 30 hours with one winding. This clock is made by the Waterbury Clock Co., stands 5 inches high, dial 2 inches. Frame is solid metal plated with pure gold, and is a very handsome ornament as well as useful timepiece.

No. 5L3050 Price........ **$1.10**

If by mail, postage extra, 17c.

$6.35 FOR THIS GUARANTEED UP TO DATE CLOCK, RUNS EIGHT DAYS WITH ONE WINDING

STRIKES THE HOURS ON A BEAUTIFUL TONED GONG AND HALF HOURS ON A NICKEL CUP BELL.

THE CASE as illustration shows is something original and entirely new, imitating the facade and general outline of an ancient Greek temple, is made of wood, enameled to imitate black Italian marble and Mexican onyx. Beautiful metal ornaments embellish the bottoms and tops of columns, feet and top of facade of the case. The dial is new, being a rococo design, perforated, allowing the numerals to stand out prominent and clear from an ivory background. The hands are of the fleur de lis Louis XV style.

THE MOVEMENT is thoroughly protected; no dust or damp will filter through. The movement, according to our opinion, is one of the most essential features of a clock. See the illustration. We want you to know exactly how the movement appears, different from any other concern, we show you the running part of our clocks. This movement is made of solid brass and oil tempered steel, the main springs are agate drawn, the pivots and pinions have all been polished, each one thoroughly timed and adjusted, both in and out of the frame.

THE FINISH of this clock is remarkable. A piece of Canton flannel slightly moistened with oil and gently rubbed over the surface every once in a while, say about nine months or a year, will keep this clock as bright as when new. This clock surely would grace any parlor, ornamental as well as practical. Stands at highest point 12½ inches, 17¾ inches wide and 5½ inches deep, is different from most of the mantel clocks now being sold. You can adjust this clock from the front, you never need touch the back and tamper with the works.

OUR GUARANTEE. With this clock we send our written binding guarantee that protects and insures you against defective material and workmanship for a term of five years.

THIS CLOCK in its entirety is American manufactured, made here in the United States by one of the great five clock companies. We cannot divulge the maker's name on account of the ridiculously close price at which we are offering these goods. They sell the same goods to wholesale jewelers at a price that would astonish the retailer, as compared to what we sell it for. Clock, boxed ready for shipment, weighs about 25 pounds.

No. 5L3660 Eight-Day Mantel Clock. Price........ **$6.35**

$3.94 FOR THIS VERY HANDSOME WOOD MANTEL CLOCK.

Stands 12½ Inches High, 17 Inches Wide at Base.

CALLED STAR OF THE NORTH

THE MOVEMENT IS A GOOD ONE. Runs eight days with one winding, strikes the hours on a cathedral gong and half hours on a cup bell. It will last you for years. This clock is manufactured with the idea of producing something ornate, attractive and large for little money. Never has such a clock value been offered before. Note the ornamentation: Six beautiful columns ornament the front of the clock and handsome metal ornaments are fixed on its sides. It is equipped with fine metal feet. The clock is actually worth double what we ask; any store would ask from $6.00 to $10.00 for it. Weight, boxed ready for shipment, about 20 pounds.

No. 5T9304 Price $3.94

$4.22 LADY ISABELLE EIGHT-DAY MANTEL CLOCK.

THINK OF IT!

We will send you this specially made, rich appearing eight-day striking mantel clock for one-half of what a similar clock would sell the world over. The ornamentation on this clock is one of its most attractive features. It consists of two side ornaments, top and bottom capped columns, feet and front and bottom ornaments. The dial is simple but rich in style. 5¾ inches in diameter. Dial sash fitted with heavy French crystal. The movement fitted in the Lady Isabelle Clock is the best clock movement we know of and is made after our own ideas on the new anti-friction principle, friction being reduced to a minimum. It runs eight days with one winding. Strikes the hours on a beautifully toned cathedral wire gong and the half hours on a brass cup bell. All parts are oil tempered, pivots all highly polished. The newest French verge escapement, metal pendulum. The case is most attractive, but the illustration does not begin to show the coloring and brass so as to give a full idea of its beauty. Stands 11 inches high, 16¼ inches wide at base, 7 inches deep, of the Corinthian style, secretly treated wood covered by hard enamel, guaranteed not to warp, chip or scale off. Comes in black and variegated colors to imitate green onyx and Italian black marble. This clock is covered by our five-year guarantee. We enclose it with every one sold and it amply protects and insures you against defective material or workmanship in this clock for a term of five years. Shipping weight, 20 pounds.

No. 5T9306 Lady Isabelle Mantel Clock. Price........$4.22

No. 5T8702 Handsome Bronze Figure, representing a cowboy on horseback throwing a lariat. This figure placed on top of the Lady Isabelle Clock makes a most beautiful parlor ornament. Shipping weight, 10 pounds. Price, figure only........78c

THIS COMPLETE MANTEL OUTFIT, INCLUDING CLOCK AND FIGURE, $5.15

The figure is of bronze, beautifully finished and represents a galloping bronco and cowboy about to cast a lasso. An animated and artistic piece of statuary. The clock runs eight days, strikes the hours on a gong, and the half hours on a cup bell. The case is rich in metal ornamentation, has beautiful French rococo designed dial, sash 5½ inches in diameter. The side ornaments and feet are of solid metal, beautifully gilded. The clock is constructed of hard black enameled highly polished wood to imitate black marble, with brown mottled trimmings to imitate Mexican onyx. A cloth slightly moistened with a non-acid oil will keep it as new for generations. The movement is a splendid piece of work, an accurate timekeeper and a good runner, made of toughened brass and oil tempered steel parts. Manufactured by the Gilbert Clock Co., a company renowned for the perfection of its product. The dimensions of this clock are very attractive; stands 19½ inches high, including figure; 17½ inches wide at base, and 8 inches deep. Observe these dimensions and you will note that the clock is large and massive, a superb ornament, and fit for any parlor. Weight, boxed ready for shipment, 25 pounds.

No. 5T9378 Price, complete with figure........$5.15

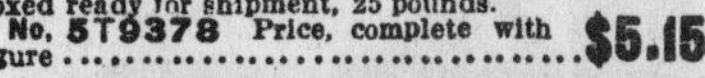

MASSIVE AND RICH APPEARING MANTEL CLOCK.

Shipping weight, 25 pounds.

This is one of our grand price defying leaders. It has been selected as the best from hundreds of clocks of the type, best both in appearance and in value. Massive and rich in appearance, will last a generation. A guaranteed clock. You are protected, you take no chance in selecting a clock where we personally guarantee it. You have an insurance that removes all the elements of chance. We guarantee it to run well for a period of five years, and warrant it against all defective material or workmanship for this period of time. It will, however, last your natural lifetime if properly cared for. It is of fine grained perfectly seasoned wood, black enameled, carefully dried in a regular kiln, will not warp, chip or peel. Columns are capped and based with gilded metal. Side ornaments and feet are of solid rich gilded metal. The dial is 5¼ inches in diameter with plain Roman numerals. The clock stands 10¾ inches high, 16½ inches wide, 7¼ inches deep. The movement runs eight days, made of solid hard rolled brass and oil tempered steel parts, strikes the hours on a soft toned gong and half hours on a sweet toned cup bell. Different from most clocks, this one can be kept new in appearance for generations. A soft piece of Canton flannel slightly moistened with sweet oil, will keep it in its pristine beauty, if occasionally applied. $9.00 would be cheap for this clock. Only on account of not using the maker's name in this advertisement and on account of a tremendous purchase are we able to make this competition defying price.

No. 5T9376 Price........$5.32

$4.38 THIS IS AN EIGHT-DAY CLOCK. OTHERS CANNOT MEET THIS PRICE.

Our new eight-day, striking, black finished, six-column Waterbury Clock for $4.38. The case is of hard, black enameled wood, not a joint, crack or crevice to be found in any part of it. It is warranted to give entire and absolute satisfaction. A woolen cloth slightly sprinkled with sweet oil lightly rubbed over this clock will keep it in its original beauty for many years. Six columns, made to imitate Mexican marble and ornamented with gilt tops and bases, ornament the sides. This is a new idea in clock ornamentation. The feet are of fine gilt metal with beautiful scroll work, which lends a richness and charm to this clock rarely equaled. The sash which holds the dial is of fine gilt brass, 5¾ inches in diameter. The dial is plain and distinctly marked with Roman numerals and fitted with fine fleur de lis hands. The clock stands 10¾ inches high; the base from foot to foot, 15½ inches wide; depth, 7 inches. The movement is trued and timed and guaranteed in every respect; runs eight days with one winding; strikes the half hours on a brass bell and the hours on a cathedral toned gong. It is made of fine hard wrought brass, oil tempered steel parts, and with care will wear and keep time for a lifetime. Weight, packed for shipment, about 20 pounds.

No. 5T9314 Price........$4.38

THE LEXINGTON EIGHT-DAY MANTEL CLOCK. $4.55

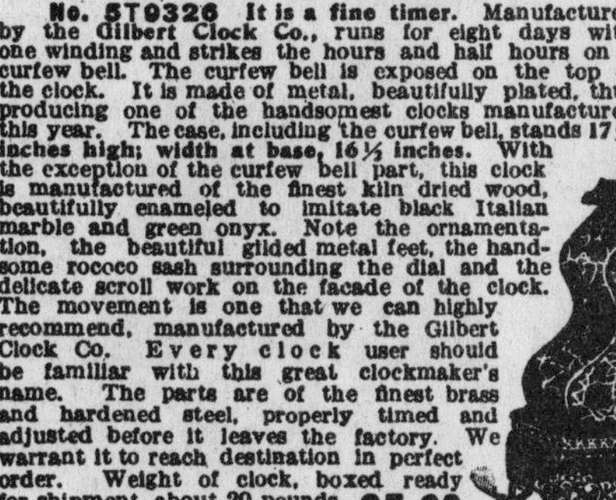

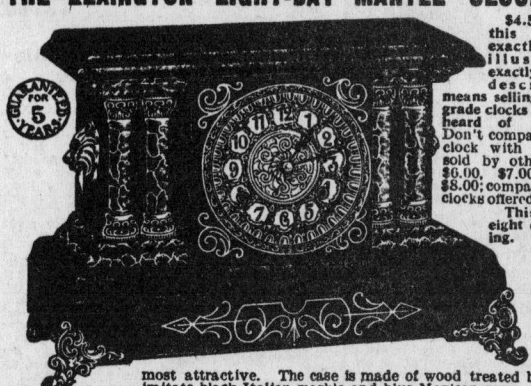

$4.55 for this clock exactly as illustrated, exactly as described, means selling high grade clocks at unheard of prices. Don't compare this clock with clocks sold by others at $6.00, $7.00 and $8.00; compare with clocks offered at $9.00 and $10.00. This mantel clock runs eight days with one winding. Strikes the half hours on a brass bell and the full hours on a beautifully toned wire cathedral gong. THE DIMENSIONS: Clock stands 11 inches high, 17 inches wide at base and 7½ inches deep. Large, massive and most attractive. The case is made of wood treated by a secret process to imitate black Italian marble and blue Mexican onyx. The feet, side ornaments, top and bottom of front columns are of hard metal heavily plated. The contrast of the gilt finish and the black marble is most pleasing.

The dial is elaborate and ornate, being a new perforated rococo design, 5¾ inches in diameter, the dial sash is fitted with a heavy French crystal glass.

The movement is the most important feature of any clock. In this clock we have fitted our special anti-friction movement. All friction has been reduced to a minimum. All pivots are polished, fine metal pendulum, latest French verge escapement, accurately run and timed before being fitted into the case. The parts are made of roll tempered brass and oil tempered steel parts.

We insure this clock. With every one of these clocks we send our written binding five-year guarantee that protects you for this term of years against faulty material or workmanship. Never before has such an offer been made by any concern and it is only possible because we know the attractive contract we have for this our Lexington Mantel Clock. Weight of clock, boxed, about 20 pounds.

No. 5T9318 The Lexington Mantel Clock. Price........$4.55

$5.32 FOR THIS HANDSOME COMBINATION METAL AND WOOD MANTEL CLOCK. $5.32

No. 5T9326 It is a fine timer. Manufactured by the Gilbert Clock Co., runs for eight days with one winding and strikes the hours and half hours on a curfew bell. The curfew bell is exposed on the top of the clock. It is made of metal, beautifully plated, thus producing one of the handsomest clocks manufactured this year. The case, including the curfew bell, stands 17½ inches high; width at base, 16½ inches. With the exception of the curfew bell part, this clock is manufactured of the finest kiln dried wood, beautifully enameled to imitate black Italian marble and green onyx. Note the ornamentation, the beautiful gilded metal feet, the handsome rococo sash surrounding the dial and the delicate scroll work on the facade of the clock. The movement is one that we can highly recommend, manufactured by the Gilbert Clock Co. Every clock user should be familiar with this great clockmaker's name. The parts are of the finest brass and hardened steel, properly timed and adjusted before it leaves the factory. We warrant it to reach destination in perfect order. Weight of clock, boxed ready for shipment, about 20 pounds.

No. 5T9326 Price.......$5.32

ACTUALLY PRICED AT ONE-HALF ITS VALUE.

Shipping weight, 35 pounds.

$5.43 for this solid iron black enameled Eight-Day Parlor Clock. Stands 10½ inches high, 15½ inches wide at base, 7 inches deep. Gilt front ornaments, gilt lion head side ornaments and gilt feet and dial sash lend a richness and artistic value to this clock unequaled by any other. The dial is its most handsome feature, having a gilt finished rim richly ornamented by a fancy rococo chased border with genuine mother of pearl inlaid figures. The dial is 6 inches in diameter. The hands are well made of blued steel. The movement fitted in this case manufactured by the celebrated New Haven Clock Co. runs eight days with one winding. Strikes the hours and half hours on a sweet toned gong.

No. 5T9334 Price........$5.43

NOTHING BETTER for time keeping qualities manufactured in clocks than the ones illustrated and described on these pages. Each one represents a wonderful saving compared with what others ask. Send for our special Clock Catalog if you desire the highest grade and artistic designs in hall clocks, French crystal, solid mahogany, genuine marble, genuine onyx, ormolu, gold plated and other styles. Restricted space will not allow illustrating and quoting these types in this catalog.

$1.46 Strike Alarm Clock.

No. 5T8574 Made by the Ansonia Clock Co., height, 6¼ inches; dial, 4½ inches, movement runs thirty hours with one winding. Different from any other alarm clock; this clock strikes the hours and half hours the same as a mantel clock. In addition it has an alarm attachment which alarms at any time set. The Ansonia Clock Co. is known for the excellent clocks which they manufacture and we guarantee this clock to be an excellent timekeeper and to give entire satisfaction. Shipping weight, 36 ounces. Price.................... $1.46

$1.96 Continuous Long Alarm Clock.

No. 5T8580 Continuous Long Alarm Clock. The case is metal, finished in bronze. The movement is made by one of the most representative clock companies in the United States, and is warranted to us by the manufacturer; we in turn guarantee it to our customers. The alarm rings for 7 minutes, but can be turned off at will by moving the lever. Height, 12 inches; width at base, 8½ inches. Shipping weight, 11 pounds. Price.................... $1.96

No. 5T8586 Nickel Plated Glass Paneled High Grade Alarm Clock. Stands 6 inches high, 4¾ inches wide at base and 3 inches deep. The dial is 2⅞ inches in diameter, has plain Roman numerals. This clock is beautified by gilt arabesque panel work in the front of the clock. The movement is manufactured by the Waterbury Clock Co. It runs thirty hours with one winding. The alarm attachment is invisible, being placed underneath the clock. This clock is not alone an alarm clock, but also strikes the hours and half hours on a bell. Weight, packed ready for shipment, about 4 pounds. Price.................... $2.30

$1.39 For an Eight-Day Gold Plated Bureau or Bedroom Clock.

No. 5T8568 Eight-Day Clock. The clock stands 3½ inches high, has a 2-inch dial with French bevel glass crystal. It is built on the order of a nickel plated alarm clock, but has no alarm, and runs eight days with one winding. Just the clock for your shelf, bureau, desk or library table. Shipping weight, 16 ounces. Price.................... $1.39

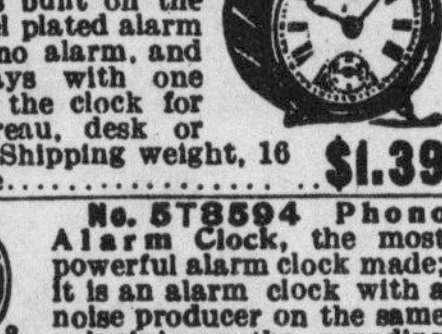

No. 5T8594 Phono Alarm Clock, the most powerful alarm clock made; it is an alarm clock with a noise producer on the same principle as the sounding disc of a telephone. Instead of the hammer striking on a bell, it strikes on a disc and a horn, similar to a phonograph horn, increases the sound and throws it directly at the sleeper. The noisiest "sleep dispeller" ever made. Copper finished, dustproof case; height 7 inches; Arabic dial, 4 inches in diameter. Shipping weight, 35 ounces. Price.................... $2.15

$2.97 For This Hanging Solid Oak Weathered Mission Eight-Day Clock.

No. 5T9026 Nothing handsomer as a wall clock for your hall, dining room, den, bedroom or parlor. The movement is a fine runner, manufactured by the New Haven Clock Co., of New Haven, Conn. The dial is exposed exactly as the illustration shows, fitted with gilt solid metal numerals and gilt solid metal hands. The entire height of the clock is 27½ inches; width at widest point, 15½ inches. The dial is 15½ inches by 15½ inches. The pendulum is likewise solid dark colored weathered oak with a fine polished brass pendulum disc, and is adjustable. The movement runs for eight days, strikes the hours and half hours on a beautiful toned wire gong. Each one has been oiled and tested. This clock, boxed for shipment, weighs about 25 pounds. Price.................... $2.97

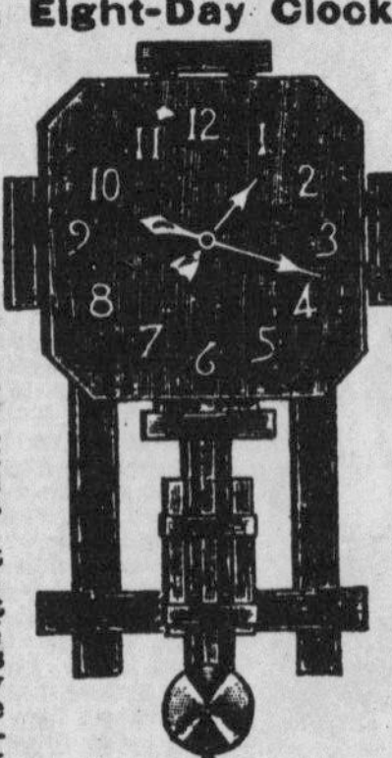

$1.83 THE ALDRICH.

Made by the Waterbury Clock Company, furnished in either oak or walnut as desired. Mention choice. Stands 22 inches high, 15 inches wide at base. Case is handsomely carved, perfectly fitted and jointed and is a marvel of value. Movement runs eight days with one winding, strikes the hours and half hours on a wire bell, has a 6-inch dial. Guaranteed to keep accurate time. Shipping weight, 16 pounds.

No. 5T9002 Strikes on a wire bell. Price.................... $1.83

No. 5T9004 Strikes on a wire bell, with an alarm attachment. Price.................... $2.30

No. 5T9008 Strikes on a gong bell, with an alarm attachment. Price.................... $2.45

$1.98 CUT PRICE. Weathered Oak Mission Style Clock.

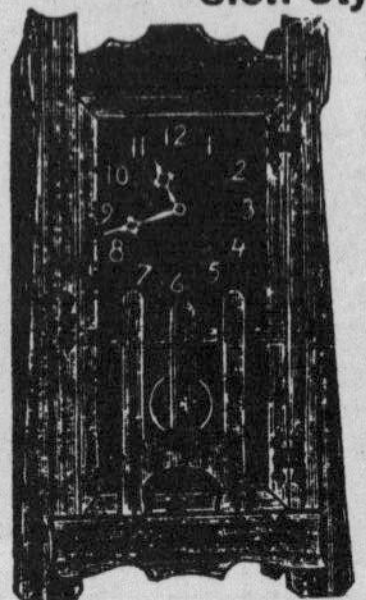

No. 5T9020 It stands at the highest point 20½ inches high; width at the base, 12 inches. The dial is plain and is also made of solid oak with bright metal numerals and bright metal hands. The movement runs for eight days with but one winding, and is manufactured by the renowned New Haven Clock Co. Strikes the hours and half hours on a sweet toned cathedral wire gong. We have contracted for an immense number; an immense quantity has made this astonishing price possible. We again offer you the advantage of the saving, adding only our own small per cent of profit to the original cost. This clock boxed, ready for shipment, weighs about 18 pounds. Price.................... $1.98

$3.40 The Rochester Fancy Ornamental Cabinet Clock,

made of solid black walnut, handsomely carved; height, 26⅝ inches. Different from any other cabinet clock, this clock has an 8-inch dial, a 2-inch larger dial than an ordinary cabinet clock, which makes it easy to see the time from any part of the room. It is fitted with an eight-day movement made by the Waterbury Clock Co., hard wrought brass and oil tempered steel parts, strikes the hours and half hours. In addition it has a calendar attachment which automatically registers the day of the month. Shipping weight, about 20 pounds.

No. 5T9032 Strikes on wire bell. Price.................... $3.40

No. 5T9038 Strikes on cathedral gong. Price.................... 3.68

$2.48 Combination Clock and Plate Rack.

No. 5T8596 $2.48 for this Combination Clock and Plate Rack, a new novelty in the clock line, a splendid ornament for any room, substantially and massively made of solid dark weathered oak, is 10½ inches high and 39½ inches long, made to hold six cups and six saucers or four fancy plates. The clock is a good running, accurate spring timer, runs for 24 hours. The dial is 5¾ inches in diameter, has solid brass numerals and brass hands, making a pretty contrast in colors, yellow brass and dark weathered oak. Boxed ready for shipment, about 18 pounds. Price.................... $2.48

$4.60 For This Beautiful Black Enameled Wood Eight-Day Clock.

No. 5T9352 Stands 10¼ inches high, 15 inches wide, 5¼ inches deep. Has four columns with bronze finished column tops and feet; runs eight days, strikes the hours and half hours on a cathedral gong. Manufactured by the New Haven Clock Co., of New Haven, Conn. One-half the price asked at cheap stores. Boxed, ready for shipment, weighs 25 pounds. Price.................... $4.60

$4.78 For This Eight-Day Gilbert Mantel Clock.

No. 5T9354 Stands 12 inches high, 18 inches wide, 8 inches deep. The case is of highly seasoned black and green enameled wood to imitate black and green onyx; has four columns with metal tops and bases, metal side ornaments and metal feet, runs eight days, strikes the hours and half hours on a cathedral gong, has beautiful rococo dial; a clock that will grace any mantel or bookcase. Boxed, ready for shipment, weighs 22 pounds. Price.................... $4.78

$4.80 For This Porcelain Eight-Day Ansonia Mantel Clock.

No. 5T9356 Stands 11¼ inches high, 8½ inches wide, 5¼ inches deep. Decorated in floral design, blended blues and yellows, the prevailing color scheme; all kiln burnt, will not wash off and will last forever. This clock runs eight days, strikes the hours and half hours on a cathedral gong; an accurate timekeeper and most beautiful ornament; will please all. Boxed, ready for shipment, weighs 20 pounds. Price.................... $4.80

$7.22 For This Beautiful Porcelain Eight-Day Clock.

No. 5T9358 Manufactured by the Ansonia Clock Co. Stands 11¾ inches high, 11¼ inches wide, 5¼ inches deep. The case is beautifully decorated with flowers in natural tints and gold lining, all kiln burnt, will not wash off and last forever. Various tints of natural green prevail in its color scheme. The movement runs eight days, strikes the hours and half hours on a cathedral gong, has plain white dial with rococo sash. Boxed, ready for shipment, weighs 18 pounds. Price.................... $7.22

$5.88 For This Genuine Ormolu Gold Plated Clock.

No. 5T9360 Stands 12½ inches high and 6¾ inches wide at its widest point. A solid gold plated, beautifully burnished clock that has been sought for by thousands, and for the first time offered at a remarkably low figure. This clock is manufactured by the New Haven Clock Co., celebrated for the perfection of its product. The movement runs eight days, very silent in action; just the kind of a clock to beautify any parlor or library. Boxed ready for shipment, weight 15 pounds. Price...... $5.88

$8.90 For This Large Size Ormolu Gold Plated Clock.

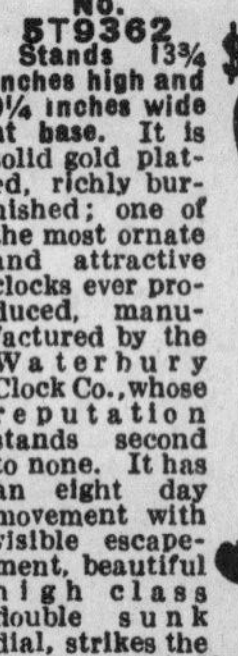

No. 5T9362 Stands 13¾ inches high and 9¼ inches wide at base. It is solid gold plated, richly burnished; one of the most ornate and attractive clocks ever produced, manufactured by the Waterbury Clock Co., whose reputation stands second to none. It has an eight day movement with visible escapement, beautiful high class double sunk dial, strikes the hours and half hours on a cathedral gong. $8.90 represents about one-half of what the regular merchant asks for this high grade clock. Boxed ready for shipment, weighs 20 pounds. Price.................... $8.90

$5.78 For This Solid Black Hard Baked Enameled Iron Clock.

No. 5T9364 Has beautiful gilt ornaments and pearl inlaid dial. Manufactured by the New Haven Clock Co., known throughout the United States for the perfection of their product. Stands 14½ inches high, 9½ inches wide, 5¼ inches deep; runs eight days, strikes the hours and half hours on a cathedral gong. Boxed, ready for shipment, weighs 38 pounds. Price.................... $5.78

$12.98 For This Exquisite Bronze Finish Mantel Clock.

No. 5T9366 Stands 15 inches, high 17½ inches wide at base, 7½ inches deep. Manufactured by the celebrated Ansonia Clock Co. Nothing handsomer, nothing grander at anywhere near this price has ever been produced. The figure of Mercury in a sitting posture, draped with beautiful cloak and armor; Syrian bronze with that beautiful green and copper colored finish, lends artistic value to this clock, unexcelled. The movement is one of the best that this company produces, runs eight days, strikes the hours and half hours on a cathedral gong; has double sunk enameled dial with exposed jewel escapement. Boxed, ready for shipment, weighs 38 pounds. Price.................... $12.98

NOTHING BETTER for time keeping qualities manufactured in clocks than the ones illustrated and described on these pages. Each one represents a wonderful saving compared with what others ask. Send for our special Clock Catalog if you desire the highest grade and artistic designs in hall clocks, French crystal, solid mahogany, genuine marble, genuine onyx, ormolu and other styles. Restricted space will not allow illustrating and quoting these fully in this catalog.

$3.94 FOR THIS VERY HANDSOME WOOD MANTEL CLOCK

Stands 12⅞ Inches High, 17 Inches wide at Base.

CALLED STAR OF THE NORTH.

THE MOVEMENT IS A GOOD ONE. Runs eight days with one winding, strikes the hours on a cathedral gong and half hours on a cup bell. It will last you for years. This clock is manufactured with the idea of producing something ornate, attractive and large for little money. Never has such a clock value been offered before. Note the ornamentation: Six beautiful columns ornament the front of the clock and handsome metal ornaments are fixed on its sides. It is equipped with fine metal feet. The clock is actually worth double what we ask; any store would ask from $6.00 to $10.00 for it. Weight, boxed ready for shipment, about 20 pounds.

No. 5R9304 Price........**$3.94**

THIS IS AN EIGHT-DAY CLOCK

OTHERS CANNOT MEET THIS PRICE. $4.38

Our new eight-day, striking, black finished, six-column Waterbury Clock for $4.38. The case is of hard, black enameled wood, not a joint, crack or crevice to be found in any part of it. It is warranted to give entire and absolute satisfaction. A woolen cloth slightly sprinkled with sweet oil lightly rubbed over this clock will keep it in its original beauty for many years. Six columns, made to imitate Mexican marble and ornamented with gilt tops and bases, ornament the sides. This is a new idea in clock ornamentation. The feet are of fine gilt metal with beautiful scroll work, which lends a richness and charm to this clock rarely equaled. The sash which holds the dial is of fine gilt brass, 5¾ inches in diameter. The dial is plain and distinctly marked with Roman numerals and fitted with fine fleur de lis hands. The clock stands 10¾ inches high; the base from foot to foot, 15½ inches wide; depth, 7 inches. The movement is trued and timed and guaranteed in every respect; runs eight days with one winding; strikes the half hours on a brass bell and the hours on a cathedral toned gong. It is made of fine hard wrought brass, oil tempered steel parts, and with care will wear and keep time for a lifetime. Weight, packed for shipment, about 20 pounds.

No. 5R9314 Price........**$4.38**

$4.22 LADY ISABELLE EIGHT-DAY MANTEL CLOCK

OUR LADY ISABELLE EIGHT-DAY CLOCK FOR $4.22. THINK OF IT!

GUARANTEED FOR 5 YEARS

We will send you this specially made, rich appearing, eight-day striking mantel clock for one-half of what a similar clock would sell the world over. **The ornamentation on this clock is one of its most attractive features.** It consists of two side ornaments, top and bottom capped columns, feet and front and bottom ornaments. The dial is simple, but rich in style, 5¼ inches in diameter. Dial sash fitted with heavy French crystal. **The movement fitted in the Lady Isabelle Clock is the best clock movement we know of and is made after our own ideas on the new anti-friction principle,** friction being reduced to a minimum. It runs eight days with one winding. Strikes the hours on a beautifully toned cathedral wire gong and the half hours on a brass cup bell. All parts are oil tempered, pivots all highly polished. The newest French verge escapement, metal pendulum.

GUARANTEED FOR FIVE YEARS.

This clock is covered by our five-year guarantee. We enclose it with every one sold and it amply protects and insures you against defective material or workmanship in this clock for a term of five years. Shipping weight, 20 pounds.

No. 5R9306 Lady Isabelle Mantel Clock. Price........**$4.22**

No. 5R8702 Handsome Bronze Figure, representing a cowboy on horseback throwing a lariat. This figure placed on top of the Lady Isabelle Clock makes a most beautiful parlor ornament. Shipping wt., 10 lbs. Price, figure only........**78c**

Our five-year guarantee against faulty material or workmanship goes with each one of them. You are insured and protected should this clock fail to perform its duties properly and by this contract you are at liberty to return it to us and have it repaired free of all cost at our expense of transportation charges. We are safe in doing this. We know that the clock will perform its duties properly and you will be entirely satisfied. The case is most attractive, but the illustration does not begin to show the coloring and brass so as to give a full idea of its beauty. Stands 11 inches high, 16¼ inches wide at base, 7 inches deep, of the Corinthian style, secretly treated wood covered by hard enamel, guaranteed not to warp, chip or scale off. Comes in black and variegated colors to imitate green onyx and Italian black marble.

$4.55 A STARTLING VALUE

THE LEXINGTON EIGHT-DAY MANTEL CLOCK.

$4.55 for this clock exactly as illustrated, exactly as described, means selling high grade clocks at unheard of prices. Don't compare this clock with clocks sold by others at $6.00, $7.00 and $8.00; compare with clocks offered at $9.00 and $10.00.

This mantel clock runs eight days with one winding. Strikes the half hours on a brass bell and the full hours on a beautifully toned wire cathedral gong.

GUARANTEED FOR FIVE YEARS.

The dimensions. Clock stands 11 inches high, 17 inches wide at base and 7½ inches deep. Large, massive and most attractive. The case is made of wood treated by a secret process to imitate black Italian marble and blue Mexican onyx. The feet, side ornaments, top and bottom of front columns are of hard metal heavily plated. The contrast of the gilt finish and the black marble is most pleasing.

The dial is elaborate and ornate, being a new perforated rococo design, 5¾ inches in diameter, the dial sash is fitted with a heavy French crystal glass. Hands of blue steel Louis XIV design, Arabic numerals, plain and distinct.

The movement is the most important feature of any clock. In this clock we have fitted our special anti-friction movement. All friction has been reduced to a minimum. All pivots are polished, fine metal pendulum, latest French verge escapement, accurately run and timed before being fitted into the case. The parts are made of roll tempered brass and oil tempered steel parts.

We insure this clock. With every one of these clocks we send our written binding five-year guarantee that protects you for this term of years against faulty material or workmanship. Never before has such an offer been made by any concern and it is only possible because we know the attractive contract we have for this our Lexington Mantel Clock. Weight of clock, boxed, about 20 pounds.

No. 5R9318 The Lexington Mantel Clock. Price........**$4.55**

$4.30 QUEEN MANTEL CLOCK AND FIGURE

Never before in the history of clock making has such a fine clock and figure been offered for the money. The case is made of fine wood, kiln dried. It is then enameled by a secret process to imitate black Italian marble with marbleized columns. The enamel is guaranteed never to crack or peel. A Canton flannel cloth sprinkled with sweet oil occasionally rubbed over the clock will make it look like new. A gilt rococo metal border ornaments the top edge of the clock. Gilt ornaments adorn the front underneath the dial, gilt bronze feet and side ornaments. Two massive marbleized columns on either side of dial. The clock is 11 inches high, 12½ inches wide at the base and 6 inches deep. The movement is made by one of the most representative clock makers in the United States; has the latest straight line verge escapement of hard wrought brass and oil tempered steel parts. Runs eight days with one winding, strikes the half hours on a brass bell and hours on a sweet toned cathedral gong. The dial is 5½ inches in diameter with gilt rococo design sash. The figure, 6⅝ inches high, represents a figure true to life, is made of bronze and finished in gilt. Our written binding guarantee for five years goes with each clock. $4.30 represents the actual cost of material and manufacturing, with only one small percentage of profit added. Order the clock and upon examination if you do not find it to be exactly as illustrated and described, the best clock value ever offered, return it to us at our expense and we will cheerfully refund your money. Shipping weight, 22 pounds.

No. 5R9310 Queen Mantel Clock, including figure. Price **$4.30**

No. 5R8704 Figure alone. Price........**.82**

GUARANTEED FOR FIVE YEARS.

$5.32 FOR THIS HANDSOME COMBINATION METAL AND WOOD MANTEL CLOCK.

No. 5R9326 It is a fine timer. Manufactured by the Gilbert Clock Co., runs for eight days with one winding and strikes the hours and half hours on a curfew bell. The curfew bell is exposed on the top of the clock. It is made of metal, beautifully plated, thus producing one of the handsomest clocks manufactured this year. The case, including the curfew bell, stands 17⅜ inches high; width at base, 16½ inches. With the exception of the curfew bell part, this clock is manufactured of the finest kiln dried wood, beautifully enameled to imitate black Italian marble and green onyx. Note the ornamentation, the beautiful gilded metal feet, the handsome rococo sash surrounding the dial and the delicate scroll work on the facade of the clock. The movement is one that we can highly recommend, manufactured by the Gilbert Clock Company. Every clock user should be familiar with this great clockmaker's name. The parts are of the finest brass and hardened steel, properly timed and adjusted before it leaves the factory. We warrant it to reach destination in perfect order. Weight of clock, boxed ready for shipment, about 20 pounds. Price........**$5.32**

ACTUALLY PRICED AT ONE-HALF ITS VALUE

$5.43 for this solid iron black enameled Eight-Day Parlor Clock. Clock stands 10½ inches high, 15½ inches wide at base, 7 inches deep. Gilt front ornaments, gilt lion head side ornaments and gilt feet and dial sash lend a richness and artistic value to this clock unequaled by any other. The dial is its most handsome feature, having a gilt finished rim richly ornamented by a fancy rococo chased border with genuine mother of pearl inlaid figures. The dial is 6 inches in diameter. The hands are well made of blued steel. The movement fitted in this case manufactured by the celebrated New Haven Clock Co. runs eight days with one winding. Strikes the hours and half hours on a sweet toned gong.

Weight, packed ready for shipment, about 35 pounds.

No. 5R9334 Price........**$5.43**

Ink Well.

No. 5R7648 Ink Well. Silver plated with beautiful ornamented figure of a horse's head. Height, 3 inches. Price........**54c** Postage extra, 12 cents.

Pin Cushion.

No. 5R7652 Silver Plated Pin Cushion with beautiful lily ornamentation. Height, 4 inches. Price........**48c** If mail shipment, postage extra, 8 cents.

Toothpick Holder.

No. 5R7650 Toothpick Holder. Silver plated. Height, 2½ inches. Price........**48c** If mail shipment, postage extra, 8 cents.

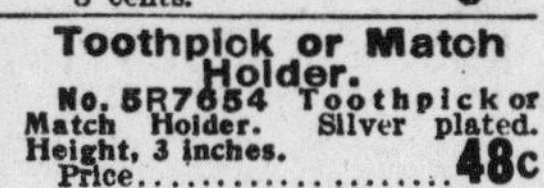

Toothpick or Match Holder.

No. 5R7654 Toothpick or Match Holder. Silver plated. Height, 3 inches. Price........**48c** Postage extra, 10 cents.

DOLLS AND TOYS

SEE INDEX, PINK PAGES 552 TO 559, TO FIND WHAT YOU WANT.

WE ACTUALLY SAVE YOU TWO PROFITS ON DOLLS

Extra Special Values in Full Jointed Dolls at Very Low Prices.

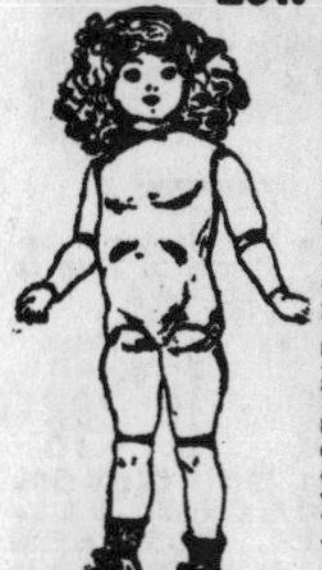

This line of Jointed Dolls has never before been offered. A good grade of papier mache dolls made in natural flesh tints, in imitation of the human body. The dolls have full elbow, wrist, hip and knee joints. Are dressed in lace trimmed chemise, have lace stockings and imitation patent leather sandals. The head is made of good quality bisque, has parted lips showing teeth, moving eyes which open and close, and side parted wig tied with ribbon. We have never before been able to offer such goodly dolls at such startlingly low prices.

Catalogue Number	Height, inches	Shipping Weight	Price, each
18L22994	10	1 lb.	$0.25
18L22996	13½	1½ lbs.	.50
18L22998	15	2 lbs.	.88
18L23000	18	4 lbs.	1.19

NOTE: No. 18L23000 has pretty eyelashes.

Our Very Finest Quality Full Jointed Dolls.

These Dolls are without doubt the best that money can buy, and we particularly recommend them to our trade. Made of heavy papier mache (light, strong and more durable than any other material) in exact imitation of the human body. The wrists, elbows, hips and knees are full ball jointed. The heads are of finest quality bisque with parted lips showing teeth. They have automatic sleeping eyes with eyelashes, and extra fine wigs, full sewed, parted, and tied with ribbons. These dolls are fitted with lace trimmed chemise, open work stockings and sateen shoes and all in all represent the highest art in doll making. Come in four sizes, carefully packed for shipping.

Catalogue Number	Height, inches	Shipping Weight	Price, each
18L23010	18	6 lbs.	$1.75
18L23012	24½	7 lbs.	2.98
18L23016	27	9 lbs.	3.89
18L23020	30	18 lbs.	4.95

Extra Large Size Genuine Kid Body Dolls.

The Dolls are well made, of good material, and are tremendous bargains at the prices quoted below. Don't confuse this line of dolls with the imitation kid dolls offered by others at our prices. Our dolls have nicely proportioned bodies, good quality bisque heads with moving eyes which open and close, nice curly wigs. Shoes and stockings. The larger the doll the better proportioned are the features and body. Come in four sizes, as follows:

Catalogue No.	H'ght, in.	Shipping Wt.	Price, each
18L23024	13	1 lb.	23c
18L23028	16	1½ lbs.	47c
18L23032	18½	2½ lbs.	73c
18L23036	21	3½ lbs.	98c

High Grade Half Jointed Kid Body Dolls.

These Dolls are made of high grade kid with riveted joints at both hips and knees, allowing the doll to assume a sitting position. The heads are bisque with moving eyes, long curly full sewed wigs, nicely parted and tied with ribbon. The lips are parted showing the teeth. Openwork stockings and sateen shoes are fitted to the doll. A splendid value at our prices, which mean a big saving to you. Come in four sizes, each nicely packed in box.

Catalogue No.	H'ght, in.	Shipping W't lbs.	Price each
18L23040	15	2	$0.59
18L23044	17	2½	.87
18L23048	20	3	1.25
18L23056	25	5	1.69

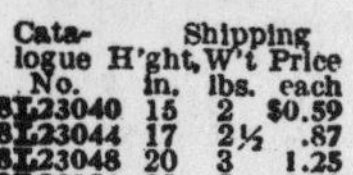

Our Columbia Half Cork Stuffed, Full Jointed, Kid Body Dolls.

To our customers who wish a fine Doll at a moderately low price we can highly recommend this quality. The entire body from shoulders to toes is made of fine quality white kid, with half cork stuffing, giving a light shapely body. The hips, knees, shoulders and elbows are nicely jointed, the forearms are of bisque. The head is of fine quality bisque with automatic sleeping and waking eyes, open mouth showing teeth, and a beautiful full sewed curly wig, neatly parted and tied with ribbons. Is fitted with openwork stockings and sateen shoes to match stockings. Quality considered, the prices quoted below are tremendous bargains. Come in four sizes, each doll carefully packed.

Catalogue Number	Height, inches	Ship'g Wt., lbs.	Price, each
18L23064	17½	2½	$1.25
18L23068	21	3½	1.88
18L23072	23	5	2.37
18L23076	27	7	2.95

Genuine Kestner Kid Body Dolls. The Standard of the World.

Absolutely the best Doll that can be bought at any price. Kestner, the manufacturer of this doll is known for the excellence of manufacture, the fine quality features, and the general superiority of his dolls. His goods are the standard by which all others are judged. The heads are of absolutely the finest quality bisque with open mouth showing teeth, and moving eyes. Fitted with long curly wig, parted on the side and tied with a bow of good quality ribbon. Has papier mache legs, tinted in natural colors, fitted with good quality removable colored lace stockings and ribbon tied sandals to match. Best quality bisque forearm. Riveted elbow, shoulder, hip and knee joints, allowing free movement of arms and legs. We buy these dolls direct from Germany and save at least one-third for you. This doll we guarantee to please you, a doll that has given satisfaction for many years. Come in five sizes, each carefully packed for shipping.

Catalogue Number	Height, inches	Shipping Wt., pounds	Price, each
18L23080	18½	3	$1.75
18L23084	20½	5	2.37
18L23088	23½	7	3.45
18L23092	25½	8	4.15
18L23096	28	11	4.98

Unbreakable Metal Head Dolls.

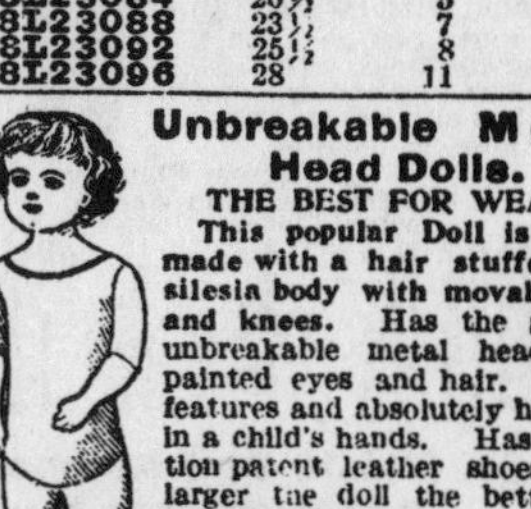

THE BEST FOR WEAR.

This popular Doll is nicely made with a hair stuffed pink silesia body with movable hips and knees. Has the genuine unbreakable metal head with painted eyes and hair. Perfect features and absolutely harmless in a child's hands. Has imitation patent leather shoes. The larger the doll the better proportioned are the heads and bodies. Come in four sizes, as follows:

Catalogue Number	Height, inches	Ship'g Wt.	Price, each
18L23100	11½	¾ lb.	25c
18L23104	14½	1 lb.	44c
18L23108	16	1¼ lbs.	57c
18L23112	18	1½ lbs.	69c

Genuine Unbreakable Metal Head Dolls With Real Curly Hair.

These hair stuffed, pink silesia body Dolls are fitted with the finest quality unbreakable metal heads, which have real curly sewed wigs, nicely parted and tied with ribbon. The eyes are of glass and the lips are parted showing teeth. The hips and knees are movable and the doll has imitation patent leather shoes. Come in three sizes as below:

Catalogue Number	H'ght, inches	Ship'g Wt.	Price, each
18L23120	14¾	1 lb.	48c
18L23124	17	2 lbs.	75c
18L23128	20	3 lbs.	95c

Genuine Kestner Bisque Babies.

A MOST POPULAR LITTLE DOLL FOR HOME DRESSING.

Made of finest quality Kestner bisque in natural flesh tints with jointed hips and shoulders. Have automatic sleeping and waking eyes and beautiful parted wigs, very long and curly. Altogether these babies are most real and lifelike and they will surely give satisfaction. The 50-cent and 98-cent sizes have natural appearing eyelashes. Come very carefully packed. We guarantee against breakage when shipped.

Catalogue Number	Height, inches	Shipping Weight	Price, each
18L23129	5	5 oz.	25c
18L23131	6½	7 oz.	50c
18L23133	10½	1 lb.	98c

Handsome Indestructible Rag Dolls at 25 and 50 Cents.

No. 18L23148 Patent Face Indestructible Rag Doll, well shaped and proportioned. Has nicely made gingham dress in bright attractive colors, with bonnet to match. Patent indestructible face, will not break or fade, making this the best appearing and most substantial rag doll obtainable, a tremendous improvement over the old style painted face. Height, 14 inches.
Price 25c
If by mail, postage extra, 10 cents.

No. 18L23150 Indestructible Rag Doll. A special value at a low price. The body is cotton stuffed, pink silesia, with removable shoes and stockings. Face is lithographed from life and is very attractive. The dress is of organdy, made very full and trimmed with lace and braid. Doll has muslin underclothes. Height, 16 inches.
Price... (Postage extra, 13 cents).... 50c

Combination Laughing and Crying Doll.

No. 18L23152 AN ATTRACTIVE AND NOVEL ARTICLE. A handsomely dressed Unbreakable Doll fitted with two heads each having a celluloid face. One face shows a smiling baby, the other a crying baby. The change is brought about by simply turning the doll upside down. The dress is of a nice quality figured flannel, lace trimmed and finished inside and out. Height, 17 inches.
Price 98c
If by mail, postage extra 12c.

Buster Brown Rag Doll.

No. 18L23160 Buster Brown Indestructible Rag Doll. A very fine imitation of the Buster Brown you read about. The doll is dressed in a red suit with white collar, cuffs and belt, has Buster Brown cap of red and white, and a large black Windsor tie. This doll will be a delight to the children on account of the popularity of Buster Brown. Length, 15 inches.
Price... (Postage, 10c.)... 25c

Infant Talking Doll.

No. 18L23164 Infant Talking Doll, dressed in long white lawn slip with lace yoke and pretty poke bonnet trimmed with ruching. Has voice which is operated by means of pullingstring. Length of body, 13 inches; entire length including dress, 18 inches. Price... 25c
Postage extra, 12c.

Unbreakable Leather Doll.

12½ INCHES HIGH ONLY 47 CENTS.

No. 18L23212 A splendid Doll for a young child, being absolutely unbreakable. Made of good clean tan colored leather with painted face and hair. The colors being absolutely fast and warranted not to come off. This is a clean wearproof article which will last for years. Height, 12½ inches.
Price.... (Postage extra, 8 cents.)... 47c

No. 18L23216 Eskimo Doll. This is a very attractive and interesting papier mache jointed doll with bisque head. The entire body is covered with white fur, all parts of the body, arms, legs and head being movable, so that you can make it assume any position. Length, 10½ inches.
Price 25c
Postage extra, 8 cents.

Infants' Doll Rattle.

No. 18L23217 Infant's Doll Rattle. Has celluloid face, lace trimmed dress with hood to match. Squeaking voice, which operates by simply shaking the doll. A splendid large rattle that will certainly amuse the young child. Size, 10¾ inches.
Price 21c
If by mail, postage extra, 3c.

Six Wonderful Value Dressed Dolls.

No. 18L23218 Pretty Dressed Doll, with full jointed arms and hips. Fancy cotton flannel dress with lace trimmed collar and hat to match. Good quality bisque head with open mouth showing teeth, moving eyes and curly wig. A doll easily worth 50 cents. Size, 13 inches. Shipping weight, 11 ounces.
Price... 25c

No. 18L23222 Young America Dressed Doll. Attractive flannelette dress nicely trimmed with plaid. The doll has good quality bisque head with parted lips showing teeth, moving eyes and curly wig. Body is jointed at hips and shoulders. Altogether a splendid value well worth 75 cents. Total height including hat, 17 inches. Shipping weight, 1½ pounds. Price.......... 48c

No. 18L23226 Special Value Dressed Doll, usually priced at $1.00. Has excellent quality bisque head. Sleeping and waking eyes and nicely curled wig. The body is full jointed at shoulders and hips. Dressed in pretty removable dress with jacket and hat to match. Lace trimmed underwear, removable shoes and stockings. Size, including hat, 16½ inches. Shipping weight 1½ pounds.
Price.......... 59c

No. 18L23230 This beautiful dressed Doll is full jointed at hips, knees, elbows and shoulders. Has fine quality bisque head, moving eyes, and nicely curled wig. Is dressed in white organdy over a colored foundation with pretty lace trimmed hat to match. Has lace trimmed underwear, and all clothes can be taken off. Height, including hat, 19 inches. Shipping weight, 2 pounds.
Price 75c

No. 18L23234 Our "Veiled Lady" Doll, with jointed arms and legs. Fine bisque head with open mouth showing teeth, moving eyes and pretty curly wig. Beautifully dressed in fancy gown, over lace trimmed underwear, all of which can be removed. Has pretty coat with hat to match and stylish drop veil. A splendid value at the price we ask. Easily worth $1.50. Size, including hat, 20 inches. Shipping weight, 2¼ pounds.
Price 98c

No. 18L23238 Our very finest American Style Dressed Doll, with full jointed hips, knees, shoulders and elbows. Finest quality bisque head with extra long curly wig, moving eyes and parted lips showing teeth. Has beautifully figured lawn dress, trimmed with ribbon sash and bows. Lace trimmed hat to match. We can particularly recommend this doll and guarantee it equal to $2.25 dolls shown by others. Comes nicely packed in box. Shipping weight, 3 pounds.
Price $1.47

YOU BUY AT FIRST COST OF MANUFACTURE PLUS ONLY OUR SMALL PROFIT

Dressed Dolls With Extra Play Clothes.

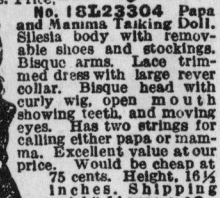

No. 18L23240 Dressed Doll with complete set of extra play clothes. The doll is made of best quality papier mache, jointed at knees, hips, elbows and shoulders. Fitted with good quality bisque head, open mouth showing teeth and moving eyes. Is dressed with underclothes, cotton flannel dress and gilt braided jacket, all of which can be removed. Has large felt hat trimmed with quill and ribbon bow. The extra outfit consists of figured wrapper with belt and sunbonnet, also a spade. One of the biggest values ever offered. Height of doll, 12½ inches. Shipping weight, 2 pounds. Price, **98c**

Unbreakable Dolls.

No. 18L23242 Indestructible Dressed Doll. Silesia body. Removable shoes and stockings. Good quality lace trimmed dress with bonnet to match. Genuine unbreakable Minerva metal head. A very pretty and at the same time unbreakable doll, which should meet with the approval of many mothers. Shipping weight, 12 ounces. Price **50c**

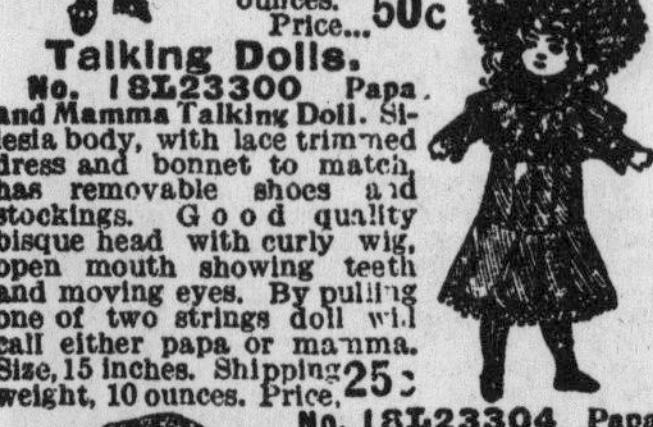

Talking Dolls.

No. 18L23300 Papa and Mamma Talking Doll. Silesia body, with lace trimmed dress and bonnet to match, has removable shoes and stockings. Good quality bisque head with curly wig, open mouth showing teeth and moving eyes. By pulling one of two strings doll will call either papa or mamma. Size, 15 inches. Shipping weight, 10 ounces. Price **25c**

No. 18L23304 Papa and Mamma Talking Doll. Silesia body with removable shoes and stockings. Bisque arms. Lace trimmed dress with large rever collar. Bisque head with curly wig, open mouth showing teeth, and moving eyes. Has two strings for calling either papa or mamma. Excellent value at our price. Would be cheap at 75 cents. Height, 16½ inches. Shipping weight, 14 ounces. Price **48c**

No. 18L23308 Extra large beautifully Dressed Talking Doll. Satin dress with large rever collar, both trimmed with lace appliqué. Lace trimmed underwear. All clothes and underwear can be removed. Has nice curly wig on extra fine bisque head with open mouth showing teeth, and moving eyes Large straw hat trimmed with coque feathers and ribbon bow. Very natural papa or mamma call is produced by pulling one of two strings. Size, 20 inches, including hat. Shipping weight, 1¾ pounds. Price **89c**

Rubber Toys.

PURE, CLEAN RUBBER TOYS IMMENSELY POPULAR. OUR VALUES AND QUALITIES ARE THE BEST.

No. 18L23312 White Rubber Doll with perfect features and limbs. Dressed in knitted yarn suit with hat to match. Positively unbreakable. Height, 8 inches. Price **25c**
If by mail, postage extra, 5 cents.

No. 18L23342 Red India Rubber Flower Girl Doll, made of the best quality red India rubber, the coloring of which will not wear off. This doll, as shown in accompanying illustration, has basket of flowers in one hand and a single flower in the other. Has German silver whistle which sounds when doll is squeezed. Size, 5¼ inches. Price............ **25c**
Postage extra, 3 cents.

No. 18L23343 Red Rubber Cat. A good and life like representation. Made of pure red India rubber, which is absolutely harmless in any child's hand. Fitted with German silver whistle. Length from tip of tail to head, 5¾ inches. Height, 3½ inches. Price (Postage extra, 5c.).... **37c**

TEDDY BEARS HAVE COME TO STAY MORE POPULAR THAN EVER

The Best Plaything Ever Invented.

THESE BEARS ARE THE MOST SENSIBLE AND SERVICEABLE

toys ever put before the public. Not a fad or campaign article, but something which has proven, true all that has ever been claimed as to their value as wearproof playthings. An article which will afford your children and even yourself great amusement and lasting pleasure. Made of the finest quality imported bear plush, they closely resemble the little cubs. They are full jointed and will assume countless different positions (four of which we illustrate). Each bear has a natural voice, produced by slight pressure on the front of body, and they are practically unbreakable. We offer these bears in four sizes. Natural cinnamon color only. The larger the size the better proportioned are the bears. These are the genuine imported toys known the world over as the very best obtainable. Our prices are wonderfully low.

No.	Size	Shipping Wt.	Price.
18L23358	10 inches high	10 ounces.	$0.75
18L23360	12 inches high	16 ounces.	1.19
18L23362	14 inches high	18 ounces.	1.69
18L23364	16 inches high	24 ounces.	2.25

Red Rubber Toys.

No. 18L23344 Red Rubber Dog. An exact representation of the Collie dog. Made of pure red India rubber, absolutely harmless to the child. Fitted with German silver whistle. Height, 4 inches. Length, 5½ inches. Price **42c**
If by mail, postage extra, 5 cents.

No. 18L23345 Water Squirting Elephant. Made of the best quality red India rubber. Has hollow trunk with hole so that it can be filled with water. By squeezing the body of the elephant the trunk will throw a thin stream of water over 25 feet. A new harmless plaything. Length from end of trunk to tail, 6¾ inches. Price......... **48c**
Postage extra, 5 cents.

Throws Water.

No. 18L23346 The new Red Rubber Teddy Bear. This is an article which has never before been offered. A very good portrayal of the popular Teddy bear standing on his hind feet. Made of the best quality pure red India rubber, fitted with German silver whistle. A very special value. Height, 5½ inches. Price **48c**
If by mail, postage extra, 5 cents.

Special Value, Horse and Soldier for 50 Cents.

50c

No. 18L23348 Red Rubber Horse and Rider. Consists of two pieces, the horse being fitted with saddle in which the rider, made up in soldier costume, sits. Both pieces have German silver whistles, and are made of the best red rubber. Size, 8 inches. Price, per set, **50c**
If by mail, postage extra, 6 cents.

Bear Family, 25 Cents.

No. 18L23366 The latest idea in bears. This family consists of one bear measuring 7¾ inches in height and two 4½ inches. The mother bear is cinnamon color and one baby is cinnamon the other white. Are made of prepared cotton on strong wire, the arms and legs being movable so that the bears will assume any position desired. These bears are practically indestructible, and no matter how roughly used by the children they can always be put back into their original shape. The value of this offer will be readily appreciated by our customers. Come put up in neat box.

Price for the entire family of 3 .. **25c**
If by mail, postage extra, 6 cents.

Two Wonderful Values in Plush Animals.

No. 18L23369 Beautiful Plush Cat. Covered with good quality plush, glass eyes, ribbon collar, bow and brass bell, also natural voice. Is very popular for the young child, being harmless and unbreakable. Entire length, 12 inches. Color, white only. Shipping weight, 8 ounces. Price........ **48c**

No. 18L23371 White Plush Covered Rabbit with Voice. A splendid value. Has ribbon collar and bow with brass bell. Natural appearing glass eyes. Large velvet and plush ears. Certainly a very popular stuffed animal. Size, 10 inches long. Color, white only. Price.... **48c**
Postage extra, 8 cents.

Very Finest Quality Kid Doll Bodies.

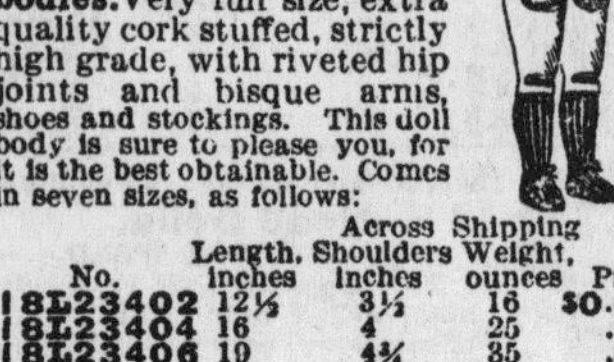

We sell only the very best make of kid doll bodies. Very full size, extra quality cork stuffed, strictly high grade, with riveted hip joints and bisque arms, shoes and stockings. This doll body is sure to please you, for it is the best obtainable. Comes in seven sizes, as follows:

No.	Length, inches	Across Shoulders inches	Shipping Weight, ounces	Price
18L23402	12½	3½	16	$0.47
18L23404	16	4	25	.69
18L23406	19	4¾	35	.88
18L23408	21½	5½	45	1.25
18L23412	23¾	6	60	1.48
18L23414	24½	6¼	65	1.69
18L23416	25½	7	75	1.98

Silesia Doll Bodies.

Hair Stuffed Pink Silesia Doll Bodies. This is a very high grade and satisfactory silesia body that will give best of wear and satisfaction; has bisque arms and removable shoes and stockings. Comes in the following sizes:

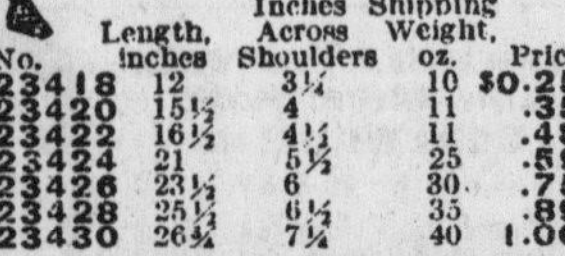

No.	Length, inches	Inches Across Shoulders	Shipping Weight, oz.	Price
18L23418	12	3¼	10	$0.25
18L23420	15½	4	11	.35
18L23422	16½	4½	11	.48
18L23424	21	5½	25	.59
18L23426	23½	6	30	.75
18L23428	25½	6½	35	.89
18L23430	26¾	7¼	40	1.00

Sewed Wig and Moving Glass Eyes.

The Metal Indestructible Minerva Doll Head with moving glass eyes. Open lips showing teeth, and very fine sewed curly wig. The metal heads, made of the best flexible sheet brass can be given to the smallest child with perfect safety, as the metal is covered with a pure, harmless paint which is manufactured especially for the purpose. Comes in sizes as follows:

No.	Height, inches	Inches Across Sh'lders	Shipping Weight, oz.	Price
18L23446	4	3	9	$0.44
18L23448	4¼	3½	11	.59
18L23450	5¾	4¾	14	.85
18L23452	6⅝	4⅞	21	1.10

Genuine Bisque Doll Heads.

IMMENSE VALUES. COMPARE OUR SIZES AND PRICES WITH OTHERS.

Bisque Doll Heads. Good quality, high grade bisque, with very beautiful moulded faces, showing teeth, with two rows, sewed wig and movable eyes. Either blondes or brunettes. Please mention choice. Comes in sizes as follows:

No.	Height, Inches	Inches Across Sh'lders	Shipping Weight, oz.	Price
18L23454	3⅞	3	9	$0.21
18L23456	4½	3½	13	.30
18L23458	5¼	4¼	15	.38
18L23460	6	5	17	.59
18L23462	7	5½	24	.88
18L23464	8¼	6¼	39	1.25
18L23466	9	6¾	42	1.68

Kestner Bisque Doll Heads.

These are the highest grade bisque heads that are manufactured. The Kestner make of dolls is wellknown, being the best make of dolls in the world. All these heads are very lifelike in appearance, having moving eyes and open mouth, showing teeth. The highest grade full sewed wig with long curls side parted and tied on side with large silk ribbon bow. We furnish these doll heads in the following sizes:

No.	Height, inches	Inches Across Shoulders	Shipping Weight, oz.	Price
18L23482	4¾	3¼	16	$0.62
18L23484	5½	4	17	.89
18L23486	6½	4¼	22	1.19
18L23488	7½	4¾	32	1.43
18L23490	8¾	6¼	36	1.96

Celluloid Doll Heads.

Celluloid Doll Heads. The celluloid doll heads, until recently, have been extremely high priced. We have succeeded in making arrangements so that they are exceptionally cheap, considering the distinct advantages this head has over the ordinary doll head. The faces are beautifully moulded. Made of the best celluloid, absolutely unbreakable, light as a feather and, at the prices we quote, will surely make them exceedingly popular. This style of celluloid doll head has painted hair and eyes, with open mouth showing teeth. Come in the following sizes:

No.	Height, inches	Inches Across Shoulders	Shipping Weight, oz.	Price
18L23500	3½	2¾	4	10c
18L23502	3¾	3	6	15c
18L23504	4¼	3½	6	29c
18L23506	5	4	8	37c
18L23508	6¼	5¼	11	50c

Celluloid Doll Heads, with glass eyes and fine curly sewed wig. The features of this doll are very beautiful. This head combines all the features of the finest bisque head, but is exceptionally light in weight, being made of the finest celluloid. They are unbreakable, making a pretty and durable doll head. We quote the following exceptionally low prices:

No.	Height, Inches	Inches Across Shoulders	Shipping Weight, oz.	Price
18L23510	3½	2¾	4	25c
18L23512	3¾	3	7	37c
18L23514	4¼	3	8	55c
18L23516	5	4	13	68c
18L23518	6¼	5¼	15	82c

Genuine Minerva Metal Doll Heads at Reduced Prices.

These Doll Heads are imported from Germany. They combine the durability of sheet metal and the beauty of bisque, are light in weight, washable, and will not chip; will stand any reasonable wear. Small children cannot injure them; larger ones love them for their unequaled beauty. The eyes are clear and tender, head flexible at the bust, and fitted with sewing holes, making it easy to adjust and fasten them to body. Comes in sizes as follows:

Catalogue No.	Height, in.	Inches Across Sh'ldrs	Ship'ng Wt., oz.	Price
18L23432	3⅝	2¾	3	14c
18L23434	3¾	3	3	21c
18L23436	4⅛	3⅜	8	28c
18L23438	4½	3⅝	8	35c
18L23440	5	4	9	40c
18L23442	6¼	4½	14	58c
18L23444	6¾	5½	17	76c

Nos. 18L23442 and 18L23444 have glass eyes and open mouth, showing teeth.

Baby Swings.

No. 29E2 Baby Swing; has hardwood seat, 11 inches square, upholstered in cretonne; intended to be hung in a doorway; furnished with cotton rope and two hooks to hang it on; has no springs.
Price........ 37c
Shipping weight, 3 pounds.

Baby Jumpers.

This Jumper combines in one article a baby swing, reclining chair, crib and jumper; strong and large enough for a child six years old; child cannot fall out. Should the baby fall asleep while in the chair it can be adjusted to a crib without disturbing the child. It is light and simple, yet substantial and perfect.

No. 29E8 Baby Jumper, complete, with springs and cotton rope and hooks, with veneered seat and back, not upholstered. Price.................. **$1.39**
Shipping weight, 12 pounds.

No. 29E12 Baby Jumper, complete, with springs, rope and hooks, upholstered in cretonne, like illustration. Price.................. **$1.75**
Shipping weight, 16 pounds.

No. 29E15
The stand is made on the best mechanical principles; will support a tested weight of 150 pounds. The only baby jumper that has a perfect reclining chair and foot rest and is adjustable. You can make a chair, cradle or crib by a single movement. All material used in the construction of the stand and chair is the best selected hardwood. Can be folded up when not in use and laid to one side. Height, ready for use, 4 feet 9 inches. You would not take three times the price and be without after having used same. Shipping weight, 30 pounds. Price..... **$3.35**

No. 29E19 Doctor Martin's Infant Exerciser. The latest and greatest success for exercising and amusing the baby. It develops the child and keeps it amused for hours at a time. Designed as a relief to the busy mother. The exerciser is an acknowledged source of pleasure to every household where there is a baby. The invention consists of a supporting jacket, adjustable so as to hold and sustain the body of any size infant, by two long shoulder straps or bands to a hook on either side of the suspension bar, which revolves under a ball bearing swivel preventing any chance of twisting and the consequence of unwinding. It may be attached to the ceiling or doorway or to the roof of piazza by means of a spiral spring with cord. Every part is made with the utmost care for strength and safety. Easily adjusted for any height so that toes of child touch the floor. Shipping weight, 3 pounds. Price..... **$2.75**

Automobiles.

No. 29E50 American Clipper Automobile. A strongly built and well finished, strongly geared vehicle with metal body and seat. The body is 13x28 inches, painted in a pretty vermilion with yellow striping, varnished inside and out. Wheels are 16 and 8 inches, with ⅜-inch rubber tires. Has special wheel steering device. Shipping weight, 40 pounds.
Price.................. **$3.95**

No. 29E52 The Winner Automobile, of same construction as above but larger size. The body is 14½x35½ inches, wheels, 18 and 12 inches, has ½-inch rubber tires. Shipping weight, 50 pounds. Price.......... **$4.50**

No. 29E54 Signal Horns for attaching to above automobiles. Shipping weight, 1 pound. Price.................. **35c**

No. 29E56 Brass Lamps to fasten on above automobiles. Shipping weight, 4 pounds. Price.................. **$1.00**

BOYS' WAGONS.

No. 29E58 Iron axles; body, 14x28 inches; wheels, 12 and 16 inches. Hardwood paneled body, landscape painting, scrolled and varnished, hub caps, high seat and dashboard. Iron braced, heavy iron axles in iron thimble skein, oval tires welded and shrunk on. Same as illustration. Shipping weight, 28 pounds. Price.................. **$1.95**

Boys' Farm Wagon, with Seat, Handle and Shafts, for $4.50.

No. 29E62 Boys' Farm Wagon, with handle and shafts. Body, 18x36 inches, with hardwood frame. The sides and ends can be taken off, leaving bed with stakes. The gearing is made like a farm wagon, having bent hawns and adjustable reach; all parts are strongly ironed and braced; wheels are 14 and 20 inches; heavy welded tires; sand boxes and hub caps; has seat, handle and a pair of hardwood shafts for dog or goat. **It is handsomely ornamented with landscapes and scroll work. This wagon is the best in the market.** Shipping weight, 54 pounds.
Price.................. **$4.50**

FOR GOAT OR DOG HARNESS, SEE INDEX.

No. 29E63 Pole and Whiffletree, to fit Farm Wagon No. 29E62.
Price.................. **.85c**

Boys' Express Wagons.

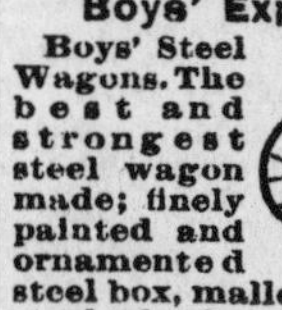

Boys' Steel Wagons. The best and strongest steel wagon made; finely painted and ornamented steel box, malleable iron gear, tinned steel wheels.

No. 29E64 Body, 12x24-inch; wheels, 8 and 12-inch. **Shipping weight, 18 pounds.** Price.................. **$1.00**

No. 29E68 Body, 14x28-inch; wheels, 10 and 14-inch. **Shipping weight, 20 pounds.** Price.................. **$1.30**

No. 29E72 Body, 15x30-inch; wheels, 12 and 16-inch. **Shipping weight, 22 pounds.** Price.................. **$1.45**

No. 29E73 Steel Wagon Body, 16x32-inch. Wheels, 14 and 18-inch. **Shipping weight, 26 pounds.**
Price.................. **$1.65**

No. 29E74 Boys' Special Steel Express Wagon. This wagon is built extra heavy and is specially adapted for heavy work. Body, 18x36 inches; wheels, 20 and 14 inches. **Shipping weight, 30 pounds.** Price.......... **$2.50**

The Little Gem Dime Savings Bank.

No. 29E155 Locks itself and registers the amount deposited. Opens automatically when $5.00 in dimes have been deposited without use of force; nickel plated, and can be carried conveniently in your vest pocket. Price, each.......... **6c**
Per dozen.................. **70c**
If by mail, postage extra, 2c.

No. 29E157 Made same as above to hold and register 50 pennies. This gives the little ones an opportunity to save their spare pennies. Price, per doz., 70c; each.. **6c**
If by mail, postage extra, each, 4c.

No. 29E159 The Seroco Savings Bank. This same bank has been adopted throughout the country by many of the savings banks who furnish them to their customers for $1.00 and they keep the key. The bank is made of the best cold rolled steel with the most perfect oxidized copper finish. Size, 4⅝x3¼x2⅝ inches. With each bank we furnish key. **Shipping weight, 1¾ pounds.**
Special price, per doz.. **$7.75**; each...... **65c**
Special price to savings banks: We put your name plate on same when ordered in lots of not less than 50, at $7.75 per dozen.

The Canary Bird Whistle.

No. 29E217 The Canary Bird Whistle. Made of metal. All the pretty notes of the canary can be imitated. Lots of fun for boys and girls.
Price, per dozen, 30c; each.......... **3c**
If by mail, postage extra, 3 cents.

The Laughing Camera.

No. 29E221 The Laughing Camera. A whole passing show. Furnishes more amusement than you would get in a circus. Your friends grotesquely photographed. Stout people look thin and thin people look stout. By getting a focus on passing pedestrians, horses, cars, etc., the most ludicrous pictures are witnessed. **The passerby takes on the swinging stride of a grand-daddy-longlegs,** horses look like giraffes.
Price, per dozen, **$1.25**; each.... **11c**
If by mail, postage extra, 5 cents.

Rattles.

No. 29E336 The Rattle Pacifier, the best rattle, teething ring and plaything ever invented for the babies. It has rubber nipple, bone shields, teething ring and bells. **Made good and strong.**
Price, per dozen, 80c; each.......... **7c**
If by mail, postage extra, 5 cents.

No. 29E338 Celluloid Rattle (with whistle), 6 inches long, come in very pretty assorted colors. Price.......... **23c**
If by mail, postage extra, 5 cents.

No. 29E340 White Celluloid Teething Ring. First quality.
Price, per dozen, 45c; each.......... **4c**
If by mail, postage extra, each, 2 cents

China Tea Sets.

No. 29E300 Toy China Tea Set, consisting of 16 pieces; cups, saucers, sugar and creamer with six extra spoons. All prettily hand decorated in fancy colors and gilt. Best value sold anywhere. Shipping weight, 16 ounces.
Price, per set.................. **25c**

No. 29E304 China Tea Set, beautifully decorated in hand painting and gilt. Consists of 18 pieces, including cups, saucers, cake dish, tea, sugar and creamer. A nice, large set. No such value sold elsewhere. Shipping weight, 30 ounces. Price, per set.......... **50c**

No. 29E308 China Tea Set. This is a particularly desirable set, made of fine, thin white china with embossed design. Extra large pieces, that can be used practically for an after dinner. Consists of six cups and saucers, one tea, one sugar and one creamer. Put up in a nice individual box. Extra $1.00 value. Shipping weight, 4 pounds.
Price, per set.................. **75c**

No. 29E312 China Tea Set. This is an elegant, large set, consisting of six cups and saucers, one tea, one sugar and one creamer. Made of very fine, thin white china, beautifully decorated in enameled picture designs taken from fairy tales; with gold traced edges, and handles relieved with floral decorations on the larger pieces. This is a very large size, for practical use, and will be very highly appreciated by the children. Regular $1.50 value. Shipping weight, 6 pounds.
Price, per set.................. **$1.00**

REMEMBER OUR PROFIT SHARING PLAN.

For every order of a dollar or more you get a certificate showing the amount of your purchase, and when these certificates amount to certain sums you can get various valuable articles ENTIRELY FREE of charge as fully explained on the last pages of this catalogue.

Britannia Tea Sets.

No. 29E316 Britannia Tea Set, consisting of about 15 pieces, silver finished tea pot, sugar bowl, sugar tongs, creamer, plates, cups, etc. Put up in neat pasteboard box. **Shipping weight, 7 ounces.** Price, per set.. **10c**

No. 29E320 Britannia Tea Set, consisting of about 23 pieces, silver finished, assortment same as above, but a little larger size. **Shipping** weight, 15 ounces. Price, per set.. **20c**

No. 29E324 Britannia Tea Set, silver finished, about 24 pieces, and still larger than above. **Shipping** weight, 28 ounces. Price, per set.. **43c**

No. 29E328 Britannia (Pewter) Tea Set. Highly silver finished, with very handsome filigree design. Large cups, saucers and other pieces. Set consists of about 23 pieces. Regular $1.25 size. Shipping weight, 40 ounces.
Price, per set.................. **80c**

The Majestic Doll.

Nothing Made to Compare With Them.

The highest grade and finest doll ever produced. The body is the human shape, made of an indestructible flesh color pressed papier mache formed by hydraulic pressure, making same exceptionally light and indestructible, ball joints, moving eyes, hips, shoulders, elbows and wrists; also moving head and moving eyes, with eyelashes, open mouth, showing teeth; the very finest quality sewed wig made of human hair; has extra quality shoes and lace stockings; comes dressed in a fine lace and ribbon trimmed chemise. The eyes are tied with strings to back of head to prevent breaking when shipped. Comes in sizes as follows:

No. 29E344 Majestic Doll, as described above. This is a special number, made to sell at an extremely low price. Length, 18½ inches. Shipping weight, 4 pounds. Price.... **$1.00**

No. 29E348 Majestic Doll, as described above. This is another extra special doll, not quite as large proportions as the regular majestic doll, but a doll equal to anything sold at $2.50 elsewhere. Length, 22½ inches. Shipping weight, 5 pounds. Price.......... **$1.40**

No. 29E352 Majestic Doll, as described above. This doll has larger proportions around body than above; extra fine finished and exceptionally pretty doll. Length, 21 inches. Shipping weight, 6 pounds. Price.......... **$2.25**

No. 29E356 Majestic Doll, as described above. Still larger proportions around body than above. Length, 24½ inches. Shipping weight, 7 pounds. Price.......... **$2.75**

No. 29E360 Majestic Doll, as described above. This is an exceptionally large and beautiful doll, a doll that regularly retails for $5.00. Length, 27½ inches. Shipping weight, 8 pounds.
Price.................. **$3.75**

No. 29E364 Majestic Doll, as described above. Extra large size body, almost life size, beautifully proportioned, extra well made in every manner. Length, 30 inches. Shipping weight, 10 pounds. Price.......... **$4.75**

Exceptional Large Size Dolls for the Money.

Not the finest quality, but well made, pretty faces, good kid bodies and very big values.

No. 29E368 Kid Body Doll, with straight hip and knee joints, fine quality bisque head, moving eyes. A doll that is usually sold by all dealers for 50 cents. Length, 14 inches. Shipping weight, 2 pounds.
Price.................. **25c**

No. 29E372 Kid Body Doll, straight hip and knee joints. Fitted with a very pretty looking bisque head, moving eyes and fine sewed wig with new style hair dressing, tied with bows of ribbon. A very full sized fat body. Length, 16 inches. Shipping weight, 3 pounds.
Price.................. **50c**

No. 29E376 Kid Body Doll, with straight hip and knee joints, as described above, with new style hair dressing, larger proportioned body. Length, 18½ inches. Shipping weight, 4 pounds.
Price.................. **75c**

No. 29E380 Kid Body Doll, with fine bisque head, fine sewed wig, new style hair dressing, as shown above. Very large sized body. An exceptionally fine doll, worth almost double our price. Length, 20½ inches. Shipping weight, 5 pounds. Price.......... **$1.00**

High Grade Kid Body Dolls.

With double riveted joints, fine bisque heads, very pretty faces, with fullsewed wigs, new style hair dressing parted in middle. This is an extra fat body and large head. The riveted joints enable an adjustment, so that the doll will sit up or assume different positions. We list this doll in six different sizes. The larger the size of the doll, the better proportioned and larger is the body.

No. 29E384 Fine Kid Body Doll, with riveted hip and knee joints, very full sized body, fine bisque head with full sewed wig, regular parting in middle. A fine grade doll. Length, 15 inches. Shipping weight, 2 pounds. Price......49c

No. 29E388 Kid Body Doll. Same quality as above, with larger proportioned body. Length, 17 inches. Shipping weight, 2½ pounds. Price....70c

No. 29E397 Kid Body Doll, riveted joints as described above, but still larger body. Length, 20½ inches. Shipping weight, 3 pounds. Price, 95c

No. 29E401 Kid Body Doll, with full sewed wig, very beautiful bisque face, showing teeth, larger proportioned body than above. Length, 23½ inches. Shipping weight, 4 pounds. Price............................$1.20

No. 29E403 Kid Body Doll, with sewed wig, riveted joints, as described above, still larger proportioned body than above. Elegant value. Length, 25 inches. Shipping weight, 5 pounds. Price............................$1.40

No. 29E405 Kid Body Doll. This is a larger size. Made as described above with a very beautiful bisque head, full sewed wig, extra large proportioned body. Length, 27½ inches. Shipping weight, 6 pounds. Price............................$1.75

Kid Body Dolls.

High Grade Cork Stuffed Kid Body Doll, with very fine extra size bisque head, moving eyes, has full sewed wig with new style hair dressing, parted in center and tied with bows of ribbon. The body has riveted hip, knee, arm and elbow joints. Also has kid legs; fitted with removable lace shoes and stockings.

No. 29E409 Kid Body Doll, as described above. Length, 17 inches. Shipping weight, 2 pounds. Price............$1.00

No. 29E411 Kid Body Doll, with riveted joints, as described above, fine extra size bisque head, with moving eyes, large size body. Length, 21 inches. Shipping weight, 2½ pounds. Price, $1.50

No. 29E420 Kid Body Doll, riveted joints as described above, larger size body and head. Length, 23 inches. Shipping weight, 3 pounds. Price............................$2.00

No. 29E424 Kid Body Doll, very large proportioned body and head. An exceptionally handsome doll. Length, 26 inches. Shipping weight, 4 pounds. Price.................$2.50

Genuine Kestner Kid Dolls.

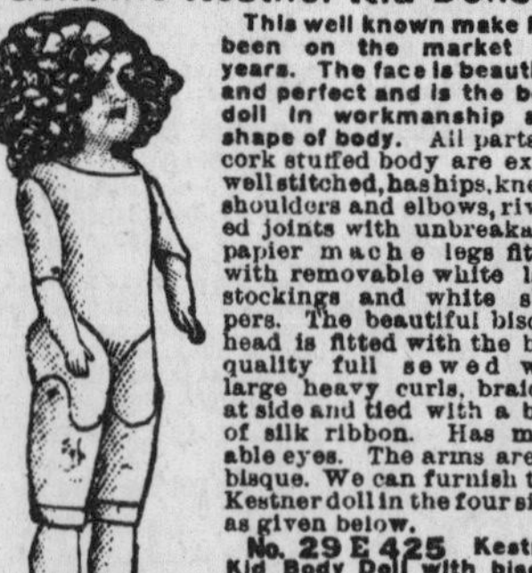

This well known make has been on the market for years. The face is beautiful and perfect and is the best doll in workmanship and shape of body. All parts of cork stuffed body are extra well stitched, has hips, knees, shoulders and elbows, riveted joints with unbreakable papier mache legs fitted with removable white lace stockings and white slippers. The beautiful bisque head is fitted with the best quality full sewed wig, large heavy curls, braided at side and tied with a bow of silk ribbon. Has movable eyes. The arms are of bisque. We can furnish this Kestner doll in the four sizes as given below.

No. 29E425 Kestner Kid Body Doll with bisque head, moving eyes, as described above. Size, 18¾ inches. Shipping weight, 2½ pounds. Price..$1.60

No. 29E426 Kestner Kid Body Bisque Doll, with moving eyes, unbreakable legs, as described above. Size, 20½ inches. Shipping weight, 3 pounds. Price...............$2.00

No. 29E427 Kestner Kid Body Doll, bisque head, moving eyes, unbreakable legs and bisque arms as described above. Length, 23⅝ inches. Shipping weight, 3½ pounds. Price............................$3.25

No. 29E429 Kestner Kid Body Doll, bisque head, moving eyes, unbreakable legs and bisque arms, as described above. Length, 26 inches. Shipping weight, 4 pounds. Price............................$4.00

NOTE—The larger size dolls come proportionately larger in body and size of head.

New Unbreakable Dolls.

Silesia Body and Minerva Metal Head.

This is a doll that has just been placed on the market after our own idea. The body is made of best quality pink silesia, hair stuffed, has reinforced knee joints, imitation stockings with shoes. Has the silesia arms in imitation of kid. **Fitted with the well known Minerva head,** made of fine sheet metal, combining the beauty of a fine bisque head and being absolutely unbreakable and harmless. This makes it absolutely the best unbreakable doll ever produced.

No. 29E436 Pink Silesia Hair Stuffed Body, fitted with Minerva metal doll head as described above. Length, 15½ inches. Shipping weight, 2 pounds. Price............................50c

No. 29E440 Pink Silesia Hair Stuffed Body, fitted with Minerva metal head, larger proportioned than above. Length, 17½ inches. Shipping weight, 3 pounds. Price...........65c

No. 29E444 Pink Silesia Hair Stuffed Body, fitted with Minerva doll head. This head has the glass eye. Larger sized body and larger sized head than above. Length, 21 inches. Shipping weight, 4 pounds. Price, 90c

Minerva Metal Head with Sewed Wig.

Unbreakable Doll.

Silesia Body Dolls with fine Minerva metal head with curly wig and glass eyes. These dolls have been recently placed on the market and have at once been a decided success. Every mother is probably familiar with the Minerva metal head and combining this feature with a fine hair stuffed silesia body, makes an unbreakable doll and at the same time a very pretty doll. These dolls, with the Minerva heads, flowing curls and glass eyes, with silesia body we furnish in the following sizes:

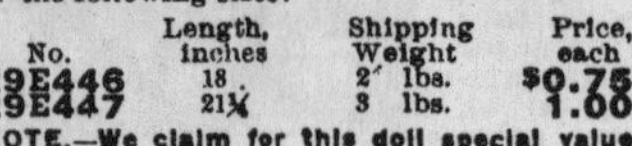

No.	Length, inches	Shipping Weight	Price, each
29E446	18	2 lbs.	$0.75
29E447	21¼	3 lbs.	1.00

NOTE.—We claim for this doll special value which cannot be equaled elsewhere.

Celluloid Dolls at Greatly Reduced Prices.

Celluloid doll babies. The celluloid dolls have become very popular, owing to their durability and light weight, and are very prettily proportioned. They are easily handled by the baby. These celluloid dolls have arm joints, so that arms can be moved in different positions. We furnish them in four sizes. The larger the size is, the larger the proportions are throughout the body.

No. 29E452 Celluloid, Featherweight Dolls, with arm joints, as described above. Length, 6¾ inches. Shipping weight, 8 ounces. Price......35c

No. 29E456 Celluloid Featherweight Dolls, with arm joints, as described above. Length, 8⅞ inches, shipping weight, 8 ounces. Price......50c

No. 29E460 Celluloid Featherweight Dolls, with arm joints, as described above. This is an exceptionally large proportioned body. Length, 10¾ inches. Shipping weight, 11 ounces. Price............................75c

No. 29E464 Red Ridinghood Rag Doll. Very prettily dressed with neat lace trimmed lawn dress and apron, red hood and cape; stuffed body. An unbreakable and durable doll, very much admired by all. Length, 16 inches. Shipping weight, 12 ounces. Price............................25c

WE DO NOT ACCEPT ORDERS FOR LESS THAN 50 CENTS. PLEASE INCLUDE OTHER GOODS IF YOU ORDER A DOLL FOR LESS THAN 50 CENTS.

Indestructible Rag Dolls.

No. 29E466 Indestructible Red Ridinghood Rag Doll. This is a very pretty and natural looking doll, dressed in the latest blouse effect in a good quality dress trimmed with lace and ruching. The doll measures 16½ inches in length and its value surpasses anything before offered at this price. Shipping weight, 1 pound. Price............50c

No. 29E468 Red Ridinghood Indestructible Doll, like above, but larger. Dressed in the latest blouse effect, dress being made of a good quality flannelette with lace and ribbon trimmings and ribbon belt. The doll has a red ridinghood bonnet of material to match dress. This doll being unbreakable and of natural appearance, will be a source of delight to any child. Shipping weight, 2 pounds. Length, 18½ inches. Price..................$1.00

Buster Brown Doll.

No. 29E478 Buster Brown Indestructible Rag Doll. A very fine imitation of the Buster Brown you read about. The doll is dressed in a red suit with white collar, cuffs and belt, has Buster Brown cap of red and white, and a large black Windsor tie. This doll will be a delight to the children on account of the popularity of Buster Brown. Length, 15 inches. Price....23c **If by mail, postage extra, 10 cents.**

No. 29E476 Infant Talking Doll, dressed in white, plain lawn dress with lace yoke, and a pretty little poke bonnet trimmed in ruching. String attachment for producing baby talk. Length of body, 13 inches. Entire length, including dress, 15 inches. Shipping weight, 12 ounces. Price............................22c

Unbreakable Leather Doll.

No. 29E516 Unbreakable Leather Doll. This is baby's friend. The leather is very fine to chew on when teething. Impossible to hurt either the baby or the doll. Stuffed with cotton and will always retain its shape. This doll will last baby and also baby's brother. Coloring matter warranted not to come off. Length, 12½ inches. Shipping weight, 15 ounces. Price.................40c

No. 29E517 Esquimaux Doll. This is a very attractive and interesting papier mache jointed doll with bisque head. The entire body is covered with white fur, all parts of the body, arms, legs and head being movable, so that you can make it assume any position. Length, 11½ inches. Price....................50c If by mail, postage extra, 8c.

No. 29E529 Very Pretty Dressed Doll, hair stuffed body, with bisque head and arms and removable shoes and stockings. The dress is made with revers pattern collar, trimmed with lace; has figured skirt and poke bonnet to match. This is excellent value. Length, 15 inches. Shipping weight, 1½ pounds. Price.......................25c

No. 29E533 Handsome Dressed Doll, with jointed neck, shoulders and hips. Dressed in style of illustration, with revers collar, trimmed with lace and good quality material. Has poke bonnet to match dress. Height, 16½ inches. This doll has removable shoes and stockings and a very pretty bisque head with long curls. Shipping weight, 2 pounds. Price...50c

White Rubber Dolls.

No. 29E560 White Rubber Dolls, dressed in knit suits and hats in assorted colors. Size, 8 inches. Price..........25c **If by mail, postage extra, 4 cents.**

No. 29E564 White Rubber Dolls, dressed in knit suits and hats in assorted colors. Fatter body and height 10½ inches. Price............................50c **If by mail, postage extra, 6 cents.**

No. 29E568 White Rubber Dolls, knit suits and hats in assorted colors, still fatter body and height 11¾ inches. Regular $1.00 value. Price.......75c **If by mail, postage extra, 8 cents.**

No. 29E572 White Rubber Dolls, knit suits and hats in assorted colors. This is a very large, fat body. Height, 13½ inches. Exceptional value. Price..............................$1.00 **If by mail, postage extra, 10 cents.**

Red Rubber Dolls.

No. 29E584 Red Rubber Doll. Has German silver whistle. Height, 7¼ inches. 75-cent quality elsewhere. Price..............50c **If by mail, postage extra, 8 cents.**

No. 29E588 Red Rubber Doll. Has German silver whistle. Height, 9¾ inches. This is good $1.00 value. Price........75c **If by mail, postage extra, 10 cents.**

No. 29E592 Red Rubber Doll. Has German silver whistle. Very large, fat body. Height, 11 inches. As sold elsewhere for $1.50. Our price. $1.00 **If by mail, postage extra, 12 cents.**

Red Rubber Animals, 50 Cents.

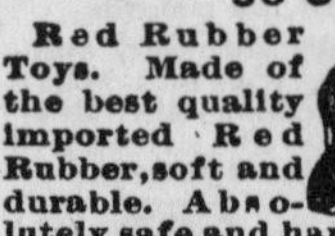

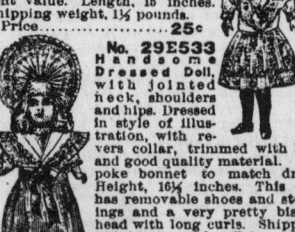

Red Rubber Toys. Made of the best quality imported Red Rubber, soft and durable. Absolutely safe and harmless for the children.

No. 29E596 Horse, fully equipped with saddle and bridle, made of the very best quality red rubber, about 6 inches long and 5 inches high. Price............................50c **If by mail, postage extra, 8 cents.**

No. 29E600 Red Rubber Cat. A very pretty design. Length, about 6 inches, height, 5 inches. Price...50c **If by mail, postage extra, 8 cents.**

No. 29E604 Red Rubber Dog, made of best quality red rubber. About 6 inches long and 5 inches high. Price............................50c **If by mail, postage extra, 8 cents.**

No. 29E608 Red Rubber Elephant, with oriental rug or saddle on back. Made of best quality red rubber. Length, about 6 inches, and height, 5 inches. Price.........................50c **If by mail, postage extra, 10 cents.**

Kid Doll Bodies.

No. 29E612 Kid Body Dolls, very full size, extra quality cork stuffed, high grade kid bodies, with riveted hip joint and bisque arms, shoes and stockings. This is a very high grade and satisfactory body. Comes in sizes as follows:

Size	Length, inches	Inches across shoulders	Shipping weight, ozs.	Price
1	12½	3½	15	$0.35
2	16	4	25	.50
3	19	4¾	35	.70
4	21½	5½	45	1.00
5	23¾	6	60	1.25
6	24½	6¼	65	1.50
7	25½	7	75	1.75

Silesia Doll Bodies.

No. 29E616 Hair Stuffed Pink Silesia Doll Bodies. This is a very high grade and satisfactory silesia body that will give best of wear and satisfaction; has bisque arms and removable shoes and stockings. Comes in the following sizes:

Size	Length, inches	Inches across shoulders	Shipping weight, ozs.	Price
1	12	3¼	10	$0.25
2	15½	4	15	.30
3	16½	4½	20	.40
4	21	5½	25	.50
5	23½	6	30	.60
6	25½	6½	35	.75
7	26¾	7¼	40	1.00

Minerva Indestructible Metal Doll Heads at Reduced Prices.

No. 29E620 These Doll Heads are imported from Germany, they combine the durability of sheet metal and the beauty of bisque, are light in weight, washable, and will not chip; will stand any reasonable wear. Small children cannot injure them, larger ones love them for their unequaled beauty. The eyes are clear and tender, head flexible at the bust, and fitted with sewing holes, making it easy to adjust and fasten them to body. Come in sizes as follows:

Style	Height, inches	Inches across sh'lders	Shipping weight, ozs.	Price
2	3⅝	2¾	5	15c
3	3¾	3	6	18c
4	4⅛	3⅜	8	25c
5	4½	3⅝	9	30c
6	5	4	10	35c
7	6¼	4½	12	50c
8	6¾	5½	14	60c

Nos. 7 and 8 have glass eyes and open mouths, showing teeth.

Sewed Wig and Moving Glass Eyes.

No. 29E624 The Minerva Indestructible Doll Head with moving glass eyes, open lips showing teeth, and very fine sewed curly wig. The Minerva heads, made of the best flexible sheet brass can be given to the smallest child with perfect safety, as the metal is covered with a pure wholesome paint which is manufactured especially for the purpose. Come in sizes as follows:

Style	Height, inches	Inches across sh'lders	Shipping weight, ozs.	Price
1	4	3	9	$0.38
3	4¾	3⅛	12	.55
5	5¾	4⅝	14	.75
7	6⅝	4⅞	16	1.00

Bisque Doll Heads.

IMMENSE VALUES. COMPARE SIZE AND PRICE.

No. 29E628 Bisque Doll Heads, first quality, high grade bisque, with very beautiful moulded faces, showing teeth, with two rows sewed wig and movable eyes. Either blondes or brunettes.

Style	Height, inches	Inches across shoulders	Shipping weight, ozs.	Price
1	3⅞	3	12	$0.19
2	4⅛	3½	24	.30
3	5¼	4¼	28	.45
4	6	5	32	.65
5	7	5½	36	.90
6	8¼	6¼	39	1.35
7	9	6⅝	42	1.65

Bisque Doll Heads, Stationary Eyes.

No. 29E632 First Quality Bisque Doll Heads, the faces are especially beautiful, showing teeth, have stationary eyes, curly flowing wigs, either blondes or brunettes.

Style	Height, inches	Inches across shoulders	Shipping weight, ozs.	Price
1	3⅞	3	12	$0.10
2	4⅛	3½	22	.18
3	5¼	4¼	26	.25
4	6	5	30	.40
5	7	5½	34	.65
6	8¼	6¼	36	.90
7	9	6⅝	40	1.25

No. 29E633 Kestner Bisque Doll Heads. These are the highest grade bisque heads that are manufactured. The Kestner make of dolls is well known, being the best make of dolls in the world. All these heads are very life like in appearance having moving eyes and open mouth, showing teeth. the highest grade full sewed wig with long curls braided in center and tied on side with large silk ribbon bow. We furnish these doll heads in the following size:

Size	Height inches	Inches across shoulders	Shipping weight, oz.	Price
3	4¾	3¼	12	$0.55
5	5½	4	26	.75
[illegible]	6½	4¼	30	1.00
[illegible]	7½	4¾	34	1.25

Celluloid Doll Heads.

No. 29E634 Celluloid Doll Heads. The celluloid doll heads, until recently, have been extremely high priced. We have succeeded this season in making arrangements so that they are exceptionally cheap, considering the distinct advantages this head has over the ordinary doll head. The faces are beautifully moulded. Made of the best celluloid, absolutely unbreakable, light as a feather, and at the prices we quote, will surely make them exceedingly popular. This style of celluloid doll head, has painted hair, glass eyes, with open mouth showing teeth. Come in the following sizes.

No.	Height, inches	Inches across Shoulders	Shipping wt., ozs.	Price
8½	3⅛	2¾	5	10c
10	3¾	3	7	15c
12	4¼	3½	9	25c
14	5	4	12	35c
16½	6¼	5¼	13	50c

No. 29E635 Celluloid Doll Heads, with glass eyes and fine curly sewed wig. The features of this doll are very beautiful. This head combines all the features of the finest bisque head, but is exceptionally light in weight being made of the finest celluloid. They are unbreakable making a pretty and durable doll head. We quote the following exceptionally low prices.

Sizes	Height, inches	Inches across shoulders	Shipping wt., ozs.	Price
8½	3⅛	2¾	5	25c
10	3¾	3	7	35c
12	4¼	3	9	50c
14	5	4	12	60c
16½	6¼	5¼	13	75c

THE SEROCO REVERSIBLE COMBINATION GAME BOARD.

THE COMPLETE OUTFIT NOW, $1.65 | **ON THIS SEROCO GAME BOARD YOU CAN PLAY 75 GAMES**

No. 29E636 This Combination Game Board with Revolving Game Board Stand and full set of rules for playing the different games.
Price, for entire outfit............ **$1.65**

THE SEROCO REVERSIBLE GAME BOARD is the best combination game board on the market, and equal to the many boards that are sold at $2.75 to $4.00. Is the only board with circles to shoot from. You can play 75 games on this elegant combination board. Made of the very best hard ash wood with three-ply veneer, which prevents the board from warping. The circles and checkerboard, stenciled on in very high colors, thoroughly rubbed and varnished, which gives the board a very artistic appearance. The board is 28⅛ inches square, with good net pockets. The illustrations show both sides of the board. **Some of the games that can be played on the board are Pyramid, Chicago, Continuous Pool, Bottle Pool and Pin Pool, Billiards, Three Ring, Carrom Game, Crokinole, Fifteen Ring Pool, Checkers, Backgammon, and almost every game that can be played on any other game board can also be played on this board.** With each board are furnished 29 nicely polished hardwood rings, two turned varnished cues, one set tenpins and extra movable back to prevent pins from being knocked off table, billiard attachment, and numbered rings for playing the different games of pool. No expense has been spared to make this board the very best. The games can be played by from two to eight persons.

THE GAME BOARD STAND for the Seroco Game Board is a firm support for the board at the proper height for players to sit on chairs. It being revolving makes it convenient. Made of best hardwood and nicely varnished. Folds up in a small compact package. The regular selling price of the game board alone is $2.75, and the regular price of the game board stand is 50 cents. By taking the entire output of a large factory, adding but our very small percentage of profit, we are enabled to place them on the market at the extremely low price for the board and stand of $1.65, which is less than the manufacturer's price to the dealer on other boards not so good.

EVERY BOARD GUARANTEED as represented and fully equal to the $3.50 and $4.00 boards sold by other concerns.

Price for set complete, board, stand, rings, cues, etc.................. **$1.65**

WE DO NOT QUOTE OR LIST OTHER ADVERTISED GAME BOARDS as we would be obliged to sell them at from $3.75 to $4.50. On the Seroco Combination Board you can play 75 games and almost any game that can be played on any of the advertised boards you can also play on the Seroco Game Board. Our board is made in the very best manner possible, equal to any board and superior to most of them, and our price for board and stand complete is only **$1.65.** Order at once. **Shipping weight, 14 pounds.**

BOOK OF INSTRUCTIONS WITH EACH GAME BOARD.

No. 29E637 Parlor Return Pool Game. A complete miniature pool table, size, 13x23 inches, including triangle, two hardwood cues, set of 15 numbered balls, also white cueball. The table has elastic cushions with brass finished corners to strengthen and beautify the table. The cushions and bed are covered with genuine green pool table cloth. The brass pockets are removable so that when playing, the balls after being shot into the open pocket, find their way into an inclined slide from which they return to the player at the front of table. Tables are finished in natural colored cherry and oak. The balls are of a red composition. Table can be set on any ordinary table and for real amusement, recreation and excitement, has no equal. Shipping weight, 4 pounds. Price. **$1.00**

No. 29E644 Folding Chess or Checkerboard. This high grade checkerboard has black and red squares 1½ inches, with gold lines ⅛ inch wide. The border is 2 inches wide in red, black and gold; covered with fine black embossed paper. Our best board. Size, 18x18 inches. Price.................**20c**
Shipping weight, 1½ pounds.

No. 29E657 Folding Backgammon Board, same style as above, squares 1½ inches, lined off with gold and varnished, with fancy illuminated paper. Fitted with complete set of checkers and two dice cups. (No dice.) Size of board, 15x15 inches. Price, per set...**20c**
Shipping weight, 1¼ pounds.

No. 29E659 Folding Backgammon Board in book form, squares 1½ inches, finished in durable embossed imitation leather. Fitted with dice cups (no dice) and complete set of checkers in separate box. Size of board, 15x15 inches. If you would pay $1.00 you could get no better board.
Price, per set........................**45c**
Shipping weight, 1½ pounds.

Please make your orders fifty cents or more. We do not accept orders for less than fifty cents as fully explained on the first pages.

No. 29E661 The finest Spanish-American Chess Men. Thirty-two pieces in set, finished in black and yellow. Put up in nice pasteboard box. Usually retail at 50 cents. Price, per set...**25c**
Shipping weight, 10 ounces.

No. 29E663 Chess Men. Good size. French pattern, made of hardwood, finished in black and white, 32 pieces in a set. Put up in nice wood box with sliding cover. Price, per set........**45c**
Shipping weight, 15 ounces.

No. 29E665 Fine Boxwood Chess Men. Staunton pattern, black and white polished; in dovetailed polished hardwood box, with sliding cover.
Price, per set........................**80c**
Shipping weight, 18 ounces.

Loaded Boxwood Chess Men.

No. 29E667 Loaded Boxwood Chess Men, in polished mahogany finished box. These are the Staunton pattern, in black and white, polished; an excellent set at the price.
Price, per set........................**$1.75**
Shipping weight, 1½ pounds.

No. 29E670 Tournament Checkers, red and black. The handsomest embossed checker ever offered at this price. Size, 1¼ inches. Price, per set....**9c**
If by mail, postage extra, 6 cents.

No. 29E672 The Yorkite Embossed Checkers, 1⅛ inches in diameter. A strong composition checker of a new and durable material, 30 to the set red and black.
Price, per set...................**20c**
If by mail, postage extra, per set, 8 cents.

No. 29E674 U.S.A. Dominoes. Black adamant dominoes, 28 pieces to the set. A durable set at this very low price.
Price, per set...(Postage extra, 10c)..**9c**

No. 29E676 Express Dominoes, double 9's. Black adamant dominoes, 55 pieces to the set with new pattern and attractive label. Many interesting complications arise when playing with a double nine.
Price, per set...(Postage extra, 12c)..**21c**

No. 29E678 Nubian Dominoes, double 9's, 55 pieces, beautiful arabesque black dominoes, packed in wood frame box. A high grade set of dominoes. Price, per set...........**40c**
If by mail, postage extra, 12 cents.

No. 29E682 Lotto, with set of embossed numbers on round blocks. Contains 12 cards, a set of embossed numbers on round blocks and box of glasses. Put up in a heavy, fancy box 4x6½ inches. The box is a bright red with gold or silver label.
Price, per set.....................**12c**
If by mail, postage extra, 8 cents.

No. 29E684 Lotto. A high grade set in wood box, covered in bright red, labels gold or silver. Contains 24 cards, round numbered blocks, cloth bag for holding same, box of glasses and chart for marking off the numbers. This is a special value. Price, per set..22c
If by mail, postage extra, 12 cents.

No. 29E686 High Grade Set of Lotto, in fine hardwood, highly polished box with beautiful lithographed design on cover. The cover is on hinges. Contains 24 cards and cloth bag containing set of embossed, colored numbers on round blocks and box of glass counters. The box has lock and key. Size, 7½x10½ inches. Shipping weight, 2 pounds.
Price, per set........................**50c**
If by mail, postage extra, 15 cents.

Large Size Ouija, or Egyptian Luck Board.

No. 29E687 Without a doubt the most remarkable and interesting and mystifying production of the age. Its operations are always interesting and sometimes invaluable; answering as it does, questions concerning the past, present and future. Full directions for operating the Ouija board accompanying each board. Packed each one in a pasteboard box. Cannot be sent by mail. Regular $1.00 size. Price...........................**75c**
Shipping weight, 3 pounds.

PLAYING CARDS.

No. 29E1864 Special Linen Finish Playing Cards, with round corners, double index, in large, plain figures, in a pretty back design. This same quality card is frequently sold at 25 cents per pack. Price, per pack......**$0.10**
Per dozen packs......................**1.10**
If by mail, postage extra, per pack, 5 cents.

No. 29E1867 Airship Superior Enamel Waterproof Playing Cards, with high radium luster finish. This card has a perfect slip and will not swell. We guarantee it equal to any card on the market. Best for professional use. Assorted backs.
Price, per pack......**$0.13**
Per dozen packs......**1.50**
If by mail, postage extra, per pack, 5 cents.

No. 29E1868 Bicycle No. 808, superior ivory, enameled finish, a variety of appropriate backs, used largely by professional and other card players throughout the world. Weight, per pack, 4 ounces.
Price, per pack..............**$ 0.15**
Per dozen packs..............**1.80**
Per gross packs..............**21.60**
If by mail, postage extra, per pack, 4c.

No. 29E1873 Angel Backs. This is a splendid high class card, pure linen stock, waterproof enamel and thoroughly known as the Squeezers. Used largely by professionals.
Price, per pack...**$0.17**
Per doz. packs ...**1.90**
Shipping weight, per pack, 4 ounces.

No. 29E1875 **The Art Series Gold Edge Cards**, made of the highest grade waterproof linen stock with gold edges. The subjects, the "Japanese" and the "Holland Girls," are very pretty designs. This card was especially designed to sell at 50 cents a pack. We offer them at the exceptionally low price per pack of............**25c**
Per dozen packs............**$2.75**
If by mail, postage extra, per pack, 4 cents.

Congress Gold Edge Cards.

No. 29E1876 Congress Gold Edge Playing Cards. A new and artistic series of backs in high, rich colors, designed especially for card parties, social and home play. Can furnish them in the following backs: Rockwood Indian, as shown in illustration; also Priscilla, The Old Mill, Rube, Rose, Autumn and Chefoo, etc. The highest grade quality linen. Put up in handsome case. Price, per pack......**$0.35**
Per dozen packs............**3.90**
If by mail, postage extra, per pack, 5c.

Fortune Telling Cards.

No. 29E1879 The Nile Fortune Telling Cards. A new pack of fortune telling cards, tinted panel faces with the signification of each card printed on each face. Can be used by everyone. Sphinx backs, printed in high colors. Gold edges. Best linen stock, double enameled. Instructions for fortune telling in each pack. Complete for playing all regular card games. Price, per pack......**$0.33**
Per dozen packs............**3.40**
If by mail, postage extra, per pack, 5c

American Whist League.

No. 29E1883 American Whist League, Waterproof. Extra enameled, half linen stock. The best enameled card made. Weight, 4 ounces.
Price, per pack............**20c**
If by mail, postage extra, 5 cents.

Barcelona Cards.

No. 29E1884 Barcelona. No. 49 Spanish Monte Cards, 48 cards in pack, assortment of backs and colors. Weight, packed, 3 ounces.
Price, per pack............**32c**
If by mail, postage extra, 5 cents.

No. 29E1886 Pinochle Cards. Good quality linen finish stock, in a pretty designed back, full double deck from 9's up.
Price, per doz. packs, **$1.60**; per pack,...**14c**
If by mail, postage extra, per pack, 5 cents.

No. 29E1888 Pinochle Cards. Full deck with sevens and eights; high grade linen cards.
Price, per pack............**33c**
If by mail, postage extra, 5 cents.

Solo Cards.

No. 29E1889 Solo Cards. Finest linen cards, highly enameled and waterproof. Regulation 36 cards.
Price, per pack............**19c**
If by mail, postage extra, 5 cents.

Skat Cards.

No. 29E1891 Skat Cards. Made of extra enameled half linen stock. A fine waterproof card.
Price, per pack............**19c**
If by mail, postage extra, 5 cents.

BUNCO

No. 29E1893 Bunco is the great card game that is having a wonderful sale. After once playing the game it fascinates and interests one and all. The game is a radical departure in get up and play from any game in the market, strictly scientific, yet highly amusing. Scientific as cribbage and as interesting as bridge whist, embodying all the features of playing card games. Easy to learn, interesting to both young and old. The cards are of the finest ivory enamel finish.
Price, per pack............**$0.35**
Per dozen packs............**4.00**
If by mail, postage extra, per pack, 5 cents.

FLINCH.

The Popular New Card Game.

No. 29E1894 Flinch. More simple than authors, more scientific than whist. Something entirely new in card games. Each pack consists of 150 cards, finest quality stock. The combinations resulting, while simple, are so intricate that the game has been pronounced by many to be more scientific than whist. Enjoyed by old and young alike.
Price, per pack............**$0.33**
Per dozen packs............**3.75**
If by mail, postage extra, per pack, 5c.

PIT.

No. 29E1896 The jolliest game ever invented for an informal good time. PIT is the latest craze and is being played by everybody, young and old. Learned in three minutes.
Price, per pack............**$0.35**
Per dozen packs............**4.00**
If by mail, postage extra, per pack, 5c

Paine's Duplicate Whist Sets.

No. 29E1898 Paine's Duplicate Whist Tray Outfit, 8-tray set.
Price............**$3.00**
Shipping weight, 4 pounds.

No. 29E1900 Paine's Duplicate Whist Tray Outfit, 12-tray set.
Price............**$4.00**
Shipping weight, 5 pounds.

No. 29E1902 Paine's Duplicate Whist Tray Outfit, 16-tray set.
Price............**$5.00**
Shipping weight, 8 pounds.

No. 29E1906 Card Case. Neat novelty in book form in exact imitation of Oxford style of binding, made of fine black seal grain leather, leather lined, closes with leather clasp and glove button catch; beautiful genuine sterling silver ornament mounted on the side. Contains a high grade deck of gilt edge playing cards. Size, 1x3x4 inches. Price............**75c**
If by mail, postage extra, 6 cents.

Poker Chips.

No. 29E1916 Composition Poker Chips. Ivory finish, warranted not to chip or warp, 1½ inches in diameter, put up 100 in a box assorted as follows: 50 white, 25 red and 25 blue, or solid colors. Shipping weight, 32 ounces.
Price, per box of 100............**$0.25**
Per 1,000............**2.40**

No. 29E1919 New Design Poker Chip, known as the Eclipse, made of composition with ivory finish. 1½ inches in diameter. A unique pattern. Come put up in boxes of 100, assorted 50 white, 25 red and 25 blue. Shipping weight, per box, 32 ounces.
Price, per 1,000, **$4.40**; per box of 100, **45c**

No. 29E1921 Corker Poker Chip. Composition, ivory finish. 1½ inches in diameter. This chip will stand hard usage. Put up in box of 100 assorted, 50 white, 25 red and 25 blue. Shipping weight, per 100, 32 ozs.
Price per 1,000, **$4.75**; per box of 100, **50c**

No. 29E1917 Good Luck Engraved Poker Chip, ivory finish. Warranted not to chip or break with ordinary usage. 1½ inches in diameter. Put up 100 to the box assorted, 50 white, 25 red and 25 blue. A new and popular pattern. Shipping weight, per box of 100, 32 ounces.
Price, per 1,000, **$5.00**; per box of 100, **55c**

No. 29E1924 Special Design Engraved Poker Chip. This is a very neat and elegant design. Made of the best quality composition, will not break easily and stack even. Size, 1½ inches in diameter. Assorted 100 in box as follows: 50 white, 25 blue and 25 red.
Price, per box of 100............**$0.60**
Per 1,000............**5.50**
Shipping weight, 30 ounces.

No. 29E1926 The American Eagle. A beautiful engraved design on composition ivory, warranted not to chip or warp. 1½ inches in diameter. Put up 100 in a box, assorted as follows: 50 white, 25 red and 25 blue, or solid colors.
Price, per box of 100............**$0.50**
Per 1,000............**4.75**
Shipping weight, 30 ounces.

Inlaid Unbreakable Poker Chips for Professional Use.

No. 29E1928 Fleur de Lis design. Inlaid celluloid on highest grade of composition ivory; 1½ inches in diameter and put up 100 to the box; assorted, 50 white, 25 red and 25 blue; or can be ordered in the solid colors, 100 to box; red, white, blue, yellow, pink or brown. Absolutely perfect in every respect, warranted to stack perfectly, and used a great deal by professionals.
Price, per box of 100............**$ 2.10**
Per 1,000............**21.00**
Shipping weight, 34 ounces.

No. 29E1929 Maltese Cross design, inlaid celluloid of the best quality composition ivory. A unique and popular pattern. Guaranteed to stack perfectly. This chip comes in white, red, blue, yellow, pink and brown. Put up 100 to the box. Used by card players and professionals. Shipping weight per 100, 34 ounces.
Price per box of 100............**$ 2.10**
Price per 1,000............**21.00**
Note. We do not sell less than 100 of a color.

Unbreakable Poker Chips.

Light, Noiseless and Easy to Handle.

No. 29E1930 Unbreakable Poker Chips made by a new process, highly polished, look just as good as the compositions but are light and better than rubber. Stack evenly and outwear any other kind made. Put up in assorted boxes 25 red, 25 blue and 50 white, or in solid colors 100 to box—red, white, blue and orange. Shipping weight, 20 ounces. Price, per box of 100....**$0.45**
Per 1,000............**4.00**

Dice.

No. 29E1932 Bone Dice. Square corners. No 6. Size, ⅜ inch.
Price, per dozen............**9c**
Price, per gross,............**95c**
If by mail, postage extra, per dozen, 3 cents.

No. 29E1934 Bone Dice. Square corners. No. 8, size, 7/16 inch.
Price, per gross, **$1.60**; per doz..**15c**
If by mail, postage extra, per dozen, 6 cents.

No. 29E1936 Bone Dice. Round corners. No. 9, size, ⅝ inch.
Price, per gross, **$2.25**; per doz..**22c**
If by mail, postage extra, per dozen, 6 cents.

No. 29E1938 Bone Dice. Square corners. No. 10, size, 11/16 inch.
Price, per gross, **$3.75**; per doz..**36c**
If by mail, postage extra, per dozen, 6 cents.

Vegetable Ivory Dice.

No. 29E1950 This is the latest style in dice, is made of the pure ivory nut. Is absolutely perfect. Size, 11/16 inch. Five in set. Per set............**$0.25**
Per dozen sets............**2.75**
If by mail, postage extra, per set, 3c.

Celluloid Dice.

No. 29E1944 Celluloid Dice, cream color, with colored spots, ⅝ inch.
Per set (five dice to set)............**28c**
If by mail, postage extra, per set of five, 3 cents.

Transparent Celluloid Dice.

No. 29E1946 Made of pure transparent celluloid. Are clear as glass; colors green, magenta or saffron. Put up five in a box. Size, ⅝ inch.
Price, per set (five dice to a set)**$0.45**
Per dozen sets............**5.00**
If by mail, postage extra, per set, 3c.

Celluloid Poker Dice.

No. 29E1940 Representing Ace, King, Queen, Jack, Ten and Nine spots. Fine ivory finished celluloid, perfect goods; size, ⅝ inch. Set of five dice.
Price, per set of five............**$0.40**
Per dozen sets............**4.75**
If by mail, postage extra, per set, 4c.

No. 29E1942 Vegetable Ivory Poker Dice. The five dice represent ace, king, queen, jack, ten and nine spots, all enameled. Size, ⅝ inch.
Price, per set of five,............**$0.25**
Per dozen sets............**2.75**
If by mail, postage extra, per set, 8 cents.

Blank Dice.

No. 29E1948 Blank Bone Dice. These dice have no spots. We can furnish blank dice in three sizes.

Nos.	8	9	10
Size, inches	7/16	½	11/16
Price, per dozen	$0.15	$0.20	$0.30
Price, per gross	1.75	2.25	3.25

If by mail, postage extra, per dozen, 4c.

Dice Cups.

No. 29E1952 Sole Leather Dice Cup, 2 inches in diameter, 3 inches deep. Natural color. Price............**19c**
If by mail, postage extra, 4 cents.

No. 29E1954 Sole Leather Dice Cup, 2 inches in diameter, 3¼ inches deep. Tan color. Price............**22c**
If by mail, postage extra, 5 cents.

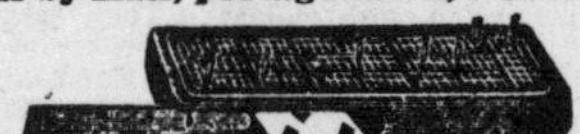

No. 29E1956 Polished Metal Nickel Plated Cribbage Board, with three double rows drilled holes, to score for three or six persons; face of polished black walnut with compartment for one pack of cards and another compartment containing nine steel cribbage pegs. Size, 2⅝x10¼ inches. Shipping weight, 20 ounces.
Price............**85c**

No. 29E4298 Fine Toilet Set, consisting of solid back ebony hair brush, ebonite mirror and comb. All finest sterling silver mounts. Put up in special box, covered with enameled paper. This set advertised elsewhere for $1.75. Shipping weight, 1¼ pounds.
Price, per set............**$1.00**

No. 29E4307 Ebonoid Military and Cloth Brush Set consisting of two 11-row solid back military and one 9-row cloth brush, all sterling silver mounted, in a heavy card board box. This set is made of the best quality bristles by one of the largest brush manufacturers in the United States and will prove satisfactory in every way. Shipping weight, 1½ pounds. Price............**$1.75**

French Stag Brush and Comb Set, $1.50.

No. 29E4344 French Stag Horn Toilet Case, consisting of brush and comb in lined leatherette box. The brush is made of white Siberian bristle. The comb is 7 inches in length and to match the brush, both mounted with heavy French gray sterling silver ornaments. This stag horn composition makes one of the most desirable toilet sets. They are unbreakable and very handsome in appearance. Shipping weight, 14 ounces.
Price, for brush and comb............**$1.50**

Brush Comb and Mirror Set, $2.65.

No. 29E4346 Genuine French Stag Horn Toilet Set, consisting of hair brush and heavy, beveled mirror; size, 2⅝x4½ inches, also 7-inch comb to match. The brush is of a fine, white, Siberian bristle. All three pieces mounted with very heavy French gray sterling silver ornaments. Put up in neat leatherette case. Shipping wt., 28 ounces. Price, per set...**$2.65**

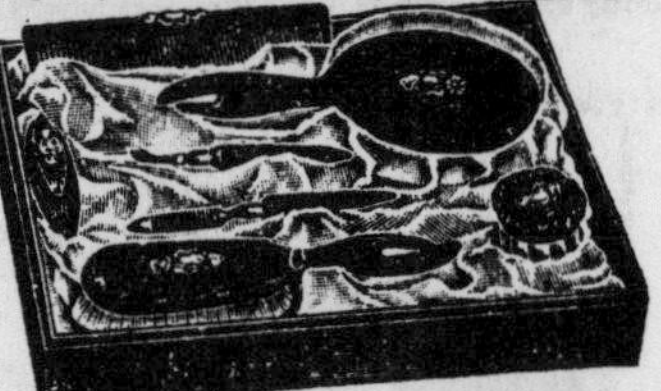

No. 29E4348 Genuine French Stag Horn Toilet Case, consisting of French stag 11-row white bristle brush, heavy plate mirror, nail file, cuticle knife, polisher, powder box and comb. All sterling silver mounted. Put up in a beautifully lined cabinet box. Will make a handsome addition to any dresser. The stag horn should be seen to be appreciated. Shipping weight, 6 pounds.
Price for this outfit............**$3.95**

No. 29E4350 French Stag Horn Manicure Outfit, consisting of stag horn handle nail file, cuticle knife, polisher and salve box. Put up in fine lined cabinet box. Each item individually retails for more than 50 cents. Shipping weight, 1½ pounds. Our price for the 4-piece set, complete............**99c**

Military Brushes, $2.50.

No. 29E4352 French Stag Horn Military Brushes. The brushes are 11-row finest white Russian bristles. The backs are mounted with very heavy sterling silver or rose gold ornaments; put up in nice leatherette case. This stag horn pair of brushes would be very much appreciated. Shipping weight, 2½ pounds.
Price, per pair............**$2.50**

No. 29E4354 Genuine French Stag Gents' Military Set and Cloth Brush. Contains one pair of military brushes, each brush set with eleven rows of best quality white Siberian bristles. The cloth brush has seven rows of extra long, best quality Siberian bristles. The tops are made of stag horn, in imitation of the real article. It is made of a composition that is absolutely unbreakable. Trimmed with sterling silver or rose gold mounts, in a new and beautiful heavy design. The set is packed in a neat lined leatherette case, and will make a beautiful and lasting present. Shipping weigh 2 pounds.
Price, per set............**$3.50**

Collar and Cuff Boxes.

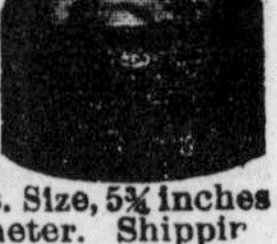

No. 29E4416 Collar and Cuff Box, round, fine black monkey grained solid metal button box with fancy purse top (patent applied for) on the cover; interior is leatherette lined, and divided into separate compartments. Size, 5¾ inches high, 6½ inches in diameter. Shipping weight, 25 ounces. Price............

THE CELEBRATED IVES MINIATURE RAILWAYS

THE FINEST QUALITY, BEST WEARING TRAINS IN THE WORLD

IN OFFERING THIS WELL KNOWN MAKE of miniature railway trains to our customers we guarantee that, price considered, they are the finest made, best wearing trains in all the world. For several years we have been anxious to display and offer for sale in our catalogue a line of track trains for boys, trains that we could honestly recommend and guarantee under the terms of our most liberal policy; a line of trains of which we could say: **If they are not satisfactory return them to us and we will cheerfully refund your money and all transportation charges or exchange for other goods.** Not until the celebrated Ives trains were brought to our attention could we fairly and honestly recommend to our customers the purchase of a track train for the boy, and rather than sell you an article which we could not recommend we have chosen in the past to omit this well known toy from our pages.

THERE IS NO PLAYTHING MADE FOR BOYS today which is so popular and absolutely safe to handle as a miniature railway system. These toys offer more than amusement to the bright boy; they offer an education also, and arouse in him the love for things mechanical and they develop his inventive brain.

THE IVES LOCOMOTIVES are not as large or showy as some made by foreign manufacturers, but they do the work. These engines are made with the best steel and brass gearing, not with the cheap stamped tin gearing found in many other makes. The springs are wider, stronger and have twice the hauling power of those of other makes in similar sizes. We found that the Ives locomotive would pull a train of cars twice as many times around a track as would a foreign made locomotive of double its size.

THESE ENGINES are guaranteed by us to be free from defects in manufacture and we will gladly replace any engine which fails to do what we claim for it. Understand, however, that we cannot be responsible for the results of rough or careless handling. We have chosen this line before all others for the reason that we always desire to sell absolutely dependable merchandise, something that we can honestly recommend to honest customers, as being well worth the money paid and that we can guarantee to give satisfaction.

No. 18N21850 Ives Mechanical Track Train with track. Consisting of heavy tin locomotive nicely decorated in colors, a tender and one passenger car. Has nine-section track, 90 inches long. This is a splendid value at a low price and carries with it a guarantee against defects. Total length of train, 14½ inches. Each train carefully tested before shipped. Instructions with every outfit. Shipping weight, 3 pounds.
Price, for complete outfit.................. **98c**

Splendid Value at $1.75

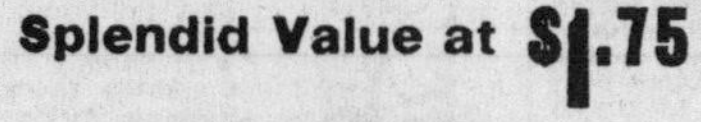

No. 18N21854 Ives Mechanical Track Train with **strictly modern design iron locomotive**, finished in the best possible manner, heavy tin tender, baggage and one passenger car. Beautifully enameled and an unusually attractive outfit, steady and even running. Guaranteed to please and give satisfaction in every way. Twelve-section track, 120 inches long, which can be arranged in various designs, also track plates for holding track securely together. Total length of train, 20 inches. Carefully tested and packed for shipment with complete instructions. Shipping weight, 4 pounds.
Price, for complete outfit.................. **$1.75**

No. 18N21858 This Ives Mechanical Track Train has a larger and heavier iron locomotive than is used in outfit No. 18N21854. Is handsomely finished in bright colors, with finely adjusted speed governor and automatic brake. Has great hauling power, which enables it to pull more cars and run longer. Has heavy tin tender, one baggage and two passenger coaches. All beautifully decorated in high colors. The track, which is 120 inches long, consists of twelve sections, including one sectional stop which when set, automatically stops the train. Track plates furnished with each section. For durability, finish and wearing qualities this train is highly recommended. The track can be set in various shapes. Total length of train, 26 inches. Is carefully tested and fully guaranteed. Complete instructions with each set. Shipping weight, 6 pounds.
Price, for complete outfit.................. **$3.48**

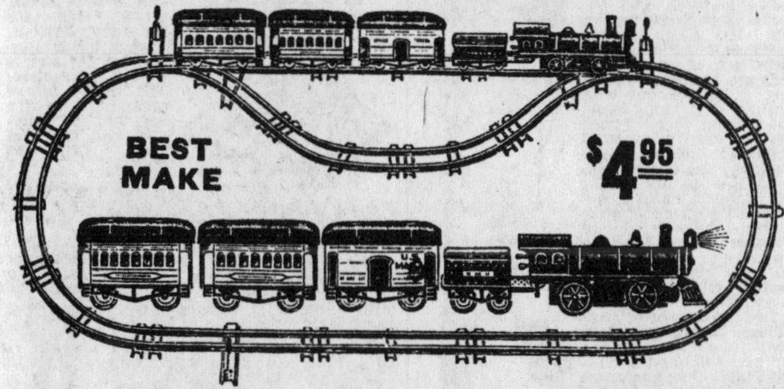

No. 18N21862 Ives Mechanical Track Train. **Our very finest and largest outfit, complete in every detail.** Extra large and heavy iron locomotive, nicely decorated in bright colors, which is fitted with automatic speed governor, throttle which starts and stops the train and reverse lever which causes the train to run backward as well as forward. This train is complete with a large tin tender, one baggage and two passenger cars. Total length of train, 27 inches. The track consists of fourteen sections, including two switches which run the train onto a side track and automatic stop which when set brings the train to a standstill. Track plates furnished with each section. Total length of track, including side track, 160 inches. Each outfit is fully guaranteed and carefully tested before shipping. Easily worth $7.50. An exceptional value at our price. Shipping weight, 7 pounds.
Price, for complete outfit.................. **$4.95**

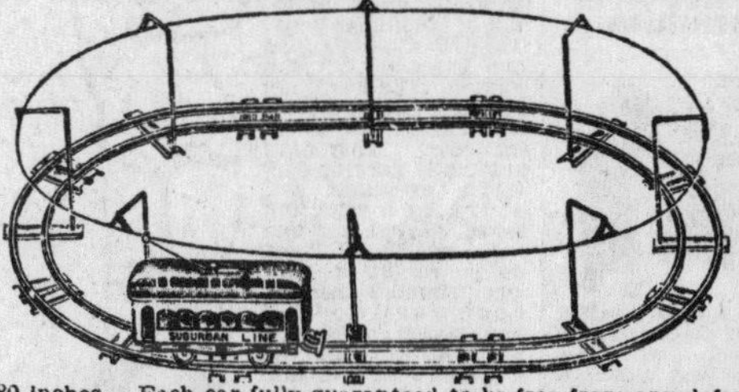

No. 18N21866 Ives Mechanical Trolley Car System. Consists of trolley car with eight-section track, together with eight trolley poles and overhead wires. The car has regulation spring trolley pole with wheel and spring tension. It runs on the track automatically, in imitation of the large electric cars. The spring motor in this car is of very good quality, which drives the car at a high rate of speed, the trolley following on the overhead wires. A splendid outfit at a very low price. Length of car, 6½ inches. Entire length of track, 80 inches. Each car fully guaranteed to be free from any defects in manufacture. Shipping weight, 3 pounds.
Price, each.................. **$1.69**

Any of the above tracks can be greatly improved and made much more interesting by the use of additional switches, cross overs, straight or curved sections, which we can furnish at prices quoted below.

No. 18N21868 Pair of Switches.
Price, per pair.................. **98c**
If by mail, postage extra, 12 cents.

No. 18N21870 Cross Over for use where one section of track crosses another.
Price, each.................. **45c**
If by mail, postage extra, 3 cents.

No. 18N21872 10-inch Straight Section of Track with track plate.
Price, per section.................. **8c**
If by mail, postage extra, 3 cents.

No. 18N21874 Curved Section of Track with track plate. Outside length, 10 inches.
Price, per section.................. **8c**
If by mail, postage extra, 3 cents.

Good Working Engine, only 98c

No. 18N21900 Miniature Portable Vertical Steam Engine and Boiler, known as the oscillating type. Has seamless brass boiler with pop safety valve and whistle. Heavy cylinder rod, crank pin and large metal fly wheel with pulley attachments so that the various miniature mechanical toys can be used with the engine. Mounted on heavy wooden base. Steams best with wood alcohol. A better engine by far than has ever before been offered at this price. Shipping weight, 1½ pounds.
Price.................. **98c**

Great Value Upright. $1.69

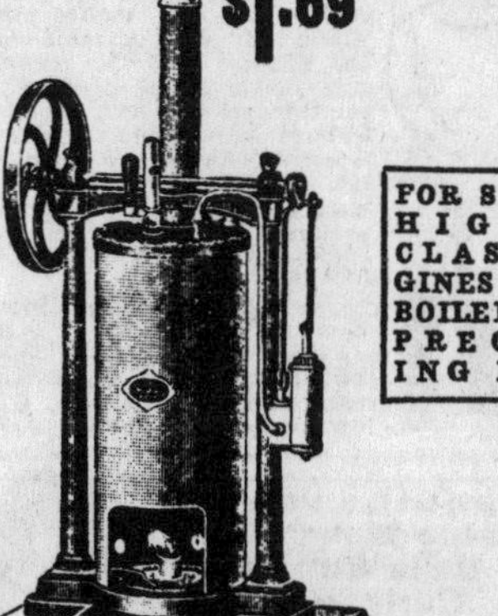

FOR STILL HIGHER CLASS ENGINES AND BOILERS SEE PRECEDING PAGE.

No. 18N21904 Special Value Miniature Portable Steam Engine and Boiler, portable oscillating type. Has heavy blue steel boiler mounted on enameled iron base with sheet iron smoke stack. Very finely adjusted having two oil cups on main shaft, pop safety valve and whistle. Large metal fly wheel with pulley wheel attached for use with the various mechanical toys. Engine is supported on the top of boiler by means of enameled metal columns. Every detail of this engine is complete. Will steam best with wood alcohol. Height, 11 inches. Shipping weight, 2 pounds.
Price.................. **$1.69**

Perfectly Adjusted and Well Made. $2.19

No. 18N21908 Horizontal Mechanical Steam Engine and Boiler, mounted on heavy wooden base. Blue steel boiler with glass water gauge, whistle and pop safety valve mounted on steel fire box, containing lamp which burns best with wood alcohol. Known as the slide valve type. Has heavy piston rod with screw adjustments, heavy metal fly wheel with pulley attachments. Engine and boiler are connected by means of nickel plated steam pipe. 8-inch metal smoke stack. Height of engine, not including stack, 7½ inches. Size at base, 6¾ x3¾ inches. A very finely adjusted, easy running toy engine, which will give the best of service. Shipping weight, 4 pounds. Price.................. **$2.19**

Weeden Make, Guaranteed. $3.00

No. 18N21912 Weeden Miniature Vertical Steam Engine and Boiler. Heavy cast steel base supporting blue steel boiler, fitted with glass water gauge and pop safety valve. Has extra heavy nickel plated fly wheel mounted on main shaft with pulley wheel for use with the various attachments. Engine is mounted on the side of boiler in such a position as to make this a very practical outfit. Entire height, 12 inches. Without doubt a most handsome engine which is guaranteed to give the best results. Steams best with wood alcohol. Shipping weight, 5 pounds.
Price.................. **$3.00**

WE ACTUALLY SAVE YOU TWO PROFITS ON DOLLS

Imitation Cut Glass Water Set.

No. 18N21780 Toy Water or Lemonade Set. Consists of seven pieces; glass water pitcher, 4½ inches high, and six glasses, each 2¼ inches high. These are made of extra heavy imitation cut glass, very nicely finished and not easily broken. Packed one set complete in box. Easily worth 60 cents. Shipping weight, 2¼ pounds. Our price **38c**

Doll Fur Set.

No. 18N21782 Doll Fur Set. Imitation ermine fur set, in white with black spots. Consists of boa 18 inches long and muff to match. Muff has silk cord by means of which it can be fastened around the neck of the doll. Will very much improve the appearance of any doll. Exceptional value at our price. Each set packed complete in lace trimmed box. Price..(Postage extra, 8c.).. **50c**

Doll Toilet Set.

No. 18N21786 Doll Toilet Set. An entirely new article, consists of dressing comb, hair brush, back comb, mirror, powder box, rattle and tooth powder bottle, also a small cake of soap. The doll's outfit will not be complete without this toilet set. Put up in neat box. Price..(If by mail, postage extra, 7c).. **49c**

Two Exceptional Values in Doll's Wooden Furniture.

No. 18N21798 Our special value Doll's Furniture Set. The four pieces consist of sideboard, chiffonier, dresser and china cabinet. Are all made in the best possible manner of natural maple varnished and polished. Sideboard is 11 inches high, 3¾ inches wide and 9¾ inches long, contains large size drawer and cupboard with two swinging doors. The china cabinet is 13 inches high by 3¾ inches wide by 8¾ inches deep, has two swinging glass doors, also drawer in bottom. Dresser, 11 inches high, contains three drawers, 8¼ inches by 3¾ inches. All drawers are finished with wooden knobs. Each piece has a mirror. Packed one set each in wooden box. Shipping weight, 15 pounds. Price.......................... **$1.29**

No. 18N21802 Doll's Bedroom Set. Consists of five pieces, folding bed, dresser, chiffonier, rocker and straight chair. Made of natural maple, varnished and highly polished in the best possible manner. A set that will not break after a few hours' use, but one that will last a long time. The bed is 9¾x7x5½ inches; dresser, 8x7x3½ inches, contains two drawers and large mirror; chiffonier, 8¾x6x3 inches, contains four drawers. Each chair is 7½ inches high by 3x3½ inches. This set is without doubt excellent value. Something that cannot be had elsewhere for less than $1.00. Shipping weight, 3½ pounds. Our price for set, complete **65c**

Doll's Parlor Sets at 88 and 50 Cents.

No. 18N21790 Doll's Parlor Set. This set is complete in every detail. Made of very strong reeds, and is without question the best set of its kind on the market. Outer reeds are black enameled ornamented with red inner reeds. The upholstering work is in velour finished with gimp to match. Set consists of table, 3 inches high by 5¼ inches long; sofa, 5 inches high, and six chairs, 5¼ inches high. Wonderful value. Shipping weight, 2 pounds. Price.... **88c**

No. 18N21794 Doll's Parlor Set. Same as above, but smaller, finished in gilt and colored materials. Table is 2½ inches high, 4 inches long and 2½ inches wide. Six chairs, each 4½ inches in height; sofa, 5 inches in height and 4½ inches in width. An attractive furniture set at a low price. Shipping weight, 1½ pounds. Price... **50c**

Extra Special Values in Full Jointed Dolls at Very Low Prices.

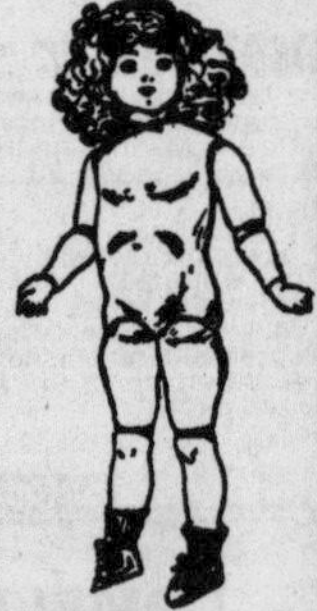

This line of Jointed Dolls has never before been offered. A good grade of papier mache dolls made in natural flesh tints, in imitation of the human body. The dolls have full elbow, wrist, hip and knee joints. Are dressed in lace trimmed chemise, have lace stockings and imitation patent leather sandals. The head is made of good quality bisque, has parted lips showing teeth, moving eyes which open and close, and side parted wig tied with ribbon. We have never before been able to offer such goodly dolls at such startlingly low prices.

Catalogue Number	Height, inches	Shipping Weight	Price, each
18N22994	10	1 lb.	$0.25
18N22996	13½	1½ lbs.	.50
18N22998	15	2 lbs.	.88
18N23000	18	4 lbs.	1.19

NOTE — No. 18N23000 has pretty eyelashes.

Our Very Finest Quality Full Jointed Dolls.

These Dolls are without doubt the best that money can buy, and we particularly recommend them to our trade. Made of heavy papier mache (light, strong and more durable than any other material) in exact imitation of the human body. The wrists, elbows, hips and knees are full ball jointed. The heads are of finest quality bisque with parted lips showing teeth. They have automatic sleeping eyes with eyelashes, and extra fine wigs, full sewed, parted, and tied with ribbons. These dolls are fitted with lace trimmed chemise, openwork stockings and sateen shoes and all in all represent the highest art in doll making. Come in four sizes, carefully packed for shipping.

Catalogue Number	Height, inches	Shipping Weight	Price, each
18N23010	18	6 lbs.	$1.75
18N23012	24½	7 lbs.	2.98
18N23016	27	9 lbs.	3.89
18N23020	30	18 lbs.	4.95

Extra Large Size Genuine Kid Body Dolls.

The Dolls are well made, of good material, and are tremendous bargains at the prices quoted below. Don't confuse this line of dolls with the imitation kid dolls offered by others at our prices. Our dolls have nicely proportioned bodies, good quality bisque heads with moving eyes which open and close, nice curly wigs, shoes and stockings. The larger the doll the better proportioned are the features and body. Come in four sizes, as follows:

Catalogue No.	H'ght, in.	Shipping Wt.	Price, each
18N23024	13	1 lb.	23c
18N23028	16	1½ lbs.	47c
18N23032	18½	2½ lbs.	73c
18N23036	21	3½ lbs.	98c

High Grade Half Jointed Kid Body Dolls.

These Dolls are made of high grade kid with riveted joints at both hips and knees, allowing the doll to assume a sitting position. The heads are bisque with moving eyes, long curly full sewed wigs, nicely parted and tied with ribbon. The lips are parted showing the teeth. Openwork stockings and sateen shoes are fitted to the doll. A splendid value at our prices, which mean a big saving to you. Come in four sizes, each nicely packed in box.

Catalogue No.	H'ght in.	Shipping W't lbs.	Price each
18N23040	15	2	$0.59
18N23044	17	2½	.87
18N23048	20	3	1.25
18N23056	25	5	1.69

Our Columbia Half Cork Stuffed, Full Jointed, Kid Body Dolls.

To our customers who wish a fine Doll at a moderately low price we can highly recommend this quality. The entire body from shoulders to toes is made of fine quality white kid, with half cork stuffing, giving a light shapely body. The hips, knees, shoulders and elbows are nicely jointed, the forearms are of bisque. The head is of fine quality bisque with automatic sleeping and waking eyes, open mouth showing teeth, and a beautiful full sewed curly wig, neatly parted and tied with ribbons. Is fitted with openwork stockings and sateen shoes to match stockings. Quality considered, the prices quoted below are tremendous bargains. Come in four sizes, each doll carefully packed.

Catalogue Number	Height, inches	Ship'g Wt., lbs.	Price, each
18N23064	17½	2½	$1.25
18N23068	21	3½	1.88
18N23072	23	5	2.37
18N23076	27	7	2.95

Genuine Kestner Kid Body Dolls. The Standard of the World.

Absolutely the best Doll that can be bought at any price. Kestner, the manufacturer of this doll is known for the excellence of manufacture, the fine quality features, and the general superiority of his dolls. His goods are the standard by which all others are judged. The heads are of absolutely the finest quality bisque with open mouth showing teeth, and moving eyes. Fitted with long curly wig, parted on the side and tied with a bow of good quality ribbon. Has papier mache legs, tinted in natural colors, fitted with good quality removable colored lace stockings and ribbon tied sandals to match. Best quality bisque forearm. Riveted elbow, shoulder, hip and knee joints, allowing free movement of arms and legs. We buy these dolls direct from Germany and save at least one-third for you. This doll we guarantee to please you, a doll that has given satisfaction for many years. Come in five sizes, each carefully packed for shipping.

Catalogue Number	Height, inches	Shipping Wt., pounds	Price, each
18N23080	18½	3	$1.75
18N23084	20½	5	2.37
18N23088	23½	7	3.45
18N23092	25½	8	4.15
18N23096	28	11	4.98

Unbreakable Metal Head Dolls.

THE BEST FOR WEAR.

This popular Doll is nicely made with a hair stuffed pink silesia body with movable hips and knees. Has the genuine unbreakable metal head with painted eyes and hair. Perfect features and absolutely harmless in a child's hands. Has imitation patent leather shoes. The larger the doll the better proportioned are the heads and bodies. Come in four sizes, as follows:

Catalogue Number	Height, inches	Ship'g Wt.	Price, each
18N23100	11½	¾ lb.	25c
18N23104	14½	1 lb.	44c
18N23108	16	1¼ lbs.	57c
18N23112	18	1½ lbs.	69c

Genuine Unbreakable Metal Head Dolls With Real Curly Hair.

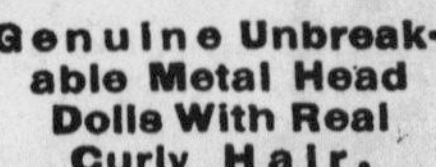

These hair stuffed, pink silesia body Dolls are fitted with the finest quality unbreakable metal heads, which have real curly sewed wigs, nicely parted and tied with ribbon. The eyes are of glass and the lips are parted showing teeth. The hips and knees are movable and the doll has imitation patent leather shoes. Come in three sizes as below:

Catalogue Number	H'ght inches	Ship'g Wt.	Price, each
18N23120	14½	1 lb.	48c
18N23124	17	2 lbs.	75c
18N23128	20	3 lbs.	95c

Genuine Kestner Bisque Babies.

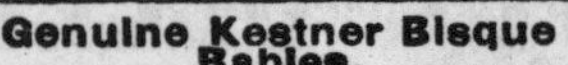

A MOST POPULAR LITTLE DOLL FOR HOME DRESSING.

Made of finest quality Kestner bisque in natural flesh tints with jointed hips and shoulders. Have automatic sleeping and waking eyes and beautiful parted wigs, very long and curly. Altogether these babies are most real and lifelike and they will surely give satisfaction. The 50-cent and 98-cent sizes have natural appearing eyelashes. Come very carefully packed. We guarantee against breakage when shipped.

Catalogue Number	Height, inches	Shipping Weight	Price, each
18N23129	5	5 oz.	25c
18N23131	6½	7 oz.	50c
18N23133	10½	1 lb.	98c

Handsome Indestructible Rag Dolls

No. 18N23148 Patent Face Indestructible Rag Doll, well shaped and proportioned. Has nicely made gingham dress in bright attractive colors, with bonnet to match. Patent indestructible face, will not break or fade, making this the best appearing and most substantial rag doll obtainable, a tremendous improvement over the old style painted face. Height, 14 inches. Price.... **25c**

If by mail, postage extra, 10 cents.

No. 18N23150 Indestructible Rag Doll. A special value at a low price. The body is cotton stuffed, pink silesia, with removable shoes and stockings. Face is lithographed from life and is very attractive. The dress is of organdy, made very full and trimmed with lace and braid. Doll has muslin underclothes. Height, 16 inches. Price... **50c**

Postage extra, 13 cents.

Buster Brown Doll.

No. 18N23160 Buster Brown Indestructible Rag Doll. The doll is dressed in a red suit with white collar, cuffs and belt, has Buster Brown cap of red and white, and a large black Windsor tie. This doll will be a delight to the children on account of the popularity of Buster Brown. Length, 15 inches. Price... **25c**

Postage extra, 10 cents.

Infant Talking Doll.

No. 18N23164 Infant Talking Doll, dressed in long white lawn slip with lace yoke and pretty poke bonnet trimmed with ruching. Has voice which is operated by means of pulling string. Length of body, 13 inches; entire length including dress, 18 in. Price.... **25c**

Postage extra, 12 cents.

No. 18N23216 Eskimo Doll. This is a very attractive and interesting papier mache jointed doll with bisque head. The entire body is covered with white fur, all parts of the body, arms, legs and head being movable, so that you can make it assume any position. Length, 10½ inches. Price. (Postage extra, 8 cents). **25c**

Unbreakable Dolls.

No. 18N23242 Indestructible Dressed Doll. Silesia body. Removable shoes and stockings. Good quality lace trimmed dress with bonnet to match. Genuine unbreakable Minerva metal head. A very pretty and at the same time unbreakable doll, which should meet with the approval of many mothers. Shipping wt., 12 oz. Price.... **50c**

Happy Hooligan Roly Poly.

No. 18N21624 Roly Poly Happy Hooligan. A great plaything for a small child. Made of papier mache pressed into the figure of the very popular Happy Hooligan. The Roly Poly is weighted at the bottom so that when upset it will roll around and automatically assume its upright position. Practically unbreakable. Height, 9½ inches. Price....... **50c**

If by mail, postage extra, 20 cents.

500 Household Necessities, 2 to 12 Cents Each. See Yellow Pages at Front of Catalog.

HIGH GRADE IMPORTED DOLLS AND SUNDRIES

Our "Little Cherub" Line.

EXTRA SPECIAL VALUES IN FULL JOINTED DOLLS AT VERY LOW PRICES.

A very good grade of papier mache dolls made in natural flesh tints, in imitation of the human body. The dolls have full elbow, wrist, hip and knee joints. Are dressed in lace trimmed chemise, have lace stockings and imitation patent leather sandals. The head is made of good quality bisque, has parted lips showing teeth, moving eyes which open and close, and side parted wig tied with ribbon. We have never before been able to offer such good dolls at such startlingly low prices.

Catalog Number	Height, inches	Shipping Wt., lbs.	Price, each
18R22994	10	1	$0.25
18R22996	13½	1½	.50
18R22998	15	2	.88
18R23000	18	4	1.19

Note:—No. 18R23000 has pretty eyelashes.

The "May Belle" Brand.

OUR VERY FINEST QUALITY FULL JOINTED PAPIER MACHE DOLLS.

These dolls are without doubt the best that money can buy and we particularly recommend them to our trade. We have even succeeded in greatly improving these dolls this year. Made of heavy papier mache (light, strong and more durable than any other material) in exact imitation of the human body. The wrists, elbows, hips and knees are full ball jointed. The heads are of finest quality bisque with parted lips showing teeth. They have automatic sleeping eyes with eyelashes, extra fine wigs, full sewed and parted and tied with ribbons. These dolls are fitted with lace trimmed chemise, openwork stockings and sateen shoes. They represent the highest art in doll making. Come in four sizes, carefully packed.

Catalog Number	Height, inches	Shipping Wt., lbs.	Price, each
18R23010	18	6	$1.75
18R23012	24½	7	2.98
18R23016	27	9	3.89
18R23020	30	18	4.95

Our "Pansy" Quality.

EXTRA LARGE SIZE GENUINE KID BODY DOLLS.

The dolls are well made, of good material, and are tremendous bargains at the prices quoted below. Don't confuse this line of dolls with the imitation kid dolls offered by others at our prices. Our dolls have nicely proportioned bodies, good quality bisque heads with moving eyes which open and close, nice curly wigs, shoes and stockings. The larger the doll the better proportioned are the features and body. Come in four sizes, as follows:

Catalog No.	H'ght, in.	Shipping Wt.,	Price, each
18R23024	13	1 lb.	25c
18R23028	16	1½ lbs.	47c
18R23032	18½	2½ lbs.	73c
18R23036	21	3½ lbs.	98c

Our "Tiny Tot" Doll.

WHEN THIS DOLL AWAKENS IT CALLS "MAMA."

No. 18R23038 This is a new patent feature which we are the first to introduce. The body is made of very high grade kid, jointed at the hips, fitted with removable shoes and lace stockings. The head is of best quality bisque fitted with curly wig. A patented mechanism is fitted inside the head which causes the doll to call "mama" when the eyes open. Well proportioned. Length, 18 inches. Originally made up to sell at $2.00. By means of a tremendous purchase we are able to offer this great value at $1.29. Shipping wt., 2½ lbs. Price............**$1.29**

The "Sunshine" Brand.

HIGH GRADE HALF JOINTED KID BODY DOLLS.

These dolls are made of high grade kid with riveted joints at both hips and knees, allowing the doll to assume a sitting position. The heads are bisque with moving eyes, long curly full sewed wigs, nicely parted and tied with ribbon. The lips are parted, showing the teeth. Openwork stockings and sateen shoes are fitted to the doll. A splendid value at our prices, which mean a big saving to you. Come in four sizes, each nicely packed in box.

Catalog No.	H'ght, In.	Shipping W't lbs.	Price, each
18R23040	15	2	$0.59
18R23044	17	2½	.87
18R23048	20	3	1.25
18R23056	25	5	1.69

Our "American Beauty."

HALF CORK STUFFED, FULL JOINTED, KID BODY DOLLS.

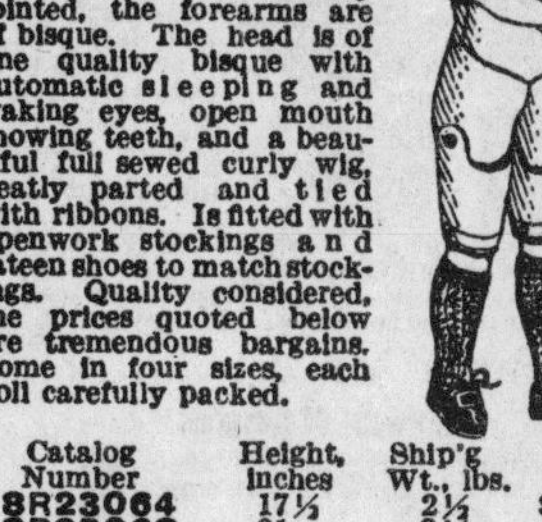

To our customers who wish a fine doll at a moderately low price we can highly recommend this quality. The entire body from shoulders to toes is made of fine quality white kid, with half cork stuffing, giving a light shapely body. The hips, knees, shoulders and elbows are nicely jointed, the forearms are of bisque. The head is of fine quality bisque with automatic sleeping and waking eyes, open mouth showing teeth, and a beautiful full sewed curly wig, neatly parted and tied with ribbons. Is fitted with openwork stockings and sateen shoes to match stockings. Quality considered, the prices quoted below are tremendous bargains. Come in four sizes, each doll carefully packed.

Catalog Number	Height, inches	Ship'g Wt., lbs.	Price, each
18R23064	17½	2½	$1.25
18R23068	21	3½	1.88
18R23072	23	5	2.37
18R23076	27	7	2.95

Our "Dainty Dorothy" Brand.

MADE BY THE CELEBRATED KESTNER OF GERMANY, THE PEER OF ALL DOLL MAKERS.

Kestner, the manufacturer of this doll, is known for the excellence of manufacture, the fine quality features, and the general superiority of his dolls. His goods are the standard by which all others are judged. The heads are of absolutely the finest quality bisque with open mouth showing teeth, and moving eyes with natural eye lashes. Fitted with long curly wig, parted on the side and tied with a bow of good quality ribbon. Has papier mache legs, tinted in natural colors, fitted with good quality, removable colored lace stockings and ribbon tied sandals to match. Best quality bisque forearm. Riveted elbow, shoulder, hip and knee joints, allowing free movement of arms and legs. We buy these dolls direct from Germany and save at least one-third for you. This doll we guarantee to please you. A doll that has given satisfaction for many years. Come in five sizes, each carefully packed for shipping.

Catalog Number	Height, inches	Shipping Wt., lbs.	Price, each
18R23080	18½	3	$1.75
18R23084	20½	5	2.37
18R23088	23½	7	3.45
18R23092	25½	8	4.15
18R23096	28	11	4.98

The "Bebe Chic" Line.

GENUINE ALL BISQUE BABIES.

A most popular little doll for home dressing. Made of finest quality bisque in natural flesh tints with jointed hips and shoulders. Have automatic sleeping and waking eyes and beautiful parted wigs, very long and curly. Altogether these babies are most real and lifelike and they will surely give satisfaction. The 50 and 98-cent sizes have natural appearing eyelashes. Come very carefully packed. We guarantee against breakage when shipped.

Catalog Number	Height, inches	Shipping Wt.	Price, each
18R23129	5	5 oz.	25c
18R23131	6½	7 oz.	50c
18R23133	10½	1 lb.	98c

Our "Knock-Out" Brand.

UNBREAKABLE METAL HEAD DOLLS. THE BEST FOR WEAR.

This popular doll is nicely made with a hair stuffed pink silesia body with movable hips and knees. Has the genuine unbreakable metal head with painted eyes and hair. Perfect features and absolutely harmless and unbreakable in a child's hands. Has imitation patent leather shoes. The larger the doll the better proportioned are the head and body. Come in four sizes, as follows:

Catalog Number	Height, inches	Ship'g Wt.	Price, each
18R23100	11½	¾ lb.	25c
18R23104	14½	1 lb.	44c
18R23108	16	1¼ lbs.	57c
18R23112	18	1½ lbs.	69c

Our "Wear Well" Line.

GENUINE UNBREAKABLE METAL HEAD DOLLS WITH REAL CURLY HAIR.

These hair stuffed, pink silesia body dolls are fitted with the finest quality unbreakable metal heads, which have real curly sewed wigs, nicely parted and tied with ribbon. The eyes are of glass and the lips are parted showing teeth. The hips and knees are movable and the doll has imitation patent leather shoes. A lifelike serviceable doll, which will stand hard use. Comes in three sizes as below:

Catalog Number	H'ght, inches	Ship'g Wt.	Price, each
18R23120	14¾	1 lb.	48c
18R23124	17	2 lbs.	75c
18R23128	20	3 lbs.	95c

Our New "Violet" Line.

KID BODY UNBREAKABLE DOLLS WITH METAL HEAD AND MOVING EYES.

This line of dolls is entirely new this season and we are introducing it on account of the immense popularity of our "Knock-Out" and "Wear Well" brands of silesia body metal head dolls. Many of our customers have asked for a fine kid body doll with metal head, so we offer this new quality. The body is made of the best white kid leather with riveted jointed hips and bisque arms. Removable shoes and stockings. Fitted with metal head with moving eyes, parted lips showing teeth, and the best quality full sewed curly wig, parted, and with ribbon bow at side. This doll, being practically unbreakable and exceptionally pretty, will certainly please the child for whom it is purchased. We can furnish in three sizes as follows:

Catalog Number	Height, inches	Shipping Wt., lbs.	Price, each
18R23125	16	1½	$0.98
18R23126	18	2	1.43
18R23127	20	2½	1.88

Our "Paragon" Line.

BEST QUALITY CELLULOID BABES.

Feather weight, celluloid babes are the most lasting for the young child. They are very light in weight and are absolutely harmless. Very natural, lifelike and well proportioned. Have movable arms. The larger the babe the better proportioned are the features and body. We can furnish these babes in five sizes as follows:

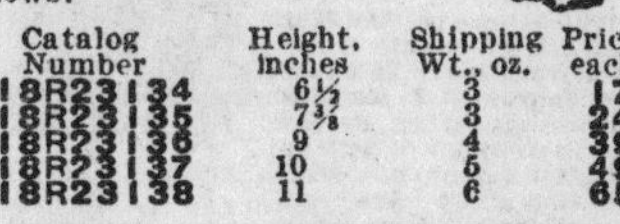

Catalog Number	Height, inches	Shipping Wt., oz.	Price, each
18R23134	6½	3	17c
18R23135	7⅜	3	24c
18R23136	9	4	39c
18R23137	10	5	49c
18R23138	11	6	65c

Infant's Doll Rattle.

No. 18R23217 Infant's Doll Rattle. Has celluloid face, lace trimmed dress with hood to match. Squeaking voice, which operates by simply shaking the doll. A splendid large rattle that will certainly amuse the young child. Size, 10¾ inches. Price............**21c**

If mail shipment, postage extra, 4 cents.

DRESSED DOLLS.

No. 18R23218 Prettily Dressed Doll. Plaited dress, ribbon trimmed, and lace collar. Lace trimmed hat to match. Fitted with bisque head, with curly wig. Doll is jointed at shoulders and hips. Size, including hat, 13 inches. A 50-cent value in most stores. Shipping wt., 12 oz. Our price.........**25c**

No. 18R23222 Dressed Doll with bisque head, moving eyes and curly wig. Pretty striped sateen dress trimmed with ribbon belt and two satin buttons. Straw hat with ribbon bow. The best and prettiest doll that we have ever offered at a low price. Size, including hat, 16 inches. Shipping wt., 2¾ lbs. Price.........**50c**

No. 18R23230 Handsome Full Jointed Dressed Doll. Neck, shoulders, arms and legs are all movable. Well proportioned, fitted with good quality bisque head, with moving eyes, open mouth and curly wig. Doll is prettily dressed in blouse style with very large trimmed hat. Has removable shoes and stockings. Size, including hat, 18 inches. Big $1.25 value. Shipping wt., 2½ lbs. Our price....**75c**

No. 18R23234 Beautiful American Style Dressed Baby Doll, full jointed, including elbow and wrist. Beautiful bisque head, with pretty face, patent sleeping eyes and curly wig. Has white mull overdress on a colored drop, lace trimmed. Very good quality underwear fastened by means of draw strings, and the dress itself is fastened with hooks and eyes, so that the doll can easily be dressed and undressed. Large mull hat made on wire frame. Regular $1.50 value. Shipping wt., 3¼ lbs. Our price.....**97c**

No. 18R23238 Handsome Doll with full embroidery dress trimmed with ribbon sash and large collar. Has large hat with two tiny ostrich feathers. The underwear is of good quality, trimmed with torchon lace. This, as well as the dress, can be taken off, being fastened by means of hooks and eyes and draw strings. The doll itself is fully jointed throughout and well proportioned, with removable shoes and lace stockings. Pretty head with curly marcelled wig; has moving eyes and parted lips showing teeth. $2.25 value. Shipping wt., 4 lbs. Our price..........**$1.48**

No. 18R23239 Our Very Finest and Largest Full Jointed Dressed Doll. Full ball jointed and made of the best quality papier mache, well proportioned throughout. Fitted with exceptionally good quality bisque head, with parted lips showing teeth, and sleeping eyes with eyelashes. Has very curly wig. The flowered organdy dress is elaborately made and trimmed. The underclothes and lingerie are very good. Large hat to match dress made on a wire frame, trimmed with ribbon and blossoms. A doll that would be sold anywhere else at $3.50. Size, including hat, 23 inches. Our price..........**$1.98**

BEST VALUES IN TOY DISHES AND FURNITURE

Big Value China Tea Sets.

Very Large and Beautifully Decorated.

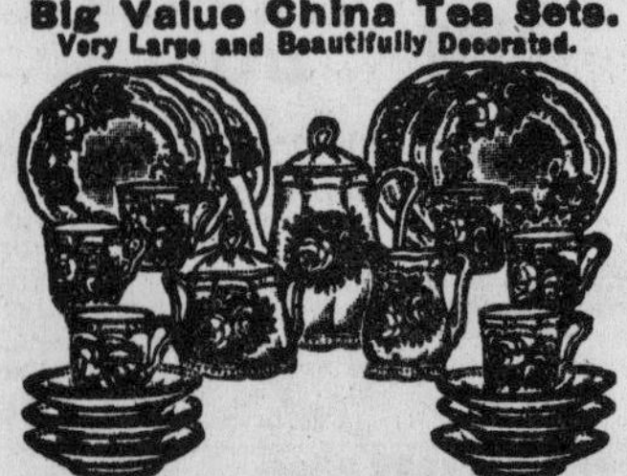

Large size high grade thin china fancy rose decorated Toy Tea Set. Consists of twenty-three extra large size pieces of the best grade imported china, hand decorated in natural color rose pattern with fancy gilt trimming. Consists of six cups and saucers, teapot and sugar bowl with covers, creamer and six 5-inch diameter fancy plates. A set that is practical and sure to please any child. Shipping wt., 8 lbs.
No. 8R700 Price.......... **$1.39**

Toy Tea Set. Same style as above, but with fancy bowl and without the six large size plates (eighteen pieces in all). A beautiful set and selling elsewhere for $1.50. Shipping wt., 6 lbs.
No. 8R701 Price.......... **$1.00**

Same as No. 8R700, but not decorated. Shipping wt., 6 lbs.
No. 8R702 Price.......... **75c**

China Tea Set. Toy china tea set consists of twenty-two pieces, including cups, saucers, sugar, creamer and six spoons, all decorated in fancy colors. An exceptional value. Shipping wt., 20 oz.
No. 8R703 Price.......... **23c**

China Tea Set. Beautifully hand decorated and finished in gilt. Consists of twenty-three pieces, including good size cups, saucers, cake dish, teapot, sugar and creamer. A very pretty set, and much better value than can be purchased at anywhere near our price. Shipping wt., 2½ lbs.
No. 8R704 Price.......... **49c**

Decorated Tin Tea Sets.

Decorated Tin Tea Set. Absolutely unbreakable. Consists of sixteen pieces, four large size cups and saucers, cream pitcher and teapot with cover, saucepan, and tray measuring 9x12 inches. All decorated in high colors on heavy metal, pictures being of animals, flowers, etc. These are very attractive sets for the younger children. Put up in heavy cardboard box. Shipping wt., 24 oz.
No. 8R710 Price.......... **47c**

Same style as above, but smaller, consists of eleven pieces, including four cups and saucers, teapot and cover and tray 6x9 inches, enameled in high colors. Put up in heavy cardboard box. Shipping wt., 16 oz.
No. 8R711 Price.......... **23c**

Britannia Tea Sets.

Britannia (Pewter) Tea Set. Highly silver finished, with very handsome filigree design. Small cups, saucers and other pieces. Set consists of about twenty-three pieces. Shipping wt., 17 oz.
No. 8R720 Our price, per set...... **19c**

Britannia Tea Set, silver finished, about twenty-four pieces, similar to above but larger. Shipping wt., 28 oz.
No. 8R721 Price, per set.......... **47c**

Britannia Tea Set, consisting of about twenty-three pieces, silver finished, assortment same as above, but a still larger size. Shipping wt., 40 oz. Good $1.25 value.
No. 8R722 Price, per set.......... **87c**

Child's Folding Tables.

These beautiful and handsomely finished birchwood tables are great favorites with children. Each table folds up flat with enameled steel spring. Well made, best materials and occupy little space when not in use.

No. 8R795 Size top, 18x26 inches; height, 18½ inches. Shipping wt., 8 lbs. Price.......... **89c**

No. 8R796 Size top, 14x20 inches; height, 15½ inches. Shipping wt., 7 lbs. Price.......... **57c**

No. 8R797 Size top, 12x18 inches; height, 14½ inches. Shipping wt., 6 lbs. Price.......... **43c**

Enameled Kitchen Sets.

Blue Enameled Kitchen Set. An outfit that will afford no end of pleasure to any girl. Consists of nineteen pieces, including all the various kitchen utensils, such as pots, pans, spoons, ladles, covers, etc. One of these outfits used in connection with our toy stove No. 8R755 will certainly please. Absolutely unbreakable, being made the same as the large, best quality enameled kitchen ware. Shipping wt., 3 lbs.
No. 8R725 Price, per set.......... **95c**

Enameled Kitchen Set. Same make as above but only nine pieces. A very attractive set at a moderate price. Shipping wt., 24 oz.
No. 8R726 Price.......... **45c**

Extra Values in Metal Doll Beds.

Complete Outfit, 98c

Every child with a doll should have a nice Doll Bed.

A child derives as much enjoyment out of a doll bed as from the doll itself. These metal doll beds are exceptionally fine, made of strong metal, finished in artistic scroll designs at the head and foot, handsome gilt finish, with excelsior stuffed mattress, two pillows and muslin sheet. All covered with good quality floral pattern silkoline spread and canopy to match. The pillows are edged with lace. Length, 25 inches; width, 12 inches. Shipping wt., 3 lbs. Good $1.50 value.
No. 8R735 Our price.......... **98c**

Doll Bed, same style and material as above, measuring 18 inches in length and 9 inches in width. Ship'g wt., 28 oz. Regular value, 75 cents.
No. 8R736 Our price.......... **49c**

Fine Doll Cradles.

The new rocking doll cradles are becoming very popular, as the child can rock the doll to sleep. Great enjoyment for your child. They are made of good heavy metal, finished in scroll designs and beautiful gilt finish. They come complete with excelsior stuffed mattress, large lace edge pillow and muslin sheet. All covered with good quality floral pattern silkoline spread and canopy to match. Length, 23 inches and 9 inches wide. Folds up for shipment and packed in nice carton. Shipping wt., 3 lbs. Regular price, $1.50.
No. 8R738 Our price.......... **97c**

Doll Cradle, same style and material as above, measuring 15 inches in length and 7½ inches in width. Shipping wt., 28 oz. Regular price, 75 cents.
No. 8R739 Our price.......... **47c**

Ta-Ka-Part Doll Houses.

An absolutely new toy. A doll house made up of very strong pressed pasteboard, but made in such a manner that it can be taken apart when not in use and occupy very small space, affording convenience in shipping. Can be put together in a few seconds. Every part perfect. Decorated doors, windows and parts being in natural color, and representing a painted house with brick foundation. Has upper and lower floors with wooden porch. It is a handy and convenient article from which a child will derive an immense amount of pleasure.

Ta-Ka-Part Doll House is a toy par excellence. Not like other wooden toys. It does not come apart; must be taken apart. It can be built up with ease, thus giving the child new interest in his plaything. Unlike most toys, the child cannot injure himself because of weight or sharp edges. **Neat and durable; a toy that is a toy indeed.** Base, 9x10 inches; height, 20 inches. Shipping wt., 4 lbs. Will easily sell for $1.50.
No. 8R745 Our price.......... **98c**

Ta-Ka-Part Doll House, same material and style as above, but not as large or complete. Has upper and lower floors, but no porch. Base, 5x15 inches; height, 15½ inches. Shipping wt., 2½ lbs.
No. 8R746 Our price.......... **47c**

Imitation Cut Glass Water Set.

38c Toy Water or Lemonade Set. Consists of seven pieces: glass water pitcher, 4½ inches high, and six glasses, each 2¼ inches high. These are made of extra heavy imitation cut glass, very nicely finished and not easily broken. Packed one set complete in box. Shipping wt., 36 oz. Easily worth 60 cents.
No. 8R750 Our price.......... **38c**

Imitation Cut Glass Punch Set.

An exceedingly popular play set for children. Consists of seven pieces: large fancy design punch bowl, size 4½x4½ inches and six glasses, each 1¼ inches high to match. Made of extra heavy imitation cut glass, handsomely finished, beautiful design, and on account of the thickness not easily broken. An immense selling item. Your child should surely have a set. Shipping wt., 36 oz.
No. 8R751 Price.......... **35c**

Imitation Cut Glass Tea Set.

Handsome in appearance and of beautiful design. Consists of a 5-inch diameter fancy edge covered butter dish, a 5-inch covered sugar bowl, a fancy creamer and a 2½-inch high spoon holder. It is a very useful item and although of heavy beautiful design, is of sufficient thickness so as not to be easily broken. One of the best selling sets ever manufactured. Shipping wt., 36 oz.
No. 8R752 Price.......... **33c**

Iron Range.

Iron Range. Nickel plate finished, with removable covers. Hot water reservoir, swinging oven door and dump grate. Without doubt the finest stove on the market at the price. Size, 11x6x6½ inches. Copper colored pan, pot, coal scuttle, shovel and lifter, and one length of stove pipe with each stove. A real fire can be built in this stove. We recommend our blue enameled granite kitchen ware No. 8R725 for use with one of these stoves as making the most instructive outfit that can be purchased for any child. Shipping wt., 9 lbs.
No. 8R755 Price, complete.......... **98c**

Doll Trunks.

Ta-Ka-Part Collapsible Doll Trunk. Easily taken apart and put away when not in use. An article that has never before been offered. This trunk is made entirely of soft heavy straw board, stronger than wood, which is finished so as to imitate the regulation brown leather trunk, trimmed with strips of the same material, to imitate natural wood. This material will not break or warp as easily as the wood heretofore used in trunks. Has extra tray of the same material and finish as the trunk itself. All beautifully lined inside. Size of trunk, 18x9½x11 inches. Shipping wt., 5½ lbs.
No. 8R730 Price.......... **95c**

Ta-Ka-Part Doll Trunk. Same style and material as above, but measuring 14x8½x7 inches. Shipping wt., 3¼ lbs.
No. 8R731 Price.......... **48c**

Child's Tea Furniture Set.

This exceedingly high class child's afternoon tea furniture set has been devised for the use of the children themselves in serving their tea parties. Made of hard wood throughout and of sufficient strength for use by the children themselves. Consists of two chairs and table made of natural oak, beautifully polished and varnished. Size chairs, 9x9x20 inches. Table 12x12x13½ inches. Every child with a tea set should also have this furniture set to serve the same. Shipping wt., 6½ lbs. Ordinary value, $1.25 to $1.50.
No. 8R790 Our price.......... **79c**

Big Value Doll Furniture Set.

Consists of 11-inch high sideboard, 11-inch dresser, 11-inch chiffonier and 13-inch china closet. All parts are 9 inches wide and 3½ inches from front to back. Made in the best possible manner of natural maple, polished and varnished. Sideboard contains a large size drawer with two swinging doors. China closet has two swinging glass doors and also drawer at the bottom. Dresser has two large and two small drawers, and chiffonier four large drawers. All finished with fancy turned wood knobs. Each piece is of sufficient size so a child can use it for the various doll clothes. Each part has fancy shaped back containing therein a circular mirror. Each set packed carefully. Shipping wt., 15 lbs. Would easily sell for $2.00.
No. 8R775 Our price.......... **$1.29**

Doll Bedroom Furniture Set.

Consists of five pieces: folding bed, dresser, chiffonier, rocker and straight chair. All parts made of natural maple, highly polished and varnished. Makes a pleasing set for any child. You will be surprised how well this little set is made, and with proper handling will last a child a long time. Bed is 9¾x6½x5½ inches; dresser, 8x7x3½ inches, and contains two drawers and large mirror; chiffonier, 8¾x6x3 inches, and contains three drawers; chair is 7½x3x3 inches and exceedingly well made, and rocking chair is 7½x4x3 inches; this is an excellent value set and will sell by others for not less than $1.00. Shipping wt., 3½ lbs.
No. 8R780 Our price, per set, complete.......... **67c**

Princess Doll Parlor Set.

This handsome little parlor furniture set is assembled for mothers desiring for their children something away above the average. The pieces are all of sufficient size that a doll can sit down, and are exceedingly well made. The three chairs are handsomely decorated on the back with heavy embossed gilt ornaments and gilt finished knobs. The four pieces are painted with white enamel which, with the gilt ornaments, gives them a handsome appearance and makes it a set of extraordinary beauty. The rocker and straight chair are 6x5½x12½ inches. The settee is 11x6x12½ inches. The table is 7½ inches wide and 8 inches high. This set, with proper handling, will last the child a long time. If you want the best set we carry, in fact, one of the best manufactured, select this item. Shipping wt., 3 lbs. Ordinary value, $1.50 to $1.75.
No. 8R785 Our price.......... **93c**

Doll Parlor Sets.

Doll's Parlor Set. This set is complete in every detail. Made of very strong reeds, and is without question the best set of its kind on the market. Outer reeds are black enameled ornamented with red inner reeds. The upholstering work is in velour, finished with gimp to match. Set consists of table, 3 inches high and 5¼ inches long; sofa, 5 inches high, and six chairs, 5¼ inches high. Wonderful value. Shipping wt., 2 lbs.
No. 8R792 Price.......... **88c**

Doll's Parlor Set. Same as above, but smaller, finished in gilt and colored materials. Table is 2½ inches high, 4 inches long and 2½ inches wide. Six chairs, each 4½ inches in height; sofa, 5 inches in height and 4½ inches in width. An attractive furniture set at a low price. Shipping wt., 1½ lbs.
No. 8R793 Price.......... **50c**

Happy Hooligan Roly Poly.

Roly Poly Happy Hooligan. A great plaything for a small child. Made of papier mache pressed into the figure of the very popular Happy Hooligan. The Roly Poly is weighted at the bottom so that when upset it will roll around and automatically assume its upright position. Practically unbreakable. Height, 9½ inches. Shipping wt., 20 oz.
No. 8R645 Price.......... **47c**

New Unbreakable Dolls.

Silesia Body and Minerva Metal Head.

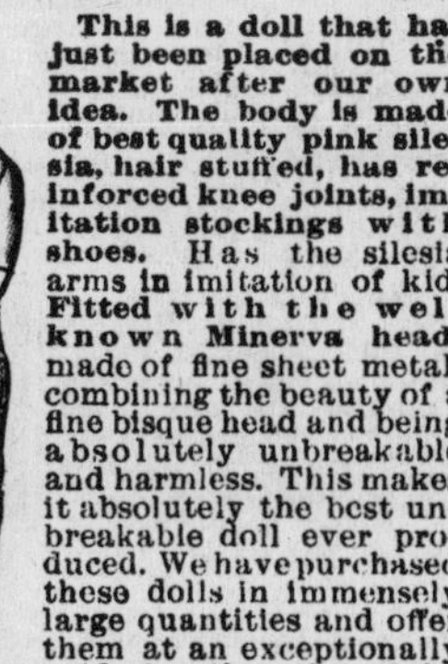

This is a doll that has just been placed on the market after our own ideas. The body is made of best quality pink silesia, hair stuffed, has reinforced knee joints, imitation stockings with shoes. Has the silesia arms in imitation of kid. **Fitted with the well known Minerva head,** made of fine sheet metal, combining the beauty of a fine bisque head and being absolutely unbreakable and harmless. This makes it absolutely the best unbreakable doll ever produced. We have purchased these dolls in immensely large quantities and offer them at an exceptionally low price, considering the value of the doll body as well as the Minerva heads. At the prices quoted they are the best doll you could buy. We offer them in five sizes, as follows:

No. 29C428 Pink Silesia, Hair Stuffed Body Unbreakable Doll, fitted with Minerva head, as described above. Length, 11½ inches. Shipping weight, 1 pound. Price..........25c

No. 29C432 Pink Silesia Hair Stuffed Body, fitted with Minerva doll head, as described above. Length, 14 inches. Shipping weight, 1½ pounds. Price..........40c

No. 29C436 Pink Silesia Hair Stuffed Body, fitted with Minerva metal doll head as described above. Length, 15½ inches. Shipping weight, 2 pounds. Price..........55c

No. 29C440 Pink Silesia Hair Stuffed Body, fitted with Minerva metal head, larger proportioned than above. Length, 17½ inches. Shipping weight, 3 pounds. Price..........70c

No. 29C444 Pink Silesia Hair Stuffed Body, fitted with Minerva doll head. This head has the glass eye. Larger sized body and larger sized head than above. Length, 21 inches. Shipping weight, 4 pounds. Price..........95c

Rag Dolls.

No. 29C468 Rag Doll, dressed in a fancy figured, short dress, with large yoke, has a pretty poke bonnet to match dress. Length, 16½ inches. Shipping weight, 14 ounces. Price..........25c

No. 29C472 Rag Doll, with short dress, made of pretty figured lawn, neatly trimmed with lace and a nice hood of the same material to match dress. Has removable shoes and stockings. This is equal to many of the $1.00 rag dolls sold elsewhere. Length, 18 inches. Shipping weight, 16 ounces. Price..........50c

No. 29C480 Reversible Rag Doll. This is a new novelty, two dolls in one. Dressed in a checked gingham dress, trimmed in lace; hood of same material, also lace trimmed. By reversing doll, you have another complete style of rag baby, which is a little **negro baby,** dressed with a red suit, having a separate white apron. This dress is also trimmed in lace, and the little colored baby has a red hood to match the dress. This is one of the biggest selling rag dolls ever placed on the market. Length, 14 inches. Shipping weight, 12 ounces. Price..........95c

Unbreakable Leather Dolls.

No. 29C516 Unbreakable Leather Doll. This is baby's friend. The leather is very fine to chew on when teething. Impossible to hurt either the baby or the doll. Stuffed with cotton and will always retain its shape. This doll will last baby and also baby's brother. Coloring matter warranted not to come off. Length, 12½ inches. Shipping weight, 15 ounces. Price..........40c

Pretty Dressed Dolls.

We Guarantee Values and Styles That Cannot Be Equaled.

We Cannot Show by Illustration How Nice They Are.

No. 29C528 Fancy Dressed Doll, full jointed body with turned bisque head, curly hair, shoes and stockings with very prettily trimmed, striped, pique dress with satin folds and sash, full frilled bonnet and pretty trimming to match dress. Shipping weight, 2 pounds. Price...25c

No. 29C532 Fancy Dressed Doll, bisque head, moving eyes, curly hair, shoes and stockings. Dressed with a fancy white lawn dress, colored silk blouse front and silk collar to match, trimmed with lace and a crepon sash. Fancy plaited bonnet to match. Shipping weight, 2½ pounds. Price.....50c

No. 29C536 Fancy Dressed Doll, full jointed body, curly hair, shoes and stockings, dressed with a corded novelty silk, fancy collar of lace and satin with braided edge and pretty shoes with fancy buckle and a showy, fancy, straw braid hat, trimmed with a plume and large bow to match the dress. This is a sleeping doll. Shipping weight, 3¼ pounds. Price..........$1.00

No. 29C540 Fancy Dressed Doll and fancy colored satin empire gown; new style collar, trimmed with lace and fancy braid, white plaited yoke with iridescent buttons, has a poke bonnet of colored satin, trimmed with lace to match the dress. This is a sleeping doll. Shipping weight, 3¾ pounds. Price..........$1.50

No. 29C544 Dressed Doll, bisque head, curly hair, shoes and stockings, dressed with a beautifully colored, fancy striped, silk gossamer empire dress, trimmed in lace and with large balloon sleeves, has a vandyke collar and cuffs of lace, rosette and sash of satin ribbon to match. Has a large picture hat of satin, elaborately trimmed with ostrich plume and rosettes. This is a sleeping doll. Shipping weight, 4 pounds. Price..........$2.25

Rubber Dolls, Figures and Animals.

White Rubber Dolls, imported high grade quality. Far superior to the domestic, which crack and do not give good satisfaction. These rubber dolls are dressed in knit woolen suits and hats in assorted colors. We guarantee these dolls as a very satisfactory article.

No. 29C560 White Rubber Dolls, dressed in knit suits and hats as described above. Size, 8 inches. Price..........25c
If by mail, postage extra, 4 cents.

No. 29C564 White Rubber Dolls, dressed in knit suits, as described above. Fatter body and height 10¼ inches. Price..........50c
If by mail, postage extra, 6 cents.

No. 29C568 White Rubber Doll, knit suit and hat as described above; still fatter body and height 11¾ inches, regular $1.00 value. Price..........75c
If by mail, postage extra, 8 cents.

No. 29C572 White Rubber Dolls, knit suits and hats as described above. This is a very large, fat body. Height, 13¼ inches. Exceptional value. Price..........$1.00
If by mail, postage extra, 10 cents.

Imported Red Rubber for Quality. Made of Pure Rubber.

No. 29C576 Red Rubber Gnome or Lilliputian Figure Doll. A very attractive little toy, made of best quality red rubber. Height, 6½ inches. Price..........25c
If by mail, postage, extra, 7c.

No. 29C580 Red Rubber Doll, made of best quality, imported red rubber, has German silver whistle. Height, 5¾ inches. Regular 50 cent value. Price..........30c
If by mail, postage extra, 7 cents.

The Red Rubber Dolls Are Pure Rubber, Harmless and Lasting.

No. 29C584 Red Rubber Doll. Has German silver whistle. Height, 7½ inches. 75-cent quality elsewhere. Price..........50c
If by mail, postage extra, 8 cents.

No. 29C588 Red Rubber Doll. Has German silver whistle. Height, 9¾ inches. This is good $1.00 value. Price..........75c
If by mail, postage extra, 10 cents.

No. 29C592 Red Rubber Doll. Has German silver whistle. Very large, fat body. Height, 11 inches. As sold elsewhere for $1.50. Our price...$1.10
If by mail, postage extra, 12 cents.

Red Rubber Animals, 55 Cents

Red Rubber Toys. Made of the best quality imported Red Rubber, soft and durable. Absolutely safe and harmless for the children. The appearance is much prettier than that of the ordinary rubber toys. We have imported this line to meet the wants of the most critical trade and at prices at least one-third less than usually sold for.

No. 29C596 Horse, fully equipped with saddle and bridle, made of the very best quality red rubber, about 6 inches long and 5 inches high. Price..........55c
If by mail, postage extra, 8 cents.

No. 29C600 Red Rubber Cat. A very pretty design. Length, about 6 inches, height, 5 inches. Price..........55c
If by mail, postage extra, 8 cents.

No. 29C604 Red Rubber Dog, made of best quality red rubber. About 6 inches long and 5 inches high. Price..........55c
If by mail, postage extra, 8 cents.

No. 29C608 Red Rubber Elephant, with oriental rug or saddle on back. Made of best quality red rubber. Length, about 6 inches, and height, 5 inches. Price..........55c
If by mail, postage extra, 10 cents.

Kid Doll Bodies.

No. 29C612 Kid Body Dolls, very full size, extra quality cork stuffed, high grade kid bodies, with riveted hip joint and bisque arms, shoes and stockings. This is a very high grade and satisfactory body. Comes in sizes as follows:

Size	Length, inches	Inches across shoulders	Shipping weight, ozs.	Price
1	12½	3½	15	$0.35
2	16	4	25	.50
3	19	4¾	35	.70
4	21½	5½	45	1.00
5	23¾	6	60	1.25
6	24½	6¼	65	1.50
7	25½	7	75	1.75

Silesia Doll Bodies.

No. 29C616 Pink Silesia Doll Bodies. This is a very high grade and satisfactory silesia body that will give best of wear and satisfaction; has bisque arms and removable shoes and stockings. Comes in the following sizes:

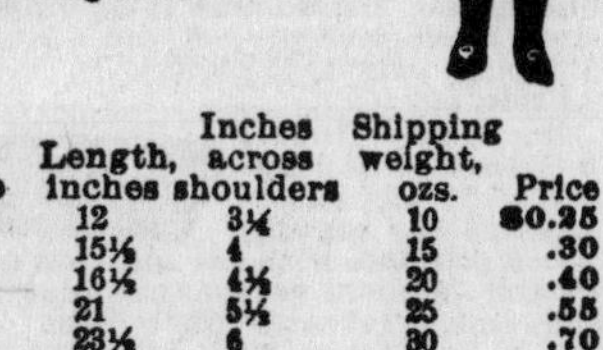

Size	Length, inches	Inches across shoulders	Shipping weight, ozs.	Price
1	12	3¼	10	$0.25
2	15½	4	15	.30
3	16½	4½	20	.40
4	21	5½	25	.55
5	23½	6	30	.70
6	25½	6½	35	.85
7	26¾	7¼	40	1.00

Minerva Indestructible Metal Doll Heads.

No. 29C620 These Doll Heads are imported from Germany, they combine the durability of sheet metal and the beauty of bisque, are light in weight, washable, and will not chip; will stand any reasonable wear. Small children cannot injure them, larger ones love them for their unequaled beauty. The eyes are clear and tender, head flexible at the bust, and fitted with sewing holes, making it easy to adjust and fasten them to body. Come in sizes as follows:

Style	Height, inches	Inches across sh'lders	Shipping weight, ozs.	Price
2	3⅜	2¾	5	18c
3	3¾	3	6	22c
4	4½	3⅜	8	30c
5	4½	3⅝	9	35c
6	5	4	10	40c
7	6¼	4½	12	60c
8	6¾	5½	14	75c

Nos. 7 and 8 have glass eyes and open mouths, showing teeth.

The Minerva Indestructible Doll Head.

Sewed Wig and Moving Glass Eyes.

No. 29C624 The Minerva Indestructible Doll Head with moving glass eyes, open lips showing teeth, and very fine sewed curly wig. The Minerva heads, made of the best flexible sheet brass can be given to the smallest child with perfect safety, as the metal is covered with a pure wholesome paint which is manufactured especially for the purpose. Come in sizes as follows:

Style	Height, inches	Inches across sh'lders	Shipping weight, ozs.	Price
1	4	3	9	$0.38
3	4¾	3½	12	.70
5	5¾	4⅜	14	.95
7	6⅝	4⅞	16	1.25

Bisque Doll Heads, Moving Eyes.

IMMENSE VALUES. COMPARE SIZE AND PRICE.

No. 29C628 Bisque Doll Heads, first quality, high grade bisque, with very beautiful moulded faces, showing teeth, with two rows sewed wig and movable eyes. Either blondes or brunettes.

Style	Height, inches	Inches across shoulders	Shipping weight, ozs.	Price
1	3⅞	3	12	$0.19
2	4½	3½	24	.30
3	5¼	4¼	28	.45
4	6	5	32	.65
5	7	5½	36	.90
6	8¼	6¼	39	1.35
7	9	6¾	42	1.65

Bisque Doll Heads, Stationary Eyes.

No. 29C632 First Quality Bisque Doll Heads, the faces are especially beautiful, showing teeth, have stationary eyes, curly flowing wigs, either blondes or brunettes, and full model bust. Sizes:

Style	Height inches	Inches across shoulders	Shipping weight, ozs.	Price
1	3⅞	3	12	$0.10
2	4½	3½	22	.18
3	5¼	4¼	26	.25
4	6	5	30	.40
5	7	5½	34	.65
6	8¼	6¼	36	.90
7	9	6¾	40	1.25

ORDER CAREFULLY

— STATING —

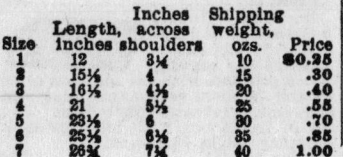

Number, Size and Price

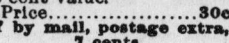

THE SEROCO REVERSIBLE COMBINATION GAME BOARD.

THE COMPLETE OUTFIT, $1.75 — **ON THIS SEROCO GAME BOARD YOU CAN PLAY 75 GAMES**

No. 29C636 This Combination Game Board with Revolving Game Board Stand and full set of rules for playing the different games. Price, for entire outfit **$1.75**

THE SEROCO REVERSIBLE GAME BOARD is the best combination game board on the market, and equal to the many boards that are sold at $2.75 to $4.00. Is the only board with circles to shoot from. You can play 75 games on this elegant combination board. Made of the very best hard ash wood with three-ply veneer, which prevents the board from warping. The circles and checkerboard, stenciled on in very high colors, thoroughly rubbed and varnished, which gives the board a very artistic appearance. The board is 28¾ inches square, with good net pockets. The illustrations show both sides of the board. **Some of the games that can be played on the board are Pyramid, Chicago, Continuous Pool, Bottle Pool and Pin Pool, Billiards, Three Ring, Carrom Game, Crokinole, Fifteen Ring Pool, Checkers, Backgammon, and almost every game that can be played on any other game board can also be played on this board.** With each board are furnished 29 nicely polished hardwood rings, two turned varnished cues, one set tenpins and extra movable back to prevent pins from being knocked off table, billiard attachment, and numbered rings for playing the different games of pool. No expense has been spared to make this board the very best. The games can be played by from two to eight persons.

THE GAME BOARD STAND for the Seroco Game Board is a firm support for the board at the proper height for players to sit on chairs. It being revolving makes it convenient. Made of best hardwood and nicely varnished. Folds up in a small compact package. The regular selling price of the game board alone is $2.75, and the regular price of the game board stand is 50 cents. By taking the entire output of a large factory, adding but our very small percentage of profit, we are enabled to place them on the market at the extremely low price for the board and stand of $1.75, which is less than the manufacturer's price to the dealer on other boards not so good.

EVERY BOARD GUARANTEED as represented and fully equal to the $3.50 and $4.00 boards sold by other concerns.

Price for set complete, board, stand, rings, cues, etc **$1.75**

WE DO NOT QUOTE OR LIST OTHER ADVERTISED GAME BOARDS as we would be obliged to sell them at from $2.75 to $4.50. On the Seroco Combination Board you can play 75 games and almost any game that can be played on any of the advertised boards you can also play on the Seroco Game Board. Our board is made in the very best manner possible, equal to any board and superior to most of them, and our price for board and stand complete is only $1.75. Order at once. Shipping weight, 14 pounds. BOOK OF INSTRUCTIONS WITH EACH GAME BOARD.

Chess and Checkerboards.

No. 29C640 Folding Chess or Checkerboard, lithographed in red and black and covered with imported morocco paper. Squares, 1 inch. Size of board, 14x14 inches.
Price, each 10c
Shipping weight, 10 ounces.

No. 29C644 Folding Chess or Checkerboard. This high grade checkerboard has black and red squares 1¼ inches, with gold lines ⅛ inch wide. The border is 2 inches wide in red, black and gold; covered with fine black embossed paper. Our best board. Size, 18x18 inches. Price **35c**
Shipping weight, 1½ pounds.

Backgammon Boards.

No. 29C648 Folding Backgammon Board. 1½-inch squares in red and black, border in red, black and white. Covered with fancy illuminated paper, fitted with dice cups (no dice) and set of checkers. Size of board, 12x12x⅞ inches.
Price, per set **10c**
Shipping weight, 10 ounces.

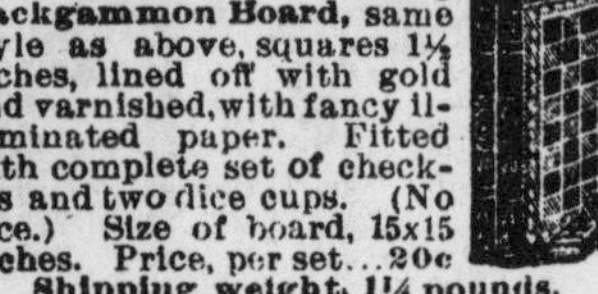

No. 29C657 Folding Backgammon Board, same style as above, squares 1½ inches, lined off with gold and varnished, with fancy illuminated paper. Fitted with complete set of checkers and two dice cups. (No dice.) Size of board, 15x15 inches. Price, per set...20c
Shipping weight, 1¼ pounds.

No. 29C659 Folding Backgammon Board in book form, squares 1½ inches, finished in durable embossed imitation leather. Fitted with dice cups (no dice) and complete set of checkers in separate box. Size of board, 15x15 inches. If you would pay $1.00 you could get no better board.
Price, per set **45c**
Shipping weight, 1½ pounds.

Spanish-American Chess Men.

No. 29C661 The finest Spanish American Chess Men. 32 pieces in the set, finished in black and yellow. Put up in nice pasteboard box. Usually retail at 50 cents. Price, per set...**25c**
Shipping weight, 10 ounces.

No. 29C663 Chess Men. Good size. French pattern, made of hardwood, finished in black and white, 32 pieces in a set. Put up in nice wood box with sliding cover. Price, per set **45c**
Shipping weight, 15 ounces.

No. 29C665 Fine Boxwood Chess Men. Staunton pattern, black and white polished; in dovetailed polished hardwood box, with sliding cover.
Price, per set **80c**
Shipping weight, 18 ounces.

Loaded Boxwood Chess Men.

No. 29C667 Loaded Boxwood Chess Men, in polished mahogany finished box. These are the Staunton pattern, in black and white, polished; an excellent set at the price.
Price, per set **$1.75**
Shipping weight, 1½ pounds.

Interlocking Checkers.

No. 29C669 Interlocking Checkers. Consisting of 30 pieces of enameled hardwood, diameter 1¼ inches. With the old style checker men you must hold both men to move a king, with these the rings interlock, and they may be moved as one man.
Price, per set **10c**
Shipping weight, 10 ounces.

The King Embossed Checkers

No. 29C671 The King Embossed Checkers. 30 pieces of hard polished wood, 1¼ inches in diameter, packed in highly polished wood box, sliding cover.
Shipping weight, 12 ounces.
Price, per set **20c**

Good Dominoes at Low Prices.

No. 29C673 Quarter Arabesque Domino, with round corners, made of selected hard maple, 28 pieces. Size, ⅜x1⅝ inches. Put up in paper box with special engraved label.
Shipping weight, 7 ounces.
Price, per set **10c**

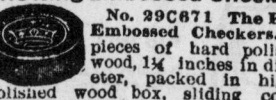

No. 29C675 Double 9 Ebony Dominoes, consisting of 55 pieces. This is an entirely new set and we do not think a double nine domino has ever been offered at the price. In heavy paper boxes. Price, per set **22c**
Shipping weight, 9 ounces.

No. 29C677 Crown Domino. Consisting of 28 pieces with fancy crown design on top. This is a special good number and put up in strong paper box with handsome lithographed label. Price, per set **25c**
Shipping weight, 12 ounces.

No. 29C679 The Magna Domino. Set of 28 pieces, 2⅛x1⅛ inches, packed in very heavy paper box. As you will notice by the dimensions this domino is of unusual size. Each piece perfect and durable.
Shipping weight, 15 ounces.
Price, per set **50c**

No. 29C681 Double 9 Domino. Consisting of 55 pieces, the same as the regular black domino, with the addition of 7's 8's and 9's; more persons can play and the game has greater possibilities. Put up in frame box with label glossed.
Shipping weight, 23 ounces.
Price, per set **75c**

Lotto.

No. 29C683 Wood frame box, size, 4¼x7½ inches, with sleeve and lift cover, 24 cards, 90 wood discs, numbered, with inside box containing glasses and counters. Covered with fine lithographed label. Price **25c**
Shipping weight, 20 ounces.

No. 29C685 Lotto, better grade than above, wood frame box, with sleeve and hinge cover, 24 large cards, 90 wood discs, numbered, pack 50 cards, counters of different colors in inside box, also separate inside box of glasses. A large elegant set. Price **50c**
Shipping weight, 2 pounds.

Large Size Ouija, or Egyptian Luck Board.

No. 29C687 Without a doubt the most remarkable and interesting and mystifying production of the age. Its operations are always interesting and sometimes invaluable; answering as it does, questions concerning the past, present and future. Full directions for operating the Ouija board accompanying each board. Packed each one in a pasteboard box. Cannot be sent by mail. Regular $1.00 size. Price **83c**
Shipping weight, 3 pounds.

PLAYING CARDS.

The Denver Plaid Back Cards.

No. 29C1862 Denver Plaid Back Waterproof Cards, round corners, double index, made in plaid, blue star, green star, Spanish wave and calico backs. Weight, per pack, 4 ounces.
Price, per pack .. **$0.06**
Per dozen .... **.70**
Per gross **8.00**
If by mail, postage extra, per pack, 5 cents.

Linen Finish Playing Cards.

No. 29C1864 Special Linen Finish Playing Cards, with round corners, double index, in large, plain figures, in a pretty back design. This same quality card is frequently sold at 25 cents per pack.
Price, per pack..... **10c**
Per dozen **$1.10**
If by mail, postage extra, per pack, 5 cents.

Waterproof Playing Cards.

No. 29C1866 Tally-Ho, Waterproof Finish, No. 9, half linen, round cornered, double index, extra enameled; large variety of handsomely designed backs in different tints and colors; **the best enameled card at the price in the market. Washable.** Price, per pack ... **$0.14**
Per dozen **1.65**
If by mail, postage extra, per pack, 5c.

Bicycle Cards.

No. 29C1868 Bicycle No. 808, superior ivory, enameled finish, a variety of appropriate backs, used largely by professional and other card players throughout the world. Weight, per pack, 4 ounces.
Price, per pack .... **$ 0.15**
Per dozen **1.80**
Per gross **21.60**
If by mail, postage extra, per pack, 4c.

Hart's Angel Back Squeezers No. 35.

No. 29C1873 Angel Backs. This is a splendid high class card, pure linen stock, waterproof enamel and thoroughly known. Used largely by professionals.
Price, per pack. **$0.17**
Per dozen **1.90**
Shipping weight, per pack, 4 ounces.

Congress Gold Edge Cards.

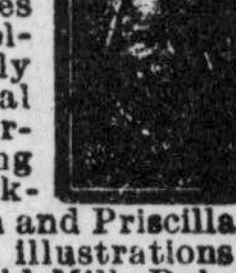

No. 29C1876 Congress Gold Edge Playing Cards. A new and artistic series of backs in high, rich colors, designed especially for card parties, social and home play. Can furnish them in the following backs: Rockwood Indian and Priscilla, as shown in illustrations; also The Old Mill, Rube, Butterfly, Chinese Dragon, etc. The highest grade quality linen. Put up in handsome case.
Price, per pack .. **$0.35**
Per dozen **3.90**
If by mail, postage extra, per pack, 5c.

Stage Cards.

Showing All the Well Known Actors.

No. 29C1877 The Stage Playing Cards, the most attractive edition of playing cards ever issued and beautiful court card designs showing portraits of world renowned celebrities of the stage. Gold edges. Finest linen stock, double enamel and highly finished. Put up in handsome, gold stamped cases. Price, per pack. **$0.38**
Per dozen packs **4.50**
If by mail, postage extra, per pack, 5c

Fortune Telling Cards.

No. 29C1879 The Nile Fortune Telling Cards. A new pack of fortune telling cards, tinted panel faces with the signification of each card printed on each face. Can be used by everyone. Sphinx backs, printed in high colors. Gold edges Best linen stock, double enameled. Instructions for fortune telling in each pack. Complete for playing all regular card games. Price, per pack... **$0.33**
Per dozen packs **3.40**
If by mail, postage extra, per pack, 5c

American Whist League.

No. 29C1882 American Whist League, Waterproof. Extra enameled, half linen stock. The best enameled card made. Weight, 4 ounces.
Price, per pack.... **20c**
If by mail, postage extra, 5 cents.

Barcelona Cards.

No. 29C1884 Barcelona, No. 49 Spanish Monte Cards, 48 cards in pack, assortment of backs and colors. Weight, packed, 3 ounces.
Price, per pack **32c**
If by mail, postage extra, 5 cents.

Pinochle Cards.

No. 29C1886 Pinochle Cards. Good quality linen finish stock, in a pretty designed back, full double deck from 9's up.
Price, per doz. packs, **$1.10**; per pack, **10c**
If by mail, postage extra, per pack, 5 cents.

No. 29C1888 Pinochle Cards. Full deck with sevens and eights; high grade linen cards.
Price, per pack **33c**
If by mail, postage extra, 5 cents.

Indestructible Rag Dolls.

No. 18R23148 Patent Face Indestructible Rag Doll, well shaped and proportioned. Has nicely made gingham dress in bright attractive colors, with bonnet to match. Has patent lifelike lithographed face, will not break or fade, making this the best appearing and most substantial rag doll obtainable, a tremendous value. Height, 14 inches.
Price........... **25c**
If mail shipment, postage extra, 10 cents.

No. 18R23150 Indestructible Rag Doll. A special value at a low price. The body is cotton stuffed, pink silesia, with removable shoes and stockings. Face is lithographed from life and is very attractive. The dress is of organdy, made very full and trimmed with lace and braid. Doll has muslin underclothes. Height, 16 inches.
Price........... **50c**
If mail shipment, postage extra, 13 cents.

Buster Brown Rag Doll.

No. 18R23160 Buster Brown Indestructible Rag Doll. A very fine reproduction of the well known character. The doll is dressed in a red suit with white collar, cuffs and belt; has Buster Brown cap of red and white, and a large black Windsor tie. This doll will be a delight to the children on account of the popularity of Buster Brown. Length, 15 inches.
Price........... **25c**
If mail shipment, postage extra, 10 cents.

No. 18R23216 Eskimo Doll. This is a very attractive and interesting papier mache jointed doll with bisque head. The entire body is covered with white fur, all parts of the body, arms, legs and head being movable, so that you can make it assume any position. Length, 10½ inches.
Price........... **25c**
If mail shipment, postage extra, 8 cents.

No. 18R23241 Unbreakable Baby Doll with knitted dress and full celluloid head. Made of a silesia covered body with very pretty full knitted dress and hat to match. The first time a full celluloid head doll has been offered for less than 50 cents. Height of doll, not including hat, 9½ inches. Shipping wt., 5 oz.
Our price........... **23c**

Talking Dolls.

No. 18R23300 Papa and Mamma Talking Doll, prettily dressed. Silesia body, with papier mache arms and removable shoes. Fitted with bisque head, with curly wig, open mouth and moving eyes. Neat lace trimmed dress with hat to match. By pulling one of two strings doll will either call papa or mamma, as desired. Size, including hat, 14½ inches. Shipping wt., 10 oz.
Price........... **25c**

No. 18R23304 Larger and Better Quality Papa and Mamma Doll than above. Silesia body, with papier mache arms, and shoes and stockings that come off. Good quality bisque head and curly wig, with sleeping eyes and open mouth, showing teeth. Very pretty dress with lace revere collar. Has hat to match. Doll will call papa or mamma, as desired. Size, including hat, 16½ inches. Shipping wt., 1½ lbs.
Price........... **48c**

Talking Doll, Only 95 Cents.

No. 18R23308 The Latest and Best Improved Papa and Mamma Dressed Doll. Made of good quality silesia, with papier mache arms, and with removable shoes and stockings. Has good quality bisque head with sleeping eyes, open mouth showing teeth, and extra quality curly wig. Fancy organdy dress, lace trimmed at bottom of skirt and around large revere collar. Good quality underwear, lace trimmed at edges. Large straw hat trimmed with ribbon and ostrich feathers. A feature of this doll is the patented concealed button under blouse; by pressing this button, the doll will alternately call papa and mamma. Entire length of doll, including hat, 19 inches. Shipping wt., 2¼ lbs. Price........... **95c**

Unbreakable Doll.

No. 18R23242 Indestructible Dressed Doll, Silesia body. Removable shoes and stockings. Good quality lace trimmed dress with bonnet to match. Genuine unbreakable Minerva metal head. A very pretty and at the same time unbreakable doll, which should meet with the approval of many mothers. Shipping wt., 12 oz.
Price........... **50c**

We Handle only the Genuine Imported All Red Rubber Toys.

ABSOLUTELY HARMLESS. WILL NOT WEAR OFF.

No. 18R23342 Flower Girl Doll, made of the best quality red India rubber. This doll has basket of flowers in one hand and a single flower in the other. Has German silver whistle which sounds when doll is squeezed. Size, 5¼ in.
Price........... **25c**
If mail shipment, postage extra, 3 cents.

No. 18R23343 Red Rubber Cat. A good and lifelike representation. Fitted with German silver whistle. Length from tip of tail to head, 5¾ inches. Height, 3¾ inches. Price........... **37c**
If mail shipment, postage extra, 5c.

No. 18R23344 Red Rubber Collie Dog. Made of pure red India rubber. Fitted with German silver whistle. Height, 4 inches. Lth., 4 in. Price........... **37c**
If mail shipment, 5 cents.

No. 18R23345 Water Squirting Elephant. Made of the best quality red India rubber. Has hollow trunk with hole so that it can be filled with water. By squeezing the body of the elephant the trunk will throw a thin stream of water over 25 feet. A new harmless plaything. Length from end of trunk to tail, 6¾ inches. Price........... **48c**
If mail shipment, postage extra, 5 cents.

Throws Water.

Special Value, Horse and Soldier for 50 Cents.

50c

No. 18R23348 Red Rubber Horse and Rider. Consists of two pieces, the horse being fitted with saddle in which the rider, made up in soldier costume, sits. Both pieces have German silver whistles, and are made of the best red rubber. Size, 8 inches.
Price, per set **50c**
If mail shipment, postage extra, 6 cents.

Plush Teddy Bears.

Plush bears are not a fad and have become one of the most staple articles in the realm of toys. Our sales are daily increasing, which is positive proof that the children like them. Our bears are absolutely the highest quality that money can buy, being of the celebrated German manufacture. They have no metal parts to harm the child and are practically indestructible. Made of finest quality imported bear plush and are absolutely true to life. All the joints are movable and bears can be made to assume countless comical positions. Each bear is fitted with comical voice. Color, natural cinnamon only. The larger the bear the better the proportion.

Catalog No.	Height, inches	Shipping wt., ounces	Price
18R23358	10	10	$0.63
18R23360	12	16	.98
18R23362	14	18	1.49
18R23364	16	24	1.98

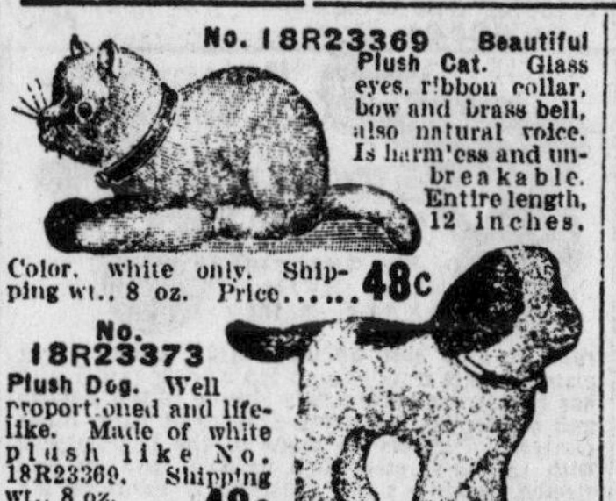

No. 18R23369 Beautiful Plush Cat. Glass eyes, ribbon collar, bow and brass bell, also natural voice. Is harmless and unbreakable. Entire length, 12 inches. Color, white only. Shipping wt., 8 oz. Price........... **48c**

No. 18R23373 Plush Dog. Well proportioned and lifelike. Made of white plush like No. 18R23369. Shipping wt., 8 oz.
Price........... **48c**

Bear Family, 19c.

No. 18R23366 The latest idea in bears. This family consists of one bear measuring 7¾ inches in height and two 4½ inches. The mother bear is cinnamon color and one baby cinnamon, the other white. Are made of prepared cotton on strong wire, the arms and legs being movable so that the bears will assume any position desired. These bears are practically indestructible. Come put up in a neat box. Price for the entire family of 3........... **19c**
If mail shipment, postage extra, 6c.

Genuine Minerva Metal Doll Heads at Reduced Prices.

These Doll Heads are imported from Germany. They combine the durability of sheet metal and the beauty of bisque, are light in weight, washable, and will not chip; will stand any reasonable wear. Small children cannot injure them; larger ones love them for their unequaled beauty. The eyes are clear and tender, head flexible at the bust, and fitted with sewing holes, making it easy to adjust and fasten them to body. Comes in sizes as follows:

Catalog No.	Height, inches	Inches Across Shoulders	Shipping Weight, ounces	Price
18R23432	3¼	2¾	3	13c
18R23434	3¾	3	3	19c
18R23436	4⅛	3⅜	8	25c
18R23438	4½	3⅝	8	31c
18R23440	5¼	4	9	37c
18R23442	6¼	4¾	14	52c
18R23444	6¾	5½	17	67c

Nos. 18R23442 and 18R23444 have glass eyes and open mouth, showing teeth.

Sewed Wig and Moving Glass Eyes.

The Metal Indestructible Minerva Doll Head with moving glass eyes. Open lips showing teeth, and very fine sewed curly wig. The metal heads, made of the best flexible sheet brass can be given to the smallest child with perfect safety, as the metal is covered with a pure harmless paint which is manufactured especially for the purpose. Comes in sizes as follows:

Catalog No.	Height, inches	Inches Across Shoulders	Shipping Weight, ounces	Price
18R23446	4⅛	3	9	37c
18R23448	4¾	3½	11	55c
18R23450	6⅛	3¾	14	79c
18R23452	6	4½	21	98c

IN ORDERING A DOLL HEAD TO FIT A BODY

be sure to measure the body from shoulder to shoulder across the top, as the sizes of our heads are measured across the shoulders in this manner. It is necessary that we have this measurement in order to fill your order correctly.

Very Finest Quality Kid Doll Bodies.

We sell only the very best make of kid doll bodies. Very full size, extra quality cork stuffed, strictly high grade, with riveted hip joints and bisque arms, shoes and stockings. This doll body is sure to please you, for it is the best obtainable. Comes in six sizes, as follows:

Catalog No.	Length, inches	Inches Across Shoulders	Shipping Weight, ounces	Price
18R23402	12½	3½	16	$0.47
18R23404	16	4	25	.69
18R23406	19	4¾	35	.88
18R23408	21½	5½	45	1.25
18R23412	23¾	6	60	1.48
18R23416	25½	7	75	1.98

Genuine Bisque Doll Heads.

IMMENSE VALUES, COMPARE OUR SIZES AND PRICES WITH OTHERS.

Bisque Doll Heads. Good quality, high grade bisque, with very beautiful molded faces, showing teeth, with two rows sewed wig and movable eyes. Either blondes or brunettes. Please mention choice. Comes in sizes as follows:

Catalog No.	Height, inches	Inches Across Shoulders	Shipping Weight, ounces	Price
18R23454	3⅞	3	9	$0.21
18R23456	4½	3½	13	.30
18R23458	5¼	4¼	15	.38
18R23460	6	5	17	.59
18R23462	7	5½	24	.88
18R23464	8¼	6¼	39	1.25
18R23466	9	6¾	42	1.65

Silesia Doll Bodies.

Hair Stuffed Pink Silesia Doll Bodies. This is a very high grade and satisfactory silesia body that will give best of wear and satisfaction; has bisque arms and removable shoes and stockings. Comes in the following sizes.

Catalog No.	Length, Inches	Inches Across Shoulders	Weight, oz.	Price
18R23418	12	3¼	10	$0.25
18R23420	15½	4	11	.35
18R23422	16½	4½	11	.48
18R23424	21	5½	25	.59
18R23426	23½	6	30	.75
18R23428	25½	6½	35	.89
18R23430	26¾	7¼	40	1.00

Celluloid Doll Heads.

Celluloid Doll Heads. The celluloid doll heads, until recently, have been extremely high priced. We have succeeded in making arrangements so that they are exceptionally cheap, considering the distinct advantage this head has over the ordinary doll head. The faces are beautifully molded. Made of the best celluloid, absolutely unbreakable, light as a feather and, at the prices we quote, will surely make them exceedingly popular. This style of celluloid doll head has painted hair and eyes, with open mouth showing teeth. Come in the following sizes:

Catalog No.	Height, inches	Inches Across Shoulders	Shipping Weight, ounces	Price
18R23500	3½	2¾	4	10c
18R23502	3¾	3	6	15c
18R23504	4¼	3½	6	25c
18R23506	5	4	8	33c
18R23508	6¼	5¼	11	45c

Kestner Bisque Doll Heads.

These are the highest grade bisque heads that are manufactured. The Kestner make of dolls is well known, being the best make of dolls in the world. All these heads are very lifelike in appearance, having movable eyes and open mouth, showing teeth. The highest grade full sewed wig with long curls side parted and tied on side with large silk ribbon bow. We furnish these dolls' heads in the following sizes:

Catalog No.	Height, inches	Inches Across Shoulders	Shipping Weight, ounces	Price
18R23482	4¾	3¼	16	$0.62
18R23484	5½	4	17	.89
18R23486	6½	4¼	22	1.19
18R23488	7½	4¾	32	1.43
18R23490	8¾	6¼	38	1.98

Bisque Finished Patented Celluloid Doll Heads.

This line of heads is by far the prettiest and most serviceable, being made of heavy celluloid and fitted with patented moving eyes that we absolutely guarantee will not fall out. They are unbreakable and bisque finished, pretty and lifelike. Wigs are of best quality, full sewed, waved and center parted, tied with ribbon bow at side. If you want the prettiest and most effective unbreakable celluloid doll head obtainable send us your order for the size you wish.

Catalog No.	Height, inches	Inches Across Shoulders	Shipping Weight, ounces	Price
18R23511	3¾	3	4	35c
18R23513	4¼	3¼	7	48c
18R23515	4¾	4	8	63c
18R23517	5½	4¾	13	85c
18R23519	6¼	5¼	15	98c

KINDERGARTEN EDUCATION AND AMUSEMENTS—ROLLER AND ICE SKATES.

Chautauqua Kindergarten Drawing Board and Writing Desk.

Without doubt the best drawing board and writing desk ever produced. Made entirely of hardwood, beautifully finished and varnished throughout, with heavy embossed, handsomely finished front. The blackboard proper is 19x20 inches, black enamel coated on one side to be used as drawing or blackboard, and the other side is finely finished for use as a writing desk. Inside of the desk has five compartments for letters, stationery, pens and drawing utensils. The top of the board contains the celebrated Chautauqua kindergarten revolving chart which contains the genuine Chautauqua subjects for instructing the young child in writing, drawing and general information. It comprises the entire alphabet in both capital and small letters in slant writing, vertical writing, German script and backhand printing, as well as the vowels, list of numbers, arithmetic signs, Roman numbers and numerical instruction for addition, subtraction, division and multiplication; various easily drawn household items, together with the name of each one; trees, animals, birds, fishes; a map of the world, face of a clock, fancy flower and scroll designs; faces, heads and general outlines; treble and base scales, together with the different kinds of notes and rests in music; train, engine and cars, mechanical engines and parts; views and landscapes; boats and marine; architectural subjects; nine lessons in shorthand; valuable interest rules and calculations; standard weights and measures; Bible quotations, and ending with the Lord's Prayer. Endorsed by the Chautauqua and without doubt the most complete, most perfect, the best board ever manufactured. When not in use can be folded against the wall, occupying a thickness of only 2½ inches. Size, 47x22 inches. Shipping wt., 21½ lbs. Regular price, $3.50.

No. 8R505 Our price........ $2.39

Combination Blackboard and Writing Desk.

A very substantial board, and although similar to the Chautauqua board is nowhere its equal. Made entirely of hardwood beautifully varnished. The blackboard proper is made of heavy sheet iron coated on one side with especially prepared black enamel and has on the other side an accurate map of the United States finely enameled in high colors. When the board is down it makes a fine writing desk and has three partitions for keeping paper, envelopes, notes, etc. The top board contains a revolving chart showing various styles of the alphabet, numbers, music, animals and other designs for the child to copy on the board. Will induce any child to study. When not in use can be folded so as to stand against the wall occupying a thickness of only 2½ inches. Height of board, 45 inches; width, 22 inches. Shipping wt., 17 lbs.

No. 8R506 Our price.......... $1.29

The Universal Spelling Board.

One of the most entertaining and educating articles for children ever put on the market; should have a place in every family having small children. The board has about fifty-six lettered blocks which are made of hardwood and very strong and serviceable. Size of board, 13½ inches long by 9½ inches wide. Shipping wt., 32 oz.

No. 8R585 Price................ 70c

Child's Folding Combination Writing Desk and Blackboard.

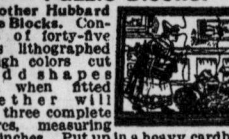

Without doubt the most unique, handy and complete writing desk and blackboard ever manufactured. The desk proper is 17x18 inches on top, hinge cover, fancy red enamel finish writing desk with reversible blackboard. Has desk slope top and is fitted inside with drawer for paper, pencils, pens, crayons, etc. Height, 26 inches. Made of the best weathered oak, natural finish. Folds up completely for shipping and can be set up in a moment. Very best in every respect and a high class article. Shipping wt., 10 lbs.

No. 8R507 Price................ 98c

Puzzle Blocks.

Old Mother Hubbard Puzzle Blocks. Consists of forty-five blocks lithographed in high colors cut in odd shapes which when fitted together will make three complete pictures, measuring 13x9 inches. Put up in a heavy cardboard box with lithographed cover, showing one of the designs that can be made with these blocks. Teach your children to put these parts together and then tell the story. Shipping wt., 20 oz.

No. 8R598 Price 23c

Story Sewing Cards.

One of the most popular and instructive pastimes for girls. Consists of twelve perforated story cards representing the leading children's stories, as follows: Mother Goose, Bo Peep, Red Riding Hood, Santa Claus, This Little Pig Went to Market, and several others equally as well known. Five assorted colors of thread are included in the box. The lines on the cards are to be sewed as represented by the printed dots. After this is completed, tell the child the story, if not already informed. Big seller. Shipping wt., 6 oz.

No. 8R660 Price................ 19c

Architectural Building Blocks.

98c

Fine Quality Hardwood Architectural Building Blocks. This style is recognized to be the best of its kind on the market. The set consists of about 150 various shaped blocks, some of which are embossed in two colors, others are turned so as to represent pillars, etc. In all, as complete a set of blocks as can be made, and one with which hundreds of designs can be made. Put up in heavy wooden box with sliding cover. Size, 9x13½ inches. Printed colored designs in each box. Shipping wt., 5 lbs.

No. 8R587 Price............... 98c

Architectural Building Blocks, same style and manufacture as above, but with only about 110 blocks, some of which are smaller in size than those in set No. 8R587. In strong wooden box measuring 8x10¾ inches. Printed designs in each outfit. Shipping wt., 3½ lbs.

No. 8R588 Price.............. 48c

Alphabet Blocks.

A very handsome set of alphabet blocks entirely new. The animals, letters, etc., on the four sides are burnt in so as to represent a good imitation of burnt wood work. On the two other sides are embossed letters and animals. Each block measures 1¾ inches in diameter. Set consists of thirty blocks, in heavy cardboard box with handsomely lithographed Christmas scene on cover. Shipping wt., 3 lbs.

No. 8R591 Price............... 49c

Alphabet Blocks. An entirely new set of thirty-five pieces, each measuring 1 inch in diameter, have two sides embossed with letters and the four other sides represent animals, figures, etc., finished in very high colors. In heavy cardboard box with handsome picture lithographed on cover. Shipping wt., 16 oz.

No. 8R592 Price 21c

ROLLER SKATES

No. 6R5821 Improved Extension Sidewalk Skates. For children and youths. Shipping wt., 42 oz. Price per pair.............................. 37c

Men's and Women's Extension Skates.

This extension skate has tops, trucks, clamps and stamping of the best cold rolled Swedish steel, finely finished. Plain bearings, heavy steel rolls. Regularly sold for $1.00 to $1.25. The skate extends to fit all sizes from 8½ to 11½ inches.

No. 6R5822 Men's Skate, with toe clamp and single heel strap, as illustrated. Price, per pair......................... 80c

No. 6R5823 Women's Skate, same as above described, with toe clamp and high heel strap as illustrated. Price, per pair....... 82c

Ball Bearing Extension Skates.

Same as above but full ball bearing. Wt., 4½ lbs.

No. 6R5825 Men's Ball Bearing Extension Skate. Price, per pair............ $2.20

No. 6R5826 Women's Ball Bearing Extension Skate. Price, per pair...... $2.24

Shipping wt. of extension skates, 64 oz.

Ball Bearing Half Clamp Rink Skates.

Ball Bearing Men's Rink Skates. Are made of the very best Swedish cold rolled steel. Foot plate is strengthened by a brace which is riveted to it, extending from the toe clamps to the back of the heel. Trucks are oscillating, with best rubber cushions, and turn in 3-foot circle. Best steel rolls. Give size of shoe worn, also length of shoe in inches. Weight, 75 ounces.

No. 6R5828 Price, per pair...... $2.65

No. 6R5831 Same as above, for women. Price, per pair...................... $2.64

Knight Roller Skates.

BRACE

The Improved Knight Roller Skate is the strongest, easiest running and best finished skate made. Foot plate is made from cold rolled machine steel, and has a rib truss brace firmly riveted to the bottom and connected with both front and back roller carriers. Carriers are made on the box pattern with the solid steel axle passing through and riveted to lower side. Cushion is made of the finest quality of rubber.

Rollers have triple thick rims. All parts of this skate are highly polished and nickel plated, suitable for both ladies and gentlemen. Give size of shoe and state whether for ladies' or men's shoe. Weight, 94 ounces.

No. 6R5837 Knight Roller Skates. Price, per pair.......................... $3.64

Rollers.

No. 6R5840 Maple Rolls. Shipping wt., per set, 8 oz. Price, per set of eight .... 12c. Postage, per set of eight, 8 cents.

No. 6R5841 Cast Iron Rolls. Plain bearing for our No. 6R5821 skate. Price, per set of eight rolls ...... 13c. Postage, per set, 18c.

No. 6R5844 Plain Bearing Steel Rolls. Price, per set of eight........ 43c

No. 6R5845 Steel Ball Bearing Rolls. Price, per set of eight 74c. Ball bearing rolls will not fit plain bearing skates. Prices are for wheels only. Postage, per set of eight, 30 cents.

No. 6R5848 3-16-inch Steel Balls. Per 100, 30c; per dozen........... 5c. Postage, per doz., 1c.

No. 6R5850 Roller Skate Keys, per dozen, 25c; each . 3c. Postage, each, 2 cents.

Skaters' Ankle Braces, 49c.

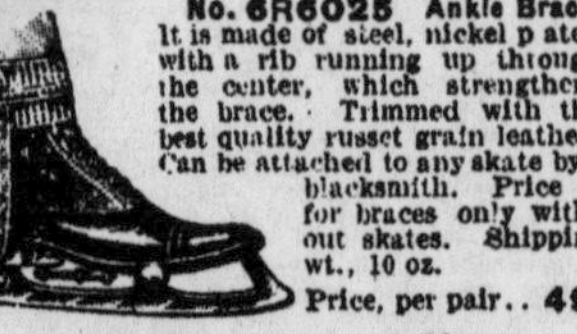

No. 6R6025 Ankle Brace. It is made of steel, nickel plated with a rib running up through the center, which strengthens the brace. Trimmed with the best quality russet grain leather. Can be attached to any skate by a blacksmith. Price is for braces only without skates. Shipping wt., 10 oz. Price, per pair.. 49c

Skate Straps and Keys.

No. 6R6030 Skate Straps, 21 inches long, ⅝-inch wide, made of good heavy black leather with buckle. Price, per pair........ 9c

No. 6R6031 24-inch Skate Straps, same as above. Price, per pair................ 11c

If mail shipment, postage extra, per pair, 3 cents.

No. 6R6033 Ice Skate Keys, nicely nickel plated. Price, each...................... 5c

If mail shipment, postage extra, each 2 cents.

ICE SKATES

When Ordering Ice Skates Give Length of Shoe in Inches.

Star Club Skates.

No. 6R5950 The runner of this skate is made of the very best cold rolled cast steel. Sizes, from 8 to 12 inches. Shipping wt., 34 to 40 oz. Price, per pair.............. 54c

When ordering give length of shoe in inches.

No. 6R5954 Hardened Skate. The steel used in this skate contains a higher percentage of carbon and the runner is carefully hardened and highly polished. Sizes, 8 to 12 inches. Shipping wt., 35 to 50 oz. Price, per pair.. 87c

When ordering give length of shoe in inches.

Racing Skates, $2.32.

No. 6R5965 Full Racer. Tops are made of selected close grain beechwood, varnished, with highly nickel plated toe, heel and center plates. Runners are made of high grade cast steel, ⅛ inch thick, and are bored, making the lightest possible skate; made with 14, 16 or 18-inch runners. Shipping wt., 40 to 48 oz. Price, per pair....................... $2.32

When ordering give length of runners desired.

Full Rocker Skates, $1.34.

No. 6R5977 Full Rocker Skate. Tops are made of selected beechwood and runners from best rolled steel. We furnish straps with every pair. Sizes, 9½ to 12 inches. Shipping wt., 36 to 48 oz. Price, per pair........................ $1.34

When ordering give length of shoe in inches.

Best Steel Hockey Skates.

No. 6R5981 Hockey Skate. All clamp. Runners best quality steel, all pairs polished and nickel plated. Lengths, 10, 10½, 11, 11½, and 12 inches. Shipping wt., 46 to 54 oz. Price, per pair....................... $1.10

When ordering give length of shoe in inches.

Tubular Racing Skates, $4.65.

No. 6R5987 Finest skate made. ⅛-inch tool steel runners, tubular caps and frames. Light weight, full nickel plated. Lengths, 10, 10½, 11, 11½ and 12 inches. Shipping wt., 45 to 50 oz. Price........................ $4.65

When ordering give length of shoe in inches.

High Grade Hockey Skates.

No. 6R5985 Hockey Skate. All clamp, welded and tempered ribbed runners with beveled edges. All parts are highly polished and heavily nickel plated. This is the best and finest finished skate made. Lengths, 10, 10½, 11, 11½ and 12 inches. Shipping wt., 43 to 52 oz. Price, per pair......................... $2.60

When ordering give length of shoe in inches.

Ladies' Strap Skates.

No. 6R5990 Ladies' Strap Skate. Runner is made of cold rolled steel highly polished. Sizes, 8 to 11½ inches. Shipping wt., 32 to 40 oz. Price, per pair.......................... 70c

When ordering give length of shoe in inches.

Ladies' Club Skates.

No. 6R5992 Ladies' Club Skate. The runner of this skate is made of cold rolled carbon steel. Heel strap is the best oak tanned russet grain leather, with tongue buckles and nickel plated heel bands. Sizes, 8 to 10½ inches. Shipping wt., 36 to 44 ozs. Price, per pair 94c

When ordering give length of shoe in inches.

Ladies' Best Club Skates.

No. 6R5993 Hardened runners, full nickel plated. The runner of this skate is made of cold rolled steel. Heel strap, best quality oak tanned russet grain leather, with tongue buckles and nickel plated heel bands. Size, 8 to 10½ inches. Shipping wt., 36 to 44 oz. Price, per pair........................ $1.20

When ordering give length of shoe in inches.

Children's Skates, 34 Cents.

No. 6R6012 The runners are so wide apart that a child can stand on them with perfect ease. They are adjustable and can be changed from a 6-inch to an 8-inch skate. Shipping wt., 24 oz. Price, per pair.......................... 34c

No. 6R6029 Skate Sharpener. It concaves a skate runner. The files are cut on four sides—two flat sides and two convex. It is nickel plated. Price.................................. 12c

If mail shipment, postage extra, 5 cents.

High Grade Jointed Kid Body Dolls.

With riveted joints, fine bisque heads, very pretty faces, sewed wigs, new style middle part. These dolls have large fat bodies, finely proportioned heads, riveted joints that enable the doll to assume any position. We list this doll in six different sizes. The larger the size of doll the better featured is the face and better proportioned body. Moving eyes.

No.	Size, inches	Shipping Weight	Price, each
18G23040	15	2 lbs.	$0.49
18G23044	17	2 lbs.	.73
18G23048	21½	3 lbs.	.98
18G23052	23½	4 lbs.	1.29
18G23056	25	5 lbs.	1.58
18G23060	27½	6 lbs.	1.87

Our Special Cork Stuffed Kid Body Dolls.

Has very fine, extra large bisque head, moving eyes; has sewed wig with new style hair dressing, parted in center and tied with bows of ribbon. The body has riveted hips, arms and elbow joints, also kid legs fitted with removable shoes and stockings. We list this doll in four sizes, all excellent values. The larger the doll the better featured the face and better the proportions of body.

No.	Size, inches	Shipping Weight	Price, each
18G23064	17	2 lbs.	$1.19
18G23068	21	2½ lbs.	1.73
18G23072	23	3 lbs.	2.37
18G23076	26	4 lbs.	2.83

Genuine Kestner Kid Body Dolls.

This well known make has been on the market for years. Face is full and perfect and the best doll in workmanship and material. Has hips, knees, shoulders and elbows riveted, papier mache legs fitted with removable colored lace stockings and slippers to match; arms of bisque. The Kestner bisque head is fitted with best quality sewed wig, has moving eyes. We can furnish this Kestner kid body doll in five sizes. The larger size dolls come proportionately larger in body and head.

No.	Size, inches	Shipping Weight	Price each
18G23080	18	2½ lbs.	$1.75
18G23084	20	3 lbs.	2.48
18G23088	23½	3½ lbs.	3.47
18G23092	26	4 lbs.	3.99
18G23096	28½	5 lbs.	5.00

Metal Head Unbreakable Dolls Are Best.

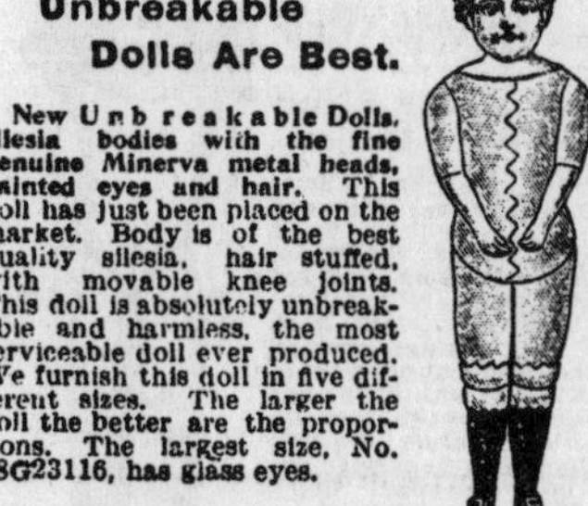

New Unbreakable Dolls. Silesia bodies with the fine genuine Minerva metal heads, painted eyes and hair. This doll has just been placed on the market. Body is of the best quality silesia, hair stuffed, with movable knee joints. This doll is absolutely unbreakable and harmless, the most serviceable doll ever produced. We furnish this doll in five different sizes. The larger the doll the better are the proportions. The largest size, No. 18G23116, has glass eyes.

No.	Size, inches	Shipping Weight	Price, each
18G23100	11½	1 lb.	25c
18G23104	14	1½ lbs.	44c
18G23108	15½	2 lbs.	59c
18G23112	17	3 lbs.	67c
18G23116	21	4 lbs.	79c

Indestructible Dolls.

No. 18G23148 Indestructible Rag Doll; well shaped and proportioned rag doll, with gingham dress, in bright and attractive colors, and bonnet to match. Indestructible cloth face of natural appearance. Size, 15 inches. Shipping weight, 10 ounces. Price 25c

No. 18G23156 Red Ridinghood Indestructible Doll, like above, but larger. Dressed in the latest blouse effect, dress being made of a good quality flannelette with lace and ribbon trimmings and ribbon belt. The doll has a red ridinghood bonnet of material to match dress. This doll being unbreakable and of natural appearance, will be a source of delight to any child. Shipping weight, 2 pounds. Length, 18½ inches. Price $1.00

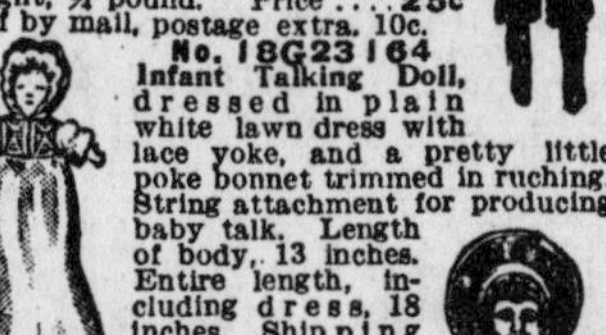

No. 18G23160 Buster Brown Indestructible Rag Doll. A very fine imitation of the Buster Brown you read about. The doll is dressed in a red suit with white collar, cuffs and belt, has Buster Brown cap of red and white, and a large black Windsor tie. This doll will be a delight to the children on account of the popularity of Buster Brown. Length, 15 inches. Shipping weight, ¾ pound. Price 25c
If by mail, postage extra, 10c.

No. 18G23164 Infant Talking Doll, dressed in plain white lawn dress with lace yoke, and a pretty little poke bonnet trimmed in ruching. String attachment for producing baby talk. Length of body, 13 inches. Entire length, including dress, 18 inches. Shipping weight, 12 ounces. Price 25c

No. 18G23168 Indestructible Farmer Boy Doll, rag body with removable shoes and stockings, dressed in red jumper and blue overalls, has celluloid face with white lawn cap; both overalls and jacket are removable, being fastened by fancy agate buttons. Size, 13½ inches. Shipping weight, 10 ounces.
Price 50c

Unbreakable Leather Doll.

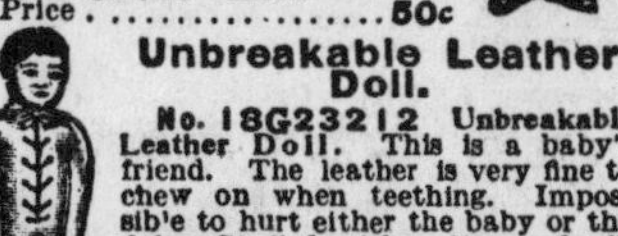

No. 18G23212 Unbreakable Leather Doll. This is a baby's friend. The leather is very fine to chew on when teething. Impossible to hurt either the baby or the doll. Stuffed with cotton and will always retain its shape. This doll will last baby and also baby's brother. Coloring matter warranted not to come off. Length, 12½ inches. Shipping weight, 15 ounces.
Price 40c

The Knit Clown Dolls.

No. 18G23224 Knit Clown Doll. Stuffed body with voice, made by pressing on body. Dressed in high colored knit suits with little bell trimmings. These knit dolls are always appreciated by the children and will not break. Size, 15 inches. Shipping weight, 10 ounces.
Price 25c

No. 18G23228 Knit Clown Doll. With stuffed body and has voice. This is a much larger size throughout, more expensively dressed in knit costume. It is a very desirable and unbreakable doll. Dresses are made in fancy colors. Size, 17 inches. Shipping weight, 15 ounces. Price...............40c

Dressed Dolls.

No. 18G23280 Dressed Doll with jointed arms and hips. Has pretty gingham dress trimmed with lace, also hat to match. Removable shoes and stockings. Height, 16 inches. Shipping weight, 12 ounces.
Price 25c

No. 18G23284 Pretty Dressed Doll full jointed throughout, with bisque head, moving eyes and natural curly wig, stylishly dressed in colored material under mull, with lace insertion. Has fancy mull hat to match dress, and removable shoes and stockings. Height, 20 inches. Shipping weight. 2 pounds

Price 75c

Unbreakable Dolls, Metal Heads, with Wigs.

Silesia Body Dolls with fine Minerva metal head with curly wig and glass eyes. These dolls have been recently placed on the market and have at once been a decided success. Every mother is probably familiar with the Minerva metal head, and combining this feature with a fine hair stuffed silesia body makes an unbreakable doll and at the same time a very pretty doll. These dolls, with the Minerva heads, flowing curls and glass eyes, with silesia body we furnish in the following sizes:

No.	Size, inches	Shipping Weight	Price, each
18G23120	14¾	1½ lbs.	$0.50
18G23124	18	2 lbs.	.75
18G23126	21¼	3 lbs.	1.00

NOTE.—We claim for this doll special value which cannot be equaled elsewhere.

Dressed Dolls.

No. 18G23286 Extra Large Dressed Doll, full jointed. Has high grade bisque head with moving eyes and natural curly wig. Is handsomely dressed with pretty colored satin dress, trimmed with lace at the yoke and the skirt. All of the doll's garments, including shoes and stockings, can be removed. Has very prettily trimmed hat with lace streamers to match dress. Height, 22 inches. Shipping weight, 3 pounds.
Price, .$1.00

No. 18G23288 Dressed Doll, full jointed body with pretty bisque head, moving eyes, long curly wig and open mouth, showing teeth. Fine satin dress beautifully designed, stylishly trimmed. All garments can be removed, including satin straw braid hat trimmed with lace. A very pretty and natural appearing doll. Height, 23½ inches. Shipping weight, 4 pounds.
Price $1.50

Knock About Dolls With Minerva Metal Heads.

No. 18G23292 Unbreakable Knock About Doll. Has genuine Minerva metal head, dressed with finely crocheted dress and cap to match. Body is of silesia. Size, 11 inches. Shipping weight, 1 pound. Price 59c

No. 18G23296 Minerva Knock About Doll. Has genuine Minerva metal head, dressed with fancy crocheted dress, trimmed with ribbon and has large crocheted hat to match. Body is of silesia. Has imitation stockings and removable shoes. Size, 13 inches. Shipping weight, 1 pound. Price............79c

No. 18G23304 Papa and Mama Dressed Dolls. With bisque Mama Dressed Dolls. With bisque head, curly hair, moving eyes, and stuffed unbreakable body. Dressed in very pretty fancy sateen trimmed gown, shoes and stockings. When you pull the cord, the doll repeats papa and mama. Fancy sateen dress, hat to match. Length, 16 inches. Shipping weight, 1½ pounds. Price..............50c

No. 18G3300 Papa and Mama Doll, like above, but smaller, 13 inches high, weight 1 pound.
Price..................................30c

Rubber Dolls, Figures and Animals.

White Rubber Dolls. Dressed in knit suits and hats in assorted colors. Larger dolls are better proportioned.

No.	Size, inches	Postage, extra	Price
18G23312	8	4 cts.	$0.25
18G23316	10½	6 cts.	.50
18G23320	11¾	8 cts.	.75
18G23324	13¼	10 cts.	1.00

No. 18G23328 Red Rubber Fat Boy. Made of best quality red rubber which will not wear off. Has German silver whistle. Size, 5 inches. Price 25c
If by mail, postage extra, 5 cents.

No. 18G23332 Red Rubber Peasant Girl. Made of finest quality red rubber, the coloring of which will not wear off. Has German silver whistle. Size, 6½ inches. Price 28c
If by mail, postage extra. 5 cents.

No. 18G23340 Red Rubber Doll. Has German silver whistle. Height, 9¾ inches. This is a good $1.00 value.
Price 75c
If by mail, postage, extra, 10c.

No. 18G23344 Red Rubber Doll. Has German silver whistle. Very large, fat body. Height, 11 inches. As sold elsewhere for $1.50.
Price $1.00
If by mail, postage extra, 12c.

No. 18G23348 Red Rubber Horse and Rider. Consists of two pieces, the horse being fitted with saddle in which the rider, made up in soldier costume, sits. Both pieces have German silver whistles, and are made of the best red rubber. Size, 8 inches.
Price, per set.......50c
If by mail, postage extra, 5 cents.

No. 18G23352 Red Rubber Elephant. Made of best quality red rubber, the coloring of which will not wear off. Has German silver whistle. Size, 6 inches.
Price 45c
If by mail, postage extra, 6 cents.

No. 18G23356 India Rubber Cat. Made of the best quality India rubber, which will not wear off. Fitted with German silver whistle. Size, 6 inches.
Price........45c
If by mail, postage extra, 6 cents.

All the Go—The Roosevelt Bears.

These bears are made of the finest imported bear plush and closely resemble the little cubs. The head, arms and legs are jointed in such a manner that any position is possible. Great fun for large and small. Come in four sizes, cinnamon color only.

No. 18G23358 Size, 10 inches.
Price........89c

No. 18G23360 Size, 12½ inches.
Price........$1.39

No. 18G23362 Size, 14 inches.
Price........$1.95

No. 18G23364 Size, 16 inches.
Price $2.59

NOTE—The larger the size, the better proportioned are the bears.

Kid Doll Bodies.

Kid Doll Bodies. Very full size, extra quality cork stuffed, high grade kid bodies, with riveted hip joint and bisque arms, shoes and stockings. This is a very high grade and satisfactory body. Comes in sizes as follows:

No.	Length	Across Shoulders	Shipping weight	Price
18G23402	12½ ins.	3½ ins.	15 ozs.	$0.35
18G23404	16 ins.	4 ins.	25 ozs.	.58
18G23406	19 ins.	4¾ ins.	35 ozs.	.79
18G23408	21½ ins.	5½ ins.	45 ozs.	1.00
18G23412	23¾ ins.	6 ins.	60 ozs.	1.26
18G23414	24½ ins.	6¼ ins.	65 ozs.	1.50
18G23416	25½ ins.	7 ins.	75 ozs.	1.75

Silesia Doll Bodies.

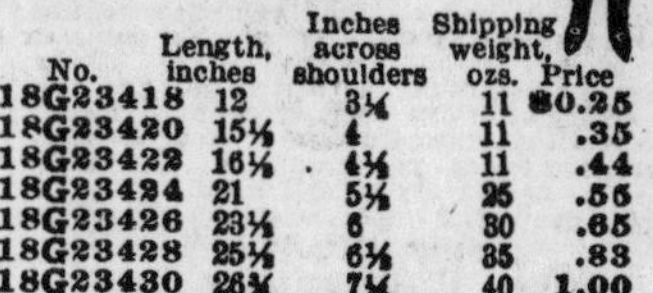

Hair Stuffed Pink Silesia Doll Bodies. This is a very high grade and satisfactory silesia body that will give best of wear and satisfaction; has bisque arms and removable shoes and stockings. Comes in the following sizes:

No.	Length, inches	Inches across shoulders	Shipping weight, ozs.	Price
18G23418	12	3¼	11	$0.25
18G23420	15½	4	11	.35
18G23422	16½	4½	11	.44
18G23424	21	5½	25	.56
18G23426	23½	6	30	.65
18G23428	25½	6½	35	.83
18G23430	26¾	7¼	40	1.00

Our Indestructible Metal Doll Heads at Reduced Prices.

These Doll Heads are imported from Germany. They combine the durability of sheet metal and the beauty of bisque, are light in weight, washable, and will not chip; will stand any reasonable wear. Small children cannot injure them; larger ones love them for their unequaled beauty. The eyes are clear and tender, head flexible at the bust, and fitted with sewing holes, making it easy to adjust and fasten them to body. Come in sizes as follows:

No.	Height, inches	Inches across sh'lders	Shipping weight, ozs.	Price
18G23432	3⅜	2¾	5	16c
18G23434	3¾	3	6	22c
18G23436	4⅛	3⅜	8	30c
18G23438	4½	3⅝	9	35c
18G23440	5	4	10	40c
18G23442	6¼	4½	12	58c
18G23444	6¾	5½	14	76c

Nos. 18G23442 and 18G23444 have glass yes and open mouths, showing teeth.

Sewed Wig and Moving Glass Eyes.

The Metal Indestructible Doll Head with moving glass eyes. Open lips showing teeth, and very fine sewed curly wig. The metal heads, made of the best flexible sheet brass can be given to the smallest child with perfect safety, as the metal is covered with a pure wholesome paint which is manufactured especially for the purpose. Come in sizes as follows:

No.	Height, inches	Inches across sh'lders	Shipping weight, ozs.	Price
18G23446	4	3	9	$0.38
18G23448	4¾	3½	12	.62
18G23450	5¾	4⅜	14	.83
18G23452	6⅝	4⅞	16	1.00

PLAYING CARDS.

No. 18G22200 Special Linen Finish Playing Cards. With round corners, double index, in large, plain figures, in a pretty back design. This same quality card is frequently sold at 25 cents per pack. Price, 3 packs for........29c
If by mail, postage extra, per pack, 4 cents.

No. 18G22204 Airship Superior Enameled Waterproof Playing Cards. With high radium luster finish. This card has a perfect slip and will not swell. We guarantee it equal to any card on the market. Assorted backs.
Price, 2 packs for........25c
If by mail, postage extra, per pack, 4 cents.

"Bee" Squeezer Playing Cards.

No 18G22212 This is a new Card and very popular in plaid backs, for professionals; also four other assorted design backs, made of pure linen stock. A very satisfactory card.
Per dozen, $1.88; 2 packs for........35c
If by mail, postage extra, per pack, 4 cents.

Angel Backs Squeezer Cards.

No. 18G22216 Angel Backs. This is a splendid high class card. Pure linen stock. Waterproof enamel and thoroughly known as the Squeezers. Used largely by professionals.
Price, 3 packs for 50c; per pack 18c
If by mail, postage extra, per pack, 4 cents.

Art Series Gold Edge Cards.

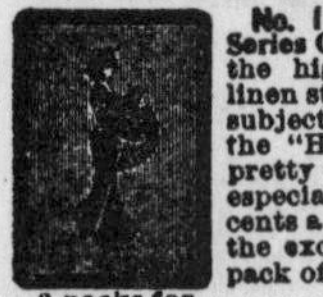

No. 18G22222 The Art Series Gold Edge Cards. Made of the highest grade waterproof linen stock with gold edges. The subjects, the "Japanese" and the "Holland Girls," are very pretty designs. This card was especially designed to sell at 50 cents a pack. We offer them at the exceptionally low price per pack of........29c
2 packs for........55c
If by mail, postage extra, per pack, 4 cents.

Fortune Telling Cards.

No. 18G22228 The Nile Fortune Telling Cards. A new pack of fortune telling cards. Tinted panel faces with the signification of each card printed on each face. Can be used by everyone. Sphinx backs, printed in high colors. Gold edges. Best linen stock, double enameled. Instructions for fortune telling in each pack. Complete for playing all regular card games. Price, per pack........34c
2 packs for........67c
If by mail, postage extra, per pack, 5 cents.

No. 18G22238 Pinochle Cards. Good quality, linen finish stock, in a pretty designed back. Full double deck from 9's up.
Price, 2 packs for 25c; per pack........14c
If by mail, postage extra, per pack, 5 cents.

Bunco.

No. 18G22280 Bunco is the great Card game that is having a wonderful sale. After once playing the game it fascinates and interests one and all. The game is a radical departure in get up and play from any game in the market, strictly scientific, yet highly amusing. Scientific as cribbage and as interesting as bridge whist, embodying all the features of playing card games. Easy to learn, interesting to both young and old. The cards are of the finest ivory enamel finish.
Price, per pack........35c
If by mail, postage extra, per pack, 5 cents.

Flinch, the Popular New Card Game.

No. 18G22284 Flinch. More simple than authors, more scientific than whist. Something entirely new in card games. Each pack consists of 150 cards, finest quality of stock. The combinations resulting, while simple, are so intricate that the game has been pronounced by many to be more scientific than whist. Enjoyed by old and young alike.
Price, 2 packs for 69c; per pack....35c
If by mail, postage extra, per pack, 5 cents.

Bridge Whist Set.

No. 18G22292 The standard game of Bridge Whist, consists of two full sets of enameled playing cards, full directions and 25 score cards. Put up in telescope box.
Price, 2 sets for 69c; per set........35c
If by mail, postage extra, 6 cents.

No. 18G22304 Playing Card Set. Book form. Fine seal grain leather, closes with fine gilt metal clasp. Interior is provided at the back with a gilt metal receptacle to securely hold a deck of cards. Contains pack of gilt edge cards. Size, 3/4x2 5/8x3 7/8 inches. Price........49c
If by mail, postage extra, 6c.

Poker Chips.

No. 18G22316 Composition Poker Chips. Ivory finish. Warranted not to chip or warp, 1 1/2 inches in diameter; put up 100 in a box assorted as follows: 50 white, 25 red and 25 blue, or solid color. State assortment wanted. Shipping weight, 32 ounces.
Price, per box of 100........$0.38
Per 1,000........3.75

No. 18G22320 New Design Poker Chip. Known as the Eclipse. Made of composition with ivory finish. 1 1/2 inches in diameter. A unique pattern. Come put up in boxes of 100, assorted 50 white, 25 red and 25 blue. Shipping weight, per box, 32 ounces.
Price, per 1,000, $5.25; per box of 100, 56c

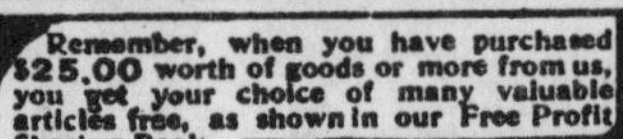
Remember, when you have purchased $25.00 worth of goods or more from us, you get your choice of many valuable articles free, as shown in our Free Profit Sharing Book.

No. 18G22324 The American Eagle. A beautifully engraved design on composition ivory; warranted not to chip or warp. 1 1/2 inches in diameter. Put up 100 in a box, assorted as follows: 50 white, 25 red and 25 blue or solid colors. State assortment wanted. Shipping weight, per box, 30 ounces. Price, per box of 100.....$0.65
Per 1,000........6.25

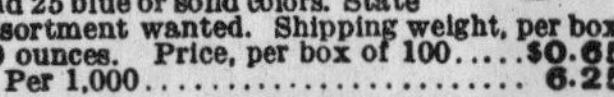

No. 18G22328 Good Luck Engraved Poker Chip. Ivory finish. Warranted not to chip or break with ordinary usage. 1 1/2 inches in diameter. Put up 100 to the box; assorted, 50 white, 25 red and 25 blue. A new and popular pattern. Shipping weight, per box of 100, 32 ounces.
Price, per 1,000, $6.60; per box of 100, 68c

Special Design Poker Chips.

No. 18G22332 Special Design Engraved Poker Chip. This is a very neat and elegant design. Made of the best quality composition; stack even and will not break easily. Size, 1 1/2 inches in diameter. Assorted 100 in box as follows: 50 white, 25 blue and 25 red. Shipping weight, 30 ounces.
Price, per box of 100........$0.70
Per 1,000........6.75

Inlaid Unbreakable Poker Chips for Professional Use.

No. 18G22336 Fleur de Lis Design. Inlaid celluloid on highest grade of composition ivory. 1 9-16 inches in diameter and put up 100 to the box; assorted, 50 white, 25 red, 25 blue; or can be ordered in the solid colors, 100 to the box, red, white, blue, yellow, pink or brown. State assortment wanted. Absolutely perfect in every respect. Warranted to stack perfectly and used a great deal by professionals. Shipping weight, 34 ounces.
Price, per box of 100........$2.05
Per 1,000........20.00

No. 18G22340 Maltese Cross Design. Inlaid celluloid of best quality composition ivory. A unique and popular pattern. Guaranteed to stack perfectly. This chip comes in white, red, blue, yellow, pink and brown. State assortment wanted. Put up 100 to the box. Used by card players and professionals. Shipping weight per 100, 34 ounces.
Price, per box of 100........$2.05
Per 1,000........20.00
Note. We do not sell less than 100 of a color.

Unbreakable Poker Chips.

No. 18G22344 Light, Noiseless and Easy to Handle. Unbreakable poker chips are made by a new process. Highly polished; look just as good as the compositions but are light and better than rubber; stack evenly and outwear any other kind made. Put up in assorted boxes 25 red, 25 blue and 50 white, or in solid colors 100 to box, red, white, blue and orange. State assortment wanted. Shipping weight, 20 ounces.
Price, per box of 100........$0.45
Per 1,000........4.00

Dice.

No. 18G22348 Bone Dice. Square corners. No. 6. Size, 1/2 inch. Price, per dozen....$0.12
Per gross........1.35
If by mail, postage extra, per dozen, 3 cents.

No. 18G22352 Bone Dice. Square corners. No. 8. Size, 9-16 inch.
Price, per dozen........20c
If by mail, postage extra, per dozen, 6 cents.

No. 18G22356 Bone Dice. Square corners. No. 9. Size, 5-8 inch.
Price, per dozen........30c
If by mail, postage extra, per dozen, 6 cents.

No. 18G22360 Bone Dice. Square corners. No. 10. Size, 11-16 inch.
Price, per dozen........45c
If by mail, postage extra, per dozen, 6 cents.

Vegetable Ivory Dice.

No. 18G22364 This is the latest style in dice. Is made of the pure ivory nut; is absolutely perfect. Size, 11-16 inch.
Price, per set (five dice to a set)........25c
2 sets for........46c
If by mail, postage extra, per set, 3 cents.

Celluloid Dice.

No. 18G22368 Celluloid Dice. Cream color, with colored spots. Size, 5/8 inch.
Price, per set (five dice to a set)........33c
2 sets for........61c
If by mail, postage extra, per set, 3 cents.

Transparent Celluloid Dice.

No. 18G22372 Made of pure transparent celluloid. Are as clear as glass. Colors, green, magenta or saffron. State color wanted. Put up five in a box.
Price, per set (five dice to a set)........47c
2 sets for........90c
If by mail, postage extra, per set, 3 cents.

Celluloid Poker Dice.

No. 18G22376 Representing Ace, King, Queen, Jack, Ten, and Nine Spots. Fine ivory finished celluloid. Perfect goods. Size, 5/8 inch. Set of five dice.
Price, per set of five..42c
2 sets for........80c
If by mail, postage extra, per set, 4 cents.

No. 18G22380 Vegetable Ivory Poker Dice. The five represent ace, king, queen, jack, ten and nine spots; all enameled. Size, 5/8 inch. Price, per set of five........25c
2 sets for........45c
If by mail, postage extra, per set, 3 cents.

Blank Dice.

Black Bone Dice. These dice have no spots. We can furnish blank dice in three sizes.

Cat. No.	Inches.	3 doz.	Per doz.
No. 18G22384	9-16	$0.55	20c
No. 18G22388	10-16	.67	25c
No. 18G22392	11-16	1.10	39c

If by mail, postage extra, per dozen, 4 cents.

Dice Cups.

No. 18G22396 Sole Leather Dice Cup. 2 inches in diameter, 3 inches deep. Natural color. Price, 2 for 28c; each........15c
If by mail, postage extra, each, 4 cents.

No. 18G22400 Sole Leather Dice Cup. 2 inches in diameter, 3 1/4 inches deep. Tan color. Price, 2 for 47c; each........25c
If by mail, postage extra, each, 5 cents.

No. 18G22404 Polished Metal Nickel Plated Cribbage Board, with three double rows drilled holes. To score for three or six persons. Face of polished black walnut with compartment for one pack of cards and another compartment containing nine steel cribbage pegs. Size, 2 3/4x10 1/2 inches. Shipping weight, 20 ounces. Price........85c

The Little Gem Dime Savings Bank.

No. 18G22408 Locks itself and registers the amount deposited. Opens automatically when $5.00 in dimes have been deposited without use of force. Nickel plated, and can be carried conveniently in your vest pocket.
Price, 2 for 15c; each........8c
If by mail, postage extra, 3 cents.

No. 18G22412 The Seroco Savings Bank. This same bank has been adopted throughout the country by many of the savings banks, who furnish them to their customers for $1.00 and bank keeps the key. The bank is made of the best cold rolled steel with the most perfect copper oxidized finish. Size, 4 5/8x3 1/4x2 3/8 inches. With each bank we furnish key. Shipping weight, 1 3/4 pounds.
Price, each........$0.65
Per dozen, $7.25; 2 for........1.25

The Canary Bird Whistle.

No. 18G22416 The Canary Bird Whistle. Made of metal. All the pretty notes of the canary can be imitated. Lots of fun for boys and girls.
Price, 3 for........10c
If by mail, postage extra, for 3, 5 cents.

Laughing Camera.

No. 18G22420 The Laughing Camera. A whole passing show. Furnishes more amusement than you would get in a circus. Your friends grotesquely photographed. Stout people look thin and thin people look stout. By getting a focus on passing pedestrians, horses, cars, etc., the most ludicrous pictures are witnessed. The passerby takes on the swinging stride of a granddaddy-longlegs, horses look like giraffes. Price, 2 for 25c; each........13c
If by mail, postage extra, each, 5 cents.

No. 18G22418 The smallest Kinematograph in the world. A positive sensation. By looking through the small eye-piece a perfect picture may be seen. Ask your friends to keep turning to see additional pictures and as soon as small knob is turned a small spray of water is released and shot into the operator's eye. Price, 2 for 45c; each..25c
If by mail, postage extra, 5 cents.

China Tea Sets.

No. 18G22424 Toy China Tea Set. Consisting of 16 pieces; cups, saucers, sugar and creamer with six extra spoons. All prettily hand decorated in fancy colors and gilt. Best value sold anywhere. Shipping weight, 16 ounces.
Price, per set........25c

No. 18G22438 Decorated Unbreakable Tea Set. Consisting of 13 pieces, 4 cups and saucers, cream pitcher, teapot with cover and sauce pan. All highly decorated on heavy tin; pictures being of landscapes, country scenes, etc. This is something new and attractive and pleasing to the children. Shipping weight, 1 1/2 pounds.
Price, 2 sets, 95c; per set........50c

Britannia Tea Sets.

No. 18G22440 Britannia Tea Set, consisting of about 15 pieces, silver finished tea pot, sugar bowl, sugar tongs, creamer, plates, cups, etc. Put up in neat pasteboard box. Shipping weight, 7 ounces. Price, per set, 12c

No. 18G22444 Britannia Tea Set, consisting of about 23 pieces, silver finished, assortment same as above, but a little larger size. Shipping weight, 15 ounces.
Price, per set........20c

No. 18G22448 Britannia Tea Set, silver finished, about 24 pieces, and still larger than above. Shipping weight, 28 ounces.
Price, per set........47c

No. 18G22452 Britannia (Pewter) Tea Set. Highly silver finished, with very handsome filigree design. Large cups, saucers and other pieces. Set consists of about 23 pieces. Regular $1.25 size. Shipping weight, 40 ounces. Price, per set........86c

Royal Jointed Dolls.

Nothing made to compare with them. The body is the human shape beautifully proportioned, made of an indestructible flesh color pressed papier mache formed by hydraulic pressure, making same exceptionally light and indestructible; ball joints, hips, shoulders, elbows and wrists; also moving head and moving eyes, with eyelashes, open mouth, showing teeth; the very finest quality sewed wig; has extra quality shoes and lace stockings; comes dressed in fine lace and ribbon trimmed chemise. The eyes are tied with strings to back of head to prevent breaking when shipped.

Come in sizes as follows:

No.	Size, inches	Shipping Weight	Price, each
18G23008	23	6 lbs.	$2.37
18G23012	24 1/2	7 lbs.	2.95
18G23016	27 1/2	8 lbs.	3.68
18G23020	30	10 lbs.	4.89

Two Special Values in Royal Jointed Dolls.

No. 18G23000 Royal Jointed Dolls. This is a special number which we sell at an extremely low price. Made of flesh colored pressed papier mache, same as above described dolls, but the bodies are not quite as large proportioned as the regular Royal doll, but they are an extremely sightly and large doll; extra value for the money. Length, 18 1/2 inches. Shipping weight, 3 lbs. Price, $1.19

No. 18G23004 Royal Jointed Dolls, described as above. This is another special number which is not proportioned quite as full as the regular Royal, but a large sized doll at a very low price. Length, 22 1/2 inches. Shipping weight, 4 lbs. Price, $1.59

Extra Large Sized Kid Body Dolls.

Extra Large Size Dolls at very low price. This line of dolls is not the finest quality, but are well made, have pretty faces, good kid bodies, and have shoulder, hip and arm joints, have fine bisque heads, moving eyes. Dolls that have never been sold within 75 per cent of the price that we ask. The larger the doll the better proportioned are the body and head. Come in four sizes; the three largest sizes have nice long sewed wig.

No.	Size, inches	Shipping Weight	Price, each
18G23024	14	2 lbs.	$0.25
18G23028	16	3 lbs.	.50
18G23032	18 1/2	4 lbs.	.75
18G23036	21 1/2	5 lbs.	1.00

No. 18G22428 China Tea Set. Beautifully decorated in hand painting and gilt. Consists of 18 pieces, including cups, saucers, cake dish, tea, sugar and creamer. A nice large set. No such value sold elsewhere. Shipping weight, 30 ounces. Price, per set........50c

No. 18G22432 China Tea Set. This is a particularly desirable set, made of fine, thin white china with embossed design. Extra large pieces, that can be used practically for an after dinner. Consists of six cups and saucers, one tea, one sugar, one creamer and bowl. Put up in a nice individual box. Extra $1.00 value. Shipping weight, 4 pounds.
Price, per set........75c

No. 18G22436 China Tea Set. This is an elegant, large set, consisting of six cups and saucers, one tea, one sugar, one creamer and bowl. Made of very fine, thin white china, beautifully decorated in enameled picture designs taken from fairy tales. With gold traced edges, and handles relieved with floral decorations on the larger pieces. This is a very large size, for practical use, and will be very highly appreciated by the children. Regular $1.50 value. Shipping weight, 6 pounds. Price, per set........$1.00

Britannia Tea Sets.

No. 18H22452 Britannia (Pewter) Tea Set. Highly silver finished, with very handsome filigree design. Large cups, saucers and other pieces. Set consists of about 23 pieces. Regular $1.25 size. Shipping weight, 40 ounces. Our price, per set **86c**

No. 18H22448 Britannia Tea Set, silver finished, about 24 pieces, similar to above. Shipping weight, 28 ounces. Price, per set **47c**

No. 18H22444 Britannia Tea Set, consisting of about 23 pieces, silver finished, assortment same as above, but a smaller size. Shipping weight, 15 ounces. Price, per set **20c**

Special Values in Full Jointed Papier Mache Dolls.

Nothing made to compare with these dolls, because of their natural appearance and beautifully proportioned human shaped bodies. Made of an indestructible flesh color papier mache formed by hydraulic pressure, making them exceptionally light weight and indestructible; ball jointed hips, shoulders, elbows, knees and wrists. These dolls have exceptionally pretty and well featured bisque heads with moving eyes and natural, long eyelashes, open mouth, showing teeth. The wig is the finest quality, full sewed. Have extra quality shoes and lace stockings which are removable. Each doll comes dressed in lace and ribbon trimmed chemise. Comes in five sizes. The larger the doll the better proportioned are the body and features.

No.	Size, inches	Shipping Weight	Price
18H23000	19	3 pounds	$1.19
18H23004	22	4 pounds	1.67
18H23012	24	7 pounds	2.88
18H23016	28	8 pounds	3.99
18H23020	30	10 pounds	4.89

Extra Large Size Kid Body Dolls.

Large Sized Dolls at very low prices. This line of dolls is not the finest quality, but the dolls are very well made and have very pretty faces. They are made of good quality genuine kid and not a poor imitation, of which most dolls at these prices are made, have fine quality bisque heads with moving eyes and very fine mohair wigs, those on the three larger sizes being full sewed and long haired. The larger the doll the better proportioned is the body and the head. We furnish this doll in four sizes.

No.	Size, in.	Shipping Weight	Price
18H23024	13	2 lbs.	$0.25
18H23028	16	3 lbs.	.50
18H23032	18½	4 lbs.	.75
18H23036	21½	5 lbs.	1.00

High Grade Jointed Kid Body Dolls.

These Dolls are made with riveted joints, fine bisque heads with moving eyes, very pretty faces, full sewed wigs with new style parting tied with ribbon. The dolls have very large, fat bodies made of the best quality kid; beautifully proportioned heads; riveted joints at hips and knees that enable this doll to assume any position. The larger the size of the doll the better featured is the face and the better proportioned is the body. We furnish this doll in four different sizes.

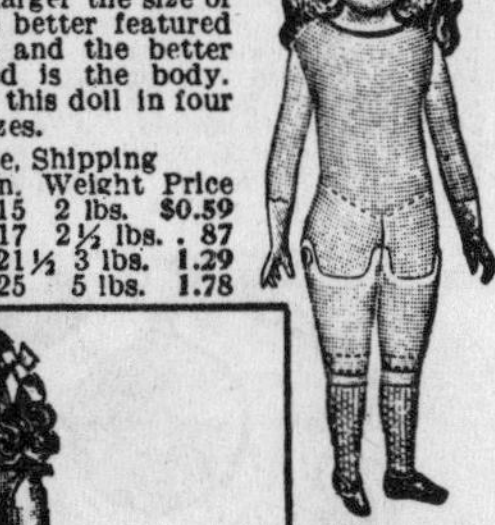

No.	Size, in.	Shipping Weight	Price
18H23040	15	2 lbs.	$0.59
18H23044	17	2½ lbs.	.87
18H23048	21½	3 lbs.	1.29
18H23056	25	5 lbs.	1.78

"TEDDY BEARS" ARE ALL THE RAGE.

The Best Plaything Ever Invented.

THESE BEARS ARE THE MOST SENSIBLE AND SERVICEABLE toys ever put before the public. Not a fad or campaign article, but something which has come to stay on merit alone. An article which will afford your children and even yourself great amusement and lasting pleasure. Made of the finest quality imported bear plush, they closely resemble the little cubs. They are full jointed and will assume countless different positions (four of which we illustrate). Each bear has a natural voice, produced by slight pressure on the front of body, and they are practically unbreakable. We offer these bears in four sizes. Natural cinnamon color only. The larger the size the better proportioned are the bears. Order one of these bears at once for your boy or girl, and you will find that no toy which you could select would give them more actual pleasure and entertainment.

No.	Size	Shipping Wt.	Price.
18H23358	10 inches high	7 ounces.	$0.75
18H23360	12 inches high	9 ounces.	1.19
18H23362	14 inches high	14 ounces.	1.75
18H23364	16 inches high	18 ounces.	2.38

Genuine Kestner Kid Body Dolls.

This well known make has been on the market for years, and their excellence of manufacture and fine quality features in general are conceded by every doll manufacturer as the standard. The face is full and perfectly featured, has very fine quality mohair wig, long curls parted and tied with ribbons; full riveted at hip, knee, shoulder and elbow; papier mache legs fitted with removable colored lace stockings and slippers to match; bisque arms; moving eyes tied in back with string which you must cut when you receive doll. We can furnish this Kestner doll in five sizes. The larger sizes of course are better proportioned than the smaller, although every number is very well proportioned and an exceptional value at our very low price.

No.	Size, in.	Shipping Weight	Price
18H23080	18½	2½ lbs.	$1.75
18H23084	20½	3 lbs.	2.37
18H23088	23½	3½ lbs.	3.48
18H23092	25½	4 lbs.	4.15
18H23096	28	5 lbs.	4.98

Metal Head Unbreakable Dolls Are Best For Wear.

New Unbreakable Dolls, silesia bodies with the fine genuine Minerva metal heads, painted eyes and hair. This doll has just been placed on the market. Body is of the best quality silesia, hair stuffed, with movable knee joints. This doll is absolutely unbreakable and harmless, the most serviceable doll ever produced. We furnish this doll in four different sizes. The larger the doll the better are the proportions.

No.	Size, in.	Shipping Weight	Price
18H23100	11½	1 lb.	25c
18H33104	14½	1½ lbs.	44c
18H23108	16	2 lbs.	59c
18H23112	18	3 lbs.	67c

Unbreakable Dolls, Metal Heads, With Wigs.

Silesia Body Dolls with fine Minerva metal head with curly hair and glass eyes. These dolls have been recently placed on the market and have at once been a decided success. Every mother is probably familiar with the Minerva metal head and combining this feature with a fine hair stuffed silesia body makes an unbreakable doll and at the same time a very pretty doll. These dolls, with the Minerva heads, flowing curls and glass eyes, with silesia body, we furnish in the following sizes:

No.	Size, in.	Shipping Weight	Price
18H23120	14¾	1½ lbs.	$0.50
18H23124	17	2 lbs.	.75
18H23128	20	3 lbs.	1.00

NOTE—We claim for this doll special value which cannot be equaled elsewhere.

Our Special Value, Half Cork Stuffed Kid Body Dolls, Full Jointed.

These dolls have very fine extra large bisque heads with moving eyes and full sewed wig with long curls and new style hair dressing, parted on the side and tied with bows of ribbon. The body is of the finest quality white kid, half cork stuffed, making it light weight and very shapely; full riveted hips, arms, elbows and knee joints, allowing the doll to assume any position, removable shoes and lace stockings. The larger the doll the better proportioned are the body and the features of the face. We can furnish this doll in four different sizes, exceptional values at our very low prices.

No.	Size, inches	Shipping Weight	Price
18H23064	17½	2 lbs.	$1.29
18H23068	21	2½ lbs.	1.88
18H23072	23	3 lbs.	2.37
18H23076	27	4 lbs.	2.99

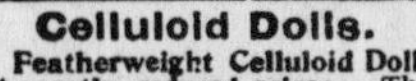

Celluloid Dolls.

Featherweight Celluloid Dolls at greatly reduced prices. The celluloid dolls have become very popular and are very prettily proportioned and handsome. These celluloid dolls have arm joints so that they can be placed in different positions. We furnish them in five sizes, the larger the size the better featured and proportioned.

No.	Size, in.	Shipping Weight	Price
18H23132	5½	6 oz.	15c
18H23134	6½	7 oz.	25c
18H23136	7	8 oz.	40c
18H23140	8½	9 oz.	65c
18H23142	10¼	10 oz.	80c

Indestructible Rag Dolls, Exceptional Values.

No. 18H23148 Indestructible Rag Doll, well shaped and proportioned. Has nicely made gingham dress in bright, attractive colors and bonnet to match. The face is photographed from life onto cloth, a tremendous improvement over the old style painted faces. Size, 15 inches high. Shipping weight, 10 oz. Price... **25c**

No. 18H23156 Red Ridinghood Indestructible Rag Doll, large size. Dressed in the latest blouse effect, dress being made of a good quality flannelette with lace and ribbon trimmings and ribbon belt. The doll has a red ridinghood bonnet of material to match dress. This doll will be unbreakable and of natural appearance will be a source of delight to any child. Shipping weight, 2 pounds. Length, 18½ inches. Price **89c**

No. 18H23160 Buster Brown Indestructible Rag Doll. A very fine imitation of the Buster Brown you read about. The doll is dressed in a red suit with white collar, cuffs and belt, has Buster Brown cap of red and white, and a large black Windsor tie. This doll will be a delight to the children on account of the popularity of Buster Brown. Length, 15 inches. Price **25c**
If by mail, postage extra, 10c.

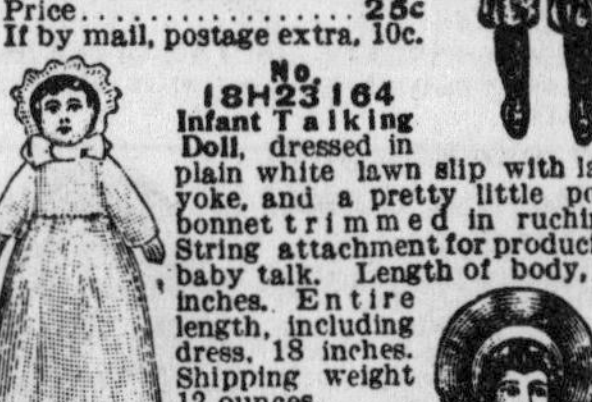

No. 18H23164 Infant Talking Doll, dressed in plain white lawn slip with lace yoke, and a pretty little poke bonnet trimmed in ruching. String attachment for producing baby talk. Length of body, 13 inches. Entire length, including dress, 18 inches. Shipping weight 12 ounces. Price **25c**

No. 18H23168 Indestructible Farmer Boy Doll, rag body with removable shoes and stockings, dressed in red jumper and blue overalls, has celluloid face with white lawn cap; both overalls and jacket are removable, being fastened by fancy agate buttons. Size, 13½ inches. Shipping weight, 10 ounces. Price **50c**

Unbreakable Leather Doll, 47 cents.

No. 18H23212 Unbreakable Leather Doll. This is a baby's friend. The leather is very fine to chew on when teething. Impossible to hurt either the baby or the doll. Stuffed with cotton and will always retain its shape. This doll will last baby and also baby's brother. Coloring matter warranted not to come off. Length, 12½ inches. Shipping weight, 15 ounces. Price, **47c**

No. 18H23216 Esquimaux Doll. This is a very attractive and interesting papier mache jointed doll with bisque head. The entire body is covered with white fur, all parts of the body, arms, legs and head being movable, so that you can make it assume any position. Length, 10½ inches. Price **25c**
If by mail, postage extra, 8c.

Wonderful Values in Dressed Dolls.

No. 18H23218 Dressed Doll with Jointed Arms and Hips. Has very pretty gingham dress trimmed with lace, also hat to match; removable shoes and stockings. Height of doll, 11½ inches; with hat, 14 inches. Shipping weight, 1 pound. Price..... **25c**

No. 18H23222 Very Pretty Sailor Doll, dressed in pretty cashmere dress with revers collar. Skirt and sailor collar very prettily trimmed with plaid. Has sailor cap to match dress; removable shoes and stockings, bisque head with natural wig; moving eyes and open mouth, showing teeth. This doll at 45c is a regular 75c value. Height of doll, 14½ inches; entire height with cap, 17 inches. Shipping weight, 2 pounds. Our price..... **45c**

No. 18H23226 A Very Pretty and Stylishly Dressed Doll with moving eyes, has jointed arms and hips. Dressed in gingham with lace trimmed skirt and revers collar, has pretty hat to match dress. The head is of best quality bisque with pretty features, sleeping eyes and natural wig. This doll is an exceptional value at our price. Height of doll, 14¼ inches; with hat, 17½ inches. Shipping weight, 2 pounds. Price **57c**

No. 18H23230 Very Pretty Dressed Doll, full jointed throughout, has well featured bisque head with moving eyes and open mouth, showing teeth, and natural wig. Dress is made of white net over colored crepe. Dress as well as underclothes are lace trimmed. Height of doll, including hat, 18½ inches. Shipping weight, 3 pounds. Price **75c**

No. 18H23234 Stylishly Dressed Doll, has dress of good quality in blouse design, lined throughout, over which is stylish removable jacket with revers collar and medallion and lace trimmed; hat of material to match dress, with drop veil. Doll is full jointed throughout; has removable shoes and stockings. Good quality bisque head with parted wig; moving eyes and open mouth, showing teeth. Entire height of doll, including hat, 20 inches. Shipping weight, 3 pounds. Price **$1.00**

No. 18H23238 Our Best Quality Dressed Doll. Very stylishly dressed in blouse design, flowered organdy dress. Full jointed throughout, has openwork stockings and sateen shoes, both removable. Lace hat trimmed with ribbon to match dress. Very well proportioned head with long natural hair, moving eyes and open mouth, showing teeth. All of the clothes can be removed, being fastened by hooks and eyes. This doll must be seen to be appreciated. Entire height of doll, including hat, 23 inches. Regular $3.00 value. Shipping weight, 5 pounds. Our price **$1.50**

Knock About Dolls, Absolutely Unbreakable.

No. 18H23242 **Unbreakable Dressed Doll.** Something for the young child who appreciates the beauty of a pretty doll and will break a doll that is not absolutely indestructible. This doll is made with a silesia, cotton stuffed body, fitted with a genuine Minerva metal doll head, making it an absolutely indestructible doll. The dress is of good quality material with lace trimmed yoke and collar; also has hat to match and removable shoes and stockings. This doll, on account of its being indestructible is a very desirable article and exceptionally low priced. Height of doll, including hat, 15 inches. Shipping weight, 1 pound. Price......49c

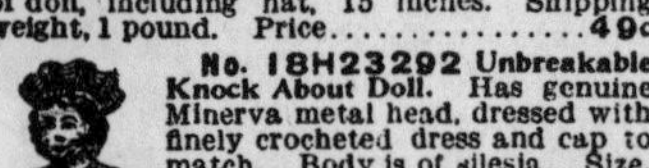

No. 18H23292 Unbreakable Knock About Doll. Has genuine Minerva metal head, dressed with finely crocheted dress and cap to match. Body is of silesia. Size, 11 inches. Shipping weight, 1 pound. Price 50c

No. 18H23296 Minerva Knock About Doll. Has genuine Minerva metal head, dressed with fancy crocheted dress, trimmed with ribbon and has large crocheted hat to match. Body is of silesia. Has imitation stockings and removable shoes. Size, 13 inches. Shipping weight, 1 pound. Price . 75c

Papa and Mama Dolls.

No. 18H23304 **Papa and Mama Dressed Dolls.** With bisque head, curly hair, moving eyes, and stuffed unbreakable body. Dressed in very pretty fancy sateen trimmed gown, shoes and stockings. When you pull the cord, the doll repeats papa and mama. Fancy sateen dress hat to match. Length, 16 inches. Shipping weight, 1½ pounds. Price 50c

No. 18H23300 **Papa and Mama Dressed Doll.** Stuffed body, bisque head, moving eyes. This is the first time a papa and mama doll has been offered at 30 cents. Neatly dressed in a pretty gown, shoes and stockings. Same as above, but smaller. By pulling cord, doll repeats papa and mama. Size, 14 inches. Shipping weight, 1 pound. Price.............30c

No. 18H23308 **Papa and Mama Dressed Dolls.** Larger and fuller stuffed unbreakable body and more elaborately dressed than above. Beautiful lace trimmed satin dress, with large poke bonnet edged with lace and lace trimmed underwear. This is a sleeping doll. Length, 18 inches. Shipping weight, 2 pounds. Price....$1.00

No. 18H23312 **White Rubber Doll,** dressed in knit suit and hat to match. This doll is a good article for the very young child, 8 inches in height. Price............25c
If by mail, postage extra, 4c.

Red India Rubber Toys.

No. 18H23328 **Red Rubber Fat Boy.** Made of best quality red rubber; red will not wear off. Has German silver whistle. Size, 5 inches. Price 25c
If by mail, postage extra, 5 cents.

No. 18H23342 **Red India Rubber Peasant Girl Doll,** made of the best quality red India rubber, the coloring of which will not wear off. This doll, as shown in accompanying illustration, has basket of flowers in one hand and a single flower in the other hand. It has German silver whistle, which is harmless to the child. Size, 5¾ inches.
Price..............28c
If by mail, postage extra, 5 cents.

Special Value, Horse and Soldier for 50c.

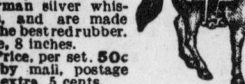

No. 18H23348 **Red Rubber Horse and Rider.** Consists of two pieces, the horse being fitted with saddle in which the rider, made up in soldier costume, sits. Both pieces have German silver whistles, and are made of the best red rubber. Size, 8 inches.
Price, per set. 50c
If by mail, postage extra, 5 cents.

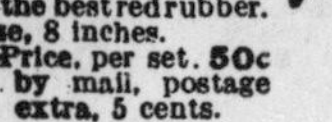

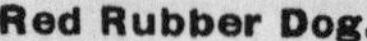

Red Rubber Dog.

No. 18H23350 **Red Rubber Dog.** Handsome representation of a dog; made of pure red India rubber; has German silver whistle, which is harmless to the child. Size, 6½ inches.
Price..............48c
If by mail, postage extra, 5 cents.

Red Rubber Cat.

No. 18H23354 **Red Rubber Cat.** A good and excellent, lifelike representation of a cat, made of pure red India rubber; has German silver whistle. Length, 5¾ inches.
Price..............37c
If by mail, postage extra, 5 cents.

Kid Doll Bodies.

Kid Doll Bodies. Very full size, extra quality cork stuffed, high grade kid bodies, with riveted hip joint and bisque arms, shoes and stockings. This is a very high grade and satisfactory body. Comes in sizes as follows:

No.	Length, inches	Across Shoulders, inches	Shipping Weight, ounces	Price
18H23402	12½	3½	15	$0.39
18H23404	16	4	25	.62
18H23406	19	4¾	35	.79
18H23408	21½	5½	45	1.10
18H23412	23¾	6	60	1.39
18H23414	24½	6¼	65	1.58
18H23416	25½	7	75	1.85

Silesia Doll Bodies.

Hair Stuffed Pink Silesia Doll Bodies. This is a very high grade and satisfactory silesia body that will give best of wear and satisfaction; has bisque arms and removable shoes and stockings. Comes in the following sizes:

No.	Length, inches	Inches Across Shoulders	Shipping Weight, oz.	Price
18H23418	12	3¼	11	$0.25
18H23420	15⅛	4	11	.35
18H23422	16⅛	4⅛	11	.44
18H23424	21	5½	25	.55
18H23426	23⅛	6	30	.69
18H23428	25⅛	6⅛	35	.83
18H23430	26¾	7¼	40	1.00

Genuine Minerva Metal Doll Heads at Reduced Prices.

These Doll Heads are imported from Germany. They combine the durability of sheet metal and the beauty of bisque, are light in weight, washable, and will not chip; will stand any reasonable wear. Small children cannot injure them; larger ones love them for their unequaled beauty. The eyes are clear and tender, head flexible at the bust, and fitted with sewing holes, making it easy to adjust and fasten them to body. Come in sizes as follows:

No.	Height, inches	Inches Across Sh'lders	Shipping Weight, oz.	Price
18H23432	3⅜	2¾	5	16c
18H23434	3¾	3	6	22c
18H23436	4⅛	3⅜	8	30c
18H23438	4⅛	3⅝	9	35c
18H23440	5	4	10	40c
18H23442	6¼	4⅛	12	58c
18H23444	6¾	5⅛	14	76c

Nos. 18H23442 and 18H23444 have glass eyes and open mouths, showing teeth.

Sewed Wig and Moving Glass Eyes.

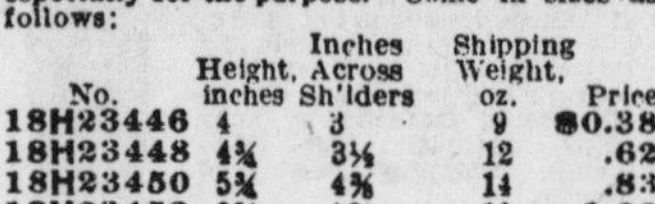

The Metal Indestructible Minerva Doll Head with moving glass eyes. Open lips showing teeth, and very fine sewed curly wig. The metal heads, made of the best flexible sheet brass can be given to the smallest child with perfect safety, as the metal is covered with a pure wholesome paint which is manufactured especially for the purpose. Come in sizes as follows:

No.	Height, inches	Inches Across Sh'lders	Shipping Weight, oz.	Price
18H23446	4	3	9	$0.38
18H23448	4¾	3⅛	12	.62
18H23450	5¾	4⅜	14	.83
18H23452	6⅝	4⅞	16	1.00

Bisque Doll Heads.

IMMENSE VALUES. COMPARE SIZE AND PRICE.

Bisque Doll Heads. First quality, high grade bisque, with very beautiful moulded faces, showing teeth, with two rows, sewed wig and movable eyes. Either blondes or brunettes. Please mention choice.

No.	Height, inches	Inches Across Sh'lders	Shipping Weight, oz.	Price
18H23454	3⅝	3	12	$0.21
18H23456	4⅛	3⅛	24	.35
18H23458	5¼	4¼	28	.45
18H23460	6	5	32	.65
18H23462	7	5½	36	.90
18H23464	8¼	6¼	39	1.35
18H23466	9	6¾	42	1.65

Kestner Bisque Doll Heads.

These are the highest grade bisque heads that are manufactured. The Kestner make of dolls is well known, being the best make of dolls in the world. All these heads are very lifelike in appearance, having moving eyes and open mouth, showing teeth. The highest grade full sewed wig with long curls braided in center and tied on side with large silk ribbon bow. We furnish these doll heads in the following sizes:

No.	Height, inches	Inches Across Shoulders	Shipping Weight, oz.	Price
18H23482	4¾	3¼	12	$0.62
18H23484	5½	4	26	.89
18H23486	6½	4¼	30	1.19
18H23488	7½	4¾	34	1.43
18H23490	8¾	6¼	36	1.96

Celluloid Doll Heads.

Celluloid Doll Heads. The celluloid doll heads, until recently, have been extremely high priced. We have succeeded in making arrangements so that they are exceptionally cheap, considering the distinct advantages this head has over the ordinary doll head. The faces are beautifully moulded. Made of the best celluloid, absolutely unbreakable, light as a feather, and at the prices we quote, will surely make them exceedingly popular. This style of celluloid doll head, has painted hair, glass eyes, with open mouth showing teeth. Come in the following sizes:

No.	Height, inches	Inches across shoulders	Shipping wt., oz.	Price
18H23500	3⅛	2¾	5	10c
18H23502	3¾	3	7	15c
18H23504	4¼	3½	9	29c
18H23506	5	4	12	37c
18H23508	6¼	5¼	13	50c

Celluloid Doll Heads. with glass eyes and fine curly sewed wig. The features of this doll are very beautiful. This head combines all the features of the finest bisque head, but is exceptionally light in weight, being made of the finest celluloid. They are unbreakable, making a pretty and durable doll head. We quote the following exceptionally low prices:

No.	Height, inches	Inches across shoulders	Shipping wt., oz.	Price
18H23510	3⅛	2¾	5	25c
18H23512	3¾	3	7	37c
18H23514	4¼	3	9	55c
18H23516	5	4	12	68c
18H23518	6¼	5¼	13	82c

Brass Wire Doll Beds.

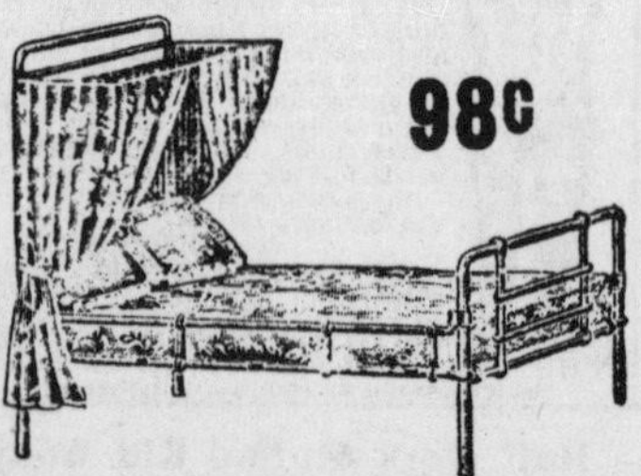

98c

No. 18H23520 **Brass Wire Doll Bed.** The frame of this doll bed is made entirely of brass finished wire, strongly put together and complete in every detail. Has mattress and two pillows covered with excellent quality floral pattern silkoline, the back and canopy being trimmed to match. Pillows are trimmed with good quality lace. Entire length of bed is 24 inches. Shipping weight, 4 pounds. This article is unmailable.
Price, for entire bed, complete with mattress, pillows and draperies..............98c

Comb and Brush Sets.

No. 18H25000 **This Genuine Ebony Brush and Comb Set** is trimmed with sterling silver mountings. Genuine ebony brush, solid back, nine-row bristle, with silver mounted comb. Strictly high grade, and put up in a nice, neat box. Shipping weight, 12 ounces. Worth double our price.
Price, per set, complete............69c

No. 18H25003 **Special value Three-Piece Toilet Set,** consisting of mahogany finished, good quality bristle eleven-row hair brush with very pretty mounting on back; 4-inch bevel plate mirror with mounting to match brush and a good quality 6½-inch rubber comb. It is only by a very large purchase that we are enabled to sell this set at the price we quote. Shipping weight, 1½ pounds. Price, entire set, put up in very neat box..............79c

$2.00 Value, Genuine Ebony Comb, Brush and Mirror Set, $1.19.

No. 18H25016 **Fine Toilet Set,** consisting of solid back genuine ebony hair brush, ebonite mirror and comb. All finest sterling silver mounted. Put up in special box, covered with enameled paper. Shipping weight, 1¾ pounds. This set advertised elsewhere for $2.00. Our price, per set........$1.19

The Best Gentlemen's Brush Set Ever Offered at $1.25.

No. 18H25019 **Imitation Ebony Sterling Silver Mounted Gentlemen's Toilet Set,** consisting of two good quality bristle, nine-row military brushes and eight-row excellent quality cloth brush to match; also 7-inch celluloid barber comb mounted to match brushes. Put up in lined box as shown in illustration.
Shipping weight, 2¼ pounds.
Price, per set..............$1.25

Special Values, Ladies' or Gentlemen's 6-Piece Toilet Sets, only $1.75.

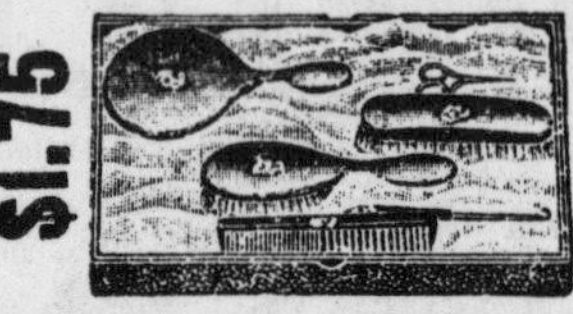

No. 18H25021 **High Grade Ladies' Ebonoid Toilet Set** in telescope box, lined with good quality grosgrain material, containing nine-row ebonoid hair brush, eight-row cloth brush and bevel edge mirror to match, ebonoid handled buttonhook, manicure scissors and a 7-inch ebonoid comb; all sterling silver mounted. A very attractive set at an exceptionally low price. Size of case, 9½x15½ inches. Shipping weight, 3 pounds. Price, per set............$1.75

No. 18H25023 **Finest Quality Gentlemen's Toilet Set,** consists of two excellent quality bristle, nine-row military brushes, a ring handled bevel edge plate mirror, ebonoid soap box, rabbit tail ebonoid handled shaving brush and good quality nail file; put up in flat telescope box with excellent quality lining; all pieces sterling silver mounted. A very attractive dresser set which any gentleman will appreciate at an exceptionally low price. Shipping weight, 3½ pounds.
Price, per set..............$1.75

SEWING MACHINES

SEWING MACHINES

GUARANTEED 20 YEARS ~ THREE MONTHS TRIAL

NEW MODELS=NEW DESIGNS=LATEST IMPROVEMENTS

OUR TWENTY YEARS' WRITTEN BINDING GUARANTEE. WE GUARANTEE THE MINNESOTA SEWING Machine for twenty years. With every sewing machine (the Homan excepted) we issue a written binding twenty-year guarantee, by the terms and conditions of which if any piece or part gives out at any time within twenty years by reason of defect in material or workmanship, we will replace or repair it free of charge. This is the longest, strongest and most binding guarantee issued by any sewing machine maker or seller, and in this way we make you absolutely secure against any possible defect of any kind. Thousands upon thousands of the machines made by the company now manufacturing our machines, from thirty to forty years ago, are still in use today. This is the best proof of quality that anyone can produce; the best recommendation that could be asked for.

CERTIFICATE No.______

CERTIFICATE OF GUARANTEE

This is to Certify that this sewing machine is warranted to be perfect in material and manufacture and to be perfect in operation if properly managed. This machine has been carefully inspected and adjusted, and there are no defects in material or workmanship. It has been delivered to the transportation company in perfect condition, carefully packed, and we guarantee it to reach your station in good order. This means that if it is damaged in transit it may be returned to us and we will pay all expenses connected with the transaction and send a new machine without extra charge.

With fair usage we hereby agree to make good any defect in material or workmanship for a period of twenty years. Natural wear and tear on any of the parts is not considered a defect in material or workmanship.

This guarantee does not apply to attachments, or the breaking of needles, shuttles, bobbins or belts.

Dated at Chicago, this______day of__________A. D., 19___ Sears, Roebuck & Co., Chicago, Ill.

OUR THREE MONTHS' TRIAL PROPOSITION. WHEN YOU SEND US YOUR ORDER FOR A Minnesota Sewing Machine, and enclose our price, we fill your order and ship the machine to you with the understanding that we give you the privilege of returning the sewing machine to us any time within three months after you receive it if for any reason you are dissatisfied with the machine (the Homan excepted), the money paid for the machine, including the freight paid by you, will be returned to you without question. This gives you the opportunity for testing and trying the machine in every way without its costing you one penny. If you are not satisfied any time within three months we agree to return not only the price of the machine but the freight charges as well.

This is to Certify that this machine is sold by us with the understanding and agreement that if it does not prove entirely satisfactory in every respect to the purchaser that it can be returned at any time within three months from date it is received, and the full amount paid for the machine, including freight charges, will be refunded to the purchaser at once.

Sears Roebuck & Co.

TO MAKE QUICK DELIVERY

WE CARRY TWO STYLES OF OUR BEST SEWING MACHINES, THE MINNESOTA NEW MODEL "A," IN WAREHOUSES IN DIFFERENT CITIES. WE HAVE THESE MACHINES IN A WAREHOUSE IN A CITY RIGHT NEAR YOU

Read What Our Customers Say About the Minnesota Sewing Machines

On this page we publish three letters from customers living in the far west, but who received their machines in a remarkably short time after ordering. We have thousands of just such letters, but unfortunately cannot publish them all. You may write to these people. Many of them have expressed a willingness to show their machines to prospective customers, and even let them test their machines, although our proposition to take our machines back any time within ninety days and refund the purchase price and freight charges is enough to convince the doubtful buyer who knows we could not afford to make such an offer unless our machines were able to stand all tests.

COLORADO: "JUST TEN DAYS AFTER I SENT YOU MY ORDER I HAD THE MACHINE IN MY HOUSE."

228 E. 3d St., Leadville, Colo.

Sears, Roebuck and Co., Chicago, Ill.

Gentlemen:—I ordered a Minnesota "A" Sewing Machine from you last month, and just ten days after I ordered it I had it in my home. It's just grand! I have used all the attachments and they are just perfect, and I also saved $40.00 in buying from you. All my friends have Singers around here and are more than surprised at the splendid machine I got for the money.

Yours respectfully,
MRS. M. D. SULLIVAN.

NEVADA: "MY MACHINE ARRIVED THROUGH THE SAN FRANCISCO WAREHOUSE TEN DAYS AFTER IT WAS ORDERED."

Sparks, Nev.

Sears, Roebuck and Co., Chicago, Ill.

Gentlemen:—After giving the Minnesota Model "A" Sewing Machine, which I ordered of you, a fair trial, I am pleased to say that it is entirely satisfactory in every way and I believe it to be fully equal to machines that are being sold here by agents for $65.00. It arrived here through your San Francisco warehouse in ten days after it was ordered, and in perfect condition. The total cost, including freight, drayage, etc., was $22.00.

Very truly yours,
FRANK HART.

CALIFORNIA: "WE RECEIVED THE MACHINE JUST TEN DAYS AFTER IT WAS ORDERED."

Sunny Vale, Cal.

Sears, Roebuck and Co., Chicago, Ill.

Gentlemen:—I am pleased very much with my sewing machine. It arrived in first class condition. I find it as good, if not better, than any other machine for which I would have had to pay more than twice as much from any local dealer. We received the machine just ten days after ordering it, which is certainly a short time. The sewing of the Minnesota is perfect and I advise anyone wishing to buy a sewing machine to get one from Sears, Roebuck and Co.

Sincerely yours,
MRS. PETER SCHAFER.

FORTY YEARS IN THE SEWING MACHINE BUSINESS. THIS IS THE LENGTH OF TIME THE FACTORY **manufacturing our machines has been in the sewing machine business.** It is one of our reasons for not hesitating about guaranteeing our machines, about giving our customers the privilege of our three months' trial.

SAFE DELIVERY GUARANTEED. WE GUARANTEE EVERY **sewing machine to reach the purchaser in the exact same perfect condition it leaves us,** and if any piece or part is broken by reason of rough handling in transit, or for any other reason, we will either replace or repair it or send you a new machine, all at our own expense.

REMEMBER, WHEN YOU SEND US AN ORDER FOR A SEWing machine and enclose our price we guarantee that the machine we send you will be wonderful value, such value as no other sewing machine manufacturer or dealer can possibly offer you, and remember, too, that you have three months' trial and every machine, with the exception of the Homan, carries our twenty-year written binding guarantee.

REPAIRS AND SUPPLIES. WE WILL ALWAYS CARry at the factory a full supply of all the different pieces and parts in which our various styles of sewing machines are made, and if you should meet with an accident of any kind and should want any part or parts of any sewing machine purchased from us, you can get these parts promptly and at actual factory cost.

LOW PRICED MACHINES

IF YOU WANT TO BUY A SEWING MACHINE and cannot afford to pay from $15.00 to $19.00 (according to the style of cabinet) for one of the best machines that money can buy (our high grade Ball Bearing Sewing Machines), see pages 677 to 704, or cannot afford to pay even $12.35 (the price of our high arm Minnesota Model "C" Machine with handsomely decorated marquetry, five-drawer, drop head cabinet), we will be pleased to accept your order for our Belmont machine at $9.84, or even our Homan machine at $8.45, and will guarantee to furnish you at these prices a far better sewing machine than you can procure from any other dealer at anywhere near the price.

WE WERE THE FIRST TO OFFER HIGH GRADE MACHINES at prices far below the old time high prices of the "agency" machines, and have through this method built up a sewing machine business of such magnitude that we can furnish today a sewing machine of the very highest grade, second to none, and by many considered the very finest sewing machine in the world, at about half the price you would be obliged to pay for a strictly high grade machine if purchased from anyone else.

A REPUTATION SUCH AS OURS CAN ONLY BE ESTABLISHED through good merchandise at money saving prices. We have come to the conclusion, after a number of years' experience in the sale of very cheap machines, that our customers and friends are not entirely satisfied with such a purchase. A sewing machine is only satisfactory when it will give the very best of service at all times, and as it is an article that in most cases is purchased but once in a lifetime, we do not consider it an economy for anyone to buy a machine that is not guaranteed for at least twenty years and will compare favorably with the best known makes of machines that have been on the market for the last forty years.

REMEMBER THAT WE WILL SELL you our Homan machine at $8.45. If you want it, just send your order accompanied by $8.45 and the machine will go to you within twenty-four hours after we receive your order. Remember, we will be glad to get your order for our Belmont machine at $9.84 if you feel that that is all you care to invest in a sewing machine, and we will take great pleasure in entering your order and will make prompt shipment and guarantee that either of these machines, by comparison with any other sewing machine at anywhere near these prices, will be far better in every way. But if you want to buy a machine that will carry our twenty-year guarantee and will prove satisfactory for the entire period of our guarantee, then

> Our Homan Machine at - - **$8.45**
> and Belmont Machine at - **9.84**
> are illustrated and described in our special Sewing Machine Catalog. SEND FOR IT. IT IS FREE AND POSTPAID.

WE RECOMMEND THAT YOU BUY OUR HIGH GRADE Ball Bearing Sewing Machine in preference to any other sewing machine made. Read the description of these machines carefully, pages 677 to 704, then order one on approval without any obligation to keep it, and satisfy yourself.

LESS THAN $1.00 A YEAR IS WHAT ONE OF OUR high grade Ball Bearing Machines will cost you. You can figure this out yourself by taking the price of the machine which you select and which is regulated by the style of cabinet you choose, and divide this amount by 20, the number of years for which we guarantee the machine. As an illustration, our most popular seven-drawer drop head automatic lift machine is priced at $17.85. If this investment were divided into 20 years it would mean only 89 cents a year. **Can you afford to invest your money in a cheap sewing machine when you realize that our high grade Ball Bearing Sewing Machine will represent such a small annual expenditure?** If you want a sewing machine that will do really fine work of all kinds, it is surely worth $1.00 a year and you cannot afford to invest your money in a sewing machine that will be likely to give you trouble and cause you annoyance and last but a comparatively short time.

NO ONE HAS A MONOPOLY ON THE ENGLISH LANGUAGE and, therefore, our statements may be, and are, repeated in practically the same words by a number of other dealers. We do not ask you to merely accept our statement of the facts regarding our ability to supply you with a far better sewing machine for the money you have to invest than any other dealer or manufacturer will, but we do ask you to order a machine from us, place it in competition with any other machines that may be offered to you and then decide for yourself after having tested them thoroughly to your entire satisfaction. We invite comparison; in fact, we will feel far better satisfied if you will only make the comparison and let the machine talk for itself.

READ WHAT OUR CUSTOMERS SAY ABOUT OUR SEWING MACHINES.

R. F. D. No. 3, Cogan Station, Pa.
Sears, Roebuck and Co., Chicago, Ill.
Dear Sirs:—I want to let you know that the sewing machine runs fine and dandy, runs light and noiseless. My wife says it sews as good as a $60.00 machine. My wife is well pleased with it. It is as fancy as any machine in this section.
Yours very truly,
S. A. BREINING.

232 Appleton St., Lowell, Mass.
Sears, Roebuck and Co., Chicago, Ill.
Gentlemen:—Received my machine all O. K., and I am more than pleased with it. Rather have it than any other make I ever saw. It is a beautiful sewer. Many thanks to you.
Sincerely,
MRS. G. G. SMITH.

Hampton, N. H.
Sears, Roebuck and Co., Chicago, Ill.
Dear Sirs:—I have received and given my new machine a good trial, and can't speak too highly of it and can recommend the Minnesota Model "A" to anyone. I can truly say I am more than pleased with it, and would advise one and all to buy a Model "A." Will you kindly send me your Wall Paper Catalog?
Yours truly,
MRS. WARREN MACE.

210 America St., Orlando, Fla.
Sears, Roebuck and Co., Chicago, Ill.
Gentlemen:—The sewing machine (Model "A," $16.50) was received a week ago or more in fine condition. We are more than pleased with same. It runs as light as any of the high priced machines and sews as well, too. It has the appearance as well as the working qualities of any of the high priced machines. Thanking you for your past courtesies, I remain,
Yours truly,
GEO. W. PHILLIPS.

IF YOU WRITE TO ANY OF THESE CUSTOMERS, BE SURE TO SEND A 2-CENT STAMP FOR REPLY.

OUR MINNESOTA $5.95 IMPROVED HAND MACHINE

No. 26T190 Price, $5.95

AT $5.95 WE FURNISH OUR MINNESOTA Hand Machine with iron base without cover, as illustrated on the left. For $7.85 we furnish the machine complete with wooden base and a fine bent wood cover. This is a very convenient machine for those who travel and for women who are unable for various reasons to operate a treadle power machine.

THIS IS A FIRST CLASS, RELIABLE MACHINE, HAVING EVERY IMPROVEMENT that is found on our high grade stand sewing machines, and capable of doing the widest range of work. It has an automatic bobbin winder, self threading vibrating steel shuttle, self setting needle clamp, tension liberator, all the latest improvements, combining simplicity, durability and strength in construction, speed and light running qualities, unequaled for ease of management and capacity for a wide range of hemming, felling, binding, tucking, ruffling, gathering, seaming, etc.; adapted to every variety of sewing, from the lightest muslin to the heaviest cloth.

Wood Base and Cover.
No. 26T195 Price, $7.85

THE BEARINGS ARE OF THE BEST HARDened steel and are adjustable. We pay as much attention to the adjustment of this machine as we do to our Minnesota Model "A," and we will not admit that this machine is equaled by any hand machine on the market, regardless of price or name. One particular point of superiority lies in its feed, which is the four-motion feed, the same that is used upon our high grade stand machine. This feed is absolutely positive, its movements being regulated by the eccentric lever bar, and does not require the use of coil springs to obtain the four movements of the feeding mechanism.

THE MAJORITY OF OTHER HAND MACHINES USE THE SPRING FEED, WHICH READILY BECOMES WEAK AND FAILS TO act properly.

THE HAND ATTACHMENT CAN BE DETACHED AND REMOVED AND THE MACHINE SET ON A TABLE OR STAND AND operated by foot power, the wheel having a groove for the belt. Other points of excellence lie in its self setting needle, positive stitch regulator, and a device by which the gearing is readily released, thus enabling the operator to wind the bobbin without operating the working parts of the machine. We furnish an instruction book and a full set of accessories free of charge with the machine. Free on board cars at Dayton, Ohio.

No. 26T190 Minnesota Hand Machine, with iron base; no cover. Price	$5.95
No. 26T195 Minnesota Hand Machine, with wood base and cover. Price	7.85
Full set of attachments, extra	.75

OUR NEW IMPROVED MINNESOTA MODEL "A"

ELEVEN STYLES — ELEVEN STYLES

FURNISHED IN THE FOLLOWING STYLES:

THE POPULAR DROP HEAD STYLES, ILLUSTRATED ON PAGES 682 TO 688.
THE FULL CABINET STYLES, ILLUSTRATED ON PAGES 689 AND 690.
THE LIBRARY TABLE SEWING MACHINE, SOLD EXCLUSIVELY BY US, ILLUSTRATED ON PAGE 691.
THE FIVE AND SEVEN-DRAWER UPRIGHT WITH DROP LEAF AND BOX COVER, ILLUSTRATED ON PAGE 692.

NEW HEAD — NEW WOODWORK — NEW STAND

THE MOST IMPORTANT PART OF A SEWING MACHINE IS THE HEAD

ON THIS AND THE FOLLOWING PAGES WE ILLUSTRATE and describe in detail the head (the works) of our Minnesota Model "A" Sewing Machine. This is the machine we recommend above all others. We make no exceptions.

THE MINNESOTA LEADS IN IMPROVEMENTS. DURING THE PAST TEN YEARS WE HAVE BEEN THE LEADERS IN SEWING machine improvements. We were among the first to introduce the ball bearing stand, the automatic lift, the independent take-up. We were the first to apply the ball bearing principle to the head. A few years ago no one thought of buying a new sewing machine for less than $40.00 to $75.00. When we advertised a sewing machine for $15.95, people could not realize the possibility of its being a serviceable article. Our liberal policy, our free trial proposition, our twenty-year guarantee, our willingness to refund not only the purchase price, but all freight charges, overcame all prejudice, all reluctance about ordering a machine at such an extraordinarily low price, so that today our sewing machines are known all over the United States, North, East, South and West. Over a million Minnesota sewing machines are in daily use throughout this country.

IF YOU TAKE OUR ADVICE AND SELECT ANY ONE OF THE different Minnesota Model "A" machines shown on the following pages, place it alongside of any other high grade sewing machine regardless of the price asked, compare it in every way, in handsome appearance, in quality of material used and class of workmanship, compare it for richness of finish, tasteful ornamentation, test it for ease of operation, for every kind of plain and fancy sewing, for absence of friction and noise in operation, you will agree with us that our Model "A" is far in advance of every other high grade sewing machine.

THE TEST OF TIME TELLS THE STORY

WE HAVE enough confidence in our machine to guarantee it for twenty years; to give our customers the privilege of using it in their own homes for three months, during which time they may test it on any and all materials, and in every way they see fit. They can put it in actual service, make practical use of it, satisfy themselves that the machine is as good or even better than we represent it to be and that it is cheaper in price by $20.00 to $40.00 than any other sewing machine that compares with it in quality and finish.

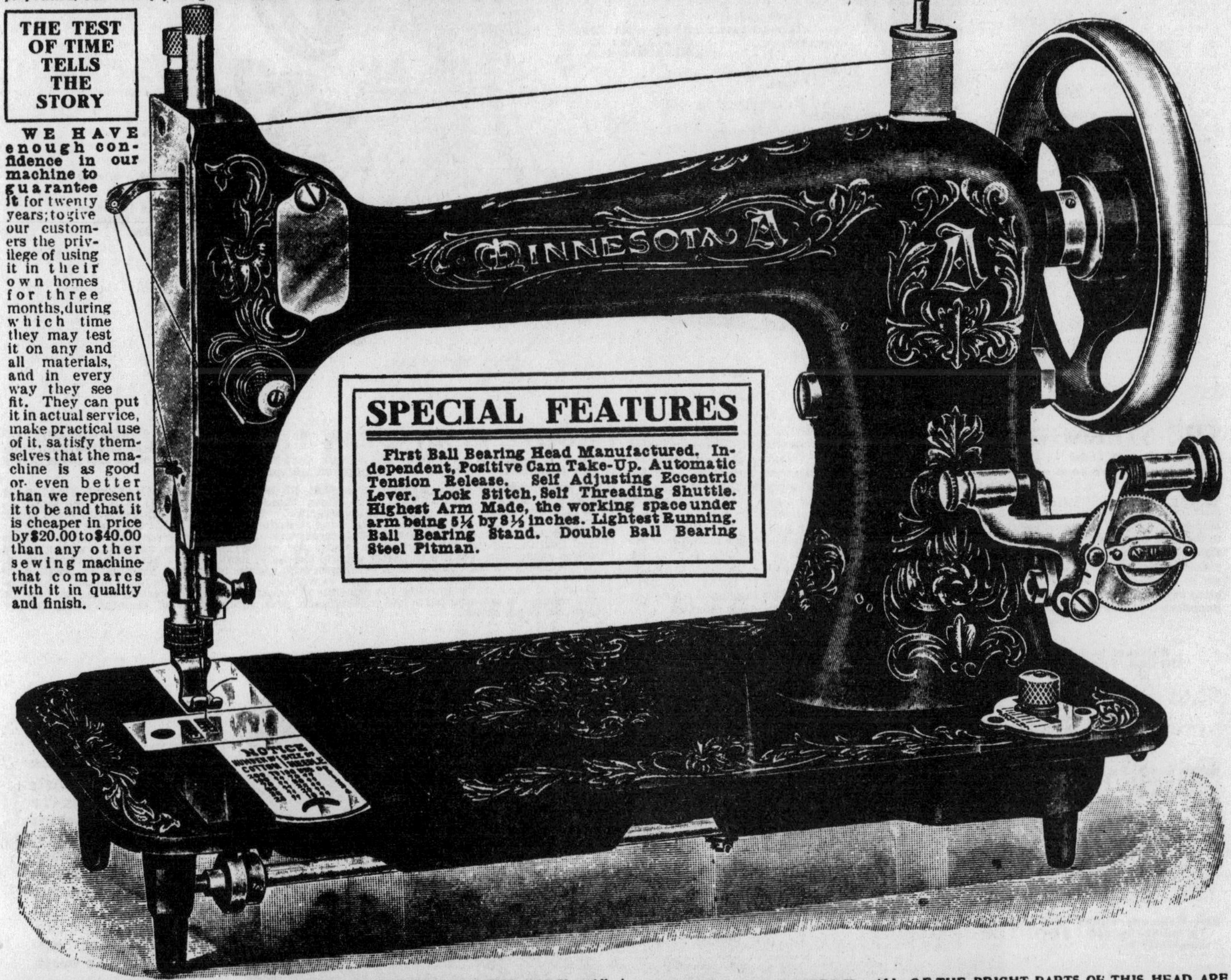

SPECIAL FEATURES

First Ball Bearing Head Manufactured. Independent, Positive Cam Take-Up. Automatic Tension Release. Self Adjusting Eccentric Lever. Lock Stitch, Self Threading Shuttle. Highest Arm Made, the working space under arm being 5¼ by 8½ inches. Lightest Running. Ball Bearing Stand. Double Ball Bearing Steel Pitman.

PLEASE NOTE FROM THIS LARGE ILLUSTRATION OF THE MODEL "A" head, its high arm, graceful appearance and beautiful ornamentation. On the next page we try to make plain the wonderful mechanical construction of the Model "A" head. The Model "A" head is ball bearing. In this new Model "A" head, the heart and vitals of the sewing machine, we have embodied a number of improvements never before carried by any sewing machine head. The Model "A" head has an extra high arm, unusually large and strong operating parts, so that this machine is fitted not only for household and domestic work, but also for the use of dressmakers, tailors and all others who require a sewing machine of the highest grade, capable of doing the greatest range of work, from extremely heavy to extremely light, both fancy and simple sewing and a machine which will also stand the wear and tear of constant usage. Unlike almost all other machines, the operation of our Minnesota Model "A" head on any weight or thickness of material and with all grades of cotton and silk thread, is perfect, rapid and easy.

DESIGN OF HEAD. THIS HEAD IS MADE AND SHAPED WITH A VIEW to the most perfect operation of the various parts, and yet not neglecting those perfect lines that make it the handsomest, most roomy and most shapely high arm sewing machine head possible to construct.

NICKEL PLATING. ALL OF THE BRIGHT PARTS OF THIS HEAD ARE heavily nickeled over copper plate, then highly polished. This insures a nickel finish that will not crack, peel, rust nor wear off. This applies to the working parts underneath the bed of the machine as well as to those parts that are exposed to view. The highly polished nickel plated parts on the outside of the head, in contrast with the rich black enamel finish, add greatly to the general handsome appearance of the machine.

COLOR ORNAMENTATION. THE MODEL "A" HEAD IS ELABorately ornamented in a special old gold design, which, in contrast with the black enameling and the elaborate nickel trimmings and graceful outlines, makes it the handsomest sewing machine head possible to produce.

THE ENAMELING. ALL THE PARTS THAT ARE NOT NICKEL PLATED are finished in black enamel. The highest grade of enamel is used, three coats being applied, each coat being separately baked on at a high temperature, rubbed down to a smooth surface by hand and finally given a coat of special varnish, baked on at a high degree of heat, making the surface extremely hard and giving the machine a rich, heavy, lasting, fast black luster. Before the machine is enameled it is treated to one coat of special anti-rust preparation which prevents the enamel from cracking, checking or peeling, which so often occurs with other makes of machines.

Detailed Construction of the Minnesota Model "A" Head

AN X-RAY PICTURE OF THE WONDERFUL MODEL "A" HEAD. NOTE THE GREAT FEATURES.

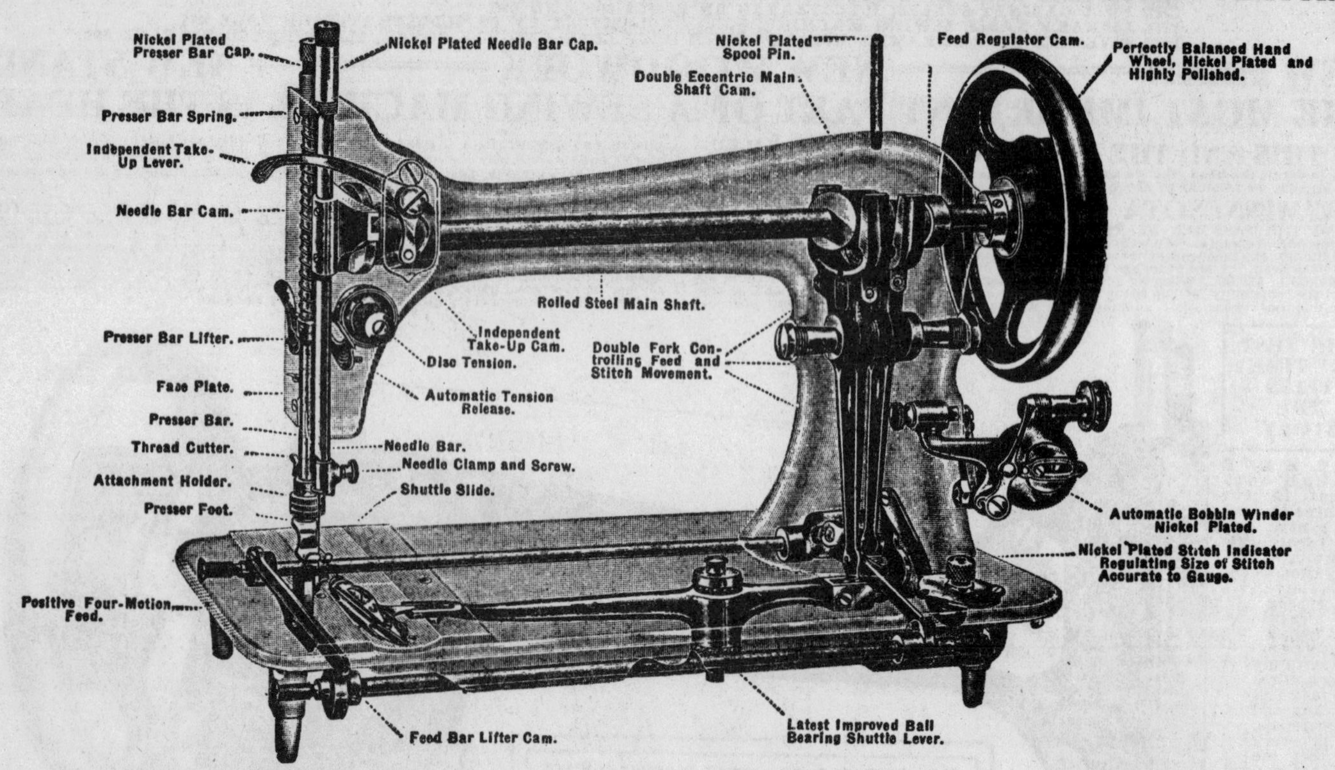

THE STRENGTH, SIMPLICITY AND CORRECTNESS OF THE mechanical principles embodied in the Minnesota Model "A" Head can be judged from these X-ray or shadowgraph pictures shown on this page. This X-ray picture shows the mechanical construction of the Model "A" Head, and if you follow it closely and read the detailed description on the next page, we are sure you will understand why the Minnesota Model "A" is so far ahead of all other sewing machines in mechanical construction, and why we so strongly recommend the selection of our Model "A". Even in these illustrations we have called attention by means of dotted lines only to the most improved features. There are many other mechanical details which go to prove the superiority of the Minnesota Model "A" which we are unable to present satisfactorily on a catalog page, and we are also unable to show you the wonderful workmanship in this machine, the manner in which every piece and part is so carefully made and finished, everything fitting and operating perfectly, a class of finest skilled workmanship that is not excelled by any fine watch or any complicated high grade mechanical device of any kind costing one hundred times as much.

ABOVE IS AN X-RAY PICTURE OR SHADOWGRAPH OF the head, and the illustration below is made from a regular photograph showing the under side of the bed plate, giving you a better view of many of the improved mechanical features.

ANY MECHANIC CAN SEE FROM THESE ILLUSTRATIONS THAT OUR Minnesota Model "A" embodies all of the very latest up to date improvements in mechanical construction. Many sewing machines, even some of the well known makes and practically all of the stenciled machines handled by other mail order houses, retain the old time complicated construction, using many rods and bars to connect the operating parts with the main shaft, also employing springs, cushions, pads, cogs and other unnecessary devices to partly control the movements of the needle, feed and take-up. When new from the factory, such machines work satisfactorily, but there is no positive assurance that the mechanism will remain in working order without frequent repair. Our constant aim has been to simplify the principle of construction by decreasing as far as possible the number of working parts and making each part independent of the others and thereby positive in its action.

Hardened Cold Rolled Steel Feed Lift Cam. This Gives the Positive Feed.

Hardened Cold Rolled Steel Feed Bar.

This Shaft Raises the Feed.

Special Bed Plate Reinforcements.

Needle Guide, Used Only On Minnesota Heads, Prevents Breaking of Needle.

Extra Strong Nickel Plated Shuttle Carrier.

Best Made and Largest Size Self Threading Cylinder Shuttle Manufactured.

BALL BEARING

BALL BEARING

Automatic Self Oiling Shuttle Race.

This Shaft Operates in Connection with the Stitch Regulator and Causes the Machine to Make the Number of Stitches to the Inch as Indicated by the Stitch Regulator.

Special Bed Plate Reinforcements.

Ball Bearing Shuttle Lever.

Frictionless Ball and Socket Joint.

Remember, this is the only family sewing machine that is made having a self adjusting main connection eccentric lever. Our Model "A" is therefore the easiest running sewing machine in the world.

THE ECCENTRIC SYSTEM IS USED IN OUR MINNESOTA MODEL "A," and all clumsy, hard working, sticky cog wheels are done away with. Less working parts are used in its makeup than in any other shuttle machine, and its transmitting power construction is exceedingly simple. All running parts, even to the bobbin winder, are supplied with operating power direct from the main shaft and act absolutely independent of one another. The eccentric at the right end of the main shaft operates both the feed and shuttle, while the shaft head at the left end of the arm drives the needle bar and take-up simultaneously. By the use of this eccentric action much less power is required to run the machine, and insures a light running, easy operating movement, harmonious action and unfailing certainty of absolute evenness in the action of the different parts, and makes it impossible for one part to be slower or quicker in movement than another. It runs smoothly, nearly noiseless and will never wear loose nor shaky.

DESCRIPTION OF MODEL "A" PARTS—Continued.

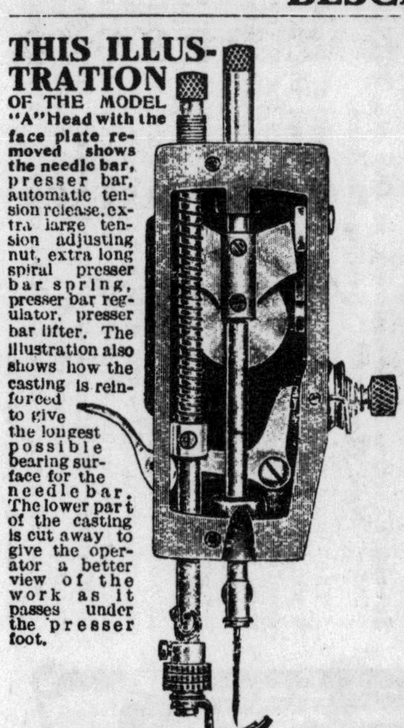

THIS ILLUSTRATION OF THE MODEL "A" Head with the face plate removed shows the needle bar, presser bar, automatic tension release, extra large tension adjusting nut, extra long spiral presser bar spring, presser bar regulator, presser bar lifter. The illustration also shows how the casting is reinforced to give the longest possible bearing surface for the needle bar. The lower part of the casting is cut away to give the operator a better view of the work as it passes under the presser foot.

MAIN CONNECTION DOUBLE FORK ECCENTRIC LEVERS.

THE MAIN CONNECTION LEVERS, as signified by the name, are the important parts of the sewing machine, because they communicate the power from the main shaft to the shuttle lever and the feed raising bar. These levers are made of the highest grade of malleable iron. The bearing surfaces are faced, hardened and ground to a perfect fit. The more perfect the adjustment of these levers the easier will the machine run and the longer will it last. This construction is an exclusive Minnesota Model "A" feature.

THE SHUTTLE.

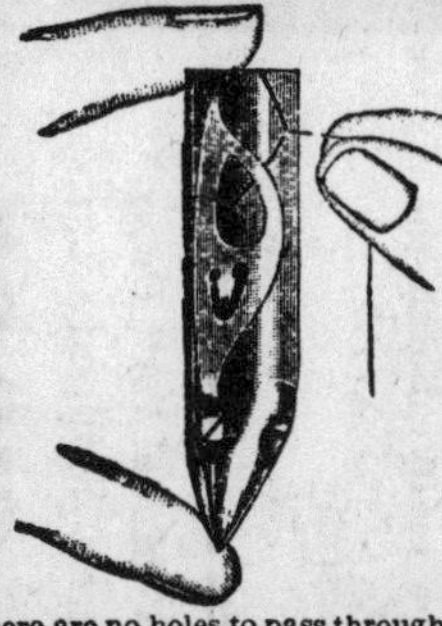

THE SHUTTLE is the most perfect self-threading cylindrical shuttle ever produced. It is extra large in size, made of the finest tool steel, hardened, ground and finished. It is absolutely selfthreading, being open at one end for inserting the bobbin, after which the thread is instantly drawn into place by two movements of the hand. There are no holes to pass through, and the shuttle can be threaded with the eyes shut. It has a perfect tension, which is practically automatic. It does not require regulating for any ordinary work. The bobbin carries a large amount of thread. The illustration shows the shuttle being held between the thumb and forefinger while threading.

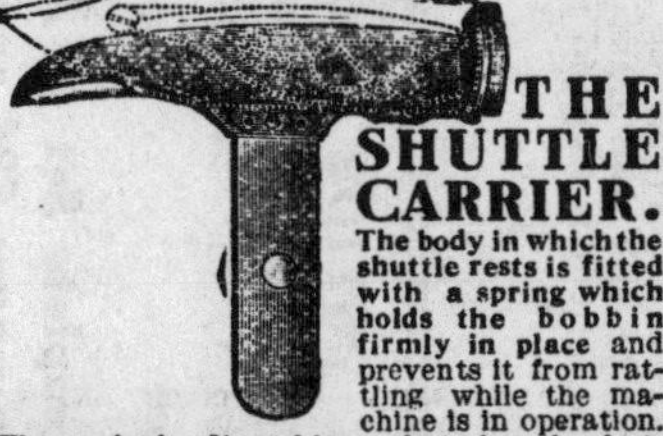

THE SHUTTLE CARRIER.

The body in which the shuttle rests is fitted with a spring which holds the bobbin firmly in place and prevents it from rattling while the machine is in operation. The carrier is adjustable, so that when the shuttle shows signs of wear, after many years of use, the carrier can be moved closer to the shuttle race, thus enabling the operator to use the same shuttle for many years, with the same satisfaction as when new.

OUR NEW SELF OILING SHUTTLE RACE FOUND ON ALL MINNESOTA MODEL "A" SEWING MACHINES.

THIS NEW IMPROVEMENT, THIS SELF oiling device for the shuttle race, solves the problem of keeping the race properly oiled without danger of getting too much oil on the race and soiling the upper and lower threads. It keeps the shuttle race always properly oiled and thereby reduces the friction of the shuttle against the race and prevents wear of the shuttle.

NEEDLE AND THREAD SCALE.

A SCALE INDICATING THE proper needle to be used with the different sizes of thread is stamped on the forward shuttle slide. Breaking of the thread and needles often occurs if incorrect sizes of needles or thread are used.

ROUND NEEDLE BAR

MADE OF COLD ROLLED steel drawn to size, hardened, straightened and then lapped to a certain gauge. In this way only can the perfect needle bar be made.

NEEDLE BAR CAM

FASTENED TO the needle bar with two screws. This cam is made with the slotted gib which insures a silent needle bar with no vibration.

SEE PAGES 694 AND 695 for illustrations showing the New Minnesota Model "A" Attachments and the many different uses to which they may be applied. Our New Model "A" Instruction Book, furnished with every Minnesota Model "A" machine, contains many more illustrations with plain, simple directions relative to the use of all the attachments, as well as complete instructions on HOW TO TAKE CARE of YOUR MACHINE.

THE NEEDLE CLAMP

HOLDS THE needle firmly in place and permits the needle to be removed in an instant when required, even though it should break accidentally in the bar where it cannot be reached by the fingers. The needles can be bought from us at factory cost. For prices see page 678.

SELF SETTING NEEDLE.

THE NEEDLE bar is constructed with a groove in which the needle shank is inserted as far as it will go, the flat side against the needle bar, so that the operation of setting the needle is absolutely automatic. It is not necessary to guess at the proper height or position of the needle.

THE PRESSER BAR

IS MADE OF COLD rolled steel and is drawn to size.

THE PRESSER BAR SPRING

IS MADE OF music wire; both ends are set square and ground. This prevents the ends of the spring from catching and twisting when adjusting the presser bar.

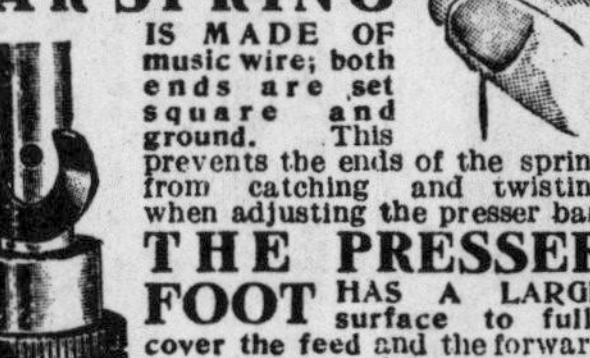

THE PRESSER FOOT

HAS A LARGE surface to fully cover the feed and the forward part nearest the operator is curved upward so that the foot will not catch in the seams of fleecy materials. The presser foot is heavily nickel plated and is highly polished.

ATTACHMENT HOLDER

IS MADE OF COLD ROLLED STEEL, is heavily nickel plated and polished. The presser foot may be removed from the attachment holder and other attachments put on without the use of a screwdriver.

THREAD CUTTER.

THIS MACHINE IS SUPplied with a steel thread cutter, conveniently attached to the presser bar, by the aid of which the thread can be easily cut, obviating the use of scissors and the danger of breaking or cutting the thread too short.

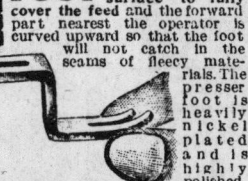

DOUBLE FEED.

THE FEED is made of the best quality tool steel; has five sets of teeth, two on one side of the needle, three on the other and so constructed that when in operation the goods must be carried forward with absolute accuracy.

FEED MOVEMENT

(FOUR-MOTION.) the feed in this machine is operated by four movements. The feed comes up, takes a firm hold on the goods, carries them forward the full length of the stitch, then it falls, releasing the goods, and comes back again toward the operator ready for the next stitch. These four movements are provided entirely by the main shaft, insuring positive action on either heavy or light work.

INDEPENDENT TAKE-UP.

THE TAKE-UP IN THIS MACHINE is driven by a rotary cam on the end of the main shaft, making it positive in its action, insuring a perfect stitch and with no springs to get out of order or break. The positive action of this take-up makes it unnecessary to alter the tensions when the length of stitch or weight of material is changed.

DISC TENSION.

THE UPper tension of this machine is of the modern disc type, and adjusts itself on all classes of work. The tension is located on the side of the cam house toward the operator. This location of the tension is not only far more convenient, but brings the point at which the tension is applied to the thread much nearer to the eye of the needle, thus reducing the amount of thread under tension and doing away, in a large measure, with the stretch in the thread, which, on old style machines, frequently causes bad stitching or skipping of stitches.

AUTOMATIC TENSION RELEASE.

THIS MACHINE IS PROvided with an automatic tension release, which separates the tension plates by merely raising the presser bar lifter so that the work can be drawn from underneath the presser foot with ease.

STITCH REGULATOR.

THE ILLUSTRATION shows the stitch regulator, which is fastened to the bed plate just in front of the arm in plain sight and within easy reach of the operator. The length of the stitch can be adjusted instantly by loosening the thumb nut and moving the pointer to the desired figure on the scale stamped on the stitch regulator plate. The stitch can be varied from seven to thirty-two stitches to the inch, thereby affording a range from the very smallest to the longest stitch.

BALL BEARING SHUTTLE LEVER

(See illustration) WHICH makes our Minnesota Model "A" the lightest running sewing machine on the market. The adjustment is perfect and positively will not get out of order. The cups and cones used in this construction are turned out of the best tool steel, they are ground out until the surface is as smooth as glass, after which all are case hardened in oil, making them PROOF AGAINST WEAR.

THE ARRANGEMENT OF the two sets of ball bearings on the shuttle lever does away with practically all the friction at this important point. Instead of friction on a 2-inch axle surface of the lever we have, by application of the ball bearings, reduced the contact surface to about one-sixteenth of an inch, the result being a machine that runs lighter, makes less noise and requires less than one-half the power to operate than any other sewing machine on the market.

All Minnesota Machines listed in this catalog use Davis Needles. On sale everywhere. For our prices see page 678.

BEARINGS.

THE BEARINGS OF this machine are of the highest mechanical type. They are either roller or ball joint bearing, or full ball bearing, according to requirement. They are automatic in their workings, have special take-up devices, doing away with all unnecessary friction, insuring an easy running and nearly noiseless machine.

ADJUSTMENT.

ALL BEARings and working parts of this machine which require adjustment are made of the finest steel that can be obtained, and after being thoroughly hardened by the latest and most improved process, are accurately ground to a perfect fit and so constructed that any lost motion, due to the slightest wear that may result after many years of use, can be easily and quickly taken up. This renders it practically indestructible and one of the most durable machines ever produced.

WE FURNISH, FREE OF CHARGE,

WITH EVERY MINNEsota Model "A" Sewing Machine, a book of instructions telling how to operate the sewing machine. This book covers every point, makes everything so plain and simple that anyone without previous experience can learn to run the machine at once and do perfect work; tells you how to get the best results, how to take care of your machine, tells you where to oil and when. It tells you how to use the different attachments, the ruffler, tucker, hemmers and binders, and contains illustrations of these attachments in use.

THE HAND WHEEL.

THE HAND WHEEL IS OF THE VERY latest pattern, with handsome nickel plated and polished rim, and is so constructed that it can be easily released and made to run free in either direction for the purpose of winding the bobbin without the necessity of removing the work from the machine and without causing the working parts to operate.

LOCK NUT.

THE LOCK NUT, which is located at the end of the shaft and used to release and tighten the hand wheel, is turned out of one piece of steel, has milled edge and is heavily nickel plated and polished. The lock nut is plainly marked with arrows showing which way it must be turned to loosen or tighten the hand wheel.

EASY TO OIL.

BY MEANS of convenient oil holes and a movable metal plate on the back of the head, all bearings are easily reached to oil. This is a most important feature, as thorough lubrication prevents friction and wear.

RUNNING SPEED.

EVERY machine, before being shipped from the factory, is put to the severest possible test, being set up and attached to a power pulley and run at a speed five times greater than it is possible to run any machine by foot power, and by this severe test we first learn that every machine is perfectly true in every particular and capable of the highest possible speed.

AUTOMATIC BOBBIN WINDER.

THE BOBBIN WINDER ON THIS MAchine is nickel plated throughout, and is the most perfect bobbin winder ever produced. It is so simple that a child can operate it, and the thread is wound on the bobbin automatically and so even and smoothly as to make the bobbin work perfectly in the shuttle, producing an even tension and greatly improving the perfection of the stitch. This also prevents the breaking of the lower thread, which is liable to occur with an unevenly wound bobbin.

BOBBIN WINDER

IS ALways in position and ready to operate. It is operated by means of the belt, which is placed in contact with the small pulley wheel of the bobbin winder.

THE ALL IMPORTANT PART

OF A SEWING MACHINE IS the head. On this and the foregoing pages we have endeavored to give you a complete description of every important piece and part entering into the construction of the New Model "A" Head. We conceal nothing regarding its manufacture. We want you to know of what material the different parts are made and from these descriptions we hope you will realize how carefully the Minnesota New Model "A" Head is made.

ALL NEW MODEL "A" PARTS

ARE EXAMINED AND MEASured before they are put in the machines. This insures uniformity of parts and is also the reason why all Minnesota parts are interchangeable.

 See Our Wonderful Guaranteed $15.00 Fitting Form for Dressmakers for $10.65.

MINNESOTA NEW MODEL "A"

DROP HEAD STYLE, AUTOMATIC LIFT, WITH LATEST DESIGN WOODWORK

Equipped with our New Swinging Inner Pocket Cabinets. The Handsomest, Most Practical and Best Finished Sewing Machine Ever Offered at Any Price. The Result of Fifty Years of Sewing Machine Experience.

FIFTEEN YEARS OF SERVICE AND NO REPAIRS.

Marcola, Oregon.

Sears, Roebuck & Co., Chicago, Ill.
Dear Sirs:—My mother has a sewing machine in her house which she bought of Sears, Roebuck & Co. fifteen years ago last January. She has never paid out a cent for repairs and it is still doing good work. I have received my new one and am well satisfied with it. I have given you orders amounting to over $100.00 this summer, and will give you a good order this fall. Several of my neighbors will order with me.

Yours respectfully,
F. S. APGER.

Compartment arranged for containing thread, needles, scissors, instruction book and various patterns.

Velvet Lined Inner Pocket Cabinet For Attachments

THE TEST OF TIME TELLS THE STORY.

No. 3 Forest Ave., Greenfield, Mass.

Sears, Roebuck & Co., Chicago, Ill.
Sirs:—It may perhaps interest you to know that the Minnesota Sewing Machine I bought of you about seven or eight years ago is doing as good work now as when we first received it.

I have made tents, motion picture screens and a lot of show stuff on it, besides the regular family sewing, dress making, etc. Have sewed heavy canvas and duck and the thinnest of silk and bunting and have really abused the machine, but it is as good today as ever.

Yours respectfully,
W. C. FOGG.

A TAPE MEASURE 18 inches long, accurately divided and beautifully colored to match the woodwork, is transferred on this table, directly in front of the head, where it is most convenient for the use of the operator.

No. 26T102
Price,
$18.95

SWINGING INNER POCKET CABINETS.

Special Features of Woodwork in Our No. 26T102 New Model "A" Sewing Machine.

The handsomest and most beautiful set of woodwork ever furnished in a sewing machine; the most practical; arranged with a particular place for everything; a convenient place for the attachments; separate places for different kinds of thread; a separate compartment for all kinds of patterns; a convenient arrangement for the bobbins filled with thread, which prevents them from becoming tangled; separate sections for the different sized needles, and in addition there are four large, roomy drawers. The drawers are hidden and are always locked when the swinging cabinets are closed. No key is necessary to open or lock the drawers. You press a button and the drawer case opens.

No. 26T102 Minnesota New Model "A" Drop Head Automatic Lift Sewing Machine. Shipped from Dayton, Ohio. Wt., about 125 lbs.
Price.............................**$18.95**

A Complete Set of Attachments as described on pages 694 and 695, 75 Cents Extra.

MINNESOTA NEW MODEL "A" SEWING MACHINE

AN ENTIRELY NEW SET OF WOODWORK IN THE POPULAR DROP HEAD AUTOMATIC LIFT STYLE

LET US SEND YOU THIS NEWEST, VERY LATEST STYLE MINNESOTA MODEL "A" Sewing Machine entirely at our risk. We guarantee it will please you. It has all the qualities of a strictly high grade sewing machine. It sews perfectly; it runs easily and with very little noise; it is furnished with a cabinet which is used exclusively by us, for the design and style of which patents have been applied for. This woodwork is an entirely new design, something out of the ordinary, different from the woodwork which you will find on all other styles of machines.

THIS IS AN EXCLUSIVE STYLE AND PATTERN, MANUFACTURED ONLY FOR US. Order one of these machines; take it home and try it. Use it for three months. Compare it with other machines, and if you are not satisfied and sure that you have greater value for $18.95 in the New Style No. 26T102 Minnesota Model "A" Sewing Machine than your neighbors have in any machine for which they have paid from $45.00 to $60.00 you may return the machine and get your money back.

DESCRIPTION OF THE NEW STYLE No. 26T102 MINNESOTA NEW MODEL "A" SEWING MACHINE

THE HANDSOMEST, MOST PRACTICAL AND FINEST FINISHED CABINET EVER USED ON A SEWING MACHINE

MATERIAL. **SPECIALLY SELECTED LARGE flaky figured quarter sawed oak and highest grade quarter sawed oak veneers are used for the** construction of this woodwork.

DESIGN. **PLEASE OBSERVE ITS SIMPLICITY and yet its richness. This design and style is made only for Sears, Roebuck and Co.** The carvings are tasteful and artistic. There is nothing gaudy or glaring to attract attention for the moment only. Every detail has been carefully considered, with the result that we not only have the most beautiful woodwork, but the most practical as well.

THE TABLE. **THE TABLES FOR OUR NEW style No. 26T102 Minnesota Model "A" woodwork are made of specially selected quarter sawed oak,** with large flaky figures. The lid is made of built-up stock, that is, there are different layers of wood, the grain of each layer running crosswise to the other, while the upper layer is specially selected quarter sawed oak with large flaky figures. For illustration showing this construction see page 687.

THE DRAWER CASES. **THE NEWEST, latest and most up to date drawer cases made. These drawer cases cover and entirely conceal the drawers.** The compartments arranged on both drawer cases are very practical and handy to get at. Every little detail has been looked after. Only the highest and most expensive grade of quarter sawed oak is used in the construction of these drawer cases. Note the gracefully curved sides of the drawer cases and the beautiful and artistic carvings on the fronts.

No. 26T102
Price, $18.95

THE DRAWERS. **BESIDES THE SPECIAL compartments in the drawer cases there are four of the regular sewing machine drawers, two on each side.** The drawers are large and roomy and the upper right hand drawer is fitted with a special compartment to hold extra bobbins and needles according to their different sizes. The drawers are made good and strong and are fitted with a neat wooden pull, capped with a brass escutcheon.

THE DRUM. **WHEN THE MACHINE IS CLOSED and not in use the head is protected from injury, dirt and dust by a metal drum,** stained in imitation of oak, giving it the same appearance as the woodwork, and which entirely encases the under part of the head, preventing the dripping of oil on the garments of the operator.

THE FINISH. **WE TAKE PARTICULAR PRIDE in the finish of this style of woodwork. It is the richest effect we have ever seen on any cabinet work.** The selected stock and the care and attention paid to the finish enable us to supply our customers with the richest and best finished set of woodwork ever supplied with a sewing machine. This woodwork is treated in the finishing department in the same manner as the highest and most expensive grades of furniture are finished. The color is a rich new shade of golden oak, a most luxurious finish.

A TAPE MEASURE, 18 inches long, accurately divided and beautifully colored to match the woodwork, is transferred on this table, directly in front of the head, where it is most convenient for the use of the operator.

Read page 693 and note what our customers say about our sewing machines.

THIS ILLUSTRATION OF THE LEFT HAND drawer case shows to what practical uses it can be applied. The upper compartment is arranged to hold a supply of spools of thread. The lower division is very conveniently arranged to hold all kinds of patterns, the instruction book, special samples of cloth, etc.

THE LARGE ILLUSTRATION shown on the page above will give you a fair idea of the finely figured and grained effect that is brought out in this woodwork, but the cabinet must be seen to be appreciated. This special style of cabinet is the result of careful observation and years of study. It is entirely different from the present and past styles of sewing machine furniture. The appearance of the machine when closed is very attractive and the illustrations do not show the beautiful finish of the woodwork. By looking at a picture of the machine you get no idea of the time and labor spent in rubbing and polishing to bring out the handsome graining effects of the quarter sawed oak. **Send for one of these machines right away.** You are not obliged to keep it if you do not like it, or if you are not satisfied in every way with your purchase. We take all the risk and will refund your money and also pay the freight charges both ways if you do not keep the machine.

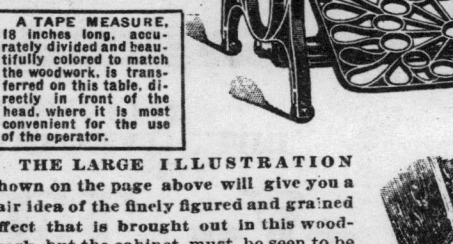

THIS ILLUSTRATION of a part of the upper right hand drawer shows the manner in which the bobbins and needles are kept in order.

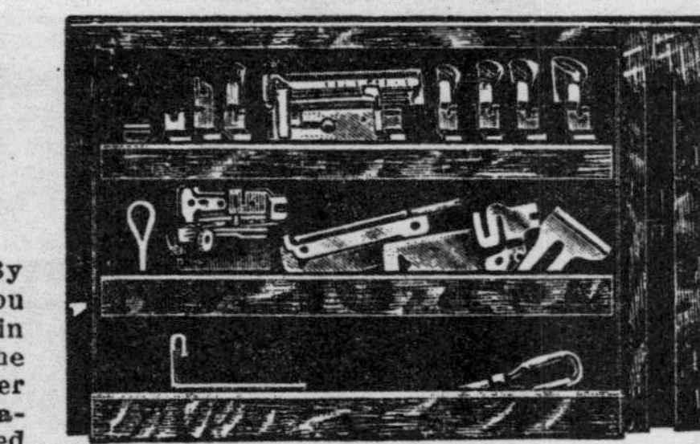

THIS ILLUSTRATION OF THE RIGHT HAND drawer case shows the orderly manner in which the attachments may be kept. The inside of this drawer case is lined with velveteen and is especially partitioned to hold all of the attachments and most of the accessories supplied with the machine. The attachments are always at hand, easily within reach, and always in plain sight.

MINNESOTA NEW MODEL "A"

SIX-DRAWER, AUTOMATIC LIFT, DROP HEAD STYLE

This Machine is Ready for Immediate Delivery in a Warehouse Near You.

Read Page 688.

Kansas: "I Received the Machine in First Class Condition Five Days From the Time I Mailed My Order on the R. F. D."

R. F. D. No. 6, Atchison, Kan.

Sears, Roebuck & Co., Chicago, Ill.

Gentlemen:—As a rule, I do not believe in giving testimonials, but I will make an exception in regard to your Minnesota "A" machine. I ordered a Minnesota "A" Six-Drawer Drop Head Machine to be shipped from your Kansas City warehouse. I received the machine in first class condition five days from the time I mailed my order on the R. F. D. The machine will compare favorably with any $40.00 machine on the market, in my estimation. I was prejudiced against the machine at first, I will admit, a Singer being my choice, but a careful examination and severe tests have removed all doubts as to the good qualities of your machine from my mind. You may use this testimonial or refer any persons or parties in this community to me.

Yours truly,

ERNEST E. KERR.

SHIPPED FROM—

Albany, N. Y.
Harrisburg, Penn.
Omaha, Neb.
St. Louis, Mo.
St. Paul, Minn.
Kansas, City, Mo.

No. 26T6 Minnesota Model "A" Six-Drawer Drop Head Automatic Lift Sewing Machine, with complete set of attachments.

Price.......... **$19.60**

The Complete Extra Set of Steel Foot Attachments is included in the above price.

SHIPPED FROM—

San Francisco, Cal.
Seattle, Wash.

No. 26T6 Minnesota Model "A" Six-Drawer Drop Head Automatic Lift Sewing Machine, with complete set of attachments.

Price.......... **$21.35**

The Complete Extra Set of Steel Foot Attachments is included in the above price.

SHIPPED FROM—

Dayton, Ohio.

No. 26T106 Minnesota Model "A" Six Drawer Drop Head Automatic Lift Sewing Machine.

Price.......... **$17.85**

A Complete Set of Attachments, 75 cents extra.

A TAPE MEASURE 18 inches long, accurately divided and beautifully colored to match the woodwork, is transferred on this table, directly in front of the head, where it is most convenient for the use of the operator.

Shipping weight, about 125 pounds.

Minnesota New Model "A" Sewing Machine

FOUR-DRAWER DROP HEAD, BALL BEARING AUTOMATIC LIFT STYLE

WITH OUR AUTOMATIC DEVICE ALL YOU do is to lift up and turn back the extension leaf, the head goes up into place ready for sewing at once; nothing further is required, and it's just one easy motion. On the old style hand lift you go through these five movements; 1—Lift up and turn back the leaf. 2—Lift up the head. 3—Lift up and adjust the narrow shelf that the head rests on. 4—Set the head down. 5—Put on the belt. In our automatic lift the one movement, the act of lifing up the leaf and turning it back, brings the head automatically into final position, and the mechanism is so adjusted and balanced that almost no effort whatever is required to lift and turn back the leaf. The weight of the head by reason of this automatic lift is not perceptible. One hand does the work. Only one operation is necessary. With the other style of hand lift drop head machine it not only requires the five separate operations, but the use of both hands is necessary. With the old hand lift machine it is necessary to remove the belt every time you raise or lower the head. With our automatic lift the belt always remains in position, and when you raise the head it is ready for sewing.

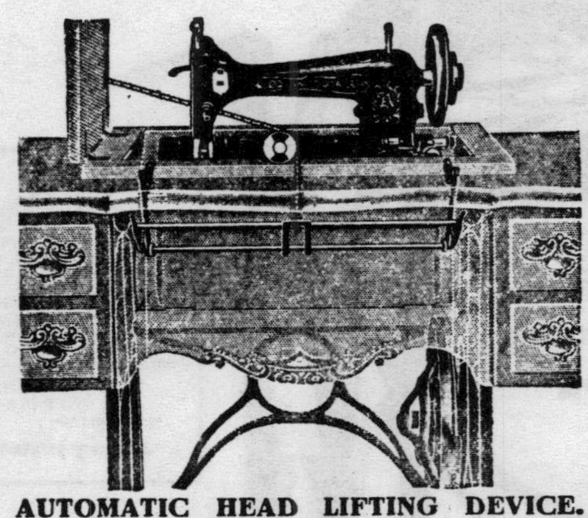

AUTOMATIC HEAD LIFTING DEVICE.

SIX-DRAWER DROP HEAD, BALL BEARING AUTOMATIC LIFT STYLE

THIS PERFECT AND SIMPLE YET EXTREMELY strong automatic lifting device is the result of years of work in improving and perfecting a lifting device. No expense has been spared in perfecting this mechanism, and its construction is of the highest class throughout. There are absolutely no springs used in this device. The chain which bears most of the strain is the strongest chain of its kind that is manufactured, the equal of the finest bicycle chain. Each link is composed of three plates, securely riveted together. This gives the chain sufficient elasticity and prevents the possibility of its breaking under any strain. By a simple arrangement the chain may be tightened or loosened, simply turning two adjusting nuts to the right or to the left, according to whether the chain is to be shortened or lengthened. The shaft to which the chain is attached, and which, when the lid is raised, forces the head in position for sewing, is made of the best grade of cold rolled steel, with a cold rolled steel roller on each end which helps to make the lifting device so easy to operate.

DESCRIPTION OF THE WOODWORK SUPPLIED WITH THE Nos. 26T104 and 26T106 FOUR AND SIX-DRAWER DROP HEAD AUTOMATIC LIFT STYLE MACHINES.

Shipping wt., about 120 lbs.

No. 26T104

No. 26T104 Minnesota New Model "A" Ball Bearing Four-Drawer Drop Head Automatic Lift Sewing Machine. Price.... **$17.35**
Shipped from Dayton, Ohio.

A Complete Set of Steel Foot Attachments, see pages 694 and 695, 75 Cents Extra.

MATERIAL. THE MINNESOTA MODEL "A" CABinets, illustrated on this page and the page above, are made of specially selected, highly figured quarter sawed oak, thoroughly air seasoned and kiln dried to prevent warping, checking or cracking. We believe that in this Model "A" woodwork we furnish the most substantial, the strongest, best finished and handsomest set of woodwork that is furnished by any sewing machine manufacturer.

DESIGN. PLEASE OBSERVE THE SIMPLICITY AND yet its richness. Note the square drawer fronts, with drawer cases and table to match, with new hand shaped wood carvings, which place this Model "A" style in a class above any other sewing machine cabinets. These designs and patterns of woodwork are exclusive with us, and cannot be secured with any other machine.

THE TABLE. THE TABLES OF THE WOODWORK used on our Model "A" machines are all made of specially selected quartered oak with large flaky figures. The Lids are all made of built-up stock; that is, there are different layers of wood, the grain of each layer running crosswise to the other, while the upper layer is highly figured specially selected quarter sawed oak. Only the highest and most expensive grades of furniture are made in this way.

THE DRAWERS. THE DRAWERS ARE ALL made to correspond in design with the table, having a square front made of quarter sawed oak. The hand shaped wood carvings, which serve as drawer pulls, also add to the ornamentation, and in that way serve a double purpose. The drawers are large and roomy, and will easily hold the attachments, accessories and all the other supplies necessary for all kinds of sewing. A strong lock is carefully fitted on each drawer so that all may be securely locked The key furnished with each machine fits the locks of all the drawers.

THE DRAWER CASES OR FRAMES ARE STRONGLY BUILT AND conform to the general style of the woodwork. The entire side of this drawer case is made of specially selected, highly figured, two-ply quartered oak veneer. On the front of the drawer case, just below the drawers, is a handsome piece of wood carving, rounding off the lower corners.

WHEN THE MACHINE IS CLOSED, AS SHOWN IN THE illustrations on this page, the head is protected by means of a wooden apron, which is forced down and against the front flap when the head is lowered. When the head is raised and in position for sewing the apron and flap rise up with the head, giving ample working space and enabling a person to assume a comfortable position while operating the sewing machine. It also serves to protect the dress from any oil which may happen to drop from the head in case too much oil is used.

THE FINISH. WE TAKE PARTICULAR PRIDE IN THE FINISH OF THIS style of woodwork. It is the richest effect we have ever seen on any cabinet work. The selected stock and the care and attention paid to the finish enables us to supply our customers with the richest and best finished set of woodwork ever supplied with a sewing machine. This woodwork is treated in the finishing department in the same manner as the highest and most expensive grades of furniture are finished. The color is a rich new shade of golden oak, a most luxurious finish. The large illustration shown on the page above will give you a fair idea of the finely figured and grained effect that is brought out in this woodwork, but the cabinet must be seen to be appreciated.

Shipping wt., about 125 lbs.

No. 26T106

No. 26T106 Minnesota New Model "A" Ball Bearing Six-Drawer Drop Head Automatic Lift Sewing Machine. Price.... **$17.85**
Shipped from Dayton, Ohio.

A Complete Set of Steel Foot Attachments, see pages 694 and 695, 75 Cents Extra.

MINNESOTA NEW MODEL "A"

In the Popular Drop Head Style. Handsome All Quarter Sawed Oak Woodwork with Artistic Carvings and Piano Polish Finish. Equipped with New Ball Bearing Stand

A TAPE MEASURE

18 inches long, accurately divided and beautifully colored to match the woodwork, is transferred on these tables, directly in front of the head, where it is most convenient for the use of the operator.

SHIPPED FROM—Albany, N. Y.; Harrisburg, Penn.; Omaha, Neb.; St. Louis, Mo.; St. Paul, Minn.; Kansas City, Mo.

No. 26T10 Minnesota Model "A" Seven-Drawer Drop Head Hand Lift Sewing Machine, with complete set of attachments. Price...................... **$18.20**

The Complete Extra Set of Steel Foot Attachments is included in the price of this machine.

SHIPPED FROM—San Francisco, Cal.; Seattle, Wash.

No. 26T10 Minnesota Model "A" Seven-Drawer Drop Head Hand Lift Sewing Machine, with complete set of attachments. Price...................... **$19.95**

The Complete Extra Set of Steel Foot Attachments is included in the price of this machine.

This Machine Shipped from Dayton, Ohio, Only.

No. 26T108 Price, $15.95

SHIPPED FROM—Dayton, Ohio.

No. 26T108 Minnesota Model "A" Five-Drawer Drop Head Sewing Machine. Price.................. **$15.95**

A Complete Set of Steel Foot Attachments, 75 cents extra.

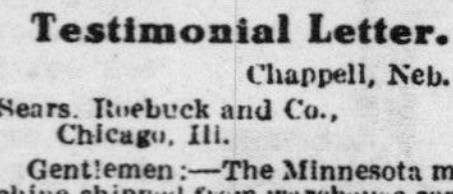

Testimonial Letter.

Chappell, Neb.

Sears, Roebuck and Co., Chicago, Ill.

Gentlemen:—The Minnesota machine shipped from warehouse compares in every way with the highest grade machine made. Am sure we saved sum more than equal to the cost of the machine. You are to be congratulated on being able to put out such a high grade machine at so low a price, and delivering same on such short notice from your branch warehouses.

Very truly,
S. C. YODER.

No. 26T110
Price, $16.45

Shipping weight, about 125 pounds.

SHIPPED FROM—Dayton, Ohio.

No. 26T110 Minnesota Model "A" Seven-Drawer Drop Head Sewing Machine.

Price, **$16.45**

A Complete Set of Steel Foot Attachments, 75 cents extra.

The New Woodwork for Our Minnesota Model "A" Sewing Machine

ENTIRELY NEW. RICH AND HANDSOME. PRACTICAL. OUR EXCLUSIVE DESIGN.

WITH THE IDEA THAT THE MINNESOTA MODEL "A" MUST ALWAYS represent, not only the highest type of mechanical construction, but that it must also present the most beautiful appearance, we have equipped our Model "A" machines with entirely new woodwork, something altogether exclusive, finer, richer and more beautiful than any woodwork that has ever been used by any other sewing machine manufacturer.

THESE NEW CABINETS ARE MADE OF CAREFULLY SELECTED quarter sawed oak, thoroughly air seasoned and kiln dried to prevent possible warping, checking or cracking. In the new Minnesota Model "A" woodwork we furnish the most substantial, the strongest, best finished and handsomest woodwork that is furnished on any sewing machine.

NOTE THE NEW DESIGNS. TEN DIFFERENT MODEL "A" styles to choose from. We wish particularly to call your attention to our style No. 26T102; something entirely new; just out, and made exclusively for us. Refer to the illustrations on pages 682 to 690, and not the appearance of the machine when closed. You will find the drawers on both sides are completely hidden by means of the drawer cases. For complete description of this particular set of woodwork refer to page 687. The other styles of woodwork are very fine and up to date. The carvings used in the construction are of the latest styles and patterns. Every little piece of carving is selected for its particular place in order to improve the appearance. The cabinets, tables, drawer cases and drawer fronts are constructed of quarter sawed oak, only the most beautiful of selected stock is used for the Minnesota Model "A" styles. The table lids are made of built-up stock, that is, thin layers of wood, the grain of each layer running crosswise or diagonally with the other, while the top layer is highly figured quarter sawed oak. Only the best and most expensive grades of furniture are made in this way.

Illustration Showing a Section of 5-Ply Built-up Stock Used in the Construction of Our Model "A" Woodwork.

This construction has been found the most satisfactory and practically insures against warping, cracking or splitting. It is the way piano cases are made and everybody knows they are made to last a lifetime. That is why we insist on this style of construction for our sewing machine woodwork, particularly the Model "A" Style.

THE DRAWER CASES ARE MADE TO correspond in design with the table. They are strongly built, the entire side being made of specially selected, highly figured quartered oak veneer. On the front of the drawer cases, just below the drawers, there is a handsome scroll wood carving rounding off the lower corners. Compare our drawer cases with the ones which are used by other manufacturers, even on machines that sell for two and three times the price of our Minnesota Model "A."

THE DRAWERS ARE ALL LARGE AND ROOMY AND ARE BUILT VERY strong. The front of each drawer is provided with a beautiful wood carving, which serves as a drawer pull. This new drawer pull gives a very rich, tasteful effect. It doesn't tarnish, neither does it break. It is not in the way and will not catch in your dress as so often happens with the old style brass or nickel plated drawer pulls. The center yoke is made with a swell front outline to correspond with the table and the drawer cases. It is handsomely decorated with wood carvings in the center and along the edges.

FULL DESK CABINETS. WE HAVE IMPROVED OUR LINE OF full desk cabinets and have added an entirely new style. For illustration and detailed description of our latest Minnesota Model "A" Cabinet, we refer you to pages 689 and 690.

THE LIBRARY TABLE. THIS STYLE CONTINUES AS POPULAR as ever. We are supplying it with the same high grade workmanship and finish as was put into this machine from the very beginning. The complete description and illustrations will be found on page 691.

THE COVER WHICH IS USED ON THE Model "A" upright machines is the full swell rounded, made from three-ply built-up veneered stock, richly carved, highly polished, beautifully finished, making the handsomest cover ever used on any upright machine.

WE TAKE PARTICULAR PRIDE IN THE FINISH OF OUR MINNESOTA MODEL "A" woodwork. It gives the richest effect we have ever seen on any cabinet work. The stock is so fine, and it is so beautifully filled, sandpapered, hand rubbed, that after the several coats of varnish are put on and then hand rubbed and polished again, the natural figure and grain of the wood is brought out with the most beautiful effect. The color is a rich new shade of golden oak; a most luxurious finish.

MINNESOTA MODEL "A" BALL BEARING STAND

NEW DESIGN. NEW CONSTRUCTION.

OUR NEW STAND SPECIALLY DESIGNED BY OUR SPECIAL DEsigner, is the neatest, best appearing and strongest stand made. These stands are molded by automatic machines, making every piece perfectly true, smooth and of unusual strength, so that when the different parts are put together they fit perfectly. Particular care and attention are paid to the finish and enameling of the stand, which is plainly evident when our Model "A" machines are compared side by side with machines which sell at two or three times the price of our Model "A."

Side View of Leg.

THE PARTICULAR FEATURE OF THIS NEW stand is the ball bearing adjustment and the manner in which the balance wheel is attached. On most other machines the wheel is attached to the leg of the machine, whereas, on the Model "A" stand the wheel is securely attached to the wheel guard, which, in turn, is secured to the leg of the machine by means of three lugs, distributed in such a manner that the wheel guard is not only securely attached to the leg of the machine, but this wheel guard acts as a brace and an extra support for the leg. On the ordinary sewing machine stand the pitman is fastened to the left of the wheel. On the Model "A" it is attached to the right of the wheel, between the balance wheel and the leg, so that it is impossible for one's clothes to come in contact with the pitman when operating the machine. This arrangement of the pitman, besides making the machine lighter running and easier to operate, allows more space between the legs of the machine, making it far more comfortable and easier to sew on our Model "A" machine than on any other machine on the market. By referring to the illustrations you will note the leg is a little wider and is designed to conform with the balance wheel. This is a point which is overlooked on most machines and for that reason the iron work on other machines has an ungainly appearance, because, as a rule, the portion of the leg where the wheel is attached is always considerably narrower and the wheel consequently projects beyond the sides of the leg.

BALL BEARING BALANCE WHEEL. ALL OUR NEW MODEL "A" MACHINES ARE EQUIPPED WITH THIS new, latest improved ball bearing hanger. The hanger is the large balance wheel and shaft fastened to the wheel guard, as shown in this illustration. As this wheel supplies the operating power to the head, the bearings on which it revolves are naturally subjected to considerable strain. By the introduction of the ball bearings all friction is removed, and the wheel revolves with the same freedom and rapidity as the ball bearing crank hanger of the bicycle. The application of the ball bearings to the balance wheel is one of the greatest improvements and the greatest aid to the light running qualities of the machine, and we have demonstrated by actual experiments and tests that our ball bearing hanger is at least 20 per cent lighter running than any ball bearing device or arrangement used on any other sewing machine made. By the aid of the ball bearings a machine is made not only lighter running, but exceedingly easy to operate and very rapid in action. The arrangement of the ball bearings with the balance wheel is the same as that on all high grade bicycles. The axle on which the wheel revolves passes through two steel cups, each of which contains eight solid steel balls, which are fitted in a patent ball retainer, which reduces friction and prevents the bearings from crowding and grinding. The cones are fitted into the balance wheel and by turning the journal to the right or the left it is possible to adjust the bearings so that the balance wheel will at all times run lightly and noiselessly. The cups and cones used on our stand are turned out of a solid bar of steel, after which they are ground out, tempered and hardened, and with proper oiling from time to time they will last a lifetime.

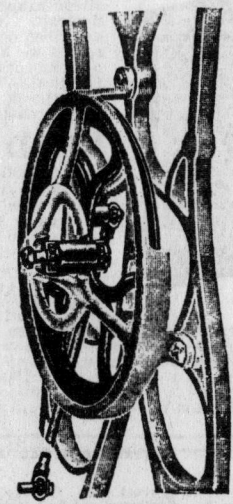

Illustration Showing Ball Bearing Arrangement on Wheel and Pitman.

NOTE. The entire wheel is protected by the guard.

THE PITMAN. ALL Minnesota Model "A" machines are equipped with our new double ball bearing nickel plated steel pitman. These pitmans have a complete set of ball bearings at each end. They are adjusted at the factory and require no more care or attention than the regular wooden pitman. The metal pitman, with ball bearings, besides reducing friction and making the machine run easier, cannot get out of order as easily as the wooden pitman.

Illustration Showing Simple Method for Perfect Treadle Adjustment.

THE BRACES. THE SIDE FRAMES OR LEGS OF THE stand are joined together by a four-armed brace, bolted at the top and bottom, making the stand absolutely rigid. This is very essential, as it lessens the vibration and so causes our machines to make less noise and last longer than those machines which are built on weak and wabbly stands.

DRESS GUARD. THE DRESS GUARDS ON THESE stands are another very strong feature. This guard covers and protects the entire wheel. This makes it impossible for the dress or apron to become caught in the wheel. Besides serving to protect the dress, it acts as a very strong brace for the leg and also acts as the anchor for the balance wheel, which is attached to the dress guard.

TREADLE. THE TREADLE IS OF THE OPENWORK STYLE, with full ends, pivot bearing, as shown by the dotted lines in the illustration; accurately trued, putting the entire machine under easy control of the operator.

OIL GUARD. THE OIL GUARD, IMMEDIATELY UNDER the treadle, extends from side frame to side frame, is securely bolted, strengthens the frame and prevents the oil from dropping on the floor or carpet.

CASTERS. WE USE THE HIGHEST GRADE SEWING MAchine casters made. They are of a large size, making it easy to move the machine from place to place, are carefully fitted and never break.

INSPECTION. ALL PARTS ARE ACCURATELY TRUED AND tested for strength; not a casting is allowed to be used that has a sand hole or defect or that isn't true to gauge. After the stand has been properly assembled, the balance wheel and treadle are operated by steam power at a very high rate of speed, whereby the balance wheel makes a great many more revolutions than any operator could possibly make. If there is the slightest flaw in the iron or in the construction or adjustment of the stand it becomes evident through this test and the stand is then rejected; and as a result, for strength, beauty, design, finish, for easy running and for perfect control of the machine by the operator, we furnish a higher grade sewing machine stand than is furnished by any other maker.

QUICK DELIVERY TO YOU

VERY LOW FREIGHT CHARGES

MINNESOTA NEW MODEL "A"

SIX AND SEVEN-DRAWER AUTOMATIC LIFT AND HAND LIFT DROP HEAD STYLES, COMPLETE WITH EXTRA SET OF STEEL FOOT ATTACHMENTS

SHIPPED FROM

ALBANY, N.Y. HARRISBURG, PENN. OMAHA, NEB. ST. LOUIS, MO. ST. PAUL, MINN. KANSAS CITY, MO.

PRICE ON CARS FROM ANY OF THE ABOVE NAMED CITIES WITH COMPLETE EXTRA SET OF STEEL FOOT ATTACHMENTS:

No. 26T6 Minnesota Model "A" Six-Drawer Automatic Lift Sewing Machine............ **$19.60**
No. 26T10 Minnesota Model "A" Seven-Drawer Hand Lift Sewing Machine............ **18.20**

PACIFIC COAST WAREHOUSES:

SAN FRANCISCO, CAL. SEATTLE, WASH.

PRICE ON CARS AT SAN FRANCISCO OR SEATTLE WITH COMPLETE EXTRA SET OF STEEL FOOT ATTACHMENTS:

No. 26T6 Minnesota Model "A" Six-Drawer Automatic Lift Sewing Machine............ **$21.35**
No. 26T10 Minnesota Model "A" Seven-Drawer Hand Lift Sewing Machine............ **19.95**

REMEMBER, IF YOU ORDER ONE OF THESE MACHINES, sending the order and money to Sears, Roebuck and Co., Chicago, you will have to pay only the small freight charge from the San Francisco or Seattle warehouse (whichever is nearest you) to your own railroad station.

TO ENABLE US TO MAKE QUICK DELIVERY, WE HAVE SHIPPED OUR SIX-DRAWER AUTOMATIC lift and seven-drawer hand lift drop head ball bearing Minnesota New Model "A," Sewing Machines in carload lots to our warehouses in the above named cities, so that we can ship you from the nearest warehouse without delay whichever of these handsome high grade machines you order so that you will receive it with but a small freight charge to pay from the warehouse nearest you to your freight station, we having paid the freight from the factory to the warehouse.

SEE LARGE ILLUSTRATION OF THIS MACHINE ON PAGE 684.

AUTOMATIC LIFT STYLE

No. 26T6

WITH ALL THE MACHINES SUPPLIED FROM THE WAREHOUSE, we include a complete set of latest improved steel foot attachments, fully described on page 694, and prepay all charges, so that the slight difference in price between what we ask for the machine at the factory and the price at the warehouse city nearest you, represents only the shipping charges from the factory to the warehouse, and when you get the machine, you have nothing to pay but the very small freight charge from the warehouse to your station.

UNDERSTAND CLEARLY THE ONLY MACHINES WE HAVE IN these different warehouses are the two most popular styles; the six-drawer and seven-drawer, drop head, Minnesota New Model "A" with automatic lift and hand lift, the exact same machines described on pages 684 to 686, catalog No. 26T106 and No. 26T110. The majority of our sewing machine customers buy our highest grade New Model "A" machine. It is the popular machine, the best seller, gives the greatest satisfaction and is a machine that we guarantee to have no superior and few equals among the sewing machines of the world.

PROMPT AND IMMEDIATE DELIVERY

If you live nearer to one of these cities than you do to Dayton, Ohio, then order one of these machines complete with full set of attachments, sending your order and money, of course, direct to Sears, Roebuck and Co., Chicago, Ill., and you will get your machine without any delay, because the machines in the warehouse are all packed and ready to be shipped the same day we notify the warehouse to ship your machine. This is a great advantage. As soon as we receive your order, we send a special delivery letter to the warehouse in the city nearest you and instruct the warehouseman to ship you a machine complete with a set of attachments, and you will get it in a day or two thereafter. There is no chance for delay, and as the distance from the warehouse to your city is very much less than from the factory, there is no long haul by railroad, just the short haul from the warehouse nearest you to your town, so there can be no delay whatever. You will be surprised and delighted with the promptness with which you will get your machine. You will be using it within a few days after you send us your order and you will get it in perfect condition.

SEE LARGE ILLUSTRATION OF THIS MACHINE ON PAGE 686.

HAND LIFT STYLE

No. 26T10

DIRECT FROM THE FACTORY (AT DAYTON, Ohio), **we ship these machines with or without the extra set of attachments as may be desired.** Nearly all of our customers order the extra set of attachments as described on page 694, at the same time that they order a machine. For this reason we have arranged to include a complete set of these high grade steel foot attachments with each machine from the warehouse. These machines are identical. They are exactly the same style, the difference in price representing only the extra set of attachments and the shipping charges from the factory to the warehouse city nearest you.

READ CAREFULLY THE DETAILED DESCRIPTION OF this machine as explained on pages 684 to 686 and we simply urge you to place your order for either the No. 26T6 six-drawer automatic lift drop head style, or No. 26T10 for the seven-drawer hand lift drop head style, and address your order to Sears, Roebuck and Co., at Chicago, because we can, in that way, ship the machine from the warehouse nearest you and you will get it within a day or two after we receive the order and the only freight you will have to pay will be the small local freight charge from the warehouse to your town.

REMEMBER THAT ALL OTHER MACHINES illustrated and described in this catalog are carefully packed and securely crated and shipped from the factory at Dayton, Ohio, and that should you desire to order any other style of machine, we can only ship it from the factory; we guarantee safe delivery and prompt shipment of any machine you may order shipped from the factory at Dayton, Ohio, but if you live any distance from Dayton, Ohio, there will be a great saving of time by ordering the New Model "A" machine shipped from warehouse, because the delivery of a single machine from Dayton to your city would naturally take longer than when shipped direct from a neighboring city.

"THE MINNESOTA MODEL 'A' ARRIVED WITHIN A FEW DAYS AFTER THE ORDER WAS MAILED."

Fort D. A. Russell, Wyo.

Sears, Roebuck & Co., Chicago, Ill.

Gentlemen:—I have received the Minnesota Model "A" Sewing Machine that I ordered from you. It arrived within a few days after I sent in my order, in fact, before I expected it. It was in first class condition in every respect, and I am satisfied that I have saved at least $40.00 on this purchase. A few days before I sent in my order an agent called on me to sell a machine and he wanted $65.00 for his machine. I find that this machine is as well made, as strong and as ornamental, and will do any of the work which his machine would, in fact, my neighbors that have some of the other machines come and use our machine when they want to do work with the attachments, claiming that your machine is superior to all. It will last a lifetime and then some. Very respectfully, H. C. SLOAN, Post Quartermaster Sergeant.

Our Minnesota Model "A"

DARK OAK ONLY

Automatic Lift, Ball Bearing, Full Desk Cabinet Machine,

GREATLY IMPROVED FOR THIS SEASON, MANY NEW FEATURES ADDED, BROUGHT RIGHT UP TO DATE

A GREAT IMPROVEMENT IN QUALITY. WE HAVE FORTUNATELY been able through our enormous sales of this particular style of cabinet work to effect a material reduction in the manufacturing cost. We have been able to make better contracts for the woodwork, have secured other advantages, have been able to save a few cents here and there by increasing the quantity of machines put through daily, and all these advantages, no matter how slight, we give our customers the benefit of by offering a cabinet sewing machine at $18.90 which will compare with cabinet machines as sold by agents and others at $40.00 and more.

WE GUARANTEE TO YOU THAT THE QUALITY OF THIS, OUR CELEBRATED Minnesota Model "A," Automatic Lift, Ball Bearing Drop Desk Cabinet Machine has been maintained in every way, in fact, if you buy a Minnesota Drop Desk Cabinet Machine from us today, you will get a better machine than you would if you had bought from our last catalog. It now embodies all our latest improvements, strengthened, improved in many small details, a better machine and handsomer woodwork than we have ever offered under this catalog number.

COMPARE OUR PRICE OF $18.90 WITH THE PRICE asked by any retail dealer, agent, or by any other catalog house for their highest grade sewing machines in a beautiful carved and decorated, all quarter sawed oak, drop desk cabinet. See if you can find anything in any catalog or in any store in the line of a fine sewing machine at anything like our price that will compare with this special Minnesota Model "A." You will not find a machine at within a good many dollars of our price. If you find it at three times the price you would not find a better sewing machine. Money cannot build a better sewing machine than the Minnesota Model "A." In all the essential points, all the features that make a fine machine in range of work of plain and fancy sewing, ease of operation, noiselessness, light running quality, the Minnesota Model "A" is really in a class by itself, not surpassed in quality by even such sewing machines that sell at $50.00 to $60.00.

WE ASK YOU TO REMEMBER THAT THE MINNESOTA MACHINE is not the kind of a sewing machine that is handled by catalog houses generally. It is a standard sewing machine, our standard for quality, the kind of article we want you to get from us and then judge us by its quality, something to use every day and serve as a reminder of our house. We guarantee every Minnesota machine for twenty years, let you take it for a full ninety days' trial in your own home, and we stand back of every machine in every way.

AS MANY OF OUR CUSTOMERS HAVE expressed a desire to purchase our Minnesota Model "A" Sewing Machine with a plainer and lighter weight cabinet than our No. 26T116, shown on page 690, we present the style shown in these illustrations, which we are confident will meet the approval of our friends who wish a tasty appearing, light weight cabinet sewing machine. The cabinet is made of the same high grade carefully selected quarter sawed oak as our No. 26T116, the bottom and back being of solid oak while the top or cover, sides and door are made of beautifully figured quarter sawed oak. The sides, back and door are paneled, which prevents cracking or splitting.

THE DESIGN OF THE CABINET WHILE PLAIN, IS VERY ATTRACTIVE, AND is strongly built; handsomely carved and ornamented. The quarter sawed oak panels on the door and sides of the cabinet are arched. The door is decorated with artistic wood carvings, which give the cabinet a very rich and elegant appearance. A compartment securely fastened to the door is arranged to contain the attachments and accessories and such other supplies as are in constant demand when sewing. This compartment, as may be seen by reference to the illustrations, is most conveniently arranged, so that it will not be necessary for the person using the machine to move her chair or even change her position when wishing to use any of the attachments or accessories contained in this compartment. Cabinet is fitted with four large wooden casters, making it very easy to move the cabinet from one part of the room to another.

THE HEAD USED ON THIS MACHINE IS THE SAME AS IS USED ON ALL OF OUR HIGHEST grade Minnesota New Model "A" Machines. For complete description of mechanical construction, attachments, etc., see pages 679 to 681.

WE FIND THE BEST ADVERTISEMENT WE CAN POSSIBLY GET IS A well satisfied customer, and we have hundreds of these in every community, and among them are quite a number in every town who have bought and are now using our sewing machines, and if you will ask anyone in your neighborhood who is using one of our machines whether they have ever seen a sewing machine furnished by any other house that will compare with the machine we sold them, either in quality or price, on their answer we are sure we will receive your order.

WE FURNISH, FREE OF CHARGE, WITH EVERY MINNESOTA MODEL "A" Sewing Machine, a book of instructions, telling how to operate the sewing machine. This book covers every point, makes everything so plain and simple that anyone without previous experience can learn to run the machine at once and do perfect work, tells you how to get the best results, how to take care of your machine, tells you where to oil and when. It tells how to use the different attachments, the ruffler, tucker, hemmers and binders and contains illustrations of these attachments in use.

A TAPE MEASURE, 18 inches long, accurately divided and beautifully colored to match the woodwork, is transferred on this cabinet, directly in front of the head, where it is most convenient for the use of the operator.

OUR BINDING GUARANTEE.

We send with every machine Our Binding 20 Years' Guarantee. Should any piece or part be found defective we will replace it free of charge, and our liberal terms of shipment, allowing you the privilege of trying and examining the machine, and if not found satisfactory, returning it to us and we will pay the freight and refund your money, will at once convince you that you run no risk in sending your order to us.

ONE ADVANTAGE IN ORDERING A SEWING machine from us is that you can be sure of getting all kinds of sewing machine repairs and supplies in the years to come and always at the very lowest cost.

This beautiful sewing machine will prove a real ornament in any home.

THIS MACHINE IS EQUIPPED WITH OUR special ball bearing hanger, which by actual use and experiment has been demonstrated to be 20 per cent lighter running than the ball bearing arrangement used in any other sewing machine. We can therefore recommend our Minnesota Model "A" Desk Cabinet Sewing Machine as very light running, exceedingly easy in operation and rapid in action, making it possible to do the work of a household in one-third less time than is required with machines fitted with ordinary non-ball bearing hanger.

THE EQUAL OF MACHINES SOLD by other dealers and agents at $40.00 to $50.00.

In ordering the machine use the following description:

No. 26T114 Minnesota Model "A" Machine one-door cabinet, dark golden oak (without attachments, but with accessories). Price...... **$18.90**

This price does not include attachments. We can furnish a complete set, as fully described on page 694, for 75 cents additional.

The machine is delivered free on board the cars at the factory in Dayton, Ohio, from which point customers pay the freight. Shipping weight, about 140 lbs.

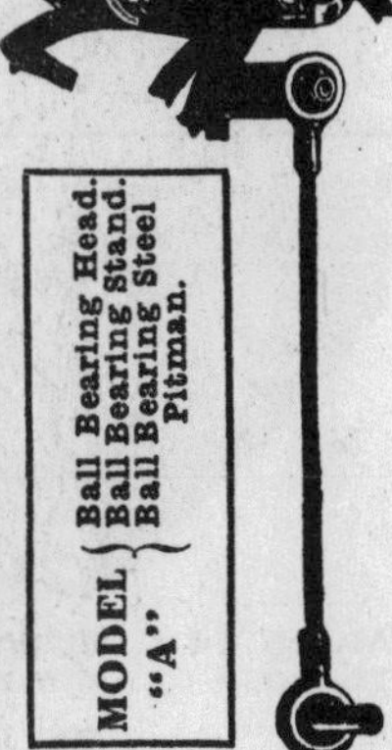

MODEL "A" { Ball Bearing Head. Ball Bearing Stand. Ball Bearing Steel Pitman.

MINNESOTA NEW MODEL "A"

AUTOMATIC LIFT, DROP DESK, ALL QUARTER SAWED OAK CABINET

SEWING MACHINE

Automatic lift chain, hinges and all hardware trimmings on the cabinet are brass plated.

THE FINEST DESK CABINET WE MAKE. THE FINEST DESK CABINET OFFERED IN THE WORLD.

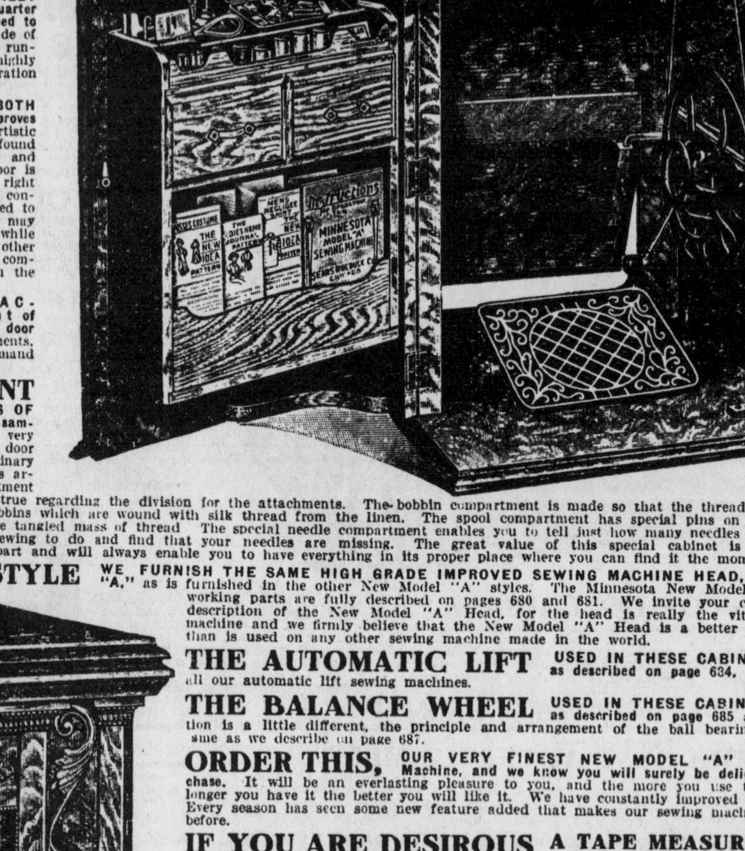

THIS IS THE VERY HIGHEST GRADE FULL DESK CABINET STYLE SEWING MAchine manufactured. It represents our very best efforts; nothing finer made in the world. This Minnesota New Model "A" Ball Bearing Sewing Machine in the very finest kind of an automatic lift drop desk cabinet, beautifully designed, richly carved and artistically decorated.

THE OAK STYLE IS MADE OF EXTRA SPECIALLY selected highly figured quarter sawed oak veneer, with large flaky figures, polished and hand rubbed to a piano finish. The doors, sides and top of this cabinet are all made of built-up stock, that is, thin layers of wood, the grain of each layer running crosswise or diagonally with the other, while the top layer is highly figured quarter sawed oak. Refer to page 687 and see the illustration showing this style of construction.

THE SUNKEN PANEL ON THE DOOR AND BOTH sides of the cabinet improves the appearance of this cabinet wonderfully. The beautiful and artistic carvings on the front and sides of the cabinet are such as are found only on the most expensive furniture. We call your particular and special attention to the construction of this cabinet; observe the door is hinged at the side of the cabinet, also that the small door at the right opens, allowing considerably more room and making it much more convenient and more comfortable for the operator. We have also added to this, our highest grade cabinet, a special ventilator feature, which may be opened or closed without getting up or changing your position while operating the machine, an improvement which is not found on any other sewing machine manufactured. This special ventilator means more comfort to the operator, especially when using the sewing machine in the summer months.

NEW DOOR CONSTRUCTION. ON ACcount of the new door construction, we have been able to attach to the door one of the most convenient cabinets for containing the attachments, accessories and all manner of supplies which are in constant demand while operating the machine.

NOTE THE SPECIAL COMPARTMENT FOR THE ATTACHMENTS, ACCESSORIES, BOBBINS, SPOOLS OF thread, needles, all kinds of patterns, instruction book and special samples of cloth, in addition to which the cabinet is fitted with two very large and roomy drawers, so that the compartment attached to the door of this cabinet will take the place of six or eight of the ordinary drawers used in sewing machine woodwork. This special cabinet is arranged so that there is a place for everything. The special compartment for the accessories is made only for the accessories. The same is true regarding the division for the attachments. The bobbin compartment is made so that the thread will not tangle, and you can always easily distinguish the different colors, also those bobbins which are wound with silk thread from the linen. The spool compartment has special pins on which the spools are fitted so that they will not roll around and unravel and become one tangled mass of thread. The special needle compartment enables you to tell just how many needles you have, and avoids the loss of time and disappointment when you have considerable sewing to do and find that your needles are missing. The great value of this special cabinet is the fact that these different and special compartments are made for every particular part and will always enable you to have everything in its proper place where you can find it the moment you want it.

IN THIS MINNESOTA CABINET STYLE WE FURNISH THE SAME HIGH GRADE IMPROVED SEWING MACHINE HEAD, OUR NEW MODEL "A," as is furnished in the other New Model "A" styles. The Minnesota New Model "A" Head and the working parts are fully described on pages 680 and 681. We invite your careful reading of the description of the New Model "A" Head, for the head is really the vital part of a sewing machine and we firmly believe that the New Model "A" Head is a better sewing machine head than is used on any other sewing machine made in the world.

THE AUTOMATIC LIFT USED IN THESE CABINETS IS THE SAME as described on page 634, and which we use on all our automatic lift sewing machines.

THE BALANCE WHEEL USED IN THESE CABINETS IS THE SAME as described on page 685 and which we use on tion is a little different, the principle and arrangement of the ball bearings is practically the sme as we describe on page 687.

ORDER THIS, OUR VERY FINEST NEW MODEL "A" CABINET SEWING Machine, and we know you will surely be delighted with your purchase. It will be an everlasting pleasure to you, and the more you use the machine and the longer you have it the better you will like it. We have constantly improved our sewing machines. Every season has seen some new feature added that makes our sewing machines better than ever before.

IF YOU ARE DESIROUS OF OWNING THE HIGHEST GRADE AND the very best sewing machine made, and we know you are, you must send to us for our New Minnesota Model "A." If we asked $10.00 more on each Minnesota New Model "A" Sewing Machine, it would still pay you well to place your order with us. $10.00 does not begin to represent the difference in quality between the Minnesota New Model "A" Sewing Machine and the sewing machines offered by other houses, particularly those shown by other catalog houses. When considering quality alone we could certainly ask $10.00 more for a machine than the prices of other dealers; but, fortunately for our customers, our policy is to ask just a narrow margin of profit on every article, and we figure our prices on the actual cost of material and labor. Do not forget that it is impossible for you to lose anything when you place your order with us. We are sure that you cannot duplicate this cabinet for less than $50.00 if you buy from any of your local dealers.

YOU HAVE THREE MONTHS IN WHICH TO GIVE THE MACHINE A THOROUGH TRIAL AND TEST, AS YOU WILL FIND BY REFERRING TO OUR LIBERAL GUARANTEE TERMS, AS EXPLAINED ON PAGE 677

A TAPE MEASURE 18 INCHES LONG, ACCURATELY DIVIDED AND BEAUTIFULLY COLORED TO MATCH THE WOODWORK, IS TRANSFERRED ON THIS CABINET, DIRECTLY IN FRONT OF THE HEAD, WHERE IT IS MOST CONVENIENT FOR THE USE OF THE OPERATOR.

Newhall, Iowa.

Sears, Roebuck & Co., Chicago, Ill.

Gentlemen:—I want to tell you how very well pleased I am with my Minnesota Model "A" Sewing Machine. I have used a number of different kinds while sewing here and there all through the country and in the city of Cedar Rapids, but never found one that comes up with this one in work and beauty, and a number of my friends and neighbors have sent for one just like mine and received them all O. K. and would not part with them for twice the price. They are ahead of the ——— and ——— for their price. These two mentioned sell for $40.00 and $45.00 in Cedar Rapids, and don't give a bit better satisfaction than the Minnesota. I cannot speak too much for it and know others will be as well pleased as I by sending to Sears, Roebuck & Co. I remain as before, Yours very truly,

MRS. CHAS. G. FREEMAN.

WE FURNISH THIS CABINET IN BLACK WALNUT, AS WELL AS IN OAK, BUT, ON ACCOUNT OF THE WALNUT LUMBER COSTING MORE THAN OAK, WE CHARGE $1.50 EXTRA FOR THIS CABINET IN BLACK WALNUT.

No. 26T118 Minnesota New Model "A" Automatic Lift OAK Cabinet Sewing Machine. Price........ $24.65

No. 26T119 Minnesota New Model "A" Automatic Lift WALNUT Cabinet Sewing Machine. Price........ 26.15

These prices do not include attachments. We furnish a complete set for 75 cents extra, as fully explained on page 694. These cabinets are shipped only from Dayton, Ohio. Shipping weight, about 140 pounds.

OUR NEW LIBRARY TABLE SEWING MACHINE

EQUIPPED WITH OUR MINNESOTA MODEL "A" SEWING MACHINE HEAD.

THE MOST WONDERFUL INVENTION IN A SEWING MACHINE. WE OFFER ON THIS PAGE an exclusive Sears, Roebuck and Co. style. Something ENTIRELY NEW in the sewing machine line. The most practical improvement made in sewing machines since the adoption of ball bearings.

THE UPPER ILLUSTRATION SHOWS A BEAUTIFUL library table made in the latest style. There is nothing about the table to indicate that it is anything else but a nicely finished and practical library table. The sewing machine is cleverly hidden and is out of the way. However, it is but the work of a moment to change your library table to a sewing machine with more table surface than any other machine. A machine which is firmer, much stronger and more substantial than any machine manufactured. There is nothing about the new Library Table Sewing Machine which is liable to get out of order. The special features which make it possible for us to successfully conceal a complete light running latest style ball bearing sewing machine in a library table are made and attached to the table in such a way that it is only necessary to touch two levers, also concealed, to bring the treadle and balance wheel into position. When these levers release the treadle and balance wheel they also lock automatically, making only one operation necessary to arrange these parts for immediate use.

THE SEWING MACHINE HEAD IS ATTACHED to the table in the same manner as the regular drop head styles, and all that is necessary to get at the head is to remove the false top of the table, which is very light but strong and substantial on account of being made of veneered stock.

FOR A COMPLETE DETAILED DESCRIPTION OF THE BALL BEARING MODEL "A" SEWING MACHINE HEAD
SEE PAGES 680 and 681

THE TABLE IS MADE OF SELECTED HIGHLY FIGURED QUARTER sawed golden oak. The legs are massive, exceptionally strong and are firmly braced by a convenient and useful lower shelf. One side of the table is fitted with a blind drawer suitable for attachments, accessories, thread, etc.

THE FINISH THROUGHOUT IS SUCH AS IS PUT ONLY ON THE FINEST furniture, being hand rubbed and highly polished, and brings out the beautiful grain of the wood as perfectly as it is possible to be shown.

THE TABLE IS CONSTRUCTED WITH A DOUBLE TOP. The upper part serves as a cover for the head and when removed can be used as a lap board, which is always a great convenience in a sewing room. As a library table it is a handsome piece of furniture and cannot be duplicated in your furniture store at less than $15.00 to $20.00, and as a sewing machine it will be superior in many ways to the ordinary style of machine on account of its being absolutely rigid and not susceptible to the usual vibrations which are unavoidable in the regular cast iron sewing machine stand.

THE LIBRARY TABLE STYLE SEWING MACHINE WHICH WE OFFER AT THE REMARKABLY LOW PRICE OF $21.95 is the latest addition to our Minnesota line, the most advanced style of sewing machine cabinet work, a machine that will not be found in any other catalog, nor offered by dealers or agents generally. It is only used on one or two of the makes of sewing machines which sell at $60.00. There is nothing richer or handsomer offered in sewing machine cabinet work, nothing more exclusive, more up to date, or that will appeal so strongly to the finest class of trade. With this new library table cabinet and its clever construction we offer a sewing machine which can go into the finest room in the house. To look at it closed, as shown by the upper illustration, you will think it is simply a very handsome piece of furniture; in fact, it represents a library table. In woodwork, graining, polishing, carving, graceful outline, etc., it favorably compares with any library table offered in any furniture store. When you consider that you have the benefit of such an attractive as well as useful piece of furniture, and in a few moments can transform it into a sewing machine ready for work, the highest grade machine at that, you can doubly appreciate what we offer in this style machine.

$21.95

No. 26T120

PRICE $21.95

ORDER BY NUMBER.

COMPLETE WITH ACCESSORIES.

ATTACHMENTS, 75 CENTS EXTRA. SEE PAGE 694.

ON BOARD CARS, DAYTON, OHIO.
SHIPPING WEIGHT, ABOUT 150 LBS.

$21.95 IS REALLY A WONDERFULLY LOW PRICE FOR THIS SEWING MACHINE. The cabinet alone, a library table of such size and quality, bought in any retail furniture store would cost you within a few dollars of our entire price for the machine complete. The sewing machine itself is the very finest, highest type of construction, our well known Minnesota Model "A," representing a fair share of the selling price in intrinsic value of the raw material and labor. $21.95 is the price that we are able to name by making a very large number of these sewing machines, as we are sure that everyone will recognize the value offered, and a big demand be created. Figuring the cost of the material and labor, and adding thereto a very small margin of profit, we are able to make the low price of $21.95, which we guarantee to be very much lower than you can buy a sewing machine and cabinet of this high quality from any other dealer.

PLEASE BEAR IN MIND THAT THE MACHINE ITSELF IS our Model "A" head and ball bearing hanger, nothing has been overlooked to make it the very best sewing machine in the world. Remember, that the cabinet is the richest product of the cabinet making art; only the highest class material is used, is beautifully fitted and finished, a piece of furniture that you will be proud to own and display.

A TAPE MEASURE, 18 inches long, accurately divided and beautifully colored to match the woodwork, is transferred on this table, directly in front of the head, where it is most convenient for the use of the operator.

PROTECTING YOU IN EVERY WAY. WE SEND YOU A SIGNED WRITTEN BINDING GUARANTEE with every machine, guaranteeing the machine from all defects for 20 years. If through accident you should need a piece or part in the years to come we can furnish it to you promptly, as we carry a full line of repairs on hand at all times, and it is our policy to furnish repairs and parts at factory cost.

NO ONE ELSE WILL OFFER YOU A SEWING MACHINE of this style or quality. You will not find this Library Table Sewing Machine offered in any other catalog. As far as competition is concerned, we could ask $35.00 or $40.00 for this sewing machine and be beyond competition and at the same time give our customers full value, but we make the price just as low as we possibly can and add to the cost of material and labor just our one small percentage of profit, and through our policy we could not take from our customers more than $21.95 for this machine.

CAN BE CHANGED FROM A LIBRARY TABLE — TO — A SEWING MACHINE IN LESS THAN A MINUTE

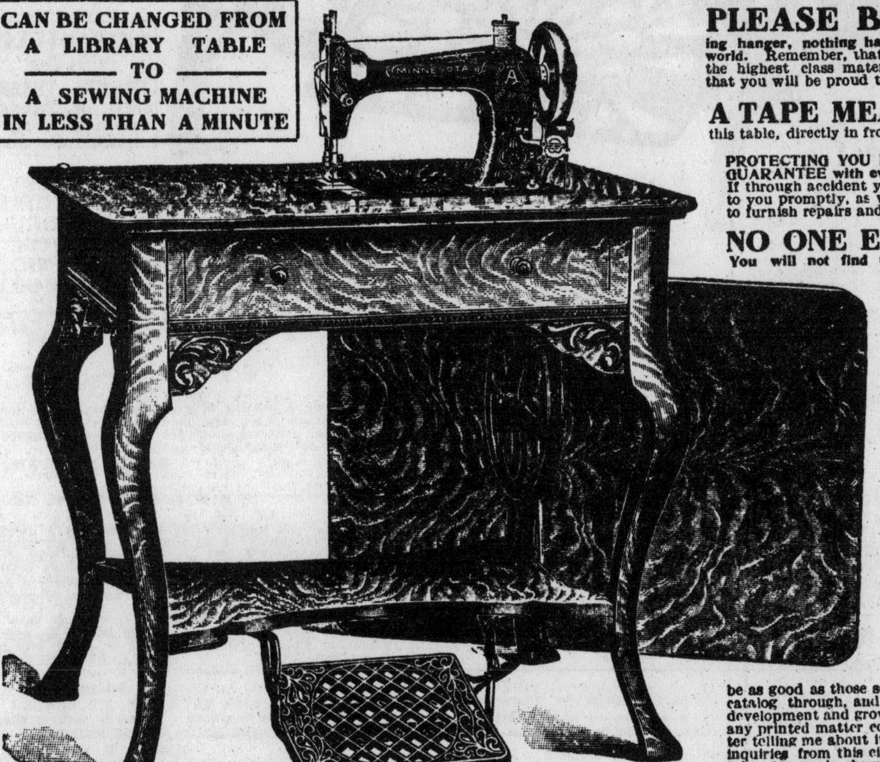

Our Minnesota Model "A" Ball Bearing Library Table Sewing Machine, Open and Ready for Work.

THE MINNESOTA MODEL "A" SEWS THE FINEST IN THE WORLD.

Buckholtz, Texas.

Sears, Roebuck & Co.

Gentlemen:—In answer to your letter, I would say my Minnesota Model "A" Sewing Machine is all O. K. It sews the finest in the world. I like the workmanship and finish of woodwork. It is easy running and I saved at least $20.00 by ordering from you. There is nothing like it in my town for the money. There were several agents to see me before I ordered from you and I would rather have my machine than their $40.00 machine.

Yours truly,

S. A. DOBBS.

THE MINNESOTA IS AS GOOD AS MACHINES SOLD AT THREE TIMES OUR PRICE.

Norfolk, Va.

Sears, Roebuck & Co., Chicago, Ill.

Gentlemen:—I received the sewing machine from you about ten days ago and it is astonishing to me to see how you can sell this machine at the price you do, as it looks to me to be as good as those sold by agents for three times that amount. I have also looked your catalog through, and as a matter of curiosity would like to know something of the origin, development and growth of such a great enterprise as your business is today. If you have any printed matter concerning it I would like to have it, or if not, I would appreciate a letter telling me about it and on what point do you attribute your success. If you have any inquiries from this city about machines you may refer them to me, and my wife and I will take pleasure in showing ours to anyone who may wish to see it, as we feel we would be doing the purchaser a greater favor than yourself. Yours truly, PAUL M. TAYLOR.

No. 26T120 Minnesota Model 'A" Ball Bearing Library Table Sewing Machine. Price.............. **$21.95**
A Complete Set of Steel Foot Attachments, 75 Cents Extra.

OUR HIGHEST GRADE BALL BEARING SPECIAL DROP LEAF AND BOX COVER

MINNESOTA NEW MODEL "A"

5-DRAWER STYLE **$15.00**

7-DRAWER STYLE (AS ILLUSTRATED HERE) **$15.45**

MANY NEW FEATURES, MANY IMPROVEMENTS, BROUGHT RIGHT UP TO DATE

EMBODYING THE LATEST IDEAS IN SEWING MACHINE CONSTRUCTION, REPRESENTING a far better value than we have been able to offer before in the matchless Minnesota New Model "A" Machine.

REMEMBER, WE POSITIVELY GUARANTEE THE NEW MODEL "A" sewing machine to be the highest grade sewing machine it is possible to build, not equaled by any other sewing machine on the market, regardless of name or price, no matter whether it is sold by agents at three to four times our prices. The Minnesota New Model "A" has all the good features, all the improvements that are found in the most expensive sewing machines sold by others, with many features of our own that are not to be found in other machines.

OUR CHALLENGE PROPOSITION. WE CHALLENGE any sewing machine manufacturer, dealer or agent to produce a sewing machine that equals the excellence of the Minnesota New Model "A." We invite our competitors to put their best machines side by side with the Minnesota New Model "A," let any competent and impartial judge test both machines, try them on all kinds of work, consider carefully the points of simplicity, ease of operation, light running quality, consider the amount of noise made by each machine, note the grade of woodwork furnished, the class of material used and the workmanship. We would indeed welcome such a comparison. We know that in such a contest the Minnesota New Model "A" Machine would be pronounced the better machine in every way. You, dear customer, can make such a comparison; if you are in doubt you need not hesitate to order a Minnesota for this purpose and send it back to us and get your money back if you find a machine that can equal it. When you consider all this, bear in mind that the Minnesota New Model "A" represents the very finest sewing machine yet produced, and remember that you are able to buy the Minnesota New Model "A" machines from us on the basis of first cost, the cost of material and labor with just our one small percentage of profit added can you afford to send your order elsewhere?

No. 26T122 PRICE, $15.45

BALL BEARING HEAD.
BALL BEARING STAND.
BALL BEARING STEEL PITMAN.
AUTOMATIC TENSION RELEASE.

ATTACHMENTS 75c EXTRA

GUARANTEED BY US FOR TWENTY YEARS SOLD ON THREE MONTHS' TRIAL

PLEASE NOTE

THE RICH, BEAUTIFUL, quartered oak cabinet we furnish for this Minnesota New Model "A" Machine. The cabinet is a product of the skill of the best cabinet makers, the material is most carefully selected, it is richly grained and rounded. The bent wood cover is also beautifully shaped and carved, and when you buy this Minnesota New Model "A" Upright Machine you will be getting as fine woodwork as is given with the sewing machines sold by agents at three to four times our price. The head is the wonderfully improved ball bearing New Model "A," more fully described on pages 680 and 681.

FOR DESCRIPTION OF STAND SEE PAGE 687.

WE PREFER THAT YOU SELECT A NEW MODEL "A" MINNESOTA Machine in preference to any other of our Minnesota models. Then we can be sure that our machine will be the very finest in your section of the country. Your neighbors will admire it, everybody will be interested in it, and many of them will surely ask the price and where you got it, and in this way our reputation for furnishing the finest goods at wonderfully low prices will spread. The sale of one sewing machine in a neighborhood usually means for us the sale of several others.

THE HEAD IS BALL Bearing, the stand is ball bearing, the pitman is steel (not wood) and double ball bearing, making the New Model "A" so easy to run, so nearly noiseless, so efficient that sewing becomes a pleasure, not a duty.

Closed View No. 26T121 $15.00

Five-Drawer Style.

No. 26T121

A TAPE MEASURE, 18 inches long, accurately divided and beautifully colored to match the woodwork, is transferred on this table, directly in front of the head, where it is most convenient for the use of the operator.

READ WHAT OUR CUSTOMERS SAY ABOUT THE MINNESOTA SEWING MACHINE.

623 Twelfth St. North, Fargo, N. Dak.
Sears, Roebuck & Co., Chicago, Ill.
Kind Sirs:—I received my Sewing Machine, and am more than pleased with it. It could not be better. I have been trading with you for the last ten years, and have always found the goods better than I expected. I am, Yours respectfully, MRS. CHAS. TORGRIM.

R. F. D. No. 1, Cycle, N. Car.
Sears, Roebuck & Co., Chicago, Ill.
Dear Sirs:—I received the Sewing Machine, which I ordered of you, and I am more than pleased with it. It works perfectly. Different parties, who have seen the machine, say it is equal to any $40.00 machine bought of agents here. I thank you very much for your prompt shipment. It reached me in perfect condition. I cannot say enough in praise of it.
Respectfully yours, DANIEL B. HARRIS.

R. F. D. No. 1, Spencer, Neb.
Sears, Roebuck & Co., Chicago, Ill.
Dear Sirs:—I received my machine in good shape, and can truly say it is certainly a dandy. It is just as nice as any machine from $40.00 up to $65.00. I have already tried all of the attachments, and they are fine. A lady in our neighborhood bought a sewing machine just after Christmas, and paid $65.00 for it. I placed my machine beside hers, and I can truly say that I would never trade my machine for hers. In beauty and workmanship, her sewing machine can never come up with mine, besides her machine is only a five-drawer drop head, and has a wooden pitman, where mine has a steel pitman.
I can truly say I am perfectly satisfied, and will use it with the best of care; will also show it to all of my friends and neighbors, so they can send to you to buy, in place of buying elsewhere. Asking you to please send me your Catalog of Pianos and Organs, and thanking you for prompt attention, I remain, Yours truly, MABLE PRENTICE.

Bridgeport, Ill.
Sears, Roebuck & Co., Chicago, Ill.
I received my machine all right. It is a beauty and does fine work. There is nothing cheap about it, and the price I am indeed well pleased with, and thank you for prompt delivery.
MRS. V. B. WICKEY.

In writing to any of these people enclose a 2-cent stamp for reply.

No. 26T121 Minnesota New Model "A" Five-Drawer, Box Cover. Price, on board cars at Dayton, Ohio........ $15.00
No. 26T122 Minnesota New Model "A" Seven-Drawer, Box Cover. Price, on board cars at Dayton, Ohio........ 15.45
The above prices do not include Attachments, a complete set of which we furnish at 75 cents additional. For complete description of New Model "A" Attachments see page 694.

What Our Customers Say About Our Sewing Machines

J. W. McALARNEY, 319 7th Ave., Juniata, Penn.

I hereby acknowledge receipt of Minnesota Model "A" Sewing Machine in good condition and wish to express my sincere thanks for same. It is a beauty and I believe I am safe in saying that, considering the prices charged for the Singer, Wheeler and Wilson or, in fact, any other make sold by dealers in this locality, I saved the difference between your price, freight and drayage, and the average price of a machine from a local dealer, about $32.53. Since the dealers have so many different prices for different people, I split the difference to find my amount that I saved. In speaking of the different prices, I can produce facts to bear out the truth of my statement. For instance, the———— people sold a machine to a friend of mine after much persuading for $35.00 cash; and again, they sold a machine to another friend for $47.00 and also had taken his old machine which was in good order and allowing him $13.00 for it, making the price of his machine (on installments) $60.00. Now, figures will not lie, and the above instances are only two of thousands. Then, it would be doing the Minnesota Model "A" a great injustice to compare it with any other machine I ever saw, since the Minnesota is a more improved, more beautiful and a more substantial machine, and therefore is not to be compared with any of the other makes which local dealers have for sale. Now, in conclusion, I wish to state that I received with this order, as well as all others which you have sent me in the past, the same "square deal" which characterizes your methods. Furthermore, I do not hesitate to recommend your goods whenever the occasion presents itself to do so.

MRS. N. M. ABBEY, Randolph, N. Y.

The Minnesota Model "A" Sewing Machine that I bought of you last spring is all you claimed for it. The attachments are **perfect.** Cannot see why one will pay from $45.00 to $60.00 for a machine that will do no better work, and I don't believe will wear any longer.

MRS. CHAS. STORTS, R. F. D. No. 1, Box 43, Groveport, Ohio.

My Minnesota Sewing Machine is all right—as good or better than I could have gotten from our home agent for double the money I paid for it. This is my second machine I purchased of you, and I knew what I was doing when I got this one. You would sell more of your machines in this community, but we have an agent here selling the———— Sewing Machine, and he goes about running down your machines, telling people all manner of things that are untrue about your machines. Tells them that all the old machines they take in exchange for their machines are sent to Sears, Roebuck & Co. and you make your new machines out of them. My sister bought one of his machines about the same time I got my machine, and I would not trade machines today with hers, and she paid $40.00 for her machine. I tried to talk her into sending with me for one of your machines, but, of course, the agent had a slicker tongue and knew better how to use it than I did; so he won the day. She is sorry now she didn't send to you. He tried his game on me and set his machine in the house. I told him I would use his machine while it was here, and when he came back he could take it away again because I was going to send to your factory for my machine. You may be sure he didn't leave it very long, and I ordered my machine while it was in the house.

MRS. C. C. WYNN, 173 Gladefield St., Pittsburg, Penn.

I bought a Model "A" Sewing Machine, 7-drawer, from you a year ago, and I will say that I would not take double the amount I paid for it unless I was positive that I could get another one like it. I let my grandson's wife sew on it, and she liked it so well that she sent and got one from Sears, Roebuck & Co., and in a short time my granddaughter in Pittsburg is going to send for one. The machine that you will sell and the one that you have sold already to my grandson, Mr. I. C. Kingan, Vandegrift, Penn., can be credited to seeing mine and the lovely stitch it makes.

CHARLES SHAUB, 330 E. Fredrick St., Lancaster, Penn.

I am pleased very much indeed with the sewing machine and everything is O. K. Saved $15.00 by getting my sewing machine from you. To tell the truth, I could not buy a machine here in the city of Lancaster under $35.00 to $50.00 and I know they would not give the satisfaction that the Minnesota Model "A" does. If we are in need of anything hereafter we will buy of Sears, Roebuck & Co., because we get the best for less money.

MRS. GEO. W. PRICE, McHenry, N. Dak.

Last November we sent for one of your two-door Automatic Model "A" Desk Cabinet Sewing Machines. I can say that I am well pleased with it. It is really better than I expected to get. It does fine work. Have run it all winter without any trouble under your instructions. Don't think I could keep house without it now. Everyone that sees it thinks it is all right. It is so light running any child could run it. I can't say enough in its praise.

J. W. HODGE, Wilmington, Cal.

Mrs. Hodge wishes me to tell you she is very much pleased with the sewing machine we ordered of you. It is giving entire satisfaction. Could not be better. You would sell more of your sewing machines in this part of the country, but there are too many sewing machine agents running around over the country misrepresenting your machines. They are mostly slick talkers and know how to get on the good side of the women; and if a woman should mention anything about your machine or your prices they come at them in about this way: "Oh, you don't want to be fooled into getting one of those machines; they are a mass of cheap, shoddy things. Why, don't you know that they can't make a first class machine for $15.00 or $20.00." Then they will tell her they sell their machines at $65.00 and that is very close for such a fine machine. They allow you $5.00, $10.00 or $15.00, as the case may be, for your old machine and will give you time on the balance if you will pay, say, $5.00 a month. "Of course, we don't do this with everybody, but we will do it with you," they say; and so on, until they make the sale.

MRS. H. W. DAHLMAN, R. F. D. No. 1, Cambridge, Minn.

Concerning the Minnesota Sewing Machine that I bought from you some time ago, I am pleased to inform you that I have given the machine a thorough test and find that it does satisfactory work in every respect. As to its appearance, it is an ornament to the house as a piece of furniture, and I am proud of it. I have shown it to my friends and neighbors and they all admired it. You would sell more of your machines in this neighborhood, but they have all been well supplied by traveling agents who come around here occasionally. They take old machines in exchange and pretend to pay a big price for same and charge an enormous price for the new machine. The agents say that the old machines are shipped to catalog houses, who in turn fix them up and distribute them among the farmers at a low price. According to that, when we send to catalog houses, we get old painted over machines. I know this is what they say, because shortly before I sent for mine, an agent was here and tried to make a deal with me. He asked me $65.00 for a common drop head. I had an old machine here that I have had for twenty years. The agent wanted $45.00 in cash and my old machine for one of his machines. I told him I was going to send to Sears, Roebuck & Co. for a cabinet machine at less than half the price he asked, and I could keep my old machine to boot. Then he told me what kind of a machine I would get for that money. If we had not been old customers I would perhaps have believed him, but I told him that we were well acquainted with your goods by this time and knew that we would not be swindled. I would not exchange with any of my neighbors who bought the $65.00 machine. That agent was certainly a clever man and made a fortune in this community. As for my part, I have said nothing but praise about my machine and others agree with me that it is a dandy.

J. P. MUNCH, 528 E. 84th St., New York, N. Y.

Enclosed you will find the three months' trial contract for a Minnesota Model "A" I bought from you, as it is no use to us. My wife said she would refuse to sell it back to you at any price and she has been used to a Domestic.

J. J. ROGERS, 4340 Maple St., Omaha, Neb.

I called at your warehouse in this city for the Minnesota Model "A" Sewing Machine. Every inch tallies with your description. In every respect where you have varied from the Singer Model you have beat; simplicity in handling, strength, style and beauty of finish and design (both metal and woodwork), free from noise, easy running, with very greatly increased space underneath. The design of iron stand is simple and beautiful and easy to clean. As I am a licensed engineer, but at present am teaching painting, frescoing and wood finishing, I have run, cleaned and repaired my own machines as well as others for thirty-five years. This is merely as proof of my capability of judging of the quality and superiority of your machines. If you care to refer anyone to me or my machine, you are at liberty to do so. I have long intended to thank you for your fair treatment, prompt service and fair dealing. I never had one reason to complain. Your system is certainly wonderful.

C. B. MINTER, Fresno, Cal.

The Minnesota Model "A" Sewing Machine Mr. Lee Neelson ordered from you arrived and his wife is well pleased. I saved them $45.00 by persuading them to buy of you instead of buying a $65.00 Singer.

MRS. ROBT. S. FULTON, R. F. D. No. 1, Danville, Va.

I received my sewing machine a few days ago and am more than pleased with it. The machine is all that you represented it to be and much nicer than I expected. Everyone who sees it says that it is equal to other machines which sell for $40.00 and $50.00. I thank you for your promptness in filling orders sent you.

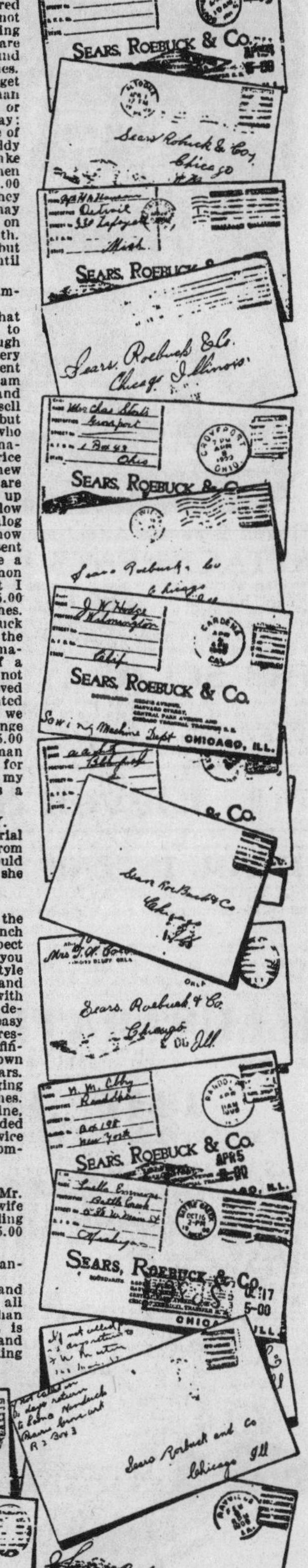

ATTACHMENTS AND ACCESSORIES

FOR OUR NEW MODEL "A" MACHINES

75 CENTS FOR A SET OF THE BEST ATTACHMENTS IN THE WORLD

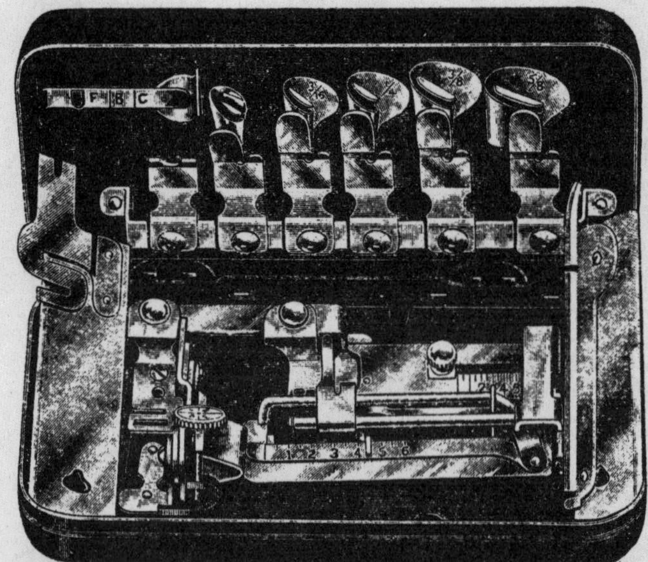

Eleven Separate Attachments as Shown Above, 75 Cents.

ATTACHMENTS

THE SET CONSISTS OF THE FOLLOWING:

- 1 RUFFLER
- 1 TUCKER
- 1 BINDER
- 1 BIAS GAUGE
- 4 HEMMERS $\frac{1}{8}$ to $\frac{5}{8}$ inch wide
- 1 SHORT BRAIDER FOOT
- 1 SHIRRING BLADE
- 1 UNDER BRAIDER

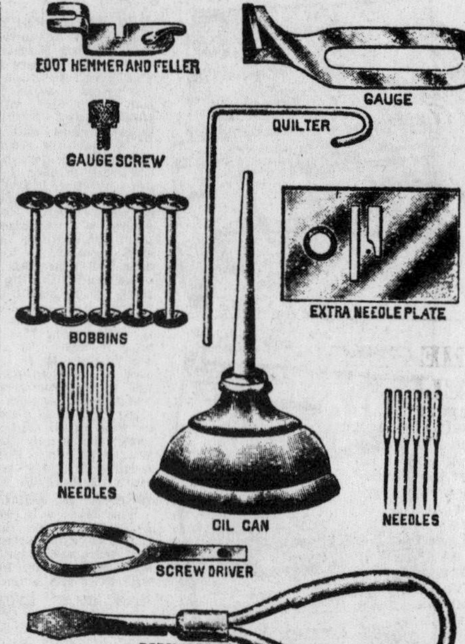

ATTACHMENTS. IT HAS BEEN CUSTOMARY IN THE PAST FOR all dealers to furnish a set of attachments with every machine, whether the purchaser required them or not. We offer our machine with or without attachments. The prices quoted in the catalog for the machines, shipped from Dayton, Ohio, are all calculated without attachments, and at 75 cents we furnish a full set of the latest patent foot attachments, as shown in the illustration herewith, packed in a handsome velvet lined metal box arranged with a place for each particular attachment. **The attachments will be furnished at 75 cents per set.** If mail shipment, postage extra, 20 cents.

THE SET OF ATTACHMENTS WHICH WE FURNISH for 75 cents, consists of one tucker, one ruffler, one shirring blade, one short braider foot, one under braider, one binder, one set of four hemmers of different widths up to ⅝ of an inch and one bias gauge. These attachments are the same style as are furnished by the largest sewing machine dealers with their highest priced machines and are guaranteed to give perfect satisfaction. The attachments are handsomely nickel plated and polished.

THE HIGHEST RECOMMENDATION THAT CAN BE GIVEN TO A SET OF attachments is that it is made by the Greist Manufacturing Company, the makers of the most complete, improved and expensive attachments on the market, whose attachments are used by all makers of well known standard machines. Our attachments are made by this concern expressly for our machines and are made of the very best tempered steel, heavily nickel plated, and will last twice as long and do double the variety of work possible with cheaper attachments. They are adjustable, very simple in construction and so easy to understand and operate that any person can quickly learn to produce a large variety of the most beautiful work. Our instruction book, furnished free with the machine, explains fully the operation of each attachment included in the set.

Eleven Separate Attachments for - - 75 Cents

IF YOU INTEND TO DO PLAIN SEWING ONLY WITH OUR MACHINES YOU NATURALLY DO NOT WISH TO BUY ATTACHMENTS, and will appreciate our departure from the old established custom of including a set of attachments with every machine at the customer's expense. If you require attachments you will nevertheless appreciate that it is unfair and unjust to force those that do not need them to receive and pay for them. If you purchase a machine without attachments and later wish to procure attachments, we can always supply you with the proper set.

ACCESSORIES. WE FURNISH WITH EVERY MINNESOTA NEW MODEL "A" Machine a complete set of accessories, such as is usually furnished with every high grade machine, consisting of one quilter, five bobbins (and one in the machine), one cloth guide, gauge and screw, a large screwdriver, one oil can filled with oil, one shuttle screwdriver, one extra needle plate, one foot hemmer, one package of needles and one instruction book. We carry in stock a full supply of needles, bobbins, shuttles, attachments, etc., which are used in the operation of our machines. We can, therefore, fill orders for repairs promptly. An order for repairs for the Minnesota New Model "A" Machine placed with us fifteen or twenty years from date would be filled as promptly as a repair order sent today. See page 678 for prices on sewing machine supplies.

ILLUSTRATIONS SHOWING A FEW OPERATIONS MADE POSSIBLE BY THE USE OF THE MINNESOTA NEW MODEL "A" ATTACHMENTS. Our instruction book furnished with each machine illustrates and gives clear and simple instructions on how to operate the machine and use all the attachments. Makes personal instruction unnecessary.

THE RUFFLER

THE RUFFLER IS, WITHOUT DOUBT, THE MOST IMPORTANT attachment used in connection with the sewing machine. It is used more than any other attachment, because it can be made to do a greater variety of work than any other. Knowing this, we have taken particular pains to procure for our customers the best ruffler made. The instructions for using the ruffler, as contained in our instruction book, are so clear that anyone, even without previous experience, learns to operate it the first time a trial is made. This is a very desirable feature and especially so for beginners. It can be operated at a high speed, but never fails to make regular, even stitches, and gathers with the same fullness.

THIS ATTACHMENT is so simple in construction that it is only necessary for the operator to place the cloth between the two operating plates and then guide the cloth, the ruffler doing the rest. This ruffler is adjustable by means of a small thumbscrew so the gathers will be full or close as desired.

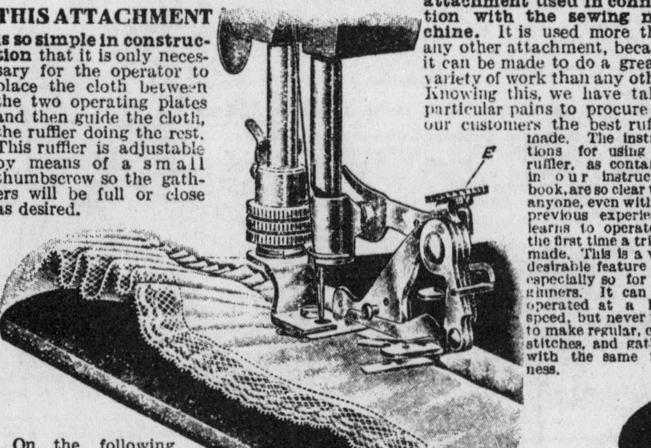

On the following page we illustrate a number of other uses of the ruffler.

THE TUCKER

THE TUCKER, ONE OF THE MOST IMPORTANT OF THE attachments, is made of the best steel, highly polished and nicely nickel plated. The explanation, how to operate it, contained in the instruction book, is so clear that anyone, even without previous experience with a sewing machine, will easily understand the working of it and be able to make the finest tucks desired.

THE ILLUSTRATION represents the tucker being used on a piece of cambric and operating on the last of a cluster of tucks. The tucker is very strong and positive in its action, cannot easily get out of order, and will operate with the same satisfaction on heavy and light goods, starched or unstarched

THE TUCKER is a great time saver. Besides the results with the tucker are far more satisfactory than without. When the folds are made by hand they are not as uniform as when marked and sewed with the tucker.

ILLUSTRATIONS OF MODEL "A" ATTACHMENTS—Continued.

THESE ILLUSTRATIONS ARE MADE FROM ACTUAL PHOTOGRAPHS SHOWING THE VARIOUS ATTACHMENTS OF THE MACHINE IN OPERATION.

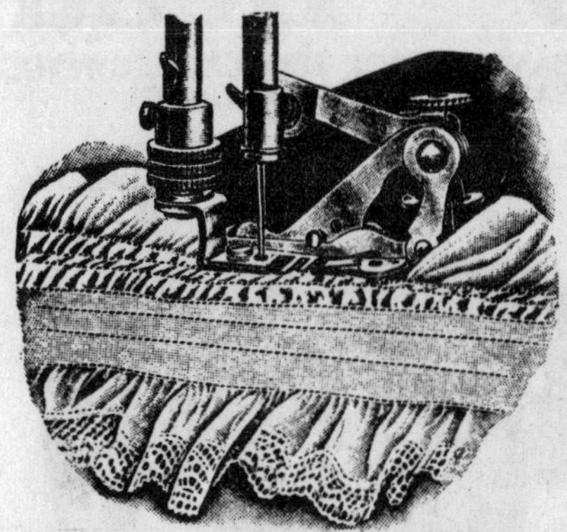

THE RUFFLER.

THIS ILLUSTRATION shows the ruffler puffing and shirring. Most sewing machine users do puffing by hand because the majority of rufflers are unable to do this work satisfactorily, but our Model "A" ruffler does puffing with more exactness and regularity than it can be done by hand. In shirring, the special shirring blade is used in connection with the ruffler, as fully described in the instruction book.

THE HEMMER AND FELLER.

THE HEMMER foot is a very important and most useful attachment. The illustration herewith shows the hemmer foot making a very narrow hem to prevent the edge of the cloth from unraveling. The instruction book tells you how to make narrow or wide hems with this attachment. It also illustrates and explains how to do felling.

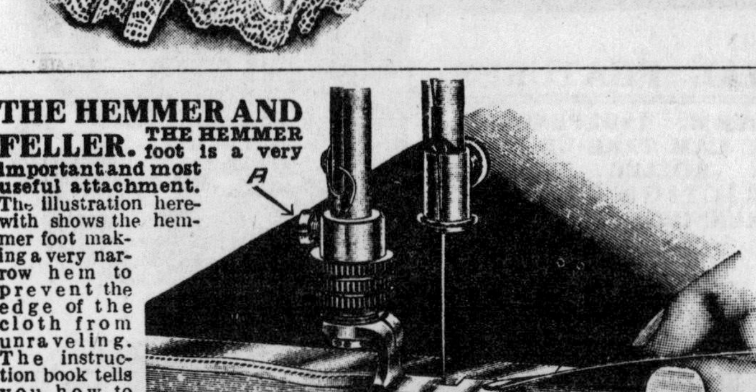

WIDE HEMMERS.

BESIDES THE NARROW foot hemmer, four hemmers of various widths, from ⅛ to ⅝ of an inch are furnished with our attachments. These hemmers are very simple and easy to operate. They are very necessary to complete the full set of attachments. The instruction book, furnished with every sewing machine, fully describes the manner in which these hemmers may be used, and enables one who has had no experience with a sewing machine to use them with the best results.

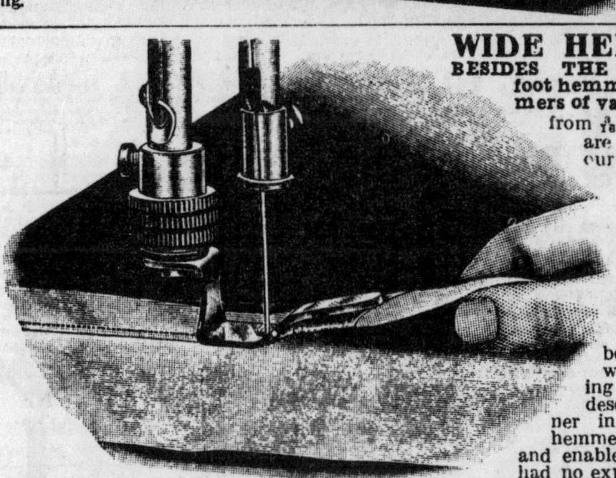

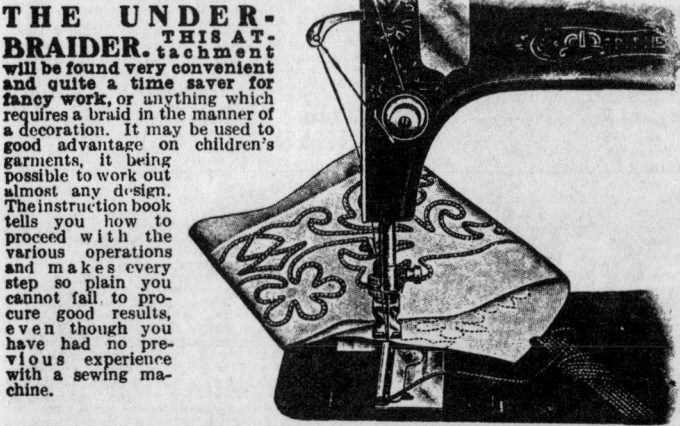

THE UNDER-BRAIDER.

THIS ATTACHMENT will be found very convenient and quite a time saver for fancy work, or anything which requires a braid in the manner of a decoration. It may be used to good advantage on children's garments, it being possible to work out almost any design. The instruction book tells you how to proceed with the various operations and makes every step so plain you cannot fail to procure good results, even though you have had no previous experience with a sewing machine.

THE RUFFLER.

THE ACCOMPANYING illustration shows another very important use of the ruffler, namely, that of ruffling, piping and sewing on heading all in one operation. The directions in the instruction book are so plain, anyone can do this work by simply following the directions.

THE HEMMER.

THIS ILLUSTRATION shows the hemmer doing two things in one operation, namely, that of making a hem and at the same time sewing on lace. This operation makes a much neater seam than if the lace were to be sewed on separately.

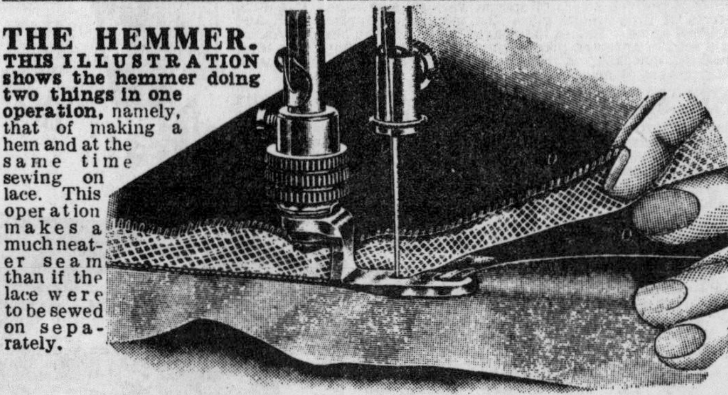

THE BINDER.

THIS ATTACHMENT seems a little more complicated than the foot hemmer and hemmers, but after following the directions contained in our instruction book, this operation becomes very simple. The binder is used in quite a number of different operations and is a great time saver. With it you can do bias binding, dress binding, make French folds and French seams. The instruction book directs and fully describes these different operations.

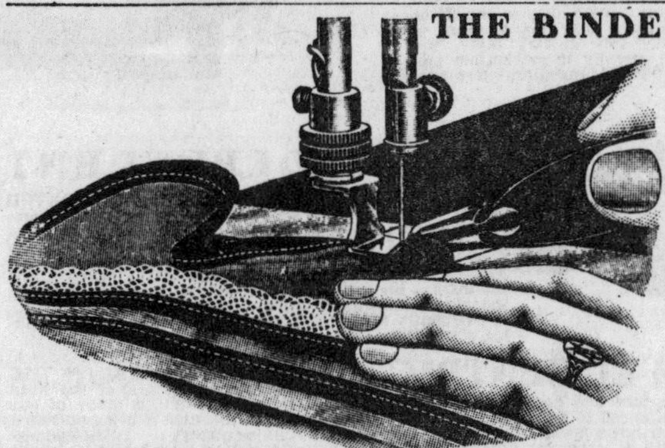

THE QUILTER.

THE MOST SIMPLE OF the attachments furnished with the sewing machine. The quilter merely acts as a gauge to enable one to sew in a straight line. It is a great time saver, because without it it would be necessary not only to mark the goods, but also to do all the stitching by hand. This is very undesirable, particularly on a large piece like a quilt, and the use of the quilter has saved many an hour and it always does the work in a satisfactory manner.

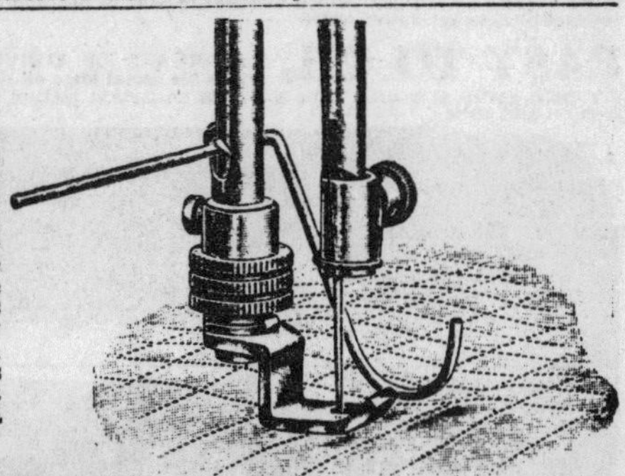

WE FURNISH,

FREE OF CHARGE, WITH EVERY MINNESOTA MODEL "A" Sewing Machine a book of instructions telling how to operate the sewing machine. This book covers every point, makes everything so plain and simple that anyone without previous experience can learn to run the machine at once and do perfect work; tells you how to get the best results, how to take care of your machine, tells you where to oil and when. It tells you how to use the different attachments, the ruffler, tucker, hemmers and binders, and contains illustrations of these attachments in use.

IF YOU HAVE TROUBLE THREADING NEEDLES, SEND FOR ONE OF OUR NEEDLE THREADERS, DESCRIBED ON PAGE 678.

THE THREAD CONTROLLER, SHOWN ON PAGE 678, IS A VERY HANDY ATTACHMENT AND MAY BE USED ALL THE TIME.

ILLUSTRATED FEATURES OF THE MECHANICAL CONSTRUCTION OF OUR

Minnesota Model "S" Head

IT WILL DO ANY WORK, LIGHT OR HEAVY, FANCY OR PLAIN SEWING, THAT CAN BE DONE ON ANY FAMILY SEWING MACHINE.

It is impossible to devise a more perfect or more suitable sewing machine for household or domestic purposes than our MINNESOTA MODEL "S." In the matter of improvements, labor and time saving conveniences, it is second only to our Minnesota New Model "A," and is built on the latest up to date principles of construction.

DESIGN. BY REFERENCE TO THE ILLUSTRATION it will be seen that the Minnesota Model "S" Head is extremely handsome and pleasing in appearance, the general design being worked out in easy curves and rounded corners so as to avoid any suggestion of harshness or angularity.

SIZE. OUR MODEL "S" HEAD IS THE REGULAR standard, high arm, family style, and measures 5¼ inches in height under the arm, 8½ inches from needle to upright part of arm and 9¾ inches from bed plate to top of the needle bar. The bed plate is 7⅛ inches wide by 14½ inches long. These measurements provide sufficient space for practically any family sewing.

FINISH. THE FINISH OF THE HEAD IS AS FINE as can be put on a sewing machine. Three coats of the highest grade of enamel are used, each coat being separately baked at a high temperature, rubbed down to a smooth surface by hand and finally beautifully decorated in an elaborate design worked out in gold and bright colors, after which it is given a coat of special varnish, also baked in a high degree of heat which gives the machine a durable, rich and lustrous finish. Before the enamel is put on, the head is treated to a coat of anti-rust preparation which prevents the finish from cracking, checking or peeling which so frequently occurs with other makes of machines.

NICKEL PLATING. ALL OF THE BRIGHT parts, including the face plate, are first copper plated, then nickel plated and finally highly polished. The nickel plating applies to the working parts underneath the bed of the machine as well as to those that are exposed to view.

LOCK STITCH. OUR MODEL "S" IS A regular lock stitch machine, which is the popular type adopted by all manufacturers of high grade family sewing machines.

OPERATING PARTS

THE OPERATING PARTS OF THE MODEL "S" Head are fully described and illustrated on this and the following page. All operating and working parts in this machine are made of the finest cold rolled steel that can be obtained, and after being thoroughly hardened by the latest and most improved process, are accurately ground to a perfect fit and so constructed that any lost motion due to the slight wear that may result after many years of usage can be easily and quickly taken up. This renders it practically indestructible and one of the most durable machines ever produced.

SPECIAL FEATURES

HIGH ARM. INDEPENDENT, POSITIVE CAM TAKE-UP. DISC TENSION. ROLLER BEARING ANTI-FRICTION FEED BAR. LIGHT RUNNING. NOISELESS.

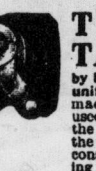

THE INDEPENDENT TAKE-UP. THE TAKE-UP IS OPERATED by a cam on the main shaft, thereby becoming absolutely positive in its action and insuring uniformity of stitch in all classes of work. In many machines, even some of the most expensive, springs are used to partly control the movement of the take-up, and the instant the spring is weakened the harmony between the take-up and other important running parts is destroyed, consequently resulting in imperfect stitches or the breaking of needles.

DOUBLE ECCENTRIC. THE DOUBLE ECCENTRIC ON THE main shaft through the arm of the head operates the shuttle, feed and needle bar mechanism. The double eccentric is made of one piece, accurately balanced so as to prevent any vibration when the machine is being operated and which also contributes greatly to its light and noiseless running qualities. This construction does away with all irregular movements and produces a shuttle and feed movement which is absolutely positive in every sense of the term. A glance at the working parts of this machine shows how remarkably simple it is. There are no springs, cushions, pads or other appliances required which necessarily add to the number of parts and the liability of the machine to get out of order.

EASY TO OIL. BY MEANS OF CONVENIENT OIL HOLES AND A movable metal plate on the back of the head, all bearings are easily gotten at to oil. This is a most important feature, as thorough lubrication prevents friction and wear.

THE NEEDLE CLAMP HOLDS THE NEEDLE FIRMLY IN place and permits the needle to be removed in an instant when required, even though it should break accidentally in the bar where it cannot be reached by the fingers. The needles can be had from us at factory cost. For prices, see page 678.

RUNNING SPEED. EVERY MACHINE BEFORE being shipped from the factory is put to the severest possible test, being set up and attached to a power pulley and run at a speed five times greater than it is possible to run any machine by foot power, and by this severe test we first learn that every machine is perfectly true in every particular and capable of the highest possible speed.

THE NEEDLE BAR IS ROUND AND MADE OF THE best quality of cold rolled steel. It is accurately fitted, insuring absolutely uniform wear at all points.

SELF SETTING NEEDLES FOR THIS MACHINE are the very best grade of flat shank needle it is possible to procure. Every needle is inspected and tested as to size, temper and position of eye. The needle bar is constructed with a groove so that the needle can only be placed in the proper position. It is not necessary to guess at the height or position when setting the needle as is the case with many other makes of machines.

NEW ROLLER BEARING FEED BAR. NEWEST and latest feature. In addition to the many improvements made on the various Minnesota Models, particularly the Minnesota Models "A" and "S," we have added a new feature to the Minnesota Model "S," making it one of the lightest and easiest running sewing machines on the market. The part of the feed bar which comes in contact with the feed lift bar has been fitted with a roller bearing. This roller bearing will make the machine run lighter and with less noise, and will also do away with the necessity for raising the feed after the machine has been in use some time.

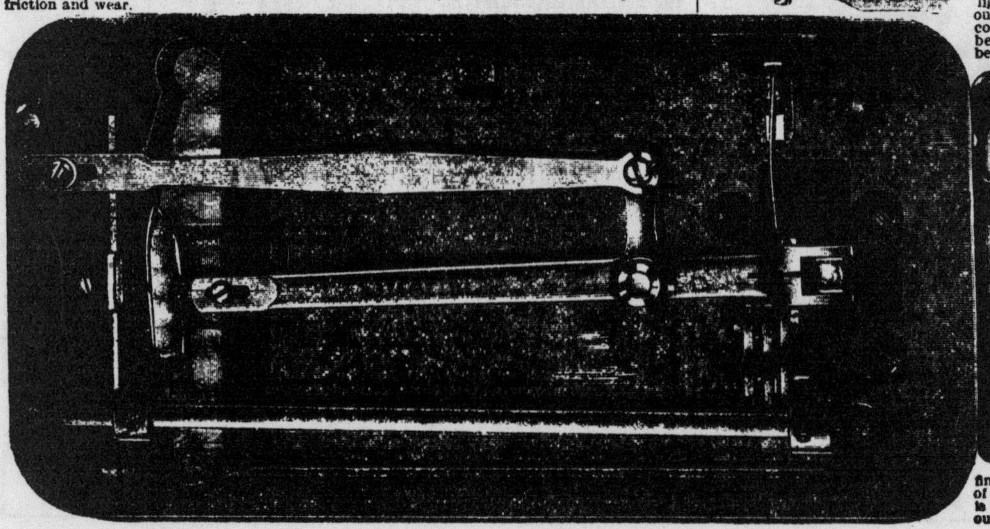

THE MINNESOTA HEAD IS CONSTRUCTED WITH FEW running or operating parts, rendering it easy to understand and operate, light running and free from vibration and noise, doing away with the liability to get out of order, common to many machines. The mechanism is so constructed that the full line of parts in the Minnesota head operate entirely independent of one another and all driving power is supplied direct from the main shaft, without the agency of the numerous connections, cogs and many unnecessary devices used in some machines to operate the feed, shuttle and needle power. The operator does not need to tamper with or adjust these parts, regardless of the weight of goods being sewed. This construction has made the Minnesota head famous as the most durable and simplest head ever produced.

ADJUSTMENT. MUCH DEPENDS upon the adjustment of the working parts, for should any part, for instance the shuttle, be adjusted 1-32 of an inch out of place, the harmony between the parts would be destroyed and imperfect work will result. The operating parts in our Minnesota machines receive the finest and most accurate adjustment, are tested on all kinds of materials, and pass other numerous inspections, so that it is practically impossible for a Minnesota machine to leave our factory, unless perfect in construction and adjustment.

DESCRIPTION OF OUR MODEL "S" HEAD—Continued.

EVERY SINGLE MACHINE WE PUT OUT IS COVERED by our written, binding twenty-year guarantee. In order that we can guarantee our sewing machines for twenty years, it is necessary that only the very finest material be used, and put together by the most skillful workmanship. You can feel assured that our sewing machines are the finest it is possible to manufacture, that we spare no effort or expense in our endeavor to produce an almost everlasting machine, since we are able to guarantee every machine for the full term of twenty years. We aim to protect you in every way and if the machine you get from us gives out in any way, by reason of any defect in material or workmanship, at any time in twenty years, we will replace it or repair it free of charge.

PRESSER FOOT. THE PRESSER foot is very large so that it will hold any weight and thickness of goods firmly in place. The edge of the foot nearest the operator is bent upward slightly so that it will not catch in fleecy material. The presser foot can be removed from the machine in an instant without the aid of a screwdriver. The illustration shows the foot being removed after the thumbscrew has been loosened.

PRESSER BAR LIFTER THE PRESSER BAR IS fitted with a steel, case hardened, nickel plated lifter, so constructed that it can be turned to the right or to the left, raising the bar to the desired height for heavy or light material.

NEEDLE AND THREAD SCALE. A SCALE INDICATING THE proper needle to be used with the different sizes of thread is stamped on the forward shuttle slide. Breaking of the thread and needles often occurs if incorrect sizes of needles or thread are used.

A SHARP STEEL THREAD CUTTER IS PLACED ON THE PRESSER bar, convenient to the operator, by the aid of which the thread can be easily cut, obviating the use of scissors and the danger of breaking or cutting the thread too short.

DOUBLE FEED. THE FEED IS MADE FROM the best quality tool steel; has four sets of teeth, two on each side of the needle, and so constructed that when in operation the goods must be carried forward with absolute accuracy.

FEED MOVEMENT. (FOUR-MOTION.) THE FEED IN THIS machine is operated by four movements. The feed comes up, takes a firm hold on the goods, carries them forward the full length of the stitch, then it falls, releasing the goods, and comes back again toward the operator ready for the next stitch. These four movements are provided entirely by the main shaft, insuring positive action on either heavy or light work.

THE SHUTTLE. THE SHUTTLE is the most perfect, self-threading, cylindrical shuttle ever produced. It is extra large in size, made of the finest tool steel, hardened, ground and finished. It is absolutely self threading, being open at one end for inserting the bobbin, after which the thread is instantly drawn into place by two movements of the hand. There are no holes to pass through, and the shuttle can be threaded with the eyes shut. It has a perfect tension, which is practically automatic. It does not require regulating for any ordinary work. The bobbin carries a large amount of thread. The illustration shows the shuttle being held between the thumb and forefinger while threading.

THE SHUTTLE CARRIER. THE BODY IN which the shuttle rests is fitted with a spring which holds the bobbin firmly in place and prevents it from rattling while the machine is in operation. The carrier is adjustable, so that when the shuttle shows signs of wear, after many years of use, the carrier can be moved closer to the shuttle race, thus enabling the operator to use the same shuttle for many years, with the same satisfaction as when new.

DISC TENSION. THE UPper tension of this machine is of the modern disc type and practically automatic on all classes of work. The tension is located on the side face plate toward the operator. This location of the tension is not only far more convenient, but brings the point at which the tension is applied to the thread much nearer to the eye of the needle, thus reducing the amount of thread under tension and doing away, in a large measure, with the stretch in the thread, which on the old style machines frequently caused bad stitching or skipping of stitches.

OUR SELF OILING SHUTTLE RACE FOUND ON all Minnesota Model "S" Sewing Machines. This new improvement, this self oiling device for the shuttle race, solves the problem of keeping the race properly oiled without danger of getting too much oil on the race and soiling the upper and lower threads. It keeps the shuttle race always properly oiled and thereby reduces the friction of the shuttle against the race and prevents wear of the shuttle.

SEE PAGE 691 FOR ILLUSTRATION AND DESCRIPTION OF THE NEW LIBRARY TABLE SEWING MACHINE

THE AUTOMATIC BOBBIN WINDER ON THIS MACHINE is nickel plated throughout and is the most perfect bobbin winder ever produced. It is so simple that any child can operate it, and the thread is wound on the bobbin automatically and so evenly and smoothly as to make the bobbin work perfectly in the shuttle, producing an even tension and greatly improving the perfection of the stitch. This also prevents the breaking of the lower thread, which is liable to occur with an unevenly wound bobbin.

THE BOBBIN WINDER IS ALWAYS IN POSITION AND READY TO operate. It is operated by means of the belt which is placed in contact with the small pulley wheel of the bobbin winder.

STITCH REGULATOR. THE illustration shows the stitch regulator, which is fastened to the bed plate just in front of the arm in plain sight and within easy reach of the operator. The length of the stitch can be adjusted instantly by loosening the thumb nut and moving the pointer to the desired figure on the scale stamped on the stitch regulator plate. The stitch can be varied from six to thirty-two stitches to the inch, thereby affording a range from the very smallest to the largest stitch.

LOCK NUT. THE LOCK NUT, which is located at the end of the main shaft and used to release and tighten the hand wheel, is turned out of one piece of case hardened steel, has milled edge and is heavily nickel plated and polished. The lock nut is plainly marked with arrows, showing which way it must be turned to loosen or tighten the hand wheel.

All Sewing Machines listed in this catalog use Davis Needles

Attachments for Our Model "S" Machines

WE USE THE CELEBRATED GREIST FOOT ATTACHMENTS.

OUR CUSTOMERS HAVE THE ADVANTAGE AND PRIVILEGE OF BEING ABLE TO PURCHASE A MACHINE WITHOUT attachments, and are not obliged to receive and pay for attachments which are not required. From our many years of experience in selling sewing machines we have found that about one-third of the sewing machine users do not need the attachments, using the machine for plain sewing only; the only necessary attachments being the shuttle, needle, bobbin, quilter, screwdriver, wrench and foot hemmer, which are always furnished with our machines at no additional charge. We have, therefore, deducted the cost of the attachments from the selling price and quote each machine without any extra attachments.

THE ATTACHMENTS FOR OUR MINNESOTA MODEL "S" SEWING Machine, furnished at 75 cents extra, are made by the Greist Mfg. Co., the largest manufacturing plant devoted exclusively to the manufacture of sewing machine attachments. This illustration shows the Model "S" attachments arranged in a velvet lined metal box. Each attachment may be kept in its particular place as provided for by the construction of the box. The complete set includes one ruffler, one shirring blade, one tucker, one under braider, one binder, one short foot and one set of four hemmers up to ⅞ of an inch wide. The attachments are made of steel, heavily nickel plated and polished.

ATTACHMENTS WILL BE FURNISHED AT 75 CENTS EXTRA. IF YOU, THE READER OF THIS CATalog, intend to use your machine for plain sewing only, and do not wish to buy extra attachments, you will appreciate our departure from the old custom of including, at the purchaser's expense, a set of attachments with every machine. If you wish to purchase a machine without attachments, and later on wish to secure attachments, we can always supply you at our lowest price.

ACCESSORIES FURNISHED FREE. WE FURNISH WITH EVERY MINNEsota Model "S" Machine a complete set of accessories, such as are usually furnished with every high grade machine, consisting of one quilter, five bobbins (and one in the machine), one cloth guide, a large screwdriver, one oil can filled with oil, one screwdriver and wrench, one foot hemmer, one package of needles and one instruction book.

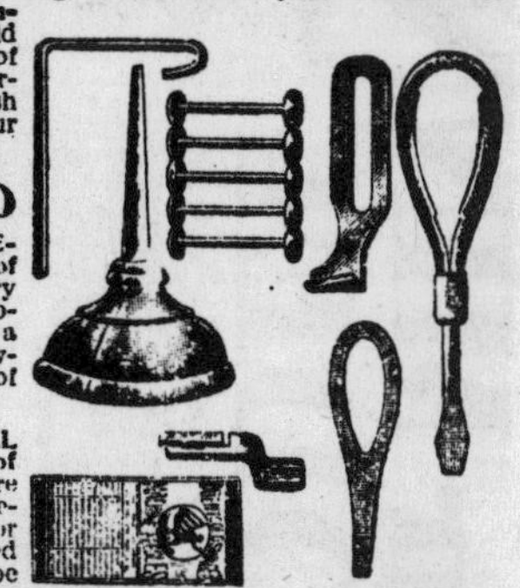

WE CARRY IN STOCK A FULL supply of needles, bobbins, shuttles, attachments, etc., which are used in the operation of our machines. We can, therefore, fill orders for repairs promptly. An order for repairs for the Minnesota Model "S" Machines, placed with us fifteen or twenty years from date, would be filled as promptly as a repair order sent us today.

WE FURNISH, FREE OF CHARGE, WITH EVERY MINNESOTA MODEL "S" SEWING MACHINE A BOOK OF INSTRUCTIONS telling how to operate the sewing machine. This book covers every point, makes everything so plain and simple that anyone without previous experience can learn to run the machine at once and do perfect work; tells you how to get the best results, how to take care of your machine, tells you where to oil and when. It tells you how to use the different attachments, the ruffler, tucker, hemmers and binders, and contains illustrations of these attachments in use.

DIRECTIONS
FOR USING THE NEW
MINNESOTA
MODEL S
SEWING MACHINE

READ WHAT OUR CUSTOMERS SAY ABOUT OUR MACHINES

HAS BEEN USING A SINGER MACHINE, FOR WHICH SHE PAID $75.00, AND CONSIDERS THE ONE SHE HAS NOW (THE MINNESOTA) EQUALLY AS GOOD IN EVERY WAY.

Sears, Roebuck & Co., Chicago, Ill. Nogales, Ariz.

Gentlemen:—The Minnesota Sewing Machine I ordered from you a few months ago came to hand promptly and has, in every respect so far, proved entirely satisfactory. I have been using a Singer machine, for which I paid $75.00, and I consider the one I have now (bought of you) equally as good in every way and not costing one-third as much as I paid for the Singer.

Respectfully, MRS. C. A. GILDEA.

WOULD NOT EXCHANGE THE MINNESOTA FOR A $60.00 MACHINE.

Sears, Roebuck & Co., Chicago, Ill. Sheridan, Oregon.

Gentlemen:—I received the sewing machine (the Minnesota) that I ordered of you in a reasonable time and I am well pleased with it in every respect. I have used the Wheeler & Wilson, also Domestic and a number of other sewing machines, but I like the Minnesota the best. One of my neighbors bought a five-drawer Singer machine in the same month I bought mine of you and my machine has seven drawers. They are both drop head machines. I would not exchange with her; she calls her machine a $60.00 machine. Yours truly,

MRS. JAS. BARNETT.

IN WRITING TO ANY OF THESE PEOPLE, ENCLOSE A 2-CENT STAMP FOR REPLY.

GREATLY PLEASED WITH THE MINNESOTA MODEL "A" SEWING MACHINE. USED TWO SINGERS FOR WHICH SHE PAID $45.00 AND $60.00, BUT THE MODEL "A" IS THE LIGHTEST AND EASIEST RUNNING OF THE THREE.

Sears, Roebuck & Co., Chicago, Ill. Campbellton, Texas.

Dear Sirs:—Having last August received a Minnesota Model "A" Sewing Machine from you, will say after using it for seven months that I am greatly pleased with it. It is a first class, up to date machine in every respect; having used two Singer machines before this, which I paid $45.00 and $60.00 for, I must say that this is the lightest and easiest running of the three, and it only cost me $18.00 with the freight. I would advise everyone in need of a sewing machine to order a Minnesota direct from you. Yours truly,

MRS. LUCY SPARKS.

USED HIS LIBRARY TABLE SEWING MACHINE AS A PARLOR TABLE AND MANY SEE IT AND THINK IT IS A PARLOR TABLE, NOT SUSPECTING THAT THERE IS A SEWING MACHINE INSIDE.

Sears, Roebuck & Co., Chicago, Ill. Dedham, Iowa.

Gentlemen:—I received the sewing machine and am more than pleased with it. I use it as a parlor table and many see it and think it is a parlor table, not suspecting that there is a machine inside. I am very much pleased with it. It takes the place of any parlor table worth at least $15.00. It runs easy, and I like it better than the Domestic. Sews well and gives entire satisfaction. I will remember your firm in the future, since I have saved at least $25.00 on the $100.00 worth of goods I bought from your firm.

Respectfully yours, REV. J. H. DRIES.

$13.95 Our MINNESOTA MODEL "S" NEW STYLE

A BETTER SEWING MACHINE FOR LESS MONEY THAN IS OFFERED BY ANY OTHER DEALER OR AGENT.

DISC TENSION. Independent, Positive Cam Take-up. Roller Bearing Anti-Friction Feed Bar.

SIZE OF HEAD WORKING SPACE UNDER ARM, 5¼x8½ INCHES.

SIZE OF BED PLATE, 7x14 INCHES.

For full and complete detailed description of woodwork and stand, see following page.

NEW CRESCENT WOODWORK, BALL BEARING STAND, NICKEL PLATED STEEL PITMAN.

WE OFFER THE MINNESOTA MODEL "S," A HIGH ARM family style sewing machine head of the vibrating shuttle type, making a double thread lockstitch, in this popular and beautiful swell front style, five-drawer, drop head cabinet, as a very much better sewing machine, superior in every way, a better head, more improvements, finer quality and workmanship, higher class woodwork than is offered by others in a similar style woodwork at very muc. higher prices.

GUARANTEED BY US FOR TWENTY YEARS. SHIPPED TO anyone subject to our liberal three months' trial plan.

WITH NEW IMPROVEMENTS. WE HAVE GREATLY IMPROVED OUR ENTIRE line of Minnesota Sewing Machines. We have carefully gone over every detail of the manufacture with a view to improving wherever possible, with the idea of adding any little changes that will make the Minnesota machine better in any detail, no matter how slight. We have succeeded in incorporating quite a few points of improvement and, splendid as our Minnesota Sewing Machines have been for the past few years, we can guarantee that the sewing machine we furnish now will give even greater satisfaction. In the large Minnesota Sewing Machine factory, adapted entirely to the manufacture of sewing machines, turning out an immense product daily, buying the material in such large quantities, with a guaranteed output, we have facilities for doing experimental work, for making tests and comparisons that enable us to constantly improve the quality of our Minnesota machines. There are any number of little features about the Minnesota machines that it is impossible to explain by illustration and description; little details that go to make perfection entirely outside of the more important mechanical features to which we have directed your attention in the preceding pages, and yet have so much to do with the superior quality of the Minnesota machines.

ORDER AND COMPARE THIS BEAUTIFUL MACHINE WITH ANY SIMILAR STYLE SEWING MAchine that you can get from anyone else, put them side by side, compare them in every piece and part, give them both a thorough working trial and test, do all kinds of plain and fancy sewing on both machines, compare the woodwork, all special features, and if you do not find our sewing machine far superior in every way, a very much better machine in all respects, very much handsomer, even though the other machine is sold at $5.00 to $8.00 more, we will not expect you to keep our machine; just return it to us at our expense, and we will promptly return all your money, including what you paid for freight charges. If you question this, if you want to prove our claims, get our sewing machine for comparison. Send for it, enclosing our price with your order, and make the comparison. If by reason of such comparison and test you desire to return our sewing machine, all your money will be promptly returned to you and you will not be out one cent by the transaction.

WE ESPECIALLY RECOMMEND OUR AUTOMATIC LIFT, BALL BEARING MINNESOTA MODEL "A" SEWING MACHINE TO ALL OUR CUSTOMERS in preference to any other sewing machine made. There is only a few dollars' difference between the cost of our Minnesota Model "S" and the highest grade sewing machine we sell, the Automatic Lift, Ball Bearing Minnesota Model "A," which is put out under guarantee that it is the highest grade sewing machine made in the world. We always feel like urging our customers to select one of our highest grade machines because the difference in price represents only the actual difference in cost, and by buying a Minnesota Model "A" you get the highest grade sewing machine construction it is possible to produce, a machine capable of doing any and all classes of family sewing, a machine that will sew the thinnest and finest fabrics as well as the heaviest and coarsest cloth, without necessitating a change in the tension. You get the lightest and easiest running sewing machine, the only family sewing machine on the market today constructed with ball bearings in the operating parts of the head. The stand is the lightest running because all the bearing parts have ball bearing adjustments. In fact, you get the very best of everything, and you get it on the basis of the actual cost of material and labor and with but one small margin of profit added.

She Has Had More Compliments on Her Sewing Machine Than on Any Other One Thing in Her House.

Sears, Roebuck and Co., Chicago, Ill. Attica, Indiana.
Gentlemen:—I have used your Minnesota Model "A" Sewing Machine quite a little and have never had any trouble whatever. I would not exchange my Minnesota Sewing Machine for any other machine I have used, such as the Domestic, the New Royal and the New Home. My sister has a ———, but comes here to do her sewing. I have had more compliments on my machine than any other one thing I have in my house. I think your Minnesota Model "A" Machine is as good, or even better than the $55.00 or $60.00 machines that are sold around here. I can recommend it to anyone, and it was through me and my machine that you sold one to Mrs. Harvey Harrington of Brazil, Indiana. Very truly yours, MRS. R. W. HICKMAN.

The Minnesota Model "A" is as Good as any $45.00 or $50.00 Sewing Machine that is Sold by Agents.

Sears, Roebuck and Co., Chicago, Ill. Park Ridge, Ill.
Gentlemen:—After one month's trial of the Minnesota Model "A" Drop Head Sewing Machine, we find that we will have no use for that three months' trial contract and I herewith return it to you. The machine is all that you claim it to be and we do not want a better one, no matter what the name may be. It is as good as any $45.00 or $50.00 machine bought of sewing machine agents. Very truly yours, WM. H. BRUEINING.

REMEMBER THAT THIS MACHINE IS GUARANTEED BY US FOR 20 YEARS with a written, binding, signed guarantee which we send you, and we guarantee to replace or repair any piece or part within 20 years that shows defective material or workmanship. When you order this machine from us you have the privilege of using it three months, and if at any time during the three months you are not perfectly satisfied, you may return it to us and we will promptly return your money, including the freight charges you paid.

SHIPPED ONLY FROM DAYTON, OHIO.

Shipping weight, about 120 pounds.

ORDER BY NUMBER

No. 26T140 Minnesota Model "S" Ball Bearing Five-Drawer Drop Head Style Sewing Machine. Price.... **$13.95**

ATTACHMENTS, SEE PAGE 697, 75 CENTS EXTRA.

MINNESOTA MODEL "S"

Description of the Woodwork.

THE WOODWORK ON OUR MODEL "S" SEWING MACHINES IS OF A very much higher grade than is usually furnished. It is made especially for our machines, under contract, by the largest manufacturer of sewing machine woodwork in the world, who supplies cabinets only for the highest grade sewing machines, therefore cannot be in any way classed with the woodwork commonly used on machines that sell generally at $30.00 or less.

MATERIALS. ONLY THE MOST SELECT GRADE OF SOLID OAK IS USED in the construction of our Model "S" woodwork. It is carefully selected with reference to grain and color and is thoroughly air seasoned and kiln dried to insure against warping, splitting or cracking.

DESIGN. THE MINNESOTA MODEL "S" CABINET IS A MODEL OF BEAUTY and artistic design, second only to our Model "A." It is made on the lines of the high grade, up to date furniture.

TABLE. THE TABLE IS MADE OF selected nicely grained solid oak. The lid is made of built-up stock. This construction has proven the most durable, being practically indestructible. The front edge of the table is handsomely shaped. When the machine is not in use the head is lowered from view, the leaf covers it, and with the drum at the bottom completely protects the head from dust. When the machine is closed it makes a very convenient stand and frequently takes the place of a table used for such purposes.

DRAWER FRAMES. THE DRAWER FRAMES IN WHICH THE side drawers are fitted are of the latest skeleton type, very handsome in appearance and made to correspond in design and style with the table and drawers.

DRAWERS. THE CRESCENT shape drawers are very large and roomy, made of nicely figured veneered oak, to harmonize with the table. The fronts are handsomely fitted with brass plated drawer pulls. The center drawer is made with double swell front, interior is partitioned off for bobbins, needles and other accessories which are in constant demand when the machine is being used. Every drawer is fitted with a lock and one key fits them all.

FINISH. IN POINT OF FINISH OUR MODEL "S" machine is strictly first class and of the very latest golden oak color, the popular finish put on high grade oak furniture. Before the finish is put on, the woodwork is most carefully sandpapered, so that the varnish, which is of the very best quality, produces a hard, glossy surface. The table is hand rubbed and polished.

NEWEST AND LATEST FEATURE. IN ADDITION TO THE MANY IMPROVEments made on the various Minnesota models, particularly the Minnesota Models "A" and "S," we have added a new feature to the Minnesota Model "S," making it one of the lightest and easiest running sewing machines on the market. The part of the feed bar which comes in contact with the feed lift bar has been fitted with a roller bearing. This roller bearing will make the machine run lighter and with less noise, and will also do away with the necessity for raising the feed after the machine has been in use for some time.

CLOSED VIEW
No. 26T140

WE FURNISH FREE A BOOK OF INSTRUCTIONS TELLING how to operate the machine; makes everything so plain and simple that anyone without previous experience can learn to run the machine at once and do perfect work; tells you how to get the best results, how to take care of your machine; tells you where to oil and when; how to use the different attachments, the ruffler, tucker, hemmers and binders, and contains illustrations of these attachments in use.

IF YOU ORDER A MINNESOTA SEWING MACHINE, AND PARTICULARLY the ball bearing Minnesota Model "S" in the beautiful drop head cabinet style, as here illustrated, you will be getting a sewing machine that will be an everlasting comfort and pleasure to you. Every time you use the machine you will find more reason to be pleased with your purchase. You will feel like writing us the same kind of a letter as thousands of other purchasers of sewing machines write us, a very few of which letters are reproduced in the various pages of this department. There is no risk whatever when you order from us, because if the sewing machine does not come up to your every expectation, and if you do not find that we have saved you money and furnished you with a machine such as has no equal, your money is awaiting you just as quick as you return the machine.

WE USE THE CELEBRATED GREIST FOOT ATTACHMENTS, MADE BY THE GREIST MANUFACTURING COMPANY of New Haven, Conn., on our Minnesota Model "S" Machine as well as our other models. The entire set is made of the very best steel of extra thickness, heavily nickel plated, and consists of the following attachments, packed in a velvet lined japanned metal box: One ruffler, one shirring plate, one tucker, one short foot, one under braider, one binder, and one set of four hemmers, different widths, up to ⅝ inch. Our price for the full set, 75 cents. Be sure to state if you wish the attachments shipped with your machine.

Description of the Stand.

OUR MODEL "S" STANDS ARE MADE FROM THE VERY BEST Birmingham, Alabama, light gray iron. These stands are molded by automatic machines, making every piece perfectly true, smooth and of unusual strength, so that when the different parts are put together they will fit perfectly. All Model "S" stand parts are filed and ground perfectly smooth, after which they are enameled by hand process. Particular pains are taken in enameling these stands and in adjusting the different parts. This special care and attention is plainly evident when our Model "S" machines are compared side by side with machines the selling price of which is two or three times as much as that for which you can buy the Model "S."

BALL BEARING BALANCE WHEEL. ALL OUR MODEL "S" Machines are equipped with ball bearing hangers. The hanger is the large balance wheel and staff fastened to the wheel guard, in the illustration. As this wheel supplies the operating power to the head, the bearings on which the wheel revolves are naturally subjected to considerable strain, but, by the introduction of the ball bearings, all friction is removed and the wheel revolves with the same freedom and rapidity as the ball bearing crank hanger of the bicycle. The application of the ball bearing to the balance wheel is one of the greatest improvements and the greatest aid to the light running qualities of the machine, and we have demonstrated by actual experience and tests that our ball bearing hanger is at least 20 per cent lighter running than any ball bearing device or arrangement used on any other sewing machine made. By the aid of ball bearings a machine is not only lighter running, but exceedingly easy of operation and very rapid in action.

THE ARRANGEMENT OF THE BALL BEARINGS ON THE BALANCE WHEEL IS the same as that used on all high grade bicycles; the axle on which the wheel revolves passes through two steel cups, each of which contains eight solid steel balls, which are fitted into the balance wheels and, by turning the journal to the right or left adjusting the bearings it is possible at all times to have the wheel run lightly and noiselessly. The cups and cones used on our stands are turned out of a solid bar of steel, after which they are ground out and hardened in oil, making them impervious to wear, and with proper oiling from time to time will make them last a lifetime.

THIS ILLUSTRATION SHOWS HOW WELL the balance wheel is protected by the dress guard which covers the entire wheel. It also shows very plainly how the ball bearing balance wheel is fastened to the dress guard. Also note the position of the pitman rod between the wheel and the side frame of the machine. With this construction it is impossible for one's dress or skirt to become entangled in the pitman or balance wheel; impossible for them to become soiled by oil from contact with these working parts of the stand. The illustration on the foregoing page shows the beautiful design of the side frame or legs of the Minnesota Model "S" stand.

DESIGN. THE MODEL "S" STAND is our own special design, made with a view of procuring a neat, graceful open effect, and at the same time furnish a most rigid and solid stand. The side frames or legs are made in the handsome open and wide ribbon pattern style. The style adopted in the side frames, besides making the stand perfectly rigid, also makes it easier to keep the stand clean and free from dust, because all parts can be reached from outside the frame.

THE BRACES. THE SIDE FRAMES OR LEGS of the stand are joined together by a four-arm brace, bolted at top and bottom, making the stand absolutely rigid. This is very essential, as it lessens the vibration and so causes our machines to make less noise and last longer than those machines which are built on weak and wobbly legs.

DRESS GUARD. THE DRESS GUARD TO THIS stand is extra large, protecting the balance wheel and belt from any possible contact with the dress, at the same time substantially bracing the side frame.

TREADLE. THE TREADLE IS OF THE OPENwork style, with full ends, pivot bearing, accurately trued.

THE TREADLE BRACE, IMMEDIATELY UNDER THE TREADLE extending from side frame to side frame, is securely bolted and strengthens the frame.

CASTERS. WE USE THE HIGHEST GRADE SEWING MACHINE CASTERS made. They are of large size, making it easy to move the machine from place to place, are carefully fitted and never break.

INSPECTION. ALL PARTS ARE ACCURATELY TRUED, TESTED FOR strength; not a casting is allowed to be used that has a defect or that isn't true to gauge. After the stand has been properly assembled, the balance wheel and treadle are operated by steam power at a very high rate of speed, whereby the balance wheel makes a great many more revolutions than any operator could possibly make. If there is the slightest flaw in the iron, or in the construction or adjustment of the stand, it becomes evident through this test, and the stand is then rejected, and, as a result, for strength, beauty, design, finish, for easy running and for perfect control of the machine by the operator, we furnish a higher grade sewing machine stand than is furnished by any other maker.

READ WHAT THESE CUSTOMERS SAY ABOUT OUR SEWING MACHINES.

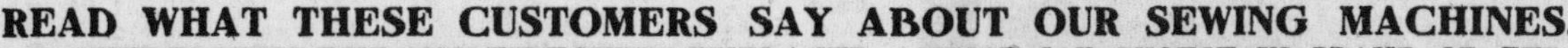

HAS PUT THE MACHINE TO EVERY TEST, SOME VERY SEVERE TESTS THAT SHE KNEW OTHER MACHINES WERE PUT TO, AND HAS NO HESITATION IN SAYING THE MINNESOTA MODEL "A" IS STRICTLY A HIGH GRADE MACHINE.

Sears, Roebuck & Co., Chicago, Ill. Mauch Chunk Road, Bethlehem, Penn.

Gentlemen:—In regard to the Minnesota Model "A" Sewing Machine sent to me some time ago I would say that I said very little in my last letter because I had very little opportunity to try the machine. Up to date, however, we have had the machine in almost constant use, and being familiar with sewing machine construction, I personally have put it to every test, and some very severe tests that I knew other machines were put to. I compared the machine with other machines of standard make, and I have no hesitation in saying that the Minnesota Model "A" is strictly a high grade machine. In operation it holds its own with any, and in range of work I find it superior to a very great number of machines. A machine very similar sells here for $45.00 on time, or $35.00 cash. Thanking you again for your very prompt attention, I remain, HERBERT V. MITMAN.

SHE CANNOT SAY ENOUGH IN PRAISE OF THE MINNESOTA MODEL "A" MACHINE. WOULD NOT TAKE TWICE WHAT SHE GAVE FOR IT IF SHE COULD NOT GET ANOTHER LIKE IT.

R. F. D. No. 1, Beaver Dams, N. Y.

Sears, Roebuck & Co., Chicago, Ill.

Dear Sirs:—I received the sewing machine which I ordered of you about the 1st of April, and I am more than pleased with it. It works perfectly, and I should have written to your company before, but have neglected doing so. Different parties who have seen the machine say it is equal to any $45.00 machine bought of agents here. I thank you very much for your prompt shipment, it reached me in perfect condition and I cannot say enough in praise of it. I would not take twice what I gave for it if I could not get another like it. Thanking you for your kindness, I remain, Very respectfully yours,

MRS. RALPH E. GOUNDREY.

IN WRITING TO THESE PEOPLE ENCLOSE A TWO-CENT STAMP FOR REPLY.

THE MINNESOTA MODEL "S"

FULL DESK CABINET BALL BEARING SEWING MACHINE

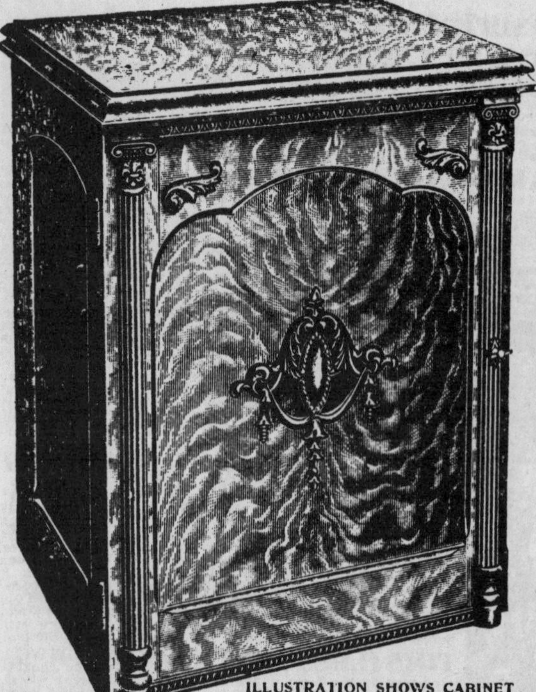

ILLUSTRATION SHOWS CABINET CLOSED.

Our Latest and Newest Design Full Desk Cabinet with Minnesota Model "S" Head

In This, OUR MINNESOTA MODEL "S" FULL DESK QUARTERED oak cabinet, full ball bearing machine, we believe we are offering not only the highest grade, but the handsomest sewing machine shown by any dealer. Our price of $15.75 for this magnificent sewing machine is figured on the basis of actual cost of material and labor with just one small profit added, and you pay nothing for wholesalers' or jobbers' profits, nothing for salesmen's or agents' expenses, for agents' profits, nothing for the expense of running accounts, collections, bad debts, etc., and as a result we can furnish you a sewing machine that if it were produced by any other dealer would cost you $30.00 to $35.00. $15.75 represents the bare cost of the material and skilled labor that enter into the construction of this machine, with just a few cents figured for our profit. See the illustrations and you will get some idea of the appearance of this handsome full cabinet Minnesota machine. One illustration shows the cabinet entirely closed, in which position it has the effect of a beautiful piece of furniture, a nice stand, table or music cabinet. The next illustration shows the machine partly closed, the head dropped down and not in use, and extension leaf folded over. The last illustration shows the machine open and ready for work. You can see how roomy it is and how convenient.

AS HANDSOME A CABINET AS HAS EVER BEEN PRODUCED BY ANY SEWING machine maker, a piece of furniture that will equal in appearance any other furniture you have in the house. The illustrations of course cannot do justice to this beautiful machine. You can see that the cabinet is beautifully carved and ornamented, and the richness of this design can only be appreciated when you see the machine itself. The cabinet is a wonderful example of the cabinet maker's art, made according to the latest design, rich but not over elaborate, a model of good taste in every way. The machine furnished in this full cabinet style is fully described on page 696, and we ask you to bear in mind that this machine is ball bearing, a feature that you will find in only the most expensive sewing machines offered by dealers and agents at $40.00 to $60.00.

THE MODEL "S" FULL DESK CABINET IS MADE OF SELECTED AIR SEASONED AND KILN DRIED quarter sawed oak. The top is of selected quarter sawed oak, finished and hand rubbed to a mirror like piano polish. Particular pains are taken in selecting the lumber used for the tops of our cabinets, and the special manner in which they are reinforced insures them against warping, cracking or splitting. The door is strongly built of quartered oak, with specially selected flaky grained quartered oak panel. The panels on both sides of the cabinet are also of specially selected quarter sawed oak. The molding on the doors, besides being handsome and ornamental, adds materially to the strength of the cabinet. The door is locked by means of a turn bolt and brass knob.

A TAPE MEASURE, 18 inches long, accurately divided and beautifully colored to match the woodwork is transferred on this table, directly in front of the head, where it is most convenient for the use of the operator.

BALL BEARING

ILLUSTRATION SHOWS HEAD WHEN NOT IN USE.

DO NOT MAKE THE MISTAKE OF THINKING THAT THE MACHINES SHOWN IN OTHER catalogs can be as good as the Minnesota Models. We are willing to compare the Minnesota Model "C," our cheaper machine, with the best offered by other catalog houses. We know that no catalog house or any other dealer offers a machine that compares in quality with our Minnesota Models "A" and "S." Our Models "A" and "S" are the very acme of sewing machine quality, as near perfection in sewing machines as has thus far been achieved. Take the best features of the very finest machines on the market offered by others, take all of the finer points from the widely advertised sewing machines sold by agents, combine all these features and you would still not have a sewing machine of the general excellence of our Minnesota Model "A" or "S." This we guarantee; and yet our price for the highest grade sewing machine it is possible to build, a sewing machine superior to anything the market offers, our price on either the Model "A" or Model "S" in any of the various styles we furnish, you will find to be about one-third, perhaps even one-fourth, of the price asked by dealers and agents of all the widely advertised machines. Is there any reason for you to pay this difference in price? If for the $20.00 extra you pay you would be getting even one dollar's worth of added value in the machine, there might be some reason for you to pay the big premium, but the $10.00 or $15.00 or $20.00 or even $30.00, which you may pay to some dealer or agent more than the price we ask for our finest machines, cannot, and does not buy for you one single degree of quality more than we give you in the Minnesota. We have exhausted the possibilities of sewing machine building in our Minnesota Models "A" and "S." We give you everything in quality; we give you everything in price. Whether you buy our cheapest sewing machine or our very finest Model "A," or whether you let us send you this beautiful Model "S" full cabinet machine, you get every advantage we can give you on the price question. You pay us the least possible price, based on the actual cost of material and labor with just our one small percentage of profit added.

BALL BEARINGS. OUR MODEL "S" FULL CABINET MACHINE IS AS LIGHT RUNNING AS EITHER the upright or the drop head style; is fitted with our celebrated bicycle ball bearing hanger, found only on our cabinet machines, which gives the same rapidity of action and ease of operation to the machine as the ball bearing arrangement to a bicycle. All wearing parts are made of case hardened ground out steel, and the steel balls are the best in the market. Simple in construction, no getting out of order. All parts are easily accessible, so that the balls or cups can be replaced at any time. All friction eliminated and operation made a pleasure.

A FULL SET OF ACCESSORIES, SEE PAGE 697, INCLUDED FREE OF COST, WITH MACHINE AT $15.75

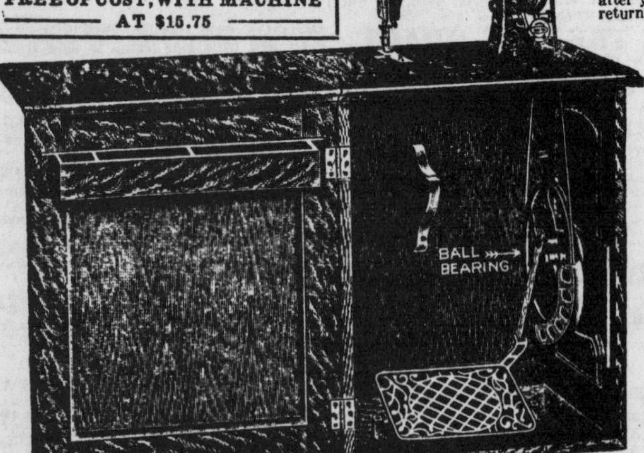

Shipping weight, about 135 pounds.

ILLUSTRATION SHOWS MACHINE OPEN AND READY FOR WORK.

REMEMBER, THE FREIGHT CHARGES ARE REALLY NOTHING. THIS MACHINE safely packed and crated for shipment weighs 135 pounds. No matter where you live, the freight charges will be a very small item compared with what you will save in price; therefore do not be afraid of the freight charges. Don't let anyone tell you that the freight will be a large item and will offset the saving you make by sending us your order. If you don't find that you have made a very great saving in price after you have paid the freight charges you can return the machine to us at our expense and we will promptly return your money, including what you paid for freight.

IF YOU ARE IN DOUBT AS TO WHETHER YOU should pay the additional cost and get this beautiful full cabinet Model "S" ball bearing machine, we would like to send it to you for trial. We know that if you could see the machine and use it we would win you over at once and there would be no doubt in your mind as to the wonderful value we are furnishing at the price. You would admit that such a handsome sewing machine was never before offered at double the money. You would say it has no rival for appearance and a trial would quickly prove to you also that it has no equal for quality. We know you would admit that as a light running machine, a machine easy to operate, perfectly simple, very easy to understand, to do any variety of work on, almost noiseless, there has never been a sewing machine offered to you or shown in your neighborhood that will compare with it.

TWENTY YEARS' BINDING GUARANTEE, THREE MONTHS' TRIAL AND TEST, EVERYTHING we can offer you in quality, the least possible price we can make, our established reliability, all combine to induce you to send us your order and really make it so that you cannot afford to buy a sewing machine elsewhere.

FOR DESCRIPTION OF MODEL "S" HEAD, ATTACHMENTS AND ACCESSORIES, SEE PAGES 696 AND 697.

Before placing your order for any machine, be sure to read the description of our Improved Minnesota New Model "A" Sewing Machines.

BALL BEARING HEAD, BALL BEARING STAND, DOUBLE BALL BEARING STEEL PITMAN.

SAVED FROM $40.00 TO $45.00 BY BUYING THE MACHINE FROM US, AS AN AGENT WOULD HAVE CHARGED NOT LESS THAN $60.00.

Port Matilda, Penna.

Sears, Roebuck and Co., Chicago, Ill.

Gentlemen:—The machine came in due time and will say I could not be more pleased than I am with this machine. Everything was satisfactory about it. I am safe in saying I have saved from $40.00 to $45.00 by buying the machine of you, as an agent would have charged not less than $60.00 for any of the new machines brought through here. A great many persons who want sewing machines have been in to see mine and they all like this one. I see Mrs. J. M. Williams has received one of the same name. She examined mine and said she would have one like it. The freight was only 66 cents, less than I expected it to be.

Yours truly,

MISS ELLA LYTLE.

SHIPPED ONLY FROM DAYTON, OHIO.

No. 26T142 Minnesota Model "S" Full Desk Cabinet, Ball Bearing Machine. Price (furnished in oak only)........ **$15.75**

The above price does not include attachments. We furnish a complete set of attachments at 75 cents additional, as fully explained on page 697.

DESCRIPTION OF THE MINNESOTA MODEL "C" HEAD

THE MINNESOTA MODEL "C" HEAD HAS BEEN CONSTRUCTED WITH A VIEW TO FURNISHING AN extra high arm machine, one that will give unqualified satisfaction, to meet the needs of our customers who desire a medium priced machine which will do a large range of work, heavy and light, equally well. While the parts are all **guaranteed absolutely first class material,** they are not of as fine construction and finish as our Minnesota Models "A" and "S" heads, but larger, stronger and better finished than our Belmont and Homan heads.

DESIGN. OUR MODEL "C" HEAD IS OF THE VERY LATEST design, with gracefully rounded lines which give it a handsome, well proportioned and strong appearance.

SIZE. THE HEAD IS EXTRA large size, having as much room under the arm as the largest family sewing machine head. Height of arm from bed plate, 5¼ inches; from needle bar to base of arm, 8½ inches; size of bed plate, 7x14 inches.

FINISH. THE HEAD IS finished with three coats of enamel, each coat being thoroughly baked and hardened before the next is put on and carefully rubbed down to a smooth surface, and finally treated to a coat of special varnish which is also baked at a high degree of heat, which makes the finish practically indestructible and of a beautiful rich black luster. Before the enamel is put on, the head is treated to a coat of anti-rust preparation which prevents the finish from cracking, checking or peeling, which so frequently occurs with other makes of machines.

DECORATION. THE ARM AND BED PLATE are decorated with handsome floral figures in a combination of silver and gold, especially designed for this machine.

NICKEL PLATING. THE RIM OF THE balance wheel, face plate, shuttle slides, tension plates, stitch regulating plate, presser bar lifter and screw heads are all heavily nickel plated and form a handsome contrast to the black enamel finish.

EQUAL TO A $45.00 MACHINE.

Malone, N. Y., L. Bx. No. 941.

Sears, Roebuck and Co., Chicago, Ill.

Gentlemen—Received sewing machine 27th inst., and find it much nicer than I expected. It came through perfectly safe, not harmed in the least. My mother (it's for her) has tried it and finds it the equal to a $45.00 machine she was thinking of buying. Thanking you for your promptness and fair dealings, I remain, dear sirs,

Yours sincerely,
JOSIAH LERO.

IN THE CONSTRUCTION OF THE MINNESOTA Model "C" head no effort or expense has been spared to make this one of the highest grade sewing machine heads in the world, combining all the best known features in sewing machine head construction, in order to produce a sewing machine head which for simplicity, ease of operation and ability to perform a large variety of work would not be excelled by any sewing machine made by any other manufacturer. Our Minnesota Sewing Machine heads throughout are built along the lines of the most advanced ideas in sewing machine construction. We have in our factory a corps of the most expert mechanics who are continually experimenting and trying out new features, new ideas, always working for the betterment of the machine, and whenever we can improve the machine in the slightest degree, such idea is immediately adopted, even if it increases the manufacturing expense. We aim to give our customers not only a sewing machine as good as they can obtain elsewhere at any price, but even a little better. We feel that our customers are entitled to the very best it is possible to produce, and therefore it is our constant effort to improve the quality of our merchandise, to make it a little better than is necessary, perhaps, so that the machine or other item of merchandise cannot fail to give satisfaction to the customer. This is the policy we have followed in the construction of our line of Minnesota Sewing Machines, and if at any time within a month or year after this catalog is issued we are able to make a still further improvement on this Minnesota machine head, you can feel sure that you will get the benefit of such improvement, and a machine embodying our very best ideas and latest improvements will be furnished you. In our line of Minnesota Sewing Machine heads we can state without fear of contradicting that we produce the highest grade sewing machine head made, of highest grade materials, and put together by more skilled mechanics and with better care than is used by other makers. This enters into the result of producing a sewing machine head, the most important part of the machine, such as cannot be compared with the sewing machine heads found on the general run of machines.

ALL BEARINGS ARE MADE OF STEEL, ESPECIALLY selected for its durable qualities, and properly fitted so as to minimize the friction and prevent wear. All bearings are fitted with adjusting devices, whereby any lost motion caused by the slight wear through years of constant use can be taken up.

OPERATING PARTS. OUR MINNESOTA MACHINES are constructed with the least possible number of running or operating parts, rendering them easy to understand and operate, light running and free from vibration and noise. To do away with the liability to get out of order, common to many machines, the mechanism is so constructed that the running parts in the Minnesota head operate entirely independent of one another and all driving power is supplied direct from the main shaft without the agency of the numerous connections, cogs and many unnecessary devices used in some machines to propel the feed, shuttle and needle bar. The operator does not have to tamper with or adjust these parts, regardless of the weight of goods being sewed. The construction has made the Minnesota head famous as the most durable head ever produced.

ADJUSTMENT. MUCH DEPENDS UPON THE ADJUSTMENT of the working parts, for should any part, for instance the shuttle, be adjusted 1/32 of an inch out of place the harmony between the parts will be destroyed and imperfect work will result. The operating parts of our Minnesota machines receive the finest and most accurate adjustment and are tested on all grades of materials and pass through numerous inspections, so that it is practically impossible for a Minnesota machine to leave our factory unless perfect in construction and adjustment.

THE NEEDLE BAR IS ROUND AND MADE TO FIT perfectly. It is absolutely positive in its action, insuring even and automatic operation on materials of any weight and thickness.

THE SELF-SETTING NEEDLES FOR THIS MAchine are the very best grade of needle it is possible to procure. Every needle is inspected and tested as to size, temper, position of the eye, etc. The needle bar is constructed with a groove so that the needle can only be placed in the proper position. It is not necessary to guess at the height or position of the needle, as is the case with many other makes of machines.

THE SHUTTLE IS CYLINDrical in shape, made of the finest cold rolled steel. It is absolutely self threading, being open at one end for inserting the bobbin, after which the thread is instantly drawn into place by two motions of the hand.

THE SHUTTLE CARRIER IS MADE of steel and is fitted with a spring lining, which holds the shuttle firmly in place and prevents it from rattling when the machine is in operation. It is adjustable, so that when the shuttle shows signs of wear it can be moved closer to the race, thus enabling the operator to use the same shuttle for many years with the same satisfaction as when new.

THREAD SCALE. THE FRONT SHUTTLE SLIDE IS stamped with a scale indicating the proper sized needles to be used with the different numbers of sewing thread.

THE DOUBLE FOUR-MOTION FEED IS MADE OF THE very best drop forged steel, hardened, constructed with four sets of teeth, two sets on each side of the needle, which carry the goods forward firmly and evenly; as the action of the feed is entirely controlled and operated by the main shaft it is strong and certain in its movements. When you get the machine the feed will be regulated for ordinary family sewing.

THE PRESSER FOOT HAS A VERY LARGE UNDER SURFACE, which extends on both sides of the needle and holds any goods firmly in place over the feed. The forward part of the presser foot nearest the operator is curved upward so that the foot will not catch in seams of fleecy materials.

THE PRESSER BAR IS ROUND AND FITTED WITH A PRESSER BAR adjuster by which the pressure on the goods is regulated. At the factory, before shipping the machine, this bar is regulated to give the proper pressure for most household materials, and it is only necessary for you to adjust this bar when sewing on extra light or extra heavy materials. The presser bar lifter can be turned to the right or to the left, producing both the high lift and the low lift. When putting on attachments or sewing bulky materials the high lift is used.

THE TAKE-UP. BOTH THE NEEDLE BAR AND TAKE-UP ARE DRIVEN by the shaft head at the left end of the main shaft, and therefore act simultaneously and in perfect harmony, insuring perfect stitching.

THE TENSION OF OUR MODEL "C" IS PLACED ON TOP OF THE ARM and consists of two flexible nickel plated steel plates, through which the thread passes. The pressure on the thread is regulated by a small thumbscrew. By pressing a small projection on the lower tension plate, called the tension release, the goods being sewed can be taken away from under the presser foot without bending the needle or breaking the thread.

STITCH REGULATOR. THE STITCH CAN BE REGULATED TO RUN from seven to twenty-four stitches to the inch by means of a regulator which is located on the bed plate just below the bobbin winder in easy reach of the operator. The stitch regulator shortens or lengthens the movement of the feed, which in turn controls the size of the stitch.

THREAD CUTTER. TO DO AWAY WITH THE NECESSITY OF USING scissors and to prevent the breaking or cutting of the thread too short, our Model "C" head is provided with a sharp steel thread cutter placed on the presser bar in such a position that the thread can instantly be cut and sufficient thread remains drawn from the needle and also from the shuttle so that the machine remains threaded and ready to sew the next piece of goods.

BOBBIN WINDER. THE BOBBIN WINDER IS AUTOMATIC IN OPERAtion. It is strongly made, well finished and well nickel plated. It is so simple a child can operate it. The thread is wound on the bobbin automatically and so evenly and smoothly as to make the bobbin work perfectly in the shuttle, producing an even tension and greatly improving the perfection of the stitch. The bobbin winder is always in position and ready to operate. It is operated by means of the belt, which is placed in contact with the small pulley wheel of the bobbin winder.

MINNESOTA MODEL "C"

Five-Drawer, Drop Head Style, Marquetry Woodwork

IN THIS MINNESOTA MODEL "C" SEWING MACHINE, FITTED IN THIS BEAUTIFULLY DECORATED FIVE-DRAWER DROP HEAD CABINET, WE BELIEVE WE HAVE ONE OF THE HANDSOMEST AND MOST ATTRACTIVE SEWING MACHINES EVER PLACED ON THE MARKET

SIZE OF =HEAD=
Working space under arm, 5¼x8½ inches. Size of bed plate, 7x14 inches.

A TAPE MEASURE
18 inches long, accurately divided and beautifully colored to match the woodwork, is transferred on this table, directly in front of the head, where it is most convenient for the use of the operator.

THE CABINET IS THE POPULAR FIVE-drawer style, two drawers on each side and one center drawer. Made of selected, nicely figured oak finished in the popular golden color, marquetry decorated, a beautiful effect not shown on any cabinet offered by any other dealer. This large illustration will give you a slight idea of the appearance of this Minnesota Model "C" Machine, but a plain black and white picture is entirely inadequate to show up the appearance of the cabinet. The decorations consist of the latest fancy colored marquetry effect, in beautiful contrast to the solid golden oak finish of the woodwork, a rich, handsome, high class effect that is sure to please you. Send us your order, and if you do not agree with us that you have never seen sewing machine woodwork to compare with this, you may return the machine to us and get your money back at once.

THE WOODWORK ON THIS, OUR MODEL "C" MACHINE, **is a much higher grade than that found on machines sold by others at double this price.** Made of well seasoned solid oak, finished in the highest art known to the trade, varnished, dried, revarnished and hand rubbed, giving not only a beautiful finish, but by reason of this treatment, a lasting effect, an almost indestructible quality which will make the cabinet absolutely perfect for years and years, impossible to peel, check, warp or split. When this machine is closed, with the head dropped from sight and the extension leaf folded over, you will have the handsomest kind of a stand or table, an ornament to any home.

THE STAND ON THIS, OUR MODEL "C" MACHINE, IS MADE FROM **the best Birmingham, Alabama, light gray iron.** Our Model "C" stands are molded by automatic machines instead of being cast by a hand process, making every piece perfectly true, smooth, and of unusual strength, so that when the different parts are put together they fit perfectly. All parts are heavily coated with black enamel. We put on a heavier, smoother, glossier, better finished and far more lasting coat of enamel than is furnished by any other sewing machine maker on a machine sold at anywhere near this price.

WE FURNISH FREE OF CHARGE, WITH EVERY MODEL "C" **sewing machine a book of instructions telling how to operate the sewing machine.** This book covers every point, makes everything so plain and simple that anyone, without any previous experience, can learn to run the machine at once and do perfect work; tells you how to get the best results, how to take care of your machine, tells where to oil and when. It tells you how to use the different attachments, the ruffler, tucker, hemmers and binders and contains the illustrations of these attachments in use.

THE ATTACHMENTS WILL BE FURNISHED WITH OR **without the machines and at cost price, 75 cents per set,** and comprise a full set of all the latest patent foot attachments, which will be furnished by no other dealer.

WE FURNISH THE FOLLOWING SET PACKED IN a handsome velvet lined metal box, as shown in the illustration: One ruffler, one shirring blade, one tucker, one short foot, one under braider, one binder and one set of hemmers, different widths up to ⅝ of an inch. Our price for the full set, **75 cents.**

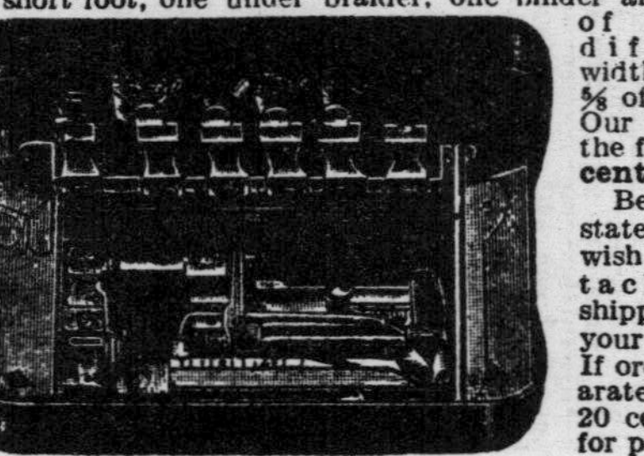

Be sure to state if you wish the attachments shipped with your machine. If ordered separately, allow 20 cents extra for postage.

ACCESSORIES FREE.
We furnish free with our Minnesota Model "C" machine a complete set of accessories such as are furnished with all high grade machines consisting of
1 quilter.
5 bobbins and 1 in the machine.
1 large screw-driver.
1 foot hemmer.
1 oil can.
1 cloth guide.
11 needles and 1 in the machine.
1 shuttle screw-driver.

No. 26T153

SHIPPED FROM DAYTON, OHIO
Shipping Weight, about 120 pounds.

SEND US $12.35

SAY YOU WANT No. 26T153 our Minnesota Model "C" Machine and we will ship it to you. You can try it in your own home for three months, compare it with any and all sewing machines, and if you are not convinced that you have received the most wonderful value, the handsomest, highest grade sewing machine that you have ever seen, better than anything offered by others, you may return the machine to us at our expense of freight charges and we will promptly return your money, including what you paid for freight.

No. 25 Russell Street, Winooski, Vermont.
Sears, Roebuck & Co., Chicago, Illinois.
Dear Sirs:—I have had and used one of your Minnesota Model "A" Sewing Machines. I have used the Singer, New Home, Standard and one or two others of the so called high grade sewing machines, but can truthfully say that the Model "A" Minnesota is a better machine in every way. I would be pleased to answer any letter that I may receive in regard to the good qualities of the Model "A" Minnesota.
Yours very truly, MRS. MERRILL McCARGAR.
NOTE—If you write to Mrs. McCargar be sure to enclose a two-cent stamp for reply.

No. 26T153 Minnesota Model "C" Marquetry Five-Drawer Drop Head Sewing Machine. Price, $12.35

OUR MINNESOTA MODEL "C"

FIVE-DRAWER DROP HEAD, WITH LATEST SWELL FRONT MARQUETRY DECORATED CABINET.

WE GUARANTEE THIS MODEL "C" DROP HEAD STYLE MACHINE SUPERIOR TO ANY SEWING MACHINE offered by any dealer at $20.00 to $25.00, the equal in every way of sewing machines offered by agents at $25.00 to $30.00. The Minnesota Model "C" Drop Head Machine is a very attractive style, a very high grade machine, it is perfect in every piece and part, embodying the very best material, put together by skilled mechanics, and is only excelled by our matchless Models "A" and "S," described on preceding pages.

PLEASE READ CAREFULLY THE FULL DESCRIPTION OF MODEL "C" HEAD AND OTHER MECHANICAL FEATURES on page 701. The Model "C" will do any and all kinds of work, it is very light running, very easy to operate and embodies all the latest improvements. **We guarantee it for twenty years.** If you order this machine you will receive our written binding guarantee, protecting you in every way for twenty years.

THE MINNESOTA MODEL "C" DROP HEAD STYLE IS A BEAUTIFUL AND GRACEFUL MACHINE, ONE THAT WOULD prove an ornament to any home. The illustration will give you some idea of its appearance, but it must really be seen to be appreciated, and only a comparison and side by side trial and test with other machines, a real working trial, will show its superior quality, its ease of operation, the many ways in which it is better than other sewing machines offered at higher prices.

WE GUARANTEE
SAFE DELIVERY
SAVING OF MONEY
SATISFACTION

Description of Marquetry Woodwork in Our Minnesota Model "C" Machines

THE WOODWORK IN OUR MODEL "C" Sewing Machines is of a very much higher grade than is usually used in sewing machines of this price. It is made especially for our machines, under contract, by the largest manufacturers of sewing machine woodwork in the world, who supply cabinets only for the highest grade sewing machines, and it cannot be in any way classed with the woodwork commonly used in machines that sell generally at $25.00 or less.

MATERIALS. ONLY THE most select grade of solid oak is used in the construction of our Model "C" woodwork. It is carefully selected with reference to grain and color, and is thoroughly air seasoned and kiln dried to insure against warping, splitting or cracking.

DESIGN. THE MINNESOTA MODEL "C" cabinet is a model of beauty and artistic design, second only to our Models "S" and "A." It is made on the lines of the high grade, up to date furniture, especially designed for us and not made for nor used on any other machines.

THE TABLE IS MADE OF SOLID oak, particular care being taken to select only nicely grained oak. The front edge of the table is handsomely shaped.

DRAWER FRAMES. THE DRAWER frames in which the side drawers are fitted are of the latest skeleton type, much handsomer in appearance and far preferable to the old fashioned solid cases.

DRAWERS. THE DRAWERS ARE very large and roomy, made with rounded corners to harmonize with the table. The fronts are handsomely decorated with marquetry of special design and fitted with nicely plated and polished ring pulls. The center drawer is made with swell front; the interior is partitioned off for bobbins, needles and other accessories which are in constant demand when the machine is being used. Every drawer is fitted with a lock and one key fits them all.

CLOSED VIEW
No. 26T153

AT OUR SPECIAL PRICE OF $12.35 WE FURNISH THIS MINNESOTA Model "C" five-drawer drop head style, marquetry decorated woodwork, on board cars at the factory in Dayton, Ohio, from which point you must pay the freight. However, the freight charges are really nothing compared with the immense saving in price. The freight on sewing machines is a small amount. No matter where you live, it will be no consideration if you think of the saving when you buy from us, when you consider the superior sewing machine you can get from us, at such a low price. Sewing machines take the first class rate of freight and this will be for a sewing machine safely crated as we ship them, about 35 cents to 50 cents for 200 miles, and 50 cents to 75 cents for 200 to 500 miles, greater or less distances in proportion. Do not let anyone discourage you from ordering by reason of freight charges. A dealer or agent might tell you that all you save in ordering from us will be eaten up by the cost of freight, but do not believe this. We know you will make a great saving even after you pay the freight charges. We guarantee it. Order your machine from us, no matter in what part of the United States you live or how far you are situated from our factory at Dayton, Ohio. After you have paid the freight, if you do not find you have made a great saving as compared with what you would be compelled to pay anyone else for a sewing machine of equal quality you may return the machine to us at our expense of freight charges and we will promptly return your money, including what you paid for freight. We promise this and we will carry out our agreement to the letter.

FINISH. IN POINT OF finish our Model "C" machine is strictly first class and of the very latest golden color, the popular finish put on high grade oak furniture. Before the finish is put on, the woodwork is most carefully sandpapered so that the varnish, which is of the very best quality, produces a hard, glossy surface.

THE DECORATION CONSISTS OF THE latest fancy colored marquetry effect, in beautiful contrast to the beautiful golden oak finish of the woodwork, a rich, handsome, high class effect that is sure to please you.

DESCRIPTION OF OUR MODEL "C" STANDS.

OUR MINNESOTA MODEL "C" STANDS ARE MADE from the best Birmingham, Alabama, light gray iron. They are molded by automatic machines instead of being cast by a hand process, making every piece perfectly true, smooth and of unusual strength, so that when the different parts are assembled they fit perfectly. All parts are heavily coated with black enamel by hand process. We put on a heavier, smoother, glossier, better finished and far more lasting coat of enamel than is furnished by any other sewing machine maker, and we furnish a stronger, better finished and handsomer sewing machine stand than is used on any other sewing machine made.

DESIGN. THE MODEL "C" STAND HAS BEEN especially designed for us with a view to procuring a neat, graceful open effect and at the same time furnishing a frame that will stand the severest test. The side frames or legs of the stand are made in the handsomest style open and wide ribbon pattern. This open design and the style in which the side frames are made make our stands the most desirable because they are so easily kept clean.

BEFORE PLACING YOUR ORDER FOR ANY MACHINE, BE SURE TO read the description of our Improved Ball Bearing Minnesota Model "A" Sewing Machine. Ball Bearing Head, Ball Bearing Stand, Double Ball Bearing Steel Pitman.

IF YOU ORDER A MINNESOTA SEWING MACHINE, AND particularly the Minnesota Model "C" in the beautiful drop head cabinet style as here illustrated, you will be getting a sewing machine that will be an everlasting comfort and pleasure to you. Every time you use the machine you will find more reason to be pleased with your purchase. You will feel like writing us the same kind of a letter as thousands of other purchasers of sewing machines write us, a very few of such letters are reproduced in the various pages of this department. There is no risk whatever when you order from us, because if the sewing machine does not come up to your every expectation, and if you do not find that we have saved you money and furnished you with a machine such as has no equal, your money is awaiting you just as quick as you may return the machine.

OTHER DEALERS AND AGENTS MAY BE ABLE TO OFFER you a sewing machine at $12.00 to $13.00, but we want to assure you that a sewing machine offered by anyone else at this price cannot compare with our Model "C" for quality. It will not have the beautiful high grade solid oak cabinet as thoroughly well made as our Minnesota cabinet, a cabinet that will never loosen up, never split or check; nor will the machine offered by anyone else compare with our Minnesota in mechanical features, in the high grade head having all the latest improvements in sewing machine head construction and in general quality, in light running quality, ease of operation. In the fundamental material and the workmanship you will find the Minnesota Model "C" outclasses any machine offered by anyone else at $20.00 to $25.00.

READ WHAT OUR CUSTOMERS SAY ABOUT THE MINNESOTA SEWING MACHINES

R. F. D. No. 1, Boothbay, Maine.
Sears, Roebuck & Co.
Gentlemen—As some time has elapsed since I received my Minnesota Model "A" Sewing Machine of you, I think I am safe in testifying to its merits. I think it is perfect in style, in workmanship and in the work it does. I have never seen any machine that I would exchange it for, although I have seen sewing machines that cost $65.00, the same style as mine, but not having the automatic lift as mine has. I am glad that I bought of you instead of buying from an agent, as I have saved so many dollars in doing so. I shall advise anyone wanting a first class sewing machine in every respect to order from you. Yours respectfully,
MRS. ALONZO F. MATTHEWS.

Sunnyside, Wash.
Sears, Roebuck & Co.
Sirs:—We ordered a Model "A" Minnesota Sewing Machine, and it's a beauty. It would be an ornament to any house. It does such nice work I would not give it for any machine I ever used. I would not take twice what we paid for it if I could not get another like it. I would advise all who want a new machine to try the Minnesota Model "A;" they can't miss a good thing. I am, as ever, a friend to the Minnesota.
Yours, etc.,
MRS. C. F. PEABODY.

Gays Mills, Wis.
Sears, Roebuck & Co.
Gentlemen:—I have had one of your sewing machines in my home over two years, and I am well pleased with it. I have used many different kinds of sewing machines, but I never sewed on one that does better work than the Minnesota. I have used all the attachments and they fit perfectly and do nice work. I think it is well worth what we paid for it. Yours respectfully,
MRS. JOHN A. HILL.

217 Fourth Ave., N., Wausau, Wis.
Sears, Roebuck & Co.
Gentlemen—Am more than pleased to tell you about the goods shipped me about March 1st. To say that I am satisfied does not begin to state the facts. One item which I was particularly pleased with is your Minnesota Model "A" Sewing Machine, which I consider the equal of any $35.00 machine on the market. All other goods were as good, if not better than represented, and if this is of any use as a testimonial you are at liberty to publish it. I shall always speak a good word for the house of Sears, Roebuck & Co. Thanking you for prompt shipment, good service, etc., I am, Truly yours,
W. W. HOWLAND.

IN WRITING TO ANY OF THESE PEOPLE ENCLOSE A 2-CENT STAMP FOR REPLY.

Our Minnesota Model "C" Sewing Machine

IN FULL CABINET STYLE. NEW AND IMPROVED CABINET.

SEE THE ILLUSTRATIONS, ONE ILLUSTRATION SHOWING THE MACHINE FULLY **closed so that it appears to be only a handsome desk cabinet;** a second illustration showing the machine open, ready for work, and a third illustration showing the machine partly closed with the head lowered and extension leaf folded over. The desk cabinet is perhaps the most beautiful style of sewing machine cabinet construction and in Model "C" cabinet style, at $14.45, we offer the lowest priced cabinet machine on the market. This style of machine must really be seen to be appreciated. It is very rich and handsome in appearance. We furnish a beautiful high grade cabinet, an extra handsome piece of woodwork, a cabinet that compares favorably with the cabinet machines sold elsewhere at double our price.

THIS HANDSOME, FULL OAK DESK CABINET IS MADE OF THE very best solid **oak, thoroughly air and kiln dried. The door is made with specially selected quarter sawed oak large panel,** ornamented with handsome design drop carvings and massive moldings and caps. Please note the rich and tasteful decorations on this woodwork. The sides are solid full oak panels. The lid is made of built-up stock with special selected quarter sawed oak top. This construction prevents warping and cracking. The inside of the door is fitted with wooden pockets to hold the oil can, bobbins, screwdriver and other accessories so they will be convenient for use when the machine is being operated. The cabinet is the product of the finest cabinet makers, finished throughout in a strictly first class manner, every piece and part is thoroughly sandpapered before it is put together, insuring perfect cabinet work. The varnish used on this cabinet is strictly high grade. It brings out the rich golden oak finish which is so popular. It is worked over and hand rubbed, giving a rich, glossy appearance, the same as the hand polished effect shown in the high grade furniture. The cabinet rests on four rollers so it can be easily moved about.

WHEN THE SEWING MACHINE IS NOT IN USE AND THE CABINET IS CLOSED, THE HEAD IS HIDDEN **entirely from view, and is also protected from dust.** The cabinet, when the machine is not in use, may be conveniently used as a stand, table or desk.

BALL BEARING

OUR MODEL "C" FULL CABINET MACHINE IS BALL **bearing. It is fitted with our celebrated bicycle ball bearing hanger,** which gives the same rapidity of action and ease of operation as the ball bearing arrangement on a bicycle. All wearing parts are made of cold rolled steel turned and hardened, and the steel balls in the bearing are the best in the market. The bearing is simple in construction, no getting out of order, all parts easily accessible so that the balls or cups can be replaced at any time in the future, if in the years to come there is reason to replace anything. By means of this ball bearing, practically all friction is eliminated and the running of the machine made a real pleasure.

IF YOU DON'T ORDER A MINNESOTA MODEL "S" OR MODEL "A" **we certainly want you to order this, our next best machine, the full desk cabinet, Model "C."** It will please you so well, look so beautiful in your home, represent to you such a great saving in price that we can anticipate how delighted you will be and how much good it will do us as an advertisement. Our only advantage in urging you to order the best machine we offer is for the additional satisfaction you yourself will get from such a purchase. It is not because we make any more profit, for we really do not. Our margin of profit is exactly the same and the additional money asked by us for a higher grade machine, the highest grade we make, buys so much in the way of superior construction, finer cabinet work, better mechanical construction, a closer approach to perfection in every feature that we feel we can conscientiously make such a recommendation. Be sure that you do not make the mistake of buying a sewing machine from anyone else before you have the opportunity of seeing and trying a Minnesota. Order any Minnesota Sewing Machine, put it side by side with the sewing machine you get from anyone else, give them both a thorough test, and if our machine is not far superior to the machine offered by anyone else at the same price, or if our sewing machine is not much lower in price than any sewing machine you can get from anyone else to equal ours in quality, then we won't expect you to keep our machine; you are perfectly welcome to return it to us at once, and we will promptly return your money, including any freight charges you may have paid.

THREE MONTHS' TRIAL

SHIPPING WEIGHT, ABOUT 135 POUNDS.

WE INVITE COMPARISON. WE URGE A TRIAL. WE **know positively that no sewing machine will excel in quality our Models "A" and "S."** We know that no sewing machines offered by others at our prices will compare in all the essential features with our other models, for we have made such side by side, piece by piece and part by part comparison that we are sure of our ground, and if we can only induce you to make a comparison we know that it will amount to a sale.

AS COMPARED WITH THE SEWING MACHINE AGENT, WE ARE IN ONE RESPECT AT A DISadvantage. He is right there on the ground with his machine and can point out all the good features of his machine, can show you its many advantages, while all we can offer you, unless you will take advantage of our liberal terms of shipment, is an illustration and description. However, we have this advantage, and that is, the agent must also tell you the price, and when he tells you the price and you compare it with our price the difference will compel you to pause and give us a fair trial before you finally place your order. We know that if you could be in the factory where our sewing machines are made for just one hour and could see the kind of material that we use, the care that is given to every detail of the manufacture, the class of skilled mechanics we employ, the tests we make; if you could see how thoroughly well made the Minnesota machines are, if you could watch our method of drying the oak, the matching and fitting, our cabinet making, the varnishing, polishing and rubbing, the drawing and shaping of the parts of the head, the plating and polishing of the bright parts, the grinding and tempering of the bearings, you would be convinced that no other manufacturer goes to such lengths to produce a perfect sewing machine. You can quickly see that every penny over and above our small margin of profit goes into the machine itself, into the cost of material and labor. You would understand why we claim that our Minnesota Sewing Machines are not at all to be compared with the sewing machines you buy from other mail order houses. There is no other mail order house whose sewing machines are made in the one factory, under the same conditions as prevail in the factory that makes the celebrated Minnesota machines. No other mail order house really knows anything about how their sewing machines are actually made, nor could they guarantee that their sewing machines are produced from the best material, the most skilled labor and under such careful supervision, which is such a great safeguard for quality in the factory that makes our machines.

SEND US YOUR ORDER FOR THE MINNESOTA MODEL **"C" full desk cabinet at $14.45. We guarantee you will receive from us a perfect machine, nothing better to be had from anyone else at anywhere near our price.** We guarantee the machine to reach you in perfect condition, the same as it left our hands. We guarantee that you will make a big saving in the price after paying the freight charges. We guarantee to return your money and pay all the expenses of the transaction if at any time during the three months' trial you have any reason to feel dissatisfied. We take all the risk. You take none.

READ OUR LIBERAL TERMS OF SHIPMENT. REMEMBER, YOU HAVE ALL THE PRIVILEGES WE OFFER. THE **three months' trial agreement is in force the moment you send us your order.** If there is any question in your mind, if you are inclined to buy a sewing machine from any agent or dealer, let us ship you a machine on three months' trial, and if you are not satisfied in every way you may return the machine and the money paid for the machine as well as freight charges will be cheerfully returned to you without any delay.

OUR PRICE OF $14.45 FOR THE FULL DESK CABINET **Minnesota Model "C" does not include attachments.** We do include a full set of accessories as shown on page 702, but we do not charge you a price to include attachments, as you may not need them if you expect to do plain sewing only. For 75 cents additional we will send you a full set of high grade attachments described on page 702. **We guarantee this machine for twenty years.**

IN ORDERING ALWAYS WRITE CATALOG NUMBER PLAINLY AND IN FULL—WRITE EVERY FIGURE AND LETTER IN THE CATALOG NUMBER.

No. 26T159 Model "C" Full Cabinet, finished in golden oak only...... **$14.45**
SHIPPED FROM DAYTON, OHIO.

ABOUT SEWING MACHINE SUPPLIES

There are a great many machines in use for which it is difficult and in some cases impossible to get new parts. The factories originally making these machines have either gone out of existence or have destroyed the tools and machinery necessary for making the different parts of their earlier models. We are in a position to supply parts for almost every sewing machine and will always supply these parts at the lowest possible price. If you want a new shuttle or an extra supply of bobbins, and you do not find the name of your machine on our shuttle list, send your old shuttle or an illustration, together with 75 cents and the extra postage and if it is at all possible we will fill your order for the shuttle, refunding to you whatever balance we can, according to the price of the shuttle. It is impossible for us to list the names of all the different sewing machines which are in use at the present time because there are so many factories making sewing machines for a great many different customers, each of whom requires a different name on the machine. If you need any bobbins for your machine either send us an illustration of the shuttle or a sample bobbin and send us the remittance according to the style bobbin which you require for your machine.

Some factories have made minor changes in the appearance of their shuttles and the shuttle which they make at the present time does not look exactly like the shuttle which we furnish with your machine, although it is made to fit the same shuttle carrier.

We are in a position to supply individual attachments for almost any make of machine. In ordering separate attachments, it is best to send a sample to us because an illustration is not sufficient. For example: The Greist attachment factory makes a ruffler for almost every well known machine and the illustration is the same for all machines, the difference in the construction of the ruffler being so slight as not to be noticeable in the illustration.

If you are ordering parts or supplies for one of our sewing machines, mention the name of the head and give the head number, which you will find stamped upon the front shuttle slide, or on the bed plate under the front slide, or upon the bed plate behind the upright part of the arm.

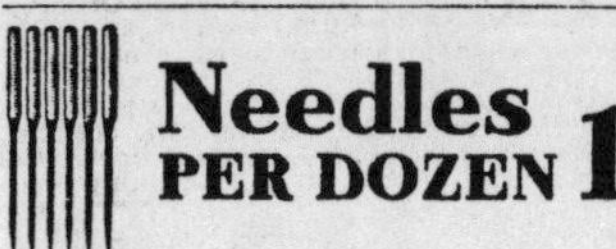

Needles PER DOZEN 15c

It is very important to use only the very best needles. A machine will not work well with poorly made needles. It is to our interest, therefore, to supply only the best and highest grade sewing machine needles made. In ordering needles, be sure to send sample, also mention name and head number of the machine. This will insure prompt attention and the proper filling of your order for needles. No order will be filled for less than 1 dozen needles. Also send cash in full with the order and allow for postage at the rate of 2 cents per dozen.

No. 26T306 Sewing Machine Needles, for all family sewing machines, regardless of name and make.
Price, per dozen..**15c**
If mail shipment, postage and packing extra, 2 cents.
No order filled for less than 1 dozen needles. **Be sure to send sample.**

BOBBINS.

All bobbins for Cylinder Shuttles (except new style White). Price, per dozen........**16c**
White New Style Cylinder Hollow Bobbins. Price, per doz. **50c**
All bobbins for Open Face Shuttles. Price, per dozen.. **16c**
All bobbins for Rotary Shuttles. Price, per dozen....**$1.00**
If mail shipment, postage extra, per dozen, on any of above bobbins, 3 cents.
We do not sell less than 6 bobbins, except Rotary Bobbins, of which we sell 3 for 25 cents.

BOBBIN CASES.

The illustrations show the bobbin cases which are now being furnished with the present styles of machines. If your bobbin case is different from the illustration you must send a sample.
Standard Bobbin Case. Price, each........................**45c**
Wheeler & Wilson Bobbin Case. Price, each..........**70c**
White Bobbin Case. Price, each............................**85c**
If mail shipment, postage extra on any bobbin case, 2 cents.

SHUTTLES.

CYLINDER STYLE. ROTARY STYLE. OPEN FACE STYLE.

All manufacturers have made changes in the styles of shuttles used in their machines and nearly every make has several different kinds of shuttles, so that in ordering, it is not only necessary to mention the name of the shuttle wanted, but to send a picture of the shuttle or the old one as sample. In addition to remitting for cost of shuttle, include 4 cents extra to pay the postage. When ordering, do not fail to send illustration or old shuttle as a sample to insure securing the proper duplicate, and wherever possible give the head number of the machine.

In many cases it will be found necessary to adjust the shuttle carrier so that the new shuttle, which is always a little larger than the worn shuttle, will fit properly.

Cat. No.		Price
26T400	Advance	50c
26T401	American (3 styles), each	65c
26T407	Arlington	75c
26T413	Belmont	50c
26T416	Burdick (4 styles) each	50c
26T423	Crown (3 styles), each	65c
26T426	Davis Vertical Feed (open face)	80c
26T429	Davis Cylinder	50c
26T432	Demorest (12 styles), each	65c
26T434	Diamond	80c
26T436	Domestic (3 styles), each	55c
26T440	Edgemere (2 styles), each	50c
26T443	Eldredge (A and B), each	50c
26T445	Eldredge (new style), each	50c
26T460	Helpmate	75c
26T461	Homan	50c
26T462	Household	60c

If mail shipment, postage extra, 4 cents.

Cat. No.		Price
26T467	Howard	50c
26T470	Iowa (4 styles), each	65c
26T475	Jennie June	70c
26T477	Kenwood	50c
26T481	Minnesota	50c
26T489	New Goodrich	50c
26T490	New Home (2 styles), each	45c
26T492	New Queen	50c
26T498	Norwood	75c
26T502	Paragon	75c
26T515	Seroco	50c
26T518	Singer N. F. and Medium (open face)	25c
26T519	Singer Oscillator (round center bobbin)	75c
26T522	Singer V. S. Cylinder (2 styles), each	50c
26T549	White Old Style (open face)	50c
26T550	White New Style (cylinder)	55c
26T551	White Rotary Shuttle	$2.00

If mail shipment, postage extra, 4 cents.

MISCELLANEOUS PARTS.

These prices apply only on the parts of sewing machines which we have listed in our catalog since the time we commenced to sell machines. In other words, these prices do no apply on parts for the Singer, Wheeler & Wilson, and other machines which were never listed in our catalog.

	Price	Postage
Attachment Holder	30c	2c
Belts	8c	2c
Bobbin Winders	65c	15c
Bobbin Winder Rubber	4c	2c
Chain for Automatic Lift	30c	6c
Feed	20c	2c
Hemmer and Feller	25c	2c
Hemstitcher	35c	3c
Instruction Book	8c	2c
Needle Bar—Flat	50c	4c
Needle Bar—Round	25c	4c
Needle Bar Cam	50c	2c
Needle Bar Cap	20c	2c
Needle Bar Clamp — Flat Bar	25c	2c
Needle Bar Clamp—Round Bar	20c	2c
Needle Plate	15c	2c
Oil Cans	5c	3c
Presser Bar	20c	2c
Presser Bar Cap	20c	2c
Presser Bar Spring	10c	2c
Presser Foot	20c	2c
Shipping Screw	10c	2c
Shuttle Carriers	20c	2c
Shuttle Slides	15c	2c
Shuttle Tension Screws	5c	2c
Shuttle Tension Spring	10c	2c
Take-up Spring	10c	2c
Tension Plates, each	10c	2c
Tension Spring	10c	2c
Thread Cutter	5c	2c

ATTACHMENTS.

A complete set, consisting of ruffler, tucker, binder, set of 4 foot hemmers, 1 under braider, 1 shirring blade, 1 short presser foot, all packed in a handsome velvet lined metal box, for any of the sewing machines ever listed in our catalog.
Price, per set..**75c**
If mail shipment, postage extra, 20 cents.

RUFFLERS AND TUCKERS.

Name of Machine—	Rufflers	Tuckers
For use on any machine ever listed in our catalogs	$0.40	$0.25
Arlington	1.00	.40
Crown	.75	.40
Davis	1.25	1.00
Domestic	1.25	1.00
Eldredge	.75	.40
Household	$0.75	$0.40
Kenwood	1.00	.40
New Home	.75	.40
Singer	1.25	1.00
Standard	1.25	1.00
White	.75	.40
Wheeler & Wilson	1.25	.40

If mail shipment, postage extra, 4 cents.

STAND PARTS FOR ANY OF OUR MACHINES.

	Price, each
Leg, right or left	75c
Brace	30c
Treadle	50c
Band Wheel, not ball bearing	50c
Band Wheel Complete, with ball bearings	75c
Dress Guard	50c
Treadle Rod	15c
Pitman	12c
Pitman, metal ball bearing	35c
Complete Set Ball Bearings, caps, cones and journal	50c

When ordering stand parts, give name and head number of sewing machine and send exact drawing of part wanted.

SCREWDRIVER.

Four and one-half-inch nickel plated and highly polished metal screwdriver.
No. 26T4049 Screwdriver. Price, each..............**5c**
If mail shipment, postage extra, 2 cents.
Price, per dozen..**45c**
If mail shipment, postage extra, per dozen, 15 cents.

SHUTTLE SCREWDRIVER.

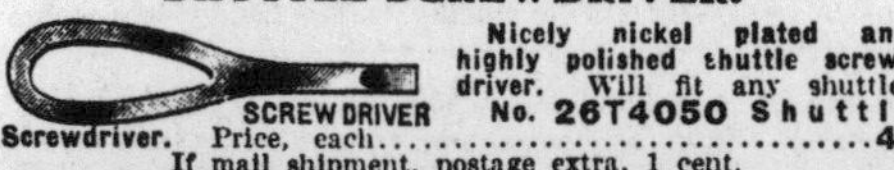

Nicely nickel plated and highly polished shuttle screwdriver. Will fit any shuttle.
No. 26T4050 Shuttle Screwdriver. Price, each..............**4c**
If mail shipment, postage extra, 1 cent.

AUTOMATIC THREAD CONTROLLER.

Will positively prevent thread from tangling, breaking of needles or spool jumping off the spindle while filling bobbins. This thread controller will fit any spool pin. The only directions are to have the spool turn to the right.
No. 26T4080 Thread Controller.
Price, each..............**10c**
If mail shipment, postage extra, 2c.
Price, per dozen........**90c**
If mail shipment, postage extra, per dozen, 15 cents.

NEEDLE THREADER.

One of the handiest attachments ever manufactured in the sewing machine needle threader, illustrated and described herewith. We have tested and compared this needle threader with all other styles on the market and find it the only satisfactory needle threader that is manufactured. There is nothing about it to get out of order, nor can it be easily broken. By means of it you can thread the needle quickly without straining your eyes and without pushing the machine from one part of the room to the other so that the light will properly strike the eye of the needle and enable you to see the eye. The attachment is simplicity itself and is always ready. People who have good eyesight have trouble in threading needles. This attachment does away with all that trouble, with all worry and annoyance in threading.
No. 26T4060 Needle Threader. Price, each........**10c**
If mail shipment, postage extra, 2 cents.
Price, per dozen..**90c**
If mail shipment, postage extra, per dozen, 6 cents.

GREIST TUCK FOLDER.

It is very strong and with reasonable care is indestructible. It is made entirely of steel, heavily nickel plated, beautiful in design and finish and perfect in workmanship. It has a capacity of from pin tucks to tucks 1 inch wide and will operate equally well upon all kinds and grades of materials, whether light or heavy, starched or unstarched, or of cotton, linen, wool or silk.

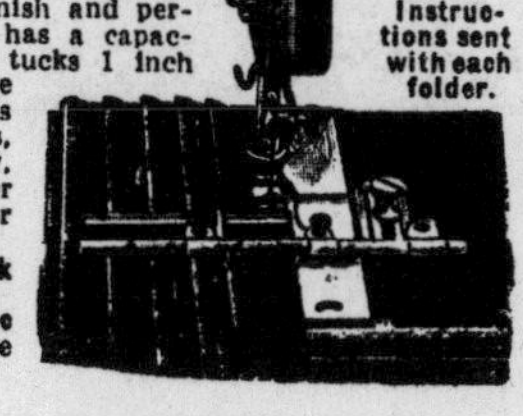

Will fit any machine. Instructions sent with each folder.

No. 26T4061 Tuck Folder.
Price, each........ **45c**
If mail shipment, postage extra, 4 cents.

DARNING ATTACHMENT.

A most useful article. Will fit any machine. This new darning attachment is very simple and fills a long felt want. With it you can darn stockings, lace curtains, table linen, towels, underwear and many other articles. A great time saver because more and better darning can be done with this attachment than is possible to do by hand. Full and complete instructions for the operation of the attachment is sent with each darner.

No. 26T4081 Darning Attachment and Spring.
Price..**10c**
If mail shipment, postage extra, 2 cents.
Extra Needle Guard Springs. Price, each..............**5c**
If mail shipment, postage extra, 2 cents.

MUSICAL INSTRUMENTS

PIANOS AND ORGANS

FULL EXPLANATION OF OUR THIRTY DAYS' FREE TRIAL OFFER. COMPLETE ILLUSTRATIONS AND DESCRIPTIONS OF THE ENTIRE LINE OF SUPERIOR BECKWITH PIANOS AND ORGANS, OUR TWENTY-FIVE YEAR FULL PROTECTION GUARANTEE, FREE LESSONS, ETC.

THIRTY DAYS' FREE TRIAL. We will ship any piano or organ of the celebrated Beckwith make for a full thirty days' free trial in your own parlor. You need not send a penny with your order or deposit a penny in advance. If you decide to order a Beckwith on trial you must read our liberal thirty days' free trial offer, explained below, for a complete understanding as to how to send your order.

SEND NO MONEY. **Deposit nothing in advance. We will ship any Beckwith Piano or Organ selected from these pages on your simple order, if it is ordered in the following manner:** Make your selection, mail the order to us without sending any money with your order, **but be sure to give us the name of the bank where you will deposit the cost of the instrument.** If you want us to pay the freight we will do so on request, but this must be included in your deposit. When the instrument arrives place the entire cost with your banker, who will hand you a bill of lading covering it. He will hold your money for you while you try the instrument for thirty days and, **at every moment of your thirty days' trial, your money will be under**

> **CERTIFICATE OF DEPOSIT**
>
> Town ———— State ———— Date ————
>
> Received from Mr. ———————— Dollars, in payment of Sears, Roebuck and Co.'s
>
> We agree to hold this money until the instrument has been received by Mr. ————, residing in ————, and has had thirty days' trial, when we shall forward the amount to Sears, Roebuck and Co. If Mr. ———— is not perfectly satisfied we will return the money on surrender of the bill of lading, showing the instrument has been reconsigned.
>
> ————————
>
> Name of bank.
>
> ————————
>
> Your banker will sign here.

your complete control. If it is not satisfactory, send it back and every penny of your money will be returned by your banker under the terms of the Certificate of Deposit shown in this column. **We guarantee to hold you free of expense, freight, cartage, and all,** if the instrument is not satisfactory. If you decide to buy it at the end of thirty days, your bank will send us the money for it. **Remember your thirty days' free trial begins only from the day you receive the instrument.** We know the quality of the Beckwith so well that we are glad to send them out on approval and guarantee that we can please you just as we have pleased thousands of others.

HAVE YOU A LOCAL FREIGHT AGENT? **If not, then give us the name of your nearest shipping point where there is an agent if you wish us to ship under our send no money offer.** The railroad companies will not accept shipments under this plan to points where they have no agent. If the money is sent with the order with a sufficient amount to cover the freight, it makes no difference whether you have an agent or not, for then we can ship in your name.

ONE-YEAR FREE TRIAL OFFER. **If you buy a Beckwith on thirty days' free trial, you have a perfect right to return it at any time within one year and get all your money if you are not entirely satisfied.** This is such absolute protection that practically all orders have the cash enclosed, for we always return all money on all goods that are not entirely satisfactory. We make this agreement a part of our guarantee, and this **one-year free trial** is such complete protection that practically everyone remits cash in full with the order, knowing that we are responsible and that we always fulfill our promises.

TO OUR CUSTOMERS. **While we make this send no money offer in good faith, we wish it understood that you are not compelled to order in this way.** You can send your order just as you are now ordering groceries, shoes and other necessities, and if you are not completely satisfied every penny will be returned, **just as we return all money on any article that does not entirely satisfy you.** Our policy of returning the money if we do not please a customer is so well known that almost always cash is sent with the order for pianos and organs, as our customers know that they take no risk, wholly relying upon us to return the money and upon our reputation of years' standing for honest dealing.

WE DON'T WANT YOUR MONEY **unless we completely satisfy you. Our success depends upon the continued patronage and support of our customers and the complete satisfaction we give them.** We know that no business can thrive where the customer's confidence is abused, and we would not forfeit your respect and confidence under any consideration. We cannot afford to.

WE CAN'T AFFORD TO MISREPRESENT ANYTHING, **no matter how great or small it might be,** and if we don't completely satisfy you with a piano or an organ we don't want your money.

THE FREIGHT CHARGE. **Our prices are for the instruments at the factory. To this price you must add the freight charge.** No matter what instrument you buy, or where you buy it, you pay the freight charge and all profits and expenses of every man who handles it on its journey to you. If anyone says if you will buy his organ you will have no freight to pay, you pay it just the same. To protect himself he **must** swell his profits so as to include the freight which he pays. The freight is a fixed charge against all pianos and organs and, under the Interstate Commerce Law, the agent pays the same amount as you do. The freight charge is absolutely nothing, however, when compared to the great saving our prices mean. We positively guarantee that after paying the freight and all expenses you will save at least one-half, if not more, on instruments of the highest grade **if you buy a Beckwith.**

THERE IS BUT ONE BECKWITH. **Anyone, no matter who he is, who pretends to offer you a Beckwith, is misleading you.** We absolutely control the sale of every instrument and it cannot be offered to you by any other dealer, agent or catalog house. Do not be misled into buying a piano or organ bearing a name **similar** to the Beckwith, but remember there is only **one** Beckwith and it can be purchased **only from us.**

A WORD OF WARNING **is especially directed against any man or woman, no matter what their business may be, who comes to you without any proof whatever, and who tells you that you will be sorry if you take a Beckwith into your parlor on trial, absolutely at our risk.** Our experience is that those who so advise against the purchase of any particular instrument do so because there is a profit or a generous commission at stake. That is why some people will advise you not to buy a Beckwith (for it is well known **we pay no commissions to anybody**), recommending you to buy another piano upon which a commission is paid. **If the Beckwith is not what we claim it to be, why don't they help you order one so as to prove what they say is true?** If the statements made by these people about the Beckwith were true, what better **proof** could they give you than to help you order one so as to show that they were **right?** Are they afraid to have you **see** one and **hear** one? Can these same people offer you as much protection as we do, or as great a saving? Can you return any instrument they recommend at any time during one year and get your money back? That is our offer and our entire institution is back of our promise.

OUR RESPONSIBILITY. We take pride in referring you to the **First National Bank of Chicago,** and while this will undoubtedly satisfy you as to our responsibility, yet the recommendation we are most proud of is the confidence reposed in us by the millions of customers who patronize use daily and who buy practically all of their supplies from us. Unquestionably you number among your neighbors and friends many who are thus favoring us with their orders, and to them we respectfully refer you.

OUR FULL PROTECTION GUARANTEE **or Bond of Indemnity is your complete and lasting protection. It runs full twenty-five years and covers every Beckwith piano or organ shipped out**

> **Bond of Indemnity**
>
> **The Beckwith Pianos and Organs**
>
> This certifies that the Beckwith is guaranteed by us for twenty-five years against defect in material or workmanship. It is sold under our guarantee that if not entirely satisfactory during one year, it may be returned at our expense, and we will replace it with another instrument or **refund the purchase price with all your expenses for freight and cartage.** Should any piece or part prove defective in material or workmanship, or should any defect manifest itself during twenty-five years that does not arise from misuse, accident, moisture or extremes of temperature, we agree to replace it or repair the instrument wholly at our expense during this entire period.
>
> SEARS, ROEBUCK AND CO.

by us. A copy of the liberal, binding, full protection twenty-five year guarantee or Bond of Indemnity is shown in this column, and we ask you to read every word of it. Under this guarantee you can return any instrument purchased at any time during one year if it is not satisfactory, and we will return every penny, freight, cartage and all. You are protected against damage arising from imperfect material or workmanship during twenty-five years. Our entire institution, our capital and resources are back of this guarantee. If other dealers have not confidence enough in their goods to guarantee them as we do, or are unwilling to protect you as we do, and will not give you a guarantee permitting you to return any instrument that is unsatisfactory during one year as we do, then why should you have enough confidence in what is offered to invest your hard earned money in it?

THE INSTALLMENT PLAN. **If we followed the dealer's method and sold on installments we would be compelled to charge very much more than we do.** You can buy practically anything on the installment plan, but what do you pay for the accommodation? Benjamin Franklin, one of the greatest minds that this country has produced, clearly saw the evil of the credit system in the early Colonial days and in his writings will be found the following: "He who sells on credit expects to lose * * * by bad debts; therefore, he charges on all he sells * * * an advance to make up that deficiency." If you buy on the installment plan you sign notes for the balance. Who holds the **notes?** **You don't know until they are presented for payment. There are concerns who make a business of buying notes at a discount.** Who pays the discount? **You do.** Does everyone pay their notes promptly? **No.** Does the dealer stand this loss? **No.** It is all figured in what he charges for his pianos. A dealer takes a risk when he sells on the installment plan and he figures his prices accordingly. That is business. You will save money if you take advantage of our low prices even if you are compelled to make some sacrifice to do it. **Don't buy on the installment plan. It costs too much in the end.**

FREE PIANO OR ORGAN CATALOG. **We will be glad to send you either our piano or organ book, whichever you may wish.** If you desire further information not found in these pages, write to the Manager of our Piano and Organ Department personally. In our special catalogs you will no doubt find finer halftone pictures, but **they are not** pictures of any different or better instruments than are shown here. There are no better inducements offered you, no more liberal terms of shipment or better prices or complete guarantee or promises. While we will gladly send either one without cost, yet you can safely order from these pages, telling us what kind of a tone you wish, putting us on our honor to give you an instrument that will **fully satisfy you,** and if it does not, return it and get your money back.

WE STRONGLY SOLICIT YOUR ORDER **from these pages. Save** the time it will take to write us for the special catalog, for all of our pianos and organs, our offers, guarantees, promises, special inducements and best prices are shown here. If you desire further information we want you to have it, and in that event we invite your correspondence. You who are reading this page are no doubt already one of our customers. If so, it is unnecessary for us to repeat that you can order from these pages in perfect safety and with a full knowledge that you will find everything just exactly as illustrated and described or if not that we will refund your money.

MUSICAL GOODS DEPARTMENT—PIANOS AND ORGANS.

OUR NEW AND REMARKABLE OFFER No. 1

So well convinced are we that our pianos and organs are among the very finest manufactured and sold anywhere that we are now making our customers an astonishing, new and liberal offer. If you wish to try one of our pianos or organs and will send us your order, it will not be necessary for you to send us one cent or deposit any money in advance. Particulars of this remarkably liberal proposition are more fully stated below.

SEND NO MONEY. Deposit nothing in advance. We will send the instrument freight charges prepaid. Just send us your order with the name of the bank with which you expect to deposit the money for the instrument, and we will make immediate shipment and notify you. We will send the instrument to you freight prepaid, so that it will not be necessary for you to send us a cent either for the price of the instrument or freight charges. When you are notified that the instrument has arrived in your town you can deposit the price, together with freight charges, with your banker and take the instrument to your home for a thorough trial and examination. You can have it in your home full 30 days from the date you receive it, during which time you can call in your friends or any musical expert that you may desire and make a thorough test of the instrument, and if you are not fully satisfied with it in every particular, and fully convinced that you have made a great saving in purchasing from us you can box the instrument up and return it to us, and the banker will refund you every cent you have deposited.

SEARS, ROEBUCK AND CO.
CHICAGO.
CAPITAL AND SURPLUS OVER FIVE MILLION DOLLARS.

Certificate of Deposit

Town______ State______ Date______
Received from Mr.______ Dollars
in payment of Sears, Roebuck & Co.'s______
We agree to hold this money until the instrument has been received by Mr.______ residing in______ and has 30 days' trial, when we shall forward the amount to Sears, Roebuck & Co., Chicago, Ill.
If Mr.______ is not perfectly satisfied with the instrument, we will refund money on surrender to us of a bill of lading showing instrument has been reconsigned to Sears, Roebuck & Co.

Name of bank.

Your banker should sign his name here.

REFERENCE BY SPECIAL PERMISSION: FIRST NATIONAL BANK CHICAGO; CORN EXCHANGE NATIONAL BANK CHICAGO; NATIONAL CITY BANK NEW YORK; SECOND NATIONAL BANK BOSTON.

Above is shown a facsimile copy of the certificate of deposit which your banker will give you when the instrument arrives in your town and you deposit the money with him.

BOND OF INDEMNITY.
THE Beckwith PIANO
STYLE OF PIANO — QUALITY — CERTIFICATE

This certifies that the Beckwith Piano of the style and certificate numbers above mentioned, is guaranteed by us for a period of 25 years against any defect in material or workmanship. This instrument is sold under our distinct agreement that if it does not prove entirely satisfactory during one year's trial, it may be returned, at our expense, and we will either replace it with another, or we will refund the purchase price, together with interest at the rate of 7 per cent per annum.

Should any piece or part prove defective in material or workmanship or should any defect manifest itself during a period of 25 years that does not arise from misuse, accident, moisture or extremes of temperature, we agree to replace the same, or to repair the instrument, wholly at our expense during this entire period.

SEARS, ROEBUCK & CO.
Dated at Chicago this......day of..........A. D.... by R. W. Sears, Pres.

WHEN ORDERING AN INSTRUMENT under this plan, be sure to send us the name of the bank where you expect to deposit the money for the instrument and freight charges, after it arrives. Immediately upon receipt of your order, we will enter it at our factory and ship it at the earliest possible date, which will be inside of a few days. Under this plan of shipment, we take absolutely all the risk, you run no risk whatever. You are not called upon to promise anything or agree to anything or to obligate yourself in any way whatever; all we ask is your permission to show you the wonderful quality represented by the Beckwith Pianos and Organs; we only ask you to test one for 30 days in your own home, and at the end of 30 days, either buy it or send it back to us at our expense. Remember, that if for any reason whatever you should return the shipment, you need not wait one moment for the return of your money in full; because all during your trial term, your money is at your own bank waiting for you.

OUR OFFER No. 2. In spite of this astonishingly liberal offer; even though we do not ask our customers to send us any money with the order, yet almost everyone prefers to do this for three reasons: In the first place they realize that with our Five Million Dollars paid up capital, our enormous forty-acre plant, our buildings and our millions of dollars' worth of merchandise, we are as strong and safe as any bank, and our reputation for honest and square dealing, our established reputation for fulfilling every agreement and promise we make, is full protection to the customer who sends the money to us.

In the second place, our friends prefer that the purchase of a piano or organ should be a confidential matter between us; they do not care for the banker or anyone else to know what they pay for this high class instrument; hence, they send the money with the order; knowing that they are amply protected under our positive agreement to refund every dollar at once, if the instrument is not satisfactory at the end of 30 days trial.

In the third place, they prefer to send the money to us, not only for the two reasons given, but also because we agree in such cases to deposit the money to their account in our Customers' Profit Sharing Department, and agree to refund the money as explained on the copy of the certificate printed below, with interest at the rate of 7 per cent per annum, in case the shipment should be returned at the end of 30 days at our expense, together with any freight charge or other cost to the customer. Our standing in the business world, our financial responsibility, our reputation for fair dealing, all invite your confidence, and if you prefer to send the money direct to us, we shall be glad to deposit the money for you in our Customers' Profit Sharing Department. If you prefer to take advantage of either offer, remember we hereby obligate ourselves to fulfill every agreement made, and to refund every dollar should you return the shipment as unsatisfactory at the end of 30 days trial.

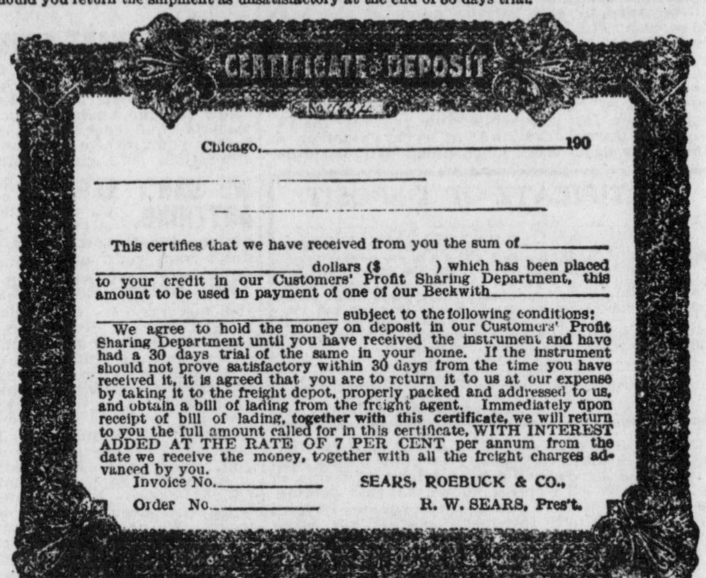

CERTIFICATE OF DEPOSIT
No. 7434

Chicago,______ 190

This certifies that we have received from you the sum of______ dollars ($____) which has been placed to your credit in our Customers' Profit Sharing Department, this amount to be used in payment of one of our Beckwith______ subject to the following conditions:

We agree to hold the money on deposit in our Customers' Profit Sharing Department until you have received the instrument and have had a 30 days trial of the same in your home. If the instrument should not prove satisfactory within 30 days from the time you have received it, it is agreed that you are to return it to us at our expense by taking it to the freight depot, properly packed and addressed to us, and obtain a bill of lading from the freight agent. Immediately upon receipt of bill of lading, together with this certificate, we will return to you the full amount called for in this certificate, WITH INTEREST ADDED AT THE RATE OF 7 PER CENT per annum from the date we receive the money, together with all the freight charges advanced by you.

Invoice No.______ SEARS, ROEBUCK & CO.,
Order No.______ R. W. SEARS, Pres't.

OUR 25 YEARS BINDING GUARANTEE is really a bond of indemnity, and this we show on the opposite side of the page. This is the strongest and most binding bond ever issued covering a piano or organ, and we are glad to show you a copy in order to remove any doubt, should doubt exist, as to the high quality of these instruments. We could not afford to offer such a strong guarantee to our customers unless we positively knew the great value and the high quality of the Beckwith.

OUR 1-YEAR TRIAL OFFER. Not only do we allow you to try the instrument in your home for a full period of 30 days, giving it a thorough test, trial and examination, but we also allow you to return it to us at any time within one year should you not be perfectly satisfied with it in every particular. In such case we will return you every cent you have paid, together with charges for freight and cartage.

OUR SPECIAL PIANO CATALOGUE. We especially recommend that you select and purchase a piano from us as illustrated and described in this big catalogue, rather than to cause a delay by writing for our free Special Piano Catalogue, since we guarantee that any piano which you may order from these pages will reach you in perfect condition, prove in every way satisfactory, and that you will find it a much better piano than you can buy elsewhere at anything like the price we offer. We also guarantee that you will make a big saving in the cost, and if you do not find this to be so, you can return the piano to us any time within thirty days and we will immediately and cheerfully refund your money and pay the freight charges both ways. If, however, you are unable to make a selection from the illustrations and descriptions shown in this catalogue, and you feel that you would like to have better illustrations and more complete descriptions, then we will be glad to send you a copy of our Special Piano Catalogue. This catalogue will be sent to you, upon request, postage prepaid, and it will only be necessary for you to send us a postal card in order to obtain it. Simply say, "Please send me your Piano Catalogue," and it will be sent by return mail.

The name "Beckwith" on a piano is an absolute guarantee of excellence. It stands for all that is represented in the word "quality." The Beckwith Piano represents the very highest attainment in the art of piano making. The Beckwith Piano is second to none regardless of name or make.

READ THIS LETTER.

THEO. A. SALVO,
Practical
Piano and Organ Tuner and Repairer,
Formerly of Chickerings

HICKORY, N. C., Sept. 19, 1905.

Sears, Roebuck & Co.,
Chicago, Ill.

Gentlemen:—

I was called upon the other day to look at a piano that you sold to Mr. J. Triplett at Goshen, N. C. The piano needed tuning and after I tuned it I must say I never was more surprised in my life. How can you make and sell such a piano as that at that extremely low price? The mechanism and material are excellent and I know if all who wish to purchase pianos could only see a Beckwith there would be lots of them sold. I have been in the business 54 years and have worked at three of the largest high grade piano factories. My knowledge of pianos and piano construction prompts me to write this unsolicited letter of praise for the Beckwith which I have just examined the second time. Again I say I am surprised that you can sell such a piano at such a low price. As I am on the road all the time following my vocation, I can and will speak to all I find who are about to purchase a piano, and advise them to give the Beckwith the first trial.

Wishing you success in this branch of business, I remain

Very respectfully,
Theo. A. Salvo.

The Beckwith Organs secured the highest award at the recent St. Louis Louisiana Purchase Exposition, as explained on page 295. The Beckwith Organs represent "quality" of the highest degree. The Beckwith is the finest organ offered regardless of name or make.

THIS WONDERFUL PIANO BOOK IS FREE

IF you do not order a piano from these pages, and from the descriptions and illustrations given herein, do not, under any circumstances, place your order elsewhere until you have written for and secured our beautiful special Piano Book, our big, SPECIAL PIANO CATALOGUE, as illustrated below. If you desire further information not contained in these pages, more complete description of any piano, just write us a letter or postal card, asking us to send our big, free Piano Book, and it will go to you immediately by return mail, all postage paid.

YOU CAN ORDER A PIANO from the following pages with absolute confidence and safety. Every instrument is exactly as illustrated and described. We take all the risk and responsibility ourselves in shipping a piano to you, and if you are in a hurry, do not hesitate to order from the following pages, because you will find every piano as it is described herein. Our entire line of pianos is thoroughly illustrated and described and our very lowest prices, and all our inducements, privileges and offers are shown in the pages of this big catalogue; but if you are not able to make a satisfactory selection, or if you wish further information on the construction of the superior Beckwith piano or if for any reason everything is not thoroughly clear to you, if you desire to learn more about the Beckwith piano before placing an order, then do not fail to write and get this big free Piano Book.

WE STRONGLY SOLICIT YOUR ORDER for a piano direct from the following pages, under our personal guarantee that we will please you in the fullest degree or immediately return your money. You do not take any risk whatever in ordering now direct from these pages for you have every privilege we extend and are fully protected in every way; yet if more information is desired, do not fail, under any circumstances, to send for this big Piano Book, free, postpaid. This handsome Piano Book is the most comprehensive work of this kind that has ever been printed or offered. The most complete piano catalogue ever issued, giving more valuable information on pianos, better illustrations, more detailed descriptions than any other ever published. It contains large handsome halftone pictures of all the Beckwith pianos, shows pictures of every piece and part, and explains why the Beckwith pianos are as fine as any in the world, why we can furnish a piano of the highest quality at prices never before attempted; tells why it is a mistaken idea to believe that a large price is a guarantee of quality, why it is that over one-half of the prices of high class fine pianos can be saved and how you can avoid this useless expense. This beautiful catalogue contains illustrations of our guarantees and certificates of deposit. All our offers are fully explained. It is the most interesting book ever issued. It shows actual illustrations in color of the San Domingo mahogany, French burled walnut and English quarter sawed oak veneers. It will tell you all that you can possibly know about the building of a good piano and will actually give you more information than you could secure from any other source.

REMEMBER when we solicit your order for a piano, whether from these pages or from our complete Piano Book, we only ask the privilege of placing it in your home on trial, with the understanding that you are to test it for thirty days, and that you and your musical friends are to judge the piano. Even if you send the money with the order, to be deposited for you in our Customers' Profit Sharing Department, as most of our friends do, we do not consider the piano sold unless you accept it and agree to keep it after the thirty days trial and test.

YOU ARE PERFECTLY SAFE in sending your order from these pages, yet if you desire further information, more detailed description of the Beckwith piano, write us a postal card now, asking us to send you this big Piano Book and we will mail the handsome work, absolutely free, postpaid

A SPLENDID MUSICAL EDUCATION FREE

A FULL COURSE OF MUSIC LESSONS ON THE PIANO, ORGAN, BANJO, MANDOLIN, VIOLIN OR CORNET GIVEN FREE TO OUR CUSTOMERS.

THE MOST WONDERFUL OFFER EVER MADE.

THIS REMARKABLE OFFER MAKES IT POSSIBLE FOR ANYONE TO ACQUIRE A MUSICAL EDUCATION, AND BECOME A FINISHED PERFORMER UPON HIS FAVORITE INSTRUMENT, ABSOLUTELY FREE OF CHARGE.

OUR OFFER

WE ARE MAKING THE ABOVE OFFER TO ALL OF OUR CUSTOMERS WHO PURCHASE MUSICAL INSTRUMENTS FROM US.

IN order to make this wonderful offer, we have not found it necessary to raise the prices on our musical instruments whatever, but give away this course of instruction absolutely free to our customers. The fact that many of our customers live in communities where musical instruction is difficult to procure, has led us to make this remarkable offer. Each course, consisting of from 10 to 96 lessons, according to the instrument purchased, is given entirely by mail by one of the best and most widely known music colleges in the country. These courses of instruction by mail, possess several advantages over the usual method of personal instruction.

THE pupil can suit his own convenience as to the time for taking his lesson, and can use his spare time only, if he desires, in securing his musical education. Another great advantage in this course is that the lessons are brought right to your home, and it is not necessary to wait on the convenience of a music teacher. The lessons are right on your instrument, waiting for you at any time when it will suit your convenience to attend to them. The courses which we offer you, place you in a position to take advantage of a large conservatory of music and the personal attention of a large corps of teachers, each one a specialist in his own line.

The Musical Education Which You Will Secure From This Course Will, Therefore, be Broad and Thorough, and Fit You Perfectly for Further Study in the Very Highest Branches of the Art.

HOW TO TAKE ADVANTAGE OF OUR GREAT FREE MUSICAL INSTRUCTION OFFER.

TO EVERY PERSON WHO PURCHASES A BECKWITH PIANO OR ORGAN, OR ANY ONE OF THE GUITARS, BANJOS, VIOLINS, MANDOLINS OR CORNETS SHOWN IN OUR CATALOGUE, WE GIVE, ABSOLUTELY FREE, A CERTIFICATE WHICH ENTITLES THE HOLDER TO A FULL COURSE OF LESSONS ON THE INSTRUMENT.

To All Who Purchase One of Our Cottage Home Organs, Boudoir Pianos at $79.45 or one of our Home Favorite Pianos at $89.00, we will give a certificate which entitles the holder to a full course of **six months lessons.** With each of the other Beckwith Pianos or Organs shown in our catalogue, we give a certificate which entitles the holder to a full course of **96 weekly lessons,** covering a period of two years. The only cost to the purchaser will be for postage, stationery and music, which we guarantee will not exceed 13 cents per week.

To Each Person Who Purchases a Violin, Guitar, Banjo, Mandolin or Cornet quoted at $3.00 or under, we send a certificate which entitles the holder to a course of instruction, consisting of 10 weekly lessons. The only cost to the purchaser will be for postage, stationery and music, which we guarantee not to exceed $1.00 for the entire course.

To Each Person Who Purchases a Violin, Guitar, Banjo, Mandolin or Cornet at prices in excess of $3.00, we will give a certificate which entitles the holder to a course of **50 weekly lessons,** covering a period of one year. The only cost to the purchaser will be for postage, stationery and music, which we guarantee not to exceed 13 cents per week.

We Wish to Call Your Attention to the fact that to all but our customers, the course of music which we are offering you free, would cost the regular terms, which are $24.00 for each course of 48 lessons. Not only is the regular fee $24.00, but the books and music used in the course ordinarily amount to over $15.00. All of this we give you free when you purchase one of our instruments. Not only do we save you the amount you would otherwise have to pay for tuition in the school, but we save you a much greater amount which you would have to pay for the personal instruction of a teacher if you took lessons in the usual way.

If You Have an Ambition to learn to play any of the musical instruments mentioned, we know you will find it to your advantage to purchase from us, because not only can we save you a large amount of money on your purchase, but we also allow you to take advantage of this magnificent offer. Our customer will receive the same personal painstaking attention on the part of the college as is given to the regular pupils who pay the regular fee. This is part of our contract with the school, and we are prepared to guarantee that all of our customers who take advantage of this offer will be perfectly satisfied with the instruction. Do not get the idea that these are all printed lessons, which are gotten up regardless of the student's ability or requirements, as this is not so. Your lessons will be suited to your ability and requirements. Any one of these courses can be taken up at any time after the customer receives the scholarship certificate, which we send when the instrument is purchased, and can be laid aside and resumed to suit his convenience. The courses are so graded that those who have now some musical knowledge can take an advanced course to suit their needs. Those who have no knowledge of music, can begin at the rudiments and thus lay a solid and broad foundation for their future musical education. The courses are so simple and everything is explained so thoroughly, that the only requisite on your part is industry—a desire to learn and an ordinary knowledge of reading and writing. Do not think that because you have not a college education you cannot acquire a musical education, as that would be a great mistake. Some of the greatest musicians that we have ever had were men of only ordinary education. If you can read and write the English language and are willing to make a conscientious effort, we will guarantee you success.

EXPERIENCE HAS DEMONSTRATED THAT MUSIC TAUGHT BY MAIL PROVES MUCH MORE SUCCESSFUL THAN WHEN ACQUIRED UNDER PERSONAL TUITION.

Because the pupil, not having a teacher present to whom he can always refer, is taught to think for himself and often thinks out many points which he would otherwise find it much easier to refer to his teacher. Knowledge acquired in this way is always more thorough and lasting. Any point which may arise about which the pupil is in doubt and which he cannot figure out for himself can always be referred by letter to the professors at the college and they will gladly explain any point which may seem to be obscure. Do not get the idea that you can learn music as well from a book of instructions as you can from one of these courses, because that would be a great error.

Bear in Mind that the receipt by you of one of these certificates places you under no obligation whatever to take the course, or if you begin you are under no obligation to continue any longer than it suits your convenience to do so. We wish to give our endorsement unreservedly to this musical course, because a careful investigation on our part has shown that wherever the lessons have been received in good faith by the pupil and a conscientious and patient effort made, it has resulted in complete success. By taking one of these courses you acquire a musical education according to the best and latest method and are in no danger of acquiring false ideas and wrong methods which would have to be gotten rid of sooner or later. You have the assurance that everything taught and every point covered is correct and according to the recognized standard of musical teaching. Having acquired a musical education in this way you will not suffer the embarrassment experienced by some players who have really fine musical ability, but have learned by methods which bring a smile to the experienced and correctly taught musician.

The Lessons are Sent to You Weekly and you are required to master each one of the lessons before you are allowed to proceed farther. The professors at the college will know at any stage of the course just exactly what proficiency you have acquired and everything given in the lessons must be thoroughly mastered and fixed in your mind. In attempting to learn music from an instruction book the tendency is to slight many important points and carry on the study in a slipshod manner so that you finally find yourself in the middle of the book with many important things unlearned which it is necessary you should know before proceeding farther. You are then in the situation of a military commander who leaves an untaken fortress behind him and finds it necessary to return and capture the stronghold before proceeding farther on the march. Of course, no good soldier will ever do this, but the temptation to do so on the part of the student who studies from a book, is very strong. You are never allowed to do this when studying music through one of these courses, but each step must be taken and each important point acquired with the view to further proficiency.

HOW TO PROCURE THE COURSE.

IN ORDER TO TAKE ADVANTAGE OF THIS GREAT OFFER IT IS ONLY NECESSARY FOR YOU TO TAKE ADVANTAGE OF ANY OF THE WONDERFUL VALUES WHICH WE ARE OFFERING IN MUSICAL INSTRUMENTS.

We Desire to Protect Our Customers in Every Way and we could not afford to offer anything to them that would be apt to prove unsatisfactory from any standpoint. Therefore, before entering into any contract with the college we personally examined into its facilities and methods and found them to be excellent in every respect. We found the officers and professors to be men of great musical ability and attainments and high character. The history of the school has been one of untiring devotion to the interests of its students, and the unswerving desire to place itself at the very head of the musical colleges of the country. That the school has been successful in its efforts is fully proved by the numerous testimonials which it has received from successful and satisfied students. We thoroughly satisfied ourselves that the institution is fully capable of living up to every contract it may make and fulfilling every promise it may give.

The Fact That We Allow a Full Year's Trial on all of the pianos and organs which we sell, and from ten to twenty days trial upon all of our other instruments, will prove to you at once that we have not sacrificed quality in order to make low prices. It has been our policy to give the customer the benefit of every reduction we could secure in the cost of the instruments to us, as we only desire to make a uniformly small profit on all of the instruments which we sell. As we have been able lately to buy our musical goods to greater advantage on account of the immense contracts which we have been able to make, we are placed in a position where we can safely offer to our customers the advantage of a splendid musical education absolutely free. If there are any questions which our customers desire to ask that will not be found answered on this page, we will be glad to answer them at any time, as we are always glad to have our customers investigate any offer which we may make them.

If You are Thinking of Buying a Piano, Organ or Any Other Musical Instrument, YOU CANNOT AFFORD TO MISS THIS GREAT OPPORTUNITY to Purchase it at an EXTREMELY LOW PRICE, and at the Same Time Secure for Yourself a THOROUGH and COMPLETE MUSICAL EDUCATION.

THE BECKWITH PIANOS.

A STANDARD LINE OF HIGH GRADE INSTRUMENTS AT PRICES LOWER THAN EVER BEFORE. A FEW POINTERS ON THE ESSENTIALS OF A HIGH GRADE PIANO.

DO NOT BE DECEIVED by the remarkably low prices at which we offer the Beckwith piano. It is a mistaken idea to measure the quality of an instrument by the amount that the manufacturer, dealer, or agent seeks to secure for it. It is not true that the more you pay for a piano, the more value you receive. The manufacturing cost of a really fine piano is not a large amount. If you are one of the few who still believe that it is necessary to pay a large price to secure a good piano, you would be doing the Beckwith an injustice to attempt to measure its quality by our low price. We would be glad to have you forget the small amount that we are willing to accept for this high grade instrument, and order one under our liberal thirty days' trial offer, with the understanding that you are to judge the instrument from the standpoint of quality alone. Remember that "fine feathers do not make fine birds," and a high price is not a guarantee of quality. It is the system under which most pianos are sold that increases the price, but not the quality. Prices above that which we ask for the Beckwith piano represents absolutely nothing of any value which is not found developed to the fullest degree in the Beckwith. In paying the larger price demanded by others, do not be deceived into the belief that you are securing a better quality, because this is not a fact; you are only paying the larger profits, commissions and expenses of jobbers, dealers, agents and others through whose hands the piano passes on its journey to you. One-half or more of the prices of pianos sold in the ordinary manner represents nothing but useless expense, profits and commissions, which can be avoided and are saved to you under our "from factory to customer" direct plan. When we place a price that we are willing to receive upon the Beckwith piano, we are asking only the bare factory cost for the high grade material and skilled workmanship entering into its construction, to which we add the same narrow margin of profit which we reserve for ourselves and are willing to accept on the sale of any ordinary merchandise. Under this plan you pay only what any high grade standard, fine, artistic and widely advertised piano is honestly worth; no more and no less. The greatest favor you can do us is to secure any one of the pianos illustrated in this catalogue on trial under our liberal terms of shipment and place it beside any other make sold at double our prices, in your own home for an actual test for quality for thirty days at the hands of yourself and any unprejudiced, disinterested person. If you will do this you will be convinced of the superiority of the Beckwith, and the fact that the ordinary price charged for a high grade piano is altogether too high, and represents a great deal more than the honest cost to make it, with one margin of profit added.

THE SCALE. In the making of a piano the drawing of a scale is one of the most important points to be considered, as it is the foundation or fundamental principle on which the construction of the piano depends. A scale may be perfect upon its first drawing, or it may be redrawn innumerable times and still be a failure. A great many piano manufacturers have redrawn the scale of their pianos, have experimented with it during the entire period of their business lives, and then have not succeeded in securing satisfactory results or a perfect scale. The scale of the piano is the correct mathematical division of each tone and semi-tone; or in other words, of each note on the entire keyboard of the piano. It can be likened to any mechanical drawing. It is a plan to be followed by piano makers in laying out the strings of the piano; it determines the proper length of each string, the exact position it must occupy across the sounding board, how far apart on each string the bridges must be set so as to secure the balance of power and uniformity of vibration which must be properly distributed throughout the whole piano. A good scale is beyond value or price. Without a good scale there is no evenness of tone, and the instrument would lack that indefinable something in the tone which not only appeals to the musical ear, but appeals also to the finer sensibilities of the hearer. Another important feature in a true scale, such as the Beckwith's, is the proper location of the striking line, or that point on the string which the hammer must strike so as to secure the proper tonal quality. In the ordinary piano, this is something that is wholly neglected, and the consequence is a coarse, raw, unrefined and unsympathetic tone which really repels and does not attract. In the artistic piano, in the piano of a higher grade, and better kind and quality, the striking line is of the first consideration and one of the first requisites. Scientific research carried on by the best piano makers in the early history of piano building and years of subsequent experience, demonstrates that by striking the string practically upon a nodal point produces the best quality of tone; the most desirable quality, the pure piano tone, is best brought out by striking the string at a point at about one-eighth of its entire length below the upper bridge. This point is exactly between two nodes, or upon a nodal point. The string vibrates in waves. These waves or curves are called nodes. If the hammer strikes on one of these waves, it will bring out a light, peculiar tone; or what is called a harmonic tone. Strange as it may seem, there is really more than one tone in a string, and unless care is used in determining the striking line more than the fundamental tone will be heard. The lighter qualities of a piano string are known as "upper partials," whereas the required tone, the true tone, is known as a "fundamental" tone. The surface of the hammer dampens or kills the "upper partials," allowing the fundamental tone to sing out in all its purity. The point of contact of the hammer on the string determines the tone quality, and experience and mathematical precision has determined in the Beckwith the one only true point of contact, and this desirable quality is found in every Beckwith piano. The scale of the Beckwith is as close to perfection as human knowledge, experience and ingenuity can make it.

THE PIANO ACTION. This is a term applied to the mechanical part of the piano, that part through the medium of which the tone is produced. From a strictly mechanical standpoint, it is that portion of the piano which conveys the motion of the keys to the hammer and thus to the strings, producing the tone. The action contains many small levers, many separate pieces of felt, etc. The levers and centers of the action must be adjusted so perfectly that they respond with the same prompt elasticity to the most delicate as well as to the most powerful touch. In a fine action, such as is in the Beckwith piano, the material used in the construction of these parts is of a very fine quality and selected with the utmost care. The stock going to make an action is composed of many different kinds of wood and several kinds of felt and metal as well. That quality known as a "repeating" quality in an action is most necessary to fine execution. When a key is struck it acts on a series of levers which communicate to the hammer, throwing it forcibly against the string. For the action to respond properly, it is necessary that the lever adjustment be perfect and that the action be properly adjusted to the keys. It must be well balanced and finely and delicately adjusted. Each and every point covered above is found in the Beckwith piano. This piano is noted for the repeating qualities of the action and for the tone produced at each stroke of the key, no matter how often the stroke is repeated. The hammers are a very important part of the action and they must be made in such a manner that they are perfectly balanced and that they respond instantly to every demand. The Beckwith piano hammer is made of genuine 14-pound felt of the very highest quality. Each hammer head is constructed of two layers of felt, the inner felt being hard so as to give a solidity to the hammer, and the outer felt being of a softer fibre, gives elasticity to the stroke and hence a fine quality to the tone. Each bearing in the action is bushed throughout with felt, and there is not one single point of contact in the entire action that is not felted, so as to prevent rattling and looseness of motion. The actions in the Beckwith are all equipped with a continuous brass flange.

There are many fine points in the construction of a piano about which the purchaser knows nothing. One of these points is the quality of the felt which enters into the instrument. This has a great deal to do with the quality of the instrument. Many cheap pianos are made without a particle of genuine piano felt entering into their construction. Some of these instruments sound very well for a time, but the tones soon become lifeless and unresponsive. The action of a piano felted in this way will rattle after being used for a time and the keys will refuse to work with that responsiveness so much desired and the piano will be altogether a disappointment. There is no remedy for this and it is simply a bad bargain. This can never happen to a Beckwith piano, as they are all thoroughly inspected before leaving the factory and are guaranteed in every way. The felts used in all of the Beckwith pianos are the finest quality of strictly high grade, all wool piano felts.

THE METAL FRAME is another important part of the piano. This frame must be so constructed as to give the least weight with the greatest amount of strength. As there is a strain of from 19 to 20 tons on the metal frame of the concert piano, tuned to international pitch, it is necessary that this frame should be constructed in the strongest possible manner so as to prevent its twisting or "buckling." It is on this frame that the strings are placed and it is securely bolted to the back and pin block in which the tuning pins are set. The strings of the piano must be of fine quality in order to produce a good tone. The scale of the Beckwith piano has a three-string unison in the treble and two-string unison in the overstrung bass. By "three-string unison" we mean three strings for every note. The bass strings are carefully wound, and all but a few of the lowest ones, which are single, are known as a two-string unison.

THE SOUNDING BOARD of the piano mellows and increases the tone of the strings and must be made of wood which is absolutely perfect and thoroughly seasoned. The sounding board in the Beckwith pianos is made of the choicest selected Canadian spruce and ribbed with braces of the same material, which insures it against warping or splitting.

THE KEY of the piano is a lever used to put the action in motion, throwing the hammer against the string and producing the tone. In order to have these keys balance perfectly they are weighted with small lead weights, inserted into the key shank back of the pivot, allowing the key, when released, to rise instantly into its former position. This requires the very nicest adjustment and is one of the most famous characteristics of the Beckwith pianos. The white keys are faced with ivory, the black keys are made of genuine ebony.

THE CASES of the Beckwith pianos are perfect in every respect and it is a fact not generally known that it takes about three months to put the finish on a good piano case. Each case is given from seven coats of varnish upward and each coat of varnish has to set from eight to ten days in order to become thoroughly dry before the next coat can be applied. These different processes, when perfectly performed, will consume from 70 to 90 days. These are points which are never slighted in the cases of the Beckwith pianos. Upon the thoroughness of this process depends the extremely high class finish for which the Beckwith piano cases are noted. In building the Beckwith piano cases the manufacturers use nothing but the best grade of richly figured sawed veneers. The case work on all these (with the exception of the Home Favorite) are double veneered inside and outside so as to provide against cracking or splitting. Anyone who is familiar with veneers and veneer work can tell by looking at the edge of either the music desk or the lower panel whether or not the piano is double veneered. If you cannot see the two layers of veneer you can rest assured that they are not there.

BUYING A PIANO.

WHEN YOU ARE READY TO PURCHASE your piano you should use great care not only to purchase a fine instrument but also to buy it from a concern which is willing to stand behind its instruments at all times. Many concerns are ready and willing to issue a guarantee with the instruments which they sell, but in nine cases out of ten the concern issuing the guarantee has not the necessary financial standing to make the guarantee of any value. It is one thing to sell a piano at a low price and quite another to guarantee it at all times. Our low prices and our guarantee go hand in hand. Our guarantee protects you against any defect which may appear in our pianos, the result of defective material or workmanship. When a local agent places a piano in your home it looks fine and the tone appears to be excellent. So far as you can see, it is a high grade piano in every way, but when the agent goes away, then the real test begins; will it be as good tomorrow, next month, and next year as it is today, and will the guarantee that the agent gives you protect you in any way? Should the instrument prove defective in any particular whom will you hold responsible and to whom will you appeal for redress? As the piano is an instrument purchased but once in a lifetime, it is certainly to your interest to use great care in selecting your piano, and as there are many points of superiority for which you have to take the word of the salesman, how necessary it is for you to purchase your piano from a house which has a standing in the business world, which has a reputation for fulfilling its promises and guarantees.

WHEN WE TELL OUR CUSTOMERS that we can save them over $200.00 on the purchase of a fine high grade piano, many of them cannot understand how this is done. People have been paying $400.00 to $500.00 for pianos for such a long time that they have grown to believe that it is necessary to pay that price in order to secure a good instrument. Some, before studying the matter fully, may doubt that we can sell them a strictly high grade piano, up to the musical standard in every way, with a splendid tone and beautiful finish for $195.00. Very few people know that the ordinary piano costs, to manufacture, less than one-half the price which the dealer asks the customer for it. They do not realize that the expenses of sale and the profits which the different dealers make through whose hands the instrument passes, make up more than one-half of the retail price of the instrument. These profits and selling expenses do not add anything at all to the quality of the piano after it leaves the factory. This being true, the customer can easily understand that if we ship our pianos from the factory direct, simply adding our one small percentage of profit to the manufacturing cost we can sell the piano for less than one-half the price which the local dealer and agent charges for identically the same grade. The dealers through whose hands the piano must pass before it reaches the customer cannot afford to handle it for nothing and a profit of $50.00 for the jobber, $50.00 for the district agent and $100.00 for the local dealer is not considered generally, a large profit to make on a single transaction; especially in view of the fact that a piano is a luxury and that the agent or dealer sells comparatively few of them. Whether he sells one or none, his expenses go on just the same and he is compelled to make a large profit on every sale to enable him to do business profitably.

BUT NOT ONLY DO WE MAKE A GREAT SAVING for our customers by cutting out the intermediate dealers' profits and expenses, but we are also able to make a great reduction in price on account of the immense buying advantage which we possess. We make contracts for thousands of pianos at one time on a spot cash basis and this places the manufacturer in a position to buy his material at the very lowest possible figure, and all of these advantages

Remember also you get a Profit Sharing Certificate if you order a piano, as fully explained on pages 1 and 2 of this book.

go to the customer in low prices. Do not be afraid of the low prices which we make on our pianos. Remember, that we are taking all the chances ourselves and do not ask you to take any risk whatever. As you have to take the dealer's word for a great many qualities of the piano, why not purchase from a concern which cannot afford to sell a poor piano or ask their customers to be satisfied with an instrument which is not up to the standard in every way? That we are not exaggerating when we tell you that we can save you $250.00 on the purchase of a Concert Grand Piano is fully proved by the testimonials which you will find on lower part of this page. We do not ask you to take our word for anything we say in favor of the Beckwith, and when we ship you a piano we do not ask you to promise anything or assume any obligations whatever, but we do ask you to believe the statements of your friends and neighbors as found in these voluntary testimonials.

BUYING FROM THE DEALER.

REMEMBER **that where a dealer buys four or five pianos on consignment,** or where he pays for them by turning in the notes at a very large discount received on other pianos sold on time, we contract for from two to three thousand pianos on a spot cash basis, therefore, at the lowest possible cost, making a great saving, all of which goes to you in the lower prices quoted.

WHEN A DEALER OFFERS YOU A PIANO, when he offers to give you good value at low prices, you must bear in mind that any low prices he can name does not represent the **legitimate value** of the instrument; it does not represent the honest factory cost with but one margin of profit added. When he offers you a piano he is not only offering you a handsome case and perhaps all that goes to make up a good piano, but he is offering you something more which, however, you cannot see, and which adds absolutely nothing to its value; he is compelled, by the very nature of things, to charge you the large profit the manufacturer made in selling the piano to the jobber, also the jobber's legitimate profit when he sells the piano to the agent. The agent must live and has expenses to meet. He cannot do business for nothing and must charge a large profit to cover his expenses, owing to the limited number of pianos he sells. The agent, in order to do business profitably, must secure what to him and to other agents and dealers may appear a legitimate profit, but it is many, many times more than the amount that we are perfectly willing to accept as our small margin of profit above the honest factory cost to make any fine piano. The dealer is under a disadvantage because his customers are few and far between, because his trade is confined, perhaps, to a village or a township or at the most, to a county. We sell pianos over the entire country, from Maine to California and from the Great Lakes to the Gulf. We enjoy an enormous purchasing power, and while we could very easily secure a great deal more for the superb Beckwith than we do, yet our policy is to reserve for ourselves always our one small margin of profit, and to give every dollar we can save to our customers, in the lower prices quoted.

STOP AND THINK **how many pianos an agent will sell each year; consider the amount of store rent he must pay;** consider how much he loses on bad debts when he sells on the installment plan; what his losses **must be** in taking various articles in exchange as part payment; figure what his honest living expenses are; the expenses of his family and the expenses of his salesmen, and bearing in mind his sales during the year, you can easily determine how much he **must make** on each piano he sells in order to meet these various expenses, without even allowing one dollar to be laid away for a rainy day.

WHEN A DEALER ASKS YOU MORE THAN $195.00 FOR A PIANO **he is simply asking you to pay him, not only the large profit which he must ask to make the business profitable,** but also the profits and selling expenses of other men through whose hands the piano passes before it comes to him. Perhaps a dealer or agent will come to you, as they have to a number of our customers and offer to sell a piano at from $165.00 to $250.00, claiming that they are equal to the Beckwith, but in every single case upon comparison such a piano offered by dealers at that price is found to be no better than the cheaper pianos we sell at $89.00 and $115.00; this has been proved time and again, and it merely upholds our claim that the ordinary piano sold in the ordinary way is sold at over twice its actual value.

A WORD ABOUT FREIGHT CHARGES.

REMEMBER **that the freight charges on a piano are exactly the same, whether they are paid by the customer or by the dealer or agent.** We guarantee that these charges will be nothing as compared to your large saving on the purchase of a Beckwith piano. Your regular dealer or agent must pay the same freight charge on any instrument he offers to you, and whether you pay this freight charge yourself on a piano purchased under our "from factory to consumer direct" plan at factory cost, with one margin of profit added, or whether you pay it to the agent or dealer in paying his prices, you pay it just the same. This freight charge must be borne by you, whether in the form of freight charge itself, or the larger prices demanded. By comparing our prices on pianos with those asked by your local dealers, and then comparing the freight charges which you will have to pay with the amount which we can save you on your purchase, you will see at once that the freight charge is but a very small amount in comparison with the amount you can save on a piano. Another advantage is, that in purchasing a piano from us you know exactly what the instrument costs you at the factory, and you know exactly what you pay in freight charges; while on the other hand, in purchasing from the local dealer, you know what the piano costs you, but do not know how much of it is his profit and how much the freight charge. The railroad companies are very reasonable in freight charges, and when you consider the fact that you have to pay the freight charges whether you buy from us or from the local dealer, we believe that you should not hesitate in giving us an opportunity to send you one of our splendid instruments under our great Thirty Days Free Trial Offer. Do not let the small amount of freight charges prove any obstacle to your purchasing one of these pianos, as we ship each one under our express promise to save you at least one-half, according to the grade of piano which you purchase.

The Profit Sharing Certificate we will send you on your purchase of a Piano will help you get valuable merchandise entirely free of charge. **See pages 1 and 2 in this book for full explanation.**

WHAT OUR FRIENDS SAY ABOUT THE MAGNIFICENT VALUES WHICH WE ARE GIVING IN PIANOS.

Voluntary Testimonials From Just a Few of Those Who Have Purchased Pianos From Us in the Last Year.

What Our Customers Say About Our Pianos is the Best Evidence of Their Splendid Finish and Magnificent Tone.

AN EXPERIENCED TEACHER IS PLEASED WITH THE BECKWITH.

The following testimonial is from Prof. J. Dempster Towne of Grand Rapids, Mich. Prof. Towne is known all over Michigan as a splendid teacher of the piano and a brilliant performer on that instrument. A word of commendation from him is doubly valuable, because he is an expert pianist, understands the mechanical construction of the instrument thoroughly and renders his judgment only after careful examination and due consideration.

Sears, Roebuck & Co., Chicago, Ill. Grand Rapids, Mich.

Gentlemen:—The Beckwith Cabinet Grand Piano which I recently bought of you is a much better piano than I expected to get for that money. This piano is fully equal, and in some respects superior to a great many pianos ordinarily sold for $300.00, and I have seen many pianos sold for $350.00 and $400.00 that were no better. During my long experience as a teacher of the piano, a great variety of pianos, of various makers and styles, have come under my observation, but I never before heard of good serviceable pianos, brand new, being sold at retail for such low prices. I have no hesitation in recommending anybody who wishes a strongly made, durable, and good looking family piano, to buy of you. I have for several years been sending to you for various articles, and have always found you willing and able to do the fair thing. In fact, I never dealt with a more reasonable, honorable or courteous house.

Very truly yours,

J. DEMPSTER TOWNE,
8 George Street.

THE BUYER DOES NOT TAKE ANY CHANCES IN ORDERING A BECKWITH.

Mr. Ebel, the writer of this letter had a good many doubts as to our ability to live up to the representations made in our catalogue. We receive many letters every day from people who say that they would like to order pianos from us, but doubt our ability to furnish a good piano at the prices charged. Where we can prevail upon these people to let us send them a piano on trial we never have any difficulty in convincing them that the instrument is everything that we claim for it, and in many cases such customers say that we do not make our claims strong enough. Mr. Ebel was prejudiced against our instruments, but he is honest and frank enough to say that the instrument cannot be duplicated for less than $400.00.

Sears, Roebuck & Co., Chicago, Ill. Moscow, Idaho.

Gentlemen:—I must say that I am surprised at the beauty of the wood, workmanship, finish and tone of the Beckwith piano I received. The tone is deep and full and the action is very responsive. I was skeptical of your ability to furnish a high grade piano at the prices you name. I went through every part of the instrument and, not wanting to rely entirely on my own judgment, I had the Rev. Father Keyser call, and both of us went through the piano very carefully I can say, as this is my third piano, and I was examining and trying most every piano around here for sale, that this instrument cannot be duplicated for less than $400.00. The buyer does not take any chances in placing an order with you. With best wishes, I am, Very truly yours, CHAS. F. EBEL.

AS GOOD AS HIS NEIGHBOR'S PIANO WHICH COST $450.00.

The customer whose testimonial appears below, took advantage of our great 30 Days Free Trial Offer, which gave him a splendid opportunity to compare his piano with the $450.00 instrument owned by his neighbor, and by reading the testimonial you will see that he found his piano in every way equal to the one purchased by his neighbor at $450.00.

Sears, Roebuck & Co., Chicago, Ill. Sterling, Nebraska.

Dear Sirs:—The Beckwith piano I received of you in January has given good satisfaction so far. We are well pleased with the same. We cannot see but what it is as good as our neighbor's, that cost $450.00. We are well pleased with the mandolin attachment. My neighbor's has no attachments. C. B. SMITH.

EQUAL TO PIANOS SOLD BY DEALERS AT $350.00 AND BETTER TONED.

Below we give another testimonial from a customer who says that the piano we shipped him is equal to pianos sold by dealers at $350.00 and is much better in tone. Bear in mind, that the customer writes this letter entirely of his own accord and without any dictation from us in any respect. We would be glad to have you write to the writer of any one of these testimonials and get his opinion of the merits of our instruments.

Sears, Roebuck & Co., Chicago, Ill. Three Rivers, Mich.

Dear Sirs:—I received the piano April 6th, all O. K. In appearance it is equal to a $350.00 Wellington, sold by a dealer here and better toned.

Yours respectfully, G. W. BARTO.

WOULD NOT PART WITH IT FOR ANY $300.00 PIANO IN TOWN.

It is the universal verdict of our customers, as gleaned from the numerous voluntary letters which we receive, that they would not exchange the pianos which we have sold them for other pianos in the neighborhood which have cost much more in price.

Sears, Roebuck & Co., Chicago, Ill. St. Cloud, Minn.

Dear Sirs:—We received our piano and must say that we are more than pleased with it. I would not part with it for any $300.00 piano in town. In fact, we are well pleased with all our goods. I wish to thank you very much. I'll advise everybody to get their goods from Sears, Roebuck & Co.

Yours very truly, MISS M. STUCKE.

EQUAL TO A KNABE AT $600.00.

We give below a testimonial from one of our enthusiastic customers, who is a business man in Columbus, Ohio, and not given to exaggeration in any way. We desire to call the attention of our customers to the difference in the two prices which the dealers made on the Knabe piano. $495.00 for cash and $600.00 on payments, being a difference of $105.00, which proves our assertion that dealers who sell instruments upon the installment plan must necessarily have their prices much higher than those who sell for cash. We do not know that we can add anything to this testimonial as it is complete in every respect. It is simply one of many which we receive from time to time.

Sears, Roebuck & Co., Chicago, Ill. Columbus, Ohio.

Dear Sirs:—I have already written you how well I like the Acme Cabinet Grand Piano, recently bought from you, but I would like again to state that according to my opinion the case is made and finished in the highest type of art. The tone is excellent and exquisite. I do not believe that I could have secured a better piano, no matter how much I paid or what I bought. That was my opinion the first day I received it, and it is still my opinion. In fact, the better I know the piano the better I like it. I would also add that the gentleman who selected the piano for me surely thoroughly understands pianos and piano construction. I do not believe that anyone else could have selected a piano for me that would suit me any better, and I thank him sincerely for the trouble to which he has gone. Miss Rose Lange, a young lady who is a fine pianist, has tried our piano very thoroughly. Last evening she told me that she liked my piano every bit as well as her own. She has a Knabe, which sells here for about $600.00 on payments, and for which she paid $495.00 spot cash. She says the case of my piano is much finer and more artistic than hers and that the action is easier and more responsive and the tone every bit as good as in her own piano If you wish a recommendation at any time, refer anyone to me, I will gladly tell them how much money they can save in buying a piano from you and how honorably you have treated me and of your very liberal terms of shipment. I will certainly recommend anyone to get one of your pianos and thoroughly try it, knowing that you can suit them so well and save them so much money.

Respectfully yours, HENRY W. MUELLER,
662 Briggs St.

$79.45

No. 46F3

OWING TO LACK OF SPACE, WE ARE UNABLE TO SHOW ANY ILLUSTRATION OF THIS PIANO.

OUR BECKWITH BOUDOIR 6-OCTAVE PIANO

Particularly suitable for small houses, summer cottages and other places where a large piano is not desirable. The tone is full and sweet, of a very pleasing quality and all that could be desired or expected in a piano of this size.

$79.45 REPRESENTS THE BARE COST to manufacture the instrument, with our usual small margin of profit added. It is the finest and most satisfactory small piano ever offered. It is built upon what is known as the F scale, beginning with the lower F and ending on the high F. Remember that the keyboard **only contains 6 octaves.** The keyboard is, therefore, one and one-third octaves shorter than the keyboard of all other Beckwith pianos. The compass is the same as in all other 6-octave pianos and is quite practical. We recommend it as the best 6-octave piano ever attempted. **THE CASE** is double veneered in genuine mahogany, with a beautiful panel effect in the upper and lower front. The trusses are square; in keeping with the balance of the case. All pilasters, trusses and mouldings are solid wood, highly polished. The piano is furnished in mahogany veneer only. **THE ACTION,** 6-octave, is of a very fine grade, responsive and repeats very nicely. The material and workmanship are of the best. **THE SCALE** is not overstrung. This piano has a straight stringing; in other words, it is strung straight up and down like a harp, and is not overstrung as is our Home Favorite Piano. There is not room enough in any 6-octave piano for the usual Beckwith overstringing. **THE PIN BLOCK** is built up in an approved manner, and cannot warp, crack or split. This construction holds the pin firmly. **THE SOUNDING BOARD** is very finely constructed of Canadian spruce pine, scientifically ribbed. **THE KEYS** are of highly polished **ivory and ebony, and not celluloid. THE PEDAL ACTION** is complete, having a loud and soft pedal and a practice pedal as well. This piano is not furnished with the mandolin attachment.

The price includes a handsome solid wood stool and complete instruction book.

THIS PIANO, THE BECKWITH BOUDOIR, in 6 octaves, is offered under our great 30 days free trial plan, as explained on page 283. All money refunded in full, together with the freight charges both ways, if you are not entirely satisfied. **We guarantee this piano for five years only.** Owing to its size and the peculiar manner of construction in all 6-octave pianos, we could not well afford to guarantee it for a longer period. If you contemplate the purchase of a 6-octave piano, you will find this the finest, the best, the most serviceable and attractive 6-octave piano ever offered.

No. 46F3 OUR BECKWITH BOUDOIR PIANO. Weight, about 400 pounds. Price **$79.45**

YOUR PARTICULAR ATTENTION IS INVITED

to the fact that this instrument is not a full size, upright piano. It is only 48 inches high, 4 feet long and 20 inches wide. It has not the usual 7⅓ octaves. It has 6 octaves only. The tone, however, and the volume of tone is all that you could possibly expect in a piano of this size. Remember, this is a Beckwith piano, and as such is sent out under our binding guarantee for quality and under the provisions of our great 30-day free trial offer.

With every purchase of this piano, we give, free, a scholarship certificate in one of the largest music schools in the United States, which entitles the holder to a course of fifty complete lessons on the piano, as fully explained on page 285.

$89.00

THE BECKWITH HOME FAVORITE PIANO

A Regular 7⅓ Octave Piano, With Overstrung Scale. A Full Size Parlor Piano, 4 Feet 6 Inches High, 5 Feet 1 Inch Long, and 2 Feet 2 Inches Deep. Weight, Boxed for Shipment, 750 Pounds.

A GUARANTEED PIANO, FULL PARLOR SIZE, FOR $89.00.

THE PRICE INCLUDES THE PIANO, a handsome solid wood stool and complete instruction book. To every purchaser of this piano we give, free, a scholarship certificate in one of the largest music schools in the United States, which entitles the holder to a six months course of instruction on the piano, as explained on page 285.

FULL DESCRIPTION.

Our HOME FAVORITE PIANO is a full size instrument, very substantially built, and is a most remarkable value at the price named.

THE CASE is of a handsome design, as the illustration, taken direct from the photograph, will show. The panel in the duet or continuous music desk is ornamented with a handsome scroll and extends the full length of the piano. It is finished in either mahogany or walnut finish, but is not veneered, therefore we can only guarantee it for five years. This piano is fitted with the latest style of rolling fall board.

THE SCALE is a regular full 7⅓ overstrung scale, the same as will be found in any piano offered by others at $200.00. It is not harp strung as is our Boudoir Piano, above described, but is overstrung in the regular manner, thus giving the greatest possible length to the string.

THE PIN BLOCK is built up of several pieces of rock maple, which holds the tuning pin firmly.

THE STRINGS are of a very fine quality, thoroughly tested, and the piano is fitted with overstrung, wound bass strings.

THE KEYS are genuine ivory and ebony, very finely polished.

THE SOUNDING BOARD is made of selected Canadian spruce, scientifically braced.

THE METAL FRAME is as strong as it is possible to have in a piano of this size, and is large enough to withstand the strain in this piano when it is tuned to pitch.

THE TONE is very full, sweet and melodious and of ample power for all ordinary requirements.

THE SIZE. Height, 4 feet 6 inches; length, 5 feet 1 inch; depth, 2 feet 2 inches. Weight, boxed for shipment, 750 pounds.

WITH THIS PIANO we will include, without any extra charge, either the mandolin attachment or the practice pedal, which is fully described on page 289. It will be necessary for you to advise us which attachment you desire, but we advise you to order the practice pedal. The price includes a substantial stool and complete instruction book.

REMEMBER, that this piano has full 7⅓ octaves, overstrung scale, ivory and ebony keys, and is the most marvelous value ever offered at this price. Owing to the size of the piano, however, the strings are not so long nor as heavy, the action is not so strong or as large as in our better grades, the case is not double veneered but is only finished, hence, we are compelled to guarantee this piano for five years only

No. 46F1 Our Home Favorite Beckwith Piano, Price, $89.00.

YOU SHARE IN THE PROFITS OF OUR BUSINESS IF YOU PURCHASE EITHER OF THESE PIANOS, AS EXPLAINED ON PAGES 1 AND 2 OF THIS CATALOGUE. SOLD UNDER OUR LIBERAL 30 DAYS FREE TRIAL OFFER, AS EXPLAINED ON PAGE 283.

$115.00 THE BECKWITH PALACE GRAND PIANO.

A VERY HANDSOME PIANO WITH A FINE TONE.

MADE OF SELECTED MATERIAL AND SOLD TO YOU AT $115.00, which represents only the bare cost at the factory, with but our one margin of profit added, the equal of any piano sold through other channels for $250.00, and offered to you for a 30 days trial in your own home under our great "send no money with order" plan. Sold under our guarantee for quality, running 25 years.

PIN BLOCK is built up of rock maple and holds pin firmly, thus preventing it from turning.

METAL FRAME is the same as used in all Beckwith pianos, but is not quite so large as in those instruments sold at a higher price, but it is just as scientifically cast.

SOUNDING BOARD is the genuine Beckwith sounding board, made of Canadian spruce of the best quality, specially prepared for this purpose, and it is ribbed in the most approved manner, which is a guarantee that the sounding board will never crack, split or warp.

FINISH. This piano can be furnished in either English quarter sawed oak, French burled walnut or richly figured mahogany veneer, very highly polished and hand rubbed. When ordering please state the veneer desired.

SIZE, 4 feet 7 inches high, 2 feet 3 inches deep, 5 feet 1 inch long. Weight, boxed for shipment, 780 pounds.

CASE is double veneered inside and outside, with cross banded, sawed veneer, and fitted with very handsome one-leg trusses, finished and polished in a beautiful manner. All mouldings, pilasters and trusses are of solid wood; a continuous music desk with handsomely raised panel in an artistic design; latest style of Boston rolling fall board. The hinges, pedals, pedal guards and metal parts are heavily nickel plated.

SCALE, full 7⅓ octaves, overstrung. Three-string unison in treble and two-string unison in bass register. Best quality Poehlmann piano wire strings. Keys of the best ivory with ebony sharps.

ACTION, very responsive, and adjusted in a most thorough manner, so that it responds to every call made upon it. All wool piano felt in the hammers and all bearings in the action properly bushed.

TONE is a full, rich Beckwith tone in all its beauty, but owing to the size of the instrument, the tone is not so full as in our Artists' Cabinet Grand Piano, but it is full and rich enough for all ordinary requirements.

THE PRICE INCLUDES a handsome stool with adjustable seat, a velour scarf, complete instruction book, and a certificate, which entitles you to ninety-six weekly lessons on the piano, covering a period of two years, as thoroughly explained on page 285.

A Profit Sharing Certificate, as explained on pages 1 and 2, will be yours if you purchase this piano.

REMEMBER, that in ordering a piano from us you do not obligate yourself in the least. We take all the risk. In shipping a piano to you we are only placing it in your parlor for examination, so you can see it and test it and know the wonderful value we are offering. We are only showing it to you so you can make up your mind whether to buy it or not. You will probably only buy one piano in a lifetime and we feel that as our prices are so remarkably low, as we can furnish you a high grade Concert Piano **for less** than others charge for a cheap piano of low grade, you ought to invest all that you can possibly spare. You ought to purchase, if you possibly can, our Special Concert Grand Piano at **$195.00** as we guarantee it is a regular **$450.00** piano of high quality.

Beckwith
Cabinet Grand
Chicago

$115.00 DEALERS ASK $250.00 FOR THE EQUAL OF THIS INSTRUMENT.

No. 46F7 Order by Number

No. 46F7 The Beckwith Palace Grand Piano, $115.00.

SEND US NO MONEY. DEPOSIT NOTHING IN ADVANCE.

We will ship this piano, freight charges prepaid, for a full 30 days free trial, as explained on page 283. Just send your trial order and write us the name of the bank where you wish to deposit the price of the piano with the freight charges **after it is received** at your local station and we will ship promptly. If the piano does not please you, send it back at our expense and the bank will refund your money. Remember that you assume no risk, because every dollar of **your money will be at your own bank waiting for you.**

PRICE. At $115.00 we furnish this piano carefully boxed, including stool, velour scarf and instruction book, all delivered on board cars at Chicago.

No. 46F7 The Beckwith Palace Grand Piano. Price....... **$115.00**

THE MANDOLIN ATTACHMENT AND THE MUFFLER OR PRACTICE PEDAL.

We furnish with all our pianos, without any extra charge, a mandolin attachment which is the best and most practical device yet invented for imitating the tones of the harp or mandolin. While this is unquestionably the best device of its character yet offered to the public, we do not advise our customers to order it in connection with their instruments. We find it necessary to furnish this mandolin attachment, as we frequently have calls for it, but in every case we advise the purchaser to substitute the practice pedal, as it is of much more practical value than the mandolin attachment. While the practice pedal muffles the tone of the instrument during practice, its use also preserves the hammers from wear and injury, while the constant use of the mandolin attachment is certain to injure the hammers to a greater or less degree, and impair the tone of the instrument in the same proportion. While we will gladly furnish the mandolin attachment to anyone desiring it, still we expressly recommend that the practice pedal be substituted for it. Teacher, pupil and the inmates of the home where music lessons are practiced will all testify to the practical value of the muffler, or practice pedal.

$138.00 THE BECKWITH ARTISTS' CABINET GRAND PIANO.

A PARLOR UPRIGHT PIANO OF STERLING QUALITY, excellent workmanship, neat and attractive case, offered under our "from factory to customer direct" plan. Guaranteed to be the equal of pianos which regularly retail at $300.00.

IT IS A PIANO OF SPLENDID QUALITY AND IS WARRANTED BY US FOR TWENTY-FIVE YEARS.

The material and workmanship are of an excellent grade and we are perfectly willing to ship it to you with the understanding that you will find it the equal of any piano regularly sold at $300.00 or it must be returned at our expense.

SEND NO MONEY. DEPOSIT NOTHING IN ADVANCE. We will ship the piano, freight charges prepaid, for a full 30 days free trial, as explained on page 283. Just send us your trial order and write us the name of the bank where you wish to deposit the price of the piano with the freight charges after it is received at your local station, and we will ship promptly. If the piano does not please you, send it back at our expense and the bank will refund your money. Remember that you assume no risk, because every dollar of your money will be at your own bank waiting for you.

CASE is made of the very best seasoned hardwood lumber, double cross band sawed veneers inside and outside. It is beautifully finished and decorated with carved pilasters and trusses; all mouldings and trusses in solid wood.

MUSIC DESK is of the continuous or duct style, extending from side to side of the piano and is very handsomely ornamented with raised design on the panel.

SIZE. 4 feet 8½ inches high, 5 feet 2½ inches wide and 2 feet 3 inches deep, and will weigh, when boxed for shipment, 800 pounds.

SOUNDING BOARD is made of the very best thoroughly seasoned Canadian spruce pine especially prepared for this purpose and universally used in only the best pianos. It is thoroughly braced by bars of the same wood. Ribs are scientifically placed, making the tone full, rich and sweet.

KEYS are tusk ivory, with ebony sharps, highly polished.

THE PRICE INCLUDES A HANDSOME SOLID WOOD STOOL, FINE SCARF AND COMPLETE INSTRUCTION BOOK.

No. 46F9

Order by Number.

The Profit Sharing Certificate we send you will help you get valuable articles free, as explained on pages 1 and 2 of this book.

FINISH. We furnish this piano either in English quarter sawed oak veneer, elegant burled walnut veneer, or richly figured mahogany veneer, as desired. The price is the same, and in ordering be sure to mention the veneer wanted.

ACTION responds instantly. It is a repeating action, built of selected materials and adjusted to a nicety. All bearings are carefully bushed with bushing felt. All hammers are genuine all wool piano felt; nickel plated action rail and brackets.

THE TONE is very full and sweet, pleasing to a wonderful degree. It is a Beckwith tone in all its purity and must be heard to be fully appreciated.

PIN BLOCK, in which the tuning pins are set, has four thicknesses of maple veneers, the grain of each running in opposite directions, making it impossible to warp or split.

FALL BOARD is of the Boston rolling pattern, the same as used on the highest grade pianos made.

SCALE is full size, 7⅓ octaves, overstrung bass, three strings to each note except wound bass strings, full length metal frame, and is so constructed as to produce a remarkably even quality of tone throughout.

WITH EVERY PURCHASE of this piano we give, free, a scholarship certificate in one of the largest music schools in the United States, which entitles the holder to ninety-six complete lessons on the piano, covering a period of two years, as fully explained on page 285.

THERE IS A REASON WHY we can offer a piano of the highest grade at a lower price than any other dealer. Our enormous purchasing power enables us to secure better prices than others for high grade pianos because where a dealer or agent buys one or two pianos and pays for them by turning in installment notes at a large discount from their face value, we contract for from two to three thousand at one time, thus securing the best possible price.

MANDOLIN ATTACHMENT. We furnish the mandolin attachment with this piano absolutely free of charge; or if the customer desires, we will furnish, as a substitute for this attachment, the Beckwith practice pedal, which muffles the tone of the instrument while the student is practicing. See what we have to say in regard to this mandolin attachment on page 289.

No. 46F9 The Beckwith Artists' Cabinet Grand Piano. Price..**$138.00**

$165.00 THE BECKWITH ACME CABINET GRAND PIANO

OFFERED UNDER OUR DIRECT FROM FACTORY TO CUSTOMER PLAN AT ONLY $165.00.

This instrument is in every essential point and feature identical with those usually sold by others at from $350.00 to $400.00, sold under our binding guarantee for quality and warranted for 25 years.

IF YOU CONTEMPLATE THE PURCHASE OF A PIANO, **the saving to you is so great when you buy a Beckwith that in justice to yourself you cannot afford to buy elsewhere before trying the Beckwith in your own home, under our liberal 30-day free trial proposition.** If at the end of the 30 days trial you should decide that you do not care to purchase the Beckwith, we would expect you to return it at our expense. We are always glad to see our customers purchase the highest grade we can offer in any line, but if you feel you do not care to buy the best piano we offer—our Special Concert Grand at $195.00, which we guarantee is the same kind of a piano as sold by others at $450.00 to $500.00—we then urge upon you the advisability of buying this, our next best instrument. It is a full size piano, but not quite so large as our Special Concert Grand. The tone is all that the Beckwith quality means, full, round, sweet and flexible. It is in every way a $350.00 to $400.00 piano. The saving that is yours in buying any Beckwith is only possible because we sell direct to you from the factory and accept a smaller margin of profit than has ever before been attempted on a piano, thus saving you every dollar that we possibly can.

SEND US NO MONEY. **Deposit nothing in advance. We will ship this piano, freight charges prepaid, for a full 30 days free trial, as explained on page 283.** Just send your trial order and write us the name of the bank where you wish to deposit the price of the piano with the freight charge **after it is received** at your local station and we will ship promptly. If the piano does not please you, send it back at our expense, and the bank will refund your money. Remember, you assume no risk, because every dollar **of your money will be at your own bank waiting for you.**

No. 46F11 Beckwith Acme Cabinet Grand Piano. Price, $165.00.

VENEERS. **Piano is furnished in beautiful San Domingo mahogany,** French burled walnut or English quarter sawed oak veneers. Mention veneer wanted.

MATERIAL AND WORKMANSHIP **are of the highest character,** and none but the finest of selected materials enter into its construction. Every piece and part finished in the most workmanlike manner.

METAL PLATE **is very strong and most scientifically cast,** and of such proportions that it makes the back of the instrument absolutely rigid.

PIN BLOCK **is built up of five layers of rock maple,** the grain of each running in opposite directions, which firmly binds on the pin and reduces the need of tuning to the minimum.

SCALE **is full 7⅓ octaves, overstrung,** three-string unison in the treble, two-string unison in the bass. All strings are of the finest quality; the bass strings are of the **best grade, copper wound.**

SOUNDING BOARD **is constructed of thoroughly seasoned, high grade, selected Canadian spruce,** especially prepared for this purpose; used in only the best pianos. It is thoroughly braced by bars of the same wood. The ribs are scientifically placed, making the tone full, rich and sweet.

TONE **is all that the most critical could wish,** of a quality absolutely lacking in a cheaper piano. It has a true Beckwith tone in all its beauty, and must be heard to be fully appreciated.

ACTION **is of a repeating style, responding instantly to every demand made upon it.** Constructed only of the finest selected material, well seasoned wood, oil tempered steel springs guaranteed extra quality of all wool piano felt, all bearings carefully bushed with bushing felt of high quality. Keys are high grade selected tusk ivory with genuine ebony sharps.

CASE **is double veneered inside and outside, crossbanded so it cannot warp, crack or split.** This case, veneered in San Domingo mahogany, quarter sawed oak or French burled walnut, is of a beautiful design. Paneled ends, beautiful hand carved design in the music desk and extremely beautiful finish. The music desk is of the duet or continuous style, extending from side to side of the piano. It has a double truss, Boston rolling fall board, continuous hinge, and all hinges, pedals, pedal guards and other metal parts are heavily nickeled and highly polished.

SIZE. **This piano is 4 feet 9 inches high, 2 feet 3½ inches wide, and 5 feet 3½ inches long.** Weight, boxed for shipment, 825 pounds.

THE PRICE, $165.00, **represents only the bare cost to manufacture the piano,** with our usual small margin of profit added, **and this price includes** a handsome, modern, solid wood stool, with adjustable seat, fine velour scarf and complete instruction book.

MANDOLIN ATTACHMENT. **We will furnish you, if you request it, without any additional charge,** a mandolin attachment, such as is advertised extensively by others, but we, by no means, recommend it, in fact, we regret to see a customer select the mandolin or instrumental attachment, because it is positively injurious to the piano. We much prefer that our customers select the muffler or practice pedal, which really has great value, in that it protects the instrument from wear and tear during the hours of practice. Please see what we say regarding the mandolin attachment and practice pedal on page 289.

TO THE PURCHASER OF THIS PIANO **we give, free, a scholarship certificate in one of the largest music schools in the United States,** which entitles the holder to ninety-six complete lessons on the piano, covering a period of two years, as fully explained on page 285.

IF YOU BUY THIS PIANO, **at the end of the 30 days trial you would receive a Customers' Profit Sharing Certificate amounting to $165.00.** You share in our profits if you order a piano, as we fully explain on pages 1 and 2 of this book.

No. 46F11 BECKWITH ACME CABINET GRAND PIANO. Price........ **$165.00**

$195.00 BECKWITH SPECIAL CONCERT GRAND PIANO.

ENTIRELY NEW IN DESIGN, BEAUTIFUL IN FINISH AND SPLENDID IN TONAL QUALITY.

A piano of the very highest possible attainment and sold by us under our great money saving method. Piano agents, retailers and other dealers easily secure from $450.00 to $500.00 for exactly the same kind of a piano.

WE OFFER THIS INSTRUMENT **as the finest type of the art of piano construction,** of the same grade and quality as the very best and most widely advertised concert pianos on the market, at a price never before attempted, and which means only the bare factory cost of the piano, with but our one usual small margin of profit added, all useless expenses of every nature being saved to you.

ONE GLANCE AT THE ENGRAVING WILL CONVINCE YOU **that so far as the appearance is concerned, this piano is equal in every respect to the very highest grade of concert pianos now on the market.** No engraving, no description, however fine, can give you an adequate idea of the beautiful finish, the artistic appearance of the piano and the splendid tonal qualities it possesses. It must be seen and heard to be fully appreciated and the opportunity of testing the instrument is yours under our great 30 days free trial, no money with order, freight prepaid plan, described on page 283.

BY CAREFULLY READING THE DETAILED DESCRIPTION **on the following page you will see that every point in the manufacture of this instrument** has received the utmost consideration and we assure you none but the finest material and the best workmanship enter into its construction. In offering this piano, our Special Concert Grand style of the celebrated Beckwith make, we are offering an instrument which represents the acme of piano perfection.

SEND NO MONEY.

Deposit nothing in advance. We will ship this piano, freight charges prepaid, for a full 30 days free trial, as explained on page 283.

Just send your trial order and write us the name of the bank where you wish to deposit the cost of the piano and the freight charges after it is received at your local station, and we will ship promptly. If the piano does not please you, send it back at our expense and the bank will refund your money. Remember, you assume no risk because every dollar of your money will be at your own bank waiting for you.

Veneered in quarter sawed oak, French burled walnut or San Domingo mahogany. Be sure to state veneer wanted.

Height, 4 ft. 10 in.
Length, 5 ft. 6 in.
Width, 2 ft. 4 in.
Shipping Weight, 1,000 pounds.

No. 46F13 The Beckwith Special Concert Grand, $195.00. Guaranteed with a written, binding guarantee for quality and workmanship for 25 years. Price includes a fine solid wood modern piano stool, also a handsome velour scarf, complete instruction book, and a full two years course of instruction, in one of the largest music schools in the country.

IN PURCHASING THIS PIANO FROM US you secure two distinct and well defined values. The first is the value which the piano takes from the high class workmanship and skill and the excellent material which enters into its construction. This is the only value for which we ask you to pay. We ask you $195.00 for this splendid piano, and this amount represents the cost of the material and labor, with but our one small profit added. Another value which you obtain is the value which the instrument takes from the genius and skill of the man who drew and perfected the scale, designed the mechanical features and combined all these points so skillfully as to make the beautiful tone of the instrument possible. **For this value we charge you absolutely nothing.** Most piano manufacturers add a large amount to every piano they sell to pay them for this value, but all we charge you for is the material and labor with a small profit added to pay us for handling the instrument. Up to the present time we are the only piano dealers who have been willing to sacrifice the profit usually made on the second of the two values above mentioned. While we do not charge our customers for this value, we absolutely guarantee that it is present in every one of these pianos and in the very highest degree.

IF YOU PURCHASE THIS PIANO, **at the end of 30 days trial you will receive a Customers' Profit Sharing Certificate to the amount of $195.00.** You will share in the profits of our business as explained on pages 1 and 2 of this book.

GIVE ONE OF THESE PIANOS A TRIAL **under our liberal send no money offer, described on page 283. Give it a thorough and impartial test for quality for full 30 days and we are certain that you will freely admit that it is in every way equal to any concert piano made, regardless of price.** It is true that you might pay all the way from $450.00 to $700.00 for one of those widely advertised pianos, but the difference in price does not indicate a difference in quality. Any amount above our prices represents nothing of any value to you. It only represents profits and commissions to jobbers, dealers, agents, etc., which is all avoided and saved to you when you buy from us. Be assured that no piano, no matter what price is asked, costs more to build than this, and no matter whether we ask $195.00 or three times our price, the fact remains that the piano could not possibly be made any better. It represents the very best in every branch of piano construction, and we will gladly send it to you under our personal guarantee that you will find it all we claim it to be, that you will find it the equal of any high grade, standard concert piano on the market or we shall expect you to return it at our expense. It is a perfect piano of beautiful tonal quality, of a flexibility and sweetness of tone which is only found in the standard pianos of the world and, under our direct from factory to customer plan, the price is but $195.00, much less than one-half what others easily secure for identically the same kind of a piano.

No. 46F13 Beckwith Special Concert Grand Piano. Price............ $195.00

THE BECKWITH SPECIAL CONCERT GRAND PIANO.

THE HIGHEST ATTAINMENT IN PIANO MAKING.

No. 46F13 Price - - - - - - - - - - - - - - - - $195.00

AS ILLUSTRATED ON OPPOSITE PAGE.

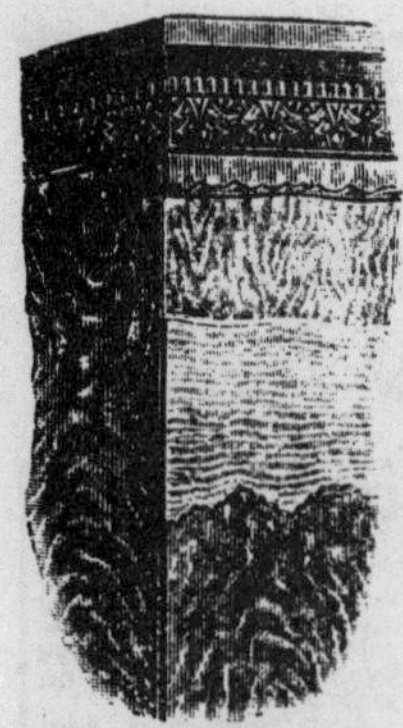

Fig. 1.

THE CASE. **The case of this piano is artistic in the highest degree. This beautiful design is entirely new, and was only adopted after the keenest competition on the part of several of the best piano designers in the country.** It is ornamented and tastefully decorated with handsomely executed genuine hand carving. There is not a particle of stained wood in the case; it is double veneered inside and outside in genuine woods and all pilasters, trusses, etc., are made of genuine solid oak, walnut or mahogany. All carvings are on natural wood. It is fitted with rolling fall cover with continuous hinges and has a handsome automatic two-thirds music desk. We believe it to be the most elegant piano that has yet been offered to the public, and will be glad to have you see it and examine it for yourself. The keyboard is supported by massive double pilasters and the pedals and pedal guards are of ornamental metallic design beautifully nickel plated and polished. The panels are very artistic and in perfect harmony with the richness of the very finely designed case. Each one of these cases is given an extremely high finish which takes from 70 to 90 days to apply. Each case is double veneered inside and out, and cross banded so that it cannot crack, warp or split. Cross banding means that the first or inner layer of veneer is glued to the base wood of the case under an enormous pressure, while the second or outer layer is glued in a like manner across the grain of the inner veneer, so that it will not be affected by climatic changes, no matter how severe. The engraving which accompanies this, marked Figure 1, shows how the veneer is placed on the piano case. These pianos are given a very high finish, each coat of varnish being allowed to become thoroughly dry, then being rubbed down before the next coat of varnish is applied. These successive coats of varnish give the case that smooth, glassy appearance so much admired in all fine pianos. As this varnish is perfectly transparent, of the very highest grade and most expensive kind, the delicate grain of the wood shows through it in all its natural beauty. In most cheap pianos the finish of the case is entirely superficial. This part of a cheap commercial piano is slighted just as all the rest of it is, and only about one-third the number of coats of varnish are applied as is applied to the Beckwith and the varnish itself is of a very low grade. **The design of these cases is everything that can be desired and will harmonize with the furnishings of any parlor.** We furnish them in English quarter sawed oak, French burled walnut, and San Domingo mahogany. Each case is thoroughly hand rubbed and carefully inspected before being turned out of the factory.

Fig 2.

THE METAL PLATE **of this piano is of the pattern known as a full metal plate.** There is no cap upon it, but it is cast in one solid piece and is of the strongest possible construction. It must be strong to resist the tension of the strings when tuned to pitch, and with the extra strong back shown in another illustration, this metal plate makes a piano of unrivaled strength and durability, powerful enough to stand, if necessary, twice the strain that is put upon it. Examine this plate closely and you will find it has bushed tuning pins, ample reinforcements and braces, and with the extra strong back it will be seen at once, by a reference to Figure 2, that with this foundation the instrument is as strongly made as human ingenuity can make it. The metal plate in this piano receives the most careful consideration. Not one single plate is accepted until it receives the most searching inspection at the hands of experts. The fault with many cheap pianos is, that, to the manufacturer, a metal plate is a metal plate and neither the quality of the workmanship or the quality of the casting receives any consideration whatever. The ordinary manufacturer of the ordinary piano is content to buy a metal plate at the lowest possible price, whereas, in the Beckwith the price is the last consideration. The quality and fitness of the plate must not only represent the highest quality in material, the most scientific casting, and be perfect in every way, but it must be the best that money can buy regardless of the price asked for it. Each plate is cast in the most approved manner and is thoroughly examined for any flaw or other imperfection. In casting the plate, allowances must be made for any tendency to warp in cooling, otherwise as the plate cools it naturally contracts, and in obedience to well defined natural laws the contraction would follow the line of least resistance and the plate would warp; this is guarded against in the casting of the perfect Beckwith plate. Should a plate be found which contains a so called blow hole, no matter how small or insignificant it might be, the plate is broken up. In the metal plate of the cheap commercial piano blow holes are numerous, because the manufacturer of such an instrument does not look upon the piano as an object of pride. To such a manufacturer the making of a piano resolves itself merely into the getting of dollars, and when an instrument has once passed out of his hands, with its many imperfections adroitly covered, it is forgotten. If a guarantee is issued with such a piano, it is of doubtful value and is more ornamental than it is useful; it is no protection to the purchaser because there is neither reputation or financial resource back of it. Not so with the Beckwith piano. This Special Concert Grand Piano is guaranteed with a written and binding guarantee running for a period of twenty-five years, backed by unlimited capital and a reputation of years of honorable dealing. We could not assume the responsibility of such a guarantee if we did not positively know that it is impossible to purchase a better grade or better quality of material than enters into its construction. The best of every thing goes into this piano. The highest priced veneers, the very best imported German steel piano strings, genuine high grade ivory and ebony keys, skilled workmanship of the best class, the highest priced and best selected piano felts and all that goes to make a recognized, standard, high grade, artistic piano. This plate is extra strong and very handsomely finished in gold bronze. From the illustration, which is necessarily small on account of our limited space, it is nevertheless easy to see how massive it is, how well it is braced and how securely it is fastened and bolted, together with the sounding board, to the extra strong foundation and frame.

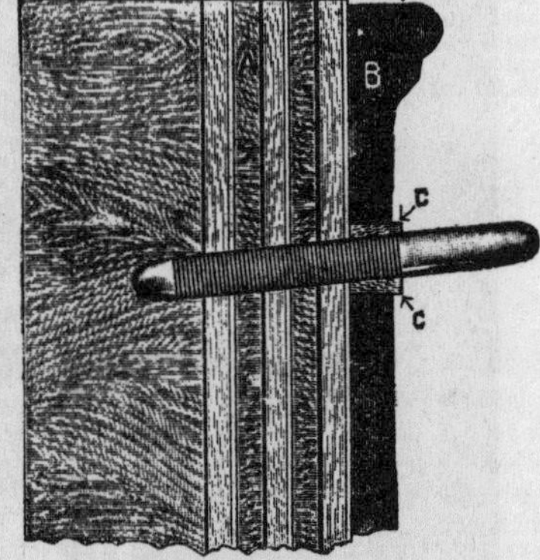

Fig. 3.
A—Built Up Pin Block.
B—Full Metal Plate.
C, C—Wood Bushing in Metal Plate.

PIN BLOCK. **The pin block is one of the most important features of a piano.** It is that part of the instrument which is built into the upper part of the foundation or back frame and into which the tuning pins are set. This pin block is also known among piano makers as a "wrest plank" and is made up of a number of separate layers of rock maple, as this is the best wood for this purpose. Each piece of wood is laid so that the grain runs in a different direction, and this in turn, presents to the tuning pins, as they go through the different layers of wood, a different face or grain. This binds the tuning pin and holds it firmly. In this piano is the very latest method of piano construction. It is equipped with what is known as "bushed" tuning pins. The metal plate of this piano is cast in one solid piece and extends from the bottom to the top of the piano, covering the pin block completely. Openings are drilled through this solid metal into which a plug, or "wood bushing" of hard maple is driven and through this bushing the heavily nickel plated, extra long tuning pin extends into the pin block. This wood bushing prevents over vibration, over brilliancy of tone, and also aids in holding the pin firmly, and by this method of construction the best tonal results are obtained. This late improvement is only found in pianos sold at $400.00 and over. The pin block in this piano is of an extra strong construction, as a glance at Figure 3 will convince you. It is necessary to make it very strong and to use an extra strong nickel plated tuning pin on account of the strain when the piano is tuned to pitch, which in this instrument is over twenty tons. It is one of the finest and most scientific pin blocks ever constructed.

SOUNDING BOARD. **This may be called the heart and soul of the piano and occupies the entire back of the instrument.** A good sounding board is made of the very choicest quality of selected materials. Over the sounding board the strings are stretched and the vibration of the strings is reinforced and the sonorousness is increased. It improves the quality of the tone and starts the vibration of the string, running through all parts of the instrument and out from it, when the string is struck by the hammer. Without the sounding board there would be no tone, the sounding board is, as you might say, the tone center. The importance of a good tone center is therefore essential. In the Beckwith piano only the finest selected spruce is used for both the sounding board itself and for the ribs or braces. Every piece of wood used in the Beckwith sounding board is carefully examined and tested. The making of a good sounding board is a delicate operation; especially constructed rooms and appliances must be used to bring out the most perfect results. The temperature is a large factor in its construction, as well as the proper consistency and the color of the glue used. Glue enters largely in the making of sounding boards and only the finest glue should be used. Furthermore in gluing the sounding boards the parts must be heated to a high degree of temperature so as to take the glue properly. In the Beckwith Piano the sounding board is of the highest type; it is thoroughly air and kiln dried until the wood from which it is made becomes as resonant as the top of an old violin. In some pianos the sounding board has a great number of ribs on it, and while these are necessary to protect it against warping or splitting, yet no more ribs should be placed on the sounding board than are absolutely necessary to protect it against these dangers. In the Beckwith pianos there are just enough ribs placed on the sounding board, no more and no less, and the exact number of these is mathematically determined by study and experience. We guarantee that the sounding board of this piano will not become weak or cracked, as is often the case with other pianos, and if this instrument is compared with other pianos costing from $450.00 to $500.00, we know that the customer will find that in volume and sweetness of tone the Beckwith is the equal of any other piano made.

THE ACTION **is that part of the piano, through the medium of which the tone is produced. It means the keys, the hammers, and all the mechanism that transmits the stroke of the keys to the hammer, and thus produces the tone.** The Beckwith piano is famous for its even tone and the remarkable quickness with which it responds to every touch of the performer. The Beckwith piano is fitted with a repeating action and the hammers come back into position ready for the repeat with marvelous rapidity. On a great many pianos it will be found that if you attempt to strike a succession of notes on one key, the hammer refuses to register any, except the first stroke, but when the same experiment is tried upon the key of a Beckwith each tone is distinctly marked, in fact it is impossible to strike the notes with such rapidity that the hammer fails to respond. **Each piece and part is selected with extreme care and is assembled only by experts.** Every bearing in the entire action is bushed with specially prepared bushing felt. All of the felt in the hammers and the action itself is of the very highest grade possible to secure of all wool piano felt. After the action is assembled and before it is placed in the piano it is given a most searching examination. Every piece and part is gone over. After it is placed in position and fastened into the piano it is then given a most severe test for responsiveness, for quick action and is adjusted and voiced to perfection.

THE SCALE. **This is the underlying or fundamental principle upon which all pianos are built.** It is a so called "lay out" of the strings, and in drawing the scale, the scale maker or designer determines, by mathematical calculation, the exact position that each particular string of the entire 7⅓ octaves must occupy across the sounding board; the exact point where the lower bridges must rest upon the sounding board, the exact curve in the upper bridge just below the tuning pins, the size and length of strings to be used for each tone; must determine exactly where each particular hammer is to strike each particular string so as to bring out the fundamental tone. If these points are not very carefully considered, the result would be an uneven scale, and there would be what is called a "dead string" here, or perhaps a "wild tone" there, and that is what you find in cheap pianos of the commercial grade. Such tones are to a piano what flaws are to a diamond, and the peerless Beckwith piano can be likened to a diamond that is absolutely flawless, as no such tone will be found in it. The scale is as clear and as liquid as running water from one end of the piano to the other. To give some idea of what is required of a scale maker in drawing or designing a perfect scale, it is necessary for him to know the number of vibrations per second of each string. For example, when pianos are pitched to international pitch, middle "A" vibrates at the rate of 435 vibrations to a second. The least number that the ear can detect runs to about 24 per second, the highest number that the human ear can detect is about forty thousand per second. All this he must know and he must proportion the strings accordingly. He must know the exact point on each string where the hammer must strike to produce the true piano tone; he must remember that sound travels at the rate of 1090 feet per second in the air and that these sound waves may be reflected, refracted, or deflected exactly as light waves are. The scale of a Beckwith piano is so perfect that you will not find a single so called "metallic" sound or an unsympathetic "woody" quality. The scale in the Beckwith piano is accurate and true and we defy the most expert performer to find a break in it from the highest to the lowest tone. The scale is the heart of the piano; it *is* the piano, and the Beckwith scale has been pronounced by eminent authorities to be perfect in every detail.

Fig. 4.

KEYS. **Figure 4 illustrates five Beckwith keys and shows how they are constructed.** A well made piano key must be made of thoroughly seasoned and kiln dried wood of perfect grain and absolutely free from any imperfection. This is the quality of wood used in the Beckwith piano keys. The ivory used is of the best grade of tusk ivory which is glued on to the wood under enormous pressure. The sharps are of genuine ebony highly polished. The keys are so evenly balanced that they fall back to their position instantly, after being struck by the performer, ready for the repeat. It is through the medium of the keys that the hammers strike the strings, or in other words, it is through the keys that the performer plays the piano, and this is one of the points of the Beckwith that receives the utmost care in construction and the most searching scrutiny and inspection when the piano is completed.

THE PIANO HAMMER **in this, our largest and best piano, is a genuine 14-pound hammer,** the greatest size and weight possible in any piano. This extra size, shown in Figure 5, is demanded by a larger sounding board area and longer and heavier strings. All these features, combined, give greater volume and purity of tone, and the increased striking surface in this hammer lessens the liability (which, however, is very slight in the Beckwith) of the felt hardening.

A hardened hammer means a hard and unsympathetic tone. The tone, and the scale, after all, is the piano, and as the hammer is what produces the tone, too much care cannot be given to it. No matter how fine a grade of string is used, the string does not vibrate unless made to do so by the striking of the hammer. The better the hammer in weight, the more nicely it is poised, the larger the striking surface, the better the quality of felt, the more perfect it is in construction, then naturally, the better the tone. It gives the string a chance to be heard to advantage. All of these essential points are combined in the hammer which is shown in the illustration and which we use in this Special Concert Grand Piano. The felt used is of the finest quality, selected for elasticity and firmness; the shank is large enough to withstand the hardest blow, but is not unwieldly and does not burden the action with superfluous weight. The illustration shows the new, special two-piece felt hammer, the very latest advancement in hammer head construction. It is the finest hammer that it is possible to make; and the peculiar quality in the felt of this special hammer head gives it an elasticity which is a large factor in producing a most beautiful quality of tone.

Fig. 5.

This improved hammer is found only in the highest priced pianos in the market; its cost prohibits its use in the cheap commercial pianos.

Fig. 6.

THE STRINGS. **This instrument has an overstrung scale, and is what is known as a three-string unison, each treble note having three strings, all of which are tuned in unison.** Figure 6 illustrates the way the instrument is strung. Each one of the strings placed in this piano is thoroughly inspected and properly tested before it is placed in position. The bass or heavier part of the scale is what is called a two-string unison. All strings in the Beckwith pianos are of the very finest quality Poehlmann piano steel wire. Each string is tested for strength, size, and perfect formation before being accepted. They must all be free from any trace of phosphorus or sulphur, otherwise they would be brittle or liable to crack. An imperfect string produces an imperfect tone, and destroys the uniformity of tone so much desired in a fine piano. **A good string is a very important part of a piano, as the string when struck by the hammer vibrates and produces the tone.** The sounding board vibrates in harmony with the string and increases the volume of tone, therefore, if the string is poor the piano will produce a poor quality of tone. The bass strings in this Special Concert Grand Piano are all copper wound.

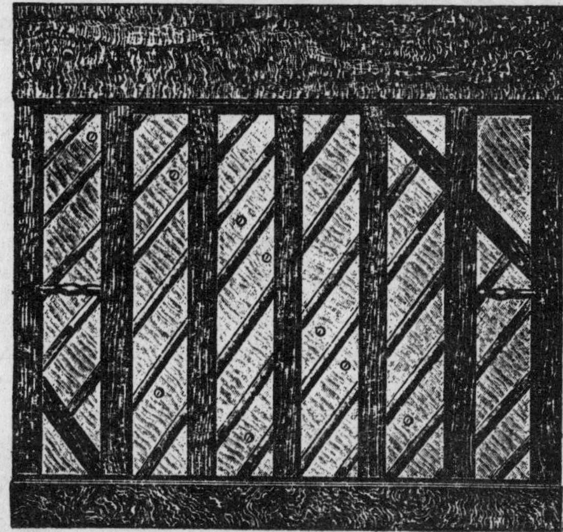

Fig. 7.

THE BACK FRAME. **This is sometimes known as the foundation and is a very important part of a piano, as it must bear its just proportion of the strain upon it when the piano is tuned to pitch.** The illustration, Figure 7, shows the seven massive uprights which are mortised into the top and bottom of the frame and shows the veneer on the two cross pieces as well as the scientifically ribbed sounding board. Into this back or foundation the pin block is built, and in a large piano, such as the Special Concert Grand, such a strong back is really essential. While the back of the piano really has nothing to do with the tonal production, yet many manufacturers give no thought to this important part and the relation it bears to the piano proper. Many piano makers use too few uprights in the back; others use too many and make them too heavy. It is unwise to burden a piano with superfluous weight, and a careful manufacturer, or one who studies this part of a piano, determines exactly the proper bracing to be used according to the size of the piano, the length of strings and other important features. The foundation or frame of a piano bears somewhat the same relationship to the instrument as a foundation of a building does to the superstructure, and therefore the maker of a high class piano bestows every consideration upon the back.

The wood in the Beckwith piano back is carefully selected and thoroughly seasoned. It really is a source of gratification to have every intending purchaser of this piano take the time and trouble to examine the back of this instrument, the uprights, the veneered upper and lower cross pieces, the general appearance of the back, the material, workmanship, finish, etc. If you will do this you will be convinced that the back receives the same loving care and attention as do the more delicate parts of the interior construction. It should do much to impress you with the quality of the piano as a whole.

REMEMBER, **you run no risk of any sort whatever in sending your order to us for a piano today, making your selection from the pages of this our general catalogue;** because we promise, agree and guarantee that you will find everything exactly as represented, illustrated and described, or we will cheerfully and willingly refund every dollar of expense on your part attending the transaction. If you are in a hurry for a piano, and you wish to have an instrument in your possession at the earliest possible date, then do not take the time to send for our free Special Piano Catalogue, but mail your order at once, making your choice from the illustrations and descriptions contained in these pages. You can safely rely upon each and every statement we make and can save valuable time in following this suggestion; but if you feel that you prefer to see our big Special Piano Book, the most complete work ever printed, if you feel there is other information that you desire before you place your order, then write us at once asking for our book, and it will be sent to you immediately free of charges.

If you are in the market for a high grade fine piano, then you cannot afford to place your order elsewhere, or consider the purchase of any other piano, no matter what the maker's name may be, before trying the high grade Beckwith of superlative quality under our great SEND NO MONEY OFFER.

THE MANDOLIN ATTACHMENT AND THE MUFFLER OR PRACTICE PEDAL.

WE FURNISH WITH ALL OF OUR PIANOS **without any extra charge, a mandolin attachment which is the best and most practical device yet invented for imitating the tones of the harp or mandolin.** While this is unquestionably the best device of its character yet offered to the public we do not advise our customers to order it in connection with their piano. We find it necessary to furnish this mandolin attachment, as we frequently have calls for it, but in every case we advise the purchaser to substitute the practice pedal, as it is of much more practical value than the mandolin attachment. While the practice pedal muffles the tone of the instrument during practice, its use also preserves the hammers from wear and injury, while the constant use of the mandolin attachment is certain to injure the hammers to a greater or less degree, and impair the tone of the instrument in the same proportion. While we will gladly furnish the mandolin attachment to anyone desiring it, still we expressly recommend that the practice pedal be substituted for it. Teacher, pupil and the inmates of the home where music lessons are practiced will all testify to the practical value of the muffler or practice pedal. Be sure and state which attachment you desire, but we urge the use of the practice pedal and advise **against** the mandolin attachment.

No. 46F13 Beckwith Special Concert Grand Piano. Price..**$195.00**

BECKWITH ORGANS

HIGHEST AWARD AT ST. LOUIS WORLD'S FAIR

A MAGNIFICENT LINE OF

REED ORGANS

WHICH FOR DURABILITY OF CONSTRUCTION, ELEGANCE OF APPEARANCE, BEAUTY OF FINISH AND MUSICAL CAPACITY IS SUPERIOR TO ANY IN THE WORLD.

ON THE FOLLOWING PAGES **you will find illustrated and described the most beautiful line of church and parlor organs ever offered to the American public.** All of these organs are manufactured under our direct supervision, fully guaranteed by us for 25 years and sold under our liberal terms of shipment as outlined and explained on page 283 of this catalogue. **The Beckwith Organ Company has established two of the largest organ factories in the world** for the purpose of manufacturing these splendid instruments. In these factories they have installed the very latest improved labor saving organ making machinery, the very best system of handling materials, employed the most skilful and experienced workmen and established the most rigid system of inspection. We take the entire output of these two immense factories and so popular have the Beckwith organs become that the capacity of these two big plants is taxed to the utmost to supply the demand. These organ factories are being enlarged and the increased capacity guarantees prompt shipment on all orders. Our immense organ business is not the result of chance or a combination of favorable circumstances, but has been built up through a careful and conscientious attention to details, untiring efforts to perfect these splendid instruments, prompt service to our customers, a careful consideration of their wants and interests and the fact that we can sell high grade splendid organs for less money than any other house in the world. If you could visit one of our great factories either at Louisville, Ky., or St. Paul, Minn., examine the great labor saving machines, the modern, up to date methods of manufacture and see the immense number of organs turned out daily you would realize at once that we are in a position to make lower prices than any other dealer in the world. If you could witness the careful attention to details, the strict system of examination and inspection and examine the high grade of material purchased by the factory for these instruments, you would not wonder that we gladly guarantee them for a quarter of a century. Upon every employe of these great factories, from the superintendent to the shipping clerk, rests the responsibility for the excellence of the instruments turned out, and so thorough is our system of inspection that should a defect appear in any organ we could immediately place our hands upon the man responsible for it. It is this strict supervision on our part which has placed the Beckwith organs upon such a high plane and made them the standard of organ value throughout the world.

OUR LOW PRICES. **Why should you be afraid of our low prices?** High prices on organs have been established and maintained for such a long time that many people are apt to believe that they cannot purchase a good organ for less than from $75.00 to $150.00, according to its grade and musical capacity. This is absolutely true under the usual method of sale, where the instruments are passed through the hands of several dealers before they reach their destination in the home; because, as each dealer has to make his profit, and as this profit must be included in the ultimate price, the amount that you are compelled to give for the organ will depend altogether upon the number of profits included in it and the amount of money you are willing to part with, rather than upon the cost of manufacturing it. Under our method of sale the instrument is shipped direct from the factory to you, and the only profit included in the price you pay is the one small profit which we add to the manufacturing cost. The price which we charge you for the organ is based upon the actual manufacturing cost and is the same to all of our customers. No other dealer can afford to sell organs at the same small margin of profit that we do, because the system under which he sells will not admit of it, and the number of organs sold is so few, as compared with our immense business, that it is necessary for him to make a large profit on each organ sold or go out of business. He must carry his organs in stock for a long time before he secures a customer, and it would be very poor business policy for him to tie up his money in this way without securing a large return on his investment. All organs become shop worn after being carried in stock for a short time, and must either be sold as second hand at a loss to the dealer or polished up and palmed off as new at a loss to the customer. Not only do we save you a large amount of money in the difference between our small profit and the several large profits which you would have to pay if you purchased your organ in the usual way, but we also make you a large saving on account of the great buying advantages which we possess. As we take the entire output of the three great Beckwith organ factories we secure these instruments at the exact manufacturing cost and sell them to you at the same figures with but our one small margin of profit added. Our inexpensive method of handling business is another point to be considered. Our organ department is but one of 63 large merchandise departments in our house, occupies but a small office space, employs very few people, never sends out any traveling men, never has to rent store rooms or store buildings for exhibition purposes and receives its business from a few inexpensive pages in this large catalogue. We give you the benefit of all of this saving. When you consider the following facts: First, that we own all of our organs at the exact cost to manufacture, because we take the entire output of the two immense Beckwith organ factories; second, that we can handle the business at a much less expense, because our organ department is only one small section of our immense institution and uses but a small space in this big catalogue, and, third, that we sell these organs in such immense quantities (having sold over 125 in a day), that a very small amount added to the manufacturing cost yields us a sufficient profit, we know you will be convinced at once that we are in a position to sell you a high grade organ at about one-half the price which any other dealer will charge you.

THE QUESTION OF QUALITY **is one which we have constantly kept in view since we first began the exclusive sale of the Beckwith organs.** The prices on our organs have never been lowered as the result of a reduction in the quality of the instruments. On the contrary, the quality of these instruments has grown higher as the prices have become lower. Labor saving machinery, skilful workmen and a great saving in buying and selling have brought about this great result. As we guarantee each one of these organs for a period of 25 years it is absolutely necessary for us to put into them the very best material and the most skilled workmanship obtainable, so that they will be certain to last and prove satisfactory during the entire period for which they are guaranteed. Our immense organ business has been built up on the basis of quality. Quality of tone, quality of finish, quality of design, quality of material and quality of workmanship have all combined to make **the Beckwith organs the standard of quality throughout the world.** With the Beckwith organs it is quality first and price second, and you are always sure of receiving the very highest quality no matter how low the price may be.

UNITED STATES OF AMERICA
UNIVERSAL EXPOSITION SAINT LOUIS MDCCCCIV
COMMEMORATING THE ACQUISITION OF THE LOUISIANA TERRITORY
THE INTERNATIONAL JURY OF AWARDS HAS CONFERRED A
MEDAL
UPON
BECKWITH REED ORGANS.

Diploma of Merit awarded the Beckwith Organs.

WE ARE SHOWING **on this page a reproduction of the great diploma of merit awarded by the St. Louis World's Fair** to the magnificent exhibit of Beckwith organs at the Louisiana Purchase Exposition. This exhibit was viewed by the thousands of visitors to the Liberal Arts Building and was a great surprise to musicians and manufacturers from all over the world. The high quality of the instruments awakened the admiration of all and the extremely low prices quoted astonished organ dealers and manufacturers alike. It was a signal triumph for the Beckwith line of organs and demonstrated to the entire world that our method of manufacturing and selling organs is the only one which will give the customer full value for his money. It was conceded from the beginning that the Beckwith organs would secure the highest prize offered for such an exhibit and the result fully confirmed these expectations, because the Superior Jury of Awards was unanimous in voting **the highest award to the Beckwith organs.** Not only were the Beckwith organs awarded the splendid diploma shown on this page, but they were also granted a medal for superior excellence of construction, great musical capacity, beauty of appearance and modern design. That the Superior Jury of Awards should grant the Beckwith organs the highest award, effectually and finally answers the question as to which is the standard line of organs of the world. When you buy one of the Beckwith organs you are not only buying an instrument which is covered by our binding 25-year guarantee, but you are also buying an instrument which the very highest authority in the world has declared to be **the unquestioned standard of organ quality.**

THE BECKWITH ORGAN FACTORIES

THE MOST MODERN, THE LARGEST AND FINEST FACTORIES EVER BUILT FOR THE MANUFACTURE OF REED ORGANS

LOUISVILLE FACTORY.

ON THIS PAGE WE SHOW PICTURES of our two immense Beckwith organ factories. These factories are built for the manufacture of reed organs exclusively, and are equipped with the most modern, up to date labor saving machinery. In these factories the Beckwith organs are built complete from top to bottom. Every known method, device or machine which will in any way reduce the cost of organ manufacture or work an improvement in their construction have been installed in these two big plants. Producing as they do, the very highest grade of organs in the world, covered by our binding guarantee which is as solid as any national bank, and sold at prices which are at least one-half lower than any other manufacturer can offer, they cannot afford to overlook any improvement in machinery or methods which will in any way better their methods of manufacture. **When you purchase one of these organs you have the assurance that it is Beckwith all the way through.** The bellows, the reeds, the stops, the valves, the couplers, the swells, and in fact everything in connection with the organ bears the stamp of Beckwith quality. Most of the organ factories throughout the country purchase their reeds, stops, bellows and other parts from different manufacturers, assemble these parts at the factory, put their name on the case and send the organ out as their own manufacture. This is the commonest method of organ making, and the result is always an instrument whose future is uncertain at the very best, which cannot be guaranteed by any reputable concern, and is sure to prove unsatisfactory to the purchaser sooner or later. The country is flooded today with organs which are manufactured in this way and sold at immense profits by irresponsible agents and dealers whose guarantee, if they venture to give any, is not worth the paper it is written on. These organs are fitted with reeds stamped out of sheet brass, dummy stops and an inferior bellows, which is bound to leak and ruin the organ sooner or later. When the organ is put in your house it looks nice; the case is handsomely finished and the tone appears to be fairly good. So far as you can see it is a good organ. But when the agent goes away the real test of the organ begins. Will it last? Will it be as good next week, next month or next year as it is today? The United States Government guarantees the money you give the agent, but who guarantees the organ the agent sells you? When the bellows gives out, the reeds break off, the top connections break or the valves get out of place and the organ begins to show the natural results of bad material and poor workmanship, to whom will you look for redress? By this time the agent is far away and the only way for you to do is to call in some local repair man and pay him to tinker it up and put it in condition—if he can. You have made a bad bargain and there is no help for it. The only way to avoid this danger is to buy your organ from a reputable dealer of sound business and financial standing whose guarantee will protect you against any defect in material or workmanship which may develop in the instrument through use. **The 25-year guarantee which we send with all of our organs is as good as a government bond.** It is backed by five million dollars of capital and surplus, buildings and appliances which are worth five million dollars more and an immense business in all classes of merchandise. an asset which cannot be estimated. This guarantee absolutely protects you against any loss and guarantees the future of your investment during every day of the twenty-five years for which it is drawn. We are safe in issuing this guarantee, because these organs are all manufactured under the strictest supervision, by the most skilful workmen that can be secured, and directly under the eyes of men in whom we have the greatest confidence.

BESIDES THE TWO IMMENSE FACTORIES, pictures of which we are showing on this page, we **have a third factory devoted exclusively to the manufacture of the celebrated Home Queen Piano-Organ.** This factory is also equipped with all of the most improved labor saving machinery for the manufacture of organs and all of our piano-organs are made complete from top to bottom under our strict supervision. Nothing but the very highest quality of material is used in the manufacture of these organs and the reeds, bellows, and every piece and part is thoroughly and carefully inspected and tested before being placed in the instrument. The numerous and valuable improvements with which the Home Queen Piano-Organ is fitted require the use of many special and very costly machines which, while they are very costly to install, prove very economical in the end. as they enable the factory to make the magnificent Home Queen Piano-Organ at much less cost than any other manufacturers can make organs of much inferior grade and quality. In the making of organs our factories have found that the installation of the very best machines and the employment of the most skilful workmen is the very best kind of economy, as skilled labor and improved machinery always improves the quality of the manufactured article and lowers the cost of production.

IN ORDER TO MAKE OURSELVES PERFECTLY SECURE under this guarantee, **every piece and part which enters into the makeup of the Beckwith Organs is manufactured complete in our factories.** The reeds are cut, bent, tuned, voiced and inspected by men who have a peculiar aptitude for this and have made a life study of the work. The cutting of the different parts, the adjustment and connection of the action and the assembling of the entire instrument are all in the hands of men who are specialists in their line, have made a study of that particular branch of organ manufacture and are especially fitted for the work.

THE LUMBER FROM WHICH WE MAKE THESE ORGANS is all cut, sized and **seasoned in our saw mills at Lyons, Ky.,** is thoroughly inspected and selected by men who have had the widest experience in this line of work, and who make a business of purchasing this material for the Beckwith organs. In fact, we have left nothing undone to make the Beckwith organs the very highest standard of quality in the world. We have found it necessary to build these factories on a very large scale in order to give our customers the very best service and make immediate shipment upon all orders. As we guarantee them a sale for every organ they make, their buyers are able to go out into the markets of the world and buy organ material in immense quantities at the very lowest limit of price. The great modern. labor saving machines with which these factories are equipped have cheapened the cost of manufacture without in any way affecting the high quality of the instruments. With their splendid equipment they can manufacture an organ of the very highest quality for one-third less than it would cost any other factory to turn out an instrument of the same grade. All of this saving goes to you in reduced prices, and together with the great saving which we make in handling and selling, enables you to purchase one of these splendid instruments at a price which no dealer can in any way approach. We established these two big factories, not for the purpose of making a greater profit for ourselves, but for the purpose of giving our customers better service and lower prices. Every employe in these factories, from the highest to the lowest, fully understands that while the cost of manufacturing these organs must be kept down the quality of the instruments must be kept up, and that every piece of wood or metal, and every bit of workmanship must measure up to the standard of our 25-year guarantee.

ANOTHER IMPORTANT POINT **is that these two great factories have been established at points which are admirably located in regard to shipping facilities.** By making our northern and western shipments from the St. Paul factory and our southern and eastern shipments from the Louisville factory, we can place these organs in the homes of our customers at the very least possible expense for freight charges. This is a great advantage, because it enables us to make the freight charges on each shipment from $1.00 to $5.00 lower than the purchaser would otherwise have to pay.

ST. PAUL FACTORY.

THIS NEW SPECIAL ORGAN CATALOGUE IS FREE

THE MOST COMPREHENSIVE, THE MOST EXHAUSTIVE AND MOST BEAUTIFUL ORGAN CATALOGUE EVER ISSUED. FILLED FROM COVER TO COVER WITH INFORMATION, FACTS AND FIGURES CONCERNING THE MAKING, BUYING AND SELLING OF REED ORGANS.

BECKWITH ORGANS

SEARS ROEBUCK & CO.

CHICAGO ILL.

WE ARE SHOWING **an illustration on this page of the complete new Special Organ Catalogue, which we are now prepared to send free to all who are thinking of purchasing one of these instruments.** This catalogue is the most complete work of its kind ever attempted, and contains everything in connection with the making and selling of reed organs. It contains 84 pages of illustrations and type matter, is printed on heavy, highly finished paper with large readable type and illustrated with the most expensive halftone engravings. The cover is made of the very heaviest grade of cover material, and is ornamented with a beautiful panel in scroll work, showing a shepherd at rest, playing on his pipes. It has large illustrations of our organ factories, showing different sections with the organs in the process of manufacture. It shows the tuning rooms, the cabinet making rooms, the varnish rooms, the packing and shipping rooms, etc. Also a large picture of the Beckwith exhibit which was given the highest award at the World's Fair, with a full and complete description. It shows facsimile letters from the First National Bank and the Corn Exchange National Bank, both of Chicago, testifying as to the soundness of our financial standing and business methods. **On page 5 you will find outlined and explained our liberal terms of shipment and the new and wonderful free trial offers which we make on our organs.** Following this you will find illustrations of the indemnity bond under which we guarantee all of our organs, also the different certificates of deposit which we use with our 30 days free trial offer. Following this you will find a complete description of the different processes in organ making from the preparation of the wood to the final tuning and inspection. This chapter will give you many valuable suggestions in regard to the general construction and the vital and important parts of an organ, and will enable you to select your instrument to much greater advantage than you could otherwise. Following this are several pages which fully explain to you how we can afford to sell such high grade organs at such extremely low prices, and also giving you an outline of the methods pursued by traveling organ agents and dealers throughout the country. These pages explain to you how agents and dealers are able to make large discounts and allowances and pay commissions on the sale of their instruments. It clearly shows to you why it is not to your advantage to purchase an organ on installments, and explains the great advantage and saving to you in buying for cash. These pages also explain and illustrate the old method of buying and selling organs and clearly show you how many hands the organ must go through from the time it leaves the factory until it reaches you, and how many large profits are necessarily included in the price you pay. Following this you will find the different Beckwith actions fully explained, the number and names of the stops given and the names and characteristic tone qualities of the different sets of reeds employed. Then follow 46 pages illustrating and describing our complete line of Beckwith organs. All of these illustrations are perfect photographic reproductions of the instruments, are etched on copper plates and reproduced on these pages with photographic exactness. The descriptions are complete, full and exact in every particular. On the back pages of the book you will find a complete table of freight rates on organs to different parts of the country, enabling you to figure out the exact freight charges to your home on any organ shown in the book; also numerous testimonial letters from satisfied and delighted purchasers.

BEFORE SENDING **for a copy of this book, we ask you to refer to the following pages of this big General Catalogue,** and see if you cannot make a selection without causing a delay by first writing for this special catalogue. You are perfectly safe in making your selection immediately from the pages of this our big catalogue, for our complete line, our lowest prices, our most liberal terms are shown on the following pages. You take no risk whatever in sending us your order immediately without waiting to get our Special Organ Catalogue, as illustrated on this page. All of the illustrations are made directly from photographs and printed from wood cuts, accompanied by complete descriptions and show our line complete. Furthermore, you can purchase the organ upon exactly the same terms as if you had the special catalogue, and as the actual examination and trial of the instrument is the final and most satisfactory test of its merits, and, as we do not ask you to pay us one cent until you are fully satisfied that the organ is everything that you desire, it is much preferable for you to order from the catalogue which is now in your hands rather than to cause any delay by writing for the special book illustrated here. If, however, you feel that you desire larger and finer illustrations and more complete descriptions of these organs, or wish to post yourself in regard to organ making and organ values before making your selection, or if you want further information about the Beckwith Organs, we will be glad to send you a copy of this book absolutely free on request. If you don't, send us your order direct from the following pages. Don't buy an organ from anyone until you first write and get this big, handsome special free Organ Catalogue with all its valuable organ information.

OUR BECKWITH HOME QUEEN PIANO-ORGAN

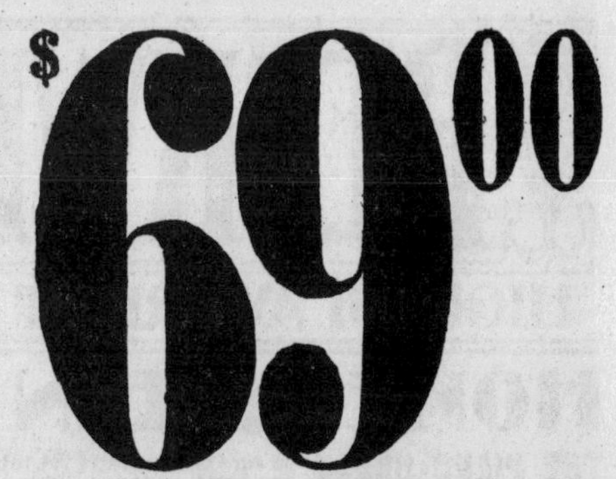

No. 46F115 ORDER BY NUMBER.

THIS is the same grade of organ which is usually offered throughout the country at $100.00 and $125.00, and we are only able to offer it to you at $69.00 because we ship it directly from the factory to you, charging you the manufacturer's price only, with our one small margin of profit added. We do not ask you to take our word for the merits of this splendid instrument as we make you the sole judge of its splendid qualities and you are the one to be satisfied in every respect. We furnish it in splendid mahogany, beautifully figured oak or rich, solid walnut. Be sure and state the veneer desired.

SEE OPPOSITE PAGE FOR DESCRIPTION.

No. 46F115 ALWAYS ORDER BY NUMBER.

SHIPPED FROM CENTRAL OHIO ONLY.

DIMENSIONS. This instrument is as large as a regular concert size piano, being 56½ inches high, 60 inches long and 26½ inches wide.

WEIGHT. Properly boxed and packed for shipment this organ weighs about 470 pounds. It is carefully packed and we guarantee it will reach you in perfect condition. We do not ask you to take any chances in this respect because we will be responsible for its safe arrival at your town. We would be glad to give you the freight charges upon request, or you can figure them up yourself by taking the weight of the instrument and consulting the table of freight rates given in the front of the catalogue.

REMEMBER, we will ship you this organ with the understanding that if you do not find, when you receive it, that you are saving from $50.00 to $75.00, at least, in comparison with the price which other dealers would ask for the same grade of organ, we will cheerfully receive it back, refund your money and pay the freight charges both ways. Our sales on these organs have been immense, owing to the extremely high qualities of the instrument, its handsome appearance and splendid tone. The piano-organ for which your dealer charges you from $100.00 to $125.00 ought not to cost any more to make than does our Home Queen. The difference in the price is made necessary by the profits made and the expenses incurred by the different dealers through whose hands this instrument must pass before it reaches you. This in many cases more than doubles the original cost of the instrument, and you have to pay the extra profits and expenses. We simply charge you the original manufacturer's price with our one small margin of profit added.

TO EVERY PURCHASER of this instrument we give a certificate which entitles him to a complete course of musical instruction on the instrument, consisting of 96 weekly lessons, covering a period of two years. In order to make this magnificent offer we have not found it necessary to add anything extra to the price of the organ.

The Finest Toned Organ He Has Ever Handled or Played On.

Mr. Foose's testimony is especially valuable because he is a thorough musician and knows what he is talking about. He was called in to test and examine the Home Queen Piano-Organ that we sent to Miss Florence Garrison, and he thinks it is the finest organ he has ever seen.

Conway, Mo.

Dear Sirs:—I want to say that I have seen the Beckwith Home Queen Piano-Organ which you sent to Miss Florence Garrison of this place and also played on it and will say that if anyone wants a beautiful piece of furniture, and an excellent musical instrument, they may send to you with perfect safety, for it is the finest toned organ I have ever handled or played on, and as soon as I can get the price I intend to buy one exactly like it. KYRTLE FOOSE.

It Beats All the Organs in His Neighborhood.

Frank Carlson thinks that the Home Queen Piano Organ is the greatest organ he has ever seen. He says that he saved at least $50.00, and there is no doubt about it, because he could not purchase an organ of this high quality anywhere else in the world for less than $125.00. Everyone of the thousands of testimonials which we receive testify to the great saving made by purchasing from us.

Ridgeway, Pa.

Dear Sirs:—We told our banker to forward the money to you on May 23d for the Home Queen Piano-Organ, which we received some time ago. We are very much pleased and like it very much in every way. It beats all the organs in our neighborhood. We feel that we have saved at least $50.00 in buying it from you.

F. CARLSON, 302 E. 2nd St.

The Home Queen Piano-Organ Better Than He Expected.

John F. Sills is a well known music teacher and has had years of experience with organs. He did not expect to receive such a beautiful instrument as we shipped him, and naturally he is surprised and delighted. His wide experience in teaching music and handling organs certainly makes him an authority upon this subject.

Follon, Wash.

Sirs:—The Beckwith Home Queen Piano-Organ was received on Nov. 21st, all in good condition. It was really better than I expected. The tone and action is good and the finish is the grandest I ever saw on an organ. The new patent octave coupler is surely one of the greatest improvements on an organ, and it is the easiest organ supplied with wind that I ever played on and I have played on a good many, as I have been teaching music for the past ten years. I believe that I am capable of expressing my judgment, as I have had years of experience in music with organs of all kinds and styles.

JOHN F. SILLS.

Likes the Home Queen Better Than a Piano.

Mr. Phelps of Pawnee, Okla., is delighted with the Home Queen Piano-Organ we shipped him. He says it has the sweetest and richest tone he has ever heard, and he knows what he is talking about, because we did not receive this testimonial from him until he had given the organ a thorough and severe test and trial.

Pawnee, Okla.

Gentlemen:—The piano-organ we purchased of you reached us on the 28th of May in perfect order without a scratch, and to say we are delighted with it is saying the least that could be said for it. It has the deepest, sweetest and richest tone I ever heard in an organ, and would be an ornament to anyone's parlor. Some of our best judges of musical instruments have seen it and say it is fine and that we surely got a bargain in it. My wife says she likes it better than a piano. With best wishes, we remain,

W. M. PHELPS.
L. G. PHELPS.

BECKWITH ORGANS

HIGHEST AWARD AT ST. LOUIS WORLD'S FAIR

MEDAL LOUISIANA PURCHASE EXPOSITION

HOME QUEEN PIANO-ORGAN

THE PIANO-ORGAN is an instrument which has become very popular in the last few years on account of its resemblance to an upright piano. This resemblance has been more or less exact, depending to a great extent upon the factory making the instrument. The piano-organs offered by other makers are all fitted with the ordinary knee swell levers which at once robs the instruments of their resemblance to a piano. This difficulty was never overcome until we fitted our Home Queen Piano-Organ with the wonderful pneumatic swell which is fully described below. A piano-organ is not an instrument which can be used both as a piano and an organ, as some people erroneously suppose, but is a reed organ placed in a piano case. We have spent much time, study and expense in perfecting this wonderful instrument and we have brought it to such a high state of perfection that it is beyond any question the very finest piano-organ ever offered. We could easily obtain a much higher price for this instrument, but it is our settled policy to sell all of our organs at the actual manufacturing cost with but one small percentage of profit added, and we are, therefore, in a position to offer you this magnificent instrument for $69.00. Do not make the mistake of judging this beautiful organ by the remarkably low price we ask for it. Bear in mind the fact that our great buying advantage, our inexpensive way of handling business and our money saving method of sale are the only things which make such a wonderfully low price possible. All of the reeds in these splendid organs are manufactured, bent, tuned and voiced with the same great care and consummate skill which characterizes the making of the reeds for all of our other organs. We sell these piano-organs under our great free trial offers as fully explained on page 283 and all we ask is an opportunity to place one of them in your home and if the instrument does not convince you of its own merits after a thorough test and trial you can return it to us at our expense and we will cheerfully refund you every cent you have paid.

This organ is unquestionably the finest instrument of its kind ever placed on the market, and at the price we offer it, $69.00, it represents a saving to the purchaser of at least $50.00 or $75.00 on the purchase. This instrument has been steadily reduced in price owing to the improving and cheapening of manufacturing processes and the reduction of selling expenses, until we are able, at the present time, to offer it at this exceedingly low price. It is made in response to a demand for a reed organ which will exactly resemble a grand piano, and the engraving will show you that we have succeeded in producing an instrument which the casual observer will not be able to distinguish from a $400.00 grand piano. In making this organ we have avoided the deadening and muffling of the tone, which is so common a fault with the ordinary piano-organ. Indeed, we have taken advantage of the shape of the case to produce in the instrument a large tone qualifying chamber, which amplifies and increases the tone of the instrument. By examining the engraving you will notice that we have avoided the necessity of placing knee swells on this instrument and their place is taken by our grand pneumatic swell.

See our wonderfully liberal terms of shipment fully outlined and explained on page 283 of this catalogue.

CASE.

The case of this organ is in every way equal to the case on an ordinary piano and can be furnished in San Domingo mahogany only. It is veneered like any piano case and given the same high finish. The wood of this case is so treated by the finisher as to show the beautiful grain through the different coats of transparent varnish with which it is covered. The carving and ornamentations are the finest ever placed on an organ case of this variety, and the design is modeled after the most approved piano design. We have been very successful in selling this instrument as it has given such universal satisfaction. It has a full duet music desk which can be pulled forward as shown in the engraving and is fitted with a regular piano fall cover. This instrument is fitted with regular piano pedals and pedal guard of regular piano design, handsomely nickel plated and polished. While the engraving gives a very good idea of the design and ornamentations of the case it falls far short of giving you an idea of its handsome appearance and beautiful finish.

CAPACITY.

The tone quality and power of this organ is far superior to the ordinary reed organ and it is fitted with three full sets of reeds and has a 7⅓-octave keyboard. It has 238 reeds in all and these can be formed into an immense number of harmonious combinations by the aid of the stops which can be seen in the engravings directly over the name of the organ. These stops are so arranged as not to be noticeable by the casual observer and do not detract from the piano effect in any way. The reeds are all the celebrated Newell reeds, are made of solid brass of the highest grade and the tongues are double riveted to the reed block. They are all tuned and bent especially for this instrument and we can guarantee their volume and sweetness of tone. The peculiar shape of the inside of the case adds to the singing quality and tone power of these reeds, and when the full power of the bellows is turned on, the effect of their different combinations is startling in its beauty.

GRAND PNEUMATIC SWELL.

This organ contains several improvements not found on any other instrument, among which is the grand pneumatic swell. This swell is placed on the organ to avoid incumbering it with knee swells. It is automatically opened by air pressure when the pedals are pumped hard and closes automatically when they are pumped lightly. When the performer desires to get more power out of the organ he naturally pumps the instrument harder and this opens the swell, allowing the full power of the organ to be heard, and when he does not desire such a volume of tone he naturally pumps the pedals with less violence and the swell closes, reducing the power of the instrument. This swell does not open suddenly, or all at once, but is opened gradually according to the power exerted on the pedals. This simple improvement will be recognized at once as being something especially fine in connection with the piano-organ, and it is not found in any other instrument on the market.

NEW PATENT OCTAVE COUPLER.

Another feature of this instrument is the new patent octave coupler operated by the middle pedal of the organ. This avoids the necessity of placing two extra stops on the organ, which would only detract from the piano effect of the case. It is an attachment whereby the tones of the instrument are coupled in both the treble and bass by pressing down the middle pedal. In order to release it, it is only necessary to press it a second time, when the coupler releases automatically. This will be recognized as a valuable addition to the instrument and will not be found on any other piano-organ on the market. The third pedal on this instrument gives the effect of a practice pedal on a grand piano, and adds to the magnificent appearance of the organ.

ACTION.

The action which we place in this organ is the very finest that can be obtained, and every bit of the material is thoroughly tested and examined before being used. Every bit of wood which enters into this action is thoroughly kiln and air dried before being worked up into the different parts for the action and so well are these things taken care of that we can guarantee our actions against defects in workmanship and material for a period of 25 years. All the different connecting parts are thoroughly felted with the best quality of wool felt, and all parts of the action intended to be air tight are covered by felt and sheepskin. In most organs the connecting parts are not felted and after they have been used for awhile they become loose and rattle. This is never found in the Beckwith organs. Every part of the action which we place in this organ is thoroughly and substantially built, so that the chances of it getting out of order are reduced to a minimum.

PIPE SWELL ATTACHMENT.

This instrument has fitted over the reeds a patent pipe swell attachment which so qualifies their tone as to make them a close imitation of the pipes on the grand pipe organ. This is an improvement much sought after by organ builders, but so far it is the only invention of its kind that has ever proven successful. It has caused the sale of a good many hundreds of these organs, and has never failed to call forth the highest praise of the performer.

BELLOWS.

This organ is fitted with the celebrated Beckwith bellows and reservoir which produces a powerful and well balanced tone. These bellows are constructed of three-ply built-up stock which cannot warp or split, and covered with fine rubber cloth which guarantees them against leaking. They are so arranged that the bellows exhausts the air in the reservoir, forming a vacuum, into which the air rushes through the reeds causing them to sound. The reservoir is fitted with our Patent Automatic Pressure Valve, which relieves the surplus air pressure and prevents the bellows being over strained by violent pumping. While these bellows have an extra large capacity the pedals are so arranged that the greatest amount of leverage is taken advantage of and the smallest child can sustain the full power of the instrument for an indefinite length of time without any great effort. By the bellows and reservoir combination which we place in this instrument, and in fact, all of our organs, we insure an easy and steady supply of air to the reeds and thus avoid that jerky, spasmodic effect which is so noticeable in other organs when the pedals are pumped violently.

THE STOPS.

All of the different sets of reeds which we place in this instrument are at all times under the control of the performer and can be worked into all sorts of harmonious combinations so as to bring out the real beauty of the instrument. These stops, or rather buttons, are easily within the reach of the player's hands and enable him to change the tone combinations of the instrument at will.

OUR OHIO FACTORY.

This splendid piano-organ is shipped direct from our factory in Central Ohio where it is made by the most improved labor saving machinery and skilful workmen. As this factory is centrally located, a great reduction in freight charges to all parts of the country is the result.

OUR 25 YEARS GUARANTEE.

We are willing to stand behind our organs, and we do not ask our customers to take any chances whatever when they purchase from us. We will ship you one of these organs with the understanding and agreement that if you should discover any defect in the workmanship or material within 25 years from the time you receive it we stand ready to make the defect good and satisfy you perfectly.

OUR 30 DAYS FREE TRIAL OFFER.

We send this organ out upon the same terms that we ship all our other organs and can place it in your home for 30 days, allow you to try it thoroughly and get the opinions of your friends before finally accepting it. How you can take advantage of this trial offer is fully explained on page 283, which we trust you will read carefully. Should you take advantage of our 30 days free trial offer, and the organ proves satisfactory within that length of time, we will then allow you one year in which time you can return the instrument at our expense and have your money refunded in case it should prove unsatisfactory. This is known as **our one-year trial offer.**

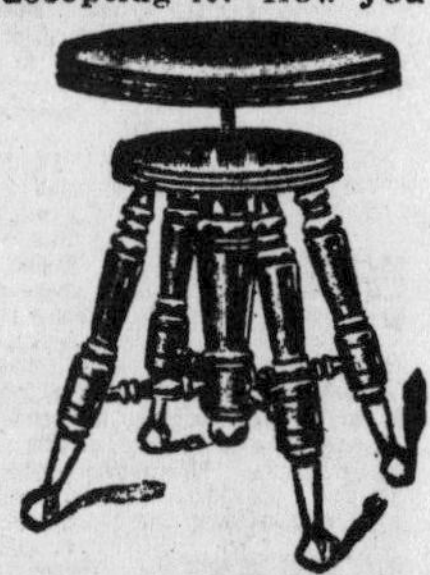

FREE.

We furnish absolutely free with this instrument a splendid stool, manufactured of wood to match the case of the organ, with handsome turned legs, brass claws and glass balls on the feet. We also furnish a handsome piano scarf, and a splendid instruction book by the aid of which anyone can learn how to play the instrument without the aid of a teacher.

YOUR MONEY WILL BE IMMEDIATELY RETURNED TO YOU FOR ANY GOODS NOT PERFECTLY SATISFACTORY.

$24.35 BUYS THE NEW BECKWITH COTTAGE HOME ORGAN

A FINE, LARGE, HANDSOME ORGAN WITH 10 STOPS AND 122 REEDS. GOLDEN OAK CASE, 78½ INCHES HIGH, 44½ INCHES LONG AND 24 INCHES DEEP. Weight, boxed for shipment, 450 pounds. Sold under our liberal terms of shipment and covered by our Binding 25-Year Guarantee.

THIS ORGAN is manufactured for those of our customers who feel that they desire an instrument in their homes and are not situated financially so that they can purchase an organ of a higher grade. To those customers we wish to say that this organ is a very satisfying instrument, and while not as fine an organ as the other instruments of our line, it is far superior to other organs placed on the market at a much higher price. We seldom advise our customers as to which organ they should purchase, but we desire to say that it is always the very best kind of economy to purchase the best organ that your circumstances will permit, because the small additional cost to you will be more than made up in the increased musical capacity of the organ which you purchase. Therefore, while we do not wish to discourage you from purchasing this organ, we suggest that you consider the other organs of our line, because every slight increase in price guarantees to you greater organ value, greater musical capacity, and a much more satisfying instrument in every respect.

No. 46F121
ALWAYS ORDER BY NUMBER.

CASE. We furnish this organ in solid oak with the case nicely finished. The carvings with which the case is ornamented are all carefully cut by hand. The case is of a good design, as shown in the engraving, and is one which will prove a fine addition to any parlor. It has a pretty canopy top, finished with hand carvings and turned ornaments and fitted with an oval top mirror. The music desk is very wide and covers a large and roomy music cabinet. The top is designed so as to provide for lamp stands and bric-a-brac shelves and gives a very pretty effect to the entire instrument. The case is fitted with handles, casters and fall cover with lock and key. The pedals are furnished with tasty metallic guards, covered with Brussels carpet and fitted with the Beckwith device for preventing the pedal straps from wearing out and breaking. The instrument is one which will appeal to every one of taste and good judgment, and if you will compare it with any organ offered by any other dealer at a much higher price we know that you will find it to be a superior instrument in every respect.

ACTION. We fit this organ with 10 stops, 122 reeds and five octaves of keys. It is furnished with two knee swells for operating the swell and grand organs, making possible a great many harmonious and musical combinations. It is furnished with the very best reeds, with vibrating brass tongues solidly double riveted to heavy brass reed blocks. All of these reeds are made at our factory; cut, riveted, inspected, bent, voiced and tuned by the most skillful workmen. A constant and steady current of air is supplied to the reeds by the celebrated Beckwith bellows with which the instrument is fitted. The ten stops are as follows: Diapason, Principal, Celeste, Cremona, Diapason Forte, Principal Forte, Treble Coupler, Bass Coupler, Dulciana and Melodia. It has four sets of reeds as follows: One set of Principal reeds, 24 notes, one set of Melodia reeds, 37 notes, one set of Diapason reeds, 24 notes and one set of Celeste reeds, 37 notes. Every piece and part of this action is fully covered by our 25-year guarantee.

THE TONE. We guarantee the tone quality of this organ, and while it has not the immense musical capacity of the other organs of our line it has a sweet and mellow tone of good volume and is very pleasing. The stop and reed combinations are those which time and experience have proved to be the very best for an organ of this character. Every stop on the organ can be used for controlling and shading the tone in some way and the organ has no dummy stops whatever. There are a vast number of organs on the market today fitted with dummy stops, 1½ sets of reeds and an inferior action which are offered at a much higher price than we ask for this organ.

WE CAN SELL YOU THIS ORGAN AT $24.35 because we give you the full benefit of every advantage which we can gain in buying, handling and selling. It is the very best organ that can possibly be made and sold at this price, and you must not make the mistake of comparing it with any other organ at the same price, because it is a physical impossibility for any dealer, not possessing our buying and selling advantages, to offer you such an instrument as this at this low price. While we are always glad to ship this organ to our customers, we would much prefer to have them purchase one of the other organs of our line, not because we would expect to make a greater profit on the sale, but because they would be sure to receive an organ which would give them much better satisfaction in every respect. As we make the same small margin of profit upon every organ that we sell, of whatever style and price, the only advantage to us in selling a higher priced instrument rests in the greater satisfaction and pleasure which the customer receives from his purchase. By all means purchase one of our higher priced organs if possible, and if not possible, then we will gladly ship you this instrument with the assurance to you that you are receiving an organ which cannot be duplicated anywhere in the world for less than double the money.

OUR GREAT 30 DAYS FREE TRIAL OFFER fully explained and outlined on page 283, makes it very easy for you to place one of these organs in your home for a full trial and examination before paying us one cent.

FREE MUSIC LESSONS. To each purchaser of this organ we give a certificate entitling the holder to a complete course of music lessons on the instrument absolutely free. This course of lessons will be given by one of the best music colleges in the country.

THE PROFIT SHARING CERTIFICATE for $24.35 goes free to every purchaser of this organ. It will entitle you to share at once in the profits of our immense business.

FREE. With this organ we give a very fine stool, made of wood and finished so as to match the case of the organ. The top is made of polished wood and so arranged that it can be raised and lowered at the convenience of the player. We also send a complete instruction book which will be of great assistance to the purchaser in learning to play the instrument.

No. 46F121 New Beckwith Cottage Home Organ. Five octaves, ten stops, oak only........$24.35

BUYS THE COTTAGE FAVORITE ORGAN

ONE OF THE LATEST AND MOST GRACEFUL DESIGNS PRODUCED BY THE CELEBRATED BECKWITH ORGAN CO.

THE BECKWITH COTTAGE FAVORITE ORGAN is a very pretty instrument in every way, and has become very popular considering the short time it has been in our catalogue. A glance at the engraving will show you that it is a very attractive instrument from the standpoint of appearance, and as we furnish it with an action of good quality it is sure to be very pleasing and satisfactory from the standpoint of quality and volume of tone. While this organ does not possess the brilliant tone, quality and great volume which is a peculiar characteristic of the higher priced organs of our line, it is an instrument which will give you good service and be very ornamental and attractive in your home. We ship it out under our 25 year binding guarantee and in order that it may last and prove satisfactory during this entire guarantee period we put into it a good grade of material and it is built by the most skilful workmen which we can secure. The Beckwith Cottage Favorite Organ is a substantial instrument in every way. The reeds are of high quality, the lumber of which it is made is thoroughly seasoned, the stop and reed combinations are adequate for the performance of any ordinary music, and we will be glad to have it compared with any organ which you may purchase from any other dealer at a much higher price. **$29.45** does not begin to represent the value contained in this instrument as compared with the prices charged by dealers all over the country for organs of the same grade. If you are looking for an organ at a moderate price, which will give you good service we strongly recommend this instrument to your attention, but if you desire an organ of great volume, with a brilliant, mellow and rich tone; an organ fitted with all the latest devices for bringing the tone under easy control of the player; an organ of beautiful design and elegant finish; an organ which never fails to surprise and delight the purchaser, we refer you to either our Royal Grand Organ or our Imperial Grand Organ, as these are certainly the most splendid instruments which have ever been offered to the American public.

CASE. **The case of this organ is of very pretty design, ornamented with neat hand carvings and covered with transparent varnish.** We furnish it in either oak or walnut and it is very durably and solidly constructed. It has a very pretty canopy top finished and ornamented in keeping with the general outline of the design, furnished with a large music cabinet so arranged that the front can be pulled outward and downward by the player when taking out or replacing music. The front of this cabinet is fitted with an oval French bevel plate mirror as shown in the engraving and the top is so arranged as to provide for lamp or bric-a-brac shelves on each side. The music desk is extra large and acts as a cover for a large and roomy music cabinet and the top of the organ is so arranged that there is room on each side of this cabinet for a lamp or music books. The entire front of the organ below the knee swells is one large panel so arranged that it can be instantly removed should it be necessary to examine the bellows for any purpose. The pedals are fitted with metallic nickel plated frames, covered with Brussels carpet and fitted with the Beckwith device for preventing the pedal straps from wearing out and breaking. The case is fitted with handles, casters, fall cover, lock and key.

ACTION. **As the tone is the most important feature of any organ** this has been well provided for in the Beckwith Cottage Favorite Organ. It is fitted with a good quality of reeds manufactured in our own factories with vibrating brass tongues solidly double riveted to heavy brass reed blocks. They are all cut, riveted, inspected, bent, voiced and tuned by the most skilful workmen. For full information in regard to the making of these reeds see page 308 of this catalogue. The stop and reed combinations are those which long experience and study have shown to be peculiarly fitted for an organ of this grade and every stop can be used in some way for controlling and qualifying the tone and there are NO DUMMY STOPS WHATEVER. For a description of the characteristic tone quality of the reeds in this organ see page 308. The celebrated **Beckwith bellows** furnishes an even and steady supply of air to these reeds, avoiding the jerky, spasmodic effect which you will notice on other organs when the pedals are pumped violently. The construction of this bellows is fully explained on page 308, of this catalogue, and we know that you will find it to your advantage to read everything that we have to say regarding it.

FREE MUSIC LESSONS. **To every purchaser of this organ we give a certificate** which entitles the holder to a COMPLETE COURSE OF MUSIC LESSONS on the instrument. This course of instructions will be given by one of the very best music colleges in the country, and will be complete and satisfactory in every particular.

FREE. **We furnish with this organ a very fine STOOL,** made and finished to match the organ. The top is made of polished wood and can be raised or lowered at the convenience of the player. We also send free with this organ **a complete instruction book,** which will prove a great help in learning to play on the instrument.

THIS IS A LARGE STANDARD SIZE ORGAN, **six feet six inches high, 44½ inches long and 24 inches deep. It weighs boxed and packed for shipment, 450 pounds.**

TO GIVE YOU AN OPPORTUNITY TO THOROUGHLY TEST AND TRY ONE OF THESE ORGANS, we offer the most Liberal Terms of Shipment, which you will find fully explained on page 283 of this Catalogue.

A PROFIT SHARING CERTIFICATE GOES TO YOU FREE **when you buy this organ. On pages 1 and 2 of this book you will find a complete list of the beautiful and valuable articles which we give in exchange for these PROFIT SHARING CERTIFICATES.**

No. 46F123 Action A, five octaves in oak. Price.......................... **$29.45**

THIS ACTION **has 11 stops as follows:** Diapason, Principal, Celeste, Cremona, Diapason Forte,. Principal Forte, Treble Coupler, Bass Coupler, Dulciana, Melodia and Vox Humana; also two knee swells, swell organ and grand organ. It has four set of reeds as follows: One set of Principal reeds, 24 notes; one set of Melodia reeds, 37 notes; one set of Diapason reeds, 24 notes; one set of Celeste reeds, 37 notes.

No. 46F124 Action C, five octaves in oak. Price............ **$33.45**

THIS ACTION **has 15 stops, as follows:** Diapason, Dulciana, Celeste, Viola, Diapason Forte, Treble Coupler, Bass Coupler, Principal Forte, Dulcet, Bourdon, Flute, Cremona, Melodia, Principal and Vox Humana; also two knee swells, swell organ and grand organ. It has six sets of reeds as follows: One set of Principal reeds, 24 notes; one set of Melodia reeds, 37 notes; one set of Diapason reeds, 24 notes; one set of Celeste reeds, 37 notes; one set of Flute reeds, 37 notes; one set of Bourdon reeds, 24 notes; 184 reeds in all.

If you desire this organ in solid walnut you must add $2.00 to the above price.

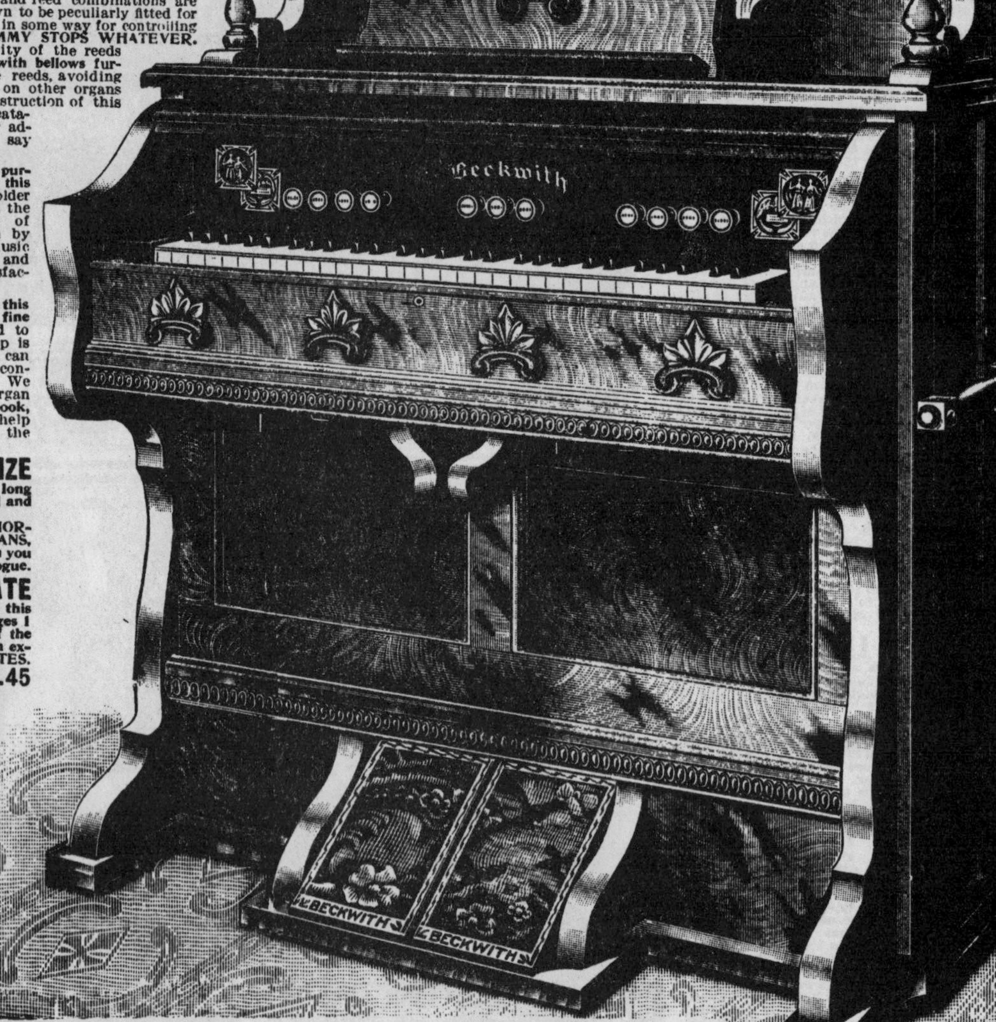

The Beckwith Cottage Favorite Organ. No. 46F123. Price, $29.45

ALWAYS ORDER BY NUMBER.

$37.35 OUR NEW PARLOR GEM ORGAN

THE FINEST LOW PRICE, SIX-OCTAVE COTTAGE ORGAN EVER PLACED ON THE MARKET.

AN ENTIRELY ORIGINAL DESIGN CONTAINING THE VERY LATEST IDEAS IN ORGAN CONSTRUCTION

81 INCHES HIGH.
54 INCHES WIDE.
24 INCHES DEEP.

Boxed and packed for shipment it weighs 530 pounds.

WHAT SOME OF THE SATISFIED PURCHASERS OF THE PARLOR GEM ORGAN HAVE TO SAY ABOUT IT.

Below you will find a few of the many testimonial letters received from customers who have purchased the Parlor Gem Organ, and if you are considering the purchase of an organ of this grade it will be to your advantage to read them.

ARE VERY PROUD OF THE PARLOR GEM ORGAN.

New Harmony, Ind.

To say that we are well pleased with the organ is to draw it mildly. The instrument came in good shape, and we are very proud of it. R. F. CARWRIGHT.

THE PARLOR GEM ORGAN A GREAT ADVERTISEMENT FOR US IN THIS COMMUNITY.

The organ we bought of you some time ago has been tested, and has proved to be a fine instrument, and the tone is very powerful. It is a great advertisement for you in this community. C. C. WALFORD.

THE PARLOR GEM AS GOOD AS ANY $65.00 ORGAN IN THE NEIGHBORHOOD.

Cedartown, Ga.

I have received my organ and am well pleased with it. Some of my neighbors say that it is as good as any $65.00 organ in the neighborhood. FRED SHAW.

THE TONE OF THE PARLOR GEM AS GOOD AS ORGANS COSTING $135.00.

Negley, Ohio.

We are very much pleased with the organ. We have had expert players to try it, and they all say it is a grand instrument. I saved from $20.00 to $25.00 in buying from you, and probably more. One player said the tone is as good as one she played on costing $135.00. JOHN BRAKRAM.

THE PARLOR GEM ORGAN IS THE FINEST IN HER LOCALITY.

Vaughns Sta., Miss.

I beg to say that my organ ordered from you is simply grand. Excellent in tone and quality and is considered to be the finest organ in my locality. MONIA MARTIN.

PARLOR GEM MAKES THE SWEETEST MUSIC OF ANY ORGAN IN THEIR NEIGHBORHOOD.

Wirtz, Va.

I have used the organ about six months and can say that I am very much pleased with it. My friends and neighbors say that it makes the strongest and sweetest music of any organ in our neighborhood, and I thought it my duty to tell you of the praise your organ receives. VIRGIE PEEL.

THE TONE OF THE PARLOR GEM AS GOOD AS AN ORGAN COSTING $80.00.

Jonesboro, Ill.

We received the organ and are very well pleased with it. It's tone is today as good as when we first got it. Everyone who sees it and hears its tone thinks it is fine. Our neighbor thought it had a tone as good as their organ and they paid $80.00 for theirs. MRS. PETER DUERCKHEIMER.

THE PARLOR GEM ORGAN BETTER THAN CAN BE BOUGHT FROM AGENTS AT DOUBLE THE PRICE.

Conesus, N. Y.

The organ came without a mar, and was just as represented. I think your organs are as good as can be bought from agents at double the price I paid. It has been tried by first class musicians and they all compare it with $75.00 and $80.00 organs. They say the tone is perfect. I will recommend your organs to all my friends. MRS. H. K. NARACON.

THE ORGANISTS ALL SAY THAT THE PARLOR GEM IS A SPLENDID INSTRUMENT.

Franks, Ind. Ty.

I had the organs tested by two good organists, and they say it is a splendid sounding instrument. I am satisfied that your company is honest and reliable, and can sincerely recommend your organ. REV. H. COLBERT.

BOUGHT THE PARLOR GEM ORGAN FOR ONE-HALF THE PRICE HE WOULD HAVE TO PAY AN AGENT.

Hogan, Ark.

I am more than pleased with the organ. It is much better than I expected. I consider that I have saved half of what I would have had to pay an agent for one, so I want to advise all my neighbors to let agents alone and patronise Sears, Roebuck & Co. I can recommend your organs to any who may want to buy. WM. HARDING.

THE PARLOR GEM ORGAN SURPASSED THEIR EXPECTATIONS IN SIZE, WORKMANSHIP AND TONE.

Vester, Ky.

We enclose you a check for the Beckwith Organ, the number and quality of which you know. The organ has proven very satisfactory in every particular. It has the sweetest, most distinct tone and has such pretty carvings. It surpassed our expectation in size, workmanship and tone. We thank you very much for kindness and accommodation shown us and we can praise you upon your integrity which will be done gladly. Everything has been fulfilled in the contract. Hoping to have a receipt from you in the near future, I remain. PEARL E. BREEDING.

No. 46F128 Beckwith Parlor Gem Organ (solid oak case). Price, oak.......... **$37.35**

If you desire the organ in walnut you must add $2.00 to the above price.

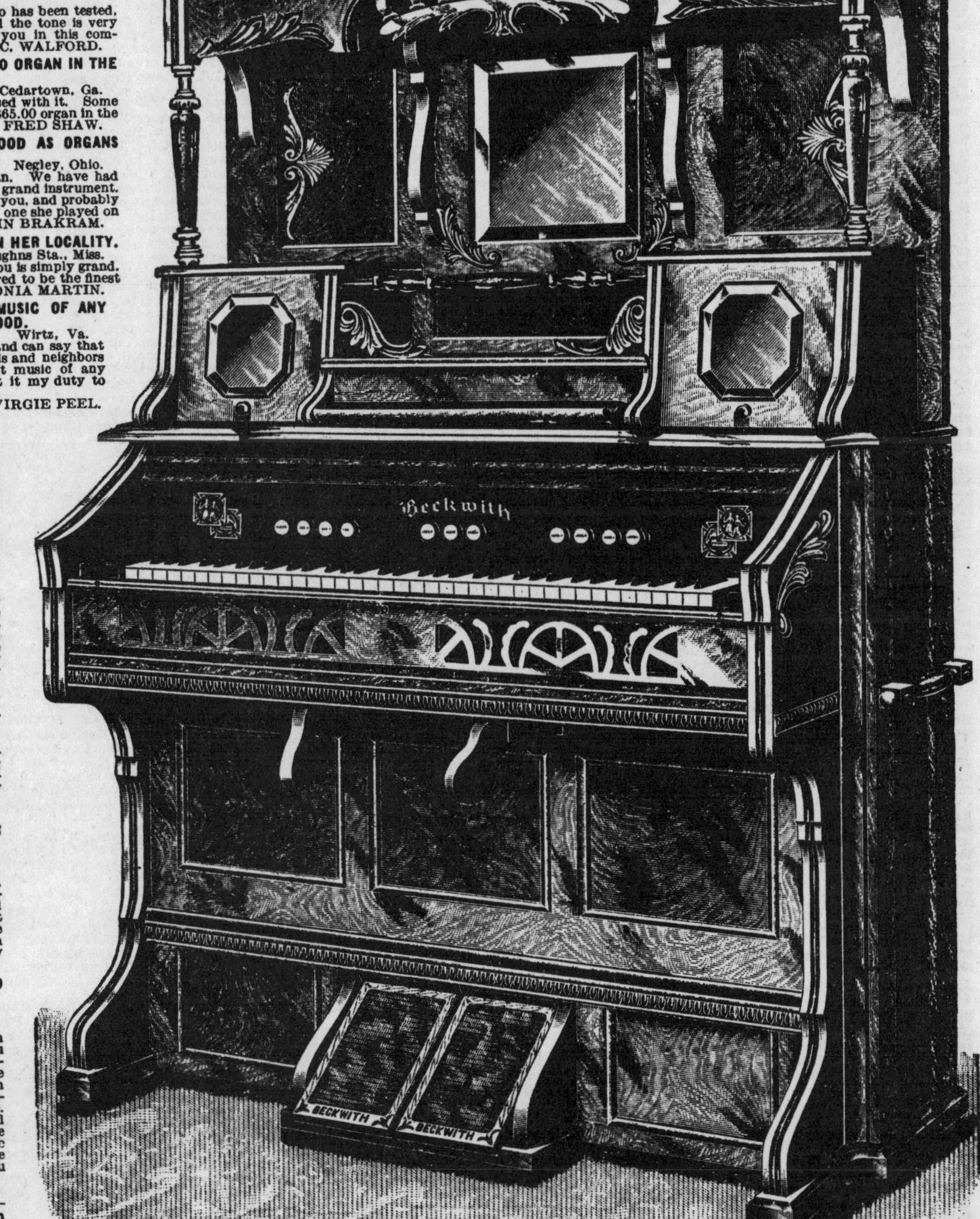

See opposite page for full description No. 46F128

BECKWITH ORGANS

HIGHEST AWARD AT ST. LOUIS WORLD'S FAIR

MEDAL · LOVISIANA PVRCHASE · EXPOSITION

BECKWITH PARLOR GEM ORGAN, $37.35

ILLUSTRATED ON OPPOSITE PAGE.

WE RECOMMEND THE BECKWITH PARLOR GEM ORGAN to all of our customers who do not feel able to purchase one of our 6-octave organs at a higher price. In fact, it is especially designed for those who are not able to purchase a six-octave instrument in our higher grades. We do not claim that this is by any means as good an instrument as either our Royal Grand or Imperial Grand Organs, but we do not hesitate to assert that you cannot purchase an organ elsewhere of the same musical capacity, the same number of octaves, the same number of reeds and the same excellent material and workmanship for less than double this price. If you do not believe that this statement is true, just give us an opportunity to place one of these splendid instruments in your home for a thorough examination and trial. Have it thoroughly tested by expert organists, compare it with any other six-octave organs in your neighborhood, and if you do not find, after such test and comparison, that it is equal, if not superior, to organs costing double the price, you can return it to us, we will cheerfully refund your money and return all the freight charges you have paid. If you have any doubt in regard to the quality of this organ, if anyone has tried to convince you that we cannot furnish a high grade six-octave organ at this price, if you have allowed any prejudice to creep into your mind, then in justice to us, the least you can do is to give us an opportunity to thoroughly satisfy you that everything we say in regard to this organ is true. We know that many prospective organ purchasers seriously doubt our ability to furnish a 6-octave organ at this price. If you are one of these persons we will simply say that we do not ask you to take our word for anything, we do not ask you to change your mind in regard to this matter, we do not ask you to alter any preconceived opinion that you may have in regard to our instruments, we simply ask an opportunity to place the organ in your home, and if the instrument itself does not convince you that every statement we have made in regard to it is true we will stand all the expenses of shipment, receive the organ back, and return your money immediately without a murmur. We will take all the risks of shipment, all the chances of rejection on your part, all of the responsibilities in every way and will not ask you to finally accept the organ until you are fully satisfied in every respect that it is just the organ you desire and up to your expectations in every way. If you are looking for a 6-octave organ at a moderate price, which will prove satisfactory under all ordinary conditions, be an ornament to your parlor and a source of entertainment and pleasure to yourself and family, we heartily recommend this instrument. **If you desire to place one of these organs in your home for a thorough trial and examination before paying us any money, you will find our wonderfully liberal terms of shipment and our great 30 days free trial offer fully outlined on page 283 of this catalogue.**

CASE. We furnish this organ either in solid walnut or oak. The case is nicely trimmed throughout with pretty designs, hand carvings and scroll work. All the carvings are made especially for this organ. The design is especially suitable for a six-octave organ and was selected from among a number offered by some of the best organ designers in the country. We put a high finish on this organ, the case being given several coats of transparent varnish through which the grain of the wood shows to splendid advantage. The case has a graceful canopy top supported by two turned spindles and trimmed with carvings of tasty design. A large French bevel plate mirror is set in the front, and the cabinets on each side of the music desk are fitted with lamp or bric-a-brac shelves. These cabinets have octagon bevel French plate mirrors and are so arranged that the doors can be raised from the bottom. There is also a very roomy music cabinet back of the music desk, which is very handy for sheet music. These are features not found upon other organs, and the great advantage of them will be seen at a glance. The key slip is ornamented with designs in scroll work backed by colored dustproof cloth. The front lower panel is all in one piece, cut into panel sections and so arranged that it can be easily removed should it be necessary to examine the bellows for any reason. The pedals are furnished with metallic nickel plated frames, covered with pretty Brussels carpet and fitted with the Beckwith device for preventing the pedal straps from wearing out and breaking. The back of the organ is so arranged that it can be instantly removed should it be necessary to examine the back of the action for any reason. The organ is fitted with handles, casters, the latest pattern of fall cover with lock and key. The entire instrument is very pleasing and the design is such that it will harmonize with the surroundings of any parlor.

ACTION. This organ is fitted with our action A six octaves, which has eleven stops as follows: Diapason, Celeste, Diapason Forte, Principal Forte, Treble Coupler, Bass Coupler, Melodia, Dulciana, Principal, Cremona and Vox Humana. Knee swells. There are no dummy stops. It has 122 reeds as follows: One set of Principal reeds, 24 notes, one set of Melodia reeds, 37 notes, one set of Diapason reeds, 24 notes and one set of Celeste reeds, 37 notes. 146 reeds in all. For a description of the characteristic tone qualities of these reeds see page 308. The reeds and stops are so arranged that they are constantly under the control of the player, and can be combined in many different ways so as to produce pleasing and harmonious combinations. Every piece and part is skillfully made and durably constructed and comes under the great 25 years' guarantee which we send out with all of our organs.

TONE. Great attention and study has been given to the tone quality of this instrument, as this, like all the other organs of our line, must measure up to the standard of Beckwith quality in this respect. The fact that all of the reeds in this organ are manufactured under our direct supervision at our factories, that they are all cut, inspected, bent, tuned and voiced by men who make a specialty of this work, fully gaurantees the tone quality of the instrument. The different combinations of reeds with which this organ is fitted are those which time and experience have proved to be the very best for an instrument of this kind. The reeds are all made of the finest quality of brass with vibrating tongues, solidly double riveted to heavy reed blocks. The celebrated Beckwith bellows furnishes an even and steady current of air to the reeds and insures a broad, deep volume of tone found in no other organ at this price. The reed and stop combinations furnish a musical capacity which is fully adequate for the performance of all ordinary music.

WE ALWAYS ADVISE OUR CUSTOMERS to purchase the very best organ that their circumstances will permit, because, as all of our prices are based upon the actual manufacturing cost, the small increase in price always means a great increase in musical capacity and genuine organ value. We aim to make the same small margin of profit upon all of our organs, based upon the actual cost of the organ at the factory, and when we ask you to pay a little higher price for one organ than another it does not mean that we are making a greater profit on that organ, but that the organ costs more to manufacture, and that the small increase in price is more than compensated for in the additional musical capacity and organ value which you receive. Under these circumstances we feel perfectly free in advising you to purchase either our Royal Grand or our Imperial Grand Organ if your circumstances will permit it, because it is the very best investment you can make in this line. The only advantage to us in the sale of a higher priced organ lies in the fact that you will receive an instrument which will be sure to give you greater satisfaction and pleasure than any you could purchase for less money.

YOUR OBJECT IN BUYING AN ORGAN is to furnish a musical instrument for your home and cultivate the musical spirit in the home circle. The primary object is to secure an organ which is a real musical instrument and not simply a fine piece of furniture fitted with a few cheap brass reeds and a lot of dummy stops. It is natural for everyone to admire an organ with a beautiful case and every organ should be fitted with a case which will prove an ornament to the home; but the musical quality of the instrument should not be sacrificed for the sake of a beautiful case. Organ purchasers are too apt to judge an instrument by its beautiful design and elegant finish. As it requires some knowledge of the mechanical construction of an organ to be a judge of its merits a large majority of those who purchase such instruments are entirely at the mercy of the agent or dealer from whom they make their purchase. They are too apt to select an instrument for its pleasing tone and beautiful case regardless of its durability of construction or musical capacity. The country is flooded with organs fitted with reeds stamped out of sheet brass and dummy stops which are entirely useless from a musical standpoint. These are things which you cannot see, and in order to avoid the danger of purchasing such an organ the only way is to buy from a reputable dealer of sound and permanent business and financial standing who will be responsible for the life and musical quality of the instrument. On page 308 of this catalogue you will find some pointers in regard to the making of a reed organ, which will undoubtedly prove very valuable to you when you are ready to make your purchase. A careful reading of that page will show you that not only are our organs fitted with the most elegantly designed and highly finished cases, but are also the very highest type of reed organs and have been selected as the standard by the Superior Jury of Awards at the St. Louis World's Fair. On page 295 you will find a facsimile reproduction of the Great Diploma of Merit awarded to the Beckwith organs by the Superior Jury of Awards at the Louisiana Purchase Exposition in 1904. This Jury of Awards is the very highest authority in the world on the question of reed organ construction, and the fact that they selected the Beckwith organs for this great honor is sufficient proof of the fact that these organs are the standard of quality for the world.

OUR SPECIAL ORGAN CATALOGUE IS FREE. We will be glad to send it to you upon request, and it will only be necessary for you to drop us a postal, saying, "Please send me your organ catalogue," and it will be sent you at once with postage prepaid. You will find a full description of this catalogue with a large illustration on page 297 of this catalogue. You are perfectly safe, however, in ordering our Beckwith Parlor Gem Organ from these pages, as the picture shown on the opposite page is printed from a wood engraving faithfully reproduced from the organ itself by photographic process, and the description given above is very full and complete. You can purchase upon the same liberal terms as if you made your purchase from the special catalogue, and we will allow you to thoroughly test and try it and satisfy yourself fully that it is a wonderful bargain and perfectly satisfactory in every way. As the real test of the organ is the examination and trial which you give it, and as it is necessary for you to see the organ and play upon it before you can decide as to whether or not it is the organ you wish, you can order from these pages as well as if you were to cause a delay by writing for the special catalogue. If, however, you should desire better illustrations and more complete descriptions than we have space for in this catalogue, then you should by all means write for this special catalogue before purchasing elsewhere. Remember, this catalogue is absolutely free, and we will be glad to send it to you on request.

THE VOX HUMANA STOP is a special feature of this organ. This stop sets in motion a fan, which gives a waving undulating movement to the tone vibrations, and produces an effect which is a very close imitation of the human voice. You will find this stop upon no other 6-octave organ but the Beckwith at this price.

FREE MUSIC LESSONS. To each purchaser of this organ we give a certificate which entitles him to a complete course of musical instruction consisting of 96 lessons and covering a period of two years, to be given by one of the best music colleges in the country, and the only expense to the customer will be the cost of music and stationery which we guarantee will not exceed 13 cents per week.

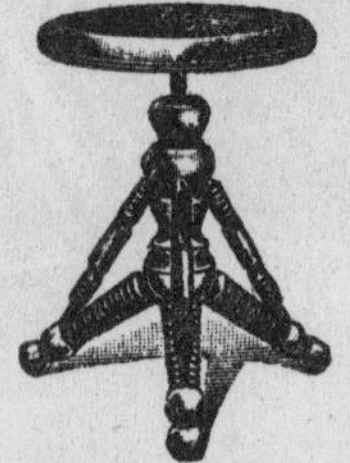

FREE. With each one of these organs we send absolutely free an elegant stool, highly finished and made in wood to match the case of the organ. This stool has a round, polished wood top, which can be raised or lowered at the will of the player. We also give a complete instruction book, which will be of great assistance in learning and playing the instrument.

WE GIVE YOU A

PROFIT SHARING CERTIFICATE FOR $37.35

WHEN YOU BUY THIS ORGAN

and you share immediately in the profits of our business. For full particulars of our Profit Sharing Offer see pages 1 and 2 of this book.

DIMENSIONS. This is a standard organ in every way, being 81 inches high, 54 inches wide and 24 inches deep. It weighs, boxed and packed for shipment, 530 pounds.

No. 46F128 Action A, Six Octaves, 11 Stops. Price, in oak..**$37.35**

If you desire the organ in walnut you must add $2.00 to the above price. Be sure to specify in your order whether you desire oak or walnut.

PROFIT SHARING ARTICLES FREE. SEE PAGES 1 AND 2.

BECKWITH ROYAL GRAND ORGAN $39.85

No. 46F140 See Opposite Page for Complete Description and Prices.

THIS IS AN UNUSUALLY LARGE AND BEAUTIFUL ORGAN, BEING 83¼ INCHES HIGH, 52½ INCHES WIDE AND 24 INCHES DEEP. IT WEIGHS, BOXED AND PACKED FOR SHIPMENT, IN FIVE OCTAVES, 450 POUNDS; IN SIX OCTAVES, 500 POUNDS.

FOR TERMS OF SHIPMENT SEE PAGE 263.

WHAT OUR CUSTOMERS SAY OF THE BECKWITH ROYAL GRAND ORGAN.

If you are thinking of buying an Organ, it will pay you to read the following letters which are just a few of the many we receive every year from the satisfied purchasers of these organs.

COULD NOT BUY AN ORGAN LIKE THE BECKWITH ROYAL GRAND IN NORFOLK FOR LESS THAN $75.00.

West Norfolk, Va.

I received the organ ordered from you and like it splendidly. It was far nicer than I expected it to be for that amount, and I do not think I could get one like it in Norfolk for less than $75.00. G. L. WILLIAMS.

CANNOT SAY TOO MUCH IN FAVOR OF THE ROYAL GRAND ORGAN.

Roscoe, Pa.

The organ reached me in due time without a scratch or blemish. Many have tried it and pronounce it good. I cannot say too much in its favor, but organs of its class will sing their own praises wherever they go. I. E. MORRELL.

CANNOT SEE HOW WE CAN SELL SUCH A HIGH GRADE ORGAN FOR SO LITTLE MONEY.

St. Charles, Idaho.

The organ is perfect, and I am well pleased with it. I had an experienced music teacher examine it and he pronounced it perfect. He could not see how it was possible for you to sell such a high grade organ for so little money. CHAS. S. PUGMIRE.

CANNOT PURCHASE AN ORGAN LIKE THE ROYAL GRAND IN THE COUNTRY FOR LESS THAN $75.00.

Echo, La.

I have taught music 31 years, and always use a good instrument. I have used many different instruments. I have sold organs for many music houses in the South, and know that your action A can't be purchased in this county or state for less than $65.00 cash, or $75.00 on installments. I have sold organs for Philip Werlein & Co. for 20 years, and several other houses, and if I can get your 46F140 for $39.85, I will save not less than $50.00. PROF. J. W. BROWN.

THE ROYAL GRAND BETTER THAN ORGANS AT $175.00.

Perryopolis, Pa.

My organ has been tested by a regular musician and he claims it is excellent. He says he never sat down to a better organ to sing by. He says he has seen $175.00 organs that he would not begin to give this one for, and it has proved satisfactory all around. MISS DILLIE M. HUFF.

OUR PRICES ONLY HALF AS MUCH AS THE AGENTS ASKED.

Logansville, Ga.

I think your organ is a bargain for the money. I came very near buying from an agent, but your price was only half as much as the agent asked for his. Mr. Bud Boss of this place bought one from an agent for $70.00, and mine sounds and looks as well as his. W. J. JOHNSON.

OUR ROYAL GRAND AS GOOD AS ORGANS AT $75.00.

Trenton, Miss.

Words fail to tell how well we are pleased with it. The tone is just simply faultless. One of our neighbors has one which they got from an agent for which they paid $75.00, and they like the tone of mine better than they do their own. I can highly recommend anyone to buy of you. ELIZA HASTINGS.

ALL THE ORGANISTS SAY THAT THE ROYAL GRAND ORGAN BEATS ANYTHING THEY EVER SAW.

Nap, Miss.

The organ is ahead of anything that I have ever seen in my travels. All the organists who have played on it say it beats anything they ever saw in every respect, and it has sold two for you. I tell the people that if I outlive my organ, I will send back to you for another one. B. W. WHITTINGTON.

DON'T SEE HOW WE CAN SEND OUT SUCH AN ORGAN FOR THE MONEY.

Benton, Tenn.

While the thirty days are not out, in which I had to try my organ, yet I am perfectly satisfied with it. I don't see how you can send out such an organ for the money. One of our neighbors has an organ which cost $72.00, and they like our organ the best. Mr. Mark Barker borrowed my catalogue the other day, and says he is going to order an organ from you. And I think you will be able to sell several organs at this place in the near future, and while it is nothing to me as to who they buy from yet, I can conscientiously recommend your company to any person who wishes to purchase an organ. JOHN S. SHAMBLIN.

WHAT YOUR FRIENDS AND NEIGHBORS SAY

is the very best evidence of the high quality of these organs. The letters printed above all come to us entirely unsolicited, and are only a very few of the many thousands we receive every year. We print these few testimonials to assist you in making your choice, and if you need any further assistance, either in the shape of advice or suggestions, we will be glad to help you. We much prefer to have you make your selection unassisted by us, but should you desire any advice or direction we will be glad to aid you to your advantage.

BECKWITH ORGANS

HIGHEST AWARD AT ST. LOUIS WORLD'S FAIR

MEDAL
LOUISIANA PURCHASE
EXPOSITION

THE BECKWITH ROYAL GRAND ORGAN.

ILLUSTRATED ON OPPOSITE PAGE.

WHEN WE OFFER THE BECKWITH ROYAL GRAND ORGAN AT $39.85, we are certainly offering you a splendid bargain. When you are ready to purchase your organ we want to ask you to consider this instrument, because it is a beautiful organ in every way, of great volume and sweetness of tone, elegant finish and graceful design. While we always advise our customers to purchase our very finest organ, the Beckwith Imperial Grand Organ, the most superb organ ever placed on the market, still we always take great pleasure in placing the Royal Grand Organ in the home of a customer, because there is no organ made today at anything like the price which can equal it in sweetness, breadth and volume of tone, beauty of appearance, durability of construction and general musical capacity. We will place this organ in your home and make you the sole judge of its merits, with the distinct understanding that it is not necessary for you to finally accept and pay for it until after a thorough trial and test you have made up your mind that it is everything you could desire in an organ and a splendid bargain in every respect. We do not claim what we cannot safely leave to your judgment, and when we claim that we are selling this organ for one-half the price usually charged for organs of this grade, we do so with the full knowledge of what other manufacturers and dealers are selling their organs for, the cost of manufacture and the exact amount of profit they make on their sales. We do not ask you to accept any of our statements in regard to our prices or in regard to the quality of material or workmanship which enter into our organs, all we ask is a chance to place one in your home. After you have thoroughly tested, tried and examined the organ, after you have received the unbiased opinions of your friends and musical neighbors, then, and not till then, do we ask you to make your final decision. For this purpose we allow you 30 days, which is ample time in which to test any musical instrument. We also allow you to return the organ to us at any time within one year should it develop any defect due to poor material or unskilled workmanship. Not only do we allow you to return the organ within one year under such circumstances but we also cover it with our written binding guarantee for 25 years which fully protects you against loss.

ON PAGE 283 OF THIS CATALOGUE YOU WILL FIND FULLY OUTLINED AND EXPLAINED THE WONDERFULLY LIBERAL TERMS OF SHIPMENT UNDER WHICH WE WILL SHIP YOU ONE OF THESE ORGANS FOR A THOROUGH TRIAL AND EXAMINATION SO THAT YOU CAN FULLY SATISFY YOURSELF THAT IT IS EVERYTHING THAT YOU DESIRE AND A WONDERFUL BARGAIN IN EVERY RESPECT.

DO NOT BE AFRAID OF OUR LOW PRICES. Remember that manufacturing processes are constantly changing as improved machinery comes into use, and that it costs less and less from year to year to produce the finished product. In former times the making of an organ was a very expensive process, and as a consequence the retail price was very high. But as more and more improved labor saving machinery has been introduced the making and finishing of the different parts have become less and less costly, and as a consequence the price of organs should become lower every year. But manufacturers and dealers generally have not found it to their interest to give the public the benefit of the reduction in cost of manufacture, and the high prices on organs are still maintained by manufacturers, dealers and agents throughout the country. In selling our organs we give you the full benefit of everything that we can save by purchasing material in large quantities, the full benefit of everything that we save by selling our organs directly from the factory to you, in fact, we give you the full benefit of all the buying and selling advantages which we possess and our sales are so enormous in consequence that we can afford to be contented with but one small margin of profit upon each organ that we sell. This is the reason why we can sell the splendid Beckwith Royal Grand Organ for $39.85.

CASE. We furnish all of these organs either in beautifully figured oak or solid walnut. The design is, next to our Imperial Grand Organ, the very finest on the market and is the result of the same careful selection and discrimination which obtained for us the designs of all of our other organs. You cannot find this design duplicated anywhere in the country, as it is fully copyrighted by us. The engraving on the opposite page is an exact photographic reproduction of the instrument, and while it will give you a good idea of the design and general appearance of the organ, it cannot possibly give you any idea of its elegant finish and beautiful tone. These cases are rubbed down with pumice stone, oil and water by hand so that all of the disagreeable gloss which comes from the varnish is toned down and the case given that deep rich finish which is characteristic of all high grade furniture. The case is ornamented throughout with elaborate and beautiful hand carvings and scroll work, and the scroll design which supports the keyboard on each side of the instrument is one of the newest ideas in organ case designing. It has a very beautiful canopy top, ornamented with hand wrought carvings, supported by graceful turned spindles and fitted with lamp stands, bric-a-brac shelves and a splendid French bevel plate mirror, 14x16 inches in size. The music desk covers a large and roomy music cabinet, on each side of which are fitted additional stands for holding lamps. The front lower panel is so arranged that it can be removed in an instant in case it should be necessary to examine the bellows for any purpose. The case is paneled and trimmed throughout with mouldings of the very latest patterns, making the entire design beautifully consistent and symmetrical. It has ornamental handles, casters and the very latest improved fall cover with lock and key. This fall cover is hung on a swinging frame so that it opens and closes without catching or binding. The back of the organ is so arranged that it can be instantly removed should it be necessary to examine the action for any reason. The pedals are covered with elegant Brussels carpet, protected by highly nickel plated metallic frames and furnished with the Beckwith patent device for preventing the pedal straps from wearing out and breaking. We do not want you to pass final judgment on this instrument from the engraving shown on the opposite page, as that would be entirely unfair to us. We would much rather place the instrument in your home at our own risk and let you examine it thoroughly and give it the most impartial test and trial before giving your final decision. We are prepared to do this with the utmost confidence that you will be both surprised and delighted when you examine it, and if you do not acknowledge that the organ is far above your expectations we will consider it a favor if you will return it to us and receive your money back.

ACTION. We furnish this organ with the Marvelous Beckwith Grand Orchestral Action, a most wonderful combination of stops and reeds which produce a wealth and volume of tone which is possible upon no other make of organ. This grand orchestral action can be thrown off and on at the will of the player by the use of the grand organ knee swell. You will find this wonderful action upon the Beckwith Royal Grand, Beckwith Imperial Grand and Beckwith Cathedral Chapel Organs only. The wonderful musical effect which it will produce can only be equaled by the largest church organ. Nothing but the most skillful workmanship and the highest grade of material enter into its construction. Every piece and part, from the pedals to the stops, is durably made and the reeds are all manufactured in our own factories of the very best quality of brass with vibrating tongues, solidly double riveted to heavy reed blocks. For a description of the characteristic tone quality of these reeds, see page 308. They are all bent, tuned and voiced especially for use in this instrument, and will produce a tone of great sweetness and beauty combined with depth and volume. The celebrated Beckwith Automatic Bellows furnishes an even and powerful current of air to the reeds, enabling the player to sustain the powerful tone of the organ indefinitely with but little effort. For a full description of this bellows, see page 308. All of our stop and reed combinations are under the perfect and easy control of the player at all times, bringing innumerable harmonious combinations within reach of even ordinary players. The combinations of reeds and stops which we place in this organ are especially designed for an instrument of this kind and are those best suited for use in a parlor organ. Every stop can be used for amplifying and controlling the tone in some way, and not a dummy stop is ever placed on this or any Beckwith Organ. The entire stop action is constructed on new principles, thus avoiding many of the complications characteristic of the old style of action. The actions placed in organs usually sold throughout the country are very complicated, are constantly getting out of order and are very difficult to adjust. The Beckwith action is very simple, it seldom gets out of order and can be placed in order and adjusted in a very few minutes by any person of ordinary intelligence. We do not claim that any organ of our line is equal in tone volume to a pipe organ, but we do claim that both our Royal and Imperial Grand Organs are far superior to any other organs on the market in the production of that beautiful mellow quality of tone, which is characteristic of the reed organ. The beautiful tone effect which is produced by the peculiar bending, tuning and voicing which these reeds receive cannot be described in words, but can only be fully appreciated after a thorough test and trial of the instrument. We are always perfectly willing to have the tone quality of our organs tested by the very best musicians and compared with the tone quality of any organ on the market.

WHEN YOU ARE READY TO BUY YOUR ORGAN there are several points which you should carefully consider. It does not always pay to be too economical in the purchase of articles which are to have a permanent place in your home. This is especially true in the purchase of an organ. You are buying something which you expect to last you a lifetime, and it will always pay you to purchase the very best organ which you can possibly afford, because the small increased price you will pay will be more than compensated for in the additional musical capacity you will secure in the organ. **How the Beckwith organs are made is fully explained on page 308 of this catalogue.** We ask you to refer to this page and read it, because it contains information which will be of value to you when you are ready to purchase your organ. Dealers and agents throughout the country are quick to take advantage of a customer's want of technical knowledge in regard to organ construction and organ value, and thousands of organs have been sold at high prices which have nothing to recommend them but a beautiful case and a certain sweetness of tone which is certain to disappear after the organ is used for a while. Every organ purchaser cannot be an expert in organ construction, but he can use ordinary care to see that he purchases his organ from a dealer of responsibility and integrity whose business and financial standing is unquestioned, who is prepared to guarantee every organ that he sells and stand behind it during the entire period of the guarantee. There is no instrument so susceptible of false valuation as a reed organ. A shrewd organ manufacturer will build a handsome organ case, fit it with cheap brass reeds and a large number of dummy stops, and to the ordinary purchaser it will look like a $150.00 organ, and in hundreds of cases would be sold at that figure. If you will read page 308 you will see what a good organ should contain. The number and kind of reeds, the number of stops, quality of material and the different musical combinations. A careful reading of this page will put you in position to purchase your organ to a much better advantage than you could otherwise, and whether you purchase from us or from some other dealer you will be less liable to be deceived in the instrument you buy. Never buy an organ without investigating carefully the standing of the dealer who signs the guarantee. It is the easiest thing in the world to guarantee an organ, but to possess the financial responsibility, which alone can give the guarantee its value, is a different proposition altogether. When you buy the Beckwith Royal Grand Organ from us you do so with the assurance that it is not only covered by our binding twenty-five year guarantee, but that it is one of the organs which the Superior Jury of Awards at the World's Fair declared to be the standard of the world.

FREE MUSIC LESSONS. With each Beckwith Royal Grand Organ we give absolutely free a certificate which entitles the holder to a complete course of musical instruction upon the instrument, consisting of ninety-six lessons and covering a period of two years. The only expense to the student will be the cost of postage, music and stationery, which we guarantee will not exceed 13 cents per week. This course of instruction will be given by one of the best music colleges in the country. This college is not one organized for the purpose of giving these lessons but is an old established school of splendid reputation.

A BEAUTIFUL ORGAN STOOL is given free with each one of these organs and is made of wood and finished to match the case of the instrument. It has brass claws and glass balls for feet and the top is so arranged that it can be raised or lowered at the convenience of the performer. We also give free a complete instruction book which will be of great assistance in learning to play on the instrument.

YOU SHARE IN OUR PROFITS

when you buy the Beckwith Royal Grand Organ, because we give you a certificate which you can exchange for one of the many valuable and beautiful articles which you will find listed on pages 1 and 2 of this book.

NUMBERS, PRICES AND ACTIONS.

No. 46F140 ACTION A, FIVE OCTAVES, ELEVEN STOPS, OAK. Price.............. **$39.85**

Four sets of reeds, as follows: One set of principal reeds, 24 notes; one set of melodia reeds, 37 notes; one set of diapason reeds, 24 notes; one set of celeste reeds, 37 notes; 122 reeds in all. These reeds are made of the finest kind of brass with tongue double riveted to reed block. They are all voiced and tuned by hand and fitted by the most expert workmen.

Eleven stops, as follows: Principal, diapason, dulciana, melodia, celeste, cremona, diapason forte, principal forte, treble coupler, bass coupler and vox humana. **If you desire the organ in walnut, you must add $2.00 to the above price.**

No. 46F143 ACTION C, FIVE OCTAVES, FIFTEEN STOPS, OAK. Price.............. **$43.85**

Six sets of reeds, as follows: One set of principal reeds, 24 notes; one set of melodia reeds, 37 notes; one set of diapason reeds, 24 notes; one set of celeste reeds, 37 notes; one set of flute reeds, 37 notes, and one set of bourdon reeds, 24 notes; 183 reeds in all. The addition of the flute and bourdon reeds adds much to the musical value of the organ, and are very useful in playing many classes of organ selections.

Fifteen stops, as follows: Diapason, principal, dulciana, melodia, celeste, viola, flute, cremona, bourdon, dulcet, diapason forte, principal forte, treble coupler, bass coupler and vox humana. **If you desire the organ in walnut, you must add $2.00 to the above price.**

No. 56F144 ACTION D, FIVE OCTAVES, SEVENTEEN STOPS, OAK. Price.............. **$45.85**

Eight sets of reeds, as follows: One set of principal reeds, 24 notes; one set of melodia reeds, 37 notes; one set of diapason reeds, 24 notes; one set of celeste reeds, 37 notes; one set of bourdon reeds, 24 notes; and one set of clarionet reeds, 24 notes; one set of cornet echo reeds, 37 notes; and one set of flute reeds, 37 notes; 244 reeds in all. The addition of the clarionet and cornet echo reeds adds immensely to the power and volume of the organ. They also increase the number of tone combinations, and place the entire range of musical interpretation entirely within the reach of the ordinary player.

Seventeen stops, as follows: Celeste, principal, dulciana, viola, melodia, diapason, flute, bourdon, clarionet, cornet, cornet echo, cremona, diapason forte, principal forte, treble coupler, bass coupler and vox humana. **If you desire the organ in walnut, you must add $2.00 to the above price.**

No. 46F146 ACTION A, FIVE OCTAVES, ELEVEN STOPS, OAK. Price.............. **$44.85**

This grade has the same action as No. 46E140, five octaves, with the additional reeds to complete the six octaves, making 146 reeds in all. If you desire the organ in walnut, you must add $2.00 to the above price.

No. 46F150 ACTION A, SIX OCTAVES, SEVENTEEN STOPS, OAK. Price.............. **$52.85**

This grade has the same action as No. 46F144, five octaves, with the additional reeds to complete the six octaves, making 292 reeds in all. If you desire the organ in walnut you must add $2.00 to the above price.

$46.75 BUYS THE BECKWITH IMPERIAL GRAND ORGAN

SEE FOLLOWING PAGES FOR COMPLETE DESCRIPTION AND PRICES.

A MARVELOUSLY LOW PRICE FOR THIS MAGNIFICENT LARGE PARLOR ORGAN

87 inches high, 46 inches long and 24 inches deep, weighing, in five octaves, 475 pounds and in six octaves 550 pounds.

WHAT OUR CUSTOMERS THINK OF THIS SPLENDID ORGAN.

As the actual examination and trial of a musical instrument is the very best evidence of its good qualities, the testimonials which we are giving below from among the many thousands we receive every year are worth reading, as they show you what purchasers of this organ think of its merits.

THE IMPERIAL GRAND IS A GOOD DEAL NICER THAN HER NEIGHBOR'S $75.00 ORGAN.

Richmond, Ky.

I have received my organ in fine order. It was simply grand. The people around here think it is the finest thing they ever saw for the money. It is a good deal nicer than my neighbor's $75.00 organ. We have visitors from all around to see it, and more compliments than enough.

MRS. S. B. TURNER.

THE EXPERT ORGANIST SAYS THAT THE IMPERIAL GRAND IS A BETTER ORGAN THAN SHE GOT FOR $90.00.

Owensville, Ind.

I must say that the organ is all right in every respect, and in perfect order. We had an expert organist to try it and she said that it was a better organ than they got for $90.00. I must say that I was surprised to see such a nice organ for so little money.

J. FRANK WILLIAMS.

THE IMPERIAL GRAND IS THE FINEST ORGAN IN THE STATE OF VIRGINIA.

Germantown, Pa.

I had my organ tested the first time I visited my home in Virginia, and everyone says that it is the finest one in the state of Virginia, for the money. I am very well pleased with it.

MISS DOROTHY CARTER,
303 Earlham Terrace.

COULD NOT BUY THE IMPERIAL GRAND ORGAN FROM A DEALER FOR LESS THAN $90.00.

Campton, Ga.

The organ came all O. K. and I am well pleased with it. I don't see how you can make them for the money. I could not buy it here from a dealer for less than $90.00. A clear saving of $56.00.

G. B. GLAZE.

THE AGENTS ASKED HIM FROM $90.00 TO $100.00 FOR AN ORGAN LIKE THE IMPERIAL GRAND.

Elbow Lake, Minn.

I am pleased to inform you that the organ gives perfect satisfaction in every respect and is equal to organs sold here by agents at $90.00 to $100.00. I would recommend it to anyone as being all you say it is, and would be pleased to have anybody going to purchase an organ refer to me either by letter or personally, and I will gladly do what I can to aid you in making sales.

C. O. KOLLE.

COULD NOT BUY AN ORGAN LIKE THE IMPERIAL GRAND FOR LESS THAN $125.00 AT HER HOME.

Sciotoville, Ohio.

I know that you have saved me at least $70.00, for I priced organs here before sending you my order, and the price was $125.00. My friends all say it is a beauty and it has a fine tone.

MISS LENA RUSS.

THE ACTION OF THE IMPERIAL GRAND ORGAN IS THE PERFECTION OF MUSICAL ART.

Bar Harbor, Maine.

I take this opportunity to try to express some of the pleasure that your organ gives. The material and workmanship are the best, but your skilful arrangement of the action seems to be the perfection of musical art. A pipe organ is expected to be capable of expressing music of an almost unlimited range, but the reed organ you sold me last April possesses this feature in a wonderful degree, and calls for a more than common expression of satisfaction.

BYRON CARTER.

AN AGENT WANTED $110.00 FOR AN ORGAN THAT WAS NOT AS GOOD AS OURS.

Cynthiana, Ky.

I am very thankful to you for sending me such a fine instrument. Several musicians have examined it and played on it and say it is far ahead of one an agent wanted $110.00 for. The tone is very beautiful, and I don't see how you can sell such an instrument for so little money.

MISS VERNIE ROBINSON.

HAS A BETTER ORGAN AT $60.00 LAID DOWN IN HIS HOME THAN HE COULD GET IN HIS TOWN FOR $85.00.

Dodson, Louisiana.

I would have written before but was waiting to give the organ a thorough test, and must say that I am more than satisfied. I have a better organ for $60.00 laid down in the house than I could get here for $85.00.

W. W. DAVIS.

The above engraving shows our No. 46F162 Imperial Grand Organ with 17 stops and 292 reeds. Price, $59.75
Same Organ with 5 octaves, 11 stops and 122 reeds (No. 46F152). Price 46.75

See opposite page for other styles.

BECKWITH ORGANS

HIGHEST AWARD AT ST. LOUIS WORLD'S FAIR

MEDAL · LOUISIANA PURCHASE · EXPOSITION

The Beckwith Imperial Grand Organ

ILLUSTRATED ON OPPOSITE PAGE.

WHEN WE SAY THAT THE BECKWITH IMPERIAL GRAND ORGAN is the very highest attainment in organ manufacture we do not make the statement simply for the purpose of inducing you to purchase the instrument, but because it is absolutely true, being based upon the decision of the Superior Jury of Awards at the St. Louis World's Fair and the testimony of thousands of satisfied purchasers. The great care and skill used in its manufacture, the wide experience and ripe judgment used in the combination of stops and distribution of the reeds, the great artistic perception exhibited in the beautiful design and handsome proportions of the case, all unite to make the Beckwith Imperial Grand Organ the very perfection of the organ maker's art. Some other dealer may offer you an organ which may seem to you to have a handsomer case, more beautiful carvings, more harmonious proportions, or greater dimensions. These are all matters of individual taste, but the real value of an organ consists in its musical capabilities and capacities, and if the instrument does not possess these qualities, no matter how handsome the design, how beautiful the proportions or how elegant the finish, it will be a dismal failure and a constant source of grief to the purchaser. It may be a beautiful piece of furniture and an ornament to your parlor, but it will always be a disappointment musically as long as it remains in your possession. While we are very proud of the beautiful designs and proportions of our organ cases, the great source of our pride is in the musical qualities of our instruments. The combinations of reeds, the disposition of the stops, the general blending of its musical qualities, and the manner in which all of these desirable qualities are placed under the easy control of the player is equaled by no other line of organs in the world. The Beckwith Imperial Grand Organ is not only a wonderfully beautiful piece of furniture, but the rich, deep tone volume, which is its great characteristic, places it upon the very highest pinnacle of organ excellence. We know that the statements we make in regard to this organ are startling, considering the low price we fix on it. They are startling because they are so unusual. You have never before known of a high class reed organ being offered at such a wonderfully low price. It is natural for you to doubt our statements as to the high quality of these instruments, and we do not ask you to accept these statements as true until you have had an opportunity to fully satisfy yourself by actual trial, test and examination. If our statements will induce you to give us an opportunity to place one of these organs in your home under our great 30 days free trial offer, as fully outlined and explained on page 283, we will be perfectly satisfied. We are willing to let the organ stand or fall on its own merits. We make you the final judge and allow you to accept or reject it entirely uninfluenced by any advice or suggestion from us.

CASE. The design for the case of the Beckwith Imperial Grand Organ was selected from among hundreds of drawings submitted to us by the best organ designers in the country. We selected it because of its harmonious proportions, its beautiful carvings the subtle beauty of its lines and another quality, which is more difficult to determine than any of these—its wearable qualities. When we say wearable qualities, we do not refer to rough usage and hard wear; but mean that the eye does not become tired of looking at it, as it always presents some new and beautiful quality, some new and pleasing detail the oftener it is examined by the purchaser. Some designs are very catchy, they please at first sight and are very attractive, but soon become wearisome and tiresome to the eye. This is not true of the Beckwith Imperial Grand Organ. The design is rich without being out of keeping with the usual furnishings of a home parlor. It possesses a simplicity along with its beauty which makes it appear always new and fresh. One of the beautiful features of the case is the handsomely hand carved griffins which support the keyboard on each side. This is a new idea in organ architecture, combines very harmoniously with the general designs of the case and is fully protected and covered by copyright. All of the carvings on these cases are wrought by hand, especially for this design. The graceful canopy top is beautifully decorated with carvings, is supported by two neatly turned pillars, fitted with lamp stands, pretty bric-a-brac shelves and a large music cabinet hid from sight by a gracefully designed door, in the front of which is a large bevel French plate mirror. All of the scroll work is cleanly and gracefully cut and backed by colored dustproof cloth. The music desk is made very wide and covers a large cabinet which can be used either for sheet music or books. The case has ornamental handles, casters, and the latest improved fall cover with lock and key. This fall cover is hung on a swinging frame at the back so that it can be opened or closed without sticking or binding. The back of the organ is so arranged that it opens like a door on hinges, making the action easily accessible should it be necessary to examine it for any purpose. The pedals are covered with very handsome Brussels carpet, bound with ornamental highly nickel plated metallic frames and fitted with the well known Beckwith device which protects the pedal straps and keeps them from wearing out and breaking. We furnish these cases either in oak highly figured with full quartered oak front or solid American black walnut. They are all very highly finished, being given several coats of highly transparent varnish and rubbed down by hand with pumice stone, oil and water. The transparent varnish allows the grain of the wood to show through in all its beauty and the rubbing by hand with pumice stone, oil and water removes the distasteful gloss of the varnish and leaves the case with a deep luster, such as is only found upon all high class furniture. The engraving of this organ, which we show on the opposite page, will give you a very good idea of its design and general appearance, but it can give you no idea whatever of its extreme beauty of finish and full rich volume of tone. You must see it and try it in your own home before you can get any adequate idea of its wonderful qualities. When you purchase this organ you have the assurance that you are placing in your home one of the very finest specimens of the organ maker's art.

ACTION. This organ is furnished with the Beckwith Grand Orchestral Action. This grand orchestral action is found upon no other organ except this, our Beckwith Cathedral Chapel and our Beckwith Royal Grand. It is made up of a series of reed combinations and stop connections which can be used at the will of the performer and produces that round, sonorous and powerful volume of tone which can be produced upon no other reed organ in the world. This wonderful combination of stops and reeds is thrown into play by means of the grand organ knee swell and should always be used in making a test either of this organ or the Beckwith Royal Grand. The addition of the grand orchestral action to these organs has made it possible for even an ordinary player to produce musical effects only excelled by the largest pipe organs. The different combinations of reeds and stops which go to make up this action are those which study and experience have proved to be the very best for an organ of this character. There is no musical composition written which cannot be played effectually upon this organ. The reeds are all manufactured in our own factory, are bent, tuned and voiced by men who have made a life study of this work, and are manipulated in such a way as to make them most suitable for use in an organ of such immense musical capacity as the Beckwith Imperial Grand. They are all made of the very best quality of brass, with vibrating tongues solidly double riveted to heavy reed blocks. Not only is the tone of the Imperial Grand Organ round, resonant and of immense power, but it is also sweet and mellow and susceptible to the most delicate variations. A steady and powerful current of air is furnished by the celebrated Beckwith Automatic Bellows which makes it possible for the player to sustain the full power of the organ for an indefinite time with but slight exertion. For a full description of these wonderful bellows, see page 308.

IF YOU ARE READY NOW TO BUY YOUR ORGAN there are some points which we desire to emphasize to you. In the first place, the fact that you order an organ from us does not mean that you are buying that organ, but simply means that you are requesting us to send the organ to your home where it can be thoroughly tried and tested by you and your musical friends so you can ascertain whether you desire to buy it or not. The instrument is placed in your home with the understanding that you are to give it a thorough examination; test and try it at every point without any suggestion or advice from us in the meantime. The matter rests entirely upon the uninfluenced judgment of yourself and your friends. You have an opportunity to examine thoroughly the finish and material of the case, the quality of the action, the number of reeds, the number of stops and fully ascertain whether or not the organ possesses the great musical capacity we claim for it. You can test the workings of the powerful bellows, you can thoroughly try the tone quality and see if the statements we have made are not absolutely true. In fact, the organ is entirely in your hands and absolutely under your control to test and try as you desire. We take all of the chances of shipment, all of the risks of rejection and return and the organ must sell itself after it reaches your home. When we say that the Beckwith Imperial Grand Organ is a wonderful instrument, that it has a handsome case and elegant finish, a rich and powerful tone, and is superior to others at double the price we do so fully appreciating the fact that the organ must prove itself to possess all of these qualities after it reaches your home, and has been thoroughly tested and tried by you. With this understanding don't you think that it would pay you to let us place one of these splendid organs in your home under our great 30 days free trial offer?

WHEN YOU BUY A BECKWITH IMPERIAL GRAND ORGAN you cannot do us a greater favor than to give it the most thorough examination, trial and test. Such a trial and test, if given impartially, will surely convince you that you have secured a splendid bargain and that you could not purchase this same organ for less than double the price you have paid for it. Remove the fall cover and examine the stop action; examine this action and see if every one of the stops are not used in some way to amplify, qualify and control the tone. Draw out the reeds and examine them. See if they are not made of the best quality of brass with the tongues solidly double riveted to heavy brass reed blocks. Count them and ascertain if the organ does not contain the exact number of reeds described in the catalogue. Remove the front and back panels of the organs and examine the wonderful Beckwith bellows. See if the wood of which the bellows are constructed is not three-ply stock with the grain running in opposite directions, solidly glued together so that it cannot warp or split. Examine the cloth with which the bellows are covered and see if it is not the very highest grade of closely woven silk rubber cloth. Open all of the stops and try the organ to its full capacity. See if it does not develop a marvelously great tone capacity. Try all of the different stop combinations, and if you do not find that this organ is the most wonderful reed organ that you ever saw and far beyond your expectations in every particular send it back to us immediately at our expense, and we will cheerfully refund your money. To assist you in making this examination and test as thorough as possible kindly refer to page 308 and read it carefully. We do not ask you to make any more thorough test of an organ purchased elsewhere than you do of the instrument purchased of us. All we ask is that you will give the other organ the same rigid test and examination that you give ours. Remember also that our instrument has no one present to speak in its favor and that it must prove its own merit without any assistance from us whatever. On the contrary the agent or dealer from whom another organ might be purchased will generally be present to assist you to see that none of the weak points in his organ are discovered and to explain away any that may become apparent upon examination. All we ask is an opportunity to place one of these splendid organs in your home for trial and examination and if it does not thoroughly convince you of its own value you can return it and get your money back immediately.

DIMENSIONS. The Beckwith Imperial Grand Organ is one of the very largest reed organs on the market, being 87 inches high, 46 inches long, and 24 inches deep, in five octaves; and 87 inches high, 52½ inches long and 24 inches deep in six octaves. It weighs, boxed and packed for shipment, in five octaves, 475 pounds, and in six octaves, 550 pounds.

FREE MUSIC LESSONS. With each Imperial Grand Organ we give absolutely free a certificate which entitles the holder to a complete course of musical instruction on the instrument, consisting of 96 lessons, covering a period of two years. The only expense to the customer will be the cost of postage and music, which we guarantee will not exceed 13 cents a week. These instructions will be given by one of the very best music colleges in the country. These lessons are all very simple and so graded and arranged that they can be understood by old and young.

FREE. We send absolutely free with each one of these organs a fine stool, made in wood to match the case of the organ, with handsome turned legs, brass claws fitted with glass balls. We also send a complete instruction book for the organ. The engraving shows you the stool which we give with this instrument.

YOU GET A PROFIT SHARING CERTIFICATE ABSOLUTELY FREE when you purchase the Imperial Grand Organ. On pages 1 and 2 of this book you will find a complete list of beautiful and valuable articles which we give in exchange for these certificates.

NUMBERS, PRICES AND ACTIONS.

No. 46F152 ACTION A, FIVE OCTAVES, ELEVEN STOPS; OAK. Price........ **$46.75**

Four sets of reeds, as follows: One set of principal reeds, 24 notes; one set of melodia reeds, 37 notes; one set of diapason reeds, 24 notes; one set of celeste reeds, 37 notes; 122 reeds in all. These reeds are made of the finest kind of brass with tongues double riveted to the reed blocks. They are all voiced and tuned by hand and fitted by the most expert workmen.

Eleven stops, as follows: Principal, diapason, dulciana, melodia, celeste, cremona, diapason forte, principal forte, treble coupler, bass coupler and vox humana. **If you desire the organ in walnut, you must add $2.00 to the above price.**

No. 46F155 ACTION C, FIVE OCTAVES, FIFTEEN STOPS; OAK. Price........ **$50.75**

Six sets of reeds, as follows: One set of principal reeds, 24 notes; one set of melodia reeds, 37 notes; one set of diapason reeds, 24 notes; one set of celeste reeds, 37 notes; one set of flute reeds, 37 notes; and one set of bourdon reeds, 24 notes; 183 reeds in all. The addition of the flute and bourdon reeds adds much to the musical value of the organ, and are very useful in playing many classes of organ selections.

Fifteen stops, as follows: Diapason, principal, dulciana, melodia, celeste, viola, flute, cremona, bourdon, dulcet, diapason forte, principal forte, treble coupler, bass coupler and vox humana. **If you desire the organ in walnut, you must add $2.00 to the above price.**

No. 46F156 ACTION D, FIVE OCTAVES, SEVENTEEN STOPS; OAK. Price........ **$53.75**

Eight sets of reeds, as follows: One set of principal reeds, 24 notes; one set of melodia reeds, 37 notes; one set of diapason reeds, 24 notes; one set of celeste reeds, 37 notes; one set of flute reeds, 37 notes; one set of bourdon reeds, 24 notes; one set of clarionet reeds, 24 notes; and one set of cornet echo reeds, 37 notes; 244 reeds in all. The addition of the clarionet and cornet echo reeds adds immensely to the power and volume of the organ. They also increase the number of the tone combinations, and place the entire range of musical interpretation entirely within the reach of an ordinary player.

Seventeen stops, as follows: Celeste, principal, dulciana, viola, melodia, diapason, flute, bourdon, clarionet, cornet, cornet echo, cremona, diapason forte, principal forte, treble coupler, bass coupler and vox humana. **If you desire the organ in walnut, you must add $2.00 to the above price.**

No. 46F158 ACTION A, SIX OCTAVES, ELEVEN STOPS; OAK. Price........ **$52.75**

This grade has the same action as No. 46F152, five octaves, with the additional reeds to complete the six octaves, making 146 reeds in all. If you desire the organ in walnut, you must add $2.00 to the above price.

No. 46F162 ACTION D, SIX OCTAVES, SEVENTEEN STOPS; OAK. Price........ **$59.75**

This grade has the same action as No. 46F156, five octaves, with the additional reeds to complete the six octaves, making 292 reeds in all. If you desire the organ in walnut, you must add $2.00 to the above price.

BECKWITH ORGANS

HIGHEST AWARD AT ST. LOUIS WORLD'S FAIR

HOW THE BECKWITH IMPERIAL GRAND ORGAN IS MADE.

Some Valuable Information Touching on the Quality of Material and Workmanship which Enter into the Construction of these Splendid Instruments.

VERY FEW ORGAN PURCHASERS possess any knowledge as to the mechanical construction and operation of reed organs. They are, therefore, entirely at the mercy of the agent or dealer from whom they make their purchase. As a general rule, they can only judge of the general appearance and finish of the case, and, to a limited extent, of the tone. As a consequence, they must pay the price the agent asks and take his word for the quality of material and workmanship which enter into the mechanical construction and operation of the instrument. In order that you may have some knowledge of these points, and be in a better position to select your organ with advantage to yourself, we are illustrating and describing on this page some of the vital points in connection with the construction of reed organ actions. If, when you are ready to purchase your organ, you will read this page carefully it will place you in a much better position to make your purchase intelligently and assure yourself that you are receiving full value for your money. Agents and dealers throughout the country too often take advantage of this want of knowledge on the part of organ purchasers and succeed in securing very high prices for worthless instruments which in a short time will have to be thrown into the junk heap. To avoid this danger, the safest way is to purchase your organ from a reputable dealer who is prepared to guarantee the instrument for a reasonable period of years. The following are some of the vital parts of an organ action:

Fig. 1

BELLOWS. One of the most vital parts of an organ is the bellows. The bellows supplies the air to the reeds, and by vibrating them, produces the tone. The celebrated Beckwith bellows, with which we furnish all of our organs, is the most perfect bellows ever placed in a reed organ. It is constructed upon the suction principle and draws the air from the outside down through the reeds instead of forcing it out from the inside. Upon the construction of these bellows depends, to a considerable extent, the life and musical quality of the instrument. The wood is all made of three-ply built up stock with the grain of the different sections running in opposite directions, these different sections being solidly glued together under enormous hydraulic pressure so that they cannot possibly warp or split. Fig. 1 shows a section of bellows stock, illustrates how the different sections of wood are glued together and shows the grain of these different sections running in opposite directions. Fig. 4 shows the bellows attached to the foundation board ready to be placed in the case. This illustration also shows the two exhausters with the exhaust valves, "AA," in position. These exhaust valves are strips of cloth nailed over circular holes; they open and close as the exhausters are worked by the pedals. These two exhausters draw the air all out of the reservoir in the back of the organ, forming a vacuum. As soon as a key is touched, it opens a valve, allows the air to rush into the reservoir through the reed, producing a tone. The cloth used on the Beckwith bellows is of the very highest quality, being tightly woven, silk rubber cloth which is very tough and elastic and is guaranteed not to wear out or leak. The pedal straps, "BB" (in Fig. 4), operate over rollers fastened to the foundation board, "HH," and connect with the pedals, thus allowing the bellows to be freely operated by the player. So well is this point taken care of that the full power of the organ can be sustained for an indefinite period with slight effort on the part of the player. These bellows are made automatic by oil tempered steel springs which never break or lose their elasticity. The excess pressure valve, "I" (in Fig. 4), opens automatically when the air has been exhausted in the reservoir and allows the air from the outside to rush in, thus preventing the bellows from being overstrained by violent pumping. The great trouble with ordinary organs is that the tone becomes jerky and spasmodic when the bellows is pumped violently. The celebrated Beckwith bellows avoids this by furnishing an even and steady supply of air at all times.

VALVES. The office of the valves is to regulate the supply of air to the reeds. Each valve covers an opening in the sound board through which the air can pass into the wind chest and thence to the reservoir. Each one of these openings must be closed perfectly when not in use or it will leak and give continual annoyance and trouble. In order that the valve may close this opening properly, it is faced with felt and sheepskin, as shown in Fig. 2. The felt and sheepskin, "A," is glued down the center by machinery allowing the edges to remain loose, as in this way it will more properly close the valve opening than if it were glued solidly to the face of the valve. In order to glue the felt and sheepskin in this way, special machinery is used and it is a much more expensive process than if the felt and sheepskin were glued solidly to the face of the valve. There are many high priced reed organs on the market today which have this facing glued flat to the valve in order to avoid the expense of gluing it properly. Such valves are bound to give trouble sooner or later, and as they are placed in the interior of the wind chest it is always a very difficult matter to reach them in order to remedy the difficulty. By examining Fig. 2, you will notice a slot in the end of the valve. This slot fits over a guide pin which holds the valve in position. Under the usual method of constructing these valves, it is quite a common occurrence for the valve to be pushed down over this guide pin. This allows the air to rush through the reeds, causing it to sound continually when the organ is pumped. It is unnecessary to say that this makes the organ absolutely useless. The only way to remedy this difficulty is to take the action entirely out of the organ, remove the wind chest and push the valve back in position. Under our method of construction this could never happen, because we place a binder over the ends of these valves, which effectually prevents them being pushed down beyond a certain point. The valves are held in position by springs which are securely fastened to the spring bar, or spring rail, on the under side of the sound board. A great many manufacturers of organs overlook the fact that while the strain of one spring is very slight, the strain of all of the springs upon this spring bar exerts a heavy and continuous pressure. One of the most usual and disheartening troubles which occur with ordinary organs is that this spring bar breaks loose, allowing all the valves to drop and causing all the reeds to sound continually when the organ is pumped. It is needless to say that under these circumstances the instrument is ruined and the only way to remedy the defect is to return it to the factory, if you can find a manufacturer who will become responsible for it. This could never happen with the Beckwith Organs, because this spring bar is so securely fastened with glue and screws that it becomes part of the sound board itself and nothing short of tons of pressure could break it loose.

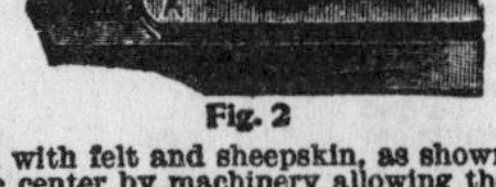

Fig. 2

THE REEDS. One of the most vital parts of an organ is the reeds. These reeds are vibrating brass tongues, securely fastened to heavy reed blocks. The tone is produced by passing the air through the slot in this reed block and vibrating the tongue. The tone of the organ is either good or bad, according to the workmanship and material which enter into these reeds. All of our reeds are manufactured under our direct supervision at our own factories. They are made out of the very highest quality of brass with the tongues all solidly double riveted to the reed blocks. They are all cut, bent, tuned and voiced according to the tone quality which they are to produce, and the particular style of organ in which they are to be used. Below we are giving the names of the different sets of reeds with which we furnish our organs, together with their characteristic tone qualities and pitch. CELESTE (sometimes called VOX CELESTE), beautifully sympathetic and expressive, 8 foot pitch; MELODIA, sweet and full, 8 foot pitch; DIAPASON, round, full and sonorous, 8 foot pitch; PRINCIPAL, free, soft and clear, 4 foot pitch; FLUTE, brilliant and clear with beautiful flute tone, 8 foot pitch; BOURDON, deep tone, substrata of the organ, 16 foot pitch; CLARIONET, a beautiful solo set of reeds, similar in tone to the clarionet, 8 foot pitch; CORNET ECHO, one of the most beautiful sets of reeds on the organ, imitating the tone of a cornet, 8 foot pitch; SUB BASS, heavy and sonorous, the most profound set of reeds on the organ, 16 foot pitch. Fig. 3 illustrates five Beckwith reeds. The first one to the left is a sub bass reed, the next, a diapason reed; the next two are flute reeds, showing one bent and one straight, and the smallest is piccolo reed. These reeds are double riveted to heavy reed blocks and are substantially and durably made in every respect. There are thousands of organs being offered for sale throughout the country fitted with reeds stamped out of thin sheet brass, voiced and tuned without regard to quality of tone or fitness for music production. These are some things that the purchaser cannot see and oftentimes is deceived through his want of knowledge of organ construction. The wonderful Beckwith tone is produced by the different combinations of the reeds we have mentioned. Our cases can be imitated, but no maker has yet succeeded in imitating the beautiful Beckwith tone.

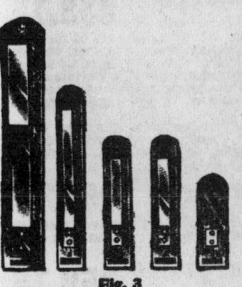

Fig. 3

THE BECKWITH ACTION. The action of an organ is that part of it which is used to produce the tone. The Beckwith action is the most perfectly constructed, most durably built and skilfully adjusted of any action known. Fig. 4 shows the front view of a Beckwith action complete, ready to be placed in the organ. "AA" shows the exhauster valves, which are fully explained under the title, "Bellows." "BB" are the pedal straps, which are also explained under the above title. "C" is the stop connections. These can be examined by removing the back of the organ, as they are easily accessible without removing any part of the action. "DD" shows the swell rods, which are operated by the knee swells and illustrate how the connections are made with the stop action. These are connected on a new principle which avoids the old complicated method and does away with the numerous troubles which arise from the pedal rod connections on other organs. "E" shows the coupler rods, which is also a new idea and avoids many of the complications incident to the coupler actions found on other organs. The illustration shows the right hand coupler board raised coupling the treble side of the instrument. In organs of other makes the coupler action is constantly giving trouble and generally falls into disuse after the purchaser has had the organ for a few weeks. "G" shows the guide pins which hold the keys in place, and "F" illustrates the tracker pins, which connect the keys with the valves of the organ. This is a very important part of the instrument, because if the organ is exposed to moisture or dampness these tracker pins are liable to swell and stick in their sockets. This is a complaint common to all organs, but is not at all serious, and will generally disappear if the organ is placed in a warm, dry room. "HH" is the foundation board which is made of three-ply built up stock, with the different layers of wood glued together so that it cannot warp or split. "I" shows the excess pressure valve, which has already been described under the title, "Bellows." Fig. 5 shows the rear view of a Beckwith action. "AA" shows the stop action, which is easily accessible after removing the back of the instrument. "B" shows the fan, operated by the Vox Humana stop, with which all of our organs are furnished and which produce the waving undulating tone which is such a beautiful imitation of the human voice in singing. "D" shows the rear end of the stops and "E" shows one of the rear swells. These swells are opened and closed by their appropriate stops and have much to do with controlling and qualifying the tone of the organ.

Fig. 4

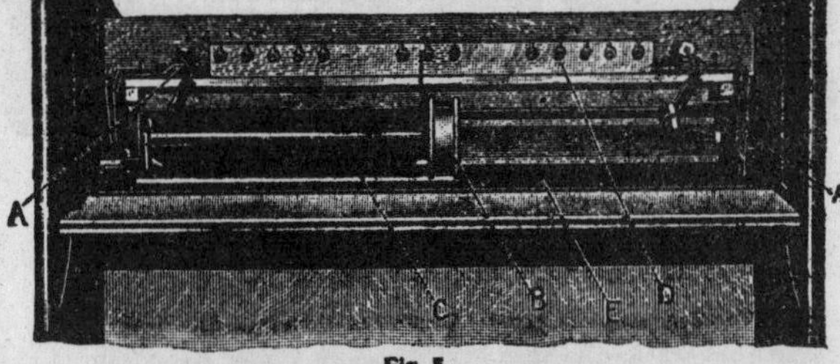

Fig. 5

SHOULD AN AGENT PLACE AN ORGAN IN YOUR HOME there are certain things that you should ascertain and know before you purchase the instrument. In order to be a thoroughly satisfactory organ, it should have at least eleven stops and all of these stops should in some way control the tone of the instrument. There should be no dummy stops or stops put in just for show. You can ascertain whether or not the stops are all necessary by removing the fall cover of the instrument and examining the top of the stop action. In order to remove the fall cover, first remove the back of the instrument and this will make the fastenings of the cover easily accessible. Having removed the cover, pull the stops in and out and you will soon be able to tell whether they are connected in any way with the reeds of the organ. **There are no dummy stops whatever on the Beckwith organs and every one is connected in some way with the reeds.** A five-octave organ with eleven stops should have four full sets of reeds, or 122 in all. By four full sets of reeds we mean two sets in front and two sets in the back. As you look into the front and back of the organ you will see one continuous row of reeds running from one end of the organ to the other. This is commonly known as four sets of reeds. An organ with eight sets of reeds has four additional sets immediately above the lower sets. If an agent tells you that his organ has eight sets of reeds, take off the back of the organ, open all of the stops and look inside. If you do not find two continuous rows of reeds, one above the other, running the full length of the organ, you will know at once that the organ he offers does not contain the number of reeds he claims for it. We receive letters every day from customers who are offered organs which appear to be the same as ours at the same, or less, prices than we quote in our catalogue, but in every instance it has been shown that the organ was deficient in reeds, stops and general musical capacity and was not by any means the same organ as ours. We want to impress the fact on your mind that it is absolutely impossible for a dealer or agent to sell organs of the grade we handle at the same, or less, prices than we ask. It is impossible because he does not buy the instruments and sell them in such enormous quantities as we do; he receives his organs after they have passed through the hands of several different dealers and the different profits charged by these dealers must be included in the price; he finds it necessary to carry an organ in stock so long before he sells it that he could not possibly be contented with the small profits we make and stay in business. If you desire to purchase an organ, it is natural for you to wish to buy the very best organ you can for the least money and we believe that a trial and examination of one of our instruments will quickly satisfy you that you cannot purchase an organ elsewhere of same grade for less than double the price we ask.

BECKWITH CHAPEL ORGANS.

AN ESPECIALLY BEAUTIFUL LINE OF ORGANS FOR CHURCHES, SUNDAY SCHOOLS AND ALL KINDS OF PUBLIC HALLS.

WE ARE ESPECIALLY PROUD of our line of chapel organs, because no other one on the market today is so well suited for the purpose of public meetings. We have made a study of the conditions under which such organs are to be used, have carefully considered the great demands which are to be made upon their musical capacities, the size of the rooms in which they are to be used, the character of the music to be played, etc., and as a consequence the Beckwith Chapel Organs have no superior on the market today. The musical qualities which a church organ must possess in order to meet all of the demands upon it and prove successful are entirely different from those required in a parlor organ. A parlor organ is, as its name suggests, for use in the parlor, which is generally a small room and does not require great depth and volume of tone. In a public hall conditions are entirely changed, and an organ for use in such a place must contain great breadth and volume of tone combined with sweetness and purity in order to come up to the requirements of such a place. The reeds which we place in these organs are all manufactured at our own factories, made out of the very best quality of brass with the tongues double riveted, bent, tuned and voiced by the most expert workmen. In preparing reeds for church organs the fact must always be kept in view that they are intended to be used in public halls and they must be prepared accordingly. In order to secure the breadth and volume of tone necessary for such purposes the reeds must be especially treated with this object in view. Very few manufacturers consider this point in building their church organs. They fit them with the same reeds, which are bent, tuned and voiced for parlor organ purposes and as a consequence the organ has a thin piping tone not at all suitable for church purposes. The manner in which we handle the reeds for all of our organs is largely responsible for the great reputation acquired by them. The care and skill which we put into this branch of organ manufacture has made the Beckwith Tone the standard of quality.

CASE DESIGNS. The designs for our church organ cases are drawn for us by some of the best designers in the country. They are all strictly new and handsome and you will find no out of date designs among them. A comparison of these cases with those offered by other dealers will convince you at once that for beauty of appearance, elegance of finish, and general fitness for public use they are far superior to any others on the market. Each one is given the finish which is most suitable for an organ of this character. They are all thoroughly and heavily covered with several coats of transparent varnish, which brings out the beautiful grain of the wood in splendid style. They are all fully covered by our wonderful 25 years guarantee, and sold under our great 30 days free trial offer. We make you and your church society the sole judge of the merits of the organ and its suitability for church use. It must prove satisfactory to you after a careful test and trial, and we do not ask you to make any decision on these points until after you have examined and tried it thoroughly.

Seminary
Norwegian Lutheran Church.

St. Anthony Park, Minn. Oct. 21, 1904

Messrs. Sears Roebuck & Co.,
Chicago, Ill.

Gentlemen:

This makes the fifth Beckwith Organ I order from you, for my pupils. Your organs give perfect satisfaction in every respect. Your prices are certainly astonishing, considering the excellency of tone and quality in these instruments. Thanking you for past favors I remain as

Yours truly
Otto Gerhard
organist & music teacher
U. C. Seminary, St. Anthony Pk. Minn.

$28.85 OUR NEW QUEEN CHAPEL ORGAN No. 46F177

One of the Very Latest and Prettiest Designs in Church Organs.

WHEN YOU ARE READY TO SELECT YOUR ORGAN we wish to call your attention to this pretty instrument. While the case of this organ is very modest it is at the same time very neat and tasty and one which will prove very satisfactory for all kinds of public services. It has sufficient volume and general musical capacity to fill any ordinary church or public hall and is fully guaranteed for 25 years. It is offered especially for those who feel that they cannot afford to buy one of our higher priced church organs, and desire an organ of good musical capacity at a moderate price. This is the organ for which your dealer is asking from $40.00 to $45.00, and we will be glad to have you compare it with any church organ which he has to offer at these prices. While this is not by any means as fine an organ as our Cathedral Chapel, yet it is an instrument which will prove very satisfactory in any ordinary size church and will prove itself much superior to other church organs for which you will pay a much higher price. When you buy this organ you are not only buying an organ which is fully covered by our binding guarantee, but one which the Superior Jury of Awards at the World's Fair declared to be the very best in the world. For a confirmation of this statement, see page 295 of this catalogue.

CASE. The design of this case is very pretty and graceful and we can furnish it either in solid oak or walnut. It is nicely hand carved, decorated and ornamented, substantially and durably constructed and well finished. It is fitted with ornamental handles, casters and the latest design of fall cover with lock and key. It has an ornamental music desk, and top railing made of turned spindles and mouldings. The back is nicely paneled and ornamented so that it can be set in any position on the platform without presenting any unfinished sides to the audience. The pedals are covered with Brussels carpet bound with metallic frames, nickel plated, polished, and are fitted with the Beckwith device which prevents the pedal straps from wearing out and breaking. The back is so arranged that it can be opened instantly should it be necessary to examine the action for any purpose. We are willing to ship you this organ with the understanding that you cannot duplicate it anywhere for less than double the price we are asking, and if after examination and comparison you find that this statement is not absolutely true we will receive the organ back at our expense and cheerfully refund your money.

TONE. The tone of this organ is everything that can be desired in an instrument of its size and capacity. The reeds are all manufactured in our factory especially for this organ. They are made from the very best quality of brass with vibrating brass tongues solidly double riveted to heavy reed blocks. They are all bent, tuned and voiced by men who have made a life study of this work, and guarantee to this organ the breadth, volume and sweetness of tone necessary for an organ of this character. The stop and reed combinations are those which experience has proved to be the very best for a church organ of this size, and the entire action is so arranged that it is at all times under the easy control of the player.

No. 46F177 Showing Front of Organ.

No. 46F177 Showing Back of Organ.

MUSIC LESSONS FREE. With each one of these organs we give a certificate, which entitles the holder to a complete course of instructions on the organ to be given by one of the very best music colleges in the country. The only expense to the student will be for music, postage and stationery, which we guarantee will not exceed 13 cents per week.

For our wonderfully liberal terms of shipment see page 283.

A WELL MADE STOOL is also given free with each one of these organs. This stool is made in wood to match the case of the organ, and nicely finished. The top is arranged so that it can be raised and lowered at the convenience of the player. We a so give free, a complete instruction book.

A PROFIT SHARING CERTIFICATE FOR $28.85 is given with each one of these organs, absolutely free. For full particulars see pages 1 and 2 in this book.

DIMENSIONS. The organ is 4 feet 5½ inches high, 2 feet deep, 3 feet 10 inches wide and weighs, boxed for shipment, 380 pounds.

No. 46F177 New Queen Chapel Organ, Action A, five octaves, oak. **$28.85**

This action has eleven stops as follows: Diapason, Principal, Celeste, Cremona, Diapason Forte, Principal Forte, Treble Coupler, Bass Coupler, Dulciana, Melodia and Vox Humana. It has four sets of reeds as follows: one set of Principal reeds, 24 notes, one set of Melodia reeds, 37 notes, one set of Diapason reeds, 24 notes, one set of Celeste reeds, 37 notes. For a full description of the characteristic tone quality of these different sets of reeds see page 308.

If you desire the organ in solid walnut you must add $2.00 to the above price.

Catalogue No. 46F185. Order by Number.
GUARANTEED FOR 25 YEARS.
THIS IS THE LONGEST, STRONGEST AND MOST BINDING GUARANTEE ISSUED WITH ANY ORGAN.
Beckwith

THE BECKWITH CHOIR GEM ORGAN

$34.65 = A VERY = BEAUTIFUL CHURCH ORGAN,

WITH RICH MELLOW TONE AND GREAT MUSICAL CAPACITY. FULLY GUARANTEED FOR 25 YEARS AND SOLD UNDER OUR GREAT 30 DAYS FREE TRIAL OFFER

WHEN YOU ARE READY TO PURCHASE A CHURCH ORGAN we want to call your attention to this beautiful instrument. This is one of the favorite organs of our line and has become very popular on account of its many splendid qualities and the extremely low price which we make on it. In fixing a price on this instrument we have followed our usual policy and cut the price down to the very limit, because as these organs are always used in public places, they act as the very best kind of advertising for our house, and the profit which we sacrifice comes back to us in the shape of increased business. We desire to place one of these organs in your church or Sunday school and allow you to place it in comparison with any church organ offered you by any other dealer, and if you do not find, after such comparison, that an organ of this same grade will cost you at least $65.00 you can box it up and return it to us at our expense and we will refund your money immediately without asking a question. All we ask is a fair and impartial trial and comparison and we are prepared to make you the sole judge of the merits of the organ. It is not fair to judge an organ by its outward appearance. It is much cheaper and easier to give an organ case a beautiful design and high finish than it is to furnish it with sufficient musical capacity to make it suitable for church purposes. It is possible that some other dealer may make you the same, or even a less price, upon an organ which appears to be the same instrument as ours, and in such case, if you will do us the justice to write us fully, stating the different claims which are made for the other organ, we will be glad to point out the different superior points in ours. In such case it will always be found that our organ has more reeds, more stops and greater musical capacity in every way than the organ offered by our competitor. As you desire to purchase the very best organ you can for the least money it will certainly pay you to give us every opportunity to prove that our organ is a superior one, because it gives you an opportunity to make your purchase intelligently and insures your receiving the very greatest amount of value for your money.

CASE. The case of this organ is furnished either in American black walnut or solid oak. It is very highly finished, is given several coats of transparent varnish and hand rubbed with pumice stone, oil and water, which removes the varnish gloss, leaving a deep, rich finish. The design is very handsome, strictly modern in every respect and will harmonize with the furnishings of any church, Sunday school or public hall. It is finished with a full paneled back, ornamented with carvings and scroll work, backed by colored dustproof cloth and so arranged that it can be removed instantly should it be necessary to examine the action for any reason. It has ornamental handles, casters, and the latest design of fall cover with lock and key. This fall cover is hung on a swinging frame and can be opened or closed without sticking or binding. The music rack is of graceful design and the top of the case is ornamented with a pretty railing, hand carvings and machine turned ornaments. The top is so arranged as to provide for lamp stand on each side of the music rack to allow ample room for placing music and hymn books. The front lower panel can be removed without difficulty in case it is necessary, and the pedals are covered with Brussels carpet, bound with metallic frames highly nickel plated and fitted with the Beckwith device for preventing the pedal straps from wearing out and breaking. The neat bench which we give with this organ is in perfect keeping with the design and is ornamental and tasty. The keyboard is supported on each side by machine turned spindles giving the entire instrument an appearance of elegance not found on other church organs at anywhere near this price.

TONE. This organ has a very sweet and mellow tone combined with sufficient volume to fill any church, Sunday school or public hall. All of the reeds are manufactured, bent, tuned and voiced in our own factories and are prepared especially for this instrument. They are all made of the very highest quality of brass with vibrating tongues solidly double riveted to heavy reed blocks. For a full description of the making of these reeds, their names and different characteristic tone qualities see page 308. A great many manufacturers do not discriminate between parlor and church organs in preparing their reeds and the consequence is that the tone of their different organs is not marked by that character which distinguishes the Beckwith line. While we place the same sets of reeds in our church organs that we do in our parlor organs they are all bent, tuned and voiced according as they are to be used for church or parlor organ. Perfectly satisfactory results cannot be secured in any other way, because church and parlor organs are used for an entirely different purpose and under entirely different conditions. In order to insure an even and powerful volume of tone this organ is fitted with the celebrated Beckwith Automatic Bellows, which is fully described on page 308.

IF YOU ARE THINKING OF PURCHASING A CHURCH ORGAN you cannot afford to make your purchase elsewhere without giving us an opportunity to send you one of these fine instruments for examination and trial. When you ask us to send you one of these organs under our liberal terms of shipment, which are fully explained on page 283, you do not take any responsibility or assume any obligations whatever. We take all the risks of shipment and assume all of the chances and responsibilities and only ask you to give the organ a perfectly impartial test and trial. We do not care how severe this test may be, if it is fair and impartial and made by disinterested parties, we will be perfectly satisfied with the result. As you and your church society are the ones who have to use the organ you should be perfectly satisfied that it is everything that you desire and an organ which will prove satisfactory with continued use; and we are perfectly confident that such trial and examination will fully convince you that you cannot purchase an organ of this grade from a local dealer for less than $65.00. We have made a special effort to make our line of church organs the very highest in quality and that we have succeeded is fully proved by the decision of the Superior Jury of Awards at the World's Fair and the thousands of testimonials we receive every year from satisfied purchasers. We are aware of the fact that local dealers are always ready to make a large discount, or allowance from their prices in order to place one of their organs in a church or Sunday school and this always looks as though they were really giving something to the society, but a little thought will show you that they are simply reducing a trifle the usually large profit which they make and that the original price of the instrument was placed at a high figure for the very purpose of making you this allowance or discount. We do even better than this. We place our original prices so low that no matter how large a discount or allowance the dealer may make he cannot make it sufficiently large to bring his price anywhere near as low as ours. We often have requests from church societies to make discounts or allowances from our catalogue prices, but we find it impossible to do so, because we are selling these organs now at such a very narrow margin of profit that any allowance we might make would result in a loss to us.

FREE MUSIC LESSONS. With every Choir Gem Organ we give a certificate which entitles the holder to a free course of musical instruction on the instrument.

A NEAT ORGAN BENCH is given free with this organ and also a complete instruction book.

YOU SHARE IN OUR PROFITS WHEN YOU BUY THIS ORGAN, because we give you a profit sharing certificate for $34.65, or $38.65, according to the organ you purchase. For a complete list of the many valuable articles which we give in exchange for these certificates, see pages 1 and 2 in this book.

DIMENSIONS. This organ is 4 feet 8 inches high, 3 feet 10¾ inches wide, 2 feet deep and weighs, boxed for shipment, about 400 pounds.

No. 46F185 Action A, Five Octaves, in oak **$34.65**

This action has eleven stops as follows: Diapason, Principal, Celeste, Cremona, Diapason Forte, Principal Forte, Treble Coupler, Bass Coupler Dulciana, Melodia and Vox Humana. It has four sets of reeds as follows: one set of Principal reeds, 24 notes; one set of Melodia reeds, 37 notes; one set of Diapason reeds, 24 notes, and one set of Celeste reeds, 37 notes.

No. 46F186 Action C, Five Octaves, in oak **$38.65**

This organ has fifteen stops as follows: Diapason, Principal, Dulciana, Melodia, Celeste, Cremona, Viola, Flute, Bourdon, Dulcet, Diapason Forte, Principal Forte, Treble Coupler, Bass Coupler and Vox Humana. It has six sets of reeds as follows: one set of Principal reeds, 24 notes; one set of Diapason reeds, 24 notes; one set of Flute reeds, 37 notes; one set of Melodia reeds, 37 notes; one set of Celeste reeds, 37 notes, and one set of Bourdon reeds, 24 notes.

Should you desire the organ in walnut, add $2.00 to the above prices

See page 283 where our great 30 days free trial offer is outlined and explained.

BACK VIEW OF OUR Choir Gem Organ.
No. 46F185
ORDER BY NUMBER.

For a detailed description of the making of a Beckwith Organ read page 308

...THE... BECKWITH CATHEDRAL CHAPEL ORGAN

No. 46F198 FOR $56.65

Without Doubt the Most Magnificent Chapel Organ Ever Placed on the Market. Splendid in Tone, Elegant in Appearance, Beautiful in Finish and Graceful in Design.

WE OFFER THIS ORGAN as being superior to any organ ever offered to the public. The design is elaborate and at the same time simple; it is handsome and at the same time solid and substantial. It has an appearance of quiet strength which is one of its distinctive features and the details of the case are very delicate and pretty. The entire design is full of original ideas so consistently worked out that the result is highly satisfactory and pleasing. We do not hesitate to advise our customers to purchase this organ to the exclusion of any other church organ made. The organ bench which we send with this instrument is made especially for it so as not to destroy the effect of unity and consistency which is such a prominent feature of this design. For churches, Sunday schools, lodges, public schools and public halls of all kinds this instrument has no equal. This is the organ for which dealers are asking from $100.00 to $150.00, and if you will give us the opportunity to ship you one of these organs, and do not find when you receive it that it is in every way equal, if not superior to any organ for which you would have to give the above mentioned price, you can return it to us at our expense, and we will gladly return your money, paying all freight charges both ways. If you are figuring on purchasing a church organ you naturally desire to secure the very best bargain you can for the money which you have to invest, and we desire to give you the fullest opportunity to thoroughly test and try one of our organs before calling upon you to make your final decision. We will be glad to place this organ in your church where it can be examined by every member of the society, where it can be inspected and tested by the most competent musicians and critics and compared impartially with any other church organs in your neighborhood of whatever price or grade, and if you are not compelled to acknowledge that our organ is the superior instrument in every respect, and the one which will give you the best service with continued use, send it back to us entirely at our expense, and we will return your money. **Please read page 283, where you will find our wonderful "Send no Money Offer" fully and clearly explained.**

CASE. An examination of the accompanying engravings will at once convince you that this is the most superb design that you have ever seen in a church organ. We secured this design at the cost of great trouble and expense, as it appealed to us as being one of the richest, most graceful and elegant we had ever seen in our long experience. Notice the simple and graceful way in which all of the carvings and scroll work have been treated, and the generally solid and massive effect which has been secured by their consistent combination. A detailed description of this design would not tell you nearly as much as one glance at the instrument itself. We furnish it either in beautiful solid oak with quarter sawed oak front, or rich American black walnut. All of the carvings are hand wrought, the scroll work is tastefully and clearly cut and not one part is slighted. The music desk is a beautiful piece of scroll work and the top is finished with machine cut designs and turned spindle railings The keyboard is supported on each side by elegant three column trusses and the key slip is ornamented with scroll work backed by colored dustproof cloth. It has ornamental handles, casters, and an improved fall cover with lock and key. This fall cover is hung on a swinging frame which allows it to open and close without sticking or binding. The back is beautifully ornamented with hand carvings and scroll work, the top being so arranged that it can be instantly removed should it be necessary to examine the action. The pedals are fitted with metallic frames highly nickel plated and polished, are covered with Brussels carpet and fitted with the well known Beckwith device for protecting the pedal straps and preventing them from wearing out and breaking.

TONE. **The tone of this organ is remarkable in every respect.** It is fitted with nine sets of reeds all manufactured in our own factories of the very best quality of brass, bent tuned, voiced and especially prepared for this organ. For a full description of the characteristic tone qualities of these reeds see page 308. We fit this organ with the Beckwith Grand Orchestral Action, the most wonderful combination of reeds and stops ever placed in an organ. This wonderful action is controlled by the grand organ knee swell and is thrown on and off at the pleasure of the player. Besides the usual reeds we supply this organ with an extra set of subbass reeds which increase the profundity of tone to a wonderful degree. The nine sets of reeds, the eighteen necessary stops and the wonderful Beckwith Grand Orchestral Action make this the most powerful reed organ ever placed on the market. In order that the full capacity of this organ may be at the command of the player at all times we fit it with an extra large automatic Beckwith bellows which enables the performer to control the full power of the instrument without difficulty. Each set of reeds can be used separately if so desired or the performer can throw on the grand orchestral action which combines all these different sets of reeds into one sonorous and profound volume of tone, which never fails to produce an effect of startling beauty. All of these splendid qualities combine to make the Beckwith Cathedral Chapel Organ an ideal church organ in every respect, and we unhesitatingly recommend it as an organ which will satisfy you in every way.

FREE MUSICAL INSTRUCTION. **With every one of these organs we give absolutely free** a certificate which entitles the purchaser to a complete course of musical instructions on the organ to be given by one of the best music colleges in the country.

FREE. **We send free a fine organ bench,** as shown in the illustration and a complete instruction book which will be of great assistance in learning to play on the instrument.

A PROFIT SHARING CERTIFICATE GOES TO YOU FREE when you buy this organ. The certificate which we give you entitles you to share at once in the profits of our business. For a complete list of the many beautiful and valuable articles which we give in exchange for these certificates, see pages 1 and 2.

DIMENSIONS. This organ is 55 inches high, 54 inches long and 24 inches wide. It weighs, boxed for shipment, 500 pounds.

No. 46F198 Action E, Five Octaves. Oak. Price.................. $56.65

No. 46F200 Action E, Six Octaves, Oak. Price.................. 63.65

This action has eighteen stops as follows: Diapason, Principal, Dulciana, Melodia, Bourdon, Clarionet, Cornet, Cornet Echo, Cremona, Flute, Viola, Celeste, Subbass, Bass Coupler, Treble Coupler, Diapason Forte, Principal Forte and Vox Humana. It has nine sets of reeds as follows: one set of Principal reeds, 24 notes; one set of Melodia reeds, 37 notes; one set of Diapason reeds, 24 notes; one set of Celeste reeds, 37 notes; one set of Flute reeds, 37 notes: one set of Bourdon reeds, 24 notes; one set of Clarionet reeds, 24 notes; one set of Cornet Echo reeds, 37 notes; one set of Subbass reeds, 13 notes; 257 reeds in five octaves; 305 reeds in six octaves.

If you desire the organ in walnut you must add $2.00 to the above prices.

Please read page 283, where you will find our wonderful "Send No Money Offer" fully and clearly explained.

BACK VIEW OF OUR CATHEDRAL CHAPEL ORGAN.

$1.95 VIOLINS $22.45

AT $1.95 TO $22.45 WE OFFER GREAT BARGAINS IN VIOLINS, EACH AND EVERY INSTRUMENT CAREFULLY TESTED AND APPROVED BY OUR VIOLIN EXPERT.

OUR LINE OF VIOLINS **was never so complete and of such high grade as at the present time.** Our prices were never so low and we were never in a position to offer greater values in these popular instruments than we are at the present time. Some dealers are offering violins as low in price as 79 cents, but we feel that in offering a violin at $1.95 we are striking the very lowest limit at which a violin can be offered containing any qualities of real merit. We could sell to our customers violins lower in price than any other dealer can offer, but we could not afford to sell and recommend to our customers violins which we know will not give satisfaction. From the very lowest to the very highest priced violin in our line each instrument is the very best value that can possibly be offered for the money. We will be glad to have you compare any instrument in our line with any violin offered by others at double the prices we are asking.

THE VALUE OF A VIOLIN **depends upon two things—workmanship and material.** The grade of workmanship and the quality of the material which enter into a violin can be fully judged by an expert only. The manager of our musical department has made a life study of violins and violin values, and has selected from among the hundreds of samples submitted, the following violins, which represent the very greatest values which can possibly be given at the prices asked. The purchase of a violin from us guarantees your receiving an instrument which cannot be duplicated for less than double the prices we are asking. The expert knowledge of the manager of this department and our great purchasing power are both entirely at the service of our customers. Should you desire a personal selection to be made for you, the manager will be glad to comply with your wishes, and select a violin for you which will represent full value and more for the price you pay. No instruments are so susceptible of false valuations, but our knowledge and experience of violin values fully protect you against any danger of loss in this respect.

OUR LIBERAL TERMS OF SHIPMENT **make it possible for you to order any violin from us for examination and comparison without entering into any obligations or making any promise to accept it** until you satisfy yourself by examination that it is the very best value that can be obtained anywhere for less than double the price we ask.

THE FITTINGS **which we send with all of our violins are in every way equal in value to the instrument itself,** and the bow which we give, free, with each instrument is not the usual cheap thrashy affair sent out with the violins sold by other dealers, but is in every way on a par with the violins themselves. **The bow** is a very important part of the outfit, and as it is good or bad, so will be the tone produced on the instrument. These are all things which you should take into consideration when figuring on the purchase of a violin. Do not be misled by the apparently lower prices offered by other dealers, as our great buying advantage and our inexpensive method of sale make it possible for us to sell our goods at lower prices than any other dealer can make. It is impossible for other dealers to undersell us on any goods without sacrificing quality to price.

FREE FURNITURE, FREE CLOTHING, Etc.

You get a PROFIT SHARING CERTIFICATE for every purchase and these entitle you to valuable articles FREE, as explained on pages 1 and 2 of this book.

OUR $3.85 CONSERVATORY VIOLIN.

$3.85 FRONT VIEW

$3.85 BACK VIEW

This violin is made after the celebrated Stradivarius model. The wood of which it is constructed is old and well seasoned material, and the entire instrument is put together with great care. It has the characteristic Stradivarius neck and scroll and the tailpiece, fingerboard and pegs are made of solid ebony. **The body of the instrument is finished in a rich, red color, shaded into amber, and covered with a beautiful transparent varnish.** It is double lined and carefully blocked. Do not class this instrument with violins which are usually sold by dealers at this price, because it is an instrument which will compare favorably with the violins usually offered for sale by other dealers at from $6.00 to $8.00. The very best material and workmanship which can possibly be furnished at this price enter into its construction, and we can recommend it as the very best value which can be obtained in a violin for less than double the price we ask. We will be glad to have you order this instrument and compare it with violins offered generally throughout the country at more than double the price, and we know you will find it superior in every way. Shipping weight, 10 pounds.

With this violin we furnish the following outfit:

	Regular Retail Price.
Our Conservatory Violin, as described above	$10.00
One Genuine Brazilwood Bow	1.00
One Case of Solid Wood, handsomely lined and finished	1.50
One Extra Set of Glendon Strings	.25
One Piece of Rosin, good quality	.05
One Winner's New American School Instruction Book	$0.50
One Fingerboard Chart, adjustable to any violin	.25
One Tuning Pipe	.10
Total Value of Outfit	$13.65

We also give a certificate which entitles the holder to a complete course of instruction on the instrument, to be given by one of the best music colleges in the country.

No. 12F215 Our Special Outfit Price $3.35

OUR $1.95 STRADIVARIUS MODEL VIOLIN.

$1.95 FRONT VIEW

$1.95 BACK VIEW

No. 12F210 In t' violin we are furnishing a genuine Stradivarius model at an extremely low price. While we always recommend that our customers buy the very best violin their circumstances will permit, still we believe you will find no instrument at this price which will give equal satisfaction. This violin is modeled very carefully after the celebrated violins of Stradivarius. It is made of selected wood, has very neat maple back and sides with top of resonant spruce. The tailpiece, fingerboard and pegs are of very fine imitation ebony and the body of the violin is finished in a brownish red color shaded into yellow. The purfling is very neatly and evenly inlaid and the entire instrument has the appearance of the $4.00 violin ordinarily sold by music dealers. Do not make the mistake ot comparing it with the violins usually sold by dealers at $1.95, as it will be found far superior in every respect. With this violin we give a certificate entitling the holder to a course of ten weekly lessons on the instrument.

Price, STRADIVARIUS MODEL $1.95

$4.35 OUR GENUINE MAGGINI MODEL VIOLIN. $4.35

FRONT VIEW

BACK VIEW

AN EXACT COPY OF THE CELEBRATED MAGGINI VIOLIN.

No. 12F216 This violin is one of the neatest violins we have to offer in our cheaper line. It is an exact copy of the celebrated Maggini violins and the characteristic Maggini double purfling gives it a very trim, graceful appearance. The back is made of two pieces of beautiful flamed maple, and the sides of the same material. The top is made of old, well seasoned spruce and the soundholes are evenly and gracefully cut. The tailpiece, fingerboard and pegs are of solid ebony and the scroll is the characteristic neat Maggini model. The body of the instrument is finished in golden red, blending into the natural color of the wood. The varnish is transparent and highly polished, bringing out the grain of the wood in a very effective manner. This is one of the very best values that we have to offer in a moderate priced violin and in beauty of appearance, excellence of tone and durability of construction it cannot be equaled by any violin on the market at anywhere near this price.

WE FURNISH WITH THIS VIOLIN a very nicely finished serviceable bow, which is in every way as good a value as the violin itself, a box of rosin, an extra set of strings, a complete instruction book, fingerboard chart and a marbleized pasteboard case. We also give a certificate which entitles the holder to a course of fifty weekly lessons on the instrument.
Price.. $4.35

$5.15 OUR STAINER MODEL VIOLIN. $5.15

FRONT VIEW

BACK VIEW

REMEMBER you not only save money on your violin purchase, but you get one of our valuable Profit Sharing Certificates also.

No. 12F218 This violin is an exact copy of the famous Stainer violins, a characteristic of which is the bulging top and back and a long flat scroll. The original Stainer violins are today much sought after by artists on account of their exceedingly beautiful tone. Great care has been used to pattern this instrument exactly after this celebrated model. The back of the instrument is made of two pieces of very highly flamed, well seasoned maple, the sides being of the same material. The top is made of well seasoned resonant silver spruce, the soundholes are graceful and very sharply and neatly cut and the purfling is accurately and evenly inlaid. The body of the violin is a deep red color blending into the natural color of the wood. The tailpiece, fingerboard and pegs are of solid ebony. If you will compare it with the violins usually sold by dealers throughout the country you will find that you cannot purchase an instrument of this grade elsewhere for less than $10.00 to $12.00.

THIS VIOLIN GOES COMPLETE with well made, durable bow of good pattern and finely finished, a complete instruction book, a box of rosin, an extra set of strings, a fingerboard chart and a very nice marbleized pasteboard case. Also a certificate which entitles the holder to a course of fifty weekly lessons on the instrument.
Price.. $5.15

$6.10 OUR STRADIVARIUS MODEL VIOLIN. $6.10

FRONT VIEW

BACK VIEW

WE SHARE our profit with you. Your PROFIT SHARING CERTIFICATE will help you get something for nothing from us.

No. 12F222 This violin is a very accurate copy of the celebrated Stradivarius violin, and is the characteristic flat pattern of this maker. The Stradivarius violins are the most gracefully made instruments of all the celebrated makes. Antonious Stradivarius unquestionably carried the art of violin making to its very highest perfection and today his violins are the most highly prized of any of the works of the great violin makers. Our $6.10 Stradivarius model violin has a two-piece back of fine grained, well flamed maple, the sides being of the same material. The top is made of old, well seasoned resonant silver spruce, and the soundholes are of the graceful Stradivarius pattern. The body of the violin is finished in rich, deep red color, shaded into a light yellowish red, and the transparent varnish brings out the grain of the wood and the color of the finish in a beautiful manner. The tailpiece, fingerboard and pegs are made of solid ebony. The edges of the top, back and scroll are finished in the natural color of the wood, giving the violin a rich, graceful appearance.

We ship this instrument complete with a durable and well finished Brazilwood bow, a complete instruction book, an extra set of strings, a box of rosin, fingerboard chart and a nicely marbleized pasteboard case. We also give free a certificate which entitles the holder to a full course of fifty weekly lessons on the instrument. Price.... $6.10

$7.25 OUR AMATI MODEL VIOLIN. $7.25

FRONT VIEW

BACK VIEW

No. 12F223 Amati Model Violin. This violin is a perfect copy of the violins of the celebrated Nicholas Amati and has the characteristic one-piece back of that celebrated maker. It is handsomely finished and gracefully outlined and contains wonderful value for the price we ask. The back is made of one piece of selected curly maple. The sides are made of maple, and the top of very old, thoroughly seasoned silver spruce. The soundholes are of the small graceful Amati pattern and the purfling is very fine and beautifully inlaid. The instrument is finished in a light chocolate brown color, and the transparent varnish with which it is coated is highly polished and brings out many beauties in the grain of the wood. The tailpiece, fingerboard and pegs are of solid ebony and the scroll is neatly cut. This is the violin for which your dealer is obtaining from $12.00 to $15.00, and we will be glad to have you compare it with any instrument at this price offered by any other dealer.
Price.. $7.25

No. 12F224 Amati Model Violin, three-quarter size. Same description as No. 12F223. Price.. $7.25

No. 12F226 Amati Model Violin, seven-eighth size. Same description as No. 12F223. Price.. $7.25

Each of the above violins is shipped complete with a well finished, durable bow, complete instruction book, box of rosin, extra set of strings, fingerboard chart and a very nice marbleized pasteboard case, also a certificate entitling the purchaser to a complete course of fifty weekly lessons on the instrument.

$8.75 OUR GUARNERIUS MODEL VIOLIN. $8.75

FRONT VIEW BACK VIEW

YOU WILL GET A PROFIT SHARING CERTIFICATE FOR $8.75, and can soon share in our profit.

No. 12F262 This violin is a fine copy of the celebrated King Joseph violins, made by Joseph Guarnerius in the best period of his career. It has a beautifully flamed two-piece back made of selected, well seasoned maple. The sides are made of maple, the top of especially selected Cremona silver spruce. The soundholes are the characteristic Guarnerius pattern and the purfling is perfectly inlaid. The edges of the top, bottom and scroll are finished in natural wood, adding greatly to the beauty of its appearance. The instrument is a deep, rich red throughout, covered with a splendid transparent amber varnish and highly polished. The tailpiece, fingerboard and pegs are of solid ebony and the scroll is accurately and gracefully cut. Order this violin and give it a thorough trial and examination, and if you do not find that it is in every way equal to any violin that you can purchase elsewhere for from $14.00 to $16.00, we will cheerfully receive it back and return you your money. This instrument is shipped complete, with a good quality Brazilwood bow, finely finished and skillfully made, complete instruction book, box of rosin, extra set of strings, fingerboard chart and a very nicely finished wooden case, also a certificate entitling the holder to a complete course of instruction on the instrument. Price........ $8.75

$9.45 OUR SPECIAL STRADIVARIUS MODEL VIOLIN. $9.45

FRONT VIEW BACK VIEW

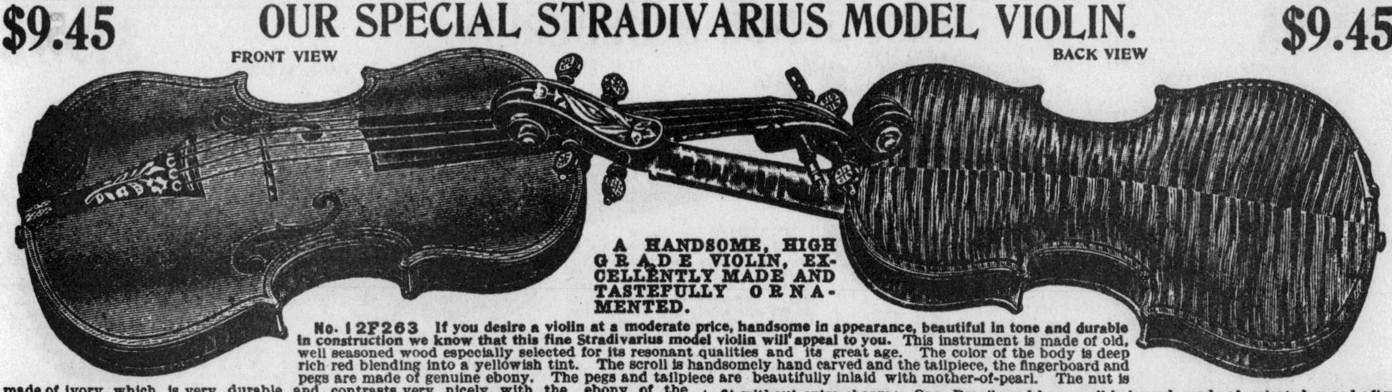

A HANDSOME, HIGH GRADE VIOLIN, EXCELLENTLY MADE AND TASTEFULLY ORNAMENTED.

No. 12F263 If you desire a violin at a moderate price, handsome in appearance, beautiful in tone and durable in construction we know that this fine Stradivarius model violin will appeal to you. This instrument is made of old, well seasoned wood especially selected for its resonant qualities and its great age. The color of the body is deep rich red blending into a yellowish tint. The scroll is handsomely hand carved and the tailpiece, the fingerboard and pegs are made of genuine ebony. The pegs and tailpiece are beautifully inlaid with mother-of-pearl. The nut is made of ivory, which is very durable and contrasts very nicely with the ebony of the fingerboard. The entire instrument is covered with beautiful transparent varnish, which shows off the grain of the wood very nicely, but the real beauty of this violin does not consist in its elegant appearance, but in its splendid tone. It is double lined throughout and blocked so as to insure the permanency of its tone. With this instrument we give the following outfit without extra charge: One Brazilwood bow, well balanced, made of selected wood after the best model, with ebony frog, German silver trimmed and inlaid with a handsome design in mother-of-pearl; one nicely finished wood case, one extra set of strings, one piece of rosin, one complete instruction book, one fingerboard chart and a certificate entitling the holder to a complete course of instruction on the instrument. Price.......... $9.45

$11.35 ANOTHER FINE STAINER MODEL VIOLIN. $11.35

FRONT VIEW BACK VIEW

REMEMBER Our Wonderful CUSTOMERS' PROFIT SHARING DEPARTMENT SHOWN ON PAGES 1 AND 2.

No. 12F264 This violin is a copy of the celebrated violins of Jacob Stainer of a higher grade than the No. 12F218, quoted on a previous page. It is a very good specimen of the expert violin maker's art and is a magnificent value at the price we ask. It has a two-piece maple back made of old, thoroughly seasoned maple, beautifully figured and flamed. The sides are maple and the top is made of carefully selected, thoroughly seasoned old Cremona spruce. It has the characteristic Stainer soundholes and the tailpiece, fingerboard and pegs are made of solid ebony. The instrument is finished in a rich wine color blending into the natural color of the wood. It is covered with beautiful transparent varnish polished to a high degree. This is an instrument which cannot be duplicated for less than from $18.00 to $20.00 anywhere in the country, and we are only able to offer it at this extremely low price on account of our inexpensive method of sale. We would be glad to send you one of these instruments under our 10 days trial proposition, and give you an opportunity to compare it with any violin in your neighborhood purchased at anywhere near this price, and if you do not find that this is superior in every way, you can return it to us, and we will cheerfully refund your money.

We ship this violin complete with a very fine Brazilwood bow, equal in quality to the violin, a complete instruction book, a box of rosin, an extra set of strings, fingerboard chart and a nicely finished well constructed wooden case; also a certificate which entitles the holder to fifty weekly lessons on the instrument, covering a period of one year. Price........ $11.35

$13.85 GENUINE DA SALO MODEL VIOLIN. $13.85

FRONT VIEW BACK VIEW

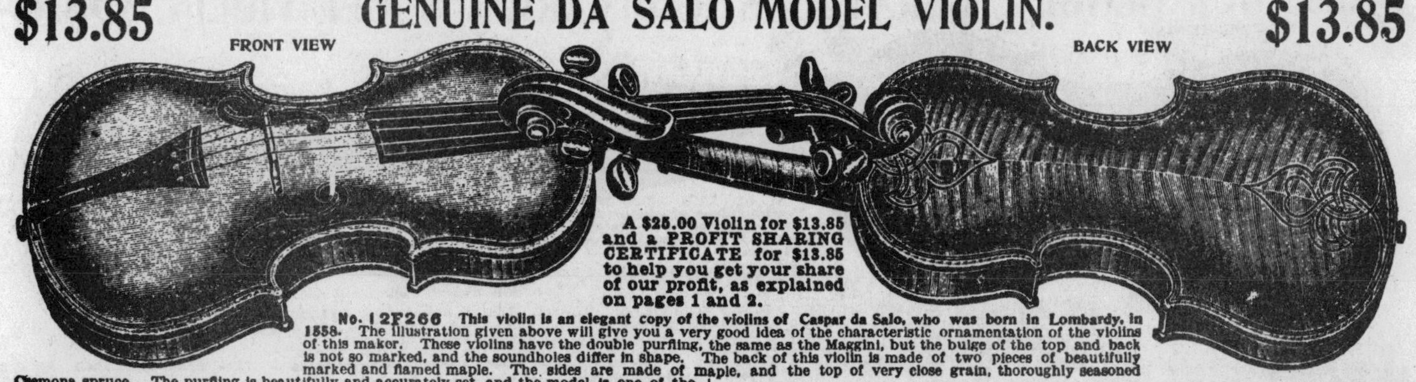

A $25.00 Violin for $13.85 and a PROFIT SHARING CERTIFICATE for $13.85 to help you get your share of our profit, as explained on pages 1 and 2.

No. 12F266 This violin is an elegant copy of the violins of Caspar da Salo, who was born in Lombardy, in 1558. The illustration given above will give you a very good idea of the characteristic ornamentation of the violins of this maker. These violins have the double purfling, the same as the Maggini, but the bulge of the top and back is not so marked, and the soundholes differ in shape. The back of this violin is made of two pieces of beautifully marked and flamed maple. The sides are made of maple, and the top of very close grain, thoroughly seasoned Cremona spruce. The purfling is beautifully and accurately set, and the model is one of the finest ever conceived. The instrument is a deep, rich red, softened by a tinge of yellow, giving the instrument a very elegant appearance. The instrument is very highly polished and covered with a coat of transparent varnish. The tailpiece, fingerboard and pegs are made of genuine ebony, and the outlines of the scroll are graceful in the extreme.

We ship this violin complete with a high quality, well balanced, Brazilwood bow, a complete instruction book, an extra set of strings, a box of rosin, a fingerboard chart and a well finished and constructed case. We also give a complete course of fifty lessons on the instrument. Price........ $13.85

$16.25 OUR PERUGINI VIRTUOSO VIOLIN. $16.25

FRONT VIEW　　BACK VIEW

No 12F271 This violin is an excellent copy of some of the very rarest of the violins of Antonious Stradivarius, which were made with one-piece back. It will be necessary for you to see this violin and examine it before its real beauty will become apparent. Its beautiful outlines show the handiwork of the violin maker who loves his profession for its own sake. The back is made of one piece of especially selected beautifully figured maple. The sides are of the same material, and the top is made of very rare old Cremona spruce. The violin gets its delicate appearance from the manner in which the purfling is inlaid, it being set very close to the outside edge of the top and bottom of the instrument. The instrument is finished in a beautiful shade of reddish brown and polished to the last degree of completion. The tailpiece and fingerboard are made of genuine ebony and the pegs of rosewood. It is double lined throughout and carefully blocked. The scroll is beautifully carved and has the word "Virtuoso" stamped upon it. This is a violin such as you will very seldom find for sale by local music dealers.

We ship this instrument complete with an exceptionally high grade Pernambuco bow with frog German silver trimmed, complete instruction book, extra set of strings, box of rosin, fingerboard chart and a well finished wooden case. Please notice that the label in each one of these violins is carefully signed with the autograph of its maker. We give with this violin a complete course of instruction on the instrument, consisting of fifty weekly lessons. Price........................ **$16.25**

$19.95 OUR GENUINE HEBERLIN. $19.95

FRONT VIEW　　BACK VIEW

No. 12F278 This violin is an exact copy of the violins made by Nicholas Amati, one of the chief characteristics of which was a one-piece back. It would be an extremely difficult matter to find a violin more beautiful in appearance than this exquisite instrument. The one-piece back is made of especially selected curled and flamed maple. The sides are made of the same material, and the top is made of very rare, old Cremona spruce. The model of the violin is very dignified and beautiful, and the body of the violin is finished in natural wood, tinged with golden yellow, blending off into a beautiful yellowish red. The instrument is double lined, carefully blocked, and the tailpiece, fingerboard and pegs are made of polished ebony. The pegs and tailpiece are ornamented with gold plated tips, which add much to the beauty of the instrument. This is an instrument which has been extensively imitated throughout the country, and we desire to caution our customers against purchasing a so called Heberlin violin, unless fully satisfied that it is genuine. We send a certificate of guarantee with each violin, signed by the maker, and each instrument has the autograph of the maker written across the label on the inside of the violin, and should anyone offer to sell you a Heberlin violin, you can easily detect the fraud by examining the label. The illustration given above will give you but a very poo idea of the real beauty of this instrument. We ship this violin complete with a very high quality Pernambuco Tourte model bow, with full German silver trimmed frog, complete instruction book, extra set of strings, box of rosin, fingerboard chart and a finely finished wooden case. We give to each purchaser of this violin a certificate which entitles the holder to a course of instruction, consisting of fifty weekly lessons. Price....., **$19.95**

$22.45 OUR LUDWIG CONCERT VIOLIN. $22.45

FRONT VIEW　　BACK VIEW

No. 12F281 This violin is a copy of the celebrated Stradivarius violin, beautifully worked out by the maker, L. Ludwig. It has a two-piece back of carefully selected, well seasoned maple, beautifully figured and flamed. The sides are maple and the top is made of carefully selected, close grained, thoroughly seasoned silver spruce. The soundholes are accurately and delicately cut, and the entire general appearance of the instrument is very handsome. The body is finished in brownish red color covered with especially prepared varnish. It is double lined throughout and carefully blocked, and the tailpiece, fingerboard and pegs are made of solid ebony. The tailpiece and fingerboard are very highly polished and the pegs and tailpiece are furnished with gold plated ornaments. Should you desire an instrument for orchestra or solo work where a powerful and sweet tone is desired we would unhesitatingly recommend this violin. Each violin bears the autograph of the maker across the label on the inside. Do not allow yourself to be deceived by imitations. This is a violin which cannot be duplicated anywhere in the country for less than $35.00 to $40.00, it will improve with age, and prove in the end a very profitable investment. We ship this violin complete with an extra quality Pernambuco wood bow, Tourte model, complete instruction book, extra set of strings, box of rosin, fingerboard chart and well finished wooden case. We also give with this violin a complete course of instruction, consisting of fifty weekly lessons. Price **$22.45**

$29.85 OUR GENUINE CURATOLI STRADIVARIUS MODEL VIOLIN. $29.85

FRONT VIEW　　BACK VIEW

An Exact Copy of one of the very best specimens of the Violins made by the celebrated Antonius Stradivarius.

No. 12F282 Antonius Stradivarius was the greatest maker of violins that ever lived. His violins are today among the very highest priced and some specimens have been sold for as high as $10,000.00. Curatoli, one of the best known modern violin makers of Italy has copied one of the choicest of these rare old violins and furnished us with a limited number of violins, which are an exact imitation of the wonderful Stradivarius violin mentioned above. Not only has he copied the model and proportions exactly, but he has also imitated the violin in every respect. The varnish and wood show the same signs of age, the top around the chinrest is worn, the color is exactly the same and so exactly has he copied the old violin that no one but the most clever expert can distinguish it from a violin worth thousands of dollars. The varnish has the same rich glow and luster, which is one of the chief characteristics of the old Cremona varnish, and, while the maker has succeeded in duplicating the old violin in appearance he has also duplicated the deep sonorous tone which gives it its great value. If you wish to be the possessor of a violin which is an exact duplicate of a $10,000.00 Stradivarius this is the instrument you are looking for. We furnish with this violin a splendid Pernambuco wood bow, Tourte model, complete instruction book, extra set of strings, box of rosin, fingerboard chart and well finished wooden case. Also a complete course of instruction consisting of 50 weekly lessons. Price........................ **$29.58**

$2.95 VIOLIN OUTFITS $23.45

AT $2.95 TO $23.45 WE OFFER A COMPLETE LINE OF HIGH GRADE VIOLIN OUTFITS

These outfits are put up for the purpose of furnishing to the customer everything necessary in connection with the violin. Every article that appears in these outfits is the very best that can be obtained, considering the price that we ask for the outfit. Each article is selected from our own stock, which is a guarantee of quality, and each violin is selected for its peculiar fitness according to the price asked.

IN ORDER TO SHOW YOU COMPARISONS between our prices and the prices generally asked for these articles, under each outfit we give the usual retail price and then quote our special bargain price for the entire outfit. Each one of these outfits is put up under the special supervision of the manager of our musical department, who is fully acquainted with the articles necessary to violin outfits, for amateur and professional alike.

WE OFFER the same liberal terms of shipment on these outfits that we are offering upon all our other violins. Each one of these violins is strictly hand made.

$2.95 BUYS A REGULAR $10.20 OUTFIT.

THIS OUTFIT IS THE BEST VALUE ever offered for the money. Anyone desiring a complete outfit for general use should not fail to examine this famous bargain. This outfit must not be compared with the outfits offered generally by dealers at this price, because an outfit of this grade is sold by dealers generally at from $10.00 to $12.00. We furnish the following articles with this outfit: One genuine Stradivarius model violin, with two-piece curly maple back, sides of the same material and top of silver spruce. Tailpiece, fingerboard and pegs are solid ebony, the body of the instrument is finished in brown shaded to yellow. The violin is double lined and blocked throughout.

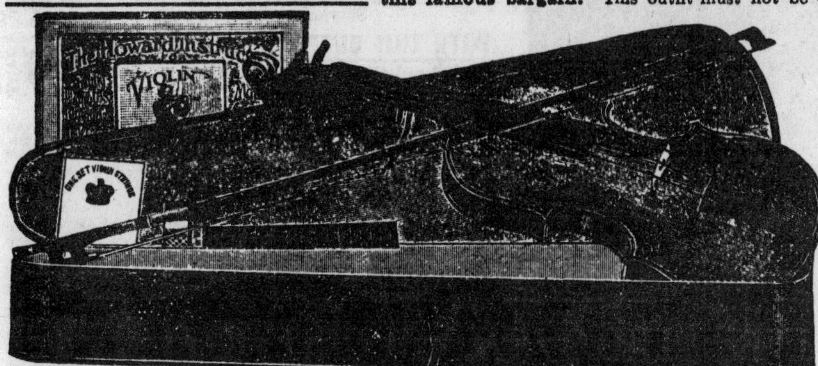

Regular retail price of this violin	$8.00
One Brazilwood bow with ebony frog inlaid with dots	.75
One marbleized pasteboard case	.40
One full set of strings	.25
One piece of rosin good quality	.05
One instructor. Simplest and most complete published	.50
One lettered fingerboard chart	.25
Total value of outfit	$10.20
No. 12F300 Price, for complete outfit	**$2.95**

Shipping weight, 7 pounds.

SEND $2.95 with your order and we will send you this outfit by express, and if you do not find it the greatest bargain you ever saw or heard of and perfectly satisfactory to you in every respect, you can return it to us at our expense and we will cheerfully refund your money. With this outfit we give a certificate which entitles the holder to a complete course of musical instruction.

OUR CHALLENGE $13.10 VIOLIN OUTFIT, $5.50.

THIS IS THE GREATEST VALUE OFFERED in a violin outfit at this price, and that this is true will be recognized at once by all who are familiar with violin values. We send this entire outfit complete, consisting of **one Maggini model violin,** instruction book, bow, rosin, case, set of strings and fingerboard chart for **$5.50. The most wonderful bargain ever offered in a violin outfit.**

THE VIOLIN which we offer with this outfit is modeled after the celebrated Maggini violin, and is very skilfully and durably made. It has the characteristic double purfling of the well known Maggini model and is the very best violin ever offered in an outfit at this price. The back is made of two pieces of very nicely flamed maple and the sides are constructed of the same material. The top is made of a carefully selected piece of thoroughly seasoned silver spruce, and the tailpiece, fingerboard and pegs are made of solid ebony. The body of the instrument is finished in a dark reddish brown, blending into the natural color of the wood. You will find this a very handsome violin and a very great bargain at this price. The neck is curly maple, very finely finished, and the scroll is neatly and gracefully cut.

One regular Maggini model violin	$10.00
One genuine Brazilwood bow	1.00
One canvas, fleece lined, leather bound case	1.00
One extra set of strings	.25
One piece of rosin	.10
One complete instruction book	.50
One fingerboard chart	.25
Total regular price of outfit	$13.10
No. 12F306 Our great bargain price for outfit	**$5.50**

Shipping weight, 7 pounds.

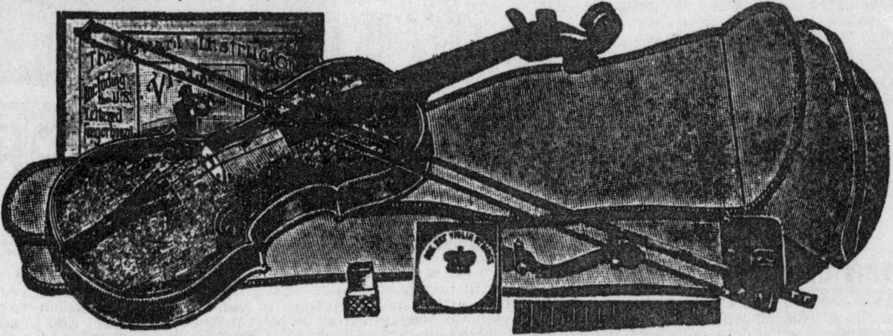

WE SHIP THIS OUTFIT to the customer with the assurance that it cannot be purchased in the regular way for less than $13.00 to $14.00. We are willing to have the purchaser compare it with anything his local dealer has to offer at these prices, and if he does not find that it is equal, and in many points superior, he can return the entire outfit to us, we will refund the money paid and pay the express charge both ways.

WITH THIS OUTFIT we give a certificate which entitles the holder to a complete course of musical instructions.

OUR HIGH GRADE CHALLENGE OUTFIT FOR $7.25.

THIS OUTFIT IS OFFERED to those who desire to invest a little more money in an outfit than we ask for the above. Every article which it contains is the very best which can possibly be supplied for the price we ask, the entire outfit has been gotten up with great care so as to insure the customer receiving something which will be perfectly satisfactory to him and fully supply his needs. **Remember, also, that you will get a Profit Sharing Certificate, and in this way you can quickly share in our profit and get something entirely free, as explained on pages 1 and 2.**

WITH THIS OUTFIT we send a certificate which entitles the customer to a full course of ir tructions on the instrument, consisting of fifty weekly lessons, covering a period of one year. This certificate costs you absolutely nothing, and the lessons are given by one of the best musical colleges in the country. You will find full particulars of this splendid offer fully outlined and explained on page 285 of this catalogue.

THIS OUTFIT is made up of one genuine Stradivarius model violin, one Brazilwood bow, case, extra set of strings, rosin, instruction book, fingerboard chart and a tuning pipe.

THE VIOLIN which we give with this outfit is a genuine Stradivarius model, very handsomely and durably made. The back is made of two pieces of beautifully curled and flamed maple. The sides are made of a very pretty piece of maple and the top of a well selected piece of close grained silver spruce. The tailpiece, fingerboard and pegs are made of solid ebony, the scroll is very nicely cut and the body of the instrument is finished a yellowish brown color very nicely blending into yellow.

Regular retail price	$12.00
The bow which we furnish with this outfit is made of Brazilwood, with ebony frog, German silver trimmed and has German silver buttons	1.50
The case is of solid wood, handsomely lined and has lock, handle and hook	1.50
One extra set of Acme strings	.75
One piece of rosin	.10
One instruction book	.50
One fingerboard chart	.25
One tuning pipe	.25
Total value of outfit	$16.85
No. 12F308 Our great bargain price	**$7.25**

Shipping weight, 12 pounds.

OUR SPECIAL CONSERVATORY OUTFIT FOR $9.85.

THIS OUTFIT is a little higher in price than those preceding it and is fully as great a bargain as any in our line. Each article which goes to make it up is carefully selected and is of the very best, considering the price of the outfit. Do not make the mistake of comparing this outfit with the outfits sold generally by dealers throughout the country at this price, as this is a regular $30.00 outfit, and cannot be purchased for less than that amount from any dealer in the country. Our buying advantage is so great that we are in a position to get the very lowest possible prices upon all classes of goods, and as we import all of these goods from Europe we are able to quote the actual importing price with but our one small percentage of profit added. Every bit of advantage we can gain, either in buying or selling, we give to our customers in low prices. That is the reason why we can sell this $30.00 violin outfit at $9.85. **The outfit contains** one special high grade Guarnerius model violin, with a beautifully flamed two-piece back made of selected well seasoned maple. The sides are made of maple and the top of especially selected Cremona spruce. The soundholes are of the characteristic Guarnerius pattern and the purfling is perfectly and tastefully inlaid. The edges of the top, bottom and scroll are finished in natural wood, adding greatly to the beauty of its finish. The instrument is a deep, rich red throughout covered with a splendid transparent amber varnish and highly polished. The tailpiece, fingerboard and pegs are of solid ebony, and the scroll is accurately and gracefully cut.

Regular retail price of violin	$20.00
One Vuillaume model bow, imitation snakewood with carved ivory frog	4.00
One solid wood case with lock, handle and spring clasps, lined with red flannel	2.75
One piece genuine Gustave Bernadel rosin, the best manufactured imported by us directly from France	.25
One Howe's Original Violin School, complete in every respect	.75
One extra set of Acme Professional strings, imported from Europe	.85
One fingerboard chart	.25
One set of violin tuning pipes	.65
One book of choice violin music	.50
Total value of outfit	$30.00

No. 12F314 Our great bargain price......$9.85
Shipping weight, 10 pounds.

WITH THIS OUTFIT WE GIVE A CERTIFICATE

Which entitles the holder to a full course of fifty weekly lessons in violin instruction, covering a period of one year. This certificate is absolutely free.

You also get your PROFIT SHARING CERTIFICATE, which entitles you to valuable articles, entirely...... FREE

OUR SPECIAL PROFESSIONAL VIOLIN OUTFIT, $13.95.

THIS OUTFIT is regularly sold by dealers throughout the country for from $45.00 to $55.00. We have been furnishing this outfit for the past five years, and it has given the greatest satisfaction to every purchaser. **We send with each outfit a certificate which entitles the holder to a complete course of instruction on the violin consisting of fifty weekly lessons covering a period of one year.** These lessons are given by one of the best music schools in the country and we charge you absolutely nothing for the certificate.

WE ARE OFFERING This outfit in response to a demand from professionals who desire an outfit for general work and do not desire to pay the usual high prices asked by dealers generally for outfits of this grade. We furnish with this outfit one special high grade Stradivarius model violin, one bow, case, rosin, instruction book, extra set of strings, fingerboard chart, tuning pipes, violin and collection of violin music. All of these articles are of the very best that can possibly be purchased at the price.

THE VIOLIN which we furnish with this outfit is a genuine Stradivarius model and is very elegant in appearance. It has two-piece back of highly flamed well seasoned maple. The sides are made of a very nice quality of maple, and the top is made of a carefully selected piece of close grain Cremona spruce. The tailpiece, fingerboard and pegs are of solid ebony, the neck is of curly maple and the scroll is carefully and tastefully cut. The body of the instrument is finished in a very rich, brownish red color. It is the most elegant violin ever offered at this price.

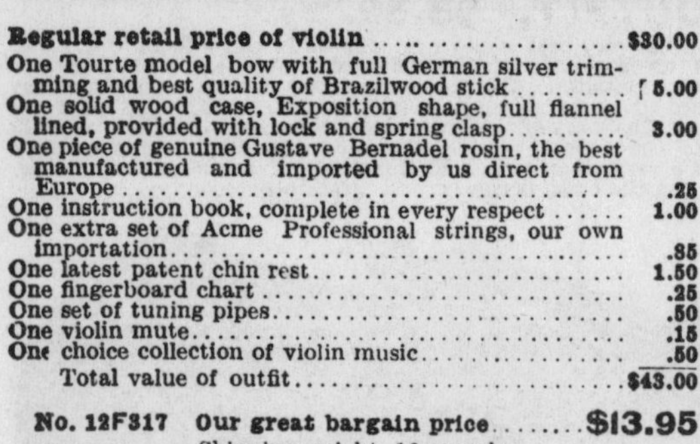

Regular retail price of violin	$30.00
One Tourte model bow with full German silver trimming and best quality of Brazilwood stick	5.00
One solid wood case, Exposition shape, full flannel lined, provided with lock and spring clasp	3.00
One piece of genuine Gustave Bernadel rosin, the best manufactured and imported by us direct from Europe	.25
One instruction book, complete in every respect	1.00
One extra set of Acme Professional strings, our own importation	.85
One latest patent chin rest	1.50
One fingerboard chart	.25
One set of tuning pipes	.50
One violin mute	.15
One choice collection of violin music	.50
Total value of outfit	$43.00

No. 12F317 Our great bargain price........$13.95
Shipping weight, 10 pounds.

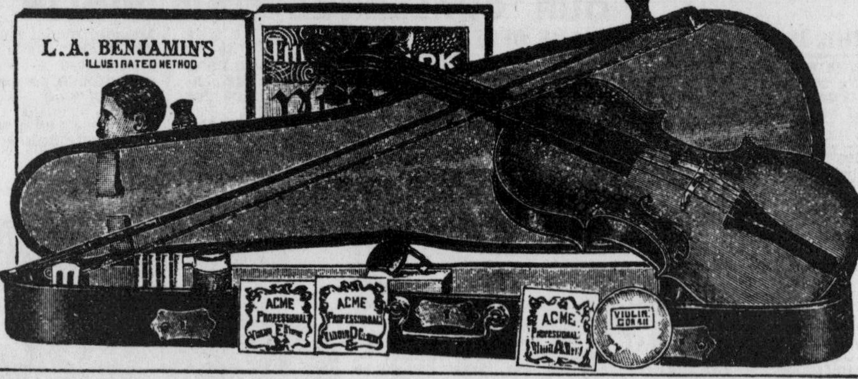

A GENUINE HEBERLIN VIOLIN OUTFIT, $17.65.

THIS OUTFIT is high grade in every respect, and every article in it is fully guaranteed by us. The maker of the violin which we send with this outfit is among the best known violin makers of Europe and we have been able to arrange with him to furnish us with a limited number of these instruments, which we can supply in an outfit at this exceptionally low price. The violin is guaranteed to be perfect in every respect and is accompanied by a numbered certificate countersigned with the autograph of the maker. Should anyone attempt to sell you a Heberlin violin you can easily detect the fraud by asking for the certificate. We are showing herewith a facsimile of the certificate which goes with every one of these violins.

THE VIOLIN is a genuine Stradivarius model, has two-piece, highly flamed maple back, nicely figured maple sides and top of old, well seasoned Cremona silver spruce. The edges of the top, bottom and scroll are finished in natural wood, adding greatly to the instrument's appearance. The fingerboard and tailpiece are of solid ebony and the pegs of rosewood. The violin is double lined throughout and carefully blocked. The body is a very deep, rich brown. An elegant instrument in every respect, and one which will please amateur and professional alike. We show below the comparison in price between this outfit at retail and our bargain price.

Regular retail price of violin	$40.00
One genuine snakewood Vuillaume model bow with handsomely carved genuine ivory frog, double pearl eye, German silver lining and ivory buttons	5.00
One violin case, covered with a durable waterproof material, made in perfect imitation of alligator skin, full lined with velvet, leather handles, nickel link clasps and nickel spring lock	5.00
One piece genuine Gustave Bernadel rosin	.25
One Henning's School for the Violin, one of the most complete instruction books published. 101 pages printed on fine paper, bound in boards	1.50
One mammoth collection of violin music with 350 selections	.75
One extra set of Acme Professional strings	.85
One latest patent violin chin rest	1.00
One violin mute	.15
One fingerboard chart	.25
One set tuning pipes	.50
Total value of outfit	$55.25

No. 12F321 Our great bargain price.......$17.65
Shipping weight, 12 pounds.

WITH THIS OUTFIT we give a certificate which entitles the holder to a complete course of instruction on the violin, consisting of fifty weekly lessons, covering a period of one year. See page 285 for full particulars.

THE PROFIT SHARING CERTIFICATE FOR $17.65 which we will send you if you buy this outfit, will enable you to share in our profit, as explained on pages 1 and 2.

OUR GENUINE L. LUDWIG OUTFIT, $18.95.

BY A SPECIAL ARRANGEMENT with this celebrated maker we are able to offer a limited number of these fine violins in these outfits. **We guarantee absolutely that each one of these outfits is genuine** and the maker's autograph will be found plainly written across the label on the inside of the instrument. This entire outfit is of exceptionally high grade and one which will satisfy anyone who desires a 1 outfit which will prove satisfactory under all conditions. If any dealer should offer to sell you an L. Ludwig violin be sure to examine the label on the inside, and if you do not find the maker's signature written across it you will know at once that it is an imitation.

Regular retail price of violin.......................**$35.00**
One Tourte model bow with full German silver trimming and best quality Brazilwood stick............ 5.00
One leather case, Exposition shape, full velvet lined, nickel trimmed, spring clasps, lock, key and leather handle.................... 5.00
One piece of genuine Gustave Bernadel rosin......... .25
One "Wichtl's Young Violinist," containing 100 exercises and celebrated violin duets............ 1.00
One extra set of Acme Professional strings........... .85
One latest patent chin rest............ 1.00
One fingerboard chart............ .25
One set of violin tuning pipes............ .50
One violin mute............ .15
One Gigantic collection violin music............ .50
Total value of outfit........................**$49.50**

No. 12F325 Our great bargain price.......**$18.95**
Shipping weight, 12 pounds.

TO EVERY PURCHASER of this violin outfit we give a certificate entitling the holder to a full course of instruction on the violin, consisting of 50 weekly lessons, covering a period of one year. These lessons will be given by one of the best known and thorough music colleges in the country.

THE VIOLIN is of the well known Stradivarius model, gracefully and carefully worked out by the maker. It is an exceptionally large instrument, and especially desirable for orchestra work, where a broad and powerful tone is desired. It has a two-piece beautifully figured and flamed maple back, and the sides are made of a fine piece of the same material. The top is made of a rare piece of genuine Cremona silver spruce, guaranteeing a deep, rich tone to the instrument. The tailpiece and fingerboard are made of solid ebony, highly polished, and the pegs of genuine rosewood. The body and scroll of the instrument are finished in rich cherry red, the edges of the top and bottom being finished in natural wood. This violin is one that we can highly recommend for its elegant appearance and beautiful tone.

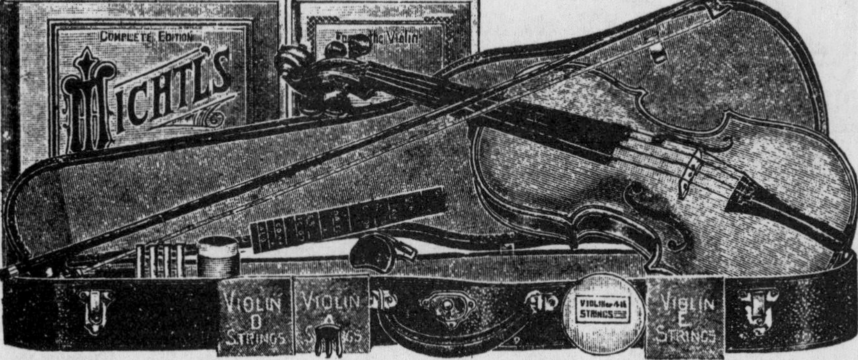

OUR GENUINE CHADWICK (LONDON) VIOLIN OUTFIT, $23.45.

THIS IS AN EXTREMELY HIGH GRADE VIOLIN OUTFIT which we have made up for the use of professionals and high class amateurs, and which we are prepared to furnish at the present time at a price never before heard of. This is one of the very best outfits we have ever offered to our customers, and its sale up to the present time proves that it is destined to become as popular as any of our other high grade outfits. If you are looking for a violin outfit which will be strictly high class in every respect and in which every article will be of the very best, you will make no mistake in purchasing this. You will not find an outfit of this grade offered for sale by any of your local dealers. The violin which we furnish with this outfit is made under the direct supervision of Chadwick, the famous London violin maker, and we guarantee its beauty of appearance, the durability of its workmanship and the quality of its tone. If you could purchase an outfit of this high grade from your local dealer it would cost you as follows: One high grade Chadwick violin, Stradivarius model, beautifully worked out by the maker. We cannot begin to describe the elegant and graceful appearance of this instrument, as it must be seen to be appreciated. The back is made of two pieces of very close grain, finely flamed maple. The sides are made of the same material and the top is made of a rare old piece of Cremona silver spruce. It is double lined throughout and carefully blocked. The tailpiece, fingerboard and pegs are made of solid ebony, and the body of the instrument is finished in deep orange yellow. This is undoubtedly the most elegant violin which we furnish with any outfit shown in our catalogue. It has the words, "The Chadwick London Violin" stamped on the back of the scroll.

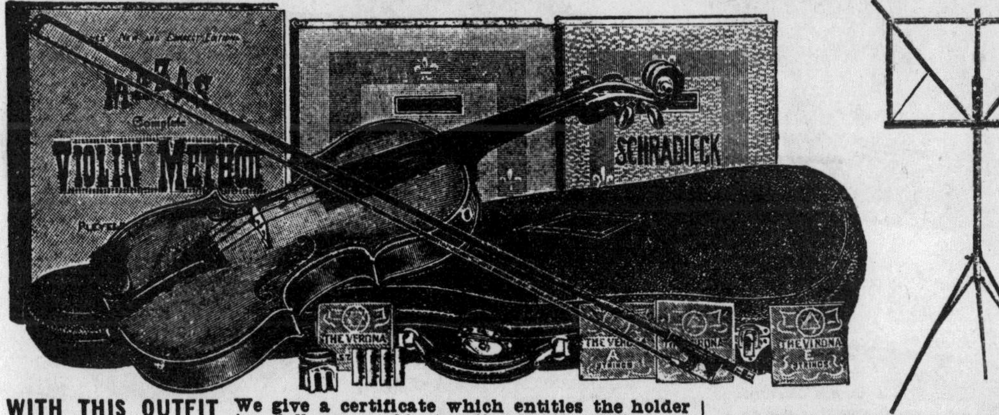

Regular retail price of violin.................**$40.00**
One Tourte model bow, full German silver trimmed, and of the very best quality Pernambuco wood........... 12.00
One pulp case, covered throughout with a fine grade of leather, velvet lined and nickel trimmed........... 8.00
One genuine Quinn telescope music stand........... 2.00
One genuine piece Gustave Bernadel rosin........... .25
One Mazas complete violin instructor........... 1.00
Two volumes of Schradieck's violin studies........... 1.00
One extra set of Verona strings. .85
One latest pattern chin rest.. 1.00
One set of tuning pipes...... .50
One violin mute........... .15
Total value of outfit.........**$66.75**

No. 12F330 Our great bargain price.......**$23.45**
Shipping weight, 14 pounds.

WITH THIS OUTFIT We give a certificate which entitles the holder to a full course of instruction on the violin, consisting of 50 weekly lessons, covering a period of one year. These lessons will be given by one of the best known and most thorough music colleges in the country, and we give you this certificate absolutely free

VIOLONCELLOS.

WEIGHT, PACKED FOR SHIPMENT, ABOUT 45 POUNDS.

Our $9.25 Violoncello with Patent Head.

No. 12F400 We furnish it complete with perfect fitting canvas bag, violoncello bow, a piece of fine rosin in pasteboard case, **one fingerboard chart,** and a complete instruction book, and the instrument is ready to play as soon as received by you. Price........................**$9.25**

No. 12F406 This instrument is of excellent quality and has handsome inlaid edges which add greatly to its general appearance. It has patent head as shown in illustration. It is fitted with a complete set of the best strings,

And with it are furnished FREE,
A Perfect Fitting Canvas Bag,
A Handsome Violoncello Bow,
An Extra Large Piece of fine Rosin and
A Valuable Instructor.

Price..**$11.20**

Our Highest Grade Violoncello with Peg or Patent Head, $15.45.

No. 12F420 This is an instrument which must be seen, examined and tested in order to fully appreciate all its merits. This violoncello is extra fine quality, beautifully polished. Solid ebony trimmings throughout, including the solid ebony fingerboard and solid ebony tailpiece. The peg head is the very best which is manufactured and the material used in the body is such as is found only in the highest grade instruments. It is made by expert workmen, and the construction is such that it produces a tone such as you would naturally expect only from instruments which retailers sell at from $25.00 to $30.00. We include a perfect fitting canvas bag, valuable instruction book, a violoncello bow and a large piece of our best rosin in a pasteboard box, so that the instrument is ready to play as soon as received. Price... ....**$15.45**

No. 12F422 Same description as our No. 12F420, but fitted with best quality patent head on brass plates. Price.............**$17.85**

DOUBLE BASS VIOLS.

EACH INSTRUMENT IS PACKED WITH GREAT CARE, AND WHEN READY TO SHIP WEIGHS 125 POUNDS.

Our $18.95 One-Half Size Double Bass Viol.

No. 12F450 At $18.95 we offer a four string Double Bass Viol, one-half size, with bow, and complete instruction book. This double bass viol is of the very best model, is dark red shaded, very highly polished, and is superior quality in every respect. Best patent head. Price........................**$18.95**

Our Three-Quarter Size Double Bass Viol.

No. 12F462 A High Grade Three-Quarter Size Double Bass Viol for $19.50. This double bass viol has four strings, finest iron patent head and is beautifully shaded and colored. In finish it is wonderfully fine, being highly polished throughout.
Price **$19.50**

$22.85 Double Bass Viol.

Three-Quarter Size.

No. 12F466 This Double Bass Viol has four strings, high grade iron patent head, solid ebony fingerboard. The inlaid purfling is very handsome and adds greatly to the attractiveness of the instrument, giving it the appearance of the most expensive and highest priced viols on the market. We furnish free with each instrument a good double bass bow and complete instruction book. Price...**$22.85**

$1.95 GUITARS $25.15

AT $1.95 TO $25.15 WE OFFER THIS MATCHLESS LINE OF HIGH GRADE GUITARS

OUR LINE OF GUITARS is more than usually complete this year, and we are glad to be able to offer to our customers such especially wonderful values in this line. We wish to say that we could offer for sale guitars as low in price as $1.25, but the reputation, which we have been so many years in building up, is much too valuable for us to sacrifice for the sake of a few cents profit on the sale of such an instrument. Do not allow yourself to be misled by the apparently lower prices offered by others upon these instruments, because a careful examination and comparison will at once convince you that such instruments are not by any means what they appear to be, and that the guitar which we offer at $1.95 is superior in every way to those offered by others at a much higher price. Each one of the following guitars from the highest to the lowest in price contains the very best material and workmanship that can possibly enter into a guitar at the price named.

THE DIMENSIONS OF THE DIFFERENT SIZES of guitars are as follows:

STANDARD SIZE—Length of body, 18½ inches; total length, 37 inches; width, small end, 9⅛ inches; width, large end, 12¼ inches; depth, small end, 3⅛ inches; depth, large end, 3⅞ inches.

CONCERT SIZE—Length of body, 18¾ inches; total length, 37¾ inches; width, small end, 9⅝ inches; width, large end, 13¼ inches; depth, small end, 3⅛ inches; depth, large end, 3⅞ inches.

GRAND CONCERT SIZE—Length of body, 19 inches, total length, 38 inches; width, small end, 10 inches; width, large end, 14 inches, depth, small end, 3⅜ inches; depth, large end, 4 inches.

AUDITORIUM SIZE — Length of body, 19½ inches; total length, 38¾ inches; width, small end, 10⅜ inches; width, large end, 14⅞ inches; depth, small end, 3⅜ inches; depth, large end, 4 inches. **The auditorium size guitars are made to order only, and require from two to three weeks' time.**

WE SELL ALL OF THESE GUITARS upon the same liberal terms upon which we sell all other musical instruments, and give every purchaser 10 days trial.

REMEMBER You get a Profit Sharing Certificate for your purchase entitling you to share in our profits as explained on pages 1 and 2.

WITH EACH GUITAR we send an extra set of strings, one magic Capo d'Astro, one book of Guckert's chords and one lettered fingerboard chart. Shipping weight, 12 pounds.

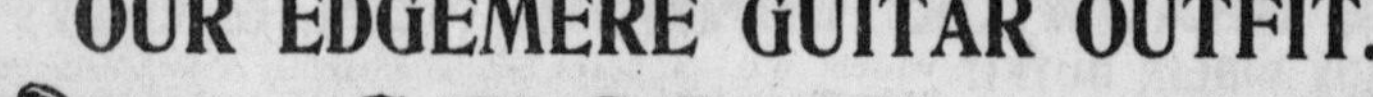

OUR EDGEMERE GUITAR OUTFIT.

$3.95
Part of the $3.95 you send us you will soon get back.
YOUR PROFIT SHARING CERTIFICATE
Will help you get something
FREE
Your share of our profit, as explained on pages 1 and 2.
See what is yours FREE on pages 1 and 2.
You will get a
PROFIT SHARING CERTIFICATE
If you buy this outfit, and will soon be able to
SHARE IN OUR PROFITS
GUCKERT'S CHORD BOOK
FRONT VIEW
BACK VIEW

This guitar is rosewood finished, being an exact imitation of the highest priced genuine rosewood. It has a spruce top, inlaid with variegated wood around the edge and soundhole, and bound with white celluloid. It is also inlaid down the back with a strip of different colored wood. The fingerboard is made of genuine rosewood with pearl position dots and raised frets. It has the best quality of American made patent head, nickel plated metal tailpiece and ebony bridge.

With this guitar outfit we give a certificate, entitling the holder to a complete course of instruction on the instrument, consisting of ten weekly lessons, given by one of the best music colleges in the country.

We offer this outfit as the very best that could possibly be put up at this price. The material and workmanship which enter into the construction of every article offered is the very best that has ever been offered at anywhere near this price. The tone and finish of the guitar is everything that could be found in an instrument sold by others at from $7.00 to $10.00

We can furnish these guitars in standard size only. Shipping weight, about 12 pounds.

With this guitar we furnish the following outfit:

	Regular Retail Price
Our Edgemere Guitar, as described	$5.00
One Canvas Case, flannel lined, leather bound	1.50
One Book of Guckert's Chords	.50
One Extra Set of Glendon Strings	.50
One Guitar Tuner	.50
One Lettered Fingerboard Chart	.25
One Thumb Pick	.10
One Magic Capo d'Astro	.25
Total value of outfit	$8.60

No. 12F605 Our bargain price.......... $3.95

No. 12F606 We can also furnish this guitar in quarter sawed oak, exactly as described above, complete with outfit. Price.......... $3.95

$1.95 THE TROUBADOUR GUITAR. | THE OAKWOOD GUITAR AT $2.35.

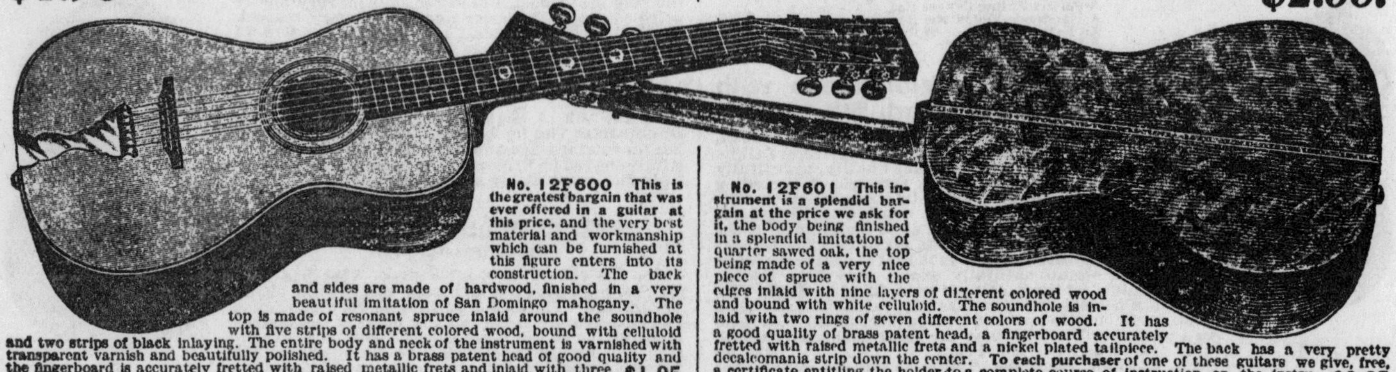

No. 12F600 This is the greatest bargain that was ever offered in a guitar at this price, and the very best material and workmanship which can be furnished at this figure enters into its construction. The back and sides are made of hardwood, finished in a very beautiful imitation of San Domingo mahogany. The top is made of resonant spruce inlaid around the soundhole with five strips of different colored wood, bound with celluloid and two strips of black inlaying. The entire body and neck of the instrument is varnished with transparent varnish and beautifully polished. It has a brass patent head of good quality and the fingerboard is accurately fretted with raised metallic frets and inlaid with three pearl position dots. Standard size only. Price.......... $1.95

No. 12F601 This instrument is a splendid bargain at the price we ask for it, the body being finished in a splendid imitation of quarter sawed oak, the top being made of a very nice piece of spruce with the edges inlaid with nine layers of different colored wood and bound with white celluloid. The soundhole is inlaid with two rings of seven different colors of wood. It has a good quality of brass patent head, a fingerboard accurately fretted with raised metallic frets and a nickel plated tailpiece. The back has a very pretty decalcomania strip down the center. **To each purchaser of one of these guitars we give, free,** a certificate entitling the holder to a complete course of instruction on the instrument. Standard size only. Price.......... $2.35

THE STANFORD GUITAR, $4.20.

Our college line of guitars represents the very highest attainment in guitar building. A trial order will satisfy you of this fact.

YOU WILL GET A PROFIT SHARING CERTIFICATE for your purchase and can soon get a valuable article entirely FREE, as explained on pages 1 and 2.

BACK VIEW

FRONT VIEW

No. 12F608 This guitar is finished in a very beautiful and tasty manner. Sides and back are made of hardwood, finished in perfect imitation of rosewood. The back has a strip of inlaid colored wood down the center and around the outside edges, the inlaying on the edges being bound with white celluloid. The top is made of eastern spruce inlaid around the soundhole with three rings of different colored wood, inlaid around the outside edge with colored wood and bound with white celluloid. It has a good quality of brass patent head, a rosewood fingerboard accurately fretted with raised metallic frets and inlaid w'th pearl position dots. It has a nickel plated tailpiece, and the body of the instrument is varnished with transparent varnish and highly polished.

WITH EACH ONE O THESE GUITARS, **we give the purchaser a certificate which entitles him to a complete course of instruction on the instrument, consisting of fifty weekly lessons, c vering a period of one year.** This course of instruction will make you a performer upon the gu'tar if you hav a fair amount of perseverance and intelligence. We will be glad to na e you compare this instrument with anything your dealer has to offer in this line at double the price we are asking you for this, as we know you will find it superior in every way. While we always recommend that our customers purchase the very best guitar of which their circumstances will admit, still, if you feel that you do not desire to pay more than $4.20 for a guitar, we would recommend this instrument to you as something especially good at this price. Standard size only.

No 12F608 Price..................................**$4.20**

THE COLUMBIA GUITAR, $6.90.

You will not find these guitars for sale by dealers. The designs are our exclusive property and can be obtained from us only.

From the lowest to the highest in price, each guitar is the very best that can be sold for the price.

BACK VIEW

FRONT VIEW

This guitar is an especially fine bargain at the price we ask, and will compare very favorably with anything your dealer has to offer at from $10.00 to $12.00. The back and sides are made of beautifully figured quarter sawed oak, inlaid down the back and around the edges with broad strips of different colored wood. The edges are bound with white celluloid. The top is made of a well selected piece of eastern spruce, inlaid around the edge with a broad strip of different colored wood and bound with white celluloid. It is inlaid around the soundhole with three rings of different colored wood, and the edge bound with white celluloid. The head is fitted with a very good quality brass patent head, and veneered on the top with rosewood. The fingerboard is accurately fretted with raised metallic frets and inlaid with diamond shaped position dots. It is fitted with a nickel plated tailpiece which takes the strain of the strings off the top, and the entire instrument is coated with transparent varnish, highly polished.

A FREE COURSE OF MUSICAL INSTRUCTION **goes absolutely free with each one of these guitars.** This course consists of fifty weekly lessons, covering a period of one year. The splendid value which we are offering in this instrument fully justifies us shipping it out under our liberal terms of shipment. It is a guitar which cannot be purchased from your local dealer for less than from $10.00 to $15.00. We can recommend this instrument as being a splendid bargain, considering the low price we ask for it.

No. 12F614 Standard size. Price..................................**$6.90**
No. 12F616 Concert size. Price..................................**7.60**

THE OXFORD, $7.85.

Give us a trial order for one of our best guitars. If you are an artist you will admire the finish. If you are a musician you will fall in love with the tone.

Nothing is quite so satisfying as a guitar with an elegant finish and beautiful tone. Our guitars never fail to satisfy the purchaser in both of these points.

BACK VIEW

FRONT VIEW

This guitar, for which your dealer is asking from $12.00 to $15.00, was formerly one of our Acme Professional style and never sold at less than $9.90. The immense increase in our business has enabled us to reduce the price on this guitar to a wonderful extent. The back and sides are made of an especially selected piece of mahogany. The back is inlaid down the center and around the outside edges with a broad strip of different colored wood, the edges being bound with white celluloid. The top is made of an especially fine piece of eastern spruce. The outside edges are inlaid with a broad strip of different colored wood and bound with white celluloid. There are five strips of different colored wood inlaid around the soundhole, and the edges bound with white celluloid. The head is inlaid on the top with rosewood, the fingerboard is accurately fretted with raised metallic frets, the bridge is ebony and celluloid, and the instrument is fitted with a very fine quality brass patent head. The entire guitar is beautifully finished and polished, covered with elegant transparent varnish.

WE GIVE ABSOLUTELY FREE **to every purchaser of this guitar a certificate which entitles him to a complete course of instruction on the instrument, consisting of fifty weekly lessons, given by one of the best music colleges in the country.** Considering the price we ask for this instrument it cannot be duplicated anywhere on the market.

No. 12F650 Standard size. Price..................................**$7.85**
No. 12F651 Concert size. Price..................................**8.55**

THE CAMBRIDGE, $8.75.

We guarantee tone, finish, durability and price. You cannot possibly make a mistake when you purchase one of these guitars.

Nothing adds quite so much elegance to your apartment as a well made, elegantly finished guitar. Our guitars are within the reach of all.

BACK VIEW

FRONT VIEW

This guitar is another very fine bargain and is the result of a very fortunate purchase on our part. The entire finishings of the instrument are plain and neat and the material and workmanship which enters into its construction are excellent in every respect. It has a genuine rosewood back and sides and the top is made of a fine piece of eastern spruce finished in natural wood. It is inlaid down the back with a broad strip of wood in three colors. The top is inlaid around the edge with a broad strip of different colored woods and bound with white celluloid. It is inlaid around the soundhole with a ring of different colored wood and bound with white celluloid. The neck is solid mahogany, the head is inlaid on the front and back with rosewood and ornamented on the front with a beautiful design inlaid in pearl. It has a fine quality of nickel plated patent head, and ebony fingerboard accurately fretted with raised metallic frets and inlaid with pearl position dots. It is an instrument which you cannot purchase generally from your dealer for less than from $15.00 to $18.00 and we would be glad to have it compared with any instrument at this price.

WE GIVE WITH THIS GUITAR **a certificate which entitles you to a complete course of instruction by one of the very best music colleges in the country.** This course consists of fifty weekly lessons, covering a period of one year.

No. 12F653 Standard size. Price..................................**$ 8.75**
No. 12F654 Concert size. Price..................................**[illegible]**
No. 12F655 Grand Concert size. Price..................................**10.25**

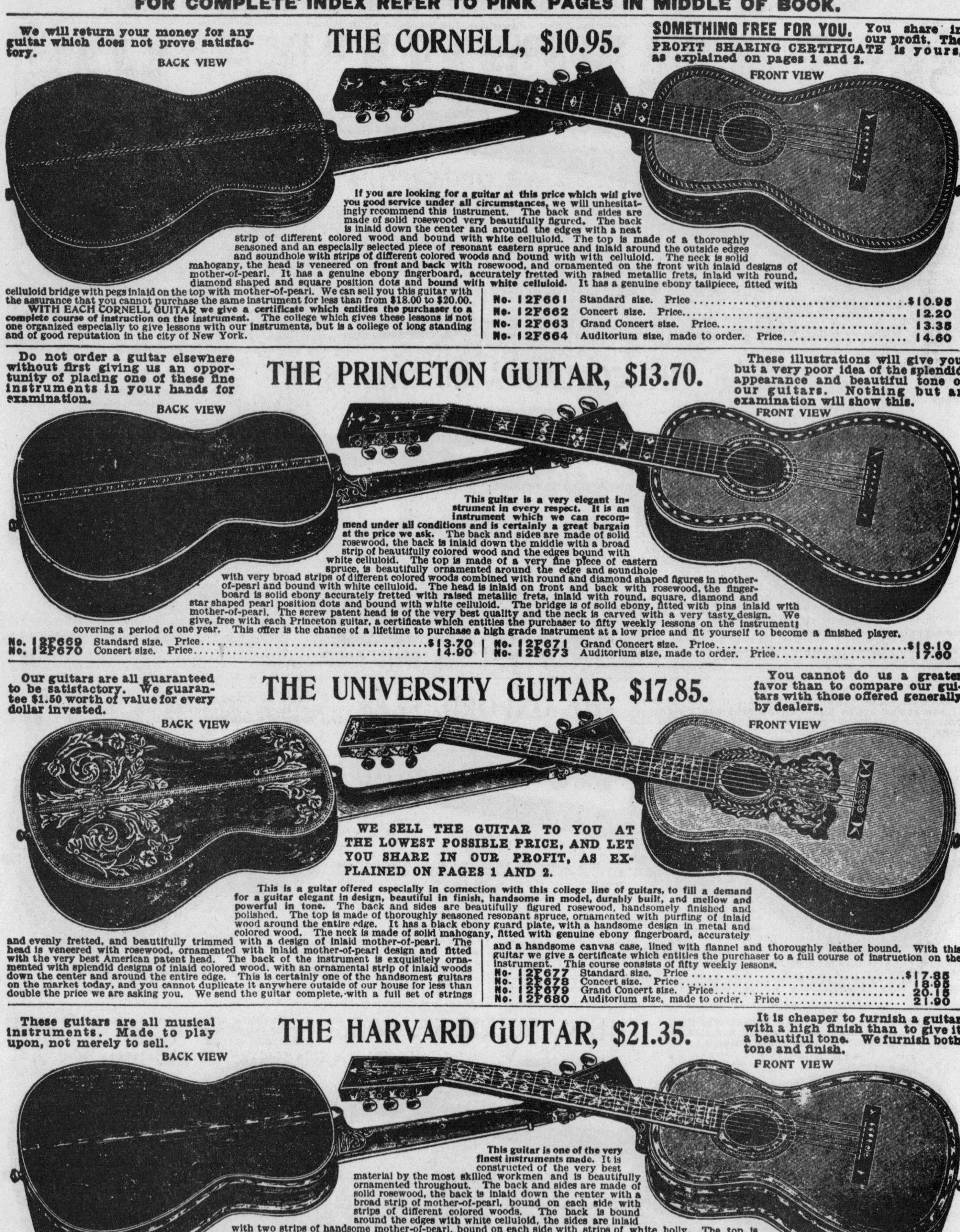

THE CORNELL, $10.95.

We will return your money for any guitar which does not prove satisfactory.

SOMETHING FREE FOR YOU. You share in our profit. The PROFIT SHARING CERTIFICATE is yours, as explained on pages 1 and 2.

If you are looking for a guitar at this price which will give you good service under all circumstances, we will unhesitatingly recommend this instrument. The back and sides are made of solid rosewood very beautifully figured. The back is inlaid down the center and around the edges with a neat strip of different colored wood and bound with white celluloid. The top is made of a thoroughly seasoned and an especially selected piece of resonant eastern spruce and inlaid around the outside edges and soundhole with strips of different colored woods and bound with with celluloid. The neck is solid mahogany, the head is veneered on front and back with rosewood, and ornamented on the front with inlaid designs of mother-of-pearl. It has a genuine ebony fingerboard, accurately fretted with raised metallic frets, inlaid with round, diamond shaped and square position dots and bound with white celluloid. It has a genuine ebony tailpiece, fitted with celluloid bridge with pegs inlaid on the top with mother-of-pearl. We can sell you this guitar with the assurance that you cannot purchase the same instrument for less than from $18.00 to $20.00.

WITH EACH CORNELL GUITAR we give a certificate which entitles the purchaser to a complete course of instruction on the instrument. The college which gives these lessons is not one organized especially to give lessons with our instruments, but is a college of long standing and of good reputation in the city of New York.

No. 12F661	Standard size. Price	$10.95
No. 12F662	Concert size. Price	12.20
No. 12F663	Grand Concert size. Price	13.35
No. 12F664	Auditorium size, made to order. Price	14.60

THE PRINCETON GUITAR, $13.70.

Do not order a guitar elsewhere without first giving us an opportunity of placing one of these fine instruments in your hands for examination.

These illustrations will give you but a very poor idea of the splendid appearance and beautiful tone of our guitars. Nothing but an examination will show this.

This guitar is a very elegant instrument in every respect. It is an instrument which we can recommend under all conditions and is certainly a great bargain at the price we ask. The back and sides are made of solid rosewood, the back is inlaid down the middle with a broad strip of beautifully colored wood and the edges bound with white celluloid. The top is made of a very fine piece of eastern spruce, is beautifully ornamented around the edge and soundhole with very broad strips of different colored woods combined with round and diamond shaped figures in mother-of-pearl and bound with white celluloid. The head is inlaid on front and back with rosewood, the fingerboard is solid ebony accurately fretted with raised metallic frets, inlaid with round, square, diamond and star shaped pearl position dots and bound with white celluloid. The bridge is of solid ebony, fitted with pins inlaid with mother-of-pearl. The screw patent head is of the very best quality and the neck is carved with a very tasty design. We give, free with each Princeton guitar, a certificate which entitles the purchaser to fifty weekly lessons on the instrument covering a period of one year. This offer is the chance of a lifetime to purchase a high grade instrument at a low price and fit yourself to become a finished player.

No. 12F669	Standard size. Price	$13.70
No. 12F670	Concert size. Price	14.90
No. 12F671	Grand Concert size. Price	$16.10
No. 12F673	Auditorium size, made to order. Price	17.60

THE UNIVERSITY GUITAR, $17.85.

Our guitars are all guaranteed to be satisfactory. We guarantee $1.50 worth of value for every dollar invested.

You cannot do us a greater favor than to compare our guitars with those offered generally by dealers.

WE SELL THE GUITAR TO YOU AT THE LOWEST POSSIBLE PRICE, AND LET YOU SHARE IN OUR PROFIT, AS EXPLAINED ON PAGES 1 AND 2.

This is a guitar offered especially in connection with this college line of guitars, to fill a demand for a guitar elegant in design, beautiful in finish, handsome in model, durably built, and mellow and powerful in tone. The back and sides are beautifully figured rosewood, handsomely finished and polished. The top is made of thoroughly seasoned resonant spruce, ornamented with purfling of inlaid wood around the entire edge. It has a black ebony guard plate, with a handsome design in metal and colored wood. The neck is made of solid mahogany, fitted with genuine ebony fingerboard, accurately and evenly fretted, and beautifully trimmed with a design of inlaid mother-of-pearl. The head is veneered with rosewood, ornamented with inlaid mother-of-pearl design and fitted with the very best American patent head. The back of the instrument is exquisitely ornamented with splendid designs of inlaid colored wood, with an ornamental strip of inlaid woods down the center and around the entire edge. This is certainly one of the handsomest guitars on the market today, and you cannot duplicate it anywhere outside of our house for less than double the price we are asking you. We send the guitar complete, with a full set of strings and a handsome canvas case, lined with flannel and thoroughly leather bound. With this guitar we give a certificate which entitles the purchaser to a full course of instruction on the instrument. This course consists of fifty weekly lessons.

No. 12F677	Standard size. Price	$17.85
No. 12F678	Concert size. Price	18.95
No. 12F679	Grand Concert size. Price	20.15
No. 12F680	Auditorium size, made to order. Price	21.90

THE HARVARD GUITAR, $21.35.

These guitars are all musical instruments. Made to play upon, not merely to sell.

It is cheaper to furnish a guitar with a high finish than to give it a beautiful tone. We furnish both tone and finish.

This guitar is one of the very finest instruments made. It is constructed of the very best material by the most skilled workmen and is beautifully ornamented throughout. The back and sides are made of solid rosewood, the back is inlaid down the center with a broad strip of mother-of-pearl, bound on each side with strips of different colored woods. The back is bound around the edges with white celluloid, the sides are inlaid with two strips of handsome mother-of-pearl, bound on each side with strips of white holly. The top is made of especially selected eastern silver spruce and is inlaid around the edge and soundhole with a very broad strip of mother-of-pearl bound with strips of different colored wood. The edges of the top and soundhole are bound with white celluloid. The neck is made of solid mahogany, the head is inlaid on the front and back with rosewood and bound with white celluloid. It is beautifully ornamented on the front with designs of mother-of-pearl. The fingerboard is made of solid ebony, accurately fretted with metallic frets, bound with white celluloid and handsomely ornamented with a vine, flowers and leaves made of inlaid metal and different colored mother-of-pearl. The bridge is made of solid ebony and has pegs of white celluloid inlaid on top with ebony. It has the very best pattern brass American patent head, and the neck is beautifully carved and capped with white celluloid. The entire instrument is handsomely finished and polished and is one of the most beautiful in design, finish and tone ever offered to the public.

No. 12F681	Standard size. Price	$21.35
No. 12F682	Concert size. Price	23.35
No. 12F683	Grand Concert size. Price	25.15
No. 12F685	Auditorium size, made to order. Price	27.15

AT $1.95 TO $19.85 WE OFFER THIS SPLENDID LINE OF MANDOLINS.

WE FEEL CONSIDERABLE PARDONABLE PRIDE in the line of mandolins which we have to show this season. Our buyer has been more than usually careful and fortunate in his work, and has succeeded in getting together a line of mandolins which we believe to be unsurpassed by any line offered for sale in the country. We could offer mandolins as low in price as $1.25, but they would be instruments which would be entirely unsatisfactory to our customers, and while they would be in every way equal to the mandolins offered by others at from $2.25 to $2.50, still, we do not feel that they are instruments which would meet with the approval of our customers, and therefore, we do not offer them for sale. Other dealers are offering mandolins a little lower in price than we are showing, but a careful comparison of our instruments with theirs will show you at once that they are far inferior to any mandolins that we are offering.

OUR TERMS OF SHIPMENT are as liberal upon our mandolins as upon all of our other instruments. We allow any mandolin purchased from us to be tried and tested for ten days, and will receive it back and cheerfully refund the price paid, together with transportation charges, if it does not prove satisfactory.

YOU WILL GET A PROFIT SHARING CERTIFICATE for every order you send us, as well as saving money on your purchase.

WITH EACH ONE OF THESE MANDOLINS we give an extra set of strings, a complete instruction book, a very nice pick, a fingerboard chart, and a complete course of instruction on the instrument absolutely free. Weight of mandolins, about 7 pounds.

BACK VIEW

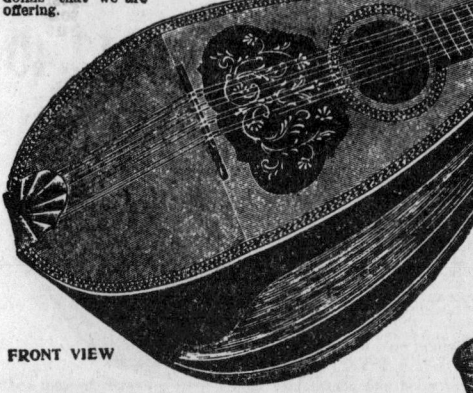

OUR EMPIRE MANDOLIN OUTFIT AT $3.95.

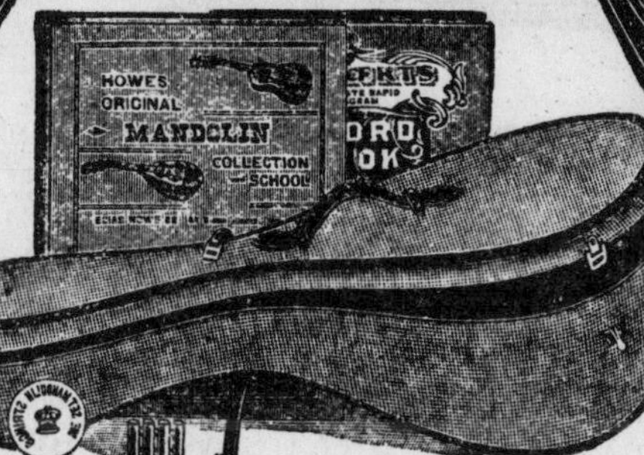

FRONT VIEW

This mandolin outfit is complete in every respect, and is on of the greatest bargains ever offered at this price. The mandolin has 11 ribs of alternate rosewood and mahogany, with strips of white holly between. It has a solid rosewood cap, top of resonant spruce, inlaid around the edge with a broad strip of different colored wood and bound with white celluloid. The soundhole has a ring of different colored wood, the guard plate is of fancy design, inlaid with a neat ornament in different colored wood. The neck is solid mahogany, the patent head is of the best screw pattern, the fingerboard is solid rosewood with raised metallic frets and genuine mother-of-pearl position dots. It has a nickel plated sleeve protector and a solid rosewood bridge. **This is the most complete mandolin outfit ever offered at this price, and is one which dealers are generally selling at from $6.00 to $8.00.**

We also give with this mandolin a complete course of instruction by one of the best music colleges in the country.

This outfit consists of the following:	Regular Retail Price
One Empire Mandolin, as described above	$ 8.00
One Extra Set of Glendon Strings..........	.50
One Lettered Fingerboard Chart..........	.25
One Complete Instruction Book..........	.50
One Guckert's Chord Book..........	.25
One Fine Canvas Flannel Lined Case, leather bound..........	1.50
One Mandolin Pick..........	.05
One Mandolin Tuner..........	.25
Total value of outfit..........	$11.30
No. 12E705 Our great bargain price......	3.95

$1.95 Our BALLINGER MANDOLIN.

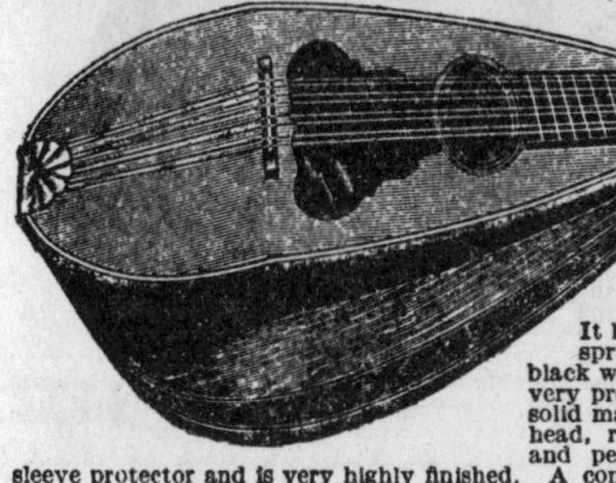

No. 12F700 This mandolin has nine ribs of alternate mahogany and maple with strips of black wood between. It has a solid rosewood cap, top of silver spruce, inlaid around the edge with a strip of black wood bound with white celluloid. It has a very pretty imitation tortoise shell guard plate, solid mahogany neck, good quality brass patent head, rosewood fingerboard with metallic frets and pearl position dots. It has nickel plated sleeve protector and is very highly finished. A complete course of musical instruction goes with this mandolin as well as the outfit described in the introduction.
Price **$1.95**

Our COMPETITION Mandolin, $2.35

No 12F703 This mandolin has nine ribs of alternate maple and mahogany with thin strips of black wood between. It has solid rosewood cap and top of silver spruce inlaid around the edge with a strip of colored wood and bound with white celluloid. It has a ring of inlaid colored wood around the soundhole and an imitation tortoise shell guard plate with a very pretty design inlaid in celluloid. The neck is solid mahogany, the patent head is of a good quality brass, the fingerboard is rosewood with raised metallic frets and inlaid pearl position dots. It has a nickel plated sleeve protector and is very highly finished. Besides the usual outfit, we give with this mandolin a complete course of musical instruction. See page 285 Price.......... **$2.35**

$3.45 Our CHALLENGE MANDOLIN.

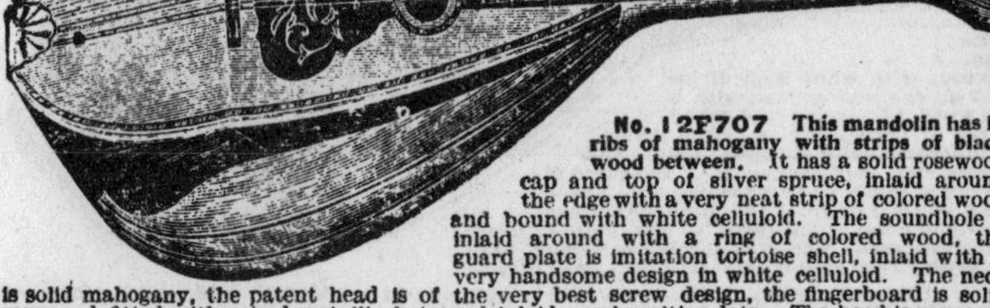

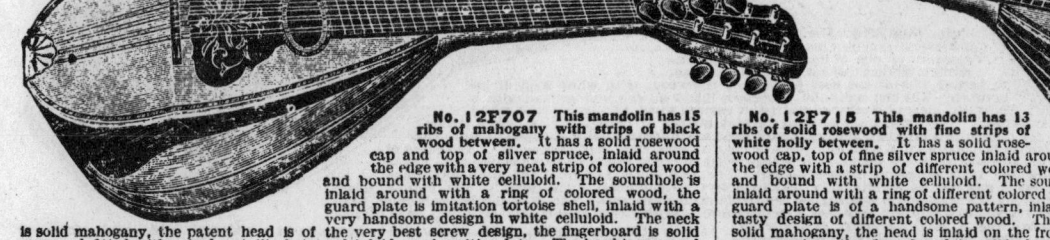

No. 12F707 This mandolin has 15 ribs of mahogany with strips of black wood between. It has a solid rosewood cap and top of silver spruce, inlaid around the edge with a very neat strip of colored wood and bound with white celluloid. The soundhole is inlaid around with a ring of colored wood, the guard plate is imitation tortoise shell, inlaid with a very handsome design in white celluloid. The neck is solid mahogany, the patent head is of the very best screw design, the fingerboard is solid rosewood, fitted with raised metallic frets and inlaid pearl position dots. The head is veneered on the front with rosewood and the sleeve protector is highly nickel plated. Besides the usual outfit mentioned above, we furnish with this mandolin a complete course of musical instruction. Price.......... **$3.45**

Our New Departure Mandolin, $4.65

No. 12F715 This mandolin has 13 ribs of solid rosewood with fine strips of white holly between. It has a solid rosewood cap, top of fine silver spruce inlaid around the edge with a strip of different colored wood and bound with white celluloid. The soundhole is inlaid around with a ring of different colored wood, the guard plate is of a handsome pattern, inlaid with a tasty design of different colored wood. The neck is solid mahogany, the head is inlaid on the front with rosewood, the patent head is of the best screw variety, the fingerboard is solid ebony, has raised metallic frets and inlaid pearl position dots. The sleeve protector is highly nickel plated and the bridge is solid ebony. **We give with this mandolin** a complete course of musical instruction absolutely free.
Price.......... **$4.65**

THE 20th CENTURY MANDOLIN.

$5.65

No. 12F718 This instrument has 21 ribs of alternate birdseye maple and rosewood, with strips of red colored wood between, making a very beautiful effect. The top is made of silver spruce, inlaid around the edge with ebony and mother-of-pearl, in alternate blocks and strips of inlaid wood. Inlaid around the soundhole with a ring of ebony and inlaid mother-of-pearl, and bound with white celluloid. The guard plate is imitation tortoise shell, inlaid with a butterfly design in mother-of-pearl. The head is veneered on the front with rosewood, the neck is solid mahogany and has the best pattern screw patent head. The fingerboard is rosewood, with raised metallic frets and pearl position dots. The sleeve protector is nickel plated and the cap, or apron, is solid rosewood. With each instrument we give a certificate for a complete course of musical instruction.
Price........ **$5.65**

THE NONPAREIL MANDOLIN.

$7.45

No. 12F724 This mandolin has 21 ribs of solid rosewood, with strips of white holly between. It has a solid rosewood cap, bound with white celluloid. The top is made of spruce, inlaid around the edge with broad strips of different colored wood and bound with white celluloid. The soundhole is inlaid around the edge with broad rings of different colored wood and the inside edge is bound with white celluloid. The head is veneered on the front with rosewood and ornamented with a pretty design in mother-of-pearl. The neck is solid mahogany and furnished with the best pattern screw patent head. The fingerboard is solid ebony, with raised metallic frets, ornamented with designs in inlaid mother-of-pearl and bound with white celluloid. It has a very handsome black guard plate, inlaid with a design in colored wood. The sleeve protector is separable and highly nickel plated. With this mandolin we furnish a free course of musical instruction. See page 285. Price........ **$7.45**

THE NEAPOLITAN.

$9.85

No. 12F752 This mandolin has 28 ribs of solid rosewood with fine strips of white holly between. It has a solid rosewood cap, bound with white celluloid. The top is of silver spruce inlaid around the edge with broad strips of different colored wood and bound with white celluloid. The soundhole has two rings of different colored wood and is bound with white celluloid. The guardplate is imitation tortoise shell inlaid with a pretty design in celluloid. The head is veneered on front and back with rosewood and ornamented on the front with star, crescent and flower shaped designs in mother-of-pearl. The neck is solid rosewood, the patent head is of the best quality with nickel plated hand carved guard and white celluloid buttons. The fingerboard is solid ebony with raised metallic frets ornamented with diamond and square designs in mother-of-pearl and bound with white celluloid. The sleeve protector is separable and highly nickel plated.

A FULL COURSE of musical instruction is given with each one of these mandolins absolutely free. Price........ **$9.85**

THE PALOMA.

$12.40

No. 12F756 This mandolin has 35 ribs of handsome rosewood with fine strips of white holly between. It has a rosewood cap bound with white celluloid. The top is made of resonant eastern spruce and has a broad strip of inlaid colored wood and mother-of-pearl around the edge and soundhole. The edges of the top and soundhole are bound with white celluloid. The guard plate is made of tortoise shell beautifully inlaid with mother-of-pearl. The neck is solid mahogany hand carved. The head is inlaid on front and back with rosewood and ornamented on the front with star, crescent and flower shaped figures inlaid in mother-of-pearl. The fingerboard is solid ebony with raised frets, diamond shaped position dots inlaid with mother-of-pearl and is bound with white celluloid. Has the best covered aluminum American patent head, hand carved, with celluloid buttons. It also has a very handsome hand carved aluminum sleeve protector.

A COMPLETE COURSE of instruction goes with this mandolin. Price........ **$12.40**

$16.95 THE SEVILLA. $16.95

SEE OUR REMARKABLE MUSICAL INSTRUCTION OFFER, on page 285.

A COMPLETE MUSICAL EDUCATION ABSOLUTELY FREE WITH EACH MANDOLIN.

FRONT VIEW

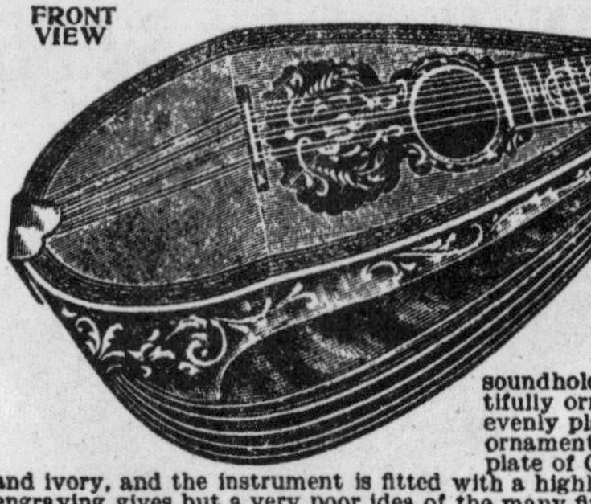

BACK VIEW

SOMETHING ESPECIALLY FINE IN A MANDOLIN.

No. 12F763 This mandolin has 21 rosewood ribs divided with thin strips of white holly, heavy rosewood cap beautifully inlaid in fancy figures made of different colored woods. The top is made of thoroughly seasoned resonant spruce and is bound with celluloid. It has an ebony guard plate beautifully inlaid with brilliant mother-of-pearl and German silver. The top has a strip of purfling made of beautifully inlaid wood, around the edge, and the soundhole is lined with celluloid. It has a genuine ebony fingerboard edged with celluliod and beautifully ornamented with a handsome design of inlaid mother-of-pearl and the frets are accurately and evenly placed. The neck is made of solid mahogany, and the head is veneered with rosewood and ornamented with a pretty design inlaid with mother-of-pearl. The back of the head has a guard plate of German silver and is fitted with a high grade patent head. The bridge is made of solid ebony and ivory, and the instrument is fitted with a highly nickel plated tailpiece and guard. The engraving gives but a very poor idea of the many fine qualities of this mandolin, and it must be seen and heard to be fully appreciated. We furnish this instrument complete with a full set of strings, mandolin pick and flannel lined, durable canvas case. We give, free, with each instrument a certificate which entitles the holder to a complete course of fifty weekly lessons on the instrument. Price........ **$16.95**

$19.85 THE CAMPANELLO. $19.85

A PROFIT SHARING CERTIFICATE IS YOURS WITH EVERY PURCHASE. YOU WILL SOON BE ABLE TO GET SOMETHING VALUABLE FREE AS YOUR SHARE OF OUR PROFIT, AS EXPLAINED ON PAGES 1 AND 2.

WE SAVE YOU ONE-HALF ON A MANDOLIN AND TEACH YOU HOW TO PLAY IT.

FRONT VIEW

BACK VIEW

No. 12F764 The purchaser of this instrument may rest assured that he is the possessor of one of the very finest instruments in this line that it is possible to produce. It has 41 ribs of the best quality of rosewood, with white holly strips between. The cap is of solid rosewood, inlaid all the way around with a beautiful strip of mother-of-pearl and colored wood, and bound with white celluloid. The top is made of the very best quality of eastern spruce, inlaid around the edge with a broad strip of mother-of-pearl and alternate strips of colored wood. The soundhole is inlaid around with four rings of colored wood and mother-of-pearl. The edges of the top and soundhole are bound with white celluloid. The guard plate is tortoise shell, inlaid with a very tasty design in mother-of-pearl. The head is inlaid on front and back with three alternate layers of rosewood and white holly, making a very elegant effect. The front of the head is inlaid with star, crescent, diamond and flower shaped designs in mother-of-pearl. The neck is solid mahogany, hand carved. The patent head is of the very best American design, with gold plated cover, beautifully hand carved. The fingerboard is of solid ebony and is ornamented with a beautiful design in metal and mother-of-pearl, representing a flower pot, vines, leaves and lilies, and has raised metallic frets and is bound with white celluloid. The bridge is of solid ebony, capped with white celluloid and the sleeve protector is gold plated, beautifully hand carved. The engraving which we show of this instrument, falls very far short of giving you any idea of its beautiful appearance and splendid tone quality.

With this mandolin we give absolutely free, a complete course of instruction on the instrument. See page 285 for full particulars. Price........ **$19.85**

$2.45 BANJOS $19.65

AT $2.45 TO $19.65 WE SHOW A SPLENDID LINE OF BANJOS, THE GREATEST VALUES EVER OFFERED.

WE WANT YOU TO MAKE A CAREFUL COMPARISON between the instruments which we are offering in this line and those offered by any other house. Such a comparison will convince you at once that no dealer can sell banjos which are in any way equal to ours at anywhere near the price we are quoting. It is not a question with us how cheap we can sell our banjos, but rather how good we can make them at the prices we quote. We could sell banjos at much lower prices than we are offering, but they could not possibly prove satisfactory to our customers, and they would prove very poor advertisements for our line of musical goods. From the highest to the lowest priced banjos in this line, each one contains the very best workmanship and material which it is possible to put into it at the price.

SEND US YOUR ORDER, enclose our price and we will send the banjo promptly; give it ten days' trial and if you are not perfectly satisfied in every way, return the instrument to us and we will promptly return your money and transportation charges. We guarantee complete satisfaction in every transaction.

A PROFIT SHARING CERTIFICATE will be sent to you when you order, and you can soon get something valuable entirely FREE.

WE FURNISH, FREE, WITH EACH BANJO one set of Glendon strings, one instruction book of chords, one lettered fingerboard chart, and a complete course of instruction on the instrument.

OUR CHALLENGE BANJO OUTFIT.

$5.75 $5.75

You share in our profit when you buy from us, as well as saving a great deal on your purchase. See pages 1 and 2.

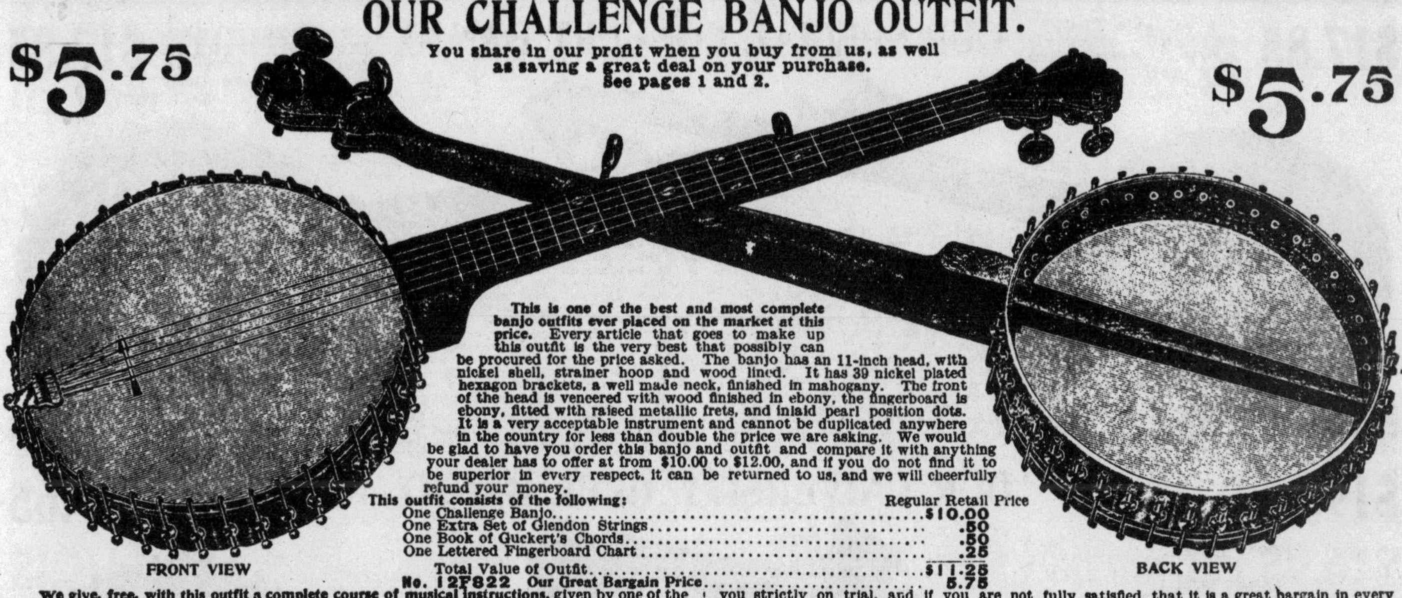

FRONT VIEW

BACK VIEW

This is one of the best and most complete banjo outfits ever placed on the market at this price. Every article that goes to make up this outfit is the very best that possibly can be procured for the price asked. The banjo has an 11-inch head, with nickel shell, strainer hoop and wood lined. It has 39 nickel plated hexagon brackets, a well made neck, finished in mahogany. The front of the head is veneered with wood finished in ebony, the fingerboard is ebony, fitted with raised metallic frets, and inlaid pearl position dots. It is a very acceptable instrument and cannot be duplicated anywhere in the country for less than double the price we are asking. We would be glad to have you order this banjo and outfit and compare it with anything your dealer has to offer at from $10.00 to $12.00, and if you do not find it to be superior in every respect, it can be returned to us, and we will cheerfully refund your money.

This outfit consists of the following:	Regular Retail Price
One Challenge Banjo	$10.00
One Extra Set of Glendon Strings	.50
One Book of Guckert's Chords	.50
One Lettered Fingerboard Chart	.25
Total Value of Outfit	$11.25
No. 12F822 Our Great Bargain Price	5.75

We give, free, with this outfit a complete course of musical instructions, given by one of the very best music colleges in the country. This course consists of fifty weekly lessons, covering a period of one year, and will be thorough and complete. Remember, that this outfit goes to you strictly on trial, and if you are not fully satisfied that it is a great bargain in every respect, we will gladly receive it back and refund every cent you have paid, including transportation charges. Shipping weight, about 12 pounds.

$2.45 OUR STUDENTS' BANJO.

No. 12F809 We would like to have you compare this banjo with any one ordinarily sold by dealers throughout the country for less than $5.00. It has a 10-inch nickel shell, wood lined. It has a well made imitation mahogany neck with fingerboard fitted with raised metallic frets. It has eleven brackets and is carefully and thoroughly made. Besides the usual outfit, we give with this banjo a complete course of instruction, consisting of ten weekly lessons, given by one of the best music colleges in the country. Shipping weight, 12 lbs. Price. $2.45

OUR EDGEMERE BANJO. $3.80

No. 12F812 This banjo is sold throughout the country by dealers generally for from $5.00 to $7.00 It has an 11-inch head with nickel shell and strainer hoops, and seventeen nickel plated hexagon brackets. It has a wooden rim, imitation mahogany neck, ebony fingerboard with raised metallic frets and inlaid pearl position dots. It is a very satisfactory instrument in every respect; a great value at the price we ask. Besides the usual outfit, we give with this banjo a complete course of instruction. Shipping weight, 12 pounds. Price........ $3.80

$4.85 Our CONSERVATORY BANJO

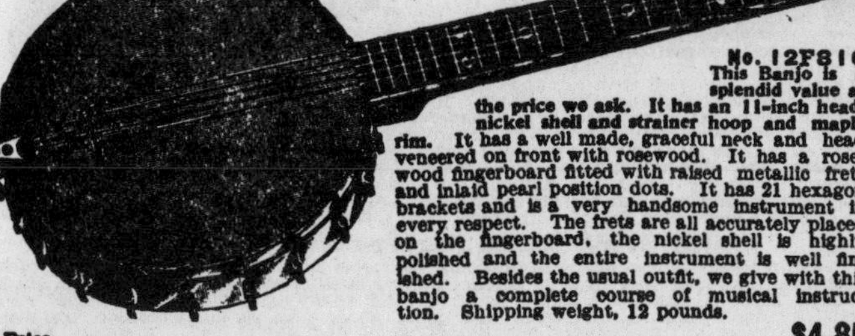

No. 12F816 This Banjo is a splendid value at the price we ask. It has an 11-inch head, nickel shell and strainer hoop and maple rim. It has a well made, graceful neck and head veneered on front with rosewood. It has a rosewood fingerboard fitted with raised metallic frets and inlaid pearl position dots. It has 21 hexagon brackets and is a very handsome instrument in every respect. The frets are all accurately placed on the fingerboard, the nickel shell is highly polished and the entire instrument is well finished. Besides the usual outfit, we give with this banjo a complete course of musical instruction. Shipping weight, 12 pounds.

Price.. $4.85

Our NEW CENTURY BANJO. $6.85

No. 12F824 This is a regular $12.00 banjo and is sold at that price generally throughout the country. It has a nickel shell and strainer hoop, and is wood lined. It has an extension removable neck with metal truss and is tightened by two ebony keys. It has 25 hexagon brackets and genuine ebony fingerboard fitted with raised metallic frets and diamond and flower shaped position dots inlaid in mother-of-pearl. The front of the head is veneered with a heavy piece of ebony, as well as the heel, and fitted with ebony pegs. We recommend this instrument as being something particularly good in a banjo at this price and we will be glad to send it to you for comparison and examination. Besides the usual outfit, we give with this banjo a complete course of instruction. See page 285 for full particulars. Shipping weight, about 12 lbs. Price. $6.85

$9.65 OUR GEM BANJO.

No. 12F858 This banjo is high class in every respect and is an instrument for which your local dealer easily receives $18.00 to $20.00. It has an 11-inch head, a heavy nickel shell and strainer hoop and has cherrywood lining. It has thirty-one nickel plated hexagon brackets with protection nuts. It has a very neatly cut extension neck held in place by two ebony keys. The head is veneered on the front with a heavy piece of ebony and inlaid with star, crescent and flower shaped designs in mother-of-pearl. It has white celluloid keys and genuine ebony fingerboard, fitted with raised metallic frets and square and diamond shaped inlaid pearl position dots.

WE CAN RECOMMEND THIS BANJO as being first class in every respect and an instrument which will give the best of satisfaction under all conditions. Besides the usual outfit, we give with this banjo a complete course of instruction, consisting of fifty weekly lessons, covering a period of one year. This is certainly the greatest value ever offered in a banjo at this price, and if you do not feel perfectly satisfied, you can return it to us entirely at our expense and we will cheerfully refund your money. Price $9.65

OUR ROYAL BANJO. $11.95

No. 12F862 This banjo is a strictly professional instrument and one which we can highly recommend to all who desire a banjo for concert purposes. It has an 11-inch head, nickel shell and strainer hoop, and is cherrywood lined. It has twenty-nine nickel plated hexagon brackets with protection nuts. The head is veneered on the front, fitted with patented friction pegs with celluloid buttons, and the head is ornamented on the front with star, crescent, diamond and flower shaped figures inlaid in mother-of-pearl. The fingerboard is of solid ebony with raised metallic frets and star and square shaped position dots inlaid in mother-of-pearl. The neck is mahogany, nicely hand carved and veneered with ebony on the heel. It is fitted with a patented extension neck appliance with swivel screw strainer and ebony keys. This is a very pleasing instrument, both from the standpoint of tone and general appearance. Besides the usual outfit, we give a complete course of musical instruction, for full particulars of which see page 285. This course of musical instruction is given by one of the best music colleges in the country. Shipping weight, about 12 pounds. Price $11.95

$17.85 OUR SPECIAL CONCERT BANJO. $17.85

A valuable PROFIT SHARING CERTIFICATE is yours when you send us your order.

Your PROFIT SHARING CERTIFICATE will help you get something valuable entirely FREE.

FRONT VIEW

BACK VIEW

No. 12F867 If you are looking for something particularly fine in a banjo, at a price which will astonish you, this is certainly the instrument you desire. We make the assertion, without fear of contradiction, that this is the handsomest banjo ever offered to the musical public. It is manufactured in response to a demand for something particularly elegant in the line of a solo banjo, to be sold by our great money saving method. This instrument is fitted with a heavy nickel 11-inch rim with wire spun edge and lined with birdseye maple. It has 25 patent hexagon brackets, and a high grade calfskin head. It has a nickel plated metallic staypiece with solid ebony keys, which prevents the neck from coming loose. The neck extension is bound with white celluloid on each of the four corners, veneered with narrow strips of ebony. The neck is made of birdseye maple and the heel is beautifully carved and tipped with a solid plate of genuine ebony. The head is veneered with six layers of wood consisting of ebony, white holly and rosewood. The fingerboard is bound with celluloid, together with narrow strips of rosewood, white celluloid and ebony and is solid ebony with handsome position ornaments of inlaid mother-of-pearl. The head is beautifully ornamented with elegant designs of inlaid mother-of-pearl. All the frets are accurately and evenly placed, and the instrument is fitted with the very highest grade of patent pegs. We furnish this banjo complete with strings, tuning key, and a handsome flannel lined, leather bound canvas case. We also give, free, a certificate which entitles the holder to a complete course of musical instruction, consisting of fifty weekly lessons on the instrument. Shipping weight, 12 pounds. Price, $17.85

$19.65 OUR UNIVERSITY GLEE BANJO. $19.65

FRONT VIEW

BACK VIEW

OUR VERY FINEST BANJO—NOTHING BETTER MADE.

No. 12F868 This banjo is artistic in every respect. It has an 11-inch head, heavy nickeled shell and strainer hoop, lined with red stained birdseye maple. It has thirty-one hexagon brackets with protection nuts. It has a patent extension neck held in place by two ebony keys and fitted with swivel strainer screw. The head and fingerboard are veneered with three layers of different colored wood capped with a heavy layer of genuine ebony. The front of the head is profusely inlaid with star, crescent and flower shaped figures in mother-of-pearl. The fingerboard is fitted with raised metallic frets and ornamented with beautiful designs inlaid in white metal and mother-of-pearl, representing a flower pot, vines, leaves and lilies running the full length of the fingerboard. The instrument is fitted with patented friction pegs with white celluloid buttons. The heel of the neck is heavily hand carved and inlaid with different layers of colored wood capped with ebony. The banjo has a genuine Joseph Rogers, Jr., calfskin head and is elegantly finished throughout. If you are looking for a banjo which will be a work of art as well as an elegant musical instrument, this is the banjo which you should buy. We would be glad to send you this instrument and give you an opportunity to compare it with anything your dealer has to offer in this line, and if you do not find, after the most critical comparison and examination, that it is much superior to anything you can buy from any local dealer for less than $40.00 to $45.00, you can box it up and return it to us and we will cheerfully refund every cent you have paid, including transportation charges. Besides the usual outfit, we give with this banjo a complete course of musical instruction, consisting of fifty weekly lessons, extending over a period of one year. This course of instruction is absolutely free and will be furnished by one of the best music colleges in the country. Price........ $19.65

Shipping weight, about 12 pounds.

For banjo strings and furnishings, see pages 342 and 344
For banjo folios and instruction books, see page 348.

$3.45 OUR MANDOLINETTO.

This is a very neat little instrument, 10 inches long and 8 inches wide. It is made of maple with beautiful rosewood finish, has light colored spruce top inlaid around the edge with a strip of different colored woods and bound with white celluloid. The soundhole has one ring of inlaid colored wood and the guard plate is beautiful imitation tortoise shell. The neck and head are neatly cut, finished in imitation mahogany and furnished with brass patent head. The fingerboard is ebony fitted with raised metallic frets and inlaid pearl position dots. It has a nickel plated sleeve protector and is highly finished and polished. It is played exactly the same as a mandolin and can be used by any mandolin player. We include without extra charge, one genuine tortoise shell mandolin pick, one complete instruction book, and one fine canvas leather bound and flannel lined case. The regular price of this outfit is $10.00.

No. 12F912 Our price........................ $3.45

No. 12F913 Same style as No. 12F912, but made of solid rosewood, celluloid bound edges, top and back; guttapercha guard plate, mahogany neck, best quality American head with the same outfit as given above. Price........ $6.25

Shipping weight, 7 pounds

OUR BANJO MANDOLIN. $6.95

No. 12F916 This little instrument is strung and played upon exactly the same as a mandolin. It has a 7-inch head with nickel shell and strainer hoop. It is lined with wood and has 17 nickel plated hexagon brackets with protection nuts. It has a neatly cut imitation mahogany neck, the front of the head is veneered with rosewood and the screw patent head is of the very best pattern. It has the regular banjo extension neck with ebony veneered heel and two ebony strainer keys. The fingerboard is solid ebony with raised metallic frets and inlaid pearl position dots. We furnish with this instrument, one genuine tortoise shell pick, one mandolin instruction book and one canvas, leather bound and flannel lined case. Regular retail price, $20.00. Shipping weight, 9 pounds. Our price........ $6.95

Our $7.85 Acme Professional Banjorine.

No. 12F914 Our Acme Professional Banjorine is 11 inches in diameter, has nickel plated rim with spun wire edge, 24 brackets, heavy band or strainer hoop, and best quality calfskin head; 12-inch neck, highly polished, solid ebony extension fingerboard, 20 raised frets, rosewood veneered head inlaid with pearl, ebony pegs, six inlaid position dots, nickel plated tailpiece, and fine canvas case, leather bound and flannel lined. A strictly high grade instrument. Shipping weight, about 15 pounds. Price........ $7.85

THE AUTOHARP

has become one of the most popular of small musical instruments. Our trade in these instruments has become enormous, and is largely due to two points: our extremely low prices and the general excellence of the instruments we handle. These are favorite musical instruments, because it require but little practice to play upon them, and the music is of the very highest order. Anyone who can read English and possesses ordinary intelligence can play upon an autoharp, because the music that we furnish is simply and plainly figured and the player will find no difficulty in following it. With each autoharp we give a complete instruction book with many different selections of music. Each one of these instruments is finished in the most beautiful manner, and carefully and durably constructed. If your time will not allow you to learn to play upon a violin, piano or other instrument of this class we would by all means, advise you to purchase one of these instruments.

$1.75

No. 12F900 Our $1.75 Autoharp has 20 strings, 3 bars and produces 3 chords. With this instrument the simpler airs and chords may be played. The best steel strings are furnished and the tone is remarkably sweet. Without a single exception, every purchaser has been delighted with this autoharp, and would not part with it at any price if another could not be secured. Weight, packed for shipment, 6 pounds.
Price............$1.75

$2.95 $4.95

No. 12F902 Our $2.95 Autoharp has 23 strings, 5 bars and produces 5 chords. The possibilities of this beautiful instrument are unbounded, and while but little practice is needed for the beginner to play nicely, constant practice will enable the performer to produce very difficult music. Weight, packed for shipment, 7 pounds.
Price............$2.95

No. 12F904 For $4.95 we offer an autoharp that is entirely new, strictly first class in workmanship and susceptible of wonderful manipulation. This special autoharp is complete with 32 strings and is fitted with 8 bars, as it has 8 chords, as follows: C major, G seventh, F major, C seventh, Bb major, B minor, A seventh and G minor. The range of different music is very great and the possibilities of the instrument are beyond that of any other of similar construction and much higher price. You cannot purchase this autoharp from any other dealer for less than from $8.00 to $10.00. Weight, packed for shipment, 9 pounds. Price............$4.95

$6.45

No. 12F906 This Autoharp is the very latest product of the manufacturers, and is destined to become the most popular style of their entire list. It has 37 strings and 12 chord bars; these bars are placed close together making the manipulation of them exceedingly easy. They produce 12 chords, as follows: G major, E seventh, C major, A minor, G seventh, E seventh, F major, D minor, C seventh, A seventh, Bb major and G minor. It is strung and tuned in a perfect chromatic scale. The finish is beautiful; highly polished ebony finish; altogether a handsome, useful musical instrument. Weight, packed for shipment, 10 pounds. Price......$6.45

$10.85

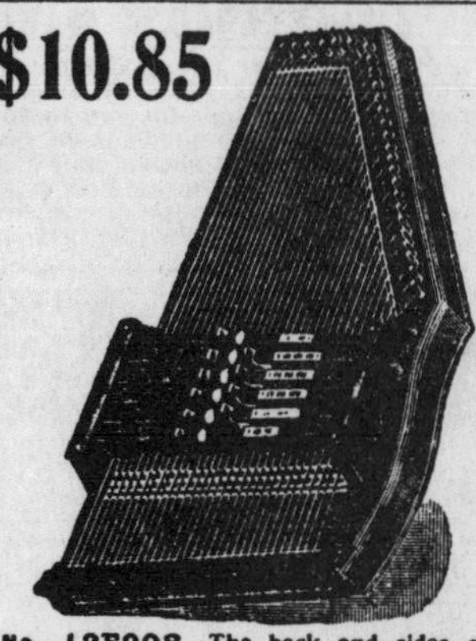

No. 12F908 The back and sides of this beautiful Autoharp are made of well seasoned hardwood and enameled in black. The top or sounding board is made of a carefully selected piece of beautifully close grain pine and finished in a light brown color. The edges are inlaid in white maple with a narrow strip of black between, giving the instrument a very elegant appearance. The bars and supporters are enameled in black and fitted with celluloid buttons for the fingers. It has six bars, by the use of which 16 chords are made possible. Weight, packed for shipment, 16 pounds.
Price............$10.85

No. 12F909 Same as above, but packed in fine black wood autoharp case, flannel lined.
Price............$11.85

GUITAR ZITHERS.

The Guitar Zither is an improved and simplified German zither, upon which may be rendered the most difficult music without the aid of a teacher. Our method of instruction is so easy that anyone can learn to play the instrument in a very short time. The bass notes are tuned in groups of chords. This is a very attractive feature because the various chords of the key are ready to be picked without effort. As an accompaniment of the voice these chords are invaluable. In connection with the violin, piano or other musical instrument, the guitar zither is especially delightful. It rewards individual skill more than any other harp in existence. These are musical instruments which charm alike the home circle and the concert audience.

$1.65

No. 12F921 The Guitar Zither at $1.65, illustrated herewith, made of maple, cherry stained and polished. It has a hand rest, 31 strings and 4 chords, namely, C, G, F major and G minor, complete with instruction book, key and ring. Lovers of music will find this a particularly fine instrument, as it is very easily learned and is delightfully entertaining. We will be glad to place this instrument in your hands for trial and examination, as we know you will find it to be an instrument which will meet your wants in every respect. Shipping weight, about 9 pounds.
Price............$1.65

$1.98

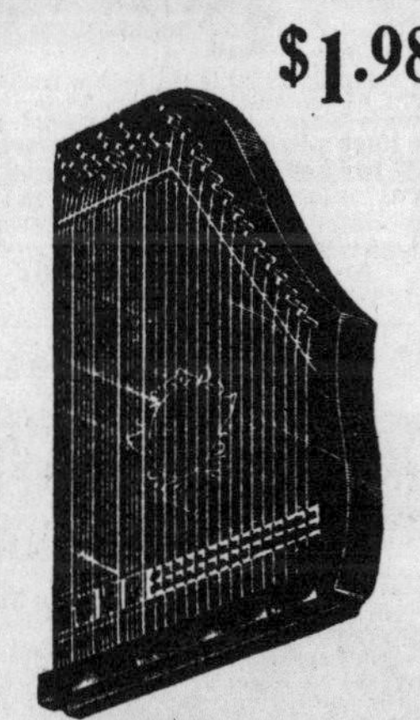

No. 12F923 This is another splendid Guitar Zither, and is made of maple, ebonized and beautifully finished. It has hand rest, and is considerably larger in size than No. 12F921. It is inlaid around the soundhole with beautiful ornamentations, has 31 strings and 4 chords, namely, C, G, F major and G minor. Complete with instruction book, key and ring. This instrument will be found by players to be handsome in every respect, and possesses a deep tone which never fails to delight the listener. It is new in our line, and we highly recommend it for its many excellent qualities. Shipping weight, about 9 pounds. Price....$1.98

$2.95

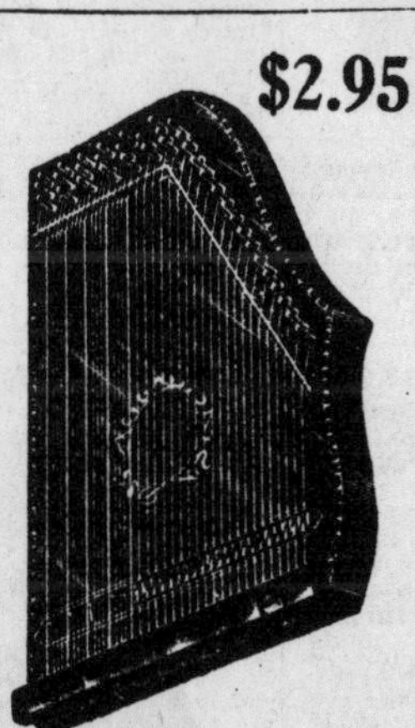

No. 12F925 This is another Guitar Zither, made of maple, ebonized and handsomely finished. It has hand rest, highly polished and is beautifully inlaid around the soundhole, has 41 strings and 5 chords, namely, C, G, F, D and A major. It is beautifully ornamented around the edge of the sounding board and is an instrument of which one may well be proud. We furnish a chart also with this instrument, which can be laid under the strings, giving the position of every note. It comes complete, with instruction book, key and ring. Shipping weight, about 9 lbs. Price $2.95

$3.95

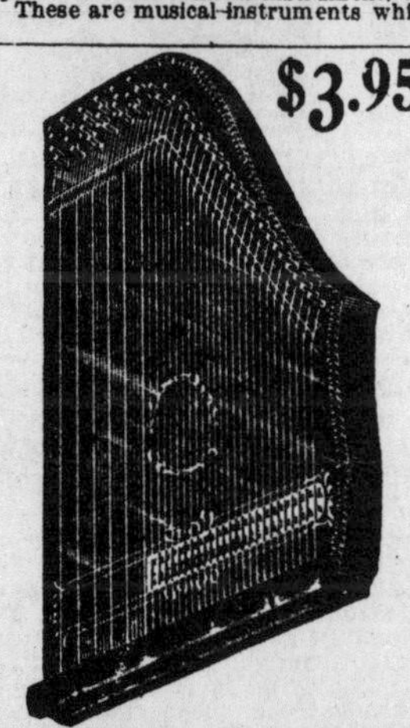

No. 12F927 This is a particularly fine instrument of great musical capacity. It is made of maple, ebonized, has hand rest, highly polished, and beautifully inlaid around the soundhole and the edge of the sounding board. Has nickel plated tuning pins, full chromatic scale with 51 strings and 6 chords, namely, C, G, F, D major and A minor. It has a deep, full, rich tone, and by the aid of the chart and instruction book which we send, it can be easily learned. We send it complete with chart, instruction book, key and ring, and the purchaser will find that it will prove a never ending source of entertainment and delight. Shipping weight, about 9 pounds.
Price............$3.95

$3.45

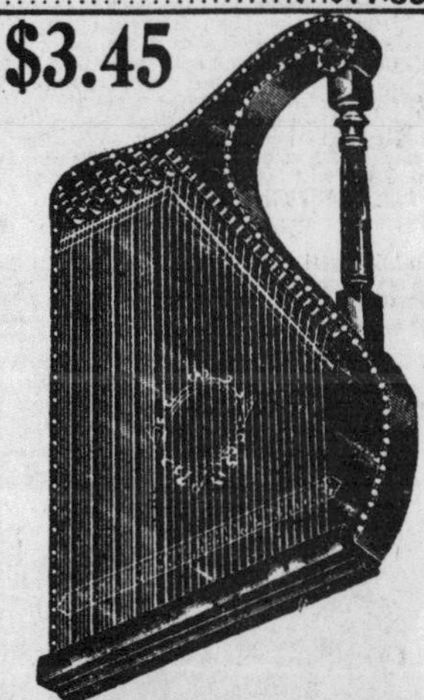

No. 12F929 Our new Harp Zither. This is the latest addition to our fine line of zithers and we know will prove very acceptable to our customers. It is beautifully made and handsomely finished in imitation ebony. In appearance it perfectly resembles a beautiful Italian harp and has 21 melody strings with 5 groups of chords, as follows: A, D, F, G and C. The illustration will give you but a very poor idea of the beautiful appearance of this instrument and nothing but a trial and test will give you a thorough appreciation of its handsome finish and exquisite tone. It has the very best quality of strings, nickel plated tuning pins, hand rest and chart for placing under the strings, showing exactly what each string and chord represents. We furnish it with tuning hammer, instruction book and extra charts. It is 25 inches wide and 23 inches high and the shipping weight, about 12 pounds.
Price............$3.45

MANDOLIN-GUITAR-ZITHER.

$3.35

No. 12F940

Three Instruments Combined at the Price of One.

No picks or rings are required to play this instrument, a patent keyboard being used instead. As you will see in the illustration, the instrument is made after the style of the guitar-zither, having treble strings on which the air is played and accompaniment strings for the accompaniment. The keyboard, which is placed over the strings, is the greatest feature with which the mandolin effect is produced. These mandolin-guitar-zithers are made of selected material beautifully ebonized and decorated with decalcomania ornamentations around the edges.

No. 12F940 Has 31 strings, 4 chords G, C and F major and G dominant 7th.
Price............$3.35
Weight, packed for shipment, 9 pounds.

No. 12F942 Has 41 strings, 5 chords C, G, F, D and A major. Price...$4.35
Weight, packed for shipment, 12 pounds.

Each packed in neat pasteboard box with instruction book and tuning key.

$4.35

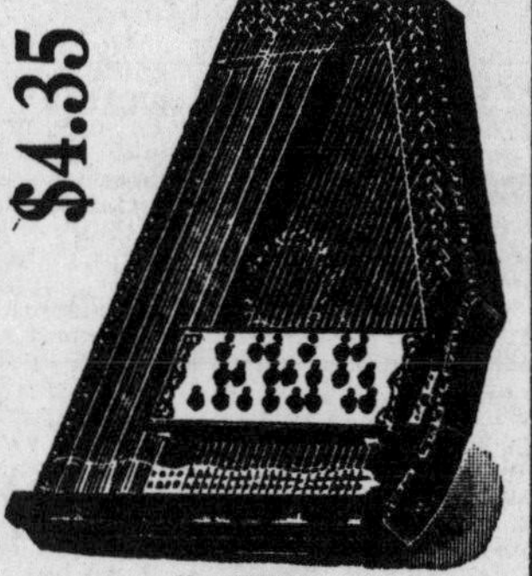

No. 12F942

THE FAMOUS MARX PIANO HARP.

$2.65

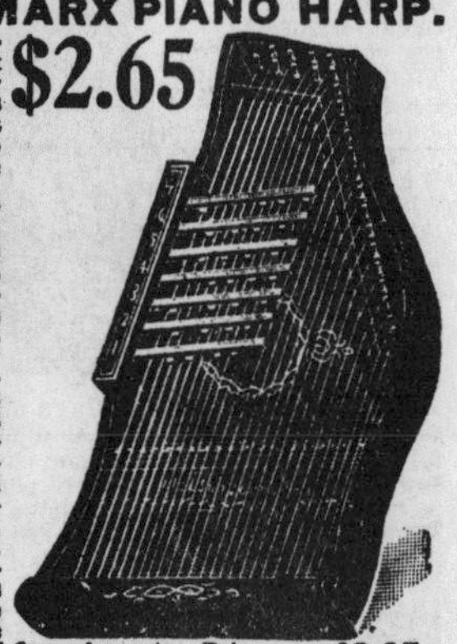

No. 12F947 This instrument is picked with the right hand, same as an ordinary autoharp, while the hammers are manipulated with the left hand. These hammers are so arranged as to produce the chords of C major, G seventh, F major, C seventh, and their relative minors. The figured music which is used on this piano harp is the simplest ever offered in any instrument of this kind. By its use anyone, even though not familiar with music, can play any tune without any previous instruction. It has 23 strings and 7 hammers. It differs from the ordinary autoharp in the important particular that there are no dead strings over which the performer has to play. It is 11 inches long and 20 inches wide, and weighs, boxed for shipment, 10 pounds. With this instrument we furnish one tuning key, one pick, one music holder and 30 pieces of figured music. Price......$2.65

OUR NEW LINE OF PRINCESS MUSIC BOXES

This well known and popular line of Music Boxes offered to the public for the first time by our great money saving method of sale.

WE HAVE SUCCEEDED IN MAKING SUCH A FAVORABLE CONTRACT WITH THE MANUFACTURERS of the well known Princess Music Boxes that we are now able to offer them for the first time by our great money saving method of sale. These boxes are all fitted with removable discs so that each box will play any number of tunes desired. We will be glad to send to anyone a list of the different discs which we can supply for these famous music boxes, and our wonderful bargain prices make it possible for you to furnish your home with music with but a very small outlay. Each one of these boxes is operated by a spring and wound up with a crank, which is shown in each illustration. If you desire to purchase something in the line of a music box which will furnish you with a never ending source of pleasure at a very small cost, we would recommend one of these boxes to you. Each box is furnished with twelve discs without extra charge.

No. 12F934 Princess Music Box. This box is a trifle larger than No. 12F932, being 16¾ inches long, 15 inches wide and 10¾ inches deep. It is handsomely finished in mahogany with all of the metallic parts nickel plated and finely polished. This is a box of great musical capacity, and it takes a disc 12¼ inches in diameter. This is a very large and handsome music box and one which will not only make a handsome ornament in the home but also prove a never ceasing source of amusement and entertainment. We would be glad to have you compare the prices which we are making on this box with the prices asked anywhere else in the country for this same kind and grade of music box, and we know you will find that our prices are very much lower than any which you can obtain elsewhere. We desire to place one of these boxes in every home in the country, and we recommend them as the greatest entertainers which we have yet offered to the public. Shipping weight, 52 pounds.
Price..**$34.45**

No. 12F930 Princess Music Box. This music box is 12½ inches long, 9½ inches wide and 7¾ inches deep. It takes a disc 8½ inches in diameter and is well and thoroughly made. The woodwork is mahogany very highly finished and the metallic parts are all beautifully finished and polished. We will be glad to have you examine anything in this line offered by other dealers and make any comparison or test you desire, and we know that you will find that this box surpasses anything else of the kind offered by other dealers at very much higher prices. Do not get the idea that because we are offering this box at this extremely low price it is not of high grade, because the very low prices which we are making are only made possible by our great buying and selling advantage. We have succeeded in making these extremely low prices without detracting in any way from the high quality of these boxes. The fact that each one of these goes to the customer under our absolute guarantee of merit will prove to you at once that the goods are of the very highest quality. Shipping weight, 24 pounds.
Price..**$13.85**

No. 12F932 Princess Music Box. This box is somewhat larger than the No. 12F930, being 13 inches long, 12 inches wide and 8¾ inches deep. It takes a disc 8¾ inches in diameter and has greater musical capacity. We can furnish extra discs for this music box which you can select from the list which we will send you on request. This music box has never before been offered to the public at anywhere near the price which we are quoting here. We will be glad to send you this box with the understanding that if you do not find that it is much superior to the same style of music box offered by your dealer at a much higher price, we will receive it back and cheerfully refund your money. It is finished in mahogany, highly polished, and all the metal parts are finished and finely burnished. It is neat and compact and occupies but very little room. We offer it to you as something very desirable in this line, and know that you will be more than pleased with it. Shipping weight, 37 pounds.
Price..**$24.95**

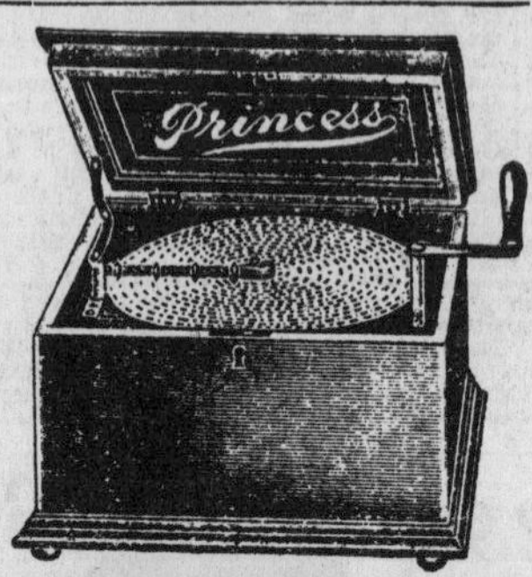

No. 12F936 Our Princess Cabinet Music Box. This is the largest Princess Music Box which we handle, and is certainly a splendid instrument in every way. It is grand concert size, being 22¼ inches long, 20 inches wide, 13 inches deep and taking a disc 15½ inches in diameter. It will play an innumerable number of tunes, as the disc is large enough to play the longest composition. The box winds on the side with a crank, as shown in the illustration, but do not get the idea that any of these boxes turn with the crank, as the crank is only used to wind them up. This is the largest Princess Music Box ever placed on the market, and at the price which we quote we have made competition absolutely impossible. The illustration will give you but a very poor idea of the beautiful finish of this box and the elegant music which it will furnish. It must be seen and heard to be appreciated. The box is finished in beautiful mahogany and all the metallic parts are nickel plated, gilt finished and highly polished. Shipping weight, 96 pounds. Price..**$59.85**

MUSIC BOXES

SELF ACTING—AUTOMATIC—CYLINDER. **These boxes are made by the best manufacturer in Switzerland, the home of the music box. It is a recognized fact that the originators and best makers of music boxes are the Swiss people. In presenting this line to our customers, we have made a very careful selection from the catalogue of one of the best known Swiss makers, and know we are offering an assortment that is unsurpassed.** Every box is made with the greatest care, and the comb and mechanism being firmly attached to the bottom (the sounding board) of the beautifully finished cases, brings forth the best possible quality of tone—that sweet, delightful tone so peculiar to the Swiss box. The mechanism is simple and will not get out of order, unless tampered with. A drop of oil occasionally in the worm of the governor keeps them running nicely, and each box is furnished with a safety catch that makes serious accidents impossible.

Our $1.59, $2.95 and $3.55 Swiss Music Boxes.

No. 12F948 This box measures 4½x3¼x2¼ inches; is a perfect little musical instrument. It plays two tunes. The case is highly finished in natural wood. The mechanism winds with a key and can be started and stopped by a small lever on the front of the box. Shipping weight, 16 ounces. Price **$1.59**

No. 12F950 This music box, as shown in illustration, is 5¼ inches long, 3¼ inches wide and 2¼ inches high. The case is made of walnut, beautifully polished and highly finished. The cylinder is 2¼ inches long; the comb has 36 teeth, plays three tunes. **It is wound with a key and changes automatically.** Shipping weight, 19 ounces.
Price..**$2.95**

No. 12F952 This box is the same as No. 12F950, shown in the illustration; the same size and finish, but plays four tunes. Shipping weight, 19 ounces. Price...**$3.55**

Our $6.25 and $7.85 Swiss Music Boxes.

No. 12F954 This box is made in imitation rosewood highly polished and handsomely decorated. The box is 13½ inches long, 7 inches wide, 5½ inches high. Has a 3½-inch cylinder. It plays six tunes and has a tune indicator, showing which selection is being played. **It is operated by a strong steel spring.** It is wound up by a lever handle; is also provided with two levers which enable you to have the box repeat any tune and the other lever to stop or start the music. The mechanism is covered by a glass lid to protect it from dust. **This box is a great bargain at the price at which we offer it.** Shipping weight, 12 pounds.
Price..**$6.25**

No. 12F956 This box is the same description as No. 12F954, but is somewhat larger. It has a 4½-inch cylinder and plays eight tunes; it is in every other detail the same as No. 12F954. Shipping weight, 15 pounds.
Price..**$7.85**

Our $22.95 Music Box.

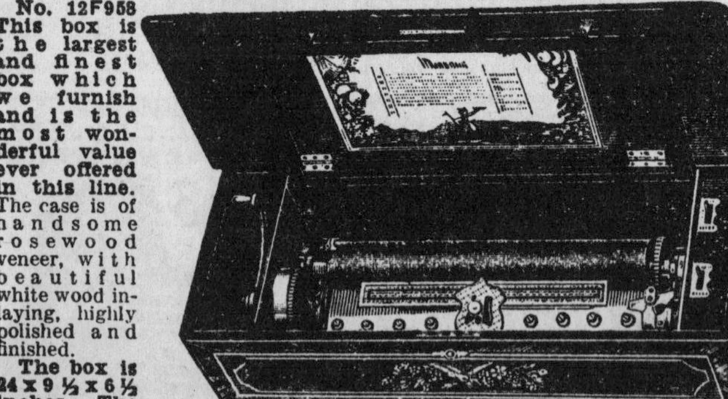

No. 12F958 This box is the largest and finest box which we furnish and is the most wonderful value ever offered in this line. The case is of handsome rosewood veneer, with beautiful white wood inlaying, highly polished and finished. **The box is 24x9½x6½ inches. The cylinder is 11 inches in length and plays 12 complete and different tunes. The tone is exceptionally pleasing,** and with the new auto-zither attachment a surprising and delightful change in tune can be made. This can be used at will by the simple moving of a lever and a very pretty effect can be secured. **PLAYS 12 TUNES.**

The box is operated by a very large strong spring, which is wound up by a lever handle. There are also two levers, one to enable you to repeat any tune desired and which can be repeated as many times as you wish, the other lever to start and stop the box. **Our price on this box is considerably less than what other dealers are obliged to ask, as we import all of our Swiss boxes direct and list them at our usual one small percentage of profit.**

No. 12F958 Price........(Shipping weight, 45 pounds)........................**$22.95**

Our Swiss Concert Music Box for $16.95.

THIS BEAUTIFUL MUSIC BOX IS MADE IN SWITZERLAND, AND, AT THE PRICE WE ASK, IS ONE OF THE BEST MUSIC BOXES ON THE MARKET.

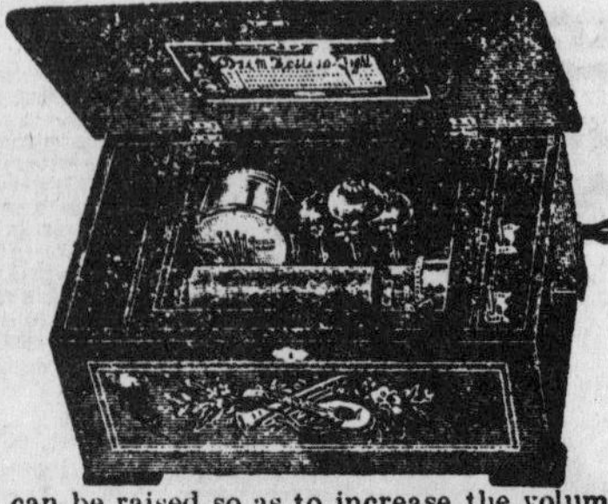

No. 12F959 This case is handsomely veneered with rosewood and has a very high piano finish. The ornaments on the case are of inlaid colored woods in handsome designs. Size, 10½ inches wide, 17 inches long and 8 inches high. The cylinder is 6½ inches long and fitted with eight of the prettiest and most popular tunes. Besides the cylinder, this box is fitted with snare drum and orchestra bells, which can be thrown on and off at pleasure by means of a lever.

It has repeat, change, stop and start levers and winds with a handle on the side.

The action is protected from dust and dirt by an extra glass cover which can be raised so as to increase the volume of tone. The comb contains 44 resonant steel tongues and the entire mechanism of the box is well and strongly made. Shipping weight, 45 pounds.
Price..**$16.95**

OUR GEM ROLLER ORGAN, $3.25

THE MOST MARVELOUS MUSICAL INSTRUMENT EVER OFFERED TO THE PUBLIC.

By contracting for the entire output of the factory we are able now to offer this beautiful Musical Instrument at the wonderfully low price of $3.25.

It is the greatest opportunity ever offered for supplying your home with a splendid musical instrument at an extremely low price.

THE GEM ROLLER ORGAN is an excellent instrument in every respect. It is durably made, beautifully finished, handsome in appearance and wonderful in tone. It is so simply arranged that a child can operate it and no previous knowledge of the music is necessary in order to play the most delightful pieces on this beautiful little organ. The music is produced by a roller which has teeth or pins like the cylinder of a regular Swiss music box. These pins operate upon valve keys allowing the air to pass through and thus producing the different tones.

ALL THE WORKING PARTS of the instrument are easily accessible, and are made of solid metal, the rollers and keys being mounted on castings. Nothing has been omitted to give these instruments their crowning qualities of extreme simplicity and durability. They are beautifully finished, making a handsome parlor ornament, and are genuine musical instruments which are recommended by good musicians. Full sized organ reeds are used, and the volume of sound will fill any ordinary sized hall.

THEY WILL PLAY hymns and popular airs with clearness and accuracy, and furnish acceptable music for any occasion. For dances, lodges, etc., they are most admirable. Perfect execution of music is obtained without the services of a skilled musician. There is no limit to either kind or quality of music they will play, and they are the most perfect mechanical musical instruments in design, operation and effect that have been produced.

WE CAN FURNISH ANY KIND OF MUSIC including sacred, Spanish, German, Norwegian and all the latest popular selections.

THE GEM ROLLER ORGAN is 16 inches long, 14 inches wide and 9 inches high.

No. 12F985 Gem Roller Organ, including three rollers. Price.......................... **$3.25**

Order by number. Shipping weight, 12 pounds.

IN ORDERING ROLLERS ALWAYS BE SURE TO GIVE A SECOND CHOICE, SO THAT IF THE FIRST IS OUT OF STOCK WE CAN SUBSTITUTE WITHOUT DELAY.

COMPLETE LIST OF THE BEST ROLLERS FOR GEM AND CONCERT ROLLER ORGANS.

Series No. 12F986 Order by Number.

Price, per dozen, $2.16; each.. 18c

If by mail, postage extra, each, 6 cents.

SACRED MUSIC.

- 1 The Sweet Bye and Bye
- 2 Nearer, My God, to Thee
- 3 I Need Thee Every Hour
- 4 From Greenland's Icy Mountain
- 6 Onward, Christian Soldiers
- 12 Hold the Fort
- 13 Just as I Am
- 14 America
- 18 He Leadeth Me
- 19 I Love to Tell the Story
- 20 The Home Over There
- 21 Is My Name Written There
- 22 Almost Persuaded
- 23 Where Is My Boy Tonight
- 24 Bringing in the Sheaves
- 25 Let the Lower Lights be Burning
- 26 Only an Armor Bearer
- 27 I Will Sing of My Redeemer
- 29 Pull for the Shore
- 30 Precious Name
- 65 What a Friend We Have in Jesus
- 67 Rock of Ages
- 68 Sweet Hour of Prayer
- 72 Pass Me Not
- 73 Jesus, Lover of My Soul
- 78 Beulah Land
- 81 We Shall Meet Beyond the River
- 90 All the Way My Saviour Leads
- 91 Rescue the Perishing
- 603 Knocking, Knocking, Who is There?
- 634 Shall We Gather at the River
- 721 Anywhere With Jesus
- 726 Glory to His Name
- 729 The Haven of Rest
- 730 Everlasting Arms
- 734 Lead, Kindly Light
- 101 Waltz—Les Roses

POPULAR SONGS, DANCES.

- 103 When the Swallows Homeward Fly
- 106 The Soldiers' Joy
- 107 When the Leaves Begin to Fade
- 108 Sweet Violets
- 109 Marching Through Georgia
- 111 Waltz—My Queen
- 112 Old Uncle Ned
- 115 Climbing Up the Golden Stairs
- 118 Meet Me in the Lovely Twilight
- 119 Vienna Polka
- 121 Old Folks at Home
- 122 Sailors' Hornpipe
- 123 Home, Sweet Home
- 124 The Marseillaise Hymn
- 127 Die Wacht am Rhine
- 132 The Dreamland Waltz
- 138 The Parade March
- 144 Nellie Gray
- 146 Annie Laurie
- 149 The Last Rose of Summer
- 150 Waltz—German Hearts
- 152 See-Saw Waltz
- 153 Polka—On the Wing
- 155 The Beautiful Blue Danube
- 156 Listen to the Mocking Bird
- 157 Then You'll Remember Me
- 161 The Blue Bells of Scotland
- 163 The Wearing of the Green
- 166 Little Old Log Cabin
- 183 The Flyaway Galop
- 190 Yankee Doodle
- 194 The Golden Slippers
- 195 The Quilting Party
- 196 Love Comes—Waltz
- 200 I, 201 II, 202 III, 203 IV, 204 V — Gay Life Quadrilles
- 205 Dixie
- 207 The Arkansas Traveler
- 209 The Kiss Waltz
- 212 When You and I Were Young
- 213 College Hornpipe
- 217 Medley Jig
- 226 Bring Back My Bonnie to Me
- 229 Tramp, Tramp
- 230 Don't Be Angry With Me, Darling
- 232 Johnny Get Your Hair Cut
- 233 Poor Old Dad
- 234 Waltz—Cricket on the Hearth
- 238 Put My Little Shoes Away
- 243 Money Musk
- 246 The Irish Washerwoman
- 247 The Devil's Dream
- 251 I'll Take You Home Again
- 254 Jennie, the Flower of Kildare
- 256 The Little Fishermaiden
- 262 Old Black Joe
- 266 Killarney
- 268 Comin' Thro' the Rye
- 270 Massa's in de Cold, Cold Ground
- 272 Grandfather's Clock
- 273 The Star Spangled Banner
- 275 Maryland, My Maryland
- 277 Hail Columbia
- 279 Red, White and Blue
- 280 Tenting on the Old Camp Ground
- 283 The Old Oaken Bucket
- 290 In Her Little Bed We Laid Her
- 293 You Never Miss the Water
- 295 The Way to be Happy—Waltz
- 297 St. Patrick's Day
- 298 Miss McLeod's Reel
- 301 The Girl I Left Behind Me
- 309 Down Went McGinty
- 335 Little Annie Rooney—Waltz
- 336 Sweetbrier Waltz
- 347 Good Luck Mazurka
- 349 Dairy Maid Waltz
- 351 Flee as a Bird
- 363 Only a Dream of My Mother
- 368 Schottische—Little Beauty
- 374 Some Day I'll Wander Back Again
- 375 Take Me Back to Home and Mother
- 390 The Battle Cry of Freedom
- 392 Come Back to Erin
- 399 John Brown
- 406 Schottische—Always Smiling
- 407 Waltz—Loves' Dreamland
- 410 Why Did They Dig Ma's Grave so Deep
- 416 Captain Jinks
- 420 Schottische—Happy-go-Lucky
- 421 My Mother's Old Red Shawl
- 423 Peep-O-Day—Polka
- 443 O My Darling Clementine
- 444 Galop—Jolly Brothers
- 446 Manhattan Polka
- 450 Clayton's Grand March
- 452 Fresh Life, Waltz
- 453 Galop—Little Fairy
- 456 Racquet Waltz
- 457 Waltz—Estudiantina
- 476 Silver Threads Among the Gold
- 480 General Grant's Grand March
- 517 Mary and John
- 527 Farewell Till We Meet Again
- 577 The High School Cadets' March
- 578 The Skirt Dance
- 600 After the Ball
- 617 God Be With You
- 635 Happy Day
- 1003 Won't You Be My Sweetheart
- 1004 The Bowery
- 1006 Two Little Girls in Blue
- 1009 The Washington Post March
- 1016 The Miner's Dream of Home
- 1019 Molly and I and the Baby
- 1020 Little Alabama Coon
- 1030 In Love With the Man in the Moon
- 1036 Sweet Marie
- 1038 The Sidewalks of New York
- 1039 The Fatal Wedding (Yard
- 1050 I Don't Want to Play in Your
- 1053 Ben Bolt
- 1054 The Honeymoon March
- 1058 Just Tell Them That You Saw Me
- 1059 Only One Girl in the World for Me
- 1061 The Sunshine of Paradise Alley
- 1069 My Old Kentucky Home
- 1070 The Darkies' Dream
- 1071 Sweet Rosie O'Grady
- 1083 Hot Time in the Old Town
- 1084 Bombasto March, Two Step
- 1086 There'll Come a Time
- 1087 All Coons Look Alike to Me
- 1090 On the Banks of the Wabash
- 1096 Stars and Stripes Forever—March
- 1100 Sunnyside Clog
- 1101 She was Bred in Old Kentucky
- 1102 Break the News to Mother
- 1107 Georgia Camp Meeting
- 1112 Hello, Ma Baby
- 1113 High Born Lady
- 1114 Smoky Mokes
- 1115 Eli Green's Cake Walk
- 1116 Whistling Rufus
- 1117 Just as the Sun Went Down
- 1118 Just One Girl
- 1119 Zenda Waltzes
- 1120 Home to Our Mountains
- 1121 Narcissus
- 1122 Intermezzo Rusticana
- 1123 The Moth and the Flame
- 1124 Sunny Tennessee
- 1125 El Capitaine—No. 1
- 1126 El Capitaine—No. 2
- 1127 Soldiers in the Park
- 1128 Holy City
- 1129 Mosquito Parade
- 1130 Good Bye, Dolly Grey
- 1131 Fishers' Hornpipe
- 1132 Creole Belle
- 1133 Tale of the Kangaroo
- 1134 Down Where the Cotton Blossoms Grow
- 1135 I Left Because I Love You
- 1136 In the Good Old Summer Time
- 1137 Mister Dooley
- 1138 Bill Bailey
- 1139 Hiawatha
- 1140 By the Sycamore Tree
- 1141 Laughing Water

OUR $7.60 CONCERT ROLLER ORGAN.

THIS ORGAN is of somewhat higher grade than the Gem roller organ, has greater musical capacity, is much better constructed and a finer instrument in every way. The cylinder and all of the mechanism are enclosed and covered with a glass door, which effectually excludes dust and dirt. It is operated in the same way as the Gem roller organ and uses the same cylinder, so that in ordering cylinders for this organ you can make your selections from the list above.

THIS IS A VERY DESIRABLE INSTRUMENT, produces delightful music and, as the cylinders are removable, a great many different pieces can be played. The tone is similar to that of a parlor organ, as the tone is produced by reeds operated by a cylinder containing teeth, which open and close the valves. It is made of genuine black walnut, nicely finished.

PART of our profit is given back to you under our **PROFIT SHARING SYSTEM** as explained on pages 1 and 2.

The Rollers Cost as Follows:

Series No. 12F986 Price, for extra rollers, each **$0.18**
Per dozen.. **2.16**

If by mail, postage extra, each, 6 cents.

Five Tunes Furnished Free With Each Concert Organ.

No. 12F988 Concert Roller Organ. Price $7.60

Weight, packed for shipment, 30 pounds.

No. 12F988

OUR BÖHM LINE OF SOVEREIGN ACCORDIONS.

A FINE LINE OF LOW PRICED ACCORDIONS. **We assure all admirers of the accordion that they will find in these instruments the greatest values ever offered in low priced accordions.** They are made especially for us by a maker who has an international reputation for manufacturing these instruments. They are all well and thoroughly made throughout, and we know that we can sell them to you at a price much lower than what other dealers will ask for the same grade of instruments. We ship them upon the same terms that we ship out other musical goods and allow full ten days' trial. They are all handsomely finished and ornamented and are instruments which we can conscientiously recommend to our customers. With each instrument we include a complete and comprehensive instruction book, by the aid of which anyone can learn to play on these instruments without the aid of a teacher. This is a line of old favorite accordions and we have been so successful in handling them that we have come to look upon them as a staple article in the accordion line. Our contract with the manufacturer of these accordions is such a favorable one that we are in a position to make prices which are lower than ever before. As a proof of this we ask you to examine the accordions shown below and compare the prices which we quote with anything any other dealer has to offer. If you are looking for an accordion of sterling merit, handsome in appearance, well made and beautifully toned at prices one-half lower than you can obtain elsewhere we will recommend any accordion in this line. Why should you go to the local dealer and purchase an accordion in the usual way, paying a price which is more than half made up of intermediate dealers' profits and selling expenses, when you can purchase just as good an accordion from us at about one-half the price?

WITH EACH ACCORDION WE GIVE A COMPLETE INSTRUCTION BOOK.

No. 12F994 This is a very fine accordion, is highly polished and finished with fancy fluted mouldings, and has double bellows with eight folds, with corner protectors and nickel clasps. It is very prettily ornamented with nickel strips on the inside of the panels and is fitted with ten keys and two sets of reeds and stops. We can recommend this accordion very highly as being a durable and splendidly made instrument. It is well built and handsomely finished throughout, and has great volume and mellowness of tone. We sell all accordions under our offer to refund your money and pay the express charges both ways should you decide that you did not care to keep it after a thorough trial and examination. It is exactly such an accordion as those for which you would be compelled to pay your local dealer from $3.50 to $4.00. We are satisfied that you will gladly admit this, if you could see it and test it, which you can do under our liberal offer. Size, 6x7x10¼ inches. Weight, boxed about 8 pounds.
Price $1.65

No. 12F995 This is a very fine accordion with fluted, ebonized mouldings and dark red panels, triple bellows, nine folds, in three alternate colors, red, black and green. Highly ornamented corner protectors, ten nickel plated keys, two sets of reeds, two stops, fancy gold paper ornamentations around the frame. Nickel plated clasps and trimmings throughout. Fitted with strips of fancy webbing. A beautiful instrument at a medium price. Should you purchase an accordion of this same grade from your local dealer he will charge you from $4.00 to $4.50 for it. Give us an opportunity of placing this splendid instrument in your hands for examination, with the understanding that we will receive it back and refund your money if it does not prove satisfactory in every particular. We guarantee the instrument to be a high class accordion in every respect. We have sold a good many thousands of these instruments, and they have given universal satisfaction. Size, 5¾x7x10½ inches. Weight, boxed, about 10 pounds.
Price $1.95

No. 12F996 Fancy fluted mouldings finished in imitation ebony. Keyboard also in imitation ebony; rich deep blue panels, with gold decorations. Triple bellows of nine folds with corner protectors, bellows and all leather work being in two colors, green and brown with rich Turkish red paper between the folds. Ten long nickel keys, clasps and trimmings, three sets of steel bronze reeds, three stops. A regular $5.00 instrument and sold for this price by dealers throughout the country. We will be glad to have you compare it with any accordion your local dealer has to offer in the same grade at double the price. We offer it to you as one of the greatest bargains that has ever been offered in such an instrument. We sell this accordion with the understanding that if you do not find when you receive it, that you have saved at least $3.00 on your purchase, that it is the greatest bargain you ever saw, you are to return it to us, and we will refund your money and pay the express charges. Size, 6x7¼x12¼ inches. Weight, boxed, about 12 pounds. Price $2.65

No. 12F997 This is undoubtedly the best double row accordion for the money yet placed on the market. It is finished with fancy fluted mouldings, highly polished ebonized keyboard, and is also furnished in imitation ebony, beautiful green panels ornamented with gold pencil design, double bellows of ten folds, and each fold is protected by metal protectors. The clasps are all nickeled, and it is trimmed in three colors, red, black and green. It contains four sets of reeds, nineteen keys, four stops and four basses. This accordion is sold under our guarantee for quality and is shipped out with the distinct understanding and agreement that if it is not all that you expect or if it is not entirely satisfactory after a thorough trial and examination, it is to be returned to us at our expense and all money paid by you is to be refunded in full. This is the offer we make on all our accordions. Size, 7½x12 inches. Weight, boxed, about 14 pounds. Price $4.25

No. 12F998 The same accordion as described above except that it has twenty-one keys. Weight, boxed, about 14 pounds.
Price $4.65

OUR WEIDLICH ACCORDIONS.

A SPLENDID LINE OF ACCORDIONS AT AN EXTREMELY LOW PRICE.

This line of accordions is manufactured by one of the best known makers of accordions in Germany, and they are all furnished for us under special contract with the manufacturers. We guarantee each instrument to be satisfactory and the purchaser has the privilege of returning any instrument he may order from us should it fail to satisfy him in any particular. These accordions are all finely finished with the metallic parts beautifully nickel plated and the frames ebonized and stained in beautiful colors. There are many imitations of these accordions on the market, but for strictly guaranteed instruments of good grade and standard reputation, our prices are far below any competition. We include, free with each instrument, a complete, valuable instruction book, by the aid of which anyone can learn this instrument without a teacher. **Your Profit Sharing Certificate** will help you get some valuable article absolutely **FREE** of cost to you.

No. 12F1001 This is the greatest bargain in our line of accordions. It is 10¼ inches high by 6½ inches wide. The case is made of imitation mahogany, beautifully polished and finished. It has ten nickel keys, two stops and two sets of reeds, and double bellows with nickel corners and clasps. Our Empress Accordions have established themselves in public favor to a wonderful extent, and this popularity is due altogether to the fact that these instruments give perfect satisfaction to all purchasers. We recommend this entire line as being something particularly fine at the extremely low prices quoted. Weight, boxed for shipment, 7 pounds. Price $1.85

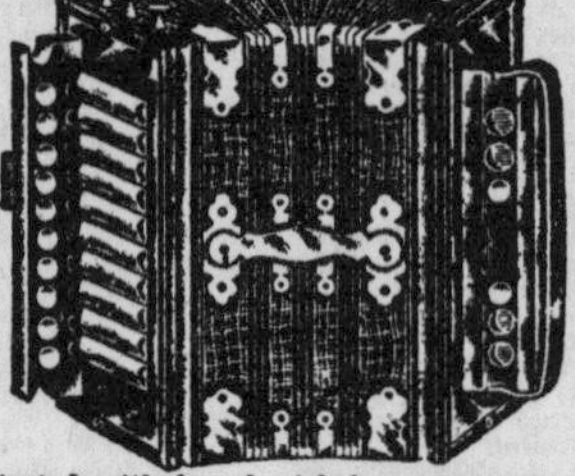

No. 12F1007 We offer this accordion as something new and particularly desirable. It has three stops, controlling three sets of powerful steel bronze reeds. It has two basses and ten keys with highly nickeled valves. It has triple bellows of nine folds furnished with nickel corner protectors. The auxiliary bellows folds are covered with green and light brown pebbled leatherette, and protected with broad nickel corner protectors. The instrument is fitted with two nickel clasps to keep it closed when not in use, and the woodwork is finished in black enamel. It measures 5½ inches in depth, is 10 inches wide and 10 inches long. It is a very powerful, sweet toned instrument, and one which we are sure will be a welcome addition to this line. Weight, boxed for shipment, 10 pounds.
Price $2.25

No. 12F1003 Genuine Celebrated Empress Accordion. It is 9x10¼x5¾ inches in size. The frame is beautifully made, with highly polished ebonized mouldings with gilt lines; has nickel corners and clasps, ten nickel keys, leather straps, two ebonized stops, powerful double bellows with the center fold protected with nickel corners. The space will not allow us to dwell with any great length upon the merits of this instrument. It has two sets of extra broad reeds, giving it a specially strong and beautiful quality of tone. Weight, boxed for shipment, about 10 pounds.
Price $2.35

No. 12F1005 Empress Accordion. This is a handsome instrument with great musical capacity and powerful tone. It has a double bellows of eight folds bound with red cloth. It has a sunken keyboard enameled in silver and the entire instrument is finished in black and yellow enameled wood, red and green cloth ornamented with silver bronze and corners fitted with nickel protectors. It has two powerful basses, ten keys fitted with elegant mother-of-pearl buttons, two stops controlling two sets of richly toned reeds, making it suitable for all kinds of concert music. This is one of the neatest accordions in our Weidlich line and we recommend it to all who desire a handsome and durable instrument at a price which is within the reach of all. If you should buy this same accordion from the dealer you would find that he would be compelled to ask you a very much higher price than we do. This instrument is 11½ inches high, 10 inches wide and 5¾ inches deep. Weight, boxed for shipment, about 10 pounds. Price $2.75

No. 12F1004 We offer this accordion in competition with any instrument you can buy elsewhere at from $4.00 to $6.00. This accordion is 13 inches in height, 6¼ inches in width, has beautiful ebonized case, fancy cut corners, handsome gilt ornaments on corners and top. Beautiful gilt beading around same. Has two stops and two sets of reeds. Open action, nickel corners and clasps. Double bellows. This is an especially handsome instrument and we have sold thousands to professionals and amateurs alike, who desire an instrument which will meet all their demands. The workmanship and material throughout is the very best that possibly can be put into an accordion at this price, and we know that the instrument will surprise and delight you, because it is one of the very best low priced accordions on the market. In tone, quality and general appearance it is in every way equal to accordions sold throughout the country at double the price. Weight, boxed, about 12 pounds.
Price $2.85

No. 12F1022 The Empress Professional Instrument. This is a large accordion, being 14½ inches high by 9 inches wide, with broad mahogany moulded frame, mahogany panels and keys, ornamented with handsome gilt and nickel ornaments. Clasps and corners are fully nickel plated, sunken open keyboard, double ribbed bellows, ten keys, eight stops, four sets of reeds, tuned in chords. Complete instruction book free. This is the best we offer, and is an instrument of great capacity and volume of tone. It is our very best Empress accordion, and is highly ornamented throughout. We will be glad to place this instrument in your hands and give you an opportunity to compare it with any accordion which your dealer has to offer at from $10.00 to $12.00. It is elegantly finished, and no accordion at this price on the market can in any way equal it in quality and volume of tone. Weight, boxed, about 15 pounds. Price $6.40

SEE OUR CUSTOMERS' PROFIT SHARING DEPARTMENT ON PAGES 1 AND 2 OF THIS BOOK.

THE CELEBRATED PITZSCHLER ACCORDIONS.

Pitzschler is recognized as one of the best manufacturers of accordions in Germany, the home of this instrument. In presenting our line of Pitzschler Accordions we have selected five of the very large number of instruments made by this celebrated maker, and by special arrangement and by contracting for a large quantity, we are able to list them at prices representing the very greatest value ever quoted in instruments of this kind. Anyone desiring to purchase an accordion should see and try our Pitzschler's before deciding to purchase elsewhere. Most remarkably superior in richness and purity of tone, ease of action as well as details of construction.

THIS LINE OF ACCORDIONS IS SO WELL KNOWN that it is not necessary for us to say much in its favor. These instruments are in universal use not only in the United States, but throughout Europe as well. An accordion player who has one of these accordions can very well feel that he is prepared for any demand which may be made upon him. We ask you to examine the accordions kept in stock by your local dealer and we know that you will see at once that we are prepared to sell you a high class instrument for about one-half the price which he would charge you. **ALL OF THESE ACCORDIONS ARE FITTED WITH PEARL BUTTON KEYS. WITH EVERY ACCORDION WE GIVE A COMPLETE INSTRUCTION BOOK.**

No. 12F1080 This accordion is 6½x7½x13 inches. Is beautifully made and highly finished; has nine folds in the bellows with nickel corners; two stops and two sets of reeds, open action, two basses. The keys are mounted in mother of pearl buttons, making them easily operated and especially adapted to the touch of the fingers. This instrument is beautifully decorated and a handsomer accordion cannot be found except at a much higher price than we ask. We include with each accordion a complete instruction book. This is the accordion which you will find in your local musical dealer's window priced at from $6.00 to $6.50. He cannot afford to sell such an instrument as this for any less than that amount, because he has not the same buying and selling advantage which we have. We sell so many thousands of these accordions that we can afford to be contented with a very small profit, and can sell them at the manufacturer's price with but our one small margin of profit added. Every instrument is carefully packed. Shipping weight, 10 pounds. Price........$3.85

No. 12F1082 This accordion measures 7x8½x13½ inches. It is of ebony finish, the moulding highly polished; has ninefold triple bellows with metal corners; three sets of reeds and open keyboard; two basses. This is an exceptionally powerful accordion and a great bargain. If you will order one of these accordions, give it a thorough trial and examination and are not convinced that you could not buy it from your local dealer for less than $10.00, you can return it to us, and we will cheerfully refund the purchase price. We include with each accordion a complete instruction book. We feel justified in recommending this accordion to our customers, as it is one of the greatest triumphs for our method of sale and is certainly a magnificent bargain in every respect. Every instrument is carefully packed. Shipping weight, 10 pounds. Price........$4.90

No. 12F1084 This accordion is one of the latest designs; measures 7x9x13½ inches. The mouldings are all finished in imitation ebony, highly polished and beautifully decorated. Has 10-fold extra broad single bellows. The end of the bellows are entirely covered with nickel and the corners are mounted with beautiful fancy brass caps, making this one of the handsomest accordions ever offered by any music dealer. This instrument has a sunken keyboard, with open action. The keys are all mounted with mother of pearl buttons. This accordion has three sets of reeds, three stops and two basses, and produces a beautiful and powerful tone. An examination of the illustration will give you some idea of the fine appearance of this accordion, but no illustration however good can give you any idea of its beautiful appearance and splendid tone. We include with each accordion a complete instruction book. Every instrument is carefully packed. Shipping weight, 11 pounds. Price........$5.80

No. 12F1086 This instrument is one of the best of the Pitzschler make. It measures 7¾x7½x13¾ inches. The mouldings are all made in imitation ebony, highly polished and decorated. Has 10-fold, double, very powerful bellows protected with nickel corners; four stops, four sets of reeds and two basses. Sunken keyboard, open action. The keys are fitted with mother of pearl buttons, making the accordion easy to play. The tone of this instrument is especially powerful and of excellent quality. Accordions of this grade are sold generally throughout the country for about $12.00, and are considered to be great bargains at that price. Our money saving method of sale enables us to sell them to you at the wonderfully low price quoted. If you will compare this accordion with any instrument offered at the same price at the music stores you will find that everything that we have told you in regard to the great saving which we offer you is absolutely true in every respect. We recommend this instrument as the finest accordion that can be purchased anywhere in the country at this price. Shipping weight, about 20 pounds. Price........$6.40

No. 12F1088 This is the finest Pitzschler Accordion we handle. It has fine fluted mouldings in imitation mahogany; panels genuine mahogany; all woodwork finely polished and finished; sunken open action keyboard; double row, nineteen nickel keys; heavy double bellows, with nickel protectors; nickel plated corners and clasps; four stops; four fine sets of reeds. Size, 14 inches by 8 inches. A complete instruction book free. Weight packed, about 20 pounds.
Price........$7.40

No. 12F1090 Genuine Pitzschler Accordion, is just the same in every way as No. 12F1088, described above, but has twenty-one nickel plated keys, as shown in the illustration. The additional three keys on this instrument increase the volume of tone to a wonderful extent and give the instrument a much greater musical capacity. The slight addition in price is more than compensated for in the greater musical value which will be obtained. Weight packed, about 20 pounds.
Price........$7.80

KALBE ACCORDIONS.

The name Imperial, together with the "double anchor" trade mark, on an accordion is a guarantee of its being of the very highest grade. While the price of these goods may be a trifle higher than others, the satisfaction derived from them, on account of the perfect workmanship and wearing qualities will amply repay for the difference in price, and they will be found much the cheapest in the end. We guarantee every one to arrive in perfect playing condition. You cannot make a mistake in buying a Kalbe Imperial for you get the very best article of the kind that is made. Attention is especially called to the patent simplex keys, which are made of heavy metal, in one piece, and are extremely durable. All of the styles of Imperial Accordions that we carry are supplied with patent metal bellows corners and patent folding clasps. Every part of these instruments is of the very best material and workmanship. The Kalbe Accordions are known throughout the world as standard instruments in every way, and we have sold an enormous number since we first begun to handle them. The name Kalbe on an accordion is an evidence of the finest grade, most thorough workmanship and most beautiful tone. **You will get a PROFIT SHARING CERTIFICATE with your purchase and can soon share in our profit, get some valuable article FREE, shown on pages 1 and 2, and in this way your Accordion will cost you even less money. At the same time our prices are as low as possible, guaranteed lower than you can get from any other dealer.**

Our Kalbe Accordion at $3.19.

No. 12F1100 This is a splendid Kalbe instrument with an ebonized maple frame very handsomely finished. It is very highly polished and is ornamented with fluted moulding. It has a powerful double bellows of eight folds, with nickel plated corner protectors. Highly polished nickel trimmings and clasps, two sets of reeds and two stops. This accordion is fitted with a tremolo or vox humana attachment, which gives the tone a wavy and undulating effect in imitation of the human voice. The tremolo can be thrown in and out of action at the will of the player by means of a lever, operated by the thumb of the right hand. The instrument is splendidly fitted throughout and will be sure to satisfy all players upon the accordion. Weight, boxed for shipment, about 10 pounds.
Price........$3.19

Our Kalbe Accordion at $3.40.

No. 12F1104 Kalbe's Imperial Miniature. Beautifully polished ebonized frame, open action, patent simplex keys, which are very durable; double bellows, with hand painted artistic design on bellows frame, patent nickel plated corners on bellows, thus protecting the weakest part of the accordion. Ten keys, two stops, two sets of reeds and patent clasps. The size of this accordion is 10¼ inches high by 6¼ inches wide. This is a very ornamental instrument, very highly finished and attractive. It has a very beautiful tone and is accurately tuned. Its good quality has caused an immense sale as it is one of the favorites in the Kalbe line. If you desire a small accordion which will be satisfactory in every way, at a price which no dealer can approach, we take pleasure in recommending this instrument to your notice. Weight, boxed for shipment, about 10 pounds.
Price........$3.40

No. 12F1112 Kalbe Imperial Accordion. This is an instrument of great sweetness and volume of tone, very rich in appearance with highly polished ebonized case. The corners are protected by fancy ornamental nickel bands and the corners of the bellows panels are protected in the same way. It is handsomely ornamented and decorated throughout, has triple bellows of eight folds. The bellows folds are ornamented in gold trimming and the entire instrument is one of the handsomest on the market. It has two sets of reeds and two stops and fitted on each side with patent clasps to keep the instrument closed when not in use. Size of instrument, 6¼ inches deep and 12½ inches wide. Weight, boxed for shipment, about 10 pounds. Price........$4.40

No. 12F1116 Kalbe Imperial Accordion. Very fine ebonized case, highly polished, beautiful nickel plated strips all around the panels. Has double bellows of ten folds, giving great volume of tone to the instrument. Has broad nickel plated corner protectors and is a handsome instrument in every respect. Three sets of reeds and three stops. This is an instrument which the purchaser will be proud to own and pleased to show to his friends. It is 6½ inches deep and 11¾ inches wide. We believe that if you will examine some of the accordions offered by different dealers throughout the country you will find that none of them are offering accordions of this grade for less than from $10.00 to $12.00. We are prepared to ship you this instrument under our distinct promise to save you at least $5.00 on your purchase, and if you do not find when you receive it that we are doing so you can return it to us and we will cheerfully refund your money. Weight, boxed for shipment, about 12 pounds.
Price........$4.95

No. 12F1120 Kalbe Imperial Accordion. This is a splendid instrument in every respect and has a very nicely finished ebonized case; has broad nickel plated corner protectors, and handsome clasps on each side to keep it closed when not in use. Has powerful double bellows of ten folds, four sets of reeds and four stops. Is very highly ornamented throughout and we guarantee it to give satisfaction. Size, 6½ inches deep by 11¾ inches wide. This is certainly one of the handsomest accordions on the market and is not only a beautiful musical instrument, but is a fine piece of workmanship as well. This accordion at $6.45 represents a wonderful saving in price to you. We could not afford to sell this magnificent instrument at this price if it were not for the fact that we buy them in such enormous quantities that we secure the lowest possible price, a price that represents the actual cost of making at the factory to which we add our one small margin of profit. Weight, boxed for shipment, about 12 pounds. Price........$6.45

OUR NEW LINE OF M. HOHNER ACCORDIONS.

Free With Each Hohner Accordion.

With each one of these accordions we send, without extra charge, a splendid carrying case, made to fit the different sizes of accordions shown on this page. These cases are made especially for us, and can be obtained with no other accordions on the market. They are made of heavy pasteboard, covered with a very durable covering of beautiful imitation of black morocco leather. They are fitted with two straps, made of a good quality of leather, fitted with buckles and a handle for carrying the case in the hand. Remember that this case can be obtained only from us and with no other line of accordions but the Hohner.

WE ARE SHOWING ON THIS PAGE OUR MAGNIFICENT LINE OF HOHNER ACCORDIONS, and we know that performers on these popular instruments will find them a welcome addition to our already large line of accordions. There are no accordions which are so thoroughly and carefully made as those which are manufactured in the Hohner factory. Every piece of woodwork is polished and finished to the last degree of completion. Every joint is accurately fitted and solidly glued. There are no ragged edges or unfinished parts, and when you purchase one of these instruments you have the assurance that you are buying the very best that can be had at any price. By special arrangement with M. Hohner each one of these accordions is made with extra care and given a special finish, which is one of their distinctive qualities. The high grade and thorough finish on these accordions take them out of the line of novelties and place them among the standard musical instruments of the world. Each instrument is fitted with the very best quality of steel bronze reeds, and it is a well known fact that no musical instruments are tuned so accurately and harmoniously as the instruments of this splendid line. From the cheapest to the most expensive instruments, each one will be found to be the very best that can possibly be made at the price asked. We will be glad to have you compare these instruments with anything that your dealer has to offer in the same line and our liberal terms of shipment give you the fullest opportunity to do this.

WE SEND A COMPLETE INSTRUCTION BOOK WITH EACH ACCORDION.

EACH ONE OF THESE INSTRUMENTS IS FITTED WITH PEARL KEYS, SO DESIGNED, ROUNDED AND FINISHED AS TO BE MOST AGREEABLE TO THE FINGERS OF THE PLAYER. THIS FEATURE IS FOUND UPON NO OTHER LINE OF ACCORDIONS

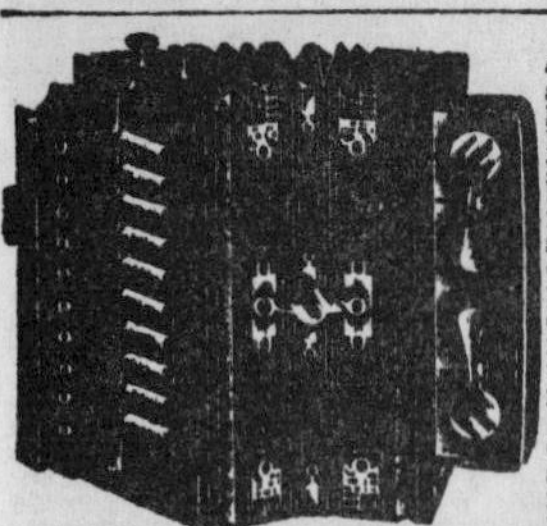

No. 12F1198 This Accordion is the latest addition to our Hohner line and is a very neat little instrument in every respect. It has a double bellows of six folds finished with light brown and plum colored leatherette. The corners are protected with the usual ornamental Hohner corner protectors, and the woodwork of the instrument is beautifully finished in black and blue enamel. It has ten keys and two powerful basses, nickel clasps and the usual pearl buttons. It has two stops controlling two sets of steel bronze reeds and is so arranged that it can easily be taken apart. It possesses the usual high grade Hohner quality of tone and we offer it as the very best value ever placed on the market at this price. It is 10 inches long, 9½ inches deep and 5½ inches wide. This is an accordion for which the local dealer will ask you from $4.00 to $6.00, and if we should be favored with your order for one of these instruments and you do not find by comparison that this is true, we will gladly receive it back and refund your money.
Price....................$2.40

No. 12F1200 Hohner Accordion. This is a very fine accordion, handsomely finished in black and red enamel and green leather. It has nickel plated guards on the corners of the bellows folds and is fitted with patent spring clasps. It has a double bellows of eight folds and two full sets of steel bronze reeds with two basses. The keys are all fitted with mother-of-pearl buttons and the valves are nickel plated. Each reed plate is separate and securely fastened with metallic fasteners. It is one of the accordions which has given M. Hohner his great reputation and an instrument which will never disappoint the purchaser. It is an instrument which will stand comparison with any accordion your dealer has to offer at more than double the price, and we recommend it to all who desire a neat, compact and durably made instrument, which will prove satisfactory under all conditions. It is 10¾ inches long, 10½ inches wide and 5¾ inches deep. See pages 1 and 2 for the valuable articles you can get FREE for PROFIT SHARING CERTIFICATES.
Price....................$3.35

No. 12F1204 M. Hohner Accordion. This instrument is a splendid concert instrument, finished in black enamel and green cloth. It has triple bellows of nine folds, finished in red with brass corners. The instrument is protected by nickel plated corners throughout and is one of the handsomest and most durable instruments in the line. The top can be taken off by simply unscrewing two thumb screws making it very easy of repair in case if anything should get out of order. It has patent spring clasps and three stops controlling three full sets of steel bronze reeds. For concert purposes it is unexcelled, as it has great depth and volume of tone and great musical capacity. It has two rich basses. It is 11½ inches high, 11½ inches long and 6½ inches deep. Price....................$4.95

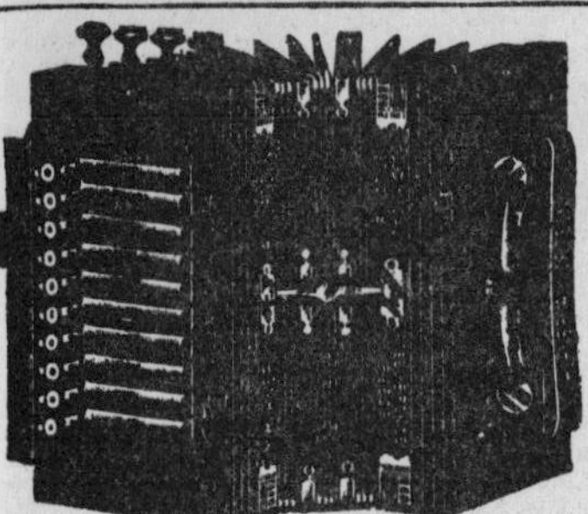

No. 12F1208 Hohner Accordion. This is another beautiful Hohner instrument, finished in rosewood and dark brown leather. It has triple bellows of nine folds finished in red with brass corner protectors. Has four stops controlling four sets of steel bronze reeds. It is fitted with two powerful basses and the keys are fitted with elegant mother-of-pearl buttons and the valves are finished in gold enamel. The reeds in this accordion are tuned to thirds, making possible a succession of beautiful chords, and wonderfully increasing the capacity of the instrument. If you will buy this accordion, and compare it with any accordion which your dealer has to offer for from $8.00 to $10.00, you will not only find that it is in every way equal, but also in many points superior. All we ask is an opportunity to place this instrument in your hands for examination and comparison, and if you are not perfectly satisfied with your bargain you can return it to us and we will cheerfully refund your money. This instrument is 12½ inches high, 11½ inches long and 7¼ inches deep.
Price....................$5.85

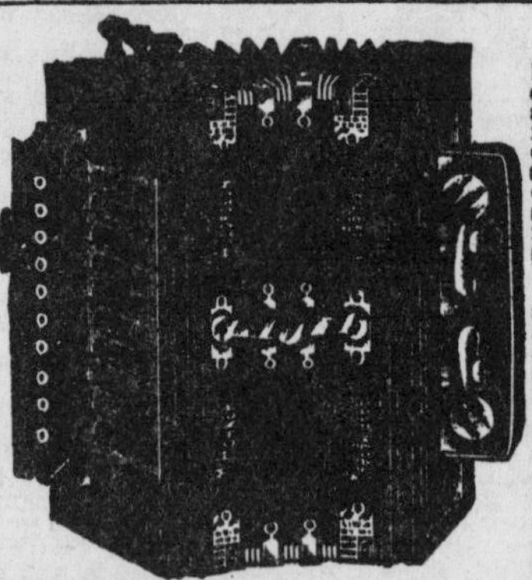

No. 12F1212 Hohner Accordion. This is another instrument a little different in style from the one previously shown, as it is fitted with a sunken keyboard finished in natural wood and black enamel. The balance of the instrument is handsomely finished in black enamel and red and green cloth. It has a powerful triple bellows of nine folds finished in red and green cloth with brass and nickel corner protectors. It is fitted with three stops controlling three full sets of steel bronze reeds, and has two powerful deep basses. The keys are fitted with elegant mother-of-pearl buttons and the valves are finished in black enamel. This is an accordion of deep mellow tone and wonderful carrying power, durably made and handsomely finished. This instrument is 13¼ inches high, 11½ inches long and 7¾ inches deep. You will also get one of our valuable PROFIT SHARING CERTIFICATES with your purchase.
Price....................$6.40

Hohner Grand Concert Accordion. This is certainly a grand concert instrument, as it is fitted with a triple bellows of nine folds, four stops controlling four sets of steel bronze reeds. It has two rows of keys, 19 in all, fitted with handsome mother-of-pearl buttons, with valves finished in gold enamel. The entire instrument is finished in black and red enameled wood and black and red cloth. The bellows folds are protected by heavy red bellows cloth and brass corner protectors. It has four powerful deep, rich basses accurately tuned with the treble reeds. The instrument is trimmed throughout with nickel plated trimmings and fitted with patent spring clasps. It is 13½ inches high, 12½ inches wide and 8 inches deep.

No. **12F1214** Grand Concert Accordion, 19 keys.
Price....................$7.95

No. **12F1216** Grand Concert Accordion, 21 keys.
Price....................8.95

No. 12F1220 Hohner Italo-Bohemian Accordion. This is a splendid Italian accordion handsomely finished in yellow and black enameled wood and black pebblecloth. It has a powerful bellows of ten folds protected by black pebble cloth and brass corner protectors. It has four basses and ten keys fitted with handsome mother-of-pearl buttons. Each end of the accordion is fastened with nickel plated catches which enable the performer to take the instrument apart instantly should any repairs be necessary. The scroll plate over the valves is lined with handsome green cloth and can be removed instantly by turning the catches shown in the engraving. The entire instrument can be taken apart in a moment and the interior construction is as carefully attended to as the outside finish. We are always glad to have this instrument compared with similar accordions offered by other dealers, because the customer is always sure to find that an instrument of this grade cannot be purchased from local dealers for less than double the price we are asking. It is certainly one of the neatest accordions on the market and it must be seen and examined to be appreciated. Our liberal terms of shipment give you a splendid opportunity to give this instrument a thorough test and examination, because we do not ask you to keep the instrument until you are fully satisfied that it is what you desire and up to your expectations in every way. This instrument is 10 inches high, 10 inches long and 5½ inches deep.
Price....................$4.55

No. 12F1224 Genuine Hohner Italian-Bohemian Accordion. It is made of a thoroughly seasoned spruce, a wood which is best known for its sonority, veneered in walnut and finished in imitation of mahogany, very highly polished. The panels are made of fancy open work of beautiful design with green cloth lining, giving the accordion a very beautiful and rich appearance. The keyboard is invisible. The keys are made of pearl, shaped like a button, making them agreeable to the touch. It has a single bellows of 14 folds, leather bound and with patent metal corner protectors. It has 21 keys, 8 basses and all trimmings are nickel plated and very highly polished. This accordion is 11½x9½x6½ inches. Weight when packed for shipment, about 15 pounds. The construction of this instrument is the same as the construction of the No. 12F1220 shown at the left and it has the same movable device by which the different complete sets of reeds can be taken from the instrument for repairs. The accordion is separable and can be taken apart instantly, should repairs be necessary.
Price....................$7.85

No. 12F1228 Hohner Special Italian-Bohemian Accordion. This is the latest creation of the Hohner factories, and is the most elegant accordion ever placed on the market by any manufacturer at any price. It is finished throughout in elegant rosewood of a deep brown shade. It is inlaid throughout in natural wood, and fitted with nickel plated trimmings. It has a large and powerful bellows of 14 folds, twelve powerful basses and 21 keys fitted with elegant mother-of-pearl buttons and has an invisible valve board. Like all our Italian accordions it is separable and can be taken apart instantly. Each reed is set on a separate plate and securely fastened without the use of wax, by means of metallic clamps. The different sets of reeds are so arranged that they can be instantly taken out of the instrument in case any repairs should be necessary. Both the outside and inside construction is the very best that has ever been placed in an accordion. The 12 basses with which this accordion is fitted together with the four sets of reeds gives it a compass and power of tone not possessed by any other accordion. It is 11½ inches high, 12¼ inches long and 6 inches deep. Price....................$9.95

THE CELEBRATED CH. WEISS HARMONICAS.

CH. WEISS IS ONE OF THE MOST CELEBRATED OF ALL HARMONICA MAKERS and his instruments are in use by professionals and amateurs alike throughout the entire world. The principal characteristics of these instruments are elegance of finish, durability of construction and beauty of tone. To both professionals and amateurs we unhesitatingly recommend this line of harmonicas as something which will prove perfectly satisfactory in every respect. The line offers a great variety from which to select and each instrument is strictly high grade. We have now been handling this celebrated line of harmonicas for some years, and the fact that we are still handling them is conclusive proof that they have given universal satisfaction. Why should you buy a harmonica in the usual way from a local music dealer when you can buy a harmonica which is in every way equal, and in many points superior to harmonicas which you will buy in that way, paying double the price which we ask? Remember, that we promise to save you at least one-quarter on your purchase and all of these harmonicas are sold under this condition. Each instrument is furnished with a beautiful case, as shown in the illustration, they are all easy blowing and accurately tuned to concert pitch. The harmonica is becoming a very popular instrument, because the musical public is beginning to realize that it is an instrument of real musical capacity and power. All of our harmonicas are beautifully and delicately tuned, are furnished with the very highest grade of bell metal reeds and are guaranteed satisfactory in every respect. The harmonica is an instrument which can be carried very handily in the pocket, and always helps to pass away the time very pleasantly. They are very easily learned and a wide range of music can be played on them.

EVERY HARMONICA IS FULLY GUARANTEED BY US. Each instrument shown in this line is suitable for the highest class of concert playing and can be used with splendid effect in playing with other instruments. Give us an opportunity to place one of these splendid instruments in **your hands for approval, and we agree that you will be so well satisfied with it that** you will recommend it to all of your friends.

YOU WILL GET A PROFIT SHARING CERTIFICATE if your total order is $1.00 or more, and can soon get something valuable entirely FREE, as explained on pages 1 and 2 of this catalogue.

No. 12F1402 The Brass Band Bell Harmonica is made by Ch. Weiss and is a splendidly finished and beautiful tuned instrument. It is fitted with tuned bells, which can be used with wonderful effect in connection with the instrument. It has ten double holes, forty finely toned reeds, accurately tuned and mounted on heavy brass reed plates. The bells are of the very best quality, made of the very best bell metal and highly polished. The tone of the instrument is very powerful and possesses that broad volume so much desired in a harmonica. 6 inches long. Furnished in A, B, C, D, E, F and G. Be sure to state key wanted.

No. 12F1402 Price..60c

No. 12F1404 Same as No. 12F1402, but has one bell, ten holes and twenty reeds. 5½ inches long. Price.........(If by mail, postage extra, 8 cents)..............30c

No. 12F1412 Our Celeste Harmonica. This harmonica is made expressly for us by the celebrated maker, Ch. Weiss. It is made of the very finest material, and is intended for those who desire an instrument of great musical capacity and a splendid volume of tone. It has heavy nickel covers decorated with hand painted flowers. The panels are gold finished and give a rich appearance to the instrument. It has a wood frame, highly enameled in beautiful imitation of ivory. It is double sided, fitted with sixteen double holes, thirty-two reeds on each side, making sixty-four reeds in all. We can furnish it in all the different keys and it comes in a splendid leatherette covered richly embossed case. This is a new instrument and one which we are prepared to recommend to all who desire something particularly fine in this line. The price which we quote on this harmonica represents simply what the harmonica costs us, with but our one small percentage of profit added, and is figured down so low that you cannot purchase a harmonica of this grade from any other dealer for less than twice the price we are making you. 5 inches long.

No. 12F1412 Price..75c
If by mail, postage extra, 15 cents.

No. 12F1414 We can furnish this instrument with eighty reeds if desired at the following price. 6¼ inches long. Price..95c
If by mail, postage extra, 15 cents.

No. 12F1428 Angel's Clarion. Manufactured by Ch. Weiss, maker of the celebrated Brass Band Harmonica. This harp resembles the Brass Band Clarion in some respects, but is so constructed as to produce a peculiar, vibrating, organ like tone not found in any other harmonica. It has twenty double holes, with forty brass reeds and mounted on heavy brass reed plates. Has the clarion pipes and nickel covers. Packed in neat case. Every harmonica player should own one of these harps. This is a neat and compact instrument suited for either amateur or professional playing, and one with which any harmonica player will be more than delighted. Our sales on this instrument have been enormous and are the best proof that it is an instrument of the very highest merit. 6¼ inches long. Furnished in A, B, C, D, E, F and G. Be sure to state key wanted.

No. 12F1428 Price.......(If by mail, postage extra, 8 cents.)..........60c

No. 12F1408 Triumph Concert Harmonica. A double instrument of powerful and pleasing tone. Has ten double holes on each edge, twenty double holes in all; eighty fine bell metal reeds, brass reed plates, nickel covers. This harmonica is furnished with a very handsome case, as shown in the illustration, and is very handy and convenient for carrying in the pocket. We recommend it to all who wish a neat, compact harmonica at an extremely low price. The fact that this harmonica is stamped with the name of Ch. Weiss is a sufficient guarantee that it is an instrument of high grade in every respect. We have handled this instrument very successfully for a number of years and it is one of the most popular harmonicas which we handle. 4½ inches long. Furnished in the following combinations: A-D, C-F, and A-E. State key wanted.

No. 12F1408 Price...........(If by mail, postage extra, 8 cents)..........65c

No. 12F1416 The Brass Band Clarion Harmonica, manufactured by Ch. Weiss, the celebrated manufacturer of the Brass Band Harmonica, the wonder harmonica of the age. A new invention in harmonicas. The brass reed plates and bell metal reeds are the same as those used in the celebrated Brass Band Harmonica which has gained such a world wide reputation. The new idea or invention is in the organ pipes, which are placed over the reeds. By means of these pipes the performer is enabled to change the tone at will, giving imitations of the flute, church organ or trumpet calls. Its construction makes it the most powerful toned harmonica as well as the easiest blowing and most attractive that has ever been placed on the market; pronounced as such by professionals throughout the country. Concert or large size harmonica has ten double holes and forty reeds. Packed in handsome heavy red leatherette case having substantial hinge and nickel plated fastener. 4¾ inches long. Furnished in A, B, C, D, E, F and G. Be sure to state key wanted.

No. 12F1416 Price..........(If by mail, postage extra, 8 cents)..........50c

No. 12F1420 Brass Band Clarion Harmonica, has ten single holes and twenty reeds. Packed in handsome red leatherette case. 4 inches long. Price.(Postage extra, 6 cents).23c

No. 12F1432 Brass Band Harmonica. The reeds are made of the finest bell metal and are extremely sensitive, producing a remarkably smooth tone. The covers are flaring at the back and are made of solid brass, heavily nickel plated and are consequently of unusual strength, thus protecting the reeds perfectly. Accurately tuned to concert pitch. The Brass Band Harmonica has ten double holes, forty bell metal reeds, brass reed plates and extension ends. We include a handsomely lined wood case, as shown in illustration. 4¾ inches long. Furnished in A, B, C, D, E, F and G. State key wanted. Retails for $1.00 and is worth every cent of it.

No. 12F1432 Price..........(If by mail, postage extra, 8 cents)..........65c

No. 12F1434 Same harmonica as No. 12F1432, but has ten holes and twenty reeds, and comes packed in a neat pasteboard case. Price..............................19c
If by mail, postage extra, 6 cents

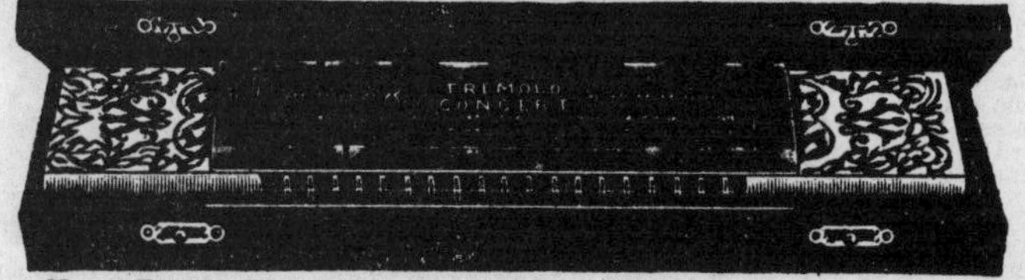

No. 12F1436 This harmonica is one of the largest, handsomest and finest toned instruments made. Coming, as it does, from Europe, direct from the factory of the celebrated maker, Ch. Weiss, is a guarantee as to its quality. The illustration gives but a faint idea of what an exceptionally fine harmonica it really is. The wood frame is 9¼ inches long, white enameled with gilt decorations. Has brass reed plates, highly polished nickel covers, forty holes on each edge, eighty best bell metal reeds accurately tuned to concert pitch, each side in a different key. As illustrated, it is packed in a handsome wood case with leatherette covering, satin lining and nickel clasps. Furnished in C-D, C-F and A-E. Be sure to state key wanted.

No. 12F1436 Price.....(If by mail, postage extra, 14 cents)........90c

No. 12F1440 This is the very latest harmonica produced by the celebrated maker, Ch. Weiss. It is made with twenty-four double holes on each side, forty-eight double holes in all, and ninety-six reeds, four heavy brass reed plates, and fancy nickel plated covers. This harp is especially constructed for the vibrato tone, which makes it very much finer in quality than most other harmonicas. No player should be without one. The two sides are tuned in different keys as follows: A-E, C-F and C-G. Be sure to state key wanted. Like all other Weiss harmonicas it is fully guaranteed. This harmonica comes in leatherette case, handsomely lined and nickel clasp.

No. 12F1440 Price.... ..(If by mail, postage extra, 15 cents) $1.15

ARE YOU INTERESTED IN BAND INSTRUMENTS?

We want to call your attention to the three magnificent lines of band instruments which we illustrate in another portion of this big catalogue. If you know of any band about to be organized, or about to purchase a new equipment of band instruments, the greatest service you can do them is to call their attention to our splendid stock of band instruments and supplies. We are the first dealers who have ever attempted to sell high grade band instruments on the same narrow margin of profit at which we sell groceries, dry goods, etc. These band instruments are all fully warranted, sold on ten days trial and guaranteed to be satisfactory in every particular. You cannot purchase these splendid instruments of any other dealer, because we are the sole American agents.

OUR SPECIAL BAND INSTRUMENT CATALOGUE, containing a complete line of brass instruments, flutes, saxophones, bassoons, oboes and band supplies, will be sent absolutely free on request. Do not overlook this magnificent opportunity to purchase a complete new set of instruments for your band at one-half the prices usually asked.

Read what we have to say in regard to our splendid lines of band instruments on page 335 of this catalogue. We have supplied hundreds of the largest bands in the country with complete outfits, and are now headquarters for all sorts of band instruments and supplies.

THE CELEBRATED HOHNER HARMONICAS.

In every trade, in every business, there can generally be found one firm that stands at the head of all the rest; and so in the small musical goods business, the firm of M. Hohner is known throughout the world as the largest manufacturers of these instruments. Not only do the Hohner goods enjoy a very large sale in the United States, but also in Europe and in all other foreign countries; and no business as extensive as the Hohner stands today, could possibly have been built up and held had not the lines laid down at the very inception—of superior quality in material and superlative excellence of workmanship—been strictly adhered to during the intervening years. Through the efforts on the part of M. Hohner, Sr., founder of the business, whose adaptability to his chosen work, coupled with sterling qualities which always command success, has established a trade of which one has every reason to feel justly proud; the name Hohner, as applied to harmonicas, has become a household word in all parts of the globe. The factories of M. Hohner stand at the head of all others in this industry, and their products are unquestionably of the best materials, expert workmanship and excel in tone. The customer can, therefore, rest assured that any instrument bearing the name of M. Hohner carries with it the same good qualities that have distinguished the Hohner harmonicas during the past half century.

M. HOHNER

During the past fifty years the Hohner Harmonicas have been leading the market as the best mouth organs made, and have grown steadily in popularity and perfection on account of their admitted excellence. This success is not the result of chance but of superior skill and conscientious work along the line of harmonica betterment. The primary efforts of these years have been to perfect the tone. With the tone perfected, it was a comparatively easy matter to obtain the most modern machinery and to carry out all improvements and new ideas. To satisfy the constantly increasing demand for these harmonicas there are employed in the main factory and its fifteen branches over 1,500 men who turn out daily over 20,500 of these instruments. We are glad to be able to announce that we are prepared to sell these harmonicas by our great money saving method of giving our customers an opportunity to purchase them at prices away below what other dealers are prepared to make. Each one of these harmonicas is sold with our absolute guarantee of merit and we recommend them to all players who desire harmonicas of beautiful appearance and splendid tone at exceedingly low prices. The engravings shown below give but a very poor idea of the handsome appearance of these instruments, and no matter how fine the illustration may be it will always be necessary for the player to thoroughly test the tone, to prove the merits of the harmonica.

No. 12F1604 M. Hohner Marine Band Harmonica. This is a beautiful little instrument, is exactly suited to performers who desire an instrument of good compass and volume to carry in the pocket. It is handsomely and durably made and accurately tuned. It has ten single holes and twenty silver toned reeds set in brass plates. It is fitted with heavy convex brass covers with open back handsomely nickel plated. We send each one of these instruments complete with neat hinged pasteboard case. 4 inches long; furnished in A, B, C, D, E, F and G. When ordering, be sure and specify key desired.
Price.......(If by mail, postage extra, 6 cents) 19c

No. 12F1606 Three Little Hohners. This is a very pretty set of three very fine Hohner harmonicas in a handsomely finished leather covered case. These harmonicas come in three different keys, which is a great advantage to the player. The case is 4½ inches long, 4 inches wide and 1 inch deep, and can be carried very nicely in the pocket. Each of these harmonicas has ten holes and twenty bell metal reeds exquisitely tuned. The reed plates are made of the very best quality of brass and the reed plate covers are highly nickel plated and polished. This is the handsomest little set of harmonicas ever placed on the market.
Price ......(If by mail, postage extra, 8 cents) 68c

No. 12F1608 Hohner's Marine Band. This is a beautiful little harmonica, 4⅛ inches long, very neatly finished and durably made. It has ten double holes, twenty reeds, brass plates, nickel plated convex covers with flat sides. We send each one of these harmonicas out in a fine leatherette pouch, which closes with button clasp, the style of which has never before been used in the harmonica line. Not only is this pouch very handy and durable, but it also keeps the mouth organ in much better condition than the old style pasteboard box. Furnished in A, B, C, D, E, F and G. When ordering, be sure to state the key desired. Price..........................45c
If by mail, postage extra, 6 cents.

No. 12F1612 Hohner's Autovalve Harp. This is absolutely a new idea in an harmonica and is fitted with a wind saving device, which is the greatest improvement that has been made in the harmonica line within the last 20 years. This improvement makes a concert harp as easy blowing as any single reed mouth organ. It has ten double holes, forty silver toned reeds, brass plates, nickel plated covers in new design, and is sent out complete in a handsome leatherette pouch shown in the engraving. 4½ inches long. Furnished in A, B, C, D, E, F and G. When ordering, be sure to state key desired.
Price....(If by mail, postage extra, 6 cents) 70c

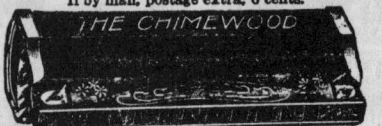

No. 12F1610 The Chimewood. This is the newest idea in harmonicas, having a hollow wooden backing giving the harmonica an almost perfect violin tone. The ends of this hollow wooden backing can be covered by the hands, thus subduing the tone at the will of the player. The wooden back is very handsomely finished and highly polished with nickel plated binding on the ends. The harmonica has ten holes and twenty bell metal reeds. The reed plates are made of the very finest brass with nickel plated covers. The harmonica is 4 inches long and one of the most exquisite little instruments ever made. Price..........................38c
If by mail, postage extra, 5 cents.

No. 12F1614 The Hohner Alpenecho. This is another new idea in harmonicas, being a double instrument with sixteen double holes on each side. It has sixty-four beautifully tuned bell metal reeds solidly riveted to heavy brass reed plates with nickel plated cylindrical covers. The horn like shape of these covers increases the tone of the instrument in a wonderful degree and make it one of the most powerful harmonicas on the market. It comes tuned in two different keys and is 5 inches in length. Price..........................62c
If by mail, postage extra, 7 cents.

No 12F1616 M. Hohner's Marine Band Tremolo Bell Harmonica. This is a splendid instrument with twenty double holes, forty reeds, brass plates, nickel covers, extension ends, fancy gilt stamp, tremolo with two extra clear toned bells. These bells are accurately tuned and a very beautiful effect can be obtained by using them in connection with music played on the reeds. This is one of Hohner's finest harmonicas and it has rapidly increased in popularity with harmonica players since its appearance on the market. For performers who do considerable concert work on the stage, this instrument is invaluable and never fails to call forth admiration and applause. Each of these harmonicas goes to the customer complete with a handsome hinged case with nickel clasps, and the instrument is very ornamental as well as of great musical value. 7½ inches long. Price 85c
If by mail, postage extra, 8 cents.

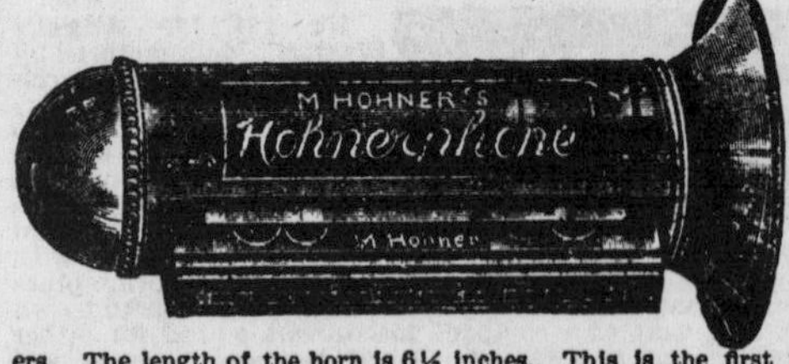

No. 12F1620 The Hohnerphone is an harmonica with a brass horn which amplifies the tone and increases it in volume. By placing the right hand over the end of the bell the finest crescendo effect can be obtained, and much more conveniently than by using a glass tumbler for the same purpose. For concert work on the stage as well as for home playing this attachment is of great importance. The harmonica has ten double holes, forty reeds, brass plates and nickel covers. The length of the horn is 6½ inches. This is the first time that this fine instrument has been offered to the public at this wonderfully low price. Our contract with the manufacturer is such that we are able to sell this instrument by our direct from the factory to customer method and thus offer it to you for about one-half the price generally asked by dealers for the same instrument. Price..........................75c
If by mail, postage extra, 10 cents.

No. 12F1624 Hohner's Triple Tremolo Harmonica. This instrument is offered in response to a demand for a harmonica which can be played in three different keys. The instrument is supplied with three sides, each tuned to a different key, and the changes from one key to another can be made instantly. The instrument is handsomely finished throughout and furnished with turning bars on each end for turning the instrument from one harmonica to the other. It has forty-eight double holes, ninety-six reeds, brass plates, nickel covers, three sides and three keys and is a wonderful instrument in many ways. The fact that this instrument is tuned in three different keys is of great importance when playing with other instruments or for accompaniments for songs. 6⅝ inches long. Price $1.25
If by mail, postage extra, 10 cents.

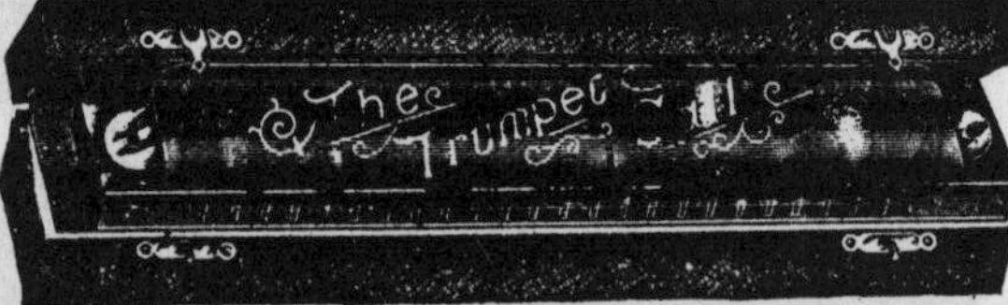

No. 12F1628 Hohner Trumpet Call. This is one of the very latest designs in the Hohner line, and it is an instrument which will be welcomed with enthusiasm by harmonica players throughout the country. It has twenty-four double holes, forty-eight bell metal reeds, extra heavy brass reed plates and heavy nickel plated covers with flaring edges. By a special construction a beautiful tremolo effect is given to the music produced on this harmonica and we recommend this instrument for all kinds of concert work. We ship this instrument to the customer in a very fine leatherette case, and guarantee it to give satisfaction in every way. 7½ inches long. Furnished in A, B, C, D, E, F and G. In ordering, be sure to specify key wanted. Price....(If by mail, postage extra, 8 cents)...58c

HOHNER'S MARINE BAND ECHO HARMONICA—ELEVEN AND ONE-HALF INCHES LONG.

No. 12F1632 This is a grand concert instrument in every respect, and is intended for those who desire an instrument of great capacity and volume of tone. It is tuned in different keys so that the performer can change instantly from one key to another. It is with a great deal of pleasure that we offer this instrument to the harmonica players of this country, and we know it will fill a long felt want and will be an instrument which will always be useful to the purchaser who requires an instrument that will meet all of the demands which may be made upon him. This instrument has sixty-four double holes, one hundred and twenty-eight reeds, brass plates, nickel plated convex covers and handsomely decorated extension ends. Each instrument comes in four keys. It goes to the customer complete with a fine case fitted with hinges and ornamented metallic clasps. We cannot recommend this instrument too highly, and desire to place it in the hands of every harmonica player who does concert playing. Like all other harmonicas which we handle, this instrument goes to the customer under our absolute guarantee of merit and with the distinct understanding that if the customer does not find, when he receives it, that he is getting an instrument of the same grade as the one for which his dealer asks double the price, it can be returned to us, and we will cheerfully refund the money paid. 11½ inches long.

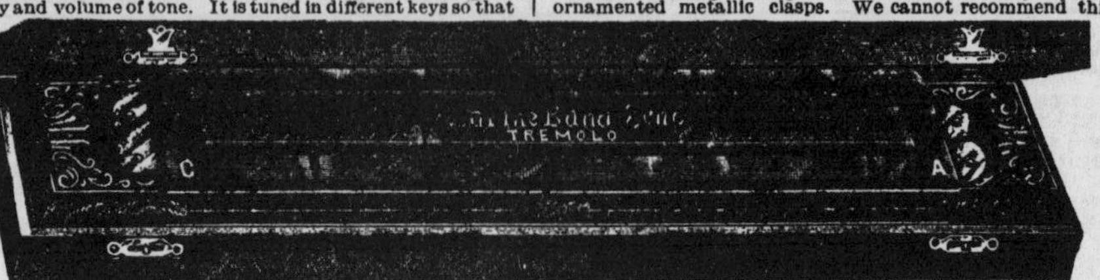

No. 12F1632 Price, $1.45
If by mail, postage extra, 12 cents.

No. 12F1804 Harmonica Holder. Will fit any harmonica not more than 4¾ inches in length. Two springs which instantly adjust themselves to any sized harmonica, thus firmly securing the same. When not in use, it may be folded into a small compass. Price..............**30c**
If by mail, postage extra 5c.

No. 12F1808 Bohm's Jubilee Harmonica, has ten single holes, twenty brass reeds, mounted on heavy brass reed plates, nickel covers. Made in imitation of organ pipes, producing an exceptionally nice quality of tone. This is a very neat little instrument and has proved a great favorite on account of being made a convenient size to carry in the pocket, 4 inches long. It comes in A, B, C, D, E, F and G. State key desired. Price, **13c**
If by mail, postage extra, 5 cents.

No. 12F1812 Bohm's Sovereign Harmonica. A rare bargain in harmonicas. This harmonica is 5½ inches long and 1½ inches wide; has sixteen double holes and thirty-two steel bronze reeds, heavy metal reed plates and beautiful fancy nickel covers. Price..**15c**
If by mail, postage extra, 8 cents.

No. 12F1816 Youth's Companion. Instead of the ordinary nickel cover the harp is made in the shape of a horn which enables the player to get the various effects which are ordinarily produced by using a tumbler. This harp has ten double holes, twenty accurately tuned brass reeds and heavy brass reed plates. 5¾ inches long. Furnished in A, B, C, D, E, F and G. State key desired. Price.....**29c**
If by mail, postage, extra, 7 cents.

No. 12F1820 Concert Harmonica, made by And. Koch, whose name is a guarantee for quality. This harmonica has ten double holes, forty bellmetal reeds, accurately tuned. Heavy brass reed plates, brass nickel plated covers, 4¾ inches long and furnished in A, B, C, D, E, F and G. Be sure to give key desired. Exceptionally sweet and powerful tone. Price.......................**23c**
If by mail, postage extra, 7 cents.

No. 12F1824 Sousa's Band, 4 inches long, 1 inch wide; ten holes and twenty brass reeds; heavy brass reed plates; handsome nickel covers. We can recommend this harmonica as being something especially fine in a low priced instrument. Furnished in A, B, C, D, E, F and G. State key desired. Price, **16c**
If by mail, postage extra, 6 cents.

No. 12F1828 Universal Favorite Harmonica, made by And. Koch, whose name is a guarantee for quality. This harmonica has ten single holes, twenty bellmetal reeds accurately tuned, fine tone, heavy brass reed plates, handsome nickel covers. Packed in a pasteboard box with hinge cover as illustrated. The illustration shown above falls far short of doing this instrument full justice. It is a neat and compact instrument and very convenient for carrying in the pocket. If you desire a harmonica which will be a constant source of pleasure, we unhesitatingly recommend this instrument. We recommend this instrument to all who are looking for a good harmonica at an unusually low price. It is 4 inches long and we can furnish it in A, B, C, D, E, F and G. State key desired. Price..........**14c**
If by mail, postage extra, 6 cents.

No. 12F1830 This is an illustration of our World's Ruler Swan Brand Harmonica, and the illustration shows an entirely new model. The instrument is fitted with twelve trumpets which carry the tone from the reeds and increase them wonderfully in volume. The instrument has a black frame highly polished. The reeds are riveted solidly to brass plates and it has nickel plated covers of very fancy artistic design. It is fitted with ten holes, twenty bellmetal extra sonorous reeds and goes to the customer complete in a fancy hinged cover box. It is 4½ inches long and 1½ inches wide at top. It comes in A, B, C, D, E, F and G. State key desired. Price..........**21c**
If by mail, postage extra, 6 cents.

No. 12F1832 This is our Finest Swan Brand Empress Harmonica. It has thirty-two holes, thirty-two resonant and strong reeds of bellmetal and heavy brass plates. It has brass covers highly nickel plated and polished. Black frame, very rich. Size, 4¾ inches long by 1 inch wide. We send this instrument complete with a very fine leatherette covered pasteboard case. It is made of convenient size to carry in the pocket and we recommend it to all who desire a fine harmonica at a low price. We furnish this instrument in seven keys, as follows: A, B, C, D, E, F and G. State key desired. Price, complete with case..(If by mail, postage extra, 7 cents.)..**26c**

No. 12F1834 This is the David's Harp Harmonica. It has a wood frame finished in rich red color, and the reeds are riveted solidly to heavy brass plates. It is fitted with twenty holes, twenty extra broad musical reeds in perfect tune. By using the hand at the bell of this trumpet the same effect can be obtained as when using a glass. On account of the shape of the harmonica the player is enabled to perform easily, as no breath is lost through the corner of the mouth; 4 inches long. We furnish it in seven different keys, as follows: A, B, C, D, E, F and G. State key desired. Price..................................**22c**
If by mail, postage extra, 6 cents.

No. 12F1836 The Tremolo Concert Harmonicas are made by And. Koch. Sixteen double holes; 7½ inches in length, 2 inches wide, two reeds to each hole, sixty-four reeds in all. Brass reed plates and nickel plated covers. The illustration gives but a very poor idea of the size and beautiful appearance of this harmonica. It is one of the best harmonicas which we handle and is a great bargain at the price which we fix upon it. We recommend it to all who desire a harmonica for general playing, as we know it will give the greatest satisfaction in every way. Comes in the following combinations of keys: A-G, C-F, A-E. State key desired. Price, **45c**
If by mail, postage extra, 6 cents.

No. 12F1840 Same as No. 12F1836, except larger. Has twenty double holes, eighty reeds in all. Price..............(If by mail, postage extra, 7 cents)..............**59c**

No. 12F1844 David's Harp. This Harmonica is 6 inches long, has 20 double holes and 40 powerful, beautifully tuned bellmetal reeds solidly riveted to heavy reed plates. The cover is elegantly nickel plated, polished and ornamented with beautiful enameled and embossed flower designs. The harmonica is made by Ch. Messner & Co. and is furnished in the keys of A, B, C, D, E, F and G. State key desired. The wood frame is finished in yellowish brown, beautifully finished and polished. Price..........(If by mail, postage extra, 5c)....**43c**

No. 12F1846 David's Harp. This is another harmonica of this well known name made by Ch. Messner & Co., with 14 double holes and 28 beautifully tuned reeds. It has heavy brass reed plates, nickel plated polished covers, ornamented with enameled flowers and tasty embossed designs. It is 4½ inches long; the wood work is finished in deep yellow and highly polished. Furnished in A, B, C, D, E, F and G. State key desired. Price.....................**29c**
If by mail, postage extra, 5 cents

No. 12F1848 The Echo Bell. This Harmonica is made by Fred Hotz, and has ten double holes and 20 exquisitely tuned reeds solidly riveted to heavy brass reed plates. The nickel plated metallic cover is so arranged as to amplify and increase the tone power of the reeds, making it an instrument which will prove very satisfactory to harmonica players. The wooden frame is finished in imitation ebony on the front and back and highly polished red on the ends. It is 4½ inches long and is a very neat looking instrument. Furnished in A, B, C, D, E, F and G. State key desired Price........(Postage extra, 5c.)........**21c**

No. 12F1850 Our New Drum Harmonica. This is one of the latest novelties in harmonicas and consists of a drum attached to a harmonica and played with the right hand as shown in the illustration. The entire instrument is very nicely finished, the metallic parts are nickel plated polished and durably made. We furnish one harmonica with this instrument with 10 double holes and 20 finely tuned reeds riveted to heavy brass reed plates. This instrument never fails to make a hit wherever exhibited and very little practice will enable the player to become very proficient in the use of the drum. It is 5½ inches long and oval in shape. Price..(If by mail, postage extra, 8c.)..**65c**

Jews' Harps.

The Jews' Harps which we list below are made by the best maker in America, and are known as the genuine E. L. American Jews' Harps and are not to be compared with the many inferior harps on the market. They are all made of white metal frames and have brass tipped tongues. If you are thinking of ordering a Jews' Harp it will pay you to buy our genuine E. L. harp. They will outlast six of the ordinary harps offered for sale by other dealers.

No. 12F2050 2-inch frame, **8c**
No. 12F2051 2¼-in. frame, **9c**
If by mail, postage extra, 3 cents.
No. 12F2052 2½-in. frame **12c**
No. 12F2053 2¾-in. frame **15c**
If by mail, postage extra, 4 cents.
No. 12F2054 3¼-inch frame..................**18c**
No. 12F2055 3½-inch frame..................**26c**
If by mail, postage extra, 5 cents.
No. 12F2056 3¾-inch frame..................**29c**
No. 12F2057 Jumbo, 4¼-inch..................**39c**
If by mail, postage extra, 6 cents.

Metronomes.

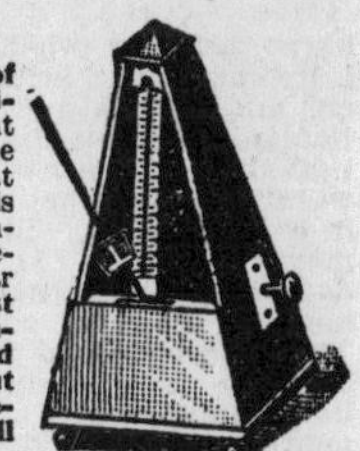

The Metronome is used by students of music, especially of the piano, to indicate the tempo or time. The upright rod moves backward and forward like an inverted pendulum, the movement being actuated by a spring which is wound up with a key. The time is indicated both to eye and ear, the movement being in sight and ticking similar to a clock. The time is regulated fast or slow by the sliding weight on the pendulum, while the latter has a graduated scale. This is an invaluable instrument for pupils of the piano and organ especially. Weight, 2 pounds. We sell only the very finest French Make.

No. 12F2207 Metronome. Genuine French make, solid mahogany case. Maelzel system. Price..............**$1.95**

No. 12F2208 Same as No. 12F2207, but with bell attachment. Price..............................**$2.95**

Ocarinas—Fiehn's Vienna Make.

No Better Ocarinas can be had at any price than these genuine imported instruments. We import these direct from Europe and own them at prices enabling us to offer them to you at about what your dealer himself pays. These instruments are easily broken and must be packed with care. We guarantee that each Ocarina leaves our hands in perfect condition. A sheet of instructions with each instrument showing exactly how it is played.

No.	Key of.	Price	No.	Key of	Price
12F2020	C, Soprano	$0.11	12F2029	Bb, Alto	$0.24
12F2021	Bb, Soprano	.11	12F2030	A, Alto	.26
12F2022	A, Soprano	.11	12F2032	G, Alto	.31
12F2023	G, Soprano	.11	12F2033	F, Alto	.41
12F2024	F, Soprano	.14	12F2035	Eb, Alto	.67
12F2025	E, Soprano	.14	12F2036	D, Bass	.67
12F2026	Eb. Soprano	.14	12F2037	C, Bass	.93
12F2027	D. Alto	.19	12F2038	Bb, Bass	1.12
12F2028	C, Alto	.21	12F2039	A, Bass	1.24
			12F2041	G, Bass	1 84

No. 12F2046 Quartettes: 1st and 2d Tenor, 1st and 2d Bass. Price, per set..............................**$2.75**
If by mail postage extra, Sopranos, each, 4 cents; Altos, each, 14 cents; Basses, each, 26 cents.

BLOW ACCORDIONS.

Flute Accordion. Substantially made, with ten bone keys, two bases and excellent reeds. Wood case with projecting bell. Weight, 20 ounces.
No. 12F2210 Price..............................**68c**

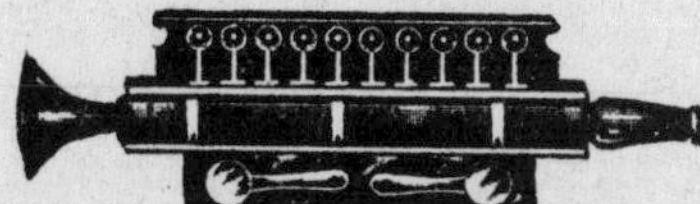

This is the newest pattern, made of black wood, polished case, projecting bell, imitation ebony, trimmed and decorated with white celluloid. Has ten keys, the same style of action as our most expensive accordions and two basses. Weight, 24 ounces.
No. 12F2214 Price..............................**82c**

The Clariophone.

A handsome little musical instrument that possesses all the necessary qualities for pleasing the ear with melodious sounds. Wood body, with fancy metal ornaments; ten keys, two basses and excellent reeds. Weight, about 28 ounces.
No. 12F2216 Price..............................**87c**

Our Finest Blow Accordion; none better made; in fact this instrument is of far better quality than blow accordions usually found in retail stores. The case is made of imitation ebony, highly polished and beautifully nickel trimmed. Has projecting bell. The action is the same as used on high grade accordions, the entire key being in one piece. Has ten keys and two basses. Weight, 30 ounces.
No. 12F2220 Price..............................**99c**

OUR BAND INSTRUMENT DEPARTMENT

THREE MAGNIFICENT LINES OF BRASS INSTRUMENTS SOLD EXCLUSIVELY BY US. A COMPLETE LINE OF WOOD WIND INSTRUMENTS, DRUMS, AND GENERAL BAND SUPPLIES

EVERY INSTRUMENT COVERED BY OUR WRITTEN BINDING GUARANTEE

OUR FREE SPECIAL BAND INSTRUMENT CATALOGUE.

THE MOST COMPLETE AND COMPREHENSIVE CATALOGUE OF BAND INSTRUMENTS EVER ISSUED WILL BE SENT TO YOU ABSOLUTELY FREE ON REQUEST.

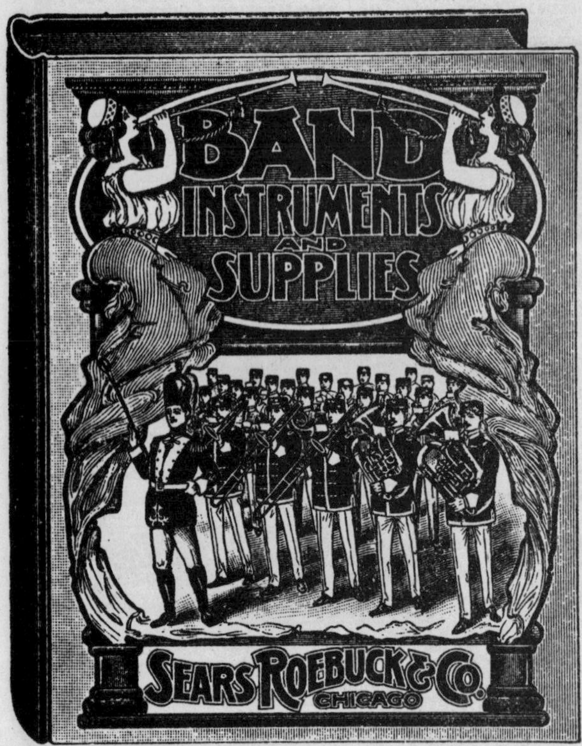

WE ARE SHOWING ON THIS PAGE an illustration of the splendid special catalogue which we are now issuing, containing illustrations and descriptions of band instruments and supplies, showing the most complete line ever offered to the bandmen of the United States. This book contains large illustrations and full descriptions of our three splendid lines of brass instruments also clarionets, saxophones, flutes, oboes, bassoons, drums and all kinds of band instrument supplies. It also tells you how to select and purchase your band instruments, how to organize and manage your band, and gives a table showing the correct instrumentation for bands of all sizes together with many suggestions in regard to the care of band instruments. This book should be in the hands of every bandman in the United States, as it marks a startling revolution in the purchase and sale of all kinds of band instruments. It fully explains the reasons why we are able to sell high class band instruments for one-half the prices asked by others. It tells you why the prices on band instruments have been so high in the past, and gives valuable information which will prove a great advantage to you when you are ready to purchase your instruments. We desire to place this book in your hands, but will say that if you are ready to make your purchase you are perfectly safe in making your selection of band instruments from the following pages, and it is much preferable for you to do so rather than cause a delay by writing for our Special Band Catalogue. The illustrations which we give on the following pages are faithful reproductions of the instruments themselves from photographs, and the descriptions are as complete as we can possibly make them in the small space allowed for this purpose. As the true and final test of any article ordered from us is the examination and trial which you give it after it is received, and as you are not asked to accept it until after a thorough trial you are fully satisfied that it is everything that you desire and a great bargain in every respect, you will see that you have the same advantages in ordering from this big catalogue that you would have in ordering from the special catalogue. If, however, you desire illustrations and descriptions of our complete line before ordering, we will be glad to send you this special catalogue, and it will only be necessary for you to send us a postal card saying, "Please send me your Special Band Catalogue," when it will be forwarded to you absolutely free. We are now the largest band instrument dealers in the world selling directly to users, and we are in a better position than any other house in the country to furnish you instruments of a high grade at the same small margin of profit which we make on groceries, dry goods, etc. If you are not particularly interested at the present time in the purchase of band instruments, we would esteem it a favor if you would send us the name of the band leader in your town, or some member of the band who will be interested in these goods. You probably know of some band about to be organized, and you will not only do us a great favor, but you will also do them a great service as well by sending us the name of the leading member, so that we may place this catalogue in his hands.

WE WANT ALL BANDMEN TO KNOW that we are now the largest band instrument dealers in the country selling directly to the user. Last year we furnished over 500 bands with complete sets of instruments besides selling an immense number of single instruments of all kinds, and this year our business will undoubtedly be doubled. The reason for the growth of this immense business is easily explained. Our methods of sale have worked the same revolution in this line of goods as in all other lines. We sell our instruments directly to the user adding but one small percentage of profit to the maker's price, and in this way the cornet which was formerly sold at $50.00 is now sold at $15.00, and a proportional saving is made throughout the entire line of band instruments. As our business has grown in this line and we have sold these instruments in greater quantities, we have been able to reduce the prices from time to time, so that now we are selling all classes of band instruments at prices ranging from one-third to one-half lower than any other dealers are able to offer. We ask you to compare all the instruments and prices shown in our catalogue with those offered by other dealers and you will find the above statement to be absolutely true in every particular. The fact that we send all of our instruments out with the understanding that the purchaser is to be the sole judge of their merits and decide for himself whether or not they are everything we claim for them and high grade instruments in every respect, will remove all doubt in regard to the truthfulness of the statements we make. It is our desire and intention to make our band instrument department headquarters for band instruments and supplies in the United States, and we certainly could not do this by misrepresenting our goods in any way. There is no class of goods so susceptible to false valuation as musical instruments. The true value of such an instrument can only be fixed by one who is expert in its manufacture or handles it constantly in buying or selling. The fact that a man is a musician does not always make him a good judge of musical instrument values. He can judge of tone or ease of execution, but as to the material and workmanship contained in the instrument he is often the poorest kind of a judge. These are points for which the purchaser has to take the dealer's word absolutely, and, as a general rule, is entirely at the mercy of the man from whom he purchases. **The value of every musical instrument which we handle is accurately determined by an expert at the time we purchase it.** We base our prices upon the value determined at that time and sell the instrument to the customer under our binding guarantee, so that the purchaser is always sure of receiving an instrument the real value of which is in proportion to the price we charge. There are many so called high class cornets on the market today for which the manufacturer is charging from $50.00 to $100.00, when as an actual fact the real cost of manufacturing the instrument does not exceed $15.00 at the outside. He is able to fix and receive this large price because he has established a reputation, possesses a monopoly and is absolutely without competition. The price is fixed without any reference whatever to the real value of the instrument, but with the idea of getting as much as the unsuspecting customer is willing to pay.

THE MARCEAU BAND INSTRUMENTS are certainly the very finest line of low priced band instruments ever offered to American bandmen. They are fully guaranteed by us, shipped under our ten days' trial offer and we ship them with the distinct understanding and agreement that the buyer must be perfectly satisfied or they can be returned entirely at our expense. They are especially suitable for beginners or amateurs who are playing a medium grade of music and desire a set of instruments which will give satisfactory service at a low price. We have sold hundreds of sets of these instruments and they have proved universally satisfactory. They are all of the very best models with French pattern silver piston valve and are thoroughly tested and inspected by us before shipping.

OUR DUPONT BAND INSTRUMENTS. This is our line of medium priced band instruments, and we are willing to have them compared with band instruments offered by other dealers and sold at more than double our prices. These instruments are especially suitable for the better grade of amateur bands and the thousands of testimonials which we receive every year sufficiently prove that they give satisfaction in every case. We have handled them for the last five years, and during that time have furnished them to hundreds of bands. They are instruments which will meet every demand made upon them, are of the very best model, and are fitted with French light action piston valves. If you are figuring on purchasing a new set of instruments for your band and desire a set of instruments at a low price, which will give satisfaction under all conditions, we especially recommend them for your consideration

TOURVILLE & CO. BAND INSTRUMENTS. This is certainly the most magnificent line of band instruments ever sold in this country. We are the sole American agents for these splendid instruments, and while we have only been selling them for about three years our sales have grown to enormous proportions. They will compare favorably with the very highest class of band instruments made in this country, and in many instances they have been selected in preference to several well known makes of instruments manufactured in this country. They are of beautiful model, handsome chased reinforced joints, splendidly made and fitted with the French light action silver piston valves. We recommend them to all bands who desire to do the very finest kind of concert playing, as they will meet every demand made upon them and prove satisfactory under all conditions. They are superb instruments in every respect and all we ask is an opportunity to place one or more of them in your hands for trial and examination, and if you do not find that they are up to your expectations in every way, and that the price you have paid is only about one-half what you would have to give any other dealer for the same grade of instruments, we will not ask you to keep them, but you can return them entirely at our expense and we will cheerfully refund your money. We have equipped some of the largest concert bands in the country with these splendid instruments, and in almost every case they have been selected in preference to well know and high priced instruments of American make. All of these instruments are of the latest improved short model, handsomely ornamented with chased bands around the joints, made of the very best material and by the most skilful workmen. They are all imported from France, the home of modern high grade band instruments. We desire an opportunity to place a set of these magnificent instruments in your hands for trial and examination.

HOW TO ORDER.

Select the instrument you want, order by number, enclose our price and we will make prompt shipment. The instrument will be sent to you with the understanding and agreement on our part that it will prove perfectly satisfactory to you in every way, just as represented by us and a wonderful value for the money; and if on receipt you do not find all this true, you are at liberty to return it to us at our expense and we will promptly return all your money including what you paid out for transportation charges.

OUR TEN DAYS TRIAL OFFER.

After the customer has received the instrument we allow him to try it for ten days, and if at any time within that period it should prove unsatisfactory, it can be returned to us and we will refund the full price paid and pay express charges both ways. This fully protects the customer against any possible loss, and we make him the sole judge of the merits of the instruments. We ship all our band instruments and musical goods upon these terms, as we desire our customers to be perfectly satisfied before finally accepting their purchase.

A COMPLETE COURSE IN MUSIC FREE.

With each cornet sold by us we give absolutely free to the purchaser a certificate which entitles him to a complete course, consisting of fifty weekly lessons, extending over a period of one year. This course of lessons is so complete and thorough that the student will have no difficulty in understanding them. The lessons will be given by one of the best music colleges in the country, the only expense to the student being the cost of the music and stationery, which we guarantee not to exceed 13 cents a week. You will find this course of lessons fully outlined and explained on page 285 of this catalogue, which we ask you to read carefully. The fact that we give this course of lessons absolutely free does not in any way affect the extremely low prices which we make on our instruments, and we shall continue to offer to our customers the very highest grade of instruments that can be secured at the very lowest possible prices.

OUR CELEBRATED MARCEAU BAND INSTRUMENTS.

GREATEST BARGAINS IN BAND INSTRUMENTS EVER OFFERED TO THE BANDMEN OF AMERICA.

THIS IS ONE OF THE FINE LINES of band instruments which we have been handling for years and which have given such immense satisfaction.

MUSIC RACKS and INSTRUCTION BOOKS are sent with all of these Instruments.

YOU GET A PROFIT SHARING CERTIFICATE WITH EVERY PURCHASE AND CAN SOON GET SOMETHING VALUABLE FREE OF COST, AS EXPLAINED ON PAGES 1 AND 2.

WE GUARANTEE EVERY INSTRUMENT in this line and sell them on the same terms that we sell all of our other band instruments. Each horn is fitted with celebrated French piston light action valves and is splendid in model and finish. On page 335 of this catalogue you will find the terms upon which we sell these instruments fully given and also estimates of bands of different sizes, which may prove of interest to you.

Marceau E Flat Cornet.

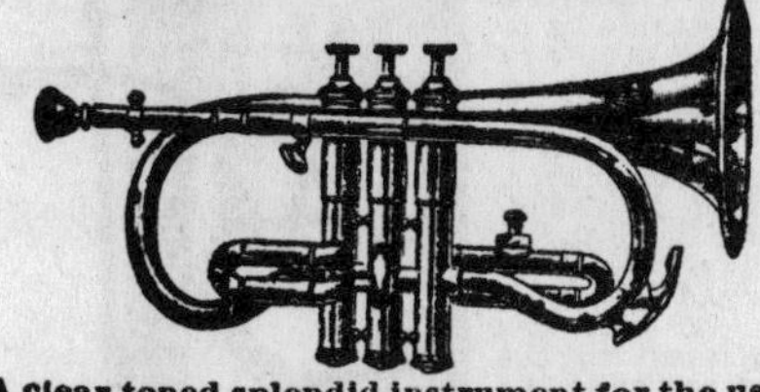

A clear toned splendid instrument for the use of leaders. Guaranteed in every way. Beautiful in model, perfect in tune and tone. The E flat cornet is never used except for playing in a band. If you wish a cornet for general playing, you should order a B flat cornet.

No. 12F7980 Brass, highly polished........$5.75
No. 12F7981 Nickel plated, highly polished 6.65

Marceau B Flat Cornet.
SINGLE WATER KEY.

This is a fine B Flat Cornet in every way and is suitable for use in either band or orchestra. We send with it an A shank for use in orchestra, and it is a splendid instrument in every way.

No. 12F7984 Brass, highly polished $5.85
No. 12F7985 Nickel plated, highly polished 6.75

Marceau C Cornet.

We can also furnish this cornet in the key of C at the following prices:

No. 12F7988 Brass. Price..............$6.05
No. 12F7989 Nickel plated. Price.......... 6.95

Marceau B Flat Cornet.
DOUBLE WATER KEY.

This Double Water Key Cornet has been a favorite with bandmen for a long time on account of its beautiful model and splendid tone. It is furnished with an A shank for use in orchestra and is a fine instrument in every way.

No. 12F7992 Brass, polished. Price......$ 7.95
No. 12F7994 Nickel plated, highly polished. Price.............................. 8.95

Marceau Solo Altos.

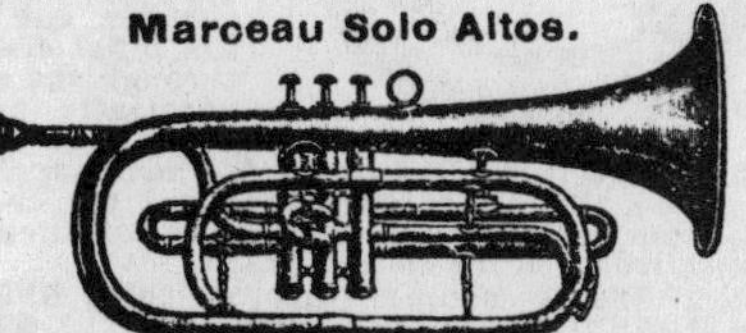

These instruments are manufactured for solo alto purposes and have been great favorites ever since their appearance. They are easy blowing, have a splendid tone and a handsome appearance.

No. 12F8011 Brass, highly polished............$ 9.25
No. 12F8012 Nickel plated, highly polished.... 10.75

Marceau E Flat Altos and B Flat Tenors.

These instruments are splendid for harmony work in a band, and we recommend them highly for those who desire fine altos and tenors at extremely low prices. They have a splendid tone, a beautiful model and a handsome appearance. They are perfect in tune and tone and so well constructed that they will last a lifetime. The action of the valves is extremely light and either one of these instruments can be used very nicely for solo purposes. We guarantee them to be satisfactory, and we believe that alto and tenor players will find in these instruments just what they desire at a very small cost. We desire to place them in the hands of all who are looking for something in this line at a moderate price, and we do not ask the customer to take any chances as we assume all the risk of shipping them.

No. 12F8013 Alto, brass, polished........$ 9.75
No. 12F8014 Alto, nickel, polished....... 11.25
No. 12F8015 Tenor, brass, polished...... 10.65
No. 12F8016 Tenor, nickel, polished...... 13.05

REMEMBER OUR WONDERFUL

PROFIT SHARING PLAN,

AS WELL AS THE ENORMOUS SAVING WHEN YOU BUY FROM US.

Marceau B Flat Baritone.

These instruments have been used with great success in all sorts of solo playing and general band work. A large number of bandmen have pronounced them the finest baritones on the market for less than double the price given below. Their tone is full and sonorous without being dull, and is light and clear without being too snappy. The model is handsome and the general workmanship on the instruments is all that can be desired. We recommend these baritones highly to baritone players throughout the country and we are always willing to have them compared with instruments offered by other dealers for twice the price.

No. 12F8017 Brass, highly polished.
Price..$12.15
No. 12F8018 Nickel plated, highly polished.
Price..$15.15

Marceau B Flat Bass.

These instruments can be used with excellent effect to fill in between the E Flat Bass and the B Flat Baritone. They are very effective when used in the bass solos which frequently occur in band selections, and they serve to balance up the instrumentation in excellent shape. Their tone is everything that could be asked for in an instrument of this nature and in model and finish they are splendid in every way.

No. 12F8019 Brass, highly polished..... $13.65
No. 12F8020 Nickel plated, highly polished.
Price...$16.95

Marceau E Flat Bass.

We wish to call your attention particularly to this instrument and will say, without fear of contradiction, that it has never been equaled, price considered. It has a deep, rich tone and furnishes an excellent fundamental bass for any brass band. It has enough volume to answer for a large instrumentation and the tone is full and sweet enough for use, if desired, in orchestras. The model is fine and the tubing is so thoroughly braced and reinforced that it will not break down undersevereuse. The valves are all quick and responsive and we guarantee the instrument to be satisfactory in every particular.

No. 12F8021 Brass, highly polished.....$19.35
No. 12F8022 Nickel plated, highly polished, 23.45

Marceau Circular Alto.

This style of alto horn has become very popular with all kinds of military and concert bands in the last few years on account of its beautiful mellow tone. It is used almost exclusively by all of the larger bands and we recommend its use to all bandmen. Its circular model makes it a very easy blowing and sensitive instrument and not only does it add to the appearance of the band but it gives the music a coloring which can be obtained in no other way. It is made by the same celebrated makers who manufacture the balance of this line, and is a valuable addition to the well known Marceau & Co. band instruments which we have handled so successfully for years. If your band does not possess altos of this model you should by all means procure them without delay, and you will find that the beautiful effect which you will obtain will much more than compensate for the small expense incurred.

No. 12F8033 Brass, highly polished.
Price..$17.95
No. 12F8034 Nickel plated. Price, 20.45

Marceau Valve Trombones.

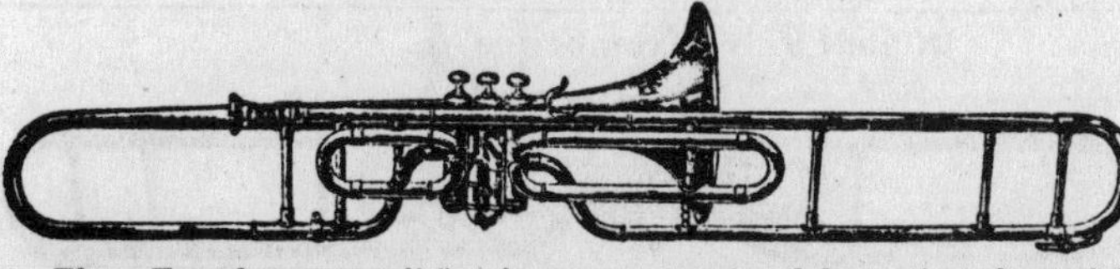

These Trombones are all fine in every respect and have that deep, rich tone so peculiar to trombones. Each band should be fitted with at least two of these, as they give a coloring harmony, which could be obtained in no other way.

No. 12F8023 E Flat Alto Trombone, brass. Price.............$ 9.75
No. 12F8024 E Flat Alto Trombone, nickel plated. Price........ 11.25

Special Hillyard Long Model Marceau Trombones.

No. 12F8029 B Flat Tenor Trombone, brass. Price...............$11.25
No. 12F8030 B Flat Tenor Trombone, nickel plated. Price...... 13.15

Marceau Slide Trombones.

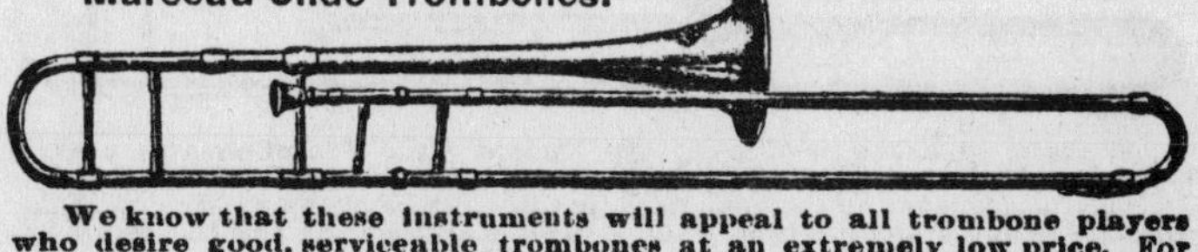

We know that these instruments will appeal to all trombone players who desire good, serviceable trombones at an extremely low price. For band and orchestra use they will be found equal to all requirements. For solo playing they have given general satisfaction. The slide works with ease and rapidity and the tone is mellow and powerful.

No. 12F8031 Brass, highly polished. Price..............................$6.65
No. 12F8032 Nickel plated, highly polished. Price...................... 8.55

OUR WORLD RENOWNED DUPONT BAND INSTRUMENTS.

Saved $200.00 on a Set of Band Instruments.

Edenville, Mich.

Sears, Roebuck & Co., Chicago, Ill.

The set of band instruments purchased of your house is giving the best possible satisfaction. I have had them examined by experts in the band business and it was hard for me to make them believe that they were bought for so little money. The valve action, taken with the ease in blowing, is simply marvelous. In finish and appearance I consider the band instruments excelled by no others in the world, regardless of price. I earnestly thank you in behalf of the band for the generous and courteous manner in which you have treated me in the purchasing of our band. Our band has cost us $300.00 and I do not believe that I could have purchased the same high grade instruments elsewhere for less than $500.00. I would earnestly recommend all interested to compare your goods and prices with those of any other firm doing band business before placing their orders.

JOHN P. LEE.

Dupont E Flat Cornet.

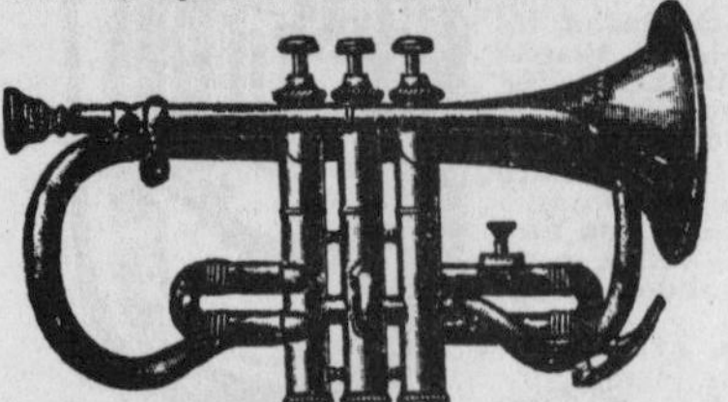

This is an especially fine instrument, and is so constructed that many of the objectionable features to be found in other E flat cornets have been entirely avoided. The E flat cornet is never used except for playing with a band. If you want a cornet for general playing you should order a B flat cornet.

No. 12F8040	Brass, polished	$ 7.95
No. 12F8042	Nickel plated	9.25
No. 12F8044	Silver plated, satin finish	12.45
No. 12F8046	Silver plated, polished	14.55

Dupont B Flat Cornet, Single Water Key.

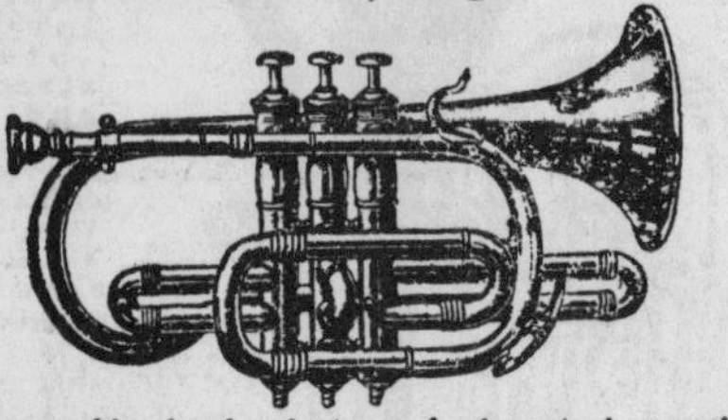

For general band and orchestra work where steady, conscientious results are required, this cornet is particularly desirable.

No. 12F8047	Brass, polished	$ 8.45
No. 12F8048	Nickel plated	9.65
No. 12F8049	Silver plated, satin finish	12.95
No. 12F8050	Silver plated, polished	15.15

Dupont C Cornet.

We can also furnish the above cornet in the key of C at the following prices:

No. 12F8039	Brass, polished	$ 8.40
No. 12F8041	Nickel plated	9.60
No. 12F8043	Silver plated, satin finish	12.90
No. 12F8045	Silver plated, polished	15.10

Dupont B Flat Cornet, Double Water Key.

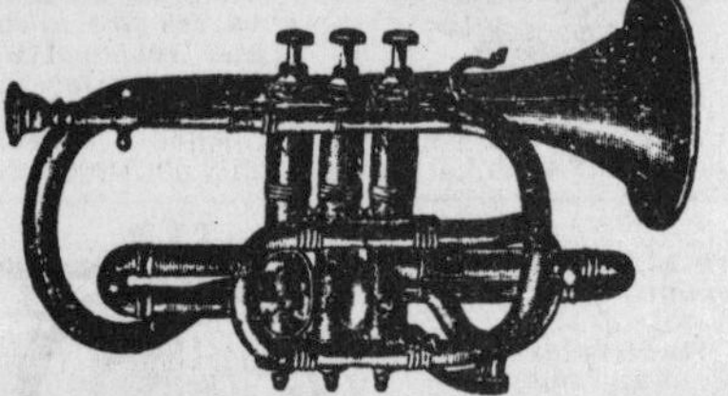

The B Flat Cornet, illustrated above, has never been excelled in playing qualities by any band instrument ever made. The material of which it is made is of the very finest, and the skill of the maker is splendidly shown in the beautiful model and excellent finish.

No. 12F8052	Brass, polished	$10.95
No. 12F8054	Nickel plated	12.15
No. 12F8056	Silver plated, satin finish	15.45
No. 12F8058	Silver plated, polished	17.65

The Best Cornet He Has Ever Seen.

Newton, Ala.

Sears, Roebuck & Co., Chicago, Ill.

I can truly say that the cornet I purchased from you is the best I have ever seen for the money. One member of our band preferred it to his $25.00 silver cornet. It is still a very fair cornet although it has been kicked about very much. I can recommend it to all my friends.

SAXON P. POYNER.

Dupont Solo Alto.

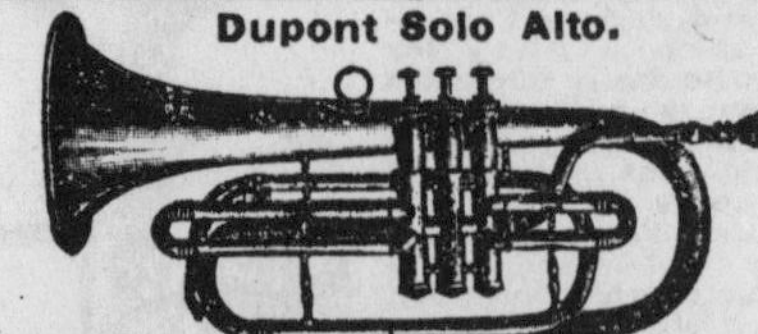

This instrument is intended for use as a solo alto, and while it can be used as a harmony instrument it is best adapted for use on solo alto parts in band music which have been so popular of late years.

No. 12F8076	Brass, polished	$11.90
No. 12F8078	Nickel plated	13.90
No. 12F8080	Silver plated, satin finish	18.90
No. 12F8082	Silver plated, polished	22.75

Dupont Concert Alto.

This is fast becoming a very popular instrument, both in bands and orchestras. It adds a dash of color to the harmony in band music, which can be obtained in no other way, and is fast supplanting the regular upright alto as an accompaniment horn. In orchestra it is considered valuable because it does not require the constant practice which is required on the French horn, and its tone is every bit as mellow and sweet. Anyone who has learned to play a cornet or alto can play this instrument, because it fingers exactly the same as a cornet and blows exactly the same as the alto. It is furnished in the key of F, with C, E flat and D crook. When used in a band it is always played in E flat, and when used in the orchestra, the F and D crooks are used. The C crook is very useful, as it throws the instrument into a key which enables the performer to play right along with the piano or organ without transposing the music. It is the beautiful French horn model and is furnished complete, with music rack, mouthpiece and instruction book. We especially recommend this instrument and we know it will prove acceptable to all band and orchestra men who use it.

No. 12F8075	Brass polished. Price	$22.45
No. 12F8077	Nickel plated. Price	24.95
No. 12F8079	Silver satin finish. Price	30.15
No. 12F8081	Silver polished. Price	37.75

Dupont Altos and Tenors.

These instruments are intended for harmony purposes and for playing accompaniment parts, but they can both be used for solo work and are excellent for that purpose. They are of fine model, made of the very highest quality of spun brass and the tubing is rolled until it is absolutely seamless. These altos and tenors are all thoroughly tested and inspected before they leave our house and we guarantee them in every respect.

No. 12F8084	E Flat Alto, brass. Price	$11.95
No. 12F8086	Nickel plated. Price	$13.95
No. 12F8088	Silver, satin finish. Price	$18.95
No. 12F8090	Silver plated. Price	$21.95
No. 12F8092	B Flat Tenor, brass. Price	$13.25
No. 12F8094	B Flat Tenor, nickel plated. Price	$15.45
No. 12F8096	B Flat Tenor, silver plated, satin finish. Price	$21.60
No. 12F8098	B Flat Tenor, silver plated polished. Price	$25.95

Dupont B Flat Baritone.

We take pleasure in bringing to the notice of baritone players the magnificent instrument shown in the engraving opposite. We have supplied these instruments to a large number of bands, and in every case they have called forth the unstinted praise of the player. The tone is round, full and deep, and in solo playing it leaves nothing to be desired. Particular care has been used by the manufacturer in the production of this instrument, and we do not hesitate to say that it is certainly one of the best baritones made today.

No. 12F8100	Brass, polished	$15.85
No. 12F8102	Nickel plated	18.55
No. 12F8104	Silver plated, satin finish	25.15
No. 12F8106	Silver plated, polished	31.45

Dupont B Flat Bass.

This instrument is particularly adapted for shading and blending the deep diapason tones of the tuba, and forms a connecting link in the harmony between that instrument and the baritone. It produces an excellent effect in the heavy bass solos of modern street marches and selections, and serves to blend and distribute the harmony of the bass section.

No. 12F8108	Brass, polished	$16.75
No. 12F8110	Nickel plated	19.35
No. 12F8112	Silver plated, satin finish	29.15
No. 12F8114	Silver plated, polished	34.75

Dupont E Flat Bass.

We do not believe that these instruments have ever been equaled for dignity and profundity of tone by any other basses ever made, where the price is taken into consideration. They are capable, in the hands of an ordinary player, of furnishing a fundamental bass for any band, and when used in an orchestra the effect is striking and grand. They possess the quality so rare in bass instruments of being in perfect tune in the upper register, and from low B flat clear up through the entire chromatic scale, every note is full, accurate and in perfect tune. We have supplied a great many bass players throughout the country with these instruments and in every instance they have called forth the loudest praise.

No. 12F8116	Medium, brass, polished	$23.25
No. 12F8118	Medium, nickel	27.45
No. 12F8120	Medium, silver, satin finish	38.25
No. 12F8122	Medium, silver, polished	46.95
No. 12F8124	Contra-Bass, brass	24.95
No. 12F8126	Contra-Bass, nickel	29.15
No. 12F8128	Contra-Bass, silver, satin finish	39.85
No. 12F8130	Contra-Bass, silver, polished	47.95

Dupont Tenor Slide Trombone.

We take pleasure in offering the Dupont Slide Trombones to players because we believe that they represent the very highest possible attainments in this line, considering the extremely low prices which we are able to make. Great care and study has been given to their manufacture, and the result has been gratifying, indeed.

No. 12F8156	Brass, polished	$ 7.95
No. 12F8158	Nickel plated	9.90
No. 12F8160	Silver plated, satin finish	13.45
No. 12F8162	Silver plated, polished	16.10

Dupont Valve Trombones.

The valve trombones of this line are made after the latest approved models and are fine instruments in every respect.

No. 12F8132	E Flat Alto Trombone, brass, polished	$11.85
No. 12F8134	E Flat Alto Trombone, nickel plated	13.85
No. 12F8136	E Flat Alto Trombone, silver plated, satin finish	18.85
No. 12F8138	E Flat Alto Trombone, silver plated, polished	23.75
No. 12F8140	B Flat Tenor Trombone, brass, polished	13.15
No. 12F8142	B Flat Tenor Trombone, nickel plated	15.35
No. 12F8144	B Flat Tenor Trombone, silver, satin finish	21.45
No. 12F8146	B Flat Tenor Trombone, silver plated, polished	25.85

OUR SPLENDID LINE OF TOURVILLE & CO. BAND INSTRUMENTS.

MADE BY TOURVILLE & CO., OF PARIS, FRANCE

AND THE ENTIRE LINE FITTED WITH THE WONDERFUL TOURVILLE LOW PITCH ATTACHMENT

AN EXAMINATION OF THE ENGRAVINGS SHOWN BELOW will show you that each one of these **splendid instruments is now fitted with a low pitch attachment,** enabling the performer to change the instrument instantly from high to low pitch. This is of immense advantage, because the performer never knows when it will be necessary for him to change his instrument from one pitch to another, and with ordinary band instruments it would be necessary to possess both a high and low pitch instrument in order to be prepared for every emergency. With this attachment only one instrument is necessary. As all pianos manufactured nowadays are tuned to low pitch, and as the large majority of band instruments used throughout the country are tuned to high pitch, a great deal of confusion arises and professional musicians have always found it necessary to own both a high and low pitch instrument in order to be fully prepared for every emergency. With the Tourville instruments this is not necessary, as the low pitch attachment makes it easy to change from one pitch to another. The engraving which we show herewith illustrates how this appliance is attached to upright horns. It adds to the appearance of the instrument and is one of the most valuable improvements ever made in brass instruments. The addition of this attachment to these instruments has not in any way affected the price, and the low prices which we have always quoted on this splendid line places this great improvement easily within your reach. **All of the cornets are fitted with extra low pitch slides** which can be inserted instantly if necessary to change from one pitch to another.

E Flat Cornet.

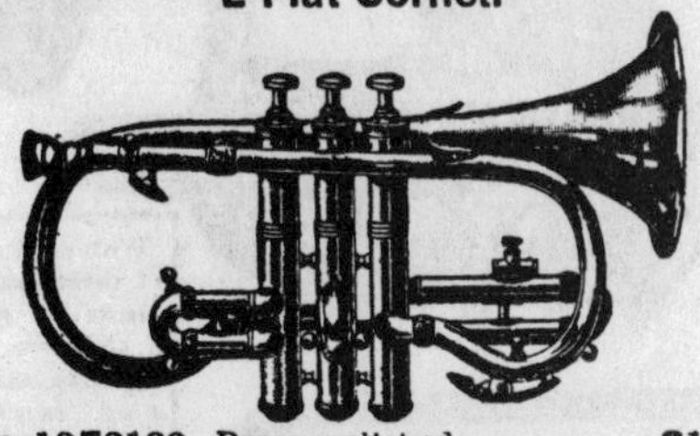

No. 12F8180	Brass, polished	$13.85
No. 12F8182	Nickel plated	15.10
No. 12F8184	Silver plated, satin finish	17.35
No. 12F8190	Silver plated, polished	19.35

Leaders' B Flat Cornet. Double Water Key.

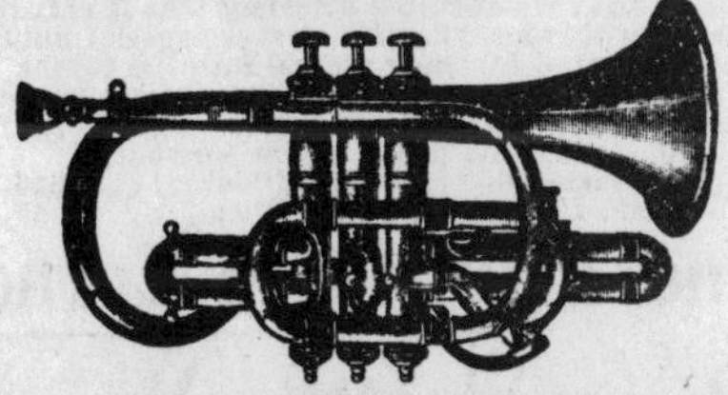

This cornet is a splendid instrument for general street and concert work, an ideal cornet for leaders who use a B flat cornet in their work.

No. 12F8201	Brass, polished	$15.95
No. 12F8202	Nickel plated	17.25
No. 12F8203	Silver plated, satin finish	19.45
No. 12F8204	Silver plated, polished	21.45

Artists' B Flat Cornet.

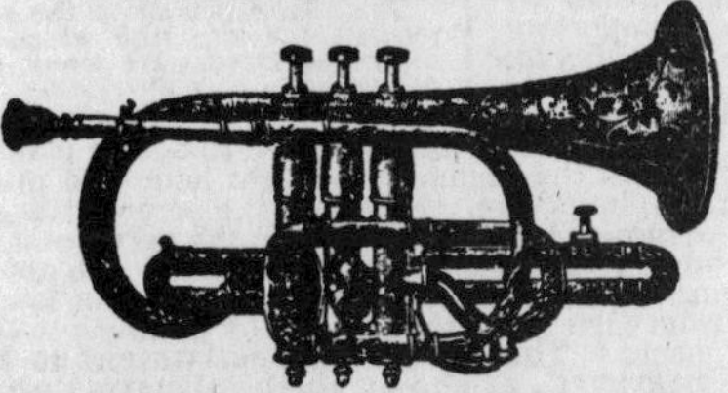

We offer this instrument as something particularly fine for soloists and those who desire a cornet of the highest possible grade in both looks and playing qualities.

No. 12F8205	Brass, polished	$18.15
No. 12F8206	Nickel plated	19.45
No. 12F8207	Silver plated, satin finish, gold lined bell	21.95
No. 12F8208	Silver plated, polished, gold lined bell	23.95

Solo E Flat Alto.

This is a favorite model with Alto players and is one which we highly recommend as handsome and durable. This instrument is easily the equal of other instruments of this line, and is very acceptable for playing solo alto parts.

No. 12F8192	Brass, polished	$15.95
No. 12F8194	Nickel plated, polished	18.45
No. 12F8196	Silver plated, satin finish	22.80
No. 12F8198	Silver plated, polished	25.95

Tenors and Altos.

These are by far the best harmony instruments ever turned out by any maker. Their tone is peculiarly adapted for accompaniment parts and is heavy enough for solo work. As great care has been used in their manufacture as is used in the manufacture of the finest cornets of this line, and we do not hesitate to say that they are the best instruments of their kind ever produced.

No. 12F8210	**Alto,** brass, polished	$16.45
No. 12F8212	**Alto,** nickel plated	$18.45
No. 12F8214	**Alto,** silver, satin finish	$22.85
No. 12F8216	**Alto,** silver, polished	$25.85
No. 12F8218	**Tenor,** brass, polished	18.25
No. 12F8220	**Tenor,** nickel plated	20.45
No. 12F8222	**Tenor,** silver, satin finish	26.55
No. 12F8224	**Tenor,** silver, polished	29.45

WE FURNISH EACH ONE OF THESE INSTRUMENTS WITH A

Music Holder and Instruction Book

AND OFFER THE COMPLETE LINE AS BEING UNSURPASSED BY ANY LINE OF BAND INSTRUMENTS ON THE MARKET TODAY.

B Flat Baritone.

Of all brass instruments the baritone is perhaps the most difficult to make, for the reason that great depth and breadth of tone are required, combined with the lightest possible action. This happy combination is fully realized in this baritone. The valve action in this instrument is the result of much special thought and experiment, and the maker has succeeded in so regulating the air pressure as to produce the lightest valve action ever known.

No. 12F8226	Brass, polished	$21.25
No. 12F8228	Nickel plated	$24.35
No. 12F8230	Silver plated, satin finish	$30.55
No. 12F8232	Silver plated, polished	$35.20

B Flat Basses.

No. 12F8234	Brass, polished	$23.45
No. 12F8236	Nickel plated	26.95
No. 12F8238	Silver plated, satin finish	35.45
No. 12F8240	Silver plated, polished	39.95

E Flat Bass.

The Tuba shown in the engraving is without any question the finest E flat bass ever made in tone, tune and finish. Too much cannot be said in its praise, but we would prefer to place it in the hands of bass players and let it speak for itself. In tone, tune and valve action it is certainly a revelation, and never fails to receive the greatest praise from all who may use it. It has that grand, sonorous and at the same time mellow tone which has been the dream of both player and manufacturer for years, and only realized in this production of the master hand.

No. 12F8242	Brass, polished	$32.25
No. 12F8244	Nickel plated	36.45
No. 12F8246	Silver plated, satin finish	48.55
No. 12F8248	Silver plated, polished	56.25

Helicon Basses.

We can furnish Helicon Basses in this line at the following prices:

No. 12F8258	Brass, polished	$46.85
No. 12F8260	Nickel plated	51.55
No. 12F8262	Silver plated, satin finish	62.95
No. 12F8264	Silver plated, polished	71.25

He Wouldn't Take $30.00 for His Cornet.

Pleasantville, N. J.

Sears, Roebuck & Co., Chicago, Ill.

The cornet is worth as much again as I gave for it, and I am well pleased. I would not take $30.00 for it now. I only gave $15.00 for it. Thanks to you for the same, and I recommend it highly.

JOHN R. RICE.

Valve Trombones.

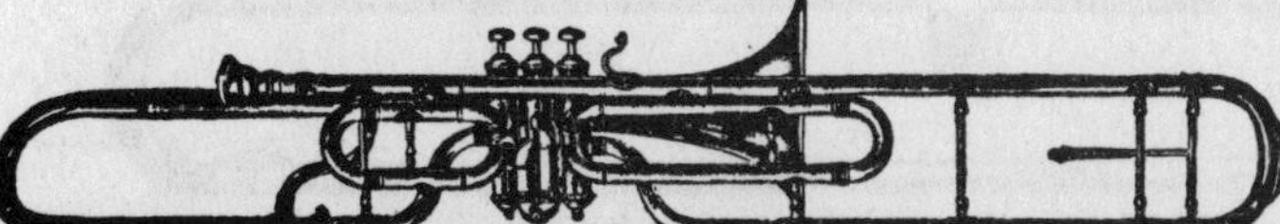

The Trombones of this line are all well balanced and easy to hold, and the model is one which has received the approval of both maker and player. Owing to the peculiarly sweet tone they possess, they are favorite instruments in all brass bands.

No. 12F8266	**E Flat Alto Trombone,** brass, polished	$16.80
No. 12F8268	**E Flat Alto Trombone,** nickel plated	18.55
No. 12F8270	**E Flat Alto Trombone,** silver plated, satin finish	22.75
No. 12F8272	**E Flat Alto Trombone,** silver plated, polished	25.80
No. 12F8274	**B Flat Tenor Trombone,** brass, polished	18.95
No. 12F8276	**B Flat Tenor Trombone,** nickel plated	21.45
No. 12F8278	**B Flat Tenor Trombone,** silver plated, satin finish	26.45
No. 12F8280	**B Flat Tenor Trombone,** silver plated, polished	28.95

Tenor Slide Trombones.

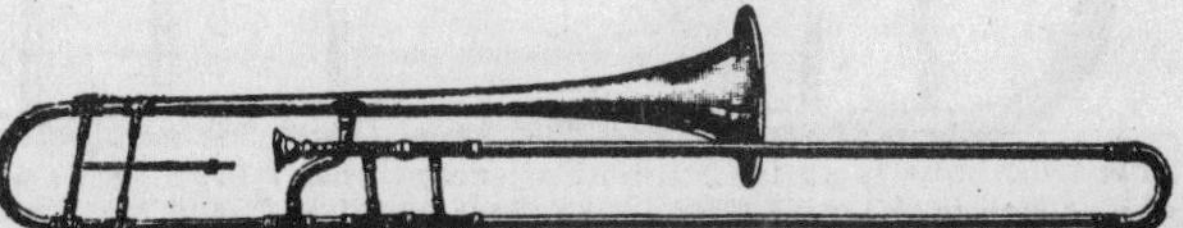

In this instrument the maker has succeeded in combining the profound tone of the old German instruments with the light, airy tones of the more recent French trombones, thus realizing a dream which has haunted both maker and player for so many years. The tone of this trombone is mellow and rich, and the style of action is perfection itself. **Wonderful saving in price, and a PROFIT SHARING CERTIFICATE with every order to help you share in our profit.**

No. 12F8282	Brass, polished	$12.35
No. 12F8284	Nickel plated	14.45
No. 12F8286	Silver plated, satin finish	17.85
No. 12F8288	Silver plated, polished	20.45

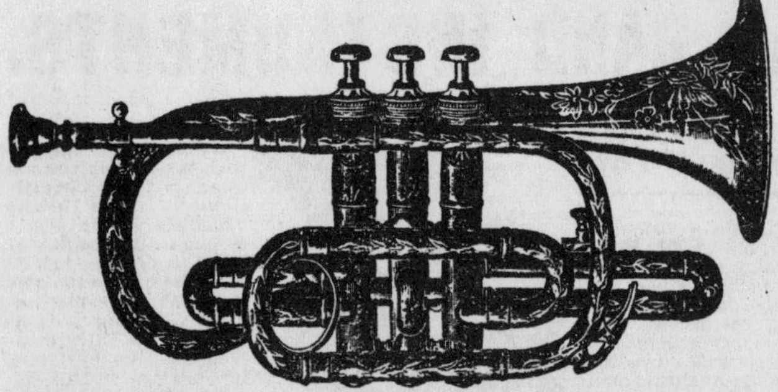

Our Engraved Marceau Bb Cornet, $8.25.

We are offering this instrument in response to a demand for a highly engraved Bb cornet at a moderate price. We can say, without fear of contradiction, that never before in the history of the band instrument business has a fully engraved Bb cornet been offered at anywhere near the price which we are quoting on this instrument. This cornet is one of our Marceau line, handsomely and completely engraved, and an instrument which is sure to please you in every way. It is fitted with French piston light action valves, the model is very handsome and the instrument is very carefully and skilfully made. If you desire a fine looking instrument, one which is easy blowing, and has a beautiful tone, we will unhesitatingly recommend this cornet to you. The engraving gives but a very poor idea of the appearance of this splendid instrument and nothing but an examination and trial will bring out all of its good qualities. Compare this instrument with any cornet of the same grade offered by any other dealer and you will find at once that we are offering it to you at one-half the price generally charged throughout the country. **Weight, packed for shipment,** 12 pounds.

No. 12F7850 Brass, polished. Price........ **$ 8.25**
No. 12F7852 Nickel plated. Price........ **9.25**
No. 12F7854 Silver plated, satin finish. Price........ **12.25**
No. 12F7856 Triple silver plated, polished. Price........ **14.95**

Our Engraved Double Water Key Marceau Cornet, $12.45

This is one of our double water key Marceau cornets, Courtois model, engraved especially in response to a demand for a cornet of handsome appearance and good tone at a moderate price. We are pioneers in offering instruments of this high grade at the exceedingly low prices quoted below. Up to the time when we began to offer these instruments to the public the prices on all engraved band instruments were exceedingly high and were so fixed and maintained by the dealers, as it was to their interest to do so. We found that by importing the instruments directly from Europe and selling them with our one small margin of profit added we could furnish these beautifully engraved instruments at prices in many cases two-thirds lower than the dealers could afford to make.

No. 12F7860 Brass, highly polished. Price........ **$12.45**
No. 12F7862 Handsomely nickel plated. Price........ **13.65**
No. 12F7864 Triple silver plated, satin finish. Price........ **17.45**
No. 12F7866 Triple plated, polished, with gold bell. Price........ **19.95**

Our Specially Engraved Marceau Slide Trombone, $9.75.

With each one of these instruments we give a complete instruction book and music holder, also a complete course of instruction free.

We have had so many calls for a slide trombone of good grade engraved throughout at a moderate price that we are now offering this instrument to the public as one of the finest trombones of this description that was ever offered. One important feature of this instrument deserves especial notice on our part, and that is the fitting and adjustment of the slide. The slides on these instruments are carefully and skilfully adjusted by being ground into the tubing until they become perfectly airtight and at the same time work absolutely without friction. The tone of this instrument is rich and mellow, and is everything that can be desired by the most critical performer. The many splendid qualities which this instrument possesses cannot be shown in an engraving, however fine it may be. We offer this instrument to bandmen with the assurance that nothing finer in this line has ever been offered at less than double the prices which we charge.

No. 12F7868 Brass, polished. Price........ **$ 9.75**
No. 12F7870 Nickel plated, polished. Price........ **11.25**
No. 12F7872 Triple silver plated, satin finish, gold lined bell........ **$15.75**
No. 12F7874 Silver plated, burnished gold lined bell. Price........ **17.25**

See pages 1 and 2 for what is yours FREE in exchange for the PROFIT SHARING CERTIFICATES you get on your purchase.

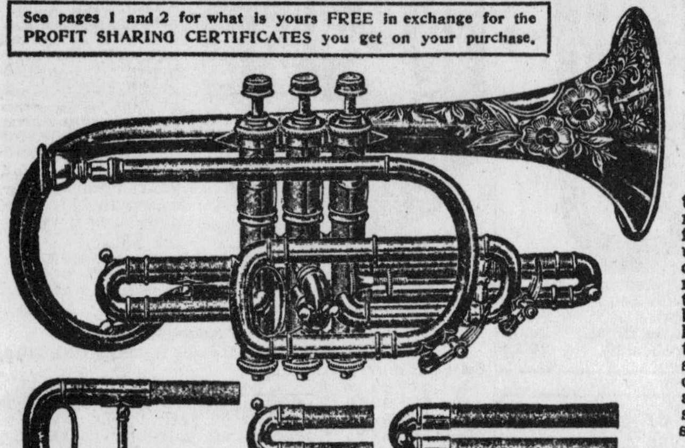

Our New HIGH and LOW Pitch Cornet, Four in One.

OUR PROFESSIONAL LAMOREAUX FRERES Bb CORNET, $22.45.

This illustration shows the screw regulating device with which this cornet is fitted. Its many good points can be seen at a glance.

This splendid instrument is the finest cornet that we have so far offered to bandmen and is manufactured in one of the finest band instrument factories in Paris, France, and imported directly by us. It has many improvements, the most important of which is the screw device shown in the engraving for regulating the pitch of the cornet. It is not necessary to carry around a Bb and A shank with this cornet, because the instrument is accurately tuned in Bb and in order to throw it into the key of A it is only necessary to reach down with the thumb of the right hand and push out the A slide by using the knob shown in the engraving. By using the screw attachment shown in the engraving the pitch of the instrument can be regulated to the very finest shade of tone, and you have a Bb and A cornet complete without the use of shanks, which are liable at any time to get lost or mislaid. We furnish also with this instrument a set of low pitch slides so that the cornet can be changed from high pitch to low pitch by pulling out the Bb slides and inserting these slides in their places. **The bell of this instrument is handsomely engraved, as shown in the illustration, and the valve buttons are decorated with beautiful pearl tips.**

No. 12F7876 Brass, polished. Price........ **$22.45**
No. 12F7878 Nickel plated. Price........ **23.70**
No. 12F7880 Silver plated, satin finish. Price, **26.95**
No. 12F7882 Silver plated, polished. Price .. **29.55**

Lamoreaux Freres Slide Trombone.

$17.45

This trombone is an instrument of exceptionally high grade and great care and skill are used in its manufacture. One of the greatest virtues of a slide trombone is that the slide shall work easily and quickly and that virtue is possessed by this instrument in the highest degree. The engraving shown above gives but a very poor idea of the beauty of this instrument and must be tested and examined before its many fine qualities can be fully appreciated. One of the important improvements that this instrument possesses is the screw attachment for regulating the pitch of the instrument. By placing the set screw in a certain position the instrument can be instantly thrown into low pitch by drawing the tuning slide. By the use of the set screw the pitch of the instrument can be regulated to the finest shade of tone. The bell of this instrument is beautifully engraved, and the instrument is highly finished throughout. It has the latest improved water key and the model is very handsome. We have no hesitation in recommending this instrument to professionals and amateurs alike, as we know that it will prove satisfactory under every condition. **We shall be glad to have you compare this instrument with anything shown you of a similar grade by other dealers,** and you will always find that our price is about one-half lower. In fact, we are prepared to ship you this beautiful trombone with the distinct understanding and agreement that if you do not find when you receive it that it is equal, and in many points, superior to instruments sold by other dealers at double the price, you can return it to us and we will cheerfully refund your money. This is a splendid instrument for presentation purposes and never fails to attract admiration when used as a solo instrument on the stage.

No. 12F7884 Brass, polished. Price........ **$17.45**
No. 12F7886 Nickel plated, Price........ **19.65**
No. 12F7888 Silver plated, satin finish. Price........ **$22.95**
No. 12F7890 Silver plated, polished. Price........ **25.95**

OUR FINE LINE OF FLUTES.

All of these Flutes are made of grenadilla wood, selected stock, accurately bored and handsomely finished. They are fitted with pure German silver keys, highly polished and we guarantee them absolutely as to tone, tune and wearing qualities. These instruments are all made by one of the most celebrated European flute makers, and we take pleasure in offering them to American musicians. Remember that we send out all of these flutes with the understanding that if they do not prove satisfactory in every way, and up to your expectations in every particular, we will refund your money and pay the express charges both ways. The prices which we make on these flutes are less than one-half the prices which other dealers are asking for instruments of inferior grade, and these prices are only made possible by the fact that we ship them directly from our house to the customer. They are suitable for bands or orchestras, and can be used right along with piano or violin if the proper key is selected. Do not class these instruments with the different cheap flutes which local dealers are offering throughout the country, because these are high class instruments in every way, and when we ship them to our customers they go with our absolute guarantee of quality. If you are looking for a good flute at a very small price, we highly recommend these instruments to your consideration. We can furnish anything in this line from one-key flutes to the very finest Boehm instrument with a guarantee to sell them for lower prices than any other dealer can make.

No. 12F9070 Genuine cocoa wood, German silver trimmed, tuning slide, 1 key. Price......**$1.45**

No. 12F9072 Grenadilla wood, German silver trimmed, tuning slide, 4 keys. A very serviceable instrument at an unusually low price. Price......**$1.95**

No. 12F9074 Grenadilla wood, tuning slide, cork joints, 6 keys, German silver caps and trimmings. A fine instrument never before offered at this price. Price......**$2.65**

No. 12F9076 Grenadilla wood, tuning slide, cork joints, 8 keys, German silver caps and trimmings. A well made, beautifully finished instrument. An exceptional bargain. Price......**$3.25**

No. 12F9078 Grenadilla wood, tuning slide, cork joints, 8 keys, German silver caps and trimmings and metal embouchure. This flute is finely trimmed, handsomely finished and well made. We recommend it as something particularly fine at this price. Price......**$3.85**

No. 12F9080 Genuine Meyer Model Flute. Key of D, 8 keys, grenadilla wood, tuning slide, cork joints, in fine morocco, velvet lined case, with joint caps, grease box, swab, pads and screwdriver. Price......**$5.45**

No. 12F9082 Genuine Meyer Model Flute. Key of D, 10 keys, grenadilla wood, tuning slide, cork joints, in fine morocco, velvet lined case with joint caps, grease box, swab, pads and screwdriver. Price......**$8.45**

No. 12F9084 Genuine Meyer Model Flute. Key of D, 10 keys, grenadilla wood, tuning slide, cork joints, genuine ivory head in velvet lined morocco case, with joint caps, grease box, swab, pads and screwdriver......**$11.45**

Paulsboro, N. J.

Sears, Roebuck & Co., Chicago, Ill.

I have bought several of your band instruments for myself and friends. I bought an upright alto horn, Dupont make, nickel plated, about a year and a half ago and used it in the band. I found that it blew easy and the valve action was good and the old bandmen said that it was the nicest toned horn in the band. Next I bought a Marceau B flat cornet, which I played in the band for a while and found it satisfactory in every way. Then I bought a slide trombone of the same make and found it satisfactory in every way; the slide works very easy and it has a good tone. Then I bought another nickel plated cornet of the same make for a Christmas present, which was satisfactory and pleasing.

WM. G. COWGILL, Jr.

Ethelfelts, Va., April 6, 1906.

Messrs. Sears, Roebuck & Co., Chicago, Ill.

The Marceau Solo Bb Cornet I bought of you at $7.95 I don't only think, but I know is a great bargain. I have it now one year, and as you know it was sent with a written guarantee for one year and I have not had the privilege of sending it to you for repairs of any kind. I have compared this horn with one sold by another company at $10.55, and it is superior to the $10.55 horn in tone, valve action and ease of blowing and of course lets the water out better, as the $10.55 horn was a single water key cornet, which you know sell about $2.00 cheaper than a double water key, the kind I got of you. So you see it would take $12.55 to get the cornet from the other company with double water key like the one I got of you. Then I'm afraid it would be behind it in some things. But this I know. I think I know what I am talking about. I ordered my brother one of those $8.95 cornets from you and it's a dandy. Double water key and nickel plated and fine enough for any man, and I would say to anyone wishing to buy band instruments that they can get as good ones, or better ones, from Sears, Roebuck & Co. as from any other place I know of and keep one-third their money in their pockets.

Yours respectfully,
W. E. ALDERMAN, (Band Leader).

P. S.—I bought 7 horns of you lately which are giving satisfaction, also 2 drums which are all right.

OUR SPLENDID LINE OF CLARIONETS.

LaFayette & Co.'s Clarionets.

The clarionets are certainly the finest line of low priced clarionets ever offered to the American bandmen. They are substantially made and well finished. They are made of grenadilla wood and all of the trimmings are pure German silver, highly polished. We promise to save the purchaser from $5.00 to $10.00 upon each one of these clarionets bought from us, and will ask our friends to compare them and the prices we ask, with the instruments and prices offered by other dealers. LaFayette & Co. have been manufacturing these clarionets for years. They have always given the greatest satisfaction.

No. 12F8850 13 keys, 2 rings, grenadilla wood, in A, Bb, C or Eb. Be sure to state key wanted. Price......**$9.95**

No. 12F8852 15 keys, 2 rings, grenadilla wood, in A, Bb, C or Eb. Be sure to state key wanted. Price......**$11.95**

Shipping weight, 50 ounces.

J. B. Martin Clarionets.

This is the line of favorite clarionets which we have handled for years, and which have given such universal satisfaction. We do not believe that there is a line of moderate priced clarionets on the American market today which in any way equals them in tone and finish. They are all made of genuine grenadilla wood, with trimmings of pure German silver, highly polished. They are bored through cleanly and evenly and are accurately made throughout. We guarantee them as to tune and tone and are prepared to take back any instrument which does not give satisfaction in every way. These clarionets, as well as the balance of our line, are fitted with the Albert system, and we can furnish them in all of the different keys. Bear in mind that you take no chances in purchasing one of these instruments, because we send them out on approval and we do not ask you to accept them unless you are perfectly satisfied in every respect. Many expert clarionet players have been surprised at the wonderful degree of superiority demonstrated by these clarionets. Bandmen desiring to furnish their reed sections with clarionets, and who are not prepared to pay a large amount for such instruments, cannot do better than purchase a set of these splendid clarionets.

No. 12F8854 13 keys, 2 rings, grenadilla wood, in A, Bb, C, or Eb. Be sure to state key wanted. Price......**$11.25**

No. 12F8856 15 keys, 2 rings, grenadilla wood, in A, Bb, C or Eb. Be sure to state key wanted. Price...**$13.25**

No. 12F8858 15 keys, 4 rings, grenadilla wood, in A, Bb, C or Eb. Be sure to state key wanted. Price......**$15.35**

Shipping weight, 13 keys, 50 ounces. Shipping weight, 15 keys, 64 ounces.

Tourville & Co.'s Universelle Clarionets.

Tourville & Co.'s Universelle Clarionets are considered by experts to be the finest in the world. We are offering these instruments in response to a demand for a line of clarionets which will be as fine as can be procured. We are willing to say without question that no clarionet, however costly, can excel these instruments in tune, tone and wearing qualities. They are used by all the finest concert bands of Europe and are meeting with an enthusiastic reception from clarionet players in this country. They are all made of the finest selected grenadilla wood, accurately and evenly bored, with the intervals absolutely perfect. The trimmings are all pure German silver, highly polished and strongly made. Because we are offering these clarionets at such extremely low prices, we do not want you to make the mistake of classing them with the different lines of low class clarionets which are offered throughout the country by dealers today. The reason we are able to make such extremely low prices upon these instruments is because we purchase them directly from the manufacturer in France, and sell them by our usual method directly to the customer. No clarionet should cost over $20.00, and when you pay a higher price than this you are simply paying for the name of the maker, which in many cases adds no value to the clarionet in any way.

No. 12F8860 13 keys, 2 rings, grenadilla wood, in A, Bb, C or Eb. Be sure to state key wanted. Price......**$13.95**

No. 12F8862 15 keys, 2 rings, grenadilla wood, in A, Bb, C or Eb. Be sure to state key wanted. Price......**16.45**

No. 12F8866 15 keys, 4 rings and 4 roller keys. Price......**19.45**

Shipping weight, 13 keys, 70 ounces. Shipping weight, 15 keys, 72 ounces.

We can ship all accessories for clarionets. For prices send for our special Free Band Catalogue.

OWING TO THE PECULIAR CHARACTER of the construction of wood wind instruments, they are liable to crack at any time, and no music dealer can give a guarantee for any length of time. We, however, guarantee that these instruments will reach you in perfect condition and should they be cracked when you receive them we will replace them with others in perfect condition. If, however, they are in perfect condition when you receive them we could not be responsible for their checking or cracking, as this depends entirely upon atmospheric conditions and is not governed in any way by the high or low quality of the material of which they are constructed.

FIFES.

Key of B Flat or C only. Be sure to state key wanted. Instruction Book, 12 cents.

No. 12F3358 Solid rosewood; brass ferrules. Price......25c

No. 12F3359 Cocoa wood; German silver. Price......27c

No. 12F3361 Solid ebony; nickel plated ferrules. Price......48c

No. 12F3362 Solid ebony; long metal ferrules. Crosby model; extra fine quality. Price......68c

If by mail, postage extra, 9 cents.

Nickel Plated Fifes.

No. 12F3363 Highly Nickel Plated Fife, for beginners, with mouthpiece adjusted all ready for playing. A very fine instrument for those who desire to learn the fife. Key of B flat or C. Be sure to state key wanted. Price......19c

If by mail, postage extra, 7 cents.

No. 12F3364 Key of B Flat or C. Nickel plated with raised finger holes, with gutta percha embouchure. Be sure to state key wanted. Price......55c

If by mail, postage extra, 9 cents.

Our Special Acme Hand Made Fife.

No. 12F3365 Metal nickel plated, strictly high grade Fife for professional players. Made in two pieces. Easy blowing, perfect in scale. None better made. Key of C or B flat. Be sure to state key wanted. Price......95c

If by mail, postage extra, 7 cents.

Flageolets.

Key of D. In Pasteboard Box.

No. 12F3376 Grenadilla; German silver trimmed; 6 keys. Price...$1.85

If by mail, postage extra, 10 cents.

Atlas Flageolets.

No. 12F3378 Atlas Flageolets, made of cast metal, nickel plated, are of French manufacture and imported by us direct from France. Is an exceptionally well made instrument, accurately tuned in key of D. Price....43c

If by mail, postage extra, 12 cents.

Piccolo-Flageolets.

Key of D.

With extra mouthpiece; can be played either as a piccolo or as a flageolet. In pasteboard box.

No. 12F3382 Boxwood; German silver trimmed; 1 key. Price....$1.15

No. 12F3383 Grenadilla; German silver trimmed; 5 keys. Price..$1.85

No. 12F3384 Grenadilla; German silver trimmed; 6 keys. Price...$1.98

If by mail, postage extra, 12 cents.

Multiflutes.

No. 12F3391 Multiflute, the latest French novelty. Is a combination instrument. It is made of cast metal, nickel plated, and has three distinct mouthpieces, as shown in the illustration. The instrument is of French manufacture and imported by us direct from France. It is accurately tuned in key of F, and is easy to play. Price......58c

If by mail, postage extra, 16 cents.

Piccolos.

Key of D or E flat. Be sure to state key wanted. In pasteboard box.

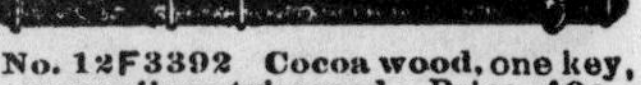

No. 12F3392 Cocoa wood, one key, German silver trimmed. Price..40c

No. 12F3394 Grenadilla wood, with tuning slide and four keys, German silver trimmed. Price......95c

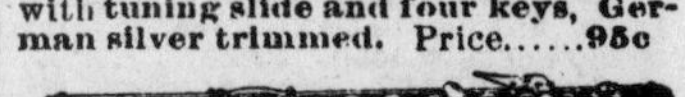

No. 12F3395 Grenadilla wood, with tuning slide, six keys, German silver trimmed, cork joints. Price......$1.35

If by mail, postage extra, 15 cents.

Meyer Pattern Piccolo.

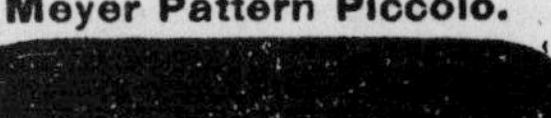

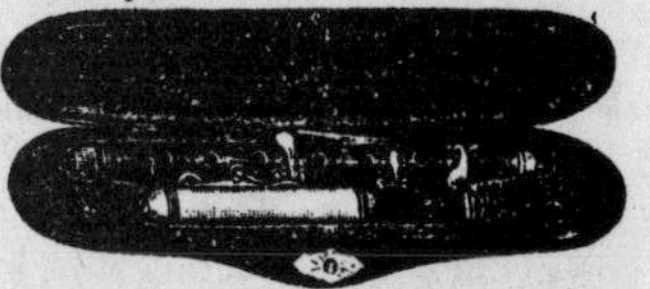

No. 12F3396 Grenadilla, ivory head, six keys, with slide cork joints and German silver trimmed, in fine velvet lined morocco case, as shown in illustration. **Key of D or E flat. Be sure to state key wanted.** Price......$3.95

If by mail, postage extra, 16 cents.

ACME PROFESSIONAL DRUMS

OUR NEW PATENT DRUM ROD AND CORD HOOK,

THE GREATEST IMPROVEMENT EVER MADE IN DRUMS.

CAN ONLY BE FOUND UPON OUR CELEBRATED LINE OF ACME PROFESSIONAL DRUMS.

THESE WONDERFUL NEW INVENTIONS are certainly the greatest improvements that have ever been made in bass and snare drums. We know that they will be gladly welcomed by drummers all over the country, and they can only be secured on our drums. A glance at the above illustration will show you at once how vast an improvement **OUR NEW PATENT DRUM ROD** is over the old fashioned device. It is stamped out of sheet steel and nickel plated. It is tightened by a double screw in the center and can be operated with almost any wrench. It fits snugly on the strainer hoops of the drum, and unlike the old fashioned drum rod does not allow the end to stick up beyond the hoop to catch on the clothing. It is very much neater in appearance than the old fashioned drum rod, and imparts a graceful appearance to the instrument which cannot be obtained with any other drum rod. One of the greatest advantages which it possesses is that it makes the drum very much lighter than when fitted with the old fashioned drum rod. This increase in lightness makes a wonderful improvement in the tone of the instrument, and adds 100 per cent to its responsiveness. **REMEMBER, you can only obtain these drum rods with our Acme Professional Drums,** and if you are thinking of purchasing a drum do not purchase elsewhere without having first given us an opportunity to place one of these instruments in your hands and demonstrate to you what a wonderful improvement these drum rods are. All of our Prussian pattern bass and snare drums are fitted with these patent drum rods, and we do not add anything extra to the price in order to give our customers the benefit of this wonderful invention.

THE NEW PATENTED DRUM HOOK is another remarkable invention for the improvement of Regulation Pattern Drums. They are made of white metal and are very durable. Like the drum rods they can be obtained only from us and will be found only upon our Acme Professional Drums. Instead of having an eye for the cord to run through, like the old fashioned drum hooks, they are furnished with an open hook, which holds the cord securely in its place. Should it be necessary to fit the drum with a new cord or repair the cord when broken it is not necessary to remove all the hooks, as with the old fashioned pattern, but it is only necessary to loop the cord over the hooks and tighten it up. **All of our Regulation Drums are fitted with this new cord hook, and you can obtain them from no one else and upon no other line of drums.**

THE ACME PROFESSIONAL TENOR OR SNARE DRUMS.

PRUSSIAN PATTERN.

Weight, packed, about 15 pounds.

No. 12F8506 Has 14-inch maple shell, 6 inches high; seven nickel rods, white metal plated hooks and trimmings, six snares, one calfskin head, one pair rosewood sticks. Price.....$4.35

No. 12F8508 Has 16-inch maple shell, is 6 inches high with eight nickel plated rods and hoops of maple, finished in imitation rosewood or ebony, with trimmings of white metal, plated, best quality calfskin head, eight rawhide snares. Price, including 1 pair of rosewood sticks $4.85

No. 12F8510 The same style of drum as No. 12F8508, with brass shell, nickel plated polished rods. Price.....$4.95

No. 12F8512 The same drum as No. 12F8508, but has two best quality calfskin heads, nickel plated polished rods. Price, including one pair of rosewood sticks..............$5.10

No. 12F8514 Same drum as No. 12F8508, but has brass shell, and two best quality calfskin heads, nickel plated polished rods. Price, including one pair rosewood sticks..............$5.20

No. 12F8516 Has 16-inch shell, is 6 inches high with **eight nickel plated polished patent rods,** hoops of maple, decorated with fancy decalcomania ornamentation, trimmings of white metal plated, best of calfskin heads, **eight rawhide snares.** Price, including one pair of rosewood sticks..............$5.35

No. 12F8518 Same description as No. 12F8516, with the exception of the shell, which is made of brass, nickel plated polished rods. Price, including one pair of rosewood sticks..............$5.45

REGULATION PATTERN.

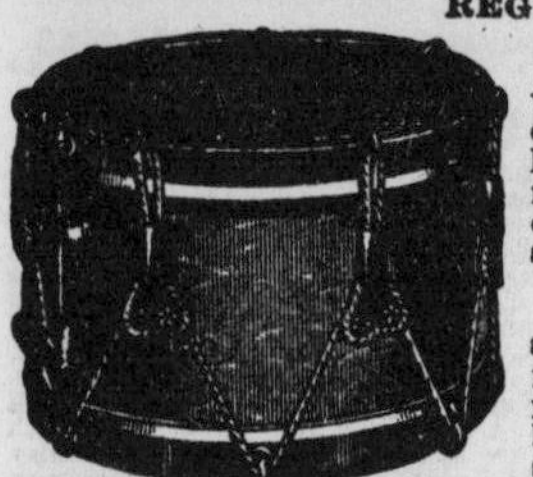

Weight, packed, about 15 pounds.

No. 12F8500 This is the regulation pattern with a shell 14 inches in diameter, made of birdseye maple, varnish finish, 8 inches high, cord hooks, with seven braces. The hoops are of maple, finished in imitation ebony or rosewood, best of calfskin heads, **six snares, new pattern snare strainer,** nickel plated hooks. Price, including one pair of sticks.......$4.85

No. 12F8502 Regulation pattern, but with a 16-inch shell, 9½ inches high, made of birdseye maple with maple hoops, finished in ebony or rosewood. Shell has fine varnish finish, **eight braces, best calfskin heads, new pattern snare strainers,** nickel plated hooks. Price, including one pair of rosewood sticks $5.25

No. 12F8504 The same description as No. 12F8502, but has a shell made of rosewood, fine varnish finish, nickel plated hooks. Price.....$5.60

OUR ACME PROFESSIONAL ORCHESTRA DRUMS.

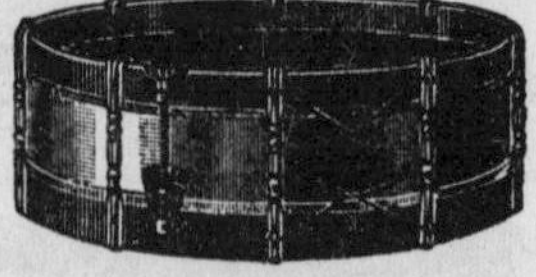

No. 12F8520 Has 16-inch brass shell, 4 inches high, maple hoops finished in imitation ebony, ten nickel plated polished rods, white metal hooks and trimmings, eight rawhide snares and two selected calfskin heads. Price, including one pair rosewood sticks..............$5.55

No. 12F8522 Same description as No. 12F8520, but with nickel plated shell..$5.95

No. 12F8524 This is our best orchestra drum. It has a 16-inch diameter, nickel plated shell, 4 inches high. Hoops are made of maple, highly finished in imitation ebony and inlaid with a very fine white metal band, ⅛ inch wide, giving the drum a very handsome and striking appearance. It has ten nickel plated rods, nickel plated hooks and trimmings, eight rawhide snares and two calfskin heads. With this drum we include, free, a pair of genuine ebony sticks. Price..............$6.45

DRUMMERS' DELIGHT—SINGLE HEADED DRUMS.

No. 12F8526 This drum has been designed to meet the requirements of drummers wishing a very sharp drum. It is quick in responding to the lightest touch of the sticks. It has a birdseye maple shell, highly polished, 14½ inches diameter, 3¾ inches high including hoop, twelve special pattern nickel plated rods, highly polished, silk snare with special patent adjuster. Best quality transparent head. The real thing for trap drummers. Easily carried. Occupies little space. Price, including a pair of genuine ebony sticks..............$6.95

OUR LINE OF DRUMS has been very carefully selected, and we have used every endeavor to improve the instruments wherever possible. Comparison of our line with drums handled by any other dealer will prove their superiority at once. The immense increase in our sales has enabled us to reduce our prices from time to time, and we have never found it necessary to increase our prices in order to recompense us for the numerous improvements which we have made in our line. If you are thinking of organizing a drum corps or a brass band in your vicinity we will be glad to make you an estimate upon complete outfits, and will guarantee to save you a large amount of money and furnish you with superior instruments in every respect.

We can furnish any of the following bass drums, either in regulation or Prussian pattern, at the same price, and when ordering be sure to state which pattern is desired:

PRUSSIAN PATTERN

No. 12F8527 Birdseye Maple Shell, finished in natural wood, 24 inches in diameter, 10 inches high, one calf and one sheepskin head. Complete, including one stick with buckskin head..............$7.45

No. 12F8529 Same as above, but two calfskin heads. Price 8.45

No. 12F8528 Same as No. 12F8527, imitation mahogany shell. Price..............$7.45

No. 12F8530 Same as above, but two calfskin heads. Price, 8.45

No. 12F8531 Birdseye Maple Shell, 28 inches in diameter, finished in natural wood, 12 inches high; maple hoops, finished in imitation ebony or rosewood, one calfskin and one sheepskin head. Complete, including stick with buckskin head. Price..............$8.90

No. 12F8533 Same as above, with two calfskin heads. Price..............$10.25

No. 12F8532 Same as No. 12F8531, imitation mahogany shell. Price..............$8.90

No. 12F8534 Same as above, with two calfskin heads. Price, 10.25

REGULATION PATTERN

No. 12F8535 Birdseye Maple Shell, 30 inches in diameter, finished in natural wood, 12 inches high; maple hoops, finished in imitation ebony or rosewood, one calfskin and one sheepskin head. Complete, including one stick with buckskin head. Price..............$9.85

No. 12F8537 Same as above, with two calfskin heads. Price..............$11.95

No. 12F8536 Same as No. 12F8535, imitation mahogany shell. Price..............9.85

No. 12F8538 Same as above, with two calfskin heads. Price..............11.95

No. 12F8539 Birdseye Maple Shell, 36 inches in diameter, 12 inches high, **finished in natural wood, two calfskin heads.** Complete, including one stick with buckskin head. Price..............$15.45

No. 12F8540 Same as above, imitation mahogany shell. Price..............15.45

OUR LINE OF BUGLES AND TRUMPETS.

These instruments are all of regulation pattern, size and key, and are fully guaranteed by us. They are all made of the very highest grade of spun brass and are tempered just to the proper point where they become the best medium for the transmission of musical sounds. They are all of good model, handsomely finished and splendid tone.

No. 12F3329 Officer's Bugle, made of brass and finely finished; key of C. Two turns. Weight, boxed, about 5 pounds. Price..............$1.25

No. 12F3330 Same, finely nickel plated. Price..............$1.65

No. 12F3334 Cavalry Bugle, brass; key of F. Two turns. Weight, boxed, 6 pounds. Price..............$1.65

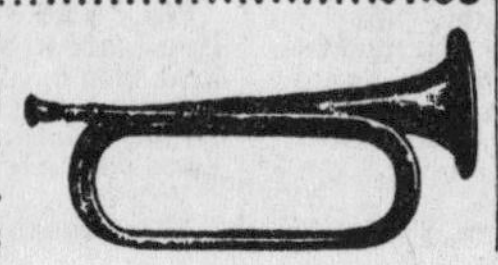

No. 12F3335 Same, nickel plated. Price..............$2.15

No. 12F3341 Infantry Bugle; brass; key of C, with B flat crook. Weight, boxed, 6 pounds. Price..............$1.85

No. 12F3342 Same, nickel plated. Price..............$2.30

No. 12F3345 Genuine Hunting Horn, brass; one turn. Price..............50c

If by mail, postage extra, 15 cents.

No. 12F3346 Genuine Hunting Horn, brass, four turns. Price..............85c

If by mail, postage extra, 15 cents.

No. 12F3347 Cavalry Trumpet, key of F, made of brass, with tuning slide. Price......$2.25

No. 12F3348 Same, nickel plated. Price..........(Weight, boxed, 8 pounds.)..........$2.70

This Cavalry Trumpet is in the key of G, but the tuning slide is long enough so that it can be tuned to F. We furnish this trumpet with two mouthpieces.

No. 12F3350 Brass polished. Price..........$2.90

No. 12F3352 Same, nickel plated. Price.... 3.45

Weight, boxed, 8 pounds.

STRINGS.

WE IMPORT DIRECT FROM EUROPEAN MANUFACTURERS and handle none but the best strings made. Not an inferior string sold by us at any price. We guarantee every one to be perfectly made of the best quality and material. WE DO NOT GUARANTEE THEM AGAINST BREAKING, but they will last as long as can be expected of the best strings made. We solicit your orders on this particular line, knowing that we can please you in the fullest degree and save you from 50 to 60 per cent on every purchase.

SILVER TONED BELL BRAND STRINGS.

Without doubt the best steel strings on the market. They are carefully and accurately made of tested materials of superior quality. The steel used is especially made, giving the strings the true tone of silver like bell quality. Each string is carefully tested, heavily silver plated and polished, wrapped in anti-tarnish ribbed silver tissue paper and enclosed in an oil paper envelope, making the strings impervious to moisture and climatic changes and preserves them against tarnish and rust. We recommend the Bell Brand strings as being strictly high grade in every particular.

Silk Violin E Strings.

No. 12F4125 Muller's Celebrated Eternelle. Most reliable string in existence. Doz. 90c; Each 8c
If by mail, postage extra, 2 cents.

Extra Quality Violin Strings.

All E strings have 4 lengths, A and D strings 2½ lengths and G strings 1 length.

No.		Doz.	Each
12F4130	E, polished	76c	7c
12F4132	E, rough finish	76c	7c
12F4134	A	76c	7c
12F4136	D	99c	9c
12F4138	G	65c	6c
12F4139	Set of four		25c

If by mail, postage extra, per set, 2 cents.

No. 12F4140 G string, extra fine quality, pure silver wire wound on gut. Each...40c
If by mail postage extra, 2 cents.

Our Special Waterproof Violin Strings.

By virtue of a special preparation these are purer in tone than the ordinary strings. They are made scientifically correct and absolutely unsusceptible to climatic influences. They are especially desirable for players who are troubled with moist fingers, as they possess extraordinary durability. Every string is fully tested and warranted. All E strings have 4 lengths, A and D strings 2½ lengths and G strings 1 length.

No.		Doz.	Each
12F4141	E	$1.28	12c
12F4142	A	1.28	12c
12F4143	D	1.52	14c
12F4144	G	.76	7c
12F4145	Set of four		45c

If by mail, postage extra, per set, 2 cents.

Our "Verona" Brand Violin Strings.

Special attention is called to this splendid line of strings, as they are unquestionably as fine as any Italian strings made. They are made of the very best quality of sheep gut, and particular attention is called to the way they are wrapped, which insures them against injury in transmission through the mails. We recommend them to all who are looking for fine violin strings at a reasonable price. All E strings have 4 lengths, A and D strings 2½ lengths and G strings 1 length.

No.		Doz.	Each
12F4146	E	$1.92	16c
12F4147	A	1.92	16c
12F4148	D	2.28	19c
12F4149	G	1.20	10c
12F4150	Set of four		61c

If by mail, postage extra, per set, 2 cents.

Extra Quality Acme Professional Violin Gut Strings.

All E strings have 4 lengths, A and D strings 2½ lengths and G strings 1 length.

No.		Doz.	Each
12F4162	E	$0.99	9c
12F4164	A	.99	9c
12F4166	D	1.20	11c
12F4168	G	.76	7c
12F4170	Set of four		36c

If by mail, postage extra, per set, 2 cents.

No. 12F4171 G string, pure silver wire wound on gut, burnished, superfine quality. Price, each...50c
If by mail, postage extra, 2 cents.

Glendon Violin Strings.

Silvered steel. Each string one full length.

No.		Doz.	½ Doz.
12F4172	E	5c	
12F4174	A	5c	
12F4176	D, covered	12c	6c
12F4178	G, covered	12c	6c
12F4180	Set of four		4c

If by mail, postage extra, per set or dozen, 2c.

Bell Brand Violin Strings.

Steel, triple silver plated and polished. Each string one full length.

No.		Doz.	½ Doz.	Each
12F4182	E	24c	12c	
12F4184	A	24c	12c	
12F4186	D, cov'ed	36c		3c
12F4188	G, cov'ed	48c		4c
12F4190	Set of four			11c

If by mail, postage extra, per set or dozen, 3c.

Extra Quality Acme Professional Banjo Gut Strings.

Each string one full length. The same string is used for both first and fifth on the banjo.

No.		Doz.	Each
12F4194	B and E	76c	7c
12F4196	G	84c	8c
12F4198	E	99c	9c
12F4200	A	65c	6c
12F4202	Set of five		35c

If by mail, postage extra, per set, 2 cents.

Glendon Banjo Strings.

Silvered steel. Each string one full length.

No.		Doz.	½ Doz.
12F4220	B and E	5c	
12F4222	G	5c	
12F4224	E	5c	
12F4226	A	24c	12c
12F4228	Set of five		5c

If by mail, postage extra, per set, 2 cents.

Bell Brand Banjo Strings.

Steel, triple silver plated and polished. Each string one full length.

No.		Doz.	½ Doz.	Each
12F4230	B and E	24c	12c	
12F4232	G	24c	12c	
12F4234	E	24c	12c	
12F4236	A	48c		4c
12F4238	Set of five			12c

If by mail, postage extra, per set, 3 cents.

Professional Guitar Strings.

The E, B and G strings are of superior quality gut and the D, A and E or 6th string are silver wire wound on silk.

All of these strings are of the very highest quality. Each string one full length.

No.		Doz.	Each
12F4240	E	$0.96	8c
12F4242	B	.96	8c
12F4244	G	1.20	10c
12F4246	D	.48	4c
12F4248	A	.60	5c
12F4250	E	.72	6c
12F4252	Set of six		41c

If by mail, postage extra, per set, 3 cents.

Extra Quality Acme Professional Guitar Gut Strings.

D, A and E strings silvered wire on silk, plush knots.

No.		Doz.	Each
12F4260	E	$0.99	9c
12F4262	B	.99	9c
12F4264	G	1.20	11c
12F4265	D	.96	8c
12F4266	A	1.08	9c
12F4267	E	1.20	10c
12F4268	Set of six		56c

If by mail, postage extra, per set, 3 cents.

Glendon Guitar Strings.

Silvered steel. Each string one full length. G, D, A and E strings silvered wire wound on steel.

No.		Doz.	½ Doz.	Each
12F4270	E		5c	
12F4272	B		5c	
12F4274	G	12c	6c	
12F4276	D	24c	12c	
12F4278	A	36c		3c
12F4280	E	48c		4c
12F4282	Set of six			12c

If by mail, postage extra, per set, 2 cents; per dozen, 4 cents.

Bell Brand Guitar Strings.

Steel, triple silver plated and polished. Each string one full length. G, D, A and E strings silvered wire wound on steel.

No.		Doz.	½ Doz.	Each
12F4283	E	24c	12c	
12F4284	B	24c	12c	
12F4285	G	48c		4c
12F4286	D	60c		5c
12F4287	A	72c		6c
12F4288	E	84c		7c
12F4289	Set of six			23c

If by mail, postage extra, per set, 3 cents; per dozen, 5 cents.

Glendon Mandolin Strings.

Silvered steel. Each string one full length.

No.		Doz.	½ Doz.
12F4290	E		5c
12F4292	A		5c
12F4294	D	12c	6c
12F4296	G	12c	6c
12F4298	Set of eight		6c

If by mail, postage extra, per set, 3 cents; per dozen, 4 cents.

Bell Brand Mandolin Strings.

Steel, triple silver plated and polished. Each string one full length.

No.		Doz.	½ Doz.	Each
12F4310	E	24c	12c	
12F4312	A	24c	12c	
12F4316	D	36c		3c
12F4318	G	48c		4c
12F4320	Set of eight			22c

If by mail, postage extra, per set or doz., 3c.

Best Quality Double Bass Strings.

The G and D strings are of high grade Italian gut, the A strings can be furnished either in plain gut or wound with silvered wire and the E strings wound with silvered wire on gut.

No.		Each
12F4321	G	$0.65
12F4323	D	.85
12F4325	A, wound	1.10
12F4327	A, plain	.95
12F4329	E	1.35

If by mail, postage extra, single string, 4 cents; per set, 12 cents.

Acme Violoncello Strings.

These strings are the very best quality and we highly recommend them in every respect.

No.		Each
12F4340	A	11c
12F4342	D	17c
12F4344	G	8c
12F4346	C	9c
12F4348	Set of four	40c

If by mail, postage extra, single string 2 cents; per set, 5 cents.

Autoharp Strings.

No.		
12F4350	Set for No. 71	20c
12F4352	Set for No. 2¾	25c
12F4354	Set for No. 72⅞, or 3, 4, 5	30c
12F4358	Set for No. 6	35c
12F4359	Set for No. 73	40c
12F4360	Steel strings	3c
12F4362	Bass or wound strings	5c

If by mail, postage extra, single string, 1 cent; per set 4, cents.

When ordering single strings always mention number of harp, letter of string, and whether bass, low, middle, high or highest.

Columbia Zither Strings.

No.		
12F4380	Set for Nos. 1 and 2	50c
12F4382	Set for Nos. 2½, 3 and 3½	70c
12F4384	Set for Nos. 3¾ and 4	90c

If by mail, postage extra, per set, 6 cents.

No.		
12F4386	Steel strings. ½ doz.	12c
12F4387	Wound or bass strings	3c

If by mail, postage extra, each, 1c; per set, 6c.

Guitar-Zither Strings.

No.		
12F4390	Set for No. 0½	48c
12F4392	Set for No. 2	48c
12F4394	Set for No. 2½	55c
12F4396	Set for No. 3½	75c
12F4398	Plain strings. Each	3c
12F4400	Wound strings	5c

Piano and Dulcimer Wire.

No. 12F5594 English Steel Wire, best quality, ½-pound coils. Sizes from 7 to 23. Be sure to state size wanted.
Price, per coil...26c

VIOLIN CASES.

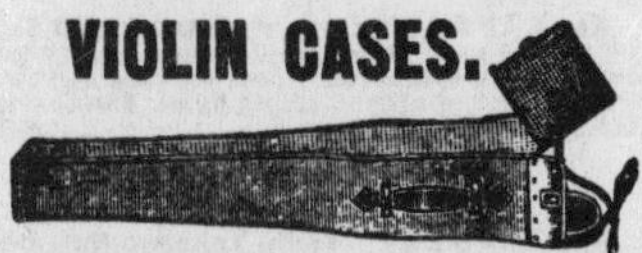

No. 12F4528 Violin Case, brown canvas. Opens at end. Leather bound edges, flannel lined, leather handle. Shipping weight, 7 pounds. Price...58c

No. 12F4529 Violin Case, common shape, well made of wood and half lined with flannel, complete with handle and hooks. Shipping weight, 8 pounds. Price...78c

No. 12F4530 Same as No. 12F4529 above, with lock. Shipping weight, 8 pounds.
Price...88c

No. 12F4533 Violin Case, of select wood, American made, black varnished, full lined with flannel, complete with nickel plated lock, handle and hook clasps. Shipping weight, 8 pounds. Price...$1.30

No. 12F4534 Violin Case, made solidly of wood, finely varnished black, exposition shape, full lined throughout with flannel; complete with lock, handle and spring clasps. Full, three-quarter or half size. Shipping weight, 8 pounds. Price...$1.68

No. 12F4535 Violin Case, covered with durable waterproof material, made in perfect imitation alligator skin, full lined with velvet, leather handle, nickel link clasps and nickel spring lock. Shipping weight, 8 pounds.
Price...$2.90

No. 12F4536 Violin Case, made of leather pulp, black finish, waterproof, fleece lined, has leather handle, nickel plated trimmings and patent spring lock. A very strong, durable and light case. Shipping weight, 8 pounds.
Price...$2.75

No. 12F4538 Violin Case, full leather covered and full lined with velvet, leather handle, nickel plated lock and hook hasps. Comes in either black or russet color. Especially good value. Shipping weight, 8 pounds.
Price...$3.45

No. 12F4541 Violin Case, seal grain leather covered, lined throughout with silk plush, has hand sewed valance, leather handle and nickel plated spring clasps. This is the best case we handle and retails regularly at $7.00 to $8.00. Comes in black only. Shipping weight, 8 pounds. Price...$5.45

Violin Bows.

If by mail, postage extra, each, 15 cents

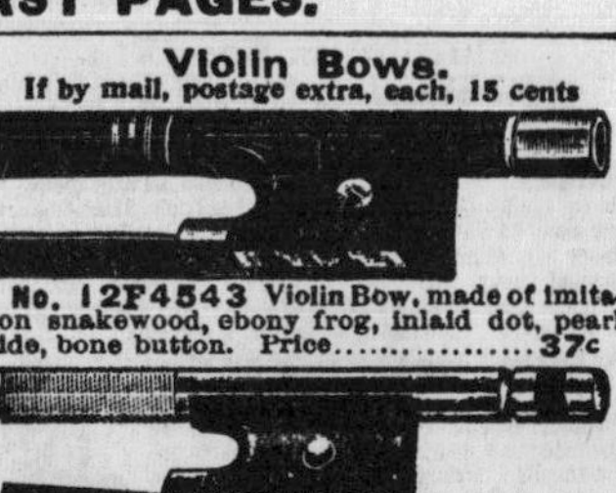

No. 12F4543 Violin Bow, made of imitation snakewood, ebony frog, inlaid dot, pearl slide, bone button. Price...37c

No. 12F4546 Violin Bow, ebony frog, pearl slide, pearl eye. German silver button, superior quality bow hair. Price...48c

No. 12F4547 Violin Bow, genuine Brazil wood, ebony frog, pearl slide, pearl dot, German silver lined, German silver button. Price, 69c

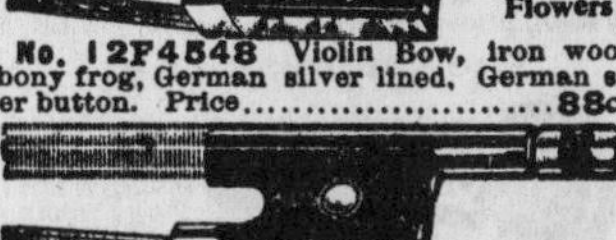

No. 12F4548 Violin Bow, iron wood, ebony frog, German silver lined, German silver button. Price...88c

No. 12F4550 Extra Wide Violin Bow, full genuine Tourte model, Brazil wood, ebony frog, full German silver lined, German silver button, best quality bow hair. Price...95c

No. 12F4552 Violin Bow, genuine Brazil wood, very carefully made, best quality ebony frog, German silver lined, extra wide frog and extra quality hair, latest style button.
Price...$1.38

No. 12F4553 Violin Bow, made of select Brazil wood, imitation of snakewood. Has imitation ivory frog and button, like No. 12F4554, double pearl eye, and is German silver lined. Best bow hair. Price...$1.03

No. 12F4554 Violin Bow, as shown in the illustration, is made of genuine snakewood, has genuine ivory frog, double pearl eye, German silver lined and ivory button. Only the finest quality of bow hair with this bow. This bow will keep its elasticity and shape under all conditions, and is one of the greatest bargains which we offer in violin bows. Price. $2.20

Genuine Pernambuco Wood Violin Bows.

No. 12F4557 Genuine Pernambuco Wood Bow, best quality, ebony frog, two pearl eyes, full German silver-lined, pearl slide, German silver button, full hair, best quality.
Price...$1.85

No. 12F4558 Genuine Pernambuco Wood Bow, octagon shape, best quality ebony frog, two pearl eyes, full German silver button, full hair, best quality, a professional bow.
Price...$2.55

Pure Silver Mounted Bows.

No. 12F4560 Genuine Pernambuco Wood Bow, finest quality ebony frog, two pearl eyes, full solid silver trimmed, pearl slide, full hair, best quality. Price...$2.85

No. 12F4561 Genuine Pernambuco Wood Bow, highly finished in natural color, best quality ebony frog, two pearl eyes, solid silver mounted, pearl slide, extra full hair, best quality. Regular retail price, $6.00.
Our price...$3.80

Our Finest High Grade Bow.

No. 12F4562 Genuine Pernambuco Wood Bow, octagon shape, pure silver mounted, finest ebony frog, pearl eyes and pearl slide, extra quality full hair. This bow retails regularly at $10.00. Our price...$4.85

Violin Bow Frogs.

No. 12F4563 Violin Bow Frog, ebony, pearl dot inlaid in sides, German silver button, pearl slide. Price...17c
If by mail, postage extra, 2 cents.

No. 12F4564 Violin Bow Frog, ebony, with pearl dot inlaid in sides; full German silver lined, German silver button, pearl slide.
Price......(Postage extra, 2 cents)......26c

Violin Bow Screws.

No. 12F4567 Bow Screw, with bone button, octagon shape, inlaying in end. Shipping weight, 1 ounce. Price...5c

No. 12F4568 Bow Screw, with ebony and German silver button, octagon shape, inlaying in end. Price...6c
If by mail, postage extra, 1 cent.

Aluminum Bow Tip.

No. 12F4569 This is a new idea and is intended for the purpose of repairing violin bows which are broken at the neck. It is so light that it does not destroy the balance or add to the weight of the bow, and makes the bow tip much stronger than if repaired in the usual way. It has a socket in the end into which the stick of the bow can be easily fitted. Price......(Postage extra, 2 cents)........29c

Violin Patent Heads.

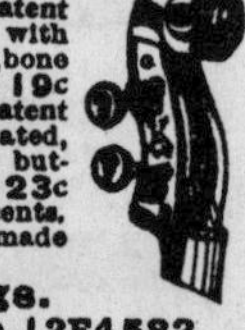

No. 12F4570 Violin Patent Head, made of solid brass, with handsome engraving on sides, bone buttons. Price, per set...... 19c

No. 12F4572 Violin Patent Head, handsomely nickel plated, fancy engraved sides, bone buttons. Price, per set...........23c

If by mail, postage extra, 4 cents.

NOTE—Patent heads are made in one size only.

Violin Pegs.

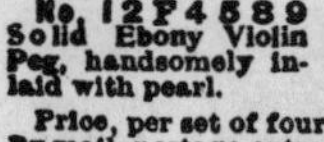

No. 12F4582 Solid Ebony Violin Peg, hollow shape, pearl dot in head. Price, each, 3c Per set of four... 10c

By mail, postage extra each, 1 cent; per set, 2c.

No. 12F4589 Solid Ebony Violin Peg, handsomely inlaid with pearl.

Price, per set of four, 64c; each........ 16c

By mail, postage extra, each, 1 cent; per set, 2c.

The Champion Key.

No. 12F4592 Genuine Celluloid Violin Peg, made of metal, nickel plated, celluloid, polished thumbpiece, white, black or amber. State color desired.

Price, per set of four, 63c; each....... 16c

If by mail, postage extra, 6 cents.

Becker Friction Pegs.

No. 12F4594 These pegs are an entirely new idea, and are so arranged that they do not injure the tone of the violin whatever. They are of great value to ladies and younger scholars especially, who find difficulty in turning up the pegs of their violin. The great advantage of these pegs is that they never slip and when the string is once tuned up to the pitch it remains there.

Price, per set.........58c

If by mail, postage extra, 6 cents.

Violin Chin Rests.

No. 12F4603 Violin Chin Rest. Gutta percha; single screw; double acting. Easily adjusted to any violin, a chin rest which has been found very satisfactory. Price.... 18c

No. 12F4604 Violin Chin Rest. Becker's celebrated patent. Ebonite and nickel. Same as No. 12F4606, but without shoulder rest.

Price... ....(Postage extra, 6 cents) 23c

Chin and Shoulder Rest.

No. 12F4606 As shown in illustration, chin and shoulder rest combined. The most perfect and complete violin rest made.

Price....57c

If by mail, postage extra, 6 cents.

The Columbia Chin Rest.

No. 12F4607 The Columbia Chin Rest. One of the most desirable features of this chin rest is that it is adjustable to any size instrument. It is made of best gutta percha with full nickel plated mountings. It is very desirable in every respect, and we consider it one of the best chin rests on the market. Price..........53c

If by mail, postage extra, 6c.

The Ideal Chin Rest.

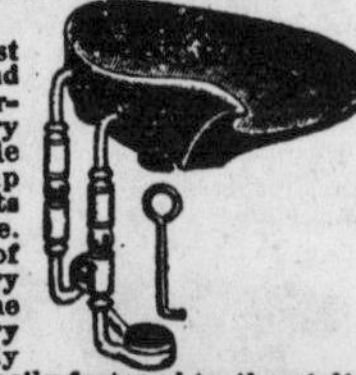

No. 12F4609 This is the very latest idea in a chin rest and one which will certainly please every violinist. It is made with a very deep cup and a horn which fits over the tailpiece. This gives the chin of the performer a very strong grip on the violin. It is very carefully and durably made, and is very easily fastened to the violin. When once attached it will not work loose. It is made of solid ebony, and has nickel plated attachments. Price.........................58c

If by mail, postage extra, 7 cents.

Violin Tailpieces.

If by mail, postage extra, each, 2 cents.

No. 12F4611 Solid Ebony Violin Tailpiece. Excellent model and finish. Fitted complete with tailpiece gut.

Price...................................9c

No. 12F4615 Solid Ebony Violin Tailpiece, New Model. Best quality. Fitted complete with tailpiece gut. Price........16c

No. 12F4617 Solid Ebony Tailpiece, highly polished, inlaid with five colored pearl flowers. Fitted complete with tailpiece gut.

Price...23c

No. 12F4618 Violin Tailpiece; is made of solid ebony, inlaid with seven pearl flowers and has pearl inlay around string holes. Complete with tailpiece gut. Price............45c

No. 12F4620 Our very finest Violin Tailpiece, made of select solid ebony, highly polished, inlaid with 11 fancy pearl flowers and bird. Pearl inlaying around string holes. Fitted with tailpiece gut. Price...........................68c

If by mail, postage extra, each, 2 cents.

Violin Tailpiece Gut.

No. 12F4621 Violin Tailpiece Gut, best quality, in 12-inch lengths to fasten tailpiece to violin. Price, per length..................2c

If by mail, postage extra, 1 cent.

Violin Bridges.

No 12F4622 Violin Bridge, made of maple, three scrolls, good quality. Price..........3c

If by mail, postage extra, 1 cent.

No. 12F4624 Violin Bridge. Vuillaume model, made of extra select maple, three scrolls, very fine quality.

Price..8c

If by mail, postage extra, 1 cent.

No. 12F4626 Violin Bridge, made of selected maple. Superfine quality, three scrolls. Made for artists' use. Price..............14c

If by mail, postage extra, 1 cent.

Violin Mutes.

No. 12F4630 Violin Mute, made of plain solid ebony.

Price...........................4c

If by mail, postage extra, 1 cent.

No. 12F4632 Violin Mute, German silver. Price..........6c

If by mail, postage extra, 1 cent.

12F4630

No. 12F4636 Violin Mute, as illustrated, is made of German silver, and has tuning pipe A and string gauge.

Price..............15c

If by mail, postage extra, 1 cent.

Violin Fingerboards.

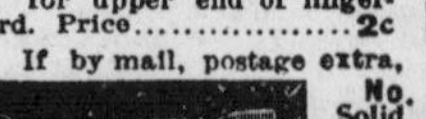

No. 12F4642 Solid Ebony Fingerboard, fine model, highly finished. Price..........14c

If by mail, postage extra, 8 cents.

No. 12F4643 Finest Quality Ebony. French polished. Price...................34c

If by mail, postage extra, 8 cents.

Chart for Violin Fingerboard.

You can learn how to play the violin without the aid of a teacher by using the patent lettered fingerboard chart. It is a great help for beginners.

No. 12F4644 This Chart is made in the shape of the fingerboard, and can be easily attached under the strings without changing the instrument, and will enable a beginner to find every note and each position readily. Retail dealers ask 25 cents for this chart. Price...4c

If by mail, postage extra, 2 cents.

Violin Nuts or Saddles.

No. 12F4646 Solid Ebony Nut for upper end of fingerboard. Price...................2c

If by mail, postage extra, 1 cent.

No. 12F4648 Solid Ebony Nut, for supporting the tailpiece string. Price.......................3c

If by mail, postage extra, 1 cent.

Violin End Pins.

No. 12F4652 Ebony, best model, pearl dot inlaid in head. Price.......3c

If by mail, postage extra, 1 cent.

Bow Hair.

No. 12F4660 Siberian, good quality, for full length bows. Price, per bunch..........9c

If by mail, postage extra, 1 cent.

No. 12F4662 French, finest quality, slightly bleached. Price, per bunch.......14c

If by mail, postage extra, 1 cent.

No. 12F4664 Russia, extra quality. Price, per bunch...........................17c

If by mail, postage extra, 1 cent.

Violin Bow Rosin.

No. 12F4672 Bow Rosin, large size cakes in oblong pasteboard box. Price..........2c

If by mail, postage extra, 2 cents.

No. 12F4673 Large Size Metal Spool, in pasteboard case.

Price...............6c

If by mail, postage extra, 2 cents.

Violin Bow Rosin.

No. 12F4674 Large Sized Cakes Bow Rosin, in neat wood case, to be used without removing from case. Price...............5c

If by mail, postage extra, 2 cents.

No. 12F4678 Genuine Gustav Bernardel Paris Rosin, put up in convenient form. Imported direct from France. Nothing better made. Price..........13c

If by mail, postage extra, 2 cents.

No. 12F4679 Same rosin as No. 12F4678, put up in fine metal box.

Price..............19c

If by mail, postage extra, 2 cents.

Violin Necks.

No. 12F4680 Violin Necks, maple, unfinished, carved scroll. Price.................................21c

If by mail, postage extra, 8 cents.

No. 12F4682 Violin Necks, maple, unfinished, fine quality, finely carved scroll.

Price..36c

If by mail, postage extra, 8 cents.

No. 12F4684 Violin Necks, curly maple, unfinished, best quality, finely carved scroll.

Price..49c

If by mail, postage extra, 8 cents.

Sound Post Setter.

No. 12F4688 Sound Post Setter. Steel, nickel plated; can be used in adjusting sound post of any violin. Price..........................19c

If by mail, postage extra, 4 cents.

Violin Tuner.

No. 12F4690 Four Tuning Pipes, E, A, D, G, combined, for tuning violin. Made of German silver and tuned to concert pitch. Price... 16c

If by mail, postage extra, 3 cents.

Double Bass Bows.

No. 12F4955 Made of Maple, red painted, light wood frog, excellent quality, common model. Shipping weight, 18 ozs. Price ..85c

No. 12F4957 Redwood, natural color, ebony frog, good quality, superior model.

Price...(Postage extra, 18 cents).......$1.65

Double Bass and Violoncello Fingerboard Chart.

No. 12F4997 This Chart is an accurate guide, having all the notes with sharps and flats in full view, and can be adjusted on any double bass fingerboard without changing the instrument. With the use of the lettered fingerboard chart, anyone can learn how to play.

Price...(If by mail, postage extra, 2c.).....9c

No. 12F5043 This Chart is similar to the Double Bass Chart No. 12F4997, but is adapted only for the violoncello. Price...............7c

If by mail, postage extra, 2 cents.

Violoncello Bags.

No. 12F5045 Perfect Fitting Canvas Bag, with button fastener. Shipping weight, 20 ounces. Price...(Postage extra, 20c.).....$1.20

Violoncello Bows.

No. 12F5064

No. 12F5062 Brazil Wood, plain ebony frog, bone button, good quality. Price.....70c

If by mail, postage extra, 17 cents.

No. 12F5064 Brazil Wood, ebony frog, pearl eye, German silver button. Price.....93c

If by mail, postage extra, 17 cents.

No. 12F5066 Brazil Wood, ebony frog, double pearl eye, full German silver lined, pearl slide, German silver button.

Price...(Postage extra, 17 cents.)......$1.65

Violoncello Bow Hair.

No. 12F5073 Fine Quality Siberian Bow Hair, each filling tied separately. Price. 14c

If by mail, postage extra, 2 cents.

Violoncello Patent Head.

No. 12F5108 Violoncello Patent Head. Made with separate brass plates, iron screws and maple pegs, each peg having a pearl inlaid dot in head. Shipping weight, 1 lb. Price, per set....$1.65

GUITAR FURNISHINGS.

Guitar Cases.

No. 12F5160 Brown Canvas, as illustrated, leather bound edges, open on end, complete with strap, buckle and handle. Standard or regular size. Weight, 5¼ lbs. Price, 82c

No. 12F5162 Same as No. 12F5160, for concert size. Weight, 5½ pounds. Price, 88c

No. 12F5163 Same as No. 12F5160, for grand concert size. Weight, 6 lbs. Price..94c

No. 12F5164 Hand Sewed Leather, embossed black or russet, very superior quality, for standard size guitar. Shipping weight, 10 pounds. Price $4.45

No. 12F5166 Same as No. 12F5164, for concert size. Shipping weight, 10 pounds.

Price..$4.85

Guitar Bags.

When ordering, give size of guitar.

No. 12F5168 Fine Green Cloth, with buttons, for standard or concert guitar. Shipping wt. 1 lb. Price, (Postage 16 cents)...40c

No. 12F5170 Green Felt, fleece lined, patent fasteners; fine quality; for standard, concert or grand concert size guitar. Shipping wt. 1 lb. Price, (Postage 16 cents.).68c

Guitar Tuners.

No. 12F5172 Six Tuning Pipes, E, B, G, D, A, E, combined, for tuning guitar. Made of German silver and tuned to concert pitch. Price. 23c

If by mail, postage extra, 5 cents.

Guitar Patent Heads.

No. 12F5174 Brass, bone buttons, fine quality. Price, per set.....................27c

If by mail, postage extra, per set, 6 cents.

No. 12F5176 Same as No. 12F5174, nickel plated. Price, per set.......................36c

If by mail, postage extra, per set, 6 cents.

Guitar Tailpieces.

No. 12F5186 This is the latest novelty in the line of Guitar Tailpieces. It is made of solid brass, beautifully nickeled, and of genuine American manufacture. Price 5c

If by mail, postage extra, 5 cents.

No. 12F5190 Brass, nickel plated, for any size guitar.

Price......37c

If by mail, postage extra, 5 cents.

Guitar Tailpiece Bridge.

No. 12F5194 Ebony, plain with German silver fret, used in connection with metal tailpiece. Price 7c

If by mail, postage extra, 2 cents.

Guitar Bridges.

No. 12F5198 Ebony, plain, best model and finish.

Price..12c

If by mail, postage extra, 4 cents.

No. 12F5200 Ebony, neat pearl inlaying at each end. Price 40c

If by mail, postage extra, 4 cents.

Guitar Bridge Pins.

No. 12F5208 Ebony, polished pearl inlaying in head. Price, per set of six 4c

No. 12F5214 Ivory, polished, pearl inlaying in head. Price, each..............3c

If by mail, postage extra, each, 1 cent.

Guitar Fingerboards.

No. 12F5218 Ebony, with frets.

Price..69c

If by mail, postage extra, 16 cents.

Guitar Fingerboard Chart.

No. 12F5220 Guitar playing made easy by using the Patent Lettered Fingerboard Chart. It is an accurate guide, having all notes, with sharps and flats, in full view, and can be easily adjusted to any guitar without changing the instrument. Price..........4c
If by mail, postage extra, 2 cents.

Guitar Capo d'Astro.

The Capo d'Astro is for the purpose of changing the key of the guitar without retuning it. This is done by simply moving the Capo d'Astro up on the neck of the guitar and tightening it. This instrument is very convenient when playing accompaniments for the voice.

The Magic Capo d'Astro.

No. 12F5222 Nickel plated, steel spring action, cork lined. The simplest and best Capo d'Astro made. Price..........7c
If by mail, postage extra, 3 cents.

No. 12F5225 Capo d'Astro. Another brass, highly nickel plated appliance for changing the key of the guitar. It is finely cork lined and the pressure bar fitted with rubber so as not to mar the finish of the neck of the guitar. Price..........13c
If by mail, postage extra, 3 cents.

Used to clamp on fingerboard to facilitate playing in flat keys,
No. 12F5226 Capo d'Astro nickel plated, spring action, felt covered clamps. Shipping weight, 3 ounces. Price..........18c
If by mail, postage extra, 3 cents.

No. 12F5230 Capo d'Astro, made of brass, polished and lacquered, cork lined clamps, improved model, extra weight and strength. Weight, 3 ounces. Price..........20c
No. 12F5232 Same, brass, finely nickel plated. Price..........25c
If by mail, postage extra, 3 cents.

Guitar End Pins.

No. 12F5242 Ebony, plain, polished head, with pearl dot inlaid. Price..........4c
If by mail, postage extra, 1 cent.

Guitar and Banjo Frets.

No. 12F5246 German Silver, in sets of eighteen. Price, per set..........14c
NOTE—We do not break sets.
If by mail, postage extra, 3 cents.

BANJO FURNISHINGS.

Banjo Cases.

No. 12F5310 Brown canvas case, superior quality, edges bound with leather, flannel lined, with handle, for any size banjo from 7 to 13 inches. Shipping weight, 6 pounds. Price..........82c

No. 12F5312 Extra fine black or russet leather case, embossed, flannel lined, open on end, complete as illustrated, with strap, buckle and handle, for 10 or 11-inch banjo. Shipping weight, 7 pounds. Price..........$4.35
No. 12F5314 Same, for 12 or 13-inch banjo. Price..........$4.55
NOTE—When ordering case for banjo, give diameter of head only.

Banjo Bags.

No. 12F5320 Fine green cloth, with buttons, for 9 to 13-inch banjo. Weight, 7 ounces. Price..........34c
No. 12F5324 Green felt, box shape, fleece lined, patent fasteners, for any size banjo. Shipping weight, 12 ounces. Price..........66c

Banjo Tuners.

No. 12F5326 Five tuning pipes, B, G sharp, E, A and E, combined, for tuning banjos. Made from German silver and tuned to concert pitch. Price..........19c
If by mail, postage extra, 4 cents.

Banjo Bridges.

No. 12F5328 Maple or rosewood; professional model. Price..........2c
No. 12F5330 Solid ebony, regular model. Price..........3c
No. 12F5334 Genuine Stewart; special professional; hand made. Price..........6c
If by mail, postage extra, 1 cent.

Banjo Tailpieces.

No. 12F5336 Plain solid ebony. Price..........3c
No. 12F5339 A very practical tailpiece. Brass, nickel plated. Price..........8c
By mail, postage extra, 2c.

No. 12F5340 Fancy design, complete with screw, bracket and nut, ready for use. Will fit any banjo. Brass, nickel plated. Price..........14c
If by mail, postage, 4 cents.

Banjo Pegs.

No. 12F5350 Imitation ebony, hollow shape, polished, pearl dot in head. Price, each..........2c
No. 12F5352 Same, but side peg. Price, each..........2c
No. 12F5354 Solid Ebony, hollow shape, pearl dot in each end, regular. Price, each..........4c
No. 12F5356 Same, side peg. Price, each..........4c
If by mail, postage extra, each, 1c; per set, 3c.

No. 12F5362 Made of metal, nickel plated, celluloid, polished thumb piece, white, black or amber. Be sure to state color wanted. Price, per set of five, 88c; each..........18c
If by mail, postage extra, per set, 3 cents.

Banjo Brackets.

No. 12F5370 Our Hexagonal Pattern Banjo Bracket is made of solid brass, highly polished, with bolt and nut. Price, per dozen, 36c; each, 3c
No. 12F5372 Same as above, but handsomely nickel plated. Price, per dozen, 48c; each, 4c
No. 12F5374 Our Ball Banjo Bracket is made of solid brass, highly polished, complete with safety nut and bolt. Price, per dozen, 48c; each, 5c
No. 12F5376 Same as above, but handsomely nickel plated. Price, per dozen, 60c; each, 6c
Weight, about 9 ounces to the dozen.
If by mail, postage extra, per dozen, 10 cents.

Banjo Thimbles.

No. 12F5386 German silver, imported pattern. Weight, 2 ounces. Price..........3c
If by mail, postage extra, 1 cent.

Banjo Wrenches.

Be sure to state size of bracket nut.
No. 12F5387 Brass, key shape. Price, 4c
No. 12F5388 As above, nickel plated. Price..........6c
If by mail, postage extra, 2 cents.

Banjo Fingerboard Chart.

No. 12F5392 With the aid of the fingerboard chart anyone can easily locate the notes. This chart can be adjusted to the fingerboard of any banjo and does not change the instrument in the least. Price..........4c
If by mail, postage extra, 2 cents.

MANDOLIN FURNISHINGS.

Mandolin Cases.

No. 12F5460 Mandolin Case, brown canvas, with leather bound edges, flannel lined, handle and patent fastenings. Shipping weight, 5 pounds. Price..........65c

No. 12F5461 Waterproof Mandolin Case, made of rubber cloth in imitation of alligator leather, flannel lined, leather handle, patent fasteners. Shipping weight, 7 pounds. Price..........$1.47

No. 12F5462 Mandolin Case, made of russet or black leather, extra quality, hand sewed, flannel lined, same as illustration. Shipping weight, 7 pounds. Price..........$3.54

Mandolin Bags.

No. 12F5464 Mandolin Bag, made of green cloth with buttons, good quality. Shipping weight, 12 ounces. Price..........28c
No. 12F5466 Mandolin Bag, made of green felt, full fleece lined, patent fasteners, superior quality. Shipping weight, 12 ounces. Price..........45c

Mandolin Tailpieces.

No. 12F5467 Especially attractive shell design Mandolin Tailpiece. Made of brass, nickel plated and highly polished. Price..........9c
If by mail, postage extra, 3 cents.

No. 12F5468 High Class Tailpiece, arm rest and sleeve protector combined; hinge pattern; made of brass, nickel plated, highly burnished. Price..........23c
If by mail, postage extra, 5 cents.

Mandolin Patent Heads.

No. 12F5469 American Made Brass Patent Head, Guitar Style; bone buttons. Price, per set..........32c
If by mail, postage extra, per set, 8 cents.

Mandolin Tuner.

See Violin Tuner No. 12F4690.

Professional Mandolin Pick.

No. 12F5478 The Patent Mandolin Pick, fastened to the finger by steel clasp, the pick proper being held between rubber discs, it is possible for it to be held more firmly and at the same time not require the tightness of clasp which is necessary with the old pick when playing soft music. By placing the thumb and index finger lightly on the disc the player will be able to play the sweetest and softest music possible, and if necessary he can tremolo a chord with the utmost ease. Price..........12c
If by mail, postage extra, 2 cents.

Mandolin Picks.

No. 12F5480 Genuine Tortoise Shell, oval shape, polished or unpolished. Price..........2c
If by mail, postage extra, 1 cent.
No. 12F5482 Same, extra large, extra quality. Price..........4c
If by mail, postage extra, 1 cent.
No. 12F5484 Genuine Tortoise Shell, triangular shape. Price..........4c
If by mail, postage extra, 1 cent.

Mandolin Bridges.

No. 12F5486 Bridges, ebony, plain finish. Price..........4c
No. 12F5490 Bridges, ebony, ivory inlaid. Price..........13c
If by mail, postage extra, 2 cents.

Mandolin Fingerboard Chart.

The Latest Patent Self Instructor.

No. 12F5498 With the aid of the Lettered Fingerboard Chart, anyone can easily locate the notes. The chart can be adjusted on the fingerboard of any mandolin, and does not change the instrument in the least. Price..........4c
If by mail, postage extra, 2 cents.

AUTOHARP FURNISHINGS.

Tuning Keys.

No. 12F5570 Tuning Keys, malleable iron. Price..........7c
If by mail, postage extra, 2 cents.

Autoharp Picks.

No. 12F5572 Picks, celluloid. Price..........2c
If by mail, postage extra, 2 cents.

No. 12F5576 Autoharp Picks, brass, spiral. Price..........2c
If by mail, postage extra, 1 cent.

Autoharp Tuning Pins.

No. 12F5578 Autoharp Tuning Pins, made of blued steel. Price, per doz..........5c
If by mail, postage extra, per dozen, 4 cents.

Autoharp Cases.

Autoharp Case, made of brown canvas, bound all around the edges with leather, flannel lined, superior model and quality, complete with handle and strap. To fit autoharp No. 71, catalogue No. 12F900; No. 2¾, catalogue No. 12F902; No. 72¾, catalogue No. 12F904; No. 73, catalogue No. 12F906; No. 6, catalogue No. 12F908.
No. 12F5584 Autoharp Case. Price..........85c

Guitar Zither Cases.

To fit guitar zither No. 0¼, catalogue No. 12F921; No. 2¼, catalogue No. 12F925; No. 3¼ catalogue No. 12F927.
No. 12F5585 Guitar Zither Case. Price..........85c

Mandolin Zither Cases.

To fit instrument style A, catalogue No. 12F940; style B, catalogue No. 12F942.
No. 12F5586 Mandolin Zither Case. Shipping weight, about 7 pounds. Price..........90c

Zither Ring.

No. 12F5627 Zither Ring, made of steel, nickel plated, new model. Sizes, 1 to 6. Price..........10c
If by mail, postage extra, 2 cents.

FLUTE AND PICCOLO FURNISHINGS.

No. 12F5650 Composition metal, adjustable with screw, for piccolo. Price..........5c
No. 12F5651 Same as No. 12F5650, but for fife. Price..........5c
No. 12F5655 Flute Mouthpiece, composition metal, adjustable with screw. Price..........9c
If by mail, postage extra, 2 cents.

No. 12F5665 The Cleaner which we show in the illustration is made of the very best worsted in variegated colors and furnished with wire covered handle. Price..........13c
If by mail, postage extra, 4 cents.
No. 12F5666 Same as No. 12F5665, but for piccolo. Price..........9c
If by mail, postage extra, 4 cents.

CLARIONET FURNISHINGS.

Reed Holders and Protectors.

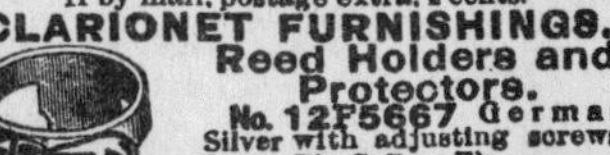

No. 12F5667 German Silver with adjusting screws, for A, Bb, C, D or Eb. Price, each..........22c
If by mail, postage extra, 6 cents.

Mouthpiece Cap.

No. 12F5674 Nickel Plated, for A, Bb, C, D or Eb mouthpieces. Price..........17c
If by mail, postage extra, 3 cents.

Reeds.

Our Clarionet Reeds are made expressly for us by a reed maker of great celebrity.
No. 12F5682 Cottereau, fine quality, for A, Bb, C, D or Eb clarionet. Price, each...4c
No. 12F5684 Barbu, superfine, for A, Bb, C, D or Eb clarionet. Price, each..........6c
No. 12F5685 Genuine Martin Freres for A, Bb C, D or Eb clarionet. Price, each..9c
No. 12F5686 Our Special Fournier Waterproof Clarionet Reeds. These reeds are strictly waterproof, and model and quality are particularly desirable. They are made for any key clarionet. In ordering, always state for what key they are desired. Price, each..11c
No. 12F5688 Artists' Cabinet Reeds, a grade of reed that is the best that can be secured at any price. Made for A, Bb, D or Eb clarionet. Price is the same. Price, each, 16c
If by mail, postage extra, 2 cents.

Clarionet Reed Cases.

No. 12F5694 Leather Pocket Case, for six reeds. Price..........22c
If by mail, postage extra, 5 cents.

No. 12F5696 This is a very neat little Clarionet Reed Case. Lined with plush, covered with genuine leather, nicely finished and fitted with nickel plated spring clasp. The reeds are held in place on a glass plate by a broad band of silk elastic. The case is deep enough to hold from 8 to 10 reeds. Price..38c
If by mail, postage extra, 8 cents.

Give Key of Clarionet.

No. 12F5702 Solid ebony mouthpiece, without reed holder. Price, each..........43c
No. 12F5704 Grenadilla mouthpiece, with German silver reed plate, but without reed holder, any key. Price, each..$1.23
If by mail, postage extra, 7 cents.

Clarionet Cases.

No. 12F5708 Clarionet Case; leather bag, lined, with handle and catch, for clarionet of any key. Shipping weight, 19 ounces. Be sure to give key of clarionet. Price..98c

No. 12F5710 Clarionet Case; valise form, leather covered, flannel lined, with handle, hooks and lock. Made to carry three clarionets. Shipping weight, 4 pounds. Price..........$2.48

Cornet Cases.

No. 12F5713 Brown or Gray Canvas, satchel form, leather bound edges, flannel lined, with shoulder strap. Shipping wgt., 6 lbs. Price........**70c**

No. 12F5715 Black or Russet Pebble Leather, very fine, satchel form, as illustrated; flannel lined, nickel plated trimmings, with shoulder strap. Shipping weight, 25 ounces. Price........**98c**

No. 12F5717 Cornet Case, valise form, made of wood covered with an indestructible waterproof material made in perfect imitation of pebbled leather, handsomely embossed, trimmed with nickel corners, leather handle, nickel spring lock, nickel link clasps and nickel hinges. Lined inside with velvet, partitioned off for cornet and various parts. One of the best cornet cases made. Shipping weight, 6 pounds. Price........**$3.15**

Folding Drum Stand.

No. 12F3600 Seroco Patent Folding Drum Stand. It is made of the best quality of steel, highly nickel plated. It is the neatest and most compact drum stand manufactured, very solid in construction yet very light. Will fit any size drum. Shipping weight, 4 pounds. Price, **$2.25**

CYMBALS.

Brass Cymbals with Leather Handles.

No. 12F3660 10-inch. Wt., 35 oz. Price, per pair...**$1.32**

No. 12F3661 11-inch. Wt., 40 ounces. Per pair........**$1.45**

No. 12F3662 12-inch. Wt., 45 ounces. Per pair........**$1.56**

No. 12F3663 13-inch. Wt., 60 ounces. Per pair...**$1.69**

No. 12F3664 Turkish Cymbals. 8-inch, composition metal. Weight, 35 ounces. Per pair...**$2.45**

No. 12F3666 Turkish Cymbals, 12-inch composition metal, with leather handles. Weight, 65 ounces. Price, per pair.....**$3.95**

Drum and Cymbal Beater.

No. 12F3668 Combined Drum and Cymbal Beater. Made entirely of metal. An important advantage of this beater is being able to play with greater rapidity and accuracy than with any other make on account of its quick action and simple construction. Easy to carry, as it is easily put together and packed. Shipping weight, 5 pounds. Price, without cymbal........**$2.53**

Bones and Clappers.

No. 12F3670 Hardwood, 5½ inches. Wt., 5 ounces. Set of four, **6c**

No. 12F3672 Rosewood, 5½ inches. Wt., 5½ ounces. Set of four **9c**

No. 12F3674 Rosewood, 7 inches long. Weight, 6 ounces. Set of four........**13c**

No. 12F3676 Solid Ebony, 5½ inches. Weight, 6 ounces. Set of four........**19c**

No. 12F3678 Solid Ebony, 7 inches long. Weight, 7 ounces. Set of four........**28c**

No. 12F3680 Clappers. Made of walnut, with patent steel spring and lead clappers. Weight, 4 ounces. Set of two........**8c**

Triangles.

Nickel Steel, with Hammer.

No. 12F3684 4-inch. Wt., 7 ounces. Price........**15c**

No. 12F3686 6-inch. Wt., 9 ounces. Price........**23c**

No. 12F3688 7-inch. Wt., 12 ounces. Price........**28c**

No. 12F3690 8-inch. Weight, 15 ounces. Price........**36c**

Triangle Beater.

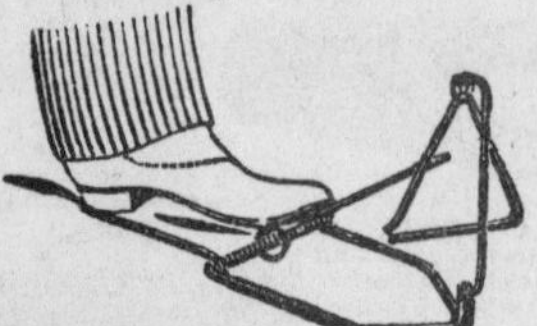

No. 12F3694 Made of nickel plated wire, very strong and durable. Used to play with foot, thus allowing both hands to be free for the use of other instruments. Shipping weight, 10 ounces.
Price, without triangle........**55c**

Tambourines.

No. 12F3696 7-inch maple rim, with tacked sheepskin head and three sets of jingles. Weight, 10 ounces. Price, per dozen, **$2.16**; each........**18c**

No. 12F3698 Same, with 8-inch head. Weight, 12 ounces. Price, per dozen, **$2.64**; each........**23c**

No. 12F3700 Same, with 10-inch head. Weight, 14 ounces. Price, per dozen, **$3.24**; each........**28c**

No. 12F3702 Maple painted rim, 8-inch tacked calfskin head, nine sets of jingles. Weight, 16 ounces. Price........**42c**

No. 12F3704 Maple painted rim, 10-inch tacked calfskin head, twelve sets of jingles. Weight, 19 ounces. Price........**55c**

Salvation Army Tambourines.

No. 12F3709 10-inch Maple Hoop, fancy painted and ornamented, 28 sets of brass jingles, calfskin head fastened with brass tacks. Weight, 28 ounces. Price........**$1.25**

No. 12F3711 Same as No. 12F3709, but with 32 sets of jingles. Weight, 32 ounces. Price........**$1.40**

No. 12F5718 Our Bb Tenor Slide Trombone Cases are made of black sole leather, very artistically embossed and lined with red flannel. They have metal end protectors, strong carrying straps and handle. Suitable for either high or low pitch instruments. Furnished with extra inside pocket for low pitch slide. Shipping weight, 6 pounds. Price........**$5.50**

We can furnish cases for instruments of all kinds. Send for Special Band Instrument Catalogue.

The Newman Professional Cornet Mute.

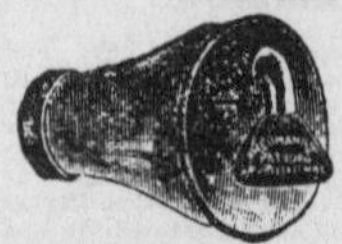

This mute is the very latest and best invention of its kind, and has several distinct advantages over the old style. It does not drive the air back into the cornet, but allows it to escape freely through the bell. It can be used without throwing the cornet out of tune, and softens the tone of the instrument to a much greater extent than the old fashioned mute. It is made of brass, durably constructed and finely finished. It is invaluable for practice purposes as well as for the mute effect in cornet solos.

No. 12F5720 Brass polish. Price, **$1.45**
No. 12F5722 Nickel plated. Price, **1.75**
If by mail, postage extra, 8 cents.

FOR TROMBONE.

No. 12F5724 Brass polish. Price, **$2.40**
No. 12F5726 Nickel plated. Price, **2.75**
If by mail, postage extra, 10 cents.

Calfskin Heads.

For Drums, Banjos and Tambourines.

No.	Size, Inches	For	Price
12F5770	12	10-inch Shell	$0.27
12F5772	13	11-inch Drum Shell	.35
12F5774	14	11½-inch Shell	.41
12F5776	15	12-inch Shell	.49
12F5778	16	13-inch Shell	.54
12F5782	18	15-inch Drum	.71
12F5783	19	16-inch Drum	.76
12F5784	20	17-inch Drum	.84
12F5785	22	19-inch Drum	.98
12F5786	28	24-inch Bass Drum	1.85
12F5787	30	26-inch Bass Drum	2.05
12F5788	32	28-inch Bass Drum	2.35
12F5789	34	30-inch Bass Drum	2.45
12F5790	36	32-inch Bass Drum	2.70
12F5792	38	34-inch Bass Drum	3.15
12F5794	40	36-inch Bass Drum	3.60

Extra Quality Special Banjo Heads.

Genuine Rogers. First Quality.

No. 12F5796 13-inch, white, for 11-inch banjo. Price........**59c**

No. 12F5797 14-inch, white, for 11½-inch banjo. Price........**73c**

No. 12F5798 16-inch, white, for 13-inch banjo. Price........**94c**

Our Special High Grade Transparent Heads.

No. 12F5802 13-inch for 11-inch shell. Price........**48c**

No. 12F5804 14-inch for 11½-inch shell. Price........**58c**

No. 12F5808 16-inch for 13-inch shell. Price........**69c**

Shipping weight, 12 to 20-inch head.. 4 ounces
Shipping weight, 22 to 28-inch head.. 9 ounces
Shipping weight, 30 to 36-inch head.. 20 ounces
Shipping weight, 38 to 40-inch head.. 24 ounces

Music Stands.

No. 12F5920 Our Special Umbrella Pattern Folding Music Stand, made of iron, handsomely japanned. Folds up into small compass. Shipping weight, 43 ounces. Price.....**24c**

No. 12F5924 Same, nickel plated. Shipping weight, 43 ounces. Price........**63c**

95c

No. 12F5925 This is the Genuine "Quinn" Telescope Music Stand. It is made of the best steel obtainable, heavily nickel plated and highly polished. It has no thumbscrews which will easily wear out, but is fitted with patent friction spring adjustments so that the stand can be easily adjusted to any height. It is the lightest, yet the strongest stand made, and is far superior in every way to similar stands offered by other dealers. Length, when folded, 17 inches. Shipping weight, 30 ounces. Regular retail price, $2.50. Our price........**95c**

Music Stand Cases.

No. 12F5926 Our Best Music Stand Case is made of sole leather and is exactly like the illustration above. It is made for folding iron stands such as we quote under Nos. 12F5920, 12F5924 and 12F5925. Shipping weight, 18 ounces. Price........**58c**

No. 12F5927 This Music Stand Case is made of black sole leather, with extra strong hand sewed handle and nickel plated rings for shoulder straps. It is 18 inches long and intended only for our stand No. 12F5925 or any other telescope stand which will not measure more than 17½ inches when closed. Shipping weight, 8 ounces. Price........**55c**

Students' Music Pad.

No. 12F5930 One Hundred Sheets of Ruled Music Paper, put up in the form of a pad, suitable for music students. Each sheet shows all signatures used in writing music, which serves as a great aid to composers. Price....(If by mail, postage extra, 8c) ... **15c**

Music Blank Books.

These books are well bound and are made of good quality paper, ready ruled for writing Music. Size, 7⅛x9¾ inches.

No. 12F5940 6 staves, 40 pages...... **8c**
No. 12F5941 8 staves, 24 pages...... **7c**
No. 12F5942 8 staves, 40 pages...... **10c**
No. 12F5943 8 staves, 64 pages...... **11c**
If by mail, postage extra, per book, 11 cents.

Music Paper.

Super Royal Music Paper. Size, 10¾x13¾ inches.

No. 12F5947 10 staves, octavo.
No. 12F5948 12 staves, octavo, or oblong.
No. 12F5949 12 staves, octavo, for vocal or piano.
No. 12F5950 14 staves, octavo, or oblong.
Price, per quire (24 sheets)........**19c**
If by mail, postage extra, per quire, 11 cents.

Gummed Paper.

No. 12F5952 French Gummed Paper, for mending sheet music. Price, per sheet. **6c**
If by mail, postage extra, 1 cent.

Ruling Pens.

No. 12F5956 Ruling Pens, with five lines for drawing staff. Price...... **8c**
If by mail, postage extra, 1 cent.

Steel Pens.

No. 12F5962 Steel Pens, with three points, for writing music, special make. Price, per dozen. (Postage extra, 1c).... **14c**

Tuning Forks.

New Standard or Low Pitch.

No. 12F3780 Steel, A or C, philharmonic. Price........**6c**

No. 12F3781 Nickel plated steel, A or C, superior quality. Price........**14c**

No. 12F3782 Blue steel, A or C, superior quality. Price........**28c**
If by mail, postage extra, 2 cents.

Tuning Pipes.

New Standard or High Pitch.

No. 12F3790 German silver, keys of A and C combined, extra fine quality, in white metal boxes. Price........**7c**

No. 12F3792 Same, keys of C and G combined. Price........**7c**
If by mail, postage extra, 2 cents.

For Violin, Mandolin and Guitar Tuners, see pages containing Violin, Mandolin, Guitar and Banjo Furnishings.

Piano Tuning Hammer.

No. 12F3801 Long rosewood handle with extension rod of steel, double head with oblong holes and single head with star holes. Extra quality, warranted. Weight, 2 pounds. Price........**$1.28**

Music Rolls, Bags and Folios.

No. 12F5990 This Music Roll is made of fine black imitation monkey grain leather; heavy leather handle, strap and buckle, bound and stitched edges. It is lined throughout and has a flap at the bottom to hold music. Size, open, 14¾x15½ inches. Price........**23c**

No. 12F5992 Our Students' Music Roll. This is a leatherette music roll, neatly and durably made and lined with cloth. It has a handle, strap and nickel plated buckle, and is furnished with a purse, the very latest convenience. This is one of the best music rolls on the market for the price. Price....(Postage extra, 5c)....**29c**

No. 12F6003 A Very Fine Imitation Seal Grain Leather Roll, has leather handle, wide strap and fancy buckle. We furnish this roll in either orange or black. Be sure to state color wanted.
Price......(Postage extra, 6 cents)......**48c**

No. 12F6004 This Music Roll has beautiful double colored imitation hornback alligator skin, heavily lined, with stitched handle, wide lined and stitched strap and fine nickel buckle. It is lined throughout, and has a flap at the bottom to hold music in place. Bound and stitched all around. Size, open, 14¾x15 inches. Price......(Postage extra, 6c)... **48c**

Leather Music Rolls.

No. 12F6005 This Music Roll has a fine solid case of leather in orange and black, beautiful creased sides, and has an inside flap to keep the music in place, wide strap and finely plated harness buckle. Be sure to state color wanted. Size, 14¾x15 inches.
Price ......(Postage extra, 6 cents).....**78c**

No. 12F6008 Our New Burnt Leather Music Roll. This is one of the tastiest music rolls ever placed on the market and is decorated with pretty designs burnt on the leather, with an imitation white rose on each end made of white velvet. We know you will like it. Fitted with strap and handsome nickel plated buckle. Leather handle ornamented with tasty design.
Price........**85c**
If by mail, postage extra, 6 cents.

No. 12F6009 This Music Roll is made of fine black buffalo grain leather, leather lined, bound and stitched edges, heavy double stitched handle, wide lined and stitched strap and fine nickel buckle. It has an inside flap at bottom to hold music in place. Size, open, 14¾x15½ inches. Price......(Postage extra, 6c)....**95c**

No. 12F6016 Genuine Seal Music Roll. This would retail at from $2.50 to $3.00. A splendid roll, 15x14½ inches, especially suitable as a present. It has leather handle, strap and buckle of the latest design; leather bound.
Price........(Postage extra, 8c)......**$1.32**

No. 12F6018 This Music Roll is made of genuine walrus seal, double stitched strap and leather covered buckle, double stitched handle, leather bound and stitched all around; grosgrain moire lining, beautiful shades, and it has an inside flap to hold music. A fine music roll and well finished. Size, 14¾x15 inches.
Price........**$2.15**
If by mail, postage extra, 6 cents.

No. 12F6021 This Music Bag is made of a new waterproof material known as Yohese, manufactured by the Japanese by a secret process, and is a perfect imitation of genuine leather. It is pressed to imitate woven basket work, has black straps, nickel plated buckle and is lined with fancy material. It opens flat and takes a full size sheet of music, which is held in place by two flaps of special design. It is bound and stitched and is the very latest article in music bags. It comes in black only. Price........**57c**
If by mail, postage extra, 12 cents.

No. 12F6022 This Music Bag is made of solid leather, is a fine imitation of walrus skin and is lined with black silk mohair. The shape is entirely original and serves the double purpose of a music bag and a shopping bag, as it has an extra pocket in which can be carried a pocketbook, handkerchief, etc. It will take a full size sheet of music which is held in place by two flaps of special design, has a handle made of steel, covered with leather and fitted with nickel plated trimmings. It is a very pretty bag in every respect, durably made and very artistic. It is bound and stitched and comes in black only. Price........**$1.87**
If by mail, postage extra, 16 cents.

No. 12F6026 This Music Case and Bag is made of a waterproof and indestructible material in imitation of beautiful walrus grained leather, heavy stitched handle, bound and stitched all around, closes with fine steel catch. So arranged as to be used for a bag or case. Comes in two colors, black or maroon. Size, open, 24½x27½ in. Size as a case, 1½x11½x14½ in. Size as a bag, 1½x6x14½ in. Price.....$1.15
State color desired when ordering.

Imitation Alligator Music Bag.

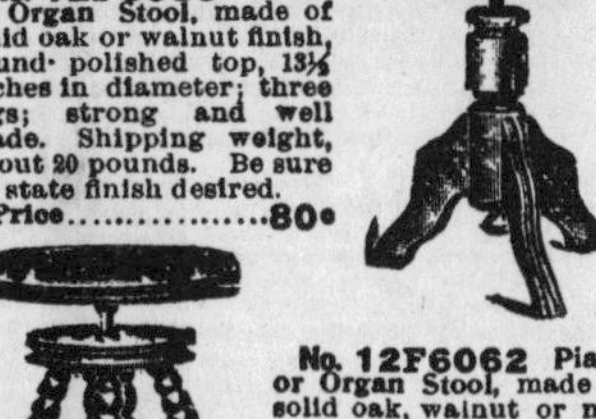

No. 12F6027 Music Bag. Perfect imitation alligator, 15 inches wide, 12 inches high. Will hold full size sheet music without folding or rolling. Has strong strap handles, reaching entirely around the bag, which adds greatly to its strength and durability. Price.....$1.15
If by mail, postage extra, 34 cents.

Piano and Organ Stools.

No. 12F6059 Piano or Organ Stool, made of solid oak or walnut finish, round polished top, 13½ inches in diameter; three legs; strong and well made. Shipping weight, about 20 pounds. Be sure to state finish desired.
Price.....80c

No. 12F6062 Piano or Organ Stool, made of solid oak, walnut or mahogany finish, round polished top, 12½ inches in diameter; three legs; very strong. Shipping weight, about 15 pounds. Be sure to state finish desired. Price.....$1.05

Special Value at $1.45.

No. 12F6068 Piano or Organ Stool, made of solid oak or in ebony, walnut, mahogany, rosewood, burl walnut or Circassian walnut finish, nicely polished round top, 13½ inches in diameter; three legs, with brass feet and glass balls. Shipping weight, about 25 pounds. Be sure to state finish desired.
Price.... $1.45

No. 12F6070 Same description as No. 12F6068, but with four legs. Price.....$1.65
Solid walnut. Price..... 2.65

The Best Piano Stool Made for the Money.

This stool is the most massive and substantially built piano stool we have ever been able to furnish. This stool is made of solid wood, has a 15-inch round polished top with shaped edges. The top is made of two pieces of wood glued together so that it becomes doubly strong. The base has a massive center post and four legs, handsomely fluted and turned, beautiful brass claw feet with glass balls. Only the best kiln dried hardwood lumber is used throughout, and only the best quality of screws, nuts and bolts enter into the construction of this stool. Weight, packed for shipment, 25 pounds.

No. 12F6071 Mahogany, rosewood, walnut or ebony finish. Be sure to state finish desired. Price.....$1.95
No. 12F6074 Solid oak. Price..... 2.15
No. 12F6076 Solid walnut. Price, 2.65

Upright Piano Scarfs.

No. 12F6081 Special Heavy Damask Scarf, in assorted colors and patterns, with extra heavy silk fringe, draped with draw cords in two places. Shipping weight, about 20 ounces.
Price.....$1.85

No. 12F6083 Fine Figured China Silk Scarf, in assorted colors and patterns, with heavy all silk fringe, draped with draw cords in two places. Shipping weight, 5 ounces.
Price.....$1.75

No. 12F6085 Special Fine Silk Damask Scarf, in assorted colors and patterns, with heavy silk fringe, draped with draw cords in two places. Shipping weight, about 15 ounces.
Price.....$2.55

No. 12F6087 Fine Velour Scarf, in assorted colors and patterns, with extra heavy silk fringe, draped with draw cords in two places. Shipping weight, 20 ounces. Price.....$1.65

No. 12F6089 Extra Fine Velour Scarf, in assorted colors and patterns, with extra heavy silk fringe, draped with draw cords in two places. Shipping weight, about 20 ounces.
Price.....$2.15

Latest Popular and Sentimental Songs.

Sheet Form Only. Order by Number and Title.

No. 12F6500 Order by this number and be sure to give name of song also.
Price, per dozen, $2.28; each.....19c
Postage extra, each, 2 cents; per dozen, 16 cents.
We Can Furnish All Popular Songs Not Herein Listed at 23c each and 2c for postage.
WE DO NOT EXCHANGE SHEET MUSIC.

Absence Makes the Heart Grow Fonder......
Always in The Way......
Break the News to Mother.....Chas. K. Harris
Come and Share Your Love With Me.....
.....Jeff T. Branen and Leo Friedman
Come Down, Miss Malinda.....
.....T. J. Faron, Jr., and Jas. M. Hollander
Dearie.....
Down in the Vale of Shenandoah.....
Down Where the Silvery Mohawk Flows.....
Farewell, Sweetheart May.....
For Sale—A Baby.....
Hello, Central.....Harris
I Live Alone For You, J.T. Branen and S. Keene
I Want to be a Soldier.....
If I Could Send This Letter C. O. D.....
.....T. J. Faron, Jr., and Wallace Smith
I'll Be There, Mary Dear.....H. Von Tilzer
I'm Trying so Hard to Forget You.....
I'm Wearing My Heart Away For You.....
In the Golden Autumn Time My Sweetheart Elaine.....
In the House of Too Much Trouble.....
.....Heeland and Helf
In the Valley of Rest.....
In the Valley That the Sunshine Never Leaves
It Wasn't a Real One, J.T. Branen & H.S. Sawyer
Just a Bunch of Wild Flowers..Branen & Ryan
Just As the Sun Went Down.....Udal
Little Girl, You'll Do.....
Mansion of Aching Hearts.....H. Von Tilzer
'Mid the Green Fields of Virginia..C. K. Harris
My Lady Bird..Jeff T. Branen and Evans Lloyd
My Little Georgia Rose.....Max S. Witt
My Old New Hampshire Home..Harry Von Tilzer
My Sunburnt Babe.....Branen and Smith
No One But You.....Horwitz & Bowers
On a Sunday Afternoon.....H. Von Tilzer
Peggy Brady.....
Rosita.....
Sing Me a Song of the South....Martin & Casey
Stay in Your Own Back Yard.....
Sweet Bunch of Daisies.....A. Owen
Sweet Maid of the Sunset Sea.....
.....Louis A. Ripley and Jas. M. Hollander
Swing on Your Own Apple Tree, Newton & Keene
The Little Rustic Cottage by the Stream
.....Heinzman
The Letter Edged in Black.....Hattie Nevada
The Maiden with the Dreamy Eyes....Johnson
The Old Postmaster.....Stern
The Song My Sweetheart Used to Sing.....
.....Jeff T. Branen and Fulton
The Spider and the Fly.....Von Tilzer
The Star and the Flower.....A. Hubbel
Tildy.....T. J. Faron, Jr., and Jas. M. Hollander
Upon a Sunday When the Church Bells Chime.....Rosenfeld & Solman
Welcome.....
When the Harvest Moon is Shining on the River
When the Sunset Turns the Ocean's Blue to Gold.....Petrie
When It's All Goin' Out and Nothing Comin' In (Coon).....Williams and Walker
When Kate and I Were Coming Through the Rye.....H. Von Tilzer
When the Frost is on the Flower.....
.....Jeff T. Branen and George H. Bramhall
When the Harvest Days Are Over...Von Tilzer
When the Fields Are White With Cotton
.....Roden and Witt
When the Convent Bells Were Ringing.....
.....Roden and Witt
Why Don't They Play With Me?.....
Would You Care?.....
You are as Welcome as the Flowers in May
.....Sullivan

No. 12F6554 Recital Folio. A new collection of 24 choice songs by favorite composers including George Rosey, John Stromburg, S. R. Henry, Richard Stahl, Harry Von Tilzer and many others. This folio is filled from cover to cover with the very finest kind of vocal music and will prove a valuable addition to the singer's library. Price.....30c
If by mail, postage extra, 6 cents.

No. 12F6560 The Cole & Johnson Dance Folio. A superior collection of quaint and classic negro songs by the famous writers, Cole & Johnson Bros. This superb collection contains the very best negro songs which have been written in the last ten years. It is in every way superior and all of the accompaniments are splendidly arranged.
Price...(If by mail, postage extra, 8c)...30c

No. 12F6570 Little Songs for Little Folks. This is a beautiful collection of catchy child songs arranged especially for children's voices. Each piece is nicely arranged so that the music in each case is exactly suited to the words. The following are some of the numbers: Good Morning Song, The Woolly Dog, The Cows and the Pigs, The Dog and the Cat, The Doctor, The Boo-La, Boo-La, The Fishes, May Day Song, Master Jack Frost and many others equally as good.
Price...(If by mail, postage extra, 8c)...30c

Good Old Songs Folio.

No. 12F6580 We guarantee every piece in this Folio to be the ORIGINAL and complete in every way. Please read carefully the contents: Alice, Where Art Thou, Comin' Thru the Rye, Annie Laurie, Ave Maria, Come Back to Erin, The Song I Love Best, Good-by, Sweetheart, Good-by, In Old Madrid, Little Annie Rooney, Nearer, My God to Thee, Juanita, Kitty Tyrrell, O, Ye Tears! O, Ye Tears! and many others as good. Price..20c
If by mail, postage extra, 8 cents.

No. 12F6590 Musical Chatterbox, No. 2. Contains both vocal and instrumental music. Every piece a popular favorite; choice, easy and medium piano pieces; beautiful songs for the young folks; just the collection for home; it contains, besides the music, eight beautiful illustrations.
Price.....25c
If by mail, postage extra, 8c.

No. 12F6601 The Crest Collection of Popular Songs, the latest and best vocal folio published, containing the following popular songs: My Gal's a High Born Lady, Picture Turned to the Wall, God Save America, Pumpkin Pies Mother Used to Make, and 28 others, any one of which retails at 50 cents per copy.
Price.....23c
If by mail, postage extra, 12 cents.

No. 12F6603 Crest Collection, No. 2. Contains latest and more up to date pieces, such as: Always, Because, Her Memory Brings Me No Regret, and 41 selections equally as good.
Price......(Postage extra, 8 cents)....23c

No. 12F6604 Palace Folio. One of the best collections of popular and standard songs published. Contains 31 songs with chorus, 12 solos arranged for different voices, 1 duet, 1 quartette, also the famous bass song "A Hundred Fathoms Deep." This folio should be in every music library.
Price.....30c
If by mail, postage extra, 8 cents.

No. 12F6606 Song Casket, a valuable collection of choice vocal music by well known authors. Contains ballads, songs with choruses, duets, quartettes, home songs, Scotch songs, etc., with piano or organ accompaniments.
Price.....30c
If by mail, postage extra, 12 cents.

No. 12F6607 Song Offering. This is a fine collection of vocal music of the highest order of merit and is printed from fine plates on heavy paper and bound with handsome cover. It contains such pieces as: Beautiful Girl of the North, Bird, Tell Winnie I Am Waiting, Eva Darling, A Good Time Coming, and a large number of others of the same high order of merit. Price.....30c
If by mail, postage extra, 12 cents.

No. 12F6608 Golden Folio. A special collection of well known vocal and instrumental selections. This folio contains a number of selected vocal duets and songs with chorus arranged for mixed voices.
Price.....30c
If by mail, postage extra, 8 cents.

No. 12F6609 Silver Folio. Companion to Golden Folio. Contains same class of music but entirely different selections. 12 vocal solos, 6 songs with chorus for mixed voices, waltzes, marches, schottisches, etc. 144 pages of good, soul reaching music.
Price.....30c
If by mail, postage extra, 8 cents.

No. 12F6615 Rag Time Folio, No. 2. A splendid collection of the latest and best negro melodies of the day by favorite composers, including My Hannah Lady, Pliny, Come Kiss Your Baby, and 20 others as good.
Price.....45c
If by mail, postage extra, 8 cents.

No. 12F6620 Sacred Songs Worth Singing. A collection of carefully selected songs which will surely please. Contains the following: Ave Maria, Mascagni; In Him Confiding; Jerusalem; Praise the Lord; The Golden Pathway; Thou Art My Guide; Come Unto Me, and twenty others as good. Publisher's price, 50c.
Our price.....30c
If by mail, postage extra, 8 cents.

No. 12F6622 Portfolio of Sacred Songs. A very fine collection of sacred selections suitable for home or church. The names of the composers are a guarantee of their excellence. Chas. Gounod, J. Faure, O. King, etc. Most of the pieces herein contained are copyrighted and are not to be found in any other similar collection.
Price.....30c
If by mail, postage extra, 8 cents.

No. 12F6624 Choice Songs for High Voice, No. 2. As ideal a collection as any singer could possibly desire, each song having been selected on its merits. Singers looking for a collection of high class songs by well known composers will be highly pleased with this book.
Price.....30c
If by mail, postage extra, 8 cents.

No. 12F6626 Choice Songs for Low Voices, No. 2. In this collection singers will find just that variety and beauty of sentiment and melody which combine to make such a book a success. Each and every song is an assured favorite.
Price.....30c
If by mail, postage extra, 8c.

VOCAL DUETS.

No. 12F6636 Brainard's Vocal Duet Folio. A collection of choice popular vocal duets. Printed from fine plates on heavy paper and securely bound. A very choice collection. 100 pages.
Price.....25c
If by mail, postage extra, 6c.

PATRIOTIC SONG BOOKS.

No. 12F6640 Songs of the Flag and Nation. No folio is more necessary on the piano rack of the patriotic American than patriotic songs and melodies. This folio is the most complete published, containing not only the standard patriotic songs, such as America and Star Spangled Banner, but a number of new choice songs also.
Publisher's price, 50c. Our price.....35c
If by mail, postage extra, 8 cents.

GRAND ARMY SONGS.

No. 12F6641 A valuable collection of war and camp songs, to which is added a selection of memorial songs and hymns for Decoration Day, etc.; choruses all arranged for male voices, organ or piano accompaniment; 100 pages; heavy paper covers. Price.....40c
If by mail, postage extra, 5 cents.

No. 12F6642 Songs of Dixie, a collection of camp, marching and plantation songs by favorite authors. Among the selections are Dixie Land, My Old Kentucky Home, Maryland, My Maryland, Our Flag, and 40 others. The book contains 71 pages, printed on fine paper, handsomely bound with linen back. Price.....38c
If by mail, postage extra, 4 cents.

QUARTETTE BOOKS.

No. 12F6643 The Pan-Collegiate Collection of Songs. This is a book of songs, quartettes, etc., and is something new in its line. The selections comprise some of the latest popular songs, comic and sentimental, and are just the thing for glee clubs, colleges, etc. It is also a jolly book to have at home and will make fun anywhere; 132 pages with handsome colored cover. Price.....23c
If by mail, postage extra, 8 cents.

No. 12F6645 Chas. Shattuck's Beautiful Male Quartette Arrangement of Chas. K. Harris' popular publications. No. 2, in book form, 32 pages. Price.....35c
If by mail, postage extra, 4c.

No. 12F6647 The Glee Club Quartette Folio. This is the finest collection of male quartettes yet issued, suitable for all occasions and arranged by the well known musician, C. F. Shattuck. We offer this folio at the low price of 30c
If by mail, postage extra 6c.

NEW SONGS FOR MALE QUARTETTES.

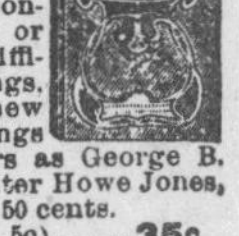

No. 12F6650 This little folio has just filled an empty niche in musical literature, where it was needed, because everyone connected with a male quartette or singing club appreciates the difficulty of getting really good songs, and has welcomed gladly this new book. It contains about 32 songs by such well known composers as George B. Nevin, Henry K. Hadley, Walter Howe Jones, and others. Publisher's price, 50 cents.
Our price....(Postage extra, 5c).......35c

COLLEGE SONGS.

No. 12F6657 The Most Popular College Songs. This is the best folio of old and familiar college songs published, for it contains not only such dear old favorites as Aunt Dinah's Quilting Party, Forsaken, Old Oaken Bucket, Jingle Bells, but also a great many new songs, which will be sure to please. Publisher's price 50 cents. Our price.....35c
If by mail, postage extra, 5 cents.

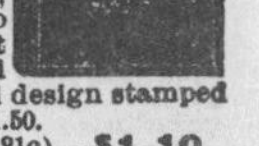

No. 12F6660 Songs of All the Colleges. If you or any of your family have attended college or any of your friends are college bred, this book will certainly have its interest for you, because it contains not only the songs which are familiar to all, but also the special ones dear to the students in every prominent university. It is strongly bound in durable cloth with a beautiful design stamped on cover. Publisher's price, $1.50.
Our price....(Postage extra, 21c)...$1.10

CHILD SONGS.

No. 12F6662 100 new Kindergarten Songs. This is the daintiest children's song book you could ask for, containing a hundred pretty little songs with melodies within the range of the little ones' voices, and with just the cutest verses which could be devised to interest the little ones. Bound in cloth. Publisher's price, $1.00. Our price........75c
If by mail, postage extra, 11 cents.

MINSTREL SONGS.

No. 12F6672 The Jolly Songster. A fine collection of 200 pieces, including comic and patriotic songs, popular ballads and favorite negro melodies. Paper cover. Price........20c
If by mail, postage extra, 5 cents.

No. 12F6678 Album of Comic Songs. This is a splendid collection of laughable songs of the highest order of merit. It contains such pieces as follows: It Tickled Me So, I Liked to Die, Johnny Morgan, Smart Young Men of Town, The Dutchman's Lament, So Nearsighted, and many others as good. Printed from fine plates on a good quality of paper bound in paper covers. Price........20c
If by mail, postage extra, 6 cents.

No. 12F6680 They're After Me; Folio of Funny Songs for the Whole World. A new collection of the very latest comic songs by the most popular song writers of every nation; very funny; 128 pages. Price........30c
If by mail, postage extra, 8c.

No. 12F6684 Old and New Popular Comic Songs. 39 of the best known and most popular comic songs. Price........30c
If by mail, postage extra, 8 cents.

No. 12F6688 Mirthful Album of Comic Songs. Containing comic, negro, Dutch, coster and Irish songs. Also a great number of comicalities by the best known comic writers of the day that have never before been published in book form. A handsome folio of 160 pages printed on fine paper and beautifully bound. Price........30c
If by mail, postage extra, 8 cents.

GOSPEL HYMNS.

Board Covers.

No. 12F6690 Consolidated, Nos. 1, 2, 3 and 4. Large type, words and music; 400 pages. Price........67c
If by mail, postage extra, 10c.

No. 12F6694 Words only. Nos. 1, 2, 3 and 4. Price....17c
If by mail, postage extra, 4c.

No. 12F6696 Gospel Hymns. No. 5, with words and music. Price........27c
If by mail, postage extra, 6 cents.

No. 12F6700 No. 6. Price........25c
If by mail, postage extra, 6 cents.

No. 12F6701 No. 6. Christian Endeavor Edition. Price........29c
If by mail, postage extra, 6 cents.

No. 12F6704 Nos. 5 and 6, combined. Price........55c
If by mail, postage extra, 8 cents.

No. 12F6706 Nos. 5 and 6. Words only. Price........18c
If by mail, postage extra, 4 cents.

No. 12F6707 Nos. 1 to 6. Complete with words and music in one volume. Bound in cloth. Price........86c
If by mail, postage extra, 20 cents.

No. 12F6709 Nos. 1 to 6. Words only, cloth cover. Price........17c
If by mail, postage extra, 3 cents.

INSTRUMENTAL FOLIOS FOR PIANO.

No. 12F6712 Easy Pieces for Young Players. The book is filled with bright sparkling music for young piano players and is so arranged as to be within easy reach of little fingers. All of the compositions are by Francois Behr and are in the composer's best style. The following are a few of the numbers: Shepherd Song, Spanish Dance, The Dawn of Spring, Pearly Dew Drops, Russian Gipsy Song, Night Song, and many others. Price......(Postage extra, 5 cents)........30c

No. 12F6714 Folio Leaves. This is a splendid collection of instrumental music for the organ or piano and every piece in it is of the very highest order of merit. It contains such selections as Christmas Bells, Clear the Track Galop, Dress Parade Polka, Florence Schottische, Idlewild Waltz, and many others of the best composers. It is plainly printed on heavy paper and bound with a handsome paper cover. Price......(Postage extra, 12 cents)........30c

No. 12F6715 Whitney's Easy Piano Folio. Very fine and desirable collection of easy piano pieces, especially adapted for beginners. Nothing hard to finger or read. Waltzes, marches and everything herein contained arranged in a very easy and progressive manner. Publisher's price, 50 cents.

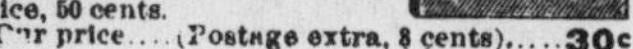

Our price....(Postage extra, 8 cents).....30c

No. 12F6718 This book contains new music of all the popular round and square dances. Plain quadrille, prairie queen quadrille, lancers, waltz-quadrille, waltz-lancers, polka, galop, schottische, gavotte, two-steps, waltzes, marches and cake walks. Price........30c
If by mail, postage extra, 8c.

No. 12F6721 Musical Friends. A choice collection of piano duets, consisting of marches, waltzes, polkas, schottisches, mazurkas, galops and popular pieces by favorite authors. Price........25c
If by mail, postage extra, 8c.

No. 12F6728 Sacred Pianoforte Album. Contains 22 beautiful selections, among which are: Angelic Hands Shall Guide Thee, Ave Maria, Dews of Heaven, Jesus, Lover of My Soul, Monastery Bells, Song of Heaven, The Palms, and other sacred compositions to suit the taste of anyone who does not care to play light, frivolous music, especially on the Sabbath. Price.......(Postage extra, 8 cents).......30c

No. 12F6730 Pretty and Easy Piano Solos. This folio is filled with brilliant and catchy music arranged in a tasty and easy manner for the piano. It is intended for players who have not made much progress on the piano but will be acceptable to those who have acquired more skill. The following are some of the numbers: Pretty Pink Primrose, On the Wave, Puss in Boots, Star Beam Waltz, Good Night, Gentle Rain Mazurka, Bohemian Girl, Song Without Words, and many others equally as pretty. Price........30c
If by mail, postage extra, 5 cents.

No. 12F6732 Whitney's Folio Gems. A choice selection of recent compositions, including marches, waltzes, polkas, schottisches, etc. by popular composers; 150 pages, sheet music size. Price........30c
If by mail, postage extra, 10 cents.

No. 12F6740 The Witmark Dance Folio, No. 1. This is a new folio, containing the hits of the day, such as waltzes, marches, schottisches, polkas, waltz-quadrilles, three steps, etc. Arranged for dance, and compiled from the latest popular songs. The finest book of its kind published. Price........23c
If by mail, postage extra, 10 cents.

No. 12F6741 Witmark Dance Folio, No. 2. A later edition than Folio No. 1. Contains, When You Were Sweet Sixteen, My Wild Irish Rose, Sing Me a Song of the South, Pullman Porters' Ball, My Blushing Rose, Stay in Your Own Back Yard, Little Sallie Brown, and thirteen more equally good pieces arranged as waltzes, marches, two steps, schottisches, and lancers. Price..(Postage extra, 10 cents)..25c

No. 12F6743 The Smart Set Dance Album. This is a collection of the very latest selections by some of the most famous writers of the present day. Among other things it contains Marie Cahill's Congo Love Song, On Lalawana's Shores, The Banana Man, I Want to Be a Soldier, When the Harvest Moon is Shining on the River, and many others. One of the best collections yet issued. Price........20c
If by mail, postage extra, 4 cents.

No. 12F6746 Pastime Dance Album. Containing twenty popular songs and instrumental hits arranged as waltzes, two steps, schottisches, polkas, marches, lancers, etc. This book includes Phrenologist Coon, The Maiden with the Dreamy Eyes, Hi-le Hi-lo, The old Postmaster, The Harlem Rag. Any one of these selections would be worth the price of the entire book. Publisher's price, 75 cents. Our price....(Postage extra, 6c)..18c

No. 12F6752 Golden Hours. A fine collection of popular piano music, consisting of a large variety of marches and miscellaneous dance music, four-hand pieces, etc., forming a select library of elegant music. 224 pages. Price........25c
Postage extra, 12c.

No. 12F6754 Folio of Pearls. A valuable collection of standard selections for the piano, dance music and easy teaching pieces. A folio that always pleases. Price........30c
By mail, postage extra, 8c.

No. 12F6761 The Golden Chord. A choice collection of favorite and modern pianoforte music. Gems for the home circle. 225 pages. The best folio published. Price........25c
By mail, postage extra, 10c.

No. 12F6769 A Collection of Easy Pieces for the Piano. By Streabog & Lichner. The best known composers of selections suitable for beginners. A folio of 119 pages, beautifully bound. Price........30c
If by mail, postage extra, 8 cents.

No. 12F6770 Easy to Play, No. 2. Another splendid collection of compositions, easily arranged. The selections in this volume are by Spindler & Behr, the celebrated composers of sparkling and interesting teaching pieces. Price....(Postage extra, 8c)....30c

No. 12F6771 Easy to Play, No. 3. In this superb collection, Lichner, Streabog, Spindler & Behr have demonstrated their skill as composers. The pieces herein contained do not only serve the best purpose of instruction, but also offer the most pleasing musical recreation. Price........30c
If by mail, postage extra, 8 cents.

No. 12F6776 Braintree's Ragtime Collection, characteristic marches, two steps, cake walks, plantation dances, etc. Price.......45c
If by mail, postage extra, 8 cents.

No. 12F6774 Pretty and Easy Piano Duets. This is one of the nicest collections of four-hand piano music yet placed on the market. Every piece is tastefully and skillfully arranged, and the technical difficulties removed. The following are some of the numbers: Dancing Flowers, The First Ball, Moss Rose Waltz, Return of the Heroes March, Two Students Polka, Waves of the Ocean, and many others. Price........30c
If by mail, postage extra, 8 cents.

No. 12F6775 Young Students' Four-hand Collections. This is another collection of very pretty four-hand pieces for the piano and will be welcomed by piano teachers and pupils as well. Each piece is arranged so as to be within easy reach of even the youngest players. The following are some of the numbers: Bloom and Blossom Waltz, Dashing Steed Galop, March of the Brave, Basket of Roses, Golden Rod March, and many others equally as good. Price........30c
If by mail, postage extra, 8 cents.

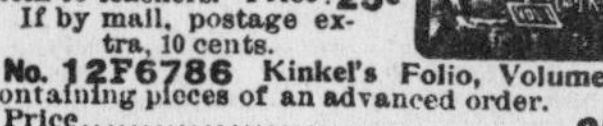

INSTRUMENTAL FOLIOS FOR PIANO AND CABINET ORGAN.

No. 12F6784 Kinkel's Folio, Volume 1. A rare collection of bright instrumental gems for young players, arranged for piano and organ. No better books for pupils can be obtained, and we especially recommend them to teachers. Price........25c
If by mail, postage extra, 10 cents.

No. 12F6786 Kinkel's Folio, Volume 2. Containing pieces of an advanced order. Price........25c
If by mail, postage extra, 10 cents.

No. 12F6796 Brainard's Collection of Marches. Suitable for use in schools and for all occasions. A book of 116 pages, printed on good paper, and handsomely bound with linen back. Any piece contained in this book if bought in sheet form would cost as much as we ask for the entire book. Price........28c
If by mail, postage extra, 8 cents.

No. 12F6800 Marches. Selected from the works of celebrated composers for pianoforte or organ; regular sheet music size. A large folio of the very best selections; 160 pages. Price........30c
If by mail, postage extra, 9 cents.

MUSIC FOR CABINET ORGANS.

No. 12F6806 Ideal Reed Organ Gems, No. 1. A collection of original compositions and arrangements for the reed or cabinet organ. A splendid folio and especially adapted to the needs of beginners. 69 pages of choice music. Price........30c
If by mail, postage extra, 8 cents.

No. 12F6807 Ideal Reed Organ Gems, No. 2. A splendid collection of sacred, popular and operatic selections, especially arranged for the cabinet organ. Like volume No. 1, sure to please. Price........30c
If by mail, postage extra, 8 cents.

No. 12F6808 Reed Organ Folio. A new collection of the best and most popular music of the day, arranged especially for the five-octave organ. Over 60 pieces, full sheet music size; paper cover. Price........25c
If by mail, postage extra, 10c.

No. 12F6810 Reed Organ at Home. A collection of reed organ music, containing favorite melodies and a variety of dance music, operatic music, etc.; 128 pages. Price........25c
If by mail, postage extra, 5c.

No. 12F6812 Whitney's Organ Folio, No. 1. A collection of standard and popular music, arranged as solos for the organ. Especially adapted for home music. Publishers' price, 50 cents. Our price........30c
If by mail, postage extra, 8 cents.

FOLIOS FOR VIOLIN AND PIANO.

No. 12F6820 Popular Duets for Violin and Piano, No. 1. This is a new collection of the very latest music, including Love's Dreamland Waltzes, Mendelssohn's Wedding March, Hornpipe Polka, etc., 24 pieces; every piece a gem; 122 pages, full sheet music size; paper cover. Price........28c
If by mail, postage extra, 10 cents.

No. 12F6822 Popular Duets for Violin and Piano, No. 2. This collection is in every way as fine as the one described above and contains many fine pieces of music of a much later date. It is in fact filled with all the latest popular music, full sheet music size and contains 128 pages. Price........28c
If by mail, postage extra, 10 cents.

No. 12F6824 Drawing Room Collection for the Violin and Piano. This book contains 121 pages of the best violin music by the most celebrated composers, and is a most desirable book for violin players. The pieces are arranged especially for beginners and amateurs. Price........30c
If by mail, postage extra, 10 cents.

No. 12F6835 The Witmark Violin and Piano Folio, No. 5. Every violinist should have this book. The best and most popular music published is contained therein. Pretty Mollie Shannon, Stay in Your Own Back Yard, I Want a Ping Pong Man, Two steps and twenty other selections of equal beauty. No piece in this book duplicated in any other folio. The greatest value ever offered. Price........23c
If by mail, postage extra, 6 cents.

No. 12F6837 Popular Selections for Mandolin and Piano. This book is filled with 128 pages of the very finest kind of music tastefully arranged for mandolin and piano. The selections are not too difficult and each number is a gem. The following are some of the numbers: Mexican Butterfly Dance, Maritana Selection, Love's Dream After Fall, The Palms, Traumerei, Intermezzo from Cavaleria Rusticana, Schubert's Serenade, Bridal Chorus from Lohengrin and many others. Price.....30c
If by mail, postage extra, 8 cents.

FOLIOS FOR VIOLIN.

No. 12F6838 The Young Violinist's Favorite, No. 1. A collection of popular music for the violin, including overtures, quadrilles and a wide selection of dance music; 50 pages. Price........25c
If by mail, postage extra, 4c.

No. 12F6840 The Young Violinist's Friend, No. 2. An entirely different edition from Folio No. 1 above, containing no duplicates. Contains 50 pages. Price........25c
If by mail, postage extra, 4 cents.

No. 12F6841 The Young Violinist's Gigantic Collection of standard and popular music. 350 pieces of the best music arranged in an easy manner, all in the first position. A valuable book to either beginner or experienced player, and the selections are so varied that it cannot fail to please and last a long time. Price........25c
If by mail, postage extra, 23 cents.

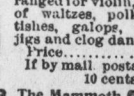

No. 12F6842 Musicians' omnibus. A book containing 1,500 pieces arranged for violin, consisting of waltzes, polkas, schottishes, galops, quadrilles, jigs and clog dances, etc. Price........68c
If by mail, postage extra, 10 cents.

No. 12F6843 The Mammoth Collection for the Violin. A companion book to the Gigantic Collection. Contains over 350 selections from the operas, dances and the latest and best music published, arranged by the best composers in an artistic manner. Price....25c
If by mail, postage extra, 25 cents.

No. 12F6846 Evening Pastime. A collection of 88 popular waltzes, polkas, marches, quadrilles, also selections from favorite operas arranged in an easy and pleasing manner for the violin alone, by John Philip Sousa. Price.......(Postage extra, 4c)........55c

No. 12F6848 Old and new Favorites for Violin. This is just what its name signifies and is a splendid collection of favorite music for the violin, both old and new. There is not a poor selection in the entire collection, and it is just the thing for violinists who do lots of miscellaneous playing. It contains over 150 pages of dance and operatic music and is bound up in the most handy form for convenient use. Price........16c
If by mail, postage extra, 5 cents.

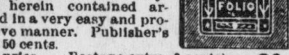

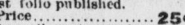

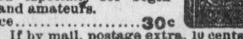

No. 12F6849 20th Century Violinist's Library. A magnificent collection of popular violin solos. A complete library of all the very best music for this popular instrument. Violinists possessing this book will never be at a loss for music to play on all occasions. It contains over 150 pages of high grade violin music. Price..........16c
If by mail, postage extra, 5 cents.

GUITAR FOLIOS.

No. 12F6854 Collegiate Guitar Folio. This folio contains eight first class songs arranged for voice and guitar and four very fine selections as guitar solos. Among others are the following: When the Sunset Turns the Ocean Blue to Gold, You're as Welcome as the Flowers in May, Big Indian Chief, Egypt, The Goo-goo Man, Peggy Brady and many others. Price..........20c
If by mail, postage extra, 3 cents.

The Witmark Folios for Guitar are filled from cover to cover with the finest kind of music and contain the latest and most popular selections for this instrument. None of the selections will be found duplicated in any two of the following numbers, and the folios are all handsomely and durably bound. The music is all printed from fine plates.

No. 12F6855 The Witmark Guitar Folio No. 1. A folio of vocal and instrumental music, containing All Coons Look Alike to Me, My Gal is a High Born Lady and 26 others just as good; 72 pages, printed on fine music paper and bound in a heavy lithographed cover. Price..........23c
If by mail, postage extra, 5 cents.

No. 12F6856 The Witmark Guitar Folio No. 2. Price..........23c
If by mail, postage extra, 5 cents.

No. 12F6857 The Witmark Guitar Folio No. 3. Price..........23c
If by mail, postage extra, 5 cents.

No. 12F6858 The Witmark Guitar Folio No. 4. Price..........23c
If by mail, postage extra, 5 cents.

No. 12F6859 The Witmark Guitar Folio No. 5. Price.....(Postage extra, 6c)......23c

BANJO FOLIOS.

No. 12F6866 Banjo Folio, by Brooks & Denton. This is a splendid banjo folio, filled with fine selections for that instrument and giving right along with the music an easy method of learning to play it. The following are some of the pieces: Congo Love Song, What is the Matter with the Moon Tonight, The Glow Worm and the Moth, The Colored Major and numerous others. Price..........30c
If by mail, postage extra, 10 cents.

The Witmark Banjo Folios are splendid collections of the latest popular music and each song is nicely arranged for banjo accompaniments. Each volume is handsomely bound and the music is printed from fine plates on heavy paper. No selection will be found duplicated in the different numbers.

No. 12F6874 The Witmark Banjo Folio No. 2. Price..........23c
If by mail, postage extra, 5 cents.

No. 12F6876 The Witmark Banjo Folio No. 3. Price..........23c
If by mail, postage extra, 5 cents.

No. 12F6878 The Witmark Banjo Folio No. 4. Price..........23c
If by mail, postage extra, 5 cents.

No. 12F6879 The Witmark Banjo Folio No. 5. Price..........23c
If by mail, postage extra, 6 cents.

MANDOLIN and GUITAR FOLIOS.

No. 12F6884 Mark Stern's Mandolin and Guitar Folio No. 4. A collection of popular successes, such as The Maiden with the Dreamy Eyes, While the Convent Bells are Ringing, and May Be. This book is arranged in very nice and easy form so that anybody can play the contents with good effect. This book is arranged for first and second mandolin and guitar and piano. In separate books.
Price of each book..........20c
If by mail, postage extra, 3 cents.

No. 12F6884½ Mark Stern's Mandolin and Guitar Folio No. 5. Contains a splendid collection of popular and operatic selections. Among the twenty-five successes we shall mention: Under the Bamboo Tree, No One But You, If You'll Be Mine, Hail to The Nation—March, Summer Moon—Gavotte. Published for first and second mandolin, guitar and piano in separate parts. Price, each book..........20c
If by mail, postage extra, 3 cents.

No. 12F6889 Brainard's Ragtime Collection for first and second mandolin, guitar and piano. The very latest collection of popular ragtime and characteristic selections, such as marches, cakewalks, two steps, plantation dances, etc. Price for each instrument..........20c
If by mail, postage extra, 3c.

No. 12F6894 The Witmark Mandolin and Guitar Folio No. 5. Just out. No mandolin club is complete without this book. Be up to date and play the latest music. It costs no more. This book contains 23 choice selections, among which are the following: Stay in Your Own Back Yard, It's for Her, Her, Her, Sweet Maggie May, I Left My Heart in Dixie. No piece in this book is found in any other mandolin and guitar folio. Price..........23c
If by mail, postage extra, 6 cents.

No. 12F6896 The George Rosey Standard Mandolin and Guitar Folio. Published in separate book form for mandolin solo, guitar accompaniment and piano accompaniment. The following are some of the pieces: Adoration Waltzes, The Anniversary March, Belles and Beaux, The Chinatown March, The Senegambian Patrol, The Scorcher, The Spirit of Liberty and many others.
Price..........20c
If by mail, postage extra, 4 cents.

CORNET AND PIANO DUETS.

No. 12F6902 Popular Duets for Cornet and Piano No. 1. A splendid collection of popular, sacred and operatic selections arranged in an easy, effective manner by the celebrated D. L. Ferrazzi. Price..........28c
If by mail, postage extra, 11 cents.

The Witmark Cornet and Piano Folios are splendid collections of the latest popular music arranged as duets for these two instruments. We can safely promise that the purchaser will be perfectly satisfied with every selection contained in any of these folios. They are all handsomely and durably bound and the music is printed from new plates on heavy paper.

No. 12F6903 The Witmark Cornet and Piano Duets No. 1. Price..........23c
If by mail, postage extra, 6 cents.

No. 12F6904 The Witmark Cornet and Piano Duets No. 2. Price..........23c
If by mail, postage extra, 6 cents.

No. 12F6905 The Witmark Cornet and Piano Duets No. 3. Price..........23c
If by mail, postage extra, 6 cents.

No. 12F6906 Par Excellence Cornet and Piano Selections. As light, interesting and brilliant solos, cornetists will find these selections all that can be desired. No cheap, raggy music, but all of the popular favorites.
Price..........30c
If by mail, postage extra, 8c

No. 12F6907 Cornet Players' Pastime. This is one of the most remarkable books of cornet solos ever issued. It contains 1,000 of the very best solos for B flat cornet. Printed very plainly on fine paper. Is strongly bound and contains 472 pages. It will be welcomed by every cornet player and is something very desirable in this line. Price..........25c
If by mail, postage extra, 23 cents.

TROMBONE AND PIANO FOLIOS.

No. 12F6908 The Witmark Trombone and Piano Folio No. 3. This is the only folio of its kind on the market containing all of the latest hits of the day. The following are a few of the twenty pieces contained in this book: Good Night, Beloved, Good Night, The Tale of a Sea Shell, Mosquito Parade. Price..........23c
If by mail, postage extra, 6 cents.

VIOLIN, CORNET AND PIANO.

No. 12F6909 Peerless Collection No. 1. Contains all the latest songs and instrumental successes of the day. The best compositions by George Rosey and Max Witt, such as First Violin Waltzes, Belle of Granada and 46 other selections, enrich this work. Published separately for either violin, cornet or piano.
Price, each book..........20c
If by mail, postage extra, 3 cents.

No. 12F6911 Peerless Collection No. 2. This is another fine collection of violin solos of the same series as No. 12F6909 filled with very fine popular music for the violin, as follows: Hail to the Nation, March; The Jolly Friars, Waltzes; Selections from the Jewel of Asia, Moonlight on the Mississippi, Oh, Didn't He Ramble, and many others as good. Price, each book..........20c
If by mail, postage extra, 3 cents.

No. 12F6914 Violin, Cornet and Piano Dance Folio by George Rosey. This folio contains 26 complete compositions by America's greatest instrumental music composer by including all of his world famous successes. All the pieces are suitably arranged for parlor or ballroom in the form of marches, schottisches, waltzes, lanciers, two-steps, cake walks, etc. Price, each book..........20c
If by mail, postage extra, 3 cents.

DANCE JOURNAL FOR BALL ROOM ORCHESTRAS.

No. 12F6916 Contra Dance Journal for Ball Room Orchestras. New and good. Thirty of the very best new and old jigs, reels and hornpipes. Arranged for first and second violin, cornet, clarinet, bass, flute, trombone and piano, alto and tuba. Every dance orchestra should have this journal. Best thing of the kind ever published.

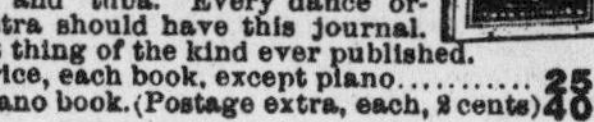

Price, each book, except piano..........25c
Piano book.(Postage extra, each, 2 cents)40c

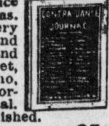

Gems of the Ball Room Series.

Each number contains thirty-two or thirty-three of the very latest and best pieces of the very latest music, all kinds, strictly up to date, arranged for orchestra of eight instruments, viz., first violin, second violin, cornet, clarinet, flute, trombone (treble clef), bass viol and piano. Each part separate.

No.		Each Orchestral Part	Each Piano Book
12F6918	Gems No. 1	36c	70c
12F6919	Gems No. 2	36c	70c
12F6920	Gems No. 3	36c	70c
12F6921	Gems No. 4	36c	70c
12F6922	Gems No. 5	36c	70c
12F6923	Gems No. 6	36c	70c
12F6924	Gems No. 7	36c	70c
12F6925	Gems No. 8	36c	70c
12F6926	Gems No. 9	36c	70c
12F6927	Gems No. 10	36c	70c

If by mail, postage extra, each, 3 cents.

In addition to the regular parts of the Gems of the Ball Room Series, we can furnish first and second mandolin and guitar parts for Nos. 9 and 10.

Beauties of the Ball Room Series.

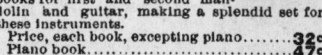

Choice selection of dance music, arranged for eight different orchestra instruments: First violin, second violin, cornet, flute, clarionet, trombone (treble clef), bass viol and piano. No duplicates to be found in any of the three numbers. No orchestra is complete without this series.

No.		Each Orchestral Part	Each Piano Book
12F6931	Beauties No. 1	36c	70c
12F6932	Beauties No. 2	36c	70c
12F6933	Beauties No. 3	36c	70c

If by mail, postage extra, per book, 3 cents.

No. 12F6942 Root's Beginner's Orchestra. A collection of easy overtures, waltzes, schottisches, etc., selected and arranged by the celebrated Professor D. S. McCosh. This is an exceptionally fine orchestral book, and is arranged for the following instruments: First violin, second violin, cornet, clarinet, bass and cello, flute, viola, trombone, first mandolin, second mandolin, guitar and piano.
Price, each book, excepting piano..........32c
Piano book..........47c
If by mail, postage extra, per book, 2 cents.

CONCERT AND PARLOR GEMS.

No. 12F6944 Concert and Parlor Gems. For concerts, entertainments and home amusements. Beautiful music. Easy, not over grade two. Particularly good for young orchestras. Books for first and second violin, cornet, clarionet, bass and cello, flute, viola, trombone and piano. Also books for first and second mandolin and guitar, making a splendid set for these instruments.
Price, each book, excepting piano..........32c
Piano book..........47c
If by mail, postage extra, per book, 2 cents.

No. 12F6945 The Wurlitzer Dance Album No. 1. A collection of choice dance music for the violin or mandolin. This is a very fine collection of popular dance music nicely arranged for the above instruments. Contains the following numbers: Imperial Grand March, Navy Blue Two-step, Bridal Rose Waltzes, Dancing in the Dew Schottische, and 19 others, arranged for 1st violin, 2nd violin, cello, bass, viola, 1st cornet, 2nd cornet, flute, clarionet, trombone, drums, piano.
Price, each book, excepting piano..........30c
Piano book..........45c
If by mail, postage extra, per book, 2 cents.

No. 12F6947 Root's Chicago Orchestra No. 1. An up to date collection of dance and concert music by well known authors. Contains 26 bright and catchy selections—waltzes, two-steps, cakewalks, mazurkas, etc., 32 pages of music. Published for 1st violin, 2nd violin, cornets, clarionets, bass and cello, flute, viola, trombones, drums, 1st mandolin, 2nd mandolin, guitar, piano.
Price of each book, except piano..........36c
Piano book..........70c
If by mail, postage extra, per book, 3 cents.

ORCHESTRA SELECTIONS.

No. 12F6948 Order by number and title. The best and newest popular pieces, arranged for full orchestra, 10 parts and piano. Price, each..........50c
If by mail, postage extra, 3 cents.

Alagazam (Characteristic Two Step)
All Hands 'Round (Lancers). Very easy..........J. Zimmerman
Anona Intermezzo (Two Step)
Because (Waltz)..........Mackie
Blaze Away (Two Step)..........Holtzman
Comedy King (March)
Creole Belles (Rag Time March)
Darktown is Out Tonight (Two Step). Intro.
Hottest Coon in Dixie. Arr. by..........R. Recker
Dearie (Waltz)
Down Where the Silvery Mohawk Flows (Waltz)
Dream of Heaven (Waltz)
Golden Echoes (Waltzes)
Hiawatha Intermezzo (Two Step)
Huckleberry Cross Roads (A Country Cake Walk)..........Robert Cone
Hunky Dory (Two Step)..........Holtzman
I Want a Real Coon (Cake Walk)..........Adler
I Want to be a Soldier (March)
Just as the Sun Went Down....Arr. by Mackie
Just One Girl (Waltz)..........Mackie
Love and Kisses (Caprice)
Ma Tiger Lily (Cake Walk)..........A. B. Sloane
March Medley—1863
Mexico (Two Step)
Mosquitoes Parade (Two Step)
My Mose Babe (Cake Walk)
On a Sunday Afternoon
Peter Piper (Two Step)
Polly Prim (Two Step)
Priscilla (Colonial Two Step)
Rambling Mose (Two Step)

ORCHESTRA SELECTIONS—Con.

The Gondolier (Two Step)
The Latest Fad (Three Step)..........Nat. D. Maine
The Steel King (March, Two Step)
The Tale of the Kangaroo (Polka)..........G. Luders
Tickled to Death (March)
Virginia Beauties (Two Step)
Voice of the Night (Waltz)
When the Harvest Moon, etc. (Waltz)
When the Sunset Turns the Ocean's Blue to Gold (Waltz)

MUSIC FOR MILITARY BANDS.

No. 12F6950 Order by number and title. The latest up to date selections of military band music, complete with 26 parts, but so arranged that they can be used for small or large bands. Price, each..........35c
If by mail, postage extra, 3 cents.

Alagazam (Characteristic Two Step)
Blaze Away (Two Step)..........Holtzman
Comedy King (March)
Creole Belle (Rag Time March)
Dearie (Waltz)
Egypt (Two Step)
Golden Echoes (Waltzes)
Hiawatha Intermezzo (Two Step)
Hunky Dory (Two Step)..........Holtzman
Just As the Sun Went Down (Waltz) Intro.
Nobody Wants Me Now. Arr. by W. H. Mackie
Just One Girl (Waltz) Arr. by..........W. H. Mackie
Love and Kisses (Caprice)
My Heart's Tonight in Tennessee (Cornet Solo, Band Accompaniment)
On a Sunday Afternoon
Peggy Brady (Two Step)
Peter Piper (Characteristic March)
Polly Prim
Rambling Mose (Two Step)
Sing Me a Song of the South (Waltz). Intro.
A Song That Would Last Evermore. Arr. by..........W. H. Mackie
The Mosquitoes' Parade. (March and Two Step)..........Howard Whitney
The Steel King (March, Two Step)
The Tale of the Kangaroo (Polka) Gustav Luders
Tickled to Death (March)
Voice of the Night (Waltz)
You Are as Welcome as the Flowers in May (Waltz)
When the Harvest Moon is Shining on the River (Cornet Solo)
When the Sunset Turns the Ocean's Blue to Gold (Cornet Solo)

ROOT'S BEGINNER'S BAND BOOK No. 1.

No. 12F6951 This book contains the natural and chromatic scales, progressive exercises and variety of easy but pleasing selections, such as two steps, waltzes, overtures, etc., also a dictionary of musical terms. Published for the following instruments: Piccolo, Eb clarionet, 1st Bb clarionet, 2nd Bb clarionet, solo Bb cornet, 1st Bb cornet, 2nd and 3rd cornet, Eb cornet, solo alto, altos, tenors, trombone, Bb bass tubas and drums. Price, ea. book, 12c
If by mail, postage extra, 2 cents.

No. 12F6952 Root's Beginner's Band Book No. 2, containing more advanced music than No. 1, with the same instrumentation.
Price, each book..........12c
If by mail, postage extra, 2 cents.

ROOT'S GEM BAND BOOK.

No. 12F6954 Root's Gem Band Book. This book contains sixteen easy and attractive pieces of medium grade, arranged for the following instruments: Piccolo, Eb clarionet, clarionets solo Bb cornet, 1st Bb cornet, 2d and 3d Bb cornets, Eb cornet, solo alto, 1st and 3d altos, tenors (treble), tenors (bass), baritone (treble), baritone (bass), Bb bass (treble), tubas, drums. Price, each book..........15c
If by mail, postage extra, per book, 2 cents.

PIANO INSTRUCTION BOOKS.

No. 12F6955 Brainard's New Easy Method for Piano. Containing complete and thorough instructions; also a choice selection of vocal and instrumental music. Regular retail price, $1.00.
Our price..........40c
Postage extra, 8 cents.

No. 12F6958 Root's New Musical Curriculum for Pianoforte Playing, Singing and Harmony. Bound in board. Publishers' price, $3.00.
Our price..........$1.95
If by mail, postage extra, 28 cents.

No. 12F6959 Whitney's Rapid Method for the Pianoforte. A thorough, progressive course of lessons presented in an easy and attractive form; with illustrations showing proper position of the hands and fingers on the keyboard. Also contains a great variety of instrumental pieces by distinguished authors. Bound in board. Regular retail price, $2.00. Our price..........80c
If by mail, postage extra, 20 cents.

THE RAPID PIANO INSTRUCTOR.

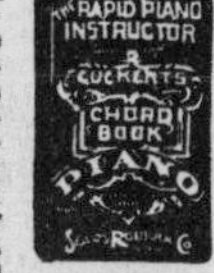

No. 12F6961 Chord Book for Piano. This book was especially compiled for us by the celebrated instructor and composer, E. H. Guckert. It contains illustrations of the piano keyboard showing the fingers to be used in each chord, besides many other valuable illustrations and instructions for the beginner or advanced pupil. This book will teach anyone how to play chords and accompaniments without the aid of a teacher. Price..........$1.00
If by mail, postage extra, 12 cents.

The Witmark Progressive Method for the Piano.

A distinctly modern book, especially desirable, as it contains a series of up to date instructive compositions instead of the old fashioned studies. It is arranged in a melodious form, making it more interesting for the pupil—a book of exceptional merit, as it starts at the first rudiments and instructs by easy stages.

No. 12F6966 Board cover. Price....80c

No. 12F6967 Paper cover. Price....65c

If by mail, postage extra, boards, 12c.; paper, 10c.

ORGAN INSTRUCTION BOOKS.

No. 12F6968 Chord Book for Organ. This book was especially compiled for us by E. N. Guckert, the celebrated instructor and composer. It contains 24 illustrations of the keyboard of the organ, showing the fingers used in each chord, besides other valuable instructions for the beginner or advanced pupil. This book will teach anyone how to play chords and accompaniments without the aid of a teacher. Price..(Postage extra, 16c.)..$1.00

No. 12F6982 White's School for the Reed Organ. One of the best methods ever offered. Contains a full and comprehensive method of instruction, also scales, studies, exercises, voluntaries, songs, marches, waltzes, polkas, opera melodies, hymns, tunes, etc., arranged expressly for the reed organ, melodeon or harmonium, by C. A. White and Charles C. Blake. Contains 152 pages. Bound in board. Price.......65c

If by mail, postage extra, 12 cents.

No. 12F6984 Karl Merz's Improved and Modern Method for the Parlor Organ. Contains complete elementary department, exercises in all keys, hints to pupils and teachers, voluntaries, preludes, popular airs and beautiful songs, to which is added a complete course of thorough bass instruction. This book retails at $2.00.

Our price.......(Postage extra, 18c.)....55c

Easy Method for the Parlor Organ.

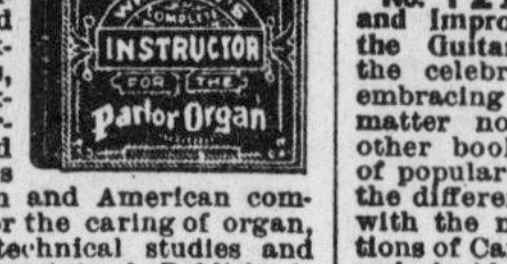

No. 12F6988 Whitney's Improved Easy Method for the Parlor Organ. New and enlarged edition. This is a new and attractive system by which the pupil may rapidly learn to play the organ. Besides a thorough course in music, this book contains a choice collection of vocal and instrumental pieces, progressively arranged. Publisher's price, $1.50. Our price.(Postage extra, 13c.).50c

No. 12F6989 Whitney's Complete Instructor for the Parlor Organ. Contains a complete graded system with pleasing exercises, easy waltzes, marches, polkas, quicksteps, schottisches, operatic airs, songs and ballads; in fact, selections from the best European and American composers. All directions for the caring of organ, explanation of stops, technical studies and transposition are herein contained. Publisher's price, $2.50. Our price, heavy board covers $1.20

If by mail, postage extra, 19 cents.

Organ and Piano Charts.

No. 12F6995 Mason's Organ Chart. This chart is the most wonderful invention of the age, for with the use of Mason's Indicator, piano and organ playing can be learned in one day. A child ten years old can understand it perfectly. Mason's Indicator is a machine which fits over the keys of a piano or organ, indicating where and how the hands are to be placed and the proper keys to strike, changing the position and the arrangement to suit the different keys. Price....(Postage extra, 3c.)....75c

VIOLIN INSTRUCTION BOOKS.

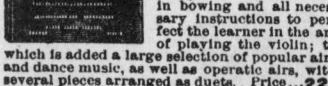

No. 12F6996 Howe's Violin Without a Master. Containing new and complete rules and exercises, with full directions in bowing and all necessary instructions to perfect the learner in the art of playing the violin; to which is added a large selection of popular airs and dance music, as well as operatic airs, with several pieces arranged as duets. Price...22c

If by mail, postage extra, 3 cents.

The Howard Violin Instructor.

No. 12F6997 A very fine instructor for this splendid instrument filled with scales and exercises in all the minor and major keys, and explains all the different parts of a violin and the best methods of studying it. It is filled with many fine musical selections of particular advantage to the student and easy to learn to play. It has a complete musical dictionary, giving an explanation of the different musical terms and also contains a fingerboard chart which will be of great assistance in learning the instrument. Price..........20c

If by mail, postage extra, 4c.

No. 12F7004 Henning's School for the Violin. Specially revised, with bow and finger marks added. In three parts, complete in one book; 101 pages, printed on fine paper, bound in board.

Price, complete........80c

If by mail, postage extra, 15c.

No. 12F7012 Mazas' Complete Violin Instructor. Contains besides a dictionary of musical terms and exercises in all positions, several of Pleyel's celebrated duets.

Price..................30c

If by mail, postage extra, 8 cents.

No. 12F7014 Benjamin's Illustrated Violin Method. This is the latest publication in the way of a violin instructor and is the best work for the beginner ever put upon the market. It contains the complete elementary course; is profusely illustrated; also contains a collection of popular music; 79 pages, sheet music size. Price........37c

If by mail, postage extra, 5 cents.

No. 12F7016 Wichtl's Young Violinist. An excellent book for beginners, as it contains the first instructions in the violin line, including one hundred progressive exercises in the first position through all intervals and keys, with the second violin part for the teacher. It contains also Pleyel's celebrated violin duets.

Price.........(Postage extra, 10c.)....38c

No. 12F7018 Howe's Original Violin School, new and enlarged edition. Contains complete rules and exercises, together with a collection of over 450 pieces of every variety. Hundreds of old familiar airs, never before published for the violin. Extra large type and fine paper.

Price..................20c

If by mail, postage extra, 4 cents.

No. 12F7020 Howe's Diamond School for the Violin, contains complete instructions, full directions for bowing and 558 pieces of dance music. Price..........20c

If by mail, postage extra, 4c.

No. 12F7021 The Violin; How to Master It. This little book is a treatise on the violin itself. It gives all the points in the art of playing the violin besides all the special instructions on position and bowing. It is also furnished with a complete fingerboard chart showing the different positions in which the violin can be played. A great help to teacher and pupil. Price..................15c

If by mail, postage extra, 3 cents.

GUITAR INSTRUCTION BOOKS.

No. 12F7030 Bowers' Standard Method for the Guitar. Positively the most popular instruction book for the guitar ever published; bound in paper.

Price..................25c

If by mail, postage extra, 4 cents.

No. 12F7033 New and Improved Method for the Guitar. By Carcassi, the celebrated guitarist embracing much valuable matter not contained in other books. The number of popular songs in each of the different keys, together with the masterly instructions of Carcassi, make this a desirable method to both teacher and scholar.

Price.....(Postage extra, 12c.)......50c

No. 12F7039 Guckert's Complete Rapid Diagram Chord Book for the Guitar. The best book of its kind published, written expressly for us by E. N. Guckert and published and copyrighted by us. Mr. Guckert claims it to be the most complete diagram self instructor published. The book contains popular guitar solos that can be played by anyone at sight, a feature not to be found in other chord books. List price, 50 cents.

Our price.......(Postage extra, 2c.).....18c

The Howard Guitar Instructor.

No. 12F7040 This is one of the best guitar instructors yet issued for this instrument, and we recommend it to all who desire to play upon the guitar without the aid of a teacher. It is filled with all sorts of exercises and plain explanations, has a splendid musical dictionary, chords in all the minor and major keys, as well as a complete set of scales. It is filled with many fine musical selections among which are the following: Sweet Hour of Prayer, Blue Bells of Scotland, Robin Adair and many fine marches and waltzes. We also enclose in this instructor a very fine finger board chart which will prove of great assistance in learning to play the instrument. Price..................20c

If by mail, postage extra, 4 cents.

BANJO INSTRUCTION BOOKS.

No. 12F7053 Witmark's Progressive Banjo Method, written and compiled by G. L. Lancing. Complete, progressive, practical, thoroughly up to date method. A great aid to the teacher. The elementary or first part will enable the pupil to progress so as to play the popular selections of today within a short time. The entire work is arranged in a most progressive and systematic manner. The book contains 88 pages. Has superior quality paper, flexible cover and linen back. Publisher's retail price, $1.00.

Our price......(Postage extra, 10c).......65c

No. 12F7055 Guckert's Complete Rapid Diagram Chord Book for the Banjo. The best book of its kind published, written expressly for us by E. N. Guckert and published and copyrighted by us. Mr. Guckert claims it to be the most complete diagram self instructor published. The book contains popular banjo solos that can be played by anyone at sight, a feature not found in other chord books. List price, 50 cents.

Our price..........................18c

If by mail, postage extra, 2 cents.

The Howard Banjo Instructor.

No. 12F7056 A very fine instructor for this instrument, with all sorts of exercises, plates and descriptions, so that the beginner can learn the instrument without the aid of a teacher. Diagrams of all the principal minor and major chords, scales and many splendid pieces of music, among which are the following: Sailor's Horn Pipe, Dixie, Irish Washerwoman, Wedding March, Waltzes, etc., plainly printed on heavy paper with a fine cover. Also includes fingerboard chart for the banjo. Price..................20c

If by mail, postage extra, 4 cents.

MANDOLIN INSTRUCTION BOOKS.

No. 12F7069 Guckert's Complete Rapid Diagram Chord Book for the Mandolin. The best book of its kind published, written expressly for us by E. N. Guckert and published and copyrighted by us. Mr. Guckert claims it to be the most complete diagram self instructor published. The book contains popular mandolin solos that can be played by anyone at sight, a feature not to be found in other chord books. List price, 50 cents.

Our price.....(Postage extra, 2c).......18c

No. 12F7070 Howe's Original Mandolin Collection and School. A very easy and comprehensive method for this beautiful instrument, containing complete theory of music, also splendid collection of 450 selections, arranged in an easy and effective manner. New and enlarged edition. Price....25c

If by mail, postage extra, 4 cents.

No. 12F7071 The Howard Mandolin Instructor. A fine instructor for the mandolin filled with all sorts of plain instructions, exercises, scales and chords in all of the principal minor and major keys. With the aid of this instructor the beginner can learn to play the mandolin without the aid of a teacher. It has a very fine musical dictionary and contains many splendid pieces of music among which are the following: I Dreamt I Dwelt in Marble Halls, La Paloma and many fine marches and waltzes. Printed on heavy paper with a handsome cover. Price..........................20c

If by mail, postage extra, 4 cents.

No. 12F7072 The Witmark Progressive Mandolin Method. A distinctively modern book, written and compiled by T. P. Trinkaus, the mandolin expert. Especially desirable, as it contains a series of simple melodies and exercises as well as a number of very fine pieces. It starts at the very first rudiments and instructs by easy stages so that by a slight effort, any person using the book can become a good player without a teacher. The book contains 105 pages, printed on a superior quality of paper, flexible cover and linen back. Publisher's retail price, $1.00. Our price..............65c

If by mail, postage extra, 10 cents.

No. 12F7077 Hamilton's Imperial Mandolin Instructor. A wonderfully simple method for the mandolin. Adapted especially for the use of beginners without a teacher; one of the most up to date and easiest methods to learn from published. In addition to its elementary department, the book contains nearly 50 pages of easy and beautiful music for mandolin with guitar accompaniment. Price..........35c

If by mail, postage extra, 6 cents.

No. 12F7078 Singer's Complete Mandolin Method. This is one of the best mandolin instructors which has appeared for some time and thoroughly and carefully explains all the technicalities in connection with the mandolin. It is not only filled with instructions and exercises but contains many beautiful tunes arranged for solos and duets. It is complete in every respect, and any student who will use it patiently and conscientiously will certainly become a thorough master of the instrument. Special attention is devoted to tuning, shifting, memorizing, sight reading, tremolo playing, double note playing and the care of the mandolin, besides other important subjects.

Price.......(Postage extra, 8c).........$1.00

MISCELLANEOUS INSTRUCTION BOOKS.

NOTE, IMPORTANT—When ordering any of the instruction books listed be sure to state for which instrument.

No. 12F7079 Sherwood's Imperial Diagram Method, for guitar, mandolin and banjo. A new method, with new ideas, easily understood. Also contains an excellent variety of carefully graded teaching pieces, studies and exercises in the various keys. Full instructions with illustrations on the manner of holding the instrument. Price..................28c

If by mail, postage extra, 5 cents.

No. 12F7081 White's Excelsior Method, for the violin, guitar, banjo, mandolin, viola, violoncello, contrabass, flute, clarionet, cornet, organ, trombone, accordion and piano. It illustrates the proper method of holding the instruments and gives a complete list of their technical parts. Not only does it deal with the technicalities of the instruments but it also gives a brief and complete instruction in the rudiments of music. Price..................30c

If by mail, postage extra, 5 cents.

No. 12F7083 National Teacher for Hohner accordion, violin, mandolin, guitar, guitar chords, banjo, mouth harmonica, fife or nightingale flageolet, accordion, slide trombone bass or treble cleff. A chart system, by which, after slight practice, anyone can play at sight all the popular airs and any music adapted for the instrument. No tedious study of notes or scales is required, as only the necessary rudiments are given in condensed form. Price.......9c

If by mail, postage extra, 3 cents.

No. 12F7098 Winner's Primary School for accordion, organ, violin, mandolin, guitar, banjo, flute, fife, violoncello, clarionet and cornet. Not condensed; unabridged. Specify for which instrument book is wanted. Price, each book.....13c

If by mail, postage extra, 3 cents.

No. 12F7119 Otto Langey's Celebrated Instructors for any Instrument. These books have a worldwide reputation as being among the finest instructors ever published, being easily understood, yet complete in every detail, so that a beginner using one of these books, can with practice easily master any instrument. Published for cornet, Eb alto, Bb tenor, bass clef; Bb tenor, treble clef; Bb tenor slide trombone, bass clef; Bb tenor slide trombone, treble clef; Bb baritone, bass clef; Bb baritone, treble clef; Bb bass, bass clef; Bb bass, treble clef; Eb bass, clarinet, flute, piccolo, violin, viola, violoncello, double bass, guitar, mandolin, banjo, saxophone, oboe, bassoon, French horn, drums, fife, tympany, orchestra bells, xylophone and piano. Coleman's edition. Regular retail price, $1.00.

Our price, each book..........................38c

If by mail, postage extra, 7 cents.

No. 12F7120 A B C Figure System for Guitar, Banjo, Violin and Mandolin. Contains a choice selection of up to date music, in a simple and original system, by which anyone can play music at sight, in five to ten minutes, and gain a perfect knowledge of the instrument with but little study, and without the assistance of a teacher. It also contains a complete diagram of the chords in major and minor keys, and their modulations, to play accompaniments at sight to any song, solo or duet, with an illustration of the fingerboard and position of the hands.

Price.........(Postage extra, 3c.)..........9c

No. 12F7121 Autoharp Instructor. By C. F. Zimmerman, containing full instructions, besides a great number of easy selections for the beginner. Price..(Postage extra, 6c.)..19c

No. 12F7123 Howe's Army and Navy Fife Instructor, containing complete course of instructions, also calls, signals and the complete camp and garrison duties as practiced in the United States army and navy, besides marches, quicksteps, waltzes, etc. Paper cover.

Price.........(Postage extra, 4c.)..........20c

No. 12F7140 Rudiments of Music. A concise and thoroughly practical course of instruction on the art of singing by note; prepared by J. R. Murray. Price..........9c

If by mail, postage extra, 2 cents.

No. 12F7146 Pronouncing Pocket Dictionary of over 500 musical terms. Price...12c

If by mail, postage extra, 1 cent.

No. 12F7148 National Self Tuner. Contains complete instructions on tuning and regulating pianos, together with a specification of defects and their remedies, for those who wish to know more about the structure or care of their instrument. Contains illustrations and examples, etc. This work is recommended by some of our best tuners and teachers. It also gives a short and concise treatise on the organ, its preservation, stops and effect, etc.

Price.........(Postage extra, 4c.)..........25c

BALL ROOM GUIDE AND CALL BOOKS.

No. 12F7150 Prof. Clendenen's Fashionable Quadrille Book and Guide to Etiquette. This book contains all the necessary instructions, both with reference to etiquette on the ball room floor, as well as description of figures and calling. New and revised edition contains the Trilby Two-Step Quadrille, Oxford Minuet, Aurora, La Veta, Chicago Glide, the latest German and 50 other popular dances; 89 pages.

Price.........(Postage extra, 2c.)..........20c

No. 12F7152 Howe's New American Dancing Master, containing 400 dances and including 100 figures of the German. The latest and most fashionable dances are included, with full explanation of the latest and most approved figures and calls for the different changes, as well as rules on deportment, toilet and etiquette of dancing; 140 pages. Price..........30c

If by mail, postage extra, 2 cents.

No. 12F7158 Gems of the Ball Room Call Book. Contains 100 pages of calls that every dance orchestra should have; 25 Plain Quadrilles, several Prairie Queens, Lancers, Waltz Quadrilles, etc. Price..........25c

By mail, postage extra, 3 cents.

For other Dancing and Call Books, see our BOOK DEPARTMENT.

TRUNKS AND SUITCASES

SUIT CASES AND TRAVELING BAGS

GUARANTEED FULLY.

$3.45 AND UP **No. 33T1232 Large Oxford Style Outseam Sewed Seal Embossed Cowhide Bag.** Dark tan shade. Covered frame to match bag leather. Brassed lock and sliding catches, round padded leather handle. Imitation leather lined; inside pocket.

Size, in.	Wt., lbs.	Price
14x7 x10¾	3	$3.45
16x7½x11½	3½	4.15
18x8 x12	4	4.85

$7.95 AND UP **No. 33T1242 Popular Three-Piece Oxford Style Bag** of black walrus. Leather lined, welted seams, satin finish brass plunger lock and sliding catches. Padded round leather handle and large pocket in lining. A wonderful value.

Size	Weight	Price
Size, 16x 9 x13 in.	wt., 5¾ lbs.	$ 7.95
Size, 18x 9¾x13¾ in.	wt., 6½ lbs.	9.35
Size, 20x10¼x14¼ in.	wt., 7 lbs.	10.75

$9.95 AND UP **No. 33T1244 Best Selected Black Walrus Grain Seal Three-Piece Oxford Style Bag.** French finished seams. English frame, leather lined. Sunken brass lock and sliding catches, leather tab name plate. Lined with fine buff leather and has capacious pockets in both sides. **State size.**

Size	Weight	Price
Size, 16x 9 x13 in.	wt., 5¾ lbs.	$ 9.95
Size, 18x 9¾x13¾ in.	wt., 6½ lbs.	11.35
Size, 20x10¼x14¼ in.	wt., 7 lbs.	12.75

$2.15 AND UP **No. 33T1230 Large Oxford Shape Black Leather Bag.** Welted seams black enameled frame, brassed lock and catches, round leather handle. Cloth lined and inside pocket. **State size.**

Size	Weight	Price
Size, 14x6¾x11 in.	wt., 2½ lbs.	$2.15
Size, 16x7¼x11½ in.	wt., 3¼ lbs.	2.55
Size, 18x8 x12 in.	wt., 4 lbs.	2.95

$8.95 AND UP **No. 33T1251 Highly Finished Russet Bridle Leather Three-Piece Oxford Style Bag.** French finished seams, English frame, leather lined. Sunken brass lock and sliding catches, round padded English leather handle. Fine buff leather lining and capacious pockets.

Size, in.	Wt., lbs.	Price
16x 9 x13	5½	$ 8.95
18x 9¾x13¾	6¼	10.35
20x10¼x14¼	6¾	11.75

59c AND UP **No. 33T1210 Alligator Embossed Brown Sheepskin Club Bag.** Cloth lined. Double hasp lock, slide catches, round leather handle. **State Size.**

Length	Weight	Price
Length, 10 inches	weight, 1 pound	$0.59
Length, 12 inches	weight, 1¼ pounds	.75
Length, 14 inches	weight, 1¾ pounds	.87
Length, 16 inches	weight, 2¼ pounds	1.12
Length, 18 inches	weight, 3 pounds	1.25

29c AND UP **No. 33T1208 Enameled Waterproof Rubber Cloth Club Bag.** Alligator embossed. Double hasp lock and cloth lined. Dark brown. **State size.**

Size	Weight	Price
Size 10 inches	weight, ¾ pound	29c
Size 12 inches	weight, 1 pound	39c
Size 14 inches	weight, 1½ pounds	45c
Size 16 inches	weight, 2 pounds	50c

98c EACH **No. 33T1302 Imitation Brown Leather Rubber Cloth Suit Case.** Made over strong steel frame. Brassed lock and catches, riveted cowhide corners and padded leather handle. Cloth lined and inside straps. Length, 24 inches.

$2.15 EACH **No. 33T1305 Practical Light Weight Olive Matting Suit Case.** Cowhide corners and straps all around. Made over strong steel frame. Strong brassed lock and padded leather handle. Dimensions, 24x13x5½ inches. Weight, 5½ pounds.

No. 33T1324

No. 33T1330

$10.65 AND UP **No. 33T1324 Our Finest Hand Boarded Cowhide Suit Case.** Rich brown or light russet. Extra deep. Linen lined. Linen Shirt fold with handkerchief pocket. Brass side lock and catches, scalloped cowhide corners and strap loops with bell rivets matching leather. Round padded sewed leather handle. **State size and color.**

Size	Weight	Price
24x13 x7 in.	11 lbs.	$10.65
26x13½x7 in.	12 lbs.	11.00

$1.37 EACH **No. 33T1307 Alligator Embossed Waterproof Keratol Suit Case.** Made over strong steel frame. Riveted cowhide corners, strong brassed lock with catches and round padded leather handle. Cloth lined and inside straps. Length, 24 inches. Weight, 7 pounds.

$6.95 AND UP **No. 33T1315 Ladies' Light Weight One-Piece Body Hand Sewed Russet Bridle Leather Suit Case.** Mercerized moire lined. Handkerchief pocket in cover, straps in body.
Dimensions, 22x13x6 inches. Weight, 6½ pounds. Price...$6.95
Dimensions, 24x13x6 inches. Weight, 7 pounds. Price...$7.15

$12.75 AND UP **No. 33T1330 Automobile or Tourists' Double Suit Case.** Extra heavy russet cowhide, reinforced underneath with heavy binders' board and made over strong steel frame. This case has the capacity of two ordinary suit cases. It opens through the center, as shown in illustration, contains strapped and removable partition with large linen bellows pocket so that each side can be packed separately. Linen lined. Full set inside straps; strong cowhide straps around outside. Improved brass lock and catches and six large bell rivets on each corner. Thoroughly sewed and riveted throughout. Has sewed double handles.

Size	Weight	Price
26x13½x8 in.	12½ lbs.	$12.75
28x14 x8 in.	13¼ lbs.	13.75
30x14½x8 in.	14 lbs.	14.75

$3.15 EACH **No. 33T1311 Genuine Grain Leather Suit Case.** Full weight sheepskin, made over strong steel frame, reinforced underneath with binders' board. Cowhide corners, round padded leather handle, brassed lock and catches. Cloth lined, straps inside. Size, 24x13x6 inches. Weight, 6½ pounds.

$1.67 EACH **No. 33T1304 Best Waterproof Imitation Brown Grain Leather Suit Case.** Made over strong steel frame. Cowhide corners, round padded leather handle, brassed lock and catches. Creased surface and cloth lined with straps inside. Length, 24 inches. Weight, 7 lbs.

49c AND UP **No. 33T1346 Leather Bound Waterproof Canvas Telescope.** Leather bound and strongly sewed and riveted. Three grain straps on large sizes. **State size.**
Size, 16x8¼x6½ inches, extended 12 inches. Wt., 2 lbs. Price...49c
Size, 20x10¼x8 inches, extended 14 inches. Wt., 3 lbs. Price...69c
Size, 24x12¼x9½ inches, extended 17 inches. Wt., 4 lbs. Price...89c
Size, 26x13½x10½ inches, extended 18½ inches. Wt., 4½ lbs. Price...$1.09

$5.85 AND UP **No. 33T1313 Selected Cowhide Bridle Leather Suit Case.** Holland linen lining and shirt fold. Fine grain full weight russet stock, made same as No. 33T1316, above described, and in addition has two strong bridle leather straps all around. **State size.**

Size	Weight	Price
24x13 x6½ in.	8 lbs.	$5.85
26x13½x6¾ in.	9 lbs.	6.10

$7.95 AND UP **No. 33T1323 Best Selected Russet Bridle Leather Suit Case.** Extra deep; linen lined. Strapped linen shirt fold with handkerchief pocket. Straps in bottom and stay straps to hold cover. Brass lock and catches; escalloped leather corners, each with six brass bell rivets. Two bridle leather straps. Padded sewed leather handle. **State size.**

Size	Weight	Price
24x13x7½ in.	9 lbs.	$7.95
26x13x7¾ in.	10 lbs.	8.30

$9.35 AND UP **No. 33T1322 English Bellows Cowhide Suit Case.** Extension side reinforced with straps around case. Holland linen lined. Full weight cowhide over steel frame. Cowhide corners, round padded leather handle, brass lock and catches. Straps in bottom and strapped partition. Bellows may be packed separate. **State Size.**
Size, 24x12½ inches, extended 10¼ inches. Weight, 9 pounds. Price.......$ 9.35
Size, 26x13 inches, extended 10½ inches. Weight, 10½ pounds. Price....... 9.85
Size, 28x13½ inches, extended 10¾ inches. Weight, 11 pounds. Price....... 10.35

$4.35 AND UP **No. 33T1316 Genuine Cowhide Bridle Leather Suit Case.** Linen lining and shirt fold. Selected full weight russet stock, made over strong steel frame; binders' board reinforced. Cowhide corners, padded English leather handle, brass lock and catches and bell rivets. Straps in body and cover **State size.**
Dimensions, 24x13 x6½ inches. Weight, 8 pounds. Price.......$4.35
Dimensions, 26x13½x6¾ inches. Weight, 8½ pounds. Price....... 4.65

No. 33T1316 No. 33T1323 No. 33T1313 No. 33T1322

FROM $1.85 STRONG VALUES IN TRUNKS UP TO $7.25

CONVENIENCE AND CAPACITY. ONLY THOROUGHLY SEASONED BASSWOOD WHICH WILL NOT SPLIT OR CHECK. REINFORCED AT EVERY DANGER POINT. REPLACED IF UNSATISFACTORY.

OUR TRUNKS ABSOLUTELY THE BEST STYLES are built like battleships, strongly protected and reinforced at every danger point, and are practically unbreakable. Our first and last consideration in their construction has been to make them as roomy, as strong and as nearly unbreakable as possible, and strongest trunks made. If you don't find the trunk you get from us far superior to what will cost you 50 per cent more if purchased elsewhere, we will willingly return both the price and any transportation charges you paid on the goods on return of the same to us. Freight charges on trunks are a small item compared to what we save you on the cost of trunks, and don't overlook the fact that you have to pay the freight just the same when you buy of your home dealer.

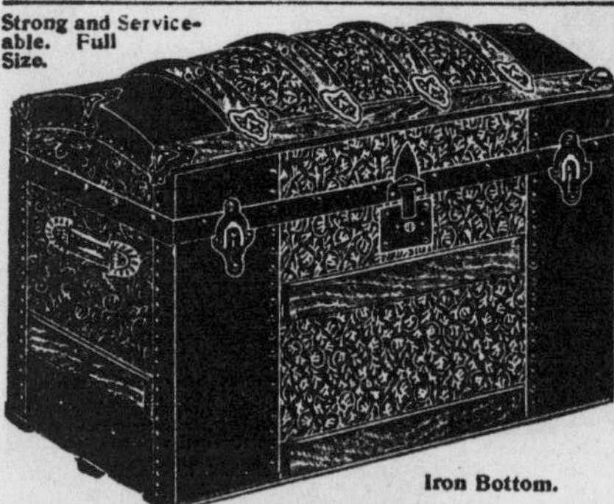

Strong and Serviceable. Full Size.

Iron Bottom.

$1.85 CRYSTALLIZED METAL COVERED TRUNK.

No. 33T2002 Substantially made Barrel Top Trunk, sheet iron bound, japanned steel end clamps, iron bottom, hardwood slats, special bar bolts, hinges, rollers, strong hasp lock and leather handles. Contains set up tray with side compartment and covered bonnet box. A full size trunk at a very low price. But we honestly advise the purchase of a better trunk, as a good trunk lasts many years and always insures safe transportation to its contents. But remember, at the price, this is the best trunk on the market. State size wanted and give correct catalog number.

Length	Width	Height	Weight	Price
26 in.	14 in.	18 in.	28½ lbs.	$1.85
30 in.	16½ in.	20½ in.	36 lbs.	2.45
34 in.	18 in.	22 in.	44 lbs.	3.05
36 in.	19½ in.	22½ in.	50 lbs.	3.35

$6.05 STEAMER TRUNK. CANVAS COVERED.

No. 33T2136 Painted Canvas Covered Wagon or Steamer Trunk. Heavy hardwood slats. Heavy brass clamps and corner bumpers, brass lock, side bolts, and valance clamps at corners where cover meets body. Tray with two compartments separately covered and muslin faced. Reinforced with heavy sole leather straps. We will replace any trunk which does not prove satisfactory. State size and catalog number.

This illustration is from an actual photograph.

Length	Width	Height	Weight	Price
32 in.	19 in.	13 in.	38 lbs.	$6.05
36 in.	20 in.	13 in.	44 lbs.	6.70
38 in.	20½ in.	13 in.	47 lbs.	7.25

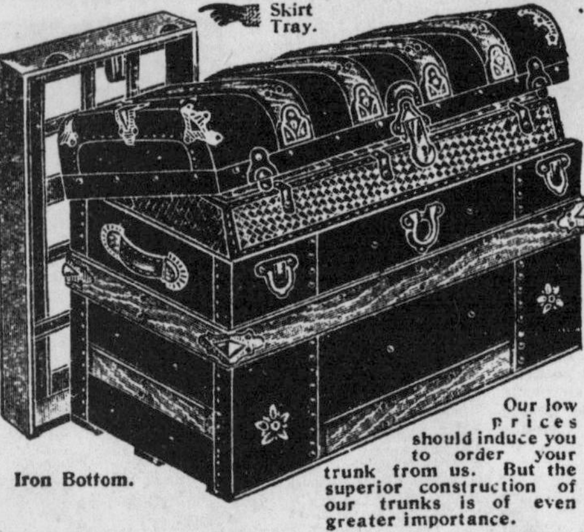

Skirt Tray.

Iron Bottom.

$3.65 MONITOR TOP TRUNK. STEEL COVERED.

No. 33T2022 Handsomely black enameled. Large box made of thick basswood, and lined with paper. Heavy hardwood bar slats, as illustrated. Heavy sheet iron bottom and is thoroughly reinforced and trimmed with metal trimmings, steel end clamps, patent bar bolts, heavy steel hinges and rollers, brass monitor lock, leather handles, and contains tray with separately covered bonnet box and side compartment, also skirt tray which fits underneath first tray and when desired can be inverted and takes up comparatively little room. A trunk that is easily worth $2.00 to $3.00 more than our low price. Be sure to state size wanted and give catalog number.

Our low prices should induce you to order your trunk from us. But the superior construction of our trunks is of even greater importance.

Length	Width	Height	Weight	Price
28 in.	15½ in.	18½ in.	36 lbs.	$3.65
32 in.	17½ in.	20½ in.	48 lbs.	4.25
36 in.	19½ in.	22½ in.	55 lbs.	4.85

HEAVIEST MONITOR TOP BLACK ENAMEL STEEL COVERED TRUNK.

ONE OF THE HANDSOMEST and STRONGEST TRUNKS MADE

Intersecting Slat Lengthwise on Top.

Extra Skirt Tray. Iron Bottom.

Extra Large Size.

$4.95

No. 33T2040 Four heavy hardwood slats over top and down side, two across each end and one lengthwise across top, intersecting cross slats. Extra heavy bolts, clamps and reinforcements, brass Excelsior lock. Rollers, hinges, stitched leather handles, etc. Contains tray with bonnet box and side compartment, fall-in-top compartment in cover, all separately covered. Has extra skirt tray which can be inverted and takes up comparatively little room. Note the heavy malleable trimmings, the number of and width and thickness of the hardwood slats, the strong reinforcements, and remember that this trunk has an iron bottom and is made on an extra large size thick basswood box. One of the handsomest and most serviceable trunks made. We are so confident of the strength and the superiority of this trunk that we will, at any time, replace any one that does not give absolute satisfaction. Be sure to state size and catalog number.

Length	Width	Height	Weight	Price
28 in.	17 in.	19½ in.	42 lbs.	$4.95
32 in.	19 in.	22 in.	54 lbs.	5.55
36 in.	21 in.	23½ in.	63 lbs.	6.35
38 in.	22 in.	24½ in.	72 lbs.	6.70

$2.95 LEADER CANVAS COVERED TRUNK.

No. 33T2055 Iron bottom, sheet iron bound edges, hardwood slats, steel clamps, knees and corner bumpers top and bottom. Brass Monitor lock, patent bolts, hinges, catches, rollers, etc., leather handles, deep tray with covered hat box. Large size box, paper lined. While this trunk for the money is guaranteed to be better than can be bought anywhere else, we strongly recommend the purchase of better trunks, as a good trunk will last indefinitely. Remember, though, that at the price we defy anyone to equal the trunk here illustrated and described and which is guaranteed to give satisfaction. State the size wanted and give catalog number.

Taken from Photograph.

Iron Bottom.

Length	Width	Height	Weight	Price
28 in.	16 in.	18½ in.	36 lbs.	$2.95
32 in.	17¾ in.	20½ in.	43 lbs.	3.65
36 in.	20½ in.	21¾ in.	49 lbs.	4.35
38 in.	21½ in.	23 in.	59 lbs.	4.70

$2.95 CANVAS COVERED STEAMER TRUNK.

No. 33T2132 Good Strong Wagon or Steamer Trunk, covered with heavy painted canvas. Iron bottom, sheet iron bound and strong iron clamps at corners. Inside tray with two compartments. While sold at the lowest price ever quoted for a steamer or wagon trunk, we will guarantee it to give satisfactory service and to be unequaled at less than double our price. State size and give catalog number.

Length	Width	Height	Weight	Price
28 in.	17 in.	12 in.	31 lbs.	$2.95
32 in.	19 in.	12 in.	37 lbs.	3.65
36 in.	21 in.	12 in.	43 lbs.	4.35

$3.65 BARREL TOP TRUNK. FANCY METAL COVERED.

We recommend canvas covered rather than metal covered trunks.

Extra Suit or Skirt Tray.

Iron Bottom and Sheet Iron Bound.

No. 33T2014 Thick seasoned basswood, paper lined, large Barrel Top Trunk with hardwood bar slats, sheet iron binding, and heavy fancy metal trimmings and reinforcements. Iron bottom, patent bar bolts and rollers, heavy steel hinges and strong end clamps. Strong brass Monitor lock, and leather handles, and contains tray with bonnet box and side compartment separately covered, also fall-in cover top compartment. Has skirt tray, which fits in underneath the upper tray and when not in use can be inverted and takes up comparatively little room. This is the greatest value ever offered in a low priced barrel top trunk, and we guarantee it to give satisfaction. Be sure to state the size wanted.

Length	Width	Height	Weight	Price
28 in.	16½ in.	19 in.	38½ lbs.	$3.65
32 in.	18½ in.	21½ in.	48½ lbs.	4.25
36 in.	20½ in.	24½ in.	58 lbs.	4.85

$5.65 WATERPROOF CANVAS COVERED STEEL BOUND TRUNK.

TWO TRAYS.

No. 33T2058 Large, full size Trunk, thick basswood box, covered with heavy waterproof canvas, entirely bound with japanned angle steel binding, heavy hardwood slats, heavy malleable iron japanned valance clamps, buckle bar bolts, corner bumpers, steel strip clamps, knees, center band and iron bottom, brass Monitor lock, sole leather straps. Contains roomy hinged upper tray with hat box and side compartments separately covered and extra skirt tray below.

Iron Bottom.

Length	Width	Height	Weight	Price
30 in.	18 in.	19½ in.	48 lbs.	$5.65
32 in.	18½ in.	20½ in.	51 lbs.	6.00
36 in.	20½ in.	22 in.	61 lbs.	6.70
38 in.	21½ in.	23 in.	68 lbs.	6.95

Fully guaranteed to give the best service and to stand unlimited rough usage. Remember to state the size wanted and catalog number.

$6.85 OUR BEST MEDIUM PRICED CANVAS COVERED TRUNK.

From photograph.

Iron Bottom.

No. 33T2070 The equal of this trunk cannot be bought anywhere else at twice our remarkably low price. Extra large size box, covered with painted waterproof canvas. Extra wide heavy hardwood slats. Heavy sheet iron bottom and binding on ends. Has heaviest and strongest malleable iron brass plated clamps and reinforcements wherever there could be chance for breakage. Buckle bar bolts. Brass Excelsior lock, brass corner bumpers and malleable valance clamps at corners where lid and body meet. Strong rollers, and is reinforced with two extra heavy sole leather straps. Contains large, roomy tray with hat box and large side compartment separately covered.

A trunk that has been thoroughly tried by us for several years and has never disappointed. If this trunk becomes broken in ordinary service or does not give satisfaction we will replace it. State size.

Length	Width	Height	Weight	Price
32 in.	20 in.	21 in.	54 lbs.	$6.85
36 in.	21½ in.	22½ in.	62 lbs.	7.55
38 in.	22¼ in.	23½ in.	67 lbs.	7.90
40 in.	23 in.	24½ in.	72 lbs.	8.25

$11.85 OUR "BATTLESHIP" TRUNK, GUARANTEED UNBREAKABLE.

TWO TRAYS.

One of the strongest trunks ever made.

No. 33T2096 Wonderful Leather and Iron Bound Trunk. "Built like a battleship," because reinforced at every danger point. Extra large and thick basswood box covered with heaviest waterproof painted canvas. Angle steel and cowhide leather binding on edges. Five heavy hardwood slats on top and three on ends and sides. Leather quarter rounds in corners, heavy leather handles and two heavy cowhide leather straps running through fancy metal and leather loops, and tips. Heavy dome set brass plated clamps, knees, corner bumpers, valance clamps, etc. Brass Excelsior lock, patent lifter bolts, socket dowel clamps on front and ends. Heavy hinges, patent rollers, iron bottom, and contains hinged tray with hat box and other compartments, each with folding lid. Additional dress tray, full cloth lined, which fits underneath main tray.

We say, "built like a battleship," and the trunk is sufficient proof of the statement. State the size wanted and catalog number.

Length	Width	Height	Weight	Price
32 in.	18½ in.	21 in.	60 lbs.	$11.85
34 in.	19½ in.	22 in.	65 lbs.	12.60
38 in.	21½ in.	24 in.	70 lbs.	14.10
40 in.	22½ in.	24½ in.	80 lbs.	14.85

OUR "GIBRALTAR" TRUNK, GUARANTEED FOR 5 YEARS

No fort is better fortified or more nearly impregnable than the fortress of Gibraltar.

No trunk is better fortified or more nearly damage proof than our solid veneer "Gibraltar" Trunk.

No. 33T2098 Our five-year guarantee trunk is the strongest trunk we know how to build and is so good that we have named it the "Gibraltar" Trunk.

Inside every trunk we put our printed guarantee covering five years of ordinary service from date of purchase. (This trunk is not guaranteed as a "sample" trunk nor for theatrical traveling purposes).

DESCRIPTION—Body of our "Gibraltar" Trunk is made entirely of extra thick three-ply reinforced veneer basswood, the strongest trunk box construction possible, as the direction of the grain in the center ply runs crosswise or opposed to the grain of the two outer plies, making it practically impossible for the veneered board to bend or break. The "Gibraltar" Trunk is made with slightly rounded extra thick veneered top and is entirely covered with thick waterproof keratol, the best trunk covering made. Heavy hardwood slats; rolled steel bottom; and all edges reinforced and bound with rawhide finish vulcanized fiber underneath heavy bronzed angle steel binding. Reinforced and fortified with vulcanized center band and full set of heavy malleable iron clamps, valance sets; dowels and corner bumpers; strongly riveted throughout (not nailed) and heavy brass plated, making them absolutely rustproof. Strong brass Excelsior lock and catches, four broad steel hinges, and two wide and heavy sole leather straps running around trunk through malleable iron and leather strap loops. Sliding leather handles. Trunk is lined throughout with durable cloth and contains deep hinged upper tray with spacious hat box and three side compartments separately arranged for linen, gloves, toilet articles, etc., all covered with folding lid. Additional tray underneath upper tray for pressed outer garments as suits, dresses, etc.

The veneer body, angle steel binding over vulcanized fiber and the riveted malleable reinforcements make Our "Gibraltar" Trunk with its five-year guarantee the greatest trunk ever put on the market at $25.00 or less.

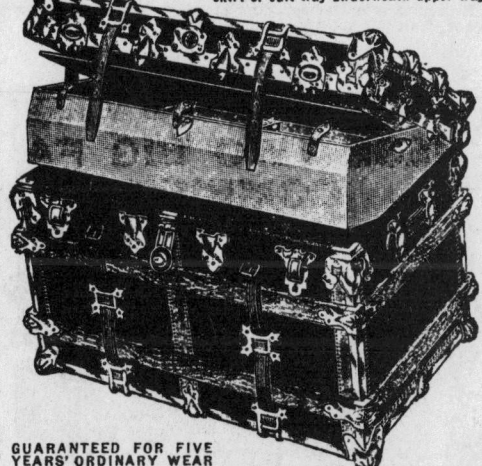

Cloth lined hinged tray with capacious hat compartment and three side compartments, all covered with folding lid. Deep skirt or suit tray underneath upper tray.

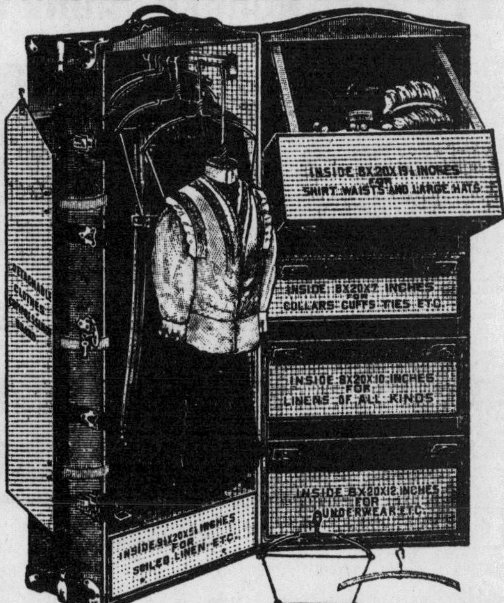

GUARANTEED FOR FIVE YEARS' ORDINARY WEAR

Length	Width	Height	Weight	Price
32 inches	20 inches	21½ inches	72 lbs.	$13.95
36 inches	22 inches	23½ inches	86 lbs.	15.45
38 inches	23 inches	24½ inches	93 lbs.	$16.95
40 inches	24 inches	25½ inches	99 lbs.	18.45

Above dimensions are actual body measurements between slats.

$17.95 STRONGEST, MOST CONVENIENT BUREAU TRUNK MADE.

No. 33T2110 Strongest and most convenient Wall Dresser Trunk made. Extra large thick basswood box covered with heavy waterproof painted canvas and reinforced and protected with bronzed angle steel binding on edges. Brass plated knees, corner bumpers, clamps. No. 4 buckle bar bolts, brass Excelsior lock, strong, heavy, malleable catches; valance clamps and strong socket dowels joining cover and body; four heavy hinges and rollers, and has heavy stitched leather handles. Reinforced with two heavy sole leather straps, protected with metal and leather strap loops. Linen lined; genuine Holland linen facing, three strapped pockets and three roomy compartments in lid of trunk. Three large, roomy drawers arranged with movable hat form, and extra compartment in bottom of trunk. For strength and durability, coupled with its many convenient features, this trunk stands without a peer among bureau trunks. Please state size wanted.

The strongest guarantee ever put on a trunk; we will replace any trunk if at any time it is proven unsatisfactory.

Taken from photograph

Accessible at all times.

Sizes as follows:

Length	Width	Height	Weight	Price
32 in.	19½ in.	24 in.	71 lbs.	$17.95
36 in.	22 in.	26 in.	85 lbs.	20.95
38 in.	23 in.	27 in.	92 lbs.	22.45
40 in.	23½ in.	27½ in.	99 lbs.	23.95

$32.50 A PORTABLE WARDROBE TRUNK.

No. 33T2120

Our great demand for a Portable Wardrobe Trunk at a reasonable price enabled us to secure the exclusive mail order selling privileges of this most convenient and useful Combined Trunk and Wardrobe, never retailed at less than $45.00 to $50.00, while our remarkably low price is only $32.50. This Wardrobe Trunk is convenient and practical as any garments, few or many, when hung in the roomy clothes compartment at the left, as in a closet, are held firmly in place without crushing by the compressing board shown outside at the left, and when removed are in perfect condition to wear.

Hangers are of assorted styles to accommodate every kind of wearing apparel: top coats, overcoats, trousers, waists, skirts, etc.

The Nickeled Sliding Hanger Rod when pulled out brings the clothes to a convenient position for hanging or removing each garment without disturbing the others.

The Compartments at the right are roomy and convenient, as shown by the dimensions and suggestions for use printed on each. Soiled linen compartment beneath the hanging garments.

The Make. Three-ply veneer basswood to combine strength and lightness. Painted canvas covered, hardwood slats, brass plated steel trimmings, brass Excelsior lock, heavy bolts, dowels and hinges, vulcanized fiber binding and center bands, sole leather handles. Solid dome top to insure setting on bottom end. **Dimensions:** Inside, 50x20x18 inches. Weight, 77 pounds. Price..........$32.50

$6.85 OUR BEST MEDIUM PRICED CANVAS COVERED TRUNK.

From photograph.

Iron Bottom.

No. 33R1070 The equal of this trunk cannot be bought anywhere else at twice our remarkably low price. Extra large size box, covered with painted waterproof canvas. Extra wide heavy hardwood slats. Heavy sheet iron bottom and binding on ends. Has heaviest and strongest malleable iron brass plated clamps and reinforcements wherever there could be chance for breakage. Buckle bar bolts. Brass Excelsior lock, brass corner bumpers and malleable valance clamps at corners where lid and body meet. Strong rollers, and is reinforced with two extra heavy sole leather straps. Contains large, roomy tray with hat box and large side compartment separately covered.

A trunk that has been thoroughly tried by us for several years and has never disappointed. If this trunk becomes broken in ordinary service or does not give satisfaction we will replace it. State size.

Length	Width	Height	Weight	Price
32 in.	20 in.	21 in.	54 lbs.	$6.85
36 in.	21½ in.	22½ in.	62 lbs.	7.[illegible]5
38 in.	22¼ in.	23½ in.	67 lbs.	7.90
40 in.	23 in.	24½ in.	72 lbs.	8.25

$11.85 OUR "BATTLESHIP" TRUNK, GUARANTEED UNBREAKABLE.

TWO TRAYS.

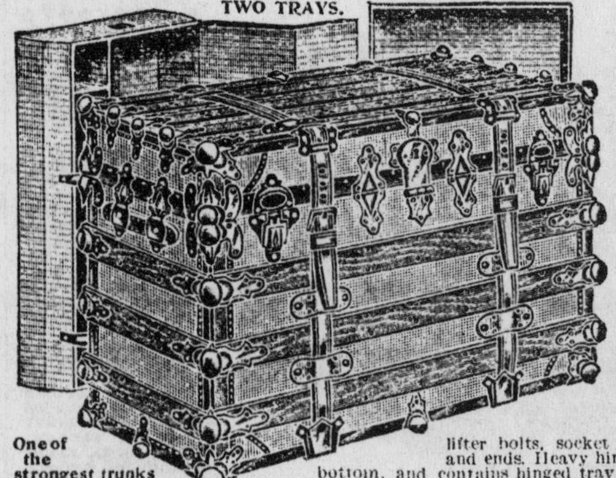

One of the strongest trunks ever made.

No. 33R1096 Wonderful Leather and Iron Bound Trunk. "Built like a battleship," because reinforced at every danger point. Extra large and thick basswood box covered with heaviest waterproof painted canvas. Angle steel and cowhide leather binding on edges. Five heavy hardwood slats on top and three on ends and sides. Leather quarter rounds in corners, heavy leather handles and two heavy cowhide leather straps running through fancy metal and leather loops, and tips. Heavy dome set brass plated clamps, knees, corner bumpers, valance clamps, etc. Brass Excelsior lock, patent lifter bolts, socket dowel clamps on front and ends. Heavy hinges, patent rollers, iron bottom, and contains hinged tray with hat box and other compartments, each with folding lid. Additional dress tray, full cloth lined, which fits underneath main tray.

We say, "built like a battleship," and the trunk is sufficient proof of the statement. State the size wanted and catalog number.

Length	Width	Height	Weight	Price
32 in.	18½ in.	21 in.	60 lbs.	$11.85
34 in.	19½ in.	22 in.	65 lbs.	12.60
38 in.	21½ in.	24 in.	70 lbs.	14.10
40 in.	22½ in.	24½ in.	80 lbs.	14.85

OUR "GIBRALTAR" TRUNK, GUARANTEED FOR 5 YEARS

No fort is better fortified or more nearly impregnable than the fortress of Gibraltar.

No trunk is better fortified or more nearly damage proof than our solid veneer "Gibraltar" Trunk.

No. 33R1098 Our five-year guarantee trunk is the strongest trunk we know how to build and is so good that we have named it the "Gibraltar" Trunk.
Inside every trunk we put our printed guarantee covering five years of ordinary service from date of purchase. (This trunk is not guaranteed as a "sample" trunk nor for theatrical traveling purposes).

DESCRIPTION—Body of our "Gibraltar" Trunk is made entirely of extra thick three-ply reinforced veneer basswood, the strongest trunk box construction possible, as the direction of the grain in the center ply runs crosswise or opposed to the grain of the two outer plies, making it practically impossible for the veneered board to bend or break. The "Gibraltar" Trunk is made with slightly rounded extra thick veneered top and is entirely covered with thick waterproof keratol, the best trunk covering made. Heavy hardwood slats; rolled steel bottom; and all edges reinforced and bound with rawhide finish vulcanized fiber underneath heavy bronzed angle steel binding. Reinforced and fortified with vulcanized center band and full set of heavy malleable iron clamps, valance sets; dowels and corner bumpers; strongly riveted throughout (not nailed) and heavy brass plated, making them absolutely rustproof. Strong brass Excelsior lock and catches, four broad steel hinges, and two wide and heavy sole leather straps running around trunk through malleable iron and leather strap loops. Sliding leather handles. Trunk is lined throughout with durable cloth and contains deep hinged upper tray with spacious hat box and three side compartments separately arranged for linen, gloves, toilet articles, etc., all covered with folding lid. Additional tray underneath upper tray for pressed outer garments as suits, dresses, etc.,

The veneer body, angle steel binding over vulcanized fiber and the riveted malleable reinforcements make Our "Gibraltar" Trunk with its five-year guarantee the greatest trunk ever put on the market at $25.00 or less.

Cloth lined hinged tray with capacious hat compartment and three side compartments, all covered with folding lid. Deep skirt or suit tray underneath upper tray.

GUARANTEED FOR FIVE YEARS' ORDINARY WEAR

Length, 32 inches. Width, 20 inches. Height, 21½ inches. Weight, 72 lbs. Price...$13.95
Length, 36 inches. Width, 22 inches. Height, 23½ inches. Weight, 86 lbs. Price... 15.45
Length, 38 inches. Width, 23 inches. Height, 24½ inches. Weight, 93 lbs. Price...$16.95
Length, 40 inches. Width, 24 inches. Height, 25½ inches. Weight, 99 lbs. Price... 18.45

Above dimensions are actual body measurements between slats.

$17.95 STRONGEST, MOST CONVENIENT BUREAU TRUNK MADE.

No. 33R1110 Strongest and most convenient Wall Dresser Trunk made, Extra large thick basswood box covered with heavy waterproof painted canvas and reinforced and protected with bronzed angle steel binding on edges. Brass plated knees, corner bumpers, clamps. No. 4 buckle bar bolts, brass Excelsior lock, strong, heavy, malleable catches; valance clamps and strong socket dowels joining cover and body; four heavy hinges and rollers, and has heavy stitched leather handles. Reinforced with two heavy sole leather straps, protected with metal and leather strap loops. Linen lined; genuine Holland linen facing, three strapped pockets and three roomy compartments in lid of trunk. Three large, roomy drawers arranged with movable hat form, and extra compartment in bottom of trunk. For strength and durability, coupled with its many convenient features, this trunk stands without a peer among bureau trunks.
Please state size wanted.

The strongest guarantee ever put on a trunk; we will replace any trunk if at any time it is proven unsatisfactory.

Taken from photograph

Accessible at all times.

Sizes as follows:

Length	Width	Height	Weight	Price
32 in.	19¼ in.	24 in.	71 lbs.	$17.95
36 in.	22 in.	26 in.	85 lbs.	20.95
38 in.	23 in.	27 in.	92 lbs.	22.45
40 in.	23½ in.	27½ in.	99 lbs.	23.95

$32.50 A PORTABLE WARDROBE TRUNK.

No. 33R1120
Our great demand for a Portable Wardrobe Trunk at a reasonable price enabled us to secure the exclusive mail order selling privileges of this most convenient and useful Combined Trunk and Wardrobe, never retailed at less than $45.00 to $50.00, while our remarkably low price is only $32.50. **This Wardrobe Trunk** is convenient and practical as any garments, few or many, when hung in the roomy clothes compartment at the left, as in a closet, are held firmly in place without crushing by the compressing board shown outside at the left, and when removed are in perfect condition to wear.

Hangers are of assorted styles to accommodate every kind of wearing apparel: top coats, overcoats, trousers, waists, skirts, etc.

The Nickeled Sliding Hanger Rod when pulled out brings the clothes to a convenient position for hanging or removing each garment without disturbing the others.

The Compartments at the right are roomy and convenient, as shown by the dimensions and suggestions for use printed on each. Soiled linen compartment beneath the hanging garments.

The Make. Three-ply veneer basswood to combine strength and lightness. Painted canvas covered, hardwood slats, brass plated steel trimmings, brass Excelsior lock, heavy bolts, dowels and hinges, vulcanized fiber binding and center bands, sole leather handles. Solid dome top to insure setting on bottom end. Dimensions: Inside, 50x20x18 inches. Wt., 77 lbs. Price....$32.50

TRUNKS AND TRAVELING BAGS

Trunks Like Battleships Reinforced at Every Danger Point—Strongest Leather Traveling Bags.

ABSOLUTELY THE BEST MATERIAL AND BEST MAKE is offered in this line. Our bags and suit cases are made of the thickest and toughest kinds of leather, sewed with heaviest waxed thread over strong steel frames, carefully riveted and handsomely finished throughout. Our trunks are built like battleships, strongly protected and reinforced at every danger point, practically unbreakable. There is integrity in every inch of these trunks and traveling bags. Our first and last consideration in their construction has been to make them as roomy, as strong and as nearly unbreakable as possible.

WE GUARANTEE THEM ABSOLUTELY in every case, and if you don't find the trunk or traveling bag you get from us far superior to what will cost you 50 per cent more if purchased elsewhere, we will willingly refund both the price and any transportation charges you paid on the goods on return of the same to us. Read carefully each description, compare every statement with illustrations shown, note carefully one by one the reinforcements, note size and weight of the trunk and the compartments and fittings in it, and last but not least, remember the IRON CLAD GUARANTEE ON THESE IRON CLAD TRUNKS. Every illustration is made from an actual photograph of the trunk, case or bag which will be found to surpass goods sold at retail at double our prices.

98c ENAMEL RUBBER CLOTH SUIT CASE.

No. 33H1302 Brown Enamel Rubber Cloth Suit Case, solid cowhide leather, riveted corners, reinforced round padded leather handle. Made over strong steel frame and riveted throughout, brass lock and bolts and cloth lined; length, 24 inches; weight, 6 pounds. The greatest value ever offered in a cheap suit case. Equal in appearance to genuine russet cowhide leather. Retail value, $1.50.
Our price, each, only........98c

59c FINE IMITATION BROWN LEATHER BAG.

No. 33H1208 Heavy Waterproof Rubber Cloth Club Style Bag, which cannot be told from genuine brown pebble leather. Has cloth lining, round padded leather handle, highly nickled lock and catches and large bell rivets in bottom. Big value at our low price. **Be sure to state length wanted.**

Length	Price
Length, 10 inches.	$0.59
Length, 12 inches.	.79
Length, 14 inches.	.95
Length, 16 inches.	1.12

$4.65 GENUINE COWHIDE SOLE LEATHER DRESS SUIT CASE.

No. 33H1312 The greatest value ever offered in a Genuine Cowhide Case of extra heavy stock. This is regular bridle leather, which has that smooth and perfect finish which distinguishes high grade cowhide leather. The leather in these cases is warranted extra heavy weight, and of the best selected stock. Made over strong steel frame with solid brass spring lock, catches and three hinges, heavy brass bell riveted sole leather corners, sewed with waxed linen thread, and reinforced throughout with brass bell rivets. Surface of case is artistically creased, has solid leather padded handle. Linen lined and finished with full set of inside traps; a beautiful case which has no equal at $2.00 more than our price. Rich, brown color.

Length, 24 inches; weight, 7 pounds. Price........$4.65
Length, 26 inches; weight, 8 pounds. Price........ 4.90

$2.95 GENUINE LEATHER DRESS SUIT CASE.

No. 33H1310 Genuine Leather Dress Suit Case, made over strong steel frame, brass riveted and sewed with waxed linen thread. Highly finished surface which gives it the appearance of finest cowhide but is of extra heavy selected sheepskin, has brass lock and catches, three hinges, round padded leather handle, solid cowhide riveted corners and is linen lined with leather straps inside. A genuine leather case, which cannot be duplicated at less than $3.50 to $4.00. Sole leather color only. Length, 24 inches, weight 7 pounds. Price........$2.95

$2.15 GENUINE GRAIN LEATHER BAG.

No. 33H1228 Genuine Russet Grain Leather Bag, in the popular Oxford shape, cloth lined. Large and roomy and very sightly. Welted seams sewed with waxed linen thread, brassed lock and catches and has five large bell rivets on bottom. The best medium priced genuine leather bag ever shown. **Be sure to state the size wanted.**

Length	Price
Length, 14 in.	$2.15
Length, 16 in.	2.55
Length, 18 in.	2.95

$3.65 EXTRA HEAVY FANCY METAL COVERED TRUNK. HARDWOOD SLATS. IRON BOTTOM.

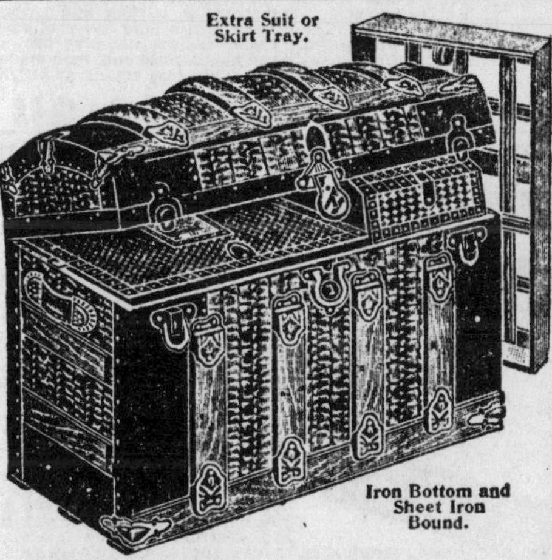
Extra Suit or Skirt Tray.
Iron Bottom and Sheet Iron Bound.

No. 33H1014 Fancy Metal Covered Trunk, large thick basswood box, paper lined, large barrel top with four heavy hardwood bar slats over top and on side, and two across each end. Heavy sheet iron bound with heavy fancy malleable trimmings and reinforcements. Iron bottom, patent bar bolts and rollers, heavy steel hinges and strong end clamps. Strong Monitor lock, fancy catches and leather handles, and contains tray with bonnet box and side compartment separately covered, also fall-in covered top compartment. Has skirt tray, which fits in underneath the upper tray and when not in use can be inverted and takes up comparatively no room. The strength and durability of which we boast is typified in this trunk which is warranted absolutely. **Be sure to state the size wanted.**

Length, 28 inches; width, 16½ inches; height, 20 inches; weight, 41 pounds. Price..$3.65
Length, 32 inches; width, 18½ inches; height, 22 inches; weight, 49 pounds. Price.. 4.25
Length, 36 inches; width, 20½ inches; height, 24 inches; weight, 60 pounds. Price.. 4.85

$1.95 CRYSTALIZED METAL COVERED TRUNK, HARDWOOD SLATS, IRON BOTTOM.

Strong and Serviceable. Full Size.
Iron Bottom.

No. 33H1002 Substantially made Barrel Top Trunk, with four hardwood slats over top and two slats on sides and one on either end. Sheet iron bound, fancy metal trimmings and reinforcements, Japanned steel end clamps, iron bottom, special bar bolts, hinges, rollers and catches and has strong hasp lock and leather handles. Contains set-up tray with covered bonnet box. A good solidly made full size trunk at a very low price. If bought in the regular retail way could not be duplicated at $1.50 to $2.00 more than we ask. But we honestly advise the purchase of a better trunk as a good trunk lasts many years and always insures safe transportation to its contents, and we recommend to you our No. 33H1014 illustrated and described on the left. Remember though, for the price this is the best trunk ever made. **State size wanted and give correct catalogue number.**

Length	Width	Height	Weight	Price
26 inches	14½ inches	17½ inches	28 pounds	$1.95
30 inches	16½ inches	19½ inches	35 pounds	2.55
34 inches	18½ inches	21½ inches	42 pounds	3.15
36 inches	19½ inches	22½ inches	47 pounds	3.45

$6.85 ELEGANTLY FITTED COWHIDE LEATHER SUIT CASE.

SELECTED COWHIDE

No. 33H1317 Extra Heavy Selected Cowhide Suit Case, hand creased and sewed with waxed linen thread, riveted throughout and finished with best brass lock, catches and hinges, heavy bell riveted cowhide corners and padded leather handle, best Irish linen lining. Has inside straps, including stay straps to hold cover when open and is fitted with hair brush, comb, soap box, tooth and nail brush in glass case and perfume bottle, each article firmly held in place by strong loops. A convenient and handsome suit case. Color, olive brown. Length, 24 inches.
Price........$6.85

$1.69 SPECIAL KERATOL SUIT CASE.

No. 33H1304 Best Waterproof Imitation Brown Grain Leather, Cloth Lined Suit Case, strongly riveted and sewed throughout, made on strong steel frame and has heavy riveted sole leather corners, round padded handle, brassed lock and catches, and three strong hinges. A handsome and sightly imitation leather case. Length, 24 inches; weight, 6 pounds. Regular price, $2.50. Our price, each, only...$1.69

$4.95 HEAVIEST BLACK ENAMEL MONITOR TOP TRUNK. STEEL AND IRON COVERED, BOUND WITH FIVE HEAVY HARDWOOD SLATS. SAVING YOU $2.50 TO 3.00.

No. 33H1040 Black Enamel Steel Covered Monitor Top Trunk. Four heavy hardwood slats over top and down side, two across each end and one lengthwise across top, intersecting cross slats. Extra heavy malleable clamps and reinforcements, corner bumpers, brass Excelsior lock, heavy patent bolts, rollers, hinges, catches, etc. Stitched leather handles, heavy iron bottom, contains tray with bonnet box and side compartments, fall-in top compartment all separately covered. Has extra skirt tray that can be inverted and takes up comparatively no room. Note the heavy malleable trimmings, the number of and width and thickness of the hardwood slats, the strong reinforcements, and remember that this trunk has an iron bottom and is made on extra large size thick basswood box. We are so confident of the strength and the superiority of this trunk that we will, at any time, replace any one of these trunks that does not give absolute satisfaction. Where is the dealer that offers this guarantee on any trunk he sells? **Be sure to state size and catalogue number.**

Intersecting Slat Lengthwise on Top.
Extra Skirt Tray. Iron Bottom.
Extra Large Size.

Length	Width	Height	Weight	Price
28 inches	17 inches	20 inches	45 pounds	$4.95
32 inches	19 inches	22 inches	55 pounds	5.65
36 inches	21 inches	24 inches	64 pounds	6.35
38 inches	22 inches	25 inches	70 pounds	6.70

$5.15 FOR COWHIDE SUIT CASE WITH SHIRT FOLD.

No. 33H1316 This case is made of Finest Heavy Cowhide Bridle Leather, over strong steel frame, solid brass plated lock and catches, bell rivets, padded leather handle, and sole leather corners, beautiful creased surface, strongly sewed with waxed linen thread, linen lined and has linen shirt pockets closed with leather straps in top as illustrated, also straps in bottom of case and stay straps at back. A remarkable value at our low price in a beautiful dark brown shade. **State size wanted.**

Length, 24 inches; weight, 7½ pounds. Price........$5.15
Length 26 inches; weight, 8½ pounds. Price........$5.40

$1.38 FOR BEST IMITATION ALLIGATOR SUIT CASE.

No. 33H1307 Finest Imitation Alligator Suit Case, highly finished surface, and can hardly be distinguished from genuine alligator. Round padded sole leather handle, riveted ends and brass plated lock and catches, strong steel frame, inside straps, cloth lined and waterproof. Length, 24 inches; weight, 7 pounds.
Price........$1.38

$1.95 CRYSTALLIZED METAL COVERED TRUNK, FLAT TOP, HARDWOOD SLATS, IRON BOTTOM.

No. 33H1010 Good Substantial Fancy Metal Covered Flat Top Trunk, with four hardwood slats across top and two on sides and one on each end, has sheet iron binding, fancy metal trimmings, japanned steel end clamps and iron bottom, made with special bar bolts and strong hasp lock, catches, rollers and hinges, and has leather handles. Contains set-up tray with covered bonnet box. A good, solid, substantial trunk, full size, at small cost. This trunk will cost $2.00 to $2.50 more if bought in the regular retail way. Yet we honestly advise that you purchase better trunks. The small difference in cost is not to be considered, as a better trunk always insures protection to contents. If interested in a better trunk, we refer you to our No. 33H1022, illustrated and described opposite, and which is thoroughly guaranteed. But remember, for a low price trunk the number here described and illustrated cannot be equaled.

Length	Width	Height	Weight	Price
26 in.	14½ in.	17½ in.	29 lbs.	$1.95
30 in.	16½ in.	19½ in.	36 lbs.	2.55
34 in.	18½ in.	21½ in.	43 lbs.	3.15
36 in.	19½ in.	22½ in.	47 lbs.	3.45

$3.75 EXTRA HEAVY MONITOR TOP STEEL COVERED TRUNK, HARDWOOD SLATS, IRON BOTTOM.

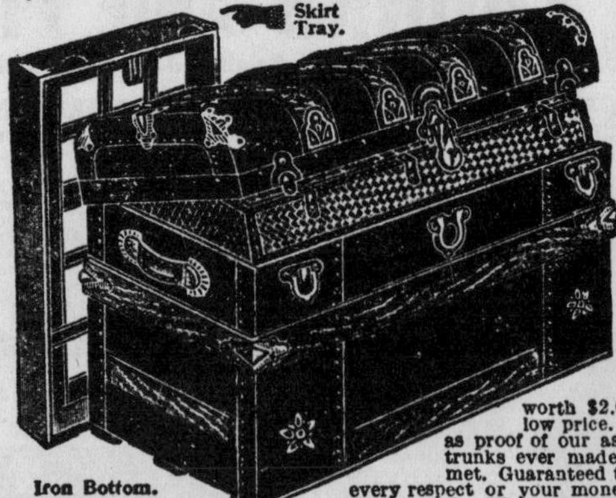

No. 33H1022 Handsome Steel Covered Black Enamel Monitor Top Trunk. Large box made of thick basswood, paper lined, has flat top with rounded edges and is finished with four heavy hardwood bar slats over top and two on sides and around ends. Heavy sheet iron bottom and is thoroughly reinforced and trimmed with metal trimmings, steel end clamps, patent bar bolts, heavy steel hinges and rollers, brass monitor lock and catches, leather handles, and contains tray with separately covered bonnet box and side compartment, also skirt tray which fits underneath first tray and when desired can be inverted and takes up comparatively no room. A trunk that is easily worth $2.00 to $3.00 more than our low price. We gladly offer this trunk as proof of our assertion of absolutely the best trunks ever made at prices which cannot be met. Guaranteed to give absolute satisfaction in every respect or your money back. **Be sure to state size wanted.** Wholesale prices as follows:

Length	Width	Height	Weight	Price
28 in.	16 in.	18½ in.	37 lbs.	$3.75
32 in.	18 in.	20½ in.	47 lbs.	4.35
36 in.	20 in.	22½ in.	58 lbs.	4.95

$6.65 FOR HEAVY QUILTED SATIN LINED, COWHIDE SUIT CASE.

No. 33H1319 Solid Cowhide Suit Case of Finest Bridle Leather, beautifully hand creased and has latest brass lock and catches. Padded leather handle and heavy bell riveted sole leather corners, lined complete with rich heavy quilted satin, stitched with silk. Leather straps in both lid and bottom, and also leather stay straps to hold cover when open. A beautiful case for ladies. Color, rich brown. Length, 24 inches.

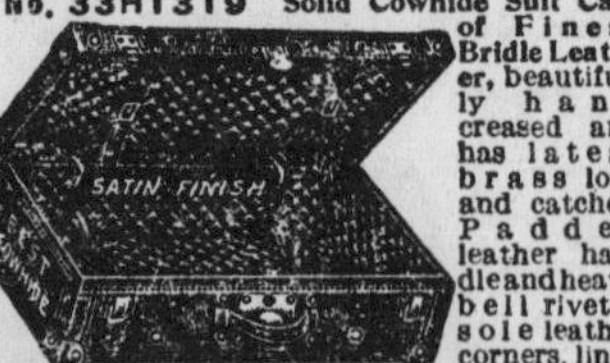

Price, each, only $6.65

$3.35 FOR GRAIN LEATHER CABINET BAG. A STAPLE STYLE.

No. 33H1240 Heavy Grain Leather Cabinet Bag, with strong japanned steel frame and brass lock, brass catches at ends. Fine cloth lining with inside pocket. Strong round padded leather handle and finished with heavy bell rivets on bottom. A bag which retails at $1.00 to $1.50 more than we ask.

Length, 16 inches. Price $3.35
Length, 18 inches. Price 3.95

$3.65 FOR GRAIN LEATHER OXFORD BAG. LEATHER LINED.

No. 33H1232 Finest Selected Heavy Grain Leather Oxford Bag, with elegant leather lining and inside pocket. A large roomy bag and will give best of service. Welted seams sewed with waxed linen thread. Best brass lock and catches, leather covered steel frame. English round padded leather handle and heavy bell rivets on bottom. **State size.**

Length, 14 inches. Price..........$3.65
Length, 16 inches. Price..........4.05
Length, 18 inches. Price..........4.45

$8.35 FOR STRONGEST, MOST ELEGANT BRIDLE LEATHER CASE.

No. 33H1321 Strongest Cowhide Bridle Leather Suit Case, highly finished and beautifully trimmed and hand creased, full leather lined. Heavy sole leather corners with six large brass bell rivets at each corner. Heaviest solid brass lock and catches, three brass hinges, and is reinforced with two continuous cowhide straps, running through wide riveted leather loops. Padded solid leather handle. Has leather shirt fold in cover, closed with two straps, two straps in bottom and leather stay straps at back, which hold cover of case when open. Color, the stylish olive brown. Undoubtedly the handsomest suit case made. **Please state size.** This case retails at $10.00 to $12.00.

Length, 26 inches. Price..........$8.35
Length, 28 inches. Price..........8.70

$4.65 FOR STRONGEST, FANCY METAL, BARREL TOP TRUNK. FIVE HEAVY HARDWOOD SLATS TOP AND SIDE. IRON BOTTOM.

No. 33H1050 Heaviest, Fancy Metal Covered Trunk, with large barrel top, five heavy hardwood barrel stave slats over top and down side, two hardwood slats across each end. Heavy, malleable trimmings and reinforcements throughout. Monitor lock, heaviest and strongest malleable iron bumpers, patent bolts, rollers, hinges, catches, etc. Leather handles, full finished hinged tray with separately covered compartment and bonnet box, also fall-in covered top compartment and extra skirt tray which fits in underneath first tray. Iron bound, made and trimmed and reinforced at every danger point exactly as illustrated. Made on extra large size, thick basswood box. One of the greatest trunks in this style trunk ever offered. We will, at any time, replace any trunk of this number which fails to give satisfaction. Where else can you get a guarantee like this on trunks? **Remember to state the size and catalogue number.**

Length	Width	Height	Weight	Price
28 in.	16½ in.	22 in.	48 lbs.	$4.65
32 in.	18½ in.	24 in.	51 lbs.	5.35
36 in.	20½ in.	26 in.	62 lbs.	6.05

$2.95 FOR OVAL TOP CANVAS COVERED TRUNK.

No. 33H1055 Painted Canvas Covered Trunk, with iron bottom, sheet iron bound edges, four hardwood slats running lengthwise on top, two slats on sides and ends. Japanned steel clamps, knees and corner bumpers top and bottom. Monitor lock, patent bolts, hinges, catches, etc., leather handles, deep tray and covered hat box. Large size box, paper lined. A low priced trunk which for service is unequaled. While this trunk for the money is guaranteed to be better than can be bought anywhere else, we strongly recommend the purchase of better trunks, as a good trunk will last indefinitely. If interested in a better trunk, we recommend to you our No. 33H1058, illustrated and described on the following page. Remember, though, that at the price we defy anyone to equal the trunk here illustrated and described and which is guaranteed to give satisfaction. **State the size and catalogue number.**

Length	Width	Height	Weight	Price
28 in.	16¾ in.	17¾ in.	38 lbs.	$2.95
32 in.	18¾ in.	19¾ in.	50 lbs.	3.65
36 in.	20¾ in.	21¾ in.	57 lbs.	4.35
38 in.	21¾ in.	22¾ in.	62 lbs.	4.70

When you buy a trunk or traveling bag of us you get the greatest possible value

22c FOR LEATHER RIVETED CANVAS COVERED TELESCOPE.

No. 33H1344 Excellent Quality Canvas Covered Telescope. Full size. Riveted leather corners. Padded, stitched and riveted leather handle and closed with three solid cowhide straps on large sizes. **State length wanted.**

Length	Width	Weight	Height	Extd.	Price
14 in.	7 in.	1½ lbs.	6 in.	12 in.	22c
18 in.	9 in.	2½ lbs.	7 in.	14 in.	42c
20 in.	10 in.	3 lbs.	8 in.	15 in.	52c
24 in.	12 in.	4 lbs.	8½ in.	17 in.	72c
26 in.	13 in.	4½ lbs.	9 in.	18 in.	92c

55c FOR FULL LEATHER BOUND CANVAS TELESCOPE.

No. 33H1346 Strongest Waterproof Canvas Telescope. Leather bound ends. Thoroughly sewed and riveted corners and ends, and broad sewed and riveted handle. Finished with three solid grain leather straps on large sizes. **State length wanted.**

Length	Width	Weight	Height	Extd.	Price
16 in.	8½ in.	2 lbs.	6½ in.	12 in.	$0.55
20 in.	10½ in.	3 lbs.	8 in.	14 in.	.75
24 in.	12½ in.	4 lbs.	9½ in.	17 in.	.95
26 in.	13½ in.	4½ lbs.	10½ in.	18½ in.	1.12

$6.10 FOR CANVAS COVERED WAGON OR STEAMER TRUNK. STRAPS AND VALANCE CLAMPS.

No. 33H1136 Painted Canvas Covered Wagon or Steamer Trunk. Four heavy hardwood slats running lengthwise across top, one heavy hardwood slat across front and back, all protected with heavy brass clamps and heavy fancy corner bumpers, brass plated lock and side bolts. Heavy valance clamps at corners where cover meets body. Tray with two compartments separately covered. Muslin lined throughout. Reinforced as illustrated and strengthened with heavy sole leather straps. Our guarantee: We will replace any trunk of this number which does not prove satisfactory. **State size and catalogue number when ordering trunk.** Following are wholesale prices:

This illustration is from an actual photograph.

Length	Width	Height	Weight	Price
32 inches	19 inches	13½ inches	36 pounds	$6.10
36 inches	20 inches	13½ inches	40 pounds	6.75
38 inches	21 inches	13½ inches	43 pounds	7.30

$6.65 FOR FINE LEATHER LINED SUIT CASE.

No. 33H1320 Handsome Brown Cowhide Leather Suit Case of heaviest, highly polished bridle leather, made over strong steel frame, finished with heavy brass bell rivets in sole leather corners and on ends, sewed throughout with waxed linen thread and handsomely creased. Solid brass lock, catches and hinges. Padded leather handle. Full leather lined body with leather shirt fold closed with two straps, also straps in bottom, and at back to hold cover.

Length, 24 inches. Price..........$6.65
Length, 26 inches. Price..........6.90

$5.95 FOR STRAPPED SOLE LEATHER SUIT CASE. From Photo.

No. 33H1313 Heavy Selected Cowhide Suit Case, hand creased surface, sewed with waxed linen thread, finished with heavy bell riveted sole leather corners, round padded leather handle, brass lock and catches, heavy rivets throughout, reinforced with two heavy straps and lined with Irish linen. Shirt fold in top with extra straps over same and in bottom. Color, rich olive brown. Length, 24 inches. Price, each, only..........$5.95

$15.50 FOR HANDSOME LEATHER BOUND, IRON BOTTOM TRUNK. THE FINEST TRUNK MADE.

TWO TRAYS.

Most beautiful trunk made.

No. 33H1100 Beautiful Painted, Olive Green Canvas Covered Trunk. Very large and thick basswood box, slightly rounded three-ply veneer top, heavy cowhide leather binding and center band, heaviest sole leather straps running through fancy metal strap loops. New dome set brass corner bumpers and clamps, riveted valance clamps, combination handle loops and dowels, brass Excelsior lock, patent lifter bolts, heavy steel hinges, rollers, deep hinged tray, hat box with secret drawer, side compartments, folding lids and dress tray all cloth lined. For beauty, coupled with serviceability cannot be matched by any trunk on the market today. We recommend this trunk and will replace any one broken in regular service, a guarantee that has never before been made on trunks. **Don't forget to state the size and our catalogue number.**

Length, 32 in.; width, 19 in.; height, 23½ in.; weight, 55 lbs. Price......$15.50
Length, 36 in.; width, 21 in.; height, 25½ in.; weight, 72 lbs. Price...... 17.50
Lehgth, 38 in.; width, 22 in.; height, 26½ in.; weight, 77 lbs. Price...... 18.50

$11.95 FOR THIS WONDERFUL LEATHER AND IRON BOUND TRUNK. BUILT LIKE A BATTLESHIP, BECAUSE REINFORCED AT EVERY DANGER POINT.

TWO TRAYS.

Strongest trunk ever made.

No. 33H1096 The Strongest Trunk Ever Made. Extra large and thick basswood box covered with heaviest painted canvas. Flat top, five painted hardwood slats running lengthwise on top, and three heavy hardwood slats running around body of trunk. Front and back angle steel binding, edges heavy cowhide leather bound with fancy leather quarter rounds in corners, heavy leather handles and two heavy cowhide leather straps running through fancy metal and leather loops and tips. Heavy dome set brass plated clamps, dowels, knees, corner shoes, valance clamps, etc. Brass Excelsior lock, patent lifter bolts, dowels on front and end. Heavy hinges, patent rollers, iron bottom, and contains hinged tray with hat box and other compartments, each with folding lid. Additional dress tray, full cloth lined, which fits underneath main tray. You cannot fail to note the thorough manner in which this trunk is made and reinforced. We say, "built like a battleship," and the trunk is sufficient proof of the statement. A great big trunk, which can never be broken in ordinary service. We will replace any trunk so broken. **Do not fail to state the size and our catalogue number.**

Length, 32 in., width, 18½ in., height, 21 in., weight, 65 lbs. Price......$11.95
Length, 34 in., width, 19½ in., height, 22 in., weight, 69 lbs. Price........ 12.70
Length, 38 in., width, 21½ in., height, 24 in., weight, 82 lbs. Price........ 14.20
Length, 40 in., width, 22½ in., height, 25 in., weight, 92 lbs. Price........ 14.95

From photograph.

$6.35 FOR GENUINE ALLIGATOR OXFORD BAG.

No. 33H1242 Genuine Alligator Leather Oxford Traveling Bag at a price never before made for a genuine alligator bag. Made over a strong steel frame, waxed linen sewed welted seams and opens full and wide, as illustrated. Latest solid brass lock and catches, heavy bell rivets on bottom. Best round padded English handle, also of genuine alligator. Finest leather lined with inside pocket. Without doubt the greatest bargain ever offered in a traveling bag. Genuine alligator which cannot wear out. This bag retails at $10.00 to $12.00. **Please state size.** Length, 14 inches. Price..$6.35
Length, 16 inches. Price........................ 7.35
Length, 18 inches. Price........................ 8.35

$9.45 FOR ENGLISH BELLOWS COWHIDE CASE. RETAILS AT $12.00 TO $14.00.

HOLDS TWICE AS MUCH

No. 33H1322 English Bellows Case. Made of rich olive brown cowhide leather, selected stock, hand creased and sewed with waxed linen thread. Double bellows side, reinforced with two heavy cowhide straps running through broad riveted leather loops, finished with solid sole leather corners, secured with heavy bell rivets. Solid brass lock and catches, padded round leather handle. Lined with finest Holland linen. Strapped partition so that bellows side can be packed entirely separate from balance of case. Straps in bottom and stay straps at back. **Be sure to state length wanted.**

Length, 24 inches; weight, 10¼ pounds. Price..$ 9.45
Length, 26 inches; weight, 11¼ pounds. Price.. 9.95
Length, 28 inches; weight, 12¼ pounds. Price.. 10.45

$9.45 FOR GENUINE BRIDLE LEATHER TRAVELING BAG.

From photograph.

No. 33H1251 Heavy Highly Finished Genuine Bridle Leather Oxford Bag. Made of 6-ounce selected cowhide, welted seams sewed with waxed linen thread. English frame which opens up full width. Satin finished, solid brass lock and catcher covered with leather flap with slot for name plate or card. Large bell rivets on bottom, and round padded English handle. Lined with fine heavy buff colored selected leather and finished with large pocket inside. Large roomy shape and will wear a lifetime. Retails at $12.00 to $15.00. **Please state size.**

Length, 16 inches. Price......................$ 9.45
Length, 18 inches. Price...................... 10.35
Length, 20 inches. Price...................... 11.25

$6.65 FOR EXTRA LARGE CANVAS COVERED TRUNK. HEAVIEST HARDWOOD SLATS. IRON BOTTOM.

From photograph.

No. 33H1070 Extra Large Size Painted Canvas Covered Trunk. Made with four extra wide and heavy hardwood slats on top, and two body slats running clear around. Heavy sheet iron bottom and binding around ends. Has heaviest and strongest malleable clamps and reinforcements at every point. Buckle bar bolts. Excelsior lock. Heavy malleable valance clamps at corners where lid and body meet. Strong rollers, and is reinforced with two extra heavy sole leather straps. Contains large roomy tray with hat box and large side compartment separately covered. A trunk that has been thoroughly tried by us for several years and has never disappointed. We will replace any trunk which does not give satisfaction. **When ordering please state size.**

Iron Bottom.

Length	Width	Height	Weight	Price
32 in.	21 in.	23½ in.	50 lbs.	$6.65
34 in.	21½ in.	24 in.	55 lbs.	7.00
36 in.	22½ in.	25 in.	60 lbs.	7.35
38 in.	23 in.	25½ in.	65 lbs.	7.70

$5.65 FOR CANVAS COVERED STEEL BOUND TRUNK. VALANCE SET, HEAVY SOLE LEATHER STRAPS.

TWO TRAYS.

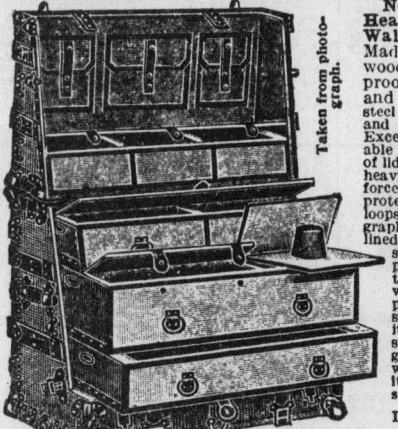

Iron Bottom.

No. 33H1058 Large, Full Size Trunk, thick basswood box, covered with heavy waterproof canvas, entirely bound with angle steel binding, heavy hardwood slats, heavy malleable iron valance clamps, buckle bar bolts, corner bumpers, steel strip clamps, knees, center band and iron bottom, brass Monitor lock, sole leather straps. Contains roomy hinged upper tray with hat box and side compartments separately covered with folding lids. Has extra skirt tray below. What can you get in the ordinary retail way that will compare in construction, reinforcements and appearance with this trunk? We warrant our trunks absolutely, and this trunk, if in any way at any time should prove unsatisfactory, we will replace without charge.

Remember the size and catalogue number when ordering.

Length, 30 in.; width, 17½ in.; height, 19½ in.; weight, 51 lbs. Price.......$5.65
Length, 32 in.; width, 18½ in.; height, 20½ in.; weight, 56 lbs. Price....... 6.00
Length, 36 in.; width, 20½ in.; height, 22½ in.; weight, 65 lbs. Price....... 6.70
Length, 38 in.; width, 21½ in.; height, 23½ in.; weight, 69 lbs. Price....... 7.05

$11.25 FOR WALL DRESSER TRUNK. SHEET IRON BOUND. IRON BOTTOM.

Illustration is made from an actual photograph.

Iron Bottom.

No. 33H1116 Special Wall Dresser Trunk, painted canvas covered, made over large thick basswood box, thoroughly reinforced and protected by heaviest malleable japanned trimmings, with No. 4 buckle bar bolts in front and ends, has brass Excelsior lock, strongest patent catches, hinges and rollers. Valance clamps at corners where cover strikes body. The most convenient style trunk ever made. Any part accessible at all times. Upper part contains three compartments with drawers in body, metal bound, resting on steel supports, cloth faced. Exactly as illustrated. This is one of the most serviceable and convenient trunks ever made. A favorite with ladies. We cannot afford to misrepresent. Your money's worth here or your money back. **Please state size wanted.**

Length	Width	Height	Weight	Price
32 in.	18½ in.	22 in.	62 lbs.	$11.25
36 in.	20½ in.	24 in.	74 lbs.	12.75
38 in.	21½ in.	25 in.	80 lbs.	13.50

$18.95 FOR MOST CONVENIENT BUREAU TRUNK MADE. ROOMY COMPARTMENTS, ALWAYS ACCESSIBLE.

Taken from photograph.

Accessible at all times.

No. 33H1110 The Strongest, Heaviest and Most Convenient Wall Dresser Trunk ever made. Made over extra large, thick basswood box, covered with heavy waterproof painted canvas, and reinforced and protected with olive enameled steel binding. Brass plated heels, bumpers and clamps, No. 4 buckle bar bolts, brass Excelsior lock, strongest and heaviest malleable catches, valance clamps at corners of lid, four heavy hinges and rollers, and has heavy stitched leather handles, and is reinforced with two heavy sole leather straps, protected with metal and leather strap loops. The illustration is an exact photographic reproduction of this trunk. Linen lined with genuine Irish linen facing, three strapped pockets and three roomy compartments in lid of trunk and has three large roomy drawers arranged with movable hat form, and extra compartment in bottom of trunk. For strength and durability, coupled with its many convenient features, this trunk stands without a peer. The strongest guarantee ever put upon a trunk; we will replace any trunk, if at any time it is proven unsatisfactory. **Please state size.** Sizes as follows:

Length	Width	Height	Weight	Price
32 in.	20 in.	24 in.	78 lbs.	$18.95
36 in.	22 in.	26 in.	88 lbs.	21.95
38 in.	24 in.	28 in.	98 lbs.	23.45

TRUNKS AND TRAVELING BAGS.

WE SELL ALL STYLES OF TRUNKS AT LOWEST PRICES. WE CAN SUIT YOU IN PRICE AND QUALITY. NO ONE CAN COMPETE WITH US IN THIS LINE.

IN TRUNKS AND BAGS, as in most other kinds of merchandise, we recommend the better grades, for they are the cheapest in the end. A dollar or two added to the price of a trunk may mean many years of additional usefulness. The particular reason why we deserve careful consideration and your order, is because we protect you from high prices, from dishonest quality and workmanship. While we sell the cheaper kinds as well as the better grades, each represents the best value of that kind at lowest possible prices. We do not offer one kind of trunk or bag at cost and then ask you to pay too much for another.

THERE IS INTEGRITY in trunks as in other merchandise. They should be made to stand the wear and tear which they are sure to get from time to time.

OUR TRUNKS AND BAGS are made under careful supervision; every nail, rivet, clamp, hinge and lock is attached with the exactness and skill of thorough workmen. THIS IS WHY WE WARRANT EVERY TRUNK AND BAG to be as represented and the best of its kind at the lowest possible price.

Crystallized or Fancy Metal Covered Trunks.

Cross Bar Slats, Iron Bottom.

No. 33G5002 Very substantially made; barrel stave top, paper lined, iron bound, cross bar slats on top, body slats, set up tray with covered bonnet box, hasp lock, leather handles, fancy tinned trimmings, iron bottom. Be sure to state size wanted.

Length	Width	Height	Weight	Price
26 in.	14½ in.	17½ in.	27 lbs...	$1.75
30 in.	16½ in.	19½ in.	34 lbs...	2.40
34 in.	18½ in.	21½ in.	41 lbs...	3.00
36 in.	19½ in.	22½ in.	46 lbs...	3.50

Crystallized Metal Covered Trunks, Flat Top.

No. 33G5010 Fancy Metal Covered Trunk. Tinned trimmings, flat top, large shape, paper lined, iron bound, cross bar slats on top; long slats on body, set up tray with covered bonnet box, iron bottom. Be sure to state size wanted.

Length	Width	Height	Weight	Price
26 in.	14½ in.	17 in.	28 lbs.....	$1.75
30 in.	16½ in.	19 in.	35 lbs.....	2.40
34 in.	18½ in.	21 in.	43 lbs.....	3.00
36 in.	19½ in.	22 in.	46 lbs.....	3.50

New Shape Up to Date Trunk, Cross Bar Slats, Iron Bottom.

No. 33G5020 Fancy metal covered, flat top, paper lined, with front and back rounded, hardwood reverse bent slats, metal corner bumpers, clamps, bottom rollers, etc. Brass lock and patent bar bolts, heavy strap hinges, tray with bonnet box. Fall-in top and side compartments, separately covered and four slats on all sizes. Be sure to state size wanted.

Length	Width	Height	Weight	Price
28 in.	16½ in.	19 in.	35 lbs.....	$3.50
32 in.	18½ in.	21 in.	45 lbs.....	3.75
36 in.	20½ in.	23 in.	56 lbs.....	4.00

Crystallized Metal Covered Trunk, $3.90.

No. 33G5024 Cross bar slats, hinge tray, iron bottom, full finish. Barrel stave top, paper lined, wide iron bound, four cross bar slats on top, malleable iron corners and shoes, etc., stitched leather handles. Brass lock, patent bolts, fancy skeleton work, covered tray with bonnet box, parasol case and side compartment, fall-in top. Be sure to state size wanted.

Length	Width	Height	Weight	Price
28 in.	17½ in.	24 in.	45 lbs...	$3.90
32 in.	19½ in.	26½ in.	48 lbs...	4.59
36 in.	21½ in.	28½ in.	59 lbs...	5.26

Our Special for $4.35.

Iron Bottom and Rosewood Finish

No. 33G5035 High Wide Trunk, paper lined, covered with heavy iron, enameled, rosewood finish. Flat top, iron bottom, round corners. **Hardwood bent slats over entire top, upright on front and end slats.** All protected with heavy metal clamps and bumpers, clamps and fancy skeleton iron work on ends. **Heavy brass lock and side bolts,** stitched leather handles, heavy hinges, covered tray, with **bonnet compartment.** Be sure to state size wanted.

Length	Width	Height	Weight	Price
28 in.	17 in.	19½ in.	39 lbs....	$4.35
32 in.	19 in.	21½ in.	47 lbs....	5.00
36 in.	21 in.	23½ in.	59 lbs....	5.65

Black Enameled Iron Trunk for $4.05.

No. 33G5040 Black Enameled Iron Round Top Trunk, paper lined, large size box covered with black enameled iron, flat top with **rounded corners,** hardwood bent slats on top, fancy clamps, rollers, leather handles, brass lock, **patent bolts,** tray with bonnet box, fall-in top, **all fancy trimmed. Iron bottom.** Be sure to state size wanted.

Length	Width	Height	Weight	Price
28 in.	17 in.	20 in.	43 lbs.....	$4.05
32 in.	19 in.	22 in.	51 lbs.....	4.70
36 in.	21 in.	24 in.	62 lbs.....	5.40

Fancy Metal Covered Trunk for $5.40.

No. 33G5050 Extra High and Wide Trunk, barrel stave top, cross bar slats on top, upright on front, malleable iron bumpers. **Brass lock,** fancy chain work, malleable iron bolts, heavy hinges, stitched leather handles, covered tray with bonnet box, **parasol case** and other compartments, cloth faced, fall-in top, **crystallized metal,** handsomely trimmed and finished. Be sure to state size wanted.

Length	Width	Height	Weight	Price
32 in.	19½ in.	24½ in.	54 lbs....	$5.40
34 in.	20½ in.	25½ in.	60 lbs....	5.80
36 in.	21½ in.	26½ in.	65 lbs....	6.20

Canvas Covered Trunk for $2.80.

No. 33G5052 A Good Canvas Covered Trunk at a very low price. Square top, painted canvas cover, hardwood slats on top and body, paper lined, protected with heavy iron clamps, heavy bottom cleats, good lock and patent bolts and heavy hinges. Set up tray with covered hat compartment. The best low priced canvas covered trunk sold. Be sure to state size wanted.

Length	Width	Height	Weight	Price
30 in.	17 in.	19¼ in.	35 lbs....	$2.80
32 in.	18½ in.	21 in.	40 lbs....	3.10
36 in.	20½ in.	23 in.	49 lbs....	3.80

Trunk for $5.25 and Up.

No. 33G5058 Large box, paper lined, covered with heavy canvas, painted brown, four heavy hardwood slats on top and two on body running full length of trunk. Heavy sole leather strap. Front and back of top and bottom and ends protected with steel binding, heavy brass corners and brassed steel trimmings, valance set, heavy dowel bolts, brass lock, large tray with hat box and side compartment separately covered. Be sure to state size wanted.

Length	Width	Height	Weight	Price
30 in.	19 in.	21 in.	49 lbs......	$5.25
32 in.	20 in.	22 in.	54 lbs.....	5.55
34 in.	21 in.	23 in.	58 lbs......	5.95
36 in.	22 in.	24 in.	63 lbs......	6.20
38 in.	23 in.	25 in.	67 lbs	6.75

Canvas Covered Trunk for $4.45.

No. 33G5060 Canvas covered, iron bottom, square top, paper lined, corners double iron bound, four hardwood slats full length of trunk, **two slats all around body,** japanned steel bumpers and clamps, large brass plated lock, **heavy bolt locks,** tray containing hat box and packing compartment, fall-in top all covered. Be sure to state size wanted.

Length	Width	Height	Weight	Price
30 in.	19¼ in.	20½ in.	41 lbs.	$4.45
32 in.	20 in.	21½ in.	44 lbs.	4.75
34 in.	20¾ in.	[illegible] in.	48 lbs.	5.00
36 in.	[illegible] in.	23½ in.	53 lbs.	5.40
38 in.	[illegible] in.	24½ in.	59 lbs.	5.95

Brass Trimmed Special Value at $6.10.

No. 33G5070 Large size box, covered with painted canvas, iron binding, four heavy hardwood slats on top, two slats running full length of trunk on body, with hardwood bottom cleats protected and strengthened with heavy metal clamps at top, bottom and sides, heavy brass corner shoes and clamps, heavy brass bolts and lock, tray with separately covered compartments, cloth faced, heavy sole leather straps. Be sure to state size wanted.

Length	Width	Height	Weight	Price
32 in.	21 in.	23½ in.	50 lbs......	$6.10
34 in.	21½ in.	24 in.	55 lbs......	6.50
36 in.	22½ in.	25 in.	60 lbs......	6.90
38 in.	23 in.	25½ in.	66 lbs......	7.45

Canvas Covered Trunks, $7.15 to $10.00.

No. 33G5078 Large, Full Sized Trunk, covered with heavy waterproof canvas, bound with enameled iron binding; hardwood slats with ends brass wrapped used entirely on this trunk. Heavy valance set buckle bar bolts, Brass lock, stitched leather sliding handles, two heavy sole leather straps. Inside arranged with roomy upper tray, with hat box and side compartments separately covered with folding lids. Extra skirt tray below. Cloth faced.

Length	Width	Height	Weight	Price
30 in.	19 in.	22 in.	47 lbs...	$ 7.15
32 in.	20 in.	23 in.	52 lbs...	7.70
34 in.	21 in.	24 in.	57 lbs...	8.25
36 in.	22 in.	25 in.	62 lbs...	8.75
38 in.	23 in.	26 in.	68 lbs...	9.35
40 in.	24 in.	27 in.	75 lbs...	10.00

Rawhide Bound, Riveted, Canvas Covered Trunk.

No. 33G5096 Covered with heavy canvas, painted; cloth lined throughout; hardwood slats, all protected with heavy brassed clamps; edges bound with rawhide, valance set, heavy brass dowel bolts, all bolts, lock and hinges are riveted; heavy sole leather straps. Brass lock, tray with hat box and other compartments, separately covered with folding lids; **dress tray cloth lined.** Be sure to state size wanted.

Length	Width	Height	Weight	Price
32 in.	19½ in.	23 in.	58 lbs..	$11.45
34 in.	20¼ in.	24 in.	62 lbs..	12.15
36 in.	21 in.	25 in.	67 lbs..	12.80
38 in.	22 in.	26 in.	75 lbs..	13.50

Wonderful Values in Bureau Trunks.

No. 33G5110 The Finest Bureau Trunk made. Steel trimmings, all riveted, Irish linen faced. Basswood box, hardwood slats, ends all brass wrapped, canvas covered, olive colored steel binding on edges of top and bottom, trimmed with brass clamps and heavy corner bumpers; all riveted; brass lock; heavy sole leather straps. Four steel hinges, Hagney bolts on ends; linen lined, with genuine Irish linen facing; all compartments are separately covered and easy of access, and arranged as shown in illustration. A veritable traveling chiffonier of great convenience. Be sure to state size wanted.

Length	Width	Height	Weight	Price
32 in.	20¾ in.	25 in.	76 lbs..	$17.55
34 in.	21½ in.	26 in.	82 lbs .	18.90
36 in.	22¼ in.	27 in.	88 lbs..	20.25
38 in.	23 in.	28 in.	95 lbs..	21.60
40 in.	23¾ in.	29 in.	102 lbs..	22.95

REMEMBER WHEN YOU HAVE BOUGHT $25.00 WORTH OF GOODS OR MORE FROM US YOU GET YOUR CHOICE OF MANY VALUABLE ARTICLES FREE, AS SHOWN IN OUR FREE PROFIT SHARING BOOK

Our $10.40 Dresser Trunk.

No. 33G5116 Our Special Dresser Trunk; all space can be utilized, and is accessible at any time; upper part contains three compartments, with three drawers in body. An excellent trunk for skirts and dresses. Covered with heavy painted canvas, hardwood slats on top and around body of trunk; brass lock, heavy steel clamps and corners, patent lever bolts on front and heavy lock bolts on ends. The only trunk for traveling, and of great convenience. Be sure to state size wanted.

Length	Width	Height	Weight	Price
32 in.	19⅛ in.	23¾ in.	62 lbs....	$10.40
34 in.	20¼ in.	24⅛ in.	69 lbs....	11.45
36 in.	21 in.	25 in.	74 lbs....	12.40

Special Quality Wagon or Steamer Trunk.

No. 33G5136 Our Special Quality Wagon or Steamer Trunk. Covered with heavy canvas, painted; four hardwood slats on top, one on body, all protected with heavy brass clamps and fancy corner bumpers; brass plated lock and side bolts. Has tray, two compartments separately covered with folding lids. Trunk is muslin lined throughout. Heavy sole leather straps. Be sure to state length wanted.

Length	Width	Height	Weight	Price
32 in.	19 in.	13½ in.	36 lbs....	$6.10
36 in.	20 in.	13½ in.	40 lbs....	6.75
38 in.	21 in.	13½ in.	43 lbs....	7.30

BAGS, GRIPS AND VALISES.

No. 33G5184 One of the most serviceable and best grade leather bags. Made of fine selected full stockgrain leather. Cloth lined, brass lock and catches. Heavy straps. Color, brown. Be sure to state length wanted.

Length, 16 inches. Price....$3.55
Length, 20 inches. Price.... 3.80
Length, 24 inches. Price.... 4.48

Fine Pebble Leather Brown Club Bag, 75 Cents.

No. 33G5208 Club Bag, selected pebble leather. Leather handle, brassed lock and catches. Cloth lined. Be sure to state length wanted.

Length, 10 inches. Price....$0.75
Length, 12 inches. Price.... .85
Length, 14 inches. Price.... .95
Length, 16 inches. Price.... 1.05

Our Special Leather Club Bag.

No. 33G5228 Our Special Leather Bag, made of good genuine grain leather, brassed lock and catches, cloth lined. Color, brown. Be sure to state length wanted.

Lgth.
14 in. Price.$2.25
16 in. Price. 2.55
18 in. Price. 2.85

Leather Lined Deep Club Bag.

No. 33G5232 Selected Full Grain Leather Bag, heavy brass trimmings, leather covered steel frame, English handle, full leather lined. Color, brown. Be sure to state length wanted.

Length.
14 in. Price.$3.25
16 in. Price. 3.75

A Good Cabinet Bag.

No. 33G5240 CabinetStyle Bag, made of genuine grain leather, japanned frame, brassed lock and catches, cloth lining and inside pockets. Color, brown. Be sure to state length wanted.

Length, 14 inches. Price.........$2.98
Length, 16 inches. Price......... 3.69

SUIT CASES.

AT PRICES far below what others ask for equal qualities. We furnish high class, guaranteed SUIT CASES for very little money. **A SUIT CASE** is a convenience; it enables you to carry clothing without wrinkling it and is easy to handle, in many respects more useful than a bag or valise.

Enameled Cloth Suit Case, 98 Cents.

No. 33G5302 Olive Enameled Cloth. Solid leather, riveted corners and handle. Steel frame. Brassed lock and bolts. Cloth lined. Length, 24 inches.
Price....................................98c

Our Special Keratol Suit Case.

No. 33G5304 Our Special Rain and Waterproof Suit Case, has the appearance of brown grain leather, heavy riveted leather corners, steel frame, cloth lined, brass lock and catches. Color, brown. Length, 24 inches.
Price....................................$1.69

Imitation Alligator Suit Case.

No. 33G5307 Imitation Alligator Suit Case, sole leather handles, brass plated bolt and lock, steel frame, cloth lined and inside straps. Looks like leather and is equal to it for wear. Length, 24 in. Price.........$1.35

Leather Dress Suit Case.

No. 33G5310 Leather Dress Suit Case, steel frame, brass lock and catches, all leather handle, solid cowhide riveted corners, linen lined, leather straps inside. This is the most remarkable value in all leather dress suit cases on the market. Sole leather color only. Length, 24 inches. Price.........$2.79

Our Special Leather Dress Suit Case, $4.80.

No. 33G5312 A most wonderful value in suit cases made of heavy brown colored cowhide leather. Steel frame, solid brass spring lock and catches, heavy sole leather corners reinforced with large brass bell rivets, linen lined, with inside straps, and artistically creased. Convenient to handle and exceedingly rich in appearance. Be sure to state length wanted.

Length, 24 inches. Price.........$4.80
Length, 26 inches. Price......... 5.05

Strap Suit Case, $6.79.

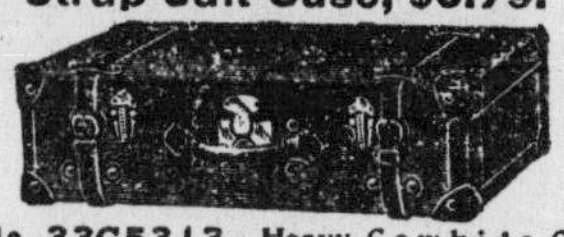

No. 33G5313 Heavy Cowhide Case Leather. Double steel frame, solid brass lock and catches, large sole leather corners reinforced with large brass rivets, two heavy sole leather straps all around outside of case. Case is lined with Irish linen, has shirt-fold in top and extra straps in bottom. Color, brown. Length, 24 inches. Price....$6.79

Leather Suit Case with Tray, $5.49.

No. 33G5314 Made of Heavy Cowhide Case Leather. Double steel frame, solid brass plated lock and catches, extra large sole leather corners reinforced with large brass bell rivets, heavy round handle, linen lined and four heavy leather straps in body. Contains linen covered drum bottom tray which can be used to great advantage. Color, brown. Be sure to state length wanted.

Length, 24 inches. Price.........$5.49
Length, 26 inches. Price......... 5.79

Leather Suit Case, $5.10.

No. 33G5316 Made of heavy fine cowhide case leather. Steel frame, solid brass plated lock and catches, large sole leather corners reinforced with brass bell rivets, heavy round handle, linen lined, with strap in body and shirt fold in top. For a sightly and durable case, this case cannot be excelled. Color, brown. State length wanted.

Length, 24 inches. Price.........$5.10
Length, 26 inches. Price......... 5.45

Elegantly Fitted Leather Suit Case, $6.79.

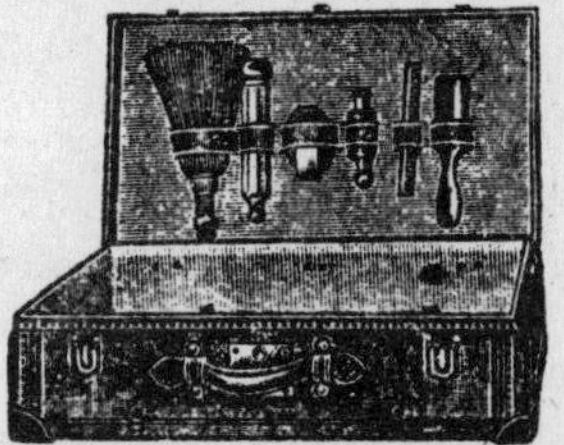

No. 33G5317 Made of Extra Quality Selected Cowhide. Solid cowhide handle and corners. New English rounded top, beautifully creased by hand and lined with the best Irish linen. Finest brass lock and catches. Fitted with whisk broom, hair brush, soap box, tooth and nail brush in glass case, perfume bottle and comb, each article firmly held in place by heavy loops. A most desirable and serviceable case and never before offered for such little money. Color, brown. Length, 24 inches. Price.........$6.79

The New Three-Pocket Suit Case, $6.79.

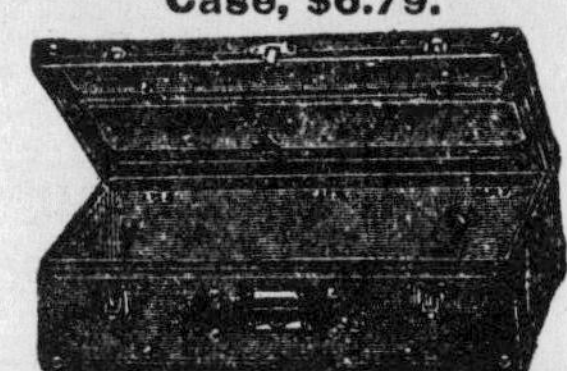

No. 33G5318 A New Suit Case with three pockets in the lid suitable for holding collars, cuffs, handkerchiefs, etc., where easily accessible. Made from select cowhide case leather, heavy leather corners, newest brass catches and lock and steel frame. Holland linen pockets and lining and inside straps. A most practical case for convenience and durability. Color, brown. Length, 24 inches.
Price....................................$6.79

All Satin Lined Suit Case $6.79.

No. 33G5319 Made of an extra quality selected cowhide, solid cowhide corners and handle. New English rounded top, beautifully creased by hand finest brass lock and catches. Lined complete with rich satin, heavily padded and stitched with silk, straps in lid and bottom of case. Without exception this is the finest case ever brought out to be sold for the money. Color, brown. Length, 24 inches. Price.........$6.79

Fine Leather Lined Suit Case.

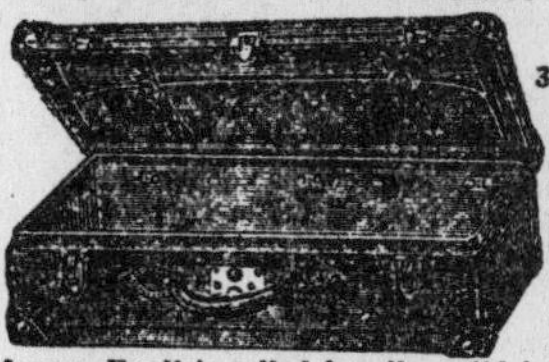

No. 33G5320 Fine Brown Cowhide Leather Suit Case, heavy, leather covered steel frame, English rolled handle, solid brass lock and catches. Heavy brass rivets, stitched ends, double corners, full leather lined body and shirt fold with straps. If you want the best and finest, this is the case you are looking for. Color, brown. State length wanted.

Length, 24 inches. Price.......$6.79
Length, 26 inches. Price....... 6.98

New English Bellows Case.

No. 33G5322 Up to Date English Bellows Case, made of brown cowhide leather. Heavy sole leather corners, reinforced with large brass bell rivets, with single accordion bellows side, reinforced with two heavy straps. Heavy roll handle attached to sole leather loops, securely riveted solid. Brass locks and bolts on this case. Selected Holland linen lined, with partition in the center. This is an exceptionally fine case and cannot help but satisfy those looking for a case of this character. State length wanted.

Length, 24 inches. Price.....$ 9.75
Length, 26 inches. Price..... 10.50
Length, 28 inches. Price..... 11.25

CANVAS TELESCOPES.

22 to 69-Cent Telescopes.

No. 33G5344 Riveted leather corners and bottom tips, heavy stitched handle; three straps on large sizes. State length wanted.

Lgth.	Width	Height	Ext'd	Price
14 in.	7 in.	6 in.	12 in..........	22c
18 in.	9 in.	7 in.	14 in..........	40c
20 in.	10 in.	7½ in.	15 in..........	51c
24 in.	12 in.	8½ in.	17 in..........	69c

Full Leather Bound Canvas Telescopes.

No. 33G5346 Heavy Canvas Leather Bound Telescope. Three grain leather straps on large sizes. State length wanted.

Lgth.	Width	Height	Ext'ed	Price
16 in.	8¼ in.	6 in.	12 in.....	$0.50
20 in.	10¼ in.	8 in.	14 in.....	.73
24 in.	12¼ in.	9½ in.	17 in.....	.86
26 in.	13¼ in.	10½ in.	18½ in.....	1.06

Extra Heavy Canvas Telescopes.

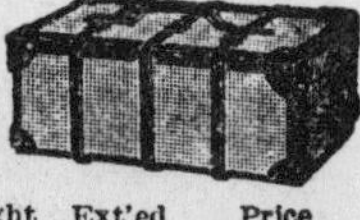

No. 33G5350 Extra heavy canvas; edges bound all around with wide leather, very heavy corner protectors; three sole leather straps. State length wanted.

Lgth.	Width	Height	Ext'ed	Price
20 in.	11¼ in.	8½ in.	15 in....	$1.49
24 in.	13¼ in.	10 in.	17 in....	1.79
26 in.	14¼ in.	10½ in.	18 in....	1.98

Shoulder or Sling Straps.

No. 33G5354 Solid Grain Leather Shoulder or Sling Straps. Price..........19c
If by mail, postage extra, 4 cents.

Shawl Straps.

No. 33G5355 Good Solid Leather Shawl Straps. Price....(Postage extra, 5 c.)... 20c

Package Handles.

No. 33G5359 Handle your package with a handle. Something new in the way of a handle for satchels. Price, per dozen, $2.25; each.......(Postage extra, each, 4 cents)...... 20c

Trunk Straps.

No. 33G5360 Very Heavy Strong Grain Leather Trunk Strap, 9 feet long, 1¼ inches wide. Price............(If by mail, postage extra, 14 cents.)........................55c

DRUGS AND COSMETICS

DRUG DEPARTMENT

IN THIS DEPARTMENT WE PRESENT A COMPLETE LINE OF

DRUGS, MEDICINAL PREPARATIONS, FAMILY REMEDIES, SOAPS, INVALID CHAIRS, NURSERY ACCESSORIES, PERFUMES, RUBBER GOODS AND SUNDRIES, ELASTIC STOCKINGS AND BELTS, BATH CABINETS, TOILET PREPARATIONS, ARTIFICIAL LEGS, TRUSSES, VETERINARY REMEDIES AND VETERINARY INSTRUMENTS.

WE CALL PARTICULAR ATTENTION to this, our very complete, thoroughly up to date and high class **Drug Department,** including everything in the line of drugs, druggists' sundries and everything in the lines mentioned above. This department includes a larger and more carefully selected line of preparations and sundries than we have ever before presented and we believe it to be the best drug department in the country.

EXPERT CHEMIST IN CHARGE. The manager of our Drug Department is a thoroughly competent, highly educated, technical chemist and pharmacist, and is a graduate of the best chemical and pharmaceutical courses in the country. In addition to this training he has also had many years' practical experience in charge of retail drug stores and drug manufacturing concerns and knows every detail of the trade. He has associated with him a large corps of registered pharmacists and chemists, all of whom have been personally examined by the Illinois State Board of Pharmacy and received certificates of proficiency in their profession. You therefore can feel assured that you are perfectly safe in entrusting us with an order for anything in this department, feeling sure that all your drug orders will be made up carefully and accurately and of absolutely pure ingredients.

DRUGS AND MEDICINES.

PROBABLY IN NO OTHER LINE is it so easy to practice adulteration as in drugs and medicines. Chemicals, of varying strength can be secured, quality can be secured to match any price, cheapened and inferior drugs and chemicals are offered by some manufacturers and strictly pure goods by others. We wish to say most emphatically that we use only the very best, purest and highest grade drugs and we carefully analyze every drug and chemical we use to ascertain its purity and prove its identity. We will not use any goods that are not strictly pure and up to a certain high standard of quality and this is your safeguard in ordering drugs from this department.

THE SAME CONDITION holds true in medicines. For example, preparations like Beef, Iron and Wine can be made to sell at all prices, from 70 cents a gallon upwards, depending upon the material used. Please remember this in comparing prices on drugs and medicines and bear in mind that a preparation like Beef, Iron and Wine may be, very much cheaper at $2.00 a gallon by reason of its efficiency than the inferior, weakened and adulterated preparations that might be sold as low as 70 cents a gallon.

WE GUARANTEE OUR PRICES THE VERY LOWEST, quality considered; **no one undersells us if the quality is only taken in consideration.** Our prices in this line and throughout our institution are based on our cost for material and labor with just our one small percentage of profit added. We ask only a uniform small profit on drugs and we guarantee that our prices are below any kind of competition, quality always, especially in this line, being taken into consideration.

OUR OWN LABORATORY. About four-fifths of the drugs and remedies sold by us are prepared in our own laboratory and so labeled. Our laboratory is known as Seroco Chemical Laboratory and it is second to none in the country. We positively guarantee every preparation from the Seroco Chemical Laboratory to be absolutely pure, positively free from any adulteration, made of the very best drugs and never cheapened in any way; in fact, with our facilities, with the most skilled chemists and pharmacists, with the facilities afforded in our big laboratory, we are in position to furnish a better and higher grade of preparations than can be furnished by any other concern. We are in better position than any retail druggist can possibly be in to thoroughly test and carefully analyze the goods we buy and sell, to know they are strictly pure and of the highest efficiency. You are sure of getting not only the highest quality, but you are also sure of getting the lowest prices, one-half the prices charged by others and many times even less than this.

THE PRICES ASKED by the manufacturers for most patent medicines make it impossible for us to save you more than from 25 to 50 per cent, whereas, from our own laboratory, the Seroco Chemical Laboratory, we can furnish you higher grade remedies on the basis of the actual cost for the ingredients, compounding, package, etc., with but our one small percentage of profit added, and as a rule, the price is from one-third to one-half that charged by retail dealers for inferior goods.

OUR POSITION ON THE PATENT MEDICINE QUESTION.

WE SELL NEARLY ALL OF THE ADVERTISED or so called patent medicines without adding our recommendation to any particular preparation. (We can furnish only the patent medicines listed on page 841.) We simply furnish our customers such advertised patent medicines as they may want and which they would buy anyway, just the same as we supply any other merchandise, giving our patrons, however, the advantage of our buying facilities and supplying this class of goods at from 25 to 40 per cent lower prices than the prices which they would have to pay at any drug store. It must be understood, however that we know nothing about the formulae or ingredients and we can, therefore, say nothing for or against the merit of such patent medicines.

IN ADDITION we furnish to our customers a selected line of household remedies, not only for the minor ills, but also for chronic diseases, and these remedies, being prepared in our own laboratory, under our own supervision, every ingredient going into these remedies being known to us and the formula itself being in every instance one used by thousands of physicians as the most reliable and efficient for the treatment of symptoms for which they are intended, we do not hesitate to guarantee them absolutely pure and harmless and to highly recommend these remedies, feeling confident that they will meet all reasonable hopes and expectations of the customer.

THESE HOUSEHOLD PREPARATIONS of ours, put up in the Seroco Chemical Laboratory, are preparations that are the result of a great deal of experience and are based on the most successful formulas and prescriptions that are recognized by practitioners as the most successful in the treatment of these certain symptoms and for the relief and cure of the disorders and diseases for which they are intended.

IN ALL CASES OF ACUTE SICKNESS, it is usually necessary, and in many cases of chronic diseases it is advisable, to employ the services of a skilled physician. The patient may not know what is ailing him; he may not be able to judge as to the nature of his symptoms, and a careful diagnosis should be made and the treatment employed should be suitable to his condition as ascertained by the physician's examination and as determined by his judgment. When you know, however, that you are suffering from indigestion or stomach trouble; when it is a question of saving for yourself inconvenience, time and expense; when you know that your ailment is a catarrh trouble, which may have become chronic and which neither by treatment of the physician or by the use of so called patent medicines has been benefited, you need not hesitate to give our household remedy for indigestion or for catarrh, as the case may be, a fair test, as it may be just the remedy that covers your condition exactly, affording quick relief and a possible cure within a comparatively short time.

EVERY ONE OF OUR HOUSEHOLD REMEDIES is considered one of the best, if not the best prescription employed by the most successful medical practitioners for the treatment of the condition for which we supply them. Of this fact you may be certain. We also wish to emphasize the fact that these remedies are prepared in our own laboratory; that we know every ingredient that goes into the preparations, and we consequently know and can assure you that they are absolutely harmless. You are not taking the slightest risk in giving our household remedies a thorough trial.

WE DO NOT CLAIM that any one of our household remedies is a "cure all," nor do we wish you to understand that we (or anybody else) can claim that without a diagnosis of your case we know beforehand that our remedy will cure you. This would be unreasonable, and you would have a perfect right to question our sincerity. What we do know is that our household remedies comprise the most valuable and highly successful prescriptions for the different ailments which they cover. We know that there is nothing harmful in any single one of our preparations. We know that they have afforded relief and even permanent cure in hundreds and thousands of cases. We know that they are prepared with the greatest care, and we know that we are able to and do offer these remedies for a fraction of the cost of what same prescription would cost put up in any drug store.

YOU CAN EASILY ASCERTAIN whether any one of the household remedies we recommend is suitable for the treatment, relief and cure of your case. You are taking no risk, for we do not ask, nor do we expect, that you should risk a single penny when making a test of these remedies. They may be the best remedies made, they may have relieved and cured thousands of men and women, which fact would ordinarily be sufficient to secure your confidence. No matter how good a remedy may be, no matter how much it has done for others, the question for you to determine is "What will it do for me?" Is it at all suitable for your particular case? To learn whether it is or not you have the privilege of ordering the first bottle or package of our household remedies with the understanding that after you have used it you find that it has not benefited your case, upon receipt of your report to that effect and the statement that you have never ordered or used the same remedy before, we will refund you the entire amount you have paid for the first package. We shall not expect you to be put to any expense or to proceed with the treatment, unless you find that the medicine is helping you and seems to be what you need for obtaining relief and a cure.

PRESCRIPTION DEPARTMENT.

OUR PRESCRIPTION DEPARTMENT is under the direct charge of one of the most able chemists and pharmacists in the country. Every prescription is compounded with the greatest care, only the very best drugs are used, and yet we are able to save our customers in nearly all cases one-half in price. If you send your doctor's prescription, or any other prescription, to us, you can rest assured it will be given professional care. There will not be any substitutions such as local drug stores are often compelled to make for want of certain drugs. The prescription will be compounded in the most scientific manner and returned to you immediately and at a saving in price on an average of more than one-half.

WE DO NOT HANDLE OR SELL SPIRITUOUS LIQUORS.

POISONOUS DRUGS. We will not fill orders for morphine, opium, laudanum or cocaine or any preparation containing them, either with or without a physician's prescription.

OUR FAMILY REMEDIES comprise the most commonly used remedies and preparations for the housewife. Remedies that should be on the shelf of every home ready for emergency and sickness. It also includes other well known sundries and appliances for household use.

NURSERY ACCESSORIES. This includes talcum powder puffs and boxes, nursing bottles, nipples, teething rings, rattles and other items for the amusement and comfort of the baby.

PERFUMES. We wish to call special attention to our perfumes. We have made arrangements with one of the most famous French perfumers, located at Grasse, France, for all our perfumes. They will be shipped to us from Grasse, France, in sealed packages, and we will bottle these elegant floral odors in small bottles and furnish them to our customers at practically cost. Every one admires an exceptional fine perfume and we assure you that the perfumes we sell at our best price are the same, or in some cases a higher grade, to what is ordinarily sold at retail stores at 65 cents to $1.00 per ounce.

TOILET PREPARATIONS. Our toilet preparations are of exceptionally fine grade and will have the effect desired. We also absolutely guarantee that no toilet or facial preparation we list contains arsenic, mercury, corrosive sublimate or any form of poisonous ingredients. Many of our face powders and rouges we import from France direct, as the French stand today as the most expert in this line of work.

RUBBER GOODS AND SUNDRIES. We carry a complete line of rubber sundries, including water bottles, fountain syringes, nipples, urinal bags, complexion bulbs, wrinkle eradicators, toilet masks, rubber gloves, finger cots, invalid rings, bandages, rubber sheeting, ice bags and nearly every item carried in the up to date rubber line.

SOAP DEPARTMENT. Our soap department includes all the finest medicated and fancy toilet soaps. They are all made by the highest grade soap manufacturers and are guaranteed as represented.

ELASTIC STOCKINGS. Our elastic stockings are made in our own house, by experienced and high salaried men, and are manufactured of the best grade rubber and lilac silk. With our large facilities we are prepared to make on short notice all kinds and sizes of elastic goods for all parts of the body at rock bottom prices.

ARTIFICIAL LEGS. We make to order any form or size of leg, stump or foot. This division is under an expert who has made this work a life study. We guarantee a perfect fit and satisfaction.

INVALID CHAIRS. Our invalid chairs are the best that can be manufactured. We carry a complete line of all forms and shapes of reclining house and street chairs, propelling chairs, reed chairs, childrens chairs, etc. Send for our special Invalid Chair Catalogue.

BODY BRACES AND SUPPORTERS. Our line of body braces, shoulder braces, abdominal belts and supporters is very complete and of the highest grade. They are of various sizes and ordered according to size.

TRUSSES. We handle nothing but the very best grades of trusses, made for us by one of the largest truss manufacturers in the world. They are fitted by experts in the line, and a perfect fit and satisfaction is guaranteed.

BATH CABINETS. We have now made arrangements whereby we are exclusive dealers in the famous Quaker Bath Cabinet. This cabinet needs no introduction, as it is the recognized best, up to date steel frame cabinet manufactured. Do not confuse the old fashioned wood frame with our new up to date steel construction frame.

ACIDS, POISONS OR INFLAMMABLE GOODS CANNOT BE MAILED.

HOW TO ORDER.

IN ORDERING state the catalogue number of the goods you want, enclose our price and your order will be carefully filled by us with the understanding and agreement that if anything does not prove perfectly satisfactory, it can be returned to us at our expense and your money will be promptly refunded. Where goods can be mailed, we state the amount of postage required with the description of the article. If you order goods to be sent by mail, don't fail to include the necessary amount of postage. Please remember also that we do not fill orders for less than 50 cents, as fully explained in the introductory pages of this book.

A SPECIAL CATALOGUE FOR PHYSICIANS AND SURGEONS FREE

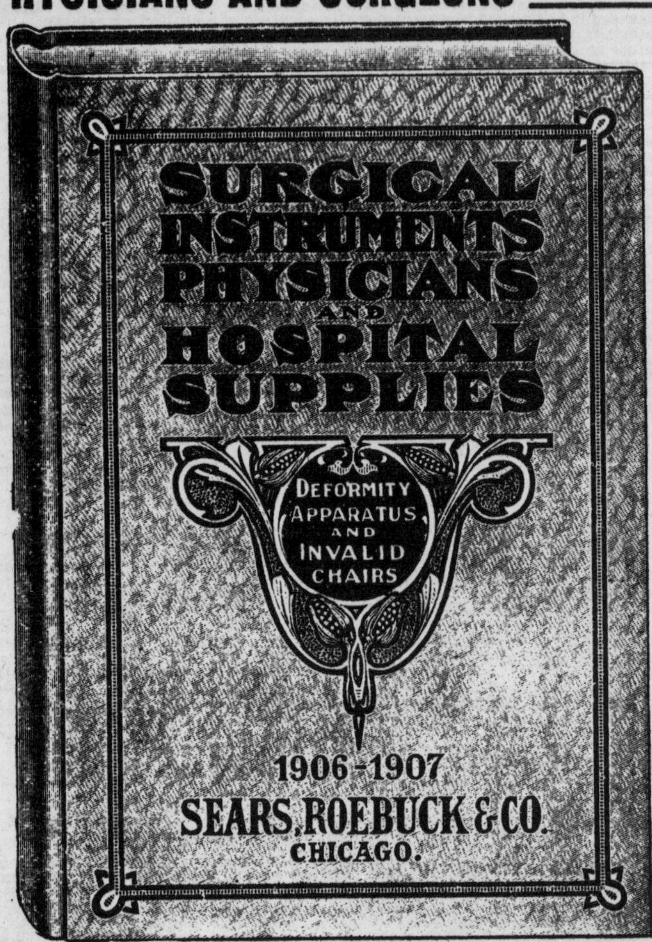

WE ISSUE A VERY COMPLETE, SPECIAL CATALOGUE of Surgical Instruments and Physicians' Supplies, which will be mailed to any physician free on application. We don't send it to anyone except physicians and surgeons, for no one else would have any use for it. This special catalogue for physicians and surgeons illustrates and describes the most complete line of surgical instruments and physicians' supplies, including everything for hospitals, etc., and all priced at very much lower prices than the same high quality of goods can be bought elsewhere. We handle only the very highest grade of instruments, appliances and supplies, everything sold subject to approval, with the understanding that if the quality is not the very best, the goods can be returned to us at our expense and the money and transportation charges will be promptly refunded.

IF YOU ARE A PHYSICIAN OR SURGEON don't pay specialty house prices for your instruments. We can save you so much money that you will be surprised and you will also be surprised at the high quality of the goods we handle in this special department.

IF YOU ARE A PHYSICIAN OR SURGEON you should write for this catalogue immediately. Just ask us to send you our free Catalogue of Surgical Instruments and it will be sent to you immediately by return mail, postpaid. It is a large book, as illustrated, containing 160 pages, fully illustrating and describing and pricing at the lowest prices ever heard of the most complete line of these goods ever offered to the profession.

DOCTOR, please don't buy another thing in this line until you first write and get our free Catalogue of Surgical Instruments and Physicians' Supplies and see what we offer you.

A SPECIAL CATALOGUE TO DENTISTS ONLY FREE

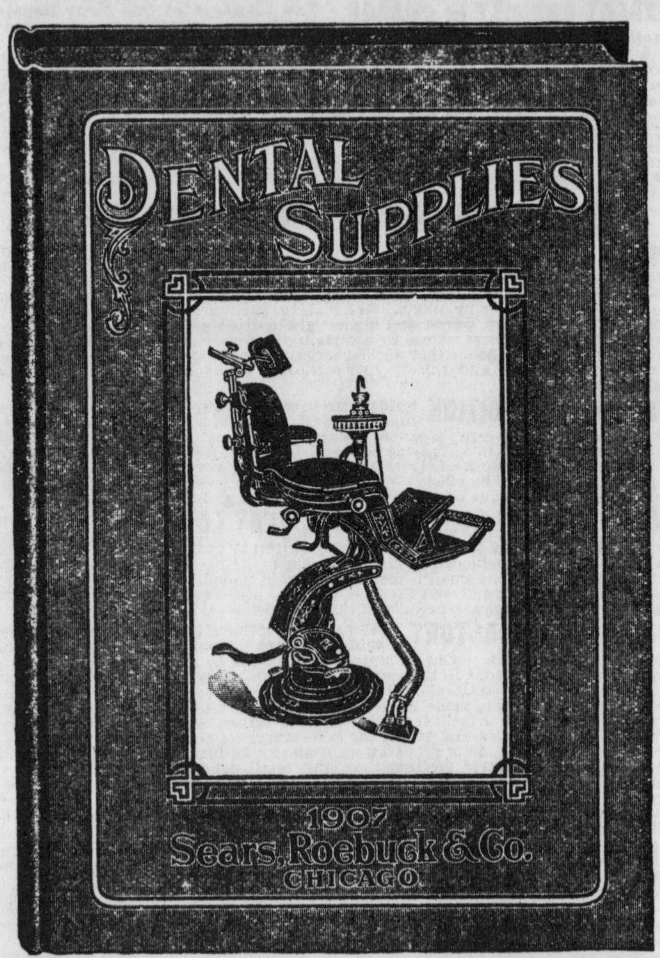

WE HAVE JUST ISSUED the most complete, comprehensive and lowest priced Catalogue of Dental Instruments and Supplies ever published, and this handsome and valuable catalogue as illustrated, we will gladly mail free to any dentist on application. Encouraged by the success we have made in selling surgical instruments of the highest quality, at prices in many instances one-half what the regular specialty houses ask for the same goods, and also in response to many inquiries as to whether we could furnish dental instruments and supplies on the same low price basis, we have established this new department of dental instruments, following the same policy that has proven so successful in our department of surgical instruments. Our lines of dental instruments and supplies are now complete and our special catalogue illustrating, describing and pricing it all is just off the press. It will prove a revelation to every dentist. These instruments and supplies have always been sold at high prices on a long profit basis, and our new plan of handling these goods is in direct opposition to the regular method. We are offering everything in the line of dental instruments and supplies, all of unquestioned quality, the very best in every class on the basis of our first cost in the largest quantities, adding only a very narrow margin of profit.

EVERY DENTIST NEEDS THIS CATALOGUE. It not only shows the complete line of dental instruments and supplies at lower prices than any concern ever dared offer direct to the dentist, but also the most complete line of artificial teeth ever presented.

IF YOU ARE A DENTIST, please write us and let us send you this new Catalogue of Dental Instruments and Supplies. Ask for our Catalogue of Dental Instruments and Supplies and it will be sent to you immediately by return mail, postpaid, everything with our compliments.

These remedies are neither patented nor secret preparations. We publish the ingredients so you may know what they contain. We positively guarantee that they contain the ingredients named and nothing else. They represent the best standard formulas in prepared form for the treatment of the conditions for which they are intended.

DR. WILDEN'S QUICK CURE FOR INDIGESTION AND DYSPEPSIA

DO YOU SUFFER FROM INDIGESTION? Do you have dyspepsia? Does your food distress you?

DO YOU SUFFER after your meals from a stuffed up, choking feeling and difficulty in breathing, pain in the chest, as if a lump were there? These are some of the easily recognized and sure symptoms of indigestion. Send for Dr. Wilden's Quick Cure for Indigestion and Dyspepsia, a stomach remedy of recognized merit. Each tablet contains in correct proportion: **Sodium Bicarbonate, Extract Rhubarb, Extract Gentian, Powdered Capsicum, Powdered Ipecac, Powdered Pancreatin, Powdered Willow Charcoal.**

OUR PRICE, ONLY **35c**
Regular Retail Price, 50 cents.

THIS VALUABLE PRESCRIPTION is furnished by us, designated as Dr. Wilden's Quick Cure for Indigestion and Dyspepsia; is put in the form of chocolate coated, easily taken tablets and highly recommended for the treatment and cure of indigestion and dyspepsia. If you suffer from only an occasional attack of indigestion, even though your stomach is out of order but seldom, keep Dr. Wilden's Quick Cure for Indigestion and Dyspepsia on hand, take a tablet after your meals as a protection against the trouble. You can then enjoy your meals without suffering from a distressed condition of your stomach. In fact, you won't know you have such an organ as a stomach, so far as any pain is concerned.

Price, only 35 cents per box, containing fifty doses, enough for fifty treatments.

FOR 35 CENTS we furnish a box of Dr. Wilden's Quick Cure for Indigestion and Dyspepsia, containing almost double the number of tablets or treatments found in boxes of other so called dyspepsia tablets that retail at 50 cents everywhere.

FOR 54 CENTS we furnish a large box containing as much as three small ones and more tablets than are contained in any other dyspepsia remedy that retails at $1.00.

DO NOT WAIT until your digestion or occasional stomach trouble has become chronic. Do not think that because you suffer from distress after meals only once in a while you should overlook it. With Dr. Wilden's tablets at hand for convenient use, you can check the trouble and at the slightest intimation of indigestion, the least fullness or uncomfortable feeling after eating, take a tablet (they dissolve easily) and in a short time you will be relieved. At the same time the stomach is toned and strengthened, better able to perform its natural functions and you are protecting yourself against after complications.

ONE TABLET OF DR. WILDEN'S QUICK CURE FOR INDIGESTION AND DYSPEPSIA helps the stomach to digest food. There is a recognized stimulating power to aid digestion in a single tablet of this stomach remedy and yet this splendid preparation does not contain one single particle of opium, calomel or any other harmful ingredient, but it nevertheless assists the stomach and strengthens the digestive organs.

YOU MAY PREFER TO HAVE YOUR PHYSICIAN take charge of your case and prescribe for you. You may wish to get information as to the merit of Dr. Wilden's Quick Cure for Indigestion and Dyspepsia, and he can judge by the printed formula and you will find that he will tell you in all fairness that this prescription is one of the best for the treatment and cure of indigestion and dyspepsia. We do not believe there is a preparation on the market that possesses more valuable properties to stimulate digestion than are found in Dr. Wilden's Quick Cure for Indigestion and Dyspepsia.

DR. WILDEN'S QUICK CURE FOR INDIGESTION AND DYSPEPSIA is the best remedy of its kind. It is, however, of importance to you to know whether it will reach your case or whether it will benefit your condition. We are, therefore, willing that you should send for a box of Dr. Wilden's Quick Cure for Indigestion and Dyspepsia, with the understanding that you can give it a trial, and if it does not benefit you, simply tell us that you received no benefit from it and that it is the first package that you have tried, and we will immediately return your money. We have great confidence in this remedy and we do not want any of our customers to suffer, if we are able to offer them the means of relief and cure. We have supplied this preparation for many years, and from reports received from our customers, we feel justified in recommending Dr. Wilden's Quick Cure for Indigestion and Dyspepsia to those that need a remedy of this kind, believing that it will do for them what it has accomplished for thousands of others who have given it a fair trial and found it satisfactory in every respect.

No. 8F1 Regular price, 50c; our price, 3 boxes for **$1.00**; per box.... **$0.35**
No. 8F2 Regular price, large box, $1.00; our price, per box........ **.54**
3 boxes for........ **1.50**
If by mail, postage extra, small box, 4 cents; large box, 8 cents.

BROWN'S VEGETABLE CURE FOR FEMALE WEAKNESS.

The Great Female Tonic and Regulator.

One 20-ounce bottle, retail price, **$1.00**; our price, per bottle..... **52c**

UNDER THE GENERAL HEADING OF FEMALE WEAKNESS are included a vast array of systemic troubles, including most derangements of the female organism and other difficulties. The term "female weakness" itself has no specific meaning and covers a multitude of ailments, in fact, given six different women with six different ailments peculiar to their sex, each one of them would be sure to characterize her trouble as female weakness. **Brown's Vegetable Cure** is a remedy that can be used with benefit in the treatment of diseases peculiar to women.

OUR PRICE, ONLY **52c**
Regular Retail Price, $1.00

This highly beneficial remedy contains the following ingredients in correct proportions: Partridge Berry, Helonias Root, Blue Cohosh, Black Haw, Golden Seal, Podophyllum, Hydro-Alcoholic Menstruum, Sugar q. s.

If you have any of the following symptoms, give this preparation a test, it may afford you prompt relief and an easy cure.

NAUSEA AND BAD TASTE IN THE MOUTH, sore feeling in lower part of bowels, an unusual discharge, impaired general health, feeling of languor, sharp pains in region of the kidneys, backache, dull pain in small of back, bearing down feeling, a dragging sensation in the groin, courses irregular, or suppressed, timid, nervous and restless feeling, fainting spells, temper irritable, a feeling of fullness, pain in the womb, swelling in front, sleep short and disturbed, headache, dizziness, morbid feeling and the blues, nerves weak and sensitive, appetite poor, spirits depressed, a heavy feeling and pain in the back upon exertion, fainting spells, etc.

IF YOU HAVE ANY OF THESE SYMPTOMS, try a bottle of Brown's Vegetable Cure and give this preparation a trial. It will be sufficient to show you whether Brown's Vegetable Cure is just the remedy you need, a remedy that will not only bring relief, but a cure, so far as a cure is possible, as it has in thousands of cases of suffering women, who have given this medicine a fair test. Invalids have found health from it. One bottle will be sufficient to convince you.

BROWN'S VEGETABLE CURE FOR FEMALE WEAKNESS is a prescription **that has proven highly efficient in a very large number of cases.** It is put up in our own laboratory, under our own supervision, and is guaranteed to contain nothing harmful, but made up of the ingredients named above, which are known to have the best effect in cases where the symptoms of female weakness are present. We offer it with every confidence and, if you are suffering, you can give this remedy a trial. If it affords you no relief, it will not harm you and we will return you your money, if you have not used this remedy before.

No. 8F4 Regular price, per bottle, $1.00; our price, per bottle....... **$0.52**
3 bottles for.....(**Cannot be mailed on account of weight**)...... **1.50**

CELERY MALT COMPOUND.

A HIGH CLASS PREPARATION.
Large 20-ounce capacity $1.00 bottles. OUR PRICE, ONLY 52c
A NERVE BUILDER, BRAIN TONIC AND STIMULANT.

CELERY MALT COMPOUND contains the following ingredients: **Celery Seed, Liquid Extract of Malt, Coca Leaves, Cinchona, Senna, Couch Grass, Rochelle Salts, Iron Phosphate, Hydro-Alcoholic Menstruum, Sugar q. s.**

CELERY COMPOUND has for years been recognized as one of the best tonics. Our celery compound is improved by the addition of malt, making it superior to other similar remedies, and being absolutely pure and unadulterated, is regarded of superior merit as compared with any other celery compound on the market, regardless of name or price.

OUR PRICE, ONLY **52c**
Regular Retail Price, $1.00

IT IS A TRUE NERVE TONIC, a genuine appetizer, a stimulant for both the young and old. We do not claim that Celery Malt Compound is an absolute specific for any chronic disease, but it has a much wider range of usefulness, as it is just the preparation required in hundreds of cases and where no chronic disease has taken hold, it is very beneficial in hundreds of ills that require a reconstructive tonic.

CELERY MALT COMPOUND IS A RECOGNIZED NERVE AND BRAIN MEDICINE. It combines the tonic and quieting effects of celery and other standard tonics with the nutritive and digestive elements of malt, and thereby gives an opportunity to secure relief in nearly every form of nerve trouble. This preparation contains in concentrated form the active medicinal properties of celery seed, well known to physicians as one of the best and most controlling agencies for the nerves, also the phosphates, as required for a strong, healthy, vigorous body, and other medicinal properties in correct proportion, the value of which have been thoroughly demonstrated in all brain and nervous affections and in emaciated conditions. In addition it contains a large percentage of malt, which creates a tendency for building up strength. All this makes it an ideal combination, and it is not only a useful tonic and stimulant but an extremely pleasant tasting preparation as well. As a brain and nerve tonic, appetizer and stimulant it has few equals in the realm of medicine. For insomnia, nervousness or mental exhaustion, loss of appetite, impoverished blood and for that tired feeling that comes from close confinement or sedentary habits, it is very effective and infinitely better than all stimulants of an alcoholic nature.

IF YOU ARE NERVOUS, EXHAUSTED, CANNOT SLEEP, DIGESTION IMPERFECT, or if you are out of sorts generally and in a low physical condition, we recommend a trial of Celery Malt Compound. As a rule it will give new life and vigor and build up the entire system.

IF YOU ARE SUFFERING you can make a trial of this preparation, under our liberal offer; order one bottle, use it and if it does not benefit you, if you do not find that it is the remedy that suits your condition and will help you, all you have to do is to notify us that you have never used the remedy before and we will refund to you, upon request, the full amount that you paid us for the first bottle of this preparation. You assume not the slightest risk in making the test. The remedy can do you no harm, and you can ascertain whether the Celery Malt Compound is the proper remedy indicated for the treatment of your condition. Large size (20-ounce bottle), sufficient for about one month's treatment.

No. 8F8 Regular price, per bottle, $1.00; our price, per bottle.... **$0.52**
3 bottles for.....(**Cannot be mailed on account of weight**)...... **1.50**

WINE OF LIFE—"VIN VITAE"—WINE OF LIFE.

A TONIC STIMULANT FOR THE TIRED, WEAK AND SICK OF ALL CLASSES; A RENEWER OF ENERGY; A STIMULANT FOR THE FATIGUED.

A STRENGTHENER FOR THE WEAK, AN EFFECTIVE AND AGREEABLE FOOD FOR THE BLOOD, BRAIN AND NERVES.

Retail price, per bottle, $1.25; our price........................**64c**

A popular medicine because it is delightful to the taste and to the stomach. Not merely a stimulant, but a genuine toner and strengthener.

A TONIC WHICH YOU WILL FIND TO REACH YOUR CASE.

WHAT IS VIN VITAE? **Vin Vitae is a preparation combining the curative, healing and strengthening powers of ingredients named below** with the invigorating tonic effects of the purest and finest wines of sunny California. The herbs supply the needed food and strength for the blood and nerves; the wine element counteracts the disagreeable, nauseous properties of the herbs and gives just the right fire and life to the preparation. It is a combination producing a pleasing and effective medicinal tonic.

VIN VITAE **is an ideal tonic and strengthener for all,** combining all the best elements of similar medicines with distinctive and peculiar advantages of its own that make it enjoyed and appreciated by all who try it. A pleasant medical tonic to strengthen and tone up the nerves, purify and enrich the blood, invigorate brain, body and muscles, regulate the system.

VIN VITAE **is an excellent tonic. It is in a class by itself.** Are you easily tired? Do you sleep badly? Are you nervous? Do you feel exhausted? Have you lost your appetite? Is your stomach weak? Are you thin? Is your circulation poor? Are you weak, either constitutionally or from recent sickness? **You should take Vin Vitae,** because it may be just the very tonic you need.

OUR PRICE, ONLY **64c** Regular Retail Price, $1.25

TAKE VIN VITAE **and the good effects will be apparent.** You will get stronger, you will feel brighter, more fresh and active; you will feel your health and strength and energy improving.

VIN VITAE MAKES WOMEN STRONG. **Weak women, easily tired, worn out by ordinary household duties, should take Vin Vitae, the Wine of Life, as a tonic.** Women sufferers from the diseases and troubles peculiar to their sex will realize benefit from the strengthening and tonic effects of Vin Vitae. It is a tonic for ailing and suffering women. Vin Vitae is giving thousands of women new health.

VIN VITAE **is compounded in our own laboratory, under the direction of our own skilled chemists, after a formula comprising the following ingredients: Coca Leaves, Iron Pyrophosphate, Gentian, Corn Silk, Senna, Port Wine.**

FOR LACK OF APPETITE, **general lassitude, worn out nerves, Vin Vitae is recommended.** It improves the appetite, assists digestion, purifies and enriches the blood, carries strength to every part of the body and induces a vigor and tone not usually obtained by the use of ordinary medicine. If you are not enjoying your usual good health, if you feel the need of a powerful tonic, you need not hesitate giving Vin Vitae a fair trial.

ORDER ONE BOTTLE **as a test of this splendid preparation. We offer it on its merits; offer it to our customers as an excellent preparation.** Everyone who is in need of a tonic should try Vin Vitae. We offer it feeling confident that if you try it you will be pleased with its agreeable and strengthing effects, and you will not fail to recommend Vin Vitae to your friends and neighbors.

IN FAIRNESS AND AS A PROTECTION **to you, you are permitted, under the terms governing the sale of our household remedies, to order a bottle of Vin Vitae, take it according to directions, and if you do not feel a decided improvement within a few days, if you do not feel that it renews your energy, soothes the nerves, improves digestion, induces restful sleep, brings back former strength; in fact, if you do not find that it does you more good than any medicinal tonic you have taken before, notify us and we will not hesitate to refund to you on the first bottle that we ever supplied to you the full amount that you have paid for it.**

No. 8F12 Price for Vin Vitae, the Wine of Life, per pint bottle.........**$0.64**
3 bottles for.......**(Unmailable on account of weight)**.......... **1.80**

FAT FOLKS, TAKE DR. ROSE'S OBESITY POWDERS

THEY REDUCE THE WEIGHT IN A COMPARATIVELY SHORT TIME.

Retail price, $1.00; our price, 3 boxes for **$1.65;** per box **58c**

TOO MUCH FAT IS A DISEASE **and a source of great annoyance to those afflicted.** It impairs the strength and produces fatty degeneration of the heart, which sometimes leads to a premature death. All people who have obesity are troubled with **sluggish circulation and labored action of the heart.** The patient feels **lazy and burdensome. There is a sluggish condition of the whole system, while they are not exactly sickly, there is a feeling that all is not right.** Nervousness, rheumatism, headache, dropsy and kidney diseases are frequent complications of obesity and, more cause to be alarmed, the heart is always affected.

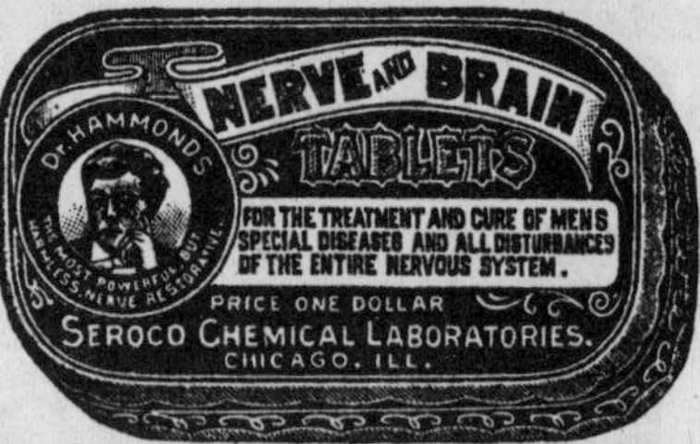

SEND AT ONCE FOR A BOX OF DR. ROSE'S OBESITY CURE. **It will reduce corpulency in a safe and agreeable manner. Perfectly harmless.** No bad results follow its use, as is the case with many other preparations. Explicit directions and valuable information for fat folks enclosed in each box.

No. 8F14 Regular price, per box, $1.00; our price, per box.....**$0.58**
3 boxes for.....**(If by mail, postage extra, per box, 7 cents)**...... **1.65**

SEROCO SPECIFIC FOR THE TOBACCO HABIT.

No matter in what form you are using tobacco, if you want to stop the habit, Seroco Tobacco Specific is the preparation you should try.

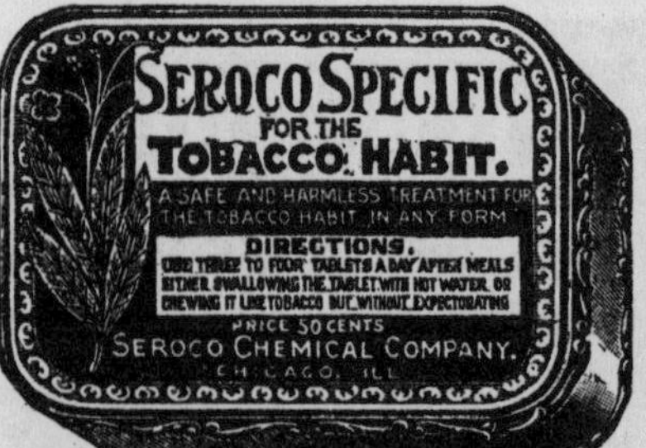

THIS SPECIFIC FOR THE TOBACCO HABIT **is a preparation that is a result of long experience in the treatment of the tobacco habit. It has proven very successful to help men break this disagreeable habit.** It acts without upsetting the nerves, without taking away your capacity for work and without disarranging your physical system. It is a preparation that, taken as directed, in many cases almost immediately helps to overcome the craving for tobacco and at the same time it has a beneficial effect upon the stomach and nervous system. It is therefore a tobacco specific which also has tonic effects. We do not hesitate to offer it to our customers under the liberal terms governing the sale of our household remedies. We believe many of our customers could get relief by giving this preparation a trial and, while we do not pretend to guarantee relief for every case, we offer the remedy for exactly what it is and nothing else. So much benefit has been derived from its use that we give everyone the opportunity of making a trial and test for himself and, if no benefit is received, and it is the first package you have tried, we will gladly refund to you your money upon receipt of your report to that effect.

OUR PRICE, ONLY **39c** Regular Retail Price, 50 cents.

THE SEROCO TOBACCO SPECIFIC **can do you no harm but only benefit when used in accordance with directions furnished. The most important ingredients which it contains are: Powdered Chamomile—Roman, Powdered Golden Seal, Powdered Natrium Muriate, Powdered Ext. Glycyrrhiza, Powdered Cypripedium, Powdered Nux Vomica, Powdered Prunus Virginiana, Powdered Ginger, Powdered Bitterwort, Sugar of Milk q. s.**

A COMBINATION **which, from many experiments made, has been demonstrated as a specific for the treatment of men addicted to the tobacco habit.**

Complete information and instructions how to get the best results from the use of Seroco Tobacco Specific are furnished with each package.

No. 8F16 Regular price, regular size box, 50 cents; our price, per box, **$0.39**
3 boxes for.. **1.10**
No. 8F17 Regular price, large box, $1.00; our price, per box....... **.67**
3 boxes for.. **1.85**
If by mail, postage extra, per small box, 3 cents; large box, 4 cents.

DR. HAMMOND'S NERVE AND BRAIN TABLETS.

A GREAT REMEDY FOR WEAK MEN.

A special prescription in a prepared form for the treatment and cure of men's special diseases and all disturbances of the nervous system. Our price, per box, only 55 cents; six boxes for $2.80.

DR. HAMMOND'S NERVE AND BRAIN TABLETS **are designated for the use of weak men and will not disappoint those who will use this treatment systematically and for a reasonable length of time,** and a test of one single box of these tablets will be entirely sufficient to show the actual merit which they possess.

THOUSANDS OF MEN IN ILL HEALTH, **or only slightly sick from other causes, yes, thousands of men who otherwise are strong and well, are suffering from a weakness which they are desirous and anxious to overcome.** In some cases, owing to the peculiar cause of the weakness, it may require the personal supervision and treatment by a reliable physician. In such cases we warn you to be careful and under no circumstances place yourself in the hands of a so called advertising physician. Be sure that you personally know the physician as a man of standing, skill and reliability. To such a man explain your case freely and without reserve, without false pride and he will either do for you what medical science can do in such cases or else frankly give you the very best advice.

OUR PRICE, ONLY **55c** Regular Retail Price, $1.00

IN MANY CASES OF MEN'S WEAKNESS **it requires, however, only a safe yet powerful stimulant; a remedy that will reach the nervous system and build up the former strength and endurance without having a disturbing effect upon the digestive organs.** There is but one prescription that has been tested for many years that will do this; but one remedy that will meet, in the majority of cases, the expectations of those who require a medical treatment of this kind; a prescription which we have sold for many years—**Dr. Hammond's Nerve and Brain Tablets.** These tablets comprise the following ingredients, in correct proportion: **Dried Sulphate Iron, Potassium Carbonate, Asafetida, Ext. Damiana, Aloin, Zinc Phosphide, Ext. Nux Vomica.**

THE MERIT OF DR. HAMMOND'S NERVE AND BRAIN TABLETS **is perhaps best illustrated by the fact that their sale has steadily increased from year to year.** Millions of these tablets are used today by men who have convinced themselves by actual test that these tablets are the best medicine for the treatment of that condition for which they are intended.

IF YOU HAVE USED THIS MEDICINE BEFORE, **you will, of course, reorder it whenever you need the stimulating benefit they afford.** If you have never tried **Dr. Hammond's Nerve and Brain Tablets,** you have the privilege of sending for one regular size box, containing about three or four weeks' treatment, use them as directed and if you are not entirely satisfied with the results, write us and we will refund to you at once the price of 55 cents which you have paid for them.

DR. HAMMOND'S NERVE AND BRAIN TABLETS **is a very carefully compounded remedy; a preparation that took years of study and experimenting to perfect,** in order to combine the elements that would restore vital force and revitalize the weakened sexual organism, and at the same time strengthen the heart action and tone up the stomach, liver and kidneys.

BUY THE BEST—**Many nerve and brain pills are offered at cheaper prices, but Dr. Hammond's Tablets cannot be sold for such figures. They are the best, and we know you want the best, and our price of 55 cents is as low as this grade of a remedy can be sold. It pays to buy the best.**

No. 8F22 Regular price, per box, $1.00; our price, per box........**$0.55**
3 boxes for.....**(If by mail, postage extra, per box, 3 cents)**...... **1.50**

HAVE YOU CATARRH?

CATARRH OF THE THROAT, NOSE, STOMACH, BLADDER, OR ANY FORM OF CATARRHAL AFFECTION?

Do you suffer from catarrh of any kind, in any of its stages or from any of its effects? If so, try Dr. Hammond's Internal Catarrh Remedy.

Retail price, $1.00; our price..51c

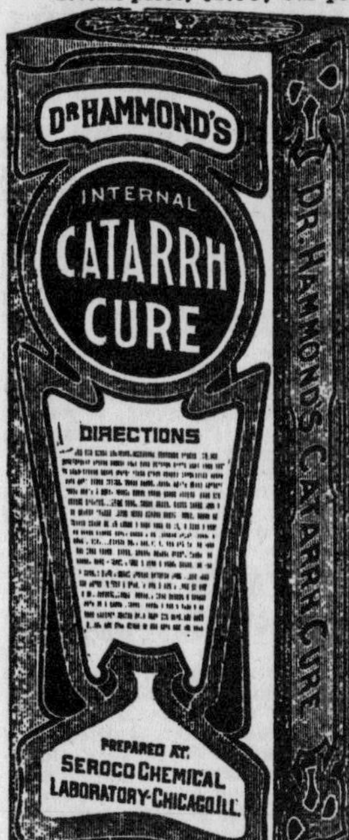

WHAT IS CATARRH? Catarrh is a congestion of the blood vessels of any mucous surface with a large increased discharge from the part, but usually speaking catarrh refers more to a catarrhal condition of nose, air passages or throat.

SYMPTOMS The symptoms of catarrh are numerous and varied, but mostly a mucous discharge from the nose, a continual cold in the head, foul breath, slight deafness, watery eyes, throat troubles, indigestion, etc. Its effects are quite similar in these instances and often deceive those so afflicted. If you have any one or more of these symptoms, you are invited to give Dr. Hammond's Internal Catarrh Remedy a trial. It is designed to go straight to the root of the malady and enables the tissues affected to throw off poisons and perform their functions perfectly.

OUR PRICE, ONLY 51c
Regular Retail Price, $1.00.

OUR CATARRH REMEDY, designated as Dr. Hammond's Internal Catarrh Remedy, is a preparation which has met with decided success in the treatment of this disease and contains the following ingredients in correct proportion: Potassium Iodide, Burdock Root, Poke Root, Couch Grass, Golden Seal, Marigold, Rochelle Salts, Hydro-Alcoholic Menstruum.

It is a highly efficient preparation and composed of ingredients known for their beneficial action upon catarrhal diseases.

IF YOU KNOW THAT YOU ARE A SUFFERER FROM CATARRH, send for a bottle of Dr. Hammond's Internal Catarrh Remedy and give it a thorough trial, according to directions. Your experience, no doubt, will be the same as that of thousands of other customers who have received benefit by the use of this remedy right from the start and obtained final relief and cure by continuing the treatment a reasonable length of time.

DR. HAMMOND'S CATARRH REMEDY is designated as internal catarrh treatment because it reaches all kinds of catarrh, whether in the head or elsewhere, for it acts through the blood, enables it to throw off diseases and to fortify the entire system against catarrhal trouble of every description.

WE HAVE SUPPLIED DR. HAMMOND'S CATARRH REMEDY for many years to thousands of customers located in every state in the Union and particularly to those residing in the localities where catarrhal diseases are most prevalent and, judging from the reports received from those who have learned of the merit of Dr. Hammond's Internal Catarrh Remedy by its use and the benefit derived from it, we feel justified in saying to you: "If you need a remedy of this kind, send for a bottle, use it in the proper manner, and if not found suitable for your particular case, if the first bottle does not benefit you to a noticeable extent, do not proceed with the treatment, but notify us and we will pay you back every cent that you paid for this remedy." We believe, however, you will, as have thousands of others, decide to proceed with the treatment of Dr. Hammond's Internal Catarrh Remedy, so that by following up this treatment you can bring the beneficial change in your condition produced by the first bottle of this medicine, if possible, to an established cure.

PLEASE UNDERSTAND, however, that we want you to be the judge. We want you to know beyond a reasonable doubt that this remedy is really benefiting you before you are expected to proceed with the treatment.

No. 8F20 Regular price, per bottle, $1.00; our price, per bottle....**$0.51**
3 bottles for..**1.45**
Unmailable on account of weight.

GLYCERINE SUPPOSITORIES.

HARMLESS, CERTAIN AND AGREEABLE AND CONTAIN 95 PER CENT GLYCERINE.

The best treatment for constipation, producing painless, prompt and copious evacuation of the bowels without disturbing the stomach and whole system. No internal taking of nauseous medicines, pills, capsules, etc. The ideal method of emptying the lower bowels. Easy to apply and will keep indefinitely. The best remedy for constipated children. Full directions with each bottle.

No. 8F23 Price, per bottle, containing 12 adult suppositories .**14c**
3 bottles for **40c**
If by mail, postage extra, per bottle, 10 cents.

Drugs, Chemicals, Pills, Extracts, Etc.

We have always in stock a full assortment of Drugs, Chemicals, Fluid Extracts, Compressed Tablets, Elixirs, Wines, Liniments, Ointments, Tinctures, Druggists' Sundries, in fact, every article that is generally kept in large, first class drug stores. You can safely send us your order for any drug or chemical, either in the crude state or prepared in the form of **extract, tincture, elixir, etc.,** and rest assured of receiving exactly what you ordered in a fresh condition and pure quality, and at a price far below what is usually charged for such articles in retail stores, which is a very important item for you to consider. **Poisons cannot be sent by mail, and a four-ounce bottle of liquid is the largest that can be mailed.** As articles in our drug department are not, as a rule, very heavy, they can be sent by express at very little cost, but the most economical method is for you to include an order for drugs when you are ordering goods from our other departments.

We will not sell any drug which we know is to be used for abortive purposes.

POISONS. **We will not sell any form of poisons as cocaine, morphine, strychnine, prussic acid, corrosive sublimate, etc., either with or without a physician's prescription.**

ALTERATIVE JUICE.

THE FAMOUS ANTISYPHILITIC AND ALTERATIVE.

Made after the formula of one of the most prominent syphilitic specialists in the United States. This preparation is now recognized by prominent physicians as the best remedy obtainable for the cure of syphilis in all its forms.

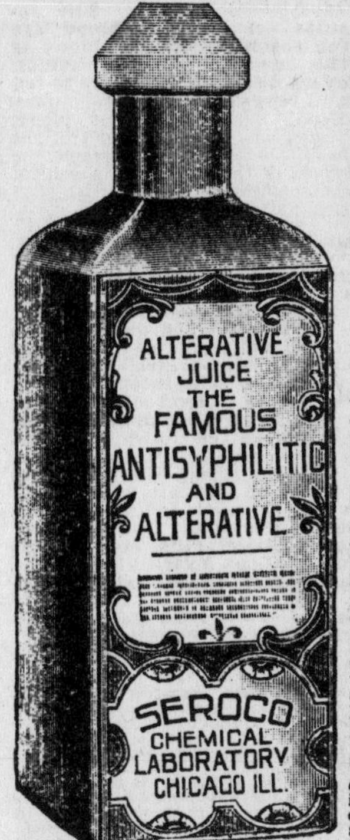

PURE JUICE FROM THE PLANTS.

Alterative Juice is the preserved fresh juices of the true medicinal plants Stillingia Sylvatica, Smilax Sarsaparilla, Phytolacca Decandra, Lappa Minor and Xanthoxylum Carolinianum. They are all collected in the proper season when the roots are at their highest stage of medicinal activity, and their juices carefully extracted by the latest and most improved methods. Each pint bottle of Alterative Juice contains in natural combination the unimpaired virtues of sixteen troy ounces of the true medicinal plants mentioned above. The virtues of these plants are extracted in such a manner that they remain perfect and unimpaired, and the patient always gets the medicinal effect desired.

OUR PRICE, ONLY $1.00
Regular Retail Price, $2.00.

ALTERATIVE JUICE stimulates all the secretions throughout the system, more especially those of the stomach, kidneys, liver and grandular systems. It increases the appetite, aids the digestion of food, tones up the kidneys and liver, purifies the blood, frees the system from secretions, aids elimination of these poisons through the kidneys, bowels and skin.

FREE FROM MERCURY OR IODIDES.

For many years Mercury Salts and Potassium Iodide have been the treatment in all serious blood disorders, but on account of their injurious effects on the stomach, they should be used with caution. Alterative Juice, on the other hand, is a purely vegetable medicine, exerting the same effect as the chemicals mentioned above, but absolutely free from any injurious properties. This being the case, Alterative Juice can be taken for any length of time, without in the least disturbing or injuring the system.

A CONSTITUTIONAL REMEDY. **Alterative Juice is the one great constitutional medicine, possessing in a** marked degree the power of eliminating specific poison from the blood, and at the same time increasing the proportion of red corpuscles in poor and poisoned blood, thus enabling the system to free itself from all this poisonous matter.

CURES SYPHILIS. **Alterative Juice, consisting of the fresh juices of medicinal roots, is Nature's great remedy for curing syphilis and freeing the system from the effects of this disease.** If, at the first appearance of the disease, Alterative Juice is promptly used, it will free the system from the disease in a much shorter time than if treatment is delayed. Alterative Juice should be persistently used from the first appearance of the chancre and if this is done, it is very seldom that any secondary symptoms will arise. As a general rule primary cases should have three to four months, secondary cases seven to nine months and tertiary cases from nine to twelve months' treatment. While this is the general rule, there are, of course, exceptions, depending upon the condition and peculiarities of the person, other disturbances in the system, effect of medicines upon the person, and the length of time since contracting the disease. It is advisable in all cases that the patient take the medicine for several months after all symptoms disappear in order to be sure the system is entirely free from the disease.

OTHER USES. **Alterative Juice is Nature's purely vegetable juices for curing poisoned blood.** Therefore, it is very beneficial for curing all forms of blood poisoning, including scrofula, pimples, eczema, and all skin diseases.

TREATMENT. **For the treatment of syphilis, a tablespoonful of the medicine should be taken before or after meals each day for three weeks out of every month** allowing the system to rest the fourth week. This treatment should be continued for eight to twelve months, depending upon the severity of the disease. As Alterative Juice is a purely vegetable remedy it can be continued for any length of time without injury. For regular blood diseases the dose is one teaspoonful before each meal.

No. 8F24 Retail price, per pint bottle, $2.00; our price, per bottle....**$1.00**
3 bottles for..............**(Unmailable)**....................**2.75**

DR. WORDEN'S FEMALE PILLS.

Female Diseases and Troubles, Peculiar to the Sex and Woman's Delicate System, Regulated by the Use of Dr. Worden's Female Pills.

PRICE, ONLY 33 CENTS PER BOX.

THIS REMEDY, designated as Dr. Worden's Female Pills, **is a combination of ingredients well known for their value and effectiveness. These pills contain in correct proportion: Extract Squaw Vine, Dried Ferrous Sulphate, Potassium Carbonate, Ext. Sumbul, Ext. Helonias, Po. Asafetida, Ext. Gentian, Ext. Viburnum.**

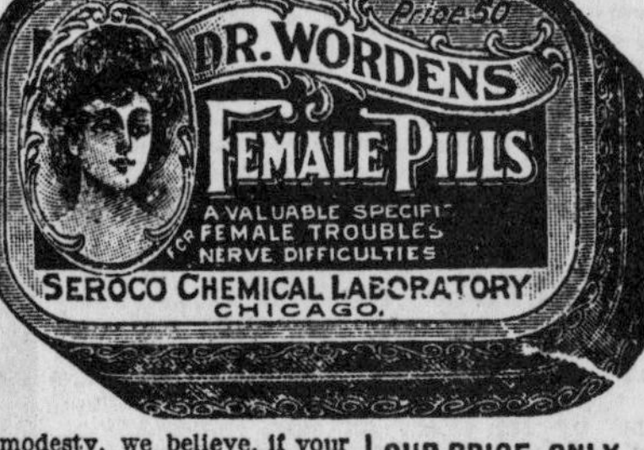

THOUSANDS OF WOMEN **suffering from ailments, peculiar to their sex, have learned to regard this remedy as a valuable treatment and peculiarly adapted to overcome the ailments from which they are suffering.**

FEMALE TROUBLE, as a rule, is **indicated by headache, nausea, weakness, sickness, depression, etc.,** the direct result of a derangement of the delicate female organism and Nature's regular functions. Nearly every woman understands the suffering her sex must undergo by what is known as female trouble, suffering which is usually borne in silence, because of the disinclination to place the case before a physician. With all due respect to your modesty, we believe, if your case is very serious and complicated, that you should not hesitate to place yourself under the treatment of a capable and responsible physician. In a number of cases a systematic treatment with Dr. Worden's Female Pills will bring the help that can be offered.

OUR PRICE, ONLY 33c
Regular Retail Price, 50c.

DR. WORDEN'S FEMALE PILLS **are for the cure of female troubles.** They **contain nothing that will injure the most delicate woman.** They are not cure alls. They are intended to relieve only the trouble peculiar to women. They can be employed in cases where leucorrhea, irregular, suppressed or painful periods, thin blood, nervousness, sleeplessness (insomnia), sick headache, weakness, anemia, chlorosis or green sickness are present. It has been demonstrated that no other prepared remedy offered to the ailing women has given better satisfaction than this remedy has in every form of female trouble.

DR. WORDEN'S FEMALE PILLS **embody the very best prescription intended for the treatment of these symptoms.** If you have used this remedy before, you will have had occasion to learn of its value and what it will accomplish in the treatment of ailments for which it is intended. If you have not used this remedy before, you can send for one box, give it a thorough trial and if you do not receive benefit and relief you need only to send us a report to that effect and we will refund to you the full amount you have paid for same; nor do we expect that you should continue with the treatment, unless you have, by the use of the first box, convinced yourself that it is just the remedy for you, that it reaches your case effectively and you have become convinced that final good results can be secured by continuing for a further reasonable length of time.

No. 8F29 Regular price, per box, 50 cents; our price, per box........**33c**
3 boxes for...........**(Postage extra, per box, 2 cents)**..........**90c**

DR. McBAIN'S BLOOD PILLS.

A Very Successful Blood Remedy in Pill Form. 27 Cents per Box.

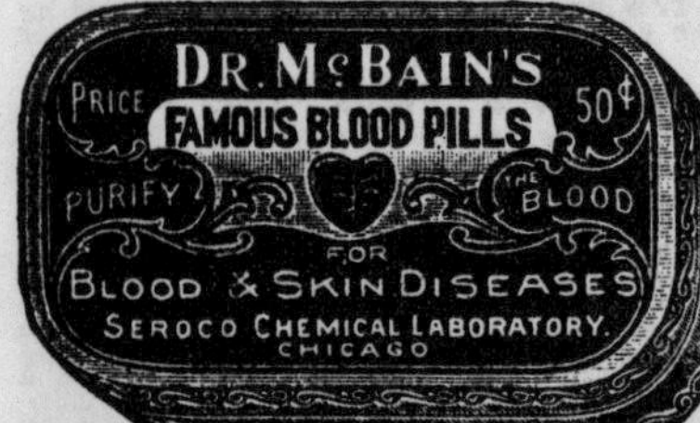

ONE-HALF OF ALL THE SICKNESS is due to impure blood. The results of impure blood are far reaching, as the blood is the medium through which every tissue of the body is fed and renewed. Therefore, impure blood, thin blood, poor blood, means lack of nourishment of the flesh, the nerves, the brain, the bones of the body and a general disorganization of the entire physical system.

OUR PRICE, ONLY **27c** Regular Retail Price, 50 cents.

GENERAL DEBILITY, GENERAL WEAKNESS, sallow or pale complexion, facial eruptions, skin diseases, loss of appetite, pain in the back, nervous headache, etc., are all troubles and diseases usually arising from humors or impurities in the blood and the impurities become worse from day to day and aggravate the troubles until the blood and entire system becomes involved.

DR. McBAIN'S BLOOD PILLS are intended as a blood cleanser and purifier. The effect of these little blood pills is very beneficial. These pills are not of the cathartic nature; they do not upset the system by violent purging, but they act upon the blood, the seat of the trouble, vitalize it, renew the red corpuscles by feeding the proper nourishment to them, thus permitting the blood to purify itself. The elements of which these pills are compounded enrich the blood and also assist digestion, regulate the bowels and act upon the liver and kidneys. Dr. McBain's Pills are invaluable to men and women alike.

This remedy, designated as Dr. McBain's Blood Pills, contains in correct proportion: Extract Iris, Extract Queen's Root, Extract Burr Seed, Extract Gentian, Extract Red Weed, Extract Couch Grass, Extract Leptandra.

THESE BLOOD PILLS are offered by us to our customers for a fair-trial and no one should overlook the opportunity we offer where so much benefit can be derived. If you are not benefited, it will not cost you one cent. If you have any trouble arising from impure blood, give this preparation a fair trial and convince yourself of the good it will do in your case.

DR. McBAIN'S FAMOUS BLOOD PILLS can be taken according to directions without any danger to either sex, and if carefully followed, will give splendid results. Weakness, poor, thin blood, sallow or pale complexion, loss of appetite, chlorosis or green sickness, pain in the back, facial eruptions, skin diseases, nervous headache, and diseases resulting from humors in the blood, which cause erysipelas, sores, swellings, are benefited by this remedy.

ONLY 27 CENTS A BOX, THREE BOXES FOR 75 CENTS, is our price for this special remedy. It usually sells at from 50 cents to $1.00 per box. Sold by us with the privilege offered by no other firm. You can send for the first box, use it and if you do not find the benefit or relief expected, notify us and we will unhesitatingly refund the amount that you have paid for same.

THE PRICE OF THIS REMEDY IS EXTREMELY LOW. Don't think that this affects the value of the remedy, for Dr. McBain's Blood Pills represent a high class blood remedy. With every box of these pills you are furnished a booklet, "How to Have Pure Blood," which is a short treatise on the blood and its diseases, with a safe, sure and convenient method of treatment for men, women and children.

No. 8F31 Regular price, 50 cents; our price, 3 boxes for **75c**; per box.... **27c**
If by mail, postage extra, per box, 3 cents.

DR. BARKER'S BLOOD BUILDER.

This remedy, designated as Dr. Barker's Blood Builder, contains in correct proportion: Stillingia, Burdock, Blue Flag, Elder Flowers, Pipsissewa, Aromatics q.s., Gran. Sugar q.s., Hydro-Alcoholic Menstruum.

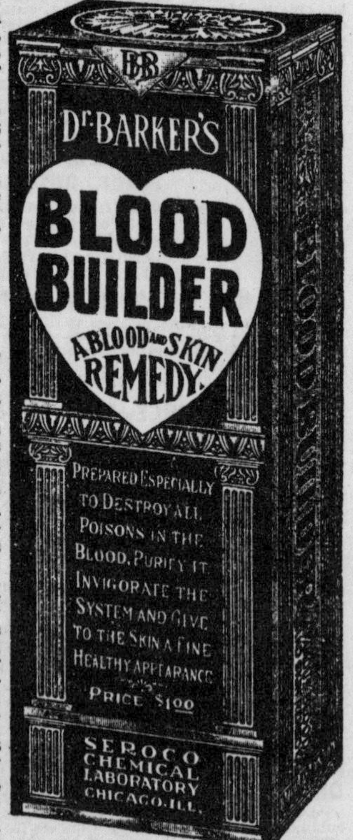

IF YOU ARE FEELING POORLY, and are not quite able to define what the trouble is, try a bottle of Dr. Barker's Blood Builder and give it a test. It is possible your blood needs nourishment and Dr. Barker's Blood Builder may prove exactly the remedy for you. It is certainly a remedy worthy of a test, for purifying the blood, building up the system and toning and strengthening every organ. It helps to eradicate and even prevent these disorders becoming chronic, when the patient is suffering from scrofula, pimples, chronic ulcers, boils and other painful and disfiguring maladies, which show themselves on the surface of the body or create serious disorders within. It purges the blood and is a remedy of merit for all forms of blood disorders, has been put to the test and many cases have yielded to its beneficial and curative influence. Dr. Barker's Blood Builder is of great value in eradicating all eruptions of the skin and face by improving the blood and by its effect on skin imperfections, helps to attain a perfect complexion. We offer you the opportunity to give this remedy a fair trial. The combination of ingredients includes some of the best known remedial agents for purifying the blood and building it up to a healthy condition and we guarantee its purity. There is nothing harmful in this preparation and it is very likely that you will receive great benefit from its use. **Order a bottle under our liberal proposition that enables our customers to receive the greatest benefit from our splendid line of household remedies, namely, with the understanding that if results are not entirely satisfactory, you can write us to that effect and if this is the first bottle you have tried, we will gladly refund your money. We have received many reports of the benefits derived by those who have suffered owing to the poor condition of their blood, and who have used Dr. Barker's Blood Builder with very gratifying results.**

OUR PRICE, ONLY **54c** Regular Retail Price, $1.00

WITH EVERY BOTTLE of Dr. Barker's Blood Builder we send free the booklet, "How to Have Pure Blood," which explains in detail the action of this remedy and also gives important hints on the care and upbuilding of the system.

No. 8F34 Regular price, $1.00; our price, 3 bottles for **$1.50**; per bottle.. **54c**
Unmailable on account of weight.

PUTS FLESH ON THIN PEOPLE.

DRINK IT AT YOUR MEALS.

$1.42 PER DOZEN.

IF YOU ARE WELL, to keep well; if you are sick, to regain your health and strength. Builds tissue and muscle and adds flesh to thin, bony figures. It strengthens as it builds.

DR. HOFFMANN'S MALT EXTRACT, guaranteed the genuine malt and hops extract, now offered for $1.42 per dozen bottles, or $2.55 per case, containing two dozen bottles.

WHAT IS MALT EXTRACT? Malt is barley that has been allowed to partially sprout and germinate and then dried, which changes the rich kernel into easily digested food. Hops are the female flowers of the Humulus Lupulus and adds the soothing tonic and stimulating properties. Malt and hops are recognized as a flesh building, strengthening combination in liquid form. It is among drinkables what beefsteak is among meats.

DR. HOFFMANN'S MALT EXTRACT is made from malt, the concentrated liquid food, and hops, a gentle nerve tonic. If you will order a dozen bottles or a case of Dr. Hoffmann's Malt Extract, take a glass at your meals and another glass before retiring and you will bring yourself up to a normal condition of health and strength.

FOR INVALIDS AND CONVALESCENTS, for those recovering from wasting fevers, for those whose system is run down, who want an agreeable, nourishing tonic to drink at their meals, there is nothing equal to Dr. Hoffmann's Malt Extract. It is very nutritious, it stimulates the appetite, it is a food as well as a tonic, and a preparation that builds up the system after fevers or other wasting diseases. **For invalids or convalescents it is especially recommended.** If there be a new baby in the house or one is expected, it will supply to the mother just the right nourishment, and plenty of it, so that baby will be strong and healthy, and no nursing bottle will be required. Dr. Hoffmann's Malt Extract contains the very best nourishment; concentrated, palatable, and easily digested. Nurses and doctors use it to keep up the strength of their patients. It will renew your energies, your strength and spirits. It helps the stomach in its work, gives new appetite, produces rich, red blood, and makes the thin stout.

IF YOU ARE WEAK OR RECOVERING FROM ILLNESS, or under weight, ask your own doctor if he would advise you to drink a good malt extract at your meals. He will no doubt answer that there is nothing better provided, of course, you get a good, carefully prepared extract. Dr. Hoffmann's Malt Extract is the best the market affords, the best that skill and care can produce.

DR. HOFFMANN'S MALT EXTRACT is especially recommended for loss of appetite. Take a small glassful a half hour before meals. It is a splendid appetizer. For sleeplessness, take a glassful on retiring at night. It produces refreshing sleep. When troubled with dyspepsia or indigestion take malt extract regularly at meals in place of coffee, tea, milk, alcoholic stimulants or other drugs. For invalids or convalescents, Dr. Hoffmann's Malt Extract is the ideal food and drink in one. For thin people, pale women, Dr. Hoffmann's Malt Extract improves the appetite, will add to the weight, build flesh, round out the figure and give new zest to life. In wasting diseases you can drink the malt as directed. It builds up and strengthens. Full directions furnished with each bottle. The usual quantity is a glassful at each meal and one before retiring at night.

No. 8F36 Price, per dozen bottles **$1.42**
No. 8F37 Per case, containing 2 dozen bottles **2.55**
No. 8F38 Per cask, containing 10 dozen bottles **11.50**

IMPORTANT NOTICE.

DURING THE WINTER MONTHS, December, January and February, and when the weather is extremely cold Dr. Hoffmann's Malt Extract is liable to freeze and during that period we cannot accept orders and ship same, excepting at the customer's risk. It will be perfectly safe to ship the extract during ordinary cold weather.

DR. HOWE'S LA GRIPPE CURE.

THE SURE CURE FOR LA GRIPPE IN ALL ITS FORMS.

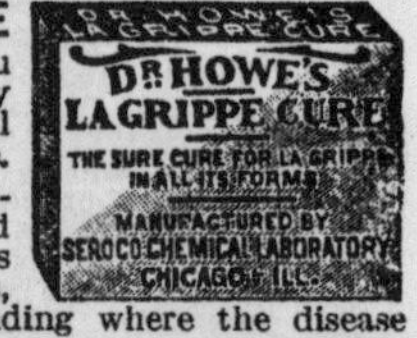

DO YOUR BONES ACHE? DO YOU HAVE CHILLS? Do you feel weak and nervous? Have you cold and then flashing spells, headache, watery eyes, discharges from the nose, etc.? If so you, in all probability, have that lingering and distressing La Grippe.

HARD TO CURE. La Grippe is recognized by physicians as hard to cure, and if allowed to run causes bronchitis or pneumonia or at least leaves the patient with some ailment, as poor hearing, sore eyes, weak lungs or stomach or may weaken any organ, depending where the disease affects.

DR. HOWE'S REMEDY CURES THE DISEASE. We guarantee Dr. Howe's tablets to quickly cure La Grippe. They are very efficient and meet all the symptoms of the disease. When taken at the very start, it can be cured in a day, but where fully developed it requires 3 to 5 days.

KEEP ON HAND. Dr. Howe's Tablets should be in every home. La Grippe comes on suddenly and you should have the treatment from the very start. They will cure the disease and have our guarantee. Full directions with each package.

No. 8F40 Retail price, 50c; our price, 3 boxes for **$1.00**; per box.. **38c**
If by mail, postage extra, per box, 4 cents.

OUR OWN COUGH CURE.

SOLD UNDER A POSITIVE GUARANTEE

Retail price.................... 50 cents and $1.00
Our price.................................32c and 53c

NEGLIGENCE ON THE PART OF PARENTS, **negligence on your own part very often permits serious sickness to overtake the children or yourself when a little caution, a trifling expense, would have saved all the worry, trouble and not infrequently spared a dear life.** We positively believe that there is among household remedies none that can prevent slight indispositions and serious illness so quickly, providing it is kept on hand, not sent for after the trouble has already developed to a certain degree, and also providing you secure the right preparation, a remedy that will not only relieve but positively cure. We mean **OUR OWN COUGH CURE.**

OUR PRICE, ONLY 32c
Regular Retail Price, 50 cents.

WE RECOMMEND OUR OWN COUGH CURE knowing that it is without question a cough remedy that will act quickly and at the same time is perfectly safe. **Order it at once, see that you have a supply of same always on hand,** so that it can be administered the moment the first signs of a cough are apparent. **A few doses will then do the work,** will prevent the cough from developing into bronchitis, pleurisy, pneumonia or other diseases of the lungs and pulmonary organs.

OUR OWN COUGH CURE **contains in correct proportions: Tar water saturated, lobelia, blood root, muriatic ammonia, chloroform, syrup. We guarantee it to be free from morphine, codeine, heroin or any form of narcotics, opiates, poisons or any other harmful ingredients. An ideal syrup for infants and children. Pleasant to take and effective in results.**

OUR OWN COUGH CURE **is not only the best to stop the cough immediately;** it is not only the best cough remedy for infants and children; it is a safe and sure treatment where a cough has become chronic, affording relief, always promptly allaying the inflammation of the bronchial tubes, and by its healing influence it will gradually restore the bronchial to normal and healthy functions and assist in removing the chronic condition within the shortest possible time.

OUR OWN COUGH CURE **is sold under a positive guarantee to possess all the elements necessary for preventing the development of a cough,** and where it has already taken hold of the patient, to quickly cure it. We personally guarantee it to be perfectly safe and harmless and to be a cough remedy that we can conscientiously recommend as being not only the cheapest but the best that can be produced. We supply Our Own Cough Cure in two sizes, the regular 50-cent size for **32 cents** and the large $1.00 size for **53 cents.**

No. 8F42 Regular price, 50 cents; our price, 3 for **90c**; each...............**32c**
No. 8F43 Regular price, $1.00; our price, 3 for **$1.50**; each...............**53c**

Unmailable on account of weight.

Our Twenty-Minute Cold Cure.

NEVER FAILS.

Retail price, 25 cents; our price..**15c**

OUR TWENTY-MINUTE COLD CURE **contains in correct proportions: Quinine sulphate, acetanilid, camphor, podophyllin, Dover's powder and tincture gelsemium.**

OUR TWENTY-MINUTE COLD CURE **is not only what its name implies, but a gentle laxative and a powerful tonic.** It acts gently on the bowels without griping, induces the liver to healthy action and assists in restoring your general health. It is a splendid tonic for the nervous system, and if once used you will never be without it. It promptly cures colds, la grippe, headache and all the symptoms usually present in a severe cold.

YOU MAY SIT IN A DRAFT, **get your feet wet, may become chilled and you will soon notice that the pores are stopped up, perhaps a slight fever starts and you begin to snuffle.** These are the signs of your getting down with a cold. This is the time to use our Cold Cure. Use one or two doses, follow it up by another dose or two in twenty minutes, and you may have cured your cold in its incipiency.

TWENTY MINUTES' TREATMENT **with our Cold Cure will very often be sufficient to stop the cold, to prevent it from** getting any further. A few doses of this preparation taken right at the beginning of the first symptoms of a cold will do the work. Don't wait a day or even an hour. Take our Cold Cure at once. Promptness is the important part.

HAVE OUR COLD CURE in the house and if away from home carry a box with you in your vest pocket. The remedy is supplied in tablet form, in neat tin boxes, convenient to be carried in that manner. In cases where the cold has already become seated before our cold cure could be obtained and used, be sure to get same as quickly as possible, use it in accordance with directions supplied with the remedy, and in connection with it Our Own Cough Cure, and you may feel assured that the combination of these two medicines will break up and cure the most severe cold and cough in the very shortest time.

No. 8F45 Our Twenty-Minute Cold Cure. 3 boxes for **40c**; per box, **15c**
If by mail, postage extra, per box, 2 cents.

WARNER'S OBESITY TABLETS

The original Warner harmless effective cure for gradually reducing obesity and over fatness.

Made after the composition of the famous Vichy and Kissingen spring waters and prepared in such a form that one or two tablets added to a glassful of water will make the exact spring water. By using Vichy tablets one day and Kissingen the next, any excessive fat will be gradually reduced without in the least endangering the patient's health. The treatment should be continued until the desired weight is obtained. Full directions given.

No. 8F46 Complete treatment of 40 tablets. Price, per box..**43c**

If by mail, postage extra, 10 cents.

HERBENA.

NATURE'S REMEDY FOR CATARRH AND KINDRED AILMENTS.

THE GREAT TONIC HERBENA **is one of the greatest tonics ever manufactured.** It has been in use for years and has given new life and strength to thousands. It is the very remedy required by all persons experiencing that tired feeling, that depression of the nervous system, irregular appetite, that sensation of fatigue.

HERBENA IS NATURE'S REMEDY, **being a combination of well known medicinal drugs and absolutely free from potassium iodide, arsenic, mercury and other remedies injurious to the stomach and general system.** It is the one remedy that should be taken at the first appearance of that languid feeling and taken according to directions. It will not only increase your appetite and tone up your system, but will make you feel like a new person, strong and ambitious and free from the depressing feeling experienced before starting Herbena.

CHANGE OF SEASONS. **With the change of seasons persons are very liable to disease.** The nerves need bracing, the brain strength and vigor and the blood purifying. Herbena is the one great remedy for this condition. Obtain a bottle at once, and take it regularly. It has helped thousands and we know it will help you.

OUR PRICE, ONLY 67c
Regular Retail Price, $1.00

CATARRHAL ORIGIN. **Many diseases are of catarrhal origin,** including affections of the head, throat and lungs as well as those of the stomach, kidneys, bladder or pelvic organs. Herbena, exerting a positive action on all mucous membranes of the body, is wonderfully beneficial in curing any disease of the mucous membrane whether in the head, lungs, stomach, kidneys, bladder or pelvic organs. La Grippe is another disease of catarrhal nature being always attended by some inflammation of the passages of the head, throat and lungs, and this is another of the many affections greatly benefited and cured by Herbena.

A SPLENDID REMEDY. **Very few remedies cover and benefit such a wide scope of diseases as Herbena.** It is equally good for men and women, old and young, and will aid in overcoming any disease of catarrhal nature wherever located. It is the one remedy for convalescents and for any person requiring tone and strength.

OUR LIBERAL OFFER. In order that you may know what benefit can be derived from Herbena and to protect you at the same time, **you are permitted under the terms governing the sale of our household remedies, to order a bottle of Herbena,** take it according to directions, and if you do not feel a decided improvement within a few days, if you do not feel that it renews your energy, soothes the nerves, improves digestion, induces restful sleep, brings back former strength, in fact, if you do not find that it does you more good than any medicinal tonic you have taken before, notify us, and we will not hesitate to refund to you on the first bottle that we ever supplied to you the full amount that you have paid for it. Full directions furnished with each bottle.

No. 8F47 Retail price, per pint bottle, $1.00; our price, **per bottle, $0.67**
3 bottles for...**1.80**

Unmailable on account of weight.

SANTAL COMPOUND PERLES.

Each Gelatine Perle contains 5 minims of a combination of Oil Sandalwood, Balsam Copaiba, Oil of Cassia and Harlem Oil of the Highest Possible Purity.

THE GREAT UNFAILING REMEDY IN ALL CATARRHAL CONDITIONS **of the genito urinary tract.** Preferable to copaiba, cubebs, etc., which are so often used, owing to the decreased stomachic disturbance.

ACTS SPECIFICALLY **on inflamed mucous surfaces, renders the urine less acrid and lessens the quantity passed, hence reduces** the inflammation.

A SPLENDID REMEDY **for chronic or acute Gonorrhea, Gleet or Catarrh of the Bladder, or all urinary inflammations.**

EASY TO SWALLOW, **quickly soluble, and easily distributed and absorbed by the system. Full directions with each bottle.**

No. 8F48 Regular price, 50 cents; our price..................................**37c**

If by mail, postage extra, 8 cents.

PRESCRIPTION DEPARTMENT.

WE HAVE UNEQUALED FACILITIES **for preparing prescriptions and family recipes. In this branch of our Drug Department we employ only registered druggists having long experience.** Our medicines are always fresh and of the best quality. Send your prescriptions and recipes to us—you can always feel well assured of having them prepared with the greatest care by **competent and skillful druggists and chemists,** using only the purest and freshest drugs, and at a price very much cheaper than you could have them prepared elsewhere. Our prices for prescriptions in general average: **For liquid preparations, 7 cents per ounce; for powders and pills, 27 cents per dozen.** These prices can be applied to the majority of prescriptions and recipes, but there are exceptional cases where the substances called for are very expensive, and hence in such cases we are compelled to charge more, but in all cases our prices are always far below retail druggists' prices.

MEXICAN HEADACHE CURE.

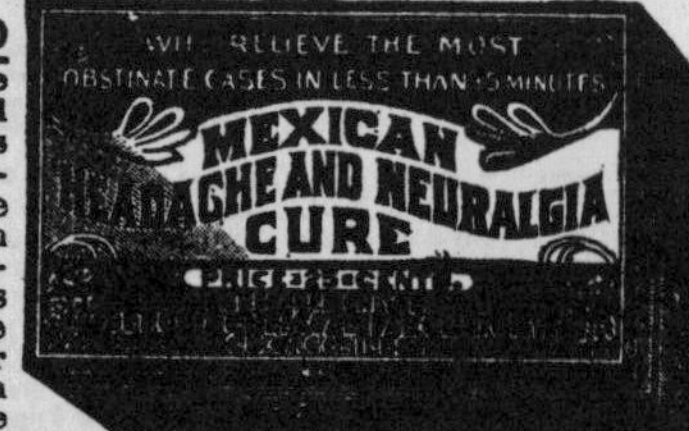

A SPLITTING HEADACHE CURED IMMEDIATELY by our positive Headache and Neuralgia Cure. Almost everyone is more or less troubled with a headache at some time or other. Some persons are hardly ever free from them, and suffer martyrdom. We confidently say to our customers that it is not necessary to suffer longer than the time it takes to get a package of our Mexican Headache Cure. We can promise relief within a short time after the first dose has been taken. A second dose is not required except in very obstinate cases. No matter from what cause, whether a nervous headache, or from the stomach, or a severe case of neuralgia, you will usually obtain complete relief. It is perfectly harmless, no bad results follow its use. Give it a trial when you suffer, and you can easily convince yourself that the Mexican Headache and Neuralgia Cure is the best and most uniformly successful headache remedy in existence.

No. 8F55 Regular price, 25 cents; our price, 3 boxes for 42c; per box..16c
If by mail, postage extra, per box, 3 cents.

OLD RELIABLE EYE SALVE.

FOR SORE, WATERY AND DISEASED EYES, STIES, INFLAMMATION AND ULCERATIONS, FOR GRANULATED EYELIDS, there is nothing better than Old Reliable Eye Salve. Has been in use for many years and nothing better has been found. Our Old Reliable Eye Salve is today one of the most reliable eye salves which will give uniform and good results. Heals quickly and permanently. Can be easily applied. Is soothing, cooling and especially valued as a quick pain reliever in cases of sore and inflamed eyes. Furnished in airtight tin boxes with full directions.

No. 8F61 Old Reliable Eye Salve. Regular price, 25 cents; our price, 3 boxes for 48c; per box 18c
If by mail, postage extra, per box, 4 cents.

LLOYD'S ENGLISH BOIL REMEDY.

A New Remedy—A Specific for Curing Boils.

LLOYD'S ENGLISH BOIL REMEDY is a discovery by an eminent English chemist of certain peculiarities in the poison which causes the formation of boils and his further discovery of the antidote. Calcium sulphide, which, when given in correct proportions, destroys this poison in the blood. It removes almost invariably the soreness in a few hours. The remedy is perfectly safe and it seems certain in its cure. No trouble, easy to take, the results are all that can be expected. Don't wait until you are tortured with a boil! Be ready for the trouble! Keep a package on hand! It never spoils!

No. 8F64 Retail price, 50 cents; our price, 3 boxes for 75c; per box...26c
If by mail, postage extra, per box, 5 cents.

CATHARTIC PILLS, ONLY 8c PER BOX.

Retail price, 25 cents; our price 8c

THIS IS THE OLD FASHIONED SUGAR COATED CATHARTIC PILL of the U. S. Pharmacopœia, containing these ingredients in correct proportions: Extract colocynth calomel, extract jalap, powder gamboge. They act principally on the liver, and move the bowels gently without griping. These pills are carefully prepared and can be thoroughly relied upon. For this reason they are much superior to many others sold at double their price.

No. 8F67 Regular price, box containing 25 pills, 25 cents; our price, 3 boxes for 22c; per box 8c
If by mail, postage extra, per box, 2 cents.

LITTLE LIVER PILLS.

Retail price, 25 cents; our price, per box 11c
Entirely vegetable in their composition. These little pills operate without disturbance to the system, diet or occupation.

It is a well known fact that a large proportion of all human sickness is due to constipation and a torpid liver. The bowels become clogged and the refuse cannot escape by the proper channels. The result is jaundice, torpid liver, biliousness, sallow skin, indigestion, foul breath, coated tongue, pimples, belching foul gases, blotches, boils, dizziness, headache, cramps, colic, etc. You can easily avoid these troubles and keep your system pure and healthy by taking from time to time one or two of our LITTLE LIVER PILLS. Whenever your stomach, liver and bowels get out of order take one or two of our LITTLE LIVER PILLS and notice the quick effect and great relief you will experience. Use them occasionally and they will keep you regular and well conditioned.

No. 8F70 Regular price, 25 cents; our price, 3 boxes for 30c; per box, 11c
If by mail, postage extra, per box, 2 cents.

INSTANTANEOUS EARACHE DROPS.

A FEW DROPS APPLIED ON A PIECE OF MEDICATED COTTON and inserted into the ear will relieve earache in a comparatively short time, removing the cause of the pain. INSTANTANEOUS EARACHE DROPS ARE VERY PENETRATING and, when properly applied, will reach all parts of the inner ear organism, removing and healing every portion in a diseased state. While earache drops are intended for relieving earache, they will also be found useful in many cases for deafness resulting from nasal catarrh, inflammation of the ear drums, unusual discharges and for removal of hardened ear wax deposits.

INSTANTANEOUS EARACHE DROPS ARE PENETRATING, HEALING, SOOTHING AND EMOLLIENT.

No. 8F71 Instantaneous Earache Drops, 2-dram vials. 3 vials for 50c; each 18c
If by mail, postage extra, per vial, 2 cents.

DR. COOPER'S MENTHOL COUGH DROPS.

UNEXCELLED for curing Coughs, Colds, Sore Throat, Hoarseness, Tickling in the Throat, etc. Pleasant to the taste and slowly dissolving in the mouth. The medicaments are so distributed that the beneficial effects continue as long as the tablet dissolves. Much better than the average cough drop. Absolutely harmless and free from all opiates or poisons. Will not stick together in summer.

No. 8F72 Price, 3 boxes for 10c
If by mail, postage extra, per box, 4 cents.

HAMMOND'S SARSAPARILLA.

Guaranteed the Best on the Market.

Retail price, $1.00; our price 46c

THIS REMEDY contains in correct proportions: Sarsaparilla, licorice root, senna leaves, sassafras, burdock, potassium iodide, aromatics, hydro-alcoholic menstrum.

DR. HAMMOND'S SARSAPARILLA combines in an agreeable form the medicinal properties of the most approved alterative and blood purifying remedies of the vegetable kingdom. Dr. Hammond's Sarsaparilla will not cure everything, but the fact that on the purity and vitality of the blood depends the vigor and health of the whole system, and that disease of various kinds is often only the sign that nature is trying to remove the disturbing cause, lead to the conclusion that a remedy which gives life and vigor to the blood and eradicates scrofula and other impurities, as this preparation undoubtedly does, must cure and prevent many diseases. Hence the field of its usefulness is a large one, and we are warranted in recommending it for all derangements caused by an unnatural state of the blood.

FOR SCROFULA Dr. Hammond's Sarsaparilla is especially recommended. It has been found to be the ideal remedy for eruptions and eruptive diseases of the skin, ulcers, tumors, erysipelas and other disorders arising from a low condition of the system or impure state of the blood. There are many sarsaparilla preparations on the market, but none of them will excel in strength and merit the one we offer. We know exactly what goes into it, for it is compounded in our own laboratory. We know that it contains only the purest and best ingredients and we can offer it to our customers with every confidence and every assurance. It has a long splendid record of satisfactory results to its credit, and if you feel that you need a preparation of this kind, we certainly recommend that you give it a trial. Remember, that you can send for a bottle of Dr. Hammond's Sarsaparilla and give it a trial, and if you do not receive benefit, you can simply write us to this effect, state that this is the first bottle you have tried, and we will cheerfully refund your money. This is a fair proposition and enables everyone to get the benefits of our meritorious line of household remedies.

> OUR PRICE, ONLY
> **46c**
> Regular Retail Price, $1.00

OUR SARSAPARILLA is a purely scientific preparation. It is carefully prepared from perfectly safe and harmless alteratives and blood purifying agents, selected from the vegetable kingdom. This preparation does not contain mercury or arsenic in any form or combination whatever. It combines the merits of all other sarsaparilla compounds with defects of none. For blood making, blood cleansing, flesh and appetite producing, our Sarsaparilla is unequaled. No family can afford to be without it. For infants, children, grown people, it should be taken regularly. Our prices are very low.

No. 8F73 Regular price, large bottle, $1.00; our price, 3 bottles for $1.30 per bottle......(Unmailable on account of weight)...... .46
NEVER RETAILED AT LESS THAN $1.00.

DR. ROSS' RHEUMATIC CURE.

The recognized cure for rheumatism and endorsed by thousands that have been cured. Retail price, $1.00; our price 59c

RHEUMATISM is a blood disease, always due to one cause, namely, the presence in the system of an excess of uric acid, which element could not be retained unless there was a defective kidney action underlying the rheumatic disease.

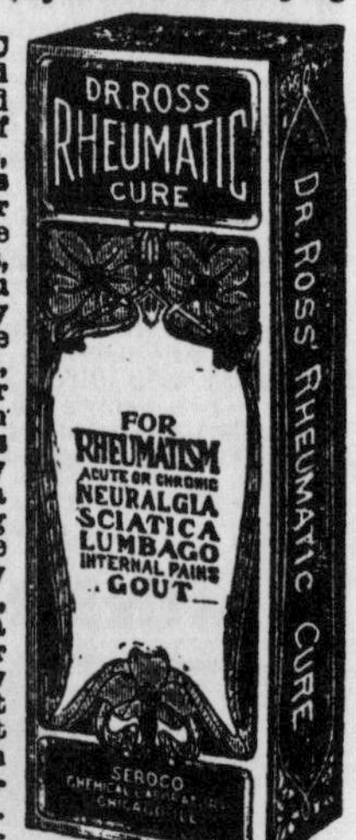

THIS REMEDY, designated DR. ROSS' RHEUMATIC CURE, is an old and time tried preparation, a combination of elements that has had success in relieving and curing this disease. So many of our customers have received great benefit from its use, that we consider it the duty of everyone who suffers from rheumatism in any form to give this remedy a fair trial. We are willing that you should send for it, take it according to directions, and then if you find you have not received any benefit and this is the first bottle you have tried, we will gladly refund your money. It has met with such great success and is so highly recommended by those who have given it a fair trial, that they bring it to the attention of those of our customers who may suffer from rheumatism, and ask them to give it a trial. It is put up in our own laboratory, under our own supervision. We know every ingredient that goes into it, we can guarantee it absolutely pure and harmless, and, we have found that there are few preparations that compare with it in effectiveness. If you have been suffering with rheumatism for years, we still recommend that you give Dr. Ross' Rheumatic Cure a fair trial. If you have rheumatic pains occasionally, it is important that you take this remedy in time, for it will, in all probability effect a permanent cure. Dr. Ross' Rheumatic Cure acts on the blood and removes from the system the uric acid upon which the disease depends. We have received many letters, describing the benefit received from the use of this preparation, and in many families it has been in use for years with uniformly good results.

> **DR. ROSS' RHEUMATIC CURE contains:**
> Colchicum Seed
> Salicylic Acid
> Potassium Acetate
> Potassium Iodide
> Black Cohosh
> Sodium Bicarbonate
> Hexamethylene Tetramine

No. 8F79 Regular price, $1.00; our price, 3 bottles for $1.65; per bottle, 59c
Unmailable on account of weight.

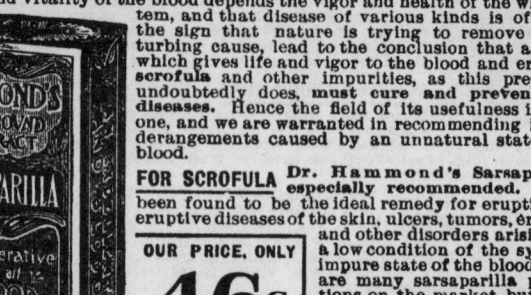

PURE NORWEGIAN COD LIVER OIL.

Retail price, $1.00; our price..........43c

GUARANTEED ABSOLUTELY PURE. Highest grade made. There are several grades of pure oil, varying largely in price. We pay from $3.00 to $5.00 more per barrel for our grade than for any other grade, but we want our customers to have the best. You will save one-half in price and get the best goods possible to put up if you place your order with us. You can't afford to buy Cod Liver Oil unless you know it is absolutely pure. If you buy from us you will have our guarantee and know it is absolutely pure and fresh, imported direct from Norway, in original packages, where it is prepared from strictly fresh livers, pure and sweet.

OUR PRICE, ONLY
43c
Regular Retail Price, $1.00

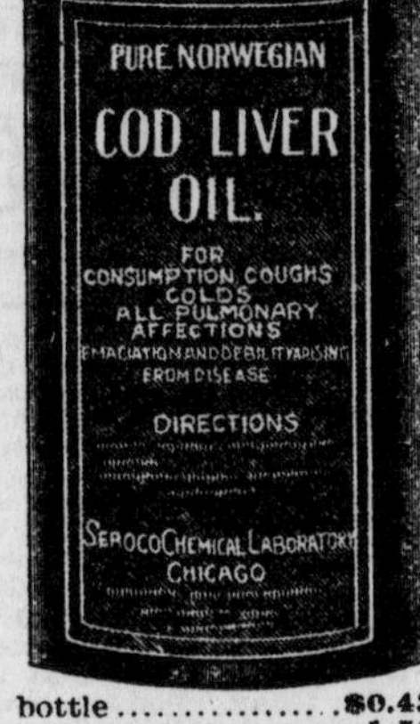

IN THE TREATMENT of wasting diseases where the body has become emaciated, where patients are losing flesh, where the system is constantly weakening and reaches a state of debility, our Pure Norwegian Cod Liver Oil will not only act as a food, increasing properly the assimilation of all food partaken of, but the medicinal properties which it contains will at the same time produce a quick restoration to general health.

For severe colds, lung and throat troubles, NORWEGIAN COD LIVER OIL should be taken regularly.

No. 8F83 Price, 3 pint bottles for $1.20; per bottle..........$0.43
No. 8F84 Price, per ½ gallon.......... 1.50
No. 8F85 Price, per 1 gallon...(Unmailable on account of weight.) 2.75

OUR COD LIVER OIL EMULSION.

(Emulsified Cod Liver Oil.)
Pure Cod Liver Oil with Hypophosphites of Lime and Soda. Palatable and easy to take.

OUR COD LIVER OIL EMULSION is free from that objectionable taste of the pure oil, so that while still containing the oil, it is in such a condition that it cannot be tasted. This preparation is considered of great value in the treatment of consumption, and it is endorsed by physicians generally. 51 cents is the lowest price at which the highest quality of Cod Liver Oil Emulsion was ever sold, and we feel sure our customers will appreciate this opportunity in giving them for 51 cents what they have heretofore been compelled to pay $1.00 or more for. This is a valuable remedy for the treatment of phthisis, colds and chronic coughs, puny children, anemia or poor condition of the blood, and general debility. It is often prescribed by physicians for consumptive patients in both first and second stages, as it usually affords great help. This preparation is without an equal for coughs and chronic colds, and serious complications and unnecessary expense can be avoided and often lung fever and other diseases averted by the use of Cod Liver Oil Emulsion. We would advise every household to have a bottle on hand always. It is invaluable for general debility and emaciation. Our Cod Liver Oil Emulsion, taken regularly after meals, will build you up to renewed strength and vigor.

OUR PRICE, ONLY
51c
Regular Retail Price, $1.00

No. 8F91 Regular price, $1.00; our price, per bottle..........$0.51
3 bottles for..........(Unmailable on account of weight.).......... 1.50

DR. HAMMOND'S HONEY AND TAR EXPECTORANT.

Retail price, 50 cents; our price..........28c

FOR THE TREATMENT OF COUGHS. colds, influenza, bronchitis, laryngitis, hoarseness, sore throat and affections of the lungs generally. Many cases of consumption have been prevented and other mild cases cured by the timely use of Dr. Hammond's Honey and Tar Expectorant. Dr. Hammond's Honey and Tar Expectorant contains in correct proportions, wild cherry, lobelia herb, glycerole tar, muriate ammonia, pure honey. It is especially beneficial in those diseases which are too often regarded as simply annoying, such as common coughs and colds, which are really dangerous in their tendencies and demand prompt and active treatment. For the more serious forms of throat and lung troubles, its value cannot be overestimated, and to anyone worn out with constant coughing and loss of sleep. In cases of pulmonary disease, Dr. Hammond's Honey and Tar Expectorant almost always brings relief and prompt cure.

OUR PRICE, ONLY
28c
Regular Retail Price, 50 cents.

No. 8F95 Price, 3 bottles for 75c; per bottle..........28c
Unmailable on account of weight.

DR. WALTER'S CELEBRATED EYE WATER.

Retail price, 25 cents; our price..........13c

Wherever this beneficial Eye Water has been introduced a marked improvement in the health of the eyes has been the result. Dr. Walter, a celebrated specialist on eye diseases, used this water 25 years in his practice, performing wonderful cures. For weakness or inflammation of the eyes it has no equal; absolutely harmless to the youngest child.

No. 8F97 Price, 3 bottles for 35c; per bottle..........13c
If by mail, postage and tube extra, 12 cents.

DR. BROWN'S ITCH CURE.

We are now manufacturing the famous itch cure according to the formula of Dr. Brown, the eminent skin specialist. If troubled with any itch on any part of the body, this remedy can be employed and immediate relief and a complete cure within a comparatively short time obtained by using the preparation according to directions, which will be furnished with each package.

No. 8F99 Price, 2-ounce tin box..........28c
3 boxes for..(If by mail, postage extra, per box, 5c)..75c

PERUVIAN WINE OF COCA.

Retail price, $1.00; our price..........63c

PERUVIAN WINE OF COCA contains in correct proportions: Peruvian bark, coca leaves, ginger, gentian, port wine, aromatics q. s.

A GENUINE RICH WINE and well known for its strengthening and nourishing qualities. It sustains and refreshes both the body and the brain and has deservedly gained its excellent reputation and great superiority over all other tonics. It is effective and rapid in its action. It may be taken for any length of time with perfect safety, without causing injury to the system, the stomach and gastric juices. Peruvian Wine of Coca also aids digestion, removes fatigue and improves the appetite, without causing constipation. For many years past it has been thoroughly tested and has received the endorsement of many who expressed their utmost satisfaction with the results obtained by using it for ailments for which it is prescribed. They recommend its use in the treatment of anemia, impurity and impoverishment of the blood, weakness of the lungs, asthma, nervous debility, loss of appetite, malarial complaints, biliousness, stomach disorders, dyspepsia, languor and fatigue, loss of forces and weakness caused by excesses, and for similar diseases of the same nature. It is especially adapted for persons in delicate health and convalescents. It is very palatable and agreeable to take and can in many cases be borne by enfeebled stomachs where everything else has failed.

OUR PRICE, ONLY
63c
Regular Retail Price, $1.00

No. 8F101 Regular price, $1.00; our price, 3 bottles for $1.75; per bottle, 63c
Unmailable on account of weight.

NUTRITIVE TONIC. BEEF, IRON AND WINE.

AN UNRIVALED STRENGTHENER FOR WORKERS, FOR ATHLETES, FOR THIN BLOODED PEOPLE. SPLENDID FOR PUNY CHILDREN.

The very essence of strength, health and vitality.

GUARANTEED HIGHEST GRADE ever produced. No family should be without a bottle of Beef, Iron and Wine. This is an old time tonic, universally known for its great strength giving and flesh producing qualities.

OUR PRODUCT CONTAINS BEEF. Many so called beef, wine and iron products are made cheap, some not even containing any beef and very little iron. These of course can be sold much cheaper than a product like our own, made of the very best extract of beef, iron and pure wine and aromatics. No product as good as our own has ever been sold at anywhere near our price. It is especially prepared for assimilating and enriching the blood.

THE BEST TONIC KNOWN to be used when suffering from extreme exhaustion, produced by overwork or other causes, brain fatigue, debility of all kinds, blood disorders, salt rheum, eruptions, anemia, scrofula and all conditions depending upon impure blood. It stimulates digestion, improves the condition of the blood, and enriches and enables it to throw off accumulated humor, and to give tone and vigor to the entire system. We have a great number of testimonials testifying to the great good this medicine has done for those who are weak, nervous and debilitated. Our prices are as low as a good article of this grade can be sold. Inferior goods are sold everywhere at nearly double our prices.

OUR PRICE, ONLY
33c
Regular Retail Price, 50 cents.

No. 8F102 Price, full pint bottles, each..........$0.33
No. 8F103 Price, ½-gallon bottle.......... 1.27
No. 8F104 Price, 1-gallon jug.......... 2.19
Unmailable on account of weight.

DR. MATHEWS' COLIC CURE.

THE ONE SURE AND HARMLESS RELIEF FOR COLIC IN INFANTS.

COLIC IN INFANTS arises mostly from indigestion, slight cold, constipation, gas on stomach or in bowels, over feeding, etc.

SYMPTONS. The many symptons of infantile colic are quite familiar to all, including crying, kicking of the legs, drawing up the knees toward stomach, rolling of the eyes, distended stomach, gas on stomach, etc.

DR. MATHEWS' COLIC CURE will relieve any case of stomachic colic. It neutralizes any acidity, tones up the stomach, throws off the gas, relieves the pain, and is a blessing to every household.

OUR PRICE, ONLY
34c
Regular Retail Price, 50 cents.

ABSOLUTELY HARMLESS. Many colic cures are very injurious to children, ruining their little stomachs and causing harm by reason of their harmful nature. Dr. Mathews' Colic Cure is free from whiskey, laudanum or other harmful substances. It is the prescription of this well known child specialist and is regarded as the best remedy for relieving this common ailment. No home with an infant can afford to be without it. Full directions with each bottle.

No. 8F106 Regular price, 50 cents; our price, per bottle.......(Unmailable on account of weight)..........34c

ORANGE WINE STOMACH BITTERS.

Retail price, $1.00; our price, each..60c

GUARANTEED ABSOLUTELY PURE, AND THE HIGHEST GRADE ON THE MARKET.

DO NOT COMPARE our Orange Wine Stomach Bitters with the bitters that are being sold generally at $1.00 to $1.50 a bottle, bitters that are made from the very cheapest ingredients. Our Orange Wine Stomach Bitters are made from the following ingredients, well known for their tonic and healing effect upon the stomach.

ORANGE WINE STOMACH BITTERS contains the following ingredients in correct proportions: Orange peel (bitter), gentian, ginger, cardamom, cinnamon, caraway, aromatic spirits ammonia, wine q. s.

OUR PRICE, ONLY **60c** Regular Retail Price, $1.00

THIS IS A PLEASANT BITTERS. Is unsurpassed as an appetizer and it is a recognized cure for dyspepsia when its use is continued for some time. As a general bracer up of the whole system there is none superior, and the taste is so pleasant that the most fastidious enjoy taking it. Owing to the intrinsic and widely established therapeutic value of its chief constituents, which are helpful to good digestion, this preparation furnishes admirable means for treating gastric ailments, indigestion, want of appetite, malarial diseases, low spirits, and nervousness; it removes that tired feeling. It exerts a most wonderful power in sustaining the system during arduous labors and journeys. It is an agreeable and wholesome stimulant, and imparts a pleasant taste with an agreeable sense of warmth which permeates the entire system.

No. 8F105 Price, per bottle........................$0.60
3 bottles for........................ 1.70
Unmailable on account of weight.

THE GENUINE GERMAN HERB LAXATIVE TEA.

Retail price, 25 cents; our price, per box........................12c

A HARMLESS VEGETABLE REMEDY and a successful treatment for constipation, with no bad after effects. It is composed of herbs and roots familiar to the peasants of Germany, especially those who nurse the sick. Through irregular living, poorly cooked food, improper habits of eating, nearly all persons are suffering more or less from constipation and the resultant sick headaches; although there may be a daily movement of the bowels, there is still much fecal matter adhering to the intestines and poisoning the blood. Our Herb Tea, made of the simple, harmless herbs, will, when taken regularly for a short time, thoroughly cleanse the stomach and bowels of all unclean matter. The blood becomes purified and the person greatly improved in health.

HERB LAXATIVE TEA contains in correct proportions: American saffron, elder flowers, senna leaves, fennel seed, licorice root, anise seed, dog grass.

No. 8F107 Price, 3 boxes for 33c; per box........................12c
If by mail, postage extra, per box, 7 cents.

BLACKBERRY BALSAM.

Retail price, 50 cents; our price, each........................20c

A RELIABLE, necessary and highly beneficial family remedy. Very agreeable to the taste, and may be given to both adults and children.

BLACKBERRY BALSAM contains in correct proportions the following: Rhubarb, pancreatin, golden seal, Jamaica ginger, cassia, potassium bicarbonate, catechu, balmony, oil peppermint, blackberry root.

OUR PRICE, ONLY **20c** Regular Retail Price, 25 cents.

IT WILL PREVENT SERIOUS ILLNESS if used promptly and often be the means of saving life. It is a pleasant, safe, speedy and effectual remedy for dysentery, diarrhea, looseness, cholera morbus, cholera infantum, summer complaint, colic, cramps, griping pains, sour stomach, sick and nervous headache, pain or sickness of the stomach, vomiting, restlessness and inability to sleep, wind in the stomach and bowels, and for all bowel affections. We have received thousands of statements from families bearing the strongest testimony in its favor.

Our Blackberry Balsam is indeed a household remedy and should be in every home. Taken at the very beginning it will save a great amount of pain and check what might become a serious ailment.

No. 8F108 Price, 3 bottles for 50c; per bottle........................20c
If by mail, postage and tube extra, 16 cents.

PURE BLACKBERRY BRANDY.

AN EXCEPTIONALLY fine and absolutely Pure Blackberry Brandy, made from the ripe blackberry, fine dark red color, heavy body, and guaranteed to be nothing but the juice of the pure large blackberry. Held by every pure food law as absolutely pure. Many grades of Blackberry Brandy are not pure, but our product is guaranteed. Used and prescribed by the best physicians as one of the simplest and most effective remedies for all derangements of the stomach and bowels. Does not constipate. Fine in taste, agreeable and tones up and invigorates the system.

No. 8F117 Price, per pint bottle........................$0.28
No. 8F118 Price, per case of 1 dozen pints........................2.85
No. 8F119 Price, per quart bottle........................48
No. 8F120 Price, per dozen quarts........................5.00
Unmailable on account of weight.

DR. ROSS' KIDNEY AND BLADDER CURE.

Retail price........................$1.00
Our price, each........................$0.58
Our price, 3 bottles for........................1.60

IF YOUR KIDNEYS ARE WEAK AND INACTIVE, if there is any bladder trouble noticeable in your case, we can recommend Dr. Ross' Kidney and Bladder remedy as a very effective preparation; one that will give prompt relief in most disorders of the kidneys and bladder.

OUR PRICE, ONLY **58c** Regular Retail Price, $1.00

DR. ROSS' KIDNEY AND BLADDER CURE contains in correct proportions: Sodium phosphate, sodium benzoate, couch grass, corn silk, potassium acetate, shepherd's purse, queen meadow, senna, hexamethylene tetramine, hydro-alcoholic menstruum, syrup.

The great value of Dr. Ross' Kidney and Bladder Cure is derived from the fact that this combination of remedies acts directly upon the organs affected, stimulating the filtering activity of the kidneys and restoring vigor and tone to the whole system. The kidneys are one of the most important parts of the digestive system and if they are in a weakened condition, if they do not perform their duties properly, every other organ of the body will feel its effect and a general break down of your health may quickly result.

WE WANT YOU TO GIVE Dr. Ross' Bladder and Kidney Cure a trial because we believe that after you have given it a test, you will find that it is the best kidney and bladder remedy on the market today. You can make this trial without any risk to yourself. There is absolutely nothing harmful in this remedy, so you can feel perfectly safe in using it as directed and experience its beneficial effects within a short time. The remedy is guaranteed to give satisfaction and if you do not receive any benefit from its use and will write us to that effect, we will promptly refund to you the full amount that you have paid for the first bottle.

No. 8F121 Price, 3 bottles for $1.60; per bottle........................58c
Unmailable on account of weight.

OUR LAXATIVE FIG SYRUP.

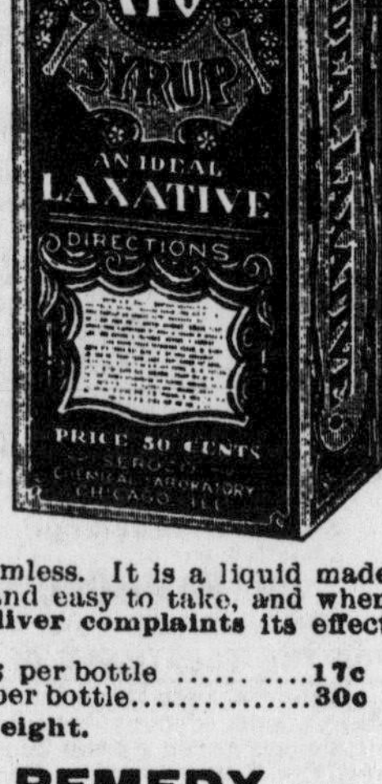

Retail price........................25c and 50c
Our price, 25c size, per bottle........$0.17
Our price, 25c size, 3 bottles for........48
Our price, 50c size, per bottle........30
Our price, 50c size, 3 bottles for........85

FOR CONSTIPATION. The great remedy of the age for this trouble. Laxative Fig Syrup was never retailed for less than 25 cents. Our special price is 17 cents. If you suffer from constipation, order a large bottle of Laxative Fig Syrup and you will find immediate relief and in time a permanent cure. It contains in correct proportions: Figs, senna, cascara sagrada, mandrake, rhubarb, tamarinds, aromatics, syrups.

OUR PRICE, ONLY **17c** Regular Retail Price, 25 Cents.

Laxative Fig Syrup is Nature's own remedy for restoring the bowels to a healthy and normal condition. Unlike pills and purgatives, it strengthens instead of weakening and enfeebling their action. For chronic constipation, to secure the best results a remedy is required that will not only act quickly on the bowels, but will produce a tone and stimulating effect upon the inner coating of the intestines, strengthen the muscular action and restore the paralyzed functions. Laxative Fig Syrup, if taken regularly, will cure constipation with its attending ills. Laxative Fig Syrup is perfectly harmless. It is a liquid made from fruits, plants and herbs, is mild in form and easy to take, and when used in cases of bowel, stomach, kidney and liver complaints its effect upon the system is marked.

No. 8F124 Price, regular size bottle, 3 for 48c; per bottle........................17c
No. 8F125 Price, large size bottle, 3 for 85c; per bottle........................30c
Unmailable on account of weight.

SPEEDY CURE PILE REMEDY.

Retail price........................50c
Our price, per box........................$0.20
3 boxes for........................50

WHY SUFFER from Piles when 20 cents spent for our Speedy Cure Pile Remedy will give relief and may perform a cure. This preparation affords immediate relief and a prompt cure in many cases. It allays at once the extreme soreness and tenderness of all parts, reduces the inflammation and heals all ulcerative conditions. It is equally serviceable for itching piles. We have sold thousands of boxes and have received splendid reports. If you have tried other remedies without getting relief, try our Speedy Cure; you will find results satisfactory.

No. 8F126 Price, per box........................20c
3 boxes for........................50c
If by mail, postage extra, per box, 4c.

BRANDY CORDIAL.

FOR MEDICINAL AND DOMESTIC USE. MADE FROM THE JUICE OF SELECTED BLACKBERRIES.

ABSOLUTELY PURE.

This is not an ordinary blackberry wine, but a sweet, wholesome cordial of the finest quality, equally useful as a medicine for bowel complaints. Also used for flavoring pastry and fruit sauces.

A VALUABLE ARTICLE FOR EVERY HOME. EXTRA FINE QUALITY AND FULL STRENGTH.

No. 8F128 Price, per pint bottle........................$0.28
No. 8F130 Per quart bottle........................48
No. 8F131 Original cases of 12 pints........................2.85
No. 8F132 Original cases of 12 quarts........................4.75
Not mailable on account of weight.

CUROLENE.

VAPORIZED CUROLENE cures while you sleep. A remedy for whooping cough, asthma, catarrh, diphtheria, croup, colds, coughs, etc.

89c

VAPORIZED MEDICINES have for years been recognized as the best means for curing all diseases of the nose, throat and lungs. By this means every particle of air becomes charged and loaded with medicine and as we breathe or inhale every part of the channel becomes coated. The vaporizing has heretofore been usually performed by means of a spray atomizer, but in doing this some liquid must be used with the remedy, and this being heavier than the air, soon settles and does not have the beneficial results as though no liquid was used. With this point in view we have devised the new aluminum Curolene Vaporizer. The Curolene liquid is placed in the small pan above the little alcohol lamp, lighted, and before long the Curolene will be converted into a vapor, the air around becomes loaded and, being heated, it rises and gives place to more air. In this way all the air becomes charged and, before long, every crevice, every nook and corner becomes filled with these beneficial and curing vapors. By this means the air is not loaded with moisture, but with nothing except the medicine itself. This will not settle, but, on the other hand, will purify every spot.

THE GERM THEORY. **It is now acknowledged by all physicians that the causes of scarlet fever, diphtheria, whooping cough, croup, asthma, etc., are from minute germs,** which, once present, grow and increase the severity of the disease until killed. To successfully accomplish this some strong and effective remedy must be used and this remedy can now be successfully accomplished by Curolene Vapors.

CUROLENE **is a strong antiseptic and germicide with marked germ destroying properties.** Curolene vapors permeate every crevice and afford the only means of quickly and surely curing all forms of germ diseases. The vapors of Curolene are pleasant, of the nature of carbolic acid, yet will not injure the youngest child. The vapors are carried to every passage and cell of the respiratory organs and this is the reason it has such a beneficial effect upon all diseases of the nose, throat and lungs.

SHOULD BE IN EVERY HOME. **A complete Curolene outfit should be in every home.** Croup, whooping cough, diphtheria and many other germ diseases arise very quickly and you should have a vaporizing outfit always ready for any emergency. It may save the life of your child. It will not deteriorate with age and the vaporizer will last a lifetime. No home with children can afford to be without it.

No. 8F140 Regular price, complete, comprising the new aluminum stand, aluminum vaporizing pan, alcohol lamp and 2-oz. bottle Curolene, $1.50. Our price ....(Not mailable)....................89c

DR. WALKER'S CELEBRATED SKIN OINTMENT.

Retail price..........................50c
Our price, each....................26c
Our price, 3 bottles for 75c

Considered one of the best remedies for all skin diseases and blemishes and superior to any other skin ointment in the market, furnished by us at less than one-half its selling value. This skin ointment is highly recommended for eruptive and skin diseases, pimples, blotches, eczema, salt rheum, erysipelas, ringworms or any scaly or scabby eruptions, often healing cracked or rough skin on the hands, face or any part of the body by a few applications. We are in a position to furnish this excellent remedy for skin diseases and blemishes for only 26 cents a box. You could obtain no remedy that is better or can equal it in healing qualities if you were to pay $1.00 per package.

No. 8F157 Dr. Walker's Skin Ointment. Price, per box..............26c
3 boxes for...........(If by mail, postage extra, 3 cents)..............75c

RELIABLE WORM SYRUP AND WORM CAKES.

YOU CAN SAVE YOUR CHILDREN **from much suffering and in many cases save their lives.** No other disease is so fatal to children as worms. Unfortunately they are seldom free from them, and as the symptoms resemble those of almost every other complaint, they often produce alarming effects without being suspected. Worms are not only a cause of disease in themselves, but by their irritation aggravate all other diseases, wandering from one part of the body to another, winding themselves up into large balls, obstructing the bowels and frequently the throat, causing convulsions and too often death.

18c

OUR RELIABLE WORM SYRUP **effectually destroys the worms and removes the nest in which their young are deposited.** It moves the bowels very gently the worms being to a greater or less extent dissolved by the action of the medicine, can scarcely be recognized in the stools, but the improvement in the health of the child will be sufficient evidence of the beneficial effects of the medicine.

EVERY MOTHER **ought to have a bottle of the syrup or a box of the cakes always in the house. The syrup and the cakes are two medicines used for the same purpose.** The syrup is more pleasant to the taste and more suitable for very young children. The cakes can be given to older people; even adults can be benefited by using them, as grown up folks, as well as children, often suffer from worms. **These reliable worm medicines are not only worm destroyers, but act as a general tonic,** destroying sourness of the stomach and producing a healthy appetite. **Mothers, keep your children healthy.**

RELIABLE WORM CAKES
PLEASANT AND EFFECTIVE
THE SAFEST AND SUREST CURE FOR WORMS IN CHILDREN

No. 8F111 Worm Syrup. Price, 3 bottles for 50c; per bottle. ..18c
If by mail, postage and tube extra, per bottle, 16 cents.
No. 8F112 Worm Cakes. Price, 3 boxes for 50c; per box..........18c
If by mail, postage extra, per box, 2 cents.

CORN AND BUNION REMOVER.

Retail price, 25c; our price 9c

THE GREAT CHINESE CORN **and Bunion Remover,** never fails to give immediate relief, and a complete cure is certain when directions are faithfully followed. **No one suffering from corns, or bunions should fail to give our great Chinese Corn and Bunion Remover a trial.** We have tried it ourselves and found relief, therefore can testify knowingly as to its great merits.

No. 8F139 Price...9c
If by mail, postage extra, 3 cents.

ANGEL'S OIL.

The Remedy for Curing Pain.

Retail price...........................50c
Our price, each.....................28c
Our price, 3 bottles for...........75c

COMPOSED OF VEGETABLE OILS. **Offers great relief** in cases of rheumatism, neuralgia, gout, sciatica, pleurisy, backache, quinsy sore throat, stiffness of the neck and joints, sprains, lumbago and swellings, inflammations, chilblains, bites and stings of poisonous insects, weak ankles and joints, sore feet, pain in the back and limbs, or any other bodily pain or ailment. **This liniment is one of those standard household remedies** which comes in handy upon many occasions where a remedy is needed quickly to afford relief and to give protection against more serious complications. After giving it a trial you will never be without a bottle in the house. We make the price very low so that every one of our customers may afford to have a bottle constantly at hand.

No. 8F142 Price, per bottle 28c
If by mail, postage and tube extra, per bottle, 14 cents.

ELECTRIC LINIMENT.

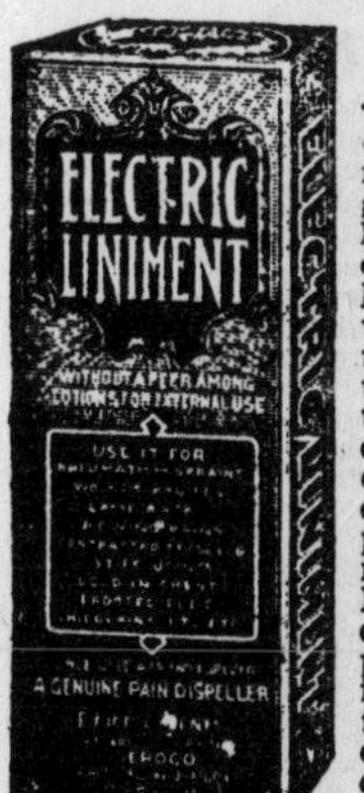

Retail price..............50c
Our price, each..........23c

THIS LINIMENT **is an excellent remedy in cases of rheumatism, sprains, old sores, bruises, growing pains, contracted muscles, lame back, stiff joints, frosted feet, chilblains, etc.** Persons suffering from lameness or cold in the arms and legs will be rendered great benefit by its use; also as an application for the throat and chest; in cases of inflammation, for stiff neck, bruised or contracted muscles and in all cases requiring external treatment great relief will be experienced with this, one of the most penetrating and best liniments ever made. We call this remedy Electric Liniment because its application produces a feeling similar to the feeling produced by a mild charge of electricity. This is a liniment that should find a place in every family. It will offer relief in hundreds of different cases. Electric Liniment once used will make for itself a place in every home.

No. 8F115 Price, 3 bottles for 60c; each..........23c
Not mailable.

INJECTION No. 7.

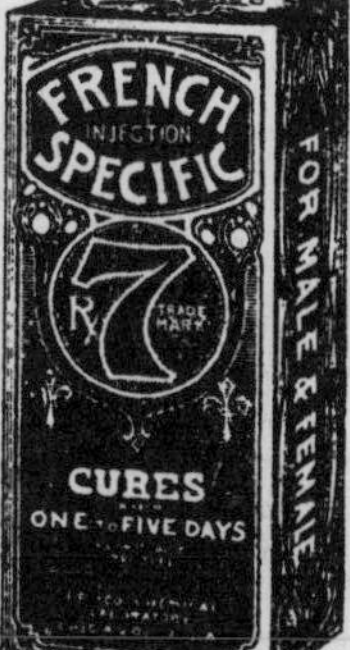

Retail price,.......$1.00
Our price, each.....59c

CURES IN ONE TO FIVE DAYS. **No other medicine required. No fear of stricture. No bad results. A French specific,** having a great reputation abroad as a reliable cure for **all troubles of the urinary organs in either male or female;** has a very quick effect and leaves no bad results. Either gonorrhoea or gleet quickly and easily cured. Full instructions and valuable information with each package.

No. 8F133 Price, each....................$0.59
3 bottles for...................................1.50
If by mail, postage and mailing case extra, each, 18 cents.

No. 8F822 Hard Rubber Syringe, to be used with this remedy. Price. (Postage, 2c extra) .16c

BROMO VICHY.

Retail price....... ......10c and 25c
Our price, 10c size, each........$0.07
Our price, 10c size, dozen.........75
Our price, 25c size, each............17
Our price, 25c size, dozen..........1.50

A Morning Bracer.
A Headache Reliever.
A Brain Clearer.
A Nerve Steadier.

EFFERVESCENT BROMO VICHY SALTS

THIS IS BY FAR THE BEST "BROMO" **preparation at present offered to the public.** One or two teaspoonfuls taken in half a tumbler of cold water will instantly dispel any sickness of the stomach, relieve a severe headache, clear up the brain and steady the nerves. **It is a thirst quencher,** and causes a pleasant feeling to prevail all through the body. It is a quick remedy for nervous headaches, neuralgia, sleeplessness, over brain work, depression following alcoholic excesses, and all nervous troubles. A little should always be on one's bureau table for use in the morning or at night.

No. 8F136 Price, 10c size,.................7c
No. 8F137 Price, 25c size,.................17c
No. 8F138 Price, 50c size,.................38c
If by mail, postage extra, small size, 4 cents; large size, 8 cents.

YOU SHARE IN OUR PROFIT

We send you a valuable PROFIT SHARING CERTIFICATE and you can soon get something valuable entirely FREE, as shown on pages 1 and 2.

WHITE STAR SECRET LIQUOR CURE.

Regular retail price.........................$2.50
Our price, complete, box of thirty treatments.............94

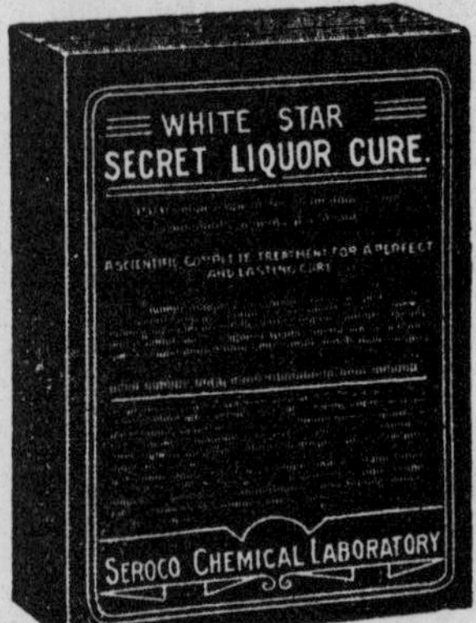

THIS EXCEEDINGLY SUCCESSFUL LIQUOR CURE is designated as a Secret Liquor Cure because it can be administered secretly without the knowledge of the drinker and can be given in tea, coffee or food, without the consent of the unfortunate victim of the drink habit.

THE WHITE STAR SECRET LIQUOR CURE contains the following ingredients in correct proportion: Gold Chloride, Ammonium Muriate, Scutellaria, Erythroxylon Coca, Ext. Cayenne, Ext. American Valerian, Cephalis Ipecac, Ext. Bleeding Heart, Saccharaum Lactis..

OUR PRICE, ONLY **94c**
Regular Retail Price, $2.50

THIS REPRESENTS an odorless and tasteless preparation in powdered form, which, given to the drinker in tea, coffee or food will not upset the patient, but by its action on the system and the tonic stimulating effect upon the nerves, it often removes that desire, that craving for intoxicating liquor, in a comparatively short time.

IT IS NOT CLAIMED that there is a liquor cure, secret or otherwise, that is absolutely infallible in all cases, but so many have been entirely cured and stayed cured, so many have been reclaimed for months or years before they suffered a relapse that it would really seem a neglect of duty not to make the attempt to help them, even save them against their will, especially when you can undertake this treatment without the slightest risk, so far as expense is concerned, without any risk whatever of harming the patient.

THE WHITE STAR SECRET LIQUOR CURE will do no harm in any case. It will always improve the general condition of the drinker to a marked degree. It is considered one of the best prescriptions to be employed secretly in the treatment of the liquor habit. Neither you nor we ourselves can tell, however, beforehand, what it can and will accomplish for the patient whose treatment you contemplate, nor do we wish you to be disappointed in the results and we therefore make you the following liberal offer.

SEND FOR A BOX of the White Star Secret Liquor Cure, which contains thirty treatments, give it according to directions, a small powder in tea or coffee. After you have made a fair trial according to instructions, if there is no benefit derived, write us. State that this is the first box that you have tried and we will promptly refund your money.

REMEMBER, the price is only 94 cents per box of thirty complete treatments.

Full directions sent with each box. Medicine sent in a plain sealed package.
No. 8F151 Price, 3 boxes for, $2.50; per box.........................94c
If by mail, postage extra, per box, 12 cents.

WINE OF COD LIVER OIL WITH LIME, IRON AND CHERRY BARK.

THIS IS A PLEASANT, ELEGANT PREPARATION, recommended and prescribed by physicians for the treatment of pulmonary affections and as a general system tonic.

WINE OF COD LIVER OIL contains the active medicinal principles of cod liver oil in a palatable form, avoiding the nauseating effect of the oil. It is preferred by many to plain cod liver oil, and at the same time admits of combining with it the very best tonics, tissue and blood builders, making the Wine of Cod Liver Oil with Lime, Iron and Cherry Bark one of the most satisfactory cod liver oil preparations obtainable.

OUR PRICE, ONLY **38c**
Regular Retail Price, 75 cents.

WINE OF COD LIVER OIL with Lime, Iron and Cherry Bark is a remedy that should always be used by patients who are constantly weakening and who are debilitated and wasting away. It is undoubtedly very valuable in the treatment of all lung troubles, colds and chronic coughs, scrofula, blood disorders and skin affections, as well as diseases of the joints and spine. It will build up the strength of the entire system, giving renewed health and vigor to the weak and debilitated, increasing the functional activity of every organ of the body.

WINE OF COD LIVER OIL with Lime, Iron and Cherry Bark is a valuable general tonic; its pleasant taste makes it very palatable. It is easily taken by the patient, who will like it and relish it. It is quickly assimilated and taken up by the system. Consequently it will improve the patient's condition almost from the first dose taken.

No. 8F160 Wine of Cod Liver Oil with Lime, Iron and Cherry Bark.
Our price, 3 bottles for $1.00; per bottle.........................38c
Unmailable on account of weight.

GENUINE ENGLISH PILE REMEDY.

Retail price.........................50c
Our price, each.........................30c
Three boxes for.........................80c

A scientifically prepared pile remedy in suppository form, soothing, healing and for the most effective curing of blind, itching or bleeding piles. Speedy in relief, safe in its action, permanent in its effect. No matter what you may have employed for the treatment of this trouble, if all else has failed to afford you relief and cure, you should send for the Genuine English Pile Remedy at once. You may have the same experience as have thousands of other sufferers troubled with different forms of this ailment, that is, you will find that the Genuine English Pile Remedy will not only promptly relieve, but establish the desired result. The remedy having been prepared in the form of suppositories, admits of easy and convenient application, and will in this manner thoroughly reach the affected parts, and by its prompt healing action will prove more satisfactory than almost any mode of treatment of piles. The preparation is furnished in regular 50-cent size boxes, which we, however, supply to our customers at the exceedingly small price of only 30 cents per box.

No. 8F163 Price, 3 boxes for 80c; per box.........................30c
If by mail, postage extra, per box, 3 cents.

CASCARA CATHARTIC TABLETS.

A VERY PLEASANT LAXATIVE.

FOR CONSTIPATION AND ALL GENERAL STOMACH, LIVER AND BOWEL COMPLAINTS.

A pleasant, efficient laxative and stimulative tonic, the most effective remedy for the quick relief and cure of constipation, jaundice, nausea, dyspepsia, biliousness and all complications resulting from a disordered condition of the stomach and bowels. **Our Cascara Cathartic Tablets are a combination of the most successful,** yet perfectly harmless remedies, recommended and used by the most eminent physicians, as a positive laxative and tonic. On account of their mild action on the bowels they are not only a valuable cathartic, but at the same time the most pleasing treatment for the cure of symptoms for which they are intended. **You will never know how easy it will be to keep yourself in a perfect and regular condition,** how quickly you can dispel those apparently unimportant yet exceedingly distressing little troubles resulting from a disturbed digestion or an irregularity of the bowels. Using two or three Cascara Cathartic Tablets for a few days will tone up the entire system, strengthen the digestive organs and bowels connected with the function of digestion and the elimination of waste matter. You will feel lighter, brighter, more restful and cheerful and free from the nervous and painful state which always follows indigestion and bowel trouble. Less valued remedies of this kind are usually sold at 50 cents in boxes containing 30 to 35 doses. Our price for 54 doses is 27 cents. **We guarantee our Cascara Cathartic Tablets to give satisfaction.**

No. 8F165 Price, large size, containing 54 doses, 3 boxes for 70c; per box.........................27c
If by mail, postage extra, per box, 4 cents.

DR. ALLEN'S ASTHMA CURE.

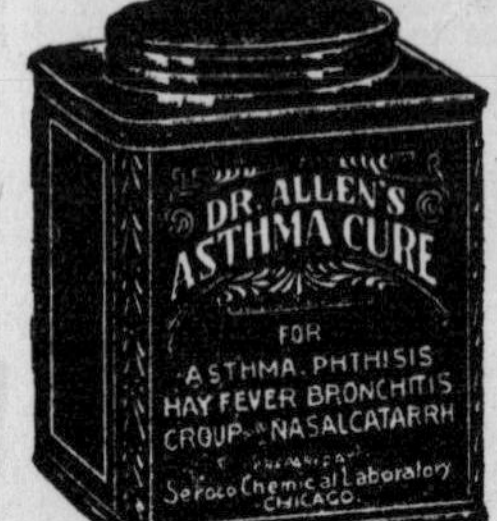

DR. ALLEN'S ASTHMA CURE is for the relief of all forms of Asthma, Hay Fever, Bronchitis, Croup and Nasal Catarrh. It is a scientific combination of oxygenating chemicals with such herbs and barks as have proven themselves effective for the relief of asthma and other affections of the respiratory organs, attended with short, difficult or spasmodic breathing. It is the result of many years' study and experiment in the treatment of diseases of the lungs and air passages, and all stages of asthma. **It has never failed to give some relief or effect a cure when a fair trial was given** and used according to directions. This remedy is used by inhalation and as its virtues reach the air passages direct, the relief obtained is instantaneous. **Plain directions and valuable information enclosed in each box,** and if the sufferer will follow these directions carefully, mild forms of asthma, hay fever, etc., **are often cured in a week or two;** but if the disease is old and deep seated and has obtained a firm hold on the system, the treatment ought to be continued for several months, even though the patient may believe himself entirely cured.

OUR PRICE, ONLY **62c**
Regular Retail Price, $1.00

No. 8F169 Full size box. Price, 3 boxes for $1.75; per box.........62c
If by mail, postage extra, per box, 5 cents.

DR. WALTERS' CHILL CURE.

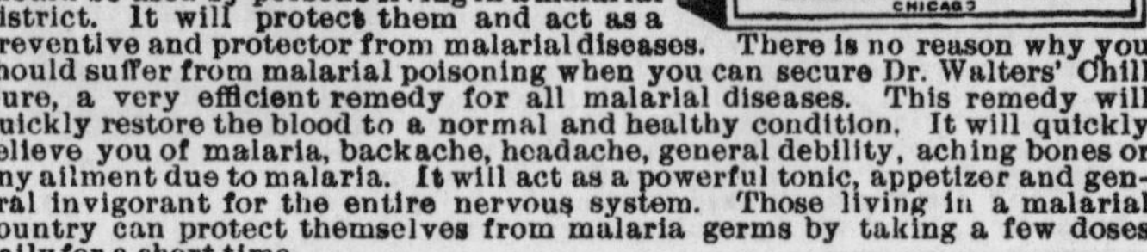

DR. WALTERS' WELL KNOWN CHILL CURE is a specific for the cure of all diseases due to malarial poisoning. It will promptly relieve intermittent fever or fever and ague, remittent fever, dumb ague, periodic headache or malaria. It completely destroys the germs of malaria in the blood, thus removing the cause of the disease from the entire system. Dr. Walters' Chill Cure should be used by persons living in a malarial district. It will protect them and act as a preventive and protector from malarial diseases. There is no reason why you should suffer from malarial poisoning when you can secure Dr. Walters' Chill Cure, a very efficient remedy for all malarial diseases. This remedy will quickly restore the blood to a normal and healthy condition. It will quickly relieve you of malaria, backache, headache, general debility, aching bones or any ailment due to malaria. It will act as a powerful tonic, appetizer and general invigorant for the entire nervous system. Those living in a malarial country can protect themselves from malaria germs by taking a few doses daily for a short time.

No. 8F171 Dr. Walters' Chill Cure.
Price, 3 boxes for 95c; per box.........................36c
If by mail, postage extra, per box, 4 cents.

CATARRH-OL SOLUTION.

A VERY HIGHLY RECOMMENDED AND BENEFICIAL TREATMENT FOR CHRONIC CATARRH.

This new local treatment for catarrh in the head or nose and throat, as well as all affections of the bronchial tubes and lungs, consists of a combination of the most powerful antiseptic and germ destroying ingredients, prepared for the purpose of preventing infectious diseases of the breathing organs and for the cure of catarrhal diseases of the head and lungs, and when applied with the Catarrh-ol Nebulizer or Vaporizer will prove of greatest benefit in the treatment of catarrh in all its different forms. **Catarrh-ol is cleanly, inexpensive and guaranteed to reach most cases in an effective manner.** Its antiseptic and curing influences when it is properly used are simply remarkable. It does not cause even the slightest irritation. It is prompt in its relief and quick results can always be assured. Catarrh-ol Solutions are furnished as Solution No. 1 and Solution No. 2. The first is of especial value in the treatment of catarrh of the nose and throat, while No. 2 is intended for bronchial trouble and lung diseases. **The Catarrh-ol Vaporizer** is the only instrument of its kind on the market, and, on account of its peculiar construction and patented features, will nebulize the solutions and carry the same over the entire surface of the mucous membrane, the seat of all catarrhal trouble, reaching every portion of the nasal passages and the air passages, the bronchial tubes and, through them, the lungs, soothing, healing and curing.

No. 8F172 Catarrh-ol No. 1. For catarrh of nose and throat. Price, 47c
No. 8F173 Catarrh-ol No. 2. For bronchial and lung trouble. Price, 47c
No. 8F174 Catarrh-ol Vaporizor. Price.........................89c
No. 8F175 Catarrh-ol Solution Treatment, including one bottle Catarrh-ol No. 1, one bottle Catarrh-ol No. 2, sufficient for three months' treatment, and one patent Vaporizer, all complete. Price.............$1.58
Unmailable on account of weight.

DR. WALTER'S CATARRH SNUFF.

The best known local catarrh remedy. Affords relief and great benefit in nine cases out of ten.

For all catarrhal affections—Headache, catarrh of the mucous membrane of the nose, cold in head, etc., nothing acts so quickly as WALTER'S CATARRH SNUFF. PERFECTLY HARMLESS. It contains no injurious drugs or chemicals. Every bottle comes supplied with blower, by means of which the healing powder can be applied directly to the inflamed parts, stopping and healing any discharges, pain or irritation. **OUR PRICE FOR THE CATARRH SNUFF IS 21 CENTS**, complete with blower. **If you have friends** who have suffered with this **dread disease**—catarrh—tell them of this **catarrh snuff**, that the price has been reduced to only **21 cents. Never sold for less than 50 cents by others.**

OUR PRICE, ONLY **21c**
Regular Retail Price, 50 Cents.

No. 8F176 Price, per bottle..................21c
3 bottles for..................55c
If by mail, postage extra, 7 cents.

DR. WALTER'S DIGESTIVE ELIXIR.

For the prompt relief of dyspepsia, indigestion and stomach complications generally.

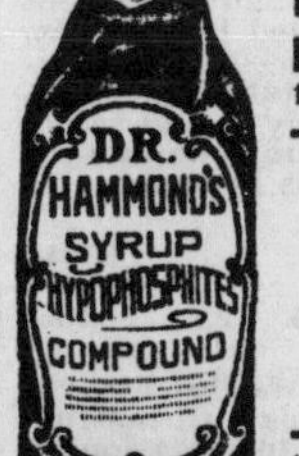

DR. WALTER'S DIGESTIVE ELIXIR contains, in correct proportions: Pepsin, diastase malt, rennin, menthol, thymol, baptisia, eucalyptol, rochelle salts, hydrochloric acid, lactic acid, elixir simplex.

DOES YOUR STOMACH DISTRESS YOU? Do you suffer with dyspepsia? Are you troubled with indigestion? Send for a bottle of Dr. Walter's Digestive Elixir. It will be furnished to you with the understanding that after you have used the first bottle and if you have not tried this remedy before, if you do not find results entirely satisfactory, all you have to do is to notify us of that fact, and the full amount that you have paid for the first bottle of this remedy will be refunded to you at once.

OUR PRICE, ONLY **52c**
Regular Retail Price $1.00

DR. WALTER'S DIGESTIVE ELIXIR increases the gastric juices, aids digestion, makes the food antiseptic, tones the system, removes all gas and makes the stomach strong, healthy and able to perform its work.

PLEASE BEAR IN MIND that Dr. Walter's Digestive Elixir is a digestive remedy; a preparation that will have a beneficial effect upon the entire digestive system by performing a portion of its work in a most natural way, thus resting the stomach when in a weakened condition and by this rest which it affords to the digestive system will strengthen these organs so that they soon can and will perform their work without any medical aid.

DYSPEPSIA is a very common and exceedingly distressing disease and as a rule manifests itself by the following symptoms: A feeling of fullness and weight in the stomach after eating, flatulency, decomposing of food from slow and imperfect digestion, which produces gases, swelling of the stomach, great discomfort or pain, constant belching, heartburn, frequent fainting, sick headache and constipation.

THE ABOVE SYMPTOMS are usually caused by a weak stomach, inability to digest the food, so that it sours in the stomach and the trouble starts.

BY USING DR. WALTER'S DIGESTIVE ELIXIR you will not only assist the digestion of the food but this remedy will gradually strengthen the stomach and the entire digestive system, resulting in the proper assimilation of the food, furnishing the right nourishment and building up your general health to a point where you can eat all kinds of food without being distressed; enjoy all your meals to the fullest measure.

DR. WALTER'S DIGESTIVE ELIXIR combines in an agreeable form some of the best medical substances used for the cure of dyspepsia and indigestion in all its forms.

ONE TEASPOONFUL of this remedy taken three or four times a day after meals will increase the gastric juices, free the stomach from all gas, aid digestion, and in a very short time you will know what it means to be free again from dyspepsia and indigestion. When using Dr. Walter's Digestive Elixir you can eat nearly everything that you like without experiencing any discomfort or ill effects in the least.

No. 8F180 Dr. Walter's Digestive Elixir, each bottle, 12-ounce capacity. Price, 3 bottles for $1.40; per bottle..................52c
Unmailable on account of weight.

DR. CURTIS' SORE THROAT CURE.

The great remedy for sore throat and all acute throat affections.

COMPOSITION. Dr. Curtis' Sore Throat Cure is the formula used by this eminent throat specialist for years in his private practice and contains in permanent solution, chlorine, ferric iron, chlorates, oxychlorides, etc., combined in such a manner as to continually liberate free chlorine, oxygen and and oxychlorides. The efficiency of these gases in sore throat and early diphtheria is well known and combined with other beneficial substances forms one of the foremost treatments for these conditions.

OUR PRICE, ONLY **32c**
Regular Retail Price, 50 Cents.

ITS USES. Dr. Curtis' Sore Throat Cure may be used locally or internally as conditions may require. The preparation is best used undiluted and should reach as nearly as possible every part of the throat. This is best accomplished by means of an atomizer, if at hand, otherwise by gargling and swallowing the quantity remaining in the mouth after each treatment.

IF YOU SUFFER FROM SORE THROAT, tonsilitis, enlargement of the tonsils, or any one of similar throat affections, we would urge you by all means to order a bottle of Curtis' Sore Throat Cure, as a trial. Use it according to directions and a severe sore throat can be prevented. It is far better to use the product as soon as possible after the soreness is noticed and before the inflammation becomes deep seated as it is then much harder to cure.

A HOUSEHOLD NECESSITY. This excellent sore throat cure should be in every household. None of us are able to tell just when we will experience a severe sore throat and then is just the time we want a good remedy. A bad sore throat should be carefully treated, otherwise diphtheria or other chronic symptoms may arise. With our liberal offer on this product you cannot afford to be without it. **Full directions with each bottle.** Regular retail price, per bottle, 50 cents.

No. 8F182 Price, three 4-ounce bottles, **80c**; per bottle..................32c
If by mail, postage and tube extra, per bottle, 19 cents.

SYRUP HYPOPHOSPHITES COMPOUND.

(Dr. Hammond.)

The Great Tonic and Reconstructive for Nervous Exhaustion, General Debility.

DR. HAMMOND'S SYRUP HYPOPHOSPHITES COMPOUND has for years been recognized as one of the very best reconstructive tonics, stimulating and toning the appetite, the functions of digestion and assimilation and the entire nervous system, while it also contains the necessary mineral constituents for supplying the required energy to aid in overcoming disease.

OUR PRICE, ONLY **64c**
Regular Retail Price, $1.00

COMPOSITION. The composition of this new but highly successful tonic comprises the hypophosphites of potassium, sodium, lime, manganese, iron and quinine. Potassium, sodium and lime serve as great constructive tonics to bone, muscle and nerve tissue. Manganese and iron supply the red color to the blood. Phosphorus, as it exists in the composition, forms a large per cent of the different parts of the body and especially the brain. Quinine, the main alkaloid of this preparation, acts as a tonic, keeping up the strength of the system, toning the appetite and improving all the functions of the body.

IN ALL AFFECTIONS OF THE BRONCHIAL TUBES, Dr. Hammond's Syrup Hypophosphites Compound should be given a trial. If used conscientiously, this syrup will diminish the tendency to consumption and may even prevent the further formation of tuberculous deposit after the disease has taken hold. In the first and second stages of tuberculosis this composition may, when rightly used, overcome the disease, and even in advanced stages great benefit will be derived from its use.

A UNIVERSAL TONIC. Dr. Hammond's Syrup Hypophosphites Compound may be considered the one universal tonic. It stimulates and increases the appetite and has a favorable influence upon the red corpuscles of the blood, tones up the functions of digestion and assimilation, strengthens the nervous system, supplies the necessary mineral constituents of the body and induces, by its tonic action on the digestive organs, regular and easy evacuation of the bowels. Patients taking this syrup, as a rule, gain flesh from the very first and it is considered to be one of the foremost tonics for use in a debilitated or weakened condition.

THIS REMEDY is sold under our liberal guarantee allowing our customer who has never used it, to order one bottle to ascertain whether this product reaches your condition and whether it will afford you benefit, otherwise the full amount paid will be refunded upon request.

No. 8F181 Price, three 16-ounce bottles for **$1.75**; per bottle..................64c
(Unmailable on account of weight)

DR. ROSE'S RED CLOVER COMPOUND.

This is a splendid remedy for worn out, tired, and exhausted conditions of the system.

This well known and highly beneficial blood purifier is in all probability better known than any other combination ever offered. It is a system builder of the highest nature.

COMPOSITION. Dr. Rose's Red Clover Compound contains in permanent syrup: Red clover blossoms, stillingia root, burdock root, berberis aquafolium, cascara amarga, prickly ash bark and potassium iodide in the proportions best suited for quick and effective results. **Red clover blossoms** is a very good blood purifier and general alterative. **Stillingia root** acts especially beneficial in syphilitic skin diseases, scrofula and bronchial affections. **Burdock root** acts upon the blood, kidneys and liver, purifying the blood and aiding in the elimination of the impurities. **Berberis aquafolium** is a tonic as well as aiding elimination of the impurities of the system through the kidneys and skin. **Cascara amarga** comprises one of the very best tonics and laxatives, especially valuable in syphilis, chronic liver troubles, eczema and consumption. It also aids elimination through the bowels. **Prickly ash bark** is an excellent stimulant tonic, highly recommended in chronic rheumatism, syphilis, liver troubles and wherever a stimulating alterative is required. **Potassium iodide** affords one of the very best remedies for syphilis, rheumatism and as a general blood purifier.

OUR PRICE, ONLY **68c**
Regular Retail Price, $1.00

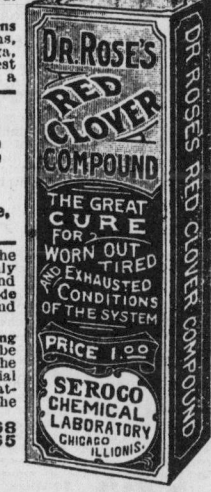

CONCLUSIONS. After studying the separate drugs entering into this valuable remedy one cannot but be impressed that Rose's Syrup Red Clover Compound is one of the very best medicines for treating all blood, skin and bronchial affections. It enriches the blood, aids elimination of waste matter, increases appetite and digestion and in general improves the entire system. **Full directions with each bottle.**

No. 8F183 Price, per bottle..................$0.68
3 bottles for..................1.65
Unmailable on account of weight.

EFFERVESCENT LIVER SALT.

PLEASANT TO TAKE AND EFFECTIVE IN RESULTS.
Promotes Health and Prevents Disease.

An excellent combination, free from all harmful ingredients, for quickly relieving all forms of liver troubles.

OUR PRICE, ONLY **34c**
Regular Retail Price, 50 Cents.

CORRECTS THE LIVER. Effervescent Liver Salt is superior to most forms for correcting all the ills arising from lack of exercise, improper food, poor digestion and irregular meals.

LIVER SALT Affords ready relief in torpid liver, jaundice, constipation, sick headache, heartburn, bad breath, biliousness, distress after eating, gout, rheumatism, dizziness, prickly heat, hives, and all conditions arising from a clogging of the liver. Put up in large amber bottles. **Full directions with each bottle.**

No. 8F184 Price, per bottle..........$0.34
3 bottles for.......... .90
Unmailable on account of weight.

COMPRESSED EFFERVESCENT LITHIA TABLETS.

LITHIA SALTS have for years been recognized as one of the standard remedies for the treatment of subacute and chronic rheumatism, gout, uric acid, irritable bladder and all kidney affections depending upon an excess of uric acid in the system. Our Lithia tablets are absolutely pure, convenient, and accurate in dosage and possess many advantages not embraced by other forms of administration. One tablet dissolved in a glass of water makes a very agreeable, refreshing and beneficial effervescing draught.

No. 8F186 Price, per bottle, 3-grain tablets, 40 in bottle, **18c**
No. 8F187 Price, per bottle, 5-grain tablets, 40 in bottle, **23c**
If by mail postage extra, 15 cents.

Family Medicine Case.

HANDY POCKET TABLET REMEDIES. **Twenty-four different remedies in large glass vials with metal screw top, will keep in every climate for years, a treatment for almost every disease for only 11 cents. For 11 cents each, 2 cents extra for postage,** we offer twenty-four different remedies, put up in neat tablet form, easy to take and convenient to be carried in vest pocket. These remedies are compounded in our own laboratory, and represent the best prescriptions of the highest medical authorities in the land, **are absolutely harmless, prepared from vegetable tinctures, herbs and roots. No mineral, mercury or poison.** These handy pocket tablet remedies will save you doctor bills and much suffering. **No family can afford to be without a supply of these remedies, and the price has been fixed so low, only 11 cents each vial, that all may be supplied.**

No. 8F199 12 Bottles of any of the following in fancy case..........**$1.20**
Medicine Case and Medical Book free.

No. 8F200 24 Bottles of any of the following in fancy case.......... **2.25**
Medicine Case and Medical Book free.

WITH EVERY ORDER **for a case of the following 11-cent remedies we will send "The Family Doctor,"** a book giving full instructions how to use these remedies and containing other valuable information for the cure of the sick, **free.** You can select any twelve of the following named remedies at **11 cents** each, and a black cloth covered case will be furnished with the same **without extra cost. For $1.20, covering the price of 12 bottles of the following listed household remedies, we will send the medicine at once, together with medicine case and medicine book free.**

If by mail, postage extra, 26 cents.

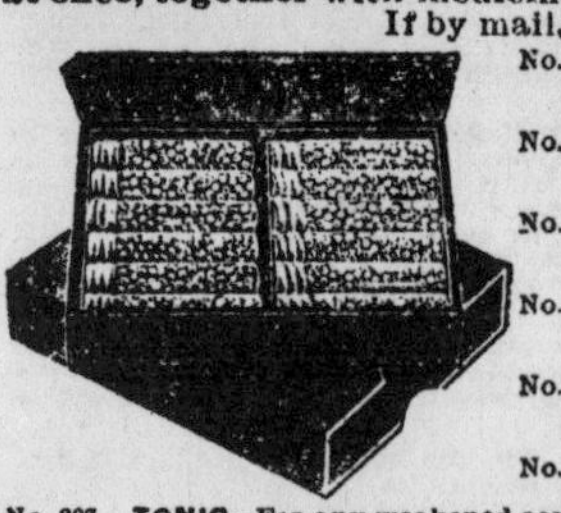

No. 201. **COLD IN THE HEAD.**—For quinsy, tonsilitis cold in the head, influenza, and many of the milder troubles arising from cold. Price..........**11c**

No. 202. **COLIC**—Very useful for all childish pains, such as cramps, colic, or for the restlessness of teething, diarrhea, etc. Price..........**11c**

No. 203. **COUGH**—Valuable in coughs, bronchitis, hoarseness and any trouble in throat and chest arising from cold. Price..........**11c**

No. 204. **CONSTIPATION**—Will relieve cases of constipation, which are often the cause of headache, biliousness, offensive breath, etc. Price..........**11c**

No. 205. **DIARRHEA**—Useful for any form of diarrhea, cholera morbus, cholera infantum, sour stomach, etc. Price..........**11c**

No. 206. **HEADACHE**—Good for headache of any sort, fever, cold, nervousness, la grippe, etc. Price..........**11c**

No. 207. **TONIC**—For any weakened condition of the system. Price..........**11c**

No. 208. **ALTERATIVE**—For impure blood, boils, scrofula, ulcers, eczema, etc. Price..........**11c**

No. 209. **DYSPEPSIA**—From any of the ordinary causes. Price..........**11c**

No. 210. **KIDNEY AND LIVER**—To remove or cure all diseases of the organs. Price..........**11c**

No. 211. **MALARIAL**—To be used when quinine fails, or when the patient cannot take it. Price **11c**

No. 212. **RHEUMATIC**—A true remedy. Price..........**11c**

No. 213. **NERVOUS TROUBLES**—Calms and soothes; will relieve nervousness in any form. Price..........**11c**

No. 214. **HEART REGULATOR**—A splendid tonic for the heart. Price..........**11c**

No. 215. **LIVER CORRECTOR**—For biliousness, jaundice, sallow complexion, sour stomach, etc. Price..........**11c**

No. 216. **KIDNEY DISORDERS**—Gently stimulates the kidneys and relieves urinary troubles in both old and young. Price..........**11c**

No. 217. **BRONCHIAL**—For difficult breathing, pain in the chest, cold in the bronchial tubes. Price..........**11c**

No. 218. **THROAT**—For hoarseness, tickling in the throat; useful for speakers and singers. Price..........**11c**

No. 219. **NEURALGIA**—For the relief of neuralgia, sciatica, etc. Price..........**11c**

No. 220. **FEVER**—For all kinds of fever, especially that arising from cold. Price..........**11c**

No. 221. **CROUP**—For children; to be given when the first symptom appears. Price..........**11c**

No. 222. **MUMPS**—Give regularly and follow instructions in our Medical Guide. Price..........**11c**

No. 223. **PLEURISY**—For pain in the chest on breathing and coughing. Price..........**11c**

No. 224. **PIMPLES**—For skin blemishes. Price..........**11c**

Our Homeopathic Remedies.

12 bottles of different Homeopathic Remedies, your own selection..........$1.39
A nice, black cloth covered Medicine Case and Instruction Sheet free.

OUR HOMEOPATHIC SPECIFICS **are prepared under the supervision of an old, experienced homeopathic physician.** Great care is taken in preparing them according to the rules laid down by the **highest authorities on homeopathy,** and only the purest drugs used. Every one of the following specifics is **a special cure for the diseases named on it. Adults take 6 pellets, children from 1 to 3, according to age,** and from two to four doses are to be taken every day, according to the severity of the case. We ask the special attention of all our customers to these **high grade remedies.** If you have them near at hand, we guarantee they **will save you many a doctor's bill, and what is of more consequence, quickly relieve any suffering member of the family and ward off more serious sickness.**

No. 8F230 12 bottles, any selection..........**$1.39**
No. 8F232 24 bottles, any selection..........**2.35**
No. 8F234 36 bottles, any selection..........**2.85**
Medicine Case and Instruction Sheet free.

A SPECIAL OFFER. **As an inducement to give these remedies a thorough trial, we will allow you to select any of the cures listed below. Make your** own selection, one or more of any kind, and we will put them in a neat case, such as we represent here, and only charge you $1.39. **The homeopathic physician book also furnished free. No family can afford to neglect this great offer.**

A 12-Box Case will save you many dollars doctors' bills in a year and may save your life. **No family should be without a case of our Homeopathic Remedies.**

		Usual Price	Our Price
No. 8F235	For treating rheumatism rheumatic pains	25c	13c
No. 8F236	For treating fever and ague, intermittent fever, malaria, etc.	25c	13c
No. 8F237	For treating piles, blind or bleeding, external or internal	25c	13c
No. 8F238	For treating ophthalmia, weak or inflamed eyes	25c	13c
No. 8F239	For treating catarrh, influenza, cold in the head	25c	13c
No. 8F240	For treating whooping cough, spasmodic cough	25c	13c
No. 8F241	For treating asthma, oppressed or difficult breathing	25c	13c
No. 8F242	For treating fevers, congestions, inflammations	25c	13c
No. 8F243	For treating worm fever or worm diseases	25c	13c
No. 8F244	For treating colic, crying and wakefulness of infants teething	25c	13c
No. 8F245	For treating diarrhea of children and adults	25c	13c
No. 8F246	For treating dysentery, griping, bilious colic	25c	13c
No. 8F247	For treating cholera, cholera morbus, vomiting	25c	13c
No. 8F248	For treating coughs, colds, bronchitis	25c	13c
No. 8F249	For treating toothache, faceache, neuralgia	25c	13c
No. 8F250	For treating headache, sick headache, vertigo	25c	13c
No. 8F251	For treating dyspepsia, indigestion, weak stomach	25c	13c
No. 8F252	For treating suppressed or scanty menses	25c	13c
No. 8F253	For treating leucorrhea, or profuse menses	25c	13c
No. 8F254	For treating croup, hoarse cough, difficult breathing, laryngitis	25c	13c
No. 8F255	For treating salt rheum, eruptions, erysipelas	25c	13c
No. 8F256	For treating ear discharge, earache	25c	13c
No. 8F257	For treating scrofula, swellings, ulcers	25c	13c
No. 8F258	For treating general debility, physical weakness, brain fag	25c	13c
No. 8F259	For treating dropsy, fluid accumulations	25c	13c
No. 8F260	For treating seasickness, nausea, vomiting	25c	13c
No. 8F261	For treating kidney disease, gravel, calculi	25c	13c
No. 8F262	For treating nervous debility, vital weakness	25c	13c
No. 8F263	For treating sore mouth and canker	25c	13c
No. 8F264	For treating urinary incontinence, wetting bed	25c	13c
No. 8F265	For treating painful menses, pruritus	25c	13c
No. 8F266	For treating diseases of the heart, palpitation	25c	13c
No. 8F267	For treating epilepsy, St. Vitus' dance	25c	13c
No. 8F268	For treating sore throat, quinsy or ulcerated sore throat	25c	13c
No. 8F269	For treating chronic congestions, headache	25c	13c
No. 8F270	For treating grip and chronic colds	25c	13c

If by mail, postage extra, per case, 26 cents; per bottle, 2 cents.

LIQUID IROZONE (FERROUS LIQUID OXYGEN)

A GERM KILLER. AN OXYGEN SUPPLIER.

Cures Germ Diseases. Strengthens, Invigorates and Cures by Furnishing that Great Life Property, Oxygen, to the Blood.

No. 8F189 Price, per bottle (commercial pint size)..........**46c**

A WONDERFUL DISCOVERY.

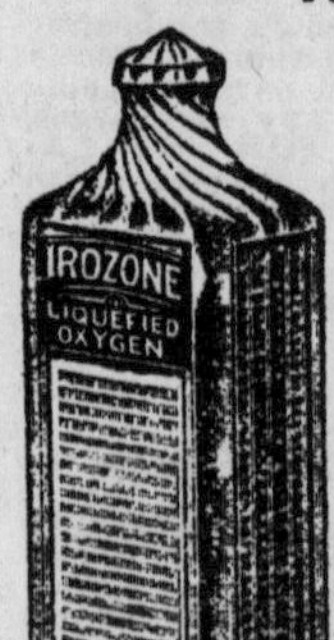

LIQUID IROZONE (**Ferrous Liquid Oxygen**) is a harmless but powerful preparation for the prompt and effectual cure of all germ diseases. It cures by supplying oxygen to the blood and thus creating healthy tissue. Germs cannot thrive or live in healthy oxygenized tissue.

MANY DISEASES **are directly caused by germ infection.** In all such cases Liquid Irozone is an ideal, positive remedy because it kills the germs, it purifies the blood by supplying oxygen and it does all this without harming tissue or organ.

OUR PRICE, ONLY
46c
Regular Retail Price, $1.00.

GREAT BENEFIT IS DERIVED **by taking Liquid Irozone even if you are not positively sick,** because it strengthens, invigorates and purifies the blood by supplying an extra quantity of oxygen, the life giving principle of the atmosphere. It is perfectly safe, wonderfully effective and positively certain, a complete destruction of all germ life wherever germs may be the real cause of disease. It is nature's own tonic, supplying to the blood that substance that the human body most vitally requires in health and in sickness, namely, oxygen, and it supplies this great life principle in a new and scientific way.

YOU KNOW, OF COURSE, **that without oxygen no human being can live.** Every second of your life you need oxygen. Nature supplies it to you in every breath of air you inhale. It reaches the blood through the lungs. It is at this stage of the circulation of the blood through the body that the oxygen is taken into the blood, immediately changing the impure dark venous blood (vein blood) into purified, healthy, bright red or arterial blood. The blood after being ozonated with oxygen becomes purified and then passes into the heart and finally into the circulation, supplying to the weakened, impoverished and diseased tissues, cells and organs an abundance of that life sustaining fluid, pure, rich and healthy blood. If the blood is liberally supplied with oxygen, in its travel through the system it destroys germ life and at the same time revitalizes every organ, every part of the body, acting as a stimulative, tonic and invigorator, sustaining life and the healthy condition of the body.

THE NORMAL QUANTITY OF OXYGEN **needed is supplied in nature by our breathing pure, fresh air.** A lack of fresh air means a diminishing of the supply of oxygen for your body. Those that live constantly in the pure, open air, feed their lungs with all the oxygen needed to maintain life and to protect them against germ diseases, but millions of men, women and children, under the modern system of living, suffer from an insufficient supply of oxygen and therefore their systems are not immune from the attack of germs, and they may already be troubled with a germ dissease in some form, or from the lack of pure air, or oxygen, they are unable to resist an attack if exposed to germ infection, no matter in what manner the infection may present itself.

BY TAKING LIQUID IROZONE **you fortify your system against sickness,** you ward off and cure all germ diseases by furnishing your system with a liberal and greater supply of oxygen. In Ferrous Liquid Oxygen we have the only liquefied oxygen that will destroy germs without destroying the tissues of the body and without creating a disturbing or distressing effect upon the digestive organs. Oxygen, as every one knows, is the vital part of air. It is the very source of vitality, the most essential element of life. **Oxygen is also nature's greatest tonic, the blood food, the nerve food, the scavenger of the blood.** It is oxygen that turns the blue blood to red in the lungs, it is oxygen that eliminates the waste tissue and builds up the new. You can therefore realize what a wonderful and valuable preparation Liquid Irozone is, how important it is that every one should avail himself of this great chemical product, Ferrous Liquid Oxygen or Ozone Liquefied.

LIQUID IROZONE **supplies to weakened, exhausted and anemic subjects,** a soluble, tasteless and non-constipating form of iron, which is so combined with purified ozone (or concentrated oxygen), as to produce a pleasant and palatable blood and tissue building tonic.

No. 8F189 Price, 3 bottles for **$1.15**; per bottle......(Unmailable)..........**46c**

Dr. Rowland's System Builder and Lung Restorer.

Large Commercial Quart Bottles.

Retail price..........$1.00
Our price, per bottle..........$0.52
Three bottles for..........1.45

A Powerful Vegetable Medicine for the thousand ailments common to the masses.

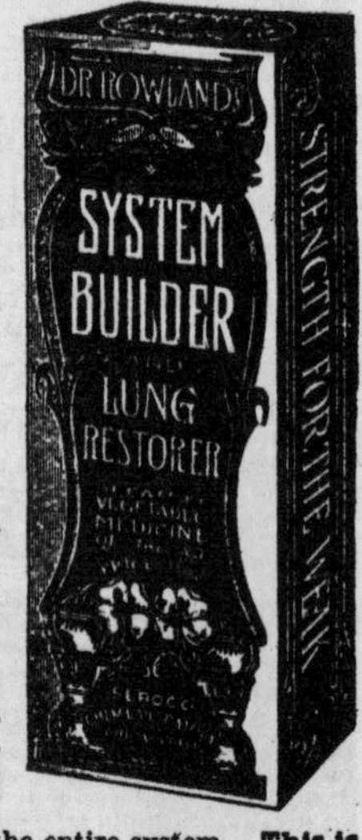

FOR THE RELIEF OF COUGHS **of all kinds, chronic and lingering, especially bronchitis, laryngitis, consumption, ulcerated throat,** ministers' or public speakers' **sore throat, hoarseness and suppression or loss of voice.** It does not nauseate or debilitate the stomach or system, but improves digestion, strengthens the stomach, builds up solid flesh when the system is reduced below a healthy standard, and **invigorates and cleanses the whole system.**

OUR PRICE, ONLY
52c
Regular Retail Price, $1.00.

As a remedy for torpor of the liver, generally termed liver complaint or biliousness, and for habitual **constipation of the bowels** it has no equal. For loss **of appetite, indigestion and dyspepsia, and for general or nervous debility or prostration,** in either sex, **it is especially recommended.** As an alterative or blood purifier, this medicine is far **superior** to any preparation of sarsaparilla, **iodide of potassium,** or any other medicine now offered for general sale. It is, therefore, very valuable in all forms scrofulous and other **blood diseases,** also for all **skin diseases, eruptions, pimples, rashes and blotches, boils, ulcers, sores and swellings,** arising from **impure blood,** and usually cured by the use of a few bottles of this compound. **Unlike** other **alteratives** or blood cleansing medicines, it does not debilitate, but strengthens the entire system. **This is a very concentrated vegetable extract.** The dose is small and pleasant to the taste. Full directions accompany each bottle.

BUILD UP YOUR ENTIRE SYSTEM by using a few bottles of this remedy. **Is your health impaired, are you overworked,** do you need a general toning up? If so, we earnestly recommend a trial of this preparation.

No. 8F190 Price, 3 large bottles for **$1.45**; per bottle..........**52c**
Unmailable on account of weight.

ANTI-CONGESTION PLASTIC DRESSING.

THE GREAT REMEDY FOR RELIEVING AND REDUCING INFLAMMATION AND SWELLINGS OF EVERY DESCRIPTION. TAKES THE PLACE OF THE OLD FASHIONED LINSEED OR BREAD POULTICES.

RECOMMENDED, USED AND PRESCRIBED TODAY BY EVERY PHYSICIAN IN THE CIVILIZED WORLD, in the treatment of diseases accompanied by external or internal inflammation or congestion.

SOLD UNDER OUR PERSONAL GUARANTEE.

IF USED AND FOUND NOT SATISFACTORY, we will return every cent you have paid us for same. NO HOUSEHOLD, whether rich or poor, should be a single day without a sufficient quantity of ANTI-CONGESTION PLASTIC DRESSING Order a supply without a moment's delay. Send for it even before you send for a physician, for it is a remedy for any and all cases, acute or chronic, where superficial or deep seated congestion exists. **DO NOT UNDER ANY CIRCUMSTANCES FAIL TO PROVIDE YOURSELF** with a package of ANTI-CONGESTION PLASTIC DRESSING and keep it in the house ready for instant use. **DO NOT WAIT** until you need it and then send for it. **IT MAY BE TOO LATE WHEN IT ARRIVES** to give you the protection it would have afforded you if it had been kept for ready use

ALTHOUGH IN CASES LIKE pneumonia, bronchitis, pleurisy, peritonitis, erysipelas, and poisoned wounds a physician should be called in, you should have Anti-Congestion Plastic Dressing on hand. In nine cases out of ten he will surely make an immediate application of an Anti-Congestion Plastic Dressing to reduce and remove the inflammation. You will, therefore, save money, worry, and perhaps the life of the patient by having this remedy on hand to meet the emergency without any delay.

BUT THIS IS NOT ALL. Simple instructions are furnished with this remedy and anyone can make the application, so that you can in critical cases apply the Plastic Dressing and do for the patient, long before the doctor arrives, the exact thing he would have advised you to do as the first step after his examination of the patient. **In anticipating the action of the physician, you have aided him as much as may lie in your power in making the sufferer comfortable and in saving the life of the sick one.**

WHAT ANTI-CONGESTION PLASTIC DRESSING WILL DO:

It is the only bland and non-irritating remedy which allays and heals inflammation and congestion. It absorbs from the tissues over which it is placed the moisture resulting from the inflamed condition. It is applicable in all stages and in all varieties of inflammation.

It acts as a complete dressing, furnishing compression, support, rest and protection for that part of the body to which it is applied; it acts as a poultice, does all any poultice can do, supplying heat and moisture, but it goes a great deal further, as it is absorbent, antiseptic, anodyne and nutrient, lasting from twelve to forty-eight hours. It does not annoy and irritate the patient, which nearly always is the case where irregular and too frequent poultice applications are made. **Anti-Congestion Plastic Dressing does not interfere with internal remedies of any kind.**

ANTI-CONGESTION PLASTIC DRESSING WILL GIVE INSTANT AND CERTAIN RELIEF IN ALL CASES OF

PNEUMONIA, PELVIC INFLAMMATION, TUMORS, FELONS, TONSILITIS, BOILS, POISONED WOUNDS, INFLAMMATORY RHEUMATISM BRONCHITIS, INFLAMED BREASTS, PERITONITIS, SPRAINS, CHRONIC ULCERS, ERYSIPELAS, PILES, DYSMENORRHEA, FROSTBITES, AND OPEN WOUNDS IN WHICH INFLAMMATION OR CONGESTION IS A FACTOR. HEED OUR WELL MEANT ADVICE AND KEEP IT ON HAND READY FOR IMMEDIATE USE.

No. 8F191	12-ounce can Anti-Congestion Plastic Dressing. Price	$0.19
No. 8F192	1-pound can Anti-Congestion Plastic Dressing. Price	.25
No. 8F193	1-pound collapsible tubes Anti-Congestion Plastic Dressing. Price	.28
No. 8F194	5-pound package Anti-Congestion Plastic Dressing. Price	1.10

Unmailable on account of weight.

COMPLETE INFORMATION AND INSTRUCTIONS will be furnished with each package.

FREMONT UNFERMENTED GRAPE JUICE.

The pure unfermented dark red juice of the best ripe Concord grapes. Delicious in taste, dark red heavy body and real grape flavor.

PURE RED JUICE. **The Fremont Grape Juice is made from the choicest Concord grapes grown in the famous Lake Erie Island vineyards of Ohio.** Only perfectly ripe fruit, carefully assorted, is used, and the juice is separated and expressed by the latest and most improved methods.

GUARANTEED. **The Fremont Grape Juice is positively guaranteed clean, pure, unfermented (non-alcoholic) and without any antiseptic or preservative in any form.** The juice after expressing is put up in crown sealed amber bottles and Pasteurized by heat—never boiled or cooked and is the only pure grape juice on the American market that will not mold in the bottle or have a heavy sediment at the bottom. We do not bleach or filter out the pulp (body of grape) in order to make the juice clear like wine, as this sacrifices good quality and nutritive value for looks only.

EFFECTS. **Taken in quantities of from one to three glasses daily it increases nutrition, promotes secretion and excretion,** improves the action of the liver, kidneys and bowels and adds to the health. The sugar of the grape requires no digestion, but is taken almost at once into the blood, where it renders up its force as required; so also the water. Taken moderately, with a suitable diet, it will not produce cathartic effects, but a more natural action of the bowels, so important to health: if taken in large quantities, it is generally laxative. As soon as this occurs, obstructions disappear, and a feeling of comfort arises which is very gratifying to the sufferer. Being absolutely free from alcohol, you may drink a quart and yet not become intoxicated. Alcoholic juices and beverages are temporary stimulants at best, while with Fremont Grape Juice, the beneficial effects are permanent and lasting. The one pure unfermented juice for medicinal, hospital and table use.

NOTHING BUT THE JUICE. **The Fremont brand of Concord Grape Juice is positively pure, and being pure conforms to the pure food laws everywhere.** This juice according to Government analysis is all Grape except outer skin and seeds, and not the transparent or watery looking kind, sometimes sold for pure grape juice.

FOR SACRAMENTAL USES. **Fremont Grape Juice is certainly the safest, purest and best that can be procured for this purpose.**

ALL CAN DRINK FREMONT GRAPE JUICE **without the slightest injury; as a chemical analysis of our JUICE shows it to contain, measure for measure, MORE NOURISHMENT than milk.** It affords a household and health beverage of the highest order, a pleasant drink and food in sickness and convalescence, in summer and winter, for the young and the aged. Not a stimulant, but nature's own true tonic, and the best that money can buy. If you want the pure unfermented dark red juice of the grape, buy this product. Satisfaction guaranteed.

OUR PRICE, ONLY 20c
Regular Retail Price, 25 cents.

No. 8F195	Price, per pint bottle	$0.20
No. 8F196	Price, per quart bottle	.38
No. 8F197	Price, per dozen pints	2.2[illegible]
No. 8F198	Price, per dozen quarts	4.25

GREATER LIBERALITY IN OUR PROFIT SHARING DEPARTMENT THAN EVER BEFORE.

OUR WONDERFUL PROFIT SHARING DEPARTMENT, **by which we share the profits of our business with our customers, and which has been so wonderfully popular the past two years, has been greatly extended by us.** The variety, the beauty, the value of our Profit Sharing Articles have been vastly improved over any previous season, and though our prices on everything catalogued in the pages of this big catalogue are lower than those named on similar qualities by any other merchandising institution in the history of the world, we have gone even further than ever before in sharing the profits of this immense business with those who send us a liberal share of their patronage, and this greatly enlarged Profit Sharing Plan so far outclasses all plans ever devised by any other concern for rewarding their customers that no possible comparison can be made.

WE HAVE ISSUED **a large beautifully illustrated Special Profit Sharing Catalogue** in which these useful and valuable Profit Sharing Articles, which we give you free are fully described, and this big free book, containing full information with reference to this wonderfully liberal Profit Sharing Plan, will be sent you by return mail upon request. Just send us a postal card, or a letter, and say, "Please send me your free Profit Sharing Catalogue," and it will go to you immediately, free and postpaid.

OUR PROFIT SHARING PLAN **has so greatly increased our business, it has so promoted the sales of all kinds of merchandise catalogued in the pages of this big book,** that our quantity purchases of merchandise have been growing so large, enabling us to purchase to greater advantage and further enabling us to reduce our prices, that we have determined to make this, our Profit Sharing Plan, much stronger than it has ever been before, and in this free Profit Sharing Catalogue, which we will be glad to send you on request, we offer hundreds of beautiful and valuable articles, such articles as we know will please you and which are wonderful values; in fact, so wonderfully liberal is this, our Profit Sharing Plan, that you will wonder at our ability to make such a liberal distribution of the profits of this business.

SEND FOR THIS FREE PROFIT SHARING CATALOGUE **containing a full explanation of this, our liberal Profit Sharing Plan,** and it will explain to you why our business is growing by leaps and bounds; why millions of families in the United States find it enormously profitable to them to send to us for the goods they need to eat, to wear and to use.

Boracine Eye Remedy.

The purest and best remedy for curing all sore and inflamed eyes and for keeping them well and strong. Modern hygienic rules as laid down by the up to date physician and specialist include the occasional cleansing of the eyes the same as the use of the bath and the daily washing of the body. In using Boracine, the purest and best remedy, a few drops at a time will remove inflammation, heal any irritation or swelling, act as a tonic to the mucous membrane of the eye and restore tired eyes to their natural condition and brilliancy.

Boracine is an eye remedy, not an eye water. Is absolutely harmless and highly beneficial when used as an eye cleanser and eye protector. It will cure all forms of sore eyes, red, inflamed or scaly, itching or granulated eyelids. Complete directions will be furnished with each bottle. Retail price, 50 cents.

No. 8F319 Price, 1-ounce bottle............32c
3 bottles for..............................85c
12 cents extra, for mailing tube and postage.

Dr. Rowland's Eczema Specific.

What is Eczema? This troublesome disease is a local inflammation, manifesting itself upon the skin in the form of a rash and eruption, and causing intense itching and suffering. This itching causes scratching and soon a red, highly inflamed rash makes its appearance and may spread to any part of the body.

Dr. Rowland's Eczema Specific is made in accordance with a special formula and is without doubt the most satisfactory and reliable remedy for the treatment and cure of this troublesome complaint.

Very few diseases are more distressing to the patient or harder to cure, but Dr. Rowland's Eczema Specific will relieve the itching at once and soothe the inflammation, killing the germs causing the disease.

Dr. Rowland's Eczema Specific will cure rash, eczema and skin eruptions of every description and should not be compared with the cheap eczema pastes on the market. We guarantee our preparation to be made from absolutely pure materials and strictly in accordance with the original formula, and it is supplied by us with the distinct understanding that the patient has the privilege of using the first package and if it does not afford relief, if there are no indications, after the treatment has been continued for a reasonable length of time, that it will afford a complete cure, all you have to do is to notify us that results are not satisfactory, stating that this is the first package that you have ever used of Dr. Rowland's Eczema Specific, and we will cheerfully refund to you every cent that you paid for same.

No. 8F311 Price, 8-ounce bottle............$0.60
3 bottles for..............................1.50
Unmailable on account of weight.

Boroseptine.

Antiseptic.

Retail price..........................35c and $1.00
Our price, regular size....................17c
Large size.................................42c

The Ideal Medicine for general household usage, pronounced by many superior to Listerine or any similar preparation.

BOROSEPTINE is an absolutely safe and powerful antiseptic made from menthol, thymol, eucalyptol, glycerine, wintergreen, benzoic and boric acids, and acts as a preventive remedy; is swift and certain in the destruction of microbes, etc., which form contagion. It does not irritate and may be applied to the most delicate tissues. Used in diluted form as a mouth and teeth wash by the most careful ladies and gentlemen. The faithful use of Boroseptine in catarrh establishes prompt and satisfactory relief, and even in chronic cases of catarrh of nose or throat, the parts if sprayed with Boroseptine night and morning will feel its immediate effect in a cooling and refreshing manner, overcoming the sore and sometimes inflamed condition of the tissues. As a mouth and throat wash, also as a gargle, it is acknowledged to be the very best remedy. Should be used as a toilet antiseptic, also after shaving. In the sick room when sprinkled upon furniture and clothing it will impart an agreeable odor, refreshing to the patient and those in attendance. There is really no more valuable general remedy than Boroseptine, the great antiseptic household remedy. It is not a luxury, but a necessity for every home.

No. 8F313 Price, regular size bottle............17c
No. 8F314 Price, large bottle, commercial pints..............................42c
If by mail, regular size bottle, postage and tube extra, 14 cents. Large size unmailable.

Seroco Menthol Inhaler.

Menthol is now a recognized and well known antiseptic, employed by inhalation as an efficient means for quickly curing fresh colds, headache, neuralgia, mild catarrh and for clearing the head, etc. The Seroco Menthol Inhaler is a beautiful, highly polished aluminum tube, with closely fitting cap, to prevent evaporation and has the menthol distributed through the tube in such a manner that best results can always be obtained by simply inhaling the menthol from time to time. Sufficient for two to three months.

No. 8F315 Price..............................15c
If by mail, postage extra, 2 cents.

Dr. Alexander's Formaldehyde Inhaler.

Dr. Alexander's Formaldehyde Inhaler is a scientific treatment for the cure of hay fever, catarrh, asthma and all germ diseases of the nose, throat and lungs. Recommended and prescribed regularly by the best physicians.

Dr. Alexander's Formaldehyde Inhaler is recognized as the only reliable cure by inhalation for nose, throat and lung affections. If you are a sufferer from hay fever and catarrh and so far have been unable to obtain relief and a cure, we recommend Dr. Alexander's Formaldehyde Inhaler, which has proved effective where all other treatments have been found inadequate for a cure.

Dr. Alexander's Formaldehyde Inhaler is a remarkable remedy and considered a specific local treatment for hay fever, catarrh and all germ diseases of the nose, throat and lungs. Furnished in a handsome aluminum tube, with a closely fitting cap to prevent evaporation. Contains a two to three months' treatment.

No. 8F316 Price..............................19c
If by mail, postage extra, 2 cents.

Dr. Swartz's Death to Microbes.

Retail price..............................$2.00
Our price, ½-gallon bottles, each.........70c

NONE GENUINE unless bearing our own label. Our special price, one-half gallon bottle, 70c. Others sell at $2.00. **This is Dr. Swartz's Microbe Killer,** one of the grandest remedies known to the present age. **It will prevent la grippe, catarrh, consumption, malaria, blood poison, rheumatism** and all diseases of the blood. Acts as an antiseptic, killing the germs which are the cause of the disease. Dr. Swartz's Microbe Killer will eradicate any form of disease and purify the whole system. By taking it regularly once or twice a day it will ward off many attacks of disease which would otherwise cause much suffering. **If you have weak lungs don't fail to keep this remedy on hand to be taken Fall and Spring and at other times when there are sudden climatic changes. If you are subject to catarrh** take this remedy once or twice a week and all trouble will be ended. **If you are subject to rheumatism it will save you all pain.** You will never again be bothered with rheumatism if you use Dr. Swartz's Microbe Killer. **If you are subject to fever and ague** take Dr. Swartz's Microbe Killer as a preventive and you will never have this trouble. **No family should be without this wonderful remedy.** It will save its cost a hundred times every year. **The price is very low.**

No. 8F322 Price, per half gallon bottle..........70c
Unmailable on account of weight

Cole's Petroleum Emulson with Hypophosphites of Lime, Soda and Potash.

A True Nutritive Tonic and Reconstructive.

Emulsion of Petroleum and Hypophosphites is today regarded as the greatest flesh builder known to medical science and rapidly replacing Cod Liver and Peanut Oil emulsions on account of its pleasing and agreeable taste.

Petroleum has been known for many years, but to get the objectionable ingredients removed without affecting the flesh building and antiseptic properties has only been successfully accomplished recently. Our oil is a special grade for internal use imported direct from Russia, and not obtainable by chemists generally.

Our Price, only 67c
Regular Retail Price $1.00

The Hypophosphites of Lime, Soda and Potash greatly increase the efficiency of this preparation and taken as a whole it is superior to any other flesh building product.

The success it has attained is wholly due to the good and lasting effect derived. It fills a long felt want in medicine, rapidly replacing other products. Thousands of people who need a strengthening and building tonic cannot take Cod Liver Oil or fatty emulsions on account of the taste as well as the nauseating effect upon the stomach. **Cole's Petroleum Emulsion,** on the other hand, is pleasant to the taste, agreeably taken and does not affect the stomach or digestion. It is easily absorbed by the blood and its beneficial strength is soon felt throughout the system.

Wasting Diseases—For all affections of the throat and lungs, especially bronchitis and consumption, general debility and wasting diseases, particularly when due to faulty nutrition, **Cole's Emulsion of Petroleum and Hypophosphites** stands without an equal. It has all the advantages of all other flesh forming emulsions and has none of their objectionable features. For the early stages of consumption, there is nothing so beneficial, as it rebuilds the wasting tissues, tends to counteract the disease and often effects a cure. For hard coughs and bronchial affections it is invaluable.

Our price of 67 cents for the $1.00 size bottle is exceptionally cheap and we hope our customers will appreciate the exceedingly low price we are able to offer.

Try a bottle of **Cole's Emulsion of Petroleum,** take it regularly after meals and if you are not more than pleased with the beneficial results obtained, we will gladly refund you the money you have paid for the first bottle.

No. 8F319 Regular price, $1.00 per bottle; our price, 3 bottles for **$1.80**; per bottle..............................67c

THE CELEBRATED
DRY POWDER FIRE FIGHTERS.

SOLD EVERYWHERE FOR $3.00 EACH. OUR PRICE ONLY 55 CENTS EACH.

WHAT HAVE YOU IN READINESS IN CASE OF FIRE?

PROTECT YOUR HOME, YOUR BARN, YOUR STABLE, YOUR SHOP, or any other valuable premises by placing within handy reach a few of the celebrated Fire Fighters, the latest improved dry powder fire extinguisher, absolutely safe in its use, instantaneous in its action, and never failing in results. Each Fire Fighter is complete, and **SUPERIOR AND MORE EFFECTIVE THAN ANY OTHER SIMILAR APPLIANCE OBTAINABLE.**

THE FIRE FIGHTER IS A DRY POWDER FIRE EXTINGUISHER, put up for use in a metallic tube 22 inches long and 2 inches in diameter. One end of the tube is fitted with a cover, held in place by natural tension and fitted with a ring by which the tube is hung from a strong hook, attached for this purpose to a wall, column, door or window frame. By grasping the tube firmly and jerking it, it will immediately be released from the cover, which remains hanging on the hook, leaving the tube open at the upper end and its contents free for immediate use. The dry powder is thrown on the floor by a sweeping motion in accordance with complete instructions furnished with each Fire Fighter. Anyone, even children, can use a Fire Fighter with perfect safety and never failing success. It will extinguish the fire, not in five minutes or ten minutes, but instantaneously by blotting it out in a few seconds after proper application of the dry powder has been made.

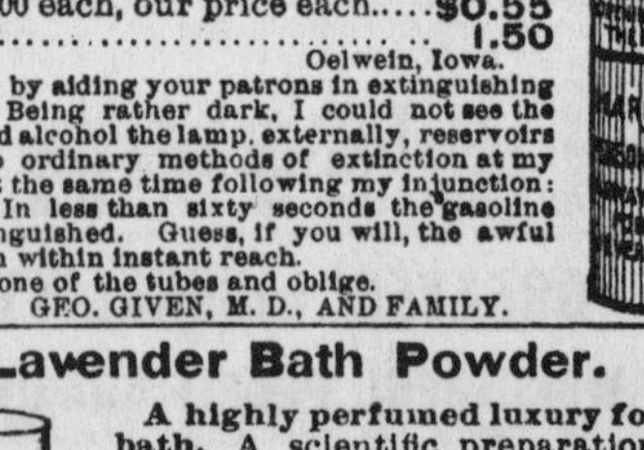

No. 8F324 Fire Fighters, retailing everywhere at $3.00 each, our price each.....**$0.55**
3 for..............................(Not mailable)..............................**1.50**

Gentlemen:— Oelwein, Iowa.

Allow me to congratulate you upon the magnificent work you are doing by aiding your patrons in extinguishing fires. The night before last I filled my gasoline lamp in my working office. Being rather dark, I could not see the gasoline was overflowing, so when, shortly afterwards, I generated with wood alcohol the lamp, externally, reservoirs and all, became one mass of flame, which paid no attention whatsoever to ordinary methods of extinction at my command. My wife called, the Fire Extinguisher, the Fire Extinguisher!!! at the same time following my injunction: Tear it from the hook and hand it to me! which she did more than quickly. In less than sixty seconds the gasoline flame (the strongest flame possibly, today known to man) was entirely extinguished. Guess, if you will, the awful results possible had that most precious yellow can, The Fire Fighter, not been within instant reach.

God knows, gentlemen, I thank you with all my heart. Send me another one of the tubes and oblige.

Gratefully, GEO. GIVEN, M. D., AND FAMILY.

Old English Wart Remover.

GUARANTEED TO GIVE SATISFACTION.

This is a very reliable and harmless remedy for the removal of all forms of warts. After the first application, the wart commences to shrink and after the treatment is continued for a reasonable length of time, the wart will drop off without leaving any scar. The treatment is perfectly painless. All that is necessary is that the patient follow directions furnished with each package. The Old English Wart Remover is guaranteed to be absolutely free from nitric, sulphuric, carbolic or salicylic acids, corrosive sublimate, chrysarobin or creosote, all of which are dangerous to be used for the removal of warts.

No. 8F318 Price..............................15c
If by mail, postage extra, 10 cents.

Lavender Bath Powder.

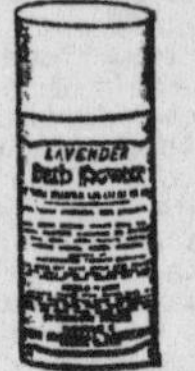

A highly perfumed luxury for the bath. A scientific preparation for softening, purifying and perfuming the water. It adds value and pleasure to the bath, by making it more agreeable and refreshing, neutralizing the germs and impurities in the water, toning and invigorating the system like an ocean bath, and at the same time leaving that exquisite fragrance of Old English Lavender about the entire body. You will never know or appreciate the real luxury of such a bath with its refreshing, stimulating and exhilarating effect until you have used this delightful toilet necessity.

No. 8F321 Price, per package..............18c
If by mail, postage extra, 10 cents.

FAMOUS YELLOWSTONE LITHIA SPRING WATER.

Absolutely the purest, softest, best and choicest of natural remedial spring waters.

Every glass a cup of vitality, health and strength.

IN PRESENTING THIS WATER we have ascertained **that it is not only above all waters in America, but is among the best in the world,** and have a standing offer of $500 for any water that equals it in certain attributes.

THE ANALYSIS herewith given indicates its worth, but a simple test of its organic and mineral purity you can make for yourself. Expose ½ gallon bottle of this natural water to the sun and light for a long period, a year or more if you please. The result—no organic or mineral deposit or any perceptible change. This is a wonderful showing. Find any other water on the market that will withstand such a test for even 30 to 60 days. They will all show both an organic and mineral deposit. This proves to you that the famous Yellowstone Lithia Water is absolutely free from all organic matter and impurities and is the purest and best water ever offered to the public.

OUR PRICE, ONLY
$3.37
Per Doz. ½ Gal. Bottles
Regular Retail Price, $4.75

THIS IS THE AGE OF MINERAL WATERS. There is today **perhaps more mineral water on the market than at any other time in the history of the world.** Some are good, some tolerable and the greater part of little value. In the highest rank, in fact the best of all, stands the now famous Yellowstone Lithia. It is pleasant to take, invigorating and strengthening, clear and sparkling, and a strictly pure, high class mineral spring water. Dame Nature has prepared this wonderful medicine in her own depths of earth, and has herself forced it to the surface of the earth that suffering humanity may drink.

The analysis of this famous water has been carefully performed by accurate analytical chemists and reported as follows:

Sulphate Potassium	1.2214 grains
Sulphate Sodium	5.5475 grains
Chloride Sodium	1.3640 grains
Bicarb. Sodium	39.9671 grains
Bicarb. Calcium	1.1402 grains
Magnesium Bicarb	0 2419 grains
Bicarb. Iron	0.0648 grains
Silica	0.4198 grains
Lithium Bicarb	7.3236 grains
Alumina	0.0784 grains
Total to gallon solid	57.3677 grains

THE ANALYSIS OF THIS WATER discloses medicinal properties that make it one of the very best remedies for Stomach, Liver and Kidney diseases, Dyspepsia, Gravel, Bright's Disease, Constipation and Rheumatism ever known. Note the predominence of Bicarbonate of Sodium (40 grains to gallon shown in analysis). Bicarbonate of Sodium is the basis of all stomach remedies. In this water you have it direct from nature. Then why should not this water be one of the greatest cures for Dyspepsia, Indigestion, etc.; very effective in results, aiding the action of the kidneys and liver and not like most stomachic remedies, having a bad effect upon the system.

NEXT NOTE the absence of Bicarbonate of Calcium (Lime) about one grain to the gallon, the mineral above all others that is undesirable in a water. There are many so called Lithia waters that are simply lime waters, containing from 25 to 75 grains of lime to the gallon, and are positively dangerous to use. There is no water in America to our knowledge so pure or that contains such a small amount of lime as the famous Yellowstone Lithia. A test will show you that you can wash in this water, it is so soft that you cannot detect it from rain water, yet it has not that flat, insipid rain water taste. Only pure, sparkling, invigorating, refreshing health. New life and enjoyment in every drop to the last.

IMPORTANT NOTICE.

DURING THE WINTER MONTHS, December, January and February, and when the weather is extremely cold, all mineral waters are liable to freeze and during that period we cannot accept orders and ship same, excepting at the customer's risk. It will be perfectly safe to ship the water during ordinary cold weather.

THIS WELL KNOWN SPRING WATER comes through over 100 feet of solid rock. The water gushes forth from Mother Earth several feet above the ground. No possible contamination can occur as the pure water is bottled by special machinery direct at the spring. The utmost cleanliness is observed in bottling, etc., the bottles and cases being washed with the water and then the clean bottles filled with the pure water which preserves the unsullied purity and the perfect natural state of this highly beneficial water.

THIS IS THE FIRST ATTEMPT ever made to supply a strictly and exceptionally high class mineral water at a price that would enable its free use by all as a pure drinking water. So many persons need a water of this kind that we trust our customers will appreciate the great opportunity we offer of obtaining one of the best and purest waters in the world at an exceptionally low price.

TREATMENT OF RHEUMATISM: The Yellowstone Lithia Water has the greatest effect in relieving rheumatism of any water known. The disease is caused by the deposit of uric acid throughout the system. The water promotes the activity of the kidneys, increases the elimination of urea and converts uric acid into a soluble form. Hence, in gout and rheumatism the continued drinking of this water will effectively allay the inflammation caused by the presence of gritty, deleterious matter in the joints, and after continued use will cure the disease. This water, being practically free from lime and having a high percentage of sodium bicarbonate, forms one of the very best preventives against rheumatism in all its forms, as it improves the digestive power, dissolves the deposits and carries them out of the system.

IN KIDNEY TROUBLES, it is the only water that should be taken. Many people are especially liable to the formation of insoluble, gritty particles of gravel, urinary calculi or stone in the bladder. This water being free from lime, will dissolve out these deposits, diminish their size and carry them out of the body.

MANY WATERS are highly advertised for this purpose, but the actual result can only be performed by a very few waters and the Yellowstone Lithia stands supreme for this purpose. Gall stones may also be kept in check and gradually diminished by drinking this beneficial water. In Bright's Disease it is of great value as it prevents the accumulation of toxic products and hence is influential in reducing albuminaria.

IN FACT the Yellowstone Lithia Mineral Spring Water is the one cure for nearly every disease. Dr. Chas. L. Dana, one of the head Professors in the New York Post Graduate Medical School, says: "Pure water should be drunk before meals or between meals, and a moderate amount at meals. At least three pints, or about six tumblerfuls should be taken daily. American neuratics do not drink enough water They have half dessicated nerves and dessication increases nervous irritability." This is merely the opinion of one medical expert and all others verify his statements. Nothing but pure lime free water should be taken and about six to eight glasses per day. The drinking of ordinary hard well waters is what causes nearly all the rheumatism, gravel stone, gall stones, etc., as the heavy amount of lime present being unable to be thrown off by the system becomes deposited in the system and soon rheumatism, gravel, stone in bladder, etc., result. Not so with Yellowstone Lithia. None of the above will ever be caused by this famous spring water. It tends to carry off what is present and always prevents their formation.

THERE IS no state of the system where the free use of this water would cause ill effects. It will build up a weak body and fortify a strong system against disease. What a blessing to invalids; the persons above all others that should have nothing but the purest organic free water.

DO NOT WAIT. Knowing the great dangers from drinking all kinds of impure and hard well waters, we feel every satisfaction in offering to our many customers this now world famous Yellowstone Lithia Mineral Spring Water and stating that there has never been offered on the market a true spring water that better deserves your every confidence than this water. We sell it at such a never before heard of price for such an elegant water, that it is within the reach of all. Nothing more desirable, whether as an aid to the recovery, or the preservation of health, or as a pure healthful and delicious table water, can be obtained anywhere in the world.

No. 8F325 1 dozen ½ gallons. Regular price, $4.75; our price. **$3.37**
No. 8F326 1 dozen quarts. Regular price, $2.50; our price ... **1.78**
No. 8F327 Our Special Offer: With every first order of 1 dozen ½ gallons Natural Yellowstone Lithia Water, for a limited time, we will pack free 1 pint Effervescent Yellowstone Lithia Water, and 1 Effervescent Aperia Split at price of No. 8F325.

EFFERVESCENT YELLOWSTONE LITHIA WATER.

The Choicest Sparkling Mineral Water, Palatable, Appetizing and Bracing.

THIS HIGHLY BENEFICIAL MINERAL WATER is carbonated at the springs, possessing marked sanitary properties and preferred by many expert critics to London Appollinaris. It is strictly a health drink and especially beneficial as a restorative in headache, nausea, flatulency, heartburn, indigestion, vertigo and other temporary indispositions. Taking into consideration all its beneficial properties, when taken in amounts sufficient for these properties to exert themselves, the effervescent Yellowstone Lithia Water is the most agreeable, far-reaching, and highly curative of all sparkling or bottled waters. Unsurpassed as a remedy for stomach disorders; gout, rheumatism; weak, inflamed or ailing kidneys, torpid liver, flatulency, diabetes, obesity, gravel, or gall stones, dropsy, melancholia, and in fact all disorders caused by improper drainage or removal of the poisons from the body. The carbonated Yellowstone Lithia Water is the one water that will satisfy and quench any thirst. It is intended to be used at meals. It quickly stimulates the glands of the stomach and promotes the flow of gastric juices, thereby assisting in the digestion of the food and assuring a perfect assimilation of the nutritious elements present. Put up in pints and quarts.

No. 8F328 Regular price, per pint, 20 cents; our price............ **$0.14**
No. 8F329 Regular price, per case of 12 pints, $2.00; our price **1.27**
No 8F330 Regular price, per quart, 25 cents; our price.......... **.19**
No. 8F331 Regular price, per case of 12 quarts, $2.75; our price.... **1.78**

APERIA SPLITS-EFFERVESCENT.

The Latest. The Best. Once Used—Always Used—Because It Does The Work.

EFFERVESCENT APERIA SPLITS has taken the place of all other laxative waters, for the reason that it is never failing in its results. It contains several laxative salts in natural combination, is made from the famous Yellowstone Lithia water, and being effervescent makes a refreshing and beneficial draught. One Aperia Split just fills an ordinary drinking glass and is one full dose. It sparkles like champagne, is very agreeable to the taste and always produces a free, easy, thorough passage. Aperia Splits furnish the ideal morning beverage. It quickly quiets the nerves, sweetens and soothes the stomach, causes the proper secretion from the liver and a mild evacuation of the bowels. This water is a mild aperient, delightful and refreshing, and gives the relief sought by thousands of persons. It is a revelation to those who have felt compelled to overcome their dislike to the flat, sickish, nauseating taste of the purgative waters commonly employed. Continued use of Aperia Splits cures constipation, biliousness, headache and all diseases or ailments caused by a torpid liver.

No. 8F332 Regular price, per bottle, 15 cents; our price............ **$0.12**
No. 8F333 Regular price, per case of 1 dozen, $1.50; our price.......... **1.18**

MEDICATED MINERAL WATERS.

Hunyadi Janos.

THE FAMOUS AND WORLD WIDE known Hunyadi Janos Natural Aperient water, collected from the springs in Hungary. For 43 years it has been regarded as of exceptionable value by the medical professon due to its peculiar natural combinatfon. It is the only natural mineral water of such favorable composition, and to this is unquestionably due the fact that its action is prompt and reliable, yet gentle and pleasant. In the treatment of constipation from whatever cause, Hunyadi Janos has no equal; in many other diseases in which an aperient is indicated, it has proven its value.

OUR PRICE, ONLY
27c
Regular Retail Price, 35 cents

No. 8F340 Regular price, per quart, 35 cents; our price.................. **27c**

FRANZ JOSEF.

The Most Palatable and Most Reliable.

THIS WELL KNOWN WATER is from the famous Aperient Springs of Budapest, Hungary, and due to the special medicinal action contained therein, permission was given by His Majesty, Emperor Franz Josef of Austria, Hungary, to bear his name. This fact alone proves that the water must hold some exceptionally fine medicinal properties. The **"Franz Josef"** water contains by far the greatest quantity of aperient sulphates and is apparently the strongest water of which we know at present. It has in its favor the **advantages of certainty of action, smallness of dose,** and the fact that the various **sulphates are present in nearly equal proportions,** which has been found by experience to produce the best results. It does not affect the appetite, is painless in its action, and, moreover, unlike most other waters, it is almost tasteless, and only presents to the palate a delicate, appetizing bitter flavor. Used and prescribed by thousands of physicians for the relief and cure of all forms of constipation.

No. 8F341 Regular price, per quart, 35 cents; our price.. **22c**

WORLD FAMOUS PITCHER'S CASTORIA.

THE OLD RELIABLE BRAND.

THE BEST REMEDY KNOWN FOR ALL STOMACH AND BOWEL COMPLAINTS OF INFANTS AND CHILDREN.

PROMOTES DIGESTION, CHEERFULNESS AND REST.

FREE FROM HARMFUL SUBSTANCES.

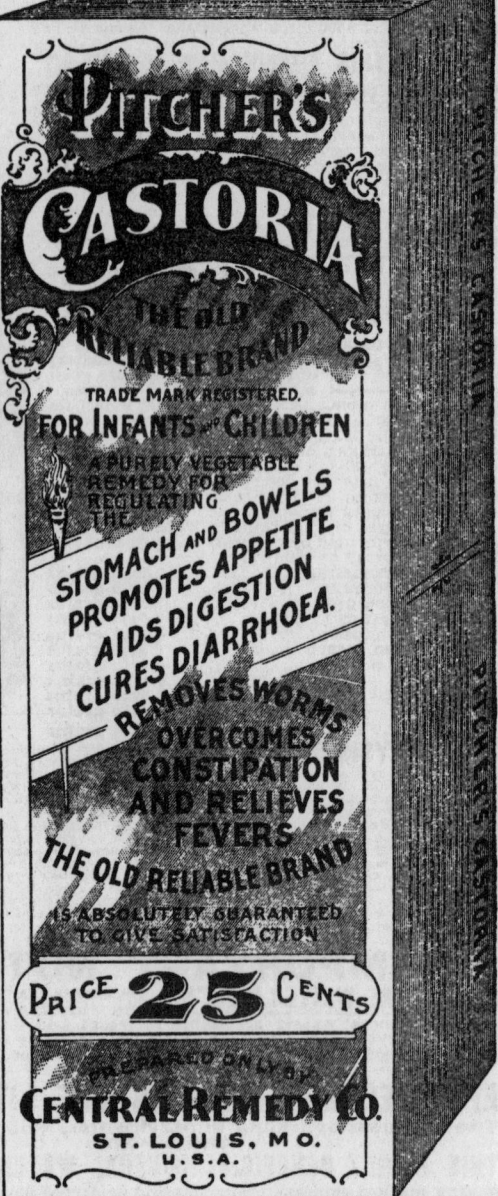

Castoria is truly a wonderful medicine for children. Doctors prescribe it, medical journals recommend it, and more than a million mothers are using it in place of Paregoric, Bateman's Drops, so called soothing syrups and other narcotic and stupefying remedies. Castoria is the quickest thing to regulate the stomach and bowels, and give healthy sleep, the world has ever seen. It is guaranteed to be perfectly harmless.

MORTALITY. **Nearly every married couple have children and every infant and child is sick more or less during the first and second years.** Infant mortality is something frightful, and we can hardly realize that 22 per cent or nearly one-fourth of all born die from stomach and bowel troubles before the age of one year. This being true, it is very essential that their young bodies be closely watched and irregularities be quickly corrected. If now one remedy was to be selected which would cure all these ills, but one name would be on every tongue, Castoria, Castoria; nothing but Castoria. The best physicians of today prescribe it, recommend it, and even go so far as to state that if a child's stomach and bowels were kept in perfect condition with some harmless remedy like Castoria, that infants and children would be free from nearly all their more serious ills. Castoria is the one remedy that meets all the requirements of children, it is the one medicine that is known the world over as **The Mothers' Blessing and the Babies' Friend.**

OUR PRICE, ONLY

18c

Regular Price, 25c.

CHILDREN CRY FOR IT. **Children cry for Castoria because they like it. No trouble to give, is beneficial and makes the child healthy and cheerful.** We do not hesitate in saying that Castoria has done more for suffering children than all other remedies combined. The least irregularity in the food of the nursing mother upsets the stomach and bowels of the child, then comes indigestion, sour stomach, wind colic, constipation, loss of sleep, etc. The child becomes cross and feverish and sickness follows. Every mother then thinks of but one remedy, Castoria; only Castoria. The popularity of this wonderful remedy has so increased until it now stands alone among druggists and physicians as the only reliable and harmless regulator of children's complaints. It is being used more and more every week, until the sales of this beneficial remedy double every three years. This proves but one thing—Castoria is very beneficial, is harmless and does the work. It is truly a Mother's Blessing, a Baby's Friend and a Father's Comfort.

WHAT IS IT? **Dr. Pitcher's Castoria is composed of the medicinal properties of Pumpkin Seed, Alex. Senna, Rochelle Salts, Anise Seed, Peppermint, Bicarbonate of Soda, Worm Seed, Clarified Sugar and Wintergreen.** A pure, vegetable preparation for assimilating the food and regulating the stomach and bowels of children and infants. Promotes digestion, cheerfulness and rest. Contains neither opium, morphine or any form of narcotic. A perfect remedy for constipation, sour stomach, diarrhea, worms, convulsions, feverishness and loss of sleep.

A FEW FACTS FOR MOTHERS.

1. **No medicine** should be given to children without knowing what you are giving. Castoria is purely vegetable, and the ingredients are given upon every package.
2. **Castoria is harmless,** is the standard prescription of Dr. Pitcher, and has been in constant use by thousands of mothers for over thirty years.
3. **Castoria** may be given to any one and at any time; it is superior in its effects to Paregoric, Castor Oil or any other cathartic or quieter. It is free from dangerous or nauseous properties.
4. **Castoria** keeps indefinitely and hence no danger of spoiling by age. The last drop is just as effective as the first one taken from the bottle.
5. **Castoria** is without doubt the best medicine for children and infants the world has ever known. In it mothers have something absolutely safe, pleasant to give, effective in results and perfectly satisfactory in every respect.
6. **Castoria** assimilates the food, regulates the stomach and bowels, and produces perfect and natural sleep. With this valuable medicine on hand, much sickness may be avoided, the child kept cheerful and robust and the parents obtain their needful sleep.
7. **Castoria** being the world's medicine for children, is grossly imitated and adulterated. Many castorias are on the market, but we handle only the well known and world famous Dr. Pitcher's Castoria. Do not allow anyone to sell you anything else on the plea that it is just as good. What you want is Dr. Pitcher's Castoria.
8. **Castoria** is usually sold for 25 to 35 cents per bottle; but now consider our exceptionally low price of 18 cents. Order now and obtain a supply. It should be in every home.

No. 8F345 Regular price, per bottle, 25 cents; our price, 3 bottles for **50c**; each.........**18c**

Unmailable on account of weight.

Pitcher's Castoria
The Old Reliable Brand
Trade Mark Registered.
For Infants and Children
A purely vegetable remedy for regulating the
Stomach and Bowels
Promotes Appetite
Aids Digestion
Cures Diarrhoea.
Removes Worms
Overcomes Constipation
and Relieves Fevers
The Old Reliable Brand
Is absolutely guaranteed to give satisfaction
Price 25 Cents
Prepared only by
Central Remedy Co.
St. Louis, Mo.
U.S.A.
Pitcher's Castoria

Murine Eye Remedy.

A Safe and Positive Cure For Eye Troubles, Reliable, Efficient and Absolutely Harmless.

Murine positively and thoroughly cures Pink Eye, Redness, Itching, Smarting, Burning, Watering, Dryness, Mattering, Irritation, Inflammation, Granulation, Blurring and Cloudiness of the Eyes. Styes, cysts, ulcers, pimples, and scales on the eye lids, restores eye lashes, makes weak eyes strong, dull eyes bright, does not smart, soothes eye pain. A favorite toilet accessory. Quickly removes redness and swelling of the eyes caused by weeping, or the excessive use of tobacco and stimulants. Endorsed by the medical and optical men everywhere; 48-page booklet on eye troubles free, with each package. Regular price, 50 cents.

No. 8F350 Our price.......**40c**

If by mail, postage extra, 10 cents.

Murine Eye Salve.

Promotes growth and prevents loss of eye lashes. A remedy for diseased eye lids. Promptly allays inflammation (redness) and irritation of the eyes and eye lids. Removes scales from eye lids, cures and prevents styes, cysts and ulcers. It is a soothing application to eyes that feel dry and smart. Regular price, $1.00.

No. 8F351 Our price.......**83c**

If by mail, postage extra, 10 cents.

Granuline.

For old and chronic cases of sore eyes, granulated lids, spots, scums, and opacities on the eyes. Old and stubborn cases which have resisted the ordinary methods of treatment and where most positive action is desired. Granuline is a tonic, antiseptic and astringent. It is a valuable collateral remedy to Murine. "Two drops" in the above conditions. Regular price, $1.50.

No. 8F353 Our price.....**$1.30**

If by mail, postage extra, 10 cents.

Banene.

Stimulates the circulation of the blood supply which nourishes the eye. An internal treatment for cloudiness or dimness of vision, floating or stationary spots or webs before the eye, poor circulation in the eyes, retinal and optic nerve diseases, affections of the choroid, sluggish action of the pupil, hemorrhage in the eyes and weakness of the ocular muscles. For lessening of the acuteness of vision from age or disease, inability to wear glasses with comfort, Banene and Murine have no equals. Murine and Banene should be in the hands of every individual who wears glasses, and Banene should be used at the first indication of discomfort. Regular price, $1.25.

No. 8F352 Our price.....**$1.10**

If by mail, postage extra, 10 cents.

IF YOU BUY FROM US, WE WILL SEND YOU A FREE PROFIT SHARING CERTIFICATE

ORANGEINE.

A harmless combination of Podophyllin, Blue Flag, Sodium Bicarbonate, Acetanilid, Nux Vomica and Caffeine, carefully balanced by years of human test and guaranteed by manufacturers not to leave any injurious effect.

Highly advertised and recommended by manufacturers for curing headache, neuralgia, colds, biliousness, rose cold and hay fever. Relieves from fatigue, nourishes and regulates the brain, nerves and stomach.

Full directions with each package.

No. 8F354 Regular 25-cent size; our price...........**19c**

No. 8F355 Regular 50-cent size; our price...........**38c**

GRANULAR EFFERVESCENT SALTS.

Headache, see Bromo, page 829

Kissingen Salt.

Each heaping teaspoonful dissolved in a half tumblerful of water forms a refreshing and agreeable draught, identical with the natural water. Highly recommended in daily alternation with Vichy, by Dr. Wm. T. Cathell, of Baltimore, for the successful treatment of obesity. The dose of Kissingen Salt is taken in water 20 to 30 minutes after each meal one day, and a similar dose of Vichy after each meal the next day, and this treatment continued week after week, until patient is relieved of the discomforts of overflesh. When near the desired weight, gradually reduce the dose and at last stop treatment entirely.

No. 8F365 Price, 12-oz. bottle..28c
Unmailable on account of weight.

Laxative Lithia.

Each dessert spoonful contains potassium citrate 30 grains, sodium phosphate 30 grains, lithium citrate 5 grains. Laxative, refrigerant, diuretic and antacid. This double salt of lithium is very efficient for relieving excess of acid existing in the secretions, and hence is indicated in rheumatism, gout, neurasthenia, cystitis, gravel and in all similar affections, arising from a uric acid diathesis.

No. 8F368 Price, 12-oz. bottle..28c
Unmailable on account of weight.

Magnesium Sulphate.

Each heaping teaspoonful contains 30 grains magnesium sulphate. Laxative, cathartic, refrigerant, antacid. This effervescent form affords a pleasant method of administering this salt. It possesses the power to render the secretions alkaline, especially those of the alimentary canal, and at the same time is agreeable to the stomach and does not in the least interfere with the appetite or digestion. For laxative effect take one or more tablespoonfuls in small glass of water and drink while effervescing. For cathartic effect take two or more tablespoonfuls in the same manner.

No. 8F370 Price, 12-oz. bottle..28c
Unmailable on account of weight.

Sodium Phosphate.

Each heaping teaspoonful contains 30 grains sodium phosphate. This well known medicinal agent is one of the very best in the treatment of liver trouble, jaundice, obesity, rickets, constipation, diarrhea of small children, and in all cases requiring a saline laxative. Dose: One or two heaping teaspoonfuls in half glass water before breakfast and teaspoonful before dinner, if necessary

No. 8F372 Price, 12-oz. bottle..28c
Unmailable on account of weight.

Sodium Sulphate.

Each heaping teaspoonful contains 30 grains sodium sulphate. Aperient, laxative, diuretic. A very efficient laxative where watery stools are required. Dose: One or two heaping teaspoonfuls in half a glass of water for laxative effect and one or two tablespoonfuls as a cathartic.

No. 8F374 Price, 12-oz. bottle..28c
Unmailable on account of weight.

Vichy.

We have taken the French governmental analysis of the famous Vichy Springs as the correct one, and have carefully and strictly followed it, adding to our product all the valuable therapeutic properties contained therein. Each teaspoonful of this salt when added to a glass of water forms a grateful and refreshing draught, identical with the natural water. Highly recommended in daily alternation with Kissingen, by Dr. Wm. T. Cathell, of Baltimore, for the treatment of obesity. The dose of Vichy Salt in water is taken 20 to 30 minutes after each meal one day, and a similar dose of Kissingen after each meal the next day, and this treatment continued week after week until patient is relieved of the discomforts of overflesh. When near the desired weight, gradually reduce the dose, and at last stop treatment altogether.

No. 8F376 Price, 12-oz. bottle 28c
Unmailable on account of weight.

DEPARTMENT OF FAMILY REMEDIES AND HOUSEHOLD PREPARATIONS

Prepared and put up by careful and experienced pharmacists and chemists in our own laboratory and sold under an absolute guarantee of highest strength and purity.

MAILING CHARGES, 2-ounce bottle, tube and postage, extra, 12 cents; 4-ounce bottle, tube and postage, extra, 16 cents; 8-ounce and 16-ounce bottles unmailable on account of weight.

Elixir Calisaya Iron and Strychnine.

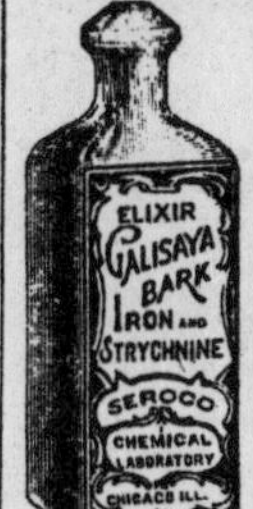

The remedy used for over fifty years as the one great Spring and Fall tonic. Increases the appetite, tones up the system and increases the strength. Used by every physician for this purpose. Full directions with each bottle.

No. 8F500 Price, 8-ounce bottle.....30c
No. 8F501 Price, 16-ounce bottle....52c

Borax.

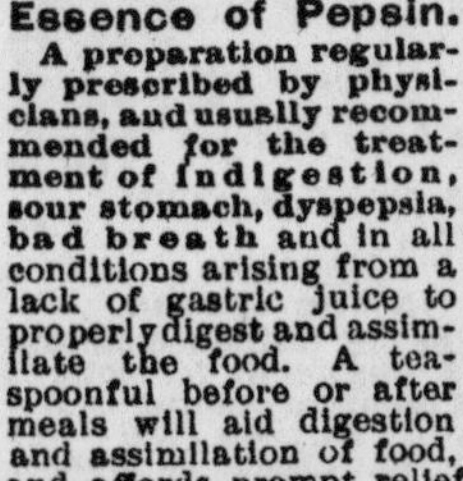

The housekeeper's friend; has more uses about the home than even that of common salt. For the laundry, the kitchen, the bath and for various medicinal uses it is indispensable. Chemically pure and finely powdered. We put it up in 1-pound boxes with complete directions for using in **washing, starching, keeping away moths, killing cockroaches, dressing wounds and bruises, arresting fermentation, cleaning clothes, etc.** You can rely on getting from us the pure powdered borax.

No. 8F505 Price, 1-pound box..10c

Paregoric.

Always useful, both for children and adults. One of the best known and most extensively used house remedies for cramps, deranged stomach, diarrhea, etc. Full directions.

No. 8F507 Price, 2-ounce bottle..........8c
No. 8F508 Price, 4-ounce bottle.........14c
Mailable sizes, see note above.

Tasteless Castor Oil.

After considerable experimenting in our laboratories, we have finally succeeded in producing a tasteless castor oil, which is without the disagreeable and nauseating odor and taste of the castor oil as it has been sold in the past, and yet it possesses all the good points that have made castor oil one of the most certain and reliable cathartics that can be used when a remedy of this kind is required. Can be taken by adults and children alike. After you have given our Tasteless Castor Oil a trial you will never use any other, and you will always keep it on hand as one of the standard cathartic and household remedies.

No. 8F510 Price, 2-oz. bottle.....11c
No. 8F511 Price, 4-oz. bottle.....19c
No. 8F512 Price, 8-oz. bottle.....29c
Mailable sizes, see note above.

Sweet Spirits of Nitre.

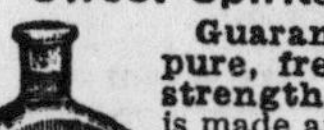

Guaranteed absolutely pure, fresh and of full strength. This medicine is made and put up in our own laboratory, and is much more reliable than that generally offered for sale in drug stores.

No. 8F515 Price, 2-ounce bottle.........10c
No. 8F516 Price, 4-ounce bottle.........18c
No. 8F517 Price, 1-pint bottle..........68c
Mailable sizes, see above note.

Essence Peppermint.

Pure, strong and of full strength. Largely used for colic in children, sickness or aching of stomach, cramps, etc. A very useful and beneficial household remedy. **Best quality for medical use.**

No. 8F520 Price, 2-ounce bottle........11c
No. 8F521 Price, 4-ounce bottle.........20c
Mailable sizes, see note above.

Essence Jamaica Ginger.

Prepared of great strength from the finest quality of Jamaica ginger. We guarantee our preparation to be absolutely pure and of full strength. Very beneficial in colic, diarrhea, cramps, etc. **Buy our genuine essence and get the full benefit of its valuable properties.**

No. 8F525 Price, 2-ounce bottle. 9c
No. 8F526 Price, 4-ounce bottle. 17c
Mailable sizes, see note above.

Essence of Pepsin.

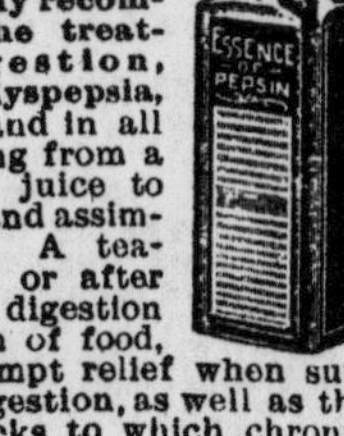

A preparation regularly prescribed by physicians, and usually recommended for the treatment of indigestion, sour stomach, dyspepsia, bad breath and in all conditions arising from a lack of gastric juice to properly digest and assimilate the food. A teaspoonful before or after meals will aid digestion and assimilation of food, and affords prompt relief when suffering from indigestion, as well as the distressing attacks to which chronic sufferers from dyspepsia are subject.

No. 8F530 Price, 8-oz. bottle...45c

Elixir Buchu, Juniper and Potassium Acetate.

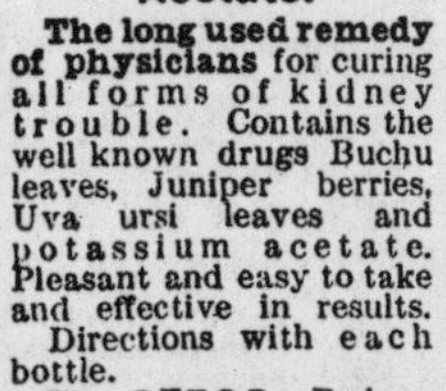

The long used remedy of physicians for curing all forms of kidney trouble. Contains the well known drugs Buchu leaves, Juniper berries, Uva ursi leaves and potassium acetate. Pleasant and easy to take and effective in results. Directions with each bottle.

No. 8F533 Price, 8-ounce bottle......30c

Neutralizing Cordial.

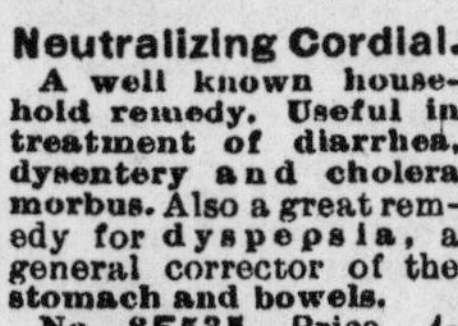

A well known household remedy. Useful in treatment of diarrhea, dysentery and cholera morbus. Also a great remedy for dyspepsia, a general corrector of the stomach and bowels.

No. 8F535 Price, 4-ounce bottle...........16c
Mailable sizes, see note above.

Castor Oil.

Cold pressed and almost tasteless.

No. 8F537 Price, 2-ounce bottle......... 6c
No. 8F538 Price, 4-ounce bottle..........10c
No. 8F539 Price, 1-pint bottle..........25c
No. 8F540 Price, per ½ gallon jug.........85c
No. 8F541 Price, per gallon jug.........$1.45
Mailable sizes, see note above.

Olive Oil (Sweet Oil).

This is a fine domestic oil, considered by many equal to imported oil. For either internal or external use. Anyone wishing to use an absolutely pure olive oil should send for this.

No. 8F545 Price, 2-ounce bottle........... 6c
No. 8F546 Price, 4-ounce bottle............10c
No. 8F547 Price, ½-pint bottle..........17c
No. 8F548 Price, per pint bottle.........37c
No. 8F549 Price, per gallon jug...........$1.75
Mailable sizes, see note above.

Spirits of Camphor.

Made from pure imported Gum Camphor and Grain Alcohol. We guarantee this article to be strictly pure and of full strength. Much used for nausea and fainting spells.

No. 8F550 Price, 2-ounce bottle.........12c
No. 8F551 Price, 4-ounce bottle..........22c
No. 8F552 Price, 1-pint bottle..............67c
Mailable sizes, see note above.

Spirits Ammonia Aromatic.

Made from Ammonia, spirits and aromatics. Largely employed in the household for fainting spells and as an agreeable odor for refreshing the sick.

No. 8F555 Price, per 2-ounce bottle.........14c
No. 8F556 Price, per 4-ounce bottle..........21c

Camphorated Oil.

An excellent article for rubbing on children's and grown up persons' chests and throats in cases of croup, difficulty in breathing, sore throat, coughs. A small quantity of pure spirits of turpentine added to it will increase its effectiveness in many cases.

No. 8F560 Price, 2-oz. bottle.....9c
No. 8F561 Price, 4-oz. bottle....17c
No. 8F562 Price, 8-oz. bottle....28c
Mailable sizes, see note above.

Spirits of Turpentine.

Spirits of Turpentine is a largely used and well known household remedy. Largely used for aiding the action of the kidneys. Warranted absolutely pure. Our turpentine has been refined, and is free from impurities of all kinds.

No. 8F565 Price, 4-ounce bottle.... ....9c
No. 8F566 Price, 8-ounce bottle...........15c
No. 8F567 Price, per pint bottle...........27c
No. 8F568 Price, per gallon jug...............89c
Mailable sizes, see note above.

Glycerine.

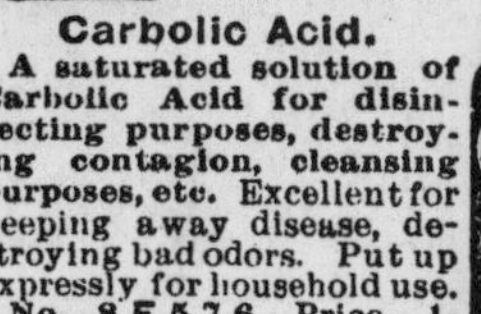

Warranted absolutely pure. Can be used either externally or internally.

No. 8F570 Price, 2-ounce bottle 9c
No. 8F571 Price, 4-ounce bottle...........12c
No. 8F572 Price, ½-pound bottle.... .....18c
No. 8F573 Price, 1-pound bottle...........30c
No. 8F574 Price, per gallon jug.............$1.95
Mailable sizes, see note above.

Carbolic Acid.

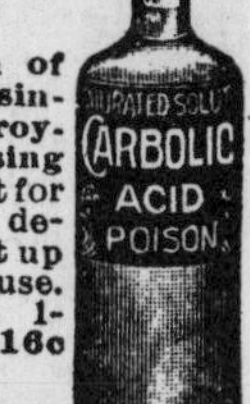
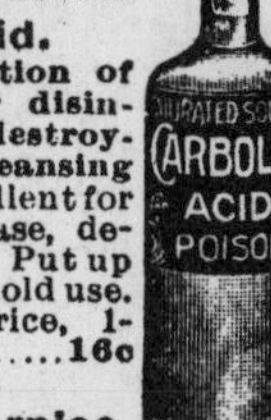

A saturated solution of Carbolic Acid for disinfecting purposes, destroying contagion, cleansing purposes, etc. Excellent for keeping away disease, destroying bad odors. Put up expressly for household use.

No. 8F576 Price, 1-pound bottle 16c
Unmailable.

Tincture of Arnica.

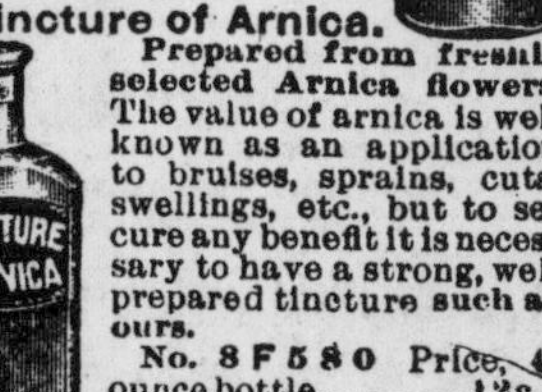

Prepared from freshly selected Arnica flowers. The value of arnica is well known as an application to bruises, sprains, cuts, swellings, etc., but to secure any benefit it is necessary to have a strong, well prepared tincture **such as ours.**

No. 8F580 Price, 4-ounce bottle..........12c
No. 8F581 Price, ½-pint bottle...........20c
No. 8F582 Price, 1-pint bottle............35c
Unmailable.

Ammonia.

Standard quality. Extra purity and strength. Put up expressly for home use. It lightens work and brightens the home. Makes the washing cleaner and polishing easier.

In pint bottles, with full directions for using in the laundry, for the toilet, and for cleaning glass, crockery, paint, taking out stains, etc.

No. 8F585 Price, per pint bottle...........................9c
No. 8F586 Price, per gallon jug.......................63c
Unmailable on account of weight.

Violet Ammonia.

For the Toilet and Bath. Violet Ammonia is a comparatively new article for toilet and bathing purposes, which has won the favor of every lady and gentleman who has given it a trial. They will never be without it. We furnish Violet Ammonia in liquid form and in the very best condition for toilet and bath. It is inexpensive and a few drops added to the water before washing will be sufficient to purify and perfume it, and to whiten the skin of the user to perfection. A small quantity added to the bath will intensify the cleansing and invigorating effects greatly, leaving a mild but lasting odor always pleasing and refreshing.

No. 8F588 Violet Ammonia. Price, 1-pint bottle....................17c

Unmailable on account of weight.

Genuine Witch Hazel Extract.

Buy Direct and Save All Retail Profits. We can save you money, save you one-half on anything in this line, and guarantee highest grade goods on the market. Our Extract of Witch Hazel, you will find to be the purest made. It is absolutely free from wood alcohol, columbian spirits, formaldehyde or any injurious ingredient. We guarantee our Witch Hazel to contain full 15 per cent of grain alcohol. **A universal all healing remedy. Should be in every household; useful for sore throat, hemorrhage, wounds, sprains, bruises, sore eyes, stiff joints, burns** and in nearly every accident that one can have. **Our price is so low** that every family can afford to keep a supply in their homes. **Look at our prices.**

No. 8F590 ½-pint bottle, retail price, 40 cents; our price..........12c

No. 8F591 1-pint bottle, retail price, 50c; our price..............22c

No. 8F592 1-quart bottle, retail price, $1.00; our price.............33c

No. 8F593 ½-gallon, retail price, $1.75; our price....................60c

No. 8F594 1-gallon, retail price, $2.50; our price......................95c

Unmailable on account of weight.

Pure Alcohol.

94 PER CENT, or 188 PROOF.

Guaranteed absolutely pure and full strength; distilled from the finest selected grain and recommended for every purpose for which pure grain alcohol is required. Our pure alcohol is undiluted, of full strength and of the highest quality.

No. 8F602 Price, per 4-ounce bottle..........$0.19

No. 8F603 Price, per pint bottle..........40

No. 8F604 Price, per quart bottle..........75

No. 8F605 Price, per gallon, can inclusive..........2.95

Carbolic Arnica Salve.

The best in the world for burns, flesh wounds, chilblains, boils, felons, sores, piles, ulcers and fever sores. Excellent for salt rheum, eczema and ringworm.

No. 8F610 Price, per box..........14c

If by mail, postage extra, per box, 4 cents.

Refined Camphor.

(GUM CAMPHOR.)

We carry only the best and purest refined camphor, imported direct from Kobe, Japan, and guarantee it to be the highest grade camphor obtainable, both for domestic and medicinal purposes.

No. 8F614 Price, 1-ounce cake..........$0.10

No. 8F615 Price, 1-pound pkg., 1.25

Subject to market changes.

Boric Acid—Pure.

(BORACIC ACID.)

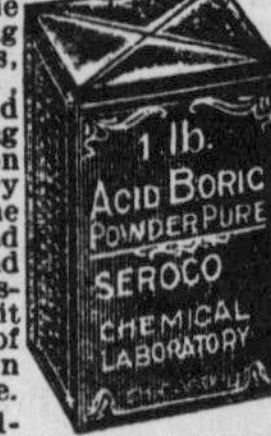

Guaranteed highest purity powder—a popular, valuable and aseptic healing dressing and protective for cuts, wounds, ulcers, sores, bruises and all inflamed and irritated surfaces, a healing and soothing application for chafed and harsh, dry or rough skin. Absorbs the odor of perspiration and renders antiseptic and agreeably smelling all diseased parts to which it may be applied. A can of boric acid should be in every well regulated home.

No. 8F620 Price, 1-pound airtight container..........20c

Powdered Alum.

This largely used chemical we guarantee of full strength and efficiency. Will immediately stop bleeding, and largely used around the home for removing canker of the mouth, a small amount placed on canker performing a cure. Also used for astringent washes and douches.

No. 8F625 Price, per pound carton..........12c

Wood Alcohol.

95 PER CENT.

Guaranteed full strength. Wood alcohol is also known as wood spirit and wood naphtha. It is used for burning in alcohol stoves and lamps and by painters and others for cutting and dissolving shellac, paint and varnish. It is poisonous if taken internally, but perfectly harmless if used for mechanical purposes and considerably cheaper than grain alcohol.

No. 8F631 Price, per pint bottle..........18c

No. 8F632 Price, per quart bottle..........$0.30

No. 8F633 Price, per gallon, can inclusive..........1.10

Not mailable.

Syrup Ipecac.

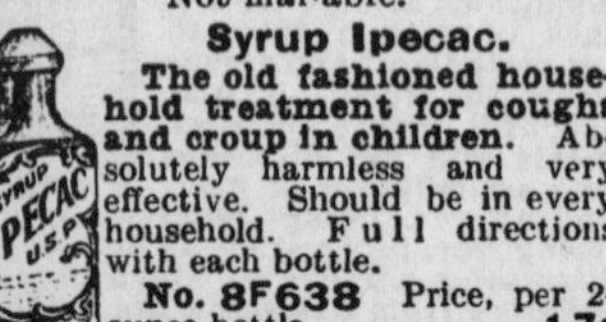

The old fashioned household treatment for coughs and croup in children. Absolutely harmless and very effective. Should be in every household. Full directions with each bottle.

No. 8F638 Price, per 2-ounce bottle..........17c

No. 8F640 Price, per 4-ounce bottle..........28c

Tincture Iodine.

For external use only. Universally recommended for reducing swelling and inflammation resulting from sprains and bruises, also highly endorsed by physicians for the treatment of goitre and erysipelas. Always apply by painting the affected parts with a camel's hair brush.

No. 8F645 Price, 2-ounce bottle..........13c

No. 8F646 Price, 4-ounce bottle..........24c

Not mailable.

Chloroform Liniment.

Highly recommended for inflamed joints, neuralgia, rheumatism, lumbago, sprains and bruises. Very beneficial for removing inflammation quickly. Is recognized as one of the most reliable counterirritants, and possesses great merit.

No. 8F650 Price, 2-ounce bottle..........10c

No. 8F651 Price, 4-ounce bottle..........18c

If by mail, postage and mailing tube extra, 16 cents.

Chemical Camphor.

Packing or Chemical Camphor. Looks and smells similar to true gum camphor, and equally good for packing purposes. It cannot be taken internally. Very effective for removing moths and other pests from fancy furs, cloth ing, and for all packing purposes.

No. 8F655 Price, per pound package..........19c

Seroco Egg Preserver.

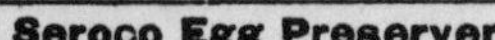

The best and most effective means for preserving eggs for an almost indefinite period of time.

Carefully conducted experiments have shown that the Seroco Egg Preserver is practically the only egg preserver today that will accomplish all that can reasonably be expected from a preparation of this kind.

An equal quantity of eggs having been treated for preserving purposes with a mixture of glycerine and salicylic acid, another in salt water, another wrapped in paper, another rubbed with salt, another coated with paraffin, another placed in alum solution, another in boiling water for a short time, another in salicylic acid solution, one lot varnished with collodion, one lot coated with silicate of potash, another lot covered with lard, another lot preserved in wood ashes, and one lot with Seroco Egg Preserver, and while in each and every instance in all other preservatives used, a larger or smaller number of the eggs were bad after a lapse of eight months, those preserved with the Seroco Egg Preserver proved to be as fresh as they were the day they were preserved. **Seroco Egg Preserver** is supplied in gallon jugs; this quantity is sufficient for the preserving of forty to fifty dozen of eggs. Complete directions furnished with each gallon of the preservative.

No. 8F665 Price, per gallon..........48c

Unmailable on account of weight.

Lightning Tanner.

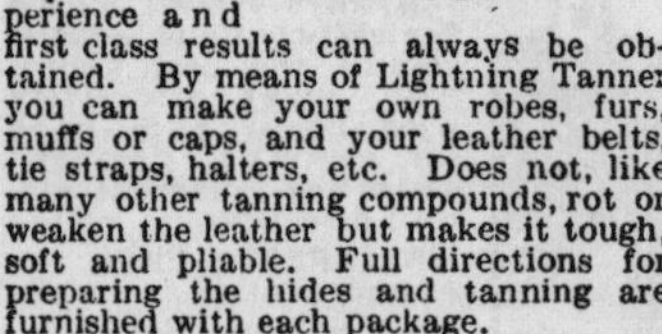

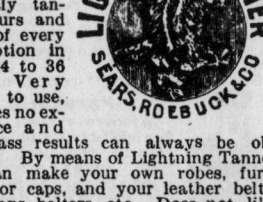

Lightning Tanner is the very latest mixture for quickly and perfectly tanning furs and skins of every description in from 24 to 36 hours. Very simple to use, requires no experience and first class results can always be obtained. By means of Lightning Tanner you can make your own robes, furs, muffs or caps, and your leather belts, tie straps, halters, etc. Does not, like many other tanning compounds, rot or weaken the leather but makes it tough, soft and pliable. Full directions for preparing the hides and tanning are furnished with each package.

No. 8F670 Box with powder sufficient to tan two raccoon skins in 36 hours..........(Unmailable)..........10c

No. 8F671 Box containing three times the above and sufficient for deer skin..........(Unmailable)..........25c

No. 8F672 Box holding about twelve times the above and sufficient for horse or cow hide..........75c

Unmailable.

Quinine Pills.

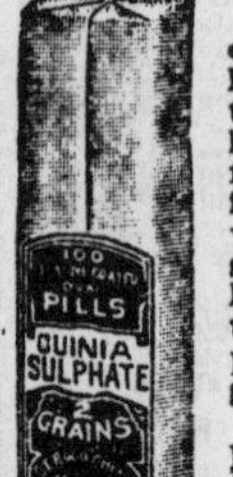

Two grains each, sugar or gelatine coated. We have made a special contract with one of the best known and largest manufacturers of quinine pills in the world to supply us with these pills made full strength and with absolutely pure quinine. Bottles containing 100 2-grain pure quinine pills, either gelatine or sugar coated.

No. 8F675 Price, per bottle..........20c

If by mail, postage extra, 8 cents.

Quinine.

(Quinine Sulphate.)

Guaranteed absolutely pure. Quinine is today a widely known tonic and especially used in the treatment of malarial diseases, colds, chills, ague, erysipelas, etc. Can be supplied in 1-ounce and 5-ounce packages.

No. 8F680 Price, 1-ounce..........40c

No. 8F681 Price, 5-ounce tin $1.95

If by mail, postage extra, per ounce, 6 cents.

Superfine Furniture Polish.

A handy and valuable household article of the greatest perfection for polishing and restoring all kinds of furniture. Quickly removes scratches, stains and marks of wear and makes the furniture look as good as new. Superfine furniture polish is easily applied and always reliable. Full directions with each bottle.

No. 8F685 Price, per bottle..........14c

If by mail, postage and mailing tube extra, 16c.

Witch Hazel Salve.

The great healing salve. Very good for all forms of cuts, bruises, sores and all kinds of abrasions of the skin hard to heal.

No. 8F690 Price, per box..........12c

If by mail, postage extra, per box 4c.

Milk Sugar—Pure.

(Sugar of Milk.)

Especially recommended for making modified milk as a food for infants. Practically indispensable in all cases where babies are brought up by the bottle. It is free from cane sugar, glucose, acids and other substances which might be disturbing or injurious. Full direction for infant feeding on each package. Furnished in airtight 1-pound packages.

No. 8F695 Price, per 1-pound package..........25c

Seidlitz Powders.

We always make our Seidlitz Powders fresh when we receive the order for them. Most of the powders bought in stores are worthless from being kept too long; they lose their strength. We guarantee all Seidlitz Powders we send out to be made from pure materials and to be full strength. Put up in boxes, containing in each 10 blue and 10 white papers.

No. 8F700 Price, per box..........14c

If by mail, postage extra, per box, 5 cents.

A Few Handy Pocket Goods in Screw Top, Air Tight Glass Vials.

No. 8F705 Aromatic Cachou Lozenges, for perfuming the breath. Make a delicious confection. Price..........7c

No. 8F707 Silver Cachous, for perfuming the breath, vest pocket size 7c

No. 8F709 Chlorate Potash Tablets, 5 grains each. For sore throat, hoarseness, etc. Price..........7c

No. 8F712 Soda Mint Tablets, for sour stomach, flatulency, nausea, etc. 7c

No. 8F715 Bronchial Troches, for coughs, colds, sore throat, hoarseness. Price.....7c

No. 8F718 Licorice Lozenges, pure, very soothing to the throat and bronchial tubes. Price..........7c

No. 8F720 Slippery Elm Lozenges. Demulcent, for roughness in the throat and irritating cough. Price..........7c

No. 8F722 Paregoric Tablets. Each tablet equals 15 drops of paregoric; dose 1 to 4, according to age. Price..........7c

No. 8F724 Pepsin Tablets, made from pure pepsin, for dyspepsia, indigestion, etc. Price, per bottle..........15c

No. 8F726 Sen-Sen. Price, per package 3c

If by mail, postage extra, each, 2 cents.

LIQUID HICKORY SMOKE.

FOR SMOKING AND CURING MEAT AND FISH IN A SIMPLE AND INEXPENSIVE MANNER.

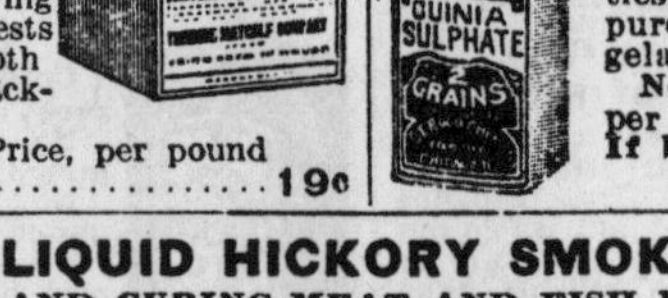

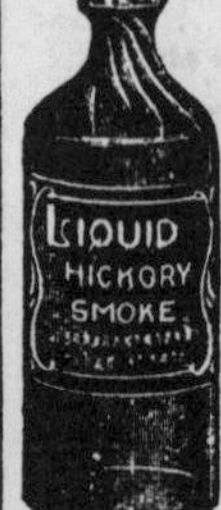

Our genuine Liquefied Hickory Smoke is not only the most perfect, reliable and absolutely harmless modern vegetable liquid meat smoker, but it imparts a true and delicious hickory smoke flavor to meats, dried beef, sausages, fish and game, which renders them at the same time wholesome and palatable. Liquid Hickory Smoke is not only a meat smoker, but a meat preserver. By using Liquid Hickory Smoke you can keep your meat solid and sweet for any length of time. Liquid Hickory Smoke will accomplish the work of weeks of smoke house smoking in a few minutes. A brush and a bottle of Liquid Hickory Smoke will do it better and quicker and the cost is almost nothing. One bottle of genuine Liquid Hickory Smoke, which we furnish you for 35 cents a quart, will smoke about 300 pounds of meat, and by this new way of smoking you will make your meats more wholesome and get a finer flavor than in the old and slow way of the smokehouse method. Full directions furnished with each bottle.

No. 8F660 Price, full quart bottles ready for immediate use..........35c

NEW SEROCO FAST AND STAINLESS DYES, ONLY 7 Cents
Dyes Evenly Cotton, Wool, Silk and Mixed Goods, All in the Same Bath.

DYES

SEROCO STAINLESS DYES
SHADE BLACK
WILL NOT STAIN THE HANDS OR SPOT THE KETTLE.
SEROCO CHEMICAL LABORATORY, CHICAGO ILL.

No more trouble with dyeing cotton and wool goods separately, as by means of the new Seroco Dyes it can all be performed together and an even color be obtained.

The best and most satisfactory dyes as well as the simplest to color, of any dyes ever offered to a customer.

For nearly ten years we have supplied to our customers the old style Dyes, up to the present time considered the best household dyes on the market, at a small price, and while they have given good satisfaction everywhere, we are pleased to be able to furnish to our customers, to the economical housewife, a new process dye, the New Seroco Fast and Stainless Dyes which are beyond any question the finest, brightest, most durable and always reliable household colors for dyeing perfectly cotton, wool, silk and mixed goods. Owing to the immense output of these dyes we have secured the control for our house exclusively and we are therefore in condition not only to supply you the best dyes made, but supply them to you at a price which is much lower than what you would pay for an inferior grade or an entirely unsatisfactory dye.

These dyes are made in our own laboratory, are the result of many years of experimenting, and knowing all about their composition we can fully guarantee them. They are simple and easy to use and will not stain the hands or the container. Will color from one to six pounds of goods according to the shade desired.

The New Seroco Fast and Stainless Dyes can be successfully used for coloring dress goods, coats, carpetrags, ribbons, feathers, yarns, silk fabrics, grass and basket material, moss, and in general for coloring all forms of material. When using the New Seroco Fast and Stainless Dyes you are always sure of obtaining bright, fadeless colors, and each package of dye is true to its name. The New Seroco Fast and Stainless Dyes are furnished in the following beautiful shades:

Pink	Wine	Orange	Cardinal	Heliotrope	Myrtle Green
Pale Blue	Seal Brown	Cerise	Lemon	Brown	Old Rose
Light Green	Navy Blue	Royal Purple	Tan	Yellow	Drab
Olive Green	Turkey Red	Black	Emerald Green	Royal Blue	Salmon

A direction booklet is furnished free with each package of dye. In it is contained a fund of valuable information, including general directions, detection of cotton from wool or mixed goods, cleaning goods before dyeing, using the dye, preparing the goods, preparing the dye bath, boiling, removing goods from bath, various shades of color, ripping the goods, drying, pressing, dyeing light shades, etc., and ending with a complete list of colors produced by dyeing over various shades of cloth. **Be sure to state color wanted.**

No. 8F730 New Seroco Dyes, fast colors only. Price, per package........ **7c**
If by mail, postage extra, 2 cents.

Liquid Skin.

A newly invented preparation to be used for all cuts, bruises and abrasions. Acts instantaneously. Better, cheaper and quicker than any other antiseptic bandage, court plaster or other method usually applied for stopping loss of blood in any open, bleeding wound. Can be applied in a few seconds, forming at once a new skin over the cut, bruise or abrasion, protecting the wound from all foreign matter and healing it without a moment's delay or danger. If promptly applied it will positively prevent forming of pus or the setting in of blood poison. No person should be without this valuable yet inexpensive remedy. It may save your life or that of your friends almost any day. Put up neatly in small vials, so it can be carried in the vest pocket ready for immediate use.

No. 8F830 Liquid Skin, vest pocket size. Price........ 9c
If by mail, postage extra, 3 cents.

Artgum Cleaner.

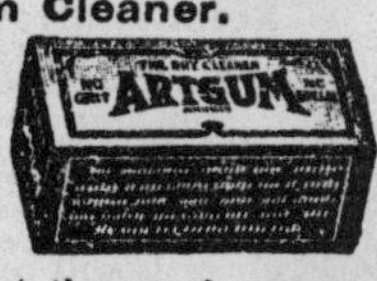

No grit, no grease, no odor, no danger from fire. It never dries out or hardens. Artgum removes surface dirt from everything without the use of water or any other liquid, and does not change the color or injure the articles rubbed with it. It does not take out grease spots or other stains which have gone below the surface. Artgum cleans gloves, white kid and suede slippers, belts, corsets, hand bags, canvas and tan shoes, felt and straw hats, coat collars and lapels, neckties, hatbands, silk and satin goods, furniture coverings, etc. Artgum renovates and cleans pictures, photographs, frescoes, wall paper, drawings, tracings, books, art specialties, burnt wood and leather work, etc. It removes pencil marks and memoranda from books and papers without erasing anything that is written or printed in ink. It cleans by picking up the dirt and rolling it up with the fine particles of artgum that crumble off the piece. It is made soft in order that it may wear away without abrading or scratching the surface of the article rubbed with it.

No. 8F835 Price, 2¼ x 1⅛ x 1⅛ inches, in carton........ 8c
If by mail, postage extra, 2 cents.
No. 8F836 Price, 3x3x2 inches, in carton........ 19c
If by mail, postage extra, 4 cents.

STRIP-IT.

This new product is a wonderful invention as it enables the housewife to take all the colors out of all goods except black and make them practically colorless without in the least injuring the goods. Equally good results on cotton, wool and silk. Dark colors can be removed, enabling the cloth to be dyed any of the lighter shades of sky blue, pink, etc. This enables the wife to change the color of cloth to any desired tint or shade. The greatest advantage for fine dyeing and obtaining beautiful bright shades ever offered to the dyer. Each package is sufficient to remove the color from 2 to 5 yards of cloth, depending upon the color and weight. Full directions with each package.

No. 8F735 Price, per package **12c**
Unmailable.

Epsom Salts.

These salts lose their strength when kept long in open drawers and boxes, as is the custom in most retail stores. **We furnish this salt always fresh and its valuable qualities unimpaired by exposure to the atmosphere.**

No. 8F740	Price, 1-lb. carton,	$ .04
No. 8F741	Price, 5-lb. pkg.	.15
No. 8F742	Price, 10-lb. pkg.	.30
No. 8F743	Price, 25-lb. pkg.	.75
No. 8F744	Price, 50-lb. bag	1.25
No. 8F745	Price, 100-lb. bag	2.50
No. 8F746	Price, barrel (375 pounds in barrel)	$5.60

Rochelle Salts.

Pure Rochelle Salts is free from the sickening taste of other salts and is an excellent cathartic. Our product is absolutely pure and fresh.

No. 8F750 Price, ¼-lb. package.... 12c
No. 8F751 Price, ½-lb. package.... 16c
No. 8F752 Price, 1-lb. package, 28c

Our Mexican Gulf Sea Salt.

For taking a genuine ocean bath at home. We have found this salt remarkable for strengthening the nerves and muscles. Toughens the skin, makes it clear and healthy, renders it impervious to skin troubles, and **we can highly recommend it in the physical development of both adults and children.**

No. 8F756 Price, 5-pound bag, 15c
No. 8F757 Price, 10-pound bag........ 25c

Sublimed Sulphur.

Can be used either internally or externally. The finest flour of sulphur, prepared especially for medicinal use. Can be used internally as a blood purifier or in combination with other ingredients as stock foods.

No. 8F760	Price, 1-lb. carton	$0.05
No. 8F761	Price, 5-lb. pkg.	.23
No. 8F762	Price, 10-lb. pkg.	.40
No. 8F763	Price, 25-lb. pkg.	.88
No. 8F764	Price, 50-lb. bag.	1.75
No. 8F765	Price, 100-lb. bag.	3.50
No. 8F766	Price, 180-lb. bbl.	5.40
No. 8F767	Price, 250-lb. bbl.	6.25

Petroleum Jelly.

This is another name for pure vaseline or cosmoline, and other titles given to it. It is one of the most valuable and also the most harmless and simple articles to have at hand in cases of **bruises, cuts, burns, chaps, roughness of the skin, etc.** For convenience, we put it in 2-ounce screw top glass jars.

No. 8F780 Price, 2-oz. glass jar, 4c
No. 8F781 Price, 1-pound can.. 16c
If by mail, postage extra, each, small, 8 cents; large, 20 cents.

Carbolized Petroleum Jelly.

This is the same as the above, with the addition of pure carbolic acid, which increases to a great extent its powers of healing.

No. 8F785 Price, 2-oz. bottle..... 8c
No. 8F786 Price, 1-pound can, 25c
If by mail, postage extra, each, small, 8 cents; large, 20 cents.

Soap Liniment.

The well known and highly recommended home treatment for sprain, bruises, swelled joints and rheumatic and gouty pains. Soap Liniment is one of the best liniments for removing inflammation and can be used with benefit in all cases requiring a liniment of this nature.

No. 8F790 Price, 2-ounce bottle........ 11c
No. 8F791 Price, 4-ounce bottle........ 19c
If by mail, postage and mailing tube extra, 16 cents.

Compound Licorice Powder.

This well known, agreeable and gentle laxative should have a place in every home. It depends for its action upon senna leaves and as they are combined with sugar and aromatics, form a mild laxative, pleasing to every one.

No. 8F795 Price, 4-ounce carton........ 15c
No. 8F796 Price, 16-ounce carton, 46c
Unmailable.

Carron Oil for Burns.

This is one of the household remedies that ought to be ordered by every housewife and kept on hand ready for immediate use.

Our Improved Carron Oil is the safest and most reliable treatment for fresh burns of every description. It stops the pain and smarting at once, prevents inflammation when used without delay, and in cases where the inflammation has started, it will reduce it quickly, healing the burns in the shortest possible time. Complete directions are furnished with each package.

No. 8F800 Price, 4-ounce bottle, Per bottle........ 17c
3 for........ 45c
If by mail, postage and tube extra, each, 16 cents.

Cleanit Liquid.

The only preparation that removes fresh paint, grease, oils, syrup, beer or wine stains from carpets, dress goods, silks and all kinds of clothing, etc., without injury to the finest fabric. It leaves the goods soft and clean, free from marks or creases. It also removes all gloss or shine caused by wear, restoring the natural luster. A preparation that is indispensable in every household.

No. 8F805 Price, 4-oz. bottle.. 14c
No. 8F806 Price, 8-oz. bottle.. 22c
No. 8F807 Price, 16-oz. bottle.. 40c
Unmailable on account of weight.

China Cement.

China Cement. The best cement for mending glass, china, ivory, shell, marble, fur, terra cotta, meerschaum, porcelain, plaster of paris, wool, alabaster and leather. Does the work well and quickly.

No. 8F810 Price, ½ ounce bottle. Per bottle........ 9c
If by mail, postage and tube extra, 8 cents.

Household Paraffine.

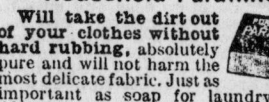

Will take the dirt out of your clothes without hard rubbing, absolutely pure and will not harm the most delicate fabric. Just as important as soap for laundry work. Also largely used to seal jams and jellies and protect them against mould. Once you use it you will never be without this household necessity.

No. 8F815 Price, per pound cake, including full directions for use.... 18c

Favorite Foot Powder.

This powder is particularly beneficial to those inclined to perspiration. For destroying bad odors and giving comfort to sore feet nothing like it has hitherto been put on the market. A little shaken in the shoes keeps the feet comfortable at all times.

No. 8F820 Price, per box........ 12c
If by mail, postage extra, 3 cents.

Moulded Beeswax.

Absolutely pure beeswax in cake form. Especially prepared for waxing thread, keeping flatirons clean, preventing them sticking when ironing, especially starched goods. The genuine J. K. McA. brand sold everywhere 5 cents per cake.

No. 8F825 Price, 3 cakes for, **10c**

MAKE YOUR TOTAL ORDER $1.00 OR MORE, SO THAT YOU WILL GET A PROFIT SHARING CERTIFICATE AND CAN SHARE IN OUR PROFITS.

Sulphur Candles.

For fumigating infected rooms and clothing in times of cholera, diphtheria, typhoid and scarlet fevers and all contagious diseases. The most powerful disinfectant known. Kills all insects. **Destroys noxious vapors.** When you wish to fumigate with sulphur, use these; no danger of fire, easily lighted, burns steadily, a most convenient article to have.

No. 8F840 Price, per candle... 8c
If by mail, postage extra, 5 cents.

Lightning Carpet Cleaner.

For cleaning and whitening carpets and rugs. Will quickly clean the carpet, restore its color, remove grease spots and at the same time act as a powerful, invaluable disinfectant and germicide. It not only leaves a freshness upon the carpet with but little work, but will also destroy disease germs very effectively without the slightest injury to the carpet or rug. Furnished in boxes with full directions, sufficient for cleaning two small or one extremely large carpet.

No. 8F850 Price, per box........ 23c
If by mail, postage extra, 10 cents.

Magic Kid Glove Cleaner.

A great money saver. Will make kid gloves almost like new. Requires but little work and always gives satisfactory results. Put up in paste form and tin boxes so it can easily be used and always handy.

No. 8F855 Price, per box.... 9c
If by mail, postage extra, 4 cents.

Copper, Brass and Nickel Polish.

Put up in paste form. No dust, no dirt, no grit, but a reliable and inexpensive preparation for cleaning and polishing copper, brass and nickel. A necessity to every particular housekeeper. Put up convenient for use in 1 and 2-ounce tin boxes.

No. 8F860 Price, 1-ounce box..15c
If by mail, postage extra, 3 cents.
No. 8F861 Price, 2-ounce box..25c
If by mail, postage extra, 5 cents.

Seroco Silver Polish.

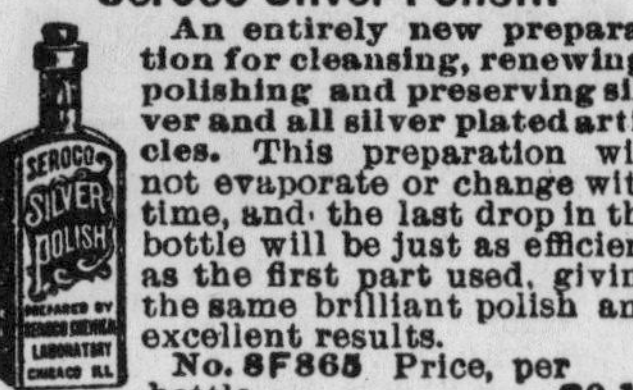

An entirely new preparation for cleansing, renewing, polishing and preserving silver and all silver plated articles. This preparation will not evaporate or change with time, and the last drop in the bottle will be just as efficient as the first part used, giving the same brilliant polish and excellent results.

No. 8F865 Price, per bottle..................$0.16
Per dozen bottles.............. 1.60
If by mail, postage and tube extra, each, 13 cents.

Plantora.

Nature's Great Plant Food.

The one great combination of nature's foods for giving life and healthy growth to all household and flowering plants, palms, ferns, vegetables, strawberries, grasses, lawns, shrubs, hot house plants, etc. The best plant and shrub food in existence. Will positively mature them from two to three weeks earlier than ordinary fertilizers. Plantora is the body, life and blood of the plant. The great quantity of nitrogen, phosphoric acid and potash in this article gives to the roots just the very substances required, and creates a healthy and vigorous growth. Used by prominent growers, expert gardeners and up to date garden specialists. Try it and be convinced. Try it on your puny fruit trees, your potatoes, lettuce, wax beans and other vegetables, sugar cane, tobacco plants, lawns, flower gardens, house plants, in green houses, etc. We cannot speak too highly of the results you will obtain with Plantora. They will certainly surprise you. Each pound package make 28 gallons of solution.

No. 8F870 Price, 1-lb. can.. **19c**
No. 8F871 Price, 5-lb. can.. **73c**

Spot and Stain Eradicator.

(NON-INFLAMMABLE.)

An absolute necessity for the careful housekeeper. The most efficient and safest liquid preparation for the prompt removal of spots and stains from clothing, carpets, linen, woolens and all kinds of fabrics. Will remove stains caused by iodine, paint, iron rust, fruit, etc. It is colorless, odorless and non-inflammable. Guaranteed to do the work quickly and thoroughly. Complete directions with each bottle.

No. 8F875 Spot and Stain Eradicator. Price, 2-ounce bottle........12c
If by mail, postage extra, 12 cents.

Metal Polishing Cloth.

ALWAYS READY, SAVES TIME AND MONEY FOR THE HOUSEWIFE.

The handy polisher for silverware and all nickel service. No polishing powder, polishing paste or polishing liquid required. Better than chamois skin and much cheaper. **With this specially prepared polishing cloth,** you can keep your tableware, gold, silver, and nickel clean and free from corrosion, tarnish, dirt, etc., by simply rubbing the articles with this cloth. **Full directions with each package.**

No. 8F880 Metal Polishing Cloth, the handy polisher. Price........ .9c
If by mail, postage extra, 2 cents.

Flake Tar Moth Destroyer.

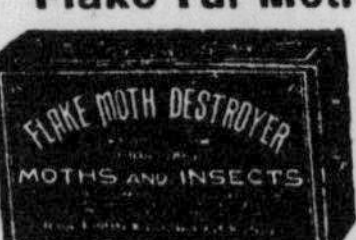

A chemically pure product of coal tar for the preservation of furs and clothing, etc., from moths. It will not injure the most delicate fabrics and is a certain preventive of moth attacks which are so destructive to winter clothing, woolen goods especially.

No. 8F885 Price, 1-lb. package. **10c**
If by mail, postage extra, 18 cents.

English Moth Balls.

The well known Pure Naphtha Moth Balls in marble form. A certain preventive to moths. Can be easily removed from clothing.

No. 8F888 Price, per 4-ounce carton........**4c**
No. 8F889 Price, per 8-ounce carton........**5c**
No. 8F890 Price, per 1-pound carton........**8c**
If by mail, 8 ounces, 12 cents; 1-pound package, 18 cents.

Bed Bug Exterminator.

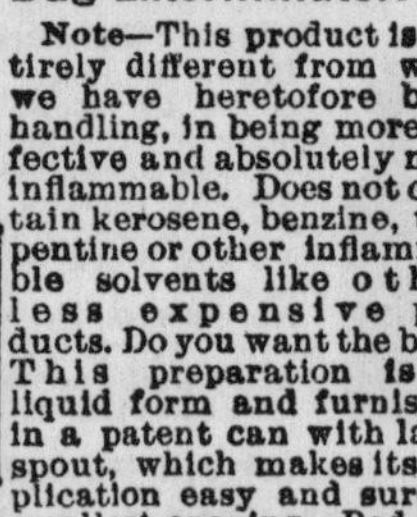

Note—This product is entirely different from what we have heretofore been handling, in being more effective and absolutely non-inflammable. Does not contain kerosene, benzine, turpentine or other inflammable solvents like **other less expensive products. Do you want the best? This** preparation is in liquid form and furnished in a patent can with large spout, which makes its application easy and sure to reach the smallest opening. Bed Bug Exterminator will not only exterminate every bed bug and roach, but rid a room or building of these little pests entirely. Full descriptions with each can.

No. 8F894 Price, ½-pint can. **$0.18**
No. 8F895 Price, one pint...... **.28**
No. 8F896 Price, one gallon.. **1.90**
Not mailable.

Strangle Food.

The surest and quickest death to bugs. It instantly strangles. Kills cockroaches, bed bugs, croton bugs, ants, moths, fleas, lice and all other vermin. Harmless to man, beast or bird.

No. 8F900 Price, per can.......................**22c**
If by mail, postage extra, 8 cents.

A New Invention Ant and Roach Trap.

A sure method for getting rid of all such pests as ants, roaches, water bugs, etc. No poison; easily used; will last for years. Get one.

No. 8F905 Price......................**10c**
If by mail, postage extra, 6 cents.

Poison Fly Paper.

Guaranteed the strongest and most effective Poison Fly Paper on the market. Put up eight sheets in each envelope.

No. 8F915 Price, three envelopes for..............**5c**
Per dozen envelopes..............**16c**
Unmailable.

THE DAISY FLY KILLER.

THE CLEANEST, BEST AND MOST EFFECTIVE FLY KILLER KNOWN.

IT IS A BEAUTY.

Will not injure or soil anything. Will effectually kill flies in a room.

HARMLESS TO PERSONS.

Will last all the season. It is cheaper than fly paper. Clean, neat, ornamental. Try it.

No. 8F910 Price, each........**$0.15**
Price, per dozen................. **1.50**
If by mail, postage extra, each, 9c.

Elastic Cement.

Mends Everything. Glass, crockery, metal, wood, leather, rubber, paper, cloth, etc. It differs from all others as it sticks closer, holds tighter and never relaxes. It is not a glue or a paste but a true cement. You will not realize the difference until you try it, then you will.

No. 8F920 Price, 10c-size... **8c**
No. 8F921 Price, 25c-size... **18c**
If by mail, postage extra, 2 cents.

Rat Killer.

The Great Vermin Destroyer.

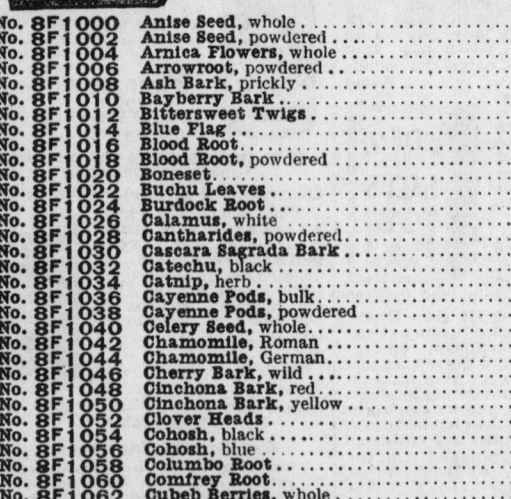

The most efficient poison for rats, mice, cockroaches, ants, flies, squirrels, crows, bed bugs, and all kinds of troublesome vermin. This is a sure destroyer. Rats and mice do not die in the house after eating it, but go outside for air and water.

No. 8F925 Price, per box.........**8c**
Unmailable.

Insect Powder.

A true Dalmatian Insect Powder, warranted free from all adulterations. **Fresh and strong. Sure death to bed bugs, croton bugs, potato bugs, cockroaches, fleas, lice, moths, flies, ants and all insects. This article is very much subject to adulteration.** Buy from us and get it pure.

No. 8F929 Price, ¼-lb. carton..**10c**
No. 8F930 Price, 1-lb. carton..**27c**
Unmailable.

Insect Powder Gun.

For using Insect Powder No. 8F930.

No. 8F934 Price.....................**5c**
If by mail, postage extra, 4 cents.

Large or Jumbo Powder Gun, holds ¼-pound of powder, **button and spout** screw off. **Large opening for filling.**

No. 8F935 Price.................**16c**
If by mail, postage extra, 6 cents.

Formaldehyde-Sulphur Fumigator for Household Use.

A new and perfect disinfectant; a combination of formaldehyde and sulphur. This is the most perfect and convenient of all fumigating devices, and, at the same time, the most powerful and far reaching in its effects, combining the fumes of sulphur and the great disinfecting and penetrating power of formaldehyde gas. Equally successful in destroying the germs of disease and vermin. This fumigator has no soldering joints to melt off and no bottle to break. It is absolutely safe and guaranteed to do the work every time.

No. 8F940 Price, complete.**20c**
Unmailable.

HERBS, FLOWERS, ROOTS, SEEDS AND BARKS.

The following list comprises our stock of fresh crude drugs, and where not otherwise specified, refers to the drug pressed in ounce packages. Always give the number as well as the name of the item wanted.

The following list comprises all we will supply.

No.	Article	Per ¼ Lb. Package.
No. 8F1000	**Anise Seed,** whole	$0.08
No. 8F1002	**Anise Seed,** powdered	.09
No. 8F1004	**Arnica Flowers,** whole	.09
No. 8F1006	**Arrowroot,** powdered	.08
No. 8F1008	**Ash Bark,** prickly	.08
No. 8F1010	**Bayberry Bark**	.08
No. 8F1012	**Bittersweet Twigs**	.08
No. 8F1014	**Blue Flag**	.08
No. 8F1016	**Blood Root**	.08
No. 8F1018	**Blood Root,** powdered	.08
No. 8F1020	**Boneset**	.08
No. 8F1022	**Buchu Leaves**	.12
No. 8F1024	**Burdock Root**	.08
No. 8F1026	**Calamus,** white	.08
No. 8F1028	**Cantharides,** powdered	.30
No. 8F1030	**Cascara Sagrada Bark**	.08
No. 8F1032	**Catechu,** black	.08
No. 8F1034	**Catnip,** herb	.08
No. 8F1036	**Cayenne Pods,** bulk	.08
No. 8F1038	**Cayenne Pods,** powdered	.09
No. 8F1040	**Celery Seed,** whole	.08
No. 8F1042	**Chamomile,** Roman	.09
No. 8F1044	**Chamomile,** German	.09
No. 8F1046	**Cherry Bark,** wild	.08
No. 8F1048	**Cinchona Bark,** red	.09
No. 8F1050	**Cinchona Bark,** yellow	.09
No. 8F1052	**Clover Heads**	.09
No. 8F1054	**Cohosh,** black	.08
No. 8F1056	**Cohosh,** blue	.08
No. 8F1058	**Columbo Root**	.08
No. 8F1060	**Comfrey Root**	.08
No. 8F1062	**Cubeb Berries,** whole (Often smoked for catarrhal trouble.)	.08
No. 8F1064	**Culver's Root**	.08
No. 8F1066	**Damiana Leaves**	.08
No. 8F1068	**Dandelion Root,** true	.08
No. 8F1070	**Dwarf Elder Root**	.09
No. 8F1072	**Elder Bark**	.08
No. 8F1074	**Elder Flowers**	.08
No. 8F1076	**Elecampane**	.08
No. 8F1078	**Elm Bark,** slabs	.08
No. 8F1080	**Elm Bark,** powdered	.08
No. 8F1082	**Eucalyptus Leaves**	.08
No. 8F1084	**Flaxseed,** whole	.05
No. 8F1086	**Fenugreek Seed,** whole	.05
No. 8F1088	**Fenugreek Seed,** powdered	.05
No. 8F1090	**Gentian Root**	.05
No. 8F1092	**Gentian Root,** powdered	.08
No. 8F1094	**Ginger Root,** African, powdered	.08
No. 8F1096	**Ginger Root,** Jamaica	.09

Continued on next page.

HERBS, FLOWERS, ROOTS, SEEDS AND BARKS—Continued from Preceding Page.

		Per ¼ Lb. Package
No. 8F1098	**Ginger Root**, Jamaica, powdered	$0.09
No. 8F1100	**Golden Seal Root**	.50
No. 8F1102	**Golden Seal**, powdered	.50
No. 8F1104	**Hellebore**, white, powdered	.08
No. 8F1106	**Hemlock Bark**	.08
No. 8F1108	**Hoarhound**, herb	.08
No. 8F1110	**Hops**, pressed	.06
No. 8F1112	**Hops**, fresh	.15
No. 8F1114	**Juniper Berries**, Italian	.05
No. 8F1118	**Ladies' Slipper**	.15
No. 8F1120	**Lavender Flowers**	.08
No. 8F1122	**Licorice Root**, XX	.08
No. 8F1124	**Licorice Root**, powdered	.08
No. 8F1126	**Lobelia**, herb	.08
No. 8F1128	**Mandrake Root**	.08
No. 8F1130	**Marshmallow Root**	.12
No. 8F1132	**Motherwort Herb**	.08
No. 8F1134	**Mullein**, herb	.08
No. 8F1136	**Nux Vomica**, buttons, powdered	.08
No. 8F1138	**Orris Root**, fingers	.40
No. 8F1140	**Orris Root**, powdered	.08
No. 8F1142	**Pennyroyal**, herb	.08
No. 8F1144	**Peppermint Herb**	.08
No. 8F1146	**Pipsissewa**	.09
No. 8F1148	**Plantain Leaves**	.08
No. 8F1150	**Poke Root**	.08
No. 8F1152	**Poplar Bark**, white	.08
No. 8F1154	**Pulsatilla**	.09
No. 8F1156	**Quassia Chips**	.07
No. 8F1158	**Queen of the Meadow**	$0.08
No. 8F1160	**Rhubarb Root**, cut, best	.35
No. 8F1162	**Rhubarb Root**, powdered	.25
No. 8F1164	**Saffron**, American ... per ounce	.20
No. 8F1166	**Saffron**, Spanish, ¼-ounce packages	.25
No. 8F1168	**Sage**, pressed	.08
No. 8F1170	**Sage**, medicinal	.08
No. 8F1172	**Sarsaparilla Root**, American	.10
No. 8F1174	**Sarsaparilla Root**, Honduras	.15
No. 8F1176	**Sarsaparilla Root**, Mexican	.08
No. 8F1178	**Sassafras Bark**	.08
No. 8F1180	**Senna Alex**	.09
No. 8F1182	**Scullcap Herb**	.08
No. 8F1184	**Skunk Cabbage Root**	.08
No. 8F1186	**Soap Tree Bark**	.07
No. 8F1188	**Spikenard Root**	.08
No. 8F1190	**Squaw Vine Leaves**	.08
No. 8F1192	**Stillingia**	.08
No. 8F1194	**Stone Root**	.08
No. 8F1196	**Stramonium Leaves**	.08
No. 8F1198	**Tansy Herb**	.08
No. 8F1200	**Unicorn Root**, false	.25
No. 8F1202	**Unicorn Root**, true	.25
No. 8F1204	**Valerian Root**	.10
No. 8F1206	**Wahoo Root**	.09
No. 8F1208	**Wintergreen Leaves**	.08
No. 8F1210	**Witch Hazel Bark**	.08
No. 8F1214	**Yellow Dock Root**	.10

PROPRIETARY AND PATENT MEDICINES.

The following list contains the principal patent medicines of the world We do not handle those not listed below.
We do not sell less than one dozen at dozen prices.

No.	Proprietary and Patent Medicines.	Retail Price	Our Price Per Doz.	Our Price Each
No. 8F1525	**Alcock's Porous Plasters**	$0.25	$1.25	$0.12
No. 8F1527	**Allen's Lung Balsam**, large	1.00	8.00	.75
No. 8F1529	**Allen's Lung Balsam**, medium	.50	4.00	.40
No. 8F1530	**Allen's Lung Balsam**, small	.25	2.00	.20
No. 8F1532	**Antifebrin**, 1-ounce boxes	.50	1.75	.15
No. 8F1534	**Antikamnia**, powdered or tablets	1.25	12.00	1.00
No. 8F1536	**Antipyrine**, per ounce	1.00		.50
No. 8F1538	**Ayer's Ague Cure**, regular size	.50	4.50	.40
No. 8F1540	**Ayer's Cherry Pectoral**, large	1.00	8.75	.75
No. 8F1541	**Ayer's Cherry Pectoral**, medium		4.75	.40
No. 8F1543	**Ayer's Hair Vigor**	1.00	8.00	.75
No. 8F1545	**Ayer's Pills**	.25	2.25	.20
No. 8F1547	**Ayer's Sarsaparilla**	1.00	8.75	.75
No. 8F1549	**Battle's Bromidia**, 4-ounce	1.00	8.75	.75
No. 8F1552	**Beecham's Pills**, Eng.	.25	2.00	.18
No. 8F1554	**Benson's Capcine Plasters**	.25	2.00	.20
No. 8F1556	**Benson's Celery and Chamomile Pills**	.50	5.00	.45
No. 8F1558	**Bromo-Seltzer**	.10	.75	.08
No. 8F1559	**Bromo-Seltzer**	.25	2.25	.20
No. 8F1560	**Bromo-Seltzer**	.50	4.00	.35
No. 8F1561	**Bromo-Seltzer**	1.00	7.50	.65
No. 8F1563	**Bucklen's Arnica Salve**	.25	2.00	.18
No. 8F1565	**Caldwell's Syrup Pepsin**	.50	4.00	.40
No. 8F1567	**Carter's Iron Pills**	.50	4.00	.35
No. 8F1569	**Carter's Little Liver Pills**	.25	1.60	.14
No. 8F1571	**Carter's Nerve Pills**	25	1.60	.14
No. 8F1573	**Cascarets**, small	.10	1.00	.09
No. 8F1574	**Cascarets**, medium	.25	2.40	.20
No. 8F1575	**Cascarets**, large	.50	4.80	.40
No. 8F1576	**Castoria**, Fletcher's	.35	2.80	.24
No. 8F1577	**Celerina**	1.00	8.85	.80
No. 8F1579	**Chamberlain's Colic, Cholera and Diarrhea Remedy**, medium	.50	4.25	.40
No. 8F1582	**Chamberlain's Cough Remedy**, med.	.50	4.00	.40
No. 8F1584	**Cuticura Ointment**, large	1.00	9.50	.80
No. 8F1585	**Cuticura Ointment**, small	.50	4.75	.40
No. 8F1587	**Cuticura Resolvent**, liquid, large	1.00	9.20	.80
No. 8F1588	**Cuticura Resolvent**, liquid, small	.50	4.60	.40
No. 8F1590	**Cuticura Resolvent Pills**	.25	2.30	.20
No. 8F1592	**Damiana Wafers**, pink or white	1.00	8.00	.70
No. 8F1594	**Danderine**, small	.25	2.00	.18
No. 8F1595	**Danderine**, large	1.00	8.00	.70
No. 8F1597	**Davis, Perry, Pain Killer**	.25	2.25	.20
No. 8F1598	**Davis, Perry, Pain Killer**	.50	4.50	.40
No. 8F1600	**Doan's Kidney Pills**	.50	4.50	.40
No. 8F1602	**Dodd's Kidney Pills**	.50	4.50	.40
No. 8F1605	**Fellow's Hypophosphites**	1.50	13.00	1.09
No. 8F1608	**Garfield Tea**, small	.25	2.10	.19
No. 8F1609	**Garfield Tea**, medium	.50	4.20	.38
No. 8F1610	**Garfield Tea**, large	1.00	8.40	.75
No. 8F1615	**Green's August Flower**	.75	5.50	.48
No. 8F1617	**Green's Nervura Tonic**	1.00	8.50	.75
No. 8F1620	**Gude's Pepto-Mangan**	1.25	10.00	.90
No. 8F1622	**Harlem Oil**, 3 h'ds	.15	.50	.06
No. 8F1625	**Hall's Lung Balsam**, large	1.00	8.00	.70
No. 8F1630	**Hall's Catarrh Cure, F. J. Cheney's**, Toledo	.75	6.00	.50
No. 8F1633	**Hall's Family Pills**	.25	2.00	.18
No. 8F1635	**Hall's Hair Renewer**	1.00	8.00	.70
No. 8F1640	**Hamburg Breast Tea**, genuine	.25	2.00	.18
No. 8F1642	**Hamlin's Wizard Oil**, small	.50	4.00	.35
No. 8F1643	**Hamlin's Wizard Oil**, large	1.00	8.00	.67
No. 8F1645	**Hood's Sarsaparilla**	1.00	8.00	.75
No. 8F1647	**Hood's Olive Ointment**	.25	2.00	.18
No. 8F1650	**Hood's Vegetable Pills**	.25	2.00	.18
No. 8F1652	**Horlick's Food for Infants**, large	.75	7.00	.60
No. 8F1654	**Horlick's Food for Infants**, small	.40	3.60	.30
No. 8F1658	**Horsford's Acid Phosphate** large	1.00	8.00	.70
No. 8F1659	**Horsford's Acid Phosphate**, small	.50	4.00	.35
No. 8F1665	**Hostetter's Stomach Bitters**	1.00	8.50	.73
No. 8F1669	**Imperial Granum**, small	.75	6.50	.58
No. 8F1670	**Imperial Granum**, large	1.00	9.50	.79
No. 8F1673	**Jayne's Alterative**	1.00	8.00	.70
No. 8F1675	**Jayne's Expectorant**	1.00	8.00	.70
No. 8F1677	**Jayne's Carminative Balsam**	.25	2.00	.18
No. 8F1680	**Jayne's Liniment**	.50	4.00	.35
No. 8F1682	**Jayne's Sanitive Pills**	.25	1.75	.18
No. 8F1685	**Jayne's Tonic Vermifuge**, small	.35	3.00	.25
No. 8F1687	**Jayne's Tonic Vermifuge**, large	.50	4.00	.40
No. 8F1690	**Kendall's Spavin Cure**, family use	.50	4.00	.35
No. 8F1691	**Kendall's Spavin Cure**	$1.00	$8.00	$0.70
No. 8F1695	**Kennedy's Medical Discovery**	1.50	13.50	1.25
No. 8F1697	**Kickapoo Indian Cough Cure**	.25	2.00	.18
No. 8F1700	**Kickapoo Indian Oil**	.25	2.00	.18
No. 8F1702	**Kickapoo Indian Sagwa**	1.00	8.00	.70
No. 8F1704	**Kickapoo Indian Salve**	.25	2.00	.18
No. 8F1706	**Kickapoo Prairie Plant**	.50	4.00	.40
No. 8F1708	**Kickapoo Worm Killer**	.25	2.00	.18
No. 8F1710	**Kickapoo Pills**	.25	2.00	.18
No. 8F1712	**King's New Discovery**, large	1.00	8.00	.70
No. 8F1713	**King's New Discovery**, small	.50	4.00	.35
No. 8F1715	**King's New Life Pills**	.25	2.00	.18
No. 8F1717	**Lane's Family Medicine**, small	.25	2.00	.18
No. 8F1720	**Lane's Family Medicine**, medium	.50	4.00	.35
No. 8F1725	**Listerine**, Lambert's, large	1.00	8.00	.69
No. 8F1727	**Listerine**, Lambert's, small	.25	2.20	.20
No. 8F1730	**Lyon's Tooth Powder**		2.00	.20
No. 8F1732	**Malted Milk Food**, small	.50	4.50	.45
No. 8F1733	**Malted Milk Food**, large	1.00	9.00	.90
No. 8F1734	**Malted Milk Food**, hospital size	3.75		3.35
No. 8F1737	**McGill's Orange Blossom**	1.00	8.00	.70
No. 8F1740	**Mellin's Infant Food**, large	.75	6.50	.58
No. 8F1741	**Mellin's Infant Food**, small	.50	4.00	.35
No. 8F1743	**Mennen's Borated Talcum Powder**	.25	2.00	.18
No. 8F1747	**Merchant's Gargling Oil**, large	1.00	7.75	.70
No. 8F1748	**Merchant's Gargling Oil**, medium	.50	4.15	.40
No. 8F1750	**Mexican Mustang Liniment**, large	1.00	8.30	.72
No. 8F1751	**Mexican Mustang Liniment**, medium	.50	4.15	.38
No. 8F1752	**Mexican Mustang Liniment**, small	.25	2.10	.20
No. 8F1753	**Orangine**	.25	2.00	.19
No. 8F1754	**Orangine**	.50	4.75	.38
No. 8F1755	**Ozomulsion**	1.00	8.00	.70
No. 8F1758	**Parker's Hair Balsam**, large	1.00	8.50	.80
No. 8F1760	**Parker's Hair Balsam**, small	.50	4.25	.40
No. 8F1762	**Petit's Eye Salve**	.25	2.00	.20
No. 8F1764	**Petit's Pile Remedy**	.25	2.00	.20
No. 8F1766	**Pinkham's Blood Purifier**	1.00	8.25	.70
No. 8F1768	**Pinkham's Liver Pills**	.25	2.00	.18
No. 8F1769	**Pinkham's, Lydia, Vegetable Liquid Compound**	1.00	8.25	.69
No. 8F1770	**Pinkham's Compound Pills**	1.00	8.25	.70
No. 8F1771	**Pinkham's Sanative Wash**	.25	2.00	.18
No. 8F1772	**Pond's Extract**, large	1.75	16.00	1.40
No. 8F1773	**Pond's Extract**, medium	1.00	8.00	.70
No. 8F1774	**Pond's Extract**, small	.50	4.00	.35
No. 8F1776	**Radway's Ready Relief Pills**	.25	1.75	.15
No. 8F1777	**Radway's Ready Relief**	.50	4.00	.40
No. 8F1778	**Ripan Tabules**	.25	2.00	.18
No. 8F1780	**Sage's Catarrh Remedy**	.50	4.00	.40
No. 8F1782	**Schenck's Mandrake Pills**	.25	2.00	.18
No. 8F1784	**Schiffman's German Asthma Cure**, large	1.00	8.50	.80
No. 8F1785	**Schiffman's German Asthma Cure**, small	.50	4.25	.40
No. 8F1787	**Sanmetto**	1.00	8.00	.70
No. 8F1789	**Scott's Emulsion**	1.00	8.00	.70
No. 8F1790	**Simmon's Liver Regulator**, liquid	1.00	8.00	.70
No. 8F1792	**St. Jacob's Oil**	.50	4.00	.35
No. 8F1794	**Stearns' Electric Paste**	.25	1.45	.15
No. 8F1796	**Stuart's Catarrh Tablets**	1.00	8.00	.70
No. 8F1797	**Stuart's Catarrh Tablets**, small	.50	4.00	.35
No. 8F1798	**Stuart's Calcium Wafers**	.50	4.00	.35
No. 8F1799	**Stuart's Charcoal Lozenges**	.25	2.00	.20
No. 8F1800	**Stuart's Dyspepsia Tablets**	.50	4.00	.35
No. 8F1801	**Stuart's Dyspepsia Tablets**, large	1.00	8.00	.70
No. 8F1804	**Swift's Specific**, (S. S. S.) large	1.75	16.00	1.39
No. 8F1805	**Swift's Specific**, (S. S. S.) small	1.00	8.00	.70
No. 8F1806	**Swift's Specific**, dry form	.50	4.00	.40
No. 8F1808	**Wakefield's Blackberry Balsam**	.35	2.50	.24
No. 8F1810	**Warner's Lithia Tablets**, Eff. 3 Gr.	.25	2.00	.17
No. 8F1812	**Warner's Lithia Tablets**, Eff. 5 Gr.	.50	3.00	.30
No. 8F1814	**Warner's Safe Kidney and Liver Cure**	1.25	8.00	.70
No. 8F1816	**Warner's Safe Pills**	.20	1.50	.14
No. 8F1818	**Warner's Safe Rheumatic Cure**	1.25	10.50	.90
No. 8F1820	**Warner's Tippecanoe**, the best	1.00	8.50	.75
No. 8F1822	**Warner's Nervine**, large	1.00	8.00	.70
No. 8F1824	**Warner's Nervine**, small	5.00	4.00	.40
No. 8F1826	**Williams' Pink Pills**	.50	4.75	.40
No. 8F1828	**Wine Cardui**	1.00	8.00	.70
No. 8F1830	**Winslow's Soothing Syrup**	.25	2.00	.20

LIQUID FORMALDEHYDE PREVENTS SMUT.

RECOMMENDED BY U. S. GOVERNMENT

AS A PREVENTIVE OF SMUT IN WHEAT, OATS, BARLEY AND OTHER GRAINS, ALSO OF THE POTATO SCAB.

VERY LOW IN COST. **A very small expense, for one pint is sufficient to use in fifty gallons (a barrel) of water.** Used in a very simple manner. Just spread your seed out on the barn floor and sprinkle with the formaldehyde after it has been diluted with water, one part of formaldehyde to ten thousand parts of water (about a pint to a barrel of water), then let the seed dry before sowing or planting. In this way, at a very small expense of a few cents, you can treat your seed and protect your crop of wheat, oats, barley, etc., from smut and your potatoes from scab in the most effective manner.

Pamphlet of instructions free with each package giving you complete information on its preparation and use.

MILLIONS OF DOLLARS SAVED FOR FARMERS. **Bulletin No. 91 of Wisconsin, states that the loss from smut in the oat crop in the year 1901 in that state alone was approximately $6,387,500.00, and that all this vast sum of money could have been saved had the farmers treated their seed with liquid formaldehyde.** Thousands of dollars are lost by the farmers every season in the loss of the crops caused by smut and other germ diseases. Formaldehyde treatment is the only preventive and cure, very much better than the poisonous sprays, has many advantages, always certain of results and is perfectly harmless. Every bushel of seed should receive this treatment before sowing as it guarantees freedom from diseases and largely increased crops in every case. Wheat, oats, corn, barley, tobacco, cotton, flax and potatoes are all subject to certain destroying diseases, and for these, formaldehyde is the only certain cure. The diseases are all caused by minute germs or spores adhering to the seeds, developing as the plant grows and maturing in the kernels of the full grown plant. Our liquid formaldehyde is the ideal remedy as it can be applied easily, effectively and very economically and with perfect safety. It is cheap enough to use extensively and it has no tendency to retard the germination of the seed; in fact it facilitates it.

IN ADDITION **to preventing smut and potato scab, liquid formaldehyde is now recognized as the best and most certain antiseptic, disinfectant and germicide.** It is far superior as an antiseptic and disinfectant to chloride of lime, carbolic acid, etc., very much cheaper, much safer and much more easily handled and applied. A few drops of the 40 per cent solution sprinkled around will prevent decomposition or putrifaction or retard it if already started, or a small amount greatly diluted with water (about two ounces to a bucket of water) can be used more freely with equally good results. It destroys all odor, and is a positive antiseptic and disinfectant. You will find a hundred uses for it in the house and around the farm, and no one should be without a full size package.

FULL 40 PER CENT SOLUTION. **We guarantee our liquid formaldehyde to contain a full 40 per cent quantity of formaldehyde gas and is so recognized by the pure food and drug laws of every state.** This cannot be said of many other formaldehyde solutions which are diluted with water and which are thereby debarred from entering certain states. We guarantee our liquid formaldehyde to be full strength.

REMEMBER, **with each package we send you a pamphlet "Usefulness of Liquid Formaldehyde on the Farm," giving the various uses and dilutions necessary for best results. Don't fail to include a bottle with your next order.**

No. 8F1995	Price, per pint	$0.24
No. 8F1998	Price, per gallon jug	1.65
No. 8F1996	Price, per dozen pints	2.60

Unmailable on account of weight.

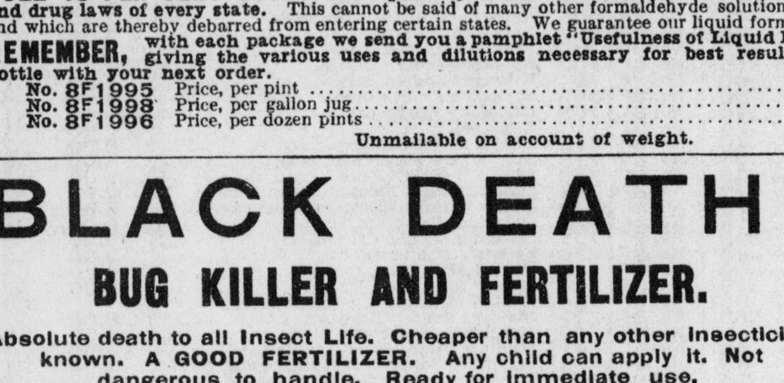

BLACK DEATH!

BUG KILLER AND FERTILIZER.

Absolute death to all Insect Life. Cheaper than any other insecticide known. A GOOD FERTILIZER. Any child can apply it. Not dangerous to handle. Ready for immediate use, no mixing or preparation required.

IT WILL POSITIVELY KILL **potato bugs, squash bugs, pumpkin bugs, watermelon bugs, rose bugs, currant worms, cabbage worms, etc.** It will kill all kinds of creeping things that eat the leaves of vegetables or plants. **Black Death** has been on the market for five years, during which time it has met with unprecedented success wherever introduced all over the United States. It has proven to be the most successful destroyer of all insects, bugs or beetles that live on vegetation. We can recommend this preparation to our customers with every confidence; we can assure them it is a better and cheaper insect powder than they have ever used and it operates with certainty.

WHAT IS "BLACK DEATH?"

IT IS AN INEXPENSIVE POWDER **as fine as flour and extremely diffusable, and completely covers, with a fine dust, all plants over which it is sprinkled.** In addition to being powerful in its effect in killing all insect life, **it is also a splendid fertilizer,** increasing the crop very materially to which it is applied. **It is superior to all other bug poisons on the market.**

A GOOD CROP OF POTATOES, CABBAGE, **or any other vegetables cannot be obtained, no matter how good your soil and seeds may be, or how favorable the weather, or how much labor or care you expend on them, unless the vines and leaves are kept vigorous and healthy.** Such a condition cannot be kept up unless all insects and bugs are destroyed as fast as they appear. Any cause that injures the leaves hurts the plants, and anything that destroys the foliage affects the roots also and poisons the crops. Nothing, therefore, is more necessary than that the growing vines and trees be kept free from the ravages of insects and bugs.

"BLACK DEATH" KILLS POTATO BUGS IMMEDIATELY. **The potato bug is the greatest enemy the potato grower has. This bug eats the leaves of the plants.** He is fitted with powerful upper and under jaws and works the greatest ravages in a field of potatoes. **"BLACK DEATH"** sprinkled on the leaves kills him with neatness and despatch. Three crops of eggs are laid each year. Prompt action is therefore necessary. **Just as soon as the potato bug makes his appearance, dust the potato vines thoroughly and carefully with "BLACK DEATH" and your plants are safe from destruction.** Kill off the first arrivals and you will have no further trouble, pursuing the same course in the case of other bugs and insects. Dust the leaves of the plants as soon as there is the slightest indication of their presence and save your crop from destruction.

THE WAY TO APPLY "BLACK DEATH."

THE BEST WAY **is to shake "BLACK DEATH" on the vines dry** (never mix with water), early in the morning when the plants are damp with the dew, or otherwise, but do not apply it when the plants are dry. It can be applied with a sifter, or can be put on with a small burlap or sack made of moderately coarse cloth. In this way the powder is not unnecessarily wasted. **Be on the lookout for the first appearance of the bugs,** as at that time a few pounds will do the work of a much larger quantity later. One application will usually exterminate all the bugs for the entire season, but sometimes two applications are necessary.

AMOUNT NECESSARY. **We recommend that you apply 10 to 15 pounds per acre for potatoes, but 20 to 30 pounds can be applied with safety and the expense of it will be returned in an increased crop.**

EVERY POTATO GROWER, **every cabbage grower, every farmer, every market gardener,** every grower of roses and flowers and plants of any kind, should give "BLACK DEATH" a fair trial. If it is once used it will always be used. **DO NOT FAIL TO GIVE IT A TRIAL.**

SPECIAL PRICES:

No. 8F20[illegible]	Black Death.	Per 5-pound package,	$0.18
No. 8F2036	Black Death.	Per 10-pound package,	.31
No. 8F2037	Black Death.	Per 25-pound package,	.74
No. 8F2038	Black Death.	Per 50-pound package,	1.47
No. 8F2039	Black Death.	Per 100-pound package,	2.93
No. 8F2040	Black Death.	Per 300-pound barrel,	8.10

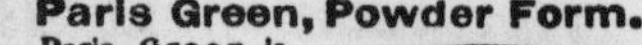

Paris Green, Powder Form.

Paris Green is recognized as one of the most important insecticides and is used for destroying insects of all kinds, either in wet or dry conditions, but in all cases it is first largely diluted. When it is used in the dry or powder form, it should be mixed with plaster, sifted wood ashes or flour. The strength of the mixture should depend upon the plants and insects to which it is to be applied, but at no time should more than one pound of Paris Green be added to 50 pounds of mixture, as that is usually sufficient.

Care should be taken when using Paris Green mixed with water that the liquid is constantly stirred up when it is used for spraying, as otherwise the Paris Green will settle and the last quantity in the bottom of the cask will be so strong as to be liable of doing serious damage.

No. 8F2002 Price, per pound...**28c**

No. 8F2003 Per 2-pound package. Price, per pound...**27c**

No. 8F2004 Per 5-pound package. Price, per pound...**27c**

No. 8F2005 Price, per pound in 14, 28 and 56-pound kits...**27c**

No. 8F2006 Price, per pound in 100-pound kegs...**26c**

The above prices are subject to market changes

Liquid Paris Green.

For spraying all kinds of fruit trees, vines and plants. Is sure death to potato bugs, cinch bugs, curculio, canker worms, etc. One bottle is sufficient for 160 gallons of water. Full instructions how to use it on every bottle.

No. 8F2010 Price, per bottle...**25c**

Liquid London Purple.

For spraying all kinds of fruit trees, vines and plants. Is sure death to potato bugs, cinch bugs, curculio, canker worms, etc. Sufficient for 100 gallons of water. Directions how to use it to the best advantage. **Not mailable on account of weight.**

No. 8F2015 Price, per bottle...**25c**

Purple Jack.

Sure death to the worm that eats the head of the cabbage or the fruit of the tomato. Not mailable on account of weight.

No. 8F2017 Price, per bottle......**25c**

Kerosene Emulsion.

For spraying and washing fruit trees, vines, plants, field crops and domestic animals. Destroys plant lice, red spiders, scales, mealy bugs, lice on cattle and hogs, tick on sheep. One can is sufficient for 50 gallons. **Not mailable on account of weight.**

No. 8F2020 Price, per can.........**30c**

Bordeaux Mixture.

Compounded from the old formula, but by an entirely new process. Prevents blight, rot, mildew and rust. Destroys all fungus growth on vegetation. One can is sufficient to dilute with 35 to 50 gallons of water. **Not mailable on account of weight.**

No. 8F2025 Price, per can.... **20c**

Seroco Sifter.

The illustration here shown represents the Seroco Sifter with which to apply the famous Black Death and other dry powder insecticides. To obtain best results fill the sifter only about half full. This sifter is positively the best on the market. Patent applied for.

No. 8F2045 Seroco Sifter. 2-quart. Price...............**23c**

Unmailable.

Hammond's Grape Dust.

A powdered fungicide which is very efficient in destroying mildew and preventing blight in greenhouses or in the open, also in destroying aphis and black fly.

No. 8F2050	Price, 5 pounds.	$0.28
No. 8F2051	Price, 10 pounds	.54
No. 8F2052	Price 25 pounds	1.23

Hammond's Slug Shot.

This is truly the vegetable growers' friend. It is a fine powder, easily applied to the plants by hand, by duster or bellows, or in water by spraying. It is harmless and **sure death** to cabbage worms, potato bugs, currant worms, lice, slugs, sow bugs, etc., and is strongly impregnated with fungicides. The 125-pound kegs contain a duster for applying the powder.

No. 8F2060 Price, 5 lbs..**24c**

No. 8F2061 Price, 10 lbs. **47c**

No. 8F2062 Price, 125-pound keg...............**$4.95**

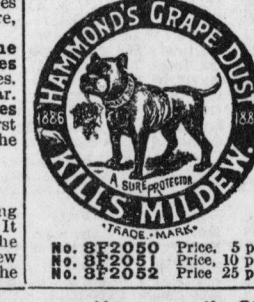

POWDERED BORAX.

The housekeeper's friend; has more uses about the home than even that of common salt. For the laundry, the kitchen, the bath and for various medicinal uses it is indispensable. Absolutely pure and highest grade.

No. 8T160 Price, per 1-pound carton......10c
Price, 5 pounds for 47c

TASTELESS CASTOR OIL.

Without the disagreeable and nauseating odor and taste of regular oil as it has been sold in the past, and yet possessing all the good points that have made castor oil one of the most certain and reliable cathartics that can be used when a remedy of this kind is required. Can be taken by adults and children alike. **After you have given our Tasteless Castor Oil a trial** you will never use any other, and you will always keep it on hand as one of the standard cathartic and household remedies.

No. 8T162 Price, 4-ounce bottle......23c
No. 8T163 Price, 8-ounce bottle......37c
Mailable sizes, see note on page 372.

SWEET SPIRITS OF NITRE.

Guaranteed absolutely pure, fresh and of full strength. Much more reliable than that generally offered for sale in drug stores.

No. 8T165 Price, 3-ounce bottle......17c
No. 8T166 Price, 1-pint bottle......75c
Mailable sizes, see note on page 372.

ESSENCE PEPPERMINT, U. S. P.

Pure, strong and of full strength. Largely used for colic in children, sickness or aching of stomach, cramps, etc. A very useful and beneficial household remedy. **Best quality for medical use.**

No. 8T168 Price, 3-ounce bottle......19c
Mailable sizes, see note on page 372.

ESSENCE JAMAICA GINGER, U. S. P.

Prepared of great strength from the finest quality of Jamaica ginger. Very beneficial in colic, diarrhea, cramps, etc. **Buy our genuine essence and get the full benefit of its valuable properties.**

No. 8T170 Price, 3-ounce bottle......19c
Mailable sizes, see note on page 372.

ESSENCE OF PEPSIN.

A preparation regularly prescribed by physicians, and usually recommended for the treatment of indigestion, sour stomach, dyspepsia, bad breath and in all conditions arising from a lack of gastric juice to properly digest and assimilate the food. A teaspoonful before or after meals will aid digestion and assimilation of food, and affords prompt relief when suffering from indigestion, as well as the distressing attacks to which chronic sufferers from dyspepsia are subject; also largely used for making junket, whey, etc., for invalids.

No. 8T172 Price, 8-ounce bottle......47c
Mailable sizes, see note on page 372.

NEUTRALIZING CORDIAL.

A well known household remedy. Useful in treatment of diarrhea, dysentery and cholera morbus. Also a great remedy for **dyspepsia,** a general corrector of the **stomach and bowels.** An ideal children's remedy for all bowel complaints.

No. 8T174 Price, 4-ounce bottle......25c
Mailable sizes, see note on page 372.

CASTOR OIL.

Cold pressed and almost tasteless. Exceptionally fine grade.

No. 8T176 Price, 4-ounce bottle......12c
No. 8T177 Price, 1-pint bottle......25c
No. 8T178 Price, per ½-gallon jug......90c
No. 8T179 Price, per gallon jug......$1.65
Mailable sizes, see note on page 372.

SPIRITS OF CAMPHOR, U. S. P.

Made from pure imported Gum Camphor and Grain Alcohol. Strictly pure and full strength. Much used for nausea and fainting spells.

No. 8T180 Price, 3-ounce bottle......19c
No. 8T181 Price, 1-pint bottle......79c
Mailable sizes, see note on page 372.

CAMPHORATED OIL, U. S. P.

An excellent article for rubbing on children's and grown up persons' chests and throats in cases of croup, difficulty in breathing, sore throat, coughs. A small quantity of pure spirits of turpentine added to it will increase its effectiveness in many cases.

No. 8T183 Price, 4-ounce bottle......22c
No. 8T184 Price, 8-ounce bottle......39c
Mailable sizes, see note on page 372.

GLYCERIN.

Warranted absolutely pure. Can be used either externally or internally.

No. 8T186 Price, 4 ounces......12c
No. 8T187 Price, ½ pound......19c
No. 8T188 Price, 1 pound......37c
No. 8T189 Price, per gallon jug......$2.42
Mailable sizes, see note on page 372.

CARBOLIC ACID SOLUTION.

A saturated solution of Carbolic Acid for disinfecting purposes, destroying contagion, cleansing purposes, etc. Excellent for keeping away disease, destroying bad odors. Put up expressly for household use.

No. 8T191 Price, 1-pound bottle......18c
Unmailable.

TINCTURE OF ARNICA, U. S. P.

The value of arnica is well known as an application to bruises, sprains, cuts, swellings, etc., but to secure any benefit it is necessary to have a strong, well prepared tincture **such as ours.**

No. 8T193 Price, 4-ounce bottle......18c
No. 8T194 Price, ½-pint bottle......35c
No. 8T195 Price, 1-pint bottle......67c
Unmailable.

HOUSEHOLD AMMONIA.

Standard quality. Extra purity and strength. Put up expressly for home use. It lightens work and brightens the home. Makes the washing cleaner and polishing easier.

In pint bottles, with full directions for use in the laundry, for the toilet, and for cleaning glass, crockery, paint, taking out stains, etc.

No. 8T197 Price, per pint bottle......10c
No. 8T198 Price, per gallon jug......75c
Unmailable.

VIOLET AMMONIA.

For the toilet and bath. Violet Ammonia is a comparatively new article for toilet and bathing purposes, which has won the favor of every lady and gentleman who has given it a trial. It is inexpensive and a few drops added to the water before washing will be sufficient to soften and perfume it, and to whiten the skin of the user to perfection. A small quantity added to the bath will intensify the cleansing and invigorating effects greatly, leaving a mild but lasting odor always pleasing and refreshing.

No. 8T200 Violet Ammonia. Price, 1-pint bottle......19c
Unmailable.

GENUINE WITCH HAZEL EXTRACT.

We guarantee our extract of Witch Hazel to contain full 15 per cent of grain alcohol, and free from formaldehyde, wood alcohol or other substances used to cheapen the same. A universal all healing remedy. Should be in every household; useful for sore throat, hemorrhage, wounds, sprains, bruises, sore eyes, stiff joints, burns, and in nearly every accident that one can have. Our price is so low that every family can afford to keep a supply in their homes. Absolutely pure, full strength and the best made. Look at our prices.

No. 8T202 ½-pint bottle, retail price, 40 cents; our price......18c
No. 8T203 1-pint bottle, retail price, 50 cents; our price......30c
No. 8T204 1-quart bottle, retail price, $1.00; our price......49c
No. 8T205 ½-gallon, retail price, $1.75; our price......75c
No. 8T206 1-gallon, retail price, $2.50; our price......$1.25
Unmailable.

GLYCERIN SUPPOSITORIES.

The best treatment for constipation, producing painless, prompt and copious evacuation of the bowels without disturbing the stomach and whole system. No internal taking of nauseous medicines, pills, capsules etc. The ideal method of emptying the lower bowels. Easy to apply. The best remedy for constipated children. 1 dozen to bottle with full directions.

No. 8T208 Price, per bottle......19c
Postage extra, per bottle, 10c.

REFINED CAMPHOR. (Gum Camphor.)

We carry only the best and purest refined camphor, guaranteed to be the highest grade camphor obtainable, both for domestic and medicinal purposes.

No. 8T210 Price, 1-ounce cake......8c
No. 8T211 Price, 1-pound package......75c
Prices subject to market changes.
Mailing charges, 2 cents per ounce.

BORIC ACID—PURE (BORACIC ACID.)

Guaranteed highest purity powder, a popular, valuable and aseptic healing dressing and protective for cuts, wounds, ulcers, sores, bruises and all inflamed and irritated surfaces, a healing and soothing application for chafed and harsh, dry or rough skin.

No. 8T213 Price 1-pound airtight container......23c

PURE POWDERED ALUM.

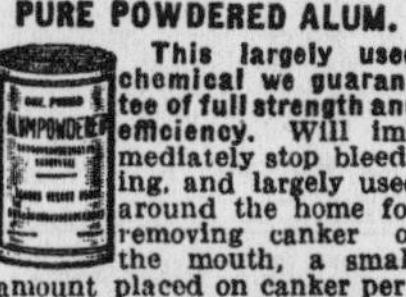

This largely used chemical we guarantee of full strength and efficiency. Will immediately stop bleeding, and largely used around the home for removing canker of the mouth. A small amount placed on canker performing a cure. Also used for astringent washes and douches.

No. 8T215 Price, per 1-pound carton......9c

CARBOLIC ARNICA SALVE.

The best family salve in the world for burns, flesh wounds, chilblains, boils, felons, sores, and fever sores. Excellent for salt rheum, eczema and ringworm. Keep it in the house.

No. 8T217 Regular price, 25 cents; our price, per box......16c
If mail shipment, postage extra, per box, 4 cents.

COMPOUND CATHARTIC PILLS.

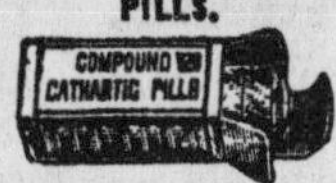

The old fashioned sugar coated Cathartic Pill of the U. S. Pharmacopoeia. They act principally on the liver, and move the bowels gently without griping.

No. 8T219 Price, per box......8c
Six boxes for......42c
If mail shipment, postage extra, per box, 2 cents.

WITCH HAZEL SALVE.

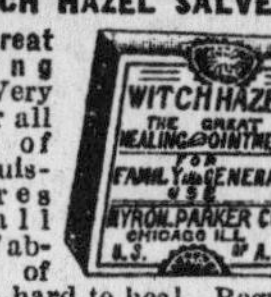

The great healing salve. Very good for all forms of cuts, bruises, sores and all kinds of abrasions of the skin hard to heal. Regular price, per box, 25 cents.

No. 8T221 Our price, per box......14c
If mail shipment, postage extra, per box, 4 cents.

REGAL FOOT POWDER.

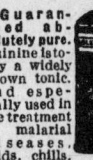

Do your feet ache or hurt you? If so, send for a bottle of Regal Foot Powder. It is a powder particularly beneficial to those troubled with foot perspiration. For destroying bad odors and giving comfort to sore feet nothing like it has hitherto been put on the market. A little shaken in the shoes keeps the feet comfortable at all times.

No. 8T223 Regular price, 25 cents; our price, per box......13c
If mail shipment, postage extra, 3 cents.

OLD ENGLISH WART REMOVER.

Guaranteed to give Satisfaction.

This is a very reliable and harmless remedy for the removal of all kinds of warts. After the first application the wart commences to shrink and after the treatment is continued for a reasonable length of time the wart will drop off without leaving any scar. The treatment is perfectly painless and harmless. Regular price, 25 cents.

No. 8T225 Our price, 18c
If mail shipment, postage extra, 10 cents.

LAVENDER BATH POWDER.

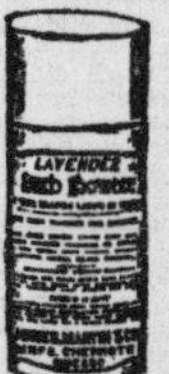

A highly perfumed luxury for the bath. A scientific preparation for softening, purifying and perfuming the water. It adds value and pleasure to the bath, by making it more agreeable and refreshing, softening and perfuming the water, toning and invigorating the system like an ocean bath, and at the same time leaving that exquisite fragrance of Old English Lavender about the entire body. You will never know or appreciate the real luxury of such a bath with its refreshing, stimulating and exhilarating effect until you have used this delightful toilet necessity.

No. 8T227 Price, per package......21c
If mail shipment, postage extra, 10 cents.

MILK SUGAR—PURE. (Sugar of Milk.)

Especially recommended for making modified milk as a food for infants. Practically indispensable in all cases where babies are brought up by the bottle. Guaranteed absolutely pure and the best made. Full directions for infant feeding on each package. Furnished in airtight 1-pound packages.

No. 8T230 Per 1-pound package......25c

SEIDLITZ POWDERS.

We guarantee all Seidlitz Powders we send out to be made from pure materials absolutely fresh, and to be **full strength.** Put up in boxes containing in each 10 blue and 10 white papers.

No. 8T232 Price, per box......17c
If mail shipment, postage extra, per box, 5 cents.

QUININE PILLS.

Two grains each, sugar or gelatine coated. Full weight and strength and **with absolutely pure quinine.**

No. 8T234 Price, per bottle of 100 pills......19c
If mail shipment, postage extra, 8c.

QUININE. (QUININE SULPHATE.)

Guaranteed absolutely pure. Quinine is today a widely known tonic, and especially used in the treatment of malarial diseases, colds, chills, ague, erysipelas, etc.

No. 8T236 Price, 1-ounce......37c
If mail shipment, postage extra, per ounce, 6 cents.

FURNITURE POLISH.

A handy and valuable household article of the greatest perfection for polishing and restoring all kinds of furniture. Quickly removes scratches, stains and marks of wear, and makes the furniture look like new. Full directions with each bottle.

No. 8T238 Price, per 4-ounce bottle......13c
If mail shipment, postage and mailing tube extra, 16 cents.

EPSOM SALTS.

We furnish this salt always fresh and its valuable qualities unimpaired by exposure to the atmosphere.

No. 8T240 Price, 1-lb. carton......7c
No. 8T241 Price, 5-lb. package......17c
No. 8T242 Price, 10-lb. package......33c
No. 8T243 Price, 25-lb. package......73c
No. 8T244 Price, 50-lb. bag......$1.20

ROCHELLE SALTS.

Pure Rochelle Salts is free from the sickening taste of other salts and is an excellent cathartic. Our product is absolutely pure and fresh.

No. 8T246 Price, ¼-lb. package......11c
No. 8T247 Price, ½-lb. package......17c
No. 8T248 Price, 1-lb. package......32c
All sizes unmailable.

SUBLIMED SULPHUR.

Can be used either internally or externally. The finest flour of sulphur, prepared especially for medicinal use. Can be used internally as a blood purifier or in combination with other ingredients as stock foods.

No. 8T250 Price, 1-lb. carton......7c
No. 8T251 Price, 5-lb. package......27c
No. 8T252 Price, 10-lb. package......45c
No. 8T253 Price, 25-lb. package......96c
No. 8T254 Price, 100-lb. bag......$3.25
No. 8T255 Price, 180-lb. bbl......$5.40
All sizes unmailable.

PETROLEUM JELLY.

One of the most valuable and also the most harmless and simple articles to have at hand in cases of bruises, cuts, burns, chaps, roughness of the skin, etc. Should be in every home.

No. 8T257 Price, 4-oz. glass jar......7c
No. 8T258 Price, 1-lb. can......17c
Postage extra, each, small, 8 cents; large, 20 cents.

CARBOLIZED PETROLEUM JELLY.

This is the same as the above, with the addition of 3 per cent pure carbolic acid which increases to a great extent its powers of healing.

No. 8T259 Price, 4-ounce bottle......7c
No. 8T260 Price, 1-pound can......17c
Postage extra, each, small, 8 cents; large, 20 cents.

IDEAL EGG PRESERVER.

One of the best and most effective means for preserving eggs for an almost indefinite period of time.

Carefully conducted experiments have shown that the Ideal Egg Preserver is practically the only egg preserver today that will accomplish all that can reasonably be expected from a preparation of this kind.

Ideal Egg Preserver is supplied in gallon jugs; this quantity is sufficient for the preserving of forty to fifty dozen of eggs. Complete directions furnished with each gallon of the preservative.

No. 8T262 Price, per gallon...(Unmailable)...75c

BEDBUG EXTERMINATOR.

Note—This product is entirely different from what we have heretofore been handling, in being more effective and absolutely non-inflammable. Does not contain kerosene, benzine, turpentine or other inflammable solvents like other less expensive products. Do you want the best? This preparation is in liquid form and furnished in a patent can with large spout, which makes its application easy and sure to reach the smallest opening. Bedbug Exterminator will not only exterminate every bedbug and roach, but rid a room or building of these little pests entirely. Full directions with each can. Unmailable.

No. 8T264 Price, ½-pint can......$0.17
No. 8T265 Price, one pint......28
No. 8T266 Price, one gallon......1.90

LEININGER'S FORMALDEHYDE INHALER.

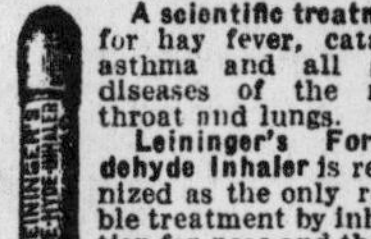

A scientific treatment. for hay fever, catarrh, asthma and all germ diseases of the nose, throat and lungs.

Leininger's Formaldehyde Inhaler is recognized as the only reliable treatment by inhalation for nose and throat. If you are a sufferer from hay fever and catarrh and so far have been unable to obtain relief, try Leininger's Formaldehyde Inhaler, which has proved so satisfactory.

No. 8T268 Price...17c
If mail shipment, postage extra, 2 cents.

CHINA CEMENT.

China Cement. The best cement for mending glass, china, ivory, shell, marble, fur, terra cotta, meerschaum, porcelain, plaster of paris, wool, alabaster and leather. Does the work well and quickly.

No. 8T270 Price, ½-ounce bottle, per bottle......9c
If mail shipment, postage and tube extra, 8 cents.

Thompson's Wild Cherry Phosphate.

A delicious beverage. For over seventeen years drank by millions the world over. Cheaper and easier made than lemonade. Rich cherry flavor, satisfying and refreshing. For daily use in the home and for parties, lodge socials, church fairs and the harvest field, nothing can equal it. Try it and you will never keep house without it.

No. 8T275 25-cent bottle (making fifty glasses.) Price. **17c**
Three bottles for........**45c**

Bromo Seltzer.

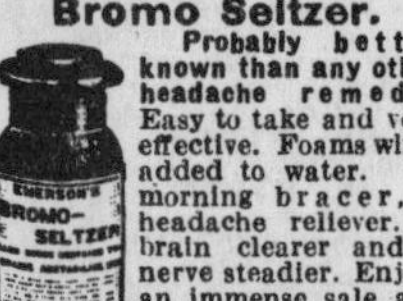

Probably better known than any other headache remedy. Easy to take and very effective. Foams when added to water. A morning bracer, a headache reliever, a brain clearer and a nerve steadier. Enjoys an immense sale and well known everywhere

No. 8T277
25-cent bottle. Our price..**20c**
No. 8T278 50-cent bottle. Our price........**40c**
No. 8T279 $1.00 bottle. Our price....(Unmailable).....**80c**

Chlorate of Potash Tablets.

Large pocket vial of pure snow white Chlorate Potash Tablets. Largely used for sore throat, hoarseness and throat irregularities.

No. 8T281
Price, per bottle..**9c**

Soda Mint Tablets.

A well known tablet for neutralizing the acidity of the stomach. Composed of sodium bicarbonate, ammonium carbonate and oil peppermint. Fine for that acid feeling and sour stomach.

No. 8T282 Price, per bottle........**9c**

Pepsin and Charcoal Tablets.

A fine stomach tablet. Pepsin aids the digestion, and the charcoal absorbs the gases and makes the stomach sweet and pure. Give these tablets a trial.

No. 8T283
Price, per bottle..**9c**

Herb Laxative Tea.

Good for old and young. Composed of roots and herbs long used for their beneficial effect in thoroughly cleansing the system and bowels of all unclean matter. They purify the blood and the person thereby becomes greatly improved in health. Made from American saffron, elder flowers, senna leaves, fennel seed, licorice root, anise seed and couch grass, all well known for their tonic and blood purifying effect. The tea made from this remedy is pleasant to take and will benefit you.

No. 8T285 25-cent package. Our price..........**9c**
If by mail, postage extra, 2 cents

Honey and Tar Cough Syrup.

A fine cough syrup for children. Made from harmless ingredients, pleasant to the taste, easily taken and very effective. An ideal cough syrup for the home. A good cough syrup is a household necessity, especially where there are children. Coughs usually come quickly, and the sooner they are treated the better. This syrup keeps indefinitely and you should always keep a bottle for ready use when needed.

No. 8T287 25-cent bottle. Our price....(Unmailable).**19c**

Stop That Cough!

Bronchial Tablets will check it. They are a pleasant tasting tablet for dissolving in the mouth. Harmless, pleasant and effective. Always keep them in the home.

No. 8T291 Price......**8c**
Postage extra 2 cents.

White Camphorated Liniment.

Every home needs a good household liniment for sprains, rheumatic pains, bruises, swellings, lame back, contracted muscles, stiffness of the neck and joints and other common everyday pain. This remedy is very good, white in color, penetrating and healing and will be found most beneficial on all occasions where a remedy of this kind is required. Once tried, will make a place for itself in every home.

No. 8T289 25-cent bottle. Our price........**19c**
Unmailable.

Granular Effervescent Salts.

SODIUM PHOSPHATE.

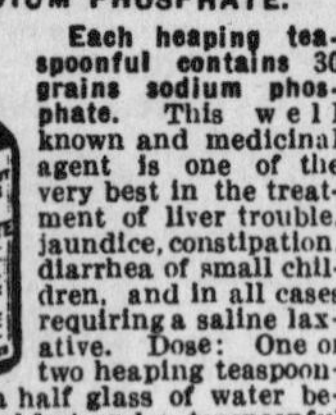

Each heaping teaspoonful contains 30 grains sodium phosphate. This well known and medicinal agent is one of the very best in the treatment of liver trouble, jaundice, constipation, diarrhea of small children, and in all cases requiring a saline laxative. Dose: One or two heaping teaspoonfuls in a half glass of water before breakfast and a teaspoonful before dinner, if necessary.

No. 8T293 Price, 4-ounce bottle........**19c**
No. 8T294 Price, 1-pound bottle........**50c**
Unmailable on account of weight.

Kissingen Salts.

Each heaping teaspoonful dissolved in half a tumblerful of water forms a refreshing and agreeable draft, identical with the natural water. Very beneficial as a table water in all cases of gout and liver derangement, and highly recommended in daily alternation with Vichy by Dr. Wm. T. Cathell, of Baltimore, for the successful treatment of obesity. Full directions on package.

No. 8T295 Price, 4-ounce bottle........**19c**
No. 8T296 Price, 1-pound bottle........**50c**
Unmailable on account of weight.

Vichy Salts.

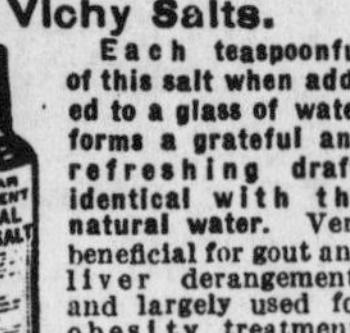

Each teaspoonful of this salt when added to a glass of water forms a grateful and refreshing draft, identical with the natural water. Very beneficial for gout and liver derangements and largely used for obesity treatment. Full directions in package.

No. 8T297 Price, 4-ounce bottle........**19c**
No. 8T298 Price, 1-pound bottle........**50c**

Laxative Lithia.

A very reliable effervescent salt for rheumatism, gout, neurasthenia, gravel, cystitis and other similar affections. Each dessertspoonful contains potassium citrate 30 grains, sodium phosphate 30 grains, and lithium citrate 5 grains. A fine laxative, refrigerant, diuretic and antacid.

No. 8T299 Price, 4-ounce bottle........**23c**
No. 8T300 Price, 1-pound bottle........**69c**
Unmailable on account of weight.

Effervescent Lithia Tablets.

Lithia Salts have for years been recognized as one of the standard remedies for the treatment of subacute and chronic rheumatism, gout, uric acid, irritable bladder and kidney affections depending upon an excess of uric acid in the system. Lithia Tablets are absolutely pure, convenient and accurate in dosage and possess many advantages not embraced by other forms of administration. One tablet dissolved in a glass of water makes a very agreeable, refreshing and beneficial effervescing draft.

No. 8T301 Price, per bottle, 3-grain tablets, 40 in bottle........**17c**
No. 8T302 Price, per bottle, 5-grain tablets, 40 in bottle........**23c**
Postage extra, 15 cents.

Effervescent Magnesium Citrate.

A largely used and well known cathartic. On account of its agreeable taste and foaming property, it is much more acceptable than Epsom salts. Prompt in action. Put up in 12-ounce bottles.

No. 8T303
Price........**19c**
Unmailable.

Rock Candy.

An absolutely pure sugar for the making of home cough syrups and remedies. Too well known to need description.

No. 8T305 String Rock Candy, 5-pound box. Price..**52c**
No. 8T306 Crystal Rock Candy, 1-pound carton. Price........**13c**
No. 8T307 Crystal Rock Candy, ½-pound carton. Price........**7c**

Blackberry Balsam.

A pleasant, safe and largely used home remedy for diarrhea, looseness of the bowels and summer complaints of children, cramps, griping pains, sour stomach and for minor bowel affections. Very agreeable to the taste and can be given alike to children and adults. Should be in every home.

No. 8T310 Price......**23c**

Laxative Cold Tablets.

A very good household tablet for all kinds of fresh colds. They are the same kind of tablets doctors use for this purpose as they not only check the cold but, possessing laxative effect, gently move the bowels as well. Colds come quickly and you should always have a reliable cold tablet in the home. One or two doses at the very start may save a doctor bill and check the cold before it gets any worse. Promptness is the important thing. Each tablet is sugar coated which makes them pleasant to take and they keep indefinitely.

No. 8T312 Price....**13c**
If by mail, postage extra, 2 cents.

Nasal Tablets.

Dr. Seiler's Formula.

The well known, long used formula of Dr. Carl Seiler. It represents probably the best known formula for dissolving in water to use as an antiseptic cleansing spray for catarrh, nasal and throat troubles, etc. They are used by physicians everywhere and are very effective as a cleansing spray and for freeing the parts of all mucus discharges and for rendering the parts antiseptic and cleanly. One tablet should be dissolved in 2 ounces of warm water and used in an atomizer. The fact that they are used by physicians the country over and in large quantities would seem to prove that they are a very satisfactory medicine for the conditions for which they are recommended. Packed 40 tablets to bottle.

No. 8T314 Price....**21c**
If by mail, postage extra, 3 cents.

Listerine.

Now recognized as a household antiseptic. Pleasant to the taste, clear in color and finds a hundred uses in the home. Largely employed as a tooth wash, gargle for sore throat, an antiseptic spray or wherever a reliable pleasant antiseptic is required. (Unmailable.)

No. 8T315 Large $1.00 bottle. Our price........**79c**
No. 8T316 25-cent size bottle. Our price........**19c**
(Unmailable.)

A Reliable Corn Remedy.

Every person suffering with corns is anxious for a reliable corn remedy. We believe this one of the very best preparations and ask you to give it a trial. Easy to apply, stops the soreness and will take out the corn. Your money back if not satisfactory.

No. 8T318
Price........**9c**

Wine of Cod Liver Oil Compound.

A pleasant, palatable liquid preparation containing the active principles of cod liver oil together with hypophosphites and cherry bark. It represents the active medicinal principles of the oil but avoiding its nauseating effect. It is preferred by many to plain cod liver oil and at the same time admits of combining with it the best tonic tissue and blood builders, making it an ideal tonic for the conditions for which it is indicated. It is undoubtedly very valuable for all debilitated and wasting conditions, for chronic coughs, blood disorders, and is a general strengthener for the entire system. Its pleasant taste makes it very palatable and we know you will like and relish it. It is quickly assimilated, taken up by the system, and gives very satisfactory results.

No. 8T320 Regular price per 12-ounce bottle, $1.00; our price........**67c**
Unmailable on account of weight.

Earache Drops.

A few drops on a piece of medicated cotton and inserted into the ear will relieve earache in a comparatively short time. Free from chloral hydrate and other harmful substances and will pass all pure food and drug requirements. Earache drops are penetrating, healing, soothing and emollient.

No. 8T322 Price, 2-dram vials........**16c**
If mail shipment, postage extra, 2 cents.

Liquid Skin.

A fine liquid court plaster preparation to be used for all cuts, bruises and abrasions. Acts instantaneously. Better, cheaper and quicker than any other antiseptic bandage, court plaster or other method usually applied for stopping loss of blood in any open, bleeding wound. Can be applied in a few seconds, forming at once a new skin over the cut, bruise or abrasion, protecting the wound from all foreign matter and healing it without a moment's delay or danger. No person should be without this valuable yet inexpensive remedy. It may save your life or that of your friends almost any day. Put up neatly in small vials, so it can be carried in the vest pocket ready for immediate use.

No. 8T324 Price, vest pocket size........**8c**
If mail shipment, postage extra, 3 cents.

Carron Oil for Burns.

One of the household remedies that ought to be ordered by every housewife and kept on hand ready for immediate use. The safest and most reliable treatment for fresh burns of every description. It stops the pain and smarting at once, prevents inflammation when used without delay, and in case where the inflammation has started, it will reduce it quickly, healing the burns in the shortest possible time. Complete directions with each package.

No. 8T325 Price, 4-ounce bottle........**9c**

Insect Powder.

A true Dalmatian Insect Powder, warranted free from all adulterations. Fresh and strong. Sure death to bedbugs, croton bugs, cockroaches, fleas, lice, moths, flies, ants and all insects. This article is very much subject to adulteration. Buy from us and get it pure.

No. 8T330 Price, ¼-pound carton........**13c**
No. 8T331 Price, 1-pound carton........**31c**
(Unmailable.)

Insect Powder Gun.

For using insect powder.

No. 8T332
Price..........**5c**
If mail shipment, postage extra, 4 cents.

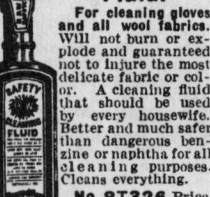

Large or Jumbo Powder Gun, holds ¼-pound of powder; button and spout screw off. Large opening for filling.

No. 8T333 Price.....**16c**
Postage extra, 6 cents.

Safety Cleaning Fluid.

For cleaning gloves and all wool fabrics. Will not burn or explode and guaranteed not to injure the most delicate fabric or color. A cleaning fluid that should be used by every housewife. Better and much safer than dangerous benzine or naphtha for all cleaning purposes. Cleans everything.

No. 8T326 Price, 8-ounce bottle...**17c**
Unmailable.

New Seroco Fast and Stainless Dyes.

DYES EVENLY COTTON, WOOL, SILK AND MIXED GOODS, ALL IN THE SAME BATH.

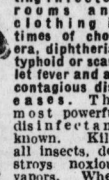

No more trouble with dyeing cotton and wool goods separately, as by means of the new Seroco Dyes it can all be performed together and an even color be obtained.

The best and most satisfactory dyes as well as the simplest to color, of any dyes ever offered to a customer. Simple and easy to use, produce bright fadeless colors and will not stain the hands or the container. Will color from one to six pounds of goods according to the shade desired.

The New Seroco Fast and Stainless Dyes can be successfully used for coloring dress goods, coats, carpet rags, ribbons, feathers, yarns, silk fabrics, grass and basket material, moss, and in general for coloring all forms of material. Furnished in the following beautiful shades: Pink, wine, orange, cardinal, heliotrope, myrtle green, pale blue, seal brown, cerise, lemon, brown, old rose, light green, navy blue, royal purple, tan, yellow, drab, olive green, turkey red, black, emerald green, royal blue, salmon. A direction booklet is furnished free with each package of dye. In it is contained a fund of valuable information, including general directions, detection of cotton from wool or mixed goods, cleaning goods before dyeing, using the dye, preparing the goods, preparing the dye bath, boiling, various shades of color, ripping the goods, drying, pressing, dyeing light shades, etc., and ending with a complete list of colors produced by dyeing over various shades of cloth. Be sure to state color wanted.

No. 8T327 Regular 10c package, our price........**8c**
Postage extra, 2 cents.

The Celebrated Dry Powder Fire Fighters.

The Fire Fighter is a dry powder fire extinguisher, put up for use in a metallic tube 22 inches long and 2 inches in diameter. One end of the tube is fitted with a cover, held in place by natural tension and fitted with a ring by which the tube is hung from a strong hook, attached for this purpose to a wall, column, door, or window frame. By grasping the tube firmly and jerking it, it will immediately be released from the cover, which remains hanging on the hook, leaving the tube open at the upper end and its contents free for immediate use. The dry powder is thrown into the fire by a sweeping motion in accordance with complete instructions furnished with each Fire Fighter. Anyone, even children, can use a Fire Fighter with perfect safety and never failing success. It will extinguish the fire, not in five minutes nor ten minutes, but instantaneously by blotting it out in a few seconds after proper application of the dry powder has been made.

No. 8T329 Fire Fighters, retailing everywhere at $3.00 each; our price........**$0.59**
3 for (Not mailable)..**1.50**

Rat Killer.

The Great Vermin Destroyer.

An efficient poison for rats, mice, cockroaches, ants, flies, squirrels, crows, bedbugs, and all kinds of troublesome vermin. This is a sure destroyer. Rats and mice do not die in the house after eating it, but go outside for air and water.

No. 8T334 Price.....**8c**
This article, being poisonous, cannot be sent through the mail.

Ratnip.

Without doubt the greatest rat exterminator ever produced. Guaranteed free from arsenic, phosphorus and strychnine. The only effective rat exterminator which is not dangerous to human beings or to dogs, cats or other animals if taken accidentally in small quantities. A clean, agreeable smelling preparation made in the form of a squash seed, the rat's favorite food. It sure bears out the claim, "Sure death to rats." If you want the best, buy this.

No. 8T335 Price.....**19c**

Sulphur Candles.

For fumigating infected rooms and clothing in times of cholera, diphtheria, typhoid or scarlet fever and all contagious diseases. The most powerful disinfectant known. Kills all insects, destroys noxious vapors. When you wish to fumigate with sulphur, use these; no danger of fire, easily lighted, burn steadily. A most convenient article to have.

No. 8T337 Price.....**8c**
If by mail, postage extra, 5 cents.

High Grade Medicinal Plasters at Popular Prices.

Celebrated Johnson & Johnson's Belladonna Plaster. Probably the best known and largest used belladonna plaster on the market. Largely used for local sprains, strains, etc. Sold by druggists everywhere at 25 cents each.

No. 8T340 Our price, **13c**
Postage extra, 2 cents.

Johnson & Johnson's Belladonna and Capsicum Plaster. Same uses as the Belladonna Plaster but combines the heating action of the capsicum. Sold by druggists everywhere at 25 cents each.

No. 8T341 Our price, **13c**
If by mail, postage extra, 2 cents.

Strengthening Plaster. Largely used for sprains, colds, etc. A warming plaster.

No. 8T344 Price.....**9c**
If by mail, postage extra, 2 cents.

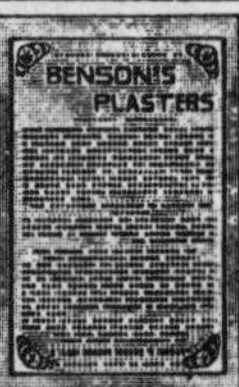

Celebrated Seabury & Johnson Benson's Plaster. For over twenty-five years the leading and best example of this form of external treatment. A great remedy for pain. Sold by druggists everywhere at 25 cents each.

No. 8T343 Our price..**9c**
If by mail, postage extra, 2 cents.

Celebrated Blue Jay Corn Plaster. The one plaster that is guaranteed to remove a corn or relieve a bunion. Made of soft fine grade blue felt with non-irritating adhesive tape for attaching to the toe. Your money back if they do not remove the corn. Seven before sold for less than 10 cents.

No. 8T346 Our price..**7c**
If by mail, postage extra, 1 cent.

Sanitary Metal Medicine Cabinet.

Built on sanitary principles and steel construction throughout. Does not soak up spilled medicines, easily cleansed and kept antiseptic. Beautiful heavy beveled 9x12-inch mirror in door. Brass hinges and of artistic design. Has three shelves for bottles. Height over all, 26 inches; depth, 6 inches; width, 17 inches. Weight, without crating, 25 pounds. Furnished in either oxidized or white enamel finish. **State finish desired.** A handsome, inexpensive and up to date cabinet.

No. 8T4030 Price........**$4.39**

Family Medicine Cabinets.

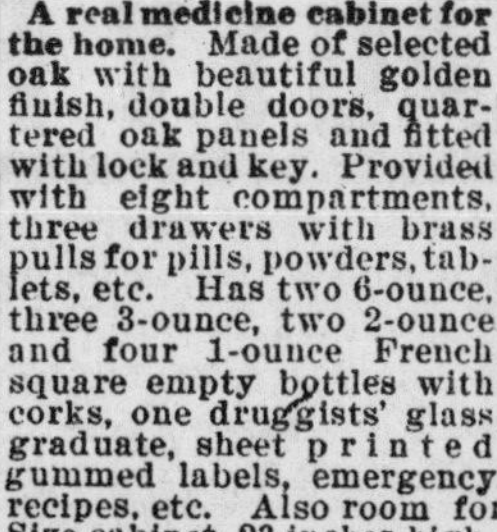

A real medicine cabinet for the home. Made of selected oak with beautiful golden finish, double doors, quartered oak panels and fitted with lock and key. Provided with eight compartments, three drawers with brass pulls for pills, powders, tablets, etc. Has two 6-ounce, three 3-ounce, two 2-ounce and four 1-ounce French square empty bottles with corks, one druggists' glass graduate, sheet printed gummed labels, emergency recipes, etc. Also room for thirty additional bottles if required. Size cabinet, 23 inches high, 21 inches wide and 6 inches deep. No mother can afford to take chances of serious errors by keeping family medicines and dangerous drugs in the cupboard, pantry or closet. Keep them in the proper cabinet and they will always be ready when wanted. Weight, about 30 pounds.

No. 8T4031 Price..............................**$4.50**

The same cabinet as above, but with beautiful 6x14-inch heavy French bevel plate mirror in each door.

No. 8T4032 Price..............................**$5.50**

Electric Sparkler Torches.

A Harmless Firework of Today. Beautiful in Appearance, Odorless and Absolutely Harmless.

For street parades, Fourth of July celebrations, picnics, lawn parties, coach parties, theatrical performances, lodge work and for all indoor and outdoor celebrations and illuminations. These torches fill the air with showers of sparkling golden stars and produce for a long time a brilliant and dazzling illumination of all surrounding objects, making a beautiful and lasting display. These are the new fireworks approved by everyone and far superior to the old kinds, which cause injury, danger and fires, **to say nothing of the loss of life itself. After once using these torches you would never use the old form of fireworks.**

Twelve-inch Sparkler Torches, burning three minutes each, packed twelve torches in neat box, with 12-inch wooden handle for holding.

No. 8T4046 Price.....**43c**
Unmailable on account of weight.

Twenty-one-inch Sparkler Torches, guaranteed to burn six minutes each, packed six to the box, with 18-inch wooden handle for holding.

No. 8T4047 Price, per box.........(Unmailable)......**43c**

INSECTICIDES

Arsenate of Lead Paste.

For the destruction of the potato bug, codling moth and green bugs on rose bushes and all leaf eating insects. Far superior to Paris Green in that it will not wash off with ordinary rains, is not injurious if applied unskillfully or in too great quantities and will not burn the most delicate foliage. Arsenate of Lead can be successfully used for killing all leaf eating insects, including the potato bug, codling moth, canker worm, green bugs on rose bushes, elm leaf beetle, gypsy and brown tailed moth, etc. A very effective article. Full directions on can.

No. 8T2010	Price, 1-lb. jar...$	0.19
No. 8T2011	Price, 2-lb. jar..	.36
No. 8T2012	Price, 5-lb. pail..	.89
No. 8T2013	Price, 12½-lb. pail	2.00
No. 8T2014	Price, 100-lb. keg.	14.25

Paris Green, Powder Form.

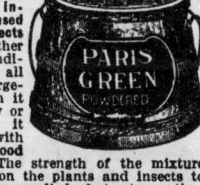

Paris Green is recognized as one of the most important insecticides and is used for destroying insects of all kinds, either in wet or dry conditions, but in all cases it is first largely diluted. When it is used in the dry or powder form, it should be mixed with plaster, sifted wood ashes or flour. The strength of the mixture should depend upon the plants and insects to which it is to be applied, but at no time should more than 1 pound of Paris Green be added to 50 pounds of mixture, as that is usually sufficient. Care should be taken when using Paris Green mixed with water that the liquid is constantly stirred up when it is used for spraying, as otherwise the Paris Green will settle and the last quantity in the bottom of the cask will be so strong as to be liable to do serious damage.

No. 8T2002 Price, per pound......**28c**
No. 8T2003 Price, per 2-pound package.............................**54c**
No. 8T2004 Price, per 5-pound package.............................**$1.35**
No. 8T2005 Price, per 14-pound kit...............................**$3.78**
No. 8T2006 Price, per 100-pound keg.................................**$26.00**

The above prices are subject to market changes.

Bordeaux Mixture.

Endorsed by leading Agricultural Experiment Stations as a reliable and superior preparation in every respect. Compounded from an old formula, but by a new process, making a usable and practical mixture, and by simply adding water and stirring it is ready for use. Destroys all fungus growth on vegetation, prevents blight, rot, mildew and rust. Should be diluted fifty times with water before using. Actual cost of spray less than 1 cent per gallon. Use little or much, remainder is always ready for use. The only Bordeaux Mixture that has stood the test of years. Do not waste your time and money on cheap and worthless products. The easiest man convinced is the one who has seen the results of spraying on his neighbor's potatoes, grape or cucumber vines. The results are very profitable. Being in concentrated paste form, it is much better and stronger than weaker solutions. Full directions on packages. **You cannot afford to be without it.**

No. 8T2025 Price, per 2-lb. jar....**25c**
No. 8T2026 Price, per 10-lb. pail..**95c**
No. 8T2027 Price, per 45-lb. pail (approximately 5 gallons)..........**$4.00**

QUICK DEATH BUG KILLER AND FERTILIZER.

INSURE YOUR CROPS AGAINST LOSS.

Absolute death to all insect life; cheaper than any other insecticide known; a good fertilizer; any child can apply it; not dangerous to handle; ready for immediate use; no mixing nor preparation required.

Quick Death is a whirlwind of destruction to potato bugs and at the same time fertilizes and invigorates the plants. This means that if you use Quick Death your potato vines will be green and growing days after those of your neighbors are dead.

Quick Death will positively kill potato bugs, squash bugs, pumpkin bugs, watermelon bugs, rose bugs, currant worms, cabbage worms, and all others of the same nature eating the leaves of vegetables or plants. **Quick Death** has been on the market for nine years, during which time it has met with unprecedented success wherever introduced all over the United States. It has proved to be the most successful destroyer of all insects, bugs or beetles that live on vegetation. We can recommend this preparation to our customers with every confidence, we can assure them it is a better and cheaper insect powder than they have ever used and it operates with certainty.

A GOOD CROP OF POTATOES, CABBAGE,

or any other vegetable cannot be obtained, no matter how good your soil and seeds may be, or how favorable the weather, or how much labor or care you expend on them, unless the vines and leaves are kept vigorous and healthy. Such a condition cannot be kept up unless all insects and bugs are destroyed as fast as they appear. Any cause that injures the leaves hurts the plants, and anything that destroys the foliage affects the roots also and poisons the crops. Nothing, therefore, is more necessary than that the growing vines and trees be kept free from the ravages of insects and bugs. Remember that every dollar invested in Quick Death may perhaps mean fifty times that amount in increased profit when the crop is harvested.

QUICK DEATH KILLS POTATO BUGS IMMEDIATELY.

The potato bug is the greatest enemy the potato grower has. This bug eats the leaves off the plants. He is fitted with powerful upper and under jaws and works the greatest ravages in a field of potatoes. **Quick Death** sprinkled on the leaves kills him with neatness and dispatch. Three crops of eggs are laid each year. Prompt action is therefore necessary. **Just as soon as the potato bug makes his appearance, dust the potato vines thoroughly and carefully with Quick Death and your plants are safe from destruction.** Kill off the first arrivals and you will have no further trouble, pursuing the same course in the case of other bugs and insects. Dust the leaves of the plants as soon as there is the slightest indication of their presence and save your crop from destruction.

THE WAY TO APPLY QUICK DEATH.

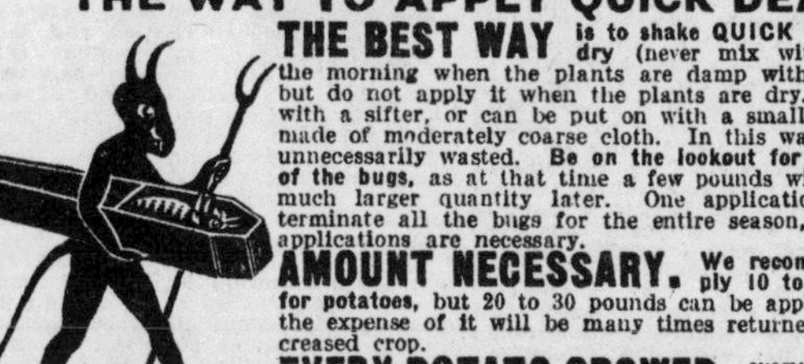

THE BEST WAY is to shake QUICK DEATH on the vine dry (never mix with water), early in the morning when the plants are damp with dew, or otherwise, but do not apply it when the plants are dry. It can be applied with a sifter, or can be put on with a small burlap bag or sack made of moderately coarse cloth. In this way the powder is not unnecessarily wasted. **Be on the lookout for the first appearance of the bugs,** as at that time a few pounds will do the work of a much larger quantity later. One application will usually exterminate all the bugs for the entire season, but sometimes two applications are necessary.

AMOUNT NECESSARY. We recommend that you apply 10 to 15 pounds per acre for potatoes, but 20 to 30 pounds can be applied with safety and the expense of it will be many times returned in the greatly increased crop.

EVERY POTATO GROWER, every cabbage grower, every farmer, every market gardener, every grower of roses and flowers and plants of any kind should give **QUICK DEATH** a fair trial. If it is once used, it will always be used. **DO NOT FAIL TO GIVE IT A TRIAL.**

SPECIAL PRICES:

No. 8T2035	Quick Death.	Per 5-pound package..	$0.22
No. 8T2036	Quick Death.	Per 10-pound package..	.41
No. 8T2037	Quick Death.	Per 25-pound package..	.89
No. 8T2038	Quick Death.	Per 50-pound package..	1.69
No. 8T2039	Quick Death.	Per 100-pound package..	3.20
No. 8T2040	Quick Death.	Per 300-pound barrel...	8.45

Lime-Sulphur Solution.

Used by thousands of fruit growers and recommended by all the leading experimental stations. Millions of fruit trees are being destroyed annually by the San Jose scale and millions of others are infested with it and are the breeding places for others. Always ready for use by simply adding water. Use what you want out of can; balance good at any time. Trees should be sprayed first time in March or April and a few weeks later go over them a second time to be sure every part is covered. Reasonable in price, effective in results, keeps permanently. **You cannot afford to be without it.**

No. 8T2015 Price, per gallon can.**$0.60**
No. 8T2016 Price, per 5-gal. can **2.50**
No. 8T2017 Price, 25-gal. barrel. **7.65**

SEE WHAT OUR WALL PAPER PAGES SAY. Don't Fail to Read Them.

Fly Spray.

A reliable preparation for keeping the flies off horses, cattle and for general use in stables, barns, corrals, stock yards, dairies, etc., and as a spray for flies, gnats, mosquitoes or other insect pests. A liquid preparation to be merely sprayed over the stock during the summer months for keeping them free from flies and is guaranteed to produce this result for twenty-four hours after spraying. It pays for its use a hundred times and a single gallon is sufficent to keep flies off of twenty head of cattle and horses a month. Saves a great amount of energy in the animal and we suggest that you give it a trial. Thousands of gallons sold last year. Non-sticky, non-irritating, easy to apply, non-poisonous and a preparation that keeps indefinitely. It is better than a fly net for your stock and far more economical and lasting. If you once try this product, you will always have it on hand. Can also be used as general stable disinfectant and purifier and as such cannot be beaten. Regular price, per gallon, $1.50. Include a can in your next order.

No. 8T1323 Price, per gallon can..**95c**
Unmailable.

Daisy Fly Killer.

The cleanest, best and most effective fly killer known. It is a beauty. Made of tin, beautifully lithographed with daisies in colors attracting the flies and they drink the poison through the small sponge in the center of each daisy. Will not injure nor soil anything. Will effectually kill flies in a room. Will last all season. It is cheaper than fly paper, clean, neat, ornamental. **Try it.**

Harmless to Persons.

No. 8T910 Price, each..........**$0.14**
Per dozen...........................**1.50**
If mail shipment, postage extra, 4 cents.

Sticky Fly Paper.

We guarantee absolutely that STICKY will catch flies all the time. It will bear exposure and remain in a fly catching condition indefinitely. Having stuck them, it holds them there. They cannot pull away. **It will not granulate nor dry up.**

No. 8T912 Packed 25 double sheets to carton. Regular price, 75 cents.
Our price, per carton...................................**34c**

Poison Fly Paper.

Four large 5-cent packages of Poison Fly Paper, each package containing eight sheets. The best brand made.

No. 8T7131 Price, 4 envelopes for.............**7c**

Insecticide Sifter.

The illustration here shown represents the insecticide Sifter with which to apply the famous Quick Death and other dry powder insecticides. To obtain best results fill the sifter only about half full. This sifter is positively the best on the market. Patent applied for.

No. 8T2045 Insecticide Sifter, 2-quart size.
Price **29c**
Unmailable.

Liquid Formaldehyde Prevents Smut.

Recommended by the United States Government as preventive of smut in wheat, oats, barley and other grains and also of the potato scab.

Liquid Formaldehyde in full 40 per cent strength has now become so well known to the average farmer that it needs little description. It is so easy to apply, each pint being merely added to a barrel of water and the seed sprinkled before sowing, that there is no reason but what every farmer in the land should use it upon the seed before planting. Millions of dollars have been saved by farmers by treating their seed with Formaldehyde before sowing. The up to date farmer of today treats his seed in this manner before sowing, as it is now recognized to guarantee freedom from disease and largely increasing the size of the crops. Wheat, oats, corn, barley, tobacco, cotton, flax and potatoes are all subject to a certain destroying disease and for these Formaldehyde is the only certain cure. Remember, with every package we send you a pamphlet, "Usefulness of Liquid Formaldehyde on the Farm," giving various uses and dilutions necessary for best results. Don't fail to include a bottle in your next order.

Liquid Formaldehyde is also a standard household disinfectant for the sick room or wherever a reliable antiseptic is required.

No. 8T1999	Price, 400-lb. barrel.	$40.00
No. 8T1998	Price, 125-lb. keg..	15.00
No. 8T1997	Price, 60-lb. keg...	9.00
No. 8T1996	Price, 1 gallon......	1.25
No. 8T1995	Price, 1 pint.......	.33

Unmailable on acount of weight.

TOILET AND BEAUTY PRODUCTS

The list of toilet and beauty products shown on these pages comprises in our opinion by far the finest list of high grade articles ever shown or ever sold. A few represent the masterpieces of the finest perfume and toilet makers of Paris, France, and the remainder the best produced in our own country. Any product we know will be satisfactory, as they have all been sold the country over for years, are well known and standard everywhere and represent in every case the best made for the purpose for which they are used. Not the cheapest but the best, and in toilet and beauty products it pays to buy the best.

DR. C. H. BERRY'S FRECKLE OINTMENT.

For the Removal of Freckles, Moth Patches, Muddy Complexion or Discolorations of the Skin.

Three freckles can make any woman forget that beauty is only skin deep. Standards of beauty in the matter of features or form differ. There is little difference of opinion in the matter of complexion. Only those endowed by nature with bewitching clear and delicate skins are affected by that great enemy of beauty, freckles. Nothing so mars a woman's beauty and it is absolutely impossible for any lady to have a real pretty face, a complexion the envy of her friends, if her face is covered with freckles. Outdoor exercise is always productive of freckles and it is highly essential that a reliable remedy be always kept on hand. Artificial means are often used to cover up defects of face and form, but heavy blotches and freckles cannot be concealed. Dr. Berry's Freckle Ointment does not cover them. It completely removes every trace of the discoloration, leaving the skin pure, white and delicate.

Dr. Berry's Freckle Ointment is an exquisitely dainty preparation in the form of a fragrant snow white cream and is easily and quickly applied. No massage is necessary. For nearly fifteen years it has been the standard of all freckle ointments in America and in all that time it has not to our knowledge injured the most delicate skin, but has given the most universal satisfaction. Try it after all else has failed and be benefited. Satisfaction guaranteed or your money back. $1.00 jar. Sufficient for the most obstinate cases.

No. 8T3073 Large $1.00 jar. Our price........................**77c**
If mail shipment, postage extra, 20 cents.

FLORAL MASSAGE CREAM.

Promotes Facial Attractiveness Through Cleanliness.

Do you wish your skin to look as soft as a baby's and have it as soft as it looks? Then buy a jar of Floral Massage Cream and cleanse and beautify the face. Mothers and fathers use it to look as fresh as their children and the daughters and sons to retain their fresh youthful appearance. Nature never intended that a person's beauty and freshness should depart with youth, and it will not if you keep the skin of your face and neck healthy, the flesh firm, the muscles plastic and the blood circulation free and active. There are many things that cannot be removed with soap and water—wrinkles, accumulations of waste matter in the skin, blackheads, pore dirt that ends in facial blemishes, etc. There is only one way to get rid of them, and that is by massaging with some good massage cream. Do it at your home. Rub Floral Massage Cream into the pores (it is quickly absorbed) and then rub it out again. You will be agreeably surprised. It carries with it all the pore dirt and waste matter, leaving the skin absolutely clean and with the healthy glow of youth that all persons desire. There is no mystery, no magic about it; the effects of Floral Massage Cream are based simply on plain common sense, and it is used in massage for removal of wrinkles, for making the cheeks, neck and bust plump, full and healthy; to bring back the color of youth, cleanse and beautify the face and remove the telltale marks of time. Wrinkles and crow's feet are driven away, sallowness vanishes, angles are rounded and double chins reduced by its use.

Floral Massage Cream is a preparation that should appeal to all ladies of refinement who are particular regarding their appearance and many prefer it to the oily massage creams so common today. It is just as necessary an adjunct to the dressing table as a bottle of fine perfume, just as important to the toilet as a tooth brush. It brings fresh bloom to faded faces; and is indeed a very necessary toilet article. Fine illustrated booklet giving directions and full information on massage accompanies each package. Shipping weight, small jar, 14 ounces.

No. 8T3110 Regular 2-ounce jar. Price........................**33c**

No. 8T3111 Large jar, holds more than three times the quantity of the smaller. Price..........**67c**

DEPILATORY PREPARATIONS.

The greatest drawback to perfect loveliness in woman is the superfluous unnatural growth of hair where nature never intended it. The prettiest face is marred or disfigured by hair on the lips, cheeks or chin. Depilatory products are used for removing these superfluous growths, and by following the directions accompanying the package every particle of hair on the face, neck or arms can be removed without the least irritation, and a perfectly clear, beautiful, smooth skin be assured. There are two kinds of depilatories on the market, namely, liquid and powder, differing in their method of application, but the final result, of course, being the same.

Toilet Liquid Depilatory.

A liquid applied to the part by means of a pellet of cotton and an orange wood stick which accompanies each package. The liquid is thoroughly rubbed on the part, allowed to remain for two or three minutes and then washed off, at which time the hair should be removed completely. Then thoroughly wash the part with plenty of warm water, dry and apply a good cold cream and no one will ever know you have been using a depilatory. Care must be used, however, not to allow the liquid to remain on the part too long, as it will surely irritate or injure the skin. If at any time you experience a burning sensation, the solution should be removed at once and the part thoroughly bathed with plenty of warm water, dried and cold cream applied, as irritation is apt to follow. It is for this reason that Foraline Depilatory Powder is so popular, as the length of time left on the part makes no difference and the final result is just as satisfactory. Regular price, per 1-ounce bottle Toilet Liquid Depilatory, $1.00.

No. 8T3105 Our price............**73c**
If mail shipment, postage extra, 12 cents.

Foraline Depilatory Powder.

Backed by the testimonials of the best physicians of the country as the best depilatory known. Used by them in all cases where it is desired to remove the hair, as in wounds, scalp cuts, etc. Will not irritate. Will always do as represented without trouble or irritation and is indeed a depilatory that can always be depended upon. Has been manufactured in Germany for twenty-five years and was eight years ago introduced in the United States with privilege of making in this country. It is a long tried product and enjoys today a wonderful sale in both this and foreign countries. The depilatory powder is merely mixed with water to form a paste, applied to the part from three to five minutes and then washed off, at which time the hair should be removed completely. We have seen it tried on so many cases and have known of many others, and we have yet to hear of a single complaint on this well known powder. This is truly remarkable considering a remedy of this kind, and we know if you want a depilatory you will make no mistake in selecting this one. Packed 3 ounces of powder in a fine tin box. Will keep indefinitely. Full directions accompany each package. Regular price, per box, $1.00.

No. 8T3106 Our price............**77c**
If mail shipment, postage extra, 5 cents.

WHITE LILY FACE LOTION.

The Reliable Face, Neck and Arm Whitener.

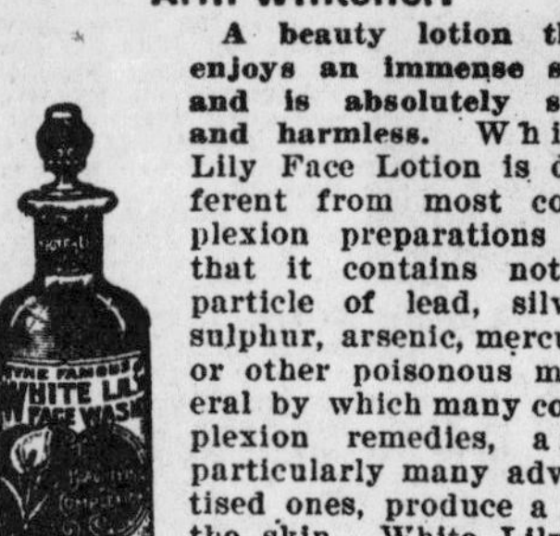

A beauty lotion that enjoys an immense sale and is absolutely safe and harmless. White Lily Face Lotion is different from most complexion preparations in that it contains not a particle of lead, silver, sulphur, arsenic, mercury or other poisonous mineral by which many complexion remedies, and particularly many advertised ones, produce a temporary smoothness and brilliancy of the skin. White Lily Face Lotion is clear and harmless as water, contains no poison, no sediment, nothing to hurt the most tender and delicate skin.

It is backed by the praise and highest testimonials of thousands of our customers and by their continued use. Its sale today is truly wonderful, but it only proves to us that an absolutely pure whitening beauty lotion is desired and truly appreciated.

The market is full of injurious beauty preparations containing corrosive sublimate, mercury preparations, etc., and are really dangerous in their effects. Run no risk in buying unknown remedies. You might ruin your complexion forever by using some poisonous face bleach. Run no risk, but buy the genuine White Lily Face Lotion, and you are sure to be safe.

If you want to use a beauty lotion, then send at once for White Lily Face Lotion; use it according to directions and we know we will have another added to our list of pleased customers. It is only truly appreciated by those giving it a trial. It is a luxury that no woman, old or young, should deny herself. Put up in 4-ounce bottles. Regular price, per bottle, 75 cents.

No. 8T3100 Our price, per bottle.... ....**47c**
If mail shipment, postage and tube extra, 14 cents.

DR. CHARLES FLESH FOOD

A Dainty, Sweet and Delicately Perfumed Toilet Luxury for Applying to the Skin to Heal, Nourish and Beautify.

Nourishes by Absorption. Dr. Charles' Flesh Food is not only a very well known but long used toilet preparation for massage use to clear the complexion, to remove wrinkles, round out thin cheeks and for developing bust, neck, shoulders and arms. It conforms to all laws of hygiene and is made on scientific principles, needs no expert to properly apply it and is so dainty and pleasing that its use is a delight.

Dr. Charles' Flesh Food has built up a very high class reputation as a fine massage ointment for rounding out and beautifying thin cheeks, shrunken chests, necks and arms. When applied to the skin it immediately begins its work of stimulating and nourishing impoverished tissues, and of refining the skin texture. Remember, old Father Time keeps plodding along and it is a duty every woman owes to herself and to her friends to develop to the fullest limit her attractive charms and to preserve as long as possible her clear, healthy, youthful 'appearance. Full directions for using accompany each package. Regular price, per box 50 cents.

No. 8T3088 Our price..**39c**
If mail shipment, postage extra, 6 cents.

"Most wonderful preparation in the world."—Dr. Monroe.
"Does more for my complexion and form than anything I have ever used."—Anna Held.

DR. CHARLES' FACE POWDER.

For the Complexion.

This exquisite powder is finely screened, delicately perfumed and reduced to the last degree of perfection. Not a trace of any deleterious substance is found in its composition. It can be used as freely as desired and will be found to have a soothing, cool and healing effect upon the irritated and roughened skin of women who have been exposed to the weather. It is indispensable in the nursery and can always be depended upon to heal baby's most delicate skin.

Should always be used after applying Flesh Food, as it leaves the skin in a much better condition and gives the face, neck and arms a softer and more delicate appearance. A single box will demonstrate its superiority and everyone who values a beautiful velvety skin should give it a trial. Furnished in white, flesh and brunette. **State color.** Regular price, per box, 50 cents.

No. 8T3089 Our price.. **37c**
If mail shipment, postage extra, 5 cents.

WOMEN! BE BEAUTIFUL

LET US SHOW YOU THE WAY.

IT IS SIMPLE WHEN YOU USE THE BEST BEAUTY PRODUCTS.

MRS. GERVAISE GRAHAM is probably as well known as any other woman in the world because of her famous beauty preparations and the wonderful good she has accomplished for women generally. Her love for the beautiful, her full appreciation of the help that beauty is to woman and her desire to aid in the accomplishment of such a power has not left her contented until she has perfected beauty products to accomplish this result, shown below, each of exceptional quality and purity. Her excellent preparations have been sold for over twenty years and are today the standard in every civilized country of the globe.

WHAT IS BEAUTY? Beauty is one of the greatest blessings that heaven has bestowed upon woman. Let no woman be ashamed of her love for the beautiful, for beauty is adorable, be it in landscape, picture, bird, flower or woman. God would never have filled this world so full of beauty if it were wrong to admire it. When beauty is of such infinite variety and form, let no woman despair of obtaining it in some degree. Among those we meet there are very few who are hopelessly homely.

KOSMEO BEAUTY CREAM.

THE FINEST OF TOILET CERATES AND UNLIKE ANY OTHER PREPARATION.

Kosmeo is valuable not only for the good it does, but for the harm it forestalls. It prevents roughness and chapping caused by harsh, cold and dusty winds. It prevents tan, sunburn and freckles, and should be used by every man, woman and child wherever the wind blows and the sun shines. No veil can afford half so much protection. Its daily use will keep the skin moist and pliable, thus preventing the fine wrinkles that always result from dryness of the skin. Kosmeo is soothing, cleansing and healing in the highest degree; it makes and keeps the flesh firm, the skin clear, soft, velvety, fine grained and close pored. It gives a clean, delicious, fresh feeling. Its use is not a task, but a delight. Its reward is not a distant promise, but is seen and felt instantly. It contains no mineral oils or animal fats and cannot promote a growth of superfluous hair. It is especially nice to use Kosmeo before applying face powder. When it is used the powder is absolutely invisible and remains longer on the face. Kosmeo, immediately allays irritation and consequently is an excellent thing for men to use after shaving. Regular price, 50 cents.

No. 8T3148 Our price..39c

If mail shipment, postage extra, 12 cents.

KOSMEO FACE POWDER.

A DAINTY, DELICATELY PERFUMED, REFINED FACE POWDER.

Kosmeo Face Powder will improve even the most beautiful complexion, and is invaluable to the woman who wishes to look her best. Not so many years ago powder was considered injurious to the complexion, and it was also considered bad form to use it, excepting on the stage; but both of these prejudices have passed away. A dainty touch of powder improves the appearance of almost every skin, and provided it is composed of soft, nonirritant and nonpoisonous materials, it does not harm the skin in the least. On the contrary, it is some protection from the weather. If a wholesome powder be used the sun will not burn nor the wind roughen the skin as much as if no powder were used. For a perfect protection from sun and wind the Kosmeo Cream should first be used, then the Kosmeo Powder, which is as soft, delicate and harmless as a rose leaf placed against the cheek; so wholesome, impalpable and dissolving in its nature that it cannot clog the pores, and thus cause pimples, comedones and the many other skin diseases that coarse, inferior powders are sure to do. It is prepared scientifically and carefully, and is the ne plus ultra of face powders. It removes the objectionable oily and shiny look so many ladies are troubled with; checks profuse perspiration and produces that rich and soft velvety appearance so seldom seen and so universally admired. It is adhesive and positively imperceptible when properly applied. Three shades, white, brunette or flesh. **State shade.** Regular price, per box, 50 cents.

No. 8T3178 Our price..39c

If mail shipment, postage extra, 5 cents.

HYGIENIC SKIN FOOD.

There are many skin foods (so called) upon the market, but not every concoction called skin food nourishes, feeds and builds up the wasted tissues of the skin. Mrs. Graham's celebrated Hygienic Skin Food is made of the finest materials and with the utmost care. The oils used are so digested and so changed by the process they undergo that they are no longer oils. The original conditions are lost, forming an amalgamated compound which feeds and nourishes the cellular glands and tissues, restoring flabby flesh and decayed muscles to a solid and firm condition. It has a wonderful effect in restoring a withered or wrinkled skin. It is used to make a thin face round and plump. It is the very best skin food on the market. Other manufacturers even try to duplicate it. Why, therefore, run any risk in buying an imitation product when we are able to offer you the genuine Gervaise Graham's Hygienic Skin Food, a $1.50 jar, for the special reduced price of $1.23 each?

No. 8T3150 Our price........(If mail shipment, postage extra, 16 cents)..........$1.23

Be Sure to Get the Genuine Quick Gray Hair Restorer.

RESTORES GRAY HAIR TO ITS ORIGINAL COLOR.

Many a man and woman has written these words, "Mrs. Graham's Quick Gray Hair Restorer makes me look ten years younger since I began its use." Gray hair gives the appearance of age. Even a younger face looks old if framed in gray, faded or lifeless looking hair. Mrs. Graham's Quick Gray Hair Restorer is absolutely harmless to the hair or health. It is easy to apply and it takes only a few days to restore to the natural color brown or black hair that is not more than half gray. It has no odor and is not oily or sticky. It makes the hair glossy and full of life. It works quietly, firmly and effectively. Its merits have made it a success. In the business world of today looks count a great deal. The person desiring a position must look young in appearance, healthy, vigorous and in the bloom of youth. Many are the cases where a man of middle age, with his hair turning gray, has been refused a position merely because the person employing thought him a man of much greater age. If he had only realized its importance and changed that gray or faded hair to its natural color he might have easily obtained the position, that on account of his looks, was refused him. Not only, therefore, from a business standpoint, but from a sincere desire to be helpful does Mrs. Graham urge upon all persons afflicted with gray or faded hair the use of her Gray Hair Restorer, so that they can obtain the relief that this preparation actually affords. Full directions accompany each package. Regular price, per bottle, $1.00.

No. 8T3155 Our price, per bottle..................(Unmailable.)...................73c

MRS. GRAHAM IS A BEAUTIFUL IDEAL.

Would you not feel certain that preparations have great merit if a woman who uses them lived and worked hard for twenty years without perceptibly aging and kept her contour girlish, her flesh firm, and maintained her beautiful, youthful complexion without a blemish and her skin without wrinkles, though she is a grandmother with a grandchild 14 years of age? This is what the preparations have done for Mrs. Graham herself. She has accomplished this seemingly impossible thing by the use of her beauty products. They will do the same for you.

WHEN A MAN MARRIES, NINE TIMES OUT OF TEN HE CHOOSES THE GIRL WHO IS CAREFUL ABOUT HER PERSONAL APPEARANCE, THE GIRL WITH THE PRETTY COMPLEXION.

You can't blame men for not being attracted to women whose faces are disfigured with pimples, blotches, blackheads or other unnecessary blemishes. It is possible for every woman to have a clear, beautiful complexion if she will devote just a few minutes each day to the care of her face. Order some of Mrs. Graham's beauty products today and commence using them at once.

BECAUSE YOU ARE MARRIED IS NO EXCUSE FOR NEGLECTING YOUR PERSONAL APPEARANCE.

"Don't care" women make unhappy homes. If you would like the admiration of your husband, children and friends, be even more particular than you were in "courting days." Don't allow yourself to look "careless." Dress your hair becomingly. Take care of your complexion; a smooth, velvety skin, free from blackheads, pimples, tan, freckles and wrinkles will make you attractive. Therefore, always keep Kosmeo in the house to retain and improve your beauty.

If you care at all for beauty, if you want your skin soft, clear and velvety, if you want your skin to look as fresh as a baby's and feel as fresh as it looks, then buy a jar of Kosmeo Beauty Cream and a jar of Hygienic Skin Food and see what they will do. All you have to do is to gently rub a little Kosmeo on your face, neck, shoulders and hands, let it stay a few moments, then wipe it off; that's all. Kosmeo will make your skin firm, smooth and velvety and your complexion beautiful. Kosmeo is your friend; it is the great beauty maker.

BEAUTY MAY BE CULTIVATED. Woman's opportunities for developing beauty are increasing every day. We know that health and beauty go hand in hand; that bright eyes, rosy cheeks, glossy hair and supple, well developed bodies can only be secured and kept by paying attention to the laws of hygiene; and the time has gone by when sensible people consider it a weakness and vanity to care for the body. To work and strive faithfully for perfection in beauty and form should be one of woman's noblest and highest ambitions.

COMPLEXION. A complexion is admirable when it pleases, like a beauteous flower; but to be charming it does not have to resemble one flower alone. Race, climate, hair and eyes determine the color fitness. If every woman could only realize how a bad complexion looks to her friends; how that skin clogged with blackheads and other destructive matter and covered with powder to try to conceal its condition looks in the bright light of day, she would surely improve every moment to make it what man admires and appreciates, the beautiful, soft delicate skin so easily obtained by care and attention. It is the duty of every woman, young, middle aged or old, to preserve to the fullest extent her youthful charm and beauty. Let every woman, therefore, spend at least ten minutes each day to improve her beauty and complexion, to free her skin from all blemishes and produce for herself that clear, fresh, velvety skin so much appreciated and admired by all.

SYSTEMATIC TREATMENT.

One reason why women do not improve more under treatment is that they expect such wonderful results in too short a time. They buy a pot of skin food or beauty cream, and use it faithfully every day for a week, watching each day for improvement and almost expecting to find the wrinkles gone after the third treatment; and at the end of a week, as they do not find very visible improvement, they are ready to give up in despair, declaring the preparation a failure and the manufacturer a fraud; or they at least weaken in the performance of their part of the work, and after the first week, instead of using the article every day, they give a little careless attention to the use of it, once in two or three days and then not for several days; yet all the time expecting improvement and feeling disappointed because they see none. How foolish of them! The complexion is not lost in a day. Wrinkles do not come in a week. Neither can the complexion be renewed nor the wrinkles erased in such an unreasonably short space of time. Daily care, systematic treatment, patience and vigilance alone will renew, restore and rejuvenate.

Mrs. Gervaise Graham's preparations are particularly good for home use. They are so meritorious that in the preparations themselves the virtue lies, rather than in the treatment of the specialist.

FACE BLEACH.

This preparation removes sallowness, sunburn, freckles, moth patches, blackheads, eruptions; indeed, all blemishes that come on the skin. It does not take from the face its natural rosy color, but bleaches out all blemishes lodged in the skin. This bleach, according to Mrs. Graham, is perfectly harmless and is always to be relied upon. It brings to the surface all face eruptions, which dry and fall off with the old cuticle. While the old skin is thus being disposed of, the new skin underneath is forming soft and smooth, pure and white, and fine in texture. The complexion is then as perfect as it can be made and nothing remains then but to keep it so by the use of Kosmeo Skin Food and Kosmeo Face Powder. From one to three bottles are required to insure perfect satisfaction. Regular price, per bottle, $1.50.

No. 8T3152 Our price, per bottle..........................$1.27

Unmailable on account of weight.

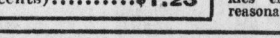

Eastman's Benzoin and Almond Lotion.

The finest lotion ever produced. Widely known as one of the most dainty preparations ever offered for preserving the skin and complexion, healing, soothing and whitening, free from injurious substances. Every lady and gent of refinement should possess a bottle for the toilet. Sweetly and delicately perfumed. Regular price, 50 cents.

No. 8T3095 Our price, per 6-ounce bottle..........**27c**
3 bottles for..............**75c**
Unmailable.

Hair Brilliantine.

A sweetly perfumed liquid for making the hair soft and glossy. Used to advantage to keep the hair in place and make it glossy. Largely used today by women wearing artificial puffs and switches for giving the soft glossy lifelike appearance. Needs no shaking, will not cause the hair to appear greasy and never turns rancid. The fine perfume in this product greatly adds to its value.

No. 8T3240 Price.....**21c**
If mail shipment, postage and tube extra, 13c.

Ruby Salve.

Ruby Salve is a refined and harmless rouge prepared in the form of a cream for tinting the cheeks, lips and fingers. leaves a perfectly natural stain or glow and cannot be detected. The majority of ladies prefer rouge in this form, as it is put up in a very convenient manner and easily applied.

No. 8T3202 Price, per box........**19c**
If mail shipment, postage extra, 5 cents.

Imported Bay Rum.

This is the genuine imported Bay Rum and far superior in every way to the cheaper home made imitations. It has a very high grade, refreshing and sweet odor, and if you desire a fine bay rum be sure to buy this genuine product. It is a very refreshing lotion for use after shaving and for general toilet purposes.

No. 8T3066 Price, ½-pint bottle..........**33c**
No. 8T3067 Price, 1-pint bottle..........**60c**
No. 8T3068 Price, 1-quart bottle..........**$1.10**
All sizes unmailable.

Eau de Cologne.

This is the finest grade of Eau de Cologne and is usually considered the gentlemen's toilet water. Largely used by men as an application after shaving, and considered by many equal to the finest imported product. It is very refreshing and of great value in the sick room for destroying odors and making the air in the room fresh and pleasant. It is delightfully perfumed and a very superior article.

No. 8T3060 Price, 3-ounce bottle..........**33c**
No. 8T3061 Price, $1.00 size bottle..(Both sizes unmailable.) **69c**

Perfect Combination Hair Dye.

This is a two-solution hair dye. Solution No. 1 is first applied to the hair to get it in shape for dyeing and will produce no color. Solution No. 2 is then carefully applied with a comb and in the strength desired for producing all tints from a light brown to a jet black. A two-solution hair dye is preferred by many to the one-liquid hair dye, although much harder to apply. Explicit and complete directions are furnished with each package.

No. 8T3242 Price..................**81c**
If mail shipment, postage extra, 17 cents.

Cream Ormonde with Peroxide Hydrogen.

Pure, creamy and delightfully fragrant. **A cream of snowy whiteness.** Nothing so adds to beauty as a clear, spotless complexion, and nothing so detracts as its absence. Cream Ormonde is not an accidental discovery. It is the result of an endless amount of work by beauty chemists and is considered today to be by far the best non-greasy beauty cream made. It is of snowy whiteness, soothing, softening and whitening to the skin, free from all forms of grease and an exceptionally fine ladies' beauty cream. It also contains peroxide of hydrogen, which greatly adds to its value as an antiseptic bleaching beauty cream. There is beauty in every jar and it leaves the face as soft and pink as a baby's, followed by the so much desired cool and restful sensation. Full directions and booklet, "How to Be An Attractive Woman," accompany each package. Put up in a beautiful opal jar. Regular price, per jar, 50 cents. Shipping weight, 13 ounces.

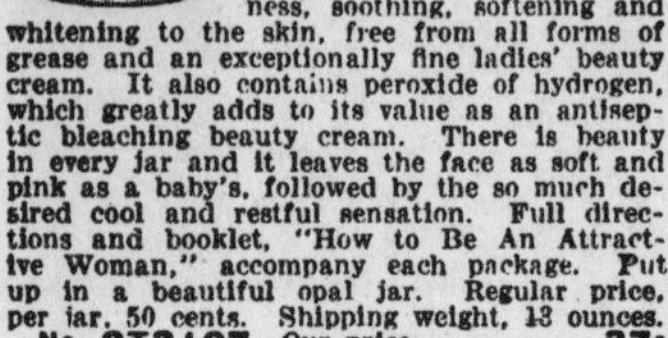

No. 8T3107 Our price..............**37c**

BOURJOIS' MANON LESCAUT TOILET PREPARATIONS.

IF YOU WANT THE BEST, BUY THESE.

These world famous toilet products have been named after the beauty heroine of France and represent in the face powder, rouge and perfume the finest and best known toilet articles manufactured by the famous perfumer Bourjois, of Paris, France. This is the line above all others that we suggest that you buy.

Perfume.

This perfume, on account of its sweet odor, high fragrance and exquisite blend, has well been called the pride of France. 1½-ounce bottle in beautiful case. Quality, not quantity. It pays to buy the best.

No. 8T2900 Price, per box..................**$1.87**
If mail shipment, postage extra, 26 cents.

Face Rouge.

The best and the finest Rouge made. Gives a beautiful healthy tint to the lips and cheeks. It cannot be detected. Six months' supply (with average use) in fine velvet lined case. Sweetly and delicately perfumed. This is the rouge to buy. It is the cheapest in the end.

No. 8T3199 Price, per box..................**$1.17**
If mail shipment, postage extra, 7 cents.

Face Powder.

The finest Face Powder made. Highly and sweetly perfumed. Made of the finest impalpable Oriental rice together with other high grade beauty products. Absolutely harmless to the most delicate complexion. Give this powder a trial. White, flesh or brunette. **State color wanted.**

No. 8T3177 Price, per box..................**$1.17**
If mail shipment, postage extra, 5 cents.

CORYLOPSIS OF JAPAN TOILET PRODUCTS.

THE PERFUME OF THE ORIENT.

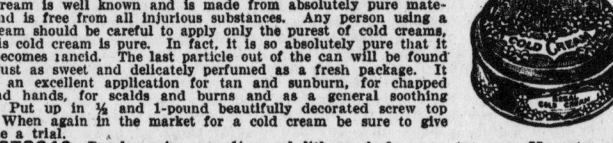

No one who uses this can forget or would forget the delicate clinging odor of the Corylopsis of Japan. The blend of the flowers of the Orient is suggestive of the luxurious fragrance of the sun kissed isles of Japan.

The Corylopsis of Japan perfumes and toilet articles are a combination of the most delicate essential oils, skillfully blended so as to emit when using the most lasting fragrance that ever graced milady's dressing table. The choicest products of the far East assembled in unique Oriental designs. Exclusively individual in their creations.

Face Powder.

Soft and velvety. An exceptionally high class powder and one that will please any lady. Flesh, white or brunette. **State color wanted.** Regular 50-cent box.

No. 8T3135 Our price...**37c**
If mail shipment, postage extra, 6 cents.

Toilet Water.

The characteristic sweet blend that has made this product famous. 3½-ounce bottle.

No. 8T3136
Price **43c**
Unmailable.

Talcum Powder.

A sweetly perfumed highest grade imported Talcum Powder. In a beautiful highly colored can.

No. 8T3137
Price **13c**
If mail shipment, postage extra, 6 cents.

Sachet Powder.

Highest grade sweetly perfumed Sachet. Spread this among your handkerchiefs and stationery and note how quickly they will absorb its sweet fragrance.

No. 8T3138
Price **17c**
If mail shipment, postage extra, 3 cents.

Perfume.

One-ounce bottle in Oriental box. 75-cent value. A very high grade perfume.

No. 8T3139
Price **43c**
If mail shipment, postage extra, 3 cents.

REGAL COLD CREAM.

A PERFECTLY PURE AND SWEETLY PERFUMED COLD CREAM.

This Cold Cream by means of its healing action upon the skin preserves that freshness and whiteness so much admired by all. The Regal Violet Cold Cream is well known and is made from absolutely pure materials and is free from all injurious substances. Any person using a cold cream should be careful to apply only the purest of cold creams, and this cold cream is pure. In fact, it is so absolutely pure that it never becomes rancid. The last particle out of the can will be found to be just as sweet and delicately perfumed as a fresh package. It affords an excellent application for tan and sunburn, for chapped lips and hands, for scalds and burns and as a general soothing agent. Put up in ½ and 1-pound beautifully decorated screw top cans. When again in the market for a cold cream be sure to give this one a trial.

No. 8T3049 Regular price, per ½-pound lithographed, screw top can, 75 cents; our price..........**31c**
No. 8T3050 Regular price, per 1-pound lithographed, screw top can, $1.25; our price..........**60c**

PAYAN'S IMPORTED PERFUMES.

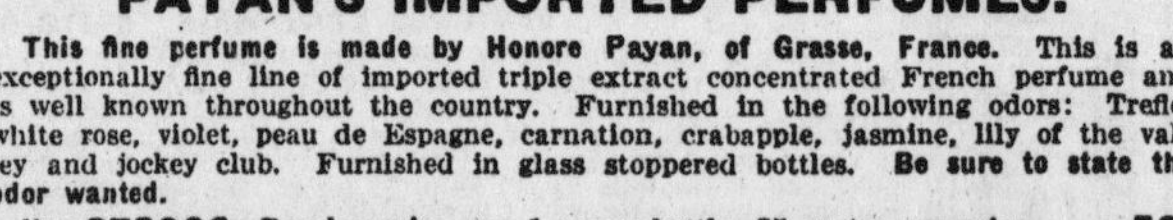

This fine perfume is made by Honore Payan, of Grasse, France. This is an exceptionally fine line of imported triple extract concentrated French perfume and is well known throughout the country. Furnished in the following odors: Trefle, white rose, violet, peau de Espagne, carnation, crabapple, jasmine, lily of the valley and jockey club. Furnished in glass stoppered bottles. **Be sure to state the odor wanted.**

No. 8T2906 Regular price, per 1-ounce bottle, 75 cents; our price.......**50c**
If mail shipment, postage and mailing tube, extra, 12 cents.
No. 8T2907 Regular price, per 2-ounce bottle, $1.25; our price..........**89c**
If mail shipment, postage and mailing tube, extra, 19 cents.

No. 8T10025 1 ounce exceptionally fine Perfume in fancy flower color embossed perfume box. Furnished in white rose, violet, carnation, lily of the valley, heliotrope and jockey club. **Specify odor.**

Price **47c**
If mail shipment, postage extra, 15 cents.

No. 8T11002 1 ounce very high class Perfume in fancy cut glass stoppered perfume bottle, packed in handsome display case. Furnished in violet, white rose, crabapple, heliotrope, carnation or lily of the valley. **Specify odor.** Price.....**67c**
If mail shipment, postage extra, 15 cents.

No. 8T2975 4-ounce bottle genuine Myron Maynard Princess Violet Perfume, with ball stoppered top. A sweet smelling and lasting quality perfume. A very popular and good grade perfume and a large 4-ounce bottle brought within the price of everyone. Worth $1.50. Our price **79c**
If mail shipment, postage extra, 16 cents.

No. 8T12001 1 ounce very best Violet Perfume in fancy oval flower and gilt embossed display case. A handsome package and very high class perfume.
Price **97c**
No. 8T12002 Same as No. 8T12001, except white rose odor.
Price **97c**
If mail shipment, postage extra, 17 cents.

Perfumed Scalp Food.

A Fine Tonic for the Scalp.

A highly beneficial and absolutely harmless hair dressing for applying to the scalp for massage treatment to stimulate the growth of hair. It is in the form of an ointment, and a small amount is all that is necessary to apply at a time. This preparation is well known and if used as directed will be found a very reliable and pleasing product. Should be applied to the scalp after each treatment of Princess Hair Tonic. It materially aids the hair tonic in performing its work and leaves the scalp and hair at all times in a clean, soft, antiseptic condition. Full directions accompany each jar. Shipping weight, 15 ounces.

No. 8T3130 Price, per jar..........**40c**

New Life Curly Hair Straightener.

An ointment to be applied to the hair in all cases where curls or kinky hair are objectionable. It is merely applied to the hair, rubbed in and the hair then thoroughly brushed. It causes the hair to straighten and lie flat to the head without injuring the hair. Nicely perfumed, keeps indefinitely, and if you desire straight instead of curly or kinky hair give this product a trial. Regular price, per jar, 50 cents.

No. 8T3231 Our price..........**37c**
If mail shipment, postage extra, 6 cents.

Novita Rouge.

This is a standard article used by the theatrical profession of today. Imported direct from France. Evenly ground, carefully put up and delightfully perfumed. A very satisfactory and easily applied rouge. Imparts a tint identical to health and one whose use cannot be detected. Regular price, per box, 75 cents.

No. 8T3198 Our price..........**39c**
If mail shipment, postage extra, 4 cents.

Imported Liquid Rouge.

This fine Liquid Rouge is made in France and contains the same coloring matter as the powder rouge, only in liquid form. It is preferred by many ladies, being claimed to be much easier applied and gives in all cases the same natural, beautiful, healthy tint. Regular price, per bottle, 75 cents.

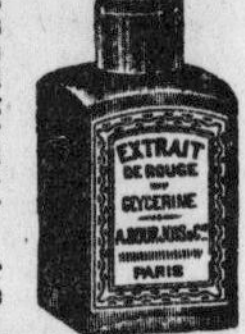

No. 8T3200 Our price **39c**
Postage extra, 12 cents.

Celebrated Cheeks Ever Blooming Liquid Rouge.

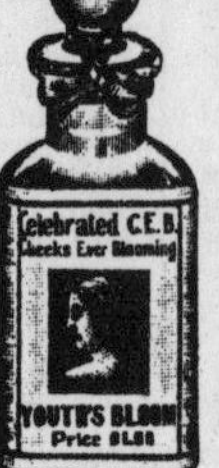

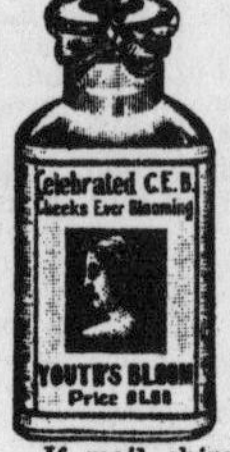

We have now made arrangements for the sale of this well known product. This is a liquid rouge that can be applied to the center of the cheek and then by means of wet cloth be evenly distributed over the entire cheek or wherever desired. In our opinion the best liquid rouge made. Keeps forever and after once using you would never again use the cheaper inferior kinds. Enough rouge for one year's use for one lady. If you want the best this is the one to buy. Regular $1.00 bottle.

No. 8T3201
Our price..........**69c**
If mail shipment, postage extra, 6 cents.

Clay's Hair Shader.

A one-solution preparation that will restore gray, faded or streaked hair to its natural color; blonde, auburn, any shade of brown or black. Absolutely harmless, easily applied. Leaves the hair soft and glossy. Antiseptic. Preserves while it beautifies. Cannot be detected. Will not wear or wash off. Full directions with each bottle.

No. 8T3218 Regular large $1.00 bottle. Our price......**73c**
Postage extra, 13 cents.

Dupre Massage Cup.

For Face, Neck and Bust.

A beautiful nickel plated suction cup for bringing color to the cheeks, removing blackheads and pore accumulations, for filling out wrinkles, for producing plump, firm cheeks and bust, and for causing easy absorption of all face, bust and beauty creams. Just as essential to the toilet as a comb or brush. Has one attachment for cheeks and face and another for neck and bust. If used a few times the toilet is incomplete without it. Regular price, $2.50.

No. 8T3183 Our price..........**$1.33**
If mail shipment, postage extra, 4 cents.

COMBS, CURLING IRONS AND HAIR BRUSHES

GENTS' AND BARBERS' COMBS.

Excelsior Barbers' Comb. An exceptionally finely polished gents' and barbers' hard rubber comb. Graduated coarse and fine teeth. Length, 7 inches.
No. 8T1000 Our price..........12c
If mail shipment, postage extra, 2 cents.

New Self Cleaning Barbers' Comb. Heavy smooth back, beautiful gilt inlay, coarse and fine teeth. Regular 25-cent grade.
No. 8T1001 Our price..........17c
If mail shipment, postage extra, 2 cents.

Gentlemen's Favorite.

Fancy Curved Back Design Barbers' Comb. Coarse and fine teeth nicely finished throughout, best material and hand finished teeth.
No. 8T1003 Our price..........33c
If mail shipment, postage extra, 2 cents.

Horn Barbers' Combs.

Fine Horn Barbers' Comb. Length, 7¼ inches, tapering design, nicely finished.
No. 8T1008 Our price..........17c
If mail shipment, postage extra, 2 cents.

The Big Value Gents' Comb.

Finest Hand Finished Horn Barbers' Comb, with coarse and fine teeth. Length, 7½ inches, tapering design, self cleaning teeth. A beauty and the one we urge you to buy.
No. 8T1009 Our price..........39c
If mail shipment, postage extra, 2 cents.

Metal Back Horn Comb. With chain attached. A very durable, high grade and convenient comb. You will always find it hung in its place. Length, 7 inches, with three feet of chain and screw at end.
No. 8T1005 Price..........14c
If mail shipment, postage extra, 6 cents.

LADIES' DRESSING COMBS.

Strong Hard Rubber Dressing Comb. Heavy square, rounded teeth, coarse and fine. Length, 8 inches.
No. 8T1002 Our price..........13c
If mail shipment, postage extra, 4 cents.

Fancy Rope Back Hard Rubber Dressing Comb. Ladies' special favorite. Heavy fancy design back and a very serviceable comb. Exceptional quality at the price. Length, 8 inches.
No. 8T1004 Our price..........22c
If mail shipment, postage extra, 2 cents.

Koh-I-Noor Unbreakable Comb. This is the finest hard rubber comb manufactured. Full 8-inch length, exceptional width, very heavy weight. Finely polished and stamped in gilt letters "Koh-I-Noor, Guaranteed Unbreakable." Guaranteed not to break with one year's wear or it will be replaced free. Has long heavy teeth. A comb made for service.
No. 8T1011 Regular 50 to 65-cent value; all coarse teeth; our price..........39c
No. 8T1012 Regular 50 to 65-cent value; coarse and fine teeth; our price..39c
No. 8T1013 Same comb, but heavier, 9-inch length. Especially adapted for long heavy hair. Ordinary 75-cent value; coarse and fine teeth; our price..........53c
No. 8T1014 Same as No. 8T1013, but all coarse teeth. Our price..........53c
If mail shipment, postage extra, 4 cents.

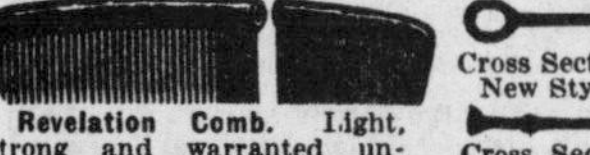

Cross Section New Style.

Cross Section Old Style.

Revelation Comb. Light, strong and warranted unbreakable. Made with hollow back; stronger than solid combs but much lighter; can be handled with ease and comfort. Eliminates superfluous weight and makes a massive beautiful looking article. Each comb guaranteed. Either coarse and fine or all coarse teeth, as desired. Length, 8¼ inches. 75-cent value.
No. 8T1006 Coarse and fine teeth. Our price..........46c
No. 8T1007 All coarse teeth, especially adapted for long heavy hair..........46c
If mail shipment, postage extra, 4 cents.

Koh-I-Noor Hard Rubber 8½-inch Dressing Comb with handle. Gives extra purchase on the comb. Much easier handled. All coarse teeth. Just the thing for heavy and thick hair. A new departure, but a ladies' comb that is always satisfactory. Ordinary 75-cent value.
No. 8T1010 Our price..........47c
If mail shipment, postage extra, 3 cents.

Ivory White Pyralin Dressing Comb. Length, 7½ inches, fancy curved back, nicely embossed with rope design. Coarse and fine teeth. A big value.
No. 8T1016 Our price..........18c
If mail shipment, postage extra, 2 cents.

Handsome Ivory White Dressing Comb. Length, 7½ inches, with fancy heavily embossed back. Coarse and fine teeth, strong and a big seller.
No. 8T1017 Our price..........33c
If mail shipment, postage extra, 2 cents.

A Special Favorite.

Large, massive, beautiful Ivory White Dressing Comb. Length, 8½ inches; latest plain curved back. Coarse and fine teeth. Just the thing for long heavy hair.
No. 8T1018 Our price..........33c
If mail shipment, postage extra, 2 cents.

Handsome Ebony Finished Celluloid Dressing Comb. Length, 7½ inches. Beautifully sterling silver mounted. Regular 50-cent value.
No. 8T1020 Our price..........33c
If mail shipment, postage extra, 3 cents.

Ladies' Favorite Comb. Without doubt the finest celluloid comb made. Very latest pattern. Fine embossed sunflower design. Just the thing for heavy or long hair. You can buy no better comb no matter what price you pay. Ordinary $1.00 value.
No. 8T1025 Our price..........73c
If mail shipment, postage extra, 2 cents.

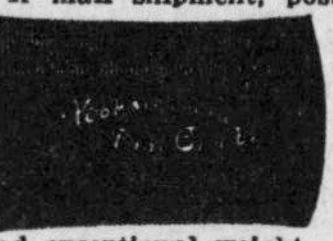

Koh-I-Noor Comb. Imported extra heavy hard rubber fine tooth comb. 3-16-inch thick. Stamped in gilt "Koh-I-Noor Fine Comb." Beautifully polished and exceptional weight. Size, 4¼x2½ inches. Regular 50-cent value.
No. 8T1015 Our price..........29c
If mail shipment, postage extra, 3 cents.

For cheaper combs than shown on this page, see 7, 17 and 33-cent bargains on pages 383 to 393.

CURLING IRONS.

Waving Iron.

Five-Prong Waving Iron, for waving the hair. Made of good quality metal fully nickel plated. Length, 9 inches. 14c
No. 8T1050 Price..........14c
If mail shipment, postage extra, 9 cents.

Marcel Hair Waver.

The Marcel Hair Waver, for making large, deep graceful waves which are so popular. Recommended by all the leading hair dressers. Made of best quality steel, heavily nickeled.
No. 8T1052 Price..........22c
If mail shipment, postage extra, 10 cents.

Grace Darling Curling Iron.

Grace Darling Curling Iron is without doubt the most artistic and best curling iron made. Highly ornamented, and heavily nickel plated on copper, enabling it to hold heat three times longer than others. Has tapering end, making hair slip off with ease. Patent spring and natural oak handles. The one it pays to buy.
No. 8T1054 Our price..........18c
If mail shipment, postage extra, 10 cents.

Lillian Russell Improved Crimping Iron.

Lillian Russell Improved Crimping Iron. A special favorite and one of the best made. Beautifully nickel plated over copper, holding heat three times longer than cheaper kinds.
No. 8T1056 Our price..........29c
If mail shipment, postage extra, 10 cents.

Perfection Hair Straightener.

A new and novel idea and the first ever introduced in any country. To all persons with curly or kinky hair, this iron is indispensable, as it enables hair dressing at all times in the latest fashion. Finely nickel plated, with natural oak handles.
No. 8T1058 Our price..........37c
If mail shipment, postage extra, 12 cents.

Curling Iron Heater.

Fits any gas jet, no leakage of gas, no blackening of iron, can be applied in a second, can be used for other purposes, and is the best heater made. Handsomely oxidized, highly polished brass tube with wire attachment for heating water, or infant foods.
No. 8T1060 Price..27c
If mail shipment, postage extra, 12 cents.

DR. SCOTT'S ELECTRIC HAIR BRUSHES.

STIMULATE BLOOD VESSELS TO YOUTHFUL VIGOR, REMOVE DANDRUFF, GIVE HEALTH TO THE SCALP AND AID GROWTH OF THE HAIR.

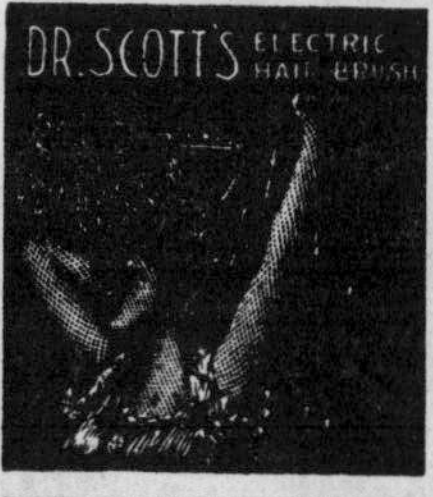

Dr. Scott's Electro-Magnetic Hair Brushes are recommended by leading physicians and are extensively known. This brush promotes blood circulation in the scalp, thus not only keeping strong and healthy the hair you have but stimulating the growth of more. The magnetism infuses new life and vigor into the hair and the hair roots are fed with nourishing blood as a result. Brush has been tried for years and fulfills every claim. Fine stiff penetrating black bristles. A compass accompanies each brush and you can see the magnetism for yourself. Furnished in three sizes, depending upon size of brush and strength.
No. 8T1185 $1.00 value. Our price...$0.79
No. 8T1186 $2.00 value. Our price... 1.39
No. 8T1187 $3.00 value. Our price... 2.17
If mail shipment, postage extra, each, 12 cents.

Alcohol Lamp Curling Iron Heaters.

Very handy article; folds up completely; always ready for use. No danger of blackening the iron or burning the handle. Occupies little space, convenient and a necessity for every woman curling her hair. Either grain or wood alcohol can be used in these lamps.

Nickel Plated Heater. Has large screw nickel plated cap over wick preventing waste or spilling of liquid. Has folding clamps for holding iron. Size, 4¾x2 inches. One of the best nickel plated heaters made.
No. 8T1090 Price..........25c
If mail shipment, postage extra, 4 cents.

Tin Finish Heater, similar to the above, but made of tin finish instead of nickel plated. Size, 5½x1¾ inches.
No. 8T1091 Price..........17c
If mail shipment, postage extra, 2 cents.

Ladies' Favorite Heater. One of the largest selling heaters manufactured. Folds up completely. Top opening up as holder for iron; 2-inch opening for flame, heating iron evenly. Beautiful gilt finish throughout. Size of heater open, 5¼x2 inches. Size closed, 3¼x2 inches.
No. 8T1092 Price..........29c
If mail shipment, postage extra, 2 cents.

SOLID BACK HAIR BRUSHES.

For cheaper brushes than shown on this page see 7, 17 and 33-cent bargains on pages 383 to 393.

A Big Value.

New Concave Back Hair Brush. Has eleven rows of heavy, stiff white Russian bristles, set in solid golden maple highly polished back. Length, 9 inches. A wonder value. Worth 75 cents.
No. 8T1105 Our price..........47c
If mail shipment, postage extra, 7 cents.

Barbers' Stiff Bristle Hair Brush. Special value. Has eleven rows of best stiff unbleached Russian bristles, set in beautiful rosewood finished and polished back. Recommended for gents and barbers desiring a stiff, penetrating brush. Regular 75-cent value.
No. 8T1106 Our price..........48c
If mail shipment, postage extra, 8 cents.

Sensible Hair Brush. Has thirteen rows of extra quality, long, firm, white China bristles. Set in oval, so called turtle back, beautifully polished back and handle. Size, 3x9 inches. Regular $1.00 brush. Furnished in either ebony or cherry finish.
No. 8T1110 Ebony finish. Our price..........67c
No. 8T1111 Cherry finish. Our price..........67c
If mail shipment, postage extra, 9 cents.

Ladies' Favorite.

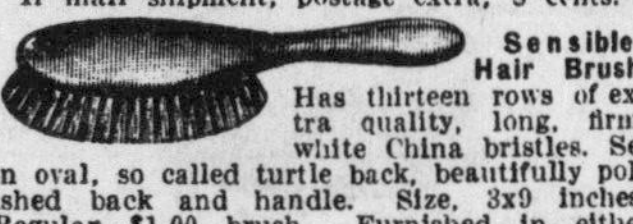

This fine Ladies' Dressing Brush is made long and narrow, having seven rows of the very best stiff Russian bristles, set in piano polished fine rosewood back and handle. With it no comb is necessary, as the bristles are stiff enough to penetrate a heavy head of hair. Remember the better the bristles, the better the brush. Will last for years. A great favorite with every woman. The kind of a brush you will recommend to your friends. Do not confuse this with the many cheaper brushes of same design.
No. 8T1112 Price..........59c
If mail shipment, postage extra, 5 cents.

French design Brush. Long, narrow concave back, fancy shaped handle, rosewood finish. Has eleven rows fine stiff penetrating white bristles. The shape and fine stock make it appreciated by everyone. Regular $1.00 value.
No. 8T1115 Our price..........69c
If mail shipment, postage extra, 7 cents.

Barbers' Black Bristle Brush. This is the regular $1.25 barber brush, but made in new design back, concave shape to fit the shape of the head. Thirteen rows best penetrating black China bristles, set in highly polished solid walnut back and handle. A high grade brush.
No. 8T1122 Our price..........89c
If mail shipment, postage extra, 9 cents.

Our Leader Brush.

This is one of the best selling brushes on the market on account of its extra quality, beauty and price. Has eleven rows extra quality, long, stiff, penetrating white bristles, set in a 9½-inch long beautifully piano polished dark rosewood back and handle. A special favorite with both ladies and gents. You will be well pleased with this brush. Regular $1.25 value.
No. 8T1124 Our price..........99c
If mail shipment, postage extra, 10 cents.

Our Big $1.00 Leader.

This is without doubt the greatest leader that has ever been offered to the brush trade. New imported pattern and a beauty. Contains eleven rows extra long, fine, firm, penetrating white bristles, firmly set in solid rosewood finished back, 2¼x9 inches.
No. 8T1130 Price..........$1.00
If mail shipment, postage extra, 10 cents.
No. 8T1131 Same as above, but in ebony finish. Price..........$1.00
If mail shipment, postage extra, 10 cents.

Our Big $1.35 Value.

This represents the best all around brush it is possible to produce. Has eleven rows extra long stiff white penetrating bristles, set in a sensible wide solid back and handle. Nothing fancy, but for quality, wear, appearance, high grade bristles and durability it cannot be duplicated. Worth $2.50. Either ebony or mahogany finish.
No. 8T1135 Ebony finish. Our price..........$1.35
No. 8T1136 Mahogany finish. Our price..........$1.35
If mail shipment, postage extra, 10 cents.

Genuine Ebony Back Brushes.

Genuine Ebony Latest Design Hair Brush, with eleven rows finest quality, long penetrating white Russian bristles; handsome sterling silver mounting on back. Suitable for ladies or gentlemen. Length, 9½ inches. A beautiful and very serviceable brush. Guaranteed $2.00 value.
No. 8T1150 Our price..........$1.29
If mail shipment, postage extra, 8 cents.

Genuine Ebony Hair Brush, with solid sterling silver mounting, with eleven rows of fine quality stiff white Russian bristles. Length, 9 inches. Regular $1.75 value.
No. 8T1151 Our price..........$1.10
If mail shipment, postage extra, 8 cents.

Real Ebony Hair Brush, with solid sterling silver mountings, nine rows finest quality imported bristles. Length, 8½ inches. A brush retailed at your jeweler's for $1.00.
No. 8T1152 Our price..........79c
If mail shipment, postage extra, 8 cents.

Genuine Ebony Military Brush with eleven rows of extra fine white bristles, extra heavy and highly finished back, with sterling silver mount. Length, 5 inches. Regular $1.50 value. A much better brush than before handled.
No. 8T1154 Our price, each....$1.19
Per pair..........2.25
If mail shipment, postage extra, 7 cents.

Genuine Ebony Military Brush, same as above, beautifully sterling silver mounted, nine rows extra fine bristles. Regular $1.25 value.
No. 8T1155 Our price..........$0.89
Per pair..........1.65
If mail shipment, postage extra, 7 cents.

The Brush of Quality.

IT PAYS TO BUY THE BEST.

This brush is especially designed for persons that are very particular regarding their brushes and desire the very finest manufactured. Latest pattern, imported from Japan, and contains thirteen rows of 1-inch extra firm, exceptional quality, high grade bristles, firmly set in an all solid genuine rosewood back and handle. These bristles cannot come out and it is a brush that will last you a lifetime. If you desire something new, something exceptionally fine, select this brush. Ordinary value, $2.75 to $3.00.

No. 8T1209 Our special leader..$2.39
If mail shipment, postage extra, 8 cents.

Celebrated Keep Clean Brush.

These brushes are well known on account of their construction. They are all ebony finished solid wood backs and have the black bristles firmly set in aluminum, which is waterproof, preventing cracking. Cannot become foul by absorbing water or oil, no veneer or holes for the collection of dirt, and is a brush easily kept clean. The materials in these brushes are all the same, differing only in size. Each brush packed in display carton.

No. 8T1175 Keep Clean Brush (Medium Size). Brush has eleven rows firm stiff black bristles. Size, 2½x9½ inches. Price..37c
If mail shipment, postage extra, 10 cents.

No. 8T1176 Keep Clean Brush (Large Size). Oval shaped back containing fifteen rows firm stiff black bristles. Size, 3¼x9¾ inches. An excellent wearing brush. Price..........59c
If mail shipment, postage extra, 12 cents.

No. 8T1177 Keep Clean Military Brushes. Eleven rows medium grade white bristles set in aluminum block, ebony finished. Come two in box. Price, per pair..89c
If mail shipment, postage extra, 12 cents.

Genuine "Very Best" Rubber Cushion Brush.

This highly advertised well known rubber cushion brush is the best of its kind manufactured. Made with the finest Siberian bristles set in elastic air cushioned base. Back and handle beautifully finished and piano polished. This construction enables scalp massage and stimulation with comparative ease. If you want the best air cushion brush this is the one to buy.

No. 8T1190 Medium size. Price..77c
No. 8T1191 Large size. Price..94c
If mail shipment, postage extra, 10 cents.

Akerley's Perfect Air Cushion Brush.

A special favorite fourteen-row Hair Brush. The wires are all nickel plated and securely set in soft rubber air cushion. Makes combing hair easy, reaches scalp without scratching, invigorating and a brush made for wear; 50 cents everywhere.

No. 8T1192 Our price..........37c
If mail shipment, postage extra, 10 cents.

Fancy Flower Design, embossed black composition back and handle. Has eleven rows of long fine white best penetrating Russian bristles. A very substantial and durable brush. Easily penetrates heavy hair and a brush made for service.

No. 8T1180 Price..............66c
If mail shipment, postage extra, 9 cents.

Infant's Celluloid Brush, with soft white camel's hair bristles and exceptionally fine white, pink or baby blue celluloid handle. Regular 65 cent value. State color wanted.

No. 8T1200 Our price..........43c
If mail shipment, postage extra, 2 cents.

Twisted Handle Brush. The old reliable twisted handle celluloid brush. Twelve rows of fine white bristles firmly set in celluloid. No danger from moisture. No cracking or warping. Regular $1.00 value.

No. 8T1205 Our price..........67c
If mail shipment, postage extra, 8 cents.

Clothes Brushes.

Black Beauty Clothes Brush. This excellent seven-row fine long black Russian bristle brush is of special value. Bristles firmly set in solid concave cherry finished 7-inch back, beautifully piano polished. The bristles are long and soft, enabling it to be used as a hat as well as a clothes brush. Very pretty and a brush built for wear. Regular 65-cent value.

No. 8T1225 Our price..........49c
If mail shipment, postage extra, 9 cents.

Curved Back Clothes Brush. Has nine rows fine long soft unbleached bristles, set in solid satinwood piano finished back. Length, 7½ inches. Very serviceable. Regular 75-cent value.

No. 8T1227 Our price..........61c
If mail shipment, postage extra, 9 cents.

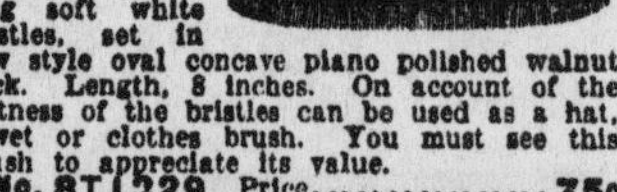

White Bristle Clothes Brush. Has nine rows exceptionally fine long soft white bristles, set in new style oval concave piano polished walnut back. Length, 8 inches. On account of the softness of the bristles can be used as a hat, velvet or clothes brush. You must see this brush to appreciate its value.

No. 8T1229 Price..............75c
If mail shipment, postage extra, 9 cents.

Ebony Clothes Brushes.

A Beauty. The finest genuine Ebony Clothes Brush ever manufactured. Has nine rows 1¼-inch long beautiful white bleached, soft, highest grade bristles, set in heavy massive style, new design back. The 1¼-inch floral design sterling silver mount makes it by far the best brush ever offered. You must see it to appreciate its value. If you want the best select this brush. Regular $3.50 value.

No. 8T1235 Price..............$1.98
If mail shipment, postage extra, 10 cents.

Solid Back New Design Genuine Ebony Clothes Brush, having nine rows of fine firm white Russian bristles, solid back, sterling silver mounted. Length, 6½ inches. Extra value.

No. 8T1237 Price..............99c
If mail shipment, postage extra, 8 cents.

Genuine Ebony Velvet or Hat Brush, with long white imported bristles, very desirable for ladies' or gents' hats or for fine cloth and velvet. Very acceptable gift for ladies or gents; solid sterling silver mounted. Length, 6 inches.

No. 8T1239 Price..............67c
If mail shipment, postage extra, 5 cents.

Flesh and Bath Brushes.

A Six-Row Bath Brush, long curved detachable varnished handle and good black and white domestic bristles. Shipping weight, 12 ounces. Regular price, 50 cents.

No. 8T1280 Our price..........39c
Unmailable.

57c

Detachable Handle Bath Brush, large firm black and white bristles, solid varnished back and long curved varnished detachable handle. Excellent value. Regular price, 75 cents.

No. 8T1282 Our price..........57c
Unmailable.

87c

Our Pride. As fine a bath brush as anyone could desire. Long black China imported bristles, firm yet fine, solid back, and long double curved detachable holly handle. Can be used without handle as flesh brush or with handle for bath and back brush. Will not mat down when wet. Will last a lifetime. Regular price, $1.25.

No. 8T1283 Our price..........87c
Unmailable.

$1.29

American Beauty. Same style brush as No. 8T1283 except much larger brush and pure white bristles, handle and back of brush the finest white holly wood. Justly called the American Beauty, as it is the best brush made. With proper care will last a lifetime. Each brush in box. Regular price, $1.50 to $1.75.

No. 8T1284 Our price..........$1.29
Unmailable.

An Excellent Flesh Brush, 5½ inches long, with strap. Large firm black and white bristles, good solid back. Can be used dry or in the bath.

No. 8T1285 Price..........29c
If mail shipment, postage extra, 7 cents.

A Home Necessity.

Celluloid Whisk Broom Holder. Fancy celluloid holder with excellent quality whisk broom. Holder made of heavy celluloid, decorated in front with beautiful painted flower design in natural colors and fastened in back by means of heavy silk cord. Length, holder and broom, 10 inches. Furnished in white, blue or pink to match the color of room. Specify color. Ordinary value, $1.00.

No. 8T1794 Our price..........55c
Postage extra, 10 cents.

Feather Dusters.

There are many grades of feather dusters, some made for show and some for wear. We carry only an exceptionally fine line. Only the best hardwood heads and handles are used and we guarantee every thread against stripping. These dusters are the best that can be produced. Each duster guaranteed exceptional value at the price quoted. They are made for wear and represent exceptional value in every case.

Handy Household Duster. Made out of turkey body feathers, well filled, extra soft and durable. Length of feathers, 7 inches; length of handle 9 inches.

No. 8T1292 Price......13c
If mail shipment, postage extra, 8 cents.

Standard Dusters, same style as No. 8T1292. Containing 100 selected wing and tail feathers. No pointers or culls and are made with black head and handles. A very serviceable duster. Best medium priced dusters made.

No. 8T1293 10-inch feathers. Price..19c
No. 8T1294 14-inch feathers. Price..39c
If mail shipment, postage extra, 16 cents.

Veri-Soft Dusters, are made of the softest known feathers, guaranteed not to scratch. Will give satisfaction for dusting fine furniture and bric-a-brac. Light in weight, easy to use and are the best made for general family use. These dusters are made with special metal base heads, will wear for years. Length of feathers, 10 inches; length of handle, 14 inches. Regular price, $1.00.

No. 8T1295 Our price..........69c
If mail shipment, postage extra, 12 cents.

The Perfect Duster. Same style duster as preceding No. 8T1295. This is the finest duster manufactured, made of exceptionally fine selected soft feathers, firmly secured; rosewood handle, hardwood head fitted with nickel plated base which absolutely prevents slitting of the head or loosening of the handle, faults that make so many ordinary dusters almost useless. The feathers are long and of exceptional softness, containing 200 selected tail feathers, or at least twice the number of the ordinary duster. Especially suitable for dusting carriages, automobiles, fine furniture and all highly polished surfaces. Length of feathers, 16 inches; length of handle, 11 inches; width over top, 19 inches. A duster that will last a lifetime. Ordinary value, $2.50.

No. 8T1296 Our price..........$1.25
If mail shipment, postage extra, 12 cents.

Flat Soft Down Duster.

Made of the very finest brown soft down, 6½ inches wide. 10½ inches long; length of handle, 16 inches. Just the thing for dusting shelving, highly polished furniture and other places where it is desired to wipe up the dust and retain in the duster. When filled can be taken out of doors and shaken clean. Enables housewives to take up dust without scattering over room. Ordinary value $1.50.

No. 8T1297 Our price..........$1.20
If mail shipment, postage extra, 8 cents.

Wool Dusters.

Made of long imported fleece dyed in bright colors. Always soft, never scratch, neat and durable. Can be washed when dirty. Largely used for dusting carriages, furniture, etc.

No. 8T1298 Length of wool, 8 inches; length of handle, 9 inches. Ordinary value, 25 cents. Our price..........19c

No. 8T1299 Same as above, length of wool 9 inches; length of handle 13 inches; ordinary value, 50 cents. Our price..........37c
If mail shipment, postage extra, 12 cents.

Plate Glass Mirrors.

Square Shape Mirrors, in hardwood frame with polished nickel stand, which can be used as a fastening to hang on the wall or a base to stand on. French beveled plate mirror in highly polished selected hardwood frame, either mahogany, oak or ebony finish. State wood desired. Exceptional values. Each packed in box to prevent breaking.

No.	Size of glass, inches.	Shipping Wt. lbs.	Price
8T1400	4x 6	1	$0.31
8T1401	5x 7	1¼	.47
8T1402	6x 8	1½	.67
8T1403	7x 9	2½	.97
8T1404	8x10	3	1.15

Unmailable.

Round Hand Mirror.

MORE POPULAR AND MUCH BETTER THAN OLD FORM OVAL MIRRORS.

Finest Quality Heavy Round French Plate Mirrors, fitted in highest grade piano polished hardwood frames. Furnished in mahogany or ebony finish. Each packed in separate box to prevent breaking. Specify wood desired. In mirrors it pays to buy the best. For cheaper grades see 7, 17 and 33-cent bargains in following pages.

No. 8T1415 Price, 5-inch mirror..........69c
No. 8T1416 Price, 6-inch mirror..........99c
No. 8T1417 Price, 7-inch mirror..........$1.25
Unmailable.

Adjustable Slide Mirror.

The handiest and most complete adjustable toilet, dressing or shaving mirror ever devised. Can be turned to any angle, meets any condition. Consists of a hardwood back, 2x11 inches, which screws on the wall, on front of which is an 8-inch beautifully nickel plated sliding rod, enabling mirror to be raised to any angle. Branching from this is an adjustable rod allowing the mirror to be turned to any position and at any angle. Mirror itself consists of a beautiful 6-inch heavy beveled glass and nickel plated rim. We believe you will be better satisfied with this mirror than any ever offered. Can easily be set up and very good for campers. Shipping weight, 2½ pounds. Regular price $2.00 to $2.50.

No. 8T1464 Our price..........$1.39

Our Leader.

Ladies' fancy Oak Leaf Mirror. A new stylish design, very finest heavy French beveled plate mirror, fancy shaped and highly polished handle. A beauty, and a present any lady would be proud of. No description can do it justice. Each mirror carefully packed in box to prevent breakage. If you want something fine, latest design, do not omit this from your order. Furnished in mahogany or ebony finish. State wood wanted.

No. 8T1425 Size glass, 4½x6½ inches; length of handle 14½ inches. Regular $3.00 value. Shipping weight, 3 pounds. Our price..$1.69

No. 8T1426 Same as above, but slightly smaller; size glass 4½ inches diameter. $2.00 value. Our price..........$1.19

Nickel Plated Toilet Mirror.

Large, handsome, nickel plated mirror. The mirror is mounted on large base on which stands a figure holding with head and arms a heavy wire frame which supports mirror from the center, giving it full swing, and allowing the user to tilt it backward or forward. A swivel in the base allows the mirror to be turned freely from side to side without removing the base itself. We furnish this mirror in two sizes.

No.	Ht., in.	Size of Glass, in.	Wt., lbs.	Price
8T1462	17	6x 8	3	$1.53
8T1463	20	8x10	4	1.89

Our Beauty Stand and Shaving Mirror.

One of the finest manufactured. Beautiful, artistic, heavy scroll design, guaranteed gold plated. Large handsome 6½x9-inch heavy oval French beveled plate mirror set in heavy beautiful flower and scroll design frame, with large, massive four-footed base, arising from which are two arms with screws supporting the mirror. By means of these adjustable screws the mirror can be tilted backward or forward or placed at any desired angle. The frame and stand are of large massive design and guaranteed gold plated throughout. A fine gift for gentleman or lady. Each in box. Shipping weight, 7 pounds. Will easily sell for $5.00.

No. 8T1465 Our price..........$2.47

Comb, Brush and Mirror Set.

This beautiful high class ebony finished toilet set is composed of a thirteen-row long fine white bristle hair brush, a 5-inch heavy French bevel plate mirror, and a 7½-inch fancy design dressing comb. Both brush and mirror have fine fleur de lis embossed mountings. Packed in fine brocade lined display box. Size, 11x10½x2 inches. Shipping weight, 2 pounds. An exceptionally high class item. Good $2.50 value.

No. 8T1701 Our price..........$1.98

Imported Palm Plants.

Extensively used for ornamenting parlors and halls. These plants are naturally prepared and very lasting. Made of best material and much better than the cheaper kinds offered at about our prices. They come packed flat, without the pots. Are easily set up. Sizes and prices are as follows:

No. 8T1796 Height, 36 inches; branches, 4 inches. Shipping wt., 6 lbs. Price, each..........69c

No. 8T1797 Height, 40 inches; branches, 5 inches. Shipping wt., 8 lbs. Price, each..........83c

No. 8T1798 Height, 45 inches; branches, 7 inches. Shipping wt., 8½ lbs. Price, each..........$1.10

No. 8T1799 Height, 60 inches; branches, 10 inches. Shipping wt., 10 lbs. Price, each..........$2.55

The 10-branch palm comes in shape of a tree with removable branches to set in tin tubes, and branches much larger size than the 4, 5 and 7-inch plants.

PYROGRAPHY OR THE ART OF WOOD BURNING

PYROGRAPHY OR WOOD ETCHING is the art of burning decorated stamped designs on wood, leather or cardboard by means of a heated platinum point. The heat is produced with the rubber bellows and attachments, as fully explained with each outfit. Pyrography is wonderfully fascinating. It requires no great amount of talent to produce very satisfactory results. When you consider the small expense for an outfit to begin in this art and the enjoyment it brings, it is worthy the efforts of anyone who has a desire to develop a natural gift in the line of art.

YOU CAN MAKE AN EXCELLENT LIVING in pyrography, as the designs and pictures are so artistic and popular they bring good prices. Articles costing but 15 cents or 25 cents when burned and stained bring as high as $1.00, which is about the proportion of profit throughout. Photo frames, fancy designed panels, table book racks, collar, cuff, handkerchief and necktie boxes, pipe and spoon holders, etc., are very popular, adding much to the artistic appearance of any home. They also make handsome presents which are always deeply appreciated, because they are the work of one's own hands.

BUY THE BEST. The main essential in this line is the best of materials. We are handling the best line manufactured, all parts being made of the finest white basswood, made in three-ply construction to prevent warping, beautifully polished and finished, and then very clearly stamped with very popular and artistic designs. Many cheap imitations are mere prints in black ink instead of brown, and upon wood of much poorer grade and finish. Brown stamps should always be used as black is very hard to follow, is indistinct and unless burned exactly as designed will leave black lines to show through and spoil the finished article. We have had all the experience in this line. Take our frank advice and select any one of the following lines you may desire and you will have the best workmanship and material in every respect. You cannot buy any better goods or material, no matter how much you are willing to pay.

This High Grade Amateur Pyrographic Outfit in Fine Basswood Box with a Reliable Platinum Point for only $1.79.

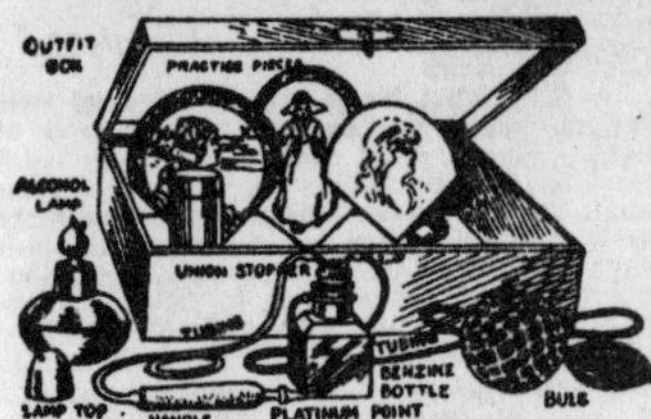

This outfit is especially intended for those expecting to do a limited amount of work. An exceptionally high grade outfit put up in a clearly stamped fine white basswood box for burning. The outfit contains a good curved platinum point, plain cork handle, medium size, imported double rubber bulb and tubing; alcohol lamp with wick complete; metal union stopper and glass bottle for benzine; three pieces stamped for practice work and full instructions for burning. Put up in a well made white basswood box, size 9x5½x3¾ inches, stamped with design ready for decorating and may be used as photo or glove box. We do not wish this outfit confused with many of the so called cheap combination outfits offered for a few cents cheaper price. Well worth $3.50. Shipping wt., 3 lbs.

No. 8T4600 Our price **$1.79**

Peerless Professional Pyrographic Outfit.

This outfit contains the most complete assortment of materials used in pyrographic decorations. In addition to the principal articles required for burning, it contains an Instruction Sheet, liquid water color outfit, transparent Pyro varnish, painting and staining brushes, and Peerless patent cork handle with controlling device by means of which the heated point can be regulated perfectly for steady low, medium or high temperature burning. The outfit consists of a large imported double rubber bulb with long tubing, benzine bottle with metal cork, glass top alcohol lamp, rubber tubing, Peerless patent cork handle, metal union stopper, liquid water color outfit, ¼ pint Pelican varnish, 1-6 pint Pelican ebony wood stain, one water color brush, one varnish brush, instructions for burning, three exceptionally fine pieces stamped for practice work, and a fine platinum point for burning. All contained in the well finished white basswood box, size 10x7x4 inches, stamped with a suitable design for burning. Regular price, $5.75 and well worth $7.50. Shipping wt., 3½ lbs.

No. 8T4610 Our price **$3.69**

Platinum Points, Stains, Bulbs and Materials.

No. 8T4625 Swivel Cork Handles, with revolving joint to prevent tubing from twisting. Price, (Postage extra, 2 cents.) .. **19c**

No. 8T4626 Cork Handle, plain style. Price .... (Postage extra, 2 cents.) **14c**

No. 8T4627 Extra Large Imported Double Rubber Bulb, with long tubing, the kind usually sold at $1.50. Our price .... **$1.00** Postage, extra, 4c.

No. 8T4628 Large Imported Double Rubber Bulb, with long tubing. Worth $1.00. Our price .... (Postage extra, 3c.) **63c**

No. 8T4629 Klean Best Eraser. Especially prepared for cleaning wood and leather articles. The best made. Price .... (Postage extra, 4 cents.) **19c**

No. 8T4630 Heavy Imported Rubber Tubing. Price, per 3-foot length .... **15c** If mail shipment, postage extra, per foot, 3c.

No. 8T4631 Metal Union T Cork. Price, each ... (Postage extra, each, 2c) ... **8c**

No. 8T4632 Alcohol Lamp. Price, **15c** If mail shipment, postage extra, 10 cents.

Pyro-Benzine. This is especially prepared for pyro work and will work much better than regular benzine. Will burn much better and save the point. Include several cans in your order.

No. 8T4633 Price, ½-pint can ..... **14c** Unmailable.

No. 8T4634 Metal T Union Stoppered Benzine Bottle. Price **10c**

Water Color Stains. Six bottles of absolutely fast colors, red, yellow, green, blue, violet and brown. Shipping wt., 1 lb.

No. 8T4640 Price, per set **35c**

Oil Stains for pyro work, mahogany, cherry, walnut, flemish and ebony. These stains are pure and strong and will not fade. Give even and best results with any finishers. Be sure to state color. Regular price, per airtight can, 35c.

No. 8T4641 Our price, 4-ounce can **21c** Shipping wt., 10 oz.

Pyro-Varnish, for finishing decorated burnt wood articles. Best preparation and greatly adds to beauty and finish. Put up in 4-ounce cans. Regular price, 40 cents.

No. 8T4652 Our price ... **27c** Postage extra, 8 cents.

BRUSHES SUITABLE FOR STAINS AND SHELLAC.

No. 8T4655 ⅛-Inch Brush **7c**
No. 8T4656 ¼-Inch Brush **9c**
No. 8T4657 ½-Inch Brush **12c**

Points.

No. 8T4670 Used for average lines and general utility work. Price **$1.00**

No. 8T4671 Used for points, delicate lines and leatherwork. Price, **$1.00**

No. 8T4672 Used for background and shading work. Price **$1.00**

No. 8T4675 Used for average lines and general utility work. Price **$1.39**

No. 8T4676 Used for points, delicate lines and leather work. Price **$1.39**

No. 8T4677 Used for background and shading work. Price, **$1.39**

Heavy Platinum Combined Scorcher and Point. To be used as a regular point or a scorcher.

No. 8T4680 Price, **$2.25** If mail shipment, postage extra on all points, each, 3 cents.

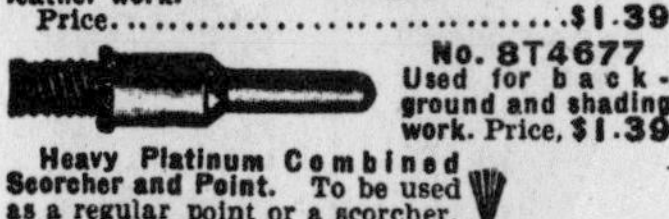

FANCY ASSORTMENTS FOR DECORATING.

These three assortments have been selected with special care. They are all made of the finest white basswood, three-ply construction, and are plainly stamped, easily burned, and make articles of exceptional beauty when finished.

Amateur Assortment.

THE GREATEST NUMBER OF REALLY HIGH GRADE PIECES EVER SOLD FOR 98c.

The outfit consists of a handkerchief box, 6x6 inches; fancy hinge cover glove box, 10½x3½ inches; oval shaped Indian Head design match holder; oval 6x12-inch football Boy plaque; square oval opening photo frame; 4x8-inch oval panel; 6-inch circular panel; one heart shaped panel and one small circular practice piece. The best outfit ever offered for anywhere near 98 cents. The items if bought separately would cost you at least $1.75. Shipping wt., 2½ lbs.

No. 8T4875 Our price **98c**

Our Big $1.59 Assortment.

This complete assortment is of the finest white basswood three-ply construction, beautifully stamped for burning and is in our opinion as all the other items shown, exceptional value. It is composed of the most popular selling pieces and if bought separately would cost you $2.50 to $2.75. The outfit consists of an exceptionally fine 7x7-inch fancy beveled edge hinge cover, fancy clasp handkerchief box; a 12x4-inch fancy beveled edge glove box, 12 inches high; fancy decorated necktie holder; 9½-inch match holder; heart shaped and circular practice pieces; the favorite club shaped whisk broom holder; an 8x10-inch fancy shaped photo frame with easel; a 12-inch fancy decorated edge celebrated Pharaoh's Horses panel, and a 11x13-inch Dog and Game dining room plaque. All carefully packed in box for shipping. Shipping wt., 4 lbs. A wonderful value. **No. 8T4880** Our price **$1.59**

Our Big 18-Piece Leader for Only $1.98.

The greatest value ever offered. An assortment for wood burning. Every piece the best and the designs the most popular. Every article burns to exceptional beauty. Assortment comprises one 16x7½-inch cover fancy extension top and bottom photo box; 4x12-inch fancy beveled edge hinge cover glove box; 7x7-inch fancy hinge cover beveled edge handkerchief box; an 8x10-inch shield shaped U. S. flag; decorated Indian Head design pipe and match holder; a 4x8-inch grape decorated oval panel; a 6-inch circular panel; two oval shaped practice pieces; two 3-inch circular practice pieces; two heart shaped 3½-inch practice pieces; three 3x5-inch oblong panels; an 8x10-inch oblong photo frame with easel; an 11x13-inch oval plaque and a special favorite souvenir postal and letter holder, which is interchangeable and can be used for either one. Each piece in the above set beautifully and clearly decorated. Shipping wt., 6¾ lbs. Packed in heavy box for shipping. Ordinary value, $4.25.

No. 8T4885 Our price **$1.98**

Gas Jet Outfit.

Comprises a wooden knob for fitting over gas jet, 5 feet rubber tubing together with wooden handle and special burning point. This is largely used by both amateurs and professionals, is very cheap in price and can be used by many persons not desiring a large bulb or more complete outfit. Each packed in fine basswood box decorated for burning. Also includes directions for attachment and burning. Ordinary value, 75 cents.

No. 8T4682 Our price .... **33c** If mail shipment, postage extra, 6 cents.

Favorite Pieces.

FANCY DECORATED PANELS.

These beautiful and clear design panels in the neat decorated border make a very easy yet artistic design for amateurs. Subjects are clear, popular and easy to burn, 12-in. size. Regular price, 50 cents. Shipping wt., 2 lbs.

No. 8T4782 Indian Head design. Our price **19c**

No. 8T4783 Stag Head design. Our price **19c**

No. 8T4784 Pharaoh's Horses design. Our price .... (Unmailable.) **19c**

Novelty Match Hangers.

Easy subjects, assorted shapes and designs, clearly stamped, and useful in any home. Contain holding and scratching attachment. Regular 25-cent value.

No. 8T4745 Our price .. **19c** If mail shipment, postage extra, 5 cents.

Photo Frames.

Fine white basswood, three-ply construction to prevent warping. Very artistic in shape and fine in finish. Fitted with glass and ring.

No. 8T4700 Fancy design Photo Frame, size 8x10 inches. Furnished in Holly, Poinsettia, Poppy or Cherry design. State design wanted. Ordinary value, 35 cents. Shipping wt., 9 oz. Our price **19c**

No. 8T4705 Square Photo Frame, with stand attachment, size 8x10 inches. Furnished in Holly, Poinsettia, Poppy or Cherry design. State design wanted. Ordinary 40 to 45 cent value. Shipping wt., 10 oz. Our price **27c**

Double Cabinet Opening Photo Frames. Fitted with glass back and standing attachment. Regular price, 85 cents to $1.00.

No. 8T4715 Size frame 9x12 inches. Furnished in either Holly or Rose design. State design wanted. Our price .... **35c** Unmailable.

Book Holder. These folding book holders have of late been very popular and are largely used on library and parlor tables for holding a few favorite books. Owl and Moon design. This book rack when properly burned and stained makes a very handsome ornament. Size, 15x6 inches. Ordinary value, 65 cents. Shipping wt., 12 oz.

No. 8T4810 Our price **43c**

Fancy Boxes.

Made in every case of the finest of white basswood, very firmly constructed. Brass clasp and hinges, and stamped with exceptionally plain, clear and beautiful designs.

No. 8T4725 Handkerchief Box, size 7x7 inches; fancy beveled edge top. Furnished in Poinsettia, Holly, Rose or Cherry design. State design wanted. Ordinary 40 to 45-cent value. Shipping wt., 11 oz. Our price **23c**

No. 8T4730 Glove and Necktie Box, size 4x12 inches, fancy beveled edge top. Furnished in Poinsettia, Holly, Rose or Cherry design. State design wanted. Regular 50-cent value. Shipping wt., 12 oz. Our price **23c**

No. 8T4740 Collar and Cuff Box, size 5x7½x7½ inches, with fine extension top and bottom. Furnished in Poinsettia, Holly, Rose or Cherry design. State design wanted. Ordinarily 65-cent value. Shipping wt., 16 oz. Our price **47c**

No. 8T4735 Photo Box, size 7½x15½ inches; fancy extension top and bottom. An exceptionally fine box. Furnished in both Rose and Holly designs. Ordinary value, 85 cents to $1.00. Shipping wt., 24 oz. Our price .... (Unmailable) **67c**

No. 8T4737 Post Card Box. A big leader, holds 200 cards. Beautifully and clearly stamped with name "Post Cards" on top. Size, 6x4x4½ inches. Regular price, 40 cents. Our price .... (Unmailable) **23c**

Skins for Decorating.

These are extra fine skins, natural shape, smooth on one side and soft velvet finish on the other. Largely used as tablethrows, den hangers or stamped for burning. Size of skins, about 7½ square feet. Colors, golden rod, light grass green, dark bottle green, mahogany, tan, dark cinnamon, ruby red, navy blue, medium gray, very light tan or olive green. When ordering, be sure to state color wanted. Shipping wt., 1½ lbs.

No. 8T4685 Price, each **$1.29**

Beautifully decorated Leather Sofa Pillow Tops. Handsome and artistic, made of best heavy velvet leather. Differently colored leather backs. Top beautifully hand pyrographically burned. Fancy cut edges and a pillow top that will last a lifetime. The same filling can be used in this as any other pillow. Size, 29 inches square. Furnished in green, tan or red leather. Specify color. Regular $5.00 to $7.00 value. Shipping wt., 2 lbs.

No. 8T4687 Stag Head. Our price **$3.75**
No. 8T4688 Indian Head. Our price **3.75**

Fancy decorated Leather Library Hangers. Full size velvet leather skins, hand burned, in both Indian and Stag Head designs. Very artistic, handsome and exceedingly popular and ornamental. Size, about 35x35 inches. Furnished in green, red or tan leather. Specify color. Regular price $4.00 to $5.00. Shipping wt., 1½ lbs.

No. 8T4689 Indian Head. Our price **$2.69**
No. 8T4690 Stag Head. Our price **2.69**

Fancy decorated Leather Table Throw. By far the most popular of any library table cover. Soft velvet skins, round shape, 19 inches diameter and with six beautiful appliqued raised Poinsettia flower decorations. Furnished in green, tan or red leather. Specify color. The rage of the season. You must see it to appreciate its value. Ornaments any home. Regular price, $2.50. Shipping wt., 12 oz.

No. 8T4691 Our price **$1.49**

7 cents each WONDERFUL VALUES IN DRUGS, NOVELTIES AND TOYS

COMPARE PRICES. Just see how much you can save. If you will only compare our prices on these articles with what they will cost you if bought anywhere else, you will soon realize what exceptional bargains they represent; then call your friends' and neighbors' attention to them and send us an order for as many as you want, but in no case order less than six. Order other goods that you need at the same time so that they can be included in your freight or express order. These about one-half regular drug prices are really wonderful and you should take advantage of them.

ORDER AT LEAST AN ASSORTMENT OF SIX OF THESE ARTICLES AT A TIME. To make up the six you can include some from the 17 and 33-cent articles shown on the following pages, but don't fail to order at least six items (either all one kind or assorted, just as you choose). We must ask our customers to observe this rule in order that we may continue to make these low prices. Look over the list very carefully, make your order as large as possible and take advantage of these values. Order as many as you need. Observe our rule about ordering not less than six articles, giving in each case the catalog number and allowing the price given upon the page from which you select the item, and help us to maintain these remarkably low prices.

No. 8T7148 4-ounce bottle fine Fountain Pen Ink.

No. 8T7149 Box best Metal Cleaning Polish ever made.

No. 8T7152 Rubber lined Sponge or Wash Rag Bag.

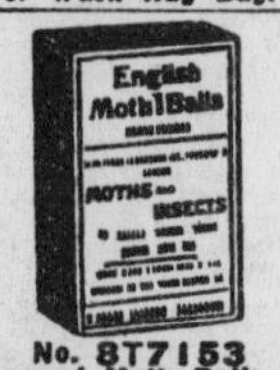

No. 8T7153 1 pound Moth Balls in carton. Should be in every home for keeping moths out of furs, clothing, etc.

No. 8T7154 Infant's Hair Comb, in ivory, pink or blue. State color wanted.

No. 8T7156 Aluminum Tooth Brush and Curling Iron Holder.

No. 8T7157 Big value roll medium grade Toilet Paper.

No. 8T7547 1,000-sheet roll finest quality satin finished tissue Toilet Paper. 15-cent value.

No. 8T7168 Box Flower and Leaf Decorated Stationery.

No. 8T7170 Beautiful satin finished aluminum 4-inch Pocket Mirror, fancy picture back. Every lady wants one.

No. 8T7172 7-inch fine rubber Ladies' Dressing Comb.

No. 8T7175 7-inch white pyralin Dressing Comb. Always white and pretty.

No. 8T7173 Fancy aluminum Soap Box. Word "Soap" embossed on top.

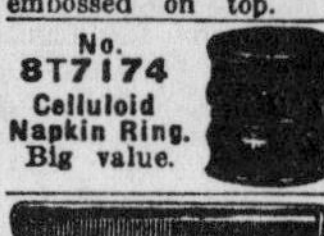

No. 8T7174 Celluloid Napkin Ring. Big value.

No. 8T7177 7-inch metal back horn Comb.

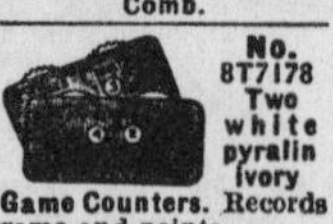

No. 8T7178 Two white pyralin ivory Game Counters. Records game and points.

No. 8T7179 Ladies' 3x5-inch Hand Mirror with handle.

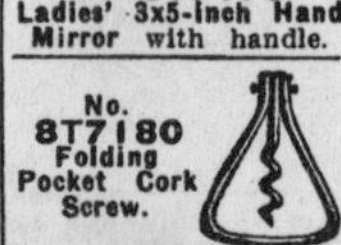

No. 8T7180 Folding Pocket Cork Screw.

No. 8T7183 Fancy hanging double shell Pin Cushion. Sells easily for 25 cents.

No. 8T7184 Fancy shell Paper Weight. A handsome ornament.

No. 8T7185 25-cent picture side pocket spring Measure. Wonderful value.

No. 8T7186 Finely polished aluminum Pocket Rule in leather case.

No. 8T7187 Pocket Toilet Mirror in leather case. Handy, fine glass and a big seller.

No. 8T7192 Two large rolls of 20 feet each, fancy Shelf Paper. White, green or red. State color wanted.

No. 8T7195 Mahogany finish Hair Brush. Great value.

No. 8T7188 Pocket Toilet Case, beveled mirror. You will be surprised at this great value.

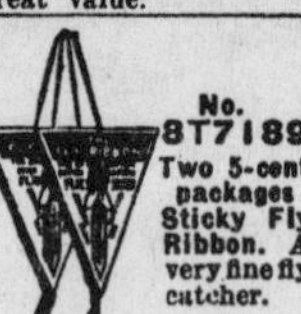

No. 8T7189 Two 5-cent packages Sticky Fly Ribbon. A very fine fly catcher.

No. 8T7197 5½-inch fancy aluminum Letter Opener.

No. 8T7198 Fancy Crepe Paper Lunch Set. Contains one tablecloth 42x56 inches and one dozen fancy flower and gilt decorated napkins. Worth 25 cents.

No. 8T7200 Fancy decorated Aluminum Pocket Memorandum Book.

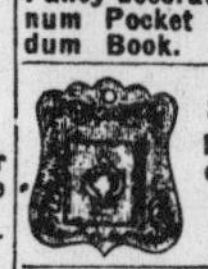

No. 8T7201 Fancy decorated aluminum Match Holder.

No. 8T7202 Big value Shoe Brush.

No. 8T7203 Metal handle Shoe Dauber.

No. 8T7205 Fancy aluminum Whisk Broom Holder.

No. 8T7208 15-cent Celluloid Whistle.

No. 8T7209 Pocket Pencil Holder and Clasp.

No. 8T7210 13-inch fine wool Duster.

No. 8T7211 Tube fine Tooth Paste.

No. 8T7212 Imported polished Clothes Brush.

No. 8T7214 9x12-inch folding paper Waste Basket. Great value.

No. 8T7215 Imported Hat and Cleaning Brush.

No. 8T7216 ¼-pound box assorted sizes and kinds of fancy Japanese Aquarium Shells.

No. 8T7219 10 yards of 2½-inch plain Gauze Bandage.

No. 8T7220 Two big rolls, 24 sheets, 12x18-inch Pure Waxed Lunch Paper.

No. 8T7221 Picture back 2-inch pocket Reducing Mirror. Shows whole face. Great value.

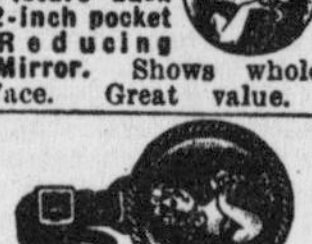

No. 8T7222 Ladies' picture front and mirror back leather Watch Fob.

No. 8T7223 One dozen assorted colors fine School Crayons.

No. 8T7224 One-half dozen hoof shaped Orangewood Sticks.

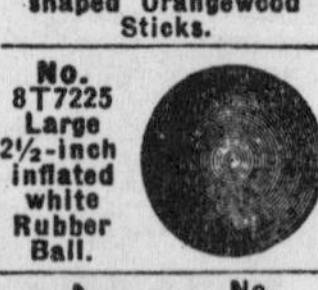

No. 8T7225 Large 2½-inch inflated white Rubber Ball.

No. 8T7261 Fruit Pin Cushion, natural color decorated.

No. 8T7262 Donkey Match Holder, metal base.

TOILET SOAPS. Extraordinary Values.

No. 8T7226 Violet Soap, 3 cakes to box.

No. 8T7227 Oatmeal Soap, 3 cakes to box.

No. 8T7228 Buttermilk Soap, 3 cakes to box.

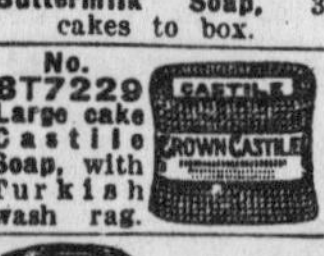

No. 8T7229 Large cake Castile Soap, with Turkish wash rag.

No. 8T7230 Cake exceptionally fine perfumed La Flora Bouquet Toilet Soap.

No. 8T7231 Two large cakes Forest Queen Soap. Wonderful value.

BIG VALUES IN CANDY

No. 8T7232 One-half pound finest high grade crystallized sugar Gum Drops. A big favorite and high quality.

No. 8T7581 One pound medium grade sugar Gum Drops. Assorted colors and flavors.

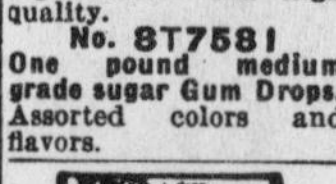

No. 8T7233 15-cent box Berry's Cream Caramels, assorted flavors.

No. 8T7234 Two 5-cent boxes Berry's fine Butter Scotch Candy.

No. 8T7235 10-cent box Chocolate dipped Marshmallows.

No. 8T7236 Large box Peanut Candy.

No. 8T7237 Box Berry's assorted Chocolates.

No. 8T7238 10-cent box Berry's Chocolate Dipped Peppermints.

No. 8T7239 Two 5-cent boxes Berry's fine Fruit Tablets, assorted flavors.

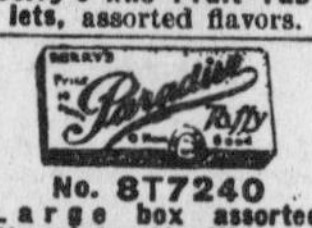

No. 8T7240 Large box assorted Chocolate, Vanilla and Strawberry Taffy. Very popular.

No. 8T7241 Berry's Chocolate Dipped Molasses Chips.

No. 8T7242 10-cent box Berry's fine Chocolate Dipped Cream Caramels.

No. 8T7264 6-inch Indian hand made Canoe, sweet grass and porcupine trimming, leather hanger and bead decorated.

No. 8T7265 Fancy Crepe Shelf Paper, tinted edge, something new, yet exceedingly popular. Decorate your shelves with this new paper. Furnished in pale blue, light pink, white or ruby red. Specify color.

No. 8T7266 Beautiful leather Watch Fob with fancy design metal automobile tip, gilt finished and worth 25 cents. Every man wants one.

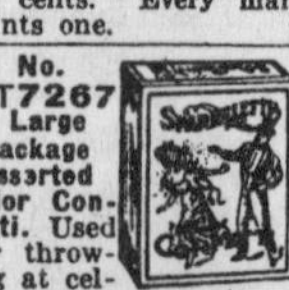

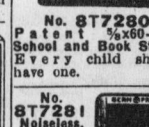

No. 8T7267 Large package assorted color Confetti. Used for throwing at celebrations, picnics, festivities, etc. Better than rice at weddings. You cannot shake it off.

No. 8T7268 Imported Eyebrow Pencil, black or brown. Specify color. A big leader. Sold by many at 25 cents.

No. 8T7269 5-inch fancy Cone Shell. Beautifully pinked and leaf cut decorated.

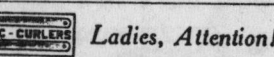

Ladies, Attention!

No. 8T7263 Magic Magnetized Steel Hair Curlers. Don't put up your hair in paper at night. Forget about curling your hair until about ten minutes before you are ready, then use Magic Hair Curlers. They curl or wave the straight hair in ten minutes without heat while you are dressing, traveling, anywhere, any time. Stylish and up to date. Do not omit them from your order. Makes the genuine marcel wave. Two curlers on card.

No. 8T7274 Two 6x9-inch mammoth Pencil Tablets, containing 120 sheets each. Wonderful value.

No. 8T7275 Two 6x9-inch Ink Writing Tablets, containing 68 sheets each. You will be surprised at the value.

No. 8T7276 Large 8x10-inch Monitor Composition Book, containing 44 sheets, very highest grade plate paper.

No. 8T7277 Two large Ink Composition Books, containing 48 sheets each, best paper.

No. 8T7278 Oakwood Linen Unruled Paper, letter size, 8x10 inches, contains 48 sheets, best high grade paper.

No. 8T7280 Patent ⅝x60-inch School and Book Strap. Every child should have one.

No. 8T7281 Noiseless, antiseptic, germproof Slate, 6½x10 inches, first quality. A great bargain.

No. 8T7283 Two leatherette covered Pocket Memorandum Books with rubber band holders. Big value.

No. 8T7288 Prestomatic Indelible Metal Pencil, vest pocket size. Sold by many as high as 25 cents each. Extraordinary value.

No. 8T7289 Eagle Fountain Pen. The only cheap pen that is reliable.

No. 8T7290 3½-inch Screw Metal Pencil.

No. 8T7291 Four fancy flower and color decorated Birthday Cards, with verse.

No. 8T7292 Imported Metal Paint Box, containing assorted colors, with brush and stick. Entertainment and education for the child.

No. 8T7293 Fancy embossed aluminum Stamp Box, hand carved top. "Stamps" embossed on cover.

No. 8T7294 7x8-inch transparent Drawing Slate with seven assorted pictures. A very instructive pastime for children.

No. 8T7295 Novelty picture front Paper Clasp.

No. 8T7296 Pencil Assortment in holly box. Everybody should have one.

No. 8T7297 Noiseless leatherette covered, felt lined Pencil Box. Much superior to the old noisy kind. Teachers hail its coming with delight.

No. 8T7298 Fish Pond Game, complete. A great pastime for children.

7 cents each — WONDERFUL VALUES IN DRUGS, NOVELTIES AND TOYS — 7 cents each

7 CENTS EACH FOR ANY ARTICLE ON THIS PAGE IN ASSORTMENTS OF SIX OR MORE.

JUST THINK of 10, 15 and 25-cent drug store items sold for only 7 cents each! Go over this page and the following bargain pages, item by item, all wonderful values; compare our prices with what you will have to pay at home. Every item is a real big bargain. While goods sold by others may look like these illustrations, we know when you compare the goods, our qualities will be better. Many merchants are buying these items from us, knowing they can make money selling them. Surely you can't fail to realize what big values they are. Look over the pages carefully and make up your order. Order at least an assortment of six items. You can make up your order of six items from our pages of 7 to 33-cent items. You can order as many more than six as you please.

No. 8T7000 Bottle Perfume in "Hello, Central" case. Very popular and great value.

No. 8T7001 ¼ pound finely perfumed Rice Powder, soft and velvety. Fine for the face and as a baby powder. Absolutely harmless.

No. 8T7002 Box fine Face Powder. Pure, soft and sweetly perfumed.

No. 8T7003 2-ounce jar fine snow white Violet Cold Cream. Easily sells for 25 cents.

No. 8T7004 Package Rose or Violet Sachet Powder. Fine for perfuming handkerchiefs, neckties and clothes generally.

No. 8T7005 Cake Beauty Complexion Soap. The beauty's favorite. Pure and harmless. Give it a trial.

TOILET SOAPS.

No. 8T7008 Box Pure Cold Cream Soap.

No. 8T7009 Box Transparent Glycerin Soap.

No. 8T7010 Box Castile Soap.

No. 8T7089 Box fine Witch Hazel Soap.

No. 8T7013 Two large cakes Brown's Old Original Pine Tar Soap. Cleaning, healing and antiseptic. One of the best made. Sold by others at 5 cents per cake.

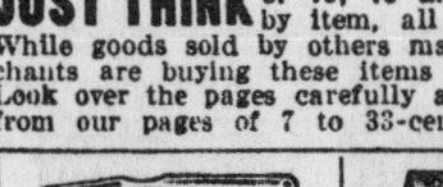

No. 8T7012 25-cent fancy sanitary back Tooth Brush.

No. 8T7017 Three 5-cent red rubber Nursing Nipples.

No. 8T7018 Two 10-cent Styptic Pencils to stop bleeding and for hardening the skin if tender after shaving.

No. 8T7019 25-cent box Albi-Denta Tooth Soap. Antiseptic, preserves while it beautifies; hardens the gums and whitens the teeth.

No. 8T7020 Two 5-cent boxes Menthol Cough Drops.

No. 8T7021 Two 5-cent boxes Hoarhound Candy.

No. 8T7022 Two 5-cent boxes Lemon Ice Candy.

No. 8T7025 Florida Water for toilet or bath use. A great favorite. 2-ounce bottle.

LADIES, NOTICE!

No. 8T7026 Cake celebrated Williams' Matinee Violets Toilet Soap. One of the best and most sweetly perfumed soaps made. Order one or two cakes and try it.

No. 8T7028 Two 5-cent packages Sen Sen Breath Perfume.

No. 8T7029 Two 5-cent boxes Candied Cherries.

No. 8T7030 Cake Toilet Pumice Stone for whitening the hands, manicuring and toilet use.

No. 8T7031 Complete Manicure Set. Comprising nail powder, emery nail files, pumice stone and cuticle stick. Big value.

No. 8T7033 Two 5-cent boxes Licorice Lozenges.

No. 8T7035 Glass Nasal Douche, in carton. Largely used for applying liquids to the nose. Should be in every home.

No. 8T7036 Package Genuine Blue Jay Corn Plasters.

No. 8T7037 2-ounce jar Hair Shampoo Jelly. Regular 25-cent size. Makes the hair fluffy and clean.

No. 8T7039 Box Camphor Ice, for chapped hands and lips and as application after shaving.

No. 8T7041 Two boxes imported Japanese Tooth Picks.

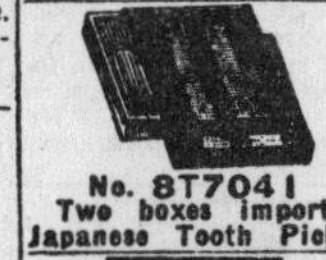

No. 8T7042 15-cent white pyralin Fine Tooth Comb. Great value.

No. 8T7043 15-cent hard rubber Fine Tooth Comb. Sells on sight.

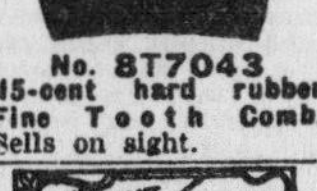

No. 8T7047 Clean your old straw hat. Akely's Powder makes it look like new. Does the work quickly and easily. Full directions on package. A big seller.

No. 8T7052 Toothache Drops. Apply into cavity of tooth to stop the ache. Reliable, quick to act and should be in every home.

No. 8T7054 3x5-inch Gents' Shaving and Stand Mirror. Wonderful value.

No. 8T7055 Quick Relief Toothache Gum. Fills up cavity and stops the toothache. Easy to apply and results certain.

No. 8T7056 Novelty Shell Bag Pipe Whistle, with fancy Job's tear and bagpipe decorations. A great novelty and you want one.

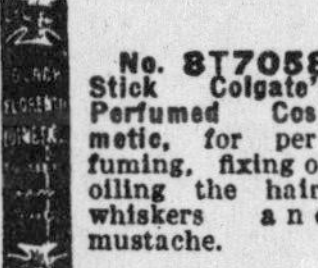

No. 8T7058 Stick Colgate's Perfumed Cosmetic, for perfuming, fixing or oiling the hair, whiskers and mustache.

No. 8T7059 Two packages best Chewing Gum.

No. 8T7060 Novelty Pipe Fan. By pulling out stem gives circular United States fan in colors. Very novel and sells on sight. Size, 13 inches.

No. 8T7061 Imported ladies' bone handle Tooth Brush.

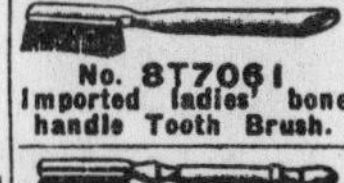

No. 8T7062 Child's fine bone handle Tooth Brush.

No. 8T7063 Imported bone handle Nail and Hand Brush.

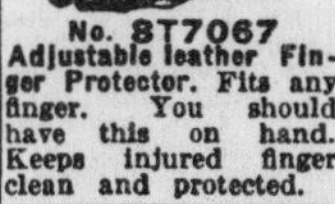

No. 8T7067 Adjustable leather Finger Protector. Fits any finger. You should have this on hand. Keeps injured finger clean and protected.

No. 8T7068 Imported bone Ear Cleaner and Sponge.

No. 8T7074 Graduated Nursing Bottle and red rubber Nipple.

No. 8T7069 3-inch best steel nickel plated Tweezers for pulling out splinters, holding small objects and has many home uses. Regular 25-cent grade.

No. 8T7072 Fine hard rubber Pocket Comb in case.

No. 8T7075 Celluloid Eye Shade. For better shade see No. 8T8475, page 389.

No. 8T7076 5-inch Nail File and Cleaner. A fine instrument and well worth 25 cents.

No. 8T7077 Box fifty assorted sizes and widths Rubber Bands.

No. 8T7078 Gents' 7-inch fine aluminum Comb.

No. 8T7171 Barbers' 7-inch fine hard rubber Comb.

No. 8T7079 Two Bell Baby Rattles.

No. 8T7081 25-cent nickel plated Blackhead and Pimple Remover with ear spoon end.

A FINE TOOTH POWDER.

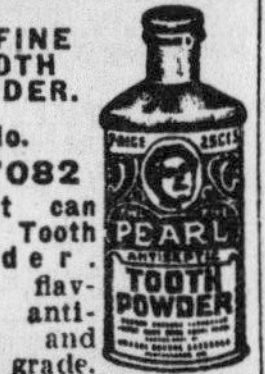

No. 8T7082 25-cent can Pearl Tooth Powder. Nicely flavored, antiseptic and high grade.

No. 8T7083 Folding nickel plated Nail File and Cleaner.

No. 8T7084 15-cent leather Wrist Supporter.

No. 8T7085 Three 5-cent packages fine Silk Court Plaster.

No. 8T7086 Two fancy pinked edge face Chamois Skins.

No. 8T7087 15-cent pinked edge white face Chamois Skin.

TWO BEAUTIFUL BIRTHDAY CARDS.

No. 8T7092 Two beautiful satin mounted, color decorated birthday Post Cards with birthday greetings. Sell at 10 cents each.

No. 8T7096 25-cent jar Orange Flower Skin Food. For beautifying the skin and keeping it soft and beautiful.

No. 8T7097 4-ounce bottle Carter's Blue Black Writing Fluid.

No. 8T7098 4-ounce jar best Mucilage with brush.

No. 8T7099 15-cent imported down Face Puff.

No. 8T7100 Two 10-cent cans fine Talcum Powder. You will make no mistake in buying a dozen cans.

No. 8T7102 Box fine Writing Paper and Envelopes. Big value.

No. 8T7103 Box (24 sheets and envelopes) fancy Juvenile Stationery.

No. 8T7104 ½-ounce bottle Royal Perfume, in violet, white rose, crabapple, lily of the valley or carnation odors. Exceptional value. State odor wanted.

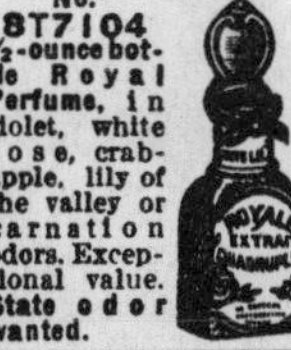

No. 8T7107 4-ounce bottle Liquid Egg Shampoo. For cleaning the hair and making it soft, healthy and fluffy. 25-cent value.

No. 8T7105 Two large cakes Genuine Force Pumice Soap for cleaning the hands and removing callous parts and all dirt and stains.

ROSE WATER AND GLYCERIN.

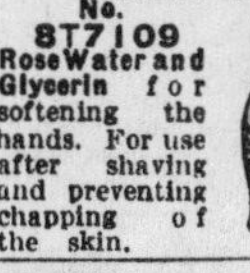

No. 8T7109 Rose Water and Glycerin for softening the hands. For use after shaving and preventing chapping of the skin.

No. 8T7111 Deck Steamboat Playing Cards. Great value.

No. 8T7115 Large house or boat cleaning Sponge.

No. 8T7108 Large fine soft bleached Bath Sponge.

No. 8T7116 Fine pyralin Baby Rattle in pink, baby blue or white. State color.

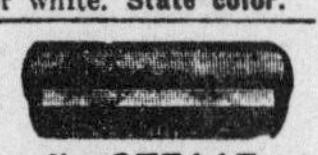

No. 8T7117 15-cent wooden handle Nail Brush.

No. 8T7119 15-cent can fine Violet Talcum Powder, soothing and healing.

No. 8T7120 14-inch Loofah Bath and Flesh Brush.

No. 8T7122 Box fine Silver Polish. Does not scratch.

No. 8T7125 2-ounce bottle Liquid Glue. Mends and sticks everything. One of the best stickers known.

No. 8T7127 Oval gilt Photo Frame. Everybody wants one.

No. 8T7128 Three good 5-cent Lead Pencils with erasers.

No. 8T7129 100 fancy Paper Napkins. 25-cent value.

No. 8T7131 Four 5-cent envelopes best Poison Fly Paper.

No. 8T7133 Fancy decorated embossed Card or Ash Tray.

No. 8T7134 Fancy imported Autograph Album, 6x9 inches. Great value.

No. 8T7136 Bottle Japanese Gold Ink. Writes beautiful gold color and keeps indefinitely. Very popular.

No. 8T7137 Cake Transparent Tar Shampoo Soap. Lathers freely and leaves hair fine, silky, clean and glossy.

CHAPPED HAND LOTION.

No. 8T7138 Lilac Hand Softener and Whitener.

No. 8T7140 2-ounce package Absorbent Cotton. Should be in every home for emergency use.

No. 8T7144 Two cakes Colgate's fine Shaving Soap.

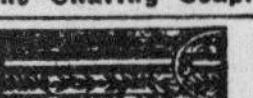

No. 8T7146 Rubber lined Tooth Brush Holder. Keeps brush clean and antiseptic.

No. 8T7151 Fancy silver plated Pocket Match Holder. 25-cent value.

POST CARD AND GAME VALUES

7 cents each

YOU CAN HAVE ANY ARTICLE ON THIS PAGE FOR 7 CENTS EACH in assortment of six or more. To make up your six items you can select any item from this page or from any of our eleven pages of 7-cent to 33-cent items. We must make this rule in order that we may be able to sell these goods at such remarkably low prices. **THESE POST CARDS, GAMES** and other articles shown on these bargain pages are wonderful values. We buy them in enormous quantities at lowest prices and sell them at our cost, plus our one small profit. Don't pay fancy prices; select your wants from these pages. See also our 47-cent, 67-cent and 97-cent bargains on the following pages. **ALSO NOTE OUR 2-CENT TO 12-CENT BARGAINS IN THE FIRST PAGES OF THIS CATALOG.**

No. 8T7299 Scroll Puzzle, assorted subjects. Forty separate pieces. A fine and very fascinating pastime for old and young.

No. 8T7300 Two 10-cent mirror back Puzzles. Amusement by the hour.

No. 8T7301 Genuine Wizard Game. A very popular outdoor game for old and young.

No. 8T7302 15-cent set 1¼-inch very finely embossed Checkers.

No. 8T7303 Set big value double six Dominoes.

No. 8T7304 Lotto Game, complete. An excellent game.

No. 8T7305 Tiddledy Winks, complete. A popular pastime for old and young.

No. 8T7306 Backgammon Board and Checkers. An enjoyable pastime for all.

No. 8T7309 Old Maid. Too well known to need description. 15-cent value.

No. 8T7310 Modern Authors. A high class and very instructive game. 15-cent value.

No. 8T7312 Jack Straws. A simple and very popular pastime. Good for old and young.

No. 8T7311 A B C Game. Game of letters and animals. Knowledge and fun for the little ones.

No. 8T7313 Flag Game. Contains flags of all nations with names and verse. Object of game to see who can take the most flags by winning the most cards. Very instructive for all.

No. 8T7314 Wild West Game. A very interesting game for boys.

No. 8T7315 Mother Goose Game. A juvenile favorite. Very entertaining and a big seller.

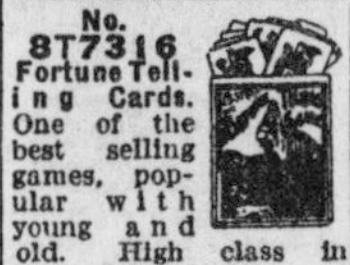

No. 8T7316 Fortune Telling Cards. One of the best selling games, popular with young and old. High class in every respect.

No. 8T7317 Peter Coddle and his Trip to New York. Comic, laughable and entertaining. Fun for everybody. Regular 15-cent value.

No. 8T7318 Comic Conversation Cards. Laugh and be merry with this popular game. Object of the game is to see which pair of players can hold the most comical conversations with each other. Everyone enjoys it.

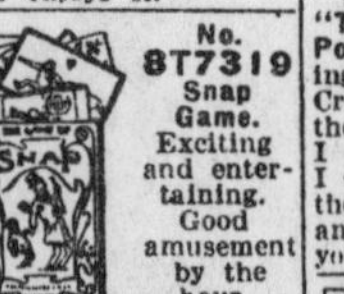

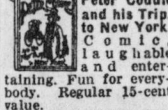

No. 8T7319 Snap Game. Exciting and entertaining. Good amusement by the hour.

No. 8T7321 Sliced Animals and Birds, complete. Give all the letters of the alphabet and descriptions of animals and birds thereon.

No. 8T7285 Ten fancy border, decorated and embossed comic Love Post Cards, with subjects, "I will always be true to you," "I am right in the swing," "Surroundings are satisfactory," etc. Big values. Sell everywhere at 2 for 5 cents.

No. 8T7286 The Ten Commandments Post Cards. A beautiful series of exquisitely colored and handsomely embossed design, illustrated commandment cards. Extremely appropriate for Sunday school distribution.

No. 8T7287 Big value Post Card Album. Holds 90 cards. Fancy decorated cover. Greatest value ever obtained. See 250-Card Album No. 8T8374, page 391. Also a wonder value.

No. 8T7505 Ten handsome natural color flower and gilt embossed Post Cards, with space for writing. A very popular and beautiful card. Regular 2 for 5 cents cards.

No. 8T7506 Ten "The Great Crowd" Post Cards, with printing beneath: "The Crowd that Met Me at the Train," "The Mob I Got Into," "Where I Got Lost," etc. Send them to your friends and show how popular you are.

No. 8T7507 Ten assorted exceedingly popular Post Cards, with words, "Hot Air Shots," "As Soon as We Get a Little Better Acquainted, I Will Tell You My Real Name," "I Would Get Married But My Wife Won't Let Me." Popular with everyone.

No. 8T7284 Twelve fancy color decorated and embossed flower Post Cards, with verse. Sells everywhere at 2 for 5 cents.

No. 8T7508 Ten assorted sentimental Love Post Cards. Just out and new. With words, "I Have Eyes for You Only," "You Look Good to Me," "I Can't See Anybody Else but You," "You Are It," etc. You surely want several packages of this card.

No. 8T7509 Twelve assorted high class Humorous and Comic Post Cards. Sell everywhere. Have fun with your friends.

No. 8T7510 Two novelty Music Roll Post Cards, with miniature roll attached which contains music and verse, "Though You Are Gone You're Not Forgotten." A good seller.

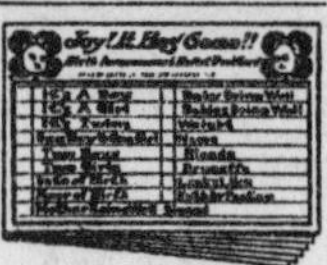

No. 8T7511 Ten Birth Announcement Post Cards, with wording, "Joy! It Has Come," and wording for all the news items. Announce baby's birth to your friends.

No. 8T7512 Eight assorted "Greetings From" Post Cards, with beautiful landscape views and space for writing in name of place. Can be used anywhere. Pretty and popular.

No. 8T7513 Three folding "Souvenir From" Post Cards. Beautiful colored front with space for name at bottom. Exceedingly comic center showing one view scene on the principal street and the other a park view. Rapid sellers. Regular price, 5 cents each.

No. 8T7522 Seven fancy color decorated Best Wishes Post Cards. A nice remembrance from a friend. Regular price, two for 5 cents.

No. 8T7515 Six assorted very fancy and exceedingly beautiful color cross series Easter Post Cards. Flower embossed and decorated. Regular 5 cents each.

No. 8T7516 Six assorted very fancy rabbit and chicks Easter Post Cards, with Easter greetings. Flower natural color embossed. A beautiful and exceedingly high class card. Regular 5 cents each.

No. 8T7517 Two satin cross mounted and embossed hand decorated Easter Post Cards, with Easter greetings. Sells at 10 cents each.

No. 8T7518 Five beautifully colored and highly embossed Birthday Post Cards, with appropriate sentiments. Regular price, two for 5 cents.

No. 8T7519 Two handsome Best Wishes and Heartiest Greetings Post Cards, with large satin embossed flower in corner. Must be seen to be appreciated.

No. 8T7520 Ten assorted views Niagara Falls in colors. Handsome, instructive and very interesting.

No. 8T7521 Ten assorted views of Yellowstone Park in natural colors. Very popular and interesting and should be in every home.

No. 8T7551 Six assorted "Don't" Post Cards with knocks witty and wise. Humorously illustrated. Big sellers.

No. 8T7553 Ten handsomely colored illustrated Post Cards, celebrated Sheridan's Ride with verse on each. Instructive, interesting and educational. A noted epoch of the Civil War.

No. 8T7554 Twelve beautiful colored Post Cards with gilt frame border illustrating the sentimental love poem of Eugene Field entitled "Lovers' Lane, Saint Jo." One of the greatest values in post cards.

No. 8T7566 Eight Arctic Series Post Cards, showing reproduction of photographic views of trip to the north pole, together with fine picture of Dr. Cook and Commander Peary.

Mother of Pearl Post Cards. One of the finest, most classical and highest grade post cards manufactured. Each with the genuine mother of pearl setting, gilt and color embossed mottos by celebrated authors. Something entirely new and exceptionally high class. You must see and examine this card to appreciate its true value. Subjects as follows:
No. 8T7562 The Value of a Friend.
No. 8T7563 Hope.
No. 8T7564 Luck.
No. 8T7565 A Wish.
Regular 10 to 15-cent value.

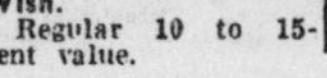

No. 8T7571 Picture Puzzle Post Cards. Fascinating, entertaining and instructive. Assorted designs. Send all your friends one of these new novelties.

No. 8T7588 Four celebrated Christie Love Series Post Cards. The best and most popular love cards of the day. 5-cent grade. Beautiful reproductions in colors of his most famous originals.

No. 8T7589 Four Christie "Beautiful American Women" Post Cards. Color reproductions from his famous paintings.

No. 8T7557 Seven beautifully colored embossed floral design Bible texts. Very popular for Sunday school work. Two for 5-cent grade.

No. 8T7558 Eight "Our National Life" Post Cards, showing the army and navy battleships, revenue service, the Mint, West Point, etc. Every person should be interested in this series. Two for 5-cent grade.

No. 8T7561 Six very fine oil painting effect "O'er Hill and Dale" Post Cards. Beautifully embossed picturesque landscapes. Send these beautiful cards to your friends. Two for 5-cent grade.

No. 8T7590 Eight beautifully colored and embossed Mother Goose Nursery Rhyme Post Cards. New and very high grade. Every mother should teach her child these illustrated verses. Two for 5-cent grade.

No. 8T7541 Fine 5x7-inch empty Passe-partout Frame. Largely used for keeping post cards, photos or pictures. Frame your favorite subjects and keep them.

No. 8T7584 Ten beautifully embossed and highly decorated Sunday school Cards with assorted Bible verses thereon. The cards now so universally used by Sunday school teachers for their classes.

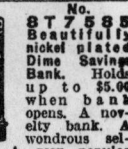

No. 8T7585 Beautifully nickel plated Dime Savings Bank. Holds up to $5.00 when bank opens. A novelty bank. A wondrous seller. A very popular home item. A great bank for children.

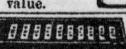

No. 8T7587 Purefoam Hand Shaving Stick, in fine patented case. A good soap and big value.

No. 8T7320 Fancy imported Tubeaphone and Hammer in box. A popular musical toy. Many tunes can be played upon it. Ten keys.

No. 8T7322 Exceptionally fine folding Chess Board. Size, 14x14 inches.

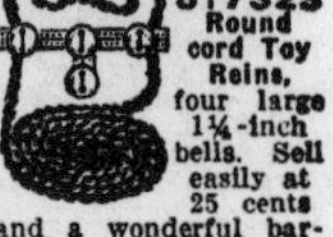

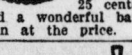

No. 8T7323 Round cord Toy Reins, four large 1¼-inch bells. Sell easily at 25 cents and a wonderful bargain at the price.

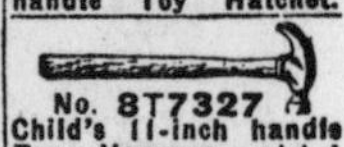

No. 8T7324 Fancy gilt finished, polished edge, 12-inch handle Toy Hatchet.

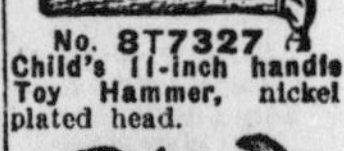

No. 8T7327 Child's 11-inch handle Toy Hammer, nickel plated head.

No. 8T7328 Muslin Pug Dog on wheels. Size, 6x7 inches.

No. 8T7330 Popgun Water Pistol. Amusement for all.

7 cents each

WONDERFUL DRUG STORE, NOVELTY AND TOY VALUES

IN ORDER THAT WE MAY SELL YOU these 10, 15 and 25-cent drug store, novelty and toy items at the price of only 7 cents each, we must ask that you order at least six items from these pages at one time. You may select them all from the 7-cent pages, all from the 17-cent pages, or the 33-cent pages, or some from each of the 7, 17 and 33-cent pages inclusive, just as you choose, so long as you order six items from these pages at one time. Select as many more as you want, but at least six (all one kind or assorted) must be ordered at one time. These wonderfully low prices have only been made possible by great economy in handling expense where six or more items are selected, and we give to our customers the benefit of these marvelously low prices by making it a rule that at least six articles must be ordered at one time. Include these goods with your orders by freight or express and we know you will be greatly surprised at the wonderful values you will receive.

No. 8T7329 Child's detachable handle Flatiron, with stand. Wonderful value.

No. 8T7331 Iron Toy Man in Sulky. Beautifully colored. A big seller.

No. 8T7333 Neverstop Top. Every boy should have one. Beautiful red, white and blue color decorated.

No. 8T7334 Japanese bamboo five-piece Child's Doll Furniture Set. Do not omit these from your order. Sells readily at 25 cents.

No. 8T7335 Japanese Roly Poly Doll. Cannot hold him down.

No. 8T7336 Child's tin Kitchen Set. Complete in box.

No. 8T7339 Child's fancy Watch and Chain, on card.

No. 8T7340 Clown toy metal Bank, 6½ inches high. Gilt and red decorated.

No. 8T7341 Boys' Tool Set. Comprising hand saw, screwdriver, pincers and hammer. Fine set for an industrious boy.

No. 8T7343 Big value Popgun, with cork, wooden handle with trigger. Length, 10 inches. Great value.

No. 8T7337 Iron U. S. Mail Box Bank, in colors, 3⅝ inches high by 2¾ inches wide and 1¾ inches deep. Greatest seller ever offered.

No. 8T7338 Horse and Bells. As the horse is pulled the bells ring. A big seller.

No. 8T7344 Set of six telescope fancy colored Paper Blocks. A fine amusement for any child.

No. 8T7345 Surprise Toy, in wooden box. Lots of fun for every child. Size box, 3½x3½x4 inches.

FRAMED PICTURES.

No. 8T7346 Beautiful Landscape and Woodland Scenes. Size, 6x8 inches. Gilt frame. Best subjects.

No. 8T7347 Beautiful Marine Scenes. Size, 6x8 inches. Fine gilt frames.

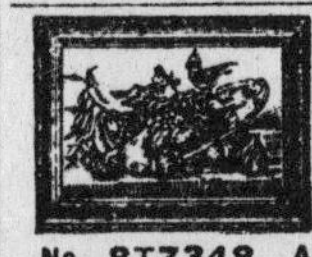

No. 8T7348 Assorted natural colored Fruit Pictures. Size, 6x8 inches. Artistic frames.

No. 8T7349 Our big leader, the famous subject, "The Young Mother." Size 6x8 inches, beautiful gilt and red wood frame. This picture easily sells for 25 cents. Should be in every home.

No. 8T7579 Beautiful Moonlight and Marine Scenes. Framed pictures, size over all 4½x11 inches. A special favorite and a wonder value.

No. 8T7578 Fancy gilt finished wooden Photo Frame with fine white mat. Size, 6x8 inches. Embossed corner decorations.

PASSEPARTOUT PICTURES.

A handsome and varied line of 5x7-inch Passepartout Pictures comprising all the latest popular, novelty and up to date subjects. Very attractive and beautifully finished. Sell everywhere at 10 to 15 cents each. Beautiful and ornamental to any room.

Famous Head Series. Best assorted subjects. Famous heads in natural colors. Each in artistically matted assorted colored paintings.

No. 8T7362 Famous Peggy Series Heads, reproduced in natural colors. Too well known to need description.

No. 8T7595 Celebrated Astic Heads. Three subjects only. Reproduced from the famous paintings in natural colors. Each with white mat and red binding.

No. 8T7596 Celebrated American Beauty Heads, assorted subjects, oval mats, pictures reproduced in colors. No description can do them justice.

No. 8T7363 Beautiful embossed oil painting effect Landscapes in natural colors. Exceptionally high class and artistic. White mat, black binding. Take our advice and buy at least one dozen of this series.

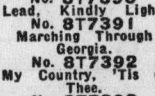

No. 8T7619 "Blow." A picture appealing to everyone. The genuine copyright picture, reproduced in colors. Beautiful white mat, black binding. Sells on sight.

Celebrated Christie Series. Best love series known. All copyright pictures. Best subjects with gray mat and white binding, as follows:

No. 8T7364 Teasing.
No. 8T7365 Sailing Close.
No. 8T7366 A Winning Hand.
No. 8T7367 Canoe Mates.
No. 8T7368 Drifting.
No. 8T7369 The World Before Them.
No. 8T7370 Excess Baggage.
No. 8T7371 The Summer Girl.
No. 8T7620 Black Eyed Susan.

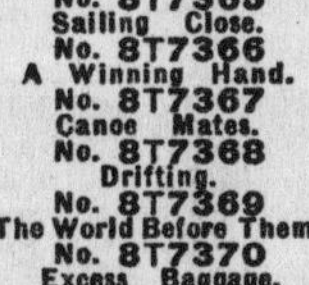

BIBLE VERSES. Flower Illustrated. Very popular, flowers in natural colors, handsome and instructive. You cannot have too many in your home. All furnished with white mat and black binding. Verses as follows:

No. 8T7372 Blessed are the pure in heart.
No. 8T7373 Happy is the people whose God is the Lord.
No. 8T7374 The Lord watch between me and thee when we are absent one from another.
No. 8T7375 Consider the lilies how they grow.
No. 8T7376 The Lord bless thee and keep thee.
No. 8T7377 Wait on the Lord.
No. 8T7378 All things work together for good to them that love God.

No. 8T7380 Marine Scenes. Different views in natural colors, white mat, black binding. Fine parlor decorations.

FAVORITE SONGS WITH VERSE. Beautifully colored and illustrated. Very instructive and ornamental. Furnished with white mat and black binding in songs as follows:

No. 8T7387 Rock of Ages.
No. 8T7388 Home, Sweet Home.
No. 8T7389 Way Down upon the Swanee River.
No. 8T7390 Lead, Kindly Light.
No. 8T7391 Marching Through Georgia.
No. 8T7392 My Country, 'Tis of Thee.
No. 8T7393 Nearer, my God, to Thee.
No. 8T7394 Coming Thru' the Rye.
No. 8T7395 The Star Spangled Banner.
No. 8T7396 Old Black Joe.

No. 8T7379 Moonlight Series. Assorted subjects, gray mat, white binding. Large sellers, handsome in appearance and the coloring beautiful. Do not omit this from your order.

No. 8T7597 A special favorite. "Love on the Square." The ideal lover's pictures. Dark mat, black binding. A beautiful picture.

No. 8T7598 High class comic picture. "Lead Us Not Into Temptation." Reproduced in beautiful brown tint. The genuine copyright picture.

No. 8T7599 "She Lufs Me; She Lufs Me Not." Copyright picture. Reproduced in colors. White mat, black binding.

No. 8T7600 Stork picture. "What's the Address?" Genuine copyright picture reproduced in beautiful brown tint. A favorite everywhere.

No. 8T7601 Comic. "Hold on, I'm a Brother Elk." Sells on sight.

No. 8T7602 "One of Us Must Die." Celebrated copyright picture. One of the most popular pictures of the day.

No. 8T7605 "Birds of a Feather." Genuine copyright picture.

No. 8T7603 "A Little Shriner Wearing His First Pin." Every Shriner wants one. Send one to your friend. He will be more than pleased with it.

No. 8T7606 "Nobody Loves Me." One of the largest selling pictures ever painted. Verse at the bottom, "Nobody loves me, I'm going into the garden to eat worms; yesterday I ate two smooth ones and one wooly one." Ordinary 15-cent value.

No. 8T7607 "Somebody Loves Me; I Ain't Going to Eat No Worms." Companion piece to catalog No. 8T7606. You surely want these two pictures in your home.

No. 8T7617 "Hear My Dolly's Prayer." Just the picture for the child's room. Picture reproduced in colors with verse.

No. 8T7618 "Mending Day." Celebrated copyright picture with verse. New and exceedingly popular. The companion piece to No. 8T7617.

No. 8T7397 German silver mounted, ebony finished Hair Curler.

No. 8T7398 German silver mounted, ebony finished Button Hook.

No. 8T7399 German silver mounted, ebony finished Cuticle Knife.

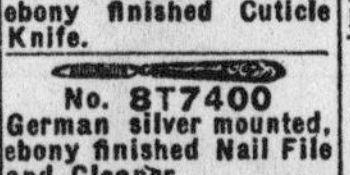

No. 8T7400 German silver mounted, ebony finished Nail File and Cleaner.

No. 8T7401 German silver mounted, ebony finished Shoe Horn.

No. 8T7402 Dr. Sickles Nail and Manicure Shears. Can be used as manicure scissors, cuticle knife, nail file, tweezers, ripper, for cutting threads or ravelings or the frayed edges of collars and cuffs. A complete useful pocket item.

No. 8T7403 Two large 2-ounce sticks Spanish Extract Licorice.

No. 8T7404 25-cent bottle Hygienic Tooth Wash.

No. 8T7405 Patented pure rubber Teething Ring. You should have this for the teething infant.

No. 8T7406 Velvet leather Lincoln head Calendar, 1910 pad. Size, 4x6.

No. 8T7407 Two Picnic Lunch Sets each comprising one collapsible sanitary picnic lunch basket, three fancy decorated crepe paper napkins, six sheets high grade wax paper, one pepper envelope and one salt envelope. You should always have these on hand.

No. 8T7408 Metal dog Ash or Pin Tray. Size, 4x5 inches. Big value.

No. 8T7409 Metal dog Pin Cushion. Size, 3½x4½ inches.

No. 8T7410 Two large Rubber Balloons, assorted colors. Just the thing to keep the children amused.

No. 8T7411 High grade Shaving Brush, exceptional value. Sold by others for 15 cents.

No. 8T7412 Beautiful flower decorated imported Shaving Mug. A beauty.

No. 8T7413 4½-inch collapsible stand Shaving Mirror. Folds up and occupies little space.

No. 8T7414 Novelty Dress Suit Case, filled with bottle perfume. A big leader.

No. 8T7415 Trick Japanese Cigar Pouch. Offer your friend a cigar and then let it snap back. Lots of fun.

No. 8T7416 12-foot roll ⅞ inch wide Paper Passepartout Binding. White, black, red, green, gilt or brown. State color.

No. 8T7417 Pair fancy decorated aluminum Salt and Pepper Shakers. Extraordinary value.

No. 8T7418 One-ounce bottle Headlight Cologne. A big leader.

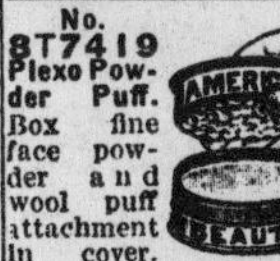

No. 8T7419 Plexo Powder Puff. Box fine face powder and wool puff attachment in cover. Complete powder set. A wonderful seller.

No. 8T7420 Jap Presto Cigar, fastens at elbow with rubber cord on cigar. Offer your friend a cigar and after releasing, slips up sleeve. You can have lots of fun with this item.

No. 8T7422 Child's complete Dinner Set, knife, fork and spoon, in tufted lined box.

No. 8T7423 Fine folding leather Calling Card Case.

No. 8T7424 15-cent imported Japanese Wind Chimes. A great novelty and you should have one in every room.

No. 8T7425 Two pure gum Nursing Nipples.

YOUR CHOICE FOR ONLY 7 CENTS EACH

7 cents each

DO YOU REALIZE what wonderful values we are offering you at only 7 cents each? Many of these articles are from France, Germany, Japan and other foreign countries, imported at a big expense, and yet we sell you your choice of these items manufactured abroad at the wonderfully low price of only 7 cents each. Every item shown on these pages at 7, 17 and 33 cents is a wonderful value and you should call your friends together and show them the bargain pages and make up and send us a large order at once. Look over each item carefully and include them in your freight and express orders to get the greatest possible saving. See also the wonder 2, 4, 6, 8 and 12-cent values shown on the first yellow pages in this catalog.

No. 8T7426 Imported Shampoo and Dandruff Comb. Used for reaching all parts of the head while shampooing the hair. A great seller.

No. 8T7427 4½x3-inch Funny Mirror. Makes the tall short and fat and the stout tall and slim. You will have lots of fun with your friends.

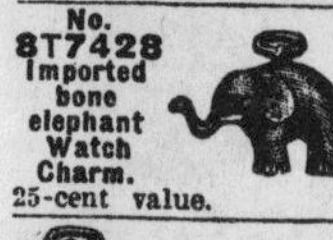

No. 8T7428 Imported bone elephant Watch Charm. 25-cent value.

No. 8T7429 Imported bone skull Watch Charm. 25-cent value.

No. 8T7430 Imported Straw Rattle. A big leader.

No. 8T7431 Dangling large size lifelike eight-legged Spider on string. You can scare your friends with this.

No. 8T7432 Dangling lifelike Darning Needle Bug. Spring wings and tail. 4x4 inches, on string. You can scare both old and young with this bug.

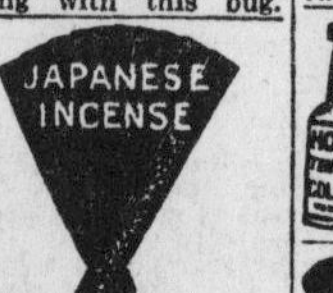

No. 8T7434 Ten envelopes Japanese Incense, eighteen sticks to envelope. Light a stick and hold it in your hand to keep away the mosquitoes.

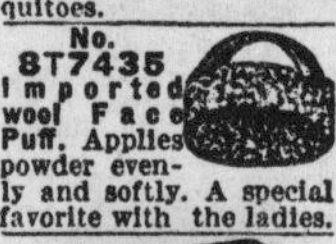

No. 8T7435 Imported wool Face Puff. Applies powder evenly and softly. A special favorite with the ladies.

No. 8T7437 Fancy decorated Japanese hinge cover lacquered Box, with fancy patent clasp. Size, 4½x2x1⅜ inches. Can be used for hairpins, jewels or trinkets. Will easily sell for 25 cents.

No. 8T7439 Fancy Japanese decorated Paper Panel. Size, 4½x54 inches. A beauty and an ornament to any room. Often sells for 25 cents each. Japanese colored flower and figure decorated.

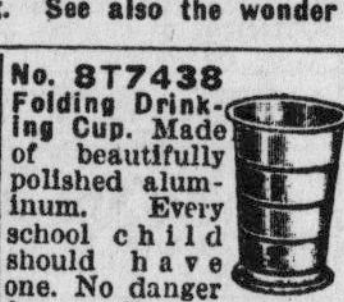

No. 8T7438 Folding Drinking Cup. Made of beautifully polished aluminum. Every school child should have one. No danger from disease. Folds up and occupies little space.

No. 8T7440 Very fine imported Harmonica. An exceptionally fine item.

No. 8T7441 Fancy imported handled Basket. Size, 7½x5x8 inches. Made of twisted willow and colored Chinese straw. A very handy item.

No. 8T7442 Fancy braided straw imported Japanese hanging Hair Receiver. A novel and very useful item.

No. 8T7444 Imported Child's Work Box. Comprises mirror, button hook, bone ripper and ribbon leader. Size, 3¾x4¾x2 inches.

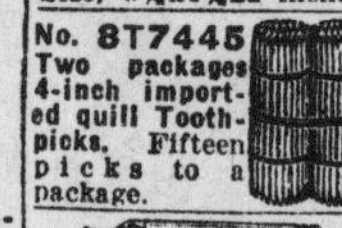

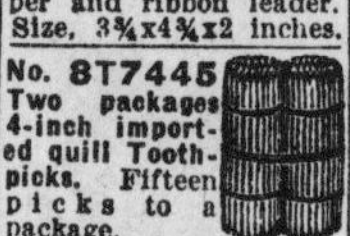

No. 8T7445 Two packages 4-inch imported quill Toothpicks. Fifteen picks to a package.

No. 8T7446 Improved glass Menthol Inhaler. A large seller.

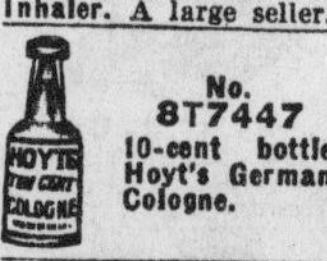

No. 8T7447 10-cent bottle Hoyt's German Cologne.

No. 8T7448 Big value Japanese finish Wire Hair Brush.

No. 8T7449 Toolever Nail Clip. A fine pocket manicure item.

No. 8T7450 Large 14-ounce can Cleanso Hand Cleaner. Keeps the hands clean and soft.

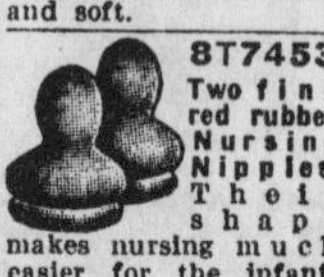

No. 8T7453 Two fine red rubber Nursing Nipples. Their shape makes nursing much easier for the infant. Cannot be torn in putting on bottle and provides natural and regular flow of milk. A child's favorite.

No. 8T7454 Leather Bag Tag. Size, 2x6 inches.

No. 8T7452 1-inch genuine Indian hand made Canoe Stick Pin on card. A novelty and a wonderful seller.

No. 8T7455 Curved stiff grooved Nail File, with cuticle knife. Big value.

No. 8T7456 Fancy shell novelty Thimble Holder.

No. 8T7457 Large tiger cowry shell sectional cut Ash or Pin Tray.

No. 8T7458 Tiger cowry shell flower decorated Match or Trinket Holder, with chain hanging attachment.

No. 8T7459 Pearl handle gilt ferrule Pen Holder and Pen.

No. 8T7461 Two dozen 6-inch lace paper Doilies, in envelope.

No. 8T7463 Exceptionally large 12-inch fancy decorated oval Japanese Lantern. 15-cent value.

No. 8T7466 Package tailors' garment mending Rubber Tissue for repairing tears and cuts in all kinds of garments. Never fails.

No. 8T7467 Black fancy design Candlestick, with handle.

No. 8T7468 4-inch white Murex Shell. Fancy and very ornamental.

No. 8T7474 Bottle Indelible Laundry Marking Ink, with pen. Every household should have one.

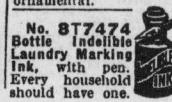

No. 8T7481 7-inch Indian hand made Sewing Basket.

No. 8T7465 One dozen Electric Sparklers. These torches fill the air with showers of sparkling golden stars and produce for a long time a brilliant and dazzling illumination of all surrounding objects, making a beautiful and lasting display. For street parades, Fourth of July, picnics, lawn parties, theatrical performances and all indoor and outdoor celebrations and illuminations. Smokeless, odorless and harmless. The ideal fireworks for everyone.

No. 8T7470 Cupid Shell Ornament. Fancy large shell back. A handsome shell novelty.

No. 8T7471 Fancy Shell Holy Water Fount with Crucifix. Size, 3x5 inches.

No. 8T7472 Rubber Stamp Inking Pad. Size, 2x3¾ inches.

No. 8T7473 One ounce Pad Ink. Green, red or black. Specify color.

No. 8T7475 Fancy decorated leather Cigar Case holding three cigars.

No. 8T7477 Fancy imported straw Whisk Broom Holder. Size, 4½x7½ inches.

No. 8T7478 Little Gem Telephone. A wonderful leader. Lots of amusement for the children.

No. 8T7480 Fancy velvet, leather decorated pants Match Scratcher, with hangers. Size, 5x8 inches.

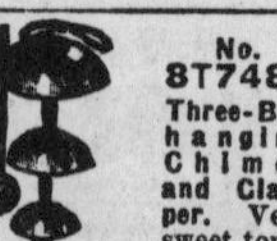

No. 8T7485 Three-Bell hanging Chimes and Clapper. Very sweet tone.

No. 8T7486 Bell Rattle, with four 1¼-inch bells. A big seller.

No. 8T7490 Thirty-six beautiful United States Flags, assorted sizes, on string. Used for celebrations, carnivals and for general decorating. A great bargain.

No. 8T7491 Magnetic Fish Pond. Lots of fun for the children. Contains twelve hand carved beautifully colored magnetic fish in glass hinge cover case with fish pole, line and magnetic hook. Most exciting and the greatest selling novelty fish pond ever invented. Can be used in water or on the table or on the floor, especially interesting for children in bath tubs.

No. 8T7492 15-inch lifelike green paper Snake on bulging attachment. More amusement and excitement for 7 cents than you ever before thought possible.

No. 8T7493 34-inch lifelike green paper Snake. The boys' favorite for carrying in the pocket and scaring people generally.

No. 8T7494 Two hemmed United States Silk Flags on 4½-inch brass pins.

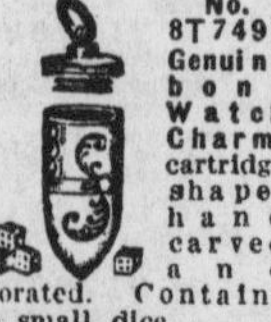

No. 8T7495 Genuine bone Watch Charm, cartridge shape, hand carved and decorated. Contains five small dice.

No. 8T7499 Three-inch Roly Polies. Coon, Dutchman and Clown. Each set in box.

No. 8T7496 Handsome mother of pearl butterfly Veil Pin. Fancy decorated, clasp attachment.

No. 8T7497 Little dangling Demon in colors. Wired head, arms, tail and legs. Lots of fun for the boys.

No. 8T7498 Beautiful hand decorated pocket knife shape bone Ear Cleaner, Letter Opener and Toothpick. Opens like a knife. A novelty and easily worth 25 cents.

No. 8T7500 Fancy novelty Japanese imported head Match Holder. Everybody wants one.

No. 8T7501 Imported Japanese toy Parachute. The child's favorite. Blow it in the air and watch it come down. Sells on sight.

No. 8T7502 Two large double ball Noisy Clappers. The noisy boy's toy. The loud ball clapper. A favorite with every boy.

No. 8T7503 Ghost Autograph Book. The great new fad. An odd and novel keepsake of your friends. Have them sign their name and make their ghost in your book. Everybody goes wild over them. Fun for old and young. Be among the first to have them. Give a ghost party in your neighborhood.

No. 8T7504 Beautiful novelty shaped murex shell Pin Cushion. A great favorite.

No. 8T7534 Twenty-two beautiful assorted Colored Views of Chicago in folder, comprising business houses, park views, residences, stock yards, etc. Every home should have views of this great city.

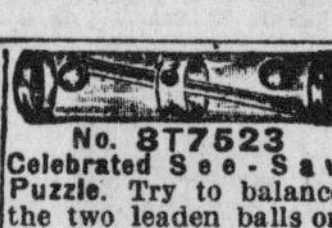

No. 8T7523 Celebrated See-Saw Puzzle. Try to balance the two leaden balls on the brass see-saw. It will keep you amused for hours.

No. 8T7524 Two Canary Bird Whistles. All the pretty notes of the canary can be imitated. Very popular.

No. 8T7525 Artgum. The well known dry cleaner. No grit, no grease. It cleans without scratching. For renovating pictures, photographs, drawing books, art work, wall paper. For cleaning gloves, dress belts, canvas and tan shoes, fancy slippers and general cleaning. No odor or danger from fire.

No. 8T7526 Rolo Bolo. The child's up to date popular toy. Roll it up one side and down the other. An amusement for any child by the hour. Finished in beautiful colors.

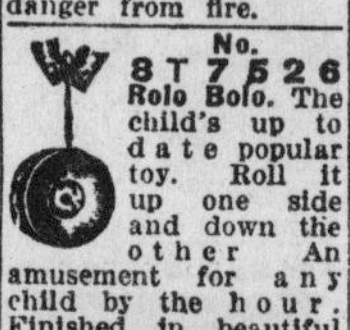

No. 8T7529 North Pole Game. An interesting, educational, amusing and absolutely new game. There is only one correct route known to the north pole. See if you can find it.

No. 8T7530 Frying Pan Rattle. An ordinary 6-inch frying pan made from highly polished steel with ball attached to each end of the steel spring wire and when shaken produces the loudest noise and rattle that you can possibly imagine. One of the greatest selling novelty rattles of the day. Just the thing for carnivals, celebrations, campaigns, street parades, etc. Every boy wants one.

No. 8T7531 The large Thunder Rattle. The loudest noise maker ever invented. Can be easily operated without any exertion. If you want to create noise, this is the one you want.

No. 8T7580 Imported Circular Work Box with cover. Five inches in diameter. Very fancy and useful.

No. 8T7592 Beautiful 14-inch snow white tissue paper Wedding or Easter Bell.

No. 8T7593 Two beautiful 9-inch snow white Wedding Bells.

No. 8T7594 Fancy snow white tissue paper Wedding Garland Decoration, 12 feet in length. Decorate the room with the bells and garlands.

No. 8T7569 Boys! Attention! Here is where you can have some fun. Large false nose, eyebrows and false mustache, together with one comic Japanese mouth toy and one Peck's Bad Boy movable tongue face. All in box. More fun for 7 cents than you ever before thought possible.

No. 8T7538 Illuminated Toy Street Car. An evening pastime for children during summer and autumn. Pulled with a string on the sidewalk after dark with lighted candle inside. Very attractive, has transparent windows and shows up beautifully. A delight to old and young. Big seller.

No. 8T7539 Beautifully colored fancy cut out shape Easter Cards. Bunny and chick decorated with "Easter Greetings." Sells everywhere for 25 cents. Each carefully packed.

No. 8T7573 Folding Silicate School Slate with pencil, comprising four slates, size 5x8 inches.

17 cents each

WONDER DRUG, SOAP AND NOVELTY VALUES

DON'T FAIL TO TAKE ADVANTAGE OF THESE BARGAINS. Include them with your order for other merchandise. You can add quite a number of such items to any freight shipment without increasing the freight charges, thus securing the full benefit of the big saving we make you. Such items as these sell in the drug stores throughout the country at 25, 35 and even 50 cents. Tell your friends and neighbors about these great bargain pages.

DON'T ORDER LESS THAN SIX OF THESE ITEMS. In order that we may continue to make these extremely low prices on such goods, we must necessarily ask you to order at least six items, but you can select the six items from any of the 11 pages of 7-cent, 17-cent and 33-cent items. Order as many more than six as you please.

No. 8T8001 25-cent box Colgate's Violet Talcum Powder, with fine imported face chamois skin.

No. 8T8014 25-cent stick Colgate's or Williams' Shaving Soap. Without doubt the two best shaving soaps on the market.

No. 8T8002 $1.00 bottle Cucumber and Elder Flower Cream Compound for beautifying the face and keeping it soft and white.

No. 8T8004 50-cent bottle Hair Curling Fluid. Keeps the hair in curl during damp weather.

No. 8T8005 50-cent bottle Regal Freckle Lotion. Every lady should use it.

No. 8T8006 50-cent bottle Regal Cream of Cucumber. A very fine chapped hand lotion.

No. 8T8007 50-cent bottle Complexion Restorer. For giving that beautiful healthful glow to the complexion.

No. 8T8008 50-cent bottle Regal Almond Cream for preserving, healing, soothing and whitening the skin and complexion. Sweetly and delicately perfumed. A sensational value.

No. 8T8011 Large 4-oz. jar very finely perfumed Orange Flower Skin Food.

No. 8T8019 Fancy Stag Metal Match and Cigar Stand. Size, 6¾x5½x4 inches. Good 50-cent value.

No. 8T8016 Celluloid Soap Box, pink, blue or ivory. State color wanted.

No. 8T8021 6-inch round Ladies' Hand Mirror, fancy chipped edge.

No. 8T8027 Hoyt's German Cologne, 25-cent bottle. A favorite everywhere.

No. 8T8030 Imported leatherette covered Autograph Album. Fine paper, gilt edge and big value.

No. 8T8031 4-ounce jar fine Shampoo Jelly for shampooing the hair. Sold by many at 50 cents.

No. 8T8032 4-piece Pocket Toilet Case. Very popular and big value.

No. 8T8033 25-cent package Ink and Spot Eradicator. A very useful item for removing ink spots, iron rust, etc. Always keep in the house.

No. 8T8035 A Plaster for removing wrinkles of all kinds. A big seller, simple to apply and harmless.

No. 8T8040 25-cent Bon Ton Manicure Set.

No. 8T8044 German silver handle Nail File and Cleaner.

No. 8T8038 Bleached sheep's wool Bath Sponge.

No. 8T8128 Ladies' exceptionally fine Toilet or Baby Bath Sponge.

No. 8T8235 Large Mexican Wool Cleaning Sponge for washing carriages, automobiles, etc.

No. 8T8041 8-ounce Bulldog Paper Weight.

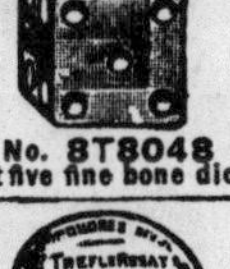

No. 8T8048 Set five fine bone dice.

No. 8T8050 Box finely perfumed imported Face Powder. Soft and velvety.

No. 8T8051 1-ounce bottle Flower Perfume in display box. Violet, white rose, crabapple and lily of the valley odors. State odor wanted.

No. 8T8054 Fancy Dog Paper Weight and Match Sets. Flower decorated. Big value.

No. 8T8055 German silver top Puff Box.

No. 8T8062 German silver Cuticle Knife.

No. 8T8095 Fancy genuine Pearl Cuticle Stick, hoof end.

TOILET SOAPS.

No. 8T8100 35-cent box Florentine Sandalwood Soap.

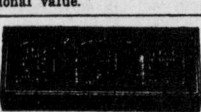

No. 8T8101 Box Fifth Ave. Bouquet Toilet Soap. Pure soap. Highly and sweetly perfumed. A great ladies' favorite.

Include one box of this wonderful value pure Castile Soap in your next order.

No. 8T8103 1 pound pure Castile Soap in cakes.

No. 8T8178 25-cent box medicated Carbolic Toilet Soap.

No. 8T8145 8 cakes fine Cocoa Toilet Soap. Lathers freely in all waters. Big and excellent value.

No. 8T8066 ½ pound Williams' Shaving Soap.

No. 8T8023 Two boxes celebrated Prof. Charles' Buttermilk Toilet Soap. Exceptional value.

No. 8T8046 25-cent box Violet Transparent Glycerin Soap. A great favorite and a sure repeater. Violet perfumed.

No. 8T8109 35-cent box Celebrated Renaissance Toilet Soap. One of the best known and largest sellers.

No. 8T8182 Box 3 cakes fine perfumed Toyland Baby Soap.

No. 8T8217 Two large boxes fine Toilet Soap, each box having one cake each cream castile, tar, cocoa and pumice soap. A big leader.

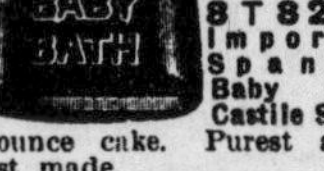

No. 8T8243 Imported Spanish Baby Bath Castile Soap. 8-ounce cake. Purest and best made.

FINE STATIONERY.

No. 8T8013 Genuine Glenure High Grade Linen Stationery (24 sheets and envelopes). Fancy slide drawer box. Big value and fine paper.

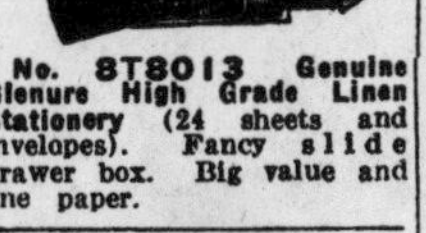

No. 8T8107 Genuine Whiting's Rozane Linen Stationery. One of the best made. Known everywhere. Exceedingly high quality.

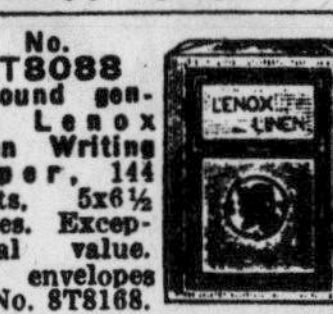

No. 8T8088 1 pound genuine Lenox Linen Writing Paper, 144 sheets, 5x6½ inches. Exceptional value. For envelopes see No. 8T8168.

No. 8T8056 Fancy decorated padded top Handkerchief Box, filled with fine high grade Linen Stationery. You will make no mistake in ordering a dozen boxes of this great value.

No. 8T8034 1 pound extra fine ruled Writing Paper, 5x8¼ inches. For envelopes see No. 8T8067 shown below.

No. 8T8067 100 fine Bond Envelopes, for paper see No. 8T8034.

No. 8T8168 100 fine Linen Envelopes, for paper see No. 8T8088.

No. 8T8069 Fine leather Wrist Supporter. A very strong and reliable support.

No. 8T8070 Two 25-cent bottles Regal Tooth Wash.

No. 8T8071 Beautifully colored Crepe Paper Lunch Set. Table cloth, 42x84 inches; 12 doilies and 12 napkins.

No. 8T8086 4 dozen beautiful gold and flower design Crepe Paper Napkins in case.

No. 8T8085 Two 25-cent tubes Regal Tooth Paste.

No. 8T8089 4-ounce jar exceptionally fine Violet Cold Cream.

No. 8T8096 Lance end, fine steel nickel plated Blackhead and Pimple Remover. 50-cent value. The professional instrument.

No. 8T8097 German silver handle Letter Seal.

No. 8T8098 German silver handle Letter Opener.

No. 8T8099 German silver handle Letter Scratcher.

No. 8T8102 25-cent package Bathasweet Bath Powder.

No. 8T8110 Fancy imported Japanese hand carved and decorated Letter Opener and Desk Ornament, well worth 50 cents.

No. 8T8111 Fancy Silk Suspensory. J. P. style. Very convenient.

No. 8T8115 Deck Outing Playing Cards. A big quality, high grade, enamel playing card.

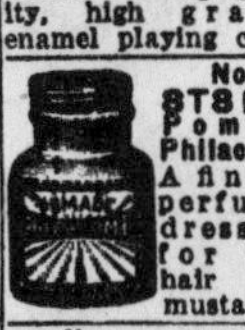

No. 8T8112 Pomade Philacome. A finely perfumed dressing for the hair and mustache.

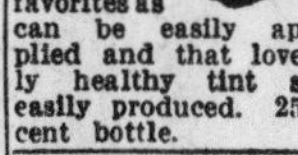

No. 8T8113 Bottle Cheeks Ever Blooming Liquid Face and Lip Rouge. One of the special favorites as can be easily applied and that lovely healthy tint so easily produced. 25-cent bottle.

No. 8T8123 25-cent bottle Lavender Smelling Salts. Refreshing and invigorating.

No. 8T8124 Satin silver Jewel Box. Satin lined.

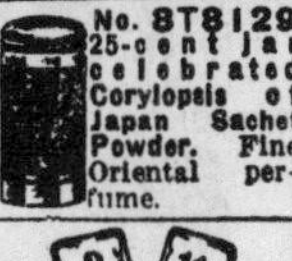

No. 8T8129 25-cent jar celebrated Corylopsis of Japan Sachet Powder. Fine Oriental perfume.

No. 8T8130 50-cent Trix Card Game. An entertaining and fascinating pastime.

No. 8T8132 11-inch fine 35-cent Whisk Broom.

No. 8T8131 ½ pound Berry's Fine assorted Chocolate Creams. Fresh and delicious.

No. 8T8134 Imported English Soft Cleaning Washable Chamois Skin. 12x14½ inches.

No. 8T8196 Imported soft white Chamois Skin, 11x14 inches.

No. 8T8139 Fancy combination Face Puff, Powder and Mirror in metal pocket case.

No. 8T8140 Imported Face and Lip Rouge. The best rouge made. Cannot be detected. Easy to apply. Keeps indefinitely.

No. 8T8149 Poultry Marker. Used for making holes in web of foot of poultry to keep track of breeds and flocks.

No. 8T8147 6-inch square beveled Shaving Mirror.

No. 8T8150 25-cent Flannel Kidney Plaster. Largely used for minor kidney disorders.

No. 8T8155 Bell's Celebrated Tooth Powder. The powder now so popular. Not the cheapest but the best. Made by Dr. V. C. Bell, professor of dentistry in New York colleges and known the country over as one of the highest authorities on mouth and teeth. If you want one of the best powders made, one we know you will like and always use hereafter, then buy this 25-cent box. Safe for old and young, snow white and exceptionally pleasant to the taste.

No. 8T8164 Exceptionally fine 25-cent imported Down Face Puff.

No. 8T8165 Imported large size Eyebrow Color Pencil.

YOUR CHOICE FOR ONLY

SEND US AN ORDER FOR SIX OR MORE of any of these items and we promise you the biggest bargains ever obtained. You can't buy these articles for less than 25 cents elsewhere and numbers of them will sell for 35 to 50 cents retail. It is necessary, however, that we make the rule that orders should not be for less than six items. We could not otherwise maintain these low prices. Certainly you can use a great many more than six items, and in making up your list of six, you can select from any of these pages of 7, 17 and 33-cent items. We are getting great numbers of orders for large quantities of these goods from people who are selling them. They are considered great bargains for fairs, church bazaars and the like throughout the entire country. Tell your neighbors and friends about these bargains. They will not be able to get such values anywhere else. You will do them a favor to call their attention to them.

No. 8T8020 35-cent hard rubber Fine Tooth Comb.

No. 8T8154 35-cent pyralin ivory Fine Tooth Comb.

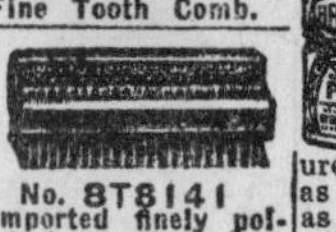

No. 8T8141 Imported finely polished wooden back Nail and Hand Brush. Great value.

No. 8T8159 5-inch fine ebony chamois Nail Buffer.

No. 8T8160 Ebony finished handle Shaving Brush and Special Shaving Soap Box in case.

No. 8T8161 Fancy silk covered, ribbon tied pocket face Puff, Powder and Chamois combined. Handy for any lady.

No. 8T8162 25-cent soft rubber Ear and Ulcer Syringe. Very useful for children.

No. 8T8169 Webster's Indexed Pocket Dictionary. Bound in morocco leather. Great value and very convenient.

No. 8T8170 Leatherette Indexed Pocket Memorandum Book.

No. 8T8171 Infants' rubber bulb Syringe.

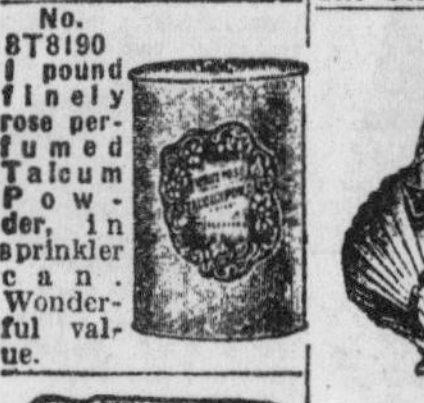

No. 8T8190 1 pound finely rose perfumed Talcum Powder, in sprinkler can. Wonderful value.

No. 8T8193 Extra high grade Nail File, Cleaner and Cuticle Knife. Best made.

No. 8T8185 8-ounce bottle Hygienic Shampoo Liquid for cleaning and shampooing the hair.

No. 8T8189 Electro-shine Silver Polish. Makes cleaning of silver ver a pleasure. Soft and smooth as cream and just as harmless. Will not scratch nor mar the finest surface. Easy to use and clean.

No. 8T8195 50-cent Gammut Card Game. Very popular. Price good while they last.

No. 8T8202 Fine glass Japanese Wind Chimes. Something new and very popular. Regular 50-cent value.

No. 8T8204 Flower embossed aluminum Puff Box.

No. 8T8179 4-ounce bottle Violet Witch Hazel. A fine toilet luxury after shaving.

No. 8T8183 1-pound jar pure antiseptic Green Soap.

No. 8T8213 25-cent Gem Nail Clipper and Cleaner. The best made.

No. 8T8208 Beautiful triple shell Pin and Needle Cushion.

No. 8T8205 Gold Plated Photo Frame, with easel.

No. 8T8206 Gold plated oval Photo Frame, with hanger.

No. 8T8209 15x11-inch fancy design paper folding Waste Basket.

No. 8T8210 Imported 3x4-inch Triplicate Mirror. Colored design back.

No. 8T8211 Double aluminum engraved Photo Frame, 6x8 inches.

No. 8T8212 Photo size aluminum engraved Photo Frame, 6x8 inches.

No. 8T8219 Beautiful flower embossed aluminum Bonbon or Card Tray.

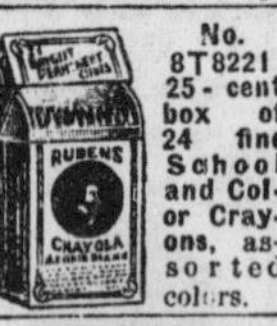

No. 8T8221 25-cent box of 24 fine School and Color Crayons, assorted colors.

No. 8T8222 Fine bone handle high grade flexible steel Nail File. Great value.

No. 8T8229 Bone handle nickel plated steel Cuticle Knife and Cleaner.

No. 8T8223 Exceptionally fine metal handle Shoe Dauber.

No. 8T8142 Ladies' 8-inch exceptionally fine hard rubber Dressing Comb.

No. 8T8136 Fine 35-cent 7½-inch Horn Ladies' Dressing Comb.

No. 8T8148 7½-inch fine aluminum Ladies' Dressing Comb.

No. 8T8121 7½-inch fancy roll top white pyralin Dressing Comb.

No. 8T8167 25-cent Horn Comb, with chain attachment.

No. 8T8172 35-cent value 9-row ebony finished fine white bristle solid back Hair Brush.

No. 8T8173 35-cent value 9-row mahogany finished solid back fine white bristle Hair Brush.

No. 8T8218 Pair ebony finished fine imported Military Hair Brushes. Great value and easily worth 50 cents.

No. 8T8220 Very fine soft Shoe Polishing Brush.

No. 8T8224 Big value soft Shoe Brush, with dauber.

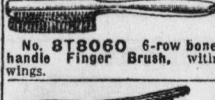

No. 8T8060 6-row bone handle Finger Brush, with wings.

No. 8T8122 Extra fine fancy handle imported Tooth Brush.

No. 8T8176 Imported Tooth Brush, for cleaning false teeth.

No. 8T8265 Fine imported Tooth Brush in glass case. Keeps it clean and dry.

No. 8T8059 Tissue Paper Flower Outfit for making artificial flowers. Complete in every detail. Furnished in roses, chrysanthemums or carnations. State flower wanted.

No. 8T8036 Paper Doll Outfit, consisting of assorted colors crepe and tissue papers, gold and silver stars, crepe lace paper, jointed dolls, crepe paper ribbon and full instructions for making and dressing paper dolls.

No. 8T8264 German silver handle, nickel plated Hair Curler. Length, 7 inches.

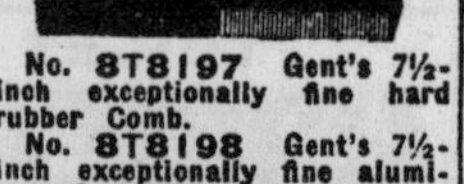

No. 8T8197 Gent's 7½-inch exceptionally fine hard rubber Comb.

No. 8T8198 Gent's 7½-inch exceptionally fine aluminum Comb.

No. 8T8233 7½-inch Barber's Tapering Horn Comb. Ordinary 35-cent value.

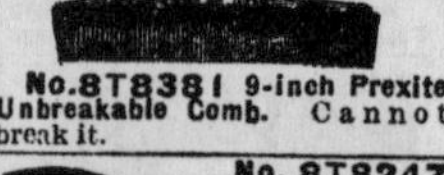

No. 8T8381 9-inch Prexite Unbreakable Comb. Cannot break it.

No. 8T8247 Folding hard rubber Pocket Comb and Mirror. Length, 5½ inches. Very popular and a big seller.

No. 8T8057 11-row ebony finished Wire Hair Brush. A big seller.

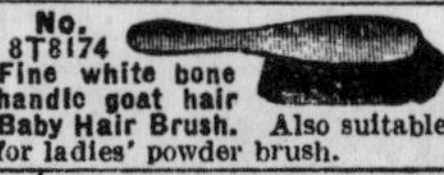

No. 8T8058 Exceptionally fine mahogany finished black bristle Hair Brush.

No. 8T8174 Fine white bone handle goat hair Baby Hair Brush. Also suitable for ladies' powder brush.

No. 8T8180 7-inch exceptionally fine pure bristle Clothes Brush. Big value.

No. 8T8045 Genuine Aseptic Tooth Brush. Reaches and cleanses all parts of the teeth. The finest made.

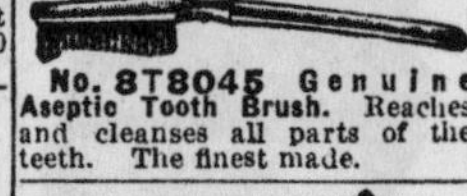

No. 8T8250 Wearwell Tooth Brush. A well known and very reliable brush.

No. 8T8439 Grace Darling Curling Iron. Not the cheapest but the best. Has tapering ends, enabling hair to be more easily removed; made of best material and beautifully nickel plated over copper, holding heat three times longer than another; has patent spring and oak handles. If you want the best, buy this.

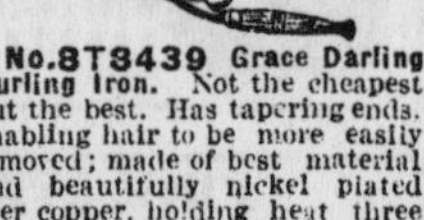

No. 8T8440 Celebrated Comb Electric Curling Iron. Beautifully nickel plated comb shape, has teeth for combing and forming curl. Sells for 50 cents.

No. 8T8482 Alcohol Curling Iron Heater. Has large screw cap over wick preventing waste or spilling of liquids. Has folding clamps for holding iron. Size, 5½x1¾ inches.

No. 8T8475 Ellis' New Folding Eye Shade. Lightest in weight. Comfortable to wear. Shades eyes from front and sides; light, made of finest opaque celluloid. The only shade for persons wanting a real protection for the eyes.

No. 8T8225 Child's beautifully polished aluminum Cup and Saucer, with name "Darling" hand carved on cup.

No. 8T8232 Feel Fine Air Heels. Make walking a pleasure. Worn inside shoe. Better in every respect than rubber heels. Take Jar off body, and once tried, always used. Furnished in ladies' and gents' and in large or small size. Specify kind and size. Great value.

No. 8T8236 Fancy ormolu gold finish swan Pin Cushion.

No. 8T8237 Fancy Japanese lacquer Bank, with lock and key.

No. 8T8238 Lightning Pin Feather Picker. Picks pin feathers from fowls quicker and easier than any other instrument. Far ahead of old knife and hand method.

No. 8T8244 Fancy color decorated Table Crumb Scraper and Tray. A very useful article.

No. 8T8245 Beautiful Copper Cigar Rest and Ash Tray, handsome nickel plated top, 3-inch diameter. Exceptional value.

No. 8T8246 25-cent Plexo Powder Puff with Powder. Fine wool puff in top. Furnished in white, flesh or pink. Specify color.

No. 8T8429 Genuine Walrus Leather Watch Fob. Nickel plated initial. As fine a watch fob as can be desired. The up to date fob. Will last for years. Very ornamental. Give initial wanted.

No. 8T8230 25-cent tube Pearlo-Dento Tooth Paste.

No. 8T8412 Ladies' curved handle, exceptionally fine white bristle Tooth Brush.

No. 8T8413 Badger hair Tooth Brush. Made for persons with tender gums.

No. 8T8420 Curved handle, white hair Table Crumb Brush.

No. 8T8240 Genuine Indian hand made sweet grass Table Mat, birchbark center, porcupine trimmed, 8-inch diameter. Nature's sweet and lasting perfume.

No. 8T8242 Stork Incense. Complete with bird, stand and incense sticks.

No. 8T8248 Fancy rustic turned wood Powder Box. Fancy color flower decorated top, very novel and something entirely new. Very ornamental.

No. 8T8249 Photograph Album, fancy design, holding eighteen small size photographs, hinge and clasp. Size, 5¼x4½ inches. Fancy colored front.

No. 8T8272 Imported Japanese lacquer, hinge cover Handkerchief Box, fancy decorated.

No. 8T8273 Fancy Shell and Novelty Box, hinge cover, handsome and very ornamental.

No. 8T8270 Handsome fancy imported straw hanging Hair Receptacle. You would buy it if you could only see it.

No. 8T8271 Imported straw Handkerchief Box, fancy silk top, beautiful colored and gilt flower painted, hinge cover. Wonderful value.

No. 8T8275 Padded top, imported hinge cover Work Box, comprising mirror, button hook, darner, needle and ripper. Size, 3¼x4¾x2¼ inches.

No. 8T8274 Japanese lacquer Card Case. Size, 5½x3½x2 inches, fancy decorated, lock and key.

No. 8T8276 Imported wood compass Watch Charm with metal screw pencil attachment.

No. 8T8277 Gent's genuine leather Calling Card Case.

No. 8T8278 Fancy German silver top, glass bowl Hair Receiver.

No. 8T8279 Exceptionally good Fountain Pen. Filler attachment.

No. 8T8282 Pair genuine Indian hand made Snow Shoes, 4x12 inches. A novelty used for decorating purposes.

No. 8T8283 Metal dog Hat Pin Holder. Height, 5 inches. A novelty readily selling for 35 to 50 cents.

17 cents each

TOYS, NOVELTIES AND GAME VALUES

17 CENTS EACH IN ASSORTMENTS OF SIX OR MORE is our price for articles on this page. Just think what this means to you. Here you find many household necessities, many novelties, many articles suitable for gifts. These are just such items as are offered in drug stores and other stores throughout the country at 25, 35 and 50 cents. Look over the list, item by item, and you are sure to find many that you will need. Compare the price with what you pay at home. Remember that in making up your order for at least six items you can select from any of the 11 pages of 7, 17 and 33-cent items. Buy as many more than six as you please.

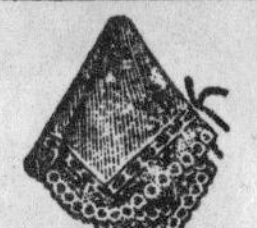

No. 8T8285 Ladies' lace trimmed imported Face Chamois Skin, baby ribbon trimmed. Size, 7½ inches square.

No. 8T8287 Fancy figure Hat Pin Holder. A great bargain, very ornamental and useful.

8T8288 Aluminum three-minute egg timer. Should be in every home.

No. 8T8289 Donkey Money Bank, with lock. A rapid seller.

No. 8T8290 Sanitary Wash Cloth, in fancy rubber lined case. A necessity for every person traveling.

No. 8T8291 Fancy celluloid top, gilt and flower decorated Eyeglass, Jewel, Collar Button or Trinket Box. Very pretty.

No. 8T8293 German silver handle Button Hook. Length, 6½ inches

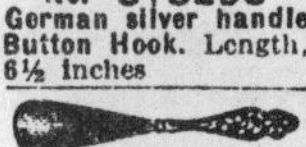

No. 8T8281 German silver handled, nickel plated shank Shoe Horn. Length, 7½ inches.

No. 8T8294 Fancy ebony finished, metal figure Crucifix. Size, 10½ x 5½ inches.

No. 8T8295 Pencil, Pen and Eraser Assortment. Big 25-cent value. In holly box.

No. 8T8297 Deception Cigars with Tray. Very close imitation of real cigars.

No. 8T8298 Double metal dog and umbrella Match Ornament. Beautiful, enameled in natural colors. Size, 1¾x2 inches.

No. 8T8299 Double paddle and canoe Match Holder, hanging attachment.

No. 8T8300 Exceptionally fine imported Japanese Lanterns, assorted shapes.

No. 8T8301 Hand decorated, ribbon trimmed, fancy Pin Cushion, hanging attachment. Size, 4½x4½ inches.

No. 8T8302 Imported Wool Puff. Regular 25-cent value.

No. 8T8303 Deception Pipe and Tray. Brass cup.

No. 8T8304 Extra fine steel blade Corn Knife, 1¾-inch blade. Also largely used as lady's ripping knife.

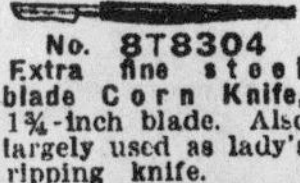

No. 8T8305 Pearl handle gilt ferrule Pen in Case. A big holiday leader.

No. 8T8308 Big 25-cent value varnished Folding Checker Board, 15x15 inches, and checkers.

No. 8T8310 Exceptionally fine set double nine embossed Dominoes.

No. 8T8332 Big value Set Child's Tin Dishes.

No. 8T8309 Box fancy 1¼-inch enamel finished Crown Checkers.

No. 8T8311 Set double six genuine crown embossed Dominoes.

No. 8T8312 Lotto Game, complete.

No. 8T8313 75-piece cut up Jig-a-Jig Wood Puzzle, assorted subjects. An exceptionally fine and instructive pastime.

No. 8T8314 Old Maid Card Game. 25-cent value.

No. 8T8315 Game of Authors. Genuine red line quality.

No. 8T8316 Celebrated Wizard Game. Enjoyed by old and young in or out of doors. A great seller.

No. 8T8317 50-cent game Sherlock Holmes. Play detective. Very interesting.

No. 8T8320 25-cent game of Tiddledy Winks. Assorted colored chips, glass bowl.

FANCY SEA SHELLS.

No. 8T8251 West India Corkscrew Shell. Sectional cut. One of the prettiest novel shells to be found. An ornament in any home. Length, approximately, 8 inches.

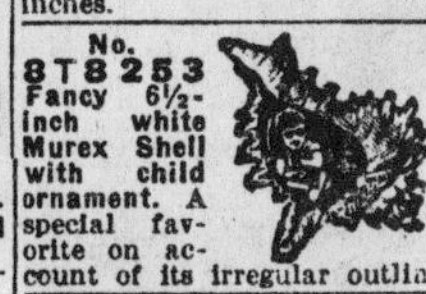

No. 8T8253 Fancy 6½-inch white Murex Shell with child ornament. A special favorite on account of its irregular outline.

No. 8T8254 Fancy Child and Vase Shell Ornament, large shell base. A handsome ornament.

No. 8T8257 Six assorted Sea Shells in package. Name of shell and place of origin printed on each shell. Sufficient novelty shells for complete mantel decoration.

No. 8T8228 Beautiful flower Painted Conch Shell.

No. 8T8306 Cameo shell Trinket and Hairpin Holder. Beautiful and very useful. Size, 4x3 inches.

No. 8T8266 Hexagon shape Work Basket, white willow interwoven with colored straw. Diameter, 9½ inches.

No. 8T8267 Tufted satin lined Work Basket. Size, 6½x9½ inches.

No. 8T8268 Kindergarten Lunch Basket, colored willow interwoven with colored straws. Reinforced handles. Very fancy. Size, 3¾x7x8 inches. This can also be used as candy or fancy basket.

No. 8T8146 Ladies' $1.00 rubber sanitary Protector. A great bargain.

No. 8T8436 Miniature Desk. One of the finest pieces of Japanese handicraft ever produced. Beautiful top inlaid and a miniature desk becoming any home. A fine den or library novelty. A miniature desk in ever respect. Size, 4¾x 2½x2¼ inches. Each in box.

No. 8T8252 Medium size Conch Shell. Fancy decorated, sectional cut. Very pretty and ornamental.

No. 8T8255 Japanese peacock Abalone Shell, 7½x 5 inches. Admired on account of the beautiful tints of the shell.

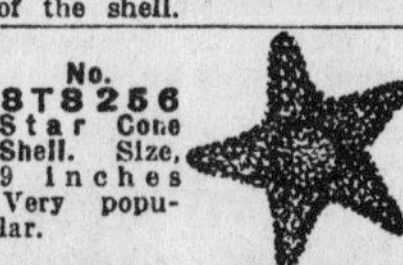

No. 8T8256 Star Cone Shell. Size, 9 inches. Very popular.

No. 8T8226 6-inch irregular design Novelty Shell.

No. 8T8227 Fancy Hanging Shell Fern Dish. Very ornamental.

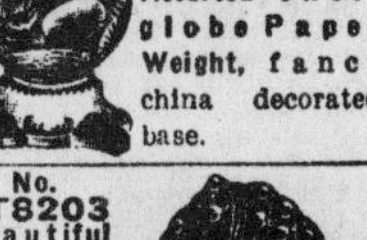

No. 8T8307 Assorted shell globe Paper Weight, fancy china decorated base.

No. 8T8203 Beautiful large Cameo Shell, 6x4 inches.

No. 8T8426 Beautiful Pearl Napkin Ring. Handsome and very ornamental. One that sells on sight.

No. 8T8200 25-cent exceptionally fine Wool Duster.
No. 8T8201 Fine soft Feather Duster.

No. 8T8262 Stag and Canoe Pipe and Match Holder. Fancy shield shape. Size, 6x10 inches. Wonderful value and an immense seller.

No. 8T8258 Fancy imported Japanese straw Glove Box, full silk top, beautifully colored and gilt flower decorated, hinge cover. Size, 10x3 inches. A great bargain.

No. 8T8259 Japanese lacquer Glove Box, hinge cover, flower and gilt decorated. Size, 10x3x2 inches.

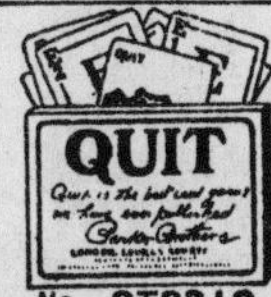

No. 8T8318 50-cent "Quit" Card Game. The large selling game of Europe. Fine playing card stock. From three to seven persons can play at one time. A wonderful value. Sold elsewhere for 50 cents.

No. 8T8319 Paris Fortune Telling Cards.

No. 8T8321 "Who" Card Game. Comical and amusing. A very enjoyable pastime.

No. 8T8323 25-cent game Jack Straws. An old and very popular game.

No. 8T8322 U. S. Puzzle Map. Size, 7½x11 inches. A very instructive pastime for children.

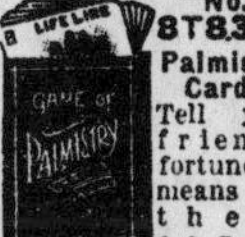

No. 8T8324 Palmistry Cards. Tell your friends' fortunes by means of these cards.

No. 8T8325 Three Roly Poly toys. One 2¾ inches, one 3¾ inches and one 5 inches. One of the greatest children's toys ever offered.

No. 8T8326 Five Russian Wooden Dolls one fitting within another. A fine novelty. Each carefully decorated. Very popular and a great amusing toy for children.

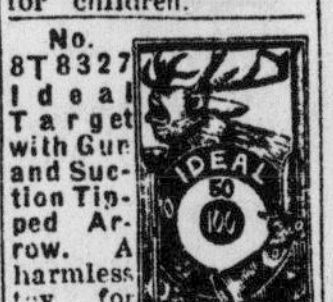

No. 8T8327 Ideal Target with Gun and Suction Tipped Arrow. A harmless toy for boys.

No. 8T8329 Big value Wooden Ark with wooden painted animals. An immense seller.

No. 8T8328 Big value Choral Singing Top. Beautifully lithographed.

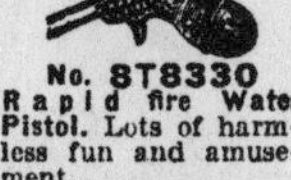

No. 8T8330 Rapid fire Water Pistol. Lots of harmless fun and amusement.

No. 8T8263 Imported imitation rabbit's foot Watch Charm with screw pencil attachment.

No. 8T8269 Imported straw Whisk Broom Holder. Very fancy.

No. 8T8333 Fancy revolving Gyroscope Top. Spins in assorted designs. Full directions with box. The most perfectly balanced top made. A big seller.

No. 8T8334 Child's nickel plated Flatiron and Stand. Detachable handle. Weight, 1¾ lbs.

No. 8T8335 10-inch red Trunk, with tray. Three slats on cover. Patent clasp, hinge cover. A neat container for dolly's clothes.

No. 8T8336 12-inch fancy painted and decorated red, white and blue Pistol Popgun with cork. A great selling boys' toy.

No. 8T8337 Gilt Watch and Chain in case. Every boy should have one.

No. 8T8338 Team of Horses and Bells. When the horses are pulled the bells ring.

No. 8T8339 Imitation cut glass Toy Condiment Set, including vinegar bottle, pepper shaker, salt dish and fancy leaf tray. No children's dinner set or playthings are complete without this set.

No. 8T8380 Toy Reins with eleven 1¼-inch bells. The greatest value in toy reins ever offered. A great favorite with children.

No. 8T8382 Nickel plated Money Bank. Size, 5½x4⅛x3 inches.

No. 8T8383 Metal Donkey and Cart, fancy color decorated. Total length, 10 inches.

No. 8T8377 Fancy Japanese bamboo Furniture Set. Comprises six pieces, four chairs, couch and table. Carefully packed in box. Every child should have one.

No. 8T8384 Set seven Telescope A B C Blocks. A special favorite for children.

No. 8T8385 Big value set Architectural Blocks with wheels for making wagon. Amusement for boys or girls by the hour.

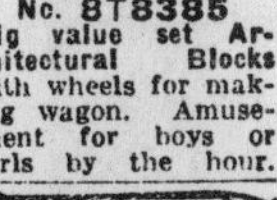

No. 8T8387 Child's rubber tired four-wheeled Iron Express Toy Wagon and Handle. Wonder value.

YOUR CHOICE FOR ONLY 17 cents each

OUR EXTREMELY LOW PRICES are based on orders of six or more items selected from the 7, 17 or 33-cent pages. Don't order less than six items, but you can select them from any of these pages of 7, 17 and 33-cent items. Order as many more as you like. A good way is to include these items with your order for other goods to be shipped by express or freight. In this way you get the full benefit of every saving made.

OUR 2 TO 12-CENT VALUES ON THE FIRST YELLOW PAGES OF OUR CATALOG WILL ALSO INTEREST YOU.

No. 8T8284 ½ pound Berry's assorted Cream Caramels.

No. 8T8286 Indian tomahawk Key Holder, leather hanger, fancy decorated. Length, 15 inches.

No. 8T8386 Sliced Pictures of Animals and Birds with A B C descriptions. Each letter of the alphabet has letter on top and description at the bottom. A very instructive item and a big seller. 25-cent value.

No. 8T8388 Child's rubber tired two-wheeled Cart and Handle. 25-cent value.

No. 8T8460 Fancy 25-cent Bunny Easter Card. Size, 3½x5½ inches. Satin perfumed sachet body with rose ivory mount, hand colored and celluloid top. Well known bunny and egg decoration in colors. An exceptionally fine Easter card. Each in box.

No. 8T8392 Birthday Card. Same size and style card as above, with the exception of being red rose center decoration. A nice birthday remembrance.

No. 8T8393 Best Wishes Card. Similar to above, with basket of flowers in beautiful colors. Kind remembrance from a friend.

No. 8T8389 Twelve cube Animal Blocks in hinge cover wooden box. Each block decorated on all sides. Instructive and entertaining.

No. 8T8396 Fancy Japanese Banner Panel. Size, 21x58 inches. Celebrated temple design. A fine house or den decoration. Readily sells at 35 to 50 cents. A wonderful bargain.

No. 8T8397 Celebrated Rembrandt Color Paint Box. Containing eighteen assorted colors inlaid with names beneath each color, stick, brush and white enamel palette. One of the best and finest colors manufactured.

No. 8T8398 Imported Tobacco Jar. Head designs with cap. Size, 3½x4 inches. Readily sells at 25 cents. Fancy color decorated.

No. 8T8399 3½-inch nickel plated Tweezers with ebony finished handle. Used by professionals.

No. 8T8401 Big value 25-cent Scroll Saw Outfit. Very entertaining and instructive pastime for children.

No. 8T8402 Cotton Bale Match or Toothpick Holder, gold plated. A fine ornament for any table.

No. 8T8403 Automatic hard rubber Screw Pencil with five extra leads. Every person needs one of these pencils.

No. 8T8404 Genuine Dr. Scott's Magnetic Plaster. 25-cent value. Used for kidney and rheumatic complaints.

No. 8T8406 Ebony finished handle child's mirror. Beveled glass, 3x4 inches.

No. 8T8407 1 pint can Extermoline Bedbug and Insect Destroyer.

No. 8T8410 Oval Photo Frame with mat and easel. Size frame, 6½x8½ inches.

No. 8T8408 4½-inch Glass Ebony Finished Handled Mirror.

No. 8T8411 25-cent celebrated Mirol Imported Nail Enamel in celluloid case. One of the best and most reliable made.

No. 8T8414 Imported fancy rose decorated luster trimmed Shaving Mug.

No. 8T8415 French bristle Shaving Brush, assorted colored handles.

No. 8T8418 Double Match Stand with Thermometer. A novelty suitable for any room.

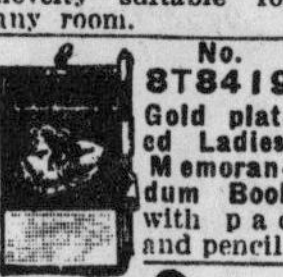

No. 8T8419 Gold plated Ladies' Memorandum Book with pad and pencil.

No. 8T8438 Genuine bone hand carved Watch Charm with Compass. Made in Japan and a novelty often sold for 50 to 75 cents each. As fine a little charm as anyone can desire.

No. 8T8423 Picture Head Dating Stamp for dating bills and letters. In addition to names, months and figures corresponding to the days and months of the year, the dater contains the words, Paid, Answered, Returned and Filled. Very convenient.

No. 8T8424 Tommy Tucker Ten Pins. 5-inch pins. A big seller.

No. 8T8452 Toy Parachute. A cloth toy parachute, securely made, with attachments. A really high grade item and one pleasing to any child. A fine outdoor exercise and a great deal of amusement.

WONDER VALUES IN FRAMED PICTURES.

No. 8T8345 Fancy rope effect gilt framed Picture. Assorted landscapes. Size frame, 4¾x14 inches. One of the best values ever offered. A fine parlor or library ornament.

No. 8T8471 Same as above, marine scenes.

No. 8T8344 Fancy gilt framed Landscape Picture. Size over all, 4x13 inches. Ornamental in any room. Will easily sell for 25 to 35 cents.

No. 8T8343 Fancy gilt embossed framed Picture with heavily ornamented corners. Size, 5¾x7¾ inches. Assorted subjects. One of the most highly ornamented framed pictures we offer.

No. 8T8346 Beautiful oval gilt framed Picture. Size, 6½x8½ inches. Assorted subjects. One of the best selling and most popular pictures of the day. Highly ornamental.

No. 8T8469 A real novelty in the picture line. Celebrated picture, "Nobody Loves Me" with verse "I am going into the garden to eat worms. Yesterday I ate two smooth ones and one wooly one." A favorite picture with everyone and one you would buy if you could only see it. Beautiful green tinted frame.

No. 8T8465 A special favorite. Well known "Village Smithy" Picture in 1¼-inch beautiful gilt frame with ornamented corners. Size, 8x10 inches. A wonderful value and a big seller.

No. 8T8468 Buy this picture for papa. An exceedingly popular picture with every household. The well known subject, "Time you Were Home, Papa," with clock showing quarter to one. Size picture, 4¼x9½ inches. Brown Mission frame.

No. 8T8374 A wonder value. Just think of a fine large post card album holding 250 cards, with decorated cover and hand sewed back for only 17 cents. Sold by others at 50 cents. The greatest bargain in a post card album ever known.

No. 8T8376 11-inch hand made Birchbark Indian Canoe. Two cross supports. Will not leak water. Sweet grass trimmed.

No. 8T8479 Faith, Hope and Charity Brooch Pin. Beautiful cream colored celluloid. 1¾ inches in width. The great Catholic motto, Faith, Hope and Charity. Easily worth 50 to 75 cents.

No. 8T8456 Parlor Croquet Set. Contains four long handled mallets, nine arches, four balls, two sticks, complete in box. A remarkable value.

No. 8T8476 Novelty Brooch Pins. Beautiful lover's rose design, latest cream tinted celluloid, heavily embossed and very pretty. Width, 2 inches. Sells in many novelty stores for 75 cents to $1.00. Clasp attachment.

No. 8T8477 Friendship Brooch Pin. Latest cream tinted celluloid, hands clasped with beautiful embossed rose decoration. Width, 1¾ inches. Clasp attachment. Big value.

No. 8T8478 The Doves of Peace celluloid Brooch Pin. Everybody's favorite. Beautiful embossed design, latest cream tinted celluloid. Very artistic. Easily worth 50 to 75 cents. Width, 1¾ inches. Clasp attachment.

No. 8T8427 Fancy Chess Board. Size, 16½x16½ inches. A very nice board.

No. 8T8378 7-inch fancy decorated Metal Head Drum. The noisy boy's favorite. Furnished complete with sticks. Every boy should have one.

No. 8T8431 Rubber Stamp Inking Pad. 2¾x4¼ inches.

No. 8T8432 Fancy Cupid Paper Weight. Gold plated. Very artistic, ornamental and useful.

No. 8T8433 Nickel Plated Snuff or Tobacco Box. Hinge cover. Convenient pocket size. A big seller.

No. 8T8481 Fine Sea Grass Child's Lunch Basket. Size, 7x5x4 inches. Fine for carrying lunch to school. 30 to 35-cent value.

No. 8T8437 Genuine Imported Japanese hand carved bone Watch Charm, with fancy inlay decoration. Latest pocketbook Netsuke style, containing five miniature well formed dice. A novelty every man would buy if he could only see it.

No. 8T8453 Fancy decorated sectional Shell Thermometer and Wall Ornament. Handsome, ornamental and very popular novelty.

No. 8T8454 Large size beautiful white 6-inch murex shell Pin Cushion. A fine ornament and a very useful novelty.

No. 8T8441 Novelty Wild Horse Race. Imported Japanese wooden box representing six horses and race. Lots of simple amusement for children, home circles or parties. Size, 3½x2 inches.

No. 8T8442 Imported fancy Japanese Circular Game, after the style of Pigs in Clover. One of the most intricate, difficult, time killing pleasure puzzles ever constructed. Wonderfully well made. Size, 4½x4½x1 inch.

No. 8T8455 Sumeda Novelty Box. Imported from Japan. Beautifully finished wood inlaid top. Can be used as collar button, jewel or trinket box, or fine rose jar. Ornamental to any home. Size, 2¾x3 inches.

No. 8T8444 Twenty beautiful national onyx Marbles in box. This is the greatest bargain in marbles ever offered. Every boy goes wild over them. The kind you have many times paid 5 cents each for at home.

No. 8T8445 Japanese Toy Parasol. Size, 14x18 inches. Every child should have one. Beautiful assorted colors.

No. 8T8435 One of the largest selling toys of the day. Three-drawer beautifully colored and decorated Japanese lacquer Cabinet. Can be used for collar buttons, jewels, trinkets or as a girl's small miniature doll bureau. Sells on sight. Easily worth 50 cents. Size, 4¼x2¼x4¼ inches. Each in box.

No. 8T8379 Pocket Stereoscope with 100 Stereopticon Views, of happy scenes of children, animals, birds, comics, etc. Affords many entertaining and delightful hours for the little folks. Size views, 1½x3 inches. Would easily sell at 50 cents.

No. 8T8459 Fancy hammered brass Finger Bowl. Exceedingly popular, very novel and entirely new. Diameter, 4½ inches. If you want something exceptionally fine, buy these.

No. 8T8472 Twenty Post Card Wonders of America. Shows assorted natural colored views of the wonders of the country. Interesting, educational and very instructive.

No. 8T8473 Twenty-five assorted Post Card Views of Chicago. A series of splendidly illustrated colored views of Chicago including parks, buildings, stock yards and other points of interest.

No. 8T8474 Twenty-five Post Card Views of America. A very interesting series, showing scenes, cities, wonders of the country and points of interest. A very popular and large selling series. Each one in beautiful colors.

No. 8T8451 Nest of six fancy children's Japanese Baskets. Assorted colored straws with handles. Size of the largest basket, 4x4x7 inches.

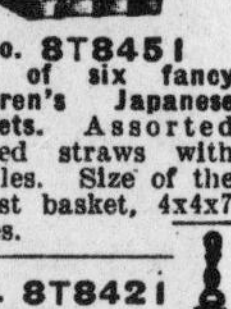

No. 8T8421 Imported nickel Watch Fob, cameo head charm. Never tarnishes.

33 cents each FOR ANY ARTICLE ON THIS PAGE

IN LOTS OF SIX OR MORE is our remarkably low price for any article on this page. You need not select six items from this page alone, but may make your selection of six items from any of our pages of 7, 17 and 33-cent items, pages 383 to 393 inclusive. We are able to quote these sensationally low prices by basing them on actual cost for large quantities and selling them six or more at a time. Just look through this list and you will see articles for which you have always paid 50 cents, 75 cents or even $1.00 in your own drug store. In ordering, be sure to give the catalog number of each item and the correct price according to the page from which you select. Buy as many as you like, only your order must be for at least six items.

No. 8T9001 Satin faced, hand painted Pin Cushion, large size.

No. 8T9002 Large size Star Sea Shell. Very ornamental as mantel, piano, den or corner decoration.

No. 8T9003 Fancy decorated Shaving Mug and Brush. A fine present.

No. 8T9004 4½-inch ebony finished beveled Hand Mirror.

No. 8T9005 Ormolu gold finished, satin lined fancy 2¼-inch Jewel Box.

No. 8T9006 6x6-in. red and white straw, hinge cover Handkerchief, Jewel or Work Basket.

No. 8T9050 75-cent pair Rheumatic Insoles. Keeps the feet warm in winter. A great seller. Give size of shoe.

No. 8T9009 50-cent deck Gypsy Witch Fortune Telling Cards. A well known and standard card.

No. 8T9012 Fancy netted bulb, decorated colored glass Perfume Atomizer.

No. 8T9015 German silver handled Tooth Brush.

No. 8T9162 German silver handled bone tipped Nail Brush.

No. 8T9018 Fancy imported Bohemian glass Puff Box.

No. 8T9019 Fine red rubber Bath Sponge. Cannot wear it out.

No. 8T9020 Sixty sheets exceptionally fine Linen Writing Paper and Envelopes.

No. 8T9022 Pair nine-row, mounted, ebony finished Military Hair Brushes. Exceptionally big value.

No. 8T9138 Pair mahogany finished, mounted Military Hair Brushes.

No. 8T9025 Four-piece ebony finished Manicure Set in fancy lined box.

No. 8T9070 Exceptionally big value flower decorated Sewing Box, comprising four pieces and mirror top. Great value.

No. 8T9029 50-cent bottle Rose Toilet Water.

No. 8T9044 50-cent bottle Violet Toilet Water.

No. 8T9114 50-cent bottle Carnation Toilet Water. An exceptionally fine toilet water.

No. 8T9030 Gold plated top, glass Hairpin or Trinket Holder. Fancy flower embossed top.

No. 8T9031 50-cent set black composition Double Six Dominoes. Finely polished and an exceptionally high class item. One of the finest sets made.

No. 8T9032 50-cent box celebrated Dora imported Face Powder. An exceptionally high class powder and one that will please any lady.

No. 8T9033 Set five fancy Vegetable Ivory Dice.

No. 8T9137 Box ⅝-inch ivory transparent pyralin Dice.

No. 8T9023 Gold plated Novelty Pin or Ash Tray. Beautiful in appearance and high class.

No. 8T9056 1 pound package absolutely pure Absorbent Cotton. 50-cent value.

No. 8T9061 13-inch exceptionally fine Whisk Broom, braided handle. Will last for years.

No. 8T9207 Beautiful embossed nickel plated Soap Box, hinge cover.

No. 8T9000 Celebrated Three Wise Monkeys Incense Burner, representing the correct method of living, "Speak no evil, see no evil, hear no evil." A motto of living that should be practiced by all. Buy this novelty statue and keep it in your home so it may impress upon you the lesson it teaches. Imported direct from Japan and made of the celebrated oxblood colored Doryake ware, and a novelty that will cost you elsewhere three to five times our price. Sells on sight. Must be really seen to be appreciated.

No. 8T9013 Hard rubber embossed eleven-row Hair Brush.

No. 8T9016 Large beautiful painted Conch Sea Shell with words "What are the Wild Waves Saying?" A large selling parlor ornament.

No. 8T9027 Three boxes Old Reliable Buttermilk Soap. Exceptionally big soap value.

No. 8T9035 Child's Comb and Brush Toilet Set. Hinge cover, lined box. A great child's favorite.

No. 8T9065 Fancy 8-inch polished back Clothes Brush. Big value.

No. 8T9038 Mission Wood Match Holder, with metal bulldog. Wonderful value. Size, 7x2½x4½ inches.

No. 8T9058 Celluloid top, hinge cover, tufted lined Glove Box. Size, 11x3x2¾ inches. For handkerchief box see No. 8T9112 on following page.

No. 8T9071 Exceptionally fine 7-inch real horn Ladies' Dressing Comb.

No. 8T9039 Mission Pipe and Match Holder, with metal stag and hanging attachment. Size, 9½x11 inches. One of the greatest values on this page.

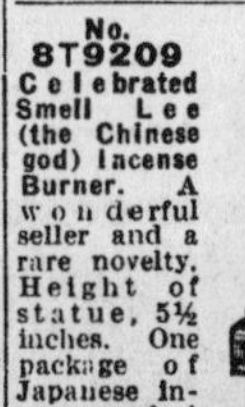

No. 8T9209 Celebrated Smell Lee (the Chinese god) Incense Burner. A wonderful seller and a rare novelty. Height of statue, 5½ inches. One package of Japanese incense and six good luck Japanese post cards accompany every package. Packed in box. Make a present to your friends of this bringer of good luck, the greatest selling novelty ever manufactured.

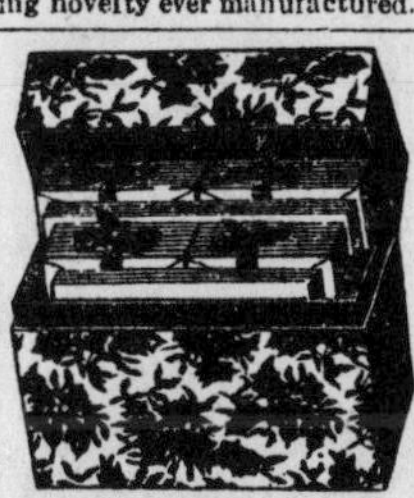

No. 8T9107 Fine Box, holding two quires fine Linen Stationery.

No. 8T9068 Ebony or bone handle fine steel, nickel plated Cuticle Knife, with ferrule attachment. The best made. One you can depend upon. State whether ebony or bone handle is wanted.

No. 8T9074 Bone or ebony handled exceptionally fine steel Nail File. 3¼-inch shank, beautifully finished. Specify handle. 50-cent value.

No. 8T9153 Fine large heavy Rubber Dressing Comb. Big value.

No. 8T9208 Fine imitation alligator leather Music Roll. Big value.

No. 8T9205 Fine Work and Handkerchief Baskets. Fancy Japanese straw, beautifully woven and decorated. Work box size, 7½x7½x3½ inches. Handkerchief size, 7x7x3 inches.

No. 8T9034 Fancy Japanese straw Glove or Necktie Box, with satin hand decorated hinge cover top and fancy Japanese straw design trimming for ribbon decoration. Size, 3½x12x2½ inches. (For handkerchief box see No. 8T9057.)

No. 8T9043 1 ounce bottle imported Perfume. Exceptionally sweet and delicate odors. Furnished in violet, rose, carnation, heliotrope and lily of the valley odors. Specify odor wanted.

No. 8T9045 Fancy embossed ivory pyralin Soap Box. Embossed, acorn decorated top

No. 8T9046 Fancy 7x9-inch cabinet size metal Photo Frames. Ormolu gold finished, assorted shapes, easel attachment.

No. 8T9047 Gold plated top Puff or Powder Box.

No. 8T9048 Gold edge, fancy color decorated back deck best Playing Cards. Big 50-cent value.

No. 8T9049 Fancy embossed natural flower top, decorated, hinge cover, imported straw Collar and Cuff Box, assorted shapes.

No. 8T9051 25-cent tube genuine Colgate's Dental Cream Tooth Paste, and 25-cent can Colgate's Violet Talcum Powder. Two well known, highly advertised specialties. Regular 50-cent value.

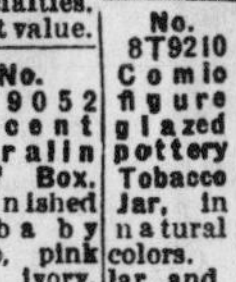

No. 8T9052 50-cent Pyralin Puff Box. Furnished in baby blue, pink or ivory. State color wanted.

No. 8T9054 Solid nickel Watch Fob with Compass Charm. A very fine and ornamental fob.

No. 8T9055 6-inch celluloid top Collar and Cuff Box with words "Collars and Cuffs" embossed on top. Big value.

No. 8T9057 Fancy Japanese straw Handkerchief Basket, with satin top, flower color decorated hinge cover. For glove box see No. 8T9034.

1-Ounce Bottle Fine Perfume in glass stoppered bottle. Packed in fancy color embossed display box. Furnished in odors as follows:

No. 8T9059 White Rose odor.

No. 8T9100 Violet odor.

No. 8T9106 Crabapple odor.

No. 8T9135 Lilac odor.

No. 8T9062 Heart shaped fancy imported Shell Handkerchief or Trinket Box, with silk pin cushion. Box completely decorated with imported fancy shells. Size 6x6x2½in.

No. 8T9159 Shell Work Box. Similar to above, having compartments for needles, thread, sewing, etc. Size, 7x7 inches. A box you cannot buy at home. A novelty.

No. 8T9069 Big value hard rubber handle Fountain Pen, with filler. A reliable item.

No. 8T9067 50-cent 4-piece Pocket Toilet Case. Very convenient. Can be carried in the pocket.

No. 8T9210 Comic figure glazed pottery Tobacco Jar, in natural colors. Very popular and an immense seller. Easily sells for 75 cents.

No. 8T9072 Fine Ladies' Silk Toilet Sponge.

No. 8T9144 Fine bleached Sheep's Wool Bath Sponge.

No. 8T9075 Imported Japanese straw, fancy hinge cover, rounded edge Work Basket. Size, 9½ x 6½ x 3 inches. Can be trimmed with ribbon and makes a handsome article.

No. 8T9053 Beautiful rubber lined Sponge Bag with draw string. Size, 6½x8 inches. Big 50-cent value.

No. 8T9204 Trip Around the World Post Cards. Fifty colored views of points of interest in this and foreign countries with description of each view. Very popular and big sellers. Worth $1.00.

No. 8T9234 Fifty beautifully colored views of Northern, Central and Southern Europe. An educational and very high class series.

No. 8T9206 "State Capitols" Post Cards. A splendid set of fifty photographic reproductions of state capitols of the Union. Produced in the latest beautiful brown tints. Cards for which you would easily give 5 cents each. Buy this set and note for yourself the difference of architecture and construction throughout the country. Educational, instructive and very interesting. Sold by others at 65 to 75 cents per set.

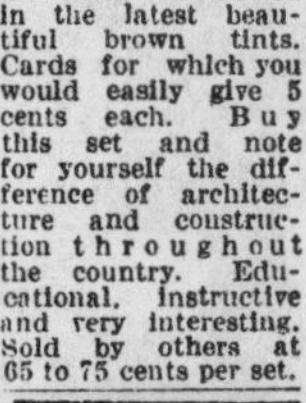

No. 8T9224 "Love on the Square" Picture. The ideal method of living and a picture that should be in every young married couple's home. Size, 7½x9½ inches.

YOUR CHOICE OF ANY ARTICLE ON THIS PAGE FOR ONLY

EXAMINE THESE PAGES CLOSELY, LOOK OVER ALL THE ITEMS LISTED. We have crowded these pages purposely in order to give you as many items to select from as possible. In order that we can sell you these ordinary 50-cent, 75-cent and $1.00 drug store and novelty items for only 33 cents each, we ask that you order at least six of the articles shown on pages 383 to 393, inclusive. You can order from any one page or select the six items from the eleven pages, just as you choose, so long as you order at least six. We believe it will pay you to go over the pages item by item and look at the illustrations closely, compare prices, just see what these goods will cost you at home, get your neighbors and friends interested, and then make up as large an order as you can. Be sure in every case, however, to order at least six items (as many more as you choose), **giving in each case the correct catalog number and allowing the price given on the page from which the article is selected.**

No. 8T9078 Folding pocket flexible Nail File in German silver embossed decorated case.

No. 8T9079 Beautiful nickel plated Cigar Rest and Ash Tray.

No. 8T9081 7x9-inch fancy chipped edge Shaving and Stand Mirror, with easel. A fine mirror.

No. 8T9082 Our big mirror value. 4-inch, gold plated edge, fancy decorated back, heavy beveled Mirror, with handle.

No. 8T9083 Gold plated ladies' slipper with silk plush Pin Cushion.

No. 8T9085 Ebony finished Shaving Brush and Soap Box, sterling silver mounted, in fancy display case.

No. 8T9087 Fine imported swan decorated hinge cover metal Jewel Box. Very fancy.

No. 8T9088 Box fifty 1-cent large sticks assorted Stick Candy, including hoarhound, peppermint, lemon, cloves, etc.

No. 8T9092 Fancy silk Jewel Bag, filled with perfume sachet, with ribbon attachment.

No. 8T9089 Fine gold lipped, beautiful luster tinted imported Shaving Mug.

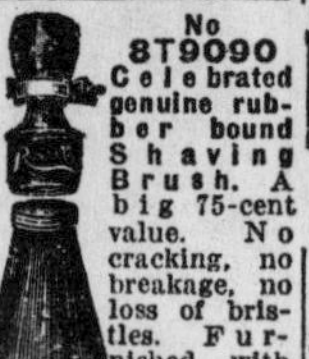

No. 8T9090 Celebrated genuine rubber bound Shaving Brush. A big 75-cent value. No cracking, no breakage, no loss of bristles. Furnished with holder attachment. Each in box.

No. 8T9093 Imported folding Cribbage Board. Folds up and occupies little space.

No. 8T9094 Fancy novelty Dagger Letter Opener and Paper Weight. Heavy embossed handle, gray silver finish. Length, 6½ inches.

No. 8T9096 German silver Dresser Set, comprising German silver top hair receiver and puff box. Fancy design and a great bargain.

No. 8T9097 Shell Cross and Crucifix, with holy water attachment. Handsome and very ornamental.

No. 8T9099 1-ounce fancy Perfume Bottle, with fancy red bulb Parisian patented perfume spray, each in box.

No. 8T9103 5-inch fancy Chamois Buffer. Beautiful celluloid top.

No. 8T9104 Fine seven-row Russian bristle Hand Brush, oval top.

No. 8T9108 1 pound Berry's Famous Assorted Chocolates.

No. 8T9105 1 pound exceptionally high class Linen Writing Paper.

No. 8T9101 Box 100 very fine Arbiter Linen Envelopes.

No. 8T9109 $2.50 Rheumatic Ring. Largely worn for rheumatism.

No. 8T9110 Mission double Match and Cigar Holder, hand flower decorated. Size, 7½x5x3½ inches.

No. 8T9111 Fine Medicinal and Toilet Atomizer.

No. 8T9112 Fine celluloid top, gilt and flower decorated hinge cover, tufted lined Handkerchief Box. Size, 6x6 inches. For glove box to match see No. 8T9058 on previous page.

No. 8T9117 Oval French Miniature Picture in oval gold mounted frame, with easel. Reproduction from famous painting. Would easily sell for 75c.

No. 8T9214 Miniature Opera Glasses, handsome in appearance. Screw extension attachment and a very good glass for the price. A high class toy. Size, 4x3½ inches. Each in box.

WONDERFUL VALUES IN FRAMED PICTURES.

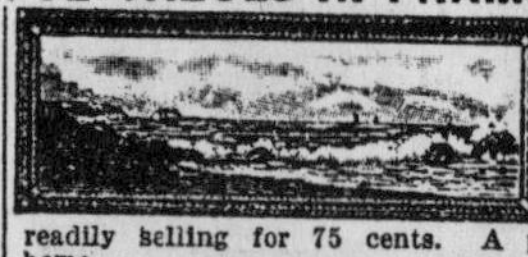

Our Wonder Leader. Handsome 6x16-inch artistic and fancy gilt framed picture. Frame artistically and heavily embossed. A picture readily selling for 75 cents. A picture suited for any home.

No. 8T9215 Assorted Marine.
No. 8T9216 Assorted Landscape and Woodland Scenes.

No. 8T9217 Celebrated Gossip Picture.
"There's so much good in the worst of us,
And so much bad in the best of us,
That it hardly behooves any of us
To talk about the rest of us."

A motto that should be in every home. A motto that applies to everyone. A motto everyone should follow. Picture in colors in fancy gilt frame. Size, 7x15 inches. 75-cent value.

No. 8T9223 Double Fruit Picture. Assorted colored fruits in double compartment picture. Brown Mission frame. Size, 7½x18 inches. A fine dining room picture. 75-cent value.

No. 8T9231 Everybody's favorite. Well known "Haying" Picture. Beautiful brown tint in 1-inch Mission round cornered frame. A beautiful picture for any room. Readily sells for 75 cents to $1.00. Size, 11½x14 inches.

Fancy brown tint Religious Pictures in beautiful oval gilt metal frames. Wonderful sellers. Pictures that sell at sight. Pictures that should be in every home. Size, 8x10 inches. Subjects as follows:

No. 8T9225 Christ in the Temple.
No. 8T9226 Christ at Thirty.
No. 8T9227 Sistine Madonna.
No. 8T9228 Christ and the Rich Ruler.
No. 8T9229 The Gleaners.
No. 8T9230 The Angelus.

No. 8T9213 Bloze Gold Bronze Outfit. A necessity for every home. Decorate the chairs, pictures, bric-a-brac and other home ornaments. Beautiful gold tint. Produces a beautiful appearance. Will not tarnish, requires neither skill nor experience. Can be used on anything anywhere. Regular 50-cent outfit.

Religious Pictures. Well known religious subjects. Brown Mission frame. Size, 11½ x14 inches. Favorites everywhere and should be in every home. Pictures that sell at sight. Wonderful value.

No. 8T9218 Christ at Twelve.
No. 8T9219 Christ in Gethsemane.
No. 8T9220 Christ and the Doctors.
No. 8T9221 Sacred Heart of Mary.
No. 8T9222 Sacred Heart of Jesus.

No. 8T9131 Big showy mahogany finished Hair Brush. Has twelve rows bristles.

No. 8T9136 Big value twelve-row white bristle ebony finished Hair Brush.

No. 8T9080 Largest size Conch Graveyard Shell, natural finish, with words "At Rest" on lip.

No. 8T9130 Acme Bulb Syringe. Exceptionally big value. White rubber, with two slip pipes.

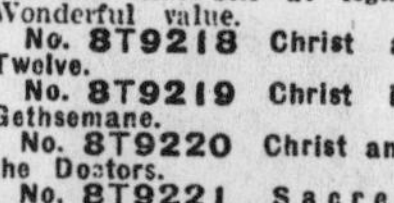

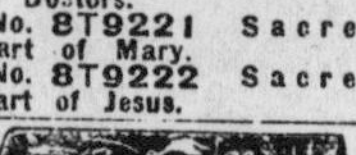

No. 8T9123 Imported Japanese lacquer Glove Box. Fancy gilt design decorated. Size, 11x3½x2¼ inches.

No. 8T9154 Fine ebony finished sterling silver mounted Comb and Brush Set. Eleven-row brush and 7-inch hard rubber comb.

No. 8T9120 Hexagon Work Basket. Fancy tufted satin lined bottom. Size, 9½x9½x6.

No. 8T9121 Market or Picnic Basket. Made of colored willow interwoven with colored straw and red rush. A very solid and useful basket. Size, 7x11x12 inches.

No. 8T9165 Sea Grass Lunch Basket. Made of very fine split willow interwoven with colored sea grass, with reinforced handles. A very solid and serviceable basket. Size, 4½x9x9½.

No. 8T9133 Big value Newspaper Rack or Wall Pocket. Made of fancy colored straw and raffia. Size, 11x13 inches.

No. 8T9134 Fancy satin lined rectangular shape hinge cover imported straw Work Box. Size, 6x4x3 inches.

No. 8T9158 Oval Willow Work Basket. Size, 9x13½ inches.

No. 8T9124 Handkerchief Box, imported Japanese lacquer. Fancy gilt design decorated. Size, 6¾ x 5¾ x 2¼ inches.

No. 8T9125 Photo Box, similar to handkerchief box above. Size, 5x8x2¼ inches.

No. 8T9102 Mission metal Cigar Holder and Ash Tray. Fancy decorated. Big value.

No. 8T9127 1½ pounds absolutely pure imported Spanish Castile Soap, the best you can buy.

No. 8T9129 Magnetic Tooth Brush with Compass. Regular 50-cent value. Highly advertised and well known.

No. 8T9132 Pyralin handle white camel's hair Infant's Brush. Furnished in pink, baby blue or white. State color.

No. 8T9126 Polished Back, fancy handled imported wood Finger and Nail Brush. Six-row, all bristle, five-row top.

No. 8T9143 Deck fine Playing Cards in leather case.

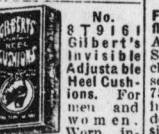

No. 8T9147 16x18-inch imported soft cleaning English Chamois Skin. Will not scratch.

No. 8T9177 14x20-inch soft imported white Chamois Skin.

No. 8T9156 Genuine Leather Dice Cup with Dice.

No. 8T9161 Gilbert's Invisible Adjustable Heel Cushions. For men and women. Worn inside the shoe. Real foot comfort. They take off the shock of walking. Are simple and durable. Specify ladies' or gents' and size of shoe.

No. 8T9182 Queen Helmet Fancy Shell, beautifully notched. A fine ornament.

No. 8T9186 Ladies' silver plated beveled miniature mirror. Size glass, 2¼ inches; length, 5 inches over all.

No. 8T9160 Big value Photograph Album. Fancy lithographed front, gilt and plush decorated. Holds twelve large size cabinets and four small pictures. Hinge clasp. Size, 7x8½ inches.

No. 8T9191 Fancy flower embossed, artistic design, gold plated Photo Frame, standing attachment. Size over all, 5x7 inches, each in box.

No. 8T9192 Oval Gold Plated Photo Frame, heavy flower embossed. Size, 4¼ x 6¼ inches.

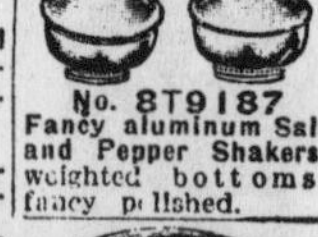

No. 8T9187 Fancy aluminum Salt and Pepper Shakers, weighted bottoms, fancy polished.

No. 8T9212 Fancy natural color flower decorated Tray. A wonder seller. Size, 13⅝x16⅝ inches. Sells wherever seen. Easily worth 75 cents. Furnished in rose and violet designs. State design wanted.

No. 8T9180 Big value Shoe Brush and Polisher.

No. 8T9211 Fancy imported Margarite style handle four-row slit back Tooth Brush. A very fine brush.

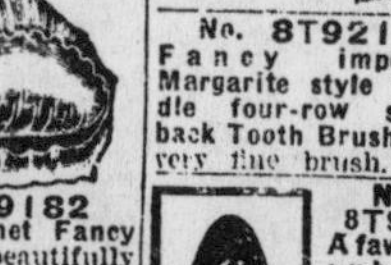

No. 8T9233 A favorite subject, "The Mother and Babe," in natural colors, oval opening. Fancy passe-partout frame, white mat. Size, 6x14 inches. Each in box. Women's favorite.

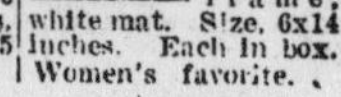

 SAVINGS ON TABLES. 6-FOOT EXTENSION, $4.75; CLAW FOOT PEDESTAL EXTENSION, $7.95; INVESTIGATE.

47 cents each IS OUR PRICE FOR ANY ARTICLE ON THIS PAGE

WONDERFUL VALUES 47 cents is the price of any article on this page. You may buy as many as you please. Most of these items will cost you 75 cents to $1.00 in your home stores. Every article is high grade and the best of its kind. Include a number of them with an express or freight shipment. You will find them better values than expected. Our guarantee of quality applies to every item.

No. 8T10000 1 pound genuine Benedetto Allegretti famous Chocolates.

No. 8T10002 Fancy netted bulb, imported, flower decorated Bohemian glass Perfume Atomizer.

No. 8T10003 Novelty metal Thermometer, animal decorated. Very artistic. Handsome and beautiful ornament for any home. Assorted shapes and designs. Size 5¼ inches wide by 8 inches high.

No. 8T10004 Fancy imported color braided straw Work Basket, oval shaped with hinge cover, full satin tufted lined. A good 75-cent value. Size, 8x5½x3½ inches.

No. 8T10005 Fancy imported leather Pocket Toilet Case, complete. Fine 2x4-inch heavy beveled mirror. Very soft heavy leather covered.

No. 8T10006 Imported fancy lacquered and decorated three-drawer Card Case or Trinket Holder. Very pretty. Size, 4½x3x5½ inches.

No. 8T10008 Very fancy and up to date imported Wall Pocket or Newspaper Rack. Fancy colored straws and raffia. Good stiff frame. Size, 13x14 in.

No. 8T10009 Fancy ormolu gold finish metal frame, 4½-inch width, Shaving or Stand Mirror.

No. 8T10011 3½-inch exceptionally high grade steel Nail Scissors with File Attachment, beautifully nickel plated.

No. 8T10012 Very fine steel 3½-inch nickel plated Cuticle Scissors.

No. 8T10013 Spring Nail Nippers, beautifully nickel plated.

No. 8T10014 Beautiful horn handled stiff tapering Nail File with cleaner end, very best steel and exceptionally high grade instrument in every respect. 3-inch shank.

No. 8T10015 Beautiful pearl handle flexible Nail File, exceptionally high class steel, well finished.

No. 8T10016 Beautiful horn handled stiff Cuticle Knife, very best steel.

No. 8T10017 Beautiful pearl handled Cuticle Knife, exceptionally high class steel.

No. 8T10023 Big value imported Rubber Sponge. Will last for years.

No. 8T10026 Fancy shaped imitation alligator covered Collar and Cuff Box. Fancy padded top, lined throughout. Size, 8x6x5 inches. Readily sells for 75 cents.

No. 8T10028 Gold lipped, fancy flower and color decorated Shaving Mug. A beautiful Christmas present.

No. 8T10030 Continuous spray, two hard rubber tipped Medicinal Atomizer. Can be used for oil or water. Nose and throat attachment.

No. 8T10032 Bronze finished metal hat and boot Cigar and Match Holder. Very novel, artistic shape and highly ornamental. Size, 5¼x4x2½ inches.

No. 8T10033 Hard rubber Fountain Pen. Big 75-cent value. Complete with filler attachment.

No. 8T10034 Gold plated metal novelty shape Photo Stand, with easel attachment. Size, 8x11 inches. Regular price, 75 cents.

No. 8T10054 9-inch circular heavy plate glass Shaving or Stand Mirror, chipped edge, easel attachment.

No. 8T10055 Circular Collar and Cuff Box, with compartment center, clasp collar button top, padded inside cover. A big value. Size, 6x5 inches.

No. 8T10060 Fancy genuine leather Card Case, containing deck of gilt edged high class playing cards

No. 8T10067 Beautiful nickel plated, handled Collapsible Drinking Cup in genuine leather heavy padded top case.

No. 8T10035 Fancy imported china Shaving Mug and Brush Set, fancy color decorated, packed in tufted lined case.

No. 8T10036 Hand carved monk head novelty shield shaped match and Pipe Holder, leather hangers, metal rings, brass cups, chain hanging attachment. One of the greatest values ever offered. Size, 8x15 inches. Good 75-cent value.

No. 8T10037 Lehmann's celebrated Autobus. Well put together. Finished in white enamel with yellow and brown decoration. Size, 8x3x5 inches. Patent spring winding attachment.

No. 8T10038 Lehmann's "Toot-Toot" Automobile. A most clever mechanical toy. Gives the familiar "toot-toot" when running along the floor. White enamel finish, red decorated, imitation rubber tires. Size, 7x3½x6½ inches.

No. 8T10039 Mechanical Flying Machine. Fastened on string and will fly around room in a most natural manner. Same construction as the regular flying machine. An educating, strong and nicely finished toy. Length, 10 inches.

No. 8T10049 A very high class Horse and Bell Toy. Horse cloth covered, fitted in metal frame, carrying bell of sweet tone between 3½-inch gilt and blue enameled colored wheels. A long lasting and reliable toy. Length, 8½ inches.

No. 8T10050 The mechanical Clown Tumbler. A simple but effective toy. Winds up by arms and tumbles around on floor, turning somersaults. Height, 8½ inches. Illustration shows different positions assumed.

No. 8T10051 Beautiful sterling silver mounted, ebony finished Comb and Brush Set. Packed in fancy display tufted lined box. A big 75-cent value.

No. 8T10052 Same as above, but mahogany finished.

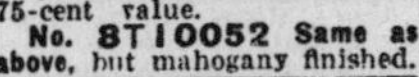

No. 8T10040 Fancy hinge cover lacquered Glove Box, fancy color decorated. Size, 4x12x2¾ inches. Furnished with lock and key. Sells readily for 75 cents.

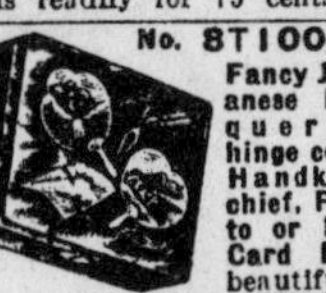

No. 8T10041 Fancy Japanese lacquered hinge cover Handkerchief, Photo or Post Card Box, beautifully decorated. Size, 7¾x6½x2¾ inches.

No. 8T10043 Celluloid top, fancy flower color decorated Dresser Set. Comprises glove box, handkerchief box and trinket, collar button or hairpin box. Imported fancy braided straw bottoms, complete set.

No. 8T10047 Glove or Handkerchief Box, holding one quire very high grade Linen Stationery, tied with beautiful lavender ribbon to match trimmings of box, packed in hinge cover beautifully flower color decorated box. Size, 5¾x9¾x2¼ inches.

No. 8T10109 Stag novelty Cigar and Match and Ash Holder, hand decorated. A showy and very useful item.

No. 8T10111 Big value Child's Comb and Brush Set in hinge cover box. Mirror inside cover, tufted lined box. Nice present for a child.

No. 8T10120 Fine black keratol (best imitation leather) Music Roll, black moire lined, fine leather handle and strap. Size, 15 inches.

No. 8T10063 Combination Work and Handkerchief Set. Fancy imported lace and fancy colored straw hinge cover. Very artistically made. Work box 6x6x4½ inches. Handkerchief box 5x5x3½ inches. This beautiful set is a great bargain.

No. 8T10064 Crucifix in shell frame. Glass cover, shell border, 5x7 inches, easel attachment. A high class crucifix.

No. 8T10069 Pair fancy sterling silver mounted, ebony finished Military Hair Brushes. Have nine rows long white 1-inch bristles. A great bargain and you would readily pay 75 cents for them. Complete in box.

No. 8T10070 Same as Military Brushes above, but mahogany finish.

No. 8T10078 Four-wheeled collapsible Doll Cart. Size, set up, 12-inch cart, 15-inch handle. Black trimmed, red cloth body, gilt wheels.

No. 8T10081 Japanese lacquer double opening Card Case, basket effect, fancy decorated, very popular. Size, 6x 4½x2½ inches.

No. 8T10082 Fancy stag novelty Match or Cigar Holder. Large size and a beautiful ornament. In box. Size, 5½x 1¼x6 inches.

No. 8T10083 16x21-inch exceptionally fine soft imported washable English Chamois Skin. Will not scratch.

No. 8T10093 Genuine Indian hand made sweet grass Handkerchief Basket, hinge cover. Every part hand made from the fragrant sweet grass of Canada. Perfumes the entire room. Pillow shaped. A rare article.

No. 8T10169 Beautiful hand decorated imported Japanese Wind Bells and Chimes. One of the greatest selling Japanese novelties of the day. Beautifully decorated in colors. Japanese designs. Makes a fine decoration for any home. A fine decoration for dens or on the porch. As the gentle breezes blow against the tiny pieces of glass it produces that favorite Oriental music so pleasing to everyone.

No. 8T10079 Four-piece ebony finished, sterling silver mounted Manicure Set, in fancy tufted lined display box.

No. 8T10084 5-inch heavy beveled long handled ebony finished Mirror. A real beauty. Carefully packed in box.

No. 8T10088 Fancy hinge cover Work Basket. Made of braided and colored imported straw. Size, 12x12x6 inches.

No. 8T10090 Gold plated heavy flower embossed Jewel Box, full satin lined, silk cord trimmed.

No. 8T10099 Fancy aluminum Salt, Pepper and Toothpick Set. Includes heavy weighted bottom salt and pepper shakers and fancy aluminum toothpick holder and tray. Beautifully decorated and burnished. Size, 6½x4x3 inches. In box.

No. 8T10100 Double deck Wall Pocket. Made of colored willow, lace and jumbo straw, reinforced edges. Size, 12x15 inches.

No. 8T10106 Folding Shaving Set, comprising nickel plated handled shaving brush, porcelain dish and 4½-inch plated mirror, nickel rim. Folds up completely and occupies little space. Can be set up and mirror tilted at angle.

No. 8T10164 Fancy imported Photograph Album, holding sixteen regular size and eight small pictures. Heavy beautiful gilt and color decorated top, plush trimmed, gilt edge, clasp attachment. Size, 7x9 inches. Big value.

No. 8T10101 Fancy hinge cover Photo Box. Fancy tufted lined, ribbon hanging attachment, beautifully decorated. Size, 5½x7½x3 inches.

No. 8T10103 Fancy decorated shell Glove Box, with hinge cover. Decorated with fancy shells from all over the world. Satin pin cushion on top. Very ornamental and a big seller. Size, 10x4x4½ inches.

No. 8T10104 Shell Handkerchief Box, similar to glove box above. Size, 6⅞x6⅞x1¼ inches.

No. 8T10165 4½-inch well made, stag finished, beautifully mounted Ladies' Beveled Hand Mirror.

No. 8T10080 Fancy comic head glazed pottery Tobacco Jar, natural color finished. Size, 4½x 1¼x6 inches.

YOUR CHOICE OF ANY ARTICLE ON THIS PAGE FOR ONLY

EXAMPLES OF MONEY SAVING. The many articles shown on this page are exceptional values and sell regularly at $1.00 to $1.25 each. Just think of the saving we offer you in giving you your choice of any of these well known, high grade items at only 67 cents each. We guarantee the quality. They are made of the very best materials and we know that no such great values have ever before been offered at such a low price as 67 cents. Send us your order, select as many items as you please. Give catalog number of each item you select and allow 67 cents for each.

No. 8T11001 Popular large size skull Match or Toothpick Holder with movable drop jaw. A wonderful selling novelty.

No. 8T11003 Two-tip metal attachment Atomizer. Cannot get out of order. Regular $1.00 value.

No. 8T11004 Mariner Shaving Mug and Brush Set. Fancy color decorated light green tinted edge. Packed in fancy display box.

No. 8T11008 Fancy imported, highly decorated shell Handkerchief Box with rococo legs, trimmed in imitation pearl paper, hinge cover, and a beauty. Size, 7x7x4 inches. each carefully packed.

No. 8T11009 Glove Box, similar to above. Size, 10½x 5x4 inches.

No. 8T11010 Fancy opal glass, fancy flower and leaf color decorated Puff or Powder Jar, with hinge cover and brass clasp. Size, 5x3½ inches. A beautiful and useful ornament.

No. 8T11014 Genuine imported English soft cleaning washable Chamois Skin. Size, 19x22 inches.

No. 8T11141 Fine soft cream colored Chamois Skin. Size, 18x25 inches. Largely used for dry polishing and as lining for winter garments.

No. 8T11015 9-inch lion novelty Paper Weight and Ornament, natural color finish, massive and very ornamental.

No. 8T11016 Virgin and child shell Holy Water Fount, sides beautifully decorated with imported shells, inside full mirror lined. Size, 5x5x7 inches. Hanging attachment.

No. 8T11017 4-inch fancy ormolu gold finish, fancy flower embossed decorated, full satin lined Jewel Box, each in box. Great value.

No. 8T11019 Fancy decorated and ornamental Three-Cigar Rest, nickel-plated top ash tray. Size, 5½x2¼ inches. Handsome. Selling elsewhere at $1.00 each.

No. 8T11020 German silver Manicure Set, comprising German silver handled cuticle knife, button hook and nail file and cleaner. Fancy lined display box. Size, 5x7 inches.

Fine Military Hair Brushes. Have eleven rows of fine long white bristles and fancy sterling silver head mount. Pair in box.

No. 8T11021 Ebony finish.

No. 8T11022 Mahogany finish.

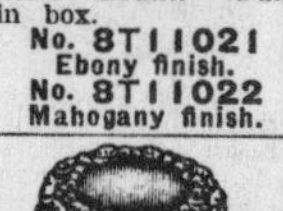

No. 8T11046 Big Shaving Leader. Comprises beautiful heavy embossed polished German silver top soap box and German silver handle good bristle shaving brush, packed in fancy tufted display box. Size box, 5x6x 3¾ inches.

No. 8T11055 Fancy gold lipped, beautiful luster and gold decorated imported china Shaving Mug.

6-inch genuine fancy leather, heavy decorated top Collar Bag, full moire lined, fancy draw strings, leather tipped. Will readily sell for $1.00 to $1.25.

No. 8T11051 Tan.

No. 8T11052 Black.

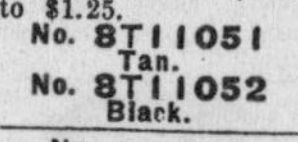

No. 8T11047 Fancy imitation bronze Bust of Lincoln. Natural and very ornamental. Size, 3½x2½x7 inches.

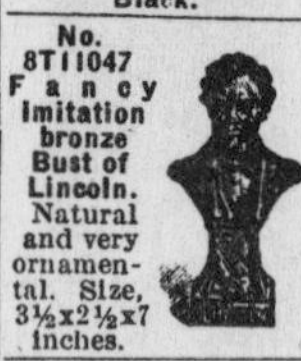

No. 8T11048 Letter Initial Press. Very serviceable, beautiful nickel plated press for placing initials on stationery, envelopes or wherever desired. Old English letters. Never gets out of order. Always ready for use. No longer necessary to buy initial paper. Make your own. Specify letter wanted.

No. 8T11054 Novelty Collar and Cuff Box, made of imported Japanese wood bamboo, beautifully polished, top fancy inlaid, compartment for collar and cuff buttons. Size, 7x4½ inches. In box. Something entirely different than you can ever buy at home.

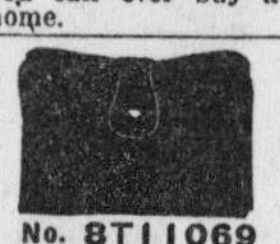

No. 8T11069 Genuine seal leather lapping edge Playing Card Case; with deck fine gold edge playing cards and two celluloid game counters.

No. 8T11058 Fancy imported hinge cover Work Basket, made of willow interwoven with white and colored fancy jumbo straw, colored willow framework. Size, 10x10x7 inches. A beauty.

No. 8T11066 Fancy imported straw, hinge cover, handled Work Basket. Full satin tufted lined. Size, 7½x7x4½ inches.

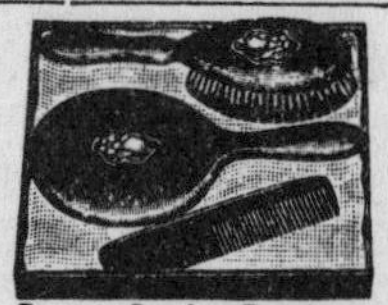

Fancy Comb, Brush and Mirror Set, containing 3½-inch beveled mirror, eleven-row hair brush and 7-inch dressing comb, packed in box. Brushes and mirror each have fancy mount.

No. 8T11026 Ebony finish.

No. 8T11027 Mahogany finish.

4½-inch very heavy French beveled plate Mirrors, long handles, exceptional quality, each in box.

No. 8T11028 Ebony finish.

No. 8T11029 Mahogany finish.

No. 8T11031 Novelty carved and decorated double cup, brass lined Pipe and Match Holder, fancy mission finish, metal ring pipe hangers, leather trimmed, chain hanging attachment. One of the greatest values we offer.

Fancy Comb and Brush Set. Beautiful tufted lined display case, nine-row long white bristle hair brush, beautifully sterling silver mounted, and 7-inch comb.

No. 8T11033 Ebony.

No. 8T11034 Mahogany.

No. 8T11036 Genuine leather 15-inch wide Music Roll, with handle and strap. Big value.

No. 8T11038 Three-quire cabinet very high class Linen Stationery, fancy decorated box, beautiful ribbon tied.

No. 8T11099 Fancy Match and Cigar Holder and Ash Tray. Highly ornamental. Contains two novelty pipes at side holding match holder secure. Gold plated and beautifully burnished. A very fine present. Size, 4½x2½ inches.

No. 8T11100 Fancy decorated celluloid top, hinge cover, fancy sateen tufted lined Glove Box. (See handkerchief box No. 8T11093.)

No. 8T11044 Gentlemen's Favorite. Double Cigar and double Match Holder. Four brass cups, mission finished, brass trimmed. Size, 8x4¼x5 inches. Will readily sell for $1.25. Handsome in appearance and exceedingly ornamental. Each carefully packed.

No. 8T11045 Fancy padded top Child's School Companion and Writing Pad. Contains nickel screw top ink well, compartments for stationery, pens, pencils, etc. Size, 8x10½x2¾ inches. Each carefully packed.

No. 8T11095 Mission Match and Cigar Set, with three brass cups, hand carved wood decoration, full brass trimmed. Size, 7¼x5½x7¾ inches. Readily sells for $1.00. A very fine present. Carefully packed.

Pair Military Hair Brushes and Comb Set. Contains pair eleven-row mounted military hair brushes and a 7-inch dressing comb in fancy tufted lined case.

No. 8T11096 Ebony finish.

No. 8T11097 Mahogany finish.

No. 8T11098 Child's Comb, Brush and Mirror Set. Contains 2½x4-inch beveled mirror, a nine-row hair brush and 7-inch dressing comb. All made of beautiful white composition, with fancy decorated backs. Packed in fancy tufted lined display case. A very fine child's present. Size, 6½ x 8½ inches.

No. 8T11042 Fancy keratol (imitation leather) oval shaped Glove Box, with hinge cover, full moire padded lining and fancy oxidized clasp. Size, 4x12x3 in.

No. 8T11043 Fancy keratol (imitation leather) covered, round shaped Handkerchief Box, with hinge cover, full padded moire lining and fancy oxidized clasp. Size, 7½x3 inches.

No. 8T11129 4-piece Manicure Set in fancy tufted lined hinge cover display box. Size, 3¾x8¼x2 inches.

No. 8T11059 Oxidized silver finish fancy leaf and scroll design Photo Frame with easel. Size, 7x11½ inches. A great bargain and very ornamental and hard to obtain.

No. 8T11061 Two-tip metal Nebulizer. Largely used for throat and nasal trouble. Cannot get out of order.

Genuine velvet leather Motto Hanger. Fancy decorated stamped and burned in following mottoes. Has heavy silk cord hanging attachment, leather tipped. Size, 8½x20 inches. Furnished in green, gray or tan leather. State color wanted. Mottoes as follows:

No. 8T11063 Aim high and believe yourself capable of great things.

No. 8T11064 Keep an even temper no matter what happens.

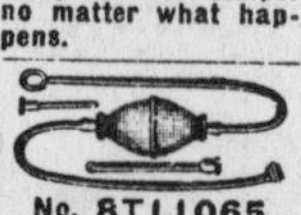

No. 8T11065 Big value red rubber Bulb Syringe, furnished with two hard rubber screw pipes. Packed in box.

No. 8T11067 Perpetual Calendar. Celluloid pad with months, days and dates. Guaranteed gold plate. Standing attachment. Size, 3½x5 inches. In box.

No. 8T11076 Oxidized silver handled Whisk Broom. Length, 11 inches. Hanging attachment.

No. 8T11128 Very best 8-inch genuine ebony beautifully polished Chamois Nail Buffer.

No. 8T11070 Standing Deer Paper Weight. Size, 8½x8 inches. Furnished in natural colors. A fine parlor, library or mantel decoration.

No. 8T11071 Ormolu gold finish top, fancy Colonial glass bowl Tobacco or Cigar Jar, sponge attachment on top. Size, 4x4x5½ inches.

No. 8T11072 Fancy imported Shell Photo Frame with velvet molding, oval opening, handsome in appearance, very ornamental and popular. Size, 7½x 10 inches. Standing and hanging attachment.

No. 8T11077 Fancy imported Combination Newspaper Rack or Wall Pocket and Whisk Broom Holder, made of raffia colored straw with fancy reinforced frame. Very ornamental. Size, 12x5x 13 inches.

No. 8T11078 Imitation leather covered wooden Photo Box, full satin tufted lined, satin ribbon raising attachment, fancy clasp. Size, 7½x5x3¼ inches.

No. 8T11081 Pair ebony finished, beautifully mounted Clothes and Hat Brushes in box.

No. 8T11126 Pair extra fine steel Nail Nippers, with fine spring, beautifully nickel plated.

No. 8T11082 The gentleman's favorite. Fancy large size pottery Skull Tobacco Jar. Represents skull in every detail. Top opens up, forming receptacle for tobacco. Sells readily at $1.00 to $1.25. Each carefully packed.

No. 8T11087 Very large pure unbleached Sheep's Wool Sponge, for cleaning carriages, automobiles, etc. Soft and will wear for years and will not scratch.

No. 8T11093 Celluloid top, fancy tufted sateen lined Handkerchief Box, clasp attachment. (See glove box No. 8T11100).

No. 8T11139 5-piece imported Baby Toilet Set. Comprising hair brush, comb, puff box, puff and ear cleaner. A fine present for any child.

No. 8T11140 Collar and Cuff Box. Fancy shaped, beautiful keratol leather covered, fancy lined, hinge cover. $1.00 value.

No. 8T11125 Beautiful square gold plated, fancy tinted Photo Frame. Oval opening fine tapestry mat. A very high class item. In box.

97 cents each FOR ANY ARTICLE ON THIS PAGE

THESE WONDER VALUES represent useful articles for about ½ their regular price. You would pay elsewhere $1.25, $1.50 or even $1.75 for them. Our price is only 97 cents each. Call the attention of your friends and neighbors to these pages. They will appreciate it. We know these values will surprise you when you see the goods. We guarantee the quality. In ordering, be sure to give the catalog number of each item you select and allow 97 cents for each. You may order as many as you please.

No. 8T12000 Fancy heavy embossed stag Shaving Mug and Brush. Very ornamental, exceedingly popular and one of the best selling sets.

No. 8T12053 Gentleman's Companion. Beautifully polished aluminum, handsomely onyx finished and decorated. Comprises shaving soap box, tooth brush holder, shaving brush holder, talcum bottle and soap box. Packed in holly box, size 6x9 x2¼ inches.

No. 8T12007 Double elephant imported Tobacco Jar. Novel, unique and something out of the ordinary. Elephant and dancing girl embossed, fancy decorated in green, gilt and brown tints. Carefully packed. Size, 3½ x 5 x 6½ inches

No. 8T12010 Five-piece German silver handled Manicure Set. Consisting of button hook, cuticle knife, nail file, powder box and chamois buffer. Tufted lined, hinge cover display box. Size, 5x7½x2 inches.

No. 8T12043 7-inch fine black India sheepskin Collar Bag, beautifully moire lined, heavy silk cord draw strings. Size, 7x6¾ inches.

No. 8T12044 Fancy 6-inch velvet leather Collar Bag. Fancy pinked edges, moire lined, silk cord draw strings. Furnished in brown, tan or green leather. Specify color.

No. 8T12014 Fancy Japanese Bamboo Collar and Cuff Box with center collar button holder. Top beautifully rustic flower and leaf design inlaid. Cannot wear it out. Size, 7½x7½x 4½ inches.

Pocket Manicure Set. Comprising high grade fine steel corn knife, cuticle knife, nail file and cleaner and tweezers in folding imitation leather case. Size case, 2½x6 inches.

No. 8T12015 Bone handled instruments.

No. 8T12016 Genuine ebony handled instruments.

No. 8T12017 Burnished oxidized, heavy flower embossed, beautifully polished Hair Receiver. Handsome and high class in every respect. Size, 4x4x 3½ inches.

No. 8T12018 Puff Box, same as No. 8T12017, with out center opening.

No. 8T12021 Genuine India Russian leather Handkerchief Case. Full satin lined, pearl button clasp. Size, 6x6 inches. Handsome, very durable and would sell readily for $1.50.

Fancy 4½-inch extra heavy beveled French plate Mirror in the new late artistic design oak leaf shape, beautifully finished and polished oval back. Sells on sight. Each carefully packed.

No. 8T12037 Ebony finish.

No. 8T12038 Mahogany finish.

No. 8T12042 Triple Reindeer Ornament, natural color finish.

No. 8T12023 Beautifully nickel plated Nail Nippers, with patent spiral Spring. $1.25 value.

No. 8T12039 Fancy Bohemian glass bowl Ash Receiver, double Cigar Rest and Match Holder, nickel plated trimmings. Size, 5½ x3¾ inches.

No. 8T12045 Fancy Imported English Chamois Skin, washable. Size, 28x 30 inches. The best made.

No. 8T12132 Beautiful Cream Colored Chamois Skin, size, 25x32 inches. Used for dry cleaning and also for lining for winter garments.

No. 8T12046 Burnished oxidized silver Crumb Tray and Scraper, heavily embossed, beautifully finished. Size, 8½x 8 inches.

Double Military Hair and Clothes Brush Set, sterling silver mounted.

No. 8T12049 Ebony finished backs.

No. 8T12050 Mahogany finished backs.

No. 8T12051 Cigar and Match Holder with Ash Tray. All parts gold plated, beautifully embossed and burnished; has 6-in tray.

No. 8T12003 Fancy ormolu gold finished, beautifully burnished, heavy flower decorated and embossed Jewel Box. Full satin lined, hinge cover. Size, 4½x3½x3½ inches. Beautiful design, very ornamental and a great seller. In box.

No. 8T12059 Home Utility Item. Comprises an 11-inch whisk broom, gilt handled, ebony finished cloth brush and a 4-inch beveled mirror, hanging attachment. Very useful. Size, 8½x11 inches.

Fancy Combination Comb, Brush and Mirror Set. Contains an eleven-row long white bristle hair brush, a 4½-inch fine beveled long handled mirror and a 7-inch fine dressing comb. Brush and mirror beautifully sterling silver mounted. Packed in fancy display tufted lined case.

No. 8T12024 Ebony finish.

No. 8T12025 Mahogany finish.

No. 8T12026 Fancy mission finish Smoker. Contains four fancy copper cups for cigars, matches and ash receiver. Fancy brass trimmed. Size, 10½x7½x4½ inches. The greatest value ever offered in a smoker.

No. 8T12027 Our big value shell Work Box. Exceedingly high class and artistic work box. Made from shells from all parts of the world. Full size mirror inside of cover. Six compartments for fancywork, has plush pin and needle cushion. Furnished with lock and key. Ornamental, handsome, useful and a great value. Size, 7½x4½x5 inches. Each carefully packed.

No. 8T12028 Our Beauty Match Holder and Pipe Hanger. Hand carved decoration. Brass cups, metal pipe hangers, arts and crafts decorations, chain hanging attachment. Size, 15x14 inches. If you want the best, buy this. Each carefully packed.

No. 8T12030 Child's Toilet Comb, Brush and Mirror Set in celluloid top, holly decorated, hinge cover box, extension base. Handsome, very useful and very popular.

No. 8T12031 Child's Sewing or Work Box. Contains six pieces, fancy mirror top, full satin lined, round edged box, full celluloid top, handsome and useful.

No. 8T12133 Beautiful Wind Chimes or Memory Bells. The largest and the best made. Every glass drilled and cord firmly tied, thereby being much superior to the cheaper pasted varieties. Made of selected high grade glass cut into artistic shapes and sizes and every piece beautifully hand painted in colors. Largely sold as a lover's remembrance, to be hung in the window where the gentle breezes may blow to and fro and the pretty painted bits of glass, with every passing breeze tingle from casement, fondly in memory of him. A charming lover's offering. A chime with memory bells, to hang in some dear friend's window that his story it may tell, and tingle and chime every morning a dainty greeting and fond remembrance.

Double Military Hair Brush, Clothes Brush and Comb Set. Contains pair fine military hair brushes, a 7-inch good value clothes brush and a gents' barber comb. Packed in fancy tufted lined case. Brushes beautifully mounted.

No. 8T12034 Ebony finish.

No. 8T12035 Mahogany finish.

No. 8T12041 Three quires highest grade Linen Stationery, beautifully ribbon tied, packed in fancy three-drawer hinge cover decorated box. Great value. A beautiful present for a friend.

No. 8T12036 Ladies' Dresser Set. Contains beautiful Bohemian glass handsomely flower color decorated puff box, pin tray and sprinkler top perfume bottle. Packed in fancy tufted lined case, beautifully covered. Something new and great value. Size box, 12½x7x4 inches.

Big value Comb and Brush Set. Contains thirteen-row long white bristle sterling silver mounted hair brush, a 7½-inch dressing comb in fancy tufted lined case.

No. 8T12096 Ebony finish.

No. 8T12097 Mahogany finish.

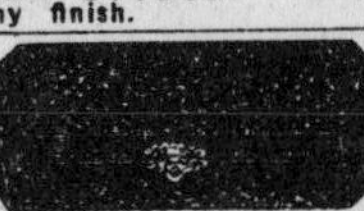

No. 8T12093 Imitation leather covered, fancy design Glove Box, with hinge cover and full satin lining. Size, 4¼x11x3 inches. For handkerchief box to match, see No. 8T12080.

No. 8T12058 Fancy pyralin ivory Child's Comb and Brush Set. A very high class item. Fancy tufted lined box, size 4¼x8½x2¾ inches.

No. 8T12064 Fancy flower and leaf color decorated, hinge cover, opaque glass Puff Box on fancy base. Size, 5x5x4½ inches.

No. 8T12061 Fancy ebony finished, heavy embossed gilt decorated Comb and Brush Holder with 3-inch fancy beveled mirror in gilt frame. Size, 3½x11x9½ inches.

No. 8T12062 Fancy genuine ebony Manicure Set, comprising nail file, scissors, button hook, salve box and buffer. Fancy tufted lined hinge cover box, size 4¼x6½x1¾ inches.

No. 8T12065 Irishman Tobacco Jar. A rare novelty. Made from large size natural coconut, including shell, hand carved and decorated. Features of face brought out in detail, including eyes, teeth, whiskers, etc. Top raises up, inside hollowed out for tobacco, hinge attachment. Admired wherever seen. Sells on sight. If you want an oddity, buy this. Size, 7x6½x10 inches. Assorted faces.

No. 8T12072 Pair beautiful heavy embossed German silver Military Hair Brushes in case.

No. 8T12078 Fancy gold plated, beautiful polished and burnished Standing Mirror. Center contains 4½x6 inch heavy bevel plate mirror. Size, 9x12 inches.

Fancy emblem Shaving Mug, gold lipped and decorated, fancy luster tinted, gold covered handle. Colored emblems as follows:

No. 8T12066 Masonic Design.
No. 8T12067 Odd Fellows Design.
No. 8T12068 Elks Design.
No. 8T12069 Knights of Pythias Design.
No. 8T12070 Mine Workers Design.
No. 8T12071 Knights of Columbus Design.

No. 8T12080 Fancy imitation leather covered Handkerchief Box, artistic design shaped, full satin tufted lined, fancy clasp. Size, 6¼x7¼x3 inches. Great value. For glove box to match, see No. 8T12093.

No. 8T12084 Imitation leather covered Jewel Box, full satin lined with removable tray and compartments, hinge clasp. Size, 7x5¾x3¼ inches.

Pair high grade Military Hair Brushes, containing fifteen rows firm white bristles, beautifully sterling silver mounted, packed in tufted lined case.

No. 8T12085 Ebony finish.

No. 8T12086 Mahogany finish.

Ladies' long handled Oval Mirror, containing 5x7 - inch heavy beveled French plate mirror.

No. 8T12087 Ebony finish.

No. 8T12088 Mahogany finish.

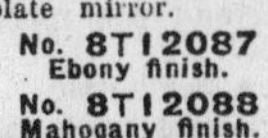

No. 8T12126 Fancy colored head decorated Comb and Brush Set, in tufted lined box. A very pretty set.

No. 8T12089 Beautiful 7-inch German silver, heavy flower embossed Clothes Brush containing nine rows soft white bristles.

No. 8T12115 Mariner beautifully decorated Shaving Mug and Brush Set, with 4½-inch circular bevel edge shaving mirror, packed in tufted lined display case. Size box, 6½x 6½x4½ inches.

No. 8T12116 Fine fancy silk covered Tourist Traveling Case, rubber lined. Contains separate compartments for traveling toilet articles. Size, 9½x15 inches. Folds up completely. A great bargain.

No. 8T12117 Fancy velvet leather, beautifully flower pyrographically decorated Table Throw, fringed edge. Size, 14x21 inches.

No. 8T12119 Big $1.25 value Writing Companion. Beautifully finished.

No. 8T12120 Folding Shaving Stand, Mug and Brush, nickel plated. 5¼-inch beveled mirror.

No. 8T12121 Fancy 8x8x4½ - inch Imported Straw Work Basket, hinge cover, full tufted satin lined. A beauty. $1.50 value.

NURSERY DEPARTMENT.

Baby Scales.

35c

No. 49F2298 Spring Baby Scales. Capacity, 15 pounds. For the small sum of only 35 cents we furnish the well known baby scale, which will last a lifetime. This scale offers the means to ascertain and watch the weight, improvement and actual development of the little baby in a very convenient manner.

Price.......................... 35c
If by mail, postage extra, 4 cents.

Lillian Talcum Powder.

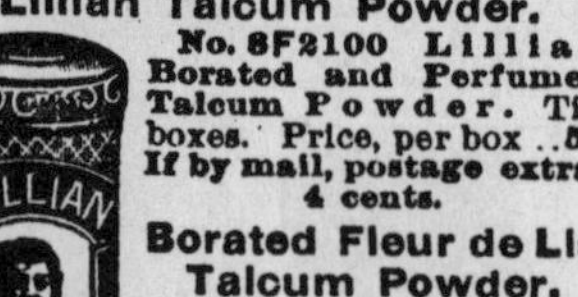

No. 8F2100 Lillian Borated and Perfumed Talcum Powder. Tin boxes. Price, per box ..5c
If by mail, postage extra, 4 cents.

Borated Fleur de Lis Talcum Powder.

An ideal baby powder for the toilet and nursery. Preserves, softens and whitens the skin. For chafing it is an excellent powder. Absorbs moisture and keeps the skin cool and soft. Nicely perfumed and put up in handsomely decorated metal boxes, with sprinkler top.

No. 8F2102 Price, per box.......8c
If by mail, postage extra, 4 cents.

La France Violette and Crushed Rose.

La Dore's Celebrated Antiseptic Talcum Powder. We furnish you the celebrated La Dore's antiseptic talcum powder, La France Violette and Crushed Rose, in 4-ounce glass jars with perforated, nickel plated screw cap. The finest talcum powder on the market, thoroughly borated and delicately perfumed. This talcum powder is absolutely antiseptic, and beyond question the acme of perfection.

No. 8F2104 La France Violette, 4-ounce glass jar, screw cap. Price...12c
No. 8F2106 Crushed Rose. Price, 12c
Not mailable.

Baby Syrup.

A blessing to parents, harmless and effectual in soothing and quieting children of any age. We guarantee it to contain no opium or morphine, or other narcotic poison, prepared from simple herbs and has a wonderful effect in soothing and quieting a child who may be cross, no matter from what reason. A great friend for mothers during teething time.

No. 8F2110 Price, per bottle...15c
If by mail, postage and tube extra, 12 cents.

Teething Rings.

No. 8F2112 White Celluloid Teething Ring. Best quality.
Price, 2 rings for...................8c
If by mail, postage extra, each, 2 cents

No. 8F2114 Rubber Teething Rings, seamless, full size, best white rubber. Price, 2 rings for...........8c
If by mail, postage extra, each, 2c.

No. 8F2116 Rubber Teething Rings, full size, seamless, best black rubber. Price, 2 rings for..............8c
If by mail, postage extra, each, 2c.

No. 8F2118 Bone Teething Ring. 1¾ inches, nicely finished. Price, 2 rings for 8c
If by mail, postage extra, each, 2c.

Small Teething Ring and Pacifier.

This New Style Teething Ring and Pacifier is a bone ring and rubber nipple combined. Has a fine silk cord to go round wrist to keep pacifier from being lost.

No. 8F2120 Price, 2 for..........6c
If by mail, postage extra, each, 2c.

New Style Teething Ring or Pacifier. The new style teething ring or pacifier is a bone ring and bone guard with a soft rubber nipple, having a silk cord for attaching to the baby's arm so the ring cannot be lost.

No. 8F2122 Price.................6c
If by mail, postage extra, 2 cents.

The Rattle Pacifier, the best rattle, teething ring and plaything ever invented for the babies. It has rubber nipple, bone shields, teething ring and bells. Made good and strong.

No. 8F2124 Price....................7c
If by mail, postage extra, 2 cents.

Combination Teething Ring or Pacifier with Bell Attachment. The combination teething ring or pacifier with bell attachment consists of a rubber ring, bone guard and soft rubber nipple. It pacifies and amuses the baby at the same time.

No. 8F2126 Price................7c
If by mail, postage extra, 2 cents.

The Whistling Bird Rattle and Pacifier.

This Rattle is made of pure white rubber, and will amuse and entertain the baby. It has a teething ring at handle end, making it doubly valuable.

No. 8F2128 Price.....8c
If by mail, postage extra, 2c

No. 8F2130 Celluloid Rattle (with whistle), 6 inches long, comes in very pretty assorted colors. Price.....20c
If by mail, postage extra, 5 cents.

Magic Painless Teething Necklace.

This well known necklace is worn around the baby's neck during the teething period and by means of the mild magnetic power generated, soothes and quiets the child. Has been used for over 20 years and was never known to fail. Cannot injure the most delicate child. The value of this wonderful discovery cannot be over estimated. It acts as a gentle stimulant to the glands and gums, relieves the baby of the pain during this period, and soothes its sleep at night. No inconvenience is caused the child, who must commence wearing it at two months of age and wear it until through teething.

No. 8F2132 Price, 2 necklaces for 80c; each.........................45c
If by mail, postage extra, 4 cents.

Rubber Nipples.

Rubber Nipples for tube fittings. White, black or maroon. State color wanted.

No. 8F2134 Price, 3 for.........5c
Per dozen............................15c
If by mail, postage extra, 2 cents.

Rubber Nipples.

Rubber Nipples to fit over bottle, white, black or maroon. State color wanted.

No. 8F2135 Price, 2 for...........5c
Per dozen.................................25c
If by mail, postage extra, 2 cents.

Health Nipples. Made from the finest Para rubber, is constructed so that the infant can obtain a strong hold and renders nursing easy.

No. 8F2136 Per doz., 35c; 3 for 10c
If by mail, postage extra, per dozen, 8 cents; each, 2 cents.

Pure Gum Combination Nipple. A very popular new nipple made from pure gum rubber and having a special combination to prevent collapsing.

No. 8F2138 Price, each............4c
Per dozen.......................................40c
If by mail, postage extra, per dozen, 8 cents; each, 2 cents.

Mizpah Valve Nipple. Making nursing easy. Allows the food to flow easily. Prevents colic.

No. 8F2140 Price, each.......4c
Per dozen...............................45c
If by mail, postage extra, per dozen, 8 cents; each, 2 cents.

Anti-Colic Nipple. The famous anti-colic nipple, has a rubber projection preventing closing at end. A very popular pure gum nipple. Non collapsible and hence prevents colic.

No. 8F2142 Price, 2 for....10c
If by mail, postage on rubber nipples extra, per dozen, 6c; each, 1c.

Nursing Flasks.

Graduated to hold 8 ounces, oval shape, straight with sloping sides. No corners, therefore easy to clean. Weight, 14 ounces.

No. 8F2144
Price 4c
Unmailable.

Graduated Nursing Bottle.

No. 8F2146 Graduated Nursing Bottle, bent neck for tube fittings.

Price..................................4c
Unmailable.

Nursing Bottles.

Nursing Bottles. Burr patent, white rubber fittings.

No. 8F2148
Price 7c
Unmailable.

S., R. & Co.'s Complete Nurser.

S., R. Co.'s Nurser. Fitted with white fittings. Complete with two brushes in box.

No. 8F2153 Price.........12c
Unmailable.

Hygeia Nursing Bottle.

The most up to date, cleanly, antiseptic nursing bottle, and the only one with a breast attachment. Easy to clean and fill. Bottle is without a neck or angle, needs no brush to clean or funnel to fill and can be wiped out like a tumbler. Rubber attachment is large, soft and yielding like the mother's breast. Babies do not detect the difference and hence can be weaned from the breast without a struggle. 6 ounces capacity. Retail price 50 cents.

No. 8F2150
Price, bottle complete........35c

No. 8F2151 Extra breasts or bottles can be supplied.
Price, each..........................19c
Unmailable.

Merwin Baby Food Warmer.

For heating and keeping milk warm or other liquid foods for infants or invalids. The greatest device ever patented for keeping baby's milk warm all night. No more starting fires at night to warm food. No more unbroken rest as a crying baby's food is always ready. The health of the child is conserved, as the temperature of the food is right at all times. Made of metal and finished in white enamel. Three tubular compartments, each containing one nursing bottle. All you have to do is fill container with boiling water at 9 p. m. Heat is so regulated that bottle No. 1 is correct temperature for feeding from 10 to 12 p. m., No. 2 from 12 to 3 a. m. and bottle No. 3 from 3 to 6 a. m. Once used, you would never be without it.

No. 8F2155 Price..........$5.00
Unmailable.

Glass Nipple Shield.

Glass Nipple Shield with white rubber nipple and bone guard.

No. 8F2160
Price.............8c
Unmailable.

Nipple Shield.

Glass Nipple Shield with long flexible rubber tube, mouth guard and rubber nipple.

No. 8F2162 Price..............9c
Unmailable.

Nursing Bottle Fittings.

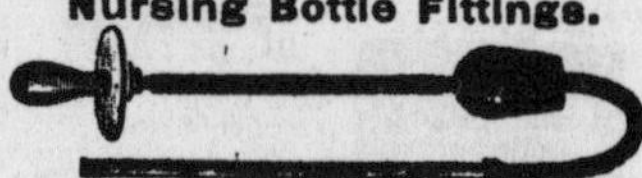

Best quality, all complete, in white, black or maroon. State color wanted.

No. 8F2164 Price, 2 for..........8c
If by mail, postage extra, each, 2c.

Bottle Brushes. For cleaning nursing bottles, etc.

No. 8F2166 Price, 3 for...............5c
If by mail, postage extra, each, 1c.

Tube Brushes. For cleaning bottle fittings and nurser tubing.

No. 8F2168 Price, 6 for.. ......5c
If by mail, postage extra, each, 1 cent.

New Yankee Idea Bottle Brush.

The New Yankee Idea Bottle Brush, made under patent No. 519948. The most ingenious, and practically constructed, general all around cleaning brush ever produced. With it you can reach and clean every bend, every corner; in fact all shapes of inner and outer surfaces of fruit jars, water bottles, milk bottles, chimneys, caster bottles, graduates, sterilizing bottles, molasses pitchers and tumblers. Sells everywhere for 15 to 25 cents.

No. 8F2170 Yankee Idea Bottle Brush.
Price.....................................9c
If by mail, postage extra, 3 cents.

RUBBER GOODS.

We present to our customers a complete line of rubber goods for bathroom, sickroom and toilet. Every article is perfect in material, workmanship and appearance. Our stock comprises all the best makes, and in syringes and water bottes are found all from medium priced to the very best manufactured. By comparison you will find all our prices far lower than others on the same grade of goods, and we offer you a much better article in every case than sold by competitors at anywhere near our prices.

SPECIAL NOTICE.

When your physician suggests the use of a 2, 3 or 4-quart fountain syringe, it is very important that the syringe bag should hold the full quantity. We are today the only house furnishing our customers full capacity fountain syringes. Compare our fountain syringes with those of other houses and you will not only find our quality superior but also that the average 2-quart bag sold by others, holds little more than 1 quart and the 3-quart bag about 2 quarts or less.

When buying a fountain syringe, always insist on full capacity bags, as otherwise the prescribed irrigation or douche may prove insufficient and ineffectual.

These bags are the very best possible values for the money and are all guaranteed for a period of one year. Will gladly replace any found defective.

English Breast Pump.

English Breast Pump, with white rubber bulb. One in box.
No. 8F2172
Price..............15c
If by mail, postage extra, 8 cents.

Swansdown Puffs.

Fine Powder Puffs for ladies' and infants' use. Satin tops, ivory handle, genuine fine down.
No. 8F2175 Price, large size...12c
No. 8F2176 Price, medium size 8c
If by mail, postage extra, 2 cents.

Wool Powder Puffs.

Made of carefully selected fine wool, with silk handle to pass over hand. Can be cleansed and washed. Applies the powder very evenly and rubs in the skin. Very popular. Once tried you would use no other.
No. 8F2178 Price, large size, 15c
No. 8F2179 Medium size...10c
If by mail, postage extra, 2 cents.

Puff Boxes.

Celluloid, in ivory, pink or blue. Be sure to state color wanted. Very light and handsome.
No. 8F2181
Price............40c
Postage extra, 8c.

White Metal Puff Boxes, handsome covers, ornamental tops.
No. 8F2182 Price...............19c
If by mail, postage extra, 8 cents.

Nursery Rubber Sheeting.

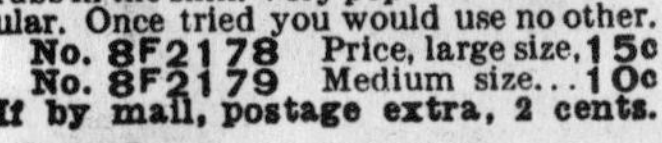

No. 8F2185 White Rubber Sheeting. Heavy weight. State width wanted.

Width, 27 inches.	Per yard......	35c
Width, 36 inches.	Per yard......	48c
Width, 45 inches.	Per yard......	62c
Width, 54 inches.	Per yard......	75c

No. 8F2186 Tan Rubber Sheeting, soft as silk, very light in weight, strong and absolutely waterproof. For hospital and nursery use, also for making bathing caps, diapers, etc. 36 inches wide. Price, per yard..............65c
If by mail, postage extra, per yd., 18c.

Antiseptic Nursery Sheeting.

No. 8F2187 This sheeting is made of very fine coated cambric, absolutely waterproof, antiseptic, soft, light and pliable. Can be washed and even boiled without injury. Will not crack or peel. A new product and regarded by many far superior to rubber sheeting.
Width, 36 inches. Per yard....48c
Width, 50 inches. Per yard....70c
If by mail, postage extra, per yd., 18c.

Rubber Tubing.

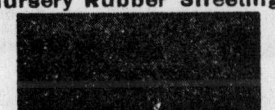

No. 8F2189 Corrugated, white, for bulb and fountain syringes.
Price, per foot, 1/4-inch 5c
If by mail, postage extra, per foot, 3c.

No. 8F2191 White, black or maroon rubber tubing for nursing bottles. Be sure to state color wanted.
Price, per foot........................3c
If by mail, postage extra, per foot, 3c.

Glass Tubes.

No. 8F2192 Glass tubes for nursing bottle fittings. Price, per dozen.....7c
If by mail, postage extra, per foot, 3c.

YOU CAN SHARE LIBERALLY IN OUR PROFITS. We not alone save you the greatest possible amount of money on your purchases, but with every purchase over $1 00 you get a **profit sharing certificate**, and these will soon enable you to get something very valuable, entirely free of charge, as explained on pages 1 and 2.

Gem Fountain Syringe.

GUARANTEED FULL CAPACITY.

(Full capacity.)

A good quality fountain syringe, has infant, rectal and vaginal hard rubber pipes. Patent shut off for stopping flow of water and fine quality of rubber tubing make syringe perfect in every respect. The water bag is full measure and guaranteed so by us. Compare the size of our syringe bag with those from other houses. Packed complete in neat, strong paper box.

While these bags are much better than can be obtained elsewhere at 25c to 50c extra, to get the greatest possible value for your money we advise you by all means to add 50c to $1.00 extra and order one of our highest priced syringes.

No. 8F2300	2 quarts.	Price.....52c
No. 8F2301	3 quarts.	Price.....62c
No. 8F2302	4 quarts.	Price.....72c

If by mail, postage extra, 16 cents.

Reliable Fountain Syringe.

GUARANTEED FULL CAPACITY.

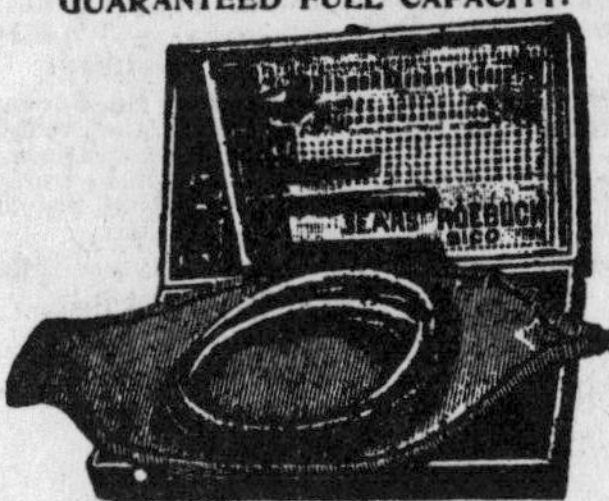

(Full capacity.)

A first quality four-pipe fountain syringe. Pipes are infant, rectal, vaginal and irrigator. Patent shut off and good quality tubing with rolled end or socket for pipes. Water bags made of heavy rubber, reinforced seams and is guaranteed full capacity. Syringe bag is of slate rubber with white trimmings and embossed in handsome diamond design. Packed complete in neat, finely polished wooden box.

While these bags are much better than can be obtained elsewhere at 25c to 50c extra, to get the greatest possible value for your money we advise you by all means to add 50c to $1.00 extra and order one of our highest priced syringes.

No. 8F2305	2 quarts.	Price..$0.88
No. 8F2306	3 quarts.	Price.. .97
No. 8F2307	4 quarts.	Price.. 1.08

If by mail, postage extra, 21 cents.

Monarch Syringe.

A Combination Syringe and Water Bottle, including hard rubber connections and infant, vaginal, rectal, irrigator and nasal screw pipes and six feet of pure rubber tubing and hard rubber combination attachment. Made from superior grade of heavy white ribbed rubber with special reinforced seams and is altogether a very superior article. Fitted with automatic shut off attachment. Packed in finely finished oak wood box.

No. 8F2320	2 quarts.	Price.....$1.20
No. 8F2321	3 quarts.	Price..... 1.30
No. 8F2322	4 quarts.	Price..... 1.40

If by mail, postage extra, 28 cents.

Our Guaranteed Rapid Flow Perfection Fountain Syringe.

GUARANTEED FULL CAPACITY.

The Rapid Flow Syringe is fitted with 1/4-inch tubing for flushing and for this reason is a special favorite. The tubing and bag are made of the finest quality rubber, four hard rubber screw pipes, infant, rectal, bent vaginal and irrigator. The bag is full capacity, made from heavy white ribbed rubber, heavily reinforced seams and fully guaranteed. It is one of the most desirable syringes on the market combining as it does all the necessary fittings for family use with unusual strength. Packed in fine box, wrapped and complete, at one-half usual price charged.

(Full measure.)

No. 8F2310	2 quarts.	Price..$0.90
No. 8F2311	3 quarts.	Price.. .98
No. 8F2312	4 quarts.	Price.. 1.08

If by mail, postage extra, 27 cents.

Imperial Rapid Flow Fountain Syringe.

GUARANTEED FULL CAPACITY.

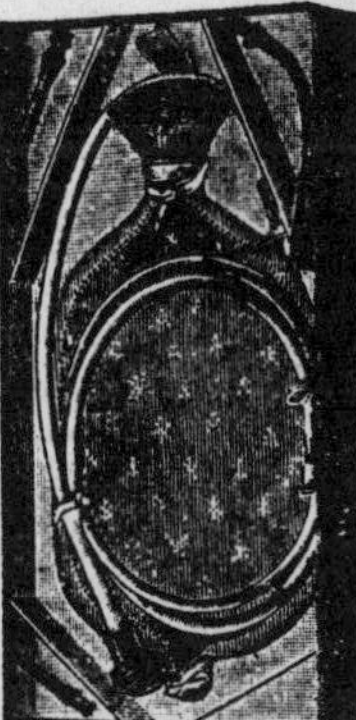

A Combination Syringe and Hot Water Bottle. Is fitted with three hard rubber rapid flow slip pipes including infant, rectal and bent vaginal pipes. Quarter-inch fine quality tubing, with rolled end or socket for the pipes. Patent shut off and hard rubber combination attachment. The hot water bottle is made of a fine quality white rubber, handsomely embossed with floral design. Each packed complete in handsome flat box with partition for pipes.

No. 8F2315	2 quarts.	Price, $1.05
No. 8F2316	3 quarts.	Price, 1.17
No. 8F2317	4 quarts.	Price, 1.28

If by mail, postage extra, 21 cents.

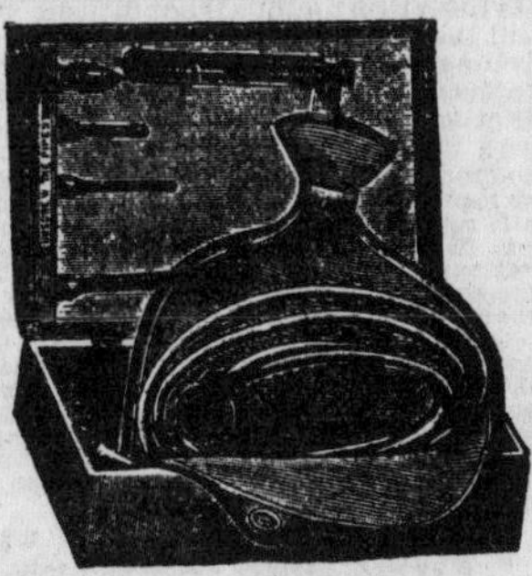

Faultless Never Leak Syringe.

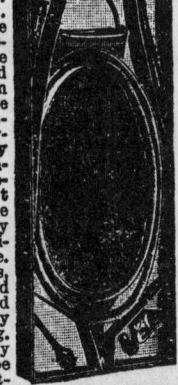

Very latest and most up to date syringe made. Perfectly sanitary. Wide opening for the water. Non-corrosive metal handle which is a splendid feature. You can hang this syringe anywhere. Very attractive in appearance. Absolutely seamless in construction, consequently cannot leak. Made of the very best quality rubber and practically indestructible. Three screw pipes, infant, rectal and vaginal. Five and one-half feet very best rubber tubing. Patent shut off. By reason of its shape and rapid flow outlet, this bag will empty quicker than any other syringe made. Just as the name indicates, faultless in every particular. Fully guaranteed.

No. 8F2325 Two Quarts. Regular price, $2.00; our price...$1.62
No. 8F2326 Three Quarts. Regular price, $2.50; our price....$1.77
If by mail, postage extra, 21 cents.

Canton Seamless Syringe.

GUARANTEED FULL CAPACITY.

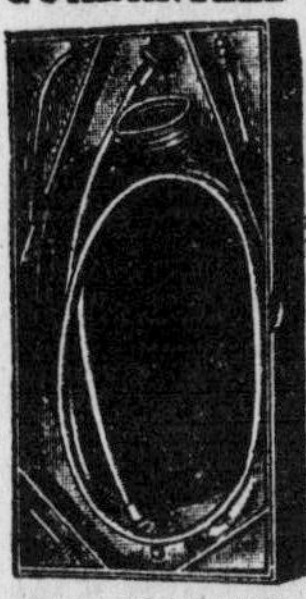

One of the very best and highest grade syringes made. It is absolutely seamless, made of the very best grade of maroon rubber, scientifically vulcanized and will last a lifetime. This article is made heavier at the bottom, as per our request, and furnishes a bottle standing any strain and guaranteed to give absolute satisfaction. Furnished with three hard screw rubber pipes, 5½ feet best rubber tubing, wide open tap, reinforced bottom and tip and as fine a syringe as any person can obtain. Each syringe packed and wrapped in a neat box.

No. 8F2330 Two Quarts. Regular price, $1.75; our price....$1.43
No. 8F2331 Three Quarts. Regular price, $2.25; our price....$1.65
If by mail, postage extra, 21 cents.

Acme Bulb Syringe.

No. 8F2335 Acme Bulb Syringe. Put up in nice pasteboard box. Good quality rubber, two hard rubber pipes. Drug store price, 50 cents for same quality.
Our price..........................23c
If by mail, postage extra, 10 cents.

Our 41-Cent Ideal Syringe.

No. 8F2340 The Celebrated Ideal Syringe, with three hard rubber pipes, put up in a neat wooden box. Druggists ask $1.00 for this syringe.
Our price.......... ....41c
If by mail, postage extra, 12 cents.

The Wonder Bent Neck Douche.

The Latest and Safest Quick Action Vaginal Syringe. The only vaginal syringe that can be used with ease, comfort and positive results in a recumbent or other position. Will fit perfectly and accomplish a thorough dilation and cleansing of all parts in the shortest possible time. Recommended by physicians for the purpose for which it is intended, and this appliance can be used without the slightest discomfort, inconvenience or harm. The advantages and merits as pointed out by leading physicians recommending the Wonder Douche to their lady patients are as follows: It is practical, safe and sanitary. It prevents injection of air. It is the only douche that can be used with ease and convenience, as the bent neck brings the bulb within reach without straining forward. It can be operated by the user while in a reclining or otherwise convenient position. It has no long, hard rubber tube to injure the delicate membranes of the vagina and the mouth of the womb. It will stand firmly on the bottom of the large bulb when filled, thereby preventing spilling of the liquid. It has a large capacity, about half a pint, and the bulb is soft and easily compressed. It will inject a solid, copious stream, which thoroughly flushes and cleanses the vagina. It will distend the vagina, thereby exposing every portion of its surface to the injection, and all secretions will be withdrawn with the injection fluid. It is the best and most perfect douche ever invented, and is invaluable to every married woman. The wholesale price of the Wonder Douche or Vaginal Syringe is $2.50, and we furnish the same to our customers with a positive guarantee that we supply the genuine Wonder Bent Neck Douche for women.

No. 8F2345 Our price....**$1.48**
If by mail, postage extra, 20 cents.

Ladies' Perfect Syringe.

The Ladies' Perfect Syringe is constructed on the latest scientific principles regarding injection and suction. Cleanses the vaginal passages thoroughly of all discharges. Recommended by the medical profession as one of the best and most efficient of any syringe ever made. Especially adapted for injections of hot water without soiling the clothing. Made of one piece of fine soft rubber.

No. 8F2350
Price **55c**
Postage extra, 17c.

The Truefrend Vaginal Spray.

The Truefrend Vaginal Spray has just been patented and this is the first time ever offered for sale. It combines all the advantages of all other bulb syringes, along with many valuable features not shared by any other. It can be regulated to any degree of force, from an energetic flow to a gentle spray. It can be carried about filled, always ready for use, being the only bulb syringe that can be made water tight. The Truefrend is free from danger of clogging and is the only bulb syringe that has a direct unimpeded flow. Can be taken apart and cleansed. Perfectly sanitary. Retail price, $5.00 each. We guarantee to furnish you this same syringe.

No. 8F2353 Our price... **$2.25**
If by mail, postage extra, 20 cents.

Dr. Tullar's Vaginal Spray.

$1.57

The latest and safest patented new ball spraying, quick action douche. Made entirely of soft and hard rubber. The one physicians always recommend. Dr. Tullar's Vaginal Spray is the latest and only reliable injection and suction bulb syringe. No other vaginal douche compares with it for convenience, safety, comfort and effectiveness. Used and preferred by every married woman that has ever seen it. **The new patent ball tip discharges a hollow or cup shaped spray. The only instant cleansing spray ever invented.** This is Dr. Tullar's new invention. In this syringe the nozzle or discharge pipe is only ⅝ inch in diameter and 5 inches long. It is made with a highly polished ball shaped tip which allows its insertion under all conditions without the slightest discomfort or harm. It is long enough to allow a ball spraying injection to come in immediate contact with and remove all secretions and discharges that have become lodged in the folds about the neck or mouth of the womb. It is furnished with a soft rubber shield which is so shaped that it will fit correctly and properly, and close the vaginal entrance, allowing the passage to be thoroughly flushed. It prevents spilling of the fluid and soiling of the clothes. The regular price of the Dr. Tullar's Ball Spraying Quick Action Douche everywhere is $3.00. We furnish the same to our customers with a positive guarantee that we supply the genuine Dr. Tullar's Ball Spray, Vaginal Douche for women at $1.57. Dr. Tullar's interesting folder, containing complete instructions and advice, sent with every Dr. Tullar's syringe free.

No. 8F2355 Our price...........**$1.57**
If by mail, postage extra, 20 cents.

The Whirlpool Syringe.

The well known and highly advertised Pneumatic Cushion Syringe. It has a heavy glass open end vaginal tube, fine rubber bulb and is the only syringe admitting of thorough cleansing and sterilizing with hot water. Will not break. The patent pneumatic cushion is adjustable on the tube, absolutely preventing the injection of air or the inserting of the tube beyond the depth desired. It overcomes all the dangers and harshness of solid rubber guards, and being so soft and pliable conforms to the size and shape of the orifice. Highly recommended by the medical profession as one of the very best and safest syringes made.

No. 8F2358 Price.......**$1.69**
If by mail, postage extra, 20 cents.

Hard Rubber Stem Syringe.

Superior to other syringes of this class and a most perfect syringe for a far reaching vaginal douche. Made with soft rubber bulb and hard rubber stem. Has no valves. Cannot corrode or get out of order. This is one of the most efficient syringes for cleansing the vagina, and is highly recommended by the best physicians to married ladies for that purpose, and for the treatment of any local disorder and female complaints.

No. 8F2360 Price......................**53c**
If by mail, postage extra, 10 cents.

Omega Syringe—Continuous Flow.

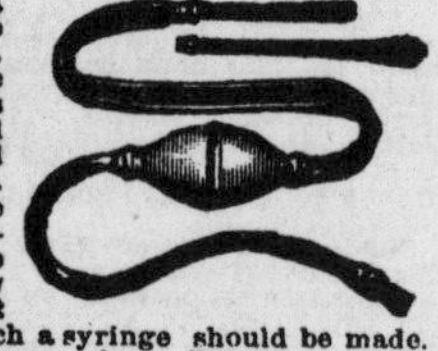

No. 8F2364 Made of pure Para rubber. Omega Syringe No. 5, continuous flow, with hard rubber vaginal and rectal pipes. The valves are secured and cannot be lost. The continuous flow is the correct principle on which a syringe should be made. Packed in neat maroon box. Price........**34c**
If by mail, postage extra, 10 cents.

No. 8F2365 Omega Syringe No. 4, continuous flow. Hard rubber vaginal and rectal pipes, **valves secured and cannot be lost. Omega No. 4 has a flattened outlet tube which is made by a specially invented process, that produces the continuous flow.** Packed in neat octagonal box. Price.........................**62c**
If by mail, postage extra, 15 cents.

No. 8F2367 Omega Syringe No. 3, continuous flow. Has hard rubber vaginal, rectal and infant pipes, noiseless and non-corrosive sinker, patented screw joint socket, by which pipes are **quickly attached** without use of threads or washers. Packed in oval box.
Price...**75c**
If by mail, postage extra, 10 cents.

Alpha Continuous Flowing Syringe.

Made of best Para rubber. All intermittent syringes inject more or less air, which is invariably drawn back into the tube while the bulb is expanding and refilling; this is often painful **as well as dangerous. Not so with the Alpha Continuous Flowing Syringe.**

No. 8F2369 Alpha E Syringe, continuous flow, hard rubber vaginal, rectal and infant pipes, noiseless and non-corrosive sinker, **valves cannot be lost.** Packed in handsome cloth covered case with nickel plated clasp.
Price.............................**$1.25**
If by mail, postage extra, 15 cents.

No. 8F2371 Alpha D Syringe, continuous flow, fitted with extra large valve chambers, hard rubber vaginal, rectal, infant and nasal pipes and improved vaginal irrigating spray, noiseless and non-corrosive sinker. Packed in nice cloth covered case.
Price..............................**$1.45**
If by mail, postage extra, 15 cents.

Dr. Thiebaud's Expanding Vaginal Bath Speculum and Douche.

Can be used in connection with all our fountain and family syringes.

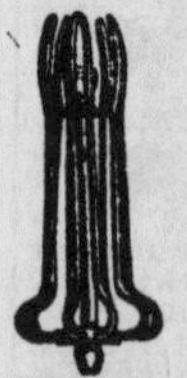

Is made with nickel plated, highly polished wire frame, with metal nozzle, and so constructed to make it collapsible. When placed in position it can be easily expanded, thus acting as a speculum and syringe at the same time. It will do what no other syringe will accomplish and will always insure a thoroughly successful douche.

Expanded. Collapsed.

No. 8F2373 Dr. Thiebaud's Expanding Vaginal Bath Speculum and Douche. Price.......................**35c**
If by mail, postage extra, 4 cents.

Bath Speculum and Douche.

No. 8F2375 Expanding Return Flow Bath Speculum and Douche. This expanding bath speculum is fitted with latest improvements, a soft rubber shield preventing the spilling of fluid, also metal base with outlet tube and is recognized today as the most hygienic, convenient and always satisfactory appliance for vaginal irrigation. Can be used with fountain syringe or irrigator. Price (Postage extra, each, 5c.) **55c**

Ear and Ulcer Syringe.

No. 8F2380 Eye, Ear, Ulcer and Abscess Syringe. Capacity, one ounce; injection pipe; is made of soft and flexible rubber. Will not injure, or pain the inflamed parts.
Price.................**12c**
If by mail, postage extra, 3 cents.

Infants' Syringe.

No. 8F2382 Infants' Syringe. Holds one ounce and is made of a soft rubber bulb, with hard rubber infants' rectal pipe. Price..................**13c**
If by mail, postage extra, 5 cents.

Hard Rubber Syringes.

No. 49F1555 Hard Rubber, Cone Point Male Urethral Syringe, ½ ounce. Price...............**14c**
If by mail, postage extra, 2 cents.

No. 49F1557 Male Urethral Syringe. Hard rubber, with soft rubber point, ⅛ ounce. Price.......... **21c**
If by mail, postage extra, 2 cents.

No. 49F1558 Hard Rubber, Long Point, Male Urethral Syringe. ⅛ ounce.
Price.....(Postage extra, 2 cents.)..**14c**

Rectal Syringe, hard rubber, ring handle.
No. 49F1560 1 oz. Price, **45c**
If by mail, postage extra, 4 cents.
No. 49F1561 2 oz. Price, **65c**
If by mail, postage extra, 5 cents.
No. 49F1562 3 oz. Price, **75c**
If by mail, postage extra, 6 cents.

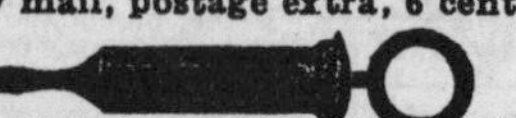

No. 8F1563 Infants' Hard Rubber Rectal Syringe, ½ ounce.
Price...............................**40c**
If by mail, postage extra, 2 cents.

No. 49F1570 Vaginal Syringe, hard rubber, 2 ounce. Price....**50c**
If by mail, postage extra, 4 cents.

Flannel Covered Water Bottles.

Our Flannel Covered Hot Water Bottles are the most perfect made. Are pure gum rubber with fine flannel cover which keeps an even temperature and will not irritate the most delicate skin. Guaranteed perfect in every respect.

No. 8F2385 2 quarts. Price..78c
No. 8F2386 3 quarts. Price..88c
No. 8F2387 4 quarts. Price..98c
If by mail, postage extra, 15 cents.

Excelsior Hot Water Bottles.

All rubber, embossed floral design, exceptional value. Each in a box. Fully guaranteed. While these bags are much better than can be obtained elsewhere at 25 to 50 cents extra, to get the greatest possible value for your money we advise you by all means to add a small advance and obtain one of our higher priced bags.

No. 8F2390 2 quarts. Price..48c
No. 8F2391 3 quarts. Price..53c
No. 8F2392 4 quarts. Price..58c
If by mail, postage extra, 2 qts., 11c; 3 qts., 13c; 4 qts., 15c.

Majestic Hot Water Bottles.

Slate rubber with white rubber reinforcements at top and bottom. Absolutely full capacity. Seams are reinforced with an inside cloth strip. Each in a flat box. Fully guaranteed. While these bags are much better than can be obtained elsewhere at 25 to 50 cents extra, to get the greatest possible value for your money we advise you by all means to add a small advance and obtain one of our higher priced bags.

No. 8F2395 2 quarts. Price..65c
No. 8F2396 3 quarts. Price..72c
No. 8F2397 4 quarts. Price..77c
If by mail, postage extra, 17 cents.

Famous Canton Hot Water Bottle.

Excellent material, seamless in construction, full capacity, handsome in appearance, with metal mouth that will not corrode. Easy to fill. Exceedingly tough, strong, pliable and soft, absolutely watertight.

No. 8F2400
2 quarts. Price.77c
No. 8F2401
3 quarts. Price.88c
If by mail, postage extra, 17c.

Hyperion Standard Shape Water Bottles.

Handsome in appearance, of highest quality and made of the very finest heavy white ribbed rubber. Absolutely full capacity. Special double reinforced seams. Each in fine flat box. Fully guaranteed. This we consider an exceptionally high grade bottle worth double the money.

No. 8F2405
2 quarts. Price...90c
No. 8F2406
3 quarts. Price.$1.00
No. 8F2407
4 quarts. Price.$1.10
If by mail, postage extra, 2 quarts, 12c; 3 quarts, 14c; 4 quarts, 16c.

Face Hot Water Bottle.

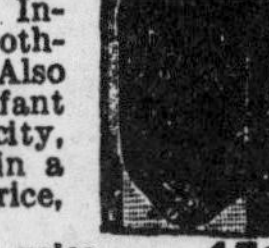

Made of pure Para rubber, red in color, with a cloth insertion, making it especially strong and durable. Invaluable in cases of toothache and neuralgia. Also largely used as an infant water bottle. Capacity, one pint. Each tied in a neat box. Regular price, 75 cents.

No. 8F2410 Our price......47c
If by mail, postage extra, 12 cents.

THE FAMOUS H. AND H. BUST FORMS.

The Only Bust Form Made Which Defies Detection.

THE CELEBRATED H. & H. BUST FORMS are now so perfect that they cannot be detected from the natural bust whether by sight or touch. Strikingly stylish, a source of relief, delight and pride to the wearer and of admiration to others. Very durable, economic and hygienic.

THESE FORMS do away with all unsightly, unhealthy and uncomfortable padding. They produce perfectly the full bust and slender waist decreed by the latest fashion. Positively the only device which perfectly simulates flesh and blood. Applied in an instant; made of white rubber, invisible with any costume; neither sight nor touch reveals their use. Worn with or without corsets. Eagerly welcomed by society women everywhere. Indorsed by leading dressmakers and ladies' tailors. They fit any figure, adapt themselves to every movement and position, take the desired size and shape, filling out ill-looking wrinkles, making the "fit" of any dress perfect and stylish. In light waists and evening dress they are worn low in the corset, forcing the natural bosom upward while they remain concealed. As a support they are a grateful relief to mothers. Made of a quality of Para rubber so amazingly tough that a strong man cannot break a piece an inch broad. They are pronounced by an eminent woman "more an inspiration than invention."

FOR BATHERS at the sea shore and lakes they are indispensable, as their buoyancy keeps the wearer's head above water and makes swimming easy. Natural as life and without the slightest inconvenience. They accurately fit the form, are enclosed in fine muslin cover, lace trimmed, cannot get out of place, and can be made any desired size.

BE ADMIRED. A fine form is admired by all. Why then wear heavy pads or be flat chested, both of which are unnatural and plainly detected, when so natural a form as this is within your reach. Light as air, takes all the motions of the body and cannot be detected. Do not delay any longer, but buy a bust form, make it the desired size and have a perfect figure.

No. 8F2475 Regular price, $1.50 to $2.00; our price......$1.39
If by mail, postage extra, 8 cents.

Hot Water Throat Bag.

This newly patented Throat Bag is an article that should be in every home. Used for quickly curing sore throat, tonsilitis or any irritation or inflammation of the throat. Contains two springs, which divide at center and fit closely around the neck. The water bottle attachment is filled with hot water, and keeps the throat warm for hours. It is far superior to any method heretofore used for this purpose. Made of the very best rubber and fully guaranteed.

No. 8F2415 Price..........62c
If by mail, postage extra, 8 cents.

Invalid Air Cushions.

The finest Air Cushion made. All one ring; softer and larger surface than the old fashioned four-piece ring. Good full width. For use in the sick room, for bed sores, etc.; it is invaluable for invalids; soft, pliable and light.

No. 8F2420 12 inches diameter. Price......$0.95
No. 8F2421 14 inches diameter. Price......$1.10
No. 8F2422 16 inches diameter. Price......$1.25
No. 8F2423 18 inches diameter. Price......$1.40
If by mail, postage extra, 20 cents.

Dusting or Bathing Caps.

Made of pure gum rubber, very strong, and will fit any head. An excellent article for protecting the hair in household work. Largely used for protection in sweeping, cleaning house, bathing, etc. Regular price, 75 cents.

No. 8F2427 Our price......43c
If by mail, postage extra, 8 cents.

Air Pillows.

Air Pillows. Made of very finest cloth covered rubber.

No. 49F1722 9x13 inches. Price..$1.20
If by mail, postage extra, 10 cents.
No. 49F1723 10x16 inches. Price.. 1.35
If by mail, postage extra, 12 cents.

Hospital Rubber Chair Cushions.

Strong and useful for persons engaged in sedentary occupations. Regular size, 17½ inches in diameter. Opening in center of cushion, when inflated, 3½ inches.

No. 8F2433 Price......$2.48
If by mail, postage extra, 35 cents.

Ice Bag.

No. 49F1672
English Ice Bag, screw cap, 8-inch.
Price.........40c
If by mail, postage extra, 6 cents.

Oval Bed Pans.

Oval Bed Pans, with outlet tube, soft rubber. The highest grade made. For ladies and men. A necessary article for the sick room.

No. 49F1702
Price.........$2.45
If by mail, postage extra, 60 cents.

Soft Rubber Urinal Bags.

For Boys and Men or Girls and Women.

For bed wetting and general incontinence of urine. For male and female children and adults. For day and night use.

Our New Safety Inner Tube Pure Gum Rubber Urinal Bag.

FOR MEN.

This Urinal Bag is constructed for day and night use, for men only, and is fitted with special double valve and inner tube, so as to prevent the return flow of the urine. This is the only urinal bag on the market for male use that can be guaranteed to prove entirely satisfactory for both day and night use. The only absolutely safe male urinal.

No. 8F2450 Price......$1.55
If by mail, postage extra, 20 cents.

Our New Safety Inner Tube Pure Gum Rubber Urinal Bag.

FOR WOMEN.

This Urinal Bag is constructed for day and night use, for women only, and is fitted with double valve and inner tube to prevent the return flow of the urine. This is the only urinal bag on the market for female use that can be guaranteed to prove entirely satisfactory for both day and night use. An absolutely safe female urinal.

No. 8F2451 Price..................$1.85
If by mail, postage extra, 20 cents.

Night Attachment for Urinal Bags.

The Night Attachment for use only in connection with Nos. 8F2450, 8F2451 and 8F2456 Urinal Bags, increases their capacity to almost double. The attachment is made of pure gum rubber, is fitted with inner valve and hard rubber connections, and fills a long felt want with those who require extra large capacity during the night. If you order either the No. 8F2450, No. 8F2451 or No. 8F2456 Urinal get this attachment for night use. The tube is attached directly to urinal and is of sufficient length to be placed without the bed.

No. 8F2452 Night Attachment.
Price..............................$1.65
If by mail, postage extra, 15 cents.

Soft Rubber Urinal Bag, the most comfortable pattern made, of the best material, for male, day or night use.

No. 8F2453 Price....................90c
No. 8F2454 Short, for boy..........75c
If by mail, postage extra, 12 cents.

Soft Rubber Urinal Bag, most improved pattern, made of the very best material, for female use.

No. 8F2455 Price....................90c
If by mail, postage extra, 12 cents.

No. 8F2456 Soft Rubber Urinal Bag, day and night use for male; improved French pattern, with waist belt ready to use without other attachments.

Price..................$1.85
If by mail, postage extra, 20c.

Rubber Massage and Complexion Bulb.

One of the latest devices for massage and complexion purposes. Very popular.

No. 8F2458
Price...........19c
If by mail, postage extra, 2 cents.

Beauty Brush for the Complexion.

It is especially constructed for improving the complexion. It removes all roughness and dead cuticle, smoothing out the wrinkles, rendering the skin soft, pliant, and tinted with a healthy glow. It is made of soft rubber — flexible, flattened end, tiny teeth and will not scratch or irritate the skin. Removes wrinkles like magic. For physical development it is recommended by the highest in the profession for improving the circulation, exercising the muscles and promoting a healthy action of the skin.

No. 8F2460 Price.......17c
If by mail, postage extra, 3 cents.

Hair Growing Fountain Comb.

For applying hair tonics, eau de quinine, bleaches, etc. The comb being hollow and with pressure on the bulb the liquid will flow through the teeth to the scalp applying the remedy to the roots of the hair where it will do the most good. The use of the comb will prevent getting tonic all through hair unless it is desired to do so. You can apply the tonic rapidly and thoroughly without soiling the hands or badly ruffling up the hair. Every lady will appreciate this advantage. The comb may be used for applying bleaches to the hair by spraying. Packed complete in neat case with full directions for using.

No. 8F2465 Scalp Sprayer. Price..65c
If by mail, postage extra, 8 cents.

The Improved Triplex Massage Roller for Self Massage.

With the Triplex Massage Roller you can massage your face, neck and bust, in fact, any part of the body in a really scientific manner without the aid of another person. This is not an ordinary massage roller, but an instrument which will take hold of the skin and massage it like the hands of a skilled massage operator. You have never seen or used anything like it, nor is there any other massage roller that will accomplish quickly so much as this little wonder will do. It is a handsome instrument and works like a charm. Shipped in a neat box together with complete instructions.

No. 8F2480 Improved Triplex Massage Roller. Price.......69c
If by mail, postage extra, 10 cents.

Wrinkle Eradicator.

This convenient little article will remove wrinkles from around the eyes and nose and any part of the face. It invigorates the skin and keeps a perfect contour of the face.

No. 8F2485 Price. 22c
If by mail, postage extra, 6 cents.

Magic Flesh Builder and Cupper.

An entirely new and scientific invention. Has no equal as a developer. Makes it possible for every lady to possess a well rounded, plump, beautiful figure. Rebuilds sunken tissues of the bust, neck, arms, and the only method which permanently removes wrinkles and makes the sunken cheeks smooth, full and developed.

No. 8F2490 Price...25c
If by mail, postage extra, 9 cents.

The Toilet Mask.

The Art of Beautifying the Complexion.

Every lady knows the value of a mask made of transparent rubber, acid cured, for the removal of freckles, liver spots, and other facial blemishes. As a bleacher it cannot be excelled, and will give any lady the fine, soft, velvety skin of a child. It is safe, simple, cleanly and effective for beautifying purposes, and never injures the most delicate complexion. Usually sold for $5.00. Made in 3 sizes, small, medium and large. Always state size desired.

No. 8F2492 Price....89c
If by mail, postage extra, 4 cents.

Seamless Para Rubber Gloves.

Seamless Para Rubber Gloves. By wearing them at night during sleep, you will obtain a hand as fair as an infant's, without the least injury. They will remove wrinkles, tan, sallowness, freckles and discolorations as if by magic. With care they will last for years. Made of the pure transparent rubber, same as face mask. Order 1 size larger than your kid glove number.

No. 8F2494 Price, per pair....65c
If by mail, postage extra, per pair, 6 cents.

Household Rubber Gloves.

These Gloves keep the hands soft and white and are unequaled for ladies' use in doing housework. They are strong, soft and pliable, and can be worn without the slightest inconvenience in doing work of the most delicate nature. Every pair fully guaranteed. Order a half size to one size larger than your kid glove number.

No. 8F2496 Price, per pair....73c
If by mail, postage extra, per pair, 3 cents.

Celebrated Net Lined Rubber Gloves.

For ladies and men. For use in rainy weather for driving or walking, and especially valuable for working about gardens and orchards and as a housework glove. They keep the hands in perfect condition, and prevent user from getting poisoned from wet weeds and poison ivy. Gloves are made in such a way that, while they are strong and durable, they are elastic and comfortable. They fit well, have a neat appearance and wear well. Made in two colors, tan and black. State color wanted.

Ladies' and Men's Net Lined Rubber Gloves. Colors, tan or black. Be sure to state size and color wanted.

No. 8F2500 Ladies' sizes, short, 7, 8 and 9. Price, per pair....63c
No. 8F2501 Men's sizes, short, 10, 11 and 12. Price, per pair....83c
No. 8F2502 Extra sizes, 13, 14 and 15. Price, per pair....93c

Ladies' and Men's Net Lined Gauntlet Rubber Gloves. Black or tan. Be sure to state size and color wanted.

No. 8F2503 Ladies' sizes, 7, 8 and 9. Price, per pair....$0.88
No. 8F2504 Men's sizes, 10, 11 and 12. Price, per pair....1.05
No. 8F2505 Extra sizes, 13, 14 and 15. Price, per pair....1.15
If by mail, postage extra, per pair, 12 cents.

Men's Heavy Rubber Mittens.

No. 8F2510 Men's Heavy Rubber Mittens. Lined with sheeting. Black only. Price, per pair....95c
If by mail, postage extra, per pair, 8 cents.

Goodyear Plant Sprinkler.

Plant Sprinkler for spraying plants and flowers without injury, for sprinkling clothing in the laundry, spraying carpets and clothing to prevent moths, spraying disinfectants in the sick room, etc.

No. 8F2512 Capacity, 6 oz. Price...50c
If by mail, postage extra, 10 cents.

Stomach Tubes.

No. 49F1657 Very Fine Maroon Soft Rubber Stomach Tube, with funnel. Price....75c
If by mail, postage extra, 10 cents.

No. 49F1653 Extra Fine Maroon Soft Rubber Stomach Tube, with funnel and bulb. Price....90c
If by mail, postage extra, 10c.

Rubber Finger Cots and Tips.

No. 49F1663 Antiseptic Finger Cots. Made of pure rubber; very light in weight. Price, 2 for....5c
If by mail, postage extra, for 2, 1 cent.

Reinforced Finger Cot.

Made of heavy gum rubber. Heavy weight at end where the wear comes.

No. 49F1660 Price, 2 for....5c
If by mail, postage extra, for 2, 2 cents.

Adjustable Finger Cot.

Made of soft flexible black leather, with adjustable back. To be used over finger where small bandage is placed to prevent injury. Can be regulated to suit small or heavy wrapping. Easy to apply, easily adjusted and very convenient.

No. 8F2520 Price....8c
Postage extra, 2 cents.

Catheters.

No. 49F167 Male Catheter, olive tip, silken linen. English scale, 3 to 18. Price....33c
No. 49F169 Male Catheter, conical tip, silken linen. English scale, 3 to 18. Price....33c
No. 49F170 Male Catheter, cylindrical tip, silken linen. English scale, 3 to 18. Price....33c
No. 49F171 Male Catheter, lisle thread. English scale, 3 to 18. Price...23c
No. 49F174 Soft Rubber Catheter, Patent velvet eye. American scale, 5 to 15. Price....15c
No. 49F190 English Catheter, with wire stilet. Price....11c

All catheters, if by mail, postage extra, 2 cents.

Chamois Skin.

Chamois skins are used as follows: Ladies use them for toilet purposes, for cleaning glass, woodwork of all kinds, carriages, silverware, or any metal, lining pockets and for chest protectors.

No. 8F2550 Our Very Fine Toilet Chamois, for applying powder, etc., to the face. Size, about 5x6 inches. Price....5c

No. 8F2551 Size, 6¼x8¾ inches. 5c
No. 8F2552 Size, 9x11 inches....9c
No. 8F2553 Size, 11x13¾ inches. 14c
No. 8F2554 Size, 15x20 inches....36c
No. 8F2555 Size, 23x26 inches....70c
No. 8F2556 Size, 28x32 inches....95c
If by mail, postage extra, each, 6 cents.

Chamois Polishing and Cleaning Brush.

A cleaning brush made entirely of chamois skin bound with linen. So soft that it may be used in cleaning and polishing the finest mirror or silver. Unequaled for rubbing down pianos and other fine furniture. Wears like leather and is washable. An article you need every day if you desire to keep your furniture free from dust and also from scratches and marks.

No. 8F2560 Chamois Polisher, Price, 3 for 60c; each....22c
If by mail, postage extra, each, 3 cents.

Sponges.

Our Sponges are obtained direct from the Mediterranean Sea, Cuba and Florida, and are the finest quality and size obtainable. Our prices are 25 per cent to 40 per cent lower than the usual prices for the same quality of goods.

No. 8F2575 Small Silk Toilet or Eye Sponge, can be used for surgical purposes, application of face lotions, shaving, etc.
Price, per dozen, 55c; each....5c

No. 8F2577 Extra Fine Elephant's Ear Sponge, a fine article for toilet and bath, specially shaped to fit the hand. Price, per dozen, $1.60; each. 14c

No. 8F2579 Baby Toilet Sponge. A fine soft silk sponge for nursery use and for shaving.
Price, per dozen, $2.50; each....22c

No. 8F2581 Ladies' Silk Sponge. A very fine special form.
Price, per dozen, $2.20; each...20c

No. 8F2583 Ladies' Extra Fine Cup Shaped Sponge. Each in a box.
Price, per dozen, $3.75; each....35c

No. 8F2585 Ladies' Superfine Cup Shaped Sponge, specially selected forms. Each in a box.
Price, per dozen, $5.60; each....50c

Sheep's Wool Fine Bath Sponges.

No. 8F2587 Larger than the Mediterranean for same price. Medium, for bath.
Price, per doz, $1.35; each...12c
No. 8F2589 Large, for bath.
Price, per dozen, $2.35; each....21c

Mediterranean Bath Sponges.

No. 8F2591 Mediterranean. Extra large, for bath.
Price, per dozen, $3.35; each....30c
No. 8F2593 Mediterranean. Extra fine, large, for bath.
Price, per dozen, $6.20; each....54c
No. 8F2595 Mediterranean. Special size. Extra fine.
Price, per dozen, $7.75; each....69c

Bleached Florida Bath Sponges.

Very durable, soft as silk and round as apples.

No. 8F2597 Medium size. A fine soft sponge for bath.
Price, per dozen, 70c; each....7c
No. 8F2600 Large size. Same as above.
Price, per dozen, $1.45; each....13c
No. 8F2602 Extra large size. Same as above.
Price, per dozen, $2.15; each....19c

Unbleached Sheep's Wool Sponges.

Used for bath or for cleaning fine carriages, automobiles or furniture. Largely used by painters and wall paper hangers for wall use. Tough, durable sponges, something you can hardly wear out.

No. 8F2604 Small.
Price, per dozen, $1.20; each....11c
No. 8F2606 Large circumference.
Price, per dozen, $4.30; each....38c
No. 8F2608 Extra large circumference.
Price, per dozen, $6.40; each....56c
No. 8F2610 Large Cleaning Sponge, 15 to 24 inches in circumference. Suitable for rough work, house cleaning, bailing boats, cleaning walls wood work, etc.
Price, per dozen, $1.00; each....10c

Patent India Rubber Bath Sponges.

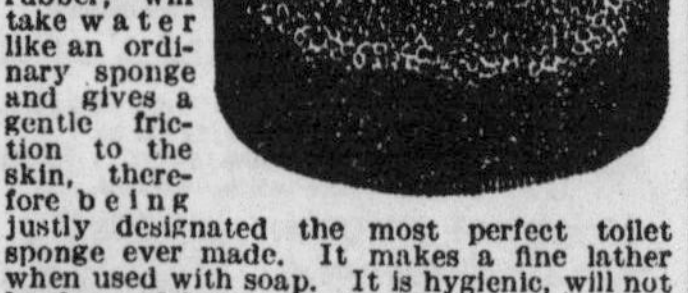

The finest, durable Bath Sponge in existence. Made of pure rubber, will take water like an ordinary sponge and gives a gentle friction to the skin, therefore being justly designated the most perfect toilet sponge ever made. It makes a fine lather when used with soap. It is hygienic, will not harden and is very durable; will last for years. We offer these sponges at nearly one-half the prices at which they are sold elsewhere. Each sponge is packed in individual waterproof boxes, especially for our trade.

No. 8F2615 Small. Price....24c
No. 8F2618 Medium. Price....42c
No. 8F2620 Large. Price....68c
If by mail, postage extra, each, 4 cents.

Rubber Soap Tray.

Rubber Soap Trays are the popular idea. Clean and unbreakable, they make a perfect article for the bath room or toilet table. Fine for travelers.

No. 8F2625 Price....17c
If by mail, postage extra, 5 cents.

Combination Sponge Bag.

Made of a high grade rubber lined satin, escalloped top, flap trimmed with red silk and fitted with patent button clasps. One side pocket for tooth brush, extra side pocket for comb, extra center pocket for brushes, extra pocket for soap holder. Size, 9 x 10 inches. A handsome article for bath or wash room equipment, and very handy when traveling.

No. 8F2630 Combination Sponge Bag. Price....44c
If by mail, postage extra, 4 cents.

Bath Thermometer.

No. 49F1992 Bath Thermometer, in wood frame.
Price (Postage extra, 4 cents), 17c

Japanese Loofah Flesh Brush.

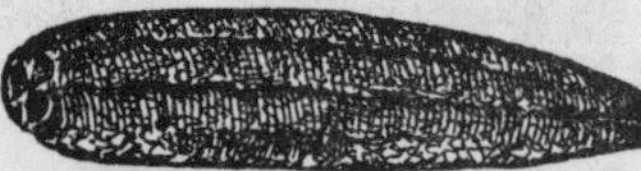

The Loofah is the fibrous part of a gourd that grows in the south of Japan. Their use gives a healthy glow to the body, removes all accumulations from the pores of the skin, increases the circulation of the blood, and leaves a pleasant sensation.

DIRECTIONS—The loofah may be used as a sponge just as it is, or to make it a trifle more handy, soak in water until it expands full size; cut lengthwise and remove the inner substance so that the loofah opens out like a cloth.

No. 8F2632 Large 14-inch size. Price....7c
If by mail, postage extra, 3 cents.

Loofah Bath Mitten.

Loofah front, with Turkish toweling back. The best bath mitten in the market.

No. 8F2635 Price....13c
If by mail, postage extra, 2 cents.

Toilet or Medicinal Atomizers.

Atomizer for either Toilet or Medicinal Use. Hard rubber nozzle, rubber bulb of fine quality. Continuous spray. Regular price, 50 cents.

No. 8F2650 Price....32c
If by mail, postage extra, 14 cents.

The Most Reliable and useful Atomizer in the world. Has three hard rubber tips. Can be used for spraying perfume, or disinfecting a sick room, or applying medicine to the throat or in the nose. It is made of the best materials, and with care will last a lifetime. Regular price, 75 cents.

No. 8F2652 Our price....58c
If by mail, postage extra, 12 cents.

Simplex Atomizer.

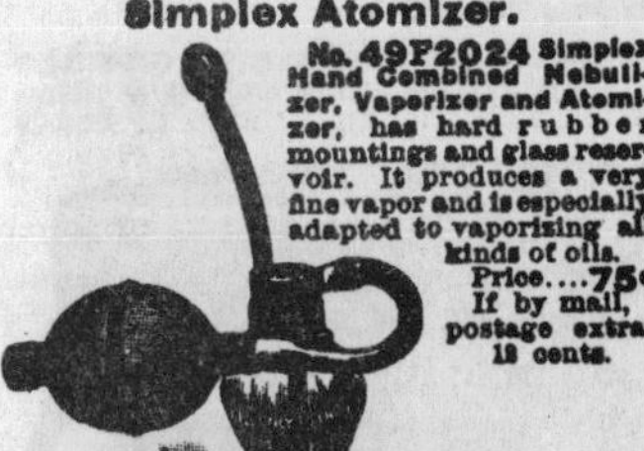

No. 49F2024 Simplex Hand Combined Nebulizer, Vaporizer and Atomizer, has hard rubber mountings and glass reservoir. It produces a very fine vapor and is especially adapted to vaporizing all kinds of oils.
Price....75c
If by mail, postage extra, 18 cents.

Success Atomizer.

For liquefying and spraying; especially for atomizing medicines and medicated oils of every description for the treatment of catarrh, bronchitis, and other affections of the respiratory organs. Large rubber bulb, strong hard rubber tube, which is detachable; metal cap, strong glass vial.
No. 8F2654 Success Atomizer.
Price....45c
If by mail, postage extra, 8 cents.

Hand Nebulizer.

No. 49F2026 Hand Nebulizer. This is the latest improved and most useful hand nebulizer offered to the public. It throws a light or profuse spray of vapor, excelling that of any other intrument of its kind on the market. Removable throat and nasal tips of hard rubber.
Price........$1.10
Not mailable.

Dr. Barcley's Hygienic Face Atomizer (Face Steamer).

For the rational and common sense treatment of the skin for the attainment of a clear, beautiful complexion. Dr. Barcley's Hygienic Face Atomizer (Face Steamer) is a handsome apparatus built on the same model as the large and expensive steaming apparatus used by dermatologists all over the country, but adapted in every detail for home use. The treatment with Dr. Barcley's Hygienic Face Atomizer will accomplish for you better results in a few weeks than you could obtain with any other steaming method in months or years. It will make the skin firm and elastic, and gives the complexion a freshness, purity, transparency, brilliancy and harmonious coloring, which could not be gained in any other way. Dr. Barcley's Face Atomizer will successfully remove blackheads, liver spots, freckles; in fact, every known facial blemish, and bring back oily and dry skins to a normal condition, make them firm, pliable and velvety, establishing at the same time that healthful hue usually designated as a natural fine complexion. Dr. Barcley's Hygienic Face Atomizer (Face Steamer) has never been sold for less than $3.50; we furnish the same to our lady customers for 95 cents, with a guarantee that we supply at this special price the genuine Dr. Barcley's Hygienic Face Atomizer complete, with full directions and instructions.
No. 8F2660 Dr. Barcley's Hygienic Face Atomizer, complete.
Price....95c
Unmailable.

YOU GET A PROFIT SHARING CERTIFICATE
WITH EVERY ORDER OF $1.00 OR MORE.

You will be able to share in our profits and get something valuable absolutely FREE, very quickly, if you send us your orders. We guarantee our prices to be lower than you can get elsewhere. The quality of the goods is the very highest, and under our PROFIT SHARING PLAN you are able to share with us in the profits of this business.

PERFUMERY DEPARTMENT.

WE OFFER THIS SEASON THE FINEST UP TO DATE IMPORTED PERFUMES IN THE LATEST ARTISTIC STYLES OF FANCY BOTTLES.

WE OFFER below the finest grade of imported perfumes manufactured. They are blended and made direct from the flowers by the best perfumers of Grasse, France, and represent in every case the true odor of the flower. Their delightful fragrance, delicate blend, lasting qualities, true representation of odors and the high quality has won for them a world wide reputation. No American perfume can compare in flower odor with those manufactured direct in France from the true flowers, and this is the only grade we sell. We import all our perfumes ourselves, obtaining them fresh from the producer. It is by this means that we can offer our customers the very best perfumes at a price much less than others charge for cheaper and inferior products. We guarantee our perfumes as pure, imported odors, unequaled for sweetness of odor, fragrance, lasting quality and true representation of the flower.

THE ILLUSTRATIONS will give you a very accurate idea of the handsome packages or bottles in which our perfumes are supplied. In sending your order, select the size and style bottle desired, state the name of the odor which you wish to receive, and we will execute your order carefully. We know that you will be more than pleased with the perfumes when you receive them.

REMEMBER that a handsome bottle of high grade perfume always makes a welcome and dainty gift.

While the bottle, of course, will add nothing to the quality of the perfume, the handsome appearance of the perfume container serves a double purpose in making the package pleasing to the eye and later the bottle can be used for different toilet purposes, if desired. **Although we supply our one-ounce perfume packages at extremely low prices, you can obtain an additional and considerable saving by ordering two ounces, four ounces, or, still better, ½-pound bottles. Wherever it is stated that perfume packages can be sent by mail, the amount of postage as stated with each item must be included, together with the price of the perfume, providing the customer wishes them forwarded in that manner.**

LIST OF IMPORTED ODORS WHICH WE ALWAYS CARRY IN STOCK:

Hyacinth,	Jasmin,
Trefle,	Crab Apple,
Violet,	Lilac Blossoms,
Carnation Pink,	Lily of the Valley,
White Heliotrope,	Peau d' Espagne,
White Rose,	Jockey Club.

NOTE—The above odors are all imported from France and are of exceptionally high grade. They are sold regularly at 50 to 85 cents per ounce.

Imported Perfumes of any Odor.

This 1-ounce genuine round Lubin bottle, with ball glass stopper, only 25 cents.

The bottle, although of simple design, is one of quiet beauty, and, when filled with any one of the above elegant odors makes a package that cannot be duplicated anywhere for less than 50 cents. We offer you this fine bottle filled with any odor perfume you may select for 25 cents. State odor wanted.
No. 8F3000 Price, 1-ounce round Lubin bottle........25c
If by mail, postage and mailing tube extra, 7 cents.

Your choice of any triple extract perfume of odors above listed, with genuine 1-ounce square Lubin bottle and sprinkler top, only 25 cents.

Usually sold in drug stores at 50 to 85 cents per ounce. Sprinkler top bottles are extremely convenient and many will prefer this style. You cannot realize what a fine grade of perfume you are receiving until you compare it with an odor sold by druggists at 50 to 75 cents per ounce. A beautiful package and a fine perfume. State odor wanted.
No. 8F3003 Price, 1-ounce square Lubin bottle, sprinkler top........25c
No. 8F3006 Price, 2-ounce square Lubin bottle, sprinkler top........45c
If by mail, postage and mailing tube extra, small, 7c; large, 12c.

No. 1 1-oz. No. 2 1-oz.

We will send you our celebrated La Dore's imported perfume, worth 50 cents an ounce, for only 30 cents, and with it your choice of either one of the handsome and attractive bottles Nos. 1 and 2, as illustrated, without extra charge. We will supply you same packed in a beautifully lithographed perfume box. These packages make a very acceptable present, welcome to and appreciated by every lady. State odor wanted.
No. 8F3009 Any of the above odors in Bottles Nos. 1 and 2, as may be selected by you. Price, 1-ounce bottle in neat paper case....30c
If by mail, postage and mailing tube extra, 15c.

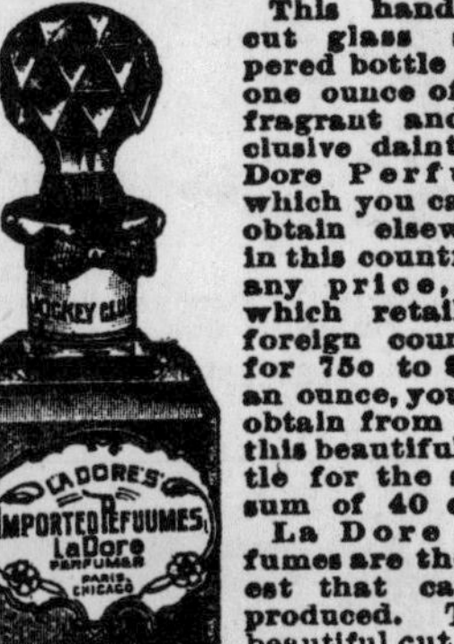

This handsome cut glass stoppered bottle with one ounce of our fragrant and exclusive dainty La Dore Perfume, which you cannot obtain elsewhere in this country at any price, and which retails in foreign countries for 75c to $1.00 an ounce, you can obtain from us in this beautiful bottle for the small sum of 40 cents. La Dore Perfumes are the finest that can be produced. This beautiful cut glass stoppered bottle, with fine La Dore perfume, for only 40 cents per bottle, is exceptional value. Shipped in neat lithographed boxes without extra charge. State odor wanted.
No. 8F3012 Price, 1-ounce beautiful cut glass stoppered bottle, filled with any odor of our imported perfumes........40c
No. 8F3013 Price, same style bottle only 2-ounce capacity, filled with any odor....60c
No. 8F3014 Price, same style cut glass stoppered bottle, 4-ounce capacity, filled with any odor....95c
If by mail, 1-ounce bottle only, postage and mailing tube extra, 8 cents. Other bottles unmailable.

Two Ounce Bottle of Triple Extract Perfume, any odor you may wish, with this handsome glass stoppered bottle, only 45 cents. Splendid value at this price and very popular with our customers. An exceedingly attractive package and extremely ornamental for the dressing table of ladies. The best perfume and the nicest display bottle ever sold at this very low price. State odor wanted.
No. 8F3015 Price, 2-ounce bottle.....45c
If by mail, postage and mailing tube extra, 13c.

This large, beautiful cut glass stoppered bottle and filled with our fine imported perfume, worth 50 to 75 cents an ounce, or $1.00 value, for 55 cents. Almost one-half the price others would ask for the perfume alone, not mentioning the costly bottle in which the perfume is supplied. There is nothing that can please people of good taste and refinement more than a faint trace of true odors of favorite flowers. Avoid cheap, coarse, diluted extracts. They have no lasting qualities and usually prove offensive. Our perfume extracts are always pleasing, elegant, lasting. Our 2-ounce cut glass stoppered bottle, filled with any odor you may select. State odor wanted.
No. 8F3018 Price, 2-oz. bottle. 55c
Unmailable on account of weight.

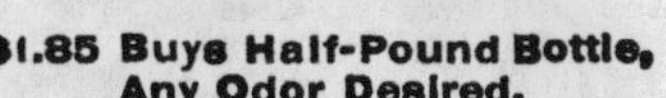

$1.85 Buys Half-Pound Bottle, Any Odor Desired.

$1.85

For only $1.85 we will send a ½-pound bottle, sufficient for a year's needs, of any of our imported perfumes, any odor you may select, including Violette and White Rose Extracts, in beautiful 8-ounce cut glass bottle with cut glass stopper as shown in this illustration. A year's supply for such a small price. The bottle is of heavy cut glass pattern and practically indestructible, and afterward may be used as a receptacle for fine toilet waters and forms one of the prettiest and loveliest dressing room ornaments imaginable. Be sure to state odor wanted.
No. 8F3030 One-half pound cut glass pattern bottle with cut glass stopper, containing any odor of our perfumes, $6.00 value. Price....$1.85
Unmailable on account of weight.

Our Leaders in Fine Packages, 63 Cents and Up.

The many requests for extra fine perfumes in fancy boxes has resulted in our offering the following three leading odors in box form: Violet De Pare, Crushed Roses, and Ze Dora. These three odors are the very finest the French perfumers can manufacture and are imported by us direct. They are the same grade perfumes ordinarily sold for $1.00 to $1.50 per ounce in plain bottles. They have many times the endurance and are as sweet and lasting odors as can be blended. One drop of Violet De Pare, for example, is equal to the perfume of one hundred violets. Ze Dora is now famous as the finest, most delicate and long lived perfume made. It is put up in a handsome cut glass stoppered bottle and is one of the very prettiest designs obtainable, filled with any one of the new leading odors, Violet De Pare, Crushed Roses and Ze Dora. Be sure to state odor wanted. The fancy box used is of special design, white interior and heavy padded exterior. A very beautiful package, and one admired and appreciated by every woman of taste and refinement. A very attractive and desirable gift. **Be sure to state odor wanted.**

No. 8F3035 1-ounce bottle in package above. Retail price, $1.00 to $1.50. Our price $0.63
No. 8F3036 2-ounce bottle in package above. Retail price, $1.50 to $1.75. Our price .... .93
No. 8F3037 4-ounce bottle in package above. Retail price, $1.75 to $2.25. Our price 1.23

Two-Bottle Case, $1.79.

To meet the many demands for a two-bottle perfume can we offer the following: A beautiful special design shouldered box, 9 inches long by 5 inches wide, fancy elevated and beveled cover with raised design. Inside of box is lined with the very best light pink satin, neatly folded and securely holding in place two handsome 1-oz. cut glass stoppered bottles of perfume. The inside cover is heavily padded and fits down tightly over the bottles, making a neatly fitting and beautiful package. The odors furnished comprise any two of the three leading blends: Violet De Pare, Crushed Rose, and Ze Dora. This is without a doubt the finest two-bottle perfume case ever offered. Its equal, regarding the sweetness and delicacy of perfume, the beautiful cut glass stoppered bottles and the very elaborate satin lined box, has yet to be produced. Each case is carefully packed in a second corrugated box to afford perfect safety in shipping. If you desire something exceptionally fine, a perfume surpassed by none, a present you may well feel proud to give, select this case. **Be sure to state odor wanted.** Regular price, $2.50.

No. 8F3040 Our price, case complete, with choice of perfumes named $1.79

Perfume Atomizers.

No. 8F3043 Fancy Shape Perfume Atomizer with raised floral design. Fitted with brass top and good red rubber bulb. Excellent value at our special price. Regular price, 35c. Our price... 25c
Unmailable.

No. 8F3044 Fancy Shaped Perfume Atomizer. Floral design. Fitted with brass top and red rubber bulb, covered with fine netting. Very pretty atomizer. Regular price, 50 cents. Our price... 37c
Unmailable.

No. 8F3045 New Patent Pump Atomizer. Made of fancy crystal glass with polished brass, heavily nickel plated top, and is an ornament to any lady's dressing table. Can be used for perfumes, toilet waters, etc. The atomizer will not get out of order and will last indefinitely. Regular price, 85c. Our price... 62c

No. 8F3047 Fancy Decorated Bohemian Glass Atomizer. Comes in beautiful assorted designs. Has the new patent upright pump. All metal parts heavily nickel plated. The atomizer especially fitted for finely spraying perfumes, toilet waters, rose water, etc. Very convenient for both ladies and gents. Properly used will last a lifetime. Regular price, $1.50. Our price 95c

No. 8F3046 New Patent Pump Atomizer. Very handsome imitation cut glass. Top is made of polished brass, heavily nickel plated. Sprays both perfumes and toilet waters. Simple in construction and easy to operate. No valves to get out of order. No rubber bulbs to wear out and break. Plunger made of heavy soft leather. A steady spray with no waste. A very attractive and ornamental atomizer. Will last a lifetime. Regular price, $1.00. Our price... 79c

No. 8F3048 Genuine Imported Very Deep Cut Glass Atomizer. With finely polished nickel plated top. This makes a beautiful ornament for the dressing table. Genuine imported cut glass and a beauty. Will last a lifetime. A beauty for a present to any young lady friend. Regular price, $2.25. Our price $1.23

TOILET PREPARATIONS

RECOGNIZING THAT UP TO DATE TOILET AND BEAUTIFYING PREPARATIONS are largely adulterated, many containing harmful ingredients and are injurious to the skin, we have taken the initial start in offering our customers an opportunity to obtain from us all the very latest beneficial standard articles free from any harmful substances. Our assortment comprises every lotion and article of merit, many being made by the famous Parisian perfumer, La Dore. Knowing all about his various lotions, and being assured that nothing but the best and purest goods are used therein, our customers can feel a sense of security in using these pure articles. All of our lotions and toilet preparations are scientifically prepared, strictly up to date, finely perfumed, possess merit and will give satisfaction when used for the purposes for which they are intended. We guarantee every product we sell, as well as giving our customers the positive assurance that in making their selection from the following list, they will obtain not only the latest and best toilet preparations, but they will save from fifty to sixty per cent in price on nearly every article.

Violet Cold Cream, Only 28 Cents Per Jar.

A Perfectly Pure and Sweetly Perfumed Cold Cream.

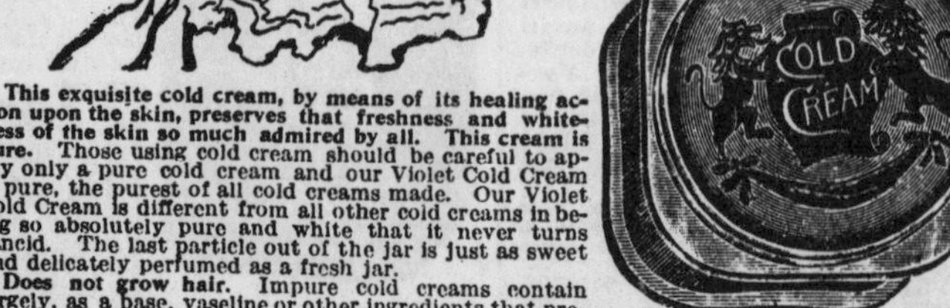

This exquisite cold cream, by means of its healing action upon the skin, preserves that freshness and whiteness of the skin so much admired by all. This cream is pure. Those using cold cream should be careful to apply only a pure cold cream and our Violet Cold Cream is pure, the purest of all cold creams made. Our Violet Cold Cream is different from all other cold creams in being so absolutely pure and white that it never turns rancid. The last particle out of the jar is just as sweet and delicately perfumed as a fresh jar.

Does not grow hair. Impure cold creams contain largely, as a base, vaseline or other ingredients that promote the growth of hair. No refined woman desires a growth of hair upon her face, neck or arms, and hence every careful woman will restrict herself to a high grade cold cream the composition of which guarantees absolute protection against this danger. Our cream contains no vaseline or other harmful ingredients. Its uses—Our Violet Cold Cream affords an excellent application for tan and sunburn, for chapped lips and hands, for scalds and burns and as a **general soothing agent.** When again in need of cold cream order a jar of our Violet Cold Cream. After you have convinced yourself of the purity and elegance of this preparation, we know you will use no other in the future. **(Unmailable on account of weight.)**

No. 8F3050 Price, per jar 28c

La Dore's Toilet Waters.

We carry nothing but the very finest grade of toilet waters, made by the famous perfumer, La Dore, direct from the flowers and in concentrated form. They are much stronger in flower odor and sweetness than the average toilet water and cannot but be appreciated wherever used. They are furnished in four odors, violet, carnation, lilac and rose. Beautiful in color, sweet and lasting odors and handsome bottles. The occasional sprinkling of a few drops of any of these waters on furniture, clothing, linen, etc., will keep these articles fresh, and owing to the highest purity and strength of the perfumes used in these waters their lasting quality is fully equal to their fragrance, thus making them more desirable and of greater value for toilet requisites than any other toilet preparations of this kind.

La Dore's Toilet Water, violet, carnation, lilac or rose. Always state plainly in your order the odor desired.

No. 8F3051 Price, 4-oz. bottle... 30c
No. 8F3052 Price, 8-oz. bottle... 45c
Unmailable on account of weight.

IF YOU BUY FROM US, WE WILL SEND YOU A FREE PROFIT SHARING CERTIFICATE.
See Pages 1 and 2.

Eastman's Toilet Waters.

We now carry in stock the famous Eastman Big 3 Toilet Waters, Verona Violette, Crushed Roses and Crushed Carnations. Their universally known high standard of excellence needs no introduction. They are as fine as can be manufactured, are in beautiful packages and always give absolute satisfaction. But a few drops on the hands, and their delicate, sweet and lasting odor causes admiration by all. Every lady and gentleman of refinement desires an article of exceptionally high merit and it is always found in the Eastman Toilet Water. **Be sure to state odor wanted.**

No. 8F3055 Regular 50-cent size; our price..........38c
No. 8F3056 Regular $1.00 size; our price..........72c
Unmailable on account of weight.

German Cologne Water.

Especially prepared by us for the toilet and handkerchief, and equal to the finest colognes in the market. It is very refreshing and of great value in the sick room, where it can be used as a disinfectant by destroying bad odors and rendering the air in the room fresh and pleasant, giving it a nice perfume.

No. 8F3060 Price, 4-ounce bottle....30c
No. 8F3061 Price, 8-ounce bottle....55c
If by mail, postage and tube extra, small, 16c; large, unmailable on account of weight.

Genuine Florida Water.

This is the finest toilet water manufactured. Can be used as a perfume, or mixed with water as a cooling and refreshing lotion for the skin. In the bath it is a luxury only known to those who have tried it. There are many imitations. Send to us and get the only **genuine quality.**

No. 8F3063 Regular 25-cent size bottle; our price......15c
No. 8F3064 Price, ½-pint bottle..........21c
Unmailable on account of weight.

Pure Bay Rum.

This is a fine quality of **Bay Rum**, being manufactured from pure oil of Porto Rico bay aromatics and pure imported rum. This is one of the very few bay rums made from genuine imported rum. Being a pure article it is very useful for toilet purposes. A refreshing lotion for the skin.

No. 8F3066 Price, ½-pint bottle..........23c
No. 8F3067 Price, 1-pint bottle..........43c
No. 8F3068 Price, 1-quart bottle..........72c
Unmailable on account of weight.

Almond Nut Cream.

An excellent face cream, cleansing and cooling. Clears the skin from wrinkles, tan, freckles and other facial blemishes, rendering the face soft and white. This Almond Nut Cream is a pure preparation made from almonds with the addition of other properly selected ingredients, making it one of the most effective creams obtainable for freckles, pimples, scaly or scabby skin. It is non-poisonous and does not contain any bleaching chemicals, which are always dangerous when used in face preparations.

No. 8F3070 Price..........40c
Unmailable on account of weight.

Violet Witch Hazel.

Is a face and hand application, a delicacy after shaving, and as a general perfumed antiseptic. Violet Witch Hazel is a comparatively new product, combining the exquisite odor of violets with the antiseptic properties of pure extract of witch hazel. **No household antiseptic can compare with extract of witch hazel, and when sweetly perfumed with odor of violets, makes an article** that has won the favor of every lady and gentleman that has ever given it a trial. When used for perfuming the hands and face, or as a delicacy after shaving, it removes inflammation, makes the parts antiseptic and leaves that exquisite odor of violets about the person.

No. 8F3072 Price, 8-oz. bottle..20c
Unmailable on account of weight.

Orange Flower Water.

This is the genuine, full strength, imported article, obtained by distillation from pure orange flower petals. An article of very fine odor and one appreciated by every lady of taste and refinement.

No. 8F3074 Price per 8-ounce bottle....25c
Unmailable.

Secret de Ninon.

THE GREAT FRECKLE LOTION.

This new French preparation is especially recommended for removing freckles, redness, blotches, tan and all imperfections of the skin, leaving same clear, soft and rich in appearance. By using Secret de Ninon you can secure a healthy, blooming complexion. Ladies exposed to the sun, wind and sudden changes of weather frequently find their delicate complexions injured from these causes, but **Secret de Ninon will quickly remove such imperfections and a satin like, smooth skin of great beauty can soon be acquired, a complexion which will be admired by everyone.**

No. 8F3076 Price, per bottle...55c
Unmailable on account of weight.

Witch Hazel Toilet Balm.

This is an elegant preparation for the skin when it is chapped and rough. A few applications well rubbed in make the skin soft and velvety. It is also recommended for removing sunburn and freckles. It will prevent the skin from chapping or coloring when exposed to the cold if used before going out. It does not leave the skin greasy or sticky. Gloves can be used immediately after each application, the balm being absorbed by the skin very quickly. The Witch Hazel Balm is a very popular healing and soothing toilet requisite for harsh, dry, cracked or rough skin. Gentlemen find it a lotion highly satisfactory for use after shaving.

No. 8F3078 Price, per bottle...18c
If by mail, postage and tube extra, each, 16 cents.

Sachet Powders.

The well known Genuine La Dore Sachet Powders in beautiful air-tight sealed envelopes, the most fragrant, delicate odors, lasting and refined. Size of envelope, 3x4 inches; furnished in the following favorite odors: Violette, crushed roses, crushed heliotrope and crushed carnation.

No. 8F3080 Sachet Powders in fancy envelope. State odor wanted. Price..........8c
If by mail, postage extra, 2 cents.

Genuine La Dore Sachet Powders in very fine screw cap glass jars. We furnish the genuine La Dore Sachet Powders in medium size glass jars, with metal screw caps. Absolutely airtight, so the sachet powder will remain fresh and fragrant for a very long time. Selection of the following odors: Violette, crushed carnation, crushed roses and crushed heliotrope.

No. 8F3081 Sachet Powder, in screw cap glass jars. State odor wanted. Price. (By mail, postage extra, 8c). 20c

Eye Brow Grower.

A harmless composition for stimulating the eye brows and aiding their growth. Merely moisten the eye brows twice per week before retiring with the liquid and rub in thoroughly.

No. 8F3085 Price, per bottle...18c
If by mail, postage extra, 8 cents.

Benzoinated Rose Water and Glycerine.

A combination of tincture benzoin, imported rose water and pure glycerine. An exceptionally fine article for facial use after shaving, chapped hands, rough skin, etc.

No. 8F3087 Price, per 4-ounce bottle..21c
Unmailable.

La Dore's Complexion Tonic.

A beautifying tonic of exceptional merit. An external application, rapidly clearing the complexion and whitening the skin. One teaspoonful of this tonic is added to a basin of hot water, the face steamed with it and then applied by cloths to the face. Very efficient and highly beneficial.

No. 8F3090 Price, per 4-ounce bottle..38c
Unmailable.

Eastman's Benzoin and Almond Lotion.

This widely known lotion is one of the most dainty preparations ever offered for preserving the skin and complexion, healing, soothing and whitening; free from injurious substances. Every lady and gent of refinement should possess a bottle for their toilet. A few applications will readily remove tan, sunburn, wrinkles, muddy and dark colored imperfections of the skin and increase the beauty of the complexion. Sweetly and delicately perfumed. A very superior article.

No. 8F3095 Price, per 6-ounce bottle..........27c
Unmailable.

English Lavender Smelling Salts.

REFRESHING AND INVIGORATING.

For faintness, headache. etc. In pretty glass stoppered bottles, a useful and handsome ornament for the dressing table.

No. 8F3135 Price, per bottle..........18c
Postage and tube extra, 10 cents.

Malaga Almond Meal.

This is the genuine Oriental Meal; much more emollient than the meal usually sold in this country. We import it direct in original bags and put it up in nice packages. It is splendid for the skin and can be used in place of soap. **Malaga Almond Meal is highly recommended to ladies who have a very sensitive skin;** one that is easily affected even by the slightest presence of acid in a toilet preparation.

No. 8F3138 Price, ¼-lb. size.....15c
No. 8F3139 Price, ½-lb. size.....25c
If by mail, postage extra, small size, 8 cents; large size, 12 cents.

Milk of Roses for the Complexion.

A great beautifier used by the most fashionable ladies in Europe, and prepared from fresh white and pale colored roses by a simple process, which, however, secures and obtains by a superior extraction, the finest odor and other portions which always have a pleasant and softening effect on the skin when used for the treatment of same, especially when the skin is not entirely free from blemishes. The process for preparing this toilet article has been secured from the French manufacturer and chemist for our exclusive control in the United States.

No. 8F3145 Price..........32c
Unmailable on account of weight.

Genuine Rose Water.

This is the genuine full strength imported article obtained by distillation from pure rose petals. Its fine odor, strength and purity, make it an exceptionally fine toilet article.

No. 8F3150 Price, per 8-ounce bottle.......18c
Unmailable on account of weight.

Genuine Juice of Lily Bulbs.

After many futile efforts we finally succeeded in obtaining the genuine and pure juice of the fresh bulbs of pond lilies, so that our customers are in a position to obtain from us the real, genuine article of this toilet preparation, recognized as one of the best in the world. When used for a limited time only this preparation always assures a clear complexion, soft and transparent, giving at the same time an extremely healthy color.

No. 8F3152 Price..........36c
Unmailable on account of weight.

Witch Hazel Glycerine Jelly.

A very fine and delicately perfumed Glycerine Jelly for chapped and rough skin. It is antiseptic, cooling and healing, and a few applications of this jelly rubbed into the skin will make it soft and velvety. **It is highly recommended as a cooling emollient** application for removing tan, sunburn and quickly curing chapped hands, lips and face. Used and rubbed into the skin it affords an excellent means of preventing chapping in the cold. **It is not greasy or sticky** and, being soon absorbed by the skin, forms a very popular toilet requisite.

No. 8F3154 Price, per jar....16c
If by mail, postage extra, 12 cents.

Creme de Marshmallow.

A very fine, fragrant, dainty toilet lotion, bland and soothing, for preserving the complexion. Especially recommended for an inflamed and irritated condition of the skin. Ladies doing domestic work will find it a perfect lotion for the skin. May be applied at any time. Quickly absorbed by the skin. **Unmailable.**

No. 8F3156 Price, 26c

Milk of Cucumber.

An astringent wash, scientifically prepared from the fresh juice of green cucumbers. Cannot be equaled for the treatment of coarse pores and oily skin. Always gives a freshness to the skin, so much desired. **Purely vegetable and perfectly harmless.** This toilet article has been in great favor the past few years, and is highly recommended by ladies having used the wash constantly, and always with the very best results.

No. 8F3158 Price..........18c
Unmailable.

OUR WHITE LILY FACE WASH

37c PER BOTTLE

THE LADIES' FAVORITE TOILET PREPARATION.

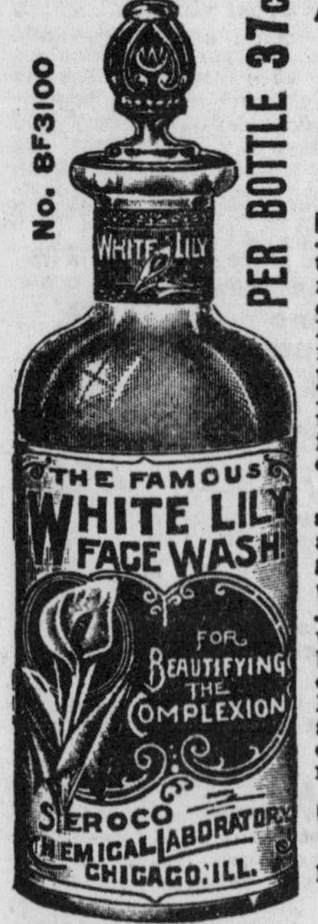

An Invaluable Remedy for Pimples, Freckles, Sallowness, Roughness, Wrinkles, Tan, Blackheads and Irritations and Imperfections of the Skin.

Retail Price, 75c. Our Price, 3 Bottles for $1.00; each, 37c

Recommended By Thousands of Beautiful Women.

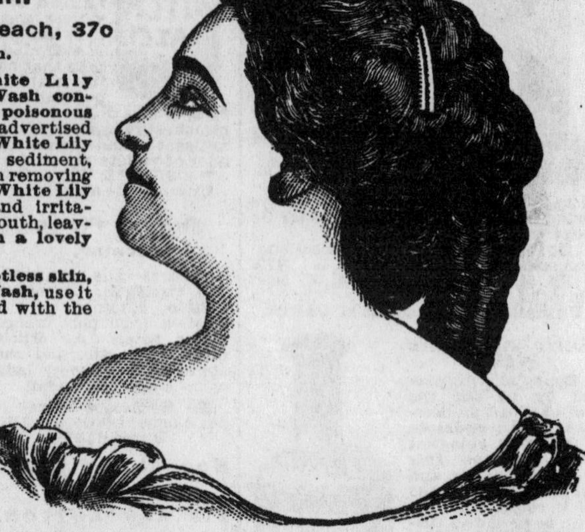

DIFFERENT FROM MOST COMPLEXION PREPARATIONS, our White Lily Face Wash contains not a particle of lead, silver, sulphur, arsenic, mercury or other poisonous mineral by which most complexion remedies, and particularly the advertised ones, produce a temporary smoothness and brilliancy of the skin. White Lily Face Wash is clear and harmless as water, contains no poison, no sediment, nothing to hurt the most tender and delicate skin. Its effect will aid in removing pimples, blackheads, freckles, roughness and tan in a short time. White Lily Face Wash smoothes out wrinkles and roughness, imperfections and irritations of the skin disappear, restores the delicate tint of girlhood and youth, leaving the skin soft and velvety. Nothing is more attractive than a lovely complexion.

DO YOU WANT TO BE BEAUTIFUL? Do you want a spotless skin, a matchless complexion? Send for a bottle of White Lily Face Wash, use it according to directions and give it a fair trial. You will be satisfied with the good results obtained.

WHITE LILY FACE WASH has a wonderful sale. The market is full of injurious complexion preparations. Many, in fact most, of these preparations contain lead, arsenic, bismuth or mercury and are really dangerous in their effects. You can protect yourself from serious skin diseases by using our White Lily Face Wash. Take no chances. Avoid all danger. Use only a preparation that is absolutely harmless, one that you can depend on for a spotless skin, a positive beautifier that has been recommended by thousands of ladies.

USE ONLY THE GENUINE WHITE LILY FACE WASH, TO SECURE FOR YOURSELF THE BEST RESULTS.

No. 8F3100 Regular retail price, per bottle, 75c; our price, 3 bottles for $1.00; each.......... **37c**

If by mail, postage and mailing tube extra, 19 cents.

FOR REMOVING SUPERFLUOUS HAIR

OUR FAMOUS PARISIAN DEPILATORY

FOR REMOVING SUPERFLUOUS HAIR

Regular retail price, each...$1.50
OUR PRICE, EACH......$0.58
3 BOTTLES FOR........1.60

THE FAMOUS
PARISIAN DEPILATORY
SEROCO CHEMICAL LABORATORY
CHICAGO, ILL.

One bottle is usually sufficient for any case.

At 58c Per Bottle We Offer Our Celebrated PARISIAN DEPILATORY. A Harmless and Successful Preparation for Removing Unsightly Hair from the Face, Neck and Arms.

WE POSITIVELY GUARANTEE OUR PARISIAN DEPILATORY NOT TO HARM THE MOST SENSITIVE SKIN OR MAR THE MOST DELICATE COMPLEXION.

Hair on the face, neck or arms, so embarrassing to ladies of refinement, can be removed without danger or chance of failure. The Parisian Depilatory instantly dissolves the hair wherever applied and removes it entirely.

THE GREATEST DRAWBACK TO PERFECT LOVELINESS in woman is a superfluous, unnatural growth of hair where nature never intended it. The prettiest face is marred and disfigured by hair on the lips, cheeks or chin. By means of our Parisian Depilatory every vestige of hair can be removed, a perfect, clean, smooth, soft, beautiful skin is assured.

NO UNPLEASANT EFFECTS. The Parisian Depilatory is not only perfectly harmless when used according to directions, but it has the additional effect of a fine depilatory cosmetic, softening the hair and removing it entirely. It leaves no burning sensation, it is entirely painless, easily applied; one application is usually sufficient.

FAR SUPERIOR TO THE ELECTRIC NEEDLE. The electric needle will remove superfluous hair by destroying the roots, but it is a very painful operation. Serious results have often followed the use of the electric needle. Parisian Depilatory is highly recommended. No matter what you have tried before or how stubborn the growth of hair is, you ought to give Parisian Depilatory a trial.

A WONDERFUL PREPARATION. Compounded in our own laboratory by a competent chemist. Every ounce is prepared under his personal supervision. The ingredients are the best and purest, carefully selected. OUR PRICE of 58 cents per bottle is the lowest price ever heard of for this genuine depilatory.

DON'T PAY $1.00, $2.00 AND $3.00 for a so called hair remover. Be careful about using the preparations of unknown concerns. Some of the hair removers widely advertised are very powerful, very corrosive; they remove the hair and often burn the skin. You can use our Parisian Depilatory with perfect safety. Leaves no marks, no ill effects, no one can tell that you are using a hair remover. No one will know the difference except in your improved appearance, the enhanced loveliness of the skin and complexion.

NO TOILET IS COMPLETE without the famous Parisian Depilatory. Ladies of refinement everywhere find the Parisian Depilatory an invaluable toilet requisite. It removes the hair only where it is applied, does not interfere with the use of cosmetics, washes; has no effect whatever on the blood, complexion, health or hair, or any part of the person, except where it is applied. If you are bothered by superfluous hair, whether on face, neck or arms, if you want perfectly smooth, clean clear skin, send for a bottle of our celebrated 58-cent Parisian Depilatory, the only absolutely harmless hair remover ever compounded.

Our Celebrated Parisian Depilatory removes all superfluous hair and other imperfections, and leaves the skin soft, smooth and velvety.

No. 8F3105 Our price, 3 bottles for $1.60; each.................(If by mail, postage and mailing tube extra, 8 cents)........... **58c**

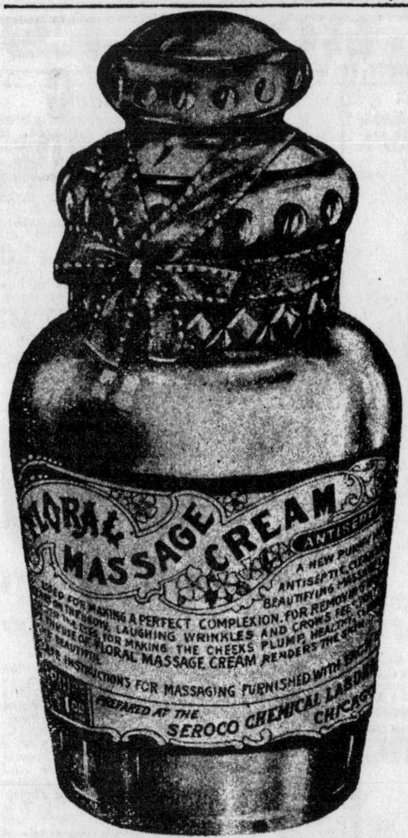

This is a life size illustration of the jar.

HOW TO BE BEAUTIFUL. FLORAL MASSAGE CREAM, THE GREAT AID TO BEAUTY

A WONDERFUL TOILET PREPARATION. A NEW PURIFYING, ANTISEPTIC, CLEANSING AND BEAUTIFYING MASSAGE CREAM. A MOST EXCELLENT PREPARATION. MAKES THE OLD YOUNG, THE PLAIN BEAUTIFUL AND REMOVES THE TELLTALE MARKS OF TIME.

Regular 50-cent size jars.................................... 32c
Extra large size jar, one-half pound, enough for 60 treatments, regular retail price $1.00 Only.................................... 55c

A BOOKLET, A COMPLETE COURSE OF INSTRUCTIONS FOR FACIAL MASSAGE, SENT FREE WITH EACH JAR.

COMPLETE DIRECTIONS for taking a complete course of massage treatment sent with each jar, a booklet written by a specialist, illustrated throughout with pictures and diagrams showing the same course of treatment society ladies receive in the fashionable city massage parlors at $1.00 per treatment. This booklet shows by pictures the exact way to massage the face, the various movements, the position of the hands, all explained by illustrations, so that anyone by following the plain and simple instructions, and the methods as shown by the pictures can get the same delightful, wonderful and improving effect from facial massage that makes this treatment so much appreciated by ladies of refinement and fashion everywhere.

WITH FLORAL MASSAGE CREAM and with the complete illustrated booklet of instructions you can do all this yourself at a mere fraction of the cost and get all the benefit and all the results that you would get if you went regularly to any of the fashionable massage parlors in large cities.

FLORAL MASSAGE CREAM is our latest and most improved toilet preparation, a standard, high grade and perfectly satisfactory facial massage cream, guaranteed by us as the very finest preparation of its kind on the market, very much superior in quality and effectiveness to the many creams and ointments on the market, many of which are widely advertised and sell through retail stores at two to three times the price that we ask for our matchless preparation.

FLORAL MASSAGE CREAM is a luxury which no woman, young, middleaged or old should deny herself. It is composed of the purest ingredients, perfectly harmless to the most delicate skin. Our Floral Massage Cream contains no grease of any kind, its emollient effects are greater, its cleansing and beautifying results more marked than can be obtained from any other combination prepared for massage purposes.

OUR FLORAL MASSAGE CREAM is based on a combination used so successfully by the leading professional masseurs in the massage parlors of the large cities, and is supplied by us exclusively to our customers for home massage. We have taken this basis of combination and by careful experiment we have refined and improved the preparation until it is now without question the most attractive and delightful toilet preparation ever offered, one that will appeal to ladies of refinement everywhere, who would not use any of the usual so called toilet preparations, cosmetics or skin preparations. Floral Massage Cream is a pure preparation, contains nothing to harm the most delicate skin, is not to be classed with cosmetics or other skin preparations. It is a preparation that no one can feel the slightest embarrassment in using. Our Floral Massage Cream is just as necessary an adjunct to the dressing table as a bottle of fine perfume; just as important to the toilet as a tooth brush.

FLORAL MASSAGE CREAM removes the horizontal lines from the brow, takes out the laughing wrinkles and crows' feet, removes the wrinkles under the eyes, makes the cheeks plump and round, cleanses the skin absolutely of all dirt, soot and impurities of all kinds, makes your complexion just what you want it to be, healthy, clear and rosy. For removing wrinkles, filling out the cheeks, clarifying the skin and bringing out that rosy color, Floral Massage Cream does indeed work wonders. It brings fresh bloom to faded faces, it smoothes away age lines and care marks. Underneath wrinkles and hollows and unbecoming flabbiness it builds firm sound healthy tissues; it is a food to the starved skin system and is absorbed with a grateful sense of delight.

HAVE YOU EVER EXPERIENCED the peculiarly delightful, stimulating and exhilarating effects upon the facial nerves and muscles produced by a scientifically prepared and properly applied massage cream? Do you know that massaging the face is now considered a function which no progressive lady omits in order to produce and preserve that healthy glow, that pink complexion which makes beautiful features more beautiful, and adds to irregular ones attractions, the effect of which is really remarkable. We all know that exercise means increased circulation of the blood, but generally exercise is not entirely sufficient to produce the right results in the fullest measure for the facial perfection. Local exercise, in other words massage of the face, becomes necessary to induce increased circulation through the facial blood vessels, but even this is incomplete unless you use in connection with it the famous Floral Massage Cream which cleanses and clears the skin, arouses to activity every facial nerve and muscle, stimulates and feeds them, removes wrinkles under the eyes, on the brow, fills out the cheeks, making them plump and round, and insures a beautiful complexion in all cases. It is not surprising that the foremost professional masseurs will use nothing else in their work but Floral Massage Cream, which can be found in every fashionable massage parlor, where it is used almost exclusively.

IT IS NOT GREASY, it does not contain any animal fats, and therefore is not subject to decomposition. It is absolutely pure, therefore harmless and cleanly. It is prepared in the most scientific manner, therefore reliable and certain in results. It is, however, not necessary that you should employ the services of a professional masseur, for with our Floral Massage Cream you can massage your face in the privacy of your own home, and at an expense of only a cent or two. We supply the regular large $1.00 size of the genuine Floral Massage Cream to our customers for 55 cents, sufficient for many months of facial massage treatment. Complete instructions are sent with each jar.

OUR FREE OFFER. Send us an order for a jar of our Floral Massage Cream, use it according to directions, and if you are not more than pleased with the result, if you find any massage cream or other toilet preparation that will compare with ours, if you do not find it strictly a high class preparation intended for people of refinement, then simply write us to this effect, tell us you are not satisfied and if it is the first jar you have ever ordered we will, without further question, refund your money. Anyone who has ever tried Floral Massage Cream will never be without it. The cost is so little, the benefit so great, one extra large size jar, which we sell at only 55 cents, lasts so long and it is, therefore, so inexpensive that anyone who has ever used it and given it a fair trial will never be without it.

No. 8F3110 Floral Massage Cream. Regular 50 cent size. Price, 2 jars, 60c; each..........(If by mail, postage extra, per jar, 14 cents).......... 32c
No. 8F3111 Large size (holding three times the quantity of 50 cent jars.) Price, per two jars, $1.00; each..........(Unmailable).......... 55c

THE PRINCESS BUST DEVELOPER AND BUST CREAM OR FOOD

Regular retail price, each.............$5.00
OUR PRICE, EACH.............1.46
With one bottle Bust Developer, and one jar Bust Food FREE.

WILL ENLARGE ANY LADY'S BUST FROM 2 TO 3 INCHES. PRICE FOR DEVELOPER, BUST EXPANDER AND BUST FOOD, COMPLETE $1.46

With every order for Princess Bust Developer and Bust Food, we furnish FREE one bottle of the FAMOUS GALEGA BUST EXPANDER and TISSUE BUILDER (retail price, 50 cents) without extra charge. This developing tonic has a world wide reputation for developing the figure, rounding out the bust, perfecting and producing the firm, rounded bosom of a perfect figure.

THE PRINCESS BUST DEVELOPER

IS A NEW SCIENTIFIC HELP TO NATURE.

COMBINED WITH THE USE OF THE DEVELOPING TONIC, BUST CREAM OR FOOD, FORMS A FULL, FIRM, WELL DEVELOPED BUST. It is designed to build up and fill out shrunken and undeveloped tissues, form a rounded, plump, perfectly developed bust, producing a beautiful figure.

THE PRINCESS BUST DEVELOPER AND CREAM FOOD is absolutely harmless, easy to use, perfectly safe and considered the most successful bust developer on the market.

IF NATURE HAS NOT FAVORED YOU with that greatest charm, a symmetrically rounded bosom, full and perfect, send for the Princess Bust Developer and you will be pleased over the result of a few weeks' use. The Princess Developer will produce the desired result in nearly every case. If you are not entirely satisfied with the result after giving it a fair trial, please return it to us and we will gladly refund your money.

Unmailable on account of weight.

PRINCESS BUST DEVELOPER.
Comes in two sizes, 4 and 5 inches in diameter. State size desired. The 4-inch Developer is the most popular as well as the most desirable size.

THE DEVELOPER is carefully made of nickel and aluminum, very finest finish throughout. Comes in two sizes, 4 and 5 inches diameter. In ordering please state size desired. The developer gives the right exercise to the muscles of the bust, compels a free and normal circulation of the blood through the capillaries, glands and tissues of the flabby, undeveloped parts, these parts are soon restored to a healthy condition, they expand and fill out, become round, firm and beautiful.

THE BUST CREAM OR FOOD is applied as a massage. So many cheap and injurious bust creams are offered to the public that we have discarded every one and now handle only the original, world famous La Dore's Bust Food. This is absolutely free from injurious ingredients and is made from the purest of materials. We are pleased to offer it to our customers as a bust food unrivalled for its purity, perfume, elegance and effect. It forms just the right food required for the starved skin and wasted tissues. It is delicately perfumed and is unsurpassed for developing the bust, arms and neck, making a plump, full, rounded bosom, perfect neck and arms, a smooth skin, which before was scrawny, flat and flabby. FULL DIRECTIONS ARE FURNISHED. SUCCESS IS ASSURED. You need no longer regret that your form is not what you would like it to be. Ladies everywhere welcome the Princess Bust Developer and Cream Food as the greatest toilet requisite ever offered.

THE PRINCESS BUST DEVELOPER AND FOOD is a treatment that will when properly used for a reasonable length of time develop and enlarge the bust, cause it to fill out to full and natural proportions, give that rounded, firm bosom which belongs to a perfect symmetrical figure.

DON'T PAY an extravagant price for a so called bust developer. Be careful of the medicines and treatments offered by various irresponsible companies. Send for the Princess Developer, complete with the Bust Food and Bust Expander, at our special reduced price of $1.46, state whether you wish the 4 or 5-inch developer, and if you are not entirely satisfied with the results, if it does not meet your expectations, without the slightest harm or inconvenience, return it, after giving it a trial, and we will refund your money. Don't put off ordering. Nowhere else can you buy a Princess Bust Developer for only $1.46.

$1.46 is our Combination Price for the PRINCESS DEVELOPER, BUST FOOD and BUST EXPANDER, Complete, the Lowest Price Ever Made on this Article.

No. 8F3115 Our Princess Bust Developer, with one bottle Galega Developing Tonic and one jar La Dore's exquisite Bust Food. Price, complete. $1.46
No. 8F3117 Galega Tissue Builder, per 4-ounce bottle. Retail price, 50 cents; our price.......... .20
No. 8F3118 Galega Tissue Builder, per 16-ounce bottle. Retail price, $1.50; our price.......... .50
No. 8F3119 La Dore's Exquisite Bust Food, per 2-ounce jar. Retail price, 75 cents; our price.......... .40
No. 8F3120 La Dore's Exquisite Bust Food, per 4-ounce jar. Retail price, $1.25; our price.......... .62
No. 8F3121 La Dore's Exquisite Bust Food, per 8-ounce jar. Retail price, $2.00; our price.......... .87
No. 8F3122 La Dore's Exquisite Bust Food, per 16-ounce jar. Retail price, $3.50; our price.......... 1.42

SYRINGES AND WATER BOTTLES

ON ACCOUNT OF THE UNCERTAINTY OF THE RUBBER MARKET, THE FOLLOWING PRICES ARE SUBJECT TO MARKET CHANGE.

Utility Fountain Syringe.

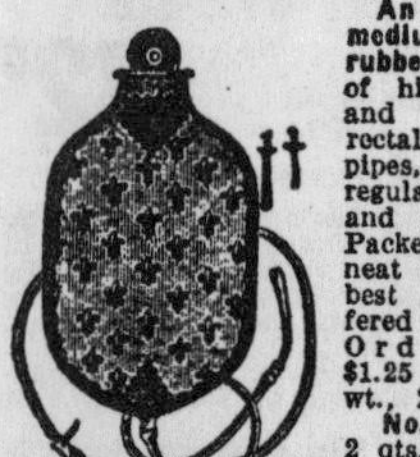

An exceptionally fine medium priced white rubber syringe. Made of high grade rubber and contains vaginal, rectal and infant slip pipes, good rubber, regular flow tubing and patent shut off. Packed complete in neat box. By far the best syringe ever offered at the price. Ordinary $1.00 to $1.25 value. Shipping wt., 21 oz.

No. 8T2313 2 qts. Our price..85c
No. 8T2314 3 qts. Our price..95c

Our Big $1.00 Leader.

A new departure in Fountain Syringes, but the latest and one of the most satisfactory for home use. The bag is made of exceptionally fine heavy white enamel instead of rubber, which enables it to be used for a lifetime with proper care. No danger of breaking, no leaking and can be washed out, boiled, cleansed and is always antiseptic. Fitted with 5½ feet of exceptionally fine rubber rapid flow tubing, newly patented hard rubber bent vaginal, infant and rectal pipes and hard rubber patented shut off. Shipping wt., 40 oz.

No. 8T2335 2 quarts. Price....$1.00
No. 8T2336 3 quarts. Price....1.10

Venus Red Rubber Syringe.

Latest design syringe, excellent material, rapid flow shape, absolutely seamless in construction, wide opening for filling, non-corrosive metal handle, and a syringe that can be hung anywhere. Five and one-half feet fine rubber tubing and infant, rectal and bent vaginal screw pipes. Patent shut off, easily regulating the flow. An excellent syringe and worth double the price asked. Packed complete in fine box and wrapped. Fully guaranteed. Retail prices, $1.75 to $2.00. Shipping wt., 21 oz.

No. 8T2325 2 quarts. Our price.$1.49
No. 8T2326 3 quarts. Our price. 1.57

Dr. Tullar Ball Spray Fountain Syringe.

SPECIAL XXX QUALITY.

New shape bag, large opening at top, easily filled and cleaned. Fitted with a patented ball spray curved vaginal douche pipe, a perfect device for spraying and cleansing the vagina, a 20-outlet straight vaginal pipe, a 3-outlet adult and infant enema pipe arranged to discharge the water obliquely and not straight like the old style rectal pipe; also 6-foot extra quick flow rubber tubing with automatic shut off. The Dr. Tullar syringe is made of the very best materials, and the newly patented pipes make it one of the very best syringes manufactured. Fully guaranteed. Furnished only in 3-quart capacity. Regular price, $3.00. Shipping wt., 21 oz.

No. 8T2332 Our price..........$2.25

Monarch Syringe and Water Bottle.

Exceptionally high grade white rubber Fountain Syringe and Water Bottle. Packed in fine hardwood case, especially adapted for home use, as the box enables all parts to be kept clean and antiseptic and always to be found when wanted. Has four hard rubber connections; namely, vaginal, rectal, irrigator and infant screw pipes, and 6 feet of pure rapid flow tubing and hard rubber combination attachment. Water bottle has reinforced seams and makes a very superior article. A large seller and a special favorite. Ordinary value, $3.00. Shipping wt., 28 oz.

No. 8T2320 2 quarts. Our price.$2.25
No. 8T2321 3 quarts. Our price. 2.35

FAIRY WHITE RUBBER LINE.

This fine line of white rubber goods is manufactured by the well known Hodgman Rubber Co. and is of exceptional quality and value. All of latest designs, heavy high grade material, proper construction, and made for service and wear. You will make no mistake in selecting any one of this well known high grade line. All fully guaranteed.

Fairy Syringe, heavy properly shaped bag, reinforced seams to prevent leaking, and rapid flow infant, rectal and bent vaginal hard rubber screw pipes. Rapid flow tubing and connections causing the bag to empty rapidly and thoroughly flush the parts desired. Regular $1.75 to $2.00 value. Shipping wt., 16 oz.

No. 8T2327 2 quarts. Our price............$1.45
No. 8T2328 3 quarts. Our price............$1.55

Fairy Water Bottle. A really first class high grade white water bottle and one that in service and appearance will please you. Fine white material, neat design, proper construction, reinforced seams. If you want a fine white water bottle, this is the one to select. Regular prices, $1.25 to $1.50.

No. 8T2398 2 quarts. Our price..............97c
No. 8T2399 3 quarts. Our price..............$1.05

Postage extra, 13c.

Fairy Combination Syringe and Water Bottle. The ideal combination for the home. Can be used alone as water bottle or with connections and tubing as a family syringe. Metal stopper connection, rapid flow tubing, three fine hard rubber screw pipes, infant, rectal and bent vaginal, and together combine the expense of water bottle and syringe at a very nominal cost. Regular prices, $2.00 to $2.25. Shipping wt., 21 oz.

No. 8T2329 2 quarts. Our price..............$1.85
No. 8T2330 3 quarts. Our price..............$1.95

HODGMAN CLOTH INSERTION LINE

OF FINE RED RUBBER GOODS

NOTE CAREFULLY THIS EXCELLENT GROUP.

THIS EXCEEDINGLY POPULAR LINE is really remarkable for its high quality, strength, general usefulness and durability. They are the latest and best products of the rubber manufacturers' skill. They have now been tested for years and have proven without doubt, to be the best wearing and most serviceable of any line ever manufactured. This cloth insertion material differs greatly from the regular rubber line. It is made of fine cloth, firmly inlaid between two layers of the finest extra quality maroon rubber, thus producing a material having all the advantages of the best rubber, together with the strength and durability added by the cloth inlaid. This line of cloth insertion goods will outwear any three of the cheaper rubber goods, and you can rest assured that it can always be depended upon when needed. You cannot possibly make a mistake in buying all or any of this trio, as your requirements demand. They will last indefinitely and the prices we name are so low that you cannot afford to be without them. All beautiful red rubber with white trimming. Fully guaranteed.

Cloth Insertion Water Bottle. A maroon colored hot water bottle that will give the service and lasting qualities of bottles costing three times as much. Practically indestructible. Handsome in appearance. Never equaled for wearing qualities and at a price within the reach of all. Retail prices, $1.75 to $2.00. Shipping wt., 16 oz.

No. 8T2400 2 quarts. Our price............$1.39
No. 8T2401 3 quarts. Our price............$1.45

Cloth Insertion Fountain Syringe and Hot Water Bottle Combined. Combines best features of the most approved style of fountain syringe together with the advantages of a durable and serviceable hot water bottle. Generous length of pure tubing, patent shut off, extra quality hard rubber pipes. Can always be depended upon. Retail prices, $2.50 to $3.00. Shipping wt., 21 oz.

No. 8T2338 2 quarts. Our price............$2.20
No. 8T2339 3 quarts. Our price............$2.27

Cloth Insertion Fountain Syringe. Latest design, rapid flow bag, 5½ feet maroon rubber tubing, infant, rectal and bent vaginal hard rubber screw pipes, patent shut off, and on the whole a very serviceable and reliable syringe. One that always gives satisfaction. Retail price, $2.00. Shipping wt., 21 oz.

No. 8T2333 2 quarts. Our price............$1.70
No. 8T2334 3 quarts. Our price............$1.80

PURE RED RUBBER LINE.

The finest, latest and most up to date line of red rubber goods it is possible to manufacture. The very best that money, excellent material and skill have been able to produce. Every article beautiful in appearance, excellent in quality and, although higher in price than most other lines, is well worth the difference.

Alpha Red Rubber Syringe. In our opinion the finest syringe made. No description can do it justice. Seamless in construction, consequently cannot leak. By reason of its shape, will empty quicker than any other syringe made. Three hard rubber, highest polished and finest manufactured pipes and rapid flow tubing. A beauty, and worth double the price quoted. Furnished only in 3-quart capacity. Regular prices, $3.00 to $3.50. Shipping wt., 21 oz.

No. 8T2341 Our price.........$2.45

Red Rubber Combination Syringe. This combination of hot water bottle and family syringe for home use comprises a fine red rubber bottle, three hard rubber exceptionally highly polished and finest grade pipes manufactured, a liberal length of pure red gum tubing and metal stopper connection. With proper care it should last for years. Regular price, $2.75 to $3.00. Shipping wt., 14 oz.

No. 8T2343 2 quarts. Our price..........$2.29
No. 8T2344 3 quarts. Our price..........$2.35

Red Rubber Water Bottle. Same as above, without tubing and pipes.

No. 8T2404 2 quarts..........$1.59
No. 8T2405 3 quarts..........$1.65

Family Water Bottle.

This is an exceptionally good low priced water bottle and is great value at the price quoted. It is made of heavy white ribbed rubber and is a bottle that with ordinary wear should last a year. While this is as good a bottle as can be obtained elsewhere for anywhere near this price, we by all means suggest that you buy as good a grade bottle as your means will allow. In rubber goods especially it pays to buy the best. Regular $1.00 value.

No. 8T2388 2 quarts. Our price..79c
No. 8T2389 3 quarts. Our price..87c

If mail shipment, postage extra, 12 cents.

Flannel Covered Water Bottle.

The Comet Flannel Covered Water Bottle is too well known to need extended description. It is the standard flannel covered water bottle of the day. The cover is of the very finest soft flannel, which makes the water bottle soft on the skin, prevents burning and will not irritate the most delicate skin. The rubber is of exceptional quality and this flannel covered bottle is guaranteed in every respect. Regular retail price, $1.25.

No. 8T2385 2 quarts. Our price.$1.00
No. 8T2386 3 quarts. Our price. 1.10

If mail shipment, postage extra, 11 cents.

High Grade Maroon Water Bottle.

This High Grade Maroon Water Bottle is handsome in appearance, of highest quality and made of the very finest heavy maroon ribbed rubber. Absolutely full capacity and a bottle that with ordinary care will last for years. Special double reinforced seams and without doubt the best value and highest grade rubber bottle at the price quoted. This is the genuine Maroon Bottle and at a price within the reach of all. You will make no mistake by selecting this bottle. Each in fine box. Shipping wt., 14 oz.

No. 8T2406 2 quarts. Price....$1.50
No. 8T2407 3 quarts. Price....1.60

Faultless Never Leak Water Bottle.

AS GOOD AS MONEY CAN BUY.

Very latest and up to date bottle made. Handsome in appearance, being made of pure gum red rubber; absolutely seamless in construction, consequently cannot leak. Perfectly sanitary, with wide opening for filling. Covers a larger surface when filled than any other water bottle made, thus giving a more uniform application of heat, which point particularly is a marked advantage. Practically indestructible; just as the name indicates, faultless in every particular. The kind you will be pleased to show and recommend to your friends. No description can do this bottle justice. Should be in every home. Regular price, $2.50. Shipping wt., 16 oz.

No. 8T2408 Our price..........$1.59

Our 73-Cent Ideal Syringe.

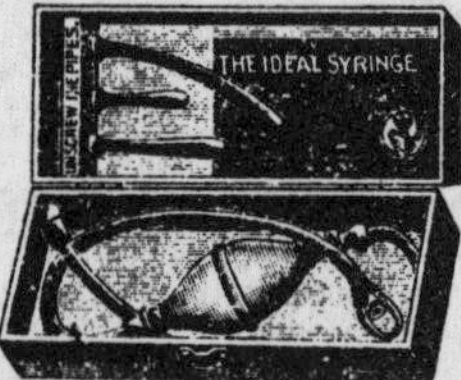

A bulb syringe covering every requirement of the home. Fine grade white rubber bulb and tubing fitted with bent vaginal, rectal and infant pipes. Put up in a neat polished wooden box. A very useful and exceedingly reasonable household necessity. This item being for personal use cannot, if once used, be returned for credit. Ordinary $1.00 value.

No. 8T2340 Our price............73c

If mail shipment, postage extra, 12 cents.

Imperial Combination Syringe and Water Bottle.

Guaranteed full capacity. This fine medium priced red rubber Combination Syringe and Water Bottle is an exceptional bargain. Made of fine soft red rubber, double reinforced seams and contains three hard rubber rapid flow slip pipes and ¼ inch rapid flow tubing with combination attachment. Ordinary value, $2.00. Shipping wt., 21 oz.

No. 8T2315 2 quarts. Our price.$1.69
No. 8T2316 3 quarts. Our price. 1.75

Rubber Tubing.

No. 8T2189 Corrugated, for bulb and fountain syringes. A very high grade red rubber tubing. Price, per 5½-foot length........**35c**
Postage extra, 15 cents.

Acme Tooth Forceps.

A Universal Tooth Forceps for home use. Will fit all teeth. The same instrument as used by dentists. Can be used for extracting with ease all children's teeth and save all dentist's fees. Finely nickel plated.
No. 8T2190 Price..............**$1.11**
If mail shipment, postage extra, 7 cents.

Air Pillows.
Fancy Sateen Covering.

This new shape Air Pillow is indeed very popular. Can be folded into a small space when not used and can be blown to the size of an ordinary pillow at a moment's notice. Is always antiseptic and affords at all times an exceedingly soft and very restful pillow. Largely used today by campers, travelers, persons sleeping out of doors, invalids, etc. With proper care will last for years. This is the genuine Hodgman pillow, guaranteed the best made. Much better than the old fashioned three-division pillow.
No. 8T2425 Size, 10x16 in. Price.**$2.59**
No. 8T2426 Size, 12x18 in. Price. **2.98**
If mail shipment, postage extra, 18 cents.

Seamless Para Rubber Gloves.

Largely used for wear while sleeping for bleaching and whitening the hands, wrists and arms. They are used to remove wrinkles, tan, sallowness, freckles and discoloration of the skin. With care they will last for years. Made of the **pure transparent rubber,** same as face mask. **Order one size larger than your kid glove number.**
No. 8T2494 Price, per pair.......**95c**
If mail shipment, postage extra, per pair, 6c.

Famous Venus Household Red Rubber Gloves.

89c

One of the very best and highest grade household gloves made. Never waste time and money on the cheap kinds. It pays to buy the best. If you ever wash dishes, scrub floors, develop photographic negatives, wash windows, trim plants, work in the garden, dye any fabrics, blacken stoves, do a hundred and one other household duties, then for your hands' sake buy a pair of Venus Red Rubber Gloves. They keep the hands soft and white and are unequaled for ladies' use in doing general housework. They are strong, soft and pliable and can be worn without the slightest inconvenience in doing work of the most delicate nature. Every pair fully guaranteed. Order one size larger than your kid glove number. These gloves are one of the best produced. Follow closely the directions for keeping them clean found on cover of each box. Especially note effect of oil and grease. Remember, gloves are sold at all prices, from 25 cents a pair up. These are the best and will outwear a dozen pairs of the cheaper kinds. Regular price, $1.25 per pair.
No. 8T2496 Our price, per pair...**89c**
If mail shipment, postage extra, per pair, 10c.

Venus Sanitary Protector.

No woman who values comfort, cleanliness and health can possibly be without this supporter. Perfect in fit. Safe in use. Waterproof, cleanly and antiseptic. This protector is made of a transparent India rubber sack which is very soft and pliable and also very strong. This sack readily admits a napkin or any other soft substance like cheesecloth or cotton and will hold it securely in the proper position. The belt is made of the very best lisle, non-elastic. The sack is fastened to belt by means of snap buckles, which afford much easier fastening and adjustment than the old fashioned kind. It is perfectly sanitary, comfortable, pliable and non-irritating; easily adjusted and readjusted and indispensable to women walking, riding or traveling. Always clean and ready for use. Feels cool in summer and protects the wearer from cold in winter. This protector will save many times its cost in washing and bleaching. **In ordering give waist measure.** Regular price, $1.00.

45c

No. 8T2466 Our price..........**45c**
If mail shipment, postage extra, 3 cents.

Invalid Air Cushions.
Genuine Hodgman Cloth Insertion.

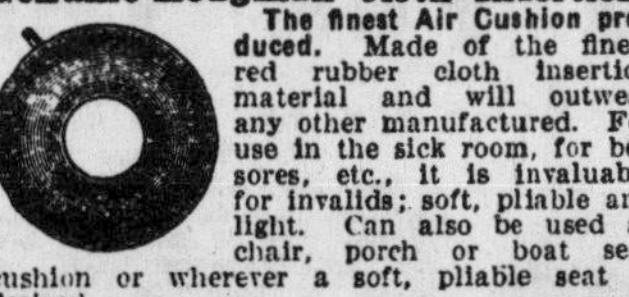

The finest Air Cushion produced. Made of the finest red rubber cloth insertion material and will outwear any other manufactured. For use in the sick room, for bed sores, etc., it is invaluable for invalids; soft, pliable and light. Can also be used as chair, porch or boat seat cushion or wherever a soft, pliable seat is desired.

		Price
No. 8T2420	12 inches diameter.	**$1.83**
No. 8T2421	14 inches diameter.	**2.17**
No. 8T2422	16 inches diameter.	**2.59**

If mail shipment, postage extra, 20 cents.

Beauty Complexion Bulb.

23c

Very beneficial for filling out the hollow of the cheeks and making them plump and rosy. One of the latest devices for massage and complexion purposes and freeing the face of blackheads, flesh worms and objectionable accumulations. The face should be thoroughly bathed in as hot water as possible and while still moist and warm use the complexion bulb for five minutes. Very popular. You will be greatly surprised at the good results. Regular price, 50 cents.
No. 8T2458 Our price...........**23c**
If mail shipment, postage extra, 2 cents.

Beauty Complexion Brush.
Worth Double the Cheaper Kind.

33c

It is especially constructed for improving the complexion and removing all forms of facial blemishes. It removes all roughness and dead cuticle, smoothing out the wrinkles, rendering the skin soft, pliant and tinted with a healthy glow; also admirably adapted for use in the bath and for wet or dry massage of the face, neck and arms. The most thorough, most sanitary and most efficient way to clean the pores of the skin is by using the well known oval shaped red rubber toilet and beauty brush. It is designed especially for this purpose, has just the right texture to soften the dirt and coax it out from its hiding places without irritating the most delicate skin. This is not the cheap kind often offered at a cheaper price, which is made square of black rubber, and a few days after use loses the teeth and becomes worthless. **Remember, your complexion is at stake, therefore buy the best.** Regular price, 50 cents.
No. 8T2460 Our price...........**33c**
If mail shipment, postage extra, 3 cents.

Famous H. & H. Pneumatic, Air Retaining Bust Forms.
Pin punctures have no effect.

Nature's Only Rival.
The only bust form made which defies detection.

Superbly Stylish, Healthful, Strikingly Lifelike, Light, Cool and Comfortable.
Durable, Economical, Cleanly, a revelation to all refined and well dressed women.

They give a fit and finish to the toilet that feminine beauty counts as one of its chief charms. If a woman is deficient in natural development it is impossible for her to appear well dressed, to meet the requirements of fashion and style, without artificial aid. She simply must adopt some means to gain the proper contour.

The celebrated H. & H. Pneumatic, Air Retaining Bust Forms are now so perfect that they cannot be detected from the natural bust, whether by sight or touch. Strikingly stylish, a source of relief, delight and pride to the wearer and of admiration to others. Very durable, economic and hygienic. These forms do away with all unsightly, unhealthy and uncomfortable padding. They produce perfectly the fashionable full bust and slender waist. Positively the only device which perfectly simulates flesh and blood. Applied in an instant; made of white rubber, invisible with any costume; neither sight nor touch reveals their use. They accurately fit the form, are enclosed in fine muslin cover, lace trimmed, cannot get out of place, and can be made any desired size. **Be admired.** A fine form is admired by all. Why then wear heavy pads, wire forms or be flat chested, all of which are unnatural, disgusting and unhealthy and plainly detected when so natural a form as this is within your reach? Light as air and takes all the motions of the body.
No. 8T2475 Celebrated H. & H. round shape ventilated bust form, absolutely sanitary, can be adjusted to fit any figure.
Price **$1.35**
No. 8T2476 Price, oblong form, which fills out the hollows under the arm and more like natural bust.....................**$1.81**
No. 8T2478 Same as No. 8T2475 with valve so same can be inflated with air to any desired size. Pin punctures will have no effect. Price..........................**$1.81**
No. 8T2479 Same style as No. 8T2476 with valve so same can be inflated to any desired size. Pin punctures will have no effect. Our price..........................**$2.29**
If mail shipment, postage extra, 8 cents.

Wrinkle Eradicator.

This convenient little article is made of heavy glass bowl 1-inch diameter, and rubber bulb. It is used after creams are applied to the face for removing wrinkles from around the eyes and nose and any part of the face. It invigorates the skin and keeps a perfect contour of the face. Regular price, 50 cents.
No. 8T2485 Our price............**22c**
If mail shipment, postage extra, 6 cents.

Flesh Builder and Cupper.

Same as the above but 1½-inch diameter glass. Much better for cheek, neck and bust massage than the smaller size above.
No. 8T2490 Our price............**22c**
If mail shipment, postage extra, 9 cents.

Toilet and Complexion Mask.
Art of Beautifying the Complexion.

Many ladies praise the value of a mask made of **pure transparent rubber,** for the removal of freckles, liver spots and other facial blemishes. **It is safe, simple, cleanly and effective for beautifying purposes, and never injures the most delicate complexion.** Usually sold for $5.00. We carry only the genuine, guaranteed not to injure the face. Beware of cheap imitations offered by others at less prices, and when received have no manufacturer's name upon the package. Made in three sizes, small, medium and large. **Always state size desired.**
No. 8T2492 Price..............**$1.00**
If mail shipment, postage extra, 4 cents.

Soft Rubber Urinal Bags.
FOR MEN, WOMEN, BOYS AND GIRLS.

For bed wetting and general incontinence of urine. For male and female, children and adults. For day and night use. **Consult your family physician before ordering, that you may purchase the proper article, because Soft Rubber Urinal Bags are for personal use and cannot be returned for credit after leaving our store. We cannot offer for sale articles of this character which have or may have been used. This is for your protection as well as our own.**

Safety Pure Gum Male Urinal Bag.
For Day or Night Use.

The best Male Urinal Bag made. Pure red rubber and much better and higher grade than the cheaper inferior kinds. The top can be removed for day use if desired, and the two combined for night use. Is fitted with special double valve and inner tube, thereby preventing return flow of urine. The long slender receptacle when worn during the day can never be detected. The only perfectly satisfactory male urinal bag on the market. Be sure to buy this bag. This is the one where the top fits next to the body and not the one with the opening upward. Note top of illustration. Regular price, $3.50.
No. 8T2450 Our price...........**$2.89**
If mail shipment, postage extra, 10 cents.

Safety Inner Tube Pure Gum Rubber Female Urinal Bag.

This Urinal Bag is constructed for day and night use, for women only, and is fitted with double valve and inner tube to prevent the return flow of the urine. This is the only urinal bag on the market for female use that can be guaranteed to prove entirely satisfactory for both day and night use. An absolutely safe female urinal. Urinals being employed for personal use cannot be returned. This is your protection as well as our own. Consult your physician before ordering. Regular price, $4.50.
No. 8T2451 Our price..........**$3.25**
If mail shipment, postage extra, 10 cents.

Soft Rubber Urinal Bag, the most comfortable pattern made, of the best material, for male, day or night use. The short bag fits closely and strap around limb holds bag in place. Consult your physician before ordering. Regular price, $2.50.
No. 8T2453 Our price...**$1.89**
No. 8T2454 Short, for boys **1.79**
Postage extra, 8 cents.

No. 8T2456 Soft Rubber Urinal Bag for day use for male; improved French pattern, with waist belt ready to use without other attachments. Very desirable pattern, as top part holds entire scrotum. Consult your physician before ordering. Regular price, $3.50.
Our price.............**$2.95**
Postage extra, 20 cents.

Rectal Ointment Pipe.

Especially constructed for applying healing ointments to the rectum in the treatment of piles, etc. Made of polished hard rubber, hollow center and with screw top connection.
No. 8T2193 Price..................**33c**
If mail shipment, postage extra, 3 cents.

Hair Growing Fountain Comb.

For applying hair tonics, eau de quinine, bleaches, etc. The comb being hollow and with pressure on the bulb the liquid will flow through the teeth to the scalp applying the remedy to the roots of the hair where it will do the most good. The use of the comb will prevent getting tonic all through hair unless it is desired to do so. You can apply the tonic rapidly and thoroughly without soiling the hands or badly ruffling up the hair. Every lady will appreciate this advantage. The comb may be used for applying bleaches to the hair by spraying. Packed complete in neat case with full directions for using.
No. 8T2465 Fountain Comb. Price.**75c**
If mail shipment, postage extra, 8 cents.

Wonder Values in Atomizers.

Very good low priced Atomizer. Hard rubber atomizer tip, white rubber bulb and glass bowl. Can be used for oil or water. 50-cent value.
No. 8T2650 Our price........**39c**
If mail shipment, postage extra, 13 cents.

Two-Tip Atomizer. Sprays oil or water continuously. Hard rubber atomizer tip that screws into the bowl, large bulb, glass bowl. Has two interchangeable tips for nose and throat troubles. 75-cent value.
No. 8T2651 Our price..........**59c**
If mail shipment, postage extra, 15 cents.

Three-Tip Hard Rubber Atomizer. A very good instrument and can be used for oil or water. Throws continuous spray. Has three interchangeable tips for reaching the various parts of nose and throat. $1.00 value.
No. 8T2652
Our price.........................**69c**
If mail shipment, postage extra, 15 cents.

Genuine Emmet Smith Atomizer. The best known and most reliable. A decided improvement over other atomizers in that it throws a much finer and better spray and is of metal construction, beautifully nickel plated. Applies oil or water liquids to the entire nasal or throat cavities without force and with equal distribution. If you want the best, buy this.
No. 8T2653
Our price..**$1.00**
If mail shipment, postage extra, 14c.

Enameled Bed Pan.

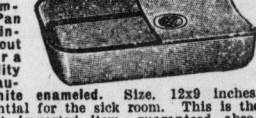

This beautifully finished Enameled Bed Pan is made inside and out of extra fine quality metal, beautifully white enameled. Size, 12x9 inches. Very essential for the sick room. This is the very finest imported item, guaranteed absolutely free from all poisonous materials. There are many grades of enameled ware on the market offered at cheaper prices, but this is the best manufactured. It pays to buy the best. Regular price, $2.00. Unmailable.
No. 8T2194 Our price..........**$1.25**

Double Bed and Douche Pan.

Enameled inside and out with four coats extra heavy white enamel and will wear a lifetime. Size, 11x3x15½ inches. This is the very finest imported item, guaranteed absolutely free from all poisonous materials. There are many grades of enameled ware on the market offered at cheaper prices, but this is the best manufactured. It pays to buy the best.
No. 8T2195 Price..(Unmailable)..**$1.49**

Fischer Bunion Protector.

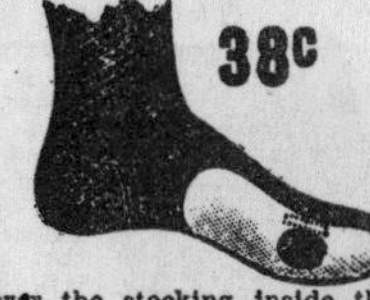

38c

Fits all feet, relieves pain instantly; cures bunions permanently, and keeps shoes in shape. Perfect comfort guaranteed. The Fischer Bunion Protector is a neat, soft leather device that goes over the stocking inside the shoe. It forms a firm wall all around the bunion, keeps it completely housed and protected. The ends of the protector are soft and pliable and fit easily over the shank and toe. Once used you would never be without them. It relieves pain instantly. It effects an absolute and permanent cure. Fits any foot and can be worn with perfect comfort. **In ordering, give size of shoe and whether right or left.** Regular price, 50 cents.
No. 8T2525 Ladies' right..............**38c**
No. 8T2526 Ladies' left...............**38c**
No. 8T2527 Men's right...............**38c**
No. 8T2528 Men's left.................**38c**
If mail shipment, postage extra, 4 cents.

EVERYTHING FOR THE BABY

Sterilized Rubber Sheeting.

Not the Cheapest but the Best. It Pays to Buy the Best.

A high class Steam Sterilized Nursery Sheeting. Cleanly, absolutely waterproof, strong, antiseptic and ready for immediate use for hospitals and nursery purposes. This is not the cheap grade usually sold for a slightly cheaper price, but is the best we can buy. This you can depend upon and will give you the service you desire. Steam sterilized, carefully wrapped and packed. The only sheeting offered where same is cleanly and steam sterilized. Cut in squares of assorted sizes and packed one square in a box. A very superior article. It pays to buy the best.

No. 8T2183 Square, ¾x¾ yd...$0.39
No. 8T2184 Square, 1x1 yd..... .63
No. 8T2184½ Piece, 1x2 yd...... 1.09
No. 8T2185 Square, 1¼x1¼ yd. 1.00
No. 8T2185½ Square, 1½x1½ yd. 1.39
No. 8T2186 Tan cambric coated with pure rubber, soft as silk, finest made, 1 yard square 84c
No. 8T2186½ Piece tan, 1x2 yds. Price (Postage extra, per yard, 18c.) $1.49

O-M-O Nursery Sheeting.

A very fine grade of snow white waterproof Sheeting. Beautiful in appearance, healthful in composition and largely used for making babies' bibs, infants' waterproof panties for slipping over diapers, for keeping infant dry and clean, and as a covering for baby's place at table. Pliable, light weight and easily cleansed.

No. 8T2187 Square, 1x1 yard. Our price $1.19
No. 8T2188 Square, 1¼x1¼ yards. Our price $1.39
If mail shipment, postage extra, 22 cents.

Absorbent Cotton.

This is the genuine Johnson & Johnson Red Cross Absorbent Cotton. Clean, pure, sterile and absorbent. Packed in a convenient aseptic container from which any quantity may be removed without contaminating the remainder. The finest, softest and purest absorbent cotton manufactured.

No. 8T2721 1-pound package. Price 39c
No. 8T2722 ½-pound package. Price 21c
Unmailable on account of weight.

Sterilized Gauze.

This is the genuine B. & B. Aseptic Sterilized Gauze. The materials used are especially selected. It is manufactured under the very latest conditions and the utmost care and attention given to every detail. This gauze is guaranteed to be absolutely sterile, eliminating every possible source of infection. It is very necessary when using items of this nature that the very best be employed and we carry none except this exceptionally high grade material. A few cents' difference in price may mean the life of the person upon whom it is used. Therefore, buy the very best and run no risk. Packed in antiseptic sterilized airproof carton ready for immediate use.

No. 8T2725 5 yards plain Sterilized Gauze in carton. Price........43c
Unmailable on account of weight.

Graduated Nursing Flasks.

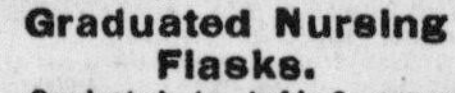

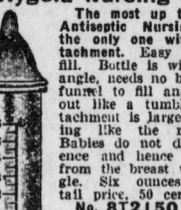

Graduated to hold 8 ounces, oval shape, straight with sloping sides. No corners, therefore easy to clean. Weight, 14 ounces. Weight makes it unprofitable by mail.

No. 8T2144 Price.......5c
No. 8T2146 Bent neck flask. Price........5c

Bottle Cleaning Brush.

Curved end, wooden handle. Just the brush for cleaning nursing bottles; will reach all corners. 11 inches long.

No. 8T2148 Price........8c
If mail shipment, postage extra, 2 cents.

Hygeia Nursing Bottles.

The most up to date, cleanly, Antiseptic Nursing Bottle, and the only one with a breast attachment. Easy to clean and fill. Bottle is without a neck or angle, needs no brush to clean or funnel to fill and can be wiped out like a tumbler. Rubber attachment is large, soft and yielding like the mother's breast. Babies do not detect the difference and hence can be weaned from the breast without a struggle. Six ounces capacity. Retail price, 50 cents.

No. 8T2150 Our price, bottle, complete........25c
No. 8T2151 Extra breasts or bottles can be supplied. Price 14c
Unmailable.

S., R. & Co.'s Complete Nurser.

No. 8T2153 S., R. and Co.'s Nurser. Fitted with good seamless nipples. Complete with bottle brush in box. Price 14c
Unmailable.

Sterilized Antiseptic Nipple.

Made of the very best material, absolutely pure gum, and by far the very best nipple ever manufactured. Each one is sterilized and packed in airproof gelatine capsule so as to keep it perfectly free from all disease germs or other contamination. By using these nipples received in this condition, you need have no fear of giving your baby any disease.

No. 8T2138 Price........9c
If mail shipment, postage extra, 2 cents.

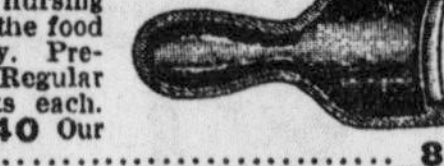

Mizpah Valve Nipple. Making nursing easy. Allows the food to flow easily. Prevents colic. Regular price, 10 cents each.

No. 8T2140 Our price, each........8c
Per dozen........75c
Postage extra, per doz., 8 cents; each, 2 cents.

For Cheaper Nipples see 7-cent Bargain Pages.

Glass Nipple Shield.

Glass Nipple Shield with white rubber nipple and bone guard.

No. 8T2160 Price.......8c
Unmailable.

Teething Rings.

New style Teething Ring and Pacifier. Best nipple, bone ring, silk cord tassel ends. The best made.

No. 8T2122 Price.9c
If mail shipment, postage extra, 2 cents.

Combination Teething Ring and Pacifier with Bell. Has rubber ring, bone attachment, best rubber nipple and bell. Amuses the baby.

No. 8T2126 Price........8c
If mail shipment, postage extra, 2 cents.

Job's Tear Necklace and Pacifier.

The old reliable kind used by your mothers. No danger of nipple dropping on the floor.

No. 8T2123 Price.8c
If mail shipment, postage extra, 2 cents.

The Whistling Bird Rattle and Pacifier.

This Rattle is made of pure white rubber, and will amuse and entertain the baby. It has a teething ring at handle end, making it doubly valuable. Regular price, 15 cents.

No. 8T2128 Our price. 10c
Postage extra, 2 cents.

Eye, Ear and Ulcer Syringe.

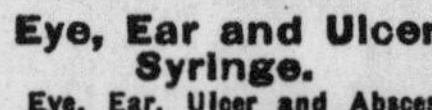

Eye, Ear, Ulcer and Abscess Syringe. Capacity, 1 ounce; injection pipe is made of soft and flexible rubber. Will not injure or pain the inflamed parts. Regular price, 25 cents.

No. 8T2380 Our price. 19c
If mail shipment, postage extra, 3 cents.

Infants' Syringe.

Infants' Syringe. Holds 1 ounce and is made of a soft rubber bulb, with hard rubber infants' rectal pipe. Regular price, 25 cents.

No. 8T2382 Our price........19c
If mail shipment, postage extra, 5 cents.

English Breast Pump.

English Breast Pump, with white rubber bulb. A good medium priced article. One in box. Regular price, 35 cents.

No. 8T2172 Our price 25c

A much better pump, with fine red rubber bulb. Packed in box. Regular 50-cent value.

No. 8T2173 Our price 39c
If mail shipment, postage extra, 8 cents.

Swansdown Puffs.

Fine Powder Puffs for ladies' and infants' use. Satin tops, ivory handle, genuine fine down. The nicest way of evenly distributing powder over the baby.

No. 8T2175 Price, 25-cent size...18c
No. 8T2176 Price, 15-cent size...10c
If mail shipment, postage extra, 2 cents.

Puff Boxes.

Celluloid, in ivory, pink or blue. The best means of keeping baby's powder clean and handy. Box is the largest size and will also hold the puff. **Be sure to state color wanted.** Very light and handsome.

No. 8T2181 Price..43c
Postage extra, 8 cents.

Infants' Celluloid Sets.

Two-Piece Set. Composed of an exceptionally fine white goat's hair celluloid brush and a fine tooth infants' comb with handle. Packed in a two-part compartment box and makes a very handy and useful gift. Size of box, 5x3x1¾ inches. Furnished in pink, blue or ivory. **State color wanted.** Ordinary value, 75 cents.

No. 8T1776 Our price........39c
If mail shipment, postage extra, 5 cents.

Three-Piece Set. This beautiful set comprises an exceptionally fine white goat's hair infants' brush, fine tooth infants' comb with handle, and a twisted handle celluloid rattle. Very tastefully tied on dispaly card with fancy white baby ribbon. A very acceptable and pleasing gift. Furnished in pink, blue or ivory. **State color wanted.** Size of box, 8½x6x2¼ inches. Ordinary value, 85 cents to $1.00.

No. 8T1777 Our price........57c
If mail shipment, postage extra, 7 cents.

Extra value Baby Toilet Set. This is an exceptional bargain. Comprises every requisite needed for an infant. It contains a very fine long white goat's hair celluloid handled brush, a fine tooth celluloid comb with handle, a beautifully colored rattle, telescope soap box, and a powder or talcum box. Every part carefully packed in separate compartment and the outfit makes an exceptionally fine gift. Ordinary value, $1.25 to $1.50.

No. 8T1778 Our price........$1.00
If mail shipment, postage extra, 15 cents.

Holdem Baby Strap.

In go-cart, chair or anywhere, it holds the baby safely there. Just what every mother is looking for. No danger of slipping out or falling. May be quickly and easily fastened anywhere and adjustable to any position. Regular price, 50 cents.

No. 8T2160 Our price........23c
If mail shipment, postage extra, 3 cents.

Baby Talcum Powders.

Colgate's Violet Talcum Powder. Probably the best known and one of the finest made. Fine imported talcum, sweetly perfumed and carefully made. Regular 25-cent can.

No. 8T2105 Our price, 3 cans for........45c
If mail shipment, postage extra, 15 cents.

Mennen's Talcum Powder. The oldest and the standard of all. Just as good and sweet as ever. Soft on baby's skin and also refreshing. Fine after baby's bath and to prevent chafing. Sold everywhere for 25 cents.

No. 8T2107 Our price, 3 cans for........45c
If mail shipment, postage extra, 15 cents.

Regal Violet Talcum Powder. A very fine imported talcum, sweetly violet perfumed, very soft and fluffy. Borated and antiseptic. Regular price, 25 cents per can.

No. 8T2108 Our price, 6 cans for........59c
If mail shipment, postage extra, 30 cents.

Jergen's Rose Talcum Powder. Large 1-pound can, filled with the best imported Italian talcum, rose perfumed and carefully borated to make it antiseptic. The prettiest can ever shown. Beautifully polished sprinkler screw top, and the proper size can for nursery use. Big 50-cent value.

No. 8T2109 Our price. 23c
If mail shipment, postage extra, 18 cents.

NOTE—For Cheaper Talcum Powders see 7-cent Bargain Pages, Catalog Nos. 8T7100 and 8T7119.

Infants' Baskets.

Imported white willow Infants' Basket, made of white straw reinforced with white straw edge. Beautifully interwoven with colored strands. Size, 12x16x5 inches. Open edge at top for fancy decorating. Fancy tufted satin lined. Not the cheap satin lined basket but the best. Regular $1.50 value.

No. 8T2130 Our price........$1.00
Not profitable mail shipment.

Infants' Basket, same size as above, but not lined and made of white straw and willow throughout. Regular 75-cent to $1.00 value.

No. 8T2131 Our price........57c
Not profitable mail shipment.

Baby Bath Sponge.

Fine soft Silk Sponge for baby's bath. This is the sponge to use.

No. 8T2132 Price 25c
If mail shipment, postage extra, 2 cents.

Imported Castile Soap.

Especially Imported Spanish Olive Oil Castile Soap. The finest, absolutely pure and the one soap that all mothers should use for baby's bath. 1½-pound bars. Shipping weight, 25 ounces.

No. 8T2133 Price........35c

Leather Stork Bag.

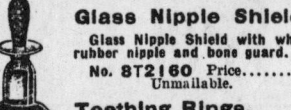

Every young mother should have one. Made of extra fine soft leather, with silk draw strings. Large opening bag containing a rubber lined diaper bag which can be removed for cleaning at any time. Outside pocket used for milk bottles or whatever desired. Double stitched leather handles and large enough to slip over arm. Size bag, 10x19 inches. Sells on sight.

No. 8T2134 Price........$1.89
If mail shipment, postage extra, 12 cents.

For Rattles see 7-cent Bargain Pages.

STEEL FRAME BATH CABINETS.

NOTE. We no longer handle the old fashioned cheap wood frame cabinets. They were used years ago before a steel cabinet could be made, but today are old-fashioned and in our opinion nowhere near as good as a steel frame. Most wood frames are clumsy, warp with steam, break easily, occupy much more room, and are much cheaper to make than the up to date steel frame cabinet. Do you want a few wooden slats nailed together or an up to date steel constructed frame? We are proud to say we do not handle old wood frame cabinets.

THE VAPOR BATH is a very reliable means for effectively opening the pores of the skin and causing proper elimination of the poisons and waste matter present. The kidneys and liver get new life and activity, the blood becomes purified, the digestive organs improve, the nerves become strengthened and the health of the person improves from the very first.

WITH A STEAM CABINET you can take a Turkish bath in the privacy of your own home just before retiring, consequently there is no exposure afterward. You avoid any danger from this source and also save much valuable time and have the bath ready for immediate use when most needed, save the expense of public baths, and, most important of all, breathe the fresh air while bathing, air not polluted with poisons exhaled from others.

IF YOU DESIRE a home treatment for opening the pores of the skin, for producing a clear, beautiful complexion, a perfect skin, a healthy body, in short, if you want perfect health buy a good bath cabinet. It is an investment you will never regret. We carry three grades of bath cabinets, depending upon the covering material and appliances desired, as follows:

PEERLESS BATH CABINET, $3.25.

THE PEERLESS BATH CABINET represents the best low priced cabinet. It is a four-wall rubber lined room fitted with galvanized steel wire frame. Size cabinet, 28x30½x42 inches. The coating is the best rubber lined muslin. We, however, will sell you this genuine Peerless Bath Cabinet for $3.25 complete with alcohol heater and vaporizing pan. While the Peerless is the best low priced cabinet made, it can in no way compare with our higher priced ones in efficiency, wear and durability. Weight, boxed, 40 pounds. Regular price, $5.00.

No. 8T4000 Peerless Bath Cabinet. Price **$3.25**

OUR LEADER BATH CABINET, $4.75.

With complete book, "THE GUIDE BOOK TO HEALTH AND BEAUTY," furnished free.

OUR SPECIAL LEADER CABINET is made of the very best material and made on the most scientific principles. It is a cabinet large enough to enable you to take a foot bath while you are taking a Turkish bath. The top of the Leader Cabinet is in two pieces. The Leader top is a very great convenience in entering as well as in cooling off. The construction of our Leader Cabinet is most substantial. The covering is of special cabinet material (rubber coating inside, checked drill outside) that never stretches, thoroughly vapor-proof. The frame is of the best steel construction, and, unlike old fashioned wood frames, does not warp or break. In cooling off, both sides of the top may be unbuttoned and thrown back. The whole cabinet is so jointed and hinged that it can be put away in the smallest possible space. When you have finished using the cabinet, simply loosen the braces, tip the frame and it folds up completely. Any child can open and close it in a minute. Shipping wt., 40 lbs. Regular price, $7.50.

No. 8T4005 Leader Bath Cabinet. Our price.. **$4.75**

THE HIGHEST GRADE PERFECTION BATH CABINET, $7.25.

FOR $7.25 we offer the highest grade bath cabinet of the celebrated Perfection grade as the very finest and highest grade bath cabinet made. There is no better bath cabinet construction possible.

OUR $7.25 BATH CABINET is constructed with double walls of the best rubber coated material that can be made, everlasting and always new. The construction of our special $7.25 cabinet is without doubt the best ever shown.

FACE STEAMER FREE. A celebrated Perfection Face Steamer, improved style, as shown in illustration below, will be included with each Perfection Bath Cabinet free. For treatment of the complexion the Perfection Face Steamer is one of the most important parts of a vapor bath cabinet. If same is wanted with other cabinets, price is $1.00 extra.

VAPOR BATHS are great for blood and skin diseases. For rheumatism and neuralgia, chronic, acute or inflammatory, our vapor baths have been known to benefit where everything else had failed to give relief. You'll be surprised and delighted at the improvement in your health, feelings and complexion. Weight, boxed, 40 pounds. Retail price, $12.00.

No. 8T4010 Perfection Bath Cabinet. Our price (without metal bath stool, as illustrated) **$7.25**

CANE SEAT CHAIRS or ordinary kitchen chairs can be employed in taking vapor baths in these cabinets. Customers wishing to order the fancy wire metal stool illustrated above can get the same from us at our very low price.

No. 8T4011 Wire Metal Vapor Bath Stool. Price **$1.45**

ADJUSTABLE BEDSIDE AND UTILITY TABLE.

A COMFORT IN HEALTH; A BLESSING IN SICKNESS.

The most useful piece of furniture ever manufactured. It can not only be used in the greatest number of ways and readily conveyed from one place to another, but will harmonize with the most artistic surroundings wherever located. It can be set up in a moment at any desired height or angle and projects over the bed without touching it, leaving patient free to move body and limbs without upsetting the dishes. It is mounted on casters and can be moved to any place or adjusted to any position required. This table is not a novelty, but a necessity at all seasons of the year. It is strong in construction, the proportions are correct and the lines are light and graceful. Will be found very convenient for writing, reading, games, drawing, music stand, sewing table, back rest, child's dining table, bedside table and a hundred other uses. When not in use can be folded up, thereby occupying but little floor space. Each table packed for shipment in a single box. Weight packed for shipment, 35 pounds.

No. 8T3895 Adjustable Bedside and Utility Table. Black enamel metal parts, with a golden oak hand rubbed oil finished top, 18x24 inches. Price **$3.45**

ADJUSTABLE ROCKER TRUCK

A fine medium priced appliance for fastening on rocker of chair enabling invalids to be wheeled about at will and affording them ease, fresh air and comfort. Made of ½-inch square steel axle with drop part for rocker. The wheels are 8 inches high with ¾-inch rubber tires. Adjustable to fit any rocking chair. More real pleasure for an invalid for $4.00 than you ever before thought possible. Weight, packed for shipment, 10 pounds.

No. 8T5304 Regular price, $6.00; our price...... **$4.00**

INVALID CHAIRS AT PRICES WITHIN THE REACH OF ALL.

MORE COMFORT AND PLEASURE FOR ALL INVALIDS FOR LESS MONEY THAN EVER BEFORE THOUGHT POSSIBLE.

SPECIAL CATALOG FREE.

We have for years carefully studied the wants and requirements of invalids, and realize that the important requirements of a perfect invalid chair are strength, comfort and ease of operation. Our chairs have been improved wherever possible until they stand today the standard of all, beautiful in appearance, perfect in construction, as good as money, science and ability are able to produce.

If you are interested in invalid chairs send at once for our special Invalid Chair Catalog, here illustrated. Contains large illustrations of some forty to fifty reclining, propelling, folding, combination, reed, car, traveling and carrying chairs, the finest line of invalid chairs offered by any firm or dealer. It gives you full and accurate information concerning each one, tells you just the purposes for which they are designed. It quotes the lowest prices ever named by any firm or individual. It gives the freight rates to various parts of every state in the Union, it answers every possible question that you might ask concerning invalid chairs. In short, this big book is an authority, and it will give you such information as you cannot obtain from any other source. We sell invalid chairs just as we sell other merchandise, that is to say, our prices represent the cost of materials and labor when made in large quantities, plus one profit. Dealers generally charge very high prices for invalid chairs, but we have changed all this, as explained in the pages of this free catalog. Write for it.

SPECIAL CATALOG FREE

REED HAND PROPELLING CHAIR. New style and a very comfortable chair. Send for our new catalog for full particulars.

A NEW HAND AND FOOT PROPELLING CHAIR. Send for our new catalog for full particulars

RECLINING ROLLING CHAIR.

WITH SWIVEL WHEEL OF LARGE DIAMETER. ONE OF OUR MOST POPULAR STYLES OF INVALIDS' RECLINING CHAIRS.

One of the easiest running chairs because of its large swivel wheel in the rear. Made of oak with a rubbed and polished finish. Fitted with hygienic cane weaving. Has the improved curved reclining back that is a perfect fit to the human body, equipped with the improved patent reclining device, so constructed that by simply turning a thumbscrew and slightly pressing against the back the occupant can assume any desired position without assistance. Footboard is adjustable, and can be laid flat against the leg rest to facilitate entering or leaving the chair, affording great comfort to rheumatic or paralytic patients. Chair equipped with hand rims, enabling the occupant to turn chair in its own space, or propel it forward or backward at will.

No. 8T5000 With Oval Steel Rim Wheels, plain bearings, without handle. Regular price, $23.00; our price........ **$15.35**

No. 8T5002 With ¾-inch Cushion Tires on Front and Rear Wheels, plain bearings, without handle. Regular price, $33.50; our price........ **$22.35**

No. 8T5004 With 1-inch Cushion Tires on Front and Rear Wheels, plain bearings, without handle. Regular price, $40.50; our price........ **$27.00**

Weight, crated ready for shipment, about 100 pounds.

For special features in the way of extras, write for our Invalid Chair Catalog.

Specify whether wide or narrow width is desired.

In determining whether to order the narrow or wide pattern, measure the width of the doorways through which the chair is to pass.

Dimensions	Wide, inches	Narrow, inches
Height of back from seat	31	31
Height of seat from floor	20	20
Height of seat from footboard	17	17
Height of arms from seat	9½	9½
Depth of seat	20	20
Width of seat between arms	19	17
Diameter of large wheels	28	28
Diameter of small wheel	14	14
Width over all	29	27

GET THE BENEFIT OF FRESH AIR WHILE YOU SLEEP.

Everybody would be benefited by the use of one of our open air window tents; the healthy that their vitality may be preserved; the sick that they may regain their health; and the tired brain worker that he may have the exhilarating effect produced by pure cold air. Especially is this tent needed by victims of throat and lung diseases.

The Perfection and Monarch Window Tents are the most sanitary window tents yet devised. They are scientifically constructed and differ from all others; are adjustable, not only to fit the window but the bed as well, and can be put up or removed on a moment's notice. Require no nails, hooks or screws to put in place, and all covering can be removed for cleansing and disinfecting by the release of a single spring. By the use of an awning and the curtain you can regulate the amount of air entering the tent and protect yourself from cold or storm.

The Perfection Window Tent in Use, with Portion of Wall Cut Away to Show the Relation of Tent to the Bed.

Open Air Window Tents are furnished in two grades as follows:

THE PERFECTION. The best open air window tent it is possible to manufacture. Highest grade material, very best connections, perfect in every detail. Satisfaction guaranteed. Weight, crated, 20 pounds. Regular price, $20.00.

No. 8T4015 Perfection Open Air Window Tent. Our price........ **$10.50**

THE MONARCH. By eliminating a few features which are incorporated in our Perfection Window Tent, without sacrificing any of the essential features, the Monarch Window Tent has been constructed. The lowest priced window tent on the market possessing real merit. Weight, crated, 15 pounds. Regular price, $15.00.

No. 8T4020 Monarch Open Air Window Tent. Our price........ **$8.50**

LAMPS AND CHANDELIERS

GAS AND ELECTRIC FIXTURES

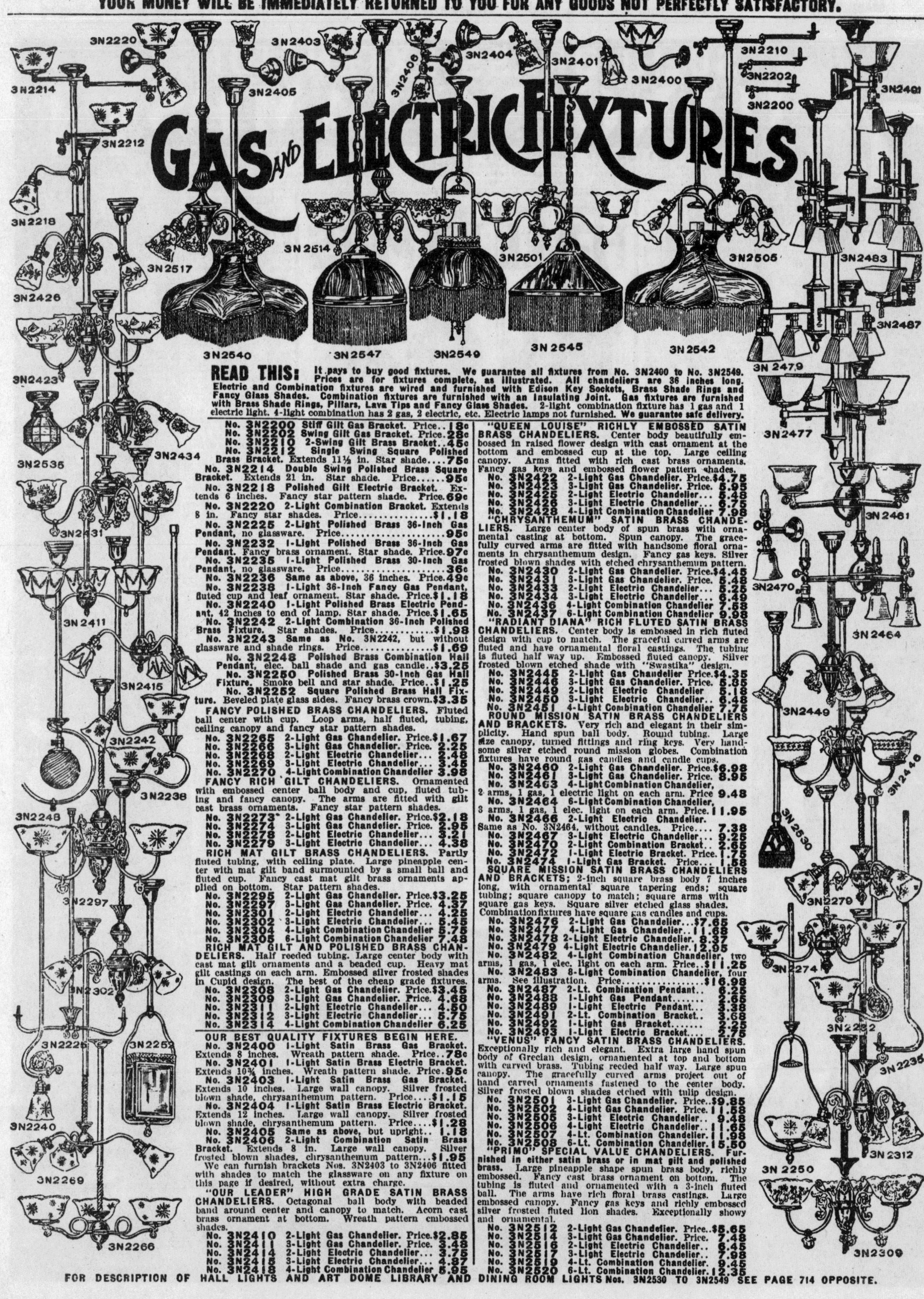

READ THIS: It pays to buy good fixtures. We guarantee all fixtures from No. 3N2400 to No. 3N2549. Prices are for fixtures complete, as illustrated. All chandeliers are 36 inches long. Electric and Combination fixtures are wired and furnished with Edison Key Sockets, Brass Shade Rings and Fancy Glass Shades. Combination fixtures are furnished with an Insulating Joint. Gas fixtures are furnished with Brass Shade Rings, Pillars, Lava Tips and Fancy Glass Shades. 2-light combination fixture has 1 gas and 1 electric light. 4-light combination has 2 gas, 2 electric, etc. Electric lamps not furnished. We guarantee safe delivery.

No. 3N2200 Stiff Gilt Gas Bracket. Price..**18c**
No. 3N2202 Swing Gilt Gas Bracket. Price.**28c**
No. 3N2210 2-Swing Gilt Brass Bracket..**45c**
No. 3N2212 Single Swing Square Polished Brass Bracket. Extends 11½ in. Star shade....**75c**

No. 3N2214 Double Swing Polished Brass Square Bracket. Extends 21 in. Star shade. Price......**95c**

No. 3N2218 Polished Gilt Electric Bracket. Extends 6 inches. Fancy star pattern shade. Price.**69c**

No. 3N2220 2-Light Combination Bracket. Extends 8 in. Fancy star shades. Price...............**$1.18**

No. 3N2225 2-Light Polished Brass 36-Inch Gas Pendant, no glassware. Price......................**95c**

No. 3N2232 1-Light Polished Brass 36-Inch Gas Pendant. Fancy brass ornament. Star shade. Price.**97c**

No. 3N2235 1-Light Polished Brass 30-Inch Gas Pendant, no glassware. Price.....................**36c**

No. 3N2236 Same as above, 36 inches. Price.**49c**

No. 3N2238 1-Light 36-Inch Fancy Gas Pendant, fluted cup and leaf ornament. Star shade. Price.**$1.18**

No. 3N2240 1-Light Polished Brass Electric Pendant, 42 inches to end of lamp. Star shade. Price.**$1.65**

No. 3N2242 2-Light Combination 36-Inch Polished Brass Fixture. Star shades. Price............**$1.98**

No. 3N2243 Same as No. 3N2242, but without glassware and shade rings. Price...............**$1.69**

No. 3N2248 Polished Brass Combination Hall Pendant, elec. ball shade and gas candle..**$3.25**

No. 3N2250 Polished Brass 30-Inch Gas Hall Fixture. Smoke bell and star shade. Price..**$1.25**

No. 3N2252 Square Polished Brass Hall Fixture. Beveled plate glass sides. Fancy brass crown.**$3.35**

FANCY POLISHED BRASS CHANDELIERS. Fluted ball center with cup. Loop arms, half fluted, tubing, ceiling canopy and fancy star pattern shades.

No. 3N2265 2-Light Gas Chandelier. Price.**$1.67**
No. 3N2266 3-Light Gas Chandelier. Price. **2.25**
No. 3N2268 2-Light Electric Chandelier... **2.48**
No. 3N2269 3-Light Electric Chandelier... **3.45**
No. 3N2270 4-Light Combination Chandelier **3.98**

FANCY RICH GILT CHANDELIERS. Ornamented with embossed center ball body and cup, fluted tubing and fancy canopy. The arms are fitted with gilt cast brass ornaments. Fancy star pattern shades.

No. 3N2273 2-Light Gas Chandelier. Price.**$2.18**
No. 3N2274 3-Light Gas Chandelier. Price. **2.95**
No. 3N2278 2-Light Electric Chandelier... **3.21**
No. 3N2279 3-Light Electric Chandelier... **4.38**

RICH MAT GILT BRASS CHANDELIERS. Partly fluted tubing, with ceiling plate. Large pineapple center with mat gilt band surmounted by a small ball and fluted cup. Fancy cast mat gilt brass ornaments applied on bottom. Star pattern shades.

No. 3N2295 2-Light Gas Chandelier. Price.**$3.25**
No. 3N2297 3-Light Gas Chandelier. Price. **4.37**
No. 3N2301 2-Light Electric Chandelier... **4.25**
No. 3N2302 3-Light Electric Chandelier... **5.45**
No. 3N2304 4-Light Combination Chandelier **5.75**
No. 3N2305 6-Light Combination Chandelier **7.48**

RICH MAT GILT AND POLISHED BRASS CHANDELIERS. Half reeded tubing. Large center body with cast mat gilt ornaments and a beaded cup. Heavy mat gilt castings on each arm. Embossed silver frosted shades in Cupid design. The best of the cheap grade fixtures.

No. 3N2308 2-Light Gas Chandelier. Price.**$3.45**
No. 3N2309 3-Light Gas Chandelier. Price. **4.68**
No. 3N2311 2-Light Electric Chandelier... **4.50**
No. 3N2312 3-Light Electric Chandelier... **5.75**
No. 3N2314 4-Light Combination Chandelier **6.25**

OUR BEST QUALITY FIXTURES BEGIN HERE.

No. 3N2400 1-Light Satin Brass Gas Bracket. Extends 8 inches. Wreath pattern shade. Price..**78c**

No. 3N2401 1-Light Satin Brass Electric Bracket. Extends 10¾ inches. Wreath pattern shade. Price.**95c**

No. 3N2403 1-Light Satin Brass Gas Bracket. Extends 10 inches. Large wall canopy. Silver frosted blown shade, chrysanthemum pattern. Price....**$1.15**

No. 3N2404 1-Light Satin Brass Electric Bracket. Extends 12 inches. Large wall canopy. Silver frosted blown shade, chrysanthemum pattern. Price....**$1.28**

No. 3N2405 Same as above, but upright.. **1.18**

No. 3N2406 2-Light Combination Satin Brass Bracket. Extends 8 in. Large wall canopy. Silver frosted blown shades, chrysanthemum pattern...**$1.95**

We can furnish brackets Nos. 3N2403 to 3N2406 fitted with shades to match the glassware on any fixture on this page if desired, without extra charge.

"OUR LEADER" HIGH GRADE SATIN BRASS CHANDELIERS. Octagonal ball body with beaded band around center and canopy to match. Acorn cast brass ornament at bottom. Wreath pattern embossed shades.

No. 3N2410 2-Light Gas Chandelier. Price.**$2.85**
No. 3N2411 3-Light Gas Chandelier. Price. **3.48**
No. 3N2414 2-Light Electric Chandelier... **3.75**
No. 3N2415 3-Light Electric Chandelier... **4.87**
No. 3N2418 4-Light Combination Chandelier **5.95**

"QUEEN LOUISE" RICHLY EMBOSSED SATIN BRASS CHANDELIERS. Center body beautifully embossed in raised flower design with cast ornament at the bottom and embossed cup at the top. Large ceiling canopy. Arms fitted with rich cast brass ornaments. Fancy gas keys and embossed flower pattern shades.

No. 3N2422 2-Light Gas Chandelier. Price.**$4.75**
No. 3N2423 3-Light Gas Chandelier. Price. **5.95**
No. 3N2425 2-Light Electric Chandelier... **5.48**
No. 3N2426 3-Light Electric Chandelier... **6.75**
No. 3N2428 4-Light Combination Chandelier **7.98**

"CHRYSANTHEMUM" SATIN BRASS CHANDELIERS. Large center body of spun brass with ornamental casting at bottom. Spun canopy. The gracefully curved arms are fitted with handsome floral ornaments in chrysanthemum design. Fancy gas keys. Silver frosted blown shades with etched chrysanthemum pattern.

No. 3N2430 2-Light Gas Chandelier. Price.**$4.45**
No. 3N2431 3-Light Gas Chandelier. Price. **5.48**
No. 3N2433 2-Light Electric Chandelier... **5.25**
No. 3N2434 3-Light Electric Chandelier... **6.49**
No. 3N2436 4-Light Combination Chandelier **7.58**
No. 3N2437 6-Light Combination Chandelier **9.98**

"RADIANT DIANA" RICH FLUTED SATIN BRASS CHANDELIERS. Center body is embossed in rich fluted design with cup to match. The graceful curved arms are fluted and have ornamental floral castings. The tubing is fluted half way up. Embossed fluted canopy. Silver frosted blown etched shade with "Swastika" design.

No. 3N2445 2-Light Gas Chandelier Price.**$4.35**
No. 3N2446 3-Light Gas Chandelier. Price. **5.85**
No. 3N2449 2-Light Electric Chandelier **5.18**
No. 3N2450 3-Light Electric Chandelier.. **6.48**
No. 3N2451 4-Light Combination Chandelier **7.75**

ROUND MISSION SATIN BRASS CHANDELIERS AND BRACKETS. Very rich and elegant in their simplicity. Hand spun ball body. Round tubing. Large size canopy, turned fittings and ring keys. Very handsome silver etched round mission globes. Combination fixtures have round gas candles and candle cups.

No. 3N2460 2-Light Gas Chandelier. Price.**$6.98**
No. 3N2461 3-Light Gas Chandelier. Price. **8.95**
No. 3N2463 4-Light Combination Chandelier, 2 arms, 1 gas, 1 electric light on each arm. Price **9.48**
No. 3N2464 6-Light Combination Chandelier, 3 arms, 1 gas, 1 elec. light on each arm. Price.**11.95**
No. 3N2466 2-Light Electric Chandelier. Same as No. 3N2464, without candles. Price.... **7.38**
No. 3N2467 3-Light Electric Chandelier... **9.25**
No. 3N2470 2-Light Combination Bracket.. **2.65**
No. 3N2472 1-Light Electric Bracket. Price.**1.75**
No. 3N2474 1-Light Gas Bracket. Price... **1.58**

SQUARE MISSION SATIN BRASS CHANDELIERS AND BRACKETS; 2-inch square brass body 7 inches long, with ornamental square tapering ends; square tubing; square canopy to match; square arms with square gas keys. Square silver etched glass shades. Combination fixtures have square gas candles and cups.

No. 3N2476 2-Light Gas Chandelier...**$7.65**
No. 3N2477 4-Light Gas Chandelier..**11.68**
No. 3N2478 2-Light Electric Chandelier. **8.37**
No. 3N2479 4-Light Electric Chandelier.**12.95**
No. 3N2482 4-Light Combination Chandelier, two arms, 1 gas, 1 elec. light on each arm. Price..**$11.25**
No. 3N2483 8-Light Combination Chandelier, four arms. See illustration. Price................**$16.98**
No. 3N2487 2-Lt. Combination Pendant.. **6.25**
No. 3N2488 1-Light Gas Pendant....... **2.65**
No. 3N2489 1-Light Electric Pendant... **3.38**
No. 3N2491 2-Lt. Combination Bracket.. **3.68**
No. 3N2492 1-Light Gas Bracket....... **2.25**
No. 3N2493 1-Light Electric Bracket.... **2.75**

"VENUS" FANCY SATIN BRASS CHANDELIERS. Exceptionally rich and elegant. Extra large hand spun body of Grecian design, ornamented at top and bottom with carved brass. Tubing reeded half way. Large spun canopy. The gracefully curved arms project out of hand carved ornaments fastened to the center body. Silver frosted blown shades etched with tulip design.

No. 3N2501 3-Light Gas Chandelier. Price..**$9.85**
No. 3N2502 4-Light Gas Chandelier. Price.**11.58**
No. 3N2505 3-Light Electric Chandelier.. **9.48**
No. 3N2506 4-Light Electric Chandelier..**11.65**
No. 3N2507 4-Lt. Combination Chandelier.**11.98**
No. 3N2508 6-Lt. Combination Chandelier.**15.50**

"PRIMO" SPECIAL VALUE CHANDELIERS. Furnished in either satin brass or in mat gilt and polished brass. Large pineapple shape spun brass body, richly embossed. Fancy cast brass ornament on bottom. The tubing is fluted and ornamented with a 3-inch fluted ball. The arms have rich floral brass castings. Large embossed canopy. Fancy gas keys and richly embossed silver frosted fluted lion shades. Exceptionally showy and ornamental.

No. 3N2512 2-Light Gas Chandelier. Price..**$5.65**
No. 3N2514 3-Light Gas Chandelier. Price. **7.48**
No. 3N2516 2-Light Electric Chandelier.. **6.45**
No. 3N2517 3-Light Electric Chandelier.. **7.98**
No. 3N2519 4-Lt. Combination Chandelier. **9.45**
No. 3N2520 6-Lt. Combination Chandelier.**12.35**

FOR DESCRIPTION OF HALL LIGHTS AND ART DOME LIBRARY AND DINING ROOM LIGHTS Nos. 3N2530 TO 3N2549 SEE PAGE 714 OPPOSITE.

SOLID BRASS EXTENSION
HANGING LAMPS
ALL OF THE LIBRARY LAMPS ARE FITTED WITH 36-INCH EXTENSIONS which allow the lamp to be raised or lowered a distance of three feet. All the metal parts of our hanging lamps, the frames, ornaments, ceiling plates, collars, smoke bells, etc., are made of solid brass (not bronze metal, a composition made in imitation of brass, costing one-third what brass costs) Weights quoted are on lamps packed for shipment.
"RADIANT BEAUTY."
No. 3R825 Solid rich gold finished brass fancy extension frame ornamented with carved brass castings in flower design. Fitted with tinted 14-inch dome shade and fount, decorated with American Beauty roses and thirty cut glass crystal prisms, embossed brass shade band, crown, collar and smoke bell, detachable brass fount 100-candle power central draft burner, No. 2 round wick and Rochester chimney. Wt., 40 lbs. Price....$7.98
"JEWEL."
No. 3R814 Polished solid brass extension frame, fitted with No. 1 Miller embossed brass fount and central draft burner. No. 1 round wick and Rochester chimney. Brass crown and smoke bell. Fitted with 14-inch plain dome shade. Wt., 30 lbs. Price..$3.38
No. 3R815 Same as No 3R814, but fitted with richly decorated shade Price..$3.75
"SUNBURST."
No. 3R817 Richly ornamented patina finish (shaded) solid brass extension frame. Removable fount, with embossed gold finished medallion ornament, embossed brass shade band, crown, collar and smoke bell, fitted complete with thirty crystal cut glass prisms, 85-candle power central draft burner, No. 2 wick and Rochester chimney and plain white 14-inch dome shade. Wt., 45 lbs. Price.......$4.68
No. 3R818 Same as No. 3R817, but fitted with richly decorated shade. Price..$5.25
HALL LAMPS
3R851
3R840
3R854
3R848
The Hall Lamps weigh about 15 lbs. each.
COLONIAL SQUARE HALL LAMP.
No. 3R851 Made of solid brass with etched glass panel sides. Patent lighting adjustment. Fitted with removable glass fount, No. 1 brass burner, chimney, wick, brass ceiling plate and smoke bell......$2.98
RUBY HALL LIGHT.
No. 3R840 Made with new shape fluted ruby globe, patent lighting adjustment, brass collar, and oil fount holder. Complete with glass fount and No. 0 burner, chimney and wick. Price..$1.48
IDEAL HALL OR DEN LIGHT.
No. 3R854 Hand wrought black iron frame, rich fluted ruby globe. Fitted complete with smoke bell and ceiling plate, glass fount, No. 0 brass burner, chimney and wick. Price..$1.95
ORIENTAL HALL OR DEN LIGHT.
No. 3R848 Fitted with 9-inch Colonial globe in imitation of leaded glass. Complete with brass collar, fount holder, ceiling plate, glass fount, No. 1 brass burner, chimney and wick. Price..$2.85
No. 3R724 Dining Room or Hall Lamp. Fancy metal bronze finish, complete with glass fount, No. 2 Banner burner, chimney and wick and 8-inch silvered glass reflector. Weight, 10 pounds. Price..........55c
No. 3R750 Highest grade Bracket Lamp. Gold finish frame with polished brass fount, 10 candle power central draft burner, No. 2 Rochester chimney and wick; 10-inch silvered glass reflector. Weight, 10 pounds. Price.........$1.85
"MIDNIGHT SUN."
No. 3R797 Elegant Library Lamp, ornamental solid brass extension frame, brass shade band, crown, collar and smoke bell. Fitted with thirty cut glass crystal prisms suspended from shade band, 14-inch plain dome shade, crystal fount, No. 3 Climax burner, No. 2 Electric chimney and No. 3 wick. Wt., 35 lbs. Price.......$4.25
No. 3R798 Same as No. 3R797, but fitted with tinted, richly decorated 14-inch dome shade and fount to match. Price, $4.65
"SUN'S RAYS."
No. 3R829 Solid Brass Extension Lamp. Fitted with decorated 14-inch dome and decorated fount to match, removable brass oil pot, No. 2 central draft burner, 85-candle power, No. 2 Rochester chimney and wick. Brass crown, collar and smoke bell. Wt., 45 lbs. Price.......$5.48
"BRILLIANT BEAUTY."
No. 3R828 Fancy Solid Brass Extension Lamp, fitted with richly embossed brass shade band, crown, collar and smoke bell. Different from the ordinary library lamp. It has a 5-inch green bead fringe suspended from the shade band instead of prisms. 14-inch dome. The shade and fount are tinted a rich green to match, and are elaborately decorated with clusters of American beauty roses. Fitted with No. 3 Climax burner, No. 2 Electric chimney and wick. Wt. 35 lbs. Price..$5.68
"EVENING STAR."
No. 3R810 Fancy solid brass extension frame. Fitted with brass crown and ceiling plate, 14-inch plain white dome shade, plain glass fount, No. 3 Climax burner, No. 2 Electric chimney and No. 3 wick. Wt., 30 lbs. Price, $2.75
No. 3R811 Same as No. 3R810, but fitted with 14-inch decorated shade and decorated fount to match. A very rich lamp. Price...........$3.15
"COMET."
No. 3R820 Solid Brass Extension Hanging Lamp. Brass shade band, crown and smoke bell, 14-inch plain white dome shade, glass fount, thirty crystal cut glass prisms, No. 3 Climax burner, No. 2 Electric chimney, No. 3 wick. Wt., 30 lbs. Price.....$3.35
No. 3R821 Same as No. 3R820, but fitted with 14-inch decorated dome shade and decorated fount to match. Price..$3.85
"OUR LEADER."
No. 3R807 Solid brass extension frame, crown and smoke bell, 14-inch plain dome shade, glass fount and No. 2 burner, No. 2 Climax chimney and wick. Wt., 35 lbs. Price..$1.78
No. 3R808 Same as No. 3R807, but fitted with decorated dome shade. Price.........................$2.18
MAMMOTH STORE LAMP.
No. 3R860 400-candle power, solid brass Juno Mammoth Store Lamp with solid brass extension. Has No. 3 central draft burner and embossed oil fount, 14-inch white opal shade and No. 3 Rochester chimney and wick. Holds one gallon of oil which burns ten hours. Wt., 35 lbs. Price...$4.98
No. 3R861 Same lamp as No. 3R860, but finished in bright nickel. Price.$5.48
DRESDEN MAMMOTH LAMP.
No. 3R800 400-candle power, solid brass satin finish extension, Juno Dresden Mammoth Lamp, 14-inch dome. A brilliant steady pure white light, surpassing electricity or gas. Gives more light and burns longer with less oil than any other lamp. Holds one gallon of oil, which burns sixteen hours. Complete with fancy brass shade band, embossed removable brass time oil fount, No. 3 Dresden central draft burner and No. 00 Belgium chimney and wick. Wt., 40 lbs. Price...$6.85
No. 3R802 Same as No. 3R800, but fitted with thirty crystal cut glass prisms and richly tinted, decorated 14-in. dome shade. Price..$7.98
JUNO STORE LAMP.
No. 3R856 Juno Solid Brass Store Lamp, highly polished, with removable brass fount and 85-candle power, No. 2 central draft burner, 15-inch tin shade (outside enameled green) and smoke bell, No. 2 wick and chimney. Comes without extension. Wt., 35 lbs. Price.........$1 98
3R825
3R814 815
3R817-818
3R810-811
3R820-821
3R860-861
3R800-802
3R856
3R807-808
3R797-798
3R829
3R828
WITH PLAIN SHADE
WITH DECORATED SHADE

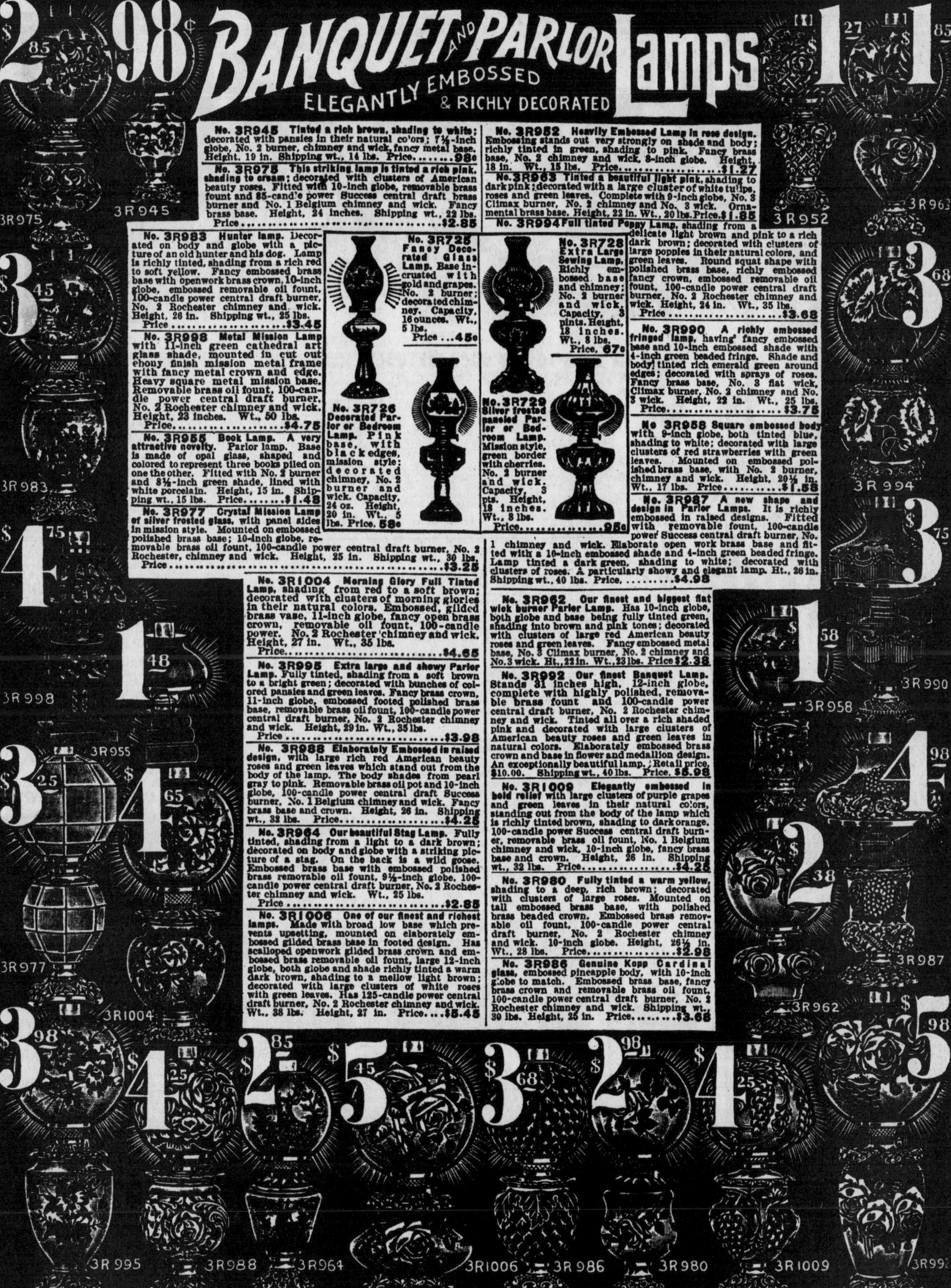

BANQUET AND PARLOR Lamps

ELEGANTLY EMBOSSED & RICHLY DECORATED

No. 3R945 Tinted a rich brown, shading to white; decorated with pansies in their natural colors; 7½-inch globe, No. 2 burner, chimney and wick, fancy metal base. Height, 19 in. Shipping wt., 14 lbs. Price........98c

No. 3R975 This striking lamp is tinted a rich pink, shading to cream; decorated with clusters of American beauty roses. Fitted with 10-inch globe, removable brass fount and 85-candle power Success central draft brass burner and No. 1 Belgium chimney and wick. Fancy brass base. Height, 24 inches. Shipping wt., 22 lbs. Price........$2.85

No. 3R952 Heavily Embossed Lamp in rose design. Embossing stands out very strongly on shade and body; richly tinted in green, shading to pink. Fancy brass base, No. 2 chimney and wick, 8-inch globe. Height, 18 in. Wt., 15 lbs. Price........$1.27

No. 3R963 Tinted a beautiful light pink, shading to dark pink; decorated with a large cluster of white tulips, roses and green leaves. Complete with 9-inch globe, No. 3 Climax burner, No. 2 chimney and No. 3 wick. Ornamental brass base. Height, 22 in. Wt., 20 lbs. Price.$1.85

No. 3R994 Full tinted Poppy Lamp, shading from a delicate light brown and pink to a rich dark brown; decorated with clusters of large poppies in their natural colors, and green leaves. Round squat shape with polished brass base, richly embossed fancy crown, embossed removable oil fount, 100-candle power central draft burner, No. 2 Rochester chimney and wick. Height, 24 in. Wt., 35 lbs. Price........$3.68

No. 3R983 Hunter lamp. Decorated on body and globe with a picture of an old hunter and his dog. Lamp is richly tinted, shading from a rich red to soft yellow. Fancy embossed brass base with openwork brass crown, 10-inch globe, embossed removable oil fount, 100-candle power central draft burner, No. 2 Rochester chimney and wick. Height, 26 in. Shipping wt., 25 lbs. Price........$3.45

No. 3R998 Metal Mission Lamp with 11-inch green cathedral art glass shade, mounted in cut out ebony finish mission metal frame with fancy metal crown and edge. Heavy square metal mission base. Removable brass oil fount, 100-candle power central draft burner, No. 2 Rochester chimney and wick. Height, 23 inches. Wt., 50 lbs. Price........$4.75

No. 3R955 Book Lamp. A very attractive novelty. Parlor lamp. Base is made of opal glass, shaped and colored to represent three books piled on one the other. Fitted with No. 2 burner and 8½-inch green shade, lined with white porcelain. Height, 15 in. Shipping wt., 15 lbs. Price........$1.48

No. 3R725 Fancy Decorated Glass Lamp. Base incrusted with gold and grapes. No. 2 burner; decorated chimney. Capacity, 16 ounces. Wt., 5 lbs. Price ...45c

No. 3R726 Decorated Parlor or Bedroom Lamp. Pink base, with black edges, mission style; decorated chimney, No. 2 burner and wick. Capacity, 24 oz. Height, 20 in. Wt., 5 lbs. Price. 58c

No. 3R728 Extra Large Sewing Lamp. Richly embossed base and chimney; No. 2 burner and wick. Capacity, 3 pints. Height, 18 inches. Wt., 8 lbs. Price. 67c

No. 3R729 Silver frosted paneled Parlor or Bedroom Lamp. Mission style, green border with cherries. No. 2 burner and wick. Capacity, 3 pts. Height, 18 inches. Wt., 8 lbs. Price........95c

No. 3R990 A richly embossed fringed lamp, having fancy embossed base and 10-inch embossed shade with 4-inch green beaded fringe. Shade and body tinted rich emerald green around edges; decorated with sprays of roses. Fancy brass base, No. 3 flat wick, Climax burner, No. 2 chimney and No. 3 wick. Height, 22 in. Wt., 25 lbs. Price........$3.75

No. 3R958 Square embossed body with 9-inch globe, both tinted blue, shading to white; decorated with large clusters of red strawberries with green leaves. Mounted on embossed polished brass base, with No. 2 burner, chimney and wick. Height, 20½ in. Wt., 17 lbs. Price........$1.58

No. 3R977 Crystal Mission Lamp of silver frosted glass, with panel sides in mission style. Mounted on embossed polished brass base; 10-inch globe, removable brass oil fount, 100-candle power central draft burner, No. 2 Rochester, chimney and wick. Height, 25 in. Shipping wt., 30 lbs. Price........$3.25

No. 3R987 A new shape and design in Parlor Lamps. It is richly embossed in raised designs. Fitted with removable fount, 100-candle power Success central draft burner, No. 1 chimney and wick. Elaborate open work brass base and fitted with a 10-inch embossed shade and 4-inch green beaded fringe. Lamp tinted a dark green, shading to white; decorated with clusters of roses. A particularly showy and elegant lamp. Ht., 26 in. Shipping wt., 40 lbs. Price........$4.98

No. 3R1004 Morning Glory Full Tinted Lamp, shading from red to a soft brown; decorated with clusters of morning glories in their natural colors. Embossed, gilded brass vase, 11-inch globe, fancy open brass crown, removable oil fount, 100-candle power. No. 2 Rochester chimney and wick. Height, 27 in. Wt., 35 lbs. Price........$4.65

No. 3R995 Extra large and showy Parlor Lamp. Fully tinted, shading from a soft brown to a bright green; decorated with bunches of colored pansies and green leaves. Fancy brass crown, 11-inch globe, embossed footed polished brass base, removable brass oil fount, 100-candle power central draft burner, No. 2 Rochester chimney and wick. Height, 29 in. Wt., 35 lbs. Price........$3.98

No. 3R988 Elaborately Embossed in raised design, with large rich red American beauty roses and green leaves which stand out from the body of the lamp. The body shades from pearl gray to pink. Removable brass oil pot and 10-inch globe, 100-candle power central draft Success burner, No. 1 Belgium chimney and wick. Fancy brass base and crown. Height, 26 in. Shipping wt., 32 lbs. Price........$4.25

No. 3R964 Our beautiful Stag Lamp. Fully tinted, shading from a light to a dark brown; decorated on body and globe with a striking picture of a stag. On the back is a wild goose. Embossed brass base with embossed polished brass removable oil fount, 9½-inch globe, 100-candle power central draft burner, No. 2 Rochester chimney and wick. Wt., 25 lbs. Price........$2.85

No. 3R1006 One of our finest and richest lamps. Made with broad low base which prevents upsetting, mounted on elaborately embossed gilded brass base in footed design. Has scalloped openwork gilded brass crown and embossed brass removable oil fount, large 12-inch globe, both globe and shade richly tinted a warm dark brown, shading to a mellow light brown; decorated with large clusters of white roses with green leaves. Has 125-candle power central draft burner, No. 2 Rochester chimney and wick. Wt., 38 lbs. Height, 27 in. Price....$5.45

No. 3R962 Our finest and biggest flat wick burner Parlor Lamp. Has 10-inch globe, both globe and base being fully tinted green, shading into brown and pink tones; decorated with clusters of large red American beauty roses and green leaves. Fancy embossed metal base, No. 3 Climax burner, No. 2 chimney and No. 3 wick. Ht., 22 in. Wt., 23 lbs. Price $2.38

No. 3R992 Our finest Banquet Lamp. Stands 31 inches high, 12-inch globe, complete with highly polished, removable brass fount and 100-candle power central draft burner, No. 2 Rochester chimney and wick. Tinted all over a rich shaded pink and decorated with large clusters of American beauty roses and green leaves in natural colors. Elaborately embossed brass crown and base in flower and medallion design. An exceptionally beautiful lamp. Retail price, $10.00. Shipping wt., 40 lbs. Price. $5.98

No. 3R1009 Elegantly embossed in bold relief with large clusters of purple grapes and green leaves in their natural colors, standing out from the body of the lamp which is richly tinted brown, shading to dark orange. 100-candle power Success central draft burner, removable brass oil fount, No. 1 Belgium chimney and wick, 10-inch globe, fancy brass base and crown. Height, 26 in. Shipping wt., 32 lbs. Price........$4.25

No. 3R980 Fully tinted a warm yellow, shading to a deep, rich brown; decorated with clusters of large roses. Mounted on tall embossed brass base, with polished brass beaded crown. Embossed brass removable oil fount, 100-candle power central draft burner, No. 2 Rochester chimney and wick. 10-inch globe. Height, 26½ in. Wt., 28 lbs. Price........$2.98

No. 3R986 Genuine Kopp Cardinal glass, embossed pineapple body, with 10-inch globe to match. Embossed brass base, fancy brass crown and removable brass oil fount. 100-candle power central draft burner, No. 2 Rochester chimney and wick. Shipping wt., 30 lbs. Height, 25 in. Price........$3.68

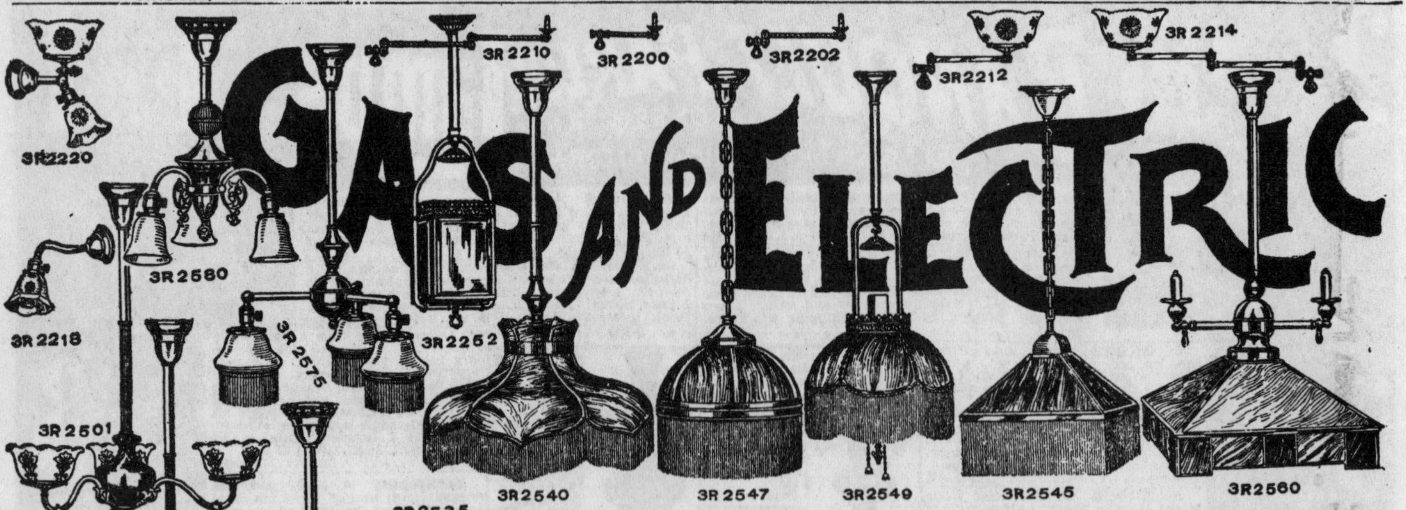

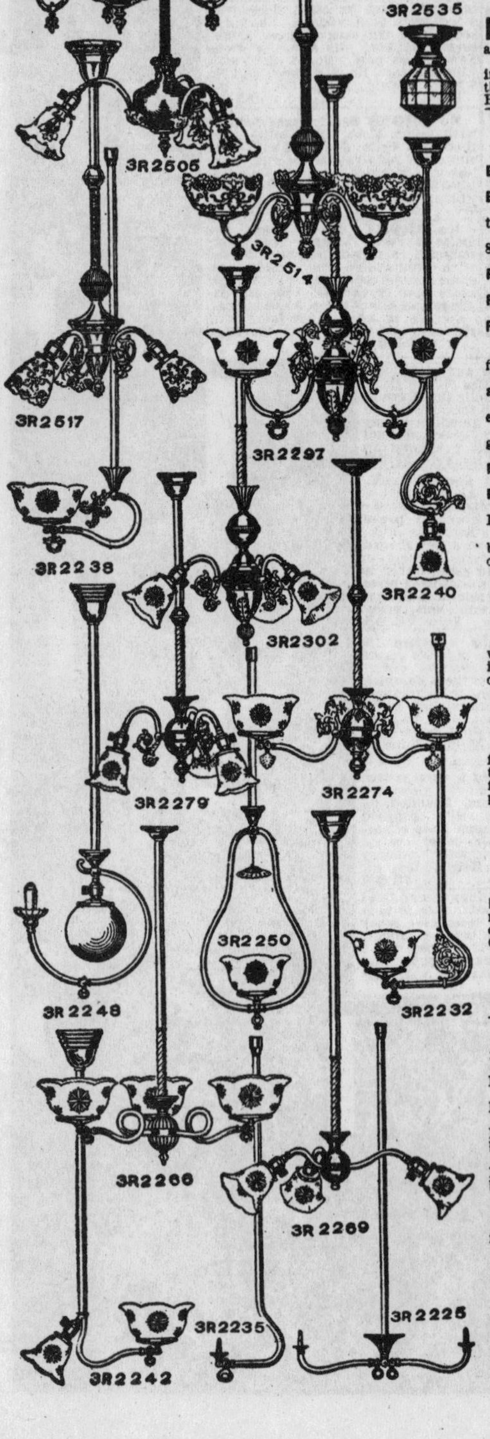

GAS AND ELECTRIC

IT PAYS TO BUY GOOD FIXTURES.

Fixtures running from No. 3R2200 to 3R2314 are the best fixtures it is possible to put up for the money we ask. They are showy and ornate, and we can guarantee that they will hold gas, are properly wired and insulated and are perfectly safe.

Fixtures No. 3R2400 to No. 3R2586. They are made of the finest quality solid brass, extra heavy gauge (weight) and are finished in rich satin brass (brush brass), buffed and polished by hand. In thoroughness of construction they are absolutely perfect. In these fixtures all connecting joints, sockets, etc., are cemented. They conform in every particular with the requirements of the Board of Insurance Underwriters. You cannot buy better made or finished fixtures at any price.

No. 3R2200 Stiff Gilt Gas Bracket, 6-Inch..18c
No. 3R2202 Swing Gilt Gas Bracket, 11-Inch.28c
No. 3R2210 2-Swing Gilt Brass Bracket....45c
No. 3R2212 Single Swing Square Polished Brass Bracket. Extends 11½ inches. Star shade........75c

No. 3R2214 Double Swing Polished Brass Square Bracket. Extends 21 inches. Star shade. Price....95c

No. 3R2218 Polished Gilt Electric Bracket. Extends 6 inches. Fancy star pattern shade. Price..69c

No. 3R2220 2-Light Combination Bracket. Extends 8 inches. Fancy star shades. Price............$1.18

No. 3R2225 2-Light Polished Brass 36-Inch Gas Pendant, no glassware. Price....................95c

No. 3R2232 1-Light Polished Brass 36-Inch Gas Pendant. Fancy brass ornament. Star shade. Price..97c

No. 3R2235 1-Light Polished Brass 30-Inch Gas Pendant, no glassware. Price....................36c

No. 3R2236 Same as No. 3R2235, 36 inches..49c

No. 3R2238 1-Light 36-Inch Fancy Gas Pendant, fluted cup and leaf ornament. Star shade. Price..$1.18

No. 3R2240 1-Light Polished Brass Electric Pendant, 42 inches to end of lamp. Star shade. Price.$1.65

No. 3R2242 2-Light Combination 36-Inch Polished Brass Fixture. Star shades. Price..........$1.98

No. 3R2243 Same as No. 3R2242, but without glassware and shade rings. Price...............$1.69

No. 3R2248 Polished Brass Combination Hall Pendant, electric ball shade and gas candle....$3.25

No. 3R2250 Polished Brass 30-Inch Gas Hall Fixture. Smoke bell and star shade. Price......$1.25

No. 3R2252 Square Polished Brass Hall Fixture. Beveled plate glass sides. Fancy brass crown....$3.35

FANCY POLISHED BRASS CHANDELIERS. Fluted ball center with cup. Loop arms, half fluted, tubing, ceiling canopy and fancy star pattern shades.

No. 3R2265 2-Light Gas Chandelier. Price.$1.67
No. 3R2266 3-Light Gas Chandelier. Price 2.25
No. 3R2268 2-Light Electric Chandelier.. 2.48
No. 3R2269 3-Light Electric Chandelier... 3.45
No. 3R2270 4-Light Combination Chandelier 3.98

FANCY RICH GILT CHANDELIERS. Ornamented with embossed center ball body and cup, fluted tubing and fancy canopy. The arms are fitted with gilt cast brass ornaments. Fancy star pattern shades.

No. 3R2273 2-Light Gas Chandelier. Price.$2.18
No. 3R2274 3-Light Gas Chandelier. Price. 2.95
No. 3R2278 2-Light Electric Chandelier... 3.21
No. 3R2279 3-Light Electric Chandelier... 4.38

RICH MAT GILT BRASS CHANDELIERS. Partly fluted tubing, with ceiling plate. Large pineapple center with mat gilt band surmounted by a small ball and fluted cup. Fancy cast mat gilt brass ornaments applied on bottom. Star pattern shades.

No. 3R2295 2-Light Gas Chandelier. Price.$3.25
No. 3R2297 3-Light Gas Chandelier. Price. 4.37
No. 3R2301 2-Light Electric Chandelier.. 4.25
No. 3R2302 3-Light Electric Chandelier.. 5.45
No. 3R2304 4-Light Combination Chandelier 5.75
No. 3R2305 6-Light Combination Chandelier 7.48

RICH MAT GILT AND POLISHED BRASS CHANDELIERS. Half reed tubing. Large center body with cast mat gilt ornaments and a beaded cup. Heavy mat gilt castings on each arm. Embossed silver frosted shades in Cupid design. The best of the cheap grade fixtures.

No. 3R2308 2-Light Gas Chandelier. Price.$3.45
No. 3R2309 3-Light Gas Chandelier. Price. 4.68
No. 3R2311 2-Light Electric Chandelier... 4.50
No. 3R2312 3-Light Electric Chandelier... 5.75
No. 3R2314 4-Light Combination Chandelier 6.25

OUR BEST QUALITY FIXTURES BEGIN HERE.

We guarantee all fixtures from No. 3R2400 to No. 3R2549 and emphasize their superior quality and beauty.

No. 3R2400 1-Light Satin Brass Gas Bracket. Extends 8 inches. Wreath pattern shade. Price....78c

No. 3R2401 1-Light Satin Brass Electric Bracket. Extends 10¾ inches. Wreath pattern shade. Price..95c

No. 3R2403 1-Light Satin Brass Gas Bracket. Extends 10 inches. Large wall canopy. Silver frosted blown shade, chrysanthemum pattern. Price....$1.15

No. 3R2404 1-Light Satin Brass Electric Bracket. Extends 12 inches. Large wall canopy. Silver frosted blown shade, chrysanthemum pattern. Price....$1.28

No. 3R2405 Same as above, but upright.. 1.18

No. 3R2406 2-Light Combination Satin Brass Bracket. Extends 8 in. Large wall canopy. Silver frosted blown shades, chrysanthemum pattern..$1.95

We can furnish brackets Nos. 3R2403 to 3R2406 fitted with shades to match the glassware on any fixture on this page if desired, without extra charge.

"OUR LEADER" HIGH GRADE SATIN BRASS CHANDELIERS. Octagonal ball body with beaded band around center and canopy to match. Acorn brass ornament at bottom. Wreath pattern embossed shades.

No. 3R2410 2-Light Gas Chandelier. Price.$2.85
No. 3R2411 3-Light Gas Chandelier. Price. 3.48
No. 3R2414 2-Light Electric Chandelier... 3.75
No. 3R2415 3-Light Electric Chandelier... 4.87
No. 3R2418 4-Light Combination Chandelier 5.95

No. 3R2530 ORNAMENTAL HALL LIGHT. Length, 36 inches; ⅞-inch satin brass tubing. Chain pull socket and art fiber shade 4½ inches, with metal finish; lined with red transparent linen and has 5½-inch ruby beaded fringe. Price........................$2.43

No. 3R2535 HALL OR PORCH CEILING LIGHT. Mission style, copper ceiling canopy and large frosted octagonal electric ball lined with black to represent leaded glass. Price............$2.95

No. 3R2537 MISSION ART GLASS HALL LIGHT. Satin brass. Length, 36 inches; ⅞-inch square tubing with square canopy to match, with 8-inch square amber colored cathedral glass shade. Mounted in cut out brass frame. Chain pull socket. Price..$5.78

No. 3R2540 THREE-LIGHT ELECTRIC ART DOME LIGHT. Length, 48 inches. The shade is 22 inches in width with eight panels of bent cathedral art glass. Either green or amber colored, with 5-inch transparent beaded fringe to match, and is equipped with fancy bent art glass crown in satin brass frame, surrounded by satin brass band. Has ⅝-inch satin brass tubing and large hand spun canopy. A truly big value. Retail price, $25.00. Our price..$16.50

No. 3R2542 GAS ART DOME LIGHT. Exactly the same as No. 3R2540, except fitted for gas instead of electricity. Complete with 80-candle power incandescent gas burner, mantle, chimney and patent by-pass, which lowers the gas without turning off. Price....$15.75

No. 3R2543 FIVE-LIGHT COMBINATION ART DOME SHADE. Exactly the same as No. 3R2540, but fitted with two round mission gas arms, projecting out of the crown of the shade, these arms fitted with round white gas candles and candle cups; three electric lights under dome shade. Price..............................$18.95

No. 3R2545 TWO-LIGHT ELECTRIC SQUARE DOME LIGHT. Length, 48 inches; 4-inch double shade of green cathedral art glass and 6-inch transparent green beaded fringe to match. Edges, top canopy and square link chain made of satin brass. Price..$14.98

No. 3R2547 TWO-LIGHT ROUND ELECTRIC DOME LIGHT with 14-inch dome shade of amber colored cathedral art glass and 6-inch transparent amber beaded fringe to match. Edges, round link chain and canopy made of satin finished brass. Price......$14.45

No. 3R2549 ROUND GAS DOME LIGHT with 14-inch dome shade of cathedral art glass mounted in embossed satin brass frame and ⅝-inch tubing, 6-inch transparent green beaded fringe. This dome is surmounted with an ornamental cut out embossed brass crown. Fitted complete with 80-candle power incandescent burner, mantle, chimney and patent by-pass. Price................$11.75

INCANDESCENT GAS BURNERS.

FOR NATURAL OR ARTIFICIAL GAS.

No. 3R2367 "SUNBEAM" UPRIGHT ADJUSTABLE GAS BURNER. Made of polished brass, complete with mica airhole, chimney, star pattern glass shade, 3¼-inch brass shade ring and mantle. Burns 1 foot of gas per hour. Price..................35c

No. 3R2368 "Sunbeam" Burner, without glass shade.....25c

No. 3R2370 "BANNER" ADJUSTABLE GAS BURNER. Polished brass. Best quality mantle and opal air hole globe. Price.45c

No. 3R2372 "SOLAR" ADJUSTABLE GAS BURNER. Highly polished brass. Gas regulated by patent air shutter. Best quality mantle and opal air hole globe. Fancy perforated body. Price..65c

No. 3R2374 "MAGIC" INVERTED BURNER. Polished brass, air regulator, mantle and half frosted glass globe. Price......48c

No. 3R2376 "EUREKA" INVERTED GAS BURNER. Highly polished, with patent side screw regulator and air adjustment. Inverted gas mantle and half frosted globe. Price................78c

No. 3R2378 "RADIANT" INVERTED GAS BURNER, satin brass. Ornamental crown detachable goose neck. Patent gas adjustment. Best quality mantle, frosted globe. Price............$1.17

No. 3R2381 PATENT BY-PASS, permitting gas to be lowered to a speck without turning off. **In ordering state catalog number of burner on which it is to be used.** Price........................35c

RAMSDELL INVERTED GAS LAMPS.

Graceful appearance, efficient in operation, simple in construction, economical and durable. Lever air shutter, no flashback.

No. 3R2394 RAMSDELL No. 7 INVERTED 65-CANDLE POWER INCANDESCENT GAS LAMP. Complete with full silver frosted globe, imported mantle, adapter, and porcelain heat deflector. Satin brass finish. Price.$1.35

No. 3R2396 RAMSDELL No. 8 BIJOU INCANDESCENT GAS LAMP. Giving 20-candle power on 1 foot of gas per hour. Complete with silver frosted shade, imported mantle and adapter, porcelain cone and bracket protector. Satin brass finish. Price.$1.08

OUR PRICES ARE FOR THE FIXTURES COMPLETE, as illustrated, ready to hang. All electric and combination brackets, chandeliers and art glass dome shades are **completely wired** and furnished with **Edison key sockets, brass shade rings and glass shades.** The gas fixtures and combination fixtures are furnished with complete brass shade rings, gas pillars, lava tips and **glass shades.** The combination fixtures are also furnished with insulating joint (which ordinarily costs you 50 cents extra). A 2-light combination fixture means one gas and one electric light; a 4-light combination fixture means two gas and two electric lights; a 6-light combination fixture means three gas and three electric lights. All chandeliers are 36 inches long. We will make them any length at a cost of 30 cents per foot or fraction of a foot. Electric lamps are not furnished with fixtures.

No. 3R2555 SIX-LIGHT COMBINATION ART DOME SHADE. Made of satin brass, fitted with 16-inch amber colored cathedral art glass with 5-inch transparent beaded fringe to match. Has four outside lights; two fancy gas arms, fitted with fancy embossed shades, and two electric arms with fancy embossed shades. There are also two electric lights inside of dome. The stem is richly ornamented. Length to bottom of fringe, 48 inches. Price....**$18.75**

No. 3R2560 FOUR-LIGHT COMBINATION SQUARE ART DOME LIGHT. Fitted with 20-inch square amber colored cathedral art glass shade, which has a 3-inch amber glass curtain around edge, instead of fringe. Curtain has green art glass corners and center squares. Satin brass frame and stem. The two electric lights are inside of glass dome. The gas lights are on outside. Round Mission arms, with round white candles and candle cups. Length to bottom of curtain, 48 inches. Price....................**$17.98**

No. 3R2565 LARGE THREE-LIGHT HEXAGON ART DOME LIGHT. Fitted with a 22-inch six-panel dome shade and six-panel art glass curtain edge. Made of amber colored cathedral art glass with red art glass corners and center squares in the curtain. Mounted in satin brass frame with satin brass canopy and link chain. Our handsomest dome light. We can furnish the shade with green instead of amber glass, if desired. Length to bottom of curtain, 48 inches. Price....................................**$21.50**

No. 3R2570 FANCY FOUR-LIGHT ART SQUARE MISSION PARLOR OR DINING ROOM CHANDELIER. Exceptionally rich and ornamental chandelier. Embodies the very newest ideas in art shade lighting. Satin brass with square body, 7 inches long. Four 8-inch square arms. At end of arm hangs an 18-inch brass chain with 8-inch amber colored cathedral glass shade mounted on cut out Mission brass frame. Chain pull sockets. Retail price $50.00. Length to bottom of shade, 48 inches. Our price..........**$29.75**

No. 3R2571 Exactly the same as No. 3R2570, but fitted with two lights only. Price....................................**$18.98**

No. 3R2575 THREE-LIGHT ROUND MISSION COLONIAL PARLOR CHANDELIER. Satin brass pattern, ornamented with large spun ball center, surmounted by an oblong ball ornament. Three 8-inch round Mission arms, with three hanging silver frosted Colonial 6-inch shades, with 4-inch transparent silver crystal fringe. Length to bottom of fringe, 46 inches. Price..............**$10.75**

No. 3R2576 Exactly the same as No. 3R2575, but with two lights only. Price....................................**$8.85**

No. 3R2580 THREE-LIGHT ELECTRIC CEILING FIXTURE. Very newest method of lighting. The chandelier is out of the way and the light is diffused over the entire room. Satin brass. Has spun pineapple shaped body, richly embossed with fancy ornament at bottom. Three stalactitic arms, ornamented with floral brass castings. Extends 18 inches from the ceiling. Has round silver frosted glass shade. Eyeless sockets. Price.....................**$6.95**

No. 3R2585 SQUARE FOUR-LIGHT MISSION ELECTRIC CEILING FIXTURE. Satin brass. Has square ceiling canopy and tubing, with large square Mission body 7 inches long, and four 8-inch arms. On each arm is a large octagon shape silver frosted glass closed bottom Mission globe. Keyless sockets. Exceptionally attractive parlor or hall chandelier. Extends 20 inches. Price....**$13.50**

No. 3R2586 Exactly the same as No. 3R2585, but fitted with two lights only. Price....................................**$9.75**

INCANDESCENT GAS MANTLES.

We handle only the best grades of mantles, guaranteed to give a bright, clear light.

No. 3R2380 No. 1. Standard Grade Mantles, 60-candle power. Price......**8½c**

No. 3R2384 No. 5. Extra Grade Mantles, 100-candle power. Price.....**13c**

No. 3R2386 No. 6. Heavy Weave, especially for high pressure gasoline lamps; 5 inches long; nothing better made....**18c**

No. 3R2390 Our Triple Weave Double Wire Mantle attached to cap is by far the longest lived mantle we sell. Cannot break by handling. Very strong. Price....**17c**

No. 3R2392 Genuine Sears Special, extra double strength, 100-candle power platinum tied, with nickel support combined with burner cap and gauze. Nothing better made at any price. Price..............**21c**

No. 3R2385 Our Special Cross Weave Inverted Gas Mantle. Made extra heavy to stand high pressure. Price..............**11c**

No. 3R2387 Best Quality Triple Weave Inverted Mantle. Extra light producing surface of exceptional durability. Price........**18c**

No. 3R2391 Highest Grade Soft Inverted Mantle. Extra strong. For artificial gas and high pressure gasoline systems. Price....**12c**

CRYSTAL GAS AND ELECTRIC SHADES.

No. 3R2316 Crystal Pebbled Glass Gas Shade in star cutting design. Fancy edge. Fits 4-inch holder. Price......**12c**

No. 3R2317 Star Pattern Electric Gas Shade. Fits 3-inch holder. Price......**9c**

No. 3R2104 Strictly high grade Pebbled Crystal Gas Shade. Beautiful wreath pattern. Fits 4-inch holder. Price....**18c**

No. 3R2102 Wreath Pattern Electric Shade. Fits 3-inch shade ring. Price. **13c**

No. 3R2106 Silver Frosted Blown Gas Shade. Etched in beautiful carnation pattern, fluted edge. Fits 4-inch holder. Price **29c**

No. 3R2107 Electric Carnation Blown Shade. Fits 3-inch holder. Price.....**25c**

"QUEEN LOUISE" RICHLY EMBOSSED SATIN BRASS CHANDELIERS. Center body beautifully embossed in raised flower design with cast ornament at the bottom and embossed cup at the top. Large ceiling canopy. Arms fitted with rich cast brass ornaments. Fancy gas keys and embossed flower pattern shades.

3R2422	2-Light Gas Chandelier. Price.	$4.75
3R2423	3-Light Gas Chandelier. Price.	5.98
3R2425	2-Light Electric Chandelier...	5.48
3R2426	3-Light Electric Chandelier...	6.75
3R2428	4-Light Combination Chandelier	7.98

"CHRYSANTHEMUM" SATIN BRASS CHANDELIERS. Large center body of spun brass with ornamental casting at bottom. Spun canopy. The gracefully curved arms are fitted with handsome floral ornaments in chrysanthemum design. Fancy gas keys. Silver frosted blown shades with etched chrysanthemum pattern.

3R2430	2-Light Gas Chandelier. Price.	$4.45
3R2431	3-Light Gas Chandelier. Price.	5.48
3R2433	2-Light Electric Chandelier...	5.25
3R2434	3-Light Electric Chandelier...	6.49
3R2436	4-Light Combination Chandelier	7.58
3R2437	6-Light Combination Chandelier	9.98

"RADIANT DIANA" RICH FLUTED SATIN BRASS CHANDELIERS. Center body is embossed in rich fluted design with cup to match. The graceful curved arms are fluted and have ornamental floral castings. The tubing is fluted half way up. Embossed fluted canopy. Silver frosted blown etched shade with "Swastika" design.

3R2445	2-Light Gas Chandelier. Price.	$4.35
3R2446	3-Light Gas Chandelier. Price.	5.85
3R2449	2-Light Electric Chandelier..	5.18
3R2450	3-Light Electric Chandelier..	6.48
3R2451	4-Light Combination Chandelier	7.75

ROUND MISSION SATIN BRASS CHANDELIERS AND BRACKETS. Very rich and elegant in their simplicity. Hand spun ball body. Round tubing. Large size canopy, turned fittings and ring keys. Very handsome silver etched round mission globes. Combination fixtures have round gas candles and candle cups.

3R2460	2-Light Gas Chandelier. Price.	$6.98
3R2461	3-Light Gas Chandelier. Price.	8.95
3R2463	4-Light Combination Chandelier, 2 arms, 1 gas, 1 electric light on each arm. Price.	9.48
3R2464	6-Light Combination Chandelier, 3 arms, 1 gas, 1 elec. light on each arm. Price....	11.95
3R2466	2-Light Electric Chandelier. Same as No. 3R2464, without candles. Price....	7.38
3R2467	3-Light Electric Chandelier..	9.25
3R2470	2-Light Combination Bracket..	2.65
3R2472	1-Light Electric Bracket. Price.	1.75
3R2474	1-Light Gas Bracket. Price..	1.58

SQUARE MISSION SATIN BRASS CHANDELIERS AND BRACKETS; 2-inch square brass body 7 inches long, with ornamental tapering ends; square tubing and canopy to match; square arms and gas keys. Square silver etched glass shades. Combination fixtures have square white gas candles and candle cups.

3R2476	2-Light Gas Chandelier......	$7.65
3R2477	4-Light Gas Chandelier......	11.68
3R2478	2-Light Electric Chandelier..	8.37
3R2479	4-Light Electric Chandelier..	12.95
3R2482	4-Light Combination Chandelier, two arms, 1 gas, 1 elec. light on each arm. Price....	$11.25
3R2483	8-Light Combination Chandelier, four arms. See illustration. Price..............	$16.98
3R2487	2-Lt. Combination Pendant..	6.25
3R2488	1-Light Gas Pendant......	2.65
3R2489	1-Light Electric Pendant...	3.38
3R2491	2-Lt. Combination Bracket..	3.68
3R2492	1-Light Gas Bracket........	2.25
3R2493	1-Light Electric Bracket....	2.75

"VENUS" FANCY SATIN BRASS CHANDELIERS. Exceptionally rich and elegant. Extra large hand spun body of Grecian design, ornamented at top and bottom with carved brass. Tubing reeded half way. Large spun canopy. The gracefully curved arms project out of hand carved ornaments fastened to the center body. Silver frosted blown shades etched with tulip design.

3R2501	3-Light Gas Chandelier. Price.	$9.85
3R2502	4-Light Gas Chandelier. Price.	11.88
3R2505	3-Light Electric Chandelier..	9.48
3R2506	4-Light Electric Chandelier..	11.65
3R2507	4-Lt. Combination Chandelier.	11.98
3R2508	6-Lt. Combination Chandelier.	15.50

"PRIMO" SPECIAL VALUE CHANDELIERS. Furnished in either satin brass or in mat gilt and polished brass. Large pineapple shape spun brass body, richly embossed. Fancy cast brass ornament on bottom. The tubing is fluted and ornamented with a 3-inch fluted ball. The arms have rich floral brass castings. Large embossed canopy. Fancy gas keys and richly embossed silver frosted fluted lion shades. Exceptionally showy.

3R2512	2-Light Gas Chandelier. Price.	$5.65
3R2514	3-Light Gas Chandelier. Price.	7.48
3R2516	2-Light Electric Chandelier..	6.45
3R2517	3-Light Electric Chandelier..	7.98
3R2519	4-Lt. Combination Chandelier.	9.45
3R2520	6-Lt. Combination Chandelier.	12.35

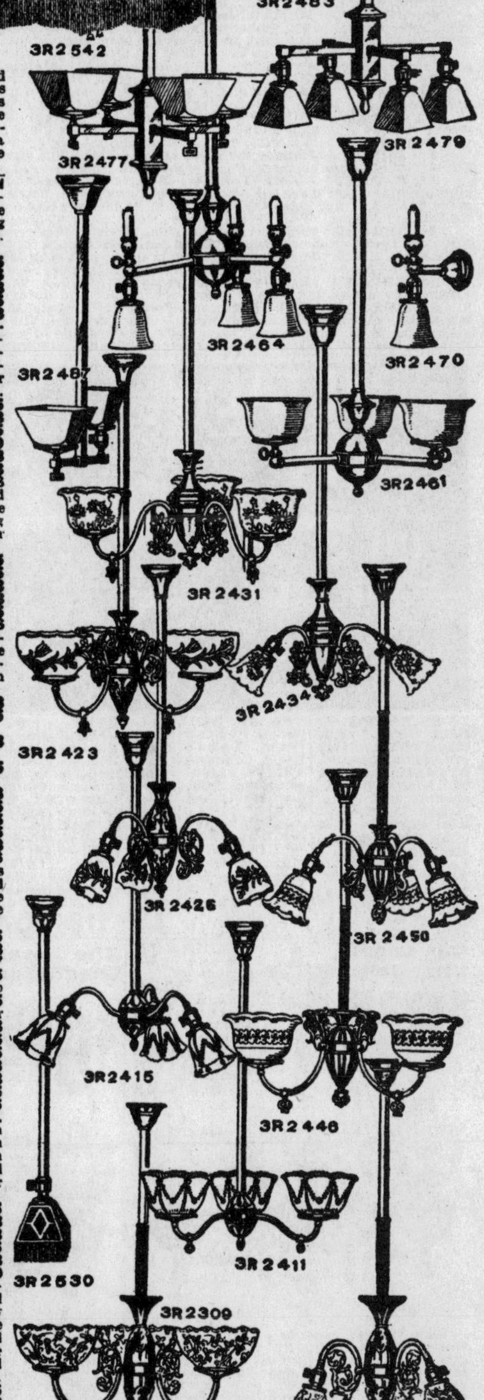

No. 3R2800 "OUR LEADER" Gas Portable. Height, 20 inches. Made of rope brass tubing with square iron base enameled black. Fitted complete with 80-candle power incandescent brass burner, tripod, shade ring, mantle, chimney and 10-inch opal dome shade, 6 feet of green mohair tubing and brass goose neck. Shipping weight, 16 lbs. Price.......**$1.48**

No. 3R2805 "PEERLESS" Gas Portable. Height, 21 inches. Made of embossed metal with fancy base, finished in a rich black, with polished brass band around center. Complete with incandescent brass burner, chimney, mantle, 10-inch porcelain lined green shade, shade ring, 4-inch beaded fringe, 6 feet tubing and goose neck. Wt., 19 lbs. Price....**$2.98**

No. 3R2810 "IDEAL" Electric Portable. Height, 18 inches. Special value. Made of satin brass with tulip leaf embossed base and 12-inch straw opalescent shade. Has 6 feet of electric cord, solid plug, Edison key socket and shade ring. Shipping wt., 18 lbs. Price, **$3.48**

No. 3R2812 Same as No. 3R2810 but fitted for gas with incandescent burner, mantle and chimney, 6 feet of gas tubing and brass goose neck. **Height, 20 inches.** Price..**$3.45**

No. 3R2815 "EMPRESS" Electric Portable. Height, 18 inches. Made of satin brass, richly embossed. Has 6 feet of silk cord, plug, chain pull Edison socket, 12-inch pink rose decorated, full tinted shade with 4-inch green beaded fringe. Wt., 20 lbs. Price....**$7.48**

No. 3R2820 "MISSION" Electric Portable. Height, 26 inches. Made of solid dark weathered oak with four metal arms, 12-inch green art glass shade, metal edges and grille work supported. 6 feet electric cord, plug and Edison key socket. Wt., 25 lbs. Price, **$3.98**

No. 3R2822 Exactly the same as No. 3R2820, but fitted for gas with incandescent burner, mantle and chimney, 6 feet of gas tubing and brass goose neck. Price....**$3.98**

No. 3R2827 'ORIENTAL" Art Electric Portable oxodized bronze finish Heavy ribbed metal stem, mounted on richly embossed base, fitted with 14-inch metal bound, green Cathedral Art glass shade. Height, 21 inches. Has 6 ft. of electric cord, plug and Edison key socket. Wt., 30 lbs Price..**$3.98**

No. 3R2830 "CUPID" Gas Portable. Height, 30 inches. An elegant, massive portable, cupid figure on an ornamental footed base. Rich copper bronze finish. Has incandescent gas burner, mantle and chimney, and richly tinted pink rose decorated 12-inch shade, 4-inch ruby beaded fringe, 6 feet of silk gas tubing and brass goose neck. Wt. 25 lbs. Price..**$7.98**

No. 3R2832 Exactly the same as No. 3R2830, but fitted for electricity, with Edison key socket and 6 feet of silk electric cord and detachable plug. Price...**$8.75**

No. 3R2835 "TULIP" Electric Portable. Height, 22 inches. Heavy solid satin brass cast column in rich rococo design. The shade is made of gracefully bent art pink glass mounted in an embossed brass frame in the shape of a tulip. Has Edison chain pull socket, 6 feet of silk electric cord and detachable plug. Shipping wt., 23 lbs. Price **$9.95**

No. 3R2837 Exactly the same portable as No. 3R2835, but fitted for gas with incandescent burner, mantle and chimney, 6 feet of silk gas tubing and brass goose neck. Shipping weight, 25 pounds. Price..**$9.95**

No. 3R2840 "REGENT" Electric Portable. Height, 25 inches. Made of extra heavy richly embossed and elaborately carved polished brass column mounted on very ornamental footed base. The shade is made of six panels of bent amber colored art glass with ornamental crown surrounded by an open cast metal band. Complete with 5-inch transparent amber beaded fringe, 6 feet of silk electric cord and detachable plug and Edison chain pull socket. Shipping weight, 26 pounds. Price..........................**$11.75**

No. 3R2842 Exactly the same as No. 3R2840, but fitted for gas with incandescent burner, mantle and chimney, 6 feet of silk gas tubing and goose neck. Price......**$11.75**

No. 3R2850 "ELK" Art Electric Portable. Best Proposition On Earth. Stands 32 inches high. A very elegant, massive and elaborate lamp. The column represents the trunk of a tree in its natural colors, and the elk is an exact reproduction with all colors true to life. The fancy metal crown and edges of the 14-inch shade are finished in a soft green. The panels are green cathedral art glass. Has 5-inch green beaded fringe, 6 feet of silk electric cord, plug and one Edison chain pull socket. Weight, 35 pounds. Price..............**$12.48**

No. 3R2855 "OUR FINEST" Electric Portable. Height, 32 inches. Made of satin brass. The beautiful 14-inch leaded shade has ten panels of cathedral glass in the softest tints. The concave base is extra large and richly carved, while the stem is ornamented with applied cast brass leaves and stems. 6 feet of silk cord, detachable plug and two Edison chain pull sockets. Shipping weight, 30 lbs. Price..................**$14.98**

No. 3R2860 Adjustable Desk Light. Length, 40 inches. Made of polished brass with heavy weighted base and spiral flexible stem which enables the light to be placed in any position desired. Fitted with 6 feet of silk cord, detachable plug, Edison key socket and green reflecting aluminum lined shade. Shipping weight, 10 pounds. Price........**$3.45**

No. 3R2875 Polished Brass Handled Candlestick. Height to top of candle, 6½ inches. Shipping weight, 1 pound. Price, complete with candle **17c**

No. 3R2880 Polished Brass Colonial Candlestick. Height to top of candle, 10 inches. Shipping weight, 1½ pounds. Price, complete with candle..................**21c**

No. 3R2890 Table Candlestick with Shade. Height, 15 inches. Polished brass Colonial design. Fitted complete with candle, shade holder and hand painted rose candle shade. The edges are of strong green fiber. Weight, 3 pounds. Price, complete................**98c**

No. 3R703 Brass Night Lamp. Fitted with revolving reflector and hanging bracket, complete with Nutmeg burner, chimney and wick. Height, 7¾ in. Wt., 8 oz. Price.....**23c**

No. 3R714 Non-Explosive Solid Brass Lamp. Guaranteed to be non-explosive, fitted with No. 1 hinge burner, chimney and wick. Height, 12 in. Wt., 1 lb.......**69c**

No. 3R730 Nickel Plated Brass Table Lamp. Complete with No. 2 burner, electric chimney and wick and 7-inch white dome shade. Height, 15 in. Wt., 12 lbs.**85c**

No. 3R731 Same as No. 3R730 but with 7-inch green dome shade. Price..**$1.19**

No. 3R734 Nickel Plated Brass Reading Lamp. With 10-inch white dome shade, No. 2 central draft burner, Rochester chimney and wick. Height, 20 in. Wt., 16 lbs.**$1.48**

No. 3R735 Same as No. 3R734, but fitted with 10-inch green dome shade ...**$1.89**

No. 3R738 Embossed Handled Reading Lamp, made of brass nickel plated, No. 2 central draft burner, with 10-inch white dome shade, No. 2 Rochester chimney and wick. Height, 19 in. Wt., 17 lbs.....**$2.28**

No. 3R739 Same as No. 3R738, but fitted with 10-inch green dome shade. Price**$2.75**

No. 3R744 Smokeless Parlor Lamp, made of solid embossed brass, No. 2 central draft burner, with patent which prevents smoking. Complete with 10-inch white shade, No. 2 Rochester chimney and wick. Height, 20 in. Wt., 16 lbs. Price ..**$1.98**

No. 3R745 Same as No. 3R744, but with 10-inch green shade. Price **$2.48**

No. 3R716 Brass Central Draft Handled Lamp, No. 1 central draft burner, 7-inch white dome shade, No. 1 Rochester chimney and wick. Height. 14 in. Wt., 12 lb.**$1.25**

No. 3R717 Same as No. 3R716, with 7-in. green dome shade..**$1.49**

No. 3R701 Brass Night Lamp, 7¾ in. high, with Gem burner, chimney and wick Wt., 6 oz. **16c**

No. 3R712 Solid Brass Monarch Hand Lamp. With No. 1 burner and wick, and No. 1 Sun chimney. Height, 11 in. Wt., 10 oz. Price ..**38c**

No. 3R707 Footed Glass Hand Lamp. Complete with No. 1 Sun burner, chimney and wick. Capacity, 12 ounces. Weight, 3 lbs. Price **21c**

No. 3R709 Glass Stand Lamp. Complete with No. 1 burner, chimney and wick. Capacity, 12 ounces. Weight, 4 lbs. Price..........**32c**

No. 3R711 Large Stand Lamp with No. 2 burner, chimney and wick. Capacity, 16 ounces. Weight, 5 lbs. Price **39c**

No. 3R710 Glass Sewing Lamp, with No. 2 burner, chimney and wick. Capacity, 32 ounces. Fine light. Price **45c**

No. 3R722 Metal Bracket Lamp with glass fount, No. 2 burner, chimney and wick, 7-inch glass reflector. Weight, 10 pounds. Price.......**44c**

No. 3R756 Juno Students' Lamp. Solid brass, nickel finish No. 0 central draft burner, chimney and wick, 7-inch white shade. Height, 21 inches. Weight, 18 pounds. Price..........................**$3.15**

No. 3R757 Same as No. 3R756, but with green shade. Price **$3.35**

No. 3R759 Ideal Students' lamp. Brass, nickel finish, No. 1 Rochester burner and wick; 10-inch white shade. Gives splendid reading light. Wt., 25 pounds. Price...**$4.98**

No. 3R760 Same as No. 3R759, but with 10-inch green shade. Price **$5.49**

OIL CHANDELIERS

Guaranteed to be made of solid brass. Fitted with patent extension. Length, extended, 60 inches. The burners of all our founts can be lighted without removing either the chimney or shade.

Our Leader Chandelier. $6.85

No. 3R822 Two-Light Chandelier. Price..**$6.85**
No. 3R823 Three-Light Chandelier. Price..**$8.98**
No. 3R824 Four-Light Chandelier. Price **$10.95**

Made of solid brass in a bright burnished finish. It is fitted with a richly embossed, pear shaped center pendant and highly polished brass arms and tubing and an embossed ceiling plate. Furnished with fancy glass founts and a No. 2 Unique burner and comes complete with 1-inch wicks, No. 2 hinge chimneys and etched shades.

This is the cheapest price at which genuine solid brass chandeliers have ever been sold.

The Jewel Chandelier. $9.85

No. 3R832 Two-Light Chandelier. Price..**$9.85**
No. 3R833 Three-Light Chandelier. Price **$11.95**
No. 3R834 Four-Light Chandelier. Price **$14.48**

It is made of solid brass in bright burnished finish, with an embossed center ring, studded with twelve colored cut glass jewels, and thirty crystal cut glass prisms suspended from it. It is fitted with fancy glass founts and No. 2 Unique burners and comes complete with 1-inch wick, No. 2 hinge chimneys and handsomely etched shades. The ribbed arms and tubing and embossed ceiling plate make this a very neat and attractive chandelier.

New Art Chandelier. $11.85

No. 3R837 Two-Light Chandelier. Price **$11.85**
No. 3R838 Three-Light Chandelier. Price **$15.98**
No. 3R839 Four-Light Chandelier. Price **$18.45**

Made of solid brass with the new brush brass finish, with the tubing, arms and supports in ribbed design. Fitted with oxidized brass ornaments on the arm supports and a fancy ceiling plate. Elegantly embossed solid brass No. 1 Miller founts with central draft, 60-candle power burners and comes complete with No. 1 Rochester chimneys, wicks and daintily etched shades.

Our Finest Chandelier. $15.85

No. 3R845 Two-Light Chandelier. Price **$15.85**
No. 3R846 Three-Light Chandelier. Price **$18.95**
No. 3R847 Four-Light Chandelier. Price **$21.48**

Made of solid brass in new patina finish (satin finish). Beautiful spun brass body, shading to a dark oxidized color, surrounded by a rich embossed crown from which hang thirty cut glass prisms, giving a brilliant effect when lighted. Ornamental supports for the arms finished in Roman yellow gold. Fancy ceiling plate. Fitted with richly embossed No. 1 Miller founts with central draft, 60-candle power burners, No. 1 Rochester chimneys, wicks and beautifully etched shades in rose design.

LAMP DEPARTMENT.

WE TAKE PLEASURE IN INTRODUCING AN ENTIRELY NEW LINE OF ALL DIFFERENT STYLES OF LAMPS.

THESE LAMPS were selected as the very best of the different grades which they represent after long and earnest investigation. We know that our prices cannot be duplicated by any other firm, style, quality and workmanship of the lamps taken into consideration. They are all packed very carefully so that we can guarantee their arrival in perfect condition. If the best of oil is used and the wick is kept clean, we guarantee the lamps to give perfect satisfaction.

All Lamp Chimneys herein quoted are made by the famous Macbeth factories and are universally known as the best in the world. They are furnished in the following grades:

Anchor Brand, made from the first quality flint glass and is the best medium price chimney made.

Zenith Brand, made of fine lead glass, oil finished and annealed. Recommended as a high grade chimney.

Macbeth Pearl Glass Chimneys, universally recognized as absolutely the best chimney made, finely annealed and oil tempered, guaranteed to stand extreme heat. Each stamped with the maker's name and number for future reference.

Alabaster Chimneys, known as the unbreakable chimney, made from extra heavy especially prepared glass and guaranteed to stand exceedingly tough usage.

All our chimneys are packed in square cartons.

Catalogue No.	Anchor Brand.	Outside Bottom, inches	Measure. Height, inches	Price, per doz.
2C600	No. 0 Sun Crimp	2	7	$0.40
2C601	No. 1 Sun Crimp	2⅛	7½	.48
2C602	No. 2 Sun Crimp	3	8½	.59
	Zenith Brand.			
2C604	No. 1 Sun Crimp	2⅛	7½	.63
2C605	No. 2 Sun Crimp	3	8½	.77
2C607	No. 1 Sun Hinge Crimp	2⅝	7½	.70
2C608	No. 2 Sun Hinge Crimp	2⅝	8¼	.90
2C609	No. 1 Rochester	2	8	.85
2C610	No. 2 Rochester	2⅝	10	.90
2C611	No. 2 Rochester	2⅝	12	1.40
2C612	No. 2 Electric	3	10	.88
	Macbeth Pearl Top and Pearl Glass.			
2C614	Macbeth No. 500 (0 Sun)			.79
2C615	Macbeth No. 502 (1 Sun)			.83
2C616	Macbeth No. 504 (2 Sun)			.95
2C640	Macbeth No. 4 (Jr. Rochester)			.85
2C620	Macbeth No. 6 (1 Rochester)			.92
2C621	Macbeth No. 12 (2 Rochester, 10 in.)			1.09
2C621½	Macbeth No. 9 (2 Rochester, 12 in.)			1.55
2C626	Macbeth No. 10 (3 Rochester)			1.95
2C624	Macbeth No. 40 (2 Electric, 10 in.)			1.10
2C625	Macbeth No. 63 (2 Electric, Slim, 10 in.)			1.12
2C630	Macbeth No. 32 (1 Belgian)			1:20
2C631	Macbeth No. 36 (00 Belgian)			1.70
2C632	Macbeth No. 50 (1 Student)			.90
2C633	Nutmeg, 3⅛ in. tall, 1⅛-in. bottom			.20
2C634	Gem, 4¾ in. tall, 1½-in. bottom			.25
	Alabaster Chimneys, extra heavy.			
2C641	No. 1 Sun, plain top			1.10
2C642	No. 2 Sun, plain top			1.30

BURNERS AND WICKS.

Genuine Banner Burner, made of solid brass. This is the best sun burner made.

No. 2C650 No. 0 Banner Burner, takes No. 0 wick and No. 0 Sun chimney. Price.......4c

No. 2C651 No. 1 Banner Burner, takes No. 1 wick and No. 1 Sun chimney. Price.......5c

No. 2C652 No. 2 Banner Burner, takes No. 2 wick and No. 2 Sun chimney. Price.......6c

GENUINE CLIMAX BURNER.

No. 2C656 Made of solid brass. Has double thread to fit either No. 2 or No. 3 lamp collar. Takes No. 3 wick, 1½ inches wide, and No. 2 Electric chimney. This is the most powerful single wick burner made. Price.......15c

AMERICAN DUPLEX BURNER.

No. 2C658 Made of solid brass. Has double thread to fit No. 2 and No. 3 lamp collar. This is a double wick burner, using two No. 3 wicks 1½ inches wide and a No. 2 Electric chimney. Gives a strong, steady light and is perfectly safe. Price.......25c

WICKS.	No.	Size		Price
No. 2C661	0	⅜-inch.	Per dozen	3c
No. 2C662	1	⅝-inch.	Per dozen	4c
No. 2C663	2	1 -inch.	Per dozen	5c
No. 2C664	3	1½-inch.	Per dozen	8c

No. 2C669 Lamp Wicks, Junior Rochester, round, 1¼ inches when flat. Price, per dozen.....14c

No. 2C670 Lamp Wicks, No. 1 Rochester, round, 1⅝ inches when flat. Price, per dozen.....16c

No. 2C671 Lamp Wicks, No. 2 Rochester, round, 2½ inches when flat. Price, per dozen.....19c

No. 2C672 Lamp Wicks, No. 3 Rochester, round, 4¼ inches when flat. Price, per dozen.....78c

No. 2C673 Lamp Wicks, No. 1 Belgian, round, 2 inches when flat. Price, per dozen.....50c

Brass Night Lamps.

No. 2C701 Brass Night Lamp. 7¼ inches high, complete. Gem burner, chimney and wick. Price.......15c

No. 2C703 Brass Night Lamp. This is the most practical night lamp made. The lamp is fitted with a revolving reflector and a bracket which enables you to hang lamp on wall. Height, 7¾ inches.

Price, complete.......33c

Wall Lamps.

No. 2C705 This Very Useful Lamp became popular at once because of its great utility and low price. It has removable glass fount and reflector, No. 2 Sun burner and chimney. Is made to hang on a wall or rest on a table, and reflector can be taken off if desired. Shipping weight, 8 pounds. Price.......25c

Hand Lamps.

No. 2C707 Plain Footed Glass Hand Lamp, complete with chimney, No. 1 Sun burner and wick. Safely packed so that it can be shipped without danger of breakage. Just the thing for carrying about the house. Guaranteed perfect in every way. Price.......24c

Large Stand Lamp made of clear pressed glass, complete with Sun burner, wick and chimney. Just the thing for bedrooms or to carry around the house.

No. 2C709 Crystal Stand Lamp, with No. 1 burner, chimney and wick. Price...35c

No. 2C711 Large Stand Lamp, like No. 2C709, with No. 2 Burner, wick and chimney. Price....43c

No. 2C713 Our Heavy Imitation Cut Glass Footed Hand Lamp complete with No. 1 Sun burner, wick and chimney. Price..33c

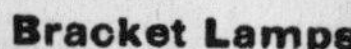

Bracket Lamps.

No. 2C722 Kitchen or Dining Room Bracket Lamp, finished in French bronze, has glass fount, No. 2 Banner burner, and 7-inch silvered glass reflector; complete with chimney as shown. Shipping weight, about 15 pounds. Price.......45c

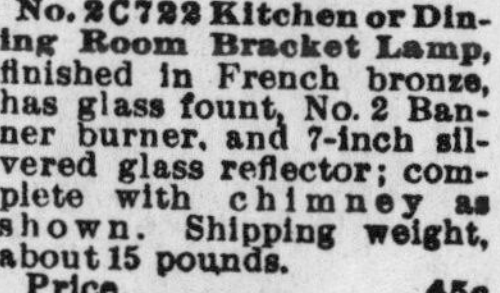

No. 2C724 Dining Room or Hall Lamp. Is the strongest and best finished on the market. We furnish it complete with glass fount, 8-inch silvered glass reflector, No. 2 Banner burner and chimney. The bracket is made of cast iron, fancy design, bronze finish. Shipping weight, 15 pounds. Price, complete, 65c

Our $1.85 Bracket Lamp.

No. 2C728 Two-Joint Church, Parlor or Bedroom Swinging Bracket Lamp, with 20-inch rope design arm. Is made of bronze metal, gold finished and has fancy crystal oil fount and shade, handsomely etched body with genuine cut glass crown design edge. Furnished complete with No. 2 Unique burner and chimney. Can be lighted without removing chimney or globe. Weight, securely packed, 20 pounds. Price.......$1.85

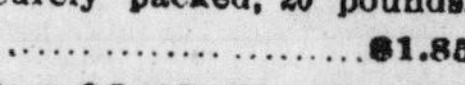

Our $2.45 Bracket Lamp.

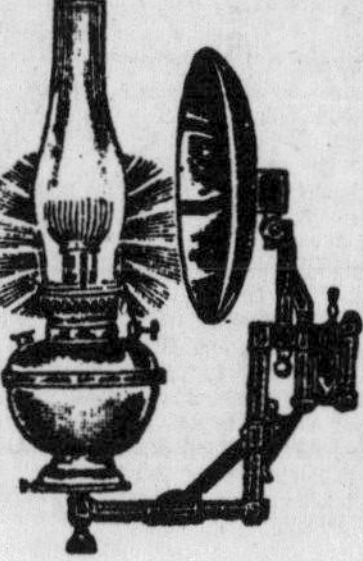

No. 2C750 Where a strong light is needed we recommend this attractive and serviceable lamp. The bracket is made of cast iron and is finished in French bronze, fount is the celebrated Royal center draft burner, giving a light equal to 100 candle power, is made of brass, highly polished, and will hold enough oil to burn eight hours. The silvered glass reflector is 10 inches in diameter and can be so adjusted as to throw light wherever needed. Shipping weight, 25 pounds. Price, complete.......$2.45

Wonderful Value for 79 Cents.

No. 2C730 At 79 cents we offer a lamp which has usually sold for twice this amount. The base is of brass, heavily nickel plated. It has a nickel plated No. 2 burner of extraordinary capillary power. It is furnished complete with wick, chimney, shade ring and a 7-inch imported white dome shade, making the best and cheapest reading lamp on the market. Shipping weight, 20 pounds. Price.......79c

No. 2C731 Nickel Lamp, exactly like above, with 7-inch imported green shade. Price.......$1.19

Reading or Table Lamps.

No. 2C734 Our Polished Nickel Reading or Table Lamp with one of the best center draft burners on the market. It will give as good light as a gas burner. It is complete with a 10-inch opal dome shade, holder, wick and chimney. This lamp is well made and shapely throughout. It gives a strong, steady, bright light and the wick can be raised or lowered instantly. It is made of plain polished metal with neat embossing at base, giving it a handsome appearance. Shipping weight, 20 pounds. Price.......$1.48

No. 2C735 Nickel Lamp, exactly like above, with 10-inch imported green shade. Price.......$1.99

No. 2C738 Parlor or Reading Lamp. This handsome, nickel center draft lamp is superior to all others because it is suitable for a parlor as well as a sewing lamp. It is very rich in pattern and for burning qualities it is unequaled. It is richly embossed and has two handles at the sides which greatly add to the appearance of the lamp. This lamp is made from solid brass and is full nickel plated throughout, and equipped with a large, high grade Royal Burner which is of an improved center draft type and is considered to be the best made. It is so simple in construction that the lamp can be easily taken apart, re-wicked and cleaned with no trouble. It is complete with a 10-inch imported white opal shade, 10-inch tripod and No. 2 Rochester chimney. Shipping weight, 20 pounds. Price.......$2.25

No. 2C739 Nickel Lamp, exactly like above, with 10-inch imported green shade. Price...$2.75

No. 2C742 Nickel Reading or Parlor Lamp, is the latest and best made, being smokeless and odorless, having a patent wick regulator which prevents the wick from being turned too high. Besides this important feature it has an oil gauge showing the quantity of oil in the lamp at all times. It is fitted with H. B. & H. No. 2 center draft burner, which gives double the light with the smallest quantity of oil. It is complete with 10-inch imported reading shade, shade holder, chimney and wick. This lamp usually retails for double the price we ask. Shipping weight when packed, 20 pounds. Price.......$1.95

No. 2C743 Nickel Lamp, as above described, with 10-inch imported green shade. Price...$2.45

STUDENT LAMPS.

Student Lamps are universally recognized as the most perfect lamp for reading and sewing, because they can be adjusted to any height and the powerful light is thrown directly upon the work, and as the oil fount is at one side there is no shadow underneath the lamp. We have handled different makes of Student Lamps for years and we find that the ones we offer below are absolutely the best upon the market, as the mechanism is so perfect that they give no trouble.

This Student Lamp is nickel plated, has center draft burner with removable fount and perfect wick attachments, Junior Rochester wick and chimney, 7-inch dome shade. It will burn nine hours with one filling. Height to top of rod 21 inches. Is perfectly safe and reliable. Packed complete in a box for shipment. Weight, 16 pounds.

No. 2C756 With white shade. Price.......$2.89

No. 2C757 With green shade. Price.......3.14

We also furnish a student lamp same style as No. 2C756, only much larger in size, which is equipped with No. 1 Rochester burner, wick and large 10-inch imported dome shade. This lamp is recommended to give double the light of the smaller size and is well worth the difference in price.

No. 2C759 Ideal Student Lamp. Price..$4.45

No. 2C760 Same as No. 2C759, with 10-inch imported green shade. Price.......$4.75

Shipping weight, 22 pounds.

BANQUET LAMPS

We take pleasure in presenting an entirely new and complete line of Banquet Lamps and Globes, which were selected with the greatest care after long and careful investigation. **We feel confident we are offering the best line of lamps made,** as every lamp is carefully tinted and decorated by the most skilled artists. Every lamp is equipped with the best quality burners, wicks and chimneys. **Our prices** are from 33 to 50 per cent less than quoted by the regular crockery dealers.

Each lamp is carefully packed in box or barrel to insure safe delivery.

No. 2F951 Rosalie Banquet Lamp. Very neat and attractive; best low priced lamp made It is richly embossed with roses and rose leaves, and has scroll panels as shown in illustration. Made of rich satin finished glass. It is 18 inches high and complete with a 7½-inch globe, No. 2 burner and wick and No. 2 electric chimney. Has a brass metal base. Shipping weight, 14 pounds. Price..............**89c**

No. 2F954 Our Beauty Banquet Lamp is beautifully decorated by hand, with white and purple chrysanthemums and foliage, as shown in illustration. The body or background is richly tinted in pink, heavily shaded at the upper and lower extremities. It is 19 inches high, and has an 8-inch globe. The foot is made of cast metal heavily plated with brass and lacquered. It is furnished complete with No. 2 Sun burner and wick, and No. 2 Electric chimney and shade ring. Shipping weight, 20 pounds. Price............**99c**

No. 2F964 Our Acme Banquet Lamp is without doubt the prettiest medium priced lamp made. Embossings form rich pannels, and are decorated with beautiful sprays of wild roses and green leaves as shown in the illustration. It is richly tinted in pink and yellow, forming a beautiful contrast which can only be appreciated when seen. Complete with No. 3 Climax burner and wick, and No. 2 Electric chimney. Height, 22 inches. It has a beautiful brass plated cast metal base. Shipping weight, 23 pounds. Price........**$1.98**

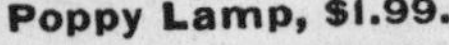

Poppy Lamp, $1.99.

No. 2F967 This Beautiful Parlor Lamp is exceptionally large and attractive. It is complete with 9-inch globe and vase, and measures 21 inches high. The decoration consists of large hand painted poppies in pink, purple and white. The globe and also the vase are delicately tinted at the top in light green and the bottom in pink. It has a heavy brass plated metal foot of scroll design. It is equipped with No. 3 Climax burner, No. 3 wick and No. 2 Electric chimney, and produces 60-candle power light. Shipping weight, 20 pounds. Price........**$1.99**

Customers living in the Central and Eastern states who order one of our lamps only, will receive it shipped direct from our factory in Pennsylvania, thus effecting a saving in transportation charges.

No. 2F968 Clematis Lamp. This lamp is the best low priced central draft lamp made. It is decorated with large sprays of pink Clematis and green leaves, which form a very pleasing design. The background is richly tinted with light green and orange. It is 23 inches high and has a 9½-inch globe. It has the latest improved Success central draft burner, 60-candle power with large removable brass oil fount, complete with a No. 1 Belgium chimney and wick. It has a heavy cast base, made of satin finish brass. Shipping weight, 22 pounds. Price........**$2.48**

No. 2F972 Cerise Beauty. This banquet lamp is made of ruby glass and when lighted produces a rich ruby glow, one of the most cheery and attractive lights which throws a ruby glow on all surroundings. It is handsomely embossed in large scrolls of floral design, and handsomely embossed satin finish cerise glass which make up an attractive and handsome lamp. It is furnished with improved Success central draft burner, 80-candle power and wick, No. 1 Belgium chimney. It has a solid brass removable fount and brass plated crown. Height, 26 inches, and has a 10-inch globe. Shipping weight, 28 pounds. Price..............**$2.96**

No. 2F976 The American Beauty Lamp, $2.98. This is one of the prettiest lamps shown this season. The globe measures 10½ inches in diameter; the vase or cylinder to match is of equal size. The lamp measures 26 inches high. The hand painted decorations consist of beautiful American Beauty roses and foliage on a blue tinted background. It has the improved Success central draft burner, and takes No. 1 Belgium chimney and round wick. It produces a strong and steady 80-candle power light. This lamp compares favorably with those sold by crockery dealers at $4.50 and $5.00. Shipping weight, 25 pounds. Price.......**$2.98**

No. 2F983 This handsome lamp is one of the latest and most up to date patterns made. It is made of satin finish glass, French etched on the inside and decorated on the outside with beautiful sprays of pansies in their natural colors and green leaves. It is complete with a large 10-inch dome shade, and solid brass ring which is trimmed with 4-inch imported beads to match. It has the latest improved Success central draft burner and wick, 100-candle power, and No. 1 Belgium chimney. The oil pot is made of solid brass. All metal parts are furnished in satin finished brass. It is 24 inches high. Shipping weight, 25 pounds. Price..............**$3.48**

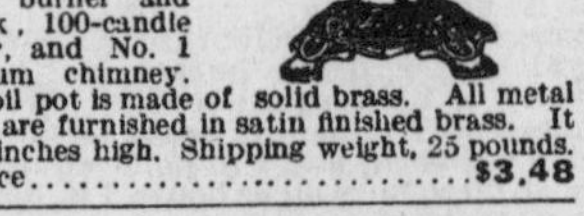

PROFIT SHARING ARTICLES

SEE THEM ON PAGES 1 AND 2.

No. 2F986 Romeo Lamp, $3.49, is one of the prettiest lamps made in a lilac design. It is large and shapely throughout. The decoration consists of large hand painted lilacs, highly enameled, with light green leaves. The lamp and globe are richly tinted in a dark green and when lighted, the beautiful lilacs appear true to life. A decoration of this kind appeals to the most critical and is sure to meet with favor everywhere. The burner, which is the highest grade central draft type, produces a 100-candle power light and is complete with No. 2 Rochester chimney and wick. This lamp stands 27½ inches high and has a large 10-inch globe and is adorned with heavy brass crown and base which is finely gold lacquered. Securely packed in a box. Shipping weight, 30 pounds. Price......**$3.49**

No. 2F980 This beautiful lamp is particularly attractive owing to the beautiful dark American Beauty roses which form the floral decorations. These roses with the green foliage are printed on the tinted green background before the last firing of the lamp in the kiln and then the large roses are put on by hand in the deep red color, making the flowers stand out distinct from the lamp. The base is of solid cast brass and the fount holder has a solid brass drawn ring. The removable oil fount is of brass and has the No. 2 100-candle power center draft burner, taking No. 2 Rochester chimney and round wick. Shipping weight, 30 pounds. Price...........**$3.55**

No. 2F1009 Our Bordeau Lamp. This is an exceptionally attractive lamp and represents the highest grade of workmanship. As illustration shows, it is elegantly embossed, bringing out the large clusters of grapes and leaves, and also panel scrolls in bold relief. The grapes and leaves are colored true to life. Body of globe and base are richly tinted in brown and shaded into dark orange. The mountings of this lamp are made of cast metal and gold plated. It has the latest imported Success central draft burner 100-candle power, and No. 1 Belgian chimney. It has a solid brass oil pot, and heavy brass gold plated crown. This lamp is one of the best values ever offered. It is 26 inches high, and has a 10-inch globe. Shipping weight, 32 pounds. Price..............................**$3.97**

No. 2F1016 Kismet Lamp, $4.88. Beautifully decorated by hand. This lamp is the work of high class artists, the decoration consisting of large white and pink chrysanthemums and light green leaves, very cleverly painted by hand and in such a manner that the beautiful flowers are true to life. The entire lamp is most handsomely tinted in pink and light green, forming a fine background for the flowers. No lamp has ever been made that can surpass it in beauty. It is extra large, measuring 26½ inches high and 11½-inch globe and 13-inch base. It has the best grade central draft burner, which produces 100-candle power light, and removable oil fount made of solid brass and is complete with No. 2 Rochester chimney and round wick. All metal parts, including the fancy cast crown and large base, are made of brass, gold plated and lacquered and will not tarnish. No better lamp made at any price. Securely packed in a barrel. Shipping weight, 40 pounds. Price..............................**$4.88**

No. 2F1017 Peony Lamp. This lamp represents one of the largest and best lamps we offer. It measures 29 inches high, and has a large 12-inch globe. The decoration consists of large pink and white peonies with green leaves with a beautifully tinted pink and green background. The shape is the newest offered this season. It has a large massive brass crown and brass feet, which forms the base. All metal parts are gold plated fully protected from wear and tarnishing by a heavy coat of lacquer. It is fitted with the latest improved Success central draft burner 100-candle power, and wick, No. 1 Belgian chimney and oil pot of solid brass richly gold plated. It is securely packed in a barrel. Shipping weight, 45 pounds. Price..............................**$4.98**

No. 2F1022 Cardinal Lamp. This is an exceptionally large and handsome lamp and is made of fine ruby glass, beautifully embossed pattern. The outer surface of the globe and cylinder are made of glossy finish; inside being French or rough etching. When lighted this lamp produces a beautiful rich ruby glow. It is completed with a large 12-inch dome shade, which is mounted on a solid brass 12-inch ring and ornamented with 5-inch imported ruby bead fringe. This is the latest creation in high grade lamps. All metal parts are heavily brass plated and gold lacquered. It is equipped with the latest imported Success central draft 100-candle power burner and wick and No. 1 Belgium chimney. The oil pot is made of solid brass richly plated and lacquered. It is 27 inches high. Shipping weight, 33 pounds. Price.........**$6.25**

Decorated Globes.

Decorated Globes for banquet or vase lamps, will fit any 4-inch globe ring. These globes are beautifully decorated by hand with large pink wild roses and green leaves on a tinted background. Furnished in three tints, pink, yellow or green. Be sure to mention color of tint and size desired.

	Diameter	Price
No. 2F1201	8 inches	55c
No. 2F1202	9 inches	73c
No. 2F1203	10 inches	98c

Shipping weight from 8 to 12 pounds.

Crystal Etched Globes for banquet or vase lamps, made of etched crystal glass, beautifully figured like illustration. Will fit any 4-inch globe ring.

No. 2F1255 Diameter, 8 inches. Price.........**57c**
No. 2F1256 Diameter, 9 inches. Price..............**68c**
No. 2F1257 Diameter, 10 inches. Price..............**99c**
No. 2F1258 Diameter, 10 inches, made of satin ruby glass. Price..........**$1.79**
Shipping weight from 8 to 12 pounds.

Banquet Lamp Globes beautifully decorated by hand with large white and pink chrysanthemums and dark green leaves on background, richly tinted in pink or light green. An exceptionally fine globe at an extremely low price. Be sure to mention the color of tinting and size desired.

	Diameter	Price
No. 2F1264	8 inches	$0.75
No. 2F1265	9 inches	.95
No. 2F1266	10 inches	1.39
No. 2F1267	11 inches	1.69

Shipping weight from 8 to 12 pounds.

SPECIAL BARGAINS IN BANQUET LAMPS.

Customers living in the Central and Eastern states who order one of our lamps only will receive it shipped direct from our factory in Pennsylvania, thus effecting a saving in transportation charges.

The Rustic Parlor Lamp, 89c.

No. 2 C 950

This Handsome Banquet Lamp is an entirely new style of decoration this year, being of shaded myrtle green and pink. It is heavily embossed, as shown in the illustration, which adds strength to the lamp as well as enhancing its appearance. It has a solid brass No. 2 burner, shade ring and No. 2 chimney. It is 17 inches high and has an 8-inch globe. At the extremely low price there is no reason why any home should not be decorated with this useful as well as ornamental lamp. Carefully packed to insure safe delivery. Shipping weight, 15 pounds.
Price 89c

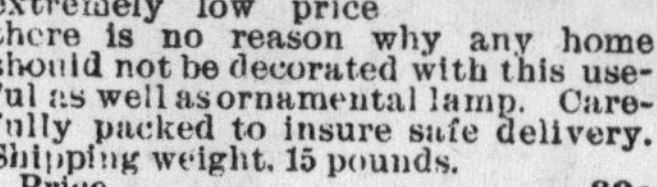

The Carmen, $1.09.

No. 2C955 This Banquet Lamp has unusually handsome decorations, consisting of large red flowers with dark green foliage on a tinted pink and white background. The bowl is heavily embossed, thus adding strength as well as attractive appearance to the lamp. It is 19 inches high and has an 8-inch globe. The metal foot is of cast brass. It is furnished with No. 2 brass Banner burner and takes a No. 2 chimney and 1-inch wick. Shipping weight 18 pounds. Price.......................$1.09

The Victor, $1.89.

No. 2C965 This Lamp is a handsome embossed design, as illustrated. The embossing is of dark green forming panels of white, which have a large red flower and foliage in the center of each. This same embossing makes the lamp very strong. The metal base of the lamp is of cast brass. It has a removable oil fount of brass which can be taken from the bowl of the lamp to be filled. It is also furnished with a No. 2 brass burner and takes No. 2 chimney and 1-inch wick. Owing to the removable fount this lamp is one of the best bargains which we furnish. It is 20 inches high and has an 8-inch globe. Shipping weight, 20 pounds. Price.......................$1.89

Our Poppy Lamp, $1.98.

No. 2C967 This Beautiful Reception or Parlor Lamp is exceptionally large and attractive. It is complete with 9-inch globe and 9-inch vase, and measures 21 inches high. The decoration consists of large hand painted poppies in pink, purple and white. The globe and also the vase are delicately tinted at the top in light green and the bottom in pink. It has a heavy brass plated metal foot of scroll design. It is equipped with No. 3 Climax burner, No. 3 wick and No. 2 electric chimney, and produces 60-candle power light. This lamp, without doubt, is the greatest value ever offered. Carefully packed in wood box. Shipping weight, 20 pounds. Price.......................$1.98

Cerise Beauty, $2.95.

No. 2C985

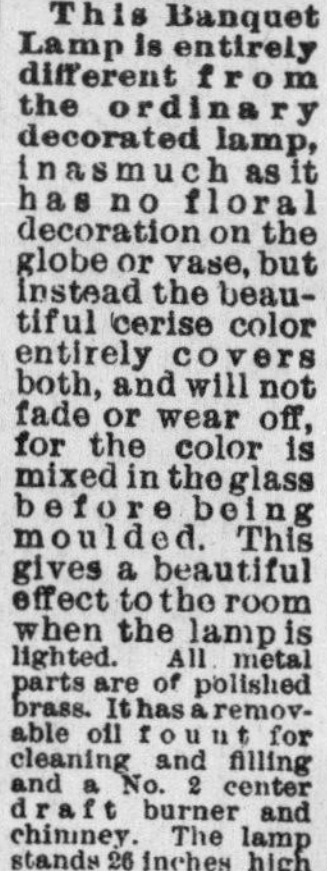

This Banquet Lamp is entirely different from the ordinary decorated lamp, inasmuch as it has no floral decoration on the globe or vase, but instead the beautiful cerise color entirely covers both, and will not fade or wear off, for the color is mixed in the glass before being moulded. This gives a beautiful effect to the room when the lamp is lighted. All metal parts are of polished brass. It has a removable oil fount for cleaning and filling and a No. 2 center draft burner and chimney. The lamp stands 26 inches high and has a 10-inch globe. Shipping weight, 25 pounds. Price......$2.95

The American Beauty Lamp.

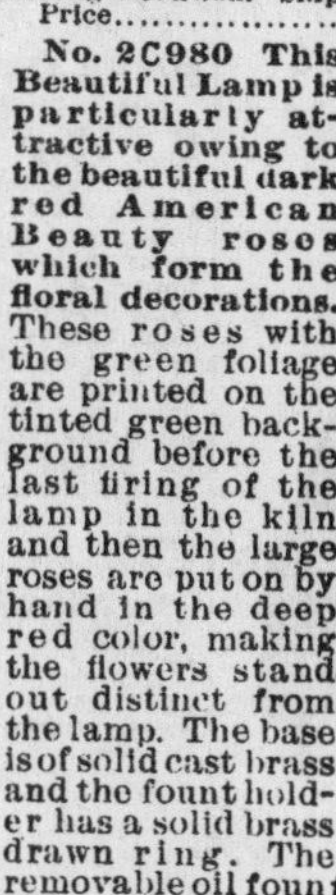

No. 2C976 This is one of the prettiest lamps shown this season. The globe measures 10½ inches in diameter, the vase or cylinder to match is of equal size. The lamp measures 26 inches high. The hand painted decorations consist of beautiful American Beauty roses and foliage, on a blue tinted background, forming a rich contrast. It is equipped with the improved Success central draft burner, and takes No. 1 Belgium chimney and round wick. It produces a strong and steady 80-candle power light. This lamp compares favorably with those sold by crockery dealers at $4.50 and $5.00. Carefully packed in strong wood box. Shipping weight, 25 pounds. Price.......................$2.98

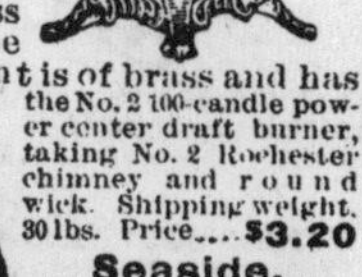

No. 2C980 This Beautiful Lamp is particularly attractive owing to the beautiful dark red American Beauty roses which form the floral decorations. These roses with the green foliage are printed on the tinted green background before the last firing of the lamp in the kiln and then the large roses are put on by hand in the deep red color, making the flowers stand out distinct from the lamp. The base is of solid cast brass and the fount holder has a solid brass drawn ring. The removable oil fount is of brass and has the No. 2 100-candle power center draft burner, taking No. 2 Rochester chimney and round wick. Shipping weight, 30 lbs. Price.......$3.20

Seaside.

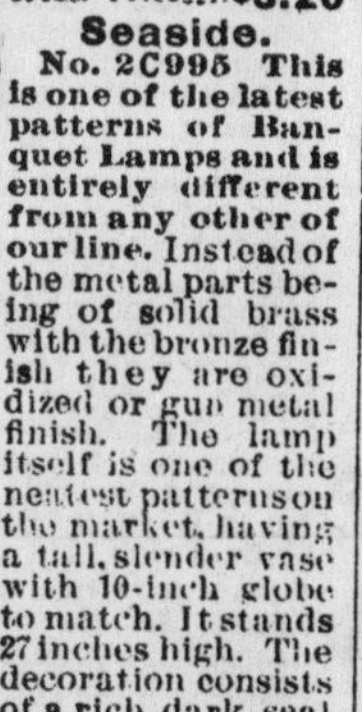

No. 2C995 This is one of the latest patterns of Banquet Lamps and is entirely different from any other of our line. Instead of the metal parts being of solid brass with the bronze finish they are oxidized or gun metal finish. The lamp itself is one of the neatest patterns on the market, having a tall, slender vase with 10-inch globe to match. It stands 27 inches high. The decoration consists of a rich dark seal brown in a cloud effect, having the sea view with ships, etc. When lighted the lamp gives a very dainty tint to the room. Shipping wgt., 25 lbs. Price, $3.65

Canary Metal Lamp, $3.78.

No. 2C1005

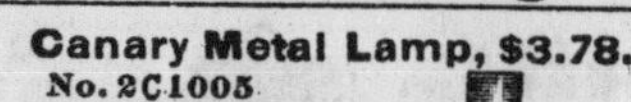

Metal Lamp. Complete base is of solid brass in the old copper finish, with polished brass handles and top ring. It has removable oil fount with 100-candle power center draft burner, and perfect attachment for raising and lowering the wick, which can be removed and renewed with no difficulty. The globe is of bright canary, ground on the inside so that it gives a very soft light and is just the lamp for reading, sewing, etc. It has No. 2 Rochester chimney and round wick. It is 20 inches high and has a 9-inch globe. Shipping weight, 30 pounds. Price.......................$3.78

The Brown Lion, $3.95.

No. 2C1010 The body of this lamp is of brown, shaded from a dark seal brown to a light tan. The eight lions' heads stand out prominently from the lamp, and, together with the embossing, form the eight panels which contain the Oriental landscapes, which are far beyond description or illustration. The mountings of this lamp are of solid brass and the removable brass oil fount has the highest grade center draft burner, which takes No. 2 Rochester chimney and round wick. It is 26 inches in height and has a 10-inch globe. It is carefully packed in a wooden box. Shipping weight, 30 lbs.
Price.......................$3.95

The Cerise Lion Lamp, $3.98.

No. 2C1030

This is one of the prettiest ruby parlor or reception lamps made. It is made from good quality ruby glass, beautifully embossed in a new and original design. The glass is carefully etched so as to produce a soft velvety effect, and casts a soft red mellow glow which greatly adds to the cheery appearance of any room. The metal parts of this lamp are gold plated and lacquered and will not tarnish. It is equipped with No. 2, large size, Royal central draft burner, with a removable oil pot, which holds one quart of oil; No. 2 Royal wick, No. 2 Rochester chimney and gives 100-candle power light. This lamp measures 26 inches high, and globe and vase measure 10½ inches in diameter. Lamps similar to our Lion Cerise usually retail at for double the price we ask. Lamp neatly packed in wooden case. Shipping weight, 30 pounds. Price.......$3.98

ALL our Banquet Lamps sold at $2.00 or more are equipped with the genuine ROYAL AND SUCCESS center draft burners, which are guaranteed to give a strong, steady light. These burners take No. 2 Rochester chimneys and No. 2 Rochester or Success wick.

The Princeton, $5.95.

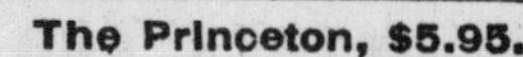

No. 2C1025 This is the largest lamp in our line, and is perfect in outline, decoration, construction and material. The globe and bowl are of deep myrtle green decorated with highly tinted red and pink flowers and green foliage. These flowers are placed on the lamp after first removing the green decoration from the background only where the flower is to appear, and then painting the decoration on the body by hand, so that when lighted the light shows clearly and brightly through the flower, thus showing off the lamp to the very best advantage. The base and crown are of solid cast brass, highly polished. The removable oil fount is of brass and has large center draft 100-candle power burner with perfect wick attachment. It comes complete with No. 2 Rochester chimney and round wick. It is 30 inches high and has 11-inch globe. It is very carefully packed in a wooden box. Shipping weight, 35 pounds.
Price.......................$5.95

The Tulip, $6.59.

No. 2C1040 The decoration is put on the lamp in the same manner as No. 2C1025, but the background is of deep red and the tulip flowers of white and orange with green leaves. The light shining through the flowers is sufficient for reading, etc., while the dark red gives the room a very deep ruby appearance. The base and crown are of solid cast brass highly polished. It has a brass removable oil fount with large center draft burner and perfect wicking device. It takes No. 2 Rochester chimney, and round wick. It is 28 inches high and has a 11-inch globe and 12-inch bowl. Packed carefully in a wooden box. Weight, 35 pounds.
Price.......................$6.59

The Nevada, $7.95.

No. 2C1045 This Lamp is decorated with beautiful variegated pink roses with deep green foliage on a tinted green background. This decoration is very high class, being strictly hand painted throughout. It is not only on the front and back of the lamp, but completely covers all parts. When lighted it looks very beautiful, giving tone and elegance to the beautiful roses. The base and crown are of solid cast brass, highly polished and plated with gold. It has a removable brass oil fount, center draft 100-candle power burner and perfect wicking device. It is furnished with No. 2 Rochester chimney and round wick. It is 28 inches high and has 11-inch globe and bowl. It is packed carefully in a barrel. Shipping weight, 50 pounds.
Price.......................$7.95

HALL, STORE AND LIBRARY LAMPS.

WE DESIRE TO CALL SPECIAL ATTEN- 'ION TO OUR ASSORTMENT OF LAMPS,

AND TO THE FACT THAT

ALL METAL PARTS OF OUR LAMPS ARE MADE OF SOLID BRASS

WITH HANDSOME LACQUERED BRONZE FINISH.

great many dealers advertise library lamps ch in appearance are similar to ours, but are de of bronze metal, which is oftentimes mis-en for brass when the lamps are new, but will not stand the wear and retain the handsome appearance of a solid brass lamp. **We guarantee every one of our lamps to stand the wear of a lifetime, and guarantee them not to tarnish.** Each lamp carefully packed to insure safe delivery.

HALL LAMPS.

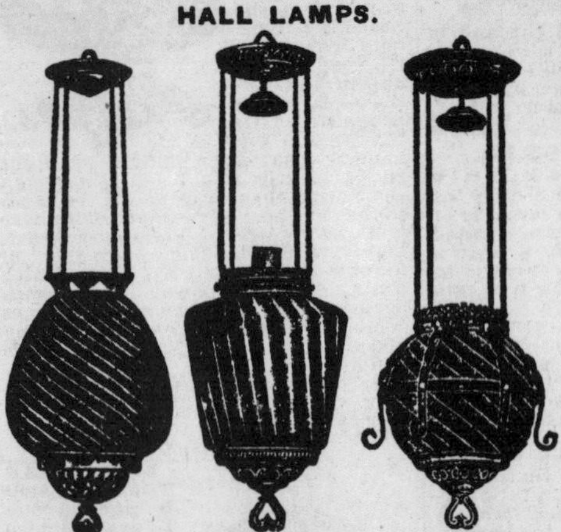

No. 2C849 No. 2C852 No. 2C854

No. 2C849 Hall Lamp, with a rich opal globe. Just the right for a hall. This is the cheapest and best hall lamp in the market. Length, 29 inches. Made of solid brass, finished in rich bronze. Packed carefully in box, with oil fount, burner and chimney complete. Ship'g weight, about 12 lbs. Price....**$1.10**

No. 2C850 Hall Lamp, exactly like No. 2C849, with rich ruby globe, which produces a rich mellow light. Shipping weight, 12 pounds. Price..........**$1.23**

No. 2C852 Hall Lamp, with rich ruby globe, complete with oil fount, burner and chimney. Finished in rich bronze metal. Length, 29 inches. Makes a soft red light, and very attractive in hall. Weight, about 14 pounds. Price..........**$1.59**

No. 2C854 Hall Lamp. A new design in hand wrought black iron frame and rich ruby globe. Just the thing for halls and dens. Length, 29 inches. Complete with oil fount, burner and wick. Packed carefully to insure safe delivery. Shipping weight, 17 pounds. Price..........**$1.98**

Store Lamps.

Juno Store Lamp. For large areas and where good light is required, only the best lamps should be procured. We guarantee every lamp we sell to give perfect satisfaction. The Juno gives a steady white light. Just the thing to throw light on a window display. Complete as illustrated with 15-inch tin shade, suitable for store or window lights, 85-candle power. Shipping weight, 40 pounds.

No. 2C856 Price, brass finish..........**$2.00**

No. 2C857 Price, nickel finish..........**$2.25**

$3.20 TO $4.95

Juno Mammoth Store and Hall Lamps.

Juno Mammoth Store and Hall Lamp. 400-candle power, the strongest and best finished lamp on the market. Wick movement is perfect. Patent lock ring to hold fount obviates all danger of fount jarring out of frame. Fount taken out from below when filling. You are taking no chances with this lamp, as we guarantee every one to give perfect satisfaction or we will replace them and pay all expenses. Complete, as illustrated, with 14-inch plain dome shade suitable for churches, halls, stores, etc., and fitted with **automatic spring extension so that it can be lowered for cleaning and lighting of lamp.** Closed, 42 inches; fully extended, 78 inches. Money cannot buy a finer constructed lamp. It is very handsome in appearance. Shipping weight, 50 pounds.

No. 2C860 Price, complete, brass finish..........**$4.70**

No. 2C861 Price, complete, nickel finish.......... **4.95**

Same lamp as above, but without automatic spring extension. You get the same service from this lamp, but you are obliged to use a step ladder or chair for lighting. Shipping weight, 40 lbs.

No. 2C862 Price, complete, brass finish..........**$3.20**

No. 2C863 Price, complete, nickel finish.......... **3.35**

No. 2C785

Our Leader at $1.79

No. 2C785 This Lamp has 14-inch plain white dome shade with No. 3 Climax burner and No. 2 chimney; wick, 1½ inches; **solid brass frame and patent spring extension.** Length, closed, 27 inches; extended, 63 inches. **This frame being of solid brass** will give much better service than the common polished bronze metal lamps, and is equal in every respect to lamps your dealer will ask $3.50 for. Weight, 40 pounds. Price, **$1.79**

No. 2C786 Same Lamp as above described, but with a beautiful 14-inch hand decorated dome shade. Shipping weight, securely packed, 40 pounds. Price, **$2.21**

No. 2C787 Library Lamp. Has extra heavy reinforced frame, made of solid brass, which will give far better service and will last longer than the ordinary bronze metal so commonly used in lamps of this style. Crystal oil fount and 14-inch plain dome shade, making a very beautiful and attractive lamp. Extra large No. 3 Climax burner and No. 2 Electric chimney; wick, 1½ inches. High grade automatic spring extension; length when closed, 30 inches; extended, 61 inches. The spring extension makes the lamp suitable for high or low ceiling. Shipping weight, about 40 pounds.
Price..........**$2.45**

No. 2C788 Same Lamp as described above, but with handsome decorated dome shade.
Price..........**$2.95**

No. 2C789 Solid Brass Library Lamp with No. 2 Juno center draft fount, 85-candle power. Fount removable for filling and cleaning. Automatic spring extension. Length, closed, 33 inches; extended, 69 inches. The base of the lamp is of beautiful embossed metal and finished in rich bronze to match the frame. This is a new design and is up to date in every way. Complete with 14-inch white dome shade. Takes No. 2 Rochester chimney and wick. Shipping weight, about 4 pounds. Price..**$3.48**

No. 2C793 Library Lamp with automatic spring extension. Length, closed, 30 inches; extended, 66 inches. Plain white dome shade, fancy glass oil fount with No. 3 Climax burner, No. 2 electric chimney and 1¼-inch wick. **Solid brass frame**, not the common bronze metal. Has 30 cut glass pendants suspended from shade band. Shipping weight, about 40 pounds.
Price..........**$3.49**

No. 2C794 Same lamp as above, but furnished with beautifully decorated dome shade. Shipping weight, about 40 pounds.
Price..........**$3.95**

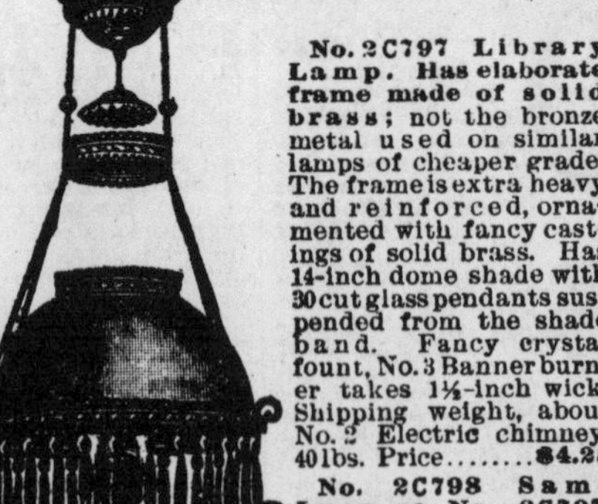

No. 2C797 Library Lamp. Has elaborate frame made of solid brass; not the bronze metal used on similar lamps of cheaper grade. The frame is extra heavy and reinforced, ornamented with fancy castings of solid brass. Has 14-inch dome shade with 30 cut glass pendants suspended from the shade band. Fancy crystal fount, No. 3 Banner burner takes 1½-inch wick. Shipping weight, about No. 2 Electric chimney. 40 lbs. Price..........**$4.25**

No. 2C798 Same Lamp as No. 2C797, described above, excepting the dome shade is handsomely decorated with flower design on tinted background.
Price..........**$4.48**

No. 2C799 Parlor Extension Lamp, fitted with No. 2 center draft burner, 85-candle power; takes No. 2 round wick, No. 2 Rochester chimney. Fount can be removed from vase for filling. Automatic extension. Length, closed, 40 inches; extended, 78 inches. Can be used in room with either high or low ceiling. All metal parts are solid brass. Fancy collar at top of fount holder. Vase and globe are beautifully decorated with hand painted floral decorations on rich tinted background. Shipping weight, about 40 lbs. Price..........**$4.86**

No. 2C801 Library Lamp with automatic spring extension. Length, closed, 30 inches; extended, 73 inches. The celebrated No. 2 Juno fount and center draft burner giving 85-candle power light. Fount can be removed for filling and cleaning. No. 2 round wick, No. 2 Rochester chimney. Extra heavy collar at top of oil fount holder. Heavy reinforced solid brass frame and beautifully decorated and tinted fount and dome with 30 cut glass prisms suspended from dome band, make this one of the most attractive lamps in our line. Shipping weight, about 40 lbs.
Price..........**$5.75**

Polka Dot Cerise Lamp

This is the latest style in a Library or Parlor Lamp. It has a fancy ruby metal vase with gold plated cupid ornaments and solid brass embossed frame, and a beautiful 14-inch ruby polka dot dome. It is constructed so as to cast a rich ruby glow in the upper part of the room, and at the same time produces a bright steady light beneath for sewing or reading purposes. It has the latest improved No. 2 center draft burner, chimney and wick and produces 100 candle power light. It is one of the most ornamental lamps made, and is trimmed with 30 cut glass prisms or pendants which greatly add to the striking beauty of the lamp.

No. 2C802 Library Lamp. Weight, 40 pounds. Securely packed in a barrel and shipped to eastern customers from our factory in Connecticut, and to western customers from Chicago.
Price..........**$5.98**

No. 2C803 Library Lamp. Has solid brass frame of most beautiful design with ornamental heavy castings. Has automatic spring extension; length, closed, 30 inches; extended, 73 inches. The part of the frame on which the lamp is suspended is made of twisted brass instead of chains. Has No. 2 Juno fount and center draft burner, giving 85-candle power light; can be removed for filling and cleaning. Has No. 2 round wick and No. 2 Rochester chimney. The fount and dome are beautifully decorated with hand painted carnations. A heavy brass collar strengthens the top of oil fount holder. Thirty cut glass pendants are suspended from the dome band. Shipping weight, 40 lbs. Price..........**$6.85**

GAS FIXTURES

LET US SAVE YOU MONEY WHEN YOU BUY YOUR GAS FIXTURES. All we ask is that you make a selection from this catalogue, and after you have received them, if you are not satisfied that you have saved 50 per cent on your purchase, return them to us at our expense and we will gladly refund your money together with all transportation charges both ways.

THE PROFESSIONAL GAS FITTER, PLUMBER OR MECHANIC will do well to buy his fixtures from us. We can save him money and at the same time furnish him with fixtures that will give satisfaction to his customers. Our exclusive designs cannot fail to please even the most critical and the fixtures have a rich, expensive appearance.

OUR GUARANTEE. We guarantee that the fixtures are made of the best quality of highly polished brass. We guarantee that these fixtures are well made, strong and durable. Every fixture is tested before leaving our house to insure against leakage. We claim our fixtures are superior in quality, finish and durability and we guarantee them to give perfect satisfaction.

NATURAL GAS AND ACETYLENE GAS TIPS. The prices quoted below are for fixtures fitted complete with tips for artificial or manufactured gas. We can furnish gas fixtures for natural gas at an extra cost of 8 cents for each tip or with acetylene tips for 25 cents each tip.

Swing Gilt Brass Gas Bracket.

Made of excellent quality of brass in ribbed design. Furnished complete with wall plate, pillar, tip, and with one or two arms; either with burner cup or with white crystal glass shade in richly cut design and brass shade holder.

No. 3H2211

No. 3H2202 Single Swing Gilt Brass Gas Bracket, with burner cup. Price, per ½ dozen, $2.25; each 39c

No. 3H2203 Single Swing Gilt Brass Gas Bracket with white crystal glass shade and brass shade holder. Price, per ½ dozen, $3.15; each....55c

No. 3H2210 Double Swing Gilt Brass Gas Bracket with burner cup. Price, per ½ dozen, $3.50; each 63c

No. 3H2211 Double Swing Gilt Brass Gas Bracket with white crystal glass shade and brass shade holder. Price, per ½ dozen, $4.50; each 80c

One and Two-Light Polished Brass Pendant.

Suitable for kitchen, cellar, back hall and other places where a fancy gas fixture is not necessary. All brass tubing nicely polished, neat and well constructed. Furnished complete with burner cup, pillar and gas tip, no globe or globe holders furnished at prices quoted below.

No. 3H2235 One-Light Pendant, 30 ins. long. Price 50c

No. 3H2236 One Light Pendant. Price........55c

No. 3H2225 Two-Light Pendant, 36 inches long. Price....$1.18

No. 3H2225

One-Light Fancy Gas Pendant Polished Brass.

One of the neatest and most artistic pendants on the market. It is made of polished brass with fluted cup and fancy carved leaf ornaments and fancy gas stop cock. The pendant is very well constructed, and is an ornament to any room. Furnished complete with brass ceiling plate, pillar and gas tip and in one length only, 36 inches. We can furnish this pendant either with or without a globe and holder.

No. 3H2234 Fancy Gas Pendant, with burner cup. Price..$1.14

No. 3H2238 Fancy Gas Pendant, fitted with white crystal shade in very rich looking design, and brass burner plate. Price..........$1.28

Hall Gas Fixture.

A very neat and effective fixture for little money. Made of highly polished brass tubing, in graceful design. Comes complete as shown in illustration with ceiling plate, pillar, gas tip, globe, globe holder and fluted ceiling protector hanging over the light. Length of fixture, 30 inches. We can furnish this light with either opalescent or red globe.

No. 3H2245 Price, with opalescent globe..........$1.60

No. 3H2246 Price, with red globe..........$2.15

$2.48 OUR LEADER HALL LIGHT

NEW DESIGN. VERY ARTISTIC. A GREAT BARGAIN.

THIS BEAUTIFUL FIXTURE is made of solid brass tubing, very highly polished with heavy weight brass ornamentation. We consider this fixture the greatest value in hall lights ever offered for the money.

A HANDSOMELY EMBOSSED CROWN is fitted around the top of the globe. On either side of the frame, just above the light, a wrought brass spray projects, adding greatly to the graceful design. A fluted ceiling protector hangs over the light, while above it is a center ornament in the form of a brass cup, and above that the brass ceiling plate. The globe is of opalescent glass, fluted in a graceful design cylinder shape. An openwork key to turn on and off gas completes the light.

THIS HALL FIXTURE IS FURNISHED COMPLETE with globe, brass globe holder, pillar, lava gas tip and ceiling plate, just as shown in the description. The fixture, when you receive it, is all complete and ready to screw into ceiling. Bear this in mind. Our price is for the fixtures complete. It includes all the parts.

No. 3H2255 Our Leader Hall Gas Fixture, just as described above. Price..........$2.48

No. 3H2256 Our Leader Hall Gas Fixture, just as described above, but with transparent red globe. Price..................$3.25

$3.48 PEERLESS GAS PORTABLE LAMP.

A high grade reading lamp for parlor and library, furnished complete, green shade and tubing, the lamp is all ready to use when you receive it. All that is necessary to do is to remove the gas tip from the fixture and slip in the gooseneck. Then turn on the gas and light it. The price we ask includes all the parts, including burner, which is of the best quality being made of polished brass; high grade cap mantle opaque chimney globe with air holes, green shade (green outside, white inside), fitted with a heavy green bead fringe to match and six feet of the best quality of mohair tubing fitted with brass gooseneck. A high grade lamp. We are able to offer our customers a high grade reading lamp, and for those desiring a high grade lamp we believe this outfit will give perfect satisfaction. The stand is made of metal, finished in a rich black color. The metal is highly ornamented and trimmed in polished brass. A lamp of this quality and finish together with all the fittings we give has never been sold before for less than $5.00 and more often at $7.50.

No. 3H2191 Peerless Lamp, complete and ready to light. Price..............$3.48

"The Star" Gas Chandelier.

$2.98

Made of highly polished brass with exceedingly attractive ornamentation. Consisting of fancy fluted ball ornament and pear shaped pendant. The curved arms project from this ring and have cast brass ornaments in dull finish. Fitted complete, as shown in the illustration, with beautiful pebbled crystal glass shades, ornamented with cut stars. It is also fitted with brass shade holders, pillar, lava gas tips and brass ceiling plate. We can furnish with two or three lights. Length of fixtures, 36 inches. Spread of arms, 19 inches.

No. 3H2275 Two-light fixture. Price..$2.98

No. 3H2276 Three-light fixture. Price..$3.95

Gilt Gas Chandelier.

$1.83

For people desiring a low price fixture this is just what they want. Made of polished brass, corrugated design with brass ball ornament in satin finish and artistic loop design. Furnished with two or three lights. Length of fixture, 36 inches. Spread of arms, 36 inches. Remember the prices quoted below are for the fixture complete with crystal glass globes in rich design, brass globe holders, pillar, gas tips and ceiling plate, all complete and ready to put up.

No. 3H2265 Two-light fixture. Price, $1.83

No. 3H2266 Three-light fixture. Price $2.49

"Au Fait" Polished Brass Gas Chandelier.

$1.95

The very best low price chandelier made. It is made of polished brass in a simple and classical design, yet at the same time most artistic. It is ornamented with two octagonal shaped balls with beaded centers, just above where the arms connect. The lower ball has a flattened octagonal top with a rounded embossed lower part; and the arm connection and keys are of dull finished brass. Furnished with either two or three lights and is complete with white crystal shades in richly cut design, brass shade holders, pillar, lava gas tips and brass ceiling plate. Length of fixture, 36 inches. Spread of arms, 19 inches.

No. 3H2270 Two-light fixture. Price, $1.95

No. 3H2271 Three-light fixture. Price, $2.58

Imperial Gas Chandelier.

$3.40

A well made finely finished chandelier, and exceedingly attractive to look at. It has a graceful design being made of extra fine brass tubing, highly polished, with fluted cup, pear shape ornaments. Around the center of the pear shape ornament runs a beaded band, from which project the arms. The arms are in graceful descending curves with solid cast brass ornaments in fern design. The delicately etched shades add greatly to the beauty of the chandelier. This fixture can be furnished with two or three lights and comes complete with etched shades, brass shade holders, pillar, lava gas tips and ceiling plate.

No. 3H2280 Two-light fixture. Price..$3.40

No. 3H2281 Three-light fixture. Price..$4.69

OUR SPECIAL EXTRA VALUE LEADER CHANDELIERS

Solid Heavy Brass Tubing, Highly Polished, Elaborately Ornamented, Satin Finish Trimmings.

$4.25

EXQUISITE IN DESIGN AND DETAIL.

Do not be deceived by the price we ask for this chandelier. The only thing cheap about it is the price.

WE GUARANTEE THIS FIXTURE to be of the best materials. It is made of heavy brass tubing, very highly polished. Part of the tubing is corrugated, giving the fixture a very rich appearance. The fixture has a fluted ceiling plate and is ornamented with a fluted cup in satin finish surmounting a ball with beaded band and large pineapple shaped pendant. This pendant is extra large and elegant, and has attached to it at the bottom a fluted ball in satin finish brass. From this ball five heavy cast brass leaves reach up and are appliqued on the pendant. A ribbed band of satin finish brass surrounds the pendant, from which band project the arms, which have a graceful downward curve and are ornamented with heavy solid cast brass ornaments in dull finish. The keys are fancy openwork in the same finish.

THE CHANDELIER IS FITTED complete with fluted brass ceiling plate, pillars, best quality of lava gas tips, brass shade holders and beautiful new swell shape silver frosted shades, with embossed edges and angel design, having delicate tracery work etched around the figures. Elegant parlor, library or dining room chandelier.

No. 3H2295 Our Leader Chandelier, with TWO lights. Price..........$4.25

No. 3H2297 Our Leader Chandelier, with THREE lights. Price..................$5.25

No. 3H2298 Our Leader Chandelier, with FOUR lights. Price..................$6.25

$4.49 OUR BORDEAU PARLOR LAMP

EXCEPTIONALLY ATTRACTIVE. HIGHEST GRADE OF WORKMANSHIP. BEAUTIFUL DESIGN IN NATURAL COLORS.

OUR BINDING GUARANTEE

WE GUARANTEE that our lamp will outwear, will give a better light and is handsomer in appearance than any other lamp of similar design.

DO NOT CONFUSE this lamp with imitations made in the same style and which look the same in an illustration. Our lamp represents the highest grade of workmanship and the very finest materials, while the cheap lamps of the same pattern are most inferior, both as regards workmanship and quality.

ELEGANTLY EMBOSSED, decorated in natural colors. This beautiful lamp is made of the very finest quality of translucent porcelain. The body of the globe and base are richly tinted in brown, which shades into dark orange. The embossing is in the form of large clusters of grapes and leaves with panel scrolls in bold relief. The grapes and leaves are colored true to life, giving an exceedingly rich and elegant appearance to the lamp. The bottom of the base and the crown on the base are made of heavy gold plated solid brass in open work filigree design. No other lamp made with so rich and elaborate trimmings.

100-CANDLE POWER Success central draft burner, No. 1 Belgian chimney. We have equipped this lamp with an extra heavy candle power burner, so as to insure it giving a brilliant and livable light. Many of the parlor lamps have small burners and many statements are made regarding the candle power, which are not borne out by using. It has a solid brass oil pot which fits in the china base, and solid brass burner. Most of the cheap parlor lamps have no oil pot. The oil is poured into the base, which sooner or later gives the base a greasy and ugly appearance.

EXTRAORDINARY VALUE. We say, without fear of contradiction, that this lamp is extraordinary value, and not only is it perfect in workmanship and design, but it is made of only the very finest and richest materials. It stands 26 inches high and is equipped with a full 10-inch globe. The lamp is carefully packed in a barrel, which insures its safe delivery. Shipping weight, 32 pounds.

No. 3H1009 Our Bordeau Parlor Lamp. Price..$4.49

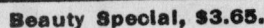

Beauty Special, $3.65.

This is the handsomest Rose Design Parlor Lamp made. This decoration consists of beautiful, dark, American Beauty roses, with their buds, leaves and stems in their natural colors in large clusters on both sides of the lamp and globe on a tinted green background. The large American Beauty roses are put on by hand in the deep red color, making the flowers stand out distinct from the lamp. The crown and base are of solid cast brass in open work design and the fount holder has a solid brass drawn ring. The removable oil fount is of brass and has the No. 2 100-candle power center draft burner, taking No. 2 Rochester chimney and round wick. Shipping weight, 30 pounds.

No. 3H980 Beauty Special Parlor Lamp. Price..$3.65

New Style Lilac, $3.99.

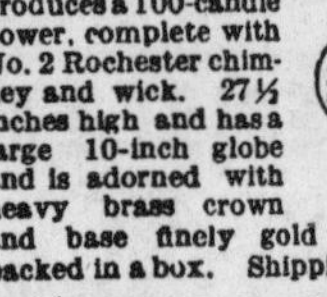

Our New Style Lilac in the Romeo shape, decorated with hand painted lilacs, is the newest and most fashionable thing in parlor lamps. It is extra large and shapely throughout. The decoration consists of large hand painted lilacs, highly enameled, with light green leaves. Richly tinted in a dark green and when lighted the beautiful lilacs appear true to life. The burner is the highest grade central draft type, produces a 100-candle power, complete with No. 2 Rochester chimney and wick. 27½ inches high and has a large 10-inch globe and is adorned with heavy brass crown and base finely gold lacquered. Securely packed in a box. Shipping weight, 30 pounds.

No. 3H988 New Style Lilac Parlor Lamp. Price..$3.99

OUR LEADER SOLID BRASS STUDENT LAMP.

SATIN FINISH—DUPLEX BURNER—IMPORTED GREEN DOME SHADE.

$6.98

THIS IS THE FINEST STUDENT LAMP MADE. It is in a new artistic design, very ornamental and strikingly handsome. Made of solid brass. Elegantly burnished in the rich French satin finish. This is the newest finish. The ornamented oil pot and the lamp proper are made in the new cone shape. The lamp is fitted with a stand made of French satin finished brass, which consists of a rod 21 inches long and an extra weighted base, so that the lamp will not upset. The lamp can be raised, lowered or turned on the rod, to any position to suit the user.

60-CANDLE POWER DUPLEX (DOUBLE WICK) BURNER.

This lamp is fitted with an extra powerful burner, with patent extinguisher. This burner will produce a 60-candle power light, which will give a light of great brilliancy, and is just the thing to save the eyes when reading. The oil pot holds 1½ pints of oil, and will burn 10 hours with one filling. The lamp is complete with a large full 10-inch elaborate green dome shade with white lining, and the finest quality genuine lead glass Duplex chimney.

BEAR IN MIND that this lamp is made of genuine solid brass. No composition or bronze metal is to be found in it, as is the case with many students' lamps usually sold at $15.00. Do not confuse this lamp with cheap students' lamps although they may try to imitate our shape. Shipping weight, 30 lbs.

No. 3H764 Our Leader Solid Brass Students' Lamp. Price..$6.98

ELEGANT EMBOSSED AND DECORATED BANQUET OR PARLOR LAMPS

WE TAKE PLEASURE IN PRESENTING AN ENTIRELY NEW AND COMPLETE LINE OF PARLOR OR BANQUET LAMPS AND GLOBES which were selected with the greatest care after long and careful investigation. **We feel confident that we are offering the best line of lamps made.** Every lamp is made of the finest quality of china, heavily embossed with **solid brass trimmings,** and is carefully tinted and decorated by the most skilled artists. Every lamp is equipped with the best quality burner, wick and chimney. **Our prices** are from 33 to 50 per cent less than quoted by the regular crockery dealers. Each lamp is carefully packed in box or barrel to insure safe delivery.

Royal Poppy, $1.99.

This beautiful Parlor or Banquet Lamp is exceptionally large and attractive for the price we ask. It is complete with 9-inch globe and vase, and measures 21 inches high. The decoration consists of large hand painted poppies in pink, purple and white. The globe and also the vase are delicately tinted at the top in light green and the bottom in pink. It has a heavy brass plated metal foot of scroll design. It is equipped with No. 3 Climax burner, No. 3 wick and No. 2 Electric chimney, and produces 60-candle power light. Shipping weight, 20 pounds.

No. 3H967 Royal Poppy Parlor Lamp. Price..$1.99

American Beauty, $3.25.

This is one of the prettiest lamps shown this season. Do not confuse this lamp with the cheap parlor lamps in American Beauty design. This one is better, handsomer, more elaborately decorated and in every way superior. The globe measures 10½ inches in diameter; the vase or cylinder to match is of equal size. The lamp measures 26 inches high. The hand painted decorations consist of beautiful American Beauty roses and foliage on a blue tinted background. The crown and bottom of base are made of richly polished brass in open work design. It has the improved Success central draft burner and takes No. 1 Belgian chimney and round wick. It produces a strong and steady 80-candle power light. This lamp compares favorably with those sold by crockery dealers at $4.50 to $5.00. Shipping weight, 25 pounds.

No. 3H976 American Beauty Parlor Lamp. Price..$3.25

Imperial Cardinal, $3.48.

This Banquet Lamp is made of ruby glass and when lighted produces a rich ruby glow. It is handsomely embossed in large scrolls of floral design, the embossing being of satin finish cardinal glass. The combination of highly polished ruby glass for the body of the lamp, and satin finish, cardinal glass embossing makes an exceedingly rich, attractive and handsome lamp. It is furnished with improved Success central draft burner, 80-candle power and wick, No 1 Belgian chimney. It has a solid brass removable fount and brass plated crown. Height, 26 inches, and has a 10-inch globe. Shipping weight, 28 pounds.

No. 3H978 Imperial Cardinal Parlor Lamp. Price..$3.48

OUR IMPERIAL PARLOR LAMP $6.48

ROSE PINK COLOR. WILD GEESE DECORATION.

GENUINE GOLD PLATED SOLID BRASS TRIMMED

THE VERY NEWEST and smartest design in parlor lamps. We are exceedingly fortunate in being able to offer our customers the very latest design, the most fashionable coloring and shape. This lamp is made of the very finest quality of translucent porcelain, tinted a delicate rose pink. This color is sometimes called old rose. Bands of Japanese ebony black encircle the top and bottom of the shade and base, with horizontal lines running up and down the shade and base.

A FULL 5-INCH FRINGE of pink translucent beads hangs from the shade ring which is 12 inches in diameter, and made of solid brass, with four heavy supports. The advantage of the fringe of beads is not only that it adds richness and elegance to the light, but that it tones down and softens the light that comes from under the shade and it also covers up the more unattractive part of the burner. The base is heavy open cast, in filigree design, and is made of the finest quality of genuine gold plated solid brass.

100-CANDLE POWER

Success central draft solid brass burner is used in this lamp, with a chimney of the very best quality of lead glass. The shade measures fully 15 inches and the lamp stands 26 inches high. It has a solid brass oil pot which fits into the china base.

SUPERB DECORATION. The decoration on this lamp consists of flying wild geese in ivory white, with feet, head and wings tinted in their natural colors. This decoration is hand painted by artists and is one of the richest and most effective decorations that we have ever seen. It cannot be adequately described or shown by the illustration. The lamp must be seen to be appreciated. Not only is this an exceptional value, but it is one of the most beautiful and graceful as well as newest designs on the market. A richer or more effective lamp when lighted, with the light streaming through the rose pink shade with ivory white decoration and through the deep fringe of opalescent pink beads, cannot be imagined. Rose color is the most becoming of any light. A regular $20.00 value.

No. 3H1025 Our Imperial Japanese Parlor Lamp. Price..$6.48

HANGING LIBRARY LAMPS

A GREAT MANY DEALERS, in order to quote a low price, advertise library lamps, which, while in appearance are similar to ours, are made out of bronze metal, which is a composition made in imitation of brass and costs one-half what brass costs. When the lamps are new this bronze metal is often mistaken for brass, but it will not stand the wear, nor retain the handsome appearance of the solid brass lamp, nor is it worth what a brass lamp is worth, either for serviceability or for looks.

WE GUARANTEE that every one of our lamps is made of genuine solid brass, in rich gold finish, handsomely lacquered. We guarantee these lamps to stand the wear of a lifetime and not to tarnish. Remember, when comparing our price and the prices quoted by other dealers, that we are quoting genuine solid brass lamps, not bronze metal.

THE EMPIRE SOLID BRASS EXTENSION LIBRARY LAMP

3 98

NEW FANCY SHAPE, RICH AND ELEGANT DESIGN.

THIS BEAUTIFUL LIBRARY LAMP is made of the finest quality, guaranteed solid brass, with rich gold finish. The lamp itself is superbly embossed in artistic design to match the frame. The frame is a double side frame with heavy cut out pull down, with heavy brass collar, ceiling protector, ceiling plate and chandelier.

85-CANDLE POWER LIGHT. This beautiful lamp is fitted with a No. 2 Juno center draft burner, 85-candle power, of the very best quality solid brass, and a No. 2 Rochester chimney and wick. The fount, which is also of solid brass, is removable, making the filling and cleaning easy and without danger of soiling the table or carpet. The lamp is fitted with an automatic spring extension, which makes it, when closed, 33 inches, and can be extended to 69 inches, being the largest extension ever given on a lamp of this price. This lamp is fitted with a full 14-inch white dome shade. Weight, packed for shipment, 40 pounds.

THIS MAGNIFICENT LAMP is exactly what you want, if you are not looking for something as elaborate and ornamental, such as No. 3H805, our leader, Royal Sunburst.

WE GUARANTEE this lamp to be made of solid brass, to conform in every particular to the description given above.

No. 3H789 Empire Solid Brass Library Lamp, fitted with plain white 14-inch dome shade. Price.....$3.98

No. 3H790 Empire Solid Brass Library Lamp, exactly as No. 3H789 described above, except that it is fitted with a 14-inch tinted dome shade, decorated with American beauty roses and foliage in their natural colors. Price $4.48

No. 3H785 This handsome lamp is equal in every respect to lamps generally sold at $3.50. It has a 14-inch plain white shade, No. 3 Climax burner, No. 2 Electric chimney, and 1½-inch wick. It has a solid brass frame and patent automatic spring extension. Length, closed, 27 inches; extended, 63 inches. Price, with plain white shade...$1.99

MADE OF SOLID BRASS

No. 3H786 Same lamp as No. 3H785 with a beautiful 14-inch hand decorated dome shade. Shipping weight, 30 pounds. Price..............................$2.43

No. 3H793 Library Lamp with automatic spring extension. Plain white 14-inch shade, crystal oil fount, No. 3 Climax burner, No. 2 Electric chimney and 1½-inch wick. Solid brass frame. Has 30 cut glass pendants suspended from shade band. Length, closed, 30 inches; extended, 66 inches. Weight, about 40 pounds. Price..$3.59

No. 3H794 Same lamp as No. 3H793 with beautifully decorated domeshade. Weight about 40 pounds. Price.....$3.99

MADE OF SOLID BRASS

No. 3H801 Library Lamp with automatic spring extension. Length, closed, 30 inches; extended, 73 inches. The celebrated No. 2 Juno fount and center draft burner giving 85-candle power light. Fount can be removed for filling and cleaning. No. 2 round wick, No. 2 Rochester chimney. Extra heavy collar at top of oil fount holder. Heavy reinforced, solid brass frame and beautifully decorated and tinted fount and dome with 30 cut glass prisms suspended from dome band, makes this one of the most attractive lamps in our line. Shipping weight, about 40 pounds. Price..$6.25

No. 3H797 Library Lamp. Has elaborate frame of solid brass. The frame is extra heavy and reinforced, ornamented with fancy castings of solid brass. Has 14-inch dome shade with 30 cut glass pendants suspended from the shade band. Fancy crystal fount. No. 3 Banner burner takes 1½-inch wick, No. 2 Electric chimney. Weight, 40 lbs. Price. $4.39

No. 3H798 Same lamp as No. 3H797, excepting that the dome shade is handsomely decorated with floral design on tinted background. Price..............................$4.69

Store Lamps.

No. 3H856 Juno Store Lamps, made of solid brass, highly polished and finely lacquered, with the latest improved Royal center draft burner, which produces a perfect white and steady 85-candle power light. It has latest wick adjusting device. Holds one quart of oil and burns twelve hours at one filling. It is complete with large 15-inch tin shade, harp and smoke bell, trimmed ready to light. Shipping weight, 15 pounds. Price...$2.10

No. 3H857 Exactly like No. 3H856, only finished in bright nickel, complete with shade and harp. Price..............$2.35

No. 3H860 The Juno Mammoth Store Lamp. The best and most economical oil lamp on the market. It is made of solid brass, handsomely finished and lacquered. It has the latest improved No. 3 Mammoth center draft burner, which produces a strong, steady 400-candle power light. It is complete with 14-inch white opal shade, No. 3 Rochester chimney and wick. Holds one gallon of oil and burns ten hours at one filling. This lamp is complete with a high grade automatic extension, which raises or lowers the lamp to any desired height. When extended it measures 78 inches and when closed measures 42 inches. We positively guarantee this lamp to be an economical burner and produce the highest capillary power of any lamp made. Shipping weight, 35 pounds. Price..........$5.49

No. 3H861 Same lamp as above, finished in bright nickel. Price..............$6.28

Same lamp as No. 3H861, but without automatic spring extension. Shipping weight, 40 lbs.

No. 3H862 Price, brass finish...$3.99

No. 3H863 Price, nickel finish...4.59

Same lamp as No. 3H862 and No. 3H863, excepting it is furnished with 20-inch tin shade, and without spring extension, making a lower priced lamp, but one which will give equally as strong a light. Shipping weight, 35 pounds.

No. 3H864 Price, brass finish....$3.57

No. 3H865 Price, nickel finish..3.89

No. 3H800 The Juno Dresden Mammoth Lamp will give 400-candle power steady white light, burns 16 hours with one filling; holds 4 quarts of oil. Most scientifically constructed, giving a light which surpasses electricity or gas. Made of solid brass in a beautiful satin finish, has an extra strong spring extension, extends 72 inches when opened and is 32 inches when closed. The lamp fount can be detached by a patent lock device passing through the ring which holds the fount. Complete with large 14-inch No. 00 Belgian chimney, smoke bell and rings. Suitable for large rooms, churches or lodge halls. Weight, packed, 31 pounds. Price... $6.98

Swinging Bracket Lamps.

No. 3H728 Two-Joint Church, Parlor or Bedroom Swinging Bracket Lamp, with 20-inch rope design arm. Is made of bronze metal, gold finished and has fancy crystal oil fount and shade, handsomely etched body with cut glass crown edge. Furnished complete with No. 2 Unique burner and chimney. Can be lighted without removing chimney or globe. Weight, securely packed, 12 pounds. Price..............$1.98

No. 3H750 Recommended where a strong light is needed. It has the celebrated Royal center draft burner, giving a 100-candle power light, and will hold enough oil to burn eight hours. The 10-inch silvered glass reflector can be so adjusted as to throw light wherever needed. Takes No. 2 Rochester chimney and round wick. Shipping weight, 20 pounds. Price $2.55

ROYAL SUNBURST SOLID BRASS EXTENSION LIBRARY LAMP

RICH GOLD FINISHED.
ELABORATELY ORNAMENTED.
HAND DECORATED SHADE.
30 PRISM CUT PENDANTS.

WONDERFUL VALUE. This exceedingly beautiful hanging lamp represents a wonderful value. You cannot get from this illustration or description an adequate idea of the great beauty and elegance of this lamp. To really appreciate what a superb lamp it is, it must be seen lighted. It is better made, of finer materials and more elaborately ornamented and decorated than any other hanging lamp sold at any price.

$8 48

MADE OF SOLID BRASS, genuine gold finish. Bear in mind that this lamp is made of genuine solid brass Not the smallest piece of it is made of composition metal. The chains, the base, the arms, the rings, the burner, everything is genuine solid massive brass. The solid brass frame is of most elaborate design, ornamented with heavy cut out solid brass trimmings. The side ornaments are in special scroll design and around the bottom of the shade is a filigree crown, from which hang thirty prism cut crystal glass pendants, each pendant composed of two pieces. Upon the top of the shade is another filigree crown, and above is an elaborate brass collar, which adds greatly to the beauty and strength of the lamp. The ceiling plate and the ceiling protector are both of heavily embossed brass.

73-INCH EXTENSION and 85-candle power burner. This beautiful lamp is equipped with a patent automatic spring extension. The lamp when closed is 30 inches high, when extended, 75 inches, being the largest extension lamp on the market. It is also equipped with 85-candle power, center draft, solid brass burner, giving an exceedingly brilliant light and a No. 2 Juno brass fount, which fits inside of the delicately tinted and decorated porcelain outside fount or cylinder. It also has a No. 2 round wick and No. 2 Rochester chimney. The fount is removable.

HAND DECORATED SHADE. The dome shade, which is of extra large size, beautifully tinted and superbly decorated by hand with flowers, in their natural colors.

No. 3H805 Our Leader, Royal Sunburst, Patent Extension, Solid Brass Hanging Lamp. Shipping weight, 45 pounds. Price....................$8.48

OUR LEADER, "THE IDEAL" HALL LAMP

NEW SWELL SHAPE—HAND WROUGHT BLACK IRON FRAME—RICH RUBY GLOBE.

$2.23 **THIS ELEGANT LAMP** is just the thing for halls and dens. It is exceedingly rich in appearance and when lighted it gives that soft glow to a hall or den that is so much to be desired. It is made in the new swell shape with a patent adjustment. Pulling down of the bottom raises the globe, which permits the taking out of the fount and filling the lamp in comfort.

SOLID BLACK WROUGHT IRON TRIMMINGS. This is the latest and smartest thing in hall or den fixtures. All the metal of the lamp is solid wrought iron, in ebony finish, and the globe is of rich ruby glass in converged fluted design. If you will look at the illustration you will note how graceful the metal work of this lamp is, how heavily embossed and delicate. The bottom of the fixture is of solid wrought iron upon which rests the oil fount, which is fitted complete with a No. 0 burner, chimney and wick, plate, ceiling protector and hook for hanging. Height of lamp is 30 inches.

DO YOU WANT A REALLY ELEGANT HALL LAMP? If so, let us send you Our Leader, "The Ideal" Hall or Den Lamp.
No. 3H854 Our Leader, "The Ideal" Hall or Den Lamp. Price....................$2.23
Weight, packed for shipment, 16 pounds.

Alpha Hall Lamp.

This is the lowest price good hall lamp that has ever been sold. It is made of solid brass, finished in bronze, and fitted with a rich opal globe in fluted design. The lamp is furnished complete with oil font, No. 0 burner, chimney and wick, ceiling cap, ceiling protector and hanging hook. The fount may be removed from the lamp and filled without taking down the fixture.
No. 3H849 Alpha Hall Lamp, fitted with opal globe. Price........$1.23
No. 3H850 Alpha Hall Lamp, exactly like No. 3H849, but fitted with a rich ruby globe. Price..$1.39
Weight, packed for shipment, 14 pounds.

The Elite Hall Lamp.

This exceptionally pretty hall lamp is made in a new shape of solid brass in bronze finish, with rich ruby globe. The globe is in a special shape in fluted design. The lamp is 29 inches in length and is furnished complete with oil fount, No. 0 burner, chimney and wick. Is fitted with patent device, whereby the fount may be removed and filled and cleaned without taking down the fixture. This lamp makes a very attractive light for a hall or den. Fitted complete with ceiling cap, ceiling protector, and hanging hook.
No. 3H852 The Elite Hall Lamp.
Price.......$1.75
Weight, packed for shipment, 14 pounds.

READING OR TABLE LAMPS—STUDENTS' LAMPS

SEE PAGE 827 FOR OUR LEADER STUDENT LAMP.

REMEMBER, our Reading or Table and Students' Lamps are made of genuine solid brass, not composition metal. Bear this in mind. We do not offer our lamps in competition with composition metal, which is used by our competitors and which is worth but one-half what brass costs. We guarantee our lamps, and every part of them, to be made only of GENUINE SOLID BRASS

EMBOSSED READING AND TABLE LAMP.

$2.85

AN EXCEEDINGLY RICH AND ELEGANT LAMP suitable for parlor, library, dining room or as a sewing lamp. It is exceedingly rich in design and its burning qualities are unequaled. **IT IS RICHLY EMBOSSED** in artistic scroll design, and has two elaborately ornamented handles on the sides, which add greatly to its appearance. The base is heavy open cast, and in filigree pattern. The handles not only make it easy to carry the lamp about, but add greatly to its appearance.

MADE OF SOLID BRASS, full nickel plated throughout. Bear in mind that our lamp is made of genuine brass, not bronze metal or plated steel. The nickel plating is of the finest quality and guaranteed not to wear off. The burner is a high grade royal center draft burner and is considered to be the best made. It is made of solid brass, handsomely lacquered. The lamp comes complete with a 10-inch white opal shade, brass tripod and No. 2 Rochester chimney and wick.

IF YOU WANT THE BEST and handsomest reading or table lamp at a price less than is usually asked for a lamp of inferior quality, send us your order for this lamp. Shipping weight, 17 pounds.
No. 3H738 Elegantly Embossed Reading and Table Lamp. Price..............$2.39
No. 3H739 Elegantly Embossed Reading and Table Lamp, exactly like No. 3H738, but fitted with 10-inch imported green shade with white lining. Price..................$2.85

No. 3H734 Polished Nickel Reading and Table Lamp. Has one of the best center draft burners made. It is complete with a 10-inch opal dome shade, holder, wick and No. 2 Rochester chimney. The lamp is well made and gives a strong, steady, bright light. By a patent device the wick can be instantly raised or lowered. It is made of plain nickel with neat embossing at the base. Shipping weight, 16 lbs. Price..........$1.65
No. 3H735 Nickel Lamp, exactly like No. 3H734, excepting that it has a 10-inch imported green shade. Price..........$2.12

No. 3H756 Juno Student Lamp, made of solid brass, finely nickeled with center draft burner and patent wick adjustment, complete with 7-inch white dome shade. Height, 21 inches. Weight, 18 pounds.
Price.......$3.29
No. 3H757 Exactly like No. 3H756 but with imported green shade. Price, $3.49
No. 3H759 Ideal Student Lamp. Same as No. 3H756 but equipped with large size Rochester burner, wick and 10-inch white dome shade. This lamp will give double the light of the smaller size. Shipping weight, 25 pounds.
Price...............$4.98
No. 3H760 Same as No. 3H759, with 10-inch imported green shade. Price, $5.59

CHANDELIERS

ALL METAL PARTS OF OUR CHANDELIERS ARE OF SOLID BRASS WITH A HANDSOME RICH GOLD FINISH. A good many dealers advertise chandeliers which in appearance are similar to ours, but are made of bronze metal or plated steel, which is often mistaken for brass when the lamps are new but will not stand the wear and retain the handsome appearance of solid brass. We GUARANTEE every one of our chandeliers to be made of genuine solid brass with a rich gold finish; we guarantee that they will stand the wear of a lifetime and warrant them not to tarnish.

GENUINE BRASS CHANDELIER FOR ONLY $6.99.

$6.99

THIS BEAUTIFUL CHANDELIER, is made of solid brass, finished in rich gold, complete with fancy glass oil founts, etched globes of very popular shape. The No. 2 unique burner is of a new design that can be lighted and filled without removing chimney or globe, thus removing the possibility of breakage in handling them. Takes 1-inch wick and No. 2 hinge chimney. It has the best patent automatic extension for raising and lowering so that it can be used with high or low ceilings. Packed complete in box to insure safe delivery.
No. 3H810 Price, two lights, complete. Shipping weight, 42 pounds..............................$6.99
No. 3H811 Price, three lights, complete. Shipping weight, 46 pounds..............................$8.93
No. 3H812 Price, four lights, complete. Shipping weight, 55 pounds..............................$11.50

PATENT EXTENSION SOLID BRASS CHANDELIER

$9.95

THIS BEAUTIFUL CHANDELIER, has patent automatic extension for raising and lowering. It is made of solid brass, finished in rich gold, with a center band studded with 12 beautifully colored cut glass jewels and 30 cut glass prisms suspended from same. This gives a very brilliant effect when lighted. Has fancy glass founts, best grade No. 2 Unique burners and handsomely etched shades. The burners can be lighted without removing chimneys or shades, which is a great convenience. Takes 1 inch wick and No. 2 hinge chimney. The fancy rope shaped arms and standards make it very neat and attractive and it is an ornament as well as a fixture.
No. 3H826 Chandelier, with two lights, complete. Shipping weight, 50 pounds. Price..............$9.95
No. 3H827 Chandelier, with three lights, complete. Shipping weight, 55 pounds. Price..............$11.95
No. 3H828 Chandelier, with four lights complete. Shipping weight, 60 pounds. Price..............$14.90

THREE AND FOUR-LIGHT CHANDELIERS.

FOR DWELLING, CHURCH AND HALL USE.

$11.65

THIS is our handsomest oil chandelier. It is equipped with patent extension apparatus, so that it may be lowered to any desired height. Length, extended, 60 inches. This chandelier is made of solid brass. Elaborately ornamented. Rich gold finished and silver finished ornaments. The center ball, the scroll work, projecting from the arms are heavily embossed and silver finished, while the balance of the ornamentation is elegantly etched and embossed in elaborate design and rich gold finish.

FANCY GLASS OIL FOUNTS, with etched crystal globes, in new bell shape in fancy design, are furnished with this chandelier. The lamps are complete, being fitted with No. 2 unique genuine brass central draft burners, which can be trimmed and lighted without removing the globe. Also fitted with a 1-inch wick and No. 2 chimney. These globes give an exceedingly strong and brilliant light.
No. 3H841 Chandelier, with three lights. Price..$11.65
No. 3H842 Chandelier, with four lights. Price.. 15.25
Weight, packed for shipment, 60 pounds.

CHURCH OR HALL CHANDELIERS. This chandelier is exactly as those described above, so far as ornamentation, quality, etc., is concerned, except that they are fitted with the celebrated solid brass, No. 1 Miller fount, with central draft 60-candle power burner. Gives an exceptionally strong and brilliant light.
No. 3H843 Chandelier, with three lights. Price..$14.89
Shipping weight, 55 pounds.
No. 3H844 Chandelier, with four lights. Price.. 17.50
Shipping weight, 60 pounds.

Lamp Department.

All Lamp Chimneys herein quoted are made by the famous Macbeth factories and are universally known as the best in the world.

All our Macbeth and Zenith chimneys are packed in square cartons.

Anchor Brand chimneys are packed in corrugated paper tubes.

Anchor Brand.

MADE FROM FLINT GLASS.

Catalogue No.	No.		Bottom Diameter, Inches	Price, per Dozen
2E600	0	Sun Crimp	2	40c
2E601	1	Sun Crimp	2½	48c
2E602	2	Sun Crimp	3	59c

Zenith Brand.

PURE LEAD GLASS.

Catalogue No.	No.		Bottom Diameter, Inches	Price per Dozen
2E604	1	Sun Crimp	2½	63c
2E605	2	Sun Crimp	3	77c
2E607	1	Sun Hinge Crimp...	2⅜	70c
2E608	2	Sun Hinge Crimp...	2⅝	90c
2E609	1	Rochester	2	85c
2E610	2	Rochester	2⅝	90c
2E612	2	Electric..	3	88c

Macbeth Pearl Top and Pearl Glass.

HIGHEST GRADE CHIMNEY MADE.

Catalogue No.	No.		Macbeth No.	Price, per Dozen
2E614	0	Sun........	500	$0.79
2E615	1	Sun........	502	.83
2E616	2	Sun........	504	.95
2E640		Jr. Rochester	4	.85
2E620	1	Rochester ..	6	.92
2E621	2	Rochester, 10 inches..	12	1.09
2E621½	2	Rochester, 12 inches..	9	1.55
2E626	3	Rochester ..	10	1.95
2E624	2	Electric, 10 inches....	40	1.10
2E625	2	Electric, Slim, 10 in	63	1.12
2E630	1	Belgian	32	1.20
2E631	00	Belgian	36	1.70
2E632	1	Student	50	.90
2E633	....	Nutmeg, 3½ in. tall, 1⅛-in. bottom.	.....	.20
2E634	....	Gem, 4¾ in. tall, 1½-in. bottom.....	.....	.25

La Bastie Chimney.

THE STRONGEST LAMP CHIMNEY MADE.

Genuine LaBastie Unbreakable Glass Lamp Chimneys, tempered by the famous LaBastie French process. These chimneys are guaranteed unbreakable and are especially recommended to those desiring an extra heavy and strong chimney. Universally sold for 25 cents each.

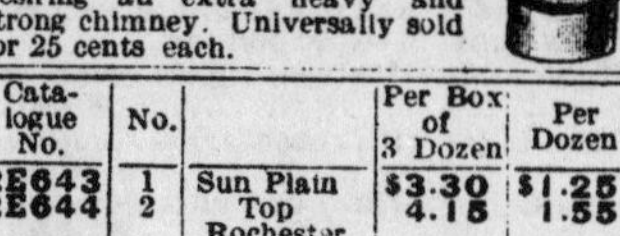

Catalogue No.	No.		Per Box of 3 Dozen	Per Dozen
2E643	1	Sun Plain	$3.30	$1.25
2E644	2	Top	4.15	1.55
2E648	2	Rochester 10 in.	4.75	1.90

Burners.

Genuine Banner Burners, made of solid brass. Best sun burner made.

No. 2E650 No. 0 takes No. 0 wick and No. 0 Sun chimney. Price........4c

No. 2E651 No. 1 takes No. 1 wick and No. 1 Sun chimney. Price..............5c

No. 2E652 No. 2 takes No. 2 wick and No. 2 Sun chimney. Price.............6c

No. 2E656 Genuine Climax Burner, solid brass. Has double thread to fit either No. 2 or No. 3 lamp collar. Takes No. 3 wick, 1½ inches wide, and No. 2 Electric chimney. This is the most powerful single wick burner made. Price..............................15c

No. 2E658 American Duplex Burner, solid brass. Has double thread to fit No. 2 and No. 3 lamp collar. This is a double wick burner, using two No. 3 wicks 1½ inches wide and a No. 2 Electric chimney. Gives a strong, steady light and is perfectly safe. Price, 25c

Lamp Wicks.

Catalogue No.		Size when Flat	Price, per Dozen
2E661	No. 0	⅜ in.	3c
2E662	No. 1	⅝ in.	4c
2E663	No. 2	1 in.	5c
2E664	No. 3	1½ in.	9c
	Round Wick		
2E669	Junior Rochester	1¼ in.	14c
2E670	No. 1 Rochester	1¾ in.	16c
2E671	No. 2 Rochester	2½ in.	19c
2E672	No. 3 Rochester	4¼ in.	78c
2E673	No. 1 Belgian	2 in.	50c

Brass Night Lamps.

No. 2E701 Brass Night Lamp, 7¾ inches high, complete with Gem burner, chimney and wick. Price.... 15c Weight, 6 oz.

No. 2E703 Brass Night Lamp. This is the most practical night lamp made. The lamp is fitted with revolving reflector and a bracket which enables you to hang lamp on wall. Height, 7¾ in. Price, 23c Weight, 8 oz.

No. 2E705 This is a very useful lamp, has a removable glass fount and polished tin reflector, No. 2 Sun burner and chimney. It is made to hang on the wall or rest on a table. Shipping weight, 4 pounds. Price..............26c

Stand Lamps.

These stand lamps are made of clear pressed glass and are complete with Sun burner, wick and chimney. Just the thing for bedrooms or to carry around the house.

No. 2E707 Plain Footed Glass Hand Lamp, complete with No. 1 Sun burner and wick, just the thing for carrying about the house. Price.....24c Shipping weight, 4 lbs.

No. 2E709 Crystal Stand Lamp, with No. 1 burner, chimney and wick. Price..............35c Shipping weight, 5 lbs.

No. 2E711 Large Stand Lamp, like No. 2E709, with No. 2 burner, wick and chimney. Price..........43c Shipping weight, 6 lbs.

Bracket Lamps.

No. 2E722 Kitchen or Dining Room Bracket Lamp, finished in French bronze, has glass fount, No. 2 Banner burner and 7-inch silvered glass reflector; complete as shown. Shipping weight, about 10 pounds. Price.......45c

No. 2E724 Dining Room or Hall Lamp. Is the strongest and best finished on the market. We furnish it complete with glass fount, 8-inch silvered glass reflector, No. 2 Banner burner and chimney. The bracket is made of cast iron, fancy design, bronze finish. Shipping weight, 10 pounds. Price........65c

No. 2E728 Two-Joint Church, Parlor or Bedroom Swinging Bracket Lamp, with 20-inch rope design arm. Is made of bronze metal, gold finished and has fancy crystal oil fount and shade, handsomely etched body with cut glass crown edge. Furnished complete with No. 2 Unique burner and chimney. Can be lighted without removing chimney or globe. Weight, securely packed, 12 pounds. Price...............$1.85

No. 2E750 This lamp is especially recommended where a strong light is needed. It has the celebrated Royal center draft burner made of solid brass, giving a 100-candle power light, and will hold enough oil to burn eight hours. The 10-inch silvered glass reflector can be so adjusted as to throw light wherever needed. Takes No. 2 Rochester chimney and round wick. Shipping weight, 20 pounds. Price, ...$2.45

Nickel Table Lamps.

No. 2E730 At 79 cents we offer a lamp which usually sells for twice this amount. It is made of solid brass, heavily nickel plated; has a nickel plated No. 2 burner and No. 2 wick, and is complete with a No. 2 Electric chimney, shade ring and 7-inch white dome shade, making the best and cheapest reading lamp on the market. Shipping weight, 15 lbs. Price..................79c

No. 2E731 Lamp exactly like above, with 7-inch imported green shade. Price..........$1.19

No. 2E734 Polished Nickel Reading and Table Lamp. Has one of the best center draft burners made. It is complete with a 10-inch opal dome shade, holder, wick and No. 2 Rochester chimney. The lamp is well made and gives a strong, steady, bright light. By a patent device the wick can be instantly raised or lowered. It is made of plain nickel with neat embossing at the base, giving it a handsome appearance. Shipping weight, 16 pounds. Price.............$1.48

No. 2E735 Nickel lamp, exactly like No. 2E734, excepting that it has a 10-inch imported green shade. Price..................................$1.99

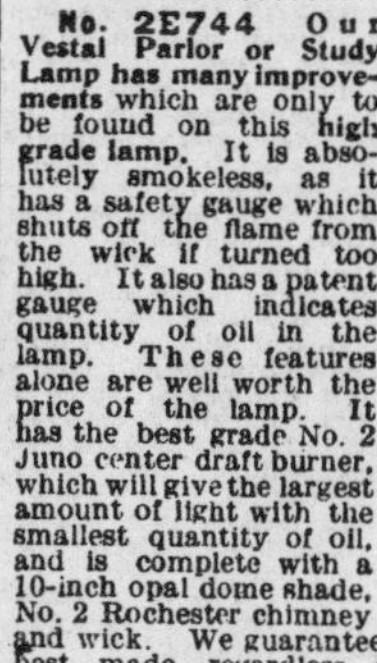

No. 2E738 This Handsome Nickel Center Draft Lamp is superior to all others, as it is suitable for a parlor as well as a sewing lamp. It is very rich in pattern, and its burning qualities are unequaled. It is richly embossed and has two handles at the sides, which greatly add to its appearance. The lamp is made of solid brass, full nickel plated throughout. The high grade Royal center draft burner is considered to be the best made. It is complete with a 10-inch white opal shade, tripod and No. 2 Rochester chimney and wick. Shipping weight, 16 pounds. Price...................................$2.25

No. 2E739 Nickel lamp, exactly like above, with 10-inch imported green shade. Price.................................$2.75

No. 2E744 Our Vestal Parlor or Study Lamp has many improvements which are only to be found on this **high grade lamp.** It is absolutely smokeless, as it has a safety gauge which shuts off the flame from the wick if turned too high. It also has a patent gauge which indicates quantity of oil in the lamp. These features alone are well worth the price of the lamp. It has the best grade No. 2 Juno center draft burner, which will give the largest amount of light with the smallest quantity of oil, and is complete with a 10-inch opal dome shade, No. 2 Rochester chimney and wick. We guarantee this lamp to be the best made, regardless of price. Shipping weight, 16 pounds.

No. 2E744 Vestal Lamp, brass finished, gold lacquered. Price $1.95

No. 2E745 Vestal Lamp, exactly like No. 2E744 above described, but furnished in bright, nickel finish. Complete with shade and chimney. Price..................$2.23

Hall Lamps.

No. 2E849 Hall Lamp, with a rich opal globe. This is the cheapest and best hall lamp in the market. Length, 29 inches. Made of solid brass, finished in rich bronze, complete with oil fount. No. 0 burner, chimney and wick. Price..................................$1.10

No. 2E850 Hall Lamp, exactly like No. 2E849, with rich ruby globe, which produces a rich mellow light. Price.........$1.23

No. 2E852 Hall Lamp, with rich ruby globe, complete with oil fount, No. 0 burner, chimney and wick. Finished in rich bronze metal. Length, 29 inches. Makes a soft red light, and is very attractive in a hall. Price..$1.59

No. 2E854 Hall Lamp. A new design in hand wrought black iron frame and rich ruby globe. Just the thing for halls and dens. Length, 29 inches. Complete with oil fount No. 0 burner, chimney and wick. Price...$1.98 Shipping weight of above lamps, about 14 lbs.

Store Lamps.

No. 2E856 Royal Store Lamps, made of solid brass, highly polished and finely lacquered, with the latest improved Royal center draft burner, which produces a perfect white and steady 85-candle power light. It has latest wick adjusting device. Holds one quart of oil and burns twelve hours at one filling. It is complete with large 15-inch tin shade, harp and smoke bell, trimmed ready to light. Shipping weight, 25 pounds. Price .$2.00

No. 2E857 Exactly like above, only finished in bright nickel, complete with shade and harp. Price..............................$2.25

No. 2E860 The Banner Mammoth Store Lamp. The best and most economical oil lamp on the market. It is made of solid brass, handsomely finished and lacquered. It has the latest improved No. 3 Mammoth center draft burner, which produces a strong, steady 400-candle power light. It is complete with 14-inch white opal shade, No. 3 Rochester chimney and wick. Holds one gallon of oil and burns ten hours at one filling. This lamp is complete with a high grade automatic extension, which raises or lowers the lamp to any desired height. When extended it measures 78 inches and when closed measures 42 inches. We positively guarantee this lamp to be an economical burner and produces the highest capillary power of any lamp made. Shipping weight, 35 pounds. Price..........$4.70

No. 2E861 Same lamp as above, finished in bright nickel. Price.................$4.95

Same lamp as above, but without automatic spring extension. You get the same service from this lamp, but you are obliged to use a step ladder or chair for lighting. Shipping weight, 40 pounds.

No. 2E862 Price, brass finish.$3.20
No. 2E863 Price, nickel finish 3.35

Same lamp as No. 2E862 and No. 2E863, excepting it is furnished with 20-inch tin shade, and without spring extension, making a lower priced lamp, but one which will give equally as strong a light. Shipping weight, 35 pounds.

No. 2E864 Price, brass finish..$2.69
No. 2E865 Price, nickel finish 2.98

Latest Improved Student Lamps.

The most perfect lamps made for reading or sewing as they can be raised or lowered to any height by patent thumb screw adjustment. These lamps are simple in construction, easily rewicked, **easy to keep clean** and constructed on improved lines which makes them entirely safe and reliable.

No. 2E756 Student Lamp, made of solid brass, finely nickeled with center draft burner and patent wick adjustment, complete with 7-inch white dome shade and Junior Rochester chimney. Holds one pint of oil; will burn nine hours with one filling. Height to top of rod, 21 inches. Weight, 18 pounds. Price...............$2.98

No. 2E757 Exactly like 2E756 but with improved green shade. Price, $3.25

We also furnish a student lamp like above equipped with large size Rochester burner, wick and 10-inch imported dome shade. This lamp will give double the light of the smaller size and is well worth the difference in price. Shipping weight, 22 pounds.

No. 2E759 Ideal Student Lamp. Price...$4.45

No. 2E760 Same as No. 2E759, with 10-inch imported green shade. Price, $4.75

No. 2E761 Duplex Study or Parlor Lamp. A new design. Very ornamental and strikingly handsome. Made of solid brass, elegantly burnished in rich satin finish. Fitted with genuine duplex burner (double wick), with patent extinguisher. It produces a strong 60-candle power light. It has a large ornamental oil pot which holds one and one-quarter pints and will burn ten hours with one filling. Completed with large 10-inch imported green dome shade, with white lining and heavy shade ring and duplex chimney. Height, to top of rod, 21 inches. Shipping weight, 25 pounds. Price $5.98

All Metal Parts of Our Lamps are Made of Solid Brass,

With Handsome Lacquered Bronze Finish.

A great many dealers advertise library lamps which in appearance are similar to ours, but are made of bronze metal, which is oftentimes mistaken for brass when the lamps are new, but will not stand the wear and retain the handsome appearance of a solid brass lamp. **We guarantee every one of our lamps to stand the wear of a lifetime, and guarantee them not to tarnish.** Each lamp carefully packed to insure safe delivery.

No. 2E785 This handsome lamp is equal in every respect to lamps generally sold at $3.50. It has a 14-inch plain white shade, No. 3 Climax burner, No. 2 Electric chimney, and 1¼-inch wick. It has a solid brass frame and patent automatic spring extension. Length, closed, 27 inches; extended, 63 inches.

Price, with plain white shade. **$1.79**

No. 2E786 Lamp as described above, with a beautiful 14-inch hand decorated dome shade. Shipping weight, 30 pounds. Price........**$2.21**

No. 2E787 Library Lamp. Is made with an extra heavy reinforced frame of solid brass, making it very strong and durable. It has a crystal oil fount, 14-inch plain white opal dome shade, No. 3 Climax burner, No. 2 Electric chimney and 1¼-inch wick, and has a high grade automatic spring extension. Length, when closed, 30 inches; extended, 61 inches. Price, with opal shade......**$2.45**

No. 2E788 Lamp, as described above with 14-inch hand decorated dome shade. Price..........**$2.95**

Shipping weight, 40 pounds.

No. 2E789 Solid Brass Library Lamp with No. 2 Juno center draft fount, 85-candle power. Fount removable for filling and cleaning. Automatic spring extension. Length, closed, 33 inches; extended, 69 inches. The base of the lamp is beautifully embossed and finished in rich bronze to match the frame. Complete with 14-inch white dome shade, No. 2 Rochester chimney and wick. Weight, 40 pounds. Price....**$3.48**

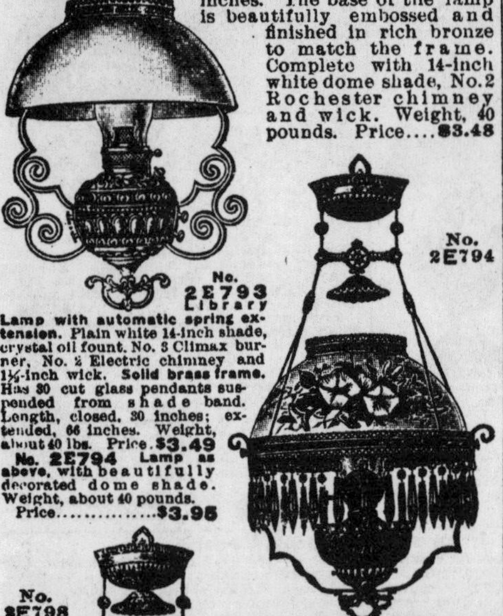

No. 2E789

No. 2E794

No. 2E793 Library Lamp with automatic spring extension. Plain white 14-inch shade, crystal oil fount. No. 3 Climax burner, No. 2 Electric chimney and 1½-inch wick. **Solid brass frame.** Has 30 cut glass pendants suspended from shade band. Length, closed, 30 inches; extended, 66 inches. Weight, about 40 lbs. Price.**$3.49**

No. 2E794 Lamp as above, with beautifully decorated dome shade. Weight, about 40 pounds.

Price..............**$3.95**

No. 2E798

No. 2E797 Library Lamp. Has elaborate frame of solid brass. The frame is extra heavy and reinforced, ornamented with fancy castings of solid brass. Has 14-inch dome shade with 30 cut glass pendants suspended from the shade band. Fancy crystal fount, No. 3 Banner burner takes 1¼ inch wick. No. 2 Electric chimney. Weight, 40 pounds. Price, **$4.25**

No. 2E798 Lamp as described above, excepting that the dome shade is handsomely decorated with floral design on tinted background.

Price..........**$4.48**

Extension Lamps.

No. 2E799 Parlor Extension Lamp, fitted with No. 2 center draft burner, 85-candle power; takes No. 2 round wick, No. 2 Rochester chimney. Fount can be removed from vase for filling. Automatic extension. Length, closed, 40 inches; extended, 76 inches. Can be used in room with either high or low ceiling. All metal parts are solid brass. Fancy collar at top of fount holder. Vase and globe are beautifully decorated with hand painted floral decorations on rich tinted background. Shipping weight, about 40 lbs. Price......**$4.86**

No. 2E799

No. 2E801 Library Lamp with automatic spring extension. Length, closed, 30 inches; extended, 73 inches. The celebrated No. 2 Juno fount and center draft burner giving 85-candle power light. Fount can be removed for filling and cleaning. No. 2 round wick, No. 2 Rochester chimney. Extra heavy collar at top of oil fount holder. Heavy reinforced solid brass frame and beautifully decorated and tinted fount and dome with 30 cut glass prisms suspended from dome band, make this one of the most attractive lamps in our line. Shipping weight, about 40 lbs.

Price......................**$5.75**

Polka Dot Cerise Lamp

No. 2E802 Library Lamp. This is the latest style in a Library or Parlor Lamp. It has a fancy ruby metal vase with gold plated cupid ornaments and solid brass embossed frame, and a beautiful 14-inch ruby polka dot dome. It is constructed so as to cast a rich ruby glow in the upper part of the room, and at the same time produces a bright steady light beneath for sewing or reading purposes. It has the latest improved No. 2 center draft burner, chimney and wick and produces 100-candle power light. It is one of the most ornamental lamps made, and is trimmed with 30 cut glass prisms or pendants which greatly add to the striking beauty of the lamp. Securely packed in a barrel and shipped to eastern customers from our factory in Connecticut, and to western customers from Chicago. Weight, 40 pounds.

Price..................**$5.98**

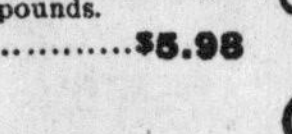

No 2E802

No. 2E803 Library Lamp. Has solid brass frame of most beautiful design with ornamental heavy castings. Has automatic spring extension; length, closed, 30 inches; extended, 73 inches. The part of the frame on which the lamp is suspended is made of twisted brass instead of chains. Has No. 2 Juno fount and center draft burner, giving 85-candle power light; can be removed for filling and cleaning. Has No. 2 round wick and No. 2 Rochester chimney. The fount and dome are beautifully decorated with hand painted carnations. A heavy brass collar strengthens the top of oil fount holder. Thirty cut glass pendants are suspended from the dome band. Shipping weight, 40 lbs. Price.........**$6.85**

ALL METAL PARTS OF OUR CHANDELIERS

ARE OF SOLID BRASS (NOT BRONZE METAL), WITH A HANDSOME BRONZE FINISH.

A great many dealers advertise chandeliers which in appearance, are similar to ours, but are made of bronze metal or plated steel, which is often mistaken for brass when the lamps are new, but will not stand the wear and retain the handsome appearance of solid brass. **We GUARANTEE every one of our chandeliers to stand the wear of a lifetime and warrant them not to tarnish.**

Two-Light Chandelier for only $6.89.

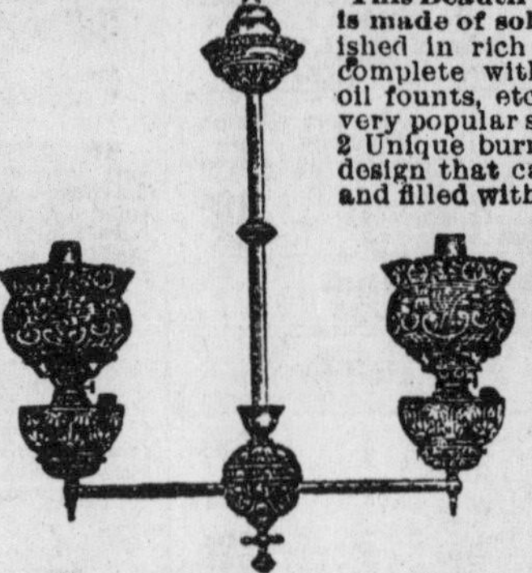

This Beautiful Chandelier is made of solid brass, finished in rich gold bronze, complete with fancy glass oil founts, etched globes of very popular shape. The No. 2 Unique burner is of a new design that can be lighted and filled without removing chimney or globe, thus avoiding all possibility of breakage in handling them. Takes 1-inch wick and No. 2 hinge chimney. It has the best patent automatic extension for raising and lowering so that it can be used with high or low ceilings. Packed complete in box to insure safe delivery. Shipping weight, 50 to 75 pounds.

No. 2E810 Price, two lights complete...**$ 6.89**
No. 2E811 Price, three lights complete. **8.65**
No. 2E812 Price, four lights complete.. **10.85**

Patent Extension Chandelier.

This Beautiful Chandelier has patent automatic extension for raising and lowering. It is made of solid brass, finished in rich gold bronze, with a center band studded with 12 beautifully colored cut glass jewels and 30 cut glass prisms suspended from same. This gives a very brilliant effect when lighted. Has fancy glass founts, best grade of No. 2 Unique burners and handsomely etched shades. The burners can be lighted without removing chimneys or shades, which is a great convenience. Takes 1-inch wick and No. 2 hinge chimney. The fancy rope shaped arms and standard make it very neat and attractive and it is an ornament as well as a fixture. Shipping weight, 70 to 100 pounds.

No. 2E826 Chandelier with two lights complete. Price..**$9.45**
No. 2E827 Chandelier with three lights complete. Price..**$10.65**
No. 2E828 Chandelier with four lights complete. Price..**$13.95**

Three and Four-Light Chandeliers for Church, Hall or Dwelling Use.

Patent Extension Chandelier. Extended 57 inches. This chandelier is solid brass, elegantly finished in rich gold, with large ball and cast ornaments in bright silver finish. The No. 2 Unique burners can be trimmed and lighted without removing the chimney or globe. Takes 1-inch wick and No. 2 hinge chimney. Furnished with fancy glass oil founts and etched crystal globes. Shipping weight of three lights, about 75 lbs.; four lights, about 90 lbs.

No. 2E841 Chandelier with three lights complete. Price..**$11.35**
No. 2E842 Chandelier with four lights complete. Price..**$13.95**

Church or Hall Chandelier. Same chandelier as above except founts. This fixture is trimmed with celebrated No. 1 Miller fount, with center draft 55-candle power burner, making a very strong light for church or hall use.

No. 2E843 Chandelier with three lights complete. Price..**$13.45**
No. 2E844 Chandelier with four lights complete. Price..**$16.85**

OIL CHANDELIERS

Made of solid brass and fitted with patent extension apparatus so that they may be raised to any desired height. Length of our chandeliers extended, 60 inches. The burners of all our founts, wheather brass or glass, can be lighted without removing either the chimey or shade, which is a great convenience and saves breakage. Full directions for lighting accompany each chandelier. A great many dealers advertise chandeliers which in appearance are similar to ours, but which are made of bronze metal or plated steel which looks like brass when the chandeliers are new but which cost the dealers much less than solid brass chandeliers and which will not stand the wear or retain the handsome appearance of solid brass. **WE GUARANTEE** that all the metal parts of our chandeliers are made of solid brass, beautifully finished, and we guarantee they will wear a lifetime.

IN ORDER TO INSURE NEW AND PERFECTLY FINISHED STOCK, THE OIL CHANDELIERS ARE SHIPPED FROM THE FACTORY IN MERIDEN, CONN.

Our Leader Chandelier.

$6.85

No. 3L822 Two-Light Chandelier. Price..$6.85
No. 3L823 Three-Light Chandelier. Price..$8.98
No. 3L824 Four-Light Chandelier. Price $10.95

Made of solid brass in a bright burnished finish. It is fitted with a richly embossed, pear shaped center pendant and highly polished brass arms and tubing and an embossed ceiling plate. Furnished with fancy glass founts and a No. 2 unique burner and comes complete with 1-inch wicks, No. 2 hinge chimneys and etched shades.

This is the cheapest price at which genuine solid brass chandeliers have ever been sold.

The Jewel Chandelier.

$9.85

No. 3L832 Two-Light Chandelier. Price..$9.85
No. 3L833 Three-Light Chandelier. Price $11.95
No. 3L834 Four-Light Chandelier. Price $14.48

It is made of solid brass in bright burnished finish, with an embossed center ring, studded with twelve colored cut glass jewels, and thirty crystal cut glass prisms suspended from it. It is fitted with fancy glass founts and No. 2 unique burners and comes complete with 1-inch wick. No. 2 hinge chimneys and handsomely etched shades. The ribbed arms and tubing and embossed ceiling plate make this a very neat and attractive chandelier.

New Art Chandelier.

$11.85

No. 3L837 Two-Light Chandelier. Price $11.85
No. 3L838 Three-Light Chandelier. Price $15.98
No. 3L839 Four-Light Chandelier. Price $18.45

This beautiful Chandelier is made of solid brass with the new brush brass finish, with the tubing, arms and supports in ribbed design. It is fitted with oxidized brass ornaments on the arm supports and a fancy ceiling plate. Furnished with elegantly embossed solid brass No. 1 Miller founts with central draft, 60-candle power burners and comes complete with No. 1 Rochester chimneys, wicks and daintily etched shades.

Our Finest Chandelier.

$15.85

No. 3L845 Two-Light Chandelier. Price $15.85
No. 3L846 Three-Light Chandelier. Price $18.95
No. 3L847 Four-Light Chandelier. Price $21.48

Made of solid brass in new platina finish (satin finish). Has a beautiful spun brass body, which shades to a dark oxidized color, surrounded by a rich embossed crown from which hang thirty cut glass prisms which gives a very brilliant effect when lighted. The ornamental supports for the arms are finished in Roman yellow gold. Has fancy ceiling plate. It is fitted with richly embossed No. 1 Miller founts with central draft, 60-candle power burners, No. 1 Rochester chimneys, wicks and beautifully etched shades in rose design.

GAS FIXTURES

LET US SAVE YOU MONEY when you buy your Gas Fixtures. If you are not satisfied that you have saved 50 per cent on your purchase when you receive your fixtures we will gladly refund your money and pay all transportation charges. The professional gas fitter, plumber or mechanic, will do well to buy his fixtures from us. We can save him money and at the same time furnish him with fixtures that will give satisfaction to his customers. Our exclusive designs cannot fail to please even the most critical, and the fixtures have a rich, expensive appearance. OUR GUARANTEE—We guarantee that the fixtures are made of the best quality of highly polished brass, well made, strong and durable. Every fixture is tested for leakage before leaving our house. NATURAL GAS AND ACETYLENE GAS TIPS—The prices quoted below are for fixtures fitted complete with tips for artificial or manufactured gas. We can furnish tips for natural gas at an extra cost of 8 cents for each tip or with acetylene tips for 25 cents each.

Gas Brackets.

No. 3L2200 Stiff Gilt Brass Gas Bracket. 6-inch, complete with wall plate, burner cup, pillar and tip. Price........18c

No. 3L2202 Single Swing Gilt Brass Gas Bracket. Complete with wall plate, burner cup, pillar and tip. Price........28c

No. 3L2203 Single Swing Gilt Brass Gas Bracket with white crystal glass shade and brass shade holder. Price........53c

No. 3L2210 Double Swing, Gilt Brass Gas Bracket. Furnished complete with wall plate, burner cup, pillar and lava tip. Price........45c

No. 3L2211 Double Swing Gilt Brass Gas Bracket with white crystal glass shade and brass shade holder. Price........59c

One and Two-Light Polished Brass Pendant.

Suitable for kitchen, cellar, back hall, etc. All brass tubing nicely polished, neat and well constructed. Furnished complete with burner cup, pillar and gas tip. No globe or globe holders furnished at prices quoted below.

No. 3L2235 One-Light Pendant, 30 inches long. Price........36c

No. 3L2236 One-Light Pendant. 36 inches long. Price........49c

No. 3L2225 Two-Light Pendant, 36 inches long. Price........95c

No. 3L2235

No. 3L2225

One-Light Fancy Gas Pendant, Polished Brass.

One of the neatest and most artistic pendants on the market. It is made of polished brass with fluted cup and fancy carved leaf ornaments and fancy gas stop cock. Furnished complete with brass ceiling plate, pillar and gas tip and in one length only, 36 inches.

No. 3L2234 Fancy Gas Pendant, with burner cup. Price........98c

No. 3L2238 Fancy Gas Pendant, fitted with white crystal shade in very rich looking design, and brass burner plate. Price........$1.18

No. 3L2234

SPECIAL EXTRA VALUE CHANDELIER.

Solid Heavy Brass Tubing, Highly Polished, Elaborately Ornamented, Satin Finish Trimmings.

$3.45

It is made of heavy brass tubing, very highly polished. Part corrugated and ornamented with a fluted cup in satin finish surmounting a ball with beaded band and large pineapple shape pendant, with heavy cast brass ornaments and ribbed band. The arms are ornamented with heavy solid cast brass ornaments and openwork keys.

The Chandelier is fitted complete with fluted brass ceiling plate, pillars, best quality of lava gas tips, brass shade holders and beautiful new swell shape silver frosted shades, with embossed edges and angel design having delicate tracery work etched around the figures.

No. 3L2295 TWO-light chandelier. Price........$3.45
No. 3L2297 THREE-light chandelier. Price........$4.68
No. 3L2298 FOUR-light chandelier. Price........$5.89

Hall Gas Fixture.

A very neat and effective fixture for little money. Made of highly polished brass tubing, in graceful design. Fitted with ceiling plate, pillar, gas tip and fluted ceiling protector hanging over the light. Length of fixture, 30 inches.

No. 3L2244 Price 95c
No. 3L2245 Fitted complete with opalescent globe and brass globe holder....$1.35
No. 3L2246 Fitted complete with red globe and brass globe holder..$1.68

Our Leader Hall Light.

This beautiful fixture is made of solid brass tubing, very highly polished with heavy weight brass ornamentations. A handsomely embossed crown is fitted around the top of the globe. On either side of the frame are wrought brass sprays. A fluted ceiling protector hangs over the light. This hall fixture is furnished complete with globe brass globe holder, pillar, lava gas tip and ceiling plate.

No. 3L2255 Our Leader Hall Gas Fixture, fitted with fluted opalescent globe$2.39

No. 3L2256 Our Leader Hall Gas Fixture, fitted with fluted ruby red globe $2.75

Big 6 Gas Light.

No. 3L2375 The Big 6 Gas Light is the simplest, most economical and best light on the market. It develops 300-candle power on a consumption of four feet of gas per hour. Furnished complete with mantle, burner and patent air hole opal glass globe, ready to fasten on the gas fixtures, for either natural or artificial gas.

Price........60c
Extra mantles for above light. 17c
Extra globes for above light. Price........16c

The Star Gas Chandelier.

ade of highly polished brass with fancy fluted ball ornament and pear shape pendant. The curved arms have cast brass ornaments in dull finish. Fitted complete with crystal glass, star cut shades, brass shade holders, pillar, lava gas tips and brass ceiling plate. Length of fixtures, 36 inches. Spread of arms, 19 in.

$2.48

No. 3L2275 Two-Light Fixture. Price $2.48
No. 3L2276 Three-Light Fixture. Price, $3.25

Imperial Gas Chandelier.

A well made, finely finished Chandelier of extra fine brass tubing, highly polished, with fluted cup and pear shape ornament, with beaded band, from which projects the arms. With graceful descending curves and solid cast brass ornaments in fern design. Furnished complete with beautifully etched shades, brass shade holders, pillar, lava gas tips and ceiling plate.

$2.75

No. 3L2280 Two-Light Fixture. Price, $2.75
No. 3L2281 Three-Light Fixture. Price. $3.85

Peerless Gas Portable Lamp.

$3.48

A high grade Reading Lamp for parlor and library, furnished complete, green shade and tubing ready to use when you receive it. The price we ask includes all the parts, including best quality brass burner; high grade incandescent mantle, opaque chimney globe, with air holes, green shade (green outside, white inside), fitted with a heavy green bead fringe to match, and six feet of the best quality of mohair tubing fitted with brass gooseneck. The stand is made of metal, finished in a rich black color. The metal is highly ornamented and trimmed in polished brass. A lamp of this quality and finish together with all the fittings we give has never been sold before for less than $5.00.

No. 3L2191 Peerless Lamp, complete and ready to light. Price......$3.48

Gilt Gas Chandelier.

$1.49

Made of polished brass, corrugated design with brass ball ornament in satin finish and artistic loop arms. Length of fixture, 36 inches. Spread of arms, 36 inches. Complete with crystal glass globes, brass globe holders, pillar, gas tips and ceiling plate, all ready to put up.

No. 3L2265 Two-Light Fixture. Price........$1.49
No. 3L2266 Three-Light Fixture. Price........$1.98

Incandescent Mantles.

We handle only the best grades of mantles and warrant them to give a bright, clear light.

No. 3L2380 No. 1. Standard Grade Mantles, 60-candle power. Price.....8½c

No. 3L2384 No. 5. Extra Grade Mantels, 100-candle power. Price........13c

No. 3L2386 No. 6. Heavy weave, especially for high pressure gasoline lamps; 5 inches long; nothing better made. Price........18c

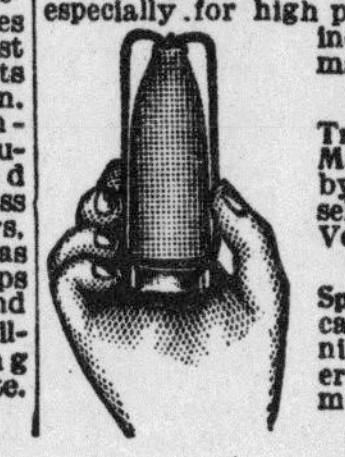

No. 3L2390 Our Triple Weave Double Wire Mantle attached to cap is by far the longest lived mantle we sell. Cannot break by handling. Very strong. Price........17c

No. 3L2392 Genuine Sears Special, extra double strength, 100-candle power platinum tied, with nickel support combined with burner cap and gauze. Nothing better made at any price. Price........21c

TELEPHONES

TELEPHONES

YOU CAN'T AFFORD TO BE WITHOUT ONE AT OUR LOW PRICES

WE SELL TELEPHONES

WITH ONLY ONE SMALL PERCENTAGE OF
PROFIT BETWEEN FACTORY AND HOME

A SALESMAN'S EXPERIENCE.

The following story is told by a traveling salesman who recently resigned his position with one of the largest telephone companies in Chicago. "Some time ago we got an inquiry on our telephones from a small town out in Kansas, and I started out to look this man up. It was a jump of several hundred miles, but the prospects for a sale looked good. When I got into town, I found that the man lived several miles out in the country, so I drove out to see him, only to discover, that he had written to us out of curiosity and had no intention of buying any telephones whatever. Of course, he said he was 'awfully sorry that I had come clear out there in answer to his letter, and he would probably need some telephones next year, but was not in the market just now, etc.' There I was with a big railroad ticket and several days' expense to pay for, and I felt pretty sore. Fortunately, I heard of another man about twenty miles further west, who was in the market, and I drove cross country to see him, hoping I could land a sale and make back some of the expense. I found the man was out of town and had to wait two days for him to return, only to learn that he had already bought his telephones and paid for them. More time wasted and a big livery bill to pay for without any sale whatever.

BIG SALARY AND EXPENSES OF SALESMAN

Just at this time I got your telegram about the new company down in Texas, and it looked particularly good. I took the night train, rode straight through, and finally had to drive twelve miles out in the country but at last succeeded in finding the man. 'Certainly,' he said, 'we are in the market for about eighty telephones, and the necessary line material.' Well after dinner we got to talking business, and I showed him our samples, and he seemed well pleased with the telephones. I felt I had that order cinched. But when he started to ask about prices and I gave him our regular list, he went straight up in the air. 'Why, great goodness, man!' he said, 'I can buy the same telephone in Chicago for about one-half what you want, and he went in the house and brought out one of Sears, Roebuck's big catalogues, and opened it up to the telephone pages. I tried every argument I could think of, but he answered them all right from the catalogue. I simply couldn't meet those prices, so there was nothing to do but to drive back to town. Before leaving the city, I called on the old telephone company there and found they were needing about thirty phones. As they had started with us in the early times, I had no trouble in selling them at our regular prices, but there were ten days' expenses and several hundred miles of railroad fare besides my salary, so that I barely broke even on the trip. When I told the general manager how things came out he looked pretty serious for a few minutes, and then said, 'There is only one thing to do, we'll have to make a telephone so cheap that they can't help buying it; but goodness help the poor fellow who buys it. We can't begin to compete with a mail order house in quality but we'll soon fix the price. I'll have a talk with our factory superintendent tomorrow morning.'"

OUR ONLY "SALESMAN" DRAWS NO SALARY.

There are no Telephones Made at Any Price That Will Talk Plainer or Farther Than Our Telephones. There are no Telephones Made at Any Price That Will Ring More Bells on a Line or That Will Ring Over a Greater Distance Than Our Telephones

OUR TELEPHONES are made with the greatest possible simplicity, all complicated parts having been eliminated. They are easy to put up and easy to keep in order after they are put up. They are easy to repair if by accident any part becomes damaged or broken. Anyone without the slightest electrical knowledge or telephone experience can put up a telephone line and install our telephones. There is nothing complicated about them —nothing hard to understand. The instruments are simple, they are right in every way, they reach you in perfect order, and they come to you with simple and easily understood directions, so that it is easy for anyone, without the slightest previous experience, to put up a line and install these instruments with perfect assurance that the line will give good service.

OUR NAME does not appear on our telephones in any way. We find that occasionally customers who would like to take advantage of the low prices and high quality of our telephones, hesitate to do so because of the antagonism of local companies or other interested parties, and for this reason we do not put any name plate or any identifying mark of any kind on our telephones. You can send us your order for telephones with perfect assurance that the transaction is in every way strictly confidential, and that no marks will appear on the telephones inside or outside to show where you bought them.

OUR GUARANTEE

AND TWELVE MONTHS' FREE TRIAL OFFER

As the astonishing low prices which we quote on these telephones may, very naturally, lead some to doubt the high quality of the instruments, we send with every telephone our signed guarantee, under the terms of which we become responsible for the quality, material and workmanship of every telephone we sell, and we accept your order with the distinct understanding and agreement that you can put the telephone up, use it for twelve months, compare it with any other telephones in your neighborhood, telephones that may have cost twice the amount that we ask you for ours, and if at the end of the year you have any fault whatever to find with this telephone, if you do not find it better than any other telephone in your locality and if you do not feel that you have secured a better telephone and saved money, you can pack it up and return it to us at our expense. We will refund without question, the entire purchase price, and reimburse you for all transportation charges.

A FARMER'S EXPERIENCE.

"Last Spring the farmers around this neighborhood decided to build a telephone line and wanted me to go in on the line. I didn't see any use for a telephone and told them I didn't believe I would need one just then. Everything went along all right till about two months ago, when I drove to town one day with the boys and left the women folks alone. We didn't start back from town till about dark, and when we got to the farm we found there was a big crowd there and most of our household goods were setting out in the yard. When I finally found the women folks I learned that one of the girls had dropped a coal oil lamp and it had started a blaze in a minute. Before they could hitch up and drive to the neighbors for any help the fire had got such headway that when the men arrived from the next farm it was almost impossible to check the flames, but they finally succeeded in getting the fire under control, but not until it had destroyed most of the house and a good part of our furniture, besides injuring some of the people who were trying to fight the fire. Well, after we got the house repaired and bought a lot of new furniture, paid all the doctor's bills, bought the women folks new dresses and borrowed some money from the bank to get things fixed up, I decided that it might be cheaper to put in a telephone after all, and you bet I did so mighty quick."

IF AN ACCIDENT SHOULD HAPPEN

This farmer's story illustrates only one of the many reasons why every farmer should have a telephone in his home. If anyone should take sick the doctor can always be called immediately by the telephone. Oftentimes it is necessary to have some small article in a hurry, but which is too small to make a special trip to the city for. With a telephone you can call up the merchant and have him mail it to you, so that you receive it the following morning. Many farmers' exchanges have adopted the plan of having "Central" read the market reports to them at a certain time each day, so that they may be able to take advantage of any market conditions that may suddenly arise. A farmer's wife can enjoy many a pleasant chat with her neighbors, who may be several miles away, while she is quietly seated in her arm chair at home. The young folks will find their social life is made far more interesting, as they can invite their friends to parties, arrange to visit each other, and can have much more delightful enjoyment than would ever be possible without the use of the telephone. There are any number of uses for the telephone in every American home, and no up to date farmer can afford to ignore the judgment of over two million farmers who have installed the telephone in their homes, and have found it to be the most profitable investment they have ever made.

YOU CAN REACH YOUR FRIENDS INSTANTLY

HOW OTHER DEALERS SELL TELEPHONES

SPLENDID OFFICES HIGH RENT.

THE SALESMAN STARTS OUT.

HE TRAVELS IN PULLMAN CARS

HE STOPS AT THE BEST HOTELS

THE FINEST RIG WHEN HE DRIVES OUT TO SEE YOU

EVER GENEROUS WITH CIGARS ETC.

WEEKLY EXPENSES
SALARY 40.00
R.R. FARE 10.00
HOTEL BILL 15.00
LIVERY " 10.00
CIGARS ETC. 20.00
COST OF $95.00 MAKING SALE

THE EXPENSE BILL YOU PAY IT ~

HOW OUR TELEPHONES ARE MADE

MADE COMPLETE IN ONE FACTORY. **There are many dealers in telephones today who pretend to be manufacturers, but who are merely assemblers,** purchasing the various parts wherever they can buy the cheapest. They buy their generators from one factory, their transmitters from another and their receivers from another. The cabinet is made in still another factory, probably a factory where nothing is known of actual telephone requirements. All the various small parts are purchased here and there, and then these odds and ends of telephone construction are assembled or put together in this so called "telephone factory." It is impossible to produce a dependable, reliable telephone in this way, because the various parts come first from one source of supply and then another. They are always subject to variation because different manufacturers never produce articles exactly alike, and the purchaser of such a telephone never knows whether he can secure repair parts, never knows whether he can replace a worn out or broken part, and if the instrument is not satisfactory he finds that he has no redress, but must accept the loss and buy another telephone from some reliable dealer. **Our telephones are made complete, from start to finish, in one factory.** The generators, switch hooks, ringers, transmitters, receivers, cabinets, everything, even the smallest screws and washers which enter into the construction of our telephones, are made in one factory. Every part is interchangeable, and we can furnish at any time in the future, ten, fifteen or twenty years from now, exact duplicates of every part. Every part is interchangeable and we can replace, at any time, any part that may wear out in service or become damaged in any way.

Our Five-Magnet Compact Bridging Telephone.

TESTS AND MATERIALS. **Every telephone we sell is tested before it leaves the factroy by ten different electrical experts.** Not an instrument is allowed to go out that does not test better by 25 per cent than the standard established by the National Interstate Telephone Association. Our lumber is all air dried for months and afterward kiln dried before it is made up into cabinets. Every lot of new material that comes to the factory is tested chemically and mechanically before it is accepted. There are no cheap materials used in our telephones. We could use American steel for the magnets of the generator, the receiver and the ringer, and make very substantial reductions in the cost, but imported magnet steel is better than American magnet steel, therefore every magnet that enters into the construction of our telephones is made from the highest grade of imported magnet steel. We use only first quality magnet wire, with double silk insulation, the most expensive magnet wire that we can buy. We use the very highest priced, the most expensive granulated carbon and carbon diaphragms that we can import. All of these things count, and count very much in determining whether a telephone is a good telephone or not. When you buy a telephone, you want one that you can rely upon all the time, under all conditions, and such a telephone must be made right all the way through. It must be put up by good workmen; it must be properly designed and it must be made throughout from the very best materials. Our telephones comply with all these requirements.

OUR FIVE-MAGNET BRIDGING TELEPHONES **are built for use on lines with from thirty to forty instruments installed, and are equally suited to smaller lines.** They are equipped with our extra powerful five-magnet generators, tested and guaranteed to ring through 125,000 ohms resistance, tested and guaranteed to ring through fifty telephones on the same line, **more power than is ever required in actual practice.** If you are building a new line, no matter how many telephones are to be installed, we advise the purchase of our powerful five-magnet 1,600-ohm compact, or 2,000-ohm Southwestern style bridging telephones, as this equipment is standard throughout the country. If you are buying telephones to put on a line already equipped, then it will be best to select instruments equipped with generators and ringers to match those already on the line. Prices on our bridging telephones, with both four and five-magnet generators and ringers of 1,000, 1,600 or 2,000 ohms resistance will be found on the following page.

THE CABINETS. Our Compact Telephones are put up in cabinets of very ornamental design, very compact and made throughout of the best selected kiln dried oak. The corners are rounded and dovetailed, the screw holes are provided with metal bushings and the finish is a fine golden oak with piano polish. This cabinet measures 23¼ inches high by 5½ inches deep by 8⅜ inches wide. We put up our Southwestern style of telephone in an extra large, substantially made cabinet, with sufficient space in the lower compartment for two full sized wet batteries. We recommend this cabinet particularly for use in engine rooms, creameries, etc., and especially in warm, dry climates, where dry batteries are not satisfactory. This cabinet measures 32 inches high, 12 inches wide and 7 inches deep. It is made throughout of the finest selected kiln dried oak, with piano polish.

Our Five Magnet Southwestern Style Bridging Telephone.

THE TRANSMITTER. **We equip all telephones with our latest improved solid back long distance transmitter, a transmitter that will talk farther and louder and plainer than any other transmitter made.** The framework is built of heavy brass castings, making it absolutely solid, and the carbon cup is turned from a solid brass bar. The carbon diaphragm and the granulated carbon are the very finest grade of carbon that we can import from Europe, and before going into the transmitter are subjected to a special process of polishing which still further improves the quality.

THE RECEIVER. **We equip all our telephones with our latest improved bi-polar receiver, a receiver that is the result of years of study, experiment and constant improvement.** It is made with concealed connections, the coils are wound with **double silk** insulated magnet wire, the magnets are made from the highest grade **imported** magnet steel, and the cords, which are made extra heavy to prevent any possibility of cord trouble, are attached with a special wide contact which cannot work loose.

THE GENERATOR. **Our generators are made from the best imported magnet steel, and are guaranteed to retain their magnetism and power longer than any other generator made. There is more steel, more wire and more power in our five-magnet generator than in any five or six-magnet generator on the market.** The steel is the best imported magnet steel. The wire on the armature is the best double silk insulated magnet wire. Our five-magnet generator weighs 10½ pounds, and this weight is made up of the best imported magnet steel, the most expensive steel that can be bought, and the best double silk insulated copper magnet wire, the best magnet wire we can buy. **There is plenty of reserve power in this generator,** more power than you will ever need in actual practice. The resistance of an ordinary line, 25 or 30 miles in length, with 30 bridging telephones installed, **even if poorly constructed and put up with small wire,** is less than 60,000 ohms, and we absolutely guarantee our five-magnet generator to ring through 125,000 ohms resistance, more than double the work which it will ever be called upon to do, and from three to four times the work which it will ordinarily be required to perform. **There is plenty of reserve power in our big five-magnet generator, and it will always ring every bell on the most heavily loaded lines.** The gear wheels are solid brass castings with milled gears and reinforced spokes, made extra wide to insure strength and durability, and the shunt springs are of heavy German silver.

SWITCH HOOK. **We equip all our telephones with our special long lever switch hook made with heavy German silver springs, and pure platinum contacts.** This hook is so constructed that no current whatever passes through the frame and there is no chance of a shock when removing the receiver from the hook. The greatest attention is paid to securing perfect connections, every joint being soldered, and the general construction and design of this switch hook is such as to prevent any possibility of trouble from this source.

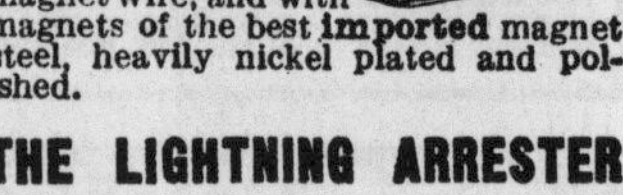

THE RINGER. **Our telephones are all equipped with the latest improved ringers,** made with adjustable armatures, the coils wound with **double silk** insulated magnet wire, and with magnets of the best **imported** magnet steel, heavily nickel plated and polished.

THE LIGHTNING ARRESTER

Our New Two-Path Carbon Lightning Arrester is the most perfect protection from lightning as well as sneak currents, that has ever been devised. This lightning arrester is made up of three heavy brass punchings, the binding posts sweated on to insure perfect contact, the carbon extra large, presenting ample surface to the ground plate, and the mica insulated washers carefully perforated so that the shortest possible air gap is maintained between the carbon and the ground plates.

5-MAGNET 1600-OHM BRIDGING TELEPHONE

Our COMPACT Style of Cabinet.

PRICES ON COMPACT BRIDGING TELEPHONES.

No. 20L5500 Five-Magnet Compact Bridging Telephone, with 1,000-ohm ringer.
Price, with two dry batteries, each..$ 9.70
6 for........ 56.45

No. 20L5501 Five-Magnet Compact Bridging Telephone, with 1,600-ohm ringer.
Price, with two dry batteries, each..$ 9.95
6 for........ 57.90

No. 20L5502 Five-Magnet Compact Bridging Telephone, with 2,000-ohm ringer.
Price, with two dry batteries, each..$10.20
6 for........ 59.36

No. 20L5506 Four-Magnet Compact Bridging Telephone, with 1,000-ohm ringer.
Price, with two dry batteries, each..$ 9.40
6 for........ 54.70

No. 20L5507 Four-Magnet Compact Bridging Telephone, with 1,600-ohm ringer.
Price, with two dry batteries, each..$ 9.65
6 for........ 56.17

No. 20L5508 Four-Magnet Compact Bridging Telephone, with 2,000-ohm ringer.
Price, with two dry batteries, each..$ 9.90
6 for........ 57.62

Shipping weight of Compact Telephones, 43 pounds.

PONY MAGNETO CALL TELEPHONE

No. 20L5570 This telephone is built for use on short lines of from 50 feet to 5 miles. It can be used with copper or iron wire or even with fence wire. It is equipped with a high grade transmitter, receiver and three-magnet pony generator. It is put up in a handsome oak case, and all parts are heavily nickel plated. We furnish an outfit complete, consisting of two telephones, four batteries, weighing 30 pounds.
Price........ $9.50

For local use in making connections from one building to another or between different rooms of the same house, our Pony Magneto Call Telephones will give the most satisfactory results in every way and will answer the requirements for this class of work as well as our higher priced telephones which are intended for use on heavily loaded bridging lines.

$9.95

ONLY THE VERY BEST MATERIALS and only the very highest class of skilled labor is employed in the construction of our telephones. They are mechanically and electrically perfect in every detail, correctly and scientifically designed. We spare no expense that will in any way improve the quality. Our object is to produce the most perfect, the most serviceable and the most satisfactory telephone that can be manufactured. Every part that enters into the make up of these telephones is as good as expert designers and skilled workmen can produce. There is not a loose joint in the entire instrument, every connection being soldered, making a solid circuit that cannot possibly get out of order. The workmen engaged in the construction of these telephones are men of the highest degree of skill—men of long and practical experience in actual telephone construction.

PROMPT DELIVERIES. We carry in stock, right here at our store in Chicago, the largest stock of telephones that is carried by any dealer or manufacturer in the United States. We have thousands of telephones on hand at all times, packed and ready for immediate shipment; and whether you send us an order for one telephone or for one hundred telephones, you may send it with perfect confidence that **shipment will be made at once and there will be no waiting, no delay.** The instruments will go forward at once, carefully packed and guaranteed to reach you in perfect condition.

SERIES TELEPHONES

No. 20L5530

SERIES TELEPHONES. Series Telephones are made for use on lines where only two instruments are to be installed or for use on lines having a switchboard and an operator at a central office. Our Series Telephones are made throughout in the same perfect manner as our Bridging Telephones; every detail has exactly the same rigid inspection, and exactly the same high standard of excellence is maintained throughout the instrument. We put up our Series Telephones with the same high grade long distance transmitter, bi-polar receiver, long lever switch hook, improved ringer, etc., exactly the same as furnished with our highest grade Bridging Telephones. Our Series Telephones are equipped with three-magnet generators and 80-ohm ringers, will talk over lines of any length, and the generators are guaranteed to ring a bell over a 30-mile single line.

No. 20L5532

No. 20L5530 Compact Series Telephone. Price, including two dry batteries, 6 for $45.40; each........ $7.80
Shipping weight, 41 pounds each.

No. 20L5532 Southwestern Style Series Telephone. Price, including two dry batteries, 6 for $47.75; each........ $8.20
Price, including two wet batteries, 6 for $49.10; each... 8.44
Shipping weight, 52 pounds each.

OUR DESK TELEPHONES

SUITABLE FOR ANY KIND OF A LINE, SERIES OR BRIDGING.

OUR DESK TELEPHONE is made with exactly the same high grade equipment as all the other styles of our telephones, either bridging or series, exactly the same high power generators, long distance transmitters, improved bi-polar receivers, etc., embodying in all essential points every good quality represented in our various types of wall telephones.

THE GENERATOR AND RINGER are mounted in a neat golden oak cabinet, made with rounded, dovetailed corners and piano polish. This cabinet can be mounted on the wall near a table or desk, or on the side or underneath the table, where it is practically out of sight.

No. 20L5550 Series Desk Telephone, three-magnet generator, 80-ohm ringer, suitable for use on single lines where only two instruments are installed and also for lines having a switchboard and central operator. It cannot be used on bridging or party lines.
Price, 6 complete for $71.00; each, with two dry batteries......$12.20

No. 20L5553 Bridging Desk Telephone, four-magnet generator, 1,600-ohm ringer, suitable for use on bridging lines when not more than 18 instruments are installed.
Price, 6 complete for $79.45; each, with two dry batteries......$13.65

No. 20L5556 Bridging Desk Telephone, five-magnet, generator, 1,600-ohm ringer, suitable for use on bridging lines with from 30 to 50 instruments installed.
Price, 6 complete for $84.10; each, with two dry batteries.......$14.45

No. 20L5560 Bridging Desk Telephone, five-magnet generator, 2,000-ohm ringer, suitable for bridging lines, with from 30 to 50 instruments installed.
Price, 6 complete for $86.15; each, with two dry batteries......$14.80
Shipping weight of desk telephones is 35 pounds.

Our SOUTHWESTERN Style of Cabinet

PRICES ON SOUTHWESTERN BRIDGING TELEPHONES.

No. 20L5515 Five-Magnet Bridging Telephone, Southwestern Style, with 1,000-ohm ringer.
Price, with two dry batteries, each, $10.20
6 for........ 59.35
Price, with two wet batteries, each, 10.44
6 for........ 60.75

No. 20L5516 Five-Magnet Bridging Telephone, Southwestern Style, with 1,600-ohm ringer.
Price, with two dry batteries, each, $10.50
6 for........ 61.10
Price, with two wet batteries, each, 10.74
6 for........ 62.50

No. 20L5517 Five-Magnet Bridging Telephone, Southwestern Style, with 2,000-ohm ringer.
Price, with two dry batteries, each, $10.80
6 for........ 62.85
Price, with two wet batteries, each, 11.04
6 for........ 64.25

No. 20L5521 Four-Magnet Bridging Telephone, Southwestern Style, with 1,000-ohm ringer.
Price, with two dry batteries, each.....$ 9.50
6 for........ 55.30
Price, with two wet batteries, each.. .. 9.74
6 for........ 56.70

No. 20L5522 Four-Magnet Bridging Telephone, Southwestern Style, with 1,600-ohm ringer.
Price, with two dry batteries, each.....$ 9.80
6 for........ 57.05
Price, with two wet batteries, each..... 10.04
6 for........ 58.45

No. 20L5523 Four-Magnet Bridging Telephone, Southwestern Style, with 2,000-ohm ringer.
Price with two dry batteries, each......$10.10
6 for........ 58.80
Price, with two wet batteries, each..... 10.34
6 for........ 60.20

Shipping weight, Southwestern Style Telephones, 54 pounds.

TELEPHONE SWITCHBOARDS

No. 20L5575 50-line Express Type, Automatic Self Restoring Drop Switchboard with five talking circuits, ten cords and plugs, five ringing out drops, switchboard generator, night alarm circuit, complete operator's set and fifteen feet of cable.
Price, without drops........$78.50

No. 20L5577 Series Drops installed.
Price, each........$1.65

No. 20L5578 Bridging Drops installed.
Price, each........$2.10

We can furnish any kind or size of switchboard wanted. Tell us what you want and we will quote prices that will save you money.

$11.25 BUYS OUR 5 MAGNET 1600 OHM COMPACT BRIDGING TELEPHONE

THERE ARE NO TELEPHONES MADE AT ANY PRICE THAT WILL TALK PLAINER OR FARTHER THAN OUR TELEPHONES. THERE ARE NO TELEPHONES MADE AT ANY PRICE THAT WILL RING MORE BELLS ON A LINE OR THAT WILL RING OVER A GREATER DISTANCE THAN OUR TELEPHONES.

OUR FIVE-MAGNET BRIDGING TELEPHONES are built for use on lines with from thirty to forty instruments installed, and are equally suited to smaller lines. They are equipped with our extra powerful five-magnet generators, tested and guaranteed to ring through 125,000-ohms resistance, tested and guaranteed to ring through fifty telephones on the same line, **more power** than is ever required in actual practice. If you are building a new line, no matter how many telephones are to be installed, we advise the purchase of our powerful five-magnet 1,600-ohm compact, or 2,000-ohm Southwestern style bridging telephones, as this equipment is standard throughout the country. If you are buying telephones to put on a line already equipped, then it will be best to select instruments equipped with generators and ringers to match those already on the line. Prices on our bridging telephones, with both four and five-magnet generators and ringers of 1,000, 1,600 or 2,000 ohms resistance will be found at the bottom of this and the following page.

THE CABINETS. **Our Compact Telephones are put up in cabinets of very ornamental design, very compact and made throughout of the best selected, kiln dried oak.** The corners are rounded and dovetailed, the screw holes are provided with metal bushings and the finish is a fine golden oak with piano polish. This cabinet measures 23¼ inches high by 5½ inches deep by 8¾ inches wide. We put up our Southwestern style of telephone in an extra large, substantially made cabinet, with sufficient space in the lower compartment for two full sized wet batteries. We recommend this cabinet particularly for use in engine rooms, creameries, etc., and especially in warm, dry climates, where dry batteries are not satisfactory. This cabinet measures 32 inches high, 12 inches wide and 7 inches deep. It is made throughout of the finest selected, kiln dried oak, with piano polish.

THE TRANSMITTER. **We equip all telephones with our latest improved, solid back long distance transmitter, a transmitter that will talk farther and louder and plainer than any other transmitter made.** The framework is built of heavy brass castings making it absolutely solid, and the carbon cup is turned from a solid brass bar. The carbon diaphragm and the granulated carbon are the very finest grade of carbon that we can import from Europe, and before going into the transmitter, are subjected to a special process of polishing which still further improves the quality.

THE RECEIVER. **We equip all our telephones with our latest improved bi-polar receiver, a receiver that is the result of years of study, experiment and constant improvement.** It is made with concealed connections, the coils are wound with **double silk** insulated magnet wire, the magnets are made from the highest grade **imported** magnet steel, and the cords, which are made extra heavy to prevent any possibility of cord trouble, are attached with a special, wide contact which cannot work loose.

SWITCH HOOK. **We equip all our telephones with our special long lever switch hook made with heavy German silver springs, and pure platinum contacts.** This hook is so constructed that no current whatever passes through the frame and there is no chance of a shock, when removing the receiver from the hook. The greatest attention is paid to securing perfect connections, every joint being soldered, and the general construction and design of this switch hook is such as to prevent any possibility of trouble from this source.

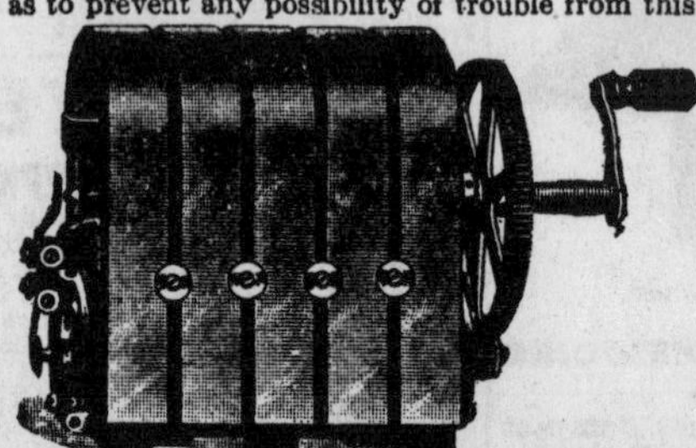

THE GENERATOR. **Our generators are made from the best imported magnet steel, and are guaranteed to retain their magnetism and power longer than any other generator made. There is more steel, more wire and more power in our five-magnet generator than in any five or six-magnet generator on the market.** The steel is the best imported magnet steel. The wire on the armature is the best double silk insulated magnet wire. Our five-magnet generator weighs 10½ pounds, and this weight is made up of the best imported magnet steel, the most expensive steel that can be bought, and the best double silk insulated copper magnet wire, the best magnet wire we can buy. **There is plenty of reserve power in this generator,** more power than you will ever need in actual practice. The resistance of an ordinary line, 25 or 30 miles in length, with 30 bridging telephones installed, **even if poorly constructed, and put up with small wire,** is less than 60,000 ohms, and we absolutely guarantee our five-magnet generator to ring through 125,000 ohms resistance, more than double the work which it will ever be called upon to do, and from three to four times the work which it will ordinarily be required to perform. **There is plenty of reserve power in our big five-magnet generator, and it will always ring every bell on the most heavily loaded lines.** The gear wheels are solid brass castings with milled gears and reinforced spokes, made extra wide to insure strength and durability, and the shunt springs are of heavy German silver.

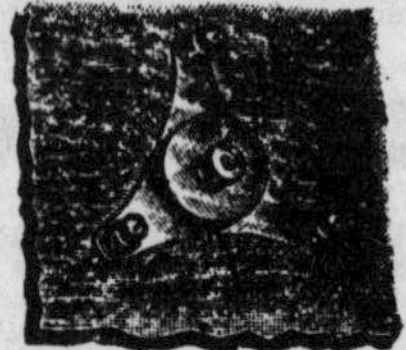

THE LIGHTNING ARRESTER **Our New Two-Path Carbon Lightning Arrester is the most perfect protection from lightning as well as sneak currents, that has ever been devised.** This lightning arrester is made up of three heavy brass punchings, the binding posts sweated on to insure perfect contact, the carbon extra large, presenting ample surface to the ground plate, and the mica insulated washers carefully perforated so that the shortest possible air gap is maintained between the carbon and the ground plates.

THE RINGER. **Our telephones are all equipped with the latest improved ringers, made with adjustable armatures, the coils wound with double silk insulated magnet wire, and with magnets of the best imported magnet steel, heavily nickel plated and polished.**

PRICES ON COMPACT BRIDGING TELEPHONES

No. 20H5500	**Five-Magnet Compact Bridging Telephone,** with 1,000-ohm ringer. Price, with two dry batteries, 6 for	$62.86;	each......$10.80
No. 20H5501	**Five-Magnet Compact Bridging Telephone,** with 1,600-ohm ringer. Price, with two dry batteries, 6 for	65.48;	each...... 11.25
No. 20H5502	**Five-Magnet Compact Bridging Telephone,** with 2,000-ohm ringer. Price, with two dry batteries, 6 for	67.22;	each...... 11.55
No. 20H5506	**Four-Magnet Compact Bridging Telephone,** with 1,000-ohm ringer. Price, with two dry batteries, 6 for	58.78;	each...... 10.10
No. 20H5507	**Four-Magnet Compact Bridging Telephone,** with 1,600-ohm ringer. Price, with two dry batteries, 6 for	60.82;	each...... 10.45
No. 20H5508	**Four-Magnet Compact Bridging Telephone,** with 2,000-ohm ringer. Price, with two dry batteries, 6 for	63.15;	each...... 10.85

Shipping weight of Compact Telephones, 43 pounds.

1907 MODELS SERIES AND BRIDGING

SEROCO TELEPHONES $9 to $12

Our 1907 No. 2 Cabinet Seroco Phone (series or bridging). Prices according to style. See Nos. 48G2105 to 48G2166.

THERE IS NOT A TELEPHONE MADE AT ANY PRICE THAT WILL TALK PLAINER OR FARTHER THAN THE SEROCO. THERE IS NOT A TELEPHONE MADE, AT ANY PRICE, THAT WILL RING AS MANY BELLS ON A LINE OR THAT WILL RING FARTHER THAN THE SEROCO.

IMPROVED MODELS FOR 1907.

ABOUT THE QUALITY. **When you buy a telephone, you want to be sure, first, that it is a good telephone.** You want to be sure that it is good all the way through; you want to be sure that nothing but the very best materials are used and nothing but the highest class of skilled labor is employed in its construction; you want to be sure that it is mechanically and electrically perfect in every detail, correctly and scientifically designed. That is the first consideration—quality. Second, you want to be sure that you buy it at the right price. There is nothing to be gained simply by paying out more money for an article than it is worth, even if it is good quality.

THERE ARE MANY DEALERS IN TELEPHONES **today who pretend to be manufacturers, but who are in reality merely assemblers,** purchasing in the open market, wherever they can buy the cheapest, all of the various parts which enter into the construction of a telephone; and these so called "manufacturers" simply assemble these parts, that is, put them together. It is impossible to produce a thoroughly dependable telephone under such a system of manufacturing, because the various parts come first from one source of supply and then another; sometimes they are good; sometimes they are bad. They are always subject to variation, because different manufacturers never produce articles exactly alike, and the purchaser of such a telephone never knows whether he can obtain repair parts, never knows whether he can replace a worn out or broken part, and in the long run such a telephone is a very expensive instrument, regardless of the original cost.

THE SEROCO TELEPHONES **are made complete from start to finish in one factory;** the generator, the switch hook, the ringer movement, the transmitter, the receiver, the cabinet; even the smallest screws, washers, etc., which enter into its construction are all made in the same factory. Every part of the Seroco Telephone is interchangeable, and we can furnish at any time in the future exact duplicates of every part. We can replace at any time any part that may wear out in service or become damaged in any way.

ALL OUR MATERIALS **are bought months in advance, to guard against possible delays, and bought in large quantities to obtain the very lowest market prices.** Our lumber is all thoroughly seasoned for months and kiln dried before it is made up into cabinets. Our carbon and steel are imported direct from Europe and shipped from the Atlantic seaboard by an all water route to secure the lowest possible freight charges. Every lot of new material as it comes to the factory is chemically tested before acceptance. The workmen engaged in the construction of the Seroco Telephones are men of the highest degree of skill; men of long and practical experience in telephone work.

TESTING. **Every one of the Seroco Telephones is tested before it leaves the factory, in ten different ways, by ten different electrical experts.** Not a telephone is allowed to leave the factory that does not test better by 25 per cent than the standard established by the National Interstate Telephone Association. The fact that every part of the Seroco Telephone is made complete in the one factory, under the general supervision of one man, gives us absolute control of every part and enables us to maintain this very high standard of excellence, something which no manufacturer can do who is compelled to depend upon outside manufacturers for parts of his telephone.

PROMPT DELIVERIES. **We carry in stock here at our store in Chicago the largest stock of telephones that is carried by any dealer or manufacturer in the United States.** We have on hand at all times, boxed, packed and ready for shipment from 1,500 to 2,000 telephones, and we have arrangements with the factory under which we receive shipments of new stock daily, thus keeping our stock rooms full at all times and enabling us to fill all orders promptly.

SIMPLICITY OF CONSTRUCTION. **The Seroco Telephones are made with the greatest possible simplicity, all complicated parts having been eliminated.** They are easy to put up and they are easy to keep in order after they are put up. They are equally easy to repair in case of accident or damage. Simplicity of construction in the telephone means simplicity of construction of the line. Anyone can put up a telephone line and install our instruments. There is nothing complicated, nothing hard to understand about it. No expert knowledge of electrical matters, no skill as a telephone man is required. The instruments are simple; they are made right in every way; they reach you in perfect order, and with the easily understood and simple directions which we send with every instrument it is easy for anyone, without the slightest previous experience, to put up a line and install the instruments satisfactorily.

ABOUT OUR PRICES. **Our prices are lower than the prices made by any other telephone manufacturer or dealer,** because, first, we are satisfied with a very much smaller percentage of profit, selling telephones on exactly the same small percentage of profit that we figure to make on the most staple merchandise; secondly, because the cost to us is figured on a basis of actual shop cost, without one cent added for general overhead expenses, which must be added to the cost of telephones marketed in the usual way. The factory which makes our telephones does no advertising, employs no salesmen, thus entirely eliminating all selling, collecting and other general expenses.

OUR GUARANTEE. **As the astonishing low prices which we make on Seroco Telephones may, in spite of our explanation, lead some to doubt the high quality of the goods, we send out with every telephone our signed guarantee,** under the terms of which we become responsible for the quality, material and workmanship of every telephone we sell. Remember that our guarantee means something, because Sears, Roebuck & Co., with their fully paid capital and surplus of over Forty Million Dollars, stand back of it. Remember that the guarantee issued by unknown and financially weak concerns, who may be out of business six months after you buy their telephone, is not worth the paper it is written on.

OUR TWELVE MONTHS' FREE TRIAL OFFER. **You may return to us, at our expense, at any time within one year from the time you receive your shipment,** any Seroco Telephone not found entirely satisfactory in every way, mechanically and electrically perfect, and we will refund your money, together with any express or freight charges you may have paid. If there are any weak points in a telephone they will certainly show up within a year, so **you assume no risk whatever in sending us your order for telephones.**

OUR BIG FREE TELEPHONE CATALOGUE **which we will be glad to send you free,** tells all about the details of the Seroco Telephones, all about the transmitters, the receivers, the switch hooks, the ringers, the generators, the lightning arresters, and the cabinets. Explains in detail just how our instruments are made and why we can sell a better telephone for less money than anyone else.

While we will gladly send you this free telephone catalogue, you need not delay to write for it, but you can order direct from these pages, which show our complete line at lowest prices. We accept your order with the understanding and agreement that if you are not fully satisfied with the goods, if you don't find our telephones the highest grade instruments in every respect and if you don't find we have saved you a great deal of money, you can return the goods at our expense and we will promptly return all the money you sent us.

WANTS SEVENTEEN MORE.

Sears, Roebuck & Co., Chicago, Ill. — Clinton, Ky.
Gentlemen:—I recently ordered of you twenty telephones and they are highly satisfactory. I now order seventeen more just like the others — Five-Magnet Bridging, 1600-ohm ringer with double battery cabinet. Yours truly, E. T. SPICER.

RINGS FORTY BOXES WITH OUR PHONE.

Sears, Roebuck & Co., Chicago, Ill. — Chico, Texas.
Gentlemen:—Our boxes came last week and I think that the goods are the best I ever saw by odds. Two of the parties on the line would not let me send their order. Sent theirs to——————— and can't ring Central with only six boxes on the line, and we have rung forty with the Seroco. Yours very truly, W. B. NORWOOD.

BEST HE EVER SAW.

Sears, Roebuck & Co., Chicago, Ill. — Coleman, Ga.
Gentlemen:—The lot of telephones which I received from you are the best that I ever saw. I don't want any other kind. Please let me know what you can sell me your express switchboard at with 100 drop capacity, and rigged up with forty drops to begin with. Yours truly, C. A. BROWN.

SEE NEXT PAGE FOR PRICES ON ALL TELEPHONES.

THIS ILLUSTRATION SHOWS OUR FIVE-MAGNET BRIDGING SEROCO PHONE WITH 1907 No. 2 CABINET. Prices, $11.20 to $11.95. See Nos. 48G2166 to 48G2168.

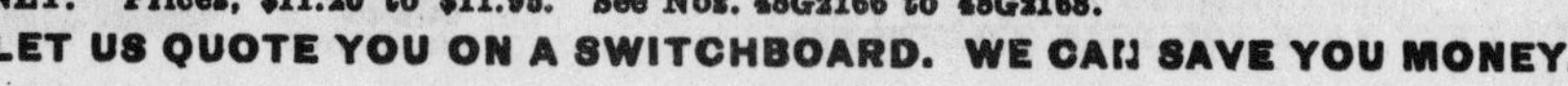
LET US QUOTE YOU ON A SWITCHBOARD. WE CAN SAVE YOU MONEY.

5 MAGNET 2000 OHM SOUTHWESTERN TELEPHONE BRIDGING $12.00

GENERAL CONSTRUCTION

ONLY THE VERY BEST MATERIALS and only the very highest class of skilled labor is employed in the construction of our telephones. They are mechanically and electrically perfect in every detail, correctly and scientifically designed. We spare no expense that will in any way improve the quality. Our object is to produce the most perfect, the most serviceable and the most satisfactory telephone that can be manufactured. Every part that enters into the make up of these telephones is as good as expert designers and skilled workmen can produce. There is not a loose joint in the entire instrument, every connection being soldered, making a solid circuit that cannot possibly get out of order. The workmen engaged in the construction of these telephones are men of the highest degree of skill—men of long and practical experience in actual telephone construction.

SIMPLE AND EASY TO INSTALL. Our telephones are made with the greatest possible simplicity, all complicated parts having been eliminated. They are easy to put up and easy to keep in order after they are put up. They are easy to repair if by accident any part becomes damaged or broken. Any one without the slightest electrical knowledge or telephone experience can put up a telephone line and install our telephones. There is nothing complicated about them—nothing hard to understand. The instruments are simple, they are right in every way, they reach you in perfect order, and they come to you with simple and easily understood directions, so that it is easy for anyone, without the slightest previous experience, to put up a line and install these instruments with perfect assurance that the line will give good service.

TESTS AND MATERIALS. Every telephone that we sell is tested before it leaves the factory by ten different electrical experts. Not an instrument is allowed to go out that does not test better by 25 per cent than the standard established by the National Interstate Telephone Association. Our lumber is all air dried for months and afterwards kiln dried, before it is made up into cabinets. Every lot of new material that comes to the factory is tested chemically and mechanically before it is accepted. **There are no cheap materials used in our telephones.** We could use American steel for the magnets of the generator, the receiver and the ringer, and make very substantial reductions in the cost, but imported magnet steel is better than American magnet steel, therefore every magnet that enters into the construction of our telephones is made from the highest grade of imported magnet steel. We use only **first quality** magnet wire, **with double silk insulation**, the most expensive magnet wire that we can buy. We use the very highest priced, the most expensive granulated carbon and carbon diaphragms that we can import. All of these things count, and count very much in determining whether a telephone is a good telephone or not. When you buy a telephone, you want one that you can rely upon all the time, under all conditions, and such a telephone **must be made right all the way through.** It must be put up by good workmen; it must be properly designed, and it must be made throughout from the very best materials. **Our telephones comply with all these requirements.**

MADE COMPLETE IN ONE FACTORY. There are many dealers in telephones today who pretend to be manufacturers, but who are merely assemblers, purchasing the various parts wherever they can buy the cheapest. They buy their generators from one factory, their transmitters from another and their receivers from another. The cabinet is made in still another factory, probably a factory where nothing is known of actual telephone requirements. All the various small parts are purchased here and there, and then these odds and ends of telephone construction are assembled or put together in this so called "telephone factory." It is impossible to produce a dependable, reliable telephone in this way, because the various parts come first from one source of supply and then another. They are always subject to variation because different manufacturers never produce articles exactly alike, and the purchaser of such a telephone never knows whether he can secure repair parts, never knows whether he can replace a worn out or broken part, and if the instrument is not satisfactory he finds that he has no redress, but must accept the loss and buy another telephone from some reliable dealer. **Our telephones are made complete, from start to finish, in one factory.** The generators, switchhooks, ringers, transmitters, receivers, cabinets, everything, even the smallest screws and washers which enter into the construction of our telephones, are made in one factory. Every part is interchangeable, and we can furnish at any time in the future, ten, fifteen or twenty years from now, exact duplicates of every part. Every part is interchangeable and we can replace, at any time, any part that may wear out in service or become damaged in any way.

PROMPT DELIVERIES. **We carry in stock, right here at our store in Chicago, the largest stock of telephones that is carried by any dealer or manufacturer in the United States.** We have thousands of telephones on hand at all times, packed and ready for immediate shipment; and whether you send us an order for one telephone or for one hundred telephones, you may send it with perfect confidence that **shipment will be made at once and there will be no waiting, no delay.** The instruments will go forward at once, carefully packed and guaranteed to reach you in perfect condition.

OUR GUARANTEE AND TWELVE MONTHS' FREE TRIAL OFFER. **As the astonishing low prices which we quote on these telephones may, very naturally, lead some to doubt the high quality of the instruments,** we send, with every telephone, our signed guarantee, under the terms of which we become responsible for the quality, material and workmanship of every telephone we sell, and we accept your order with the distinct understanding and agreement that you can put the telephone up, use it for twelve months, compare it with any other telephones in your neighborhood telephones that may have cost twice the amount that we ask you for ours, and if, at the end of the year, you have any fault whatever to find with this telephone, if you do not find it better than any other telephone in your locality and if you do not feel that you have secured a better telephone and saved money, you can pack it up, and return it to us at our expense. We will refund, without question, the entire purchase price, and reimburse you for all transportation charges.

OUR NAME **does not appear on our telephones in any way.** We find that occasionally customers who would like to take advantage of the low prices and high quality of our telephones, hesitate to do so because of the antagonism of local companies or other interested parties, and for this reason we do not put any name plate or any identifying mark of any kind on our telephones. You can send us your order for telephones with perfect assurance that the transaction is in every way strictly confidential, and that no marks will appear on the telephones inside or outside, to show where you bought them.

PRICES ON SOUTHWESTERN STYLE BRIDGING TELEPHONES.

No. 20H5515 Five-Magnet Bridging Telephone, Southwestern Style, with 1,000-ohm ringer.
Price, with two dry batteries, 6 for **$65.48**; each $11.25
Price, with two wet batteries, 6 for **$66.87**; each 11.49

No. 20H5516 Five-Magnet Bridging Telephone, Southwestern Style, with 1,600-ohm ringer.
Price, with two dry batteries, 6 for **$67.80**; each 11.65
Price, with two wet batteries, 6 for **$69.20**; each 11.89

No. 20H5517 Five-Magnet Bridging Telephone, Southwestern Style, with 2,000-ohm ringer.
Price, with two dry batteries, 6 for **$69.84**; each 12.00
Price, with two wet batteries 6 for **$71.24**; each 12.24

No. 20H5521 Four-Magnet Bridging Telephone, Southwestern Style, with 1,000-ohm ringer.
Price, with two dry batteries, 6 for **$61.40**; each 10.55
Price, with two wet batteries, 6 for **$62.50**; each 10.74

No. 20H5522 Four-Magnet Bridging Telephone, Southwestern Style, with 1,600-ohm ringer.
Price, with two dry batteries, 6 for **$63.44**; each 10.90
Price, with two wet batteries, 6 for **$64.84**; each 11.14

No. 20H5523 Four-Magnet Bridging Telephone, Southwestern Style, with 2,000-ohm ringer.
Price, with two dry batteries, 6 for **$65.77**; each 11.30
Price, with two wet batteries, 6 for **$67.16**; each 11.54

Shipping weight, Southwestern Style Telephones, 54 pounds.

SERIES TELEPHONES. **Series Telephones are made for use on lines where only two instruments are to be installed or for use on lines having a switchboard and an operator at a central office.** Our Series Telephones are made throughout in the same perfect manner as our Bridging Telephones; every detail has exactly the same rigid inspection, and exactly the same high standard of excellence is maintained throughout the instrument. We put up our Series Telephones with the same high grade long distance transmitter, bi-polar receiver, long lever switch hook, improved ringer, etc., exactly the same as furnished with our highest grade Bridging Telephones. Our Series Telephones are equipped with three-magnet generators and 80-ohm ringers, will talk over lines of any length, and the generators are guaranteed to ring a bell over a 30-mile single line.

No. 20H5530 Compact Series Telephone. Price, including two dry batteries, 6 for **$49.50**; each $8.50
Shipping weight, 41 pounds each.

No. 20H5532 Southwestern Style Series Telephone. Price, including two dry batteries, 6 for **$52.70**; each 9.05
Price, including two wet batteries, 6 for **$54.10**; each 9.29
Shipping weight, 52 pounds each.

No. 20H5532

No. 20H5530

SEE NEXT PAGE FOR DESK TELEPHONES.

OUR DESK TELEPHONES.

SUITABLE FOR ANY KIND OF A LINE, SERIES OR BRIDGING.

THE CONVENIENCE and neat appearance of a desk telephone appeals to every telephone user, and our Desk Telephone is not only electrically and mechanically a perfect instrument, but it is, at the same time, of the most handsome and ornamental design.

OUR DESK TELEPHONE is made with exactly the same high grade equipment as all the other styles of our telephones, either bridging or series, exactly the same high power generators, long distance transmitters, improved bipolar receivers, etc., embodying in all essential points every good quality represented in our various types of wall telephones. The frame is made of solid cast brass, the stand is of heavy brass tubing, octagonal in shape, and the connecting cords, both for the instrument and the receiver, are made extra heavy. The entire instrument is heavily nickel plated and highly polished.

THE GENERATOR AND RINGER are mounted in a neat golden oak cabinet, made with rounded, dovetailed corners and piano polish. This cabinet can be mounted on the wall near a table or desk, or on the side or underneath the table, where it is practically out of sight.

WHEN ORDERING DESK TELEPHONES, remember that the generator and ringer must correspond in size and resistance to those of the instruments already on the line. If you are buying instruments for a new line, we advise the purchase of telephones with standard equipment, five-magnet generators and 1,600-ohm ringers.

No. 20H5550 Series Desk Telephone, three-magnet generator, 80-ohm ringer, suitable for use on single lines where only two instruments are installed and also for lines having a switchboard and central operator. It cannot be used on bridging or party lines.
Price, each, with two dry batteries $12.20
Six, complete for 71.00

No. 20H5553 Bridging Desk Telephone, four-magnet generator, 1,600-ohm ringer, suitable for use on bridging lines when not more than 18 instruments are installed.
Price, each, with two dry batteries $13.65
Six, complete for 79.45

No. 20H5556 Bridging Desk Telephone, five-magnet generator, 1,600-ohm ringer, suitable for use on bridging lines with from 30 to 50 instruments installed.
Price, each, with two dry batteries $14.45
Six, complete for 84.10

No. 20H5560 Bridging Desk Telephone, five-magnet generator, 2,000-ohm ringer, suitable for bridging lines, with from 30 to 50 instruments installed.
Price, each, with two dry batteries $14.80
Six, complete for 86.15
Shipping weight of desk telephones is 35 pounds.

Pony Magneto Call Telephone.

No. 20H5570 This telephone is built for use on short lines of from 50 feet to 5 miles. It can be used with copper or iron wire or even with fence wire. It is equipped with a high grade transmitter, receiver and three-magnet pony generator. It is put up in a handsome oak case, and all parts are heavily nickel plated. We furnish an outfit complete, consisting of two telephones, four batteries, weighing 30 pounds.
Price $9.50

Telephone Parts.

No. 20H5600 Our Solid Back Transmitter, the best long distance transmitter on the market. Our transmitters talk. Each one guaranteed. Price, each $1.20
If by mail, postage extra, 24 cents.

No. 20H5605 Our Bipolar Receiver is the result of twenty years' experience. They are in use on 150,000 telephones today. Each one guaranteed. Price, each 90c
If by mail, postage extra, 20 cents.

No. 20H5610 Five-magnet Bridging Generator, guaranteed to ring through 100,000 ohms. Made of the best imported steel. Price, each $3.95

No. 20H5612 Four-magnet Bridging Generator, guaranteed to ring through 50,000 ohms. Made of the best imported steel. Price, each $3.30

No. 20H5614 Three-magnet Series Generator, guaranteed to ring through 25,000 ohms. Made of the best imported steel. Price, each $2.40

No. 20H5619 80-ohm Series Ringer. Silk wound coils, imported steel magnet. Easily adjusted and fully guaranteed. Price, each 95c

No. 20H5621 1,000-ohm Bridging Ringer. Silk wound coils, imported steel magnet. Easily adjusted and fully guaranteed. Price, each $1.60

No. 20H5623 1,600-ohm Bridging Ringer. Silk wound coils, imported steel magnet. Easily adjusted and fully guaranteed. Price, each $1.85

No. 20H5625 2,000-ohm Bridging Ringer. Silk wound coils, imported steel magnet. Easily adjusted and fully guaranteed. Price, each $2.30

No. 20H5635 Nickel plated Gongs and Stands.
Price, per set 20c

No. 20H5640 Long Lever Switch Hook. German silver springs, platinum contacts. All nickel plated.
Price, each 50c

No. 20H5655 250-ohm Induction Coil. Silk wound, square fiber ends. Price, each 45c

No. 20H5657 500-ohm Induction Coil. Silk wound, square fiber ends. Price, each 60c

Extension Bells, as an additional call for noisy places, and in other rooms away from the telephone, must be same size as telephone ringer.

No. 20H5670 80-ohm Extension Bell.
Price, each $1.50

No. 20H5671 1,000-ohm Extension Bell.
Price, each 2.50

No. 20H5672 1,600-ohm Extension Bell.
Price, each 2.65

No. 20H5673 2,000-ohm Extension Bell.
Price, each 2.85

No. 20H5680 Adjustable Arm with transmitter and coil, all complete. Price, each $2.10

No. 20H5685 Receiver Cords, worsted, 36 inches long.
Price, per pair 16c

No. 20H5690 Telephone Mouthpieces. Male or female thread. Price, each 11c
If by mail, postage extra, 3 cents.

No. 20H5725 Single Pole Fuse Block with Carbon Lightning Arrester. Porcelain base and brass mountings, upright carbons, with mica insulation. Western Union or Postal style.
Price, each, with one dozen copper fuses 25c

No. 20H5727 Double Pole Fuses Blocks with Carbon Lightning Arrester, either Western Union or Postal style.
Price, each, with one dozen copper fuses 35c

No. 20H5729 Veribest Glass Inclosed Fuses, for Western Union fuse blocks.
Price, per 100 .... $1.40; each 1½c

No. 20H5731 ¼-Ampere Fuses, tipped with tinfoil, Western Union or Postal style.
Price, in lots of 100 .... $1.00; per dozen 12c

No. 20H5733 ¼-Ampere Fuses, tipped with copper. Western Union or Postal style.
Price, in lots of 100 .... $1.25; per dozen 15c

Galvanized Telephone Wire.

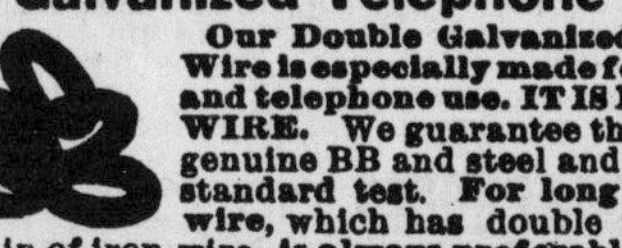

Our Double Galvanized Steel Line Wire is especially made for telegraph and telephone use. IT IS NOT FENCE WIRE. We guarantee this wire to be genuine BB and steel and to stand any standard test. For long spans, steel wire, which has double the breaking strain of iron wire, is always preferable. The No. 10 wire will weigh about 275 pounds to the mile, the No. 12, 165 pounds, and the No. 14 about 96 pounds.

This wire is sold in half-mile coils only. Prices subject to change without notice. All shipments made direct from our factory in Central Indiana.

	B.W.G. Gauge	Price, per 100 pounds on BB Iron Wire	Price, per 100 pounds on Steel Line Wire
No. 20H5750	No. 10	$3.87	$3.62
No. 20H5751	No. 12	4.00	3.75
No. 20H5752	No. 14	4.12	4.00

Write for special prices on large quantities.

We do not recommend fence wire for telephone use, but can furnish it at the lowest market price. Write for quotations.

Rubber Covered Telephone Wire.

No. 20H5760 Double Conductor Rubber Covered, braided, twisted, and covered with a saturated braid No. 19. Price, per hundred feet ... $1.57

No. 20H5765 Rubber Covered Braided, twisted pair telephone wire No. 19, for inside use.
Price, per hundred feet $1.35

Office and Annunciator Wire.

No. 20H5770 Annunciator Wire, No. 18, in ½ and 1-pound coils.
Price, per pound 40c

No. 20H5772 Office Wire, No. 18, in 1-pound coils. Price, per pound 42c

Magnet Wire, B. & S. Gauge.

No. 20H5775 Belden Double Cotton Covered Magnet Wire. One piece only on a spool. Insulation and wire is perfectly uniform.

Size	1-oz. Spool	2-oz. Spool	4-oz. Spool	8-oz. Spool	1-lb. Spool	5-lb. Spool per lb.
16	....	.....	.....	.....	$0.57	$0.53
18	....	.....	.....	.....	.64	.60
20	....	.....	.....	$0.42	.74	.70
21	....	.....	.....	.47	.83	.77
22	....	.....	.....	.48	.86	.81
23	....	.....	.....	.50	.90	.85
24	....	.....	$0.27	.52	.97	.92
25	....	.....	.30	.58	1.06	1.01
28	....	$0.25	.33	.63	1.15	1.10
30	$0.25	.27	.45	.87	1.62	1.56
32	.27	.31	.52	.99	1.87	1.80
34	.30	.40	.70	1.36	2.52	2.42
36	.40	.50	.95	1.83	3.45	3.30

Note—Above prices include the spool and cost of spooling. The wire is furnished only on sized spools given. We can furnish single cotton, single and double silk covered in 5-pound lots. Prices on application.

Insulators, Brackets, Etc.

No. 20H5800 Pony Glass Insulator for telephone, telegraph and fire alarm work. Packed 400 in a barrel. Weight, per barrel ready for shipment, 300 pounds.
Price, per barrel, 400 insulators .. $6.30
Price, each, in less than barrel lots .01¼

No. 20H5805 Double Groove Pony Glass Insulator for telephone transposition work, packed 400 in a barrel. Weight, per barrel, ready for shipment, 300 pounds. Price, per barrel, 400 insulators . $6.30
Price, each, in less than barrel lots .... .01¼

No. 20H5810 Porcelain Insulator No. 4½, new code; requiring 1 inch space between bottom and groove. Height, 1⅜ inches; diameter, 1⅛ inches; hole, $\frac{7}{16}$ inch; groove, $\frac{7}{16}$ inch.
Price, per 100 .... 70c
Price, per standard package of 1,000 .... $6.65

No. 20H5815 Porcelain Insulator No. 5½, new code; requiring 1 inch space between bottom and groove. Height, 1$\frac{5}{16}$ inches; diameter, 1 inch; hole, ¼ inch; groove, $\frac{5}{16}$ inch. Price, per 100 .... $0.42
Price, per standard package of 1,000 .... 3.90

No. 20H5820 Pony Oak Telephone Bracket, painted and dipped, weight 1 pound each. Price, per sack containing 250 brackets $3.30
Price, each, in less than sack lots .01½

No. 20H5825 1¼-inch Pony Oak Pins, for telephone work, painted and dipped. Price, per sack, containing 250 pins $1.98
Price, each, in less than sack lots ..... .01

No. 20H5835 Black Insulating Friction Tape, will not vulcanize with heat, nor crack nor harden and become defective by exposure and use; ¾ inch wide.
Price, per pound 36c

No. 20H5840 Standard Soldering Salts, for making soldering acid. Mixed with water only. Will not corrode the finest metal. Directions on bottle. In ½-pound bottles. Price, per bottle 21c

No. 20H5845 Soldering Stick, a soldering flux in solid form, superior to any style of acid, very portable, used by applying on heated joint.
Price, per stick 14c

No. 20H5850 Soldering Paste, 2-ounce box.
Price, per box 9c

No. 20H5855 Wire Solder, for ordinary electric work.
Price, per pound 37c

Baby Knife Switches.

FOR TELEPHONE AND BATTERY WORK.

No. 20H5875 15-ampere, single pole, single throw.
Price 25c

No. 20H5877 15-ampere, single pole, double throw.
Price 33c

No. 20H5879 15-ampere, double pole, single throw.
Price 30c

No. 20H5881 15-ampere, double pole, double throw.
Price 40c

Tackle Block Wire Stretcher.

87c

No. 20H5900 Tackle Block Wire Stretcher. Self locking at any point. This stretcher is provided with all malleable iron grapples for stretching barbed wire strands and woven wire fencing and telephone wire. It is also a complete safety rope hoist for ordinary use with which one man can raise 500 pounds. Weight, 4½ pounds.
Price, complete with 16 feet of ⅝-inch rope .. 87c

Bull Dog Wire Grip.

No. 20H5905 Bull Dog Wire Grip. The more you pull, the tighter it grips. Used with a tackle block with an ordinary wire stretcher, or with a hand spike and chain. It never slips, and does not injure the wire. Price, per pair of two grips 40c

Linemen's Tools.

No. 20H5910 The Elgin Adjustable Linemen's Wrench. Made of the very best tool steel, heavily nickel plated. It will hold pipe nipples, collars, round or square rods and square, hexagon or round nuts. Guarantee with each wrench. Length, 7 inches. Weight, 10 ounces. Price 75c

No. 20H5915 Extra jaws for above. Price 25c

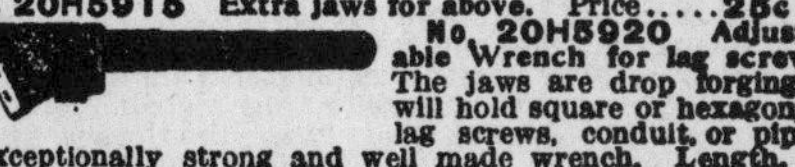

No. 20H5920 Adjustable Wrench for lag screw. The jaws are drop forgings; will hold square or hexagonal lag screws, conduit, or pipe. An exceptionally strong and well made wrench. Length, 9 inches. Price 62c

No. 20H5925 Combination Wrench for either square, round or hexagonal lag screw or bolts. Made of the best tool steel, with drop forged jaws, one side of which is plain, to be used as a hammer for starting the screw. Length, 7½ inches.
Price 65c

No. 20H5930 Linemen's Clamps or Connectors. Made from electro boracic Swedish steel. Spring tempered handles with round edges; will not wear out clothes. The best that mechanical skill can produce. Fully warranted. Length, 11 inches; full polished; for No. 3 wire and smaller, B. & S. gauge. Two oval and two round holes.
Price $1.35

No. 20H5935 Linemen's Clamps; same grade as above. Length, 11 inches; full polished; for No. 3 wire and smaller, B. & S. gauge. Four round holes. Price $1.35

No. 20H5940 Linemen's Side Cutting Pliers. Made of the best tool steel properly tempered, raised cutters, polished finish.
Price, 8-inch .... $1.15; 7-inch 95c

Hargraves' Climbers.

We guarantee these climbers to be made of the very best steel, perfectly tempered, finely finished, the very best, strongest and safest climbers made. We carry these climbers in standard lengths, namely, 15, 15½, 16, 16½, 17 and 17½ inches in stock. State length wanted. No straps are furnished with our climbers at prices as listed below.

No. 20H5945 Hargraves' Climbers, Eastern Pattern. Price, per pair, with spurs $1.85

No. 20H5946 Extra Spurs, for Eastern Pattern Climbers. Price, per pair with rivets 38c

No. 20H5950 Climber Straps. These straps are furnished with a large leather pad, which prevents the climber from digging into the knee. Can be used with any make of climber, either Eastern or Western. Price, per set of four $1.10

Iron Box Bells.

No. 20H6000 3-inch Iron Box Bell for door and call bell use. The box is made of stamped sheet metal, has cast gong and German silver contacts. Will ring 50 feet on one cell of battery.
Price, each 28c
If by mail, postage extra, 10 cents.

No. 20H6002 4-inch Iron Box Bell. This bell is larger and heavier than the 3-inch and is intended for use where a louder call is necessary.
Price, each 38c
If by mail, postage extra, 14 cents.

SERIES AND BRIDGING SEROCO TELEPHONES $7.70 TO $11.15

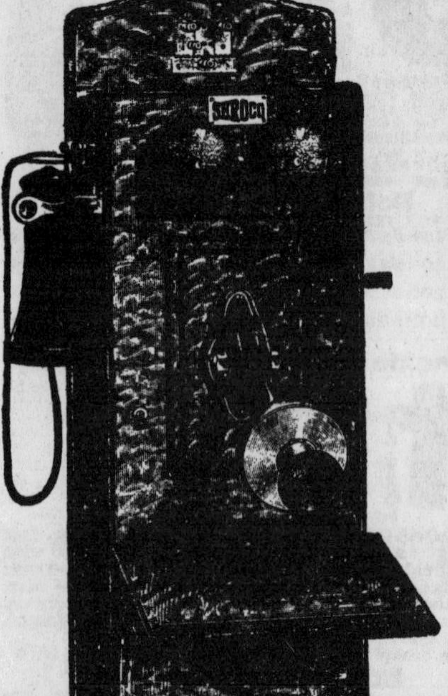

Our Compact Cabinet Series or Bridging Seroco Phone. Prices. $7.70 to $10.30, according to style. See Nos. 48F2101 to 48F2173.

THERE IS NOT A TELEPHONE MADE AT ANY PRICE THAT WILL TALK PLAINER OR FARTHER THAN THE SEROCO. THERE IS NOT A TELEPHONE MADE, AT ANY PRICE, THAT WILL RING AS MANY BELLS ON A LINE OR THAT WILL RING FARTHER THAN THE SEROCO.

AS TO PRICES, WE WANT YOU TO ASK OTHER DEALERS FOR QUOTATIONS BEFORE ORDERING, THEN YOU WILL KNOW THAT WE SAVE YOU MONEY.

ABOUT THE QUALITY. **When you buy a telephone, you want to be sure, first, that it is a good telephone.** You want to be sure that it is good all the way through; you want to be sure that nothing but the very best materials are used and nothing but the highest class of skilled labor is employed in its construction; you want to be sure that it is mechanically and electrically perfect in every detail, correctly and scientifically designed. That is the first consideration—quality. Second, you want to be sure that you buy it at the right price. There is nothing to be gained simply by paying out more money for an article than it is worth, even if it is good quality.

THERE ARE MANY DEALERS IN TELEPHONES **today who pretend to be manufacturers, but who are in reality merely assemblers,** purchasing in the open market, wherever they can buy the cheapest, all of the various parts which enter into the construction of a telephone; and these so called "manufacturers" simply assemble these parts, that is, put them together. It is impossible to produce a thoroughly dependable telephone under such a system of manufacturing, because the various parts come first from one source of supply and then another; sometimes they are good; sometimes they are bad. They are always subject to variation, because different manufacturers never produce articles exactly alike, and the purchaser of such a telephone never knows whether he can obtain repair parts, never knows whether he can replace a worn out or broken part, and in the long run such a telephone is a very expensive instrument, regardless of the original cost.

THE SEROCO TELEPHONES **are made complete from start to finish in one factory;** the generator, the switch hook, the ringer movement, the transmitter, the receiver, the cabinet; even the smallest screws, washers, etc., which enter into its construction are all made in the same factory. Every part of the Seroco Telephone is interchangeable, and we can furnish at any time in the future exact duplicates of every part. We can replace at any time any part that may wear out in service or become damaged in any way.

ALL OUR MATERIALS **are bought months in advance, to guard against possible delays, and bought in large quantities to obtain the very lowest market prices.** Our lumber is all thoroughly seasoned for months and kiln dried before it is made up into cabinets. Our carbon and steel are imported direct from Europe and shipped from the Atlantic seaboard by an all water route to secure the lowest possible freight charges. Every lot of new material as it comes to the factory is chemically tested before acceptance. The workmen engaged in the construction of the Seroco Telephones are men of the highest degree of skill; men of long and practical experience in telephone work.

TESTING. **Every one of the Seroco Telephones is tested before it leaves the factory, in ten different ways, by ten different electrical experts.** Not a telephone is allowed to leave the factory that does not test better by 25 per cent than the standard established by the National Interstate Telephone Association. The fact that every part of the Seroco Telephone is made complete in the one factory, under the general supervision of one man, gives us absolute control of every part and enables us to maintain this very high standard of excellence, something which no manufacturer can do who is compelled to depend upon outside manufacturers for parts of his telephone.

PROMPT DELIVERIES. **We carry in stock here at our store in Chicago the largest stock of telephones that is carried by any dealer or manufacturer in the United States.** We have on hand at all times, boxed, packed and ready for shipment from 1,500 to 2,000 telephones, and we have arrangements with the factory under which we receive shipments of new stock daily, thus keeping our stock rooms full at all times and enabling us to fill all orders promptly.

SIMPLICITY OF CONSTRUCTION. **The Seroco Telephones are made with the greatest possible simplicity, all complicated parts having been eliminated.** They are easy to put up and they are easy to keep in order after they are put up. They are equally easy to repair in case of accident or damage. Simplicity of construction in the telephone means simplicity of construction of the line. Anyone can put up a telephone line and install our instruments. There is nothing complicated, nothing hard to understand about it. No expert knowledge of electrical matters, no skill as a telephone man is required. The instruments are simple; they are made right in every way; they reach you in perfect order, and with the easily understood and simple directions which we send with every instrument it is easy for anyone, without the slightest previous experience, to put up a line and install the instruments satisfactorily.

ABOUT OUR PRICES. **Our prices are lower than the prices made by any other telephone manufacturer or dealer,** because, first, we are satisfied with a very much smaller percentage of profit, selling telephones on exactly the same small percentage of profit that we figure to make on the most staple merchandise; secondly, because the cost to us is figured on a basis of actual shop cost, without one cent added for general overhead expenses, which must be added to the cost of telephones marketed in the usual way. The factory which makes our telephones does no advertising, employs no salesmen, thus entirely eliminating all selling, collecting and other general expenses.

OUR GUARANTEE. **As the astonishing low prices which we make on Seroco Telephones may, in spite of our explanation, lead some to doubt the high quality of the goods, we send out with every telephone our signed guarantee,** under the terms of which we become responsible for the quality, material and workmanship of every telephone we sell. Remember that our guarantee means something, because Sears, Roebuck & Co., with their fully paid capital and surplus of over Five Million Dollars, stand back of it. Remember that the guarantee issued by unknown and financially weak concerns, who may be out of business six months after you buy their telephone, is not worth the paper it is written on.

OUR TWELVE MONTHS' FREE TRIAL OFFER. **You may return to us, at our expense, at any time within one year from the time you receive your shipment,** any Seroco Telephone not found entirely satisfactory in every way, mechanically and electrically perfect, and we will refund your money, together with any express or freight charges you may have paid. If there are any weak points in a telephone they will certainly show up within a year, so **you assume no risk whatever in sending us your order for telephones.**

OUR BIG FREE TELEPHONE CATALOGUE **which we will be glad to send you free,** tells all about the details of the Seroco Telephones, all about the transmitters, the receivers, the switch hooks, the ringers, the generators, the lightning arresters, and the cabinets. Explains in detail just how our instruments are made and why we can sell a better telephone for less money than anyone else.

While we will gladly send you this free telephone catalogue, you need not delay to write for it, but you can order direct from these pages, which show our complete line at lowest prices. We accept your order with the understanding and agreement that if you are not fully satisfied with the goods, if you don't find our telephones the highest grade instruments in every respect and if you don't find we have saved you a great deal of money, you can return the goods at our expense and we will promptly return all the money you sent us.

SEE NEXT PAGE FOR PRICES ON ALL TELEPHONES.

THIS ILLUSTRATION SHOWS OUR FIVE-MAGNET BRIDGING SEROCO PHONE WITH COMPACT CABINET.

Prices, $9.70 to $10.30.

See Nos. 48F2171 to 48F2173.

WANTS SEVENTEEN MORE.

Sears, Roebuck & Co., Chicago, Ill. — Clinton, Ky.

Gentlemen:—I recently ordered of you twenty telephones and they are highly satisfactory. I now order seventeen more just like the others — Five-Magnet Bridging, 1600-ohm ringer with double battery cabinet.

Yours truly, E. T. SPICER.

RINGS FORTY BOXES WITH OUR PHONE.

Sears, Roebuck & Co., Chicago, Ill. — Chico, Texas.

Gentlemen:—Our boxes came last week and I think that the goods are the best I ever saw by odds. Two of the parties on the line would not let me send their order. Sent theirs to———— and can't ring Central with only six boxes on the line, and we have rung forty with the Seroco.

Yours very truly, W. B. NORWOOD.

BEST HE EVER SAW.

Sears, Roebuck & Co., Chicago, Ill. — Coleman, Ga.

Gentlemen:—The lot of telephones which I received from you are the best that I ever saw. I don't want any other kind. Please let me know what you can sell me your express switchboard at with 100 drop capacity, and rigged up with forty drops to begin with.

Yours truly, C. A. BROWN.

LET US QUOTE YOU ON A SWITCHBOARD. WE CAN SAVE YOU MONEY.

Seroco Series Telephones.

Our Seroco Series Telephones are made with 80-ohm ringers and powerful series generators guaranteed to ring through 25,000 ohms resistance. This generator is made with extra long heavy laminated armature wound with silk insulated wire, wide noiseless gear and automatic shunt, highest grade bi-polar receiver, long distance solid back transmitter, self contained long lever switch hook and two-path lightning arrester and switch. The best series telephone that can be made regardless of price.

Series Telephone with Compact Cabinet.

No. 48F2101 Series Telephone, as described above, with latest style compact cabinet. Price, each......$ 7.70
Per dozen.................. 88.70

Series Telephone with Double Battery Cabinet.

No. 48F2106 Series Telephone, as described above, with large double battery cabinet.
Price, each...................$ 8.20
Per dozen.................. 94.25

Two dry batteries are included with each series telephone at above prices. If wet batteries are wanted instead of dry batteries add 26 cents to the price of each phone. Wet batteries can be used only with the double battery cabinet. Weight of one telephone when packed, about 50 pounds.

Seroco Bridging Telephones.

These telephones are used on party lines where a number of instruments are installed, and no switchboard or central office is necessary. Our bridging telephones are equipped with a special high grade ringer, designed especially for bridging work, and extra powerful four-magnet or five-magnet generators. The generators, transmitters, receivers, ringers, switch hooks, lightning arresters and cabinets are all of the highest grade. We guarantee our bridging telephones to be the best that skilled labor, money and expert electrical knowledge can produce.

Four-magnet Bridging Telephones.

These telephones, equipped with four-magnet generators, are adapted to party lines having twenty or less instruments.

With Compact Cabinets.

No. 48F2151 Four-magnet Bridging Telephone, with compact cabinet; 1000-ohm ringer. Price, each, $ 9.25
Per dozen.................. 106.15

No. 48F2152 Four-magnet Bridging Telephone, with compact cabinet; 1600-ohm ringer. Price, each, $ 9.50
Per dozen.................. 109.30

No. 48F2153 Four-magnet Bridging Telephone, with compact cabinet; 2000-ohm ringer. Price, each, $ 9.80
Per dozen.................. 112.50

Two dry batteries are included with each of our four-magnet bridging telephones at above prices. Weight of one telephone when packed, about 50 pounds.

With Double Battery Cabinets.

No. 48F2156 Four-magnet Bridging Telephone, with double battery cabinet; 1000-ohm ringer. Price, each...$ 10.00
Per dozen.................. 116.85

No. 48F2157 Four-magnet Bridging Telephone, with double battery cabinet; 1600-ohm ringer. Price, each...$ 10.25
Per dozen.................. 118.70

No. 48F2158 Four-magnet Bridging Telephone, with double battery cabinet; 2000-ohm ringer. Price, each...$ 10.50
Per dozen.................. 121.70

Two dry batteries are included with each of these bridging telephones at above prices. The double battery cabinet, however, is large enough to accommodate two wet batteries, and if preferred we will include wet batteries for 26 cents extra per telephone.
Weight of one telephone when packed, about 50 pounds.

Five-magnet Bridging Telephones

These telephones, equipped with extra powerful five-magnet generators, are adapted to lines on which from twenty to forty instruments are installed.

With Compact Cabinets.

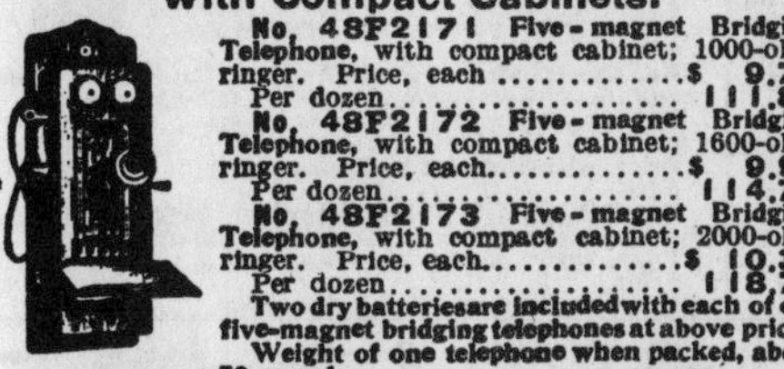

No. 48F2171 Five-magnet Bridging Telephone, with compact cabinet; 1000-ohm ringer. Price, each..............$ 9.70
Per dozen.................. 111.80

No. 48F2172 Five-magnet Bridging Telephone, with compact cabinet; 1600-ohm ringer. Price, each..............$ 9.95
Per dozen.................. 114.75

No. 48F2173 Five-magnet Bridging Telephone, with compact cabinet; 2000-ohm ringer. Price, each..............$ 10.30
Per dozen.................. 118.70

Two dry batteries are included with each of our five-magnet bridging telephones at above prices.
Weight of one telephone when packed, about 50 pounds.

With Double Battery Cabinets.

No. 48F2176 Five-magnet Bridging Telephone, with double battery cabinet; 1000-ohm ringer. Price, each...$ 10.60
Per dozen.................. 121.70

No. 48F2177 Five-magnet Bridging Telephone, with double battery cabinet; 1600-ohm ringer. Price, each...$ 10.85
Per dozen.................. 124.90

No. 48F2178 Five-magnet Bridging Telephone, with double battery cabinet; 2000-ohm ringer. Price, each...$ 11.15
Per dozen.................. 128.00

Two dry batteries are included with each of these bridging telephones at above prices. The double battery cabinet, however, is large enough to accommodate two wet batteries, and if preferred we will include wet batteries for 26 cents extra per telephone.

Seroco Portable Desk Set.

For use on desks and tables. Made up the same as our high grade telephones.

No. 48F2200 Series Desk Set. Price, complete..............$9.45

No. 48F2201 Four-magnet 1000-ohm Bridging Set. Price, complete..............$11.25

No. 48F2202 Four-magnet 1600-ohm Bridging Set. Price, complete..............$11.50

No. 48F2203 Four-magnet 2000-ohm Bridging Set. Price, complete..............$11.75

No. 48F2204 Five-magnet 1000-ohm Bridging Set. Price, complete..............$11.85

No. 48F2205 Five-magnet 1600-ohm Bridging Set. Price, complete..............$12.10

No. 48F2206 Five-magnet 2000-ohm Bridging Set. Price, complete..............$12.40

Pony Magneto Call Telephone.

No. 48F2270

This telephone is built for use on short lines of from 50 feet to 5 miles. It can be used with copper or iron wire or even with fence wire. It is equipped with a high grade transmitter, receiver and three-magnet pony generator. It is put up in a handsome oak case, and all parts are heavily nickel plated. We furnish an outfit complete, consisting of two telephones, four batteries, weighing thirty pounds.
Price..............................$9.50

Telephone Switchboards.

Our express type, automatic, self restoring drop switchboard is of the very latest design and most approved pattern. We can furnish a fifty-drop board, complete with five talking circuits, ten cords and plugs, five ringing out drops, switchboard generator, night alarm circuit, complete operator's set and fifteen feet of cable.

No. 48F2300 Price, as described..............$71.50
No. 48F2310 **Series drops installed.** Price, each, 1.40
No. 48F2320 **Bridging drops installed.**
Price, each.............................. 1.90

We can furnish any kind or size of switchboard wanted. Tell us what you want and we will quote prices that will save you money.

No. 48F2544 Single Pole Fuse Block with Carbon Lightning Arrester. Porcelain base and brass mountings, upright carbons, with mica insulation. Western Union or Postal style. Price, each.............11c

No. 48F2545 Double Pole Fuse Blocks with Carbon Lightning Arrester, either Western Union or Postal style.
Price, each..............................18c

No. 48F2548 Veribest Glass Inclosed Fuses, for Western Union fuse blocks. Price, per 100, $1.40; each.......1½c

Telephone Parts.

No. 48F2375 Our Solid Back Transmitter, the best long distance transmitter on the market. Our transmitters talk. Each one guaranteed.
Price, each..............................$1.05
If by mail, postage extra, 24 cents.

No. 48F2385 Our Bi-polar Receiver, is the result of twenty years' experience. They are in use on 150,000 telephones today. Each one guaranteed.
Price, each..............................85c
If by mail, postage extra, 20 cents.

No. 48F2400 Five-magnet Bridging Generator, guaranteed to ring through 100,000 ohms. Made of the best imported steel. Price, each..........$3.35

No. 48F2403 Four-magnet Bridging Generator, guaranteed to ring through 50,000 ohms. Made of the best imported steel. Price, each..........$2.60

No. 48F2405 Three-magnet Series Generator, guaranteed to ring through 25,000 ohms. Made of the best imported steel. Price, each..........$2.00

No. 48F2430 Eighty-ohm Series Ringer. Silk wound coils, imported steel magnet. Easily adjusted and fully guaranteed, Price, each..........75c

No. 48F2435 1000-ohm Bridging Ringer. Silk wound coils, imported steel magnet, easily adjusted and fully guaranteed. Price, each..........$1.45

No. 48F2440 1600-ohm Bridging Ringer. Silk wound coils, imported steel magnet. Easily adjusted and fully guaranteed. Price, each..........$1.55

No. 48F2445 2000-ohm Bridging Ringer. Silk wound coils, imported steel magnet, easily adjusted and fully guaranteed. Price, each..........$1.70

No. 48F2450 Nickel Plated Gongs and Stands.
Price, per set..............................20c

No. 48F2489 Long Lever Switch Hook. German silver springs, platinum contacts. All nickel plated.
Price, each..............................35c

No. 48F2490 250-ohm Induction Coil. Silk wound square fibre ends. Price, each..........35c

No. 48F2492 500-ohm Induction Coil. Silk wound square fibre ends. Price, each..........50c

Extension Bells, as an additional call for noisy places, and in other rooms away from the 'phone, must be same size as telephone ringer.

No. 48F2500 80-ohm Extension Bell.
Price, each..............................$1.30

No. 48F2505 1000-ohm Extension Bell.
Price, each..............................$2.00

No. 48F2510 1600-ohm Extension Bell.
Price, each..............................$2.25

No. 48F2515 2000-ohm Extension Bell.
Price, each..............................$2.50

No. 48F2528 Adjustable Arm with transmitter and coil, all complete. Price, each..........$1.80

No. 48F2534 Receiver Cords, worsted, 36 inches long. Price, per pair..........12c

No. 48F2546 Telephone Mouthpieces. Male or female thread. Price, each..........9c
If by mail, postage extra, 3 cents.

Galvanized Telephone Wire.

Our Double Galvanized Steel Line Wire is especially made for telegraph and telephone use. IT IS NOT FENCE WIRE. We guarantee this wire to be genuine BB and steel and to stand any standard test. **For long spans,** steel wire, which has double the breaking **strain of iron wire, is always preferable.** The No. 10 wire will weigh about 275 pounds to the mile, the No. 12, 165 pounds, and the No. 14 about 96 pounds.

This wire is sold in half-mile coils only. Prices subject to change without notice. All shipments made from our factory in Central Indiana.

	B.W.G. Gauge	Price, per 100 pounds on B.B. Iron Wire	Price, per 100 pounds or Steel Line Wire
No. 48F2600	No. 10	$3.25	$3.00
No. 48F2601	No. 12	3.37	3.12
No. 48F2602	No. 14	3.67	3.25

Write for special prices on large quantities.

We do not recommend fence wire for telephone use, but can furnish it at the lowest market price. Write for quotations.

Rubber Covered Telephone Wire.

No. 48F2610 Double Conductor Rubber Covered, braided, twisted, and covered with a saturated braid No. 19. Price, per hundred feet. $1.63

No. 48F2612 Rubber Covered Braided, twisted telephone wire for inside use.
Price, per hundred feet..............$1.75

Office and Annunciator Wire.

No. 48F2625 Annunciator Wire, No. 18, in ½ and 1-pound coils.
Price, per pound..............30c

No. 48F2630 Office Wire, No. 18, in 1-pound coils. Price, per pound..........32c

No. 48F2940 Morris Hard Fibre Cleats. Made with two grooves, especially adapted for putting up office and telephone wire, only one screw necessary to hold the cleat firmly in position. Size, ¾ x 1⅜ x ¼ inch; groove, ⅛ x ⅛-inch.
Price, per 1000, $4.25; per 100..............50c

Magnet Wire, B. & S. Gauge.

No. 48F2705 Belden Double Cotton Covered Magnet Wire. One piece only on a spool. Insulation and wire is perfectly uniform.

Size	1-oz. Spool	2-oz. Spool	4-oz. Spool	8-oz. Spool	1-lb. Spool	5-lb. Spool per lb.
16	....	......	......	.....	$0.35	$0.32
18	....	......	......	.....	.36	.34
20	....	......	......	$0.30	.45	.40
21	....	......	......	.35	.50	.45
22	....	......	......	.40	.55	.50
23	....	......	......	.45	.60	.55
24	....	......	$0.30	.50	.70	.65
25	....	......	.35	.55	.80	.75
26	....	$0.25	.45	.65	.90	.85
30	$0.18	.35	.55	.85	1.30	1.25
32	.18	.35	.55	.95	1.50	1.45
34	.25	.40	.70	1.20	2.15	2.10
36	.35	.50	.90	1.70	3.25	3.00

NOTE—Above prices include the spool, and cost of spooling. The wire is furnished only on sized spools given. We can furnish single cotton, single and double silk covered in 5-pound lots. Prices on application.

Insulators, Brackets, Etc.

No. 48F2755 Pony Glass Insulator for telephone, telegraph and fire alarm work. Packed 400 in a barrel. Weight, per barrel, ready for shipment, 300 pounds.
Price, per barrel, 400 insulators..$5.74
Price, each, in less than barrel lots .01¾

No. 48F2760 Double Groove Pony Glass Insulator for telephone, transposition work, packed 400 in a barrel. Weight, per barrel, ready for shipment, 300 pounds. Price, per barrel, 400 insulators $5.74
Price, each, in less than barrel lots....... .01¾

No. 48F2765 Porcelain Insulator No. 4½, new code; requiring 1 inch space between bottom and groove. Height, 1⅞ inches; diameter, 1¼ inches; hole, 5/16 inch; groove, 5/16 inch.
Price, per 100..............................50c
Price, per standard package of 1,000..........$4.60

No. 48F2770 Porcelain Insulator No. 5½, new code; requiring 1 inch space between bottom and groove. Height, 1 5/16 inches; diameter, 1 inch; hole, ⅜ inch; groove, 5/16 inch. Price, per 100..........$0.45
Price, per 1,000.............................. 4.10

No. 48F2830 Pony Oak Telephone Bracket, painted and dipped, weight 1 pound each. Price, per sack containing 250 brackets..............$2.50
Price, each, in less than sack lots .01½

No. 48F2835 1¼-inch Pony Oak Pins, for telephone work, painted and dipped. Price, per sack, containing 250 pins..............................$1.70
Price, each, in less than sack lots.. .01

No. 48F2900 Black Insulating Friction Tape, will not vulcanize with heat, nor crack or harden and become defective by exposure and use; ¾ inch wide.
Price, per pound..............28c

No. 48F2910 W. E Soldering Salts, for making soldering acid. Mixed with water only. Will not corrode the finest metal. Directions on bottle. In ½-pound bottles. Price, per bottle.......14c

No. 48F2915 Soldering Stick, a soldering flux in solid form, superior to any style of acid, very portable, used by applying on heated joint.
Price, per stick..............................15c

No. 48F2920 Soldering Paste, 2-ounce box.
Price, per box..............................9c

No. 48F2925 Wire Solder, for ordinary electric work.
Price, per pound..............................27c

SERIES AND BRIDGING TELEPHONES $7.80 TO $10.80

COMPACT BRIDGING TELEPHONES.

No. 20R5500 Five-Magnet Compact Bridging Telephone, with 1,000-ohm ringer.
Price, with two dry batteries, each..$ 9.70
6 for.. 56.45

No. 20R5501 Five-Magnet Compact Bridging Telephone, with 1,600-ohm ringer.
Price, with two dry batteries, each..$ 9.95
6 for.. 57.90

No. 20R5502 Five-Magnet Compact Bridging Telephone, with 2,000-ohm ringer.
Price, with two dry batteries, each..$10.20
6 for.. 59.36

No. 20R5506 Four-Magnet Compact Bridging Telephone, with 1,000-ohm ringer.
Price, with two dry batteries, each..$ 9.40
6 for.. 54.70

No. 20R5507 Four-Magnet Compact Bridging Telephone, with 1,600-ohm ringer.
Price, with two dry batteries, each..$ 9.65
6 for.. 56.17

No. 20R5508 Four-Magnet Compact Bridging Telephone, with 2,000-ohm ringer.
Price, with two dry batteries, each..$ 9.90
6 for.. 57.62

Shipping weight of Compact Telephones, 43 pounds.

PROMPT DELIVERIES. **We carry in stock, right here at our store in Chicago, the largest stock of telephones that is carried by any dealer or manufacturer in the United States.** We have thousands of telephones on hand at all times, packed and ready for immediate shipment; and whether you send us an order for one telephone or for one hundred telephones, you may send it with perfect confidence that **shipment will be made at once and there will be no waiting, no delay.** The instruments will go forward at once, carefully packed and guaranteed to reach you in perfect condition.

TWO PHONES FOR $9.50.

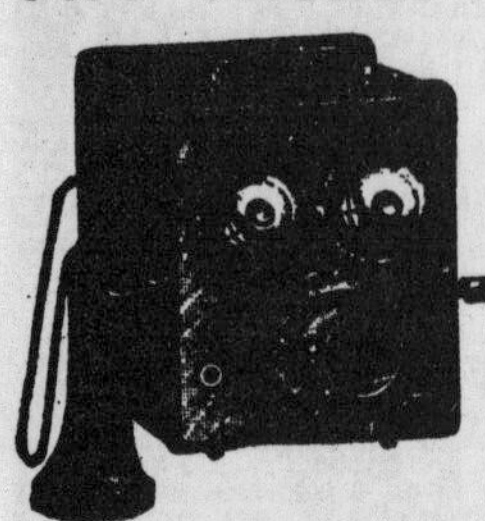

No. 20R5570 This Magneto Call Telephone is built for use on short lines of from 50 feet to 5 miles. It can be used with copper or iron wire or even with fence wire. It is equipped with a high grade transmitter, receiver and three-magnet pony generator. It is put up in a handsome **oak case,** and all parts are heavily nickel plated.
Price, per pair (two telephones).......$9.50
Four batteries are included with each pair.
Shipping weight, 46 pounds.

HOW OUR TELEPHONES ARE MADE.

FIRST, they are made complete from start to finish, under one roof, in one factory. The generators, switch hooks, ringers, transmitters, receivers, cabinets, everything, even the smallest screws and washers which enter into the construction of our telephones, are made in one factory. Every part is interchangeable, and we can furnish at any time in the future, ten, fifteen or twenty years from now, exact duplicates of every part. Every part is interchangeable and we can replace, at any time, any part that may wear out in service or become damaged in any way.

TRANSMITTER. We equip all telephones with our latest improved solid back long distance transmitter, a transmitter that will talk farther and louder and plainer than any other transmitter made. The framework is built of heavy brass castings, making it absolutely solid, and the carbon cup is turned from a solid brass bar. The carbon diaphragm and the granulated carbon are the very finest grade of carbon that we can import from Europe, and before going into the transmitter are subjected to a special process of polishing which still further improves the quality.

RECEIVER. We equip all our telephones with our latest improved bi-polar receiver, a receiver that is the result of years of study, experiment and constant improvement. It is made with concealed connections, the coils are wound with **double silk** insulated magnet wire, the magnets are made from the highest grade **imported** magnet steel, and the cords, which are made extra heavy to prevent any possibility of cord trouble, are attached with a special wide contact which cannot work loose.

GENERATOR. Our generators are made from the best imported magnet steel, and are guaranteed to retain their magnetism and power longer than any other generator made. There is more steel, more wire and more power in our five-magnet generator than in any five or six-magnet generator on the market. The steel is the best imported magnet steel. The wire on the armature is the best double silk insulated magnet wire. Our five-magnet generator weighs 10½ pounds, and this weight is made up of the best imported magnet steel, the most expensive steel that can be bought, and the best double silk insulated copper magnet wire, the best magnet wire we can buy. **There is plenty of reserve power in this generator,** more power than you will ever need in actual practice. The resistance of an ordinary line, 25 or 30 miles in length, with 30 bridging telephones installed, **even if poorly constructed and put up with small wire,** is less than 60,000 ohms, and we absolutely guarantee our five-magnet generator to ring through 125,000 ohms resistance, more than double the work which it will **ever** be called upon to do, and from three to four times the work which it will ordinarily be required to perform. The gear wheels are solid brass castings with milled gears and reinforced spokes, made extra wide to insure strength and durability, and the shunt springs are of heavy German silver.

SWITCH HOOK. We equip all our telephones with our special long lever switch hook made with heavy German silver springs and pure platinum contacts. This hook is so constructed that no current whatever passes through the frame and there is no chance of a shock when removing the receiver from the hook. The greatest attention is paid to securing perfect connections, every joint being soldered, and the general construction and design of this switch hook is such as to prevent any possibility of trouble from this source.

RINGER. Our telephones are all equipped with the latest improved ringers, made with adjustable armatures, the coils wound with **double silk** insulated magnet wire, and with magnets of the best **imported** magnet steel, heavily nickel plated and polished.

LIGHTNING ARRESTER. Our New Two-Path Carbon Lightning Arrester is the most perfect protection from lightning, as well as sneak currents, that has ever been devised. This lightning arrester is made up of three heavy brass punchings, the binding posts sweated on to insure perfect contact, the carbon extra large, presenting ample surface to the ground plate, and the mica insulated washers carefully perforated so that the shortest possible air gap is maintained between the carbon and the ground plates.

PUSH BUTTONS AND CONDENSERS.

FOR 20 CENTS extra per telephone, we will equip any of our bridging telephones with a simple push button attachment, by means of which you can ring any subscriber on your line without ringing central, or you can ring central without ringing the bell of any other subscriber.

FOR 40 CENTS extra per telephone, we will equip any of our bridging telephones with condensers, which enable you to ring any party you want, no matter how many receivers are off their hooks.

FOR 55 CENTS extra per telephone, we will equip any of our bridging telephones with both push button and condenser.

SERIES PHONES, $7.80 AND $8.20.

No. 20R5530

Series Telephones are made for use on lines where only two instruments are to be installed or for use on lines having a switchboard and an operator at a central office. Our Series Telephones are made throughout in the same perfect manner as our Bridging Telephones; every detail has exactly the same rigid inspection, and exactly the same high standard of excellence is maintained throughout the instrument. We put up our Series Telephones with the same high grade long distance transmitter, bi-polar receiver, long lever switch hook, improved ringer, etc., exactly the same as furnished with our highest grade Bridging Telephones. Our Series Telephones are equipped with three-magnet generators and 80-ohm ringers, will talk over lines of any length, and the generators are guaranteed to ring a bell over a 30-mile single line.

No. 20R5532

No. 20R5530 Compact Series Telephone. Price, including two dry batteries, 6 for **$45.40;** each......................$7.80
Shipping weight, 41 pounds each.

No. 20R5532 Southwestern Style Series Telephone. Price, including two dry batteries, 6 for **$47.75;** each..............$8.20
Price, including two wet batteries. 6 for **$49.10;** each... 8.44
Shipping weight, 52 pounds each.

SOUTHWESTERN TYPE BRIDGING TELEPHONES.

Our SOUTHWESTERN Style of Cabinet.

No. 20R5515 Five-Magnet Bridging Telephone, Southwestern Style, with 1,000-ohm ringer.
Price, with two dry batteries, each, $10.20
6 for.. 59.35
Price, with two wet batteries, each, 10.44
6 for.. 60.75

No. 20R5516 Five-Magnet Bridging Telephone, Southwestern Style, with 1,600-ohm ringer.
Price, with two dry batteries, each, $10.50
6 for.. 61.10
Price, with two wet batteries, each, 10.74
6 for.. 62.50

No. 20R5517 Five-Magnet Bridging Telephone, Southwestern Style, with 2,000-ohm ringer.
Price, with two dry batteries, each....$10.80
6 for.. 62.85
Price, with two wet batteries, each.... 11.04
6 for.. 64.25

No. 20R5521 Four-Magnet Bridging Telephone, Southwestern Style, with 1,000-ohm ringer.
Price, with two dry batteries, each.....$ 9.50
6 for.. 55.30
Price, with two wet batteries, each..... 9.74
6 for.. 56.70

No. 20R5522 Four-Magnet Bridging Telephone, Southwestern Style, with 1,600-ohm ringer.
Price, with two dry batteries, each.....$ 9.80
6 for.. 57.05
Price, with two wet batteries, each..... 10.04
6 for.. 58.45

No. 20R5523 Four-Magnet Bridging Telephone, Southwestern Style, with 2,000-ohm ringer.
Price with two dry batteries, each......$10.10
6 for.. 58.80
Price, with two wet batteries, each..... 10.34
6 for.. 60.20

Shipping weight, Southwestern Style Telephones, 54 pounds.

TELEPHONE SWITCHBOARDS

No. 20R5575 50-Line Express Type Automatic Self Restoring Drop Switchboard with five talking circuits, ten cords and plugs, five ringing out drops, switchboard generator, night alarm circuit, complete operator's set and 15 feet of cable.
Price, without drops.......................$78.50

No. 20R5577 Series Drops installed.
Price, each.. 1.65

No. 20R5578 Bridging Drops installed.
Price, each.. 2.10

We can furnish any kind or size of switchboard wanted. Tell us what you want and we will quote prices that will save you money

SOME FACTS ABOUT TELEPHONE WIRE

ROEBLING'S WIRE IS BEST

The manager of a telephone company knows that wire exposed to the weather becomes rusty and weak unless protected. Ordinary fence wire should not be purchased for use on telephone lines, as it is almost entirely unprotected. Furthermore, the distance between fence posts is usually about sixteen feet, while the distance between telephone poles is 90 to 120 feet or more, consequently the strain on the wire is much greater. This requires the wire to be very much heavier and stronger and fully protected against the action of the weather, so it will not break because of rusting.

We sell Roebling Double Galvanized Telephone Wire in standard coils, bearing the genuine Roebling seal. It has an extra heavy coating of nearly pure zinc, covering every part of the wire and protecting it against rust and corrosion. It will last longer, give better results and prove much cheaper in the end than any other kind of telephone wire, regardless of price. The No. 10 wire weighs about 275 pounds to the mile, No. 12 about 165 pounds and the No. 14 about 96 pounds. This wire is sold in coils of about one-half mile each. We cannot make shipment of less than standard half-mile coils.

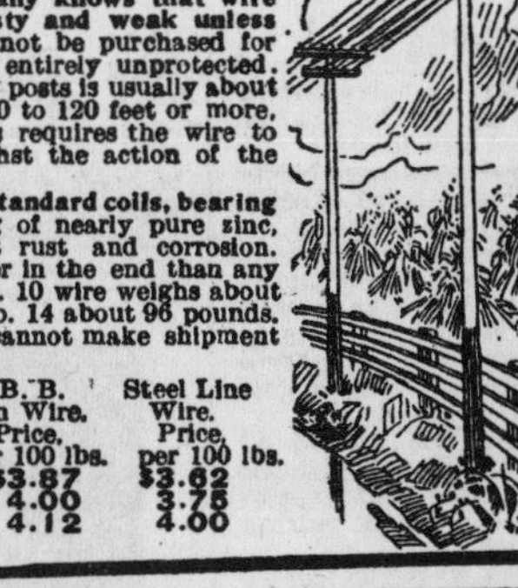

Be sure to state plainly whether **iron** or **steel** wire is wanted.

		B. W. G. Gauge	B. B. Iron Wire, Price, per 100 lbs.	Steel Line Wire, Price, per 100 lbs.
No. 20R5750	Roebling Wire.	No. 10	$3.37	$3.62
No. 20R5751	Roebling Wire.	No. 12	4.00	3.75
No. 20R5752	Roebling Wire.	No. 14	4.12	4.00

ADJUSTABLE WRENCH.

No. 20R5910 The Elgin Adjustable Linemen's Wrench. The Lineman's Made of the very best tool steel, heavily nickel plated. It will hold pipe nipples, collars, round or square rods and square, hexagonal or round nuts. Guarantee with each wrench. Length, 7 inches. Weight, 10 ounces. Price....75c

No. 20R5915 Extra jaws for above. Price....25c

COMBINATION WIRE AND SLEEVE CLAMPS.

No. 20R5926 Combination Wire and Sleeve Clamps made of forged tool steel, properly tempered and will not bend out of shape. Polished head, black handle, 10½ inches long, five holes for Nos. 6, 8, 10, 12 and 14 wire; 8, 10, 12 and 14 sleeves. Price, each........$1.58
If by mail, postage extra, 23c.

No. 20R5927 Combination Wire and Sleeve Clamps. Same as above but full polished. Price, each........$1.77
If by mail, postage extra, 23c.

SPLICING CLAMPS.

No. 20R5931 Linemen's Splicing Clamps. Made of best bar tool steel and warranted against flaws or false temper. The handles have spring temper and will not bend out of shape after being closed on the wire. Full polished, length, 10½ inches, for Nos. 8, 10, 12 and 14 wire. Price, each............$1.35
If by mail, postage extra, 20c.

No. 20R5936 Linemen's Splicing Clamps. Same as above but with two round and two oval holes for Nos. 4, 6, 8 and 9 wire. Price, each............$1.35
If by mail, postage extra, 21 cents.

SIDE CUTTING PLIERS.

No. 20R5940 Linemen's Side Cutting Pliers. Made of the best tool steel properly tempered, raised cutters, polished finish.
Price, 8-inch...78c
Price, 7-inch....65c

TACKLE BLOCK WIRE STRETCHER.

78c

No. 20R5900 Tackle Block Wire Stretcher. Self locking at any point. This stretcher is provided with all malleable iron grapples for stretching barbed wire strands and woven wire fencing and telephone wire. It is also a complete safety rope hoist for ordinary use with which one man can raise 500 pounds. Weight, 4½ pounds.

Price, complete, with 16 feet of ⅜-inch rope............78c

Bull Dog Wire Grip.

No. 20R5905 Bull Dog Wire Grip. The more you pull the tighter it grips. Used with a tackle block with an ordinary wire stretcher, or with a hand spike and chain. It never slips, and does not injure the wire.

Price..................19c

Linemen's Climbers.

These climbers are especially designed for linemen who want the very best climbers made at any price.

We guarantee these climbers to be made of the very best steel, perfectly tempered, finely finished, the very best, strongest and safest climbers made. We carry these climbers in standard lengths, namely, 15, 15½, 16, 16½, 17 and 17½ inches, in stock. State length wanted. No straps are furnished with our climbers at prices as listed below.

No. 20R5945 Linemen's Climbers, Eastern Pattern. Price, per pair, with spurs..........$1.65

No. 20R5946 Extra spurs, for Eastern Pattern Climbers. Price, per pair with rivets..........38c

No. 20R5950 Climber Straps. These straps are furnished with a large leather pad, which prevents the climber from digging into the knee. Can be used with any make of climber, either Eastern or Western. Price, per set of four.....$1.10

Insulating Friction Tape.

No. 20R5835 Black Insulating Friction Tape, will not vulcanize with heat, nor crack nor harden and become defective by exposure and use; ¾ inch wide.

Price, per pound..................36c

10 Pounds Wire Solder for $1.98.

No. 20R5855 Wire Solder, best grade, for all electrical work. Price, per pound..........$0.21
Per 5-pound coil, $1.00; per 10-pound coil..........1.98

GLASS INSULATORS.

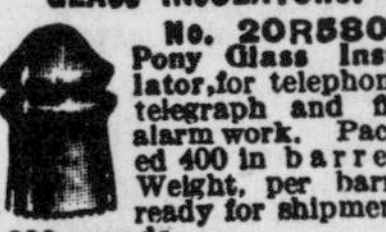

No. 20R5800 Pony Glass Insulator, for telephone, telegraph and fire alarm work. Packed 400 in barrel. Weight, per barrel ready for shipment, 300 pounds.
Price, per barrel, 400 insulators..........$6.05
Price, each, in less than barrel lots..........1¾c

No. 20R5805 Double Groove Pony Glass Insulator, for telephone transposition work, packed 400 in a barrel. Weight, per barrel, ready for shipment, 300 pounds. Price, per barrel, 400 insulators.......$6.05
Price, each, in less than barrel lots..........1¾c

PORCELAIN INSULATORS.

No. 20R5810 Porcelain Insulator No. 4½, new code; requiring 1 inch space between bottom and groove. Height, 1⅞ inches; diameter, 1½ inches; hole, 5-16 inch; groove, 7-16 inch.
Price, per 100..........70c
Price, per standard package of 1,000..........$6.65

No. 20R5815 Porcelain Insulator No. 5½, new code; requiring 1 inch space between bottom and groove. Height, 1 3-16 inches; diameter, 1 inch; hole, ¼ inch; groove, 5-16 inch.
Price, per 100......42c
Price, per standard package of 1,000 ......$3.90

PONY OAK PINS.

No. 20R5825 1¼-inch Pony Oak Pins, for telephone and telegraph line construction. Best quality. For use on cross arms, etc. Painted and dipped. Price, per sack, containing 250 pins.$1.44
Price, each, in less than sack lots..........¾c

PONY OAK BRACKETS.

No. 20R5820 Pony Oak Telephone Brackets, for telephone and telegraph line construction. Can be fastened to side of pole or house. Do not require the use of cross arms. Painted and dipped, weight, 1 pound each. Price, per sack, containing 250 brackets..........$2.25
Price, each, in less than sack lots..........1c

TELEPHONE PARTS

No. 20R5600 Our Solid Back Transmitter, the best long distance transmitter on the market. Our transmitters talk. Each one guaranteed. Price, each..........$1.20
If mail shipment, postage extra, 24 cents.

No. 20R5605 Our Bipolar Receiver is the result of twenty years' experience. They are in use on 150,000 telephones today. Each one guaranteed. Price, each......90c
If mail shipment, postage extra, 20 cents.

No. 20R5609 Generators. Same as used on our telephones.

Three-Magnet Series Generator.	Price	$2.40
Four-Magnet Series Generator.	Price	3.25
Four-Magnet Bridging Generator.	Price	3.30
Five-Magnet Bridging Generator.	Price	3.95

No. 20R5618 Ringers. Same as furnished with our telephones.

80-ohm Series Ringer.	Price	$0.95
1000-ohm Bridging Ringer.	Price	1.60
1600-ohm Bridging Ringer.	Price	1.90
2000-ohm Bridging Ringer.	Price	2.30

No. 20R5635 Nickel plated Gongs and Stands. Price, per set..........20

No. 20R5640 Long Lever Switch Hook. German silver springs, platinum contacts. All nickel plated. Price, each..........50c

No. 20R5655 250-ohm Induction Coil. Silk wound, square fiber ends. Price, each..........45c

No. 20R5657 500-ohm Induction Coil. Silk wound, square fiber ends. Price, each..........60c

Extension Bells.

Extension Bells, as an additional call for noisy places, and in other rooms away from the telephone, must be same ohms resistance as telephone.

No. 20R5670 80-ohm Extension Bell. Price, each..........$1.50

No. 20R5671 1,000-ohm Extension Bell. Price, each..........2.50

No. 20R5672 1,600-ohm Extension Bell. Price, each..........2.65

No. 20R5673 2,000-ohm Extension Bell. Price, each..........2.85

No. 20R5680 Adjustable Arm with transmitter and coil, all complete. Price, each..........$2.10

No. 20R5685 Receiver Cords, worsted, 36 inches long. Price, per pair..........16c

No. 20R5690 Telephone Mouthpieces. Male thread. Price, each..........11c
If mail shipment, postage extra, 3 cents.

Fuse Blocks with Carbon Lightning Arrester.

No. 20R5725 Single Pole Fuse Block with Carbon Lightning Arrester. Porcelain base and brass mountings, upright carbons, with mica insulation, Western Union or Postal style.
Price, each, with one dozen copper fuses..........25c

No. 20R5727 Double Pole Fuse Block with Carbon Lightning Arrester, either Western Union or Postal style.
Price, each, with one dozen copper fuses..........35c

One-Quarter Ampere Fuses.

	Per 100	Per Doz.
No. 20R5731 Western Union, Tin Foil Tip	$0.90	11c
No. 20R5732 Postal, Tin Foil Tip	.90	11c
No. 20R5733 Western Union, Copper Tip	1.12	14c
No. 20R5734 Postal, Copper Tip	1.12	14c

No. 20R5729 Veribest Glass Inclosed Fuses, for Western Union fuse blocks.
Price, per 100, $1.40; each..........1½c

Rubber Covered Telephone Wire.

No. 20R5760 Double Conductor Rubber Covered, braided, twisted and covered with a saturated braid, No. 19. Price, per hundred feet..........$1.67

No. 20R5765 Rubber Covered, Braided, twisted pair telephone wire, No. 19, for inside use. Price, per hundred feet..........$1.35

Annunciator Wire.

No. 20R5770 Annunciator Wire, No. 18, in ½ or 1-pound coils (150 feet to the pound).
Price, per pound.......29c

No. 20R6030 ½-inch Brass Bell Wire Staples. Sold in 1-pound packages only.
Price, per pound.......12c

No. 20R5772 Office Wire, No. 18, in 1-pound coils. Price, per pound..........27c

Magnet Wire, B. & S. Gauge.

No. 20R5775 Belden Double Cotton Covered Magnet Wire. One piece only on a spool. Insulation and wire is perfectly uniform.

Size	1-oz. Spool	2-oz. Spool	4-oz. Spool	8-oz. Spool	1-lb. Spool
16	......	......	......	......	$0.54
18	......	......	......	......	.59
20	......	......	......	$0.39	.63
22	......	......	......	.44	.72
24	......	......	$0.27	.49	.85
30	$0.13	$0.22	.40	.75	1.25
32	.14	.25	.46	.87	1.45
36	.23	.42	.80	1.56	2.70

Note—Above prices include the spool and cost of spooling. The wire is furnished only on size spools given.

Baby Knife Switches.

FOR TELEPHONE AND BATTERY WORK.

No. 20R5875 15-ampere, single pole, single throw. Price..........25c

No. 20R5877 15-ampere, single pole, double throw. Price..........33c

No. 20R5879 15-ampere, double pole, single throw. Price..........30c

No. 20R5881 15-ampere, double pole, double throw. Price..........40c

Iron Box Bells at 19 Cents.

No. 20R6000 3-Inch Iron Box Bell for door and call bell use. The box is made of stamped sheet metal, has cast gong and German silver contacts. Will ring 50 feet on one cell of battery.
Price, each......(Postage extra, 13c.).......19c

No. 20R6002 4-Inch Iron Box Bell. This bell is larger and heavier than the 3-inch and is intended for use where a louder call is necessary.
Price, each........(Postage extra, 16c.).......29c

Ecco Buzzers.

No. 20R6006 Ecco Buzzer No. 0. A very small buzzer. Size, 1¼x¾ inches. Dust and bug proof, with spring cover, fully nickel plated, finely finished throughout. Platinum contact points. Will operate equally well on one or ten cells of battery. Price, each......(Postage extra, 5c.).......38c

No. 20R6008 Ecco Buzzer No. 4. Same as above, but larger. Size, 1⅝x3¼ inches. Japann finish. Price ..38c
If by mail, postage extra, 9 cents.

Skeleton Bells.

Skeleton Bell, for fire and burglar alarm and other purposes requiring loud and strongly made bells.

No. 20R6010 Skeleton Bell, with 4-inch gong. Price, Class A, $1.40; Class B...$1.10

No. 20R6011 Same as above, with 6-inch gong. Price, Class A, $2.16; Class B...$1.65

No. 20R6012 Same as above, with 8-inch gong. Price, Class A, $3.60; Class B...$3.00

Electric Bell Outfits.

For Door and Call Bell Service.

No. 20R6022 Electric Bell Outfit, consists of one Red Label dry battery, one bronze push button, one 3-inch iron box bell, 75 feet of annunciator wire and necessary staples. Weight, 3½ pounds when packed. Price.......60c

No. 20R6024 Electric Bell Outfit, consists of one cell of Special battery, one bronze push button, one 3-inch iron box bell, 75 feet of annunciator wire and necessary staples. Weight, 4¾ pounds when packed. Price.75c

BATTERIES.

Our Special Wet Battery.

No. 20R6040 Our Special Wet Battery is a strictly first class open circuit battery for door bells, telephones, surgical and dental outfits, etc., easily recharged when exhausted, consists of round carbon, square zinc and jar and one charge of sal ammoniac. Price, complete..........28c
Weight, 4½ pounds when packed. Cannot be sent by mail.

No. 20R6041 Square Zinc, for battery No. 20R6040. Price, per dozen, 35c; 3 zincs.....10c

No. 20R6042 Sal Ammoniac. Price, per pound, 15c; per charge..........5c

No. 20R6043 Carbon, for our Special Wet Battery. Price..........15c

Gravity Battery.

The Gravity Battery is a closed circuit battery used almost entirely for telegraph work. It can be used for operating electric bells, small motors, etc. Each battery requires about three pounds of blue vitriol or blue stone to charge it. Full directions for charging are given in the Manual of Telegraphy, sent with each telegraph instrument.

No. 20R6060 Gravity Battery. Size, 5x7 inches, consisting of jar, copper and zinc. Weight, 5 pounds.
Price, complete..........42c

No. 20R6061 Gravity Battery. Size, 6x8 inches; consisting of jar, copper and zinc. Weight, 6 pounds. Price, complete 55c

NOTE—Blue Vitriol is not furnished with these batteries. It is always sold extra. Gravity batteries cannot be sent by mail.

No. 20R6062	Battery Jar, glass, 5x7. Price	1[illegible]
No. 20R6063	Battery Jar, glass, 6x8. Price	[illegible]
No. 20R6064	Zinc, for 5x7 battery. Price	2[illegible]
No. 20R6065	Zinc, for 6x8 battery. Price	34c
No. 20R6066	Copper, for 5x7 battery. Price	7c
No. 20R6067	Copper, for 6x8 battery. Price	7c
No. 20R6068	Blue Vitriol. Price, per pound	10c

TELEPHONES.

Our Seroco Compact Cabinet Telephone.

OUR CONTRACT IS THE LARGEST ever placed by any one house for high grade telephones, enables the manufacturer to figure the cost to us on a basis of actual material and labor.

THE PRICES at which telephones have heretofore been sold have necessarily been greatly in excess of the actual cost, because under the usual system of marketing such goods, a large percentage had to be added to the actual cost to cover such items as traveling salesmen's expenses, advertising, general office, selling and collecting expenses. All such items are absolutely eliminated from our prices on telephones.

THE COST TO US is figured on a basis of actual shop cost, without one penny added for general overhead expenses, which form so large a part of the selling price under ordinary conditions.

WE DO NOT ENDEAVOR to make as cheap a telephone as can be produced, because we know that a telephone cheapened by the use of inferior materials or unskilled labor, is dear at any price.

Our aim is first, to make the best telephone that can be produced, and secondly, to sell such a telephone at a lower price than has ever before been possible.

A FEW REASONS WHY YOU NEED A TELEPHONE Time is money. A telephone saves time. It is easier and quicker to talk than to walk or ride. Government statistics show that in the year 1903 there were SIX HUNDRED THOUSAND TELEPHONES in use by farmers in the United States. It is estimated by telephone manufacturers that more than two hundred thousand new telephones were installed by farmers during the year 1904. No progressive farmer can afford to be without a telephone to keep him in close communication with the world and its markets.

WITH A TELEPHONE IN YOUR HOUSE YOU CAN KNOW EVERY NIGHT HOW THE MARKET CLOSED and always take advantage of the highest prices for your products.

YOU CAN GET THE VERY LATEST ELECTION RETURNS without leaving your home.
YOU CAN ORDER YOUR SUPPLIES FROM TOWN and save time and the use of your team.
YOU CAN HIRE YOUR HELP without losing your own time driving about.
YOU CAN CALL THE DOCTOR without dangerous delay or personal inconvenience.
YOU CAN KEEP CLOSELY IN TOUCH with your neighbors and with the outside world.
YOU CAN PROTECT YOUR HOME. Tramps and the telephone do not stay near each other.

THE TELEPHONE GIVES YOU INSTANT COMMUNICATION WITH

THE RAILROAD OFFICE. THE BANK OR YOUR LAWYER.
THE TELEGRAPH OFFICE. THE POSTOFFICE.

In a few minutes' conversation over the telephone you can transact business that otherwise would necessitate a trip to town with the team that could be used to better advantage in the field.

THE TELEPHONE brings country people more closely together, helps them in their work, makes life pleasanter and more profitable and, above all, SAVES TIME AND MONEY.

THE COST of installing a telephone line is very small, but even though it cost five times as much as it does, it would be a profitable investment for any community of progressive up to date farmers.

Our Seroco Double Battery Cabinet Telephone.

IT IS EASY to put up a telephone line, no technical knowledge is required.

BRIDGING OR PARTY LINES are lines on which a number of telephones are installed and no central office or switch board is used.

SERIES TELEPHONES are used on regular exchange systems where there is a central office with operators in charge.

OUR GUARANTEE.

As the astonishingly low prices which we make on telephones may lead some to doubt the high quality of the goods, we send out with every telephone our signed guarantee, under the terms of which we become responsible for the quality, material and workmanship of every telephone we sell.

REMEMBER that our guarantee means something, because SEARS, ROEBUCK & COMPANY stand back of it.

REMEMBER that a guarantee issued by unknown and financially weak concerns, who may be out of business six months after you buy your telephone, is not worth the paper it is written on.

OUR 30 DAYS' FREE TRIAL OFFER.

You may return to us, at our expense within 30 days from the time you receive your shipment any telephone not found entirely satisfactory, and we will refund your money together with any express or freight charges you have paid. You assume no risk whatever in sending us your order for telephones.

Series Telephones.

Our Series Telephones are made with 80-ohm ringers and powerful series generators guaranteed to ring through 25,000 ohms resistance. This generator is made with extra long heavy laminated armature wound with silk insulated wire, wide noiseless gear and automatic shunt, highest grade bi-polar receiver, long distance solid back transmitter, self contained long lever switch hook and three-path lightning arrester. The best series telephone that can be made regardless of price.

Series Telephone with Compact Cabinet.

No. 48E2101 Series Telephone, as described above, with latest style compact cabinet. Price, each......$ 7.70
Per dozen...... 88.70

Series Telephone with Double Battery Cabinet.

No. 48E2106 Series Telephone, as described above, with large double battery cabinet.
Price, each......$ 8.20
Per dozen...... 94.25

Two dry batteries are included with each series telephone at above prices. If wet batteries are wanted instead of dry batteries add 26 cents to the price of each phone. Wet batteries can be used only with the double battery cabinet. Weight of one telephone when packed, about 50 pounds.

Portable Desk Telephone.

No. 48E2200 Our Portable Desk Telephone is of the very latest pattern. It is equipped with our high grade standard receiver, our own solid back transmitter, designed especially for long distance work, induction coil mounted in the base, self contained switch hook and conducting cords. The base is of cast brass, the standard is of the best steel tubing, the springs have platinum contacts, and the entire instrument is heavily nickel plated. The ringer and generator used with a desk telephone must be the same size as used with the telephones on the line to which it is connected. Our desk telephone can be used on any line and we can furnish the generator and ringer to attach to any line. The price of the desk set complete with ringer and generator is $1.25 more than the price of the Double Battery Telephone of the same generator capacity and ringer resistance.

Bridging Telephones.

These telephones are used on party lines where a number of instruments are installed, and no switchboard or central office is necessary. Our bridging telephones are equipped with a special high grade ringer, designed especially for bridging work, and extra powerful four-magnet or five-magnet generators. The generators, transmitters, receivers, ringers, switch hooks, lightning arresters and cabinets are all of the highest grade. We guarantee our bridging telephones to be the best that skilled labor, money and expert electrical knowledge can produce.

Four-magnet Bridging Telephones.

These telephones, equipped with four-magnet generators, are adapted to party lines having twenty or less instruments.

With Compact Cabinets.

No. 48E2151 Four-magnet Bridging Telephone, with compact cabinet; 1000-ohm ringer. Price, each.$ 9.25
Per dozen...... 106.15

No. 48E2152 Four-magnet Bridging Telephone, with compact cabinet; 1600-ohm ringer. Price, each, $ 9.50
Per dozen...... 109.30

No. 48E2153 Four-magnet Bridging Telephone, with compact cabinet; 2000-ohm ringer. Price, each. $ 9.80
Per dozen...... 112.50

Two dry batteries are included with each of our four-magnet bridging telephones at above prices. Weight of one telephone when packed, about 50 pounds.

With Double Battery Cabinets.

No. 48E2156 Four-magnet Bridging Telephone, with double battery cabinet; 1000-ohm ringer. Each $10.00
Per dozen......$116.85

No. 48E2157 Four-magnet Bridging Telephone, with double battery cabinet; 1600-ohm ringer. Each $10.25
Per dozen......$118.70

No. 48E2158 Four-magnet Bridging Telephone, with double battery cabinet; 2000-ohm ringer. Each $10.50
Per dozen......$121.70

Two dry batteries are included with each of these bridging telephones at above prices. The double battery cabinet, however, is large enough to accommodate two wet batteries, and, if preferred we will include wet batteries for 26 cents extra per telephone.

Weight of one telephone when packed, about 50 pounds.

Five-magnet Bridging Telephones.

These telephones, equipped with extra powerful five-magnet generators, are adapted to lines on which from twenty to forty instruments are installed.

With Compact Cabinets.

No. 48E2171 Five-magnet Bridging Telephone, with compact cabinet; 1000-ohm ringer. Price, each, $ 9.70
Per dozen...... 111.80

No. 48E2172 Five-magnet Bridging Telephone, with compact cabinet; 1600-ohm ringer. Price, each, $ 9.95
Per dozen...... 114.75

No. 48E2173 Five-magnet Bridging Telephone, with compact cabinet; 2000-ohm ringer. Price, each, $ 10.30
Per dozen...... 118.70

Two dry batteries are included with each of our five-magnet bridging telephones at above prices.

Weight of one telephone when packed, about 50 pounds.

With Double Battery Cabinets.

No. 48E2176 Five-magnet Bridging Telephone, with double battery cabinet; 1000-ohm ringer.
Price, each......$ 10.60
Per dozen...... 121.70

No. 48E2177 Five-magnet Bridging Telephone, with double battery cabinet; 1600-ohm ringer.
Per dozen, $124.90; each, $10.85

No. 48E2178 Five-magnet Bridging Telephone, with double battery cabinet; 2000-ohm ringer.
Per dozen, $128.00; each, $11.15

Two dry batteries are included with each of these bridging telephones at above prices. The double battery cabinet, however, is large enough to accommodate two wet batteries, and if preferred we will include wet batteries for 26 cents extra per telephone.

WANTS A DOZEN MORE.

Sears, Roebuck & Co., Chicago, Ill. Bladen, Ohio.

Gentlemen:—We have given your telephones a thorough trial and they prove to be good instruments, even better than Stromberg telephones. You will please send us a dozen more of the same kind at your earliest convenience. Yours very truly,

J. C. WILLS, Secy.

OUR SPECIAL CATALOGUE OF TELEPHONES in which we show larger illustrations of our instruments, more complete descriptions, together with illustrations and descriptions of all the various parts which enter into their construction, will be mailed to any address, free. THIS SPECIAL CATALOGUE shows also our complete line of electrical goods, the largest and most complete line of electrical goods shown in any mail order catalogue, all offered at astonishingly low prices.

WHAT ANOTHER CUSTOMER SAYS.

Sears, Roebuck & Co., Chicago, Ill. Hess, Oklahoma.

Gentlemen:—We are all highly pleased with your telephones. We now have over fifty of your 5-bar 2,000-ohm bridging telephones in use on our Rural Telephone Line; built on a barb wire fence, and they are giving entire satisfaction. I will have to order fifty more by next fall, for our barb wire line is so cheap and easily built that every farmer is wanting a telephone. Your telephones are the best in this part of the country. They beat the Bell telephones that are used here. These last four telephones that I am ordering are for Mr. Ben Flowers, of Elmer, Oklahoma Territory. He has a Chartered Company Telephone Line and is throwing aside the instruments now in use and putting in your telephones. Yours truly,

J. W. COLLIER, M. D.

It takes a good telephone to give satisfactory service anywhere, but it takes a MIGHTY GOOD TELEPHONE TO GIVE SATISFACTORY SERVICE ON A HEAVILY LOADED BARB WIRE FENCE LINE.

Our telephones are equal to any requirements, no matter how severe.

Gem Battery, $2.65.

No. 48C1610 The Gem Battery is the best medical battery on the market. It uses a dry cell, thus doing away entirely with the annoyance of acids or other liquids, and is contained in a very handsome polished wood case. **The compact form, ease of operation,** handsome appearance and strong, even current of this battery, make it a universal favorite. All metal parts are finely nickel plated. With each battery is furnished: **One pair silk battery cords, wood handle, one pair metal handles, one nickel plated foot plate, one pair sponge electrodes, one copy "Medical Electricity at Home,"**, a complete guide to the use of electricity in the treatment of diseases. Weight, 6½ pounds.
Price........................ **$2.65**

Davis & Kidder Magneto Battery.

$7.25

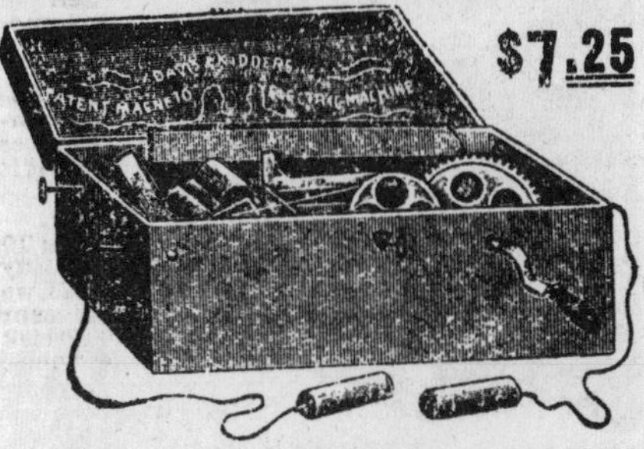

No. 48C1625 This is the genuine Davis & Kidder Battery and not the cheap imitation which is so extensively sold at present. **Operated without the use of chemicals or batteries of any kind.** The electric current is produced by the revolving of fixed electro magnets by turning a handle from the outside of the case. This machine produces a very powerful current **and will last a lifetime if properly cared for. Every one absolutely guaranteed.** Complete, with cords and metal handles, ready for use, and our complete instructor **"Medical Electricity at Home."** Weight, 7 pounds. Price.......... **$7.25**

Improved Double Cell Battery.

$6.95

No. 48C1630 This Medical Battery is an extra large and powerful instrument, made in accordance with our own plans. It is furnished with two high grade dry cells in a case of highly polished hardwood, strongly made and handsomely finished. In addition to adjustments for regulating strength of current from either mild to very strong, it has an improved pole changer, by means of which the current may be changed from positive to negative, or vice versa. It is also furnished with a special rheotome or adjustable vibrator, for treatment of various muscular diseases, such as rheumatism, paralysis, etc. By means of this adjustable vibrator, the current, either the primary or secondary, or a combination of them, can be applied with slow or rapid vibrations. The vibrator on this instrument is of the latest improved type and has very fine adjustments. The coil is very high grade. All metal parts are nickel plated. The battery is provided with an electric hair brush, metallic foot plate, one pair of metallic hand electrodes, one pair of silk covered cords, one pair wood handles, one pair sponge electrodes, one metallic securer and our book, **"Medical Electricity at Home,"** explaining the proper method of using electricity for any kind of disease. Weight, 10 pounds. Price, complete........ **$6.95**

Medical Battery Supplies.

We can furnish special electrodes, extra cords and other supplies. Send for our Special Electrical Catalogue.

The Sure Waker Alarm Clock.

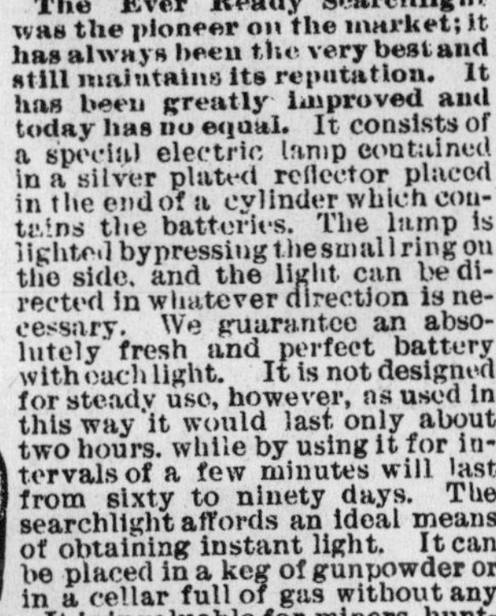

No. 48C1750 This is an Alarm Clock which, when placed in the circuit of an ordinary bell outfit, using a switch in place of a push button, will wake the soundest sleeper. Price, of clock only.................. **98c**
If by mail, postage extra, 24 cents.

No. 48C1752 The Sure Waker Alarm Clock Outfit consists of our Sure Waker alarm clock, 3-inch iron box bell, one wood base switch, one cell of Seroco dry battery and 75 feet of annunciator wire with necessary staples. The diagram shows the method of connection, which is very simple and can be made by anyone. **Just the thing for the farmer,** who can place the bell anywhere in the house and wake the occupant of the room at the same time he awakens. The bell will continue to ring until the switch is shut off. Weight, 5 pounds.
Price, all complete.................. **$1.56**

Famous Ever Ready Searchlight.

The Ever Ready Searchlight was the pioneer on the market; it has always been the very best and still maintains its reputation. It has been greatly improved and today has no equal. It consists of a special electric lamp contained in a silver plated reflector placed in the end of a cylinder which contains the batteries. The lamp is lighted by pressing the small ring on the side, and the light can be directed in whatever direction is necessary. We guarantee an absolutely fresh and perfect battery with each light. It is not designed for steady use, however, as used in this way it would last only about two hours, while by using it for intervals of a few minutes will last from sixty to ninety days. The searchlight affords an ideal means of obtaining instant light. It can be placed in a keg of gunpowder or in a cellar full of gas without any danger whatever. It is invaluable for miners, hunters, farmers, or, in fact, anyone who is out at night. It is beautifully finished with a black leatherette case and full nickel plated trimmings. This is no imitation but is the Ever Ready lamp.

No. 48C1800 No. 1 Ever Ready Searchlight, 8½ inches long, 1½ inches in diameter, good for from 4,000 to 5,000 flashes. Weight, 1 pound.
Price..**(If by mail, postage extra, 24 cents.) $1.80**
No. 48C1801 Extra battery for No. 1 Ever Ready. Price...**(If by mail, postage extra, 14 cents)..24c**
No. 48C1802 Extra lamp for No. 1 Ever Ready. Price.....**(If by mail, postage extra, 2 cents)..34c**
No. 48C1806 No. 3 Ever Ready Searchlight. 1½x13 inches, contains a 5½-volt lamp; the most powerful searchlight of its kind on the market. Weight, 2 pounds. Price...................... **$2.95**
If by mail, postage extra, 32 cents.
No. 48C1807 Extra battery for No. 3 Ever Ready. Price..**(If by mail, postage extra, 20 cents.)** **.42c**
No. 48C1808 Extra lamp for No. 3 Ever Ready. Price.....**(If by mail, postage extra, 2 cents.)..36c**

The Ever Ready Electric Vest Pocket Light.

Can be carried in the vest pocket, has a fine imitation morocco covered case with polished nickel trimmings. This lamp gives instant light when you press the button. No chemicals, oil, smoke or odor. It is always ready. No wires to go wrong, cannot be put out by the wind. Indispensable to those who make night calls or for farmers who go into dark stables, granaries, etc., for the housewife who has to search in dark corners or down into dark trunks. For farmers, railroad employes and in fact, everyone who is out at night. Used in the United States and British navies and in many other branches of the government service. Size, 1 x 2¾ x 3¼ inches. Weight, 10 ounces.
No. 48C1825 Vest Pocket Searchlight, strong metallic case, with black seal grain covering. Price, complete.............. **95c**
If by mail, postage extra, 15 cents.
No. 48C1826 Extra battery. Price.............. **24c**
If by mail, postage extra, 10 cents.
No. 48C1827 Extra bulb. Price................ **32c**
If by mail, postage extra, 2 cents.

Electric Scarf Pins.

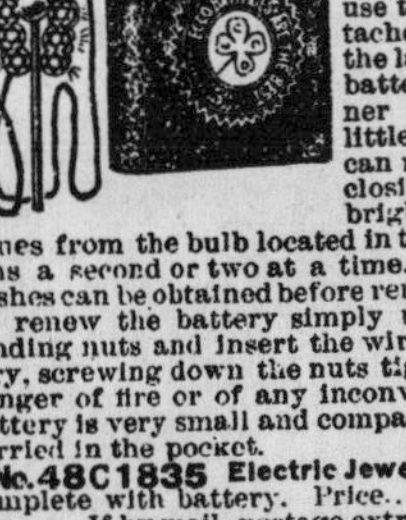

We handle three different styles of electric scarf pins, the Jeweled Horseshoe Pin, the Scull Pin and the Elk's Head Pin. To use these, the pin is attached to the scarf or to the lapel of the coat, the battery placed in an inner pocket, with the little switch where you can reach it easily. By closing the switch a bright, strong light issues from the bulb located in the pin. Using these pins a second or two at a time, from 1,500 to 2,000 flashes can be obtained before renewing the battery. To renew the battery simply unscrew the small binding nuts and insert the wires on the new battery, screwing down the nuts tightly. There is no danger of fire or of any inconvenience. The dry battery is very small and compact and can easily be carried in the pocket.

No. 48C1835 Electric Jeweled Horseshoe Pin, complete with battery. Price........... **$1.20**
If by mail, postage extra, 16 cents.
No. 48C1836 Electric Scull Pin.
Price...................... **$1.65**
If by mail, postage extra, 16 cents.
No. 48C1837 Electric Elk's Head Pin. Price.. **$2.00**
If by mail, postage extra, 16 cents.
No. 48C1840 Battery for any style of scarf pin.
Price.......(If by mail, postage extra, 12 cents)........ **25c**
No. 48C1844 Extra Lamp, Cord and Switch for use with any style of pin. Price.... .(Postage extra, 2 cents.)...... **80c**

SEROCO TELEPHONES.

Series Telephones.

Our Series Telephones are made with 80-ohm ringers and powerful four-magnet series generators guaranteed to ring through 25,000 ohms resistance. This generator is made with extra long heavy laminated armature wound with silk insulated wire, wide noiseless gear and automatic shunt, highest grade bi-polar receiver, long distance back transmitter, self contained long lever switch hook and Maltese lightning arrester. The best series telephone that can be made regardless of price.

Series Telephone with Compact Cabinet.

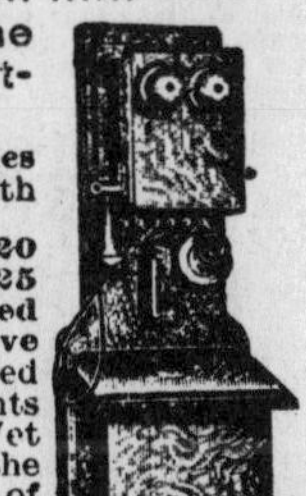

No. 48C2101 Series Telephone, as described above, with latest style compact cabinet. Price, each.... **$ 7.70**
Per dozen.............. **88.70**

Series Telephone with Double Battery Cabinet.

No. 48C2106 Series Telephone, as described above, with large double battery cabinet.
Price, each.............. **$ 8.20**
Per dozen.............. **94.25**

Two dry batteries are included with each series telephone at above prices. If wet batteries are wanted instead of dry batteries add 26 cents to the price of each phone. Wet batteries can be used only with the double battery cabinet. Weight of one telephone when packed, about 50 pounds.

Bridging Telephones.

These telephones are used on party lines where a number of instruments are installed, and no switchboard or central office is used. Our bridging telephones are equipped with a special high grade ringer, designed especially for bridging work, and extra powerful four-magnet or five-magnet generators. The generators, transmitters, receivers, ringers, switch hooks, lightning arresters and cabinets are all of the highest grade, exactly as illustrated and described below and on next page. We guarantee our bridging telephones to be the best that skilled labor, money and expert electrical knowledge can produce.

Four-Magnet Bridging Telephones.

These telephones, equipped with four-magnet generators, are adapted to party lines having twenty or less instruments.

With Compact Cabinets.

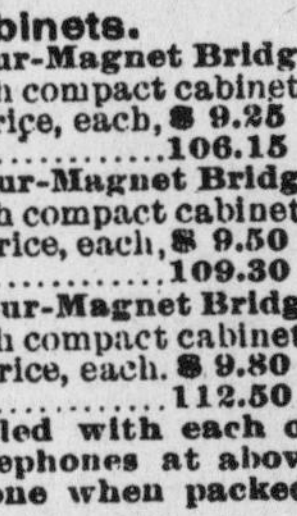

No. 48C2151 Four-Magnet Bridging Telephone, with compact cabinet; 1000-ohm ringer. Price, each, **$ 9.25**
Per dozen.............. **106.15**
No. 48C2152 Four-Magnet Bridging Telephone, with compact cabinet; 1600-ohm ringer. Price, each, **$ 9.50**
Per dozen.............. **109.30**
No. 48C2153 Four-Magnet Bridging Telephone, with compact cabinet; 2000-ohm ringer. Price, each. **$ 9.80**
Per dozen.............. **112.50**

Two dry batteries are included with each of our four-magnet bridging telephones at above prices. Weight of one telephone when packed, about 50 pounds.

With Double Battery Cabinets.

No. 48C2156 Four-Magnet Bridging Telephone, with double battery cabinet; 1000-ohm ringer. Each **$10.00**
Per dozen.............. **$116.85**
No. 48C2157 Four-Magnet Bridging Telephone, with double battery cabinet; 1600-ohm ringer. Each **$10.25**
Per dozen.............. **$118.70**
No. 48C2158 Four-Magnet Bridging Telephone, with double battery cabinet; 2000-ohm ringer. Each **$10.50**
Per dozen.............. **$121.70**

Two dry batteries are included with each of these bridging telephones at above prices. The double battery cabinet, however, is large enough to accommodate two wet batteries, and if preferred we will include wet batteries for 26 cents extra per telephone.
Weight of one telephone when packed, about 50

SEROCO TELEPHONES IMPROVED MODELS FOR 1907

No. 1 Cabinet, With Battery Box.

OUR No. 1 CABINET is the smallest and most compact cabinet that is made, measuring only 8½ inches high by 10½ inches wide, by 11 inches deep. This small cabinet is just as carefully made as any of our other styles, made from specially selected kiln dried quarter sawed oak; all screw holes with metal bushings; all corners rounded and dove tailed; the finish a beautiful dark golden oak. This cabinet contains the entire mechanism of the telephone—the generator, ringer, etc.—but there is no space provided for the batteries. If desired, we can furnish an extra box for the batteries as shown in the illustration, and this box can be mounted on the wall at the side of the telephone or in any other location that may be considered convenient. The battery box may, if preferred, be entirely dispensed with and the batteries placed in some out of the way place—in the basement or on a shelf.

Remember, the battery box, as shown in the illustration, is not furnished unless ordered extra.

No. 2 Cabinet.

OUR No. 2 CABINET is of very ornamental design, very compact and so constructed that all the principal parts, including the ringer, generator, induction coil, etc., are contained in the same chamber. The arrangement of the parts in this No. 2 cabinet is very clearly shown in the illustration on the preceding page. There is sufficient space in the lower part of this cabinet for two dry batteries which are placed in an upright position. This cabinet, like all of our other cabinets is made from the best selected kiln dried quarter sawed oak, with all corners rounded and dovetailed, the screw holes provided with metal bushings; finish a golden oak with fine piano polish. This cabinet measures 9½ inches high, by 28 inches wide, by 10 inches deep.

No. 3 Cabinet.

OUR No. 3 CABINET is made extra large and the battery compartment has sufficient space for two full size wet batteries. We recommend this cabinet particularly for use in engine rooms, creameries, etc., and especially in warm, dry climates where the use of dry batteries is not satisfactory. This cabinet measures 30 inches high, the greatest width is 12 inches, and the greatest depth is 12 inches. We find that this cabinet is especially popular throughout the Southwest, where the warm, dry weather makes the use of wet batteries necessary. This cabinet is made throughout from the finest selected quarter sawed and kiln dried oak, all corners are rounded and dovetailed; screw holes are made with metal bushings; the finish is a dark golden oak, with piano polish.

The Generator.

THE GENERATOR, especially in a bridging telephone, is one of the most important parts. If the generator is not right, and right in every way, good service is impossible. In our generators the laminated armature is extra long, has more laminations, and is wound with more magnet wire than any other generator made. This wire is the best double silk insulated magnet wire all the way through.

BEST IMPORTED MAGNET STEEL. Our generators are made from the best imported magnet steel and are guaranteed to retain their magnetism and power longer than the magnets of any other generator made. The magnets are painted with aluminum paint as a protection from rust, and as a further protection each magnet is covered with a special, nickel plated shield.

MORE STEEL, MORE WIRE, MORE POWER. There is more steel in our five-magnet generator than in any five or six-magnet generator made, and moreover it is the best imported magnet steel. There is more wire on the armature than on any other generator made, and it is all **double silk insulated** magnet wire.

Our Five-Magnet Generator weighs 10½ pounds.

PLENTY OF RESERVE POWER. Our generators have ample reserve power. Our five-bar generator is absolutely guaranteed to ring through 125,000 ohms resistance. An ordinary line, twenty-five or thirty miles in length with thirty telephones installed, no matter what size generators, has a total resistance, even allowing for poor construction, small wire, etc., of less than 60,000 ohms. The output of our generator is sufficient to ring the bells through double this amount of resistance.

THE GEAR WHEELS ARE SOLID BRASS CASTINGS, with milled gears and reinforced spokes, made extra wide to insure strength and wearing quality. The shunt springs are of heavy German silver.

The Transmitter.

OUR SOLID BACK, LONG DISTANCE TRANSMITTER will talk further and louder than any other transmitter made. The framework is built up of heavy brass castings, making it absolutely solid. The carbon cup is turned from a solid brass bar. The carbon diaphragm and the granulated carbon are the best that we can import, and are [illegible]

The Receiver.

OUR IMPROVED BIPOLAR RECEIVER, with concealed connections, is one of the features of our telephone. The coils are wound with silk insulated magnet wire, the magnets are of the best imported magnet steel, and the cords are attached with an especially wide contact which cannot work loose. To prevent any possibility of cord trouble our cords are made extra heavy.

The Switch Hook.

OUR LONG LEVER SWITCH HOOK is made with heavy German silver springs and platinum contacts. This hook is so constructed that no current whatever passes through the frame and there is no chance of a shock when taking the receiver from the hook.

The Ringer.

OUR RINGER is of the latest improved pattern, with adjustable armature; the coils are wound with silk insulated magnet wire; the magnet, made of the best imported magnet steel, is heavily nickel plated and polished.

The Wiring.

SEROCO TELEPHONES are wired absolutely without loose joints, every connection being soldered, which makes a solid circuit that cannot get out of order.

The Lightning Arrester.

OUR LIGHTNING ARRESTER is of the regular two-path ground wire switch type. Years of practical experience have proven the advantage of this type of lightning arrester over all other types, and our lightning arrester constitutes the best insurance against lightning or sneak currents that a telephone can have.

The Induction Coil.

OUR INDUCTION COILS are wound throughout with silk insulated magnet wire, and are accurately tested and standardized by standard Weston instruments. Every coil is guaranteed absolutely perfect.

PRICES.

SEROCO FIVE-MAGNET BRIDGING TELEPHONES.

Standard Instruments of the Highest Grade.

FURNISHED WITH No. 1, No. 2 OR No. 3 CABINETS.

OUR FIVE-MAGNET BRIDGING TELEPHONES are built for use on lines where from thirty to forty instruments are installed. They are equipped with our extra powerful, five-magnet generator, which is guaranteed to ring through 125,000 ohms resistance. Every one of these generators is tested to ring through 125,000 ohms resistance before it leaves the factory, and is absolutely guaranteed to give this output. This five-magnet generator is guaranteed to ring through fifty telephones on the same line.

IF YOU ARE BUILDING A NEW LINE, no matter how many telephones are to be installed, we advise the purchase of instruments with five-magnet generators and ringers of 1,600 ohms resistance, as this equipment is rapidly becoming standard throughout the country. If you are buying telephones to put on a line already equipped, then you must select instruments equipped with generators as powerful or more powerful than those already on the line, and you must select ringers of the same resistance (1,000 ohm, 1,600 ohms or 2,000 ohms) as the ringers already on the line.

YOUR CHOICE OF CABINETS. We put up our five-magnet bridging telephones in No. 1, No. 2 or No. 3 cabinets, as illustrated and described above. The equipment, including the generator, transmitter, receiver, ringer, etc. is exactly the same in all styles, regardless of of the cabinet.

WITH No. 1 CABINETS.

No. 48G2136 Five-Magnet Bridging Telephone with No. 1 Cabinet, 1,000-ohm ringer.
Price, each, with two dry batteries .... **$ 9.75**
6 for **56.75**

No. 48G2137 Five-Magnet Bridging Telephone with No. 1 Cabinet, 1,600-ohm ringer.
Price, each, with two dry batteries **$10.15**
6 for **59.10**

No. 48G2138 Five-Magnet Bridging Telephone with No. 1 Cabinet, 2,000-ohm ringer.
Price, each, with two dry batteries **$10.50**
6 for **61.15**

Shipping weight of five-magnet telephones with No. 1 Cabinet is 24 pounds. **Above prices do not include the battery box which is shown in the illustration of the No. 1 Cabinet.**

No. 48G2139 Battery box, for No. 1 Cabinet, golden oak, with rounded and dovetailed corners, holds two dry batteries. Price, 6 for **$2.30**; each **40c**

No. 48G2140 Battery box, for No. 1 Cabinet, same as No. 48G2139, but larger; holds two wet batteries.
Price, 6 for **$3.15**; each **55c**

(Continued on next page.)

FIVE-MAGNET BRIDGING TELEPHONES—Continued.

WITH No 2 CABINETS.

No. 48G2166 Five-Magnet Bridging Telephone, with No. 2 Cabinet, 1,000-ohm ringer.
Price, each, with two dry batteries.............. $11.20
Six for.............. 65.20

No. 48G2167 Five-Magnet Bridging Telephone, with No. 2 Cabinet, 1600-ohm ringer.
Price, each, with two dry batteries.............. $11 55
Six for.............. 67.20

No. 48G2168 Five-Magnet Bridging Telephone, with No. 2 Cabinet 2,000-ohm ringer.
Price, each, with two dry batteries.............. $11.95
Six for.............. 69 55

Shipping weight of five-magnet telephones with No. 2 Cabinet is 50 pounds.

WITH No. 3 CABINETS.

No. 48G2186 Five-Magnet Bridging Telephone, with No. 3 Cabinet, 1,000-ohm ringer.
Price, each, with two dry batteries.............. $11.25
Six for.............. 65.50
Price, each, with two wet batteries.............. 11.49
Six for.............. 66.90

No. 48G2187 Five-Magnet Bridging Telephone, with No 3 Cabinet, 1,600-ohm ringer.
Price, each, with two dry batteries.............. $11.65
Six for.............. 67.80
Price, each, with two wet batteries.............. 11.89
Six for.............. 69.20

No. 48G2188 Five-Magnet Bridging Telephone, with No 3 Cabinet, 2,000-ohm ringer.
Price, each, with two dry batteries.............. $12.00
Six for.............. 69.85
Price, each, with two wet batteries.............. 12.24
Six for.............. 71.25

Shipping weight of five-magnet telephones with No. 3 cabinet is 45 pounds.

SEROCO FOUR-MAGNET BRIDGING TELEPHONES.

FURNISHED WITH No. 2 CABINETS ONLY.

FOUR-MAGNET TELEPHONES are built for short lines when not more than eighteen telephones are installed. They are equipped with our four-magnet generators, which are guaranteed to ring through 20 telephones on the same line.

IF YOU ARE BUILDING A NEW LINE, we advise the purchase of Five-Magnet, 1600 ohm, telephones, as this is now practically standard equipment, but if you are adding telephones to lines already in operation, then you must select instruments with generators and ringers to match those already on the line.

OUR FOUR-MAGNET TELEPHONES are in every way equal to our Five-Magnet instruments, except in the power of the generator. Talking quality, finish and workmanship are exactly the same.

No. 48G2161 Four-Magnet Bridging Telephone, with No. 2 Cabinet. 1,000-ohm ringer.
Price, each, with two dry batteries.............. $10.50
Six for.............. 61.10

No 48G2162 Four-Magnet Bridging Telephone, with No. 2 Cabinet, 1,600-ohm ringer.
Price each, with two dry batteries.............. $10 85
Six for.............. 63 15

No. 48G2163 Four-Magnet Bridging Telephone, with No 2 Cabinet, 2,000-ohm ringer.
Price, each, with two dry batteries.............. $11.25
Six for.............. 65 50

Shipping weight of four-magnet telephones with No. 2 Cabinet is 45 pounds.

SEROCO SERIES TELEPHONE.

FURNISHED WITH No. 2 CABINETS ONLY.

SERIES TELEPHONES are built for use on lines where only two instruments are to be installed, or for use on lines having a switchboard and central operator. Our Series telephones are equipped with three-magnet generators, 80-ohm ringers, and high grade, long distance transmitters, bipolar receivers, long lever switch hooks, improved ringers, etc. exactly the same as all the latest 1907 Seroco telephones. Our Series telephones will talk over lines of any length, and the generators are guaranteed to ring the bell over a 30-mile single line.

No. 48G2105 THREE-MAGNET SERIES TELEPHONE, with No. 2 cabinet, 80-ohm ringer.
Price, each, with two dry batteries.............. $ 9.00
Six for.............. 52.40

Shipping weight, 35 pounds.

THIS BOY'S SUIT FREE

For only $25.00 in Profit Sharing Certificates, we will send you absolutely free of all cost this splendid two-piece double breasted knee pants suit for any boy between eight and fifteen years old. The amount in Profit Sharing Certificates which we ask for this suit is so small that by sending to us from time to time for any needed articles for yourself or family, in just a little while you are certain to be entitled to this suit absolutely **free** of charge in addition to the vast saving which you will make on every item in your order. Remember, you do not have to order $25.00 worth of goods at any one time, as we send you a certificate with every order for $1.00 or more and the total of $25.00 worth of certificates may be made up of any number of orders. This suit is such as would cost you a goodly sum from your home clothing dealer, being up to the minute in style, exactly as illustrated and made of strong quality Union Cashmere in a neat striped pattern, substantially lined and tailored; in fact such a suit as you would buy if you want your boy to appear well dressed. Our Profit Sharing Plan brings you this and many other articles absolutely **free** of charge. In order to secure these articles as quickly as possible it is only necessary to consult our big General Catalogue whenever you are in need of anything. The Profit Sharing Certificates made out for the full amount of your order every time you buy from us will accumulate rapidly and you will soon be enabled to choose from the amazing variety of beautiful and useful articles contained in our latest revised **free** Profit Sharing Book which we send you **free** and postpaid upon application.

SEROCO DESK TELEPHONES.

SUITABLE FOR ANY KIND OF A LINE, SERIES OR BRIDGING.

THE CONVENIENCE and neat appearance of a desk telephone appeals to every telephone user, and the Seroco Desk Telephone is not only electrically and mechanically a perfect instrument, but it is, at the same time, of the most handsome and ornamental design.

THE SEROCO DESK TELEPHONE is made with exactly the same high grade equipment as all the other styles of Seroco telephones, either bridging or series, exactly the same high power generators, long distance transmitters, improved bipolar receivers, etc., embodying in all essential points every good quality represented in our various types of wall telephones. The frame is made of solid cast brass, the stand is of heavy brass tubing, octagonal in shape, and the connecting cords, both for the instrument and the receiver, are made extra heavy. The entire instrument is heavily nickel plated and highly polished.

THE GENERATOR AND RINGER are mounted in a neat golden oak cabinet, made with rounded, dovetailed corners and piano polish. This cabinet can be mounted on the wall near a table or desk, or on the side or underneath the table, where it is practically out of sight.

WHEN ORDERING DESK TELEPHONES, remember that the generator and ringer must correspond in size and resistance to those of the instruments already on the line. If you are buying instruments for a new line, we advise the purchase of telephones with standard equipment, five-magnet generators and 1,600-ohm ringers.

No. 48G2200 Series Desk Telephone, three-magnet generator, 80-ohm ringer, suitable for use on single lines where only two instruments are installed and also for lines having a switchboard and central operator. It cannot be used on bridging or party lines.
Price, each, with two dry batteries.............. $12.20
Six, complete for.............. 71.00

No 48G2202 Bridging Desk Telephone, four-magnet generator, 1,600-ohm ringer, suitable for use on bridging lines when not more than 18 instruments are installed.
Price, each, with two dry batteries.............. $13.65
Six, complete for.............. 79.45

No. 48G2203 Bridging Desk Telephone, five-magnet generator, 1,600-ohm ringer, suitable for use on bridging lines with from 30 to 50 instruments installed.
Price, each, with two dry batteries.............. $14.45
Six, complete for.............. 84.10

No 48G2206 Bridging Desk Telephone, five-magnet generator, 2,000-ohm ringer, suitable for bridging lines, with from 30 to 50 instruments installed.
Price, each, with two dry batteries.............. $14.80
Six complete for.............. 86.15

Shipping weight of desk telephones is 35 pounds.

Pony Magneto Call Telephone.

No. 48G2270

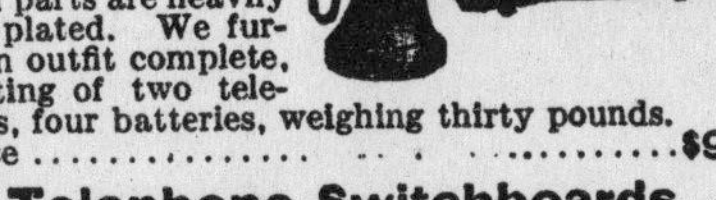

This telephone is built for use on short lines of from 50 feet to 5 miles. It can be used with copper or iron wire or even with fence wire. It is equipped with a high grade transmitter, receiver and three-magnet pony generator. It is put up in a handsome oak case, and all parts are heavily nickel plated. We furnish an outfit complete, consisting of two telephones, four batteries, weighing thirty pounds.
Price.............. $9.50

Telephone Switchboards.

Our express type, automatic, self restoring drop switchboard is of the very latest design and most approved pattern. We can furnish a fifty-drop board, complete with five talking circuits, ten cords and plugs, five ringing out drops, switchboard generator, night alarm circuit, complete operator's set and fifteen feet of cable.

No. 48G2300 Price, as described.............. $71.50
No. 48G2310 Series drops installed. Price, each. 1.40
No. 48G2320 Bridging drops installed.
Price, each.............. 1.90

We can furnish any kind or size of switchboard wanted. Tell us what you want and we will quote prices that will save you money.

No. 48G2544 Single Pole Fuse Block with Carbon Lightning Arrester. Porcelain base and brass mountings, upright carbons, with mica insulation. Western Union or Postal style. Price, each.............. 12c

No 48G2545 Double Pole Fuses Blocks with Carbon Lightning Arrester, either Western Union or Postal style.
Price, each.............. 20c

No. 48G2548 Veribest Glass Inclosed Fuses, for Western Union fuse blocks. Price, per 100, $1.40; each 1½c

Telephone Guide.

A complete book on telephones, explaining how to build telephone lines, install bridging and series of telephones, how to inspect telephone material and correct telephone troubles; fully illustrated. Bound in cloth. Size, 5½x7½ inches, 226 pages.

No. 3G04765 Price.............. 69c
If by mail, postage extra, 13 cents.

Telephone Parts.

No. 48G2375 Our Solid Back Transmitter, the best long distance transmitter on the market. Our transmitters talk. Each one guaranteed.
Price, each.............. $1.20
If by mail, postage extra, 24 cents.

No. 48G2385 Our Bipolar Receiver, is the result of twenty years' experience. They are in use on 150,000 telephones today. Each one guaranteed.
Price, each.............. 90c
If by mail, postage extra, 20 cents.

No. 48G2400 Five-magnet Bridging Generator, guaranteed to ring through 100,000 ohms. Made of the best imported steel. Price, each.............. $3.95

No. 48G2403 Four-magnet Bridging Generator, guaranteed to ring through 50,000 ohms. Made of the best imported steel. Price, each.............. $3.30

No. 48G2405 Three-magnet Series Generator, guaranteed to ring through 25,000 ohms. Made of the best imported steel. Price, each.............. $2.40

No. 48G2430 80-ohm- Series Ringer. Silk wound coils, imported steel magnet. Easily adjusted and fully guaranteed, Price, each.............. 95c

No. 48G2435 1,000-ohm Bridging Ringer. Silk wound coils, imported steel magnet, easily adjusted and fully guaranteed. Price, each.............. $1.60

No. 48G2440 1,600-ohm Bridging Ringer. Silk wound coils, imported steel magnet. Easily adjusted and fully guaranteed. Price, each.............. $1.85

No. 48G2445 2,000-ohm Bridging Ringer. Silk wound coils, imported steel magnet, easily adjusted and fully guaranteed. Price, each.............. $2.30

No. 48G2450 Nickel Plated Gongs and Stands.
Price, per set.............. 20c

No. 48G2489 Long Lever Switch Hook. German silver springs, platinum contacts. All nickel plated.
Price, each.............. 50c

No. 48G2490 250-ohm Induction Coil. Silk wound square fiber ends. Price, each.............. 45c

No. 48G2492 500-ohm Induction Coil. Silk wound square fiber ends. Price, each.............. 60c

Extension Bells, as an additional call for noisy places, and in other rooms away from the telephone, must be same size as telephone ringer.

No. 48G2500 80-ohm Extension Bell.
Price, each.............. $1.50

No. 48G2505 1,000-ohm Extension Bell.
Price, each.............. 2.50

No. 48G2510 1,600-ohm Extension Bell.
Price, each.............. 2.65

No. 48G2515 2,000-ohm Extension Bell.
Price, each.............. 2.85

No. 48G2528 Adjustable Arm with transmitter and coil, all complete. Price, each.............. $2.10

No. 48G2534 Receiver Cords, worsted, 36 inches long. Price, per pair.............. 16c

No. 48G2546 Telephone Mouthpieces. Male or female thread. Price, each.............. 11c
If by mail, postage extra, 3 cents.

Galvanized Telephone Wire.

Our Double Galvanized Steel Line Wire is especially made for telegraph and telephone use. IT IS NOT FENCE WIRE. We guarantee this wire to be genuine BB and steel and to stand any standard test. **For long spans, steel wire, which has double the breaking strain of iron wire, is always preferable.** The No. 10 wire will weigh about 275 pounds to the mile, the No. 12, 165 pounds, and the No. 14 about 96 pounds.

This wire is sold in half-mile coils only. Prices subject to change without notice. All shipments made direct from our factory in Central Indiana.

	B.W.G. Gauge	Price, per 100 pounds on B. B. Iron Wire	Price, per 100 pounds on Steel Line Wire
No. 48G2600	No. 10	$3.62	$3.37
No. 48G2601	No. 12	3.75	3.50
No. 48G2602	No. 14	4.00	3.75

Write for special prices on large quantities.

We do not recommend fence wire for telephone use, but can furnish it at the lowest market price. Write for quotations.

Rubber Covered Telephone Wire.

No. 48G2610 Double Conductor Rubber Covered, braided, twisted, and covered with a saturated braid No. 19. Price, per hundred feet. $1.57

No. 48G2612 Rubber Covered Braided, twisted pair telephone wire No. 19 for inside use.
Price, per hundred feet.............. $1.35

Office and Annunciator Wire.

No. 48G2625 Annunciator Wire, No. 18, in ½ and 1-pound coils.
Price, per pound.............. 40c

No. 48G2630 Office Wire, No. 18, in 1-pound coils. Price, per pound..... 42c

Magnet Wire, B. & S. Gauge.

No. 48G2705 Belden Double Cotton Covered Magnet Wire. One piece only on a spool. Insulation and wire is perfectly uniform.

Size	1-oz. Spool	2-oz. Spool	4-oz. Spool	8-oz. Spool	1-lb. Spool	5-lb. Spool per lb.
16	....	......	......	.....	$0.57	$0.53
18	....	......	......	.....	.64	.60
20	....	......	......	$0.42	.74	.70
21	....	......	......	.47	.83	.77
22	....	......	......	.48	.86	.81
23	....	......	......	.50	.90	.85
24	....	......	$0.27	.52	.97	.92
25	....	......	.30	.58	1.06	1.01
26	....	$0.25	.33	.63	1.15	1.10
30	$0.25	.27	.45	.87	1.62	1.56
32	.27	.31	.52	.99	1.87	1.80
34	.30	40	.70	1.36	2.52	2.42
36	.40	.50	.95	1.83	3.45	3.30

Note—Above prices include the spool, and cost of spooling. The wire is furnished only on sized spools given. We can furnish single cotton, single and double silk covered in 5-pound lots. Prices on application.

GUNS AND PISTOLS

THE BEST GUN MADE ONLY $5.95

OUR CHALLENGE COMPARISON TEST OFFER.

SEND US $5.95, give length of barrel which you prefer and we will send you this, our new improved 1906 Model, Genuine A. J. Aubrey Hammerless Single Barrel Automatic Ejector Shotgun, with the understanding and agreement that if you do not find it in every way the highest grade single barrel shotgun you ever saw, if you do not say it is worth a dozen of any other single barrel guns on the market, regardless of name, make or price, if you do not say it is far cheaper at $5.95 than any other single gun would be for just one dollar, if you do not find it smoother, handsomer, better shooting, stronger, higher grade in every way, if you do not say that it carries an individuality, a finish, a workmanship, a style, a high grade effect not found in any other single gun made, if you do not find in this single gun every up to date feature that you will find in the highest grade double barrel hammerless ejectors that sell at $50.00 to $100.00 each, if it has not every earmark of every $100.00 double barrel, automatic ejector hammerless gun, if it does not outclass, in every particular, any single gun yet produced, return it to us at our expense, and we will immediately return your money. Do not buy any kind of a single barrel gun until you see this. If all other makes of single barrel guns were sold at $1.00 each, you could not afford to buy one even at $1.00 until you had seen this new A. J. Aubrey hammerless single gun. Nothing like it was ever produced before, nothing on the market that resembles it, nothing that begins to approach it; it stands in a class by itself, higher grade in every detail, better in every piece and part than anything yet produced in a single barrel shotgun.

GENUINE ARMORY STEEL

WE SELL SINGLE BARREL BREECH LOADING SHOTGUNS as low as $2.65; we sell hammerless ejector single barrel guns as low as $3.92, and they are standard guns of good quality, they are the equal of shotguns sold by others at one to three dollars more money. You will find them illustrated and described in this catalogue, but we sell no single gun in which we give so much value for the money, we or no other house sell any single gun that will in any way compare with this, the new improved A. J. Aubrey Single Barrel Ejector Hammerless Shotgun which we offer at $5.95.

IT IS DIFFERENT FROM ANY SINGLE BARREL HAMMERLESS AUTOMATIC SHELL EJECTING BREECH LOADING SHOTGUN YOU EVER SAW.

YOU CANNOT COMPARE it in any particular with any other single gun on the market. You really can compare it in quality only with the highest priced double barrel ejector guns, guns that retail at $100.00 or more, in short, it has every feature found in the highest grade $100.00 double hammerless guns, the same safety device, same style of frame, bolt action, lock work, finish and general mechanism, the same water table construction; it is a gun in a class by itself. This A. J. Aubrey Single Barrel Hammerless Automatic Shell Ejecting Shotgun is made in our own factory, a factory we own, control and operate, the Meriden Fire Arms Company, of Meriden, Conn. The gun is designed, modeled and made by that celebrated gunmaker, Mr. A. J. Aubrey, vice-president and general manager of the Meriden Fire Arms Company, the designer of a number of the highest grade guns on the market, a recognized authority as a maker of the highest grade fire arms produced.

TAPER CHOKE BORED

A J AUBREY

DETAILED DESCRIPTION

A Few of the Many Special Features of the A. J. Aubrey Hammerless Single Barrel Breech Loading Shotguns.

FRAME. The frame is made of steel, with water table, the lugs of the barrel fitting strongly into the same, so that it will stand the maximum amount of shooting; no possibility of shooting loose. So far as we know, it is the only single barrel construction of the kind on the market, and such as you will find on $100.00 double barrel ejector guns.

BARREL. The barrel is made from the best quality armory steel, Taper choke bored by the celebrated Taper system, fitted with automatic shell ejector, which throws the shell automatically with the opening of the gun, and it is the strongest, most positive, perfect acting, most effective and best made automatic shell ejector ever used in a single gun, equaled only by the most expensive shell ejector systems found in $100.00 double barrel guns.

TOP LEVER. The top lever is of the new design, invented by Mr. Aubrey, and constructed with a cam motion, that by opening the gun, it simultaneously cocks the hammer, working very smoothly and easily, a feature not to be found in any other gun made.

THE LOCK. The lock is fitted on the trigger plate, which may be removed with the aid of a screwdriver in a few seconds, for oiling or repairing, by removing the two screws in the trigger plate and the two screws in the tang under and back of the top lever. This alone more than doubles the value of this gun over any other single gun made.

BARREL LUG. The barrel lug is made of the best steel, which will wear longer than any ordinary iron lug, such as is used on other single guns.

FORE END. The fore end may be taken off or put on the same as any double barrel shotgun, and is held fast to the fore end lug by two side springs; a feature of fore end fastening not to be found on any other single gun made. The fore end design is a novel feature, the shape of which is pleasing to the eye and more easily removed than any other fore end made, the wood part of which is made from well seasoned, straight grained walnut in a handsome diamond design checkering.

STOCK. The stock is made from well seasoned walnut lumber, with a handsome checkered pistol grip, with ornamented cap, shaped and aligned on the order of regular $100.00 double barrel guns, and, in fact, in appearance, general outline, hang, construction and all is on the lines of the $100.00 double hammerless gun.

LUG AND OILING DEVICE. All the lock parts are made of the very best tool steel, and with ordinary care should last the owner a lifetime. The main spring is a "V" shaped spring, which acts in combination as a hammer spring as well as a sear spring.

WATER TABLE. The water table construction is a feature that is distinctive in the Aubrey single barrel gun only, a feature of construction that you will find only on the most expensive double guns that sell at $100.00 each and upwards.

SHOOTING QUALITIES. This gun is built with a view to giving you in a single gun, in shooting quality, in penetration, in pattern, in long range shooting, in fact, in every particular all the results that can possibly be attained in the highest priced double barrel hammerless ejector shotgun made, a gun that you would pay a $100.00 or more for, and we guarantee this gun to shoot as far, to give pattern and penetration equal to any gun made, single or double, regardless of name, make or price, and if you order this gun and do not find it all this, you can return it to us at our expense, and we will immediately return your money.

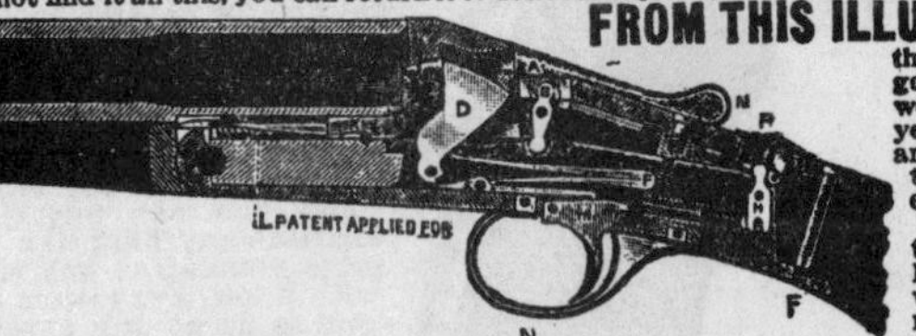

FROM THIS ILLUSTRATION of the working parts of the Aubrey single gun you can get just a little idea of how far we have gone beyond anything yet produced in single guns, and how closely we approach the highest priced double guns ever made.

The pushing to the right of the top lever "A" causes the cocking lever "B" to have a swinging motion, which gives to the locking bolt "C" a sliding motion, which causes the hammer "D" to be thrown into a cocked position and held there by the sear "E", which is released from the notch of the hammer "D" by the trigger "M." The letter "J" represents the safety slide, which, by being pushed forward, causes the safety lever "H" to be swung backwards in such a manner as to draw the safety rod "I" from its locked position on the trigger. The automatic safety rod "G" raising against the locking bolt "C" at one end and the safety lever "H" at the other, will automatically lock the gun by being thrown rearward, with the sliding motion of the locking bolt "C" when the gun is being cocked. The letter "K" represents the automatic ejecter, which has a notch at its forward end which engages with a pin driven through the lug, which holds it in position until the gun is opened far enough for the shell to pass over the top of the frame, when it is released by being pushed from the pin in the lug by the end of frame when opening the gun.

FIGURE 3 shows the manner in which the lock, cocking and safety mechanism is fastened to the trigger plate.

FIG. 3

PAT. APPLIED FOR

THE ABOVE ILLUSTRATION AND DESCRIPTION of the working parts of the $5.95 Aubrey Single Gun will give you just a little idea of the wonderful mechanism worked out in this most wonderful gun.

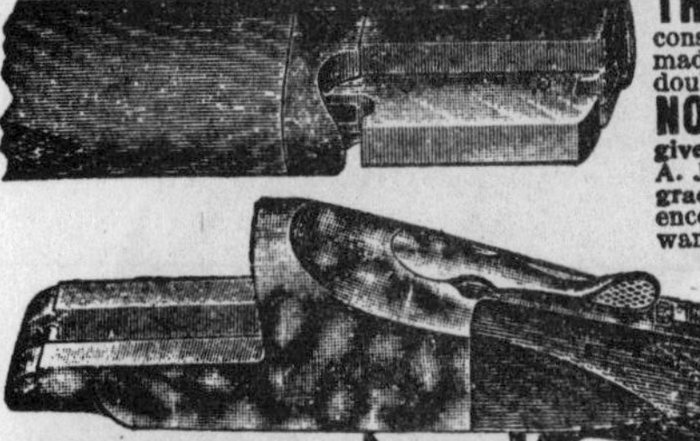

THESE ILLUSTRATIONS show the water table construction on the frame and lug, the water table construction on the barrel, a construction found on no other single gun made, the same construction as is used on the highest priced ejector double hammerless guns, guns that sell generally at $100.00 and upwards.

NO ILLUSTRATIONS, NO DESCRIPTIONS, no explanation will give you any idea of the difference in the real value between this wonderful A. J. Aubrey hammerless ejector single gun and any of the many other grades of single guns on the market. There is no comparison; the difference in quality is many times the difference in price, therefore, if you want a single gun that outclasses anything heretofore produced, by all means send for this, our A. J. Aubrey single ejector. Let us send it to you with the understanding and agreement that it must prove perfectly satisfactory to you, you must feel that this gun is cheaper at our special price of $5.95 than any other single gun made would be at one-fourth the price, and remember, our $5.95 price barely covers the cost of material and labor in our own factory, with but our one small percentage of profit added.

Be sure to state length of barrel wanted.

OUR PATENT GLOBE SIGHT FREE WITH THIS GUN.

DON'T BUY A CHEAP SINGLE BARREL GUN. By all means select this A. J. Aubrey gun. While we sell cheaper single barrel guns at lower prices, as good guns as others sell at prices much higher than ours, for the slight difference in cost you will get ten times the difference in value if you order this A. J. Aubrey at $5.95. If you could see and compare this with any other single gun made before buying, you would have no other. It contains every high grade feature of every high grade double barrel ejector hammerless breech loading shotgun, with the defects of none, and is entirely free from any of the earmarks of cheapness, common to all other single barrel shotguns and common with the cheaper grades of double guns.

WANT OF SPACE prevents our going into detail as to the mechanical construction, the workmanship, the finish and more than a hundred little points of superiority in this gun over any other single gun made. We tell you what we can in the limited space, and urge that you let us send you this gun to see, examine and test in every way; of course, with the understanding, that if it is not perfectly satisfactory, you can return it to us at our expense, and we will immediately return your money, together with any express charges paid by you.

Catalogue No.	Grade	Style of Barrels	Gauge	Length of Barrels, Inches	Weight, Pounds	PRICE
6F424	A. S.	Genuine Armory Steel	12	30 or 32	6½	$5.95
6F425	L. S.	Genuine Laminated Steel	12	30 or 32	6½	6.75

Weight, packed for shipment, about 10 pounds.

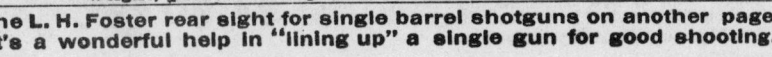

NOTICE the L. H. Foster rear sight for single barrel shotguns on another page. It's a wonderful help in "lining up" a single gun for good shooting.

No. 6F424

THE WORLD'S CHALLENGE AUTOMATIC EJECTOR, $4.30

A GENUINE TWIST BARREL, FANCY CHECKERED FULL PISTOL GRIP, AUTOMATIC SHELL EJECTING, SINGLE BARREL BREECH LOADING SHOTGUN FOR ONLY $4.30.

NOTE THE SPECIAL STRONG POINTS OF EXCELLENCE.

No. 1. Genuine twist barrel. See our booklet explaining how twist barrels are made, and do not compare the genuine twist barrel with any of the plain steel barrels usually found in single guns. This is a genuine twist barrel, sometimes known as laminated steel.
No. 2. Case hardened frame. The frame used in the **World's Challenge Ejector** is the very latest style, extra heavy and strong, beautifully mottled, case hardened finish effect, accurately milled and nicely fitted.
No. 3. Full pistol grip. The World's Challenge Ejector has a good straight grained walnut stock and a full pistol grip. The stock is nicely shaped, close and firmly fitted, with the result that the gun hangs beautifully.
No. 4. Checkered grip. The full pistol grip on the **World's Challenge Ejector** is nicely checkered by hand. Note the fancy checking as shown in the illustration, and bear in mind that none of the cheaper single barrel guns are finished in this way.
No. 5. Taper Choke Bored. The **World's Challenge Ejector** is choke bored by the celebrated taper system. The barrel is so taper choke bored as to confine all the gas behind the charge, insuring the greatest possible penetration, and the barrels being twist or laminated steel, are of the very greatest strength, hence are perfectly safe for the use of either smokeless or black powder.

THE WORLD'S CHALLENGE AUTOMATIC EJECTOR...

which we offer at $4.30, is made in our own gun factory at Meriden, Conn., the most complete, up to date, thoroughly modern gun factory in America. We started this factory with a view of turning out a uniformly high grade of guns and revolvers, and by employing the most modern type of automatic gun making machinery, and buying our material in large quantities for cash, reduced the cost of manufacture, so that after adding our one small percentage of profit, we could furnish our customers direct from our own factory the

HIGHEST GRADE GUNS AND REVOLVERS

at but a fraction of the price charged by other makers. In our own factory at Meriden, using nothing but the most modern type of automatic gun making machinery, having no traveling salesmen, no high salaried officers, making no losses by bad debts, we can produce and sell direct to our customers the highest grade guns and revolvers at about one-half the price charged by others.

DON'T COMPARE THIS GENUINE twist or laminated steel single barrel, checkered grip, automatic shell ejecting, breech loading shotgun with any of the many cheaper grades of single barrel shotguns of which there are many on the market. **This single barrel gun is made in our own factory at Meriden, Conn., and the barrels, frame, action, stock, in fact all the parts, all the material and workmanship are calculated to give our customers a higher grade single barrel breech loading shotgun than they could get from any other factory.** If you want a cheaper single barrel breech loader, and yet a thoroughly reliable gun, select our **Long Range Winner Automatic Shell Ejector at $2.96,** shown on another page; but if you want one of the highest grade single barrel guns made, a genuine twist or laminated steel barrel, a single barrel automatic shell ejector, combining the good points of all single barrel shotguns made with the defects of none, then pay a little more; add $1.34 more to the price of our $2.96 Long Range Winner and select this, the **World's Challenge Ejector at...... $4.30**

Examine the Foster Rear Sight for single guns, on page 155. It is a wonderful adjunct to a single barrel gun.

THE ILLUSTRATION does not do the gun justice, since by picture we are unable to show the difference between a twist barrel and the plain steel barrel. We are unable to show satisfactorily the difference between this and a cheaper frame. The many points of excellence in this, **OUR WORLD'S CHALLENGE EJECTOR,** can only be appreciated when you have seen and examined the gun and compared it with other single guns, and particularly after you have put it through the test of long range shooting, and more particularly after it has stood the test of years of service.

TAPER CHOKE BORED

$4.30

WE FURNISH FREE

with every WORLD'S CHALLENGE EJECTOR at $4.30 our own patent Globe Sight as illustrated.

THIS GLOBE SIGHT IS OWNED BY US and can be had only from us, and is furnished free with every World's Challenge Ejector at $4.30. You cannot afford to buy a single barrel shotgun from any other house when you can get our **World's Challenge Ejector at $4.30 and our patent Globe sight attachment FREE.** With this globe sight you can do wing shooting which it would be impossible to do without the sight. By the aid of this sight the most swift winged game can be instantly targeted, and, unless you are an expert wing shot, you will with this attachment, get three birds where you would not get more than one without it.

Order our $4.30 World's Challenge Ejector Gun and we will send it to you with the understanding and agreement that you can give it ten days' free trial, during which time you can put it to every test; you can compare it with other guns for long range shooting, for target and for penetration, for quality of barrels, for workmanship and finish, for strength and durability, and if you do not find our World's Challenge Ejector better than any single gun you can buy elsewhere at anything like the price, you can at any time within ten days return the gun to us at our expense and we will immediately return your money, together with any express charges you may have paid; further, we guarantee every piece and part of the material that goes into the construction of the gun. Any part proving defective by reason of defective material or workmanship within one year will be replaced or repaired free of charge.

DETAILED DESCRIPTION.

THE BARREL. The barrel of the World's Challenge Ejector is twist, which is sometimes known as laminated steel, and is made by hand by skilled workmen, who have spent years of their lives learning this art, and no machine has ever been invented which could do this work. It is made by a hand welding process of iron and steel, which makes one of the strongest barrels conceivable, free from flaws and defects. All barrels in the World's Challenge Ejector are made with a view of using black or nitro smokeless powder.

STOCK. The stocks are made from carefully selected straight grain, well seasoned walnut, turned out and finished from the solid plank, and the full pistol grip is handsomely checkered.

FORE END. The fore end is made from the same grade of material as the stock.

PARTS. All the parts which go into this gun are made accurate and true to gauge and are interchangeable, so if you accidentally break a hammer top lever or similar part, it may be replaced without the assistance of a gunsmith.

CHOKE BORED. The World's Challenge Ejector Gun is choke bored on the latest scientific principles, choke bored by the taper system, which insures the best possible target at the longest possible range.

BUTT PLATE. Each gun is fitted with a handsome fancy butt plate of neat design.

EJECTING DEVICE. Our ejecting device is made with the fewest possible parts, which renders it less liable to get out of order than any other ejecting device made, and throws out the shell automatically when opening the gun.

HAMMER. The hammer is rebounding and comes back to half cock, so the gun may be opened without cocking the hammer.

GAUGE. The World's Challenge Ejector comes in 12-gauge only, and is bored for either black, nitro or smokeless powder.

LENGTH OF BARREL. These guns come in 30 or 32-inch barrel. **When ordering, state which you prefer.**

OUR PROFIT SHARING PLAN enables you to get back part of your money. Consider what you get FREE as shown on the first pages.

REMEMBER OUR LIBERAL TERMS by which you can give this gun ten days' free trial, and if not found satisfactory you can return it to us at our expense and have your money returned to you. Remember, this is a genuine twist barrel gun, not a plain steel barrel gun. Note that

IT HAS A CHECKERED FULL PISTOL GRIP...

not a plain half pistol grip. REMEMBER, WE GUARANTEE it combines the good points of all high grade single barrel automatic ejectors, with the defects of none. It is, in short, the only single barrel shotgun to buy. There is no need of paying more money for any single barrel ejector made.

THE MAIN POINTS to be considered when buying a single barrel breech loading shotgun are these: Are the barrels bored true to gauge, so they will shoot well? Are they so strong, they will withstand black, nitro or smokeless powder? Are the stocks well seasoned so they will not open in the grain after being fitted on the gun? Is the frame case hardened and strong? Is the hammer rebounding, and does it come back to half cock so you do not have to raise it every time you wish to open the gun? Is the **automatic ejector simple, so that the gun can be taken apart to be cleaned?**

ALL THESE POINTS are covered in the World's Challenge Ejector, and we are satisfied that if you send us your order for one of these guns you will not part with it for three times the cost if you could not get another. Read our booklet of Useful Information to Shooters so you will become familiar with fire arms and the explosive nature of powder, as we wish our customers to have no accidents whether you buy guns of us or other houses.

Loaded Shells, $1.32 per 100. See page 164.

WEIGHT, PACKED FOR SHIPMENT, ABOUT 10 POUNDS. No. 6F422

No. 6F422 Our World's Challenge Ejector. 12-gauge, 30 or 32-inch barrel, as desired; state length wanted; every barrel guaranteed genuine twist. Weight, about 6½ pounds. Price, including our Globe Sight... **$4.30**
Weight, packed for shipment, about 10 pounds.

$2.96 BUYS THE LONG RANGE WINNER

AT $2.96, reduced from $5.50, our original price, and afterward reduced to $4.45, we now offer the genuine Long Range Winner as one of the highest grade automatic shell ejecting, single barrel breech loading shotguns made for white or black powder.

Our Globe Sight is Free with this Gun.

$2.96 barely covers the cost of material and labor in our own gun factory with but our one small percentage of profit added. It is lower than dealers can buy in any quantity, a gun the equal of guns that retail everywhere at from $7.00 to $10.00.

OUR $1.00 OFFER. While nearly all of our customers send cash in full with their orders, we will, on receipt of $1.00, send this gun to any address by express C. O. D., subject to examination, the balance of $1.96 and express charges to be paid after the gun is received and found perfectly satisfactory and in every way as represented. We recommend that you send the full amount of cash with your order, as we guarantee the gun to reach you in perfect condition. We guarantee every part and piece that enters into the construction of the gun to be absolutely perfect, and if you do not find it equal to any automatic, single barrel, long range gun that retails at $7.00 to $10.00, you may return the gun to us immediately at our expense of express charges both ways and we will return your money.

COMPARE THIS, OUR $2.96 LONG RANGE WINNER, with any of the single barrel, automatic shell ejecting, breech loading guns on the market, those catalogued by other houses at $4.50 to $6.00, those that retail generally at $7.00 to $10.00, and if you do not find our Long Range Winner at $2.96 the equal of any other shell ejecting breech loader, you can return the gun to us at our expense of express charges both ways and we will immediately return your money.

HOW WE MAKE THE PRICE $2.96.

WE OWN THE FACTORY in which these guns are made and control the entire output. The cost to us is gotten down to merely the cost of the raw material and labor, and to this we add our one small percentage of profit, naming the heretofore unheard of price of $2.96. This gun is made in our own factory at Meriden, Conn., and the factory is in charge of one of the best single gun makers in the world, and we believe under his management, utilizing the modern machinery we do, that we produce a better automatic shell ejecting single barrel shotgun at a lower cost than any other factory.

WE MAKE AND FINISH MORE BARRELS of this kind than any other maker, thus reducing the cost. On the item of barrels alone there is a saving to us in the cost of every gun over other manufacturers of about 50 cents. Where nearly all makers of single guns import the barrels, the barrels being made in Belgium, we make our barrels in our own factory from solid bars of genuine Armory steel. To make the barrels we buy the highest grade of genuine Armory steel in solid bars of about 12 foot lengths. We cut this steel up into lengths of 30 and 32 inches, and in a new improved automatic barrel boring machine we bore two barrels at a time, and by this process we not only reduce the cost of the barrels about 50 cents each, but we furnish a higher grade, truer, stronger, better finish, and hence a better shooting barrel than is furnished on any single gun made.

BY OUR SYSTEM each barrel is choke bored for strong and long range shooting, made and bored to shoot either white, nitro or black powder, is more highly polished, better finished and blued than any similar gun on the market. We have installed special machinery for making every screw, every piece and every part for the milling, cutting, polishing, shaping, making and fitting of stock, the most economical and finest case hardening plant, everything combined to turn out a perfect gun at the very minimum of cost, and to this actual cost we add our one small percentage of profit, and quote the ridiculously low price of $2.96.

WE LOCATED OUR SINGLE GUN FACTORY at Meriden as a matter of economy and efficiency of labor. Meriden, Conn., is located in the very center of the gun and revolver making industry of America. Within a short radius of our factory, nearly all the American gun and revolver factories are located, hence we have the most skilled labor concentrated and always at our disposal. The supply usually being in excess of the demand of other factories, we are able to build this gun at a lower wage scale at Meriden than at any other point in the country.

ALL THIS HELPS TO MAKE POSSIBLE OUR SPECIAL $2.96 PRICE.

ALWAYS STATE LENGTH OF BARREL WANTED.

GENUINE ARMORY STEEL.

TAPER CHOKE BORED

$2 96

Notice our Proposition on Pointer Shells,

SEE PAGES 298 and 299.

SPECIAL POINTS OF EXCELLENCE.

We claim for the Long Range Winner superiority over other single barrel guns, especially on the following points: First, genuine Armory steel barrels, choke bored and finished in our own factory, smoother, stronger and better than other makers furnish, and bored for nitro or black powder.

AUTOMATIC SHELL EJECTOR, stronger, more sure, and less liable to get out of order than any other single barrel, shell ejecting device made.

LOCKING BOLT. The heaviest, strongest and best locking bolt used on any single gun.

FRAME AND ACTION. The strongest, handsomest, most simple, neatest and best finished case hardened frame and action used on a single barrel ejector.

SHOOTING QUALITIES. Above all, we claim for our $2.96 Long Range Winner the best shooter of any single barrel gun of this type on the market. Our barrels and frames are made and the gun is hung in a way that insures a better target at longer range than you will get from any single barrel gun you can buy from any other house at $1.00 to $3.00 more money.

UNDERSTAND, we accept your order and money with the agreement to immediately return your money to you and pay the express charges both ways if the gun is not found perfectly satisfactory.

$2.96

Loaded Shells, $1.32 per 100. See page 300.

Illustration shows the action of our Long Range Winner

T is the Hammer.
U is the Top Lever.
V is the Top Lever Spring.
W is the Locking Bolt.
X is the Mainspring.
Y is the Trigger Spring.
Z is the Trigger.
G is the Stock.
1 is the Extractor Cam Spring.
2 is the Extractor Cam.
3 is the Extractor Hook.
4 is the Fore End.
5 is the Trigger Guard.
5 is the Screw Key.

DETAILED DESCRIPTION.

THE BARREL is bored from a solid bar of the highest grade, extra fine, thoroughly tested genuine Armory steel, choke bored by the celebrated taper system, each barrel is blued, decarbonized finish, fitted with automatic shell ejector, one of the strongest, positive, perfect working automatic shell ejectors made, so constructed that when you open the gun the empty shell is automatically thrown clear from the gun.

The illustration shows the action of the shell as it is being automatically ejected. By this device there is no stopping to remove the shell by hand, it being thrown clear from your way ready to receive the new loaded shell. This makes possible very rapid firing; in fact, you can load and unload very much faster than with the ordinary extractor gun. The device is only appreciated by those who have used automatic shell ejecting guns, and such people would have no other; in fact with this single barrel automatic shell ejecting gun you shoot almost as rapidly and do almost the same execution that you can accomplish with a double barrel hammer breech loading shotgun.

FRAME. The $2.96 Long Range Winner has one of the very strongest solid steel frames, made extra heavy, reinforced at all parts, nicely shaped, perfectly finished. It is given a handsome mottled finish on the outside. It has the latest rebounding hammer, positive springs, the very latest top snap break. The gun is the latest type of take-down or detachable model. By simply removing the thumbscrew the barrel and fore end can be detached from the frame.

STOCK. This gun is fitted with an extra quality, thoroughly seasoned straight grain walnut stock, with pistol grip as illustrated, and the stock is fitted with a fancy butt plate. The fore end is of selected straight grained seasoned black walnut.

GENERAL FINISH. This gun is gotten up to present a more symmetrical, shapely and in every way a better general appearance than the ordinary single barrel gun. With its neat stock, handsome butt plate, beautifully decarbonized frame and trimmings, highly finished blued barrel, nicely proportioned parts and fittings throughout, even at our special $2.96 price it is one of the handsomest single guns on the market.

GAUGE. This gun comes in 12-gauge only, and being made and bored for white or black powder, made extra strong throughout, the gun is suitable for any kind of shooting where any shotgun can be used, suitable for game, geese, ducks, chickens, partridge, quail, snipe, rabbits, squirrels, etc.

LENGTH OF BARREL. The barrel is either 30 or 32 inches in length as desired. When ordering be sure to state the length of barrel wanted.

You Share in our Profit

We send you a valuable PROFIT SHARING CERTIFICATE and you can soon get something valuable, entirely FREE, as shown on last pages.

ABOUT THE EXPRESS CHARGES

The gun weighs, packed for shipment, about 10 pounds and you will find the express charges will amount to next to nothing as compared with what we will save you in price. The express charges will average for 300 miles, 40 cents; for 500 miles, 50 to 65 cents; 1,000 miles and upwards 75 cents to $1.00.

OUR $2.96 GUN weighs about 6¾ to 7 pounds, making a light gun to carry, very convenient and at the same time one of the strongest shooting guns made, and in this respect is more convenient than a double barrel gun, for it is in shooting qualities equal to a double barrel gun that would weigh from 8 to 10 pounds. Weight, packed for shipment, about 10 pounds.

NO. 6E401 ORDER BY NUMBER

No. 6E401 LONG RANGE WINNER, 12-gauge, 30 or 32-inch barrel. Weight, about 6¾ to 7 pounds. Price.......................... **$2.96**

EXAMINE THE FOSTER REAR SIGHT ON PAGE 291.

OUR COMBINATION SINGLE BARREL SHOTGUN AND OUTFIT, COMPLETE, $3.98.

FOR $3.98 we offer the High Grade Genuine American Made Pistol Grip Breech Loading Shotgun, such a gun as retails generally at $6.00 to $8.00, together with a complete gun outfit, such an outfit as every owner of a breech loading shotgun must have, an outfit that would retail anywhere at from $3.00 to $5.00. We furnish the entire outfit, gun, implements and all, for only $3.98.

Give waist measure when ordering.

SEND US $3.98 and we will send you this gun and complete outfit, exactly as illustrated and described, and it will go to you with the understanding and agreement that you can give the gun ten days' trial, during which time you can shoot it and put it through every test, compare it with guns that retail at from $5.00 to $8.00, compare the implements and supplies with those of any other outfit which you could buy at home from $3.00 to $4.00, and if you do not find this gun and outfit satisfactory in material, workmanship, finish, if it is not satisfactory in every way, and you do not find that you have made a big saving in cost, you can return the gun and outfit to us at our expense and we will immediately refund the $3.98, together with any express charges you may have paid.

THE PRICE, $3.98, is made possible because, first, we are one of the largest manufacturers of guns and sporting goods in the world and these guns are made in our own factory in Meriden, Conn., and through our own factory we are able to contract with other factories on more favorable terms than any other buyer or seller of guns and sporting goods. No such price has ever before been attempted nor could any other concern think of making such an offer.

The gun is strictly high grade, one of the best American made single barrel breech loading shotguns on the market. The tools and implements are also of the highest standard of quality, the very best, and fully guaranteed.

DESCRIPTION OF THE GUN.

The gun is 12-gauge and the barrel is made from genuine armory steel, made especially strong so that either smokeless or black powder can be used. They are choke bored by the celebrated taper system. They have the latest style of shell extractor (not ejector), beautifully blued finish, guaranteed for long range hard shooting, make a close target and the gun has wonderful penetrative powers.

FRAME. The frame is extra heavy and is fitted with the strongest kind of lock work, beautifully finished with a decarbonized mottled effect, has the latest style top snap break. It is made with a selected walnut stock. Made with pistol grip, fancy butt plate and selected walnut fore end.

We furnish it in 30-inch barrel and the gun goes out under our binding guarantee for quality, durability and excellent shooting qualities.

THE OUTFIT illustrated above, which is furnished with the gun, all for $3.98, includes one reloading block, which retails generally at from 25 cents to 50 cents; a handsome jointed cleaning rod, which retails at from 30 cents to 50 cents; a shell crimper, one of the best made, such as retails at from 50 cents to $1.00; one loader and decapper, which retails at from 20 cents to 40 cents; one recapper, japanned, which retails at from 10 cents to 20 cents; one interchangeable powder and shot measure, which retails at from 10 cents to 25 cents; one extractor, retail price 10 cents to 25 cents; one wad cutter, retail price 10 cents to 25 cents; one genuine Victoria canvas gun cover, retail price 50 cents to $1.00; one genuine web shell belt, retail price 50 cents to $1.00; one box of twenty-five loaded shells, retail price 40 cents to 50 cents.

All of the above outfit, eleven valuable and needed accessories, and the gun complete, can be furnished for only $3.98. Send us $3.98, mention the number of the outfit as given below, and the gun and outfit will go to you under our binding guarantee, and if it is not entirely satisfactory and does not mean a big saving to you, return it at our expense and get your money back at once. Our price for the complete outfit, gun and all, is only $3.98.

No. 6E410 Our High Grade Single Barrel Shotgun, in 12-gauge, with 30-inch barrel, and the outfit as illustrated and described above, for **$3.98**

Weight, packed for shipment, about 16 pounds.

Examine the Foster Rear Sight for single guns, on page 291. It is a wonderful adjunct to a single barrel gun.

OUR $3.39 NEW WHITE POWDER WONDER AUTOMATIC EJECTOR.

OUR $3.39 PRICE is made possible by reason of our building this gun in our own factory. We started the manufacture of these guns with a view of giving our customers something better than the regular grade of single barrel guns turned out by factories generally. We started our own factory that we might produce a gun free from all the weak points of the many guns that are being manufactured under competitive conditions that compel the manufacturer to slight vital parts in order to meet the price made by other makers.

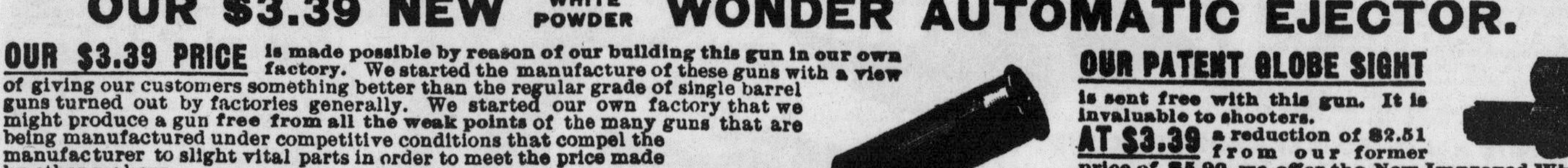

OUR PATENT GLOBE SIGHT is sent free with this gun. It is invaluable to shooters.

AT $3.39 a reduction of $2.51 from our former price of $5.90, we offer the New Improved White Powder Wonder Ejector, a gun with all the very latest improvements brought right up to date, one of the highest of high grade single barrel shotguns. We especially recommend to you for your consideration our New Model White Powder Wonder Automatic Ejecting Single Barrel Breech Loading Shotgun at only $3.39.

WE HAVE SUCCEEDED in turning out in our New White Powder Wonder Ejector, a gun combining the good points of all strictly high grade guns with the defects of none, and yet on a basis of the actual manufacturing cost, the cost of material and labor with but our one small percentage of profit added.

SOME PROFIT GOES BACK TO YOU. We send you a PROFIT SHARING CERTIFICATE for every purchase.

No.6E414 Order by Number

LOADED SHELLS, $1.32 PER 100. See page 300

FROM THE ILLUSTRATION, engraved by our own artist from a photograph, taken direct from our $3.39 New White Powder Wonder Ejector, you can form some idea of the appearance of this gun, but you must see this gun, examine it, compare it with others, must put it to the test of its shooting qualities, compare its target, penetration, long range, killing effect, to realize fully what we have, from our own factory, from the material we ourselves control, from the workmanship we put on the gun by employing the very finest automatic machinery, attained in this justly termed New White Powder Wonder Ejector; THE ONLY WHITE POWDER EJECTOR AMERICAN GUN OFFERED AT $3.39.

SPECIAL POINTS OF SUPERIORITY in the New Model White Powder Wonder Ejector over the many other single guns made: Genuine highest grade full armory steel barrel, bored for black or white nitro powder, choke bored by the celebrated taper system; more perfect and more positive action; stronger built and lock mechanism; highest grade automatic shell ejector made; greater strength, accuracy and better finished frame; interchangeable and better finished parts; longer range, better target and more carefully tested. All these very essential points in the shooting and lasting qualities of a gun go to make our New Model White Powder Wonder Ejector superior to any of the regular factory made ejectors now on the market.

BROKEN PARTS ALWAYS REPLACED. If by accident or otherwise, any part should get broken or become lost, being interchangeable they can be readily replaced and can always be had from us at a very nominal charge.

OUR BINDING GUARANTEE. Every New White Powder Wonder Ejector offered at $3.39, is sent out under our binding guarantee, by the terms and conditions of which if any piece or part gives out by reason of defect in material or workmanship within one year from date of purchase, we will replace or repair it free of charge.

DETAILED SPECIFICATIONS Genuine armory steel barrel bored from the solid bars, choke bored by the celebrated taper system; very finest automatic ejector, heavy bolted, self locking, self compensating, interchangeable parts, beautifully case hardened; reinforced frame; barrel detachable fr n frame; rebounding hammer, latest top snap break, fine selected straight grain full pistol grip walnut stock, fancy butt plate to stock. Weight, about 6½ pounds.

No. 6E414 Automatic Ejector, case hardened frame, 12-gauge only, 30 or 32-inch barrel. State length of barrel wanted. Price.................... **$3.39**

Weight, packed for shipment, about 10 pounds.

$5.75 LONG BARREL BIG GAME GUN

This is a special, extra long barreled gun, barrel 6 to 10 inches longer than any regular length of barrel, barrel made extra long for very long range shooting for big game, a gun really wonderful for birds at very long distances, just the gun for big game at short range, a gun to kill at distances that cannot be reached by any 30 or 32-inch barreled gun.

A GREAT DEMAND **has come for these exceedingly long barreled guns, especially from those who hunt the larger game, such as geese, turkeys and even ducks at exceedingly long range, jack rabbits, etc.** While especially adapted for a gun that will reach out and kill larger game and a gun that will show a telling effect at distances three to six rods greater than any of the regular length barrel, it is also equally suitable for all kinds of smaller game. With this extra long barreled gun, shooting the smaller game, such as partridges, quail, chickens, rabbits, etc., it is advisable to let your game get several yards farther away from you than with the ordinary gun before shooting, lest at ordinary distances you might injure the game by shooting it to pieces.

OUR GREAT FREE TRIAL OFFER

AS A GUARANTEE **that this extra long barrel will meet your requirements in every way for extra long range shooting, we make you this free trial proposition:** Send us your order, enclose our price, $5.75, if you wish a 36-inch barrel gun, $6.25 if you wish a 40-inch barrel gun, and we will send you this new improved 1907 model breech loading shotgun, with the understanding and agreement that you can give it ten days' trial, during which time you can put it to every reasonable test, you can try it out for exceedingly long range shooting, try it as you like, and if at any time during the ten days' trial you have reason to feel it is not just exactly the gun you want, you will be under no obligations to keep the gun; on the contrary, you can return the gun to us at any time within ten days, at our expense, and immediately we receive the gun we will pay the express charges and return the money you have sent us, together with any express charges you may have paid.

For an extra long barrel, an extra long distance gun, for a gun that will kill game that you could not reach with any ordinary gun, we especially recommend this, our new 1907 model.

HOW WE CAME TO HAVE THIS 36 AND 40-INCH BARREL MADE ESPECIALLY FOR US

FROM DIFFERENT SECTIONS OF THE COUNTRY **we have had many inquiries from customers for a gun that would shoot farther, kill at greater distances than any ordinary gun and yet a gun that was not exceedingly heavy or did not use an exceedingly large shell, like an 8 or 10-gauge.** These inquiries have come from people who have found it impossible to kill game such as ducks, geese and game wild and flying very high, a distance that they cannot reach and kill with the ordinary gun; the demand, too, has come from sections of the country where a shotgun is used for larger game; and to meet this demand we have, after considerable experiment, developed for this very proposition these exceedingly long barrels, 36 and 40 inches long, and we are pleased to say with most wonderful results, results that have satisfied the most exacting on the question of unusually long range.

CUSTOMERS **have written us that at certain seasons of the year, when the duck or goose flight was on, particularly in the fall of the year,** this game would pass over them in large numbers and that any ordinary gun would not bring them down. We are glad to report in these, our 36 and 40-inch barrel guns, guns with barrels 6 to 10 inches longer than the ordinary gun, we have been able to place in the hands of our customers requiring this special service a gun that fills every requirement.

THIS, OUR SPECIAL, LONG RANGE, EXTRA LONG BARREL GUN **has been remodeled for 1907, improved in many respects, strengthened in the frame and lock work.** The barrel has been made somewhat heavier, stronger and we believe better, and yet our contract this season, placed with a large New England maker of single guns, enables us, after adding our one small percentage of profit, to offer you this gun in the 36-inch barrel for only $5.75 and in the 40-inch barrel for $6.25.

IF THE ORDINARY 30 OR 32-INCH BARRELED GUN **will not meet your requirements, if you feel you must have a gun that will do about the same execution at several rods greater distance,** if you need a gun for unusually long range shooting, then you will be safe in ordering one of these extra long barreled guns, and we would especially recommend in such a case that you order the 40-inch barreled gun, which we offer at $6.25.

GENERAL DESCRIPTION.

THIS IS AN EXTRA STRONG, EXTRA WELL MADE GUN, **made by one of the best makers in New England, made under special contract for us and can be had only from us.** The barrel is made from genuine armory steel, made extra heavy, it comes either 36 or 40 inches in length as desired, it is choke bored by the celebrated taper system, and being unusually long, most extra care is exercised in boring it to a perfect taper and to give it a choke effect that will insure perfect execution at the greatest possible distance. The barrel is made unusually strong and heavy at the breech. The frame is extra heavy, made from solid steel, the frame, the barrel, the jointing and the whole construction being made with a view to shooting either nitro, smokeless or black powder. The gun is fitted with an extra quality walnut stock of perfect grain, it has full pistol grip, the pistol grip nicely checkered by hand; every gun is equipped with the strongest automatic ejector device, by which when you open the gun the empty or discharged shell is automatically thrown clear from the gun; the frame and trigger guard are case hardened and beautifully finished, the hammer is hung in the center of the frame so as to strike the primer squarely, the butt plate is of a neat design and the gun can be taken down by simply removing the patent fore end. We have endeavored to have this gun built on lines that, even though it be an extra long gun, 6 to 10 inches longer than the average gun, by reason of the very long barrel, yet a gun that will handle almost as easily as the standard 30 or 32-inch barreled gun.

THIS GUN **has every up to date feature of all standard grade single barrel, hammer, automatic shell ejecting guns,** the best known shell ejector, patent top snap break, fancy case hardened mottled finishing, rebounding locks, everything thoroughly complete.

THIS GUN FILLS A SPECIAL PLACE, **it stands in a class by itself; therefore, if you want a special gun of this kind for a special purpose,** there is no other gun in our catalogue that we could especially refer you to or recommend for the special purpose you desire. It's a gun that is adapted to all purposes that the standard length of guns are adaptable to; in other words, a gun that can be used for all kinds of game, big or small, at either medium or very long range distances. The only care necessary in shooting ordinary game at a close range or ordinary distance is that you must remember to wait a little until the game gets some distance from you, for remember in this you have a gun with a terrific reach, with a killing power at great distance. In referring you to any other single barrel breech loading shotgun in our line, any regular standard gun for all around purposes, a standard length of barrel, 30 or 32-inch, we wouldn't pass without calling your attention especially to the A. J. Aubrey guns, and if you want a single gun, especially to the A. J. Aubrey Hammerless Automatic Shell Ejecting Flat Water Table Gun, shown on another page in this book and offered at only $7.95, for this Aubrey gun is positively the highest grade single barrel gun made in America, and it's the only gun made on the same lines as the highest grade double barrel hammerless breech loading shotgun, and if you are wanting any regular style of a single gun, any gun coming in the regular lengths, 30 or 32-inch barrels, then as compared to any gun we have in our entire line, any single gun you can buy from us, or anyone else at home or elsewhere and at any price, however low or however high, we would urge you in your own interest to get the highest grade gun made, the $7.95 Aubrey, illustrated and described on another page; but this particular gun we are here describing, the extra long barreled gun, made extra long for a special purpose, for wonderfully long range shooting, a gun while filling the place of a shotgun in some measure approaches the rifle, a gun that for special purposes sort of fits in between the rifle and a shotgun, it leans toward the rifle in that it approaches many rifles in the distance it will carry and kill; on the other hand, it fills the purpose of a shotgun, inasmuch as it can with care (lest you destroy the game by shooting it to pieces) be used for as small game as can any single shotgun made.

THIS ILLUSTRATION **will give you an idea of the general appearance of our Globe Sight, which we furnish free with every one of these guns.** This sight is instantly attachable and detachable to any single gun. In a fraction of a minute you can slip it on and fasten it to the end of the gun barrel and you can very quickly remove it, but it adapts itself more especially to this long barrel gun than to any other single barrel gun made, since the longer the barrel the more difficult it is to get a quick sight, especially on birds when flying, but with the addition of our Globe Sight, which we illustrate hereon, and which we furnish free with this gun, you will have no trouble even with the 40-inch barreled gun in getting a quick line or sight on the swiftest flying birds; in short, with this single barrel gun and our Globe Sight attached it makes it easy, for even the comparatively inexperienced, to make a wonderful target in the field on wing game, and having the advantage over everyone shooting a 30 or 32-inch barrel, you will get many shots that will be entirely out of the range of your associates shooting a shorter barreled gun, and when the game is flying especially high you will then find that you will get a good bag from a single barrel gun while those all around you with a double gun will be unable to reach and bring down the game. Your advantage in long carrying, in killing at exceedingly long distances, in reaching up into the very skies several rods farther than anyone in your party can reach with other standard guns, will in many instances result in your getting more game from the one single barrel gun than the balance of your party, no matter what guns they may carry.

Catalogue No.	Grade	Style of Barrel	Gauge	Length of Barrel, inches	Weight of Gun, lbs.	Price
6H510A	Ejector	Genuine Armory Steel	12	36-in. choke bored	7 to 7¼	$5.75
6H510B	Ejector		16	36-in. choke bored	6¾ to 7	
6H511A	Ejector		12	40-in. choke bored	7¼ to 7½	6.25
6H511B	Ejector		16	40-in. choke bored	7 to 7¼	

WEIGHT, PACKED FOR SHIPMENT, ABOUT 14 POUNDS.

IF ONE OF THESE **very long range, hard shooting guns, guns made especially for the purpose with 36 or 40-inch barrel,** will be useful to you, then kindly send us your order and enclose our price. Remember, for the special purpose they are intended we really recommend the 40-inch barrel, the $6.25 gun, and remember, if it doesn't please you, you can return it to us at our expense, and we will immediately return your money. We furnish these guns in the different lengths at prices quoted herewith.

YOUR MONEY WILL BE IMMEDIATELY RETURNED TO YOU FOR ANY GOODS NOT PERFECTLY SATISFACTORY.

OUR NEW LONG RANGE SINGLE BARREL 10-GAUGE GOOSE GUNS, $13.50.

The Best Low Priced Gun for Long Range Shooting Ever Made.

For Geese and Large Game.

36-Inch Laminated Steel Barrels.

No. 6H520

10-GAUGE

$13.50

OUR PATENT GLOBE SIGHT IS FREE WITH THIS GUN. At $13.50 for 10-gauge we will furnish you our celebrated Long Range Goose Guns. These guns are made especially for us and all guns are TESTED BEFORE THEY LEAVE OUR STORE.

COMPARE OUR GOOSE GUNS WITH ANY OTHER, and you will find them better made and better finished than any goose guns on the market. All have top snap break, checkered pistol grip stock and rebounding hammer.

No. 6H520 Our Heavy Long Range, 10-Gauge, Single Barrel Gun, adapted to heavy shooting. A very popular goose gun for long range, hard shooting. All parts made with a view to securing a strong, lasting gun. Choke bored, fine laminated steel barrel, 36 inches long; weight, 9 pounds. With our patent Globe Sight. Price............... **$13.50**

Weight, packed for shipment, 14 pounds.

OUR 16-GAUGE ARMORY STEEL AND TWIST BARREL AUTOMATIC EJECTOR SINGLE GUNS.

12-GAUGE LOADED SHELLS, $1.49 PER 100. See page 697.

Our Patent Globe Sight is furnished FREE with these Guns.

Guaranteed Genuine Armory Steel and Genuine Twist Barrel.

Choke Bored. 16-gauge only. 30-inch barrel. Weight, about 6½ pounds.

$4.38 and $5.05

CHOKE BORED

BORED FOR NITRO POWDER.

No. 6H535

Our $4.38 gun is fitted with genuine armory steel barrel and our $5.05 16-gauge Ejector. Single Gun is fitted with a genuine twist barrel; all have walnut pistol grip stock, walnut fore end, bored smooth and true to gauge, choke bored for field shooting and have fancy butt plate. The hammer is hung in the center so as to strike the cartridge squarely. The automatic ejector device is very strong and simple and cannot get out of order. The barrel is detachable, making it convenient to carry the gun apart in a Victoria style gun case. It has rebounding hammer, top snap break, and the frame and trigger guard are case hardened and beautifully finished. The shell is thrown out automatically when you open the gun.

Catalogue Number	Grade	Style of Barrel	Gauge	Length of Barrel	Weight, about	Price
6H534	No. 1	Armory Steel	16	30 inches	6½ pounds	$4.38
6H535	No. 2	Genuine Twist	16	30 inches	6½ pounds	5.05

Weight, packed for shipment, about 10 pounds.

OUR LADIES' LITTLE BREECH LOADING DOUBLE BARREL SHOTGUN.

$10.10

A 44-Caliber, or 40-85 Caliber Shotgun.

No. 6H541

We have had this little gun built for ladies or boys who like to hunt and for whom a 12-gauge gun kicks too hard. It is very effective for squirrels, birds or small game, and is made to take the 44 XL shot cartridge No. 6H2717. It can also be furnished to take the 40-85 primed shell, which is about 3 inches long, and can be loaded heavier than the 44 XL shot cartridges are loaded. We cannot furnish the 40-85 shells loaded. The 40-85 shells are large enough to take about 40 grains of black powder and ½-ounce of shot, while the 44 XL will use only about one-half as much powder and shot. This little breech loader is fitted with 25-inch barrels and weighs about 4 pounds. Our patent Globe Sight is not made small enough for this gun.

This gun is fitted with twist finished barrels, checkered pistol grip stock and checkered fore end, rebounding locks, top snap break, extension rib; a neat, well made and good looking, small, double barrel breech loader, suitable for small game such as quail, squirrels, etc.

Catalogue Number.	ARTICLE	Caliber	Quantity	Price
6H541	Our Ladies' Breech Loader................	44 or 40-85	Each	$10.10
6H2717	Shot Cartridges...........................	44 XL	Per 100	1.50
6H3230	Empty Brass Shells (not loaded)...........	40-85	Per 100	2.50
6H977	Loading Tools, consisting of Recapper, Decapper, Wad Cutter and Charge Cup......	40-85	Per Set	.55

This gun alone when packed for shipment, weighs about 8 pounds.

A HIGH POWER 6-SHOT SMOKELESS BIG GAME REPEATING RIFLE FOR ONLY $7.25.

$7.25

A RIFLE FOR BIG GAME.

A HIGH POWER RIFLE AT A LOW PRICE.

We have purchased from the Swiss Government for cash a large quantity of genuine Vetterli repeating high power rifles, such as were used by the Swiss Government and known as the Model 1881, which we have transformed into sporting rifles, as illustrated above.

The Vetterli Repeating Rifles, as they came to us from the Swiss Government, weighed about 12 pounds, had 33-inch barrels and were only 12 inches from the trigger to the center of the butt plate, which is too short a stock for the average man, and we have transformed these rifles by cutting off the barrel to 26 inches, fitting new stocks, making them 13½ inches from trigger to center of butt, revamped the fore end and transformed it into a 6-shot repeating rifle weighing about 8 pounds, which is very much more desirable and balances much better and looks much better than the original Vetterli rifles when they reached us from Switzerland. **For $7.25 we furnish this Vetterli Repeating Rifle, and 20 rounds of cartridges go free with each rifle,** making an outfit ready to hunt big game at a very low price. Remember, this is not a cheap rifle. It is a rifle which originally cost the Swiss Government at least $16.00 to make, is made from the best high grade material that money can buy, has the Mauser type bolt lever repeating action, one of the strongest bolt actions made, carries five cartridges in the magazine and one in the chamber, making it a 6-shot repeating rifle, and shoots the 41-caliber Swiss smokeless powder cartridges, which may be compared in power to the 30-30 smokeless cartridges, but the bullet is 7-16 inch diameter, weighs 300 grains and strikes a very powerful blow. You will notice the 30-30 bullet is 5-16 inch in diameter and weighs 160 grains. **Remember, $7.25 is our price** for the genuine Vetterli smokeless high power rifle, and with each rifle we send 20 cartridges free; also remember, this is not the heavy, clumsy Vetterli rifle which we purchased from the Swiss Government, but is the transformed Vetterli rifle, which is much more shapely, much better balanced, longer stock, and in every way much more up to date and more desirable.

No. 6H650 Our Vetterli Smokeless High Power Repeating Rifle, with 20 cartridges. Price..............(Weight, packed for shipment, about 14 pounds.)..............$7.25

No. 6H652 Extra Smokeless Cartridges, 41-caliber Swiss, for the above rifle. Price, per 100...$2.00

WINCHESTER REPEATING SHOTGUNS, MODEL 1897.

$20.00

No. 6H550

Model 1897. 12-Gauge, 30-inch Barrel.

$21.60

No. 6H560

THE PRICES on these goods are fixed by the manufacturers, and we are compelled to sell them at these prices. Every Winchester Gun is doubly guaranteed, both by the factory and ourselves, and in addition to the rigid examination given them by the factory, they are furthermore carefully inspected by our inspectors, and every Winchester Gun we sell is guaranteed to be perfect in material, workmanship and mechanical construction.

THIS IS THE IMPROVED MODEL WITH DOUBLE EXTRACTORS, constructed so that accidental discharge is impossible. The gun is operated by the sliding forearm, which, when pushed back, unlocks the breech box, ejects the empty shell, places another shell in the carrier, and cocks the hammer. To open gun when full cocked, press button at right side of frame. The stock is 13¾ inches long, 2½-inch drop. The gun is fitted with blued steel barrel, chambered for 2¾-inch and 2⅝-inch shells. The takedown gun can be taken apart in a moment's time, and as quickly assembled. There are no screws to lose, as when taken apart, the gun is in two parts, namely, the barrel and magazine, and stock and frame.

Catalogue No.	GRADE	Length of Barrel	Number of Shots	Weight	Price
6H550	Model 1897, Solid Frame	30 inches	6	7¾ pounds	$20.00
6H560	Model 1897, Take Down	30 inches	6	7¾ pounds	21.60

TARGET RIFLES 22-CALIBER.

OUR QUACKENBUSH JUNIOR RIFLE, $3.26.

$3.26

The Quackenbush Junior Rifle is practically the same as the Quackenbush Safety Rifle No. 6H676, except it has a nickel plated or blued steel 18-inch barrel, skeleton stock and metal fore end, as shown in the illustration, otherwise the rifle is identical with the Quackenbush Safety Rifle. The Junior rifles are no longer made and we will have no more after our stock is sold.

No. 6H672 Quackenbush Junior Rifle, 22-caliber, 18-inch blued steel barrel, with open sights, as illustrated. Price..$3.26

No. 6H672½ The same rifle with nickel plated barrel. Price.............. 3.36

Shipping weight, 9 pounds.

Notice our prices on Rifle Rods. It saves the rifle to keep it clean.

QUACKENBUSH SAFETY CARTRIDGE RIFLE.

$3.90 WITH 22-INCH BARREL.

21 CENTS PER 100 FOR 22-CALIBER SHORT CARTRIDGES. See page 700.

B

Our new model safety has fine steel barrel, automatic cartridge extractor. Stock is black walnut, handsomely finished, and so fastened to the barrel that the two may be easily and quickly separated, making the rifle handy to carry in a trunk, valise or package. The barrel is rifled and durably blued, except the breech block, which is case hardened in color. **Whole length, 33 inches,** has 22-inch barrel, 22-caliber. Shoots cartridges Nos. 6H2336, 6H2338, 6H2340, or 6H2535; good for 35 to 100 yards. Plain open sights, as shown in illustration. Weight, about 4½ pounds. Guaranteed good shooter. We have discontinued selling this rifle with an 18-inch barrel, as the 22-inch costs only a few cents more and is the best all around rifle.

OUR NEW No. 4 REMINGTON TAKE DOWN RIFLE, $5.00.

21 CENTS PER 100 FOR 22-CALIBER SHORT CARTRIDGES. SEE PAGE 700.

These are the Genuine Remington Take Down Rifles. Don't buy imitations offered by many houses. They are worthless. All Remingtons have walnut stock, case hardened frame and mountings, open front and rear sights. As finely rifled as any rifle in the market, and made of the very best rifle material. Perfectly accurate and every one warranted as represented. Weight, about 4½ pounds. 22-caliber. RIM FIRE.

Cat. No.	Caliber	Barrel	Shoots Cartridge	Good for	Price
6H678	22 Short or Long Rim Fire	22½ in.	No. 6H2336	35 to 100 yards	$5.00
6H680	32 Short or Long.........	24 in.	No. 6H2340	100 to 125 yards	5.00

Weight, packed for shipment, about 8 pounds.

Notice our prices on Rifle Rods. It saves the rifle to keep it clean.

RUSTED AND DAMAGED GUNS. Do not return to us a gun, revolver or rifle which is rusted, pitted or has the finish worn off, for we have no way of selling these guns. If you have a gun, revolver or rifle which needs repairing, first write us fully describing the article and what is broken, as we may be able to send you the part necessary, thus saving the express charges on the gun both ways.

Catalogue No.	Caliber	Barrel, inches	Shoots Cartridge	Good for	Price
6H676	22 Rim Fire	22	No. 6H2336 No. 6H2338 No. 6H2340 No. 6H2535	35 to 100 yards	$3.90

Weight, packed for shipment, about 8 pounds.

Notice our prices on Rifle Rods. It saves the rifle to keep it clean.

21 CENTS PER 100 FOR 22-CALIBER SHORT CARTRIDGES, SEE PAGE 70

ATLAS MODEL OF 1908

$1.98

$1.98 BUYS THIS NEW IMPROVED TAKE DOWN MODEL OF 1908

22 caliber, 22-inch barrel, accurately rifled, full finished rifle, exactly as illustrated. Please note this is a 22-inch barrel. The barrels are 22 inches long and are full rifled, rifled after exactly the same style and method as the rifling in the highest priced rifles, features not found on any other rifle sold at a low price.

COMPARE THIS RIFLE with any rifle you can buy anywhere at anything like this price, any rifle you can buy at from $2.00 to $4.00, and you will find the barrels of other rifles are shorter, usually 18 to 20 inches, and they are not rifled by the same accurate process. They will differ in alignment and general finish, differ in accuracy of target and in general shooting qualities.

OUR $1.98 PRICE for the improved take down 1908 model Atlas Rifle barely covers the cost of material and labor, with but our one small percentage of profit added. This rifle is made for us under contract by one of the largest Connecticut factories. We have a contract with this factory for 200 rifles per day (60,000 rifles per year), and our contract calls for these rifles to pass a certain rigid inspection, our contract controls the quality of material that goes into the barrels, the stock and all the parts, our contract exacts a certain high standard of workmanship, and every piece and part of every finished rifle is, under our contract, compelled to pass a test and a rigid inspection, and our contract for 60,000 Atlas rifles a year (200 per day) provides also that these rifles shall cost us only the actual cost of material and labor, plus one small agreed percentage of profit to the manufacturer; therefore, after adding our one small percentage of profit, which makes a figure of $1.98 (our special price to you, $1.98), you buy a better rifle in this new 1908 Model Take Down Atlas Rifle from us than you could buy elsewhere at double the price.

FROM THIS ILLUSTRATION, engraved by our artist from a photograph, you can get a general idea of the rifling of the barrel, but you must see, examine and compare this rifle with rifles made by others and sold at prices ranging from $3.00 to $5.00 to appreciate the superiority of the 1908 Atlas over the ordinary rifles on the market. This rifle barrel is rifled by a special machine, designed by an expert mechanic on rifles, and it approaches the same fine effect, the same graduated rifling work and finish as is found on the highest grade rifles made. The result is, in the Atlas rifle you get a better target, more accurate shooting and a stronger shooting rifle than in any of the many cheap rifles on the market.

OUR BINDING GUARANTEE.

With every Atlas rifle at $1.98 we furnish a written binding guarantee, by the terms and conditions of which if any piece or part gives out by reason of defect in material or workmanship, we will replace or repair it free of charge.

OUR FREE TRIAL AND FREE TARGET PRACTICE OFFER

IN ORDER THAT YOU MAY TEST the Atlas Rifle we make you this offer: Send us $1.98 and we will send you the Atlas Rifle and we will also send you free twenty-five of our celebrated Stoll paper rifle targets. Use the Atlas Rifle for thirty days, use as many of the twenty-five targets we send you as you like, try the rifle for yourself, compare it with any rifle you can buy anywhere at two to three times the price, and if for any reason you are dissatisfied with your purchase, you can return the Atlas Rifle to us with the unused targets which we send free with the rifle, and we will immediately return your $1.98, including any express charges you may have paid.

HOW YOUNG MEN AND BOYS CAN MAKE MONEY WITH THIS RIFLE.

When you send us $1.98 for this Atlas Rifle we will send free with the rifle twenty-five of our celebrated Stoll paper or shooting gallery targets, targets made especially for galleries, shooting practice and shooting contests, as illustrated and described on this page. When you order the rifle at $1.98 you should also order at least 100 or, better still, several hundreds of our 22 short powder cartridges, which we furnish at only 21 cents per hundred, as shown on another page. When you receive the rifle take one of the twenty-five targets we furnish you free, set it up against a board or wall, or any substantial background which you may build up with boxes or boards, set the target about fifty feet from the shooting stand, then from the point that you expect to shoot place a box, a fair size dry goods box, which you can borrow, or a little platform, which you may build with a board and four stakes, or sticks will answer the purpose nicely, a common kitchen table will do very well, arrange these to suit yourself. Now while it is customary in all shooting galleries to furnish target, rifle and ammunition at the rate of from two to three shots for five cents, in order to make your effort exceedingly attractive and interesting to all the young men and boys who are old enough and grown men as well, we would suggest that you offer to furnish the ammunition, cartridges and all, at the rate of six shots for five cents, or one cent per single shot. This will be at the rate of one-half to one-third the price usually charged in shooting galleries, and you will be surprised how every one who passes your gallery will be induced to patronize you, and at the price you will find dozens will be interested, and will not only shoot six times, but will shoot several times six times, trying to better their target. Figure out how this will make money for you. Remember, you have to buy the 22 short rim fire cartridges from us at 21 cents per hundred, or five cartridges for a cent; you will sell them to your patrons through the use of the targets we furnish you free at one cent per shot or one cent for each shell, $1.00 for every hundred shots, $1.00 for every hundred shells; therefore, for every hundred shells you buy from us for 21 cents you will make 79 cents profit. It is nothing uncommon in the first day for a young man to make the cost of the rifle several times over from the little home made gallery and the outfit we furnish free.

NO. 6H664 PRICE.

$1.98

DETAILED DESCRIPTION

BARRELS—These Atlas rifle barrels are 22 inches long, and please note that you cannot get a 22-inch rifle barrel elsewhere excepting at two to four times the special $1.98 price we offer. You will observe all rifles sold at $4.00 and under have short and light barrels as compared with the Atlas. These Atlas barrels are made extra heavy, made from genuine Crystal Carbon Rifle Drill Steel, the same grade of steel as is used in the highest priced rifle barrels made; in short, one of the Atlas Rifle barrels in quality of material, in finish, boring, rifling, targeting, etc., is worth a half a dozen of the cheap target rifle barrels on the market. These barrels are especially prepared, they are extra well finished, beautifully blued. The barrels are bored to shoot 22 short caliber cartridges or BB caps, and in the boring it is rifled by the same process, with the same care, the same accuracy and finish as the boring and rifling in the most expensive rifles made. Therefore, for target shooting, target practice, for small game, such as squirrels, rabbits, birds, etc., it is the equal of any rifle made.

BB Round | BB Conical | 22 Short

These illustrations show the different sizes of 22-caliber that can be used in the Atlas model of 1908. We furnish the BB caps for 16 cents per hundred, the 22 short rim fire cartridges for 21 cents per hundred, as shown on another page.

BREECH LOADING DEVICE—The breech loading, or locking, extracting and loading mechanism is as strong and as positive as any loading and extracting mechanism made on any breech loading rifle. The lock parts being all made true to gauge, interchangeable and strong, having an exceedingly strong spring construction and a positive locking mechanism, therefore a misfire is impossible, an explosion is impossible and the breech loading mechanism is so much firmer than on any other rifle on the market at within two to three times the price, that you get a better penetration and a more accurate target. The extractor, a very ingenious device, is positive in its action and no cartridge can stick in the barrel that cannot be quickly extracted by the positive extractor device.

RAPID SHOOTING—The breech loading construction of the Atlas Rifle is such that you can load or reload with great rapidity. As soon as you become accustomed to the handling of this little breech loader you will have no desire for a repeating rifle, since it is not only one of the strongest, safest and most accurate rifles made, but by its construction is possible to load, fire and reload with wonderful rapidity.

SPECIAL FEATURES—This rifle is made with a front and rear sight, carefully gauged; has a strong trigger guard which is nicely blued and finished, has the latest Atlas lock, half and full cocked trigger and locking device.

STOCK—The stock is made of selected, full seasoned, straight grained black walnut, nicely finished, and the alignment is perfect, making it an easy gun to handle, quick at sight and accurate in the shooting.

TAKE DOWN SYSTEM—This is one of the best take down rifles made. One screw in the fore end of the stock immediately in front of the trigger guard removes and the barrel is then free from the stock.

25 STOLL TARGETS FREE

WE FURNISH YOU FREE with the Atlas Rifle at $1.98 twenty-five of these celebrated Stoll white paper rifle targets, targets that are especially suitable for indoor and outdoor practice. These are the genuine Stoll heavy white paper targets, the best paper target made, and we furnish them free only with the Atlas Take Down $1.98 Rifle. In order to get a supply of twenty-five of these Stoll paper targets free of any cost you must order the $1.98 Atlas rifle. Remember, with every order for an Atlas Rifle at $1.98 you receive enough targets to start a shooting gallery for money making, an ample supply for a thorough test.

YOU MAY SET UP A GALLERY at or near your home, or, better still, you may get permission from a friend to put up a little gallery on a vacant lot in the main part of the village or town, alongside of a store or postoffice, convenient, perhaps, to a busy corner in the village, and you may be fortunate enough to make from five to ten dollars a day from the very start, although we don't feel like holding out this sort of encouragement, and yet if you get the right location you will be surprised how busy you will be loading and unloading for your patrons. The way the cartridges will go, the rapidity with which box after box will be emptied, every box showing you a net profit of about 40 cents, will certainly surprise and please you, and on occasions, such as days when there is a picnic, fair, circus or other occasion in the town that calls together a large number of people, you will have no trouble at a good stand in taking in in a single day and showing a profit to yourself of many times the cost of the rifle and the complete target and gallery outfit that we furnish with it. The twenty-five Stoll white paper gallery or target practice targets which we furnish free with every Atlas rifle sold at $1.98 are furnished to give the young man an opportunity to make a trial of running a shooting gallery outfit at a profit. After you have set the targets up, fixed things convenient for the purpose, and you have given the work a few days' trial and you have accumulated several dollars in profit—five, ten, fifteen or twenty dollars—you may then want a more permanent target, such a target as is used in the best shooting galleries in large towns and cities.

IF YOU BUY THIS RIFLE FOR THE PURPOSE OF SETTING UP A SHOOTING GALLERY

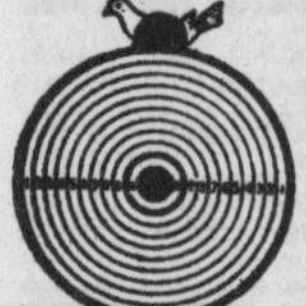

after you have accumulated a few dollars' profit and then want to get a substantial, everlasting, high grade steel target, you can order the target shown in this picture and which we furnish for $1.45 under No. 6H4541. This is a steel target, 12 inches in diameter, made extra heavy, it rings when the bull's eye is hit, the bull's eye is ½ inch or ¾ inch in diameter, as desired, the target weighs 15 pounds, and for $2.20, under No. 6H4543, we furnish the exact same target with the addition that a bird, as pictured at the left, is thrown up and the bell rings when the bull's eye is hit, after which you may reset with a rope from the shooting stand. The latter, the $2.20 target, is the one used in large shooting galleries in Chicago, New York and other large cities. Remember, the twenty-five Stoll heavy white paper targets are furnished free with the Atlas Rifle at $1.98, whether you wish to start a shooting gallery or not, whether or not you wish to devote your spare time to adding a few dollars each week to your earnings or whether you simply wish to buy the rifle for pleasure, for target shooting at home, indoors and outdoors, for hunting or for any other purpose. For whatever purpose you buy this gun you will find the twenty-five Stoll paper targets will be most convenient, and you will be sure to derive a great deal of pleasure in their use, and, remember, these twenty-five Stoll paper targets are furnished free and can be had only with the Atlas Rifle at $1.98, and with every box containing an Atlas rifle is packed at the factory twenty-five of the celebrated Stoll heavy white paper regulation targets.

BOYS AND YOUNG MEN ATTENDING SCHOOL make money by devoting their spare time nights and mornings in running home galleries, using our Acme Rifle and gallery outfit. It is used very largely for gallery work and money making by old men who have become too old for hard work. Especially is it used by people who have otherwise become incapacitated for hard work. Many bright, active, hustling young men use the Atlas Rifle, first, with our free paper targets and later with our high grade steel targets for money making, putting in all their time, going about in different towns in the county, a day or two in this town, a day or two in another town and so on, visiting and setting up their little shooting gallery outfit at picnics, fair grounds and outing places and resorts in their immediate neighborhood. While the Atlas Rifle which we furnish at $1.98, together with our target outfit, free gallery and practice proposition, is especially suited to beginners who wish to start a home or local shooting gallery, it is, of course, adapted to every purpose that a 22-caliber, accurately rifled, strong shooting rifle can be used, good for target practice, good for shooting all kinds of game that can be killed with 22-caliber ammunition, such as partridges, ducks, chickens, doves, squabs, quails, and especially for squirrels, rabbits, gophers, rats, etc., etc. **Always clean the rifle with a cleaning rod and oiled rag after every twenty-five shots.** It will shoot much better.

No. 6H664 Our special price for the rifle all complete, exactly as illustrated, breech loading, single shot, 22-caliber, 22-inch barrel; weight, 2¾ pounds.......... **$1.98**

If by mail, postage extra, 64 cents.

THE AUBREY ELABORATELY ENGRAVED.

Made in our own factory, the Meriden Fire Arms Co., Meriden, Conn., under the personal supervision of Mr. A. J. Aubrey, one of the foremost gun makers in this country.

Illustration showing the Gun Lock used in our Aubrey Double Barrel Hammerless Shotguns. You will notice it is strong and simple, having but four pieces, namely, hammer, sear, main spring and bridle.

$19.35

BORED FOR BLACK OR SMOKELESS POWDER.

Be sure to state length of barrels wanted.

FOR $19.35 in the highest grade twist or laminated steel barrel or for $22.35 in the genuine two-blade Damascus barrel, with the elaborate fine line scroll and game hand engraving on the locks, frame, guard, etc., the quality is equal to any gun made; with special finish throughout, with specially selected and elaborately finished stock and fore end, with every new and up to date high grade feature, we furnish you this genuine A. J. Aubrey Hammerless Double Barrel Breech Loading Shotgun, exactly as shown in the illustration, under our guarantee that it is in every way the equal of any hammerless double barrel breech loading shotgun you can buy elsewhere for $50.00. We will gladly accept your order and, in fact, we especially urge that you let us send you this gun to examine. We will send the gun to you with the understanding and agreement that you can use it for ten days, during which time you can put it to every test, compare it with any gun made for long range shooting, penetration, target, for mechanical construction, and if you do not find it perfectly satisfactory, the equal of any double barrel hammerless gun you could buy elsewhere for $50.00, if you do not find the bolting mechanism, the locking device and all essential parts superior to any other hammerless gun on the market, regardless of name, make or price, if you do not feel you have saved from $20.00 to $30.00 by sending your order to us, if you are not convinced you have gotten one of the highest grade double hammerless guns made, if you cannot see wherein this gun is worth double that of any of the cheaper grades of double hammerless guns on the market, you can return the gun to us at our expense and we will immediately return your money.

THIS SPECIAL, high grade, elaborately engraved A. J. Aubrey Hammerless Double Barrel Shotgun, which we furnish at $19.35 and $22.35, according to the barrels, has every late improvement, every up to date feature, is put out under our binding guarantee. We especially urge that you send us your order for this gun, enclosing the full amount of cash, and if the gun isn't perfectly satisfactory you can return it to us at our expense and we will immediately return your money. Weight, packed for shipment, about 15 pounds.

FOR FULL DESCRIPTION of bolting mechanism, of barrels, locks, frame and mechanical construction throughout, see preceding pages, or the description of the $13.85 gun. All Aubrey guns are in mechanical construction alike, and whether you buy the cheapest Aubrey double barrel gun at $13.85 or the one illustrated and described hereon at $19.35 or $22.35, or the highest grade Aubrey gun we make, the $69.00 gun, the mechanical construction, the shooting qualities, the durability are exactly the same. The difference in the price represents only the difference in the barrels, the difference in the elaborate engraving and finish, and in these more elaborately finished guns we actually furnish you from three to five times as much value for your money as you could possibly get elsewhere.

THIS GUN comes in 12-gauge only, in 30 or 32-inch barrels, the finest twist or laminated steel barrels or genuine two-blade Damascus barrels, as desired. Weight, packed for shipment, about 15 pounds.

THIS GUN is made by the Meriden Fire Arms Company, of Meriden, Conn., under the personal direction of Mr. A. J. Aubrey, maker of the highest grade shotguns made in America. It combines every new, high grade, up to date feature of every other high grade double barrel hammerless shotgun made, with the defects of none.

Cat. No.	Grade	Style Barrels	Gauge	Length of Barrels	Weight	Finish	Price
6F50	A. S. E.	Genuine Laminated Steel	12	30 or 32-in.	7¼ to 7¾ lbs.	Fine Line Scroll & Game Engraving	$19.35
6F52	D. S. E.	Genuine two Blade Damascus	12	30 or 32-in.	7¼ to 7¾ lbs.		22.35

NOTICE OUR PRICES ON AMMUNITION, especially Shotgun Shells. We beat all competitors, wholesale or retail; none can compete with us.

KNICKERBOCKER HAMMERLESS GUN, $15.50.

Made by the American Gun Co., of New York, factory in Connecticut.

12-GAUGE ONLY
Bored for Nitro or Black Powder.
Our Patent Globe Sight is FREE with this GUN.

ALIGNMENT. The Celebrated Knickerbocker Hammerless Double Barrel Shotgun, as turned out by the American Gun Co., possesses perfect alignment, in fact, the alignment is equal to that of any gun made, regardless of name, make or price.

Every minute feature has been studied with a view of producing a gun which "handles" and "hangs" nicely, which is a comfort to the shooter, a gun that makes a good pattern, has excellent shooting qualities and one which is bound to become a favorite with hunters or trap shooters.

The above illustration is engraved direct from a photograph of the gun itself by our artist and will give you some idea of its appearance, but you should see the gun and examine it and compare it with high priced guns in order to get a proper idea of the gun. We recommend this gun very highly and know that you will be pleased with it. THIS IS THE LATEST HAMMERLESS SHOTGUN ON THE MARKET. It is made from the best material that money can buy—made on fine lines, balances perfectly and is a neat, attractive and serviceable gun.

DESCRIPTION. The Knickerbocker is fitted with top snap break, laminated steel or genuine Damascus barrels, strong bar locks, beautifully matted L-shape Edwards' extension rib, double bolt locks, straight grained walnut stock and fore end handsomely checkered, Deeley & Edge patent fore end, full pistol grip capped with ornamental rosette, choke bored for close shooting; a good, sound, honest, hammerless gun. Wt., packed for shipment, about 14 lbs.

Catalogue Number	Grade	Style of Barrels	Gauge	Length of Barrels	Weight of Guns	Price
6F100	No. 7	Laminated Steel	12	30 or 32 in.	7½ to 8 lbs.	$15.50
6F102	No. 8	Genuine Damascus	12	30 or 32 in.	7½ to 8 lbs.	17.50

LOADED SHOTGUN SHELLS, $1.32 per 100. See page 164.

THE NEW FOREHAND DOUBLE BARREL HAMMER GUN.

12-GAUGE ONLY

$12.45

BORED FOR NITRO OR BLACK POWDER.

For $12.45 we offer this season the celebrated Forehand Double Barrel Hammer Gun, fitted with fine laminated steel or twist barrels, low circular hammers, patent nitro cross bolt in the extension rib which locks the gun firmly when the barrel is closed. Straight grain walnut stock and fore end nicely checkered, rebounding hammers, patent top lever, fancy butt plate, elegantly case hardened frame and lock works, choke bored for close, hard shooting; a well made, good shooting, well balanced gun and one that is bound to give satisfaction. The factory price on this gun with laminated steel or twist barrels is $19.50, but owing to a large contract which we have made for them we are able to make you a reduced price of $12.45 this season, and it is certainly a great bargain at this price. All Forehand Arms Company's product is now manufactured by Hopkins & Allen Manufacturing Company, who purchased the entire plant of the Forehand Arms Company, including patents, machinery, tools, etc., about seven years ago.

Catalogue Number	Grade	Style of Barrels	Gauge	Length of Barrels	Weight of Gun	Price
6F103	T. P.	Laminated Steel	12	30 or 32 in.	7½ to 8 lbs.	$12.45

Weight, packed for shipment, 14 pounds.

$1.32 PER 100 FOR HIGHEST GRADE LOADED SHELLS. SEE PAGE 164.

NOTICE. All our guns are tested with heavy loads and cannot burst unless by carelessness or improper loading of nitro or dense powders. Read how gun barrels burst on another page so you will avoid accidents.

ENGRAVED, SPECIALLY FINISHED HAMMERLESS GUN, $13.30 AND $15.30.

$13.30

IN OUR OWN FACTORY WE MAKE THE HIGHEST GRADE OF GUNS AND REVOLVERS AND OFFER THEM DIRECT TO OUR CUSTOMERS ON THE BASIS OF FIRST COST OF MATERIAL AND LABOR WITH BUT OUR ONE SMALL MANUFACTURING PROFIT ADDED.

YOU WILL SHARE IN OUR PROFIT if you send us an order from this department. We send you a profit sharing certificate showing the amount of your purchase for every order, and when these certificates amount to certain sums you can get various kinds of goods entirely free of charge, as explained in the first pages of this book.

HOW WE CAN MAKE THE PRICE $13.30 As explained on other pages, we own, control and operate our own gun factory, and this factory is equipped with every high grade, up to date, labor saving gun making machine, tool and device, and it is the only gun factory that runs every working day in the year at full capacity, the only gun factory with practically no overhead expense, no expense for traveling salesmen, no expense for collection, none of the big office and officers expense common to other gun factories. This is one gun factory in which practically every dollar expended goes into raw material and pay roll, the only factory where the cost of the finished gun can be figured by the cost of the original raw material and the labor.

Illustration of No. 6F106

Be Sure to State Length of Barrels Wanted.

THE HAND ENGRAVING. From the illustration you can get an idea of the beautiful scroll and floral effect worked out in this hand engraved design, a full engraving covering the sides and top of frame, top lever, the guard and the fore end connection. The hand engraving alone that we show on this gun would not be furnished by any other maker much short of an extra charge of $13.30, our price for the complete gun.

FOR $13.30 we offer this specially finished, extra well made, elaborately engraved and decorated, double barrel, hammerless breech loading, 12-gauge shotgun with laminated steel barrels, and for $15.30 we furnish it with genuine Damascus barrels, as illustrated, under our guarantee for quality, workmanship, material, finish, shooting qualities, pattern, penetration. Your money back if it isn't in every way superior to any double barrel. hammerless shotgun you can buy elsewhere at less than $20.00 to $25.00.

BARRELS. We furnish this gun either in genuine laminated steel or twist barrels for $13.30, or in extra high grade two-blade Damascus steel barrels for $15.30. We would especially recommend that in selecting one of our guns that you select the highest grade double barrel breech loading shotgun we make, the specially finished, hand engraved gun with the genuine two-blade Damascus steel barrels at $15.30. You will find it such a gun as you could not buy elsewhere at less than $30.00 to $40.00. Our barrels are all especially well made, they are made from the highest grade barrel steel. They are bored true to gauge, they are taper choke bored by the celebrated taper system, they have an especially finished, shaped, trued and matted rib; they are accurately sighted, made for extra long and extra hard shooting. They are all 12-gauge and will take 12-gauge shells only. They are made with extra long, heavy, full extension rib; have the latest patent shell extractor and extra strong lug.

FRAME. The frames are made from the best quality steel. They are beautifully mottled and finished, they are elaborately engraved by hand, as shown in the illustration, fitted with a top snap break, and with patent safety.

ACTION. The action includes the locking, cocking, safety double lever, the sears, triggers and main spring of the mechanism, and we say, without fear of contradiction, that in this we have the simplest, strongest, safest action, less liable to get out of order, than any other gun action made.

STOCK. The stocks are made of carefully selected walnut, beautifully finished, fancy checkered pistol grip and fore end, fancy butt plate. At our special price of $13.30 for twist barrel, $15.30 for two-blade Damascus barrel, we furnish the gun complete under our binding guarantee. We guarantee the gun to reach you in the same perfect condition it leaves us, and if there is a defect of any kind, or if the gun doesn't prove perfectly satisfactory, return it to us at our expense and we will immediately return your money. This gun is the same identical gun as described on the following page, the Chicago Long Range Wonder, except it is highly engraved by hand and highly finished, otherwise, in general detail, it is the same.

Catalogue Number	Grade	Style of Barrels	Gauge	Length of Barrels	Weight of Guns	Finish	Price
6F104	T. E.	Laminated Steel	12	30 or 32 in.	7¾ to 8 lbs.	Engrav'd	$13.30
6F106	D. E.	Two-Blade Damascus	12	30 or 32 in.	7¾ to 8 lbs.		15.30

Weight, packed for shipment, about 14 pounds.

OUR STRICTLY AMERICAN HAMMERLESS SHOTGUN. THIS GUN IS KNOWN AS THE BOX FRAME SHOTGUN.

AT $9.95 WITH ARMORY STEEL IT IS THE WORLD'S WONDER.

$9.95 buys the now justly celebrated, high grade, 12-gauge, Chicago Long Range Wonder, Double Barrel Breech Loading Hammerless Shotgun, with Armory Steel Barrels, a double barrel hammerless gun, which in gun making is indeed the "World's Wonder."

OUR OWN PATENT GLOBE SIGHT FURNISHED FREE WITH THIS SHOTGUN.

OUR GLOBE SIGHT is a wonderful invention, for it makes possible more accurate and far more rapid wing shooting than would otherwise be possible. Can be quickly put on or taken off from any gun. When aimed at a bird on the wing (flying ever so fast) it defines a big circle, and when the bird appears within that circle (as it will even if you are a poor shot) pull the trigger and you kill the bird every time. THIS SIGHT DOUBLES THE VALUE OF ANY SHOTGUN, but we furnish it free with this gun and all other shotguns.

YOU CANNOT ESTIMATE THE VALUE OF OUR PATENT GLOBE SIGHT.

Don't Buy a Gun Without It.

HOW A $9.95 PRICE IS MADE POSSIBLE.

The manager of our gun department being convinced that high grade hammerless shotguns, such as are usually offered, were being sold at prices unreasonably high, conceived the idea of establishing a strictly up to date modernized gun factory of our own, where a high grade gun, embodying all the good points of other high grade guns could be made and offered to our customers at a price that would barely cover the cost to make and leave us our one small percentage of profit. To accomplish this we secured as manager of our gun factory one of the best gun makers in America, a gentleman who has for years been in charge of several of the best gun and revolver factories in this country. We also secured the services of a number of expert gun machinists, gun and gun tool makers. These gentlemen, in charge, selected and had built for our factory the very highest types of gun making machinery, machines built with marked improvements of their own over the machines employed by other gun factories. Ample time was taken for the making of all special tools, dies, patterns, jigs, chucks, gauges, etc., everything essential to the accurate making and finishing of every part of the gun was completed and perfected before any start was made to get out guns. All this machinery, all necessary tools and appliances were perfectly placed in one of the most modern gun plants in this country. A competent corps of selected mechanics, the best men picked from the best factories, where they had formerly been in charge, were engaged and detailed to take charge of, operate and make the different parts that go into our **$9.95 LONG RANGE WONDER** so that when the factory was opened for the production of the Long Range Wonder, every piece came out with a nicety and perfectness of shape and finish to be found only on the highest grades of guns made, a gun with a general outline, weight, shape, proportion, dimensions, style, finish, fit, strength, durability, long and hard range shooting, simplicity of action such as can be equaled only by the most expensive guns on the market.

$9.95

ABOUT THE SAFETY OF HAMMERLESS GUNS.

Many hunters who have always used hammer guns are under the impression that hammerless guns are dangerous. We would like to say in regard to this, that hammerless guns are just as safe as hammer guns, in fact they may be considered safer for it is possible to lock a hammerless gun by the safety slide so that it is absolutely impossible to pull off the hammers, whereas with a hammer gun it has often happened that when the hammer was at half cock, something coming in contact with the hammer has discharged a shell accidently. This is not possible with a hammerless gun, for the hammer is concealed within the frame, and it is impossible for it to come in contact with anything. Remember every time you open a hammerless gun you cock it and it is ready to shoot.

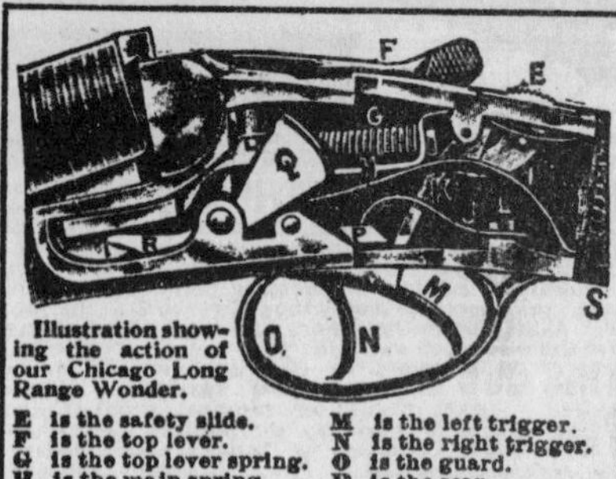

Illustration showing the action of our Chicago Long Range Wonder.

E is the safety slide.
F is the top lever.
G is the top lever spring.
H is the main spring.
I is the safety guide.
K is the safety rocker.
J is the sear spring.
L is the trigger spring screw.
M is the left trigger.
N is the right trigger.
O is the guard.
P is the sear.
Q is the hammer.
R is the cocking lever.
S is the stock.

DETAILED DESCRIPTION.

BARRELS. We furnish this gun with either blued steel at $9.95, genuine twist or laminated steel barrels at $10.45, or genuine Damascus barrels at $13.80, as desired.

THE TWIST OR LAMINATED STEEL BARRELS we use in these guns are the highest grade of genuine laminated steel, and should not be compared with the many imitations and so called laminated steel barrels that are not safe for high explosive powders. Our barrels are made for the highest explosive gun powders used, such as white or nitro powder. The Damascus barrels are extra high grade, beautifully finished. The method of making Damascus barrels is illustrated and described on another page. These barrels are all beautifully browned and given an extra high finish. They are the highest strength barrels of the kind made, and are made with handsome heavy matted rib, tapering from breech to muzzle, as found only on the most expensive guns made. The matting is especially fine, of neat design. The rib is extra heavy and beautifully finished. The barrels are made with a strong Edwards extension rib. They are taper choke bored, by the celebrated Taper system, to insure the strongest long range shooting qualities, the best possible target, the highest possible penetration, and being made in the proper proportion of heft at the butt, the minimum of recoil is obtained. The barrels are flatted at the breech with a genuine flat water table, found only on the most expensive guns made. They have a very heavy self locking steel lug, the strongest fore end lug used on any gun made.

FRAME. The frame is made of the best quality steel, case hardened beautifully mottled and finished. It is thoroughly machined and accurately fitted, and made especially strong at the points where the recoil acts in order to insure perfect safety. In design it is one of the handsomest hammerless shotgun frames made, smooth, symmetrical, strong at every part, perfect fitting and highly polished.

ACTION. This includes the locking, cocking safety double lever, the concealed hammers, sears, triggers and main spring of the mechanism with which the gun is operated, and these parts are made from the very best material procurable. Positive, accurate, yet simple in construction, made interchangeable so that if the parts should break (which rarely happens) they can be immediately replaced at a very slight expense. The action will, in simplicity of construction, strength, durability, in finish and every essential feature, compare favorably with the action furnished on the highest priced hammerless shotguns made.

STOCK. The stock is handsomely shaped, pistol grip, handsomely checkered in a neat design, fancy checkered butt plate. The stock is made from carefully seasoned selected walnut, hand finished and hand polished, and fitted to the gun by one of the best gun stock fitters in the country.

FORE END. The fore end is made from carefully selected walnut, handsomely finished and polished, beautifully checkered in a neat design, made with a special patent spring fastener.

SAFETY. We offer in our $9.95 Long Range Wonder Hammerless Gun one of the best safety devices used on any gun. It is positive and automatic in its action and renders an accident next to impossible, as the gun always stands on safe when loaded, unless pushed forward ready to shoot. Standing on safe the triggers are locked and the gun cannot be discharged. By a very ingenious mechanical device, we feel we have the best automatic safety made.

GENERAL FINISH. This gun is not only honestly built from the best material procurable, by skilled makers, but in finish you will find it has none of the ear marks of cheapness common to hammerless guns that sell for from $20.00 to $30.00, on the contrary, in finish it is given all the appearance of a high priced hammerless gun such as sells at $30.00 and upwards. The beautiful browning effected on the barrel, the case hardening of the frame and trigger guards, bringing out a clear handsome mottled effect unequaled by any other maker; the high finish given to stock and fore end, the artistically finished checkering, the taper extension rib (a special mark of high grade) and the generally well proportioned outlines of the gun throughout gives you in this gun at $9.95 all the show and style, as well as all the essential features, everything that you would get in a hammerless shotgun that cost three times the money.

SHOOTING QUALITIES. This all essential point has been the foundation from which the manufacturer has built this gun up, to furnish a gun that would not shoot loose, that would be the equal of any gun made for durability and a gun that could be relied upon for close, hard shooting at long range, and one in which white or nitro powder could be used as safely as the regular black powder. This gun has been built on lines to insure all this in the highest degree. The barrels are made gauged and bored (choke bored by the celebrated Taper system) to effect the best possible target, the longest range that it is possible for white or black powder to throw shot, and no matter what make or what price you may pay for a gun you will get no gun that will shoot stronger or better.

WEIGHT, LENGTH, GAUGE, ETC. These guns are **MADE IN 12-GAUGE ONLY.** They can be furnished in no other gauge. They are made in 30 or 32-inch barrels as desired, and can be furnished in weights ranging from 7¾ to 8 pounds, as desired. In ordering, be sure to state length of barrel and weight wanted.

ABOUT BROKEN PARTS OR REPAIRS. While this gun is built with a view of making repairs or replacements unnecessary, in case by accident or otherwise, any piece or part should get broken or lost, we wish to say that from our factory we can at any time to come furnish at a comparatively small expense to the purchaser any piece or part to replace any part that may break or get lost. This should be quite an object to the purchaser of a gun, for it may mean the saving to you of quite an expense at some future date.

AN ALL PURPOSE GUN. We are manufacturing this gun to meet the general demand throughout the country for a thoroughly reliable, high grade hammerless all purpose double barrel breech loading shotgun, and it is suitable for all kinds of game that can be hunted with any shotgun—geese, ducks, prairie chickens, partridges, squirrels, quails, snipe, rabbits—in fact it is an all around general purpose, high grade, up to date guaranteed, double barrel, hammerless, breech loading shotgun.

We make the price, $9.95, a very small percentage above the actual cost to produce in our own factory, the cost of material and labor, for we must depend upon our customers, upon the illustrations and descriptions given on this page to consume the entire output of our factory.

AT $9.95

we know we are offering a hammerless gun with genuine Armory steel barrels that once seen, you would have no other. If you are about to select a cheap foreign made gun at $10.00 to $20.00, a single barrel gun at $5.00 to $15.00 or a high priced gun at $30.00 to $50.00, and could first see our Hammerless Long Range Wonder at $9.95, you would instantly accept this gun in preference to any other gun made.

BUILT IN OUR OWN FACTORY

under the direct supervision of one of the most skilled gun makers in America, utilizing the highest types of automatic gun making machinery, buying only the highest grades of raw gun material, we produce the finished hammerless, double barrel shotgun as illustrated, at a net shop or factory cost that enables us to undersell almost any other maker by half, and quote the astonishingly low price of $9.95.

THE $9.95 LONG RANGE WONDER, with genuine Armory steel barrels, is a hammerless gun that must be seen to be appreciated, a gun that is seldom equaled even by the most expensive guns, in its perfect proportion, in its beautiful case hardened finish, in all those lines so much appreciated by the lover of a fine hammerless shotgun.

EXAMINE OTHER CATALOGUES. Ask your dealer for prices on double barrel hammerless shotguns and you will find no one can quote within 25 to 50 per cent of our prices, gun for gun and quality for quality, besides every gun goes out under our binding guarantee for quality, and if you do not find it the greatest gun value you have ever seen, return it to us at our expense of transportation charges both ways and we will return your money.

THIS ILLUSTRATION, which is engraved from a photograph taken direct from our $10.45 Chicago Long Range Wonder, which is exactly the same as the $9.95 gun, except it has laminated steel barrels instead of Armory steel, and will give you some idea of the appearance of this handsome gun, but it must be seen and compared with other hammerless shotguns to appreciate the value we are giving.

Illustration of No. 6F112½

$1.32 PER 100 BUYS HIGHEST GRADE BLACK POWDER LOADED SHELLS MADE. See Page 164.

ORDER BY CATALOGUE NUMBER IN FULL AND BE SURE TO STATE LENGTH OF BARRELS WANTED.

Catalogue No.	Grade	Style of Barrels	Gauge	Length of Barrels	Weight of Gun	Price
6F110½	C.L.W.	Armory Steel	12	30 or 32 in.	7¾ to 8 lbs.	$9.95
6F112½	C.L.W.	Laminated Steel	12	30 or 32 in.	7¾ to 8 lbs.	10.45
6F114½	C.L.W.	2-Blade Damascus	12	30 or 32 in.	7¾ to 8 lbs.	13.80

Weight, packed for shipment, about 14 pounds.

We have at present a capacity of about 40 guns a day, or 12,000 a year, and to insure our selling every gun we make, we have really made the price ridiculously low, namely, $9.95. Understand, you send us your order, we taking all the risk, guaranteeing the gun to you in every respect, guaranteeing it to reach you in the same perfect condition it leaves us, and further, if not found perfectly satisfactory to you, to be returned to us at our expense of transportation charges both ways, we to return your money at once.

THE NEW AMERICAN MADE DOUBLE BARREL BREECH LOADER, $11.89.

MADE IN 12-GAUGE ONLY.

THIS GUN HAS GENUINE TWO-BLADE DAMASCUS BARRELS AND IS STRICTLY OF AMERICAN MAKE.

Manufactured by the American Gun Co., New York.

30 OR 32-INCH BARRELS.

$11.89

Loaded Shells, $1.32 per 100. See page 164.

GENERAL DESCRIPTION of our $11.89 New American Double Barrel Breech Loader. It is fitted with genuine two-blade Damascus barrels, the celebrated Crescent top snap break, strong steel bar rebounding locks, with hardened parts well made and well fitted, rebounding circular hammers, Crescent style extension rib beautifully engine turned and matted, straight grained and well seasoned walnut stock and fore end handsomely checkered, full pistol grip with ornamental rosette, double bolt locks for locking the barrel to the frame, nitro firing pins, flat top rib, left barrel full choke bored and right barrel modified choke for field shooting, all barrels bored smooth and true to gauge for black or smokeless powder, frame and lock plates of best steel and beautifully case hardened, and the lock plates hand engraved with chased line engraving, fitted with Deeley & Edge patent fore end. Order by catalogue number and state length of barrel wanted.

All are fitted with Deeley & Edge fore end.

Our GLOBE SIGHT sent Free with this Gun.

NOTICE—The lock parts of these guns are hardened. The screws and top lever parts, also the lock parts and hammers, being made by machinery, are practically interchangeable. Remember, a Profit Sharing Certificate is yours, when you order this Gun.

Catalogue No.	Grade	Style of Barrels	Gauge	Length of Barrels	Weight, pounds	Price
6F343	No. 3	Genuine Damascus	12	30 or 32 in.	7¾ to 8	$11.89

Weight, packed for shipment, about 14 pounds.

THE BARRELS on these guns are all genuine Damascus, and not imitation Damascus as sold by some houses. We guarantee them just as represented or money refunded. No other house will give you such a guarantee on a gun at the price which we offer you this gun, and it is certainly the best value offered by any house in the United States. Each gun is made and bored to shoot any proper load of black, white or nitro powder.

OUR SPECIAL HIGH GRADE, HAND ENGRAVED, AMERICAN DOUBLE GUN WHICH WE QUOTE AT $12.98.

MANUFACTURED BY THE AMERICAN GUN CO., NEW YORK.

WE KNOW IN OUR HIGH GRADE AMERICAN GUNS we are offering such value as was never before offered, such guns as you could not get elsewhere at less than double the price. We know you would be so well pleased with any one of these guns you order that you would show it to your friends, recommend our house and we will be sure to receive more orders from your neighborhood.

THE GUN IS MADE OF THE VERY BEST MATERIAL THROUGHOUT. It has a strong steel frame, beautifully case hardened steel parts and locks. Every part in this gun is machine made and interchangeable.

BORED FOR NITRO POWDER.

OUR GLOBE SIGHT IS SENT FREE WITH THIS GUN.

DETAILED DESCRIPTION of our $12.98 New American Double Barrel Breech Leader. It is fitted with genuine laminated steel barrels, celebrated Crescent top snap break, strong bar rebounding locks with hardened parts well made and well fitted. Crescent style extension rib, engine turned and handsomely matted, rebounding shapely circular hammers, straight grained and well seasoned walnut stock and fore end handsomely checkered, full pistol grip with ornamental rosette, double bolt locks (the strongest made, and seldom found on guns at this price), nitro firing pins, flat top rib, left barrel full choke bored and right barrel modified choke bored for field shooting, all barrels bored smooth and true to gauge for black or smokeless powder. The frame, locks, guard and fore end iron are handsomely hand engraved; the design is laid out in scroll pattern, and this gun is fitted with the celebrated Deeley & Edge patent fore end, as shown in illustration. Order by number and state length of barrel wanted.

No. 6F344

The above illustration shows our NEW, HIGH GRADE, HAND ENGRAVED, DOUBLE BARREL BREECH LOADING SHOTGUN; our special $12.98 American made gun.

THE BARRELS on these guns are all genuine laminated steel and not imitation laminated steel as sold by some houses. We guarantee them just as represented or money refunded.

NO OTHER HOUSE will give you such a guarantee on a gun at the price which we offer you this gun, and it is certainly the best value gun offered by any house in the United States.

THIS GUN IS HANDSOMELY HAND ENGRAVED and decorated; it is a gun the equal of American guns that sell everywhere at double the price; there is no better shooting or stronger gun made at any price. ALWAYS STATE LENGTH OF BARREL WANTED.

Catalogue No.	Grade	Style of Barrels	Gauge	Length of Barrels, inches	Weight, pounds	Price
6F344	No. 4	Laminated Steel	12	30 or 32	7¾ to 8	$12.98

Weight, packed for shipment, about 14 pounds.

OUR REMINGTON AUTOMATIC SELF LOADING MAGAZINE SHOTGUN, $28.75.

FOR $28.75 we will furnish you this standard Remington Automatic Loading and Automatic Cocking Single Barrel Magazine Shotgun, manufactured by the celebrated Remington Arms Co., of Ilion, N. Y., one of the oldest manufacturers of firearms in the United States, a company whose guarantee goes out with every gun and rifle which it makes, a company which is well known to all hunters, trap shooters and sportsmen as well as all governments of the world. They have not only made firearms for the hunter and trap shooter, but they have made rifles for a great many foreign governments, and have made thousands of rifles and revolvers for the United States Government during the Civil War. This $28.75 Remington Automatic Shotgun is the latest creation in firearms. The gun was invented by Mr. Browning, of Ogden, Utah, and is now being made exclusively by the Remington Arms Co., under the Browning patents for the United States trade. This $28.75 Remington Automatic Self Loading, Self Cocking Shotgun is exactly as its description implies. It is a 5-shot self loading shotgun. You place four loaded shells in the magazine and one in the chamber, then press the little button on the right hand side and the breech block closes. After you fire your first shot, the recoil of the shell opens the breech block, throws out the empty shell, places a new shell in the chamber from the magazine and closes the breech block, and all you have to do is to pull the trigger each time you fire a shot. When the last shell leaves the magazine and is fired, the breech block remains open, which tells you that there are no more shells in the magazine.

OUR $28.75 Remington Automatic Self Loading and Self Cocking Magazine Single Barrel Shotgun is fitted with well seasoned, straight grained, pistol grip, imported walnut stock, and the fore end is made of the same quality walnut. The frame is finished in a military blue of the very best quality workmanship, is bored and machined out of a solid bar of extra quality of steel and is beautifully matted on the top to guide the eye to the front sight. The barrel is of standard length, which is, in this gun, 28 inches long, beautifully tapered from the breech to the muzzle, giving the most metal at the breech; choke bored on the celebrated Remington system, and the gun weighs about 7¾ pounds. It is fitted with a patent safety device in front of the trigger, so that the trigger can be locked or unlocked instantly, as the shooter may desire. We predict a large sale for these guns, and for rapid shooting at the trap or in the field they have no equal, since you can shoot as fast as you can pull the trigger.

No. 6F349 Our No. 1 Grade Remington Automatic Self Loading Shotgun is made in 12-gauge only, 28-inch barrel, weight about 7¾ pounds, 5-shot; factory price, $40.00. Our price $28.75

Weight, packed for shipment, about 14 pounds.

HOW DAMASCUS GUN BARRELS ARE MADE.

The above illustration shows, as near as possible, how the Damascus gun barrels are made. The three strips, A, B and C, each consist of from 40 to 60 layers of iron and steel welded together into one square strip, then they are twisted (D) while hot and rewelded into one strip about ⅝-inch wide, and ⅛-inch thick: the object being that if any one of these numerous layers of iron or steel has a flaw, the welding process entirely eliminates the flaw. After these numerous layers of iron and steel are twisted and rewelded into one strip, the strip is twisted around a mandrel and welded together as shown in the illustration. These barrels are all hand made by skilled mechanics who have spent years in learning this art. They cannot be made by machinery. When a barrel is made from three strips it is called three-blade Damascus, when made from two strips it is called two-blade Damascus, and when make from one strip it is called twist or laminated steel. The more strips used in making the barrel, the finer is the figure of the barrel, and the more costly to make.

OUR BELGIAN MUZZLE LOADING DOUBLE BARREL SHOTGUN, WITH POWDER FLASK AND SHOT BELT, FOR ONLY

$3.15

We have just bought at a forced sale for cash a large quantity of these Belgian bar lock muzzle loading double barrel shotguns, fitted with imitation wire twist barrels, genuine (not imitation) patent breech, bar side plate locks, stained and varnished stock, metal butt plate, wood ramrod with brass tip and reversed wormer. The locks on these muzzle loading guns are what is known as the hook locks, which, by being removed occasionally and adding a drop of oil to the tumbler, will make them last a long time. As above stated, we have bought these guns at a forced sale for cash, and they are guns that could not be imported for less than $4.50 to $5.00, but in offering these guns we do it the same as we do all other merchandise, based on the cost to us with our narrow small margin of profit added.

SIZES. The sizes vary, 12, 14 or 16 gauge in bore, and 30 to 32-inch in barrel and 6½ to 7¾ pounds in weight. When ordering state length, gauge and weight wanted.

No. 6F350 Our Special Belgian Bar Lock Muzzle Loading Double Gun, with Powder Flask and Shot Belt. Price $3.15

State size wanted. Weight, packed for shipment, about 12 pounds.

OUR BELGIAN MUZZLE LOADING DOUBLE BARREL SHOTGUN, WITH POWDER FLASK AND SHOT BELT, ONLY

$6.95

No. 6F367

These guns are imported direct from Belgium, and all have the Belgian Government test same as our breech loaders.

Our Bar Lock Gun has genuine patent breech, genuine twist barrels, case hardened bar lock plates, checkered pistol grip stock, wood ramrod, German silver escutcheons, iron butt plate, case hardened and blued mountings. This illustration is made from a photograph of the gun and is an exact copy. With each gun we give free, one Powder Flask and one Leather Shot Belt. These guns are made in 12 and 14-gauge, 34-inch barrels and weigh 7½ to 8 pounds.

No. 6F367 The Gun, a Powder Flask and a Shot Belt (three articles). Mention length and gauge wanted. Price $6.95

Weight, packed for shipment, about 13 pounds.

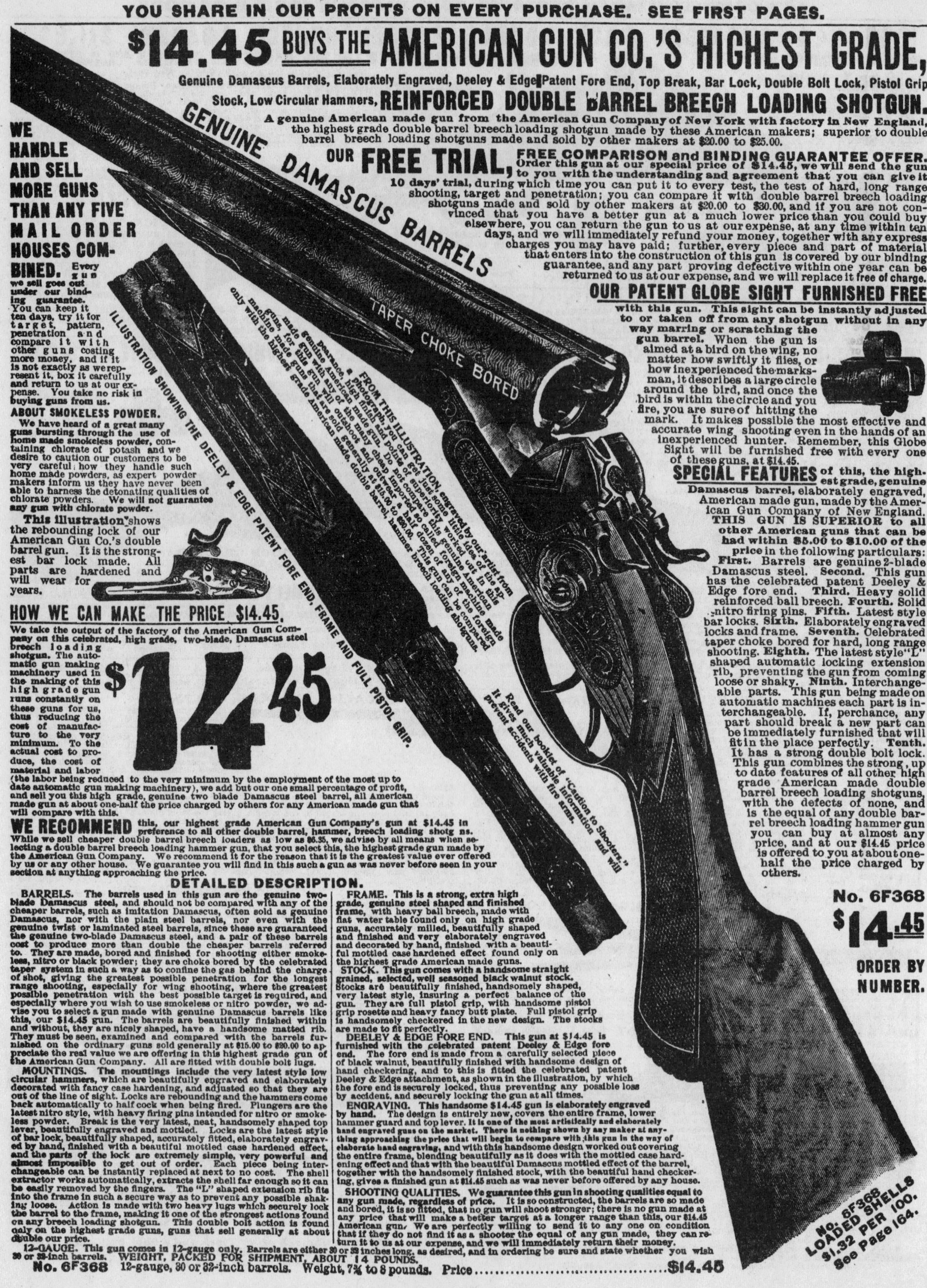

$14.45 BUYS THE AMERICAN GUN CO.'S HIGHEST GRADE,

Genuine Damascus Barrels, Elaborately Engraved, Deeley & Edge Patent Fore End, Top Break, Bar Lock, Double Bolt Lock, Pistol Grip Stock, Low Circular Hammers, **REINFORCED DOUBLE BARREL BREECH LOADING SHOTGUN.**

A genuine American made gun from the American Gun Company of New York with factory in New England, the highest grade double barrel breech loading shotgun made by these American makers; superior to double barrel breech loading shotguns made and sold by other makers at $20.00 to $25.00.

OUR FREE TRIAL, FREE COMPARISON and BINDING GUARANTEE OFFER. Order this gun at our special price of $14.45, we will send the gun to you with the understanding and agreement that you can give it 10 days' trial, during which time you can put it to every test, the test of hard, long range shooting, target and penetration; you can compare it with double barrel breech loading shotguns made and sold by other makers at $20.00 to $30.00, and if you are not convinced that you have a better gun at a much lower price than you could buy elsewhere, you can return the gun to us at our expense, at any time within ten days, and we will immediately refund your money, together with any express charges you may have paid; further, every piece and part of material that enters into the construction of this gun is covered by our binding guarantee, and any part proving defective within one year can be returned to us at our expense, and we will replace it free of charge.

WE HANDLE AND SELL MORE GUNS THAN ANY FIVE MAIL ORDER HOUSES COMBINED. Every gun we sell goes out under our binding guarantee. You can keep it ten days, try it for target, pattern, penetration and compare it with other guns costing more money, and if it is not exactly as we represent it, box it carefully and return to us at our expense. You take no risk in buying guns from us.

ABOUT SMOKELESS POWDER.

We have heard of a great many guns bursting through the use of home made smokeless powder, containing chlorate of potash and we desire to caution our customers to be very careful how they handle such home made powders, as expert powder makers inform us they have never been able to harness the detonating qualities of chlorate powders. We will not guarantee any gun with chlorate powder.

This illustration shows the rebounding lock of our American Gun Co.'s double barrel gun. It is the strongest bar lock made. All parts are hardened and will wear for years.

HOW WE CAN MAKE THE PRICE $14.45.

We take the output of the factory of the American Gun Company on this celebrated, high grade, two-blade, Damascus steel breech loading shotgun. The automatic gun making machinery used in the making of this high grade gun runs constantly on these guns for us, thus reducing the cost of manufacture to the very minimum. To the actual cost to produce, the cost of material and labor (the labor being reduced to the very minimum by the employment of the most up to date automatic gun making machinery), we add but our one small percentage of profit, and sell you this high grade, genuine two blade Damascus steel barrel, all American made gun at about one-half the price charged by others for any American made gun that will compare with this.

$14.45

OUR PATENT GLOBE SIGHT FURNISHED FREE

with this gun. This sight can be instantly adjusted to or taken off from any shotgun without in any way marring or scratching the gun barrel. When the gun is aimed at a bird on the wing, no matter how swiftly it flies, or how inexperienced the marksman, it describes a large circle around the bird, and once the bird is within the circle and you fire, you are sure of hitting the mark. It makes possible the most effective and accurate wing shooting even in the hands of an inexperienced hunter. Remember, this Globe Sight will be furnished free with every one of these guns, at $14.45.

SPECIAL FEATURES of this, the highest grade, genuine Damascus barrel, elaborately engraved, American made gun, made by the American Gun Company of New England. **THIS GUN IS SUPERIOR to all other American guns that can be had within $5.00 to $10.00 of the price in the following particulars: First.** Barrels are genuine 2-blade Damascus steel. **Second.** This gun has the celebrated patent Deeley & Edge fore end. **Third.** Heavy solid reinforced ball breech. **Fourth.** Solid nitro firing pins. **Fifth.** Latest style bar locks. **Sixth.** Elaborately engraved locks and frame. **Seventh.** Celebrated taper choke bored for hard, long range shooting. **Eighth.** The latest style "L" shaped automatic locking extension rib, preventing the gun from coming loose or shaky. **Ninth.** Interchangeable parts. This gun being made on automatic machines each part is interchangeable. If, perchance, any part should break a new part can be immediately furnished that will fit in the place perfectly. **Tenth.** It has a strong double bolt lock. This gun combines the strong, up to date features of all other high grade American made double barrel breech loading shotguns, with the defects of none, and is the equal of any double barrel breech loading hammer gun you can buy at almost any price, and at our $14.45 price is offered to you at about one-half the price charged by others.

No. 6F368
$14.45
ORDER BY NUMBER.

WE RECOMMEND this, our highest grade American Gun Company's gun at $14.45 in preference to all other double barrel, hammer, breech loading shotg ns. While we sell cheaper double barrel breech loaders as low as $6.35, we advise by all means when selecting a double barrel breech loading hammer gun, that you select this, the highest grade gun made by the American Gun Company. We recommend it for the reason that it is the greatest value ever offered by us or any other house. We guarantee you will find in this such a gun as was never before seen in your section at anything approaching the price.

DETAILED DESCRIPTION.

BARRELS. The barrels used in this gun are the genuine two-blade Damascus steel, and should not be compared with any of the cheaper barrels, such as imitation Damascus, often sold as genuine Damascus, nor with the plain steel barrels, nor even with the genuine twist or laminated steel barrels, since these are guaranteed the genuine two-blade Damascus steel, and a pair of these barrels cost to produce more than double the cheaper barrels referred to. They are made, bored and finished for shooting either smokeless, nitro or black powder; they are choke bored by the celebrated taper system in such a way as to confine the gas behind the charge of shot, giving the greatest possible penetration for the longest range shooting, especially for wing shooting, where the greatest possible penetration with the best possible target is required, and especially where you wish to use smokeless or nitro powder, we advise you to select a gun made with genuine Damascus barrels like this, our $14.45 gun. The barrels are beautifully finished within and without, they are nicely shaped, have a handsome matted rib. They must be seen, examined and compared with the barrels furnished on the ordinary guns sold generally at $15.00 to $20.00 to appreciate the real value we are offering in this highest grade gun of the American Gun Company. All are fitted with double bolt lugs.

MOUNTINGS. The mountings include the very latest style low circular hammers, which are beautifully engraved and elaborately decorated with fancy case hardening, and adjusted so that they are out of the line of sight. Locks are rebounding and the hammers come back automatically to half cock when being fired. Plungers are the latest nitro style, with heavy firing pins intended for nitro or smokeless powder. Break is the very latest, neat, handsomely shaped top lever, beautifully engraved and mottled. Locks are the latest style of bar lock, beautifully shaped, accurately fitted, elaborately engraved by hand, finished with a beautiful mottled case hardened effect, and the parts of the lock are extremely simple, very powerful and almost impossible to get out of order. Each piece being interchangeable can be instantly replaced at next to no cost. The shell extractor works automatically, extracts the shell far enough so it can be easily removed by the fingers. The "L" shaped extension rib fits into the frame in such a secure way as to prevent any possible shaking loose. Action is made with two heavy lugs which securely lock the barrel to the frame, making it one of the strongest actions found on any breech loading shotgun. This double bolt action is found only on the highest grade guns, guns that sell generally at about double our price.

FRAME. This is a strong, extra high grade, genuine steel shaped and finished frame, with heavy ball breech, made with flat water table found only on high grade guns, accurately milled, beautifully shaped and finished and very elaborately engraved and decorated by hand, finished with a beautiful mottled case hardened effect found only on the highest grade American made guns.

STOCK. This gun comes with a handsome straight grained, selected, well seasoned black walnut stock. Stocks are beautifully finished, handsomely shaped, very latest style, insuring a perfect balance of the gun. They are full pistol grip, with handsome pistol grip rosette and heavy fancy butt plate. Full pistol grip is handsomely checkered in the new design. The stocks are made to fit perfectly.

DEELEY & EDGE FORE END. This gun at $14.45 is furnished with the celebrated patent Deeley & Edge fore end. The fore end is made from a carefully selected piece of black walnut, beautifully finished with handsome design of hand checkering, and to this is fitted the celebrated patent Deeley & Edge attachment, as shown in the illustration, by which the fore end is securely locked, thus preventing any possible loss by accident, and securely locking the gun at all times.

ENGRAVING. This handsome $14.45 gun is elaborately engraved by hand. The design is entirely new, covers the entire frame, lower hammer guard and top lever. It is one of the most artistically and elaborately hand engraved guns on the market. There is nothing shown by any maker at anything approaching the price that will begin to compare with this gun in the way of elaborate hand engraving, and with this handsome design worked out covering the entire frame, blending beautifully as it does with the mottled case hardening effect and that with the beautiful Damascus mottled effect of the barrel, together with the handsomely finished stock, with the beautiful hand checkering, gives a finished gun at $14.45 such as was never before offered by any house.

SHOOTING QUALITIES. We guarantee this gun in shooting qualities equal to any gun made, regardless of price. It is so constructed, the barrels are so made and bored, it is so fitted, that no gun will shoot stronger; there is no gun made at any price that will make a better target at a longer range than this, our $14.45 American gun. We are perfectly willing to send it to any one on condition that if they do not find it as a shooter the equal of any gun made, they can return it to us at our expense, and we will immediately return their money.

12-GAUGE. This gun comes in 12-gauge only. Barrels are either 30 or 32 inches long, as desired, and in ordering be sure and state whether you wish 30 or 32-inch barrels. WEIGHT, PACKED FOR SHIPMENT, ABOUT 14 POUNDS.

No. 6F368 12-gauge, 30 or 32-inch barrels. Weight, 7¾ to 8 pounds. Price **$14.45**

SEE INDEX, PINK PAGES 598 TO 607, TO FIND WHAT YOU WANT.

THE IMPROVED NEW MODEL WHITE POWDER WONDER

$3.64

AN AUTOMATIC SHELL EJECTING SINGLE BARREL BREECH LOADING SHOTGUN, AS ILLUSTRATED AND DESCRIBED HEREON, COMPLETE WITH OUR GLOBE SIGHT, AS ALSO ILLUSTRATED HEREON, IS NOW OFFERED FOR ONLY $3.64.

THE NEW IMPROVED WHITE POWDER WONDER as offered on this page, is now made for us under contract by a New England maker, made on the general lines of our $2.59 and $2.89 single barrel guns shown on another page, but a better gun throughout, a better quality of barrel and a general improvement in gunsmith making from beginning to end, and our $3.64 price barely covers the cost to us, with but our one small percentage of profit added.

$7.00 was the old price of the White Powder Wonder. We afterwards were able to reduce the price to $4.40, but now and under our latest contract we can offer the new model gun, with a number of improvements, as furnished us by the famous New England gun maker for only $3.64. If you want to buy a good single barrel shotgun at a low price, and you want something a little better, stronger, safer, better made and better finished than the ordinary single barrel shotgun that is being sold generally at retail at $5.00 to $7.00 and $8.00, it will certainly pay you to accept the following liberal offer, a liberal offer on this, our New Model White Powder Wonder Gun which we offer at $3.64.

GENUINE ARMORY STEEL

CHOKE BORED

NEW WHITE POWDER WONDER

OUR OFFER

SEND US $3.64, say whether you wish the barrel 30 or 32 inches long, we will send this gun to you and include with it free our removable globe sight, as illustrated hereon, you can examine the gun and use it for ten days, compare it with other guns that you can buy at within several dollars of our price, and if you are not perfectly satisfied with your purchase, you can return the gun to us at our expense, and we will immediately return your money together with any express charges you may have paid.

IN CONTRACTING with the New England Gun Company for this gun, we have asked them to get away from the more common guns and to use a higher grade of steel in the barrel, to give us a stronger, better made and better finished gun throughout than the more common single guns on the market, and this they have certainly done in our New Model White Powder Wonder, and as between this, the New Model White Powder Wonder, and a cheaper gun which we are able to offer you on another page, for durability, for strength, lasting qualities, for shooting, penetration, safety, for general service in every way, for the slight difference in price, the difference between the lowest price we are able to make on an automatic shell ejecting single gun, as shown on another page, $2.89, and this, our special price of $3.64 on the White Powder Wonder, a difference of only 75 cents, we certainly would advise you to pay the 75 cents extra and send us your order for this, our New Model White Powder Wonder at only $3.64.

IN YOUR OWN INTEREST, and before you buy a single gun of any kind from us or any other house, any make at any price, please let us call your attention to the Aubrey Hammerless Flat Water Table Automatic Shell Ejecting Breech Loading Shotgun, shown on another page in this catalogue, and offered by us for $7.95.

THIS $7.95 AUBREY HAMMERLESS EJECTOR SINGLE GUN so far outclasses in every possible respect any and every single barrel breech loading shotgun we have ever seen that we honestly feel it our duty, before presenting any other single gun, to call our customers' attention to this most extraordinary gun value. Really, it's the only single gun made that we know of that is made on exactly the same lines, the same qualities of material, the same workmanship and finish, the same safeguarding, the same strength, the same wonderful shooting qualities as mark the highest grade double barrel hammerless breech loading shotguns; therefore, when about to buy a single gun, even though you do not at first feel like paying more than $2.89 or $2.59, the prices we are able to make on our lowest priced single guns, or if you are considering this, the White Powder Wonder at $3.64, which, by the way, is a much better gun than the more common single barrel guns, we, however, urge you to think seriously of our $7.95 Aubrey, try to add the few additional dollars and see how much more you will get for your money, and if you do this and you are not pleased, if you don't think you have made a wonderful investment in the Aubrey gun, if you don't think it is worth more than twice as much as any other single gun made, return it to us any time within sixty days at our expense and we will immediately return your money, together with any express charges paid by you.

WE KNOW THESE GUNS, know them all, we have examined them, we have had them all apart, we know all the guns made in America and in Europe, our Gun Department has gone over them in every detail, we, therefore, know what the Aubrey guns are, the single and the double. We know if anyone wants a single gun the Aubrey gun is really on its merit the only gun to buy. If anyone is in the market for a double gun, hammer or hammerless, we know the Aubrey Double Hammerless is the only gun to buy. However, if you don't feel like investing as much as $7.95 in a single gun and getting the best single gun ever made, then let us send you this $3.64 gun, our White Powder Wonder, and if it isn't perfectly satisfactory, if you are not convinced you have gotten a much better single gun for $3.64 than you could have gotten elsewhere at two or three dollars more, of course, we want you to return it to us at our expense and we will immediately return your money.

THIS GLOBE SIGHT, which can be instantly attached and removed, and which is a wonderful aid in shooting, especially wing shooting, is furnished free with this, our White Powder Wonder at $3.64.

WHEN DECIDING on a single barrel shotgun as between this, the New Model White Powder Wonder, furnished us by a New England maker, and the cheaper grade automatic ejector guns shown on another page, which we furnish for only $2.89, we would advise in your own interest that you pay the slight difference of 75 cents more and order the White Powder Wonder and get something better than the ordinary single barrel shotgun; but still better, and greatly to your interest, don't forget what we have to say here and throughout the book about the Aubrey guns, and if you want a single gun, don't overlook the $7.95 Aubrey single gun shown on another page. Quality considered, the Aubrey is, in fact, really the only high grade single gun standing in a class by itself, and as for use as compared with any of the more common guns worth even twice the $7.95 price we ask.

PLEASE READ ALL ABOUT THE AUBREY GUN AS SHOWN ON A PAGE BY ITSELF ELSEWHERE IN THIS DEPARTMENT.

ILLUSTRATION SHOWS THE ACTION OF OUR WHITE POWDER WONDER.

T is the Hammer.
U is the Top Lever.
V is the Top Lever Spring
W is the Locking Bolt.
X is the Mainspring.
Y is the Trigger Spring.
Z is the Trigger.
G is the Stock.
1 is the Extractor Cam Spring.
2 is the Extractor Cam.
3 is the Extractor Hook.
4 is the Fore End.
5 is the Screw Key.
6 is the Trigger Guard.

ABOUT SMOKELESS POWDER. We have heard of a great many guns bursting through the use of home made smokeless powder, containing chlorate of potash, and we desire to caution our customers to be very careful how they handle such home made powders, as expert powder makers inform us they have never been able to control the detonating qualities of chlorate powders. We will not guarantee any gun with chlorate powder.

DETAILED DESCRIPTION

THE FRAME of this $3.64 White Powder Wonder is made extra strong. The frames are solid steel, made heavy and they are reinforced, neatly shaped, well finished, given a mottled finish on the outside, made with rebounding hammer, positive springs, latest top snap break, latest style of takedown or detachable model; by simply removing the thumbscrew the barrel and fore end can be detached from the frame.

BARREL—The barrel is made from a solid bar of high grade steel, thoroughly tested, choke bored by the Swage system, each barrel is blued with a decarbonized finish, each barrel is fitted with an automatic shell ejector, one of the strongest, positive, perfect working automatic shell ejectors made, so constructed that when you open the gun the empty shell is automatically thrown clear from the gun. The illustration shows the action of the shell as it is being automatically ejected or thrown by the force of the ejector free from the gun. By this device there is no stopping to remove the shell by hand, it being thrown clear from your way ready to receive the new loaded shell. This makes possible very rapid shooting; in fact, you can load and unload much faster than with the ordinary extractor gun. This device is appreciated only by those who have used automatic shell ejecting guns and such people would have no other; in fact, with the single barrel automatic shell ejecting gun you shoot almost as rapidly and do almost the same execution that you can accomplish with a double hammer breech loading shotgun.

STOCK—The stock is made from a good quality, plain, thoroughly seasoned, straight grain walnut, made with pistol grip and fancy butt plate, the fore end is of plain walnut, well finished.

GENERAL FINISH—This gun is gotten up to present a more symmetrical, shapely and in every way better appearance than the ordinary single barrel gun, and in this respect, of course, excels our $2.89 gun. With its neat stock and butt plate, nicely decarbonized frame and trimmings, polished blued barrel and well proportioned parts and fittings throughout, even at our special $3.64 price, it outclasses most single guns retailed generally at $5.00 to $8.00.

GAUGE—The White Powder Wonder comes in 12-gauge only, and being made and bored for white or black powder, made extra strong throughout, the gun is suitable for any kind of shooting where any shotgun can be used, suitable for small game, also geese, ducks, partridge, quail, snipe, rabbits, squirrels, etc.

LENGTH OF BARRELS—The barrel comes in 30 or 32-inch length, as desired. When ordering be sure to state length of barrel wanted.

THE GUNS are made with especially selected steel barrels, bored from solid bar steel, choke bored, best automatic ejector, self bolted, self locking, self compensating, interchangeable parts, well case hardened, reinforced frame, barrel is detachable from frame, rebounding hammer, latest top snap break, selected straight grain full pistol grip walnut stock. The gun weighs about 6½ pounds, and at our special $3.64 price we furnish it as follows:

No. 6H414 SPECIAL SELECTED STEEL BARREL, 30 OR 32 INCHES AS DESIRED; WEIGHT, ABOUT 6½ POUNDS. OUR SPECIAL PRICE............ $3.64

Weight, packed for shipment, about, 12 pounds.

Read our booklet of Useful Information to Shooters, so you will familiarize yourself with fire arms, and you will have no accidents.

$4.55
WORLD'S CHALLENGE
AUTOMATIC EJECTOR SINGLE BARREL SHOTGUN
A GENUINE TWIST BARREL, FANCY CHECKERED FULL PISTOL GRIP, AUTOMATIC SHELL EJECTING, SINGLE BARREL, BREECH LOADING SHOTGUN AT AN ASTONISHINGLY LOW PRICE.
GENUINE LAMINATED STEEL.
TAPER CHOKE BORED
THE NEW ENGLAND GUN COMPANY who are furnishing us this, the celebrated World's Challenge Automatic Ejector, Breech Loading Single Shotgun under contract, made some quite substantial improvements in this gun for this season, and yet our contract is so large, in spite of the advance in the price of materials generally, in spite of the tendency all the time to a higher wage scale, and notwithstanding gun makers generally are and have been of late rapidly advancing the selling price of their fire arms, we are able this season, with the many improvements, to still offer you this, the World's Challenge Ejector Single Gun, at the very lowest price we have yet been able to make, only $4.55.
WE HAVE ENDEAVORED to make our line of single guns most complete. Beginning with the grade of single guns commonly sold and commonly made, and which represent perhaps at least four-fifths of all the single guns manufactured and sold today, we offer you on another page in this catalogue a good, strong, single barrel shotgun for $2.59, another one at $2.89, and still another, the White Powder Wonder, with several substantial improvements for this season, at $3.64, as shown on another page, and as our highest grade, regular size, hammer ejector, 12-gauge, single barrel breech loading shotgun, we are still able to name you the astonishingly low price of only $4.55 on this, the World's Challenge Automatic Ejector.
NOTE HOW THIS GUN DIFFERS FROM THE CHEAPER SINGLE BARREL GUNS WHICH WE OFFER AT LOWER PRICES ON PRECEDING PAGES.
BARRELS. Please note that this gun has genuine laminated steel or twist barrels. These barrels are made for us in Europe under contract, the only place where reliable twist barrels can be made. They are not made from a solid bar of steel as are the cheaper steel barrels, but they are made by a twisting process, which is explained in another page of this catalogue. This necessarily is a much more expensive process of making barrels, and tends to make a stronger and better barrel than is possible to be made from a straight bar of solid steel. The comparatively slight difference in cost between the plain steel barrel and the twist barrel at once recommends for your most favorable consideration this World's Challenge Automatic Ejector.
STOCK. Note the specially shaped and finished walnut stock, with the full pistol grip, the pistol grip being neatly checkered by hand, as shown in the illustration. When you stop to consider that every one of these little diamond checks on both sides of the hand hold, as illustrated hereon, must be cut out by hand, you can understand it must take some time and adds considerably to the cost, a cost that is money paid out for labor; but certainly it adds to the finish and appearance of the gun and, too, is most practical in that it gives you a better grip or better hold on the gun.
FINISH. Special attention has been given to the finish of the World's Challenge Ejector as compared with the cheaper guns, therefore, when considering a single barrel hammer gun, please note the very considerable difference in the construction and the finish of this, our World's Challenge Ejector, as compared with the guns offered by us on other pages at lower prices, and you may wish, and we would advise you, to try to make up the difference in price and get the better gun.
YOU TAKE NO RISK
UNDERSTAND, you take no risk in deciding as between two guns, and especially do you take no risk if you decide to get the better gun, because the few dollars more we pay for a better article is really seldom considered if we are very much pleased with the article we buy, and we always have the satisfaction of knowing that we got something that pleased us and we soon forget the slight difference in cost. Under any circumstances, however, you take no risk in ordering this or any other gun from us, because in our offer all we ask you to do is to send us your order, enclose our price, and we will send the gun to you with the understanding and agreement that if it isn't perfectly satisfactory after giving it any part of ten days' trial, you can return it to us at our expense and we will immediately return your money, together with any express charges you may have paid.
JUST ONE MOST IMPORTANT WORD OF ADVICE
JUST BEFORE YOU PLACE YOUR ORDER for any single gun, before you send your money to us or to any other house, or pass your money over the counter for a single gun, please consider the A. J. Aubrey Hammerless Single Gun, illustrated and described on another page in this catalogue. We advise you to consider this, for while the gun will cost you a few dollars more in the start, it is positively the highest grade single barrel shotgun made, and the only single barrel shotgun made on the same high grade lines in every particular, same as the highest grade double barrel hammerless shotguns are made. Before buying a single gun please read fully all we have to say on another page about the $7.95 Aubrey gun. True, it's a few dollars more, but until you have seen the Aubrey gun you cannot begin to measure what those extra dollars will mean to you, what they will bring to you in additional value and satisfaction, in pleasure, in comfort and in safety, in more and better game as long as you own and shoot the gun.
DESCRIPTION OF OUR WORLD'S CHALLENGE AUTOMATIC EJECTOR
WHICH WE OFFER HERE AT $4.55 AND WHICH WE GUARANTEE EQUAL TO GUNS THAT ARE RETAILED GENERALLY AT ABOUT DOUBLE THE PRICE.
THE BARREL—The barrel of the World's Challenge Ejector is twist, which is sometimes known as laminated steel, and is made by hand by skilled workmen, who have spent years of their lives learning this art, and no machine has ever been invented which would do this work. It is made by a hand welding process of iron and steel, which makes one of the strongest barrels conceivable, free from flaws and defects. All barrels in the World's Challenge Ejector are made with a view of using black or nitro smokeless powder.
STOCK—The stock is made from carefully selected, straight grained, well seasoned walnut lumber, turned out and finished from the solid planks, and the full pistol grip is handsomely checkered by hand.
FORE END—The fore end is made from the same grade of material as the stock, nicely finished.
PARTS—All the parts which go into this gun are made accurate and true to gauge and are interchangeable, so if you accidentally break the hammer, top lever or similar part, it may be replaced without the assistance of a gunsmith at a small cost.
CHOKE BORING—The World's Challenge Ejector Gun is choke bored on the latest scientific principles, choke bored by the taper system, which insures the best possible target at the longest range.
BUTT PLATE—Each gun is fitted with a handsome fancy butt plate of neat design.
SAFETY DEVICE—Our safety device is made with the fewest possible parts, which renders it less liable to get out of order than many other ejectors, the ejector throwing it automatically.
HAMMER—The hammer is rebounding and comes back to half cock, so the gun may be opened without cocking the hammer.
GAUGE—The World's Challenge Ejector comes in 12-gauge only, and is bored for either black or nitro smokeless powder.
LENGTH OF BARREL—These guns come in 30-inch barrel.
THIS GLOBE SIGHT IS FREE. It can be instantly attached to or removed from any single gun and aids wonderfully when shooting on the wing; in fact, for accurate shooting in the hands of anyone but an expert, these sights, owned exclusively by us, are practically indispensable. With every gun we send this sight free with our compliments.
THIS IS ONE OF THE STRONGEST AND ONE OF THE VERY BEST hammer, single barrel, automatic shell ejecting, breech loading shotguns on the market. It is made exceedingly strong in every particular, made for long range, hard shooting. It's a gun that will make an exceedingly deep penetration, a close pattern, and will certainly in every respect outshoot any of the cheaper or more common single barrel, breech loading shotguns on the market.
IF YOU ARE THINKING OF BUYING a regular model hammer, shell ejecting, single barrel, breech loading shotgun, then by all means, in preference to the cheaper made guns, select our World's Challenge Ejector. Send us $4.55; we will send the gun to you at once with the understanding and agreement that if it isn't perfectly satisfactory you can return it to us at any time within ten days, using any part of these ten days to try the gun thoroughly, and we will immediately return your money, together with any express charges you may have paid.
No. 6H422 Our World's Challenge Ejector, 12-gauge, 30-inch barrel. Remember, every barrel is guaranteed high grade, genuine twist, beautifully finished showing the twist figure. The gun weighs about 6½ pounds, and remember, the price includes our own patent Globe Sight. Weight, packed for shipment, about 12 pounds. Our special price....... $4.55

$7.65 AMERICAN DOUBLE BARREL SHOTGUN

We have discontinued the sale of all cheap imported or Belgian guns, which we have heretofore sold at $6.75 to $9.00, and which are sold generally at prices running from $9.00 to $15.00.

WE HAVE DISCONTINUED selling these cheap imported Belgian guns for the reason that we are able in the New England Gun Company's gun factory, that makes only for us, to produce a hammer double barrel breech loading shotgun that is really worth twice as much as any of the cheap imported Belgian guns, and yet sell the gun at a lower price than you can buy even the common double barrel breech loading Belgian or foreign gun from any other house. The first two guns which we offer you on this page at $7.65 and $8.95 are different from all cheap Belgian guns that others sell, in that they are safer, stronger, handsomer, better finished, far better shooting, better fitting, will last longer, easier to handle, and in every way vastly better than any of the cheap Belgian guns, and you positively cannot buy an American made gun from any other house at anything like the special prices here offered of $7.65 and $8.95.

WHILE WE, of course, advise you in your own interest to by all means buy one of our higher grade double guns, either the New England or, better still, the genuine A. J. Aubrey at $12.59, as shown on another page, still, remember, in this, our cheapest gun, you get an American made gun that is really worth double the price of any cheap Belgian gun on the market.

THIS IS A GENUINE BAR LOCK GUN, not a back action gun, remember; a top snap break, not a side snap; a pistol grip stock, not a straight stock; has choke bored barrels, not straight cylinder barrels; therefore it will shoot close and strong, will not shoot loose and scatter, like the other cheap guns. Comes in 12-gauge only, 30-inch barrels, rebounding locks, extension rib, checkered pistol grip and fore end; a genuine American made New England gun offered for only $7.65.

No. 6L70 Style of barrels, plain blued steel; length, 30 inches; weight, 7½ to 8 pounds. Price........ **$7.65**

$8.95 GENUINE AMERICAN GUN

THIS IS A REINFORCED BOLT ACTION genuine New England American made double barrel hammer breech loading shotgun, and in your own interest, if you do not feel you can afford as much as $10.95 for the best New England Gun, or, better still, $12.59 for a genuine A. J. Aubrey, then we advise you in your own interest to get this New England American gun, and we promise you that you will find it worth twice as much as any of the cheap imported Belgian guns on the market.

THE $7.65 NEW ENGLAND GUN offered above is worth twice as much as any of the cheap imported Belgian guns, but this, our $8.95 gun, is a better gun for you to buy than the $7.65 gun shown above. It is better in that this gun has reinforced barrels at the breech, has reinforced breech bottom at the barrels; it has a strong bolt and forged lug; it has a wider spread, better shell extractor; it has genuine nitro firing pins and is choke bored by the taper system, and has an extra long extension rib; has special low circular hammers; it has the highest grade break and lever action; it has genuine Armory steel barrels; a higher grade of steel than the cheaper gun.

THIS GUN is made by a New England gun company, one of the oldest and best makers in America. It is easily worth several dollars more than any Norwich American gun that we have ever been able to sell at less than $11.00.

DETAILED DESCRIPTION.

Fine Armory steel barrels, choke bored, good extractor, extension rib, matted top rib, steel frame, flat water table, double bolts, top snap lever, low circular hammers, bar locks, full checkered pistol grip, checkered fore end, 12-gauge only. 30 or 32-inch barrels; weight, 7½ to 8 lbs. Our special price for this thoroughly reliable New England American made, interchangeable parts, gun, **$8.95**

IF YOU FEEL YOU DO NOT CARE to pay more than $8.95 for a double barrel breech loading shotgun, then let us suggest this: Rather than buy a cheaper gun which we offer at $7.65, and, vastly more to your interest, rather than buy an imported Belgian gun at from $7.00 to $12.00 that you might buy elsewhere, send us $8.95, and let us send you this gun with the understanding and agreement that you can give it ten days' trial, during which time you can test it out; you can compare it with guns sold by others at double our price, compare it especially with any cheap gun you can buy from anyone, either in Chicago, at home or elsewhere, and especially compare it with any Belgian guns on the market, and if you are not satisfied that you have gotten better gun value from us than you could possibly get elsewhere, if you are not convinced that it is to your interest to pay the $8.95 in preference to the $7.65, and as compared with any gun you can buy elsewhere at the same money, $8.95, if you are not satisfied that you have gotten twice as much for your money as anyone else would give you, you can return the gun to us at our expense and we will immediately return your money.

No. 6L73 Carbon steel barrels; 12-gauge; 30 or 32 inches; 7½ to 8 lbs. Price... **$8.95**

COMBINATION SHOTGUN AND RIFLE $14.80

Formerly sold for $16.62

WE HAVE SUCCEEDED IN REDUCING THE PRICE of this double purpose reliable fire arm from $16.62 to $14.80. The reduction of $1.82 in our selling price represents the difference in cost to us, and we have been able to make this heretofore unheard of price of $14.80, this liberal reduction of $1.82 in this combination gun, by reason of a much larger purchase contract with the manufacturers than ever before. No sellers of guns in America buys or sells as many of these combination guns as we do, and our big contract puts us in a position to make a lower price contract than ever before, and we now give you the benefit of this in the low price of only $14.80.

IF YOU WOULD LIKE TO SEE, examine and fully understand the advantages of the Universal Combination Shotgun and Rifle, and will send us your order, enclosing $14.80, we will send the gun to you with the understanding and agreement that you can give it ten days' trial, during which time you can put it to every reasonable test, and if for any reason you are not perfectly satisfied with your purchase, you can return it to us at our expense, and we will immediately return your money.

REALIZING, as we did, that there was a demand for such a combination fire arm, we were the first to get out this wonderful gun. It is made for us under contract by one of the largest gun makers in Europe and is much higher grade, entirely out of the class of the ordinary grade of Belgian guns.

OUR NEW IMPROVED $14.80 Universal Combination Shotgun and Rifle is an invaluable fire arm in territories where large game as well as birds are found, and it is so constructed that if you do not wish to use the rifle barrel you can easily remove it and have both barrels for 12-gauge shotgun shells. In case you go hunting for game birds and expect to find a moose, elk, bear, or other large game during the hunt, you can use one barrel as a rifle and the other barrel as a shotgun, and you are ready for any kind of game which may come your way.

DETAILED DESCRIPTION. Our Universal Shotgun and Rifle is a new departure in this line, in that the rifle is auxiliary and may be removed in a minute and both barrels may be used for shotgun shells. It is fitted with Scott action top snap break; fine imported double blade laminated twist steel barrels, with extra heavy reinforced Diana style breech, strong bar rebounding locks, elevated, matted and engine turned rib, fitted with sporting rear and sporting front sights, Edwards' L shape extension rib, rebounding circular hammers, straight grained walnut stock and fore end, nicely checkered full pistol grip with shield inlaid, patent snap fore end, nitro firing pin, right barrel choke bored, left barrel cylinder bored, case hardened forged frame and lock plates. The 38-55 cartridge is suitable for heavy game, such as deer, moose, elk, bear, etc.

TWO GUNS IN ONE. This is the best two-in-one gun on the market. In this you have a combination of a high grade 12-gauge breech loading shotgun and a strong and thoroughly reliable rifle, using 38-55 caliber cartridge. The special rifle barrel attachment which goes with this two-in-one shotgun can be instantly removed, so that you have a double barrel shotgun, both barrels shooting the regulation 12-gauge shells, but in an instant, in less than a minute, you can insert the rifle barrel into the left barrel, and you are then equipped with one shotgun barrel and one accurately rifled, perfectly trued, dependable rifle barrel, and the gun being equipped with an adjustable rear rifle sight and a high grade front rifle sight you have every advantage in the one arm of a high grade, accurate, perfect rifled single barrel rifle and a high grade dependable single barrel shotgun. In countries where you occasionally run across big game, and especially at long range, game such as deer, bear, or even wild turkeys, geese, etc., where the game is wild and where it is impossible to approach within shotgun range, then this two-in-one fire arm is most valuable, as you have at once one of the strongest shooting shotguns made in the right hand barrel, while the left hand barrel can be changed in a fraction of a minute with our attachment into one of the strongest shooting, most accurate and best all around 38-55 caliber rifles made. The gun is exceedingly popular, and our special $14.80 price is about one-half the lowest price at which this high grade two-in-one combination shotgun and rifle has ever been sold; and, by the way, this two-in-one combination shotgun and rifle is a big improvement over all previous attempts, inasmuch as when you have no use for one rifle barrel, you can, in a fraction of a minute, convert it into a shotgun barrel, and you are then equipped with a high grade double barrel shotgun.

This illustration is just one-half the size of a 38-55 cartridge used in the rifle barrel of this gun.

No. 6L79 We furnish this high grade double barrel shotgun and rifle as follows: Caliber of rifle, 38-55 C. F., takes cartridge No. 6L2432; barrels are fine twist finished steel. Shotgun, 12-gauge; length of barrels, 30 inches; weight of gun, 9 to 9¼ pounds. Our special price........ **$14.80**

NEW ENGLAND WONDER

$10.95

WE CHALLENGE ANY GUN MAKER

OR GUN SELLER IN AMERICA TO PRODUCE THE EQUAL OF THIS AMERICAN GUN WITHIN $5.00 OF OUR PRICE

PAY $25.00 FOR A GUN

ANYWHERE ELSE, AND THEN COMPARE IT WITH THIS, OUR NEW ENGLAND $10.95 GUN, AND YOU WILL FIND OURS A FAR SUPERIOR GUN IN EVERY PIECE, PART AND WAY.

FOR SEVERAL YEARS we have been handling the Norwich double barrel breech loading shotgun which we have been able to offer at prices ranging from $11.72 to $16.10. The Norwich gun is a thoroughly reliable gun, so long as we handled it, far better in value than any double hammer gun we were able to buy and offer our customers, but with a view to making our hammer guns still much higher in grade, determined to give our customers still much more for their money than ever before, we arranged at our own factory (the Meriden Fire Arms Company of Meriden, Conn.,) to build a full line of the highest grade hammer double barrel breech loading shotguns made, the A. J. Aubrey line, and these we show on other pages in this department at prices ranging from $12.59 upward; then to get another gun that we could sell at a lower price and yet outclass in quality the Norwich guns we have sold in the past, we arranged with a New England maker, who also makes for us our $11.95 hammerless gun, to make for us a strictly high grade double barrel hammer gun, following the lines of the famous A. J. Aubrey, and as a result, we can offer you in this New England gun at $10.95, a vastly better double barrel breech loading shotgun than we have ever before been able to offer at even $15.00. It is made along the same lines as the A. J. Aubrey, and while in the making of this New England gun we do not employ the same skilled mechanics or give that rigid inspection and beautiful finish found only in the Aubrey, still we have made it in its various parts almost identical with the Aubrey, and in this New England factory employ the same grade of gun mechanics and workmen, use the same grade of machine tooling, finishing, etc., as is used in practically all gun making factories outside of the Meriden Fire Arms Company, so while this, our special $10.95 gun, will compare in workmanship, finish, fit, etc., with guns made by other American makers that sell even at double this price, it combines all of the high grade mechanical advantages of the A. J. Aubrey, making it a wonderful improvement over any gun on the market that you can buy elsewhere at anything like the price.

THIS $10.95 NEW ENGLAND GUN is made so good that we extend with this gun the same liberal guarantee and the same liberal free trial offer that we extend with all of the famous A. J. Aubrey guns.

IF YOU SEND US YOUR ORDER for this, our new improved 1908 model New England Wonder Hammer Breech Loading Shotgun, we will send it to you with the understanding and agreement that you can give it a free test, compare it with any gun you can buy elsewhere at double the price, and if you are not perfectly satisfied with your purchase, if you are not convinced you have gotten far more value for your money than you could have gotten elsewhere, you are at liberty to return the gun to us at our expense, and we will immediately return your money.

LIKE THE FAMOUS A. J. AUBREY DOUBLE HAMMER GUN

SHOWN ON THE FOLLOWING PAGES AT $12.59 AND UPWARD, THIS NEW ENGLAND GUN HAS THE FOLLOWING SPECIAL STRONG AND VALUABLE FEATURES:

BARRELS—The barrels are made from the very finest crystal barrel steel, highly polished and finished, and a grade of steel, that when finished, will not rust, pit or mark like the cheaper grade guns. The barrels are beautifully tapered, they are reinforced at the breech, they have extra heavy top and bottom rib, the top rib is matted, tapered, beautifully shaped and accurate in alignment. The reinforcing of the breech makes the gun an ideal gun for smokeless powder as well as black powder, and reduces the recoil or kick to the very minimum, putting the entire force of the powder into the penetration of the shot. The barrels are beautifully finished and they are accurately choke bored by the taper system, which guarantees a pattern, target, penetration and long distance killing not effected by any of the cheaper guns.

EXTRACTOR—These barrels are fitted with the very latest shell extractor, which is positive in its action.

HEAVY BOLT ACTION—These barrels are fitted with extra heavy bolts, made very strong, thus insuring a perfect lock and strength by which the gun, even with the use of black or white powder, cannot wear loose or shaky. The bolt action of this gun cannot be in any way compared with the cheaper guns on the market.

FRAME—This gun is made with one of the heaviest, strongest and most durable drop steel forged frames made; extra strong and heavy in every part, well finished, case hardened and handsomely colored. It has the latest Norwich firing pins, handsomely shaped, perfect acting top snap break, neat low circular hammers, very strong, genuine bar locks with steel hardened interchangeable parts, perfectly finished and all points of contact are made of case hardened tool steel.

STOCK—Stock is made from carefully selected straight grained walnut, thoroughly seasoned, perfectly shaped. The stock is fitted to the frame by an automatic stock fitting machine, which insures a perfect fit, and the frame and stock are so constructed in points of contact as to insure the strongest kind of a stock where many guns are weak. This stock is full pistol grip and comes with a handsomely ornamented butt plate as illustrated.

FORE END—This, our $10.95 gun, is fitted with a self locking beautifully finished and checkered walnut fore end, strong steel tip and steel tang.

SAFE AND DURABLE—First, in considering hard, long range shooting, extra penetration, extra target, the question of strength, durability and safety has not been overlooked, and while it is not safe to use white or nitro powder in many of the cheap American made guns, this gun is built for shooting either white, black or nitro powder. It has been built extra strong of the best material, strongly locked, strongly reinforced, especially strong where many guns are weak, all with a view of giving you a gun that will be always safe, always reliable, a gun that will last for years and give the very best of satisfaction.

THE HIGH GRADE AUBREY FEATURES that are carried out in this, our $10.95 gun, are the bolt locking mechanism, the special interchangeable bar locks, the reinforcing of the barrels at the breech, the crystal barrel steel used in the barrels, the barrel finishing and the choke boring, the beautiful alignment, the hang, the shape, that perfect balance, that means when you bring the gun to your shoulder and cast your eye over the matted rib between the two barrels you catch the sight instantly, and even though it be on fast wing shooting, this sight instantly gets in line with the game, and this is all effected by the higher art of scientific gun making, which has been devoloped by Mr. A. J. Aubrey, and introduced and used in this $10.95 gun for the purpose of putting this gun in a class by itself. The Aubrey ideas of wonderful barrel construction, perfect milling, extra heavy, rigid, everlasting drop steel forged frame, strong at every point, a gun that will not shoot loose, a gun with none of the earmarks of cheapness, a gun that will shoot as well as any gun made, regardless of name, make or price; you will find all these features in this new improved 1908 model New England Wonder.

WITH EVERY ONE OF THESE $10.95 NEW ENGLAND DOUBLE BARREL BREECH LOADING SHOTGUNS WE ISSUE A

WRITTEN BINDING 20-YEAR GUARANTEE

BY THE TERMS AND CONDITIONS OF WHICH IF ANY PIECE OR PART GIVES OUT WITHIN 20 YEARS, BY REASON OF DEFECT IN MATERIAL OR WORKMANSHIP, WE WILL REPLACE OR REPAIR IT FREE OF CHARGE.

TAKE OUR ADVICE

IF YOU DON'T BUY a genuine A. J. Aubrey, then buy this gun, the New England make, made on the A. J. Aubrey lines, and believe us, it isn't to your advantage to buy a cheaper gun, for in this and the A. J. Aubrey guns you get so much more for your money than we or any other house can possibly offer you in any other gun made, and, remember, we send this gun to you on the same conditions with the Aubrey guns, with the understanding and agreement that you can give the gun sixty days' trial, during which time you can put it to every reasonable test, and if, at any time during the sixty days, you should become dissatisfied with your purchase, you can return the gun to us at our expense, and we will immediately return your money, together with any freight or express charges you may have paid. We also guarantee this gun under a written binding guarantee for twenty years.

IF AT ANY TIME in the years to come you should want any piece or part to repair one of these guns, we will always carry it in stock, and will supply it to you at actual factory cost, plus only our one small percentage of profit, and if it comes within the limits of our guarantee we will furnish such parts free of cost to you.

$10.95

No. 6L81 We furnish this gun exactly as illustrated and described under our 20-year written binding guarantee, 12-gauge only, 30 or 32-inch barrels, as desired, combining every high grade feature of every gun with the defects of none, weighing 7½ to 8 pounds, complete with the very finest genuine crystal barrel steel barrels, beautifully finished throughout. Be sure to state length of barrels wanted. Price.................... **$10.95**

No. 6L81

YOUR MONEY WILL BE IMMEDIATELY RETURNED TO YOU FOR ANY GOODS NOT PERFECTLY SATISFACTORY.

A. J. AUBREY HAMMERLESS DOUBLE BARREL BREECH LOADING SHOTGUN $13^{85}

ILLUSTRATIONS AND DESCRIPTIONS OF SOME OF THE PARTS OF THE AUBREY HAMMERLESS DOUBLE BARREL BREECH LOADING SHOTGUN

JUST A FEW FEATURES are shown hereon to give you an idea of the individuality of this gun, how all essential parts have been cared for in the matter of strength, workmanship and finish, an opportunity for you to compare the general mechanical construction and design of the Aubrey hammerless with any other hammerless gun made, a chance for you to see for yourself that the Aubrey Hammerless Double Barrel Breech Loading Shotgun is indeed the highest grade double barrel breech loading shotgun made. The limited space does not permit of our going into all the details. To know and to fully appreciate what an Aubrey Double Barrel Hammerless Breech Loading Shotgun really is, and how much better it is than an ordinary hammerless double gun, why and wherein it is better than any other double hammerless gun on the market, you must see, examine and compare the Aubrey Hammerless Double Barrel Breech Loading Shotgun with others to appreciate the value we are giving, how much it is possible for us to furnish you from our gun factory at Meriden, Conn., when we name a price based on the actual cost of material and labor in our own factory, with but our one small percentage of profit added.

Illustration No. 1.

ILLUSTRATION No. 1 will give you a little idea of the breech construction of the double Aubrey hammerless. All Aubrey barrels are reinforced at the breech and made extra strong. They are bored by the taper system, reinforced, and are, therefore, specially adapted to white or smokeless powder as well as black powder. The Aubrey breech construction is not matched by any other gun on the market.

This illustration also shows the new extension rib used on the Aubrey Double Hammerless Guns. This rib, you will note from the illustration, is deeper, heavier and stronger than the ordinary extension rib. Note the heavy slot cut in the rib, which engages with the solid steel cross bite in the top lever, firmly locking the barrel and frame, preventing any possibility of this gun shooting loose. We have tested this extension rib lock thoroughly. In testing this extension rib lock we have taken out the bottom bolts and shot over 1,000 shells with just this extension rib lock holding the barrels to the frame. After shooting 1,000 shells we found the gun just as rigid and as strong as ever.

Bear in mind that, in addition to this extension rib cross bite locking device, you also have two bolts engaging with the lugs in the bottom of the barrel, making this the strongest bolted gun on the market.

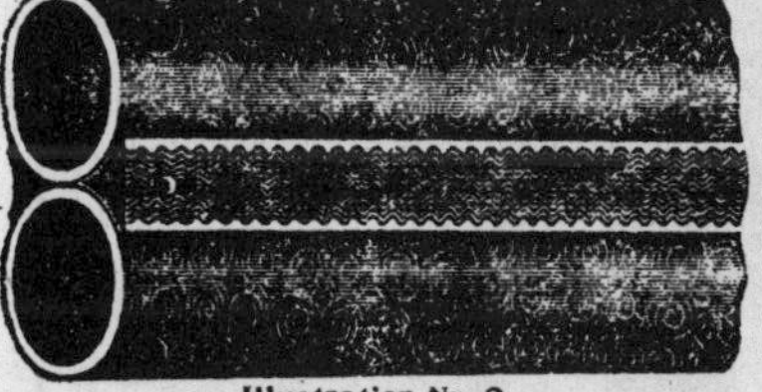

ILLUSTRATION No. 2 shows the style of the full taper shaped and finished matted rib which is used on all Aubrey Hammerless Double Barrel Breech Loading Shotguns. This is undoubtedly the handsomest, most shapely and truest matted rib construction made.

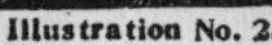

Illustration No. 2.

ILLUSTRATION No. 3, engraved from a photograph of the interior of one of the locks, will give you some idea of the simplicity, the strength and the positiveness of action of the Aubrey lock, which is a full shaped, full finished bar lock, and undoubtedly the highest grade gun lock used on any double hammerless gun made.

Illustration No. 3.

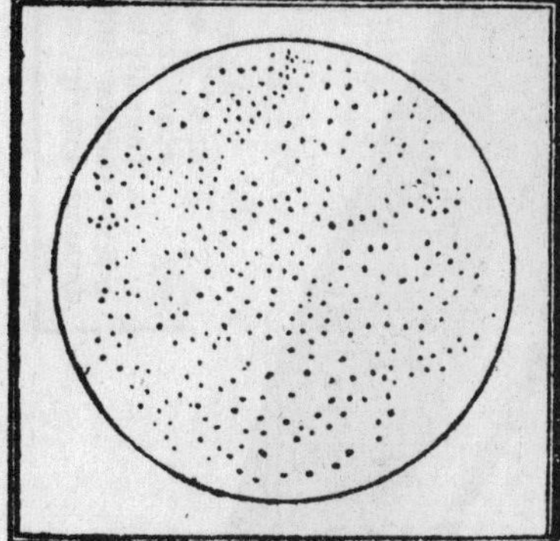

Illustration No. 4.

ILLUSTRATION No. 4 is a reproduction of an average target made by the A. J. Aubrey Hammerless Gun. This target was made at a distance of 40 yards, shooting at a 30-inch circle, with 3¼ drams powder, 1⅛ oz. No. 8 shot. Note the excellence of the pattern, how uniformly the shot is distributed. This illustration tells you far better than words possibly could of the wonderful shooting qualities of these A. J. Aubrey Guns, choke bored on the celebrated Aubrey system.

ILLUSTRATION No. 5, engraved from a photograph taken direct from the safety device on the Aubrey gun will give you an idea of the Aubrey safety construction as used on this gun, unquestionably the simplest, handsomest and strongest safety mechanism used on any hammerless breech loading barrel made, a mechanism that is positive in its action, putting the gun always under the control of the shooter, rendering accidental discharge impossible and insuring for you far greater safety than is possible in a hammer gun; no triggers to slip from your fingers, an unmatchable safety construction.

Illustration No. 5.

ILLUSTRATION No. 6 shows a portion of the frame construction, the flat water table, the double bolt, a portion of the lock construction and the cocking bolts. Little idea of the superiority brought out in this construction can be had except by a comparison of this, the Acme frame and bolt and locking action, with other hammerless guns.

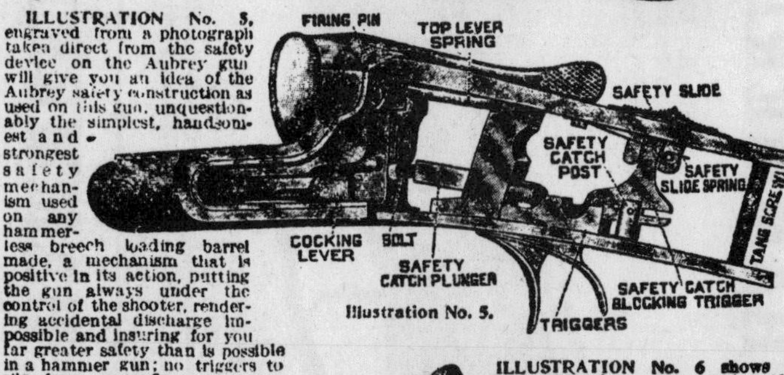

Illustration No. 6.

ILLUSTRATION No. 7 shows you the two heavy double steel lugs with their treble lock construction, the flat table, the reinforced barrel connection construction, the extractor and the bottom view of the slotted self locking extension rib.

Illustration No. 7.

Illustration No. 8.

ILLUSTRATION No. 8 will give you simply a little idea of the shapely appearance of the fore end used on the Aubrey hammerless gun. It is, of course, made of carefully selected walnut stock, nicely checkered ornamentation, is very shapely, as the illustration shows. It has the best automatic locking mechanism known, by which it locks automatically squarely to the barrel.

ILLUSTRATION No. 9 shows the bottom of the fore end. You can see the locking device, the fancy metal tip and the general scheme of fore end construction as used on the Aubrey gun.

Illustration No. 9.

IN PRESENTING THE AUBREY GUN to you in the different grades, we wish it clearly understood that the quality of workmanship, the strength, the endurance, in fact, in every essential way, one gun is like the other; the $13.85 grade will last as long, shoot as well and give as good satisfaction as the highest priced Aubrey gun we offer. They differ only in the barrels and in the special finish given them. These guns are 12-gauge, they come with either 30 or 32-inch barrels, as desired (in ordering state length of barrels preferred); they weigh from 7½ to 8 pounds.

UNDERSTAND, all frames are made from the highest grade drop steel forgings, all accurately milled, cut and finished, all barrels are given a specially high finish, beautifully browned.

ALL PARTS BEING INTERCHANGEABLE, we can, in case you should want any part to replace another, even in the years to come, always furnish you these parts from stock, and will gladly furnish any part to any owner of an Aubrey gun at actual factory cost, plus only our one small percentage of profit, a mere fraction of what you would have to pay others for a similar part to another gun; further, if it comes within the limits of our twenty years' binding guarantee any such part will, of course, be furnished to you free of cost.

UNDERSTAND, with every gun we send a written binding twenty years' guarantee, by the terms and conditions of which, if any piece or part gives out within twenty years, by reason of defect in material or workmanship, we will replace or repair it free of charge.

No. 6L18 Genuine crystal barrels, 12-guage; length, 30 or 32 inches (state length preferred); weight, 7½ to 8 pounds; handsome line engraving. Price, only........ **$13.85**

No. 6L20 Genuine imported Liege steel twist barrels, 12-guage; length of barrels, 30 or 32 inches (state length preferred); weight, 7½ to 8 pounds; beautiful line engraving. Price........ **14.85**

No. 6L22 Genuine double blade imported Liege Damascus full finished steel barrels; 12-guage; length of barrels, 30 or 32 inches (state length preferred); weight, 7½ to 8 pounds; beautiful line engraving. Price........ **17.00**

A. J. AUBREY DOUBLE BARREL HAMMERLESS SHOTGUN
This picture shows our $13.85 A. J. Aubrey Double Barrel Hammerless Shotgun. Its fine points of design, workmanship and finish are all fully described on page 595.
This A. J. Aubrey Double Barrel Hammerless Shotgun is backed by a twenty-year guarantee and a sixty-day free trial offer that shows you what we think of it. Read the full detailed description on page 595 and send us your order today.
A.J.&Aubrey
No. 6L18
$13.85
From the plain steel barrel shotguns here shown at $13.85 to the most beautifully engraved, checkered and finely finished gun at $38.50 these A. J. Aubrey Double Barrel Hammerless Shotguns are leaders; each and every one represents the highest shooting quality, the finest workmanship, and the very greatest value to the purchaser. The most positive statement that we can make concerning them would be but feeble compared with the merits of the guns themselves. Read all about them on pages 594 to 600.
A. J. AUBREY SINGLE BARREL HAMMERLESS SHOTGUN
This is a picture of the A. J. Aubrey Single Barrel Hammerless Shotgun at $7.95. A tremendous value. We tell you all about it on page 617.
There is no single barrel hammerless shotgun on the market today that in any way compares with this A. J. Aubrey Single Barrel Hammerless Shotgun in mechanical construction, symmetrical proportion, finish or shooting qualities. Look for the complete description on page 617.
A.J.&Aubrey
No. 6L424
$7.95
An actual photograph of our A. J. Aubrey Single Barrel Hammerless Shotgun at $7.95 was used as the basis of this illustration. To say that it is in a class apart from all others tells only a very small part of the story. It is positively the only single barrel hammerless shotgun made today that embodies in outline, in construction and in finish the features of the highest grade double barrel shotgun. Read the detailed description carefully on page 617 and send us your order at once.

A. J. AUBREY DOUBLE BARREL HAMMER SHOTGUN

This is an exact picture of the celebrated A. J. Aubrey Double Barrel Hammer Shotgun, the very best shotgun in the world. For complete detailed description see page 603.

Do you want the very best double barrel hammer shotgun made? Read the full detailed description of this gun, our celebrated A. J. Aubrey, on page 603 and then send us your order at once.

No. 6L82

$12.59

We make the positive claim that the A. J. Aubrey guns are the most perfect all around guns made, and thousands of shooters all over the world back up our statement. The above is a picture of our special $12.59 Double Barrel Aubrey Hammer Shotgun, positively reliable and guaranteed to you every day of the year for twenty years Read the detailed description on this and other A. J. Aubrey hammer guns on pages 603.

A. J. AUBREY SINGLE BARREL HAMMER SHOTGUN

This is a picture of our special A. J. Aubrey $5.95 Single Barrel Hammer Shotgun; the best that fine material and perfect workmanship can produce. Read the detailed description on page 615.

You or your friends or their friends cannot afford to buy a single barrel hammer shotgun of any other make or at any other price. This is the very best single barrel hammer shotgun made in the world and the price is very modest, $5.95; this is the factory cost with one small margin of profit added. Read the full detailed description on page 615.

No. 6L426

$5.95

This A. J. Aubrey is the only single barrel hammer shotgun in the world made with a safety which will prevent accidental discharge; the only perfectly reliable shotgun of its class on the market guaranteed every day in the year for twenty years. Do not look for or expect anything better at $15.00 to $25.00. This A. J. Aubrey Single Barrel Hammer Shotgun is the best. It is the limit of high quality; the best material and the finest workmanship can do no more. Read the detailed description on page 615 and send us your order at once.

A. J. AUBREY HAMMERLESS DOUBLE BARREL SHOTGUN

IMPROVED MODEL CROSS BITE EXTENSION RIB, TREBLE BOLTED

$19.35 IS OUR PRICE **for this high grade A. J. Aubrey Hammerless Gun with beautiful and elaborate hand engraved locks and frame, fitted with genuine twist barrels.** In this gun at $19.35 for the genuine twist barrel gun, or $22.35 for the same gun fitted with fine two-blade Damascus barrels, we offer you value which you could not duplicate for less than $30.00 or more in any other American made gun. The engraving on these guns is better than that found on any of the $50.00 or $60.00 guns on the market. The finish, the inside lock work and the close, fine checkering on the full pistol grip stock and on the finely shaped walnut fore end, are better and handsomer than those found on almost any other make of gun, regardless of price. These guns have been made to supply a demand for a high grade gun of beautiful design and finish at a popular price, a price of about one-half of what you would ordinarily have to pay for a gun of this design and quality.

THE VALUE **of the A. J. Aubrey Hammerless Gun in comparison with any other make gun, either hammer or hammerless,** can hardly be estimated, as the Aubrey gun is so much better in finish, shooting qualities, alignment, choke boring, construction, so distinctive in itself, that a comparison with any other make of gun, either hammer or hammerless, would convince even the novice that, considering the price at which our guns are sold, we would be justified in asking more than treble the prices we now ask for these guns.

THE MATERIAL, **design, workmanship, shooting qualities and general construction of the Aubrey guns** are so far in advance of the other guns, the prices we ask for the Aubrey guns are so incomparably low that when these guns are thoroughly introduced and the value embodied in them is well known, no man will buy a gun other than the A. J. Aubrey.

WE HAVE AT MERIDEN, CONN., **one of the largest gun factories in the world. We have surrounding this factory many acres of land to enable us to enlarge this already enormous plant to take care of the growing demand.** Our output today in double hammerless guns, single guns and revolvers, is larger than that of any factory in the country, which is marvelous, when you stop to consider the few years that these guns have been on the market as compared with standard makes of guns which have been on the market for the last twenty or thirty years. To build up a business in this short space of time so as to be able to dispose of the output of the largest fire arms factory of its kind in the world, certainly speaks well of the wonderful value of these guns. Never in the history of the gun business has any line of fire arms shown the rapid growth in sales that the A. J. Aubrey goods have shown. We know that as these guns become better known, the sales will double and treble, making it necessary to keep on increasing our already enormous factory.

THE MANAGEMENT, **equipment and system of manufacturing are such that we are able to manufacture a thousand guns with the same care and attention to detail as if we were manufacturing but one hundred.** The factory is so thoroughly divisionized; every step in the manufacture of these guns is under the watchful eye of a careful, trained inspector. The machine work performed by the highest grade automatic machines is so accurate to the thousandth part of an inch, the parts are so strictly interchangeable, that you will find that not the slightest detail in the construction of the guns has in any way been overlooked or neglected.

OUR LIBERAL SIXTY-DAY FREE TRIAL OFFER, **as fully given on page 592, and our binding twenty-year guarantee** fully protect you in the purchase of one of these guns. If you are desirous of purchasing a gun, send us your order for an A. J. Aubrey, and if you do not find it all we claim it to be, a better gun than you could obtain elsewhere at any price, if you are not satisfied with its shooting qualities, its construction, or, in short, if you are not pleased with your purchase, return the gun to us, and we will cheerfully refund the price you paid, as well as any express charges.

THE RANGE OF PRICES **on Aubrey guns is large; the guns are graded to suit everyone who wishes to purchase a gun, the prices ranging from $13.85 for the blued steel barrel gun to $38.50 for three-blade Damascus barrel gun;** and although there is a considerable range of prices, as stated, the quality in all Aubrey Guns is uniform. The $13.85 gun will shoot just as well and wear just as well as the $38.50 gun. The mechanical construction is the same and the mechanism is identical in the cheapest gun as in the highest priced. The difference in price is accounted for entirely by the difference in the cost of the various grades of barrels and the additional work put on the guns, the checkering and engraving, and the special selected imported stocks with which the higher priced guns are fitted, and whether you buy an A. J. Aubrey Gun at $13.85 or any of the higher grades, you are assured of getting a gun that will give you absolute satisfaction, a gun that will shoot better and last longer than any other gun you could possibly buy and such value as you could not possibly obtain in the purchase of any other gun.

SEE PAGE 595 **for illustrations and full descriptions of the various parts entering into the construction of the A. J. Aubrey Hammerless Gun.** By studying these illustrations and descriptions carefully, you will appreciate to some small extent the wonderful construction of this great gun. We want you to know all about this gun, as the more you know about it, the more certain we are of receiving your order. We have endeavored to describe these guns carefully, have given a description in detail of each and every part. We show, as stated, illustrations on another page taken from photographs of the various parts, so that you, in making your selection, will know just what to expect, so that you will be in a position to make a selection to your best interest, and remember, you are fully protected by our most liberal and binding guarantee and 60 days' free trial offer, as fully given on page 592.

GUARANTEED 20 YEARS
60 DAYS' FREE TRIAL

THE HAND ENGRAVING

EVERY LINE OF THIS ENGRAVING **is done by an artist by hand, at the bench.** The locks, as illustrated, are most elaborately engraved by hand; the frame, body, top and sides, the trigger guard, the tang, the break, the whole is most beautifully finished.

IF YOU WANT A MOST EXTRAORDINARY GUN, **something entirely out of the ordinary in beautiful lines and hand engraved finish, then we would especially like to receive your order for this our high grade Aubrey.** Send us your order, enclose our price, $19.35, if you wish genuine laminated steel barrels; $22.35, if you wish genuine two-blade Damascus steel barrels (of course, you will state whether you wish barrels 30 or 32 inches long), we will send the gun to you by express, with it we will send our written binding 20-year guarantee, by the terms and conditions of which if any piece or part gives out by reason of defect in material or workmanship within 20 years, we will replace or repair it free of charge. We will also send the gun to you with the understanding and agreement that it must reach you promptly, must reach you in perfect order, and after you have received it you have the privilege of giving it 60 days' thorough test, and during this time you can compare it with other guns as to its shooting qualities, the penetration it will make, the target and the pattern you can get, its long range shooting qualities; compare it in any way you may like, you be the sole judge, if at any time during the 60 days you decide you don't want to keep the gun, you can return it to us at any time within 60 days at our expense, without explanation or reason from you of any kind and the day we receive the gun we will pay the express charges and immediately return to you all the money you may have sent us, including any express charges you may have paid.

BE SURE TO MENTION LENGTH OF BARREL WANTED.

$19.35

DESCRIPTION

Read the description of our $13.85 Aubrey Gun, as appearing on one of the preceding pages, and you have all the description of this, our highest grade Aubrey Gun except for the elaborate hand engraving; otherwise the guns are alike. This has the treble bolt, our cross bite extension rib, it is taper choke bored by the celebrated Aubreyized taper system, built on an alignment giving it such a perfect balance, such a perfect hang, such beautiful control, making it a gun that will come to the shoulder with the stock tight to the shoulder, with the barrel so balanced that you catch the top of the sight and quickly line it with the game, do it as you can do it on no other gun. Built, as we say, exactly the same as the $13.85 gun, except for the hand engraved finish, put out under our binding guarantee, is the Aubrey Hammerless Double Barrel Breech Loading Shotgun, which we most earnestly advise you to consider when about to buy a gun, whether you have been thinking of buying a hammer or hammerless from us or anyone else of any make, at any price.

WE FIT THIS HIGHER GRADE OF GUN **with an extra fine English walnut stock,** using great care in selecting the wood for the stock and fore end so as to use only the most beautiful grain. The stock and fore end are made additionally attractive by the beautiful hand checkering, which is of a beautiful design, if you will note the illustration. It is all done by hand with very fine tools, requiring twice the time ordinarily required to checker an ordinary gun. All in all, in this, our best grade Aubrey Gun, we aim to combine beauty with strength and to realize how successful we have been in this respect you really have to see the gun, for which an opportunity is afforded you by our liberal sixty-day free trial offer, as fully given on page 592.

WE GIVE AWAY FREE with every one of these Guns **OUR IMPROVED GLOBE SIGHT**

which is a big help to the shooter for wing shooting. This sight is patented and is manufactured and controlled exclusively by us. This sight can be instantly attached or detached from the gun, and the regular front sight of the gun does not in any way interfere with the use of this globe sight. **Every one of these guns bears the name, A. J. Aubrey,** the strongest guarantee on the highest quality, material and workmanship ever embodied in a shotgun of any kind. The name "A. J. Aubrey" on this gun means more to you than the name on any other gun. It means that you are getting the highest quality and the greatest value it is possible to produce. It further means that you are fully protected for a period of twenty years against defective material or construction by a binding guarantee.

No. 6L52

Catalogue No.	Grade	Style Barrels	Gauge	Length of Barrels	Weight, Pounds	Finish	Price
6L50	A. S. E.	Genuine Twist	12	30 or 32 in.	7½ to 8	Fine Line Scroll and Game Engraving.	$19.35
6L52	D. S. E.	Genuine Two-Blade Damascus	12	30 or 32 in.	7½ to 8		22.35

WEIGHT PACKED FOR SHIPMENT, ABOUT 14 POUNDS.

WHEN ORDERING **give catalogue number, length of barrels and weight desired.** We will send you a gun in accordance with your wishes, a gun that we know will please you in every particular.

$26.75 AUBREY HAMMERLESS SPECIAL

AMONG THE TRAP AND FIELD SHOOTERS and especially among the professional trap shooters there are a great many gun fanciers, those who want something exceedingly fine in finish, some specially fine, very elaborate hand engraving, engraving where an artist must be employed and where in some instances to execute some special orders, we have been compelled to employ the most skilled artist at as high as five or six dollars a day for a full week, where a very elaborate, beautiful, fine and artistic engraving design would have to be carried out, and occasionally some professional trap shooter or other customer may want something most elaborate, a special kind of grain in a fine Italian stock. He may call for a special weight, a special drop, irregular length, and to accommodate all these, as explained in the introductory on page 592, Mr. Aubrey is always ready to figure on anything special, on a gun made to order for $50.00 or more, and those wishing to figure with him on such guns can write him direct, addressing their letters to Mr. A. J. Aubrey, President Meriden Fire Arms Company, Meriden, Connecticut.

CARRYING THESE HIGH GRADE GUNS IN STOCK, where they heretofore were made only to order enables us to manufacture them in quantities with considerable saving and offer them to you at prices from $10.00 to $15.00 less than we have ever been able to offer them heretofore, and from $25.00 to $40.00 less than you could purchase a gun of similar quality from any other manufacturer. In placing these guns in stock, we have not in any way detracted from the finish or the elaborate checkering and engraving that we placed on these guns when they were made to order. These guns are beautifully engraved, exactly as shown in the illustration. This engraving is all done by hand, requiring from two to three days of a first class artist's time. The checkering is very fine and in harmony with the beautiful engraving. The finish of the entire gun is thoroughly in keeping with the idea of presenting in these guns the most artistic and beautiful work that can be embodied in the construction of a double barrel shotgun. These special high grade guns at $26.75 to $38.50 are designed particularly for the shooter who wants the best from an artistic as well as a mechanical standpoint, and are made to compete with other high grade guns sold for $50.00 to $150.00.

Remember, these guns are all sold under our binding 20-year guarantee.

UNDERSTAND, YOU CAN HAVE SIXTY DAYS' FREE TRIAL

We will be glad, on receipt of the price, to send you any one of the guns shown on this page, with the understanding and agreement that you can give it sixty days' free trial, during which time you can put it to every test, and if you are not satisfied with your purchase you can return the gun to us at our expense, and we will immediately return your money.

Understand, every gun carries with it **OUR WRITTEN BINDING TWENTY YEARS' GUARANTEE,** by the terms and conditions of which if any piece or part gives out within twenty years, by reason of defect in material or workmanship, we will replace or repair it free of charge. Understand also, this gun is in every detail of construction exactly the same as the $13.85 Aubrey, 12-gauge only, 30 or 32-inch barrels **(be sure to state length of barrels wanted),** treble bolt action, wedge automatic self locking and bolting mechanism, which bolts the barrel through the matted extension rib to the frame, highest grade safety, the very best of everything.

THE PAST YEAR the demand for special guns at the prices we have been able to quote, ranging from about $30.00 to $50.00, has been so great that we decided to catalogue the guns shown on this page, which are higher grade in finish than we have ever before offered, and which are designed to supply the wants of many of those who heretofore have been going to Mr. Aubrey for something in this line of special finish in guns made to order. By getting out these special, high grade finished styles shown on this page in large quantities, several hundred of each at a time, we can very materially reduce the cost as against getting them out singly to special order; in other words, the guns we offer you on this page at $26.75 to $38.50 if gotten out singly, special to order as heretofore, could not be furnished direct from the factory at less than $10.00 to $15.00 more money each.

No. 6L55

This is the exact same gun as all A. J. Aubrey Hammerless Guns shown on preceding pages. It differs only in its most elaborate finish, quality of stock and special engraving and checkering

WHILE THE BARRELS IN THIS SPECIAL GUN which we offer at $26.75 are plain steel barrels, they are made from the finest carbon gun barrel steel that money can buy, they have been given a finish that is indescribable, something you really must see to appreciate. The elaborate and beautiful finish of this gun is represented more especially in the very handsome hand engraving, the work of a famous artist, engraving that covers the locks, frame, guards, break, etc., in the beautiful imported buried walnut stock, in the elaborate checkering, beautiful decorating, the high polish and finish throughout; in short, the difference in price between this, our special Aubrey gun at $26.75, and the cheapest Aubrey gun we offer, which is $13.85. The difference of $12.90 represents but little more than the actual difference in labor that has gone to make this the beautiful gun it is.

DURING THE PAST YEAR following the directions of the customers, mostly professional trap shooters, Mr. Aubrey has made singly to specific orders a large number of these guns, and almost without exception from every buyer he has received the most flattering testimonials.

HAVING MADE SO MANY OF THESE GUNS to special order, almost identical with the gun here shown, and being compelled by reason of making them singly to order to charge from $40.00 to $45.00 in order to cover the expense where made singly to order and allowing a small manufacturing profit, we decided this season to bring them out in one hundred lots, taking them through every part of the factory, otherwise in a most special way, but at the same time give our customers the benefit of all the saving by taking these guns through the factory in one hundred lots instead of one gun at a time. Figuring out this saving as carefully as we can, it amounts to about $15.00 a gun, or going over the actual cost of producing this gun as shown on this page, the cost of material and labor, carefully calculated through every part of the factory, and then adding only our one small percentage of profit, we find we can offer it for $26.75.

IF YOU WANT A DOUBLE BARREL hammerless breech loading shotgun that is entirely out of the ordinary, a beautiful thing to look at, as fine a shooting gun as was ever made, something that will be a joy forever, something that will be in appearance, in fact, in every way handsomer and better than you would be likely to find in a party of a dozen hunters, then we advise you to order one of these finest special made guns.

No. 6L55 12-gauge, 30 or 32-inch barrels of XX carbon steel. Weight, 7½ to 8 pounds........ **$26.75**

No. 6L56 The exact same gun, 12-gauge, 30 or 32-inch, 7½ to 8 pounds, with the very finest imported three-blade, full finished Damascus steel barrels........ **30.75**

$38.50 AUBREY SPECIAL DAMASCUS BARREL SHOTGUN

AT $38.50 WE FURNISH THIS beautifully engraved, extra highly finished Aubrey Special Hammerless Shotgun, fitted with three-blade Damascus steel barrels, one of the most beautiful guns ever turned out in an American factory. This is the highest priced Aubrey gun carried in stock by us, and compares in finish, workmanship and material with guns sold by other manufacturers at prices ranging from $100.00 to $150.00. We originally only made these guns to special order, one at a time, and in so doing were compelled to charge not less than $60.00 for this very same grade of gun, but the demand for these guns was so large, every gun sent out brought so many returns, that we decided to stock this quality of gun, and in manufacturing them in quantities where we heretofore made them one at a time, we are able to sell it to you at the remarkably low price of $38.50.

UNDERSTAND, this gun will shoot no better, last no longer and give no better satisfaction as a shooting arm than the $13.85 Aubrey shown on a preceding page, for the machine parts are identical throughout. This, like the $13.85 Aubrey, is the best shooting gun made in the world. No gun made at any price will shoot farther, kill at longer range, give better target, better balance or safety. The only object in buying a specially fine finished gun like this, in fact, the only inducement we can offer you is, that you will have not only the best mechanical and the best shooting gun possible to build but you will also have something entirely out of the ordinary, a handsomer and better gun than any in your neighborhood. You can match it up, if you please, with any gun made to order by any other maker, even at $100.00 or $150.00 or more. There's a world of work; days and days of hand labor at the hands of the most skilled artist have gone into this gun to make it the thing of beauty that it is. The very elaborate hand engraving on the lock plates, the frame, the break, the guards, etc.; the buried imported Italian walnut wood that has gone into the stock has been selected with great care, the beautiful three-blade imported Liege full Damascus steel barrels have been selected with great care, all parts have been very highly polished and finished; in short, this gun has been gotten out practically without regard to expense. It's Mr. Aubrey's masterpiece, by far the finest gun we carry in stock, and the price we name, $38.50, barely covers the cost of material and labor in our own factory, with but our one small percentage of profit added. It is no doubt a handsomer and better gun than many special made to order guns that are sold at $100.00 to $150.00.

READ WHAT ONE OF OUR CUSTOMERS SAYS OF THE FINEST AUBREY GUN.

Sears, Roebuck & Co. Milford, Conn.

Dear Sirs:—I take pleasure in writing a few lines to let you know that I am very much pleased with my special order A. J. Aubrey gun, which I received direct from the factory. I have given it a good, fair trial and it outshoots and outpatterns (with various sized shot ranging from No. 6 to No. 12) any other gun that I own, and I own four high priced American made guns which aggregate sixteen times as much in cost as my Aubrey, and I consider the Aubrey far superior in design and workmanship to any one of them and a finer balanced gun, also showing a higher art of scientific gun making. Several years ago I worked as a machinist and tool maker and also on gun work, so I think that my judgment ought to be good, as I have been a hard man to please in the matter of guns. I think your Mr. A. J. Aubrey one of the most competent men to provide for the special needs and fancies of trap and field shots. Wishing you every success, I remain,

Very truly yours, C. E. BACKER, V. M. D.

No. 6L58

IF YOU ARE DESIROUS OF OWNING THE FINEST GUN IN YOUR NEIGHBORHOOD, a gun that is a work of art, that is particularly well finished, which is made and finished with the same care and attention to the most minute details as a high priced watch, a gun that is most beautifully engraved by hand and fitted with the highest quality imported walnut stock, a gun, in short, that possesses everything that would tend to make a gun beautiful and mechanically perfect, then we would advise that you purchase this special Aubrey gun at $38.50.

THIS GUN IS MADE IN 12-GAUGE ONLY, 30 AND 32-INCH BARRELS CARRIED IN STOCK (26 and 28-inch made to special order, requiring several weeks' delay), weight, 7½ to 8 pounds, regular stock full choke bored (can be furnished cylinder bored, one barrel cylinder, one barrel choke, as desired, to special order), full pistol grip stock, fitted with finest imported three-blade Damascus barrels. State length of barrels wanted.

No. 6L58 Price........ **$38.50**

THE NEW 1908 MODEL T. BARKER SHOTGUN
FORMERLY SOLD FOR $16.35 NOW
$12.45
This is the old favorite T. Barker Double Barrel Shotgun, a gun which we have sold for a great many years and which is probably better and more favorably known than any double barrel imported shotgun on the market. This gun from the start was identified by its sterling qualities and through the fact that it was a better gun than any of the Belgian guns offered in competition. While we have greatly reduced our line of Belgian guns, we have decided to continue handling this famous gun because of its sterling qualities and the fact that it has thousands of friends throughout the United States who would sooner shoot a T. Barker Shotgun than any other double barrel imported hammer gun.
HOW WE WERE ABLE TO IMPROVE THE QUALITY OF THIS GUN AND REDUCE OUR PRICE. It is probably impossible for you to understand how we can improve the quality of a gun without raising our price, much less lowering it as we have in this instance, the T. Barker Gun having been sold for $16.35 during the season of 1906 and we are now offering the improved gun for $12.45.
AS YOU WILL NOTE, in going through our catalogue, we have greatly reduced our line of imported guns and in reducing our line we have figured to concentrate the business on double barrel hammer guns on our new line of high grade American guns and this, our Improved Model T. Barker Gun. After carefully considering the matter, comparing the various valuable features embodied in Belgian hammer guns formerly catalogued by us and those embodied in this T. Barker Gun, we found that by improving the T. Barker Gun we could embody all the valuable features of the other Belgian guns in this gun, as well as retain such features as are peculiar to itself, and by doing this, by concentrating our business on imported guns to a large extent on this T. Barker Gun, and taking into consideration the enormous business-we have had on this gun during the past season, we were able, for the season of 1908, to contract for these guns in quantities twice as large as ever before, and in making this contract, we were able to demand certain improvements and certain changes for the better in this gun without suffering any increase in cost; in fact, this enormous quantity has enabled us to obtain the improved model gun at even a lower cost than we were obliged to pay for the old model gun, of which reduction in cost we give you full benefit in our reduced price of $12.45.
IN RECOMMENDING A GUN TO YOU, without wishing to detract in any way from the value of this most excellent gun, we ask that you, before making your selection, read carefully the description given of the A. J. Aubrey Hammer and Hammerless Guns, fully described and illustrated elsewhere in this catalogue. Understand, we do not mean to detract from the value of this T. Barker Gun, for if it were not a good gun, we would not devote space to it, nor would we handle it, but we want you to know about the A. J. Aubrey guns, as we believe that these guns are the most wonderful guns ever manufactured. They are distinctive in their construction, they have many features peculiar to themselves which add to their value; in fact, in design, finish and mechanical construction they are entirely different from any other double barrel hammer or hammerless gun, and therefore, whether you buy this T. Barker Gun at $12.45, or an A. J. Aubrey Gun, or any other gun, we want you to know about these guns. Whatever gun you order will be shipped to you under our binding guarantee with the assurance that if you do not find the gun entirely satisfactory in every respect, you have the full privilege of returning it to us after giving it a thorough and careful trial, and your money, as well as any transportation charges you may have paid, will be immediately returned to you.
THIS T. BARKER GUN, as we offer it today at $12.45, is a better gun than any previous model. At $12.45 we are offering you the improved model gun, a better gun than that for which we were formerly compelled to ask $16.35.
ILLUSTRATION SHOWING THE PATENT FORE END FRAME AND INLAID FULL PISTOL GRIP.
T. BARKER
DESCRIPTION.
BARRELS—The barrels are made from an extra fine quality of steel, bored true to gauge, all barrels are choke bored. Different from the cheaper Belgian guns, all barrels are reinforced to give them great strength and to make them ideal barrels for either smokeless or black powder. These barrels are given the highest possible genuine Damascus finish and in this respect present an appearance similar to the highest priced guns. All barrels have heavy extension rib, the highest grade shell extractor, they are bored for long, hard shooting, have wonderful force, penetration and power, and make an exceptionally good pattern.
FRAMES—The frames are all made of the highest grade drop steel forgings, they are carefully machined, and being made where labor is cheap there is a vast amount of hand labor put on the finishing.
LOCKS—The locks are all extra strong made from the highest grade of material, given a vast amount of hand finish to insure a perfect fit and perfect work. The locks are all rebounding, all fitted with low circular hammers, the frame is made with a long, strong tang; neat top snap break, beautifully shaped trigger guard and triggers.
STOCK—The stocks are genuine imported walnut stocks, carefully selected, beautifully finished, full pistol grip, fancy butt plate and grip plate, pistol grip and fore end are checkered by hand.
ENGRAVING—This is one of the most elaborately hand engraved guns made, in fact, if it were not for the low price for skilled labor (professional engravers) in Liege, it would not be possible to put the elaborate engraving on this gun, as the engraving alone would be worth the price we ask for the complete gun. Unfortunately, no illustration or description we can show here will do this engraving justice. You must see it, examine it and compare it with other guns to appreciate the elaborate hand engraved finish on this gun.
SILVER INLAYING—The locks are ornamented with a beautiful silver inlaid dog. The small illustration does not in any way do it justice. You will note the picture of the dog on one lock immediately back of the circular hammer. This stands out conspicuously and effects a beautiful finish in the gun when you see it.
GENERAL CONSTRUCTION, STRENGTH AND SHOOTING QUALITIES.
THIS T. BARKER GUN AT $12.45 is without doubt the most wonderful value ever offered in an imported gun, and its value lies greatly in the above qualities. This gun was built specially for the use of nitro powder or smokeless powder The breech is heavy and specially reinforced; the bolts are made of solid steel, extra heavy; the top lever connects directly with the barrel bolt, making a positive and direct action; the doll's head extension rib locks firmly in the frame, giving this gun a strength and solidity not found in any of the lower grade guns offered by other dealers at far more money. The shooting qualities of this T. Barker Gun are excellent. The gun is choke bored on the taper system, which means that the choke extends from breech to muzzle, instead of what is known as the jug choke, which means that the barrels are choke bored only 6 inches from the muzzle. The taper choke extends the full length of the barrel, meaning that the barrels have to be built and bored specially, making this the most expensive method of choke boring a gun, but at the same time, insuring pattern and penetration such as it would be impossible to find in a gun choke bored by any other method than the taper system.
THE VARIETY OF HAMMER GUNS we offer is very large, and you ought not have any trouble in making a suitable selection. You will find double barrel hammer guns ranging in price from $7.65 and higher, all of which are fully guaranteed to give you satisfaction and to be excellent value for the money. Remember that when you buy a gun of us you are fully protected by our binding guarantee, a guarantee which insures you satisfaction or your money refunded, a guarantee far more liberal in its terms than any other house ever offered. There is not a gun that we sell in our entire line that is not absolutely safe, and which we do not feel perfectly free in recommending to you, therefore, in making your selection you can be guided entirely by your choice of style or construction, and by the amount you are able to invest.
OUR GREAT FREE TRIAL OFFER
SEND US YOUR ORDER give gauge and length as listed below, enclose price, and we will send you the T. Barker Gun by express or freight, as you may direct, with the understanding and agreement that you can give the gun ten days' trial, during which time you can put it to every test, you can test it for long range killing (don't be afraid to add two or three rods to the range you have been able to reach with killing effect with any of the cheaper grades of imported or American guns), give it a thorough test, try it out in every way, try it out with smokeless and with black powder, test it for penetration, for target, for accuracy of gauge, test as you like in your own way, compare it with other guns sold at anything like the price, and if at any time during the ten days you become dissatisfied for any reason whatever, you are at liberty, to return the gun to us at our expense, and we will immediately return your money together with any express or freight charges you may have paid.
SPECIAL FEATURES
BARRELS. These barrels are given a royal Damascus finish. Unfortunately, illustrations printed on this paper will give you but very little idea of the finish of these barrels, but in finish they at least approach, if not equal, the most expensive genuine Damascus barrels made, and so far as strength is concerned, they are as strong as it is possible to make barrels with the highest grade of steel obtainable, and remember, they are exceedingly strong barrels, guaranteed for either black or smokeless powder.
HAND ENGRAVING. For this, the model of 1908, we have demanded from the manufacturers a finer job of hand engraving, and as a result we present to you this season in the T Barker a most elaborately hand engraved gun.
SPECIAL FINISHED STOCKS. For 1908 we have given special attention to the stocks, and every stock is guaranteed genuine imported walnut, walnut grown in Europe, carefully selected, beautifully grained, full pistol grip, and fore end handsomely checkered by hand, fancy rubber butt plate butt and pistol grip.
OUR SPECIAL REDUCED PRICE,
$12.45
No. 6L111A

Catalogue No.	Grade	Style of Barrels	Gauge	Length of Barrels	Weight of Gun, pounds	Finish	Price
6L111A	No. 678	2-Blade	12	30 or 32 in.	7½ to 8	Hand Engraved	$12.45
6L111B	No. 678	Royal	16	30 in.	6¾ to 7	Hand Engraved	12.60
6L111D	No. 678	Damascus	10	32 in.	8¾ to 9½	Hand Engraved	12.95
6L113E	No. 678	Finish	12	36 in.	8 to 8¼	Hand Engraved	14.15

Weight, packed for shipment, about 14 pounds. Always state length of barrels wanted.

L. C. SMITH HAMMERLESS GUNS

MADE BY THE HUNTER ARMS CO., FULTON, N. Y.

PRICES—THE MANUFACTURER FIXES THE SELLING PRICE OF THESE GUNS AND WILL NOT ALLOW US OR ANY OTHER HOUSE TO SELL THEM LOWER.

OUR BINDING GUARANTEE. EVERY GUN WHICH WE SELL IS COVERED BY OUR BINDING GUARANTEE, WHICH MEANS THAT IF ANY PIECE OR PART GIVES OUT BY REASON OF DEFECTIVE MATERIAL OR WORKMANSHIP WITHIN ONE YEAR, WE WILL REPLACE IT FREE OF CHARGE. You may order any gun of us, and if you do not find it satisfactory, or as represented, you may return it to us at our expense of transportation charges both ways and we will immediately refund your money.

GENERAL DESCRIPTION. All L. C. Smith Hammerless Guns are full choke bored, have English walnut pistol grip stock, tapered matted rib, case hardened locks and frame, rubber butt plate, compensating extension rib and fore end and patent safety slide. OUR PATENT GLOBE SIGHT is furnished free with all Smith guns.

ARMOR STEEL BARRELS.

Globe Sight free with this gun.

BORED FOR NITRO POWDER.

$25.00

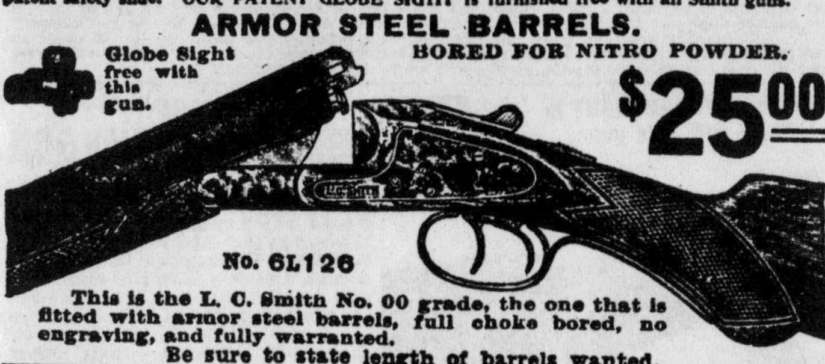

No. 6L126

This is the L. C. Smith No. 00 grade, the one that is fitted with armor steel barrels, full choke bored, no engraving, and fully warranted.

Be sure to state length of barrels wanted.

Catalogue Number	Grade	Style of Barrels	Gauge	Length of Barrels	Weight	Price
6L126	No. 00	Armor Steel	12	30 or 32 inches	7½ to 8 lbs.	$25.00

Weight, packed for shipment, about 14 pounds.

NOTICE. All our guns are tested with heavy loads and cannot burst except by carelessness, obstruction in the barrel or improper home loaded shells with nitro or dense powder. We are not responsible for burst gun barrels.

DAMASCUS BARRELS.

GLOBE SIGHT free with this gun.

BORED FOR NITRO POWDER.

$35.25

No. 6L140

The No. 0, No. 1 and No. 2 grades are all fitted with Damascus barrels of three qualities. All of them are very good, but the figure varies in size; for example, the figure of the three-blade is much finer than in the plain Damascus. The No. 0 is plain finished, the No. 1 has line engraving and the No. 2 has fine scroll and game engraving on the lock plates. All are choke bored for black or nitro powder and fully warranted by the factory. **Be sure to state length of barrels wanted.**

Catalogue Number	Grade	Style of Barrels	Finish	Gauge	Length of Barrels	Weight, Lbs.	Price
6L132	No. 0	Damascus	Plain	12	30 or 32 in.	7½ to 8	$35.25
6L136	No. 1	2-Blade Damascus	Plain Line Engraving	12	30 or 32 in.	7¾ to 8	45.00
6L140	No. 2	3-Blade Damascus	Game and Scroll Engraving	12	30 or 32 in.	7¾ to 8	60.00

Weight, packed for shipment, about 14 pounds.

REMINGTON AUTOMATIC SHOTGUN $29.00

GENUINE REMINGTON AUTOMATIC SHOTGUN

$29.00

MANUFACTURED BY THE REMINGTON ARMS CO., ILION, N. Y., under the Browning Patent. This gun is a five-shot, self loading, magazine gun, holding four shells in the magazine and one in the chamber. After firing the first shot, the recoil opens the breech block, automatically throws the empty shell, carries the new shell from the magazine into the chamber and closes the breech block. In other words, to shoot the five shells, it is simply necessary to pull the trigger five times. The gun is made with a solid breech, and is absolutely safe. The barrel is made of the highest quality carbon steel with reinforced breech; the frame and barrel are finished in military blue. Length of barrel, 28 inches, beautifully tapered from breech to muzzle, with matted top; choke bored. This gun is fitted with pistol grip, selected walnut stock and walnut fore end.

No. 6L161 **Remington Automatic Self Loading Shotgun**, 12-gauge only, 28-inch barrel, weight, 7¾ pounds. Price.................... **$29.00**

Weight, packed for shipment, about 14 pounds.

REMINGTON "K" GRADE DOUBLE BARREL HAMMERLESS SHOTGUN

Globe Sight FREE with this Gun.

PRICED AT **$23.00**

The "K" Grade Remington Double Barrel Hammerless Shotgun is a plain, well built, substantial gun, built for service, and like all Remington guns the greatest care is given to every piece and part. It is fitted with blue armory steel barrels, matted nitro extension rib, top snap action; strong forged frame beautifully case hardened, straight grained walnut stock and fore end nicely checkered; a plain finished gun but a good one. State length of barrels wanted. Weight, packed for shipment, about 14 pounds.

Cat. No.	Grade	Style of Barrels	Style of Extractor	Gauge	Length Barrels	Weight, Lbs.	Price
6L166	K	Blued Armory Steel	Regular	12	30 or 32 in	7¼ to 7¾	$23.00

No. 3 GRADE REMINGTON DOUBLE BARREL SHOTGUN

PRICED AT **$24.85**

GLOBE SIGHT free with this Gun.

DESCRIPTION.

All No. 3 Grade Remington Double Barrel Shotguns have two-blade Damascus barrels, matted rib, double bolt locks, extension rib, rebounding hammers, checkered pistol grip stock and fore end, top snap action, choke bored on the latest improved system for nitro or black powder, frame beautifully case hardened. All parts are interchangeable. All hammer guns have Deeley & Edge patent fore end. State length of barrels wanted. Order by catalogue number in full.

Catalogue Number	Grade	Style of Barrels	Gauge	Length Barrels	Weight	Price
6L167A	No. 3	Damascus	12	30 or 32 inches	7¼ to 8 lbs.	$24.85
6L167D	No. 3	Damascus	10	32 inches	9 to 9¾ lbs.	

Weight, packed for shipment, about 14 pounds.

REMINGTON AUTOMATIC SHELL EJECTING DAMASCUS BARREL GUN $31.00

MADE BY THE REMINGTON ARMS CO., OF ILION, N. Y.,

one of the oldest and most reliable manufacturers of arms in the world. This gun at $31.00, is fitted with the finest two-blade Damascus barrels, choke bored on the Remington system, with finely matted rib with nitro bite on the extension, automatic cocking device which cocks the hammer when opening the gun, and improved safety attachment. The frame is made of heavy drop steel forging, beautifully mottled and case hardened, fitted with a well seasoned, imported walnut stock, checkered pistol grip and fine walnut, patent snap fore end.

THE AUTOMATIC EJECTOR OF THIS GUN is very simple and is absolutely positive. It works independently, and will throw out either one or two shells. In case but one shell is fired it will throw out the empty shell, and in case both are fired, will eject the two empty shells simultaneously. If the gun is loaded but not fired, the ejector works as a positive extractor, and will not eject the loaded shells, but will extract them from the chamber, the same as in an ordinary gun. If you want a shotgun with a positive automatic ejector, fine two-blade Damascus barrels, we would advise the purchase of this gun, for at our price of $31.00, it is exceptional value.

GENUINE 2-BLADE DAMASCUS

CHOKE BORED

$31.00

No. 6L172

Cat. No.	Grade	Style of Barrels	Style of Extractor	Gauge	Length of Barrels	Weight, Lbs.	Price
6L172	K E D	2-Blade Damascus	Automatic	12	30 in.	7½ to 8	$31.00

Shipping weight, about 14 pounds when packed.

YOUR MONEY WILL BE IMMEDIATELY RETURNED TO YOU FOR ANY GOODS NOT PERFECTLY SATISFACTORY.

OUR LINE OF IMPORTED DOUBLE BARREL SHOTGUNS.

WE IMPORT OUR OWN GUNS direct from Belgium thereby saving the profit of the importer and jobber which enables us to offer imported guns at less money than dealers pay for them. Our principle is to sell imported guns as we do all other merchandise at one small narrow margin of profit from the maker to the consumer. We handle more goods than any house in the United States selling to the consumer and by comparing our prices with other houses you will find that we are 10 per cent to 25 per cent below any competition.

In our line of imported guns we desire to call your attention to our Double Barrel Breech Loader, our T. Barker, our Special Greener Action Guns, and our high grade machine guns. We are in a position to make you prices on this class of goods below any competition, and if you will favor us with your order we know you will be so well pleased that you will not only give us your future orders, but recommend our house to your friends. Think also of our **PROFIT SHARING PLAN.**

HOW OUR IMPORTED GUNS are tested by the Belgian Government. All our imported guns are tested by the government of Belgium in the following manner: After the barrels are first made and before they are brazed together, reamed or chambered, they are sent to the government proof house where a plug is screwed into the breech of the barrel and it is loaded with 11 drams of good quality black powder and a bullet weighing 1 ounce. After this test they are brazed together and tested again with 7 drams of good black powder and a bullet weighing 1 ounce. After this second test is made, the frame, or breech, is fitted to the barrels and they are tested for the third time with 6⅛ drams of powder and 1⅛ ounces of shot. You will see that the test is very severe, and each and every Belgian gun which we sell, from the cheapest to the best, is put through this same test, so if you buy a Belgian gun of us you are assured that you are getting a gun which has been thoroughly tested for Sears, Roebuck & Co. with more powder and more shot than you can possibly put into a shell. In order to put such a heavy charge into the barrels, the government must load from the muzzle, and any gun you buy from us is safe, as you will see by the foregoing rigid tests.

AN IMPORTED EXTENSION RIB GUN

10, 12 and 16-Gauges.

$6.35

Our Patent GLOBE SIGHT is FREE with this gun.

No. 6F237A

The above illustration, engraved from a photograph, will give you an idea of the appearance of this gun.

Order by catalogue number in full and be sure to state length of barrel wanted.

—OUR— $6.35 BACK ACTION GUN

We offer you a high grade, imported double barrel shotgun at $6.35 which cannot be duplicated elsewhere for less than $8.00 to $10.00. We import these guns direct, and you save the wholesale and retail dealers' profit. The result is you buy a gun for less than one-half the retail price, 20 to 40 per cent cheaper than other houses advertise, and far below the price you would pay for a poorer gun from other houses. We guarantee every gun to have barrels of best Raleigh steel.

Catalogue No.	Grade	Style of Barrels	Gauge	Length of Barrels	Weight	Price
6F237A	No. 559	Laminat'd	12	30 or 32 in.	7¼ to 8 lbs.	$6.35
6F237B	No. 559	steel	16	30 inches	6¾ to 7 lbs.	6.60
6F237D	No. 559	finish	10	32 inches	8¼ to 9¾ lbs.	6.85

Weight, packed for shipment, about 14 pounds.

GENERAL DESCRIPTION. This gun is fitted with top snap break, laminated steel finished barrels, made of best Raleigh steel, strong back action rebounding locks, L-shaped Edwards' extension rib, rebounding hammers, straight grain walnut stock and fore end nicely checkered, pistol grip stock, patent snap fore end, flat plain rib, left barrel choke bored, right barrel cylinder bored, nitro firing pins, case hardened lock plates and frame.

RUSTED AND DAMAGED GUNS OR RIFLES. Do not return to us a gun, revolver or rifle which is rusted, pitted or has the finish worn off, for we have no way of selling these guns. If you have a gun, rifle or revolver which needs repairing, first write us, fully describing the article and what is broken and we may be able to send you the part necessary, thus saving the express charges on the gun both ways.

OUR HIGHLY ENGRAVED DIANA STYLE BREECH SHOTGUN.

30 OR 32-INCH, **$7.85** | 38-INCH, **$9.78**

ENGRAVED LOCKS, MATTED RIB, TOP SNAP, 12-GAUGE ONLY, PISTOL GRIP, PATENT FORE END.

Send 10 cents for our Booklet of Useful Information to Shooters.

WE FURNISH OUR PATENT GLOBE SIGHT FREE WITH EVERY SHOTGUN.

Doubles the Value of any Shotgun.

No. 6F238

This illustration, engraved from a photograph, will give you some idea of the gun. All our imported guns are thoroughly tested for safety (see our Belgian government test above), and we have no hesitation in saying that they are superior to any guns in the market. Don't buy guns known as seconds when you can buy first quality guns of us.

CASE HARDENED FRAME, 30, 32 OR 38-INCH BARRELS.

WE CHARGE YOU NOTHING FOR BOXING AND PACKING GUNS FOR SHIPMENT.

DESCRIPTION. This gun is fitted with top snap break, back action locks, two-blade Damascus finished barrels, Edwards' L-shaped extension rib, handsomely matted, rebounding circular hammers, straight grained seasoned walnut stock and fore end nicely checkered, pistol grip stock, nitro firing pins, patent snap fore end, case hardened frame and lock plates, Diana style breech, the frame and locks being highly engraved, and the barrels are bored smooth and true to gauge for black or smokeless powder. The left barrel is choke bored and the right barrel cylinder bored. Always state length of barrel when you order.

Catalogue Number	Grade	Style of Barrels	Gauge	Length Barrels	Weight	Price
6F238	No. 569	Two-blade Da-	12	30 or 32 in.	7¼ to 8 lbs.	$7.85
6F239	No. 569	mascus finish	12	38 inches	8 to 8¼ lbs.	9.78

Weight, packed for shipment, about 14 pounds.

$1.32 per Hundred Buys Highest Grade Loaded Shells Made. SEE PAGE 164.

Our Patent Globe Sight Furnished Free with this Gun.

FOR $8.38 we offer you a GENUINE BAR LOCK DOUBLE BARREL BREECH LOADER.

OUR CELEBRATED SAM HOLT GUNS FOR $8.38.

CASE HARDENED MOUNTINGS. EXTENSION RIB. BAR LOCKS.

12-Gauge Only.

THIS IS A LOWER PRICE for a bar lock gun than most houses in this country ask for a back action lock double barrel breech loader. All these guns have been put through the Belgian government rigid test and for strength, durability and finish they are superior to any bar lock gun ever offered by any other house.

LOADED SHELLS $1.32 per 100. **See page 164.**

Notice our prices on SMOKELESS POWDER SHELLS

We beat all competitors.

No. 6F247

The Celebrated **SAM HOLT GUN** is made especially for us under season contract and will be found to give entire satisfaction for field shooting. THE BARRELS are made from celebrated Raleigh steel and the frame from best forgings. The barrels are bored smooth and accurate and are chambered to gauge.

DESCRIPTION. Our Sam Holt Gun is fitted with top snap break, strong bar locks, laminated steel finished barrels, Edwards' L-shaped extension rib nicely fitted, rebounding circular hammers, straight grain well seasoned checkered stock and fore end, pistol grip stock, nitro firing pins, patent snap fore end, chase engraving on the locks, case hardened frame and lock plates, bored smooth and true to gauge for black or smokeless powder. The left barrel is choke bored and the right barrel is cylinder bored for field shooting. Always state length of barrels wanted in your order.

Catalogue Number	Grade	Style of Barrels	Gauge	Length Barrels	Weight	Price
6F247	No. 659	Laminated	12	30 or 32 in.	7¼ to 8 lbs.	$8.38

Weight, packed for shipment, about 14 pounds.

WE GUARANTEE ALL OUR SHOTGUNS FOR BUCKSHOT WHEN LOADED AS FOLLOWS:

This illustration shows how buckshot should be loaded in a shell.

1st—put in the powder; 2d—put in a card wad; 3rd—put in two felt wads; 4th—put in a layer of buckshot; 5th—a card wad, then another layer of buckshot and a card wad. Always put a card wad between each layer of buckshot and if you wish you may sprinkle sawdust around the buckshot or in cold weather you may use lard or paraffin around the buckshot instead of sawdust.

RULE FOR LOADING BUCKSHOT. The following rule is for Raymond shot which we have tested. You may use other shot, but if you do it must be the same size as Raymond, so the pellets will lie flat and not pile up on the wad, otherwise they will strain the muzzle of the gun.

A **12-gauge shell** should take three No. 4 buck, four No. 6 buck or five No. 8 buckshot in each layer. Don't vary from this. Notice, these are all even numbers of buckshot.

A **10-gauge shell** should take three No. 3 buck, four No. 5 buck or five No. 7 buckshot in each layer. Notice, they are all uneven numbers.

A **16-gauge shell** should take three No. 5 buck or four No. 7 buckshot in each layer. **Don't try to use larger sizes or you may injure the barrel and we will not be responsible for same.**

HOW A SHOTGUN BARREL IS CHOKE BORED. For the benefit of our customers who are not familiar with choke boring, we give here illustration of how a shotgun barrel is choke bored. From the illustration you will imagine that a shotgun barrel has been cut in two the entire length, and you are looking at the inside of the barrel. You will notice that the chamber is large, the rest of the bore (cylinder bore) is smaller and of the same diameter until you come to about 1 inch from the muzzle, which is smaller than the cylinder bore from the chamber to the choke. This is known as taper choke; that is to say, the diameter is the same after it leaves the chamber until it meets the choke about 1 inch from the muzzle, when it tapers slightly, leaving the muzzle about one or two gauges smaller than the diameter of the cylinder bore from the chamber forward. It requires fine reamers and skill to taper choke a shotgun barrel. The difference between the cylinder and choke bore is hardly great enough to notice with the naked eye and the philosophy of choke bore is that the shot travels normally until it meets the choke when it becomes concentrated while leaving the barrel, and being concentrated puts a larger number of pellets in a 30-inch circle than if the shotgun was cylinder bored. Cylinder bored shotguns are similar, except that they are not smaller at the muzzle, the bore being the same from the chamber to the muzzle end of the barrel.

Chamber Choke

THE CELEBRATED THOMAS BARKER DOUBLE BARREL BREECH LOADING SHOTGUN, $9.80

Made in 16-gauge, 6½ to 7 pounds. 30-inch barrels.
20-gauge, 6¼ to 6½ pounds. 30-inch barrels.
The illustration will give you some idea of the appearance of this gun.
Over 50,000 now in use.

GENERAL DESCRIPTION. Our Thomas Barker gun is made with top snap break, Scott action, strong bar locks, laminated steel finished barrels, extension rib beautifully matted, rebounding circular hammers, straight grained walnut stock and fore end nicely checkered, full pistol grip stock with shield inlaid, nitro firing pins, patent snap fore end, chased engraving on locks, case hardened frame and lock plates, left barrel full choke bored, right barrel cylinder bored; all barrels bored smooth and true to gauge. A wonder for the money and a gun that will shoot black or smokeless powder. Always state length of barrel and gauge wanted. They come in 10, 12, 16 and 20-gauge. One of the best guns made for field shooting. Mention gauge wanted. Weight, packed for shipment, about 14 pounds.

Our Patent Globe Sight furnished free with this gun. Doubles the value of any shotgun for wing shooting.

LEFT BARREL CHOKE BORED.

No. 6F249A
12-GAUGE LOADED SHELLS, $1.32 per 100.
See page 164.

Catalogue No.	Grade	Style of Barrels	Gauge	Length of Barrels	Weight of Gun	Price
6F249A	No. 659 MD	Laminated Steel Finish	12	30 or 32 in.	7½ to 8 lbs.	$ 9.80
6F249B	No. 659 MD		16	30 in.	6½ to 7 lbs.	9.90
6F249C	No. 659 MD		20	30 in.	6¼ to 6½ lbs.	9.95
6F249D	No. 659 MD		10	32 in.	8¾ to 9¼ lbs.	10.15

Always look through the barrels before putting in a new shell, to avoid accident.

OUR PATENT GLOBE SIGHT FURNISHED FREE WITH THIS GUN. Our sight adds many dollars' value to the shooting possibilities of a gun, but we furnish it FREE with this gun.

LOADED SHELLS $1.32 PER 100. SEE PAGE 164.

OUR $9.42 IMPORTED DOUBLE BARREL BREECH LOADER, WITH ENGRAVED LOCKS.

FOR $9.42 we offer you this genuine BAR LOCK DOUBLE BARREL BREECH LOADER

THIS IS A LOWER PRICE than most houses ask for a common plain back action lock double barrel breech loader. All these guns have been put through the Belgian government rigid test, and for strength, durability and finish they are superior to any bar lock guns ever offered by any other house and present a handsome appearance.

No. 6F250

THIS GUN is made especially for us under season contract and will be found to give entire satisfaction for field shooting. THE BARRELS are made from celebrated RALEIGH STEEL and the frame from best forgings. The barrels are bored smooth and accurate and are chambered to gauge.

Catalogue No.	Grade	Style of Barrels	Gauge	Length of Barrels	Weight of Gun	Price
6F250	No. 639 ME	2-Blade Damascus Finish	12	30 or 32 in.	7¼ to 8 lbs.	$9.42

Weight, packed for shipment, about 14 pounds.

DETAILED DESCRIPTION. Our engraved lock guns fitted with Scott action, top snap break, strong bar locks, two-blade Damascus finished barrels, rebounding circular hammers, straight grained well seasoned walnut stock and fore end nicely checkered, full pistol grip stock with inlaid shield, patent snap fore end, nitro firing pins, scroll engraving on the lock plates, case hardened frame and lock plates, bored smooth and true to gauge for black and smokeless powder, left barrel choke bored, right barrel cylinder bored, suitable for black or smokeless powder. Always mention length of barrel wanted.

Our Patent Globe Sight furnished free with this gun. Worth the price of the gun for wing shooting.

OUR CARVED STOCK DOUBLE BARREL BREECH LOADING SHOTGUN, $10.98

We sell more guns to the consumer than any five mail order houses combined.

AT $10.98 we offer you this handsome double barrel genuine bar lock breech loading shotgun, fitted with our hexagon matted breech and two-blade Damascus finished barrels.

DESCRIPTION. Our Carved Stock Shotgun is fitted with Scott action top snap break, bar locks. Damascus finished barrels with matted hexagon breech beautifully matted as shown in the illustration. Extension rib, Edwards' patent, rebounding circular hammers, straight grained walnut stock and fore end beautifully carved in leaf design, pistol grip stock, nitro firing pins, patent snap fore end, case hardened frame and lock plates, left barrel choke bored, right barrel cylinder bored, bored true to gauge for black or smokeless powder. Always mention length of barrels wanted.

No. 6F257
Order by Number.

Send 10 cents for our Booklet of Useful Information to Shooters.

Catalogue No.	Grade	Style of Barrels	Gauge	Length of Barrels	Weight of Gun	Price
6F257	No. 669O	Damascus Finish	12	30 or 32 in.	7¼ to 7¾ lbs.	$10.98

Weight, packed for shipment, about 14 pounds.

OUR CELEBRATED EBONIZED DOUBLE BARREL BREECH LOADING SHOTGUN, $10.69

Our Globe Sight FREE with this gun.

MADE IN 12-GAUGE ONLY. LEFT BARREL CHOKE BORED.

AN IMPORTED GUN, MADE IN LIEGE, BELGIUM.

FOR $10.69 we furnish our celebrated ebonized black stock and black fore end double barrel hammer breech loading shotgun, one of the most attractive and well made shotguns ever offered by any house, a gun that must be seen to be appreciated, as it is so different from the regular walnut stock and fore end usually applied to shotguns.

WE ARE THE LARGEST IMPORTERS in the United States, selling goods from the manufacturers to the consumer. We import all our own foreign guns direct from Liege, Belgium, which is probably the largest gun making center in the world, and all our imported guns have the Belgium Government test, as explained on another page of this catalogue. When you buy a Belgium gun from us you do not pay a wholesaler's, jobber's, or retail dealer's profit, but you buy the gun at one small profit from the manufacturer to the consumer, thus making a great saving on your purchase.

OUR CELEBRATED EBONIZED STOCK and fore end double barrel breech loading shotgun is fitted with a forged breech, lock plates are nicely polished and handsomely nickeled, elegantly engraved in scroll design, as shown in the illustration. The barrel is finished in two-blade Damascus pattern with handsome matted rib, latest style Edwards' extension rib, bored smooth and true to gauge, the right barrel is cylinder bored and the left barrel is choke bored for field shooting.

THE LOCKS are of the bar lock type with rebounding hammers, which fly back to half cock after the gun is fired. The butt plate and top lever are nickel plated to conform with the frame and locks of the gun. The stock is beautifully finished in black ebonized color, checkered in diamond design with German silver pins in the diamonds; has scroll carving on the outer edge of the diamond field, as shown in the illustration. The general appearance of the ebonized stock, engraved nickel plated frame, locks and top lever, nickel plated butt plate and the two-blade Damascus finished barrels makes a combination of contrast pleasing to the eye. Always mention length of barrel wanted.

Catalogue No.	Grade	Style of Barrels	Gauge	Length of Barrels	Weight of Gun	Price
6F258	No. 739	2-Blade Damascus Finish	12	30 or 32 in.	7¼ to 8 lbs.	$10.69

Weight, packed for shipment, about 14 pounds.

FREE FURNITURE, FREE CLOTHING. See our PROFIT SHARING PAGES for what is yours FREE WHEN YOU BUY GOODS FROM US.

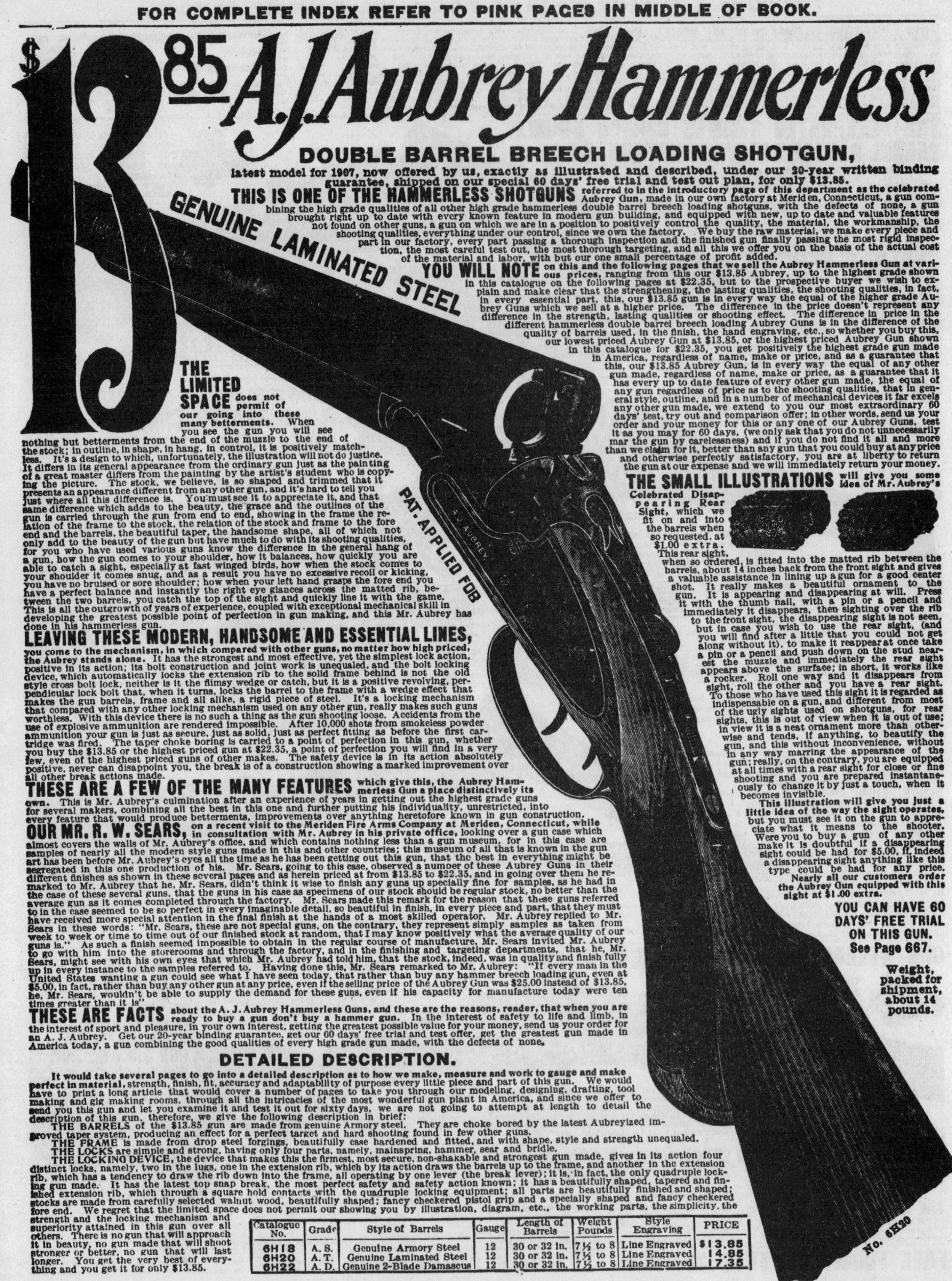

$13.85 A. J. Aubrey Hammerless

DOUBLE BARREL BREECH LOADING SHOTGUN,

latest model for 1907, now offered by us, exactly as illustrated and described, under our 20-year written binding guarantee, shipped on our special 60 days' free trial and test out plan, for only $13.85.

THIS IS ONE OF THE HAMMERLESS SHOTGUNS referred to in the introductory page of this department as the celebrated Aubrey Gun, made in our own factory at Meriden, Connecticut, a gun combining the high grade qualities of all other high grade hammerless double barrel breech loading shotguns, with the defects of none, a gun brought right up to date with every known feature in modern gun building, and equipped with new, up to date and valuable features not found on other guns, a gun on which we are in a position to positively control the quality, the material, the workmanship, the shooting qualities, everything under our control, since we own the factory. We buy the raw material, we make every piece and part in our factory, every part passing a thorough inspection and the finished gun finally passing the most rigid inspection, the most careful test out, the most thorough targeting, and all this we offer you on the basis of the actual cost of the material and labor, with but our one small percentage of profit added.

YOU WILL NOTE on this and the following pages that we sell the Aubrey Hammerless Gun at various prices, ranging from this our $13.85 Aubrey, up to the highest grade shown in this catalogue on the following pages at $22.35, but to the prospective buyer we wish to explain and make clear that the strengthening, the lasting qualities, the shooting qualities, in fact, in every essential part, this, our $13.85 gun is in every way the equal of the higher grade Aubrey Guns which we sell at a higher price. The difference in the price doesn't represent any difference in the strength, lasting qualities or shooting effect. The difference in price in the different hammerless double barrel breech loading Aubrey Guns is in the difference of the quality of barrels used, in the finish, the hand engraving, etc., so whether you buy this, our lowest priced Aubrey Gun at $13.85, or the highest priced Aubrey Gun shown in this catalogue for $22.35, you get positively the highest grade gun made in America, regardless of name, make or price, and as a guarantee that this, our $13.85 Aubrey Gun, is in every way the equal of any other gun made, regardless of name, make or price, as a guarantee that it has every up to date feature of every other gun made, the equal of any gun regardless of price as to the shooting qualities, that in general style, outline, and in a number of mechanical devices it far excels any other gun made, we extend to you our most extraordinary 60 days' test, try out and comparison offer; in other words, send us your order and your money for this or any one of our Aubrey Guns, test it as you may for 60 days, (we only ask that you do not unnecessarily mar the gun by carelessness) and if you do not find it all and more than we claim for it, better than any gun that you could buy at any price and otherwise perfectly satisfactory, you are at liberty to return the gun at our expense and we will immediately return your money.

THE LIMITED SPACE does not permit of our going into these many betterments. When you see the gun you will see nothing but betterments from the end of the muzzle to the end of the stock; in outline, in shape, in hang, in control, it is positively matchless. It's a design to which, unfortunately, the illustration will not do justice. It differs in its general appearance from the ordinary gun just as the painting of a great master differs from the painting by the artist's student who is copying the picture. The stock, we believe, is so shaped and trimmed that it presents an appearance different from any other gun, and it's hard to tell you just where all this difference is. You must see it to appreciate it, and that same difference which adds to the beauty, the grace and the outlines of the gun is carried through the gun from end to end, showing in the frame the relation of the frame to the stock, the relation of the stock and frame to the fore end and the barrels, the beautiful taper, the handsome shape, all of which not only add to the beauty of the gun but have much to do with its shooting qualities, for you who have used various guns know the difference in the general hang of a gun, how the gun comes to your shoulder, how it balances, how quickly you are able to catch a sight, especially at fast winged birds, how when the stock comes to your shoulder it comes snug, and as a result you have no excessive recoil or kicking, you have no bruised or sore shoulder; how when your left hand grasps the fore end you have a perfect balance and instantly the right eye glances across the matted rib, between the two barrels, you catch the top of the sight and quickly line it with the game. This is all the outgrowth of years of experience, coupled with exceptional mechanical skill in developing the greatest possible point of perfection in gun making, and this Mr. Aubrey has done in his hammerless gun.

LEAVING THESE MODERN, HANDSOME AND ESSENTIAL LINES, you come to the mechanism, in which compared with other guns, no matter how high priced, the Aubrey stands alone. It has the strongest and most effective, yet the simplest lock action, positive in its action; its bolt construction and joint work is unequaled, and the bolt locking device, which automatically locks the extension rib to the solid frame behind is not the old style cross bolt lock, neither is it the flimsy wedge or catch, but it is a positive revolving, perpendicular lock bolt that, when it turns, locks the barrel to the frame with a wedge effect that makes the gun barrels, frame and all alike, a rigid piece of steel. It's a locking mechanism that compared with any other locking mechanism used on any other gun, really makes such guns worthless. With this device there is no such a thing as the gun shooting loose. Accidents from the use of explosive ammunition are rendered impossible. After 10,000 shots from smokeless powder ammunition your gun is just as secure, just as solid, just as perfect fitting as before the first cartridge was fired. The taper choke boring is carried to a point of perfection in this gun, whether you buy the $13.85 or the highest priced gun at $22.35, a point of perfection you will find in a very few, even of the highest priced guns of other makes. The safety device is in its action absolutely positive, never can disappoint you, the break is of a construction showing a marked improvement over all other break actions made.

THESE ARE A FEW OF THE MANY FEATURES which give this, the Aubrey Hammerless Gun a place distinctively its own. This is Mr. Aubrey's culmination after an experience of years in getting out the highest grade guns for several makers, combining all the best in this one and further putting his individuality, unrestricted, into every feature that would produce betterments, improvements over anything heretofore known in gun construction.

OUR MR. R. W. SEARS, on a recent visit to the Meriden Fire Arms Company at Meriden, Connecticut, while in consultation with Mr. Aubrey in his private office, looking over a gun case which almost covers the walls of Mr. Aubrey's office, and which contains nothing less than a gun museum, for in this case are samples of nearly all the modern style guns made in this and other countries; this museum of all that is known in the gun art has been before Mr. Aubrey's eyes all the time as he has been getting out this gun, that the best in everything might be segregated in this one production of his. Mr. Sears, going to this case, observed a number of these Aubrey Guns in their different finishes as shown in these several pages and as herein priced at from $13.85 to $22.35, and in going over them he remarked to Mr. Aubrey that he, Mr. Sears, didn't think it wise to finish any guns up specially fine for samples, as he had in the case of these several guns, that the guns in his case as specimens of our stock should be regular stock, no better than the average gun as it comes completed through the factory. Mr. Sears made this remark for the reason that these guns referred to in the case seemed to be so perfect in every imaginable detail, so beautiful in finish, in every piece and part, that they must have received more special attention in the final finish at the hands of a most skilled operator. Mr. Aubrey replied to Mr. Sears in these words: "Mr. Sears, these are not special guns, on the contrary, they represent simply samples as taken from week to week or time to time out of our finished stock at random, that I may know positively what the average quality of our guns is." As such a finish seemed impossible to obtain in the regular course of manufacture, Mr. Sears invited Mr. Aubrey to go with him into the storerooms and through the factory, and in the finishing and targeting departments, that he, Mr. Sears, might see with his own eyes that which Mr. Aubrey had told him, that the stock, indeed, was in quality and finish fully up in every instance to the samples referred to. Having done this, Mr. Sears remarked to Mr. Aubrey: "If every man in the United States wanting a gun could see what I have seen today, that rather than buy any hammer breech loading gun, even at $5.00, in fact, rather than buy any other gun at any price, even if the selling price of the Aubrey Gun was $25.00 instead of $13.85, he, Mr. Sears, wouldn't be able to supply the demand for these guns, even if his capacity for manufacture today were ten times greater than it is"

THESE ARE FACTS about the A. J. Aubrey Hammerless Guns, and these are the reasons, reader, that when you are ready to buy a gun don't buy a hammer gun. In the interest of safety to life and limb, in the interest of sport and pleasure, in your own interest, getting the greatest possible value for your money, send us your order for an A. J. Aubrey. Get our 20-year binding guarantee, get our 60 days' free trial and test offer, get the greatest gun made in America today, a gun combining the good qualities of every high grade gun made, with the defects of none.

THE SMALL ILLUSTRATIONS will give you some idea of Mr. Aubrey's Celebrated Disappearing Rear Sight, which we fit on and into the barrels when so requested, at $1.00 extra. This rear sight, when so ordered, is fitted into the matted rib between the barrels, about 14 inches back from the front sight and gives a valuable assistance in lining up a gun for a good center shot. It really makes a beautiful ornament to the gun. It is appearing and disappearing at will. Press it with the thumb nail, with a pin or a pencil and immediately it disappears, then sighting over the rib to the front sight, the disappearing sight is not seen, but in case you wish to use the rear sight, (and you will find after a little that you could not get along without it), to make it reappear at once take a pin or a pencil and push down on the stud nearest the muzzle and immediately the rear sight appears above the surface; in short, it works like a rocker. Roll one way and it disappears from sight, roll the other and you have a rear sight. To those who have used this sight it is regarded as indispensable on a gun, and different from most of the ugly sights used on shotguns, for rear sights, this is out of view when it is out of use; in view it is a neat ornament more than otherwise and tends, if anything, to beautify the gun, and this without inconvenience, without in any way marring the appearance of the gun; really, on the contrary, you are equipped at all times with a rear sight for close or fine shooting and you are prepared instantaneously to change it by just a touch, when it becomes invisible.

This illustration will give you just a little idea of the way the sight operates, but you must see it on the gun to appreciate what it means to the shooter. Were you to buy a gun of any other make it is doubtful if a disappearing sight could be had for $5.00, if, indeed a disappearing sight anything like this type could be had for any price. **Nearly all our customers order the Aubrey Gun equipped with this sight at $1.00 extra.**

YOU CAN HAVE 60 DAYS' FREE TRIAL ON THIS GUN. **See Page 667.**

Weight, packed for shipment, about 14 pounds.

DETAILED DESCRIPTION.

It would take several pages to go into a detailed description as to how we make, measure and work to gauge and make perfect in material, strength, finish, fit, accuracy and adaptability of purpose every little piece and part of this gun. We would have to print a long article that would cover a number of pages to take you through our modeling, designing, drafting, tool making and gig making rooms, through all the intricacies of the most wonderful gun plant in America, and since we offer to send you this gun and let you examine it and test it out for sixty days, we are not going to attempt at length to detail the description of this gun, therefore, we give the following description in brief:

THE BARRELS of the $13.85 gun are made from genuine Armory steel. They are choke bored by the latest Aubreyized improved taper system, producing an effect for a perfect target and hard shooting found in few other guns.

THE FRAME is made from drop steel forgings, beautifully case hardened and fitted, and with shape, style and strength unequaled.

THE LOCKS are simple and strong, having only four parts, namely, mainspring, hammer, sear and bridle.

THE LOCKING DEVICE, the device that makes this the firmest, most secure, non-shakable and strongest gun made, gives in its action four distinct locks, namely, two in the lugs, one in the extension rib, which by its action draws the barrels up to the frame, and another in the extension rib, which has a tendency to draw the rib down into the frame, all operating by one lever (the break lever); it is, in fact, the only quadruple locking gun made. It has the latest top snap break, the most perfect safety and safety action known; it has a beautifully shaped, tapered and finished extension rib, which through a square hold contacts with the quadruple locking equipment; all parts are beautifully finished and shaped; stocks are made from carefully selected walnut wood, beautifully shaped; fancy checkered pistol grip and a specially shaped and fancy checkered fore end. We regret that the limited space does not permit our showing you by illustration, diagram, etc., the working parts, the simplicity, the strength and the locking mechanism and superiority attained in this gun over all others. There is no gun that will approach it in beauty, no gun made that will shoot stronger or better, no gun that will last longer. You get the very best of everything and you get it for only $13.85.

Catalogue No.	Grade	Style of Barrels	Gauge	Length of Barrels	Weight Pounds	Style Engraving	PRICE
6H18	A. S.	Genuine Armory Steel	12	30 or 32 in.	7½ to 8	Line Engraved	$13.85
6H20	A. T.	Genuine Laminated Steel	12	30 or 32 in.	7½ to 8	Line Engraved	14.85
6H22	A. D.	Genuine 2-Blade Damascus	12	30 or 32 in.	7½ to 8	Line Engraved	17.35

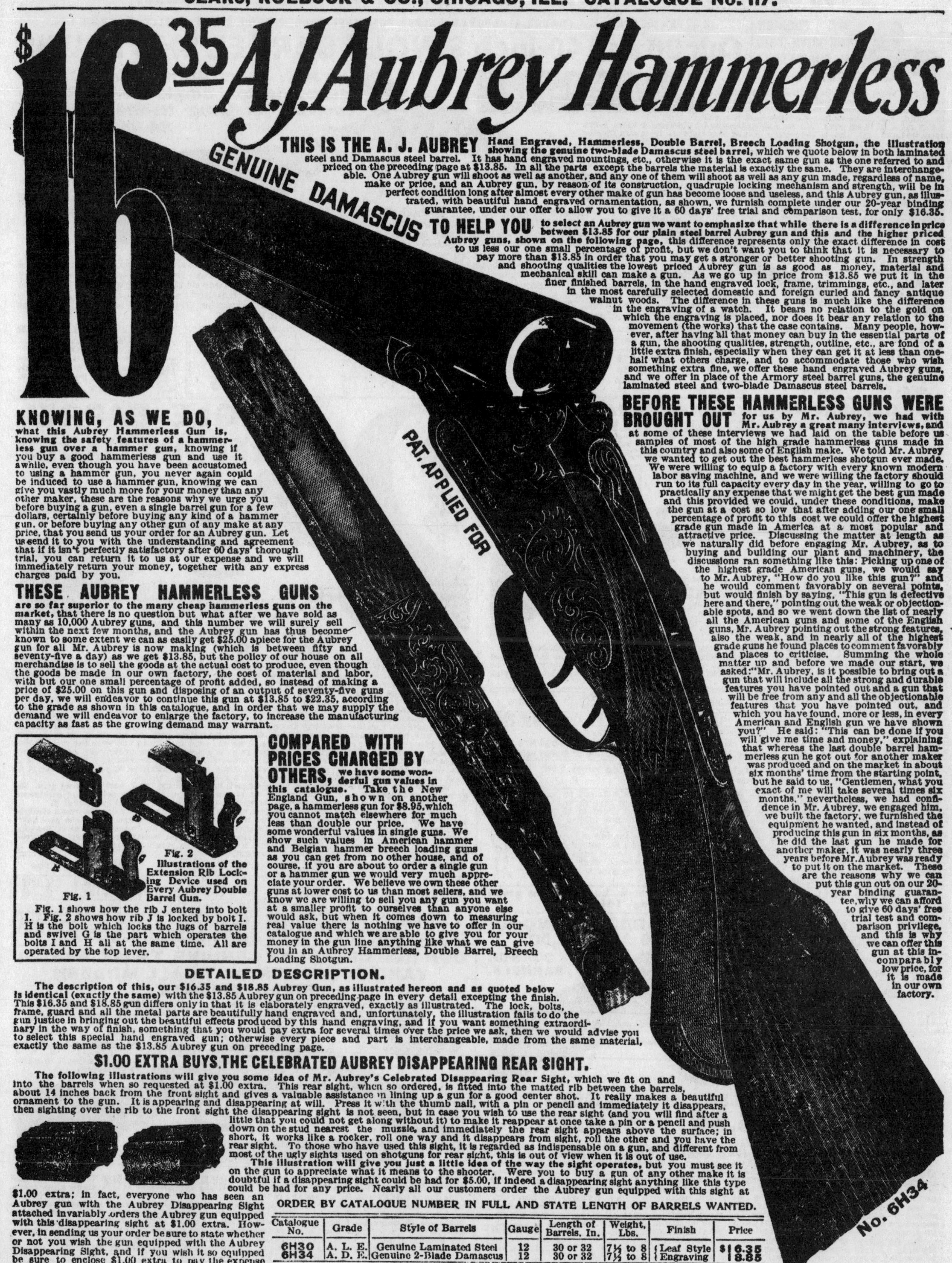

$16.35 A. J. Aubrey Hammerless

THIS IS THE A. J. AUBREY Hand Engraved, Hammerless, Double Barrel, Breech Loading Shotgun, the illustration showing the genuine two-blade Damascus steel barrel, which we quote below in both laminated steel and Damascus steel barrel. It has hand engraved mountings, etc., otherwise it is the exact same gun as the one referred to and priced on the preceding page at $13.85. In all the parts except the barrels the material is exactly the same. They are interchangeable. One Aubrey gun will shoot as well as another, and any one of them will shoot as well as any gun made, regardless of name, make or price, and an Aubrey gun, by reason of its construction, quadruple locking mechanism and strength, will be in perfect condition long after almost every other make of gun has become loose and useless, and this Aubrey gun, as illustrated, with beautiful hand engraved ornamentation, as shown, we furnish complete under our 20-year binding guarantee, under our offer to allow you to give it a 60 days' free trial and comparison test, for only $16.35.

TO HELP YOU to select an Aubrey gun we want to emphasize that while there is a difference in price between $13.85 for our plain steel barrel Aubrey gun and this and the higher priced Aubrey guns, shown on the following page, this difference represents only the exact difference in cost to us less our one small percentage of profit, but we don't want you to think that it is necessary to pay more than $13.85 in order that you may get a stronger or better shooting gun. In strength and shooting qualities the lowest priced Aubrey gun is as good as money, material and mechanical skill can make a gun. As we go up in price from $13.85 we put it in the finer finished barrels, in the hand engraved lock, frame, trimmings, etc., and later in the most carefully selected domestic and foreign curled and fancy antique walnut woods. The difference in these guns is much like the difference in the engraving of a watch. It bears no relation to the gold on which the engraving is placed, nor does it bear any relation to the movement (the works) that the case contains. Many people, however, after having all that money can buy in the essential parts of a gun, the shooting qualities, strength, outline, etc., are fond of a little extra finish, especially when they can get it at less than one-half what others charge, and to accommodate those who wish something extra fine, we offer these hand engraved Aubrey guns, and we offer in place of the Armory steel barrel guns, the genuine laminated steel and two-blade Damascus steel barrels.

KNOWING, AS WE DO, what this Aubrey Hammerless Gun is, knowing the safety features of a hammerless gun over a hammer gun, knowing if you buy a good hammerless gun and use it awhile, even though you have been accustomed to using a hammer gun, you never again could be induced to use a hammer gun, knowing we can give you vastly much more for your money than any other maker, these are the reasons why we urge you before buying a gun, even a single barrel gun for a few dollars, certainly before buying any kind of a hammer gun, or before buying any other gun of any make at any price, that you send us your order for an Aubrey gun. Let us send it to you with the understanding and agreement that if it isn't perfectly satisfactory after 60 days' thorough trial, you can return it to us at our expense and we will immediately return your money, together with any express charges paid by you.

THESE AUBREY HAMMERLESS GUNS are so far superior to the many cheap hammerless guns on the market, that there is no question but what after we have sold as many as 10,000 Aubrey guns, and this number we will surely sell within the next few months, and the Aubrey gun has thus become known to some extent we can as easily get $25.00 apiece for the Aubrey gun for all Mr. Aubrey is now making (which is between fifty and seventy-five a day) as we get $13.85, but the policy of our house on all merchandise is to sell the goods at the actual cost to produce, even though the goods be made in our own factory, the cost of material and labor, with but our one small percentage of profit added, so instead of making a price of $25.00 on this gun and disposing of an output of seventy-five guns per day, we will endeavor to continue this gun at $13.85 to $22.35, according to the grade as shown in this catalogue, and in order that we may supply the demand we will endeavor to enlarge the factory, to increase the manufacturing capacity as fast as the growing demand may warrant.

Fig. 1

Fig. 2 Illustrations of the Extension Rib Locking Device used on Every Aubrey Double Barrel Gun.

Fig. 1 shows how the rib J enters into bolt I. Fig. 2 shows how rib J is locked by bolt I. H is the bolt which locks the lugs of barrels and swivel G is the part which operates the bolts I and H all at the same time. All are operated by the top lever.

COMPARED WITH PRICES CHARGED BY OTHERS, we have some wonderful gun values in this catalogue. Take the New England Gun, shown on another page, a hammerless gun for $8.95, which you cannot match elsewhere for much less than double our price. We have some wonderful values in single guns. We show such values in American hammer and Belgian hammer breech loading guns as you can get from no other house, and of course, if you are about to order a single gun or a hammer gun we would very much appreciate your order. We believe we own these other guns at lower cost to us than most sellers, and we know we are willing to sell you any gun you want at a smaller profit to ourselves than anyone else would ask, but when it comes down to measuring real value there is nothing we have to offer in our catalogue and which we are able to give you for your money in the gun line anything like what we can give you in an Aubrey Hammerless, Double Barrel, Breech Loading Shotgun.

BEFORE THESE HAMMERLESS GUNS WERE BROUGHT OUT for us by Mr. Aubrey, we had with Mr. Aubrey a great many interviews, and at some of these interviews we had laid on the table before us samples of most of the high grade hammerless guns made in this country and also some of English make. We told Mr. Aubrey we wanted to get out the best hammerless shotgun ever made. We were willing to equip a factory with every known modern labor saving machine, and we were willing the factory should run to its full capacity every day in the year, willing to go to practically any expense that we might get the best gun made and this provided we could, under these conditions, make the gun at a cost so low that after adding our one small percentage of profit to this cost we could offer the highest grade gun made in America at a most popular and attractive price. Discussing the matter at length as we naturally did before engaging Mr. Aubrey, as to buying and building our plant and machinery, the discussions ran something like this: Picking up one of the highest grade American guns, we would say to Mr. Aubrey, "How do you like this gun?" and he would comment favorably on several points, but would finish by saying, "This gun is defective here and there," pointing out the weak or objectionable spots, and so we went down the list of nearly all the American guns and some of the English guns, Mr. Aubrey pointing out the strong features, also the weak, and in nearly all of the highest grade guns he found places to comment favorably and places to criticise. Summing the whole matter up and before we made our start, we asked: "Mr. Aubrey, is it possible to bring out a gun that will include all the strong and durable features you have pointed out and a gun that will be free from any and all the objectionable features that you have pointed out, and which you have found, more or less, in every American and English gun we have shown you?" He said: "This can be done if you will give me time and money," explaining that whereas the last double barrel hammerless gun he got out for another maker was produced and on the market in about six months' time from the starting point, but he said to us, "Gentlemen, what you exact of me will take several times six months," nevertheless, we had confidence in Mr. Aubrey, we engaged him, we built the factory, we furnished the equipment he wanted, and instead of producing this gun in six months, as he did the last gun he made for another maker, it was nearly three years before Mr. Aubrey was ready to put it on the market. These are the reasons why we can put this gun out on our 20-year binding guarantee, why we can afford to give 60 days' free trial test and comparison privilege, and this is why we can offer this gun at this incomparably low price, for it is made in our own factory.

DETAILED DESCRIPTION.

The description of this, our $16.35 and $18.85 Aubrey Gun, as illustrated hereon and as quoted below is identical (exactly the same) with the $13.85 Aubrey gun on preceding page in every detail excepting the finish. This $16.35 and $18.85 gun differs only in that it is elaborately engraved, exactly as illustrated. The lock, bolts, frame, guard and all the metal parts are beautifully hand engraved and, unfortunately, the illustration fails to do the gun justice in bringing out the beautiful effects produced by this hand engraving, and if you want something extraordinary in the way of finish, something that you would pay extra for several times over the price we ask, then we would advise you to select this special hand engraved gun; otherwise every piece and part is interchangeable, made from the same material, exactly the same as the $13.85 Aubrey gun on preceding page.

$1.00 EXTRA BUYS THE CELEBRATED AUBREY DISAPPEARING REAR SIGHT.

The following illustrations will give you some idea of Mr. Aubrey's Celebrated Disappearing Rear Sight, which we fit on and into the barrels when so requested at $1.00 extra. This rear sight, when so ordered, is fitted into the matted rib between the barrels, about 14 inches back from the front sight and gives a valuable assistance in lining up a gun for a good center shot. It really makes a beautiful ornament to the gun. It is appearing and disappearing at will. Press it with the thumb nail, with a pin or pencil and immediately it disappears, then sighting over the rib to the front sight the disappearing sight is not seen, but in case you wish to use the rear sight (and you will find after a little that you could not get along without it) to make it reappear at once take a pin or a pencil and push down on the stud nearest the muzzle, and immediately the rear sight appears above the surface; in short, it works like a rocker, roll one way and it disappears from sight, roll the other and you have the rear sight. To those who have used this sight, it is regarded as indispensable on a gun, and different from most of the ugly sights used on shotguns for rear sight, this is out of view when it is out of use.

This illustration will give you just a little idea of the way the sight operates, but you must see it on the gun to appreciate what it means to the shooter. Were you to buy a gun of any other make it is doubtful if a disappearing sight could be had for $5.00, if indeed a disappearing sight anything like this type could be had for any price. Nearly all our customers order the Aubrey gun equipped with this sight at $1.00 extra; in fact, everyone who has seen an Aubrey gun with the Aubrey Disappearing Sight attached invariably orders the Aubrey gun equipped with this disappearing sight at $1.00 extra. However, in sending us your order be sure to state whether or not you wish the gun equipped with the Aubrey Disappearing Sight, and if you wish it so equipped be sure to enclose $1.00 extra to pay the expense of such equipment.

ORDER BY CATALOGUE NUMBER IN FULL AND STATE LENGTH OF BARRELS WANTED.

Catalogue No.	Grade	Style of Barrels	Gauge	Length of Barrels, In.	Weight, Lbs.	Finish	Price
6H30	A. L. E.	Genuine Laminated Steel	12	30 or 32	7½ to 8	Leaf Style	$16.35
6H34	A. D. E.	Genuine 2-Blade Damascus	12	30 or 32	7½ to 8	Engraving	18.85

Weight, packed for shipment, 14 pounds.

WE FURNISH FREE WITH THIS GUN OUR PATENT GLOBE SIGHT.

$1.32 PER 100 FOR BLACK POWDER, $1.49 FOR SMOKELESS, BUYS BEST GRADE 12-GAUGE LOADED SHELLS. SEE PAGE 1.64.

Our 36 and 40-inch SINGLE BARREL SHOTGUNS

BORED FOR NITRO POWDER

Our New 36 and 40-Inch Barrel, Automatic Ejector, Single Barrel Breech Loaders, for Long Range Shooting, $4.85 and $5.35.

Several years ago we had a number of inquiries from the south and west for long barrel single guns, and we equipped to make some of these guns to supply our customers. We have sold a great many more of these guns than we anticipated, and by reason of these large sales we have been able to reduce our cost of manufacture from our former price of $5.95 for the 36-inch, and our former price of $6.55 for the 40-inch, to the present prices, thereby giving our customer the benefit of the reduction, which was made possible by our largely increased sales. It is always our principle that whenever we are able to effect a saving, either by a reduction in the raw material or labor or by increased volume of manufacture, we always give our customers the benefit of any saving which we make in this way and which we know is appreciated.

36 AND 40 INCH GENUINE ARMORY STEEL BARRELS

CHOKE BORED

No. 6F510A

ORDER BY CATALOGUE NUMBER.

$4.85 AND $5.35

These Special 36 and 40-inch Barrel Guns are made of the best material throughout, with automatic shell ejectors, made on the latest improved principle, **choke bored by the latest taper system,** fine quality of walnut stock, nicely checkered, and fore end nicely shaped and finished, as shown in the illustration; and bored for nitro or black powder. The automatic ejector device is very strong and simple and less liable to get out of order than any other device known. The frame is made from the best material that money can buy; the barrel from Wilson's best quality of Armory steel, and we consider it one of the best guns that was ever put upon the market. The frame and trigger guard are case hardened and beautifully finished; all are made with pistol grip walnut stocks, hand checkered. The hammer is hung in the center of the frame so as to strike the primer squarely, the butt plate is of ornamental design and the gun can be taken down by removing the patent fore end.

Catalogue No.	Grade	Style of Barrel	Gauge	Length of Barrel, inches	Weight of Gun, pounds	Price
6F510A	Ejector	Genuine	12	36	7 to 7¼	$4.85
6F510B	Ejector	Armory	16	36	6¾ to 7	
6F511A	Ejector	Steel,	12	40	7¼ to 7½	5.35
6F511B	Ejector	choke bored	16	40	7 to 7¼	

WEIGHT, PACKED FOR SHIPMENT, ABOUT 12 POUNDS.

THINK of the wonderful, liberal Profit Sharing Plan we offer you.

THE GENUINE REMINGTON SEMI-HAMMERLESS, AUTOMATIC EJECTING, SINGLE BARREL BREECH LOADING SHOTGUN.

ALL HAVE AUTOMATIC EJECTORS.

$6.75

BEWARE OF IMITATIONS. All Genuine Remington Guns Bear the name "REMINGTON ARMS CO., ILION, N.Y."

No. 6F515

This gun has been on the market for many years, is very popular

HANDSOME AND WELL MADE. CAN YOU MATCH IT?

REMINGTON GUNS ARE UNSURPASSED FOR STYLE, FINISH, MATERIAL AND WORKMANSHIP.

The Remington Semi-Hammerless Single Barrel Breech Loading Shotgun, top lever break, the best break made, blued armory steel barrel, choke bored, side choking lever, case hardened frame and butt plate, pistol grip stock, rebounding lock. The material, finish and shooting qualities are the same high standard as the Remington double barrel gun. Every gun is warranted perfect and a strong shooter. They are all put to a test before leaving the factory and none are allowed to go out until a perfect pattern has been shown. You take no risk in buying the old and reliable Remington.

Catalogue No.	Grade	Style of Barrel	Gauge	Length Barrel, inches	Weight, about	Price
6F515	No. 9	Armory Steel	12	30	6½ lbs.	$6.75

Weight, packed in box, about 10 pounds.

BEWARE OF IMITATIONS. Many houses are selling guns that are similar, but not genuine. **We guarantee our guns to be as represented or money refunded.**

Examine the Foster Rear Sight for single guns on page 155. It is a wonderful adjunct to a single barrel gun.

TESTING SHOTGUNS. When testing a shotgun do not attempt to test it on a target 12 inches square, but take three or four sheets of newspaper, rest the muzzle on some solid object, and shoot at 40 yards. This will give you a chance to see how the shot groups and will not deceive you in case you shoot to one side of the target, which often happens, and shows only about half the pellets. After you get the target, draw a 30-inch circle around the shot, and you will find, as a rule, that any gun you get from us will make a satisfactory target. Always remember that the shot begins to fall at 40 yards. It cannot remain in the air. When a gun puts 60 per cent of the entire charge in a 30-inch circle it is considered a good shooting gun. If you live in Canada, the duty on guns is 30 per cent when shipped from the United States.

$1.32 per 100 for black powder, $1.49 for smokeless, buys the best grade 12-gauge loaded shells. See page 164.

OUR LONG RANGE SINGLE BARREL 8 AND 10-GAUGE GOOSE GUNS, $15.50 AND $12.50.

The Best Low Priced Gun for Long Range Shooting Ever Made.

For Geese and Large Game.

36-INCH BARRELS.

8-GAUGE	10-GAUGE
$15.50	**$12.50**

AT $15.50 FOR 8-GAUGE AND $12.50 FOR 10-GAUGE we will furnish you our celebrated Long Range Goose Guns. These guns are made especially for us and all guns are TESTED BEFORE THEY LEAVE OUR STORE.

COMPARE OUR GOOSE GUNS WITH ANY OTHER, and you will find them better made and better finished than any goose guns on the market. All have top snap break, checkered pistol grip stock and rebounding hammer.

No. 6F518 8-Gauge Heavy, Long Range, Single Barrel Goose Gun, adapted to heavy shooting. A very popular goose gun for long range, hard shooting. All parts made with a view to securing a strong, lasting gun. Choke bored, fine laminated steel barrel, 36 inches long; weight, 10 pounds. Our patent Globe Sights are not made in 8-gauge. Price.. **$15.50**

No. 6F520 Our Heavy Long Range, 10-Gauge, Single Barrel Gun, adapted to heavy shooting. A very popular goose gun for long range, hard shooting. All parts made with a view to securing a strong, lasting gun. Choke bored, fine laminated steel barrel, 36 inches long; weight, 9 pounds. With our Patent Globe Sight. Price............... **$12.50**

Weight, packed for shipment, 14 pounds.

$2.28 SINGLE BARREL BREECH LOADER

OTHERS ASK $3.00 TO $5.00

FOR $2.28 WE OFFER YOU THIS NEW 1906 MODEL 12-gauge, hammer single barrel breech loading shotgun under our guarantee that it is in every way equal to single barrel breech loading shotguns that are being widely advertised and sold by other houses at $3.00 to $5.00.

If you want to buy a thoroughly reliable single barrel breech loading shotgun, a gun that is bored for smokeless or black powder, one that will kill at long range, a gun that is choke bored by the celebrated Taper system, then we especially urge that you select one of our higher grade guns, either our $2.96 Long Range Winner, as shown on page 147, our White Powder Wonder, as shown on page 148, or, better still, our celebrated World's Challenge Ejector, as shown on page 149, which we furnish for only $4.30, complete with genuine twist barrels, checkered grip, automatic shell ejector, all the very latest improvements, a better gun than you could buy elsewhere at less than double our price. However, if you want a single barrel breach loading shotgun at a low price, rather than buy any gun now being advertised by other houses at $3.00 or less, or sold by retail dealers generally at $3.00 to $5.00, then send us an order for this single barrel gun, enclose our special price, $2.28, and we will send the gun to you with the understanding and agreement that if you do not find it satisfactory, and in every way equal to any single barrel breech loading shotgun you can buy from any other catalogue house at $3.00 or less, the equal of single barrel guns that retail dealers sell at $3.00 to $5.00, you can return it to us at our expense and we will immediately return your money.

In your own interest, to give you the strongest, best shooting and best wearing gun, the greatest value possible for your money, we especially urge that you select our celebrated World's Challenge Automatic Ejector, as shown on page 149, and as offered by us at $4.30.

This, our **$2.28** gun, has blued steel barrel, strong frame and breech, top snap break, straight grained black walnut stock, pistol grip, black walnut fore end, ornamental butt plate, case hardened frame, rebounding hammer, comes in either 12 or 16-gauge, as desired, offered in 12-gauge at $2.28, in 16-gauge at $2.48, under our guarantee that it is equal to any single barrel gun advertised by any other house at $3.00 or less, equal to guns sold by retail dealers at $3.00 to $5.00.

Catalogue No.	Grade	Style of Barrel	Gauge	Length of Barrel	Weight of Gun	Price
6F530A	N. V.	Blued	12	30 inch	6½ to 6¾ lbs.	$2.28
6F530B	N. V.	Steel	16	30 inch	6¼ to 6½ lbs.	2.48

Weight when packed for shipment about 10 pounds.

Understand, we furnish this gun at **$2.28**, guaranteeing it equal to guns that others advertise at $3.00 and dealers sell at $3.00 to $5.00; but to get the most possible for your money, we urge you to select our World's Challenge Automatic Ejector, shown on page 149, which we sell at $4.30 under our guarantee that it is the equal of guns others sell at double the price or more.

OUR 1906 CRESCENT GENUINE TWIST BARREL TAKE DOWN GUN, WITH ALL MODERN IMPROVEMENTS.

Our Patent Globe Sight is Furnished FREE with this Gun

16-GAUGE ONLY.

READ THE DESCRIPTION.

Choke Bored......$4.08

Examine the Foster Rear Sight for single guns on page 155. It is a wonderful adjunct to a single barrel gun.

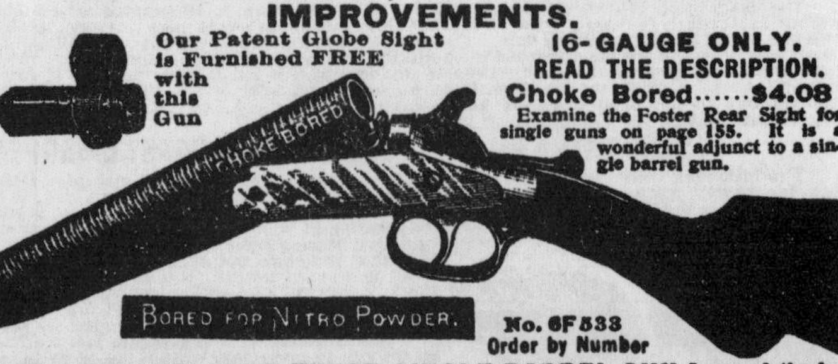

BORED FOR NITRO POWDER.

No. 6F533
Order by Number

OUR NEW CRESCENT TWIST SINGLE BARREL GUN Is one of the best single guns made. This gun is made on modern lines and in the most approved manner to shoot any proper load of black or smokeless powder. It has fine laminated steel or twist barrel, center hammer, patent top lever break, pistol grip stock, rebounding hammer, fancy butt plate, and is choke bored. These new guns, as now made for us, leave absolutely nothing that is to be desired in a first class single gun, as they are a combination of every real improvement of merit. The barrels used are genuine laminated steel or twist of the best quality, imported especially for them. These guns make an average target of 250 pellets in a 30-inch circle at 40 yards. Load used, 2¾ drams black powder, 1 ounce of No. 8 shot. Weight, packed in box, about 10 pounds.

No. 6F533 16-gauge, 30-inch barrel; weight, 6½ pounds. Price...............**$4.08**

12-GAUGE LOADED SHELLS, $1.32 PER 100. SEE PAGE 164.

OUR 16-GAUGE ARMORY STEEL AND TWIST BARREL AUTOMATIC EJECTOR SINGLE GUNS.

12-GAUGE LOADED SHELLS, $1.32 PER 100.

See page 164. Our Patent Globe Sight is furnished FREE with these Guns.

Guaranteed Genuine Armory Steel and Genuine Twist Barrel.

Choke Bored.

16-gauge only. 30 or 32-inch barrel. Weight, about 6½ pounds.

$3.78 and $4.55

BORED FOR NITRO POWDER.

Our $3.78 Gun is fitted with genuine armory steel barrel and our $4.55 16-gauge Ejector Single Gun is fitted with a genuine twist barrel; all have walnut pistol grip stock, walnut fore end, bored smooth and true to gauge, choke bored for field shooting and has fancy butt plate. The hammer is hung in the center so as to strike the cartridge squarely. The automatic ejector device is very strong and simple and cannot get out of order. The barrel is detachable, making it convenient to carry the gun apart in a Victoria style gun case. It has rebounding hammer, top snap break, and the frame and trigger guard are case hardened and beautifully finished. The shell is thrown out automatically when you open the gun. State length of barrel.

Catalogue Number	Grade	Style of Barrel	Gauge	Length of Barrel	Weight, about	Price
6F534	No. 1	Armory Steel	16	30 or 32 inches	6½ pounds	$3.78
6F535	No. 2	GenuineTwist	16	30 or 32 inches	6½ pounds	4.55

Weight, packed for shipment, about 10 pounds.

HOW GUN BARRELS BURST AND CAUTION TO SHOOTERS.

FOLLOW THESE INSTRUCTIONS and you will never have a burst gun or rifle barrel. Do not accidentally put two charges of smokeless powder in the shell, always look through the barrels before loading and see that there is nothing in them. Don't ram the wad edgewise into the powder, nor crimp the shell more than ¼ of an inch.

DON'T USE A MALLET for ramming the powder, use hand pressure. Don't rest the muzzle on the ground, nor leave the gun in the bottom of a boat or buggy, for something is liable to get into the barrel in this way. When using 12-gauge brass shells use 10-gauge wads, so they will not get loose in the shell and bulge the barrel. If you get a bullet stuck in the barrel don't try to shoot it out or you may bulge the barrel. No manufacturer is held responsible for a burst gun or rifle barrel, because barrels are made to withstand a greater bursting strain than you can possibly get from any factory loaded ammunition. When a gun barrel bursts at the breech or chamber it is caused by an overload of nitro powder, and when it bursts forward of the chamber it is caused by some obstruction, such as a dent, snow, water, moss, mud, etc., and will generally show a distinct ring inside the barrel. Nitro powder should only be used by people familiar with it; and dense nitro powder should be weighed by an apothecary's scale and not measured. Chlorate of potash powder should never be used. We will not guarantee any gun with chlorate powders.

GUN AND RIFLE BARRELS can only burst by having some obstruction in the barrel or by overloading with nitro powder. We would like our customers to read this, for it will prevent accidents.

PLEASE OBSERVE THE FOLLOWING CAUSES, for we are extremely anxious that our customers have no accidents with firearms, whether they buy them from us or some other house. Every gun or rifle which we offer for sale is bought from reliable manufacturers, made from the very best materials that money can buy, and is made to stand any proper load of nitro or black powder, but no matter how good or how strong the material is, you can burst the very strongest barrels by misuse or improper loading. Even an army cannon may be burst in this way. A strong rifle barrel, such as made by the Winchester Arms Co., which has a bursting strain limit of 40,000 to 80,000 pounds to the square inch, can be burst by misuse or carelessly loading smokeless powder, but no barrel will ever burst by using factory loaded ammunition, providing there is no obstruction or foreign substance inside the barrel.

FREE FURNITURE! READ OUR PROFIT SHARING PLAN See how easily you can share in our profits. Buy everything you need from us, save money on everything you buy, get it from us at a lower price than anyone else offers, and in addition get your PROFIT SHARING CERTIFICATES. Save your CERTIFICATES and get the FREE FURNITURE and other valuable articles shown in our PROFIT SHARING DEPARTMENT ON FIRST PAGES.

OUR BOX FRAME SINGLE BARREL HAMMERLESS AUTOMATIC EJECTOR, $3.92

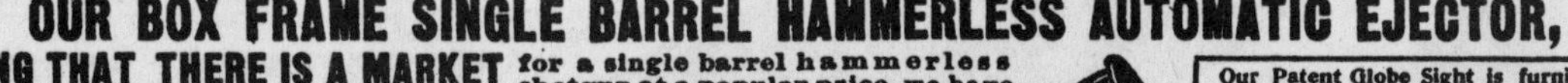

REALIZING THAT THERE IS A MARKET for a single barrel hammerless shotgun at a popular price, we have closed a contract with an eastern manufacturer for a large quantity of Box Frame Single Barrel Hammerless Shotguns with automatic ejector, and we are giving our customers the benefit of our large contract by furnishing this gun at the manufacturing cost, adding our one small percentage of profit.

IN ORDER TO GIVE OUR CUSTOMERS better value and a better gun than can be had from any other house at $3.92, we have stipulated these must be manufactured from the best material that money can buy, the barrels must be made from the very best armory barrel steel and all other parts of the gun must be proportionately good in quality.

THE BARREL is made from the best quality of armory barrel steel, taper choke bored for black or smokeless powder at $3.92, and for 75 cents more we furnish the same gun with genuine laminated steel or twist barrel.

THE STOCK is made from well seasoned walnut, the pistol grip is fitted with an ornamental cap on the pistol grip, nicely checkered, and the butt is fitted with an ornamental butt plate. The fore end is also fitted with well seasoned straight grained walnut, nicely finished and nicely shaped, as shown in the illustration.

$3.92

Our Patent Globe Sight is furnished free with this gun. It is a remarkable assistance in shooting game on the wing.

THIS WELL MADE AND WELL FINISHED hammerless single barrel automatic ejecting shotgun is made on the box frame type, as shown in the illustration. The automatic ejecting device is a recent improvement on automatic ejectors and is very positive in its action. The cocking device is operated from the fore end, so that every time you open the gun to insert a shell the hammer cocks itself automatically and the gun is ready to shoot by pushing forward the safety slide just back of the top lever. The fore end is made on the spring locking principle, which may be removed in order to take down the gun and is fitted with a metal joint where it connects with the frame.

TAPER CHOKE BORED

No. 6F537

THE FRAME is made of steel and the lock works are easy of access. The top lever is so constructed that it is next to impossible for it to get out of order.

WHILE WE HIGHLY RECOMMEND this gun as being positively the best hammerless single gun upon the market at $3.92, a gun that will give you good satisfaction, a gun that is good value in every way, a gun that has strong shooting qualities and good penetration and a gun which we know will please you at our popular price of $3.92 with armory steel barrels, or 75 cents extra for genuine laminated steel or twist barrels; but if you wish a very high grade gun, one that handles and is lined up very much like a double barrel gun, we refer you to the A. J. Aubrey single barrel hammerless gun, which we illustrate and describe on another page, as the A. J. Aubrey single barrel gun which is positively the highest grade single gun made, regardless of name, make or price. It is impossible to make a higher grade gun at any price.

Catalogue No.	Grade	Style of Barrel	Gauge	L'gth Barrel, inches	Weight, about	Price
6F537	A. S.	Armory Steel	12	30 or 32	7 lbs.	$3.92
6F538	L. S.	Laminated Steel	12	30 or 32	7 lbs.	4.67

Weight, packed for shipment, about 14 pounds.

WINCHESTER MODEL 1897. REPEATING SHOTGUN, PRICED AT $16.10

THIS GUN IS KNOWN AS THE WINCHESTER PUMP GUN. MODEL 1897.

For an extra inducement on this gun, equal to a BIG DISCOUNT, see Profit Sharing Dept. on first pages. While we will gladly furnish this Winchester Repeater for only $16.10, since we can furnish you the celebrated Take Down Model Marlin Repeating Shotgun, a gun we consider worth $10.00, more for only 40 cents additional for a take down gun, only $16.50, as shown at bottom of page, No. 6F580. If you want a repeating shotgun we would advise by all means that you order the Marlin Take Down Repeater, No. 6F580, at $16.50.

Choke Bored.

No. 6F550 Order by Number.

Operated by sliding fore arm below the barrel. When the hammer is down, the backward and forward motion of this slide unlocks and opens the breech block, ejects the cartridge or fired shell and replaces it with a fresh cartridge. The construction of the arm is such that the hammer cannot fall on the firing pin and strike cartridge until the breech block is in place and locked fast; while the hammer stands at the full cock notch the gun is locked against opening. In this position the firing pin must be pushed forward to open the gun. When the hammer stands at half cock, the gun is locked both against opening and pulling the trigger.

All our Winchester Shotguns have the factory serial number, and the Winchester Arms Company, New Haven, Conn., guarantees such guns.

We furnish our Patent Globe Sight free with this gun. It is a wonderful help toward making good shots.

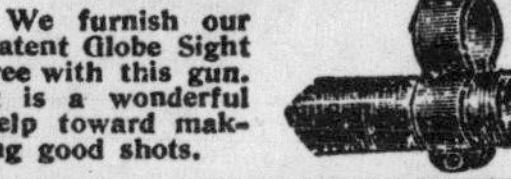

Catalogue No.	Grade	Style of Barrel	Gauge	Length of Barrel	Number of Shots	Weight	Price
6F550	Model 1897 Solid frame	Rolled Steel Choke Bored	12	30 inches	6	7¾ lbs.	$16.10
6F560	Model 1897 take down	Rolled Steel Choke Bored	12	30 inches	6	7¾ lbs.	17.50
6F565	Brush Gun take down	Rolled Steel Cylinder Bared	12	26 inches	5	7½ lbs.	19.00

Weight, packed for shipment, about 14 pounds.

FLOBERT RIFLES.

NOTE. We do not recommend or guarantee Flobert Rifles. Buy a good rifle. It will pay in the end. We recommend Nos. 6F695, 6F697 and 6F698. We do not guarantee Flobert Rifles, but handle them because many of our customers insist on having them.

WARNANT SYSTEM FLOBERT RIFLE.

22-CALIBER $2.25 and $2.65.

See page 165. **19 Cents per 100 for 22-Caliber Short Cartridges.**

Warnant or Springfield action, polished medium or heavy octagon barrel, pistol grip stock, fancy butt, trigger guard, checkered stock, dark mountings, 22 and 24-inch barrel. Weight, about 4½ to 6 pounds. Uses 22-caliber short or long rim fire cartridges No. 6F2336 or No. 6F2338. See note above.

No.	Caliber	Barrel	Shoots Cartridge	Weight	Price
6F658	22 Short or Long Rim Fire	22 inches	No. 6F2336	4½ pounds	$2.25
6F659	22 Short or Long Rim Fire	24 inches	No. 6F2338	6 pounds	2.65

Weight, packed for shipment, about 8 pounds.

NEW MODEL WARNANT ACTION FLOBERT RIFLE.

32-CALIBER $2.75.

Our New Model Warnant Action. Oiled walnut stock, checkered pistol grip, 24-inch octagon barrel, 32-caliber short, rim fire, shell extractor; barrel very finely finished. Weight, 6½ pounds. Shoots cartridges No. 6F2352. See note above.

No. 6F663 Our cash with order price.......................**$2.75**

Weight, packed or shipment, about 10 pounds.

NOTICE. 22 caliber short cartridges are good for 35 yards. 22-caliber long cartridges are good for 50 yards, and 22-caliber long rifle cartridges are good for 100 yards.

MARLIN 6-SHOT REPEATING TAKE DOWN SHOTGUNS, $16.50.

The Marlin Take Down Repeating Shotgun, model 1898, can be taken apart and put together very quickly and easily. Made in 12-gauge, 30-inch barrel only. Weight, about 7 pounds. Barrel made of blued smokeless steel, choke bored, guaranteed for nitro powder. Pistol grip stock. This gun has been tried and thoroughly tested by the best shooters in the country and found to be perfect in every detail. Magazine holds five shells, and one in the chamber, making six shots.

Catalogue Number	Grade	Style of Barrel	Gauge	Length of Barrel	Weight	Price
6F580	A	Smokeless Steel	12	30 inches	7 pounds	$16.50

Weight, packed for shipment, 14 pounds.

A FEW WORDS ABOUT MARLIN SHOTGUNS AND RIFLES. Mr. Marlin was the original maker of the Ballard Rifle, which was so very popular many years ago. No Ballard Rifle was allowed to leave the factory unless it was absolutely perfect in every detail, and this policy has been pursued by the Marlin Company ever since. Later on the company made repeating rifles which immediately became popular with hunters, and in 1898 they put this present shotgun on the market, which has been growing more and more popular ever since. We cannot recommend Marlin goods too highly. None but the best material enters into the construction and only the best skilled workmen are employed in the factory. If you wish a repeating take down shotgun, by all means order this gun.

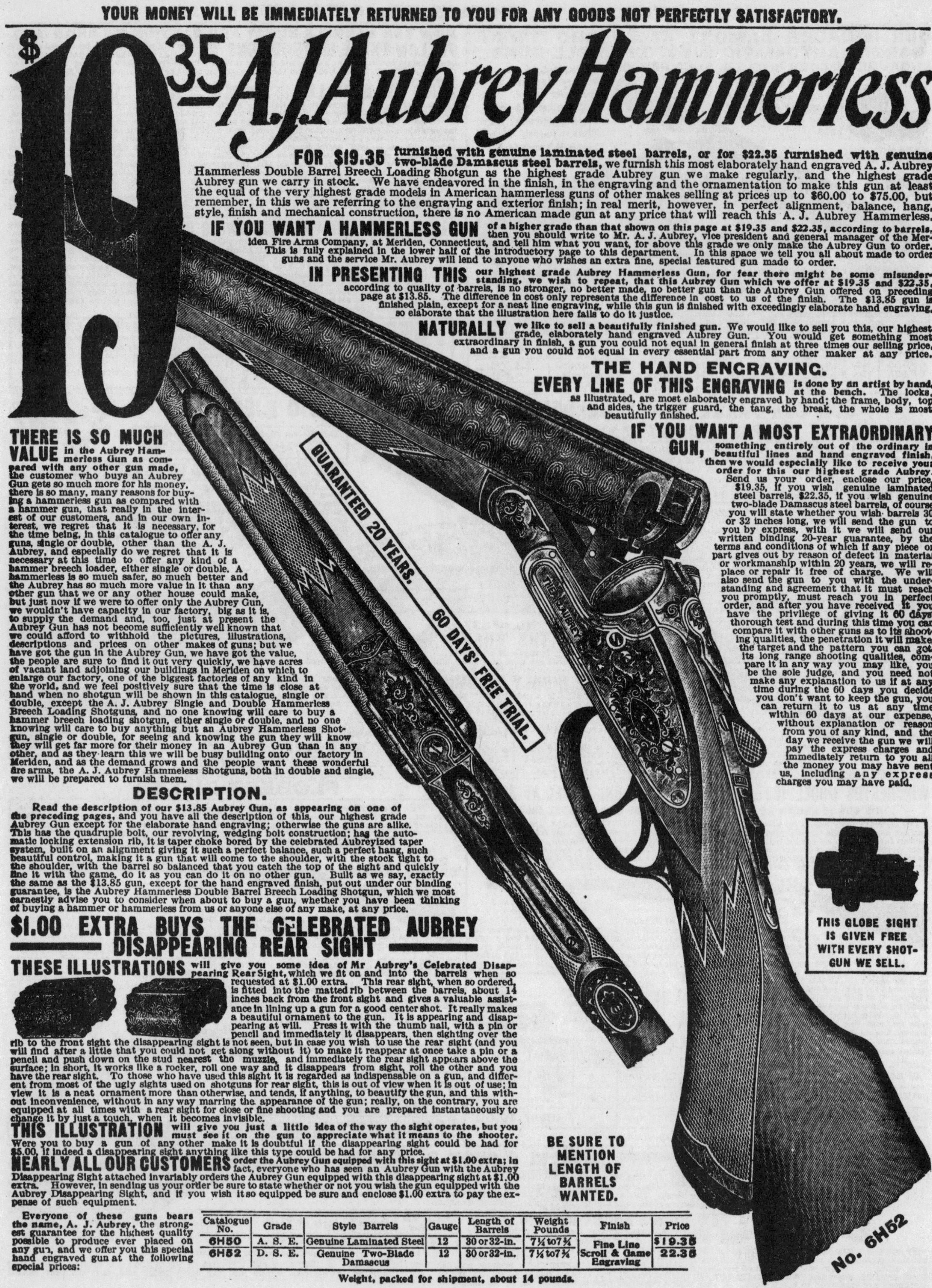

$19.35 A. J. Aubrey Hammerless

FOR $19.35 furnished with genuine laminated steel barrels, or for $22.35 furnished with genuine two-blade Damascus steel barrels, we furnish this most elaborately hand engraved A. J. Aubrey Hammerless Double Barrel Breech Loading Shotgun as the highest grade Aubrey gun we make regularly, and the highest grade Aubrey gun we carry in stock. We have endeavored in the finish, in the engraving and the ornamentation to make this gun at least the equal of the very highest grade models in American hammerless guns of other makes selling at prices up to $60.00 to $75.00, but remember, in this we are referring to the engraving and exterior finish; in real merit, however, in perfect alignment, balance, hang, style, finish and mechanical construction, there is no American made gun at any price that will reach this A. J. Aubrey Hammerless.

IF YOU WANT A HAMMERLESS GUN of a higher grade than that shown on this page at $19.35 and $22.35, according to barrels, then you should write to Mr. A. J. Aubrey, vice president and general manager of the Meriden Fire Arms Company, at Meriden, Connecticut, and tell him what you want, for above this grade we only make the Aubrey Gun to order. This is fully explained in the lower half of the introductory page to this department. In this space we tell you all about made to order guns and the service Mr. Aubrey will lend to anyone who wishes an extra fine, special featured gun made to order.

IN PRESENTING THIS our highest grade Aubrey Hammerless Gun, for fear there might be some misunderstanding, we wish to repeat, that this Aubrey Gun which we offer at $19.35 and $22.35, according to quality of barrels, is no stronger, no better made, no better gun than the Aubrey Gun offered on preceding page at $13.85. The difference in cost only represents the difference in cost to us of the finish. The $13.85 gun is finished plain, except for a neat line engraving, while this gun is finished with exceedingly elaborate hand engraving, so elaborate that the illustration here fails to do it justice.

NATURALLY we like to sell a beautifully finished gun. We would like to sell you this, our highest grade, elaborately hand engraved Aubrey Gun. You would get something most extraordinary in finish, a gun you could not equal in general finish at three times our selling price, and a gun you could not equal in every essential part from any other maker at any price.

THE HAND ENGRAVING.

EVERY LINE OF THIS ENGRAVING is done by an artist by hand, at the bench. The locks, as illustrated, are most elaborately engraved by hand; the frame, body, top and sides, the trigger guard, the tang, the break, the whole is most beautifully finished.

IF YOU WANT A MOST EXTRAORDINARY GUN, something entirely out of the ordinary in beautiful lines and hand engraved finish, then we would especially like to receive your order for this our highest grade Aubrey. Send us your order, enclose our price, $19.35, if you wish genuine laminated steel barrels, $22.35, if you wish genuine two-blade Damascus steel barrels, of course you will state whether you wish barrels 30 or 32 inches long, we will send the gun to you by express, with it we will send our written binding 20-year guarantee, by the terms and conditions of which if any piece or part gives out by reason of defect in material or workmanship within 20 years, we will replace or repair it free of charge. We will also send the gun to you with the understanding and agreement that it must reach you promptly, must reach you in perfect order, and after you have received it you have the privilege of giving it 60 days' thorough test and during this time you can compare it with other guns as to its shooting qualities, the penetration it will make, the target and the pattern you can got, its long range shooting qualities, compare it in any way you may like, you be the sole judge, and you need not make any explanation to us if at any time during the 60 days you decide you don't want to keep the gun, you can return it to us at any time within 60 days at our expense, without explanation or reason from you of any kind, and the day we receive the gun we will pay the express charges and immediately return to you all the money you may have sent us, including any express charges you may have paid.

THERE IS SO MUCH VALUE in the Aubrey Hammerless Gun as compared with any other gun made, the customer who buys an Aubrey Gun gets so much more for his money. there is so many, many reasons for buying a hammerless gun as compared with a hammer gun, that really in the interest of our customers, and in our own interest, we regret that it is necessary, for the time being, in this catalogue to offer any guns, single or double, other than the A. J. Aubrey, and especially do we regret that it is necessary at this time to offer any kind of a hammer breech loader, either single or double. A hammerless is so much safer, so much better and the Aubrey has so much more value in it than any other gun that we or any other house could make, but just now if we were to offer only the Aubrey Gun, we wouldn't have capacity in our factory, big as it is, to supply the demand and, too, just at present the Aubrey Gun has not become sufficiently well known that we could afford to withhold the pictures, illustrations, descriptions and prices on other makes of guns; but we have got the gun in the Aubrey Gun, we have got the value, the people are sure to find it out very quickly, we have acres of vacant land adjoining our buildings in Meriden on which to enlarge our factory, one of the biggest factories of any kind in the world, and we feel positively sure that the time is close at hand when no shotgun will be shown in this catalogue, single or double, except the A. J. Aubrey Single and Double Hammerless Breech Loading Shotguns, and no one knowing will care to buy a hammer breech loading shotgun, either single or double, and no one knowing will care to buy anything but an Aubrey Hammerless Shotgun, single or double, for seeing and knowing the gun they will know they will get far more for their money in an Aubrey Gun than in any other, and as they learn this we will be busy building onto our factory in Meriden, and as the demand grows and the people want these wonderful fire arms, the A. J. Aubrey Hammeless Shotguns, both in double and single, we will be prepared to furnish them.

DESCRIPTION.

Read the description of our $13.85 Aubrey Gun, as appearing on one of the preceding pages, and you have all the description of this, our highest grade Aubrey Gun except for the elaborate hand engraving; otherwise the guns are alike. This has the quadruple bolt, our revolving, wedging bolt construction; has the automatic locking extension rib, it is taper choke bored by the celebrated Aubreyized taper system, built on an alignment giving it such a perfect balance, such a perfect hang, such beautiful control, making it a gun that will come to the shoulder, with the stock tight to the shoulder, with the barrel so balanced that you catch the top of the sight and quickly line it with the game, do it as you can do it on no other gun. Built as we say, exactly the same as the $13.85 gun, except for the hand engraved finish, put out under our binding guarantee, is the Aubrey Hammerless Double Barrel Breech Loading Shotgun, which we most earnestly advise you to consider when about to buy a gun, whether you have been thinking of buying a hammer or hammerless from us or anyone else of any make, at any price.

$1.00 EXTRA BUYS THE CELEBRATED AUBREY DISAPPEARING REAR SIGHT

THESE ILLUSTRATIONS will give you some idea of Mr Aubrey's Celebrated Disappearing Rear Sight, which we fit on and into the barrels when so requested at $1.00 extra. This rear sight, when so ordered, is fitted into the matted rib between the barrels, about 14 inches back from the front sight and gives a valuable assistance in lining up a gun for a good center shot. It really makes a beautiful ornament to the gun. It is appearing and disappearing at will. Press it with the thumb nail, with a pin or pencil and immediately it disappears, then sighting over the rib to the front sight the disappearing sight is not seen, but in case you wish to use the rear sight (and you will find after a little that you could not get along without it) to make it reappear at once take a pin or a pencil and push down on the stud nearest the muzzle, and immediately the rear sight appears above the surface; in short, it works like a rocker, roll one way and it disappears from sight, roll the other and you have the rear sight. To those who have used this sight it is regarded as indispensable on a gun, and different from most of the ugly sights used on shotguns for rear sight, this is out of view when it is out of use; in view it is a neat ornament more than otherwise, and tends, if anything, to beautify the gun, and this without inconvenience, without in any way marring the appearance of the gun; really, on the contrary, you are equipped at all times with a rear sight for close or fine shooting and you are prepared instantaneously to change it by just a touch, when it becomes invisible.

THIS ILLUSTRATION will give you just a little idea of the way the sight operates, but you must see it on the gun to appreciate what it means to the shooter. Were you to buy a gun of any other make it is doubtful if the disappearing sight could be had for $5.00, if indeed a disappearing sight anything like this type could be had for any price.

NEARLY ALL OUR CUSTOMERS order the Aubrey Gun equipped with this sight at $1.00 extra; in fact, everyone who has seen an Aubrey Gun with the Aubrey Disappearing Sight attached invariably orders the Aubrey Gun equipped with this disappearing sight at $1.00 extra. However, in sending us your order be sure to state whether or not you wish the gun equipped with the Aubrey Disappearing Sight, and if you wish it so equipped be sure and enclose $1.00 extra to pay the expense of such equipment.

THIS GLOBE SIGHT IS GIVEN FREE WITH EVERY SHOTGUN WE SELL.

BE SURE TO MENTION LENGTH OF BARRELS WANTED.

Everyone of these guns bears the name, A. J. Aubrey, the strongest guarantee for the highest quality possible to produce ever placed on any gun, and we offer you this special hand engraved gun at the following special prices:

Catalogue No.	Grade	Style Barrels	Gauge	Length of Barrels	Weight Pounds	Finish	Price
6H50	A. S. E.	Genuine Laminated Steel	12	30 or 32-in.	7¼ to 7¾	Fine Line Scroll & Game Engraving	$19.35
6H52	D. S. E.	Genuine Two-Blade Damascus	12	30 or 32-in.	7¼ to 7¾		22.35

Weight, packed for shipment, about 14 pounds.

No. 6H52

L. C. SMITH HAMMERLESS AND HAMMER GUNS

MADE BY THE HUNTER ARMS CO., FULTON, N.Y.

OUR BINDING GUARANTEE. EVERY GUN WHICH WE SELL IS COVERED BY OUR BINDING GUARANTEE, WHICH MEANS THAT IF ANY PIECE OR PART GIVES OUT BY REASON OF DEFECTIVE MATERIAL OR WORKMANSHIP WITHIN ONE YEAR, WE WILL REPLACE IT FREE OF CHARGE. You may order any gun of us, and if you do not find it satisfactory, or as represented, you may return it to us at our expense of transportation charges both ways and we will immediately refund your money. PRICES—THE MANUFACTURER FIXES THE SELLING PRICE OF THESE GUNS AND WILL NOT ALLOW US OR ANY OTHER HOUSE TO SELL THEM LOWER.

GENERAL DESCRIPTION. All L. C. Smith Hammerless Guns are full choke bored, have English walnut pistol grip stock, tapered matted rib, case hardened locks and frame, rubber butt plate, compensating extension rib and fore end and patent safety slide. OUR PATENT GLOBE SIGHT is furnished free with all Smith guns.

ARMOR STEEL BARRELS.

GLOBE SIGHT free with this gun.

BORED FOR NITRO POWDER.

$25.00

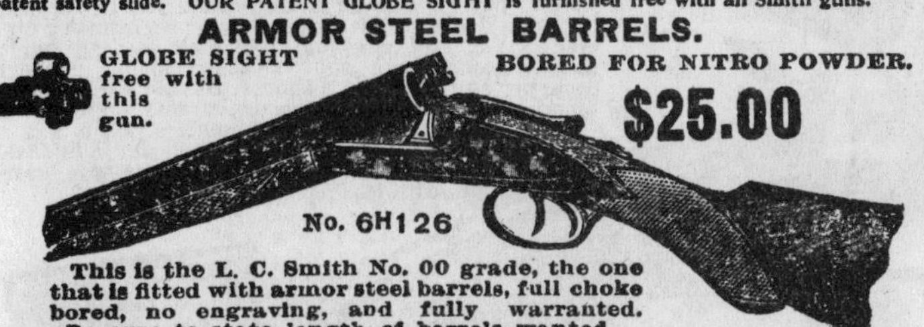

No. 6H126

This is the L. C. Smith No. 00 grade, the one that is fitted with armor steel barrels, full choke bored, no engraving, and fully warranted. Be sure to state length of barrels wanted.

Catalogue Number	Grade	Style of Barrels	Gauge	Length of Barrels	Weight	Price
6H126	No. 00	Armor Steel	12	30 or 32 inches	7½ to 8 lbs.	$25.00

Weight, packed for shipment, about 14 pounds.

DAMASCUS BARRELS.

GLOBE SIGHT free with this gun.

BORED FOR NITRO POWDER.

$32.90

ILLUSTRATION OF No. 0 GRADE

No. 6H132

The No. 0, No. 1 and No. 2 grades are all fitted with Damascus barrels of three qualities. All of them are very good, but the figure varies in size; for example, the figure of the three-blade is much finer than in the plain Damascus. The No. 0 is plain finished, the No. 1 has line engraving and the No. 2 has fine scroll and game engraving on the lock plates. All are choke bored for black or nitro powder and fully warranted by the factory. **Be sure to state length of barrels wanted.**

Catalogue Number	Grade	Style of Barrels	Finish	Gauge	Length of Barrels	Weight, Lbs.	Price
6H132	No. 0	Damascus	Plain	12	30 or 32 in.	7½ to 8	$32.90
6H136	No. 1	2-Blade Damascus	Plain Line Engraving	12	30 or 32 in.	7¾ to 8	42 00
6H140	No. 2	3-Blade Damascus	Game and Scroll Engraving	12	30 or 32 in.	7¾ to 8	56.00

Weight, packed for shipment, about 14 pounds.

OUR L. C. SMITH HAMMER GUNS.

The L. C. Smith Hammer Guns have the patent cross bolt locks, top snap action, compensating fore end, rebounding bar locks, circular hammers, best American walnut stock and fore end, checkered pistol grip, fancy butt plate, case hardened frame, and are choke bored for black or smokeless powder. These guns are too well known and too popular to require an exhaustive description, for you probably know the L. C. Smith guns have as many friends among the shooters as any guns made.

Globe Sight free with this gun.

$18.50

We have had numerous inquiries within the last two years for the celebrated L. C. Smith Hammer Guns, and are now prepared to furnish them in the following specified grades.

Be sure to state length of barrels wanted.

Catalogue Number	Grade	Style of Barrels	Gauge	Length of Barrels	Weight	Price
6H149	F. T.	Laminated Steel	12	30 or 32 inches	7½ to 8 lbs.	$18.50
6H151	F. D.	Damascus	12	30 or 32 inches	7½ to 8 lbs.	23.00

Weight, packed for shipment, about 14 pounds.

NOTICE. All our guns are tested with heavy loads and cannot burst except by carelessness, obstruction in the barrel or improper home loaded shells with nitro or dense powder. We are not responsible for burst gun barrels.

HOW DAMASCUS GUN BARRELS ARE MADE.

The above illustration shows, as nearly as possible, how the Damascus gun barrels are made. The three strips, A, B and C, each consist of from 40 to 60 layers of iron and steel welded together into one square strip, then they are twisted (D) while hot and rewelded into one strip about ⅜ inch wide and ⅛ inch thick; the object being that if any one of these numerous layers of iron or steel has a flaw, the welding process entirely eliminates the flaw. After these numerous layers of iron and steel are twisted and reweided into one strip the strip is twisted around a mandrel and welded together as shown in the illustration. These barrels are all hand made by skilled mechanics who have spent years in learning this art. They cannot be made by machinery. When a barrel is made from three strips it is called three-blade Damascus, when made from two strips it is called two-blade Damascus, and when made from one strip it is called twist or laminated steel. The more strips used in making the barrel, the finer is the figure of the barrel and the more costly to make.

OUR PATENT GLOBE SIGHT FURNISHED FREE with this gun. Worth the price of the gun for wing shooting.

OUR HEXAGON MATTED BREECH DOUBLE BARREL BREECH LOADING SHOTGUN,

We sell more guns to the consumer than any five mail order houses combined. **$12.35**

OUR HEXAGON BREECH GUN as we are getting it out this season, is one of the handsomest double barrel breech loading shotguns on the market.

AT $12.35 we offer this, our Hexagon double barrel shotgun, the equal of any gun made, and superior to guns offered by any other house at 25 per cent more money. We have placed a large order for these guns and the terms and conditions of our order stipulate that they must be good shooters as to long range, good penetration and good pattern, and each and every gun is carefully constructed and tested before it leaves the factory.

DESCRIPTION. Our Hexagon Matted Breech Shotgun is fitted with Scott action top snap break, bar locks, Damascus finished barrels, with matted hexagon breech beautifully matted as shown in the illustration, extension rib, Edwards' patent rebounding circular hammers, straight grained walnut stock and fore end beautifully carved in leaf design, pistol grip stock, nitro firing pins, patent snap fore end, case hardened frame and lock plates, left barrel choke bored, right barrel cylinder bored, bored true to gauge for black or smokeless powder.

No. 6H257

Order by Number.

Send 10 cents for our Booklet of Useful Information to Shooters.

ABOUT 30 AND 32-INCH BARRELS.

We have tested this gun with 30 and 32-inch barrels, with the selfsame ammunition in each gun, and we fail to find the slightest difference in the pattern, penetration or velocity between one and the other, and as a 30-inch gun in 12-gauge makes the best proportioned and best handling gun, we have concluded to handle this gun with 30-inch barrels only, since 95 per cent of all the 12-gauge guns sold in the United States are sold with 30-inch barrels.

Catalogue No.	Grade	Style of Barrels	Gauge	Length of Barrels	Weight of Gun	Price
6H257	No. 669C	Damascus Finish	12	30 inches	7¼ to 7¾ lbs.	$12.35

Weight, packed for shipment, about 14 pounds.

OUR CELEBRATED EBONIZED DOUBLE BARREL BREECH LOADING SHOTGUN, "THE BLACK BEAUTY"

AN IMPORTED GUN, MADE IN LIEGE, BELGIUM.

$11.25

ELABORATELY ENGRAVED AND CARVED. MADE IN 12-GAUGE ONLY. LEFT BARREL CHOKE BORED

Our GLOBE SIGHT FREE with this Gun.

FOR $11.25 we furnish our celebrated ebonized black stock and black fore end, elaborately carved and engraved double barrel hammer breech loading shotgun, one of the most attractive and well made shotguns offered by any house, a gun that must be seen to be appreciated, as it is so different from the regular walnut stock and fore end usually applied to shotguns.

No. 6H266

WE ARE THE LARGEST IMPORTERS in the United States selling goods from the manufacturers to the consumer. We import all our own foreign guns direct from Liege, Belgium, which is probably the largest gun making center in the world, and all our imported guns have the Belgian Government test, as explained on another page of this catalogue. When you buy a Belgian gun from us you do not pay a wholesaler's, jobber's, or retail dealer's profit, but you buy the gun at one small profit from the manufacturer to the consumer, thus making a great saving on your purchase.

OUR CELEBRATED EBONIZED STOCK and fore end double barrel breech loading shotgun is fitted with a forged breech; lock plates are nicely polished and handsomely nickeled, elegantly engraved in scroll design, as shown in the illustration. The barrel is finished in two-blade Damascus pattern with handsome matted rib, latest style Edwards' extension rib, bored smooth and true to gauge, the right barrel is cylinder bored and the left barrel is choke bored for field shooting.

THE LOCKS are of the bar lock type with rebounding hammers, which fly back to half cock after the gun is fired. The butt plate and top lever are nickel plated to conform with the frame and locks of the gun. The stock is beautifully finished in dead black ebonized color, has scroll carving in leaf and dragon design, very beautiful, as shown in the illustration. The general appearance of the ebonized stock, the engraved nickel plated frame, locks and top lever, nickel plated butt plate and the two-blade Damascus finished barrels make a combination of contrast pleasing to the eye. Always mention length of barrels wanted.

Catalogue No.	Grade	Style of Barrels	Gauge	Length of Barrels	Weight of Gun	Price
6H266	No. 937	2-Blade Damascus Finish	12	30 in.	7½ to 8 lbs.	$11.25

Weight, packed for shipment, about 14 pounds.

NOTICE OUR PRICES ON LOADED SHELLS. WE BEAT ALL COMPETITORS.

$4.92 BUYS A COMPLETE SINGLE BARREL SHOTGUN OUTFIT

12-GAUGE AUTOMATIC EJECTOR, WORTH $10.00

OUR PRICE OF $4.92 for this high grade single barrel automatic ejector shotgun and outfit is less by $2.00 to $3.00 than you would have to pay for a shotgun alone were you to purchase it from a dealer. With this shotgun we furnish a high grade set of gun cleaning and shell loading implements, powder and shot measure, loader, rammer, decapper and recapper, crimper, 20-hole shell loading block, wad cutter and extractor, a fine quality web shell belt with shoulder strap, a box of 25 machine loaded shells and a fine take down Victoria style canvas gun cover with leather handle.

OUR PATENT GLOBE SIGHT IS FREE WITH THIS GUN

TO APPRECIATE THE WONDERFUL VALUE we are offering in this combination shotgun and outfit, we suggest that you take this outfit item by item and price it according to the prices you would have to pay any other house for the single items. For the gun you would have to pay anywhere from $5.00 to $8.00; the loading tools purchased singly from any dealer would cost you approximately $3.00; the canvas gun cover could not be duplicated for less than 50 cents to $1.00; the shell belt would retail for about 50 cents: the 25 loaded shells of a quality equal to those we furnish would cost you not less than 50 cents.

HOW WE ARE ABLE TO MAKE SUCH AN EXTRAORDINARY OFFER Our business in shotguns is the largest gun business in the world today. Our sales on guns exceeds the combined sales on guns of all the mail order houses in the United States. We own and control at Meriden, Conn., the largest gun factory of its kind in the world. We further contract for guns with other factories in quantities five times as great as any other house. Selling such enormous quantities of guns gives us the minimum cost, a cost far lower than that enjoyed by any other concern. This enormous saving in the cost of our guns results in your direct benefit, as we ask but one small margin of profit over the actual cost, thereby furnishing you a gun for less than half of what you would have to pay elsewhere for a gun of equal grade. We also manufacture all of the gun cleaning and shell loading implements we sell. We are the only concern in the country today manufacturing its own gun cleaning and loading implements. Our selling price on these goods is less than your local dealer's cost. We control the output of one of the largest manufacturers of hunting clothing, gun cases and canvas goods in the United States. It is these conditions that make it possible for us to give you $10.00 value for $4.92.

OUR LIBERAL TRIAL OFFER.

SEND US $4.92 and we will send you this complete outfit as described and illustrated herewith, with the full understanding and agreement that you can give the gun ten days' trial, during which time compare it with other guns sold for more than you paid for the complete outfit, test its shooting qualities, note the pattern and penetration, compare the finish, workmanship and construction with that of any other single barrel gun in your neighborhood, examine the outfit carefully, and if you, for any reason, are not satisfied with the gun or the outfit, if you are not pleased with your purchase, if you do not think you have received the greatest possible value, if you do not think that this outfit fulfills our description, or in other words, if you are dissatisfied in any way with your purchase, return this gun and outfit to us at our expense, and we will immediately refund the $4.92, together with any express charges you may have paid.

DESCRIPTION OF THE GUN.

THE GUN is furnished in 12-gauge only. THE BARREL is made of the highest quality armory steel, bored specially for nitro powder. This gun is bored on the celebrated taper system, insuring uniform target and enormous penetration. THIS GUN is fitted with an improved Automatic Shell Ejector, the strongest ejector ever placed on a single barrel gun, and absolutely positive in its action; will automatically throw the shell clear of the breech when the gun is opened. THE FRAME of this gun is a heavy drop forging, beautifully case hardened and finished. THE MECHANISM is the simplest, yet strongest, found in any single barrel gun on the market. Improved top snap action. THE BOLT is of a special design, particularly adapted for the use of nitro powder. This gun is bolted so that it will not shoot loose. THE STOCK is of fine quality walnut, fitted with a neat, shapely pistol grip. THE FORE END is of neat design and finely finished. SHOOTING QUALITIES—This gun is guaranteed to outshoot any single barrel gun on the market today ranging in price from $5.00 to $8.00. Special attention has been paid to the shooting qualities of this gun, and we know that after you have had an opportunity to try and test this gun you will be more than pleased with its shooting qualities.

THE OUTFIT which accompanies this gun is first class in every respect; nothing cheap or shoddy in the entire outfit. The gun cleaning and loading implements are all made in our own factory, of the very best material, and are better goods than you could purchase at retail at any price.

UNDERSTAND, if you purchase this outfit at our price of $4.92 and are for any reason dissatisfied, you have the privilege of returning it to us and your money and charges will be refunded. It is sent you under our binding guarantee, which fully protects you in case you are for any reason dissatisfied with your purchase.

No. 6L411 Our high grade Single Barrel Shotgun and Outfit, 12-gauge, with 32-inch barrel. Price, complete **$4.92**
Weight, packed for shipment, about 16 pounds.

NEW ENGLAND SINGLE BARREL AUTOMATIC EJECTOR SHOTGUN

$3.25

FOR $3.25 we offer this New England Single Barrel Shotgun, fitted with automatic ejector and a fine steel barrel, a better gun than you could purchase elsewhere for $4.50 to $5.00. This gun is made especially for us under contract by a large New England manufacturer, and is guaranteed to be a first class gun in regard to strength, durability, shooting qualites and construction.

WE WILL SHIP YOU one of these guns with the distinct understanding and agreement that if, after giving it a ten-day trial, it is not found satisfactory in every respect, if you do not think it excellent value for the money and a better gun than you could obtain elsewhere for $4.50 or $5.00, if you are not satisfied with the shooting qualities—for that matter, if you are in any way not pleased with your purchase, you may return it to us, and your money and any transportation charges you may have paid will be cheerfully refunded.

THIS GUN is well made, nicely finished, and, as stated, compares with any $4.50 or $5.00 single barrel gun sold elsewhere. Of course, it is not so good a gun as our A. J. Aubrey Hammer or our A. J. Aubrey Hammerless Single Guns described elsewhere in our catalogue, these being the highest grade single barrel guns made. Such being the case, we ask that before buying this gun, or any other gun, you read carefully the description and note the illustrations given of the various parts of these wonderful A. J. Aubrey Single Barrel Guns, both hammer and hammerless. If you want one of the finest single barrel guns made, the greatest value for your money, a single barrel gun that is entirely different from anything else on the market, then we would advise that you purchase an A. J. Aubrey gun, but if you cannot afford to pay more than $3.25 for a gun and are satisfied with a gun of ordinary construction such as you would have to pay any other dealer $4.50 to $5.00 for, we recommend this New England Single Barrel Gun at $3.25 as being excellent value for the money. With every one of these guns we furnish one of our Improved Patent Globe Sights.

No. 6L404 New England Single Barrel Automatic Ejector Shotgun, 12-gauge, 30 or 32-inch, special blued steel barrel, weight, about 6¾ pounds. (State length of barrel wanted.) Price **$3.25**

GENUINE TWIST BARREL SINGLE GUN,

$4.00

12-GAUGE, AUTOMATIC EJECTOR, 30 AND 32-INCH.

FOR $4.00 we offer this automatic ejector, single barrel shotgun, 12-gauge, fitted with genuine twist barrel, manufactured especially for us under contract by one of the largest eastern manufacturers, a gun such as you could not duplicate elsewhere within $2.00 to $3.00 of our price. Never before has a single barrel gun with genuine twist barrel been sold at such a ridiculously low price. We have succeeded in obtaining a large quantity of these guns at a price which enables us, with one small margin of profit added, to offer you for $4.00 a gun such as you would have to pay from $6.00 to $8.00 for if purchased elsewhere.

THIS GUN is made in 12-gauge, fitted with 30 and 32-inch barrels; barrels are genuine imported twist, finely finished, choke bored to give a close, even pattern, fitted with automatic ejector which throws the shell clear of the gun, the frames are finely finished, accurately machined, beautifully case hardened, fitted with a strong positive bolt, operated by improved style top lever, rebounding hammer, fine selected walnut stock, with full checkered pistol grip, rubber cap and fancy rubber butt plate. The fore end is securely fastened to the barrel, is made of selected walnut and is finely finished. This is a high grade gun. If you are looking for a single barrel gun with genuine twist barrel at a low price, this is certainly the gun to buy.

WE PARTICULARLY ASK that you compare this gun at $4.00 with guns sold by other dealers at far higher prices, and you will find that in durability, construction, finish and shooting qualities it is a far better gun. Should you buy one of these guns and not find it all we claim it to be, or if for any reason you find it unsatisfactory, if you are disappointed in its shooting qualities, or if for any reason whatsoever you are not pleased with your purchase, you may return it to us, after giving it a thorough ten-day trial, and your money and any transportation charges you may have paid will be promptly returned to you.

WE INCLUDE with each of these guns at $4.00 one of our Improved Globe Sights, which shooters find a great aid in both field and trap shooting. These Globe Sights are patented, the patent is owned by us, and no other house is able to furnish you with one of these special Globe Sights at any price.

No. 6L406 Genuine Twist Barrel Single Gun, 12-gauge, 30 or 32-inch barrel. (State length when ordering.) Price **$4.00**

OUR LATEST 1908 IMPROVED MODEL WHITE POWDER WONDER

$3.92

AN AUTOMATIC SHELL EJECTING SINGLE BARREL BREECH LOADING SHOTGUN, AS ILLUSTRATED AND DESCRIBED HEREON, COMPLETE WITH OUR GLOBE SIGHT, AS ALSO ILLUSTRATED HEREON, IS NOW OFFERED FOR ONLY $3.92.

THE NEW IMPROVED WHITE POWDER WONDER as offered on this page, is now made for us under contract by a New England maker, made on the general lines of our $3.25 single barrel guns shown on another page, but a better gun throughout, a better quality of barrel and a general improvement in gun making from beginning to end, and our $3.92 price barely covers the cost to us, with but our one small percentage of profit added.

$7.00 was the old price of the White Powder Wonder. We afterwards were able to reduce the price to $4.40, but now and under our latest contract we can offer the new model gun, with a number of improvements as furnished us by the famous New England gun maker, for only $3.92. If you want to buy a good single barrel shotgun at a low price, and you want something a little better, stronger, safer, better made and better finished than the ordinary single barrel shotgun that is being sold generally at retail at $5.00 to $7.00 and $8.00, it will certainly pay you to accept the following liberal offer, a liberal offer on this, our New Model White Powder Wonder Gun which we offer at $3.92.

OUR OFFER

SEND US $3.92 say whether you wish the barrel 30 or 32 inches long, we will send this gun to you and include with it free our removable globe sight, as illustrated hereon, you can examine the gun and use it for ten days, compare it with other guns that you can buy at several dollars above our price, and if you are not perfectly satisfied with your purchase, you can return the gun to us at our expense, and we will immediately return your money together with any express charges you may have paid.

IN CONTRACTING with the New England Gun Company for this gun, we have asked them to get away from the more common guns and to use a higher grade of steel in the barrel, to give us a stronger, better made and better finished gun throughout than the more common single guns on the market, and this they have certainly done in our New Model White Powder Wonder, and as between this, the New Model White Powder Wonder, and a cheaper gun which we are able to offer you on another page, for durability, for strength, lasting qualities, for shooting, penetration, safety, for general service in every way, for the slight difference in price, the difference between the lowest price we are able to make on an automatic shell ejecting single gun, as shown on another page, $3.25, and this, our special price of $3.92 on the White Powder Wonder, a difference of only 67 cents, we certainly would advise you to pay the 67 cents extra and send us your order for this, our New Model White Powder Wonder at only $3.92.

WHEN PURCHASING A GUN a shooter has several essential things in mind, namely, safety, shooting qualities, value and construction. Different guns answer these requirements in various ways, more or less satisfactorily. Of all the single barrel guns made, there are no single barrel guns at any price in which the features of safety, shooting qualities, value and construction are so well attained as in the celebrated A. J. Aubrey Hammer and Hammerless Shotguns, quoted elsewhere in this catalogue at $5.95 and $7.95.

WITHOUT WISHING IN ANY WAY TO DETRACT from the merits of this White Powder Wonder Shotgun at $3.92—it is an excellent gun, a better gun than you could obtain from you local dealer for $5.00—we refer attention to the A. J. Aubrey Single Barrel Guns as being the finest single barrel guns made. **The man who wants a single barrel hammer gun** is certainly serving his interests best by purchasing one of the A. J. Aubrey Single Barrel Hammer Guns at $5.95 for the steel barrel or $6.95 for the twist barrel. The safety feature of the A. J. Aubrey Hammer Gun, which absolutely prevents accidental discharge, the hammer not coming in contact with the firing pin at any time, is alone worth the difference in price between $5.95 and $3.92, the price of this gun, or any of the lower priced guns. In addition, the A. J. Aubrey Hammer Gun embodies the finest mechanism, which is absolutely reliable at all times, and in shooting qualities it exceeds any other gun on the market.

THE BARREL IS CHOKE BORED on the celebrated Aubrey system, and in outline and finish this gun exceeds any single barrel gun made, regardless of name make or price. It is the handsomest, hardest shooting, safest single barrel hammer gun made, and at our price of $5.95 is unquestionably the greatest value ever offered. We ask that before buying a single barrel gun, you carefully read the description of the celebrated A. J. Aubrey gun given on another page of this catalogue.

THIS GLOBE SIGHT which can be instantly attached and removed, and which is a wonderful aid in shooting, especially wing shooting, is furnished free with this, our White Powder Wonder at $3.92.

WHEN DECIDING on a single barrel shotgun as between this the New Model White Powder Wonder, furnished us by a New England maker, and the cheaper grade automatic ejector guns shown on another page, which we furnish for only $3.25, we would advise in your own interest that you pay the slight difference of 67 cents more and order the White Powder Wonder and get something better than the ordinary single barrel shotgun; but still better, and greatly to your interest, don't forget what we have to say here and throughout the book about the Aubrey guns, and if you want a single gun, don't overlook the Aubrey single guns shown on other pages. Quality considered, the Aubrey is, in fact, really the only high grade single gun standing in a class by itself, and as for use as compared with any of the more common guns worth even twice the price we ask.

PLEASE READ ALL ABOUT THE AUBREY GUN AS SHOWN ON A PAGE BY ITSELF ELSEWHERE IN THIS DEPARTMENT.

ILLUSTRATION SHOWS THE ACTION OF OUR WHITE POWDER WONDER.

T is the Hammer.	G is the Stock.
U is the Top Lever.	1 is the Extractor Cam Spring.
V is the Top Lever Spring	2 is the Extractor Cam.
W is the Locking Bolt.	3 is the Extractor Hook.
X is the Mainspring.	4 is the Fore End.
Y is the Trigger Spring.	5 is the Trigger Guard.
Z is the Trigger.	

ABOUT SMOKELESS POWDER. We have heard of a great many guns bursting through the use of home made smokeless powder, containing chlorate of potash, and we desire to caution our customers to be very careful how they handle such home made powders, as expert powder makers inform us they have never been able to control the detonating qualities of chlorate powders. We will not guarantee any gun with chlorate powder

DETAILED DESCRIPTION

THE FRAME of this $3.92 White Powder Wonder is made extra strong. The frames are solid steel, made heavy and they are reinforced, neatly shaped, well finished, given a mottled finish on the outside, made with rebounding hammer, positive springs, latest top snap break, latest style of takedown or detachable model; by simply removing the thumbscrew the barrel and fore end can be detached from the frame.

BARREL—The barrel is made from a solid bar of high grade steel, thoroughly tested, choke bored by the Swage system, each barrel is blued with a decarbonized finish, each barrel is fitted with an automatic shell ejector, one of the strongest, positive, perfect working automatic shell ejectors made, so constructed that when you open the gun the empty shell is automatically thrown clear from the gun. The illustration shows the action of the shell as it is being automatically ejected or thrown by the force of the ejector free from the gun. By this device there is no stopping to remove the shell by hand, it being thrown clear out of your way ready to receive the new loaded shell. This makes possible very rapid shooting; in fact, you can load and unload much faster than with the ordinary extractor gun. This device is appreciated only by those who have used automatic shell ejecting guns and such people would have no other; in fact, with the single barrel automatic shell ejecting gun you shoot almost as rapidly and do almost the same execution that you can accomplish with a double hammer breech loading shotgun.

STOCK—The stock is made from a good quality, plain, thoroughly seasoned, straight grain walnut, made with pistol grip and fancy butt plate, the fore end is of plain walnut, well finished.

GENERAL FINISH—This gun is gotten up to present a more symmetrical, shapely and in every way better appearance than the ordinary single barrel gun, and in this respect, of course, excels our $3.25 gun. With its neat stock and butt plate, nicely decarbonized frame and trimmings, polished blued barrel and well proportioned parts and fittings throughout, even at our special $3.92 price, it outclasses most single guns retailed generally at $5.00 to $8.00.

GAUGE—The White Powder Wonder comes in 12-gauge only, and being made and bored for white or black powder, made extra strong throughout, the gun is suitable for any kind of shooting where any shotgun can be used, suitable for small game, also geese, ducks, partridge, quail, snipe, rabbits, squirrels, etc.

LENGTH OF BARRELS—The barrel comes in 30 or 32-inch length, as desired. When ordering be sure to state length of barrel wanted.

THE GUNS are made with especially selected steel barrels, bored from solid bar steel, choke bored, best automatic ejector, self bolted, self locking, self compensating, interchangeable parts, well case hardened, reinforced frame, barrel is detachable from frame, rebounding hammer, latest top snap break, selected straight grain full pistol grip walnut stock. The gun weighs about 6½ pounds, and at our special $3.92 price we furnish it as follows:

No. 6L414 SPECIAL SELECTED STEEL BARREL, 30 OR 32 INCHES AS DESIRED; WEIGHT, ABOUT 6½ POUNDS. OUR SPECIAL PRICE............................ $3.92

Weight, packed for shipment, about 12 pounds.

Read our booklet of Useful Information to Shooters, so you will familiarize yourself with fire arms, and you will have no accidents.

$2.59 —NON— EJECTOR NEW ENGLAND SINGLE BARREL BREECH LOADING SHOTGUN

THIS GUN is made for us under contract by a New England maker of single barrel breech loading shotguns, and is offered by us on the basis of our one small percentage of profit above our actual cost, under contract, for only $2.59.

This is the exact same style of SINGLE BARREL BREECH LOADING SHOTGUN that retails generally at $5.00 to $7.00, and such a single barrel gun as is not being advertised by any other house, to our knowledge, at less than $4.00, and from that price upward.

WHILE THIS IS A GOOD, STRONG, AMERICAN MADE SINGLE BARREL BREECH LOADING SHOTGUN and the same standard of quality as most of the single guns on the market, and especially those retailing at $6.00 and under, we would be very glad to receive your order for this gun, and if you will send us $2.59 we will send you this gun exactly as illustrated and described and include with it our Globe Sight FREE, as illustrated below, and ship the gun to you with the understanding and agreement that if you don't find it perfectly satisfactory, you can return it to us and we will cheerfully refund your money; still, in your own interest, if you want a thoroughly reliable, in fact, an extra high grade single barrel shotgun; in short, if you are thinking of buying a single barrel breech loading shotgun of any kind at any price, we would especially refer you to our A. J. Aubrey Gun, shown on another page of this catalogue, and which we offer at $7.95, for if you will consider all the features in this Aubrey Gun, if you will stop to consider it is the only high grade single barrel breech loading shotgun on the market that carries with it all the features of the highest grade double barrels made, every saf guard, every point of strength and accuracy, for the few dollars difference in price, we are sure you will decide to buy this, the only extra high grade single barrel gun made. So far as the percentage of profit is concerned, it makes no difference to us, but for the sake of our reputation, for the advantage to us in selling higher grade goods than you could possibly buy elsewhere, and at prices, quality considered, not approached by anything on the market, we feel, in your own interest, it is our duty to call your attention especially to our single barrel Aubrey at $7.95, and urge in your interest if you do buy a single gun, buy the Aubrey and get the very best.

IF YOU FEEL YOU DO NOT WISH TO PAY MORE THAN $2.59 for a single barrel gun, we are pleased to say to you that we believe this gun the equal of any you can buy elsewhere at $5.00 and such a gun as is often sold at $6.00 to $8.00. It has a strong frame, strong plain blued steel barrel, the barrel is 32 inches long. Comes in 12-gauge only, the barrel is choke bored by the swage system; it has a top snap break, it is made with a plain walnut stock, with a plain semi-pistol grip, as illustrated, plainly finished walnut fore end, it is fitted with a shell extractor, but you will note, not a shell ejector. By a shell extractor we mean when you open the gun the shell is extracted a fraction of an inch from the barrel so that you can easily, with your hand, remove the empty shell from the barrel. Not like the gun following, however, it does not automatically eject or throw the empty shell from the barrel. It's a good, fair shooting gun, but, of course, at the price, like all the single guns that sell at low prices, it must go out with a limited amount of finish, yet it's a good strong arm, gives generally good satisfaction in shooting qualities and surely at our special price should give satisfaction.

PATENT GLOBE SIGHT.

This, our special Globe Sight, owned, made and controlled by us, will be furnished free with this New England Single Barrel Breech Loading Shotgun at our special $2.59 price. Understand, the sight can be immediately attached or removed at will from the gun, and will be found an invaluable addition to any single gun, and we furnish it free with all the single guns we sell.

We furnish this gun at $2.59 under the following specifications:

No. 6H402 Plain Blued Steel Barrel, 12-gauge, length of barrel, 32 inches. Weight, about 6¾ pounds.
Our special price $2.59
Weight, packed for shipment, about 12 pounds. Order by catalogue number.

AUTOMATIC SHELL EJECTING SINGLE BARREL BREECH LOADING SHOTGUN $2.89

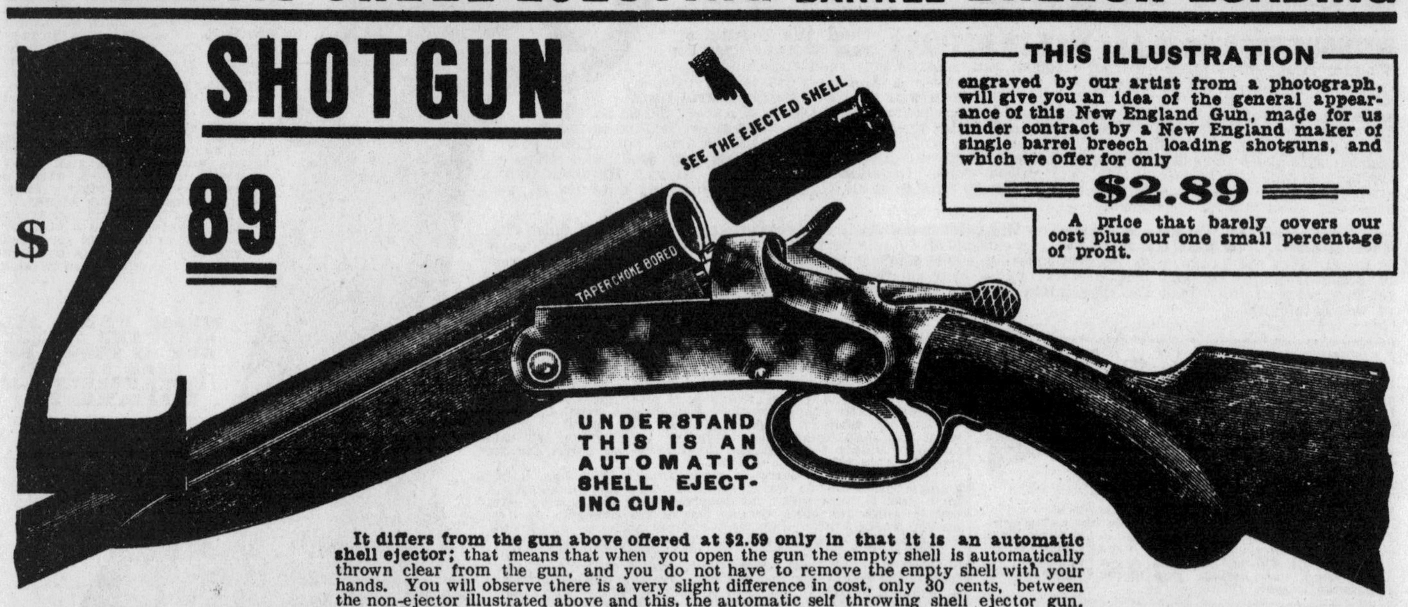

THIS ILLUSTRATION engraved by our artist from a photograph, will give you an idea of the general appearance of this New England Gun, made for us under contract by a New England maker of single barrel breech loading shotguns, and which we offer for only

$2.89

A price that barely covers our cost plus our one small percentage of profit.

It differs from the gun above offered at $2.59 only in that it is an automatic shell ejector; that means that when you open the gun the empty shell is automatically thrown clear from the gun, and you do not have to remove the empty shell with your hands. You will observe there is a very slight difference in cost, only 30 cents, between the non-ejector illustrated above and this, the automatic self throwing shell ejector gun.

Therefore, as between the non-ejector offered above and this, the ejector gun offered at $2.89, we would in your own interest strongly advise that you order this, the $2.89 gun.

ONE WORD IN YOUR OWN INTEREST AND BEFORE YOU ORDER A SINGLE GUN

OF COURSE, as these low prices would indicate, these are the ordinary single barrel breech loading shotguns which are generally on the market and sold generally at prices ranging from $5.00 to $8.00, sold regularly in this way you cannot expect an extra well finished or a high grade gun, but you will find them in every way equal to guns that retail generally at $5.00 to $8.00, but in your own interest, if you are about to buy a single barrel gun, either one of the guns shown on this page or any other single gun from us or any other maker or seller, by all means first read what we have to say on another page about our $7.95 Aubrey Hammerless Shell Ejecting Single Barrel Breech Loading Shotgun, a gun which is positively the highest grade single barrel shotgun made, and the only single barrel shotgun made which is built on the same lines, with the same high grade of workmanship as is found in the highest grade double barrel hammerless breech loading shotguns, a gun which in real value (intrinsic) is cheaper by far at $7.95 than is any of the ordinary single barrel shotguns even at one-third of $7.95. In short, if just before you decide to buy a cheaper single barrel shotgun you will let us send you our $7.95 Aubrey on our special sixty days' offer, we are confident that after having used the Aubrey Gun for a few days for your own use, for the real worth of the gun you wouldn't trade it for a half dozen of any other single barrel guns made. With this word of advice it will help you to decide and select as between the best single gun made, the Aubrey at $7.95 and our other guns, we are pleased to say in behalf of this our $2.89 New England Single Barrel Breech Loading Shotgun, that like the $2.59 gun described above, it has a strong, solid frame, a plain walnut stock, a plain finished semi-pistol grip, plain finished fore end, good, strong, plain blued steel barrel, choke bored by the swaged system, the top snap break, the frame and bright parts are neatly case hardened with mottled finish, the guns are strong, they are good average shooters, they have a good ordinary finish, the finish will outlast that of any of the ordinary single guns on the market, guns that retail generally at $5.00 to $8.00. If you feel you do not wish to pay more than $2.89 for a shotgun, send us $2.89 and we will send you this gun, and will include with it our new detachable Globe Sight free. It will go to you with the understanding and agreement that if it isn't found perfectly satisfactory in every way, if you don't find it all and more than we claim for it, the equal of guns that retail generally at $5.00 to $8.00, you can return the gun to us at our expense and we will cheerfully refund your money.

No. 6H403 We furnish this gun exactly as illustrated and described, in 12-gauge only, plain blued steel barrel, barrel 32 inches long, gun weighing about 6¾ pounds, all complete, and included with the gun free our detachable Globe Sight, at our special price of........ $2.89
Weight, packed for shipment, about 12 pounds. Order by catalogue number.

PATENT GLOBE SIGHT.

This detachable Globe Sight, which can be instantly attached to or taken from the gun and which aids greatly in the shooting of any single gun, is furnished free with this and all our single guns at the special prices named.

YOUR MONEY WILL BE IMMEDIATELY RETURNED TO YOU FOR ANY GOODS NOT PERFECTLY SATISFACTORY.

THE GREAT NORWICH GUN
NOW ONLY $16.10
GENUINE DAMASCUS BARRELS
AS OUR GREATEST LEADER, our greatest value in a hammer double barrel breech loading shotgun, for one of the highest grade hammer double barrel breech loading shotguns on the market, an all American gun, we offer you this season the great Norwich Gun, a gun made for us by a Norwich gun company at Norwich, Connecticut, and we offer you this gun on the basis of the actual cost to us, a price we have been able to secure from the Norwich maker by reason of an enormously large contract, we offer it at the exact cost to us plus only our one small percentage of profit.
REFERRING TO GREATER VALUE we refer to the A. J. Aubrey hammerless double barrel breech loading shotguns offered at $13.85 and upward, as illustrated and described on 667 to 671 in this catalogue.
BEFORE you decide to buy a hammer breech loading shotgun, we would advise you, in your own interest, to refer to the pages illustrating and describing the double barrel Aubrey hammerless gun, and note the few points among the many where we point out the great advantages of a hammerless shotgun over a hammer gun, and remember, in the Aubrey gun we guarantee it the highest grade gun made in America. This gun we make in our own factory and, therefore, can offer it to you on the basis of the actual cost to produce, plus our one small percentage of profit, and, therefore, in the Aubrey gun we are in a position to give you greater value than it is possible to give in any gun we buy from any other factory. However, if after reading what we have to say about the Aubrey hammerless gun you still feel that you prefer a hammer gun, then by all means try and add a few dollars, if necessary, to the amount you contemplate paying for a gun, and give us your order for this, the highest grade double barrel breech loading shotgun that this great Norwich (Connecticut) factory turns out.
OUR PATENT GLOBE SIGHT.
With every $16.10 gun we send FREE our patent Globe Sight, a sight which we own and control, a sight on which we have bought the patents in order to control it, a sight that is a wonderful help in shooting, goes FREE with the gun.
THE NORWICH FACTORY that makes this gun has been in the fire arms business for a great many years. It is one of the best equipped and best managed gun factories in America. They have had all the benefits that accrue from years of practical experience, and year by year, in the development of gun making they have improved their guns where improvement has been possible. When explosive ammunition, like smokeless powder, came out, they were the first to bring out the reinforced and double strengthened gun, adapting it to the use of smokeless powders. They were among the first to use the low circular hammers and solid plungers, the extension rib construction, the top snap break action, and as makers of the most dependable hammer double barrel breech loading shotguns they have gained such a reputation that we feel we have a right to some pride when we can offer you the highest grade gun they make, with genuine Damascus barrels, hand engraved throughout, for only $16.10.
CHOKE BORED
Remember Our 10 Days' Free Trial Offer on this Gun.
You can send your order to us for this gun, and if it is not perfectly satisfactory after you have given it a ten days' thorough test and comparison you are at liberty to return it to us at our expense and we will immediately return your money, together with any express charges you may have paid.
ILLUSTRATION SHOWING THE DEELEY & EDGE PATENT FORE END, FRAME AND FULL PISTOL GRIP.
IF YOU HAVE DECIDED TO BUY A DOUBLE BARREL BREECH LOADING SHOTGUN,
and you have decided that you wish a hammer gun instead of a hammerless, and you feel you can afford to pay as much as $16.10 for a thoroughly reliable high grade gun, then we advise you in your own interest, as compared with any other hammer breech loader we show in this catalogue, or as compared with any double barrel breech loading hammer shotgun, that you can buy elsewhere we strongly advise you to select this, the highest grade gun made by this Norwich maker.
IN SELECTING A GUN we want you to look our catalogue over carefully, and if you decide on a hammer gun in place of a hammerless, and you feel you cannot afford to pay as much as $16.10, or even as much as $10.00, you will find a number of double barrel hammer breech loading shotguns in our catalogue at exceedingly low prices, namely, from $6.75 up, and such values as you could not get elsewhere at anything like the price; but since it is always best in selecting a gun to give preference to the higher grade, we have in this catalogue, in the interest of our customers, in aiding them to make their selection, advised them, first, in buying a hammer gun to try and make up their minds to pay as much as $13.89 the price at which we offer the celebrated T. Barker gun, as shown on a preceding page; but, better still, and in your own interest, we advise you to pay even a little more, pay $16.10, and get this, the highest grade hammer double barrel breech loading shotgun made by this Norwich company.
THIS IS THE HIGHEST GRADE BREECH LOADING SHOTGUN, this Norwich (Connecticut) gun company makes. They make several lower grade guns that are good, reliable fire arms, but this gun which we offer at $16.10 is the highest grade, the finest, the best that is turned out of their factory. At the price, $16.10, you get the gun exactly as illustrated, although, unfortunately, no illustration will do it justice. You get it with their highest grade genuine two-blade Damascus steel barrels, full finished, you get their highest grade frame and lock construction, the highest grade and best finished stock and fore end, and you get this elaborately engraved gun, a gun that is elaborately engraved by hand, the locks, hammers, frame, guards, tang, snap, etc., etc. You get, in our judgment, the greatest gun value, the most for your money in the way of a high grade hammer breech loading shotgun that goes out of any factory in America; in short, there is to our knowledge only one gun made in America in which we can offer you greater value for your money than is offered in this celebrated Norwich gun at $16.10.
No. 6H365 $16.10
OUR FREE TRIAL OFFER
IF YOU DECIDE TO ACCEPT OUR ADVICE, and if you have also decided to buy a hammer breech loader, and you will send us either $14.85 or $16.10 for this gun, depending on the barrels you select, whether laminated steel or genuine Damascus, as quoted below, we will be pleased to send this gun to you with the understanding and agreement, that after it is received you can give it ten days' trial, during which time you can put it to every possible test; you can test it for long range, hard shooting, extra long distance killing, for penetration, for pattern, for strength, for beauty, for durability, etc., and if for any reason you are dissatisfied with your purchase, you can return the gun to us at any time within ten days and we will cheerfully return your money, together with any express charges you may have paid.
Detailed Description of the Celebrated Norwich Hammer Double Barrel Breech Loading Shotgun.
The Highest Grade Gun Turned Out by this Famous Norwich (Connecticut) Gun Factory.
BARRELS—The barrels of this Norwich gun the $16.10 gun are genuine two-blade Damascus steel barrels, while the $14.85 gun has the genuine laminated steel barrels, both of which are especially bored for black or smokeless powder, bored for long range extra pattern and extra penetration. They are handsomely finished, polished and browned, fitted with what is known as the rifle extension rib, beautifully matted on a machine, built especially for this work and equal to the barrels generally furnished on fine hammerless guns costing more than three times the price we ask for this gun.
FRAME—The frame of this gun is made from solid steel forgings, worked up, milled, drilled, shaped, profiled and polished, and then the frame and locks are beautifully case hardened and mottled.
STOCK—The stock of this Norwich gun is made from the very best quality of selected well seasoned, straight grained black walnut, beautifully shaped and handsomely checkered; has a full pistol grip capped with a rosette, fancy butt plate and well fitted to the frame. FORE END—The fore end is made from the same quality black walnut stock, handsomely checkered and fitted, and it is fitted with a genuine Deeley and Edge patent fore end fastening, a fastening found only on high grade guns. TOP LEVER—The top lever is one of the strongest and simplest top levers made and one which cannot possibly get out of order. The lever operates the locking bolts in the frame, so that when you turn it to the right the gun is unlocked and ready for shells. THE LOCKING BOLTS—Our $16.10 Norwich gun has two locking bolts in the frame, which is known as a double bolt locking construction, a construction found only on high grade guns. LOCKS—The locks of the Norwich gun are made non-destructible, practically impossible to get out of order, simple and strong. They are rebounding, so that the hammer falls back to half cock after the trigger is pulled. They are fitted with spiral mainsprings, the best made, beautiful case hardened lock bolts, and all wearing parts are hardened, so as to render them practically everlasting. ALIGNMENT—The alignment of this Norwich gun is equal to any gun made, regardless of price; the gun handles and comes up nicely, a feature which is much appreciated by hunters, trap shooters and marksmen generally. ENGRAVING—This $16.10 genuine Norwich gun is laid out in neat scroll and matted design, engraved throughout by hand. The lock plates, the low circular hammers, the tang the break, the guards, the bottom frame all elaborately engraved by hand; in fact, it is in finish, workmanship, material and construction throughout the highest grade gun made by this great Norwich maker. GAUGE AND LENGTH—These guns are made in 12-gauge only. They come with barrels either 30 or 32 inches long, as desired, and the gun weighs from 7¾ to 8 pounds.
IF YOU ARE ABOUT TO BUY A DOUBLE BARREL SHOTGUN look this catalogue over carefully. Note we sell double barrel hammer breech loading shotguns as low as $6.75, we have another at $8.60, and quite a variety under $12.00. We have an exceedingly high grade Liege (Europe) imported shotgun, the famous T. Barker, and a gun that we recommend highly at $13.89, shown in a full page illustration on a preceding page, and we have, as shown in the fore part of the gun section of this catalogue, the New England hammerless double barrel breech loading shotgun for as low as $8.95; but unless you decide to buy the genuine A. J. Aubrey Hammerless Double Barrel Breech Loading Shotgun, the highest grade gun made in America, and the greatest value we or any other house have ever offered; in short, if you have decided to buy a hammer double barrel breech loading shotgun, by all means get the best, the greatest value for your money, buy this, the highest grade hammer double barrel breech loading shotgun made by this celebrated Norwich maker, made in our own country, made with American tools, by American labor, the best that this factory turns out, this celebrated full hand engraved Norwich gun at either $14.85 or $16.10, according to the quality of the barrels you select.
We furnish this, the highest grade hammer double barrel breech loading shotgun that this Norwich factory makes, in the following styles at the following special prices: When ordering state length of barrels you prefer to have.
No. 6H364 Imported Liege Laminated Steel Barrels, 12-gauge. Length of barrels, 30 or 32 inches. Weight, 7¾ to 8 lbs. Price..$14.85
No. 6H365 Genuine Two-Blade Damascus Barrels, 12 gauge. Length of barrels, 30 or 32 inches. Weight, 7¾ to 8 lbs. Price.. 16.10
Weight, packed for shipment, about 14 pounds.

OUR COMBINATION SHOTGUN AND RIFLE, $14.76

Our Globe Sight FREE with this gun.

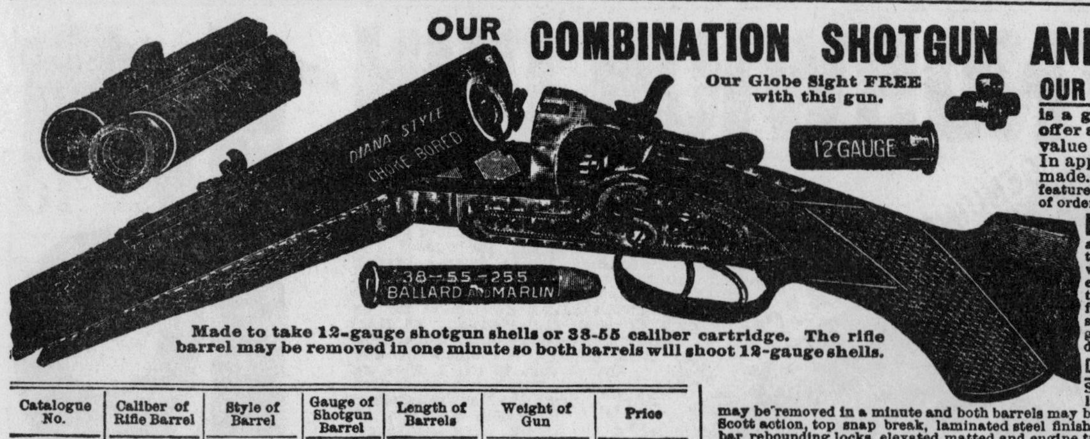

Made to take 12-gauge shotgun shells or 38-55 caliber cartridge. The rifle barrel may be removed in one minute so both barrels will shoot 12-gauge shells.

OUR $14.76 BELGIAN COMBINED RIFLE AND SHOTGUN is a gun equal to what retail gun stores offer at $25.00 to $30.00; it is such a gun value as has never before been offered. In appearance one of the handsomest guns made. Combines every strictly high grade feature, easily handled. A gun that cannot get out of order, a gun that will last a lifetime.

EVERY $14.76 GUN we put out will be a big advertisement for us. Everyone who sees the gun will admire it; every true sportsman will appreciate its splendid qualities, and every dealer in sporting goods will realize the wonderful value we are offering in this fieldpiece at only $14.76. On this basis we solicit your order, feeling confident we will give you such a gun at the price as cannot be duplicated elsewhere.

DETAILED DESCRIPTION. Our Combination Shotgun and Rifle is a new departure in this line, in that the rifle barrel is auxiliary and may be removed in a minute and both barrels may be used for shotgun shells. It is fitted with Scott action, top snap break, laminated steel finished barrels with Diana style breech. Strong bar rebounding locks, elevated matted and engine turned rib fitted with sporting rear and sporting front sight, Edwards' L-shape extension rib; rebounding circular hammers, straight grained walnut stock and fore end nicely checkered, full pistol grip with shield inlaid, patent snap fore end, nitro firing pins, left barrel choke bored, right barrel cylinder bored, case hardened forged frame and lock plates, suitable for birds and heavy game. The 38-55 cartridge is suitable for heavy game such as deer, moose, etc.

Catalogue No.	Caliber of Rifle Barrel	Style of Barrel	Gauge of Shotgun Barrel	Length of Barrels	Weight of Gun	Price
6F259	38-55 C. F. Takes cartridge 6F2432	Laminat'd Steel Finish	12	30 in.	9 to 9¼ lbs.	$14.76

Weight, packed for shipment, about 14 pounds.

OUR HIGHLY ENGRAVED DIANA STYLE BREECH, DOUBLE BARREL BREECH LOADER FOR ONLY $9.98

Our Patent Globe Sight furnished free with this gun. Doubles the value of any shotgun for wing shooting.

12-GAUGE LOADED SHELLS, $1.32 per 100. See page 164.

MADE IN 12-GAUGE ONLY.

No. 6F270
The above illustration, engraved from a photograph, will give you some idea of the appearance of this gun.

Read our booklet "Information to Shooters" so you will have no accidents with fire arms.

This gun is made in Europe by one of the oldest and most reliable makers there, and we offer it for the first time at the remarkably low price of $9.98. Don't be deceived by anyone into buying any of the many cheap imitations. By reason of a large contract, which we have made for a quantity of these guns, we have gotten the manufacturer to figure the price down to the lowest point, and by paying cash for the goods we are able to obtain them based on the actual cost of labor and material, and by adding our one small percentage of profit we are enabled to name you this heretofore unheard of price on the highly engraved Diana Style Breech, Double Barrel Breech Loading Shotgun.

MINUTE DESCRIPTION. Our Diana Style Breech Gun is fitted with top snap break, laminated steel finished barrels, strong bar rebounding locks, L-shape Edwards' extension rib, rebounding circular hammers, imported walnut stock and fore end nicely checkered; full pistol grip with inlaid shield, patent snap fore end, nitro firing pins, flat matted rib, left barrel choke bored, right barrel cylinder bored; both barrels bored smooth and true to gauge for black and smokeless powder; case hardened forged frame and lock plates. A beautiful gun at a low price. Order by catalogue number and state length of barrels wanted.

Catalogue Number	Grade	Style of Barrels	Gauge	Length Barrels	Weight	Price
6F270	No. 839N	Damascus Finish	12	30 or 32 in.	7½ to 8 lbs.	$9.98

Weight, packed for shipment, about 14 pounds.

CELEBRATED GREENER ACTION BREECH LOADING SHOTGUN... $11.95

12-GAUGE ONLY

DESCRIPTION of our Greener Action Cross Bolt Shotgun. It is fitted with Scott action, top snap break, Damascus finished barrels, strongest bar action locks, with rebounding circular hammers, nicely matted extension rib with Greener action cross bolt in the extension; straight grained walnut stock and fore end nicely carved; pistol grip of inlaid design, giving the grip a handsome appearance; patent snap fore end, handsomely carved scroll engraving on the lock plates, left barrel choke bored, right barrel cylinder bored for field shooting; bored smooth and true to gauge for black and smokeless powder. Order by catalogue number and state length of barrels wanted.

You will get a PROFIT SHARING CERTIFICATE and will quickly get your share of our profit.

Notice our prices on J. C. Hand Traps

$11.95 BUYS A CROSS BOLT GUN

With handsomely carved stock and fore end.

The barrels of this gun are made of Wilson's best steel.

12-GAUGE LOADED SHELLS, $1.32 PER 100. SEE PAGE 164.

OUR PATENT GLOBE SIGHT furnished free with this gun. Worth the price of the gun for wing shooting.

We import all our guns direct from Europe and give our customers the benefit of all the saving we make by doing so.

Catalogue Number	Grade	Style of Barrels	Gauge	Length Barrels	Weight	Price
6F272	No. 865	Damascus Finish	12	30 or 32 in.	7½ to 8 lbs.	$11.95

Weight, packed for shipment, about 14 pounds.

OUR LADIES' LITTLE BREECH LOADING DOUBLE BARREL SHOTGUN.

$9.93

44-Caliber, or 40-85 Caliber Shotgun.

No. 6F276

We have had this little gun built for ladies or boys who like to hunt and for whom a 12-gauge gun kicks too hard. It is very effective for squirrels, birds or small game, and is made to take the 44 X. L. shot cartridge No. 6F2717. It can also be furnished to take the 40-85 primed shell which is about 3 inches long, and can be loaded heavier than the 44 X. L. shot cartridges are loaded. We cannot furnish the 40-85 shells loaded. The 40-85 shells are large enough to take about 40 grains of powder and ⅝-ounce of shot while the 44 X. L. will use only about one-half as much powder and shot. This little breech loader is fitted with 25-inch barrels and weighs about 4 pounds. Our patent Globe sight is not made small enough for this gun.

Cata. No.	ARTICLE	Caliber	Quantity	Price
6F276	Our Ladies' Breech Loader	44 or 40-85	Each	$9.93
6F2717	Shot Cartridges	44 X.L.	Per 100	1.50
6F3232	Empty Brass Shells (not loaded)	40-85	Per 100	2.50
6F277	Loading Tools, consisting of Recapper, Decapper, Wad Cutter and Charge Cup	40-85	Per Set	.55
57F4716	Gun Cover, 18-ounce canvas		Each	.71

This gun alone when packed for shipment, weighs about 8 pounds.

GIANT 8-GAUGE GOOSE GUN, 36-INCH BARRELS.

$21.10

Our 8-Gauge Double Barrel Goose Gun for Long Range Shooting. Strong French action. The illustration represents our new 8-gauge Lefeaucheaux Breech Loading Gun. This gun has bottom lever, genuine laminated steel barrels, best double key fore end, pistol grip stock, case hardened frame, fancy butt plate, rebounding locks, checkered grip; made for long range shooting. Our 8-gauge Goose Gun is made especially for us under contract and nothing but the best material and the best barrels are used in the construction of this gun. We realize the importance of having guns intended for 8-gauge charges strong at every point, and we have covered these points in the manufacture of these goose guns. Our Globe Sight can only be fitted to 10, 12 and 16-gauge guns.

No. 6F282 The Giant Goose Gun. Made 8-gauge, 36-inch barrels; weight, 12 to 14 pounds. Cylinder bored for buckshot. Price.............. $21.10

OUR AUXILIARY RIFLE BARREL, CALIBER 38-55, FOR 12-GAUGE SHOTGUNS, $4.95.

WITH THIS AUXILIARY RIFLE BARREL you can transform a double barrel shotgun into a combination rifle and shotgun by inserting the auxiliary barrel into the shotgun barrel and it will enable you to shoot a shot shell with the one barrel and a rifle cartridge with the other. It may also be used in a single barrel shotgun, but it is not intended to be used in magazine repeating shotguns.

UNDERSTAND, that for fine target shooting this barrel is impracticable, but for large game shooting a hunter can, with little practice, bring down large game at a distance of 50 to 100 yards by using the shotgun front sight and sighting over the rib of the gun instead of using a rear sight.

No. 6F284 Auxiliary Rifle Barrel, 38-55 caliber, to fit a 30 or 32-inch 12-gauge shotgun. State which length is wanted. Weight, 1¾ to 2 pounds. Price..................$4.95

If by registered mail, postage extra, 40 cents.

$11.22 BUYS THE CELEBRATED T. BARKER

Royal Damascus Finish, Elaborately Engraved, Silver Dog Inlaid, Bar Lock, Double Barrel Breech Loading Shotgun, in 10, 12 or 16-Gauge and $13.35 Buys a 36-inch Barrel 12-Gauge Gun.

Don't Order a Low Priced Double Barrel Shotgun.

WHILE WE SELL double barrel breech loading shotguns of the latest style as low as $6.35, and a number of others at prices lower than this, our celebrated T. Barker Royal Damascus finished gun, we especially urge that you order one of our higher grade guns, either this, our highest grade T. Barker Royal Damascus finish double barrel breech loader, or one of our American Gun Company's high grade, double barrel, breech loading shotguns. You will be much better satisfied by selecting this or a higher grade gun. You will find such a selection much cheaper in the end. In the shooting qualities, wearing qualities and general satisfaction, it pays to select one of our double barrel guns at from $11.22 and upward.

OUR OWN PATENT GLOBE SIGHT

FURNISHED FREE WITH THIS GUN.

This Globe Sight, which makes wing and fast shooting easy, a sight which can be quickly put on or taken off the gun, is furnished free with every T. Barker gun at $11.22. If you order this gun at $11.22 you will get with the gun, free of any cost, our own special patent Globe Sight as illustrated.

Loaded Shells, $1.32 per 100. See page 164.

THIS HANDSOME GUN is gotten out especially for us, following our own detailed specifications, with a view of giving our customers a higher grade, handsomer and better finished shotgun than can possibly be had elsewhere at anything approaching the price.

A NUMBER OF GUNS have been gotten out by various makers in imitation of this, our celebrated T. Barker gun, but you will find any gun offered by any other house bearing the appearance of this our T. Barker Special, will suffer by comparison; in other words, if you will order this gun from us and then order any of the imitations offered by others, and will compare them side by side, you will find that they do not in any way compare with this. We have sold over 10,000 of these guns since 1900.

OUR SPECIAL T. BARKER GUN AT

$11.22

ILLUSTRATION SHOWING THE PATENT FORE END, FRAME AND INLAID FULL PISTOL GRIP.

FROM THE LARGE ILLUSTRATION, engraved by our artist from a photograph, we have endeavored to give you just a little idea of the beautiful finish, the elaborate appearance and the new up to date lines produced in this gun and OFFERED AT ONLY.............. **$11.22**

THE ROYAL DAMASCUS FINISHED BARRELS are thoroughly reliable as to quality and have all the handsome appearance of the most expensive barrels made, and each barrel is branded on the rib, Royal Damascus. These barrels are made and bored especially for field shooting, the right barrel being cylinder bored for an open target, and the left barrel choke bored for a close target. The locks and frame are elaborately engraved; the gun is full pistol grip, the grip and fore end neatly checkered. It is finished with a handsome German silver shield or medallion in the full pistol grip. In short, the gun has been gotten out according to our own specifications on lines more up to date, handsomer, more modern and in every way better than anything shown by any maker

AT ANY PRICE APPROACHING OUR $11.22 PRICE.

OUR FREE TRIAL GUARANTEE OFFER. As a guarantee that this is in every way a better gun than any gun you can buy elsewhere at the price, we will accept your order and ship the gun to you with the understanding and agreement that you can give it ten days' trial, during which time you can put it to any test and if for any reason you become dissatisfied with your purchase, you can return it to us at our expense and we will return your money, together with any express charges paid by you.

DETAILED DESCRIPTION.

BARRELS—The Royal Damascus finished barrels. Each pair of barrels is branded on the rib "Royal Damascus." The right barrel is cylinder bored and the left barrel choke bored. The barrels have all the beautiful finish effect of the most expensive Damascus barrels made. They are finished with shell extractor, "L" shaped extension rib, making a strong locking device. They are fitted with heavy lugs, locking securely into the frame; they are nicely shaped and finished, have a neat, handsome matted rib and they are bored for either black, nitro or smokeless powder.

FRAME—The frame is solid steel, strong, beautifully finished, elaborately engraved, handsomely case hardened, made extra strong and of the latest model.

MOUNTINGS—The gun is mounted with neat low circular hammers, adjusted so that they are out of the line of sight; handsome top snap break; the locks are the latest type of bar lock, each lock branded "T. Barker," and the left lock inlaid with a handsome solid silver hunting dog, which in connection with the hand engraving on the lock represents a strikingly beautiful appearance; has the latest style trigger guard, elaborately engraved; neatly shaped triggers; strong, heavy nitro firing pins; locks are rebounding and come back automatically to half cock on being fired.

STOCK—Stock is made from carefully selected and well seasoned black walnut, beautifully finished, made full pistol grip. The pistol grip is finished with a handsome German silver shield, grip is handsomely decorated as illustrated, fancy butt plate to stock; stock is beautifully shaped, giving the gun an even balance. Comes complete with handsome selected black walnut patent fore end, which is handsomely checkered and beautifully finished.

GAUGE—Our T. Barker gun is furnished in 10, 12 or 16-gauge as desired.

Our $11.22 price barely covers the cost of material and labor, with but our one small percentage of profit added. It is the greatest value ever shown in a gun at the price; it is such a gun as can be had from no other house for only $11.22

ABOUT SMOKELESS POWDER.

We have heard of a great many guns bursting through the use of home made smokeless powder, containing chlorate of potash and we desire to caution our customers to be very careful how they handle such home made powders, as expert powder makers inform us they have never been able to harness the detonating qualities of chlorate powders. We will not guarantee any gun with chlorate powder.

WE TAKE ALL THE RISK. Could anything be more fair? We want you to see the gun, examine it, compare it with other guns, test it for pattern, penetration and shooting qualities, alignment, general appearance and workmanship. We also send our booklet of Useful Information to Shooters with every gun.

FROM THE ILLUSTRATION engraved by our artist direct from a photograph, you can get just a little idea of the appearance of the gun, although you must see and examine this gun and compare it with guns sold by others at higher prices to appreciate the real value we are offering, yet the picture will give you just a little idea of the HANDSOME EFFECT WORKED OUT IN THESE ROYAL DAMASCUS FINISHED BARRELS, in the elaborate engraving of the frame and locks, of the solid silver dog inlaid in the lock, of the general handsome outlines of this

NEW, UP TO DATE, BEAUTIFULLY FINISHED SHOTGUN.
ALWAYS STATE LENGTH OF BARRELS WANTED

Catalogue No.	Grade	Style of Barrels	Gauge	Length of Barrels	Weight of Gun, pounds	Finish	Price
6F292A	No. 678	2 Blade Damascus Finish	12	30 or 32 in.	7½ to 8	Hand Eng'ved	$11.22
6F292B	No. 678		16	30 in.	6¾ to 7	Hand Eng'ved	11.45
6F292D	No. 678		10	32 in.	8¾ to 9½	Hand Eng'ved	11.65
6F293E	No. 678		12	36 in.	8 to 8¼	Hand Eng'ved	13.35

Weight, packed for shipment, about 14 pounds.

WHILE THE PROFIT IS THE SAME TO US, just our one small percentage of profit above the actual cost of material and labor, and the prices on all our guns are very much lower than you can buy from any other house, wholly in the interest of our customers we urge you to select one of our higher grade guns, a double barrel breech loading shotgun at $11.22 and upward. You will get such gun value as was never before given, you will get such a gun as was never seen in your section at anything approaching the price, and, remember, every gun is sent to you subject to your thorough test trial and approval, sent to you with the understanding that you can give it TEN DAYS' TRIAL, during which time you can put it to every test; you can compare it with guns made and sold by others, and if you are not convinced that we are giving you a better gun at a lower price than you can buy elsewhere, you can return the gun to us at our expense, and we will immediately

RETURN YOUR MONEY

together with any express charges you may have paid.

WE ARE THE LARGEST IMPORTERS and handlers of guns and sporting goods in the United States selling direct to the consumer. We sell guns and sporting goods as we do all other merchandise at one small margin of profit above the cost to manufacture, and we save you the importers, wholesalers and dealers' profit.

REMEMBER, with this and all our high grade guns PART OF THE PROFIT IS YOURS. We will send you a Profit Sharing Certificate and you can soon get a Fine Article entirely

FREE

AS EXPLAINED ON THE FIRST PAGES.

OUR SPECIAL PRICE,

$11.22

for 30 or 32-inch barrels or

$13.35

for 12-gauge gun with 36-inch barrels.

LOADED SHELLS. $1.32 per 100. See page 164.

No. 6F292A
ORDER BY NUMBER
Price, $11.22

MARLIN'S MODEL 20 TAKE DOWN REPEATING RIFLE, $11.50.

22-CALIBER.

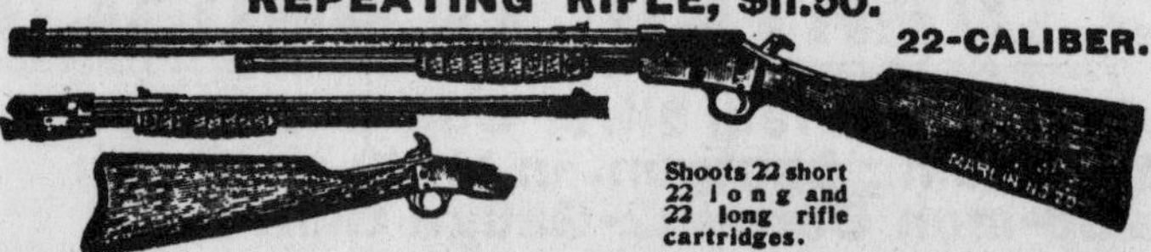

Shoots 22 short 22 long and 22 long rifle cartridges.

AT $11.50 we furnish the New Model No. 20 Pump Action Marlin Take Down Repeating Rifle, the lat t product of the well known Marlin Fire Arms Co., New Haven, Conn. This New Model No. 20 Repeating Rifle is fitted with ivory bead front sight and Marlin's new patent sporting rear sight, the latter being the best rear sight ever placed upon any rifle. It is made to adjust with a small screw and when once set to range, cannot be changed except at the wish of the shooter. The No. 20 rifle is fitted with 22-inch octagon steel barrel, of the best Marlin rifle steel, accurately bored, chambered and rifled for fine shooting up to 200 yards; the frame is made from a special quality of gun frame steel, nicely blued, finely machined and finished in every particular. The take down action is similar to the popular model 1897, and is taken down by pulling hammer to half cock and unscrewing the knurled screw on the right side of the frame. The stock is made from very best straight grained, well seasoned and selected walnut, the fore end is also made from well seasoned, straight grained selected walnut. All the working parts are accurately milled, drilled, fitted and tempered, and should last a lifetime with the proper care. It is the only pump or fore-end action repeater on the market which shoots the 22 short, 22 long and 22 long rifle rim fire cartridges in the same rifle. The magazine has a capacity to hold fifteen 22 short cartridges, twelve 22 long cartridges, or eleven 22 long rifle cartridges. The cartridges are extracted from the side of the frame and it is the only pump action rifle which has an ivory bead front sight and the celebrated special Marlin rear sight.

Catalogue Number	Caliber	Barrel	Weight	Shoots Cartridge Number	Number of Shots	Price
6L736	22 Rim Fire	22-inch octagon	4¼ lbs.	6L2336 6L2338 6L2340	15 12 11	$11.50

Weight, packed for shipment, about 10 pounds.
For fitting Lyman Sights, add 25 cents to cost of sights for fitting.
Nos. 6L4698, 6L4701 and 6L4716 Covers fit any the above rifles. See page 637.

MARLIN REPEATING RIFLES, MODEL 1892.

All Model 1892 Rifles have BLUED FRAMES, Sporting rear sights, Rocky Mountain front sights.

$12.15 $13.16

FOR SMALL GAME AND TARGET WORK.

Made in 22-caliber rim fire, 32-caliber rim fire and 32-caliber center fire.

In the 22-caliber rifles any or all of the following rim fire cartridges may be used; 22-short, 22-long and 22-long rifle. The Model '92, the Model '97 and Model 20 Marlin are the only repeaters that will do this. Other systems require two or three rifles to do this same work. This model takes entirely to pieces without tools, allowing of perfect cleaning. The magazine holds 25 cartridges 22-short, 20 cartridges 22-long and 18 cartridges 22-long rifle.

All 32-caliber rifles are sent out with two firing pins. This rifle is so made that in the same rifle may be used 32-short rim fire, 32-long rim fire cartridges, and by changing the firing pin, 32-short and 32-long center fire cartridges may be used. The magazine holds 18 cartridges 32-caliber short and 15 cartridges 32-caliber long. This ammunition is cheap, and as compared to repeaters using the 32-20 cartridge will save the entire cost of the rifle on first 2,000 cartridges. Always clean your rifle after shooting. It will last longer. A rifle cleaning rod is a good investment.

Catalogue Number	Caliber	Length of Barrel	Shoots Cartridges	Good for	Weight	Price
6L740 6L741	22 rim fire 22 rim fire	24-in. Octagon 24-in. Round	6L2336 6L2338 6L2340	35 to 100 yds. 35 to 100 yds.	5¾ lbs. 5¼ lbs.	$13.16 12.15
6L742	32-caliber rim or center fire.	24-in. Octagon	6L2352 6L2353	100 to 200 yds.	6 lbs.	$13.16
6L743	32-caliber rim or center fire.	24-in. Round	6L2380 6L2381	100 to 200 yds.	6 lbs.	12.15

Weight, packed for shipment, 14 pounds.
For fitting Lyman Sights, add 25 cents to the cost of the sights for fitting.

MARLIN REPEATING RIFLES, MODEL 1894.

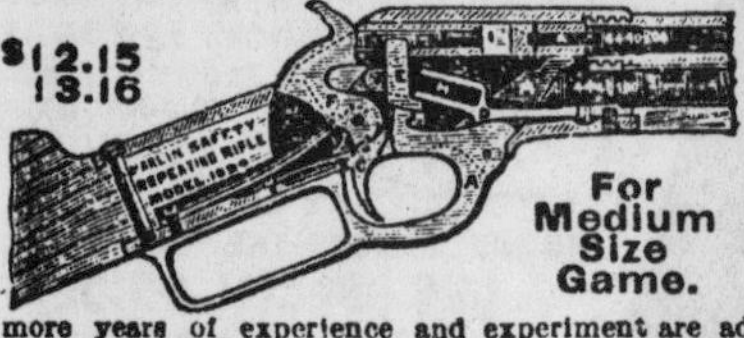

$12.15 13.16

For Medium Size Game.

ALL HAVE CASE HARDENED FRAMES

This illustration shows the action of the Model 1894 Marlin Repeating Rifle. This is the latest and most improved repeating rifle to use the popular 25-20, 32-20, and 38-40 caliber center fire cartridges, and is the natural successor to the well known Model 1889. In the Model 1894 rifle every desirable feature of the 1889 which tended to make that arm the sportsman's favorite wherever used, is retained and the improvements suggested by five more years of experience and experiment are added. This rifle is practically the Model 1893 rifle adapted to the shorter cartridges and good for 100 to 300 yards. Always clean your rifle after shooting. It will last longer. A rifle cleaning rod is a good investment.

Catalogue No.	Caliber	Barrel	Using Cartridge No.	Weight	No. of Shots	Price
6L750	25-20	Octagon, 24-inch	6L2374	6⅞ lbs.	14	$13.16
6L751	25-20	Round, 24-inch	6L2374	7¼ lbs.	14	12.15
6L752	32-20	Octagon, 24-inch	6L2384	6⅞ lbs.	14	13.16
6L753	32-20	Round, 24-inch	6L2384	7¼ lbs.	14	12.15
6L754	38-40	Octagon, 24-inch	6L2396	6⅞ lbs.	14	13.16

Weight, packed for shipment, 14 pounds.
For fitting Lyman Sights, add 25 cents to the cost of the sights for fitting.

MARLIN REPEATING RIFLES, MODEL 1893.

$12.15 TO $15.53

THE BEST RIFLE FOR BIG GAME.

The Model 1893 Rifle is made to take the 32-40, 38-55 and 30-30-caliber cartridges, both black and smokeless. The 30-30 rifle is fitted with smokeless steel barrels and is intended principally for smokeless cartridges, although the 32-40 and 38-55 styles will shoot smokeless cartridges just the same as Winchester or other rifles, the only difference being that the 30-30 rifle is fitted with a smokeless steel barrel, which is somewhat harder than the regular steel barrel, and will shoot more metal patched bullets without injuring the rifling than the regular steel barrel rifle. If you intend to shoot black powder cartridges most of the time and wish to shoot smokeless occasionally, the regular rifle will answer the same purpose as the smokeless steel barrel rifle. From all the information which we can gather the smokeless steel barrel is intended to shoot about 1,000 rounds of metal patched cartridges before the rifling begins to wear, while the regular steel barrel will shoot about 600 or 700 rounds before the rifling begins to wear.

Catalogue Number	Caliber	Style Steel Barrels	Using Cartridge No.	Weight	Good for Yards	No. of Shots	Price
6L758	32-40	Octagon, 26-inch	6L2429	7¾ lbs.	100 to 400	10	$13.16
6L759	32-40	Round, 26-inch	6L2429	7¾ lbs.	100 to 400	10	12.15
6L760	38-55	Octagon, 26-inch	6L2432	7¾ lbs.	100 to 400	10	13.16
6L761	38-55	Round, 26-inch	6L2432	7¾ lbs.	100 to 400	10	12.15
6L766	30-30	Octagon, 26-inch	6L2607	7¾ lbs.	100 to 600	10	15.53

Weight, packed for shipment, 14 pounds.
For fitting Lyman Sights, add 25 cents to the cost of the sights for fitting.
Always clean your rifle after shooting. It will last longer. A rifle cleaning rod is a good investment.

THE NEW WINCHESTER 22-CALIBER RIFLE, MODEL 1902, $3.50.

$3.50

The New Winchester Single Shot, Model 1902 is one of the latest products of the Winchester Repeating Arms Company. The rifle is guaranteed to shoot as well as any 22-caliber rifle made and is adapted to the 22-short or 22-long rim fire cartridges. 18-inch round barrel, 12¾-inch stock, 2¾-inch drop and fitted with plain front and rear sights. **This rifle cannot be furnished any other way.** The rifle can be taken apart in an instant by simply unscrewing the thumbscrew on the fore end, so that it can be carried in a trunk or a grip. Shoots cartridges Nos. 6L2336, 6L2338 or 6L2535. Good for 35 to 100 yards. **Weight, packed for shipment, about 6 lbs.**

No. 6L778 Price, 18-inch barrel; weight, 3 pounds............ **$3.50**

WINCHESTER REPEATERS, MODEL 1906, $8.50.

20 CENTS PER 100 FOR 22-CALIBER SHORT CARTRIDGES. SEE PAGE 631.

Made in 22-Caliber Short only.

The Standard Shooting Gallery Rifle.

The Model 1906 Winchester Take Down Rifle is one of the most popular 22-caliber repeating rifles on the market. The rifle is cocked and loaded by a sliding action of the fore arm and is fitted with 20-inch round barrel, adjustable, Model 1906, rear sight, weighs about 5 pounds, can be easily and quickly taken apart by unscrewing a thumbscrew on the left side of the frame, is made in 22-caliber short rim fire only and is a very popular shooting gallery rifle. The 22-caliber short is good for 35 yards.

THE MODEL 1906 RIFLE is similar to the Model 1890 except it has a plain fore end, round barrel, 20 inches long instead of octagon barrel 24 inches long and shotgun butt instead of rifle butt. Otherwise it is identical with the Model 1890. These rifles cannot be furnished in any other way.

Catalogue Number	Model	Caliber all Rim Fire	Barrel	Weight	Shoots Cartridge Number	Number of Shots	Price
6L781	1906	22-Short	20-in. Round	5 lbs.	6L2336 only	15	$8.50

Weight, packed for shipment, 14 pounds.
For fitting Lyman Sights on any of the above rifles, add 25 cents to the cost of sights for fitting. We box and pack guns free of cost to you. Some houses charge extra for this.

WINCHESTER 22-CAL. AUTOMATIC RIFLE, MODEL 1903, $16.88.

$16.88

Ten-Shot Automatic Hammerless Take Down Rim Fire Rifle. Shoots 22-caliber automatic smokeless cartridges with greaseless bullet (catalogue No. 6L2540). After first cartridge is fired the recoil automatically ejects the empty shell, places a new cartridge in the chamber and cocks the hammer. Ten shots can be fired as fast as the trigger can be pulled. Fitted with trigger lock safety, blued trimmings, plain walnut stock and fore end, 22-inch round barrel with open front and rear sights, 13¼-inch stock, 1¾-inch drop. Length over all, 36 inches. No. 6L2540—22 Cal. Automatic Smokeless Cartridges 54c a 100.

Catalogue No.	Model	Caliber	Barrel	Weight	Shoots Cartridge No.	Number of Shots	Price
6L782	1903	22 Automatic	22-inch, round	5¾ lbs.	6L2540	10	$16.88

WINCHESTER REPEATING RIFLE, MODEL 1890.

Made in 22-Caliber only.

$10.80

Winchester Model 1890 Take Down 22-Caliber Rifle, one of the most popular pump action rifles on the market. This rifle is cocked and loaded by the action of the fore arm; fitted with 24-inch blued octagon barrel; adjustable rear sight, sporting front sight. The rifle is quickly taken apart by unscrewing thumbscrew on the left side of frame. Made in 22-caliber rim fire only, and although made for three different sizes of 22-caliber rim fire cartridges, one rifle will chamber but one size cartridge. A rifle chambered for 22-short cartridges will not take 22-long.

Catalogue No.	Model	Caliber	Barrel, Inches	Weight	Shoots Cartridges Number	No. of Shots	Price
6L784	1890	22-Short	24, Octagon	5¾ pounds	6L2336	15	$10.80
6L786	1890	22-Long	24, Octagon	5¾ pounds	6L2338	12	10.80
6L788	1890	22 Winch. Special	24, Octagon	5¾ pounds	6L2344	10	10.80

Weight, packed for shipment, 14 pounds.
Nos. 6L4698, 6L4701 and 6L4716 Covers fit the above rifle. See page 637.

WINCHESTER MODEL 1892 REPEATING RIFLE.

$12.15 $13.16

The Model 1892 Winchester Repeater superseded the old model 1873. It is an improvement over the original 1873 model. The rifle is operated with finger lever; the empty shell is ejected and new shell carried from magazine to chamber by the operation of the lever. This gun is light, strong and handsome, and the range varies from 200 to 400 yards, according to caliber.

Catalogue Number	Caliber	Barrel	Weight	Shoots Cartridges Number	No. of Shots	Price
6L790	44-40 W. C. F.	Octagon, 24 in.	6¾ lbs.	6L2409	15	$13.16
6L792	38-40 W. C. F.	Octagon, 24 in.	6¾ lbs.	6L2396	15	13.16
6L794	32-20 W. C. F.	Octagon, 24 in.	6¾ lbs.	6L2384	15	13.16
6L796	25-20 W. C. F.	Octagon, 24 in.	6¾ lbs.	6L2374	15	13.16
6L797	25-20 W. C. F.	Round, 24 in.	6½ lbs.	6L2374	15	12.15

WINCHESTER MODEL 1894.

$13.16 $16.54

High Power Winchester Rifle, blued frame, blued octagon barrel, fitted with sporting rear and sporting front sight. This model rifle is too well known to require any introduction. The 25-35 and 30-30 rifles have nickel steel barrels and are fitted with express rear sight and sporting front sight.

Catalogue Number	Caliber	Barrel	Weight	Shoots Cartridges Number	Number of Shots	Price
6L830	32-40 C. F.	Octagon, 26 in.	7½ lbs.	6L2429	10	$13.16
6L832	38-55 C. F.	Octagon, 26 in.	7½ lbs.	6L2432	10	13.16
6L836	30-30 Winch.	Octagon, 26 in.	7½ lbs.	6L2607	10	16.54
6L838	25-35 Winch.	Octagon, 26 in.	7½ lbs.	6L2601	10	16.54

WINCHESTER MODEL 1907 SELF LOADING RIFLE.

.351-Caliber. High Power.

$18.90

This rifle shoots a cartridge .351 caliber with a 180-grain bullet, having a muzzle velocity of 1861 feet per second. It will penetrate a steel plate ¼ inch thick or twenty-six ⅞-inch pine boards. This is a high power rifle of the latest type, powerful enough for the largest game. The working parts of this rifle are few and strong. There are no moving projections on the outside of the rifle, no pins or screws to work loose. The barrel is stationary like that of an ordinary rifle. The recoil of the exploded cartridge ejects the empty shell, cocks the hammer, and feeds a fresh cartridge from the magazine into the chamber. This rifle is provided with a trigger lock, allowing it to be carried with the hammer at full cock. The take down feature of this rifle is simple. By giving the screw at the rear of the receiver a few turns, the rifle is separated into two parts. This rifle is fitted with a 20-inch round nickeled steel barrel, with sporting front and rear sights.

Catalogue Number	Caliber	Barrel	Weight	Shoots Cartridges Number	Number of Shots	Price
6L841	.351 High Power	20-in. Round	7¾ lbs.	6L2587 6L2588	6	$18.90

Nos. 6L4698 or 6L4701 Covers fit this rifle. See page 637.

A HIGH POWER 6-SHOT SMOKELESS BIG GAME REPEATING RIFLE, NOW ONLY

$7.00

A RIFLE FOR BIG GAME.

A HIGH POWER RIFLE AT A LOW PRICE.

We have purchased from the Swiss Government for cash a large quantity of genuine Vetterli repeating high power rifles, such as were used by the Swiss Government and known as the Model 1881, which we have transformed into sporting rifles, as illustrated above.

The Vetterli Repeating Rifles, as they came to us from the Swiss Government, weighed about 12 pounds, had 33-inch barrels and were only 12 inches from the trigger to the center of the butt plate, which is too short a stock for the average man, and we have transformed these rifles by cutting off the barrel to 26 inches, fitting new stocks, making them 13½ inches from trigger to center of butt, revamped the fore end and transformed it into a 6-shot repeating rifle weighing about 8 pounds, which is very much more desirable and balances much better and looks much better than the original Vetterli rifles when they reached us from Switzerland. For $7.00 we furnish this Vetterli Repeating Rifle, and 20 rounds of cartridges go free with each rifle, making an outfit ready to hunt big game at a very low price. Remember, this is not a cheap rifle. It is a rifle which originally cost the Swiss Government at least $16.00 to make, is made from the best high grade material that money can buy, has the Mauser type bolt lever repeating action, one of the strongest bolt actions made, carries five cartridges in the magazine and one in the chamber, making it a 6-shot repeating rifle, and shoots the 41-caliber Swiss smokeless powder cartridges, which may be compared in power to the 30-30 smokeless cartridges, but the bullet is 7-16 inch diameter, weighs 300 grains and strikes a very powerful blow. You will notice the 30-30 bullet is 5-16 inch in diameter and weighs 160 grains. Remember, $7.00 is our price for the genuine Vetterli smokeless high power rifle, and with each rifle we send 20 cartridges free; also remember, this is not the heavy, clumsy Vetterli rifle which we purchased from the Swiss Government, but is the transformed Vetterli rifle, which is much more shapely, much better balanced, longer stock, and in every way much more up to date and more desirable. Weight, packed for shipment, about 14 pounds.

No. 6L850 Our Vetterli Smokeless High Power Repeating Rifle, with 20 cartridges. Price.......... **$7.00**

No. 6L852 Extra Smokeless Cartridges, 41-caliber Swiss, for the above rifle. Price, per 100.......... **1.95**

OUR 45-70 CALIBER SPRINGFIELD GOVERNMENT BREECH LOADING RIFLE, REDUCED TO $2.75.

$2.75 With Leaf Sight and 20 Rounds of Ammunition Free With Each Rifle.

FOR $2.75 we offer you this Genuine Springfield Government Breech Loading Rifle and we give 20 rounds of ammunition free with each rifle. This rifle cost originally from $12.00 to $15.00 to produce. They were made by the United States Government and bear the government stamp. We have just bought a large lot of these guns direct from the U. S. Government Arsenal at Rock Island, Ill., for cash, and while they last we will sell them at $2.75. These are the Genuine Springfield Breech Loading Rifles, taking the 45-70 caliber government cartridge, and any of our customers who have been in the civil war will know that there are no better rifles made at any price, for these are the same rifles that were used in our civil war.

These Genuine Springfield Rifles have 33-inch steel barrels; the empty shell is thrown out when you open the breech block, ready for a new cartridge; they are fitted with sling swivels; the very best quality walnut stock; have the finest quality steel barrels; can be had with or without angular or rod bayonets at the same price in case some of our customers wish to use them for G. A. R. purposes. In case you do not wish the bayonet mention it in your order. These rifles will kill all kinds of game, and our special $2.75 price is within the reach of everybody. You cannot afford to be without a rifle at this price, and we would advise you to send your order early as we anticipate a heavy sale on this new lot of rifles and we may not be able to get any more after these are sold. Order by number. Weight, packed in box ready for shipment, about 18 pounds.

No. 6L886 Our Springfield Breech Loading Rifle, with 20 rounds of government ammunition free with each rifle, gives you an outfit ready to go hunting. Price.......... **$2.75**

Buy a rifle cleaning rod. It saves the rifle to keep it clean.

OUR SPRINGFIELD SPORTING RIFLE. REDUCED PRICE, $3.75

A RIFLE FOR BIG GAME AT A SMALL PRICE.

This, our $3.75 Springfield Breech Loading Sporting Rifle, takes the 45-70 government cartridge and is made from the regular Springfield government musket. We have taken the 45-caliber Springfield breech loading musket, which has a 33-inch barrel and weighs 9¼ pounds and transformed it by cutting the barrel down to 26 inches, which is the regular sporting length, cut off the fore stock in such a manner as to make a neat appearing sporting rifle, fitted a sporting front sight instead of the musket sight, and in this manner we have reduced the weight to about 8 pounds, which is a more desirable weight for hunting purposes, especially for big game. The above illustration will give you a good idea of the appearance of our Springfield breech loading sporting rifle, which we offer for only $3.75. It is without exception the best value ever offered. We bought them direct from the government for cash at a price which permits of our offering this very superior rifle, which could not be duplicated for three times the price we ask, by any factory, and with this rifle we furnish free, twenty rounds of cartridges, making an outfit ready to go hunting for big game at a popular price of only $3.75.

No. 6L888 Our Springfield Breech Loading Sporting Rifle, 26-inch blued steel barrel, weight, about 8 pounds and twenty rounds of government cartridges. Price for rifle and cartridges only ....(Weight, packed for shipment, about 14 pounds) .. **$3.75**

Buy a rifle cleaning rod. It saves the rifle to keep it clean.

AIR RIFLES

THE NEW QUACKENBUSH AIR RIFLE $3.00

This Quackenbush No. 6 Air Rifle, very latest model, while not finished as handsomely as their higher priced model, is of practically the same construction, and is just as strong, will shoot as hard and as accurately, and will in every way give as good satisfaction as the higher priced rifles. This rifle is 39 inches long, weighs 43 ounces, shoots either darts or slugs. The outside barrel is made of steel, nicely blued; the inside barrel is of brass; the stock is made of black walnut, neatly finished. No cast iron or soft metal used in this rifle. This rifle shoots size 17-100 darts and slugs. Each rifle is packed in a neat paper box, with six steel darts, three paper targets and one cleaning rod.

No. 6L905 No. 6 Air Rifle, blued finish. Price.......... **$3.00**

No. 6L912 Caliber 17-100 Darts, for above rifle. Price per dozen.......... **23c**

No. 6L914 Slugs, caliber 17-100, for Quackenbush Air Rifle. Price per 100.. **9c**

THE NEW MODEL KING AIR RIFLE, SINGLE SHOT, 64 CENTS.

Our King Rifles we Guarantee the Highest Grade Made.

All metal, nickel plated, shoots BB shot. Length of barrel, 19 inches; length over all, 31 inches. Weight, 1⅜ pounds. The New Model King Air Rifle shoots common BB shots accurately and with sufficient force to go through ½-inch soft pine. The barrel and all working parts are made from the best material possible; no castings to break in case it falls to the ground. Each gun is sighted with movable sights.

No. 6L932 The New Model King Air Rifle. Price.......... **64c**

If by mail, postage extra, 35 cents.

No. 6L3615 BB Shot for this Air Rifle. Per pound.......... **13c**

THE COLUMBIAN 1,000-SHOT AIR RIFLE, $1.22.

The Columbian 1,000-Shot Air Rifle, as now made, with improved lock parts and magazine, is a rifle which will give universal satisfaction. The loading device is similar to the old model air rifle, that by pushing the sleeve "A" forward you fill the magazine with BB shot, and to operate the rifle place the butt under your right knee, pull lever upward until the trigger catches. This rifle will hold about 1,000 pellets of BB shot, and every time the lever is pulled forward one of the shots is placed automatically in the barrel. Should an imperfect shot get into the barrel, it can easily be removed by cocking the rifle and inserting a wire from the muzzle, which pushes the shot into the chamber, from which it can be easily removed. The entire length of the Columbian 1,000-Shot Air Rifle is 35 inches; the barrel is nickel plated and the frame is japanned; the stock is of good seasoned hardwood. This rifle weighs about 4½ pounds. It looks like a Winchester, works like a Winchester and pleases the boys. Cannot be sent by mail, as the postoffice will not take anything over 4 pounds.

No. 6L946 The Columbian Air Rifle. Price.......... **$1.22**

No. 6L3615 BB Shot for this Air Rifle. Per pound.......... **13c**

COMBINATION No. 1 REAR SIGHTS.

No. 6L1005 Our Rifleman's Combination, Rear Sight No. 1 is the best rear sight made. Anyone can attach it to the tang of the rifle in a few minutes with the assistance of a screwdriver. If they don't "pitch" right, place a piece of writing paper under them. When ordering, state the name of your rifle, also the caliber and model of same, as these sights are made to fit each particular model and caliber of rifle. When using this sight the regular rear sight should be removed and blank piece No. 6L1030 should be used. Price.......... **$2.00**

Extra for fitting sight to rifle, allow... **.25**

If by mail, postage extra, 6 cents.

TO REMOVE SIGHTS drive from left to right, facing the muzzle, and use a brass or copper punch so that it will not deface the sight. To put on a sight, drive from right to left.

This illustration shows how game appears to the hunter when using the Lyman Patent Combination Rear Sight when sighting. It resembles a ring or hoop and when using one of these sights it is not necessary to get a real fine sight, as is the case with open sights, in order to get the game. When the game is seen in the ring or hoop, like the illustration, pull the trigger and you generally get it.

NOTICE

WHEN ORDERING, GIVE THE NAME AND CALIBER OF YOUR RIFLE, ALSO, IF POSSIBLE, GIVE THE MODEL OF SAME SO WE CAN SEND YOU THE CORRECT SIGHTS.

No. 6L1009

No. 6L1010

No. 6L1012

No. 6L1013

No. 6L1015

No. 6L1030

No. 6L1034

No. 6L1036

No. 6L1048

NOTICE—Always mention caliber, brand and model of rifle when ordering.

Catalogue Number	Factory Number	Name of Sight	Kind of Sight	Notice	Price of Sight	Postage, extra
6L1009	20	Ivory Jack Sight	Front	Always mention caliber, brand and model of Rifle when ordering Sights.	69c	2 cents
6L1010	3	Ivory Bead Sight	Front		69c	2 cents
6L1012	4	Ivory Hunting Sight	Front		34c	3 cents
6L1013	10	Ivory Shotgun Sight	Front		30c	2 cents
6L1014	11	Ivory Shotgun Sight	Rear		30c	2 cents
6L1015	5	Ivory Folding Globe	Front		69c	3 cents
6L1030	12	Blank Piece, to replace rear sight	Rear		15c	3 cents
6L1034	S. R. S.	Coin Silver Bead	Front		50c	2 cents
6L1035	S. R. G.	Solid Gold Bead	Front		70c	2 cents*
6L1036	S. R.	Sporting Rear	Rear		48c	2 cents
6L1048	K. B.	German Silver Rocky Mountain	Front		45c	2 cents

NOTICE—The Coin Silver and Solid Gold Bead Sights are much used by Rocky Mountain hunters. They are very effective in the woods, open country as well as for dark days and twilight shooting. The diameter of bead is about 3-32 of an inch.

No. 6L1055 Our Own Patent Globe Front Sight for single barrel shotguns, a wonderful help to shooters. Made for 10, 12 and 16-gauge guns. Price.......... **38c**

If by mail, postage extra, 2 cents.

No. 6L1057 Our Own Patent Globe Front Sight for double barrel shotguns, a sight which is greatly appreciated by shooters. For 10, 12 and 16-gauge double barrel breech loaders. Price.......... **40c**

If by mail, postage extra, 2 cents.

THE L. H. FOSTER REAR SIGHT FOR SINGLE BARREL SHOTGUNS.

No. 6L1060 Our L. H. Foster Rear Sight for Single Barrel Shotguns is a wonderful assistance to shooters. It helps you to "line up" a single barrel shotgun in a straight line with the object, whereas you now cast your eye down the barrel, which is not always effective and causes you to shoot to the right or left unless you are an expert shot. To attach the sight, place it 12 to 14 inches back of the front sight in a straight line, as shown in the illustration, and fasten it in position with the screw.

Price, each, for all 12 and 16-gauge single guns...(If by mail, postage extra, 1 cent).. **20c**

SPORTING GOODS DEPARTMENT.

ON RECEIPT OF $1.00 we will ship any gun or revolver by express C. O. D., subject to examination, the balance to be paid upon receipt of the goods, if found entirely satisfactory; but we recommend that you send cash in full with your order, thereby saving the extra charge on a C. O. D. shipment. Nearly all of our customers send cash in full with their orders, as we agree to promptly refund your money for anything not entirely satisfactory. All we ask is that you keep goods in perfect condition. Ammunition, Tents and Seines will not be shipped C. O. D.

ENGRAVED, SPECIALLY FINISHED HAMMERLESS GUN, $13.40.

FOR $13.40

We offer this SPECIALLY FINISHED, EXTRA WELL MADE, ELABORATELY ENGRAVED AND DECORATED, DOUBLE BARREL, HAMMERLESS, BREECH LOADING, 12-GAUGE SHOTGUN UNDER OUR GUARANTEE FOR QUALITY, WORKMANSHIP, MATERIAL, FINISH, SHOOTING QUALITIES, PATTERN, PENETRATION. YOUR MONEY BACK IF IT ISN'T IN EVERY WAY SUPERIOR TO ANY DOUBLE BARREL HAMMERLESS SHOTGUN YOU CAN BUY ELSEWHERE AT LESS THAN $25.00.

MADE IN OUR OWN FACTORY. This special, high grade, engraved gun is made in our own factory at Hopkinton, Mass. There has been a demand for a hammerless shotgun with extra finish, with special engraving and decoration, and to satisfy this demand we have gotten out this special hand engraved hammerless shotgun. You will note that our price for this gun is but $1.50 more than the price of the same gun in plain finish with twist barrels, $1.50, the difference in cost, represents the exact difference in cost of manufacture. The material is the same through and through, all specially selected, all extra high grade, but this, our special $13.40 hammerless gun is given an especially high finish. The frame, the locks, the action, the guard, the barrels, the stock, all are given an extra high finish and then the gun is elaborately engraved by hand, as shown in illustration.

THE HAND ENGRAVING. From the illustration you can get an idea of the beautiful scroll and floral effect worked out in this hand engraved design, a full engraving covering the sides and top of frame, top lever, the guard and the fore end connection. The hand engraving alone that we show on this gun would not be furnished by any other maker much short of an extra charge of $13.40, our price for the complete gun.

HOW WE CAN MAKE THE PRICE $13.40. As explained on other pages, we own, control and operate our own gun factory at Hopkinton, Mass., and this factory is equipped with every high grade, up to date, labor-saving gun making machine, tool and device, and it is the only gun factory that runs every working day in the year at full capacity, the only gun factory with practically no overhead expense, no expense for traveling salesmen, no expense for collection, none of the big office and officer expense common to other gun factories. This is the one gun factory in which practically every dollar expended, goes into raw material and pay roll, the only factory where the cost of the finished gun can be figured by the cost of the original raw material and the labor.

WE REDUCE THE COST of every piece and part, first, by getting the material in large quantities from first hands; secondly, by doing the work on the highest type of automatic and self acting labor saving machines and devices.

THIS PATENT GLOBE SIGHT FURNISHED FREE WITH THIS GUN.

REMEMBER, with every shotgun you buy from us you get our celebrated Patent Globe Sight, a sight that can be had only from us, a sight that is invaluable to anyone for wing shooting. If you are not an expert wing shot use our Globe Sight, which can be instantly attached and is quickly detached from any shotgun, and you will find that your shooting will be as effective as the most expert. **REMEMBER, these Globe Sights can be had only from us.** We own the patents, we own the tools and materials for making them, they are absolutely controlled and made by us, and can be had only from us, and they are furnished free with every shotgun we sell.

From the illustration you can get some idea of the appearance of this, our specially finished, extra high grade, elaborately engraved, $13.40 hammerless, breech loading shotgun but it is a gun you must see, examine and compare with hammerless shotguns sold by others at $25.00 and upward to appreciate the value we are offering.

HOW WE GET BETTER BARRELS AT LOWER COST THAN ANY OTHER FACTORY.

OUR STEEL BARRELS ARE MADE IN OUR OWN FACTORY, FROM THE HIGHEST GRADE OF BARREL STEEL THAT CAN BE PRODUCED, which steel we buy direct from the rolling mills in long bars in carload lots, the same being bored true to shape, finished, choked and targeted in our own factory. We are one of the few factories that furnishes a steel barrel complete, made direct from the original, solid, full length bar of steel as it comes from the rolling mills.

OUR TWIST AND DAMASCUS BARRELS ARE MADE BY THE LATEST and most approved process and, like our steel barrels, are the highest grade barrels made, yet the cost is reduced to merely the cost of material and labor.

OUR WALNUT STOCKS.

We turn out better finished, stronger and handsomer gun stocks than any other factories can produce at much higher cost. The reason for this is, we buy our walnut lumber in carload lots, we have specially devised machinery for cutting, milling and shaping. It works automatically, turns the stock out true to gauge, gives it a shape, style, finish and hang that you will seldom find on other guns, and yet, by the use of automatic cutting, shaping and turning machinery, we reduce the cost to a fraction of the cost of most other factories.

FRAME, LOCK, ACTION, ETC. By the marvelously clever genius of our Mr. Fyrberg, head of our gun plant, a number of ingenious cutting, milling and shaping machines have been built in our own factory, one machine doing several operations, machines operating automatically, and only requiring the attention of one young man to five or six machines, to take away the finished part and feed in the raw material. By utilizing these wonderful machines which are found only in our factory, we get each part accurate, every part interchangeable, true to gauge to the 1000th part of an inch, and we reduce the cost of these parts to a mere fraction of what similar parts cost other factories. To the actual cost to us, the cost of material and labor, we add our one small percentage of profit; hence it is possible for us to offer you this specially finished, extra high grade, full hand engraved, double barrel, hammerless, breech loading shotgun for only $13.40.

$13.40

OUR GUARANTEE AND COMPARISON TEST, TARGET TEST AND MONEY REFUND OFFER.

SEND US $13.40, OR, IF YOU PREFER, SEND $1.00 (BALANCE PAYABLE AFTER RECEIVED), AND WE WILL SEND THIS HAND ENGRAVED, SPECIALLY FINISHED, HIGH GRADE, DOUBLE BARREL BREECH LOADING, HAMMERLESS SHOTGUN TO YOU. It will go to you with the understanding and agreement that you can give it ten days' trial, during which time you can test it for target, test it for penetration, test it for long range, hard shooting, satisfy yourself that it will shoot as strong and kill as far as any shotgun made, compare it with double barrel hammerless shotguns sold by others at double the price, and if you are not perfectly satisfied with your purchase, if you are not satisfied that this gun is equal to guns sold by others at double the price, you can return the gun to us at our expense and we will immediately return your money, together with any express charges paid by you.

HAMMERLESS VERSUS HAMMER. PLEASE NOTE THIS IS A HAMMERLESS DOUBLE BARREL SHOTGUN, NOT A HAMMER GUN. In comparing our prices with others be sure you compare with hammerless shotguns. Most gun manufacturers ask from $10.00 to $20.00 more for a hammerless shotgun than they do for the corresponding grade in a hammer shotgun, and in our judgment for all around shooting, everything considered, even at this big difference in cost a hammerless shotgun is well worth the difference over a hammer shotgun. The advantage of safety and quick firing are most important. With the hammerless shotgun, equipped with our patent automatic safety device, accidental discharge is practically impossible. All danger from accident by accidental discharge is practically done away with, and for rapid firing there is no comparison between the hammer and the hammerless gun, for with the hammerless gun there is no cocking of hammers, the lock and firing device is on the inside of the gun and it all works automatically. Understand, you do not carry the gun cocked unless you so desire. It is all operated with the rig[illegible] hand thumb by the little ingeniously contrived safety device immediately b[illegible] of the top lever. Don't think of buying any kind of a double barrel shotgun from any other house until you have at least seen one of our own make and especially one of our double barrel hammerless shotguns, and more especially this, our specially finished, hand engraved, double barrel, breech loading, hammerless shotgun, which we make in our own factory at Hopkinton and which we offer complete as illustrated for only $13.40.

BARRELS. We furnish this gun either in genuine twist or laminated steel barrels for $13.40, or in extra high grade two-blade Damascus steel barrels for $16.40. We would especially recommend that in selecting one of our guns that you select the highest grade double barrel breech loading shotgun we make, the specially finished, hand engraved gun with the genuine two-blade Damascus steel barrels at $16.40. You will find it such a gun as you could not buy elsewhere at less than $30.00 to $40.00. Our barrels are all especially well made, they are made from the highest grade barrel steel. They are bored true to gauge, they are taper choke bored by the celebrated taper system, they have an especially finished, shaped, trued and matted rib, they are accurately sighted, made for extra long and extra hard shooting. They are all 12-gauge and will take 12-gauge shells only. They are made with extra long, heavy, full extension rib; have the latest patent shell extractor and extra strong lug.

FRAME. The frames are made from the best decarbonized steel. They are beautifully finished, they are elaborately engraved by hand, as shown in the illustration, fitted with a top snap break, and with patent safety.

ACTION. The action includes the locking, cocking, safety double lever, the sears, triggers and main spring of the mechanism, and we say, without fear of contradiction, that in this we have the simplest, strongest, safest action, less liable to get out of order than any other gun action made.

STOCK. The stocks are made of carefully selected walnut, beautifully finished, fancy checkered pistol grip and fore end, fancy butt plate. At our special price of $13.40 for twist barrel, $16.40 for two-blade Damascus barrel, we furnish the gun complete under our binding guarantee. Comes in 30 or 32-inch barrels, weighs 7½ to 8 pounds. We guarantee the gun to reach you in the same perfect condition it leaves us, and if there is a defect of any kind, or if the gun doesn't prove perfectly satisfactory, return it to us at our expense and we will immediately return your money.

No. 6C4½ Chicago Long Range Wonder. Hand engraved, extra finish, genuine laminated steel or twist barrels, 12-gauge, 30 or 32-inch barrels, weight, 7½ to 8 pounds. Weight, packed for shipment, about 13 pounds. Price........ **$13.40**

No. 6C6½ Chicago Long Range Wonder. Hand engraved, extra high grade two-blade Damascus steel barrels, 12-gauge, 30 or 32-inch barrels; weight, 7½ to 8 pounds. Weight, packed for shipment, about 13 pounds. Price........ **16.40**

A. J. AUBREY SINGLE BARREL HAMMER SHOTGUN $5.95

THE SAFEST SINGLE BARREL HAMMER GUN MADE

ACCIDENTAL DISCHARGE ABSOLUTELY PREVENTED BY OUR FAMOUS FIRING PIN BLOCK SAFETY

This A. J. Aubrey Single Barrel Hammer Gun is distinctly different from any single barrel hammer gun made. The difference lies entirely in its superior and unique construction. It is the only single barrel hammer gun on the market finished in the same high grade manner as the best double guns made, with flat water table frame; the barrel, instead of being round where it joins the frame, is made with a flat, heavy reinforced water table, set firmly on the frame, as shown in the illustration. This gun has the same breaking and bolting mechanism as the highest grade double barrel breech loading shotgun. In building this gun we have followed closely the lines of our famous A. J. Aubrey Hammerless Shotgun, sold at $7.95. The high class workmanship embodied in this famous gun, the wonderful sale it has had, and the fact that there is a large demand for high grade single hammer guns, convinced us that if we placed a high grade gun on the market, a gun entirely different in every respect than any other single barrel hammer gun, a gun built on the same lines, finish and construction as the highest grade double gun, a gun that would possess individuality and be something entirely different, that it would meet with an enormous sale, would answer a demand that, up to the introduction of this A. J. Aubrey Safety Hammer Gun, has never been met. In offering this A. J. Aubrey Single Barrel Hammer Gun at $5.95, we know that we are offering you value such as could not be duplicated in any other single barrel hammer gun made, we are giving you something that you could not get elsewhere at any price, a high grade gun that is absolutely safe at all times, a gun with which accidental discharge is absolutely impossible, and a gun which, in finish, construction and material, is not exceeded by any gun double or single, on the market today regardless of price.

IF YOU WANT A SINGLE BARREL BREECH LOADING SHOTGUN, want the best gun made, for after all, the best is the cheapest, we would advise you, for your own interest, to purchase this A. J. Aubrey Safety Hammer Shotgun at $5.95, or if you want a hammerless single gun, our A. J. Aubrey Hammerless at $7.95. There are cheaper guns on the market than these two guns; we sell single barrel guns as low as $3.25, and they are excellent guns for the money, better guns than you could obtain elsewhere by paying from $4.00 so $5.00; but if, as stated, you want the best gun made, a gun that will outshoot any other single barrel gun, a gun bored on the famous Aubrey Taper System, a gun that is absolutely safe against accidental discharge, safe with any reasonable load of bulk or dense smokeless powder, a gun that is ready and reliable at all times and that will last a lifetime, a gun that not only possesses durability, strength and the highest shooting qualities, but which is finished in the highest possible manner and which is handsomer in finish and appearance than any other single barrel gun made; a gun that possesses the simplest and safest locking mechanism, a gun in which the lock work contains fewer parts than any other single barrel gun, which is easy of access and can be repaired by any novice—in other words, if you want a gun that is entirely different from any other single barrel gun made, if you want the finest single barrel hammer gun on earth then we would advise that you purchase this A. J. Aubrey Single Barrel Safety Hammer Shotgun at $5.95 for the crystal steel barrel, and $6.95 for the twist barrel.

THIS ILLUSTRATION GIVES YOU AN IDEA of the excellent construction of this gun. It is particularly intended to bring out the safety feature, which is not found in any other single barrel gun. Accidental discharge with this gun is impossible. Should the hammer slip it will not strike against the firing pin; but will strike the solid frame above the firing pin, as you will note by referring to the illustration. In case your hands are cold, and in attempting to cock the hammer your thumb slips, there will be no discharge to probably injure your companion or yourself, as would be the case with any other single barrel hammer gun, as the hammer cannot come in contact with the firing pin until the trigger is pulled. No danger of shooting yourself or your friend in pulling the gun out of a boat, climbing over a fence or in case of an accidental fall. No danger of accidentally knocking the hammer, causing a discharge; in fact, "Danger" is absolutely eliminated in the construction of this gun. As you will note by referring to the illustration, the only manner in which this gun can be discharged is by pulling the trigger, which raises the safety block on a level with the firing pin, and as the hammer is released it strikes the safety block against the firing pin and discharges the shell. Unless the trigger is pulled the safety block cannot be raised, consequently the hammer does not strike the firing pin, but strikes the solid frame immediately above it. The feeling of comfort and safety in using this gun by reason of this safety device is alone worth the price we ask for this gun.

WERE IT NOT FOR THE FACT that we are making this gun in our own factory at Meriden, Conn., one of the largest fire arm factories in the world, and enjoy the minimum cost on material and labor, that this gun is only one gun from the large line of fire arms we are making in this factory, that, therefore, our expense in manufacturing this gun is proportionately small, and that we are content with but one small margin of profit over the cost of material and labor, we would not be able to offer you this gun for less than double our price of $5.95.

THE ILLUSTRATIONS shown on this page will give you but a faint idea of the wonderful lines and proportions of this excellent gun. The lines are all continuous, running from muzzle to butt plate, there are no short broken lines anywhere; it is a gun that tapers beautifully from end to end, and adding the beautiful finish of the frame, barrel, stock and fore end to this artistic outline, makes this gun, without question, the most beautiful single barrel hammer gun ever made.

OUR 60 DAYS' FREE TRIAL OFFER

As a guarantee that this is by far the best single barrel gun ever made, that it is far cheaper at $5.95 than any of the ordinary single barrel guns would be even at $2.00 apiece, as a guarantee that it is in every way the equal of the highest grade double barrel breech loading shotgun, we make you this offer:

SEND US YOUR ORDER FOR THIS GUN, enclose $5.95, we will send the gun to you with the understanding and agreement that you can give it sixty days' trial, during which time you can put it to every possible test, try it for long range killing, long distance shooting, for target, pattern and penetration, compare it with any double guns for shooting, compare it with any of the ordinary single barrel guns which you can buy for $3.50 to $8.00, and if you don't think it is worth a dozen of the cheaper grades, in short, if you are not perfectly satisfied with your purchase in every way, you can return the gun to us at our expense, and we will immediately return your money.

OUR 20-YEAR BINDING GUARANTEE

Every one of these hammer single barrel breech loading shotguns is covered by our written, binding twenty-year guarantee, by the terms and conditions of which, if any piece or part gives out within twenty years, by reason of defect in material or workmanship, we will repair or replace it free of cost to the buyer or owner.

If you are contemplating buying your boy a Single Barrel Shotgun, buy him a gun which absolutely insures his safety under all conditions.

DETAILED DESCRIPTION

FRAME—The frame of this gun is made extra heavy and is strongly reinforced. The lines are graceful. The best proportioned frame ever placed on a single barrel gun. It is finished throughout. Made with a flat water table, as shown in the illustration, fitted with a positive automatic bolting mechanism, Scott top lever, same as used on the highest priced double guns. The trigger guard is well proportioned and sightly, no ugly screws or pins to mar its appearance. The frame is beautifully case hardened. Every frame bears the stamp of quality in the name "A. J. Aubrey" which appears thereon.

THE STOCK is made of selected, seasoned walnut, handsomely finished, high piano finish, made with full pistol grip stock with fancy rubber cap and fancy rubber butt plate. The stock is well proportioned. Particular attention is paid to the drop and length. It is beautifully checkered by hand, as shown in the illustration.

THE FORE END is made of walnut, checkered to match the stock, is our own design, very neat and graceful, fitted to a finely finished fore end iron, securely attached to the barrel by our special Aubrey patent snap fore end, as illustrated on page 617.

THE BARRELS of these guns are either crystal steel or twist. The crystal steel barrels are a special grade of steel made especially for us and bought by us in the rough bar and turned, bored and finished in our own factory by the most experienced barrel makers in the United States. The twist barrels are imported direct from Europe, as there are no good twist barrels made in this country and we desire only the best material to enter into the construction of these guns. The barrels are made 12-gauge only, 30 and 32 inches long.

BORING—These guns are all choke bored on the Aubrey Taper System. The shooting quality is guaranteed to be superior to that of any other single barrel hammer gun on the market, regardless of price. There are no better shooting guns made than the A. J. Aubrey. Special attention is paid to the boring. We absolutely guarantee these guns for target and penetration.

We furnish this gun exactly as illustrated and described, under our twenty-year binding guarantee and sixty days' free trial offer, for $5.95 and $6.95, according to grade of barrels, as listed below.

No. 6L426 Gun, complete with special crystal steel, full finish, blued barrel, 12-gauge; length of barrel, 30 or 32 inches (state length wanted); weight, about 6½ pounds. Price........ **$5.95**

No. 6L429 The exact same gun furnished with genuine imported two blade, twist steel barrel, 12-gauge; length of barrel, 30 or 32 inches (state length wanted); weight, 6½ pounds. Price........ **6.95**

Weight, packed for shipment, 14 pounds.

For general illustration of the parts of this special $5.95 gun, see page 617, showing parts of the $7.95 Aubrey Hammerless, for in most respects these parts are interchangeable and identical.

$18.50 OUR HIGHEST QUALITY A. J. AUBREY DOUBLE BARREL HAMMER SHOTGUN

IN OFFERING THIS GUN, we feel that we are offering something entirely out of the ordinary, a gun that is distinctly different from any other double hammer gun in finish, construction, mechanism and quality. This gun is of the same high grade construction as our Aubrey Double Hammer Gun at $12.59, embodies the same mechanism, the same automatic wedge extension rib, with barrel double bolted to frame, the highest grade bar lock, with double tumblers, special nitro firing pins, hardened steel bearings, the most artistic alignment, and the same beauty of outline. In this respect this gun at $18.50 resembles the lowest priced Aubrey gun at $12.59. We decided in building this gun that we would furnish a gun that in the engraving, checkering, ornamentation, fitting and finish would outclass any double hammer gun on the market, even sold at double or treble our price of $18.50. A gun of this kind was originally suggested by the large demand we had for double hammer guns of extra high grade finish, something different than the ordinary hammer gun, which demand we for some time were referring direct to our factory and which they were supplying one gun at a time, made specially to order. As this demand continued to increase and as it developed that it would be impossible to satisfy it by making one gun at a time to special order, we decided to stock these highest grade double hammer guns, and by so doing, in manufacturing these guns in quantities, we are able to offer you from our stock this beautiful gun at the price of $18.50, which is fully $10.00 less than we have heretofore been able to make it, building these guns one at a time, and is less than one-half of what any other manufacturer would charge you for a gun of equal finish which would in any way compare with our gun. It is impossible for us to describe or illustrate this gun in a manner that will give you, at the best, but a faint idea of its beauty. The engraving on the lock work, the frame and the trigger guard is all done by hand by artists and takes several days' time. The checkering on the stock and fore end is very fine, special tools are used, and it requires fully three times as much time to checker one of these guns as is consumed in checkering an ordinary gun. The case hardening on the frame and hammers is not done in the ordinary way. It is done by a special process to bring out the contrasting colors and to properly show up the elaborate hand engraving. The barrels are beautifully finished. The browning of the barrels is most carefully done and very critically inspected, and what would be ordinarily considered a first class job on any ordinary $25.00 or $30.00 gun, would be rejected on this special A. J. Aubrey gun at $18.50. The stock is fitted by hand by most experienced stock makers. The lines of the stock are continuous, there are no short broken lines anywhere, and it tapers beautifully from the frame to the butt plate. The stock is finished entirely by hand, and when completed, has a luster and finish found only in guns that are ordinarily sold for double the price we ask. All this has been done on this gun with practically no addition in price, as compared with what others would charge for similar work.

BEAR IN MIND that although this is a beautiful gun, is sold for more money than the lower priced A. J. Aubrey gun at $12.59, in shooting qualities and mechanism it is not a better gun than the A. J. Aubrey gun which we sell at $12.59. The difference between the price of this gun at $18.50 and our lower priced gun at $12.59 is accounted for, not by the difference in quality, but entirely by the additional finish and the special hand work we employ on this, our special A. J. Aubrey hand finished gun. Whether you buy this gun at $18.50 or our lower priced gun at $12.59, you are guaranteed satisfaction by our binding 20-year guarantee. For shooting qualities, durability of construction, general outline and absolute satisfaction, one Aubrey gun is exactly like another, but if you want the finest double hammer gun made, a gun that you will be proud to show to your friends, a gun that will excite favorable comment at any trap shoot, a gun that combines beauty with safety and durability, a gun that is a work of art, a gun that is distinctly different from any other gun made, then we advise purchasing of one of these special A. J. Aubrey Double Barrel Hammer Shotguns at $18.50 for the crystal steel barrels, $19.50 for the twist barrels, and $22.50 for the very finest two-blade Damascus barrels.

IF YOU HAVE DECIDED to buy a double barrel breech loading shotgun, then by all means select an Aubrey. If you don't select an Aubrey hammerless, select one of these Aubrey hammer guns. Understand, whether you select the lowest priced Aubrey double gun, whether it be a hammer or hammerless gun, the shooting qualities, the strength, the design and parts are exactly alike. The difference in the price of the Aubrey guns is only the difference in the barrels, and in the hand finish on the outside of the gun. You should select an Aubrey; first, because you have the privilege of giving it 60 days' trial, during any of which time you can, if you are not perfectly satisfied with your purchase, return the gun to us at our expense, and we will immediately return your money. You should select an Aubrey gun as compared with any gun made, because you get more than twice as much real value for your money as you could get in any other gun made, regardless of name, make or price; you get a gun made in our own factory at a price to you that barely covers the cost of material and labor with but our one small percentage of profit added; you get a gun covered by a written binding 20-year guarantee; you get a gun that combines the good qualities of every other high grade gun made, with the defects of none.

No. 6L95 Very finest crystal steel barrels; 12-gauge; 30 or 32-inch barrels; weight, 7½ to 8 pounds. Price **$18.50**
No. 6L96 Very finest imported two-blade Liege twist steel barrels; 12-gauge; 30 or 32-inch barrels; weight, 7½ to 8 pounds. Price **$19.50**
No. 6L97 Very finest imported Liege two-blade Damascus steel barrels, full finished; 12-gauge; length of barrels, 30 or 32 inches; weight 7½ to 8 pounds. Price. **22.50**

For illustrations of parts of this gun see preceding pages.

$11.72 GREENER CROSS BOLT ACTION

THIS IS A GENUINE GREENER ACTION, cross bolt, automatic, self acting, self locking imported Liege double barrel hammer breech loading shotgun, which we are offering for only $11.72

THIS GUN IS PATTERNED AFTER THE FAMOUS original Greener Gun made in England, which sold as high as $500.00. The distinctive feature of the original Greener Gun was this cross bolt mechanism, which is exactly duplicated in this Greener Cross Bolt Action Gun of ours at $11.72. In other words, this gun of ours at $11.72 embodies the same identical features as the famous original Greener Cross Bolt Gun manufactured in England and sold at prices ranging from $200.00 to $500.00.

THIS GENUINE LIEGE GUN, with its Greener cross bolt, self locking, self acting mechanism, is a gun that is usually sold in this country at from $25.00 to $30.00. It is a gun that cannot be compared in any way with the ordinary Belgian guns on the market that sell generally at prices ranging from $9.00 to $15.00, for it differs from the ordinary or cheap grade guns, first, in its Greener action, with its cross bolt, self acting, self locking mechanism; it differs, too, in that it is not cylinder bored, it will not scatter the shot, but, on the contrary, both barrels are choke bored, the left barrel, a very close choke, the right barrel, a medium choke. The gun is also reinforced at the breech and also has a genuine steel frame, case hardened. With its automatic rigid locking mechanism to the Greener action you have a gun that is true, strong, a gun in which the recoil or kick is reduced to the minimum, a gun that will make an excellent target, a long range shooting arm, something thoroughly strong and safe, perfectly safe for any kind of powder used in any gun, either white, smokeless or black. You have in this gun the regular Liege full bar lock, with low circular hammers, it is neatly engraved by hand, the barrels are given a specially fine finish, in fact a genuine Damascus finish. While giving the barrels all the appearance, all the beauty of the most expensive genuine Damascus barrels, still, of course, it should be understood the barrels are not genuine Damascus. They are made of fine armory steel, beautifully finished on the inside, accurately choke bored and then given that most elaborate, full, fine Damascus finish on the outside, a Damascus outside finish that so far they have been able to produce only in Liege, and as a result, with these imported, full Damascus finished barrels, with the Greener action and the cross bolt, self locking, self acting mechanism, with the hand engraved locks, frame, guards, etc., with the fine imported walnut stock which is nicely finished, with full pistol grip, checkered fore end and fancy butt plate, you have a gun that has all the appearance of a gun that sells generally at a much higher price, and you have at the same time a thoroughly strong, reliable, safe, strong shooting double barrel breech loading shotgun.

HOW WE CAN MAKE THE PRICE ONLY $11.72

UNDER A CONTRACT with the famous Liege maker we take all the guns that this great maker makes for the American trade. Formerly the maker who furnishes us these guns, made exclusively for the European and South African trade, and our gun buyer, visiting Liege for the purpose of making the best possible arrangement, went to all the different gun makers in this great gun making city, to find where the very best guns were made, and he found that the very best guns made in Liege were made by the maker of this gun, but none were made for the American market. He built exclusively for the European and South African trade, but we succeeded in making an arrangement with him to build for us and only us in America; therefore we are the first and the only concern in this country who are able to get guns from this famous maker, and under our contract we take all he makes for America. We have made a most favorable contract, taking advantage of the low labor cost in Liege, and the actual cost to us for these guns laid down here, plus our one small percentage of profit, is the price we make you, only $11.72, and if you were to go to your dealer at home for a gun you would pay at least double our price for any gun that would in any way compare with the gun we here offer you for only $11.72.

Small Sectional Illustration of Greener Action.

FROM THIS ILLUSTRATION, engraved by our artist direct from a photograph, you can get some idea of the Greener action, with its self acting, self locking mechanism, by which, when the gun is broke or open, it releases the barrels; when closed it automatically, with its rigid steel cross bolt, locks through the extension rib, thereby locking the barrel securely to the frame, making it an ideal gun for smokeless powder, a gun that cannot shoot loose, a gun in which there is very little recoil or kick, a gun that gives you wonderful results at long distances.

THIS GREENER ACTION GUN has an extra strong reinforced breech; the breech is made extra strong and reinforced, adapted especially to white or smokeless powder as well as black powder, to reduce the recoil or kick to the very minimum, and to guard against any possibility of the gun shooting loose.

Small Illustration of Breech Showing the Thickness of the Breech.

WE FURNISH THIS GUN EXACTLY AS ILLUSTRATED WITH ITS GREENER ACTION, self acting, self locking cross bolt mechanism, beautiful Damascus finished barrels, hand engraved trimming throughout, fine imported walnut stock, full finished, full pistol grip with fancy checkered grip and fore end, fancy rubber butt plates, reinforced breech, top snap break, fine Damascus finished, choke bored, close shooting barrels; 12-gauge only; length of barrels, 30 inches; weight, 7½ to 8 pounds.

No. 6L101 Our special price **$11.72**

LONG RANGE SINGLE BARREL GUN

36 AND 40-INCH BARRELS, 12 AND 16-GAUGE

$5.70

WE WERE THE FIRST TO MEET THE DEMAND for a high grade single barrel gun with an extra long barrel for long range shooting. These guns are made with 36 and 40-inch barrels, full choke bored, and are particularly adapted to such sections of the country where a gun of extreme long range is required for shooting geese, turkeys and jack rabbits. Where the game is shy and cannot be readily approached a gun of exceptionally hard shooting qualities is required to obtain results. We have sold this style gun for several years with great success. The guns have invariably given the best of satisfaction. **The gun we are offering this year** is an improved model and is quite unlike any of the guns of this pattern we have sold in previous seasons. We have greatly improved the lines of this gun. The frame is heavily reinforced and the stock and fore end are made on more shapely lines; the gun is choke bored on the improved system, insuring greater shooting qualities than ever before. We predict for this long barrel gun, branded **"Long Tom,"** a sale more than three times as great as that experienced in any previous season. We know that this gun at $5.70 for the 36-inch barrel and $6.20 for the 40-inch barrel is such extraordinary value, will give such great satisfaction, its graceful lines are so pleasing to the eye—in spite of its long barrel it balances nicely—that one of these guns in any community will bring orders for many more.

FOR EXTREME LONG DISTANCE SHOOTING, for a gun which will kill game where you could not reach it with an ordinary gun, we especially recommend our Improved 1908 Model Long Barrel Gun.

OUR GREAT FREE TRIAL OFFER

We shall be pleased to ship one of these guns to you upon receipt of our catalogue price, with the full understanding and agreement that if you do not find this gun all we claim it to be, do not find its shooting qualities are as good or better than we claim they are, if you do not find this gun outshoots any single barrel gun in your neighborhood, or if you, after giving it ten days' trial for penetration and target, are in any way dissatisfied with it, return the gun to us any time within ten days at our expense, and we will, immediately upon the receipt of the gun, refund you your money together with any express charges you may have paid.

GENERAL DESCRIPTION

THIS GUN IS DOUBLY REINFORCED, made with the expectation that it will be used with heavy loads of black and nitro powder and built accordingly. The barrel is made of the highest quality armory steel with an extra heavy reinforced breech, choke bored on the taper system, which insures perfect target and enormous penetration. The barrel lugs are extra heavy and solid. The bolt engages directly with the heavy, solid lug and is carefully fitted. This gun will not shoot loose. The frame is extra heavy drop forging, a far stronger frame than is used on the ordinary single barrel guns. The barrel is fitted with a positive automatic shell ejector, which throws the shell clear out of the gun when the barrel is opened. The frame and trigger guard are beautifully case hardened. This gun is fitted with a patent snap metal tip fore end, differing in this respect from the single barrel guns which are made with a key or screw, it being but a moment's work to remove the fore end and take the gun apart for packing. The stock is made of selected clear grained walnut; pistol grip finely checkered. The fore end is also made of selected walnut. We particularly call your attention to the graceful lines of the fore end, frame and stock. Compare the lines of this gun with those of single barrel guns sold throughout the country, and you will, in a measure, appreciate what an up to date gun this really is. This gun, by reason of its long barrel, is in a class all by itself, as the 36-inch and 40-inch barrels give this gun a great advantage in shooting qualities over the ordinary gun. For the man who wants a gun for long distance shooting, for the man who lives in a locality where game is scarce, where the game has been hunted a great deal and is, therefore, very shy, we recommend these special long barrel guns.

REMEMBER that if you order one of these guns it will be shipped to you with the understanding, that if it does not please you, you may return it at our expense and we will immediately return your money.

WE FURNISH FREE at our price of $5.70 for the 36-inch barrel gun and $6.20 for the 40-inch barrel gun, our Special Globe Sight, which is manufactured and controlled exclusively by us. This sight can be instantly attached or detached from the gun barrel, and does not in any way interfere with the regular sight on the barrel. There are several thousands of these sights now in use, as we have been furnishing shooters with them for a number of seasons; and, the majority of shooters who have once used this sight depend on it entirely, claiming that the use of this sight improves the marksmanship from 33⅓ per cent to 50 per cent. This sight is of particular value on this long barrel gun, as it enables you to center your game directly in the globe of the sight, giving you a direct line that you would not obtain sighting in the ordinary way. This sight, as stated, is furnished free with these single barrel guns.

OUR SPECIAL GLOBE SIGHT

Catalogue Number	Grade	Style of Barrel	Gauge	Length of Barrel	Weight of Guns	Price
6L510A	Ejector	Genuine Armory Steel	12	36 inches, Choke Bored	7 to 7¼ lbs.	$5.70
6L510B	Ejector		16	36 inches, Choke Bored	6¾ to 7 lbs.	5.70
6L511A	Ejector		12	40 inches, Choke Bored	7¼ to 7½ lbs.	6.20
6L511B	Ejector		16	40 inches, Choke Bored	7 to 7¼ lbs.	6.20

Weight, packed for shipment, about 14 pounds.

DEAD SHOT 22-CALIBER RIFLE

SHOOTS 22-CALIBER SHORT, LONG OR LONG RIFLE CARTRIDGES, either black or smokeless powder. An entirely new rifle, manufactured exclusively for us by one of the largest fire arm manufacturers in the United States. This rifle is entirely unlike any other rifle on the market. It is unique in its construction, and contains fewer parts than any other 22-caliber rifle made. We formerly sold a rifle known as the Atlas Rifle at a very low price. It was a good rifle and gave satisfaction. We have discontinued the Atlas Rifle because this Dead Shot Rifle is so much superior in every way that we contracted for a quantity so large that we are able to sell this new model Dead Shot Rifle, which is worth from $1.00 to $2.00 more than the old Atlas, at practically the same price.

THIS RIFLE IN SHOOTING QUALITIES, QUALITY OF MATERIAL, FINISH AND CONSTRUCTION COMPARES WITH RIFLES SOLD BY OTHER HOUSES AT PRICES RANGING FROM $3.00 TO $5.00.

DON'T FORGET that this rifle shoots 22-short, 22-long or 22-long rifle cartridges, either black or smokeless powder.

WE GUARANTEE

every Dead Shot Rifle at $1.52 to be free from mechanical defects; we guarantee the material to be first class; we guarantee the shooting qualities of the rifle to be equal to any $3.00 or $5.00 rifle on the market. After testing this rifle for ten days, if you are in any way dissatisfied with it and do not think that you have obtained the greatest possible value for your money, or if you are displeased with it in any way, return it to us at our expense and we will cheerfully refund you the amount you paid, together with any transportation charges.

GENERAL DESCRIPTION

BARREL—22 inches long, heavy at breech, tapering gradually toward the muzzle, rifled in identically the same manner as the highest priced rifles on the market. The rifling is deeper than in the ordinary 22-caliber rifle. It will not foul so readily. The barrel is made of special high carbon steel, is handsomely blued and fitted with stationary accurately fitted front and rear sights.

THE EXTRACTOR (note illustration) is the most positive and the simplest ever placed on a 22-caliber rifle. It consists of but two parts, the extractor and the spring. The action in extracting a shell is direct. Simply pulling the extractor forward positively ejects the shell. There are no parts to get out of order. There are no links or cams to break. Made with a coiled spring which lasts forever, instead of a flat and poorly tempered spring, such as is used in almost all other 22-caliber rifles.

THE STOCK is made of selected straight grain, seasoned walnut, nicely finished, fitted with a heavy trigger guard of special design, which gives a firm grip; in fact most shooters prefer this straight stock with the special trigger guard to a pistol grip stock.

THE TAKE DOWN FEATURE is extremely simple. To take the rifle apart, move the screw in front of the trigger guard and the rifle can be taken down in two pieces. No small parts to become lost, no breech block to become misplaced.

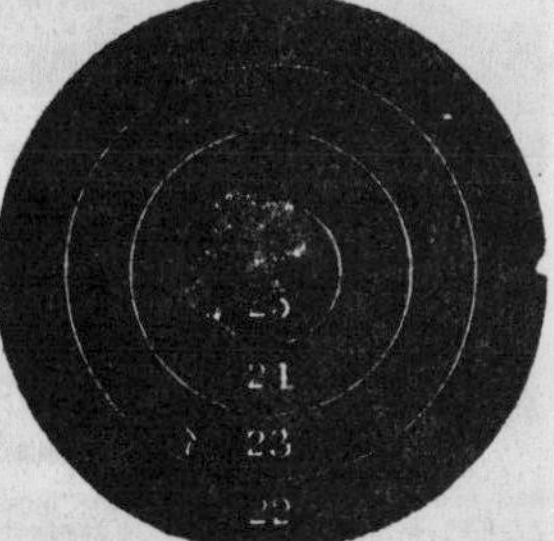

The above illustration is taken from a photograph of a target made by F. A. Schneider, score 125, using a Dead Shot 22-caliber rifle and Meriden 22-short cartridges. This target speaks well for the accuracy of this excellent little rifle.

THIS RIFLE IS ESPECIALLY ADAPTED for small game, such as birds, squirrels and rabbits. It will shoot as accurately and give as good satisfaction as any 22-caliber rifle on the market, regardless of name, make or price. Each rifle is packed in a neat paper box, complete with cleaning rod. Weight, rifle, 3 pounds; weight, packed for shipment, 4½ pounds

No. 6L661 Dead Shot 22-Caliber Rifle, 22-inch barrel. Price........ **$1.52**

TARGET RIFLES, 22-CALIBER

QUACKENBUSH SAFETY CARTRIDGE RIFLE.

$3.90 WITH 22-INCH BARREL.

20 CENTS PER 100 FOR 22-CALIBER SHORT CARTRIDGES. See page 631.

Our new model safety has fine steel barrel, automatic cartridge extractor. Stock is black walnut, handsomely finished, and so fastened to the barrel that the two may be easily and quickly separated, making the rifle handy to carry in a trunk, valise or package. The barrel is rifled and durably blued, except the breech block, which is case hardened in color. Whole length, 33 inches, has 22-inch barrel, 22-caliber. Shoots cartridges Nos. 6L2336, 6L2338, 6L2340, or 6L2535; good for 35 to 100 yards. Plain open sights, as shown in illustration. Weight, about 4½ pounds. Guaranteed good shooter. We have discontinued selling this rifle with an 18-inch barrel, as the 22-inch costs only a few cents more and is the best all around rifle.

Catalogue No.	Caliber	Barrel, inches	Shoots Cartridge	Good for	Price
6L676	22 Rim Fire	22	No. 6L2336 No. 6L2338 No. 6L2340 No. 6L2535	35 to 100 yards	$3.90

Weight, packed for shipment, about 8 pounds.
Notice our prices on Rifle Rods. It saves the rifle to keep it clean.
No. 6L4716 Cover fits this rifle. See page 637.

OUR NEW NO. 4 REMINGTON TAKE DOWN RIFLE, $4.90.

20 CENTS PER 100 FOR 22-CALIBER SHORT CARTRIDGES. SEE PAGE 631.

These are the Genuine Remington Take Down Rifles. Don't buy imitations offered by many houses. They are worthless. All Remingtons have walnut stock, case hardened frame and mountings, open front and rear sights. As finely rifled as any rifle in the market, and made of the very best rifle material. Perfectly accurate and every one warranted as represented. Weight, about 4½ and 5½ pounds. 22 and 32-caliber. RIM FIRE.

Cat. No.	Caliber	Barrel	Shoots Cartridge	Good for	Price
6L678	22 Short or Long Rim Fire	22½ in.	No. 6L2336 No. 6L2340	35 to 100 yards	$4.90
6L680	32 Short or Long..........	24 in.	No. 6L2352 No. 6L2353	100 to 125 yards	4.90

Weight, packed for shipment, about 8 pounds.
Notice our prices on Rifle Rods. It saves the rifle to keep it clean.
No. 6L4716 Cover fits this rifle. See page 637.

OUR NEW No. 6 REMINGTON TAKE DOWN RIFLE, $2.95

The New Remington No. 6 Take Down Rifle is placed upon the market with the view of giving the best possible value at a low price. This new No. 6 Remington Rifle is made from the best material that money can buy, and the shooting quality is of a high order, and each rifle is bored and rifled with the same accuracy and precision that follows the entire line of Remington rifles, which have become famous for their shooting qualities. It is made in 22-caliber only, shoots the 22-caliber cartridges Nos. 6L2336 or 6L2338, and is good for 35 yds.

No. 6L681 Remington Rifle No. 6, 22-caliber, 20-inch round barrel; weight, 3¼ pounds; walnut stock and fore end; case hardened frame; take down model. Weight, packed for shipment, about 8 pounds. Price.......... **$2.95**

Nos. 6L4698 and 6L4716 Covers fit these rifles. See page 637.

RUSTED AND DAMAGED GUNS.

Do not return to us a gun, revolver or rifle which is rusted, pitted or has the finish worn off, for we have no way of selling these guns. If you have a gun, revolver or rifle which needs repairing, first write us fully describing the article and what is broken, as we may be able to send you the part necessary, thus saving the express charges on the gun both ways.

HOPKINS & ALLEN TAKE DOWN RIFLE, $2.35.

For $2.35 we offer you the latest model Hopkins & Allen Take Down Rifle, factory No. 722. Description—This Hopkins & Allen Take Down Rifle has a finely rifled steel barrel. The frame, breech and trigger guard, as well as all working parts, are case hardened, making them durable. The stock and fore end are of selected straight grain walnut. The rifle is fitted with fancy butt plate and plain open sights. In order to take the barrel from the frame, remove the screw in front of the trigger guard.

No. 6L695 Hopkins & Allen Rifle, 22-caliber, suitable for cartridges Nos. 6L2336 and 6L2338, 19-inch barrel, weight, about 3¼ pounds. Weight, packed for shipment, about 8 pounds. The factory price, $3.50 our price.......... **$2.35**

Notice our prices on Rifle Rods. It saves the rifle to keep it clean.

THE OLD RELIABLE HOPKINS & ALLEN JUNIOR RIFLE, $4.50.

The Hopkins & Allen Junior Rifle is one of the most popular 4½ to 5-pound rifles that has ever been placed on the American market.

GENERAL DESCRIPTION. The Hopkins & Allen Junior Rifle is made with the celebrated vertical sliding breech block, similar to that used on the Sharps rifles in past years, which is conceded to be one of the strongest breech block systems ever invented and which made the Sharps rifles so popular in the large calibers years ago. The Hopkins & Allen Junior Rifle is made in the take down model, so that by unscrewing the bolt in front of the guard lever the barrel may be detached so it may be carried in a Victoria style gun cover. The hammer of this rifle is rebounding, a feature very seldom found on rifles and one which commends itself to the user. The barrel is made from the very best quality crucible steel, bored true to gauge, well rifled with the proper amount of twist and the proper depth of rifle grooves to give the very best possible execution and the most accuracy, and the empty shell is ejected by throwing the lever forward.

The stock and fore end are made from well seasoned straight grained lumber, finished and fitted accurately and perfectly, and the stock is also fitted with rubber butt plate.

SIGHTS. The Hopkins & Allen Junior Rifle is fitted with sporting rear and sporting front sights, a special feature which has been added to the old original rifle, and a feature which makes it far better than any rifle made at this price.

Cat. No.	Grade No.	Caliber	Barrel	Shoots Cartridge	Good for	Price
6L697	922	22 Rim Fire	22 inches	No. 6L2336 No. 6L2340	35 to 100 yds.	$4.50
6L698	932	32 Rim Fire	22 inches	No. 6L2352	100 to 200 yds.	

Weight, packed for shipment, about 8 pounds.
Buy a Rifle Cleaner. It saves your rifle to keep it clean inside.
Nos. 6L4698 and 6L4716 Covers fit this rifle. See page 637.

HOPKINS & ALLEN LATEST REPEATING RIFLE, 22-CALIBER.

$7.75

For $7.75 we will furnish you the Hopkins & Allen Junior Repeating Rifle, the latest creation of the Hopkins & Allen Arms Co. of Norwich, Conn.

General Description—The Barrel. The quality of the barrel is precisely the same as the quality which goes into the Junior Single Shot Rifle, is made from the very best decarbonized barrel steel, true and accurately bored, chambered and rifled, fitted with sporting rear and sporting front sight and is handsomely blued and military finish.

The Stock is made from well seasoned, selected, straight grained walnut, handsomely polished and finished, fitted with metal butt plate. The fore end is made from the same quality of lumber and finished in the same manner.

The Action. The action is what is known as the military style bolt action and works very much like the action of the Mauser rifles which were used so successfully in the Spanish-American war. To operate the action, turn the bolt lever up, as shown in the illustration, draw the bolt back toward the butt plate, then push it forward toward the muzzle and turn to the right to lock it, and the rifle is ready to shoot.

The Take Down Feature. The take down feature of this $7.75 repeating rifle is the simplest take down feature yet produced. A small knurled screw at the left hand side of the receiver is all there is to the take down action. By simply turning the screw to the left a few times, you release the barrel from the receiver and it is ready to take down.

Safety. This $7.75 Hopkins & Allen Junior Repeating Rifle has a patent safety device, whereby the trigger cannot be pulled until the breech bolt is home, seated and locked.

The Magazine. The magazine will hold sixteen 22-caliber short cartridges and twelve 22-caliber long rifle cartridges. To load the rifle, pull out the magazine tube about 13 inches, to uncover the cartridge receiver, insert the cartridges, bullet pointing toward the muzzle, then replace the tube in the same way you found it.

Catalogue Number	Caliber all Rim Fire	Round Barrel	Weight	Shoots Cartridge No.	Number of Shots	Price
6L700	22 Short 22 Long 22 Long Rifle	22 inches	5¾ lbs.	6L2336 6L2338 6L2340	12 to 16	$7.75

Weight, packed for shipment, about 15 pounds.
Buy a rifle cleaning rod. It saves the rifle to keep it clean.

STEVENS' FAVORITE RIFLE WITH DETACHABLE BARREL.

All our Stevens' Favorite Rifles are carefully selected for finish, accuracy and workmanship, and we do not send out any rifle which has not passed a rigid inspection at the factory. The manufacturer fixes the price at which we shall sell these rifles, and will positively not allow our house to sell them cheaper. The prices are guaranteed to be as low as offered by any reliable house in the United States, and should you be offered these rifles lower by any dealer, you will confer a great favor by advising us, to give us an opportunity of adjusting the prices.

20 CENTS PER 100 FOR 22-CALIBER SHORT CARTRIDGES. SEE PAGE 631.

$5.40

THE FAVORITE

is guaranteed as well finished and rifled a barrel as found in the most costly rifles. Entirely new model. The barrel is held to stock by a set screw, and is easily separated or put together. Rifling and quality of barrel same as the higher cost rifle. All have case hardened frames, walnut stock, finely finished, warranted accurate; all shoot rim fire cartridges and are fitted with sporting rear sight. The Favorite has 22-inch barrel and weighs about 4½ pounds.

Catalogue No.	Caliber	Barrel	Shoots Cartridge	Good for	Price
6L708	22 Rim Fire	22 inches	No. 6L2336 No. 6L2338 No. 6L2340	35 to 100 yards	$5.40
6L709	25 Rim Fire	22 inches	No. 6L2346	75 to 150 yards	
6L710	32 Rim Fire	22 inches	No. 6L2352	100 to 125 yards	

Weight, packed for shipment, about 8 pounds.
For fitting Lyman sights, add 25 cents to cost of sights.
ANY DEVIATION FROM THIS CATALOGUE MAY CAUSE A DELAY IN YOUR ORDER.
Buy a Rifle Cleaner. It saves your rifle to keep it clean inside.

STEVENS' LATEST MODEL IDEAL RIFLE.

The Ideal Rifle is manufactured by the Stevens Arm & Tool Co., Chicopee Falls, Mass. The barrel is made so that it can be instantly detached from the frame and put into a Victoria gun cover. The rifling in the barrel is equal to any rifle made, regardless of price, and the Ideal Rifle, as made for us, will be found extremely accurate. Finish—The barrel is blued and fitted with sporting rear and Rocky Mountain front sight; the frame is handsomely case hardened, and the lock works are hardened to insure them being good wearing parts; stock and fore end are made from selected straight grain well seasoned walnut, and in fact, the Ideal Rifle is all that its name implies, an Ideal Rifle. The manufacturer fixes the price at which we shall sell these rifles and will not allow us to sell them cheaper. NOTE OUR PRICES ON POINTER SMOKELESS SHELLS. NO HOUSE CAN COMPETE WITH US.

20 CENTS PER 100 FOR 22-CALIBER SHORT CARTRIDGES. SEE PAGE 631.

$8.25

STEVENS' IDEAL No. 44.

This rifle meets the demand for a 7 to 7¼ pounds reliable and accurate rifle at a moderate price. It is recommended by us and fully guaranteed by the maker. All have half-octagon barrel, oiled walnut stock and fore end, rifle butt, sporting rear and Rocky Mountain front sights.

Catalog No.	Grade No.	Caliber	Length Barrel	Shoots Cartridge	Good for	Weight about	Price
6L718	44	22 Rim Fire	24 inch.	6L2336 6L2338 6L2340	35 to 100 yds.	7¼ lbs.	$8.25
6L720	44	25-20 C.F.S.S.	26 inch.	6L2373	200 to 300 yds.	7 lbs.	

Weight, packed for shipment, about 12 pounds.
If wanted with Lyman Sights, add 25 cents to cost of sights, for fitting.
We quote 38-40 caliber at $7.25 as long as our stock holds out. They are no longer made.
Buy a Rifle Cleaner. It saves your rifle to keep it clean inside.

MARLIN TAKE DOWN MODEL 1897 RIFLE, $14.85

FITTED WITH IVORY BEAD FRONT SIGHT AND SPORTING REAR SIGHT. 22-CALIBER.

22-Caliber

The New Marlin Model '97 Take Down Rifle is the latest 22-caliber arm of its class on the market. This rifle is practically the model '92 with the addition of the "take down" feature and many other valuable improvements. It has finely tapered barrel and a neat rubber butt plate; the receiver is made of special steel, same as is used in the high power smokeless rifles, and is finely case hardened. This rifle is very easily cleaned: simply removing the side plate (by use of the thumbscrew for the purpose), makes ready access to the inside of this rifle. It comes in 22-caliber only Magazine holds 25 cartridges 22-caliber short, 20 cartridges 22-caliber long, and 18 cartridges 22-caliber long rifle. Shoots cartridges No. 6L2336, No. 6L2338 or No. 6L2340.

Catalogue Number	Caliber	Length of Barrel	Shoots Cartridge	Number of Shots	Good for	Weight	Price
6L734	22 rim fire	24-inch Octagon	6L2336 6L2338 6L2340	25 20 18	35 to 100 yards	5¾ lbs.	$16.20
6L735	22 rim fire	24-inch Round			35 to 100 yards	5½ lbs.	14.85

Weight, packed for shipment, 14 pounds.
For fitting Lyman Sights, add 25 cents to the cost of the sights.

OUR UNIVERSAL SHOTGUN AND RIFLE, $16.62

$16.62

Our Globe Sight FREE with this gun.

Realizing that there is a demand for a Universal Shotgun and Rifle combined in one fire arm, we have made a contract with one of the largest gun manufacturers in Europe for a large quantity of this Universal Combination Shotgun and Rifle, which we offer at $16.62.

OUR $16.62 Universal Combination Shotgun and Rifle is an invaluable fire arm in territory where large game, as well as game birds are found, and it is so constructed that if you do not wish to use the rifle barrel you can easily remove it and have both barrels for 12-gauge shotgun shells. In case you go hunting for game birds and expect to find a moose, elk, bear, or other large game during your hunt, you can use one barrel as a rifle and the other barrel as a shotgun, and you are ready for any kind of game which may come your way.

Made to take 12-gauge shotgun shells or 38-55 caliber cartridge. The rifle barrel may be removed in one minute so both barrels will shoot 12-gauge shells.

IF YOU WISH to realize what wonderful value we are offering in this Universal Gun at $16.62, look at other catalogues, ask your local dealer, or write to any gun, sporting goods or hardware house anywhere in the United States and you will find that our $16.62 price is at least 50 per cent below any price that you can get from any other house.

Catalogue No.	Caliber of Rifle Barrel	Style of Barrel	Gauge of Barrels	Length of Barrels	Weight of Gun	Price
6H259	38-55 C. F. Takes cartridge 6H2432	Laminat'd Steel Finish	12	30 in.	9 to 9¼ lbs.	$16.62

Weight, packed for shipment, about 14 pounds.

DETAILED DESCRIPTION.

Our Universal Shotgun and Rifle is a new departure in this line, in that the rifle barrel is auxiliary and may be removed in a minute and both barrels may be used for shotgun shells. It is fitted with Scott action top snap break, laminated steel finished barrels with Diana style breech. Strong bar rebounding locks, elevated matted and engine turned rib, fitted with sporting rear and sporting front sight, Edwards' L-shape extension rib, rebounding circular hammers, straight grained walnut stock and fore end nicely checkered, full pistol grip with shield inlaid, patent snap fore end, nitro firing pins, left barrel choke bored, right barrel cylinder bored, case hardened forged frame and lock plates, suitable for birds and heavy game. The 38-55 cartridge is suitable for heavy game such as deer, moose, elk, bear, etc.

TWO GUNS IN ONE. This is the best two in one gun on the market. In this you have a combination of a high grade, 12-gauge, breech loading shotgun and a strong and thoroughly reliable rifle, using 38-55 caliber cartridges. The special rifle barrel attachment which goes with this two in one shotgun can be instantly removed so that you have a double barrel 12-gauge shotgun, both barrels shooting the regulation 12-gauge shells, but in an instant, in less than a minute, you can insert the rifle attachment, the rifle barrel, which inserts into the left hammer or barrel, and you are then equipped with one shotgun barrel and one extra strong, accurately rifled, perfectly trued, dependable rifle barrel, and the gun being equipped with extra high grade, adjustable, short, medium, long and extra long range adjustment for rifle shooting, an adjustable rear rifle sight and a high grade front rifle sight, you have every advantage in the one arm of a high grade, accurate, perfectly rifled single barrel rifle and a high grade dependable single barrel shotgun. In countries where you occasionally run across big game, and especially at long range, game such as deer, bear, or even wild turkey, geese, etc., where the game is wild and where it is impossible to approach within shotgun range, then this two in one fire arm is most valuable, as you have at once one of the strongest shooting shotguns made in the right hand barrel, while the left barrel can be changed in a fraction of a minute, with our attachment, into one of the strongest shooting, most accurate and best all around 38-55 caliber rifles made. **This gun is exceedingly popular, and our special $16.62 price is about one-half the lowest price at which this high grade two in one combination shotgun and rifle has ever been made,** and, by the way, this combination two in one shotgun and rifle is a big improvement over all previous attempts, inasmuch as when you have no use for one rifle barrel you can, in a fraction of a minute, convert it into a shotgun barrel and you are then equipped with a high grade double barrel shotgun.

$10.60 DIANA STYLE

NOTE THE DIANA STYLE BREECH OF BARRELS.

No. 6H270

LOOK AT THE ILLUSTRATIONS OF THE BARRELS and note the color in the finish of the barrels changes about 4 inches from the breech where the Diana style finish begins. Note the small separate illustration showing the Diana style breech, the extra heavy, thick, strong, sound Diana style breech construction. This Diana style finish and construction is the great feature of this gun. Don't overlook it.

ANOTHER FEATURE. Note the length of barrels. This gun is not only furnished in regular standard length barrels, which is 30 inches, but where so wanted is also furnished in a very special extra long length. Note 38-inch barrels, for most extraordinarily long distance killing. When shooting at very great distances this gun with its Diana style finish for smokeless or black powder and its 38-inch barrels 8 inches longer barrels than regular length guns, gives it a far reaching, long distance killing power that puts it in a class by itself.

We furnish this genuine Liege Diana style breech loading double barrel hammer shotgun, complete with our Globe sight free, in either 30 or 38-inch barrels at the special prices as quoted below.

THIS DIANA STYLE HAMMER DOUBLE BARREL BAR LOCK BREECH LOADING SHOTGUN is also a genuine Liege gun, and our special price is based on the actual cost to us plus our one small percentage of profit. This gun has extra strong barrels, extra heavy Diana style breech, extra strong bar rebounding lock, "L" shaped Edwards' extension rib, rebounding circular hammers, selected imported walnut stock and fore end, stock has full pistol grip, grip and fore end fancy checkered by hand, pistol grip is finished with inlaid shield, the gun is made with patent snap fore end, smokeless powder firing pins, has a full finished flat mottled rib. This gun is made with left barrel choke bored for long, hard range shooting and for close target; the right barrel is cylinder bored so as to give a wider target or to scatter somewhat more than the left barrel. Both barrels are bored true to gauge for smokeless or black powder. Is made with case hardened forged steel frame and lock plates, elaborately finished. The frame, locks and mountings have deep line engraving, has very strong bolt construction. The barrels, while made of genuine Liege barrel steel perfectly bored and made extra strong, built on the special Diana style as described, are at the same time given the most elaborate genuine Damascus finish, presenting a finish equal to guns that sell at several times our special price.

REMEMBER OUR LIBERAL TERMS. We will send you this gun with the understanding and agreement that if it is not perfectly satisfactory after you have given it a ten days' trial, you can return the gun to us at our expense and we will immediately return you your money, and in selecting a double barrel gun don't overlook the special features we offer with our several guns and the advantage of paying just a little more money than is necessary to buy the cheapest gun, and for this slight difference in cost get a gun that you will value so much as long as you use it.

THIS IS THE ONLY DOUBLE BARREL GUN in our entire line that we furnish in extra long or 38-inch barrels. Please note throughout our entire line of guns there are 12 that we furnish in extra long barrels. This, our Diana style gun, we furnish in 38-inch barrels for $12.62, and our highest grade T. Barker, shown on another page, we furnish in 36-inch barrels for $15.39, and remember, these extra long barrels that can be had only from us, are intended for guns where it is necessary to kill at a great distance, where you wish to reach out several rods farther than is possible with the standard length barrel of 30 inches.

No. 6H270 Style of barrels, genuine Liege steel, Damascus finish, 12-gauge, length of barrels, 30 inches; weight, 7½ to 8 pounds. Price.............. **$10.60**

No. 6H271 Style of barrels, genuine Damascus steel, 12-gauge, length of barrels, 38 inches; weight, 8¼ to 8½ pounds. Price.............. **12.62**

GENUINE GREENER CROSS BOLTS AUTOMATIC, SELF ACTING, SELF LOCKING ACTION $11.95 IN THIS GENUINE LIEGE DOUBLE BARREL HAMMER BREECH LOADING SHOTGUN.

Note the Greener Cross Bolt Action.

THE SMALL ILLUSTRATION is intended to give you an idea of the working mechanism of this celebrated Greener Action. Until recently the Greener Action was used only and could be had only on the most expensive hand made English Hammerless Guns which sold at $100.00 upward, but now we can offer the same high grade Greener action on this genuine Liege gun, the complete gun with Greener action all for only $11.95.

THE GREENER ACTION. The small illustration will show you how a cross bolt runs crosswise clear through the frame of the gun, also through the long extension rib of the barrel. When you open the gun to remove the empty shells, the cross bolt automatically closes, running back through the frame and through the extension rib. Note the round hole in extension rib. In this way, when closed ready to shoot, your gun has really a quadruple, wedged bolt, lug and cross bolt lock; so locked it is rendered absolutely safe for any powder, and it can't shoot loose. This Greener automatic self acting, self locking action, by which the barrel is automatically locked through the extension rib, is a valuable feature which you cannot afford to overlook in this gun, which we offer for only $11.95.

No. 6H272

THIS, OUR PATENT GLOBE SIGHT IS FURNISHED FREE WITH EVERY ONE OF THESE GREENER ACTION GUNS.

REMEMBER, THIS GUN this is a genuine Liege gun, and our special $11.95 price barely covers the cost of material and labor, with but our one small percentage of profit added. comes in 12-gauge only and in 30-inch barrels. The barrels are made of special Liege steel, are given a beautiful Damascus finish, and really have all the appearance of the highest priced Damascus barrels; has handsome matted rib, both barrels are choke bored for close, hard shooting, has a deep extension rib for the Greener ejector bolt to pass through.

THE FRAME is made of heavy solid steel, beautifully finished, and is fitted with the Greener cross bolt mechanism as described; has low circular hammer, top snap break; the locks, frame and mountings are nicely finished, have hand engraved decoration, and are neatly case hardened.

THE STOCK is a very special stock, is a genuine improved walnut wood, full pistol grip, the pistol grip and fore end are beautifully hand engraved with scroll effect. Unfortunately, in this respect, the illustration does not do it justice.

AT OUR SPECIAL $11.95 PRICE we will send you this Greener action double barrel hammer breech loading shotgun on our famous ten days' free trial plan, with the understanding and agreement that you can give the gun ten days' trial, during which time you can put it to every test, and if for any reason you are dissatisfied with your purchase, you can return the gun to us at any time within ten days, and we will cheerfully return your money together with any express charges you may have paid.

WE FURNISH THIS GREENER ACTION, cross bolt, genuine Liege double barrel hammer breech loading shotgun with beautiful Damascus finished barrels at $11.95, as listed below.

No. 6H272 Style of barrels, genuine Damascus finish, 12-gauge; length of barrels, 30 inches; weight, 7½ to 8 pounds. Our special price.................. **$11.95**

YOUR MONEY WILL BE IMMEDIATELY RETURNED TO YOU FOR ANY GOODS NOT PERFECTLY SATISFACTORY.

OUR LINE OF FOREIGN DOUBLE BARREL BREECH LOADING SHOTGUNS.

WE ARE THE LARGEST DEALERS IN FOREIGN DOUBLE BARREL SHOTGUNS SELLING DIRECT TO THE CONSUMER.

WE SELL MORE GUNS than any five mail order houses combined, and being large buyers in the market we are able to command the lowest possible prices, to which we add our one narrow margin of profit and are thus able to offer you imported breech loading shotguns at lower prices than you can possibly get from any other house. By comparing our prices with those of other houses you will notice we are from 10 to 35 per cent below any competition, and we sell guns as we do all other merchandise, on the very smallest margin of profit.

HOW OUR IMPORTED GUNS are tested by the Belgian government. All our imported guns are tested by the government of Belgium in the following manner: After the barrels are first made and before they are brazed together, reamed or chambered, they are sent to the government proof house where a plug is screwed into the breech of the barrel and it is loaded with 11 drams of good quality black powder and a bullet weighing 1 ounce. After this test they are brazed together and tested again with 7 drams of good black powder and a bullet weighing 1 ounce. After this second test is made, the frame, or breech, is fitted to the barrels and they are tested for the third time with 6½ drams of powder and 1½ ounces of shot. This test is very severe, and each and every Belgian gun which we sell, from the cheapest to the best, is put through this same test.

BY IMPORTING OUR GUNS direct from the largest manufacturers in Europe we save you the profit which the importer, the wholesaler and the retail dealer would charge you, so you can readily see that you will be making a big saving by sending us your order for any of the following guns.

DOUBLE BARREL HAMMER BREECH LOADER.

$6.75

THIS hammer, double barrel, bar lock, top snap break, breech loading shotgun, which we offer for only $6.75, has plain bluedsteel barrels, plain cylinder bored, has a good, strong, plainly finished frame, plain bar locks, plain American walnut stock, pistol grip, plain walnut fore end.

No. 6H242

We furnish it in 30-inch barrels only. 12-gauge only; weight, 7½ to 8 lbs.

SIX DOLLARS AND SEVENTY-FIVE CENTS shows how low it is possible to go in price and yet leave us our small percentage of profit, and still furnish a reasonably good gun, a gun that gives generally fair satisfaction and a gun surely worth at least $2.00 more than many guns we have seen advertised by others at $8.00 to $10.00, a better gun than many that retail at $10.00 to $15.00. To help you to get an idea where the difference in quality comes in to make the difference in cost between this $6.75 gun and our next higher grade at $8.65 we will tell you it differs in many ways, principally in the following:

THIS $6.75 GUN has a single bolt construction, the $8.65 gun double bolt; this has plain blue cylinder bored steel barrel, while the $8.65 gun has genuine Damascus finished armory steel barrels, each barrel choke bored. There is a difference in the general finish, a difference in the frame, lock and general construction. So while there is but $1.90 difference in the cost, there really is a vastly greater difference in the quality. For example, our $6.75 gun, while generally sold for at least several dollars more than our $6.75 price, it is nearly always represented as a gun suitable for and plenty strong enough for either black or smokeless powder. No doubt it would stand smokeless powder for all time, and yet since you can buy from us a gun of so much stronger construction, made especially for either smokeless or black powder and for so very little more money, we do not feel like recommending this gun for any powder other than black.

IN COMPARING THIS, our $6.75 double barrel, hammer, breech loading shotgun, with shotguns offered by others at anything like our price, please be particular to compare, first, the locks, and note that ours are bar locks and not a back action lock gun which can be built for $1.00 less money, and please note, while this gun is offered for only $6.75, still we give you the latest top snap break, the low circular hammers and the full bar lock action and bar lock frame construction.

THIS $6.75 GUN is by no means the cheapest gun on the market and it will give satisfaction in every way, and we will be glad to receive your order, sending the gun to you with the understanding and agreement that if it isn't perfectly satisfactory, you can return it to us at our expense, and we will immediately return your money: however, in your own interest, we would especially suggest that if you want to buy a cheap gun, a double barrel gun at a low price, please note that for only $1.90 difference, for only $8.65 instead of $6.75, we furnish a much higher grade gun in the next gun following this illustration and description, a gun that we furnish for only $8.65.

No. 6H242 Style of barrels, plain blued steel; 12-gauge; length of barrels, 30 inches only; weight, 7½ to 8 pounds.
Price $6.75

DOUBLE BOLT BURDICK HAMMER BREECH LOADER

CHOKE BORED, SMOKELESS OR BLACK POWDER SHOOTER

In selecting a double barrel gun, before you place your order, don't overlook the celebrated A. J. Aubrey hammerless guns shown on the first pages of this department.

$8.65

Our Patent Globe Sight furnished FREE with this gun. Doubles the value of any shotgun for wing shooting.

CHOKE BORED

No. 6H246

WHILE WE SELL a double barrel, hammer, bar lock, single bolt, breech loading shotgun as low as $6.75, a gun made and bored for black powder, yet a better gun than many sell and recommend for either smokeless or black powder, and it would be possible by giving you this same $6.75 gun in a back action lock instead of a genuine bar lock to make the price as low as $5.75, we offer you in this Burdick hammer, bar lock, double barrel, breech loading shotgun for $8.65 the lowest priced double barrel, breech loading shotgun we have to offer, which we can recommend and guarantee for either smokeless or black powder, a genuine double bolt, bar lock, reinforced, drop forge steel frame construction, a thoroughly reliable breech loader and the equal of guns that retail generally at double the price.

IF YOU WANT TO BUY a safe, strong, reliable, hammer, breech loading shotgun at a low price, we advise you in your own interest not to buy a single bolt construction, not to buy a cast frame construction or a cheaper gun than this Burdick double barrel breech loader at $8.65.

WE FURNISH this gun at $8.65, a price based on the cost to us, purchased under long season contract, plus only our one small percentage of profit. It's the equal of guns that sell generally at retail at about double our price.

AS A GUARANTEE that this gun is better than any gun you can buy from any other house at within several dollars of our price we make you this offer:

RATHER THAN BUY A CHEAPER GUN send us $8.65, let us send you this gun, we will send it to you with the understanding and agreement that if it isn't perfectly satisfactory to you after you have given it a ten days' trial, if it isn't a better gun than you could buy from any other house at $10.00, a better gun than double hammer guns usually sold at $12.00 to $15.00, you are at liberty to return the gun to us at our expense, and we will immediately return your money.

OUR PERCENTAGE OF PROFIT is almost exactly the same throughout the entire line; therefore, in your own interest, and to give you something that will satisfy, to give you the best satisfaction possible for your money, we advise you not to order a cheaper gun, but take advantage of our guarantee, comparison and return offer on this $8.65 Burdick if you are looking for a low priced gun.

THIS GUN COMES IN 12-GAUGE ONLY, 30-inch barrels, barrels are made of specially finished barrel steel, they are choke bored, the outer finish of the barrels is a genuine Damascus finish, the barrels have neat matted rib, extension rib, shell extractor, frames are made from drop steel forgings, well finished, extra strong, it has double bolt construction, made heavy and reinforced, made for either smokeless or black powder, has low circular hammers, full shaped and fitted bar locks, long tang, top snap break, has a good selected black walnut stock, full size pistol grip, fancy checkered grip and fore end, rebounding locks, the locks, frame, lock plates and all are nicely case hardened. This is a good, strong shooting gun, worth two of the cheaper grade Belgian guns on the market. We furnish this gun as follows:

No. 6H246 Style of barrels, special steel, Damascus finish; 12-gauge; barrels, 30 inches long; weight, 7½ to 8 pounds. Price $8.65

THE CELEBRATED THOMAS BARKER DOUBLE BARREL, BREECH LOADING SHOTGUN, $9.80.

THE VALUE LEADER OF THIS PAGE.

WE CONSIDER THIS, the genuine Thomas Barker Liege Double Barrel Breech Loader, the greatest value offered on this page; in other words, the slight difference in cost between this Thomas Barker gun and the two guns illustrated and described above at $6.75 and $8.65 is more than made up in the difference in the quality of the gun. First, this is the Barker model, which distinguishes this gun from the others. It has especially beautiful barrels, giving the highest laminated steel finish, has an extra reinforced breech, the strongest double lock mechanism, a handsome full capped pistol grip, the alignment is such as you will not find on cheaper guns, therefore, in your own interest, if you are considering one of the three guns on this page, we would especially recommend this, the genuine Thomas Barker at $9.80.

IF YOU HAVE ANY DOUBT as to the real value of this gun as compared with the first two, note the slight difference in price and then accept the following special offer: You will observe the difference in price between this gun and the Burdick gun above illustrated is only $1.15, and the difference in price between this and the cheapest gun illustrated at the top is only $3.05, but the real difference in strength, lasting qualities and shooting qualities is much greater than the difference in price, and for this reason we especially call your attention to this offer. If you are about to select one of these three guns, order this, the Thomas Barker, at $9.80, enclose our price, we will send the gun to you with the understanding and agreement that you can give it ten days' trial, during which time you can put it to every test, and if you are not satisfied that it is the greatest value ever offered at $9.80, and it is much to your advantage to buy this, the genuine Thomas Barker at $9.80 rather than one of our cheaper double guns, you can return the gun to us at our expense and we will immediately return your money.

Note especially that this gun comes in 12-gauge, also in 10, 16 and 20-gauge, and it is the only gun shown in this catalogue that is furnished in four different gauges.

THE 16 AND 20-GAUGE are especially recommended for boys, women and girls, and also for men who wish an extremely light, reliable double gun for small game, such as quail, snipe, rabbits, prairie chicken and other small game, while the 10-gauge is recommended for large game, such as ducks, geese, turkey, deer, etc., and the 12-gauge gun is recommended as an all purpose gun for small, medium and large game, for every general purpose for which a double barrel breech loading shotgun is used.

AGAIN, in your own interest, as between the three guns shown in this page quoted at $6.75, $8.65 and $9.80, we especially recommend that you order this, the Thomas Barker at $9.80, as the greatest value offered on this page.

$9.80

Our Patent Globe Sight furnished free with this gun. Doubles the value of any shotgun for wing shooting.

LEFT BARREL CHOKE BORED.

MADE IN 10, 12, 16 AND 20-GAUGES.

The illustration will give you some idea of the appearance of this gun. Over 50,000 now in use.

GENERAL DESCRIPTION. Our Thomas Barker gun is made with top snap break, Scott action, strong bar locks, laminated steel finished barrels, extension rib beautifully matted, rebounding circular hammers, straight grained walnut stock and fore end nicely checkered, full pistol grip stock with shield inlaid, nitro firing pins, patent snap fore end, chased engraving on locks, case hardened frame and lock plates, left barrel full choke bored, right barrel cylinder bored; all barrels bored smooth and true to gauge. A wonder for the money and a gun that will shoot black or smokeless powder. Always state gauge wanted. They come in 10, 12, 16 and 20-gauge.

CHOKE BORED

T. BARKER

No. 6H249A

12-GAUGE LOADED SHELLS, $1.60 per 100.
See page 697.

One of the best guns made for field shooting. Mention gauge and length of barrels wanted. Weight, packed for shipment, about 14 pounds. Always look through the barrels before putting in a new shell, to avoid accident.

Catalogue No.	Grade	Style of Barrels	Gauge	Length of Barrels	Weight of Gun	Price
6H249A	No. 659 MD	Laminated Steel Finish	12	30 in.	7½ to 8 lbs.	$ 9.80
6H249B	No. 659 MD		16	30 in.	6½ to 7 lbs.	9.90
6H249C	No. 659 MD		20	30 in.	6¼ to 6½ lbs.	9.95
6H249D	No. 659 MD		10	32 in.	8¾ to 9¼ lbs.	10.15

OUR REMINGTON AUTOMATIC SELF LOADING MAGAZINE SHOTGUN $30.00

FOR $30.00 we will furnish you this standard Remington Automatic Loading and Automatic Cocking Single Barrel Magazine Shotgun, manufactured by the celebrated Remington Arms Co., of Ilion, N. Y., one of the oldest manufacturers of firearms in the United States; a company whose guarantee goes out with every gun and rifle which it makes; a company which is well known to all hunters, trap shooters and sportsmen as well as all governments of the world. They have not only made firearms for the hunter and trap shooter, but they have made rifles for a great many foreign governments, and have made thousands of rifles and revolvers for the United States Government during the Civil War. This $30.00 Remington Automatic Shotgun is the latest creation in firearms The gun was invented by Mr. Browning, of Ogden, Utah, and is now being made exclusively by the Remington Arms Co., under the Browning patents for the United States trade. This $30.00 Remington Automatic Self Loading, Self Cocking Shotgun is exactly as its description implies. It is a 5-shot self loading shotgun. You place four loaded shells in the magazine and one in the chamber, then press the little button on the right hand side and the breech block closes. After you fire your first shot, the recoil of the shell opens the breech block, throws out the empty shell, places a new shell in the chamber from the magazine and closes the breech block, and all you have to do is to pull the trigger each time you fire a shot. When the last shell leaves the magazine and is fired, the breech block remains open, which tells you that there are no more shells in the magazine.

$30.00

OUR $30.00 Remington Automatic Self Loading and Self Cocking Magazine Single Barrel Shotgun is fitted with well seasoned, straight grained, pistol grip, imported walnut stock, and the fore end is made of the same quality walnut. The frame is finished in a military blue of the very best quality workmanship, is bored and machined out of a solid bar of extra quality of steel and is beautifully matted on the top to guide the eye to the front sight. The barrel is of standard length, which is, in this gun, 28 inches long, beautifully tapered from the breech to the muzzle, giving the most metal at the breech; choke bored on the celebrated Remington system, and the gun weighs about 7¾ pounds. It is fitted with a patent safety device in front of the trigger, so that the trigger can be locked or unlocked instantly, as the shooter may desire. We predict a large sale for these guns, and for rapid shooting at the trap or in the field they have no equal, since you can shoot as fast as you can pull the trigger.

No. 6H161 Our No. 1 Grade Remington Automatic Self Loading Shotgun is made in 12-gauge only; 28-inch barrel; weight, about 7¾ pounds, 5-shot. Factory price, $40.00; our price $30.00

Weight, packed for shipment, about 14 pounds.

HOW GUN BARRELS BURST AND CAUTION TO SHOOTERS.

FOLLOW THESE DO NOT'S and you will never have a burst gun or rifle barrel. Do not accidentally put two charges of smokeless powder in the shell; always look through the barrels before loading and see that there is nothing in them. Don't ram the wad edgewise into the powder, nor crimp the shell more than ⅛ inch.

DON'T USE A MALLET for ramming the powder; use hand pressure. Don't rest the muzzle on the ground, nor leave the gun in the bottom of a boat or buggy, for something is liable to get into the barrel in this way. When using 12-gauge brass shells use 10-gauge wads, so they will not get loose in the shell and bulge the barrel. If you get a bullet stuck in the barrel don't try to shoot it out or you may bulge the barrel. No manufacturer is held responsible for a burst gun or rifle barrel, because barrels are made to withstand a greater bursting strain than you can possibly get from any factory loaded ammunition. When a gun barrel bursts at the breech or chamber it is caused by an overload of nitro powder, and when it bursts forward of the chamber it is caused by some obstruction, such as a dent, snow, water, moss, mud, etc., and will generally show a distinct ring inside the barrel. Nitro powder should only be used by people familiar with it; and dense nitro powder should be weighed by an apothecary's scale and not measured. Chlorate of potash powder should never be used. We will not guarantee any gun with chlorate powders.

GUN AND RIFLE BARRELS can only burst by having some obstruction in the barrel or by overloading with nitro powder. We would like our customers to read this, for it will prevent accidents.

REMINGTON "K" GRADE DOUBLE BARREL HAMMERLESS SHOTGUNS

Globe Sight FREE with this Gun.

The "K" Grade has patent snap fore end.

Priced at $23.25

The "K" Grade Remington Double Barrel Hammerless Shotgun is a plain, well built substantial gun built for service, and like all Remington guns the greatest care is given to every piece and part. It is fitted with blue armory steel barrels, matted nitro extension rib, top snap action; strong forged frame beautifully case hardened, straight grained walnut stock and fore end nicely checkered; a plain finished gun but a good one. State length of barrels wanted. Weight, packed for shipment, about 14 pounds.

Cat. No.	Grade	Style of Barrels	Style of Extractor	Gauge	Length Barrels	Weight, Lbs.	Price
6H166	K	Blued Armory Steel	Regular	12	30 or 32 in	7¼ to 7¾	$23.25

No. 3 GRADE REMINGTON DOUBLE BARREL SHOTGUNS PRICED AT $23.25

GLOBE SIGHT free with this Gun.

DESCRIPTION.

All No. 3 Grade Remington Double Barrel Shotguns have two-blade Damascus barrels, matted rib, double bolt locks, extension rib, rebounding hammers, checkered pistol grip stock and fore end, top snap action, choke bored on the latest improved system for nitro or black powder, frame beautifully case hardened. All parts are interchangeable. All hammer guns have Deeley & Edge patent fore end. State length of barrels wanted. Order by catalogue number in full.

Catalogue Number	Grade	Style of Barrels	Gauge	Length, Barrels	Weight	Price
6H167A 6H167D	No. 3 No. 3	Damascus Damascus	12 10	30 or 32 inches 32 inches	7¼ to 8 lbs. 9 to 9¾ lbs.	$23.25

Weight, packed for shipment, about 14 pounds.

ITHACA NEW MODEL BREECH LOADING SHOTGUNS.

MANUFACTURED BY THE ITHACA GUN CO., ITHACA, N.Y.

The manufacturer fixes the selling price of these guns and will not allow us or any other house to sell them lower.

ILLUSTRATION shows the heavy breech of Ithaca guns. This illustration is intended to show our customers the double thick breech of Ithaca guns. All guns made for us by the Ithaca Gun Co. have this reinforced breech and are made extra strong for any proper load of black or nitro powder. We charge you nothing for boxing guns for shipment, as some houses do.

ITHACA FIELD GRADE HAMMERLESS SHOTGUN

Our Patent Globe Sight free with these guns

Bored for Black or Nitro Powder.

$18.00

No. 6H174A

THE ITHACA FIELD GRADE HAMMERLESS SHOTGUN is the latest creation of the Ithaca Gun Co., Ithaca, N. Y., and is put on the market with a view of giving our customers a lower priced gun, and at the same time a good, honest, substantial gun at a lower price than we have heretofore been able to offer. The lock, working parts and frame are essentially the same as on the high grade guns and the principal difference between the Field grade and the No. 1 grade is the style of barrel. The Field grade is fitted with smokeless steel barrels, while the No. 1 grade is fitted with the twist barrel, and we heartily recommend the Field grade gun as one of the best medium priced hammerless shotguns made. State length of barrels wanted. Weight, packed for shipment, about 14 pounds.

Catalogue Number	Grade	Style of Barrels	Gauge	Length Barrels	Weight	Price
6H174 A 6H174 D	Field Field	Smokeless Steel Smokeless Steel	12 10	30 or 32 inches 32 inches.	7⅛ to 8 lbs. 9 to 9¾ lbs.	$18.00

RUSTED AND DAMAGED GUNS. Do not return to us a gun, revolver or rifle which is rusted, pitted or has the finish worn off, for we have no way of selling these guns. If you have a gun, revolver or rifle which needs repairing, first write us, fully describing the article and what is broken, as we may be able to send you the part necessary, thus saving the express charges on the gun both ways.

OUR REMINGTON AUTOMATIC SHELL EJECTING DOUBLE BARREL SHOTGUN, ONLY $31.50

GLOBE SIGHT FREE with this Gun.

REMEMBER, these are the genuine Remington Shotguns, manufactured by the Remington Arms Company, of Ilion, N. Y., one of the oldest and most reliable manufacturers of arms; a company which has made arms a study for many years; a company which has manufactured arms for the hunter as well as for the United States and other governments, and the name Remington on a firearm is a guarantee of first class workmanship, high grade rifles and shotguns and arms which can be depended upon.

AT $31.50 we furnish this celebrated Remington Double Barrel Hammerless Shotgun, fitted with top snap break, genuine two-blade Damascus barrels; nicely milled engine turned matted rib, with nitro bite on the extension, making it safe for black, smokeless or nitro powder; strong cocking device which cocks the hammers when opening the gun; patent safety slide, making the gun perfectly safe until you are ready to shoot, bored true and smooth to the Remington gauge and taper choke bored for black or nitro powder; steel forged frame beautifully mottled and case hardened; well seasoned, straight grained walnut stock with the pistol grip nicely checkered; walnut patent snap fore end, also checkered and fitted with the Remington latest patent automatic shell ejector.

Send 10c for our booklet, Useful Information to Shooters.

$31.50

GENUINE 2-BLADE DAMASCUS

CHOKE BORED

$31.50

No. 6H172

The above illustration, engraved by our artist direct from a photograph, will give you some idea of this celebrated Remington Automatic Shell Ejecting Hammerless Shotgun.

$31.50 is the lowest price ever named on a standard, hammerless, double barrel, breech loading shotgun, fitted with an automatic shell ejector and genuine two-blade Damascus barrel.

ABOUT THE AUTOMATIC SHELL EJECTOR. The Remington Automatic Shell Ejector is constructed with a "split extractor," so when you open the gun it ejects only the shell which is fired and the unfired shell remains in the gun. If you fire both shells, the gun ejects both upon opening it. In addition to this the ejector is so constructed that should anything happen to the automatic ejector device, the gun will act as a plain extractor, pushing the shells out far enough so that they can be removed by the thumb and first finger. This is an improvement which very few ejector guns have. Don't miss this opportunity to buy a high grade gun at a low price. Mention sight wanted when ordering.

Cat. No.	Grade	Style of Barrels	Style of Extractor	Gauge	Length of Barrels	Weight Lbs.	Price
6H172	KED	2-Blade Damascus	Automatic	12	30 in.	7¼ to 8	$31.50

Shipping weight, about 14 pounds when packed.

OUR GLOBE SIGHT free with every Ithaca gun.

ITHACA HAMMER GUN.

Illustration of No. 6H175A

GENERAL DESCRIPTION. All of our Ithaca guns are fitted with the best grade of selected barrels, nicely case hardened breech, beautiful matted rib, top snap action, selected walnut stock, extension rib, blued mountings, compensating patent fore end, and choke bored for trap and long range shooting. The shooting qualities of the Ithaca guns cannot be surpassed, and for penetration and long range shooting are equal to any guns, regardless of price. All are bored for black or nitro powder and all barrels have heavy breech. Shipping weight, when packed, about 14 pounds. State length of barrels desired.

Catalogue Number	Grade	Style of Barrels	Gauge	Length Barrels	Weight	Price
6H175A	A	Stub Twist	12	30 or 32 inches	7½ to 8 lbs.	$19.00
6H175D	A	Stub Twist	10	32 inches	9 to 9¾ lbs.	
6H177A	AA	Damascus	12	30 or 32 inches	7½ to 8 lbs.	21.00
6H177D	AA	Damascus	10	32 inches	9 to 9¾ lbs.	

All Bored for Nitro or Black Powder.

ITHACA HAMMERLESS SHOTGUNS.

$24.00 AND $29.50

Globe Sight free with this gun.

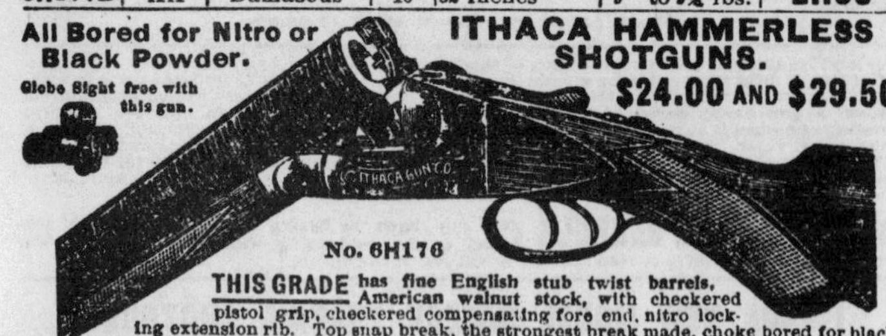

No. 6H176

THIS GRADE has fine English stub twist barrels, American walnut stock, with checkered pistol grip, checkered compensating fore end, nitro locking extension rib. Top snap break, the strongest break made, choke bored for black or nitro powder and long range shooting, fancy tapered and matted rib. A good, strong, honest gun in every way. All barrels are bored and guaranteed for all proper loads of smokeless powder. The No. 1½ grade is the same as the No. 1 grade, but fitted with Damascus barrels. Weight, packed for shipment, about 14 pounds. Mention length of barrels desired.

Catalogue Number	Grade	Style of Barrels	Gauge	Length Barrels	Weight	Price
6H176	No. 1	Stub Twist	12	30 or 32 inches	7½ to 8 lbs.	$24.00
6H178	No. 1½	Damascus	12	30 or 32 inches	7½ to 8 lbs.	29.50

NEW IMPROVED BAKER BREECH LOADING SHOTGUNS.

MADE BY THE BAKER GUN AND FORGING CO., BATAVIA, N. Y.

PRICES—The manufacturer makes the selling price of these guns and will not allow us nor any other house to sell them lower.

Our patent Globe Sight free with this gun.

IMPROVED BAKER HAMMER SHOTGUN.

$20.00

No. 6H183A

ALL BAKER GUNS have nitro cross bite matted rib, beautiful case hardened breech and locks, selected walnut pistol grip stocks, top snap action, compensating patent fore end, and each and every gun is choke bored and thoroughly tested before leaving the works, and no gun is allowed to go out that will not make a good target. All are bored for black or nitro powder. State length of barrels preferred.

Catalogue Number	Grade	Style of Barrels	Gauge	Length of Barrels	Weight of Gun	Price
6H183A	Hammer	Twist	12	30 or 32 ins.	7½ to 8 lbs.	$20.00

IMPROVED BAKER HAMMERLESS SHOTGUNS.

The Batavia Leader, Reduced to $19.50

Our Patent Globe Sight furnished free with this and other shotguns. It positively doubles the shooting value of any shotgun.

No. 6H186

Bored for Nitro Powder.

The Leader is a plain finished, but a good strong shooting gun (See the above illustration.) The frame, guard, lock plates and lever are made from drop forgings. The rib is beautifully matted and has a nitro cross bite in the extension to take up wear of the top lever and patent safety slide to prevent accidental discharge. The stock is of imported walnut, fully checkered in a neat design. The checkering is laid out in handsome pattern and is of a high class workmanship.

Catalogue Number	Grade	Style of Barrels	Gauge	Length of Barrels	Weight of Gun	Finish	Price
6H186	Leader	Twist	12	30 inches	7½ to 8 lbs.	Plain	$19.50

THE IMPROVED BAKER HAMMERLESS SHOTGUNS.

$31.00

This illustration from a photograph by our artist will give you some idea of the Model B Baker Hammerless Double Barrel Shotgun.

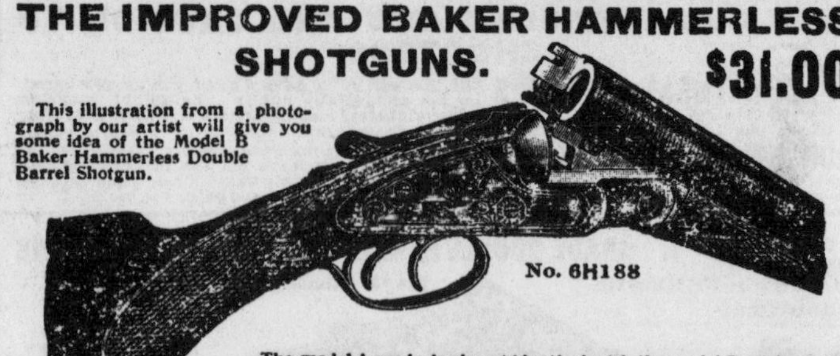

No. 6H188

The model A grade is almost identical with the model B grade except that it is fitted with beautiful four-blade Damascus barrels instead of laminated steel barrels and the design of the engraving varies slightly.

As is well known by all hunters, the Baker gun is an old reliable, good, honest, well made gun. The fitting, the workmanship, the alignment, the general appearance, the balance and the general construction of the Baker gun is equal or superior to any hammerless gun made regardless of name, make or price.

The Model B gun is fitted with celebrated Baker nitro bite extension rib, which is made to take up the wear for years, and any hunter will tell you that Baker guns will stand more hard usage and not shoot loose than any gun made.

The Model B gun is fitted with the celebrated block safety device, so that if the hammer accidentally falls before you are ready to shoot, the hammer falls on the safety block instead of on the firing pin, a feature which has made the Baker model A and B grades very popular.

The Model B grade is fitted with finest laminated steel barrels, beautifully matted and tapered rib, celebrated Baker bar locks, imported English walnut stock and fore end, beautifully checkered, patent safety device which makes the gun always ready to shoot but can be made inoperative to lock the triggers by pushing the safety slide backward, fitted with Baker top lever, fine artistic hand engraving on the locks and frame as shown in the illustration, well fitted, well made, well balanced and well lined up, a gun that comes up to the shoulder as easily and as comfortably as any gun made. Weight, packed for shipment, about 15 pounds. In ordering state length of barrels preferred.

Catalogue Number	Grade	Style of Barrels	Gauge	Length of Barrels	Weight of Gun	Finish	Price
6H188	Model B	Twist	12	30 or 32 ins.	7½ to 8 lbs.	Engr'd	$31.00
6H190	Model A	Damascus	12	30 or 32 ins.	7½ to 8 lbs.	Engr'd	36.50

WE ARE NOT RESPONSIBLE FOR BURST GUN BARRELS

Gun barrels can only burst either by overloading nitro powder or having an obstruction in the barrel. For full information on this subject see article on another page. We nor any other house are **not responsible for burst gun or rifle barrels.**

THE ILLINOIS ARMS CO.'S HAMMERLESS REPEATING TAKE DOWN SHOTGUN, $15.96

$15.96 BUYS THE NEW MODEL ILLINOIS ARMS CO.'S REPEATING TAKE DOWN SHOTGUN.

FOR $15.96 we offer you this latest improved model 1907 Illinois Arms Co.'s repeating take down shotgun as the best value ever offered by any house on a repeating shotgun, shooting six shells without reloading, magazine holding five shells and one in chamber, making six; a gun built by one of the largest manufacturers in the United States; and owing to our placing a large contract, we have succeeded in obtaining a price which enables us to offer a first class up to date repeating shotgun for only $15.96.

A FEW SPECIAL FEATURES OF THIS $15.96 REPEATING TAKE DOWN SHOTGUN.

THE FRAME is made from a solid steel forging, the best decarbonized steel which money can buy, and is fitted with a telescope sliding cover, something not found on any other repeating shotgun made, so when operating the gun the slide does not come back and cut the shooter's thumb like most repeating shotguns where either the slide or the breech block goes back far enough to come in contact with the shooter's thumb.

In our $15.96 gun we have telescoped the extractor slide so that it only protrudes about three-fourths of an inch beyond the frame and is entirely out of the way of the shooter's thumb, as you will notice by the above illustration. If you have ever hunted with a repeating shotgun you may have had the experience which we have eliminated on this, the Illinois Arms Co.'s repeating shotgun, which we sell for only $15.96. THE BARREL—The barrel on the Illinois Arms Co.'s repeating take down shotgun is made from the very best barrel steel obtainable, regardless of cost; nothing but the best barrel steel is used in making the barrel for this gun; all are accurately bored and true to gauge, choke bored by the celebrated taper system, which insures a greater penetration, better target, longer range than bored by any other system; the barrel is so made and fitted with a lock nut where it enters the frame so that if by constant shooting the barrel should become loose in the thread the lock nut will take up the wear, and with this adjunct you will always have a gun where the barrel is solid in the frame. THE BREECH BLOCK—The breech block is made on the order of the old Spencer breech block, which is considered one of the strongest and safest breech blocks ever put onto a gun of any kind, and it is so constructed that the accidental discharge is absolutely impossible until the breech block is up in place against the head of the shell, therefore, we claim that we have one of the safest repeating take down shotguns made. THE STOCK is made from thoroughly selected straight grain walnut, handsomely designed, nicely shaped and checkered full pistol grip, fitted with ornamental butt plate, and the general design and alignment is pronounced correct in every particular. To unload the magazine you do it by pressing the little button on the right hand side of the frame upward with the thumb; you can manipulate the unloading of the magazine without touching the hammer or trigger. COCKING LEVER—In case of misfire and for safety on the Illinois Arms Co.'s repeating take down shotgun, you have a cocking lever in front of the trigger so that you can cock the hammer to try it on the same primer without manipulating or unloading the gun, a feature much appreciated by hunters. ALIGNMENT—The above illustration of our $15.96 gun will give you some idea of the alignment, which is equal to the alignment on any gun made, regardless of the price, and the gun handles and comes up to the shoulder beautifully, is well balanced and well proportioned in every way. THE GAUGE—It is made in 12-gauge only, fitted with 30-inch barrel, which is the most desirable and most popular length barrel, since there is really no advantage in having any other length, as the results of shooting between 30-inch barrel and 32-inch barrel guns are precisely the same, and we think our customers will find a 30-inch barrel gun makes the best proportioned and best looking gun, so we have gotten it out in this way only. THE HAMMERLESS FEATURE—This, the Illinois Arms Co.'s repeating take down shotgun, is, strictly speaking, a hammerless magazine shotgun. When the fore end slide is forward the gun is entirely closed, which prevents dirt, snow or other elements of the weather from getting into it, and this is a point which we think will be greatly appreciated by our customers.

OUR BINDING GUARANTEE. Each one of these guns is sent out with our binding guarantee, under the terms and agreement of which it must be satisfactory to our customers or they may return it at once at our expense and we will refund your money.

THE TAKE DOWN FEATURE.

1st—Cock the hammer by the cocking lever "F" in front of the trigger. 2nd—Pull the small milled slide "A" at the forward end of the magazine away from the barrel with the thumb. 3rd—Push the wood fore end slide "B" forward toward the muzzle, which releases the magazine from the frame. 4th—By giving the gun a jar, let the breech block "D" fall below the lower part of the frame as it looks in the above illustration. 5th—Pull the extractor side slide "C" back toward the rear end of the frame. 6th—Unscrew the frame from the barrel by holding the barrel in the left hand and turning the stock to the right with the other hand.

TO ASSEMBLE THE GUN.

1st—Cock the hammer by the cocking lever "F" in front of the trigger. 2nd—See that the magazine and fore end slide are free from the frame. 3rd—Screw the barrel into the frame by turning the stock to the left or toward you. 4th—Push the extractor slide "C" forward until it closes the frame at the point where the shell is extracted. 5th—Raise the breech block "D" with the second and third fingers of the right hand and hold it up in the frame. 6th—See that the little slide locking pin on the extractor slide "C" is seated in the slot on lower side of the frame where the shell is extracted when the gun is in operation. 7th—Insert the magazine into the frame by pressing on end "A." 8th—Snap the hammer and the gun is ready to load and shoot.

Catalogue Number	Grade	Style of Barrel	Gauge	Length of Barrel	Weight	Price
6H206	No. U.F.	Best Quality Steel	12	30 inches	7½ pounds	$15.96

Weight, packed for shipment, about 14 pounds.

$2.50 NEW ENGLAND REVOLVER

AUTOMATIC SHELL EJECTING, DOUBLE ACTION, NICKEL PLATED.

FOR $2.50 WE OFFER THESE GENUINE NEW ENGLAND AUTOMATIC REVOLVERS, a price lower than you are able to buy an ordinary double action bull dog revolver from any dealer. These automatic double action revolvers are well made and are guaranteed to be safe and give satisfaction. They are not so well finished nor so finely made as the Eastern Arms Co. Revolvers shown on the following pages, but they are wonderful value for the money, and safe and reliable arms.

32 AND 38-CALIBER

WHY WE ARE ABLE TO NAME SO LOW A PRICE

WE HAVE CONTRACTED FOR A QUANTITY OF THESE REVOLVERS so large as to take the entire output of the factory, enabling the manufacturer to get his cost on material and production down to the lowest notch, and as we are content with but a small profit over the cost of material and labor, we are able to name you a price of $2.50 for these automatic revolvers, which price is way below what you would have to pay elsewhere for a revolver of similar grade. These revolvers are furnished nickel plated or blued, the cylinders are nicely fluted, fitted with front and rear sights, and barrel is rifled. The revolver is fitted with neatly scored black rubber handles, well finished throughout, and as compared with prices asked throughout the country for ordinary double action revolvers, it is well worth double our price of $2.50.

THE 32-CALIBER REVOLVER has a 3-inch barrel, and the 38-caliber revolver has a 3¼-inch barrel. The cylinders are chambered for the regular 32 and 38 Smith & Wesson cartridges.

PRICES WITH RUBBER HANDLES.

Catalogue Number	Caliber	Length of Barrel	Finish	No. of Shots	Weight, ounces	Shoots Cartridge	Price
6L1061	32 C.F.	3 inches	Nickel Plated	5-shot	12	6L2377	$2.50
6L1062	38 C.F.	3¼ inches	Nickel Plated	5-shot	15	6L2388	
6L1063	32 C.F.	3 inches	Blued Steel	5-shot	12	6L2377	2.75
6L1064	38 C.F.	3¼ inches	Blued Steel	5-shot	15	6L2388	
6L1065	32 C.F.	5 inches	Nickel Plated	5-shot	15	6L2377	3.00
6L1066	38 C.F.	5 inches	Nickel Plated	5-shot	18	6L2388	
6L1067	32 C.F.	5 inches	Blued Steel	5-shot	15	6L2377	3.25
6L1068	38 C.F.	5 inches	Blued Steel	5-shot	18	6L2388	

PEARL HANDLES can be fitted on these revolvers at an additional charge of $1.00 over the price of the revolver with rubber handles.

NEW ENGLAND ARMS CO. ENGRAVED, AUTOMATIC SHELL EJECTING, DOUBLE ACTION REVOLVERS $3.00

NEVER BEFORE HAS AN ENGRAVED, automatic, double action, shell ejecting, center fire revolver been sold at any such price. We take the entire output of the factory on this revolver and are able to sell it at a price $2.00 to $3.00 below the market, compared with prices other houses get for common double action revolvers.

THESE REVOLVERS ARE OF THE SAME CONSTRUCTION as those above described, except that they are full engraved. The barrel, cylinder and frame are all engraved by hand.

THIS ILLUSTRATION, TAKEN FROM A PHOTOGRAPH, will give you an idea of the style of the engraving. This revolver comes in 32 and 38-caliber, blued steel or nickel plated.

WE SHOULD BE PLEASED TO RECEIVE YOUR ORDER for one of these New England Revolvers with the understanding and agreement that if it is not perfectly satisfactory when received, you may return it to us, and we will immediately return your money. Understand, we do not claim this to be as good a revolver as our Eastern Arms Co. Revolver, described on the following pages, but it is a first class revolver for the money and will give satisfaction.

Catalogue Number	Caliber	Length of Barrel	Finish, All Hand Engraved	No. of Shots	Shoots Cartridge	Weight, ounces	Price
6L1101	32 C.F.	3 inches	Nickel Plated	5	6L2377	12	$3.00
6L1102	38 C.F.	3¼ inches	Nickel Plated	5	6L2388	15	
6L1103	32 C.F.	3 inches	Blued Steel	5	6L2377	12	3.25
6L1104	38 C.F.	3¼ inches	Blued Steel	5	6L2388	15	

PEARL HANDLES can be fitted on these revolvers at an additional charge of $1.00 over the price of the revolver with rubber handles.

$3.15 NEW ENGLAND HAMMERLESS REVOLVER

AUTOMATIC SHELL EJECTING, DOUBLE ACTION, CENTER FIRE, BLUED OR NICKEL PLATED

WE ARE NOW ABLE TO OFFER the New England Revolver in hammerless and sell a hammerless revolver at a price lower than you can buy an ordinary double action automatic. These hammerless revolvers are the same quality, made on the same lines as the New England Automatic Revolvers above described. They are carefully and neatly made, and, at our price of $3.15, are, without doubt, extraordinary value.

IF YOU WANT A HAMMERLESS AUTOMATIC REVOLVER AT A LOW PRICE, a revolver that is well worth the money, and, while not so well finished and so carefully made as our Eastern Arms Co. Revolver, described on the following pages, will give satisfaction, if you want the greatest possible value for your money, as compared with what you would have to pay elsewhere, we recommend that you purchase this New England Hammerless Revolver at our price of $3.15. These revolvers have fine rifled steel barrels, fitted with front and rear sights, automatic barrel catch, the cylinder is neatly fluted and finished, the mechanism consists of very few parts and is not liable to get out of order, neatly finished, either blued or nickel plated, shoots the regular Smith & Wesson center fire cartridges, fitted with nicely scored black rubber handles, and each revolver comes packed separately in a neat paper box.

32 AND 38-CALIBER

THE ILLUSTRATION WILL GIVE YOU A GENERAL IDEA of the neat appearance of this revolver. If you want a first class, high grade revolver, something a little better than the ordinary revolver, then we would advise that you purchase our Eastern Arms Co. Revolver, described on the following pages. The Eastern Arms Co. Revolver compares with any standard hammerless revolver on the market today. We, however, do not wish to detract from the merits of this New England Revolver. It is a good revolver, excellent value for the money, and will give you satisfaction. If you buy one of these revolvers and are not pleased with it, you may return it to us at our expense, and your money and transportation charges will be immediately refunded.

When ordering, be sure to give catalogue number, caliber and finish wanted.

Catalogue Number	Caliber	Length of Barrel	Finish	No. of Shots	Weight, ounces	Shoots Cartridge	Price
6L1130	32 C.F.	3 inches	Nickeled	5	12	6L2377	$3.15
6L1131	38 C.F.	3¼ inches	Nickeled	5	15	6L2388	
6L1132	32 C.F.	3 inches	Blued	5	12	6L2377	3.35
6L1134	38 C.F.	3¼ inches	Blued	5	15	6L2388	
6L1135	32 C.F.	5 inches	Nickeled	5	15	6L2377	3.65
6L1136	38 C.F.	5 inches	Nickeled	5	18	6L2388	
6L1137	32 C.F.	5 inches	Blued	5	15	6L2377	3.90
6L1138	38 C.F.	5 inches	Blued	5	18	6L2388	

Pearl handles, extra $1.00
If by mail, postage extra, 32-caliber, 18 to 22 cents.
If by mail, postage extra, 38-caliber, 22 to 26 cents.

EASTERN ARMS CO.

NEW MODEL AUTOMATIC DOUBLE ACTION SHELL EJECTING REVOLVER

$3.50

32 AND 38-CALIBER, 3, 3¼ AND 5-INCH BARREL, NICKEL PLATED OR BLUED.

THIS ILLUSTRATION, taken from a photograph of this latest model Eastern Arms Co. Revolver, represents the very latest automatic revolver on the market, a revolver possessing all the latest improvements, built on improved lines, and which, at our price of $3.50, is unquestionably the greatest value ever offered in a revolver of this type. We have secured the entire output of the factory on this revolver. No other house is able to furnish these revolvers, and our price of $3.50 represents but one small margin of profit over the actual cost of material and labor.

WE ILLUSTRATE AND DESCRIBE in this catalogue a large line of revolvers of all makes, styles and prices, and if you are in the market for a revolver of any particular style or model, you will have no trouble in making a selection from our large line shown in this catalogue, but if you haven't any decided opinion as to what you want, but want a first class, serviceable revolver, a revolver that can be depended upon at all times, a revolver that operates smoothly, shoots accurately, that is well finished and well made throughout, if you want the greatest value for your money, we would advise that you purchase one of these Eastern Arms Co. Revolvers, either 32 or 38-caliber, as herewith described.

OUR FREE TRIAL OFFER

IF YOU ORDER ONE OF THESE REVOLVERS, it will be sent to you with the understanding and agreement that you can give it a sixty-day trial, during which time you can put it to every reasonable test and compare it with any revolver you can buy elsewhere at even double the price, compare it with any of the so called "Standard" revolvers, test it for sure fire and accuracy—in fact, test it in any way—and if you are dissatisfied with your purchase, if you think we have not given you greater value for your money than you could get elsewhere, you are at liberty, within the sixty days, to return the revolver to us at our expense, and we will immediately return your money, together with any transportation charges you may have paid.

REMEMBER, if you buy one of these revolvers and are in any way dissatisfied with your purchase, if you do not feel that you have received the greatest value for your money, if you are dissatisfied for any reason whatever, you may return the revolver to us any time within sixty days, and your money, together with any transportation charges you may have paid, will be immediately returned to you.

COMPARING THIS REVOLVER WITH OTHER STANDARD MAKES for finish, shooting qualities and mechanical construction, you will readily admit that this Eastern Arms Co. Revolver at $3.50 (as compared with the prices asked for standard revolvers that are in no way superior—in fact, in a great many ways inferior—to these excellent revolvers) is unquestionably the best revolver and the greatest value ever known in a revolver of this type. We particularly ask you to compare this revolver carefully in every conceivable way with the other so called "Standard" makes, as a comparison of this kind will convince you more strongly than anything we can say of the excellence of this revolver and the wonderful value it represents at our ridiculously low price of $3.50.

WE SELL MORE REVOLVERS OF ALL MAKES than any other house in the United States. Our business on revolvers of all kinds is enormous, and by concentrating a large share of this business on one make of revolvers, we were able to contract for these excellent revolvers in quantities so large as to take the entire output of the factory, a quantity so large as to enable the manufacturer to enjoy the lowest cost on material, and to operate his factory the year around at a great saving in the cost of production. In offering you these revolvers at $3.50, we have added but one small margin of profit, giving you an automatic shell ejecting revolver at a price lower than the wholesale dealer can buy any of the standard revolvers of similar construction direct from the manufacturer.

PEARL STOCKS

At an additional charge of $1.00, we will furnish any Eastern Arms Co. Revolver fitted with a pair of beautiful pearl stocks instead of the regular rubber stocks, as illustrated above. These pearl stocks are made specially for these revolvers; they are guaranteed first quality, beautifully tinted, and when fitted to one of these handsome Eastern Arms Co. Revolvers add greatly to its beauty.

PEARL STOCK $1.00 EXTRA

TARGET STOCKS

We can furnish any Automatic Eastern Arms Co. Revolver described on this page with special target stocks, as herewith illustrated, at an additional cost of 40 cents per pair over the cost of the revolver. For example the 32 caliber 3-inch nickel plated revolver, catalogue No. 6L1111, fitted with target stocks, would cost you $3.90. These stocks extend beyond the frame, are made extra large and full, the same as a Colt's revolver stock, making a full grip, particularly desirable for revolvers used for target practice. These grips are 1¾ inches wide at the butt, taking the place of the regular stock without requiring any special finish. As stated, we can furnish any of the Eastern Arms Co. Revolvers described on this page with these target grips at an additional charge of 40 cents over the regular price of the revolver.

Target Stocks 40 Cents Extra.

CARTRIDGES		Price, per box of 50	Price, per 100
No. 6L2377	32 S. & W. center fire	37c	70c
No. 6L2388	38 S. & W. center fire	47c	90c

DETAILED DESCRIPTION

THE FRAMES, as you will note from the illustration, are well proportioned, beautifully shaped, strongly reinforced, finely finished, and accurately fitted to the barrel.

THE BARRELS are bored from solid steel, have a high top rib, and are fitted with a special sight such as is found on no other revolver. The barrles are finely rifled on an improved method, insuring the greatest penetration and accuracy.

THE BARREL AND CYLINDER CATCH is of improved design, absolutely positive and reliable. The barrel catch sets flush with the top of the barrel, is out of the line of sight, works smoothly, and when locked, holds the barrel rigidly in place.

THE SHELL EXTRACTOR is strong and positive, ejecting shells clear of the cylinder, as shown in the small illustration, and is fitted with well finished, accurately milled ratchet. The extractor is exceedingly simple in its construction and is not liable to get out of order. No danger of sticking or failing to extract the shell.

THE MECHANISM of the Eastern Arms Co. Revolver is exceedingly simple. It contains but a few parts, and is, therefore, less liable to get out of order. The parts are all accurately made, true to the gauge, are strictly interchangeable and work with an evenness and smoothness not found in revolvers sold for almost double the price.

FINISH—These revolvers are given the highest possible finish. The nickel plated revolvers are all heavily plated on copper, highly buffed and polished. The blued revolvers are handsomely finished with dull blue by a special process, and are guaranteed not to rust near so easily as revolvers blued in the ordinary manner.

The Shooting Qualities of these revolvers are most excellent. We guarantee these revolvers to shoot as accurately and to have as great penetration as any revolver made, regardless of price.

Catalogue Number	Caliber	Length of Barrel	No. of Shots	Weight Ounces	Shoots Cartridge	Price, Rubber Handles	
						Nickel Plated	Blued Finish
6L1111	32 C. F.	3 inches	5-shot	12	6L2377	$3.50	$3.75
6L1112	38 C. F.	3¼ inches	5-shot	15	6L2388	3.50	3.75
6L1115	32 C. F.	5 inches	5-shot	15	6L2377	3.95	4.20
6L1116	38 C. F.	5 inches	5-shot	18	6L2388	3.95	4.20

If by mail, postage extra, 32-caliber, 18 to 22 cents; 38-caliber, 22 to 26 cents. If by insured mail, add 5 cents to postage rate and say, "Ship by insured mail."

These revolvers are regularly furnished with finely scored, polished black rubber handles, but can be furnished with special target stocks at an additional charge of 40 cents per pair, or with pearl stocks at an additional cost of $1.00.

REVOLVERS

PRICES REDUCED

A VERY COMPLETE LINE of revolvers of all makes, calibers and descriptions will be found on this and the following pages. In selecting these revolvers we have been careful to select only such makes, styles and sizes as we know are practical and will give satisfaction.

OUR GUARANTEE. Every revolver we sell is carefully inspected and examined by experienced gunsmiths, and we guarantee every revolver sold by us, regardless of price, against defective material or workmanship. It is sold with the understanding that if not entirely satisfactory in every way, it may be returned to us at our expense, and we will return your money and any transportation charges you may have paid.

INSURED MAIL. We advise where a revolver only is ordered, that you have the revolver sent by insured mail, which guarantees delivery, and which costs but 5 cents extra over the regular postage for each revolver under $5.00, and 10 cents extra over the regular postage for a revolver costing over $5.00. For high priced revolvers, such as the Smith & Wesson and Colt, we recommend express or registered mail. Registered mail costs 10 cents over the regular rate of postage. We quote the regular postage under each description. Add cost of insured or registered mail to it.

REMEMBER that the postoffice does not guarantee delivery on revolvers or any other goods lost in the regular mail, but by sending goods either by insured or registered mail, delivery is guaranteed.

DOUBLE ACTION SELF COCKING REVOLVERS.

No. 6T1182

The revolvers shown below are the best self cocking revolvers made. They are the product of such famous factories as the Harrington & Richardson Co. and Hopkins & Allen Arms Co., and they are really too well known to require an introduction. These revolvers are not excelled in workmanship, material or construction by any double action revolvers made today. They have octagon rifled barrels, are full nickel plated, and are fitted with neat rubber stocks, and the cylinders are nicely fluted. By pulling the trigger, the revolver is cocked automatically.

22-CALIBER DOUBLE ACTION REVOLVERS, RIM FIRE.

Cat. No.	Length of Barrel	No. of Shots	Shoots Cartridge No.	Weight, Ounces	PRICE Rubber Stocks	PRICE Pearl Stocks	If mail shipment, postage extra,
6T1181	2½ in.	7	6T2336 6T2338 6T2535	12	$2.34	$3.25	15c
6T1182	6 in.	7	6T2336 6T2338 6T2535	13	2.95	3.85	16c

See remarks about insured and registered mail at top of page.

32 AND 38-CALIBER DOUBLE ACTION REVOLVERS.

$2.34

See above for detailed description of these revolvers. They are the product of the famous Harrington & Richardson and Hopkins & Allen factories. Finely nickel plated and polished.

If mail shipment, postage extra, on Nos. 6T1195 and 6T1206, 18 cents each; on Nos. 6T1200, 6T1201 and 6T1212, 22c each.

Cat. No.	Caliber	Length of Barrel	No. of Shots	Shoots Cartridge No.	Weight, Ounces	PRICE Rubber Stocks	PRICE Pearl Stocks
6T1195	32 c. f.	2½ in.	6	6T2377	15	$2.34	$3.25
6T1200	32 c. f.	4½ in.	6	6T2377	19	2.59	3.55
6T1201	32 c. f.	6 in.	6	6T2377	19	2.84	3.85
6T1206	38 c. f.	2½ in.	5	6T2388	15	2.34	3.30
6T1212	38 c. f.	6 in.	5	6T2388	19	2.85	3.85

DOUBLE ACTION REVOLVERS WITH SAFETY HAMMER.

$2.34

These revolvers, the same as those above described, are the product of the celebrated Harrington & Richardson and Hopkins & Allen factories, but are fitted with the safety hammer, which is preferred by some people, as there are no projections to catch in pocket, enabling this revolver to be pulled more quickly than the regular style. These revolvers, the same as those above described, are full nickel plated and have fancy rubber handle and rebounding hammer.

Cat. No.	Caliber	Length of Barrel	No. of Shots	Shoots Cartridge No.	Weight, Ounces	PRICE Rubber Stocks	PRICE Pearl Stocks
6T1217	32 c. f.	2½ in.	5	6T2377	15	$2.34	$3.25
6T1218	38 c. f.	2½ in.	5	6T2388	15	2.34	3.25

If mail shipment, postage extra, each, 18 cents.
See remarks about insured and registered mail at top of page.

THE NEW LIBERTY 22-CALIBER REVOLVER.

$1.29

In order to fill a large demand for a low priced revolver, we have gotten out the New Liberty Single Action 7-shot 22-caliber Revolver, with 2½-inch smooth bored barrel, full nickel plated and fancy rubber handles. Shoots 22-caliber short rim fire cartridges (No. 6T2336). Weighs about 7 ounces. Total length, 5¾ inches. Sells regularly for $1.50 to $2.00.

No. 6T1489 Price..........$1.29

If mail shipment, postage extra, 10 cents. Insured mail, 15 cents.

IMPROVED BABY HAMMERLESS

$2.00

22-CALIBER REVOLVER.

Manufactured by Henry M. Kolb, Philadelphia, Pa. The smallest practical 22-caliber revolver made; can be carried in vest pocket, the same as a watch. Length over all is 4 inches. Folding trigger, 1¼-inch rifled steel barrel, fancy rubber stock, fluted cylinder, chambered for six cartridges, loaded from the side, full nickel plated and polished. Shoots 22-caliber rim fire cartridges No. 6T2336.

Cat. No.	Caliber	Length of Barrel	Finish	No. of Sh'ts	Shoots Cartridge No.	Handle	Price
6T1249	22 r. f.	1¼ in.	Nickel	6	6T2336	Rubber	$2.00
6T1250	22 r. f.	1¼ in.	Plated	6	6T2336	Pearl	2.60

If mail shipment, postage extra, 8 cents.

THE STEVENS' TIP UP PISTOL, $2.45

22-CALIBER CARTRIDGES, 20c PER 100. SEE PAGE 843

$2.45 22-caliber only. 3½-in. barrel.

Stevens' Single Shot Pistol. Tip up barrel, nickel plated finish, 3½-inch blued steel barrel, 22-caliber only, rim fire. No better material put in rifles. A fine target pistol. Rifled barrel and well made throughout.

No. 6T1343 For 22-caliber short cartridge No. 6T2336.
Price..........$2.45
Postage extra, 15c

STEVENS DIAMOND MODEL TARGET PISTOL.

$4.05

The Celebrated Stevens Target Pistol, the best pistol made for fine close shooting. It has fine blued barrel, nickel plated frame, rosewood stock, 6-inch tip up barrel; fitted with fine globe or open target sights, 22-caliber, rim fire. Shoots either 22 long rifle or 22 short cartridges; good for 50 yards, 22-caliber, 6-inch barrel.

No. 6T1344 Diamond model, globe and peep sights. Price..........$4.04
No. 6T1345 The same pistol, but with open sights. Price...(If mail shipment, postage extra, 15c).....$4.05

STEVENS OFF-HAND TARGET PISTOL.

$6.00

Shoots Cartridges Nos. 6T2336, 6T2338, 6T2340.

A heavier pistol than the Diamond Model. It has weight and balance, permitting of accurate shooting without a rest. 6-inch barrel with octagon breech, sporting rear and beaded front sights, frame nickel plated, walnut stocks and single action trigger; wt., 1 lb. 6 oz. 22-caliber.

No. 6T1346 Stevens Off-Hand Target Pistol, 6-inch barrel. Price..........$6.00
If mail shipment, postage extra, 26 cents.

NEW MODEL HARRINGTON & RICHARDSON

22-Caliber **$4.80**

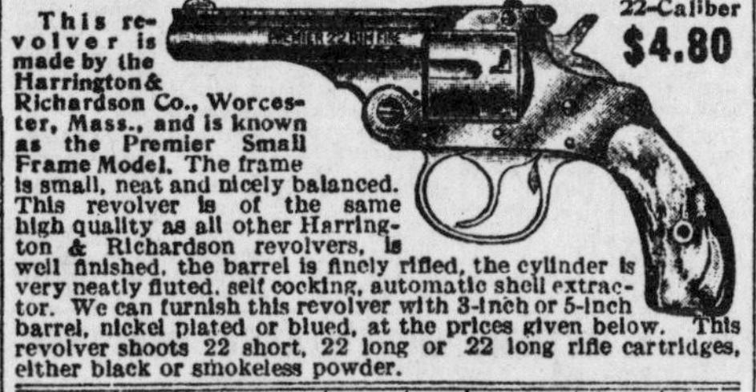

This revolver is made by the Harrington & Richardson Co., Worcester, Mass., and is known as the Premier Small Frame Model. The frame is small, neat and nicely balanced. This revolver is of the same high quality as all other Harrington & Richardson revolvers, is well finished, the barrel is finely rifled, the cylinder is very neatly fluted, self cocking, automatic shell extractor. We can furnish this revolver with 3-inch or 5-inch barrel, nickel plated or blued, at the prices given below. This revolver shoots 22 short, 22 long or 22 long rifle cartridges, either black or smokeless powder.

Cat. No.	Caliber	Length of Barrel	Finish	No. of Shots	Shoots Cartridge No.	Price, with Rubber Stocks	Price, with Pearl Stocks
6T1370	22 r. f.	3 inches	Nick'l	7	6T2336 6T2535	$4.80	$5.80
6T1371	22 r. f.	3 inches	Blued	7	6T2338 6T2340	5.00	6.10

H. & R. PREMIER.

5-INCH BARREL

$5.32

Same revolver as above, fitted with 5-inch barrel.

22-CALIBER CARTRIDGES, 20. CENTS PER 100. SEE PAGE 843.

Cat. No.	Caliber	Length of Barrel	Finish	No. of Shots	Shoots Cartridge No.	PRICE Rubber Stocks	PRICE Pearl Stocks
6T1374	22 r. f.	5 inches	Nick'l	7	6T2336 6T2535	$5.32	$6.35
6T1375	22 r. f.	5 inches	Blued	7	6T2338 6T2340	5.60	6.70

Postage extra, 22 cents. See top of page for insured mail.

HARRINGTON & RICHARDSON TARGET PISTOL

22-CALIBER 5-INCH BARREL

This is the Premier Model Pistol, same as No. 6T1374, above described, 22-caliber, 5-inch barrel, fitted with special target grips. These grips are full, large sized, 1 inch longer than the regular grip, 1¾ inches wide at butt, making a large, full, hand fitting grip for target practice.

No. 6T1376 22-caliber, 5-inch, nickeled, 7 shots. Price, with target stocks..........$5.75
No. 6T1377 Same as above blued finish 6.10
If mail shipment, postage extra 24 cents.

Target grips can be fitted on any of the regular Harrington & Richardson Automatic Revolvers at an additional charge of 75 cents.

IVER JOHNSON HAMMER REVOLVERS.

32 and 38-Caliber.

$4.79

Hammer the Hammer

70c and 90c per 100 for Cartridges. See page 843

This revolver is manufactured by the Iver Johnson Arms & Cycle Co., of Fitchburg, Mass., and is widely known and widely advertised as the "hammer the hammer" revolver. It is known as an automatic shell ejecting hinge revolver, so when you open the barrel at the top the shells are automatically extracted by the shell extractor. Fitted with a rifled steel barrel, fluted cylinder, front and rear sights, full nickel plated throughout, fancy rubber handle, may be fitted with pearl handle at the price quoted below; shoots cartridges caliber 32 S. & W., our No. 6T2377, or 38 S. & W., our No. 6T2388, and no other cartridges can be used in this revolver. It is safe, reliable and a good shooter.

Catalog Number	Caliber	Length of Barrel	Finish	No. of Sh'ts	Shoots Cartridge No.	Weight, Ounces	Price
6T1253	32 c.f.	3 in.	Nickel	5	6T2377	13	$4.79
6T1254	38 c.f.	3¼ in.	Plated	5	6T2388	18	
6T1255	32 c.f.	3 in.	Blued	5	6T2377	13	5.00
6T1256	38 c.f.	3¼ in.	Blued	5	6T2388	18	

If fitted with pearl handle, extra..........$1.00
Postage extra, 17 to 22 cents. See top of page about insured mail.

IVER JOHNSON HAMMERLESS REVOLVERS AT REDUCED PRICES.

$5.40

32 and 38-Caliber.

This illustration will give you an idea of the Iver Johnson Hammerless Revolver, manufactured by the Iver Johnson Arms & Cycle Works, Fitchburg, Mass., and is very similar to the Iver Johnson automatic hinge revolver, except it is made hammerless and is very popular as a pocket revolver.

Catalog Number	Caliber	Length of Barrel	Finish	No. of Sh'ts	Shoots Cartridge No.	Weight, Ounces	Price
6T1263	32 c.f.	3 in.	Nickel	5	6T2377	13	$5.40
6T1264	38 c.f.	3¼ in.	Plated	5	6T2388	18	
6T1265	32 c.f.	3 in.	Blued	5	6T2377	13	5.75
6T1266	38 c.f.	3¼ in.	Blued	5	6T2388	18	

If fitted with pearl handle, extra..........$1.00
Postage extra, 17c to 22c. Read top of page about insured mail.

H. & R. AUTOMATIC REVOLVERS.

70 AND 90 CENTS PER 100 FOR CARTRIDGES. SEE PAGE 843.

32 and 38-Caliber.

Hinge Revolvers are not intended for smokeless powder.

This revolver is manufactured by the Harrington & Richardson Arms Co., of Worcester, Mass., and is known as the H. & R. Automatic Shell Ejecting Hinge Revolver. It is made from first class material throughout; has a steel rifled barrel, front and rear sights, fluted cylinder; all working parts are tempered, case hardened and interchangeable. Full nickel plated or blued steel finish throughout, fitted with fancy hard rubber handle. A good, safe, reliable revolver, which takes the 32 S. & W. cartridge, our No. 6T2377, or the 38 S. & W. cartridge, our No. 6T2388. The 32-caliber is 6-shot and the 38-caliber is 5-shot and no other cartridges will fit this revolver, so if you order cartridges with the revolver, be sure to state that the cartridges are for this revolver.

Catalog Number	Caliber	Length of Barrel	Finish	No. of Sh'ts	Shoots Cartridge	Weight, Ounces	Price
6T1385	32 c. f.	3¼ in.	Nickel	6	6T2377	18½	$4.80
6T1386	38 c. f.	3¼ in.	Plated	5	6T2388	18½	
6T1387	32 c. f.	3¼ in.	Blued	6	6T2377	18½	5.00
6T1388	38 c. f.	3¼ in.	Steel	5	6T2388	18½	

Pearl handle on above revolvers, extra..........$1.20
If mail shipment, postage extra, 20 cents.

H. & R. HAMMERLESS REVOLVERS.

32 or 38-Caliber. Adapted to S. & W. Cartridges.

70 AND 90 CENTS PER 100 FOR CARTRIDGES. SEE PAGE 843.

$5.40 AND 5.75

The H. & R. Hammerless manufactured by the Harrington & Richardson Arms Co., of Worcester, Mass. Same as above, only hammerless. A good, safe, reliable revolver, which takes the 32 S. & W. cartridge, our No. 6T2377, or the 38 S. & W. cartridge, our No. 6T2388. 32-caliber has a small, light frame, making it a fine, good, convenient pocket size.

Notice our 75-Cent Rifle Revolver Stock, No. 6T1488.

Catalog Number	Caliber	Length of Barrel	Finish	No. of Sh'ts	Shoots Cartridge	Weight	Price
6T1411	32 c. f.	3 in.	Nickel	5	6T2377	13 oz.	$5.40
6T1412	38 c. f.	3¼ in.	Plated	5	6T2388	18 oz.	
6T1413	32 c. f.	3 in.	Blued	5	6T2377	13 oz.	5.75
6T1414	38 c. f.	3¼ in.	Steel	5	6T2388	18 oz.	

Pearl handle on above revolvers, extra..........$1.20
If mail shipment, postage extra, 18 to 24 cents.

SEND FOR OUR FREE AMMUNITION PRICE LIST QUOTING LOWEST PRICES ON ALL AMMUNITION

COLT'S AUTOMATIC PISTOLS AND REVOLVERS

COLT'S AUTOMATIC PISTOL, 25-CALIBER, 7-SHOT, $12.00.

The latest automatic pistol produced by the Colt's Patent Fire Arms Co. This pistol is very small and compact. It shoots the 25-caliber rimless, smokeless, center fire, metal patched cartridge with great accuracy and penetration. All parts are accurately machined and rifled; the mechanism is simple; the pistol can be taken apart without the aid of any tools; the magazine holds six cartridges, and one in the chamber, making seven shots in all. By pulling the trigger, the cartridge is fired, the empty shell is ejected and a new cartridge is loaded into the chamber. Fitted with slide lock safety, also grip safety, making it necessary that the pistol be firmly held in the hand before the trigger can be pulled and positively preventing accidental discharge. Length of barrel, 2 inches; entire length, 4½ inches; weight, 13 ounces; blued finish.

No. 6T1495 Colt's Automatic Pistol, 25-caliber, 2-inch barrel, blued finish. Price $12.00

No. 6T2563 25-Caliber Smokeless Metal Patched Cartridges for this pistol. Price, per box of 50 .... $0.63
Price, per 100 .... 1.26

COLT'S AUTOMATIC MAGAZINE PISTOL, 32-CALIBER, 9-SHOT, $15.00.

The entire pistol is made from the very best grade of crucible steel; the parts are simple and strong; the barrel is finely rifled for long range shooting; all metal parts are handsomely blued; fancy rubber handle, latest improved safety on the grip; the entire length of the Colt's Automatic Pistol is 7 inches, the weight is 24 ounces, will hold eight cartridges in the magazine and one in the barrel, making it a nine-shot pistol, is accurate up to 300 yards, and will penetrate five 1-inch pine boards at a distance of 15 feet. Each shot throws out the shell and puts in a new cartridge. All you have to do is pull the trigger.

No. 6T1500 Colt's Automatic Pistol, 32-caliber, 4-inch barrel. Weight, 24 ounces, 9-shot. Price $15.00
If fitted with pearl handle, extra 1.75
Extra magazine for the above pistol. Price .... .90
If registered mail shipment, postage extra, 40 cents.
Mention registered mail when ordering.

No. 6T2560 32-Caliber Automatic Smokeless, Rimless Cartridges with metal patched bullet. Price, per box of 50, 72c
Cartridges cannot be sent by mail.

COLT'S AUTOMATIC POCKET PISTOL, 38-CALIBER, 8-SHOT MODEL. $20.00

One of the strongest pistols ever produced, eight shots may be fired in two seconds, has a range of 500 to 1,000 yards, shoots the latest 38-caliber Colt's Automatic high pressure cartridge, and has a velocity of 1,050 feet per second, and will penetrate nine 1-inch pine boards. The magazine is in the handle, and it has no cylinder, wherein it differs from revolvers. To operate this pistol, place seven cartridges in the magazine and one in the chamber, raise the hammer, and all you have to do after that is to pull the trigger, for the pistol cocks itself by its own recoil after each shot is fired. The Colt's Automatic Pocket Pistol has 4½-inch barrel.

Catalog Number	Caliber	Length of Barrel	Finish	No. of Sh'ts	Shoots Cartridge	Weight	Price
6T1503	38 Aut.	4½ in.	Blued	8	6T2580	31 oz.	$20.00

Extra for pearl handle fitted to the above pistol $2.00
Extra magazines for above pistol. Each 1.35
If registered mail shipment, postage extra, 54 cents.
Mention registered mail when ordering.

No. 6T2580 38-Caliber Automatic Smokeless Cartridges with metal patched bullets. Price, per box of 50 .... $1.03

COLT'S MILITARY MODEL AUTOMATIC PISTOL, 38-CALIBER.

The same as above described, 6-inch barrel, square butt, with ring.

Catalog Number	Caliber	Lgth. of Barrel	Finish	No. of Sh'ts	Shoots Cartr'ge No.	Wt. oz.	Price
6T1505	38 Auto.	6 in.	Blued	8	6T2580	35	$21.00

COLT'S NEW SERVICE DOUBLE ACTION REVOLVER. 45-Caliber

The Colt's New Service Revolver, manufactured by the Colt's Patent Fire Arms Co. Has a good grip, which is a leading feature with all Colt's revolvers. The New Service Double Action Revolver is made on the jointless solid frame type, has the simultaneous side ejector, rebounding hammer, fluted and chambered cylinder, barrel made of the best rifle steel, finely rifled, all parts interchangeable. Fitted with fancy rubber handle (pearl handle may be fitted at price quoted below), blued steel finish throughout, takes the 45-caliber Colt's cartridge, is a 6-shooter, weighs about 36 ounces and is one of the most powerful shooting revolvers made shooting black powder cartridges.

Catalog Number	Caliber	Length of Barrel	Finish	No. of Sh'ts	Shoots Cartridge No.	Wt., Oz.	Price
6T1563	45 c.f.	7½ in.	Blued Steel	6	6T2413	36	$16.75

If fitted with pearl handle, extra $5.50
If registered mail shipment, postage extra, 62 cents.
Mention registered mail when ordering.

COLT'S POLICE POSITIVE REVOLVERS. 32 and 38-Caliber.

The Colt's Police Positive Revolver is made on the solid frame, side ejecting, jointless pattern, the same as the Colt's New Army and New Navy. Has the side ejecting device for extracting the shells from the cylinder, patent safety lock device in the frame, made so that the firing pin cannot strike the primer of the cartridge until you pull the trigger. It is a 6-shooter made to take the 32 short Colt's center fire, 32 long Colt's center fire or 38 Smith & Wesson cartridges. The 32-caliber revolver weighs about 18 ounces and the 38-caliber revolver weighs about 20 ounces. Has a splendid grip, smooth working action, blued steel finish, with fancy rubber handle, but may be fitted with pearl handle for $2.00 extra, and is the revolver which is adopted by the city police departments of New York and other large cities.

Catalog No.	Caliber	Lgth of Brl.	Finish	No. of Shots	Shoots Cart'ge	Weight	Price
6T1511	32 c. f.	4 in.	Blued	6	6T2380, 6T2381	18-oz.	$14.00
6T1513	38 c. f.	4 in.	Blued	6	6T2388	20-oz.	

If fitted with pearl handle, extra $2.00
If registered mail shipment, postage extra, 35 to 37 cents.
Mention registered mail when ordering.

COLT'S POLICE POSITIVE SPECIAL.

The same as the Police Positive above described, but heavier on account of the larger frame, adapted to larger size cartridges. Shoots 32-20 rifle cartridges and 38 long Colt. Six-shot; blued finish.

Catalog Number	Caliber	Le'th of Barrel	Finish	No. of Sh'ts	Shoots Cartr'ge No.	Wt. oz.	Price
6T1514	32-20	6 in.	Blued	6	6T2384	22	$14.00
6T1515	38 c. f.	6 in.	Blued	6	6T2392	24	

If fitted with pearl handle, extra $2.00
If registered mail shipment, postage extra, 37 cents.

COLT'S ARMY SPECIAL REVOLVERS, MODEL 1908, 32-20 and 38 Caliber. $15.50

This revolver supersedes the model 1892 Colt's Army and the New Navy Revolvers, the manufacture of which has been discontinued. This revolver is made in two calibers, 32-20-caliber, using the regular rifle cartridge, and 38-caliber, using either the 38 short or 38 long Colt's cartridges. The cylinder is chambered for six shots. Made with two lengths of barrel, 4½-inch and 6-inch, finished with a dark blue finish. Weight with 4½-inch barrel, 32 ounces; length over all with 4½-inch barrel, 9¾ inches. The cylinder of this revolver revolves to the right, insuring tightness and perfect alignment. The revolver is fitted with Colt's positive lock, which absolutely prevents accidental discharge.

Double Action Swing Out Cylinder Solid Frame.

Catalog Number	Caliber C. F.	Le'th of Barrel	Finish	No. of Shots	Shoots Cartr'ge No.	Wt. oz.	Price
6T1524	38	4½ in.	Blued	6	6T2392	32	$15.50
6T1526	38	6 in.	Blued	6	6T2392	32	
6T1528	32-20	4½ in.	Blued	6	6T2384	32	15.50
6T1529	32-20	6 in.	Blued	6	6T2384	32	

COLT'S OFFICERS' MODEL TARGET REVOLVER. 38-Caliber. $18.50

This revolver is designed for target shooting and where extreme accuracy is desired. It is generally adopted by army officers and is used in all target shoots. Made with jointless solid frame, swing out cylinder, stocks and trigger finely checked. Particular attention is paid to the action, which is hand finished and operates with great smoothness and excellence of pull. Sights specially adapted for target shooting. Front sight has adjustable elevation; rear sight has an adjusting screw, adjustable for windage. Six shots; length, 6 or 7½ inches; caliber, 38 long Colt or 38 S. & W. Special (either one of these cartridges may be used in the same revolver). Finish, full blued; fitted with finely checked full walnut stocks. Weight, 32 ounces. Length over all, 11½ inches.

Catalog No.	Caliber	Length of Barrel	No. of Shots	Shoots Cart'ge No.	Weight, ounces	Price
6T1625	38 Long Colt	6 in.	6	6T2392	32	$18.50
6T1626		7½ in.	6	6T2392	36	

If registered mail shipment, postage extra, 54 cents.
Mention registered mail when ordering.
Weight, packed for shipment, 3 pounds.

COLT'S SINGLE ACTION BISLEY MODEL.

The Colt's Bisley Model Revolver is patterned after the Colt's Single Action Army Revolver, but has a longer handle and a different shape hammer. The frame is case hardened and the barrel and cylinder are blued. This revolver embodies all the high grade workmanship of the famous Colt's revolvers. We carry this revolver regularly in 32-20 caliber, but can furnish it in 45-caliber to special order.

Catalog Number	Caliber	Length of Barrel	Finish	No. of Sh'ts	Shoots Cartridge No.	Weight Ounces	Price
6T1610	32-20	5½ in.	Blued Steel	6	6T2384	40	$15.50
6T1611	32-20	7½ in.		6	6T2384	40	

Pearl stocks, per pair, extra $6.50
If registered mail shipment, postage extra, 62 cents.
Mention registered mail when ordering.

COLT'S SINGLE ACTION COWBOYS' FRONTIER ARMY REVOLVERS. 32-20, 44-40 and 45-Caliber. $15.50

This is the old reliable Cowboys' Gun, and our price is $15.50 for all calibers and lengths of barrels; furnished in blued steel finish only. Colt's Single Action Army Revolver is a 6-shooter, rubber handle, solid frame, the best quality of steel and finish; warranted perfect and accurate in every detail. Barrel, 5½ or 7½ inches; 32, 44 or 45-caliber, as desired. We can furnish these in blued finish only.

Catalog Number	Caliber C. F.	Length of Barrel	Finish	No. of Sh'ts	Shoots Cartridge No.	Wt. Oz.	Price
6T1571	32-20	5½ in.	Blued Steel	6	6T2384	40	$15.50
6T1573	32-20	7½ in.		6	6T2384	40	
6T1581	44-40	7½ in.	Blued Steel	6	6T2409	40	15.50
6T1583	45 c. f.	5½ in.		6	6T2413	40	
6T1585	45 c. f.	7½ in.		6	6T2413	40	15.50

Pearl handle on any of the above revolvers, extra ..$4.00
If registered mail shipment, postage extra, 62 cents.
Mention registered mail when ordering.

COLT'S SPECIAL PEARL HANDLE REVOLVERS.

Single Action Frontier. This is our Special Cowboys' Six-Shooter with pearl handle. The right handle has an ox head carved in raised design and makes a handsome revolver. This illustration is engraved from a photograph of the revolver and will give you some idea of its appearance. Made in blued steel finish only. We handle these regularly in 32-20 and 44-40-calibers, but can furnish them on special order in caliber 41 c. f. or 45 Colt's c. f. with 5½ or 7½-inch barrel at prices quoted below. Weight, 41 ounces. When ordering say which length barrel you prefer.

Cat. No.	Caliber C. F.	Length of Barrel	Finish	No. of Sh'ts	Shoots Cartridge No.	Wt., Oz.	Price
6T1587	32-20	5½ in.	Blued	6	6T2384	41	$22.50
6T1589	32-20	7½ in.	Steel	6	6T2384	41	
6T1591	44-40	5½ in.	Blued	6	6T2409	41	22.50
6T1593	44-40	7½ in.	Steel	6	6T2409	41	

If registered mail shipment, postage extra, 61 to 71 cents.
Mention registered mail when ordering.
Weight, packed for shipment, 3 pounds.

LUGER AUTOMATIC PISTOL, 30-CALIBER, 8 SHOTS. $23.95

Modeled after the celebrated Maxim gun, automatically reloads and cocks as long as there is a cartridge in the chamber. Absolutely safe against accidental discharge. Eight shots can be fired in less than five seconds. This pistol can also be used as single loader for target practice. The Luger pistol has the endorsement of the United States and several foreign governments. Very simple to operate; has few parts. The pistol can be dismounted without the aid of any tools in a few seconds' time, and as easily assembled. Shoots special 30-caliber Luger smokeless cartridges, either soft point or metal patched bullets. Range, over 1,500 yards. Weight, 1 pound 13 ounces. Length over all, 9 inches. Length of barrel, 4¾ inches.

No. 6T1640 30-Caliber Luger Automatic Pistol, with one extra magazine. Price $23.95
If registered mail shipment, postage extra, 48 cents.

No. 6T2582 30-Caliber Luger Cartridges, soft point. Price, per box of 50 .... $1.00

No. 6T2583 30-Caliber Luger Cartridges, metal patched. Price, per box of 50 .... $1.01

MELIOR AUTOMATIC 25-CALIBER PISTOL.

A high grade, guaranteed automatic pistol. All working parts are made of the finest tool steel. Reliable, accurate and an excellent pocket arm. It automatically ejects and loads. Made hammerless style. Shoots 25-caliber Colt's Automatic Cartridges (No. 6T2563). Blued finish, positive safety; entire length, 4½ inches; weight, 13½ ounces. The magazine contained in the handle holds six cartridges, and one in the chamber makes this a seven-shot pistol.

Catalog Number	Caliber	Length of Barrel	No. of Shots	Shoots Cartr'ge No.	Weight, ounces	Price
6T1643	25 Auto.	2 inches	7	6T2563	13½	$10.18

If registered mail shipment, postage extra, 29 cents.

No. 6T2563 25-Caliber Automatic Smokeless Metal Patched Cartridges. Price, per box of 50 .... 63c

AMMUNITION.

Don't fail to include a quantity of ammunition with your order for a revolver or pistol, as our ammunition is guaranteed to be the highest quality, and our prices are far below those asked by others.

Remember, ammunition can be shipped with a revolver by express. It will pay you to include 100 or more cartridges with your order for a pistol or revolver.

Do not ruin a good revolver by neglecting to buy a first class holster. Whether you carry the revolver in your pocket, on a belt or keep it at home, it ought to be protected with a good holster. Our line of holsters is complete and consists of the very finest goods made. Made especially for us of special stock. We guarantee our holsters to excel in quality those sold by others, and, quality considered, to be at least 25 per cent lower in price. A full line of holsters and cartridge belts is shown on page 850.

COLT'S OFFICERS' MODEL TARGET REVOLVER.

38-Caliber.

$18.50

This revolver is designed for target shooting and where extreme accuracy is desired. It is generally adopted by army officers and is used in all target shoots. Made with jointless solid frame, swing-out cylinder, straps and trigger finely checked. Particular attention is paid to the action, which is hand finished and operates with great smoothness and excellence of pull. Sights specially adapted for target shooting. Front sight has adjustable elevation; rear sight has an adjusting screw, adjustable for windage. Six shots; length, 6 inches; caliber, 38 long colt or 38 S. & W. Special (either one of these cartridges may be used in the same revolver). Finish, full blued; fitted with finely checked full walnut stocks. Weight, 32 ounces. Length over all, 11½ inches.

Catalogue No.	Caliber	Length of Barrel	No. of Shots	Shoots Cart'ges No.	Weight, ounces	Price
6L1625	38 Long Colt	6 inches	6	6L2392	32	$18.50

If by registered mail, postage extra, 52 cents. Mention registered mail when ordering. Weight, packed for shipment, 3 pounds.

LUGER AUTOMATIC PISTOL, $24.45

30-CALIBER, 8 SHOTS.

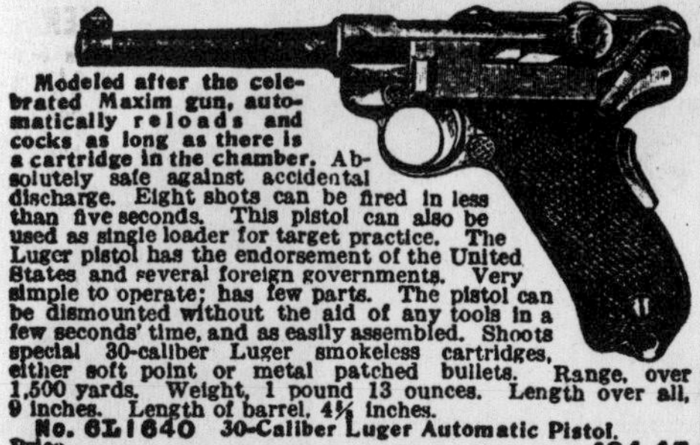

Modeled after the celebrated Maxim gun, automatically reloads and cocks as long as there is a cartridge in the chamber. Absolutely safe against accidental discharge. Eight shots can be fired in less than five seconds. This pistol can also be used as single loader for target practice. The Luger pistol has the endorsement of the United States and several foreign governments. Very simple to operate; has few parts. The pistol can be dismounted without the aid of any tools in a few seconds' time, and as easily assembled. Shoots special 30-caliber Luger smokeless cartridges, either soft point or metal patched bullets. Range, over 1,500 yards. Weight, 1 pound 13 ounces. Length over all, 9 inches. Length of barrel, 4¾ inches.

No. 6L1640 30-Caliber Luger Automatic Pistol. Price $24.45

If by mail, postage extra, 48 cents.

No. 6L2582 30-Caliber Luger Cartridges, soft point. Price, per box of 50........................$1.03

No. 6L2583 30-Caliber Luger Cartridges, metal patched. Price, per box of 50........................$1.04

GENUINE SMITH & WESSON REVOLVERS.

OUR 22-CALIBER SMITH & WESSON SIDE EJECTING REVOLVER.

This revolver is double action has fluted cylinder, rifled steel barrel, rebounding hammer, rubber handle, blued steel or nickel plated finish; made in 22-caliber, taking rim fire cartridges. This is the latest Smith & Wesson revolver, and the highest grade 22-caliber revolver made.

Catalogue Number	Caliber	Length of Barrel	Finish	No. of Sh'ts	Shoots Cartridge No.	Wgt. Oz.	Price
6L1700	22 Rim	3½ in.	Nickel	7	6L2336 or 6L2338	10	$11.85
6L1701		3½ in.	Blued	7		10	

If fitted with pearl handle, extra 90c

If by registered mail, postage extra, 25 cents. Weight, packed for shipment, about 1 pound.

S. & W. DOUBLE ACTION REVOLVERS.

$12.74

These revolvers are warranted genuine Smith & Wesson. All are self cocking and double action, with automatic shell extractor, finely rifled steel barrel, fine rubber stocks, nickel plated or blued steel finish. Made of the finest material that money can buy and the workmanship is equal in finish to that of any ordinary watch. If you want the best work for your money buy a Smith & Wesson.

Catalogue No.	Caliber	Length Barrel	Finish	No. of Shots	Shoots Cart'ge	Weight	Price
6L1724	32 c.f.	3½ in.	Nickel	5-shot	6L2377	13 oz.	$12.74
6L1725	32 c.f.	3½ in.	Blued	5-shot	6L2377	13 oz.	
6L1726	32 c.f.	6 in.	Nickel	5-shot	6L2377	15 oz.	12.75
6L1727	32 c.f.	6 in.	Blued	5-shot	6L2377	15 oz.	
6L1732	38 c.f.	4 in.	Nickel	5-shot	6L2388	18 oz.	13.83
6L1733	38 c.f.	4 in.	Blued	5-shot	6L2388	18 oz.	
6L1734	38 c.f.	5 in.	Nickel	5-shot	6L2388	19 oz.	13.84
6L1735	38 c.f.	5 in.	Blued	5-shot	6L2388	19 oz.	
6L1736	38 c.f.	6 in.	Nickel	5-shot	6L2388	20 oz.	13.85
6L1737	38 c.f.	6 in.	Blued	5-shot	6L2388	20 oz.	

FIRST QUALITY PEARL HANDLE, EXTRA.......$1.00

If by registered mail, 32-caliber, 30 cents; 38-caliber, 35 cents. Mention registered mail when ordering. Weight, packed for shipment, about 2 pounds.

S. & W. SIDE EJECTING REVOLVERS.

32-38 Caliber.

The Side Ejecting Smith & Wesson Revolver is self cocking, and being the side ejecting type makes a strong, substantial revolver. It is center fire, 6-shot, with solid frame, swing-out cylinder. This revolver is Smith & Wesson's latest creation and is a revolver that is built for business. It will withstand hard usage. They are highly recommended for target shooting, and made in blued steel or nickel plated finish, fitted with rubber handle.

Catalogue No.	Caliber	Length Barrel	Finish	No. of Shots	Shoots Cart'ge	Weight	Price
6L1704	32 c.f.	4¼ in.	Nickel	6-shot	6L2376	19 oz.	$13.80
6L1705	32 c.f.	4¼ in.	Blued	6-shot		19 oz.	
6L1706	32 c.f.	6 in.	Nickel	6-shot	6L2376	20 oz.	13.85
6L1707	32 c.f.	6 in.	Blued	6-shot		20 oz.	
6L1714	38 c f	5 in.	Nickel	6-shot	6L2392	30 oz.	14.98
6L1715	38c.f.	5 in.	Blued	6-shot		30 oz.	
6L1716	38 c.f.	6½ in.	Nickel	6-shot		32 oz.	15.00
6L1717	38 c.f.	6½ in.	Blued	6-shot	6L2392	32 oz.	

FIRST QUALITY PEARL HANDLE ON THE ABOVE, EXTRA, 32-caliber, $1.00; 38-caliber............$2.00

If by registered mail, postage extra, 32-caliber, 35c; 38-caliber, 48c.

We cannot furnish Smith & Wesson Revolvers for 38-40 and 32-20 cartridges.

SMITH & WESSON HAMMERLESS.

$13.80

Made by Smith & Wesson, Springfield, Mass. Latest type new model hammerless, automatic shell ejector, patent safety catch, self cocking rebounding hammer double action, blue steel or nickel plated finish, fitted with rubber handle. This is positively the best hammerless revolver made.

Improved Safety Trigger Locking Device which automatically releases as trigger is pulled. Accidental discharge impossible.

Catalogue No.	Caliber	Length Barrel	Finish	No. of Shots	Shoots Cart'ge	Weight	Price
6L1756	32 c.f.	3½ in.	Nickel	5-shot	6L2377	15 oz.	$13.80
6L1757	32 c.f.	3½ in.	Blued	5-shot	6L2377	15 oz.	
6L1762	38 c.f.	4 in.	Nickel	5-shot	6L2388	18 oz.	14.90
6L1763	38 c.f.	4 in.	Blued	5-shot	6L2388	18 oz.	
6L1764	38 c.f.	5 in.	Nickel	5-shot	6L2388	19 oz.	14.91
6L1765	38 c.f.	5 in.	Blued	5-shot	6L2388	19 oz.	
6L1766	38 c.f.	6 in.	Nickel	5-shot	6L2388	19 oz.	14.92
6L1767	38 c.f.	6 in.	Blued	5-shot	6L2388	19 oz.	

FIRST QUALITY PEARL HANDLE, EXTRA.....$1.00

If by registered mail, postage extra, 32-caliber, 30 cents; 38-caliber, 37 cents. ☞ See our prices on cartridges.

OUR IMPROVED RIFLE REVOLVER STOCK. 75c

Our Rifle Revolver Stock converts a revolver into a repeating rifle by attaching this skeleton stock to the butt of any revolver, which can be instantly done by giving the screw on the skeleton stock a few turns to the right. You can shoot at short range as accurately with an ordinary pistol as you can with any rifle. With the aid of this stock and any ordinary revolver, you can have all the enjoyment of shooting a repeating rifle at a cost at least $5.00 lower than you could purchase the cheapest rifle for. The jaws of this stock are covered with leather, so they will not mar the revolver. The stock is nicely nickel plated and finished. Length of stock 14½ ins.; weight of stock, 16 oz. This stock will not take a Colt's Automatic Pistol on account of the magazine in the handle of this pistol. No. 6L1488 Revolver Rifle Stock...Price, for stock only, 75c

If by mail, postage extra, 20 cents; insured mail, 25 cents.

LOADED SHOTGUN SHELLS $1.48

BLACK POWDER. 10, 12, 16 AND 20-GAUGE.

AT $1.48 PER HUNDRED we furnish the highest quality black powder loaded shotgun shells. No better black powder shells made at any price. We ask that you compare this price of $1.48 and up with the prices asked by other dealers for various grades of black powder shells, and if you will furthermore avail yourself of the opportunity of comparing the quality of our shells with those sold by others, you will realize that our shells at our prices are the greatest value ever offered in this line. These extraordinary prices, quality considered, are only made possible by the fact that we are the largest handlers of shotgun and rifle ammunition selling direct to the consumer in the world. Our sales in loaded shells, both black and smokeless, are greater than the combined sales of any ten retail houses or catalogue houses.

YOU ARE BENEFITED DIRECTLY by this low cost, for at our prices, ranging from $1.48 up, we have added but one small profit over the actual cost of material and labor, furnishing you these shells, quality considered, from 50 cents to 75 cents a hundred less than you could purchase shells of like quality elsewhere.

Powder.

IN THESE BLACK POWDER SHELLS we use a special black powder of a hard grain, which burns rapidly and leaves far less residue in the barrel than any other black powder. It has enormous penetration with a minimum breech pressure, and is really the cleanest, strongest and safest black powder ever used in shotgun ammunition. These shells are all loaded by automatic machinery, and one shell is identically like the other. One of the valuable features of these shells is their great uniformity. The good results you get with one shell you can get with the other 24 in the box, or the other 499 out of the same case.

ANTICIPATE YOUR WANTS IN SHOTGUN SHELLS. Do not wait until the season is here before you order, as our business in shells is enormous, and while we guarantee to take care of your order at any time, still we desire that you place your orders early, for with the opening of the shooting season, our business in shotgun ammunition takes an enormous increase, at times testing the utmost capacity of the factory.

Goods Shipped by Freight.

OWING TO THE WEIGHT OF SHOTGUN SHELLS, we strongly advise sending all shells by freight instead of express, as freight is far cheaper, and it is very easy for you to make up an order of 50 or 100 pounds for a freight shipment, as there are doubtless many other things in our large book that you need, any you will thereby get the minimum freight rate, and the transportation charges on each item will amount to practically nothing.

Our Guarantee.

WE ABSOLUTELY GUARANTEE every loaded shotgun shell we sell against misfire, hang fire or blow backs. We guarantee the maximum of penetration and the greatest possible uniformity in pattern. We further guarantee that our shells will give better satisfaction and are better value than those you can buy elsewhere, and to give you an opportunity of satisfying yourself that our shells are the best made, we will accept your order for 100 or more shells, and you can shoot one full box of them, and if you have any fault to find with these shells, if you do not find they have greater penetration, make a better target and give better results in every way, you may return the balance to us at our expense, and your money and any transportation charges you may have paid will be refunded.

NUMBER OF PELLETS TO ONE OUNCE OF SHOT.

We give below the number of pellets to one ounce of shot. The number is approximate. It may vary ten or more pellets.

Size of Shot	No. 10	No. 9	No. 8	No. 7½	No. 7	No. 6	No. 5	No. 4	No. 3	No. 2	No. 1	BB
1 ounce contains pellets	850	570	390	335	290	220	170	130	105	85	70	60

OUR LINE OF BLACK POWDER LOADED SHELLS.

Why not get your friends to join with you and buy shells by the case or 1,000 and ship by freight? It will save you money on freight charges, besides they are cheaper in case lots.

OUR CASE PRICE is for one size and one gauge in a case, just as it comes to us from the factory. We cannot sell less than a case at the case price, nor can we assort the case with different loads.

A case of 500 shells, 12-gauge, weighs about 65 pounds.
A case of 500 shells, 10-gauge, weighs about 75 pounds.
A case of 500 shells, 16-gauge, weighs about 53 pounds.
Our terms on loaded shells are cash with order.

We have taken great pains to select loads which are suitable for most purposes and these loads should meet all requirements.

WE DO NOT SEND SHELLS C. O. D.

ALWAYS GIVE CATALOGUE NUMBER WHEN ORDERING.

12-GAUGE

LOADED WITH SPECIAL BLACK POWDER.

Catalogue No.	Drams of Powder	Oz. of Shot	Size of Drop Shot	Price per Box of 25 Shells	Price per 100 Shells	Price per case of 500 Shells	Price per 1000 Shells
6L2006 6L2008	3	1	6 8	38c	$1.48	$7.05	$14.10
6L2014 6L2016 6L2018	3	1⅛	4 6	40c	1.57	7.45	14.90
6L2022 6L2024 6L2025 6L2026 6L2027	3¼	1⅛	2 4 5 6 7	41c	1.61	7.65	15.30
6L2034 6L2036	3½	1⅛	4 6	42c	1.65	7.85	15.70
6L2040B	3¾	1⅛	BB	48c	1.89	9.05	18.10

ALWAYS GIVE CATALOGUE NUMBER WHEN ORDERING.

10-GAUGE

LOADED WITH SPECIAL BLACK POWDER, $1.75.

Catalogue No.	Drams of Powder	Oz. of Shot	Size of Drop Shot	Price per Box of 25 Shells	Price per 100 Shells	Price per case of 500 Shells	Price per 1000 Shells
6L2072 6L2074 6L2076 6L2077	4¼	1⅛	2 4 6 7	46c	$1.75	$8.25	$16.50
6L2078 6L2079	5	1⅛	8 BB	50c	1.90	9.25	18.50

ALWAYS GIVE CATALOGUE NUMBER WHEN ORDERING.

16-GAUGE

LOADED WITH SPECIAL BLACK POWDER, $1.55.

Catalogue No.	Drams of Powder	Oz. of Shot	Size of Drop Shot	Price per Box of 25 Shells	Price per 100 Shells	Price per case of 500 Shells	Price per 1000 Shells
6L2084 6L2086 6L2088	2¾	1	4 6 8	40c	$1.55	$7.50	$15.00

ALWAYS GIVE CATALOGUE NUMBER WHEN ORDERING.

20-GAUGE

LOADED WITH SPECIAL BLACK POWDER, $1.80.

Catalogue No.	Drams of Powder	Oz. of Shot	Size of Drop Shot	Price per Box of 25 Shells	Price per 100 Shells	Price per case of 500 Shells	Price per 1000 Shells
6L2096 6L2098	2½	⅞	6 8	46c	$1.80	$8.80	$17.60

ALWAYS GIVE CATALOGUE NUMBER WHEN ORDERING.

EASTERN ARMS CO. AUTOMATIC ENGRAVED REVOLVER

AT $4.00 we furnish this Eastern Arms Co. Automatic Shell Ejecting Double Action Revolver, elaborately hand engraved, beautifully finished, either blued or nickel plated, 32 or 38-caliber. Compare this handsome automatic engraved revolver at $4.00 with any of the plain finished automatic revolvers offered in competition and sold for almost double our price, and you will realize to some extent what wonderful value we are offering in this revolver at this price, which represents actual factory cost on material and labor with but one small margin of profit added. It is to your interest to purchase one of these Eastern Arms Co. Revolvers, either in the plain finish, or engraved, in preference to buying a cheap double action revolver or one of the ordinary automatic revolvers, when at $3.50 for the plain finished and $4.00 for the engraved, you can procure one of the safest, most reliable and finest finished revolvers ever made, sold under a binding twenty-year guarantee.

LATEST MODEL AUTOMATIC REVOLVER ON THE MARKET

$4.00

THESE REVOLVERS are identical in construction, shape and finish with our regular Eastern Arms Co. Revolver quoted on a previous page, the only difference being that these revolvers are handsomely engraved by hand, as shown in the illustration. They are sold under our sixty-day free trial offer and are covered by our binding guarantee. This illustration of this full hand engraved, improved model Eastern Arms Co. Revolver cannot do this beautiful revolver justice. In order to realize what an excellent revolver it really is, both in appearance, construction and shooting qualities, it is necessary that you see it, handle it and test it, for which an opportunity is afforded you, as explained in our free trial offer on a previous page.

DETAILED DESCRIPTION

These revolvers are identical with those described on a previous page, the difference being only in the elaborate hand engraving, as shown in the illustration. This engraving is all done by hand by artists. Every line, every figure is cut with a sharp tool in the hands of an artist engraver. The engraving is neat—it is not gaudy—and greatly adds to the appearance of these already handsome revolvers. There are no revolvers made that will in any way compare with this beautiful hand engraved revolver sold by us at $4.00.

Extra for pearl handles on any of the above revolvers................$1.00

If by mail, postage extra, 32-caliber, 18 cents; 38-caliber, 22 cents.

If by insured mail, add 5 cents to pay postage insurance, and say, "Ship by insured mail."

Catalogue Number	Caliber, Center Fire	Length of Barrel	Finish, All Hand Engraved	Number of Shots	Shoots Cartridge No.	Weight, Ounces	Price, Rubber Handles
6L1121	32 C. F.	3 inches	Nickel Plated	5	6L2377	12	$4.00
6L1122	38 C. F.	3¼ inches	Nickel Plated	5	6L2388	15	4.00
6L1123	32 C. F.	3 inches	Blued Steel	5	6L2377	12	4.25
6L1124	38 C. F.	3¼ inches	Blued Steel	5	6L2388	15	4.25

EASTERN ARMS CO. HAMMERLESS REVOLVER

$4.25 IS OUR PRICE for this latest improved model revolver known as the Eastern Arms Co. Revolver, made by one of the largest and best known firearm factories in the United States. This revolver is the latest improved type, something entirely new, possessing the good features of all the well known standard revolvers with the defects of none. Made in 32 and 38-caliber, shooting the regular Smith & Wesson Cartridges, automatic shell ejecting, self cocking, made and finished in a better manner than the revolvers you could purchase elsewhere for almost double our price. No other house is able to offer any such value in a hammerless revolver. We absolutely control the output of the factory making this revolver. There are none of them to be had elsewhere at any price. These revolvers are made especially for us under contract and are billed to us at a price based on the actual cost of material and labor, enabling us to sell them at a price of $4.25, which is from $2.00 to $3.00 below what you would have to pay any dealer for a revolver of a grade that would in any way compare with these excellent Eastern Arms Co. Hammerless Revolvers. We predict for these new model revolvers an enormous sale, knowing that after they have once become known and their sterling qualities appreciated, and the trade learns what wonderful revolvers these are, what extraordinary value they represent at our price of $4.25, we will be overwhelmed with orders, for there is nothing made in a hammerless revolver today which in any way compares with these revolvers sold by us at $4.25.

LATEST MODEL, IMPROVED DESIGN, 32 OR 38-CALIBER

$4.25

SEND US YOUR ORDER for one of these revolvers, enclose $4.25, and we will send you the revolver by express with the understanding that if, any time within sixty days, you are dissatisfied with your purchase, if you do not think this revolver is the greatest value you have ever seen in a hammerless revolver, if you are not satisfied with the shooting qualities, if for any reason whatsoever you are not pleased with your purchase, return the revolver to us at our expense, and we will cheerfully refund you the price you paid, as well as the transportation charges.

IF YOU INTEND TO BUY A HAMMERLESS REVOLVER, we advise you to purchase this Eastern Arms Co. Revolver, as in so doing you would procure a revolver which is absolutely safe under all conditions, a revolver that is guaranteed sure fire, a revolver whose shooting qualities are absolutely the best, you would be protected by our binding twenty-year guarantee, and you would receive such a value for your money as would be impossible for you to obtain elsewhere.

THE ILLUSTRATION shown on this page will give you a good idea of its beautiful proportion and general outline, but in order to realize what a wonderful revolver this is, in order to appreciate its superiority over other hammerless revolvers sold for far more money, in order to satisfy yourself that it is all and more than we claim it to be, it is necessary that you handle and test it. We shall be pleased to receive your order and ship one of these revolvers to you with the distinct understanding and agreement that if, upon receipt, you are in any way dissatisfied with it for any reason whatsoever, you may return it, and your money and transportation charges will be immediately refunded.

Catalogue Number	Caliber	Length of Barrel	Finish	Handles	No. of Shots	Weight, Ounces	Shoots Cartridge No.	Price
6L1141	32 C. F.	3 inches	Nickel Plated	Rubber	5	12	6L2377	$4.25
6L1142	38 C. F.	3¼ inches	Nickel Plated	Rubber	5	15	6L2388	4.25
6L1143	32 C. F.	3 inches	Blued Steel	Rubber	5	12	6L2377	4.50
6L1144	38 C. F.	3¼ inches	Blued Steel	Rubber	5	15	6L2388	4.50
6L1145	32 C. F.	5 inches	Nickel Plated	Rubber	5	15	6L2377	4.75
6L1146	38 C. F.	5 inches	Nickel Plated	Rubber	5	18	6L2388	4.75
6L1147	32 C. F.	5 inches	Blued Steel	Rubber	5	15	6L2377	5.00
6L1148	38 C. F.	5 inches	Blued Steel	Rubber	5	18	6L2388	5.00

THE MATERIAL EMPLOYED IN THE CONSTRUCTION of this revolver is absolutely the best that can be obtained. The barrels are bored from the finest steel and are rifled in an improved manner. We call particular attention to the neat, attractive front sight on these revolvers. The cylinders are finely fluted and accurately finished to line up true with the barrel. The mechanism is made on the latest improved machines, true to gauge, it is absolutely interchangeable, it is simple and strong and is not liable to get out of order. The finish of this revolver is high grade and compares favorably with the finish on revolvers sold for double our price of $4.25.

Pearl handles, extra..$1.00

If by mail, postage extra, 32-caliber, 18 to 22 cents; 38-caliber, 22 to 26 cents.

REVOLVERS

WE ARE THE LARGEST HANDLERS OF REVOLVERS IN THE WORLD SELLING DIRECT TO THE CONSUMER

YOU WILL FIND on the following pages a very complete line of revolvers of all makes, calibers and descriptions. In selecting the revolvers shown on the following pages, we have been careful to select only such makes, styles and sizes as we know are practical and will give satisfaction.

OUR GUARANTEE. Every revolver we sell is carefully inspected and examined by experienced gunsmiths, and we guarantee every revolver sold by us, regardless of price, against defective material or workmanship. It is sold with the understanding that if not entirely satisfactory in every way, it may be returned to us at our expense, and we will refund your money and any transportation charges you may have paid.

INSURED MAIL. We advise where a revolver only is ordered, that you have the revolver sent by insured mail, which guarantees delivery, and which costs but 5 cents extra over the regular postage for each revolver under $5.00, and 10 cents extra over the regular postage for a revolver costing over $10.00. High priced revolvers, such as Smith & Wesson and Colt's, we recommend being sent by registered mail, which costs 8 cents over the regular rate of postage, or by express.

REMEMBER that the postoffice does not guarantee delivery on revolvers or any other goods lost in the regular mail, but by sending goods either by insured or registered mail, delivery is guaranteed.

DOUBLE ACTION SELF COCKING REVOLVERS.

No. 6L1182

The revolvers shown below are the best double action, self cocking revolvers made. They are the product of such well known and famous factories as the Harrington & Richardson and Hopkins & Allen. There are no double action revolvers made today that excel these we herewith show in workmanship, material or construction. The Harrington & Richardson and Hopkins & Allen goods are so well known that they hardly require any introduction. These revolvers all have octagon rifled barrels, are full nickel plated and fitted with neat rubber stocks, and the cylinders are all nicely fluted. By pulling the trigger, the revolver is cocked automatically.

22-CALIBER DOUBLE ACTION REVOLVERS.

See above for full description of these revolvers.

Cat. No.	Caliber	Length of Barrel	Style of Barrel	No. of Shots	Shoots Cartridge No.	Weight, Ounces	Price
6L1181	22 r. f.	2½ in.	Octagon	7	6L2336 6L2338 6L2535	12	Rubber Stocks $2.34 Pearl Stocks $3.30
6L1182	22 r. f.	6 in.	Octagon	7	6L2336 6L2338 6L2535	13	Rubber Stocks $2.95 Pearl Stocks $3.85

If by mail, postage extra, on No. 6L1181, 15 cents.
If by mail, postage extra, on No. 6L1182, 16 cents.
See remarks about insured and registered mail at top of page.

32-CALIBER DOUBLE ACTION REVOLVERS

$2.34

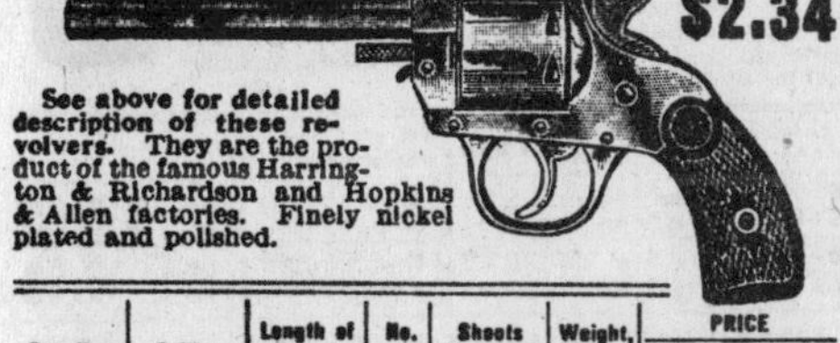

See above for detailed description of these revolvers. They are the product of the famous Harrington & Richardson and Hopkins & Allen factories. Finely nickel plated and polished.

Cat. No.	Caliber	Length of Barrel	No. of Shots	Shoots Cartridge No.	Weight, Ounces	PRICE Rubber Stocks	PRICE Pearl Stocks
6L1195	32 c. f.	2½ in.	6	6L2377	15	$2.34	$3.30
6L1200	32 c. f.	4½ in.	6	6L2377	19	2.59	3.55
6L1201	32 c. f.	6 in.	6	6L2377	19	2.84	3.85

If by mail, postage extra, No. 6L1195, 18 cents.
If by mail, postage extra, No. 6L1200, 22 cents.
If by mail, postage extra, No. 6L1201, 22 cents.
See remarks about insured and registered mail at top of page.

38-CALIBER DOUBLE ACTION REVOLVERS

$2.34

These revolvers, the same as the 32 and 22-caliber revolvers above described, are made by the well known Hopkins & Allen and Harrington & Richardson Companies, the manufacturers of the best double action revolvers on the market today. See above for further description of these revolvers.

Cat. No.	Caliber	Length of Barrel	No. of Shots	Shoots Cartridge No.	Weight, Ounces	PRICE Rubber Stocks	PRICE Pearl Stocks
6L1206	38 c. f.	2½ in.	5	6L2388	15	$2.34	$3.30
6L1210	38 c. f.	4½ in.	5	6L2388	19	2.59	3.55
6L1212	38 c. f.	6 in.	5	6L2388	19	2.85	3.85

If by mail, postage extra, No. 6L1206, 18 cents.
If by mail, postage extra, No. 6L1210, 22 cents.
If by mail, postage extra, No. 6L1212, 22 cents.
See remarks about insured and registered mail at top of page.

DOUBLE ACTION REVOLVERS WITH SAFETY HAMMER.

$2.34

These revolvers, the same as those above described, are the product of the celebrated Harrington & Richardson and Hopkins & Allen factories, but are fitted with the safety hammer, which is preferred by some people, as there are no projections to catch in pocket, enabling this revolver to be pulled more quickly than the regular style. These revolvers, the same as those above described, are full nickel plated and have fancy rubber handle and rebounding hammer.

Cat. No.	Caliber	Length of Barre	No. of Shots	Shoots Cartridge No.	Weight, Ounces	PRICE Rubber Stocks	PRICE Pearl Stocks
6L1217	32 c. f.	2½ in.	5	6L2377	15	$2.34	$3.30
6L1218	38 c. f.	2½ in.	5	6L2388	15	2.34	3.30

If by mail, postage extra, each, 18 cents.
See remarks about insured and registered mail at top of page.

IVER JOHNSON REVOLVERS. $4.80

32 and 38-Caliber.

70c and 90c per 100 for Cartridges. See page 631

Hammer the Hammer

This revolver is manufactured by the Iver Johnson Arms & Cycle Co., of Fitchburg, Mass., and is widely known and widely advertised as the "hammer the hammer" revolver. It is known as an automatic shell ejecting hinge revolver, so when you open the barrel at the top the shells are automatically extracted by the shell extractor. It is manufactured from the best material money can buy, fitted with a rifled steel barrel, fluted cylinder, front and rear sights, full nickel plated throughout, fancy rubber handle, may be fitted with pearl handle at the price quoted below; all working parts are tempered, case hardened and interchangeable, so if you accidentally break a part you can order it from the factory at a small cost; shoots cartridges caliber 32 S. & W., our No. 6L2377, or 38 S. & W., our No. 6L2388, and no other cartridges can be used in this revolver. It is safe, reliable and a good shooter.

Catalogue Number	Caliber	Length of Barrel	Finish	No. of Sh'ts	Shoots Cartridge No.	Weight, Ounces	Price
6L1253	32 c.f.	3 in.	Nickel Plated	5	6L2377	13	$4.80
6L1254	38 c.f.	3¼ in.	Nickel Plated	5	6L2388	18	$4.80
6L1255	32 c.f.	3 in.	Blued	5	6L2377	13	5.17
6L1256	38 c.f.	3¼ in.	Blued	5	6L2388	18	5.17

If fitted with pearl handle, extra.....................$1.00
Postage extra, 17 to 22 cents. See top of page about insured mail.

IVER JOHNSON HAMMERLESS REVOLVERS AT REDUCED PRICES.

$5.43

32 and 38-Caliber.

This illustration will give you an idea of the Iver Johnson Hammerless Revolver, manufactured by the Iver Johnson Arms & Cycle Works, Fitchburg, Mass., and is very similar to the Iver Johnson automatic hinge revolver, except it is made hammerless and is very popular as a pocket revolver.

Catalogue Number	Caliber	Length of Barrel	Finish	No. of Sh'ts	Shoots Cartridge No.	Weight, Ounces	Price
6L1263	32 c.f.	3 in.	Nickel Plated	5	6L2377	13	$5.43
6L1264	38 c.f.	3¼ in.	Nickel Plated	5	6L2388	18	$5.43
6L1265	32 c.f.	3 in.	Blued	5	6L2377	13	5.80
6L1266	38 c.f.	3¼ in.	Blued	5	6L2388	18	5.80

If fitted with pearl handle, extra.....................$1.00
Postage extra, 17 to 22c. Read top of page about insured mail.

IMPROVED BABY HAMMERLESS

$2.00

22-CALIBER REVOLVER.

Manufactured by Henry M. Kolb, Philadelphia, Pa. The smallest practical 22-caliber revolver made; can be carried in vest pocket, the same as a watch. Length over all is 4 inches. Folding trigger, 1¼-inch rifled steel barrel, fancy rubber stocks, fluted cylinder, chambered for seven cartridges, loaded from the side, full nickel plated and polished, shoots 22-caliber rim fire cartridges No. 6L2336.

Cat. No.	Caliber	Length of Barrel	Finish	No. of Sh'ts	Shoots Cartridge No.	Handle	Price
6L1249	22 r. f.	1½ in.	Nickel Plated	7	6L2336	Rubber	$2.00
6L1250	22 r. f.	1½ in.	Nickel Plated	7	6L2336	Pearl	2.60

If by mail, postage extra, 8 cents.

REMINGTON DERRINGERS.

$4.90

This is genuine Remington Double Derringer. Don't buy imitations. The Remington Double Derringer, 41-caliber short, rim fire, takes cartridge No. 6L2360; checkered rubber stock; length of barrel, 3 inches; entire length of pistol, 5 inches; nickel plated.

No. 6L1347 Price, nickel plated $4.90
No. 6L1348 Same blued, price.......
If fitted with pearl handle, extra.......$1.00
If by mail, postage extra, 17 cents.

THE STEVENS' TIP UP PISTOL, $2.45

22-CALIBER CARTRIDGES, 20c PER 100. SEE PAGE 631.

$2.45

22-caliber only. 3½-inch barrel.

Stevens' Single Shot Pistol. Tip up barrel, nickel plated finish, 3½-inch blued steel barrel, 22-caliber only, rim fire. No better material put in rifles. A fine target pistol. Rifled barrel and well made throughout.

No. 6L1343 For 22-caliber short cartridge No. 6L2336.
Price........$2.45
Postage extra, 15c.

STEVENS' DIAMOND MODEL TARGET PISTOL.

22-CALIBER CARTRIDGES, 20 CENTS PER 100. SEE PAGE 631

$4.06

The Celebrated Stevens' Target Pistol, the best pistol made for fine close shooting. It has fine blued barrel, nickel plated frame, rosewood stock, 6-inch tip up barrel; fitted with fine globe or open target sights, 22-caliber, rim fire. Shoots either 22 long rifle or 22 short cartridges; good for 50 yards, 22-caliber, 6-inch barrel.

No. 6L1344 Diamond model, globe and peep sights. Price.................$4.04
No. 6L1345 The same pistol, but with open sights. Price.......(If by mail, postage extra, 15c).....$4.06

NEW MODEL HARRINGTON & RICHARDSON 22-CALIBER REVOLVERS.

$4.80

This revolver is made by the Harrington & Richardson Co., Worcester, Mass., and is known as the Premier Small Frame Model, being the very latest production in a 22-caliber revolver. The frame is small, neat and nicely balanced. This revolver is made of the same high quality as all other Harrington & Richardson revolvers, is well finished, the barrel is finely rifled, the cylinder is very neatly fluted, self cocking, automatic shell extractor. We can furnish this revolver with 3-inch or 5-inch barrel, nickel plated or blued, at the prices as given below. This revolver shoots 22 short, 22 long or 22 long rifle cartridges, either black or smokeless powder.

Cat. No.	Caliber	Length of Barrel	Finish	No. of Shots	Shoots Cartridge No.	Price, with Rubber Stocks	Price, with Pearl Stocks
6L1370	22 r. f.	3 inches	Nick'l	7	6L2336 6L2535	$4.80	$5.80
6L1371	22 r. f.	3 inches	Blued	7	6L2338 6L2340	5.12	6.10

5-INCH BARREL

REDUCED TO $5.32

Same revolver as above, fitted with 5-inch barrel.

Cat. No.	Caliber	Length of Barrel	Finish	No. of Shots	Shoots Cartridge No.	Price, with Rubber Stocks	Price, with Pearl Stocks
6L1374	22 r. f.	5 inches	Nick'l	7	6L2336 6L2535	$5.32	$6.35
6L1375	22 r. f.	5 inches	Blued	7	6L2338 6L2340	5.68	6.75

Target Stocks, 50 cents extra.

If by mail, postage extra, 22 cents. See top of page for insured mail.

HARRINGTON & RICHARDSON TARGET PISTOL

22-CALIBER

5-INCH BARREL

This is the Premier Model Pistol, same as No. 6L1374 above described, 22-caliber, 5-inch barrel, fitted with special target grips. These grips are full, large sized, 1 inch longer than the regular grip, 1⅜ inches wide at butt, making a large, full, hand fitting grip, making an excellent revolver for target practice.

No. 6L1376 22-caliber, 5-inch, nickeled, 7 shots. Price, with target stocks..........$5.75

Target grips can be fitted on any of the regular Harrington & Richardson Automatic Revolvers at an additional charge of 50 cents.

H. & R. AUTOMATIC REVOLVERS.

70 AND 90 CENTS PER 100 FOR CARTRIDGES. SEE PAGE 631.

32 and 38-Caliber.

OUR $4.80 H. & R. AUTOMATIC REVOLVER.

Hinge Revolvers are not intended for smokeless powder.

This revolver is manufactured by the Harrington & Richardson Arms Co., of Worcester, Mass., one of the oldest revolver manufacturers in the United States and is known as the H. & R. Automatic Shell Ejecting Hinge Revolver. It is made from first class material throughout; has a steel rifled barrel, front and rear sights, fluted cylinder; all working parts are tempered, case hardened and interchangeable, so that if you accidentally break one of them it may be replaced at a small cost by writing to the manufacturers. Full nickel plated or blued steel finish throughout, fitted with fancy hard rubber handle. A good, safe, reliable revolver, which takes the 32 S. & W. cartridge, our No. 6L2377, or the 38 S. & W. cartridge, our No. 6L2388. The 32-caliber is 6-shot and the 38-caliber is 5-shot and no other cartridges will fit this revolver, so if you order cartridges with the revolver, be sure to state that the cartridges are for this revolver.

Catalogue Number	Caliber	Length of Barrel	Finish	No. of Sh'ts	Shoots Cartridge	Weight, Ounces	Price
6L1385	32 c. f.	3¼ in.	Nickel Plated	6	6L2377	18½	$4.80
6L1386	38 c. f.	3¼ in.	Nickel Plated	5	6L2388	18½	$4.80
6L1387	32 c. f.	3¼ in.	Blued Steel	6	6L2377	18½	5.12
6L1388	38 c. f.	3¼ in.	Blued Steel	5	6L2388	18½	5.12

Pearl handle on above revolvers, extra..............$1.20
If by mail, postage extra, 20 cents.
See top of page for insured mail.

44-CALIBER FRONTIER REVOLVERS.

$3.75

Takes Cartridge 6T2409

This revolver is known as the imported Frontier Revolver, shoots the 44-40 caliber cartridge, and is the only low priced revolver taking this cartridge. We cannot recommend this revolver as highly as we can the Colt's revolver, for it is a much cheaper revolver, consequently not so good, but it is the only cheap revolver which we can buy that shoots the 44-40 cartridge. It is made with a solid frame, as shown in the illustration, has 5½-inch barrel, is a 6-shooter; fancy rubber handle, full nickel plated or blued steel finish throughout, and for a person who does not do very much shooting, this revolver will probably answer the purpose of a large caliber, low priced revolver, but if you are so situated that you do considerable shooting, we recommend by all means that you purchase a Colt's revolver, either the Single Action Army or the Bisley Model, which are built for hard use.

Catalog Number	Caliber	No. of Shots	Finish	Length of Barrel	Price
6T1434	44-40	6	Nickeled	5½ in.	$3.75
6T1436	44-40	6	Blued	5½ in.	3.95

If registered mail shipment, postage extra, 42 cents. Insured mail, 45 cents.

REMINGTON DERRINGERS.

$5.00

This is genuine Remington Double Derringer. Don't buy imitations. The Remington Double Derringer, 41-caliber short, rim fire, takes cartridge No. 6T2360; checkered rubber stock; length of barrel, 3 inches; entire length of pistol, 5 inches; nickel plated.

No. 6T1447 Price, nickel plated **$5.00**
No. 6T1448 Same blued, price ....
If fitted with pearl handle, extra $1.00
If mail shipment, postage extra, 17 cents.

OUR IMPROVED RIFLE REVOLVER STOCK.

75c

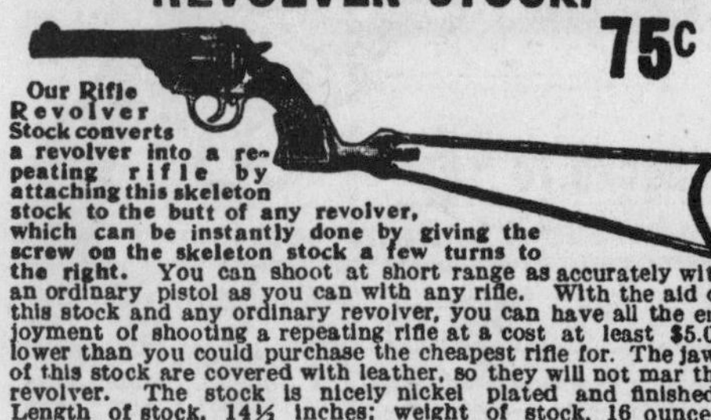

Our Rifle Revolver Stock converts a revolver into a repeating rifle by attaching this skeleton stock to the butt of any revolver, which can be instantly done by giving the screw on the skeleton stock a few turns to the right. You can shoot at short range as accurately with an ordinary pistol as you can with any rifle. With the aid of this stock and any ordinary revolver, you can have all the enjoyment of shooting a repeating rifle at a cost at least $5.00 lower than you could purchase the cheapest rifle for. The jaws of this stock are covered with leather, so they will not mar the revolver. The stock is nicely nickel plated and finished. Length of stock, 14½ inches; weight of stock, 16 ounces. This stock will not take a Colt's Automatic Pistol on account of the magazine in the handle of this pistol.

No. 6T1488 Revolver Rifle Stock. Price, for stock only **75c**
If mail shipment, postage extra, 20 cents; insured mail, 25 cents.

GENUINE SMITH & WESSON REVOLVERS

22-CALIBER SMITH & WESSON SIDE EJECTING REVOLVERS

$11.00

This revolver is double action, has fluted cylinder, rifled steel barrel, rebounding hammer, rubber handle, blued steel or nickel plated finish; made in 22-caliber, taking rim fire cartridges. This is the latest Smith & Wesson revolver, and the highest grade 22-caliber revolver made.

Catalog Number	Caliber	Length of Barrel	Finish	No. of Sh'ts	Shoots Cartridge No.	Wgt. Oz.	Price
6T1700	22 Rim	3½ in.	Nickel	7	6T2336 or 6T2338	10	$11.00
6T1701	22 Rim	3½ in.	Blued	7	6T2336 or 6T2338	10	$11.00

If fitted with pearl handle, extra 90c
If registered mail shipment, postage extra, 27 cents.
Weight, packed for shipment, about 1 pound.

S. & W. SIDE EJECTING REVOLVERS.

32 or 38 Caliber.

The Side Ejecting Smith & Wesson Revolver is self cocking, and being the side ejecting type, makes a strong, substantial revolver. It is center fire, 6-shot, with solid frame, swing-out cylinder. This revolver is Smith & Wesson's latest creation and is a revolver that is built for business. It will withstand hard usage. They are highly recommended for target shooting, and made in blued steel or nickel plated finish, fitted with rubber handle.

Catalog No.	Caliber	Length Barrel	Finish	No. of Shots	Shoots Cart'ge	Weight	Price
6T1704	32 c.f.	4¼ in.	Nickel	6-shot	6T2376	19 oz.	$12.99
6T1705	32 c.f.	4¼ in.	Blued	6-shot	6T2376	19 oz.	
6T1706	32 c.f.	6 in.	Nickel	6-shot	6T2376	20 oz.	13.00
6T1707	32 c.f.	6 in.	Blued	6-shot	6T2376	20 oz.	
6T1714	38 c.f.	5 in.	Nickel	6-shot	6T2392	30 oz.	14.98
6T1715	38 c.f.	5 in.	Blued	6-shot	6T2392	30 oz.	
6T1716	38 c.f.	6½ in.	Nickel	6-shot	6T2392	32 oz.	15.00
6T1717	38 c.f.	6½ in.	Blued	6-shot	6T2392	32 oz.	

FIRST QUALITY PEARL HANDLE ON THE ABOVE, EXTRA. 32-caliber, $1.00; 38-caliber $2.00

If registered mail shipment, postage extra, 32-caliber, 37 cents; 38-caliber, 50 cents.

We cannot furnish Smith & Wesson Revolvers for 38-40 and 32-20 cartridges.

SEE OUR LINE OF HOLSTERS AND BELTS ON PAGE 850. OUR HAND CARVED HOLSTERS ARE THE FINEST IN THE COUNTRY.

S. & W. DOUBLE ACTION REVOLVERS.

$12.00

These revolvers are warranted genuine Smith & Wesson. All are self cocking and double action, with automatic shell extractor, finely rifled steel barrel, fine rubber stocks, nickel plated or blued steel finish. Made of the finest material that money can buy and the workmanship is equal to that of any ordinary watch. If you want the best work for your money, buy a Smith & Wesson.

Catalog No.	Caliber	Length Barrel	Finish	No. of Shots	Shoots Cart'ge	Weight	Price
6T1724	32 c.f.	3½ in.	Nickel	5-shot	6T2377	13 oz.	$12.00
6T1725	32 c.f.	3½ in.	Blued	5-shot	6T2377	13 oz.	
6T1726	32 c.f.	6 in.	Nickel	5-shot	6T2377	15 oz.	12.00
6T1727	32 c.f.	6 in.	Blued	5-shot	6T2377	15 oz.	
6T1732	38 c.f.	4 in.	Nickel	5-shot	6T2388	18 oz.	12.99
6T1733	38 c.f.	4 in.	Blued	5-shot	6T2388	18 oz.	
6T1734	38 c.f.	5 in.	Nickel	5-shot	6T2388	19 oz.	13.00
6T1735	38 c.f.	5 in.	Blued	5-shot	6T2388	19 oz.	

FIRST QUALITY PEARL HANDLE, EXTRA $1.00
If registered mail shipment, postage extra, 32-caliber, 32 cents; 38-caliber, 37 cents.

SMITH & WESSON HAMMERLESS.

$13.00

Made by Smith & Wesson, Springfield, Mass. Latest type, new model hammerless, automatic shell ejector, patent safety catch, self cocking rebounding hammer, double action, blued steel or nickel plated finish, fitted with rubber handle. This is positively the best hammerless revolver made.

Improved Safety Trigger Locking Device which automatically releases as trigger is pulled. Accidental discharge impossible.

Catalog No.	Caliber	Length Barrel	Finish	No. of Shots	Shoots Cart'ge	Weight	Price
6T1756	32 c.f.	3½ in.	Nickel	5-shot	6T2377	15 oz.	$13.00
6T1757	32 c.f.	3½ in.	Blued	5-shot	6T2377	15 oz.	
6T1762	38 c.f.	4 in.	Nickel	5-shot	6T2388	18 oz.	13.99
6T1763	38 c.f.	4 in.	Blued	5-shot	6T2388	18 oz.	

FIRST QUALITY PEARL HANDLE, EXTRA $1.00
If registered mail shipment, postage extra, 32-caliber, 32 cents; 38-caliber, 39 cents. See our prices on cartridges.

LOADED SHOTGUN SHELLS $1.48

BLACK POWDER. 10, 12, 16 AND 20-GAUGE.

AT $1.48 PER HUNDRED we furnish the highest quality black powder loaded shotgun shells. No better black powder shells made at any price.

POWDER.

IN THESE BLACK POWDER SHELLS we use a special black powder of a hard grain, which burns rapidly and leaves far less residue in the barrel than any other black powder. It has enormous penetration with a minimum breech pressure, and is really the cleanest, strongest and safest black powder ever used in shotgun ammunition.

GUARANTEE.

WE ABSOLUTELY GUARANTEE every loaded shotgun shell we sell against misfire, hang fire or blow backs. We guarantee the maximum of penetration and the greatest possible uniformity in pattern. We further guarantee that our shells will give better satisfaction and are better value than those you can buy elsewhere.

OUR LINE OF BLACK POWDER LOADED SHELLS.

Why not get your friends to join with you and buy shells by the case or 1,000 and ship by freight? It will save you money on freight charges, besides they are cheaper in case lots.

OUR CASE PRICE is for one size and one gauge in a case, just as it comes to us from the factory. We cannot sell less than a case at the case price, nor can we assort the case with different loads.

A case of 500 shells, 12-gauge, weighs about 65 pounds.
A case of 500 shells, 10-gauge, weighs about 75 pounds.
A case of 500 shells, 16-gauge, weighs about 53 pounds.
Our terms on loaded shells are cash with order.

We have taken great pains to select loads which are suitable for most purposes and these loads should meet all requirements. WE DO NOT SEND SHELLS C. O. D.

12-GAUGE

LOADED WITH SPECIAL BLACK POWDER.

Catalog No.	Drams of Powder	Oz. of Shot	Size of Drop Shot	Price per Box of 25 Shells	Price per 100 Shells	Price per case of 500 Shells	Price per 1000 Shells
6T2006 6T2008	3	1	6 8	38c	$1.48	$7.05	$14.10
6T2014 6T2016	3	1⅛	4 6	40c	1.57	7.45	14.90
6T2024 6T2025 6T2026	3¼	1⅛	4 5 6	41c	1.61	7.65	15.30
6T2034 6T2036	3½	1⅛	4 6	42c	1.65	7.85	15.70
6T2040B 6T2044	3¾ 3½	1⅛	BB 4Bk	48c	1.89	9.05	18.10

10-GAUGE

LOADED WITH SPECIAL BLACK POWDER, $1.75.

Catalog No.	Drams of Powder	Oz. of Shot	Size of Drop Shot	Price per Box of 25 Shells	Price per 100 Shells	Price per case of 500 Shells	Price per 1000 Shells
6T2072 6T2076 6T2077	4¼	1⅛	2 6 7	46c	$1.75	$8.25	$16.50
6T2079	5	1⅛	BB	50c	1.90	9.25	18.50

ALWAYS GIVE CATALOG NUMBER WHEN ORDERING.

16-GAUGE

LOADED WITH SPECIAL BLACK POWDER, $1.55.

Catalog No.	Drams of Powder	Oz. of Shot	Size of Drop Shot	Price per Box of 25 Shells	Price per 100 Shells	Price per case of 500 Shells	Price per 1000 Shells
6T2084 6T2086	2¾	1	4 6	40c	$1.55	$7.50	$15.00

ALWAYS GIVE CATALOG NUMBER WHEN ORDERING.

20-GAUGE

LOADED WITH SPECIAL BLACK POWDER, $1.80.

Catalog No.	Drams of Powder	Oz. of Shot	Size of Drop Shot	Price per Box of 25 Shells	Price per 100 Shells	Price per case of 500 Shells	Price per 1000 Shells
6T2096 6T2098	2½	⅞	6 8	46c	$1.80	$8.80	$17.60

MALLARD SMOKELESS LOADED SHELLS, 12-GAUGE ONLY, $1.62 Per 100.

An excellent shell, second only to our Pointer, shown on the opposite page 842, guaranteed equal to shells sold throughout the country at prices ranging from $2.23 to $3.00 per hundred. Guaranteed against misfire and hangfire, and to have maximum penetration and to give satisfaction. Can be furnished in 12-gauge only, and only in the loads specified below.

Prices on Mallard Smokeless Loaded Shotgun Shells, 12-Gauge Only.

Give catalog number and load number when ordering.

Catalog Number	Load No.	Drams of Powder	Wt. of Shot	Size of Shot	PRICE 100	Case of 500	1,000
6T2100 Drop Shot	3014	3	1 oz.	4	$1.62	$8.00	$16.00
	3016	3	1 oz.	6	1.62	8.00	16.00
	3018	3	1 oz.	8	1.62	8.00	16.00
	3184	3	1⅛ oz.	4	1.75	8.60	17.20
	3186	3	1⅛ oz.	6	1.75	8.60	17.20
	3484	3¼	1⅛ oz.	4	1.85	9.00	18.00
	3486	3¼	1⅛ oz.	6	1.85	9.00	18.00
6T2103 Chilled Shot	C3186	3	1⅛ oz.	6 Chilled	1.90	9.32	18.64
	C3187	3	1⅛ oz.	7½ Chilled	1.90	9.32	18.64

A Case of 500 shells weighs about 65 pounds.

GUNS REPAIRED.

We have a completely equipped gun repair shop, employ a corps of experienced gunsmiths and are in a position to do all kinds of repairing on guns, rifles and revolvers. Barrels reblued and rebrowned, guns restocked, revolvers renickeled and mechanism repaired at lowest prices consistent with high grade workmanship.

We issue a booklet containing prices of repair parts for all standard makes of fire arms, also prices on parts in the rough, and if interested, we shall be pleased to send you this free booklet of gun repairs.

POINTER LONG BRASS SMOKELESS SHOTGUN SHELLS

THE LONG BRASS CUP PROTECTS THE SHELLS, KEEPS OUT MOISTURE AND MAKES THEM BETTER, STRONGER, SAFER.

WE ABSOLUTELY GUARANTEE these shells against misfire and hangfire and to have penetration and pattern equal to any shell made, regardless of name or price. If you purchase a case of the Pointer Shells, and, after trying a box of 25, for any reason find them unsatisfactory, return the remaining 475 shells to us at our expense, and we will return you the price you paid for the 500 shells, together with the freight charges.

POINTER SHELLS are the only shells sold under so liberal a guarantee. We have so thoroughly tested out the quality of these shells, as compared with other shells, that we know we are not assuming any risk in making this guarantee and trial offer, as there is no question whatsoever about your being more than pleased with the shells and finding them to be even better than we claim and better than any shells you have ever used.

BULK SMOKELESS POWDER imported from England is used in loading the Pointer Shell. We had dozens of American powders to select from, such as are used in all other makes of shells, but we preferred this English powder, although it is far more expensive than the ordinary American smokeless, the duty and freight charges alone amounting to almost as much as the price of some of the cheaper domestic powders. We were determined to furnish a smokeless shell with which there could be absolutely no fault found, and assuming that the loading machinery is up to date, everything is then dependent on the powder. Pattern, penetration, misfire and hangfire are all dependent on the quality of the powder used, and we were determined that none of these complaints should exist in our 1910 Pointer Shell, so contracted for the very best powder obtainable. These shells are primed with a No. 3 nitro primer set in a battery cup, which overcomes all danger of blowbacks and loss of gases and absolutely insures instantaneous ignition and discharge. The long brass cup on the Pointer Shell gives it a great advantage over all ordinary smokeless shells. This long brass cup more than doubles the strength of the shell and absolutely overcomes all danger of cut-offs and swelling, making it the ideal shell for use in repeating guns. If you have a Winchester, Stevens, Marlin or Remington pump gun, you will obtain the best results by using the Pointer Long Brass Smokeless Shells.

Cheyenne, Wyo.
Sears, Roebuck and Co., Chicago, Ill.

Gentlemen:—Received order for Improved Pointer Long Base Shells O. K., 500 of them, and am very much satisfied with them. I have tried nearly every shell made. I gave the Pointer Shell, No. 6 shot drop, a fair trial. I shot into a bunch of wild ducks 90 yards away and killed three with the first shot. I have a Winchester shotgun, 12-gauge. I shall never use any other shell than the Pointer.

Very truly yours,
PETER HANSEN.

Franklin Park, Ill.
Sears, Roebuck and Co., Chicago, Ill.,

Gentlemen:—I have just finished an exhaustive test of your Pointer Shotgun Shells, and for closeness of pattern and unusual penetration, they are the peer of any shell I have ever used. This, together with their cleanliness, makes them the equal of any other shell on the market, and at 45 cents to 50 cents per box, a saving of from one-fourth to one-third the cost.

Yours very truly,
BYRON E. BEEBE.
(Member Chicago Gun Club.)

PRICES ON POINTER SMOKELESS SHELLS

ALWAYS GIVE CATALOG NUMBER

Please notice we furnish only one size and one load in a case, just as they come to us from the factory, at the case price. Order by catalog number in full.

WEIGHT OF SHELLS IN CASE.

A case of 500 shells, 12-gauge, weighs about 65 pounds.
A case of 500 shells, 10-gauge, weighs about 75 pounds.
A case of 500 shells, 16-gauge, weighs about 53 pounds.

POINTER SMOKELESS SHELLS, LOADED WITH DROP SHOT.

Always give catalog number and state size of shot load wanted.

12-GAUGE LOADED WITH SMOKELESS POWDER.

Catalog No.	Grains of Smokeless Powder Equal to	Wt. of shot	Size of Drop Shot	Price, per Box of 25 Shells	Price, per 100 Shells	Price, per Case of 500 Shells	Price, per 1,000 Shells
6T1920	3 Drams	1 Oz.	No. 4, No. 6, No. 8	46c	$1.84	$9.00	18.00
6T1920	3 Drams	1 1/8 Oz.	No. 2, No. 4, No. 5, No. 6, No. 7, No. 8	48c	$1.92	$9.50	19.00
6T1920	3 1/4 Drams	1 1/8	No. 4, No. 6	51c	$2.04	10.00	20.00

Always give catalog number and state size of shot load wanted.

10-GAUGE LOADED WITH SMOKELESS POWDER.

Catalog No.	Grains of Smokeless Powder Equal to	Wt. of shot	Size of Drop Shot	Price, per Box of 25 Shells	Price, per 100 Shells	Price, per Case of 500 Shells	Price, per 1,000 Shells
6T1921	3 1/4 Drams	1 1/8 Oz.	No. 2, No. 4, No. 6, No. 8	56c	$2.24	11.00	22.00

16-GAUGE LOADED WITH SMOKELESS POWDER.

Catalog No.	Grains of Smokeless Powder equal to	Oz. of shot	Size of Drop Shot	Price, per Box of 25 Shells	Price, per 100 Shells	Price, per Box of 500 Shells	Price, per 1,000 Shells
6T1922	2 1/2 Drams	1	No. 4, No. 6, No. 8	49c	$1.96	$9.60	19.20

POINTER SMOKELESS SHELLS, LOADED WITH CHILLED SHOT.

Shells loaded with smokeless powder and chilled shot give better penetration and more even patterns than drop shot. Loaded in 12-gauge only. The No. 7½ shot is our celebrated trap load. Order by catalog number and state size of shot load wanted.

12-GAUGE LOADED WITH SMOKELESS POWDER.

Catalog No.	Grains Smokeless Powder equal to	Oz. of shot	Size of Chilled Shot	Price, per Box of 25 Shells	Price, per 100 Shells	Price, per Case of 500 Shells	Price, per 1,000 Shells
6T1923	3 Drams	1 1/8	No. 4, No. 6, No. 7½, No. 8	53c	$2.12	10.40	20.80
6T1923	3 1/4 Drams	1 1/8	No. 4, No. 6	55c	$2.20	10.80	21.60
6T1923	3 1/4 Drams	1 1/4	No. 7½	57c	$2.28	11.20	22.40

Always give catalog number and state size of shot load wanted.

8-GAUGE HAND LOADED WITH SMOKELESS POWDER.

Catalog No.	Grains Smokeless Powder equal to	Oz. of shot	Size of Drop Shot	Price, per Box of 25 Shells	Price, per 100 Shells	Price, per Case of 500 Shells	Price, per 1,000 Shells
6T1924	5 1/2 Drams	1 3/4	BB	$1.37	$5.48	$25.55	$51.10

ALWAYS GIVE CATALOG NUMBER AND STATE SIZE OF SHOT LOAD WANTED.

46c A BOX OF 25

$1.84 A HUNDRED

$9.00 A CASE OF 500

This illustration shows one of our Pointer Smokeless Shells cut open and gives you an idea of the high grade manner in which these shells are loaded. The shells are all loaded by the most improved automatic machinery. One shell is exactly like another. We claim for our Pointer Shells more uniform loading than any other shells made. Therefore, in shooting Pointer Smokeless Shells you are guaranteed more uniform results than could be obtained through the use of any other make of shells.

PAINT. THE PAINT PAGES OF OUR BIG GENERAL CATALOG SAVE YOU MONEY. INVESTIGATE.

FREIGHT CHARGES ON A CASE OF SHELLS.

We herewith give you the approximate freight charges on a case of 500 shells, weighing 65 pounds, to the various central points in the East, Middle West, South, Southwest, West and North. By taking the town nearest to where you live, you can approximately determine what the charges would be on a case of shells shipped to your town. You will note that after adding the freight charges to our prices on shells, you will still effect a great saving as against what you would have to pay elsewhere.

FREIGHT CHARGES ON 500 LOADED SHELLS, WEIGHT, 65 POUNDS.

From Chicago to—	Freight Charges	From Chicago to—	Freight Charges
Denver, Colo.	$1.25	Kansas City, Mo.	$0.45
Atlanta, Ga.	1.33	Albany, N. Y.	.72
Indianapolis, Ind.	.32	Pittsburg, Penn.	.45
Dubuque, Iowa	.25	Memphis, Tenn.	.85
New Orleans, La.	1.10	Dallas, Texas	1.45
Detroit, Mich.	.37	Houston, Texas	1.45
Minneapolis, Minn.	.40	Milwaukee, Wis.	.25
St. Paul, Minn.	.40		

THE POINTER LONG BRASS SHELL.

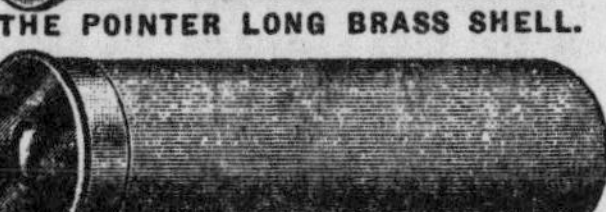

AN ORDINARY SMOKELESS SHELL.

These illustrations show the difference between the Pointer Smokeless Shell and the ordinary shell sold throughout the country at $2.25 a hundred and upward. Note the long brass reinforcement on our Pointer Shell against the short cup on the shells offered in competition. The advantages are many and it will pay you to read what we say about them.

COLT'S NEW NAVY REVOLVER.

Illustration showing the revolver open. 38 and 41-caliber.

Colt's New Navy side ejecting, double action revolver has been adopted by the U. S. navy, and every one must pass a rigid inspection and test. This Colt's New Navy double action, self cocking, side shell ejecting revolver is fitted with rubber stock, beautifully finished, and made of finest material, length about 12½ inches; six shooter; weight, 2 lbs.; blued steel finish. The 38-caliber takes cartridges No. 6E2392, and the 41-caliber takes cartridges No. 6E2400 or No. 6E2401.

This revolver is very similar to the New Army, differing slightly in the handle.

Catalogue Number	Caliber	Length of Barrel	Finish	No. of Sh'ts	Shoots Cartridge No.	Weight Ounces	Price
6E1521	38 c.f.	4½ in.	Blued	6	6E2392	32	$13.90
6E1523	38 c.f.	6 in.	Blued	6	6E2392	32	
6E1525	41 c.f.	4½ in.	Blued	6	6E2400 or 6E2401	32	13.90
6E1527	41 c.f.	6 in.	Blued	6		32	

If fitted with pearl stocks, extra.........................$2.75

If by mail, postage extra, 40 cents.

COLT'S DOUBLE ACTION REVOLVER.

38 and 41-Caliber.

Colt's Double Action, sliding side ejector. Every one warranted. 38 or 41-caliber. It is a 6-shooter using center fire cartridges, made of best revolver steel throughout, fitted with rubber handles, blued steel finish. This is the old reliable Colt double action which has been popular for many years. The 38-caliber takes cartridges No. 6E2392, and the 41-caliber takes No. 6E2400 or No. 6E2401.

Catalogue Number	Caliber	Length of Barrel	Finish	No. of Sh'ts	Shoots Cartridge No.	Weight Ounces	Price
6E1531	38 c.f.	4½ in.	Blued	6	6E2392	28	$11.60
6E1533	38 c.f.	6 in.	Blued	6	6E2392	28	
6E1537	41 c.f.	6 in.	Blued	6	6E2400 or 6E2401	28	12.95

If fitted with pearl stocks, extra. $2.75

If by mail, postage extra, each, 40 cents.

COLT'S NEW ARMY MODEL 1892.

38 and 41-Caliber.

Colt's New Army Model 1892. Double action, self cocking, side ejecting revolver. Weight, 2 pounds, 6-shooter, 38 or 41-caliber, length of barrel, 4½ or 6 inches. Blued steel finish, rubber handles. The 38-caliber takes cartridges No. 6E2392 and the 41-caliber takes No. 6E2400 or No. 6E2401. This revolver is very similar to the New Navy, differing slightly in the handle.

Catalogue Number	Caliber	Length of Barrel	Finish	No. of Sh'ts	Shoots Cartridge No.	Wgt. Oz.	Price
6E1541	38 c.f.	4½ in.	Blued	6	6E2392	32	$13.90
6E1543	38 c.f.	6 in.	Blued	6	6E2392	32	
6E1545	41 c.f.	4½ in.	Blued	6	6E2400 or 6E2401	32	13.90
6E1547	41 c.f.	6 in.	Blued	6		32	

If fitted with pearl stocks, extra.............................$2.75

If by mail, postage extra, each, 40 cents.

WE RECOMMEND THE FOLLOWING CALIBERS OF COLT'S REVOLVERS:

For small game, 32 short, 32 long and 41 short.
For medium size game, 32-20, 38 short; 38 long and 41 long.
For deer, bear, etc., 44-40 and 45-caliber.
For quantity of powder and weight of bullet in each above caliber, see central fire cartridges, loaded with black powder, on another page.

COLT'S NEW SERVICE DOUBLE ACTION REVOLVER.

45-Caliber.

The New Service Double Action, side ejecting revolvers, have jointless solid frame, combined with simultaneous ejector, using 45-caliber Colt's double action cartridges; 7½-inch barrel, rubber handles, blued steel finish only. Weight, about 2 pounds. They are powerful shooters and take cartridges No. 6E2413.

Catalogue Number	Caliber	Length of Barrel	Finish	No. of Sh'ts	Shoots Cartridge N	Wgt. Oz.	Price
6E1563	45 c.f.	7½ in.	Blued Steel	6	6E2413	36	$16.20

If fitted with pearl stocks, extra.............................$5.50

If by mail, postage extra, 44 cents.

SEND 10 CENTS for our Booklet of Useful Information to Shooters. It tells how gun barrels burst and gives interesting data to shooters.

COLT'S SINGLE ACTION "COWBOY" FRONTIER ARMY.

32, 41, 44 and 45-Caliber.

This is the old reliable Cowboys' Gun, and our price is $13.90 for all calibers and length of barrels; furnished in blued steel finish only. Colt's single action army revolver is a 6-shooter, rubber stock, solid frame, the best quality of steel and finish; warranted perfect and accurate in every detail. Barrel 5½ or 7½ inches: entire length, 12½ inches; 32, 41, 44 or 45-caliber, as desired. We can furnish these in blued finish only.

Catalogue Number	Caliber C. F.	Length of Barrel	Finish	No. of Sh'ts	Shoots Cartridge No.	Wgt. Oz.	Price
6E1571	32-20	5½ in.	Blued Steel	6	6E2384	40	$13.90
6E1573	32-20	7½ in.		6	6E2384	40	
6E1575	41 c.f.	5½ in.	Blued Steel	6	6E2401	40	13.90
6E1577	41 c.f.	7½ in.		6	6E2401	40	
6E1579	44-40	5½ in.	Blued Steel	6	6E2409	40	13.90
6E1581	44-40	7½ in.		6	6E2409	40	
6E1583	45 c.f.	5½ in.	Blued Steel	6	6E2413	40	13.90
6E1585	45 c.f.	7½ in.		6	6E2413	40	

Pearl stocks on any of the above revolvers, extra......$4.00

If by mail, postage extra, 44 cents.

Nickel Plated Colt's Revolvers are not carried in stock, but we ship these from factory. Send cash in full with order, as we cannot send C. O. D.

COLT'S SPECIAL PEARL HANDLE REVOLVER.

SINGLE ACTION FRONTIER.

This is our special. Cowboy's Six Shooter with pearl handles. The right handle has an Ox Head carved in raised design and makes a handsome revolver. This illustration is engraved from a photograph of the revolver and will give you some idea of its appearance. Made in blued steel finish only. We handle these regularly in 32-20 and 44-40-calibers but can furnish them on special order in caliber 41 c. f. or 45 Colt's c. f. with 5½ or 7½-inch barrel at $20.00 each. Weight. 41 ounces. When ordering, say which length barrel you prefer.

Catalogue Number	Caliber C. F.	Length of Barrel	Finish	No. of Sh'ts	Shoots Cartridge No.	Wgt. Oz.	Price
6E1587	32-20	5½ in.	Blued Steel	6	6E2384	41	$20.00
6E1589	32-20	7½ in.		6	6E2384	41	
6E1591	44-40	5½ in.	Blued Steel	6	6E2409	41	20.00
6E1593	44-40	7½ in.		6	6E2409	41	

Above may be had in 41 and 45-calibers or in blued steel to special order, cash with order.

If by mail, postage extra, 46 cents.

COLT'S SINGLE ACTION BISLEY MODEL.

The Colt's Bisley Model Revolver is patterned after the Colt's Single Action Army Revolver, but has a longer handle, a different shape hammer, and the lockwork is somewhat different, and it makes a good smooth working revolver. The frame is case hardened, and the barrel and cylinder are blued. This revolver embodies all the high grade workmanship of the famous Colt's revolvers. We carry this revolver regularly in 32-20 and 38-40 calibers, but can furnish it in 45 caliber to special order.

Catalogue Number	Caliber	Length of Barrel	Finish	No. of Sh'ts	Shoots Cartridge No.	Weight Ounces	Price
6E1610	32-20	5½ in.	Blued Steel	6	6E2384	40	$13.90
6E1611	32-20	7½ in.		6	6E2384	40	
6E1612	38-40	5½ in.	Blued Steel	6	6E2396	40	$13.90
6E1613	38-40	7½ in.		6	6E2396	40	

If by mail, postage extra, 45 cents.

GENUINE SMITH & WESSON REVOLVERS.

OUR 22-CALIBER SMITH & WESSON SIDE EJECTING REVOLVER, $10.00.

This revolver is double action, has fluted cylinder, rifled steel barrel, rebounding hammer, rubber stock, blued steel or nickel plated finish; made in 22-caliber, taking rim fire cartridges Nos. 6E2336 or 6E2338; weighs about 10 ounces and is 7-shot. This is the latest model Smith & Wesson Revolver, and the highest grade 22-caliber revolver made.

Catalogue Number	Caliber	Length of Barrel	Finish	No. of Sh'ts	Shoots Cartridge No.	Wgt. Oz.	Price
6E1700	22 Rim	3½ in.	Nickeled	7	6E2336	10	$10.00
6E1701		3½ in.	Blued	7	6E2338	10	

If fitted with pearl handles, extra...........................90c

If by mail, postage extra, 14 cents.

GENUINE SMITH & WESSON REVOLVERS.

S. & W. SIDE EJECTING 32 AND 38-CALIBER, $12.00 AND $14.00.

This is double action and center fire, 6-shot, with solid frame, swing-out cylinder and side ejecting mechanism; 32-caliber has 4¼ and 6-inch barrel, the 38-caliber has 5 and 6½-inch barrel; blued steel or nickel plated finish; using 32 S. & W. long No. 6E2376 and 38-caliber long Colt DA cartridge No. 6E2392. This revolver is Smith & Wesson's latest creation and is a revolver that is built for business. It will withstand hard usage and the 38-caliber has a movable firing pin on the nose of the hammer, which absolutely closes the firing pin hole and prevents any possible gas from going back of the frame. They are highly recommended for target shooting, and made in blued steel or nickel plated finish, fitted with rubber handles.

Catalogue No.	Caliber	Length of Barrel	Finish	No. of Shots	Shoots Cart'ge	Weight	Price
6E1704	32 c f	4½ in.	Nickel	6-shot	6E2376	19 oz.	$12.00
6E1705	32 c f	4½ in.	Blued	6-shot		19 oz.	
6E1706	32 c f	6 in.	Nickel	6-shot	6E2376	20 oz.	12.00
6E1707	32 c f	6 in.	Blued	6-shot		20 oz.	
6E1714	38 c f	5 in.	Nickel	6-shot	6E2392	30 oz.	14.00
6E1715	38 c f	5 in.	Blued	6-shot		30 oz.	
6E1716	38 c f	6½ in.	Nickel	6-shot	6E2392	32 oz.	14.00
6E1717	38 c f	6½ in.	Blued	6-shot		32 oz.	

FIRST QUALITY PEARL STOCKS ON THE ABOVE, EXTRA. 32-caliber, $1.00; 38-caliber..........................$2.00

If by mail, postage extra, 32-caliber, 25 cents; 38-caliber, 40c

We cannot furnish Smith & Wesson Revolvers for 38-40 cartridges.

S. & W. DOUBLE ACTION REVOLVERS.

These revolvers are warranted genuine Smith & Wesson. Manufactured by Smith & Wesson, Springfield, Mass. All are self cocking and double action, with automatic shell extractor, finely rifled steel barrel, fine rubber stocks, nickel plated or blued steel finish. Made of the finest material that money can buy and the workmanship is equal in finish to that of any ordinary watch. If you want the best work for your money buy a Smith & Wesson. The 32-caliber takes cartridge No. 6E2377 and the 38-caliber takes cartridge No. 6E2388.

Catalogue No.	Caliber	Length of Barrel	Finish	No. of Shots	Shoots Cart'ge	Weight	Price
6E1724	32 c f	3½ in.	Nickel	5-shot	6E2377	13 ozs.	$11.00
6E1725	32 c f	3½ in.	Blued	5-shot	6E2377	13 ozs.	
6E1726	32 c f	6 in.	Nickel	5-shot	6E2377	15 ozs.	11.00
6E1727	32 c f	6 in.	Blued	5-shot	6E2377	15 ozs.	
6E1730	38 c f	3¼ in.	Nickel	5-shot	6E2388	18 ozs.	12.00
6E1731	38 c f	3¼ in.	Blued	5-shot	6E2388	18 ozs.	
6E1732	38 c f	4 in.	Nickel	5-shot	6E2388	18 ozs.	12.00
6E1733	38 c f	4 in.	Blued	5-shot	6E2388	18 ozs.	
6E1734	38 c f	5 in.	Nickel	5-shot	6E2388	19 ozs.	12.00
6E1735	38 c f	5 in.	Blued	5-shot	6E2388	19 ozs.	
6E1736	38 c f	6 in.	Nickel	5-shot	6E2388	20 ozs.	12.00
6E1737	38 c f	6 in.	Blued	5-shot	6E2388	20 ozs.	

FIRST QUALITY PEARL STOCKS, EXTRA..........$1.00

If by mail or prepaid express, 32-caliber, 18 cents; 38-caliber, 24 cents.

SMITH & WESSON HAMMERLESS.

Made by Smith & Wesson, Springfield, Mass. Latest type new model hammerless, automatic shell ejector, patent safety catch, self locking rebounding locks, double action, blued steel or nickel plated finish, fitted with rubber handles. This is positively the best hammerless revolver made. "A thing of beauty is a joy forever." If you own one of these revolvers you are certain to own one of the best revolvers made and one which always has a market value. The 32-caliber takes cartridge No. 6E2377 and the 38-caliber takes cartridge No. 6E2388.

Catalogue No.	Caliber	Length of Barrel	Finish	No. of Shots	Shoots Cart'ge	Weight	Price
6E1756	32 c f	3½ in.	Nickel	5-shot	6E2377	15 oz.	$12.00
6E1757	32 c f	3½ in.	Blued	5-shot	6E2377	15 oz.	
6E1760	38 c f	3¼ in.	Nickel	5-shot	6E2388	17 oz.	13.00
6E1761	38 c f	3¼ in.	Blued	5-shot	6E2388	17 oz.	
6E1762	38 c f	4 in.	Nickel	5-shot	6E2388	18 oz.	13.00
6E1763	38 c f	4 in.	Blued	5-shot	6E2388	18 oz.	
6E1764	38 c f	5 in.	Nickel	5-shot	6E2388	19 oz.	13.00
6E1765	38 c f	5 in.	Blued	5-shot	6E2388	19 oz.	
6E1766	38 c f	6 in.	Nickel	5-shot	6E2388	19 oz.	13.00
6E1767	38 c f	6 in.	Blued	5-shot	6E2388	19 oz.	

FIRST QUALITY PEARL STOCKS, EXTRA..........$1.00

If by mail, postage extra 18 to 30 cents. ☞ See our prices on cartridges.

THE IMPORTED AUTOMATIC DOUBLE ACTION REVOLVER.

$4.35 AND $4.65

This illustration, engraved from a photograph by our artist, will give you some idea of the revolver. It is central fire and has 5½-inch barrel, finished in blued or nickel plated. Made in 44-40-caliber only. It is 6-shot, has rebounding hammer, rubber stock, weighs 35 ounces and is automatic shell ejecting. This revolver takes the same cartridge as the Winchester Rifle, 44-caliber (No. 6E2409), so that a man who has a 44-caliber rifle can use the same ammunition in both the rifle and this revolver. We have contracted for a large lot of these revolvers in order to get the price so we can sell them with our one small percentage of profit at these figures.

If by mail, postage extra, 45 cents.

If by registered mail, 45c extra.

Takes No. 6E2409 Cartridges.

Catalogue Number	Caliber C. F.	Length of Barrel	Finish	No. of Sh'ts	Shoots Cartridge No.	Weight, Ounces	Price
6E1780	44-40	5½ in.	Nickeled	6	6E2409	35	$4.35
6E1781	44-40	5½ in.	Blued	6	6E2409	35	4.65

FOR COMPLETE INDEX REFER TO PINK PAGES IN MIDDLE OF BOOK.

THE NEW IMPROVED POINTER LONG BASE SMOKELESS SHELLS REDUCED PRICES

$1.80 PER 100 | $8.50 PER CASE OF 500 | 45c PER BOX OF 25

TRIUMPH,
the New Smokeless Powder.

THE HIGHEST QUALITY SHOT-GUN SHELLS MADE.

GREATER PENETRATION,
BETTER TARGET,
MORE UNIFORM RESULTS

than in any smokeless powder shot-gun shell ever made, regardless of name, make or price.

THE NEW POINTER SHELL is entirely different from the old Pointer Shell. It is similar in name only. We have improved the old Pointer Shell over 100 per cent. The old Short Base Pointer Shell was a good shell, was a better shell than you could have obtained elsewhere for considerably more money, and with this in mind you will appreciate what an excellent shell this New Improved Long Base Pointer Shell is, and what wonderful value we are offering in these shells at $8.50 per case of 500 shells.

THE ADVANTAGES OF THE LONG BRASS CUP

THIS SPECIAL LONG BRASS CUP makes our Pointer Shell the safest shell to use. This cup of heavy brass, extending almost half the length of the entire shell, prevents bursting of shell and obviates all possibilities of the paper pulling away from the head, as occasionally occurs with the short cup shell. The long cup guards against blow-outs and obviates entirely the swelling of the shell after being shot and sticking in chamber, making this the ideal shell for repeating guns as well as all double and single barrel guns. Considering the construction of our Pointer Shells, this shell at 25 per cent more than our price would be the most economical shell to use, as it is so strongly constructed that it can be loaded far oftener than any other shell on the market.

THE PAPER IN OUR POINTER SHELLS is a strong, tough paper, especially made for this purpose, thoroughly waterproof, and is the very best that money can buy.

THIS PAPER is made for us on special contract, and is a far better paper than is ordinarily used. The paper is fully protected by the extra long brass cup, making cut-offs and blow-outs impossible, thereby making this shell particularly desirable for repeating shotguns. These shells operate better in repeating shotguns than any other shells. The primer used in these shells is a special, strong, quick primer, absolutely guaranteed against hang or misfire. You will find the Improved Pointer Shells are quicker than most other shells. It is not necessary that you lead your bird near so much with the Pointer Shells as with shells of other makes.

THE WADS IN OUR POINTER SHELLS are made of the finest elastic felt, seated squarely over the powder with uniform pressure.

SHOT. Every grain guaranteed a perfect sphere, loaded by special machines with the greatest possible uniformity, and we invite you to cut open one of our Pointer Shells and compare the arrangement of shot with that of any other shell. The manner in which our shot is loaded in the shells largely accounts for the evenness of the pattern made by the Pointer Shell.

HOW WE ARE ABLE TO IMPROVE THE QUALITY OF OUR SHELLS AND REDUCE OUR PRICE

OUR SALES on the original Low Base Pointer Shells were the largest ever known in the ammunition business. We specified for these shells in quantities of 10,000,000 and over, handling during the season as high as three and four carloads a day. While the old Pointer Shell was an excellent shell, was a better shell than you could obtain elsewhere for from 50c to 75c a hundred more, we were not entirely satisfied, and we determined to improve the quality, estimating that if we could improve the quality of our Pointer Shells and make them without question the finest shells ever produced, we would more than treble our already enormous business, and with this in mind, we specified for a quantity of the New Improved Pointer Shells greater than the combined sales of any ten houses handling ammunition, a quantity so enormous as to enable the factory to run the year around, supplying us with shells. This enormous quantity has enabled our factory to purchase raw material such as paper, brass, copper, lead and felt, in quantities three times as great as they were able to purchase them heretofore, with a consequent reduction in the price of the raw material. This enormous quantity has further enabled us to reduce the overhead expense at the factory, so that with these economies and savings in manufacturing in mind, we are able to furnish you the New Improved Long Base Pointer Shell, loaded with Triumph powder, at a price which represents a substantial reduction from what we formerly asked for our Low Base Pointer Shell, a price 25 per cent to 50 per cent below that asked by other dealers for a shell that would in no way stand comparison with our high grade Pointer Shell.

TRIUMPH POWDER.

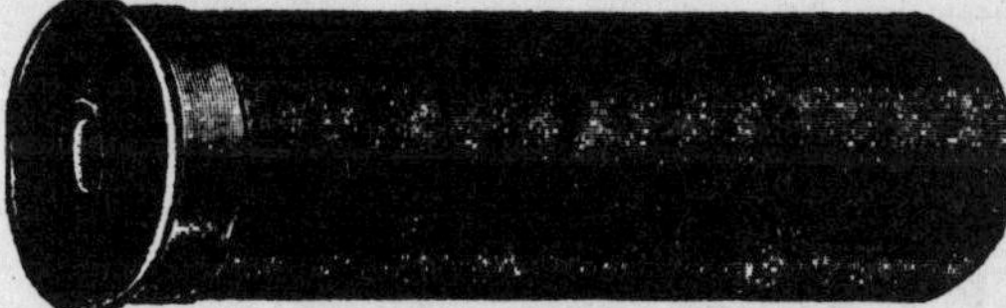

The Ordinary Smokeless Shell.

The Pointer Long Base Shell.

These illustrations show the difference between the Pointer Smokeless Shell and the ordinary shells sold throughout the country at $2.25 a hundred and upward. Note the long brass reinforcements on our Pointer Shell against the short cup on the shells offered in competition. The advantages are many and it will pay you to read what we say about them.

THE NEW IMPROVED POINTER PAPER SHELLS are loaded with the famous Triumph powder. This powder is manufactured for and controlled exclusively by us. There are no loaded shells made other than our Pointer Shells loaded with Triumph powder. This powder is far superior to most of the standard grades of bulk and dense powder, and as powder is one of the most important items, we have spared no expense in getting what we were satisfied was the best smokeless powder made. We feel safe that in offering you this Triumph powder in our loaded shells, we are giving you a better powder than you could possibly obtain in any other shell, regardless of name, make or price.

TRIUMPH POWDER IS A BULK POWDER and is far superior to the dense powders used so extensively by most manufacturers. There is no acid in Triumph to eat your gun barrel or to create an enormous breech pressure, which is apt to endanger your life. The advantages a bulk powder has over a dense powder are many, and as Triumph is the finest bulk powder made, you can appreciate that in our New Improved Long Base Pointer Shells we are giving the very best that money can buy. Triumph has a very hard grain; does not absorb moisture; there is no disagreeable odor attending the use of this powder, and no unburned particles to blow back in the face of the shooter. We guarantee that Triumph does not contain any gun cotton or nitro glycerine, and we claim that this powder has greater penetration with less breech pressure than any powder made. This being a bulk powder, and owing to the hard, fine grain the combustion is uniform, and there is less recoil to Pointer Shells than to any others.

YOU CANNOT AFFORD TO SHOOT BLACK POWDER SHELLS when you can get Pointer Smokeless Loaded Shells at $1.80 a hundred, nor can you afford to use any of the common grades of smokeless shells when we offer you the Pointer Shell at these prices, shells which will outshoot any other on the market, regardless of price.

YOU WILL BE SURPRISED AT THE RESULTS you will obtain from the use of Pointer Shells. You will be able to drop birds that you formerly thought out of range. Your marksmanship will improve from 25 to 50 per cent, depending on your present ability, with the use of Pointer Smokeless Shells.

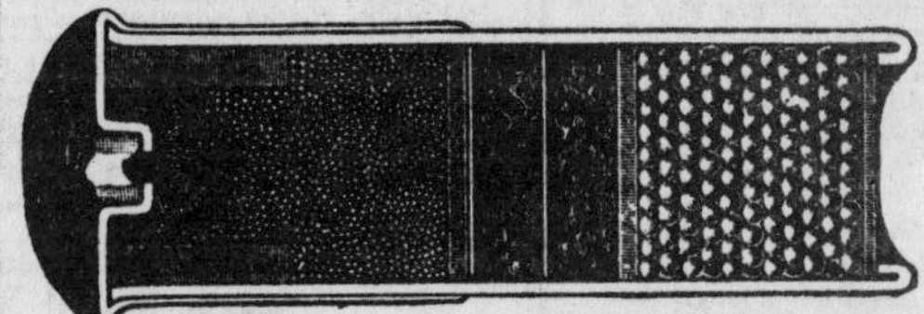

This illustration shows one of our Pointer Smokeless Shells cut open and will give you an idea of the high grade manner in which these shells are loaded. The shells are all loaded by the most improved automatic machinery. One shell is exactly like another. We claim for our Pointer Shells more uniform loading than any other shells made. Therefore, in shooting Pointer Smokeless Shells you are guaranteed more uniform results than could be obtained through the use of any other make of shells.

UNIFORM RESULTS ARE ABSOLUTELY GUARANTEED

WITH POINTER SMOKELESS SHELLS

ONE SHELL IS GUARANTEED TO BE LIKE THE OTHER. What you can do with one shell you can do with the other 24 out of the same box, or the other 999 out of the same case. With our special automatic loading machines absolute regularity and uniformity is obtained in the loading of shells, and we guarantee for our Pointer Smokeless Shells greater penetration, better pattern, instantaneous and complete combustion, and longer range than can be obtained through the use of any other shells.

ONE BOX FREE

OUR TERMS: FREE TRIAL, COMPARATIVE TEST AND GUARANTEE OFFER ON ORDER FOR ONE CASE OF 500 OR MORE.

SEND US AN ORDER FOR 500 SHELLS OR MORE, and we will send the shells to you with the understanding and agreement that you can shoot one box of 25 shells for careful test, and, if you do not find them by far the best shells you ever used, you can return the balance to us by freight at our expense and we will immediately return your money, including any freight charges you paid, and we will make no charge for the 25 shells you used for test; these 25 shells will be FREE to you.

This illustration shows a box of 25, the way in which our Pointer Shells are put up, 25 in a box, each box sealed with a handsome colored lithographed label. Always look for the Pointer dog on the label to get the genuine. The label is registered in Washington, D. C. Inside, outside, in appearance, finish, safety, regularity, comfort, shooting qualities, in every particular Pointer Smokeless Shells stand ALONE.

SEE NEXT PAGE FOR COMPLETE ASSORTMENT OF LOADS AND PRICES

THE NEW IMPROVED POINTER LONG BASE SMOKELESS LOADED SHELL

LOADED —WITH— TRIUMPH

THE NEW BULK SMOKELESS POWDER

This case contains 500 shells, 20 boxes of 25 shells each. Average weight of a case of 500 shells, 65 pounds.

REDUCED PRICE $17.00 PER 1,000

THESE SPECIAL PRICES ARE OFFERED TO DEALERS, GUN CLUBS, MARKET HUNTERS, OR ANY SHOOTER WHO WISHES TO TAKE ADVANTAGE OF OUR SPECIAL QUANTITY PRICES

WE ADVISE EVERY SHOOTER to order at least one case of 500 shells, even though he does not use this quantity for some time, as thereby he gets the advantage of our special quantity price, and these shells will keep indefinitely. They are not subject to climatic changes, and you will get as good results from these shells after you have had them a year as you would if you used them the day you receive them. It is, therefore, to your interest to buy them in quantities of 500 or more and obtain the benefit of our special price of $8.50 a case. If you cannot use the entire quantity, get your neighbors to help you make up a quantity order of 500 or 1,000 shells, and divide the saving you effect among yourselves.

THE NEW IMPROVED POINTER SHELL is loaded with Triumph, the highest quality bulk smokeless powder known. These shells are absolutely guaranteed against misfire, hangfire or blow backs.

Regardless of what success you have had with other shells, and regardless of the satisfaction the original Pointer shells doubtless gave you, the New Improved Pointer Shell as herewith described, illustrated and quoted, will give you better satisfaction and better results. It is absolutely the best shell on the market regardless of price.

THE NEW IMPROVED POINTER SHELL AT $17.00 per thousand for shells loaded with 3 drams of powder, 1 ounce of shot, is, considering the quality of the shell, certainly the greatest value ever offered in shotgun ammunition. This price of $17.00 per thousand is made only when shells are ordered in full case lots. We will not split cases of shells at these prices. Dealers can handle these shells to their best advantage, as the demand for them is greater than for any other known brand of shells, and they can be sold at a good profit to the dealer. Our name does not appear in any way on the boxes or the labels. The cases and boxes are marked exactly as shown in the illustrations on these pages.

THE NEW IMPROVED POINTER SHELL IS PRIMED WITH A No. 7 PRIMER AND IS ABSOLUTELY GUARANTEED AGAINST MISFIRES, HANGFIRES OR BLOW BACKS

2558 W. 32d Ave.
Denver, Colo.
Sears, Roebuck & Co.,
Chicago, Ill.
Gentlemen:
Having used your Pointer Shell quite extensively in the Remington Automatic No. 12-gauge shotgun, find it particularly adapted to that gun. Have shot your Pointers without a single shell breaking or sticking or in any manner interfering with the mechanism. You are probably aware that a great deal of inconvenience is caused by the breaking of certain grades of shells in this gun; in fact, almost every make of shell. Have been using your Pointer, 1-ounce No. 8 drop shot, for trap shooting. My object in writing you is to ascertain if you can furnish me with a load conforming more to the regulation trap load. Quote price and shipping charges. Will thank you for an early reply.
Yours truly,
L. F. NELL.

Mr. Wilt says our Pointer Shells kill at longer range, and are the best shells on the market.

Portage, Pa.
Sears, Roebuck & Co.,
Chicago, Ill.
Gentlemen:
Your smokeless shells are number ONE. I shall use no other make as long as I can get the Pointer shell. Have tried all other makes and find the Pointer shell the best for long range and dead shot; have killed birds from 80 to 100 yards with No. 5 shot. Your shells make better pattern and greater execution, will kill at longer range than any shell I have used before, they are the best shell on the market. Shall order more in next order.
Yours respectfully,
THOMAS WILT.

Twin Lakes, Minn.
Sears, Roebuck & Co.,
Chicago, Ill.
Gentlemen:
I bought from you some time ago the Pointer Smokeless Shotgun Shells. I must say that I was well pleased with what I received from you. I have used the highest priced shells made, the Winchester Leader, U. M. C., Arrow, etc., but cannot find a shell I like better than the Pointer made by the Meriden Fire Arms Company.
Yours, ever a customer,
H. G. DALE.

POINTER SHELLS ADOPTED BY BIG GUN CLUB.

Sears, Roebuck & Co., Chicago, Ill. Johnstown, Pa.
Gentlemen: I purchased a case of Pointer shells from you about a month ago. I have given the shells a thorough test, as we have several others, and we unanimously agree that they are superior to any shells we have ever used. I distributed the shells among my friends, also among all the trap shooters of my acquaintance, and they all agree with me that they are the best shells we ever used, barring none. We were so impressed with the shooting qualities of the shells that we called our newly organized club the Pointer Club. We shot the Winchester Leader shell against the Pointer shell and the Pointer shell won out. We are going to use the Pointer shells exclusively and we want you to give us the rock bottom club prices on the different loads. The captain of our club, Mr. Clarence Thomas, sent you an order for 1,000 Pointer shells last Friday. After trying the Pointer shells myself and finding them superior to all others I used my untiring efforts to show their real value and I am very well pleased with the foothold I have given the Pointer shells in our town. I believe that I am the first man to introduce them in Johnstown. I found that the shooters at first considered the shells too cheap to be good and they did not want to bother trying them. I insisted that they try them, which they did, and were so pleased with the results that they insisted on having Pointer shells. Write a return as soon as you can, giving us your very lowest club prices on all the different loads.
Yours truly, JOHN E. GREEN, 621 Highland Ave.

PRICES ON POINTER SMOKELESS SHELLS

ALWAYS GIVE CATALOGUE NUMBER.

Please notice we furnish only one size and one load in a case, just as they come to us from the factory, at the case price. Order by catalogue number in full.

WEIGHT OF SHELLS IN CASE.
A case of 500 shells, 12-gauge, weighs about 65 pounds.
A case of 500 shells, 10-gauge, weighs about 75 pounds.
A case of 500 shells, 16-gauge, weighs about 53 pounds.
Our terms on loaded shells are cash with order. We do not ship them C. O. D.

16-GAUGE
LOADED WITH SMOKELESS POWDER.

Cat. No.	Grains of Smokeless Powder equal to	Oz. of shot	Size of Drop Shot	Price per box of 25 Shells	Price per 100 Shells	Price per box of 500 Shells	Price per 1,000 Shells
6L1922	2½ Drams	1	4 6 8	48c	$1.92	$9.04	18.08

POINTER SMOKELESS SHELLS, LOADED WITH DROP SHOT.

Always give catalogue number and state size of shot load wanted.

12-GAUGE
LOADED WITH SMOKELESS POWDER.

Cat. No.	Grains of Smokeless Powder Equal to	Wt. of shot	Size of Drop Shot	Price per box of 25 Shells	Price per 100 Shells	Price per Case of 500 Shells	Price per 1,000 Shells
6L1920	3 Drams	1 Oz.	No. 4 No. 6 No. 8	45c	$1.80	$8.50	17.00
6L1920	3 Drams	1⅛ Oz.	No. 2 No. 4 No. 5 No. 6 No. 7 No. 8	47c	$1.88	$9.20	18.40
6L1920	3¼ Drams	1⅛	No. 4 No. 6	50c	$2.00	$9.75	19.50

Always give catalogue number and state size of shot load wanted.

10-GAUGE
SHORT BASE POINTER SMOKELESS SHELLS.

Cat. No.	Grains of Smokeless Powder Equal to	Wt. of shot	Size of Drop Shot	Price per box of 25 Shells	Price per 100 Shells	Price per case of 500 Shells	Price per 1,000 Shells
6L1921	3¼ Drams	1⅛ Oz.	No. 2 No. 4 No. 6 No. 8	55c	$2.00	$9.90	19.80

Always give catalogue number and state size of shot load wanted.

POINTER SMOKELESS SHELLS, LOADED WITH CHILLED SHOT.

Shells loaded with smokeless powder and chilled shot give better penetration and more even patterns than drop shot. Loaded in 12-gauge only. The No. 7½ shot is our celebrated trap load. Order by catalogue number and state size of shot load wanted.

12-GAUGE, CHILLED SHOT
LOADED WITH SMOKELESS POWDER.

Cat. No.	Grains of Smokeless Powder equal to	Ozs. of shot	Size of Chilled Shot	Price per box of 25 Shells	Price per 100 Shells	Price per case of 500 Shells	Price per 1,000 Shells
6L1923	3 Drams	1⅛	No. 4 No. 6 No. 7½ No. 8	51c	$2.04	$9.90	19.80
6L1923	3¼ Drams	1⅛	No. 4 No. 6	53c	$2.12	10.15	20.30
6L1923	3¼ Drams	1¼	No. 7½	55c	$2.20	10.75	21.50

Always give catalogue number and state size of shot load wanted.

8-GAUGE
HAND LOADED WITH SMOKELESS POWDER.

Cat. No.	Grains of Smokeless Powder equal to	Oz. of shot	Size of Drop Shot	Price per box of 25 Shells	Price per 100 Shells	Price per case of 500 Shells	Price per 1,000 Shells
6L1924	5½ Drams	1¾	BB	$1.37	$5.48	$25.55	$51.10

Always give catalogue number and state size of shot load wanted.

Mr. Fisher says our Pointer Shells at 45 cents are far better than Peters' Shells sold at 60 cents per box.

Sunny Side, N. J.
Sears, Roebuck & Co.,
Chicago, Ill.
Gentlemen:
I received some of your special smokeless powder shotgun shells (the Pointer). I am greatly pleased with them for various reasons. First, they have a good penetration; second, they will kill at longer range; third, they have but little jar; fourth, they are quick and sure fire; fifth, they are much cheaper in price than any shells I have ever seen or bought. Your shells sell at 45 cents per box, while the Peters' Cartridge Company shells sell at 60 cents and are not so good a grade of goods. In fact, the Pointer shells are a better shell in every respect than any other shells I have ever used.
Yours respectfully,
JAMES R. FISHER.

Mr. Tice gets better results from our Pointer Shells than any shells he ever used.

Buford, N. D.
Sears, Roebuck & Co.,
Chicago, Ill.
Gentlemen:
I am well pleased with the Pointer Smokeless Shells I received from you. They will carry a great deal farther and give much better penetration than any shell I have ever used. I have been using U. M. C., Nitro Club and Winchester Leader, and had no luck at all with them, as they would not carry far enough, so I gave your Pointer shells a trial, and have been more than pleased with the results I get. I remain,
Ever your customer,
WALTER TICE.

Mr. Gates likes our Pointer Shells better than the Winchester, U. M. C. or Peters'.

Columbia Cross Roads, Pa.
Sears, Roebuck & Co.,
Chicago, Ill.
Gentlemen:
The Pointer shells I got from you are the best shells I ever used. I have tried all kinds of shells, the Winchester, U. M. C., Peters' and several other makes, but I like Pointer shells the best for penetration and pattern, especially the three-dram and 1⅛-ounce shot load. Will order some more as soon as I need them.
Yours truly,
G. W. GATES.

WE DO NOT DEEM IT WISE TO ADVERTISE HEAVIER LOADS, SINCE HEAVIER LOADS PRODUCE TOO MUCH HEAT AND ARE LIABLE TO "BALL" THE SHOT OR CAUSE THE SHELL TO BREAK OFF AT THE BRASS WHEN SHOOTING AND GIVE VERY POOR PATTERNS.

NOTICE OUR PRICES ON METALLIC AMMUNITION, GUNS, RIFLES AND REVOLVERS. OUR PRICES ARE BELOW ALL COMPETITION.

FLINT LOCK PISTOL, ONLY $2.75.

F is the flint.
C is cover of powder pan.

For $2.75 we offer you our special Flint Lock Pistol. Many people supposed that there were no more of these pistols to be had, but our European buyer succeeded in finding a small lot of them in Europe, and has sent them to us.

No. 6E1778 Flint Lock Pistol, 14-gauge, 9-inch barrel, weight about 2¼ pounds; a good relic. Price............**$2.75**

PARTS FOR GUNS, RIFLES OR REVOLVERS.

When ordering parts for guns, rifles or revolvers, always give the name, caliber, gauge of gun, rifle or revolver, or mail us the broken part. This will save us from writing you for this information.

HOW TO TAKE APART REVOLVERS.

The average revolver is usually taken apart by **First**—Removing the stocks. **Second**—Removing the main spring. **Third**—Removing the hammer. **Fourth**—Removing the pins which hold the guard. **Fifth**—Removing the pin which holds the trigger. The average revolver can be taken apart in this manner.

THE REMINGTON BULL DOG SINGLE SHOT PISTOL, $2.90.

For $2.90 we offer you this genuine Remington Single Shot Pistol, manufactured for the United States Government from the best material money can buy, all parts and pieces are made from the best steel procurable, made with a view of combining excellent workmanship and strength, made to shoot the old reliable Government 50-caliber pistol cartridge, and we give 20 cartridges free with each pistol, a pistol that was made to be used in the United States navy, and when they were used they were used with great effect.

DESCRIPTION.—Our Remington Single Shot Bull Dog Pistol is fitted with 8-inch accurately rifled steel barrel, handsomely blued, forged steel frame beautifully case hardened, straight grained walnut handle which is so constructed as to give a good grip, straight grained walnut fore end, the celebrated Remington safety breech block which cannot fly open when the hammer is down. The Remington breech block is a feature which made the Remington arms very popular in the past. In addition to shooting the 50-caliber Remington pistol cartridge, we have had these pistols chambered so they will take the 50-70-caliber primed shells, which can be loaded with about 40 grains of black powder, a cardboard wad and half an ounce of shot, which will make a good pistol for home defense, as well as a pistol for which you can load your own shells and use it to shoot small game, if you wish to do so.

No. 6E1790 Our Reliable Remington Single Shot Bull Dog Pistol, 50-caliber, 8-inch barrel. Weight, 36 ounces.
Price, including 20 rounds of bullet cartridges..........**$2.90**

No. 6E2415 Bullet Cartridges, .50-caliber, for the above pistol. Price, per hundred..........**$1.50**

No. 6E3230 Primed Shells, 50-70-caliber Government, for the above pistol. Price, per hundred..........**$2.00**

No. 6E277 Caliber 50-70 Reloading Tools, consisting of recapper, cap extractor, powder measure and wad cutter.
Price, per set..........**56c**
Weight, packed for shipment, about 5 pounds.

ATTENTION, BOYS!

Look at These Prices on AIR RIFLES.

THE NEW MODEL KING AIR RIFLE, SINGLE SHOT.

Our King Rifles we Guarantee the Highest Grade Made.

57 CTS. All metal, nickel plated, shoots BB shot. Length of barrel, 19 inches; length over all, 34 inches. Weight, 2 pounds. The New Model King Air Rifle shoots common B B shot accurately and with sufficient force to go through ¼-inch soft pine. The barrel and all working parts are made from the best material possible; no castings to break in case it falls to the ground. Each gun is sighted with movable sights.

No. 6E1832 The New Model King Air Rifle. Price....**57c**
If by mail, postage extra, 35 cents.

THE COLUMBIAN 1,000-SHOT AIR RIFLE. $1.09

The Columbian 1,000-Shot Air Rifle, as now made, with improved lock parts and magazine, is an air rifle which will give universal satisfaction. The loading device is very similar to that of the old model air rifle, that by pushing the sleeve forward you fill the magazine with BB shot, and to operate the rifle, hold the gun in the left hand, turn the muzzle toward the ceiling, throw the lever forward, same as you would with the Winchester rifle, and the gun loads itself. Every time you throw the lever you put a shot in the barrel. It is best to shoot after you load the gun or you will get several pellets in the barrel. Should an imperfect shot get into the barrel, it can easily be removed by cocking the gun and inserting a wire from the muzzle, which pushes the shot into the chamber, from which it can easily be removed. The Columbian Repeating Air Rifle will hold about 1,000 pellets of BB shot in the magazine and can be shot repeatedly until the magazine is empty. The entire length of the Columbian 1,000-shot Air Rifle is 34½ inches; the barrel is nickel plated and the frame is japanned; the stock is of good seasoned hardwood. The gun weighs about 4½ pounds. It looks like a Winchester, works like a Winchester and pleases the boys.

No. 6E1846 The Columbian Air Rifle. Price......**$1.09**
Cannot be sent by mail.

OUR BLACK POWDER LOADED SHOTGUN SHELLS.

LOADED SHOTGUN SHELLS $1.32 PER HUNDRED AND UP for the highest grade loaded shotgun shells made, in both black and white powder, prices heretofore unknown. 12-gauge black powder shells ranging from **$1.32** to **$1.60** per hundred, and other sizes at proportionately low prices. We direct your attention to our illustrations, descriptions and incomparable low price quotations on the highest grade loaded shotgun shells made.

EVERY LOADED SHELL COVERED BY OUR BINDING GUARANTEE. We guarantee our loaded shells to be superior to any other loaded shotgun shell on the market, regardless of price.

WHILE OUR PRICES ARE VERY MUCH LOWER than you can buy elsewhere, we use a higher grade empty shell than other makers use, and if you wish to reload them, they will stand more reloading than any other paper shell made. No swelling, no sticking in the gun, the strongest, smoothest and best empty shell on the market.

QUALITY OF POWDER USED. We use a higher grade of black and smokeless powder than is used in any other machine loaded shell on the market, and we guarantee our shells, loaded with the high grade powder we use, under our special system of loading and wadding, to give better penetration, better target, in short, to kill at longer range than any other machine loaded shell made, regardless of price

WE HAVE TESTED OUR LOADED SHELLS by the Chronograph Testing Machine with all other so called reliable makes of machinery shells, and have found, by the most accurate test, that the shot from our shells goes with greater rapidity, hence it shoots farther, gives more penetration, and more perfect target than any other machine loaded shell on the market. There is less recoil, no misfires; in short, there are no other machine loaded shells made that will in durability, safety and shooting qualities compare with ours.

ABOUT OUR LOW PRICES. The price we name barely covers the cost of material and labor, with but our one small percentage of profit added; hence, we can furnish loaded shotgun shells of a higher grade than you can buy elsewhere, and yet at a price very much lower than any other house can furnish you.

BUY EARLY. We aim to carry on hand at all times, one to three millions of loaded shells in the sizes which we advertise, but in the early spring and fall when hunting is at its height, it sometimes happens that we receive hundreds of orders in one day, from all parts of the United States, for the self same load, which temporarily exhausts our stock, and in these two seasons all loaded shell manufacturers are taxed to their utmost capacity, and even then are unable to supply the demand, so if you can give us a second choice of load number, when ordering, it will oftentimes assist us in filling your order promptly in case we are out of the particular load which you prefer. We advise buying shells early when you can do so.

THE VELOCITY OF OUR SHELLS. The velocity of our shells means that the shot travels a certain number of feet per second after leaving the shell. We have repeatedly tested our shells on the electrical chronograph, which is an electrical machine constructed to measure the number of feet that shot will travel per second, and our average velocity for black powder shells is 960 feet per second, and for smokeless powder shells is 1,050 feet per second; while other makes of shells which we have tested of the same size load as our own, do not in most cases come up to this average.

THE CHRONOGRAPH is a scientific electrical instrument made for testing velocity, and shells are tested with a chronograph as follows: One electric wire is attached from the chronograph to the trigger of the gun, and another electric wire is attached from the chronograph to a metallic target. As soon as the trigger is pulled the chronograph registers and when the shot strikes the target the chronograph ceases to register, which gives us the exact velocity of the shell

SEND GOODS BY FREIGHT. We advise sending goods by freight, as it is cheaper than by express. If you order a gun or a rifle, and you include enough needed goods from our big catalogue to make a shipment of 50 to 100 pounds, the entire shipment will be very near as cheap by freight as the gun alone would cost you by express When shipping 50 to 100 pounds or more by freight, it makes the freight cost practically next to nothing on each item.

NUMBER OF PELLETS TO ONE OUNCE OF SHOT.

We give below the number of pellets to one ounce of shot. The number is approximate. It may vary ten or more pellets.

Size of shot......	No. 10	No. 9	No. 8	No. 7½	No. 7	No. 6	No. 5	No. 4	No. 3	No. 2	No. 1	BB
Contains pellets.	850	570	390	335	290	220	170	130	105	85	70	60

OUR LINE OF BLACK POWDER LOADED SHELLS.

Why not get your friends to join with you and buy shells by the case or 1,000 and ship by freight? It will save you money in freight charges.

OUR CASE PRICE is for one size and one gauge in a case, just as it comes to us from the factory. We cannot sell less than a case at the case price, nor can we assort the case with different loads.

A case of 500 12-gauge shells weighs about 65 pounds.
A case of 500 10-gauge shells weighs about 75 pounds.
A case of 500 16-gauge shells weighs about 53 pounds.
Our terms on loaded shells are cash with order. We do not ship them C. O. D.
Order by catalogue number and load number.

Catalogue No. 6E2212 — 12 Gauge — LOADED WITH BLACK POWDER.

Load No.	Drams of Black Powdr	Oz. of Shot	Size of Dr'p Shot	Price per box of 25 Shells	Price per 100 Shells	Price per case of 500 Shells	Price per 1,000 Shells
76 78 70	3	1	6 8 10	34c	$1.32	$6.55	$13.10
84 86 88	3	1⅛	4 6 8	36c	$1.40	$6.95	$13.90
112 114 115 116 117 118	3¼	1⅛	2 4 5 6 7 8	37c	$1.43	$7.10	$14.20
144 146	3½	1⅛	4 6	38c	$1.45	$7.18	$14.36
17BB	3¾	1⅛	BB	42c	$1.59	$7.90	$15.80
5B	3½	1⅛	4 Buck	43c	$1.60	$7.95	$15.90

Catalogue No. 6E2210 — 10 Gauge — LOADED WITH BLACK POWDER.

Load No.	Drams of Black Powdr	Oz. of Shot	Size of Dr'p Shot	Price per box of 25 Shells	Price per 100 Shells	Price per Case of 500 Shells	Price per 1000 Shells
282 284 286 288	4¼	1⅛	2 4 6 8	42c	$1.59	$7.90	$15.80
19BB	5	1⅛	BB	47c	$1.80	$8.95	$17.90

Catalogue No. 6E2216 — 16 Gauge — LOADED WITH BLACK POWDER.

Load No.	Drams of Black Powdr	Oz. of Shot	Size of Dr'p Shot	Price per box of 25 Shells	Price per 100 Shells	Price per Case of 500 Shells	Price per 1000 Shells
416 418	2¾	1	6 8	38c	$1.45	$7.20	$14.40

Catalogue No. 6E2220 — 20 Gauge — LOADED WITH BLACK POWDER.

Load No.	Drams of Black Powdr	Oz. of Shot	Size of Dr'p Shot	Price per box of 25 Shells	Price per 100 Shells	Price per Case of 500 Shells	Price per 1,000 Shells
4206 4208	2½	⅞	6 8	39c	$1.48	$7.35	$14.70

We have taken great pains to select loads which are suitable for most purposes and these loads should meet all requirements. WE DO NOT SEND SHELLS C. O. D.

RUSTED AND DAMAGED GUNS.

Do not return to us a gun, revolver or rifle which is rusted, pitted or has the finish worn off, for we have no way of selling these guns. If you have a gun, revolver or rifle which needs repairing, first write us, fully describing the article and what is broken, and we may be able to send you the part necessary, thus saving the express charges on the gun both ways.

Empty Pin Fire Paper Shells.

We cannot furnish these loaded. Order your ammunition and reloading tools from us and load your own shells to your own liking. These shells come 100 in a box and we cannot sell less than a box.

Catalogue No.	Gauge	Weight Per 100	Price Per 100
6E2250 6E2252 6E2253	20 Pin Fire 16 Pin Fire 12 Pin Fire	1½ pounds 1¾ pounds 2 pounds	53c 54c 62c

Shells cannot be sent by mail.

Pin Fire Primers for Above Paper Shells.

No. 6E2256 Primers for Pin Fire Paper Shells. Cannot be sent by mail. Price, per box of 100........................**19c**

First Quality Empty Brass Shells.

Not loaded. We cannot furnish brass shells loaded. These shells come in two qualities, first quality and second quality; the first quality shell is a trifle heavier than the second quality shell, but they are both good, durable and serviceable shells and may be reloaded many times. These shells come put up 25 shells in a paper box and all use the No. 2 primer and cannot be used in the magazine of repeating shotguns.

Catalogue Number	Gauge of Shell	Length of Shell	Wt. Per Box of 25	Price Per Box of 25
6E2301 6E2303 6E2304 6E2307 6E2308	8 10 12 16 20	3 in. 2⅞ in. 2⅝ in. 2½ in. 2½ in.	2 lbs. 1¾ lbs. 1¾ lbs. 1½ lbs. 1¼ lbs.	$2.00 1.15 1.10 1.10 1.10

Brass shells cannot be sent by mail.

Second Quality Empty Brass Shells.

Catalogue Number	Gauge of Shell	Length of Shell	Wt. Per Box	Price Per Box of 25
6E2316 6E2318	12 10	2⅝ in. 2⅞ in.	1½ lbs. 1½ lbs.	75c 75c

Brass shells cannot be sent by mail.

Something free to you under our

PROFIT SHARING PLAN.

You can soon get Something Valuable
ENTIRELY FREE.

SUPERIOR AMMUNITION

OUR HIGH GRADE LOADED PISTOL AND RIFLE CARTRIDGES AT LOWEST PRICES EVER KNOWN.

COMPARE OUR PRICES WITH OTHERS. NONE CAN COMPETE WITH US ON THESE GOODS.

WE GUARANTEE our Dominion rifle and pistol cartridges to be equal or superior to any cartridges made regardless of make, name or price. SEND US YOUR ORDER FOR CARTRIDGES, and if you find them otherwise, you may return them at our expense of transportation charges and we will return your money. COULD ANYTHING BE MORE FAIR?

LOADED METALLIC CARTRIDGES.

COMPARE OUR PRICES WITH OTHER HOUSES.

REMEMBER, our terms are cash with order on ammunition. These are the leading and popular selling cartridges. Cartridges can be shipped with other goods by express or freight, but cartridges cannot be sent by mail, because they are explosive. Prices subject to change without notice. Our ammunition is always fresh. We buy metallic and shotgun ammunition in carload lots. We sell large quantities, consequently have no old stock on hand. These illustrations are one-half size of the cartridges. In case you are in doubt about the correct caliber, send us a sample shell which has been shot, with your order, or send the cover of the box. Rim fire cartridges cannot be reloaded.

OUR HIGH GRADE RIM FIRE CARTRIDGES.

LOADED WITH BLACK POWDER.
Cannot be sent by mail.

No. 6E2331 No. 6E2332 No. 6E2336 No. 6E2338 No. 6E2340 No. 6E2342

No. 6E2344 No. 6E2346 No. 6E2348 No. 6E2352 No. 6E2353 No. 6E2356

No. 6E2357 No. 6E2360 No. 6E2363 No. 6E2366

No. 6E2367 No. 6E2368

Our ammunition is always fresh and loaded with first class powder. OUR TERMS ARE CASH WITH ORDER. WE CANNOT SEND C. O. D.

No.	CARTRIDGES Cannot be sent by mail. Caliber	Good for Yards	Grains of Powder	Grains of Lead	Weight per 100	Price for 50	Price for 100	Price for 1,000
6E2331	B. B. Caps (Round ball).....	15	....	21	7 oz.	......	$0.14	$1.35
6E2332	B. B. Caps (Conical ball) ...	20	....	24½	8 oz.	......	.17	1.60
6E2336	22 Short....................	35	3	30	9 oz.	10c	.19	1.90
6E2338	22 Long.....................	50	5	29	11 oz.	15c	.28	2.60
6E2340	22 Long Rifle..............	100	5	40	14 oz.	15c	.28	2.60
6E2342	22 Extra Long..............	125	6	30	15 oz.	......	.43	4.10
6E2344	22 Rim Special (Model 1890)..	125	7	45	18 oz.	22c	.43	4.10
6E2346	25 Stevens..................	150	11	65	29 oz.	35c	.70	6.65
6E2348	30 Short....................	75	6	55	20 oz.	22c	.44	4.30
6E2352	32 Short....................	100	9	82	27 oz.	24c	.48	4.56
6E2353	32 Long.....................	125	13	90	30 oz.	28c	.55	5.23
6E2356	38 Short....................	150	18	130	43 oz.	38c	.76	7.22
6E2357	38 Long.....................	200	21	148	48 oz.	43c	.86	8.17
6E2360	41 Short Rem. Derringer....	125	13	130	40 oz.	38c	.75	7.25
6E2363	44 Flat.....................	300	28	200	64 oz.	57c	1.14	10.83
6E2364	44 Long Ballard.............	300	28	220	4½ lbs.	60c	1.20	11.40
6E2366	56-50 Spencer	400	45	350	7 lbs.	99c	1.95	19.00
6E2367	56-52 Spencer	400	45	386	7 lbs.	99c	1.95	19.00
6E2368	56-56 Spencer	400	45	350	6¾ lbs.	99c	1.95	19.00

Cartridges cannot be sent by mail because they are explosive.

CENTRAL FIRE PISTOL AND RIFLE CARTRIDGES.

LOADED WITH BLACK POWDER. Explosives cannot be sent by mail.

These illustrations are half the size of cartridges. If you are in doubt about the caliber, send a sample shell which has been shot, with your order, or send the cover of the box.

No. 6E2371 No. 6E2373 No. 6E2374 No. 6E2376 Hand Eject'r

No. 6E2377

No. 6E2380

No. 6E2381

No. 6E2384

No. 6E2388 No. 6E2392 No. 6E2396 No. 6E2401

No. 6E2405 No. 6E2406 No. 6E2409 No. 6E2413

CARTRIDGES CANNOT BE SENT C. O. D.

No.	CARTRIDGES Cannot be sent by mail. Caliber for following Rifles or Revolvers	Good for Yards	Grains of Powd'r	Grains of Lead	Weight per 100	Price for 50	Price for 100	Price for 1,000
6E2371	22 C. F. Single Shot Rifles	125	13	45	1½ lbs.	54c	$1.07	$10.17
6E2373	25-20 Single Shot Rifles..	200	19	86	2½ lbs.	68c	1.35	12.83
6E2374	25-20 Repeating Rifles....	200	17	86	2½ lbs.	57c	1.14	10.83
6E2376	32 Smith & Wesson Long.	125	13	98	2¼ lbs.	48c	.95	9.00
6E2377	32 Smith & Wesson	75	9	85	1½ lbs.	35c	.70	7.00
6E2380	32 Short Colt's Revolver.	75	9	82	1½ lbs.	39c	.78	7.41
6E2381	32 Long Colt's Revolver.	125	13	90	2 lbs.	46c	.91	8.08
6E2384	32-20 Repeating Rifles...	200	20	115	3 lbs.	57c	1.14	10.83
6E2388	38 Smith & Wesson.......	100	14	145	3¼ lbs.	46c	.91	9.10
6E2392	38 Long Colt's Revolver..	175	19	150	3¼ lbs.	52c	1.03	9.79
6E2396	38-40 Repeating Rifles....	300	40	180	4½ lbs.	68c	1.35	12.83
6E2401	41 Long Colt's Revolver.	175	21	200	4¼ lbs.	62c	1.24	11.78
6E2405	44 S. & W. American.....	200	25	205	4¼ lbs.	68c	1.35	12.83
6E2406	44 S. & W. Russian	175	23	255	5 lbs.	71c	1.42	13.49
6E2409	44-40 Repeating Rifles....	300	40	200	5 lbs.	68c	1.35	12.83
6E2413	45 Colt's Revolver.......	300	40	250	5½ lbs.	79c	1.57	14.92
6E2415	50 Remington Pistol.	75	20	500	7 lbs.	75c	1.50	14.00

The above cartridges are reloadable and may be reloaded with Ideal or Bridgeport Gun Implement Co.'s loading tools.

DOMINION CENTER FIRE MILITARY AND SPORTING CARTRIDGES

LOADED WITH BLACK POWDER.

No. 6E2429

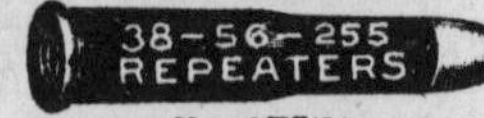

No. 6E2434

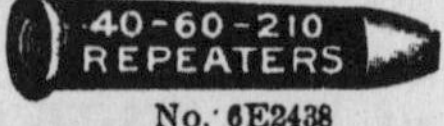

No. 6E2438

No. 6E2474

These illustrations are one-half size of cartridges. If you are in doubt about the correct caliber, send a sample shell, which has been shot, with your order, or send the cover of the box. Cartridges cannot be sent by mail.

CARTRIDGES CANNOT BE SENT C. O. D.

No. 6E2432 No. 6E2439 No. 6E2440 No. 6E2490

ALL THESE CARTRIDGES have lead bullets only, and are good for 200 to 500 yards. Explosives cannot be sent by mail. Cartridges cannot be sent C. O. D.

No.	Cartridges cannot be sent C. O. D. Caliber Kind	Grains of Powd'r	Grains of Lead	Weight per 100	Price for 20	Price for 100
6E2429	32-40 Ballard and Marlin	40	165	6 lbs	42c	$1.96
6E2432	38-55 Ballard and Marlin......	55	255	7 lbs	51c	2.40
6E2434	38-56 For Repeating Rifles.....	56	255	8 lbs	51c	2.40
6E2438	40-60 For Winchester Rifles....	62	210	7½ lbs	51c	2.32
6E2439	40-60 Marlin and Colt's Rifles.	60	260	8½ lbs	51c	2.40
6E2440	40-65 For Repeating Rifles.....	65	260	8 lbs	51c	2.40
6E2458	40-82 For Repeating Rifles....	82	260	9½ lbs	56c	2.63
6E2474	45-70-500 Government..........	70	500	12¼ lbs	58c	2.76
6E2490	50-70 Government..............	70	450	11½ lbs	57c	2.69

The above cartridges may be reloaded with Ideal tools, No. 6E4294.

SMOKELESS CARTRIDGES.

Metallic Cartridges, loaded with Smokeless Powder, are all the same shape and size as regular Black Powder Cartridges, but have less grains of Powder than Black Powder Cartridges.

30-30-160 Bullet. 30-30-160 Bullet.

Before Shooting. These Cartridges are not loaded with Black Powder.

After Shooting.

These two illustrations show a soft point bullet before and after shooting. The soft point bullets have a metal patch or jacket to the point, and when the bullet strikes it spreads at the point, as shown in illustration. **The full metal patched bullets** have a metal jacket covering the entire bullet and keep their shape after shooting. **We recommend soft point bullets for hunting purposes, but for powerful shooting, full metal patched are better;** for instance, a 30-caliber Army metal patched bullet will go through 58 pine boards, ⅞-inch thick, 15 feet from the muzzle of the rifle. A 30-30 caliber metal patched bullet will go through 35 boards, ⅞-inch thick, in the same distance, while a lead bullet would go through only about one-half as many boards.

RIM FIRE SMOKELESS. COME WITH LEAD BULLETS ONLY.

These illustrations are half size of cartridges. If you are in doubt about correct caliber, send us a sample shell, which has been shot, with your order, or send cover of box.

No. 6E2535 No. 6E2539

No.	Rim Fire Smokeless Cartridges are not guaranteed for accuracy. Caliber	Grains of Powd'r	Grains of Lead	Weight per 100	Price for 50	Price for 100
6E2535	22 Short, Rim Fire............	1½	30	10 oz.	13c	26c
6E2539	22 Long, Rim Fire.............	2½	35	12 oz.	18c	36c

CENTER FIRE SMOKELESS CARTRIDGES. RIFLE AND PISTOL SIZES.

CARTRIDGES CANNOT BE SENT BY MAIL NOR C. O. D.

All Smokeless Cartridges are the same style and size as Black Powder Cartridges, but they have less grains of powder than Black Powder Cartridges.

No. 6E2555 No. 6E2566

No. 6E2575

No. 6E2580

NOTICE: M. P. means Metal Patched Bullet. S. P. means Soft Point Bullet. Cartridges cannot be sent by mail.

The powder weight which we quote is Laflin & Rand's and it may vary in other brands.

No.	Cartridges cannot be sent C. O. D. Caliber Kind	Grains of Powd'r	Grains of Lead	Weig't per 100	Price for 50	Price for 100
6E2555	25-20 For Repeating Rifles......	3	86 Lead	2½ lbs.	$0.78	$1.56
6E2560	32 Colt's Automatic Pistol......	3¾	71 M.P.	2½ lbs.	.72	1.44
6E2566	32-20 For Repeating Rifles......	4	115 M.P.	3 lbs.	.83	1.65
6E2568	32-20 For Repeating Rifles......	4	115 S. P.	3 lbs.	.83	1.65
6E2573	38-40 For Repeating Rifles......	12	180 M.P.	4 lbs.	.99	1.98
6E2575	38-40 For Repeating Rifles......	12	180 S. P.	4 lbs.	.99	1.98
6E2580	38 Colt's Automatic Pistol......	8	105 M.P.	3 lbs.	1.07	2.14

REMEMBER you not only save money at our prices but you get your **PROFIT SHARING CERTIFICATES** and can soon get something valuable **FREE**—a wonderful plan for our customers to share in our profits.

SMOKELESS SPORTING RIFLE AND MILITARY CARTRIDGES

FOR LARGE GAME HUNTING.

All smokeless cartridges are the same style and size as black powder regular cartridges, but they have less grains of powder than black powder cartridges. Cartridges cannot be sent by mail.

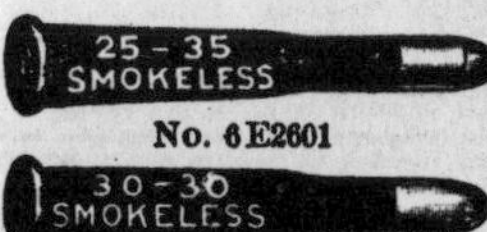

No. 6E2601

No. 6E2605

These illustrations are half size of cartridges. If you are in doubt about the correct caliber, send us a shell which has been shot with your order, or send the cover of the box with the label on it.

No. 6E2603

No. 6E2608

No. 6E2613

No. 6E2619

No. 6E2624

Cartridges cannot be sent by mail.

No. 6E2633

SEE OUR PRICES ON LOADED SHELLS.

NOTICE.
M. P. means Metal Patched Bullet.
S. P. means Soft Point Bullet.
The powder weight, which we quote is Laflin & Rand's. It may vary in other brands.

No.	Cartridges cannot be sent C. O. D. Caliber Kind	Grains of Powd'r	Grains of Lead	Weig't per 100	Price for 20	Price for 100
6E2601	25-35 For Winchester Rifles....	19	117 S. P.	4¼ lbs	$0.59	$2.88
6E2603	25-36 Marlin Winchester Rifle.	19	117 S. P.	4¼ lbs	.59	2.88
6E2605	30-30 For Repeating Rifles.....	23	160 M. P.	6 lbs	.55	2.75
6E2607	30-30 For Repeating Rifles	23	160 S. P.	6 lbs		
6E2608	303 Savage Repeating Rifle...	27	180 M. P.	6¼ lbs	.55	2.75
6E2609	303 Savage Repeating Rifle...	27	180 S. P.	6¼ lbs		
6E2613	30 U. S. Army..................	34	220 M. P.	7½ lbs	.88	4.37
6E2614	30 U. S. Army..................	34	220 S. P.	7½ lbs	.88	4.37
6E2619	32-40 For Repeating Rifles....	12	165 M. P.	5½ lbs	.50	2.45
6E2620	32-40 For Repeating Rifles....	12	165 S. P.	5½ lbs		
6E2623	38-55 For Repeating Rifles....	14	255 M. P.	7 lbs	.60	2.91
6E2624	38-55 For Repeating Rifles....	14	255 S. P.	7 lbs		
6E2633	40-70 For Repeating Rifles....	17	330 M. P.	9 lbs	.75	3.75

We handle only fresh ammunition, loaded with best grades of powder. Cartridges cannot be sent by mail. They must be sent by express or freight.

We cannot send cartridges C. O. D.

SHOT CARTRIDGES.

Loaded with shot instead of ball. For use in rifles and revolvers.

Cannot be sent by mail.

Catalogue No.	Caliber	Weight per 100	Price per 100	Price per 50
6E2710	22 Long, R. F......	¾ lb.	$0.45	$0.25
6E2712	32 S. & W. C. .F.....	1½ lbs.	.80	.40
6E2717	44 XL. C. F.........	5 lbs.	1.50	.75

How to Load Paper Shells to Get the Best Results.

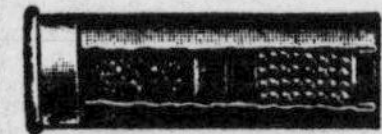

Illustration showing how a shell should be loaded.

Our experience is that the loading of shells is largely responsible for good or poor targets. Some guns will make a good pattern with a certain size of shot, and a poor pattern with another size, but nearly all guns will do better when the shell is properly loaded. Try the following rules if you load your own shells: For black powder—first, put in the powder; second, one thick cardboard wad; third, two ½-inch felt wads; fourth, another card wad; fifth, the shot; sixth, one thin card wad. Test load for 12-gauge, 3 drams black powder, 1⅛ ounces No. 8 shot. For nitro powder use the same rules, except put a thin card wad, or a wad which is free from grease, over the powder instead of a thick card wad. When loading nitro powder don't put in a heavier charge than the directions on the can. Guns are usually tested on a 30-inch circle, at forty yards distance.

OUR BLACK POWDER EMPTY PAPER SHELLS, SUITABLE FOR BLACK POWDER LOADING.

GUARANTEED TO BE AS GOOD AS ANY PAPER SHELLS MADE

These shells come packed 100 shells in a box and we cannot sell less than 100 shells of one size at a time. All theso shells take No. 2 primer. If you wish to shoot smokeless powder in these shells put 2 grains of black powder into the shell before you put in the smokeless powder. Two grains is about half as much as a 22-caliber rim fire cartridge shell will hold. This is called "priming shell" with black powder. **Empty shells cannot be sent by mail.**

Catalogue No.	Gauge	Length of Shell	Weight per 100	Takes Primer	Price, per 100
6E2728	12	2⅝ in.	3 lbs.	No. 2	57c
6E2729	10	2⅞ in.	3 lbs.	No. 2	64c
6E2730	14	2 9-16 in.	2⅝ lbs.	No. 2	60c
6E2731	16	2 9-16 in.	2½ lbs.	No. 2	60c
6E2732	20	2½ in.	2¼ lbs.	No. 2	60c

PRICES—Our prices are ROCK BOTTOM. Positively no reduction made for quantity.

OUR SMOKELESS POWDER EMPTY PAPER SHELLS FOR BULK SMOKELESS POWDER.

These shells are especially adapted to smokeless powder, all have a quick primer. They come put up 100 in a paper box, and we cannot sell less than a 100 of a size, except the 8-gauge, which come 50 in a box.

These shells cannot be sent by mail.

Catalogue No.	Gauge	Lngth of Shell	W'g't per 100	Price per 100
6E2733	12	2⅝ in.	3 lbs.	$0.76
6E2734	10	2⅞ in.	3 lbs.	.89
6E2735	16	2 9/16 in.	2½ lbs.	.75
6E2736	8	3¼ in.	5 lbs.	2.00

SEND 10 CENTS FOR OUR BOOKLET OF USEFUL INFORMATION FOR SHOOTERS.

BLANK CARTRIDGES.

Primed with regular powder charge, but without bullets. For 4th of July and celebrations. **Cannot go by mail.**

Catalogue No.	Caliber	For	Weight, per 100	Price, per 100
6E2762	22 Rim	Pistols	4 ounces	$0.13
6E2764	32 S. & W.	Pistols	12 ounces	.50
6E2765	38 S. & W.	Pistols	15 ounces	.63
6E2767	50 Govt.	Rifles	4 pounds	2.00

A FEW WORDS ABOUT RELOADING RIFLE CARTRIDGES.

The only economical way to reload rifle or pistol cartridges is to buy the cartridges and after being shot, remove the primer as quickly after shooting as possible, for the fulminate of the same is liable to bring about a corrosion of the brass.

When reloading bottle neck shells, our customers should use a shell resizing tool in order to resize the neck of the shell properly, but this is not always necessary on straight shells.

Extreme caution should be exercised when reloading smokeless cartridges so that they do not get too much smokeless powder in the shell, which will either burst the rifle or destroy the barrel for accuracy. Most smokeless powders generate a terrific heat when the shell is overloaded and this causes the bullet to lead the barrel and rifling; at the same time it is liable to deteriorate the metal of the barrel. So when loading smokeless powder always follow the directions of the manufacturer whose powder you use, and be sure to weigh the powder on an apothecary's scale to get the proper amount of grains in the shell. We have seen a shell which had been overloaded with smokeless powder, the heat of which was so intense, it actually melted the head of the shell. By all means do not load as much smokeless powder in a cartridge as you would of black powder, for you will surely have an explosion if you do, for example the 32-40 caliber black powder cartridges take forty grains of black powder while the same cartridge loaded with smokeless powder it takes only about twelve grains of Laflin & Rands sharpshooters smokeless powder, so you can readily see that if you put forty grains of smokeless powder into the shell, you will surely have an explosion and probably a wrecked rifle.

To keep your empty shells in good condition, always remove the primer as soon after shooting as possible, wash them in hot soda water or soap suds, and rinse them with hot water immediately. Do not dry them in an oven. The hot water will dry them of its own accord. Order by catalogue No. 6E3230.

PRIMED EMPTY RIFLE AND PISTOL SHELLS.

These shells have the primer, but have no powder and bullets. All center fire. Shells cannot be sent by mail. Order by number, caliber, model of gun and style. Small sizes come 50 in a box. Sporting rifle and military sizes come 25 in a box. **No. 6E3230**

Style	Caliber and Kind	Weight per 100	Price per 100
G	32-44 Smith & Wesson, target........	1 lb.	$1.00
AA	25-35 Winchester....................	2¼ lbs.	1.50
BB	25-36 Marlin........................	1 lb.	1.50
CC	30-30 Winchester....................	2½ lbs.	1.80
DD	30-40 U. S. Army....................	3 lbs.	2.00
EE	32-40..............................	2¼ lbs.	1.50
FF	38-55..............................	2¾ lbs.	1.80
GG	38-56 Winchester....................	2¼ lbs.	1.80
PP	303 Savage..........................	2½ lbs.	1.85
QQ	40-85 3-in. long, for Gun No. 6E276	4 lbs.	2.50
OO	50-70 Government	3½ lbs.	2.00

AN EXPLANATION ABOUT PRIMERS.

There are at least fifty to sixty styles of primers manufactured, and it becomes confusing to customers as to which style of primer to order. **When ordering primers advise us for which name and brand of shells the primers are wanted** and you will assist us greatly, for there are ever so many different styles of primers, and unless you give us the name and brand we are obliged to guess at what you want; but if you can tell us the maker's name of the shells, and whether they are wanted for black or smokeless powder, we can generally send you the right size.

PRIMERS AND GUN CAPS.

Illustrations show the exact size of caps and primers. Caps and primers cannot be sent by mail.

No. 1

No. 2 and No. 2½

No. 6W

No. 3

No. 4

Explosives cannot go by mail.

NOTICE—When ordering primers tell us if you want them for Winchester, U. M. C., or other shells or cartridges and state caliber, gauge and make of your shells or cartridges. The primers are different for each kind, except No. 2. All No. 2 primers are alike in size and are used for black powder paper or brass shells.

Catalogue No.	Factory No.	For Powder	Primers, per box	Price per box	Price, per 1,000
6E3201	No. 2	Black	100	$0.15	$1.30
6E3207	No. 2½	Black	250	.40	1.60
6E3208	Nos. 1 & 1½	Black	250	.40	1.60
6E3209	No. 3	Smokeless	100	.15	1.40
6E3212	Nos. 6½, 7, 7½ and 8½	Smokeless	250	.40	1.60
6E3222	Winch. No 1 W., 1½ W., 2½ W. 3, 4, 5 and 6	Smokeless	100	.16	1.60

GUN CAPS.

For Muzzle Loaders and Muskets.

No. 6E3226

No. 6E3227

Catalogue No.	Kind of Gun Caps	For	Price per 100	Price per 1000
6E3226	Trimmed Edge.	Guns.	5c	48c
6E3227	U. S. Musket.	Muskets.	7c	65c

A FEW WORDS ABOUT GUN WADS.

There is considerable difference of opinion among shooters about the best method of loading shells, with reference to the wadding. We have gone into this matter extensively and our experience is as follows: That if you place one cardboard wad next to the powder, then use one or two ¼-inch black edge wads (according to the length of the shell), after this put another cardboard wad over the black edge wads, then put in your shot and a thin cardboard wad over the shot, leaving about ¼-inch of the shell to be crimped, you will get as good results as you will from any fancy loading, all other things being equal.

The main scientific principle in shooting is to confine the gas generated by the burning powder behind the shot. If loading as above mentioned does not give the proper pattern we advise you to try one size larger felt wads. For instance, if you do not get good results with No. 12 black edge wads, try No. 11 wads, for it sometimes happens that the diameter of one gun barrel is a mere trifle larger than another. **If you are doing rapid shooting,** enough so as to cause the barrel of your gun to become heated, bear in mind that this heating process expands the bore of the gun, though not enough to notice it with the naked eye, still enough to impair the shooting qualities.

CARDBOARD GUN WADS.

Made from specially prepared cardboard. To be used next to the powder, but may be used over the shot also. Mention gauge wanted when ordering. They come 250 in a box.

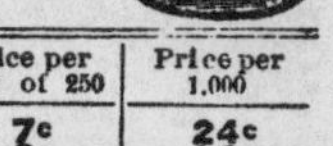

Catalogue Number	Gauge	Weight per box	Price per box of 250	Price per 1,000
6E3300	7 or 8	7 oz.	7c	24c
6E3300	9 or 10	6 oz.	6c	20c
6E3300	11 to 20	5 oz.	5c	16c

If by mail, postage extra, 1 cent per ounce.

THIN CARDBOARD WADS.

Thin Cardboard Wads to use over the shot. Made from specially prepared paper. **Mention gauge wanted.** They come 250 in a box.

Catalogue Number	Gauge	Weight per box	Price per box of 250	Price per 1,000
6E3320	9 or 10	4 oz.	6c	20c
6E3320	11 or 12	4 oz.	5c	16c

If by mail, postage extra, 1 cent per ounce.

BLACK EDGE GUN WADS.

BLACK EDGE

For use over black or smokeless powder. See above instructions about loading. Always put a card wad next to the powder. They come 250 wads in a box. Made in ⅛-inch and ¼-inch thickness. **Mention gauge wanted.**

Catalogue Number	Gauge	Thickness	Weight per box	Price per box of 250	Price per 1,000
6E3330	6	⅛ in.	10 oz.	30c	$1.14
6E3330	7 or 8	⅛ in.	9 oz.	19c	.74
6E3330	9 or 10	⅛ in.	8 oz.	16c	.64
6E3330	11 to 20	⅛ in.	7 oz.	14c	.55
6E3340	9 or 10	¼ in.	9 oz.	24c	.95
6E3340	11 or 12	¼ in.	9 oz.	21c	.82

If by mail, postage extra, 1 cent per ounce.

☞ **NOTICE—In 12-gauge brass shells, use 10-gauge wads.** In paper shells, use wads the same size as shell. **Always put the wad down to place flat and evenly, otherwise the shooting qualities of your gun will be greatly impaired.**

OUR GUN SHOP is equipped with first class, up to date milling machines, forge, grinders, drill press, turret lathe, tools, etc., and we are prepared to give estimates on almost any kind of repair work. Tell us the make, name, style, model, caliber, gauge of your shotgun, rifle or revolver, say what is broken and the manager of our gun shop will estimate the cost of repairing same and will advise you if it is necessary to send the firearm to us or if he can make or furnish the part or parts necessary so you need not return the firearm to us. We always aim to save you the transportation charges of sending the firearm to us if we can do so.

YOU SHARE IN OUR PROFITS

Why not buy everything you use from us? You will save money on every purchase. We guarantee our prices the lowest in the world and you will get your

PROFIT SHARING CERTIFICATES

Which entitles you to valuable goods

FREE

OUR APOTHECARY SCALE With Weights. FOR SMOKELESS POWDER.

Will weigh from 2 grains to 120 grains. The little weights made of sheet brass are the grain weights, weighing from 2 to 6 grains; the 10-grain weights are made of aluminum and stamped 10 grains. In addition to the above weights we also furnish the regular apothecary scruple and dram weights for druggists, 1 scruple being equal to 20 grains. These scales have 2-inch pans and come put up in a box 5½ inches long, 2½ inches wide and 1¾ inches deep.

No. 6E3451 Price 35c
If by mail, postage extra, 6 cents.

DYNAMITE BLACK AND SMOKELESS POWDER.

In order to conform with the laws of the City of Chicago, and as a necessary economy in the way of getting a low rate of fire insurance, WE ARE UNABLE TO HANDLE, BUY OR SELL ANY KIND OF POWDER OR DYNAMITE.

Understand, this does not apply to loaded ammunition, such as shotgun shells and metallic cartridges. These we carry in immense stocks in a great variety of styles, which we sell in any quantity at much lower prices than you can buy elsewhere.

BULLETS FOR SMOKELESS CARTRIDGES.

S. P. means soft point.
M. P. means full metal patched bullets. Order by catalogue number and style number.

Style No.	Catalogue No. 6E3460 and Caliber.	W'ght of Bullet. Grains	Wgt per 100, lbs.	Price per 100.
7A	25-35 Winchester, M. P.	117	1¼	$0.42
8A	25-35 Winchester, S. P.	117	1¼	.42
9A	25-36 Marlin, M. P.....	117	1¼	.42
1B	25-36 Marlin, S. P.....	117	1¼	.42
2B	30-30 Winchester, M. P.	160	2½	.50
3B	30-30 Winchester, S. P.	160	2½	.50
4B	30-40 U. S. Army, M. P.	220	3¼	1.30
5B	30-40 U. S. Army, S. P.	220	3¼	1.30
6B	32-40 Marlin, M. P.....	165	2½	.70
7B	32-40 Marlin, S. P.....	165	2½	.70
8B	38-55 Marlin, M. P.....	255	3¾	.90
9B	38-55 Marlin, S. P.....	255	3¾	.90
5C	303 Savage, M. P......	180	2¾	.90
6C	303 Savage, S. P......	180	2¾	.90

SHOT AND BAR LEAD.

Subject to market changes without notice.

Drop Shot.

Chilled and dropped shot in sacks of 5 pounds and 25 pounds at lowest market rates. We do not sell less than a sack. The price of shot fluctuates so much that we cannot quote permanent prices. Prices are subject to change without notice. Always mention size wanted. WE CANNOT SELL SHOT IN 5-POUND SACKS AT 25-POUND SACK RATE.

Catalogue Number	Kind of Shot	Size of Shot	Weight of Sack	Price, per Sack
6E3601	Drop	1 to 10	25 lbs.	$1.75
6E3603	Drop	1 to 12	5 lbs.	.42
6E3605	Chilled	1 to 10	25 lbs.	2.00
6E3607	Chilled	1 to 10	5 lbs.	.47
6E3609	Buck Drop	8 to 4	25 lbs.	2.00
6E3610	Buck Drop	8 to 4	5 lbs.	.47
6E3611	Buck Drop	BB	25 lbs.	2.00
6E3612	Buck Drop	BB	5 lbs.	.47

In case of fluctuation chilled shot is always 25 cents higher in 25-pound sacks and 5 cents higher in 5-pound sacks than drop shot. We will always bill shot at the lowest market rates.

No. 6E3613 Bar lead for running bullets at market price; average price about 7 cents per pound.

No. 6E3615 BB Shot in 1-pound packages for air rifles. Price, per pound............10c

We always bill at lowest market prices.

We guarantee lowest market price on cartridges, shells, primers, wads, shot, etc. Prices are subject to change without notice.

B. G. I. LOADING TOOLS, 45c.

These Reloading Tools, made by the Bridgeport Gun Implement Co., Bridgeport, Conn., consist of the following articles, and the bullet mould alone is worth as much as we ask for the complete set. No. 1 is the recapper; No. 2 charge cup; No. 3, decapper; No. 4, bullet mould for the 32-20, 38-40 and 44-40 calibers, and No. 6, is the base block. They come in the following sizes only: state caliber wanted.

No. 6E4279

Caliber	For	Price Per Set
32 S & W	Revolver Cartridges......	45c
38 L C F	Colts' Revolver Cartr'dgs	
32-20.....	Repeating Rifle Cartr'dgs	
38-40.....	Repeating Rifle Cartr'dgs	
44-40.....	Repeating Rifle Cartr'dgs	

If by mail, postage extra, per set, 18 cents.

IDEAL RELOADING TOOL, NO. 1. $1.43.

This tool is nicely nickel plated. All parts necessary to load the cartridge and make bullets are combined in this one tool.

No. 6E4288 Order by catalogue number and state caliber wanted, also name of revolver or rifle.

Caliber (All are Center Fire)	For	Price, Per Set
22 C. F.	Winchester	$1.43
32 Long	Colt's Revolver	1.43
32 S. & W.	Revolvers	1.43
38 Long	Colt's Revolver	1.43
38 S. & W.	Revolvers	1.43
41 Long	Colt's Revolver	1.43

If by mail, postage extra, per set, 23 to 25 cents.

Note—If you want to load S. & W. Cartridges buy S. & W. tools. No other tool will load them

IDEAL RELOADING TOOL No. 4, $1.65 AND $1.68.

This Tool is Nicely Nickel Plated.

All parts necessary to load the cartridge and cast bullets are combined in this one tool. State which caliber is wanted and give name of rifle or revolver.

No. 6E4291 Order by catalogue number and state caliber wanted, also name of rifle or revolver.

Caliber	For	Price, Per Set
25-20	Single Shot	$1.68
25-20	Repeaters	1.65
32 S.&W.	Long, Hand Ejector	1.65
32-20	Repeaters	1.65
38-40	Repeaters	1.65
44-40	Repeaters	1.65
44 Russ.	S. & W. Revolvers	1.68
44 Am.	S. & W. Revolvers	1.68
45 C.F.	Colt's Revolvers	1.65

If by mail, postage extra, per set, 28 to 30 cents.

IDEAL TOOL No. 6, ADJUSTABLE, $1.99.

Ideal Reloading Tool No. 6, adjustable, complete with bullet mould. This tool is substantially the same as No. 6E4294, with an adjustable chamber to accommodate various lengths of shells, and contains all the necessary appliances to make bullets, decap and recap shells, load and seat the bullets, and is without doubt the best tool made. The mould will cast grooved bullets only. Order by catalogue number. State caliber wanted.

Catalogue No.	Caliber	For	Price, per set
6E4293 A	25-36	Marlin......	$1.99
6E4293 B	25-35	Winchester.	1.99
6E4293 C	30-30	Marlin......	1.99
6E4293 D	30-30	Winchester.	1.99
6E4293 E	303	Savage......	1.99
6E4293 F	32-40	Marlin......	1.99
6E4293 G	32-40	Winchester.	1.99
6E4293 H	38-55	Marlin......	1.99
6E4293 J	38-55	Winchester	1.99

If by mail, postage extra, per set, 32 cents.

IDEAL TOOL No. 6, $1.99.

Ideal Reloading Tool No. 6, complete with bullet mould. This tool contains all the necessary appliances to make grooved bullets, decap and recap shells, load and seat the bullets, and is without doubt the best tool made. Order by catalogue number. State caliber wanted.

Catalogue No.	Caliber	For	Price, per set
6E4294 A	38-56	Winchester.	$1.99
6E4294 B	40-65	Winchester.	1.99
6E4294 C	40-82	Winchester.	1.99

If by mail, postage extra, per set, 32 cents.

Catalogue No.	Caliber	For	Price, per set
6E4294 G	45-60-300	Winchester.	$1.99
6E4294 H	45-70-405	Government	1.99
6E4294 J	50-70-450	Government	1.99

If by mail, postage extra, per set, about 39c.

TO PRESERVE SHELLS, always wash them out with hot soapsuds or hot soda water and take out the primers as soon after shooting as possible.

Shell Reducer and Resizer.

No. 6E4296 Shell Reducer and Resizer for any size from 25 to 35, and larger; resize shells which have become bulged. Shipped from New Haven, Conn. Allow for postage. State size wanted.

IDEAL SHELL RESIZING TOOL

Price, each.............................$1.34
If by mail, postage extra, 15 cents.

WINCHESTER MAKE LOADING TOOLS, $1.25.

No. 6E4298 Order by catalogue number.

Caliber	Style	Price
38- 90	Express	$1.25
40- 90	Sharp's Straight............	1.25
40-110	Express	1.25
44	Webley........................	1.25
50- 95	Express	1.25
25- 35	Winchester, without mould.	1.00
30- 40	Army, without mould.	1.00

If by mail, postage extra, 45 cents.

Bullet Moulds.

Be sure and give the size wanted, also give the name of the rifle or revolver. For all sporting and military size cartridges, of regular weight bullets, 1 part tin (or solder) and 40 parts of lead makes a good bullet. If bullet is too soft, add more tin. These moulds are all made specially and we require cash with order. Shipped from New Haven, Conn. Allow for postage.

No. 6E4300 To make grooved bullets. State caliber wanted. Price, each...............74c

No. 6E4302 B. G. I. Bullet Mould, with iron handle instead of wood, in 38-40, 44-40, 38 long C. F., 45-60 Winchester, 45-70 Winchester, 45-70-405. Price.............................40c

Give caliber of mould when ordering.
If by mail, postage extra, 15 cents.

Our Supplemental Chamber.

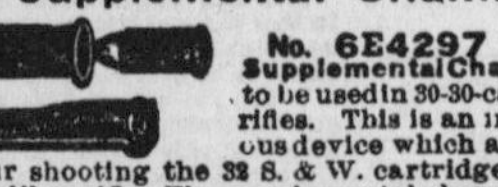

No. 6E4297 Our Supplemental Chamber to be used in 30-30-caliber rifles. This is an ingenious device which admits of your shooting the 32 S. & W. cartridge in a 30-30-caliber rifle. The supplemental chamber is made exactly like a 30-30 caliber shell, and it is chambered to take a 32-caliber S. & W. cartridge, so that if you own a 30-30-caliber rifle you can insert a 32 S. & W. cartridge in this supplemental chamber, put it in the barrel and use your rifle for short range practice at much less expense than shooting 30-30-caliber cartridges. In other words, with this chamber you can shoot a 32-caliber S. & W. cartridge in a 30-30-caliber rifle. These supplemental chambers take the regular 32 S. & W. cartridges, No. 6E2377. Price.......................................59c
If by mail, postage extra, 2 cents.

No. 6E4307 Ideal Dipper for running bullets. Price..................35c
If by mail, postage extra, 7 cents.

No. 6E4308 Ideal Melting Pot for melting lead. Weight, packed, 25 ounces. Price 35c
If by mail, postage extra, 26 cents.

No. 6E4309 Adjustable Cover, to fit any stove, for Ideal melting pot. It is 9¼ inches in diameter and weighs about 24 ounces. Price.............................36c
If by mail, postage extra, 25 cents.

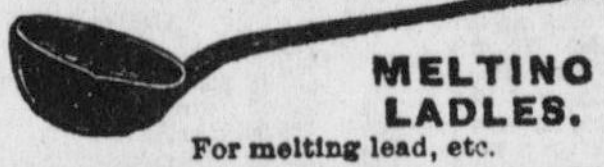

MELTING LADLES.

For melting lead, etc.

Catalogue No.	Diameter of bowl	Weight	Price, Each.
6E4311	3 inches	12 ounces	18c
6E4312	4 inches	15 ounces	28c
6E4313	5 inches	20 ounces	38c
6E4314	6 inches	24 ounces	48c

If by mail, postage extra, per ounce, 1 cent.

Cast Steel Wad Cutters.

Catalogue Number	Gauge or Caliber	Price, each	Postage Extra
6E4318	7 Gauge	21c	5c
6E4319	8 or 9 Gauge	11c	5c
6E4320	10, 11, 12, 14, 15, 16, 19, 20 Gauge	9c	5c
6E4321	32, 38, 44, 45 or 50 Caliber	29c	3c

Always mention gauge or caliber wanted. These Special Reloading Tools are the Highest Grade.

OUR AMERICAN PEDOMETER.

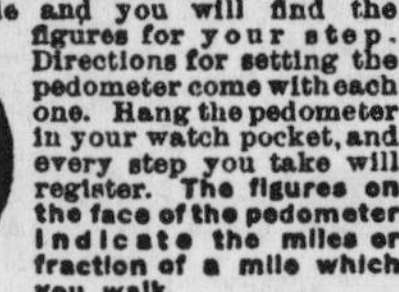

This little instrument looks like a ladies' watch, but it tells how far you walk. To operate our American Pedometer take off the back bezel with a knife blade and you will find the figures for your step. Directions for setting the pedometer come with each one. Hang the pedometer in your watch pocket, and every step you take will register. The figures on the face of the pedometer indicate the miles or fraction of a mile which you walk.

No. 6E4328 The American Pedometer. Registers ten miles and repeats. Price.....75c

No. 6E4329 Is the same with a dial like the second hand on a watch and registers 100 miles and repeats. Price.........................99c
If by mail, postage extra, 4 cents.

SHELL LOADERS.

Shellac finished Rammer, Cap and Base with polished nickel spun tube. Mention gauge wanted.

No. 6E4330A 12-gauge. Price.....14c
No. 6E4330¼ 10-gauge. Price.....14c
No. 6E4330½ 16-gauge. Price.....16c
No. 6E4330¾ 12-gauge. Price.....16c
No. 6E4930E 8-gauge. Price.....44c

If by mail, postage extra, each 4 cents.

NOTE—The decapper, or expelling pin, will be found in all loaders by taking the knob off the rammer—see illustration.

The Paragon Recappers.

Black Japanned Recapper, neat and handy for recapping shells.

Catalogue No.	For Shells	Price	Postage Extra
6E4350A	12-gauge	6c	3c
6E4350¼	10-gauge	6c	3c
6E4351	16-gauge	7c	3c
6E4351¼	20-gauge	7c	3c
6E4351E	8-gauge	35c	4c

OUR EXCELSIOR PAPER SHELL CRIMPER.

In order to give our customers an extra fine paper shell crimper at a low price, we have arranged to manufacture them ourselves. Nearly all cheap and medium grade crimpers are manufactured of common cast iron, with common crimping cups, no expelling pin to discharge the shell from the crimper after being crimped, a short chamber, and in many respects not properly gauged. On our own paper shell crimper, which we ourselves manufacture we have covered and improved all the weak points of cheap crimpers, by making our levers and cranks of the very best malleable iron which money can buy; our crimping cups are made of hard brass, with steel crimping pins, which last longer and do better work than the ordinary brass cups. Each and every crimper which we make is fitted with an expelling pin and long chamber, all are handsomely japanned, and they are by far the best crimpers ever offered by any house at the following prices. We furnish them in 10, 12, 16 and 20 gauge as desired. Order by catalogue number and state gauge wanted.

Catalogue Number	For Shells	Price, each	Postage extra
6E4357A	12-gauge	$0.30	18c
6E4357¼	10-gauge	.31	18c
6E4357½	16-gauge	.32	18c
6E4357¾	20-gauge	.33	18c
6E4357E	8-gauge	1.00	28c

NOTICE—To make a good crimp, turn fast and feed slowly.

GOLD BRONZED PAPER SHELL CRIMPER.

Our Excelsior Paper Shell Crimper, gold bronzed, japanned handle, expelling pin; a good, strong crimper.

To produce perfect crimp, turn fast and feed slowly.

Catalogue Number	For Shells	Price, each	Postage, extra
6E4358A	12-gauge	40c	18c
6E4358¼	10-gauge	41c	18c
6E4358½	16-gauge	42c	18c
6E4358¾	20-gauge	43c	18c

The New Ideal Diamond Square or Round Crimp Closer.

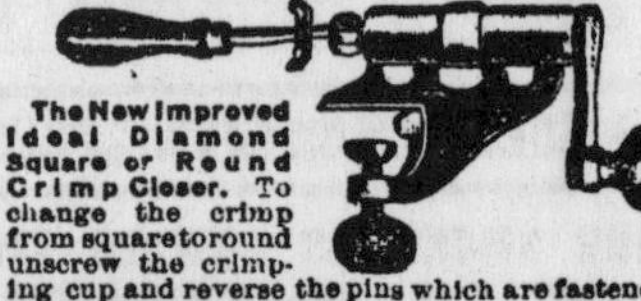

The New Improved Ideal Diamond Square or Round Crimp Closer. To change the crimp from square to round unscrew the crimping cup and reverse the pins which are fastened by small screws. It has a new straight feed lever, with steel grip. The only tool that will crimp every shell alike, no matter what variations of load may be. The only tool having an automatic plunger that prevents the end of the shell from spreading over the wad. All wearing parts and cups are of steel. The best crimper ever made.

SQUARE CRIMP

Showing style of square crimp.

Catalogue Number	For Shells	Price, each	Postage, extra
6E4360A	12-gauge	$1.47	32c
6E4360¼	10-gauge	1.48	32c
6E4360½	16-gauge	1.49	32c

TO LUBRICATE BULLETS, Dip the bullets in lubricant and set them on a board till lubricant is hard in the grooves. Good lubricant can be made from beef tallow with enough vaseline to soften it, or pure vaseline with enough paraffin to harden it. Never use fat which has salt or acid in it. It is liable to rust or pit the barrel.

NOTICE. For information on casting bullets, etc., send 3 cents to pay the postage on our Handbook of Useful Information.

SHELL LOADING BLOCKS 85c.

Our 50-Hole Shell Loading Block. Made of white wood, holes bored with shoulder to fit the entire length of shell. The top of hole is reamed out to act as a wad starter; shell does not come within ½ inch from top of block; shells cannot bulge or break down. With this block you can load 50 shells in half the time than the old way, and no danger of upsetting the shells when half loaded. Weight, about 3 pounds.

Catalogue No.	Holds	Gauge	Price
6E4362A	50 shells	12	85c
6E4362B	50 shells	10	
6E4362C	50 shells	16	

If by mail, postage extra, 53 cents.

SHELL LOADING BLOCK, 18c

No. 6E4363 Our 20-Hole Block is 1 inch deep, holds twenty shells, and made in 10, 12 and 16-gauge only. You will not upset shells while loading when using a block. State gauge wanted. Price, each.....18c
If by mail, postage extra, 9 cents.

GUN CLEANING IMPLEMENTS.

No. 6E4364 Our Jointed Cleaning Rods, made of beech or maple wood; patent brass joints and three implements, swab, scratch brush and wiper; 10, 12 or 16-gauge. Weight, packed, 13 ounces. Full length 36 inches.
Price per set. (Postage extra, 10 cents)....21c
No. 6E4365½ The same rod 48 inches long. Price.....30c

COCOBOLO JOINTED CLEANING RODS

No. 6E4366 Our New Fancy Cocobolo Jointed Cleaning Rod is made in three joints, as shown in the above illustration. It is made of cocobolo wood, with nickel plated joints and trimmings, universal thread for implements which take any of the standard swabs, slots or wire scratch brushes. The rod when joined is 37 inches long, and when disconnected, each joint is 13 inches long. It is a very handsome cleaning rod, and each rod is accompanied by a wire scratch brush, wool swab and a slotted wiper. Price, per set.....64c
If by mail, postage extra, 13 cents.

Attachments for Jointed Rods.

No. 6E4375 No. 6E4376 No. 6E4377

Catalogue Number	Article	For Rods No.	Price each	Postage extra
6E4375	Wool Swab	6E4365 or 6E4366	5c	4c
6E4376	Double Wiper		8c	4c
6E4377	Wire Brush		5c	4c

No. 6E4378A The Celebrated Ferris Gun Cleaner. The best cleaner on the market. It can be attached to jointed cleaning rods. 10 or 12-gauge. Excellent for removing lead or burnt powder from the barrel.
Price, each...(Postage extra, 5 cents.)..35c

The Tomlinson Gun Cleaner.

The Tomlinson Gun Cleaner for Shotguns; wire gauze cleaner; this is the best cleaner on the market; fits any standard jointed cleaning rod.
No. 6E4379A 12-gauge. Price.....44c
No. 6E4379B 10-gauge. Price.....44c
If by mail, postage extra, 5 cents.
No. 6E4379F Extra wire gauze to replace sides. Price, per pair.....10c
If by mail, postage extra, 1 cent.

THE A B C SHOTGUN CLEANER.

No. 6E4380 This is the latest and one of the best shotgun cleaners made. It has broad, sharp blades covering the entire circumference of gun barrel, which instantly cuts out all lead and burnt powder. Is made of brass, nickeled, will not harm the finest barrel. When used for holding cloth for wiping, and brass strainer cloth for burnishing, it is the finest burnisher made. Constant use only makes it sharper. Turning thumb nut adjusts it to 10 or 12-gauge.
Price, nickel plated.....37c
If by mail, postage extra, 4 cents.

Brass Wire Brushes.
10, 12, 16 or 20-Gauge.

No. 6E4381 Brass Wire Brush for removing lead, powder caking and rust spots; can be attached to any jointed rod; 10, 12, 16 or 20-gauge. Order by gauge, as one brush will fit but one gauge. Price.....37c
If by mail, postage extra, 2 cents.

McMillan's Shell Extractor.

No. 6E4383 The Universal Shell Extractor will extract any shell from 22-caliber to 8-gauge. Nickel plated. Price.....8c
If by mail, postage extra, 1 cent.

Ring Shell Extractors.

Catalogue Number	Gauge	Price	Postage Extra
6E4385A	12	5c	1c
6E4385B	10	5c	1c
6E4385C	16	6c	1c
6E4385D	20	6c	1c

Hickory Rods.

No. 6E4386 Our Hickory Cleaning Rod, with ball handle and jag on end. 28 inches long, 7-16 inch diameter; for shotguns and large caliber rifles.
Price .....(Postage extra, 5 cents.)......10c

Powder and Shot Measure

No. 6E4388 Interchangeable Powder and Shot Measure Combined; enameled handle, polished nickel finish; the same measure will answer for powder or shot. Price.....10c
If by mail, postage extra, 3 cents.

Revolver Cleaner Brush.

No. 6E4390 Twisted Wire and Bristle Revolver Brushes. State caliber and length of barrel when ordering. Comes in 22, 32, 38 or 44-caliber. Price.....6c
If by mail, postage extra, 1 cent.

Rifle Cleaning Rod.

No. 6E4391 Twisted wire, bristle brush on end. 22-caliber. 24 inches long. Price..6c
If by mail, postage extra, 5 cents.

Brass Rifle Brushes.
22 to 50-Caliber.

No. 6E4396 Brass Wire Brush to fit No. 6E4398 Cleaning Rod. Brass shank especially made for cleaning rust and burnt powder out of rifles. Made in 22, 25, 30, 32, 38, 40, 44, 45 and 50-calibers. State caliber wanted. Price.....14c
If by mail, postage extra, 2 cents.

Brass Cleaning Rods, 25c.

No. 6E4398 Four-jointed Brass Cleaning Rods; can be carried in the pocket. This rod has a revolving handle so the brush or cleaning rag follows the rifling grooves. Made in 22, 30, 32, 38, 44, 45 and 50-caliber. State caliber wanted. Price.....25c
If by mail, postage extra, 10 cents.

U. S. Government Cleaner.

No. 6E4400 Consists of a bristle brush and slotted wiper, with detachable cord and weight for dropping through barrel; a separate slotted wiper for drawing through a dry cloth and for oiling. The No. 6E4396 brush in 32, 38, 44 and 50-caliber may be used with this cleaner. Made in 22, 32, 38, 45 or 50-caliber. State caliber wanted. Price.....(Postage extra, 4c)....22c

GUN IMPLEMENT SETS

OUR 8-PIECE LOADING SET $1.00.

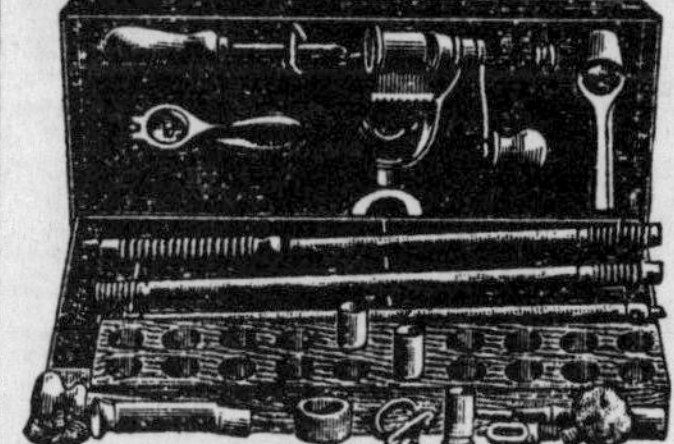

This complete Gun Implement Set for loading paper shells and cleaning a gun as illustrated and described contains eight articles, and comes in a strong pasteboard box. Size, 5x13 inches; neatly divided into compartments for each article, and each implement is made of good material and recommends itself to every owner of a breech loading shotgun. The best ever offered for the money. No house can compete with us on these goods; in fact if you bought these goods one at a time from regular stores you would have to pay about the following prices.

1 Shell Loading Block, with 20 holes.....$0.25
1 Jointed Cleaning Rod, with attachments .35
1 Paper Shell Crimper Japanned, with Expelling Pin.....45
1 Combined Powder and Shot Measure.....15
1 Rammer, Decapper (take off the knob to find decapper pin) and Nickel Loading Tube.....20
1 Shell Recapper, japanned.....15
1 Ring Shell Extractor, nickeled.....15
1 Steel Wad Cutter.....15
Eight pieces, making a total of.....$1.85

While our price for the complete 8-piece 12-gauge set is $1.00 or nearly one-half what you would have to pay, and the quality of our set is much better than offered by others, our closers are malleable iron while others are gray iron, etc.

Our Prices for the Above 8-Piece Sets.

Order by catalogue number and state gauge wanted. If sent by mail, allow for postage.

Catalogue No.	Gauge	Weight of Set	Price, per Set	Postage extra
6E4401A	12	42 oz.	$1.00	45c
6E4401B	10	42 oz.	1.01	45c
6E4401C	16	37 oz.	1.02	40c
6E4401D	20	41 oz.	1.03	44c

OUR 7-PIECE LOADING SET, 75c.

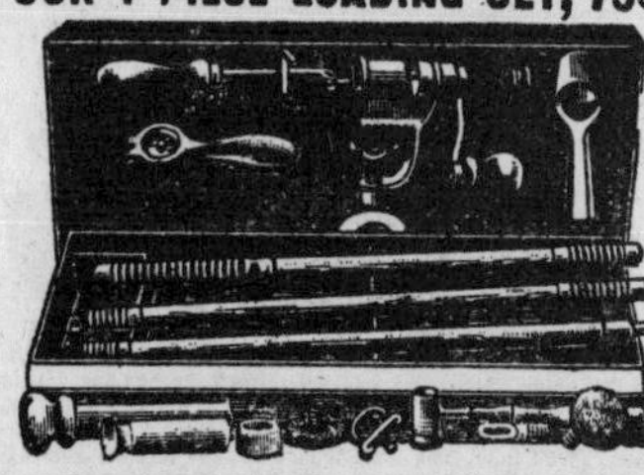

Our 7-piece Loading and Cleaning Set is put up in a nice box 5x13 inches and is practically the same quality in every way as our 8-piece set, with the exception that it has no shell loading block, otherwise it is as high grade and of the same exceptional value. We would like you to compare our loading tools in quality and price with other houses and convince yourself that we are headquarters on these goods. We show below how much you would have to pay for an outfit of this kind if you bought it at a regular store.

1 Jointed Cleaning Rod with Attachments.$0.35
1 Paper Shell Crimper with Expelling Pin .45
1 Combined Powder and Shot Measure.....15
1 Rammer, Decapper (take off knob to find decapper pin) and Loading Tube.....20
1 Shell Recapper.....15
1 Ring Shell Extractor.....15
1 Steel Wad Cutter.....15
Seven pieces, making a total of.....$1.60

While our price for a better quality outfit is only 75 cents. REMEMBER, we give you the best quality outfit that you can get anywhere in the United States and for less money than you can buy elsewhere.

Our Prices for the Above Described and Illustrated Set.

Order by catalogue number and mention gauge wanted. If sent by mail, allow for postage.

Catalogue No.	Gauge	Weight per Set	Price per Set	Postage Extra
6E4403A	12	33 oz.	75c	35 cents
6E4403B	10	33 oz.	76c	35 cents
6E4403C	16	33 oz.	77c	35 cents
6E4403D	20	33 oz.	78c	35 cents

Amateur Trapper and Trap Makers' Guide.

By Stanley Harding. A new work based upon the experience of the most successful trappers, trap makers and hunters, containing plain directions for constructing the most approved traps, snares, nets and dead falls; the most successful baits for attracting all kinds of animals, birds, etc. Chapters for preparing skins and furs for the market and for tanning them for future use; with concise and comprehensive instructions for preserving and stuffing specimens of birds, animals, etc. Illustrated.
No. 3E096124 Paper covers. Price..18c
No. 3E096125 Cloth. Price.....27c
If by mail, postage extra, paper, 3c., cloth, 6c.

OUR 6-PIECE LOADING SET.

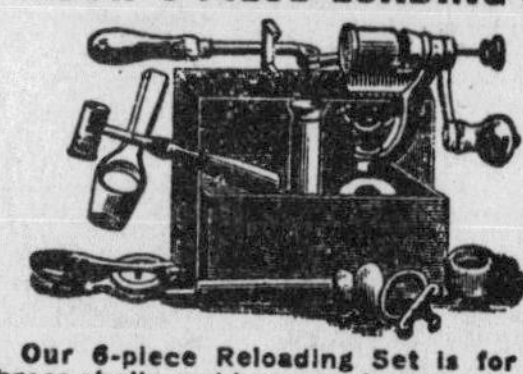

50c

Our 6-piece Reloading Set is for paper or brass shells and has no cleaning implements nor loading block, otherwise it is of the same high quality as our 7 and 8-piece sets. We will give you here a list of the prices which regular stores would charge you for an outfit if you bought it separately. No doubt many of our customers have bought these goods and can verify our figures.

1 Paper Shell Crimper with Expelling Pin.....$0.45
1 Combined Powder and Shot Measure. .15
1 Rammer, Decapper (take off knob to find decapper pin) and Loading Tube. .20
1 Shell Recapper.....15
1 Ring Shell Extractor.....15
1 Steel Wad Cutter.....15
Six pieces, making a total of.....$1.25

While our price for a better outfit is but less than half this price. The outfit comes put up in a neat paper box made especially for it as illustrated.

Our Prices on This 6-piece Outfit.

Order by catalogue number and mention gauge wanted. If by mail, allow for postage.

Catalogue No.	Gauge	Weight per Set	Price per Set	Postage Extra
6E4406A	12	21 oz.	50c	22 cents
6E4406B	10	24 oz.	51c	26 cents
6E4406C	16	20 oz.	52c	23 cents
6E4406D	20	20 oz.	53c	22 cents

POWDER FLASKS.

No. 6E4415 Holding 4 ounces black powder. Price.....14c
No. 6E4416 Holding 8 ounces black powder, with cord, common top. Price.....18c
No. 6E4417 Holding 12 ounces black powder, with cord, common top. Price.....24c
No. 6E4418 Holding 16 ounces black powder, with cord, common top. Price.....30c
If by mail, postage extra, 6 to 9 cents.

LEATHER SHOT POUCHES.

No. 6E4420 Embossed Leather Pouch with lever charger, for holding 2½ to 3 pounds shot. Price.....25c
No. 6E4421 Embossed Shot Pouch with lever charger, solid leather, holding 4 to 5 lbs. of shot. Price.....35c
If by mail, postage extra, 8 to 10 cents.

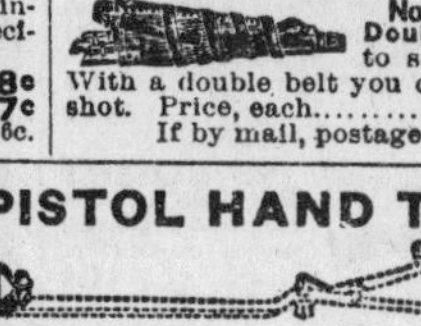

No. 6E4422 Double Leather Shot Belt to sling over shoulder. With a double belt you can carry two sizes of shot. Price, each.....28c
If by mail, postage extra, 11 cents.

OUR NEW J. C. PISTOL HAND TRAP.

$1.65

The above illustration, engraved direct from a photograph, will give you some idea of our J. C. Hand Trap, which we formerly sold at $3.25. Believing that we could manufacture this trap cheaper than the former manufacturer, we have made a contract with him whereby we obtain the right to manufacture these traps on a royalty, and under this contract we can offer this trap to our customers on our policy of one small percentage of profit above the cost of production, at $1.65.

No. 6E4423 This is the latest and most novel contrivance ever invented for trap shooters. It weighs but 6 pounds and will throw any standard target, such as blue rocks, white flyers, etc., as far as any stationary trap. The trap when sprung is 39 inches long, and when it is set for shooting is 24 inches long. The carrier is made adjustable and the mainspring is made so that it can be tightened or loosened for fast or slow birds as the shooter may desire. This J. C. Pistol Trap is made of malleable iron. The carrier is made of steel stampings, and the entire trap resembles a pistol, as you will notice by the above illustration, and the main feature of this trap is that you can do trap shooting anywhere with it. Two or more friends can go out together and you do not have to stop and fasten down the trap, as you must do with an expert trap, as it is always ready, and it will throw targets at any and all angles. All you have to do is to point the trap the way you wish the target to fly; for throwing at unknown angles, let the trapper stand behind you. When throwing targets let the trap swing forward about 4 to 6 inches after pulling trigger to obtain the best results and to reduce vibration. Weight, packed for shipment, about 9 pounds.
Price on this J. C. Pistol Trap.....$1.65

Empire Expert Trap For Expert Shooting, $5.00.

No. 6E4424 Our Empire Expert Trap. This trap will be found more substantial and more compact than others now in use; all the working parts being large, strong and bearings well fitted, assuring positive action in every detail. The Empire Expert Trap is constructed with a lever trigger pull, which allows the trap to be changed to any desired angle without interfering with the pulling device, and the ropes always have the same length and tension of the pull. These traps will throw any standard target, such as the blue rock, white flyer, black bird and others, at all angles. Weight, packed for shipment, 40 pounds. Price.....$5.00

Our White Flyer Targets.

The Latest and Best Target Made.

NOTE OUR PRICES of $1.99 for 500, $3.95 for 1000, and you will observe our price is below all others. Our terms are cash with order on these goods.

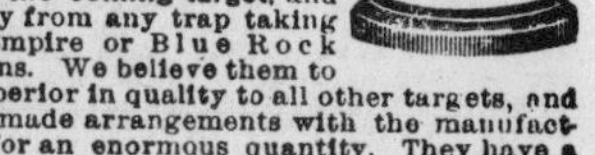

No. 6E4426 This is no doubt the coming target, and will fly from any trap taking the Empire or Blue Rock pigeons. We believe them to be superior in quality to all other targets, and have made arrangements with the manufacturer for an enormous quantity. They have a white rim, make a lighter colored target than the others, which will be a great advantage on gloomy days. Try a barrel of White Flyers and you will surely want more. Weight, per barrel (500 targets), 148 pounds.
Price, per barrel (500).....$1.99
Price, per 1000.....3.95

Our terms are cash with order on these goods.

Shooting Gallery Targets.

Round Steel Face Plain and Figure Targets.

No. 6E4433

No. 6E4431 Steel Target, 12-inch diameter, heavy, for 22 or 32 caliber rim fire cartridges. Without the bird figure, but it rings when bull's eye is hit. Weight, 15 pounds. Price............**$1.48**

No. 6E4433 12-inch diameter, steel face, ¼-inch thick. Bird is thrown up and bell rings when bull's eye is hit. May be reset with rope from the shooting stand. Intended for cartridges not larger than 32 long rim fire. Weight, 12½ lbs. Price......**$2.49**

No. 6E4434 Our new skeleton face steel target, 12 inches in diameter. Made of sheet steel ¼ inch thick and adapted to 22 caliber cartridges. When the bull's eye is hit a bell rings and the face of the target turns down, showing a skeleton head, where the face of target was. The target being swiveled on each side. The skeleton head may be removed and you can use any other figure or an advertisement to take its place. The target may be reset from the shooting stand and the skeleton is not in view to the shooter, which creates quite a little amusement when the shooter first hits a bull's eye and then sees the skeleton head facing him. Weight, about 12 pounds. Price....................**$2.55**

Gun Grease, Gun Oil, Etc.

American Gun Grease.

No. 6E4543 The American Gun Grease is the best rust preventer manufactured. For any steel or polished iron surface, and for inside or outside of gun or rifle barrels, it has no equal. Put up in neat metallic tubes. Price, per tube........**9c**
If by mail, postage extra, per tube, 5 cents.

Good Quality Gun Oil.

No. 6E4546 S., R. & Co.'s Sperm Gun Oil; put up exclusively for guns, gunlocks and fine machinery, prevents rust and will not gum.
Price, per 2-ounce bottle.........**7c**
If by mail, postage extra, 8 cents.

DUCK, TURKEY AND SNIPE CALLS.

No. 6E4560 Allen's Latest Improved Wood Duck Caller, the most natural toned and easiest blowing. Used on the duck pass by the best duck shooters in America. With a little practice you can call crows fairly well with the Allen. Price............................**34c**
If by mail, postage extra, 6 cents.

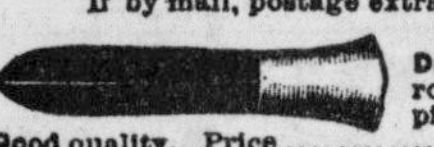

No. 6E4563 Duck Calls, with rosewood mouthpiece, horn tip.
Good quality. Price..............................**18c**
If by mail, postage extra, 4 cents.

Our Latest Turkey Caller.

No. 6E4564 Our Turkey Caller is made from well seasoned wood, adapted to make the proper sound for decoying turkeys. Hold the caller in the left hand, as shown in the illustration, and with the right hand rub the slate on the side of the caller, either with the edge or with the flat side, and after a little practice you will be able to decoy turkeys successfully. This caller is 4½ inches long, 2½ inches wide, and may be carried in the pocket. Price.......**44c**
If by mail, postage extra, 3 cents.

Horn Turkey Call.

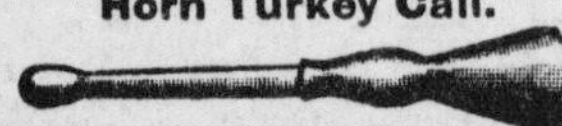

No. 6E4565 Turkey Calls, horn tip with rosewood mouthpiece. Calls by sucking into it. Price. (If by mail, postage extra, 4c)...**19c**

No. 6E4567 Snipe Calls, made of best horn and a perfect snipe call.
Price....(If by mail, postage extra, 2c)...**14c**

Our Hawk Call, 43 Cents.

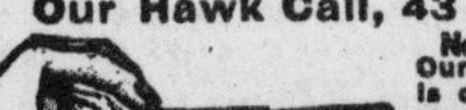

No. 6E4568 Our Hawk Call is designed and manufactured by a man who has had much trouble by hawks killing his chickens, and the hawk caller pays for itself many times over every time a hawk is killed. Hold the caller in the left hand, as shown in the illustration, and by blowing through it you can soon become expert in decoying hawks toward you.
Price..**43c**
If by mail, postage extra, 2 cents.

Wild Goose Caller.

No. 6E4570 Fuller's Metallic Wild Goose Caller. Very good.
Price...(If by mail, postage extra, 6c).....**71c**

CEDAR WOOD DECOY DUCKS.

In making these decoys great care has been used to select only sound white cedar for their construction and to secure a perfect balance. They are light, substantial and naturally painted. They will not sink if you shoot them. $2.45 and $3.65 per dozen. Each dozen contains 8 drakes and 4 females. We cannot furnish them any other way except by special order, which causes delay. Decoys below these prices cannot be properly made and painted to look natural. For highest grade wood decoy ducks, these prices are BELOW ANY COMPETITION.

They come in mallard, canvasback, redhead, bluebill, teal or sprigtail. Weight, 35 to 40 pounds per dozen. State which style you wish.

REMEMBER—We can only furnish 8 drakes and 4 females in each dozen.

No. 6E4595 No. 1, our best decoy ducks, nicely painted in natural colors with glass eyes. State which style you wish.
Price, per dozen, **$3.65**; each.........**35c**

No. 6E4596 No. 2, good decoy ducks, nicely painted in natural colors, but with painted eyes. State which style you wish.
Price, per dozen, **$2.45**; each.........**25c**

No. 6E4597 Anchors with cord for decoys.
Price, per dozen.................................**39c**

Collapsible Canvas Ducks.

No. 6E4600 Collapsible Canvas Decoy. A good imitation of the natural duck. Made of the best canvas, beautifully painted in natural colors, waterproofed, inflated with air, and when not in use the air can be let out and ducks folded. Weight, 4 ounces each. Packed one dozen in a neat box, 7x16x9 inches, and a dozen when packed will weigh 8 pounds. We sell in any quantity. We handle these decoys in Mallard species only. To inflate, put cork in mouth, inflate and adjust the cork with the tongue.
Price, per dozen...............................**$5.40**

Grass Suits Reduced to 84c.

84c PER SUIT is our price and thousands are being worn by sportsmen everywhere.

No. 6E5112 For wild goose, duck and all kinds of shore bird shooting; made of long, tough imported marsh grass into a cape coat with hood. They weigh about five pounds and are convenient to wear and shoot from. Make good waterproofs in rainy weather, are easily packed and carried. Hunters appreciate the value of these suits, as no blind or bough house is necessary when shooting on marshes. Weight, about 5 pounds.
Cannot be sent by mail. Price, per suit..**84c**

REPAIR PARTS FOR FLOBERT RIFLES.

NOTICE—These parts are not fitted. They are in a filed state and must be fitted by a gunsmith or mechanic. If possible send us the broken part and we will try to match it as near as we can.

Flobert Breech Blocks.

These parts are not fitted.

No. 6E7300 Remington Action Breech Blocks. Filed, cut nose, not fitted. Price..............................**23c**
If by mail, postage extra, 2 cents.

No. 6E7301 Remington Action Breech Blocks. Filed, pointed nose, not fitted. Price..............................**20c**
If by mail, postage extra, 2 cents.

Warnant Breech Blocks.

No. 6E7303 For Light Warnant Action Floberts weighing about 4½ pounds, not fitted. Price.........**30c**

No. 6E7304 For Heavy Warnant Floberts weighing about 8 pounds, not fitted. Price..............................**34c**
If by mail, postage extra, 6 cents.

Improved Warnant Breech Blocks.

No. 6E7305 For Light Improved Warnant Action, like our No. 6E658, not finished. Price..............**35c**

No. 6E7306 For Heavy Improved Warnant Action, like our Nos. 6E659 or 6E663, not finished. Price..............................**40c**
If by mail, postage extra, 5 cents.

Flobert Extractors.

No. 6E7307 No. 6E7308

No. 6E7307 Filed for Side Extractor Floberts, not finished. Price..............**14c**

No. 6E7308 Filed for Remington Action Floberts, not finished. Price..............**11c**

No. 6E7309 Filed for Warnant Action Floberts (to go with No. 6E7303), not finished.
Price..**18c**

No. 6E7310 Filed for Heavy Warnant Action Floberts (to go with No. 6E7304), not finished. Price...(Postage extra, 2 cents)....**22c**

Flobert Hammers, Filed.

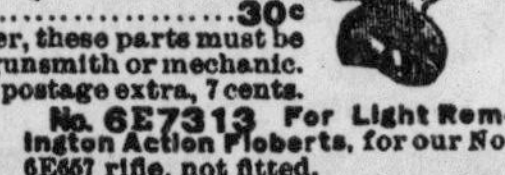

No. 6E7311 For Side Extractor Floberts, for our No. 6E655 rifle, not fitted. Price......**27c**

No. 6E7312 For Light Warnant Action Floberts, old style, not fitted, to go with No. 6E7303.
Price...**30c**
Remember, these parts must be fitted by a gunsmith or mechanic.
If by mail, postage extra, 7 cents.

No. 6E7313 For Light Remington Action Floberts, for our No. 6E657 rifle, not fitted.
Price...**29c**

No. 6E7314 For Improved Warnant Action Floberts, for our No. 6E658 rifle, not fitted. Price, **25c**

No. 6E7315 For Heavy Improved Warnant Floberts, for our No. 6E659 or No. 6E663 rifle, not fitted. Price.............................**30c**
If by mail, postage extra, 5 cents.

No. 6E7316 Hammer Swivels, for Flobert hammers, filed, not fitted. Price......**5c**
If by mail, postage extra, 1 cent.

Flobert Main Springs.

No. 6E7317 Flobert Main Springs, suitable for all styles of Floberts, not fitted.
Price...**17c**
If by mail, postage extra, 2 cents.

No. 6E7318 Flobert Trigger Springs, suitable for all Floberts, not fitted. Price..............................**9c**
If by mail, postage extra, 2 cents.

No. 6E7319 Flobert Front Sights, filed, not fitted. Price.....**9c**

No. 6E7320 Flobert Rear Sights, filed, not fitted. Price....**10c**
If by mail, postage extra, 1 cent.

Flobert Triggers.

No. 6E7321 Flobert Triggers, filed, not fitted. Price..............................**13c**
Postage extra, 2 cents.

Flobert Screws.

Catalogue No.	For	Price
6E7323	Fore End	7c
6E7324	Trigger Springs	8c
6E7325	Breech Blocks	9c

If by mail, postage extra, 1 cent.

Nipple Wrench.

No. 6E7326 Nipple Wrench, polished.
Price..............................**24c**
If by mail, postage extra, 5 cents.

WHEN ORDERING PARTS for guns, rifles or revolvers, always give the name, caliber or gauge of the gun, rifle or revolver. This will save us from writing for this information.

GUN TUBES FOR MUZZLE LOADERS.

Number of Threads to the Inch:
The English have 28 threads.
The Belgian have 30 threads.
The Springfield have 24 threads.
The Enfield have 20 threads.
The nipples have the following threads to the inch and of the specified diameter.

	Threads	Diameter
Enfield	20 per inch	5-16 inch
Springfield	24 per inch	5-16 inch
Belgian	30 per inch	¼ inch
English	28 per inch	15-64 to 20-64

When ordering English nipples always give diameter or send the old nipple.

Catalogue No.	Style	Polished	Price, Each	Postage Extra
6E7330	English	Shank	5c	1c
6E7331	English	Outside	8c	1c
6E7332	English	Bottom	10c	1c
6E7333	English	Inside	15c	1c
6E7334	Belgian	Medium	10c	1c
		For		
6E7336	Springfield	Musket Caps	10c	1c
6E7337	Springfield	Gun Caps	12c	1c
6E7338	Enfield	Musket Caps	10c	1c
6E7339	Enfield	Gun Caps	12c	1c

MUZZLE LOADING GUN LOCKS.

THESE GUN LOCKS are finished, but will have to be fitted to your gun. No two guns are exactly alike and therefore we cannot furnish gun locks to fit exactly. Measure the length of your gun lock and tell us how long it is, or send us a drawing of the lock plate, and we will send you the nearest we have to it. We usually send them a trifle longer because it is easy to cut out the stocks a little more to make them fit. Gun locks usually measure 4½ to 5 inches from end to end.

BACK ACTION, POLISHED.

FOR MUZZLE LOADERS.

Mention Length Wanted.

Cat. No.	Style	Kind	Length, inches	Price each
6E7340	Back	Rt. hand	4½, 4¾, 5	48c
6E7341	Action	Left hand	4½, 4¾, 5	50c

If by mail, postage extra, 6 cents.

ALWAYS INCLUDE POSTAGE if you wish goods sent by mail.

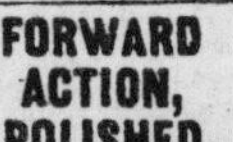

FORWARD ACTION, POLISHED.

FOR MUZZLE LOADERS

Mention Length Wanted.

Cat. No.	Style	Kind	Length, inches	Price each
6E7342	Forward	Rt. hand	4½, 4¾, 5	49c
6E7343	Action	Left hand	4½, 4¾, 5	51c

If by mail, postage extra, 6 cents.

FOR MUZZLE LOADERS

No. 6E7345 C. P. American Forward Action, cut for plug, right hand, for muzzle loading rifles, 4½, 4¾ or 5 inches long; give length wanted.
Price..**65c**
If by mail, postage extra, 6 cents.

FULL BAR ACTION GUN LOCKS.

FOR MUZZLE LOADERS.

Mention Length Wanted.

Cat. No.	Style	Kind	Length, inches	Price each
6E7346	Bar	Rt. hand	4½, 4¾, 5	55c
6E7347	Action	Left hand	4½, 4¾, 5	57c

By mail, postage extra, 6 cents.

HAMMERS FOR MUZZLE LOADING GUNS.

Muzzle Loading Hammers, 1½ to 1¾ inches from middle of nose to center of hole. State size wanted.

Catalogue No.	Side	Size, inches	Price each
6E7353	Right	1½ to 1¾	23c
6E7354	Left	1½ to 1¾	24c

If by mail, postage extra, 2 cents.

ROUGH TURNED WALNUT GUN STOCKS.

No. 6E7361 Rough Turned Gun Stocks, turned to shape, leaving the square end 1¾ inches wide and 2 inches from top to bottom, length 16¼ inches, butt measure 5¼x1¾ inches. Made of good American walnut, not fitted, just shaped, for double barrel breech loading guns. Weight, 20 ounces. Price..............**47c**
If by mail, postage extra, 27 cents.

NEW STOCKS AND FORE ENDS FITTED TO GUNS.
When stocks of double guns are broken so you can't repair them with glue, a new one will have to be fitted by hand and we can do this work all the way from $8.00 to $12.00, according to the quality of wood and amount of labor required. Fore ends fitted to back action guns from $2.75 to $4.00; to bar lock guns from $3.00 to $4.00. You to pay transportation charges both ways on the gun.

No. 6E7365 Worms for Ram Rods, reversed, medium size. Price..............**12c**
If by mail, postage extra, 2 cents.

TUMBLER PINS.

No. 6E7369 Tumbler Pins, threaded, for muzzle loading locks. Send sample, showing size, so we can match it. Price..............................**5c**
If by mail, postage extra, 1 cent.

No. 6E7370 Tumbler Pins, threaded for American made guns. Mention for which gun it is wanted. Price..............................**15c**
If by mail, postage extra, 1 cent.

SIDE PINS.

No. 6E7371 Side Pins, threaded for muzzle loading locks. Price..............................**5c**
If by mail, postage extra, 1 cent.

CROSS PINS.

No. 6E7372 Cross Pins for muzzle loading guns.
Price..**10c**

No. 6E7373 Cross Pins, for breech loading guns. Price..............................**12c**
If by mail, postage extra, 1 cent.

INSIDE LOCK SCREWS.

No. 6E7374 Inside Lock Screws, threaded. Price..............**8c**
If by mail, postage extra, 1 cent.

No. 6E7375 Tumbler Swivels, filed, single horn, not fitted. Price..............**5c**
If by mail, postage extra, 1 cent.

NICKEL PLATING REVOLVERS.

While we do not recommend nickel plating rusty revolvers, as it never makes as good a job as a new revolver, nor can an old revolver be made to look like new, we are, however, equipped to do this work if our customers wish it done, at prices ranging from $1.25 to $1.50 each for pocket size, and $1.50 to $1.75 for belt size. Add postage at the rate of 1 cent per ounce.

TOP LEVER SPRINGS.

Order by Number. Catalogue No. 6E7376

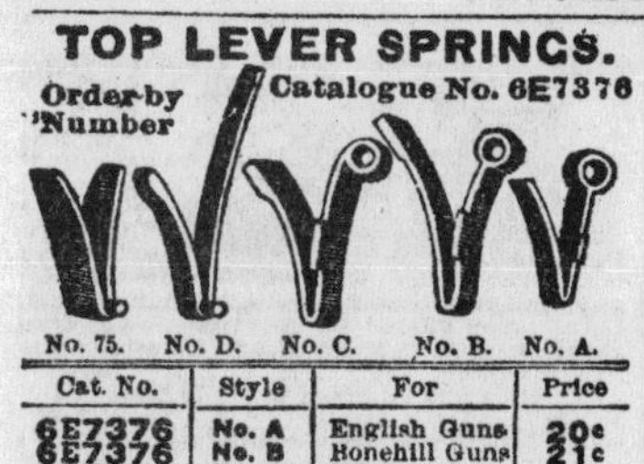

Cat. No.	Style	For	Price
6E7376	No. A	English Guns	20c
6E7376	No. B	Bonehill Guns	21c
6E7376	No. C	English Guns	22c
6E7376	No. D	Tolley Guns	23c
6E7376	No. 75	Belgian Guns	14c

If by mail, postage extra, 2 cents.

SEAR SPRINGS, FILED.

Cat. No.	For Locks	Side	Price
6E7377	Back Action	Rt. Hand	9c
6E7378	Back Action	Left Hand	9c
6E7381	Bar Action	Rt. Hand	10c
6E7382	Bar Action	Left Hand	10c

If by mail, postage extra, 1 cent.

Front Sights for Double Guns.

No. 6E7383 Made of Brass, Threaded for Double Guns.
Price.........(postage extra, 1 cent)......5c

NOTICE—This material is not finished nor ready to put into guns. It has to be fitted by a gunsmith or mechanic. If possible, send us the broken part, so we can better match it.

BREECH LOADING GUN HAMMERS.

No. 6E7384 Flat Body. No. 6E7386 Round Body. No. 6E7390 Circular Plain. No. 6E7392 Circular Concave.

Hammers are measured from center of hole to middle of nose. State which size and which hand you wish.

Catalogue No.	Style Body	Size	Hand	Price
6E7384	Flat	1 to 1¼ in.	Right	19c
6E7385	Flat	1 to 1¼ in.	Left	20c
6E7386	Round	1 to 1¼ in.	Right	22c
6E7387	Round	1 to 1¼ in.	Left	23c
6E7390	Circular	1 to 1¼ in.	Right	24c
6E7391	Plain	1 to 1¼ in.	Left	25c
6E7392	Concave	1 to 1¼ in.	Right	35c
6E7393	Plain	1 to 1¼ in.	Left	36c

If by mail, postage extra, 2 cents.

SPRING PLUNGERS.

No. 6E7395 For Old Style Spring Plunger Guns, not fitted. Price, each......9c

No. 6E7396 For Zulu Guns, not fitted.
Price, each......15c
If by mail, postage extra, 1 cent.

NITRO FIRING PINS.

No. 6E7397 For Latest Style Belgian Guns, not fitted.
Price, each......10c
If by mail, postage extra, 1 cent.

STEEL FIRING PINS.

Catalogue No.	Diameter of Head	Length, inches	Price, each
6E7398	8-32 inch	1¼ in.	11c
6E7399	9-32 inch	1¼ in.	12c
6E7400	10-32 inch	1¼ in.	13c
6E7401	11-32 inch	1½ in.	14c

If by mail, postage extra, 1 cent.

Special Firing Pins made to order. Send the broken one when ordering. Price, when they resemble the above in style, each......25c

Plunger Springs.

No. 6E7402 Taper, for Old Style Double Guns. Price, each......9c
No. 6E7403 For Zulu Guns. Price, each......11c
If by mail, postage extra, 1 cent.

Plunger Seats.

No. 6E7404 For English Guns, 6-cornered shoulder, not fitted.
Price, each......18c
No. 6E7405 For Belgian Guns, 6-cornered shoulder, not fitted.
Price, each......17c
If by mail, postage extra, 1 cent.

No. 6E7404

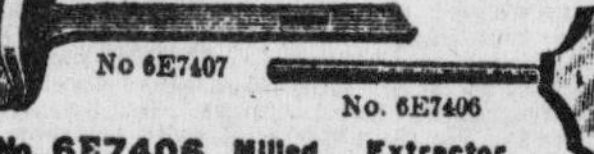

No. 6E7406 Milled Extractor, in filed state, not fitted. Price......34c
No. 6E7407 Fore End Iron, milled for the frame of double guns, not fitted.
Price......32c
If by mail, postage extra, 4 to 5 cents.

TRIGGERS.

No. 6E7408 Right Hand, Filed Trigger, not fitted. Price, each...7c
No. 6E7409 Left Hand, Filed Trigger, not fitted. Price, each...8c
If by mail, postage extra, 1 cent.

TOP LEVERS.

No. 6E7410 Top Levers for Old Style Belgian Guns, filed, not fitted.
Price, each......50c

No. 6E7412 Top Levers for New Style Belgian Guns, filed not fitted.
Price, each......60c
If by mail, postage extra, 2c.

CHOKE BORING TOOLS.

No. 6E7413 The Batchelor Choke Boring Tool, made of a brass socket, with two cutting blades as shown in illustration, and a bevel thumbscrew to expand the cutters gradually, as the operation requires. They have a rod 34 inches long, with a shank, so the tool can be used in a brace; made in 10 or 12-gauge. Weight, 2½ pounds. Price......$3.90
If by mail, postage extra, 45 cents.

BREECH LOADING GUN LOCKS.

We can only furnish the following breech loading gun locks in the sizes which we mention. As gun locks vary so much in size we have put in stock the sizes which are most generally used. These locks are all finished complete and are probably large enough to fit almost any gun where new locks are necessary.

When ordering locks give us the length of your old lock, or if you can do so, make a drawing of it on a piece of paper and attach it to your order, and we will send you as near as we can a lock to match it; but you must not expect a lock that will fit exactly in your gun. It may fit exactly or it may require some little work to make it fit your gun. When ordering **do not forget to give us the size or a drawing of your gun lock.**

No. 6E7414 Breech Loading, Back Action Gun Lock, complete with hammer. Right hand, 4½ inches long, 1 inch wide at hammer. For breech loaders. Price......98c

No. 6E7415 Back Action Gun Locks, complete with hammer. Left hand, 4½ inches long, 1 inch wide at hammer. For breech loaders.
Price......99c
If by mail, postage extra, 7 cents.

No. 6E7416 Breech Loading, Bar Lock, complete, with hammer. Right hand, 4½ inches long, 1 inch wide at hammer. For breech loaders. Price......$1.25

No. 6E7417 Bar Lock, complete, with hammer. Left hand, 4½ inches long, 1 inch wide at hammer. For breech loaders. Price......$1.26
If by mail, postage extra, 7 cents.

MAIN SPRINGS FOR BREECH LOADERS.

If possible send a drawing of the spring, or the old one, so we can match it best. Mark the place where stud goes into the lock plate.

Catalogue No.	For Locks	For Side	Price, each
6E7420	Back Action	Right Hand	24c
6E7421	Back Action	Left Hand	25c
6E7424	Bar Locks	Right Hand	35c
6E7425	Bar Locks	Left Hand	36c

If by mail, postage extra, 2 cents.

BREECH LOADING SWIVEL TUMBLERS.

Must be fitted by a gunsmith or mechanic.

Catalogue No.	For Locks	For Side	Price, each
6E7430	Back Action	Right Hand	25c
6E7431	Back Action	Left Hand	26c
6E7432	Bar Locks	Right Hand	30c
6E7433	Bar Locks	Left Hand	31c

If by mail, postage extra, 2 cents.

SEARS FOR GUN LOCKS

Must be fitted by a gunsmith or mechanic.

Catalogue No.	For Locks	For Side	Price, each
6E7434	Back Action	Right Hand	14c
6E7435	Back Action	Left Hand	15c
6E7436	Bar Locks	Right Hand	16c
6E7437	Bar Locks	Left Hand	17c

If by mail, postage extra, 2 cents.

RUBBER BUTT PLATES.

No. 6E7439 Rubber Butt Plates for breech or muzzle loading guns; not fitted. Send drawing of size on a sheet of paper. Price, each......29c
If by mail, postage extra, 3 cents.

Trigger Guards for Breech Loaders.

No. 6E7440 Breech Loading Guards, filed and threaded, not fitted. Price, each..39c

TRIGGER PLATES FOR BREECH LOADERS.

No. 6E7441 Breech Loading Trigger Plates, filed and tapped; not fitted. Price......45c
If by mail, postage extra, 5 cents.

Trigger Springs for Revolvers.

No. 6E7442 No. 14. Trigger Springs for double action revolvers, 22, 32 or 38-caliber. State for which caliber you wish it and give name of the revolver. Price, each......10c

No. 6E7443 No. 26. Trigger Springs for automatic revolvers made by Harrington & Richardson, 22, 32 or 38-caliber. State caliber wanted and give name of revolver.
Price, each......10c

No. 6E7444 Trigger Springs for Smith & Wesson double action revolvers. Price....20c

No. 6E7445 Trigger Springs for Smith & Wesson hand ejectors. Price, each......40c

No. 6E7446 Trigger Springs for Iver Johnson revolvers. Send broken one and mention caliber. Price...(Postage extra, 1c)..15c

REVOLVER MAIN SPRINGS.

No. 6E7447 Revolver Main Springs for Harrington & Richardson or Iver Johnson double action and automatic revolvers, 22, 32, 38 and 44-caliber. When ordering state the name of revolver and caliber, or send the broken spring so we can match it. Each 16c
If by mail, postage extra, 2 cents.

No. 6E7448 Main Springs for Smith & Wesson revolvers, 32, 38 or 44-caliber. State caliber wanted. Price, each..(Postage extra, 2c)..28c

No. 6E7449 Main Springs for Forehand Arms Co. revolvers. Give caliber and name of make, say if wanted for automatic or double action, when ordering. Price, each......15c
If by mail, postage extra, 3 cents.

REVOLVER HANDS.

No. 6E7450 Hands for revolving the cylinder of revolvers. Mention name, make, style and caliber of revolver. Price......20c

No. 7450½ For Smith & Wesson and Colt Revolvers..(Postage extra, 1c.).. 30c

Main Springs Air for Rifles.

No. 6E7451 Main Springs for King, Daisy, Rapid, Cycloid and Rival air rifles. Must be fitted by customer. Price, each....(Postage extra, 2c)...9c

Winchester and Marlin Main Springs.

No. 6E7452 Main Springs for Winchester Rifles. Mention caliber and model wanted.
Price, each......30c

No. 6E7453 Main Springs for Marlin Rifles. Mention caliber and model wanted.
Price, each......(Postage extra, 2c)......30c

MAIN SPRINGS OR GUN SPRINGS.

Any main or gun springs not described or listed in this catalogue, will have to be made by hand, and especially to order, and if you will send us the broken spring we will try to have a new one made for you, which will cost on any ordinary spring 40 to 50 cents, and for a main spring which is very difficult to make, the price will be higher, according to how long it takes our spring maker to make the spring. Do not forget to send the broken sample, and if possible tell us the name and caliber or gauge of the gun, revolver or rifle, for which you want the spring.
Price of ordinary springs....40c to 50c
Complicated springs.....75c to $1.25

Rubber Revolver Handles.

No. 6E7454 Rubber Stocks for All Double Action and Automatic Revolvers, except Colt, 22, 32, 38 and 44-caliber. When ordering, state name of the revolver and whether right hand or left hand is wanted, also state the caliber.
Price, each (not a pair)......25c

No. 6E7454½ Rubber Stocks for Colt's Revolvers, each......35c
If by mail, postage extra, 2 cents.

Marlin Stocks and Fore Ends.

No. 6E7455 Stocks for No 6E580 grade Marlin Shotguns. Price......$2.50
No. 6E7456 Fore Ends for No. 6E580 grade Marlin Shotguns. Price......85c
If by mail, postage extra, 10 to 20 cents.

STEVENS' RIFLE PARTS.

Cat. No.	Name of Parts	For	Price Each
6E7461	Extractor	Crack Shot	25c
6E7462	Breech Block Screw	Crackshot	10c
6E7463	Firing Pin	Crackshot	15c
6E7464	Main Spring	Crackshot	15c
6E7465	Main Spring	Favorite	15c
6E7466	Main Spring	Ideal	20c
6E7467	Hammers	Crackshot	45c
6E7468	Breech Block	Crackshot	45c
6E7469	Side Levers	Crackshot	25c

If by mail, postage extra, 2 cents.

COLT'S REVOLVER REPAIRS.

Mention name and caliber of revolver when ordering.

Cat. No.	Name of Parts	For	Price Each
6E7470	Main Spring	New S'rvce	70c
6E7471	Main Spring	Oth'r Mdls.	50c
6E7472	Trigger Spring	Dbl. Action	25c
6E7473	Sear and Bolt Spring	Sgl Action	15c
6E7473½	Cylinder Bolt	Dbl. Action	30c
6E7474	Cylinder Bolt	Sgl. Action	30c

If by mail, postage extra, 2 cents.

QUACKENBUSH RIFLE PARTS.

Cat. No.	Name of Parts	For	Price Each
6E7475	Main Spring	No. 1 Air Rifle	30c
6E7476	Main Spring	Safety Rifle	10c
6E7477	Firing Pin	Safety Rifle	15c

If by mail, postage extra, 2 cents.

PIEPER RIFLE PARTS.

Cat. No.	Name of Parts	For	Price Each
6E7480	Main Spring	22 Caliber	15c
6E7481	Extractors	22 Caliber	25c
6E7483	Firing Pin	22 Caliber	10c

If by mail, postage extra, 2 cents.

REMINGTON GUN SPRINGS.

Send broken spring so we can match it.

Cat. No.	Name of Parts	For	Price Each
6E7485	Top Lv. Sp'ngs	Semi-H'less	25c
6E7486	Main Springs	Semi H'less	40c
6E7489	Top Lv. Sp'ngs	Dbl. Hammer	25c
6E7490	Top Lv. Sp'ngs	Dbl. H'm'less	50c
6E7495	Main Springs	Rifles No. 2, 3, 4 and 6	40c

If by mail, postage extra, 2 cents.

ITHACA GUN SPRINGS.

Cat. No.	Name of Parts	For	Price Each
6E7501	Main Springs	Hammer	35c
6E7502	Main Springs	Hammerless	35c
6E7505	Sear Springs	Double Guns	25c

If by mail, postage extra, 2 cents.

DAVIS GUN SPRINGS.

Cat. No.	Name of Parts	For	Price Each
6E7510	Main Springs	Dbl. Hammer	50c
6E7511	Main Springs	Dbl. H'm'less	50c
6E7512	Top Lv. Sp'ngs	Dbl. Guns.	25c

If by mail, postage extra, 2 cents.

FOREHAND SINGLE GUN.

Cat. No.	Name of Parts	For	Price Each
6E7525	Main Springs	Hammerless	30c
6E7526	Cocking Lever	Hammerless	50c

If by mail, postage extra, 2 cents.

REVOLVER HAMMERS.

Prices vary according to style of revolver and caliber. State caliber and style wanted.

No. 6E7530 Revolver Hammers for Colt's revolvers cost......$1.00 to $1.50
No. 6E7531 Revolver Hammers for Smith & Wesson revolvers cost......50c to 75c
No. 6E7532 Revolver Hammers for Harrington & Richardson revolvers cost, 40c to 50c
No. 6E7533 Revolver Hammers for Forehand revolvers cost......40c to 60c
No. 6E7534 Revolver Hammers for Iver Johnson revolvers cost......35c to 40c
If by mail, postage extra, 2 cents.

AMERICAN GUN CO. GUN PARTS.

Send broken parts so we can match them, for the models were changed several times.

	Price
No. 6E7550 Top Lever Springs.	20c
No. 6E7551 Main Springs, right or left......	40c
No. 6E7552 Butt Plates. Send drawing of size......	30c
No. 6E7555 Sears, right or left..	30c
No. 6E7557 Firing Pins......	20c
No. 6E7558 Top Lever......	60c

If by mail, postage extra, 2 to 4 cents.

Long Range Winner, White Powder Wonder, Gold Medal Wonder and World Challenge Ejector Single Gun Parts.

These Guns Were Made by Three Different Factories.

Send broken parts so we can match them, for the models were changed several times.

	Price
No. 6E7574 Butt Plate. Send drawing of size on paper......	25c
No. 6E7575 Main Springs......	20c
No. 6E7577 Top Lever Springs......	8c
No. 6E7578 Locking Bolt......	30c
No. 6E7580 Barrel Keys......	25c
No. 6E7582 Top Levers......	35c
No. 6E7585 Firing Pins......	15c

If by mail, postage extra, 2 to 3 cents.

No. 6E7586 Stock. Wood part and butt plate. Give name of gun or factory name......$1.25
If by mail, postage extra, 25 cents.
No. 6E7587 Fore End. Wood part only......40c

Chicago Long Range Wonder Hammerless Double Gun.

Finished, Ready to Put in the Gun.

	Price
No. 6E7600 Butt Plate. Send drawing of size on paper......	30c
No. 6E7601 Main Springs. Right or left side. Send sample......	20c
No. 6E7603 Trigger Springs. Right or left side. Send sample......	20c
No. 6E7605 Hammer. Right or left side. Send sample......	35c
No. 6E7607 Sears. Right or left side. Send sample......	30c
No. 6E7609 Top Lever......	35c
No. 6E7610 Top Lever Spring......	15c
No. 6E7611 Firing Pins......	15c

If by mail, postage extra, 2 to 5 cents.

No. 6E7612 Stock. Wood part only......(Postage extra, 25c)......$2.00
No. 6E7613 Fore End. Wood part only, finished. (Postage extra, 5c). .75
No. 6E7614 Fore End. Complete. 1.50
If by mail, postage extra, 15 cents.

Money Belts.

No. 57E4495 Money Belts, made of soft chamois skin; to be worn around the waist, under the clothing; the safest way to keep money. It is soft and comfortable, and made with three compartments. Price.........34c
If by mail, postage extra, 3 cents.

No. 57E4496 Money Belts. Made of soft tanned horsehide: same style as above. Strong and durable. Price.........54c
If by mail, postage extra, 3 cents.

No. 57E4498 Money and Gold Dust Belts. Four inches wide; made of the very finest oil tanned calfskin; very soft and pliable; will never get stiff and is just the thing to carry money or gold dust in; it is double stitched all around; made with three compartments; the center pocket is 8 inches long; the two end pockets are 5 inches long, each; the outside cover folds over very closely and is fastened by snap buttons. This is the finest belt on the market for the purpose. Price.........$1.05
If by mail, postage extra, 8 cents.

Rubber Cushion Leather Recoil Pads.

Give length of butt plate.

No. 57E4503 S. R. & Co.'s Rubber Cushion Recoil Pad. Solid leather, with lacing, will not become loose; has patent rubber cushion pad to rest against the butt plate to prevent recoil of gun from bruising the shoulder. Give length of butt plate when ordering. Price...42c
If by mail, postage extra, 10 cents.

No. 57E4505 The Acme Pure Red Rubber Recoil Pad. The best pad in the market. Lined with elastic cloth so it will not stick to the varnish on the gun stock. Give length of heel plate on gun for which you want the pad. They come in three sizes: No. 2 is 5 inches long; No. 3 is 5½ inches long and No. 4 is 5½ inches long. Mention length of butt plate. Price.........59c
If by mail, postage extra, 7 cents.

Heike's Hand Protector.

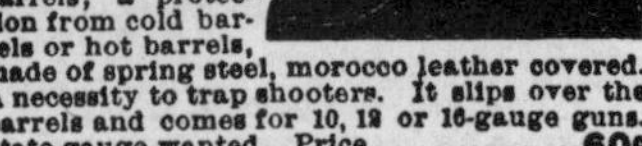

No. 57E4510 Heike's Hand Protector, for shotgun barrels; a protection from cold barrels or hot barrels, made of spring steel, morocco leather covered. A necessity to trap shooters. It slips over the barrels and comes for 10, 12 or 16-gauge guns. State gauge wanted. Price.........60c
If by mail, postage extra, 3 cents.

Our Combined Leather Cheek and Recoil Pad.

Give length of butt plate.

No. 57E4512 The Combined Leather Cheek and Recoil Pad, made of soft russet leather oil tanned, will protect the stock and at the same time protect the cheek and shoulder of the shooter. It will fit any gun stock. This pad is fitted with a corrugated rubber cushion, the same as that used on the best recoil pads. The cheek pad on the comb of stock is left open at one end so that the shooter can remove or add padding as he desires. Price.........60c
If by mail, postage extra, 4 cents.

Our Arkansaw Bowie Knife.

No. 57E4515 Bowie Knife, buckhorn handle, 6-inch steel clip blade, leather sheath, with loop to attach to belt; entire length, 11 inches. Price.........65c

No. 57E4516 Bowie Knife, with 7-inch blade. Price, with leather sheath.........75c

No. 57E4517 Bowie Knife, with 8-inch blade. Price, with leather sheath.........85c
If by mail, postage extra, 10 cents.

Our Montana Hunting Knife.

No. 57E4518 Our Montana Hunting Knife, nicely checkered handle, 6-inch blade, leather sheath with loops to attach to a belt. The best hunting knife on the market for the money. Price.........47c
If by mail, postage extra, 9 cents.

Deer Foot Hunting Knives.

No. 57E4519 Hunting Knife, deer foot handle, 6-inch clip blade, leather sheath, nickel bolster and hilt. Price.........$1.00

No. 57E4520 Hunting Knife, deer foot handle, 7-inch clip blade, best steel, leather sheath, with loop to attach to belt, nickel bolster and hilt. Price.........$1.10
If by mail, postage extra, 12 cents.

Hunters' Pocket Knife.

No. 28E0920 T. T. C. Hunters' Pride Knife. It has stag handle, long, heavy German silver bolsters, cap and shield, brass lining, highly finished inside and out. The blades open and close freely without wearing. The knife blade is always true in the center, and it is these little points to which we pay so much attention, that cause our knives to give better satisfaction than those you can procure from any other dealer. Length of handle, 4½ inches; length with large blade open, 8 inches. Price.........60c
If by mail, postage extra, 5 cents.

For a full line of pocket cutlery, see our Cutlery Department.

Sportsmen's Folding Lock Blade Knife.

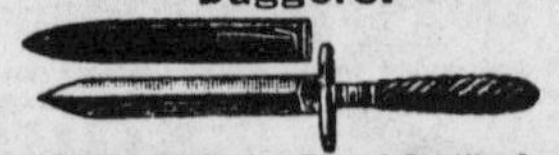

No. 57E4521 Sportsmen's Folding Lock Blade Knife, with 3⅞-inch (scimiter) blade of finest steel and 4½-inch genuine deer foot handle, making the entire length, when open, 8½ inches. It has dagger hilt, with German silver bolster, patent lock, which holds the blade either open or closed, and a corkscrew in the handle. Just the knife for camping. Price.........$1.40
If by mail, postage extra, 12 cents.

Pearl and Stag Handle Daggers.

No. 57E4523 Our Finest Quality Ladies' Dagger. This is a little beauty, with the very finest quality of steel in blade. Length of blade, 4 inches, both edges sharp, with beautiful pearl handle and dagger hilt, furnished with fancy leather sheath. This is the finest quality of a dirk knife, and the metal is warranted. Price. (Postage extra, 8c)..$1.05

No. 57E4524 Our Stag Handle Dagger, 4-inch blade of good quality steel, with leather sheath. Price......(Postage extra, 8c).....60c

Hunting Knife Sheath.

No. 57E4530 Leather Hunting Knife Sheaths.

For 6-inch Bowie..20c	For 8-inch Bowie..28c
For 7-inch Bowie..24c	For 9-inch Bowie..32c

If by mail, postage extra, 4 cents.

No. 57E4771 Leather Belts, for knife sheaths, 1¼ inches wide. Price.........18c
If by mail, postage extra, 8 cents.

Hunters' Axes.

No. 57E4533 Hunters' Axe, with handle, extra cast steel blade, weight, 1¾ pounds; with heavy russet leather sheath, as per illustration. A very convenient tool; makes a light axe or a heavy hatchet for putting up tents, etc., when camping. Weight, with sheath, 2 pounds. Price, with carrying sheath.........78c

Thomas' Nipper No. 4.

No. 57E4552 Thomas' Nipper, nicely finished and nickel plated. This nipper locks automatically when it is put on the prisoner's wrist. Price.........$1.70
If by mail, postage extra, 8 cents.

Detectives' Double Lock Handcuffs.

These handcuffs are adjustable to any size wrist and lock automatically, but cannot be unlocked without a key. They are made of forged steel, strong and durable.

No. 57E4553 Nicely polished and finished. Price, per pair.........$2.90

No. 57E4554 Nicely polished and nickel plated. Price, per pair.........$3.50
If by mail, postage extra, 20 cents.

Police Permanent Lock Handcuffs.

These handcuffs unlock with a key but lock automatically and are adjustable to any size wrist. They are made of good quality steel, are light, and used generally by detectives and other officers of the law.

No. 57E4555 Nicely polished and finished. Price, per pair.........$2.70

No. 57E4556 Nicely polished and nickel plated. Price, per pair.........$3.15
If by mail, postage extra, 16 cents.

DARK LANTERNS—See our Hardware Department.

Police Billies.

No. 57E4573 Plaited Billy, leather covered head. Weight, about 7 ounces, hand made. Price.........17c
If by mail, postage extra, 7 cents.

No. 57E4576 Leather Billy, sewed down the side, loaded with shot, made of the best material and cannot be equaled for the price. Length, 9 inches. Weight, about 9 ounces. Price...(If by mail, postage extra, 9c)....32c

No. 57E4577 Russet Leather Billy, 8½ inches long, with sliding leather handle, filled with shot, sewed down the side and well made. Weight, about 12 ounces. Price.........60c
If by mail, postage extra, 14 cents.

The most necessary part of a hunter's equipment is a good canteen. See No. 57E4796 for a description of the best canteen made, endorsed by the U. S. army officers.

Canvas Shell Bags for Carrying Loaded Shells.

No. 57E4665 10-oz. Brown Canvas Bags, leather bound, with pocket. To hold 50 shells. Price...24c
To hold 75 shells. Price.........27c
To hold 100 shells. Price.........30c
If by mail, postage extra, 10 to 14 cents.

OUR GUN AND RIFLE COVERS.

We have selected the following line of gun and rifle covers and placed a large season contract for them, so as to enable us to give you the best possible value for the least amount of money in this line of goods. When you order a gun cover from us you are getting it at a price based on the actual cost of material and labor with only our one small percentage of profit added. You will assist us materially when ordering these goods if you will give us the name of your gun or rifle, also length of barrel, and advise us whether it is a single barrel, double barrel, repeating shotgun or rifle for which you want the cover; this will enable us to furnish you the exact cover you wish without any delay. For special lengths not mentioned in this catalogue allow us one week's time to make them.

NOTICE. 8-oz. canvas means a yard weighs 8 oz. 10-oz. canvas means a yard weighs 10 oz. 12-oz. canvas means a yard weighs 12 oz. The more ounces to the yard, the heavier the canvas.

Mention length of barrel and name of gun or rifle when ordering a gun cover.

Our 39-Cent Leather Bound Cover.

No. 57E4695 Rifle and Gun Cover, best 8-ounce brown canvas, leather bound, leather sling, cotton flannel lined, best quality. For 24, 26, 28, 30 or 32-inch barrels. Mention length of barrel when ordering and say if you wish it for a rifle or shotgun. Price.........39c
If by mail, postage extra, 13 cents.

Special Value for 64 Cents.

No. 57E4698 Heavy Tan 18-ounce Duck Cover, for rifles and shotguns. Full leather bound, with heavy sole leather lock and muzzle protector, with handle and sling. For 24, 26, 28, 30 or 32-inch barrels. Price.........64c
If by mail, postage extra, 16 cents.

Our $1.40 Leather Rifle and Shotgun Cover.

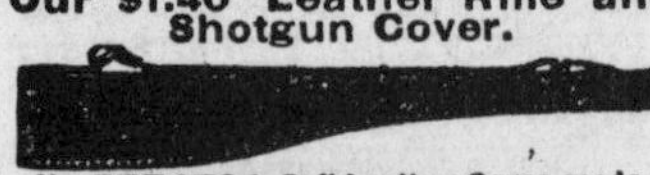

No. 57E4701 Soft Leather Cover, made of heavy, soft russet bag leather, with combined sling and handle. Bright trimmings. For 24, 26, 28, 30 or 32-inch barrels; give length of barrel and name of gun or rifle when ordering. Absolutely waterproof. The finest gun cover made. Price.........$1.40
If by mail, postage extra, 25 cents.

Give name of rifle or shotgun and length of barrel when ordering.

Our Victoria Gun Case 98c

No. 57E4707 Victoria Gun Case, heavy 18-ounce waterproof canvas, reinforced with leather lock and muzzle protector, with pocket cleaning rod; also shell bag to hold 50 shells. The most complete cover offered to sportsmen and trap shooters. For 28, 30 or 32-inch barrels. State length wanted. Price.........98c
If by mail, postage extra, 35 cents.

8-Ounce Duck Gun Case, 43c.

No. 57E4713 Tan Colored Duck Gun Case, for take down shotguns, with rod pocket, made of 8-ounce canvas. For 28, 30 or 32-inch barrels. Weight, 9 ounces. Give length of barrel. Price.........43c

Our 18-Ounce Canvas Victoria Rifle Case for Take Down Rifles, only 71 Cents.

No. 57E4716 Heavy 18-ounce tan duck, with lock and muzzle protector, rod pocket on the side, Victoria style, flannel lined, well made. This case is made for take down rifles only and the Ladies' Little Double Gun. When ordering state for which gun or rifle you wish it, and say if barrel is 24, 26 or 28 inches long. Give length of barrel and model and name of rifle when ordering. Weight, about 20 ounces. Price.........71c

IF YOU OWN A FINE GUN it pays to have a sole leather cover, as it protects the gun from bruises, dents, etc., when carrying it in a wagon, etc. For special lengths, not mentioned in this catalogue, allow us a week's time to make.

Our Sole Leather Victoria Gun Case, $2.20.

No. 57E4726 Victoria Gun Case, made of heavy russet leather, embossed, strongly stitched, with rod pocket, making it very strong and durable. For 28, 30 and 32-inch barrels. State length wanted. Weight, about 42 ounces. Price.........$2.20

English Victoria Gun Case.

$2.75

No. 57E4731 English Victoria Gun Case, leg of mutton shape, oak tanned sole leather, flannel lined, handle and sling, lock buckle, name plate. The best case on the market for the money. For 30 or 32-inch barrels. State length wanted. Weight, about 50 ounces. Price.........$2.75

French Style Gun Cases.

No. 57E4736 French Style Leather Gun Case. This is the latest style case and is the most compact, neatest sole leather case ever placed on the market. This case is made of oak tanned sole leather, fitted with lock buckle, heavy leather handle and sling, lined with Canton flannel, with partition for barrels, adapted for any take down gun whether single barrel, double barrel or repeater. This case at the large end is 6½ inches high by 3½ inches wide. Made for 28, 30 or 32-inch barrels. State length wanted. Weight, about 50 ounces. Price.........$2.70

Our U. S. Leather Mail Bag, $2.50.

No. 57E4750 An ideal mail bag for rural mail carriers, hotels, merchants and manufacturers. This bag is made from regular mail bag leather, welted seams and sides and bottom, four loops with leather strap fastener, as shown in the illustration. The strap is made with a hasp so it may be locked with a padlock on the reverse side, round leather handle extra strongly stitched, riveted throughout. Size, 21 inches long, 13 inches wide. This same bag could not be duplicated by other dealers for less than $4.00. Weight, 1¾ pounds. Price.........$2.50
If by mail, postage extra, 30 cents.

Rifle and Carbine Sheath.

No. 57E4703 Rifle Sheath, made of best russet leather, for sporting rifles. These sheaths are not full length covers, but are intended for carrying rifle on saddle, leaving stock of rifle exposed so it may be easily grasped when needed. Be sure to give name of rifle, model and length of barrel when ordering, as different makes require different sheaths. We furnish these for 24, 26 and 28-inch barrel rifles only. Price.........$1.20
If by mail, postage extra, 30 cents.

No. 57E4704 The same identical sheath for carbines. State name of carbine and length of barrel when ordering. We furnish these for 20 and 22-in. barrel carbines only. Price.$1.15
If by mail, postage extra, 25 cents.

Give name of rifle or shotgun and length of barrel when ordering.

REVOLVER AND PISTOL HOLSTERS.

Our Line of Revolver Holsters.

By taking advantage of the leather market and laying in a supply of leather before the advance, we are enabled to make you the following prices. When you order holsters of us you are buying them on our system of one small percentage of profit from the maker to the consumer, and we are sure you will agree with us, that, quality considered, our prices are below any competition. When ordering holsters, always give the name of your revolver, length of barrel and caliber, to enable us to give you the exact size, for these holsters vary in size, according to caliber and length of barrel.

Our Acme Rubber Pocket Holsters.

Made of black rubber and lined with drilling, soft and pliable, with nickel plated clasp to hook to pocket, and made for pocket size revolvers only up to 4-inch barrel. Order by catalogue number in full.

Catalogue Number	Caliber of Revolver	Length of Barrel, Inches	Price, Each	Postage Extra
57E4755B	32	3 to 4	20c	5c
57E4755E	38	3½ to 4	22c	5c
57E4755G	44	4 to 5	25c	6c

Our Leather Flap and Open Top Holsters.

Made of best quality russet leather, nicely embossed, with loop for belt. When ordering, state make, caliber and length of barrel of your revolver. Order by catalogue number in full.

Flap Holster No. 57E4756

Open Top Holster No. 57E4761

For Young America revolvers.

Caliber of Revolver	Length of Barrel, Inches	Catalogue No. 57E4756 Flap Holster Price, each	Catalogue No. 57E4761 Open Top Holster Price, each	Postage Extra
22	2	21c	16c	4c
22	6	22c	16c	4c

For Smith & Wesson, Harrington & Richardson, Hopkins & Allen, Forehand, Iver Johnson, Colt's New Pocket, Colt's Police and our own revolvers. Order by catalogue number in full.

Caliber of Revolver	Length of Barrel, Inches	Catalogue No. 57E4756 Flap Holster Price, each	Catalogue No. 57E4761 Open Top Holster Price, each	Postage Extra
32	3 to 4	23c	17c	6c
32	4½ to 5	24c	18c	6c
32	5½ to 6	25c	19c	6c
38	3½ to 4	26c	20c	6c
38	4½ to 5	27c	21c	7c
38	5½ to 6	28c	22c	7c

For Colt's New Navy, Colt's New Army, Colt's Double Action and Smith & Wesson Military revolvers. Order by catalogue number in full.

Caliber of Revolver	Length of Barrel, Inches	Catalogue No. 57E4756 Flap Holster Price, each	Catalogue No. 57E4761 Open Top Holster Price, each	Postage Extra
38 or 41	4½ to 5	33c	22c	8c
38 or 41	5½ to 6	34c	23c	8c

For large frame revolvers, such as Colt's Frontier, Army, Single Action and Double Action, 32-20, 38-40, 44 and 45 caliber. Order by catalogue number in full.

Caliber of Revolver	Length of Barrel, Inches	Catalogue No. 57E4756 Flap Holster Price, each	Catalogue No. 57E4761 Open Top Holster Price, each	Postage Extra
32-20 to 45	4½ to 5	35c	24c	10c
32-20 to 45	5½ to 6	36c	25c	10c
32-20 to 45	7½	37c	26c	10c

Our Hand Carved Mexican Style Cowboy Holsters.

Made of heavy russet saddle leather, to match our fancy cowboys' saddle. These holsters are all hand carved, and are not to be compared with the holsters that other houses sell as the fine cowboy holster, which are embossed under a large press; but these are the most handsome and best holsters in the market.

The following holsters are made to fit the Smith & Wesson, Harrington & Richardson, Hopkins & Allen, Forehand, Iver Johnson, Colt's New Pocket and New Police and our own make revolvers in 38 caliber only. They are not made for 32 caliber revolvers. When ordering, give the catalogue number in full.

Catalogue Number	Caliber of Revolver	Length of Barrel, Inches	Price, Each	Postage Extra
57E4767E	38	3½ to 4	$0.90	8c
57E4767F	38	4½ to 5	.95	8c
57E4767G	38	5½ to 6	1.00	8c

The following holsters are made to fit the Colt's Double Action, Colt's New Navy and New Army revolvers and Smith & Wesson Military and Police revolvers.

Catalogue Number	Caliber of Revolver	Length of Barrel, Inches	Price, Each	Postage Extra
57E4767H	38 or 41	4½ to 5	$1.10	10c
57E4767J	38 or 41	5½ to 6½	1.15	10c

The following holsters are made to fit the large Frontier and Army frame revolvers, 32-20, 38-40, 44-40 and 45 caliber.

Catalogue Number	Caliber of Revolver	Length of Barrel, Inches	Price, Each	Postage Extra
57E4767K	32-20 to 45	4½ to 5	$1.20	10c
57E4767L	32-20 to 45	5½ to 6	1.25	10c
57E4767M	32-20 to 45	7½	1.35	10c

Texas Shoulder Holster.

Keeps revolver always safe and ready. Made of fine soft russet leather, nicely embossed, with leather strap to pass around the chest to hold holster on shoulder, as shown in the illustration. When ordering, always give catalogue number in full and state the make and style of your revolver, give length of barrel, and we will fit your revolver.

No. 57E4768A For 22-Caliber Young America Revolvers. Mention length of barrel wanted. Price. . .(Postage extra, 5c.).....**40c**

For Smith & Wesson, Harrington & Richardson, Hopkins & Allen, Forehand, Iver Johnson, Colt's New Pocket and New Police and our own revolvers.

Catalogue Number	Caliber of Revolver	Length of Barrel, Inches	Price, Each	Postage Extra
57E4768B	32	3 to 4	45c	5c
57E4768C	32	4½ to 5	46c	5c
57E4768D	32	5½ to 6	47c	5c
57E4768E	38	3½ to 4	48c	5c
57E4768F	38	4½ to 5	48c	5c
57E4768G	38	5½ to 6	49c	5c

To fit Colt's Double Action New Navy and New Army, 38 and 41 caliber, and Smith & Wesson Military and Police revolvers.

Catalogue Number	Caliber of Revolver	Length of Barrel, Inches	Price, Each	Postage Extra
57E4768H	38 or 41	4½ to 5	50c	8c
57E4768J	38 or 41	5½ to 6½	51c	8c

To fit large frame 44 or 45 caliber revolvers.

Catalogue Number	Caliber of Revolver	Length of Barrel, Inches	Price, Each	Postage Extra
57E4768K	32-20 to 45	4½ to 5	52c	8c
57E4768L	32-20 to 45	5½ to 6	53c	8c
57E4768M	32-20 to 45	7½	54c	8c

OUR HOLSTER AND CARTRIDGE BELTS.

We would like you to compare our line of belts with any line offered by any other house, and, quality considered, we think you will find that our prices are equal to those paid by the largest dealers. Our leather goods are the best in the market. Always give waist measure and caliber when ordering.

Plain Leather Belts and Cartridge Belts.

No. 57E4771 Belts only, russet leather, 1½ inches wide, finely embossed, without loops for cartridges. Length, 32 to 40 inches. Give length wanted. Price..........**18c**

If by mail, postage extra, 5 cents.

No. 57E4772 Belts only, russet leather, nicely embossed edge, with loops for cartridges; 22, 32, 38, 41 or 44 caliber, 1½ inches wide, plain roller buckle, 30 to 40 inches long. Give length and caliber wanted. Price..........**26c**

If by mail, postage extra, 5 cents.

Russet Leather Cartridge Belt.

No. 57E4773 Belt only, fine russet leather, nicely embossed edge, with loops for cartridges, 32, 38, 44 or 45 caliber; 2¼ inches wide, large nickel plated buckle, 32 to 40 inches long. Give length and caliber wanted. Price..........**44c**

If by mail, postage extra, 10 cents.

Combination Cartridge and Money Belts.

Mexican Combined Cartridge and Money Belt. Made of the very best soft russet leather; belt is 3 inches wide; soft and pliable and will not get hard and crack; neatly embossed. Mention caliber wanted.

No. 57E4774 38-caliber, give waist measure. Price..........**95c**

No. 57E4774½ 38-caliber, give waist measure. Price..........**95c**

No. 57E4774½ 44 or 45 caliber, give waist measure. Price..........**95c**

No. 57E4774½ 50-caliber, give waist measure. Price..........**95c**

Don't forget to state caliber wanted, also waist measure.

If by mail, postage extra, 15 cents.

No. 57E4775 The Cowboy Combined Cartridge and Money Belt. Made of heavy russet tanned leather; strong and durable; nicely embossed; edges double stitched; designed to match our cowboy scabbard and holster; 32, 38, 44 or 45 caliber. Mention caliber wanted and give waist measure. Price..........**$1.15**

If by mail, postage extra, 18 cents.

Web Cartridge Belts.

No. 57E4776 Web Belts, for rifle and pistol cartridges; 32, 38, 44 or 45 caliber. Made of heavy web with loops for cartridges. A very strong and durable belt, not impaired by any kind of weather. Mention caliber and waist measure wanted when ordering. Price..........**35c**

If by mail, postage extra, 5 cents.

Shell Belts for Shotgun Shells.

Shell Belts with loops for carrying shotgun shells. Made of web and russet leather and with shoulder straps to go over the shoulder. Order by number and give waist measure.

No. 57E4786

Catalogue Number	Made of	Size Gauge	Price	Post'g extra
57E4786A	Web	12	30c	8c
57E4786B	Web	10	30c	8c
57E4786C	Web	16	30c	8c
57E4786D	Web	20	30c	8c
57E4787A	Rus. Leather	12	45c	10c
57E4787B	Rus. Leather	10	45c	10c
57E4787C	Rus. Leather	16	45c	10c
57E4787D	Rus. Leather	20	45c	10c
57E4787F	Rus. Leather	8	62c	16c

YOU GET A

Profit Sharing Certificate

with every order of $1.00 or more. You will be able to share in our profits, and gets something valuable absolutely **FREE** very quickly if you send us your orders. We guarantee our price to be lower than you can get elsewhere, the quality of goods the very highest, and under our **PROFIT SHARING PLAN** you are able to share with us in the profits of this business.

The New Anson Mills Woven Shell Belts.

No. 57E4791 In these Mills belts, the loops are woven into the belts, making them very strong and durable in all kinds of weather; 10 or 12-gauge, with shoulder strap and game hooks. Mention gauge wanted. Price**$1.18**

If by mail, postage extra, 22 cents.

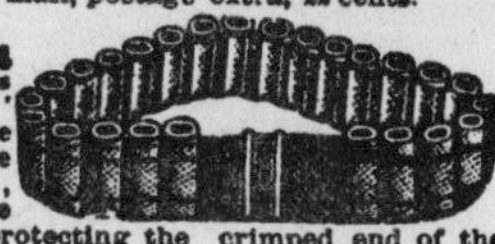

No. 57E4794 Anson Mills Hunters' Belt. The loops are woven, closed at the bottom, protecting the crimped end of the shell; no sewing whatever on the belt; 10, 12 or 16-gauge. Mention gauge wanted. Price..**79c**

If by mail, postage extra, 20 cents.

For Indian Snow Shoes

See Our Shoe Department.

The Lanz Canteen.

No. 57E4796 The only canteen which will keep water in palatable condition in any climate. With the Lanz Canteen a doctor can always have a cool drink of water in summer, or warm coffee or tea in winter, when making long rides through the country.

With it, the farmer and ranchman always have a cool drink at hand, when at work in the field, or upon the prairie.

Automobile tourists' or sportmen's tongues never parch when carrying a Lanz Canteen.

Where water in an ordinary canteen would freeze solid, under like conditions water in this canteen would not fall below a temperature of 60 degrees. The same theory applies to this canteen used in hot climates. Where water in an ordinary Government canteen would reach a temperature of 125 degrees, water in this canteen would not exceed a temperature of 82 degrees. Endorsed by doctors, explorers, soldiers and government officials. The canteen is made of heavy tin covered with a layer of felt, which in turn is covered with a removable canvas cover. Fitted with an adjustable web sling strap. The canteen is 9 inches in diameter, holds 45 fluid ounces, weighs about 1 pound. Price..........**$1.00**

If by mail, postage extra, 20 cents.

OUR HUNTING CLOTHING.

We are the largest handlers of hunting clothing selling direct to the consumer in the United States, and we know that we are offering greater value in this line of goods than it is possible for you to obtain elsewhere. Our hunting clothing is guaranteed to be made of the highest grade full weight canvas, full size, made with the same care and finish found in tailor made goods. **Quality, both in material and workmanship, considered, our prices cannot be equaled, as they are** based on our one small profit, manufacturer to consumer plan, and by reason of our enormous trade in this line, our cost of production is far smaller than that experienced by other manufacturers. In ordering, state number of inches around the chest under the arms, and state what size dress coat you wear. **Special sizes not mentioned in the following descriptions, will have to be made specially, and will cost 35 per cent more than the prices named below.**

NOTICE: DO NOT FAIL TO GIVE SIZE. Hunting clothing should be ordered one size larger than regular clothing to allow plenty of freedom.

Our Best 12-ounce Army Duck Coat, $3.80.

No. 57E5135 Our Very Best Quality Hunting Coat, made of the very best quality 12-oz. army duck, dead grass color, double stitched throughout, lined throughout the entire back with best quality 8-ounce army duck, sleeves lined with Walker's sateen, corduroy collar and adjustable cuffs lined with corduroy, **reinforced waterproof padded leather shoulder pieces,** leather bound throughout, including the pocket flaps; silk crow's foot stitching at the pockets and silk stitched buttonholes. **Note the gusset under the arms, as shown in the illustration. This enables you to freely raise your arms without feeling the weight of shells and game in the pockets.** The pockets are made on the cut in principle, with large flaps, which is very neat, and the game pockets are made so as to be accessible from the front and at the side seams, as shown in illustration. This is our best hunting coat, has six outside pockets and three spacious game pockets, with best quality of horn buttons, and no pains have been spared to make this hunting coat the best canvas hunting coat on the market, and is as nearly waterproof as a canvas coat can be. It comes in sizes of 36 to 46 inches. Give measure when ordering. Price..........**$3.80**

Cannot be sent by mail, as it weighs over 4 pounds. 12-ounce canvas weighs 12 ounces to the yard.

NOTICE — DO NOT FAIL TO GIVE SIZE. Hunting clothing should be ordered one size larger than regular clothing to allow plenty of freedom. . . .

Our 10-ounce Army Duck, Leather Bound Hunting Coat, $2.25.

No. 57E5137 Best quality 10-oz. army duck, dead grass color, lined with 8-oz. army duck, full pattern, reinforced shoulders, corduroy collar, corduroy lined adjustable cuffs, six outside pockets with flaps, three game pockets with entrance from front edge and side seam, double stitched throughout; leather bound all around. Sizes, chest measure, from 36 to 46 inches. Give chest measure when ordering. Price......**$2.25**

If by mail, postage extra, 45 to 55 cents.

Our 10-ounce Canvas Special Value Coat for $1.82.

No. 57E5139 Hunting Coat, made of 10-oz. duck, dead grass color, three-quarter drill lined, corduroy collar and adjustable corduroy lined cuffs, shoulders reinforced, double stitched throughout, five outside shell pockets with flaps, reinforced, three game pockets with entrance from front edge and side seam, fancy stitching around entrance to game pockets. Sizes, chest measure, from 36 to 46 inches. Give chest measure when ordering. Price..........**$1.82**

If by mail, postage extra, 35 to 45 cents.

ORDER YOUR HUNTING COAT ONE SIZE LARGER THAN YOUR DRESS COAT, TO ALLOW PLENTY OF FREEDOM.

BOOKS, STATIONERY AND TYPEWRITERS

BOOK DEPARTMENT

Please include your order for books with your order for other merchandise, if possible, and thus SAVE on TRANSPORTATION CHARGES.

Standard Fiction, History, Biography, Poetry, Essays and Classics.

High class books by standard well known authors, substantially bound in cloth, printed on good quality paper, guaranteed complete and unabridged, just as originally written by the author. Each book is 5½x7½ inches, containing from 200 to 500 pages, equal in every way to books sold by regular dealers at from two to three times our price.

PRICE, EACH, 12c. ANY 12 FOR $1.35. ANY 24 FOR $2.60.

Mrs. Alexander.

Admiral's Ward
By Woman's Wit
Forging the Fetters
Freres, The
Maid, Wife or Widow

Bertha M. Clay.

Between Two Sins
Dora Thorne
For Life and Love
Gilded Sin, A
Golden Heart, A
Her Martyrdom
Her Mother's Sin
Her Only Sin
Lady Damer's Secret
Mad Love
Shadow of a Sin
Squire's Darling
Thorns and Orange Blossoms
Wedded and Parted
Wife in Name Only

J. Fenimore Cooper.

Last of the Mohicans
Pathfinder
Precaution
Water Witch

Charles Dickens.

Child's History of England
Chimes, The
Christmas Carol
Cricket on the Hearth
Dombey and Son
Oliver Twist

Sir A. Conan Doyle.

Beyond the City
Micah Clarke
Sign of the Four
Study in Scarlet

Fiction.

Abbe Constantin. Ludovic Halevy
Beside the Bonnie Brier Bush Ian Maclaren
Beulah. Augusta J. Evans
Black Rock. Ralph Connor
Charlotte Temple. Susannah Rawson
Corinne. DeStael
Countess of Lascelles. Reynolds
Dead Past, A. Cameron
Deemster, The. Hall Caine
Derrick Vaughan, Novelist. Edna Lyall
Doctor Rameau. Ohnet
Doom of the Burker Reynolds
Duchess, The. Mrs. Hungerford
East Lynne. Mrs. Wood
Elaine. Chas. Garvice
Esther. Rosa N. Carey
Evil Eye, The. Theophilo Gautier
Evil Genius. Wilkie Collins
Fallen Idol. F. Anstey
Far From the Maddening Crowd Hardy
Farmer Holt's Daughter J. M. Barrie
Fatal Love, A. Arias
Frozen Pirate, The. W. Clark Russell
Gold Elsie. E. Marlitt
Hardy Norsemen. Edna Lyall
Heir of Linne, The. Robert Buchanan
Her Playthings, Men. Cahill
Her Shattered Idol. Belle V. Logan
Household Angel in Disguise. Mrs. M. Leslie
House of the Wolf Stanley J. Weyman
Humphrey Clinker. Smollet
Ideala. Sarah Grand
In Chase of Crime. Du Boisgobey
Inez. Augusta J. Evans
In the Forecastle. Cleveland
Ishmael. Mrs. E. D. E. N. Southworth
Island, The. R. Whiteing
Jackanapes, and the Story of a Short Life. Mrs. Ewing
Jane Eyre. Charlotte Bronte
John Halifax. Mrs. Mulock
Joshua. Ebers
Juliette. Mrs. Madaline Leslie
Lady Audley's Secret. Braddon
Lady Brankesmere. "The Duchess"
Lady Grace. Mrs. Henry Wood
La Veuve. Octave Feuillet
Living or Dead. Hugh Conway
Life Sentence, A. Adeline Sargeant
Little Minister. J. M. Barrie
Little Queen of Tragedy, The. Laura B. Marsh
Lost Heiress. Mrs. E. D. E. N. Southworth
Lotus Eating. G. W. Curtis
Love's Recompense. Gates
Madam Sans-Gene Victorien Sardeau
Maid Ellice. Theodore Gift
Man in Black. S. J. Weyman
Marriage of Elinor, The. Mrs. Oliphant
Matter-of-Fact Girl, A. Theodore Gift
Mayor of Caste-bridge. Hardy
Mischief of Monica, The. L. B. Walford
Miss Milne and I. Author of "Iota"
Mistletoe Bough, The. Miss Braddon
Monte Cristo. Alexander Dumas
Mortgage Foreclosed, The. E. H. Thayer
Mountain Tragedy, A. Lincoln
Mrs. Caudle's Curtain Lectures. Douglas Jerrald
My Lady's Money. Wilkie Collins
Mysterious Juror. Du Boisgobey
Mystery of a Hansom Cab. F. W. Hume
My Sweetheart. Francis Maitland
Nameless Love. Chas. Lomon
Octoroon, The. Miss Braddon
Old California Days. Jas. Steele
Old Maid's Love, An. Maarten Maartens
Old Mamselles' Secret. E. Marlitt
Only a Girl. Miss Braddon
Oriole's Daughter. Jessie Fothergill
Our Bessie. Rosa N. Carey.
Our Village. Mary Russell Mitford
Picciola. X. B. Saintine
Pretty Miss Bellew. Theo. Gift
Prue and I Geo. W. Curtis
Rasselas. Johnson
Real Good Thing, A. Kennard
Rogue, The. W. E. Norris
Roland Cashel. Lever
Romance of a Poor Young Man. Octave Feuillet
Romance of Two Worlds. Marie Corelli
Sappho. Alphonse Daudet
Self Raised. Mrs. E. D. E. N. Southworth
Sentimental Journey, A. Laurence Sterne
She's All the World to Me. Hall Caine
Ships That Pass in the Night Beatrice Harraden.
Singularly Deluded. Sarah Grand
Slings and Arrows. Hugh Conway
Song of Miriam. Corelli
Stickit Minister. S. R. Crockett
Stronger than Death. Emile Richelbourg
Ten Nights in a Bar Room. T. S. Arthur
Terrible Temptation. Chas. Reade
Thaddeus of Warsaw Jane Porter
Timar's Two Worlds. Jokai
The Son. Paul Bourget
True Hero A. Reed
Twenty Thousand Leagues Under the Sea. Jules Verne
Two Orphans. R. D. Emery
Tour of the World in Eighty Days. Jules Verne
Uncle Tom's Cabin. Harriet Beecher Stowe
Unwedded Wife, An. Calhoun
Vashti and Esther. Author of "Belles Lettres"
Wagner the Wehr-Wolf. Reynolds
White Heather William Black
White Ladies. Mrs. Oliphant
White Rocks, The A. F. Hill
Woman's Face, A. Warden
Yellow Aster. Iota

History and Biography.

Columbus, Life of. Wilkie
Great Rebellion, History of Moore
Our Planet, Its Life History. Gunning
Scottish Chiefs. Jane Porter
Scott, Sir Walter, Life of
Washington, Life of. Townsend

Miscellaneous.

Attic Philosopher in Paris. E. Souvestre
Aurette Henry Greville
Brown's Bible Dictionary
Children of the Abbey. Roche
Dodo. E. F. Benson
Don Quixote. Cervantes
Elizabeth and Her German Garden
English Men of Letters. Morley
Esther Waters. Geo. Moore
Faust and the Demon. Reynolds
Footprints of the Creator. Miller
Forbidden Fruit. Dion Boucicault
Four Destinies. Gautier
Handy Andy. Lover
Hypatia. Kingsley
In His Steps. Rev. Chas. M. Sheldon
Knowledge of Living Things. Bell
Kilpatrick and Our Cavalry. Moore
Last Days of Pompeii. Bulwer-Lytton
Matrimony. W. E. Norris
Merry Men. R. L. Stevenson
Ocean Tragedy Russell
Paul and Virginia. Saint Pierre
Pierre's Soul. George Ohnet
Poe's Weird Tales. Edgar Allan Poe
Practical Letter Writer
Prisoners and Captives. H. S. Merriman
Rab and His Friends. Dr. J. Brown
Reveries of a Bachelor. Ik Marvel
Rip Van Winkle and Sleepy Hollow. Washington Irving
Scenes and Legends of Scotland. Hugh Miller
Sketch Book. Washington Irving
Slave of the Lamp, The. Henry S. Merriman
Strange Case of Henry Tiplass. J. W. Postgate
Strange Story. Bulwer Lytton
Tales and Sketches. Hugh Miller
Tales from Alsace. Saint Hilaire
Testimony of the Rock. H. Miller
Treasure Island. R. L. Stevenson
Vicar of Wakefield. Oliver Goldsmith
Wee Macgreegor. Bell

Poems and Essays.

Browning's (Robt.) Poems
Dream Life. Ik Marvel
Emerson's Poems
Emerson's Essays
Favorite Poems
Locksley Hall and other Poems. Tennyson
Lowell's Poems J. R. Lowell
Natural Law in the Spirit World. Henry Drummond
Old Portraits and Modern Sketches. Whittier
Pleasures of Life. Sir John Lubbock
Representative Men. Ralph Waldo Emerson
Tennyson's Poems
Whittier's Poems

H. Rider Haggard.

Cleopatra
Dawn
Jess
Witch's Head
King Solomon's Mines
Mr. Meeson's Will
She

Nathaniel Hawthorne.

Blithedale Romance
Grandfather's Chair
Legends of the Province House
Marble Faun
Scarlet Letter
Tanglewood Tales
Wonder Book

Mary J. Holmes.

Aikenside
Bad Hugh
Cousin Maude
Curse of Clifton
Darkness and Daylight
Dora Dean
English Orphans
Ethelyn's Mistake
Edith Lyle's Secret
Homestead on the Hillside
Tempest and Sunshine
What Will the World Say?
What Would You Do, Love?
Leighton Homestead
Maggie Miller
Marion Gray
Meadow Brook
Mildred
Millbank
Miss McDonald
Rector of St. Mark's
Rosamond
Rose Mather

Rudyard Kipling.

American Notes
Courting of Dinah Shadd
In Black and White
Plain Tales from the Hills
Light that Failed
Min Own People
Phantom Rickshaw

Henry Wadsworth Longfellow.

Courtship of Miles Standish
Evangeline
Golden Legend
Hiawatha
Longfellow's Poems

John Ruskin.

Crown of Wild Flowers
King of the Golden River
Mornings in Florence
Queen of the Air
St Mark's Rest

Sir Walter Scott.

Bride of Lammermoor, The
Ivanhoe
Talisman, The
Lady of the Lake
Old Mortality
St. Ronan's Well

Young People's Standard Classics.

Adventures of a Brownie. Miss Mulock
Aesop's Fables
Alice in Wonderland
Andersen's Fairy Tales
Arabian Nights
Black Beauty
Brownies, The. Mrs. Ewing
German Fairy Tales Trans. by Chas. A. Dana
Grimm's Fairy Tales
Gulliver's Travels
Palmer Cox's Brownie Book
Pilgrim's Progress
Robinson Crusoe
Swiss Family Robinson
Through the Looking Glass
Tom Brown's School Days

No. 3F100 Price, each, any title $0.12
Any 12 for 1.35
Any 24 for 2.60

If by mail, postage extra, per book, 7 cents.

ANY 6 FOR $1.28. ANY 12 FOR $2.49. ANY 24 FOR $4.85.

Standard Fiction, History, Biography, Poetry, Essays, Science and Classics.

These books comprise the works of the world's most celebrated authors, each volume substantially bound in cloth, printed on good paper with gilt tops, making a most durable and substantial book. Sizes, each volume, 5½x7½ inches, containing from 200 to 800 pages.

WONDERFUL VALUE.

Handsome, attractive, well made and satisfactory books. The equal of these books has never been offered for less than double the price we ask. Sold in all the big stores as special bargains at 50 cents each.

ORDER AT LEAST A DOZEN AND HAVE THEM COME WITH YOUR NEXT FREIGHT SHIPMENT.

Abbe Constantin. Halvey
Adam Bede. George Eliot
Aesop's Fables
Age of Fable. Bulfinch
Alkenside. Mary J. Holmes
Alhambra, The. Washington Irving
Alice. Lord Lytton
Alice in Wonderland. Lewis Carroll
Andersen's Fairy Tales. Hans Andersen
Arabian Night's Entertainment
Ardath. Marie Corelli
Aunt Diana. Rosa N. Carey
Autocrat of the Breakfast Table, The. O. W. Holmes
Averil. Rosa N. Carey
Bacon's Essays. Francis Bacon
Bad Hugh. Mary J. Holmes
Bailiff's Maid. E. Marlitt
Banned and Blessed. E. Werner
Bay Path. J. G. Holland
Beside the Bonnie Brier Bush. Ian Maclaren
Beulah. Augusta J. Evans-Wilson
Bible Dictionary. Smith
Bill Nye's Sparks
Biographical Dictionary. Wheeler
Bitter Sweet. J. G. Holland
Black Beauty. Anna Sewall
Black Rock. Ralph Connor
Black Tulip, The. Alex. Dumas
Bleak House. Charles Dickens
Blithedale Romance. Hawthorne
Bondman, The. Hall Caine
Bracebridge Hall. Washington Irving
Bride's Fate, The. Mrs. E. D. E. N. Southworth
Broken Wedding Ring. Bertha M. Clay
Bryant's Poetical Works
By Order of the King. Victor Hugo
California and Oregon Trail. Francis Parkman
Camille. Alexander Dumas
Capitola's Peril. Mrs. E. D. E. N. Southworth
Changed Brides. Mrs. Southworth
Chaplain's Daughter, The. Heimburg
Character. Samuel Smiles
Charlatan, The. Robert Buchanan
Chaucer, Spencer, Milton, Cowper, Southy (English Men of Letters). Morley
Charles O'Malley. Lever
Children of the Abbey. Regina Roche
Child's History of England. Charles Dickens
Child Wife. Mayne Reid
Christmas Pudding, and other Brownie Stories. Palmer Cox
Christmas Stories. Chas. Dickens
Classical Quotations, Dictionary of
Cloister and the Hearth. Chas. Reade
Columbus, Life of. Wilkie
Comedy of Sentiment. Max Nordau
Conduct of Life. R. W. Emerson
Conquest of Peru. William H. Prescott
Corinne. Madame de Stael
Count of Monte Cristo, The. Alex. Dumas
Countess of Monte Cristo, The. Alex. Dumas
Courting of Dinah Shadd. Rudyard Kipling
Courtship of Miles Standish. Longfellow
Cousin Maude. Mary J. Holmes
Crabb's Handy Cyclopedia. Mrs. Gaskell
Cricket on the Hearth. Charles Dickens
Crucifixion of Philip Strong. Chas. M. Sheldon
Cruel as Grave. Southworth
Daniel Deronda. George Eliot
Darkness and Daylight. M. J. Holmes
Data of Ethics. Spencer.
David Copperfield. Chas. Dickens
Deemster, The. Hall Caine
Deerslayer, The. J. F. Cooper
DeFoe, Johnson, Goldsmith, Scott, Thackeray (English Men of Letters). Morley
Descent of Man. Darwin
Dombey and Son. Charles Dickens
Donovan. Edna Lyall
Don Quixote. Cervantes
Dora Deane. Mary J. Holmes
Dora Thorne. Charlotte M. Braeme
Dream Life. Ik Marvel
Drummond's Addresses. Henry Drummond
Duke's Secret. C. M. Braeme
Duty. Samuel Smiles
East Lynne. Mrs. Henry Wood
Edith Lyle's Secret. Mary J. Holmes
Edmund Dantes. Alexander Dumas
Education. Spencer
Egyptian Princess, An. Geo. Ebers
Eighth Crusade, The. Alex. Dumas
Elizabeth and Her German Garden. Arnim
Eliot's Essays
Elsie Venner. O. W. Holmes
Emerson's Essays (1st Series). R. W. Emerson
Emerson's Essays (2d Series). R. W. Emerson
English Orphans. Mary J. Holmes
English Traits. Emerson
English Woman's Love Letters
Epictetus
Ernest Maltravers. Bulwer-Lytton
Esther Waters. George Moore
Ethlyn's Mistake. Mary J. Holmes
Evangeline. Henry W. Longfellow
Fairyland of Science. Buckley
Familiar Quotations. Bartlett
Family Pride. Mary J. Holmes
Felix Holt. George Eliot
Fifteen Decisive Battles. Creasy
Firm of Girdlestone. A. Conan Doyle
First Violin. Jessie Fothergill
Floating Island. Jules Verne
Flower Fables. Louise May Alcott
Footprints of the Creator. Millers
Foul Play. Chas. Reade
Free Lances. Mayne Reid
French Revolution. Carlyle
Frivolous Cupid. Anthony Hope
From Out the Gloom. Bertha Clay
Gates of Dawn, The. Fergus Hume
Gertrude's Marriage. W. Heimburg
Gold Elsie. E. Marlitt
Golden Butterfly. Besant and Rice
Grandfather's Chair. Nathaniel Hawthorne
Great Expectations. Chas. Dickens
Grimm's Fairy Tales. Grimm
Gulliver's Travels. Dean Swift
Handy Andy. Samuel Lover
Hardy Norseman, A. Edna Lyall
Harry Lorrequer. Lever
Heart of Midlothian. Scott
Her Martyrdom. Bertha M. Clay
Her Tragic Fate. Sienkiewicz
Hiawatha. H. W. Longfellow
Hidden Hand, The. Mrs. Southworth
History of a Crime. Victor Hugo
Holmes, Oliver Wendell, Life of
Holy War. John Bunyan
Holy Living. Jeremy Taylor
Homestead on the Hillside. Mary J. Holmes
House of Seven Gables. Nathaniel Hawthorne
House of the Wolf. Stanley Weyman
How Women Love. Max Nordau
Humphrey Clinker. Smollet
Hunchback of Notre Dame. Victor Hugo
Hypatia. Chas. Kingsley
Idle Thoughts of an Idle Fellow. Jerome K. Jerome
In Darkest England. Gen. Booth
Inez. Augusta Evans-Wilson
In His Steps. Chas. M. Sheldon
In the Golden Days. Edna Lyall
In the Schillingscourt. E. Marlitt
Ishmael. Mrs. E. D. E. N. Southworth
Ivanhoe. Sir Walter Scott
Ivan the Serf. Sylvanus Cobb, Jr.
Jane Eyre. Charlotte Bronte
John Halifax. Miss Mulock
Kenilworth. Sir Walter Scott
Kipling's Barrack Room Ballads and Poems
Knickerbocker History of N. Y. Washington Irving
Knight Errant. Edna Lyall
Lady Audley's Secret. Braddon
Lady of the Lake. Scott
Lady of the Rubies, The. E. Marlitt
Lamplighter, The. Maria Cummins
Last Days of Pompeii. Bulwer Lytton
Last of the Mohicans. J. F. Cooper
Legends of the Province House. Nathaniel Hawthorne
Leighton Homestead, The. Mary J. Holmes
Lena Rivers. Mary J. Holmes
Les Miserables. Victor Hugo
Life of Christ. Geikie
Life of Christ, Earlier Years and Ministry in Galilee. Hanna
Life of Christ. Close of the Ministry and Passion Week. Hanna
Life of Christ. Last Day of Our Lord's Passion and Forty Days After the Resurrection. Hanna
Little Minister. J. M. Barrie
Longfellow's Poems.
Lorna Doone. R. D. Blackmore
Louise de la Valliere. Alexander Dumas
Lucile. Owen Meredith
Macaria. Augusta Evans-Wilson
Maggie Miller. Mary J. Holmes
Man in Black. Stanley J. Weyman
Man in the Iron Mask, The. Alex. Dumas
Man's Place in Nature. Huxley
Marble Faun, The. Hawthorne
Marian Grey. Mary J. Holmes
Martin Chuzzlewit. Chas. Dickens
Mary St. John. Rosa N. Carey
Masterpieces from Eliot
Masterpieces from Kingsley
Meadowbrook Farm. Mary J. Holmes
Merle's Crusade. Rosa N. Carey
Merry Men. R. L. Stevenson
Micah Clarke. A. Conan Doyle
Michael Strogoff. Jules Verne
Middlemarch. George Eliot
Millbank. Mary J. Holmes
Mildred. Mary J. Holmes
Mill on the Floss. George Eliot
Mine Own People and Other Stories. Rudyard Kipling
Minister's Wooing, The. Mrs. Stowe
Misjudged. W. Heimburg
Monte Cristo's Daughter. Alex. Dumas
Mosses from an Old Manse. Nathaniel Hawthorne
Mysterious Island, The. Jules Verne
Mysteries of Paris. Eugene Sue
Mystery of a Hansom Cab. Fergus W. Hume
Natural Law in the Spiritual World. Henry Drummond
Napoleon and His Marshals. Headley
Nicholas Nickleby. Chas. Dickens
Ninety-Three. Victor Hugo
No Quarter. Mayne Reid
Not Like Other Girls. Rosa N. Carey
Officer's Bride. Octave Feuillet
Old Curiosity Shop. Chas. Dickens
Old Mamselle's Secret. E. Marlitt
Oliver Twist. Chas. Dickens
Only the Governess. Rosa N. Carey
Origin of Species. Chas. Darwin
Other Worlds than Ours. Proctor
Our Bessie. Rosa N. Carey
Our Mutual Friend. Chas. Dickens
Our Planet, Its Life History. Gunning
Our Village. Mary Russell Mitford
Outre-Mer. Henry W. Longfellow
Pathfinder. J. F. Cooper
Paul and Virginia. St. Pierre
Phantom's Rickshaw. Rudyard Kipling
Pickwick Papers. Chas. Dickens
Pillar of Fire. Rev. J. H. Ingraham
Pilot, The. Cooper
Pilgrim's Progress. John Bunyan
Pioneers, The. J. F. Cooper
Plato on the Immortality of the Soul
Pleasures of Life. Sir John Lubbock
Plutarch's Lives
Poe's Tales. Edgar Allen Poe
Popular Geology. Hugh Miller
Prairie, The. J. F. Cooper
Pride and Prejudice. Jane Austen
Prince of the House of David, The. Rev. J. H. Ingraham
Princess of the Moor. E. Marlitt
Professor at the Breakfast Table. Holmes
Prue and I. Geo. W. Curtis
Put Yourself in His Place. Chas. Reade
Quo Vadis. Henryk Sienkiewicz
Rector of St. Mark's. M. J. Holmes
Representative Men. Emerson
Reveries of a Bachelor. Ik Marvel
Robinson Crusoe. Daniel DeFoe
Rogue's Life, A. Wilkie Collins
Romance of a Poor Young Man. Feuillet
Romance of Two Worlds. Corelli
Romola. George Eliot
Rosamond. Mary J. Holmes
Rose Mather. Mary J. Holmes
Samantha at Saratoga. Holley
Sartor Resartus. Thomas Carlyle
Scarlet Letter. Nathaniel Hawthorne
Scenes of Clerical Life. George Eliot
Scottish Chiefs. Jane Porter
Second Wife, The. E. Marlitt
Self Help. Samuel Smiles
Self Raised. Mrs. Southworth
Sesame and Lillies. John Ruskin
Shadow of a Crime. Hall Caine
Shadow of a Sin. C. M. Braeme
Shakespeare, Life of
She's All the World to Me. Hall Caine
Silas Marner. George Eliot
Silence of Dean Maitland. Maxwell Gray
Simple Life. Chas. Wagner
Single Heart and Double Face. Chas. Reade
Singularly Deluded. Sarah Grand
Sketch Book. Washington Irving
Snow Image. Hawthorne
Soldiers Three and Plain Tales from the Hills. Kipling
Song of Miriam, The. Marie Corelli
Son of Hagar. Hall Caine
Son of Monte Cristo. Dumas
Son of Porthos. Dumas
Spanish Gypsy. Eliot
Spy, The. J. F. Cooper
Stepping Heavenward. Prentiss
Stickit Minister. S. R. Crockett
Stories from Virgil. Church
Stories of the Persian Wars. Church
Swiss Family Robinson
Taine's English Literature
Tale of Two Cities. Dickens
Tales from Scott
Tales from Shakespeare. Chas. Lamb
Tanglewood Tales. Hawthorne
Tempest and Sunshine. Mary J. Holmes
Tennyson's Poems
Ten Nights in a Bar Room. Arthur
Thaddeus of Warsaw. Porter
Three Guardsmen, The. Alex. Dumas
Three Men in a Boat. Jerome
The Light that Failed. Kipling
Thelma. Marie Corelli
Theophrastus Such. George Eliot
Thorns and Orange Blossoms. Braeme
Thrift. Samuel Smiles
Throne of David. Rev. Ingraham
Through the Looking Glass—and What Alice Found There. Lewis Carroll
Thrown on the World. Bertha M. Clay
Toilers of the Sea. Hugo
Tom Brown's School Days. Thomas Hughes
Tom Brown at Oxford. Thomas Hughes
Tom Burke of Ours. Lever
Tom Jones. Henry Fielding
Tour of the World in Eighty Days. Jules Verne
Treasure Island. Robert Stevenson
Tried for Her Life. Southworth
Twenty Thousand Leagues Under the Sea. Jules Verne
Twenty Years After. Alex. Dumas
Twice Told Tales. Hawthorne
Two Admirals. J. F. Cooper
Uarda. George Ebers
Uncle Tom's Cabin. Mrs. H. B. Stowe
Under Two Flags. Ouida
Undine and Sintram. Fouque
Vanity Fair. Wm. M. Thackeray
Vendetta. Marie Corelli
Very Hard Cash. Chas. Reade
Vicar of Wakefield and Rasselas. Goldsmith and Dr. Johnson
Views Afoot. Bayard Taylor
Viscount de Bragelonne. Alex. Dumas
Wanda. Ouida
Wandering Jew. Eugene Sue
Washington and His Generals. Headley
Water Babies. Charles Kingsley
Water Witch. J. F. Cooper
Week on the Concord and Merrimac Rivers. A. Thoreau
Wee Wifie. Rosa N. Carey
We Two. Edna Lyall
Westward Ho! Chas. Kingsley
When a Man's Single. J. M. Barrie
White Company, The. A. Conan Doyle
Whittier's Poems
Wide, Wide World, The. E. Wetherell
Widow Bedott Papers. Whitcher
Wife of Monte Cristo. Alex. Dumas
Wigwam and Cabin. Simms
Window in Thrums, A. J. M. Barrie
Wing and Wing. J. F. Cooper
Won by Waiting. Edna Lyall
Wooed and Married. Rosa N. Carey
Wooing O'T. Mrs. Alexander
Wormwood. Marie Corelli

WORLD'S BEST LITERATURE, IN SPECIAL LIBRARY EDITION, JUST AS ILLUSTRATED AND DESCRIBED ABOVE

No. 3F199 Price, each, any title	$0.22	Price, any 12 for	$2.49
Price, any 6 for	1.28	Price, any 24 for	4.85

If by mail, postage extra, per volume, 9 cents.

ANY 2 FOR 94c

ANY 6 FOR $2.70

ANY 12 FOR $5.25

Regular $1.50 New Popular Novels at 48 Cents.

For those popular books, the cream of up to date literature, the best stories by the most noted authors, we ask only 48 cents. Your dealer wants $1.08 to $1.50. For your own reading table or as a gift they are bound to please. Cloth bound. Size, 5½x7¾ inches. 250 to 600 pages.

If by mail, postage extra, each, 8 cents.

Adventures of Brigadier Gerard. A. Conan Doyle
Adventures of Sherlock Holmes. A. Conan Doyle
Albert Gate Mystery, The. Louis Tracy
Alice of Old Vincennes. Maurice Thompson
Amateur Cracksman. E. Hornung
A Mysterious Disappearance. Gordon Holmes
Aristocrats, The. Gertrude Atherton
Ashes of Empire. Robert W. Chambers
Barabbas. Marie Corelli
Barlasch of the Guards. Henry Merriman
Battle Ground, The. Ellen Glasgow
Beautiful Joe's Paradise. Marshall Saunders
Before the Dawn. J. A. Altsheler
Between the Lines. Illustrated. Capt. Charles King
Black Friday. F. S. Isham
Black Wolf's Breed, The. Illustrated. Harris Dickson
Bob, Son of Battle. Alfred Ollivant
Boss Tom. Jas. Ball Naylor
Bosses, The. Alfred Henry Lewis
Brewster's Millions. George Barr McCutcheon
Bright Face of Danger, The. Illustrated R. N. Stephens
Buell Hampton. Willis George Emerson
By Order of the Prophet. Alfred H. Henry
By Right of Sword. A. W. Marchmont
Caleb West, Master Diver. F. Hopkinson Smith
Call of the Wild. Jack London
Calumet "K." Merwin and Webster
Captain in the Ranks, A. George Carey Eggleston
Captain Ravenshaw. R. N. Stephens
Captain's Wife, The. W. Clark Russell
Cardinal's Snuff Box, The. H. Harland
Castaways, The. Hallie Erminie Rives
Castle Craneycrow. George Barr McCutcheon
Cecilia. F. M. Crawford
Celebrity, The. Winston Churchill
Checkers. H. M. Blossom, Jr.
Children of the Ghetto. I. Zangwill
Choir Invisible. James Lane Allen
Christian, The. Hall Caine
Chronicles of Count Antonio. Anthony Hope
Circular Study, The. Anna Katherine Green
Climax, The. C. F. Pidgin
Colonial Free Lance, A. Chauncey C. Hotchkiss
Coin of Edward VII, A. Fergus Hume
Common Lot, The. Robert Herrick
Comrades in Arms. General Charles King
Conqueror, The. G. F. Atherton
Consequences. Egerton Castle
Credit of the Country, The. W. E. Norris
Crimson Blind, The. Fred M. White
Damnation of Theron Ware. H. Frederic
Dash for a Throne, A. A. W. Marchmont
Daughter of the Sioux, A. General Chas. King
Deliverance, The. Ellen Glasgow
Dodo. E. F. Benson
Dorothy Vernon of Haddon Hall. Charles Major
Downfall, The. Emil Zola
Eben Holden. Irving Bacheller
Enemy to the King, An. Robert Neilson Stephens
Fables in Slang. George Ade
Fillibusters, The. Cutliffe Hyne
Filigree Ball, The. A. K. Green
For Love or Crown. Illustrated. A. W. Marchmont.
Forsaken Inn, The. Detective Story. Anna Katherine Green
For the Freedom of the Sea. C. T. Brady
Forest Lovers, The. M. Hewlett
Four Feathers, The. A. E. W. Mason
Gentleman from Indiana, The. Booth Tarkington
Gentleman Player, A. Robert Neilson Stephens
Girl at the Half Way House. Emerson Hough
Grafters, The. Illustrated. F. Lynde
Great Mogul The. Louis Tracy
Green Diamond, The Arthur Morrison
Grey Cloak, The. H. MacGrath
Heart of Rome, The. F Marion Crawford
Helmet of Navarre, The. B. Runkle
Heritage of Unrest. Gwendolen Overton
History of David Grieve. Mrs. Humphrey Ward
Honorable Peter Stirling. Paul Leicester Ford
Hope Hathaway. F. V. Parker
Hope Loring. Lillian Bell
Hound of the Baskervilles, The. A. Conan Doyle
If I Were King. J. H. McCarthy
If Sinners Entice Thee. William Le Queux
In the Bishop's Carriage. Miriam Michelson
In the Palace of the King. F. M. Crawford
In the Name of a Woman. Arthur W. Marchmont
Jessamy Bride, The. F. F. Moore
John Burt. Frederick Upham Adams
Kate Bonnet. Frank R. Stockton
King of Diamonds, The. L. Tracy
King's Mirror, The. Anthony Hope
Law of the Land, The. Emerson Hough
Lazarre. Illustrated. M. H. Catherwood
Letters of a Self Made Merchant Geo. H. Lorimer
Leopard's Spots, The. Illustrated. Thomas Dixon, Jr.
Light of Scarthey, The. Egerton Castle
Lightning Conductor, The. C. N. and A. M. Williamson
Long Straight Road. George Norton
Making of a Marchioness. F. H. Burnett
Man from Glengarry, The. Ralph Connor
Manders. Elwyn Barron
Manxman, The. Hall Caine
Man on the Box, The. H. MacGrath
Man Who Dared, The. John P. Ritter
Marcella. Mrs. Humphrey Ward
Master Christian, The. Marie Corelli
Master of Craft, A. W. W. Jacobs
Master Craftsman, The. Sir Walter Besant
Master of Warlock, The. G. C. Eggleston
Mantle of Elijah. I. Zangwill
Matter of Millions. A Detective Story. Anna Katharine Green
Medal of Honor, The. General Charles King
Millionaire Baby, The. Anna Katharine Green
Mississippi Bubble, The. Emerson Hough
Monsieur Beaucaire. Booth Tarkington
Monk's Treasure, The. Illustrated. George Horton
Motor Pirate, The. G. S. Paternoster
Mr. Dooley in Peace and War. F. P. Dunne
Mr. Dooley in the Hearts of His Countrymen. F. P. Dunne
Mr. Isaacs. F. M. Crawford
My Friend Prospero. Henry Harland.
My Lady Cinderella. Mrs. C. N. Williamson
Mystery of Murray Davenport. Robert Neilson Stephens
None But the Brave. Hamblen Sears
Octopus, The. Frank Norris
On the Face of the Waters. Flora Annie Steel
Peggy O'Neal. Illustrated. Alfred Henry Lewis
Pillar of Light, The. Louis Tracy
Pioneer, The. Geraldine Bonner
Pit, The. Frank Norris
Prisoner of Zenda. Anthony Hope
Pride of Jennico, The. A. and E. Castle
Prodigal Son, The. Hall Caine
Puppet Crown, The. Harold MacGrath
Quest of the Golden Girl, The. R. LeGallienne
Quo Vadis. Henrik Sienkiewicz
Raffles. E. Hornung
Ralph Marlowe. James Ball Naylor
Real World, The. Robert Herrick
Red Keggers, The. Eugene Thwing
Red Triangle, The. Detective Story. Elliott Flower
Red Window, The. Detective Story. Fergus Hume
Redemption of David Corson, The. C. F. Gross
Resurrection. Count Leo Tolstoi
Revenge. Robert Barr
Richard Rosny. Maxwell Gray
Road Builders, The. Samuel Merwin
Road to Paris, The. Robert Neilson Stephens
Robert Orange. Oliver Hobbes
Rupert of Hentzau. Anthony Hope
Sant Ilario. F. M. Crawford
Saracinesca. F. M. Crawford
Sea Wolf, The. Jack London
Second Thoughts of an Idle Fellow. J. K. Jerome
Secret Passage, The. Detective Story. Fergus Hume
Senator North. Gertrude Atherton
Sentimental Tommy. J. M. Barrie
Sherlock Holmes. Illustrated. Theatre Edition. A. Conan Doyle
Sherrods, The. George Barr McCutcheon
Singular Life, A. Elizabeth Stuart Phelps
Sir Henry Morgan, Buccaneer. Cyrus Townsend Brady
Slaves of Success, The. Elliott Flower
Soldiers of Fortune. Richard Harding Davis
Soul of Lilith. Marie Corelli
Spenders, The. Harry Leon Wilson
Spoilsmen, The. Elliott Flower
Stephen Holton. Chas. Felton Pidgin
Tales of the Ex-Tanks. L. C. Cullen
Temporal Power. Marie Corelli
That Mainwaring Affair. Illustrated. A. M. Barbour
Third Degree, The. Detective Story. Chas. Ross Jackson
Thirteenth District. Brand Whitlock
Thompson's Progress. G. J. C. Hyne
Those Black Diamond Men. W. F. Gibbons
Thyra Varrick. A. E. Barr
To Have and to Hold. Mary Johnson
Tommy and Grizel. J. M. Barrie
Two Captains, The. Cyrus Townsend Brady
Two Vanrevels, The. Booth Tarkington
Via Crucis. F. M. Crawford
Voice of the People, The. Ellen Glasgow
Warwick of the Knobs. Illus. John Uri Lloyd
Watchers of the Trails, The. Illustrated. Chas. L. Bull
Westerners, The. Stewart Edward White
Wheels of Chance, The. G. H. Wells
Whirlpool, The. George Gissing
Who Goes There. B. K. Benson
Wings of the Morning. Louis Tracy
Wolfville Days. A. H. Lewis
Woman Intervenes, A. Robert Barr
Woman of the World, A. Ella Wheeler Wilcox
Yellow Holly, The. Detective Story. Fergus Hume
Young April. Agnes and Egerton Castle
Zelda Dameron. Meredith Nicholson
Ziska. Marie Corelli

No. 3F300 New Fiction, latest copyrighted novels, beautifully printed, bound in cloth with handsome cover designs. Just as illustrated and described above. Price, any 12 for **$5.25**; any 6 for **$2.70**; any 2 for **94c**; per volume **48c**
If by mail, postage extra, per volume, 11 cents.

Hearts Courageous, 48 Cents.

By **Hallie Erminie Rives.** A novel descriptive of Virginia life in the days immediately preceding the Revolution. Full of incident and adventure growing out of the difference of political opinion. Contains 407 pages, printed on excellent quality of paper. Bound in cloth with stamped cover design, and beautifully colored inlay. Size, 5½x7¾ inches.
No. 3F302 Price **48c**
If by mail, postage extra, 10 cents.

Janice Meredith, 48 Cents.

By **Paul Leicester Ford.** A story of the Revolution. With illustrations. The most popular historical novel of the past decade. Janice, her pretty coquetries overlaying the sterling qualities of her character, is a most lovable and interesting figure. Contains 536 pages, excellent quality of paper. Bound in cloth with title and cover design embossed on side and back. Size, 5½x7¾ inches.
No. 3F304 Price.......... **48c**
If by mail postage extra, 11 cents.

The Crisis, 48 Cents.

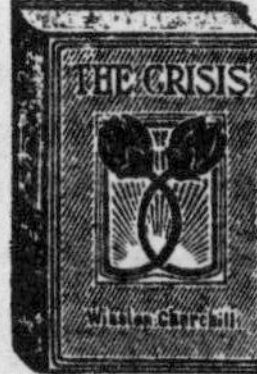

By **Winston Churchill.** Illustrations by Howard Chandler Christy. The best novel founded on the Civil War period that has yet been published. No more realistic and sympathetic study of Mr. Lincoln has been made than that which is presented in this book, and the figure grows upon the reader. Contains 522 pages, best quality of paper. Bound in cloth with cover design. Size, 5½x7¾ inches.
No. 3F306 Price.......... **48c**
If by mail, postage extra, 12 cents.

The Virginian, 48 Cents.

A Horseman of the Plains. By Owen Wister. With illustrations by Arthur Keller. No one writes of the frontier with more interest than this young author, and no one writes more essentially American. In The Virginian he has put forth a book that will be remembered. Contains 504 pages, excellent quality of paper. Bound in cloth with original cover design. Size, 5½x7¾ inches.
No. 3F308 Price **48c**
If by mail, postage extra, 12 cents.

Blennerhassett, or The Decrees of Fate, 48 Cents.

By **Charles Felton Pidgin.** A romance founded upon the events of American History. With illustrations. A fascinating tale of the time of Aaron Burr and Alexander Hamilton. Throughout the clever chain of the events of Aaron Burr's dramatic life runs the thread of a unique love story, a golden thread that gives its gleam to sombre realities. Contains 442 pages, excellent quality of paper. Bound in cloth. Size, 5½x7¾ inches.
No. 3F310 Price.......... **48c**
If by mail, postage extra, 10 cents.

Quincy Adams Sawyer, 48 Cents

By **Charles Felton Pidgin.** A picture of New England home life. With illustrations from the play. Full of interesting incidents, quaint sayings, healthy sentiment and a certain irresistible humor that will appeal to readers who are tired of the conventional novel. Contains 474 pages, excellent quality of paper. Bound in cloth. Size, 5½x7¾ inches.
No. 3F312 Price, **48c**
If by mail, postage extra, 11 cents.

St. Elmo, 48 Cents.

By **Augusta J. Evans.** Sold for the first time at a popular price, only a limited number and when these are sold, no more can be had. This novel is the best known of Mrs. Evans works. The most successful American novel ever written. Towns, yachts, country homes, etc., have been named in its honor, so widespread has been its success. Contains 565 pages, printed on excellent quality of paper. Bound in cloth with embossed cover design and photographic inlay. Size, 5½x7¾ inches.
No. 3F313 Price.......... **48c**
If by mail, postage extra, 11 cents.

When Knighthood Was in Flower, 48 Cents.

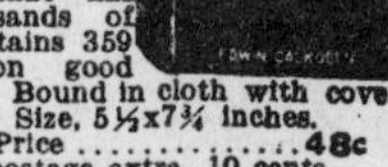

Or, the Love Story of Charles Brandon and Mary Tudor, the King's Sister, and Happenings in the Reign of His August Majesty King Henry the Eighth. Taken from the memoirs of Sir Edwin Caskoden by Charles Major. The present edition is superbly illustrated with numerous scenes from the play. A novel that has entertained thousands of readers. Contains 359 pages, printed on good quality of paper. Bound in cloth with cover design embossed. Size, 5½x7¾ inches.
No. 3F314 Price.......... **48c**
If by mail, postage extra, 10 cents.

The Hoosier Schoolmaster, 48 Cents.

By **Edward Eggleston.** A story of backwoods life in Indiana. Revised, with an introduction and notes on the district by the author, with character sketches by F. Opper and other illustrations by W. E. B. Starkweather. This book now ranks among the classics of American literature. Its wholesome tone and genuine fun, as well as its happy delineation of the characteristics of the pioneers of the time, making it a volume that should be found on the shelves of the library in every home. Contains 281 pages, printed on excellent quality of paper. Bound in cloth with title stamped on back and side, and embossed design on cover. Size, 5½x7¾ inches.
No. 3F316 Price.......... **48c**
If by mail, postage extra, 10 cents.

The Eternal City, 48 Cents.

By **Hall Caine,** author of The Christian. This famous book which was dramatized and played throughout the country with so much success by Edward Morgan, cannot fail to prove of interest to the most casual reader. Life with its intrigues, its love and hate, was never so well depicted by that master artist, Hall Caine. Illustrated throughout with photographs from the play. This edition is in every respect equal to the $1.50 edition. Contains 449 pages, printed from large type on the best quality of paper. Bound in cloth with original cover design stamped in green. Size, 5½x7¾ inches.
No. 3F318 Our price.......... **48c**
If by mail, postage extra, 11 cents.

Graustark, 48 Cents.

By **George Barr McCutcheon.** A story of love behind a throne. This work has been and is today one of the most popular works of fiction of this decade. The meeting of the Princess of Graustark with the hero, while traveling incognito in this country, his efforts to find her, his success, the defeat of conspiracies to dethrone her, and their happy marriage, provide entertainment of which every type of reader never wearies. Contains 457 pages, printed on excellent quality of paper. Bound in cloth with cover design stamped in white. Size, 5½x7¾ inches.
No. 3F320 Price.......... **48c**
If by mail, postage extra, 11 cents.

David Harum, 48 Cents.

By **Edward N. Westcott.** It is unnecessary to describe this well known book. Any one who has read David Harum wants to read it again, and those who have not, should not fail to purchase a copy. David Harum with his quaint humor, his big heart, his generosity hid under a blustering appearance, cannot fail to come very close to the reader. This book is in every respect equal to the $1.50 edition. Contains 389 pages, printed on the best quality of paper, with illustration frontispiece. Bound in cloth with beautiful cover design stamped in red and green. Size, 5½x7¾ inches.
No. 3F322 Our price.......... **48c**
If by mail, postage extra, 10 cents.

The Fat of the Land, 48 Cents.

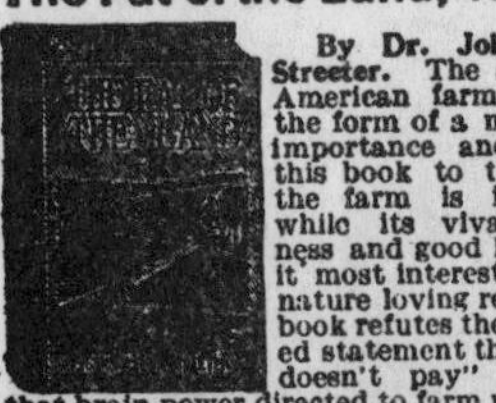

By Dr. John William Streeter. The story of an American farm, written in the form of a novel. The importance and value of this book to the man on the farm is incalculable, while its vivacity, frankness and good humor make it most interesting to the nature loving reader. The book refutes the oft repeated statement that "farming doesn't pay" and shows that brain power directed to farm management will be as liberally recompensed as when put to work in any other line. Contains 406 pages printed on excellent quality of paper and bound in cloth with original design stamped on cover. Size, 5½x7¾ inches.

No. 3F326 Price 48c
If by mail, postage extra, 10 cents.

Pathfinders of the West, 48 Cents.

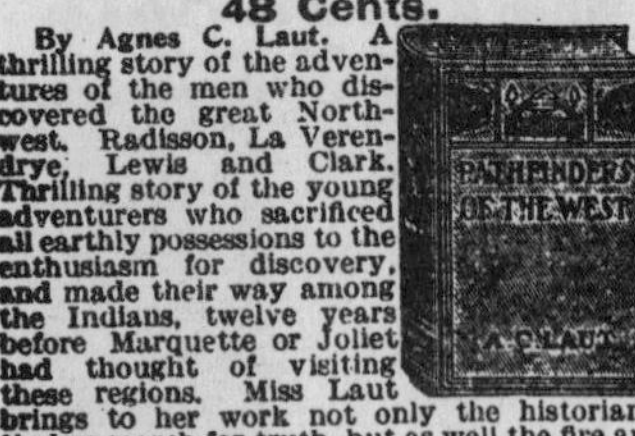

By Agnes C. Laut. A thrilling story of the adventures of the men who discovered the great Northwest. Radisson, La Verendrye, Lewis and Clark. Thrilling story of the young adventurers who sacrificed all earthly possessions to the enthusiasm for discovery, and made their way among the Indians, twelve years before Marquette or Joliet had thought of visiting these regions. Miss Laut brings to her work not only the historian's tireless search for truth, but as well the fire and imagination and creative power of a novelist and poet. Contains 380 pages, printed on excellent quality of paper; illustrations by Remington, Goodwin, Marchand and others. Bound in cloth with stamped cover design and title. Size, 5½x7¾ inches.

No. 3F328 Price 48c
If by mail, postage extra, 14 cents.

Buccaneers and Pirates of Our Coast, 48 Cents.

By Frank Stockton. Stories of the rise and decline of buccaneering and piracy in our West Indian waters. Spanish exactions grew so monstrous in the seventeenth century that English French and Dutch combined against their excesses. The buccaneers who were the result of the combination became later pirates for private gain. Mr. Stockton's quaint humor brightens the stories of their dark deeds. Contains 325 pages. Printed on excellent quality of paper. Illustrations by George Varian and B. West Clinedinst. Bound in cloth, with original cover design. Size, 5½x7¾ inches.

No. 3F330 Price 48c
If by mail, postage extra, 11 cents.

The Jungle, $1.08.

By Upton Sinclair. The most talked of book of the year. A terrible book. One that has caused an upheaval in this country. It was due to this book that the investigation of the packing houses was instituted by President Roosevelt, which disclosed the fact that the terrible, unhealthy, filthy conditions of the packing houses so vividly described in The Jungle were true. The Jungle is the story of a Lithuanian family in Chicago's "Packingtown." More than this, it is a blazing indictment of conditions existing among the working classes in the big cities in this country, which no American can read without experiencing a desire to do something. One noted writer describes this book as "the Uncle Tom's Cabin of wage slavery." Some have declared it the greatest novel written in America in fifty years. Bound in green silk cloth with original cover design. 413 pages. Size, 5½x7¾ inches.

No. 3F350 Price $1.08
If by mail, postage extra, 12 cents.

Works of Rev. E. P. Roe.

Cloth bound. 250 to 500 pages. Size, 4½x6½ inches.

A Day of Fate
An Original Belle
Barriers Burned Away
Brave Little Quakeress
Found, Yet Lost
From Jest to Earnest
He Fell in Love with His Wife
His Sombre Rivals
Knight of the 19th Century
Miss Lou
Opening a Chestnut Burr
The Hornet's Nest
Unexpected Results
What Can She Do
Young Girl's Wooing

No. 3F410 Price, per volume.....30c
If by mail, postage extra, 5 cents.

Works of Mrs. Rice.

(Alice Caldwell Hegan.)

Mrs. Wiggs of the Cabbage Patch. The story of a cheerful Christian woman who looks only on the bright side of life. One of the most successful books of the day. 16 mo. 153 pages.

Lovey Mary. For fun and pathos, for crisp wit and severe philosophy, Lovey Mary is as notable as Mrs. Wiggs. 16 mo. 197 pages.

Sandy. The best story Mrs. Rice has yet written. 16 mo. 312 pages.

No. 3F430 Mrs. Wiggs of the Cabbage Patch, Lovey Mary or Sandy. Be sure to state title desired. Price, per volume...$0.75
The 3 books for...............2.15
If by mail, postage extra, per volume, 6 cents.

Works of Gen. Lew Wallace.

Ben Hur. Cloth. Size, 5½x7¼ inches.
Price $0.96
Fair God, The
Price 1.05
Boyhood of Christ
Price 2.48
Prince of India
Price 1.78

Order by No. 3F450 and do not fail to state name of book wanted.
If by mail, postage extra, per volume, 12 cents.

Works of Augusta J. Evans.

The dramatic fervor of these stories endears them to every reader. Having read one, you will read all. Size, 5¼x7½ in.

Beulah
Inez
Macaria

No. 3F455 Price, per volumne..............25c

At the Mercy of Tiberius
Infelice
St. Elmo
Speckled Bird
Vashti

No. 3F460 Price, per volume......96c
If by mail, postage extra, per volume, 13 cents.

Fine Two-Volume Library Sets, 68 Cents.

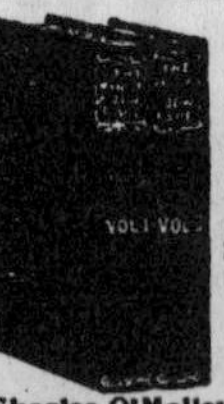

Two-Volume Edition of Standard Fiction. Printed on excellent quality of paper, and bound in ribbed cloth with title stamped on back in gold. Size of each volume, 5⅛x7½ ins. Each set comes boxed. Retail price of these sets is $1.50. We are making a special price of 68 cents per set. We do not think that you can do better than buy these beautiful sets, which will not only be a pleasure to read, but beautiful to look at.

Charles O'Malley. Vols. 1 and 2. By Charles Lever
Cloister and the Hearth. Vols. 1 and 2. By Charles Reade
Count of Monte Cristo. Vols. 1 and 2. By Alexander Dumas
Indian Tales. Vols. 1 and 2. By Rudyard Kipling
Les Miserables. Vols. 1 and 2. By Victor Hugo
Pendennis. Vols. 1 and 2. By Wm. Thackeray
Tales of Sherlock Holmes. Vols. 1 and 2. By A. Conan Doyle
The Life of Christ. Vols. 1 and 2. By F. W. Farrar
The Three Guardsmen. Vols. 1 and 2. By Alexander Dumas
The Wandering Jew. Vols. 1 and 2. By Eugene Sue
Tom Brown's School Days. Tom Brown at Oxford. By Thomas Hughes
Essays. Vols. 1 and 2. By Ralph Waldo Emerson.
On the Heigths. Vols. 1 and 2. By Berthold Auerbach.

No. 3F999 Price, per set (2 volumes) (Postage extra, per set, 20 cents)......68c

Uncle Tom's Cabin.

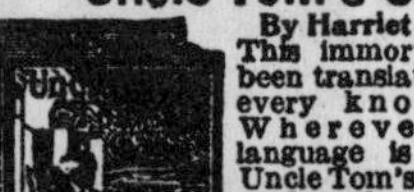

By Harriet Beecher Stowe. This immortal classic has been translated into almost every known language. Wherever the English language is known, there Uncle Tom's Cabin has been read and will be read for years to come. Cloth. Illustrated. 502 pages. Size, 5½x8 inches.

No. 3F501
Price..............45c
If by mail, postage extra, 14 cents.

No. 3F502 Uncle Tom's Cabin. Memorial edition. A special edition of this wonderful story, profusely illustrated with original drawings by celebrated artists, bound in silk finish cloth, with handsome cover design in gold and colors, printed on fine paper. 680 pages. Size, 7x9½ inches. Price...80c
If by mail, postage extra, 25 cents.

THREE QUARTER LEATHER DELUXE EDITIONS 48¢ EACH ANY 2 FOR 94c

STANDARD AUTHORS
GOLD TOPS LEATHER BOUND MARBLE SIDES.

ANY 6 FOR $2.69 ANY 12 FOR $4.98 ANY 24 FOR $9.60

THESE SPECIAL DE LUXE EDITIONS of the World's most famous books, are made as well as books can be made. Paper, type and printing are the very best. The binding is the richest of all bindings, genuine three-quarter morocco leather, stamped with handsome design and title in pure gold leaf on the back, gold tops with head bands, handsome marbled sides, genuine de luxe editions in every respect.

THESE ARE ALL BOOKS OF GREAT MERIT, books by the most famous writers the world has known. Every book in this list ought to be in every home in the land, and in offering these special de luxe editions at only 48 cents each, we are presenting to you a most unusual opportunity to place the world's best books on your shelves, at prices heretofore unknown for books of this high quality.

ALL OF THE VOLUMES in this big list are of uniform size and uniform style of binding, all bound in three-quarter leather of various colors, red, blue and green, so that an assortment of these books on your shelves presents a most attractive appearance.

WE ESPECIALLY URGE you to select as many as possible of these books. Pick out at least a dozen, or two dozen, or even more, because the opportunity to purchase these most interesting, high class books, at so low a price, put up in such beautiful bindings and so well printed may never come to you again.

Adam Bede. Eliot
Age of Fable. Bulfinch
Andersen's Fairy Tales.
Arabian Nights.
Autocrat of the Breakfast Table. Oliver Wendell Holmes
Bacon's Essays.
Barnaby Rudge. Dickens
Beulah. Augusta J. Evans
Bondman. Hall Caine
Bracebridge Hall. Irving
Bride of Lammermoor. Scott
California and Oregon Trail. Francis Parkman
Child's History of England. Dickens
Conduct of Life. Emerson
Confessions of an English Opium Eater. DeQuincey
Conquest of Peru. Prescott
Count of Monte Cristo. Dumas
Cranford. Mrs. Gaskell
Daniel Deronda. Eliot
Data of Ethics. Spencer
David Copperfield. Dickens
Descent of Man. Darwin
Dombey and Son. Dickens
Education. Spencer
Egyptian Princess. Ebers
Elsie Venner. O. W. Holmes.
Emerson's Essays.
English Traits. Emerson
Fair Maid of Perth. Scott
Familiar Quotations. Bartlett
Felix Holt. Eliot
First Violin. Jessie Fothergill
Great Expectations. Dickens
Grimm's Fairy Tales.
Holy Roman Empire. Bryce
Hunchback of Notre Dame. Hugo
In His Steps. C. M. Sheldon
Ivanhoe. Scott
Jane Eyre. Bronte
John Halifax. Mulock
Kenilworth. Scott
Koran of Mohammed.
Lamplighter. Cummins
Last Days of Pompeii. Bulwer
Last of the Mohicans. Cooper
Les Miserables. Hugo
Longfellow's Poetical Works.
Lorna Doone. Blackmore
Macaulay's Speeches.
Marble Faun. Hawthorne
Meadow Brook. Mary J. Holmes
Middlemarch. Eliot
Mill on the Floss. Eliot
Minister's Wooing, The. Stowe
Mosses from an Old Manse. Hawthorne
Napoleon and His Marshals. Headley
Old Curiosity Shop. Dickens
Oliver Twist. Dickens
Origin of Species. Darwin
Other Worlds than Ours. Proctor
Pickwick. Dickens
Plutarch's Lives.
Poe's Prose Tales.
Prince of the House of David. Rev. Prof. J. H. Ingraham
Professor at the Breakfast Table. Oliver Wendell Holmes
Prue and I. Geo. Wm. Curtis
Quo Vadis. Sienkiewicz
Representative Men. Emerson
Robinson Crusoe. Defoe
Rob Roy. Scott
Romola. Eliot
Scarlet Letter. Hawthorne
Sketch Book. Irving
Soldiers Three and Plain Tales from the Hills. Kipling
Stepping Heavenward. Prentiss
Tale of Two Cities. Dickens.
Tales from Shakespeare. Lamb
Tennyson's Poems.
Thelma. Marie Corelli
Tom Brown at Oxford. Hughes
Tom Brown's School Days. Hughes
Twice Told Tales. Hawthorne
Uncle Tom's Cabin. Stowe
Under Two Flags. Ouida
Vanity Fair. Thackeray
Vicar of Wakefield. Goldsmith
Washington and His Generals. Headley
Waverly. Scott
Week on the Concord and Merrimac Rivers. Thoreau
Whittier's Poetical Works

No. 3F700 Price, 24 for $9.60; 12 for $4.98; 6 for $2.69; 2 for 94c; per volume.........48c
If by mail, postage extra, per volume, 12 cents.

COMPLETE SETS, STANDARD AUTHORS.

NEW ILLUSTRATED LIBRARY EDITION.

Sold in sets only. An entirely new line of standard sets, printed from new clear type on the best quality of paper in uniform size and style of binding. Each volume contains a photogravure frontispiece, with printed tissue, together with numerous beautiful halftone illustrations and rubricated title page. Tastefully bound in silk ribbed cloth, stamped with author's signature on side. Full gold tops. Head bands. Size of each volume, 5½x8½ inches. Fine binding. Beautifully made books in every way. Fine paper. The handsomest library edition published. Made by Dana, Estes & Co. and T. Y. Crowell & Co.

No. 3F1001 Honore de Balzac. Complete works in 18 vols. Price, per set.$12.60
No. 3F1003 Charlotte Bronte. Complete works in 6 vols. Price, per set...$4.20
No. 3F1006 Bulwer-Lytton. Complete works in 13 volumes. Price, per set...$9.10
No. 3F1009 Thomas Carlyle. Complete works in 10 volumes. Price, per set...$7.00
No. 3F1012 James Fenimore Cooper. Complete works in 6 volumes. Price, per set.........$4.20
No. 3F1015 Daniel Defoe. Complete works in 16 volumes. Price, per set.$11.20
No. 3F1018 Charles Dickens. Complete works in 15 volumes. Price, per set..$10.50
No. 3F1021 Alexander Dumas. Complete works in 10 vols. Price, per set..$7.00
No. 3F1023 George Eliot. Complete works in 7 volumes. Price, per set,..$4.90
No. 3F1026 Henry Fielding. Complete works in 7 volumes. Price, per set....$4.90
No. 3F1029 Guizot's France. Complete works in 8 volumes. Price per set...$5.60
No. 3F1031 Nathaniel Hawthorne. Complete works in 7 vols. Price, per set..$4.90
No. 3F1034 Victor Hugo. Complete works in 8 volumes. Price, per set...$5.60
No. 3F1037 Washington Irving. Complete works in 10 vols. Price, per set,..$7.00
No. 3F1041 Charles Lamb. Complete works in 5 volumes. Price, per set...$3.50
No. 3F1043 T. B. Macaulay. Complete works in 3 volumes. Essays. Price, per set.........$2.10
No. 3F1046 Edgar Allen Poe. Complete works in 6 volumes. Price, per set, $4.20
No. 3F1049 Charles Reade. Complete works in 12 volumes. Price, per set, $8.40
No. 3F1052 John Ruskin. Complete works in 13 volumes. Price, per set, $9.10
No. 3F1054 Frederick Schiller. Complete works in 4 vols. Price, per set. $2.80
No. 3F1057 Sir Walter Scott (Waverly Novels). Complete works in 12 volumes. Price, per set...............$8.40
No. 3F1060 William Shakespeare. Complete works in 12 vols. Price, per set, $8.40
No. 3F1063 Tobias Smollett. Complete works in 12 vols. Price, per set....$8.40
No. 3F1066 Wm. M. Thackeray. Complete works in 10 vols. Price, per set, $7.00
No. 3F1069 Leo Tolstoi. Complete works in 12 volumes. Price, per set, $8.40
Each volume in the above sets weighs 2 lbs.

EVERYMAN'S LIBRARY SERIES.

Per Volume, 40 cents; Two for 78 cents; Six for $2.28; Twelve for $4.32.

FOR THE LOVER OF GOOD BOOKS, WELL MADE ATTRACTIVE BOOKS; to those who wish to collect a library of the best in the world's literature, printed and bound in such a manner that it will be a pleasure to pick up a copy; for those who do not buy a book in the cheapest possible edition, and yet who cannot afford the expensive hand made half leather books, EVERYMAN'S LIBRARY is the greatest value ever offered.

EVERYMAN'S LIBRARY is a collection of books in uniform binding. Not confined to any one department of literature, but including Biography, Classics, Belles Lettres, Fiction, History, Philosophy, Poetry, etc. A different color of cloth is used on each of the sections, for example: history is bound in red cloth, science in gray, poetry in green, etc.

EVERYMAN'S LIBRARY affords unusual opportunity for the gradual accumulation of high class books in uniform bindings at the lowest possible cost. You get one book at a time or as many as you please. You buy only the titles you want and only as you want them. But what you buy is in keeping with what you have already bought, and thus an opportunity is afforded for the gradual accumulation of a collection of standard works in uniform binding without incurring heavy financial obligations or acquiring books not specially desired, the thing most to be desired in collecting a library.

EACH VOLUME measures 4½x7 inches, 1 inch thick, and is bound in the best quality of cloth with full gilt back, with title and delicate design stamped in gold. The books are printed in London on the best quality of paper, delicately thin and fine, but absolutely opaque; printed from new extra heavy and clear type. Each book has a title page and frontispiece which is a facsimile of those in rare editions of the same book. The library as a whole is edited by Prof. Ernest Rhys, with introductory notes to the separate volumes by such famous writers as Swinburne, Lord Avebury, T. Watts-Dunton, Andrew Lang, etc.

ADDITIONAL TITLES will be added to this library at the rate of one hundred volumes each year until the best of the world's literature has been produced.

Biography.

Benvenuto Cellini.
Boswell's Life of Johnson. Vol. 1.
Boswell's Life of Johnson. Vol. 2.
Lockhart's Life of Napoleon.
Lockhart's Life of Scott.
Pepy's Diary. Introduction by Dr. Garnett, Vol. 1.
Pepy's Diary. Introduction by Dr. Garnett. Vol. 2.
Southey's Nelson.

Children's.

Andersen's Fairy Tales. Illustrated by the Brothers Robinson.
Canton's Child's Book of Saints. Illustrated by J. H. Robinson
Frossiart's Chronicles.
Grimm's Fairy Tales. Illustrated by R. Anning Bell.
Gulliver's Travels. Illustrated by Arthur Rackham.
Hawthorne's Wonder Book and Tanglewood Tales.
Kingston's Peter the Whaler.
Kingston's The Three Midshipmen.
Lamb's Tales from Shakespeare. Illustrated by Arthur Rackham.
Robinson Crusoe. Illustrated by J. A. Symington.
Tom Brown's School Days.

Classical.

Aeschylus' Lyrical Dramas.
Euripedes Plays. 2 Vols. Vol. 1.
Marcus Aurelius' Meditations. Introduction by W. H. D. Rouse.
Plato's Republic. Translated by Spens. Introduction by Dr. Garnett.

Essays and Belles Lettres.

Bacon's Essays. Introduction by Oliphant Smeaton.
Coleridge's Biographia Literaria. Edited by Arthur Symons.
Emerson's Essays. First and Second Series.
Essays of Matthew Arnold. Introduction by C. K. Chesterton.
Froude's Essays in Literature and History. Introduction by Hilaire Belloc.
Hazlitt's Lectures on Shakespeare.
Lady Montague's Letters.
Lamb's Essays of Elia. Introduction by Augustine Birrell.
Walton's Complete Angler.

Fiction.

Austen's (Jane) Emma.
Austen's (Jane) Mansfield Park.
Austen's (Jane) Northanger Abbey and Persuasion.
Austen's (Jane) Pride and Prejudice.
Austen's (Jane) Sense and Sensibility.
Balzac's Wild Ass's Skin. Introduction by George Saintsbury.
Cooper's Deerslayer.
Cooper's Last of the Mohicans.
Cooper's Pathfinder.
Defoe's Captain Singleton.
Dickens' Barnaby Rudge.
Dumas' Three Musketeers.
Edgar's Cressy and Poictiers. Introduction by Ernest Rhys.
Eliot's Adam Bede.
Kingsley's (H.) Ravenshoe.
Kingsley's Westward Ho! Introduction by A. H. Grieve.
Lytton's Harold. Introduction by Ernest Rhys.
Lytton's Last Days of Pompeii.
Lytton's Last of the Barons. Introduction by Prof. R. G. Watkin.
Marryatt's Midshipman Easy.
Manning's Sir Thomas Moore. Introduction by Ernest Rhys.
Mrs. Gaskell's Cranford.
Mrs. Henry Wood's The Cannings.
Reade's (Chas.) The Cloister and the Hearth. Introduction by A. C. Swinburne.
Scott's Fortunes of Nigel.
Scott's Ivanhoe. Introduction by Ernest Rhys.
Scott's Waverly.
Scott's Woodstock.
Thackeray's Esmond.
Trollope's Barchester Towers.

History.

Burnett's History of His Own Times.
Carlyle's French Revolution. Introduction by H. Belloc. Vol. 1.
Carlyle's French Revolution. Introduction by H. Belloc. Vol. 2.
Finlay's Byzantine Empire.
Macaulay's History of England. 3 Vols. Vol. 1.
Macaulay's History of England. Vol. 2.
Macaulay's History of England. Vol. 3.
Motley's Dutch Republic. Vol. 1.
Motley's Dutch Republic. Vol. 2.
Motley's Dutch Republic. Vol. 3.
Stanley's Memorials of Canterbury.
Strickland's Queen Elizabeth.

Philosophy and Theology.

Butler's Analogy. Introduction by the Rev. Ronald Bayne.
Law's Serious Call.
Robertson's (F. W.) Sermons. Introduction by Canon Barnett.
Robertson's (F. W.) Sermons. Vol. 1. Religion and Life.
Robertson's (F. W.) Sermons. Vol. 2. Bible Subjects.
Robertson's (F. W.) Sermons. Vol. 3. Christian Doctrine.
Sermons by Hugh Latimer. Introduction by Canon Beeching.
The New Testament. Arranged in supposed chronological order by Lindsay.

Poetry and Drama.

Browning's (R.) Poems. 1833-1864. Introduction by Arthur Waugh. Vol. 1.
Browning's (R.) Poems. Vol. 2.
Burns' Songs and Poems. Introduction by James Douglas.
Golden Book of Coleridge. Edited by Stopford A. Brooke.
Keats' Poems.
Palgrave's Golden Treasury. Appendix by Edward Hutton.
Shakespeare's Works. 3 Vols. Vol. 1.
Shakespeare's Works. Vol. 2.
Shakespeare's Works. Vol. 3,
Shelley.
Sheridan's Plays.
Tennyson's Poems. 1830-1863.

Romance.

Le Morte D'Arthur. Introduction by Prof. Rhys. Vol. 1.
Le Morte D'Arthur. Introduction by Prof. Rhys. Vol. 2.
The Mabinogion. Translated by Charlotte Guest.

Science.

Huxley's Essays. Introduction by Sir Oliver Lodge.
Tyndall's Glaciers of the Alps. Introduction by Lord Avebury.
Withe's Natural History of Shelborne. Introduction by Principal Windle.

Travel.

Borrow's Wild Wales. Introduction by Theodore Watts-Dunton.
Cook's Voyages.
Speke's Sources of the Nile.

Oratory.

Free Trade Speeches. By Bright, Cobden, Gladstone. Introduction by D. Lloyd George, M.P.
Lincoln's Speeches.

No. 3F1100 Price, 12 for $4.32; 6 for $2.28; 2 for 78c; per volume........40c
If by mail, postage extra, per volume, 7 cents.

THIS $25.00 SET OF THEODORE ROOSEVELT'S WORKS FOR $8.95

Fourteen superb volumes, special de luxe edition, magnificently bound in heavy red crushed levant leather, with marbled sides. Uncut edges, gold tops, finest book paper. Printed from new, clear type. Size, 5¼x7¼ inches. The finest, the most beautiful and the rarest edition of Roosevelt's works. We have only a few hundred of these sets and when they are sold there will be no more at any price.

Vol. I American Ideals. With a Biographical and Critical Memoir by Gen. Francis Vinton Greene.
Vol. II Administration—Civil Service.
Vol. III The Wilderness Hunter.
Vol. IV Hunting the Grizzly.
Vol. V Hunting Trips of a Ranchman.
Vol. VI Hunting Trips on the Prairie and in the Mountains.
Vol. VII The Winning of the West. Part I.—The Spread of the English Speaking Peoples.
Vol. VIII The Winning of the West. Part II.—In the Current of the Revolution.
Vol. IX The Winning of the West. Part III.—The War in the Northwest.
Vol. X The Winning of the West. Part IV.—The Indian Wars, 1784-1787.
Vol. XI The Winning of the West. Part V.—St. Claire and Wayne.
Vol. XII The Winning of the West. Part VI.—Louisiana and Aaron Burr.
Vol. XIII Naval War of 1812—Part I.
Vol. XIV Naval War of 1812—Part II.

No. 3F750 Works of Theodore Roosevelt. Fourteen volumes just as illustrated and described. Never before sold for less than $25.00.
Our price.......................................$8.95

Shipping weight, 24 pounds.

SPECIAL FIVE-VOLUME SETS AT 65 CENTS.

These Five-Volume Sets of Standard Authors, Nos. 3F801 to 3F807, are substantially bound in silk finish cloth with titles stamped on the back in gold. Printed from new, clear type on good quality paper. Size, each book, 5½x7 inches. Average weight, per set, packed for shipment, 5 pounds.

G. A. Henty.

Stirring Stories for Young and Old,
Jack Archer
The Boy Knight
The Young Buglers
The Young Colonists
With Lee in Virginia

No. 3F801 Price, per set, 65c

Henry W. Longfellow's Poetical Works.

Book of Poems
Courtship of Miles Standish
Evangeline
Tales of a Wayside Inn.
Hiawatha

No 3F804 Price, per set....65c

Edna Lyall.

Romances and Novels.
Donovan
In the Golden Days
Knight Errant
We Two
Won by Waiting

No. 3F802 Price, per set, 65c

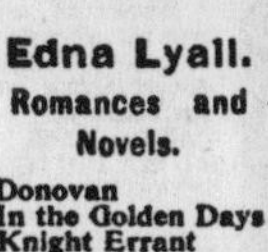

Cooper's Sea Tales.

Red Rover
The Pilot
The Two Admirals
The Water Witch
Wing and Wing

No 3F806 Price, per set, 65c

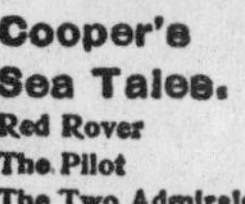

Mary J. Holmes' Choicest Writings.

English Orphans
Homestead on the Hillside
Meadowbrook Farm
Lena Rivers
Tempest and Sunshine

No. 3F803 Price, per set, 65c

Cooper's Leather Stocking Tales.

The Deerslayer
The Last of the Mohicans
The Pathfinder
The Pioneers
The Prairie

No. 3F807 Price, per set....65c

The Imperial Galaxy of Classic Masterpieces.

In Literature, Art and Philosophy. All the most famous productions from the Genius of Mankind. It is a splendid and noble luxury for every household. 1,000 classic masterpieces of the world's treasury of poetry and prose. 300 reproductions of the world's greatest art masters. Educational inspiration and wisdom for family and home. It is a superb library volume for reading and reference in the world's choicest productions of thought. Bound in cloth with attractive cover design in gold stamped on back and side. Extra large size, 8½x10¾ inches; 1¾ inches thick. 608 pages. Retail price, $2.50.

No. 3F1140 Our price........$1.18
If by mail, postage extra, 40 cents.

Famous Authors and Best Literature of England and America.

Choice selections from the writings of the great poets of England and America, famous novelists, distinguished essayists and historians, humorists, popular writers for young people, great orators, and public lecturers. Including the lives of English and American authors in story form, their portraits, their homes and their personal traits; how they work and what they wrote. Profusely illustrated with original drawings by Chas. Dana Gibson. Full page halftone pictures; photographs of their homes and other illustrations. Presentation page and colored frontispiece. Bound in cloth with elaborate cover design stamped in red and silver. Contains 606 pages. Size, 7¼x9¾ inches. Retail price, $2.50.

No. 3F1145 Our price.........78c
If by mail, postage extra, 28 cents.

BOOKS FOR LITTLE PEOPLE.

Taine's History of English Literature.

Handy Edition. Complete in one volume. The standard history of English literature from the earliest times to the present day. Recognized by all colleges and universities of both this country and England as the established authority. Printed on good paper. Bound in cloth. Blank lines stamped on front and back covers, and title on back in gold. Over 1,300 pages. Size, 5¾x7¾ inches.
No. 3F1150 Price............**85c**
If by mail, postage extra, 18 cents.

San Francisco's Horror of Earthquake and Fire.

Regular $1.50 book at 58c. By James Russell Wilson. Identically the same book (binding, number of pages, number of illustrations, paper) as offered to you by subscription agents for $1.50. Contains a vivid description of the most overwhelming and most appalling disaster of modern times. Immense loss of life and hundreds of millions of dollars worth of property destroyed. Heartrending scenes attending the disaster that shocked the civilized world, vividly depicted in this wonderful volume. The reader is held spellbound by the terrors of earthquake and fire. The terrified inhabitants rushed from their dwellings, while the flames burst forth on all sides. The ripping and rocking of the earth leveled immense buildings. Contains 400 pages, profusely illustrated with numerous pictures taken on the scene. Bound in cloth. Size, 7¼x9¾ inches. Regular price, $1.50.
No. 3F1160 Our price............**58c**
If by mail, postage extra, 24 cents.

War Songs and Poems of The Southern Confederacy.

Arranged and edited with personal reminiscences of the war by H. M. Wharton, D. D., private in General Lee's Army. A collection of the most popular and impressive songs and poems of war times dear to every Southern heart. With the poems are many incidents and stories of war times told by the author as seen when they occurred. The heroes of the South and their gallant deeds are immortalized in the verses of many poets. The author carried his gun under Gordon and Lee until the last day of Appomattox. Profusely illustrated with rare and beautiful pictures. Over 500 pages. Handsomely bound in silk finished cloth. Size, 7x9½ inches.
No. 3F1165 Price............**98c**
If by mail, postage extra, 22 cents.

The Devil of Today.

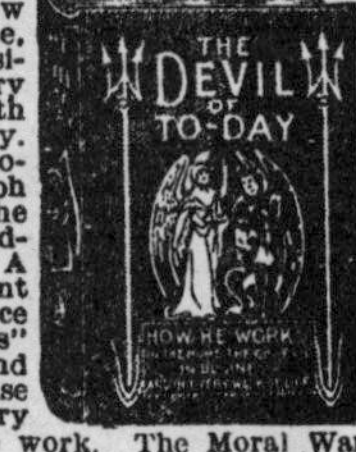

By Rev. I. M. Chambers, I. M., D.D. How he works in the home, in the church, in business, in society, in every walk of life. Set forth in a wonderful allegory. Entertaining as a romance. The triumph of goodness and the overthrow of wickedness portrayed. A thrilling book for saint and sinner. Not since "Pilgrim's Progress" has man conceived and written a more intense and powerful allegory than this remarkable work. The Moral War in Modern Life. By words that burn and thrill, it exposes wickedness which leads men and women into sin and ruin, and it does so in a living, moving play of tragedy and comedy that makes a lasting and wholesome impression. Contains over 500 large octavo pages, measuring 6x9 inches. Beautifully illustrated by numerous full page photo engravings. Bound in cloth with impressive cover design stamped with white, black and gold.
No. 3F1170 Price............**$1.25**
If by mail, postage extra, 15 cents.

Home Sweet Home.

By Rev. J. M. Hamilton. The book is to help us make a good home and be happy in it. It is a mine of good things; being replete with appreciative tributes from the poets, philosophers, novelists, theologians and citizens of the world, who delighted to honor and dignify, to exalt and immortalize the Home—The Sacred Refuge of Our Life. The only book of its kind devoted wholly to the single purpose of helping us to make a home, and indicating the easily acquired methods to be happy within it. Large quarto size, 7¼x10 inches. 550 pages. 100 full page engravings. Bound in cloth. Stamped in gold and colors. Retail price, $2.50.
No. 3F1175 Our price............**98c**
If by mail, postage extra, 25 cents.

Extra High Grade Toy Books.

Made in London. The most wonderful value in children's toy books ever offered. Each book contains 12 pages, all full of pictures; size, 7½x8½ inches, of which four are illustrated in colors, in addition to front and back covers in colors. The colored illustrations are not the cheap pictures usually found in children's books, but each illustration is a work of art, beautiful and instructive. Be sure to give names of books wanted.

Bible Stories	Red Indians
Country Cousins	Ride a Cock-Horse
Four Legs and Two	Stories of Bible Children
Frolic and Fun	
Hide and Seek	Stories for Sunday
Merry Old Rhymes	To Banbury Cross
Noah's Ark	What's O'Clock
Old Testament Stories	When Jesus Was a Child
Once Upon a Time	
Pick-a-Back	Wild Beast Show

No. 3F1300 Price, 6 for **32c**; 3 for **18c**
If by mail, postage extra, for three, 3 cents.

Our Special Toy Books.

Made by Thos. Nelson & Sons, of London, and imported especially for us. The most beautiful toy books made, are extra large, measuring 8½x11¼ inches. Contains from 16 to 20 pages, of which from 4 to 18 pages are illustrated in colors, and in addition to these colored illustrations there are numerous line drawings. The covers of these books are beautifully lithographed in colors, each cover having an individual design. We are confident that these toy books cannot be equaled for double the price. Be sure to give titles of books wanted.

A-B-C of Games and Toys	Fur Coats
All Sorts of Animals	Little Piggy-Wiggy's A-B-C
Alphabet of Children's Names	No End of Fun
	Our Darlings' Pictures
Beaks and Bills	Our Pets' Pictures
Bible Alphabet	Red Riding Hood's Picture Book
Can't You Talk	
Farmyard A-B-C	The Doll's House

No. 3F1305 Price, 2 for............**28c**
6 for............**78c**
If by mail, postage extra, for two, 5 cents.

Paint Books for Children.

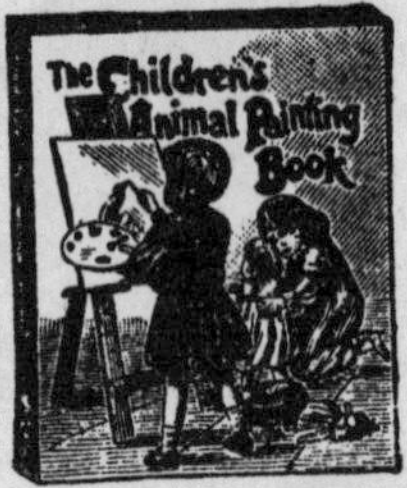

Books of outline pictures to be colored. Unique, entertaining and instructive. A paint book is something in which every child will take unbounded delight. These books contain clear, simple sketches, with many colored illustrations, showing just how the sketches should be colored. Size, 9x11 inches. Contains 24 pages.

Flags of the World
Flowers to Paint
Mother Goose Post Card Painting Book
The Children's Animal Painting Book
The Doll's Painting Book
The Nursery Rhyme Painting Book
The Soldier Painting Book

No. 3F1321 Price, each............**29c**
2 for............**55c**
If by mail, postage extra, each, 5 cents.

Pictures to Cut Out.

The Model Series of Toy Books Something new and unique. A young child is most interested and best entertained when he is doing something with his hands. Each of these books contains 20 pages, including 6 plates of pictures to be cut out in small parts and pasted together, making complete animals, soldiers, dolls, etc. These pictures are beautifully stamped in natural colors and printed on heavy paper, which makes it hard to tear, and will wear very well. Each book contains full descriptive matter and also amusing verses for children. Size, 10¼x12 inches. We do not know of anything that would please the children more than these model books.

Model Book of Trains
The Animal Model Book
The Doll's House Model Book
The Model Book of Dolls
The Model Book of Soldiers
The Model Book of the Zoo
The Model Maker

No. 3F1325 The Model Series of Toy Books. Price, 2 for **55c**; each............**29c**
If by mail, postage extra, each, 5 cents.

Linen Toy Books (Untearable).

"They may be washed
And the colors will not run;
A child may chew them,
And have lots of fun."

When dirty wash with the clothes.

These books are printed on soft linen in exceedingly bright and variegated colors. The baby can put the leaves into his mouth, and the colors will not come off or the book be soiled the least bit. The print is clear and easily read. These are books which every child will take unbounded delight in, for the simple reason that they do not need to be careful with them for fear of spoiling or tearing them. Published in three sizes.

No. 3F1335 Series 1. Linen Toy Books; size, 4½x6 inches; 12 pages.
Baby's Pets — Mother Goose Favorites
Baby's Toys — Tiny Tot's A-B-C Book
Price, 2 for............**20c**
The complete set of 4 for............**39c**
If by mail, postage extra, for two, 2 cents.

No. 3F1336 Series 2. Linen Toy Books; size, 5¾x9 inches; 12 pages.
Fairy Friends — Nursery Pets
My Playmate's A-B-C — On The Nursery Stairs
Price, 2 for, **37c**; each............**20c**
The complete set of 4 for............**68c**
If by mail, postage extra, for two, 3 cents.

No. 3F1337 Series 3. Linen Toy Books; size, 8x9 inches; 16 pages.
Baby's Doings — My A-B-C Book
Baby's Friends — Who Killed Cock Robin?
Price, any 2 for less **69c**; each............**$0.38**
The complete set of 4 for............**1.30**
If by mail, postage extra, each, 3 cents.

Board Books for Children at 20 Cents.

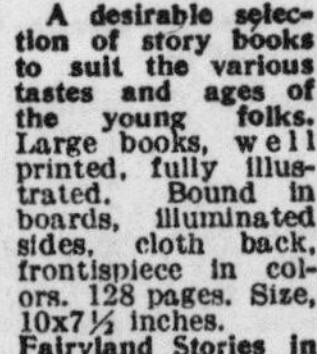

A desirable selection of story books to suit the various tastes and ages of the young folks. Large books, well printed, fully illustrated. Bound in boards, illuminated sides, cloth back, frontispiece in colors. 128 pages. Size, 10x7½ inches.

Fairyland Stories in Rhyme for the Little Ones
Grandma's Old, Old Fairy Tales
Kris Kringle's Merry Book — Santa Claus' A, B, C Book
Mother Goose's Nursery Rhymes — Story Book for Boys and Girls

No. 3F1350 Price, each............**20c**
2 for............**35c**
If by mail, postage extra, each, 10 cents.

Mother Goose.

Containing nursery rhymes and a collection of alphabet tales and jingles, with illustrations. Printed in two colors. The only attractive board edition of this famous book published. 288 pages. Size, 7x9 inches.
No. 3F1359
Price, board.....**34c**
If by mail, postage extra, 16 cents.

Mother Goose. Complete unabridged collection of Mother Goose nursery rhymes, of all her memorable writings, tales, jingles and rhymes. Fully illustrated with over 400 engravings and frontispiece in colors. Contains over 300 pages, printed in large, clear type on good quality of paper. Substantially bound in cloth with attractive cover design stamped in gold and colors. Size, 7x9 inches. Retail price, $1.00.
No. 3F1360 Our price............**49c**
If by mail, postage extra, 20 cents.

Fun for the Little Folks.

Contains charming stories and amusements, including tales of animals and pets, youthful sports and adventure, and choice reading for the little ones, together with picture alphabet, illustrated numbers, etc. Lithographed board cover. Size, 6½x9¼ inches.
No. 3F1368
Price............**18c**
If by mail, postage extra, 9 cents.

Palmer Cox's Brownies.

By Palmer Cox. Filled with quaint stories for children, of these quaint people. Stories of their mischievous pranks and humorous doings. Colored board cover. 176 pages. Size, 7¾x10 in.
No. 3F1370
Price............**24c**
Postage extra, 15 cents.

Aunt Amy's Animal Stories at 28 Cents.

A series of stories told by animals to Aunt Amy Prentice. Each illustrated with many pictures and a colored frontispiece; bound in cloth with attractive cover design cover. Delightful animal stories for children. Retail price, 50 cents each. Size, 5x7½ inches.

Billy Goat's Story	Micky Monkey's Story
Brown Owl's Story	Mouser Cat's Story
Bunny Rabbit's Story	Plodding Turtle's Story
Croaky Frog's Story	Quacky Duck's Story
Frisky Squirrel's Story	Speckled Hen's Story
Gray Goose's Story	Towser Dog's Story

No. 3F1375 Our price, each............**28c**
Any 2 for............**50c**
If by mail, postage extra, each, 5 cents.

Big Half Vellum Children's Books at 22 Cents.

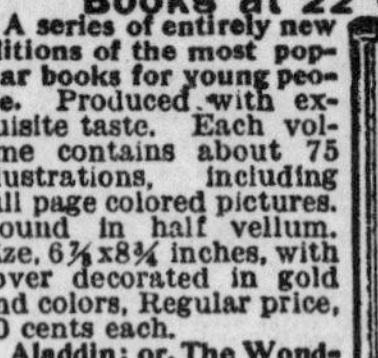

A series of entirely new editions of the most popular books for young people. Produced with exquisite taste. Each volume contains about 75 illustrations, including full page colored pictures. Bound in half vellum. Size, 6¾x8¾ inches, with cover decorated in gold and colors, Regular price, 50 cents each.

Aladdin; or, The Wonderful Lamp
Beauty and the Beast
Bird Stories for Little People
Cinderella; or, The Little Glass Slipper
Jack and the Bean Stalk
Jack the Giant Killer
Little Red Riding Hood
Little Bo-Peep
Little Miss Muffet
Mary Had a Little Lamb
Mary, Mary, Quite Contrary
Our Animal Friends
Puss in Boots
Polly, Put the Kettle On
Ride a Cock-Horse
Sing a Song of Sixpence
The House that Jack Built
The Sleeping Beauty
Who Killed Cock Robin?
Where are You Going, My Pretty Maid?

No. 3F1379 Our price, per volume, **22c**
2 for............**38c**
If by mail, postage extra, per volume, 6c.

Little People's Stories at 39c.

By Mary E. Wilkins, Marion Harland, Geo. C. Eggleston, George Cooper, etc. These books are made up of delightful stories and poems for little people; including stories of adventures, wonderful fairy tales; an account of many boyish and girlish trials and joys. Profusely illustrated and bound in cloth with individual cover designs. Each book contains 200 pages. Size, 7¼x9¼ inches.
Little Lads — Our Boys
Little Lassies — Our Girls
No. 3F1381 Price, per volume..**39c**
Any 2 for............**74c**
If by mail, postage extra, per volume 12c.

Twilight Stories.

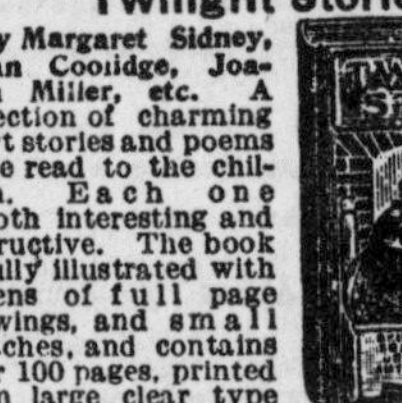

By Margaret Sidney, Susan Coolidge, Joaquin Miller, etc. A collection of charming short stories and poems to be read to the children. Each one is both interesting and instructive. The book is fully illustrated with dozens of full page drawings, and small sketches, and contains over 100 pages, printed from large clear type on the best quality of paper. Bound in cloth with attractive cover design. Size, 7¼x9¼ inches. Retail price, 75 cents.
No. 3F1383 Our price............**45c**
If by mail, postage extra, 12 cents.

Puzzle Boxes.

Each box contains three beautiful cut out puzzle pictures, size, 6½x8¾ inches, together with guide pictures for putting them together. Each box has cover stamped in full colors, with the same design as one of the puzzle pictures. We do not know of a better way to amuse the children than by putting one of these puzzle boxes in their hands.

No. 3F1390 Price, per box, three cut out puzzle pictures............**21c**
2 boxes (six pictures, all different) for **39c**
If by mail, postage extra, per box, 5 cents.

Large Puzzle Boxes. Same as described above, but larger and with four cut out puzzle pictures and guide pictures for same. Size, 9¼x7½ inches. Put up in handsome boxes with lithographed cover design, same as one of the puzzle pictures.
No. 3F1391 Price, per box.....**36c**
2 boxes (ten pictures, all different) for............**69c**
If by mail, postage extra, per box, 14 cents.

BOOKS FOR YOUNG PEOPLE—BOYS AND GIRLS.

Price, per Volume, 25 Cents. Any Three for 69 Cents. Any Six for $1.32.

ILLUSTRATED YOUNG PEOPLES' LIBRARY.

A new series of choice literature for young people, selected from the best and most popular works. Handsomely printed on fine supercalendared paper, from large clear type. Profusely illustrated by the most famous artists, the handsomest and most attractive series of juvenile books ever offered. Bound in fine English cloth with handsome new cover designs stamped in colors. Size, 5¼x6¾ inches.

A Child's Garden of Verses, by Robert Louis Stevenson. 100 illustrations.
A Child's Life of Christ. 49 illustrations.
A Child's Story of the Bible. 72 illustrations.
Adventures of a Brownie. 18 illustrations.
Adventures in Toyland. 70 illustrations.
Aesop's Fables. 62 illustrations.
Alexander the Great, King of Macedon, by Jacob Abbott. 51 illustrations.
Alfred the Great, of England, by Jacob Abbott. 40 illustrations.
Alice's Adventures in Wonderland. 42 illustrations.
Andersen's Fairy Tales. 75 illustrations.
Animal Stories for Little People. 50 illustrations.
Arabian Nights Entertainments. 130 illustrations.
Aunt Martha's Corner Cupboard, by Mary and Elizabeth Kirby. 54 illustrations.
Battles of the War for Independence, by Prescott Holmes. 70 illustrations.
Battles of the War for the Union, by Prescott Holmes. 80 illustrations.
Black Beauty, by Anna Sewell. 50 illustrations.
Bunyan's Pilgrim's Progress. 46 illustrations.
Christopher Columbus and the Discovery of America. 70 illustrations.
Cyrus the Great, the Founder of the Persian Empire, by Jacob Abbott. 34 illustrations.
Darius the Great, King of the Medes and Persians, by Jacob Abbott. 34 illustrations.
Dicken's Child's History of England. 60 illustrations.
Exploration and Adventure in Africa. 80 illustrations.
Flower Fables, by Louisa M. Alcott. 50 illustrations.
Grandfather's Chair, by Nathaniel Hawthorne. 68 illustrations.
Grimm's Fairy Tales. 50 illustrations.
Gulliver's Travels. 50 illustrations.
Hannibal, the Carthagenian, by Jacob Abbott. 37 illustrations.
Hernando Cortes, the Conqueror of Mexico, by Jacob Abbott. 30 illustrations.
Heroes of the United States Navy. 60 illustrations.
Josephine, Empress of France, by Jacob Abbott. 40 illustrations.
Julius Caesar, the Roman Conqueror, by Jacob Abbott. 44 illustrations.
King Charles the First, of England, by Jacob Abbott. 41 illustrations.
King Charles the Second, of England, by Jacob Abbott. 38 illustrations.
Lives of the Presidents of the United States. With portraits and illustrations.
Little Lame Prince. 24 illustrations.
Madame Roland, a Heroine of the French Revolution, by Jacob Abbott. 42 illustrations.
Marie Antoinette, Queen of France, by John S. C. Abbott. 41 illustrations.
Mary, Queen of Scotts, by Jacob Abbott. 45 illustrations.
Military Heroes of the United States 80 illustrations.
Mixed Pickles. 31 illustrations.
Mother Goose's Rhymes, Jingles and Fairy Tales.
Pyrrhus, King of Epirus, by Jacob Abbott. 45 illustrations.
Queen Elizabeth, of England, by Jacob Abbott. 49 illustrations.
Rip Van Winkle, by Washington Irving. 46 illustrations.
Romulus, the Founder of Rome, by Jacob Abbott. 49 illustrations.
Swiss Family Robinson. 50 illustrations.
Tales from Shakespeare, by Chas. and Mary Lamb. 65 illustrations.
The Adventures of Robinson Crusoe. 70 illustrations.
The Sleepy King. 77 illustrations.
The Story of the Frozen Seas. 70 illustrations.
Through the Looking Glass and What Alice Found There. 50 illustrations.
Uncle Tom's Cabin. 90 illustrations.
Vic; the Autobiography of a Fox Terrier, by Marie More Marsh. Illustrated.
Water Babies, by Charles Kingsley. 84 illustrations.
William the Conqueror, of England, by Jacob Abbott. 43 illustrations.
Wood's Natural History. 80 illustrations.
Xerxes the Great, King of Persia, by Jacob Abbott. 39 illustrations.
Young People's History of the War with Spain. 50 illustrations.

No. 3F1405 Price, each.....$0.25
Any 3 for..........................69
Any 6 for.........................1.32
If by mail, postage extra, per volume, 6 cents.

Peerless Series.

Large illustrated books issued in uniform size and printed on good quality of paper. Bound in cloth with cover design stamped in white and beautiful inlay center design. Each book is written or edited by distinguished writers for young people. Large octavo size, 7½x9¾ inches. 250 pages with colored frontispiece and numerous illustrations. Regular $1.00 books.

Beautiful Stories About Children. All the beautiful child characters from Dickens' famous novels. By Charles Dickens.
Child's Story of the Nations. By Chas. Morris.
Lives of the Presidents. From Washington to Roosevelt. By Charles Morris.
Child's Story of America. By Chas. Morris.
True Stories of Royal Children. How they live and what they do in palaces. By Charles Morris.
True Stories of Great Americans. Lives of men and women who have made America great. By Elbridge S. Brooks.
Child's Story of the Gospel. Easy explanations of the New Testament. By Rev. Ingram Cobbin, D.D.
Historical Stories of American Pioneer Life. Five Leather Stocking Tales, condensed. By J. Fenimore Cooper.
Story of the Bible. By Rev. Jesse Lyman Hurlbut, D.D.
Pilgrim's Progress in Words of One Syllable. By John Bunyan.
Child's Story of a Beautiful Life. Life of Christ. By Hesba Stretton.
Mother Goose and Fairyland. A collection of most beautiful stories and rhymes.
True Stories of the American Indians. A great book of thrilling Indian stories. By Edward S. Ellis.

No. 3F1408 Price, per volume....38c
Any 2 for.............................69c
If by mail, postage extra, per volume, 15 cents.

The Swiss Family Robinson.

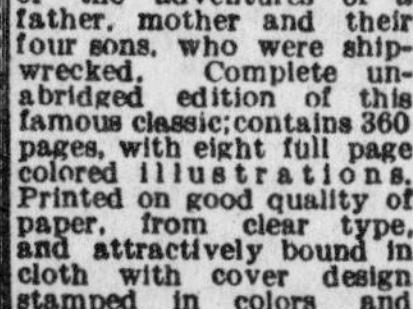

Swiss Family Robinson, or the adventures of a father, mother and their four sons, who were shipwrecked. Complete unabridged edition of this famous classic; contains 360 pages, with eight full page colored illustrations. Printed on good quality of paper, from clear type, and attractively bound in cloth with cover design stamped in colors and name on back and side in gold. Swiss Family Robinson cannot fail to interest any healthy minded boy or girl. Size, 5¼x8 inches.

No. 3F1422 Price..............48c
If by mail, postage extra, 13 cents.

Gulliver's Travels.

By Dean Swift. This book was written in 1720, and it is as popular today as it was when Swift first wrote it. Every child that has ever read Gulliver's Travels has never forgotten it. It is one of the most interesting stories that has ever been written. Describes his visit to the Lilliputians and to the giants of Brobdingnag, and his many other interesting experiences. 225 pages. Size, 5½x8 inches.

No. 3F1423 Board. Price......20c
No. 3F1424 Cloth. Price......45c
If by mail, postage extra, board, 8c; cloth, 18c.

Little Colonel Series.

By Anna Fellows Johnson. These are beautiful little stories that appeal not only to children but will be appreciated by all who feel their joys and sorrows. They are most particularly adapted for reading aloud in the family circle. Cloth. Size, 4¼x6 inches.

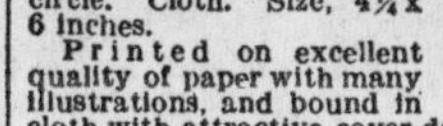

Printed on excellent quality of paper with many illustrations, and bound in cloth with attractive cover design. Size, 5x7¼ inches.

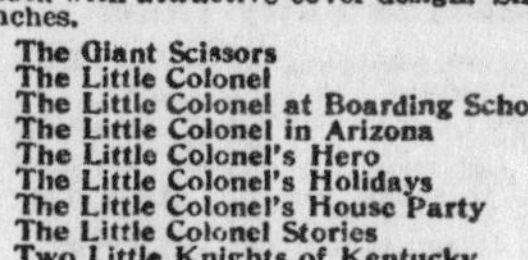

The Giant Scissors
The Little Colonel
The Little Colonel at Boarding School
The Little Colonel in Arizona
The Little Colonel's Hero
The Little Colonel's Holidays
The Little Colonel's House Party
The Little Colonel Stories
Two Little Knights of Kentucky

No. 3F1425 Price, per volume...48c
Any 2 for.........................89c
If by mail, postage extra, per volume, 7 cents.

Robinson Crusoe.

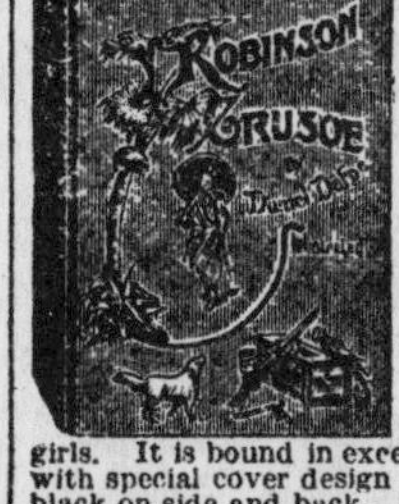

Jumbo Edition, by Daniel Defoe. Complete unabridged edition of this famous classic. Large quarto size, 7¼x9¾ inches. 466 pages. Contains over 100 illustrations, including colored frontispiece. The wonderful experiences of the shipwrecked sailor on the island of Juan Fernandez have always had a charm and fascination for boys and girls. It is bound in excellent quality of cloth with special cover design stamped in gold and black on side and back. Retail price, $1.25.

No. 3F1426 Our price..........65c
If by mail, postage extra, 25 cents.

Alice in Wonderland and Through the Looking Glass.

Two stories in one volume, with 16 illustrations in colors by Blanch McManus. This is one of the most beautiful editions of these two complete classics ever published and has the great advantage of two complete books in one volume. Printed on attractive paper, beautifully illustrated and substantially bound in cloth with original cover design in colors. Contains over 250 pages. Large quarto. Size, 7½x10 inches.

No. 3F1436 Price..............68c
If by mail, postage extra, 16 cents.

The Water Babies.

A new and beautiful edition of this famous story, written by Chas. Kingsley. Printed on the very best quality of paper with 8 full page illustrations in colors; chapter headings and a designed title page. Undoubtedly the best edition of this famous work on the market. Size, 7½x10 inches.

No. 3F1438
Price........68c
If by mail, postage extra, 16 cents.

Black Beauty.

Black Beauty is the autobiography of a horse and is a pathetic recital of man's inhumanity to "man's best friend," and a beautiful sermon against cruelty to animals. Has a beautiful lithographed cover and lithographed frontispiece, with fifty full page illustrations. Board cover. This book contains 192 pages. Size, 7¼x10 inches.

No. 3F1440 Price...........20c
If by mail, postage extra, 8 cents.

HIGH GRADE POPULAR EDITION. 200 pages, printed on best quality of paper with 22 original illustrations, some of them full page color engravings. Lithographed sides, cloth back with colored inlay of Black Beauty on cover. Size 7x9 inches.

No. 3F1445 Price..............48c
If by mail, postage extra, 20 cents.

Leisure Hours.

Cheery chats and pleasing pictures for young people. The largest book of its kind ever published. 400 pages. 7¾x10 inches, 1¾ inches thick. Contains innumerable illustrations—one to every page with many full page colored plates scattered through the book. This book cannot fail to bring joy to the heart of every young person.

No. 3F1448 Price..............48c
If by mail, postage extra, 25 cents.

Little Lord Fauntleroy.

By Frances Hodgson Burnett. This is an exceptionally pretty and beautiful story and has probably been more widely read than any other book for young people published in recent years. The story is attractive in form, and will be found interesting for older persons. Cloth. Illustrated. Size, 5x7 inches.

No. 3F1449
Price...................95c
If by mail, postage extra, 12 cents.

Famous Chatterbox Picture Books.

These large quarto picture books, consist of stories and pictures from "Chatterbox," the famous juvenile year book. Many of the pictures are by Harrison Weir, the best animal painter in the world. The stories are printed on fine toned and calendered paper from big type, and the material is all copyrighted. The largest and most attractive picture books for children ever issued for the price. Colored frontispiece in each volume. Retail price, $1.00.

Chatterbox Circus
Chatterbox Menagerie
Chatterbox Natural History
Chatterbox Picture Book
Chatterbox Wild West
Chatterbox Zoo

No. 3F1452 Price, per volume..60c
If by mail, postage extra, per volume, 28 cents.

Three Famous Books.

250,000 copies of these books have been sold and they need no further description. These books teach the great lesson, to love God's creatures and not to hurt, maim or enslave them. Size, 3¼x6 inches.

Beautiful Joe. Biography of a real dog. 360 pages, illustrated. By Marshall Saunders.
Dickie Downie. Biography of a bird. 200 pages. Full of interest. By Virginia Patterson.
Pussy Meow. The biography of a cat. Touching and beautiful. 250 pages. By Louise Patterson.

No. 3F1460 Price, for the 3 volumes..........69c
If by mail, postage extra, per set, 14 cents.

Young Folk's Standard Histories.

A series of 10 complete histories written especially for young folks, but at the same time interesting and instructive to the older people. These are not children's histories dealing with only a few incidents, but each one is an entire, complete history, and as good a history as ever was written. Each one contains over 600 pages, well illustrated with full page engravings and many smaller ones. Bound in cloth with title stamped on side and back in gold. Size, 5¼x7½ inches.

History of America	History of Mexico
History of China	History of the Netherlands
History of the Civil War	History of Spain
History of Egypt	History of Switzerland
History of India	History of Russia

No. 3F1470 Price, per volume, $0.48
Any 2 for.............................84
The entire set (10 volumes) for ..3.48
If by mail, postage extra, per volume, 12 cents.

Patriotic America.

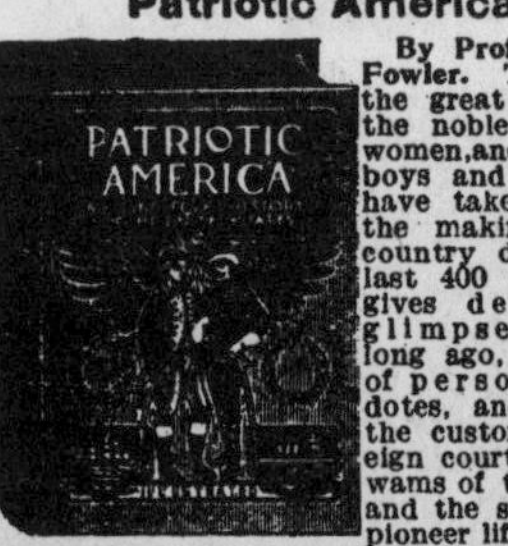

By Prof. Allen E. Fowler. Tells about the great events, the noble men and women, and the brave boys and girls who have taken part in the making of our country during the last 400 years. It gives delightful glimpses into the long ago, by means of personal anecdotes, and tells of the customs of foreign courts, the wigwams of the Indians and the struggles of pioneer life. It tells the story of our flag and thousands of other important events that have occurred in America. 388 large, handsomely printed and profusely illustrated pages. Bound in cloth, illuminated side stamp in colors and gold. Large quarto size, 7x9¾ inches.

No. 3F1473 Price..................58c
If by mail, postage extra, 23 cents.

Young People's History of the World.

By Henry Davenport Northrop, the famous historian. Contains a complete and heroic account of the marvelous deeds of the heroes of the world, including great battles and the rise and fall of the nations, the famous explorations, etc. Superbly embellished with a great number of full page engravings and numerous smaller ones. Contains 448 pages, printed on excellent quality of paper. Frontispiece. Bound in cloth with embossed cover design in colors and gold. Large quarto size, 7x9¾ inches.

No. 3F1476 Price..................59c
If by mail, postage extra, 22 cents.

Young People's Library of Entertainment and Amusement.

A book to delight, entertain, amuse and instruct both young and old. Especially prepared for all social and home occasions. Six great departments in one book.

1. Choicest Gems from the World's Best Poets
2. Choice Selections for all Occasions. Wit and humor to delight the fun loving. Dialogues, charades and plays.
3. Games. Old and new for social occasions, selected from many sources to please all tastes.
4. Development of the Body. Practical instructions for easy and delightful exercises for both pleasure and profit.
5. Practical Guide to Etiquette. How to behave well, talk and write well on all occasions and on all subjects.
6. Facts Which are Wonderful.

This book contains the newest and most fascinating information on all subjects. Beautifully illustrated throughout. The pictures have been made by special artists, and tell how the entertainments and amusements are to be performed. 450 double column pages. Bound in cloth, elaborate cover design. Containing photographic inlay and silver stamping. Size, 7¼x9¾ inches. Retail price, $1.50.

No. 3F1478 Our price..........60c
If by mail, postage extra, 22 cents.

Jim Crow Tales.

By Burton Stoner. A book on the order of "Br'er Rabbit" tales. Jim Crow, captured by a farmer and becoming his pet, tells of his friends, and their doings—the fox, the beavers, the bears, the squirrels, raccoons, woodchucks, alligators, etc. Each story complete in itself, yet all having to do with the wild life of forest and stream. Every boy will want it, whether he lives in the city or country. Dozens of full page beautiful halftone illustrations, showing the animals in their favorite haunts, and numerous smaller illustrations. Printed on beautiful quality of paper and bound in attractive cover design, stamped in colors. Size, 8x9¼ inches.

No. 3F1480 Price..................78c
If by mail, postage extra, 18 cents.

The Adventures of Two Dutch Dolls and a Golliwogg.

By Florence K. Upton. One of the most extravagantly funny books for young people ever published. Profusely illustrated in colors on one side of every page, and on the other side full of ridiculous and laughable verses. Oblong quarto, size, 8¾x11 inches. Bound in boards, with lithographed cover design in colors. Retail price, $1.25.

No. 3F1482 Our price..........43c
If by mail, postage extra, 12 cents.

Nonsense.

Written by A. Nobody. Running over with genuine fun. Full of the most comical pictures and nonsensical jingles, all printed in finest lithographic color work on pebbled paper. This book is for old as well as young. Parents as well as children will be convulsed with the pictures and funny rhymes. Quarto size, 8½x12 inches. Bound in boards, cloth back, with cover design lithographed in colors. Retail price, $1.00.

No. 3F1484 Our price..........38c
If by mail, postage extra, 10 cents.

Famous Buster Brown Books.

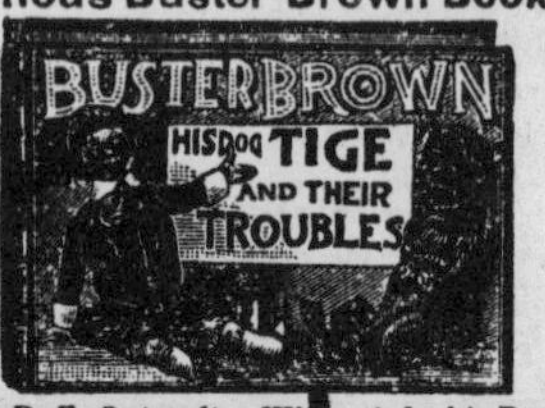

By R. F. Outcault. Without doubt, Buster Brown is the best known and the most comical little boy ever created. These pictures are all taken from the original drawings by Outcault (not the poor imitations now running in some of the comic papers). Exact reproductions of the original in size and color. In this line are included the very latest Buster Brown books, just out, July 1st. Any one of the following titles will amuse both the young and the old. Size, 11½x12½ inches.

Buster Brown's Pranks
Buster Brown, His Dog Tige, and Their Troubles
Buster Brown and His Resolutions
Buster Brown, His Dog Tige and Their Jolly Times
Buddy Tucker and His Friends

No. 3F1490 Price, per volume....45c
If by mail, postage extra, per volume, 13 cents.

Comic Picture Books.

Some of the best known cartoons that have appeared in the comic supplements of the Sunday newspapers appear in these books, being exact reproductions of the originals in size and color. Just the thing to amuse the young folks, and of particular interest to the old. Size, 8x14 inches.

Alphonse and Gaston
Foxy Grandpa's Frolics
Happy Hooligan
Katzenjammer Kids
Lulu and Leander
Latest Adventures of Foxy Grandpa
Naughty Adventures of Mr. Jack
Por' Li'le Mose
The Merry Pranks of Foxy Grandpa
The New Adventures of Foxy Grandpa

No. 3F1492 Price, per volume....45c
Any 2 for..........................85c
If by mail, postage extra, per volume, 13c.

The Wonderful Wishes of Jacky and Jean.

By Mary A. Dickerson. With 6 illustrations in colors. The stories are told with quaint humor, delightfully contrasting Jacky's love for the supernatural and Jean's matter of fact point of view. Printed on best quality of paper. 150 pages. Bound in cloth with original cover design stamped in colors. We do not know of a more attractive book for young people. Size, 7½x10 in.

No. 3F1494 Price..................69c
If by mail, postage extra, 14 cents.

FAIRY TALES AND FABLES.

Andersen's Fairy Tales.

No. 3F1510 By Hans Christian Andersen. Quaint, fascinating stories for boys and girls. They never tire of their recital or cease to long for the possession of a copy of their own. Beautifully illustrated with colored pictures. Size, 7x9 inches. Bound in boards.
Price..................20c

No. 3F1511 Andersen's Fairy Tales, complete unabridged edition. Bound in cloth, profusely illustrated. Size, 5½x8 inches.
Price..................45c
If by mail, postage extra, boards, 8c; cloth, 18c.

Grimm's Fairy Tales.

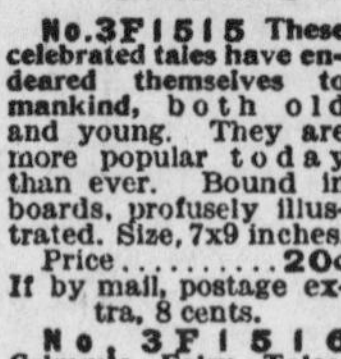

No. 3F1515 These celebrated tales have endeared themselves to mankind, both old and young. They are more popular today than ever. Bound in boards, profusely illustrated. Size, 7x9 inches.
Price..........20c
If by mail, postage extra, 8 cents.

No. 3F1516 Grimm's Fairy Tales, complete unabridged edition. Bound in cloth with beautiful cover design stamped in colors; printed on best quality of paper. Profusely illustrated, lithographed frontispiece in colors. Size, 6x8¼ inches. Price..................45c
If by mail, postage extra, 18 cents.

The Blue Fairy Book.

A splendid collection of classical fairy tales, well printed and profusely illustrated, including lithographed frontispiece in 10 colors. Durably bound in heavily varnished boards, lithographed in colors and gold. Size, 7½x10 inches. 146 pages. Cloth back.

No. 3F1520
Price.......33c
If by mail, postage extra, 12 cents.

Famous Fairy Tales.

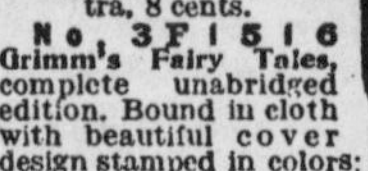

Contains "Babes in the Woods," "House that Jack Built," "Jack, the Giant Killer," "Rip Van Winkle," and many others retold in simple language for our little boys and girls. Beautifully illustrated in colors. 250 pages. Lithographed board cover in colors. Size, 7½x9½ inches.

No. 3F1525
Price..........35c
If by mail, postage extra, 15 cents.

Aesop's Fables.

This book has given delight, joy and happiness to millions of boys and girls, and should be read by everyone before they grow up.

No. 3F1530 Aesop's Fables, printed on good quality of paper and bound in boards, profusely illustrated. Size, 7x9 inches.
Price..........20c
If by mail, postage extra, 8 cents.

No. 3F1531 Aesop's Fables, complete unabridged edition, printed on best quality of paper, beautifully illustrated with full page engravings and colored frontispiece. Bound in green cloth with attractive cover design on side and back stamped in colors. Size, 5½x8 inches. Retail price, $1.00.
Our price..................45c
If by mail, postage extra, 18 cents.

The Woggle-Bug Book.

By L. Frank Baum. It will be enjoyed with delightful laughter, by everyone—men, women and children. Different from any other book. Novel in story, pictures, size, printing and general makeup. Illustrated on every other page with full page pictures in colors, while opposite page contains the text, with illustrations forming the border around it. This is one of the most amusing books ever published. Bound in stiff cardboard with cloth back. Handsome cover design stamped in colors. Size, 15x11 inches.

No. 3F1550 Price..................58c
If by mail, postage extra, 16 cents.

Dickon Bend-the-Bow and Other Wonder Tales.

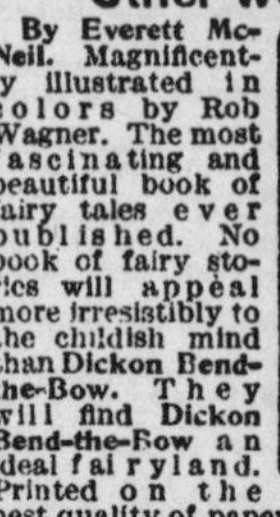

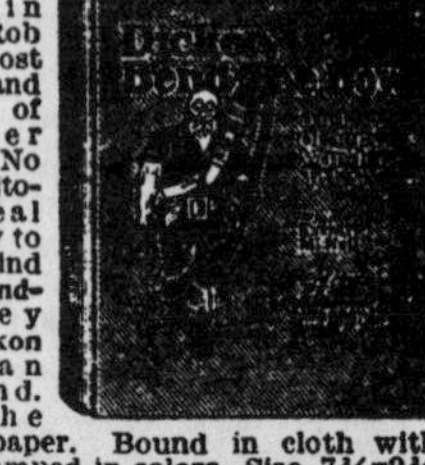

By Everett McNeil. Magnificently illustrated in colors by Rob Wagner. The most fascinating and beautiful book of fairy tales ever published. No book of fairy stories will appeal more irresistibly to the childish mind than Dickon Bend-the-Bow. They will find Dickon Bend-the-Bow an ideal fairyland. Printed on the best quality of paper. Bound in cloth with cover design stamped in colors. Size, 7¼x9¾ inches. Retail price, $1.50.

No. 3F1555 Our price..........78c
If by mail, postage extra, 16 cents.

Wizard of Oz.

By L. Frank Baum. Pictures by W. W. Denslow. An entirely new edition of this famous book, which has amused thousands of readers and theatre goers. Printed on tinted paper and lavishly illustrated in brilliant colors. Numerous full page illustrations. Bound in cloth with scarecrow cover design stamped in colors. Large quarto size, 7x9¼ inches. The story of Dorothy's remarkable travels with the Scarecrow, the Tin Woodman and the Cowardly Lion, has become a classic, and is by all odds the most popular book for children of all ages published in the last ten years.

No. 3F1560 Price..................98c
If by mail, postage extra, 17 cents.

Arabian Nights Entertainments.

The most famous story tellers of the world were the Arabs, and the most famous book of stories in the world is the Arabian Nights Entertainments. Every child and grown person should read these wonderful tales. The stories are always interesting, amusing and entertaining.

No. 3F1540 Arabian Nights Entertainments. Bound in boards, profusely illustrated. Size, 7x9 inches. Price..................20c
If by mail, postage extra, 8 cents.

No. 3F1541 Arabian Nights Entertainments, complete unabridged edition. Bound in cloth with beautiful cover design stamped in colors, printed on best quality of paper. Profusely illustrated, lithographed frontispiece in colors. Size, 5¾x7¾ inches.
Price..................45c
If by mail, postage extra, 18 cents.

Our Finest and Handsomest Children's Books.

Far superior to anything of the kind ever before presented to the little men and women. Sure to attract and delight them beyond measure. Original, forceful, captivating, witty and exceedingly funny; profusely illustrated in brilliant colors, halftone engravings, line drawings, by famous artists. Printed on the finest plate paper with cover elaborately stamped in colors. The retail price of each one of these books is $1.25.

DADDY DINKS. By Louise Mervyn. 100 pages of illustrated verses printed in bright colors; size, 9x11¼ inches.

JINGLEMANJACK. By James O'Dea. A book of pictures and rhymes of the various occupations of the day, showing the workmen at their particular tasks, the tools used, etc. Full page illustrations on every other page. 120 pages. Size, 9x11¼ inches.

BILLY WHISKERS. By Francis Trego Montgomery. 6 colored illustrations by W. H. Fry. Size, 9x11¼ inches. The biography of a goat, including his funny adventures in a circus.

HISTORY IN RHYME AND JINGLES. By A. C. Flick. Old history, newly told. 190 stories told in verse in the words of childhood, telling of the beautiful myths of the people of long ago, wonderful adventures of brave men and women. Profusely illustrated. Size, 9x11½ inches.

No. 3F1496 Our price, each..................78c
If by mail, postage extra, each, 16 cents.

SEE INDEX, PINK PAGES 603 TO 610, TO FIND WHAT YOU WANT.

HENTY'S STORIES FOR BOYS

OLIVE EDGE EDITION, Each **16c**

ANY SIX FOR... **89c**

ANY TWELVE FOR.. **$1.70**

By Geo. A. Henty.

This new edition is fully illustrated, printed from new plates on a good quality of paper with olive edges, and bound in cloth. Assorted colors. Each cover is stamped with an individual design in colors, on side and back. Size, 7½x5 inches.

Among Malay Pirates. A Story of Adventure and Peril.
Bonnie Prince Charlie. A Tale of Fontenoy and Culloden.
Boy Knight, The. A Tale of the Crusades.
Bravest of the Brave, The. With Peterborough in Spain
By England's Aid; or, The Freeing of the Netherlands. (1585-1604.)
By Pike and Dyke. A Tale of the Rise of the Dutch Republic.
By Right of Conquest; or With Cortez in Mexico.
By Sheer Pluck. A Tale of the Ashanti War.
Captain Bayley's Heir A Tale of the Gold Fields of California.
Cat of Bubastes The. A Story of Ancient Egypt.
Cornet of Horse, The. A Tale of Marlborough's Wars.
Dragon and the Raven; or The Days of King Alfred.
Facing Death. A Tale of the Coal Mines.
Final Reckoning, A. A Tale of Bush Life in Australia.
For Name and Fame; or, Through Afghan Passes.
For the Temple. The Fall of Jerusalem.
Friends, Though Divided. A Tale of Civil War in England.
Golden Canon, The. A story of adventure.
In Freedom's Cause. A Story of Wallace and Bruce.
In the Reign of Terror. The Adventures of a Westminster Boy.
In Times of Peril. A Tale of India.
Jack Archer. A Tale of the Crimea.
Lion of St. Mark, The. A Story of Venice in the 14th Century.
Lion of the North, The. A Tale of Gustavus Adolphus and Wars of Religion.
Lost Heir, The.
Maori and Settler. The New Zealand War.
One of the 28th. A Tale of W. terloo.
Orange and Green. A Tale of the Boyne and Limerick.
Out On the Pampas. A Tale of South America.
St. George for England. A Tale of Cressy and Poitiers.
Sturdy and Strong; or How George Andrews Made His Way.
Through the Fray. A Story of the Ludditef Riots.
True to the Old Flag. A Tale of American War of Independence.
Under Drake's Flag. A Tale of the Spanish Main.
With Clive in India; or, The Beginning of an Empire.
With Lee in Virginia. A Story of the American Civil War.
With Wolfe In Canada; or, The Winning of a Continent.
Young Buglers, The. A Tale of the Peninsular War.
Young Carthagenian, The. A Story of the Times of Hannibal.
Young Colonists, The. A Story of Life and War in South America.
Young Franc-Tireurs, The. A Tale of the Franco-Prussian War.
Young Midshipman, The. A Tale of the Siege of Alexandria.

No. 3F1601 Henty's Books.
Price, per volume..........$0.16
Per half dozen..........89
Per dozen..........1.70
If by mail, postage extra, per volume, 8 cents.

THE FAMOUS ALGER BOOKS.

OLIVE EDGE EDITION, Each **16c**

ANY SIX FOR... **89c**

ANY TWELVE FOR.. **$1.70**

By HORATIO ALGER

These books of spirited popular stories are put up similar to the Henty books. These two complete series will make a splendid boys' library. The Alger books are fully illustrated, printed from new plates on a first class paper, with full olive edges, bound in cloth, with individual cover designs stamped in colors, on back and sides. Size, 7½x5 inches. Retail price, 35 cents.

Adrift in New York; or, Tom and Florence Braving the World.
Andy Gordon; or, The Fortunes of a Young Janitor.
Andy Grant's Pluck; and How He Won Out.
Bob Burton; or, The Young Ranchman of Missouri.
Bound to Rise; or, Up the Ladder.
Brave and Bold; or, The Fortunes of Robert Rushton.
Cash Boy; or, Frank Fowler's Early Struggles.
Chester Rand; or, The New Path to Fortune.
Do and Dare; or, A Brave Boy's Fight for Fortune.
Driven From Home; or, Carl Crawford's Experience.
Erie Train Boy; or, Fred's Railroad Adventures.
Facing the World; or, The Haps and Mishaps of Harry Vane.
Hector's Inheritance; or, The Boys of Smith Institute.
Helping Himself; or, Grant Thornton's Rapid Rise in New York.
Herbert Carter's Legacy; or, The Inventor's Son.
In a New World; or, Among the Gold Fields of Australia.
Jack's Ward; or, The Boy Guardian.
Jed, the Poor House Boy; or, From Poverty to Title.
Julius, The Street Boy; or, Out West.
Luke Walton; or, The Chicago Newsboy.
Making His Way; or, Frank Courtney's Struggle Upward.
Only an Irish Boy; or Andy Burke's Fortune.
Paul, the Peddler; or, The Adventures of a Young Street Merchant.
Phil the Fiddler; or, The Story of a Young Street Musician.
Ralph Raymond's Heir; or, James Cromwell's Triumph.
Risen From the Ranks; or, Harry Walton's Success.
Sam's Chance; and How He Improved It.
Shifting for Himself; or, Gilbert Greyson's Fortune.
Sink or Swim; or, Harry Raymond's Resolve.
Slow and Sure; or, From the Street to the Top.
Store Boy; or, The Fortunes of Ben Barclay.
Strive and Succeed; or, The Progress of Walter Conrad.
Strong and Steady; or, Paddle Your Own Canoe.
Tin Box; or, What It Contained.
Tom, the Bootblack; or, A Western Boy's Success.
Tony, the Tramp; or, Right is Might.
Try and Trust; or, Abner Holden's Bound Boy.
Young Acrobat; or, The Great North American Circus.
Young Outlaw; or, Adrift in the Streets.
Young Salesman; or, Scott Walton's Early Struggles.

No. 3F1609 Alger's Books.
Price, per volume..........$0.16
Per half dozen..........89
Per dozen..........1.70
If by mail, postage extra, per volume, 8 cents.

SEE PAGES 897 AND 898 FOR A FULL LINE OF YOUNG PEOPLE'S BOOKS.

THE AMERICAN LIBRARY FOR BOYS.

THE MOST FAMOUS BOOKS BY FAMOUS AUTHORS FOR BOYS,

Cooper, Ellis, Optic, Reid, Verne, Trowbridge, etc.

$1.29 BUYS ANY SIX. 68 CENTS BUYS THREE. 24 CENTS BUYS ONE.

These books are printed from new plates, on superior quality paper, fully illustrated, and bound in first class binders' cloth, assorted colors. Stamped with individual designs and title in colors, on back and side. Some of the books have a special inlay in colors and from three to seven colored illustrations. These stories are deeply interesting and attractive to boys. Size, 5½x7½ inches. The regular retail price of these books is 50 cents per volume.

Admiral J., of Spurwink. Otis
Adventures of a Special Correspondent in Central Asia. Verne.
Adventures on the Mosquito Shore; or, Life in the American Tropics. E. G. Squier
All Aboard. Oliver Optic
Amazons of South America, The. C. M. Stevens
Andersen's Fairy Tales. Hans Christian Andersen
Arabian Knights' Entertainment.
Astounding Adventures Among the Comets. Jules Verne
Boat Club. Oliver Optic
Boone, Daniel, Life of. Edward S. Ellis
Boy Hunters. Mayne Reid.
Boy Slaves. Mayne Reid
Boy Tar. Mayne Reid
Buccaneers and Their Reign of Terror. C. M. Stevens.
Capital For Working Boys. Mrs. Julia E. McConaughy
Captives of the Kaid. B. Marchant
Cast Up By the Sea. Sir Samuel W. Baker
Child's History of England. Chas. Dickens
Coral Island. R. M. Ballantyne
Crockett, David, Life of. Edward S. Ellis
Cruise of the Midge. Michael Scott
Cudjo's Cave. J. T. Trowbridge
Dick Onslow. W. H. G. Kingston
Don Quixote. Cervantes
Ethan Allen and the Green Mountain Heroes of '76. De Puy
Facing the Flag. Jules Verne
Famous American Naval Commanders. Edward S. Ellis
Feats of the Fjord. Harriet Martineau
Fighter of Today, A. H. S. Canfield
Fight For the Green and Gold; A tale of Irish Liberty. Haggerty
Floating Island. Jules Verne
Flower of the Family. Mrs. Prentiss
Found in the Philippines. Gen'l Chas. King
French Fairy Tales.
From Cottage to Castle. The story of Gutenberg, inventor of printing. Mrs. E. C. Pearson
From the Earth to the Moon. Jules Verne
Fun With the Magic. Geo. Brunel
Giraffe Hunters. Mayne Reid
Golden Rock. Edward S. Ellis
Gorilla Hunters. R. M. Ballantyne
Green Mountain Boys. Thompson
Grimm's Household Series. Brothers Grimm
Gulliver's Travels. Dean Swift
Gunmaker of Moscow. Sylvanus Cobb
Held by Rebels. Tom Bevan
Home Sunshine C. D. Bell
Indoor Games and Amusements.
In School and Out. Oliver Optic
In the Forecastle. Cleveland
In the Saddle With Gomez; A tale of Cuban Liberty. Carrillo
Jack Fraser's Adventures. Herbert Haynes
Jinny and His Partners. Jas. Otis
Joan of Arc, Maid of Orleans, Life of. David Bartlett
Josiah in New York. James Otis
Jungle Fugitives, The. Edw. S. Ellis
King's Pardon. Robert Overton
Land of Mystery. Edw. S. Ellis
Last of the Mohicans. Cooper
Lights Out. Robert Overton
Little By Little. Oliver Optic
Little Merchant. Oliver Optic
"Little Phil" the Brave Soldier. Faulkner
Lone Ranch. Capt. Mayne Reid
Manco, the Peruvian Chief. W. H. G. Kingston
Marion, the Patriot Hero. Brigadier-General Horry
Martin Rattler. R. M. Ballantyne
Masterman Ready. Capt. Marryat
Mickey Finn, or Stories and Scenes of Irish Life. Jarrold.
Mysterious Island. Jules Verne
Ned Meyers. J. Fenimore Cooper
Now or Never. Oliver Optic
Old Hickory; the Hero of New Orleans. Alexander Walker
Old Ironsides; the Hero of Tripoli and 1812. Edward S. Ellis
Old Lieutenant and His Son. Norman McLeod
Pathfinder. J. F. Cooper
Paul Jones; the Naval Hero of '76. Lieut. J. T. Burden
Peter the Whaler. W. H. G. Kingston
Pioneers. J. F. Cooper
Poor and Proud. Oliver Optic
Prairie. J. F. Cooper
Proud and Lazy. Oliver Optic
Quest of the Luck. Louis Ramsden
Rich and Humble. Oliver Optic
Rifle Rangers. Mayne Reid
Robin Hood and his Merry Men.
Robinson Crusoe. Daniel DeFoe
Sailor Boy, The. Oliver Optic
Scalp Hunters. Mayne Reid
Settlers in Canada. Capt. Marryat
Soldier Boy, The. Oliver Optic
Six Nights in a Block-House. Henry C. Watson
Spy, The. J. F. Cooper
Stories from the Adirondacks. Young
Stories of the Railroad. John A. Hill
Standard Fairy Tales. Aladdin
Success and its Achievers. Thayer
Swiss Family Robinson. J. D. Wyss
Taking Manila. H. L. Williams
Tales of the Telegraph. J. E. Brady
Tales from Shakespeare. C. and M. Lamb
Three Midshipmen. W. H. G. Kingston
Tom Brown at Oxford. Hughes
Tom Brown's School Days. Hughes
Tour of the World in Eighty Days. Jules Verne
Treasure Island. Stevenson
True Stories of the Days of Washington.
Try Again. Oliver Optic
Twenty Thousand Leagues Under the Sea. Jules Verne
Two Years Before the Mast. R. H. Dana, Jr.
Washington and his Generals. Headley.
Webster, Daniel, Life of
Wee Willie Winkie. Kipling
Wetzel, the Scout and Indian Fighter. R. C. V. Meyers
Will of the Mill. J. Manville Fenn
Winning the Victoria Cross. L. Thompson
With Columbus in America. Falkenhorst
With Cortez in Mexico. Falkenhorst
With Pizarro in Peru. Falkenhorst
Wonders and Curiosities of the Railway. Wm. Sloane Kennedy
Wood Island Light. Jas. Otis
Wounded Name, A. Gen'l Chas. King
Young Pioneers. Dr. C. H. Pearson
Young Voyagers. Capt. Mayne Reid

No. 3F1614 The New American Library of Boys' Books, just as illustrated and described above. Price, any 6 for $1.29; any 3 for 68c; per volume..........24c
If by mail, postage extra, per volume, 8 cents.

FAMOUS BOOKS BY FAMOUS AUTHORS.

Copyright Edition.

Price, Per Volume.... 38c	Any 3 for...... 98c	Any 6 for..... $1.90

The latest stories by the most famous boys' authors. Each one of these books is copyrighted. This is the only edition in which the books can be obtained and on account of the very favorable arrangements we have made with the publishers, the additional cost of the copyright to our customers is very little. These books are a new edition beautifully bound in the best grade of binder's cloth. Each book has an individual cover design stamped on back and side in colors. Printed on an excellent quality of paper. Clear type. Well illustrated. Size, 7½x5 inches.

Rival Bicyclists, or, Fun and Adventures on the Wheel. By Capt. Ralph Bonehill.
Young Oarsmen of Lake View, or, The Mystery of Hermit Island. By Capt. Ralph Bonehill.
Leo, the Circus Boy, or, Life Under the Great White Canvas. By Capt. Ralph Bonehill.
Gun and Sled, or, The Young Hunters of Snow Top Island. By Capt. Ralph Bonehill.
Young Hunters in Porto Rico, or, The Search for a Lost Treasure. By Capt. Ralph Bonehill.
Poor but Plucky or, The Mystery of a Flood. By Arthur M. Winfield
By Pluck, not Luck, or, Dan Granbury's Struggle to Rise. By Arthur M. Winfield.
Rescued by a Prince. Life among the canibals. By Clement Eldridge (Capt. Nautilus).
The Castle of the Carpathians. Story of a haunted castle. By Jules Verne.
Teddy. How Teddy helped to raise the mortgage on his mother's home. By James Otis.
Telegraph Tom's Venture. An excellent detective story. By James Otis.
Messenger No. 48. A faithful messenger boy who ferreted out a band of criminals who for years had baffled the police and detectives. By James Otis.
Down the Slope. Young boy "breaker" in a coal mine. By James Otis.
Struggle for a Fortune. The story of an orphan boy. By Harry Castlemon.
Forge and Furnace. A story of the iron mills. By Victor St. Clair.
Winged Arrow's Medicine, or, The Massacre at Fort Phil Kearney. A fascinating tale of the Sioux Indians. By Harry Castlemon.
The First Capture, or, Hauling Down the Flag of England. A thrilling story of the Revolutionary war. By Harry Castlemon.
Far Past the Frontier. Adventures of two boys in the wilderness. By James A. Braden.
Connecticut Boys in the Western Reserve. A tale of the Moravian Massacre of 1791, and a sequel to "Far Past the Frontier." By James A. Braden.
The Last Cruise of the Electra. A story of a pirate submarine boat. By Charles C. Chipman.
Larry Barlow's Ambition, or, The Adventures of a Young Fireman in New York City. By Arthur M. Winfield.
A Young Inventor's Pluck, or, The Mystery of the Willington Legacy. By A. M. Winfield.
The Boy Land Boomer, or, Dick Arbucle's Adventures in Oklahoma. By Capt. Ralph Bonehill.
Three Young Ranchmen, or, Daring Adventures in the Great West. A story of three boys in Idaho. By Capt. Ralph Bonehill.
Captives, Three A thrilling story of Indian lawlessness. By James A. Braden.

No. 3F1622 Famous Books by Famous Authors, as illustrated and described. Price, any six for $1.90; any 3 for 98c; per volume...(Postage extra, per volume, 8 cents.)...38c

Log Cabin to White House Series.

Each book with a distinctive design. Entirely new edition of this famous series of celebrated men. This series is carefully printed on paper of fine quality, and handsomely bound in English vellum de luxe cloth, with attractive individual covers stamped in three-color ink combination in perfect harmony. Printed jackets to match covers. Large 12mo. Size, 5¼x7¾ inches. Retail price, 75 cents.

1. **From Boyhood to Manhood.** Life of Benjamin Franklin. By William M. Thayer.
2. **From Farm House to White House.** Life of George Washington. By William M. Thayer.
3. **From Log Cabin to White House.** Life of James A. Garfield, with eulogy by Hon. James G. Blaine. By William M. Thayer.
4. **From Pioneer Home to White House.** Life of Abraham Lincoln, with eulogy by Hon. George Bancroft. By William M. Thayer.
5. **From Ranch to White House.** Life of Theodore Roosevelt. By Edward S. Ellis.
6. **From Tannery to White House.** Life of Ulysses S. Grant. By William M. Thayer.

No. 3F1631 Log Cabin to White House Series.
Our price, 2 for **75c**; per volume........................$0.39
The entire set of 6 books for........................2.15
If by mail, postage extra, per volume, 9 cents.

The Boys' Own Author Series.

Regular $1.50 copyrighted books at 48 cents.

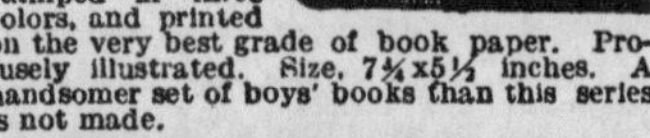

Fascinating Stories by Otis, Ober, Costello, Coffin and other famous writers for boys. Under special arrangements with the publishers we are enabled to offer these regular $1.50 books at only 48 cents each. They are put up exactly the same as the $1.50 edition, bound in the finest grade of buckram with cover design embossed and stamped in three colors, and printed on the very best grade of book paper. Profusely illustrated. Size, 7¾x5½ inches. A handsomer set of boys' books than this series is not made.

A Tar of the Old School. By F. H. Costello
Boy Captain. By James Otis
Captain Tom, the Privateersman. By James Otis
Dan of Milbrook. By C. C. Coffin
My Days and Nights on the Battlefield. By C. C. Coffin
Ned, Son of Webb: What He Did. By William O. Stoddard.
On Fighting Decks in 1812. By F. H. Costello
The Apprentice Boy. By Frank M. Bicknell
The Armed Ship America. By James Otis
The Boy Duck Hunters. By Frank E. Kellogg
The Cruise of the Comet. By James Otis
The Days of Chivalry. By W. H. Davenport Adams
The Gold Hunters of Alaska. By Willis Boyd Allen
The Land of the Incas. By W. H. Davenport Adams
The Lost City. By Joseph E. Badger Jr.
The Rulers of the Sea. By Edmond Neukomm
The Voyage of the Charlemange. By William O. Stoddard
The Young Moose Hunters. By C. A. Stephens
Two American Boys in Hawaii. By G. Waldo Browne
Two Boys in the Blue Ridge. By W. Gordon Parker
Under the Cuban Flag. By Fred A. Ober
Under the Rattlesnake Flag. By F. H. Costello

No. 3F1641 The Boys' Own Author Series. Price, per volume...........$0.48
Any 2 for **90c**; 6 for...............2.48
If by mail, postage extra, per volume, 10 cents.

The Stories of American History Series.

By James Otis.

17 original illustrations, by L. J. Bridgeman, in each volume. Large books, size, 8x6 inches. Beautifully bound in buckram with very handsome cover designs in four colors. These spirited stories make ideal boys' books. Mr. Otis takes for his subjects the most exciting and momentous events in our national history. Regular retail price, per volume, 75 cents.

Defending The Island. A story of Bar Harbor in 1758
When We Destroyed The Gaspard
Boston Boys of 1775
When Dewey Came to Manila
Off Santiago With Sampson
When Israel Putnam Served the King
The Signal Boys of '75. A Tale of the Siege of Boston
Under The Liberty Tree. A Story of the Boston Massacre
The Boys of 1745. At the Capture of Louisburg
An Island Refuge. Casco Bay in 1676
Neal the Miller. A Son of Liberty
Ezra Jordan's Escape, from the Massacre at Fort Loyal

No. 3F1650 Stories of American History Series. Our price, per volume...........40c
Any 2 for...........................75c
The complete set of 12 books for... 4.25
If by mail, postage extra, per volume, 7 cents.

The Boys' Book of Sports.

By Maurice Thompson. The aim of this book is to give the boys and the youths of America a volume full of health ul, amusing, as well as useful instruction. Teaches them how to use a gun, how to use a bow and arrow, how to fish (the best way to catch various kinds of fish), how to boat, (how to make a boat and use it), how to swim, toboggan, etc., etc. Contains 350 pages. Innumerable cuts, full-page engravings, drawings, illustrations, etc., with many working diagrams. Bound in cloth with attractive cover design stamped in colors, and title stamped in gold. Size, 6¾x9¼ inches.

No. 3F1660 Price............$1.59
If by mail, postage extra, 18 cents.

Allan Pinkerton's Detective Stories.

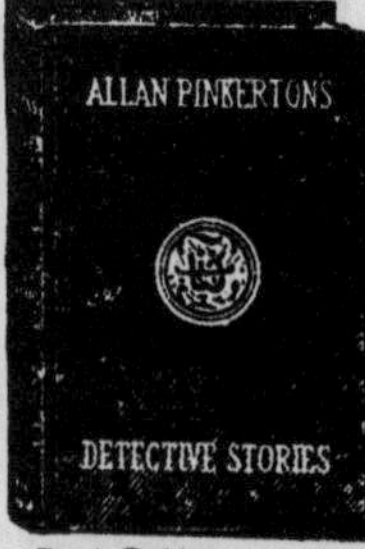

These stories were written by Allan Pinkerton, the world's greatest detective. Each story recounts the actual experiences of the great detective in running down some particular criminal case. Each one of these stories makes most exciting and delightful reading. This is a new edition, bound in best quality of binders' cloth with original stamped cover design. Size, 5x7½ inches.

Bank Robbers
Burglar's Fate, The
Criminal Reminiscences
Double Life, A
Expressmen and Detectives, The
Gypsies and Detectives, The
Mississippi Outlaws, The
Mollie Maguires, The
Professional Thieves
Railroad Forger, The
Spiritualists and Detectives, The
Spy of the Rebellion, The
Thirty Years a Detective

No. 3F1655 Allan Pinkerton's Detective Stories. Our price, per volume........$0.78
Any 2 for.......................... 1.48
The complete set of 13 volumes for.. 8.98
If by mail, postage extra, per volume, 11 cents.

United States Army Physical Exercises.

Revised for the use of the civilian by Professor Donovan. The various movements as practiced by all soldiers in garrison in order to retain a proper set-up and to keep the muscles supple. Profusely illustrated from original photographs, posed expressly for this work. Size, 5¼x7½ inches.

No. 3F1657 Price...**39c**
If by mail, postage extra, 6 cents.

Circus Day.

By George Ade. The famous humorous author. Illustrated by John T. McCutcheon, the great cartoonist. The story of two little boys who are greatly excited over the coming of the circus to their village, and they plan how to obtain the necessary funds for admittance and the great day they will have. A book which will delight every boy. Printed on best quality of plate paper. Bound in cloth in clown cover design, stamped in brilliant colors. Size, 5¾x7¼ inches.

No. 3F1665 Price.............**43c**
If by mail, postage extra, 5 cents.

Toby Tyler; or, Ten Weeks with a Circus.

By James Otis. A tale of a boy who ran away with a circus. A good, clean, high class story, intensely interesting and full of humor. Fully illustrated. 265 pages. Size, 5x7 inches.

No. 3F1667 Price, **45c**
If by mail, postage extra, 10 cents.

American Boys' Life of Theodore Roosevelt.

By Edward Stratemeyer. The life of Theodore Roosevelt is one well worth studying by every American boy who wishes to make something of himself, and this book is one of the best biographies of Roosevelt, covering his entire life from his birth to his recent western trip. 311 pages. Fully illustrated. Size, 5½x7 inches. Bound in cloth.

No. 3F1669 Price............ **95c**
If by mail, postage extra, 12 cents.

═STORIES FOR GIRLS═

GIRLS' OWN LIBRARY, BY SUCH AUTHORS AS MRS. L. T. MEADE, MRS. J. H. EWING, ROSA N. CAREY, MISS MULOCK, E. MARLITT, MRS. MOLESWORTH, ETC.

Price, each = 24c
Any three for 69c
Any six for $1.35

A carefully selected series of books for girls, written by popular authors. These are charming stories, well told. Every book is interesting and wholesome. Their simplicity, tenderness, healthy, interesting motives, vigorous action, and character painting will please all girl readers. Ornamented cloth binding; side, covers and back stamped in colored designs. Size, 7½x5 inches. Retail price, 50 and 75 cents.

A Bachelor Maid and Her Brother. I. T. Thurston
Aimee. Agnes Giberne
Alice in Wonderland. Lewis Carroll
All Aboard. Fannie E. Newberry
Almost a Genius. Adelaide L. Rouse
Annice Winkoop, Artist. Story of a Country Girl. A. L. Rouse
Annie Price; or, Grandmama's Sunshine. A. Maria Hall
Adventures of a Brownie. Miss Mulock
Aunt Diana. Rosa N. Carey
Averil. Rosa N. Carey
Bad Little Hannah L. T. Meade
Barbara Heathcote's Trial. Rosa N. Carey
Benhurst Club, The. Howe Benning
Bek's First Corner. Jennie M. Drinkwater
Bertha's Summer Boarders. Linnie S. Harris
Billow Prairie. A Story of Life in the Great West. Joy Allison
Black Beauty. Anna Sewell
Bordentown Story Tellers. Hezekiah Butterworth
Bubbles. Fannie E. Newberry
Bunch of Cherries, A. L. T. Meade
Children's Kingdom, The. Story of a Great Endeavor. L. T. Meade
Cousin Geoffrey and I. Caroline Austin
Cuckoo Clock, The. Mrs. Molesworth
Daddy's Girl. L. T. Meade
Deane Girls, The. A Home Story. Adelaide L. Rouse
Dr. Rumsey's Patient. L. T. Meade
Do Somethings. Oliver Optic
Duxberry Doings. A New England Story. Caroline B. Le Row
Edith's Ministry. McKeever
Esther Rosa N. Carey
Esther's Charge. Ellen Everett Green
Fairy Book. Miss Mulock
Fairy Tales and Wonder Stories. Dr. Thomas Dunn English
Fairy Tales Far and Near. A. T. Quiller-Couch (Q)
Fanny, the Flower Girl. Bunbury
Fifteen. Jennie M. Drinkwater
Flat-Iron for a Farthing. Ewing
From Dawn to Daylight; or, the Simple Story of a Western Home. Harriet Beecher Stowe
Gianetta. A Girl's Story of Herself. Rosa Mulholland
Gilly Flower. By Author of Miss Toosey's Mission
Girl in Ten Thousand, A. Meade
Girls of the True Blue L. T. Meade
Girl Neighbors. Sarah Tytler
Girl of Today. Ellinor Davenport Adams
Gold Elsie. E. Marlitt
Grandfather's Chair. Hawthorne
Growing Up. The Girlhood of Judith Mackenzie. J. M. Drinkwater
Happy Discipline, A. Elizabeth Cummings
Heidi. From the German Spyri. Translated by H. A. Melcon
Helen Beaton, College Woman. Adelaide L. Rouse
History of My Pets. Grace Greenwood
Hope Darrow. A Little Girl's Story. Virginia F. Townsend
In The Golden Days. Edna Lyall
Jackanapes. Mrs. J. H. Ewing
Jan of the Windmill. Mrs. J. H. Ewing
Jessica's First Prayer. Hesba Stretton
Joanna Darling. Townsend
Joyce's Investments. Fannie E. Newberry
Kathleen. Frances H. Burnett
Katie Robertson. A Girl's Story of Factory Life. M. E. Winslow
Kitty Landon's Girlhood. Armstrong
Lady of the Forest. L. T. Meade
Lamplighter, The. Maria S. Cummins
Light o' the Morning. L. T. Meade
Lindsay's Luck. Frances H. Burnett
Little Jeanneton's Work. A Chronicle of Breton Life. C. A. Jones
Little Lame Prince. Miss Mulock
Margaret Warner; or, The Young Wife at the Farm. Macleod
Margery Keith. Townsend
Margery Merton's Girlhood. Alice Corkran
Marigold. Jennie M. Drinkwater
Mary St. John. Rosa N. Carey
Maud and Miriam. McKeever
Meg's Friend. Alice Corkran
Mellicent Raymond. Fannie E. Newberry
Merle's Crusade. Rosa N. Carey
Merry Girls of England. Meade
Minister's Wooing, The. Stowe
Miss Ashton's New Pupil. A School Girl's Story. Mrs. S. S. Robbins
Miss Charity's House. Howe Benning
Miss Fenwick's Failures. Esme Stuart
Miss Malcolm's Ten. Margaret E. Winslow
Miss Nonentity. L. T. Meade
Miss Prudence. A Story of Two Girls' Lives. Jennie M. Drinkwater
Mixed Pickles. Mrs. E. M. Field
Not for Profit. Fannie E. Newberry
Not Like Other Girls. Rosa N. Carey
Odd One, The. Fannie E. Newberry
One Girl's Way Out. Howe Benning
Only a Girl. A Tale of Brittany. C. A. Jones
Our Bessie. Rosa N. Carey
Our Village. Mary Russell Mitford
Owl's Nest. E. Marlitt
Palace Beautiful, The. L. T. Meade
Polly. A New Fashioned Girl. L. T. Meade
Pretty Polly Pemberton. Frances H. Burnett
Prince of the House of David. Rev. Professor J. H. Ingraham
Princess and the Goblin. George Macdonald
Princess of the Moor. E. Marlitt
Pythia's Pupils. A Story of a School. Eva Hartner
Queechy. Susan Warner
Queenie's Whim. Rosa N. Carey
Rebels of the School. L. T. Meade
Recollections of My Childhood. Grace Greenwood
Robin Redbreast. Mrs. Molesworth
Ruth Prentiss. Marion Thorne
Rutledge. Miriam Coles Harris
Sara, A Princess. Fannie E. Newberry
Schonberg-Cotta Family. Mrs. Andrew Charles
Silver Threads. McKeever
Six Little Princesses. Prentiss
Six to Sixteen. Juliana Horatia Ewing.
Stories and Legends of Travel and History. Grace Greenwood
Stories and Sights of France and Italy. Grace Greenwood
Stories for Home-Folks. Grace Greenwood
Stories from Famous Ballads. Grace Greenwood
Stories of Many Lands. Grace Greenwood
Story of a Short Life. Juliana Horatia Ewing
Sweet Girl Graduate, A. L. T. Meade
Tessa Wadsworth's Discipline. J. M. Drinkwater
Their Little Mother. L. T. Mead
Theo. Frances H. Burnett
Three Bright Girls. A. E. Armstrong
Three Years at Glenwood. A Story of School Life. M. E. Winslow
Three Young Women. Jennie E. Drinkwater
Through the Looking Glass, and What Alice Found There. L. Carroll
Time of Roses, The. L. T. Meade
Twice Crowned. McKeever
Uncle Max. Rosa N. Carey
Under False Colors. A Story from Two Girls' Lives. Sarah Doudney
Vara; or, the Child of Adoption. Emily Strattford
Very Naughty Girl, A. L. T. Meade
Very Odd Girl, A; or, Life at the Gabled Farm. Annie E. Armstrong
Water Babies. Charles Kingsley
We and The World. Mrs. J. H. Ewing
Westbrook Parsonage. McKeever
Wide, Wide World. Susan Warner
Wild Kitty A Story of Middleton School. L. T. Meade
Wonder Book, A. Hawthorne.
World of Girls, A. A Story of School. L. T. Meade
Young Mutineer, A. L. T. Meade

No. 3F1700 Girls' Own Library Series, as illustrated and described above. Price, per volume........................$0.24
Any three titles for.. .69
Any six titles for.. 1.35
Any twelve titles for........................(If by mail, postage extra, each, 9 cents)........................ 2.65

LOUISA M. ALCOTT'S WORKS.

LITTLE WOMEN SERIES.

Eight famous books by the greatest of girls' authors, Louisa M. Alcott. The regular retail price of these books is $1.50 per volume. Bound in cloth with attractively stamped cover design. Printed on excellent quality paper. Size, 4¾x7 inches.

An Old Fashioned Girl
Eight Cousins
Jack and Jill
Jo's Boys
Little Men
Little Women
Rose in Bloom
Under the Lilacs

95c

No. 3F1703
Price, per volume..$0.95
Any 2 for.......... 1.85
Price for series (8 books)..........$7.25
If by mail, postage extra, per volume, 10 cents.

CHILDREN'S FRIEND SERIES.

By Louisa M. Alcott. Illustrated handy volumes. Size, 5x7½. Each volume contains about 40 pages. Delightful little books for children.

A Christmas Dream
A Hole in the Wall
Candy Country
Little Button Rose
Marjorie's Three Gifts.
May Flowers
Morning Glories
Mountain-Laurel and Maidenhair
Pansies and Water-Lilies
Poppies and Wheat
The Doll's Journey
The Little Men Play
The Little Women Play

No. 3F1704 Price, per volume...$0.35
Any 2 for.......... .68
Any 6 for.......... 1.95
If by mail, postage extra, per volume, 7 cents.

Famous Elsie Books.

By Martha Finley. These books are too well known to need a description. Entertaining and attractive stories. Our mothers have read them, which is their best recommendation. Attractively bound in cloth with stamped cover design. Frontispiece. Printed on excellent quality of paper. Size, 4¾x7 inches.

Elsie Dinsmore
Elsie's Holidays at Roseland
Elsie's Girlhood
Elsie's Womanhood
Elsie's Motherhood
Elsie's Children
Elsie's Widowhood
Elsie's New Relations
Christmas with Grandma Elsie
Grandmother Elsie
Elsie at Nantucket
The Two Elsies
Elsie's Kith and Kin
Elsie's Friends at Woodburn
Elsie and the Raymonds
Elsie Yachting with the Raymonds
Elsie's Vacation
Elsie at the World's Fair
Elsie's Young Folks

No. 3F1706 The Elsie Books.
Price, per volume..........$0.74
Any 2 for.......... 1.45
Any 6 for.......... 4.25
If by mail, postage extra, per volume, 10 cents.

The Mildred Books.

POPULAR PRICE EDITION.

By Martha Finley. A companion series to the Elsie books, and published for the first time at a popular price. Each book is bound in cloth, attractively decorated and printed on first class quality of paper. Illustrated. Size, 4¾x7 inches. Three delightful books for girls.

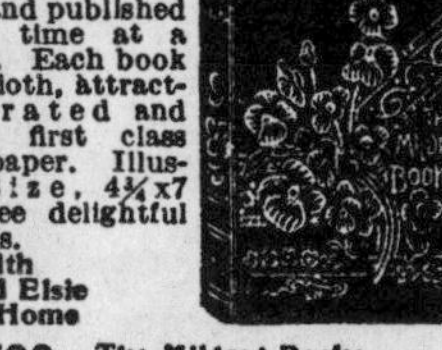

Mildred Keith
Mildred and Elsie
Mildred at Home

No. 3F1709 The Mildred Books.
Price, per volume..........35c
For series (3 books)..........98c
If by mail, postage extra, per volume, 10 cents.

Pepper Books.

By Margaret Sidney. Five Little Peppers and How They Grew. 16mo edition. Size, 6½x6½ inches. New edition bound in bright cloth with decorated cover. Fully illustrated. This is the only title in the Pepper books that is issued at this low price.

No. 3F1712 Price, 33c
If by mail, postage extra, 9 cents.

We also offer the other Pepper books in the regular edition.

Ben Pepper
Five Little Peppers' Abroad
Five Little Peppers and How They Grew
Five Little Peppers and Their Friends
Five Little Peppers at School
Five Little Peppers Midway
Five Little Peppers Grown Up
Phronsie Pepper
The Adventures of Joel Pepper
The Stories Polly Pepper Told

No. 3F1713 The Pepper Books.
Price, per volume..........99c
If by mail, postage extra, per volume, 13 cents.

When Grandmamma Was Fourteen.

By Marion Harland. This story has all the charms of manner which are characteristic of the author. A delightfully charming book, interesting and entertaining. Handsomely bound in cloth with gold stamping, and attractive cover design. Fully illustrated and printed on the best quality of paper. Size, 5¼x7½ inches.

No. 3F1718
Price..........98c
If by mail, postage extra, 10 cents.

Six Girls.

By Fanny Belle Irving. This is a new edition of this famous book, printed on the finest grade of paper from new plates, with eight beautiful full page illustrations by A. G. Learned. Bound in cloth with unique and handsome cover design in colors. Size, 5½x7¾ inches. We do not know of a more attractive book for girls or a more interesting story than "Six Girls." Retail price, $1.25.

No. 3F1723 Our price..........89c
If by mail, postage extra, 13 cents.

Business Openings for Girls.

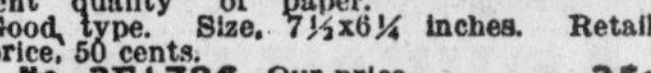

By Sally Joy White. An interesting and earnest talk with girls, enumerating and describing the various opportunities and positions that are open to girls, such as saleswomen, cash girls, stenographers, preserving and pickling, professional mending, etc. This is an excellent book for any girl who is ambitious to be self supporting. Bound in cloth, gold stamping, cover design in colors. Printed on excellent quality of paper. Good type. Size, 7½x6¼ inches. Retail price, 50 cents.

No. 3F1726 Our price..........35c
If by mail, postage extra, 8 cents.

What Women Can Earn.

Positions that are open to women, and the compensation paid. Essays on all the leading trades and professions in America in which women have demonstrated their ability to fill, including clerks, companions, dramatic art, factory work, professions, librarians, musicians, saleswomen, teaching, stenographers, typewriters and a hundred other lines of work with information as to the compensation paid in each particular field of labor. We heartily recommend this book to every ambitious woman. 354 pages, printed on best quality of paper. Bound in cloth with attractive cover design. Size, 5¼x7½ inches.

No. 3F1729 Price..........85c
If by mail, postage extra, 9 cents.

Three Hundred Things a Bright Girl Can Do.

By Lilia Elizabeth Kelley. A complete treasury of suggestions of handiwork, embroidery, sewing, cooking, candy making, home decoration, sloyd, pyrography, physical culture, scientific experiments, games, indoor sports, method of entertaining friends and evening companies, ways of making money and of helping others. Unequaled for variety, amusement, bright and original style, happy atmosphere and practical usefulness. 700 illustrations. The numerous suggestions are numbered and indexed that they will be readily available. Bound in cloth, printed on finest grade of paper. Size, 5¾x8½ inches. Retail price, $1.75.

No. 3F1731 Our price..........$1.38
If by mail, postage extra, 18 cents.

A Little Cook Book for A Little Girl.

This is a book which has long been needed. It explains how to cook so simply that anyone can fully understand every word. For girls of from 8 to 12 years of age, who are learning to make plain and pretty dishes and who are discouraged by the confusing recipes in ordinary cook books, it will be indispensable. Tells how to prepare cereals and eggs, fish and meats, soups, salads, vegetables, desserts and ices and candy, as well as light luncheons for carrying to school. Contains 180 pages full of recipes, printed on excellent quality of paper. Bound in cloth with attractive cover design. Size, 5¼x7½ inches.

No. 3F1735 Price..........65c
If by mail, postage extra, 7 cents.

NATURAL HISTORY BOOKS FOR YOUNG PEOPLE.

Wood's Natural History for Children.

Complete unabridged edition. By Rev. J. G. Wood. Adapted for juveniles by Douglas Dawson. Profusely illustrated. It contains pictures of almost every known animal, both on land and sea. Jumbo edition. Contains 432 pages. Size, 7½ x 9¼ inches. Bound in cloth with attractive cover design stamped in gold and silver.

No. 3F1752
Price..........65c
If by mail, postage extra, 28 cents.

Written in simple, easily understood language. Beautifully lithographed cover. 195 pages. Cloth back. Size, 7¼x10 inches.

No. 3F1750 Abridged edition.
Price..........22c
If by mail, postage extra, 15 cents.

Child's History of Animals.

This book is beautifully illustrated in black and white and colors, and in simple language gives the history of all the animals dear to the heart of every boy and girl, including elephants, monkeys, lions, etc. 250 pages. Lithographed board cover, in colors. Size, 7½x9½ inches.

No. 3F2453
Price..........39c
If by mail, postage extra, 15 cents.

Marvelous Story of Man.

By G. Dallas Lind, M.D. Intensely interesting; instructive and historical. Embracing the origin of man, his inadequate primitive condition, language, peculiarities, superstitious customs, etc. Describes the advent of man, the stone, bronze and iron age; the mound builders; the cliff dwellers; origin of language and titles. Deals with marriage customs, burial customs, etc., also the religion of the ancients. Contains 622 pages, profusely illustrated and is bound in tan cloth with attractive cover design stamped in colors. Size, 6½x8½ inches.

No. 3F1754 Price..........45c
If by mail, postage extra, 18 cents.

Our Animal Friends in Their Native Homes.

By Phoebe W. Humphreys. A natural history for young people. Told in story, told in picture. Is a history of animals, including mammals, birds and fishes. Written in words of easy language and describing their manner of living, characteristics, etc. Over 150 pictures, many being colored plates and halftones. A book that will gladden the heart of any young child. 272 pages. Size, 7x9½ inches. Substantially bound in boards with lithographed cover in many colors. Retail price, $1.00.

No. 3F1756 Our price..........35c
If by mail, postage extra, 14 cents.

Museum of Wonders.

By Henry Davenport Northrop. Containing marvels of natural history, with graphic descriptions of monsters of the ancient world, wild animals of forest and plain, beautiful birds and insects, wonderful trees, flowers and plants, sublime natural scenery, etc., including thrilling stories of the polar and tropical regions, remarkable traits of strange people, etc. 500 pages. Cloth. Size, 8x10 inches.

No. 3F1757 Price..........79c
If by mail, postage extra, 22 cents.

Forest and Jungle.

By P. T. Barnum. Thrilling adventures in all quarters of the globe. A complete illustrated history of the animal kingdom, written in an easy and instructive manner, embracing vivid descriptions of the manner of capture and taming of wild beasts, birds and reptiles for the menageries and zoological gardens of the world. Including an account of the last African expedition sent out by Mr. Barnum. The largest and greatest illustrated history of the animal kingdom ever published. Contains hundreds of large illustrations; printed from large, clear type. Finely bound in scarlet cloth with cover design stamped in black and silver. Large size, 7½ inches wide by 12 inches long by 2 inches thick. 502 pages. Regular retail price, $2.00.

No. 3F1758 Our price..........65c
If by mail, postage extra, 30 cents.

Living Pictures From The Animal Kingdom.

By Dr. L. Heck, director of the celebrated Berlin Zoological Garden. A superb pictorial, showing reproductions of photographs of the rarest and finest specimens of the animal kingdom, taken from life. Animal pictures of the size given in this volume, 11x14 inches, are a novelty. The foot notes by Dr. Heck, describing the habits, appearance, homes, etc., of the originals of the lifelike illustrations greatly increase the value of the book, and will be found to be exceedingly interesting. This magnificent volume will prove a never failing source of delight and information to young and old. Substantially bound in cloth with emblematic design stamped in two colors. Size, 11x14 inches; over 200 pages; printed on heavy enameled paper.

No. 3F1760 Price..........65c
If by mail, postage extra, 32 cents.

The Child's Story of Birds, Beasts and Reptiles.

By Frederick Lonnkvist, Ph.D. A natural history for the young. Contains description of animals as seen in the zoological gardens or in their wild state described with stories telling of their homes and habits in an entertaining and instructive way. Over 100 beautiful illustrations, including full page colored picture and full page halftone engravings. Contains 240 pages. Bound in cloth with animal cover design in colors. Size, 7¼x9¾ inches. Retail price, $1.00.

No. 3F1762 Our price..........45c
If by mail, postage extra, 15 cents.

Homes, Haunts and Habits of Wild Animals.

By Isaac Thorne Johnson, A.M. Young People's Natural History. A popular story of animals, birds, reptiles, fishes and insects, describing their structure, habits, instincts, dwellings, etc., with thrilling stories of adventure and amusing anecdotes of wild and tame animals. Illustrated with five full page beautiful pictures in colors. 32 full page halftones, and more than 150 other illustrations. Contains 434 pages. Bound in cloth with handsomely decorated cover with colored photographic inlay. Size, 7¼x9¾ inches.

No. 3F1764 Price..........65c
If by mail, postage extra, 28 cents.

World's Natural History

Or, Living Creatures on Land and Sea. Contains graphic descriptions of wild animals of the forest, beautiful birds, curious denizens of the deep. This book is a vast museum of all that is marvelous in natural history, including adventures of hunters of lions and of other ferocious animals. Contains 608 pages, with hundreds of superb phototype engravings and many full page colored pictures. Bound in best quality of cloth with photographic inlay and gold stamping on cover. Size, 7¼x10 inches. Retail price, $2.00.

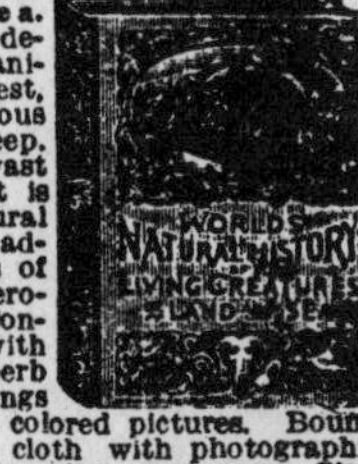

No. 3F1766 Our price..........75c
If by mail, postage extra, 32 cents.

Nature Stories for Little Folk.

"The Crooked Oak Tree and the Life of the Dragon Fly."
"Curly Head and His Neighbors and the Dirty Puddle."

Beautifully bound stories of birds, animals and plants for little people. Beautifully illustrated with colored pictures. Bound in boards with very handsome cover designs in colors. Each book has about 60 pages, printed on fine white paper, with large type. Size, 5x7½ inches. Delightful stories that will fascinate the little people and arouse their interest in the birds and trees, the insects and animals.

No. 3F1768 Price, each..........19c
Per set, 2 books..........35c
If by mail, postage extra, each, 4 cents.

RELIGIOUS BOOKS FOR CHILDREN.

Aunt Charlotte's Bible Stories.

By Charlotte M. Yonge. This is a new and original book that will commend itself to parents. Beginning with the very dawn of creation, every historical event of the Bible is brought out in beautiful narrative, arranged in the order of their happenings, thus leading the little ones along the pleasant ways on Sunday. Arranged for fifty-two Sunday readings. Illustrated with eight colored pictures. Cloth. Size, 7¼x9¼ inches.

No. 3F1775 Price..............39c
If by mail, postage extra, 18 cents.

Boys of the Bible.

By Thomas A. Handford. From the first chapter to the very last, every line is exceedingly interesting, and the language used adapted to the young reader. Every boy admires a hero, and this is a book full of heroes; it is not dull reading, as religious books are supposed to be, but full of accounts of exciting deeds, noble acts, and examples of bravery. Attractively bound in cloth. Contains 315 pages; 27 full page illustrations. Size, 8¼x7 inches.

No. 3F1777 Price..............35c
If by mail, postage extra, 16 cents.

Child's Life of Christ.

By Hesba Stretton. New edition of this beautiful story, profusely illustrated, showing the pathways trodden, the scenes visited, the burdens borne, the help rendered, the blessings bestowed and the lessons taught by Jesus, the Christ, when on His earthly pilgrimage from the manger to the throne. Cloth. 256 pages. Size, 9¾x7½ inches.

No. 3F1779 Price..............38c
If by mail, postage extra, 18 cents.

Young Peoples' Bible Stories Series.

By Josephine Pollard. A series of four volumes containing historic incidents from the Bible. All are works of untold interest, and will prove a powerful influence for good in every home. The wonderful parables and miracles are described in language which all children can comprehend. Profusely illustrated, colored frontispiece; printed in large, clear type on super-calendered paper. Elaborate cover designs stamped in three brilliant colors; title stamped in gold. Size, 7½x9¼ inches. 280 pages.

Bible Stories for Children.
History of the Old Testament.
History of the New Testament.
Sweet Story of God.

No. 3F1783 Price, per volume....48c
Any 2 for.............................94c
If by mail, postage extra, per volume, 26 cents.

Beautiful Stories from the Bible Series.

These two superb books, size 7x8½ inches, are printed on heavy plate paper, large type, with 45 full page illustrations each. Each contains over 100 pages, bound in half vellum with illuminated sides, representing religious scenes, colored frontispiece. These superb books will delight any child's heart and make a beautiful gift.

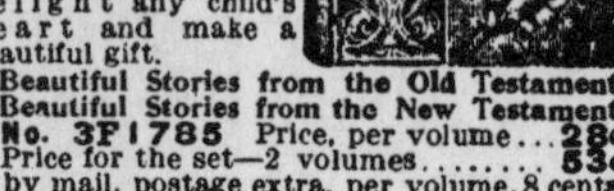

Beautiful Stories from the Old Testament.
Beautiful Stories from the New Testament.

No. 3F1785 Price, per volume....28c
Price for the set—2 volumes........53c
If by mail, postage extra, per volume, 8 cents.

One Syllable Bible Story Series.

Popular Religious Books, arranged for young folks, in words of one syllable. Printed from large, clear type on fine paper, and fully illustrated. Handsomely bound in cloth, elaborately stamped with gold and illuminated side, representing a Biblical scene. The handsomest line of one syllable religious books for young children ever published. Size, 5½x7¾ inches. Retail price, 50 cents each.

A Child's Life of Christ. 49 illustrations.
A Child's Story of the Old Testament. 33 illustrations.
A Child's Story of the New Testament. 40 illustrations.
Bible Stories for Little Children. 41 illustrations.
The Story of Jesus. 40 illustrations.

No. 3F1787 One Syllable Bible Story Series. Our price, per volume.........23c
Any 2 for.............................43c
If by mail, postage extra, per volume, 8 cents.

Bible for Young People.

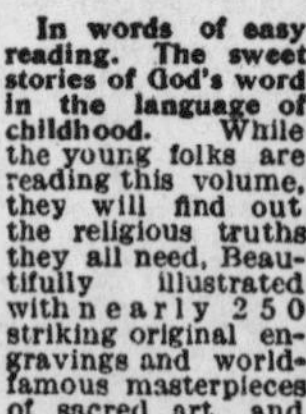

In words of easy reading. The sweet stories of God's word in the language of childhood. While the young folks are reading this volume, they will find out the religious truths they all need. Beautifully illustrated with nearly 250 striking original engravings and world-famous masterpieces of sacred art, and with magnificent colored plates. Complete in one sumptuous, massive, nearly square octavo volume, containing over 500 pages. Bound in cloth with beautiful cover design stamped on side and back in colors and gold. Size, 7½x9¼ inches.

No. 3F1789 Price..............65c
If by mail, postage extra, 30 cents.

Pilgrim's Progress.

By John Bunyan. Superfine illustrated edition with explanatory notes by Rev. Robert Macquire, D.D., together with a complete account of the life of John Bunyan, or God's Abounding Grace Toward the Greatest of Sinners, written by himself. Contain 130 beautiful engravings, 16 superbly tinted plates. 548 pages, marbled edges. Bound in blue cloth with attractive cover design. Title stamped on back and side in gold. Size, 7¼x10 inches.

No. 3F1791 Price..............75c
If by mail, postage extra, 25 cents.

Hurlbut's Story of the Bible.

Told for young and old by Rev. Jesse Lyman Hurlbut. Giving in simple language of today, in continuous form, the great truths and important facts of the English Bible. 168 stories, each complete in itself, forming a collective narrative of the Holy Scriptures. Profusely illustrated with 16 full page colored plates. Nearly 200 halftone engravings. Hurlbut's Story of the Bible is the most complete, the most sumptuously illustrated and the most beautiful story of the Bible ever issued and is of equal interest to old and young. Dr. Hurlbut facinates, instructs and entertains in this wonderful book. Contains 757 pages. Bound in cloth with elaborate cover design stamped in gold and colors on back and side. Size, 7x9½ inches. Retail price, $2.50.

No. 3F1793 Our price.......$1.28
If by mail, postage extra, 30 cents.

BOOKS OF ADVENTURE.

Wild Indians and Their Daring Deeds.

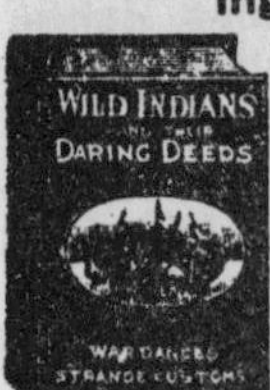

By Ellen Hines Stratton. A full account of their customs, traits of character, superstitions, modes of warfare, traditions, etc., including fantastic war dances, mysterious medicine men, desperate Indian braves, torture of prisoners, daring deeds, adventures of the chase, etc., together with thrilling incidents, bloody wars, strange marriage customs, famous chiefs, etc. Illustrated. Cloth. 500 pages. Size, 7½x9¼ inches.

No. 3F1800 Price..............68c
If by mail, postage extra, 26 cents.

Indian Horrors.

By H. D. Northrop. Startling descriptions of fantastic ghost dances; mysterious medicine men; desperate Indian braves; scalping of helpless settlers; burning their houses, etc. Illustrated with fine engravings printed in colors—battles, massacres, and other thrilling scenes among the Indians. Bound in cloth, marbled edges. Size, 6¼x8½ inches. 600 pages.

No. 3F1805 Price..............49c
If by mail, postage extra, 13 cents.

Brant and Red Jacket.

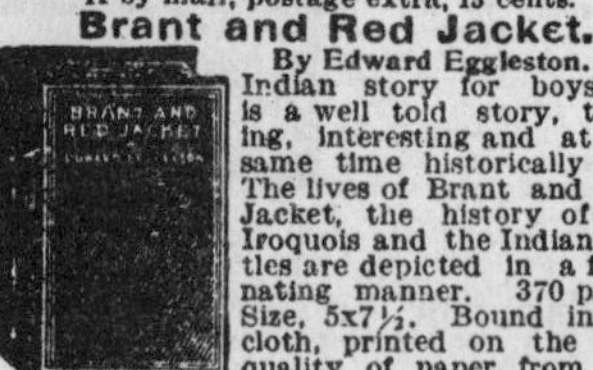

By Edward Eggleston. An Indian story for boys. It is a well told story, thrilling, interesting and at the same time historically true. The lives of Brant and Red Jacket, the history of the Iroquois and the Indian battles are depicted in a fascinating manner. 370 pages. Size, 5x7½. Bound in silk cloth, printed on the best quality of paper from new plates, with frontispiece engraving of Brant. Gilt top.

No. 3F1810 Price..............75c
If by mail, postage extra, 10 cents.

With Rogers on the Frontier.

A story of 1756, by J. Macdonald Oxley, B. A., with four full page illustrations. A stirring story of war and adventure, dealing with the French and English wars; wars with the Indians, massacres, brave deeds of the frontiersmen. A book that will interest and make the heart of every true American boy beat fast. Contains 353 pages. Printed on best quality of paper. Bound in green silk cloth, with attractive cover design in colors. Size, 5¼x7¼ inches. Retail price, $1.50.

No. 3F1811 Our price..........58c
If by mail, postage extra, 10 cents.

Calkins' Tales of the West.

By Frank W. Calkins, Exciting frontier sketches, Indian tales, and hunting stories. The most interesting tales of narrow escapes, brave deeds and strategy ever published. Every story is well told. For the boy who likes adventure and brave deeds there is no book that we can more highly recommend. Contains 403 pages with numerous illustrations. Bound in cloth, stamped with attractive cover design. Size, 6x9 inches. Retail price, $1.00.

No. 3F1812 Our price..........45c
If by mail, postage extra, 15 cents.

Deeds of Daring.

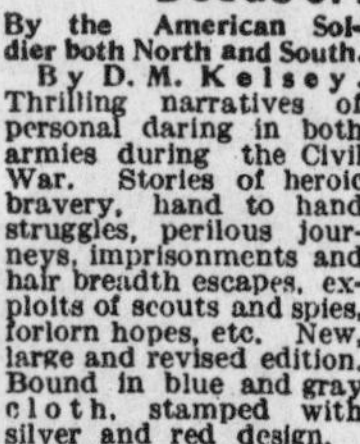

By the American Soldier both North and South. By D. M. Kelsey. Thrilling narratives of personal daring in both armies during the Civil War. Stories of heroic bravery, hand to hand struggles, perilous journeys, imprisonments and hair breadth escapes, exploits of scouts and spies, forlorn hopes, etc. New, large and revised edition. Bound in blue and gray cloth, stamped with silver and red design. Contains 672 pages. 61 different, complete stories. Profusely illustrated. Size, 9¼x6½ inches. Retail price, $1.50.

No. 3F1813 Our price..........85c
If by mail, postage extra, 30 cents.

Marching Through Georgia.

By E. Y. Headley Being pen pictures of everyday life in General Sherman's Army, from the beginning of the Atlanta Campaign to the close of the war. Introduction by Charles Walter Brown, A. M. Illustrations by F. L. Stoddard. Dedicated by permission to Mrs. John A. Logan. Autograph letter from General Sherman. 500 pages bound in cloth with cover design in colors. Retail price, $1.00. Size, 6x9 inches.

No. 3F1814 Our price..........48c
If by mail, postage extra, 18 cents.

The Adventures of Buffalo Bill.

By Col. W. F. Cody. Buffalo Bill (Col. Cody), for years one of the best loved heroes of boys, here writes of his actual adventures, scouting on the plains and fighting with the Indians. An absorbingly interesting book for boys which possesses the additional merit of being true. 156 pages. Size, 5x7 inches. Bound in cloth.

No. 3F1820 Price..............48c
If by mail, postage extra, 9 cents.

History of Our Wild West.

A record of exciting events on the western borders, massacres, desperate battles, extraordinary bravery, grand hunts, adventures by flood and field, curious escapes, etc., and the melange of incidents that make up the melodramas of civilization in the march over mountains and prairies to the Pacific. A history of Boone, Crockett, Carson, Buffalo Bill and others. 766 pages. 250 illustrations. Cloth. Size, 7x9 inches.

No. 3F1815 Price..............45c
If by mail, postage extra, 20 cents.

Story of the Wild West.

By Buffalo Bill (Hon. W. F. Cody). A full and complete history of the renowned pioneer and buffalo hunter by himself. Replete with graphic descriptions of wild life and thrilling adventures by famous heroes of the frontier. A record of exciting events on the western borders. 760 pages. 250 illustrations. Cloth. Size, 7x9 inches.

No. 3F1825
Price..............56c
If by mail, postage extra, 26 cents.

Our Western Border.

By Charles McKnight. Contains a true account of western border life and struggles and thrilling narratives of daring deeds and marvelous adventures of American pioneers more than a century ago, embracing desperate conflicts with the Indians, tales of captivity, stories of massacres, marvelous escapes, adventures of famous scouts, hunters, travels, pioneer women, brave boys and Indian chiefs of the early days in American history. Illustrated. Over 700 pages. Size, 6½x9 inches.

No. 3F1830 Price..............65c
If by mail, postage extra, 25 cents.

Famous Frontiersmen, Pioneers and Scouts.

By E. G. Cattermole. A thrilling narrative of the lives and marvelous exploits of the most renowned heroes, trappers, explorers, adventurers, scouts and Indian fighters, from Boone to Buffalo Bill, including Custer's Last Fight. 540 pages. Cloth. Size, 6x9 inches.

No. 3F1835
Price..............38c
If by mail, postage extra, 19 cents.

Daring Exploits of Scouts and Spies.

By Gen. Lafayette C. Baker. A graphic history of daring exploits, exciting experiences, perilous adventures, hair breadth escapes and valuable services rendered by the secret service bureau of the United States army. Full account of the origin and organization of that department and its scouts, spies and heroes. 400 pages. Illustrated. Bound in cloth, attractive cover design in colors. Size, 6½x9 inches. Retail price, $1.50.

No. 3F1837 Our price..........48c
If by mail, postage extra, 14 cents.

Cowboy Life in Texas.

A realistic and true recital of wild life on the boundless plains of Texas. The extraordinary experience of twenty-seven years of the exciting life of a genuine cowboy among the roughs and toughs of Texas. Fully illustrated. Contains 290 pages. Cloth. Size, 5¼x7¼ inches.

No. 3F1840
Price..............39c
By mail, postage extra, 12c.

Pioneer Heroes and Daring Deeds.

By D. M. Kelsey. Thrilling experiences and daring deeds of the Wild West. Lives and the famous exploits of Boone, Crockett, Custer, Buffalo Bill, Sitting Bull, General Miles and other hero explorers. 542 pages. Over 150 illustrations. Size, 6x9 inches. 2 inches thick. Retail price, $1.50.

No. 3F1842
Our price.......48c
If by mail, postage extra, 18 cents.

The Blue and the Gray.

Or, the Civil War, as Seen by a Boy. A true story of camp life, daring adventure, footsore marching, heartrending battles. It tells of battle scenes, of farewell requests, hair breadth escapes, the picket charges, rough rides, death and destruction on the battlefield, etc. Illustrated with 150 war photographs. Cloth. Size, 7½x9½ inches.

No. 3F1850
Price..............65c
If by mail, postage extra, 18 cents.

The Boys of '61.

By Charles Carlton Coffin. "The Boys of '61; or, Four Years of Fighting." Written in an absolutely impartial spirit, interesting alike to North and South. A book to make real the scenes of the mighty struggle. This famous war story is written from personal observation with the Army and Navy, from the first Battle of Bull Run to the Fall of Richmond. Entirely new edition containing 180 illustrations; printed on the finest grade of plate paper. This is, without doubt, the best and most interesting story of the Civil War for young and old ever written. This book is finely gotten up for library or for presentation, and no expense has been spared in making it as beautiful as possible. Contains 572 pages, bound with silk cloth, with attractive cover, stamped in white, blue and gold. Size, 7x9¼ inches. Retail price, $4.00.

No. 3F1852 Our price.........**$1.48**
If by mail, postage extra, 22 cents.

Camp Fire Stories.

By Edward Anderson. This is a collection of short stories about the Civil War, telling in an interesting and vivid manner the various scenes in army life. It portrays in glowing words fun and pathos, the drama and the tragedy, as well as everyday scenes of soldier life in camp and on the battlefield, on the march, etc. Illustrated. Cloth. Gilt top. Size, 5½x7¾ inches.

No. 3F1865 Price.............**48c**
If by mail, postage extra, 13 cents.

The Gallant Deeds of Our Naval Heroes.

By Charles Morris, LL.D. A thrilling story of America's Navy, including the adventures of Captain Paul Jones, Commodore Perry, Commodore Decatur, Admiral Farragut, Admiral Dewey and many others of America's brave sailors. Also a story of the ships made famous by great battles, and great captains. 100 beautiful illustrations, 3 color plates, and every page illustrated with two-inch ornamental border depicting naval scenes, at top and side. 256 pages, bound in cloth. Size, 7¼x9¾ inches. Retail price, $1.50.

No. 3F1867 Our price...........**39c**
If by mail, postage extra, 14 cents.

Thrilling Stories of the War.

By Returned Heroes. Contains vivid accounts of personal experiences by officers and men. Daring deeds of our brave regulars and volunteers at Santiago, in Porto Rico and the Philippine Islands. Admiral Dewey's report of the famous naval battle at Manila. Graphic account by Admiral Schley of the naval battle at Santiago. Glowing descriptions of the battles by the officers of the vessels engaged, etc., Contains also a collection of war poetry. 766 pages, profusely illustrated. Frontispiece in colors. Bound in cloth, marbled edges. Size, 7x9¼ inches. Retail price, $2.00

No. 3F1869 Our price..........**65c**
If by mail, postage extra, 20 cents.

Heroes of History.

By Henry Davenport Northrop. "Heroes of History and Their Grand Achievements" is a graphic account of men and women whose daring deeds have given them world wide fame. Comprising heroes of land and sea, including pioneers and their thrilling adventures; explorers in the tropics and polar regions; heroines of the battlefield and hospital; life savers on our tempestuous coasts. This great work should have a place in every American home. 600 large pages, embellished with hundreds of superb phototype and line engravings. Presentation frontispiece. Bound in fine cloth. Attractive design; marbled edges. Size, 7½x10 inches. Retail price, $2.50.

No. 3F1871 Our price.............**98c**
If by mail, postage extra, 30 cents.

Careers of Danger and Daring.

By Cleveland Moffett. Profusely illustrated with full page illustrations and drawings. It describes the steeple climbers, the deep sea divers, the bridge builder, the city fireman, the wild beast tamer, the locomotive engineer, etc. Printed on the very finest quality of paper, containing 419 pages. Not only intensely interesting, but practical and instructive. Size, 5¼x7½ inches.

No. 3F1873 Price...........**$1.18**
If by mail, postage extra, 13 cents.

BOOKS OF TRAVEL.

A Journey Around the World With Prof. Glee.

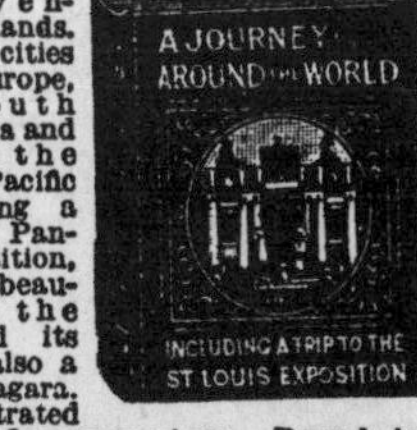

Interesting adventures in many islands. Visiting famous cities and places of Europe, Asia, Africa, South America, Australia and many islands of the Atlantic and Pacific Oceans, including a week at the Pan-American Exposition, describing the beautiful buildings, the midway, and its strange shows, also a side trip to Niagara. Profusely illustrated with nearly 200 fine engravings. Bound in silk cloth. 450 pages. Size, 7½x9¾ inches. Retail price, $2.00.

No. 3F2001 Our price...........**63c**
If by mail, postage extra, 22 cents.

Glimpses of the World.

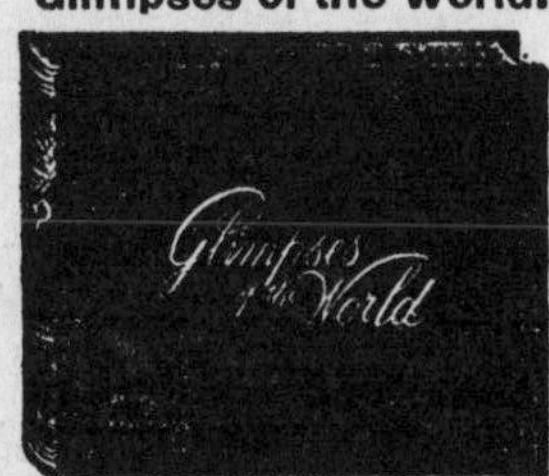

By John L. Stoddard. Contains hundreds of full page halftone views of scenes all over the world, selected by the traveler and lecturer, John L. Stoddard. Each picture is fully described by him in graphic language. Only one side of each leaf is used. 550 pages. Paper of the richest and highest quality. Size, 11x14 inches.

No. 3F2006 Glimpses of the World. Bound in buckram, stamped in silver. Retail price, $5.00; our price...........**$1.75**
Weight, packed for shipment, 9 pounds.

No. 3F2007 Glimpses of the World. Bound in full morocco, gold stamping, gilt edges. Retail price, $8.00; our price..**$3.45**
Weight, packed for shipment, 9 pounds.

Around the World on $60.00.

By Robert Meredith. A most interesting and humorous account of a man's trip around the world, traveling on his wits and a very slim purse. As entertaining as any novel. It gives a full description of the lands visited, and thousands of facts in regard to customs and habits of the people. The author started from Oscaloosa, Iowa, with only $60. Read this book and find out how he got around the world. Bound in cloth. 372 pages. Size, 6¼x8 inches. Retail price, $1.50.

No. 3F2011 Our price..........**48c**
If by mail, postage extra, 14 cents.

Explorations and Adventures of Henry M. Stanley.

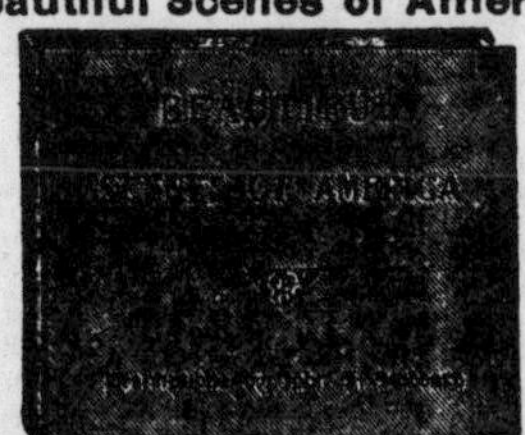

Thrilling accounts of famous expeditions, miraculous escapes, and wonderful discoveries, in the wilds of Africa. A thrilling narrative of this remarkable adventurer's terrible experiences in the Dark Continent. His explorations of the Congo, the relief of Emin Bey, with its terrible experiences of slavery, misery and death are told in the most graphic manner. Contains also the explorations and adventures of other world renowned travelers, including Livingstone, Du Chaillu, Anderson, etc. 848 pages, with 200 striking illustrations. Bound in cloth, with beautiful cover design. Printed on fine quality of paper. Size, 6¾x9 inches. Marble edges. Retail price, $2.00.

No. 3F2014 Our price...........**65c**
If by mail, postage extra, 22 cents.

Beautiful Scenes of America.

From Battery Park to the Golden Gate. Described by the famous traveler and lecturer, John L. Stoddard. The pictures include mountain and river scenery, characteristic city scenes, monuments, battlefields, colleges, statues, wonderful bridges, etc. Contains 256 photographs with appropriate descriptions under each. Bound in cloth with stamped cover. Size, 11x14 inches. Retail price, $2.00.

No. 3F2021 Our price...........**65c**
If by mail, postage extra, 20 cents.

Travels in the East;

Or, China and Japan. By Henry Davenport Northrop. Complete history, manners, customs and peculiarities of the people; superstitions; idol worship; industries; full description of their cities; modes of travel; natural scenery, birds, animals, etc. Profusely illustrated with many superb illustrations and printed on the best quality of book paper. New plates. Bound in pearl gray cloth with cover design stamped in gold and black. 512 pages. Size, 8x10 inches. Presentation frontispiece. Retail price, $2.50.

No. 3F2024 Our price...........**85c**
If by mail, postage extra, 28 cents.

The Land of Christ.

A series of magnificent illustrations, showing the country in which Christ was born, where he labored and was crucified. Comprising pictures of all the principal cities and villages which he made memorable. 320 photographic halftone views, with descriptive text under each. Printed on best grade coated paper, bound in cloth. Size, 11x14 inches. Retail price, $2.50.

No. 3F2028 Our price..........**95c**
If by mail, postage extra, 28 cents.

Lost in the Jungle.

By Paul Du Chaillu. An absorbingly interesting story of travel through the wilds of Central Africa, by the celebrated explorer. It graphically describes his perilous adventures and his hairbreadth escapes. No other white man ever penetrated into the wilds of Africa as did Du Chaillu. Superbly illustrated. Bound in best quality of silk cloth. 260 pages. Size, 5½x7½ inches. Retail price, $1.50.

No. 3F2035 Our price.........**98c**
If by mail, postage extra, 12 cents.

A Tour Through Northern Europe.

The famous cities, parks, buildings, palaces, etc., as seen and described by John L. Stoddard. A rare and elaborate collection of 130 halftone photographic views, with descriptive text under each. Includes England, Ireland, France, Germany, Norway, Sweden, Denmark, Holland, Belgium, Austria, etc. Only one side of each leaf is used. Paper of the richest and highest quality. Bound in cloth. Size, 11x14 inches. Retail price, $2.00.

No. 3F2040 Our price.........**98c**
Weight, packed for shipment, 6 pounds.

BEAUTIFULLY BOUND BOOKS FOR GIFTS.

Padded Leather Gift Books.

As gifts these padded leather books cannot be equaled. They are handsomely bound in embossed seal leather and have a beautiful title page. Red under gold edges, round corners, with silk ribbon bookmark. Size 4½x6½ inches. 175 to 280 pages.

Abbe Constantin. Ludovic Halevy
Autocrat of the Breakfast Table. Oliver W. Holmes
Beside the Bonnie Brier Bush. Ian Maclaren
Black Beauty. Anna Sewell
Black Rock. Ralph Connor
Browning's Poems. Robert Browning
Browning's Poems. Mrs. Browning
Bryant's Poems. William Cullen Bryant
Burns' Poems. Robert Burns
Courtship of Miles Standish. Henry W. Longfellow
Cranford. Mrs. Gaskell
Dickens' Short Stories. Chas. Dickens
Dream Life. Ik Marvel
Drummond's Addresses. Henry Drummond
Elizabeth and Her German Garden. Countess von Armin
Emerson's Essays. Ralph W. Emerson
Emerson's Poems. Ralph W. Emerson
Evangeline. Henry W. Longfellow
Favorite Poems. St. Elmo
Grandfather's Chair. Nathaniel Hawthorne
Hiawatha. Henry W. Longfellow
Holmes' Poems. Oliver W. Holmes
House of the Seven Gables. Nathaniel Hawthorne
Idle Thoughts of an Idle Fellow. Jerome K. Jerome
Imitation of Christ, On the. Thomas A Kempis
In His Steps. Chas. Sheldon
In Memoriam. Tennyson

John Halifax. Dinah Mulock (Craik)
Kept for the Master's Use. Frances R. Havergal
Lady of the Lake. Sir Walter Scott
Lalla Rookh. Thomas Moore
Longfellow's Poems. Henry W. Longfellow
Lorna Doone. R. D. Blackmore
Lowell's Poems. James R. Lowell
Lucile. Owen Meredith
Milton's Poems. John Milton
Paradise Lost. John Milton
Pilgrims' Progress. John Bunyan
Poe's Poems. Edgar Allen Poe
Princess, The. Alfred Lord Tennyson
Prince of the House of David. Rev. J. H. Ingraham
Prue and I. Geo. W. Curtis
Rab and His Friends. John Brown
Reveries of a Bachelor. Ik Marvel
Rubaiyat of Omar Khayyam. Edward Fitzgerald
Scarlet Letter, The. Nathaniel Hawthorne
Sesame and Lilies. John Ruskin
Simple Life. Chas. Wagner
Sketch Book. Washington Irving
Songs and Ballads of the American Revolution
Stepping Heavenward. Prentiss
Tales from Shakespeare. Lamb
Tanglewood Tales. Nathaniel Hawthorne
Ten Nights in a Bar Room. T. S. Arthur
Tennyson's Poems. Alfred Tennyson
Twice Told Tales. Hawthorne
Uncle Tom's Cabin. Harriet Beecher Stowe
Vicar of Wakefield, The. Oliver Goldsmith
Whittier's Poems. John G. Whittier
Wonder Book. Hawthorne

No. 3F2700 Price, boxed, per vol..**48c**
Any 6 for **$2.70**; any 2 for.........**93c**
If by mail, postage extra, per vol., 7 cents.

The Jewel Series.

A series of exquisite little volumes containing selected poems from the works of our most noted authors. Beautifully printed in tint on enameled paper, with marginal illustrations, together with a colored portrait and eleven elegant full page colored plates of floral designs, done in finest lithography. Bound in white satinette, covers padded and illuminated with appropriate designs in gold and colors. Tinted edges. In neat box. Size 5¼x7¼ inches.

Diamonds from Sir Walter Scott — **Pearls from John G. Whittier**
Emeralds from Thomas Moore — **Rubies from Lord Byron**
Opals from Oliver Wendell Holmes — **Sapphires from Robert Burns**

No 3F2720 Price, set of 6, **$1.58**; any 2 for **59c**; per vol..**32c**
If by mail, postage extra, per vol., 5 cents.

Padded Marbled Leather Edition of the Poets.

The handsomest padded edition ever made. The books are extra large, 5¼x7¾ inches, printed on excellent quality of paper with red under burnished gold edges. Bound in padded marbled leather (the most beautiful binding you ever saw), with title stamped in gold, also delicate flower in gold in one corner. These books average between 300 and 400 pages each. Retail price, $1.50.

Browning, Mrs.	**Holmes, Oliver Wendell**
Browning, Robert	**Keats**
Bryant	**Kipling, Rudyard**
Burns	**Longfellow**
Byron	**Love Poems**
Dante	**Lowell**
Emerson, Ralph Waldo	**Meredith**
Favorite Poems	**Milton**
Goethe	**Moore**
Golden Leaves from the American Poets	**Poe, Edgar Allen**
	Pope
Golden Leaves from the British Poets	**Proctor**
	Schiller
Golden Leaves from the Dramatic Poets	**Scott**
	Shakespeare
Golden Leaves from the English Poets	**Tennyson**
	Whittier
Goldsmith	**Wordsworth**

No. 3F2705 Our price, per vol..**$0.69**
Any 6 for **$3.78**; any 2 for.....**1.33**
If by mail, postage extra, per vol., 10 cents.

American Authors' Gems.

Beautiful gift books, of 36 pages each, 18 of which are printed in full colors and gold, and contain extracts from famous authors for every day in the month. Bound in moire antique silk, padded. Size, 5¼x6¼ inches.

Gems from Bryant
Gems from Emerson
Gems from Holmes
Gems from Lowell
Gems from Riley
Gems from Whittier

No. 3F2710 Price, boxed, per volume **$0.28**
Any 2 for.........**.53**
Set of 6 books.......**1.49**
If by mail, postage extra, per vol., 5 cents.

GIFT BOOKS—Continued.

Decorated Gift Books.

The most beautifully artistic books ever made. Originally published by Macmillan & Co., at $1.50. There is a decoration on every page and numerous full page decorations in the quaint old fashioned style. These, together with the dainty text, make a gift book that will be appreciated by all lovers of the beautiful in poetry and art. Bound in cloth.

No. 3F2735 Book of Old English Love Songs. With an introduction by Hamilton Wright Mabie, and decorative drawings. Size, 5¼x7¾ inches. Price......49c
If by mail, postage extra, 10 cents.

No. 3F2736 Book of Old English Ballads. With introduction by Hamilton Wright Mabie, and descriptive drawings. Size, 5¼x7¾ inches. Price......49c
If by mail, postage extra, 10 cents.

This Is for You.

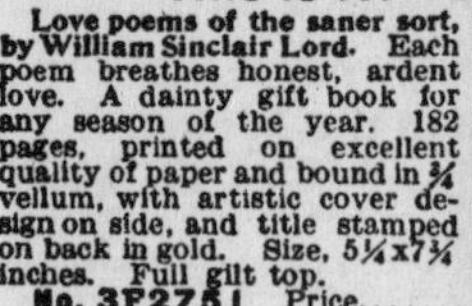

Love poems of the saner sort, by William Sinclair Lord. Each poem breathes honest, ardent love. A dainty gift book for any season of the year. 182 pages, printed on excellent quality of paper and bound in ¾ vellum, with artistic cover design on side, and title stamped on back in gold. Size, 5¼x7¾ inches. Full gilt top.

No. 3F2751 Price......78c
If by mail, postage extra, 9 cents.

To Comfort You.

Poems of Comfort, selected by Ella W. Peattie. A selection of the best poems of comfort. Bound and put up same as "This is for You."

No. 3F2752 Price......78c
If by mail, postage extra, 9 cents.

Because I Love You.

A choice collection of love poems, edited by Anna E. Mack. For sweetheart or friend. What lover is there who will not welcome the beautiful little white and gold volume of love verses under the satisfied title, "Because I Love You"? Love is ever an excuse for right or wrong doing, but in this case the result is so beautiful that no excuse is needed. Bound in ivory white cloth, with title stamped on back and side and appropriate design in gold. Size, 5x7¾ inches. Full gilt top, deckled edge. 228 pages. Each book in slip case.

No. 3F2770 Price......98c
If by mail, postage extra, 10 cents.

Our Wedding Record.

Eight full page colored plates and all the other pages elaborately decorated with appropriate and attractive designs. Has place for bride and groom's portrait, marriage record, description of dress, date of engagement, presents, list of guests, bridesmaids, etc. Size, 5⅜x6⅞ inches. Bound in finest quality of white cloth, heavily padded, with orange blossoms in colors on cover. Words, "Our Wedding Record," stamped in gold. Retail price, $1.50.

No. 3F2831 Our price......65c
If by mail, postage extra, 8 cents.

Bridal Souvenir.

One of the handsomest bride's books made. Has eleven full page illustrations in colors. Bound in the finest quality of ivory white cloth, padded sides, with spray of orange blossoms stamped on cover, with words, "Bridal Souvenir," in gold. Full gold edges. Every page elaborately decorated with scroll work. Contents same as No. 3F2831, but enlarged. Size, 6½x7¾ inches. Retail price, $2.00.

No. 3F2832 Our price......98c
If by mail, postage extra, 8 cents.

Record of Our Baby.

Has eight full page illustrations in colors and numerous other illustrations on every page. A record of birth, weight, christening day, photographs, first Christmas, first tooth, learning to walk, etc., all accompanied by appropriate verses and illustrations. Bound in white cloth with padded cover design of flowers stamped in colors and words, "Record of Our Baby," in gold. Size, 5⅜x6⅞ inches.

No. 3F2841 Price......65c
If by mail, postage extra, 7 cents.

Our Baby's History.

One of the most beautiful baby books ever made. Made of the finest quality of silk cloth, heavily padded, with violet design stamped in colors and gold on cover, and words, "Our Baby's History," stamped in gold. Full gold edges top, side and bottom. 11 full page illustrations of babies. Numerous other illustrations with appropriate verses. Contents same as No. 3F2841, but enlarged. Size, 6½x7¾ inches.

No. 3F2842 Price......98c
If by mail, postage extra, 7 cents.

The Sands of Time.

Compiled by Thomas W. Hanford. A book of birthday gems, containing a sentiment and a proverb for each day in the year. Selected from the works of 150 different authors. With blank spaces for autographs. Superbly illustrated with thirteen full page engravings. Printed on calendered paper. Cloth, stamped in colors. Size, 4x5½ inches. Retail price, $1.00.

No. 3F2860 Our price......53c
If by mail, postage extra, 11 cents.

Unique Birthday Books.

An entirely new idea in Birthday Books, each containing 96 pages, 12 of which are full page colored pictures. Each page contains quotations from the authors. Bound in moire antique silk, padded covers. Size, 4¼x4⅞ inches. State which book wanted.

Bible Birthday Books		
Dickens	Longfellow	Tennyson
Havergal	Shakespeare	

No. 3F2865 Price, per volume......28c
Any 2 for......53c
If by mail, postage extra, per volume, 5 cents.

The Heart of a Boy.

By Edmondo de Amicis. Beautiful holiday edition of this famous book that is loved and admired the world over. This is a book that is for young as well as old. A book that can never become old fashioned. There are few finer things in the world's literature. De luxe edition. Contains 290 pages with 32 full page halftones and 26 smaller ones. Bound in red silk cloth with full gilt top. Size, 6¼x8½ inches. Each book in a box. Retail price, $1.25.

No. 3F2870 Our price......78c
If by mail, postage extra, 22 cents.

Love Sonnets of an Office Boy.

By S. E. Kiser, the well known humorist. Illustrated with 12 drawings by John T. McCutcheon, of the Chicago Tribune. These sonnets will prove a source of joy to all people with a true sense of humor. They are irresistibly funny, delightfully humorous, side splitting and a joy forever. Bound in boards with original cover design. Size, 4¾x6¼ inches.

No. 3F2876 Price......39c
If by mail, postage extra, 3 cents.

Illustrated Devotional Series.

Daintily and durably bound in handy volume size, illuminated title page. Bound in full vellum, elaborately stamped in gold. Each volume with waxed paper jackets and in slip case. Size, 2½x3¼ inches. State which volume wanted. Regular retail price, 50 cents.

- Abide in Christ. Murray
- Beecher's Addresses
- Best Thoughts. From Henry Drummond
- Bible Birthday Book
- Brooks' Addresses
- Buy Your Own Cherries. Kirton
- Changed Cross, The
- Christian Life. Oxenden
- Christian Living. Meyer
- Coming to Christ. Havergal
- Daily Food for Christians
- Drummond's Addresses
- Evening Thoughts. Havergal
- Gold Dust

No. 3F2878 Illustrated Devotional Series. Our price, per volume......24c
Any 2 for......45c
If by mail, postage extra, per volume, 2 cents.

Imitation of Christ.

By Thomas a Kempis. This famous book has been gotten up in entirely new gift edition in a volume size. Printed on best quality of paper. Contains 285 pages, large, clear type. Bound in cloth, with attractive ascension lily cover design stamped in white. Title on side and back. Size, 3¾x5½ inches.

No. 3F2882 Price......32c
If by mail, postage extra, 5 cents.

The Words and Mind of Jesus and the Faithful Promiser.

By Rev. J. R. McDuff, D.D. This well known book has been gotten up as a companion to Imitation of Christ, described above, in same size and style.

No. 3F2884 Price......32c
If by mail, postage extra, 5 cents.

Immortality.

By Joseph Jefferson, the famous actor. A charming poem, concerning the after life, written by the great actor a short time before his death. A handsome souvenir book, attractively decorated by H. H. Bennett. Fancy border pictures on each page in an artistic and most charming style, with beautiful emblematic cover design of ascension lilies, on pebbled cloth. A book you will want to give to your friends, and want them to give to you. Size, 5¼x7½ inches. Boxed in individual boxes.

No. 3F2886 Price......75c
If by mail, postage extra, 7 cents.

Dore Illustrated Masterpieces.

These are the original celebrated poems of Dante and Milton, embellished with beautiful reproductions in halftone illustrations of the celebrated Dore paintings that hang in the famous European art galleries. The poems are translated by the Rev. Henry Francis Cary. Cloth. Size, 9½x11¾ inches. State which volume wanted.

Bible Gallery	Parade Lost
Inferno, Visions of Hell	Purgatory and Paradise

No. 3F2890 Price, per volume...82c
If by mail, postage extra, per volume, 30 cents.

Christmas in Manyland Series.

A dainty series of "Tales of Christmastide" from the literature of many nations. In this new series each volume consists of a charming Christmas story typical of some particular country people. Attractively written, and abound in those little touches of pathos and humor suited to such literature. Printed on heavy plate paper, copiously and beautifully illustrated from original drawings, in tints, set into the text. Delicately bound in white vellum cloth, with appropriate, beautifully colored inlay on cover. Size, 5¾x7⅝ inches. State which volume wanted.

- **Dulce's Promise.** Christmas in England.
- **Jean Noel.** Christmas in France.
- **Lischen and the Fairy.** Christmas in Germany.
- **Round the Yule Log.** Christmas in Norway.
- **The Forest Fairy.** Christmas in Switzerland.
- **The Little Musician.** Christmas in Italy.
- **The Parson's Miracle.** Christmas in America.

No. 3F2892 Price, per volume..$0.30
Any 2 for......55
Entire set, 7 volumes, boxed......1.78
If by mail, postage extra, per volume, 4 cents.

Twelve Gift Booklets for 38c.

These beautiful little Booklets are suitable for all occasions. Made with beautifully embossed covers, with richly colored flower designs, containing eight pages. Tied with silk cord and tassel, in assorted colors. Size, 3x3¾ inches. Each package contains six religious and six secular booklets. Suitable for gifts on all occasions. Each package contains 12 envelopes for mailing the booklets.

No. 3F2905 Price, per package (12 booklets and 12 envelopes)......38c
Price, for 2 packages (24 booklets and 24 envelopes)......69c
If by mail, postage extra, per package, 3 cents.

Six Art Gem Booklets, 28c.

These beautiful little Booklets are made with handsomely colored and embossed covers, in assorted landscapes and flower designs, and each contains eight pages of appropriate verses, beautifully printed. Tied with silk cord and tassel. They are suitable for gifts on any occasion and in any season. Each package contains 6 booklets, all different. Each booklet with envelope, for mailing. Size, 3x5 inches.

No. 3F2910 Price, per package (6 booklets and 6 envelopes)......28c
Price, for 2 packages (12 booklets and 12 envelopes)......50c
If by mail, postage extra, per package, 2 cents.

Religious Gift Booklets, 14 Cents Each.

These beautiful Booklets are made with fancy covers, embossed in gold and colors of various designs, flowers and landscapes, and each booklet contains five richly colored illustrations. Size, 4¾x6½ inches. State which volume wanted. Furnished in six different titles, as follows:

- Bright Leaves
- Faithful Promise
- He Leadeth Me
- In His Keeping
- Lead, Kindly Light
- Psalm of Life

No. 3F2915 Religious Booklets, in any of the above titles, complete, with mailing envelope. Price, any 2 for 25c; each, 14c
Price, for the entire set of 6, complete with mailing envelopes......69c
If by mail, postage extra, each, 2 cents.

Twenty-five Imported Christmas Cards 15 Cents.

Beautifully colored designs, including landscapes, flowers, etc., varying in size from 2¼x3½ to 2¾x3⅞ inches.

No. 3F2930 Price, 2 packages (50 cards), 28c; per package (25 cards) for 15c
4 packages (100 cards) for......50c
If by mail, postage extra, per package, 2 cents.

Twenty-four Handsome Christmas Cards, 18 Cents.

Assorted designs and shapes; beautiful colors; many of them handsomely embossed and all with appropriate Holiday Greetings. Average size, 3¼x4⅜ inches.

No. 3F2932 Price, 4 packages (48 cards) for 35c; 2 packages (24 cards) for 18c
If by mail, postage extra, per package, 2 cents.

Twelve Embossed Christmas Cards 19 Cents.

Large size, 3½x5½ inches, beautifully colored embossed designs, representing flowers, landscapes, children, etc.; all with appropriate Holiday Greetings. Genuine imported cards.

No. 3F2934 Price, per package (12 cards)......19c
2 packages (24 cards) for......35c
4 packages (48 cards) for......65c
If by mail, postage extra, per package, 2 cents.

Twelve Folding, Beautifully Embossed, Christmas Cards with Envelopes, 30 Cents.

Assorted designs, including flowers, birds, children landscapes, etc.; all with handsomely lettered Christmas Greetings on the inside. Average size, 3¼x4 inches.

No. 3F2936 Price, per package (12 cards and 12 envelopes)......30c
Price, for 2 packages (24 cards and 24 envelopes)......55c
Price, for 4 packages (48 cards and 48 envelopes)......98c
If by mail, postage extra, per package, 3 cents.

Six Folding Christmas and New Year's Cards, 23 Cents.

Beautifully embossed designs of flowers, richly colored, each card with verse on the inside and appropriate Christmas or New Year's Greeting. Average size, 4x5½ inches; each card with envelope.

No. 3F2938 Price, per package (6 cards and 6 envelopes)......23c
Price, for 2 packages (12 cards and 12 envelopes)......43c
Price, for 4 packages (24 cards and 24 envelopes)......80c
If by mail, postage extra, per package, 3 cents.

POETRY

Library of Poets.

Including the most popular English and American poets. Nothing is as pleasant to read and nothing more beautiful than poetry.

Arnold (Matthew)
Browning (Mrs.)
Browning (Robert)
Bryant
Burns
Byron
Cary's Poems
Chaucer
Courtship of Miles Standish
Dante
Dryden
Eliot
Emerson
Goethe's Poems
Goldsmith
Hemans
Holmes
Hood
Keats
Longfellow
Lowell
Lucile
Milton
Moore
Poe
Pope
Rubaiyat
Schiller
Scott
Shakespeare's Poems
Shelley
Swinburne
Tennyson
Virgil
Wordsworth.
Whittier

No. 3F3015 Library of Poets' Series; titles as listed above. Printed from new, large type plates on good quality paper and bound in cloth with title stamped on back in gold. A very sensible and satisfactory edition. Size, 5¼x7½ inches. Price, each..**32c**
Any 2 for........................**59c**
If by mail, postage extra, each, 10 cents.

No. 3F3016 Gilt Edge Edition, Library of Poets; titles as listed above. Printed on fine quality of paper with full gilt edges, top, side and bottom. Bound in green silk cloth with design in gold on back and side, making a beautiful library or gift edition. Each book contains a sketch of the author and photogravure frontispiece. Size, 5¼x7¼ inches.
Price, any 2 for **$1.18**; each..........**64c**
If by mail, postage extra, each, 12 cents.

Standard One Volume Edition of the Poets.

This edition is put up in an unusually attractive manner. Printed in double column on excellent quality of paper, and bound in cloth with ornamental cover design and lettering. Size, 7¼x10 inches. Regular retail price, $2.00 each.

Complete Poetical Works of William Wordsworth Illustrated.
Poetical Works of Robert Burns. Illustrated.
Poetical Works of Lord Byron. Illustrated.
Poetical Works of Felicia Hemans. Illustrated.
Poetical Works of John Milton. With Life by Rev. John Mitford. Illustrated.
Poetical Works of Thomas Moore. Illustrated.
Poetical Works of Alexander Pope. With Life by Dr. Johnson. Illustrated.
Poetical Works of Sir Walter Scott. Illustrated.
Poetical Works of Percy Bysshe Shelley. Illustrated.
Reliques of Ancient English Poetry. Collected by Thomas Percy, D. D. Illustrated.
Works of Samuel Taylor Coleridge.
Works of William Cowper and James Thomson. Illustrated.

No. 3F3020 Our price, each....**$0.85**
Any 2 for..........................**1.59**
If by mail, postage extra, each, 36 cents.

Works of Alfred Lord Tennyson.

The only complete and unabridged one-volume edition published. Contains all the later copyrighted poems and the Foresters. Heretofore published at $1.75. Macmillan & Co. own the copyright on some of Tennyson's works and are the only publishers who can publish a complete edition—no matter what other publishers say. This is the Macmillan edition, published by Grosset & Dunlap, and offered by us by special arrangement with them at a very low price. Size, 5¾x8 inches.

No. 3F3030 Price..............**59c**
If by mail, postage extra, 18 cents.

Ella Wheeler Wilcox's Poems.

The following books of Mrs. Wilcox are bound in cloth and contain her complete and best known works. Size, 5x7 inches.

Erring Woman's Love
Kingdom of Love
Maurine
Men, Women and Emotions
Poems of Passion
Poems of Pleasure
Poems of Power
Three Women

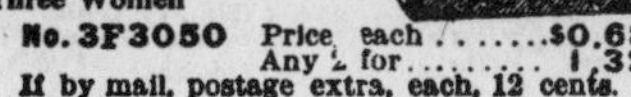

68c

No. 3F3050 Price, each.......**$0.68**
Any 2 for..........**1.32**
If by mail, postage extra, each, 12 cents.

Poems That Never Die.

Compiled and edited by Margaret M. Browning. Golden thoughts from the world's best authors, comprising poems on mother, home, heaven, the fireside, friendship, love, matrimony, sentiment, reflection, parting, absence, sorrow, religion, death, nature, patriotism, freedom, peace, war, labor, temperance, fancy, etc. An ideal gift book. Illustrated. Cloth, stamped in gold and colored inks. Size, 7x9½ inches.

No. 3F3055 Price..............**89c**
If by mail, postage extra, 24 cents.

Eugene Field's Poems.

Printed on excellent quality of paper; beautifully bound in cloth with unique design stamped on cover in four colors. Gold stamping. 12mo size.

The CLINK OF THE ICE and Other Poems. Including stories of inimitable wit and humor, with lullabies and sketches of everyday scenes that made the writer famous.

HOOSIER LYRICS. This is a series of pathetic, amusing and entertaining poems in Indiana dialect on notable Hoosier scenes, containing Eugene Field's parodies on many of James Whitcomb Riley's poems.

IN WINK-A-WAY LAND. Especially selected and arranged for the little folks.

JOHN SMITH, U. S. A. The romantic poetry-story of John Smith; also includes many other poems.

No. 3F3060 Eugene Field's Poems. Titles as listed and described above.
Price, each..........................**$0.39**
Price, for the complete set (4 vols.). **1.48**
If by mail, postage extra, per volume, 6 cents.

Works of James Whitcomb Riley.

Illustrated gift editions. He is a poet laureate of America. Our Hoosier poet. What he has said of the common aspects of life have endeared him. These books are printed on the finest quality of paper, elaborately illustrated with full page engravings and pen and ink drawings. Bound in green silk cloth with individual cover design stamped in colors and gold. Size, 5½x8 inches. Each volume has about 200 pages.

RILEY'S SONGS O' CHEER. With over 100 Hoosier pictures in colors and black and white, by Will Vawter. A book to scatter smiles and laughter.

RILEY'S FARM RHYMES. With over 100 country pictures, by Will Vawter.

RILEY'S CHILD RHYMES. With over 100 Hoosier pictures, by Will Vawter. A collection of Riley's delightful songs of childhood and children.

RILEY'S LOVE LYRICS. With numerous illustrations by William Buckingham Dyer. Containing all the favorites of Mr. Riley's dainty, tender and loving poems.

No. 3F3065 James Whitcomb Riley's Books, any of above titles.
Price, each........................**$0.98**
Price, for the complete set (4 vols.). **3.75**
If by mail, postage extra, per volume, 8 cents.

Leaves of Grass.

By Walt Whitman. Each poem has been compared with previous editions and all changes in readings given in foot notes. Together with a department of "Gathered Leaves," being a collection of poems discarded from the earlier edition. Contains an autobiography in facsimile, and four portraits. Printed on excellent quality of paper. Bound in cloth with original cover design. Gilt top, uncut edges. Size, 5¾x8¼ inches.

No. 3F3070 Price..............**95c**
If by mail, postage extra, 14 cents.

The Man With the Hoe.

And other poems. By Edwin Markham. This book of poems, by the most famous of latter-day American poets, cannot fail to appeal to all lovers of beautiful poetry. Contains over 70 poems, printed on the best quality of paper and bound in silk cloth. Deckle edge. Green top. Title stamped on back and side in gold. Size, 5¼x7¾ inches.

No. 3F3072 Price..............**95c**
If by mail, postage extra, 6 cents.

War Poems.

Collected and arranged by J. H. Brownlee. Two handsome books; the first containing poems and prose relating to the Civil War; the second containing poems and prose of the Spanish-American War. Each volume has over 200 pages printed on excellent quality of paper, and bound in cloth with cover design stamped in gold and colors. Size, 5½x7¾ inches.

Marshall Recitations. Pathetic and humorous, for the veteran's camp fire.

War Time Echoes. Patriotic poems, heroic and pathetic, humorous and dialectic, of the Spanish-American War.

No. 3F3075 War Poems. Either of above titles. Price per volume.........**48c**
2 volumes for..................................**89c**
If by mail, postage extra, per volume, 11 cents

The International Book of Song.

Sweet Melodies for the Home. The choicest selections from the greatest masters and composers, including all the popular favorites, whose music is perennial pathos, love, humor, religion, patriotism and national songs. Music for the family circle, school and all private and public occasions. Beautifully illustrated with portraits of eminent composers of song, with interesting biographies. Contains both words and music for every song, 440 pages. Bound in cloth, with photographic inlay and silver stamping on cover. Size, 7½x9¾ inches. Retail price, $1.50.

No. 3F3078 Our price..........**59c**
If by mail, postage extra, 22 cents.

The Song Lovers' Treasury.

A musical library of popular songs and music, for music lovers. Words and music to each song in sheet music size, 9¾x12 inches. Master pieces of both hemispheres with the choicest melodies and the most popular songs of the world's famous composers. Complete accompaniment for the piano or organ, to which is added a supplement of choice instrumental music. Profusely illustrated with numerous engravings. Printed on excellent quality of paper. Portraits and pictures and biographies of the most distinguished and popular musicians and composers. 320 pages. Retail price, $2.25. Size, 9¾x12 inches.

No. 3F3080 Our price..........**98c**
If by mail, postage extra, 30 cents.

Our Poets, their Portraits and Poems.

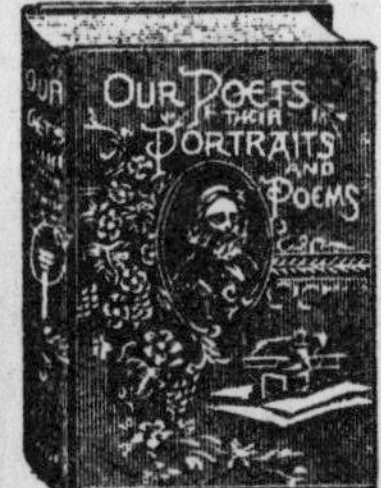

Poems we love, containing gems for the fireside, beautiful descriptions of scenes in nature, poems of love and friendship, pathos and religion, lyrics of patriotism, heroism and adventure, etc., including jewels of sentiment and reflection. Gems of wit, humor, and tragedy, childhood and youth. Pictures of the sea, rural life, etc. This is a vast treasury of the choicest selections of the most celebrated authors of the old world and the new, including biographies of the authors. Contains over 500 pages, profusely embellished with full page engravings and colored frontispiece. Bound in red cloth with cover design stamped in gold. Large quarto size, 7¼x10 inches. Marbled edges. Retail price, $2.00.

No. 3F3082 Our price..........**60c**
If by mail, postage extra, 22 cents.

Shakespeare.

Pocket Edition. Each play complete in one volume. Has the most approved text, embracing an introduction with a complete summary and story of each play. Cloth, gold title on back. Size, 4x5⅝ inches.

All's Well that Ends Well
Anthony and Cleopatra
As You Like It
Comedy of Errors
Hamlet
Julius Caesar
Macbeth
Measure for Measure
Merchant of Venice
Merry Wives of Windsor
Midsummer-Night's Dream
Much Ado About Nothing
Othello
Romeo and Juliet
Taming of the Shrew
Tempest
Twelfth Night
Winter's Tale

No. 3F3100
Price, per volume..............**15c**
Any 2 for......................**28c**
Any 6 for......................**79c**
If by mail, postage extra, per volume, 4 cents.

Shakespeare's Complete Works.

Edited by Charles Knight. Nearly 400 illustrations by Sir John Gilbert. The entire works of Shakespeare complete in one volume. Contains 1100 double column pages. Bound in ornamental cloth, with attractive cover design stamped in colors. Size, 7x9¾ inches.

No. 3F3105
Price.........**88c**
If by mail, postage extra, 36 cents.

Shakespeare's Complete Works, 8 Volumes, $2.05.

FALSTAFF EDITION.

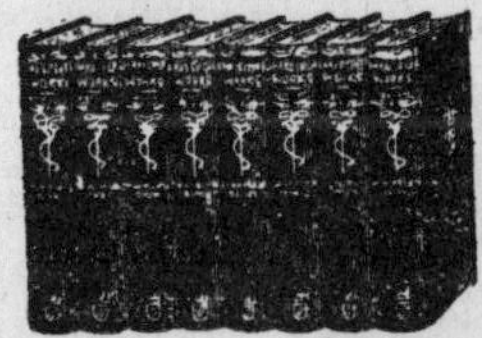

William Shakespeare, complete in eight volumes. Containing all the tragedies, comedies, poems and sonnets, and embracing a history of the early drama, an exhaustive biography, Shakespeare's will, an introduction to each play, names of actors and actresses of Shakespeare's day, index of characters, glossary of obsolete words, notes on each play, etc. Edited by George Long Duyckinck. Suitable for teachers, students, clubs and homes. Uniform in size and style of binding, 32 full page illustrations. Cloth, stamped in gold. Size of volume, 4¾x7¼ inches.

No. 3F3115 Price, per set.......**$2.05**
Weight, packed for shipment, 10 pounds.

Shakespeare's Complete Works, 13 Volumes, $4.59.

STRATFORD EDITION.

This beautiful edition contains the complete Dramatic and Poetical Works of Shakespeare complete in 13 volumes. Makes an ideal library or presentation edition. Each volume contains preface, glossary and notes by Israel Gollancz to each play. There are 40 illustrations in the entire set. This set is bound in cloth with back elaborately stamped in gold. Medallion of Shakespeare in gold on side, gold top, silk book mark and excellently well printed from large, clear type. Each volume has decorated title page and frontispiece illustration. Size of each volume, 4¼x6½ inches, making it a delightful size to handle. Each set comes in heavy green leatherette box, hinge top. Weight, packed for shipment, 10 pounds.

No. 3F3120 Price, per set....**$4.59**

No. 3F3121 Full Morocco, Flexible, full gilt edges, 40 illustrations, otherwise same as No. 3F3120. Price, per set.....**$9.98**

IF YOU BUY FROM US, WE WILL SEND YOU A FREE PROFIT SHARING CERTIFICATE.
SEE PAGES 1 AND 2

HUMOROUS BOOKS

Bill Nye's Comic History of the U. S.

By Edgar W. Nye (Bill Nye). A complete history of our own country, written in Bill Nye's peculiar style. He intensifies our interest in solid historical facts by making them glow with his delicious humor. A narrative of sustained interest, with Nye's unique characterizations, and full of fun from cover to cover. Fully illustrated by F. Opper, the world's greatest comic cartoonist. Fun and knowledge combined, the latter "sugar coated" with delicious humor. Printed on good paper, 329 pages, 140 illustrations. Bound in cloth. Size, 6½x8½ inches. Sold by agents everywhere at $5.00.

No. 3F3200 Our price..........58c
If by mail, postage extra, 16 cents.

Bill Nye's Remarks.

By Edgar W. Nye. One of the humorous books of the nineteenth century, containing 191 of this famous humorist's funniest stories; 504 pages; over 150 illustrations. Bound in cloth, with handsome cover design, stamped with gold and ink. Size, 6¾x8½ inches.

No. 3F3205
Price..........43c
If by mail, postage extra, 16 cents.

Wit and Humor.

By Edgar W Nye (Bill Nye) and James Whitcomb Riley. The yarns in this book are by the inimitable humorist, Bill Nye, and the poems are by the lovable Hoosier Poet, James Whitcomb Riley. A happy combination of wit and humor, melody and pathos and you may be sure in advance that this book will please you; 238 pages. Bound in cloth. Size, 5¾x8 inches.

No. 3F3210 Price..........43c
If by mail, postage extra, 11 cents.

Peck's Uncle Ike and the Redheaded Boy.

By George W. Peck. This famous humorist's two latest works, bound complete in one large volume, the newest, brightest and wittiest book of humor on the market. Nothing has equaled it since "Pecks Bad Boy" was written. What the bad boy does to his pa, isn't in it with some of the tricks he plays on his Uncle Ike and the redheaded boy is just as funny as the other bad boy. Fully illustrated. Bound in cloth. Size, 6½x8½ inches.

No. 3F3212 Price..........48c
If by mail, postage extra, 18 cents.

Peck's Bad Boy and His Pa, and Peck's Sunshine.

By George W. Peck. Two of Mr. Peck's most famous books, bound in one big volume. This is the first, the genuine and the only complete edition of this famous book, the book which for downright, solid fun has never been equaled. "Peck's Bad Boy and His Pa" has made thousands laugh, and the stories today are just as fresh as when they were originally written. Peck's Sunshine" is a collection of articles generally calculated to throw sunshine instead of clouds on the faces of those who read them. Remember, when you order this book you get two complete books from the pen of this most famous comic writer, "Peck's Bad Boy and His Pa" and "Peck's Sunshine," both complete in one volume. Substantially bound in cloth; 522 pages, with 100 original illustrations by True Williams; Size, 6½x8½ inches.

No. 3F3215 Price..........38c
If by mail, postage extra, 18 cents.

Peck's Bad Boy Abroad.

By George W. Peck. The "Bad Boy," who has been in more mischief and created more fun, than any other boy in the world, accompanies his dad on a tour around the world, which the latter takes for his health. They visit all the foreign lands, and call on many crowned heads. The bad boy is just as full of fun as ever, and keeps up his mirth provoking pranks in every land. Every line is a laugh; every page is a roar. Bound in cloth; 471 pages, 126 comic illustrations. Size, 6¾x8½ inches.

No. 3F3216 Price..........65c
If by mail, postage extra, 20 cents.

How Private Peck Put Down the Rebellion, and Peck's Boss Book.

By George W. Peck. Two of Mr. Peck's most humorous books, bound in one big volume. This is an exceedingly humorous account of the experiences of a raw recruit. It is written in the most mirth provoking style of this famous humorist, full of laughable stories of camp life, smuggling and scouting. "Peck's Boss Book" is a collection of over fifty of Mr. Peck's most humorous short stories, including The Troubles of a Bridal Party, Breaking Up A School, Did Eve Ever Receive Callers, The Discreet Conductor, Tale of a Shirt. Bound in cloth; 488 pages. Size, 7x8½ inches.

No. 3F3223 Price..........48c
If by mail, postage extra, 18 cents.

Peck's Bad Boy with the Circus.

By Hon. George W. Peck. This book relates the experiences of the bad boy and his dad during their travels with the circus. The bad boy gets his dad into hot water in every conceivable way, and plays jokes and pranks on everyone from the clown to the manager, and from the monkey to the elephant. Rip-roaring, side-splitting fun from beginning to end. Lots of comic illustrations; about 450 pages. Size, 7x8½ inches. Bound in cloth.

No. 3F3225 Price..........58c
If by mail, postage extra, 20 cents.

Hot Stuff.

By Famous Funny Men. Wit, humor, pathos, ridicule, satire, puns, conundrums, riddles, charades, jokes and magic. The very best stories from such famous humorists as Josh Billings, Eli Perkins, Mark Twain, Bob Burdette, Bill Nye, Artemus Ward, M. Quad, George W. Peck, Bret Harte, and more than fifty others; the funniest stories that the funniest writers have ever written. Bound in cloth, with marble edges, 774 pages. Size, 6½x9 inches.

No. 3F3240 Price..........63c
If by mail, postage extra, 18 cents.

Shams.

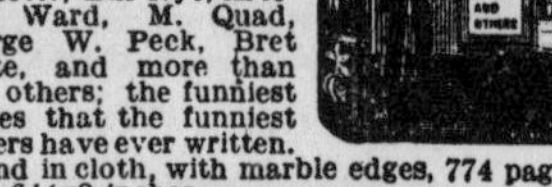

By John S. Draper. "Shams, or Uncle Ben's Experiences with Hypocrites," humorous and entertaining pictures of every day life and incidents in the rural districts, with Uncle Ben's trip to the City of Chicago and to California, and his experiences with shams and sharpers. A delightful, humorous and entertaining book, illustrated with over 100 original and humorous illustrations. Substantially bound in cloth; 412 pages. Size, 6½x8½ inches.

No. 3F3245 Price..........40c
If by mail, postage extra, 18 cents.

The Troubles of Mr. Bowser.

By G. B. Lewis (M. Quad). In The Life and Troubles of Mr. Bowser, we find this celebrated humorist at his very best. Mr. Bowser is always looking for trouble, and usually finds it. Between Mrs. Bowser, the cat, and his desire for information, he is always up against it. Mr. Bowser's troubles will make you forget your own. Bound in cloth; 441 pages, fully illustrated. Size, 6½x8½ inches.

No. 3F3247 Price..........48c
If by mail, postage extra, 15 cents.

JACKSON'S FUNNY BOOKS.

ON A SLOW TRAIN THROUGH ARKANSAS. By Thos. W. Jackson. 1,500,000 copies sold since January 15, 1906, and the game isn't called yet. Funny railroad stories, sayings of the Southern darkies, and the latest and best minstrel jokes of the day. "Then the Brakeman got in and hollered, 'Take your partners for the tunnel.'" Paper bound; 96 pages. Size, 5¼x7½ inches.

No. 3F3250 Price..........19c
If by mail, postage extra, 4 cents.

THROUGH MISSOURI ON A MULE. Thos. W. Jackson's second book, just as funny as "On a Slow Train Through Arkansas." Paper bound; 96 pages. Size, 5¼x7½ inches.

No. 3F3251 Price..........19c
If by mail, postage extra, 4 cents.

THOS. W. JACKSON ON A FAST TRAIN. Jackson's third book. If you have read one of Jackson's books, you will want to read them all. Size, 5¼x7½ inches.

No. 3F3252 Price..........19c
If by mail, postage extra, 4 cents.

Special Offer.

No. 3F3253 All three of Jackson's famous funny books, "On a Slow Train Through Arkansas," "Through Missouri On a Mule," and "Thos. W. Jackson On a Fast Train." Price, for the three books..........50c
If by mail, postage extra, 10 cents.

Irish Wit and Humor.

For sarcastic keenness, for gracefulness and for red hot scornfulness, nothing is more effective than Irish wit and humor as told in this little book. It contains the best sayings of all Irish speakers and the best efforts of the most famous Irish humorists and dialect writers. Substantially bound in cloth; 151 pages. Size, 4½x6¾ inches.

No. 3F3256 Price, 20c
If by mail, postage extra, 4 cents.

Jack Henderson Books.

By Benj. F. Cobb. Mirthful books in up to date slang. A series of stories written in the catchy, slang vein, which is so popular today. These books are among the very best humorous stories ever written, fairly blossoming with wit and humor. They are substantially bound in cloth, with gilt top, printed on fine book paper, each volume illustrated with seven full page humorous pictures. Size, 4½x6 inches.

Jack Henderson Down East
Jack Henderson Out West
Jack Henderson Down South
Jack Henderson on Matrimony
Jack Henderson on Experience
Jack Henderson on Tipping

No. 3F3260 Price, per volume..$0.30
Any 2 volumes..........58
Price for entire set, six volumes.....1.65
If by mail, postage extra, 4 cents.

The Foolish Dictionary.

By Gideon Wurdz. Just a collection of foolish definitions about everything under the sun, and is one of the most laughable books that has been written. The definitions are such as will keep a room full of people laughing for hours at a time. Cloth. Fully illustrated. Size, 4½x6 inches.

No. 3F3280 Price..68c
If by mail, postage extra, 6 cents.

Twenty Years of Hustling.

By John P. Johnston. A book bubbling with merriment, overflowing with fun, full of ridiculous incidents, and replete with comic situations. The story of twenty years of a man's life, more interesting than fiction, yet every word of it true, portraying peculiar and amusing incidents, laughable situations, failures and successes of a man who tries almost every sort of business and finally wins. 48 full page illustrations, 664 pages. Bound in cloth. Size, 6x8 inches.

No. 3F3300 Price..........47c
If by mail, postage extra, 14 cents.

What Happened to Johnston.

Sequel to "Twenty Years of Hustling," by John P. Johnston. A most humorous and interesting book, complete. The personal experiences of a man who in the making and losing of one large fortune and many smaller ones never gives up. Just as funny and just as interesting as this writer's first book, "Twenty Years of Hustling." Full of wit and humor from cover to cover. 55 funny and laughable illustrations, 459 pages. Handsomely bound in silk finish. Size, 6x8 inches.

No. 3F3303 Price..........50c
If by mail, postage extra, 14 cents.

How to Hustle.

By John P. Johnston. The latest of this famous humorist's irresistibly funny books, combining good, sound, money-making advice with the rarest humor. If you have read "Twenty Years of Hustling," or "What Happened to Johnston," you will surely want to read this new book by the same author. Every chapter is full of snap, with the funniest of funny stories and the most laughable incidents. Fully illustrated. Bound in cloth; 421 pages. Size, 6x8 inches.

No. 3F3304 Price..........50c
If by mail, postage extra, 14 cents.

Lincoln's Yarns and Stories.

By Col. Alex. K. McClure. The story of Lincoln's life told by himself, in his stories of wit and humor of the war, the courts, the backwoods and the White House. A complete collection of the funny and witty stories that made Lincoln famous as America's greatest storyteller. Illustrated with 100 original drawings by special artists. Substantially bound in cloth; 416 pages. Size, 6½x8½ inches.

No. 3F3320 Price..........60c
If by mail, postage extra, 15 cents.

Helen's Babies.

By John Habberton. One of the funniest books ever written. This story comprises some of the cutest an l wittiest of childish sayings and pranks, all at the expense of a bachelor uncle. There are many editions of this famous book, and ours is one of the best. Printed on fine book paper, with 50 full page illustrations, and dozens of smaller ones, several smaller ones, several colored illustrations. Bound in cloth. 170 pages; extra large. Size, 7¼x9 inches.

No. 3F3350 Price..........75c
If by mail, postage extra, 16 cents.
No 3F3352 Popular Edition.
Price..........30c
If by mail, postage extra, 8 cents.

Samantha at Saratoga.

By Marriette Holley (Josiah Allen's Wife). The funniest book of all. Funny hits, funny pictures, written amid the whirl of fashion at Saratoga, with takeoffs on the follies, flirtations, low neck dresses, dudes, pug dogs, water craze, tobogganing, etc., in the author's inimitable, mirth provoking style. 100 funny pictures by F. Opper. An ever fresh and inviting feast of fun. Bound in cloth; 272 pages. Size, 5¾x7¾ inches

No. 3F3355 Price..........40c
If by mail, postage extra, 15 cents.

Around the World With Josiah Allen's Wife.

By Marietta Holley (Josiah Allen's Wife). Another new book by this famous author, telling in her irresistibly humorous, quaint way, the story of her trip around the world with Josiah. Beautifully illustrated. Printed on fine book paper; 471 pages. Size, 6¼x8½ inches.

No. 3F3356
Price..........$1.25
By mail, postage extra, 18c.

Samantha at the St. Louis Exposition.

By Marietta Holley (Josiah Allen's Wife.) A story full of wit, pathos, eloquence and common sense. The Exposition is discussed and moralized over by Samantha in her inimitable way. Samantha and Josiah went to the Fair "took it all in" and Samantha relates their experiences in her well known quaint and humorous style. 312 pages. Size, 6x8½ inches.

No. 3F3357 Price..........$1.25
If by mail, postage extra, 16 cents.

Mark Twain's Books.

Everybody knows Mark Twain, the greatest of American humorists. We offer his best books, substantially bound in cloth, printed on fine book paper, fully illustrated. The latest and best copyright editions as published by Harper's. Size, 5½x8 inch.

No. 3F3366 Tom Sawyer Abroad. 410 pages.
Price..........$1 40
If by mail, postage extra, 15 cents.

No. 3F3367 The Adventures of Huckleberry Finn. 388 pages. Price.....$1.40
If by mail, postage extra, 14 cents.

No. 3F3368 Puddin' Head Wilson and Those Extraordinary Twins. 323 pages.
Price..........$1.40
If by mail, postage extra, 14 cents.

No. 3F3369 The Jumping Frog. 66 pages.
Price..........80c
If by mail, postage extra, 6 cents.

No. 3F3370 The Adventures of Tom Sawyer. 328 pages. Price..........$1.40
If by mail, postage extra, 13 cents.

No. 3F3371 The Innocents Abroad. 823 pages. Price..........$1.60
If by mail, postage extra 15 cents.

Artemus Ward's Works.

The complete comic writings of this famous humorist. Revised edition, with biographical sketch by Eli Perkins. 28 full page humorous illustrations, and photogravure frontispiece. No country ever produced a genius like Artemus Ward. No one can fail to appreciate his wonderful humor. He will always be funny. He saw the humor of everything at a glance, and his manner of relating these laughter provoking absurdities, is original and fetching. Beautifully bound in cloth, with gilt top, printed on the finest book paper. 449 pages. Size 5½x8 inches.
No. 3F3380 Price............$1.50
If by mail, postage extra, 18 cents.

Bill Nye's Red Book.

By Edgar W. Nye. Bill Nye says of this book, "I had long hoped to publish a larger, better, and, if possible, a redder book than my first. This book is the result of that hope and wish. It is my greatest and best book." The Red Book contains all of Bill Nye's best stories, jokes and brightest funny sayings. Bound in cloth, over 400 pages, more than 100 illustrations. Size 7x8½ inches.
No. 3F3411 Price............58c
If by mail, postage extra, 18 cents.

Uncle Josh Weathersby's Pumpkin Center Stories.

By Cal. Stewart. Nearly everybody has heard at least a few of the famous Uncle Josh Weathersby famous laughing stories on the phonograph. This book contains all of the famous Uncle Josh Weathersby stories, told by the same man who told them to the talking machines, that have made millions laugh. They are brimful of sunshine and simplicity, the greatest package of wit and humor ever published. Handsomely bound in cloth. 170 pages. Size, 6x8¾ inches.
No. 3F3452 Price............35c
If by mail, postage extra, 11 cents.

Uncle Jeremiah and His Neighbors at the St. Louis Exposition.

By C. M. Stevens. This is one of the funniest books ever published. The old gentleman from the country and his neighbors see all the sights at the Exposition, and get into a good deal of trouble. Every place of note is visited and described by the old gentleman, or one of his neighbors, whose mistakes make the readers roar with laughter. 80 comic illustrations by R. W. Taylor. 332 pages. Size, 6x8½ inches.
No. 3F3460 Price............38c
If by mail, postage extra, 13 cents.

Library of Wit and Humor.

By Eli Perkins and others. A book of spice and variety. The best stories and wittiest sayings of the world's greatest humorists. Among the writers of the funny stories in this great book of wit and humor are such men as Mark Twain, Robert Burdette, Josh Billings, Alexander Sweet, Artemus Ward, Bret Harte, Bill Nye, etc. 30 full page original illustrations. Bound in fine silk cloth. 438 pages. Size, 6½x9 inches.
No. 3F3463 Price............45c
If by mail, postage extra, 16 cents.

Four Hundred Laughs.

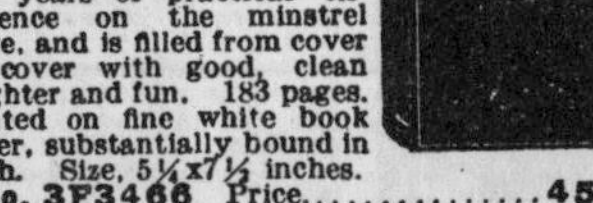

Edited by John R. Kemble. An encyclopedia of jests, toasts, eccentric rhymes, witty sayings, etc. Fun without vulgarity. This book represents more than thirty-two years of practical experience on the minstrel stage, and is filled from cover to cover with good, clean laughter and fun. 183 pages, printed on fine white book paper, substantially bound in cloth. Size, 5¼x7½ inches.
No. 3F3466 Price............45c
If by mail, postage extra, 7 cents.

Brainy Bowers and Drowsy Dugan.

A book that pleases both old and young. The most fun ever. Stories told in pictures. The side splitting stunts which first appeared in cartoons on the comic page of the Chicago Daily News. More than 300 of the most laughable stories, told in pictures to make their telling short. Bound in cloth. 155 pages. Size, 5¼x7¾ inches.
No. 3F3468 Price............39c
If by mail, postage extra, 7 cents.

A Bundle of Sunshine.

By Press Woodruff. A volume of healthful humor. An avalanche of mirth. A barrel of smiles, hearty laughs, and masterly character delineations; a barrel of oil for the troubled waters of life; a barrel of healing balm for wounded souls; a barrel of cement for cracking hearts. The troubled reminiscences of a peregrinator, whose life has been one of calamity, hard luck, accidents and fun. Bound in cloth, nearly 400 pages, with over 100 humorous illustrations. Size, 6x8½ inches.
No. 3F3469 Price............48c
If by mail, postage extra, 16 cents.

Josh Billings' Old Farmers' Allminax.

A reproduction of the famous comic almanacs which were published from 1870 to 1880. Millions of copies were sold, and it has always been one of the most popular of all comic books. Handsomely bound in cloth, printed on the best book paper, with gilt top; 200 pages. Size, 5½x7½ inches.
No. 3F3473 Price, 98c
If by mail, postage extra, 11 cents.

That Reminds Me.

A new book of the latest funniest stories. If you want a supply of the latest and the funniest kind of stories with which to amuse your friends or yourself, you will find them in this little book which, as the author states, is "A collection of tales worth telling." Printed on the very best of book paper; 230 pages. Size, 5x6½ inches.
No. 3F3475 Price...65c
If by mail, postage extra, 5 cents.

The Complete Tribune Primer.

By Eugene Field. Contains 75 original drawings by F. Opper. The most amusing book ever written. Brimful of rich humor, amusing for young and old, man or woman. Illustrations by F. Opper, the famous New York cartoonist. Contains 143 pages bound in green silk cloth. Cover design stamped in white. Size, 5x7¼ inches.
No. 3F3480
Price............55c
If by mail, postage extra, 7 cents.

The Fun Doctor.

The funniest book in the world. Fun is better than physic, and more pleasant to take. Fun about babies, twins, little children, bad boys, love and kissing. This book will help you to "laugh and grow fat." Substantially bound in cloth. 115 pages. Size, 5¼x7¾ inches.
No. 3F3485
Price............39c
If by mail, postage extra, 7 cents.

1001 Riddles.

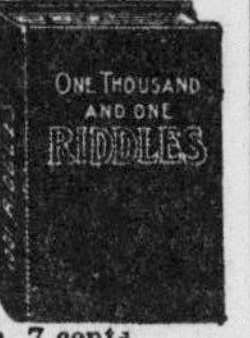

The best collection of riddles ever made. For one who enjoys reading riddles (and nothing is more amusing) we heartily recommend this book. There are 1001 laughs contained within these covers, and it is warranted to drive away the blues. Contains 1001 riddles, bound in cloth, with title stamped in colors. Size, 5¼x7¾ inches.
No. 3F3490 Price, 32c
If by mail, postage extra, 7 cents.

BOOKS ON COOKING, HOME WORK AND ETIQUETTE.

THE HOUSEHOLD COOK BOOK.

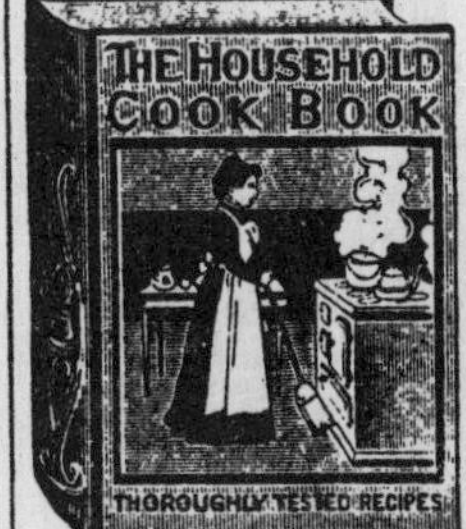

Containing all the Latest Approved Recipes in every Department of cooking; instructions for selecting meats and carving; descriptions of the best kitchen utensils, etc., to which is added hygienic and scientific cooking; rules for dinner giving; use of the chafing dish; menu cards for all special occasions; cooking for invalids; valuable hints for economical housekeeping, etc.; including 2100 Famous Recipes used by the leading chefs of the best hotels in the United States, the whole forming a standard authority on the culinary art, compiled by Maud C. Cooke, author of "Social Etiquette," etc., etc.; superbly embellished with engravings in colors and numerous full page phototype illustrations and many small engravings. The compilation of over 2100 recipes which have been thoroughly tested by experienced cooks, together with the general articles on household subjects, makes this the most valuable and complete book on this subject ever published. It also contains 16 blank pages on which to write miscellaneous recipes which all housekeepers take pride in collecting. The bills of fare for each month in the year which are included in the contents of the Cook Book are a great comfort to the new and inexperienced housekeeper, and also suggest to those who have had years of experience some new dishes with which to surprise the family. It is printed in large, clear type so that the recipes can be easily followed when the book is placed on the back of the table out of the way; it is so bound that it will remain open at any desired place. The binding is white oil cloth, which may be easily cleaned with a damp cloth. Size, 7¾x9¾ inches.
No. 3F3500 Price............48c
If by mail, postage extra, 24 cents.

Mrs. Rorer's Cook Book.

This cook book is alphabetically arranged, making it the easiest of all books in which to locate a recipe, and each recipe is written so plainly that a beginner may successfully make any dish contained in this book. All of these recipes have been tested by Mrs. Rorer herself, thus insuring a book of good working recipes. Bound in waterproof cloth and can be cleaned repeatedly. 581 pages, red edges, with attractive cover design stamped in colors. Size, 5⅝x7½ inches.
No. 3F3508 Price............98c
If by mail, postage extra, 13 cents.

Cook Books by Mrs. Rorer.

These books are as complete as Mrs. Rorer knows how to make them. Anyone who has read her famous articles in The Ladies' Home Journal knows what a help each one of these books is to every housewife. Cloth. Size, 5x7½ inches.

Bread and Cake Making
Canning and Preserving
Home Candy Making
Hot Weather Dishes
Made Overs
New Salads

No. 3F3526 Price, per volume...38c
Any 2 for...73c
If by mail, postage extra, per volume, 5 cents.

Housekeepers' Handy Book.

The most complete, authentic reliable and best recipe book published. The only complete ready reference book which is especially adapted to the home. It embraces every known subject of value pertaining to housekeeping, such as cooking, what to eat and how to prepare it, care of the health, teeth and complexion, how to remove freckles, sunburn, etc. Size, 5x7 inches.
No. 3F3550 Paper. Price......25c
No. 3F3551 Cloth. Price......45c
If by mail, postage extra, paper, 4c; cloth, 15c.

Practical Etiquette.

A strictly modern book on politeness. Just what one needs to keep in touch with what is "correct" at the present time. Hints on politeness and good breeding, sensible talks about etiquette for home, visiting; sensible talks about parties, evening entertainments, social intercourse, dress, etc. No part in daily conduct has been omitted. The immense popularity of this little book is attested by its enormous sales. It is an invaluable adjunct to any home and will be found exceedingly helpful in the hands of parents and teachers as well as young people of both sexes. 160 pages. Bound in cloth. Size, 4¾x7 inches.
No. 3F3577 Price............21c
If by mail, postage extra, 5 cents.

Social Etiquette.

Or, Manners and Customs of Polite Society. Including rules of etiquette for all occasions, including cards, invitations for weddings, receptions, dinners and teas; etiquette of the street and public places. Is a complete guide to self culture, the art of dressing well, conversation, courtship, etiquette for children, letter writing, artistic home and interior decoration, etc. All persons should know how to appear to the best advantage in polite society. A brand new book, right up to date, covering the whole field of etiquette for all occasions. Printed on fine quality of paper. 524 pages, embellished with superb phototype engravings. Presentation frontispiece. Bound in green cloth with photographic inlay and white, black and gold stamping on cover design. Size, 7x9¼ inches.
No. 3F3584 Price............55c
If by mail, postage extra, 22 cents.

Bright Ideas for Entertaining.

By Mrs. Herbert B. Linscott. 209 forms of amusement or entertainment for social gatherings of all kinds, parties, clubs, socials, church entertainments, etc., with special suggestions for birthdays, wedding anniversaries, Hallowe'en, April Fools' Day, Christmas, New Year and other holidays. 229 pages. Size, 5¼x7 inches. Cloth bound.
No. 3F3600 Price............40c
If by mail, postage extra, 9 cents.

Dainty Work for Pleasure and Profit.

With chapters on materials, embroidery, stamping, stitching, dainty trifles, brush and pallet, lace stitches and designs, knitting and crocheting. Hundreds of illustrations. 460 pages. Size, 7x9 inches. Cloth binding.
No. 3F3635 Price............55c
If by mail, postage extra, 21 cents.

MEDICAL BOOKS.

The Lightning Doctor.

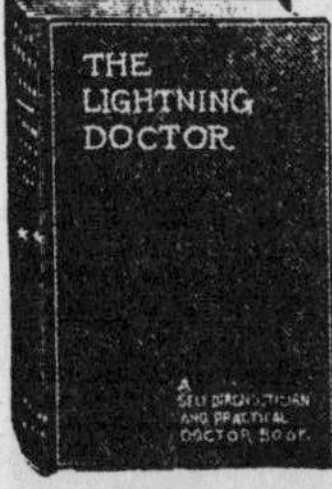

By Benj. F. Weaver, M. D. A self diagnostician and practical doctor book for private families, students and physicians. Right up to date in every particular. The object of this book is to save you doctors' bills and by looking up your symptoms in this book by means of the elaborate charts and text, you can discover at once what your trouble is, and find a reliable adequate remedy. The Lightning Doctor will diagnose your own case and will give you the prescriptions or remedies, all written out. The Lightning Doctor takes the place of a physician and will save you hundreds of dollars. Of inestimable value to those not within easy reach of the physician. Written by a prominent physician with years of practical experience to his credit. 484 pages and numerous halftone illustrations, showing where various pains might be located, and what each one indicates, or of what disease it is a symptom. Size, 6½x9¾ inches. Retail price, $3.00.
No. 3F3735 Our price........$1.48
If by mail, postage extra, 22 cents.

Dr. Gunn's New Family Physician or Home Book of Health.

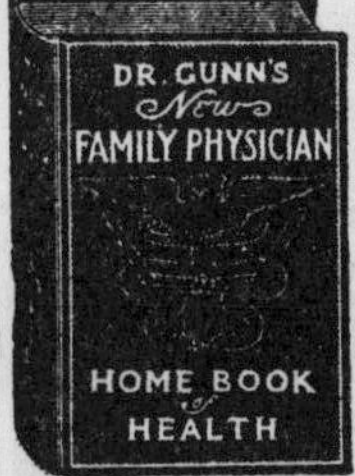

A new, revised and enlarged edition, containing full information upon new diseases as well as old diseases, new remedies and treatment, many colored charts, printed from new plates on fine book paper, handsomely bound. The latest, most complete and authentic medical book ever published. In plain language it answers thousands of questions—the causes, symptoms, prevention, remedies, and methods of treatment for every disease to which mankind is subject. Relating to all the delicate and wonderful matters pertaining to the nature and relation of the sexes. Here are answered in plain language a thousand questions that occur in the minds of both young and old, but about which they feel a delicacy in consulting their physician. The remedies set forth in Dr. Gunn's New Family Physician are of the most simple kind, and ordinarily such as can be easily obtained with but little trouble or expense. Many diseases, which have made their appearance within the last few years, are herein fully discussed, while other so called medical works do not even mention them—such as tonsilitis, tuberculosis, etc. The book also contains much valuable information heretofore held as the special and private knowledge of physicians or medical students. **A complete family medical guide—a doctor always in the house**—ready to be consulted at any time, when sudden sickness or accidents render immediate relief necessary. **A book for the people.** The result of the lifetime study and labor of one of the most noted medical writers of the country, who had an active practice extending through a period of forty years, and who held numerous medical diplomas from colleges of his own and foreign countries. **It is the plain duty of every one,** especially heads of families, to become familiar with the ways of preventing disease, preserving health and prolonging life. Handsomely and substantially bound; a book which will stand the every day wear and tear to which it will be subjected; cover design and title heavily embossed in white and green; over one thousand pages; beautiful colored charts; portrait of the author as frontispiece; a complete index, making it an easy matter to locate any particular subject. Size, 7x10 inches. Weight, packed for shipment, 5 pounds.
No. 3F3698 Bound in cloth. Regular subscription price, $4.50. Price...$1.45
No. 3F3699 Bound in full sheep. Regular subscription price, $6.00. Price 2.10

RECITATIONS, SPEAKERS, ENTERTAINMENTS AND AMATEUR THEATRICALS.

American Family Physician, New.

A popular guide for the household management of diseases, giving the history, cause, means of prevention, and symptoms of all diseases and the most approved methods of treating, with plain instructions for the care of the sick, full and accurate directions for treating wounds, injuries, poisoning, etc. Illustrated with lithographic manikins of the body and of the head, etc. Contains an index of symptoms, enabling one to determine the illness. Complete list of medicines telling what each is good for. All illustrations of the female reproductive organs are in a pamphlet which accompanies the book, so that this book can be put with safety within reach of children. Cloth. 1157 pages. Size, 7x9½ inches.

No. 3F3700 Price..............$1.29
Weight, packed for shipment, 5 pounds.

Dr. Hood's Common Sense Medical Advisor.

Relating to All the Delicate and Wonderful Matters Pertaining to the Nature and Relation of the Sexes.

It explains everything. No man or woman who anticipates a bright future and wishes to enjoy married life in its fullest sense can afford to be without a copy of this valuable work. Here are answered in plain language a thousand questions that occur in the minds of both young and old, but about which they feel a delicacy in consulting their physician. It tells in a matter of fact, easily understood way, the thousand and one questions that occur to the minds of both young and old, divulges all secrets known to medical science. It treats of the natural relations of men and women to each other; society, courtship, love and marriage, parentage, children, nursing and care of the sick, prescriptions, indications of diseases, domestic surgery, hygiene, skin diseases, etc. It covers thousands of other subjects, among which are valuable suggestions to those contemplating marrying, factors to be considered in entering the marriage relation. Bound in cloth cover design in color. 1080 pages. Size, 7¼x9¾ inches.

No. 3F3705 Price..............98c
Weight, packed for shipment, 7 pounds.

Nursing Self Taught.

By S. Levis. Every household has its serious illnesses, but few families can afford a professional nurse. A careful study of this book and by following its simple instructions anyone can be enabled to care for the sick in most every case. The fullest particulars are given for caring for the sick in the simple as well as the serious illnesses of life. Cloth. Size, 3x4½ inches. 75 pages.

No. 3F3720 Price..............38c
If by mail, postage extra, 5 cents.

Home Nursing.

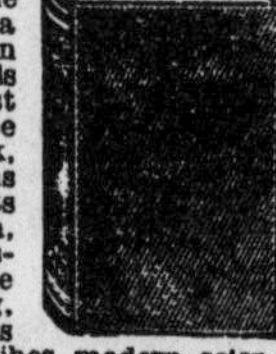

By Evelyn Harrison. This work is published in the hope that it will be a help and comfort in the home life. It is composed of the simplest rules and remedies, to be used in the care of the sick, and some general directions regarding the nourishments that should be given, especially during convalescence. Contains simple recipes for invalid cooking, grouped under the headings of the diseases; also describes modern scientific methods for the sick room. In short, this work is intended for those homes where the "expensive luxury" of a trained nurse is out of reach of the purse strings, and their place is to be supplied by the loving mother, wife or daughter. Contains 229 pages, printed on best quality of paper. Bound in cloth, title on back. Size 5¼x7¾ inches.

No. 3F3722 Price..............48c
If by mail, postage extra, 8 cents.

The Care of Children.

By Elizabeth Robinson Scovill. A complete treatise on the successful care of children, including chapters on nursing, feeding, diet for young babies, for school children, and in illness, baby's wardrobe, beds, toilet, baths, care of the teeth, eyes, ears, ailments, etc. 360 pages. Size, 5x6¾ inches. Bound in cloth.

No. 3F3724 Price..............85c
If by mail, postage extra, 10 cents.

First Aid to the Injured.

By F. J. Warwic. This book tells in simple and easily understood language what to do in case of accident as well as in first stages of illness. A little study of this book with practice of the easy principles which it teaches will enable anyone to act intelligently in case of accident, etc. Cloth. Size, 6x4½ inches. 75 pages.

No. 3F3730 Price..............38c
If by mail, postage extra, 5 cents.

Complete Library of Entertainment, Amusement and Instruction.

Suitable for every occasion. Designed to cultivate sociability and good fellowship. Embracing nine instructive books in one volume.

Book 1—Home Amusements.
Book 2—Church Entertainment.
Book 3—School Exercises.
Book 4—Outdoor Sports and Games.
Book 5—Literary Games and Exercises.
Book 6—Entertainments of Socialist Societies.
Book 7—Palmistry, Charades, Tricks, etc.
Book 8—Dainty Work for Girls; Boys' Workshop.
Book 9—The Home Book of Health, Grace, Beauty, Manners, etc.

The whole comprising the greatest book of general information ever published. Embellished with over 150 engravings. Containing nearly 500 pages, bound in silk cloth with cover design stamped in gold. Size 7½x9¾ inches.

No. 3F3801 Price..............75c
If by mail, postage extra, 22 cents.

The Fraternal and Modern Banquet Orator.

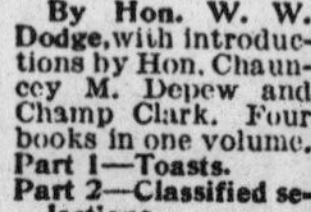

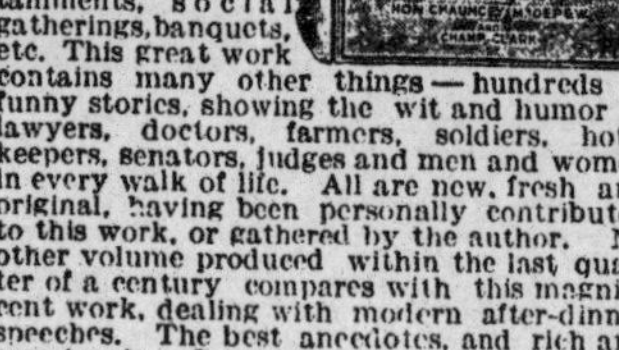

By Hon. W. W. Dodge, with introductions by Hon. Chauncey M. Depew and Champ Clark. Four books in one volume.

Part 1—Toasts.
Part 2—Classified selections.
Part 3—Anecdotes.
Part 4—Addresses.

An original book of useful "helps" for assembly of fraternal orders, college entertainments, social gatherings, banquets, etc. This great work contains many other things—hundreds of funny stories, showing the wit and humor of lawyers, doctors, farmers, soldiers, hotel keepers, senators, judges and men and women in every walk of life. All are new, fresh and original, having been personally contributed to this work, or gathered by the author. No other volume produced within the last quarter of a century compares with this magnificent work, dealing with modern after-dinner speeches. The best anecdotes, and rich and rare toasts. Contains 525 pages and 32 full page halftone portraits. Bound in green cloth with cover design stamped in gold and colors. Marbled edges. Size, 7½x9¾ inches.

No. 3F3803 Price..............78c
If by mail, postage extra, 25 cents.

The Modern Elocutionist.

By Guy Steeley. A popular speaker, comprising a choice collection of recitations and readings; descriptive, dramatic, pathetic, humorous selections suitable for schools, lodges, public entertainments, Sunday schools, together with rules of gestures, expression and cultivation of the voice. Especially adapted for home study and self teaching. Useful to every teacher; necessary to every student. Embellished with numerous halftone illustrations, illustrating various gestures, positions, etc. Bound in cloth with attractive cover design stamped in colors. Size, 6½x8½ inches; 1¾ inches thick. 449 pages. Retail price, $1.75.

No. 3F3806 Our price..............58c
If by mail, postage extra, 22 cents.

White House Handbook of Oratory.

Edited by Chas. E. Chadman. A carefully selected collection of patriotic speeches and essays; gems of literature—prose and poetry—adapted for readings and recitations, at home and on public occasions, together with an exhaustive summary of the principles of elocution and oratory, of exercises in voice and gesture. This book is not only interesting, but thoroughly instructive, and is illustrated with full page drawings depicting the proper pose and gesture to make when indicating either accusation, commanding, defiance, salutation, mimicry, etc. Contains 284 pages. Bound in best grade of pebbled cloth with White House stamped on back and side in white. Size, 5¾x8 inches.

No. 3F3808 Price..............65c
If by mail, postage extra, 15 cents.

The New Select Speaker.

Suitable to all ages. Contains more material, more pages, has prettier illustrations and gives more pleasure and instruction than any other speaker. Containing the best readings and recitations for all occasions, by the most celebrated authors, including grave, pathetic, moral, didactic, dramatic, descriptive, religious and humorous selections; programmes for special occasions, together with a treatise on elocution, cultivations of the voice; chapter on composition, letter writing, physical culture, subjects by famous orators, how to organize and conduct literary societies, etc.

It answers all requirements for readings, recitations and dialogues. Contains 464 double column pages of text with 48 full page illustrations, making 512 pages. Bound in cloth with cover design stamped in colors, and photographic inlay of Maxine Elliott. Presentation frontispiece. Size, 7¼ x 9¾ inches. Marbled edges. Retail price, $2.25.

No. 3F3811 Our price..............75c
If by mail, postage extra, 22 cents.

The Dramatic Reciter.

By Richard Linthicum. A modern book of elocution, readings, dialogues and plays for home and school and all public and social entertainments. Special lesson talks by Marvin Victor Hinshaw, of the Hinshaw school of oratory and music. This book is not only entertaining but instructive. 463 pages. Profusely illustrated with photographs and pictures from life, which will be found most instructive and helpful to the reciter. Bound in crimson silk cloth, stamped in gold and colors, with an inlay on front cover of a handsome picture in colors. Red edges. Size, 7½x9 inches. Retail price, $1.50

No. 3F3813 Our price..............75c
If by mail, postage extra, 22 cents.

New American Star Speaker.

A new Speaker, Educator and Entertainer. For young and old. New, revised and greatly enlarged edition, by Henry Davenport Northrop, the famous historian. Being a standard work on composition and oratory. Contains rules for expressing written thoughts in a correct and elegant manner, model selections from the most famous authors, subjects for compositions and how to treat them. Descriptive, pathetic and humorous recitations, together with a collection of readings, including programmes for special occasions, the whole forming an unrivaled self educator; teaching science and art of elocution, how to read and speak, etc. Suitable for all ages. 448 pages, double column, together with a large number of original engravings and eight full page colored halftones. Presentation frontispiece. Bound in red cloth. Size, 7¼x9¾ inches. Photographic inlay and elaborately stamped in gold. Retail price $1.75.

No. 3F3816 Our price..............65c
If by mail, postage extra, 22 cents.

Boys' and Girls' Speaker.

A new speaker for our little folks. A book of choice readings and recitations for boys and girls in home and school. Including programmes for special entertainments Christmas, Easter and other days; dialogues and character sketches, concert exercises, patriotic speeches, children's songs and music. Nearly 500 selections in verse and prose for all occasions with practical suggestions for delivery from platform or in the home. This book has a twofold purpose. It is a speaker and reader which will not only give pleasure, but helps the teacher and the scholar. Size, 7½x9¾ inches. Contains 238 pages, illustrated with halftones and line drawings, with colored frontispiece. Bound in cloth, with attractive cover design stamped in colors.

No. 3F3818 Price..............39c
If by mail, postage extra, 14 cents.

Comic Recitations and Readings.

Contains some of the best efforts of such world renowned humorists as Mark Twain, Josh Billings, Artemus Ward, Ezra Kendall, Bret Harte, Bill Nye, Ben King, George Thatcher, Lew Dockstader, William S. Gilbert, James Whitcomb Riley and others. Suitable for recitations in drawing room entertainments and amateur theatricals. Size, 4½x6½ inches. 200 pages. Bound in cloth.

No. 3F3822 Price..............21c
If by mail, postage extra, 5 cents.

Dutch Dialect.

If you want to know the latest and best Dutch stories, and learn how to tell them in the funny German way, buy this book.

Jokes and Recitations, as told by our foremost vaudeville stars, Weber and Fields, Rogers Brothers, Ezra Kendall, Gus Williams and others. Size, 4¼x6¾ inches. 130 pages. Bound in cloth.

No. 3F3832 Price..............21c
If by mail, postage extra, 5 cents.

Choice Dialect and Vaudeville Stage Jokes.

A new collection of readings, recitations, jokes, gags, monologues in Irish, Dutch, Scotch, Yankee, French, Italian, Spanish, Chinese, negro, and other dialects, representing every phase of sentiment from the keenest humor or the tenderest pathos to that which is strongly dramatic. Size, 4¼ x 6½ inches. 200 pages. Bound in cloth.

No. 3F3842 Price. 21c
If by mail, postage extra, 5 cents

Patriotic Recitations.

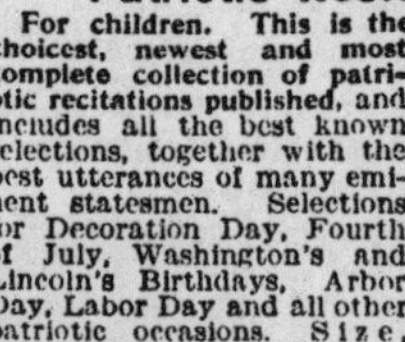

For children. This is the choicest, newest and most complete collection of patriotic recitations published, and includes all the best known selections, together with the best utterances of many eminent statesmen. Selections for Decoration Day, Fourth of July, Washington's and Lincoln's Birthdays, Arbor Day, Labor Day and all other patriotic occasions. Size, 4¾x6½ inches. 200 pages. Bound in cloth.

No. 3F3852 Price..............21c
If by mail, postage extra, 5 cents.

Little Folks' Speaker.

Containing cute and catchy pieces for small children ten years and much younger, including speeches of welcome and short dialogues for opening and closing children's entertainments. The subjects are such as delight the infantile mind, and the language, while childlike, is not childish. Size, 4¼x6¾ inches. 128 pages. Bound in cloth.

No. 3F3862 Price, 21c
If by mail, postage extra, 5 cents.

Little Folks' Dialogues.

A collection of original dialogues and dramas by various authors. Sprightly and sensible, particularly adapted for little people from 3 to 12 years old, on subjects and ideas fitted to their age, and developing the germs of mimicry and appropriate action, so often observed in even children of tender age. Size, 4¼x6¾ inches. 180 pages. Bound in cloth.

No. 3F3867 Price..............21c
If by mail, postage extra, 5 cents

Tricks with Coins.

By T. Nelson Downs. Have you ever seen anyone take a coin from the pocket and perform some simple little trick? Want to know how it is done? This book explains and illustrates how to do it and will enable you to keep your friends guessing. 170 pages. Size, 4½x6¾ inches. Bound in cloth.

No 3F3890 Price..............21c
If by mail, postage extra, 5 cents

Card Tricks and How to Do Them.

Principles of Sleight of Hand, by Professor A. Roterberg. Illustrated. Explains all card tricks in such a way that after reading the book you can entertain and mystify your friends for hours with clever tricks. Explains many games of solitaire with expose of how gamblers win. 170 pages. Bound in cloth. Size, 4½x6¾ inches.

No. 3F3922 Price. 21c
If by mail, postage extra, 5 cents.

Herrmann's Book of Magic.

By Prof. Herrmann. If you want to be able to entertain your friends with tricks of conjurors and sleight of hand performances, this book will fully explain how to do it. Contains an endless variety of coin, card, handkerchief, hat and ball tricks, any of which can be easily performed in the home. Illustrated. Bound in cloth. Size, 4½x 6¾ inches. 164 pages.

No. 3F3927 Price..............21c
If by mail, postage extra, 6 cents.

Modern Magician.

Do you want to know how to perform feats of magic, and the tricks, sleights and illusions that make magicians famous, or do you want to know how to perform in the home feats of shadowgraphy on the wall? Then buy this book, as it explains in detail for the benefit of the amateur just what is to be done. Illustrated. Cloth. Size, 5½x8 inches. 440 pages.

No. 3F3930 Price..............74c
If by mail, postage extra, 18 cents.

Practical Ventriloquism.

By Robert Ganthony. Who has not had a desire at some time in their life to become a ventriloquist and be able to fool their friends by throwing the voice and making them believe that someone is talking whom they cannot see? This book fully explains how to accomplish these results, and the application of the main principles given here and the practice of a few simple rules will enable you to become an adept in the art. Bound in cloth. 200 pages. Size, 4¼x6¾ inches. Illustrated.

No. 3F3937 Price..............21c
If by mail, postage extra, 5 cents.

Conundrums and Riddles.

Containing upward of 4,000 choice, new, intellectual conundrums and riddles. They are always a source of great amusement and pleasure, whiling away tedious hours and putting everyone in a good humor. Any person with this book may take the lead in entertaining a company and keep them in roars of laughter for hours. Bound in cloth. 160 pages. Size, 4¼x6½ inches.

No. 3F3942 Price..............21c
If by mail, postage extra, 5 cents.

Standard Drill and Marching Book.

By Edwin Ellis. Containing an endless variety of new, original drills and marches with music for young people. Each being illustrated with diagrams easy to understand. No form of entertainment has proved itself more amusing, healthful or popular than "Standard Drills and Marches." The very latest and most amusing drills and marches known. Bound in cloth. 160 pages, 30 illustrations. Size, 4¼x6¾ inches.

No. 3F3944 Price..............21c
If by mail, postage extra, 5 cents.

Negro Minstrels, Stump Speeches and Black Face Monologues.

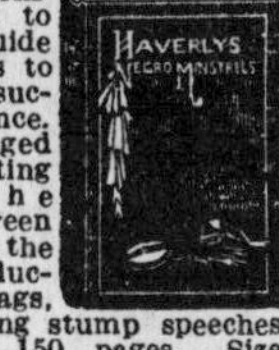

By Jack Haverly. A complete handbook written to encourage, help and guide amateurs in their efforts to form troupes and give a successful evening's performance. An entire program is arranged with full details, consisting of a first part with the brightest dialogue between "Tambo," "Bones," and the "Middleman," the introduction of ballads, songs, gags, conundrums, side splitting stump speeches, etc. Bound in cloth. 150 pages. Size, 4¼x6¾ inches.

No. 3F3950 Price..............21c
If by mail, postage extra, 5 cents.

Toasts and After Dinner Speeches.

Compiled and edited by William Young Stafford. How many times have you been called upon to respond to some toast or speech? The book contains Presentation Speeches, At and After Dinner Speeches, Political Speeches, Welcomes, Congratulations, School Commencement Valedictories, etc. Also toasts and welcomes on various subjects. Send for a copy and prepare yourself. The experienced orator will find many good suggestions. Bound in cloth. 180 pages. Size, 4¼x6¾ inches.

No. 3F3955 Price..............21c
If by mail, postage extra, 5 cents.

Graphology.

The Science of Character Reading in Handwriting.

By Henry Frith. It teaches one the secret of how to read one's friends' or strangers' characters in their handwriting. Contains 125 pages with numerous illustrations of handwriting. Bound in cloth with attractive cover design. Size, 4¼x6¾ inches.

No. 3F3965 Price..............43c
If by mail, postage extra, 5 cents.

PLAYS

We include only plays of the highest quality and greatest merit, and none in which there is in any way anything that is objectionable. We have endeavored to provide for all varieties of talent and sentiment, as well as number of people and time required to present them. The figures in the columns at the right denote the number of characters; "M," male; "F," female.

One Act Farces and Comedies.

	Characters M	F
The Assessor. This is great	3	2
Aunt Charlotte. Very amusing	3	3
April Fools. Funny situations	3	
Burglars. Extremely humorous	2	
A Bad Job. Ludicrous	3	2
Hypnotizing a Landlord	2	
Betsy Baker. Full of action	2	2
Pair of Lunatics. Lots of go	1	1
Billy's Mishaps. Decidedly rich	2	3
Poor Pilicody. Laugh a minute	2	3
A Borrowed Luncheon. Most clever		5
Trick Doctor. A big hit	4	3
Box and Cox. Old favorite	2	1
Try it On	5	2
A Breezy Call. A crackerjack	2	1
Great Medical Dispensory	6	
Cabman, No. 93. Comical	2	2
The Case Against Casey. A screamer	23	
Initiating a Granger	8	
A Convention of Paris. Excellent	7	
Madam Princeton's Temple of Beauty		6
Country Justice. Rich fun	8	
Not a Man in the House. Always takes		5
Documentary Evidence. Extremely witty	1	1
Two Aunts		4
A Dude in a Cyclone. Roaring farce	4	2
A First Class Hotel. Decided hit	4	
Fun in a Photograph Gallery. Amusing	6	10
The Great Pumpkin Case. Funny trial	12	
Hans von Smash. A great Dutchman	4	3
Is the Editor In? Very lively	4	2
A Kiss in the Dark. Laughable	2	3
The Kansas Immigrants. Big hit	5	1
The Limerick Boy. Irish fun	5	2
The Little Black Devil. Funny	2	1
Lucy's Old Man. Capital piece	2	3
The Love Potion. Funny complications	3	3
Mrs. Carver's Fancy Ball. Sure to please	4	3
My Wife's Relation. Plenty of fun	4	6
Outwitting the Colonel. A winner	3	2
Only Cold Tea. Temperance play	3	3
Pat, the Apothecary. A laugh a minute	6	2
A Regular Fix. Sure to please	6	4
Too Much of a Good Thing. Humorous	3	6
A Treasure From Egypt. Fine action	4	1
Turn Him Out. Never a failure	3	2
Two Aunts and a Photo. Enjoyable		4
Two Gentlemen in a Fix. All fun	2	
Two Ghosts in White. Great success		8
Uncle Dick's Mistake. Very sprightly	3	2
Wanted, a Correspondent. Great favorite	4	4
Wanted, a Hero. Abundant humor	1	1
Which Will He Marry? Simply immense	2	8
The Woman Hater. Always takes	2	1
Yankee Peddler. Brimful of fun	7	3

No. 3F3990 Price, each........$0.12
Per dozen........1.30
If by mail, postage extra, each, 1 cent.

Comedies and Dramas.

(Two acts or more.)

	Characters M	F
The Danger Signal. Strong play	7	4
Louva, the Pauper	9	4
The New Woman. Rich humor	3	6
Odds With the Enemy. Very excellent	7	4
An Only Daughter. Laughter and tears	5	2
Out in the Streets. Temperance	6	4
Pet of Parson's Ranch. Western life	9	2
A Soldier of Fortune. A winner	8	3
Ten Nights in a Bar Room	7	4
Under the Laurels. Has delighted thousands	5	4
The Yankee Detective. Will go	8	3

No. 3F3993 Price, each........$0.12
Per dozen........1.30
If by mail, postage extra, each, 1 cent.

Vaudeville Sketches.

These are the sketches that have made thousands laugh in the larger cities, and have been the greatest successes ever produced. For one or two people they are the best that have been devised for amusement purposes.

	Characters M	F
Breakfast Food for Two. Up to date	1	1
Doings of a Dude. Cyclone of fun	2	1
Fresh Timothy Hay. Ludicrous lines	2	1
Hey, Rube. Farmer act	1	
Is It Raining? Dutch and soubrette	1	1
Killarney Blarney. Irish puns	1	
Marriage and After. Rare hits	1	
An Oyster Stew. Puns and retorts	2	
Pickles for Two. Dutch team	2	
The Recruiting Office. Irish team	2	
Si and I. Country girl		1
A Swift Proposition. Rich lines	1	
A Tramp With a Tramp. Tramp act	1	
The Troubles of Rozinski. Jew act	1	
Wives Wanted in Squashville	3	

No. 3F3996 Price, each........$0.12
Per dozen........1.30
If by mail, postage extra, each, 2 cents.

Chas. K. Harris' Complete Songster.

Containing 150 latest popular songs—successes of Mr. Harris and his staff of famous composers. Never before would Mr. Harris allow all of his songs to be sold in one single volume on account of their ever ready sale singly, but through the untiring efforts of the publishers, at a great expense, we are now prepared to offer this superb collection of 150 popular songs at a price within the reach of all. 200 pages. Size, 4¼x6¾ inches.

No. 3F3960 Price..............21c
If by mail, postage extra, 5 cents.

BOOKS ON DANCING, LOVE AND COURTSHIP.

Dancing.

By Marguerite Wilson. A complete instructor, beginning with the first positions and steps, and leading up to the square and round dances. It contains also a full list of calls for all of the square dances, and the appropriate music for each figure, the etiquette of the dances and 100 figures for the German. Illustrated. Cloth. Size, 4½x6 inches. 90 pages.

No. 3F4000 Price..............38c
If by mail, postage extra, 5 cents.

Modern Quadrille Call Book and Complete Dancing Master.

By A. C. Wirth. Contains all the new, modern square dances and tabulated forms for the guidance of the leader or others in calling them. Full and complete directions for performing every known square dance, such as plain quadrilles, polka quadrilles, cake walk quadrille, Old Dan Tucker, money musk, waltz lanciers, waltz quadrille, the German, etc. In the round dances a special feature consists of the Wirth and other new methods of teaching the steps of the waltz, etc. 160 pages. Size, 4¼x6¾ inches. Bound in cloth.

No. 3F4007 Price..............21c
If by mail, postage extra, 5 cents.

Because I Love You.

The book of love, courtship and marriage. With the aid of this book you can learn all there is to know about this fascinating subject. Tells when to begin courting, what to say, how to propose, how to create love, how to select a wife or husband; in fact, it tells everything. Nothing is omitted. 200 pages. Size, 4¼x6¾ inches. Bound in cloth.

No. 3F4022 Price..............21c
If by mail, postage extra, 5 cents.

Curiosities of Kissing.

By Alfred Fowler. This book is a story of the wit and humor, story and anecdote of the question that is uppermost in a great many people's minds. The present practice of kissing commenced with our first parents and has gained many devotees from year to year. Contains the folklore of kissing, and in fact, everything known about this fascinating subject. Paper bound. 125 pages. Fully illustrated. Size, 5x7 inches.

No. 3F4025 Price..............22c
If by mail, postage extra, 5 cents.

Lovers' Guide and Manual.

Explains all about love, courtship, influence of matrimony, marriage, etiquette of courtship, essence of good breeding, proposals, language of flowers, code of flirtations, fortune telling, and character reading, including rules for good society, handkerchief, parasol, fan, hat, postage stamp, cigar, glove, eye, whip, pencil flirtation and love making. Paper cover. 80 pages. Size, 4½x6¾ inches.

No. 3F4030 Price..............18c
If by mail, postage extra, 2 cents.

North's Book of Love Letters; or, How to Write Love Letters.

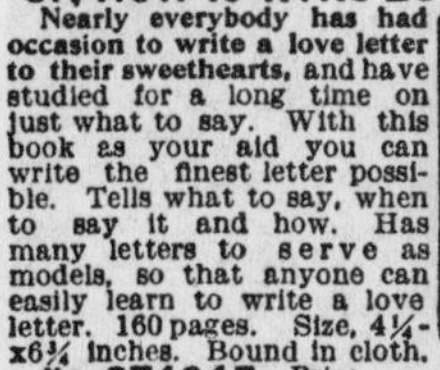

Nearly everybody has had occasion to write a love letter to their sweethearts, and have studied for a long time on just what to say. With this book as your aid you can write the finest letter possible. Tells what to say, when to say it and how. Has many letters to serve as models, so that anyone can easily learn to write a love letter. 160 pages. Size, 4¼x6¾ inches. Bound in cloth.

No. 3F4047 Price..............21c
If by mail, postage extra, 6 cents.

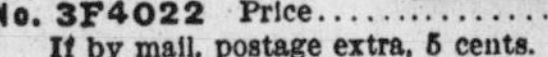

ASTROLOGY, PALMISTRY, CLAIRVOYANCY AND FORTUNE TELLING.

Practical Astrology.

By Comte C. De Saint Germaine. Do you want to learn from the stars what your future is, what possibilities you have and what dangers beset your path? If you do, this book is in language that can be easily understood, and is simple, instructive and elevating. Fully illustrated. Size, 5¼x7½ inches. 292 pages. Bound in cloth.

No. 3F4102 Price..............21c
If by mail, postage extra, 12 cents.

Zancig's Complete Palmistry.

By Zancig. Do you want to know how to read the lines in the hands of your friends, sweetheart, or acquaintances? Do you want to know from your own hand your future, your past and your present? This book fully explains in simple language just how to accomplish these results. Illustrated. Size, 5½x7½ inches. 183 pages. Bound in cloth.

No. 3F4106 Price..............21c
If by mail, postage extra, 5 cents.

How to Be a Clairvoyant.

If you want to become a clairvoyant and understand how to hypnotize and mesmerize people, with a full knowledge of being able to read the future for your friends, this book will fully explain. The explanations and system are easily understood, and a little practice will enable the student to reach perfection. 500 pages. Size, 4¼x6¾ inches. Illustrated. Bound in cloth.

No. 3F4112 Price..............21c
If by mail, postage extra, 5 cents.

Egyptian Secrets;

Or, White and Black Art for Man and Beast. By Albertus Magnus. Being the approved, verified, sympathetic and natural. Special edition. The book of nature and the hidden secrets and mysteries of life unveiled; being the forbidden knowledge of ancient philosophers. By that celebrated student, philosopher, chemist, naturalist, psychomist, astrologer, alchemist, metallurgist, sorcerer, explanator of the mysteries of wizards and witchcraft; together with recondite views of numerous arts and sciences—obscure, plain, practical, etc. 208 pages. Size, 5½x8 inches. Bound in cloth.

No. 3F4116 Price..............38c
If by mail, postage extra, 8 cents.

Original Gypsy Fortune Teller.

Now for the first time made public. A complete revelation of the art of fortune telling by cards, palmistry and signs of the zodiac, as practiced by the wandering gypsies for centuries past; with signs, tokens, spells and other marvelous instructions in the famed black art of witches, seers and astrologists. It also contains a complete dictionary of dreams, the art of palmistry, a full collection of charms, spells, incantations and much other material relating to the occult arts. 210 pages. Size, 4½x7 inches. Bound in cloth.

No. 3F4117 Price..............21c
If by mail, postage extra, 5 cents.

How to Tell Fortunes by Cards.

By Mme. Zancig. How often have your friends asked you to tell their fortune with cards? You would like to do so but are forced to say that you don't know how. If you will read this book and follow the simple instructions that are given, you can surprise your friends and your sweetheart by reading the past, present and future for them. 150 pages. Illustrated. Size, 4½x6¾ inches. Bound in cloth.

No. 3F4122 Price..............21c
If by mail, postage extra, 5 cents.

Fortune Telling Cards.

By Mme. Le Normand, the original gypsy witch. This is really a wonderful pack of cards, with which anyone can tell their own fortune, or can by their use read the future for their friends. Much fun and amusement can be secured from these cards as well as some really astonishing truths that will surprise anybody. Each pack contains 53 cards.

No. 3F4125 Price, per pack.....20c
If by mail, postage extra, 5 cents.

Gypsy Witch Dream Book.

Everybody at some time in their life has had a dream, and then have thought of it the next morning, wondering just what it meant. This book of 208 pages, fully illustrated, will tell you what any dream means, as it covers fully everything known on the subject. Also contains full information about lucky days, and gypsy omens. Size, 4¼x6¾ inches. Bound in cloth.

No. 3F4129 Price..............21c
If by mail, postage extra, 5 cents.

BOOKS FOR CARPENTERS, BUILDERS AND ARCHITECTS.

Sixth and Seventh Books of Moses.

These two books of Moses are given word for word as they were first written many centuries ago, contains 125 seals, signs, emblems, etc., used by Moses, Aaron, the Israelites, etc. Contains also the white and black art, together with the ministering spirits which were hidden from David. Fully illustrated. Bound in paper. Size, 5¼x7 inches. 190 pages.

No. 3F4130 Price..............**33c**
If by mail, postage extra, 4 cents.

Practical Character Reader.

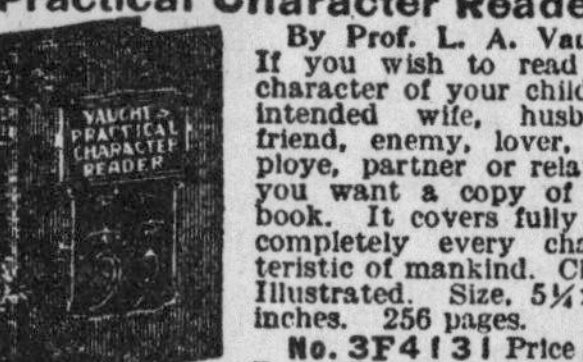

By Prof. L. A. Vaught. If you wish to read the character of your children, intended wife, husband, friend, enemy, lover, employe, partner or relative, you want a copy of this book. It covers fully and completely every characteristic of mankind. Cloth. Illustrated. Size, 5¼x7½ inches. 256 pages.

No. 3F4131 Price **59c**
By mail, postage extra, 10c.

Card Sharpers.

Their Tricks Exposed; or, the Art of Always Winning. By Robert Houdin. This volume was expressly written to enlighten the dupes, and there will be no more cheating. In unveiling the tricks of card sharpers, the author and editor have included everything practiced by gamblers of all countries, they have spent years in following every crooked or cheating move made by them, which is fully explained in diagrams. The book when read will inspire no thought beyond that of guarding the reader against the card tricks of sharpers. 200 pages, 24 illustrations. Size, 4½x7 inches. Bound in cloth.

No. 3F4134 Price..............**22c**
If by mail, postage extra, 5 cents.

The Expert at the Card Table.

Without doubt the very best and most up to date treatise on the numerous sleight used by gamblers, concluding with a thoroughly interesting chapter on card sleights and tricks with cards. Among the various new gamblers' sleights will be found many which will prove of excellent service to the progressive conjuror. 205 pages. 101 illustrations. Size, 4½x7 inches. Bound in cloth.

No. 3F4135 Price..............**21c**
If by mail, postage extra, 5 cents.

The Complete Palmist.

By Niblo. This is the only complete and thoroughly exhaustive work on the study of Chirognomy and Chiromancy published. Practically all of the modern treatises on Palmistry and kindred subjects are adapted from this great work by Niblo, which contains over 80,000 words. There are 711 marginal notes, uniformly arranged throughout the 48 chapters. The glossary, which contains about 3,000 subjects, will enable anyone to master the study in a very short time. Large quarto volume. Size, 8½x10¼ inches. Handsomely bound in white cloth.

No. 3F4140 Price..............**98c**
If by mail, postage extra, 24 cents.

What's in a Dream?

By Gustavus Hindman Miller. A scientific and practical interpretation of dreams. It interprets over 10,000 dreams. The most complete and exhaustive work that has ever been written on this subject. The author has used material from the Bible, classical sources, and medieval and modern philosophers. The preface is a valuable feature of the book and touches in an interesting way on the metaphysical New Thought School. Contains 600 pages printed on finest quality of paper. Bound in cloth with cover stamped in gold and colors. Size, 5¼x7½ inches.

No. 3F4145 Price..............**75c**
If by mail, postage extra, 12 cents.

Hypnotism.

Theories and Experiments of Practical Hypnotism by Comte C. de Saint-Germain. From the works of the famous hypnotists and teachers of hypnotism. Illustrated with full page illustrations. Contains 260 pages which explain fully and unveil the mystery of hypnotism. Bound in silk cloth with beautiful cover design stamped in colors. Size, 5¼x7¾ inches. Retail price, $1.00.

No. 3F4150 Our price..............**49c**
If by mail, postage extra, 10 cents.

Modern Carpentry.

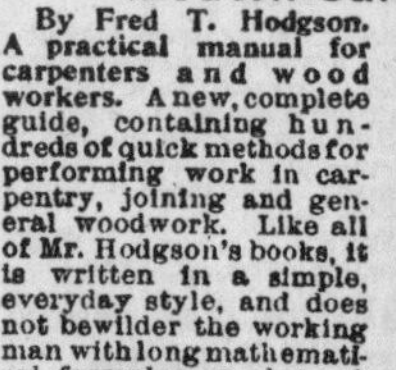

By Fred T. Hodgson. A practical manual for carpenters and wood workers. A new, complete guide, containing hundreds of quick methods for performing work in carpentry, joining and general woodwork. Like all of Mr. Hodgson's books, it is written in a simple, everyday style, and does not bewilder the working man with long mathematical formulas or abstract theories. The illustrations, of which there are many, are explanatory, so that anyone who can read, will be able to understand them easily and to follow the work in hand without difficulty. This book contains methods of laying roofs, rafters, stairs, floors, hoppers, bevels, joining mouldings, mitering, coping, plain handrailing, circular work, splayed work, and many other things the carpenter wants to know to help him in his everyday vocation. It is the most complete and very latest work published, being thorough, practical and reliable. One which no carpenter can afford to be without. It also contains perspective views and floor plans of 50 low price American homes.

The work is printed from new, large type plates on a superior quality of cream wove paper, durably bound. 250 pages. 200 illustrations. Size, 5¼x7¾.

No. 3F4300 Price..............**58c**
If by mail, postage extra, 11 cents.

Modern Carpentry, Advanced Series.

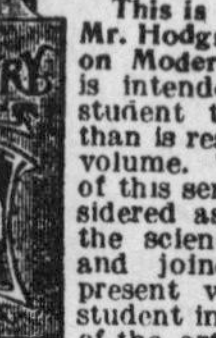

This is a continuation of Mr. Hodgson's first volume on Modern Carpentry and is intended to carry the student to a higher plane than is reached by the first volume. The first volume of this series may be considered as the alphabet of the science of carpentry and joinery, while the present volume leads the student into the intricacies of the art and shows how certain difficult problems may be solved with a minimum of labor. Every progressive workman—and especially those who have purchased the first volume of this series—cannot afford to be without this volume, as it contains so many things necessary the advanced workman should know, and that is likely to crop up at any time during his daily labors. The work is well illustrated with over one hundred diagrams, sketches and scale drawings which are fully described and explained in the text. Many puzzling working problems are shown, described and solved. This is truly a valuable aid and assistant for the progressive workman. Bound in cloth. 300 pages, over 100 illustrations. Size, 5½x7½ inches.

No. 3F4301 Price..............**85c**
If by mail, postage extra, 11 cents.

How to Measure Up Wood Work for Buildings.

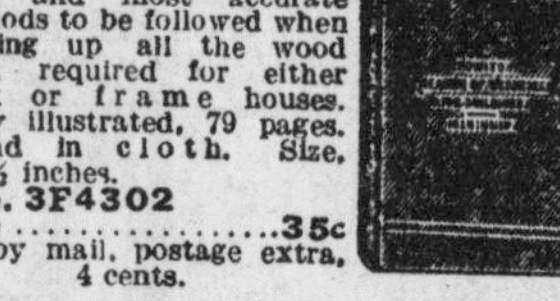

By Owen B. Maginnis. This book describes the simplest and most accurate methods to be followed when figuring up all the wood work required for either brick or frame houses. Fully illustrated, 79 pages. Bound in cloth. Size, 5x7½ inches.

No. 3F4302 Price..............**35c**
If by mail, postage extra, 4 cents.

Roof Framing Made Easy.

By Owen B. Maginnis. A practical and easily understood system for laying out and framing roofs, adapted to modern construction. The methods described in this book are made clear and intelligible by nearly 100 engravings and extensive explanatory text. This is a revised and enlarged edition, brought thoroughly up to date, contains 164 pages, bound in cloth. Size, 5¾x8 inches.

No. 3F4303 Price..............**65c**
If by mail, postage extra, 7 cents.

The Steel Square and Its Uses.

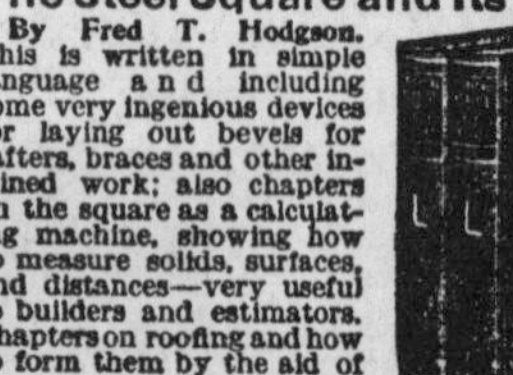

By Fred T. Hodgson. This is written in simple language and including some very ingenious devices for laying out bevels for rafters, braces and other inclined work; also chapters on the square as a calculating machine, showing how to measure solids, surfaces, and distances—very useful to builders and estimators. Chapters on roofing and how to form them by the aid of the square. Chapters on heavy timber framing, showing how the square is used for laying out mortises, tenons, shoulders, etc. The work also contains a large number of diagrams, showing how the square may be used in finding bevels, angles, etc. 350 pages in each volume. Cloth. Illustrated. Size, 5½x7 inches.

No. 3F4305 Volume 1. Price...**$0.58**
No. 3F4306 Volume 2. Price... **.58**
No. 3F4307 Two Vols. Price... **1.10**
If by mail, postage extra, per volume, 9c.

Steel Square Pocket Book.

By Dwight L. Stoddard. This book, (copyrighted in 1904, insuring it being up to date), is written in plain language, illustrated, and will be found to fully explain in simple, easily understood words how to use the steel square to gain the best practical results. Cloth bound. Size, 3½x5¼ inches. 109 pages.

No. 3F4315 Price..............**38c**
If by mail, postage extra, 7 cents.

The Handyman's Book of Woodworking.

By Paul N. Hasluck. A most comprehensive treatise on tools, materials and processe employed in woodworking. A practical book on practical handicraft in wood and the most exhaustive book on the subject ever written. It combines accurate information with clear and definite instruction, appealing not only to the restricted requirements of the amateur, but also making a direct appeal to the professional carpenter, joiner and cabinet worker. An invaluable book for ready reference, especially useful to persons in out of the way places, as it is filled with practical hints and details that are of the greatest value to those whose very existence often depends on their ability to use woodworking tools. 2545 illustrations and working drawings. 760 pages, bound in cloth. Size, 7x9¼ inches.

No. 3F4320 Price..............**$1.90**
If by mail, postage extra, 32 cents.

Hodgson's Stair Building.

By Fred T. Hodgson. The systems outlined in this book are new, simple, plain, and are such as are employed by the most successful carpenters. It contains the simplest system of stair building, and gives instructions for their building, planning, and decorations, also outlines the best methods known in the art of hand railing, with complete instructions for laying out and working handrails suitable for any kind of stairs. Cloth. 196 pages. Size, 5¼x7¾ inches.

No. 3F4340 Price..............**58c**
If by mail, postage extra, 9 cents.

Hodgson's Low Cost Homes.

By Fred T. Hodgson. This book contains perspective views and floor plans of one hundred houses, churches, schoolhouses and barns. The plans shown have been built from, and many of them duplicated many times over. All are practical, the creation of the well known author and many other architects throughout the United States and Canada. Cloth. 200 pages, 200 illustrations. Size, 5½x7¾ inches.

No. 3F4365 Price..............**58c**
If by mail, postage extra, 10 cents.

Hodgson's Practical Bungalows and Cottages.

By Fred T. Hodgson. The book contains perspective wash drawings and floor plans of 125 choice homes, ranging in price from $500 to $2,000, and is invaluable to the home builder, furnishing many new and up to date ideas and suggestions in modern architecture. Each plan illustrated will show by the complete working plans and specifications that we give you designs that will work out to the best advantage and will give you the most for your money; besides, every inch of space has been utilized to the best advantage. Every plan advertised is made by a licensed architect and been built from to the entire satisfaction of the builder and within the estimated cost invariably. We are prepared to furnish blue prints at a very moderate cost, ranging from $5.00 to $10.00, according to the cost of erection, consisting of floor, roof and foundation plans, front, side and rear elevations, with complete typewritten specifications. Size, 5½x8 inches. Bound in cloth. 250 pages.

No. 3F4367 Price..............**60c**
If by mail, postage extra, 12 cents.

Radford's Ideal Homes.

If you are thinking of building a home and want modern and up to date plans you will find this book completely describes just what you want. Contains illustrations and plans of houses, summer cottages, churches, barns, etc., at prices ranging from $550 to $6,500, giving all the comforts and conveniences, suited to every location, want, etc. Cloth. Size, 7½x10½ inches. Over 200 pages.

No. 3F4370 Price..............**68c**
If by mail, postage extra, 9 cents.

Radford's American Homes.

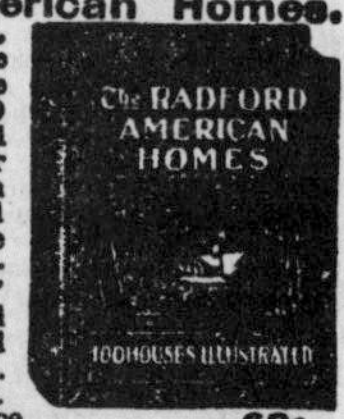

This is the latest, complete, up to date book of modern house plans. Contains 100 designs of medium and low priced houses never before illustrated. An entirely new book and continuation of the work begun in "Radford's Ideal Homes." The designs are all original, practical and artistic. Cloth bound. Size, 8¼x6 in. 256 pages.

No. 3F4375 Price..............**68c**
If by mail, postage extra, 9 cents.

IMPORTANT.—We can furnish any blue print or plan in any book listed in this catalogue at 15 per cent less than the prices asked by the publisher. When ordering, do not fail to give number of blue print wanted.

Modern House Building.

By Fred T. Hodgson. When the low price is considered, this is the best book on house plans and specifications published. Adapted to all conditions of town and country, with accurate estimates of material and cost. Contains over 50 plans and specifications of dwellings, cottages, barns, etc. Prices ranging from $450 to $6,200. Size, 4½x6¾ inches. 115 pages. Bound in cloth.

No. 3F4382 Price..............**21c**
If by mail, postage extra, 5 cents.

Hodgson's Contractors' Guide.

By Fred T. Hodgson. Contains a simple explanation of the various methods of estimating builders' work by the square, by the cubic foot, in rough quantities, accurate quantities and other methods. The mason, plasterer, carpenter, bricklayer, contractor, painter and plumber will find rules and methods given in this volume for estimating the cost of work, to which is added rules and tables showing quick methods for obtaining results in estimating. 300 pages, fully illustrated. Cloth. Size, 5½x7¾ inches.

No. 3F4385 Price (Postage, 12c) **98c**

Builders' Architectural Drawing Self Taught.

By Fred T. Hodgson. This work is especially designed for carpenters, architects and other woodworkers who desire to learn drawing at home. Over 300 fine line engravings made especially for the work with eighteen large double folding drawings with full explanation for each. Also contains perspective views and floor plans of 50 low and medium priced houses. Cloth. Size, 5¼x7¾ inches. 300 pages.

No. 3F4400 Price..............**$1.35**
If by mail, postage extra, 14 cents.

Architectural Drawing.

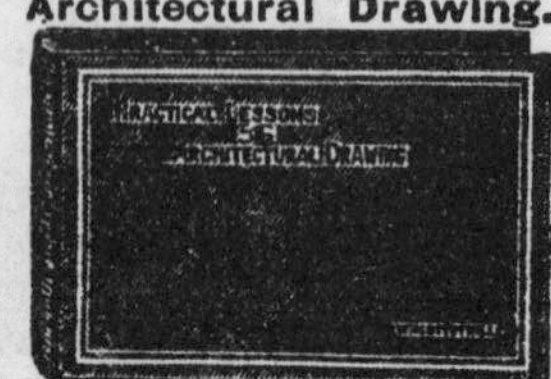

By William T. Tuthill. If you are interested in becoming a practical draftsman and want to learn drawing at home, this book will explain in detail all that you desire to know. It is suited to the wants of all those who desire to acquire a thorough knowledge of architectural drawing and construction. Cloth. Size, 11½x7½ inches. Number of pages, 60.

No. 3F4405 Price..............**$1.78**
If by mail, postage extra, 12 cents.

Concretes, Cements, Mortars, Plasters and Stucco.

By Fred T. Hodgson. As far as it has been possible to avoid chemical descriptions of limes, cements and other materials, and theories of no value to the workman, such has been done, and nothing has been admitted into the pages of the work that does not possess a truly practical character. Concretes and cements have received special attention, and the latest methods of making and using cement building blocks, laying cement sidewalks, putting in concrete foundations, making cement casts and ornaments, are discussed at length. Plastering and stucco work receive a fair share of consideration and the best methods of making and using are described in the usual simple manner so characteristic of Mr. Hodgson's style. The book contains a large number of illustrations of tools, appliances and methods employed in making and applying concretes, cements, mortars, plasters and stucco, which will greatly assist in making it easy for the student to follow and understand the text. Size, 5¼x7½ inches, 300 pages, fully illustrated. Bound in cloth.

No. 3F4410 Price..............**90c**
If by mail, postage extra, 12 cents.

BOOKS FOR MECHANICS AND ENGINEERS.

Practical Pointers For Patentees.

By F. A. Cresse. Contains valuable information and advice on the sale of patents, and illustrations of the best methods employed by the most successful inventors in handling their inventions. Published by the Scientific American. 144 pages, bound in cloth. Size, 5x7½ inches.

No. 3F4495 Price............88c
If by mail, postage extra, 6c

Appleton's Cyclopedia of Applied Mechanics.

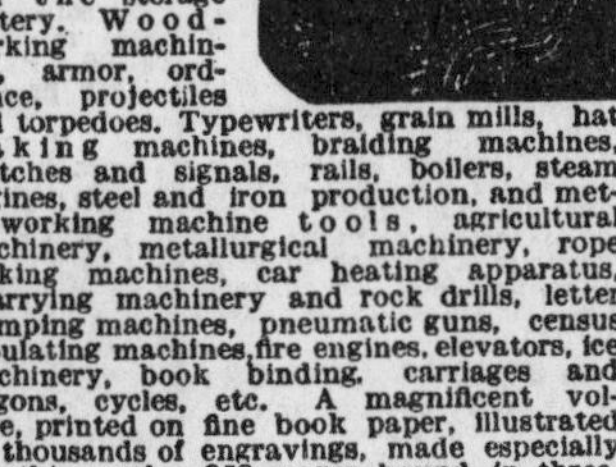

A practical treatise on machines, motors, and the transmission of power. Special chapters on electric welding, aluminum, cotton spinning machinery, water wheels, dynamo electric machines, electric motors, electric transmission of power and the storage battery. Woodworking machinery, armor, ordnance, projectiles and torpedoes. Typewriters, grain mills, hat making machines, braiding machines, switches and signals, rails, boilers, steam engines, steel and iron production, and metal working machine tools, agricultural machinery, metallurgical machinery, rope making machines, car heating apparatus, quarrying machinery and rock drills, letter stamping machines, pneumatic guns, census tabulating machines, fire engines, elevators, ice machinery, book binding, carriages and wagons, cycles, etc. A magnificent volume, printed on fine book paper, illustrated by thousands of engravings, made especially for this work. 959 pages, bound in three-quarters morocco leather, with marbled sides; a complete mechanical library in itself. Size, 7½x10½ inches.

No. 3F4497 Price............$3.75
Weight, packed for shipment, 5 pounds.

Moore's Universal Assistant and Complete Mechanic.

Contains industrial facts, calculations, recipes, processes and trade secrets for every known business. Also 200,000 items for gas, steam, civil and mining engineers, machinists, plumbers, miners, assayers, woodworkers, etc.; information for engineers, firemen, boilermakers, engine and car builders, watchmakers, jewelers, gilders, platers, silversmiths, opticians, etc. Cloth. Illustrated. 1,016 pages. Size, 5¼x7½ inches.

No. 3F4500 Price 69c
If by mail, postage extra, 21 cents.

Brookes' Twentieth Century Machine Shop Practice.

By L. Elliott Brookes. Arithmetic, practical geometry, mensuration, applied mechanics, properties of steam, the indicator, horse power, electricity, measuring devices, machinists' tools, shop tools, machine tools, auxiliary machines, portable tools, miscellaneous tools, plain and spiral indexing machines, notes on steel, gas furnaces, shop talks, shop kinks, medical aid, tables. Over 400 illustrations, 631 pages. Bound in cloth. Size, 5¼x8 inches.

No. 3F4503 Price.............$1.39
If by mail, postage extra, 18 cents.

Machine Design.

By J. G. A. Meyer. Being a complete treatise on the elementary principles of machine design, embracing the properties of connecting rods, piston rods, cotter joints, screw wrenches, etc. With instructions for setting a plain sliding valve and eccentric, and practical hints for making of necessary calculations and working drawings. Cloth, 100 pages. Size, 5x7½ inches.

No. 3F4505 Price. 75c
If by mail, postage extra, 6 cents.

Mechanical Appliances and Novelties of Construction.

By Gardiner D. Hiscox. An encyclopedia of mechanical movements and mechanical appliances, including many novelties of construction used in the arts of manufacturing and engineering, including an explanatory chapter on the leading conceptions of perpetual motion existing during the last three centuries. Hundreds of illustrations, 396 pages. Bound in cloth. Size, 6¼x9¼ inches.

No. 3F4510 Price..............$2.25
If by mail, postage extra, 23 cents.

Practical Pattern Making.

By F. W. Barrows. A thoroughly practical work on the art of making patterns, containing detailed descriptions of all necessary materials—tells how to use them—describes all necessary tools, both hand tools and machine tools, with special chapters on the lathe, band saw and circular saw, numerous illustrated examples of pattern work, with many pages of metal pattern work, gating and plate work, and finally the cost, marking and record of patterns, is explained and illustrated. 326 pages. Bound in cloth. Size, 5½x7½ inches.

No. 3F4514 Price..............$1.50
If by mail, postage extra, 12 cents.

American Tool Making and Interchangeable Manufacturing.

By Jos. V. Woodworth. A treatise upon the designing, constructing, use and installation of tools, jigs, fixtures, devices, special appliances, sheet metal working processes, automatic mechanisms and labor saving contrivances, together with their use in the lathe, milling machine, turret lathe, screw machine, boring mill, power press, sub press, drop hammer, etc., for the working of metals, the production of interchangeable machine parts, and the manufacture of repetition articles of metal. Illustrated with 600 engravings, 535 pages. Bound in cloth. Size, 6¾x9¾ inches.

No. 3F4525 Price..............$3.00
If by mail, postage extra, 26 cents.

Shop Kinks.

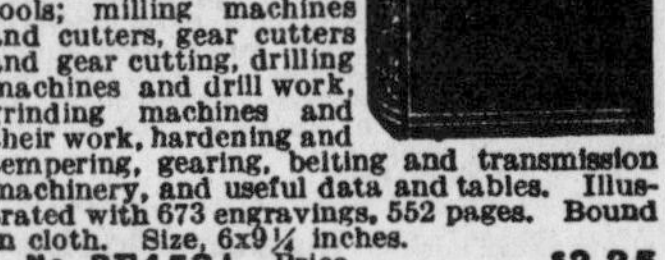

By Robert Grimshaw. This is an exceedingly popular book, entirely different from any other on machine shop practice showing special ways of doing work better, more cheaply and more rapidly than usual, as done in fifty or more leading shops in America. Full of valuable and helpful suggestions regarding things that can be applied to shop practice. Illustrated with 222 new and original engravings. Fourth edition, 393 pages. Bound in cloth. Size, 5½x8 inches.

No. 3F4528 Price............$1.88
If by mail, postage extra, 12 cents.

Modern Machine Shop Tools.

By Wm. H. Vandervoort. A practical treatise describing in every detail, the construction, operation and manipulation of both hand and machine tools. There are chapters on filing, fitting and scraping surfaces, on drills, reamers, taps and dies. The lathe and its tools; planers, shapers and their tools; milling machines and cutters, gear cutters and gear cutting, drilling machines and drill work, grinding machines and their work, hardening and tempering, gearing, belting and transmission machinery, and useful data and tables. Illustrated with 673 engravings, 552 pages. Bound in cloth. Size, 6x9¼ inches.

No. 3F4531 Price..............$2.25
If by mail, postage extra, 23 cents.

Dies, Their Construction and Use.

By Jos. V. Woodworth. A treatise on the design construction and use of dies, punches, tools, fixtures and devices, together with the manner in which they should be used in the power press for the cheap and rapid production of sheet metal parts and articles. Comprises fundamental designs and practical points by which sheet metal parts may be produced at the minimum of cost and maximum of output, with special reference to the hardening and tempering of press tools, the use of files, and to the classes of work which may be produced to the best advantage by the use of dies in the power press. Hundreds of illustrations, 384 pages. Bound in cloth. Size, 6x9 inches.

No. 3F4533 Price..............$2.25
If by mail, postage extra, 20 cents.

Plumbers' Handy Manual.

By John W. Johnson. A manual for plumbers and gas fitters. New 1906 revised and enlarged edition. Treats of steam and hot water heating, plumbing and gas fitting. For building small heating or gas plants this book will be found indispensable. Care of pumps made easy. Measurements of all kinds arranged conveniently in tables. Fully illustrated with cuts and building plans. Cloth bound. Size, 4½x6¾. 203 pages.

No. 3F4534 Price..............68c
If by mail, postage extra, 7 cents.

Home Mechanics for Amateurs.

By Geo. M. Hopkins. Scientific American Series. This book deals with woodworking, household ornaments, metal spinning, silver work, making model engines, boilers and water motors; making telescopes, microscopes and meteorological instruments, electrical chimes, cabinets, bells, night lights, dynamos, motors, electric lights and an electrical furnace. It is a thoroughly practical book by the most noted amateur experimenter in America. 320 illustrations. Bound in cloth. 370 pages. Size, 6x8¼ inches.

No. 3F4535 Price............$1.30
If by mail, postage extra, 15 cents.

Sheet Metal Workers' Instructor.

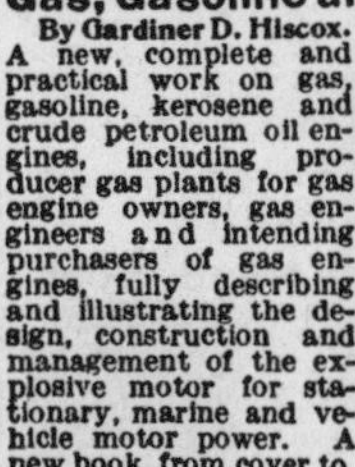

This work consists of useful information for sheet metal workers in all branches of the industry, and contains practical rules for describing the various patterns for sheet iron, copper and tin work. Geometrical construction of plane figures. Examples of practical pattern drawing. Tools and appliances used in sheet metal work. Examples of practical sheet metal work. Geometrical construction and development of solid figures. Soldering and brazing. Tinning. Retinning and galvanizing. Materials used in sheet metal work. Useful information. Tables, etc. Bound in cloth. Size, 6x8 inches, 300 pages, profusely illustrated.

No. 3F4537 Price............$1.20
If by mail, postage extra, 14 cents.

Modern Blacksmithing.

By J. G. Holstrom. An entirely new work on rational horseshoeing and wagon making. Written by a man of thirty years' experience. Contains nothing but elementary rules, thus avoiding technical terms and enabling the young man to master the principles without unnecessary delay and study. The book is filled with rules and recipes of great value to farmers, horseshoers, wagon makers, machinists, liverymen, well drillers and manufacturers. Illustrated. Cloth. Size, 5¼x7¼ ins.

No. 3F4550 Price..............55c
If by mail, postage extra, 12 cents.

Gas, Gasoline and Oil Engines.

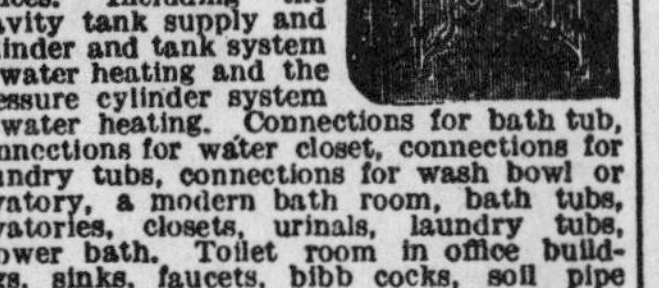

By Gardiner D. Hiscox. A new, complete and practical work on gas, gasoline, kerosene and crude petroleum oil engines, including producer gas plants for gas engine owners, gas engineers and intending purchasers of gas engines, fully describing and illustrating the design, construction and management of the explosive motor for stationary, marine and vehicle motor power. A new book from cover to cover, entirely reset, revised and enlarged. 351 engravings, 442 pages. Substantially bound in cloth. Size, 6¼x9½ inches. The latest and most comprehensive work on this subject.

No. 3F4570 Price............$1.87
If by mail, postage extra, 22 cents.

Gas and Oil Engines.

By L. E. Brookes. Gives full and clear instructions on all points relating to the care and repair of stationary or portable gas and oil engines. This book is intended to furnish practical information regarding gas, gasoline and kerosene engines, for the use of operators and any others who may be interested in their construction and management. Over 200 pages, with complete diagrams and illustrations. Size, 5x6¼ inches.

No. 3F4575 Cloth. Price..........60c
No. 3F4576 Full leather. Price..88c
If by mail, postage extra, 12 cents.

Practical Up to Date Plumbing.

By George B. Clow. A practical up to date work on Sanitary Plumbing, comprising useful information on the wiping and soldering of lead pipe joints and the installation of hot and cold water and drainage systems into modern residences. Including the gravity tank supply and cylinder and tank system of water heating and the pressure cylinder system of water heating. Connections for bath tub, connections for water closet, connections for laundry tubs, connections for wash bowl or lavatory, a modern bath room, bath tubs, lavatories, closets, urinals, laundry tubs, shower bath. Toilet room in office buildings, sinks, faucets, bibb cocks, soil pipe fittings. Drainage fittings. Plumber's tool kit, etc. Bound in cloth. Size, 6x8 inches, 200 pages.

No. 3F4580 Price..................90c
If by mail, postage extra, 14 cents.

Hot Water Heating, Steam and Gas Fitting.

By Wm. Donaldson. A modern treatise on hot water, steam and furnace heating, and steam and gas fitting, which is intended for the use and information of the owners of buildings and the mechanics who install the heating plants in them. It gives full and concise information with regard to steam boilers and water heaters and furnaces, pipe systems for steam and hot water plants, radiation, radiator valves and connections, systems of radiation, heating surfaces, pipe and pipe fittings, damper regulators, fitters' tools, heating surface of pipes, installing a heating plant and specifications. Plans and elevations of steam and hot water heating plants are shown and all other subjects in the book are fully illustrated. Size, 6x8 inches, 200 pages, over 100 illustrations. Bound in cloth.

No. 3F4585 Price..............90c
If by mail, postage extra, 14 cents.

Steam Boilers.

By C. F. Swingle. This book was written in 1904, and is complete and modern, fully describing with illustrations the steam boilers of various types. Tells all about boiler troubles, with catechism, such as pressure, steam pumps, combustion, strength, boiler settings and mechanical stokers. Fully illustrated. Over 200 pages. Bound in full leather. Size, 5x6¾ inches.

No. 3F4600 Price............$1.10
If by mail, postage extra, 12 cents.

Engineers' New Handy Book For Steam Engineers and Electricians.

Roper Handy Book Series.

Contains complete and practical information as to the running of stationary, locomotive, marine, gas and gasoline engines; also chapters on electricity, and explanations of dynamos, motors, batteries, switchboards, telephones, bells, annunciators, alarms, etc.; also rules for calculating sizes of wires. Contains also all questions most likely to be asked before being licensed as an engineer. Nearly 900 pages. 325 illustrations, 222 tables. Leather. Size, 4¾x6¾ inches. Retail price, $3.50.

No. 3F4620 Our price........$2.10
If by mail, postage extra, 5 cents.

Instructions and Suggestions for Engineers and Firemen.

ROPER'S HANDY BOOK SERIES.

Brimful of just such information as persons having charge of machinery need. Full of suggestions and instructions. Leather. 66 pages. Size, 4x6 inches. Retail price, $2.00.

No. 3F4625
Our price $1.20
If by mail, postage extra, 5 cents.

Farm Engines and How to Run Them.

Revised and enlarged by William L. Webber. Simple and reliable chapters about the farm engines and their troubles, with clear explanations about traction engines, threshers and all farm machinery. Contains 200 questions and answers for farm engine engineers, firemen, etc. Cloth. 215 pages. Illustrated. Size, 5¼x8 inches.

No. 3F4630 Price..............58c
If by mail, postage extra, 10 cents.

Engine Runners' Catechism.

By Robert Grimshaw, M.E. Latest edition. To young engineers this catechism will be of great value, especially those who may be preparing to go forward to be examined for certificates of competency, and to engineers of advanced standing many practical points are given. 336 pages. Illustrated. Cloth. Size, 4¼x5¾ inches. Retail price, $2.00.

No. 3F4635 Our price $1.48
If by mail, postage extra, 8 cents.

Steam Engine Catechism.

By Robert Grimshaw, M.E. A series of direct practical answers to direct practical questions. Not only intended for young engineers and for examination questions, but a handy volume for everyone interested in steam. Also contains formulas and worked out answers for all the problems that appertain to the operation and management of the steam engine. 413 pages. Illustrated. Cloth. Size, 4½x5¾ inches.

No. 3F4640 Price..........$1.48
If by mail, postage extra, 8 cents.

BOOKS FOR MECHANICS AND ENGINEERS—Continued.

The Traction Engine.

Every traction engine owner, farmer, mechanic or anyone who has anything to do with threshing or operating a traction engine should own a copy of this book. It treats of the use and abuse of traction engines and traction engine troubles. It was entirely rewritten and revised in 1904 and is one of the most up to date books on this engine published. Over 200 pages. Fully illustrated. Size, 4¾x6½ inches.
No. 3F4645 Price 55c
If by mail, postage extra, 6 cents.

New Catechism for Steam Engineers and Electricians.

Roper's Handy Book Series.

Upon the construction and management of steam engines, steam boilers and electrical apparatus. This catechism is particularly adapted to the needs of engineers preparing to pass examinations for license. Fully illustrated. Cloth. Size, 4½x6 inches. 357 pages.
No. 3F4655 Price..........$1.20
If by mail, postage extra, 5 cents.

Questions and Answers For Steam Engineers and Electricians.

Roper's Handy Book Series.

New Edition. Contains all the questions that an engineer will be asked when undergoing an examination for the purpose of procuring a license, with the answers to the same, couched in language so plain that any engineer or fireman can in a short time commit them to memory. Leather. Size, 4x6 inches. 306 pages. Retail price, $2.00.
No. 3F4660 Our price..........$1.20
If by mail, postage extra, 5 cents.

Twentieth Century Hand Book for Steam Engineers and Electricians.

By C. E. Swingle, M. E. A compendium of useful knowledge appertaining to the care and management of steam engines, boilers and dynamos. Thoroughly practical, with full instructions in regard to making evaporation tests on boilers. The adjustment of the slide valve, corliss valves, etc., fully described and illustrated, together with the application of the indicator and diagram analysis. The electrical division is written by engineers for engineers and is a clear and comprehensive treatise on the principles, construction and operations of dynamos, motors, lamps, etc. 512 pages, 275 illustrations. Bound in full leather. Size, 5x6⅝x1 inches.
No. 3F4665 Price..............$1.85
If by mail, postage extra, 12 cents.

Modern Locomotive Engineering.

By. C. E. Swingle. This is the most simple and concise self educating work on locomotive engineering published. It will be found an excellent guide for beginners who are ambitious to be something more than firemen, and will prove of great assistance to older and more experienced engineers. Contains also complete questions and answers. It is the most complete locomotive engineering book published, and contains also chapters and illustrations on third rail electric work and the turbine engine. 650 pages. Over 300 illustrations. Bound in full leather. Size, 5x6¾ inches.
No. 3F4680 Price $1.85
If by mail, postage extra, 12 cents.

Locomotive Catechism.

By Robt. Grimshaw. This book gives in plain language, with full, complete answers, not only all the questions asked by the examining engineer, but those which the young and less experienced would ask the veteran, and which old hands ask as "stickers." It is a veritable encyclopedia of the locomotive, free from mathematics, easily understood and thoroughly up to date. Contains 1,600 questions with their answers. 223 illustrations and 12 folding plates; nearly 450 pages. Bound in cloth. Size, 5¼x7½ inches.
No. 3F4683 Price..........$1.50
If by mail postage extra, 12 cents.

Handbook of the Locomotive.

Roper's Handy Book Series.

A valuable treatise on the subject of the locomotive. Written in plain language and easily understood. Leather. Size, 4½x6 inches. 324 pages. Retail price, $2.50.
No. 3F4686 Our price $1.50
If by mail, postage extra, 5 cents.

Modern Air Brake Practice

By Frank H Dukesmith. The new air brake book. Invaluable to engineers, firemen, electric motormen and mechanics, with questions and answers for locomotive engineers and electric motormen. Part one explains the various parts of the air brake equipment. Part two treats of the various defects and their remedies. Part three treats of the philosophy of the air brake handling, together with tables and rules for computing brake power, leverage, etc. Profusely illustrated. Every device now in use in the Westinghouse and New York air brake system is fully explained. Bound in cloth. 400 pages. Size, 5¾x8 inches.
No. 3F4690 Price..............90c
If by mail, postage extra, 12 cents.

Up to Date New York Air Brake Catechism.

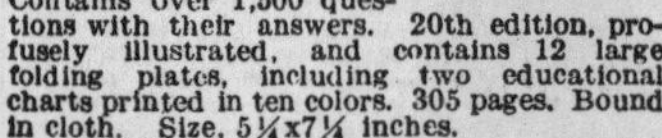

By Robt. H. Blackal. The only complete treatise on the New York air brake and signalling apparatus, giving a detailed description of all the parts, their operation, troubles and the method of locating and remedying same. Fully illustrated. 254 pages. Bound in cloth. Size, 5¼x7½ inches.
No. 3F4692
Price 75c
If by mail, postage extra, 9 cents.

Westinghouse Air Brake Catechism.

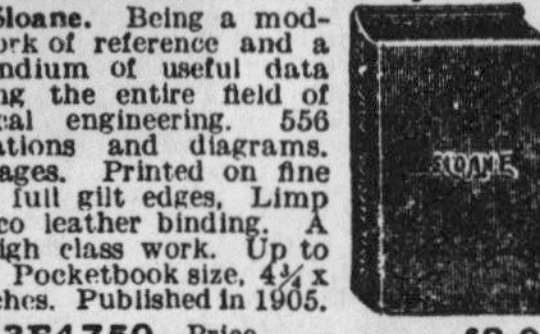

By Robt. H. Blackall. A complete study of the Westinghouse Air Brake equipment, the operation of all the parts explained in detail, and the practical art of finding their peculiarities and defects, with the proper remedy, is given. It includes the necessary information to enable a railroad man to pass a thoroughly satisfactory examination on the subject of air brakes. Contains over 1,500 questions with their answers. 20th edition, profusely illustrated, and contains 12 large folding plates, including two educational charts printed in ten colors. 305 pages. Bound in cloth. Size, 5¼x7¼ inches.
No. 3F4694 Price $1.50
If by mail, postage extra, 11 cents.

The Motormen's and Conductors' Compendium.

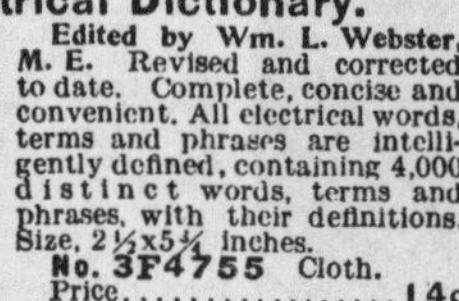

By G. H. Gayelty. Tells how to run an electric car, care and troubles of car motor, explanation of controlling stand, with questions and answers. Cloth. Illustrated. Size, 4¼x6½ inches. 113 pages.
No. 3F4720 Price..33c
If by mail, postage extra, 8 cents.

The Electrician's Handy Book.

By Sloane. Being a modern work of reference and a compendium of useful data covering the entire field of electrical engineering. 556 illustrations and diagrams. 760 pages. Printed on fine paper, full gilt edges, Limp morocco leather binding. A very high class work. Up to date. Pocketbook size, 4¾x6½ inches. Published in 1905.
No. 3F4750 Price $2.98
If by mail, postage extra, 15 cents.

Electrical Dictionary.

Edited by Wm. L. Webster, M. E. Revised and corrected to date. Complete, concise and convenient. All electrical words, terms and phrases are intelligently defined, containing 4,000 distinct words, terms and phrases, with their definitions. Size, 2½x5¼ inches.
No. 3F4755 Cloth.
Price..............14c
No. 3F4756 Full leather.
Price..............28c
If by mail, postage extra, either style, 3 cents.

Telephone Guide.

A complete book on telephones, explaining how to build telephone lines, install bridging and series of telephones, how to inspect telephone material and correct telephone troubles; fully illustrated. Bound in cloth. Size, 5½x7½ inches. 226 pages.
No. 3F4765
Price..............70c
If by mail, postage extra, 13 cents.

The Telegraph Instructor.

By G. M. Dodge. The best book published on this subject. Terms used are simple, concise and comprehensive. Universally endorsed. 263 pages. Descriptive illustrations. Bound in cloth. Size, 4¾x7 inches.
No. 3F4770 Price..65c
If by mail, postage extra, 8c.

Dynamo Tenders' Instruction Book.

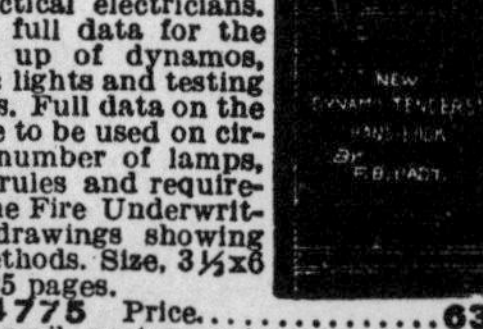

By F. B. Badt. A neat and complete book in cloth binding for practical electricians. It contains full data for the connecting up of dynamos, motors, arc lights and testing instruments. Full data on the sizes of wire to be used on circuits, the number of lamps, etc. Also rules and requirements of the Fire Underwriters, with drawings showing the best methods. Size, 3½x6 inches. 225 pages.
No. 3F4775 Price..............63c
If by mail, postage extra, 4 cents.

Easy Electrical Experiments.

By L. B. Dickinson. An elementary handbook, explains in simple language everything about galvanometers, batteries, magnets, induction coils, volt meters, dynamos, storage batteries, telephones, telegraph instruments, etc. It fully illustrates and explains how to make electrical toys and perform easy experiments. Bound in cloth. Size, 4½x6 inches. 204 pages.
No. 3F4780
Price..........68c
If by mail, postage extra, 12 cents.

Electricity and Magnetism.

By Sylvanus P. Thompson. This book is an excellent work on electricity and magnetism. It affords beginners a clear and accurate knowledge and explains a number of simple experiments to illustrate magnetism and electricity. This is a first class reference or text book. Contains 456 pages. Bound in cloth. Size, 5x7½x1½ inches.
No. 3F4785
Price 58c
If by mail, postage extra, 12 cents.

American Watchmaker and Jeweler.

By Henry G. Abbott. Compiled from the best and most reliable sources. Contains complete directions for using all the latest tools, attachments and devices for watchmakers and jewelers. Chapters on watch repairing, cleaning, etc. A treatise on wheels and pinions and hundreds of miscellaneous recipes, formulas, and hints on all kinds of work of great value to every jeweler. 367 pages. 288 illustrations. Cloth bound. Size, 5½x7½ inches.
No. 3F4860 Price............$1.10
If by mail, postage extra, 12 cents.

Watch Repairing.

By N. B. Sherwood. A practical book, written in a practical manner by a practical man. Contains complete information about the bench and its accessories. Full information about all the tools necessary to watch repairing. Illustrated. 63 pages. Paper bound. Size, 5¼x7¾ inches.
No. 3F4865 Price..............28c
If by mail, postage extra, 5 cents.

The Signist's Modern Book of Alphabets.

By F. Delamotte. Plain and ornamental, ancient and mediaeval, from the eighth to the twentieth century, with numerals. Including German, Old English, Saxon, Italic, Perspective, Greek, Hebrew, Court Hand, Engrossing, Tuscan, Riband, Gothic, Rustic and Arabesque, with several Original Designs and an Analysis of the Roman and Old English Alphabets, Large, Small, and Numerals, Church Text, Large and Small; German Arabesque, Initials for Illumination, Monograms, Crosses, etc., for the use of Architectural and Engineering Draftsmen, Surveyors, Masons, Decorative Painters, Lithographers, Engravers, Carvers, etc. Size, 6½x9¼ inches. 208 pages. Bound in cloth.
No. 3F4895 Price..............90c
If by mail, postage extra, 13 cents.

Painter, Gilder and Varnisher.

By William G. Brannt. Twenty-seventh edition, revised, enlarged and rewritten. A complete treatise comprising the manufacture and test of pigments, the arts of painting, graining, marbling, staining, sign writing, varnishing, glass staining, together with coach painting and varnishing and the principles of harmony and contrast of colors. Bound in cloth, 395 pages. Size, 5¼x7½ inches.
No. 3F4903 Price $1.15
If by mail, postage extra, 12 cents.

Practical Graining and Marbling.

By Paul N. Hasluck. This book contains comprehensive information on the general principles and practice of graining and marbling, with chapters on the necessary tools and materials, graining in oil, graining in spirit and water colors, oak, maple, mahogany, pitch pine, walnut and fancy wood graining, imitation of various woods and inlaid woods, imitatons of marble etc. 160 pages. Bound in cloth. Size, 5x7 inches.
No. 3F4904 Price..............37c
If by mail, postage extra, 6 cents.

Carriage and Wagon Painting.

Full instructions and detailed directions in plain language for painting carriages, wagons and sleighs, including lettering, scrolling, ornamenting, striping, varnishing and coloring, with numerous recipes for mixing colors. 177 pages. Illustrated. Cloth. Size, 5½x7½ inches.
No. 3F4905
Price..............65c
If by mail, postage extra, 10 cents.

How to Draw and Paint.

Contains instructions in outline, light and shade, perspective, sketching from nature, figure drawing, artistic anatomy, landscape, marine and portrait painting, the principles of coloring applied to painting, etc., 100 engravings. 151 pages. Cloth. Size, 4½x7½ inches.
No. 3F4910 Price..33c
If by mail, postage extra, 7 cents.

Everybody's Paint Book.

This book is especially designed to teach people how they may do their own house painting and save the expense of a professional painter. Contains full directions for mixing and applying paints, varnishes, polishing, staining and calcimining, etc. Cloth. 183 pages. Size, 5½x7½ inches.
No. 3F4915
Price..............59c
Postage extra, 11 cents.

Hardwood Finishing.

By Fred T. Hodgson. Gives rules and directions for finishing in natural colors, and in antique, mahogany, cherry, birch, walnut, oak, ash, redwood, sycamore, pine and all other domestic woods; also staining, polishing, dyeing, gilding and bronzing. 206 pages. Cloth. Size, 5x7½ inches.
No. 3F4920
Price..............59c
If by mail, postage extra, 8 cents.

The Painters' Encyclopedia.

By F. B. Gardner. Chapters on plain and artistic painting, with details of practice in carriage, house, sign and ornamental painting including graining, marbling, staining, varnishing, lettering, stenciling, gilding, bronzing. This is an invaluable book for every painter, no matter with what branch of the art he may be connected. 427 pages. Cloth. Size, 5½x7½ inches.
No. 3F4925 Price..............98c
If by mail, postage extra, 12 cents.

Paper Hangers' Companion.

By James Arrowsmith. A new, thoroughly revised and much enlarged edition, treating fully of tools, pastes, preparatory work, selection and hanging of wall paper, distemper painting and cornice tinting, stencil work, replacing sash cord and broken window panes, with scores of useful wrinkles and recipes. Fully illustrated. 150 pages. Bound in cloth. Size, 5¼x7½ inches.
No. 3F4950 Price..............89c
If by mail, postage extra, 7 cents.

Greatest Things in the World.

Contains history's most remarkable events, men's mightiest achievements, nature's marvels, famous explorations and discoveries, wonderful architectural creations, loftiest mountains, largest rivers, lakes, canals, bridges, etc. 600 pages. Illustrated. Cloth. Size, 7¾x9¾ inches.
No. 3F5000
Price..............95c
If by mail, postage extra, 39 cents.

AGRICULTURE, LIVE STOCK, POULTRY AND DAIRYING

Practical Farming and Gardening.

Edited by Willis MacGerald. The largest, the most complete and the most valuable general work on farming and gardening ever sold at a moderate price. There is more solid, authentic and valuable information crowded into the 500 pages of this book than is to be found in many of the largest and most expensive works on farming and gardening. This book is written for that class of farmers who put brains into the management of soil, plants and animals. Every line of work taken up and described in this book is written by a specialist in that particular line. For example: Everything pertaining to Soil Fertility and Crops is written by Joseph J. Edgerton. Topics pertaining to Gardening and Trucking, by Arthur T. Erwin. Fruits and Forestry, by Levi R. Taft. Injurious Insects and Plant Diseases, by E. S. G. Titus. Animal Husbandry, by Herbert W. Mumford. Diseases of Farm Animals, by R. A. Craig. Other sections in this big book are written by other equally well known authorities, making it an invaluable working guide and reference book to everybody interested in any way in farming or gardening. There are chapters on modern ideas in Soil Treatment and Tillage, Field Crops, their adaptations and economic relations, with specific cultural directions; Vegetable Garden and Trucking Crops, Fruit Culture and Forestry, Important Injurious Insects and Diseases Affecting Field and Garden Crops, Fruits and Shade Trees, Selecting and Feeding Farm Animals for Profit, Beef Making, Feeding Native Cattle for Beef, Feeding Range Cattle for Beef, Diseases of Farm Animals, The Silo in Modern Agriculture, Making Poultry Pay, Handy Rules and Useful Information and Wholesome Cooking Without Waste. Substantially bound in cloth. Printed on the best grade of book paper. Profusely illustrated. Most of the illustrations from original photographs. 500 pages. Size, 6½x8 inches.

No. 3F5290 Price..............**75c**
If by mail, postage extra, 16 cents.

The First Book of Farming.

By Charles L. Goodrich. Published by Doubleday, Page & Co., so you may know it is good. Treats fully of the general principles of plant culture, soils, cultivation, fertilizers, drainage, etc. 86 illustrations. 260 pages. Size, 5¼x7¼ inches. Bound in cloth.

No. 3F5300 Price..............**95c**
If by mail, postage extra, 12 cents.

Farmers' Cyclopedia of Agriculture.

By Earley Vernon Wilcox and Clarence Beaman Smith. A compendium of agricultural science and practices on farm, orchard and garden crops and the feeding and diseases of farm animals. A new, practical and complete presentation of the whole subject of agriculture in its broadest sense. It is designed for agriculturists who want up to date, reliable information on all matters pertaining to crops and stock. It contains detail directions for the culture of every important field, orchard and garden crop grown in America, together with descriptions of insect pests and fungus diseases, and means for their control. It contains accounts of modern methods in feeding and handling all farm stock, including poultry. Diseases of different farm animals are described and the most recent remedies suggested. A vast mass of new and useful information, authoritative, practical and easily found. Over 6,000 topics are covered, and the book is illustrated by nearly 500 superb halftone and other original illustrations, making it the most perfect cyclopedia of agriculture ever attempted. Strongly and substantially bound in silk finish cloth. Printed on the best quality of book paper. 619 pages. Size, 7x9½ inches.

No. 3F5303 Price............**$2.95**
Weight, packed for shipment, 5 pounds.

Magner's Farmers' Encyclopedia.

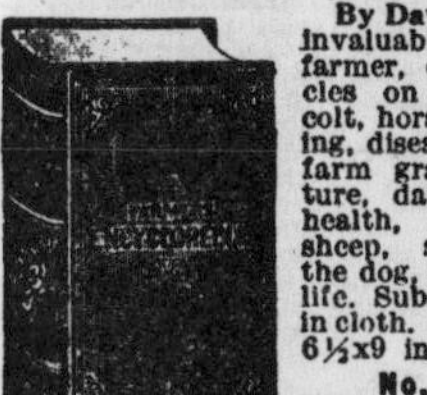

By David Magner. An invaluable book to every farmer, embracing articles on the horse, the colt, horse habits, shoeing, diseases of the horse, farm grasses, fruit culture, dairying, cookery, health, cattle, calving, sheep, swine, poultry, the dog, toilet, and social life. Substantially bound in cloth. 636 pages. Size, 6½x9 inches.

No. 3F5306 Price..............**78c**
If by mail, postage extra, 30 cents.

The Home Encyclopedia of Useful Information.

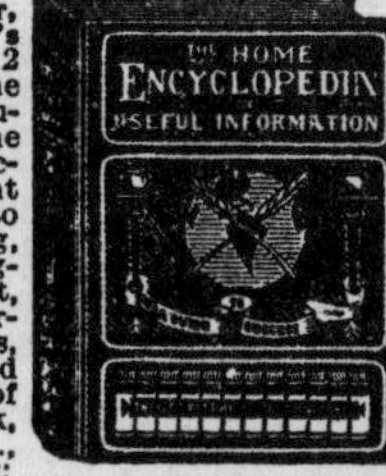

By D. Magner, author of Magner's Horse Book. 12 great books in one volume. Particularly adapted to the farmer. Embracing all important subjects of how to succeed at farming, how to grow vegetables and fruit, and how to exterminate insects, management and treatment of horses, live stock, farm animals, etc., butter making; also home remedies for health and beauty, how to make money, self instruction in bookkeeping, shorthand, penmanship, and law without a lawyer. Royal octavo book of over 700 double column pages, nearly 600 pen drawings and 64 full page halftones. Size, 7¼x9¾ inches, 2 inches thick. Bound in cloth with cover design stamped in gold and colors; marbled edges. Retail price, $2.50.

No. 3F5309 Our price...........**85c**
If by mail, postage extra, 32 cents.

Spraying Crops.

By Clarence M. Weed. Why, when and how to do it. A complete manual that will enable you to use your spraying machine to the best possible advantage. Thoroughly up to date, published in 1903. Fully illustrated. 136 pages. Size, 5x7½ inches. Bound in cloth.

No. 3F5325 Price, **39c**
If by mail, postage extra, 7 cents.

Fumigation Methods.

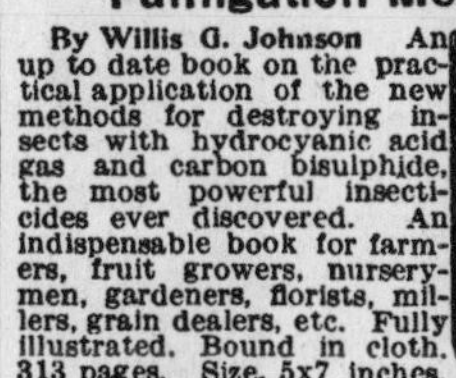

By Willis G. Johnson. An up to date book on the practical application of the new methods for destroying insects with hydrocyanic acid gas and carbon bisulphide, the most powerful insecticides ever discovered. An indispensable book for farmers, fruit growers, nurserymen, gardeners, florists, millers, grain dealers, etc. Fully illustrated. Bound in cloth. 313 pages. Size, 5x7 inches.

No. 3F5328 Price..............**85c**
If by mail, postage extra, 10 cents.

The Potato.

By Samuel Fraser. A practical treatise on the potato, its characteristics, plant cultivation, harvesting, storing, marketing, insect enemies, diseases and their remedies, etc. You can make more money out of potatoes after you have read this book. 51 illustrations. 185 pages. Size, 5x7½ inches. Bound in cloth.

No. 3F5370 Price..............**60c**
If by mail, postage extra, 9 cents.

Tobacco Leaf.

By J. B. Killebrew. A practical handbook of the most approved methods in growing, harvesting, curing, packing and selling tobacco, with an account of the operations in every department of tobacco manufacture. Based on actual experience in the field, curing barn, packing house, factory and laboratory. 150 original engravings. Bound in cloth. 506 pages. Size, 5x7 inches.

No. 3F5372 Price............**$1.70**
If by mail, postage extra, 15 cents.

Asparagus.

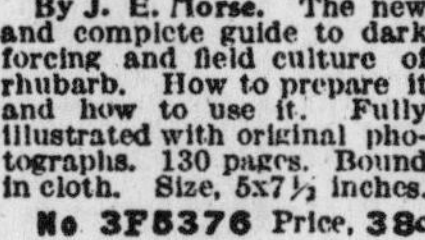

By F. M. Hexamer. A practical treatise on the planting, cultivation, harvesting, marketing and preserving of asparagus. 166 pages. Size, 5x7½ inches. Cloth.

No. 3F5373 Price, **38c**
If by mail, postage extra, 8 cents.

Rhubarb Culture.

By J. E. Morse. The new and complete guide to dark forcing and field culture of rhubarb. How to prepare it and how to use it. Fully illustrated with original photographs. 130 pages. Bound in cloth. Size, 5x7½ inches.

No. 3F5376 Price, **38c**
If by mail, postage extra, 6 cents.

New Onion Culture.

By T. Greiner. A new edition of this well known book, thoroughly rewritten and enlarged. Tells you how you can make big money in onions. Fully illustrated. 114 pages. Size, 5x7½ inches. Bound in cloth.

No. 3F5379 Price, **38c**
If by mail, postage extra, 7 cents.

The Book of Corn.

By Herbert Myrick, assisted by Shamel, Burnett, Fulton, Snow and other most capable specialists. A complete treatise upon the culture, marketing and uses of corn in America and elsewhere. For farmers, dealers and others. Fully illustrated. Bound in cloth. 372 pages. Size, 5x7 inches.

No. 3F5381 Price............**$1.25**
If by mail, postage extra, 11 cents.

Manual of Corn Judging.

By Archibald Dixon Shamel. An invaluable book in the various schools of corn judging, farmers' institutes, fairs and like places where corn is studied. Fully illustrated with photographs by the author. 72 pages. Size, 5x7¼ inches. Bound in cloth.

No. 3F5382 Price..............**38c**
If by mail, postage extra, 6 cents.

The Cereals in America.

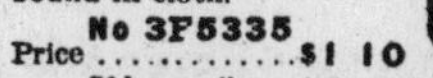

By Thos. F. Hunt. With chapters on the improvement of field crops; wheat, corn, oats, barley, rye, rice, sorghum, buckwheat, etc. Thoroughly up to date, published in 1905. The best book we have ever seen on the subject. 421 pages. Size, 5½x8 inches. Cloth binding.

No. 3F5330 Price............**$1.40**
If by mail, postage extra, 16 cents.

Grasses and How to Grow Them.

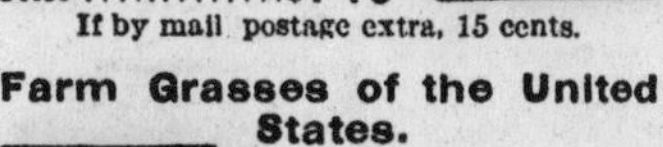

By Thomas Shaw. One of the most complete books written on the subject, with chapters on all the different kinds of grasses, pastures, meadows, hay making, etc. Fully illustrated. Right up to date, published in 1903. 453 pages. Size, 5½x7½ inches. Very substantially bound in cloth.

No. 3F5335 Price.............**$1.10**
If by mail, postage extra, 15 cents.

Farm Grasses of the United States.

By William Jasper Spillman. A practical treatise on the grass crop, seeding and management of meadows and pastures, of the best varieties, the seed and its impurities, grasses for special conditions, etc. Published in 1905 and right up to date. 54 illustrations, 248 pages. Size, 5¼x7½ inches. Cloth.

No. 3F5340 Price..............**82c**
If by mail, postage extra, 10 cents.

Forage Crops Other Than Grasses.

By Thomas Shaw. A complete treatise on the cultivation, harvesting and uses of other forage crops besides grasses, including rape, corn, sorghum, various varieties of clover, cereals, millet, root crops and miscellaneous plants. Fully illustrated. 280 pages. Size, 5x7½ inches.

No. 3F5345 Price..............**80c**
If by mail, postage extra, 12 cents.

Alfalfa.

By F. D. Coburn. Contains a fund of practical information on the production, qualities, worth and uses of alfalfa in the United States and Canada. 163 pages. Fully illustrated. Size, 5x7½ inches.

No. 3F5350 Price..............**38c**
If by mail, postage extra, 8 cents.

Prize Gardening.

By G. Burnap Fiske. This book gives the actual experiences of successful prize winners in the American Agriculturist garden contest. Every line is from actual experience, based on real work; a mine of practical information, comprising the Grand Prize gardener's methods gardening for profit, farm gardens, the home acre, town and city gardens, etc., etc. Fully illustrated with original photographs. Bound in cloth. 320 pages. Size, 5x7 inches.

No. 3F5358 Price..............**85c**
If by mail, postage extra, 11 cents.

Vegetable Gardening.

By Samuel B. Green. A manual on the growing of vegetables for home use and marketing. With chapters on the vegetable garden, irrigation, fertilizers, tillage, seeds, green houses, injurious insects, etc. A very complete work with 123 illustrations. Thoroughly up to date, published in 1905. 252 pages. Size, 5½x7½ inches. Bound in cloth.

No. 3F5360 Price..............**75c**
If by mail, postage extra, 12 cents.

The Seed Grower.

By Charles Johnson. The only book published giving full instructions for the successful growing of seeds and bulbs for the market. It tells you where to find your market, how to grow the best vegetable and flower seeds; how to dry and clean them; how to sort them; what the average crop yield per acre should be for each variety; tells the usual market price for seeds; tells how to keep seeds, how long they retain their vitality, how to raise new varieties and how to obtain fancy prices for them. It also explains the real or true names of many so called "novelties." Bound in cloth. 187 pages. Size, 5x7½ inches.

No. 3F5365 Price..............**69c**
If by mail, postage extra, 9 cents.

Cauliflower, Cabbages, Etc.

By C. L. Allen. A complete guide to the culture of cauliflower, cabbages and allied plants, from seed to harvest. With chapters on diseases, injurious insects, etc. Very fully illustrated. 125 pages. Size, 5 x 7½ inches. Bound in cloth.

No. 3F5385 Price, **38c**
If by mail, postage extra, 7 cents.

Ginseng.

By M. G. Kains. Being a complete guide to the cultivation, harvesting, marketing and market value of this big money maker. Fortunes have been made in ginseng and there is no reason why you should not do the same. This book tells you how. Fully illustrated. 144 pages. Size, 5x7 inches. Bound in cloth.

No. 3F5390 Price, **35c**
If by mail, postage extra, 7 cents.

Mushroom Culture.

By Wm. Robinson. A complete treatise on the culture of mushrooms, with chapters on suitable places for growing mushrooms, culture, preparation of materials, spawn, etc., together with modes of cooking, and descriptions of some of the most common and useful edible mushrooms. Bound in cloth. 171 pages. Size, 5x7 inches.

No. 3F5394 Price..............**40c**
If by mail, postage extra, 5 cents.

Mushrooms; How to Grow Them.

By William Falconer. The profits made by mushroom growers makes this subject one of vital interest to everyone in position to engage in this work. This book is a complete treatise on the subject, constituting a thoroughly good, reliable guide in every way. Fully illustrated. 169 pages. Size, 5x7½ inches. Cloth binding.

No. 3F5395 Price..............**80c**
If by mail, postage extra, 7 cents.

Successful Fruit Culture.

By Samuel T. Maynard. A practical guide to the cultivation and propagation of fruits. Thoroughly up to date. 274 pages. Size, 5x7½ inches. Cloth.

No. 3F5425 Price..............**80c**
If by mail, postage extra, 10 cents.

AGRICULTURE, LIVE STOCK, POULTRY AND DAIRYING—Continued.

Fruit Harvesting, Storing, Marketing.

By F. A. Waugh. A practical guide to the picking, storing, shipping and marketing of fruit, covering the fruit market, fruit picking, sorting and packing, fruit storage, evaporating, canning, statistics of the fruit trade, package laws, commission dealers, cold storage, etc. Fully illustrated. Bound in cloth. 232 pages. Size, 5x7 inches.

No. 3F5428 Price..............85c
If by mail, postage extra, 8 cents.

Amateur Fruit Growing.

By Samuel B. Green. A practical guide to the growing of fruit, both for home use and the market. With very complete chapters on strawberries, raspberries and blackberries, currants and gooseberries, grapes, Juneberries, apples, plums and cherries. With complete instructions for budding and grafting. 125 pages. Size, 5½x7½ inches. Bound in cloth.

No. 3F5430 Price..............39c
If by mail, postage extra, 7 cents.

Systematic Pomology.

By F. A. Waugh. This is the first book in the English language that really constitutes a complete and comprehensive treatment of systematic pomology. It presents clearly and in detail, the whole method by which fruits are studied. Fully illustrated. Bound in cloth. 288 pages. Size, 5x7 inches.

No. 3F5435 Price, 85c
If by mail, postage extra, 10 cents.

The Orchard and Fruit Garden.

By E. P. Powell. This new and complete work deals with the planting and cultivation of fruit, fruit bearing trees and bushes. Every known variety of fruit grown in America is considered. General advice as to the nature, excellence and defects of each fruit is given, and a list of those likely to do best in various localities, with many valuable hints on cultivation. It is a thoroughly practical volume, embodying all the valuable information on the selection of fruit. Bound in cloth. Printed on extra fine book paper. Profusely illustrated. 322 pages. Size, 6x8 inches.

No. 3F5438 Price..............$1.35
If by mail, postage extra, 16 cents.

The Grape Culturist.

By Andrew S. Fuller. In our opinion the very best book published on the culture of the hardy grapes, with full directions for all departments of propagation, culture, etc. 150 excellent engravings, illustrating method of planting, training, grafting, etc., thoroughly revised and brought up to date. 282 pages. Bound in cloth. Size, 5x7 inches.

No. 3F5440 Price..............$1.25
If by mail, postage extra, 10 cents.

Home Floriculture.

By Eben E. Rexford. A practical guide to the treatment of flowering and other ornamental plants in the house and in the garden. A new and very complete book, right up to date, published in 1904. Fully illustrated. 300 pages. Size, 5x7½ inches. Bound in cloth.

No. 3F5450 Price, 80c
If by mail, postage extra, 10 cents.

Flowers.

By Eben E. Rexford. Every woman loves flowers, but few succeed in growing them. With the help so clearly given in this volume, no one need fail. It treats mainly of indoor plants and flowers; those for window gardening; all about their selection, care, light, air, warmth, etc. Bound in cloth. 176 pages. Size, 4¾x6 inches.

No. 3F5452 Price..............38c
If by mail, postage extra, 5 cents.

Land Draining.

By Manly Miles. A book for farmers on the principles and practice of draining, giving the results of the author's extended experience in laying tile drains. The directions for the laying, use and construction of tile drains will enable the farmer to avoid the errors of imperfect construction and the disappointment that necessarily follows such errors. Fully illustrated. Bound in cloth. 200 pages. Size, 5x7 inches.

No. 3F5465 Price..............85c
If by mail, postage extra, 8 cents.

Irrigation Farming.

By Lucius M. Wilcox. A hand book for the practical application of water in the production of crops. The most complete work on irrigation ever published. This is a new edition, revised, enlarged and completely rewritten, based on the author's twenty-five years of actual experience in the field. Fully illustrated. 500 pages. Bound in cloth. Size, 5x7 inches.

No. 3F5468 Price..............$1.70
If by mail, postage extra, 15 cents.

Soiling Crops and the Silo.

By Thos. Shaw. How to cultivate and harvest crops; how to build and fill a silo; how to use silage; newest and most valuable of all books for the dairyman. It tells all about growing and feeding all kinds of soiling crops; tells the climate and soil to which they are adapted, rotation, sowing, cultivating and feeding. Also about building and filling silos, what to use and how to fill and feed it. Fully illustrated. Bound in cloth. 366 pages. Size, 5x7 inches.

No. 3F5472 Price..............$1.25
If by mail, postage extra, 12 cents.

Science of Threshing.

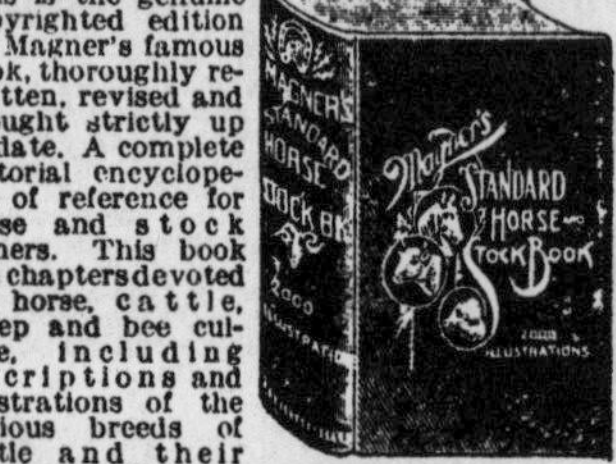

By G. F. Cooper. A complete manual, treating of the operation, management and care of threshing machinery. The only complete copy on this important subject. Besides covering fully the subject of threshing and threshing machinery, the book contains 19 chapters on traction and portable engines. Fully illustrated. Bound in cloth. 175 pages. Size, 5½x7¾ inches.

No. 3F5476 Price..............75c
If by mail, postage extra, 8 cents.

Farm Appliances.

Edited by Geo. A. Martin. This book describes numerous useful and labor saving appliances, which will be found very valuable in every department of farm work. 250 illustrations. Bound in cloth. 192 pages. Size, 5x7 inches.

No. 3F5479
Price..............40c
If by mail, postage extra, 6 cents.

Hedges, Windbreaks, Etc.

By E. P. Powell. A practical treatise on the management of hedge plants, giving accurate directions concerning hedges, how to plant, how to treat them, and especially concerning windbreaks and shelters. Fully illustrated. Bound in cloth. 140 pages. Size, 5x7 inches.

No. 3F5482 Price, 42c
If by mail, postage extra, 6 cents.

Magner's Standard Horse and Stock Book.

By David Magner. This is the genuine copyrighted edition of Magner's famous book, thoroughly rewritten, revised and brought strictly up to date. A complete pictorial encyclopedia of reference for horse and stock owners. This book has chapters devoted to horse, cattle, sheep and bee culture, including descriptions and illustrations of the various breeds of cattle and their breeding. It gives many valuable recipes and secrets hitherto unknown on taming, training, controlling and educating the horse, with chapters on feeding, stabling and the teeth, also full treatment in sickness and accidents. It treats fully of the diseases of cattle, dairying, butter and cheese making, sheep raising, care and management of swine, and their diseases, the poultry interest, the dog and his ailments, bee culture and fruit culture. This book is printed on finely finished paper, handsomely and substantially bound in cloth. 17 special full page plates, showing structure of the foot, etc. Understand, this is the genuine copyrighted Magner's Standard Horse and Stock Book. 1,181 pages. Nearly 2,000 illustrations. Size, 8x10 inches.

No. 3F5520 Price..............$1.35
Weight, packed for shipment, 6 pounds.

Animal Breeding.

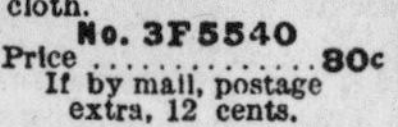

By Thomas Shaw. A new book on this important subject, published in 1905. Constituting a complete treatise on breeding of live stock, covering the subject in every detail. Fully illustrated. 406 pages. Size, 5x7 inches. Bound in cloth.

No. 3F5525
Price..............$1.15
If by mail, postage extra, 12 cents.

The Study of Breeds; Cattle, Sheep and Swine.

By Thomas Shaw. Being a brief and concise treatise on pedigreed breeds of cattle, sheep and swine, and the only book written on the study of breeds as such. An invaluable work for the stock breeder. Profusely illustrated. Right up to date, published in 1905. 370 pages. Size, 5x7½ inches. Bound in cloth.

No. 3F5530
Price..............$1.15
If by mail, postage extra, 14 cents.

How to Tell the Age of a Horse.

By Prof. J. M. Heard. A pocket manual giving full information of the methods employed by professional horsemen in determining the age of a horse, with numerous illustrations showing the shape of the teeth at different ages, and a chapter on horse character, or how to determine the disposition of a horse. In this little book the tricks of horse traders, who doctor up the teeth of old horses to make them look young, is exposed. The most practical book of the kind ever published. Bound in cloth. 58 pages. Size, 3½x5 inches.

No. 3F5533 Price..............25c
If by mail, postage extra, 2 cents.

Feeding and Management of Live Stock.

By Thomas Shaw, of the University of Minnesota. A new book, strictly up to date, and written in such a manner that anyone can get the facts without reading unnecessary matter. It is a complete guide, covering 436 subjects on everything known or that can be thought of with reference to the feeding of live stock. Cloth. Size, 5½x8 inches. 100 pages.

No. 3F5535 Price, 78c
If by mail, postage extra, 5 cents.

Harris on the Pig.

By Joseph Harris. Being a complete treatise on the breeding, rearing, management and improvement of swine. The only up to date book on this subject, and the only really good, complete treatise on pigs. 318 pages. Size, 5¼x7¾ inches. Bound in cloth.

No. 3F5540
Price..............80c
If by mail, postage extra, 12 cents.

Diseases of Swine.

By Robert A. Craig. A practical guide to the prevention and treatment of diseases of swine. The first part treats of general diseases, their diagnosis and remedies. The second part of surgical diseases, the third part of infectious diseases and the fourth part of parasitic diseases. Technical and strictly professional terms are carefully avoided, making the work just as valuable to the practical stock raiser as to the veterinary surgeon. Bound in cloth. 186 pages. Size, 5x7 inches.

No. 3F5542 Price..............40c
If by mail, postage extra, 7 cents.

Home Pork Making.

By A. W. Fulton. A complete guide for the farmer and the country butcher, in all that pertains to hog slaughtering, curing, preserving, storing pork product, from the scalding vat to the kitchen table and dining room. 125 pages. Size, 5x7½ inches. Bound in cloth.

No. 3F5545
Price..............40c
If by mail, postage extra, 7 cents.

Horse Taming.

By William Mullen. Everything about breaking, educating and handling all kinds of horses, with special instructions about colts, teaching horses to drive and for use under the saddle. An invaluable assistant to farmers, stockmen and all who handle horses. Cloth. Size, 5¼x8 inches. 107 pages.

No. 3F5575
Price..............60c
If by mail, postage extra, 11 cents.

Farm Blacksmithing.

By G. M. Drew. A complete treatise on the work which a farm blacksmith will be called upon to do. There are chapters on furnishing the shop, iron and steel, practice work, making of staples, chains, chain hooks, clevises, bolts, heading tools, welding, tongs, etc., with many useful tables and figures. 100 pages, fully illustrated. Bound in cloth. Size, 5¼x7½ inches.

No. 3F5557 Price..............39c
If by mail, postage extra, 5 cents.

Diseases of Live Stock.

By W. B. Miller. A popular guide for the medical and surgical treatment of all domestic animals, including horses, cattle, cows, sheep, swine, fowl, dogs etc., giving in brief and plain language the description of all the usual diseases to which these animals are liable, and the most successful treatment. Cloth. 9x6x2½ inches. 523 pages.

No. 3F5580 Price..............$1.30
If by mail, postage extra, 28 cents.

The People's Horse, Cattle, Sheep and Swine Doctor.

Containing in four parts, clear and concise descriptions of the diseases of horses, cattle, sheep and hogs, with the exact doses of medicine for each. A valuable book for every stock raiser. 334 pages. Size, 5½x7½ inches. Cloth binding.

No. 3F5585
Price..............65c
If by mail, postage extra, 12 cents.

Gleason's Veterinary Hand Book.

Contains a new and complete system of horse training and exhaustive treatise on veterinary science, including diseases of horses, cattle, swine, sheep, poultry, dogs, birds, etc. Written in simple language, without technical terms, so that anyone can apply the remedies. Cloth. Size, 5¼x7½ inches. 520 pages.

No. 3F5600 Price..............52c
If by mail, postage extra, 14 cents.

Dadd's Modern Horse Doctor.

By Geo. H. Dadd, M.D. V.S. Containing practical observations on the causes, nature and treatment of diseases and lameness of horses, embracing the most recent and improved methods for the preservation and restoration of health. Fully illustrated. Bound in cloth. 432 pages. Size, 5x7 inches.

No. 3F5605
Price..............85c
If by mail, postage extra, 13 cents.

Dadd's American Cattle Doctor.

By Geo. H. Dadd, M.D. V.S. To help every man to be his own cattle doctor, giving the necessary information for preserving the health and curing the diseases of oxen, cows, sheep and swine, with a great variety of original recipes of farming and dairy management. Bound in cloth. 359 pages. Size, 5x7 inches.

No. 3F5606
Price..............85c
If by mail, postage extra, 13 cents.

Gleason's Horse Book.

By Prof. Oscar R. Gleason. The only authorized work by America's "King of Horse Tamers." Comprising history of breeding, training, breaking, buying, feeding, grooming, shoeing, doctoring, telling the age and general care of the horse. This book is profusely illustrated and substantially bound in cloth. Contains 488 pages. Size, 6½x8½ inches.

No. 3F5610 Price..............45c
If by mail, postage extra, 20 cents.

Standard Poultry Book.

By C. C. Shoemaker. The recognized standard work on poultry; adopted by the Poultry Breeders' Association. It contains a complete description of all the varieties of fowls, including turkeys, ducks and geese; how and what to feed them, how to market them; also full directions for operating incubators and brooders. Fully illustrated. Size, 4½x6½ inches. Bound in cloth. 185 pages.

No. 3F5627 Price..............21c
If by mail, postage extra, 5 cents.

Profitable Poultry Keeping.

WITH ORIGINAL ILLUSTRATIONS.

By Stephen Beale. An excellent book to all who are practically interested in keeping poultry. The author is a practical man, gifted with rare common sense, and with the most comprehensive knowledge of his subject. Bound in cloth. 278 pages. Size, 5½x7½ inches.

No. 3F5629
Price..............80c
If by mail, postage extra, 12 cents.

AGRICULTURE, LIVE STOCK, POULTRY AND DAIRYING—Continued.

The New Egg Farm.

By H. H. Stoddard. A practical, reliable manual upon producing eggs and poultry for the market, as a practical business enterprise; telling all about how to feed and manage, breed and select, incubators and brooders, labor saving devices, etc. Bound in cloth, with 140 illustrations. 331 pages. Size, 5x7 inches.

No. 3F5631 Price..............80c
If by mail, postage extra, 11 cents.

Turkeys and How to Grow Them.

By Herbert Myrick. A treatise on the natural history of turkeys, the various breeds, and the best methods to insure success in the business of turkey growing. Fully illustrated. Bound in cloth. 154 pages. Size, 5x7 inches.

No. 3F5633
Price..............85c
If by mail, postage extra, 7 cents.

Poultry Feeding and Fattening

By George B. Fiske. A new and up to date book on this subject, including chapters on preparations for marketing; special finishing methods as practiced by American and foreign experts, handling of capons, water fowls, etc. 160 pages. Size, 5x7½ inches. Fully illustrated. Cloth binding.

No. 3F5635 Price, 39c
If by mail, postage extra, 8 cents.

Poultry Appliances and Handicraft.

By George B. Fiske. How to make and use labor saving devices, with descriptive plans for food and water supply, building and miscellaneous needs, with chapters on incubators and brooding. A reliable, up to date book on these subjects. 118 pages. Size, 5x7½ inches. Cloth binding.

No. 3F5640 Price, 40c
If by mail, postage extra, 7 cents.

Poultry Architecture.

By George B. Fiske. A practical guide for the construction of poultry houses, coops and yards. An invaluable work to the man who raises poultry on a large scale. Profusely illustrated. 130 pages. Size, 6x7½ inches. Bound in cloth.

No. 3F5645 Price, 39c
If by mail, postage extra, 7 cents.

Profitable Dairying.

A practical guide to successful dairy management. Separate chapters are devoted to the dairy, secretion of milk, future of dairying, dairy breeds, selections of breeds, the dairy cow and the dairy sire; care of the dairy cow, care of the calf; milk, feeds and their value, care of milk, devices for ripening cream, churning and marketing butter, the barn, silo and silage, miscellaneous topics, necessary appliances, dairy remedies, etc. A most complete, comprehensive and reliable book on this subject. Fully illustrated. Cloth. 174 pages. Size, 5x7 inches.

No. 3F5650 Price..............60c
If by mail, postage extra, 7 cents.

How to Keep Bees.

By Anna B. Comstock. A new and up to date book on this important subject. Valuable as a complete guide and text book for the beginner in bee keeping, and equally valuable to the experienced bee keeper as a book of reference. Very fully illustrated with drawings and photographs by the author. 228 pages. Size, 5¼x7½ inches. Bound in cloth.

No. 3F5655 Price..............90c
If by mail, postage extra, 12 cents.

Quinby's New Bee Keeping.

By L. C. Root. The mysteries of bee keeping explained, combining the results of fifty years experiences with the latest discoveries and inventions, and presenting the most approved methods, forming a complete guide to money making methods in bee keeping. Fully illustrated. Bound in cloth. 271 pages. Size, 5x7 inches.

No. 3F5657 Price..............85c
If by mail, postage extra, 10 cents.

Bee Hives and Appliances.

By Paul Hasluck. This little book of 157 pages and 155 illustrations covers completely the subject of bee hives and bee keepers' appliances. The chapters on honey extractors, wax extractors and furnishing and stocking of hives are most complete and easily understood. Cloth bound. Size, 4¼x6¾ inches.

No. 3F5674 Price..............38c
If by mail, postage extra, 8 cents.

Barn Plans and Outbuildings

Published by the Orange Judd Company. Contains 257 illustrations, and is full of ideas, hints, suggestions, plans, etc., for the construction of barns and outbuildings, by practical writers. There are chapters devoted to the erection and use of barns, horse barns, cattle barns, grain barns, sheep barns, corn houses, smoke houses, ice houses, pig pens, granaries and also bird and dog houses, tool sheds, ventilators, roofs and roofing, doors and fastenings, work shops, poultry houses, barnyards, etc. 225 pages. Bound in cloth. Size, 5x7 inches.

No. 3F5689 Price..............80c
If by mail, postage extra, 12 cents.

Barns and Stock Sheds.

A new work, with plans, for the construction of barns and outbuildings. Special chapters on erection and use of grain houses, cattle and sheep barns, corn, smoke and ice houses, etc. Cloth. Size, 7½x5¼ inches. 235 pages.

No. 3F5690 Price..............88c
If by mail, postage extra, 10 cents.

Fences, Gates and Bridges.

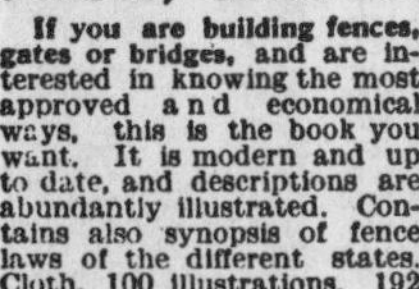

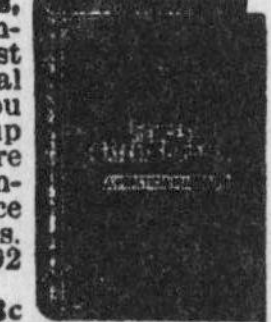

If you are building fences, gates or bridges, and are interested in knowing the most approved and economical ways, this is the book you want. It is modern and up to date, and descriptions are abundantly illustrated. Contains also synopsis of fence laws of the different states. Cloth. 100 illustrations. 192 pages. Size, 5x7 inches.

No. 3F5691 Price..43c
If by mail, postage extra, 10 cents.

BOOKS ON BUSINESS MATTERS.

How to Do Business.

By Seymour Eaton. Brimful of money making ideas, prepared to meet the wants of all who wish to extend the range of their business, and add to their profits. Contains a great variety of unique illustrations and hundreds of modern business ideas not known outside of the concerns which originated them. Special chapters are devoted to banking secrets, transportation, insurance, foreign trade, correspondence, mechanics, arithmetic, valuable hints for corresponding clerks, slips in grammar corrected, communication by telegraph, how to earn and get a good situation, New York pointers on margin trading, how big concerns keep their books, modern bookkeeping ideas, 99 short cuts in figures, etc., 100 illustrations, many of them in colors. Printed on heavy plate paper, bound in linen cloth. Cover design stamped in colors. Size, 6x8¾ inches. 430 pages.

No. 3F5801 Price..............56c
If by mail, postage extra, 16 cents.

Ropp's Commercial Calculator.

A book that saves labor, time and money; simple, rapid, reliable; adapted to all kinds of business, trades and professions. Size, 4¼x6½ inches. 128 pages.

No. 3F5807 Cloth.
Price..............10c

No. 3F5808 Cloth with flap and pocket. Silicate slate and account book. Price.........24c

No. 3F5809 Elegant leather flap and pocket, silicate slate and account book.
Price..............63c

No. 3F5810 Fine seal grain, gilt edges, flap and pocket, silicate slate and account book. Price..............79c

If by mail, postage extra, any style, 3 cents.

Gaskell's Compendium of Forms.

A book of social, legal and commercial forms. Embracing a complete course of self teaching in penmanship and bookkeeping, together with the laws and by-laws of social etiquette, business laws and commercial forms. Contains a political dictionary; the government of the United States; the states and territorial governments; also manual of agriculture, mechanics and mining; full and complete guide to parliamentary practice, etc. Size, 8¾x10¾ inches. 650 pages.

No. 3F5816 Cloth. Price......$1.15
No. 3F5817 Half Russia. Price. 1.35
If by mail, postage extra, either style, 40c.

Hill's Manual of Social and Business Forms.

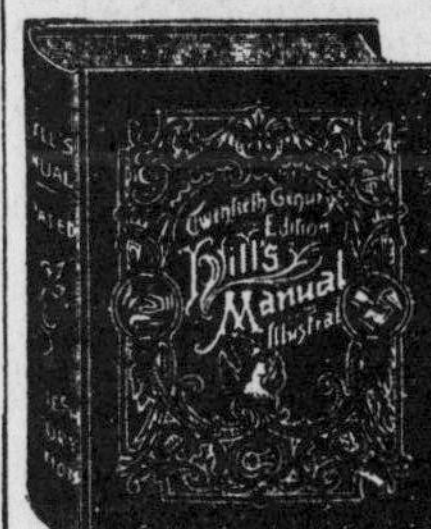

The 20th Century Edition of Hill's Manual of social and business forms. Revised. Greatly enlarged. Profusely illustrated. Hill's Manual is such a vast storehouse of information, containing so many thousand subjects of everyday use and importance that a complete description is here impossible. An examination will show you that it is suited to the needs of everyone. It is conceded to be the most comprehensive and reliable ready reference book in the world. Printed on excellent paper and bound in cloth with emblematic cover design. Gold stamping. Contains 504 pages. Large quarto size, 8¼x10½ inches. Retail price, $3.00.

No. 3F5819 Our price........$1.25
Weight, packed for shipment, 6 pounds.

Improved Ready Reckoner.

Showing at a glance the value of any number of pounds, gallons, yards, feet, etc., of any article from 1 to 1,000, at ¼ of a cent up to $10.00. Measurement of lumber, interest tables, postage rates, business forms, notes, due bills, etc. Boards, cloth back. Size, 3¼x5½ inches.

No. 3F5813 Price....19c
If by mail, postage extra, 3 cents.

Business Letter Writer.

By C. W. Brown, A. M. Gives full instructions for writing, and specimens of business letters, legal forms, leases, deeds, wills, contracts. Also leading synonyms. It will tell you everything you really need in the way of a letter. You will find this book invaluable. 208 pages Bound in cloth. Size, 4½x7 inches.

No. 3F5822 Price..21c
Postage extra, 5 cents.

Lee's Home and Business Manual.

Practical chapters on penmanship, letter writing, bookkeeping, banking, every day law, social forms, mercantile and technical terms, speeches for all occasions, and many others. Size, 4¼x5½ inches.

No. 3F5824 Flexible cloth.
Price..........17c

No. 3F5825 Stiff silk cloth.
Price..........30c

Postage extra, either style, 6 cents.

Civil Service Manual.

A detailed history, aims, opportunities, rules, regulations and requirements of the Civil Service Law. Tells how to prepare for examinations, how to obtain positions, giving questions for examinations, etc. Vest pocket size, 2½x5½ inches.

No. 3F5828 Cloth.
Price..........16c

No. 3F5829 Leather.
Price..........32c

Postage extra, either style, 4c.

Conklin's Reference Books.

The practical value of these volumes can hardly be overestimated for business men, students, mechanics and readers generally. These are vest pocket editions, each size, 2½x5½ inches. Written by Prof. George W. Conklin, and are authorities on the questions on which they deal.

Argument Settler
Civil and Business Law
Commercial Calculator — 18c
Familiar Quotations
Five Hundred Ways to Make Money
Synonyms and Antonyms
The Way to Think
Writing Desk Book
Who Wrote That (poetic selection)
Who Said That
50,000 Word Speller and Letter Writer's Manual
World's Best Proverbs and Epigrams.

No. 3F5831 Bound in cloth.
Price, each..........18c

No. 3F5832 Bound in leather.
Price, each..........30c

If by mail, postage extra, either style, 2c.

Twentieth Century Manual of Business.

By Prof E. C. Mills, and a corps of specialists. A simplified treatise on the grammar of the English language, rapid business writing, money in business bank and banking, the science of accounts, everyday law, rapid calculation, the world of science, practical mechanics, and the care of farm and stock, etc. A most valuable book, and now offered by us at a very low price. Profusely illustrated with full page halftone engravings and innumerable specimen pages. 250 double column pages. Bound in cloth, with original cover design stamped in colors. Size, 7½x9¾ inches.

No. 3F5834 Price..........39c
If by mail, postage extra, 14 cents.

Roberts' Rules of Order.

Revised edition. The standard of parliamentary authority. Experienced legislators, leading newspapers and prominent critics pronounce Roberts' Rules of Order the best parliamentary guide in the English language. Cloth. Size, 4x6 inches.

No. 3F5840 Price....54c
If by mail, postage extra, 5c.

Cushing's Manual.

By Luther S. Cushing. Revised to date by John James Ingalls, president of the United States Senate, 1887-1891. A manual of parliamentary practice, containing rules for proceeding and debating in deliberative assemblies; also an appendix containing the Constitution of the United States, Declaration of Independence and a complete index. Contains 240 pages, with paragraph headings in bold faced type. Bound in cloth. Do not confuse this with cheap, low priced editions. Size, 3⅝x5¾ inches.

No. 3F5842 Price..........32c
If by mail, postage extra, 4 cents.

Business Man's Adviser.

Instructions for everybody in all the legal and commercial affairs of life. Forms are given for every description of legal documents in common use, such as agreements, bonds, deeds leases, mortgages, wills, etc. Also a dictionary of legal terms and tables for the computation of interest and for making a variety of other calculations, as well as valuable miscellaneous information. Contains over 500 pages. Bound in boards. Size, 5¼x7¼ inches.

No. 3F5850 Price..........65c
If by mail, postage extra, 8 cents.

Interest Tables.

Breband's Interest Tables. Showing at a glance the interest on any sum from $1.00 to $10,000 for any number of days from one day to 366 days at 3, 3½, 4, 4½, 5, 5½ and 6 per cent. Also at any rate from 6 to 24 per cent. It is a correct, prompt and useful manual of interest for bankers, merchants, canvassers, clerks, farmers and all others who are compelled at any time to figure interest. Fourteenth edition, revised. Bound in cloth. The lowest priced correct and standard interest tables on the market. Size, 6x8¾ inches.

No. 3F5860 Price..........$3.48
If by mail, postage extra, 13 cents.

Standard American Business Guide.

By E. T. Roe, L. L. B. Assisted by specialists in every department. Contains business law, facts and forms, penmanship and correspondence, tables, short cuts and ready reckoner, etc. Special chapters are devoted to farming, lumbering and all trades, with legal papers and rules for same; wills, contracts and all forms needed by the ordinary business or laboring man; also helpful tables, short cuts in figures for rapid calculation, etc. All arranged systematically with appropriate heading, with index commencement words printed in bold faced type. 480 pages. Bound in cloth. Size, 5¼x7¾ inches. Regular price, $1.50.

No. 3F5865 Our price..........45c
If by mail, postage extra, 13 cents.

HISTORY.

Ridpath's History of the United States.

Complete history of the United States of America. Never before has there been published a book so rich in historical incident, so instructive in its method of presentation and so brilliant and fascinating in its narrative. Profusely illustrated with sketches, portraits and diagrams. A magnificent volume with over 800 pages, 300 illustrations. Size, 10¾x7½x2½ inches.

No. 3F6000 Price..............**89c**
If by mail, postage extra, 34 cents.

Pictorial History of the United States.

By Bishop Jas. D. McCabe. Revised and brought down to the present time by Henry Davenport Northrop, the well known historian. Two volumes with over 500 superb engravings. A complete history from the discovery of the American continent to the present time. Containing accounts of the discoveries and explorations of the Norsemen, Spaniards, English and French; the mound builders; the American Indians; the settlement of the New World; the French and Indian Wars; the struggle of the Revolution; the War of 1812; the history of the Civil War; War with Spain; subjection of the Philippines; also a full description of our new possessions. Marbled edges. Size, 7¾x10¼ inches. 1,050 pages. 500 illustrations. Each set put up in separate box.

No. 3F6002 Two volumes, bound in silk cloth with gold stamping on back and gold decorations. Price, per set..........**$1.65**

No. 3F6003 Deluxe Edition. Two volumes, bound in three-quarters morocco, stamped in gold with marbled sides and edges. Price, per set..........................**$2.25**
Weight, per set, packed for shipment, 10 lbs.

Pictorial History of the World.

By James D. McCabe. Complete in three big volumes. Brought down to the present time by Henry Davenport Northrop. Embracing full and authentic accounts of every nation of ancient and modern times. A full and comprehensive history of the rise and fall of the Greek and Roman Empires, the growth of the nations of modern Europe, the middle ages, the crusades, the feudal system, the reformation, the discovery and settlement of the New World, with sketches of the leading characters in the world's history. Embellished with over 650 fine engravings of battles and other historical scenes, portraits of the great men of ancient and modern times, views of the cities of the world, etc. Contains over 1,400 pages. Fully illustrated. Size, 7¾x10¼ inches. Each set boxed.

No. 3F6006 Three volumes, bound in cloth, silk finish, marbled edges. Price, per set **$1.98**
Weight packed for shipment, 12 pounds.

No. 3F6007 Deluxe Edition. Three volumes. Bound in three-quarter red morocco, marbled sides and edges. Decorated on back with gold stamping. Price, per set...**$2.75**
Weight, packed for shipment, 12 pounds.

History and Conquest of the Philippines and our Other Island Possessions.

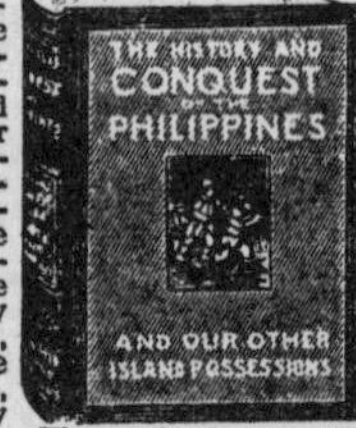

By Alden March, A.M. Embracing authentic history of the Spanish War, prepared from official government reports and naval officers. Our war with the Filipinos in 1898, together with a complete history of these islands, from the earliest times to the present. The history of Cuba, Porto Rico, the Ladrone and the Hawaiian Islands, from their discovery to the present time. The book contains 497 pages richly embellished with over 100 full page halftone and other engravings. Also frontispiece map. Bound in cloth, with attractive cover design. Gold stamping. Size, 7½x9¾ inches. Retail price, $2.00.

No. 3F6008 Our price **65c**
If by mail, postage extra, 22 cents.

Massacres of Christians by Heathen Chinese and Horrors of the Boxers.

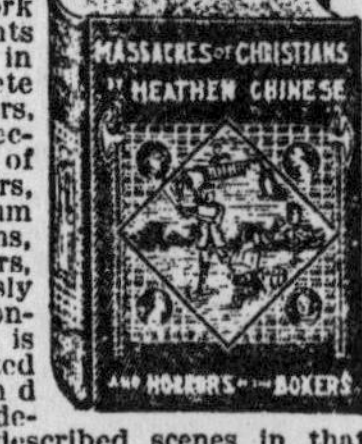

By Harold Irwin Cleveland. This work contains full accounts of recent atrocities in China and complete history of the boxers, the Tia-Ping insurrection and massacres of the foreign ministers, idol worship, the opium habit, superstitions, oriental splendors, etc. This marvelously interesting work contains 612 pages, and is profusely illustrated with halftones and other engravings; depicting the above described scenes in that wonderful and terrible country. Size, 6¾x9¾ inches. Retail price, $2.00.

No. 3F6013 Our price..........**85c**
If by mail, postage extra, 28 cents.

Famous Battles of the 19th Century.

Complete in three volumes, containing 1,256 pages, with 42 full page halftone stirring war pictures. These battles are described by the most famous writers of war stories, including Archibald Forbes, George A. Henty, Major Arthur Griffith, and other well known authors. These books are different from any other historical books in that they are given over entirely to the description of battles. Every lover of history and of brave deeds should read these books. Size, 5½x8¼ inches. Bound in cloth, with cover design in colors. Best quality of paper. Clear, large type.

No. 3F6014 Price, per set, three volumes **$2.98**
Weight, per set, packed for shipment, 6 lbs.

History of Our Own Times.

By Justin McCarthy, M. P. In two volumes. This history covers a period from 1837 to 1880. One of the most momentous periods in this world's history. The author is a famous historian, and in his style of English is above criticism. 1,200 pages. Size, 5½x7½ inches. Each set boxed.

No. 3F6015 Bound in silk cloth, gold stamping on back. Price, per set..........**70c**
If by mail, postage extra, 24 cents.

Superbly Illustrated Home Book of the World's Great Nations.

Edited by Thomas Powell. Geographical, historical and pictorial. Intensely interesting descriptions and beautiful illustrations. Scenes, events, manners, customs of many nations, from the dawn of civilization to the present time. This is a delightful book, interesting to the young and old, contains 670 pages, with over 1,000 illustrations, many of them full page. Size of book, 9½x11 inches. 1¾ inches thick. Bound in fine English red cloth. Retail price, $5.00.

No. 3F6020 Our price **98c**
Weight, packed for shipment, 6 pounds.

Pictorial History of the Civil War.

By John Laird Wilson. This book contains a full and authentic account of battles by sea and land, with graphic descriptions of heroic deeds achieved by armies and individuals. Narratives of personal adventure. Life in camp, field and hospital. The great Civil War has never been so graphically described. Illustrated. Cloth bound. 950 pages. Size, 8x10 inches.

No. 3F6025 Price..............**98c**
If by mail, postage extra, 30 cents.

Macaulay's History of England

Complete in five volumes. This history of England is probably more widely read than any other. Macaulay's History of England is famous for its fascinating contents, its beautiful style and its perfect English. No library is complete without it. Each set boxed.

No. 3F6030 Macaulay's History of England. Five volumes. Bound in cloth. Size, 5½x7½ inches. Price..................**98c**
If by mail, postage extra, per set, 48 cents.

No. 3F6031 Macaulay's History of England. Unabridged edition. Five volumes. Bound in green silk cloth, with gold stamping on back. Printed on very fine quality of paper. Size, 5½x7½ inches. Over 3,000 pages, illustrated with engravings and etchings. The finest cloth edition made.
Price, per set **$3.40**
Weight, per set, packed for shipment, 12 lbs.

No. 3F6032 Macaulay's History of England. Same as No. 3F6031, but bound in half calf, with gold stamping. Price, per set..**$4.98**
Weight, per set, packed for shipment, 12 lbs.

Conquest of Mexico.

By Wm. H. Prescott. Complete in three volumes, with a preliminary view of the ancient Mexican civilization. Includes also the life of the conqueror, Hernando Cortez. Contains over 1,280 pages. Bound in silk cloth with gold stamping on back. Size, 5¼x7½ inches. Each set boxed.

No. 3F6060 Price, per set **98c**
Weight, packed for shipment, 6 pounds.

Conquest of Peru.

By Wm. H. Prescott. Complete in two volumes. This is the standard history of Peru. Printed on best grade of paper with new clear type. Bound in cloth, with gold stamping on back. Contains 900 pages. Size, 5¼x7½ inches. Each set boxed.

No. 3F6062 Price, per set............**78c**
If by mail, postage extra, 24 cents.

Gibbons' Roman Empire.

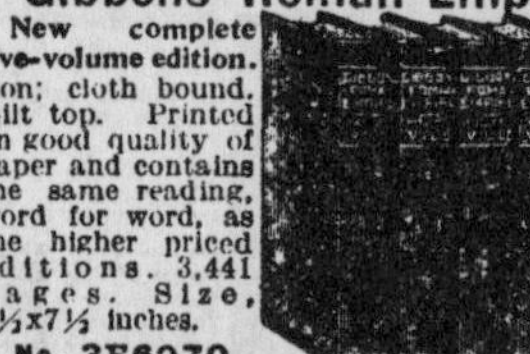

New complete five-volume edition. Unabridged edition; cloth bound. Gilt top. Printed on good quality of paper and contains the same reading, word for word, as the higher priced editions. 3,441 pages. Size, 5½x7½ inches.

No. 3F6070
Price, per set of five volumes..........**$1.70**
Weight, packed for shipment, 8 pounds.

History of Greece.

By Geo. Grote. Complete in four volumes. It is complete, word for word, as originally written and is the best and standard history of Greece. Illustrated. Cloth, gilt top. 3,335 pages. Size, 5½x7½ inches.

No. 3F6080
Price, per set **$2.89**
Weight, per set, packed for shipment, 8 lbs.

Rollins' Ancient History.

Complete unabridged edition of this standard work in four volumes. Bound in cloth. Contains full descriptions of all the nations of ancient civilization. This work is recognized as the best ancient history ever written. 3,146 pages Size, 5¼x7½ inches.

No. 3F6150
Price, per set, four volumes.....**$1.35**
Weight, packed for shipment, 8 pounds.

Green's History of the English People.

By John Richard Green. Complete in four volumes. This set contains his complete works with notes. 1,900 pages. Cloth. Size of volumes, 5x7½ inches.

No. 3F6022
Price, per set of four volumes **95c**
Weight, per set, packed for shipment, 6 pounds.

Green's Long History of the English People.

Four volumes, bound in silk cloth and printed on fine paper. This is the complete unabridged edition of this famous work. Size, 5x7½ inches. Retail price, $4.00. Each set boxed.

No. 3F6023 Our price, per set, **$1.65**
Weight, packed for shipment, 6 pounds.

Spanish-American War and Battles in the Philippines.

By James Rankin Young. A full and graphic account of Dewey's victory at Manila; sinking of the Spanish fleet at Santiago, battle of San Juan and El Caneye, surrender of Santiago and invasion of Porto Rico, including battles with the insurgents at Manila, and all important events, including treaty of peace with Spain, etc. Cloth. Illustrated. Size, 6½x8¼ inches. 800 pages.

No. 3F6100 Price **52c**
If by mail, postage extra, 21 cents.

War Between Russia and Japan.

By Murat Halstead. Complete and thrilling account of the war between Russia and Japan up to the battle of Mukden. It gives first, a history of the reason for this great conflict and then describes the various battles by sea and land with narratives of personal adventure, superb heroism and daring exploits of Oyama, Oki, Kuroki, Kuropatkin and others. Cloth bound. Fully illustrated with scenes of battles on land and sea. 600 pages. Size, 7x9 inches.

No. 3F6125 Price............**75c**
If by mail, postage extra, 25 cents.

Rowlinson's Ancient Egypt.

By George Rawlinson. The standard history of ancient Egypt. Two volumes. Contains over 600 pages with many hundred illustrations, showing famous Egyptians, temples, mummies, scarabaeus, Egyptian writing, etc. Bound in silk cloth, gilt top. Size, 5¼x7½ inches. Retail price, $2.50.

No. 3F6130
Our price..........**$1.48**
If by mail, postage extra, 24 cents.

Works of Flavius Josephus.

Complete in one volume. Comprising the histories and the antiquities of the Jews, with the destruction of Jerusalem by the Romans, to which are added the seven dissertations concerning Jesus Christ, John the Baptist, John the Just, God's Command to Abraham, Sacrifice of Isaac, together with a discourse on Hell, etc. 790 pages. Size, 6x9 inches.

No. 3F6135 Cloth. Price...**$0.70**
No. 3F6136 Full sheep. Price. **1.18**
If by mail, postage extra, either style, 30c.

Household edition of Flavius Josephus' History of the Jews, in three volumes. Bound in silk cloth, full gilt top. Twelve illustrations. Printed on best quality of paper. Size, 5x7½ inches. Retail price, $3.00.

No. 3F6137 Our price, per set.**$1.50**
Weight, packed for shipment, 5 pounds.

De Luxe Edition, in three volumes, same as No. 3F6137, but with full gold tops. Bound in half morocco. Best quality of paper. Twelve illustrations. Retail price, $5.00.

No. 3F6138 Our price, per set.**$2.75**
Weight, packed for shipment, 5 pounds.

The Rise of the Dutch Republic.

By John Lothrop Motley. Two volumes. A splendid picture of one of the most dramatic periods in the history of modern Europe. A time that bred heroes. Descriptive of the heroic struggle for religious freedom. Brilliantly written. Bound in silkcloth. Size, 5½x7½ inches. Retail price, $2.

No. 3F6140 Our price, per set, boxed (two volumes)..........**$1.15**
Weight, packed for shipment, 6 pounds.

The French Revolution.

By Thos. Carlyle. Two volumes. The greatest description of the most stupendous event in the world's history.

No. 3F6145 Household edition. Two volumes. 900 pages. Printed on good quality of paper. Large, clear type. Bound in cloth, with ornamental gold back stamp. Size, 5½x7½ inches. Each set boxed. Publisher's price, $2.00. Our price, per set, two volumes **65c**

No. 3F6146 Library Edition. Size, 5½x7½ inches. Bound in fine silk cloth, full gilt top. Printed on fine quality paper. Gold stamping. Leather labels. Retail price, $2.25. Our price, per set, two volumes, **95c**

No. 3F6147 Deluxe Edition. Size, 5½x7½ inches. Bound in three-quarter green crushed morocco, marbled sides and end leaves. Uncut edges, gold tops. Title and back design stamped in gold. The most beautiful books made.
Price, per set, two volumes..........**$2.35**
If by mail, postage extra, per set, 30 cents.

BIOGRAPHY.

The International Library Series of Biography.

Biographies of famous men by famous authors. If any one desires to purchase a first class biography at a very reasonable price, we recommend either of the following editions. The list covers the lives of the makers of this country as well as some of the greatest Europeans. Absolutely the best series of biographies made at a moderate price.

Adams, John Quincy, Life of. By William H. Seward.
Boone, Daniel, Life of. By Edward S. Ellis
Catherine II, Empress of Russia, Life of. By Samuel M. Schmucker
Celebrated Female Sovereigns. By Mrs. Jameson
Clay, Henry, Life of. By Epes Sargent and Horace Greeley
Crockett, David, Life of. By Sir Walter Scott
Cromwell, Oliver, Life of. By Herbert
Duchess of Orleans, Life of. By Marquesse de H.
Grey, Lady Jane, Life of. By David W. Bartlett
Harrison, William Henry, Life of. By H. Montgomery
Henry VIII and His Six Wives, Lives of. By Henry William Herbert
Henry, Patrick, Life of. By William Wirt
Jackson, Andrew, Life of. By John S. Jenkins
Joan of Arc, Maid of Orleans. By David W. Bartlett
Josephine, Empress, Life of. By Cecil B. Hartley
Napoleon and His Marshals
Life of Napoleon. By M. A. Arnault
Queens of American Society. By Mrs. Ellet
Taylor, Zachary, Life of. By H. Montgomery
Washington, George, Life of. By Bancroft
Washington and His Generals
Webster, Daniel, Life of. By B. F. Teft

No. 3F6298 International Library Series of Biography. Each book carefully printed on excellent paper. Contains from 300 to 600 pages. Substantially bound in cloth with elaborate and effective acorn cover design stamped in colors. Colored inlay. Size, 5¼x7½ inches.
Price, for any 3, 79c; each..........28c
Price, for the entire set, twenty-two volumes, constituting a splendid library of biography..........$4.98
If by mail, postage extra, per volume, 9 cents.

Life of Washington.

By George W. P. Custis. This is a complete story of the life of Washington and displays new phases of his character. We see him as a private citizen, plain farmer, as the head of a family, as general of the army and as president of these United States. Fully illustrated. Cloth bound. Size, 7x9½ inches. Over 500 pages.
No. 3F6300 Price..........38c
If by mail, postage extra, 18 cents.

Washington's Life and Military Career.

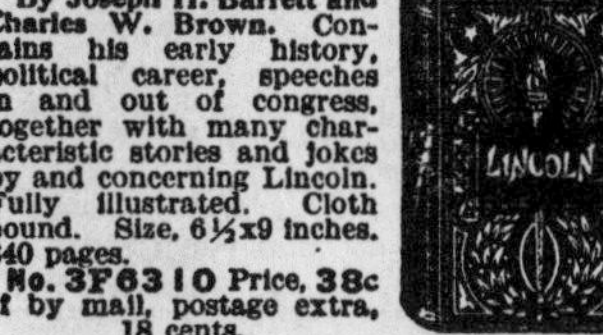

Edited and compiled by Morris H. Hancock, using Irving's Life of Washington as a basis. A complete life of this great general. Battles of the Revolutionary War; noted generals; surrender of Cornwallis, Washington as president; his closing days at Mt. Vernon; his farewell address; detailed account of his death and final resting place. Illustrated with 32 full page halftones. 593 pages. Bound in green crushed levant. Cloth sides, full gilt top. Gold stamping on back. Superb library edition. Uncut pages. Size, 6x8 inches. Retail price, $2.00.
No. 3F6302 Our price..........59c
If by mail, postage extra, 20 cents.

Life of Lincoln.

By Joseph H. Barrett and Charles W. Brown. Contains his early history, political career, speeches in and out of congress, together with many characteristic stories and jokes by and concerning Lincoln. Fully illustrated. Cloth bound. Size, 6½x9 inches. 840 pages.
No. 3F6310 Price, 38c
If by mail, postage extra, 18 cents.

Story of Abraham Lincoln.

The journey from the log cabin to the White House, including his jokes and anecdotes, by Elinor Gridley. Here are interwoven in a charming story his boyish hopes and hardships, his youthful aspirations and privations, his struggles for knowledge, his home life and public services. Contains 334 large pages. Illustrated with numerous engravings and beautifully bound in silk cloth with gold and colored emblematic stamping on cover. Size, 7¼x9¾ inches. Retail price, $1.50.
No. 3F6312 Our price..........58c
If by mail, postage extra, 18 cents.

Life of General U. S. Grant.

By Hon. Ben. Perley Poore and the Rev. O. H. Tiffany, D.D. An account of the hardships and struggles of his youth, its poverty and following his glorious and victorious career from West Point to the head of the army; comprising his many victories that crowned his later years, as president of the United States. 594 pages. Cloth. Size, 6½x9 inches.
No. 3F6315 Price..........38c
If by mail, postage extra, 18 cents.

Theodore Roosevelt.

By J. M. Miller, assisted by Hon. William Loeb, secretary to the president. An inspired narrative of his wonderful career, written by men high in public life, embracing a complete account of his early history, together with a complete history of the republican national campaign of 1904. Illustrated. Contains also history of the Vice-President, Hon. Charles W. Fairbanks. 375 pages. Size, 7x9 inches. Cloth.
No. 3F6330 Price..........75c
If by mail, postage extra, 20 cents.

Life and Sayings of Theodore Roosevelt.

By Thomas W. Hanford. Introduction by Chas. Walter Brown, A.M. An ideal American, the pride of the Roughriders. Containing complete biography and symposium of brilliant thoughts and stirring words from essays and orations of President Roosevelt. With classified index; 320 pages; new plates; numerous illustrations. Bound with silk finished cloth, with portrait inlay and ink stamping on cover. Size, 5½x7¾ inches.
No. 3F6332 Price..........55c
If by mail, postage extra, 12 cents.

Famous Americans.

By Marshall Everett. The thrilling experiences of many famous Americans, and astonishing stories of bravery and personal experiences in the lives of the heroes of the United States. Superbly illustrated with a series of one hundred portraits of famous Americans from Washington to Roosevelt. Cloth bound. Size, 7½x9½ inches. Over 400 pages.
No. 3F6335 Price. 75c
If by mail, postage extra, 12 cents.

Life of President McKinley.

The only authentic life of our late martyred president, together with a life sketch of Theodore Roosevelt, by Alexander K. McClure and Chas. Morris. Beautiful memorial edition thoroughly revised and authentic in every particular. Over 500 pages. Printed on finest grade of paper. Profusely illustrated. Bound in cloth with cover design stamped in gold and special inlay portrait of the president, mounted in center of flag. Size, 6¾x9 inches. Subscription price, $3.00.
No. 3F6345 Our price..........68c
If by mail, postage extra, 20 cents.

Life of Pope Leo XIII.

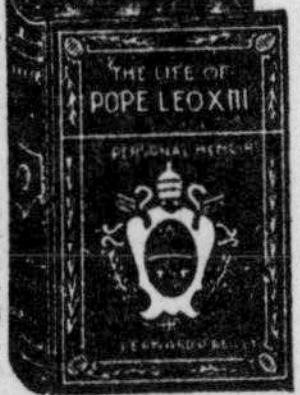

By Rt. Rev. Bernard O'Reilly, Domestic Prelate of His Holiness. This life is compiled from the authentic memoir and written with the encouragement and approbation of His Holiness. Contains over 800 pages, printed from clear type on good paper. Handsomely illustrated with over 100 beautiful pictures, including 64 pages of full page halftones and many fine text illustrations. Bound in extra fine quality cardinal cloth. Elegantly and elaborately stamped in gold on back and side. Emblematic design. Size, 6½x9¼ inches. Retail price, $3.00.
No. 3F6348 Our price..........$1.48
If by mail, postage extra, 28 cents.

Military Career of Napoleon.

By Montgomery B. Gibbs. An account of the remarkable campaigns of the "Man of Destiny." Authentic anecdotes of the battlefield as told by the famous marshals and generals of the first empire. Contains 32 full page illustrations; nearly 600 pages. Half leather binding with silk cloth sides and design and title stamped in gold on back. Size, 5½x7¾ inches. Retail price, $1.25.
No. 3F6352 Our price..........65c
If by mail, postage extra, 14 cents.

Napoleon from Corsica to St. Helena.

A pictorial work, illustrating the remarkable career of the most famous military genius the world has ever known. 256 pages, 331 half tone pictures, bound in green linen, with Napoleonic coat of arms in silver embossed on cover. John L. Stoddard, the famous lecturer and traveler, describes each picture with a foot note, which adds immensely to the interest and the value of the work. Size, 11x14 inches. Retail price, $3.00.
No. 3F6353 Our price..........90c
Weight, packed for shipment, 6 pounds.

Memoirs of Napoleon.

By Bourrienne, his private secretary. The truest, greatest, most authentic and the most interesting life of Napoleon ever written. Who could write so intimately or so truly of Napoleon as his private secretary, who never left his side throughout his career. He is depicted as a soldier, a statesman, an organizer, a politician, a general and a man. In two volumes. Beautiful de luxe edition, bound in three-quarter green crushed morocco with marbled sides and edges. Size, 5½x8 inches. Full gold top, decorated on back with design stamped in gold. Beautifully printed on the best quality of paper. Fully illustrated. Retail price, $4.00.
No. 3F6354 Our price, per set, 2 volumes, boxed..........$2.45
If by mail, postage extra, per set, 32 cents.

The Life of Gladstone.

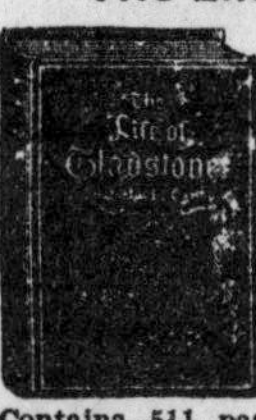

By Justin McCarthy. Revised and enlarged edition. Mr. McCarthy is one of the most picturesque, graphic and engaging of modern authors. His work as reporter of the House of Commons gave him a thorough knowledge of English politics, and he has been associated in one way and another with many of the leading figures in English life. He is the author of "A History of Our Own Times." Contains 511 pages. Bound in cloth with title stamped on back. This is McMillan & Co. regular $1.75 edition. Size, 5½x8 inches.
No. 3F6361 Price..........58c
If by mail, postage extra, 14 cents.

Plutarch's Lives.

Plutarch's lives of illustrious men. Translated from the Greek by John Dryden and others. An authenticated edition. The whole carefully revised and corrected, to which is prefixed a Life of Plutarch.
No. 3F6380 Plutarch's Lives, in three volumes, 300 pages to a volume. Abridged edition. Substantially bound in cloth. Size, 5x7½ inches.
Price, per set..........69c
Weight, packed for shipment, 5 pounds.
No. 3F6381 Plutarch's Lives, in three volumes. Unabridged edition. Over 550 pages to a volume. Bound in finest grade silk cloth, leather labels, gold stamping, full gilt top. Best quality paper.
Price, per set..........$1.35
Weight, packed for shipment, 6 pounds.

Personal Recollections of General Nelson A. Miles.

The wonderful career of a self made man. How he rose from a second lieutenant to the rank of a commander-in-chief of the United States Army. Embracing the thrilling story of his famous Indian campaigns. Every page bristles with interest. An ever changing panorama. A history in itself, distinctive, thrilling and well nigh incredible. A massive volume of 600 pages; with nearly 200 superb engravings, by Frederic Remington, etc. Attractively bound in cloth. Size, 7¾x10 inches. Regular price, $4.00.
No. 3F6392 Our price..........$2.25
If by mail, postage extra, 38 cents.

Handy Dictionary of Biography.

By Charles Morris. New and revised edition. Contains a short biography of every important person. This work has confined its scope to notable persons whose names are likely to be frequently met with in reading. These biographies are sufficiently long to give an intelligent idea of their career. Special attention has been given to the names of individuals of recent date, who have won prominence in our own day, and information concerning whom is not to be found in the older works. Retail price, $2.00. Size, 6x8½ inches.
No. 3F6397 Our price..........$1.18
If by mail, postage extra, 18 cents.

Famous Men and Great Events of the 19th Century.

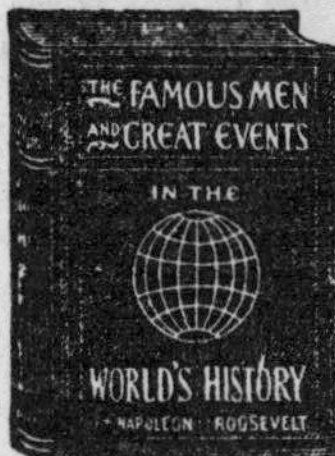

By Chas. Morris, LL.D. The achievements of 100 years, embracing descriptions of the decisive battles of the century and the great soldiers who fought them. The rise and fall of nations, changes in the map of the world, discoverers, explorers, inventors, progress of religion, morals, science and art. Contains 667 pages, with nearly 100 full page halftone engravings, illustrating the greatest events of the century, portraits of the most famous men in the world. Bound in cloth, with cover design stamped in silver. Size, 7½x9¾ inches. Subscription price, $3.00.
No. 3F6399 Our price..........98c
If by mail, postage extra, 34 cents.

BOOKS ON ECONOMICS, POLITICS AND FINANCE.

The Science of Political Economy.

"I AM FOR MEN."

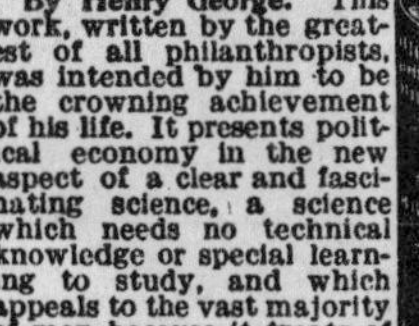

By Henry George. This work, written by the greatest of all philanthropists, was intended by him to be the crowning achievement of his life. It presents political economy in the new aspect of a clear and fascinating science, a science which needs no technical knowledge or special learning to study, and which appeals to the vast majority of men because it treats of the burning problem—the getting of a living. Divided into five divisions. Contains 545 pages, printed on the best quality of paper and bound in cloth with title in gold on back. Gilt top. Size, 5½x8¼ inches.
No. 3F6500 Price..........$1.98
If by mail, postage extra, 19 cents.

Jesus Christ and the Social Question.

By Prof. Francis G. Peabody. An examination of the teachings of Jesus in its relation to some problems of modern social life. Professor Peabody considers the social principles of this teaching, its relation to the family, to the rich, to the care of the poor, to the industrial order. It is vital, searching, comprehensive. The Christian reader will find it an illumination; the non-Christian, a revelation. Contains 374 pages. Bound in cloth with title stamped on back. Size, 5½x7¾ inches.
No. 3F6505 Price..........48c
If by mail, postage extra, 10 cents.

Kidd's Social Evolution.

By Benjamin Kidd. New edition, revised. A study of the whole development of humanity in a new light, sustained and strong and fresh throughout. It marks out new lines of study and is written in that calm and resolute tone which secures the confidence of the reader. It is undoubtedly the ablest book on social development that has been published. Contains 404 pages. Bound in cloth. Size, 5½x7¾ inches.
No. 3F6515 Price..........**48c**
If by mail, postage extra, 10 cents.

The Modern Bank.

By Amos K. Fiske. A book for every banker, banker's clerk, and those who desire practical information and instruction regarding the bank and banking. It gives a clear idea of what an up to date bank does and how it is done, and describes in plain terms the various functions of the present day bank and its officers. 348 pages, with many facsimiles of checks, drafts, leaves, from ledgers, etc. Bound in silk cloth. Size, 5½x7¾ inches
No. 3F6518 Price..........**$1.38**
If by mail, postage extra, 15 cents.

The Life Insurance Company.

By William Alexander. This book is written for the junior officers, heads of departments and canvassers of insurance companies, whose efficiency and progress may depend to some extent upon an intelligent grasp of the subject of life insurance as a whole. Illustrated with specimen policies of all kinds and descriptions. Contains 290 pages. Bound in cloth. Size, 5½x7¾ inches.
No. 3F6519 Price..........**$1.38**
If by mail, postage extra, 15 cents.

Monopolies and Trusts.

By Richard T. Ely. Probably no man is better acquainted with the serious and all important question of today—Trusts. This book might be said to be suggestive explicit in a word. A capital text book for the student, for the man of business, and for the man or woman who thinks. Contains 284 pages. Bound in cloth. Size, 5½x7¾ inches.
No. 3F6522
Price..........**58c**
If by mail, postage extra, 9 cents.

Poverty.

By Robert Hunter. Settlement worker of New York. Probably no book so well describes, as this one, the dependent and vicious classes which numbers among its members the unskilled, underpaid, underfed, poorly housed workers. Mr. Hunter points out certain remedical actions which society may wisely undertake. Every student of sociology and every thinking man and woman should read this book. In its pages they will find food for thought. Bound in cloth. 382 pages. Size, 5½x7¾ inches.
No. 3F6525 Price..........**58c**
If by mail, postage extra, 10 cents.

Social Institutions of the United States.

By James Bryce. Author of the "American Commonwealth." The reputation of Mr. Bryce as an author on economic and social subjects, will commend this book to both general reader and student. This work takes up our social institutions, dissects them and presents them to the reader in a clear, concise, instructive and brilliant manner. A book that every thinker should read. Contains 298 pages. Bound in cloth. Size, 5¼x7¾ inches.
No. 3F6530 Price..........**48c**
If by mail, postage extra, 11 cents.

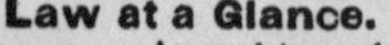

Law at a Glance.

A complete work, embracing every known subject, among which are the following: Affidavits, agents, agreements, arbitration, assignments, power of attorney, bankruptcy, bills of lading, exchange and sale, chattel mortgages, co-partnership, corporations, damages, debts, deeds, frauds, forms of guarantee, injunction, injury, insolvency, insurance, judgments, sales; husband and wife, their relations, divorce, losses, etc. Cloth, 150 pages. Size, 5½x7½ inches.
No. 3F6705 Price..........**58c**
If by mail, postage extra, 12 cents.

BOOKS ON LAW.

THE HOME LAW SCHOOL SERIES.

Complete in twelve carefully prepared volumes, covering the elements of twenty branches of American law. The Home Law School Series presents to you a practical, inexpensive and comprehensive plan whereby you will know how to read and study law, and further shows you what to read and study; at the same time furnishes in compact form, all the reading necessary to obtain a practical knowledge of law, enabling you to pass every examination required to gain admission to the bar in any state or territory.

THE BOOKS OF THIS BIG SET are designed especially for young men. Never before has a complete education in one of the noblest and most practical of all the sciences been brought within the reach of every young man. The possession and use of this set of books will enable every young man to push forward and bring out the best that is in him, attaining a more honored and higher standing in life than he could hope to attain without them. There is a great demand for young men that have a knowledge of law, and young men can learn law at home with the aid of our Home Law School Series.

EVERY BUSINESS MAN, EVERY FARMER, EVERY REAL ESTATE MAN, EVERY BROKER should have this set of law books in his library or in his office for constant reference. This set of books is indorsed by the bench, the bar and law schools, and constitutes a complete library of law.

THE PUBLISHERS AND AUTHORS of these books guarantee that by their use students of law may prepare themselves for admission to the bar in any State in the Union. Every business man, every citizen of the United States, needs these valuable books, containing the elements of jurisprudence and business forms of great value. Each volume contains from 200 to 300 pages, beautifully bound especially for us, in tan buckram, with titles stamped in gold on the backs. Size, 5¼x7¾ inches. The complete set consists of the following volumes:

- I How to Study Law
- II Constitutional Law — Federal and State
- III Personal Rights and Domestic Relations
- IV Contracts and Partnerships
- V Agency and Bailments, including Common Carriers
- VI Negotiable Instruments and Principal and Surety
- VII Wills and Settlements of Estates
- VIII Personal Property and Equity or Chancery Law
- IX Public Corporations and Private Corporations
- X Real Property and Pleading Practice
- XI Criminal Law, Criminal Procedure and Evidence
- XII Public International Law and Legal Ethics. This book will also include a complete Index to the Series.

No. 3F6717 Price, for complete set, twelve volumes..........**$8.90**
No. 3F6718 Price, for any one volume..........**75**
If by mail, postage extra, per volume, 11 cents.

GENUINE WEBSTER'S DICTIONARIES.

THE DICTIONARIES which we describe on this page are the genuine Webster's Dictionaries, authorized and copyrighted by the G. & C. Merriam Co., the latest 1906 editions, all thoroughly revised and brought right up to date. Everyone knows that the G. & C. Merriam Co. publish the **genuine Webster's Dictionaries**, the kind that are used in the schools, universities, courts and by the government. **The Webster is the standard of English word value.**

Webster's International Dictionary, $8.50.

The Standard Dictionary of the World. Without an equal.
Royal quarto, 2,380 pages, 5,000 illustrations

The latest enlarged 1906 edition, with 25,000 new words and phrases, completely revised gazetteer of the World, and completely revised biographical dictionary. Prepared under the direct supervision of W. T. Harris, Ph. D., LL.D., United States Commissioner of Education, assisted by a large corps of competent specialists and editors. Constitutes the most accurate, practical and scholarly vocabulary of the English language, and in addition, the following valuable features:
Colored Plates (8 pp.), reproductions of flags and arms of various nations, state seals, etc.
Memoir of Noah Webster
List of Authors Quoted
Brief History of the English Language
Guide to Pronunciation
Principles of Orthography, with important rules for spelling, list of words variously spelled.
Dictionary of Noted Fictitious Persons and Places often mentioned in literature.
Completely Revised Pronouncing Gazetteer of the World with over 25,000 titles
Completely Revised Pronouncing Biographical Dictionary containing 10,000 names
Pronouncing Vocabulary of Scriptural Names
Pronouncing Vocabulary of Greek and Latin Names
Vocabulary of Christian Names with Pronunciation, derivation, meaning, nicknames, etc.
Quotations from Foreign Languages translated into English
Abbreviations and Contractions
Arbitrary Signs
Classified Selection of Illustrations

No. 3F6801 Webster's International Dictionary. Bound in full sheep, marbled edges. Size, 9½x12 inches. Price..........**$8.50**
No. 3F6802 Same as No. 3F6801, but with double thumb index cut on edge.
Price..........**$9.25**
Shipping weight, either style, 18 pounds.

Webster's Collegiate Dictionary, $2.55.

Entirely new from cover to cover. The largest of the several abridgments of the famous International, upon which it is based. Especially valuable and convenient for the student and the busy man. An authoritative dictionary of the English language, complete in contents, convenient in size, easy to consult. Retains all the essential features of the International. It has a sizable vocabulary, complete definitions, adequate etymologies and indicates pronunciation by familiar diacritical marks and respellings. It has over 1,100 pages and 1,400 illustrations. Its appendix contains vocabularies of names, rhymes and foreign words, tables of arbitrary signs, also a valuable glossary of Scottish words and phrases. Size, 7x10 inches.
No. 3F6806 Webster's Collegiate Dictionary. Bound in cloth with double thumb index cut on edge. Price..........**$2.55**
No. 3F6807 Webster's Collegiate Dictionary, same as No. 3F6806, but bound in full sheep. Price..........**$3.40**
If by mail, postage extra, either style, 46 cents.

Webster's Unabridged Dictionary, $2.25.

Genuine G. & C. Merriam Co., new 1906 edition.

This edition of Webster's Unabridged has been revised and enlarged by supplementary matter until it contains 1,764 pages and has over 118,000 words and meanings. It is illustrated throughout the text with more than 3,000 pictures and besides has 68 full pages of illustrations; 4 great color pages. It also contains an explanatory and pronouncing vocabulary of the names of noted fictitious persons, places, etc.; new census tables of principal countries and cities of the world; United States census for 1900; vocabularies of Scriptural proper names, modern geographical names, common English Christian names, nicknames, etc.; 2,500 quotations, words, phrases, proverbs and colloquial expressions; abbreviations and contractions; brief history of the English language; principles of pronunciation; orthography; rules for spelling, etc. Size, 11x9½x4 inches.
No. 3F6812 Webster's Unabridged Dictionary. Bound in full law sheep, with patent thumb index cut on edge. Retail price, $5.00. Our price..........**$2.25**
Weight, packed for shipment, 9 pounds. If by mail, postage extra, 72 cents.

Webster's Unabridged Dictionary, $1.48.

G. & C. Merriam Co., special edition.

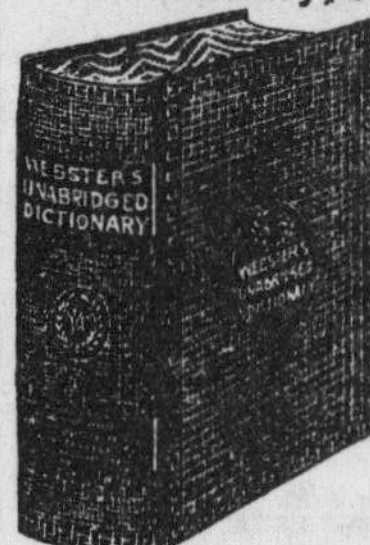

While the regular edition of the unabridged dictionary, No. 3F6812, has largely eliminated the sale of the spurious photographic "reprints" trading on the name of "Webster" there is yet a demand for them on account of their low price which is made possible by the cheap manner in which they are manufactured. They are advertised as "genuine," although they are, word for word, the same as the 1847 edition, which is out of date and worthless. This special edition is aimed to take the place of these obsolete books. While printed on cheaper paper than the regular edition, No. 3F6812, and somewhat reduced in size, the special edition is, page for page, the same as the regular 1906 edition, No. 3F6812. The difference between the two books is that of manufacture. The special edition is bound in tan sheep, with double thumb index, marbled edges. Size, 6½x11x3½ inches. Weight, packed for shipment, 6½ lbs.
No. 3F6816 Webster's Unabridged Dictionary, special edition. Price..........**$1.48**
If by mail, postage extra, 52 cents.

Webster's Condensed Dictionaries, 85 Cents to $1.35.

For Home, Office and School.

Authorized and copyrighted by G. & C. Merriam Co., 1906 edition. A dictionary of the English language, with copious etymological derivations, accurate definitions, pronunciations, spelling, and appendices of general reference, derived from Webster's Unabridged Dictionary. **Webster's Condensed Dictionary** contains 46,297 defined words (25 to 40 per cent more than any dictionary of its class), 1,500 text illustrations, with color maps and charts. **The Condensed** is strictly up to date, containing latest words and meanings and their derivations, with an appendix containing a pronouncing vocabulary, abbreviations in writing and printing, arbitrary signs, metric system of weights and measures, etc., printed on high quality paper. Size, 5¾x7¾ inches.
No. 3F6821 Webster's Condensed Dictionary. Bound in extra silk finish cloth, with side and back stamping in gold, marbled edges, double thumb index cut in edge. Weight, packed for shipment, each book, 36 ounces. Publisher's price, $1.25 Our price..........**85c**
If by mail, postage extra, 18 cents.

No. 3F6822 Webster's Condensed Dictionary. Bound in half genuine morocco, side and back stamping in gold, marbled edges, with double thumb index cut in edge. Size, 5¾x8 inches. Publisher's price, $1.75. Our price..........**98c**
If by mail, postage extra, 18 cents.
No. 3F6823 Webster's Condensed Dictionary. Bound in genuine flexible morocco gold side and back stamping, rounded corners, marbled edges, with double thumb index. Size, 5¾x8 inches. Publisher's price, $2.25. Our price..........**$1.35**
If by mail, postage extra, 18 cents.

Webster's Practical Dictionaries, 25 Cents to 58 Cents.

HANDY SIZE EDITIONS.

Authorized and copyrighted by G. & C. Merriam Co., 1906 edition. The Practical is all that its name implies—a practical dictionary of the English language, embodying 31,465 words in practical usage. While this dictionary is an abridgment of the well known **Webster's Condensed Dictionary**, it carries more words than any other handy sized dictionary claiming the Webster name, not to speak of its better illustrations and its definitions of later words.

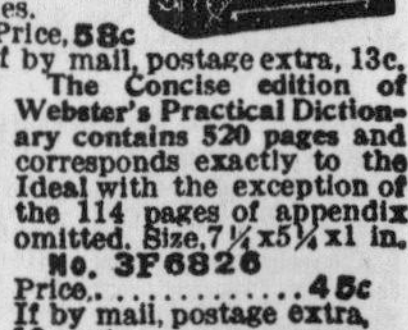

The Ideal edition of Webster's Practical Dictionary contains 634 pages, including the dictionary proper with its 1,200 illustrations and appendix of 114 pages. The appendix contains a pronouncing vocabulary, alphabetical list of abbreviations, arbitrary signs, the metric system, etc. Printed on extra book paper. Bound in fine cloth. Size, 7¼x5¼x1¼ inches.
No. 3F6825 Price, **58c**
If by mail, postage extra, 13c.

The Concise edition of Webster's Practical Dictionary contains 520 pages and corresponds exactly to the Ideal with the exception of the 114 pages of appendix omitted. Size, 7¼x5¼x1 in.
No. 3F6826
Price..........**45c**
If by mail, postage extra, 10 cents.

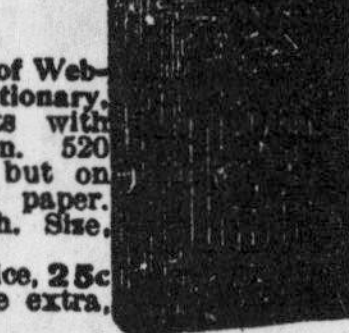

The Popular edition of Webster's Practical Dictionary, identical in contents with the Concise edition. 520 pages, well printed, but on a cheaper grade of paper. Bound in durable cloth. Size, 7¼x5¼x1 inch.
No. 3F6827 Price, **25c**
If by mail, postage extra, 8 cents.

Vest Pocket Dictionary.
Contains 45,800 Words.

A Webster Vest Pocket Dictionary and complete vest pocket library. Five books in one volume: 1. A Dictionary. 2. A Gazetteer. 3. Parliamentary Manual. 4. Expert Calculator. 5. Literary Guide. Contains 45,800 words. Absolutely full pronunciation; synonyms; plural forms; compound words; 5,000 difficult words; proper names; geographical statistics; large cities business forms; social forms; capitals; punctuation; postal regulations; etc. Thoroughly reliable throughout. Size, 2¾x5½ inches. Bound in full morocco leather.

No. 3F6828 Price..............21c
If by mail, postage extra, 2 cents.

Foreign Dictionaries.

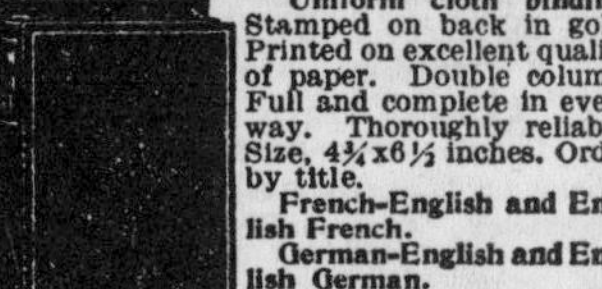

Uniform cloth binding. Stamped on back in gold. Printed on excellent quality of paper. Double column. Full and complete in every way. Thoroughly reliable. Size, 4¾x6½ inches. Order by title.

French-English and English-French.
German-English and English-German.
Spanish-English and English-Spanish.
Swedish-English and English-Swedish.
Italian-English and English-Italian.
Latin-English and English-Latin.

No. 3F6835 Price, each 45c
If by mail, postage extra, each, 8 cents.

Cassell's School Dictionaries.

Newly edited and revised. Each containing over 1,000 pages. Cloth. Size, 5x8 inches. Order by title.

French-English and English French.
German-English and English-German.
English-Latin and Latin-English.
English-Polish and Polish-English.

No. 3F6837 Price, each..............$1.05
If by mail, postage extra, each, 16 cents.

Vest Pocket Foreign Language Dictionaries.
Order by Title and Number.

Spanish-English and English Spanish.
Latin-English and English-Latin.
French-English and English-French.
German-English and English German.
Italian-English and English-Italian.

No. 3F6840 Bound in flexible cloth. Size, 2¾x5½ inches. Price, each..............19c
No. 3F6841 Bound in full leather. Price, each..........................29c
If by mail, postage extra, either style, 3 cents.

Encyclopedia of Quotations.

Compiled and arranged by Adam Woolever. A treasury of wisdom, wit, and humor, odd comparisons and proverbs. Selections from 731 authors, 1,392 subjects and contains 10,299 quotations. Its contents are so various as to appeal to all tastes and comprehensions. It deals with all manner of topics as treated by all manner of men. Contains an appendix of lighter humor and profounder wisdom. 527 pages. Printed on excellent quality of paper. Bound in cloth with cover design stamped in gold and colors. Size, 6¾x9½ inches.

No. 3F6851 Price...............88c
If by mail, postage extra, 26 cents.

Dictionary of Phrase and Fable.

By E. Cobham Brewer, LL. D. New revised and enlarged edition, giving the derivation, source or origin of common phrases, allusions and words that have a tale to tell, to which is added a concise bibliography of English literature. Contains nearly 1,500 pages. A book for every student, scholar and teacher. A book that should be in everybody's library. Bound in cloth with imitation morocco back. Title stamped on back in gold. Size, 5¾x8 in.

No. 3F6853 Price...............95c
If by mail, postage extra, 22 cents.

100,000 Synonyms and Antonyms.

By Rt. Rev. Samuel Fallows, A.M., D.D. A complete dictionary of synonyms and antonyms, or synonyms and words of opposite meaning, with an appendix embracing a dictionary of Briticisms, Americanisms, colloquial phrases, etc., in current use; grammatical uses of prepositions and prepositions discriminated; a list of homonyms and homophonous words; a collection of foreign phrases, and a complete list of abbreviations and contractions used in writing and printing. 512 pages, bound in brown cloth. A most valuable reference book. Size, 5¼x7 inches.

No. 3F6855 Price..............65c
If by mail, postage extra, 12 cents.

THE AMERICAN STANDARD ENCYCLOPEDIA AND ATLAS OF THE WORLD $9.95

8 MAGNIFICENT VOLUMES; HALF CALF LEATHER BINDING.

NEW ILLUSTRATED SUBSCRIPTION EDITION. The latest, the most complete, the most scholarly, the most authoritative work in print, regardless of price.

WHEN YOU PAY $40.00 for an encyclopedia your money is simply divided up among a long list of middlemen, head agents, sub agents and famous authors who may write a little short preface and charge the publishers a big price for the privilege of printing their names on the title page.

THE BOOK AGENT who comes to your door would charge you $40.00 for the American Standard Encyclopedia and Atlas of the World, and his commission on the sale would be $10.00. His "easy payment plan" means that you would help to pay the enormous losses arising from those customers who do not complete their payments, and this is another $10.00 item entering into the cost of the set when purchased from agents. The various losses of the installment firm, selling encyclopedias on the easy payment or subscription plan, are all put into the price of the books. Lost sets, disputed accounts, interest on the investment, advertising, head agent's commissions, sub agent's commissions, traveling expenses, collecting, auditing—all these and many other items, some large, some small, must enter into the cost of an encyclopedia or any other book or set of books bought from an agent on the easy payment subscription plan.

OUR METHOD OF SELLING this set of encyclopedia direct to the user, with only one small profit between the actual manufacturing cost and our selling price, enables us to offer the set to our customers at less than one-fourth the price which the publishers charge when selling the exact same set in the ordinary way through agents on the subscription plan. Our business methods enable us to eliminate all the losses and heavy expenses which occur in the ordinary way of selling subscription books.

WHAT THIS ENCYCLOPEDIA CONTAINS. The American Standard Encyclopedia and Atlas of the World presents to its readers clearly and concisely the sum total of the world's information, contributions of hundreds of educators, representing every great university and college. There are special articles from the most noted authorities in the field of art, literature, science, mechanics and commerce.

SIX THOUSAND YEARS OF HISTORY, extending back from the actual present through the entire period of man's activity. Practically a history of the world from the earliest times of which we have any record right down to every day occurrences of the present, such as the close of the Russian-Japanese war, the Morocco boundary dispute, the seating of the new king of Denmark, the new president of the Republic of France, the death of the merchant prince, Marshall Field, the statesman, John Hay, and the soldier, Gen. Wheeler.

IN BIOGRAPHY the American Standard Encyclopedia is most complete, embracing the lives and histories of nearly forty thousand notable men and women, both of the past and the present.

VITAL STATISTICS form the entire contents of Volume 8. This is a most important feature, covering thousands upon thousands of facts, large and small, which are so often neglected by other encyclopedias. Everything pertaining to the census, foreign and domestic, is to be found. All kinds of statistics in reference to farming, stock raising, railroading, national debts, imports, exports, labor, etc.; all are most fully and elaborately covered.

TRADES AND PROCESSES. More than five hundred important industries and processes by which they exist are fully treated. Electricity in all its phases, aeronautics, steam engineering, steel industries, mining, wireless telegraphy, photography, engraving, transportation; in fact, all that man has done and is doing.

SIXTY-FIVE THOUSAND ENCYCLOPEDIA TOPICS are embraced in this great reference library, and every topic is placed in its proper alphabetical position, making it very easy to refer instantly to any desired subject.

A COMPLETE ATLAS OF THE WORLD covering every foot of space on the globe, both land and water, showing every country, every empire, every republic, both ancient and modern, is a feature of this great reference library. Every map is new and up to date, made under the direction of the International Geographical Survey.

ILLUSTRATIONS. There are more than 3,500 illustrations, many of which are full page half tone reproductions of the great industries of the world, views of the large cities, portraits of statesmen, poets, authors and soldiers. There are also a large number of colored charts on special subjects, such as horses, fish, natural history topics, etc.

THE AMERICAN STANDARD ENCYCLOPEDIA AND ATLAS OF THE WORLD is composed of eight large magnificent volumes, each volume measuring 11¼x14 inches, the largest encyclopedia page printed. The type is large, clear and easy to read, printed on a high grade of book paper. The binding is half calf, with leather protected corners and strong pebbled cloth sides, a style of binding that is not only handsome in appearance but strong and durable; a binding that will stand the wear and tear of a lifetime of ordinary usage. Ordinarily an encyclopedia containing as much matter as the American Standard Encyclopedia would be printed in fifteen, twenty, or even twenty-five volumes, but by printing this encyclopedia with extra large pages, using a comparatively thin, but very high quality paper, we are able to put up the entire set, all complete, in only eight volumes, and in this way we reduce the manufacturing cost to the lowest possible figure.

No. 3F6905 The American Standard Encyclopedia and Atlas of the World. Eight volumes. Bound in half calf. Price, per set................................$9.95
Weight, packed for shipment, 50 pounds.

Crabb's English Synonyms.

By George Crabb, M.A. English synonyms explained in alphabetical order, with copious examples and quotations drawn from the best writers explanatory of the text. This book is the standard authority on synonyms and no other work can take its place. Its object is to assist the inquirer in ascertaining the force and comprehension of the English language. This is the original English edition, printed by George Rutledge & Sons, on the best quality of paper. Contains 650 pages. Bound in red cloth with title stamped on back. Size, 5¼x8 inches.

No. 3F6857 Price..............98c
If by mail, postage extra, 13 cents.

Pronunciation of 10,000 Proper Names.

By M. S. Mackey. Gives famous geographical and biographical names, names of books, works of art, characters in fiction, foreign titles, etc. This is the only handy volume dictionary of pronunciation, and, in addition, contains many names not in the larger works. This is invaluable to both the student and the teacher and everyone will be surprised how often they will consult it if they have a copy in their library. Contains 294 pages. Printed on best quality of paper and bound in cloth. Size, 4½x6¾ inches.

No. 3F6859 Price..............78c
If by mail, postage extra, 8 cents.

The New Noyes Dictionary and Book Holder.

A perfect book holder. Combines strength, beauty and convenience. The entire base is made from cold rolled steel; consequently is nondestructible. Can be easily set up. This holder is adjustable to any height or angle and pivoted to turn to any position. With revolving shelf, finished in bronze, nickel trimmings. Casters.

No. 3F6895 Single Adjustable Book Holder. Price..........$1.98
No. 3F6896 Double Adjustable Book Holder. Otherwise same as No. 3F6895. Price.....$2.98
Weight, packed 18 lbs.

The New Little Giant Cyclopedia of Ready Reference.

One million facts and figures. The model of compactness and comprehensiveness. A real treasury of ready reference. This book settles more arguments and answers more of the questions and problems of today than any other encyclopedia published, whether in one or thirty volumes. Contains over 500 pages. Profusely illustrated with full page maps in colors, diagrams, drawings, etc. Bound in limp leatherette. Red edges. Size, 4½x6⅛ inches

No. 3F6899 Price.............65c
If by mail, postage extra, 5 cents.

Everett's Encyclopedia of Useful Knowledge.

A complete library of universal knowledge, condensed in one volume, showing the newest and most wonderful inventions and the world's great progress in science and commerce. A culmination of centuries of human efforts; the great industries of the world photographed and explained, showing the wonderful mechanical works of this century, including a complete index and valuable list of review questions for home study. Superbly illustrated with a vast number of engravings. Innumerable full page photographs and many smaller ones. 336 pages, double column, printed on the best quality of plate paper. Bound in cloth with cover design elaborately stamped in gold. Size, 7x9¾ inches.

No. 3F7012 Price.............68c
If by mail, postage extra, 20 cents.

A Book of Curious Facts.

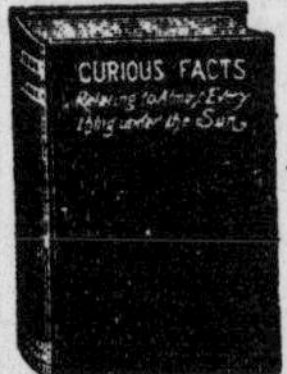

Compiled and edited by Henry Williams. A book of general interest, relating to almost everything under the sun. This book not only is intensely interesting from cover to cover, but is most instructive, and we feel sure that if anyone starts to read it they will not lay it down until they have completed it. It is impossible for us to give a list of the thousand curious facts set forth in its pages. 340 pages printed on the best quality of paper. Bound in blue cloth with title stamped on back and side in white. Size, 5¼x7½ inches.

No. 3F7015 Price..............48c
If by mail, postage extra, 8 cents.

Standard Library of Knowledge and Universal Educator for Home Study.

Containing concise and exhaustive articles upon science, arts, mechanics, automobiles, aerial transportation, cinematograph, air and submarine navigation, pneumatic tubes, wireless telegraphy, war balloons, etc., etc. All of the latest discoveries and inventions; ship building; petrified forests; gold products of the world; curious facts: wonders of electricity; history and travels; X Ray, etc. A complete treasury of knowledge, including best selections from the writings of hundreds of men renowned in science, invention and discovery, such as Edison, Marconi, Tripler, etc., etc. Containing over 600 pages. Superbly embellished with hundreds of phototype and line engravings. Bound in cloth with elaborate cover design stamped in gold and colors. Royal quarto size, 7¼x9¾ inches. Marbled edges. Retail price, $2.50

No. 3F7018 Our price..........**98c**
If by mail, postage extra, 26 cents.

The Home Cyclopedia of Necessary Information.

Embracing five separate and complete books in one volume: A Home Maker, A Question Answerer, A Health Keeper, A Business Guide, A Money Saver. Every book by an eminent authority and specialist.

Book 1. Home Cyclopedia of General Information. By Prof. Chas. Morris.

Book 2. Home Cyclopedia of Business and Commerce. By Prof. Collins and Prof. E. C. Mills.

Book 3. Home Cyclopedia of Geography and History. By Chas. Morris.

Book 4. Home Cyclopedia of Cooking and Housekeeping. By Alice Johnson and Mrs. Janet McKensie Hill.

Book 5. Home Cyclopedia of Health and Medicine. By Dr. Henry Hartshorne.

Illustrated with over 300 engravings and halftone pictures. 21 colored statistical charts, 8 pages of historical charts in colors, 3 colored anatomical plates and the flags of all nations in colors. Bound in cloth. Size, 7¼x9¾ inches. 1¾ inches thick.

No. 3F7021 The Home Cyclopedia in one big volume. Our price............**98c**
If by mail, postage extra, 32 cents.

Imperial Atlas of the World.

Rand, McNally & Co.'s edition. Contains the 1900 census, maps of every country, and special county maps of each state in the United States, maps of large cities, etc. Also a brief historical, descriptive, statistical and political review of the United States. 175 pages. Cloth. Size, 11½ x 14½ inches.

No. 3F7065 Price............**$1.30**
If by mail, postage extra, 24 cents.

New Twentieth Century Atlas.

Combination Atlas, Gazeteer, Encyclopedia and Pictorial History of the World. The latest census, description of the different people of the world, their civilization, religion, etc. Cloth. Size, 12x17 inches. 388 pages.

No. 3F7070
Price.......**$2.10**
If by mail, postage extra, 76 cents.

Boyd's Shorthand Instructor.

Easily learned in one month. A new system of shorthand in which the characters represent syllables, and are so arranged that when the student learns sixteen syllables he knows how to write eighty syllables. This new system is capable of much greater speed than the older systems, is simpler, briefer and more easily learned, and can be mastered in one month. Cloth. 70 pages. Size, 5x7 inches

No. 3F7250 Price..........**85c**
If by mail, postage extra, 10 cents.

The Correspondent's Manual.

By William E. Hickox. A text book for stenographers, typewriter operators and clerks, comprising practical information on letter taking and letter writing. Hints how to do it and how not to do it. 128 pages. Size, 4½x6½ inches. Bound in cloth.

No. 3F7255 Price.....**40c**
If by mail, postage extra, 5 cents.

How to Become an Auctioneer

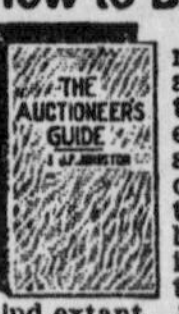

By Chas. Johnson. There is no money making occupation which admits of greater advantages than auctioneering. Auctioneers are in constant demand, and are needed in every line of merchandise. The field is large and the opportunities great. This book starts you on the right road; it gives ideas, and is the only thoroughly practical work of the kind extant. Size, 5x7 inches. 115 pages.

No. 3F7260 Paper. Price......**18c**
No. 3F7261 Cloth. Price......**30c**
If by mail, postage extra, paper, 5c; cloth, 11c

EDUCATIONAL AND SELF TEACHING BOOKS

GENUINE WEBSTER'S $10.00 INTERNATIONAL DICTIONARY .. FREE

WITH SHERWIN CODY'S GOOD ENGLISH BOOKS.

Cody's Good English Books, on the Art of Writing and Speaking the English Language, are the latest and highest authority on practical English and the best methods in business letter writing.

We recommend these books as the best that money can buy for home or school text book use.

WITH AN ORDER FOR 100 of the Cody books, as listed below, we give, absolutely free of charge, one genuine Webster's International Dictionary, very latest edition, bound in sheep, the regular $10.00 edition.

WITH AN ORDER FOR 30 of the Cody books, as listed below, we give, absolutely free of charge, one genuine Webster's Collegiate Dictionary, very latest edition, bound in cloth, the regular $3.00 book.

WITH EVERY ORDER FOR 10 of the Cody books, as listed below, we give, absolutely free of charge, one copy of Cody's Dictionary of Errors, latest revised edition, regular 75-cent value.

WITH VOLUMES I, II, III "GOOD ENGLISH FORM BOOK," we give, absolutely free of charge, in addition, under any of the above offers. Special Text Exercise books with each volume purchased.

Cody's Good English Books.

Vol. I. Word Study. The principles of the dictionary in a nutshell. The only home study spelling book published. 127 pages. Size, 4x5½ inches.

Vol. II. Grammar and Punctuation. Simplified and made practical so that by studying it one can really get skill in writing and speaking correctly in the shortest possible time. 127 pages. Size, 4x5½ inches.

Vol. III. Composition and Rhetoric. Franklin's method of getting the knack of using words effectively. Teaches you to imitate the great masters and catch their skill. 127 pages. Size, 4x5½ inches.

Vol. IV. Story Writing and Journalism. Zangwill says, "This is the most sensible treatise on the practical art of writing short stories that has yet appeared in England or America." 127 pages. Size, 4x5½ inches.

Vol. V. Dictionary of Errors. This book is five handy little reference books rolled into one—Errors of Grammar (with all the rules), Points on Letter Writing, Words Often Mispronounced, Words Often Misspelled (with every known device to fix the right form in memory), and Words Often Misused (including synonyms). Here are 25,000 errors you are making every day without knowing it, yet you can run through the book in an evening and [brush up. 136 pages. Size, 4x5½ inches.

Vol. VI. How to Read and What to Read. Chapters on What Constitutes a Great Poem, Essay, or Novel. A Complete Training Course in English Literature for home study, with authoritative lists of the best poems, essays, and novels. 130 pages. Size, 4x5½ inches.

No. 3F7201 Cody's Good English Books. Any of the above six titles. Price, each..**45c**
If by mail, postage extra, each, 3 cents.

Cody's Good English Form Book in Business Letter Writing.

"The best brief manual on letter writing and the only good dictation book for stenographers in existence." Here are 100 model letters of all kinds, written in the very latest and best business style, with points on correct English, good business usage, spelling, etc. 125 pages. Size, 5x7½ inches.

No. 3F7202 Price............**55c**
If by mail, postage extra, 5 cents.

No. 3F7203 Sample set of the four free exercise books. Price..........**90c**
If by mail, postage extra, 10 cents.

Algebra Self Taught.

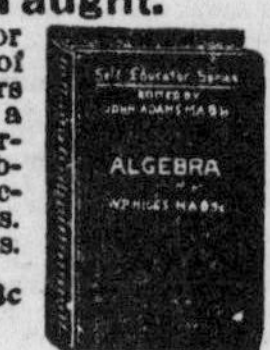

By W. Paget Higgs. For home study. For the use of mechanics, young engineers and home students. As a guide and helper in the perplexities of algebraic problems, this book can be recommended. 104 pages. Cloth. Size, 5½x7½ inches.

No. 3F7205
Price..........**58c**
If by mail, postage extra, 12 cents.

Grammar Without a Master.

By William Cobbett. Carefully revised and annotated by Alfred Ayers. Persons who studied grammar when at school and failed to comprehend its principles as well as those who have never studied grammar at all, will find the book especially suited to their needs. Cloth, with index. 254 pages. Size, 4¾x6½ inches.

No. 3F7210
Price..........**75c**
If by mail, postage extra, 10 cents.

The Self Educator Series.

Edited by John Adams. Each book begins with the beginning of every subject and carries the student far enough to enable him to continue his studies intelligently and successfully on his own account.

Self Educator in French
Self Educator in Latin
Self Educator in German
Self Educator in Chemistry
Self Educator in English Composition

The following five titles are edited by Prof. C. M. Stevens, A.M.:

Self Educator in Norwegian
Self Educator in Danish
Self Educator in Spanish
Self Educator in Swedish
Self Educator in Italian

No. 3F7215 Cloth. Size, 5x7¼ inches. Any 2 for **90c**; Price, per volume....**48c**
If by mail, postage extra, per volume, 10 cents.

Journalism and Newspaper Work.

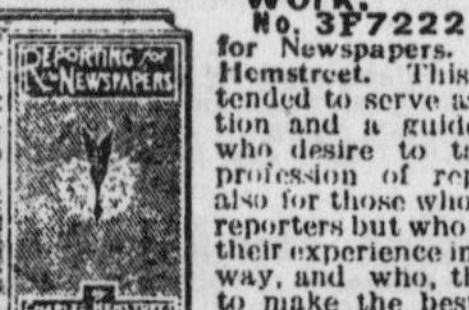

No. 3F7222 Reporting for Newspapers. By Chas. Hemstreet. This work is intended to serve as a foundation and a guide for those who desire to take up the profession of reporting, and also for those who are already reporters but who have gained their experience in a desultory way, and who, therefore fail to make the best use of it. 140 pages. Size, 4½x6½ inches. Price..........**59c**
If by mail, postage extra, 5 cents.

Advice to Singers.

By Frederick J. Crowest. This is a simple and practical book upon the subject of singing, describing in full how to obtain the best results and how to give the greatest tone and volume to one's voice. This book should prove indispensable to those who sing and who are about to take up singing. 125 pages. Size, 5x7½ inches.

No. 3F7224 Price..........**40c**
If by mail, postage extra, 5 cents.

Modern Penmanship.

For home study. A complete course in penmanship, explaining the muscular or free arm movement. The only system by which a graceful, rapid and legible style of penmanship can be obtained. Contains 28 specimen plates of up to date business and fancy writing; also a skeleton outline of letters. 80 pages. Cloth. Size, 8x10½ inches.

No. 3F7225
Price..........**65c**
If by mail, postage extra, 11 cents.

100 Lessons in Business.

By Seymour Eaton. Safe business rules, hints and helps for corresponding purposes, for accountants, for advertisers; something about business figures and how to handle them; decimal numbers and what they are for; making out accounts, percentages, receipts, orders, due bills, trade discounts, invoices, etc. Cloth. Size, 6x9¼ inches.

No. 3F7230
Price..........**32c**
If by mail, postage extra, 11 cents.

Bookkeeping Self Taught.

By Phillip C. Goodwin. A complete self instructor in bookkeeping, for students, clerks, tradesmen and merchants. With accounts in illustration, exercises for practice and a glossary of commercial terms. An entirely new departure from all other methods of self instruction and one which can be studied systematically and alone by the student with quick and permanent results. Cloth. Size, 5x7 inches. 127 pages.

No. 3F7235 Price..........**65c**
If by mail, postage extra, 12 cents.

Bryant's Practical Bookkeeping.

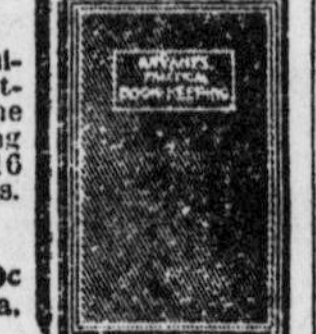

By H. W. Bryant, President of Bryant and Stratton's Business College. The best book on bookkeeping that we know about. 116 pages. Sizes, 6¾x9½ inches. Cloth binding.

No. 3F7245
Price..........**90c**
If by mail, postage extra, 8 cents.

Practical Journalism.

No. 3F7223 By E. L. Shumen. A complete and comprehensive treatise on Journalism, being a complete manual of the best newspaper methods. Not only is this work a most interesting one, but contains the best and most practical information of the subject, and is of immense value to either the beginner or the experienced reporter. Contains 255 pages, printed on best quality of paper and bound in cloth. Size, 5½x7¾ inches.
Price..........(If by mail, postage extra, 10 cents.)..........**$1.15**

Debating and How to Learn It.

By Charles Walter Brown, A. M. Not only a manual of parliamentary usages, but a complete guide pertaining to matters of organization. Debating clubs will find this book unequaled. It gives full debates, so that the inexperienced speaker may know about what he is expected to say. 160 pages. Size, 4¼x6¾ inches.

No. 3F7265 Bound in cloth. Price..........**21c**
If by mail, postage extra, 5 cents.

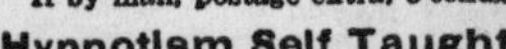

Hypnotism Self Taught.

By Prof. L. W. DeLaurence. If you want to be able to hypnotize your friends and acquaintances, and to convince them that your will power is stronger than theirs, the practical lessons in this book will teach you how to accomplish this. It is a common sense system for beginners as well as more advanced students. Illustrated. Size, 5¼x7¾ inches. 261 pages.

No. 3F7270 Paper. Price.....**28c**
No. 3F7271 Cloth. Price.....**60c**
If by mail, postage extra, paper, 7c; cloth, 12c.

Hoyle's Card Games.

With rules and methods of playing. A manual of games and an instructor of methods and systems. Contains rules for playing every known card game. Size, 2½x5½ inches.

No. 3F7275 Cloth.
Price..........**18c**
No. 3F7276 Full leather.
Price..........**30c**
If by mail, postage extra, 4 cents.

Careers For the Coming Men.

By twenty-three of the best known business, and literary men of the days. A practical and authoritative discussion of the various callings the success to be attained in each, remuneration, experience, etc., etc. Covers a wide range of subjects, as follows: the Army, Teaching, the Navy, the Commercial Life, the Church, Medicine, Railroading, Architecture, Electricity, Mechanical Engineering, Law, Mining Engineering, Civil Engineering, Real Estate, Life Insurance, Public Service, Advertising, Farming, Journalism, The Stage, Publishing, Authorship, Banking. Contains 245 extra large pages, printed on best quality of paper. Handsomely bound in green cloth with attractive cover design and title on back and side in green and gold. Size, 5½x8¾ inches.

No. 3F7312 Price..........**55c**
If by mail, postage extra, 12 cents.

The Making of An American.

An Autobiography, by Jacob A. Riis. This book has proved the most popular biography for many years. It has been in demand at the public libraries more regularly than any other book, even including fiction. It is the story of how a friendless, uneducated boy worked his way up by sheer courage and nobility of spirit until he won the record of having done more for the good of the city of New York than any other individual. Contains 443 pages. Profusely illustrated; contains portraits. Bound in cloth with title stamped on back. Size, 5½x7¾ inches.

No. 3F7317 Price..........**49c**
If by mail, postage extra, 16 cents.

SCIENTIFIC BOOKS.

Prospectors' Field Book and Guide.

By Prof. H. S. Osborne, L. L. D. A complete treatise on the search for and the easy determination of ores and their useful minerals, including gems and gem stones. This edition is thoroughly revised and enlarged. The very best book on this subject ever published. It is provided with alphabetical table of contents, making reference to any subject prompt and easy. Illustrated with 66 special engravings. 346 pages. Bound in cloth. Size, 5½x7½ inches.

No. 3F7336 Price............$1.28
If by mail, postage extra, 10 cents.

Progress of Invention in the 19th Century.

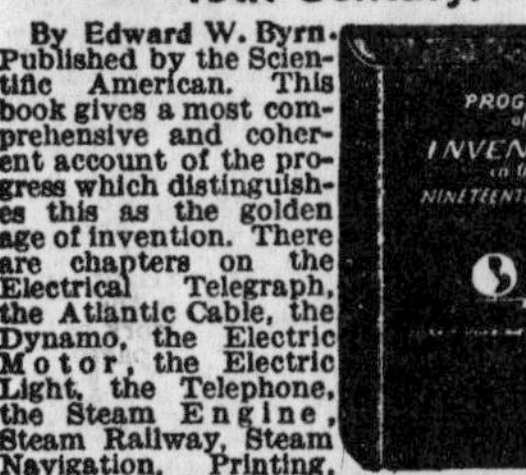

By Edward W. Byrn. Published by the Scientific American. This book gives a most comprehensive and coherent account of the progress which distinguishes this as the golden age of invention. There are chapters on the Electrical Telegraph, the Atlantic Cable, the Dynamo, the Electric Motor, the Electric Light, the Telephone, the Steam Engine, Steam Railway, Steam Navigation, Printing, the Typewriter, the Sewing Machine, the Reaper, Chemistry, Food and Drink, Medicine, Surgery and Sanitation, the Automobile, the Phonograph, Optics, Photography, the X Rays, Civil Engineering, Wood Working, Metal Working, Fire Arms, Explosives, Textiles, Liquid Air, etc. 35 complete chapters, 300 beautiful illustrations, printed on the finest paper and substantially bound in cloth. 480 pages. Size, 7x9½ inches.

No. 3F7341 Price............$2.60
If by mail, postage extra, 26 cents.

Experimental Science.

By Geo. M. Hopkins. Twenty-fifth edition. Revised and greatly enlarged. Published by the Scientific American. Since this book was last published, there have been such wonderful developments in electrical science and various other branches of natural philosophy, that the author decided it would be necessary to prepare an entirely new edition of this work, in order that the many wonderful discoveries of modern times might be fully described. The increased size of the work has made it necessary to divide it into two volumes, and this book stands today as the most complete, most interesting, and most authoritative work on Experimental Science ever published. The two big volumes are finely bound in cloth, containing over 1,100 pages and 200 illustrations. Size of each volume, 6¼x9¼ inches.

No. 3F7344 Two volumes. Price for the set............$4.15
Weight, packed for shipment, 7 pounds.

The Scientific American Boy.

By A. Russell Bond. This is a story of outdoor boy life, and suggests a large number of diversions, which, aside from affording amusement, will stimulate in boys the creative spirit. In each instance complete instructions are given for building various articles. There are directions for making camping outfits, sleeping bags and tents; also such other shelters as trees, houses, straw huts, log cabins and caves. There are instructions for making six kinds of skate sails and eight kinds of snow shoes and skis, besides ice boats, scooters, sledges, toboggans, and the Swedish contrivance called "rennwolf." Among other subjects covered are surveying, wig-wagging, heliographing and bridge building and miscellaneous devices such as scows, canoes, land yachts, windmills, water wheels and the like. 340 fine illustrations. Substantially bound in cloth. 320 pages. Size, 6x8¼ inches.

No. 3F7346 Price............$1.68
If by mail, postage extra, 16 cents.

Astronomy for Everybody.

By Simon Newcomb. The authority on astronomy. A popular exposition of the wonders of the heavens, with chapters on the motions of the celestial bodies, astronomical instruments, the sun, earth and moon, the planets and their satellites, comets, meteoric bodies, and the fixed stars. 60 illustrations. 333 pages. A complete treatise on astronomy, without the use of obscure technical language. Thoroughly up to date, published in 1904. Size, 5¾x8 inches.

No. 3F7348 Price............$1.90
If by mail, postage extra, 19 cents.

Scientific American Reference Book.

Compiled by Albert A. Hopkins and A. Russell Bond. The result of the queries of three generations of correspondence of the Scientific American is crystalized in this book, which has been in course of preparation for a long time. It deals with matters of interest to everybody, contains fifty thousand facts, and is much more complete and more extensive than anything of the kind which has ever been attempted. It has been revised by eminent statisticians. Information has been drawn from over a ton of government reports. It is a book for everyday reference, more useful than an encyclopedia, because you will find just what you want in more condensed form. Bound in cloth. 516 pages. Fully illustrated, including six colored plates. Size, 5½x8 inches.

No. 3F7349 Price............$1.30
If by mail, postage extra, 16 cents.

Scientific American Cyclopedia.

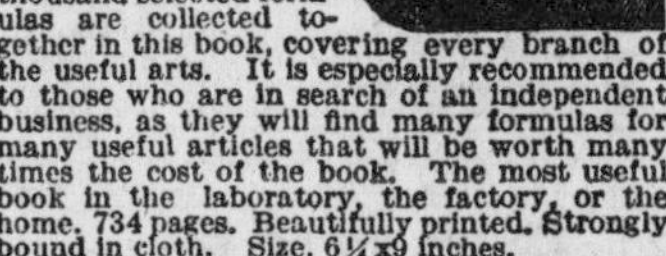

This book consists of a careful compilation of the most useful recipes and information which have appeared in the Scientific American for more than half a century. This is the twenty-fifth revised edition, brought thoroughly up to date, the latest and most complete volume on the subject of recipes ever presented. Over fifteen thousand selected formulas are collected together in this book, covering every branch of the useful arts. It is especially recommended to those who are in search of an independent business, as they will find many formulas for many useful articles that will be worth many times the cost of the book. The most useful book in the laboratory, the factory, or the home. 734 pages. Beautifully printed. Strongly bound in cloth. Size, 6¼x9 inches.

No. 3F7351 Price............$4.15
If by mail, postage extra, 38 cents.

Darwin's Works.

By Charles Darwin. These two famous books by the greatest of all scientists should be in everybody's library. The edition in which these are published is printed on excellent quality of paper and bound in cloth with title stamped on back in gold, and full gilt top. Over 500 pages each. Size, 5¼x7½ inches. Regular price, $1.00 each.

Descent of Man
Origin of Species

No. 3F7353 Our price, each............48c
Price, for set, both volumes............89c
If by mail, postage extra, per volume, 12 cents.

Books of Mythology.

Mythology is so intimately connected with the works of the greatest poets, that it will continue to be interesting, as long as classical poetry exists, and must form an indispensable part of the education of the man of literature and of the gentleman. Whether as a manual for reference, a text book for school use, or for the general reader, these books will be found very valuable and interesting. Bound in cloth, stamped in gold and printed on the best quality of paper.

No. 3F7356 Manual of Mythology. By Alexander C. Murray. Size, 5¼x8 inches. 465 pages. 200 illustrations and index. Price, 55c
If by mail, postage extra, 14 cents.

No. 3F7357 The Age of Fables; or, Beauties of Mythology. By Thomas Bulfinch. 448 pages. Size, 5¼x8 inches. 200 illustrations and complete index. Price............55c
If by mail, postage extra, 14 cents.

The Amateur Trapper, and Trap Makers' Guide.

By Stanley Harding. A complete and carefully prepared treatise on the art of trapping, snaring and netting, containing plain directions for making the best traps, snares, nets and dead falls, and how to use them. The most successful baits for all kinds of animals or birds, together with practical recipes for preparing skins and furs for market and for tanning, and comprehensive instructions for stuffing specimens of birds and animals. Fully illustrated. Bound in cloth. 134 pages. Size, 5x7 inches.

No. 3F7741 Price............35c
If by mail, postage extra, 4 cents.

The Trapper's Guide.

By S. Newhouse. This is the best book on trapping ever written, giving full descriptions of all the animals which the American trapper is likely to meet with; tells how they live, how to trap them and how to care for and cure their pelts. Gives complete descriptions of traps adapted to the capture of all kinds of animals, explaining fully the best way to use them. Finely bound in silk finish cloth. Fully illustrated. 207 pages. Size, 5½x8¼ inches.

No. 3F7743 Price............85c
If by mail, postage extra, 11 cents.

BOOKS FOR SPORTSMEN AND NATURE LOVERS.

Bird Life.

By Frank M. Chapman. This book is filled with beautifully colored pictures, showing birds as they are. It gives the portraits and names of the familiar birds of Eastern and North America, with accurate and interesting descriptions. Cloth. Size, 5¼x8 inches.

No. 3F7600 Price............$1.90
If by mail, postage extra, 18c.

History of Birds.

By Rev. W. Bingley, A.M. Containing complete accounts of their varieties and habits, and comprising sketches of hundreds of species of birds in all climes; illustrating their uses, value and culture. 526 pages. Hundreds of illustrations. Substantially bound in cloth. Size, 6x9 inches.

No. 3F7604 Price............48c
If by mail, postage extra, 18 cents.

History of Animals.

By Rev. W. Bingley, A.M. Complete account of their varieties and oddities. Comprising graphic descriptions of nearly all known species of beasts and reptiles the world over, illustrating their varied habits, mode of life, distinguishing peculiarities. Size, 6x9 inches. 586 pages.

No. 3F7606 Price............48c
If by mail, postage extra, 18 cents.

Methods in the Art of Taxidermy.

By Oliver Davie. This book describes fully all of the most practical methods in this art. It teaches, in detail, the skinning and stuffing of birds, mammals, crustaceans, fishes and reptiles, together with illustrations of forms and attitudes of the animal kingdom. Contains 90 full page engravings, 500 smaller pictures, illustrating modes of procedure in the art, including many reproductions from photographs of actual work by celebrated American taxidermists. Printed on best quality of book paper. 359 pages. Full olive edges. Substantially bound in cloth. Extra large size, 7¾x10½ inches.

No. 3F7710 Price............$1.90
If by mail, postage extra, 28 cents.

Boat Building for Amateurs.

By Adrian Nelson, C.E. Contains full and complete instructions for designing and building all manner of sailing boats, such as punts, skiffs, canoes, rowing and sailing boats. Embraces all that anyone will require, save the simplest tools and necessary materials to build any desired boat. 100 illustrations. Cloth. 136 pages. Size, 5½x7¾ inches.

No. 3F7750 Price............58c
If by mail, postage extra, 8 cents.

Canoe and Boat Building.

By W. P. Stephens. This is the eighth edition of this standard work on canoe and boat building, fully revised and extended to date. It is a complete manual for boat builders and amateurs, containing plain and comprehensive directions for the construction of canoes, row boats, sail boats and hunting craft. Canoe building is treated in detail, as the processes involved are common to all boat building, only requiring greater care and skill than ordinary work, and the principles may be applied to any of the simpler craft, such as arrow boats and skiffs. This book is profusely illustrated and in addition is accompanied by 50 plates of working drawings, printed on bond paper too large to be bound with the book and therefore furnished in a separate package. Bound in cloth, 263 pages. Size, 5x7½ inches.

No. 3F7715 Price complete, including the 50 plates of working drawings......$1.80
If by mail, postage extra, 12 cents.

Universal Natural History.

By Alfred H. Miles. With anecdotes, illustrating the habits of animals, birds, fishes, reptiles, insects, etc. Profusely illustrated with beautiful colored plates, which show the animal as it really is. This book covers North and South America, Europe, Asia, Africa and Oceanica, 385 pages. Printed on best quality of paper. Bound in silk cloth with cover design, stamped in black and gold. Size, 5¾x8 inches.

No. 3F7721 Price............$1.18
If by mail, postage extra, 15 cents.

Wood's Popular History.

The popular natural history by the Rev. J. G. Wood, M.A. 600 illustrations by Wolf, Zwecker Weir, Coleman and other celebrated artists of animal life. This is a complete unabridged edition with full text. This book needs no description as it is acknowledged the greatest general work on natural history ever written. Printed from new plates on best quality of paper. Contains 600 pages. Bound in silk cloth and with attractive animal cover design stamped in colors and gold. Size, 6x8 inches.

No. 3F7723 Price............85c
If by mail, postage extra, 22 cents.

Kingdom of Nature.

Edited by Mrs. Frank Leslie. Produced at a cost of over $50,000. Illustrated museum of the animal world. An interesting account of the most valuable facts of natural history, from original research and careful study, to the most reliable works, in various languages, forming a pictorial encyclopedia of a complete library of the marvels of animated nature. Has over 1,000 elegant illustrations by best artists. It has never been equaled, it can never be excelled. Folio size, 9½x11½ inches. Beautifully bound in cloth. Elaborately stamped in black and gold. Retail price, $2.50.

No. 3F7726 Our price............87c
If by mail, postage extra, 44 cents.

The Complete Sportsman's Guide.

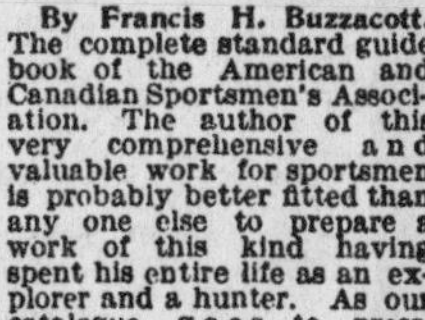

By Francis H. Buzzacott. The complete standard guide book of the American and Canadian Sportsmen's Association. The author of this very comprehensive and valuable work for sportsmen is probably better fitted than any one else to prepare a work of this kind having spent his entire life as an explorer and a hunter. As our catalogue goes to press, Mr. Buzzacott is just leaving on his third trip to the Arctic regions; this time as a member of the Wellman-Record-Herald Polar Expedition. Crowded into this book is more solid information, more matters of real interest and value to the sportsman than is to be found in any other book ever published. Practically everything of interest to the hunter, the fisherman, the trapper or the camper is covered. The book is made as small and compact as possible, so that it may be added to your outfit and carried into the woods, thus making this vast fund of valuable information always accessible, even in camp. Substantially bound in cloth, containing hundreds of illustrations. 514 pages. Size, 4½x6¼ inches.

No. 3F7736 Price............75c
If by mail, postage extra, 11 cents.

Camp Fires of the Wilderness.

By E. W. Burt. This volume treats of a multitude of matters of interest to the camper who, unless he is made comfortable by the exercise of a little expert knowledge and thoughtfulness, may find himself when in camp the most miserable of mortals. The man with experience makes himself as comfortable in camp as at home, while the free and independent life, the fresh air in which he works, eats and sleeps renders him so comfortable that every hour is likely to be a joy. This book tells what to take into camp in the way of bedding, tents, camp equipage, cooking utensils, food, medicine and fishing tackle. It gives advice about camp locations, camp life, cooking and travel. Profusely illustrated and substantially bound in cloth, with cover design stamped in silver. 221 pages. Size, 5½x7¾ inches.

No. 3F7739 Price............$1.10
If by mail, postage extra, 10 cents.

Camp Life in the Woods and the Tricks of Trapping and Trap Making.

By W. Hamilton Gibson. Comprehensive hints on camp shelter of all kinds, boat and canoe building, valuable suggestions on the trappers' food, etc., with extended chapters on the trappers' art, containing all the tricks and valuable bait recipes of the profession. Full directions for the use of the steel trap, and for the construction of traps of all kinds: detailed instructions for the capture of all fur bearing animals; valuable recipes for the curing and tanning of fur skins, etc. Cloth. Illustrated. 300 pages. Size, 5x7 inches.

No. 3F7740 Price............78c
If by mail, postage extra, 10 cents.

Canoe and Camp Cookery.

By "Seneca." The object of this book is to give to the canoeist, the cruiser and the camper some practical recipes for simple, but substantial dishes in such a manner that a novice in the art of cooking may prepare palatable foods with no more utensils than are consistent with light cruising and camping. The recipes given have been obtained from trappers and hunters, from army and navy cooks, etc., and all have been practically tested in camp. Bound in cloth. 96 pages. Size, 5x7½ inches.

No. 3F7751 Price..............85c

If by mail, postage extra, 4 cents.

American Game Fishes.

Edited by G. W. Shields. This is a sportsmen's book, written by sportsmen and is a complete guide to the art of angling. The information contained in its pages is not confined to a limited species of fishes, nor to those of any one locality, but embrace the entire United States and Canada. It is an exhaustive treatise on the finny tribe, giving full directions for making and using fishing tackle, how, when and where to angle for all kinds of fishes, their habits, habitat and peculiarities and a detailed description of the angler's camp outfit. This book is profusely illustrated, including portraits of all the fishes described and two special color plates, giving the natural colors of flies commonly used in angling. Bound in cloth. 580 pages. Size, 5¾x7¾ inches.

No. 3F7753 Price............$1.25

If by mail, postage extra, 20 cents.

Wild Fowl Shooting.

By W. W. Leffingwell. Contains scientific and practical descriptions of wild fowl, their resorts, habits, flights and most successful method of hunting them. This book treats fully of the selection of guns for wild fowl shooting; retrievers, their characteristics, how to select and how to train them. The practical suggestions in this book make it invaluable to the hunter, while the anecdotes and genuine nature studies make the book intensely interesting to the average reader. Printed on fine paper. Fully illustrated. Substantially bound in cloth, with cover design stamped in gold. 373 pages. Size, 5½x7¾ inches.

No. 3F7775 Price..........$1.30

If by mail, postage extra, 16 cents.

Field, Cover and Trap Shooting.

By Captain Adam H. Bogardus, champion wing shot of the world. A most complete book by this celebrated marksman, with chapters on guns and their proper charges, pinnated grouse shooting; late pinnated grouse shooting; quail shooting in the west; ruffled grouse shooting; shooting the woodcock, the snipe and snipe shooting; golden plover, curlew and gray plover; wild ducks and western duck shooting; wild geese, cranes and swans; wild turkeys and deer shooting. The art of shooting on the wing. Shooting dogs, breeding and breaking. Pigeon shooting; trap shooting. Bound in cloth. Fully illustrated. 444 pages. Size, 5½x7½ inches.

No. 3F7778 Price..........$1.50

If by mail, postage extra, 10 cents.

American Big Game Hunting.

Edited by Theodore Roosevelt and George Bird Grinnell. The book of the Boone and Crockett Club. Contents: A Buffalo Story, The White Goat and His Country, A Day with the Elk, Old Times in the Black Hills, Big Game in the Rockies, Coursing the Prongbuck, After Wapiti in Wyoming, In Buffalo Days, Nights with the Grizzlies, The Yellowstone Park as a Game Reserve, A Mountain Fraud, Blacktails in the Bad Lands, Photographing Big Game, Literature of American Big Game Hunting, Our Forest Reservations. Bound in cloth. 345 pages. Size, 6x8¼ inches.

No. 3F7783 Price..........$1.98

If by mail, postage extra, 14 cents.

The Dog.

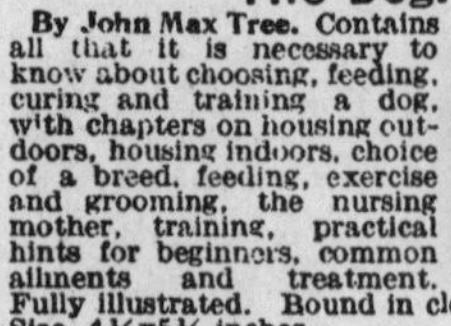

By John Max Tree. Contains all that it is necessary to know about choosing, feeding, curing and training a dog, with chapters on housing outdoors, housing indoors, choice of a breed, feeding, exercise and grooming, the nursing mother, training, practical hints for beginners, common ailments and treatment. Fully illustrated. Bound in cloth. 140 pages. Size, 4¾x5¾ inches.

No. 3F7790 Price..............38c

If by mail, postage extra, 5 cents.

Practical Dog Training.

By S. T. Hammond. Practical Dog Training, or Training vs. Breaking, is a book for dog owners who by the instructions here plainly given can successfully train their hunting dogs. This is a new and revised edition, written after the author's 35 years of successful experience with the methods described, in which he teaches how to bring out the intelligence of the dog by an entirely new method in which kindness is substituted for the whip. Finely bound in cloth. 165 pages. Size, 5x7½ inches.

No. 3F7792 Price..............85c

If by mail, postage extra, 6 cents.

Wild Animals I Have Met.

By Frederick Seymour. A book of natural history by a world renowned naturalist. This book is a complete description of various animals, their physical appearance, their habits and mode of life, and at the same time is highly entertaining with stories of travel and adventure. Illustrated from actual photographs of wild animals. 540 pages. Cloth bound. Size, 7½x10 inches.

No. 3F7800 Price...........80c

If by mail, postage extra, 24 cents.

Botany.

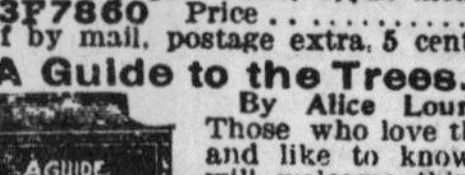

By Julian McNair Wright. A concise and accurate account of the phenomena of plant life, divided into twelve chapters, each chapter devoted to the plant life of one of the twelve months of the year. The scientific study of botany is here made as interesting as a fairy tale. Not only is the subject treated with botanical accuracy but there is given much practical information pertaining to the care and treatment of plants and flowers. Fully illustrated. Bound in cloth. 208 pages. Size, 4¾x6 inches.

No. 3F7860 Price...............38c

If by mail, postage extra, 5 cents.

A Guide to the Trees.

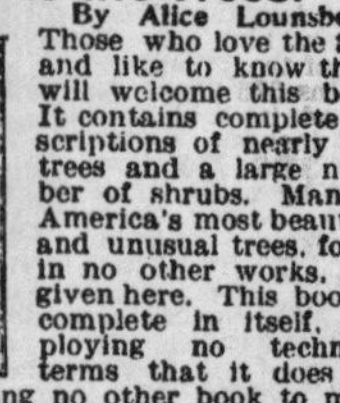

By Alice Lounsberry. Those who love the trees and like to know them, will welcome this book. It contains complete descriptions of nearly 200 trees and a large number of shrubs. Many of America's most beautiful and unusual trees, found in no other works, are given here. This book is complete in itself, employing no technical terms that it does not define and requiring no other book to make it intelligible. It is beautifully illustrated by Mrs. Ellis Rowan, the world's greatest painter of wild flowers, whose pictures are not only artistic and beautiful, but at the same time technically correct. Substantially bound in cloth. Profusely illustrated, containing 64 beautiful full page colored plates, 100 full page black and white plates, 64 engravings, 55 diagrams, etc. Bound in cloth. Printed on the finest book paper. 313 pages. Size, 5½x7¾ inches.

No. 3F7862 Price........$1.65

If by mail, postage extra, 14 cents.

American Duck Shooting.

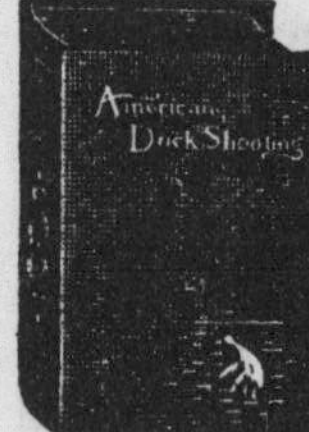

By George Bird Grinnell. An intensely interesting and valuable book to all sportsmen. Divided into three parts; the first part containing a general description of the duck family, with full descriptions of all the various varieties of ducks found in America. Part two is devoted to duck shooting, with chapters on pass shooting, timber shooting, river shooting, in the wild rice fields, etc. Part three is devoted to the gunner's equipment, with chapters on blinds, batteries, sink boxes, decoys, etc. A most complete and authentic work, illustrated with 58 portraits of North American ducks, geese and swans; 8 halftone reproductions from Audubon's plates, 50 smaller illustrations; plans of blinds, batteries, etc. Finely bound in silk finish cloth, with cover design stamped in gold. Printed on extra quality book paper. 627 pages. Size, 6x9 inches.

No. 3F7781 Price...........................$2.90

If by mail, postage extra, 32 cents.

A Guide to the Wild Flowers.

By Alice Lounsberry. A companion to A Guide to the Trees. Illustrated by Mrs. Ellis Rowan, the world's greatest painter of wild flowers. 64 beautiful full page color plates showing 79 different plants and 100 black and white plates showing 103 plants, together with 54 diagrams. Most profusely illustrated book of wild flowers published. This book contains descriptions of many beautiful and unusual flowers that are described in no other popular work. Wherever it is necessary to use technical terms, they are fully defined, making the book very easy to understand. Bound in cloth. Over 300 pages. Size, 5½x7¾ inches.

No. 3F7870 Price.........(If by mail, postage extra, 14 cents.).......$1.65

RELIGIOUS BOOKS.

Pictorial History of the Bible.

By William Smith. Author of Smith's Bible Dictionary. A full and complete account of the events narrated in the Sacred Scriptures, to which is added the history of the Jews after the dispersion, from the taking of Jerusalem, by Titus, down to the present time. Contains 904 pages. Profusely illustrated. A beautiful history for the home. Cloth. Size, 6¾x9¼ inches.

No. 3F8200 Price..............85c

If by mail, postage extra, 24 cents.

From Eden to Calvary.

By Grandpa Reuben Prescott. Especially arranged to take the reader through the Bible in a year, there being fifty-two appropriate chapters, one for each Sunday, in which the Bible stories from Genesis to Revelations are represented in a fascinating manner, and furnish entertainment and instruction for the young people during the long Sabbath afternoons. 254 pages. Cloth. Size, 7¼x9¾ inches.

No. 3F8205 Price...............37c

If by mail, postage extra, 13 cents.

The Teachings of Jesus and the Lives of the Apostles.

The sacred teachings of Jesus is brought before the reader in the order of the books of the New Testament in such a manner as to charm the eye, instruct the mind and move the heart. This book is adapted to the needs of the teacher, student or child, and all who desire a fuller knowledge and better understanding of God's word. Illustrated with numerous halftones of Thorwalden's statues of Christ and the Apostles, Hoffman's famous gallery of religious illustrations and many drawings and smaller engravings throughout the text. Contains 518 pages. Bound in cloth, with the most elaborate cover design stamped in colors and silver. Size of book, 7¼x9½ inches.

No. 3F8210 Price..............59c

If by mail, postage extra, 24 cents.

The Story of a Beautiful Life.

By Canon Farrar. This beautiful story, written by one of the best known men in religious circles, is the most complete and connected story of the life of Christ published. This book contains also a complete gallery of religious paintings, making a complete pictorial life of Christ. Cloth bound. 540 pages. Over 200 illustrations. Size, 7½x9¾ inches.

No. 3F8215 Price..............75c

If by mail, postage extra, 12 cents.

In His Steps; or, What Would Jesus Do?

By Chas. M. Sheldon, the noted Christian Endeavor worker and evangelist. This great and justly famous book needs no description. To those who have not read it we can only say, do not miss obtaining a copy at once. Contains 301 pages. Bound in cloth, with attractive cover design stamped in colors and gold. Size, 5¼x7½ inches.

No. 3F8218 Price..............25c

If by mail, postage extra, 9 cents.

The Christian's Secret of a Happy Life.

By Hannah W. Smith. To commend this work would seem superfluous and yet to young and old Christians, who may not know it, we cannot refrain from saying, buy this book and keep it with your Bible for constant study until you have thoroughly mastered in your own experience the secret which it tells. It will transform the dark days of your life as it has transformed thousands before you, into days of heavenly life. 250 pages. Size, 5x7¼ inches. Bound in cloth with original cover design stamped in colors. Retail price, 75 cents.

No. 3F8233 Our price..........30c

If by mail, postage extra, 6 cents.

The Life of Christ.

FROM THE MANGER TO THE CROSS.

By Canon Farrar, D.D., F.R.S., of Westminster. Being a captivating narrative of the thrilling scenes and events in the life of our Savior, comprising the birth, infancy and early life of Jesus; His baptism and public ministry; beautiful parables and discourses; journeys in Galilee and Judea; wonderful miracles; pathetic scenes of suffering and His sublime victory over death, including the descriptions of the manners and customs and traditions of the Israelites; the whole forming a complete and graphic record of the life and teachings of our Lord and Savior Jesus Christ. Embellished with many full page, fine phototype engravings. Printed on excellent quality of paper from large, clear type. Bound in cloth with embossed cover design. Title printed on side and back in gold. Marbled edges. 620 pages. Size, 8¾x10¾ inches.

No. 3F8225 Price..............79c

Weight, packed for shipment, 6 pounds.

The Kingship Series.

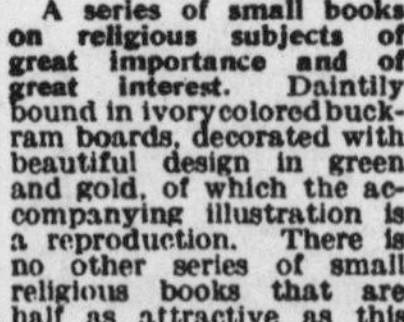

A series of small books on religious subjects of great importance and of great interest. Daintily bound in ivory colored buckram boards, decorated with beautiful design in green and gold, of which the accompanying illustration is a reproduction. There is no other series of small religious books that are half as attractive as this one. Each book contains over 50 pages, printed on the best quality of paper. Size, 5x7¼ inches. Retail price, 30 cents.

Christie's Old Organ. By Mrs. O. F. Walton

For Christ and the Church. By Charles M. Sheldon

How the Inner Light Failed. By N. D. Hills

Lend a Hand. By Charles M. Sheldon

The Kingship of Self Control. By William George Jordan

The Majesty of Calmness. By William George Jordan

Unto Him. Bishop John H. Vincent

Where Kitty Found Her Soul. By Mrs. J. H. Walworth

No. 3F8228 Our price, each......21c

Any 2 for......................38c

If by mail, postage extra, each, 3 cents.

The Home Beyond; or, Views of Heaven.

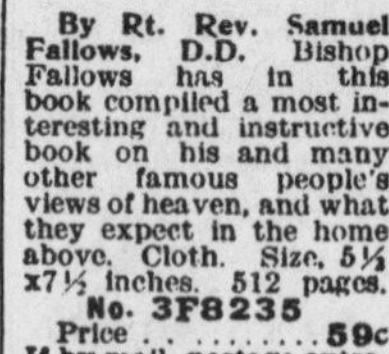

By Rt. Rev. Samuel Fallows, D.D. Bishop Fallows has in this book compiled a most interesting and instructive book on his and many other famous people's views of heaven, and what they expect in the home above. Cloth. Size, 5¼x7½ inches. 512 pages.

No. 3F8235 Price.........59c

If by mail, postage extra, 20 cents.

Making the Most of Life.

By J. R. Miller. This book is written with the hopes of stimulating those who read it to earnest and worthy living. It is to teach us how to make the most of life God has entrusted to us. Life is God's most sacred trust. It is a solemn thing and not ours to do with as we please. It must be accounted for, every particle, every power, every possibility of it. This powerful book contains 275 pages. Size, 4½x6¾ inches. Printed on the best quality of paper and bound in new style binding, board sides and cloth back

No. 3F8238 Price...........64c

If by mail, postage extra, 6 cents.

Quiet Talks on Prayer.

By S. D. Gordon. Every line is vital and arresting. It has special references to the hindrances, human and satanic, bringing it very near to the troubled heart and the seeker after God. 234 pages.

No. 3F8242 Price..69c

If by mail, postage extra, 8c.

The Royal Path of Life.

By Rev. J. S. Kirtley, D.D. This is an original and rare treatment of all questions that are of vital importance to young men and women. A helpful book from every view point. 600 pages. Size, 8x10 inches. Cloth. Illustrated.

No. 3F8245 Price...........87c

If by mail, postage extra, 23 cents.

RELIGIOUS BOOKS—Continued.

The Gospel for an Age of Doubt

By Henry Van Dyke. New revised edition. Its aim is to accentuate the truth that the question, "What to Preach," comes first, and the question, "How to Preach," comes afterward; to tell the men who were studying for the ministry that they must not be educated out of sympathy with the modern world and to show that there is a message of religion especially fitted to meet the needs of the times. Bound in cloth, with title stamped on side and back. Size, 5¼x7¾. Regular $1.50 edition.
No. 3F8248 Price.......................48c
If by mail, postage extra, 9 cents.

Sermons by Dr. Talmage.

Live Coals, or Truths that Burn. Delivered by him in the Brooklyn Tabernacle and elsewhere. The keenest and most vigorous specimens of oratory. Every page burning with eloquent entreaty for a better and purer life. They possess an intense soul absorbing interest to all who desire an advancement and higher development of the human race. Contains 675 pages. Bound in silk cloth. Title stamped in gold on back and sides. Size 6½x9 inches.

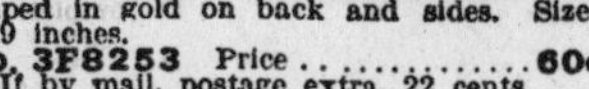

No. 3F8253 Price.......................60c
If by mail, postage extra, 22 cents.

Spurgeon's Sermons.

One hundred and forty-four different sermons by this prince of preachers. Printed in 12 fine cloth bound volumes. Size, each, 5½x8½ inches. Twelve sermons in each volume. Be sure to state title of volume wanted.

12 Christmas Sermons
12 Missionary Sermons
12 Revival Sermons
12 Sermons on Faith
12 Sermons on Belief
12 Sermons on Unbelief
12 Sermons on the Prodigal Son
12 Sermons on the Holy Spirit
12 Sermons on Prayer
12 Sermons on the Plan of Salvation
12 Sermons on the Resurrection
12 Sermons on Christian Work
12 Sermons on Heaven

No. 3F8260 Price, per volume. $0 40
Any 2 volumes for .75
Any 6 volumes for 2.28
The entire 12 volumes for 4.45
If by mail, postage extra, per volume, 5 cents.

A Common Sense Hell.

By Arthur Richard Rose. Being the practical thought of a business man about the future condition of the wicked, contained in letters to his son. His idea is that hell is terrible, but that there is no fire there. Its substitute is terrible enough. A hell of fire arouses our fears, but is flouted by our reason. This book is fascinating from cover to cover and in it we see the idea that most of our business men, financiers and capitalists hold concerning the hereafter. Cloth bound. Size, 5¼x7½ inches. 176 pages.
No. 3F8263 Price.......................89c
If by mail postage extra 9 cents.

Dwight Lyman Moody.

By Charles Francis Adams, D.D. Memorial edition. The great evangelist of the nineteenth century. Containing descriptions of the last scenes in the life of this great character also a number of generous tributes, with copious selections from his impressive utterances. Fully illustrated and contains portrait frontispiece. Fully bound in cloth with cover design stamped in aluminum and colors. Size, 5¼x7½ inches. 318 pages.
No. 3F8270 Price.......................58c
If by mail, postage extra, 11 cents.
No. 3F8275 Anecdotes, illustrations and incidents in the life of D. L. Moody. This is the latest and only authorized collection of anecdotes, etc., regarding the noted evangelist. Contains 126 pages, printed on the best quality of paper and bound in silk cloth with title stamped on back and sides. Size, 5¾x7¾ inches. Price.......................29c
If by mail, postage extra, 9 cents.

Sankey's Story of the Gospel Hymns.

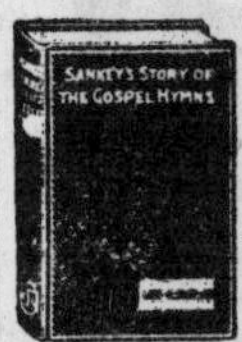

By Ira D. Sankey. It contains Mr. Sankey's story of his own life and many reminiscences of D. L. Moody, with whom he was so intimately connected for many years. Over 200 pages of incidents connected with the use of well known gospel hymns in soul winning throughout the world. Full page portrait of Mr. Sankey, another of Mr. Moody. 264 pages. Size, 5x7½ inches. Printed on the best quality of paper; bound in red cloth, full gilt top.
No. 3F8280 Price.......................58c
If by mail, postage extra, 9 cents.

The Story of Churches.

A history of the Presbyterians, the Baptists, the Methodists, the Congregationalists, and Episcopalians. The stories of the churches is a series of popular histories of the various denominations, written for the average church member, by the leading historians of each denomination. The books were designed to answer the oft asked questions, "What is a Baptist? What is a Presbyterian," etc., and to clear up many errors from the opinions of the members of one denomination regarding the history and creed of the other sects, or even of their own. The authors, Drs. Addison, Bacon, Faulkner, Veeder and Thompson, are recognized as the most pungent writers of the day of their respective religions. Each book averages between 250 and 300 pages, printed on the best quality of paper and bound in cloth with elaborate cover design. Size, 4¾x7½ inches.
No. 3F8285 Our price, each....$0.85
Price for set (5 volumes).......... 3.98
If by mail, postage extra, per volume, 9 cents.

Smith's Bible Dictionary.

By the eminent scholar, William Smith. This is the standard dictionary of the Bible and contains its antiquities, biography, geography and natural history, with numerous illustrations and maps. 778 double column pages, printed with black faced type on first class quality of paper. Bound in cloth with title stamped on back in gold. Size, 5½x7¾ inches.
No. 3F8290 Price.......................80c
If by mail, postage extra, 16 cents.

Teachers' Edition of Smith's Bible Dictionary.

Revised and edited by Revs. F. N. and M. A. Peloubet. This most valuable edition has been revised and brought up to date. It contains 8 colored maps and 440 illustrations. Also the latest researches and references to the revised version of the New Testament. Printed on heavy plate paper and bound in cloth with original cover design and title stamped on back and side with gold. Contains 817 double column pages. Retail price, $2.00. Size, 5½x7¾ inches.
No. 3F8293 Our price.............$1.48
If by mail, postage extra, 22 cents.

500 Bible Studies.

By Rev Harold F. Sayles. Dr. Sayles has endeavored to gather together into this small volume a great variety of large, sharp, clean cut Bible studies. The selection covers a large range of subjects and will be found useful in private study of the Word of God as well as in the preparation of material for public work. Especially valuable to those who are called upon to conduct meetings on short notice. Bound in canvas with cover design stamped in black. Size, 5¼x7½ inches.
No. 3F8300 Price.......................18c
If by mail, postage extra, 3 cents.

Bible Readers' and Christian Workers' Self Help Hand Book.

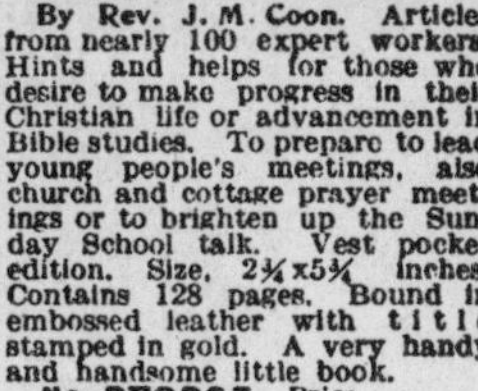

By Rev. J. M. Coon. Articles from nearly 100 expert workers. Hints and helps for those who desire to make progress in their Christian life or advancement in Bible studies. To prepare to lead young people's meetings, also church and cottage prayer meetings or to brighten up the Sunday School talk. Vest pocket edition. Size, 2¾x5¾ inches. Contains 128 pages. Bound in embossed leather with title stamped in gold. A very handy and handsome little book.
No. 3F8305 Price.......................25c
If by mail, postage extra, 2 cents.

Cruden's Concordance.

By Alexander Cruden, M.A. New edition. A complete concordance of the Holy Scriptures, both Old and New Testaments, with a list of proper names, by Rev. Alfred Jones, M.A. Contains 757 three-column pages, printed on first class quality of paper from clear new plates. Bound in cloth. Title stamped on back in gold. Size, 6½x9¼ inches.
No. 3F8310 Price.......................78c
If by mail, postage extra, 24 cents.

Bible Commentary.

Jamieson, Faussett and Brown's Popular Commentary on the New and Old Testaments. Critical, practical and explanatory. Two volumes, 8 vo. A new edition; contains complete unabridged notes in clear type on good paper, with copious index, numerous illustrations and maps and dictionary complete from Dr. Smith's standard works. C. H. Spurgeon says: I think it is the best commentary upon the Bible which has been issued within the last fifty years." Size, 5¾x8 inches.
No. 3F8315 Two-Volume Set, 8vo. Boxed. Price.......................$2.25
No. 3F8317 Four-Volume Set, 8vo. Boxed. Price.......................$5.98
If by mail, postage extra, per volume, 16c.

Episcopal Prayer and Hymn Books.

Combination sets. The book of common prayer, conforming to the new standard adopted by the General Convention of the Protestant Episcopal Church in 1892, and published under certificate of approval from the Custodian of the Standard Prayer Book, together with the Hymnal, revised and enlarged. Superbly printed on fine white paper. MINION TYPE. 48MO. Size, 2¾x3¾ inches.
No. 3F9000 Seal Grained Cloth. Red cross; red edges. Price.......................69c
No. 3F9003 Imitation Morocco, limp. Gold monogram; round corners; gold edges. Price.......................98c
No. 3F9006 French Seal, limp. Gold cross; round corners; red under gold edges. Price.......................$1.30
No. 3F9009 Padded French Morocco. Blind tooled ties; gold I.H.S.; round corners; gilt edge. Price.......................$1.40
If by mail, any of the above, postage extra, 5c.
No. 3F9012 Oxford India Paper Edition. The combined set measures only ⅜ inch in thickness. French Morocco, limp. Red under gold edges; gold roll. Price.......................$1.98
If by mail, postage extra, 5 cents.
BOURGEOIS TYPE, 32MO. OLD FOLKS' LARGE TYPE PRAYER AND HYMNAL. Size, 5x3¼ inches.
No. 3F9020 Imitation Morocco. Illuminated lettering; gold monogram; round corners; gold edges. Price.......................$1.28
No. 3F9023 French Seal, limp. Gold monogram round corners; gold edge. Price.......................$1.58
If by mail, postage extra, either style, 7c.
No. 3F9026 Oxford India Paper Edition. Combined set measures only ¾ of an inch thick. French Seal, limp. Gold cross, round corners; red under gold edges. Price...$2.28
If by mail, postage extra, either one, 5 cents.

Standard Catholic Prayer Books.

Approved by His Eminence, Cardinal Gibbons, and the Most Reverend Archbishop Ryan.

CHILD'S CATHOLIC PRAYER BOOKS. 48MO.

New and complete edition. Large clear type, with 36 full page illustrations of the Holy Mass. Size, 3¼x3¾ inches; 5-16 inch thick. Contains 288 pages.
No. 3F9050 American Seal, limp. Gold title and monogram on side; red under gold edges. Price.......................30c
No. 3F9053 Imitation Ivory Sides. White leather back, stamped in gold; beautiful monogram in colors on side; nickel rims; gold edges. Price.......................45c
If by mail, postage extra, either style, 2c.

Keys of Heaven.

48mo.

New large type edition with Epistles and Gospels. The most complete prayer book of its size ever placed before the Catholics of this country. Size, 2½x3½ inches ½ inch thick. 669 pages.
No. 3F9056 American Seal, limp. Gold title and monogram on side, red under gold edges. Price.......................33c
No. 3F9059 Best American Seal. Padded sides. Neat gold I H S. in center red under gold edges. Price.......................48c
No. 3F9062 Imitation ivory sides and back; round corners; beautiful colored picture of Sacred Heart of Jesus on outside cover. Very pretty. Red under gold edges. Price.......................78c
No. 3F9065 English Morocco, padded. Large fancy gold monogram in center. Beautiful pictures of St. Anthony with prayers to St. Anthony printed in gold inside of both front and back covers. Red under gold edges. Just the book for those devoted to this great saint. Price..75c
No. 3F9068 Persian Morocco, padded. Gold title with fancy gold and blind monogram design. Beautiful Crucifix of Pearl and indulgenced prayer inside of front cover. An elegant and appropriate gift book. Red under gold edges. Price.......................98c
If by mail, postage extra, any style 3c.

Key to Heaven. 32mo. Old Folks' Key.

Large type with Epistles and Gospels. A complete manual of prayers by the Right Reverend J. Milner D.D. Size, 2¾x4¼ inches. ½ inch thick. 548 pages.
No. 3F9071 American Seal, limp. Gold monogram in center, red under gold edges. Price.......................48c
No. 3F9073 Best Venetian Seal, padded. Gold title and monogram on side; red under gold edges; gold roll. Price..95c
If by mail, postage extra, either style, 3 cents.

The Vest Pocket Manual of Devotions.

With Epistles and Gospels. Complete in one volume. A manual of small and compact size, containing all necessary prayers, made to fit the upper vest pocket. Size, 2¾x4¼, 5-16 inch thick. 380 pages.
No. 3F9076 American Seal, limp. Gold title and monogram on side; red under gold edges. Price.......................35c
No. 3F9079 Best Egyptian Seal, extra limp. Leather lined; silk sewed; plain sides; red under gold edges. Extra fine. Price..95c
If by mail, postage extra, either style, 2 cents.
For a full line of rosaries and other ecclesiastical goods refer to page 122.
If by mail, postage extra, 5 cents.

Testaments.

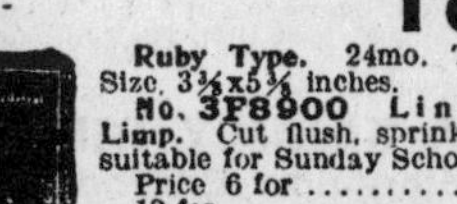

Ruby Type. 24mo. Testament. Size, 3¾x5⅜ inches.
No. 3F8900 Linen Cloth, Limp. Cut flush, sprinkled edges, suitable for Sunday School.
Price 6 for.......................35c
12 for.......................68c
If by mail, postage extra for six 6c.
Ruby Type. 12mo. Testament. Size, 2⅝x 3¾ inches.
No. 3F8902 Skytogen. Square corners; red edges. Price.......................18c
No. 3F8904 French Seal, limp. Gilt edges, square corners, gold side title. Price.......................23c
No. 3F8906 French Morocco. Divinity circuit, round corners; red under gold edges; extra grained lining. Self pronouncing text. Price.......................38c
No. 3F8908 Imitation Ivory with Gold and Silver Illuminated floral sides, round corners, gilt edge and gold rims and clasp, with full gilt back. The handsomest fancy Testament made. Price.......................45c
If by mail, postage extra, any style, 3 cents.
The Vest Pocket Holman Self Pronouncing New Testament, and Self Pronouncing New Testament and Psalms. Authorized version. Nonpareil 32mo. long Size 2⅝x 4½ inches Handiest and prettiest edition ever published. It is printed from the largest type ever used in a small edition of the Testament and the plates being entirely new the impression is clean, sharp and wonderfully clear.
No. 3F8918 French Morocco, limp. Gold side title round corners; red under gold edges. Price.......................28c
No. 3F8920 French Morocco. Divinity circuit, gold side title; red under gold edges. Price.......................39c
If by mail postage extra either style, 2 cents.

Red Letter Edition of the Vest Pocket Holman Self Pronouncing New Testament.

Words of Christ printed in red.
No. 3F8922 French Morocco, limp. Gold side title, round corners red under gold edges. Price.......................44c
No. 3F8924 French Morocco. Divinity circuit; gold side title; red under gold edges. Price.......................58c
If by mail postage extra, any style 2c.

Minion Type, 12mo. Self Pronouncing New Testament.

Size, 4x6¼ inches. All proper names are accented and divided into syllables for quick and easy pronunciation.
No. 3F8930 Morocco, limp. Gilt edges round corners. Price.......................43c
No. 3F8932 French Morocco. Divinity circuit; round corners; red under gold edges; extra grained lining. Price.......................57c
If by mail, postage extra either style, 4 cents.

Combination Self Pronouncing, Illustrated New Testament and Psalms.

Words of Jesus in bold-faced type. Nonpareil type. Size, 4⅞x6⅜ inches. This edition is self pronouncing, and in addition to containing the combination feature, which shows in simple form the changes, additions and omissions made by the revisers, is profusely illustrated throughout.
No. 3F8936 Fine Cloth. Embossed gold back and side title; red edges. Price.......................32c
No. 3F8938 French Morocco, limp. Gold back and side title; round corners, gold edges. Price.......................56c
No. 3F8940 Imperial Seal. Divinity circuit, gold back and side title, linen lined, making the cover non-tearable; red under gold edges. Price.......................72c
If by mail, postage extra, any style, 6 cents.

Oxford, India Paper Edition.

Testament and Psalms. Minion, 32mo. Size 4½x3½ inches. An ideal Testament for the pocket. Thin, light and beautifully made and printed.
No. 3F8944 Venetian Morocco, limp. Round corners red under gold edges. Price.......................63c
No. 3F8946 French Morocco. Divinity circuit, linen lined, making the cover non-tearable round corners; red under burnished gold edges. Price.......................95c
If by mail, postage extra, either style, 3 cents.

OUR PROFIT SHARING PLAN
ENABLES YOU TO GET BACK PART OF YOUR MONEY. CONSIDER WHAT YOU GET FREE AS SHOWN ON PAGES 1 AND 2.

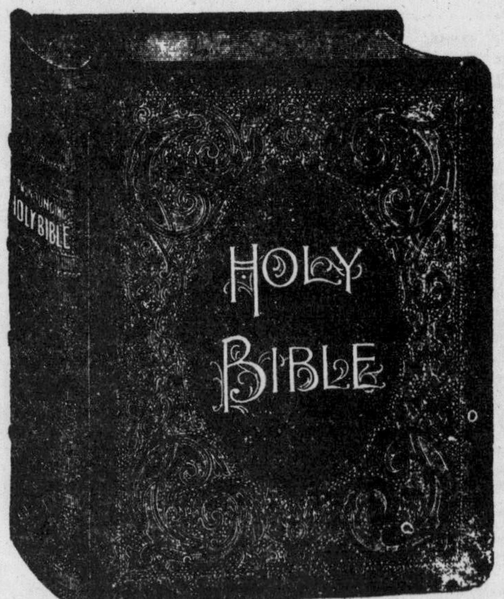

THIS $12.00 SELF PRONOUNCING FAMILY BIBLE $3.60

THE MOST WONDERFUL BARGAIN OFFERED IN OUR CATALOGUE. Never before has a Bible, half the value of this one, been offered for what we ask—$3.60. Our study of the wants of the people has shown us that there is a desire for elegance and merit in a family Bible, at a price that is within the reach of all. We feel that our customers desire a family Bible that is beautiful as well as useful, but that they are not disposed to pay $10.00 to $15.00 for such a Bible, as they are compelled to do to canvassers and small dealers. We have, therefore, at great expense prepared this magnificent Bible to equal in every respect any $12.00 Bible on the market.

It is strong, handsome and durable. Magnificently executed engravings; fine paper; thorough excellence in manufacture. More recent and instructive features and Bible aids, more maps, illustrations, tables and collateral matter than is to be found in almost any other Bible. Acknowledged by ministers, Bible students, able critics and all those who have seen this book, to be superior to any other Bible ever published at double the price we ask. **This Bible is printed on the best quality of paper** from new clear plates with extra heavy type, so that it is equally readable by old and young. The edges are red under burnished gold, and one of its particular features is the binding. Instead of having flat, hard covers, it is bound with heavily padded sides, inside edges of cover, hand tooled with pure gold. Beautifully embossed, and the words, "Holy Bible," stamped in pure gold on sides and back, thus giving this Bible an elegance in appearance not obtainable in any other Bible. Contains two steel frontispiece engravings (worth $1.00 apiece) before the New and Old Testaments, respectively. Title page in brilliant colors and the Bible is elaborately illustrated with full page engravings and colored plates. Presentation page in colors.

The type is self pronouncing, showing how proper names should be pronounced, and the Bible has the well known combination feature which enables the reader to see at a glance the difference between the King James and the revised versions. Copious marginal references and many important and valuable aids to the study of the Holy Scriptures. Want of space prevents us from describing the beauty merits and superiority of the book in full.

Full and copious helps and practical information. Containing history of the translation of the English Bible. Contents of the Bible. Eight full page colored maps. Comprehensive and critical history of all the books of the Bible, compiled expressly for this edition, from the readings of William Smith, LL.D.; this history profusely illustrated with 46 three-quarter page engravings (three-quarter page illustrations). A gallery of scripture illustrations, showing the manners and customs, religious rites, sermons, etc. of the nations mentioned in the Bible. An account of the wanderings of the Israelites in the wilderness. Smith's complete and practical household dictionary of the Bible, comprising its antiquities, biography, geography and natural history, embellished with over 500 appropriate illustrations and maps. Key to the self pronouncing Bible; and a self pronouncing dictionary of proper names in the Bible. A table of passages in the Old Testament, quoted by Christ and his Apostles in the New Testament. Complete chronological index to the Holy Bible; 4,000 questions and answers on the Old and New Testaments intended to open up the scriptures; a complete and practical concordance of the Old and New Testaments; an elegant ring marriage certificate in colors, together with marriage, birth and death record, and family temperance pledge in colors. From the few details of this wonderful book that we have given above, you can readily see what a superb edition it is, but even if you still doubt, the sight of this book will at once convince you. Send us an order and if, when you receive this Family Bible, you do not feel that you have saved from $5.00 to $8.00 and that it is one of the most beautiful Bibles made, and does not in every way please you, return it to us at our expense and we will cheerfully refund what you have paid for it, together with the transportation charges both ways. Could anything be fairer? Could anything show you more clearly the unbounding faith that we have in this book? Size, 10¼x12½ inches. Retail price, $12.00.

No. 3F8950 Our price $3.60

Weight, packed for shipment, 15 pounds.

PICTORIAL SELF PRONOUNCING FAMILY BIBLE.

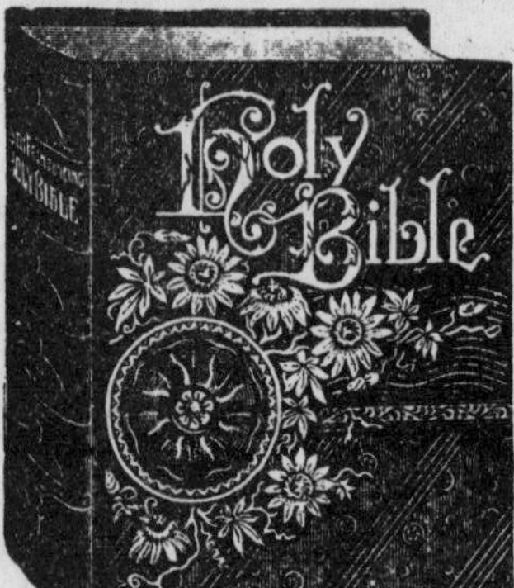

A genuine self pronouncing, beautifully illustrated Family Bible at a wonderfully low price. This splendid edition is printed from new plates with large clear type. Copious references. All proper names are divided and accented according to the standard authorities, showing how they should be pronounced. Has frontispiece and title page printed in gorgeous colors; illustrated with full page pictures, many of them in colors. Contains marriage certificate, marriage, birth and death records and family temperance pledge records, printed in brilliant colors and inserted between the Old and the New Testaments. Eight full page maps in colors and many recent and instructive features and Bible aids, such as Bible stories for the young; profusely illustrated; self pronouncing dictionary of proper names; history of the religious denominations of the world; chronological and other valuable tables, forming a complete Biblical history. Strong, handsome and durable binding; heavily embossed with gold leaf; excellent in manufacture. In fact, a wonderful bargain for the money. Size of book, 10x12 inches. Two inches thick. Weight, packed for shipment, 7 pounds.

No. 3F8955 Imitation leather, elaborately stamped in gold, gold titles, marbled edges. Retail price, $3.00; our price 98c

No. 3F8956 Genuine black calf, elaborately stamped in gold, gold title, full gold edges. Contents same as No. 3F8955. Retail price, $5.00; our price $1.89

Weight, packed for shipment, 7 pounds.

GENUINE MOROCCO LEATHER FAMILY BIBLE.

Self Pronouncing Illustrated Combination Edition.

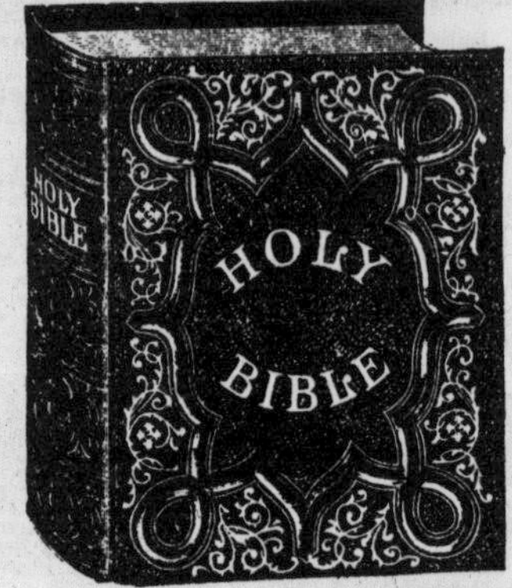

This beautiful Bible is bound in real leather with contents printed from large, clear type on excellent quality of paper. Copious references. This Bible contains the famous combination feature, which will show to the reader in simple form at a glance the difference between the King James and the revised versions. This great edition of the Bible is acknowledged by ministers, students and able critics to be the most satisfactory low priced real leather Family Bible published. The cover design is heavily and elaborately embossed and the title is stamped in gold on back and sides. Gold edges. Contains full page colored frontispiece; numerous full page phototype illustrations, engravings and colored plates and an introductory history of the Holy Bible. Contains history of the English Bible, also gallery of scripture illustrations and an account of forty years sojourn of the Israelites on the desert; a complete and practical household dictionary of the Bible, profusely illustrated with maps, engravings and plates. Self pronouncing dictionary of proper names of the Bible; marriage certificate, marriage, birth and death records and temperance pledge lithographed in brilliant colors. Chronological index and complete practical Concordance; also Psalms of David in meter. Size, 10x12½ inches. Over two inches thick. Retail price, $5.00.

No. 3F8960 Our price $2.45

Weight, packed for shipment 10 pounds.

RED LETTER ART EDITION. $2.75

Combination Self Pronouncing Family Bible.

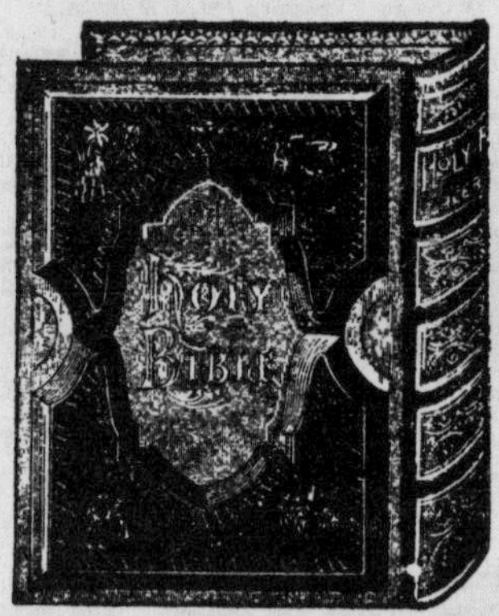

The wonderful teachings and marvelous interest in the Bible story center around the living words of Jesus. It is therefore most important that these beautiful living words should stand out in bold relief. **The Red Letter Combination Edition of the Bible** arouses interest wherever it is shown. This edition will meet with the wants of students, teachers and families. All the words of Jesus stand out vividly conspicuous, printed in red, which catches the eye and adds greatly to the value of this superb edition of the Holy Scripture.

This edition also contains the unique combination feature, showing in simple form all changes, additions and omissions made by the revisers and enabling the reader to see at a glance wherein the two versions differ. The King James version is the basis and this version is read straight along from the text in combination with the foot notes. These notes give all words and passages of the revised version where it differs from the King James version.

This Bible contains full self pronouncing text. All proper names are divided and accented according to the standard authors. This feature is especially valuable as it defines the pronunciation of the many difficult words which occur throughout the scriptures.

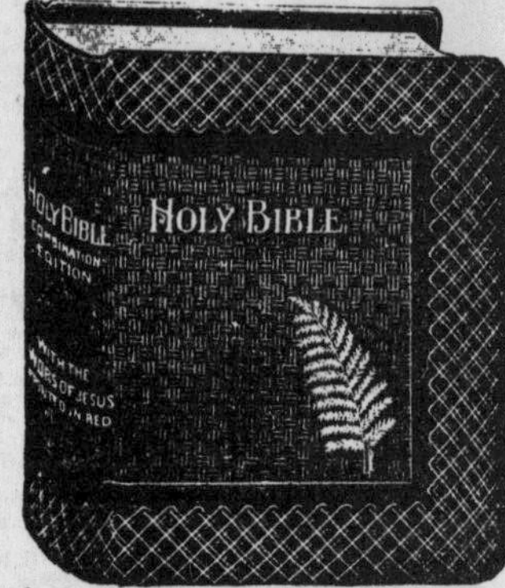

In addition, this Bible contains many beautiful full page engravings, colored maps of Palestine and the Holy Land; illuminated lithographed plates; the Lord's Prayer and the Ten Commandants in rich colors; artistic family record with pages for recording marriages, births, deaths, and a ring marriage certificate in colors; Smith's illustrated dictionary of the Bible comprising 112 pages; chronological tables; illustrated history of the books of the Bible; dictionary of the proper names, natural history of the Bible, complete concordance, etc.

No. 3F8965 Bound in black seal grained moroccotol with raised panel sides. Back and sides embossed in gold in elaborate design. Gold edges. Retail price $6.00; our price $2.89

No. 3F8966 Bound in genuine black American calf, padded sides, round corners, cover stamped in new interlaced and leaf design gold back, side, title and fern leaf. Burnished gold edges. Retail price, $9.00. Price $3.15

Weight, packed for shipment, 12 pounds.

THIS $15.00 DE LUXE EDITION

Self Pronouncing Combination Family Bible For $6.58

The Most Beautiful Family Bible Made. Contains Ten Steel Engravings, each one a Work of Art and Worth $1.00 each. An Ornament to Any Home.

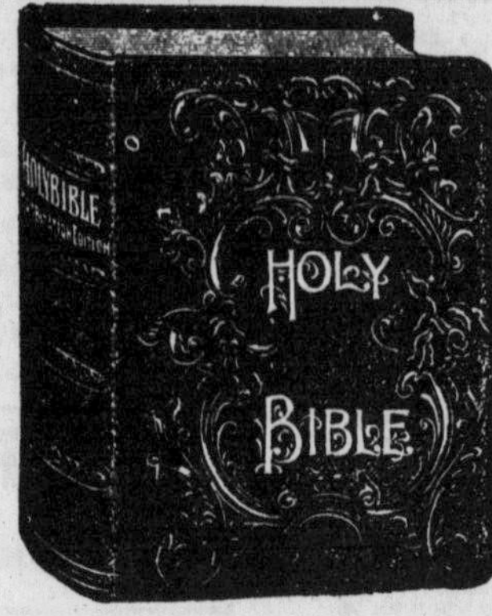

To obtain a correct idea of the value of this Bible read carefully the following, which describes some of the features that it contains. Many other features, on account of lack of space, we are unable to enumerate. It has the unique combination feature showing in simple form at a glance wherein the King James and revised versions differ. Has presentation page and steel engraving frontispiece. Emblematical title page handsomely printed in colors. History of the translations of the Bible order and contents of the books of the Old and New Testaments. Eight beautiful illustrative full page maps in colors. A comprehensive and profusely illustrated history of the books of the Holy Bible, containing 46 three-quarter page illustrations. History of the various religious denominations down to the present time. A comprehensive and critical description of the Israelitish Tabernacle and its sacred frniture, with four full page colored plates. Chronological and other valuable miscellaneous tables; natural history of the Bible containing descriptions of the animals, birds, insects and reptiles that are mentioned in the Holy Scriptures, with 27 illustrations. Trees, plants, flowers, and fruits of the Bible, with full description of each, with 17 illustrations. Illustrations and descriptions of ancient money. Parables of our Lord, with illustrations and explanations. Complete dictionary of the Bible by William Smith, LL.D., comprising its antiquities biography, geography and natural history, embellished with over 500 appropriate illustrations and maps. Captivating Bible stories for young people, profusely illustrated. A self pronouncing dictionary of Scripture proper names. Marriage certificate, family record and temperance pledge in colors. Biography and histrory of the holy apostles and evangelists. The beautiful Hoffman gallery of monotint illustrations. Complete Bible concordance. Psalms of David in metre.

This Bible is printed on the best quality of paper from large, clear type, with numerous full page engravings, line drawings and colored plates. The binding is very elegant, having heavy cushion padded sides, round corners and edges. Red under burnished gold edges. Cover heavily embossed in rich design. Inside edges of cover hand tooled with pure gold. Words, "Holy Bible," stamped on back and sides in pure gold. **A superb Bible in every particular.**

No. 3F8970 Bound in French morocco, stamped in pure gold. Retail price, $15.00; our price $6.58

No. 3F8971 Bound in genuine levant; the finest binding made. Stamped in pure gold. Retail price, $20.00; our price $7.68

Weight, packed for shipment, 16 pounds.

GENUINE ALASKA SEAL TEACHERS' BIBLE $1.35

SELF PRONOUNCING. LARGE BOURGEOIS TYPE. FULL HELPS.

$1.35 is a price never before made on a Bible of this quality, a strictly high class Bible, put up in the very best way all through; strong and durable binding, finest Bible paper, large, clear type. A most beautiful book in appearance, and made for actual service; a Bible that will last a lifetime. Our Teachers' Bible contains 1,337 pages of text, 325 pages of helps, a total of 1,662 pages, each page measuring 5¼x7⅞ inches, and the weight is 37 unces.

THE BINDING. We bind this Teachers' Bible in full genuine Alaska Seal, the best and most durable binding known for Bibles, FULL DIVINITY CIRCUIT, with extra grained lining, the entire cover interlined from edge to edge with a special grade of strong linen, making it absolutely untearable and practically indestructible. The leather with which we bind this Bible is an extra quality of leather, most carefully selected, a leather that will not peel off nor get rough from rubbing, a very different quality of leather from that used in all Bibles sold at low prices heretofore.

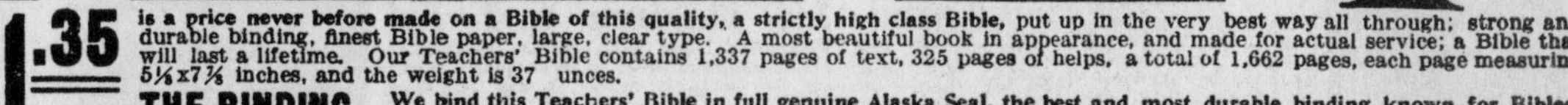

SELF PRONOUNCING TEXT. Our Teachers' Bible is printed from new, clear type, the largest bourgeois type made (really a long primer type), and the text is self pronouncing, in which all proper names are accented and divided into syllables for clear and easy pronunciation, and there are more than 60,000 center marginal references.

THE ILLUSTRATIONS. Our Teachers' Bible is profusely illustrated, including a beautiful halftone frontispiece, reproduced from the famous painting, "Suffer little children to come unto Me," 16 full page halftone reproductions from photographs of actual scenes in the Holy Land, 32 full page halftone reproductions of photographs and famous paintings, illustrating the respective articles wherein they appear. Each of these illustrations is accompanied by descriptions written according to the latest information from researches and discoveries in Assyria, Babylonia, Egypt and Palestine. Scores of other plates and pictures illustrating the text, ancient monuments, money, signs, ancient inscriptions, the languages and writings of the Bible.

David prepareth for the I. CHRONICLES, 22. *building of the temple.*

Ôr'-năn looked and saw Dā'-vĭd, and
went out of the thrĕshingfloor, and
bowed himself to Dā'-vĭd with *his*
face to the ground.
22 Then Dā'-vĭd said to Ôr'-năn,
²Grant me the place of *this* thresh-
ingfloor, that I may build an altar
therein unto the LORD: thou shalt

B. C. 1017.
ᵍ Deut. 12. 5. 2 Sam. 24. 18. ch. 21. 18, 19, 26, 28. 2 Chr. 3. 1.
² Heb. *Give.*
ˢ 1 Kin. 9. 21.

THEN Dā'-vĭd said, ᵍThis *is* the
house of the LORD God, and
this *is* the altar of the burnt offering for Ĭs'-rā-ēl.
2 And Dā'-vĭd commanded to gather together ˢthe strangers that *were*
in the land of Ĭs'-rā-ēl; and he set
masons to hew wrought stones to

This shows the exact size and style of type in our Teachers' Bible.

THE FULL TEACHERS' HELPS. Our Teachers' Bible has 325 pages of "Helps to the Study of the Bible," comprising compendious explanatory notes and tables illustrative of scriptural history and antiquities; a complete chronology and harmony of the gospels, together with a dictionary of scriptural proper names, a complete biblical concordance, based on Cruden, a subject index and a new series of twelve maps in colors with index. These Helps supply in condensed and easily accessible form all the latest information about the Bible, its writers and its language.

No. 3F8401 Our Teachers' Bible, self pronouncing, bound in genuine Alaska seal, full divinity circuit, extra grained lining with linen interlining, nontearable, red under burnished gold edges, round corners, silk sewed, head band, silk marker; a regular $3.50 Bible. Our price..........(If by mail, postage extra, 22 cents)..........**$1.35**

No. 3F8402 Our Teachers' Bible, same as No. 3F8401, but with patent thumb index cut in edge. Price..........(If by mail, postage extra, 22 cents)..........**$1.48**

RED LETTER EDITION OF OUR TEACHERS' BIBLE.

No. 3F8405 Our Teachers' Red Letter Bible. Exactly the same as No. 3F8401, except that all the words spoken by Christ are printed in red. A regular $4.50 Bible. Our price..........(If by mail, postage extra, 22 cents)..........**$1.55**

No. 3F8406 Our Teachers' Red Letter Bible, same as No. 3F8405, but with patent thumb index cut in edge. Price........(If by mail, postage extra, 22 cents)......**$1.69**

GENUINE INDIA PAPER EDITION OUR TEACHERS' BIBLE $2.38

NEVER BEFORE has a genuine India paper Bible been sold at less than double the price at which we offer this beautiful book. UNDERSTAND, this is our regular Teachers' Bible, just as illustrated and described above, bound in genuine Alaska seal, self pronouncing, large bourgeois type, with all the Helps and all the beautiful illustrations, exactly the same Bible except that it is printed on GENUINE INDIA PAPER, the toughest, the thinnest, the softest, the finest paper in all the world. There is no other paper so exactly suited to Bible making, no other paper which combines to such a marvelous degree the qualities of lightness and thinness with strength, durability, opacity and agreeable tone.

No. 3F8410 India Paper Edition, Our Teachers' Bible, exactly the same as No. 3F8401, except that it is printed on genuine India paper. Thickness only 13-16 of an inch. Regular price, $6.00. Our price.......(If by mail, postage extra, 16 cents).......**$2.38**

No. 3F8411 Indexed India Paper Edition, Our Teachers' Bible. Exactly the same as No. 3F8410, but with patent thumb index cut in edge. Price..........(If by mail, postage extra, 16 cents)..........**$2.55**

TEXT BIBLES.

Pearl Type Text Bibles.

The smallest readable type Bible made. Contains the King James or authorized version of the Old and New Testaments. Without references or helps. The size of this Bible makes it very handy for the pocket. Contains five maps and is printed on the best quality of paper. Size, 3¼x5⅜ inches. Only ¾ in. thick.

No. 3F8416 Imitation Roan; red edges; round corners; gold side title. Price..........**28c**

No. 3F8417 French Morocco limp Burnished gold edges; round corners; gold side title. Price..........**48c**

No. 3F8419 Venetian Morocco. Divinity circuit; round corners; gold edges. Price..........(If by mail, postage extra, 7 cents.)..........**57c**

Nelson's Illustrated Text Bible, Ruby Type.

Made by Thomas Nelson & Sons, of London. Contains 164 halftone illustrations, distributed throughout the text of the Bible, and near the verses referring to them, so that they not only interest the eye, but truly illustrate the text. The illustrations are all reproduced from original photographs, and are therefore truly trustworthy. Size, 3⅞x5½ inches. Contains 6 colored maps.

No. 3F8440 Black Cloth. Burnished red edges; round corners; side title. Price..........**45c**

No. 3F8442 French Morocco, limp. Linen lined; round corners; red under gold edges. Price..........**72c**

No. 4F8444 Egyptian Seal. Divinity circuit; round corners; red under gold edges. Price..........**90c**

If by mail, postage extra, any style, 11 cents.

International Self Pronouncing, Minion Type, Text Bible.

Containing the King James or authorized version of the Old and New Testaments and six maps printed in colors. All proper names are accented and divided into syllables for quick and easy pronunciation. The most satisfactory text Bible, with large type in small compass, made. Clear print on extra quality of paper. Size, 4x6½ inches.

No. 3F8453 Morocco grained cloth, limp. Burnished red edges; round corners. Price..........**48c**

No. 3F8455 French Morocco, limp; Burnished gold edges; round corners; silk markers. Price..........**83c**

No. 3F8457 Assyrian Morocco. Divinity circuit; grained lining, with linen interlining to edge, making the cover absolutely non-tearable; round corners; red under gold edges, silk head band and marker. Price..........**98c**

If by mail, postage extra, any style, 12 cents.

International Long Primer Type, Self Pronouncing Text Bible.

Containing the King James or authorized version of the Old and New Testaments, and six colored maps. Clear print; extra quality of paper; all proper names throughout the text are accented and divided into syllables for quick and easy pronunciation. Size, 4⅝x7½ inches. Long primer is an ideal type to read and very restful to the eye.

No. 3F8460 Morocco grained cloth, limp. Burnished red edges; round corners; embossed bands; side title. Price..........**85c**

No. 3F8462 French Morocco, limp; full gilt edges; round corners; silk marker; gold side title. Price..........**$1.10**

No. 3F8464 Assyrian Morocco. Divinity circuit; extra grained lining, with linen interlining to edge, making cover absolutely nontearable. Round corners; red under gold edges; silk head band and marker. Price..........**$1.48**

If by mail, postage extra, any style, 16 cents.

Oxford Long Primer Type, 8vo. Text Bible.

Size, 7½x5 inches. The most beautiful and satisfactory text Bible made. Has large, clear, black type. For family prayers and general reading, we recommend any of the following Oxford Bibles.

No. 3F8471 French Morocco, limp; round corners; red under gold edges. Price..**$1.23**

No. 3F8473 Arabian Morocco. Divinity circuit; linen lining; making absolutely non-tearable cover; red under gold edges. Price..........**$1.57**

No. 3F8475 Arabian Morocco. Same as No. 3F8473, but leather lined. Price....**1.98**

If by mail, postage extra, any style, 20 cents.

No. 3F8477 Argentine Levant. Oxford India paper edition (the finest and thinnest paper in the world). Divinity circuit; leather lined to edge; silk sewed; round corners burnished red under gold edges. Price ....(If by mail, postage extra, 11 cents)...**$3.80**

SAMPLES OF BIBLE TYPE.

The following samples of type show the actual sizes and styles used in our Bibles. WHEN BUYING A BIBLE, one of the most important features is the size of type. In order that our customers can see just what size is used in each Bible, we are illustrating below a specimen of each kind of type in the actual size it appears in the Bible.

SAMPLE OF PEARL TYPE.

THEY that trust in the LORD *shall be* as mount Zion, *which* cannot be removed, *but* abideth for ever.
2 *As* the mountains *are* round about Jerusalem, so the LORD *is* round about his people from henceforth even for ever.
3 For the rod of the wicked shall not rest

SAMPLE OF RUBY TYPE.

ing, Jō'sĕph, thou son of Dā'vĭd, fear not to take unto thee Mā'rȳ thy wife: for that which is conceived in her is of the Hō'lȳ Ghōst.
21 And she shall bring forth a son, and thou shalt call his name JĒSUS: for he shall save his people from their sins.

SAMPLE OF MINION TYPE.

before they came together, she was found with child of the Hō'lȳ Ghōst.
19 Then Jō'sĕph her husband, being a just *man*, and not willing to make her a publick example, was minded to put her away privily.
20 But while he thought on these

SAMPLE OF LARGE MINION 8 vo TYPE

Aaron's first offerings. LEVI

30 And Mō'-sĕs took of the anointing oil, and of the blood which *was* upon the altar, and sprinkled *it* upon Aă'-rŏn, *and* upon his garments, and upon his sons, and upon his sons' garments with him; and sanctified Aă'-rŏn, *and* his garments, and his sons, and his sons' garments with him.

SAMPLE OF LONG PRIMER 8 vo. TYPE.

18 ¶Now the birth of Jē'sus Christ was on this wise: When as his mother Mā'rȳ was espoused to Jō'sĕph, before they came together, she was found with child of the Hō'lȳ Ghōst.
19 Then Jō'sĕph her husband, being a just *man*, and not willing to make

REFERENCE BIBLES.

International Minion Type, Self Pronouncing Reference Bible.

Contains the King James or authorized version of the Old and New Testaments, with 60,000 references in center column and maps printed in colors. Extra quality thin Bible paper; superior bindings. Size, 4⅝x6¾ inches. With all proper names accented and divided into syllables for quick and easy pronunciation.

No. 3F8500 Morocco grained cloth, limp; red edge; embossed design. Price..........**53c**

No. 3F8502 Morocco; limp; red under gold edges; round corners; silk head band and markers. Price..........**85c**

No. 3F8504 Alsatian Morocco. Divinity circuit; extra grained lining, interlined to edge with linen, making non-tearable cover; round corners; red under gold edges. Price..........**98c**

If by mail, postage extra, any style, 11 cents.

Oxford Large Minion 8vo. Self Pronouncing Reference Bible.

The largest minion type Bible made. Size, 8x5½ inches. Contains 12 maps. This Bible has the largest minion type made.

No. 3F8510 Egyptian Seal. Divinity circuit; round corners; red under gold edges. Price..........**$1.20**

No. 3F8511 Egyptian Seal. Same as No. 3F8510, with patent cut thumb index on edge. Price..........(If by mail, postage extra, any style, 14 cents.)..........**$1.35**

Oxford India Paper Edition.

The finest minion 8vo. Reference Bible in the world. With 12 maps and index to maps.

No. 3F8525 French Morocco. Divinity circuit; linen lined to edge; Oxford India paper; round corners; red under gold edges. Price..........**$2.20**

No. 3F8526 French Morocco. Same as No. 3F8525, with patent cut thumb index on edge. Price..........(If by mail, postage extra, any style, 9 cents.)..........**$2.35**

International Illustrated Long Primer Self Pronouncing Reference Bible.

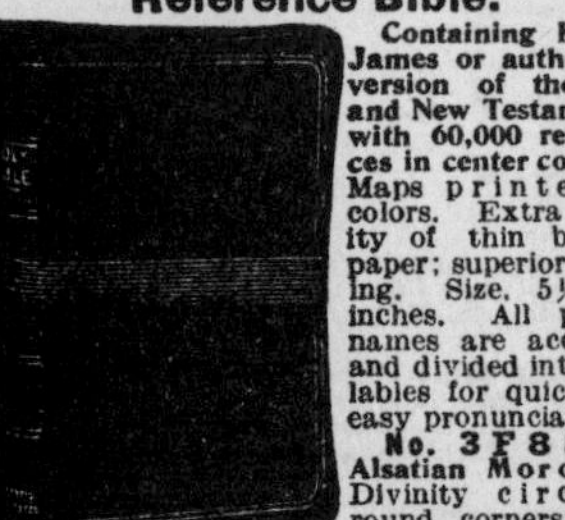

Containing King James or authorized version of the Old and New Testaments, with 60,000 references in center column. Maps printed in colors. Extra quality of thin bible paper; superior binding. Size, 5½x8½ inches. All proper names are accented and divided into syllables for quick and easy pronunciation.

No. 3F8544 Alsatian Morocco. Divinity circuit; round corners; red under gold edges; silk head band and marker, extra grained lining; interlined with linen to edge, making an absolutely nontearable cover. Price............$1.45

No. 3F8546 Alsatian Morocco. Same as No. 3F8544, with patent thumb index on edge. Price............$1.60

If by mail, postage extra, either style, 20 cents.

Oxford Long Primer, Self Pronouncing Reference Bible.

No. 3F8550 Oxford Edition. Egyptian Seal. Divinity circuit; round corners; red under gold edges. Contains 12 maps. Price............$1.50

No. 3F8551 Same as No. 3F8550, Oxford Edition. Egyptian Seal, with patent index on edge. Price............$1.65

No. 3F8553 Oxford Edition. Arabian Morocco. Divinity circuit; leather lined to edge; silk sewed to edge; red under gold edges. Price............$2.00

No. 3F8554 Oxford Edition. Arabian Morocco. Same as No. 3F8553, with patent thumb index on edge. Price............$2.15

If by mail, postage extra, any style, 21 cents.

Oxford India Paper Edition.

The Thinnest Long Primer Reference Bible in the World. Contains 12 maps and index to maps. Size, 8½x6 inches. Only 13-16 of an inch thick.

No. 3F8560 French Morocco. Divinity circuit; linen lined, (making nontearable cover) round corners; red under gold edges; contains 12 maps. Price............$2.98

No. 3F8561 French Morocco. Same as No. 3F8560, with patent thumb index on edge. Price............$3.13

If by mail, postage extra, either style, 13 cents.

Old Folks' International Self Pronouncing Bible.

Sample of small pica type.

18. *He intercedeth for Sodom.*

nation, and all the nations of the
earth shall be [b] blessed in him?
19 For I know him, [d] that he will
command his children and his

Small Pica Type Reference Bible with 60,000 references. This Bible contains extra large type so as to be perfectly readable for those with even the weakest eyes. It has the King James or authorized version of the Old and New Testaments, with maps printed in colors. Extra quality of paper and superior bindings. Size, 6⅛x9 inches. All proper names are accented and divided into syllables for quick and easy pronounciation.

No. 3F8580 Morocco grained cloth. Gilt side and back stamp, red edges; round corners. Price............98c

No. 3F8582 French Morocco, limp. Gilt edges; round corners. Price............$1.45

No. 3F8584 French Morocco. Divinity circuit; round corners; red under gold edges; silk head band and marker; extra grained lining with linen interlining to edge, making cover nontearable. Price............$1.95

If by mail, postage extra, any style, 28 cents.

Nelsons' Old Folks' Bible.

Small Pica Type Reference Bible. Size, 6¾x9¾ inches. Printed on superfine paper. Heavy faced small pica type; has family record and 12 index maps, 60,000 center marginal references, 32 halftones. This is the handsomest and most readable old folks' Bible made. Printed from largest type made. A finer old folks' Bible cannot be bought. These are beautiful Bibles.

No. 3F8590 Decorated cloth. Round corners; burnished red edges. Price....$1.25

No. 3F8592 Egyptian Seal, limp. Round corners; red under burnished gold edges. Price............$1.80

No. 3F8594 Egyptian Seal. Divinity circuit; interlined with linen to edge, making cover nontearable; round corners; red under gold edges. Price............$2.40

If by mail, postage extra, 28 cents.

Old Folks' Testament.

PICA SQUARE TYPE.

The largest type testament made. Pica square type. 16mo. Size 4½x7¾ inches. Clear black faced type edition. This book is particularly adapted to old people. The type is absolutely readable, even with the most infirm eyes. These beautiful testaments are made by William Collins & Co., of London, and are printed on extra quality of thin bible paper. Handsomely bound.

New Testament Only.

No. 3F8601 Imitation Roan, flexible. Round corners; red burnished edges; gold side title. Price............48c

No. 3F8603 French Seal, limp. Red under gold edges. Round corners; gold side title. Price............78c

No. 3F8605 French Morocco. Divinity circuit. Round corners; red under gold edges. Extra grained lining. Price..98c

If by mail, postage extra, any style, 9 cents.

Testament and Psalms.

No. 3F8613 French Seal, limp. Red under gold edges; round corners; gold side title. Price............85c

If by mail, postage extra, 11 cents.

OXFORD BREVIER BIBLES.

Large, black face type. Just issued. An astonishing feat. Large, clear type. Bible in a handy size. Superbly printed on the famous Oxford paper. This has solved the problem of making a large, readable type Bible in a handy size. These Oxford brevier 16mo Bibles are the most beautiful Bibles ever made at any price. The most appropriate Bible for presentation purposes or personal use. No one who loves a well made, beautiful Bible could fail to appreciate these superb books.

Sample of Oxford brevier black faced type.

of God's chosen.

with an arrow; suddenly [a] shall
they be wounded.
8 So they shall make [a] their
own tongue to fall upon themselves: all that see them shall
flee away.
9 And all men shall fear, and

Oxford Brevier Text Bible.

16mo. Size, 6½x4½ inches.

No. 3F8775 French Morocco, limp; round corners, red under burnished gold edges. Price............$1.47

If by mail, postage extra, 12 cents.

No. 3F8777 French Morocco. Divinity circuit; round corners; red under burnished gold edges. Price............$1.80

If by mail, postage extra, either style, 12 cents.

No. 3F8779 French Morocco. Oxford India paper edition. Only 1 inch thick. Divinity circuit; linen lined; round corners; red under burnished gold edges. Price............$2.40

If by mail, postage extra, 9 cents.

Oxford Brevier Reference Bible.

Printed on the famous Oxford India paper. Contains references, 12 maps and index to maps. Size, 7x4⅞ inches. 1 inch thick.

No. 3F8782 French Morocco. Divinity circuit; linen lined; round corners; red under burnished gold edges. Price......$2.40

If by mail, postage extra, 10 cents.

Oxford Brevier Teachers' Bible.

Printed on the famous Oxford India paper. Containing the cyclopedic concordance, the famous Oxord new up to date 20th century helps, arranged under one alphabet. Size, 7x4⅞ inches. Only 1⅛ inches thick.

No. 3F8788 French Morocco. Divinity circuit; linen lined; bound corners; red under burnished gold edges. Price.$3.20

No. 3F8790 Genuine Levant. Divinity circuit; calf lined to edge; silk sewed; round corners; red under burnished gold edges. The most beautiful Bible ever made. Price............$5.95

If by mail, postage extra, either style, 12 cents.

Oxford Brevier Testaments.

Size, 6⅜x4 inches. Black faced type, making the most readable testament published

No. 3F8792 French Seal, limp; round corners, red under burnished gold edges. Price............60c

No. 3F8794 French Morocco. Divinity circuit; linen lined (absolutely nontearable cover); round corners; red under gold edges. Price............72c

If by mail, postage extra, either style, 4 cents

Testament and Psalms.

Famous Oxford India Paper Edition.

No. 3F8797 Venetian Morocco, limp; round corners; red under burnished gold edges. Size, 6¾x4½ inches. Only 5-16 inch thick. Price............$1.40

If by mail, postage extra, 4 cents.

TEACHERS' BIBLES.

Minion 8vo Full Teachers' Bible.

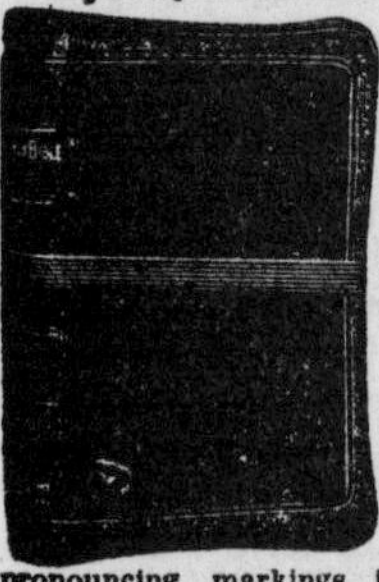

Printed on good quality of paper with 60 thousand side marginal references. Bound in Florentine Seal; Divinity Circuit; grained linings; red under gold edges; with head band and marker. Full helps and references; concordance complete. Contains 17 plates, 12 colored maps and 32 pages of illustrations. Regular retail price $3.00.

No. 3F8649 Our special price........98c

If by mail, postage extra, 19 cents.

Oxford Teachers' Bibles. With Cyclopedic Concordance.

New and up to date helps arranged under one alphabet; including index, concordance, glossary, weights, measures, coin, botany, etc., etc. Composing, in fact a complete and practical bible dictionary arranged under one alphabet with innumerable; new illustrations; the whole forming the famous new Oxford cyclopedic, concordance. The text is self pronouncing, practical, clear, simple. The self pronouncing markings in these books go further than in any other teachers' bibles, and in addition to accenting and dividing into syllables the proper names, it indicates the pronounciation of certain other words which cannot be called proper names, but which might be difficult to an unskilled reader.

Oxford Large Minion Type. 8vo Self Pronouncing Teachers' Bible.

Model line of self pronouncing editions. Size 8x5¼ inches. With full page plates.

No. 3F8650 French Morocco. Divinity circuit; round corners; extra grained lining; red under gold edges. Price............$1.20

No. 3F8651 French Morocco. Same as No. 3F8650 with patent thumb index on edge. Price............$1.35

If by mail, postage extra, either style, 19 cents.

No. 3F8658 Arabian Morocco. Oxford India Paper Edition. Only one inch thick. Divinity Circuit; leather lined to edge; round corners; red under gold edges. Price....$3.40

No. 3F8659 Arabian Morocco. Oxford India Paper Edition. Same as No. 3F8658, with patent thumb index on edge. Price............$3.55

If by mail, postage extra, either style, 12 cents.

Oxford Long Primer 8vo. Self Pronouncing Teachers' Bibles

The largest type self pronouncing Teachers' Bibles in the smallest compass made. Size, 8½x6 inches.

No. 3F8680 French Morocco. Divinity Circuit; round corners; red under gold edges. Price............$1.60

No. 3F8681 French Morocco. Same as No. 3F8680, with thumb index on edge. Price............$1.75

No. 3F8683 Arabian Morocco. Divinity Circuit; leather lined; round corners; red under gold edges. Price............$1.95

No. 3F8684 Arabian Morocco. Same as No. 3F86836, with thumb index on edge. Price............$2.10

If by mail, postage extra, any style, 24 cents.

Oxford India Paper Edition.

LONG PRIMER 8VO. SELF PRONOUNCING TEACHERS' BIBLE.

The marvel of printing. Bible only 1⅛ inches thick.

No. 3F8690 French Morocco. Divinity circuit, linen lined (nontearable cover); round corners; red under gold edges. Price..$4.00

No. 3F8691 French Morocco. Same as No. 3F8690, with patent thumb index on edge. Price............$4.15

If by mail, postage extra, any style, 16 cents.

Nelson's Teachers' Bibles.

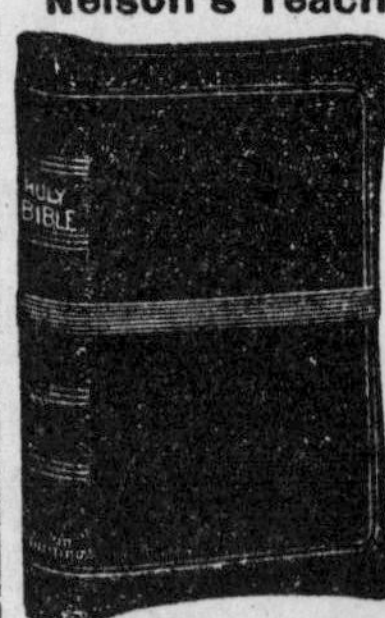

Contains illustrated Bible treasury, with 350 illustrations, including concise Bible Dictionary, combined Concordance and 12 maps, indexed. Copyright edition. These are the most complete helps ever published, and contain more pages and more actual information than any other helps. They are literally an encyclopedia. Profusely illustrated with beautiful halftones made from recent photographs and famous pictures. Also maps, diagrams, etc., all of which truly illustrate the articles in which they appear. These helps have been written by the leading scholars in America and Great Britain, and supplies in tn. most convenient form the very latest information about the Bible: its writers, its language, various versions, etc.

MINION 8VO TEACHERS' BIBLE.

Large page; size, 5¼x8 inches, with full illustrated helps.

No. 3F8700 Egyptian Seal. Divinity Circuit; extra grained lining, round corners; interlined to edge with linen, making nontearable cover; red under gold edges. Price............$1.40

No. 3F8701 Egyptian Seal. Same as No. 3F8700, with patent thumb index on each. Price............$1.55

If by mail, postage extra, either style 20 cents.

Teachers' Long Primer 8vo Self Pronouncing Bible.

Self Pronouncing Edition. Accented according to the latest revision of Webster's dictionary, making it very easy to read and pronounce all the difficult names and words in the bible. Beautifully printed from bold type on fine white paper, with full illustrated helps.

No. 3F8715 Egyptian Seal. Divinity Circuit. Grained lining; interlined to edge with linen, making nontearable cover. Bound corners; red under gold edges. Size, 5¾x8¾ inches. Price............$1.68

No. 3F8716 Egyptian Seal. Same as No. 3F8715, with patent thumb index. Price............$1.83

No. 3F8718 Oregon Seal. Divinity circuit. Leather lined to edge. Bound corners; red under gold edges. Price...$2.40

No. 3F8719 Oregon Seal. Same as No. 3F8718, with patent thumb index on edge. Price............$2.55

If by mail, postage extra, any style, 28c.

Teachers' Combination Self Pronouncing Minion Bible.

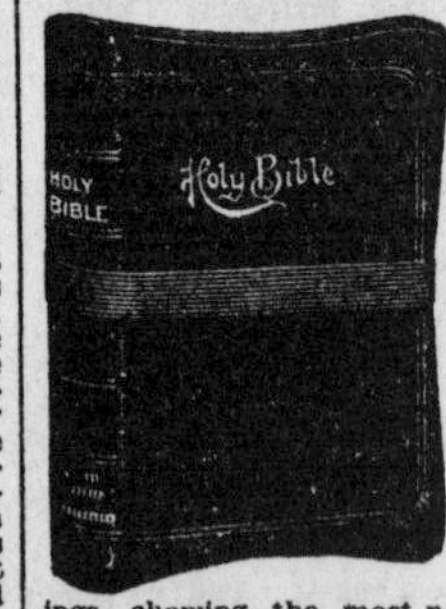

Showing in the simplest form all changes and additions made by the revisers, enabling the reader to see at a glance wherein the two versions differ. The text is the authorized King James version, unchanged. The foot notes contain all the changes made in the revised version. Readers need not refer to the foot notes unless they wish to see what changes were made by the revisers. The latest and best standard helps to the study of the Bible embellished with a complete series of new maps, illustrating the geography of Palestine and the surrounding countries in the earliest times, and embodying the most recent discoveries. Contains over 40,000 references and 4,000 questions and answers. Many superb phototype engravings, showing the most noted places mentioned in the Bible, as they appear today. All proper names throughout the text divided into syllables and accented, the same as an unabridged dictionary. This is really two Bibles in one. The old and revised versions on the same page, without increasing the size or weight of the book.

Teachers' Self Pronouncing Minion Type Combination Bible.

No. 3F8750 French Seal. Divinity circuit; round corners; red under gold edges; extra grained leather; interlined with linen to edge, making non tearable cover. Price............$1.39

No. 3F8751 French Seal. Same as No. 3F8750, with patent thumb index. Price............$1.54

If by mail, postage extra, any style, 20 cents.

Teachers' Self Pronouncing Bourgeois Type Combination Bible.

No. 3F8760 French Seal. Divinity circuit; round corners; red under gold edges; extra grained lining, interlined to edge with linen, making cover nontearable. Price.....$1.68

No. 3F8761 French Seal. Same as No. 3F8760, with patent index on edge. Price............(If by mail, postage extra, 28 cents.)............$1.83

AMERICAN STANDARD REVISED BIBLE

The Bible in plain English. Published by Thomas Nelson & Sons, London, and authorized by the American Revision Committee, whose endorsement appears on the back of the title page. It is admitted by all Bible scholars that the American Standard Edition gives the meanings of the original better than any other translation of the Scriptures. It is not a new Bible. The American Standard is simply the great book made plain for every reader. It is not the Bible that is being revised; it is man's fallible translations from one human language into another, that are capable of constant improvement in order to better convey the Father's message. The American Standard is a new translation of the Bible and represents thirty years of devout study, consideration and preparation by the most eminent biblical scholars of all evangelical denominations. The King James version was made in 1611. Since that time words have changed their meaning and examination of authorities and the revelation of modern archaeology have shown that there are many inaccuracies and many errors in the textual reading in the St. James version.

All great nations have had new translations of their Bible during the past half century and in no language has this been so necessary as in the English language, because the changes in it have been so numerous. The American Standard Revised Bible is the most accurate translation, the most thorough, simplest in expression, giving a clearer expression of the thought than any translation yet produced. It does not require a scholar to read this Bible, though it required many scholars to make it.

Text Edition of the American Standard Revised Bible.

Minion Type. 24mo. Size, 4x6½ inches.

No. 3F8800 Egyptian Seal. Divinity circuit; round corners; red under gold edges. Price .... If by mail, postage extra, 13 cents. 98c

Reference Edition of the American Standard Revised Bible.

Bourgeois Type. 8vo. Size, 5¼x8 inches, with 12 indexed maps.

No. 3F8805 Egyptian Seal. Divinity circuit; round corners; red under gold edges, extra grained lining. Interlined with linen to edge, making absolutely nontearable cover. Price $1.75

No. 3F8806 Egyptian Seal. Divinity circuit. Same as No. 3F8805, with patent thumb index on edge. Price $1.90

If by mail, postage extra, either style, 19 cents.

Teachers' Edition of the American Standard Revised Bible.

Contains the famous Nelson Concise Bible Dictionary. A new Combined Concordance of this revised version, and 12 maps with index. The Concise Bible Dictionary which forms a help to teachers. It supplies in the most convenient form all the latest information about the Bible, etc. The Combined Concordance is entirely new and is made expressly for the American Standard Edition. The maps are beautifully colored. There is also a complete index to every place noted on the maps.

BOURGEOIS TYPE. 8vo. Size, 5¼x8 inches.

No. 3F8815 Egyptian Seal. Divinity circuit; round corners; red under gold edges; extra grained lining with linen interlining to edge, making nontearable cover. Price... $2.18

No. 3F8816 Egyptian Seal. Same as No. 3F8815 with patent index on edge. Price $2.33

No. 3F8818 Persian Seal. Divinity circuit. Leather lined to edge, making nontearable cover; round corners; red under gold edges. Price $2.75

No. 3F8819 Persian Seal. Same as No. 3F8818 with patent index on edge. Price .... If by mail, postage extra, any style 22 cents $2.90

American Standard Edition of the Revised New Testament.

Minion type. 32mo. Size, 3¼x4½ inches.

No. 3F8830 Egyptian Seal, Limp; Tur-key grained; round corners; red under gold edges. Price 48c

No. 3F8832 Egyptian Seal. Divinity circuit; round corners; red under gold edges. Price .... If by mail, postage extra, either style, 6 cents 62c

RED LETTER BIBLES

Nelson's Long Primer Type Self Pronouncing Red Letter Teachers' Bible.

The best Red Letter Bible published. Printed by Lewis Klopsch, proprietor of the "Christian Herald" and originator of the red letter idea, especially for Thomas Nelson & Sons. Dr. Klopsch is the authority on red letter bibles, and his bibles are more thorough, more complete, and more accurate, and cover a greater field than any other red letter bible made. In these bibles the passages and incidents in the old testament quoted or referred to by our Lord and Savior are printed in red. In the new testament the words recorded as having been spoken by our Lord and Savior are printed in red; and in the old testament the passages generally regarded as prophetic of our Savior are indicated by a red star. Printed from large black faced type on the best quality of Bible paper. Contains 60,000 references and full teachers' helps. Size, 5½x8 inches. A really beautiful edition.

No. 3F8870 Arabian Morocco. Divinity circuit; extra grained lining; red under gold edges; round corners. Price, $2.15

No. 3F8871 Arabian Morocco. Same as No. 3F8870, with patent thumb index on edge. Price $2.30

No. 3F8873 Arabian Morocco. Divinity circuit; leather lined; round corners; red under gold edges. Price...... $2.40

No. 3F8874 Arabian Morocco. Leather lined. Same as No. 3F8873, with patent thumb index on edge. Price.. $2.55

If by mail, postage extra, any style, 26 cents.

Nelson's Red Letter Testaments.

BOURGEOIS TYPE.

All the words spoken by Christ are printed in red. Bourgeois type. 24mo. Size, 3¾x5¾ inches. These are the most beautiful and perfectly printed red letter testaments published.

No. 3F8880 Grained Cloth, limp. Round corners, burnished red edges. Price 40c

No. 3F8882 French Morocco, limp. Round corners, red under gold edges. Price 72c

No. 3F8884 French Morocco. Divinity circuit, round corners, red under gold edges, extra grained lining. Price 88c

If by mail, postage extra, any style, 4 cents.

SUNDAY SCHOOL SCHOLARS' SELF PRONOUNCING BIBLE.

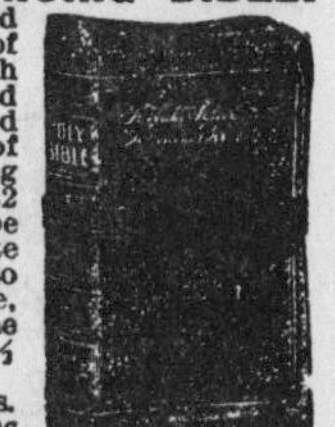

Large Minion Type. 12mo. Self pronouncing text. A Bible arranged on the plan of a Teachers' Bible, except that the aids to the study of the scripture are in simple language, and contains subjects in which young students find interest. This Bible is printed from easily read large minion type, with all proper names or hard words accented and divided into syllables, thereby facilitating pronunciation. An aid of supreme importance to young people. The only self pronouncing large type Minion Sunday School Bible made. Illustrated with 32 new pictures, which are so appropriate that they cannot fail to be most instructive to young people; together with new and complete valuable helps to bible studies, which include explanation of how to study the bible, young people's bible history, weights, measures, people, etc., etc. Also a calendar for daily reading, by which the reading of the whole bible can be completed in one year—365 readings. Size, 4x6½ inches.

No. 3F8890 Grained Cloth, limp. Red edges, round corners. Price 60c

No. 3F8892 French Morocco, limp. Red under gold edges, round corners, silk marker. Price 98c

No. 3F8894 French Morocco. Divinity circuit, round corners, red under gold edges, silk head band and marker, extra grained lining. Price $1.12

If by mail, postage extra, any style, 12 cents.

STATIONERY DEPARTMENT.

$1.98 BUYS $5.84 WORTH OF USEFUL STATIONERY.

ONE YEARS SUPPLY of STATIONERY $1.98

JUST THE STATIONERY NEEDED IN EVERY HOME. Send us an order for this big outfit, and be sure of a good, big, generous supply of everything you will need in the way of writing paper, envelopes, pencils, pens, box paper, etc., for the next year, and so make a big saving by getting about three times as much for your money as you would get if the various items were purchased separately. From the picture shown hereon and from the list of the many articles given, you can get just some little idea of the wonderful values we are giving in this enormous outfit, this great aggregation of useful stationery and supplies for only $1.98.

EVERY HOME, every grown person has use for writing paper, envelopes, pencils, stationery and the various articles shown in this illustration and in this list, a list of goods that would cost you in any retail store in the country at least $5.84 and which we offer you for only $1.98. If you are about to buy anything in the line of stationery, paper, pads, envelopes, tablets, pens, pencils or other stationery, take advantage of this most extraordinary offer. Enclose $1.98 and let us send you this big regular $5.84 outfit. It will go to you with the understanding and agreement that it must be perfectly satisfactory to you, you must find it the greatest value you ever saw or heard of, otherwise we will expect you to return it to us at our expense and get your money back.

THE GOODS shown in this big assortment as illustrated and listed are all high class, extra high grade quality, especially selected. The assortment is made up with great care by experts in the line with a view to giving our customers an ideal assortment of all kinds of useful stationery, paper and envelopes in a great variety, pencils, tablets and the various stationery as shown hereon.

OUR SPECIAL $1.98 PRICE barely covers the cost to us when bought in immense quantities and put up in special assortments, giving you every advantage of every economy that we can work out, with simply our one small percentage of profit added. About twice as much in staple stationery as you could buy at wholesale and about three times as much as you could buy at retail for the money in any store in the country.

IF YOU ARE IN NEED OF ANYTHING in the line of stationery don't overlook this most extraordinary offer. Enclose $1.98, let us send you this outfit with the understanding and agreement that you can return it to us at our expense and get your money back if you are not perfectly satisfied.

The outfit contains the following items:	Regular retail price.
500 Envelopes	$2.00
1 Box of Paper (linen finish)	.15
1 Box of Persian Silk (white wove)	.15
1 Box of Winchelsea Vellum	.25
1 Box of Daffodil (cream wove)	.25
1 Box of Holland (cloth finish)	.25
1 Box of Broughton Plate	.25
¼ Ream Jack Rose	$0.25
1 Dozen Blotters	.10
1 London Bond Tablet	.25
1 Elite Tablet (cream wove)	.10
1 Birchmont Linen Tablet	.15
1 Pencil Sharpener	.05
1 Bottle Red Ink	.05
1 Bottle Black Ink	.08
1 Bottle Mucilage	.10
1 Bottle Black Ink	.10
1 Ink Well (pressed glass, fancy design)	$0.25
1 Eraser, Pen and Pencil	.05
1 Dozen Pens (Esterbrook Bank)	.10
1 Dozen Pens (Judge's Quill)	.10
1 Dozen Pens (Gillott No. 604 E. F.)	.10
2 Pencils (No. 517 Autograph)	.05
2 Pencils (No. 2 Sphinx)	.05
2 Pencils (Tortoise Shell No. 998)	.10
2 Pencils (Electric No. 462)	.10
2 Pencils (Imperial No. 2842)	.05
2 Pencils (Blaisdell No. 520)	$0.05
1 Penholder (Cedar, metal tip)	.05
1 Penholder (Ebony handle, nickel tip)	.03
1 Penholder (Red handle, nickel tip)	.03
1 Penholder (Self ejector)	.10
1 Penholder (Pneumatic)	.10
Would cost you at retail	$5.84

No. 3F12000 Special Stationery Outfit, just as illustrated and described above, all complete. Price **$1.98**

WRITING PAPER. In this line will be found one or more boxes of every kind of writing paper that is made, put up in the newest shapes. The most popular and fashionable paper this year is fabric (cloth) finish, and we are therefore offering a great selection of this particular style. The designs on the boxes are all new. They are stamped or embossed in bright colors. They will make attractive glove, crava and handkerchief boxes. It is unprofitable to ship boxes of writing paper by mail. We would advise you to include books or other stationery, sufficient to make up an express or freight shipment. Weight, packed for shipment, 15 pounds.

No. 3F12010 Cheap Box Paper, cream wove, ruled, 20 sheets; size, 4½ x 7 inches, with 20 Baronial envelopes to match. Put up in pink box with lithographed picture in colors on cover.
Price, 6 boxes for **22c**; 3 boxes for.... **12c**
If by mail, postage extra, for 3 boxes, 22 cents.

No. 3F12020 Sweet Sixteen Box Paper. Good quality white wedding plate writing paper, ruled, contains 24 sheets, new shape, 5x6 inches, tied with white silk ribbon and bow, and 24 wallet flap envelopes with lithographed bands. Box lithographed in gold and colors, representing a winter scene.
Price, 4 boxes for **26c**; 2 boxes for... **14c**
If by mail, postage extra, for 2 boxes, 18 cents.

No. 3F12030 Society Stationery. Box Paper, 24 sheets, newest shape, 5 x 6 inches, 24 envelopes, wallet flap. High grade cloth finish writing paper, either ruled or plain. Paper and envelopes banded with embossed bands in red and gold; put up in ivory white box with elaborately embossed coat of arms on cover in red and gold.
Price, 2 boxes for **20c**; per box...... **11c**
If by mail, postage extra, per box, 8 cents.

Ruled Writing Paper.

No. 3F12040 Unwritten History. Put up in a book shaped box, imitation morocco binding, gold edged. Size of paper, 4½x7 inches.
Price, per box **12c**
3 boxes for **35c**
If by mail, postage extra, per box, 10 cents.

No. 3F12050 Box of Decorated Paper. Contains 24 sheets of superfine cream wove writing paper, ruled, 7x4½ inches, tied with baby silk ribbon, and 24 envelopes, Baronial shape. Each sheet is decorated with a spray of flowers in colors. White box, stamped with fancy design in colors.
Price, 2 boxes for **22c**; per box...... **12c**
If by mail, postage extra, per box, 9 cents.

No. 3F12060 One pound box of writing paper, containing 60 sheets cream wove, smooth finish, fine quality ruled octavo note paper. Baronial envelopes to match; put up in tinted box. Size of paper, 4x7 inches.
Per box.... **14c**
2 boxes for (two pounds)...... **25c**

No. 3F12070 One-pound box of cloth finished linen paper, 60 sheets, ruled, and 50 envelopes; put up same as No. 3F12060.
Price, per box, one pound.............. **19c**
2 boxes for............................ **35c**
If by mail, postage extra, per box, 20 cents.

No. 3F12080 Perfumed Writing Paper, put up in extra large box, 5¼ x 10 inches. Contains 24 sheets first class linen paper ruled; size, 4¾x6 inches; tied with baby blue silk ribbon, and 24 envelopes wallet flap, bound with decorated bands. Is delicately perfumed and makes attractive writing paper.
Retail price, 25 cents; our price...... **15c**
2 boxes for............................ **27c**
If by mail, postage extra, per box, 11 cents.

No. 3F12090 King's Bond Box Paper. Fine grade of bond writing paper. Contains 24 sheets, ruled or plain, newest shape, 5¼ x 6½ inches, with 24 envelopes, deep pointed flap. Bound with decorated bands, and put up in the most attractive red box, stamped in blue, gold and yellow in baronial design. Price, per box.................. **14c**
2 boxes for............................ **25c**
If by mail, postage extra, per box, 9 cents.

No. 3F12110 Box of Gentlemen's Writing Paper. 25 envelopes, tied with white silk ribbon, and 48 single sheets of high grade plate paper, vellum finish. Ruled or plain. State preference. White or blue. State color wanted. Put up especially for us in a gray box, 6¼x10¾ inches, on the cover of which is the picture of the fencing girl in short skirt. Makes nice glove or cravat box. Price, per box.......... **30c**
2 boxes for............................ **55c**
If by mail, postage extra, per box, 14 cents.

No. 3F12120 Oxford Lawn Box Paper. 4¾ x 7¼ inches, stands 5½ inches, high. Attractively decorated. Contains 24 sheets paper, one tablet 40 sheets, and 48 envelopes of Oxford Lawn high grade cloth finished writing paper.
Retail price, 75 cents; our price, per box. **45c**
If by mail, postage extra, per box, 11 cents.

Foreign Correspondence.

No. 3F12130 Whiting's Overland Mail. Made especially for foreign correspondence, of a very fine grade extra thin writing paper. The advantage of using this paper when writing to your friends and relatives abroad, is that it saves postage, and you can send twice the number of sheets for the same amount of postage than if you use regular writing paper. Can furnish in either white or blue. State color wanted. Containing 24 sheets, size, 5¾x6¾ inches, and 24 envelopes to match. Price, per box.............. **20c**
2 boxes for............................ **38c**
If by mail, postage extra, per box, 7 cents.

Highland Linen.

Eaton and Hurlbut's Finest Paper. This is the highest grade fabric finished linen writing paper made. We can furnish it in three sizes and three colors of paper, white, blue or gray. Put up in ivory white boxes, top handsomely embossed in red, gold and green. Containing 24 sheets and 24 envelopes bound with elaborately embossed bands.

No. 3F12140 Castleton, Eaton & Hurlbut's Highland Linen, regent. Size, 4½x5¾ inches. Wallet flap envelopes. Colors, white, blue or gray. State color wanted. Retail price, 35 cents; our price.............. **23c**
2 boxes for............................ **42c**
If by mail, postage extra, per box, 11 cents.

No. 3F12150 Clovelly, Eaton & Hurlbut's Highland Linen. Note. Size, 5¾x5¾ inches, with square cornered extra deep wallet flap envelopes. Colors, white, blue or gray. State color wanted. Retail price, 40 cents; our price........................ **26c**
2 boxes for............................ **49c**
If by mail, postage extra, per box, 12 cents.

No. 3F12160 Chilton, Eaton & Hurlbut's Highland Linen. Invitation and note. Size, 5¾x5¾ inches. With square cornered extra deep wallet flap envelopes. The newest and most fashionable shape paper and envelopes. Colors, white, blue or gray. State color wanted. Retail price, 50 cents; our price, per box........................ **30c**
2 boxes for............................ **55c**
If by mail, postage extra, per box, 12 cents.

No. 3F12170 Eaton & Hurlbut's Highland Linen Bond. The finest bond paper made. Fabric finish, 24 sheets, size 5¼ x 6½ inches. 24 envelopes, wallet flap, put up same as Highland linen. Can furnish in either white, blue or gray. State color wanted. Retail price, 35 cents; our price...... **24c**; 2 boxes for **45c**
If by mail, postage extra, per box, 10 cents.

Fancy Gift Boxes.

No. 3F12190 Box Paper. Handsome flowered paper covered box, 14½x5¼ inches. Contains 24 sheets of fabric finish two-fold white writing paper, 4½x10½ inches and 24 envelopes to match, bound with bands of flowered paper. Box covers in assorted designs, stamped in the natural colors.
Price, per box.. **28c**
2 boxes for.... **50c**
If by mail, postage extra, 18 cents.

No. 3F12200 Box Paper. Beautiful plush box, cover lined with sateen, with hinges and clasp. Contains crochet hook, bodkin, stiletto and one quire of cream wove square note paper, ruled, with envelopes to match. Box fitted with ball feet. Size of box, 8 x 2¾ x 5¾ in. Price, per box...... **47c**
If by mail, postage extra, 16 cents.

No. 3F12220 Box Paper, upright cabinet; covered with green satin finish paper, stamped with holly design in natural colors. Size, 3½x7¾ inches. Stands 6 inches high. Contains two quires of very fine quality cloth finish writing paper in two sizes, 4½x7 inches and 5¾x7 inches, with 48 envelopes to match, wallet flap. Each quire of paper and every 12 envelopes are tied with red silk cord and green tassels. Regular retail price, $1.00.
Our price, 2 boxes for **$1.05**; per box. **60c**
If by mail, postage extra, per box, 25 cents.

No. 3F12230 Box Paper Superb; extra large box 11½x15 inches, made of flowered kid finish paper, with elaborately embossed and carved appliqued top in center of which is a beautiful picture in colors. The box contains two quires of club size cloth finish paper, 5¾x7 inches, and 48 wallet flap envelopes to match. The two packages of paper and the four packages of envelopes are tied with white silk cord and tassels. Regular price, $2.00; 2 boxes for **$1.75**; our price, per box **98c**
If by mail, postage extra, per box, 35 cents.

Writing Paper For Children.

No. 3F12240 Gilt Box with flower design lithographed on cover in colors. Top lifts up on hinge, has pull drawer for envelopes. Contains 24 sheets of ruled high grade cream wove Juvenile writing paper 3¾x5¾, and 24 envelopes bound with decorated bands.
Price, 2 boxes for **25c**; per box...... **14c**
If by mail, postage extra, per box, 8 cents.

No. 3F12250 Child's Piano Box of writing paper. Box shaped like a piano, contains 24 sheets of fine grade ruled cream wove writing paper, and 24 envelopes, banded.
Price, 2 for **25c**; each.. **15c**
If by mail, postage extra, per box, 5 cents.

Children's Plush Work Boxes.

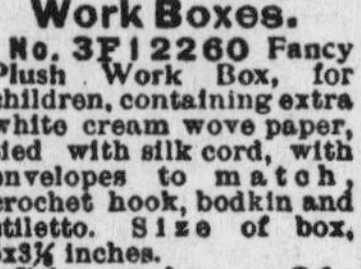

No. 3F12260 Fancy Plush Work Box, for children, containing extra white cream wove paper, tied with silk cord, with envelopes to match, crochet hook, bodkin and stiletto. Size of box, 5x3¾ inches.
Price, per box...... **21c**
If by mail, postage extra, 7 cents.

AURORA STATIONERY.

Box Paper and Tablets

The Aurora writing paper put up in both tablet form and in fancy boxes with envelopes to match, in various styles and sizes, but in one quality only, the best. It is the highest grade paper that the most expert paper makers can produce. It is made in the latest and most stylish shapes and designs, the most fashionable finishes, and the most beautiful tints.

Paper of this quality is sold in the largest cities at two and three times the prices we quote, and is not to be had at any price in the smaller cities and towns. Do not fail to send us an order for Aurora Stationery. We know that you will be pleased and we want to save you money.

Aurora Box Paper.

The Aurora Box Papers are the height of elegance in writing papers, the highest grade paper made, put up in the latest style and designs, each style in five different finishes: white wedding plate, superfine cream wove, white bond, white real Irish linen, and white, blue or gray cloth finish. The boxes are works of art, covered with heavy pale green ivory finished paper, elaborately stamped with beautiful and artistic design, in dark green and gold. The handsomest and most ornamental box made.

When ordering the Aurora Box Paper be sure to state whether you wish cloth finish, wedding plate, cream wove or bond.

No. 3F12470 Aurora Box Paper. Regular shape 4½x7 inches. One quire of paper, 24 pointed flap envelopes banded with decorated band, put up in elaborately decorated box. Furnished in cloth finish (white, blue or gray), linen, wedding plate, cream wove or bond. State preference when ordering.
Price, 2 boxes for **34c**; per box.... **18c**
If by mail, postage extra, per box, 11 cents.

No. 3F12475 Aurora Box Paper. Newest and most fashionable letter shape. Size, 5¼ x6½ inches. One quire of paper and 24 envelopes, with square corners, deep wallet flaps, banded with decorated bands, put up in handsomely decorated box, suitable for handkerchiefs, etc. Furnished in cloth finish (white, blue or gray), linen, wedding plate, cream wove or bond. State preference when ordering.
Price, 2 boxes for **35c**; per box.... **19c**
If by mail, postage extra, per box, 14 cents.

No. 3F12480 Aurora Box Paper. One quire of new shape letter size paper, 5¼x6½ inches, and 24 envelopes, in separate packs of six, banded with decorated bands. 12 envelopes having deep wallet flaps, round corners, and 12 with wallet flap, deep point. In extra large handsomely decorated box. Size, 11¼ x 7¼ inches, with hinge top. Furnished in cloth finish (white, blue or gray), linen, wedding plate, cream wove, or bond. State preference when ordering. Price, 2 boxes, **40c**; per box. **22c**
If by mail, postage extra, per box, 15 cents.

No. 3F12485 Aurora Special Box Paper. Two quires, in cloth finish, only. New style paper, large page, 5¼x6½ inches, and 48 envelopes to match. One quire of paper white and one quire blue. Four packs of envelopes, with square corners, deep wallet flaps, two blue and two white, tied with silk ribbon. Put up in handsome large box, size, 11¼x7¼ inches, two inches deep with hinge top. Retails regularly for 75 cents. Our price, per box... **39c**
2 boxes for............................ **68c**
If by mail, postage extra, per box, 26 cents.

Aurora Ink Tablets.

The Aurora Tablets are made in four different sizes; note, packet, Gladstone and letter size; each size in five different finishes: Wedding Plate, Superfine Cream Wove, Bond, Real Irish Linen and Cloth Finish, all in one quality, only, the best, with beautiful art covers stamped in gold and two shades of green. The highest grade tablets made.

No. 3F12490 Aurora Ink Tablet, note size, 5 x 8 inches, 70 sheets permanently bound, blotter attached. Furnished either ruled or plain in cloth finish, linen, wedding plate, cream wove or bond. State kind of paper desired.
Price, each............ **9c**
3 for.................. **24c**
If by mail, postage extra, each, 8 cents.

No. 3F12491 Envelopes to match the note size Aurora tablets.
Price, per 100, **30c**; per package (25), **8c**
If by mail, postage extra, per package, 5c.

No. 3F12495 Aurora Ink Tablet, packet size, 5½ x9 inches, 50 sheets, permanently bound, blotter attached. Furnished either ruled or plain in cloth finish, linen, wedding plate, cream wove or bond. State kind of paper desired
Price, each..........**9c**
3 for..........**24c**
If by mail, postage extra, each, 6 cents.

No. 3F12496 Envelopes to match the packet size Aurora tablets.
Price, per 100, **30c**; per package (25).. **8c**
If by mail, postage extra, per package, 5c.

No. 3F12500 Aurora Ink Tablets. Gladstone size, 6½x10 inches, 42 sheets, permanently bound, blotter attached. Furnished either ruled or plain in cloth finish, linen, wedding plate, cream wove or bond. State kind of paper desired.
Price, 3 for **24c**; each, **9c**
If by mail, postage extra, each, 7 cents.

No. 3F12501 Envelopes to match the Gladstone size Aurora tablet.
Price, per pkg. (25)... **8c**
Per 100..........**30c**
If by mail, postage extra, per package, 5 cents.

No. 3F12505 Aurora Ink Tablet. Letter size, 8x10 inches. 40 sheets, permanently bound, blotter attached. Furnished either ruled or plain in cloth finish, linen, wedding plate, cream wove or bond. State kind of paper desired.
Price, each..........**11c**
3 for..........**29c**
If by mail, postage extra, each, 7 cents.

No. 3F12506 Envelopes to match the letter size Aurora tablet.
Price, per 100, **30c**; per package (25).. **8c**
If by mail, postage extra, per package, 5 cents.
When ordering the Aurora Tablets be sure to state whether you wish them ruled or plain and also the finish, whether cloth finish, wedding plate, linen, cream wove or bond.

Pencil Tablets.

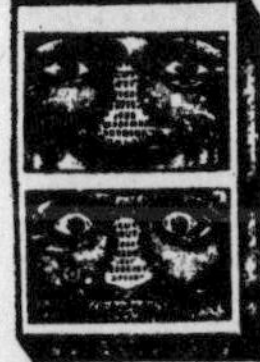

No. 3F12515 "False Face" Pencil Tablet. Cover contains two false faces, handsomely lithographed in colors. They can be cut out and used by children with great pleasure. Assorted designs. Tablet is permanently bound and contains 240 pages (120 leaves) of the best quality ruled pencil paper, size 6x9 inches.
Price for 6 tablets.. **20c**
Per dozen.......... **38c**
Weight, per doz., packed for shipment, 8 lbs.

No. 3F12525 The Flag Girl Pencil Tablets. 12 different designs representing 12 leading countries of the world. Each design shows girls dressed in national costume holding the Nation's flag. Coat-of-arms of each nation shown in the corner. These covers are superbly lithographed in many colors. Each tablet has 300 pages (150 leaves) of the best quality ruled pencil paper. Size, 6x9 inches. Price, for 6 tablets.... **23c**
Price, per dozen (12 different designs). **42c**
Weight, per doz., packed for shipment, 9 lbs.

No. 3F12535 Columbia Pencil Tablet. Permanently bound with handsome patriotic cover, beautifully embossed in red, white, blue, and gold. 240 pages (120 leaves) of best quality ruled pencil paper, size, 6x9 inches, in three colors; ⅓ of tablet is red, ⅓ white and ⅓ blue.
Price for 6 tablets... **22c**
Per dozen.......... **40c**
Weight, per dozen, packed for shipment, 7 pounds.

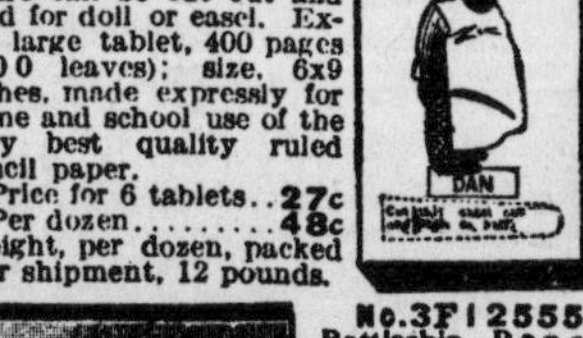

No. 3F12545 Coon Easel Pencil Tablet. Assorted cover designs. The figure can be cut out and used for doll or easel. Extra large tablet, 400 pages (200 leaves); size, 6x9 inches, made expressly for home and school use of the very best quality ruled pencil paper.
Price for 6 tablets.. **27c**
Per dozen.......... **48c**
Weight, per dozen, packed for shipment, 12 pounds.

No. 3F12555 Battleship Pencil Tablet. Covers in assorted designs, lithographed in colors, representing the battleships of our navy. 240 pages (120 sheets); size, 8 x10 inches; best quality ruled pencil paper. Price for 6 tablets.......**28c**
Per dozen.... **50c**
Weight, per dozen, packed for shipment, 12 lbs.

No. 3F12565 Pencil Box Tablet. Latest novelty in tablets. Size, 8x10 inches. Contains 200 pages (100 leaves) best quality ruled pencil paper. At the top is a pencil box, which is inserted in the head of the tablet, and which will hold pencils, erasers, etc. Permanently bound; very durable. Price for 6 tablets. **30c**
Per dozen.......... **55c**
Weight, per doz., packed for shipment 8 lbs.

Ink Tablets.

No. 3F12575 Old Glory Ink Tablet. Contains 140 pages, (70 leaves) of ruled white note paper with blotter attached. Permanently bound. The cover design represents our flag beautifully embossed in red, white, blue and gold. Size, 5x8 inches.
Price for 6 tablets.... **23c**
Per dozen.......... **44c**
Weight, per dozen, packed for shipment, 5 pounds.

No. 3F12576 Envelopes, to match. Price, per 100.......... **12c**
If by mail, postage extra, per 100, 18 cents.

No. 3F12585 Our Special Ink Tablet. A cloth finish paper at a price less than is asked for ordinary paper. Contains 100 pages (50 leaves) ruled, with blotter attached. Size, 5x8 inches. Permanently bound. A handsomely embossed cover with coat-of-arms design in green, red, gold and blue.
Price for 6 tablets..... **20c**
Per dozen.......... **38c**
Weight of 6 tablets, packed for shipment, 3 lbs.

No. 3F12586 Envelopes to match.
Price, per 100.......... **17c**
If by mail, postage extra, per 100, 18 cents.

No. 3F12595 "Square Deal" Linen Finish Ink Tablet. This tablet, like the picture of Roosevelt on its cover stands for a square deal. It represents the greatest value ever offered for the money. 200 pages (100 sheets) of high grade ruled linen paper. Size, 5x10 inches, with blotter attached. Cover is pale blue, beautifully stamped in gold and picture of Theodore Roosevelt in center.
Price, per dozen, **52c**; for 6 tablets, **28c**
Weight of 6 tablets, packed for shipment, 4 lbs.

No. 3F12596 Square Deal Ink Tablet. Same as No. 3F12595, but packet note. Size, 5½x9 inches; 144 pages (72 leaves).
Price, per dozen, **52c**; for 6 tablets, **28c**
Weight of 6 tablets, packed for shipment, 3 lbs.

No. 3F12597 Square Deal Ink Tablet. Same as No. 3F12595, but letter size. Size, 8x10 inches; 80 pages (40 sheets).
Per dozen, **52c**; for 6 tablets.......... **28c**
Weight of 6 tablets packed for shipment, 4 lbs.

No. 3F12605 Envelopes to match.
Price, per 100.......... **16c**
If by mail, postage extra, 18 cents.

No. 3F12645 Rural Route Ink Tablet. Contains 100 pages (50 sheets) best quality white ruled writing paper, with blotter attached. Size, 5x8 inches. Each sheet is decorated with a picture and is stamped "Rural Route," leaving a place for number, date, etc.
Price, 3 for.......... **13c**
Per half dozen.......... **24c**
If by mail, postage extra, for three, 15 cents.

No. 3F12646 Rural Route Decorated Envelopes to match. 25 in pack.
Price, per 100.......... **15c**
If by mail, postage extra, per package, 5c.

No. 3F12655 Postal Card Ink Tablet. The prettiest novelty in tablets ever made. Each tablet contains eight souvenir postal cards, lithographed in colors, showing the important points of interest in this country, such as the White House, Military Academy, Naval Academy, Capitol, etc. Each postal card can be cut off the tablet and mailed. 100 pages (50 sheets) of the very best ruled cream wove writing paper. Size, 5x8 inches.
Price, per half dozen, **48c**; 2 for..... **18c**
If by mail, postage extra, for two, 16 cents.

No. 3F12656 Envelopes to match tablet.
Price, per 100.......... **15c**
If by mail, postage extra, per package, 5c.

No. 3F12665 Common Sense Ink Tablet. Just the thing for old people and those whose eyesight is not as good as it used to be. Contains 150 pages (75 leaves) of extra fine quality white writing paper with special heavy ruling, thus enabling anyone to write straight without straining to see the lines. Blotter attached.
Price, 2 for.......... **19c**
Per half dozen.......... **50c**
If by mail, postage extra, for two, 18 cents.

No. 3F12666 Envelopes to match. 25 in pack.
Price, per 100.......... **16c**
If by mail, postage extra, per package, 5c.

Composition Books.

No. 3F12865 Roosevelt Combination Pen and Pencil Composition Book. Size, 6¾ x8¼ inches. Contains 172 pages (86 leaves) of good quality ruled paper. Permanently bound, in fancy lithographed cover, decorated with picture of President Roosevelt and the American flag.
Price, 3 for.... **12c**
Per half dozen.......... **22c**
If by mail, postage extra, for three, 30 cents.

No. 3F12625 Berwick Wedding Plate Ink Tablet. Size, 5x8 inches. Contains 160 pages (80 leaves) high grade pure white plate paper, extra fine finish; ruled or plain with blotter attached. Permanently bound with elaborate cover lithographed in green, red and gold; attractive design.
Price, 2 for **14c**; 6 for (If by mail, postage extra for two, 10c.).... **38c**

No. 3F12626 Berwick Wedding Plate Ink Tablet. Same as No. 3F12625, but commercial note. Size, 5½x9 inches; 120 pages (60 leaves).
Price, 2 for **15c**: 6 for (If by mail, postage extra for two, 14c.).... **40c**

No. 3F12627 Berwick Wedding Plate Ink Tablet. Letter size. Size, 8x10 inches; 80 pages (40 sheets).
Price, 2 for **16c**; 6 for (If by mail, postage extra for two, 20c.).... **44c**

No. 3F12628 Envelopes to match.
Price, per 100 (If by mail, postage extra, 18 cents.).......... **16c**

No. 3F12875 Circus Day Ink Composition Book. Size, 6¾x8½ inches. Contains 96 pages (48 leaves) of extra heavy white ruled ink writing paper, bound in cardboard covers, lithographed in colors, with picture representing a circus day parade.
Price, 3 for..... **14c**
Per half dozen.. **25c**
If by mail, postage extra, for three, 20 cents.

No. 3F12885 Work and Play Ink Composition Book. Extra size book containing 100 pages (50 sheets) 8x10 inches, of the very best quality extra heavy pure white ruled writing paper. Bound in cardboard with lithographed design on both covers in colors. Cloth binding.
Price, 2 for.. **12c**
Per half doz. **30c**
If by mail, postage extra, for two, 18 cents.

No. 3F12895 Imitation Leather Bound Ink Composition Book. Size, 7x8½ inches. Contains 144 pages (72 leaves) high grade pure white ruled ink writing paper. The cover is made of imitation leather.
Price, 2 for...... **18c**
Per half dozen... **50c**
If by mail, postage extra, for two, 20 cents.

Plain Visiting Cards.

No. 3F13245 Visiting Cards, superfine, satin finished, highest quality. Size, 2¼x3¾ inches; put up 100 cards to the package.
Price, per package.......... **18c**
If by mail, postage extra, per package, 9c.

Sealing Wax.

No. 3F13250 Sanford's Red Express Sealing Wax; four 4-ounce sticks to pound or eight 2-ounce sticks to pound.
Price, four 2-ounce sticks for.......... **16c**
Price, two 4-ounce sticks for.......... **16c**
Price, per pound (either size).......... **30c**

No. 3F13255 Perfumed Sealing Wax, for use in fine correspondence; five sticks assorted colors in box. Price, per box **15c**
If by mail, postage extra, per box, 5 cen

No. 3F13260 Taper Sealing Wax. Has a wax taper running through the center from end. By using this wax there wil wasted wax or burnt fingers. Light e same as you would a candle. Length of 4 inches. Price, 2 sticks for.......... 1
If by mail, postage extra, 3 cents.

Initial Seal Letters.

No. 3F13265 Init. Seal, for use with sealing wax; length, 3 inches; black enamel handle, nickeled metal die, with Old English initial letter. In ordering be sure and mention initial letter desired. Price.......... **9c**
If by mail, postage extra, each 3 cents.

ENVELOPES.

	PRICE, PER BOX OF 100	250	500	1,000
No. 3F13095 Manila (buff color) Envelopes, No. 5, XXX stock; size, 3 1-16x5½ inches; high cut; made from best jute stock. Weight, per box (500 in box), 3 pounds.	....	$0.15	$0.27	0.50
No. 3F13100 Manila (buff color) Envelopes, No. 6, XXX stock; high cut; made from best jute stock; size, 3⅝x6 inches. Weight, per box (500 in box), 60 ounces.	....	.16	.28	.54
No. 3F13105 White Envelopes, special grade, manufactured expressly for us; No. 5; size, 3 1-16x5½ inches; XXX stock. Weight, per box (250 in box), 32 ounces.	....	.19	.36	.68
No. 3F13110 White Envelopes, same quality as No. 3F5086, but No. 6; size, 3⅝x6 inches; XXX stock. Weight, per box (250 in box), 35 ounces.	....	.22	.41	.78
No. 3F13115 Duplex Envelopes, white outside, blue inside; writing cannot show through; No. 5, XX stock, extra quality, high cut; size, 3 1-16x5½ inches. Weight, per box (250 in box), 32 ounces.	....	.25	.48	.92
No. 3F13120 Duplex Envelopes, white outside, blue inside; writing cannot show through; No. 6, XX stock, high cut, superior quality; size, 3⅝x6 inches. Weight, per box (250 in box), 37 ounces.	....	.28	.54	1.03
No. 3F13125 White Wove Envelopes, extra quality, high cut, No. 5, XX stock; size, 3 1-16x5½ inches. Weight, per box (250 in box), 33 ounces.	....	.17	.32	.61
No. 3F13130 White Wove Envelopes, No. 6, XX stock, high cut, good quality; size, 3⅝x6 inches. Weight, per box (500 in box), 66 ounces.	....	.27	.51	.97
No. 3F13135 Cream Wove Envelopes, No. 5, XXX stock, superior quality, commercial high cut; size, 3 1-16x5½ inches. Weight, per box (500 in box), 5 pounds.	....	.26	.49	.93
No. 3F13140 Cream Wove Envelopes, No. 6½, XXX stock, superior quality, commercial high cut; size, 3⅝x6½ inches. Weight, per box (500 in box), 5¾ pounds.	$0.15	.35	.66	1.26
No. 3F13145 Cream Wove Envelopes, baronial high cut, No. 5; size, 4⅛x5⅛ inches; XXXX stock. Weight, packed, per box (250 in box), 30 ounces.	.16	.36	.69	1.32
No. 3F13150 Cream Wove Envelopes, baronial, high cut, No. 4; size, 3⅝x4⅝ inches; XXXX superior stock. This envelope is suitable for general purposes, especially for ladies' correspondence. Weight, packed, per box (250 in box), 34 ounces.	.17	.40	.77	1.47
No. 3F13155 White Bond Envelopes, high cut, No. 6; size, 3⅝x6 inches: XXX extra stock. A good envelope for all purposes, especially invitations, etc. Weight, packed, per box (250 in box), 44 ounces.	.12	.27	.52	1.00
No. 3F13160 Linen Envelopes, high cut, No. 5; size, 4⅛x5⅛ inches; XXX stock, genuine linen envelopes, suitable for commercial and general use. Weight, packed, per box (250 in box), 33 ounces.	.15	.35	.67	1.27
No. 3F13165 Marlborough style, safety seal, wedding flap, high class envelopes for general correspondence, especially for weddings, invitations, parties, etc. No. 6¼; size, 3½x6 inches; XXX superior stock. Weight, packed, per box (250 in box), 33 ounces.	.18	.42	.81	1.55
No. 3F13170 White Wove Official Envelopes, No. 10, best grade paper; size, 4⅛x9½ inches; XX stock, commercial, high cut. Weight, per box (500 in box), 3 pounds.	.26	.60	1.16	2.21
No. 3F13175 Manila (buff color) Official Envelopes, No. 10; size, 4⅛x9½ inches; XX extra heavy stock, suitable for general commercial purposes. Weight, packed, per box (500 in box), 7½ pounds.	.13	.29	.55	1.06
No. 3F13180 Coin Envelopes, first quality, No. 1, Manila (buff color) paper; size, 2¼x3½ inches. Weight, per box (500 in box), 24 ounces.	....	.16	.30	.58
No. 3F13185 Manila (buff color) Envelopes, drug use, No. 3; size, 2 5-16x3¾ inches. Weight, packed, per box (1,000 in box), 46 ounces.	....	.14	.26	.49
No. 3F13190 Cloth Finish Envelopes, finest quality white paper, wallet flap. No. 5½ size, 3⅛x5½ inches. An excellent envelope for fine correspondence. Weight, per box of 250, 40 ounces.	.19	.45	.86	1.67
No. 3F13195 Cloth Finish Envelopes, best grade white paper, regular flap. No. 6¾ size, 3⅝x6½ inches. Weight, per box of 250, 40 ounces.	.18	.42	.81	1.58

PENCILS.

We do not list every pencil made, but we do offer below the very best pencils, in the respective grades, that are on the market today. These pencils represent the greatest value for the money. It is unprofitable to ship them by mail and we would therefore advise including books and other stationery with your order, to make an express or freight shipment.

No. 3F13470 No. 1040 Dickens Pencil. Round, cedar polish, blind stamp, rubber eraser inserted in end. 7 inches long.
Price, for six dozen, **55c**; per dozen... **10c**
If by mail, postage extra, per dozen, 4 cents.

No. 3F13475 Blaisdell No. 999. Self Sharpening Paper Pencil, polished, rubber tip, finest grade lead. Each pencil may be sharpened 30 times, by detaching end of paper with penknife or any sharp pointed instrument.
Price, per dozen **12c**
If by mail, postage extra, per dozen, 7 cents.

No. 3F13480 The Universal Detachable Rubber Tip Pencil. Hexagon shape, Maroon polish; 7 inches long. An excellent pencil for school children. Price, per dozen, **13c**
If by mail, postage extra, per dozen, 5 cents.

No. 3F13485 Beats All Pencil. Round highly polished maroon finish with gilt stamp nickel tip with inserted rubber eraser. No. 2 lead. An excellent medium priced pencil. Length, 7½ inches. Price, per dozen... **14c**
If by mail, postage extra, per dozen, 5 cents.

No. 3F13490 Herald No. 2 Lead Pencil Fitted with movable patent clasp for holding rubber eraser, rosewood finish, round, gilt stamping. No. 2 and No. 3 lead.
Price, per half dozen **14c**
Per dozen **25c**
If by mail, postage extra, per ½ dozen, 3 cents.

No. 3F13495 Fresco Decorated Pencil. Round, highly polished ebony finish, with delicate leaf design traced on the wood. Has ..t top and rubber eraser. Gilt stamp. 7½ ..s long, No. 2 lead.
..e, per half dozen **12c**
..ozen **22c**
..ail, postage extra, per dozen, 5 cents.

3F13500 Triumph. The cheapest ..gon Pencil on the market. Silk finish, ..ral color, highly polished, stamped in ..r. Nickel tip with rubber eraser. High ..de quality of No. 2 lead. Writes smooth and black. Length, 7½ inches.
Price, per half dozen **14c**
Per dozen **26c**
If by mail, postage extra, per dozen, 5 cents.

No. 3F13505 Eagle Pencil Co. Diagraph No. 817 Pencil, with eraser, incased in nickel plated tip; natural polish, stamped in silver. We especially recommend it for accountants, bookkeepers and correspondents. No. 2 and No. 3 lead.
Price, per half dozen **15c**
Per dozen **28c**
If by mail, postage extra, per dozen, 5 cents.

No. 3F13510 Mecca. Hexagon shaped, highly polished. New style, canary yellow finish, stamped in gilt, gilt metal tip with inserted best quality rubber eraser. 7¼ inches, No. 2 and No. 3 lead.
Price, per half dozen **18c**
Per dozen, special packing **33c**
If by mail, postage extra, per dozen, 6 cents.

No. 3F13515 Black Knight. Round, highly polished, golden rod finish. Stamped in silver. Contains a soft lead of extra large diameter, producing an unusual black effect, and is very easy writing. Excellent for checking, marking, sketching, drafting, outlining and freehand drawing. Length, 7 inches. Price, 3 for **12c**
Per half dozen, **21c**; per dozen **39c**
If by mail, postage extra, per dozen, 5 cents.

No. 3F13520 Velvet Pencil, hexagon shape, walnut glass finish. Superfine polish, stamped in silver, gilt metal top, with band of blue enamel, with finest grade imported red rubber eraser. This is the best domestic pencil made. Price, 3 for **13c**
Per half dozen **24c**
Per dozen, special packing **44c**
If by mail, postage extra, per dozen, 5 cents.

No. 3F13525 Stars and Stripes. A new style pencil, showing the colors emblematic of our national flag. Containing a superior quality of medium grade lead, nickel tip and rubber eraser. One-half gross in box.
Price, per dozen, **26c**; per half dozen, . **15c**
If by mail, postage extra, per dozen, 6 cents.

No. 3F13530 Polka Dot. The polish on this pencil is a reproduction of the fashionable polka dot silk. In assorted colors. 7½ inches long. Gilt stamp, gilt metal tip with red rubber eraser. No. 2 and No. 3 high grade quality of lead.
Price, per half dozen **19c**
Per dozen, special packing, assorted colors **34c**
If by mail, postage extra, per dozen, 6 cents.

No. 3F13535 Jewel Pencil. Round shape, polished in assorted colors, highly finished gilt top in which a jewel is artistically set. Contains best quality No. 3 lead. Length, 7¼ inches.
Price per doz., **39c**; 6 for **22c**; 3 for... **12c**
If by mail, postage extra, for three, 3 cents.

No. 3F13540 Program Pencil. Round, thin, assorted colors, gilt tip and tassels. Suitable for balls, card parties, etc.
Price, per dozen **15c**
If by mail, postage extra, per dozen, 3 cents.

No. 3F13545 Checking Pencil. Only hexagon shaped colored pencil on the market at a moderate price. Extra large diameter, highly polished, colored enamel finish, gilt stamp. 7 inches long. Can furnish either blue, red or red and blue. State color desired.
Price, per half dozen **21c**
Per dozen, special packing, individual box **39c**
If by mail, postage extra, per half dozen, 5c.

No. 3F13550 Rob Roy Slate Pencils, made of cedar, with highly polished Rob Roy finish. Plain stamp, 7 inches long.
Price, per dozen **11c**
If by mail, postage extra, per dozen, 5 cents.

INDELIBLE COPYING INK PENCIL.

No. 3F13555 Madura 79c. It is undoubtedly the best and most durable pencil made in this or the old country. For duplicating, manifolding and all general purposes it is conceded by pencil manufacturers to have no equal. Violet polished, silver stamped, violet ink lead, with enameled mouthpiece. Length, 7 inches.
Price, per dozen, **42c**; per half dozen... **22c**
If by mail, postage extra, per dozen, 6 cents.

MEPHISTO COPYING INK PENCILS.

No. 3F13560 Hardtmuth's Copying Ink Pencil, for duplicating, manifolding and all general purposes; violet polished, silver stamped; violet ink lead. The most perfect copying ink pencil made. Price, per half dozen **21c**
Per gross, **$4.32**; per dozen **40c**
If by mail, postage extra, per dozen, 3 cents.

No. 3F13565 Hardtmuth's Copying Ink Pencil, with enameled mouthpiece, made expressly for trainmen, conductors and travelers; otherwise same as No. 3F13560.
Price, per half dozen **23c**
Per gross, **$4.68**; per dozen **43c**
If by mail, postage extra, per dozen, 4 cents.

No. 3F13570 Hardtmuth's Famous Koh-i-Noor, compressed lead ink copying pencil, yellow polished, gold stamp.
Price, per half dozen **48c**
Per gross, **$10.00**; per dozen **90c**
If by mail, postage extra, per dozen, 4 cents.

Carpenters' Pencils.

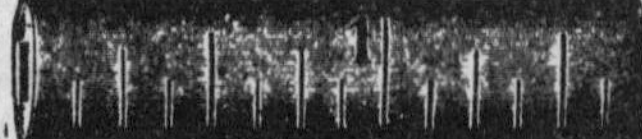

These pencils contain the best grade No. 2 lead, oval polished cedar, with correct rule stamped on reverse side.

No. 3F13575 Carpenters' Pencil, 7 inches long. Price, per half dozen **11c**
Per dozen **20c**
If by mail, postage extra, per dozen, 7 cents.

No. 3F13576 Carpenters' Pencil, 9 inches long. Price, per half dozen **13c**
Per dozen **23c**
If by mail, postage extra, per dozen, 8 cents.

No. 3F13577 Carpenters' Pencil, 12 inches long. Price, per half dozen **16c**
Per dozen **29c**
If by mail, postage extra, per dozen, 10 cents.

Tortoise Shell Carpenters' Pencils.

Octagon Cedar Pencil with tortoise glass finish, gilt stamp, contains best grade of No. 2 black lead. Very handsome and showy pencil.

No. 3F13585 7 inches long.
Price, per dozen, **39c**; per half dozen, **21c**
If by mail, postage extra, per half dozen, 10c.

No. 3F13586 9 inches long.
Price, per dozen, **44c**; per half dozen, **24c**
If by mail, postage extra, per half dozen, 13c.

No. 3F13590 Perpetual Pencil. Highly polished metal, nickel finish. When the lead wears out, pressure on the top gives a new sharp point. Saves time, does away with sharpening. The pencil is filled from the top with sharpened leads.
Price, 2 for **19c**; each **11c**
If by mail, postage extra, 1 cent.

PENHOLDERS.

No. 3F13790 Latest Improved Pen Holder. Swell cedar handle, japanned tip, 6¾ inches long, Price, 2 for **5c**
Per half dozen **13c**
If by mail, postage extra, each, 1 cent.

No. 3F13795 Highly polished swell japanned handle, assorted finishes in natural silk, red or black. Double nickel tip. State color wanted.
Price, per half dozen, **15c**; 2 for **6c**
If by mail, postage extra, each, 1 cent.

No. 3F13800 Cork Tip Tapering Pen holder, medium size, made of cedar in highly polished natural silk finish. Silver stamp. End completely covered with cork.
Price, per half dozen, **20c**; 2 for **8c**
If by mail, postage extra, each, 1 cent.

No. 3F13805 Pneumatic Anti-Nervous Pen Holder. Length, 7 inches. Made of cedar wood, with highly polished olive green finish, silver stamp and has pneumatic rubber tip which yields to the pressure of the hand, thus avoiding cramps in writing. A most agreeable pen holder. Price, 2 for **9c**
Per half dozen **24c**
If by mail, postage extra, each, 1 cent.

No. 3F13810 New Patented Pen Ejecting Pen Holder. Will hold any size pen. Long tapering cedar handle, olive green finish, highly polished, soft fluted green rubber tip, nickel mountings. By sliding the rubber tip back it ejects the pen without soiling the fingers. Price, 2 for **9c**
Per half dozen **24c**
If by mail, postage extra, for two, 3 cents.

Glass Writing Pens.

No. 3F13815 Point made of twisted glass, and is inserted in nickeled barrel. Mounted on ebony finish holder. This is a smooth writer, excellent for where carbon copies are wanted and for marking linen.
Price, per dozen, **48c**; per half dozen, **25c**
If by mail, postage extra, per ½ dozen, 5 cents.

No. 3F13820 Automatic Shading Pens, for engrossing, fancy lettering, card writing, etc. 7¼ inches long. Be sure to state size and number wanted.

Nos.	0	1	2	3
Width	1/16-in.	3/32-in.	1/8-in.	3/16-in.
Nos.	4	5	6	8
Width	5/16-in.	1/4-in.	5/8-in.	3/8-in.

Price, 2 for **18c**
If by mail, postage extra, each, 2 cents.

Ink for Automatic Shading Pens.

No. 3F13825 Shading Pen Ink. Prepared especially for use with automatic shading pens, in wide mouth, round flint 1½-ounce glass bottles. Colors, red, violet, blue, green, black or gold. Be sure to state color. Price, 2 for. **18c**
If by mail, postage and mailing tube extra, 13c.

Book on Pen Lettering and Designs.

No. 3F13830 A Compendium of Automatic Pen Lettering and Designs. For the beginner, teacher and artist. Contains instructions, alphabets, mottoes, display and business cards, beautiful and elaborate designs, monograms, hat and book marks, Christmas and New Year calling cards; also many halftone engravings. Price **85c**
If by mail, postage extra, 8 cents.

No. 3F13833 Myograph. Made from superior spring brass, nickel plated with pen holder and pen attached. Prevents the finger movement and develops the muscular movement in writing. Keeps pen and hand in correct position. Prevents writers' cramp.
Price, per half dozen, **98c**; each **19c**
If by mail, postage extra, each, 3 cents.

No. 3F13835 Combination Pen and Pencil Case and Pencil Lengthener. Made of fancy embossed gilt metal. Is fitted with gilt end tips; one tip when reversed is fitted with lead pencil, and other tip with high grade rubber eraser and steel pen. Length of case, 5 inches.
Price, per half dozen, **48c**; 2 for ... **17c**
If by mail, postage extra, each, 1 cent.

STEEL PENS.

The illustrations show the exact size of pens. We quote a varied line and warrant every pen. Order by number and give quality and price.

Spencerian Steel Pens.

No. 3F14035 Vertical, No. 37M, particularly adapted for schools and correspondents.
Price, per ¼ gross (36 pens) **23c**
Per gross **90c**
If by mail, postage extra, per ¼ gross, 3 cents.

No. 3F14040 Congressional, No. 28, silverine, point blunt and circular, easy quill action, extra long wearing.
Price, per ¼ gross (36 pens) **23c**
Per gross **90c**
If by mail, postage extra, per ¼ gross, 3 cents.

No. 3F14045 College, No. 1. The best pen made; point fine, elastic, action perfect, largely used by the best penmen of this country, Canada and England.
Price, per ¼ gross (36 pens) **20c**
Per gross **72c**
If by mail, postage extra, per ¼ gross, 3 cents.

Esterbrook Steel Pens.

No. 3F14050 Falcon, No. 048. Medium point, gray finish. An excellent pen for general business purposes.
Price, per ¼ gross (36 pens) **15c**
Per gross **55c**
If by mail, postage extra, per ¼ gross, 3 cents.

No. 3F14055 Lady Falcon, No. 182. Fine and easy action. Especially adapted for ladies. Gray finish.
Price, per ¼ gross (36 pens) **15c**
Per gross **55c**
If by mail, postage extra, per ¼ gross, 3 cents.

No. 3F14060 Bank (No. 14), bronze finish, medium point, an excellent and popular pen for business use.
Price, per ¼ gross (36 pens) **15c**
Per gross **55c**
If by mail, postage extra, per ¼ gross, 3 cents.

No. 3F14065 Short Nib Engrossing or Stub (No. 161F), bronze finish, medium fine stub, very popular.
Price, per ¼ gross (36 pens) **19c**
Per gross **72c**
If by mail, postage extra, per ¼ gross, 3 cents

No. 3F14070 Ball Pointed Scribe, No. 516F, gray finish, extra fine point.
Price, per ¼ gross (36 pens) **$0.28**
Per gross **1.05**
If by mail, postage extra, per ¼ gross, 3 cents.

Gillott's Steel Pens.

No. 3F14075 Magnum Quill. (No. 601 E.F.) extra fine point, for fine and ordinary writing, very popular for general use.
Price, per ¼ gross (36 pens) **23c**
Per gross **88c**
If by mail, postage extra, per ¼ gross, 3 cents.

3F14080 Double Elastic (No. 604 EF), extra fine point. The original double elastic pen, a favorite with professors of penmanship and teachers in business colleges.
Price, per ¼ gross (36 pens) **21c**
Per gross **79c**
If by mail, postage extra, per ¼ gross, 3 cents.

No. 3F14085 Diamond Stub, No. 1008F. A very desirable pen for commercial use. Used by bankers and business men.
Price, per ¼ gross (36 pens) **16c**
Per gross **59c**
If by mail, postage extra, per ¼ gross, 3 cents.

No. 3F14090 Gillott's Famous Principality Pen (No. 1), bronze finish, extra fine points, an excellent pen for flourishing and ornamental work.
Price, per ¼ gross (36 pens) **27c**
Per gross **98c**
If by mail, postage extra, per ¼ gross, 3 cents.

Compass and Divider.

No. 3F14290 Eagle Compass and Divider, reliable in its work and useful for school children, mechanics, artists, draftsmen and architects; nickel plated, regulated by spring end screw adjustment, each in neat box, with nickel box containing six extra leads. Price....................18c
If by mail, postage extra, 4 cents.

Pantagraph for Enlarging Purposes.

Full Instructions Accompany Each Outfit.

No. 3F14295 Style A. A simple mechanical apparatus, which, without any instruction, enables one to enlarge portraits, using ordinary cabinet sized pictures. Maps, ornamental designs, music, monograms and patterns can be enlarged or reduced to any size by the use of this instrument. Price....................9c
If by mail, postage extra, 5 cents.

No. 3F14296 Style B. Has very neat and substantial trimmings, clean cut figures. Price, in box....................29c
If by mail, postage extra, 10 cents.

No. 3F14297 Style C. Brass Mounted, with brass elbow joint wheel, pencil holder and movable point. Price, in box....................98c
If by mail, postage extra, 10 cents.

No. 3F14298 Style D. Heavily mounted, with nickel plated elbow joint wheel, pencil holder and exchangeable point. Price, in box....................$1.67
If by mail, postage extra, any style, 12 cents.

The Diamond Handy Pencil Holder.

No. 3F14305 Handy Pencil Holder, leatherette, plush lined, with double joint metal spring and pin back. Can be worn on shirt. Best pencil pocket made. Will hold four pencils. Price....................8c
If by mail, postage extra, 2 cents.

The "Au Fait" Pencil Holder.

No. 3F14310 Latest improved Pencil Holder. Can be attached to pocket, suspenders or trousers band; nickel plated. Has double barrel, which may be adjusted to hold any size lead pencil, penholder or fountain pen. Clamp securely attaches holder to garment. Price, 7c
If by mail, postage extra, each, 2 cents.

Simplex Pencil Sharpener.

No. 3F14315 Simplex Pencil Sharpener. "Do not turn the sharpener but turn the pencil." Made of gilt metal. Has handle, which keeps the fingers clean and the sharpener held securely. The blade is of highly tempered carbonized steel and retains a sharp edge. Price, 2 for 21c; each..12c
If by mail, postage extra, 1 cent.

New Acme Pencil Sharpener.

No. 3F14320 With double edge blade. When one edge becomes dull the blade can be reversed, thus there is an equivalent of two blades with each sharpener. Combines simplicity with perfection. Price....................18c
If by mail, postage extra, 3 cents.

Combination Knife and Pencil Sharpener.

No. 3F14325 Magic Automatic Combination Knife and Pencil Sharpener. The easiest knife in the world to open. The blade is made of high grade steel, and moves out or in when pressure is applied on the opposite end. Highly polished, black handle, gilt stamp. Price....................19c
If by mail, postage extra, 2 cents.

No. 3F14390 Erasit, the great substitute for rubber erasers. Far better than rubber. It will erase pencil marks, dirt, etc., quicker, and neater, and leave the paper cleaner than the best rubber eraser. Will also clean gloves, books, materials, etc.
Price, 3 pieces for....................12c
Per box of one dozen pieces....................42c
If by mail, postage extra, for 3 pieces, 2 cents.

Ink and Pencil Eraser.

No. 3F14395 Combined Ink and Pencil Eraser. Wood center, best quality erasive rubber.
Price, 2 for....................13c
If by mail, postage extra, 5 cents.

New Style Eraser.

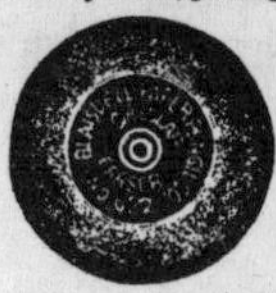

No. 3F14400 New Style Eraser, beveled ends. Contains a superior quality of best erasive rubber.
Price, per ½ dozen....18c; 3 for....................10c
If by mail, postage extra, per dozen, 7 cents.

Circular Eraser.

No. 3F14405 Circular Eraser, for type writer, ink or pencil. The circular eraser is very convenient, giving a sharp, continuous edge for use until worn out.
Price, ½ doz....................16c
If by mail, postage extra, 10 cents.

Rubber Bands.

No. 3F14455 Assortment of superior quality Rubber Bands, for office and home use, packed in a box 1⅝x3½x6½ inches. Weight, 6 ounces. Price, per box....................20c
If by mail, postage extra, per box, 7 cents.

No. 3F14460 Gray Thread Bands of superior quality, made from best elastic rubber stock. We do not sell less than one ounce, packed in a box. When ordering be sure to state whether No. 10, No. 12 or No. 14 is wanted. No. 10, 1½ inches long, 290 bands, one ounce; No. 12, 1⅞ inches long, 225 bands, one ounce; No. 14, 2 inches long, 165 bands, one ounce.
Price, per ounce....................18c

No. 3F14465 Gray Rubber Bands, ⅛-inch wide. No. 000½, 3 inches long, 24 bands, one ounce; No. 0000½, 3½ inches long, 20 bands, one ounce. Price, per ounce, either size....................18c
We do not sell less than one ounce.

No. 3F14470 Gray Rubber Bands, ¼-inch wide. No. 00½, 2½ inches long, 18 bands, one ounce; No. 000½, 3 inches long, 15 bands, one ounce; No. 0000½, 3½ inches long, 12 bands, one ounce. Price, per ounce (either style)....18c

No. 3F14475 Gray Rubber Bands, ⅜-inch wide. No. 000⅜, 3 inches long, 12 bands, one ounce; No. 0000⅜, 3½ inches long, 10 bands, one ounce. Price, per ounce....................16c
Postage extra on all rubber bands, 2c per oz.

SCHOOL CRAYONS

We list the celebrated Crayola School Crayons. The crayons that received the award at the St. Louis exposition. They are permanent, waterproof colors, that are not injurious to the hands, and will not soil the clothes. These crayons can be used on almost any surface, and will make bright, clear, permanent colors.

No. 3F14525 Crayon No. 51B. For coloring maps or pictures, sketches, etc. Contains twenty-eight assorted waterproof crayons, 2½ inches long, in cardboard box.
Price, per box....................8c
If by mail, postage extra, per box, 5 cents.

No. 3F14530 Crayola No. 100. Fourteen assorted waterproof colors. 2½ inches long, each crayon in paper jacket. For coloring maps, pictures and general school work. Price, per box....................5c
If by mail, postage extra, per box, 5 cents.

No. 3F14535 Crayon No. 97. Eight assorted waterproof colors. 4 inches long, in cardboard box, together with a series of outline pictures for drawing and coloring.
Price, per box....................7c
If by mail, postage extra, per box, 5c.

Staonal Marking Crayons.

No. 3F14540 Staonal No. 3. Waterproof. For marking on leather, lumber, tin, barrels, cases, delivery parcels, checking way bills, newspaper and bulletin work, glass, canvas, etc. Length, 4 inches. Made in red, black or blue.
Price, per dozen, 18c; 3 for....................5c
If by mail, postage extra, for 3, any color, 3 cents.

No. 3F14545 Staonal No. 2. Marking Crayon. Waterproof. For marking lumber, paper, tinware, etc. 5 inches long, made in blue, red and black.
Price, per dozen, 27c; 2 for....................5c
If by mail, postage extra, for two, 3 cents.

Le Page's Fish Glue.

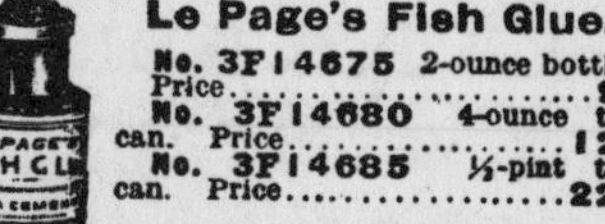

No. 3F14675 2-ounce bottle. Price....................9c
No. 3F14680 4-ounce tin can. Price....................12c
No. 3F14685 ½-pint tin can. Price....................22c

Carter's Mucilage.

No. 3F14690 4-ounce bottles. Price, per bottle....................8c
No. 3F14695 ½-pint bottles. Price, per bottle....................15c
Unmailable on account of weight.

Waterproof Transparent Glue.

No. 3F14699 Waterproof Transparent Glue. The only strictly waterproof glue in the world; neither heat, dampness nor water will affect it. Will mend china, glass, wood, leather, crockery, etc. Ready for use.
Price, per bottle....................12c
Unmailable on account of weight.

INKS.

Carter's Blue Black Ink.

No. 3F14745 Two 2-ounce bottles. Price....................7c
No. 3F14746 Two 4-ounce bottles. Price....................12c
No. 3F14747 ½-pint bottles. Price....................15c
Unmailable on account of weight.

Carter's Red Ink.

No. 3F14755 Two 1¼-ounce bottles. Price....................8c
No. 3F14760 Two 2-ounce bottles. Price....................14c
No. 3F14770 ½-pint bottles....................45c
Unmailable on account of weight.

Carter's Black Ink.

No. 3F14775 Two 2-ounce glass bottles. Price....................7c
No. 3F14780 Two 4-ounce bottles. Price....................12c
No. 3F14785 ½-pint bottles....................18c
Unmailable on account of weight.

Carter's Green Ink.

No. 3F14790 Two 2-ounce bottles..8c
Unmailable on account of weight.

Carter's Fountain Pen Ink.

No. 3F14795 4-ounce bottles, with patent stopper and filler. Price, per bottle, 18c
Unmailable on account of weight.

No. 3F14800 White Ink. Best grade pure white ink for ornamental writing and flourishing. Put up in 1-ounce flint glass bottles. Two 1-ounce bottles....................18c
If by mail, postage extra, per bottle, 11 cents.

No. 3F14805 Japanese Gold Ink, for corresponding, designing, decorating, etc.; a brilliant gold ink which writes fluently with a common steel pen. In ½-ounce bottles.
Price, two bottles....................18c
If by mail, postage extra, per bottle, 11 cents.

No. 3F14810 Chinese Silver Ink, for corresponding, decorating, etc. 1-ounce bottles.
Price, two bottles....................18c
If by mail, postage extra, per bottle, 7 cents.

No. 3F14815 Invisible Ink. An invisible ink, or secret ink, made readable by application of heat to the paper after the ink is dry, disappearing again when it is cold.
Price, two bottles....................18c
If by mail, postage extra, per bottle, 11 cents.

No. 3F14820 Ink Powders. Put up in wooden boxes. Each box contains enough powder to make one pint of good ink; blue, green, purple, red or black. In ordering, be sure to give the color wanted.
Price, 1 set, four boxes assorted colors..23c
If by mail, postage extra, per box, 2 cents.

No. 3F14825 Carter's Indelible Ink for marking linen. Complete with stretcher, pen and penholder and ink.
Price, for complete outfit....................18c
If by mail, postage extra, 5 cents.

Ink Eradicator.

No. 3F14850 Collins' Original Standard Ink Eradicator. For correcting and removing the ink blots from books, letters, etc.; also coffee, fruit, wine, tobacco and rust stains from clothing and other fabrics. Weight, packed for shipment, 10 ounces.
Price....................15c
Unmailable on account of weight.

INKSTANDS.

Common Sense Inkwell.

No. 3F15100 Common Sense Inkwell, for commercial and general use. No evaporation, no spilling of ink. The most practical and useful inkwell made; 2 inches high. Price....................7c
If by mail, postage extra, 12 cents.

No. 3F15105 Common Sense Inkwell, same as No. 3F15100, but with rubber cork in bottom; easier to clean. Price....................10c
If by mail, postage extra, 12 cents.

Automatic Inkwell.

No. 3F15110 Automatic Inkwell. Always ready for use. Automatically inks the pen, leaving all surplus ink, and does not soil the fingers. Moulding and evaporation are impossible. Size, 2½x3 inches. We can furnish with red or black funnel suitable for red or black ink. Makes a handsome desk set. State kind wanted.
Price, each....................24c
Per pair, red and black funnel....................45c
If by mail, postage extra, each, 18 cents.

The Sweesy Automatic Inkstand.

No. 3F15115 The Famous Sweesy Automatic Inkstand. "Liberty Bell" design. Height, 3 inches, diameter at base, 3 inches. Made of pressed glass with a vulcanized rubber automatic top. Is airtight and will save 80 per cent of your ink. Can furnish with red or black funnel. State kind wanted. Regular retail price, 35 cents.
Our price, each....................28c
Per pair, red and black funnel....................52c
If by mail, postage extra, each, 14 cents.

The Royal Automatic Inkstand.

No. 3F15120 New Patent Automatic Inkstand, made of the best extra heavy crystal glass with triple bottom, preventing it from upsetting or breaking. Has patent vulcanized hard rubber top, with either red or black funnel. We recommend this inkstand. It is dustproof, non-evaporating and keeps ink fresh forever. The glass part is decorated at the top and bottom with fine grooved lines. 3¼ inches high. Retails everywhere for 50 cents. Our price....39c
Per pair, red and black funnel....................73c
If by mail, postage extra, each, 14 cents.

Library Inkstands.

No. 3F15125 Enameled Library Inkstand, containing two heavy flint glass bottles, mounted on an all iron rack. Size, 4¾x4 inches.
Price....37c
If by mail, postage extra, 24 cents.

No. 3F15130 Library Inkstand, consisting of two clear cut crystal inkwells, 2½ inches high, with fancy prism tops and one pressed glass, fancy cut design sponge cup or pin bowl, mounted on highly polished oak base 12 inches long and 5½ inches wide, ornamented with carved pen racks. Regular $2.00 value. Our price....................94c
If by mail, postage extra, 56 cents.

Ladies' Aluminum Inkstand.

No. 3F15135 Removable Imitation Cut Glass Inkstand with aluminum top on beautifully embossed aluminum tray, satin silver finish in flower design, 4¼x4¼ inches. A most attractive inkstand. Retail price, 50 cents.
Our price....................21c
If by mail, postage extra, 8 cents.

Fancy Aluminum Inkstand.

No. 3F15140 Fancy Desk Inkstand, made of solid aluminum with a silver finish, in the shape of a crab with elaborate bright cut engraving. Lift up the back of the crab and underneath, in the body, is a glass inkwell. The claws are used for a pen holder. Retail price, $2.00.
Our price....................98c
If by mail, postage extra, 8 cents.

Elk's Head Aluminum Inkstand.

No. 3F15145 Extra Heavy Satin Silver Finish Aluminum Elk's Head Inkstand. Beautifully carved. Inkwell is made of imitation cut glass in fluted design, and surmounted by embossed aluminum top. The inkwell itself sits back of the head on a heavy aluminum base, carved in oak leaf and acorn design. The elk's horns are the penholders, and are of extra heavy silver finished aluminum, with six prongs each, and stretch back over the ink well. Price....................$1.50
If by mail, postage extra, 28 cents.

Paper Weights.

No. 3F15150 Crystal Glass Paper Weight with round oval top. Three inches in diameter, with a recess in the bottom in which may be mounted photographs, pictures, etc.
Price, 3 for....................22c

No. 3F15155 Crystal Glass Paper Weight, oblong, flat top. Size, 3½x4 inches, with recess in the bottom in which may be mounted photographs, pictures, etc. Price, 3 for.....24c
If by mail, postage extra, either style, each, 4c.

Photo Fan.

No. 3F15300 Photo Fan, made of the finest mat board, decorated with silk ribbon and artistically finished throughout. Will hold five photographs. Size of fan when open, 22x12 inches.
Price....19c
If by mail, postage extra, 5 cents.

No. 3F15305 Tray for desk or table, 4½ inches in diameter. Made of crystal glass with picture under it. The back is covered with red felt. For pins, ashes, stamps, etc. Price....................18c
If by mail, postage extra, 7 cents.

FOUNTAIN PENS.

We guarantee our Fountain Pens as follows: First; that the pen is solid 14 karat gold, tipped with iridium, and the exact size stated in the description. Second; that the holder and cap is made of the best India rubber, vulcanized and non-corrosive. Third; that our pens will not leak. Leakage is due to inferior workmanship and every one of our pens is tested before delivery, and not an imperfect pen is allowed to leave our establishment.

This $3.50 Pen for 98 cents.

No. 3F15355 Our Leader Fountain Pen, the greatest value ever offered for the money. Extra large, hand chased barrel and cap of the best quality hard rubber, fitted with large 14 karat gold pen, and a newly patented under feed. The workmanship is absolutely perfect and we guarantee it to be non-leakable. State whether you desire pointed, medium or stub pen. Price....98c

If by mail, postage extra, 5 cents.

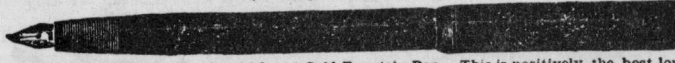

No. 3F15360 Eureka, 14 karat Gold Fountain Pen. This is positively the best low priced fountain pen. Hard rubber barrel of good quality and finish, 14 karat gold pen, ribbed section, under feed. Smooth and easy writer. Packed complete in cardboard case with filler and directions. State whether you desire pointed, medium or stub pen. Price....58c

If by mail, postage extra, 5 cents.

No. 3F15365 The Elite. A high grade Fountain Pen, fitted with 14 karat No. 3 gold pen; has chased case, under feed. Usually retails for $2.50. Packed one pen in a cardboard case with filler and directions. State whether you want pointed, medium or stub pen. Price....89c

If by mail, postage extra, 5 cents.

Perfection Fountain Pens.

Absolutely perfect. These pens cost more to make than any other pen sold. All this cost goes into the material and the workmanship, and not into ornamentation. The barrels are hand made. This insures perfect proportions. Of the finest grade vulcanized hard rubber. The gold pens are solid 14 karat gold, extra heavy and extra long, under feed, and the construction and interior mechanism of the highest order. The best fountain pen made regardless of price. State whether you want pointed, medium or stub pen.

No. 3F15370 Fitted with No. 3 (as large as other manufacturers' No. 4) 14 karat gold pen. Price....$1.05

No. 3F15371 Fitted with No. 4 (as large as other manufacturers' No. 5) 14 karat gold pen. Price....$1.25

No. 3F15372 Fitted with No. 5 (as large as other manufacturers' No. 6) 14 karat gold pen. Price....$1.50

No. 3F15373 Fitted with No. 6 (the largest 14 karat gold pen made.) Price....$1.90

If by mail, postage extra, each, 5 cents.

The Peerless Gold Mounted Fountain Pens.

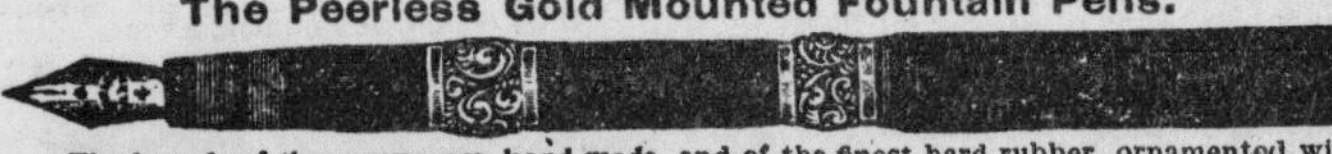

The barrels of these pens are hand made, and of the finest hard rubber, ornamented with two gold bands. Has patent under feed and is fitted with 14 karat extra large gold pen. State whether you desire pointed, medium or stub pen.

No. 3F15380 Fitted with No. 2 14 karat gold pen. Price....$1.15
No. 3F15381 Fitted with No. 3 14 karat gold pen. Price....1.50
No. 3F15382 Fitted with No. 4 14 karat gold pen. Price....1.98

If by mail, postage extra, each, 5 cents.

Gentlemen's Fancy Fountain Pen.

Makes a beautiful gift for anyone, but especially suited for gentlemen. This pen has a hand made hard rubber case. Handsomely decorated with two broad gold bands and a 1¼-inch swell oriental pearl post. Fitted with No. 3 14 karat gold pen and self feed. These pens usually sell for $7.50. State whether you desire pointed, medium or stub pen.

No. 3F15390 Price....$3.25

If by mail, postage extra, 5 cents.

No. 3F15395 Correspondents' Non-Leakable Fountain Pen, fitted with a 14 karat gold pen, and chased hard rubber barrel. Guaranteed non-leakable. Made with under feed, and patented detachable reservoir, which unscrews from the bottom, making the pen easy to fill, and absolutely non-leakable. State whether you desire pointed, medium or stub pen. Price....$1.10

No. 3F15396 Same as No. 3F15395, but handsomely ornamented with two heavy gold bands. State whether you desire pointed, medium or stub pen. Price....$1.50

If by mail, postage extra, each, 5 cents.

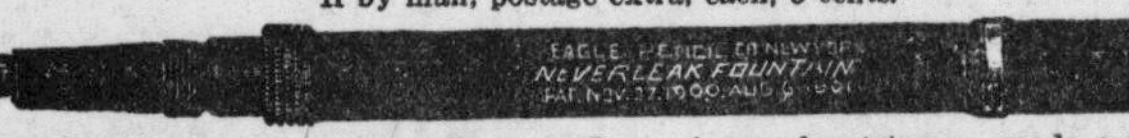

No. 3F15400 Never Leak Fountain Pen. A new fountain pen, made expressly for ladies. It can be carried with safety in pocket book, shopping bag or pocket. Guaranteed non-leakable. Fitted with No. 2 14 karat solid gold medium point pen. Packed complete in cardboard case, with filler and directions. Price....79c

If by mail, postage extra, 5 cents.

No. 3F15405 Ladies' Fancy Gold Fountain Pen. Makes a superb present. Hand made barrel of finest hard rubber, decorated with superbly embossed gold case, 3 inches long. Fitted with No. 3 14 karat gold pen. Hand feed. Regular price, $8.00; our price....$4.50

If by mail, postage extra, 5 cents.

Excelsior Self Filling Fountain Pen, 98 Cents.

No. 3F15410 A High Grade Self Filling Fountain Pen, at one-half the lowest pric ever made by any dealer. The barrel is extra large and made of the best quality hard rubber, fitted with No. 2 14 karat gold pen with self feed. The simplest self filling pen made. There is no better self filling pen made at any price. Price....98c

If by mail, postage extra, 5 cents.

Nosac Self Filling Fountain Pen.

Nosac, the pen of merit. No inside rubber sac to rot or take up room that could be used for ink. It is in this respect that we claim superiority for the "Nosac" over any other self filling fountain pen using the rubber sac. The life of a rubber sac at the best is not over one year. This pen fills itself by a very simple patent device. Holds 70 drops of ink; other self filling fountain pens hold only 40 drops.

No. 3F15415 Fitted with No. 1 solid gold pen....$2.00
No. 3F15420 Same as above, but fitted with No. 2 gold pen....2.50
No. 3F15425 Same as above, but fitted with No. 3 gold pen....3.00

If by mail, postage extra, each, 5 cents.

State whether you desire pointed, medium or stub pen.

Self Filling Fountain Pen.

No. 3F15430 "Flash" Self Filling Fountain Pen fills and cleans itself. Does away entirely with the old fashioned fountain pen dropper. Any child can fill it, as there is no intricate mechanism, no dropper, no smearing of fingers and desk, no overflowing, and no taking apart to clean. Extra heavy 14 karat No. 2 solid gold pen, iridium point. Regular length. Retail price, $2.50; our price....$1.45

If by mail, postage extra, 5 cents.

Stylographic Pens.

No. 3F15435 Stylographic Fountain Pen. Made of vulcanized hard rubber, tapering to a round point, platinum tip with flow regulated by a steel needle. This is the best and most practical pen made for carbon copy work and addressing. Will make impression through three carbons. Does not leak or blot. Each packed in a separate box with glass filler and directions.

Price, per dozen, $5.50; each....48c

If by mail, postage extra, each, 5 cents.

The "Always Ready" Stylographic Fountain Pen.

No. 3F15440 A Stylographic Pen, with one year's supply of indelible ink. This sack that produces the ink is in the barrel. The pen needs to be filled with water only to produce the best non-erasable ink possible.

Price, per dozen $11.40; each....$1.00

If by mail, postage extra, each, 5 cents.

Typewriter Supplies.

No. 3F15865 Typewriter Ink. Colors, black, blue, green, purple or red. Be sure to state color wanted. Put up in ¼-ounce bottles.

Price, per bottle....10c

If by mail, postage extra, including wooden case, 8 cents.

No. 3F15870 Standard High Grade Typewriter Ribbons, for the Crandall, Draper, Chicago, Smith Premier, Oliver, Caligraph, Hammond, Remington and any other standard machine. When ordering be sure to state whether blue, green, black or copying ribbon is wanted; also give name of machine.

Price, each....28c

If by mail, postage extra, each, 4 cents.

No. 3F15875 Typewriter Oil. ¼-ounce bottle. Price, per bottle....7c

If by mail, postage extra, 10 cents.

No. 3F15880 Typewriter Cleaning Brush. Price....8c

If by mail, postage extra, 3 cents.

Typewriter Paper.

Matchless Brand for all standard typewriters. 500 sheets to a ream.

No. 3F15885 Size, 8½ x 11 inches. Plain white paper.
Price, per ream, 45c; per ½ ream....24c

No. 3F15886 Size, 8½ x 13 inches. Plain white paper.
Price, per ream, 58c; per ½ ream....30c

No. 3F15890 Size, 8½ x 11 inches. Linen laid extra paper.
Price, per ream, 73c; per ¼ ream....20c

No. 3F15891 Size, 8½ x 13 inches. Linen laid extra paper.
Price, per ream, 89c; per ¼ ream....23c

Typewriter paper unmailable on account of weight.

No. 3F15895 Typewriter Carbon Paper. Blue, black or purple. For manifold work and copying purposes, put up in neat mailable packages containing 3 sheets. Size, 8½x10 or 8½x13 inches. Mention size and color when ordering.

Price, per package, either size....10c

If by mail, postage extra, per package, 2 cents.

No. 3F15900 Stenographers' Note Book. Good quality ruled pencil paper. Size, 6x8½ inches. 150 pages. Price, 3 for....12c

If by mail, postage extra, for 3 tablets, 6c.

No. 3F15905 Duplicator for making copies from pen or typewritten originals. Copies are exactly the same as original and 100 or more clear impressions can be made in 20 minutes. The beauty of this duplicator is that it does not require the complicated means of removing the ink from the surface, as all other duplicators do. About two hours after the original has been transferred to the surface of this duplicator, the ink will entirely disappear, and it is again ready for use. It is so simple that a child can operate it. Invaluable for making circulars, examination papers, bills of fare, postal cards and other notices. Size of copying surface, 9x14 inches.

Price, complete with bottle of purple copying ink, sponge and full instructions..$1.98

Weight, packed for shipment, 4 pounds.

LEATHER WRITING COMPANIONS.

No. 3F15940 Electric Grained Case with button lock, padded cover, gusseted pocket inside of flap, contains three compartments, one for pens, stamps, etc., one containing a glass ink well, with screw cap, and a large compartment for letters. Size, 2x6¼x10½ inches. Price....78c

If by mail, postage extra, 20 cents.

No. 3F15945 Brown Alligator Grained Writing Companion, strap with button lock. Three compartments, gusseted pockets, covered pen box, patent nickel top spring catch ink well. Compartment for writing paper, blotter, etc. Size, 8x12 inches, 2 inches high. Price....$1.38

If by mail, postage extra, 25 cents.

No. 3F15950 Black Seal Leather Case, strapped with button lock. Gusseted pocket, covered pen box, embossed gun-metal top, spring catch ink well and compartment for stationery and blotter. On the underside, the blotting pad is provided with loops and a set of ebony handle fittings, consisting of polished steel eraser, paper cutter, penholder and pen, lead pencil and a celluloid stamp book and calendar. Size, 8x12, inches, 1¾ inches high. Price $1.98

If by mail, postage extra, 25 cents.

No. 3F15955 Real Red Russian Leather Writing Companion. Made of the finest grade of real red leather, beautifully grained. Flap with button lock. Three compartments, gusseted pockets of moire silk, leather covered pen box, compartment for stationery, blotter with real leather corners and nickel top spring catch ink well. Price....$2.35

If by mail, postage extra, 25 cents.

No. 3F15960 Desk Box. Made of colored linen cloth, ornamented with white stamping, and has a locked compartment with tray for stamps, cash, etc. On one side of the compartment is a perforated tablet for memoranda, with a cloth cover, and on the other side are three cloth bound note books. Price....73c

If by mail, postage extra, 14 cents.

RUBBER TYPE OUTFIT.

This picture illustrates the style in which all our type is packed. Each outfit put up in substantial box, ready for mailing, and holding the contents in steady position. Type will not become loose or scattered in transit. The rubber used in our type is extra quality hard rubber and will last a lifetime. Each sample of type shown is the exact size and style of type in the outfit.

No. 3F16100 2A3a font of Type, solid rubber, containing 150 pieces, consisting of large and small letters, figures, fancy stars, signs, punctuation marks, etc., two-line holder 3 inches long and pad, and tweezers. Price....37c

AAaaaBBbbbCCcccDDddd12

If by mail, postage extra, 10 cents.

AAAAAaaaaaaB3

No. 3F16105 5A6a font of Solid Rubber Type, containing 285 pieces, consisting of large and small letters, three sets of figures, fancy designs, punctuation marks, and following words: "For sale," "By," "From;" a four-line holder 3 inches long, self inking pad and metal tweezers. Price....83c

If by mail, postage extra, 15 cents.

AAAAAaaaaaaBBBB

No. 3F16110 5A6a font of Solid Rubber Type, containing 285 pieces, four sets of figures, two large and two small, punctuation marks, dollar and percentage signs, stars and brackets for fancy work, tweezers, improved self inking pad and type holder for setting up four lines of matter. In addition this outfit contains the following sign words and sentences: "&," "and," "For Sale," "From," "Return in 10 days to," pad and holder. Price....68c

If by mail, postage extra, 20 cents.

AAaaaBBbbbCCcccDD12

No. 3F16115 Success Rubber Type Outfit, 2A3a; contains 102 pieces consisting of two sets of figures, bottle of indelible ink, one-line holder and ink pad, tweezers, quads, etc. Price.........................(If by mail, postage extra, 5 cents)..........35c

AAaaaBBbbbCCcccDDddd12

No. 3F16120 Special Printing Card Outfit, 2A3a font, containing 150 pieces, two-line holder and pad, is especially convenient for printing calling cards, stationery, etc. Price..........35c
If by mail, postage extra, 10 cents.

AAaaaBbCcDdEe12345

No. 3F16125 2A3a font of Script Type, as shown in illustration; solid rubber, containing complete alphabets, small and capital letters, two sets of figures, with punctuation marks, etc.; also holder and pad. Price..........93c
If by mail, postage extra, 10 cents.

AAaaaBBbbbCCcccDDdddE

No. 3F16130 Linen Marker's Rubber Type Outfit, 2A3a font; contains large and small letters of Old English type, punctuation marks, type for fancy work, pad, one-line holder and pair of tweezers. Price..........38c
If by mail, postage extra, 10 cents.

Extra Holders for Rubber Type Outfits.

No. 3F16135 Single-Line Holders. Price..........11c
No. 3F16136 Two-Line Holders. Price..........13c
No. 3F16137 Four-Line Holders. Price..........15c
If by mail, postage extra, each, 5 cents.

Harvard Printer.

No. 3F11680 Contains 5 alphabets, 3 sets of figures, punctuation marks, etc., for marking books, linen, printing name cards, etc., consisting of three sets of alphabets, two sets of figures, ornaments, three-line holder, ink pad and tweezers. Price..........18c
If by mail, postage extra, 5 cents.

Boys' Printing Outfit.

No. 3F16185 Contains 120 rubber letters, including 3 alphabets, figures, etc., ink pad, bottle of ink, one-line holder and tweezers. This is one of the most complete boys' printing outfits made. Can be used in printing invitation cards, etc. Price..........20c
If by mail, postage extra, 10 cents.

Excelsior Stamping Outfit.

No. 3F16190 Excelsior Indelible Linen Stamping Outfit. Complete with one-line hand stamp (your own name), felt pad, brush and ¼-ounce tube of indelible ink; can be applied to linens, etc. Price..........15c
If by mail, postage extra, 5 cents.

Sign Marking Outfits.

No. 3F16225 Sign Marker. Contains one set of capitals ¾-inch high and one set of figures ¾-inch high; also ½, ¼, $ and c marks; punctuation marks. Ink pad and ruler. Packed neat, attractive box. Price..........25c
If by mail, postage extra, 10 cents.

No. 3F16230 Speedy Sign Marking Outfit, for making display signs of all kinds. Complete set of rubber stamps, 1 inch high, consisting of the alphabet, figures including ¼, ½, ¾, $, and c marks, punctuation points, a bottle of indelible ink, index hand, self inking pad and gauge. Weight, packed for shipment, 2½ pounds. Price, for complete outfit..........58c

No. 3F16235 Rapid Sign Marking Outfit, for making display signs of all kinds. Contains two complete sets of the alphabet, capital letters ⅞ inch high, small letters, ½ inch high, figures from 1 to 0, including ¼, ½ and ¾, $ and c marks. Also the words For, Per, Reduced to, Each, Only; four ornaments, two fists, tube of indelible ink, one ink pad; also one patented gauge and one 14-inch ruler. Put up in a solid wooden case. Weight, packed for shipment, 5 pounds. Retail price, $3.00. Our price..........$1.20

Circus Rubber Stamps.

Hours of Amusement.

Make your own circus, each figure is mounted on an individual block; each character in outline, thus making a perfect impression.

No. 3F16245 Circus Outfit, consisting of ten pieces, animals, clowns, cages, horses, etc., with ink and pad. Price..........22c
If by mail, postage extra, 7 cents.

No. 3F16246 Circus Outfit, consisting of seventeen pieces: animals, clowns, dancers, etc., with ink and pad. Price..........38c
If by mail, postage extra, 12 cents.

No. 3F16247 Large Circus Outfit, consisting of thirty-five pieces, including elephants, band wagons, dancers, clowns, etc., with ink and pad. Price..........75c
If by mail, postage extra, 17 cents.

Fancy Initial Letters.

No. 3F16250 Fancy Initial; rubber, mounted on wood. Any letter, for marking linen, stationery, books, etc. Complete with indelible ink, and a tube of bronze ready for use. Be sure to mention letter desired. Price..........10c
If by mail, postage extra, 5 cents.

Two-Letter Monograms.

No. 3F16260 Any combination of two letters made into a monogram, like illustration, to be used for stamping note paper, envelopes, books, linen, music, etc. Mounted. Complete with ink pad ready for use. When ordering be sure to mention letters wanted. Made to order. Takes 1 to 3 days. Price..........15c
If by mail, postage extra, 5 cents.

Three-Letter Monograms.

No. 3F16265 Three-Letter Monogram, like illustration. Can be used for marking linen, stamping stationery, books, music, etc. The complete outfit, including ink pad, with ink (any color). Made to order. Takes 1 to 3 days. Price..........23c
When ordering be sure to give initials.
If by mail, postage extra, 3 cents.

Hand Stamps.

No. 3F16280 Hand Stamp, with your name, business or home address, town and state; for stamping envelopes, letter and bill heads, advertising matter, etc. On wood mount, polished base and handle. Lines not to exceed 3 inches in length. In ordering state clearly what wording is wanted on stamp. Made to order. Takes 3 to 5 days.
Price, one line..10c
Price, for each additional line, extra..10c
Two-line stamp costs..........20c
A three-line stamp costs..........30c
If by mail, postage extra, per stamp, 3 cents.
No. 3F16281 Same style as No. 3F16280, but on cushion mount. Price, one line..12c
Price, for each additional line, extra..12c
If by mail, postage extra, per stamp, 3 cents.

Automatic Self Inking Rubber Stamps.

Always ready for immediate use. With your name and address, town or state. Be sure to give your name and address clearly and distinctly to avoid error in spelling. Made to order. Takes 3 to 5 days.

No. 3F16290 Will print 1⅜x½ inches. Price, two lines only..45c
No. 3F16291 Will print 1⅞x½ inches. Price, two lines only..55c
No. 3F16292 Will print 2x11-16 inches. Price, two lines only..65c
No. 3F16293 Will print 2 7-16x13-16 inches. Price, three to six lines only..80c
If by mail, postage on above, extra, each, 5c.
No. 3F16294 Will print 2¼x1 inches. Price, three to six lines only..90c
If by mail, postage extra, 7 cents.
No. 3F16295 Will print 2¼x17-16 inches. Price, three to six lines only...$1.20
If by mail, postage extra, 10 cents.

Adjustable Dater.

No. 3F16320 Combination Changeable Dater and Name Stamp, with sufficient space on face of dater for two lines: your own wording. Consisting of a pad, one box of changeable type, containing figures from 1 to 31, days, months and years. Tweezers and stamp. Made to order. Takes 3 to 5 days. Price..........55c
If by mail, postage extra, 11 cents.

Automatic Pen and Pencil Pocket Stamp.

With Your Name and Address for 18 Cents.

18c

No. 3F16330 Self Inking Pocket Stamp. Made of polished metal. Length, 4½ inches. Is neat and strong. Each stamp contains lead pencil and pen on one end, and your name and address on the other (two lines only). Made to order. Takes 3 to 5 days. Price..........18c
If by mail, postage extra, 4 cents.

Handy Pocket Self Inking Name Stamp.

18c

No. 3F16335 New Vest Pocket Stamp. Made expressly for stamping letter heads, postal cards, envelopes, linen, etc. The name is mounted on cushion rubber, encased in metal case, highly polished. (Two lines only.) Made to order. Takes 3 to 5 days. Price..........18c
If by mail, postage extra, 5 cents.
When ordering No. 3F16330 or No. 3F16335 be sure to write your name and address clearly and distinctly to avoid error in spelling.

Excelsior Self Inking Pads.

Each size comes in the following colors: red, blue, green, violet, black. Mention color when ordering.

No. 3F16350 Little Gem. Size, 1½x2⅞ inches. Price 7c
No. 3F16351 Jumbo. Size, 2x3¾ inches. Price..........9c
No. 3F16352 No. 1. Size, 2¾x4½ inches. Price..........13c
No. 3F16353 No. 2. Size, 3¼x6¼ inches. Price..........17c
If by mail, postage extra, each, 5 cents.

Ink for Rubber Stamps and Pads.

Permanent colors, red, blue, green, violet and black.

No. 3F16365 Half-ounce bottle. Price..........8c
No. 3F16366 One-ounce bottle. Price..........12c
When ordering, be sure to specify color wanted.
If by mail, postage extra, each, 7 cents, including mail tube.

Notary Public Seals.

No. 3F16400 Official Seal. Weight, 2¼ pounds, diameter of seal 1⅝ inches. Made with any lettering, but without design. Price..........$1.25
No. 3F16402 Official Seal. Same as No. 3F16400, but larger; weight, 3½ pounds; diameter of seal, 1¾ inches. Price..........$1.40
No. 3F16404 Official Seal. Weight, 2¼ pounds; diameter of seal, 1⅝ inches. Made with any lettering and any stock emblematic design such as used by secret societies, lodges and other regular organizations. Price, $2.45
No. 3F16406 Official Seal. Same as No. 3F16404, but larger; weight, 3½ pounds; diameter of seal, 1¾ inches. Price..........$2.60
No. 3F16408 Official Seals. Weights, 2¼ or 3½ pounds; diameter, 1⅝ or 1⅞ inches, with any special design made to order at less than half other makers' prices. Send exact design and we will quote price.

Convenient Dater, only 15c.

No. 3F16425 A metal holder, provided with revolving rubber type and figures so arranged that by its use it is an easy matter to stamp the date on all bills and letters. In addition to the names of the months and the figures corresponding to the days of the month, and the years from 1905 to 1911, the dater contains the following words: Rec'd, Ans'd, Paid. Price..........15c
If by mail, postage extra, 3 cents.

The New Practical Typewriter, $3.48.

No. 3F16635 A Strong, Handsome Steel Nickel Plated Typewriter, suitable for business and private use. Is easily and quickly operated without previous instructions, and the simplicity of the machine is such that it is rarely out of order.

A Typewriter Strongly Made of Steel and Iron, capable of a speed of 30 words per minute, and as practical as the name implies for the man with a limited correspondence. It has a key for each letter, writing in sight, automatic inking device, automatic letter spacer, a complete paper carriage for paper or cards up to 8½ inches wide, and for any length of sheet, paper feed rollers with line spacing ratchet, a paper guard with cam attachment to automatically grip or release the paper, so that the paper may be released or adjusted to any point as desired or rolled from the beginning, line by line with the line spacing ratchet.

The New Practical No. 3 has capacity and strength in the most compact form, with a directness and ease of action, making it equally serviceable in the business offices, at home, or in traveling. Price..........$3.48
Weight, packed for shipment, 5 pounds.

The Little Gem Typewriter for 65 Cents.

65c

No. 3F16630 A practical machine for the household, and a kindergarten instructor of merit. Simple of operation, adjustable to single or double spacing, easily inked, and may be used to write on a book, package or any other object as well as ordinary typewriter paper. Price..........65c
If by mail, postage extra, 12 cents.

Gem Postal Scale.

No. 3F16745 Made of best cold rolled steel. Finished in black enamel, hand striped, oxidized copper lacquer. Guaranteed correct. It registers by half ounces, and shows the exact cost in cents on all classes of mail matter. Weighs up to 1 pound. The most useful and best scale of its kind made. 4½ inches high, 3 inches wide, 4½ inches long. Weight, packed for shipment, 10 ounces.
Price, per dozen, $7.75; each..........70c
If by mail, postage extra, each, 10 cents.

Ideal Postal Scale.

No. 3F16750 Same as No. 3F16745, but weighs up to 2 pounds, is 6 inches high, 4 inches wide, 6½ inches long. Weight, packed for shipment, 22 ounces. Price..98c
If by mail, postage extra, 22 cents.

Perfection Adding Machine.

No. 3F16780 A practical article, beautifully and substantially made of nickel, for adding figures. It will add figures, proving your trial balance, while you can carry on a conversation at the same time. It will enable experts to add more rapidly and with the certainty of getting the correct results at the first computation. It makes experts of those who could never have mastered ordinary addition. Price..........48c
If by mail, postage extra, 5 cents.

The Adder.

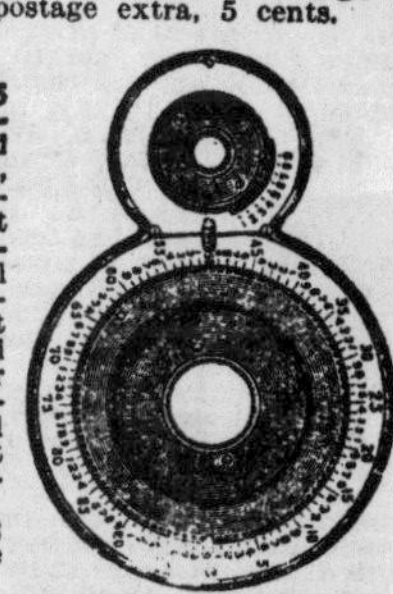

No. 3F16785 A thoroughly practical, simple and durable instrument, beautifully finished in nickel. It is mechanically perfect, made of metal throughout, indestructible, will last a lifetime. It will add any number of columns of figures, one, two and three columns at a time, with positive accuracy.
Price..........$2.68
If by mail, postage extra, 18 cents.

The B. & S. Calculator.

Always in Your Reach, but Never in Your Way.

A perfect and complete adding machine; adds and subtracts mechanically. You take it right to your work. Fits your pocket or pigeon hole. Has seven dials. Cannot get out of adjustment. Cannot make a mistake. Will perform any mathematical problem. Light, simple, handy, practical, durable. Built for hard use and long service. In taking off a trial balance, footing sales, checks, ledger accounts, deposit slips, etc., with a little care, it absolutely avoids mistakes and saves one-half the time. Retail price, $10.00
No. 3F16790 Our price..........$5.00
If by mail, postage extra, 14 cents.

Crepe Paper.

No. 3F16900 Put up in 10-foot rolls, 20 inches wide. Assorted colors. When ordering, be sure to mention color wanted.

American Beauty	Emerald Green
Black	Gold
Blue, dark	Grass Green
Blush Pink, dark	Heliotrope
Blush Pink, light	Moss Green
Canary	Nile Green
Celestial Blue	Purple
Cerise	Ruby Red
Coral, dark	Virgin White

Price, two rolls for..........14c
Six rolls for..........38c
If by mail, postage extra, per roll, 5 cents.
FREE—With a purchase of 12 rolls, we will include free of charge, a complete book on the art and decoration in crepe paper.

Lamp Shade Frames.

No. 3F16920 Wire Frames for use in making crepe paper lamp shades. 14 to 18 inches across. Shipping weight, 28 ounces. Price, 2 for... **18c**
If by mail, postage extra, for two, 12 cents.

No. 3F16925 Tissue Paper and Flower Material. An outfit containing crepe paper, tissue paper, assorted colors, leaves, buds, petals, rubber stems, etc., and a book of instructions for making all styles of shades and decorative articles, etc.
Price, 2 outfits for........ **25c**
If by mail, postage extra, 15 cents.

Crepe Paper Doll Outfit.

No. 3F16930 An outfit containing assorted tissue paper, crepe paper, jointed dolls, trimmings, etc. Also a book of instructions. For children or adults it is entertaining and instructive. Put up in boxes, fancy cover. Size, 8x14 inches. Price............. **18c**
If by mail, postage extra, 5 cents.

Paper Napkins.

No. 3F16950 Paper Napkins. Printed in two colors (new patterns). The finest white silk tissue paper, guaranteed fast colors, assorted, ten patterns to a thousand. We do not sell less than 100 of a pattern. Size, 14x14 inches. Price, per 500.............. **27c**
If by mail, postage extra, per 100, 10 cents.

No. 3F16955 Japanese Crepe Paper Napkins. A good quality soft napkin. Size, 14x14 inches. Price, per 100........... **15c**
Price, per 500............ **72c**
If by mail, postage extra, per 100, 14 cents.

Crepe Paper Lunch Sets.

No. 3F16960 A new and novel idea. Put up in boxes 8x14 inches, each box containing decorated crepe paper table cloth, 3x6 feet, 12 crepe paper napkins and 12 doilies. For picnics, socials or home luncheons, it is just the thing. Price, per set.......... **18c**
2 sets for.............. **34c**
If by mail, postage extra, 5 cents.

Fancy Shelf Paper.

No. 3F16965 Extra Heavy Grade of Smooth Finish Shelf Paper, fancy cut out border, embossed and perforated, 12 inches wide and 10 yards long. When ordering be sure to give the color wanted, whether white, blue, pink, yellow or green. Price, per half dozen pieces..... **25c**
If by mail, postage extra, per 10 yds., 7 cents.

MEMORANDUM BOOKS.

No. 3F17180 Vest Pocket Memorandum Book. Bound in fine levant grain with "Crest" stamped in silver on cover. Turned in covers. Contains 48 leaves (96 pages) of extra quality white wove water marked paper. Ruled in dollars and cents. Side opening. Size, 2½x4½ inches.
Price, per half dozen, **40c**; 2 for...... **16c**
If by mail, postage extra, for two, 3 cents.

No. 3F17190 Vest Pocket Memorandum Book. Bound in Russia leather. Side opening. Turned in covers. Contains 40 leaves (80 pages) of fine quality white wove paper. Quadrille ruling. Size, 2½x5½ inches.
Price, 2 for.............. **15c**
Per half dozen............ **39c**
If by mail, postage extra, for two, 3 cents.

No. 3F17200 Memorandum Book. Bound in Russia leather. Turned in covers; 60 leaves (120 pages). Contains fine quality of white water marked ledger paper, ruled in dollars and cents. Side opening. Size, 3¾x6 inches.
Price, per half doz. **60c**; 2 for **22c**
If by mail, postage extra, for two, 7 cents.

No. 3F17201 Memorandum Book. Indexed through. Otherwise same as No. 3F17200. Price, each......... **17c**
Per half dozen........... **90c**
If by mail, postage extra, each, 4 cents.

No. 3F17260 Pocket Receipt Book. Has best grade pressed board covers, cloth back, stub perforated. Contains fifty receipts. Size, 2x6½ inches, of good quality white paper.
Price, per dozen, **29c**; per half dozen.. **16c**
If by mail, postage extra, each, 2 cents.

No. 3F17265 Pocket Rent Receipt Book. Otherwise same as No. 3F17260.
Price, per dozen, **29c**; per half dozen, **16c**
If by mail, postage extra, each, 2 cents.

No. 3F17270 Receipt Book. Size, 3¼x11 inches. Otherwise same as No. 3F17260.
Price, per dozen, **51c**; per half dozen.. **28c**
If by mail, postage extra, each, 4 cents.

No. 3F17275 Rent Receipt Book. Size, 3¼x11 inches. Otherwise same as No. 3F17265. Price, per half dozen....... **28c**
Per dozen.............. **51c**
If by mail, postage extra, each, 4 cents.

No. 3F17280 Draft Book. Size, 3¼x12 inches. Otherwise same as No. 3F17260.
Price, per dozen, **51c**; per half dozen, **28c**
If by mail, postage extra, each, 4 cents.

No. 3F17285 Check Book. Size, 3¼x12 inches. Otherwise same as No. 3F17260.
Price, per dozen, **51c**; per half dozen, **28c**
If by mail, postage extra, each, 4 cents.

No. 3F17290 Note Book. Size, 3¼x12 inches. Otherwise same as No. 3F17260.
Price, per dozen, **51c**; per half dozen, **28c**
If by mail, postage extra, each, 4 cents.

No. 3F17295 Standard Scale Book. Contains 500 weight forms. Printed on an extra quality of good paper, with stubs attached; marbled paper sides and cloth back. Very durable. Size, 8½x11 inches. Price, each, **$0.22**
Per half dozen............ **1.18**
If by mail, postage extra, each, 12 cents.

Wagon and Order Books.

No. 3F17300 Wagon or Record Books. Bound in black waterproof oilcloth, turned in covers, has a flap which laps over and protects the edge. Also has a gusseted pocket inside of cover, and a pencil loop containing a good grade No. 2 pencil. Size of book, 4x8½ inches. Contains 150 leaves (300 pages) of extra fine, heavy white wove paper, ruled in dollars and cents.
Price, per half dozen, **68c**; 2 for...... **25c**
If by mail, postage extra, for two, 28 cents.

No. 3F17305 Same as No. 3F17300, but without flap or gusseted pocket.
Price, per half dozen, **49c**; 2 for...... **18c**
If by mail, postage extra, for two, 28 cents.

No. 3F17310 Pocket Order Book. Bound in black heavy oilcloth, turned in covers, has a pencil loop containing a No. 2 medium grade pencil. Contains 150 leaves (300 pages) of extra quality white paper. Ruled in dollars and cents. Size of book, 4¼x7 inches. Price, 2 for............... **22c**
Per half dozen.............. **62c**
If by mail, postage extra, for two, 28 cents.

BLANK BOOKS.

IMPORTANT—In ordering blank books do not fail to state distinctly catalogue number, ruling and number of pages wanted.

Bookkeeping Blanks.

No. 3F17480 For practice in schools and colleges. Excellent quality of white paper, blank book finish, ruled as follows: Day book, record, journal, cash and sales book, double entry ledger and trial balance, colored press board covers, 36 pages to book. Size, 8½x14 inches. Always mention kind of ruling wanted.
Price, any 6 for.... **28c**
If by mail, postage extra for three, 19 cents.

No. 3F17485 Crown Folio Size. Bound in full duck with imitation Russia corners and green edges. Contains a fine grade of white wove paper. Size of book, 8½x12¾ inches. Ruled in cash, day, journal, record and single or double entry ledgers.

No. of pages..	100	200	300	400	500	600
Price, per book.	14c	24c	32c	40c	49c	58c

State style of ruling wanted. Average weight, per 100 pages, 1 pound.

No. 3F17500 Crown Folio Size. Bound in slate duck, has imitation Russian ends and bands, hubs, spring back and green edges. Contains an extra quality of white wove water marked paper. Size of book, 8½x12¾ inches. Ruled in cash, day, journal, record and single or double entry ledgers.

No. of pages....	200	300	400	500	600
Price, per book.	48c	59c	75c	89c	$1.05

State style of ruling wanted. Average weight, per 100 pages, 1½ pounds.

No. 3F17505 Demy Folio Size. Bound in full sheep with Russia ends and bands; has hubs, spring back and green edges; strong and neatly made. Contains a superfine quality of heavy smooth finished white ledger paper. Size of book, 9½x14 inches. Ruled in cash, day, journal, record and single or double entry ledgers.

No. of pages....	300	400	500	600
Price, per book.	$1.44	$1.59	$1.75	$1.89

State style of ruling wanted. Average weight, per 100 pages, 2 pounds.

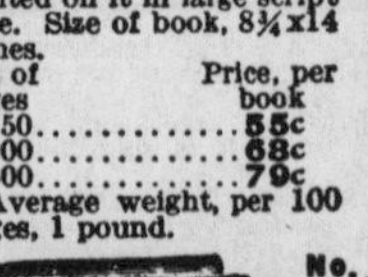

No. 3F17510 Cash Book. Bound in slate duck with Russia corners. Contains a fine quality of heavy white wove paper. Each page has the word "Cash" printed on it in large script type. Size of book, 8¾x14 inches.

No. of pages	Price, per book
150	55c
200	68c
300	79c

Average weight, per 100 pages, 1 pound.

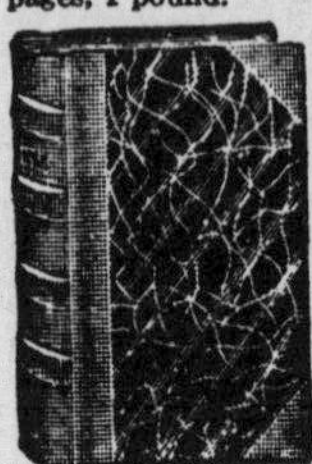

No. 3F17565 Invoice Book. Has hubs, back and corners bound in heavy slate duck, marbled paper sides. Contains best quality heavy manila paper. Size of book, 12x16 inches.

No. of pages	Price, per book
200	$0.98
250	1.18
300	1.38
400	1.98
500	2.38

Average weight, per 100-page book, 2½ pounds.

Malleable Iron Letter Press.

Malleable Iron Letter Press, highly enameled in black. Warranted against imperfections in material and workmanship.

No. 3F17615 Size of follower, 10x12½ inches.
Price...... **$3.75**
Weight, packed for shipment, 67 lbs.

No. 3F17620 Size of follower, 10x15 inches. Price.. **$4.50**
Weight, packed for shipment, 78 pounds.

No. 3F17625 Size of follower, 11x16 inches. Price.................. **$7.35**
Weight, packed for shipment, 90 pounds.

No. 3F17700 Russia Leather Holder, with 100 leaves. Dollars and cents ruling. Size of leaf, 3x5½ inches, ⅝-inch rings. Side opening. Price...... **78c**
If by mail, postage extra, 15 cents.

Extra Tab Index for above........... **20c**
If by mail, postage extra, 3 cents.

Extra Sheets, 2 packages (100 sheets each)........................ **38c**
If by mail, postage extra, 10 cents.

No. 3F17705 Russia Leather Holder, with 100 leaves. Dollars and cents ruling. Size of leaf, 3¾x6⅞ inches. ⅝-inch ring, side opening. Price.............. **98c**
If by mail, postage extra, 15 cents.

Leather Tab Index for above.......... **25c**
If by mail, postage extra, 3 cents.

Extra Sheets, 2 packages (100 sheets each)........................ **38c**
If by mail, postage extra, 10 cents.

No. 3F17710 Russia Leather Holder, with 100 leaves. Dollars and cents ruling. Size of leaf, 5x7⅞ inches. ⅝-inch ring, side opening. Price................ **$1.15**
If by mail, postage extra, 15 cents.

Leather Tab Index for above.......... **30c**
If by mail, postage extra, 3 cents.

Extra Sheets, 2 packages (100 sheets each)........................ **50c**
If by mail, postage extra, 10 cents.

SCHOOL BAGS, STRAPS AND PENCIL BOXES.

No. 3F17920 Waterproof School Bag. Made of black oilcloth, bound and stitched, with stitched shoulder straps. Size, 10x13¾ inches.
Price.............. **10c**
If by mail, postage extra, 6 cents.

No. 3F17925 Heavy Brown Canvas School Bag, with gusset, bound with tape, fitted with two fancy straps and buckles, extra heavy leather shoulder straps with buckle. Size, 9x11½ inches. Price........... **25c**
If by mail, postage extra, 12 cents.

No. 3F17930 School Bag. High grade, made of fine quality Scotch plaid cloth, lined with canvas and trimmed in leather. Has a 36-inch leather shoulder strap with buckle. Also has a 3-inch overlapping flap with buckles. Size of bag, 11x15 inches. On the outside of bag there is a pouch with a 3-inch flap and buckle. Size of pouch, 5x6½ inches. Price...................... **48c**
If by mail, postage extra, 10 cents.

No. 3F17950 School Book Case. An exact imitation of a dress suit case, made of heavy waterproof fibre in imitation of leather. Has brass clasp and leather handles. Size of case, 8½x11x3½ inches. Just the thing for school children. Price...... **25c**
If by mail, postage extra, 16 cents.

School Straps.

No. 3F17955 Book Straps, flexible leather handle, 36 inches long.
Price, each. **$0.09**
Per dozen.. **1.05**
If by mail, postage extra, each, 5 cents.

No. 3F17960 Book or Skate Strap, flexible leather, grained finish. 40 inches long.
Price..................... **6c**
If by mail, postage extra, 5 cents.

Pencil Boxes.

No. 3F18010 Japanese Ebony Pencil Box, with lithograph Japanese scene in colors on top. Has lock and key. Is divided into three compartments and is fitted with glass ink well with metal top and wooden inch measure. Size, 8½x2½x1½ inches. Price....... **12c**
If by mail, postage extra, 6 cents.

No. 3F18015 Swivel Pencil Box, size, 9½x2½x1⅜ inches. Polished hardwood, natural finish, with flowered chromo top, in colors. Is fitted with lock and key. Made double decker with six compartments. Contains pencil penholder, pen and rubber eraser.
Price, 2 for **30c**; each.............. **18c**
If by mail, postage extra, each, 10 cents.

Policeman's Club Pencil Box with Complete Outfit.

THE LATEST NOVELTY IN PENCIL BOXES.

No. 3F18120 This Pencil Box is made in the form of a policeman's club, being the same length and made of the same material as the clubs used by policemen throughout the big cities. Comes complete with pencil, penholder, eraser and steel pen.
Price...................... **14c**
If by mail, postage extra, 5 cents.

Portable Blackboards.

No. 3F18065 Portable Blackboards of cloth with best black liquid slating surface, mounted with hook and complete for hanging.

Size	Price	Size	Price
2x2 feet......	$0.38	4x4 feet......	$1.05
3x3 feet......	.52	4x5 feet......	1.27
3x4 feet......	.62	4x6 feet......	1.47
3x5 feet......	.90	4x7 feet......	1.67
3x6 feet......	1.35		

Slated Cloth for Blackboards.

No. 3F18075 Excellent for any flat surface. Black surface of best liquid slating. Easily fastened to the wall with tacks or paste containing a little glue.
Cloth, 3 feet wide, slated one side.
Price, per yard.................. **$0.32**
Per roll, 12 yards................ **3.69**
Cloth, 4 feet wide, slated one side.
Price, per yard.................. **.45**
Per roll, 12 yards................ **5.24**
Unmailable.

Liquid Slating for Blackboards.

No. 3F18090 Best Alcohol Black Liquid Slating; may be applied to hard finished plaster, paper, boards, or to old blackboards of any kind. A gallon will cover about 250 square feet, three coats. Cannot be sent by mail.
Price, per pint................ **$0.28**
Per ½-gallon can.................. **.75**
Per 1-gallon can.................. **1.48**

No. 3F18095 Flat Brush, for applying liquid slating, 3 inches wide. Price..... **35c**

Favorite Letter File.

Alphabetically Indexed. Will hold 3,000 letters adjusting itself in thickness proportionately to the number of papers it contains. Papers may be returned without tearing or defacing. Indispensable for every office, home and school.

No. 3F18145 Note Size, 6x11¼ inches. Price........ **23c**
If by mail, postage extra, 13 cents.

No. 3F18146 Letter Size, 9x11½ inches. Price.................... **23c**
If by mail, postage extra, 15 cents.

No. 3F18147 Invoice Size, 9¼x? inches. Price.................. **45c**
If by mail, postage extra, 19 cents.

Falcon Letter File.

No. 3F18150 The only complete file made. It opens automatically. Will stand alone, allowing the free use of both hands for filing letters. Indexed both right and left. Size, 10x12 inches. Price...................... **45c**
If by mail, postage extra, 34 cents.

No. 3F18170 Combination Perforator and File. Will punch holes 4 inches apart. Price........ **15c**
If by mail, postage extra, 6 cents.

No. 3F18175 Home Bill Receipt File. Bound in linen. Consists of ten pockets, properly labeled for household bills, enabling one to find a bill instantly. Size, 7x9 inches.
Price............ **48c**
If by mail, postage extra, 8 cents.

No. 3F18177 Housekeeper's Recipe File. Same as above, but with pockets properly labeled for recipes for cooking. Invaluable for the housekeeper. Price..... **48c**
If by mail, postage extra, 8 cents.

Striped Wood Board Clips.

Nickeled Clip, with brass wire spring, improved metal shoulder for papers to square against and metal eye to hang up by.

No. 3F18180 Note Size. Weight, 14 ounces.
Price.................. **27c**

No. 3F18181 Letter Size. Weight, 14 ounces.
Price.................. **30c**

No. 3F18182 Cap Size. Weight, 22 ounces.
Price.................. **33c**
Unmailable.

Carved Leather Set.

This beautiful set, consisting of writing companion, pen and ink tray, picture frame and scrap basket, is made entirely from imported imitation carved leather. **The Writing Companion is beautifully carved**, with design representing a scene in Japan, showing storks, lotus flowers and Japanese girls, with mountains and sea in the background. It is lined with leatherette, fitted with blotter and flap for pen. Size, 10x12½ inches.

The Picture Frame is carved, with a graceful flower and figured design, fitted with glass front and easel back and is made to hold the regulation cabinet size photograph.

The Pen and Ink Tray is made with handsomely carved and embossed design of a beautiful girl's head and flowers and fitted with pressed glass ink well with glass top attached by gilt hinge and made with gilt band decoration. Size, 9x2½ inches.

The Scrap Basket is the largest and handsomest piece in the set, beautifully carved and embossed, with a design representing a Japanese girl in a garden. Around the top and bottom are heavy bands of leatherette studded with brass headed nails, giving added strength and beauty. This basket is 13 inches high and 7½ inches in diameter.

No. 3F18384 Carved Leather Set, just as illustrated and described, four pieces, writing companion, picture frame, pen and ink tray and scrap basket, complete.
Price $2.15

PRICES ON SEPARATE PIECES.

No. 3F18385 Writing Companion only.
Price 64c
If by mail, postage extra, each, 22 cents.

No. 3F18386 Picture Frame only.
Price 33c
If by mail, postage extra, each, 12 cents.

No. 3F18387 Pen and Ink Tray only.
Price 49c
If by mail, postage extra, each, 10 cents.

No. 3F18388 Scrap Basket only.
Price 94c
Weight, packed for shipment, 3 pounds.

Picture Frames.

No. 3F18395 "Lincrusta" Photograph Frame, beautiful floral design, embossed in relief. Square cut cabinet opening in center with glass front. The frame is light brown, beautifully finished and has easel back. Size, 7½x9½ inches.
Price, each..15c
2 for 25c
If by mail, postage extra, each, 8 cents.

No. 3F18400 Imitation Carved Leather Photograph Frame, superbly embossed, medallion design. Square cut cabinet opening with glass front. This picture frame is the newest thing in that line and is an ornament to any room. Comes in assorted colors and has easel mount. Size, 7¼x9½ inches.
Price, 2 for 70c; each 38c
If by mail, postage extra, each, 12 cents.

No. 3F18405 Beautiful Picture Frame, made of pure aluminum, hand engraved, fitted with easel back and glass front. Size, 5¾x7½ inches. Regular cabinet opening; a little gem for the money. Will look beautiful on the piano, table or mantel piece. Retail price, $1.00.
Our price.....48c
Postage extra, 6 cts.

No. 3F18410 Wrought Metal Picture Frame, burnished, gold finish, with easel back and glass. This is the newest and most beautiful style of picture frame. The metal is beautifully carved in artistic design and the finish is guaranteed not to tarnish. Size of frame 11¾x8¾ inches. Regular cabinet opening. Retail price, $1.00.
Our price....75c
If by mail, postage extra, 12 cents.

No. 3F18415 Made of same material as above, but in oval shape and has standard oval cabinet opening. Retail price $1.00.
Our price.....75c
Weight, packed for shipment, 12 pounds

$2.98 BUYS THIS REGULAR $10.00 EASEL ALBUM.

THIS ILLUSTRATION will give you some idea of the general appearance of our special $2.98 silk plush and celluloid easel album, but to really appreciate the beautiful design and the brilliant colors, the features which make it so highly ornamental and attractive, it must be seen.

DECORATED GOLDEN CELLULOID FRONT. The golden celluloid front of this easel album is most artistically decorated in beautiful colors, the design representing the doorway of an old thatched cottage, with doves and birds, butterflies, green vines and brilliantly colored flowers, the colors forming a most delightful contrast with the delicately figured golden background. The corners are decorated with gracefully embossed designs, the raised portions tinted with metallic shades of green and red.

GREEN SILK PLUSH. The back and other parts of this album are covered with a fine quality of beautifully figured silk plush, the design wrought in three shades of green, making the predominating colors of the album gold and green, relieved by the brilliant red poppies which form the most prominent part of the floral design.

HOLDS 54 CABINET PHOTOGRAPHS. This easel album contains 27 pages, gold edges, each page with two regular cabinet size openings, thus giving the album a capacity of 54 cabinet pictures, and in addition the drawer may be used for smaller pictures or pictures of unusual shapes, which do not fit the regular size openings. The drawer is ornamented with green silk plush and golden celluloid front panel with design of tea roses in colors, handsomely embossed.

THIS EASEL ALBUM stands on a substantial brass ox yoke easel, 14½ inches high and the album itself measures 9½ inches wide by 11½ inches long, and is made with heavy brass extension clasp. The leaves are made with full gold edges, embellished with floral design in gilt around the picture openings. Easel albums are the latest, most stylish and most popular albums made, and thousands of this exact same style and quality are sold this season by agents at $10.00 each. If you want an album for your own use we know this one will please you, and as a gift it is sure to please the lucky recipient.

No. 3F18640 Silk Plush and Celluloid Easel Album. Complete and just as illustrated and described. Our price $2.98
Weight, packed for shipment, 7 pounds.

Celluloid Front Album, $1.19.

No. 3F18645 Flat, 20-Page, (10-leaf) Album, with a real celluloid front, made to resemble wood bark, on which is gracefully stamped a bouquet of narcissus. The four corners are embossed and touched with gilt The binding and back cover is made of high grade figured velour; has full gilt edges, fancy extension gilt clasp. The leaves of the book on the inside are decorated with gold stamping. Size, 8½x10½ inches. This is a regular $2.50 album.
Our price $1.19
Weight, packed for shipment, 4 pounds.

High Grade Leather Album, $1.98.

No. 3F18650 The Finest Leather Album made. Size, 8½x10½ inches. Made only of the best black Bible leather, seal grained, beautifully embossed with thistle design; real gold edges. Inside margin of cover hand tooled with gold; gilt metal extension clasp; fly page, 24 photograph pages (12 leaves), in dull gray finish, decorated with gold trace work. A really beautiful album and a wonderful value for the price. Price, $1.98
Weight, packed for shipment, 5 pounds.

Exceptional Value, All Silk Plush, Acorn Design, Only $2.18.

No. 3F18655 This album has a variegated all silk plush front and back, richly ornamented with four heavy gilt metal corners; stamped in the graceful acorn and oak leaf design. In the center on the front cover is a large gilt metal acorn frame in which is a beautiful medallion in colors of a woman's head. This album is 10½x8½ inches and is 2¼ inches thick, has extra heavy gilt extension clasp and full gilt edges; 24 elaborately gilt decorated pages (12 leaves), extra fly leaf. Sold by agents for $5.00.
Our price $2.18
Weight, packed for shipment, 5 pounds.

The Theodore Roosevelt Album, $2.48.

No. 3F18660 Would you not like to have an album with the latest picture of our President beautifully embossed in colors on an elaborately decorated celluloid cover? Above this picture floats "Old Glory" from a topmast, and on each side on the yard arms stand two beautiful boys in sailor suits—the future pride and defense of our country. The picture frame and four corners are beautifully embossed in colors. The back is of the highest grade figured silk plush. Has an extra heavy fancy gilt metal clasp, gold edges and 28 pages (14 leaves). Size, 8½x10½ inches. Retail price, $8.00.
Our price $2.48
Weight, packed for shipment, 5 pounds.

Royal Quarto Size Medallion Center All Silk Plush Album, Only $2.88.

No. 3F18665 This very beautiful royal quarto size Double Cabinet Album is made of the finest variegated silk plush with padded front and back. It has four heavily embossed gold metal corners in conventional design, and in the center there is a beautiful medallion in colors of two young girls in fancy dress, mounted in an extra heavy fancy embossed gilt frame. Has embossed extension gilt clasp, 30 pages (15 leaves), gold edges and decorated on the inside with fancy gold stamping. Two photographs to a page and in some cases, four. Size of album, 10x12 inches. Sold by agents for $10.00.
Our price $2.88
Weight, packed for shipment, 6 pounds.

Mirror Medallion, Silk Plush Musical Album, Only $4.45.

No. 3F18675 A Superb Double Cabinet Musical Album 12¾x10¼ inches, standing 4½ inches high, made of the best quality figured silk plush, mounted on a slanting silk plush covered base, decorated with four embossed gold metal corner ornaments. On the cover is a fine, large French plate glass mirror mounted in an elaborately designed gold metal frame and two gold metal corners. Plays two airs. Music apparatus in base under transparent isinglass. Stands on four gilt ball feet. Has 28 mahogany finished gilt decorated pages (14 leaves), with gold edges. Double cabinet opening on each page. Retail price, $8.00.
Our price $4.45
Weight, packed for shipment, 7 pounds.

Musical Disc Album, $6.35.

No. 3F18680 A Superb, Oblong Shaped Double Cabinet Musical Disc Album, made of polished transparent celluloid in richly colored flower design, with large beautiful picture mounted in center, representing a singing girl in a Roman palace. Cover handsomely embossed; full gilt corners; fancy gilt metal clasp; slanting celluloid base, similarly decorated with large embossed gold metal corner ornaments. Plush back binding. Has 32 double cabinet pages (16 leaves), decorated, full gold edges. The base contains a fine musical box which plays six times from interchangeable discs. Each album contains six discs. Each disc plays a different tune. Size, 13¾x11¼ inches. Stands 4¼ inches high. Retail price, $15.00.
Our price $6.35
Weight, packed for shipment, 10 pounds.

The Lady's Easle Album, $4.98.

No. 3F18705 Every lady in the country should have one of these beautiful albums in her room. This album is the newest shape. It stands 15¾ inches high and is 16¼ inches wide at the base; is made of the highest grade silk plush. The album itself drops forward, disclosing a pocket, back of album, for extra photographs. Handsomely decorated with two imitation cut glass perfume bottles and stoppers, two French plate glass mirrors in embossed gilt metal frames and gilt metal ornaments on legs and top. Has country scene in colors in frame above the album. The front of the album is transparent embossed celluloid with portrait of beautiful young girl on a floral background. Has extension embossed gilt metal clasp and 24 gilt decorated gold edge pages (12 leaves). Price....................$4.98
Weight, packed for shipment, 10 pounds.

Special Musical Album, $2.98.

No. 3F18670 The greatest bargain ever offered. A beautiful musical album, playing two airs, for less than is usually charged for an ordinary flat album. Embossed, flowered celluloid top with colored picture, "The Lovers," in the center. Silk plush binding, slanting flowered base on four gilt ball feet; embossed gilt metal extension clasp, 24 pages (12 leaves), with full gilt edges. Interior decorated with gilt stamping, 3¾ inches high. Size, 12x9¼ inches.
Price..$2.98
Weight, packed for shipment, 6 pounds.

Our Leader Easel Album, $1.70.

No. 3F18685 Detachable Cabinet Album on gilt easel. Handsomely embossed transparent celluloid front flower design, with full size colored fancy dress picture, "The Game of Love." Binding and back of high grade padded variegated velour. Has 24 gold decorated gilt edge pages (12 leaves), embossed gilt metal clasp. Size, 10½x8¼ inches. Stands on an easel 13 inches high. Retail price, $3.50. Our price $1.70
Weight, packed for shipment, 6 pounds.

$1.70

Liberty Bell Embossed Silk Velour Easel Album, $2.28.

No. 3F18690 A Beautifully Embossed Silk Velour Album, with the Liberty Bell design. A choice metal design of the bell surrounding a German plate beveled mirror beautifies the cover of this album, and smaller bell designs decorate the upper corners. Mounted on a genuine brass ox yoke easel. Easel is fitted with a silk plush box drawer with gilt metal drawer pull for extra photographs. Has 28 double cabinet pages (14 leaves), extra thick, with extension embossed gilt clasp. Size, 9¼x11½ inches. Stands on easel 13½ inches high. Retail price, $5.00. Our price $2.28
Weight, packed for shipment, 6 pounds.

Martha Washington Easel Album, $3.48.

No. 3F18695 Superb Detachable Double Cabinet Easel Album, mounted on new style extension base, ornamented and embossed with gilt metal trimmings. Made of dark brown figured plush with large embossed celluloid panel in imitation of mahogany, on which is stamped in colors a beautiful picture of Martha Washington in fancy dress. The base is of flowered plush and imitation mahogany celluloid, having drawer for extra photographs, with gilt metal drawer pull. The back of the album projects in graceful curved outlines, on the corners of which are embossed gilt metal decorations. Has extension gilt metal clasp, 28 gilt decorated gold edged pages (14 leaves). Size, 9¼x11½ inches. Stands on easel 14 inches high. The handsomest easel album ever offered. Retail price, $8.00. Our price $3.48
Weight, packed for shipment, 7 pounds.

Religious Album, $4.68.

No. 3F18700 This Beautiful Album in ecclesiastical design is made of velour plush and celluloid. It stands on a solid base 3½ inches high. The front and back of the album are celluloid and on the front is a beautiful portrait in colors of His Holiness, Pope Pius IX. The album is a drop front and the back of the stand opens up disclosing statuettes in tinted bisque of the Virgin Mary holding the infant Christ, and of St. Joseph, also a font for holy water with a crucifix above it. This compartment is lined with two plate glass mirrors and cerise sateen. Surmounting the back is a cross of velour, richly ornamented with gilt metal. The back cover of the album is of white celluloid, on which is stamped a beautiful picture of an angel carrying flowers, and below this is a bouque of flowers. The base measures 6½x12¼ inches. Stands 17 inches high. This album combines deep reverence with great beauty. The retail price is $10.00 to $15.00. Weight, packed for shipment, 12 pounds.
Our price $4.68

Combination Toilet Upright Easel Album, $5.95.

No. 3F18710 This Beautiful Extension Base Album is made of pure white imitation ivory celluloid. The interior of the base is lined with fancy red sateen, the upper compartment of which contains a three-piece embossed white imitation ivory toilet set consisting of brush, comb and hand mirror, fitted with French plate glass. The lower drawer is for extra photographs and toilet articles. The album itself swings on a pivot. On the front cover is a large panel picture in colors of a beautiful woman. On the rear cover is a large stationary mirror. The album and stand are elaborately decorated and embossed in gold. This album can be cleaned as often as desired by wiping with a damp cloth. The album contains 28 double cabinet mahogany finish gold decorated pages (14 leaves), full gold edges. Base measures 14x6½ inches and the outfit stands 14 inches high; a beautiful gift. Retail price, $15.00. Weight, packed for shipment, 12 pounds $5.95

AUTOGRAPH ALBUMS.

No. 3F18815 Autograph Album. Made of leatherette, elaborately stamped in gold with a medalion of a farm scene in colors on cover. Has 40 extra large tinted pages with lithographed frontispiece. Full gilt edges. Size, 9¼x6 inches. Price 22c
If by mail, postage extra, 4 cents.

No. 3F18820 Autograph Album, made of heavily padded velour plush with word "Autograph," inscribed on cover in cut metal. Contains 68 tinted pages, full gilt edges with lithographed frontispiece. Size, 4x6¼ inches. Price 38c
If by mail, postage extra, 6 cents.

No. 3F18825 Autograph Album, made of figured velour with gorgeous front made of gold and celluloid, elaborately embossed and decorated with flowers in their natural colors. In the center of this cover is a medalion head of a beautiful boy holding a dove. Contains nearly 100 pages, one-half white and one-half blue of the best quality of water marked paper. Full gilt edges. Size 7¾x5 inches. Price 68c
If by mail, postage extra, 12 cents.

SCRAP BOOKS.

No. 3F18880 Extra Large Scrap Book Album, bound in red leatherette, elaborately stamped in gold, with two farm scenes medallioned on cover. Contains 33 tinted pages. Size, 10¾x13¾ inches. Price 28c
If by mail, postage extra, 20 cents.

No. 3F18885 Nonpareil Scrap Book, made of the best quality of silk cloth with word, "Scrap Book," stamped in white on cover. Contains 60 pages of gray cartridge paper. Size, 8¾x11 inches. Back, 1½ inches wide; plugged so that bulky articles may be pasted in the book. This is the cheapest, most durable scrap book made. Price 49c
If by mail, postage extra, 22 cents.

No. 3F18890 Scrap Book, contains 96 leaves, (192 pages) of finest grade heavy white unruled scrap book paper. Back and corners bound in roan leather and has combed marble paper sides. Size of book, 8½x9½ inches. Price 48c
Weight, packed for shipment, 2 pounds.

No. 3F18891 Scrap Book. Size, 9½x12½ inches. Otherwise same as No. 3F18890. Price 59c
Weight, packed for shipment, 3 pounds.

GLOBES.

No. 3F19115

For the home, schoolroom or library. We have listed the best line of globes that can be found anywhere and at prices that are from 40 to 50 per cent below what anyone else is offering these goods. The spheres are made with great care and are warranted not to check or crack. Every improvement in engraving printing, coloring and mounting the maps has received critical attention. We believe you will be well satisfied with any one of these globes which you might order.

No. 3F19095 Wire Mounted Globe, 6 inches in diameter, strongly made. The details of the globe are the same as on the more expensive ones. Retail price, 50 cents.
Our price 23c
If by mail, postage extra, 16 cents.

No. 3F19100 This Globe is mounted on oxidized copper stand, the printing standing out clear and accurate. This globe is 16½ inches high, and the diameter of the ball is 8 inches. It has no movable meridian. Weight, packed for shipment, 9¾ pounds. Retail price, $5.00. Our price $1.60

No. 3F19105 Same as No. 3F19100, but with movable meridian. Weight, packed for shipment, 17 pounds. Price $3.98

No. 3F19110 This is a very handsome Globe, mounted on oxidized copper stand. Height of globe 19 inches, diameter of ball, 12 inches. This is our most popular globe for school purposes. This globe does not have movable meridian. Weight, packed for shipment 25 pounds. Retail price, $10.00.
Our price $3.80

No. 3F19115 Same as No. 3F19110, described above, but with movable meridian. Weight, packed for shipment, 33 pounds. Retail price, $16.00. Our price $4.85

No. 3F19120 A Light Library Oxidized Metal Stand Globe, unique in style and handsome in finish. Height of stand complete, 36 inches. Diameter of globe, 12 inches. This globe comes complete with movable meridian. Weight, packed for shipment, 50 pounds. Retail price, $25.00.
Our price $7.95

Wall Maps.

New, accurate and thoroughly up to date maps, suitable for schools, drawing rooms and libraries. This is absolutely the best and most complete series of wall maps published. Each map is 41x52 inches.

Western Hemisphere, Eastern Hemisphere, United States, North America, South America, Europe, Asia, Africa.

No. 3F19125 Mounted on heavy cloth, ready to hang on the wall. Weight, packed for shipment, 2 pounds.
Our price, any map 98c

No. 3F19126 Each map in diamond (wooden) case. Weight, packed for shipment, 12 pounds. Our price $1.95

No. 3F19127 Any four maps in globe case. Weight, packed for shipment, 30 pounds. Our price $7.80

No. 3F19128 The complete set (8 maps) in globe (wooden) case. Weight, packed for shipment, 50 pounds. Our price... $9.95

Indexed State Maps.

Rand & McNally's Pocket State Maps show the entire railroad system, the express companies doing business over each road, and accurately locates all the cities, towns, postoffices, railroad stations, villages, islands, lakes, rivers, etc. The population is also given according to the latest official census. We can furnish any state map wanted. When ordering, give name of state. These maps are 14x21 inches.

No. 3F19135 Price, each 16c
If by mail, postage extra, each, 2 cents.

PRINTING PRESSES.

Nonpareil Printing Press.

In offering to our customers our Nonpareil Hand Power Job Presses we desire to call attention to a few of the many advantages they possess.

They are superior to any press we have ever offered, and we invite comparison with corresponding product of other manufacturers.

They are practical presses, capable of producing all kinds of printing in a satisfactory manner, and while the price is verylow, they have proved to be the best press for the money ever offered to the trade.

They are simple in mechanical construction, perfect in distribution of ink, and inking forms can be easily adjusted to give heavier and lighter impressions when necessary, and all parts are made in such a manner that when the wear is not taken out by the machine itself, it can be quickly adjusted and any defect in action removed. These presses are especially pleasing to the eye, and are built in such a manner that their operation is perfectly smooth, without jerks or jars.

They will print anything from a single letter to a full form without causing trouble. With proper usage they will last a life time, all parts being interchangeable. Should one be broken by accident, they can easily be replaced without extra expense. Many printers who possess the most expensive job presses now possess the **Nonpariel printing press,** as they find it to be economical for certain purposes, and very valuable for helping out in short runs when the other presses are all busy.

These presses are shipped direct from our factory near Chicago.

A complete outfit goes with each press, and each outfit is made in proportion to the press and contains rollers, leads, slugs, spaces, quoins, quads, wood furniture, wood stick, type case, 100 cards, tweezers, silver and gold bronze, powder and a tube of ink.

No. 3F19350 Will print a form 3x4½ inches and contains a 6A10a font of standard metal type. Dimensions of press, 13½ inches high, 12½ inches deep, 9 inches wide.
Price, complete $11.98
Weight, packed for shipment, 45 pounds.

No. 3F19355 Will print a form 4x6 inches. Dimensions of press, 17 inches high, 21 inches deep, 12 inches wide. Otherwise, same as No. 3F19350.
Price, complete $18.75
Weight, packed for shipment, 75 pounds.

No. 3F19360 Will print a form 5x7½ inches. Dimensions of press, 21 inches high, 21 inches deep, 17 inches wide. Contains a 9A15a font of standard metal type. Otherwise same as No. 3F19350.
Price, complete $27.89
Weight, packed for shipment, 115 pounds.

No. 3F19365 Will print a form 6x9 inches. Dimensions of press, 24 inches high, 24 inches deep, 17 inches wide. Contains a 9A15a font of standard metal type. Otherwise same as 3F19350.
Price, complete $38.25
Weight, packed for shipment, 150 pounds.

STOVES AND RANGES

DEPARTMENT OF STOVES.

WE OPERATE THE LARGEST STOVE FOUNDRY IN THE WORLD AND CONTROL ITS ENTIRE OUTPUT

THIS ENORMOUS MANUFACTURING PLANT is located at Newark, Ohio, and there every day in the year, running at its fullest capacity, without cessation, except on Sundays and holidays, is manufactured the entire line of magnificent stoves and ranges illustrated and described in the pages of this Big Catalogue. The location for the development of an enormous stove making industry could not have been more fortunate than this of the Newark Stove Works. Raw materials of every sort are at our doors and, being practically in the center of the iron industry of the United States, we are able to command all those special facilities so necessary, as well as having immediately at hand men who have spent all their working years in the iron industry. There are hundreds of stove foundries throughout the United States and the world, but there is not another one that compares in extent, in perfection of equipment, in economy of operation, in quality of output with the Newark Stove Works, which is owned and controlled by us. Every pound of metal which enters these works, every pattern that is made therein, is used in the manufacture of the most complete, the most up to date, the most satisfactory stoves offered by any firm or individual, and every stove made in these enormous works is

MADE FOR US, AND SOLD ONLY BY US

LARGEST IN THE WORLD

OUR STOVE FOUNDRY AT NEWARK, OHIO.

THIS ENORMOUS STOVE FOUNDRY, birdseye view of which is given on this page, is the largest stove foundry in the world, covering thirty acres of ground in the beautiful little city of Newark, Ohio, where it is known as the Newark Stove Works, and it comprises the largest moulding room of any stove foundry in existence, the largest warehouses used for the storage of stoves and ranges, miles and miles of tracks, hundreds of the most modern, up to date machines designed to facilitate the manufacture of stoves and ranges and to reduce the manufacturing cost to the lowest possible minimum. Every process of manufacture is so reduced to an exact science, so systematized that there is not an ounce of wasted material, not a moment of wasted time, not a single useless step, and so thoroughly is this great business organized and conducted that we have revolutionized the stove making industry, and are thereby enabled to offer our customers the highest grade stoves and ranges, the very latest improvements possible to procure.

THE ILLUSTRATIONS shown in the following pages of this Big Catalogue will convey to you some idea of the beauty of these stoves and ranges. You will note the grace of outline, the fine proportions, the taste displayed in ornamentation, and if you will compare these illustrations with those shown in catalogues issued by other stove manufacturers and dealers, you will quickly admit that our stoves and ranges are the most beautiful you have ever seen. Our output is so enormous, the demand for each stove that we make is so large, that where others manufacture but a few of each stove we manufacture thousands and hundreds of thousands, and for this reason we are able to employ the highest priced artists, modelers and draftsmen, so that a pattern which costs us $5,000.00 really adds but five or six cents to the cost of each stove; whereas, smaller manufacturers with their limited output would be compelled to add $5.00 and upwards to the cost of each stove were they to use the same class of skilled labor in their pattern department. What is true of our pattern department, is also true of every other department of these great works. We employ only the highest type of skilled mechanics.

THESE GREAT STOVE WORKS as you see them in this picture, give employment to an army of people, and running at their full capacity throughout the year, no workman worthy of his place is ever discharged or laid off for an indefinite period. Our workmen know that their connection is permanent, and there is every reason, therefore, why they should devote their best energies to the development of the best that is possible to produce in stoves and ranges. This is one of the reasons why stoves manufactured by the Newark Stove Works excel the stoves of all other manufacturers. The men who make them put into their construction something more than mechanical effort, that intangible something which makes for perfection, and which enables us from day to day and month to month to keep so far in advance of all other stove manufacturers.

IF IT WERE POSSIBLE for every prospective stove buyer to visit this vast stove making plant, we could quickly convince him that no stove could possibly be made better, if as well, in any other foundry. If he could see the workings of this enormous plant, if he could follow the making of a stove from the time the pig iron enters the foundry yard, and witness the various processes through which it passes until the finished stove is ready to go to the cars; if he could see the care that is taken at every step, to insure the highest quality, if he could witness the careful test of the molten iron, the perfect moulding, the test of castings, the polishing, the grinding, the trimming, fitting, nickeling, asbestos lining, mounting, bracing; if he could see all these manufacturing processes as they are used in this, the largest stove foundry in the world, he would be convinced that no stove could be quite so well made as ours, he would be impressed with the marvelous facilities adopted for reducing cost; he would be overwhelmed with the magnitude of the plant, with its labor saving machinery, conveyers, and mechanical devices introduced to take the place of hand labor, and thus reducing largely the expense attached to operation. Such a visit to this biggest stove foundry in the world would absolutely convince the prospective buyer, that the cost of manufacture has been reduced to the very minimum, and the quality of production has been brought to the very highest possible standard. No prospective stove buyer who thus visits our foundry and witnesses the marvelous manufacturing processes in daily use therein would fail to give us his order; in fact, if every prospective buyer were first to visit this wonderful stove foundry, no other manufacturer or dealer could ever again get an order from him for a stove.

THIS GREAT FOUNDRY with its enormous output, and its systematized operation having brought the cost of manufacture to the lowest possible minimum is what has enabled us to save hundreds of thousands of our customers such enormous sums of money whenever they have been in the market for stoves. But if the product of this large foundry was marketed in the usual way, that is to say, through jobbers, wholesalers, retailers and other middlemen, the price the purchaser would have to pay would be very much in excess of the prices you will find quoted in the pages of this book. Given the lowest manufacturing cost possible in the manufacture of our stoves and ranges, by our wonderful selling organization we are enabled to bring these perfect, up to date, and satisfactory stoves and ranges to you at a price so low, a price so much lower than other manufacturers and dealers ask for stoves and ranges, which do not compare with these in quality, that our prices are really astonishing. Of course, you know the larger the quantity of any given article made at one time, the lower the proportionate cost of each individual article. The fewer hands this article passes through in its transition from raw material to the finished product and in being marketed, the lower its final cost to you. We manufacture our own stoves, and we sell our own stoves, and between us and the customer there is no intervening agency. To the remarkable lowness of manufacturing cost we add but our one small profit, and shipping our stoves from foundry direct to you we save you from a third to a half of the profits and transportation charges you are compelled to pay when you buy from other dealers.

MANY DEALERS BUY THESE STOVES from us because the prices at which we offer them to our customers is so much lower than the wholesale prices asked by other manufacturers and dealers, and our qualities are so much higher and give so much better satisfaction in the hands of the purchaser. For this reason every stove bears the name "Newark Stove Works, Chicago." Our name and address does not appear on any of the stoves we sell, nor on the tag or crate. Therefore, if you are a dealer and wish to buy to sell again, or a dealer and you wish to buy a stove for your own use, we do this to protect you; we also do it to protect the party who does not want to have his employer, or his neighbor, or his friend, who may be a dealer in stoves, criticise him for sending to us to get a stove at a lower price.

OUR BINDING GUARANTEE.

SEARS, ROEBUCK AND CO.
CHICAGO
CAPITAL STOCK FORTY MILLION DOLLARS

Certificate No.

Certificate of Guaranty

This is to Certify that this STOVE or RANGE is warranted perfect in material and manufacture and to be perfect in operation if correctly put up to a good flue and properly managed. This stove has been carefully inspected and there are no defects in material or workmanship. It has been delivered to the transportation company in perfect condition and we guarantee it to reach your station in good order. This means if it is damaged by bad handling on the railroad do not hesitate to accept the stove. Have the agent mark your freight bill damaged. Send it to us with a careful description of the parts needed to put in perfect condition and we will promptly forward them free and prepaid. Fire box linings and grates are natural wear and tear and not guaranteed.

If you have occasion to write us be sure to give this certificate number. When you desire to purchase new fire box linings in future years be sure to give name and number of stove in full.

Dated at Chicago, this ____ day of ________ A.D. 190__

Name of stove ____________

Size ________

SEARS, ROEBUCK & CO.

REFERENCE BY SPECIAL PERMISSION: FIRST NATIONAL BANK CHICAGO; CORN EXCHANGE NAT'L BANK CHICAGO; NATIONAL CITY BANK NEW YORK; SECOND NATIONAL BANK BOSTON.

WE GUARANTEE every piece and part that enters into the stove we sell you to be perfect in material, perfect in manufacture, perfect in operation, and unequaled by any other stove or range of its class in durability and beauty, in economy in the consumption of fuel, and if you do not find it so, you may return it to us at our expense, and we will immediately return your money, together with all the transportation charges paid by you.

WE FURTHER GUARANTEE every stove you order from us to reach you in perfect condition. We are very careful in preparing our stoves for shipment, they are very securely crated, every loose part is properly attached to the stove or enclosed, and we know that it will reach you in the same perfect condition in which it leaves our hands. If, however, when the stove reaches your station and is examined by you, you find that any piece or part is cracked, broken, or damaged in any way whatsoever, remember that we will replace or repair such cracked, broken, damaged or missing part free of any cost to you. Cases of this kind are extremely rare, we are glad to say, as not in one instance in a hundred does a customer have any occasion to complain to us of the condition in which a stove reached him.

THE WAY WE CRATE THEM.

An Acme Range strongly crated for a short or long journey.

OUR WRITTEN BINDING GUARANTEE is sent with every stove sold by us. Note the very broad scope of this guarantee as shown in the facsimile opposite. We will correct, without any expense to you, any defect of any nature whatsoever, which by any accident may have escaped the rigid inspection at the foundry, and which develops when the stove is put in use. No other stove manufacturer stands behind his product as we do. Please remember that a guarantee is no better than the concern that makes it, and that when we give a guarantee on any merchandise it means that all the resources of this responsible mercantile institution are behind it.

IT IS OUR AIM to build the highest grade stoves it is possible to create, the most modern, the best heaters, the best bakers, the most economical users of fuel, stoves that others are striving to equal, stoves when sold to you and used by you will be found to be so much better than you have hoped for, so satisfactory from every standpoint that we will secure your lasting good will and patronage. No concern in the world can succeed in business on first orders alone, and it has been our purpose to so excel all the manufacturers of stoves and ranges that not a single customer shall ever have occasion to criticise the merchandise we send him or find fault with the manner in which we deal with him, and our six million satisfied customers throughout the United States is proof of our ability to give the highest qualities and the best values of any supply house in existence.

SO SURE ARE WE that the stoves we sell are unapproached by those manufactured by any other stove concern in the world, so sure are we that it is impossible to produce better stoves and ranges than those we offer, so positive are we that in price and quality comparison we stand absolutely alone as stove manufacturers and dealers, that we are willing to have our product stand side by side with the product of any other stove manufacturer or dealer and have you submit them to every test, to have you judge of their merits in practical operation, to have you say whether all our claims and more are not absolutely proven and established by a thorough test in your own home.

UNDER THESE LIBERAL TERMS, and in view of our binding guarantee of quality, our guarantee of satisfaction, our free trial offers, certainly you cannot afford to send to any other manufacturer or dealer for a stove or range until you have first sent for one of the high class stoves or ranges manufactured by us in the largest and best equipped stove foundry in the world.

YOUR MONEY WILL BE IMMEDIATELY RETURNED TO YOU FOR ANY GOODS NOT PERFECTLY SATISFACTORY.

READ THIS PAGE CAREFULLY. GIVES FULL DETAILED DESCRIPTION OF

Our New Improved 1908 Acme Royal-Redwood

SIX-HOLE COMBINATION COAL AND WOOD OR EXCLUSIVE WOOD BURNING RANGE

BURNS ANYTHING, HARD COAL, SOFT COAL, COKE, WOOD OR CORNCOBS.

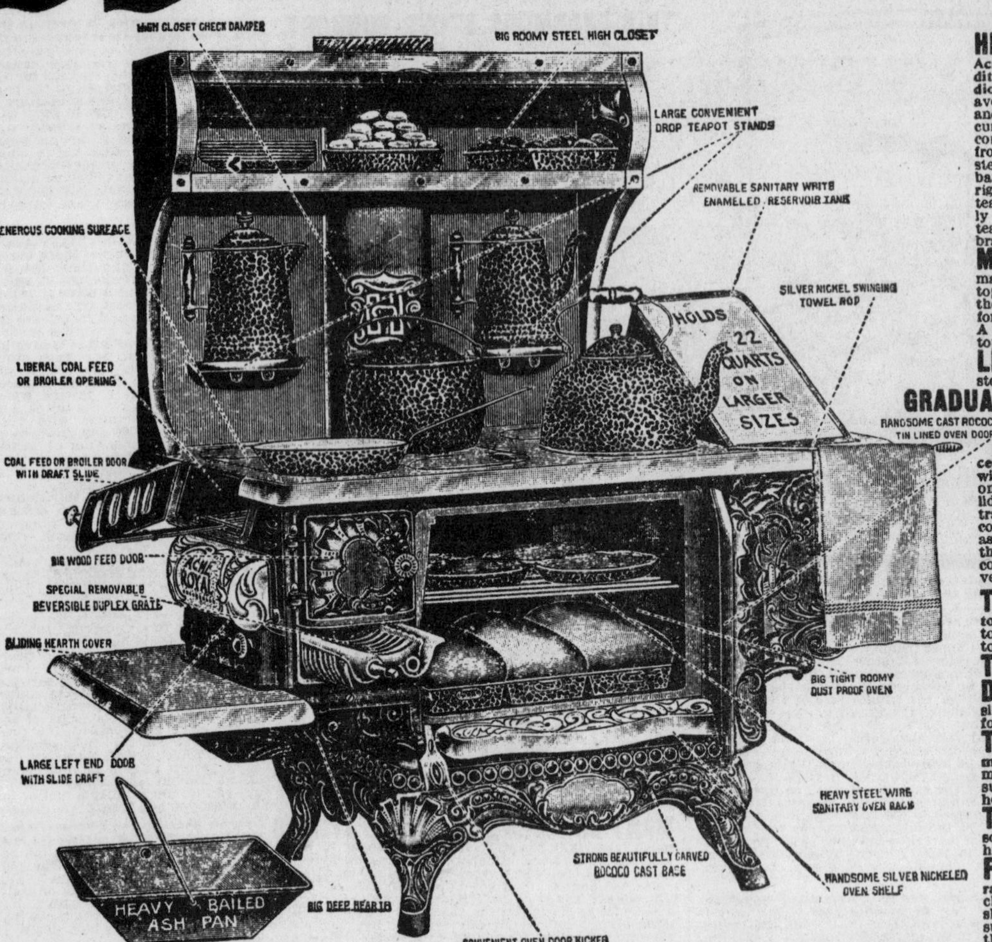

The cooking utensils shown are not furnished with range at prices quoted

DESCRIPTION.

HIGH WARMING CLOSET. The steel warming closet for our Acme Royal-Redwood Range is a new feature and a big addition at a very small cost, and will be found both commodious and convenient. It is just the right height for the average person to easily reach. The roll front rolls back and into the top of the closet after the manner of the curtain of a roll top desk, without interfering with the commodious space inside. The top, sides, back and roll front for the high closet are made of the highest grade sheet steel. It is fully nickeled, trimmed with nickeled steel bands along the front, as shown in illustration. To the right and left of the closet pipe are elaborately designed teapot holders, beautifully nickeled, which may be quickly utilized by bringing them down to a level, so that teapot or other cooking utensils may be placed upon the bracket, as shown to the right of the closet pipe.

MAIN TOP is made of best quality gray iron, cast in sections and connected again in a manner to prevent warping, with the assurance that the top will always remain level. The centers are strong, the castings serve as braces, plenty of allowance is made for expansion and contraction, joints are smoketight. A handsome silver nickeled band all around the main top gives the range an elegant, finished appearance.

LIDS. This range is furnished with five solid lids and one sectional nest lid, made from the best stove plate.

GRADUATED LID OR NEST COVER. Every Acme Royal-Redwood Range with the exception of size 7-18 is fitted with five solid covers, and the one nest cover or graduated lid, as shown in the illustration. This is a very convenient little device, as the varying sizes of the openings in the cover will be found very useful.

TOWEL ROD. A handsome silver nickel plated (never hot) Alaska wire handle towel rod is fitted at the right hand corner of the main top, which will be found very convenient for drying towels and clothing.

THE COMBINATION BROILER OR FEED DOOR is mounted on substantial hinge pins to the left of the main top and supplied with check slide to control the fire, and it will also be found desirable for feeding coal, broiling steaks, toasting, etc.

THE ASH PIT DOOR below the feed or broiler door is substantially mounted on extra heavy hinge pins, beautifully ornamented with handsome nickeled name plate. It opens sufficiently wide for the removal of the ashes in the extra heavy ash pan.

THE WOOD FIRE DOOR is the full size of the fire box, handsomely carved design, substantially mounted on nickeled hinged pins.

FIRE BOX. We have given this feature, which is the most important part of a stove or range, the most careful study, and have perfected a fire chamber that is, without question, correct in principle, shape and size and unequaled for economy of fuel consumption. It is wide, holds an abundance of fuel, just the right depth so that no heat can be wasted whether a large or small fire is burning.

DUPLEX GRATE. This handsome Acme Royal-Redwood Range is equipped with our patent duplex grate, the best made, giving free access of air to all parts of the fuel, permits the dropping of the ashes and clinkers without loss of live coals and can be quickly converted into either a wood burning or coal burning grate at will and giving equally good satisfaction in burning either coal or wood.

THE HEARTH is generously proportioned, ornamented with nickeled bands, top slides, leaving a full opening so that the ash pan is easily removed.

FLUES. The excellent and perfect flue construction in this range insures the highest quality of cooking and baking, by reason of the properly proportioned size of flues to the capacity of the fire box, which, carrying all the heat over and under the oven, prevents any heat from being wasted.

OVEN. Perfectly square, surrounded by heavy iron plates that absorb and radiate the heat, keeping a uniform temperature even with an unsteady fire. To demonstrate its unusual baking qualities, we have made repeated tests of this oven by placing a biscuit in each of the four corners, and in every instance all of them have baked alike. The handsome nickeled oven shelf, together with the silver nickeled ornamentation and silver nickeled knob adds to the rich and massive appearance of the range itself.

OVEN THERMOMETER. A good, sensitive, quick working oven thermometer adds much to the comfort and convenience of those who do the baking. It measures heat just as a clock measures time; tells you when your oven has reached the degree of heat desired, and makes good baking easy to the inexperienced. Every Acme Royal-Redwood Range is equipped with our special oven thermometer. The greatest convenience and fuel saver ever attached to a range.

THE OVEN DOOR. Handsomely designed, ornamented with a beautiful silver nickeled medallion and (never hot) Alaska wire door knob. Extending from the bottom of the oven is a silver nickeled oven shelf. The door is supplied with a kicker or foot opener, to prevent the necessity of bending over to open it.

THE RESERVOIR is quick heating, made of the best iron, fitted with removable porcelain lined reservoir tank, which is easy to keep clean and will not rust. The reservoir covers are black japanned.

BASE. The entire range is supported on a solid, independent, scroll carved base, having handsome carved, massive legs, and beautifully designed deep skirt strips on all four sides.

THIS HANDSOME, newly remodeled, rich rococo pattern, cast iron range, with full equipment, exactly as illustrated on preceding page, neat high warming closet, deep porcelain lined reservoir, all nickel trimmed throughout, is offered with all its improvements under our binding guarantee to please you, under our guarantee to reach you in perfect condition, under our guarantee to save you a big percentage in cost, offered at from $22.29 to $26.99, according to size, as listed under illustration of range on preceding page.

THIS, THE ACME ROYAL-REDWOOD Nickel Trimmed Combination Wood and Coal or Exclusive Wood Burning Range, is made in our own foundry at Newark, Ohio, the largest stove foundry in the world, made from new patterns, made by the most skilled mechanics, put up under our binding guarantee that you will find it the highest grade cast iron coal and wood or exclusive wood burning range on the market, and our prices to you barely cover the cost of material and labor, with but our one small percentage of profit added.

HIGHEST GRADE STOVE PLATE AND CASTING MADE.

IT WILL INTEREST YOU to know that every particle of pig iron we use throughout our entire line of stoves and ranges is subjected to the most careful analysis by our chemist before it is put into the cupola to be melted.

THE SEVERAL GRADES required for the different lines of castings are each carefully weighed and mixed in proportion to the different chemicals contained therein, such as silicon, sulphur, carbon, etc., as for covers, centers and top sections a different mixture or composition is required than for the linings, grates, etc. After the mixtures have all been melted, a batch of molten iron is run from the cupola and put through a most severe test by our expert chemist, and, if found not to stand the test to which it is subjected, it is again melted, mixed and tested until the proper strength is obtained, which may be relied upon to a certainty. NO OTHER STOVE FOUNDRY IN THE WORLD exercises the same care to produce absolutely flawless castings. No other stove foundry in the world gives each piece and part entering into the construction of ranges such rigid inspection as is employed in our foundry at Newark, Ohio, the largest stove foundry in the world.

NOW THAT THE STOVE BUYING SEASON will soon be in full blast and to those who contemplate buying a big, heavy, cast iron combination coal and wood or exclusive wood burning range, let us urge you to send us your order, enclosing our price for one of our wonderful bargains—our Acme Royal-Redwood Six-Hole Nickel Trimmed Combination Coal and Wood or Exclusive Wood Burning Range, and the big range will go forward to your station, with the privilege that you may look thoroughly into the principles of construction, its general merits, and if it does not prove to be a wonderful bargain in every way and the world's greatest and biggest cast iron range, return it to us at our expense of freight charges both ways and we will immediately refund your money.

SOLD DIRECT TO USER. Please remember, our Big Acme Royal-Redwood Six-Hole Nickel Trimmed Combination Coal and Wood or Exclusive Wood Burning Range, like all the other stoves and ranges illustrated and described in this catalogue, is sold direct from foundry to user, under our binding guarantee, with our one small margin of profit added, thus eliminating all dealers', jobbers', agents' and peddlers' profit.

$19.95 BUYS OUR BIG ACME GRAND SIX-HOLE RANGE

— FOR —
COAL, WOOD, COKE, COBS, OR ANY KIND OF FUEL.

PRICE REDUCED. QUALITY IMPROVED.

IMPROVED FOR 1908 with latest style steel warming oven and dependable oven thermometer, and yet we are able to offer it at a lower price than last season.

HIGH WARMING CLOSET. The steel warming closet for our Acme Grand Range is a new feature and will be found both commodious and convenient. It is just the right height for the average person to easily reach. The roll front rolls back and into the top of the closet after the manner of the curtain of a roll top desk, without interfering with the commodious space inside.

MAIN TOP, COVERS AND CENTERS. The top plates are strong and braced in the best known way so as to withstand the contraction and expansion of the heat without warping or breaking. Furnished with five solid lids and one sectional or nest lid, made from the best stove plate.

THE BROILER OR FEED DOOR is substantially mounted on hinge pins to the left of the main top, and is supplied with check slide to control the fire.

THE ASH PIT DOOR below the feed or broiler door is substantially mounted, and the pan is sufficiently large for holding a considerable quantity of ashes. The hearth top slides, leaving a full opening so that the large, reinforced ash pan may be easily removed.

Water Fronts for Acme Grand Ranges, Price, extra, $2.00. Can be furnished at any time and are easily fitted in fire box by simply removing front lining. Do not mistake water fronts for water reservoirs. Water fronts are used only where there is a water supply furnished with constant pressure, through pipes, which can be obtained only in large towns and cities with waterworks, or from an elevated pressure tank. See page 20 about hot water fronts. A big stock of all sizes always on hand, crated ready for immediate shipment.

FLUE CONSTRUCTION. The modern improved sheet flue in this range insures the highest quality of cooking and baking, by reason of the properly proportioned size to the capacity of the fire box, which carries the heat over and under the oven, preventing any heat from being wasted. It heats the oven at the base as well as the sides.

THE BIG SQUARE OVEN is extra large and the upper half is as serviceable as the lower. All oven plates are smooth and of uniform thickness. Each oven plate is especially arranged to prevent warping or cracking. Has deep nickel plated outside oven shelf.

CLEAN OUT is large and convenient, fastened underneath the oven shelf with a substantial turn key.

RESERVOIR has removable lift-out porcelain lined tank. The reservoir casing is made of heavy casting, completely surrounds the tank, forming a chamber, and by operation of the special reservoir damper the heat is forced in and around the reservoir, heating the water. Reservoir covers are japanned and highly polished, made in two parts with lift-out hinge center.

THE FIRE BOX with large fire chamber is of correct shape to give wonderful service, so constructed that it is not necessary to have a big fire to heat the cooking surface.

$19.95 TO $22.41

DUPLEX GRATE. Our patented Duplex Grate is absolutely the best made, gives free access of air to all parts of the fuel; ashes and clinkers may be easily and quickly removed from the fire with no effort, and this grate will burn coal only, or both coal and wood. An extension lengthens the fire box when end coal linings are removed and very long wood can be burned. One half turn of shaker crank reverses the grate for wood.

REPAIR PARTS. We always carry a complete stock of repairs and repair parts and even ten years hence we will be able to deliver you any piece or part to replace or repair any part which, perchance, has become defective from long usage or breakage, and this at actual cost—a mere fraction of what other dealers charge.

Prompt shipment guaranteed.

No. 22H330 to No. 22H332

THE OVEN DOOR is handsomely carved with handsomely nickeled name plate and door knob, is substantially mounted with hinge pins, provided with kicker or foot opener, thereby avoiding the inconvenience of stooping over to open it. It is equipped with our Special Oven Door Thermometer, which measures heat just as a clock measures time, or a steam gauge measures steam pressure. Tells you when your oven has reached the degree of heat desired, makes it easy to maintain a uniform temperature and makes good baking easy to the most inexperienced. This magnificent range and dependable thermometer do away with "bad luck" when baking, which is very often due to improper heat in the oven more than any other cause.

Prices with Reservoir and High Warming Closet, delivered strongly crated on the cars at our Newark, Ohio, foundry:

Catalogue Number	Range No.	Size of Lids	Size of Oven, inches	Size of Top, Measuring Reservoir	Size of Fire Box, inches: Length for Coal	Width	Depth	Length for Wood	Capacity of Reservoir in Quarts	Height to Main Top, inches	Height to Warming Closet, ins.	Size of Pipe Collar, ins.	Shipping Weight, pounds	Price
22H330	8-19	No. 8	18x18 x12	43½x27	15	9½	5½	20	17	29½	26½	7	439	$19.95
22H331	8-21	No. 8	20x19¾x12½	46 x28½	17½	9½	5½	21½	17	30½	26½	7	488	22.11
22H332	9-21	No. 9	20x19¾x12½	46 x28½	17½	9½	5½	21½	17	30½	26½	7	488	22.41

OUR $17.42 ACME GRAND without reservoir, as shown in the small illustration. This is the exact same range as the one above excepting it is without the reservoir, having the extension end shelf instead. Always state the fuel to be used. Made in three sizes as listed below. Prices without reservoir, delivered strongly crated on the cars at our foundry in Newark, Ohio:

Catalogue Number	Range No.	Size of Lids	Size of Oven	Size of MainTop	Size of EndShelf	Size of Fire Box, inches: Length for Coal	Width	Depth	Length for Wood	Height to Main Top	Height of Warming Closet, inches	Pipe to Fit Collar	Shipping Weight	Price
22H335	8-19	8	18x18 x12	43½x27	7x27	15	9½	5½	20	29½	26½	7	375 lbs.	$17.42
22H336	8-21	8	20x19¾x12½	46 x28½	7x28½	17½	9½	5½	21½	30½	26½	7	420 lbs.	18.92
22H337	9-21	9	20x19¾x12½	46 x28½	7x28½	17½	9½	5½	21½	30½	26½	7	430 lbs.	19.22

If wanted without warming closet, deduct $2.25 from prices listed above.

$17.42

No. 22H335 to No. 22H337

DESCRIPTION OF ACME TRIUMPH STEEL RANGES.

THE BODY OF BLUE POLISHED STEEL PLATE.

The material from which our Acme Triumph Steel Range is made needs no commendation from us, as it is the product of the world famous Wellsville Rolling Mills, and is known to all steel buyers as "Wellsville Polished Steel." This steel is the standard of the world, and its beautiful surface and high quality were only secured by persistent, intelligent and conscientious labor. This steel requires neither blacking, enameling or japanning, as, in the process of manufacture, it is passed and repassed through ponderous rollers, which polish and repolish it until a permanent and beautiful blue color is obtained. These steel sheets are handled and rehandled in oil at the rolling mill and at our foundry in Newark, which preserves the beautiful color from spots and markings as it passes through the hands of the workmen. It also protects the beautiful finish from all exposure of the weather in shipping, so that when you receive the range the blue polished steel plate is just as perfect as when it was first finished. Wipe off the surface of the steel with a soft cloth and the deep blue color of this matchless material becomes a delight to the eye and a satisfaction to the housewife, and it requires no further attention. Its beautiful surface will not burn off. If you should leave home for a vacation or place your range in storage, simply oil the surface of the range with common natural oil, vaseline, petroleum jelly or any other oil free from salt, and when it is required for use again, rub this oil off and its beautiful blue surface is as good as new. If you will follow these instructions this fine blue surface will never become impaired.

ALL THE HEAVY PARTS **are made of the very highest grade stove plate, the only dependable metal which** can be used in any steel range for those parts which are exposed to the direct action of the fire. We make our own stove plate from the very best grade of pig iron and guarantee it to be the equal of that used in any other high grade range made.

HIGH WARMING CLOSET. **This has become an almost indispensable attachment to this article of kitchen furniture, and the high warming closet of the Acme** Triumph Steel Range is both commodious and convenient. It is at just a proper height for the average person to easily reach; the roll front door rolls back and into the top of the closet, after the manner of the curtain of a roll top desk, without interfering with the commodious space inside. This warming closet door is so carefully counter-balanced that it works very easily, the weight of the hand being sufficient to open it. The top, sides, back and roll front of the high closet are made of the same beautiful blue polished steel used in the body of the range. It is trimmed with nickel steel bands along the front, as shown on preceding page. The upper nickel steel band is in broad relief to its parallel band at the bottom. The right and left corner pieces are full silver nickeled. The medallion or panel on the front of the closet, together with its door handle, are made of our world renowned silver nickeling on cast designs. Connecting the high closet with the main top of the range and supporting the high closet are our openwork rococo design closet brackets which are full silver nickeled. A capacious smoke pipe connecting with the main top of the stove passes up through the closet, going out at the closet top, as shown. This clear joint of smoke pipe passing through the closet is made of Wellsville polished steel plate and on its front below the closet is a circular register draft check handsomely silver nickeled, which may be opened to reduce the draft when necessary.

TEA POT HOLDERS. **To the right and left of the high closet pipe are elaborately designed tea pot holders, handsomely silver** nickeled, which may be easily and quickly utilized by dropping them down so that the tea pot or other cooking utensil may be placed upon the bracket.

COAL FEED POUCH AND BROILER DOOR. **On the left end of the range we provide a capacious coal feed pouch with a lift on the cover or door, as shown in the larger illustration on this page.** Our designer, in moulding this feature of the Acme Triumph Steel Range, has given us a combination coal feed and broiler door at the same time. Lift the feed cover and a broiler may be inserted through the opening. All the fumes of the broiling are carried up the smoke flue while the steaks or chops broiled over the bed of red coals remain sweet and wholesome. This combination pouch feed and broiler door extends downward to the draft registers, and is part of the same stove plate casting. There is no japanning to burn off, and it requires no more attention to keep it in beautiful condition than do the main top, covers and centers. It does away with moving cooking utensils and lifting off lid covers to feed the fire. The door is heavy, it is hung on the main top with strong lugs, it is easy to operate, and forms a good chute for coal.

THE WOOD FEED DOOR. **The wood feed door swings to the left and is lined so as to prevent ashes from piling against the inside and fall**ing to the floor when the door is opened. From the illustrations of the range you can see that the doors are of beautiful design, ornamented with elaborate carving and finished with our everlasting silver nickel polish. Each door is carefully ground and fitted perfecly tight, touching on every edge. When closed the doors are held secure by latches or turnkeys and are very easy to operate.

TOWEL ROD. **A handsome silver nickel towel rod is mounted on the right side of the main top.** This towel rod is a great improvement over the weak, wobbly rods made from small wire which is generally furnished with high priced steel ranges.

DUPLEX GRATE. **It is almost unnecessary to describe the merits of this grate because it is a standard construction,** too well known to need our praise. Our best mechanics construct this grate and it always operates perfectly, and with our poker device and crank shaker it is easily and quickly cleaned. A half turn will drop all large ashes and clinkers into the ash pan and return the grate to its proper position again without the loss of a particle of the fire. **For burning hard coal** with our duplex grate, which is furnished with this range, the grate should always have the concave or open side up. This allows the draft to circulate through the opening and gives proper circulation. **For soft coal,** the grate is left in the same way as for burning hard coal. With the large flues we put in this range it is impossible for them to choke up with any kind of fuel, and therefore soft coal can be burned with economy by simply regulating the drafts. **For burning wood,** always be sure to reverse the grate. Simply give it a turn with the shaker. This gives you an entirely new design of grate, made especially for burning wood. When the range is used for burning wood, the two end linings should be removed, thus giving a larger fire box so that a long stick of wood can be used. All other fuel can be burned as economically as coal and wood.

Wood Fire Box.

THE FIRE BOX. **This is the most important part of any range, and it is here that we give the greatest care in constructing our steel ranges.** It must not be too deep, nor too wide, nor the linings too heavy. The fire box has been the subject of constant consideration in our great foundry, and we have produced beyond question a fire box that is guaranteed to be a great fuel saver and one that will give absolute satisfaction. The linings are of proper weight to withstand the heat, and with just ordinary care are guaranteed to give long service. Our illustration of the fire box will convey to you a very clear understanding of the wide adaptability of this range to every sort of fuel. The picture shows the coal fire box with duplex grate and end linings in proper position. By a simple device of our own invention you are able to instantly convert this coal fire box into a wood fire box. A simple turn of the wrist inverts the grate bars so that you have a solid level grate bottom for wood burning. The end linings are then removed and the fire box then appears as shown in the illustration above. The wonderful construction of this duplex grate gives us in the Acme Triumph Steel Range the simplest method ever devised for the quick conversion of a perfect coal burning fire box to a perfect wood burning fire box, with an extra space for the reception of long sticks of wood. The length of this wood burning fire box with end linings removed and with extension attached is 26 inches in all sizes of the Acme Triumph Steel Range.

Coal Fire Box.

Prices do not include tea pot, kettle, etc., shown in above illustration. For cooking utensils see pages 919 to 927.

OUR ACME TRIUMPH Six-Hole STEEL RANGE is unequaled in design and finish, the very handsomest steel range made.

RESERVOIR TANKS. **The large reservoir tanks are lined with porcelain, making the inside as clean as a china dish.** They are easily removable, easily kept clean, and we have taken especial pains to make them of large capacity—a feature we feel sure will be appreciated. The reservoir capacity of the Triumph Range is 22 quarts. By turning the reservoir damper heat is thrown under the reservoir, heating the water boiling hot. The two reservoir covers are beautifully designed, highly japanned, the japan finish being baked on by our new and original process. No detail of construction, no matter how small, has been overlooked by us in our effort to produce the best.

COMMODIOUS ASH DOOR **By reference to the illustration of the range you will notice that the ash door is unusually large,** that it extends the full width and height of the ash pit and provides ample room for an unusually large ash pan, which will hold the accumulated ashes of one day's use, thus lessening the labor and dirt which go with the removal of the ashes.

ASH PAN. **The ash pan is extra large, has a strong wire handle or bale, is wired around the top and is made of the highest grade refined steel.** It is so constructed and fits so perfectly that the ashes shoot direct to the pan from the grate, and do not dribble over the pan to be dragged out on the floor when the ash pan is taken out. The door of the ash pit is independent of the pan, and is fitted in place so that drafts at this point may not interfere with the control of the fire.

THE LARGE OVENS. **All sizes of the Acme Triumph Steel Range are equipped with an oven 21 inches deep and 14 inches high.** The width of the oven is 16, 18 or 20 inches, according to the size of the range selected. We have put a great deal of care and skill on the oven of the Acme Triumph Steel Range, and by a special arrangement of the flues it has been possible for us to bring this oven to the highest degree of perfection and to make them quick and even and satisfactory bakers. The oven bottom of our steel ranges is made of the highest grade selected stock sheet steel. So constructed, bolted braced and reinforced that we guarantee it to always remain level and it will not buckle warp or sag. Cast oven bottoms are easily subject to firecrack, and the construction of our reinforced, bolted and braced steel oven bottom insures more heat in the oven with less fuel and better satisfaction throughout. The oven top is protected with a corrugated cast plate, which also serves to distribute the heat evenly to all parts of the oven. The oven in this handsome range is ventilated so that no dead air is retained in it. The steel wire oven rack is light, clean and substantial, and very superior to any other style.

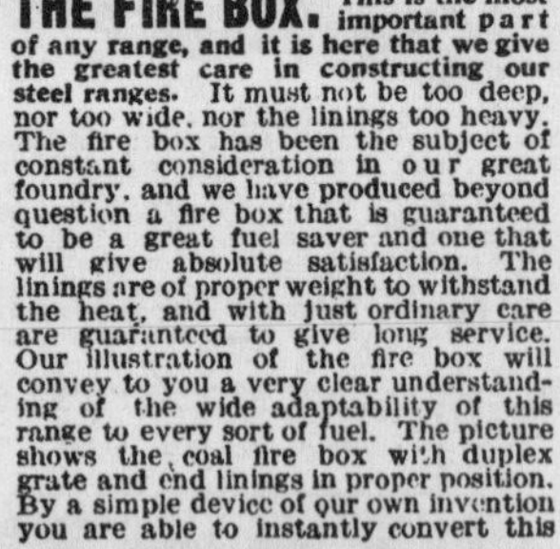

Top Oven Plate.

Bottom Oven Plate.

THE OVEN DOOR **is strong, solid and so accurately balanced that it cannot shut suddenly. It is handsomely silver nickel plated and opens even with the oven** bottom, thus forming an extension or shelf, which makes it possible to draw out and turn a roast without having to lift it, a convenience which will be appreciated. Oven door handles will not get hot, but remain as cool and comfortable to the touch as they are beautiful to the sight.

OVEN THERMOMETER. **This handsome range is equipped with the celebrated Pequabuck Oven Door Thermometer,** which will be found a great convenience and an unsurpassed fuel saver. The temperature of the oven and the consequent rate of speed at which the joint or loaf is cooking, is shown accurately without opening the oven door and makes the maintenance of an even temperature a very simple matter, insuring cooking of uniform standard of excellence, even to the most inexperienced. The indicator is in plain sight all the time, and indicates not only the progress and rate of baking, but also the condition of the fire and necessity for replenishing the fuel and warns of the cooling of the oven so destructive to good pastry baking.

FLUE CONSTRUCTION. **The Acme Triumph Range is constructed with cast flues of ample depth to prevent them from becoming easily clogged up.** They are so proportioned around the oven that any kind of fuel may be used with perfect satisfaction. The flue under the oven has a heavy flue strip riveted to both top and bottom of flue. This strip throws the heat to the front, where it circulates and passes to the back of the range.

THE POKER DOOR. **The poker door gives ready access to the entire surface of the grate,** and when it is opened it is very easy to loosen or remove a clinker that may be fastened in the grate bars, and which it has been found impossible to remove in the ordinary poking operation. If you have used other ranges you know how much trouble you have sometimes experienced with clinkers, and this fine feature of the Acme Triumph Steel Range will commend itself to you.

FOR FURTHER DETAILED DESCRIPTION OF THE ACME TRIUMPH AND OUR BIG FREE PROFIT SHARING OFFER SEE NEXT PAGE.

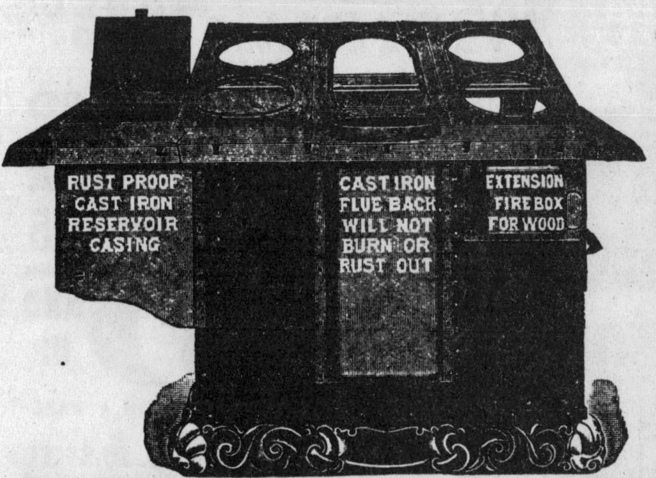

MAIN TOP, COVERS, CENTERS AND ANCHOR PLATES. All of these important parts are made of the finest cast stove plate, in the manufacture of which we use only the purest Birmingham pig iron. These plates are not to be compared with the cheap malleable iron main tops, covers, centers and anchor plates some manufacturers use in their so called "steel" ranges. Malleable iron melts at a lower temperature than first class stove castings, and for this reason the latter, which we use in the Acme Triumph Steel Range, are more durable for use where the parts come in direct contact with the fire. You will never have any trouble due to the cracking or warping of these parts when you buy and use the Acme Triumph Steel Range. Every piece of casting that we use is carefully tested. We guarantee that not a piece of scrap iron of any sort, nor any mixture of metals of doubtful quality enters into the manufacture of our castings, and that we produce only the best stove plate. In making the stove plate used in the construction of the Acme Triumph we make provision for the expansion and contraction which comes with the daily use of the range and our castings retain their shape as long as the range is in use.

THE LIDS. The Acme Triumph Steel Range is fitted with five solid lids and one sectional or nest lid, all made from the best stove plate. The nest lid is very convenient, as any one or all of the rings may be lifted out at will. If you wish to place a small vessel on the range and have it come in direct contact with the fire, you may take out one or all of the sections and expose as much or as little of the bottom of the cooking vessel to the fire as you wish.

RESERVOIR CASING. Every part of our reservoir and casing is made of cast iron stove plate. Steel or sheet iron reservoir casings, used on ranges by many manufacturers, are found not to be practical for they soon corrode and rust out from creosote and moisture. We call your particular attention to the extension reservoir of the Acme Triumph Steel Range, made from the finest grade of stove plate and embodying every improvement, and we guarantee it never to rust or burn out.

CAST IRON FLUE BACK. The large, well constructed back flue (as shown in illustration) is one solid piece of cast iron, guaranteed not to rust or burn out. When sheet steel is used for a flue back, as is the case in most steel ranges now on the market, the creosote drippings from the pipe act chemically upon the steel and eat out the flue within a short time. You will notice that whenever any part of the Acme Triumph Steel Range comes in direct contact with the fire we have substituted the best stove plate castings for steel, as it is the best class of material and is more satisfactory and more durable.

SCREW DRAFT REGISTER. It is fitted with a drop door, which gives free access to the bottom of grate for convenience in lighting the fire or poking the grate when that is necessary.

OVEN CLEAN-OUT. On this range we have put the best oven clean-out chute ever before devised for steel ranges; see the illustration. It is located underneath the handsome nickel oven door. It is large, convenient, and a liberal opening through which the space under the oven can be cleaned out thoroughly and quickly. The door is handsomely nickel plated by our silver nickel process, and is easily removed and adjusted.

BOTTOM EDGE. All of our steel ranges are reinforced by heavy steel which is run around the entire bottom of the range and is strongly riveted to the steel plates of the range body. This is just another of the many special features employed in our foundry in Newark, Ohio, the largest foundry in the world, giving our steel ranges a solid, substantial construction.

CAST END. By referring to the illustration you will note the construction of the end of all our steel ranges, a construction which forms a casting for the fire box. This whole end is a handsome piece of heavy cast stove plate work that will never burn out, warp, sag or buckle.

ROCOCO CAST BASE OR FOUNDATION. Every Acme Triumph Steel Range is placed upon an ornamental and elaborately designed base, which is made of the highest quality of stove plate casting, finished in the best manner known to stove manufacturing, and trimmed at each corner with nickel corner pieces. This heavy cast iron skirt or base, which goes clear around the base and raises the range from the floor 2½ inches, leaves an air chamber under the range and protects the floor from scorching and therefore there is no need of a stove board. We guarantee our ranges to be better constructed, more durable and to outwear any other range manufactured, and therefore we spare no pains or expense in any way, shape or manner to sustain this guarantee.

THE DIRECT DRAFT DAMPER is located in the back flue and cannot be reached by the flame; consequently it does not warp or burn out and cannot be clogged with ashes. When the oven is to be heated for baking the damper is pulled up as far as possible. We again call your special attention to the large flue at the back of the range, being made in one piece of the best cast stove plate, which we guarantee not to rust or burn out.

SILVER NICKELING. The silver nickel plated parts on our steel ranges are not only the highest quality but also the best finished, and produce the most attractive range on the market. Our process of nickeling gives our castings an indestructible luster. Each piece is put through our wonderful silver nickeling process, then polished to the highest finish. The front edge of the main top is bound with a silver nickeled band; the wood fire door, the removable grate panel, the ash door, the oven door and the oven door handle, the oven door medallion and the flue cover name plate are all made by our silver nickeling process, which gives beautiful ornamentation—a process which we have been using a number of years and which has become famous wherever our Acme stoves are used. Order one of these Acme Triumph Ranges, set it up in your own home, and after a trial of thirty days if you do not find that it is by far the best range and you do not find that you have saved a big sum on the purchase price, return the range at our expense and we will gladly pay the freight charges both ways and refund your money in full.

SEE WHAT WE GIVE YOU FREE IF YOU ORDER AN ACME TRIUMPH STEEL RANGE FROM US

The Profit Sharing Certificates which we will send you upon receipt of your order for an Acme Triumph Steel Range in any one of the five sizes mentioned on page 848 will entitle you to your choice of many articles enumerated in our latest Profit Sharing Catalogue in exchange for $25.00 in Profit Sharing Certificates.

ON THIS PAGE WE SHOW ONLY A FEW OF THEM. There are many others which we have not room to illustrate and describe, but which are equal in desirability and value to those here shown. Bear in mind that we positively guarantee our Acme Triumph Steel Range to be the very greatest range bargain ever offered. If you bought it at our price without any other inducement you would still be getting the most remarkable range value ever offered. You will be getting a better range for less money than you could possibly secure from any other dealer. But the advantage of ordering an Acme Triumph Steel Range from us does not stop there. We give you more than wonderful value, we give you more than remarkably low prices. In addition to these advantages we give you **absolutely free of any** cost your choice of these articles shown on this page and others shown in our Profit Sharing Catalogue as your share of our profits. We make it clear that you are not paying for these Profit Sharing Articles, either directly or indirectly, by the fact that our prices on the Acme Triumph Steel Range in its various sizes are far lower than you can obtain from any other dealer and you can easily satisfy yourself on this point by comparing our prices with those quoted elsewhere. The Acme Triumph Steel Range, like all the other stoves and ranges in this big catalogue, is made in our own stove foundry, the very largest stove foundry in the world, and our prices to you represent the actual manufacturing cost in the world's largest stove foundry with just one small profit added, and out of this profit we return to you a liberal share in the form of our Profit Sharing Certificates, which we issue for the full amount of your order as soon as we receive it. When we receive your order for an Acme Triumph Steel Range, the Profit Sharing Certificate, no matter what size range you order, will be more than enough to entitle you to your choice, **absolutely free**, of any of the articles we give free for only $25.00 in Profit Sharing Certificates. If you order other supplies from us for the household, for the farm, for the shop, or for the factory in addition to the Acme Triumph Steel Range, your Profit Sharing Certificates will, of course, reach a much larger amount and you will be entitled to choose from other and more valuable articles as well as from those we give for only $25.00 in certificates. These you will find fully illustrated and described in the latest revised edition of our Customers' Profit Sharing Catalogue, which is a larger, handsomer and more liberal book than we have ever before published. **We will send this latest Profit Sharing Catalogue FREE and postpaid on application.**

This Man's Raincoat FREE in exchange for $25.00 in Profit Sharing Certificates.

This Ladies' Raincoat FREE in exchange for $25.00 in Profit Sharing Certificates.

This Boys' Double Breasted Knee Pants Suit FREE in exchange for $25.00 in Profit Sharing Certificates.

This splendid Banquet Lamp FREE in exchange for $25.00 in Profit Sharing Certificates.

This Photograph Album FREE in exchange for $25.00 in Profit Sharing Certificates.

This handsome Turned Glass Bowl and Twelve Cups FREE in exchange for $25.00 in Profit Sharing Certificates.

This beautiful Cobbler Seat Rocker FREE in exchange for $25.00 in Profit Sharing Certificates.

This beautiful Mantel Clock FREE in exchange for $25.00 in Profit Sharing Certificates.

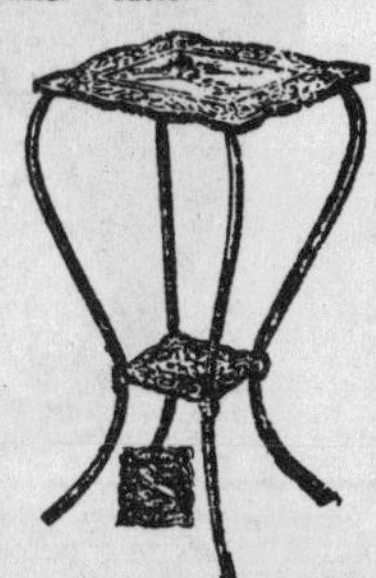

This handsome Gilt Parlor Stand FREE in exchange for $25.00 in Profit Sharing Certificates.

SEE INDEX, PINK PAGES 552 TO 559, TO FIND WHAT YOU WANT.

UNEQUALED IN MECHANICAL PERFECTION.

WEHRLE MODEL No. 20 SIX-HOLE FULL NICKELED BLUE POLISHED STEEL RANGE

$25.95 AND UP

BURNS ANY KIND OF FUEL, HARD OR SOFT COAL, WOOD, COKE OR CORN COBS.

WONDERFULLY QUICK SHIPMENT FROM A WAREHOUSE VERY NEAR YOU.

TO GET THIS WEHRLE MODEL No. 20 STEEL RANGE, exactly as illustrated, complete with reservoir and warming closet, in just a day or two, or at the farthest, a few days after we receive your order, we have it stored and securely crated in all sizes, ready for immediate shipment, from a warehouse in the following cities. You will have no freight to pay excepting the little bit of freight charges from the warehouse nearest you to your railroad station.

ST. LOUIS, MO.
FARGO, N. DAK.
KANSAS CITY, MO.
SIOUX FALLS, S. D.
ST. PAUL, MINN.
WATERLOO, IA.
DAVENPORT, IA.
MILWAUKEE, WIS.
OMAHA, NEB.
WICHITA, KAN.
NEWARK, OHIO
HARRISBURG, PA.
CHICAGO, ILL.
ALBANY, N. Y.
GRAND RAPIDS, MICH.

GUARANTEED RUSTPROOF CAST IRON RESERVOIR CASING.

CAST IRON LEFT END, GUARANTEED NOT TO WARP, BUCKLE OR BURN OUT.

Be sure to get a range that is adapted to your purpose and needs and one large enough to do its work right. By referring to the table of sizes you will find Catalogue No. 22L9, range No. 7-14, is the smallest **Wehrle Model No. 20** range we make, having six 7-inch cooking holes and a 14-inch oven. Catalogue No. 22L10 is the next smallest **Wehrle Model No. 20** range, having six 7-inch cooking holes and a 16-inch oven. Be sure to select a range large enough to answer your requirements and to fit your cooking utensils.

Water Fronts for Wehrle Model No. 20 Steel Range, $2.50 extra. Do not mistake water fronts for water reservoirs. See page 371 about Hot Water Fronts.

Prices for the Wehrle Model No. 20 6-Hole Steel Range, Complete With Reservoir and High Warming Closet: Made in seven sizes, securely crated ready for immediate shipment from our foundry at Newark, Ohio, or a warehouse very near you. Prices do not include pipe or cooking utensils. For cooking utensils see pages 419 to 422.

Catalogue No.	Range No.	Size of Lids	Size of Oven, inches	Main Top Including Reservoir, inches	Height to Main Top, inches	Height of Warming Closet, in.	Size Pipe to Fit Collar, inches	Capacity of Reservoir, qts.	Shipping Weight, pounds	PRICE
22L9	7-14	7	14x21x14	43x28½	31	27	7	10½	500	$25.95
22L10	7-16	7	16x21x14	45x28½	31	27	7	13½	505	28.45
22L11	8-16	8	16x21x14	45x28½	31	27	7	13½	505	29.39
22L12	8-18	8	18x21x14	47x28½	31	27	7	17	525	30.83
22L13	9-18	9	18x21x14	47x28½	31	27	7	17	525	31.13
22L14	8-20	8	20x21x14	49x28½	31	27	7	22	545	32.23
22L15	9-20	9	20x21x14	49x28½	31	27	7	22	545	32.53

On above sizes fire box is 8¾ in. wide, 8½ in. deep. Its length for coal is 18 in. and for wood 26 in.

If wanted without High Closet but with Reservoir, deduct $3.00 from the price of any size.
If wanted without Reservoir but with High Closet, deduct $3.00 from the price of any size.
If wanted without Reservoir or High Closet, deduct $6.00 from the price of any size.

ON PAGES 374 TO 376 YOU WILL FIND DETAILED DESCRIPTION OF OUR WEHRLE MODEL No. 20 SIX-HOLE BLUE POLISHED STEEL RANGE.

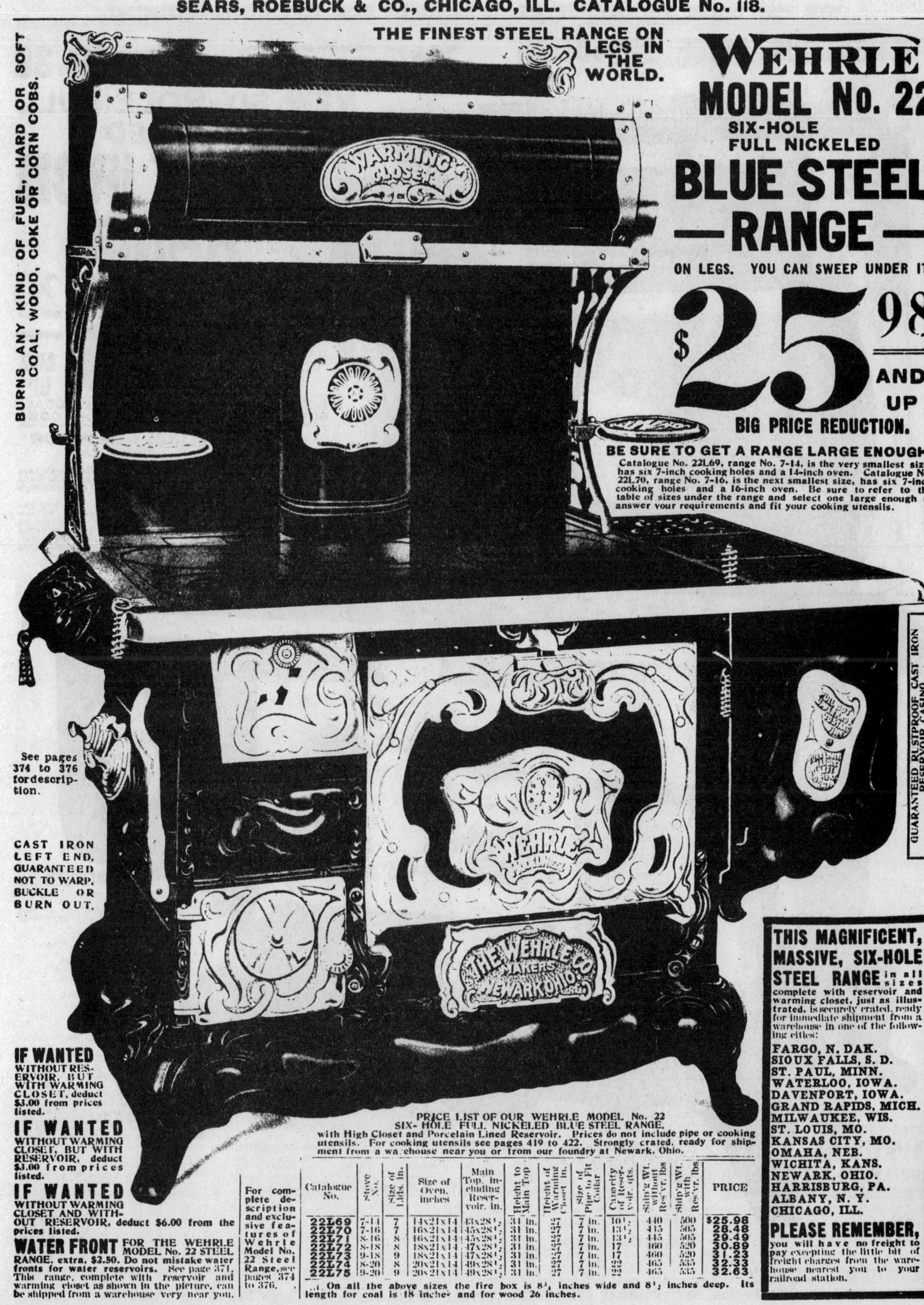

BURNS ANY KIND OF FUEL, HARD OR SOFT COAL, WOOD, COKE OR CORN COBS.

THE FINEST STEEL RANGE ON LEGS IN THE WORLD.

WEHRLE MODEL No. 22

SIX-HOLE FULL NICKELED BLUE STEEL —RANGE—

ON LEGS. YOU CAN SWEEP UNDER IT.

$25.98 AND UP

BIG PRICE REDUCTION.

BE SURE TO GET A RANGE LARGE ENOUGH. Catalogue No. 22L69, range No. 7-14, is the very smallest size, has six 7-inch cooking holes and a 14-inch oven. Catalogue No. 22L70, range No. 7-16, is the next smallest size, has six 7-inch cooking holes and a 16-inch oven. Be sure to refer to the table of sizes under the range and select one large enough to answer your requirements and fit your cooking utensils.

See pages 374 to 376 for description.

CAST IRON LEFT END, GUARANTEED NOT TO WARP, BUCKLE OR BURN OUT.

GUARANTEED RUSTPROOF CAST IRON RESERVOIR CASING.

IF WANTED WITHOUT RESERVOIR, BUT WITH WARMING CLOSET, deduct $3.00 from prices listed.

IF WANTED WITHOUT WARMING CLOSET, BUT WITH RESERVOIR, deduct $3.00 from prices listed.

IF WANTED WITHOUT WARMING CLOSET AND WITHOUT RESERVOIR, deduct $6.00 from the prices listed.

WATER FRONT FOR THE WEHRLE MODEL No. 22 STEEL RANGE, extra, $2.50. Do not mistake water fronts for water reservoirs. See page 371. This range, complete with reservoir and warming closet as shown in the picture, can be shipped from a warehouse very near you.

PRICE LIST OF OUR WEHRLE MODEL No. 22 SIX-HOLE FULL NICKELED BLUE STEEL RANGE, with High Closet and Porcelain Lined Reservoir. Prices do not include pipe or cooking utensils. For cooking utensils see pages 419 to 422. Strongly crated, ready for shipment from a warehouse near you or from our foundry at Newark, Ohio.

For complete description and exclusive features of Wehrle Model No. 22 Steel Range, see pages 374 to 376.

Catalogue No.	Stove No.	Size of Lids, in.	Size of Oven, inches	Main Top, including Reservoir, in.	Height to Main Top	Height of Warming Closet, in.	Size of Pipe to Fit Collar	Capacity of Reservoir, qts.	Ship'g Wt. without Res'vr, lbs	Ship'g Wt. with Res'vr, lbs	PRICE
22L69	7-14	7	14x21x14	43x28½	31 in.	27	7 in.	10½	440	500	$25.98
22L70	7-16	7	16x21x14	45x28½	31 in.	27	7 in.	13½	445	505	28.48
22L71	8-16	8	16x21x14	45x28½	31 in.	27	7 in.	13½	445	505	29.49
22L72	8-18	8	18x21x14	47x28½	31 in.	27	7 in.	17	460	520	30.89
22L73	9-18	9	18x21x14	47x28½	31 in.	27	7 in.	17	460	520	31.23
22L74	8-20	8	20x21x14	49x28½	31 in.	27	7 in.	22	465	535	32.33
22L75	9-20	9	20x21x14	49x28½	31 in.	27	7 in.	22	465	535	32.63

On all the above sizes the fire box is 8¾ inches wide and 8½ inches deep. Its length for coal is 18 inches and for wood 26 inches.

THIS MAGNIFICENT, MASSIVE, SIX-HOLE STEEL RANGE in all sizes complete with reservoir and warming closet, just as illustrated, is securely crated, ready for immediate shipment from a warehouse in one of the following cities:

FARGO, N. DAK.
SIOUX FALLS, S. D.
ST. PAUL, MINN.
WATERLOO, IOWA.
DAVENPORT, IOWA.
GRAND RAPIDS, MICH.
MILWAUKEE, WIS.
ST. LOUIS, MO.
KANSAS CITY, MO.
OMAHA, NEB.
WICHITA, KANS.
NEWARK, OHIO.
HARRISBURG, PA.
ALBANY, N. Y.
CHICAGO, ILL.

PLEASE REMEMBER, you will have no freight to pay excepting the little bit of freight charges from the warehouse nearest you to your railroad station.

TREMENDOUS PRICE REDUCTION

WEHRLE MODEL No. 30
NEW SIX-HOLE FULL NICKELED CAST IRON RANGE

$26.20 AND UP

BURNS ANY KIND OF FUEL, HARD COAL, SOFT COAL, WOOD, COKE OR CORN COBS

ENTIRELY NEW FOR 1909

Absolutely the handsomest, most elaborate and highest grade cast iron range made in the world. A long step ahead of others in high art stove making.

JUST LOOK what we are doing. We are furnishing you this magnificent Wehrle Model No. 30 new six-hole full nickeled cast iron range, in all sizes complete with reservoir and warming closet, just as illustrated, beyond question of doubt the highest grade cast iron range made in the world, delivered from a warehouse in one of the cities named below.

FOR DETAILED DESCRIPTION AND EXCLUSIVE FEATURES. SEE PAGES 374 TO 376

REMEMBER you have no freight to pay excepting the little bit of freight charges from a warehouse, the one nearest you, to your railroad tion.

FARGO, N. DAK.
SIOUX FALLS, S. DAK.
ST. PAUL, MINN.
WATERLOO, IOWA
DAVENPORT, IOWA
MILWAUKEE, WIS.
ST. LOUIS, MO.
KANSAS CITY, MO.
OMAHA, NEB.
CHICAGO, ILL.
WICHITA, KAN.
NEWARK, OHIO
HARRISBURG, PA.
ALBANY, N. Y.
GRAND RAPIDS, MICH.

PRICES FOR THE WEHRLE MODEL No. 30 SIX-HOLE CAST IRON RANGE.

Complete as illustrated, with high warming closet and porcelain lined reservoir, and drop oven shelf door, securely crated, delivered on cars at our foundry at Newark, Ohio, or at a warehouse very near you. Prices do not include pipe or cooking utensils. For cooking utensils see pages 419 to 422.

WATER FRONT FOR WEHRLE MODEL No. 30 Cast Iron Range, extra, $2.50. Do not mistake water fronts for water reservoirs. See page 371 about hot water fronts.

Catalogue Number	Stove No.	Size of Lids	Size of Oven, inches	Main Top Including Reservoir, inches	Size of Fire Box, Inches				Height to Main Top, in.	Height of Warming Closet, in.	Size Pipe to Fit Collar, in.	Capacity of Reservoir, quarts	Shipping Weight, pounds	Price
					Length for Coal	Width	Depth	Length for Wood						
22L214	7-14	7	14x21x14	43x28½	15½	8½	7½	19½	31	27	7	10½	500	$26.20
22L215	7-16	7	16x21x14	45x28½	16¾	9	7½	20½	31	27	7	13½	520	28.70
22L216	8-16	8	16x21x14	45x28½	16¾	9	7½	20½	31	27	7	13½	520	29.95
22L217	8-18	8	18x21x14	47x28½	17½	9½	7½	21½	31	27	7	17	550	31.45
22L218	9-18	9	18x21x14	47x28½	17½	9½	7½	21½	31	27	7	17	550	31.75
22L219	8-20	8	20x21x14	49x28½	18	10	7½	22½	31	27	7	22	595	32.85
22L220	9-20	9	20x21x14	49x28½	18	10	7½	22½	31	27	7	22	595	33.15

If wanted without warming closet, but with reservoir, deduct $3.00 from prices listed. If wanted without reservoir, but with warming closet, deduct $3.00 from price listed. If wanted without warming closet and without reservoir, deduct $6.00 from prices listed.

FOR COMPLETE DESCRIPTION AND EXCLUSIVE FEATURES OF WEHRLE MODEL No. 30 CAST IRON RANGE SEE PAGES 374 TO 376.

METHOD OF CONSTRUCTING Our WEHRLE Model No. 65 U-SO-NA Rust-Resisting Range

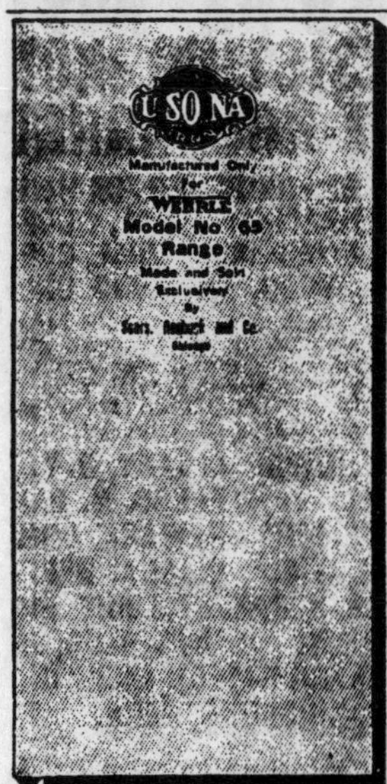

BODY. Realizing the possibilities for a practical non-corrosive rust-resisting iron for building range bodies, we had one of the large furnaces make experiments and produce for us a sheet that would absolutely resist corrosion better than steel. Working along the lines of the earliest known process of producing iron, the Catalan Forge, from which was developed the Cementine Process, and later charcoal iron, Bessemer steel and open hearth steel, the results obtained from the analysis of these metals enabled our chemist and the steel furnace metallurgist making these experiments to introduce an entirely new secret process, by which impurities in the metal are reduced to a minimum and the result of these experiments gives us an iron, the peer of all rust-resisting sheets made from iron. To identify this material as an exclusive product for building our Wehrle Model No. 65 Range, and to distinguish it from common steel sheets, charcoal iron, etc., because U-SO-NA IRON is a purer and better product, made possible by a new process, the name U-SO-NA RUST-RESISTING IRON was most correctly adopted for this product, for it is the purest iron made anywhere.

THE ILLUSTRATIONS BELOW made from a photograph of the different metals, show a comparative corrosion test between U-SO-NA RUST-RESISTING IRON, charcoal iron and sheet steel, and were made in accordance with the specifications of the American Society for Testing Metals. In this test genuine charcoal iron and the best sheet steel corroded sixty times as fast as U-SO-NA RUST-RESISTING IRON.

The original samples were suspended in a relatively large vessel containing a relative quantity of sulphuric acid solution. This solution was exactly 20 per cent chemically pure sulphuric acid and distilled water. When they were removed they were thoroughly dried and weighed as before the loss showing the comparative corrosion resisting qualities.

The result of this test is authentic in every detail, and the illustrations show the samples as they appeared after the test, demonstrating forcibly the remarkable resistance to corrosion of U-SO-NA RUST-RESISTING IRON, even excelling genuine charcoal iron.

This test proves that U-SO-NA RUST-RESISTING IRON is the purest manufactured. It is equal to the old fashioned iron that always gave satisfaction and resisted corrosion.

Duration tests have also been made on U-SO-NA RUST-RESISTING IRON, charcoal iron and steel by submerging them in a saturated solution of salt water containing 2 per cent of sulphuric acid for four months, with the following results: Loss due to corrosion: U-SO-NA, .271 per cent; charcoal, .541 per cent; steel, .409 per cent.

U-SO-NA IRON. Charcoal Iron. Steel.

The lower half of these illustrations show results of a sulphuric acid test made with different kinds of iron used in building range bodies and clearly proves that U-SO-NA IRON resists corrosion to a degree never before attained even by the old time iron sheets. U-SO-NA IRON HAS NO EQUAL.

For this reason we positively guarantee U-SO-NA RUST-RESISTING IRON, as it is now made, to be 99.94 per cent pure, and we ask you to compare this percentage with the percentage of the highest grade material made anywhere, and you will realize why U-SO-NA RUST-RESISTING IRON will and does resist corrosion. You will also understand why it is so eminently satisfactory for building ranges.

WE ALL KNOW the body is practically the life of a range, and the life of a range depends upon the material of which it is made. Wehrle Model No. 65 Ranges are made of U-SO-NA RUST-RESISTING IRON, and no other range in the world is made of this material. It costs us considerably more than steel, but in bringing out this new Wehrle Model Range we never considered cost when we saw a chance to produce a range that would last two or three times as long as a steel range.

ASBESTOS LINING. The heavy, thick insulation extends entirely under the bottom of the oven flue, preventing the heat from burning the floor and retaining the heat in the oven. When no reservoir is attached it also extends entirely over the right end of the range and, with reservoir, the lower half only is insulated. The back and all flues are similarly insulated. The asbestos, being fireproof and a non-conductor, retains the heat, and adds wonderfully to its baking qualities, making it easy to control and an economical fuel consumer.

MAIN TOP, COVERS, CENTERS AND ANCHOR PLATES must not be compared with the cheap malleable top, covers, centers and anchor plates some manufacturers use. Malleable iron will buckle, warp and burn out more easily than gray iron castings. It is impractical to use malleable iron in a range where it is exposed as directly to the fire as in fire boxes, tops, covers and centers. Gray iron castings will resist the heat longer and much better than malleable iron. Malleable iron melts at a lower temperature than gray iron castings, and for this reason the latter (which we use in our Wehrle Model No. 65 U-SO-NA Rust-Resisting Iron Range) are more durable for use where the parts come in direct contact with the fire. This range is fitted with five solid covers and one nest or graduated lid, a very convenient little device, as the varying sizes of the openings in the cover will be found very useful. You will never have any trouble due to cracking or warping of these parts when you buy and use a Wehrle Model No. 65 U-SO-NA Range, as we have made provision for expansion and contraction of the iron which comes with the daily use of the range, and our castings retain their shape as long as the range is in use.

THE HINGED TOP. This illustration shows how easy it is to lift up the top of the stove and broil meat or toast bread without having to stand over the red hot fire. By means of a silver nickel lifter the top or anchor plate directly over the fire can be easily raised and held in place by ratchets at two different heights. This is an easy way to lay the fire, as well as to spread coal over the fire without removing the lids and sliding them around over the top of the range and having the smoke pour into the room, and insures a more even heat with less fuel.

BLUE POLISHED FULL NICKEL STEEL WARMING CLOSET extends along the full length of the range body. It is the proper height for the average person to reach. The roll front door rolls back like the front of a roll top desk, out of the way, permitting the whole of the interior of the closet to be exposed. It will warm and keep the food wholesome without drying it up. Has beautiful silver nickel trimmed steel guard rail across the full length of the back and top of warming closet.

TEAPOT HOLDERS. Beautifully silver nickeled swinging teapot stands hang on double brackets at each side of the high closet. They are lifted quickly and easily to attach to either front or back holder at will. An exclusive point.

The hinged top showing the extra heavy lids and centers, the easy way to lay the fire and spread coal. You can broil meat or toast bread without having to stand over the hot fire.

RESERVOIR TANK is made of the highest grade stove plate, white porcelain lined, easily kept clean and easily lifted out. Capacity is from 13½ to 22 quarts, according to size. Reservoir Casing is made of the best cast iron stove plate. It will never rust nor burn out.

SOMETHING WORTH KNOWING ABOUT FIRE BOXES.

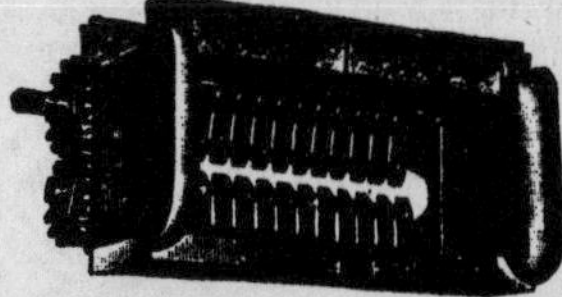

Hard Coal Fire Box, with firebrick linings and Dockash grate for burning hard (anthracite) coal.

HARD (ANTHRACITE) COAL AND WOOD FIRE BOX. No effort has been spared to equip our Wehrle Model No. 65 U-SO-NA Range with a most substantial firebrick lined fire box and Dockash grate for the use of hard (anthracite) coal. The fire box and grate conform with each other in shape and operate perfectly, leaving no dead corners for ashes or clinkers to form and there is always an even fire, proving that combustion is perfect. The fire box will retain the fire all night if the dampers are properly adjusted. A large fire box for burning wood is secured by removing the end linings and, with the extra heavy cast iron extension, gives a firebox for long sticks of wood, as shown in the table of sizes under the illustration of each range. We furnish an extra bottom grate for burning wood, which is easily dropped into place on top of the Dockash grate. When ordered for hard coal and wood the left end of these ranges appears as shown in the small picture below.

DOCKASH GRATE for hard (anthracite) coal is of the most approved pattern Dockash construction and clears the fire of ashes by a half turn of the shaker. The cog wheels which revolve the grate bars are outside of the fire box and cannot be affected by the heat or become clogged by ashes. A silver nickeled shaking crank is furnished with each range and a half turn of this shaker adjusts the grate, turning the reverse side to the fire, although the surface remains the same.

To make sure that we send you the right kind of fire box for the fuel to be used, be sure to tell us whether you burn hard (anthracite) coal and wood, soft coal and wood, or wood only.

SOFT COAL AND WOOD FIRE BOX is positively guaranteed to be the most economical and durable made in any range. The cast iron linings are made exceedingly heavy, are corrugated to prevent warping and are constructed to allow ample circulation of air behind them to prevent burning out. This is the only fire box made with a free and constant circulation of air around it and produces better combustion than ever before obtained in a range.

Soft Coal Fire Box, with Cast Iron Linings and Anti-Clinker Duplex Grate for burning soft coal.

Fire Box for burning wood only, with cast iron extension for long sticks of wood. Coal will not burn in the exclusive wood fire box.

DUPLEX ANTI-CLINKER GRATE FOR SOFT COAL AND WOOD is made in two parts. A half turn of the shaker cuts out all the dead ashes and clinkers, dropping them into the ash pan without disturbing the temper of the operator. It will burn soft coal, wood or corn cobs. For burning soft coal the grate should always have the concave or open side up. This allows the draft to circulate through the opening and gives proper combustion. For burning wood be sure to reverse the grate. Simply give it a turn with our perfected shaker crank. Wood requires less draft than coal; therefore the ribbed side of the grate should be up for burning wood and the slotted side down. When used for burning wood the two end linings are removed, giving a larger fire box so that a long stick of wood can be used. Corn cobs can be burned as economically as coal and wood.

COAL FEED POUCH AND BROILER DOOR is hinged on the left end. We provide a capacious coal feed pouch with an "always cold" lift on cover or door. On the hard coal range the broiler door drops down instead of lifting up, as shown in small illustration.

DRAFT DOOR is attached at the left of the range and directly below the feed and broiler door. It is made unusually long and has two draft registers, insuring a perfect bed of fire with no dead corners. When furnished for hard coal the range has a slide draft with knob instead of drop door with screw registers, as shown in illustration below.

WOOD FEED DOOR next to the oven on the soft coal and wood range drops down. When furnished for hard coal the door swings to the left instead of dropping down.

LARGE OVEN has been constructed with great care, so that it will bake to perfection with the least possible labor and fuel. Our ovens are made of extra heavy steel, hand riveted. No oven ever baked more evenly or quickly. **OVEN DOOR** is strong, solid and extra heavy, cannot shut suddenly and drops flush with the oven bottom, forming an extension shelf on which to draw out and turn a roast without having to lift it.

CAST IRON OVEN BOTTOM. We are using the highest grade cast stove plate for the oven bottom, which gives more heat in the oven with by far less fuel and more quickly than with a steel oven bottom. It will always remain level and will not warp nor buckle as a steel oven bottom is almost sure to do unless thoroughly braced. **OVEN RACK** is made of wrought steel rods and cannot be easily broken.

View showing left end of Wehrle Model No. 65 U-SO-NA Range for hard coal and wood, with swing wood feed door and shaking arrangement.

OVEN THERMOMETER is built right in the oven door, thus insuring absolute and even accuracy. A great convenience and an unsurpassed fuel saver.

FIRE BOX FOR WOOD ONLY is large and roomy, as shown in the table of sizes, under the large illustrations, on pages 930 to 933. When ordered for wood only, we furnish a set of extra heavy fire box linings and our improved grate for burning wood exclusively, as above illustrated. The extension is made of heavy cast iron securely bolted to the end of the fire box, no steel being exposed to the fire. **Coal will not burn in the wood fire box.**

CLEAN OUT CHUTE is located under the oven door. It is of good size so the space under the oven can be cleaned out thoroughly and quickly. The panel covering the clean out chute is handsomely nickeled, easily removed and adjusted.

This picture shows left end of the Wehrle Model No. 65 U-SO-NA Range for burning wood only, coal feed door is omitted, as the wood is fed through the end fire door to the left of the oven

OVEN DOOR HANDLE AND CATCH. The handle is made of hard-wood, beautifully polished, with a double catch. The catches have two notches, so that the oven door can be left open for cooling or ventilating. The handle is set out from the range in such a manner that it does not become hot, as oven door handles usually do. The oven door can be let down or raised without the hand coming in contact with anything except the handle on the catch.

HANDY LEVER for direct draft damper is a feature to be found in Wehrle Model Ranges only and used exclusively by us. The damper rod and "always cold" silver nickeled handle controlling the direct draft oven damper are located to the right and under the main top in front of the range, as is also the reservoir damper. You need not reach over the hot stove top to open or close either damper.

GAS ATTACHMENT. We can furnish the Wehrle Model No. 60 U-SO-NA Range in all sizes with gas attachment (as shown in illustration), but without reservoir, at $4.00 extra. Has one combination giant and simmering burner and one star burner, galvanized iron drip pan, silver nickeled supply pipe and air mixers. Grates and burner top are removable and easily cleaned. The top surface of gas attachment is 12x21 inches, can be connected to gas supply with rubber tubing or iron pipe. **Gas attachment cannot be used with gasoline or acetylene gas. If wanted with gas attachment be sure to say, "With Gas Attachment."** State whether you use natural or manufactured gas. Price for gas attachment is $4.00 in addition to price when ordered without reservoir. Shipped from our Newark, Ohio, foundry only when ordered with gas attachment.

ACCORDING TO SIZE AND FUEL USED

The exact same range as shown on page 930, with reservoir omitted and in its place is furnished an end extension shelf.

Has our improved Dockash grate and heavy brick linings of superior quality for hard (anthracite) coal, cobs and wood.

Duplex grate and cast iron linings for burning soft coal, cobs and wood.

Special grate and heavy linings for burning wood only.

BE SURE TO STATE FUEL USED

See Page 931 for Special Points of Construction and Detailed Description.

WEHRLE MODEL No. 65 U-SO-NA RUST RESISTING IRON SIX-HOLE RANGE

CAN BE FURNISHED FOR HARD (ANTHRACITE) COAL, COBS AND WOOD, SOFT COAL, COBS AND WOOD, OR WOOD ONLY

Say whether you want the range with or without water front, give catalog number and size, enclose our price, and we will ship it exactly as illustrated from one of the following warehouses:

**DAVENPORT, IOWA — ALBANY, N. Y.
CHICAGO, ILL. — FARGO, N. DAK.
KANSAS CITY, MO. — NEWARK, OHIO.
MILWAUKEE, WIS. — OMAHA, NEB.
SIOUX FALLS, S. DAK. — ST. LOUIS, MO.
ST. PAUL, MINN. — WATERLOO, IA.
GRAND RAPIDS, MICH.
HARRISBURG, PENN.**

You will have only the little bit of freight charges to pay from the warehouse nearest you to your railroad station.

FOR $2.50 EXTRA WE FURNISH THIS WEHRLE MODEL No. 65 U-SO-NA RANGE WITH HOT WATER FRONT, tested to stand 200 pounds pressure. Used in connection with pressure boilers, supplying hot water to kitchen sinks, bathrooms and chambers where there is a water supply with constant pressure, for instance city water works or elevated pressure tanks of rural districts. We can put in the water front for you when you buy the range, or you can put one in at any time thereafter yourself. Holes for the water pipe are bored at the foundry and are covered with a solid plate of iron when a water front is not ordered.

U-SO-NA IRON

COMPARE THE WEHRLE MODEL No. 65 U-SO-NA RUST RESISTING IRON RANGE, part against part, feature against feature, design against design, material against material, with any range, regardless of name or make, selling at almost double our price, and if you are conscientious in the comparison and your purchase is influenced thereby, we will get your order.

WEHRLE MODEL No. 65 THE WEHRLE CO NEWARK OHIO MAKERS

OUR NINETY-DAY TRIAL PLAN.

WEHRLE MODEL No. 65 U-SO-NA IRON RANGES are securely built, honestly represented, sold at very low prices on broad, liberal terms, making the customer the judge of the range and the one to decide whether everything is as represented and the range worth every dollar invested in it. After it arrives give it ninety days' trial, compare it with ranges of other makes selling for almost double our price. If you are not satisfied in ninety days, write us and we will instruct you how to send the range back. No questions will be asked. Your money will be refunded, together with all the freight charges you have paid.

PRICES FOR THE WEHRLE MODEL No. 65 U-SO-NA RUST RESISTING IRON SIX-HOLE RANGE, with warming closet, made in seven sizes, securely crated, ready for immediate shipment from our foundry at Newark, Ohio, or a warehouse very near you. Prices do not include pipe or cooking utensils. For cooking utensils see page 986.

Catalog No.	Stove No.	Size of Lids	Size of Oven, inches	Main Top Without End Shelf, inches	Shipping Weight, Pounds	Price for Soft Coal and Wood	Price for Hard (Anthracite) Coal and Wood	Price for Wood Only
22T44	7-14	No. 7	14x21x14	33x27	470	$25.95	$26.95	$25.70
22T45	7-16	No. 7	16x21x14	35x29	480	29.20	30.20	28.95
22T46	8-16	No. 8	16x21x14	35x29	480	30.48	31.48	30.23
22T47	8-18	No. 8	18x21x14	37x29	495	32.27	33.27	32.02
22T48	9-18	No. 9	18x21x14	37x29	495	32.52	33.52	32.27
22T49	8-20	No. 8	20x21x14	39x29	505	33.57	34.57	33.32
22T50	9-20	No. 9	20x21x14	30x29	505	33.88	34.88	33.63

FIRE BOX FOR HARD (ANTHRACITE) COAL AND WOOD on all sizes is 7¼ inches wide and 7 inches deep; its length for coal is 17¼ inches and for wood 25¼ inches.

FIRE BOX FOR SOFT COAL AND WOOD on all sizes is 9 inches wide and 7½ inches deep: its length for coal is 18½ inches and for wood 26 inches.

FIRE BOX FOR WOOD ONLY on all sizes is 10 inches wide, 8 inches deep and 27 inches long.

All sizes take 7-inch pipe. The height of warming closet, including back guard, is 31¼ inches on all sizes.

ACME LEHIGH NEW MODEL SIX-HOLE CAST IRON RANGE $23.60 AND UP

WITH HIGH SHELF AND RESERVOIR. Burning Hard (Anthracite) Coal or Wood.

Blackened, Beautifully Polished, Ready to Set Up and Use.

THE EXACT SAME RANGE as the one shown on the preceding page, excepting it has the ornamental, double capacity high shelf instead of the roll top warming closet. See full page illustration on preceding page. The handsomest, strongest and best hard coal range ever built. Fitted with the same brick linings, the same reservoir with large copper water tank holding 18½ to 25 quarts, according to size; same hi h art trimmings; broad top cooking surface; capacious oven and oven thermometer, heavily brick lined fire box and our famous Acme Dockash grate, all of which is fully described on the preceding page. Our friends in the anthracite fields of Pennsylvania, New York, New England and the East, and other locations burning anthracite coal appreciate our efforts to construct an exclusive anthracite coal and wood burning range, and nothing has ever gone out of our house for which we have received so many letters of praise.

Prices do not include pipe or cooking utensils. For cooking utensils see page 968.

We can always furnish repairs for Acme and Wehrle Model Stoves and Ranges. See page 916 about how to order stove repairs when needed in future years.

Height from stove top to top of high shelf, 28 inches.

Fitted with our dependable oven door thermometer without extra cost.

Prices are for range strongly crated and delivered on cars at our Newark, Ohio, foundry. Made in five sizes, as listed below.

Catalog No.	Range No.	Size of Lids	Size of Oven, inches	Size Top, Including Reservoir, inches	Height to Main Top	Shipping Wt., lbs.	Price, for Hard (Anthracite) Coal & W'd	Price, for Wood Only
22T310	7-16	No. 7	16 x15x11	42x24½	31 in.	475	$23.85	$23.60
22T311	7-18	No. 7	17½x17x11½	45x27	32 in.	520	26.19	25.93
22T312	8-18	No. 8	17½x17x11½	45x27	32 in.	520	26.55	26.30
22T313	8-20	No. 8	20 x19x11½	46x28	32 in.	590	28.89	28.64
22T314	9-20	No. 9	20 x19x11½	46x28	32 in.	590	29.22	28.96

For size of fire box for both wood and coal, also capacity of reservoir, see description and table of sizes of the Acme Lehigh on preceding page. All sizes take 7-inch pipe.

OUR NEW MODERN ACME LEHIGH SIX-HOLE HARD (ANTHRACITE) COAL RANGE $22.12 AND UP

WITHOUT RESERVOIR, AS SHOWN IN ILLUSTRATION, BUT OTHERWISE THE EXACT SAME RANGE AS THE ONE SHOWN ON THE PRECEDING PAGE.

THE FINEST AND BEST HARD COAL RANGE MADE.

ESPECIALLY BUILT for the hard (anthracite) coal trade in Pennsylvania, New York and New England States, and everywhere that hard coal is used. Will ornament any kitchen, and the satisfactory service it will render will make its use a pleasure to the housewife. Easy to clean and easy to operate. **The Acme Lehigh burns hard (anthracite) coal or wood.**

This range is fitted with the same high art trimmings, roll top high warming closet, broad top cooking surface, big ovens, brick lined fire box and Acme Dockash grate for hard (anthracite) coal and heavy cast iron linings for wood, as fully described on preceding page; in every respect the exact same range, but without the reservoir.

All nickel edges and nickeled medallion panels are applied or detached at your pleasure, enabling you to clean or black the stove without soiling them, and replacing them so simply that any child can do it.

Prices do not include pipe or cooking utensils. For cooking utensils see page 968.

The best style for hot water fronts. Used only where there is water furnished with constant pressure through pipes, which can only be had in towns or cities having water works or from an elevated or pneumatic water supply tank.

Water fronts for Acme Lehigh Ranges, each, $2.00.

Height from stove top to top of high closet, 29 inches.

Fitted with our dependable oven door thermometer without extra cost.

Prices are for range strongly crated and delivered on cars at our Newark, Ohio, foundry. Made in five sizes, as listed below.

Catalog No.	Range No.	Size of Lids	Size of Oven, inches	Size of Top Without End Sh'f inches	Size of End Shelf, inches	Height to Main Top	Shipping Wt., lbs.	Price, for Hard (Anthracite) Coal & W'd	Price, for Wood Only
22T305	7-16	No. 7	16 x15x11	30x24½	8x24½	31 in.	440	$22.37	$22.12
22T306	7-18	No. 7	17½x17x11½	33x27	8x27	32 in.	495	24.72	24.47
22T307	8-18	No. 8	17½x17x11½	33x27	8x27	32 in.	495	25.07	24.82
22T308	8-20	No. 8	20 x19x11½	35x28	8x28	32 in.	545	27.39	27.20
22T309	9-20	No. 9	20 x19x11½	35x28	8x28	32 in.	545	27.74	27.49

For size of fire box for both wood and coal, please see description and table of sizes of the Acme Lehigh on preceding page. All sizes take 7-inch pipe.

OUR NEW MODERN ACME LEHIGH RESERVOIR SIX-HOLE RANGE $21.62 AND UP

FOR HARD (ANTHRACITE) COAL OR WOOD. THIS ELEGANT RESERVOIR RANGE IS OFFERED, AS THE EXACT SAME RANGE WE SHOW ON THE PRECEDING PAGE, BUT WITHOUT THE HIGH CLOSET.

THE BACK TOP is finished with a handsome tea rail and in every way is as capacious, efficient and thoroughly attractive, trimmed in exactly the same manner, excepting for the absence of the high closet. The illustrations we show cannot do justice to this elegant article of kitchen furniture. It has the same detachable nickel edges; oven door medallion panel, the same long sweeping, full nickeled outside oven shelf and broad, deep base skirting, and the exact same fire box arrangement for hard (anthracite) coal and wood. For very large illustration, showing clearly every detail, nickel trimming, etc., see big illustration on preceding page. Prices do not include pipe or cooking utensils. For cooking utensils see page 968.

We can always furnish repairs for Acme and Wehrle Model Stoves and Ranges. See page 916 about how to order stove repairs when needed in future years.

Our Stoves and Ranges are blackened and polished ready to set up and use.

Fitted with our dependable oven door thermometer without extra cost.

Prices are for range strongly crated and delivered on cars at our Newark, Ohio, foundry. Made in five sizes as listed below.

Catalog No.	Range No.	Size of Lids	Size of Oven inches	Size Top, Including Reservoir, inches	Height to Main Top	Shipping Wt., lbs.	Price, for Hard (Anthracite) Coal & W'd	Price, for Wood Only
22T320	7-16	No. 7	16 x15x11	42x24½	31 in.	440	$21.87	$21.62
22T321	7-18	No. 7	17½x17x11½	45x27	32 in.	485	24.21	23.96
22T322	8-18	No. 8	17½x17x11½	45x27	32 in.	485	24.56	24.31
22T323	8-20	No. 8	20 x19x11½	46x28	32 in.	555	26.89	26.66
22T324	9-20	No. 9	20 x19x11½	46x28	32 in.	555	27.24	26.95

For size of fire box for both wood and coal, also capacity of reservoir, see description and table of sizes of the Acme Lehigh on preceding page. All sizes take 7-inch pipe.

OUR NEW MODERN ACME LEHIGH SIX-HOLE CAST IRON RANGE $21.10 AND UP

FOR HARD (ANTHRACITE) COAL OR WOOD. WITHOUT RESERVOIR, WITH HIGH SHELF.

DELIVERED ON BOARD THE CARS AT OUR FOUNDRY IN NEWARK, OHIO. THIS IS THE EXACT RANGE AS No. 22T310, AND QUOTED AT $23.60, BUT, AS ILLUSTRATED, IS WITHOUT RESERVOIR.

IT HAS ALL THE MODERN FEATURES fully described on the preceding page. Each and every Acme Lehigh is carefully fitted and inspected before being crated ready for shipment. It can be set up, connected to stove pipe, ready for fire in a very few minutes' time.

All nickel edges and nickeled medallion panels are applied or detached at your pleasure, enabling you to clean or black the stove without soiling them, and replacing them so easily that any child can do it.

Our friends in anthracite coal burning districts cannot afford to buy any other make of range when they can obtain any of this assortment of our Acme Lehigh for such wonderfully low prices as we quote.

This range is one of the latest products of our big Newark, Ohio, stove foundry, an entirely new design, gotten up especially for the section of the country where anthracite coal or wood is burned.

Prices do not include pipe or cooking utensils. For cooking utensils see page 968.

The best style for hot water fronts. Used only where there is water furnished with constant pressure through pipes, which can only be had in towns or cities having water works or from an elevated or pneumatic water supply tank.

Water fronts for Acme Lehigh Ranges, each, $2.00.

THE BEST HARD COAL RANGE MADE IN ANY FOUNDRY.

Height from stove top to top of high shelf, 28 inches.

Fitted with our dependable oven door thermometer without extra cost.

Prices are for range strongly crated and delivered on cars at our Newark, Ohio, foundry. Made in five sizes as listed below.

Catalog No.	Range No.	Size of Lids	Size of Oven, inches	Size of Top Without End Sh'f inches	Size of End Shelf, inches	Height to Main Top	Shipping Wt., lbs.	Price, for Hard (Anthracite) Coal & W'd	Price, for Wood Only
22T315	7-16	No. 7	16 x15x11	30x24½	8x24½	31 in.	430	$21.35	$21.10
22T316	7-18	No. 7	17½x17x11½	33x27	8x27	32 in.	485	23.70	23.45
22T317	8-18	No. 8	17½x17x11½	33x27	8x27	32 in.	485	24.07	23.82
22T318	8-20	No. 8	20 x19x11½	35x28	8x28	32 in.	535	26.39	26.17
22T319	9-20	No. 9	20 x19x11½	35x28	8x28	32 in.	535	26.72	26.47

For size of fire box for both wood and coal, please see description and table of sizes of the Acme Lehigh on preceding page. All sizes take 7-inch pipe.

OUR NEW MODERN ACME LEHIGH SIX-HOLE HARD COAL RANGE WITHOUT RESERVOIR $19.13 AND UP

DELIVERED ON THE CARS AT OUR FOUNDRY IN NEWARK, OHIO.

BURNS HARD (ANTHRACITE) COAL OR WOOD. Excepting for the reservoir, this is the exact same range as No. 22T320 at $21.62, and in every way meets the requirements of those who do not need the extension reservoir or the high closet. It has the same oven capacity, the same modern construction, high art trimmings, large oven, brick lined fire box and Acme Dockash grate for hard (anthracite) coal and heavy cast iron linings for wood. Closely fitted and thoroughly made in every particular. All nickel edges and nickeled medallion panels are applied or detached at your pleasure, enabling you to clean or black the stove without soiling them, and replacing them so simply that any child can do it.

In ordering this or any of our ranges, you have our absolute guarantee that if it does not reach you in perfect condition or when you have set it up in the kitchen and examined it thoroughly, cooked on it for 30 days, and it does not please you in every particular, you are at liberty to return it to us and we will return your money, together with any freight charges you may have paid.

IT TAKES JUST A FEW DAYS to get any stove to you; and freight charges amount to nothing compared with what you save in price. We guarantee safe delivery, and if the stove doesn't please you, return it and get your money back.

Prices do not include pipe or cooking utensils. For cooking utensils, see page 968.

Water fronts for Acme Lehigh Ranges, each, $2.00. We can always furnish repairs for Acme and Wehrle Model Stoves and Ranges. See page 916 about how to order stove repairs when needed in future years.

Prices are for range strongly crated and delivered on board cars at our Newark, Ohio, foundry. Made in five sizes as listed below.

Catalog No.	Range No.	Size of Lids	Size of Oven, inches	Size of Top Without End Shelf	Size of End Shelf	Height to Main Top	Shipping Weight	Price, for Hard (Anthracite) Coal & Wood	Price, for Wood Only
22T325	7-16	No. 7	16 x15x11½	30x24½ in.	8x24½ in.	31 inches	395 lbs.	$19.38	$19.13
22T326	7-18	No. 7	17½x17x11½	33x27 in.	8x27 in.	32 inches	450 lbs.	21.72	21.47
22T327	8-18	No. 8	17½x17x11½	33x27 in.	8x27 in.	32 inches	450 lbs.	22.05	21.80
22T328	8-20	No. 8	20 x19x11½	35x28 in.	8x28 in.	32 inches	500 lbs.	24.40	24.16
22T329	9-20	No. 9	20 x19x11½	35x28 in.	8x28 in.	32 inches	500 lbs.	24.74	24.49

For size of fire box for both wood and coal, please see description and table of sizes of the Acme Lehigh on preceding page. All sizes take 7-inch pipe.

Our Stoves and Ranges are Blackened, Beautifully Polished, Ready to Set Up and Use

Fitted with our dependable oven door thermometer without extra cost.

WEHRLE MODEL No 85 BIG SIX HOLE CAST IRON RANGE

A PERFECT BEAUTY ~ HIGHEST QUALITY ~ LOWEST PRICES

CAN BE FURNISHED FOR HARD COAL, WOOD AND COBS OR SOFT COAL, WOOD AND COBS OR ANY KIND OF FUEL

POSITIVELY THE LOWEST PRICE EVER MADE ON A HIGH GRADE CAST IRON RANGE

$21.18 AND UP ACCORDING TO SIZE AND FUEL USED.

STEEL WARMING CLOSET will be found both commodious and convenient. It is just the right height for the average person to easily reach. The roll front rolls back into the top of the closet without interfering with the commodious space inside.

TO MAKE SURE THAT WE FURNISH YOU THE RIGHT KIND OF FIRE BOX FOR THE FUEL TO BE USED, DO NOT FAIL TO STATE IN YOUR ORDER THE FUEL YOU BURN; SAY WHETHER HARD COAL AND WOOD, SOFT COAL AND WOOD OR WOOD ONLY

WATER FRONT for Wehrle Model No. 85, extra, $2.00. Do not mistake water fronts for water reservoirs. Water front can be easily fitted into the fire box at any time by simply removing the front lining. Water fronts are only used where there is a water supply furnished with a constant pressure through the pipes, which can only be obtained in towns and cities having water works or from an elevated pressure tank. See page 916 about hot water fronts.

BROILER OR FEED DOOR is substantially mounted to the left end of the main top and is supplied with check slide to control the fire.

MAIN TOP, COVERS AND CENTERS are strong and braced in the best known way so as to withstand the contraction and expansion of the heat without warping or breaking. Has five solid lids and one sectional or nest lid made from the best stove plate. Main top has nickel band on front edge.

ASH PIT DOOR below the feed or broiler door is substantially mounted; the ash pan is sufficiently large for holding a considerable quantity of ashes. The hearth top slides, leaving a full opening, so that the large reinforced ash pan may be easily removed.

SOFT COAL FIRE BOX with large fire chamber is of correct shape to give wonderful service, so constructed that it is not necessary to have a big fire to heat the cooking surface.

DUPLEX SOFT COAL GRATE is the best made; gives free access of air to all parts of the fuel; ashes and clinkers may be easily and quickly removed from the fire with no effort; this grate will burn soft coal only or both soft coal and wood. An extension lengthens the fire box when end coal linings are removed and very long wood may be burned. One half turn of the shaker crank reverses the grate for wood.

HARD COAL FIRE BOX is made of very heavy fire-brick linings of superior quality and is equipped with Dockash grate for the use of hard coal. A half turn of the shaker adjusts this grate, turning the reverse side to the fire, although the surface remains the same. By this means both sides of the grate are used and, of course, it will not burn out as quickly as it would if the same side were always to the fire.

PROMPT SHIPMENT GUARANTEED

WITH EVERY WEHRLE MODEL No. 85 RANGE ordered for hard coal and wood we furnish, free, a bottom grate for burning wood which may be easily put in place.

SEE OPPOSITE PAGE for prices and illustrations of Wehrle Model No. 85 Big Six-Hole Cast Iron Range, either with or without reservoir or warming closet.

A new compactly built, plain finish, "easily cleaned" large, massive perfect baking six-hole cast iron range. With ordinary care will last a life-time and give efficient service all the time.

Shipped from Newark, Ohio, blackened, beautifully polished, ready to set up and use. Look where you will and you cannot duplicate this range at double our price.

A PLAIN RANGE with SMOOTH CASTINGS, EASILY CLEANED. When you buy this WEHRLE MODEL No. 85 Big Six-Hole Cast Iron Range from us you get the best stove for the money that it is possible to produce in any foundry, a range built on principles that are absolutely correct and designed to meet the growing demand for a range with perfectly plain castings, very little nickel, and one quickly and easily cleaned. We guarantee it to last longer, bake better, use less fuel than ranges of the same kind selling at double our price. You can try this WEHRLE MODEL No. 85 Big Cast Iron Six-Hole Range in your own kitchen thirty days, and if you do not find it perfectly satisfactory, exactly as represented and the peer of any range you ever saw, regardless of name or make, selling at double our price, ship it right back to us and we will not only return your money but will return all the freight you have to pay.

BIG SQUARE OVEN is extra large and the upper half is as serviceable as the lower. All oven plates are smooth and of uniform thickness. Each oven plate is specially arranged to prevent warping or cracking. Has deep nickel plated outside oven shelf.

OVEN DOOR is handsomely carved with nickel name plate and door knob; is substantially mounted with hinge pins, provided with kicker or foot opener, thereby avoiding the inconvenience of stooping over to open it. Has our special oven door thermometer, which measures heat just as a clock measures time or a steam gauge measures steam pressure.

CLEAN OUT is large and convenient, fastened underneath the oven shelf with a turnkey.

RESERVOIR has removable lift out porcelain lined tank. The reservoir casing is made of heavy castings and completely surrounds the tank, forming a chamber, and by operation of the special reservoir damper the heat is forced in and around reservoir, heating the water. Reservoir covers are japanned, highly polished, made in two parts with lift out hinge center.

PRICES, WITH RESERVOIR AND HIGH WARMING CLOSET, DELIVERED STRONGLY CRATED ON THE CARS AT OUR NEWARK, OHIO, FOUNDRY.

Catalog No.	Range No.	Size of Lids	Size of Oven, inches	Size of Main Top, Including Reservoir	Height to Main Top, inches	Size of Fire Box, inches: Length for Coal	Width	Depth	Length for Wood	Capacity of Reservoir in quarts	Shipping Weight	Price for Soft Coal and Wood	Price for Hard Coal and Wood	Price for Wood only
22T350	82-19	No. 8	18x18x11	26½x42½ in.	29½	15	8½	7	20	13½	430 lbs.	$21.43	$22.44	$21.18
22T351	82-21	No. 8	20x20x12	28½x46 in.	30½	17½	8½	7	21½	17	480 lbs.	23.74	24.75	23.47
22T352	92-21	No. 9	20x20x12	28½x46 in.	30½	17½	8½	7	21½	17	480 lbs.	24.08	25.10	23.83

THE HEIGHT OF WARMING CLOSET ON ALL SIZES IS 27 INCHES, AND ALL SIZES TAKE 7-INCH PIPE.

FOR COMPLETE INDEX REFER TO PINK PAGES IN MIDDLE OF BOOK.

$11.81 BUYS OUR NEW IMPROVED HIGH GRADE FOUR-HOLE ACME GLOBE COOK STOVE

COMPLETE WITH PORCELAIN LINED RESERVOIR, EXACTLY AS ILLUSTRATED BELOW.

A RESERVOIR COOK STOVE FOR COAL OR WOOD. BURNS ANYTHING—HARD COAL, SOFT COAL, COKE, WOOD, OR ANYTHING USED FOR FUEL.

The Acme Globe is a Wonder at the Price.

Smyrna, Del.

Sears, Roebuck & Co., Chicago.

Dear Sirs:—I received the Acme Globe stove in good condition, and I am well pleased with it. No fault to find with it. I think it is just grand. A friend of mine wants one. Have you any more at the same price, Acme Globe? If so please let me know at once.

ISAAC H. RIDER.

Hoping to hear from you by return mail.

$11.81 TO $13.81

Our stoves are all more than we claim for them and are sold direct to you from our foundry.

OUR 30 DAYS' FREE TRIAL OFFER. As a guarantee that you will find after you have paid the freight and added same to our selling price that you have received a better stove than you could get from your dealer at home and at a much lower price, all stoves are shipped with the understanding and agreement that they can be given thirty days' trial in your own home, and if you do not find, after using the stove thirty days, that it is better than any stove you could buy from your dealer at home and perfectly satisfactory in every way, you can return the stove to us at our expense and we will immediately return your money, together with any freight charges paid by you.

THE ACME GLOBE reservoir stove, as illustrated, is one of our big leaders. It is one of the greatest values that goes out of our foundry, the equal of stoves that sell generally at about double our price.

WE GUARANTEE THE QUALITY HIGHER than any other stove works make. Our foundry being much larger than any other stove foundry, we can delegate certain pieces to certain mechanics who work month in and month out making or finishing the one piece or part, thereby becoming very proficient, doing a higher grade of work at a lower cost than any other foundry. Our castings will be found smoother and tougher, our fittings, lining, interlining, bolting and bracing better, our stove will come out smoother, more economic in the consumption of fuel, more lasting and handsomer than any similar style of stove work made by any other maker.

WE HAVE SOLD MORE THAN TEN THOUSAND of these reservoir coal and wood burning Acme Globe Cook Stoves. No doubt some of your neighbors are using them, and if so we invite you to examine the stove, ask how the owner is pleased with it, how she considers it compared with stoves of other makes, how much money she saved by ordering from us, and ask if she would advise you to order from us.

DESCRIPTION

MAIN TOP is fitted together in a manner to overcome warping, has heavy cut centers, supported by post, with heavy corners.
ASH PIT DOOR is substantially mounted, with nickeled name plate, supplied with check draft to control the fire.
THE HEARTH. Full draw hearth, sufficiently large for the easy removal of the large ash pan.
FIRE BOX. Has heavy linings, with very heavy sectional fire back, and is fitted with a convenient and substantial flat dump grate, and with every stove we include, free of all cost, an extra flat dump grate and fire back for wood. Can be easily converted for burning coal or wood.
THE FIRE DOOR is large and opens the full size of the fire box.
THE POUCH FEED, mounted to the front of the main top is very convenient for putting in coal, when coal is used as fuel.
THE OVEN will be found unequaled in baking and roasting qualities, is well constructed and well fitted, and finished with handsome oven shelf.
OVEN DOORS. The Acme Globe has two oven doors, tin lined, handsomely nickeled door knobs. The right hand door has foot trip, by the use of which the door may be opened while the hands are full.
THE RESERVOIR. The reservoir casing is made of extra quality stove plate and the tank is porcelain lined.

From above illustration, which has been engraved by our artist from a photograph, you can get some idea of the appearance of this handsome new pouch feed coal and wood burning reservoir cook stove which we furnish at $11.81 to $13.81, according to size. The most popular size of this stove is the 8-18 size, which we furnish at **$13.56**, and you will note this stove weighs full 343 pounds. Our price is therefore less than 4 cents per pound. In this size you get a top 24x44 inches, an oven 18x17x11 inches, an economically arranged smooth top good size cook stove at about one-half the price charged by dealers generally.

We furnish this handsome new Acme Globe Reservoir Wood and Coal Burning Cook Stove in four sizes as listed at the prices named. Securely crated and delivered on the cars at our foundry at Newark, Ohio.

Catalogue No.	Stove No.	Size of Lids	Size of Oven, inches	Size of Top Including Reservoir, inches	H'ght, inches	Pipe to fit Collar, inches	Size of Fire Box, inches: Length for Coal	Width	Depth	Length for Wood	Capacity of Reservoir in quarts	W'ght lbs.	Price
22H555	7-16	No. 7	16x14½x10	22x40	26½	6	14	6½	5	17	11½	294	$11.81
22H556	8-16	No. 8	16x14½x10	22x40	26½	6	14	6½	5	17	11½	294	12.06
22H557	8-18	No. 8	18x17 x11	24x44	28½	7	16	7	5½	19	13½	343	13.56
22H558	9-18	No. 9	18x17 x11	24x44	28½	7	16	7	5½	19	13½	343	13.81

If you do not use coal at all, order the Acme Elm from page 45.

OUR $8.44 ACME GLOBE. FOR COAL OR WOOD.

AT FROM $8.44 TO $11.58 according to size as listed below, we furnish this new Improved Acme Globe Cook Stove without reservoir, exactly as illustrated, designed to burn all kinds of fuel—hard coal, soft coal, coke, wood or anything used for fuel. Our very low price figures less than 4 cents per pound for this finished stove, and if you will consider the market price of the highest grade Birmingham pig iron at the furnaces in Alabama, then consider that we must pay the freight on this iron to our Ohio foundry, melt it, cast it, finish the castings, make all the nickel trimmings and mountings, furnish all the boltings, bracings, all the trimmings, furnish all the labor to complete this stove and all at less than 4 cents per pound for the finished stove, you must admit that we have the most economical manufacturing plant, that the cost to us of making stoves is much lower than other makers, and that we must necessarily be content with a fraction of the profit asked by other makers and sellers of stoves. **Our special prices, $8.44 to $11.58, barely cover the cost of material and labor, with but our one small percentage of profit added.**

OUR GUARANTEE IS ABSOLUTE. We guarantee every piece and part that enters into this stove. We guarantee the stove to reach you in the same perfect condition it leaves us. We send every stove with the understanding that it can be used thirty days in your own home and if, after putting the stove to every test, you are not convinced you have received a better stove than you could get elsewhere and at a much lower price, return the stove to us at our expense and we will immediately return your money. **We can always furnish repairs for Acmes. See page 20 about how to order repairs.**

No. 22H560 to No. 22H564

$8.44 TO $11.58

THIS HANDSOME COAL AND WOOD BURNING STOVE is a very popular design. We have sold thousands of these stoves the past few years; hundreds have gone into every state. No doubt some of your neighbors are using an Acme Globe. We are able to furnish a higher quality at a lower cost than other stove makers by reason of the enormous demand for the stove, which enables us to give but one piece of this stove, like a bottom, oven or hearth, to one moulder, who works on this and this alone. The same way in the mounting, polishing and finishing, the lining and various parts, and in this way each man working on one piece becomes very proficient, turns out a higher grade of work and at low cost to us, and all this makes possible our very low price. The Acme Globe is made with extra large flues, cut tops, heavy cut centers supported by post, heavy covers, heavy linings, extra heavy sectional fire back, large ash pan, full draw hearth, outside oven shelf, pouch feed, oven door kicker, nickel plated name plate on front door, nickel plated door knobs and tin lined oven doors. When ashes are removed from under the oven they are scraped into the hearth, avoiding all possibility of spilling the ashes on the floor when cleaning the stove. Each stove is furnished with a lifter, shaker and scraper for removing the ashes from under the oven. **Prices do not include pipe or cooking utensils. For cooking utensils see pages 341 to 346.**

FOR A MEDIUM or small cook stove, to burn all kinds of fuel, wood or coal, a stove that can be guaranteed in every way and offered at a very low price, we especially recommend our Acme Globe. Understand, at our price we furnish the stove carefully crated and delivered on board the cars at our foundry in Ohio, from which point you must pay the freight; but you will find the freight will amount to next to nothing as compared to what you save in price.

We furnish this handsome cook stove, the Acme Globe, in five sizes at prices as listed, securely crated and delivered on the cars at our foundry at Newark, Ohio.

Catalogue Number	Stove No.	Size of Lids	Size of Oven, inches	Size of Top, not measuring Shelf, inches	Size of Shelf, inches	Height, inches	Size of Pipe to fit Collar, inches	Size of Fire Box, inches: Length for Coal	Width	Depth	Length for Wood	Weight, pounds	Price
22H560	7-14	No. 7	13¾x13 x 9	20½x27½	20½x7	24	6	12	6	4½	15	215	$ 8.44
22H561	7-16	No. 7	16 x14½x10	22 x29½	22 x7	26½	6	14	6½	5	17	239	9.54
22H562	8-16	No. 8	16 x14½x10	22 x29½	22 x7	26½	6	14	6½	5	17	239	9.81
22H563	8-18	No. 8	18 x17 x11	24 x33	24 x7	28½	7	16	7	5½	19	288	11.31
22H564	9-18	No. 9	18 x17 x11	24 x33	24 x7	28½	7	16	7	5½	19	288	11.58

If you do not use coal at all, order the Acme Elm from page 45.

STEEL COOK STOVE, ONLY $6.98

ACME ROVER GENUINE STEEL, FOUR-HOLE, COAL AND WOOD STOVE, WITH RESERVOIR, MODEL OF 1908.

THREE SIZES, DIRECT FROM OUR FOUNDRY, OFFERED AT $6.98, $7.98 AND $8.98, ACCORDING TO SIZE AS LISTED BELOW.

COMPARE THE PRICES with any prices you have ever seen or heard of in either a steel or cast iron reservoir cook stove and you will find the price we are offering on this reservoir steel cook stove less than one-half what others charge, and it is positively THE GREATEST STOVE VALUE THE WORLD HAS EVER SEEN.

HOW WE CAN DO THIS. We have known for years that there would be a big demand for a steel cook stove if it could be reliably produced for as little, or, better still, for less money than any cast iron reservoir cook stove. We know this for the reason that thousands of people prefer a steel cook stove or steel range to any cast iron cook stove or range made. Steel cook stoves and ranges possess many advantages over cast iron stoves and ranges. For example: Steel stoves are practically unbreakable and, with the proper care, they are everlasting, non-destructible. They are also wonderful bakers, extremely economical in the consumption of fuel, wonderful in their fire control, because, being light as compared with cast iron, they are extremely quick to heat and quick to act. Steel cook stoves are very easy to operate. They never get out of order, and they are by far more responsive than any cast iron stove made. In short, steel stoves are the world's greatest bakers and cookers. There is no baker, no cooker, no stove in the kitchen that will take the place of a steel cook stove or a steel range, and with the proper care they are everlasting, non-destructible, never-breaking.

THIS HERETOFORE UNHEARD OF PRICE of $6.98, $7.98 and $8.98, according to size, complete with reservoir, is made possible, first, because we operate our own stove foundry at Newark, Ohio (the largest stove foundry in the world); second, because we are the largest buyers and users of heavy sheet steel, the highest grade made for the manufacture of steel ranges and steel cook stoves. Then, to still further reduce the cost of this stove and cut the cost of production down to the very lowest penny, in short, minimize the cost of handling every sort, size and shape of steel plate in our stove foundry, we have, at a cost of a great many thousand dollars, equipped our foundry with the best possible facilities for automatically stamping, punching, shaping, bending and general handling of all the weights and sizes of light, medium and heavy steel plate. By the introduction in this department of enormous punch presses, benders, conveyers, cutters, etc., we are able to take a piece of sheet steel, just as it comes from the rolling mill to us, made and cut at the rolling mill to the exact size of the particular stove we wish to make, and put it into one of our automatic machines and in the one operation practically finish this entire piece of sheet steel, putting it at once into the permanent shape in which it will go into the stove, with all bolt and rivet holes, with all openings, all shapings, all cutting, bending, etc., done automatically, done perfectly, done as it could not be done by hand, done only as it is possible to do on the automatic machines we have, and then, practically without cost. Then this sheet steel goes through our sheet steel working department (this department is filled with automatic punches, drawing, shaping, bending, and stove making machines) and goes from this department by automatic conveyers to the mounting department practically a finished stove, nothing left to be done but the bolting of the stove together.

COMPARED WITH THE LOWEST PRICES we could possibly make you on any of our cast iron reservoir cook stoves, we save you easily from $4.00 to $7.00, and compared with any other steel cook stove we could sell you, we show you a saving of from $6.00 to $8.00; and compared with any price any other maker or dealer could offer you, we show you a saving in cost on this OUR ACME ROVER STEEL COOK STOVE WITH RESERVOIR, of easily $7.00 to $15.00.

THE GREATEST STOVE VALUE THE WORLD HAS EVER SEEN

HOW THIS STEEL COOK STOVE compares with other steel goods we make. In comparing this steel cook stove with our Acme Progress Steel Cook Stove or with our other steel ranges—the Acme Triumph, Acme Regal, Acme Charm, Acme Renown and others, please remember that while this is a thoroughly reliable stove that will give absolute satisfaction in every way, is offered at the lowest price ever known, at but one-half the price others charge for light stoves, of course, the higher priced stoves offered in this catalogue are heavier, stronger, and will last much longer, and therefore, if you feel that you can afford to pay more money, if you can afford to pay $15.67 for our big heavy reliable Acme Progress Steel Cook Stove, or $20.39 for our new model Acme Charm with reservoir and high warming closet, we would then urge you, in your own interest, by all means to select the highest grade steel cook stove or range that we make. If, on the other hand, you want to get a stove that would give satisfaction and you want to buy it at the lowest possible cost, we can recommend this stove and guarantee it to you in every way.

EVERY STOVE CAREFULLY INSPECTED, BEFORE WE PACK FOR SHIPMENT.

This illustration, engraved by our artist from a photograph, shows our new 1908 model Acme Rover Four-Hole, Reservoir, All Steel Cook Stove, which we offer at $6.98, $7.98 and $8.98, will give you a good general idea of the appearance of this stove.

REPAIR PARTS. We will always carry a complete stock of repairs and repair parts in years to come; even ten years hence we will be able to deliver you any piece or part to replace or repair any defective part and this at actual cost, a mere fraction of what other stove dealers charge.

THE BODY is made of the highest grade sheet steel, thoroughly bolted, braced, reinforced throughout, the very best oven construction; our new special flue, draft, damper and circulating system, made to burn hard coal, soft coal or wood. With each stove we furnish a special grate for wood; has a cast top—the exact same grade of top that we use in our highest grade stoves and ranges; four lids, cut centers; supported by our own special system of construction. At the special price named, the stove is furnished with a detachable or removable reservoir, as shown in illustration. In shipping the stove we pack the reservoir inside of the oven and the stove is crated in a way that there is no chance of its reaching you in bad condition—in fact, the stove is really unbreakable.

WE HAVE A LARGE STOCK OF these stoves on hand, ready for immediate shipment. It will just take a few days for your order to reach us and the stove to reach you. The stove being made of sheet steel is comparatively light and the freight charges will amount to next to nothing. This stove can be shipped from 100 to 500 miles at from 35 cents to 75 cents; from 500 to 1,000 miles at from 50 cents to $1.00; greater or lesser distances in proportion.

DETAILED DESCRIPTION.

THE BODY is built of heavy smooth steel plate, is substantially put together, riveted with wrought iron rivets, strongly reinforced and braced in every part. The heavy plates are well riveted and jointed.

THE MAIN TOP. In manufacturing this, our Acme Rover, we have constructed the main top and covers of good stove plate. It has four cooking holes and with ordinary care and usage the main top and covers will last years. All parts of the main top are carefully fitted, with sufficient allowance for heat expansion.

THE LARGE FIRE BOX. It has an extra large fire box, provided with practical cast iron linings, with shaking and dumping grate. With every stove we include, free of cost, an extra grate for wood, so you can burn hard coal, soft coal or wood.

THE FIRE DOOR is beautifully designed and swings to the left.

THE ASH PIT is large and roomy and is provided with a large ash pan.

THE DRAFT SLIDE is in front, of more than usual capacity.

THE OVEN is of very generous proportions, perfectly square, is a very satisfactory, quick and even baker, and is furnished with a steel wire oven rack.

THE OVEN DOOR is on the right side (the left side left blank). It is our latest swing pattern, attractive rococo design, steel lined, perfectly square, and fits snug to the body of the stove, thus retaining all the heat in the oven.

THE FLUES are ample and provided with cleanout in rear of ash pit, which is reached from the front of the stove.

THE RESERVOIR is made of galvanized iron, heats by direct contact with the side of the stove, is removable and can be used on either end or rear side at pleasure, or can be used on top of stove as occasion requires.

GOOD SERVICE. The long looked for steel cook stove for practical people, neat, compact, serviceable and cheap. No such value in a cook stove ever offered before. This, our Acme Rover Steel Cook Stove is shipped ready to set up, the four legs and all other loose parts packed inside. When received you have only to put on the legs, pipe and other loose parts, when it is ready for fire, the same as if you were moving an old stove from one room to another.

PRICES FOR OUR ACME ROVER STEEL COOK STOVE, FOR COAL AND WOOD, WITH RESERVOIR, FOUR COOKING HOLES, DUMPING GRATE, LARGE ASH PAN, STEEL OVEN RACK, GALVANIZED RESERVOIR ADJUSTABLE TO EITHER END, SIDE OR BACK.

Catalogue Number	Range Number	Size of Lids	Size of Oven, inches	Main Top including Reservoir	Height of Main Top, inches	Size of Pipe to Fit Collar, inches	Size of Fire Box, inches			Capacity of Reservoir	Price
							Length	Width	Depth		
22H565	7-12	No. 7	12x16x10	35 x19 inches	25	6	16½	6½	4	14 quarts	$6.98
22H566	8-14	No. 8	14x18x10½	37½x21 inches	25½	6	17	6½	4½	18 quarts	7.98
22H567	8-16	No. 8	16x18x11	40½x21½inches	26½	6	17½	7	5	21 quarts	8.98

IF DESIRED WITHOUT RESERVOIR, BUT WITH END SHELF, DEDUCT 50 CENTS FROM ABOVE PRICES.

ACME HUMMER SIX-HOLE STEEL RANGE $17.52

A REDUCED PRICE

OUR LARGE STOCK INSURES PROMPT SHIPMENT

Cast Iron Left End Guaranteed not to Warp, Buckle or Burn Out.

BURNS ANY KIND OF FUEL, HARD OR SOFT COAL, COKE, WOOD OR CORN COBS.

THE STANDARD OF POPULAR PRICED STEEL RANGES. GREATLY IMPROVED FOR 1909.

COMPLETE AS ILLUSTRATED. Our great and improved Acme Hummer Six-Hole Steel Range is designed and made by us to supply our customers with a very high class, full standard steel range, complete with reservoir and warming closet, at an extremely moderate price, and nowhere else in the pages of this catalogue is our ability to produce a high grade steel range at an extremely low price so thoroughly demonstrated as it is on this page.

THIS, OUR ACME HUMMER STEEL RANGE, is put up throughout in the most substantial form, the bending, punching, riveting and forming in general being accurate and the riveting close, firm and tight. Wherever in the structure the fire comes in contact with it, cast plates are worked in for protection. Other features of the range are: Extra and original dampers, the fire box construction, which is an original one and offers many conveniences and advantages; the body is manufactured from selected cold rolled steel of a heavier, stronger gauge than is used by manufacturers of similar ranges at double our prices; the fire and oven doors are ground and closely fitted; the oven door drops flush with the oven bottom, forming a convenient shelf; in short, the range is built on excellent lines throughout. By reason of our unequaled method and system we are enabled to produce this elegant range to meet the demands of those who are inclined to spend a small amount and yet get an honestly built range that has good material in all its parts and is constructed in a most satisfactory manner, and offer it at $17.52 to $21.99 complete, according to size, with reservoir and warming closet, under our written binding guarantee, as explained on page 371.

DETAILED DESCRIPTION.

THE BODY is manufactured from selected cold rolled sheet steel of a heavier and stronger gauge than is used in ranges that retail at much higher prices. It is thoroughly put together, riveted with wrought iron rivets, strongly reinforced and braced in every part. HIGH CLOSET is of generous proportions. It is just at the right height and has a balanced door. MAIN TOP, covers and centers are made of the highest grade gray iron, which stands the heat better and is less liable to crack or warp than any other material. This range is furnished with five solid lids and one sectional or nest lid, made from the best stove plate. It has long cut centers and all loose parts of top are carefully fitted with sufficient allowance for heat expansion. THE FIRE BOX is of our well known type with famous Acme Duplex grate which is instantly converted into a coal burning grate or a wood burning grate at the will of the operator. THE OVEN is of very generous proportions, with spring balanced drop oven door, and it is an extremely quick and even baker.

WE RECOMMEND the Acme Hummer to those who cannot afford our Acme Triumph or Acme Charm Steel Ranges. But, if you can add a few more dollars to the purchase price of the Acme Hummer, turn to the pages describing the Acme Triumph Steel Range, which is unapproached in any respect by the ranges offered by other manufacturers or dealers at from $50.00 to $60.00, and if you can afford to pay the few dollars additional, necessary to secure one of these highest grade ranges, we would strongly advise that you do so.

WATER FRONTS for the Acme Hummer, price $2.50. These can be easily fitted into the fire box at any time. (See page 371 about hot water fronts.)

MADE IN FOUR SIZES AS LISTED BELOW.

With high warming closet and porcelain lined reservoir. For hard coal, soft coal, coke, wood or corn cobs. Prices do not include any pipe or cooking utensils. For pipe and cooking utensils, see pages 419 to 422. Prices, strongly crated and delivered on the cars at our foundry at Newark, Ohio.

Catalogue No.	Range No.	Size of Lids	Size of Oven, inches	Main Top, including Reservoir	Height to Main Top, inches	Height of Warming Closet, in.	Size of Pipe to Fit Collar	Shipping Weight	Price
22L225	8-19	No. 8	18x20¾x12	42⅛x29 in.	29½	26⅛	7	410	$17.52
22L226	8-21	No. 8	20x21 x14	47 x28 in.	30½	26½	7	498	21.62
22L227	9-19	No. 9	18x21 x14	45 x28 in.	30½	26½	7	490	20.69
22L228	9-21	No. 9	20x21 x14	47 x28 in.	30½	26½	7	498	21.99

WITHOUT HIGH WARMING CLOSET but with reservoir, deduct $2.50 from the price listed. When ordered without warming closet, this range is equipped with a handsome guard rail along the back edge of the main top.

WITHOUT WATER RESERVOIR but with warming closet, deduct $2.50 from the price listed. When ordered without reservoir, the range is equipped with a handsome end shelf, which is easily bolted to the right end of the main top.

On all the above sizes, with the exception of catalogue No. 22L225, range No. 8-19, the fire box is 9 inches wide and 6½ inches deep; its length for coal is 18 inches and for wood 25 inches. Capacity of reservoir, 22 quarts. Catalogue No. 22L225, range No. 8-19, the fire box is 8 inches wide, 5½ inches deep, length for coal 17 inches, and for wood 24 inches. Capacity of reservoir, 13½ quarts.

ACME BOOMER SIX-HOLE STEEL RANGE $11.98

REDUCED IN PRICE

AS A WONDERFUL ILLUSTRATION of what we can do in our Newark Stove Foundry, the largest stove foundry in the world, and as proof positive of our ability to build better stoves and ranges and sell them at lower prices than the prices asked by any other manufacturer or dealer in the world, we made this, our Acme Boomer Range, which we offer at $11.98, complete with reservoir and high warming closet. Ranges have been widely advertised by other foundries and dealers at prices ranging from $18.00 to $22.50, and in those advertisements representations have been made that the ranges are strictly high grade in every respect. To show our customers how cheaply constructed those advertised ranges are, and how much greater value we offer in the stoves and ranges made by us in our Newark foundry, we purchased samples of the ranges widely advertised at $18.00 to $22.50, and after getting these samples, we had our expert range builders make an exact duplicate of these ranges, that is to say, taking the best features of every one of them and putting them into this range to show at what price we would be able to build and sell a range in every respect the equal of the cheaply built ranges offered by others at from $18.00 to $22.50.

UNDERSTAND, WE DO NOT OFFER this Acme Boomer as a high grade range because it is not the equal of any other steel range shown in our catalogue, but we do guarantee it to be just as good as stoves and ranges offered by others at from $18.00 to $22.50. It is a very satisfactory baker, economical in the consumption of fuel, quick to heat and quick to act. In making it we have constructed the main top and covers of good stove plate. It has six cooking holes, and with ordinary care and usage the main top and covers will last for years. It has a convenient warming closet.

THIS, OUR ACME BOOMER, IS MADE IN ONE SIZE ONLY. This stove 8-16; the oven 16x18x11 inches, has six No. 8 cooking holes. Size of cooking top, 30½x21½ inches. Height from floor to main top 26

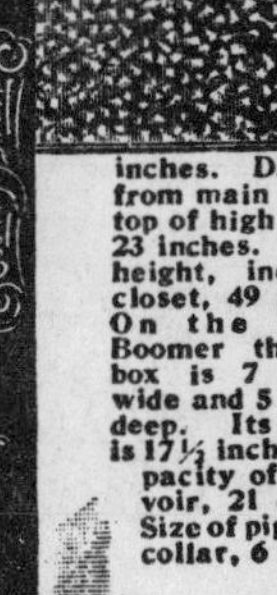
inches. Distance from main top to top of high closet, 23 inches. Total height, including closet, 49 inches. On the Acme Boomer the fire box is 7 inches wide and 5 inches deep. Its length is 17½ inches. Capacity of reservoir, 21 quarts. Size of pipe to fit collar, 6 inches.

DETAILED DESCRIPTION.

THE BODY is manufactured from cold rolled sheet steel of a heavier and stronger gauge than is used by other foundries and dealers at prices ranging from $18.00 to $22.50.

THE MAIN TOP. In manufacturing this, our Acme Boomer Range, we have constructed the main tops and covers of good stove plate. It has six cooking holes and, with ordinary care and usage, the main top and covers will last for years. All parts of the main top are carefully fitted, with sufficient allowance for heat expansion.

HIGH WARMING CLOSET is of generous proportions, is just at the right height, and will be found very convenient. The height of warming closet is 23 inches.

FIRE BOX. The fire box in our Acme Boomer Steel Range is an improved fire box, equipped with our flat dump style grate, which grate is lighter than our perfect duplex grate as used in the highest grade ranges made by us. With every range we ship we include, free of cost, an extra grate for wood, so that you can burn either hard coal, soft coal or wood.

THE ASH PAN is made of cold rolled steel with handsome draw out handle.

THE OVEN is of very generous proportions, perfectly square, is a very satisfactory, quick, even baker, and is furnished with a steel wire oven rack and convenient clean out directly under the oven door.

THE OVEN DOOR is our latest swing pattern, attractive rococo design, steel lined, perfectly square and fits snug to the body of the range, thus retaining all the heat in the oven.

THE RESERVOIR is made of galvanized iron and heats by direct contact with the end of the range. It can be adjusted to either end and, if so desired, can also be used on top of the range. Being made of galvanized iron, it will not rust or corrode and is by far a better reservoir than that on ranges offered for $18.00 to $22.50 by other dealers. This is the only steel range we build without cast iron reservoir casing. It is simply made of galvanized iron and will not last as long as the cast reservoir casing which is used by us on all our other ranges. In shipping this range we pack the reservoir inside the oven. It is easily attached to the right or left end of the range.

THE FLUE BACK which conducts the heat from the flue beneath the oven to the stove pipe is made of the highest grade cast iron stove plate. This is a very important feature. Nearly all steel ranges sold for more than double the price we ask for this, our Acme Boomer Range, are made with a thin sheet steel flue back, which easily rots out.

Prices, strongly crated and delivered on the cars at our Newark, Ohio, foundry.

No. 22L200 Square top range, without high closet or reservoir, shipping weight, 185 pounds. Price.......$ 9.60
No. 22L201 Reservoir range, without high closet, but with reservoir, shipping weight, 190 pounds. Price.......10.35
No. 22L202 Square top range, without reservoir, but with high closet, shipping weight, 215 pounds. Price.......11.62
No. 22L203 Steel range complete, just as illustrated, with high closet and reservoir, shipping weight, 220 pounds. Price.......11.98

THESE PRICES DO NOT INCLUDE PIPE OR COOKING UTENSILS. WE DO NOT FURNISH WATER FRONT FOR THE ACME BOOMER RANGE.

READ THE DETAILED DESCRIPTION OF OUR IMPROVED ACME CHARM SIX-HOLE STEEL RANGE

IT'S ON LEGS--BUILT UP FROM THE FLOOR

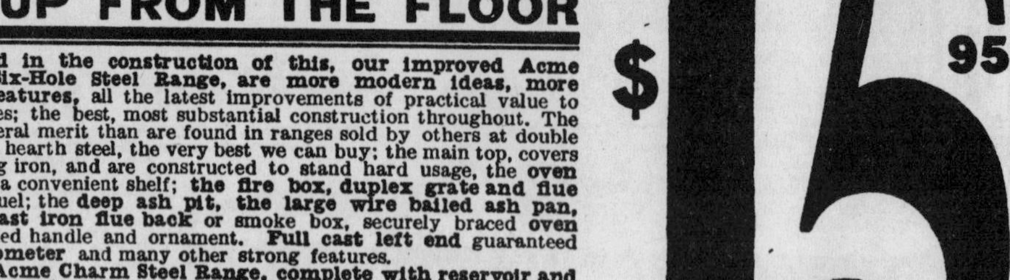

$15.95

AND UPWARD ACCORDING TO EQUIPMENT.

REDUCED IN PRICE

A RANGE OF QUALITY Combined in the construction of this, our improved Acme Charm Six-Hole Steel Range, are more modern ideas, more special features, all the latest improvements of practical value to steel ranges; the best, most substantial construction throughout. The oven is a perfect baker. In short, it has more points of general merit than are found in ranges sold by others at double our price. **The body** is made from Wood's cold rolled open hearth steel, the very best we can buy; the main top, covers and centers are made from the highest grade Birmingham pig iron, and are constructed to stand hard usage, the **oven door** is evenly balanced; drops flush with the oven, forming a convenient shelf; **the fire box, duplex grate and flue construction** are built for economy in the consumption of fuel; the **deep ash pit, the large wire bailed ash pan, large pouch feed door** with Alaska nickel wire handle, **cast iron flue back** or smoke box, securely braced **oven bottom, high closet** with roll top door, handsomely nickeled handle and ornament. **Full cast left end** guaranteed not to warp or buckle; our **dependable oven door thermometer** and many other strong features.

LET US HAVE YOUR ORDER for this big Six-Hole Acme Charm Steel Range, complete with reservoir and warming closet and oven door thermometer, at the astonishingly low price of $21.95, enclosing this amount with your order, addressed direct to Sears, Roebuck & Co., Chicago, Ill. This range will go to you direct from a warehouse very near you, or from our foundry at Newark, Ohio, without any delay, with the understanding and agreement that if it is not the biggest stove value you have ever seen, if it is not all and even more than we claim for it, and if you are not fully convinced that you have made a big saving of money, you can return the big range to us at our expense of freight charges both ways and we will immediately return your money.

WONDERFULLY QUICK DELIVERY from a warehouse very near you, explained on preceding page. Please remember, you have nothing to pay beyond our price for the range, complete with reservoir and warming closet as illustrated on preceding page, excepting the small freight charges from the warehouse nearest you to your railroad station.

IN VIEW OF THIS ASTONISHING LOW PRICE, a price much lower than we have ever made for this our Acme Charm Six-Hole Steel Range, let us urge you to order this range from us; let us ask you to go to your postmaster, R. F. D. carrier, express agent or banker and get a money order drawn for $21.95 in our favor, enclosing it in your letter addressed direct to Sears, Roebuck & Company, Chicago, Illinois, and we will immediately send your order, by special delivery, to our stove warehouse, the one nearest you, or our foundry at Newark, Ohio, and order the stove shipped to your railroad station on your order at once. By this arrangement we have brought the range very near you, and let us again repeat that you have nothing to pay beyond the price named for the range as illustrated on the preceding page and the small freight charges only from the warehouse nearest you or our foundry at Newark, Ohio, to your nearest railroad station.

DURABILITY. Our Big Acme Charm Six-Hole Steel Range, with full equipment of reservoir and warming closet, is extra heavy and will outweigh and outclass and outlast steel ranges sold by other dealers at double our price. Not only the steel body, but all the castings, main top, centers and fire box linings are built to last. For illustration, note the heavy cast iron flue back at the back of range, through which all products of combustion pass to chimney. Examine other makes of ranges and you will generally find this flue back of sheet steel. This material will not stand the strain and will soon rust out. The high principles of honest workmanship, the dependable high grade cast reservoir casing and the advanced and original ideas of design and art of stove building have made this range construction famous as a thoroughly dependable, powerful fuel saving range, which brings to the user every luxury and the self same pleasure enjoyed by those possessing a range at double the price we ask for our big Acme Charm, complete with reservoir and warming closet.

30 DAYS' FREE TRIAL. Send us your order, enclosing our price of $21.95 for the big Acme Charm Six-Hole Steel Range, complete with Reservoir, Warming Closet and Oven Door Thermometer, and the big range will be shipped immediately direct to your station from our warehouse nearest you, with the full understanding and agreement that you may use the big range in your own home for thirty days, during which time you may put it to every possible test that may be devised, examine it and observe its long rangy lines, cook, bake and roast on it, then you will fully appreciate why our big Acme Charm Six-Hole Steel Range is without a peer among ranges selling at double the prices we ask.

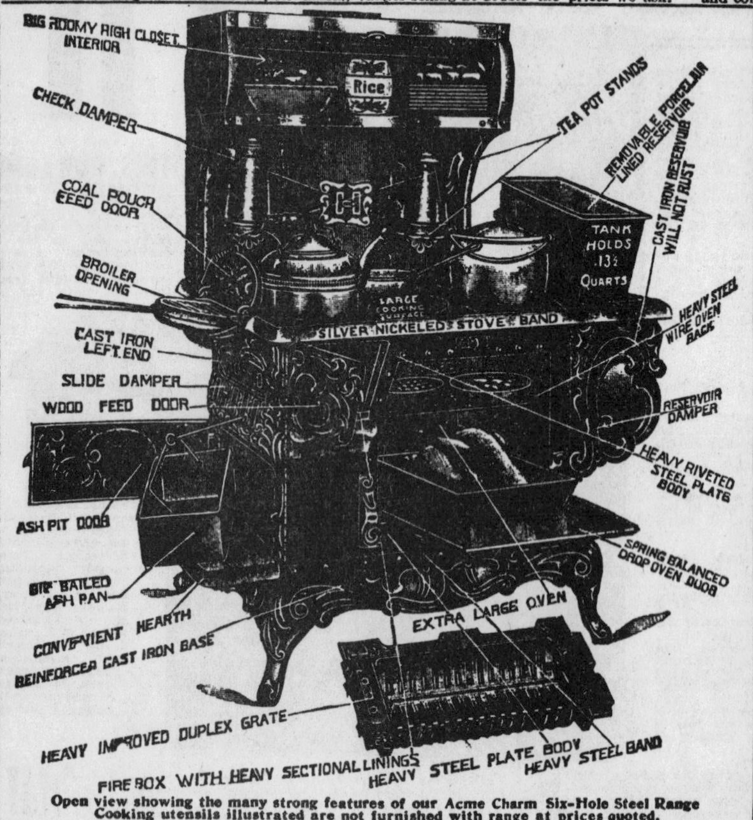

Open view showing the many strong features of our Acme Charm Six-Hole Steel Range
Cooking utensils illustrated are not furnished with range at prices quoted.

THE BODY. The most important part of our steel range is the body. The body of our Acme Charm is built like a boiler and made from Wood's cold rolled open hearth steel, the very best that we can buy, strongly put together with wrought rivets and bands, reinforced at every part. The body is given a high black finish. It is constructed by skilled workmen from heavy steel, which is rigid, airtight and durable; no seams or joints to rust out, leak ashes, or permit the escape of heat. Has full cast iron left end. Guaranteed not to warp, buckle or burn out.

ASBESTOS LINING. All parts of the steel body exposed to direct action of the fire are lined with asbestos, particular care being taken in doing this work. This protects and insures the steel body from either burning or rusting out. The asbestos being fireproof and a nonconductor retains the heat, adds greatly to the life of the stove, adds wonderfully to its baking possibilities, makes it easy to control and makes an economical fuel consumer.

HIGH WARMING CLOSET. The large, commodious roll top closet and shelf are made of cold rolled sheet steel, beautifully shaped and handsomely finished. The closet and shelf have highly polished nickel handle and bands and the closet door is so carefully counterbalanced that it works very easily, the weight of the hand being sufficient to open it. It is trimmed with nickel steel bands along the front, as shown in illustration. The teapot holders to the left and right are handsomely nickeled and conveniently arranged.

MAIN TOP, COVERS AND CENTERS. The sectional main top and centers are cut and braced in exactly the same manner as our highest grade ranges, and are constructed to stand hard usage for many years and to prevent cracking from excessive heat. We furnish this range with six 8-inch lids, including one graduated or sectional lid, made from the best stove plate. Has long cut center supported by posts.

FIRE BOX. The fire box is of large size and correctly proportioned to the size of flue so as to give the best results for a minimum amount of fuel consumed, and is easily adapted for the consumption of hard or soft coal, wood, coke or corn cobs. The linings are heavy and so constructed that they will give long service, they are sectional and easily removed and protected by an air space behind them. It is furnished with an extension at the back end of the fire box which permits the use of wood 23 inches in length.

DUPLEX GRATE. This Big Acme Charm Steel Range is fitted with our special Duplex Grate, as shown in illustration, extra heavy, the most satisfactory grate made, and designed for any kind of fuel. It is simple and very easy to operate. One movement of the shaker cuts out all cinders and dead ashes. Reversing the grate forms a perfect fire box for a wood fire, and thus it will be seen that our special duplex grate can be used either for coal or wood.

THE OVEN of this range is made of the best quality of smooth cold rolled steel, securely riveted and braced to the body of the range in such a manner as to make all the joints perfectly tight. All seams and joints are carefully riveted airtight. The oven is made in one size only and measures 18x20¾x12 inches, and is furnished with steel slide oven rack which cannot be broken.

OVEN BOTTOM. The oven bottom of this handsome range is made of the highest grade, best selected sheet steel stock, so constructed, bolted, braced and reinforced that we guarantee it to always remain level and never to buckle, warp or sag.

OVEN TOP. The oven top is properly protected by a corrugated cast plate extending back from the fire box, which makes the heat in the oven uniform.

COAL FEED POUCH AND BROILER DOOR. On the left end of the range we provide a capacious coal feed pouch with an Alaska nickel wire lift on the door, as shown in the illustration. It can be used for putting in fuel when coal is used, also for broiling purposes. This is an ideal arrangement and one which will be found very convenient.

ASH PAN. Extra large, heavy, reinforced ash pan, with wire handle. Ash pit provided with guards, which make all ashes fall into the ash pan.

FLUE BACK. The flue back, which conducts the heat from the flue beneath the oven to the stove pipe, is made of the highest grade cast iron stove plate. This is a very important feature. Nearly all ranges sold for even double the price of our Acme Charm are made with a thin sheet steel flue back, which easily rots out by condensation or creosote moisture which sometimes runs down the chimney into the flue back. We guarantee our cast iron flue back never to burn or rust out.

THE RESERVOIR CASING. This is entirely new and original. Every part of the casing is handsomely carved and made of cast iron stove plate. The steel or sheet iron reservoir casings used on ranges of other manufacturers are found not to be practical or serviceable, for they soon corrode and rust out from creosote and moisture and we do not use them. A depression in the bottom of the casing receives and holds all condensation until it is absorbed by the heat. The reservoir tank is removable, porcelain lined and holds 13½ quarts of water. By turning the reservoir damper, heat is thrown under the reservoir, heating the water boiling hot. The two covers are heavily japanned and operate on center divide hinges.

OVEN THERMOMETER. We equip our Acme Charm with a dependable Oven Thermometer. It is mounted in the oven door and it accurately shows the temperature of the oven without the necessity of opening the door. Fully illustrated and described on page 375.

GAS HOT PLATES FROM $1.48 to $2.53, GAS COOKERS FROM $4.87 to $5.92

GAS HOT PLATES.

$1.48 TO $2.13

This Gas Hot Plate with two or three burners can be placed on a table or on the top of your cooking stove and connected with the gas light fixture by the rubber tube quoted below as Nos. 22L562 and 22L563. It will cook over each burner just as well as over the burner on the highest priced gas range; the two-burner measures 9x18 inches and weighs 10 pounds and the three-burner measures 9x26¼ inches and weighs 16 pounds. Frame is 5¾ inches high, aluminum finished with nickel legs. A high grade stove. Material and workmanship the best. Will last a lifetime. The burners give a hot flame with two rings of jets, which are directed so as to have the most effect on the cooking utensils above.

			For Manufactured Gas	For Natural Gas
No. 22L558	Two burners.	Price	$1.48	$1.53
No. 22L559	Three burners.	Price	2.08	2.13

This Gas Hot Plate is a handsomer pattern than the one shown above and has a larger top. It is made with two or three burners as desired; the two-burner measures 11x20½ inches and weighs 14 pounds, and the three-burner measures 11x30 inches and weighs 18 pounds. Frame is 7 inches high, black japanned with nickel legs and levers. The top surface is large and so arranged that pots and pans can be slid over it in any direction. The burner has a loose cap and gives two rings of flame.

$1.78 TO $2.53

			For Manufactured Gas	For Natural Gas
No. 22L560	Two burners.	Price	$1.78	$1.83
No. 22L561	Three burners.	Price	2.48	2.53

Always state whether stoves are intended to be used for natural or artificial gas when writing your order. These gas stoves cannot be used with acetylene or gasoline gas.

For ovens to use on hot plates, see page 417.

GAS STOVE TUBING.

No. 22L562 Flexible Patent End Gas Stove Rubber Tubing. Covering is made of braided mohair; will not crack or break. Comes in 4, 5, 6, 8 and 10-foot pieces. Price, per foot......4c

No. 22L563 Pure Rubber Gas Stove Tubing. Guaranteed against leakage for two years. Inner tube is made of pure rubber, outer cover is silk finished webbing. This is the very best tubing made, and will outlast the ordinary kind several years. Comes in 4, 6, 8 and 10-foot lengths. Price, per foot......8c

NEW IDEA GAS COOKERS, $4.87 TO $5.92.

THESE COOKERS are handsome in appearance and substantially built. The top is made of stamped steel, tastefully japanned, supplied with convenient removable back shelf, and is ornamented with an attractive nickel name plate on the front edge.

THE COOKING HOLES are furnished with open grates.

THE TOP BURNERS are made of the highest grade gray iron, producing an intensely hot flame with two rings of jets which are directed so as to have the most effect on the cooking utensils above. They are guaranteed non-leaking, easy to regulate and easy to clean.

THE OVEN BURNERS are made of cast iron, cored, in one piece.

THE BURNER VALVES. The top burners are fitted with lever handles, positive in action, non-leaking and absolutely safe in operation. They will not get out of order.

THE OVEN is thoroughly constructed of polished steel, with self-adjusting, strongly braced, drop door, forming an extension or shelf which makes it possible to draw out or turn a roast without having to lift it. It is full flued, bright corrugated tin lined, perfectly ventilated and first class in every particular. The top is protected with a galvanized iron casing. Oven is provided with two racks. The heat is evenly distributed, baking the top of articles as thoroughly as the bottom without change of position; in brief, everything done in this oven comes out sweet, clean and wholesome.

$4.87 TO $5.92

THESE STOVES are of a convenient height and we feel sure they will fill a long felt want for an inexpensive stove, will be found very practical, and will do the same work, but on a smaller scale, as our gas ranges.

No. 22L555 Stove No. 2, as shown in illustration. Height, 29¾ inches. Top, 14x21 inches. Oven, 18 inches wide, 12 inches high and 12 inches deep. With two burners on top and one one-piece cored cast iron burner under oven. Weight, crated, 55 pounds. Price, for manufactured gas, $4.87; for natural gas......$4.92

No. 22L556 Stove No. 3. Height, 29¾ inches. Top, 14x31 inches. Oven, 18 inches wide, 12 inches high and 12 inches deep. With three burners on top and one one-piece cored cast iron burner under oven. Weight, crated, 70 pounds. Price, for manufactured gas, $5.87; for natural gas......$5.92

Always state whether stoves are intended to be used for natural or artificial gas when writing your order. These gas stoves cannot be used with gasoline or acetylene gas.

DETAILED DESCRIPTION OF WEHRLE MODEL No. 80 Colonial Cast Front Gas Ranges

ILLUSTRATED AND LISTED ON THE OPPOSITE PAGE

OUR WEHRLE MODEL NO. 80 GAS RANGES make gas, beyond question, the most satisfactory of all fuels. Our valves, our burners, our ovens, our flue system, in short, our entire construction make our Wehrle Model No. 80 Gas Ranges absolutely perfect in operation, embodying the following strong features: Strength, Durability, Economy, Cleanliness, Quickness, Convenience, Attractiveness, Simplicity and Reliability.

YOUR GAS COMPANY will connect any of our Wehrle Model Gas Ranges for you at the same small charge they always make and they will not ask you any more because the stove is not bought from them. Gas companies are always glad to connect our ranges, as they are desirous of selling their product of gas and are not anxious to be dealers in gas stoves. They were compelled to go into the gas stove business because the stove and hardware dealers asked such high prices that the people would not buy a gas stove. In this way the use of gas was greatly restricted, but our prices on gas stoves are so low and we sell so many gas stoves and ranges that the gas companies are very friendly to us and connect the stoves for our customers for the same small fee they charge when they sell a stove or range and you will find the gas companies recommend our stoves and ranges everywhere as the most economical, durable and efficient stoves and ranges to be found.

THEY ARE BUILT IN OUR NEWARK, OHIO, Stove and Range Foundry—the largest in the world. We own our own natural gas wells in Newark and use natural gas in our works and our offices. Our superintendent and workmen use it in their homes, giving us the advantage—in being located in a natural gas town—of building natural gas ranges where we can test every range we build before shipping.

SOLD TO YOU UNDER OUR BINDING GUARANTEE that if they are not all and even more than we claim for them and, after a thorough test, if you do not find our Wehrle Model No. 80 Gas Ranges the best constructed, the best bakers, the quickest way, the safest way, the cheapest way and, by far, the cleanest way of cooking, and if the gas range that we send you is not satisfactory in every way and the greatest bargain you have ever heard of, you can return it to us at our expense and we will promptly refund your money, including what you paid for freight charges. The illustrations show our latest original designs sold direct to the customer at actual foundry cost with but our one small percentage of profit added, thereby eliminating all dealers', jobbers' and middlemen's profits.

THE OVEN DOOR is equipped with our Special Oven Door Thermometer, as illustrated, which measures heat just as a clock measures time, or a steam gauge measures steam pressure. Tells you when your oven has reached the degree of heat desired, makes it easy to maintain a uniform temperature and makes good baking easy to the most inexperienced.

THESE RANGES bake cakes, pies, bread and broil with same fire. Heat water and cook with same fire. Have special burners for slow cooking. Have special burners for fast cooking.

THE RANGE BODIES are constructed of Wellsville polished steel. Double protected asbestos lined oven walls to keep the heat where it belongs. No japan or other paint used on the bodies to burn off, and the smooth surface of the steel makes the range easy to keep clean.

EVERY HOUSEKEEPER will immediately appreciate the advantages of our Oven Thermometer which we furnish free with our Wehrle Model Gas Ranges and will find it one of the most necessary and valuable parts.

THE SAME COOKING UTENSILS used on your coal and wood burning stove can be used on any of our gas stoves with equally good results.

THE OVEN insulation is perfect and consists of an outer steel body, asbestos lining and air space, an inner steel lining and a hot air flue. This construction prevents any loss of heat by radiation through the sides of the stove into the room. The oven top is of heavy sheet steel, double reinforced and lined with asbestos. The construction of the oven flues is such that the oven is evenly heated and perfectly ventilated and the burning of foods at the bottom is prevented. The oven rack is of wire, insuring cleanliness.

THE OVEN FLUES force the heat to travel a greater distance and cover more surface than is possible with any other gas range made, so that every unit of heat is utilized and the oven evenly heated without dead corners, on a small amount of gas, and will "bake even," top and bottom, the most delicate cake or pastry on either the upper or lower rack, or both at the same time.

OVEN BOTTOM is made of cast iron stove plate. We call special attention to this original feature in our entire line of Wehrle Model Gas Ranges as being far superior to steel. The cast iron bottom always remains level and will not buckle or warp as a steel bottom is sure to do when it comes in direct contact with the gas flame and also has the advantage of retaining 80 per cent more heat than steel oven bottoms found in other gas ranges.

MATCH SCRATCHER on the main front will be found very convenient and satisfactory. Does away with the necessity of defacing your walls, range or floor when ready to light burners for cooking.

Patented Safety Oven Lighter.

OVEN DOOR is carefully spring poised, so that it may be opened or closed without jarring the range, thus protecting it. When open, the door forms a most convenient shelf flush with the oven bottom. The oven door balancing spring is very simple and effective.

THE LOWER OR BROILING OVEN has pressed steel drip pan with strong wire rack open at one corner to baste meat with spoon. The bottoms are double, with circulating air space, and prevent excessive heat near the floor.

OVEN AND BROILER BURNERS are very powerful and give four lines of flame. They are provided with a patent oven lighter, as illustrated. This lighter is one of our latest improvements. It is simple, quick, effective and years ahead of the old pilot lighter in general use on other makes. Mica light gives you easy view of the oven broiler burners.

TOP BURNERS. All of these ranges are equipped with four top burners made from the finest gray iron, cored and cast in one piece. This is the only material standing continued hard use in burning gas, and the one-piece burner is the only one that is absolutely proof against leakage.. Three of these burners are single burners, as illustrated, and produce 40 jets of hot flame. One of the burners is a giant burner of triple capacity, with simmering burner in the center, as illustrated, and produces 80 jets of hot flame. The giant burner produces quick heat; the simmering burner produces slow heat. Each burner has nickel plated adjustable air mixers, which economically provide for the mixture of air and gas in the ratio of 80% air to 20% gas. These burners lift out without loosening a bolt, leaving the top open and clear for cleaning. These burners can't leak, are easy to regulate and easy to keep clean

Single Burner.

Giant Burner.

THE OVEN AND BROILER BURNERS on the entire line of Wehrle Model Gas Ranges are made of cast iron, cored and in one piece. Ordinary gas range burners are often made in two pieces, causing leaks and wasting gas, and we can only caution you to beware of such cheap construction.

BURNER VALVES. All burners are fitted with heat resisting ebonized wood handled lever valves as illustrated. These are positive in action, non-leaking and absolutely safe in operation and have been proven by experience to be the only valves which will not get out of order.

Burner Valve.

WATER HEATERS. Our Nos. 22L547, 22L548, 22L551 and 22L552 ranges are furnished with a water heater to connect with a pressure boiler. For price on the pressure boiler see page 527. Water heaters and pressure boilers are used only where there is a supply furnishing constant pressure through pipes which can only be obtained in towns and cities having water works or where you have an elevated water pressure tank. The water heater is of large capacity and will furnish an abundance of hot water at a minimum cost of fuel. The water heater burners are provided with a lighter. Two cooking holes with lids are provided over water heaters.

CAREFUL INSPECTION. Every gas range and gas heater we build is set up complete and thoroughly inspected and tested before being crated for shipment, thus insuring perfect operation and accurate fitting of all parts.

Better ranges for the money could not be made, and more satisfactory ranges to use cannot be found. They are guaranteed the greatest values ever offered in gas ranges.

SEE INDEX, PINK PAGES 552 TO 559, TO FIND WHAT YOU WANT.

WEHRLE MODEL No. 80 GAS RANGE

$13.93 TO $15.93

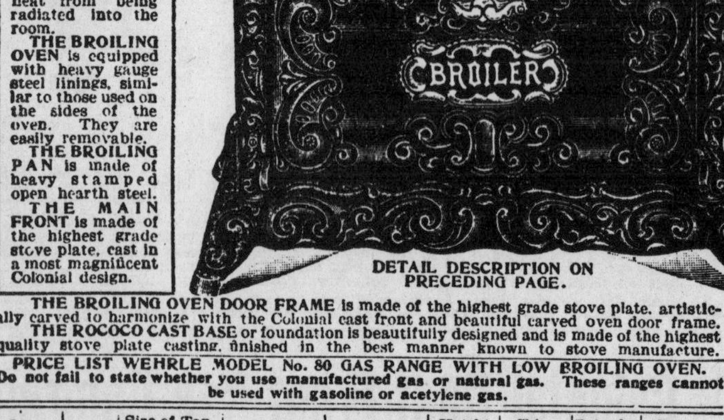

DETAIL DESCRIPTION ON PRECEDING PAGE.

Improved New Design for 1909 With Low Broiling Oven.

WE OFFER this Drop Door Gas Range with low broiler, one giant burner of triple capacity, three single burners and one simmering burner, in competition with the highest priced gas ranges in the world. Everything that is durable and practical is embodied in this range. The body is made of Wellsville polished steel, with a fine smooth surface, the kind that will not rust, chip or peel and is easy to keep clean. All cast iron parts are made from the highest grade Alabama and Tennessee pig iron.

A NOTICEABLE FEATURE in the construction of our entire line Wehrle Model No. 80 Gas Ranges is the interior oven linings, which are perfect in every detail. They are made in one section so that they can be easily and almost instantly removed from place. The whole interior oven in all ranges, including the sides and oven bottom, can be taken out for cleaning and replaced in a moment's time, without removing a bolt, nut or screw.

THE BAKING OVEN is made square with special ventilating flue construction, insuring perfect baking and the greatest economy in gas consumption.

THE OVEN RACKS are made of strong steel wire, light, convenient, easily adjusted and removable. **THE OVEN BOTTOM** is made of cast iron stove plate and is guaranteed not to warp or buckle.

OVEN SAFETY LIGHTER. A very important feature to which we call particular attention is our Safety Oven Burner Lighter, illustrated on page 44. The oven burners cannot be lighted without opening the door. When the gas is turned on at the right end of range a match is applied to an opening in the oven bottom, thus avoiding all popping or explosion in connection with the operation. It is beyond question of doubt the safest and simplest device ever used.

THE OVEN DOOR is spring balanced, dropping flush with the oven bottom, forming a convenient shelf and is equipped with our ever dependable oven door thermometer, which is a great aid in baking.

THE BEAUTIFUL OVEN DOOR FRAME is made entirely of cast iron in a handsomely carved design, ornamented with a highly silver nickeled handle and name plate.

THE OVEN LININGS are made of heavy gauge steel with broad guides or flanges, which form the sides for the oven racks.

ASBESTOS MILL BOARD. We place between the inner sides and main outside body of every Wehrle Model No. 80 gas range heavy linings of Asbestos Mill Board, which effectually retains the heat in the oven and which also aids in preventing the heat from being radiated into the room.

THE BROILING OVEN is equipped with heavy gauge steel linings, similar to those used on the sides of the oven. They are easily removable.

THE BROILING PAN is made of heavy stamped open hearth steel.

THE MAIN FRONT is made of the highest grade stove plate, cast in a most magnificent Colonial design.

THE BROILING OVEN DOOR FRAME is made of the highest grade stove plate, artistically carved to harmonize with the Colonial cast front and beautiful carved oven door frame.

THE ROCOCO CAST BASE or foundation is beautifully designed and is made of the highest quality stove plate casting, finished in the best manner known to stove manufacture.

IN SHORT, WEHRLE MODEL No. 80 GAS RANGES with oven and broiler, as shown in the large illustration, and Wehrle Model No. 80, with baking oven, broiler, water heater extension and water coil, with two extra cooking holes, as shown in the small illustration, are ranges without an equal and recommended to the wide awake housekeeper for economy in doing any kind of cooking and sold at the heretofore unheard of prices for such elegant gas ranges at $13.93 to $15.93, and $18.06 to $20.06, according to size and attachments.

THE SMALL ILLUSTRATION shows the same range as Catalogue Nos. 22D549 and 22D550 at $13.93 to $15.93, with the exception of a water heater extension. It shows the range with water heater section containing water coil to be connected with range boiler having city water pressure and will heat a 30-gallon range boiler at a minimum cost for gas. With this equipment the range has six cooking holes on top and at the same time that the water is being heated the lids over the coil can be used for cooking. The small illustration shows the range ready for manufactured gas. When ordered for natural gas we furnish this range with a closed top.

Every range is thoroughly inspected and tested before shipment.

PRICE LIST WEHRLE MODEL No. 80 GAS RANGE WITH LOW BROILING OVEN. Do not fail to state whether you use manufactured gas or natural gas. These ranges cannot be used with gasoline or acetylene gas.

Catalogue No.	Range No.	Size of Top, Including End Shelves, inches	Baking Oven, inches	Broiling Oven, inches	Height from Floor, inches	Shipping Weight, pounds	Price for Manufactured Gas	Price for Natural Gas
22L549	26P	35½x22¼	16x16¼x11	16x16¼x8	32½	181	$13.93	$14.43
22L550	28P	37½x22¼	18x16¼x11	18x16¼x8	33½	193	15.43	15.93

PRICE LIST WEHRLE MODEL No. 80 LOW BROILING GAS RANGE, INCLUDING WATER HEATER EXTENSION AND WATER COIL. Do not fail to state whether you use manufactured gas or natural gas. These ranges cannot be used with gasoline or acetylene gas.

Catalogue No.	Range No.	Size of Top, Including Water Heater and End Shelf, ins.	Baking Oven, inches	Broiling Oven, inches	Height from Floor, inches	Shipping Weight, pounds	Price for Manufactured Gas	Price for Natural Gas
22L551	26W	39½x22¼	16x16¼x11	16x16¼x8	32½	205	$18.06	$18.56
22L552	28W	41½x22¼	18x16¼x11	18x16¼x8	33½	225	19.56	20.06

WEHRLE MODEL No. 80 —SINGLE OVEN— GAS RANGE WITH COUNTER-BALANCED DROP OVEN DOOR.

AT $11.08 TO $12.88 we offer this famous single oven gas range as shown in the large illustration at prices lower than the lowest, lower than anyone can offer them, lower than any gas company cares to sell them, so low that gas companies are buying them from us and are proud to connect them for you at a small fee, and so low that it relieves them of the expense and trouble of trying to sell gas ranges, for we are selling them so fast they are kept busy increasing their facilities and capacity for supplying gas. Handsomely designed removable cast end shelves. Closely fitted and even baking oven fitted with our dependable oven door thermometer, which accurately indicates the proper heat for baking, and saves gas bills. Handsomely carved oven door frame with genuine silver nickel plated oven door handle and name plate, and silver nickeled valve line. **Note the full description on preceding page.** Has three standard star burners, one triple capacity giant burner with simmering burner in center and lighting separately. Four-line burner for oven and oven lighter. The illustration shows it ready for natural gas. When ordered for artificial gas we furnish it with open top grates. We can always furnish repairs for our gas ranges.

CAREFUL INSPECTION. Every gas range and gas heater we build is set up complete and thoroughly inspected and tested before being crated for shipment, thus insuring perfect operation and accurate fitting of all parts.

THE SMALL ILLUSTRATION shows the exact same range as catalogue Nos. 22L545 and 22L546 at $11.08 to $12.88, with the exception of a water heater. It shows the range with water heater section containing water coil to be connected with range boiler having city water pressure, and will heat a 30-gallon range boiler at a minimum cost for gas. With this equipment the range has six cooking holes on top and at the same time that the water is being heated the lids over the coil can be used for cooking. The small illustration shows the range with open top grates for manufactured gas. When ordered for natural gas, we furnish the range with closed lids or griddle covers.

DETAIL DESCRIPTION ON PRECEDING PAGE.

One lid is made in two sections to accommodate different size utensils.

The illustration shows the range ready for natural gas. When ordered for artificial gas we furnish it with open top grates.

30 DAYS' TRIAL

Remember, we have a large stock on hand, all crated and ready for immediate shipment, and accept your order for one of our very highest grade Wehrle Model No. 80 Gas Ranges with the understanding and agreement that you can give it thirty days' trial and if, during that time, you have any reason to feel dissatisfied, if it does not operate perfectly, if you find it is not by far the most wonderful labor saving and fuel saving range you have ever used, and if you find you have not made an immense saving in every way, and that we have furnished you one of our Wehrle Model No. 80 Gas Ranges at just half the price such a range would cost you from any other dealer, you are at perfect liberty to return the range to us at our expense, and we will immediately refund your money, including the transportation charges you have paid.

PRICE LIST WEHRLE MODEL No. 80 SINGLE OVEN GAS RANGE, including water heater extension and water coil. Do not fail to state whether you use manufactured gas or natural gas. These ranges cannot be used with gasoline or acetylene gas.

Catalogue No.	Range No.	Size of Top, Including Water Heater and End Shelf, inches	Size of Oven, inches	Height from Floor, inches	Shipping Weight, pounds	Price for Manufactured Gas	Price for Natural Gas
22L547	16W	39½x22¼	16x16¼x11	30	170	$15.13	$15.63
22L548	18W	41½x22¼	18x16¼x11	30	185	16.38	16.88

PRICE LIST WEHRLE MODEL No. 80 SINGLE OVEN GAS RANGE. Do not fail to state whether you use manufactured gas or natural gas. These ranges cannot be used with gasoline or acetylene gas.

Catalogue No.	Range No.	Size of Top, Including End Shelves, inches	Size of Oven, inches	Height from Floor, inches	Shipping Weight, pounds	Price for Manufactured Gas	Price for Natural Gas
22L545	16P	35½x22¼	16x16¼x11	30	162	$11.08	$11.58
22L546	18P	37½x22¼	18x16¼x11	30	170	12.33	12.88

WEHRLE MODEL No. 76 GAS RANGE

$19.48 For Manufactured Gas

$19.98 For Natural Gas

BAKING AND BROILING ON A LINE WITH THE EYE. NO STOOPING. NO BACK BREAKING.

A NEW CABINET GAS RANGE FOR 1909

IT CONTAINS EVERY FEATURE OF CONVENIENCE IN GAS RANGES AND IS BY FAR THE MOST COMPLETE AND HIGHEST GRADE GAS RANGE EVER BUILT, AN IDEAL CONSTRUCTION, MOST SATISFACTORY AND THE GREATEST GAS SAVER YOU CAN BUY. THE ELEVATED OVEN AND BROILER ALLOWS THE USER TO STAND ERECT NATURALLY AND COMFORTABLY WHILE COOKING. NO STOOPING OR BACK BREAKING WHEN USING ONE OF OUR IMPROVED CABINET WEHRLE MODEL GAS RANGES ILLUSTRATED ON THIS PAGE.

WE ASK YOU to turn to page 412 and carefully read the detailed description of our gas ranges. Read about the material we use, the highest grade pig iron used in making the cast iron parts and Wellsville polished steel for the body—how every piece and part entering into the construction of gas ranges is made in our foundry at Newark, Ohio, and used only after being carefully inspected and tested by experts.

THE BODY. The sides and back are made of Wellsville polished steel. The front is made of the highest grade cast iron stove plate, carved in a most magnificent design.

ASBESTOS LINING. Linings of asbestos millboard are placed between the inside and the main outside body. It retains the heat in the oven most effectually and also aids in preventing the heat from being radiated into the room.

THE OVEN BOTTOM is made of cast iron stove plate, is easily removed and is guaranteed not to warp or buckle.

THE OVEN PARTS. The interior of the oven, including the sides and racks and the oven bottom can be removed in less than a minute's time without removing a bolt, nut or screw.

THE OVEN DOOR. When open, the oven door drops and forms a most convenient shelf flush with the oven bottom.

THE OVEN THERMOMETER is right before you, placed in the door of the oven.

THE BROILER DOOR is made of cast iron, of artistic design, and drops flush with the bottom of the broiler.

PATENT SAFETY LIGHTER. All our Wehrle Model Gas Ranges are equipped with a patent safety lighter, illustrated and described on page 412.

THE POWERFUL BURNERS. The heat for the oven and broiler is furnished by powerful burners as described on page 412.

REMOVABLE STEEL DRIP PAN, heavily galvanized to prevent rust, is placed under the cooking top burners.

A CONVENIENT SHELF UNDER THE BODY for cooking utensils makes this Cabinet Gas Range perfectly rigid and firm on the floor.

THE STEEL SHELF. There is a high bracketed shelf at the upper left hand side (as shown in illustration) which is also convenient for dishes or cooking utensils to be kept right before you as you are using the range.

THE WARMING CLOSET above the baking oven will be found very useful. It has a roll front door which rolls back into the top of the closet without interfering with the space inside; makes a convenient and indispensable receptacle. It is so perfect in construction that it warms and keeps the food wholesome without drying it up. The Main Top is made of high grade stove plate.

PRICE LIST WEHRLE MODEL No. 76 GAS RANGE, COMPLETE WITH WARMING CLOSET AND TOP SHELF EXACTLY AS ILLUSTRATED.

DO NOT FAIL to state whether you use manufactured gas or natural gas. These ranges cannot be used with acetylene or gasoline gas.

Catalogue No.	Stove No.	Size of Top Including End Shelf, inches	Baking Oven, inches	Broiling Oven, inches	Height from Floor to Cooking Top, inches	Total Height from Floor to Top of Elevated Oven	Floor Space, inches	Pipe to Fit Collar, inches	Shipping Wt., lbs.	Price for Manufactured Gas	Price for Natural Gas
22D542	76	22x29	18x20x11	18x20x8	28	54 inches	26x45	5	325	$19.48	$19.98

IF WANTED WITH WATER HEATER but without end shelf, add $3.50 to prices quoted. When furnished with water heater this Wehrle Model No. 76 Gas Range has six No. 7 cooking holes on top, and at the same time the water is being heated the lids over the coil can be used for cooking. Shipping weight with water heater, 370 pounds.

HANDSOME HIGH OVEN AND BROILER GAS RANGE, WEHRLE MODEL No. 75

$17.45 For Manufactured Gas

$17.95 For Natural Gas

AT $17.45 AND $17.95 we offer this, our entirely New Wehrle Model No. 75 Gas Range, complete with 18-inch elevated oven, broiler, four cooking holes and our special oven thermometer, a range which will certainly command the attention of many by reason of the oven being elevated, so the user can do the baking and broiling on a line with the eye, thus obviating the necessity of stooping in order to watch the cooking process.

THE OVENS. By referring to the illustration to the right you will notice how conveniently the baking and broiling ovens are elevated and located. They allow the user to stand erect, naturally and comfortably, making it possible to do all the baking and broiling on a line with the eye. The ovens are large and roomy, and are supplied with two extra large burners extending the entire length of the ovens, each one controlled by independent wood handle lever valves, enabling the user to use either one or both burners as may be required. A convenient Safety Pilot Lighter for the oven burner is located on the right hand.

THE OVEN DOOR of this, our Wehrle Model No. 75 Gas Range, is securely mounted on hinge pins and swings to the left. It is of handsome rococo design, ornamented with a beautiful heavily silver nickeled panel holding in view our dependable oven thermometer, which tells you how to manage the fire and indicates accurately the temperature of the oven without the necessity of opening the door, and is furnished with a "never hot" nickel door knob.

THE BROILER DOOR is supplied with silver nickeled handle, drops flush with the bottom of the broiler, forming a convenient shelf.

HIGH ART BRACKETS. The elevated baking oven and broiler are supported by a pair of massive high art brackets, made of the highest grade stove plate in artistic design; the front edges of which are beautifully ground and highly polished, adding greatly to the general appearance of the stove.

CONVENIENT MATCH SCRATCHER. Has a convenient match scratcher in front of main top.

THE MAIN TOP. When equipped for natural gas, this Wehrle Model No. 75 Gas Range has solid covers; for artificial gas has open top grates, and the cooking top measures 23x24 inches and is supplied with five hardwood handle valves, silver nickeled air mixers and silver nickeled supply pipe.

THE BURNERS. This Wehrle Model No. 75 is equipped with four regular burners and one giant and simmering burner, fitted with nickel air mixers, made from the very finest gray iron, acknowledged to be the only material standing continued hard use in burning gas. Pipe collar for 5-inch pipe.

SOLD UNDER BINDING GUARANTEE of satisfaction or all your money refunded together with freight you pay.

The same cooking utensils used on your coal and wood burning stove can be used on any of our gas stoves with equally good results

For water heater extension and water coil add $3.50 to prices listed. Water heater section contains water coil to be connected with a range boiler having city water pressure, and has a large roomy top with two 7-inch lids. It is fitted with hardwood handle lever valves, silver nickeled air mixers. Measures 11x23 inches. With this equipment the range has six cooking holes on top and at the same time the water is heated the lids over the coil can be used for cooking. Shipping weight, with water heater, 355 pounds.

Gas Companies connect our gas ranges at same low fee charged for their own. See page 412.

Baking and Broiling on a line with the eye. No stooping. No back breaking.

THE BASE. The base of our Wehrle Model No. 75 Gas Range is of the latest skeleton pattern. The entire range is supported on artistically carved cast iron legs with a roomy and very convenient shelf 12 inches from the floor, which can be easily utilized for holding cooking utensils.

PRICE LIST WEHRLE MODEL No. 75 GAS RANGE, COMPLETE AS ILLUSTRATED.

Do not fail to state whether you use manufactured gas or natural gas. These ranges cannot be used with acetylene or gasoline gas.

Catalogue Number	Stove No.	Size of Top, Including End Shelf, inches	Baking Oven, inches	Broiling Oven, inches	Height from Floor to Cooking Top, inches	Total Height from Floor to Top of Elevated Oven, inches	Floor Space, inches	Pipe to Fit Collar, inches	Shipping Weight, Without Water Heater, pounds	Price for Manufactured Gas	Price for Natural Gas
22L541	75	24x45	16x18x12	16x18x6½	28	64	26x30	5	300	$17.45	$17.95

Add $3.50 to prices quoted if you want water heater extension and water coil. Shipping weight with water heater 345 pounds.

DESCRIPTION OF ACME TRIUMPH STEEL RANGES

THE BODY OF BLUE POLISHED STEEL PLATE. **The material from which our Acme Triumph Steel Range is made needs no commendation from us,** as it is the product of the world famous Wellsville Rolling Mills, and is known to all steel buyers as "Wellsville Polished Steel." This steel is the standard of the world, and its beautiful surface and high quality were only secured by persistent, intelligent and conscientious labor. This steel requires neither blacking, enameling or japanning, as in the process of manufacture it is passed and repassed through ponderous rollers, which polish and repolish it until a permanent and beautiful blue color is obtained. These steel sheets are handled and rehandled in oil at the rolling mill and at our foundry in Newark, which preserves the beautiful color from spots and markings as it passes through the hands of the workmen. It also protects the beautiful finish from all exposure of the weather in shipping, so that when you receive the range the blue polished steel plate is just as perfect as when it was first finished. Wipe off the surface of the steel with a soft cloth and the deep blue color of this matchless material becomes a delight to the eye and a satisfaction to the housewife, and it requires no further attention. Its beautiful surface will not burn off. If you should leave home for a vacation or place your range in storage, simply oil the surface of the range with common natural oil, vaseline, petroleum jelly or any other oil free from salt, and when it is required for use again, rub this oil off and its beautiful blue surface is as good as new. If you will follow these instructions this fine blue surface will never become impaired.

ASBESTOS LINING. **All parts of the steel body exposed to direct action of the fire, are lined with asbestos, particular care being taken in doing this work.** This protects and insures the steel from either burning or rusting out. By this process of lining with heavy asbestos the heat is closely confined almost entirely within the range, so that the Acme Triumph Steel Range is a quick, even baker, and yet it does not heat up the kitchen and house in the hot summer months as do the wood and coal burning stoves and ranges of other makes.

REMOVABLE GRATE. **This illustration of the fire box end of the Acme Triumph Steel Range shows you how simply the grate of this range may be removed,** either for the purpose of making repairs or for giving it any attention it may require. By turning the thumb knob the grate door may be removed and the grate pulled forward. Like all other features of this economical range, the method of placing the grate in the stove is simplicity itself.

THE POKER DOOR. **The poker door gives ready access to the entire surface of the grate,** and when it is opened it is very easy to loosen or remove a clinker that may be fastened in the grate bars, and which it has been found impossible to remove in the ordinary poking operation. If you have used other ranges you know how much trouble you have sometimes experienced with clinkers and this fine feature of the Acme Triumph Steel Range will commend itself to you.

DUPLEX GRATE. **It is almost unnecessary to describe the merits of this grate because it is a standard construction,** too well known to need our praise. Our best mechanics construct this grate and it always operates perfectly, and with our poker device and crank shaker it is easily and quickly cleaned. A half turn will drop all large ashes and clinkers into the ash pan and return the grate to its proper position again without the loss of a particle of the fire.

COAL FEED POUCH AND BROILER DOOR. **On the left end of the range we provide capacious coal feed pouch with a lift on the cover or door, as shown in the larger illustration on this page.** Our designer, in moulding this feature of the Acme Triumph Steel Range, has given us a combination coal feed and broiler door at the same time. Lift the feed cover and a broiler may be inserted through the opening. All the fumes of the broiling are carried up the smoke flue while the steaks or chops broiled over the bed of red coals remain sweet and wholesome. This combination pouch feed and broiler door extends downward to the draft registers, and is part of the same stove plate casting. There is no japanning to burn off, and it requires no more attention to keep it in beautiful condition than do the main top, covers and centers.

ADAPTABLE FIRE BOX FOR COAL OR WOOD. **We show herewith two illustrations which will convey to you a clear understanding of the wide adaptability of this range to every sort of fuel.** The picture shows the coal fire box, with duplex grate and end linings in proper position. By a simple device of our own invention you are able to instantly convert this coal fire box into a wood fire box. By inverting the duplex grate you have a solid, level grate bottom for wood burning. The end linings are then removed and you have the wood burning fire box, as shown in the illustration below. By these operations we have, in the Acme Triumph Steel Range, the simplest method ever devised for the conversion of a perfect coal burning fire box to a perfect wood burning fire box with its extra space for the reception of long sticks of wood. The length of this wood burning fire box, as shown in the illustration below with end linings removed and wood extension attached is 26 inches in all sizes of the Acme Triumph Steel Range.

WATER FRONT.

If you have pressure water from your city or town waterworks or an elevated pressure water tank of your own this range can be supplied with a water front to which the supply pipes may be attached, and with these advantages the extension reservoir is not required. The water front is a very desirable attachment as it will supply you with hot water throughout the house whenever the range is in use. On page 955 we show a small illustration of the Acme Triumph Steel Range without extension reservoir and attached to a kitchen boiler, illustrating the method of heating 30 or 40 gallons of water for circulation to the bathroom, lavatory or kitchen of your home.

MAIN TOP, COVERS, CENTERS AND ANCHOR PLATES. **All of these important parts are made of the finest cast stove plate,** in the manufacture of which we use only the purest Birmingham pig iron. These plates are not to be compared with the cheap malleable iron main tops, covers, centers and anchor plates some manufacturers use in their so called "steel" ranges. Malleable iron melts at a lower temperature than first class stove castings, and for this reason the latter, which we use in the Acme Triumph Steel Range, are more durable for use where the parts come in direct contact with the fire. You will never have any trouble due to the cracking or warping of these parts when you buy and use the Acme Triumph Steel Range.

EXTENSION RESERVOIR. **We call your particular attention to the extension reservoir of the Acme Triumph Steel Range.** The reservoir case is made of fine cast stove plate and the reservoir proper is of cast stove plate, white porcelain lined. A common fault in most steel ranges is the building of the extension reservoir casing of the same steel that is used in the frame of the range and then lining it with asbestos. When the water in the inner reservoir in ranges so constructed becomes sufficiently heated a sweating process results and dampness between the asbestos lining and the steel plates quickly rusts out the reservoir casing. Our new cast extension reservoir overcomes this fault and is a very decided improvement.

SCREW DRAFT REGISTERS. **The draft supply of the Acme Triumph Steel Range is obtained through two screw draft registers below the coal feed pouch and broiler door, a style of register which permits of the absolute control of the fire at all times.** These draft registers may be opened or closed airtight by an eccentric cam, a device of our own invention. These screw draft registers are really a part of the poker door as you will observe by consulting the illustration in the upper right hand corner showing the left end view of the range.

THE LARGE OVENS. **All sizes of the Acme Triumph Steel Range are equipped with an oven 21 inches deep and 14 inches high.** The width of the oven is 16, 18 or 20 inches, according to the size of the range selected. We have put a great deal of care and skill on the oven of the Acme Triumph Steel Range, and by a special arrangement of the flues it has been possible for us to bring this oven to the highest degree of perfection and to make them quick and even and satisfactory bakers. Oven bottom is strongly braced on under side and is guaranteed not to warp or buckle. Oven top is protected with a corrugated cast plate, which also serves to distribute the heat evenly to all parts of the oven.

FLUE CONSTRUCTION. **The Acme Triumph Range is constructed with a cast flue of ample depth to prevent it from becoming easily clogged up.** With this construction the heat is evenly distributed, consequently the oven bottom will never warp and will always bake the same in every part.

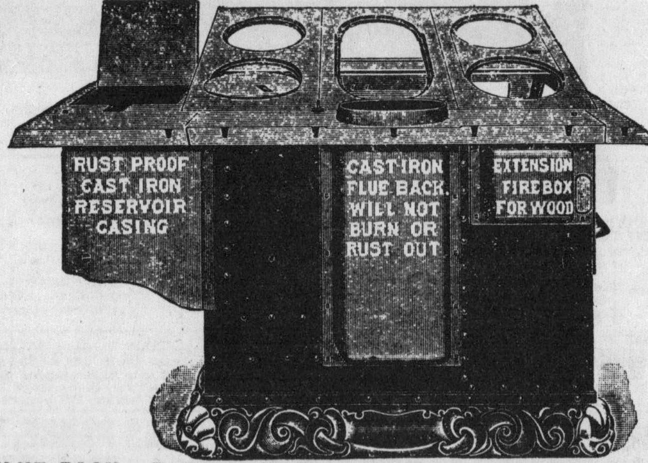

FLUE BACK. **The flue back of the Triumph Steel Range is not made of steel as is the case in most steel ranges now on the market,** but instead we construct it of the best stove plate castings. You will notice that wherever any part of the Acme Triumph Steel Range comes in direct contact with the fire we substitute the best stove plate castings for steel as it is the best class of material and gives more satisfactory and more durable service.

GRADUATED LID OR NEST COVER. **Every Acme Triumph Steel Range is fitted with five solid covers,** and the one nest cover or graduated lid, as shown in the illustration. This is a very convenient little device, as the varying sizes of the openings in the cover will be found very useful.

SILVER NICKELING. **The front edge of the main top is bound with a silver nickel steel band,** the wood fire door, the removable grate panel, the ash door, the oven door and the oven handle, the oven door medallion and the flue cover name plate are all made by our silver nickeling process, which gives beautiful ornamentation, a process which we have been using for a number of years and which has become famous wherever our Acme Stoves are used.

COMMODIOUS ASH DOOR. **By reference to the illustration of the range you will notice that the ash door is unusually large,** that it extends the full width and height of the ash pit and provides ample room for an unusually large ash pan, which will hold the accumulated ashes of one day's use, thus lessening the labor and dirt which go with the removal of the ashes.

ROCOCO CAST BASE. **Every Acme Triumph Steel Range is placed upon an ornamental and elaborately designed base,** which is made of the highest quality of stove plate casting, finished in the best manner known to stove manufacturing and trimmed at each corner with nickel corner pieces. This solid base adds immensely to the looks and beauty of this range and gives a finishing touch to what we regard as the one and only high class steel range on the market.

HIGH WARMING CLOSET. **This has become an almost indispensable attachment to this article of kitchen furniture,** and the high warming closet of the Acme Triumph Steel Range is both commodious and convenient. It is at just a proper height for the average person to easily reach; the roll front door rolls back and into the top of the closet after the manner of the curtain of a roll top desk without interfering with the commodious space inside. This warming closet door is so carefully counterbalanced that it works very easily, the weight of the hand being sufficient to open it. The top, sides, back and roll front of the high closet are made of the same beautiful blue polished steel used in the body of the range. It is trimmed with nickel steel bands along the front, as shown on preceding page. The upper nickel steel band is in broad relief to its parallel band at the bottom. The right and left corner pieces are full silver nickeled. The medallion or panel on the front of the closet, together with its door handle, are made of our world renowned silver nickeling on cast designs. Connecting the high closet with the main top of the range and supporting the high closet are our open work rococo design closet brackets which are full silver nickeled. A capacious smoke pipe connecting with the main top of the stove passes up through the closet, going out at the closet top, as shown. This clear joint of smoke pipe passing through the closet is made of Wellsville polished steel plate and on its front below the closet is a circular register draft check handsomely silver nickeled, which may be opened to reduce the draft when necessary. To the right and left of this closet pipe are elaborately designed teapot holders elegantly nickeled, which may be quickly utilized by bringing them down to a level so that a teapot or other cooking utensil may be placed upon the bracket.

SEE PRICE LIST AND ILLUSTRATION ON OPPOSITE PAGE

THE HIGHEST GRADE STEEL RANGE WE BUILD

$21.52 TO $23.90

FOR HARD COAL, SOFT COAL OR WOOD

THIS IS THE ACME TRIUMPH BLUE POLISHED STEEL RANGE, EQUIPPED WITH RUSTPROOF CAST IRON RESERVOIR CASING, PORCELAIN LINED WATER TANK. THE BEST EVER BUILT. EXACTLY THE SAME RANGE AS IS SHOWN IN THE FULL PAGE ILLUSTRATION ON PRECEDING PAGE, BUT WITHOUT THE WARMING CLOSET.

YOU WILL NOTE this range is equipped with high back shelf and reservoir, and except for the warming closet, as shown in the large full page illustration on preceding page, it is the exact same range, and equipped as you see it with high shelf and deep porcelain lined reservoir, we furnish it all complete from $21.52 to $23.90, according to size.

UNDERSTAND, our Acme Triumph Steel Ranges are made of blue polished steel in the natural color, not enameled, painted or in any way colored. The rich blue polish is produced by passing and repassing the steel plate through ponderous rollers until a permanent beautiful blue color is obtained. The steel plate is produced by the famous Wellsville Rolling Mills, and Wellsville polished steel is the standard of the world. The sheets are handled in oil at the mills and at our steel range factory, preserving the beautiful color from all exposure to the weather in shipping. **At the slight difference in cost between the blue polished Wellsville steel, which is used in this and all our Acme Triumph stoves,** and a regular standard black enameled steel, we would especially recommend and urge that you buy the Acme Triumph blue polished steel range, for in this range it is possible to bring out a lasting effect, a beauty of finish and general appearance not obtainable in any black enameled steel range. **With the elaborate nickel plated trimmings** standing out in contrast to the variegated blue polished effect in steel, we produce a richness of appearance not duplicated by any stove from any other foundry.

Cast Iron Left End, guaranteed not to warp, buckle or burn out.

Guaranteed Rustproof Cast Iron Reservoir Casing.

THE ACME TRIUMPH has the highest grade of nickel trimmings throughout. This nickeling is done in our own foundry, in our own nickeling department. Every part is highly polished before the nickel is applied, and we use a heavier nickel plate than is usually used on stove plate by other makers, and our system of polishing and buffing brings out a high luster seldom seen in stove work. The Acme Triumph stoves, in all their different styles, have the fullest nickel equipment, including a very heavy nickel plated front band, nickel reservoir panel, nickel side shelves and bands, nickel oven door trimmings, bands, medallions, catches, hinges, etc., nickel front doors, corners, drafts, medallions, etc., all built on a heavy rococo base. **All Acme Triumph blue polished steel ranges are made for hard coal, soft coal or wood, all equipped with duplex grate, screw draft registers, poker door, commodious ash door,** all made with extra large ovens and with unusually large porcelain lined reservoirs. All have the very latest style coal feed pouch and broiling door.

YOU WILL APPRECIATE an Acme Triumph in any style you may order, for it requires no blackening, enameling or japanning. Simply wipe off the surface of the steel with a soft cloth and you immediately have that deep blue color of this matchless material. Should you go away for a long vacation or store away the range, simply oil the surface with any common oil, free from salt, and when you return rub it off, and you will have the same perfect surface as the day you received the stove.

IF YOU ARE THINKING OF BUYING a steel range we know we are placed at a great disadvantage, for you may be more than a thousand miles from our foundry at Newark, Ohio. We know you can go to your dealer at home and select a steel range from his stock; very likely he will offer to set the range up in your house, furnish you the stove pipe and let you take the range on trial, he may tell you there is no hurry about paying for it, saying you can pay for it in thirty days or in three or six months. Of course, he will tell you all about the good qualities of the range, but we have this satisfaction, he must tell you the price, and, quality for quality, his price will be almost double the price we ask. **If you are thinking about buying a steel range, of course, we have only this picture or description to aid you in selecting,** whereas your dealer at home shows you the stove and gives you a chance to compare it with other stoves; and again you may raise the question, "How much will the freight amount to?" We want you to remember that this big steel range can be shipped to any point within 100 to 1,000 miles of Newark, Ohio, for from 50 cents to $3.00. Greater or less distances in proportion. We also want to assure you that we can get the stove to you in just a few days after we receive your order. We want to promise you that it will go to you in perfect condition, and if any piece or part is broken, we will replace or repair it free of charge promptly or send you a new range. We also want to assure you that in the years to come we will furnish you any piece or part that you may need for repairs, and on the shortest possible notice. We also want to assure you that anyone can set the stove up; you, the buyer, can do it as well as anyone, and then, please, remember that we guarantee to please you, guarantee to make you a big saving in cost. If you order this range from us we will send it to you with the understanding and agreement that you can set it up yourself in your own home and give it thirty days' trial, during which time you can put it to every test, compare it with the stoves you have looked at at home and thought of buying, even though the price asked you is possibly double the price we ask for this range, and if you are not satisfied that you have saved about one-half in price and gotten the best range it is possible to build; remember, you are at liberty to return the range to us at our expense, and we will immediately return your money together with any freight charges paid by you.

Price List of the Acme Triumph Six-Hole Polished Steel Plate Range, with High Shelf and Porcelain Lined Reservoir. Strongly crated and delivered on board cars at foundry in Newark, Ohio.

Catalogue Number	Range No.	Size of Lids	Size of Oven, inches	Main Top including Reservoir	Height to Main Top	Pipe, Collar	Shipping Weight, pounds	Price
22F25	8-16	No. 8	16x21x14	46x29 in.	30½ in.	7 in.	513	$21.52
22F26	8-18	No. 8	18x21x14	48x29 in.	30½ in.	7 in.	523	22.55
22F27	8-20	No. 8	20x21x14	50x29 in.	30½ in.	7 in.	534	23.65
22F28	9-18	No. 9	18x21x14	48x29 in.	30½ in.	7 in.	523	22.80
22F29	9-20	No. 9	20x21x14	50x29 in.	30½ in.	7 in.	534	23.90

Oven Door Thermometer, as described on page 951, $1.00 extra.

On all the above sizes the fire box is 10 inches wide and 7 inches deep, its length for coal is 19 inches and for wood 26 inches. Capacity of reservoir, 22 quarts.

EVERY RANGE bears the name, "Acme Triumph, Newark Stove Works, Chicago." We especially recommend this range to stove dealers who buy to sell again. Our name does not appear on the range. If you buy it to sell again the party to whom you sell it will not know where you got it or what you paid for it. Set it up in your home and even though your employer may be a retail stove dealer he need not know that you bought the stove from us, or that you bought it for about one-half the price that you would have to pay your retail dealer.

DON'T OVERLOOK OUR PROFIT SHARING DEPARTMENT.

REMEMBER, if you send us an order for a stove, part of your money comes back in the shape of your share of the profit, as explained in pages 1 and 2 of this catalogue.

A Fuel Saver and Half the Price Others Ask.

Sears, Roebuck & Co., Chicago, Ill. Columbia, Mo.

Gentlemen:—The Acme Triumph Range I purchased from you was received in good condition, and is in every way as you represented. It is a beauty, a good range, and takes but little fuel. I have had it almost a year and have found no fault with it. I could not have purchased a stove like it here for less than double the price. I am well pleased.

Respectfully, MRS. G. W. KELLEY. R. F. D. No. 2.

THE HIGHEST GRADE STEEL RANGE MADE, IN ANOTHER STYLE.

$19.00 TO $21.39

FOR HARD COAL, SOFT COAL OR WOOD.

THIS IS OUR POLISHED STEEL, nickel trimmed, rococo cast base Acme Triumph Reservoir Steel Range, the exact same range as the one shown in the above illustration, the same range as is shown in the large full page illustration on preceding page. It only differs in the equipment. This range is furnished as you see it with the deep white enamel lined reservoir, but without high back, top shelf or closet. Furnished in this style and offered at from $19.00 upwards according to size as listed below.

THE DESCRIPTION of this is the description of the two preceding steel ranges, everything the very best, the best of material, workmanship and finish, the highest grade six-hole, blue polished steel, nickel trimmed, steel range made, a range embodying the good points of every high grade steel range on the market with the defects of none, made to burn hard coal, soft coal or wood.

AT THE SPECIAL PRICE NAMED we furnish the range delivered on board the cars at the foundry at Newark, and the freight charges will amount to next to nothing compared with what you will save in price. 50 cents to $3.00 will pay the freight to any point from one hundred to one thousand miles. Greater or less distances in proportion.

OUR 30 DAYS' FREE TRIAL OFFER.

REMEMBER, the range will go to you with the understanding and agreement that you can give it thirty days' trial in your own home, during which time you can put it to every test, and if you are not convinced it is the highest grade range made, much better in quality and much lower in price than you can buy elsewhere, you can return it to us at our expense, and we will immediately return your money. We guarantee it to reach you in perfect order. When we send you the stove we send you a book on repairs, so that in the years to come if you should want any piece or part to repair a broken part, refer to the booklet we send you and you will know exactly what to order by number, and the price named opposite each number is a price that barely covers cost at the factory, a mere fraction of what others charge, and any time in the years to come just say you want number this or that, as the case may be, and the repair will go to you immediately.

SEE PAGE 951, SHOWING HOW STRONGLY WE CRATE OUR STOVES

DON'T HESITATE to send us your order for an Acme Triumph Steel Range or other stove, fearing the freight charges will be too high or it will take too long to get the stove, or that the stove will not be found all or even more than you expected when received.

IT WILL TAKE but a very few days for your order to reach us and the stove to reach you. We carry an immense stock of these stoves on hand at our Newark, Ohio, foundry and can ship your order immediately, to be loaded in solid cars for junction points, so that a stove will reach a customer a thousand miles away in a very few days from the time it is shipped and we ship immediately on receipt of the order. Have no fear of its reaching you in other than perfect condition, for we ship them guaranteeing them to reach you in perfect condition. Don't fear about the freight. Remember, the biggest stove we make can be carried from one hundred to a thousand miles at from 50 cents to $3.00. Greater distances in proportion. Lighter stoves proportionately lower.

DON'T THINK you cannot set the stove up. You will find this easy. The stove comes all ready to set up. Simply attach the loose parts, put up the pipe and you are ready for a fire. Don't feel that it will not work perfectly for, remember, it has been perfectly adjusted before leaving the foundry. Don't think that if a part should break, or at any time in the years to come, if you should want to replace any piece or part you would have any trouble in doing so, for we guarantee to supply these parts in the years to come at actual factory cost. We furnish you a book showing exactly what the parts are so you can order intelligently. Then, too, remember you take no risk for we agree to take the stove back and pay the freight charges both ways if not found entirely satisfactory.

REMEMBER OUR PROFIT SHARING PLAN. This is all explained in pages 1 and 2 of this catalogue. If you order a stove from us you get a liberal part of your money back in the shape of the division of profit, a system made plain in pages 1 and 2 of this book.

IF YOU HAVE NEVER DEALT WITH US ask your neighbors about us. Fully one-half of all your neighbors are buying from us and if they advise you to send us your order, do so. If they have not been pleased with the goods they bought from us, if we haven't saved them money, then we cannot expect your order. We are willing to be governed by the experience of your neighbors.

Price List of the Acme Triumph Six-Hole Polished Steel Plate Range, with Porcelain Lined Reservoir, Strongly crated and delivered on the cars at our foundry in Newark, Ohio

Catalogue Number	Range No.	Size of Lids	Size of Oven, inches	Main Top including Reservoir	Height to Main Top	Pipe, collar, inches	Shipping Weight, pounds	Price
22F30	8-16	No. 8	16x21x14	46x29 in.	30½ in.	7	458	$19.00
22F31	8-18	No. 8	18x21x14	48x29 in.	30½ in.	7	470	20.09
22F32	8-20	No. 8	20x21x14	50x29 in.	30½ in.	7	482	21.14
22F33	9-18	No. 9	18x21x14	48x29 in.	30½ in.	7	470	20.34
22F34	9-20	No. 9	20x21x14	50x29 in.	30½ in.	7	482	21.39

Oven Door Thermometer, as described on page 951, $1.00 extra.

On all the above sizes the fire box is 10 inches wide and 7 inches deep, its length for coal is 19 inches and for wood 26 inches. Capacity of reservoir, 22 quarts.

Grandest Range He Ever Saw.

Sears, Roebuck & Co., Chicago, Ill. Arcadia, Wis.

Dear Sirs:—We have received the Acme Triumph Range all in good order. And must say it's the grandest range we ever saw. We saved $30.00 buying this range from you. They charge here from $55.00 to $60.00 for ranges like it. And not as nice looking as the one we have now.

Respectfully, L. J. MICHALSKI.

THE ADVANCE GASOLINE STOVES.

WE ILLUSTRATE AND DESCRIBE BELOW OUR ADVANCE GASOLINE VAPOR STOVES, WHICH WE THINK WILL MEET THE DEMAND FOR MODERATE PRICED GASOLINE STOVES.

THEY ARE GUARANTEED absolutely safe and are entirely free from the serious objections of smoke and odor. In designing these stoves, the important features, safety, simplicity and durability were carefully considered and a careful reading of the descriptive points of this line will, we believe, convince anyone that we have been successful in making a stove which embodies these features.

CONSTRUCTION. All stoves have full cabinet frame, as illustrated, and are compact, neat and perfectly rigid. They are handsome in appearance, being finely japanned and tastefully decorated.

BURNERS. The Advance stove is fitted with individual generating burners, scientifically constructed, and which will generate a powerful blue flame without smoke or odor in from one to one and one-half minutes. These burners are simple in construction, cannot get out of order if properly handled, and being made in a substantial manner, will last for years. All step stoves are fitted with a double burner on step, which insures thorough and uniform baking when an oven is used. The burners used on these stoves will produce more heat from a given amount of gasoline than any other burner on the market.

SAFETY. All stoves are furnished with safety lay down tank, which cannot be filled while in an upright position. The tank does not have to be removed to refill, as feed pipe is connected to stove with a swivel joint, allowing the tank and pipe to drop level with stove, extinguishing the flame, thus

REMOVING ONE OF THE CHIEF CAUSES OF DANGER

which in the past has attended the use of gasoline stoves. This is an important feature and we offer our stoves at the same or a lower cost than the many cheap stationary tank gasoline stoves which are sold by most dealers and which are unsafe for family use.

TAKING ALL POINTS into consideration, we believe our Advance stove will come nearer meeting the demands for a first class moderate priced stove in every particular than any yet offered to the public. It will do the work more economically and more satisfactorily. There is little or no chance for it to get out of order and if ordinary care is taken, it will last for years. If, however, by accident or otherwise, you should ever require any piece or part, we will always supply it to you at the actual factory cost. A simple card of directions is attached to every stove.

We accept every stove order to be shipped with the understanding and agreement that if it is not perfectly satisfactory after giving **30 DAYS' TRIAL,** you can return it to us at our expense and WE WILL IMMEDIATELY RETURN YOUR MONEY, together with any freight charges paid by you.

$3.13

$4.25

FOR PRICES —ON— Drop Door Steel Ovens

for use on these stoves, see page 40, Nos. 22C534 and 22C535.

$3.93

No. 22C540 Two-Burner Stove. Size of top, 14x22 inches; height, 14 inches. Shipping weight, 25 pounds. Price......$3.13

No. 22C541 Three-Burner Stove. Size of top, 14x32 inches; height, 14 inches. Shipping weight, 33 pounds. Price......$4.25

No. 22C542 Two-Burner Stove, with high frame. Size of top, 14x22 inches; height, 24 inches. Shipping weight, 34 pounds. Price......$3.93

EACH AND EVERY ONE IS GUARANTEED to be perfect in operation and workmanship, or your money will be refunded.

Below we show our

...ADVANCE STOVE...

with step attachment. This is a great convenience, as the step can be used for heating a wash boiler, or for baking with our No. 22C534 oven without interfering with the use of top burners for cooking purposes.

No. 22C543 Three-Burner Stove with high frame. Size of top, 14x32 inches; height, 24 inches. Shipping weight, 43 pounds. Price......$4.80

No. 22C544 Step Stove. Two burners on top and one double burner on step. Size of top, 14x22 inches; size of step, 14x14 inches; height, 24 inches. Shipping weight, 60 pounds. Price......$7.00

No. 22C545 Step Stove. Three burners on top and one double burner on step. Size of top, 14x32 inches; size of step, 14x14 inches; height, 24 inches. Shipping weight, 70 pounds. Price......$8.13

OUR WONDERFUL NEW WICKLESS KEROSENE OIL-GAS STOVES

A MONEY SAVER FOR ANY HOME

WE CALL SPECIAL ATTENTION to the substantial framework of the Acme Kerosene Oil-Gas Stoves. Note the heavy rolled edge of the top—this means stability. Note further the heavy tube steel supports—that means rigidity. Another important feature, the tops of all Acme Wickless Kerosene Oil-Gas Stoves and Ranges present a perfectly smooth, flat surface, with no bolts or screws protruding to catch the wiping cloth. All Acme Wickless Kerosene Oil-Gas Stoves are made full cabinet and of heavy gauge stock, and the dead black japan is relieved by the handsome, full nickeled trimmings.

ALWAYS A BLUE FLAME. Whether you open the valve too wide or remove it altogether, the flame in the Acme Wickless Kerosene Oil-Gas Stove will go to the right height and no further, but you may quickly reduce the flame whenever you desire to do so by partially closing the valve.

THE RESERVOIRS are double and the upper supply tank, which holds 2½ quarts of kerosene oil, may be removed for filling, without necessitating the extinguishing of the fire, as the lower tank holds a sufficient quantity of oil to feed the flame.

THE BURNERS as shown in accompanying illustration, are extra large and powerful and will, without exception, generate the hottest blue flame of any burner made. Their combustion is superior and the process by which the oil vapor and air are mixed in the generating chamber is so perfect that the combustion of the stove is absolutely sweet and clean. The perfect blue flame cannot smell or smoke, and perfect combustion means fuel expense reduced to the lowest possible terms.

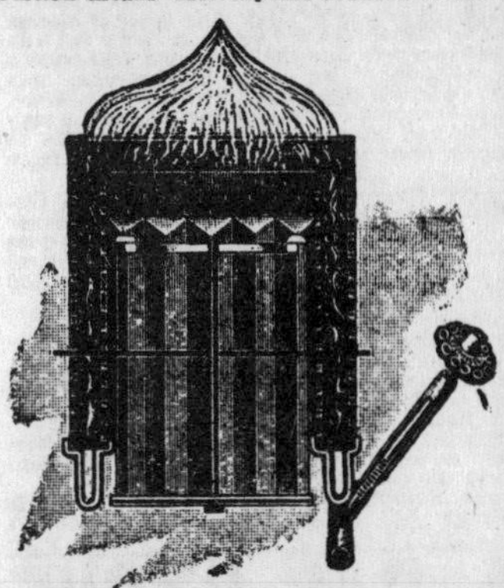

THIS IS A PICTURE OF THE BURNER SECTION of one of our Acme Wickless Kerosene Oil-Gas Stoves. The flame is shown arising from the perforated burner section which rests upon the oil cup which holds the oil and lighting ring, furnishing the oil-gas, which mixes with just enough air coming through the perforations in the chimney to form the blue flame of proper combustion.

THE LIGHTING RINGS which fit in the oil bowl are made of asbestos and are practically indestructible; they grow hard after being used a while, for all the impurities of the oil collect on them, consequently they will not light as readily after being used for quite a while as when new. It is principally a matter of your own convenience, but we would recommend that the lighting rings be renewed every six weeks or two months if the stove is used regularly, and we suggest that you order an extra dozen with your range or stove.

THIS IS OUR NEW Watershed Steel Corrugated Cooking Disc, furnished free with every Wickless Kerosene Oil-Gas Stove or Range. It fits on the open grates over the burner and prevents the contents of a vessel boiling over into the burner below.

Acme High Frame Wickless Blue Flame Kerosene Oil Stove, $8.64.

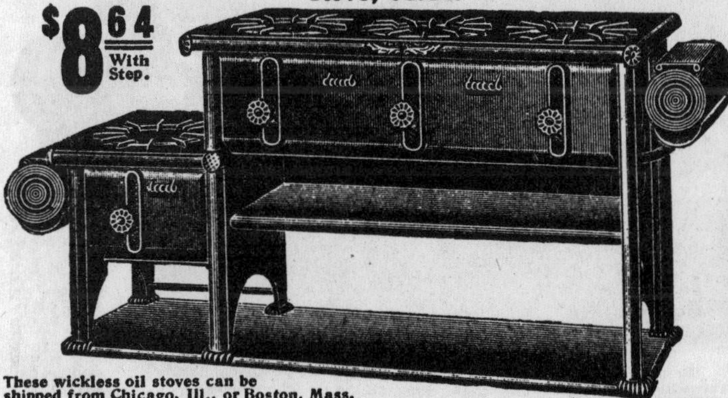

$8.64 With Step.

These wickless oil stoves can be shipped from Chicago, Ill., or Boston, Mass.

No. 22T581 Step Stove No. 533, as illustrated. Price....$8.64

For those who require a slightly different type of stove from our ordinary 2-burner and 3-burner Comet illustrated on page 958, and Acme Wickless Kerosene Oil-Gas Stove shown on this page, we commend this 1910 model. It has three burners on top and one burner on step. This style of construction is the same and its method of operation, economy in fuel consumption and perfection in operation are the same as distinguish the entire line of our Acme Wickless, Odorless Blue Flame Kerosene Oil-Gas Stoves. Its top size is 33x15½ inches. Size of step is 12x15½ inches. Height from floor to top of stove is 24 inches. The step attachment is very convenient, as it can be used for heating a wash boiler or for baking with oven without interfering with the use of the top burners for cooking. IF BAKING OVEN IS DESIRED, our portable drop door steel oven, illustrated and described on this page, placed over the burners, will be found very economical and convenient. Weight, crated, 66 pounds.

No. 22T582 Step Stove No. 532, with two burners on top and one on step. Price, $7.44

The exact same stove as catalog No. 22T581, Step Stove No. 533. Identical in every particular with the single exception that it has but two burners on top. The size of top is 22½x15½ inches. Size of step, 12x15½ inches. Height from floor to top of stove, 24 inches. Weight, crated, 56 pounds. Be sure to include a portable, drop door steel oven, illustrated on this page, when ordering a wickless oil-gas stove.

2-BURNER LOW FRAME ACME KEROSENE OIL STOVE, $4.24

We offer in this full cabinet, two-burner oil-gas stove one of the greatest stove values in our line, a stove which will give entire satisfaction to any housewife, and we put into it qualities which no stove offered by any other dealer can approach.

Characterized by the same perfect construction that enters into our entire line of Acme Wickless Kerosene Oil-Gas Stoves. It has the same full cabinet steel frame with drop front wind shield, has all of the special features, in fact, is just exactly the same stove as the catalog No. 22T585, except that it has only two burners instead of three. It is the smallest of our celebrated Acme Wickless Kerosene Oil-Gas Stoves. It will work to fine advantage with one of our Acme Drop Door Portable Steel Ovens, illustrated at right on this page, and we strongly recommend that you include one in your order. This stove has two full size burners; its top measurement is 22½x15 inches and its height 13½ inches. In general design this stove is very attractive. Shipping weight, 31 pounds.

No. 22T586

$4.24

No. 22T586 No. 512, Acme Two-Burner Wickless Kerosene Oil-Gas Stove. Price, $4.24

These wickless oil stoves can be shipped from Chicago Ill., or Boston, Mass.

SPECIAL OVENS. We offer a special oven, designed for use on these stoves, illustrated and fully described at the bottom of this page. We guarantee them to be of perfect construction and to give absolute satisfaction.

PROMPT SHIPMENT. We have a large stock on hand, crated, ready for immediate shipment, and when you send us your order, enclose our price, and the stove will be sent direct to you without any delay whatever.

A WORD ABOUT FREIGHT CHARGES. The freight charges on one of our Acme Wickless Kerosene Oil-Gas Stove will amount to next to nothing in comparison to what you save in price. Any one of them Stoves can be shipped to almost any point in Ohio, Indiana, West Virginia or Kansas for from 25 cents to $1.25; other states in proportion, according to distance.

Every stove is thoroughly inspected and tested before shipment.

Before ordering an Acme Wickless Kerosene Oil-Gas Stove, please see preceding page for Acme Kerosene Oil-Gas Ranges.

Acme High Frame Wickless Blue Flame Three-Burner Cabinet Kerosene Oil-Gas Stove, $5.96.

These wickless oil stoves can be shipped from Chicago, Ill., or Boston, Mass.

No. 22T583 Strongly constructed, perfectly operating, it has strong steel cabinet frame with closed front wind shield, handsomely finished, high grade in every respect. It is supplied with all the improved features that have made our Acme line standard. This stove is exactly the same as catalog No. 22T581 as described on this page, with the only exception that it does not have the step attachment. The top size is 33x15½ inches. Height from floor to top of stove, 24 inches. Weight, crated, 49 pounds.

No. 22T583 High Stove No. 523, as illustrated. Price....$5.96

No. 22T584 High Stove No. 522 with two burners on top. Price....$4.70

This is exactly the same stove as catalog No. 22T583 as above illustrated and described, with the single exception that it has but two burners on top instead of three. Its top size is 22½x15½ inches. Height from floor to top of stove is 24 inches. It is well made, having full cabinet steel frame, handsomely japanned and ornamented, in short, possesses all the valuable features common to our full line of Acme oil stoves and is offered at an exceedingly low price. Weight, crated, 40 pounds.

If baking oven is desired, our drop door portable steel oven, illustrated and described at the bottom of this page, placed over the burners, will be found convenient and economical.

3-BURNER LOW FRAME ACME KEROSENE OIL STOVE, $5.64

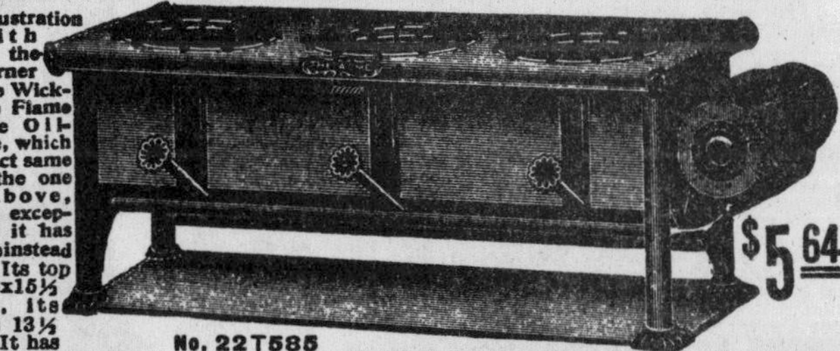

$5.64

No. 22T585

The illustration herewith shows the three-burner size Acme Wickless Blue Flame Kerosene Oil-Gas Stove, which is the exact same stove as the one shown above, with the exception that it has low frame instead of high. Its top size is 33x15½ inches, its height is 13½ inches. It has the strong, well made full cabinet steel frame with adjustable cabinet shield, double reservoirs and new process burners. If your requirements are such that the two-burner will not supply your needs, this three-burner stove will be found in every way desirable. You will note by the illustration that it is attractively designed and that every portion of the stove and its cabinet frame are easily accessible. It is no trouble at all to keep it in first class condition. There are no complicated parts to get out of order, it is simplicity itself, and it will be found a strictly first class, satisfactory stove in every respect.

WE GUARANTEE these Acme Wickless Blue Flame Kerosene Oil-Gas Stoves to give perfect satisfaction, and if you do not find that they are all that you desire in a cooking stove, if they are not in every way the best blue flame oil-gas cook stoves that you can get at the price, and much better than the stoves offered by other dealers at anywhere near the price, you may return them to us at our expense and we will immediately return your money, including the freight charges paid by you. Weight, crated, 40 pounds.

No. 22T585 No. 513, Three-Burner Acme Wickless Kerosene Oil-Gas Stove. Price, $5.64

ASBESTOS LIGHTING RINGS.

Asbestos Lighting Rings or Kindlers, as shown in the illustration, for the Acme Wickless Blue Flame Oil-Gas Stoves are made in two sizes. All high and low frame stoves and the top burners on step stoves sold previous to 1906 take the small size lighting rings. All burners on 1907 and 1908 Acme stoves take the large size lighting rings. Lighting rings for our Comet, Mascot and Security stoves are small size. We cannot furnish lighting rings for stoves not made or sold by us.

No. 22T591 Asbestos Lighting Rings, small size, 3½ in. in diameter. Price, per doz....72c

No. 22T592 Asbestos Lighting Rings, large size, 4 in. in diameter. Price, per doz....84c

ACME DROP DOOR PORTABLE STEEL OVEN, $1.83

This is a special oven which we have made particularly for our gas, gasoline and oil-gas stoves. No better oven is on the market; in fact, we consider it the best oven in every respect that is manufactured. We have spared no trouble or expense in producing these beautiful and perfect portable ovens. They are thoroughly constructed of polished steel, with drop door and they are larger than other ovens on the market, with a great deal of room inside, and wide space between the grates, so roomy that they will receive the largest loaves of bread or roasts of meat without touching the upper grate. They are full flued, bright corrugated, tin lined, perfectly ventilated, and are first class in every respect. They have heavy wire racks and Alaska "Never Hot" wire handles. Everything done in them comes out sweet, clean and wholesome. The heat is evenly distributed, baking the tops of articles as thoroughly as the bottoms without change of position. These ovens come in two sizes, as follows:

Can be shipped from Chicago, Ill., Boston, Mass., Milwaukee, Wis., or Newark, Ohio.

No. 22T593 Size, outside measurements, 13x20x18 inches. Can be used over one or two burners. Weight, crated, 17 pounds. Price....$1.83

No. 22T594 Size, outside measurements, 13x13½x18 inches. To be used over one burner. Weight, crated, 14 pounds. Price....$1.50

$3.09 OUR WONDERFUL NEW WICKLESS OIL-GAS STOVE

AN ASTONISHINGLY LOW PRICE FOR THE NEW 1910 COMET TWO-BURNER, BLUE FLAME, WICKLESS, ODORLESS OIL-GAS STOVE

THE MOST WONDERFUL STOVE OF THE CENTURY, THE MOST ECONOMICAL, THE MOST SATISFACTORY, THE SAFEST COOKING STOVE SOLD AND THE FIRST PERFECT OIL-GAS STOVE INVENTED.

Can be shipped from Chicago, Ill., or Boston, Mass.

No. 22T587
Two-Burner Comet Oil-Gas Stove. Price, $3.09

THIS NEW COMET MAKES ITS OWN GAS. This wonderful new stove manufactures its own gas from common kerosene (coal) oil and air. It has a new process burner in which the oil is mixed with enormous quantities of air, and gives you the cheapest and the best fuel in the world. Just think of it! The oil is automatically mixed with air, producing enough gas to cook for hours, an intensely hot flame, at an expense of only a fraction of a cent. This wonderful burner of the Comet Oil-Gas Stove burns 19,750 gallons of air (which costs you nothing) to one gallon of kerosene oil (common coal oil), costing about ten cents. It is practically an air burning stove, its consumption of oil being so small that the expense for fuel is next to nothing.

THE PROCESS by which the Comet Oil-Gas Stove converts kerosene oil and air into fuel gas, which produces a hot blue gas flame at the burner, at the very spot where it is required to do the cooking or baking, is very simple. Just fill the reservoir with common kerosene oil, turn the knob so that the oil may run into the burner bowl, touch a match to it, the gas begins to generate, and passing through the mixing chamber, is properly mixed with air at the ratio of one barrel of air to one spoonful of oil, giving perfect combustion and an intense heat at the burner. A slight turn of the knob one way or the other gives the amount of heat required. That is all you have to do. You light the Comet Oil-Gas Stove just as you would light a lamp; turning the knob makes the flame high or low. No trouble at all; it is self regulating; it requires no more attention from you and will remain the same, hour after hour. You will be surprised at the simplicity of the Comet Stove and how quickly and thoroughly it converts this common coal oil into a cheap fuel, giving a blue gas flame of intense heat without dust, dirt, soot or odor—a perfect heat under absolute control—a stove with all the objectionable features of all other stoves wiped out.

EVERY WOMAN NEEDS A COMET OIL-GAS STOVE. She needs it oftener than any other article she uses in housekeeping. Just think of the millions of carpet sweepers sold that are used but once a day, millions of washing machines and wringers used once a week, millions of ice cream freezers used only occasionally in the summer time, tens of millions of sewing machines which stand idle for weeks at a time. Yet here is an article more necessary, more valuable to the household economy of every home, which you may have for only $3.09, that saves a woman's health, her looks, labor, time and temper, that cuts the fuel bills to next to nothing, that is ready at a moment's notice, summer or winter, to do all that a stove can do and more than any other stove has ever done.

NO STOVE IN THE WORLD EQUALS THE COMET Blue Flame, Wickless, Odorless, Oil-Gas Stove for use in the warm summer months. All the heat it generates is right at the burner where it is required for cooking and baking, and it does not heat up the kitchen as do other stoves. You can cook in comfort on a Comet Oil-Gas Stove in the hottest weather. Remember, also, it requires no kindling of fire; simply turn the knob and light the match and the cooking operation begins. When the meal is prepared turn it off and the heat stops.

DESCRIPTION. Our Wonderful New Comet, Two-Burner, Blue Flame, Wickless, Oil-Gas Stove is just like the illustration. It is 14 inches high, of medium weight, and may be set upon a table, shelf or cabinet in almost any out of the way niche in the kitchen. Its top size is 14x22 inches, and it has two grates, each 8 inches in diameter. The 4-inch burners are protected by black japanned outer drums, affording absolute protection against gusts of wind from open doors or windows. They facilitate the generation of gas, and their use on the Comet Oil-Gas Stove reduces the consumption of oil, and fuel bills. The Comet has full cabinet frame (closed back and sides), is very strongly put together and finished in baked black japan, nicely ornamented with handsomely nickel plated name plate and nickel plated valve handles. The operating valves are very conveniently located, and every part of the stove is accessible without removing any other part, so that it may be easily kept clean. There are double reservoirs finished in brass and connected with the burners with aluminated pipe line, and full aluminized oil bowls. The workmanship is first class in every respect, all the connections so carefully made that you will never have trouble from leaks of any nature. The upper reservoir, which holds two and a half quarts of kerosene oil, may be removed for filling without affecting the temporary operation of the stove, as the lower reservoir carries sufficient oil to feed the flame. Asbestos kindler is new metal woven, 1910 patent, made only by us, and is practically indestructible. With each stove we furnish a corrugated steel disc, as shown in accompanying illustration. It prevents the contents of a vessel boiling over into the chimney bowl.

No. 22T587 Two-Burner Comet Oil-Gas Stove. Shipping wt., 30 lbs. Price.....$3.09
No. 22T591 Extra Asbestos Lighting Rings. 3½ inches in diameter, for Comet Oil-Gas Stoves. Price, per dozen.....72c

$4.13 OUR NEW COMET THREE-BURNER OIL-GAS STOVE

A REMARKABLY LOW PRICE AT WHICH WE SELL THIS NEW 1910 COMET THREE-BURNER BLUE FLAME WICKLESS, ODORLESS OIL-GAS STOVE.

THE SAME IDENTICAL STOVE DESCRIBED ABOVE IN EVERY PARTICULAR WITH THE SINGLE EXCEPTION THAT IT HAS THREE BURNERS INSTEAD OF TWO. It is 14 inches high and its top size is 32x14 inches. The illustration is an exact reproduction of the Comet Three-Burner Stove, which we are offering at a price lower than many dealers and manufacturers are asking for their unsatisfactory, imperfect two-burner oil stoves. Corrugated steel disc, as shown above, goes with the three-burner without additional charge.

WE DO NOT SELL skeleton frame stoves. All the gas, gasoline and oil stoves sold by us have enclosed backs and sides, because this full cabinet frame gives strength and durability, and adds to the appearance of the stove a hundred per cent. If you will examine the low priced stoves offered by others you will discover that they have the skeleton frame construction, a cheap, undesirable and out of date style. The wonderfully low price we quote on the Comet Oil-Gas Stove is so low, lower in fact than other dealers quote on so called blue flame oil stoves of this inferior skeleton construction, that there is now really no reason whatever why you should buy a stove without the full cabinet frame.

No 22T588
Three-Burner Comet Oil-Gas Stove. Price, $4.13
Can be shipped from Chicago, Ill., or Boston, Mass.

BE SURE TO INCLUDE A DROPDOOR PORTABLE STEEL OVEN SHOWN ON PRECEDING PAGE, WITH YOUR ORDER FOR AN OIL STOVE

THERE ARE THOUSANDS of oil stoves, many of them burning a wick on the principle of a lamp. These stoves burn only the oil and the wick and give off a bad odor which is not only annoying but injurious to the health. These stoves are expensive in operation and invariably unsatisfactory. There are others which are alleged to be blue flame oil stoves. They are better than the wick stoves and will cook and bake, but are not what you want. They have faults, many of them serious faults, and the users of these stoves are continually in trouble. The Comet Oil-Gas Stoves are just as far in advance of so called blue flame oil stoves sold by other dealers as the ordinary blue flame stove is in advance of the wick burning stove. The Comet stoves do better work. They reduce the cost of fuel, because the wonderful new burners on these stoves in the process of manufacturing gas from common coal oil burn much more air than oil. **In fact, when you use a Comet Oil-Gas Stove you take most of the fuel from the atmosphere.** This is a demonstrated, proven fact, and if you will send us $3.09 for one of the two-burner Comets, or $4.13 for one of the three-burner Comets, we know that your verdict after thirty days' trial will be an unqualified indorsement of all that we have said of the marvelous qualities of these stoves.

No. 22T588 Three-Burner Comet Oil-Gas Stove. Shipping weight, 40 pounds. Price.....$4.13

OUR NEW HANDSOME LINE OF "CLOVER" SMOKELESS, ODORLESS, SAFE OIL HEATERS.

The drums are made of American planished steel and can at all times be easily kept clean. They have our SAFETY REMOVABLE FOUNTS AND BURNERS, used on the Clover Heater, which are so scientifically constructed that two air spaces separate the burning wick from the oil fount. Also a large air chamber passes through the burner, thereby guaranteeing not only perfect combustion but absolute safety. The oil is always kept cold and explosions are impossible. Don't be backward about ordering one on account of the disagreeable features of other oil heaters, which smell and smoke, as you will be pleasantly surprised with one of these stoves. If not found all we claim, the purchase price will be returned upon request. The top is handsomely nickeled and is removable, leaving openings in the disc for the purpose of quickly heating anything placed thereon. All sizes have center mica section which reflects a brilliant light when stove is in use. They cost less money and produce more heat than any other oil heaters in the market.

No. 22T595 Height, bail down, 23 inches; diameter of steel drum, 7 inches; tank holds 2 quarts; takes 8-inch circular wick. Weight, crated, 11 pounds. This size will heat a small bedroom or bathroom nicely. Price.....$3.15
No. 22T596 Extra wicks for above, each.....09
No. 22T597 Height, bail down, 25 inches; diameter of steel drum, 7¾ inches; tank holds 3 quarts; takes 10-inch circular wick. Weight, crated, 13 pounds. This size will heat a good sized room very comfortably. Price.....$3.85
No. 22T598 Extra wicks for above, each.....10
No. 22T599 Height, bail down, 28 inches; diameter of steel drum, 9½ inches; tank holds 4 quarts; takes 15-inch circular wick. Weight, crated, 20 pounds. This size will heat a large room or suite of small rooms. Price.....$5.35
No. 22T600 Extra wicks for above.....12

ACME SMOKELESS-WICKLESS OIL RADIATORS.

Has one of our powerful burners producing a most intensely hot blue flame. Radiator top contains a double row of radiator tubes—five in each row—made of planished iron, having a radiating surface equal to a cylinder over 3 feet in circumference. **Removable Radiator top**, especially designed to leave a lamp stove for cooking purposes. Removable reservoir holds 2½ quarts, burning about seven hours. Dimensions: Total height, 25 inches; size of top, 7x12 inches, height of cooking section, 10 inches; height of radiator, 15 inches. Shipping weight, 37 pounds.

No. 22T603 Acme Wickless Radiator, No. 10. Price.....$4.69

Acme Wickless Radiator, $6.96.

Contains two powerful wickless, blue flame burners. The radiator top contains the equivalent of 21 radiating tubes. This gives a radiating surface equal to a drum cylinder 84 inches in circumference. **The radiator top is removable**, leaving a most complete and effective cooking stove. Removable reservoir holds over one gallon, permitting both burners to be operated at fair flame nearly ten hours. Dimensions: Total height, 30 inches; size of radiator, 8x16 inches; size of cooking top, 12x16 inches. Height of cooking stove section, 10 inches; height of radiator section, 20 inches. Shipping weight, 54 pounds.

No. 22T605 Acme Wickless Radiator No. 20. Price.....$6.96
Guaranteed to please or your money returned.
No. 22T592 Extra Asbestos Lighting Rings or Kindlers, 4 inches in diameter, for the above radiators. Price, per dozen.....84c

ALL OUR STOVE ILLUSTRATIONS ARE MADE FROM ACTUAL PHOTOGRAPHS, AND WHEN YOU SEE THE STOVES YOU WILL FIND THEM EXACTLY AS REPRESENTED

WE GUARANTEE ANY STOVE YOU ORDER FROM US TO REACH YOU IN PERFECT CONDITION, BLACKENED AND POLISHED, READY TO SET UP AND USE

OUR POPULAR ACME HUMMER SIX-HOLE STEEL RANGE $17.52 AND UP

CAN BE FURNISHED FOR HARD (ANTHRACITE) COAL, SOFT COAL, COKE, WOOD OR CORN COBS

OUR LARGE STOCK INSURES PROMPT SHIPMENT

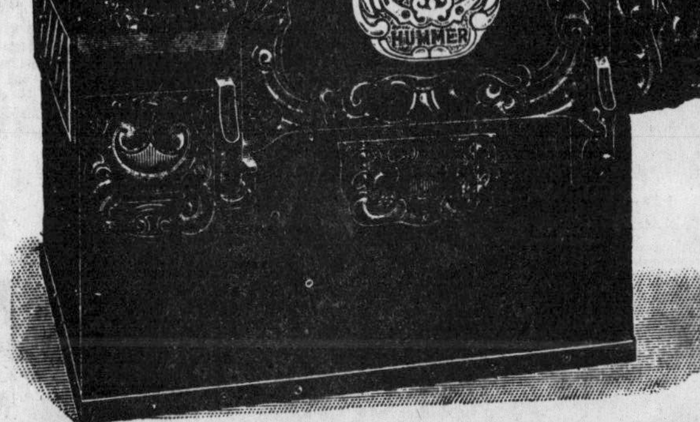

Cast Iron Left End Guaranteed not to Warp, Buckle or Burn Out.

This, our popular Acme Hummer Six-Hole Steel Range is designed and made by us to supply those who want a strong, heavy, well built range that will last and give satisfactory service and can be bought at an extremely low price. Nowhere else in the pages of this catalog is our ability to produce a high grade steel range at such an extremely low price so thoroughly demonstrated as it is on this page. The range is built on excellent lines throughout, and wherever the fire comes in contact with the construction, cast plates are worked in for protection. The different fire boxes for hard or soft coal or wood offer many conveniences and advantages and the body is manufactured from selected cold rolled steel of a heavier and stronger gauge than is used by manufacturers of similar ranges offered at double our prices.

DETAILED DESCRIPTION.

THE BODY is manufactured from selected cold rolled sheet steel of a heavier and stronger gauge than is used in ranges that retail at much higher prices. It is thoroughly put together, riveted with wrought iron rivets, strongly reinforced and braced in every part. **HIGH CLOSET is of generous proportions.** It is just at the right height and has a balanced door. **MAIN TOP, covers and centers are made of the highest grade gray iron,** which stands the heat better and is less liable to crack or warp than any other material. This range is furnished with five solid lids and one in three sections, made from the best stove plate. It has long cut centers, and all loose parts of top are carefully fitted with sufficient allowance for heat expansion. **THE FIRE BOX is equipped with heavy cast iron linings and Duplex grate for soft coal and wood,** and firebrick linings and Dockash grate for **hard coal and wood.** The Duplex grate is easily and quickly converted into a coal burning grate or a wood burning grate at the will of the operator. **WHEN ORDERED FOR HARD COAL, an extra wood bottom grate will be furnished free.**

THIS STOVE IS No. 82-19. **The oven is 18x20¾x12 inches, has six No. 8 cooking holes. THE OVEN DOOR drops flush with the oven bottom.** forming a convenient shelf. Top cooking surface with reservoir extension is 42½x29 inches; without reservoir, including end shelf, 39½x28½ inches. Height from floor to main top, 29½ inches. Distance from main top to top of warming closet, 26½ inches. Total height, including closet, **56 inches. THE FIRE BOX is 8 inches wide, 5½ inches deep.** Its length for coal is 17 inches and for wood 24 inches. Size pipe to fit collar, 7 inches. **Furnished with large steel ash pan.** Capacity of reservoir, 13½ quarts.

ACME HUMMER STEEL RANGE.
Without reservoir, but with warming closet.
Catalog No. 22R197
$15.37 for soft coal and wood.
$16.38 for hard coal and wood.

REPAIR PARTS **We always carry a complete stock of repairs and repair parts, and in** years to come, even ten years hence we will be able to deliver you any piece or part to replace or repair any which, perchance, has become defective from long usage or breakage, and this at actual cost, a mere fraction of what other dealers charge.

ACME HUMMER, MADE IN ONE SIZE ONLY, for hard coal and wood, soft coal and wood, and cobs. Prices, strongly crated and delivered on the cars at our foundry at Newark, Ohio, ONLY. (Prices do not include pipe or cooking utensils. For cooking utensils see page 997.)

	Price for Soft Coal and Wood	Price for Hard Coal and Wood (Anthracite)
No. 22R198 Price for range complete, as illustrated, with warming closet and reservoir. Shipping wt., 410 lbs..	$17.52	$18.53
No. 22R197 Price for square top range, without reservoir, but with warming closet, as shown in the small illustration. Shipping wt., 355 lbs.	15.37	16.38
No. 22R196 Price for reservoir range, without warming closet, but with reservoir. Shipping wt., 355 lbs.	15.12	16.13
No. 22R195 Price for square top range, without warming closet or reservoir. Shipping wt., 300 lbs.	12.62	13.63
WATER FRONT FOR ACME HUMMER		2.50

See page 943 about hot water fronts.

TO MAKE SURE THAT WE FURNISH YOU THE RIGHT KIND OF FIRE BOX FOR THE FUEL TO BE USED, DO NOT FAIL TO STATE IN YOUR LETTER OR ORDER THE FUEL YOU BURN. SAY WHETHER HARD COAL AND WOOD, SOFT COAL AND WOOD, OR WOOD ONLY.

$15.58 FOR OUR NEW 1910 ACME PROGRESS FOUR-HOLE STEEL COOK STOVE

BURNS ANY KIND OF FUEL, HARD OR SOFT COAL, WOOD, COKE OR CORN COBS.

WE OFFER this wonderful new 1910 pattern Acme Progress Steel Cook Stove as the very latest and very highest grade steel cook stove offered on the market, the equal of any steel cook stove you can buy at double our price. It is sold to you under our positive binding guarantee of satisfaction or your money back.

DESCRIPTION.

THE BODY of the Acme Progress Steel Cook Stove is made of heavier steel than is used by other makers. The heavy steel plates are accurately cut and punched for riveting and are hand riveted and thoroughly braced. The bottom edge is reinforced with heavy steel, which is run around the entire body of the stove and strongly riveted to the steel plates of the body. **THE MAIN TOP, covers and centers are made of the very finest cast stove plate from the purest pig iron,** and should not be confused with malleable top ranges which other manufacturers sometimes call "steel" with the deliberate purpose of deceiving you. No malleable iron top can compare in lasting quality with the cast stove plate tops used in the manufacture of our stoves and ranges. **THE FIRE BOX is of proper depth and width to provide enough heat for the oven without waste of fuel.** With the two end pieces removed and the cast iron extension attached, the fire box is easily prepared for burning wood, making the length of the fire box for wood 23½ inches. We equip the Acme Progress with Duplex grate, which can be used for hard or soft coal, wood or any other fuel. **THE OVEN is very quick and perfect,** and bakes most satisfactorily. It is of very generous proportions, being 17½x20x12 inches in size, Has one steel spring counterbalanced drop oven door on the right side, with rococo cast frame and handsomely nickeled medallion center plate and handle. The door opens downward, the same as on our steel ranges, forming a large, commodious shelf. (The left side of stove is blank.) **THE OVEN BOTTOM of our Progress Steel Cook Stove is made of the highest grade selected stock sheet steel,** so constructed, bolted, braced and reinforced that it will always remain level and there is absolutely no possibility of its buckling, warping or sagging. **The oven top** is protected with heavy asbestos mill-board, bolted securely by means of a center post, which also serves to distribute the heat to all parts of the oven. **ITS COOKING SURFACE has four holes and the size of the top,** including extension reservoir, is 42½x26 inches. The height from floor to main top is 30½ inches. Length of fire box for wood is 23½ inches; size of pipe to fit collar, 7 inches.

POUCH FEED. The Acme Progress Steel Cook Stove has a large pouch feed for feeding coal or coke and will also permit of the insertion of a broiler over the fire. **WOOD FEED DOOR swings to the left and is constructed to prevent ashes from piling against the inside and falling to the floor** when the door is opened. **THE ASH DOOR is extra large. THE ASH PAN is made of fine steel,** fits the large, roomy hearth under the ash door, which prevents the ashes from spilling on the floor when being removed.

WITHOUT RESERVOIR.

IF WANTED WITHOUT RESERVOIR BUT WITH END SHELF, JUST LIKE SMALL ILLUSTRATION, DEDUCT $2.00 FROM PRICE OF EITHER SIZE.

THE LARGE RESERVOIR TANK is made of the best grade of cast iron, white porcelain lined to prevent rusting. Easily kept clean and removable. Capacity of reservoir, 13½ quarts.

SOLD UNDER OUR BINDING GUARANTEE

Prices, strongly crated and delivered on cars at our foundry at Newark, Ohio, ONLY.

No. **22R205** Price, No. 8-20, with reservoir and 8-inch lids, 20-inch oven..$15.58
No. **22R206** Price, No. 9-20, with reservoir and 9-inch lids, 20-inch oven.. 15.88
On these stoves the fire box is 8½ inches. Capacity of reservoir, 13½ quarts. Ship- coal is 18 inches and for wood 23½ inches. Capacity of reservoir, 13½ quarts. Shipping wt., 345 lbs. Prices do not include pipe or cooking utensils. For cooking utensils see page 997.

ACME BOOMER SIX-HOLE STEEL RANGE WITH RESERVOIR AND WARMING CLOSET $11.98

BURNS ANY KIND OF FUEL. HARD COAL, SOFT COAL, WOOD, COKE OR CORN COBS.

AS A WONDERFUL ILLUSTRATION of what we can do in our Newark Stove Foundry, the largest stove foundry in the world, and as proof positive of our ability to build better stoves and ranges and sell them at lower prices than the prices asked by any other manufacturer or dealer in the world, we made this, our Acme Boomer Range, which we offer at $11.98, complete with reservoir and high warming closet. Ranges have been widely advertised by other foundries and dealers at prices ranging from $18.00 to $22.50, and in those advertisements representations have been made that the ranges are strictly high grade in every respect. To show our customers how cheaply constructed those advertised ranges are, and how much greater value we offer in the stoves and ranges made by us in our Newark foundry, we purchased samples of the ranges widely advertised at $18.00 to $22.50, and after getting these samples, we had our expert range builders make an exact duplicate of these ranges, that is to say, taking the best features of every one of them and putting them into this range to show at what price we would be able to build and sell a range in every respect the equal of the cheaply built ranges offered by others at from $18.00 to $22.50.

UNDERSTAND, WE DO NOT OFFER this Acme Boomer as a high grade range, because it is not the equal of any other steel range shown in our catalog; but we do guarantee it to be just as good as stoves and ranges offered by others at from $18.00 to $22.50. It is a very satisfactory baker, economical in the consumption of fuel, quick to heat and quick to act. In making it we have constructed the main top and covers of good stove plate. It has six cooking holes, and with ordinary care and usage the main top and covers will last for years. It has a convenient warming closet.

THIS, OUR ACME BOOMER, IS MADE IN ONE SIZE ONLY. This stove 8-16; the oven 16x18x11 inches, has six No. 8 cooking holes. Size of cooking top, 30½x21½ inches. Height from floor to main top 26 inches. Distance from main top to top of high closet, 23 inches. Total height, including closet, 49 inches. On the Acme Boomer the fire box is 7 inches wide and 5 inches deep. Its length is 17½ inches. Capacity of reservoir, 21 quarts. Size of pipe to fit collar, 6 inches.

DETAILED DESCRIPTION.

THE BODY is manufactured from cold rolled sheet steel of a heavier and stronger gauge than is used by other foundries and dealers at prices ranging from $18.00 to $22.50.

THE MAIN TOP. In manufacturing this, our Acme Boomer Range, we have constructed the main tops and covers of good stove plate. It has six cooking holes and, with ordinary care and usage, the main top and covers will last for years. All parts of the main top are carefully fitted, with sufficient allowance for heat expansion.

HIGH WARMING CLOSET is of generous proportions, is just at the right height, and will be found very convenient. The height of warming closet is 23 inches.

FIRE BOX. The fire box in our Acme Boomer Steel Range is an improved fire box, equipped with our flat dump style grate, which grate is lighter than our perfect duplex grate as used in the highest grade ranges made by us. With every range we ship we include, free of cost, an extra grate for wood, so that you can burn either hard coal, soft coal or wood.

THE ASH PAN is made of cold rolled steel with handsome draw out handle.

THE OVEN is of very generous proportions, perfectly square, a very satisfactory, quick even baker, and is furnished with a steel wire oven rack and convenient clean out directly under the oven door.

THE OVEN DOOR is our latest swing pattern, attractive rococo design, steel lined, perfectly square and fits snug to the body of the range, thus retaining all the heat in the oven.

THE RESERVOIR is made of galvanized iron and heats by direct contact with the end of the range. It can be adjusted to either end and, if so desired, can also be used on top of the range. Being made of galvanized iron, it will not rust or corrode and is by far a better reservoir than that on ranges offered for $18.00 to $22.50 by other dealers. This is the only steel range we build without cast iron reservoir casing. It is simply made of galvanized iron and will not last as long as the cast reservoir casing which is used by us on all our other ranges. In shipping this range we pack the reservoir inside the oven. It is easily attached to the right or left end of the range.

THE FLUE BACK which conducts the heat from the flue beneath the oven to the stove pipe is made of the highest grade cast iron stove plate. This is a very important feature. Nearly all steel ranges sold for more than double the price we ask for this, our Acme Boomer Range, are made with a thin sheet steel flue back, which easily rots out.

Prices, strongly crated and delivered on the cars at our Newark, Ohio, foundry.

No. 22R200 Square top range, without high closet or reservoir, but with end shelf. Shipping wt., 185 pounds. Price....$ 9.60
No. 22R201 Reservoir range, without high closet, but with reservoir. Shipping wt., 190 pounds. Price....10.35
No. 22R202 Square top range, without reservoir, but with high closet and end shelf. Shipping wt., 215 pounds. Price....11.62
No. 22R203 Steel range complete, just as illustrated, with high closet and reservoir. Shipping wt., 220 pounds. Price....11.98

THESE PRICES DO NOT INCLUDE PIPE OR COOKING UTENSILS. WE DO NOT FURNISH WATER FRONT FOR THE ACME BOOMER RANGE.

ACME ROVER GENUINE STEEL FOUR-HOLE COAL AND WOOD STOVE $6.74 AND UPWARD

GREATEST STOVE VALUE EVER OFFERED

WITH RESERVOIR MODEL OF 1910 ONLY

Three sizes, direct from our foundry, offered at $6.74, $7.74 and $8.74 without reservoir, as shown in small illustration, and $7.75, $8.75 and $9.75 with reservoir, according to size, as listed below.

COMPARE THE PRICES with any prices you have ever seen or heard of, in either a steel or cast iron cook stove, and you will find the price we are offering on this steel cook stove less than one-half what others charge, and it is positively THE GREATEST STOVE VALUE THE WORLD HAS EVER SEEN.

COMPARED WITH THE LOWEST PRICES we could possibly make you on any of our cast iron cook stoves we save you easily from $4.00 to $7.00, and compared with any other steel cook stove we could sell you we show you a saving of from $6.00 to $8.00; and compared with any price any other maker or dealer could offer you we show you a saving in cost on this, OUR ACME ROVER STEEL COOK STOVE, of easily $7.00 to $15.00.

THE BODY is made of high grade sheet steel, thoroughly bolted, braced, reinforced throughout; the best oven construction; our new special flue draft damper and circulating system, made to burn hard coal, soft coal or wood. With each stove we furnish a special grate for wood. Has a cast top, the exact same grade of top that we use in our highest grade stoves and ranges; four lids, cut centers, supported by our own special system of construction. In shipping the stove with reservoir we pack the reservoir inside of the oven, and the stove is crated in such a way that there is no chance of its reaching you in bad condition; in fact, the stove is unbreakable.

$6.74 to $8.74 ACME ROVER. WITHOUT RESERVOIR.

WE HAVE A LARGE STOCK OF these stoves on hand, ready for immediate shipment direct from our foundry at Newark, Ohio. It will just take a few days for your order to reach us and the stove to reach you. The stove being made of sheet steel is comparatively light and the freight charges will amount to next to nothing. This stove can be shipped from 100 to 500 miles at from 35 cents to 75 cents; from 500 to 1,000 miles at from 50 cents to $1.50; greater or lesser distances in proportion.

REPAIR PARTS. We will always carry a complete stock of repairs and repair parts for years to come; even ten years hence we will be able to deliver you any piece or part to replace or repair any worn part, and this at actual cost, a mere fraction of what other stove dealers charge.

BE SURE TO SELECT A STOVE LARGE ENOUGH to meet your requirements. Catalog No. 22R210, stove No. 7-12 is the smallest Acme Rover Steel Cook Stove we make. It has four 7-inch lids and a small 12-inch oven. Refer to the sizes below, noting the stove number, size of lids, size of oven, and select a stove large enough to fit your cooking utensils.

DETAILED DESCRIPTION.

THE BODY is built of heavy smooth steel plate, is substantially put together, riveted with wrought iron rivets, strongly reinforced and braced in every part. The heavy plates are well riveted and jointed. The size of pipe to fit collar is 6 inches on all sizes.

THE MAIN TOP. In manufacturing this, our Acme Rover, we have constructed the main top and covers of good stove plate. It has four cooking holes and with ordinary care and usage the main top and covers will last years. All parts of the main top are carefully fitted, with sufficient allowance for heat expansion.

THE LARGE FIRE BOX. It has an extra large fire box, provided with practical cast iron linings, with shaking and dumping grate. With every stove we include, free of cost, an extra grate for wood, so you can burn hard coal, soft coal or wood.

THE FIRE DOOR is beautifully designed and swings to the left.

THE ASH PIT is large and roomy and is provided with a large ash pan.

THE DRAFT SLIDE is in front, of more than usual capacity.

THE OVEN is of very generous proportions, perfectly square, is a very satisfactory, quick and even baker, and is furnished with a steel wire oven rack.

THE OVEN DOOR is on the right side (the left side left blank). It is our latest swing pattern, attractive rococo design, steel lined, perfectly square, and fits snug to the body of the stove, thus retaining all the heat in the oven.

THE FLUES are ample and provided with clean out in rear of ash pit, which is reached from the front of the stove.

THE RESERVOIR is made of galvanized iron, heats by direct contact with either end or left side of the stove, lifts out easily and can be used on either end or rear side at pleasure (as shown by the dotted line in illustration) or can be used on top of stove as occasion requires.

GOOD SERVICE. The long looked for steel cook stove for practical people, neat, compact, serviceable and cheap. No such value in a cook stove ever offered before. This, our Acme Rover Steel Cook Stove, is shipped ready to set up, the four legs and all other loose parts packed inside. When received you have only to put on the legs, pipe and other loose parts, when it is ready for fire, the same as if you were moving an old stove from one room to another.

PRICES, DELIVERED ON BOARD THE CARS AT OUR FOUNDRY IN NEWARK, OHIO, FOR OUR ACME ROVER STEEL COOK STOVE, FOR COAL AND WOOD, FOUR COOKING HOLES, DUMPING GRATE, LARGE ASH PAN, STEEL OVEN RACK. WHEN ORDERED WITHOUT RESERVOIR AN END SHELF IS FURNISHED.

Catalog Number	Stove Number	Size of Lids	Size of Oven, inches	Main Top, including Reservoir	Main Top, without Reservoir and without End Shelf	Size of End Shelf	Height of Main Top, inches	Size of Fire Box, inches			Capacity of Reservoir	Weight, with Reservoir	Weight, without Reservoir	Price, without Reservoir	Price, with Reservoir
								Length	Width	Depth					
22R210	7-12	No. 7	12x16x10	35 x19 inches	26 x19 inches	5 x14½	25	16½	6½	4	14 quarts	135 lbs.	120 lbs.	$6.74	$7.75
22R211	8-14	No. 8	14x18x10½	37½x21 inches	28 x21 inches	5½x16	25½	17	6½	4½	18 quarts	155 lbs.	140 lbs.	7.74	8.75
22R212	8-16	No. 8	16x18x11	40½x21½ inches	30½x21½ inches	6 x17½	26½	17½	7	5	21 quarts	170 lbs.	160 lbs.	8.74	9.75

YOUR MONEY WILL BE IMMEDIATELY RETURNED TO YOU FOR ANY GOODS NOT PERFECTLY SATISFACTORY.

ACME TRIUMPH SIX-HOLE STEEL RANGE, $25.77

THE WONDER OF THE STOVE WORLD

BURNS ANY KIND OF FUEL, HARD OR SOFT COAL, WOOD, COKE OR CORN COBS.

WARMING CLOSET

ACME TRIUMPH

NEWARK STOVE WORKS CHICAGO

Cast Iron Left End, Guaranteed Not to Warp, Buckle or Burn Out.

Guaranteed Rustproof Cast Iron Reservoir Casing.

THIS IS OUR 1907 ACME TRIUMPH SIX-HOLE STEEL RANGE, the largest, the handsomest, and in every way the highest grade steel range we build. It is the wonderful steel range which we have sold to thousands upon thousands of our customers. It is the steel range which has brought consternation to the ranks of the stove builders of the world; the steel range which others are striving now to imitate, but without success; the steel range which has proven the greatest efficiency in baking; the steel range which is unapproached in economy of fuel consumption; the steel range which, for grace of outline, elegance of design, generous proportions, taste in ornamentation, quality of materials and workmanship, is the very best steel range that money can buy. In short, the Acme Triumph Steel Range has every attachment, every improvement which adds to ease of operation and high efficiency.

THIS WONDERFUL STEEL RANGE is the highest product of the stove maker's art, and its every part is made in our great stove works at Newark, Ohio, where the most skillful workmen, the master minds of stove building, devote their best talents and energies to its perfection. In this steel range will be found the heaviest and the highest grade steel plate used by any steel range manufacturer. Every piece of material which enters into the construction of this steel range, every process through which the various parts pass in our great foundry is so closely inspected, so carefully designed, that the Acme Triumph Steel Range goes to you as a perfect steel range, a range so far in advance of the average range offered at from two to three times the price we ask, that there is no possible comparison between them. When you buy this Acme Triumph Steel Range at the wonderfully low price we name, you not only get all that any other stove manufacturer CAN POSSIBLY GIVE YOU AT ANY PRICE, BUT MORE IMPROVEMENTS AND BETTER MATERIALS, MORE PERFECT CONSTRUCTION THAN YOU CAN POSSIBLY GET WHEN YOU BUY ANY OTHER STEEL RANGE MANUFACTURED.

FREIGHT CHARGES on this stove will amount to next to nothing. It can be shipped to almost any point in Ohio, Indiana, Illinois, Michigan, Kentucky, Tennessee, West Virginia, Pennsylvania or New York for from 50 cents to $1.50.

THIS ILLUSTRATION is a faithful reproduction of the Acme Triumph Steel Range, but like all pictures it does not do justice to its subject. Note the clean cut lines of this beautiful range, its generous cooking surface and large reservoir, the ample warming closet, the convenient arrangement of drafts, coal, fire, grate and ash doors, the high, wide oven, the top of which is protected with corrugated cast flame plate which insures equal distribution of heat to all parts of the oven, preventing the oven top from burning out, warping or breaking, the artistic base, the Pequabuck oven thermometer and the numerous other features which make this the most attractive steel range on the market. This is without doubt the most popular steel range ever offered, and it comes to you just as shown in this picture with its full equipment; a range that we know will please you, a range that will give you the best service that you can possibly ask or expect, a range that will satisfy the most particular housewife. It is shipped direct to you from our foundry, giving you the benefit of all reductions in price.

MADE IN FIVE SIZES AS LISTED BELOW.

Price List of the Acme Triumph 6-Hole Polished Steel Plate Range with High Closet and Porcelain Lined Reservoir. Strongly crated and delivered on the cars at our Newark, Ohio, foundry. Prices do not include pipe or cooking utensils. For cooking utensils see pages 919 to 927.

Catalogue Number	Range Number	Size of Lids	Size of Oven, inches	Main Top, including Reservoir	Height to Main Top, inches	Size of Pipe to Fit Collar, inches	Shipping Weight, lbs.	PRICE
22G20	8-16	No. 8	16x21x14	46x29	30½	7	532	$25.77
22G21	8-18	No. 8	18x21x14	48x29	30½	7	544	26.82
22G22	8-20	No. 8	20x21x14	50x29	30½	7	556	28.23
22G23	9-18	No. 9	18x21x14	48x29	30½	7	544	27.09
22G24	9-20	No. 9	20x21x14	50x29	30½	7	556	29.50

IF YOU WANT THE BEST STEEL RANGE it is possible to build, regardless of price, if you want a range that is adapted to the use of hard or soft coal or wood, a range that will save you its first cost many times over in its economic consumption of fuel, a range that is a perfect baker, a range that has all the good points of every high grade steel range made, with the defects of none, we would especially urge that you select this Acme Triumph Steel Range with its equipment as illustrated herewith. Remember, we sell the Acme Triumph absolutely on its merits, and we shall be glad to accept your order for this range to be sent to you with the understanding and agreement that you can give it thirty days' free trial in your own home, that you may submit it to every trial and test possible for thirty days, permitting you to judge whether all the claims we make for this range are true or false, and if at the end of that time you are not thoroughly convinced that you have gotten a better stove than you could buy elsewhere at anywhere near the price, you may return it to us at our expense, and we will immediately return your money, together with all the freight charges paid by you. On all the above sizes the fire box is 10 inches wide and 9 inches deep, its length for coal is 19 inches and for wood 26 inches. Capacity of reservoir, 22 quarts.

INSTRUCTIONS ON HOW TO ORDER STOVES OR RANGES.

ALL COOK STOVES AND RANGES are variously numbered as follows: 7-17; 8-18 and 9-21, etc. The first number given denoting the size of griddle covers or lids and the last two figures the width of the oven in inches. Do not order a No. 9 stove if your cooking utensils are No. 8, as they will not fit.

BE SURE YOU SELECT A STOVE LARGE ENOUGH for your requirements. Measure the oven and the top of your old stove or one of your neighbor's stoves, if it is about the size you want, and then compare it with the measurements given in our catalogue.

IF YOU USE WOOD ONLY AS FUEL, always select a stove from among those offered for wood, thus obtaining a larger fire box than is furnished with a combination wood and coal burner. If steel range is wanted be sure to state whether for coal or wood. If you use coal as fuel do not make the mistake of selecting a stove which is offered to burn wood only, or of ordering a heating stove for soft coal when we offer it as a hard coal burner only.

WE CAN ONLY FURNISH OUR STOVES as illustrated and described in catalogue. Do not ask us to send you a range with fire box on the opposite end from that shown in illustration or to leave off or put on more nickel, as we cannot do it. We do not furnish stove pipe or cooking utensils with our stoves at prices quoted. Neither does your dealer unless he charges you enough for the stove to allow him to include them free.

IF AFTER READING DESCRIPTIONS CAREFULLY you still desire information regarding any of our stoves it will be promptly and cheerfully furnished upon receipt of your inquiry.

DON'T ORDER THE CHEAPEST STOVE we list and expect it to be the equal of the highest priced stove your dealer has. We can save you from 25 to 50 per cent of the purchase price, size for size and style for style, over the price your dealer asks for the stove he offers you.

AFTER WRITING YOUR ORDER, check it over closely to see that you have written down correctly, catalogue number, fuel used, name and size of stove wanted and correct price.

OUR 30 DAYS' FREE TRIAL OFFER.

TO PROVE TO YOU that we will furnish you with a handsomer, a better, a stronger made and better finished and more lasting and more economical fuel consuming stove than you could buy anywhere else, and at a big saving in cost to you, we make you this most liberal 30 days' free trial offer, an offer which enables you to find out, without expense to you, just what we mean when we say that we are selling the world's leaders in stoves and ranges.

SELECT ANY ONE OF OUR STOVES as illustrated, described and priced in the pages of this catalogue, send us the price of the stove which you would like to test, and we will send it to you with the understanding and agreement that you may use the stove in your own home for 30 days, during which time you may put it to every possible test that may be devised. You may compare it with any other stove you have used, and the stoves used by your friends and neighbors, and the stoves that other dealers are anxious to sell you, and if you do not find after this 30 days' trial that it is in every way better than any stove you can buy from your dealer at home or elsewhere, if you are not absolutely convinced that you have made a big saving in cost, and that you have received just the sort of a stove that you have been anxious to secure, you may return the stove to us at our expense, and we will immediately return your money, together with all the transportation charges paid by you.

NO FAIRER OFFER COULD BE MADE by any firm or individual than this 30 days' free trial offer; it gives you every opportunity that could be asked to investigate the merits of our stoves and we are able to make an extremely liberal offer because we know our stoves so well, because we know that the stoves we sell are themselves the best argument that could possibly be made for them. They really sell themselves, and when we have secured an order in a town or locality it is no uncommon thing to receive innumerable additional orders from the same town or locality as a result of the splendid advertising this stove does for us.

ABOUT THE FREIGHT CHARGES.

THE PRICES QUOTED in this catalogue are for the stove delivered on board the cars at our foundry in Newark, Ohio, from which point you must pay the freight charges. Stoves are accepted by the railroad companies at a very low freight rate (third class) and you will find the freight charges amount to next to nothing in comparison to what you will save in price. We have shipped stoves as far as California, and have received letters from our customers declaring that when the freight charges were paid by them for this long haul they even then saved as much as $25.00 on a high class steel range. You must remember that you have to pay the freight charges just the same when you buy from the home dealer, because he adds it to the cost price of the stove to him, and in many instances the dealer having purchased his stock through jobbers or wholesalers, the freight charges which you pay when you buy from him are several times what they would be if you bought your stove from us, and paid the freight charges from Newark, Ohio. Refer to pages 15 to 19 of this book and you will find that we quote the third class (stove) freight rate per hundred pounds to several points in your state. Take the rate quoted to the point nearest you and then from the weight of the stove which we give under each description you can tell almost to a penny what the freight to your town will amount to.

TAKE, FOR EXAMPLE, our very largest Acme Triumph Steel Range, weighing 556 pounds, or our largest Sunburst hard coal base burner, weighing 465 pounds. Either of these stoves could be shipped from 100 to 500 miles for a freight charge amounting to from 50 cents to $1.50, according to the distance. Our lighter weight stoves would be proportionately lower, so that you can very readily see that the freight charges are next to nothing.

YOUR MONEY BACK IF YOU ARE NOT SATISFIED.

YOU TAKE NO RISK whatever in sending us your order. If the stove we send you doesn't prove perfectly satisfactory in every way and the greatest bargain in this line you ever saw or heard of, you can return it to us at our expense and we will promptly return your money, including what you paid for freight charges. Remember also, you have 30 days' trial, during which time you can assure yourself that you have obtained from us the greatest possible value for your money. If you feel dissatisfied at any time during the 30 days you can return the stove and your money will be promptly refunded.

IN ORDERING, please note what we say on the preceding page about how to select the stove you need. Write your order on one of our regular order blanks or any plain sheet of paper. Be sure to state the catalogue number and enclose our price. You can send us a postoffice money order, an express money order, a bank draft, or send the money in a registered letter. State the amount of money you enclose and in what form. Be sure to sign your name, address and give us shipping instructions and the stove will go to you promptly and, as before stated, under our guarantee of "Your money back if you are not satisfied," and with the additional privilege of 30 days' free trial.

STOVE PIPE AND COOKING UTENSILS ARE EXTRA.

WHEN YOU ORDER STOVES at the prices quoted in this catalogue, please understand that we furnish only the stove as illustrated and described, and no stove pipe and no cooking utensils are furnished with it. If you desire any stove furniture, pipe or cooking utensils, they should be selected from either this big catalogue or our tinware catalogue. The stove furniture and pipe will be shipped from our stock in Chicago, while the stove will be sent to you direct from our foundry at Newark, Ohio, thus making two shipments, one from the foundry and one from our store. For this reason we especially urge you to make your order for cooking utensils large enough to make the purchase profitable to you, remembering that 50 to 100 pounds will, as a rule, go by freight from Chicago for as little freight charge as would 10 pounds. By consulting the pages of this catalogue you will quickly discover that every sort of stove and kitchen utensil is carried in stock by us, and our quality and price inducements are the best offered by any firm or dealer or individual, and we suggest that you turn to these pages now and note what an elegant line of iron, steel, and enameled ware we handle, and see the generous equipment a few dollars will purchase from these pages.

HOW TO GET REPAIRS FOR OUR STOVES.

ACMES SELDOM NEED REPAIRS. Our stoves do not often need repairs but when breakage occurs or parts wear out, and repairs are needed, they always fit. The fact that today we are able to furnish repairs for every stove we have ever sold, makes our guarantee doubly valuable. We handle repairs on an entirely different basis from that of other dealers, because we supply you with the needed part at foundry cost, a mere fraction of what is usually charged by others for such repairs.

WHEN YOU BUY A STOVE FROM US we send you a repair list to make it easy for you to order any piece or part you may need in the years to come. For example, if in the course of the next five or ten years a piece or part should break by accident or otherwise, by referring to the little repair book we send you, you may instantly tell by number just what piece or part you need. Order this part from us by number taken from the booklet; the booklet we send you gives the prices, which is a mere fraction of what others would charge for similar parts, and we will get the needed part to you immediately.

ANOTHER IMPORTANT FEATURE of our stove repairs and parts lies in the fact that all of them are made interchangeable and it will be no trouble at all for you to make the repairs in your own home without the assistance of anyone else. You will find that no grinding or filing will be necessary to get the new part in place. In short, we take the best possible care of our customers that we know how to take, and when you buy a stove from us, you may do so with the assurance that our interest in you and the article we sell does not end when we have received your money and the stove has been delivered to you.

IN ORDERING REPAIRS FOR STOVES, it is very important to give your purchase invoice number or the most complete and explicit information possible. By strictly adhering to the following rules, a great deal of annoyance, expense and delay may be averted. 1st. State whether stove is for coal only, for wood only, or a combined wood and coal burning construction. 2d. If cook stove or range, say if square top or with reservoir. 3d. The back of the stove is at the pipe collar. Stand facing the hearth on a cook stove or facing the oven door of a range. 4th. Give full number, shown on outside of main top. In many instances the same size of griddle holes are placed on different stove bodies, namely, 7-18, 8-18 8-20, 9-20, etc., and the single No. 7, 8 or 9 in this instance would be no indication of the correct size of the stove. 5th. Be particular to furnish all dates of patents. 6th. When legs are desired, say if stove is supplied with legs only or on leg base. 7th. Give name of stove in full. A strict observance of these directions will be mutually advantageous.

OUR STEEL RANGE DEPARTMENT GREATLY ENLARGED.

WE HAVE MADE TREMENDOUS STRIDES FORWARD in the manufacture of steel ranges. We have added new special machinery for working the heaviest kind of steel plate, and these machines, together with our new asbestos lining department and with our greatly enlarged facilities throughout every department of the steel range making section of our great stove works at Newark, Ohio, a department occupying one of the large buildings shown in the illustration, leads us to say that we are not overstating the case when we claim without fear of proven contradiction that we are now not only making more steel ranges than are made in any other two steel range making buildings in the world, but we are also producing a higher grade of steel range than comes out of any other stove foundry in America. We have spared no expense in securing and installing special machinery for the drawing, punching, shaping, bending, and handling of heavier steel plate than it is possible to handle in a like manner in any other foundry or factory, and it is for these reasons that in higher grade steel ranges like the Acme Triumph and the Acme Regal steel ranges we use a heavier and better quality of steel plate than is used in any other steel range manufactured, no matter what its name, make or price.

WHILE WE HAVE BROUGHT OUT SOME CHEAPER RANGES than our Acme Triumph, making them a little less ornate and without cast base and some other features, but without sacrificing in any way whatever the essential qualities necessary to a thoroughly reliable and lasting range, by which process we have produced the Acme Hummer which we offer at $12.35 and upward according to equipment; and the Acme Renown, which we offer at $16.20 and upward according to equipment; we nevertheless recommend our highest grade steel ranges, the ranges made from the heaviest and best steel plate ever worked up into steel ranges, the black enameled steel in the Acme Regal at $17.15 and upward according to equipment, and the blue polished steel in the Acme Triumph at $19.15 and upward as illustrated, described and quoted in this catalogue. In these two magnificent ranges, the Acme Regal and the Acme Triumph, we offer to you the highest grade steel range construction possible to produce, and offer them to you at prices based on the actual cost of material and labor in the largest and most economically operated stove works in the world, with every known equipment for economic and high grade results, with our one small percentage of profit added. While you will find the cheaper steel ranges, the Acme Hummer and the Acme Renown, in every way better, stronger, handsomer and more satisfactory than the cheaper grades of steel ranges that are offered by many makers, and in every way equal to ranges that are being sold generally at double our own prices, nevertheless, for the highest grade steel range work possible to produce we would most strongly recommend that you select either our Acme Regal or our Acme Triumph, which are the highest type of steel ranges built by us, ranges that cannot be surpassed by the product of any other stove foundry in the world.

IT IS A SHEER WASTE OF MONEY to pay more than we ask for our Acme Regal or our Acme Triumph steel ranges. Remember that when you pay more than the prices we ask you get no better stove than we offer you; indeed, it is not possible to get so good a stove no matter what the price you pay, and if you pay more than the prices named in this catalogue, the difference between our prices and those asked by other dealers represents the profit you are compelled to pay other manufacturers with their obsolete equipment and limited product, the jobber, the wholesaler and the retailer, all of which we save you when you buy from us.

DUPLEX GRATE.

WITH EVERY STEEL RANGE WE BUILD we furnish a very heavy duplex grate for either hard or soft coal or wood, so arranged that it can be changed to a wood grate instantly. The duplex grate can be drawn out of front of range without disturbing the fire linings. When our Acme steel range is used for wood only, we furnish an extension fire box, which allows a longer stick of wood to be used in the stove, so when you order a steel range from us do not fail to state whether it is for wood or coal, or for both wood and coal. FOR BURNING HARD COAL, the Duplex grate should always be used with the concave or open side up. This gives the draft necessary for perfect combustion. FOR BURNING SOFT COAL, the grate is used in exactly the same way as when burning hard coal. Our ranges have extra large flues so that it is impossible to choke the grate with any kind of coal therefore soft coal may be burned economically, the draft being very easily regulated by means of the draft registers. FOR BURNING WOOD, however, reverse the grate by giving it a turn with the shaker. This turns up the smooth side of the grate which is made especially for wood. When burning wood, the two end linings should be removed, which will give you a larger fire box taking a longer stick of wood. With this Duplex grate, any kind of fuel may be burned just as economically as you can burn coal or wood, and we are sure that you will find this grate the best that has ever been put in any range or cook stove.

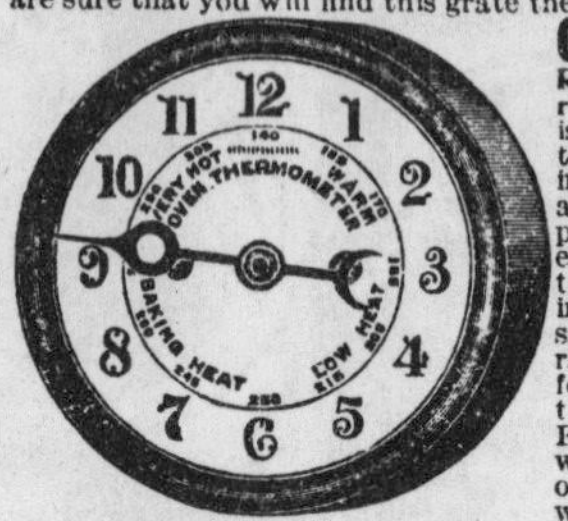

OVEN THERMOMETERS. We equip our Acme Triumph, Acme Regal, Acme Lehigh, Acme Liberty and Acme Kenwood ranges with a Cooper Pequabuck Oven Thermometer. It is mounted in the oven door and it accurately shows the temperature of the oven without the necessity of opening the door. These thermometers measure heat just as a clock measures time or a steam gauge measures steam pressure, and it is a great convenience. This thermometer is the best on the market. You can bring your oven to just the right temperature for either roasting or baking. It insures economical consumption of fuel, it saves a great deal of trouble in the management of the range, it makes it possible for you to maintain a uniform temperature and contributes to much better results than can be obtained with any range not so equipped. Every housekeeper will appreciate the many advantages which this thermometer gives, and anyone using one of our ranges equipped with a Pequabuck thermometer would not be satisfied to go back to the old "hit or miss" method of roasting and baking.

YOU SHARE IN THE PROFITS OF OUR BUSINESS when you buy a stove from us. Turn to pages 1 and 2 of this catalogue, and see there the full particulars of our wonderful Profit Sharing Plan, by which we share with our customers the profits of this great business. Whenever you buy a stove or other merchandise from us we send you a Profit Sharing Certificate for the full amount of money you send us. Keep these certificates and when they amount to $25.00 or more you may send them in to us to exchange for these Profit Sharing Articles without any additional expense to you. If you buy our highest grade steel range or our highest grade base burner, the certificate we send you will be almost sufficient to enable you to secure at once one of the many valuable articles illustrated and described on pages 1 and 2 of this big book. It will be very easy for you to get the number of additional certificates required to secure the article you want free by turning over the pages of this catalogue, noting the extremely low prices at which we quote every conceivable sort of merchandise, and ordering from these pages many of the articles you need every day in your home or on the farm. In other words, part of the money you send us for a stove or for other merchandise comes back to you in this Profit Sharing Plan of ours, as shown on pages 1 and 2 of this catalogue, the most wonderful, the most liberal plan ever devised by a mercantile institution.

HOT WATER FRONTS.

ALL OUR STEEL RANGES and all our cast iron ranges for coal can be furnished with a water front to connect with a pressure boiler as shown in this illustration, and priced on each page with the ranges. For price on the pressure boiler and stand see catalogue Nos. 42G1081 to 42G1085—see page 575. Water fronts and pressure boilers are used only where there is a supply furnished with constant pressure through pipes, which can only be obtained in towns or cities having waterworks, or where you have an elevated water pressure tank. The hot water front gives such ample supply of hot water that you would only require a square range as shown in illustration on the left, instead of one with the extension reservoir shown in the illustration on the right. However, water fronts can be fitted in either style range.

COOK WITH KEROSENE (COAL) OIL

THIRTY DAYS' TRIAL

TO PROVE THIS STOVE SUPREME OVER ALL OTHERS

F. B. Q.—FINEST BEYOND QUESTION.

$20.75

COMPLETE AUTOMATIC WICKLESS KEROSENE OIL RANGE WITH OVEN, BROILER AND WARMING CLOSET

View showing the F. B. Q. Automatic Wickless Oil Range with oven section removed. The big Cooking top makes an ideal arrangement for heavy work, such as boiling water for wash days, canning fruits, making jellies, preserves, etc.

AUTOMATIC BURNERS. The F. B. Q. Automatic Wickless Kerosene Oil Stove has the pipe line running across the front side and carrying five of our well known automatic burners which have been doing such successful work. Three of them are directly over the pipe line and stationary, excepting that they are full automatic and move up and down for operation; whereas, two of them operate from the same pipe line, but are supported by a branch or arm and swing on the center. The burners swing to either side, forming a group of four which, for some big work like a wash boiler or something you wish to give an unusually strong cooking, gives you great facilities for doing so. Each burner is provided with a silver nickeled lever to control the flow of oil. The indicator plainly shows when the flame is too low or out. The burner bowl is raised or lowered at will.

LIGHTING RINGS. The old style wick stove is out of date since our line of Wickless Kerosene Oil Stoves and Ranges has been on the market. Everything about them is simple, easily understood and durable. Plain, simple directions are sent with every stove. In fact, these wonderful stoves are ideal and are the only absolutely satisfactory wickless oil-gas stoves ever made. THE LIGHTING RINGS, which fit in the oil bowl, are made of asbestos and are practically indestructible. They grow hard after being used a while, for all the impurities of the oil collect on them; consequently they will not light as readily after being used for quite a while as when new. It is simply a matter of your own convenience, but we would recommend that the lighting rings be renewed every six weeks or two months if the stove is used regularly, and we suggest that you order an extra dozen with your range.

MAIN TOP is prettily covered with removable open grate sections. Made of the best quality gray iron. Provision for the different positions of the burners has been made without the grate bars interfering with the flame.

WARMING OR HOT CLOSET has a lift door which when open rests upon top of oven. Will be found most desirable for keeping dishes warm that have been cooked or for heating plates. There is no expense connected with heating the hot closet, for the waste heat which passes up the flue when the oven is being used heats the closet.

BAKING AND BROILING OVENS. They are conveniently located and allow the user to stand erect naturally and comfortably. The burners are so arranged that slow baking and broiling, toasting bread, or things of that sort can be done to perfection. Every unit of heat is utilized and the oven heated without any dead corners, with a very small amount of fuel. Will bake evenly top and bottom the most delicate cake or pastry on either the upper or lower rack, or both at the same time.

OVEN RACKS are substantially made of steel wire. Easy to handle and do not absorb or obstruct the heat.

OVEN DOOR. Heavy stamped steel, beautifully ornamented with a silver nickeled name plate. Drop pattern and when open forms a shelf flush with the bottom of the oven. The entire oven section can be easily lifted from the stove, giving a big amount of additional cooking space.

CONVENIENT HIGH SHELF securely fastened to main back of stove and supported with two silver nickeled brackets.

ADJUSTABLE CABINET SHIELD. The burners are provided with a shield to protect the flame from drafts, from open windows or doors. Their use also contributes to the concentration of heat at the burner and gives the largest and hottest blue flame of any oil stove made.

DOUBLE OIL RESERVOIRS. Of large capacity, and may be removed for filling without extinguishing the fire, as sufficient oil remains in the lower reservoir to temporarily feed the flame. This is an excellent feature, as there is not the slightest danger of accident for the reason that the reservoir must be removed in order to fill it, and there is no possibility of an overflow of oil.

OUR F. B. Q. AUTOMATIC WICKLESS KEROSENE OIL STOVE is extremely attractive in appearance and our very latest production in an up to date oil-gas range, a range designed and sold only by us. It has the very latest features and is the strongest and most durable, and by far the most convenient and superior range ever produced. Absolutely nothing better on the market. Made full cabinet of the best quality extra heavy gauge steel throughout, the black japanned finish is relieved by the handsome full silver nickeled trimmings. The main body and edges of the range present a perfectly smooth surface with no bolts or screws protruding to catch the wiping cloth.

THE IDEAL SUMMER STOVE. For hot weather the F. B. Q. Automatic Wickless Oil Stove is unequaled. Its use means a cool kitchen. No bother carrying kindling, coal or wood. No emptying ashes. It saves work, dirt, and its use means well cooked meals and a happy family. No delay. Quick fire. Ready in a few moments whenever you want it. No delays for meals. It is simple in construction, easily understood and operated. Does its work well and economically.

This is a burner section of one of our F. B. Q. Automatic Wickless Kerosene Oil Stoves. The flame arises from the perforated burner section, No. 3, which rests upon the oil cup, No. 2, holding the oil and lighting ring and furnishes the oil-gas, which mixes with just enough air coming through the perforations in the chimney to form a blue flame of proper combustion. No. 1 shows the controlling lever and indicator. Each burner is provided with a wrench and lock nut to prevent them from leaking, as shown in figure No. 4.

WONDERFUL, ISN'T IT, WHEN YOU THINK OF IT? A stove that makes its own gas from common kerosene (coal) oil and air. It has the new process burners in which the oil is mixed with enormous quantities of air and gives you the cheapest and best fuel in the world. It burns this cheap fuel safely and economically. Just fill the reservoir with common kerosene oil, raise the lever so that the oil may run into the burner bowl, touch a match to it. The gas begins to generate, and, passing through the mixing chamber is properly mixed with air, giving perfect combustion and intense heat.

View showing the large convenient oven and warming closet of our F. B. Q. Automatic Wickless Kerosene Oil Stove.

THIRTY DAYS' TRIAL Sold under our binding guarantee of satisfaction or your money back. We will accept your order for this range with the understanding and agreement that you can give it a thirty days' trial, and if, during that time, you have any reason to feel dissatisfied; if it does not operate perfectly; and if you find it is not by far the most wonderful labor saving and fuel saving stove you have ever used; furthermore, if you do not find that you are able to keep the house cleaner and tidier without extra work; and if you do not find it the most convenient stove for cooking and baking of all kinds, canning fruits, making jellies, preserves, etc., without the annoyance of standing over an insufferably hot coal or wood stove, especially during the summer months, a stove always ready for use and that we have furnished you one of our wonderful F. B. Q. Automatic Kerosene Oil Stoves at just half the price such a stove would cost you from any other dealer, simply write us, and we will instruct you how to return the stove to us and immediately return your money, together with the freight charges you have paid. There will be no fuss, no quibbling. If you are dissatisfied, we want you to return it. We do not ask you to accept these statements on our mere say so. We want you to have every opportunity to prove them to your own satisfaction, and for this reason we will ship upon receipt of our price our **F. B. Q. Automatic Kerosene Oil Stove** on thirty days' trial, and if not perfectly satisfactory to you we will pay freight both ways without any expense to you.

WE TEST EVERY F. B. Q. AUTOMATIC WICKLESS KEROSENE OIL STOVE BEFORE PACKING IT FOR SHIPMENT, so we know they leave the factory in perfect order, ready for use as soon as unpacked. **PLAIN PRINTED DIRECTIONS ARE SENT WITH EACH STOVE,** and on account of their simplicity of construction they are easily understood, and by following our plain directions there should be no difficulty in operating the stove with the greatest success from the very start.

THE WORLD FAMOUS ACME KEROSENE OIL COOKING RANGE

CAREFULLY NOTE THE EXCELLENT FEATURES

NO. 22T580

$13.65

ALWAYS READY FOR USE, DAY OR NIGHT.

WE LEAD ALL COMPETITION in the oil stove business with our Acme Wickless, Smokeless Blue Flame Kerosene Oil Stoves shown on the following pages. But, although they are the standard of America, we are ever striving to improve the quality, realizing that inasmuch as people must eat, anything which is needed to aid in the preparation of their foods is a household necessity. For this reason we brought out this highest grade Acme Wickless Smokeless Oil Range which we now offer.

NEW AND IMPROVED FOR 1910. For originality, convenience, compactness and beauty it blazes the way of progress. For sheer merit and work it is without a peer in stovedom. Simple, convenient and handsome; it is all that and more; it is efficient and inexpensive to operate beyond any other fuel. Experience has proved that the Acme is an eminently satisfactory and desirable article, and at the extremely low prices which we are able to make it is a wonderfully profitable and economical investment.

EVERY WOMAN ENJOYS A STOVE that will do good cooking and baking without any fuss, and therefore she will appreciate and ought to have our Acme Oil Cooking Range, which will perform any feat of cooking or baking that any kind of stove will do, and at a fraction of the cost, too. Besides, it does away with all the annoyance of coal and ashes. The same cooking utensils used on your coal and wood burning stove can be used on any of our oil-gas stoves with equally good results.

SOME WOMEN have come to dread baking day, but they need no longer do so when they own an Acme Range. It's ready at an instant's notice, without dumping any ashes or without breaking your back by lugging hods full of coal; and the beauty of it all is that it does the cooking just as well and quicker.

WE OFFER IN OUR ACME Cabinet, Wickless, Smokeless Kerosene Oil Cooking Range a stove not only attractive in design but one that will prove economical in use and a perfectly satisfactory cooking stove. Using kerosene oil for fuel and converting this cheap product into gas by the use of our new process burners, by burning more air than oil, we place within the reach of every housewife, no matter how far removed from the conveniences of the city, all the advantages the city users of gas may have, at a mere fraction of the charge for gas. Indeed, so economical is this stove in its consumption of fuel that hundreds of them have taken the place of gas ranges in the cities and towns.

FOR ALL AROUND USE the Acme Wickless, Smokeless Kerosene Oil Range will be found an almost indispensable cooking stove. All the heat generated is at the burner, where it is required for cooking and baking. As it is unnecessary to light the fire until you are ready to begin cooking or baking, and the flame is instantly extinguished when the cooking or baking is completed, it is the most satisfactory stove for all around use on the market. It is no longer necessary to swelter in an overheated kitchen if you use an Acme Cabinet, Wickless, Smokeless Oil Range.

IN CONSTRUCTION this Acme Kerosene Oil-Gas Range is the very best product of skilled labor in one of the largest and best equipped stove foundries in the world. It has a very strong steel cabinet frame, finished in baked black japan, and is handsomely ornamented with elegantly designed corner brackets, nickel plated valve handles, brass finished reservoirs and nickel plated name plate. Every joint of the Acme Oil Stove is made solid and strong by electric welding. The bowls and T pipes are welded together, likewise the stand pipes to the main pipe lines.

CLEANLY. There are no complicated parts. By simply removing the grates and chimneys, every part of the Acme is easily accessible for cleaning. This appeals to the particular housewife.

ITS DISTINGUISHING FEATURE IS THE OVEN. This important feature has been very carefully constructed and the double burners beneath it give ample heat for the most difficult baking. The flues are so constructed that the heat is very evenly distributed, and it is impossible for the products of combustion to enter the baking chamber. This makes it possible to bake the most delicate cake and brown top and bottom without the slightest danger of contamination from the flames of burning oil, as in other stoves. The oven door and the oven bottom may be removed when so desired, and it is therefore possible to use the two oven burners for cooking purposes. This converts the two-burner stove into a four-burner for cooking purposes and the three-burner into a five-burner cooking stove. This is a feature which cannot be found in any other range on the market.

THE NEW PROCESS BURNERS which we use on all our wickless, odorless, Blue Flame Kerosene Oil-Gas Stoves have so simplified and perfected the vaporizing of common kerosene oil that these stoves produce a perfect fuel gas by converting air and oil into the cheapest fuel it is possible to use in cooking stoves.

Cooking Utensils not furnished.

$11.25

Illustration shows the broad general utility of these ranges.

No. 22T579

DOUBLE RESERVOIRS. The cooking burners and the oven burners are provided with double reservoirs, and the main reservoir may be removed for filling without extinguishing the fire, as sufficient oil remains in the lower reservoir to temporarily feed the flame. This is an excellent feature, as there is not the slightest danger of accident, for the reason that the reservoir must be removed in order to fill it.

FRONT VALVES. It will be noticed by consulting the illustration that all the valves on the Acme Cabinet Kerosene Oil-Gas Range are at the front of the stove. This overcomes the danger of the operator's clothes catching fire from reaching over the flame, as it is necessary to do when operating the kerosene oil-gas stoves manufactured and sold by many other dealers.

WARMING SHELF. The Acme Cabinet Kerosene Oil-Gas Range has a generous warming shelf built with a warm air flue running to the top of the shelf, which makes it possible to keep anything desired thoroughly warm. This is a feature not to be found in any other oil-gas stove on the market.

ADJUSTABLE CABINET SHIELD. The burners are provided with a shield which protects the blue flame from drafts of air from open windows and doors; their use also contributes to the concentration of heat at the burner and gives the largest and hottest blue flame of any oil stove made.

ACCESSIBILITY. Please note that every part of the Acme Cabinet Kerosene Oil-Gas Range is easily reached for cleaning purposes without removing any other parts. It is a very simple matter to clean the Acme Kerosene Oil-Gas Range and you will find it a decided labor saver in the kitchen.

PROMPT SHIPMENT. We have a large stock on hand, crated, ready for immediate shipment from Chicago or our factory near Boston, Mass., and when you decide to send us your order, enclose our price and the stove will be sent direct to you without any delay whatever.

THE SMALL PICTURE TO THE LEFT shows the broad general utility of these ranges. It is catalog No. 22T579 and is just the same as catalog No. 22T580, shown in the big picture, except that it has only two burners on top instead of three.

30 DAY'S TRIAL. Remember, we accept your order for one of our Acme Wickless Kerosene Oil Stoves with the understanding and agreement that you can give it thirty days' trial, and if during that time you have any reason to feel dissatisfied, if it does not operate perfectly, if you find it is not by far the most wonderful labor saving and fuel saving stove you have ever used, and if you find you have not made an immense saving in every way, and that we have furnished you one of our Acme Wickless Kerosene Oil Stoves at just half the price such a stove would cost you from any other dealer, you are at perfect liberty to return the stove to us at our expense, and we will immediately return your money, including the transportation charges you have paid.

PRICE OF OUR ACME CABINET, WICKLESS, KEROSENE OIL RANGE, STRONGLY CRATED, DELIVERED ON CARS AT CHICAGO, ILL., OR BOSTON, MASS.

Catalog No.	Size Top, Inches	Height, Inches	Size Oven, Inches	Burners on Top	Burners under Oven	Shipping Weight	Price
22T580	17x37½	36	18½x11½x11½	3	2	100 pounds	$13.65
22T579	17x26½	36	18½x11½x11½	2	2	86 pounds	11.25

No. 22T592 Asbestos Lighting Rings for above large burners. Price, per dozen........84c

The range catalog No. 22T579, shown in the small illustration is just exactly the same as No. 22T580, shown in the big picture, except that it has only two burners on top instead of three.

$24.73 FOR OUR ACME LIBERTY

WITH HIGH CLOSET, BUT WITHOUT RESERVOIR. HOT BLAST, SMOKE CONSUMING, SOFT COAL OR WOOD RANGE.

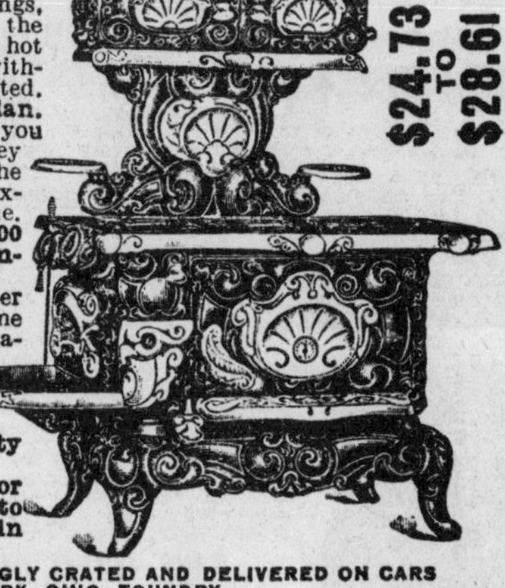

$24.73 TO $28.61

AT $26.23 we offer this as the exact same range shown on the preceding page as 22E131 at $28.25, with the same ornate high art trimmings, the same magnificent high closet, the same oven door thermometer, the same hot blast smoke consuming device, but without the extension reservoir, as illustrated.

Remember our profit sharing plan. If you send us your order for a stove you will share in our profits. Part of the money you send us will go back to you in the shape of your share of the profit, as explained in the last pages of this catalogue.

See page 716 for our liberal $1.00 to $5.00 C. O. D. subject to examination offer.

If you do not use coal at all, order the Acme Kenwood, the exact same range, built for wood only, from catalogue Nos. 22E272 to 22E277.

Prices do not include pipe or cooking utensils. For cooking utensils, see pages 517 to 534.

Water Fronts for Acme Liberty Ranges, each, $2.00.

We can always furnish repairs for Acmes. See page 721 about how to order stove repairs when needed in future years.

PRICES ARE FOR RANGE STRONGLY CRATED AND DELIVERED ON CARS AT OUR NEWARK, OHIO, FOUNDRY.

Catalogue Number	Range Number	Size of Lids	Size of Oven	Size of Top, without End Shelf	Size of End Shelf	Length of Fire Box when used for Wood	Height to Main Top	Shipping Weight	Price
22E138	7-18	No. 7	17x17x12	33x27	7x27	21	31 in.	568 lbs.	$24.73
22E139	8-18	No. 8	17x17x12	33x27	7x27	21	31 in	568 lbs.	24.98
22E140	8-20	No. 8	19x19x12½	36x30	7x30	23	32 in.	635 lbs.	26.23
22E141	8 22	No. 8	21x21x13	38x32	7x32	24	32 in.	665 lbs.	28.33
22E142	9-20	No. 9	19x19x12½	36x30	7x30	23	32 in.	635 lbs.	26.49
22E143	9-22	No. 9	21x21x13	38x32	7x32	24	32 in.	665 lbs.	28.61

AT $22.65 WE OFFER THIS, OUR ACME LIBERTY

WITH HIGH SHELF BUT WITHOUT RESERVOIR, FOR SOFT COAL OR WOOD.

$22.65 —TO— $26.51

THIS IS THE EXACT SAME RANGE as the one shown as No. 22E145 at $26.15, but is without the reservoir. It has the same massive high shelf, the same ornate high art nickeled trimmings, as all the line of Acme Liberty ranges shown on this and the preceding page. Its hot blast smoke consuming fire box is its leading feature, and its gorgeous trimmings make it the most complete and attractive range money can buy.

Send us your order for any of these ranges and if it does not please you in every respect, and you do not admit it to be the finest article at the lowest price, and that you have made a large saving even after paying the freight, you can set it up in your kitchen for 30 days, try it thoroughly, and if not fully satisfied, you can return it to us, and your money will be refunded, including any freight you may have paid.

See page 716 for our liberal $1.00 to $5.00 C. O. D. subject to examination offer.

If you do not use coal at all, order the Acme Kenwood, the exact same range, built for wood only, from catalogue Nos. 22E286 to 22E291.

Prices do not include pipe or cooking utensils. For cooking utensils see pages 517 to 534.

Water Fronts for Acme Liberty Ranges, each, $2.00.

We can always furnish repairs for Acmes. See page 721 about how to order stove repairs when needed in future years.

PRICES ARE FOR RANGE STRONGLY CRATED AND DELIVERED ON CARS AT OUR NEWARK, OHIO, FOUNDRY.

Catalogue Number	Range Number	Size of Lids	Size of Oven	Size of Top without End Shelf	Size of End Shelf	Length of Fire Box when Used for Wood	Height to Main Top	Shipping Weight, pounds	Price
22E152	7-18	No. 7	17x17x12	33x27	7x27	21	31	498	$22.65
22E153	8-18	No. 8	17x17x12	33x27	7x27	21	31	498	22.90
22E154	8-20	No. 8	19x19x12½	36x30	7x30	23	32	565	24.15
22E155	8-22	No. 8	21x21x13	38x32	7x32	24	32	595	26.25
22E156	9-20	No. 9	19x19x12½	36x30	7x30	23	32	565	24.41
22E157	9-22	No. 9	21x21x13	38x32	7x32	24	32	595	26.51

OUR ACME LIBERTY SOFT COAL RANGE

WITH RESERVOIR AND HIGH SHELF FOR BURNING SOFT COAL OR WOOD

$26.15 —TO— $30.53

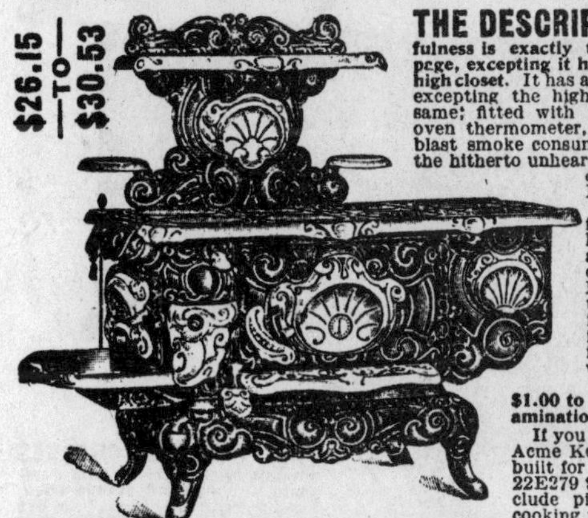

THE DESCRIPTION of this magnificent article of kitchen usefulness is exactly the same as on the preceding page, excepting it has the high shelf instead of the high closet. It has all the indispensable advantages, excepting the high closet. Trimmed exactly the same; fitted with the same famous Pequabuck oven thermometer, has the same large oven, hot blast smoke consuming fire box, and is offered at the hitherto unheard of price of $26.15 delivered on the cars at our foundry in Newark, Ohio.

In our wonderful stove foundry at Newark, Ohio, we have facilities for making stoves and ranges such as are not enjoyed by any other foundry. Practically every piece and part that goes in the stove are made in our own foundry, and all this is done to get the highest quality at the lowest cost, and this we give you the benefit of.

See page 716 for our liberal $1.00 to $5.00 C. O. D subject to examination offer.

If you do not use coal at all, order the Acme Kenwood, the exact same range built for wood only, from catalogue Nos. 22E279 to 22E284. Prices do not include pipe or cooking utensils. For cooking utensils, see pages 517 to 534.

Water Fronts for Acme Liberty Ranges, each, $2 00. We can always furnish repairs for Acmes. See page 721 about how to order stove repairs when needed in future years.

PRICES ARE FOR RANGE STRONGLY CRATED AND DELIVERED ON CARS AT OUR NEWARK, OHIO, FOUNDRY.

Catologue Number	Range No	Size of Lids	Size of Oven	Size of Top Including Reservoir	Length of Fire Box when Used for Wood	Height to Main Top	Ship'ing Weight, Lbs.	Price
22E145	7-18	No. 7	17x17x12	46x27	21	31 in	516	$26.15
22E146	8-18	No. 8	17x17x12	46x27	21	31 in.	516	26.40
22E147	8-20	No. 8	19x19x12½	50x30	23	32 in.	670	27.65
22E148	8-22	No. 8	21x21x13	52x32	24	32 in.	695	29 76
22E149	9-20	No. 9	19x19x12½	50x30	23	32 in.	670	27.92
22E150	9-22	No. 9	21x21x13	52x32	24	32 in.	695	30.53

OUR ACME LIBERTY

SOFT COAL RESERVOIR AT $23.00, DELIVERED ON THE CARS AT OUR FOUNDRY IN NEWARK, OHIO.

$23.00 —TO— $27.39

MADE ESPECIALLY for soft coal and readily changed to a wood burner. It is the exact same range as the one illustrated and fully described on preceding page, as No. 22E131 at $28.25 excepting it is without the high closet, but has a tee rail back guard and swinging teapot holders as shown. Its gorgeous silver nickeled trimmings are just the same, its large reservoir, its capacious fire box, its large hearth, smoke consumer, and all the other features contained in this wonderful line of ranges.

Remember we guarantee to please you, we guarantee that we will save you 25 to 50 per cent of the price you would pay any other dealer and if you are not satisfied of all this when you receive the stove from us, you can return it at our expense of freight charges both ways and we will promptly return your money.

See page 716 for our liberal $1.00 to $5.00 C. O. D. subject to examination offer.

If you do not use coal at all, order the Acme Kenwood, the exact same range, built for wood only, from catalogue Nos. 22E293 to 22E298.

Prices do not include pipe or cooking utensils. For cooking utensils, see pages 517 to 534.

Water Fronts for Acme Liberty Ranges, each, $2.00.

We can always furnish repairs for Acmes. See page 721 about how to order stove repairs when needed in future years.

PRICES ARE FOR RANGE STRONGLY CRATED AND DELIVERED ON CARS AT OUR NEWARK, OHIO, FOUNDRY.

Catalogue Number	Range Number	Size of Lids	Size of Oven	Size Top Including Reservoir	Length Fire Box when Used for Wood	Height to Main Top	Ship'ing Weight, pounds	Price
22E159	7-18	No. 7	17x17x12	46x27	21 inches	31 inches	508	$23.00
22E160	8-18	No. 8	17x17x12	46x27	21 inches	31 inches	508	23.25
22E161	8-80	No. 8	19x19x12½	50x30	23 inches	32 inches	615	24.50
22E162	8-22	No. 8	21x21x13	52x32	24 inches	32 inches	640	27.12
22E163	9-20	No. 9	19x19x12½	50x30	23 inches	32 inches	615	24.76
22E164	9-22	No. 9	21x21x13	52x32	24 inches	32 inches	640	27.39

OUR ACME LIBERTY WITHOUT RESERVOIR AT $19.50.

DELIVERED ON THE CARS AT OUR FOUNDRY IN NEWARK, OHIO. BURNS SOFT COAL OR WOOD.

THIS IS THE SIMPLEST FORM OF THIS SPLENDID RANGE, and is exactly the same as the one illustrated as No. 22E159, at $23.00, but is without reservoir, having the extension end shelf instead. We cannot say too much to the credit of this magnificent line of ranges, and urge upon you a careful study of the features fully described in the preceding page. Select the form, size or style of this range you require, send us the catalogue price or even deposit of $1.00 if you live north of Tennessee or east of the Rocky Mountains, and we will ship you the range you select, with the understanding and guarantee that if it does not prove to be exactly as we describe it, or does not satisfy you in every particular, you can return it to us, and we will refund you the amount you have paid, including any freight charges, even if you have had it in use in your own kitchen for 30 days, that you may give it a good trial. The price you pay us for a stove is less than your dealer can buy it for. You save the wholesaler's, jobber's and retailer's profit and get your stove from us at foundry cost with just our one narrow profit added. **See page 716 for our liberal $1.00 to $5.00 C. O. D. offer.** If you do not use coal at all, order the Acme Kenwood, the exact same range, built for wood only, from catalogue Nos. 22E300 to 22E305. Prices do not include pipe or cooking usensils. For cooking utensils, see pages 517 to 534. **Water fronts for Acme Liberty Ranges, each, $2.00. We can always furnish repairs for Acmes. See page 721 about how to order stove repairs when needed in future years.**

$19.50 to $23.36

PRICES ARE FOR RANGE STRONGLY CRATED AND DELIVERED ON CARS AT OUR NEWARK, OHIO, FOUNDRY.

Catalogue Number	Range Number	Size of Lids	Size of Oven	Size of Top, without End Shelf	Size of End Shelf	Length of Fire Box when Used for Wood	Height to Main Top	Shipping Weight	Price
22E166	7-18	No. 7	17x17x12	33x27	7x27	21	31 inches	443 pounds	$19.50
22E167	8-18	No. 8	17x17x12	33x27	7x27	21	31 inches	443 pounds	19.75
22E168	8-20	No. 8	19x19x12½	36x30	7x30	23	32 inches	510 pounds	21.00
22E169	8-22	No. 8	21x21x13	38x32	7x32	24	32 inches	540 pounds	23.10
22E170	9-20	No. 9	19x19x12½	36x30	7x30	23	32 inches	510 pounds	21.26
22E171	9-22	No. 9	21x21x13	38x32	7x32	24	32 inches	540 pounds	23.36

YOUR MONEY WILL BE IMMEDIATELY RETURNED TO YOU FOR ANY GOODS NOT PERFECTLY SATISFACTORY.

NEW 1906 PATTERN ACME LEHIGH

FOR HARD COAL (ANTHRACITE) OR WOOD.

THIS STOVE, AN ENTIRELY NEW MODEL, brand new for 1906, is designed and made expressly for hard coal. It is essentially an eastern stove, for Pennsylvania, New York and New England and the East, where hard coal is burned almost exclusively, at the same time popular in every locality where a hard coal or wood burning range is desired. It is not intended to burn soft coal. It is designed and made exclusively for anthracite (hard coal), and is put out under our guarantee as positively the newest, highest grade, and in every way the best hard coal or wood burning range ever made. This hard coal or wood burning range embodies every high grade, up to date feature of every other high grade hard coal or wood burning range made, with the defects of none. Everything brought right up to date. Everything known in stove building is embodied in this new range.

$24.75

COMPARED with any combination soft and hard coal burner or any combination coal and wood burning range, this range, for the use of hard coal or wood, will last twice as long, will use 25 per cent less fuel, will hold the fire as no combination soft and hard coal burner can, will be found a much more even baker, in fact, so far as we know, it is the only style of a stove in which hard coal can be used as conveniently as any other fuel can be used in any other stove made, and is positively the best hard coal or wood burning stove on the market.

SPECIAL FEATURES

HEAVY COPPER RESERVOIR.

OVEN THERMOMETER. The world famous Pequabuck Thermometer. The only dependable oven thermometer made.

FIRE BOX with heavy brick lining, with a special Dockash grate, with fire box constructed for the exclusive burning of hard coal.

DESIGN. Entirely new, rich, swell rococo pattern with elaborate rococo base.

NICKEL TRIMMINGS. The most elaborate nickel trimmed hard coal range on the market.

WARMING CLOSET. Special design, extra large, elaborately nickel trimmed and beautifully finished.

INTERIOR CONSTRUCTION. So built, so lined, so braced, made, stayed and finished, so arranged as to draft, fire box, oven, bottom and top construction that it forms the most ideal facility for the handling of hard coal exclusively, giving you perfect control of the draft, perfect distribution of heat, perfect control of the fire, and a stove that is built to last a lifetime.

We can always furnish repairs for Acmes. See page 721 about how to order stove repairs when needed in future years.

IF YOU LIVE IN THE EAST, in New York, Pennsylvania, or New England and burn hard coal, or if you live in any other section and burn hard coal, or wish to burn hard coal, and you have been using a combination stove that will "burn hard coal, soft coal or wood," you cannot begin to appreciate the great advantage you will find in this, an exclusive hard coal burner. If you do not use coal at all see our Acme Kenwood, built for wood only, catalogue Nos. 22E265 to 22E270.

IT IS OUR

NEW MODEL FOR 1906

When we decided to get out a hard coal or wood burning stove for New York, New England and the East and other sections where they wished to burn hard coal exclusively, we employed the most skilled draughtsman obtainable. We placed the drawings with the best stove pattern makers in the country, and every pattern and part was gotten out under the supervision of one of the most skilled stove makers in America. We carefully examined every other first class hard coal burning range on the market with a view of using only the best ideas found in all, omitting all the weak points, and as a result we present to you in our Acme Lehigh Hard Coal or Wood Burner a hard coal range embodying every good feature of every other hard coal range made, with the defects of none.

THE OVEN DOOR is fitted with the world famous Pequabuck oven thermometer, as illustrated, set in another gorgeous detachable applique silver nickeled medallion panel, and extending inside the oven door the proper distance to obtain the best possible contact with the oven heat, and registering on the outside dial the exact temperature, enabling the housekeeper to put in the food at the proper time and remove it exactly at the time when done. A good, sensitive, quick working oven thermometer adds to the comfort and happiness of those who do the baking.

THE FREIGHT CHARGES amount to next to nothing compared with what you save in price. The stove can be shipped from our foundry at Newark, Ohio, to any point in Pennsylvania for from $1.25 to $1.75, about the same to New York or New England. Other points in proportion.

IF YOU ORDER THIS RANGE we guarantee it to reach you promptly in perfect condition, and you can return it to us at any time within 30 days, if you are not perfectly satisfied, and get your money back. We bargain and agree to furnish you any repairs in the years to come at actual factory cost.

GENERAL DESCRIPTION.

Very latest handsome rococo design throughout. Oven is 20 inches wide at the door opening 19 inches deep, without the swell of the oven door, is 11½ inches high inside.

MAIN TOP. The main top and cooking surface has six cooking holes and is sectional to allow for expansion or contraction without fire cracking.

Nos. 22E172 to 22E176

☞ SEE THERMOMETER IN OVEN DOOR.

HIGH CLOSET. It is equipped with the highest grade high closet made, roll front, blue polished sheet steel, strengthened at each end with handsome nickeled castings, as illustrated.

FIRE BOX. The fire box is heavily brick lined and fitted with our famous Dockash grate, the best hard coal burning grate in existence. The coal feed and broiler door drops outward and downward, making a convenient door for inserting a broiler over the surface of the hot coals, as well as being a capacious coal feed door. This fire box can be quickly changed to a wood burner. A full set of wood burning fixtures is packed in every stove. It has a large ash pit so arranged that the ashes fall within the deep ash pan. The large inside tank is made of cold rolled copper heavily tinned on the inside and holds 24 quarts. The heating of the water in the reservoir is quickly governed by turning the reservoir damper.

TRIMMINGS. Elaborately nickel trimmed throughout, with handsome nickel plated bands on top, back, shelves and closet, nickel plated hearth bands on oven shelf, medallions, ornamentations and trimmings. Everything the best that can possibly be built, and every stove goes out under our binding guarantee, covering every piece and part that enters into the construction.

If you do not use coal at all order our Acme Kenwood, built for wood only, from catalogue Nos. 22E265 to 22E270.

PRICES ARE FOR RANGE STRONGLY CRATED AND DELIVERED ON CARS AT OUR NEWARK, OHIO, FOUNDRY.

Catalogue Number	Range Number	Size of Lids	Size of Oven	Size of Top, Including Reservoir	Size of Fire Box when Used for Wood	Pipe to Fit Collar	Height to Main Top	Shipping Weight	Price
22E172	7-16	No. 7	16x15x11 in.	42x24½ inches	18x8 x7 inches	6 inches	31 inches	563 pounds	$24.75
22E173	7-18	No. 7	18x17x12 in.	45x27 inches	20x9 x8 inches	7 inches	32 inches	600 pounds	25.75
22E174	8-18	No. 8	18x17x12 in.	45x27 inches	20x9 x8 inches	7 inches	32 inches	600 pounds	26.00
22E175	8-20	No. 8	20x19x11½ in.	46x28 inches	22x9 x8 inches	7 inches	32 inches	635 pounds	27.25
22E176	9-20	No. 9	20x19x11½ in.	46x28 inches	22x9 x8 inches	7 inches	32 inches	635 pounds	27.56

$15.16 WOOD BURNER

NEW 1907 MODEL ACME EMPRESS

in the latest rococo design, with heavy rococo base, complete with deep porcelain lined reservoir, high back shelf, tea shelves, etc. The great wood burner for only $15.16, less than 4 cents per pound, only the cost of material and labor, with but our one small percentage of profit added.

This stove is made to burn wood only and it has an exclusive wood fire box. It is the equal of any range on the market regardless of price.

WE FURNISH THIS RANGE with or without reservoir, this large illustration showing this wood burning range complete with deep porcelain lined reservoir. The small illustration at the bottom shows the exact same range but without reservoir, with neat extension shelf instead, and in this style we furnish it at from $12.01 to $13.84, according to size.

DETAILED DESCRIPTION

This stove is made from the very best Birmingham pig iron, made from new patterns by one of the best pattern makers in the country, the latest rococo design with rich swell front, swell base, four-hole top with cut centers, supported by posts. Comes with the latest style high ornamental back and shelf as illustrated, adjustable tea shelves attached. The fire box is extra large, is heavily lined, made expressly for wood, made with removable fire back and removable fire bottom, the oven is extra large, oven door is tin lined, is equipped with oven door shelf, oven door kicker or opener, fancy nickel plated medallions, knobs, ornamentations, etc., has the very best type of damper and draft regulation and construction, perfect fitting castings, embodies every high grade, up to date feature of every other high grade exclusive wood burning stove made, with the defects of none.

IF YOU WISH AN EXCLUSIVE WOOD BURNING RANGE YOU WILL MAKE NO MISTAKE IN SELECTING THE ACME EMPRESS.

THE TWO RANGES SHOWN HEREON ARE IDENTICALLY THE SAME, the large illustration showing the range complete with reservoir, the small illustration showing the range without reservoir.

UNDERSTAND; EVERY STOVE IS COVERED BY OUR WRITTEN BINDING GUARANTEE.

WE BARGAIN AND AGREE that in case you want any piece, part or repair in the years to come, **WE WILL FURNISH IT TO YOU PROMPTLY AND AT ACTUAL FACTORY COST.**

Nos. 22F343 to 22F345

DON'T THINK THE FREIGHT CHARGES WILL AMOUNT TO MUCH. THEY AMOUNT TO NOTHING COMPARED WITH WHAT YOU SAVE IN PRICE. For from 25 cents to $2.50, according to distance, one of these stoves can be shipped to any customer within one hundred to one thousand miles of our Newark, Ohio, foundry.

IT IS EASY TO ORDER. No matter if you never sent an order away in your life, you won't make any mistake. Select the stove you want from the illustrations and descriptions, fill out an order blank or on a plain piece of paper, in your own way, say what stove you want. Give the number of stove, enclose our price (this you do by buying a money order from your R. F. D. carrier, postmaster or any express agent, or by a draft from your bank, enclose it in the envelope with your letter or order addressed to us), and in a few days you will get your stove. It takes but a few days for your letter to reach us and the stove to reach you. We guarantee the stove to reach you promptly, in perfect order, you have the privilege of setting it up in your own home, giving it 30 days' trial, during which time you can put it to every test, and if you are not convinced you have gotten such a stove as you could not get elsewhere at anything like the price, return the stove to us at our expense, and we will immediately return your money, together with any freight charges paid by you.

ASK YOUR NEIGHBORS ABOUT US; ESPECIALLY THOSE WHO HAVE PURCHASED STOVES FROM US. ASK THEM HOW MUCH MONEY WE SAVED THEM, how much freight they had to pay, how many days it took for their orders to reach us and the stove to reach them. If, perchance, they ever sent to us for a repair part ask them how many days they had to wait to get it and how much it cost them. Investigate a little, if you will, and we know you will take advantage of OUR INCOMPARABLY LOW PRICES.

IF YOU LIVE IN A WOOD COUNTRY AND HAVE NO USE FOR COAL, AND WANT ONE OF THE BEST BAKERS, THE BEST HEATERS, A STOVE THAT CANNOT BE EXCELLED AS AN ECONOMIC FUEL CONSUMER, a stove to take all kinds of wood, soft wood, hard wood, knots, etc., we can then especially recommend this, our **ACME EMPRESS**, in either the reservoir style as shown in the large illustration or without reservoir as shown at the bottom of the page.

SIMPLY ORDER BY NUMBER. YOU TAKE NO RISK, FOR WE GUARANTEE EVERYTHING.

SEND US YOUR ORDER, enclose our price, and if the stove is not all or even more than you expect, return it to us at our expense of freight charges both ways, and we will promptly return all your money.

We can always furnish repairs for Acmes. See page 951 about how to order repairs. Prices do not include pipe or cooking utensils. For cooking utensils, see pages 370 to 381.

WE FURNISH THE ACME EMPRESS FOUR-HOLE TOP, WOOD BURNING RANGE exactly as shown in the large illustration, complete with deep porcelain lined reservoir, in the various sizes, at the following special prices. If desired without high shelf, deduct $1.00.

PRICES, STRONGLY CRATED AND DELIVERED ON THE CARS AT OUR FOUNDRY AT NEWARK, OHIO.

Catalogue Number	Range No.	Size of Lids	Size of Oven, inches	Size of Top, including Reservoir	Height to Cooking Top, inches	Pipe to Fit Collar	Size of Fire Box, inches			Reservoir Capacity in quarts	Shipping Weight	Price
							Length	Width	Depth			
22F343	8-18	No. 8	18x18x12	38 x26 in.	31	7 in.	20	9	5	13½	409 lbs.	$15.16
22F344	8-20	No. 8	20x20x12½	39½x27 in.	31½	7 in.	22	9	5½	17	444 lbs.	17.27
22F345	9-20	No. 9	20x20x12½	40½x27 in.	31½	7 in.	22	9	5½	17	444 lbs.	17.73

THE ACME EMPRESS exactly as shown in the small illustration, without reservoir, otherwise the same as shown in the large illustration, this stove we furnish under our binding guarantee to please or refund the money in the different sizes at the special prices as listed below:

PRICES, STRONGLY CRATED, WITHOUT RESERVOIR, DELIVERED ON THE CARS AT OUR NEWARK, OHIO, FOUNDRY.

Catalogue Number	Range No.	Size of Lids	Size of Oven, inches	Top, not including End Shelf	End Shelf, inches	Height to Cooking Top, inches	Pipe to Fit Collar	Size of Fire Box, inches			Shipping Weight	Price
								Length	Width	Depth		
22F347	8-18	No. 8	18x18x12	29x26 in.	8x26	31	7 in.	20	9	5	347 lbs.	$12.01
22F348	8-20	No. 8	20x20x12½	30x27 in.	8x27	31½	7 in.	22	9	5½	379 lbs.	13.58
22F349	9-20	No. 9	20x20x12½	30x27 in.	8x27	31½	7 in.	22	9	5½	379 lbs.	13.84

Nos. 22F347 to 22F349

IF DESIRED WITHOUT HIGH SHELF, DEDUCT $1.00.

LATEST IMPROVED BIG ACME IMPERIAL COOK STOVE $14.31

THIS HANDSOME, big square oven, nickel trimmed and nickel finished rococo design, four-hole cast iron cook stove, built to burn hard coal, soft coal, wood or coke, is offered at from $14.31 to $19.52 in the reservoir style, as shown in this large illustration, in the various sizes as listed below, and the exact same stove without reservoir but with handsome extension shelf instead, as shown in the small illustration at the bottom of the page, is offered at from $12.51 to $16.63, according to size, a little more than 4 cents per pound for one of the handsomest, best made, best fitted and most lasting combination coal and wood burning stoves on the market.

THESE STOVES are made of the highest grade Birmingham iron, melted with 72-hour coke, giving us the strongest and best finished stove plate castings made; handsome rococo pattern, large square oven door, large square oven, highly polished nickel plated trimmings throughout, beautifully ornamented and decorated; has large porcelain lined reservoir, large nickel plated oven shelf, large nickel plated panels on oven doors, handsome nickel name plate, Alaska nickel plated "Always Cold" door knobs throughout.

WE HAVE THE BEST DAMPER and fire control construction known in stove work, insuring an even distribution of heat, economy in fuel consumption, a perfect baker and an almost everlasting stove. Also has nickel teapot holder.

While this stove is designed especially for coal, we furnish it with our combination duplex grate, which can be changed to a wood burner by a half turn of the shaker crank. It is therefore suitable for hard coal, soft coal, wood or coke.

ALL THE STOVES shown in this edition of our catalogue are new. They are either from newly modeled and newly made patterns, or the highest class patterns, exclusive of our own, remodeled and brought right up to date, new for the winter season of 1907, so that every stove embraces every high grade feature of every other stove of like size and kind, with the defects of none.

TO GIVE YOU AN IDEA OF THE EQUIPMENT we employ for the manufacture of the highest grade stoves made in America, we will call your attention to a few words concerning the building and growth of our foundry.

THE BUILDING OF THE LARGEST STOVE FOUNDRY IN THE WORLD.

THIS WE HAVE BEEN EIGHT YEARS IN DOING. Starting in a small way, year by year we have added grounds, buildings, machinery and organization until our plant now covers 30 acres of ground. More than 2,500 men are employed. We melt daily from eight large cupolas, where nearly every other stove foundry in the country has but one. We have our own electric light and power plant, wonderful machines, miles of our own railroad track, elevated and surface trolley line. All this has been done to reduce cost and improve quality. You will find in our foundry every feature, every up to date labor saving and quality giving machine, appliance, device and facility that you will find in any other stove foundry in the world, all combined in the one, and many advantages in our foundry not to be found in any other foundry in America. Whether you order one stove or a carload from us you get the benefit of all this. You get the stove at the actual cost to produce in our own foundry, with but our one small percentage of profit added. Every stove bears the name "Newark Stove Works, Chicago," making it an ideal stove for dealers to buy to sell again. We have thousands of big dealers on our books. Our price is the same to all whether you order one stove or a carload, and that price the lowest price ever made for like style, weight and grade.

IF YOU HAVE A FRIEND LIVING IN NEWARK write him and ask him about our foundry. Learn from a resident of Newark, Ohio, if it isn't the biggest foundry in the world, and if we don't make the highest grade stoves made in the world, and if our prices are not recognized as being far below those of any other stove maker.

ORDER ANY STOVE from this book, order by name or number, enclose our price (postoffice or express money order, bank draft or the money in a registered letter), we will send the stove to you guaranteeing it to reach you promptly and safely, and after giving it thirty days' trial if you are not perfectly satisfied with your purchase, you can return the stove to us at our expense, and we will immediately return your money, together with any freight charges paid by you. We bargain and agree to always be prepared to furnish you parts or repairs in the years to come and at actual factory cost. You will find the freight charges will amount to next to nothing. One of these big stoves will be carried by the railroad company to points from one hundred to a thousand miles of our foundry at Newark, Ohio, for from 50 cents to $3.00, according to distance. It rarely ever happens that a stove breaks while on the road and if it does we replace it with a new one immediately. Don't think it takes too long. It takes but a few days for your order to reach us and the stove to reach you, and we guarantee prompt shipment.

YOU WILL SHARE IN THE PROFITS of our business if you send your order to us. This is fully explained on pages 1 and 2 of this catalogue. It is the most liberal offer ever made by any maker or seller.

We furnish this big, handsome, four-hole top combination coal and wood burning stove, exactly as illustrated, with deep porcelain lined reservoir, all complete, strongly crated and delivered on board the cars at our foundry, in the various sizes as listed below.

Catalogue Number	Stove No.	Size of Lids	Size of Oven, inches	Top including Reservoir	Size of Fire Box, inches: Length for Coal	Width	Depth	Length for Wood	Capacity of Reservoir in quarts	Pipe to fit Collar	Height, inches	Shipping Weight	Price
22P350	7-18	No. 7	17½x14½x11½	22x42 inches	12½	7½	6½	18	13½	7 inches	28	388 lbs.	$14.31
22P351	8-18	No. 8	17½x14½x11½	22x42 inches	12½	7½	6½	18	13½	7 inches	28	388 lbs.	14.56
22P352	7-20	No. 7	19½x16½x12	23x45 inches	15	8½	7	19	22	7 inches	30	445 lbs.	16.49
22P353	8-20	No. 8	19½x16½x12	23x45 inches	15	8½	7	19	22	7 inches	30	445 lbs.	16.75
22P354	9-20	No. 9	19½x16½x12	23x45 inches	15	8½	7	19	22	7 inches	30	445 lbs.	17.03
22P355	8-22	No. 8	21½x18½x12½	25x46 inches	17	8½	8	21	22	7 inches	31	489 lbs.	19.24
22P356	9-22	No. 9	21½x18½x12½	25x46 inches	17	8½	8	21	22	7 inches	31	489 lbs.	19.52

WITHOUT RESERVOIR, BUT WITH END SHELF INSTEAD, AS SHOWN IN THE SMALL ILLUSTRATION, othewise the exact same stove as shown in the large illustration, the latest 1907 model four-hole Acme Imperial square oven, nickel trimmed and nickel mounted combination coal and wood burning stove.

Prices, strongly crated and delivered on the cars at our foundry in Newark, Ohio.

Catalogue Number	Stove No.	Size of Lids	Size of Oven, inches	Top, not measuring End Shelf	Size of End Shelf	Size of Fire Box, inches: Length for Coal	Width	Depth	Length for Wood	Pipe to fit Collar	Height inches	Shipping Weight	Price
22P357	7-18	No. 7	17½x14½x11½	22x31 in.	8x22 in.	12½	7½	6½	18	7 in.	28	332 lbs.	$12.51
22P358	8-18	No. 8	17½x14½x11½	22x31 in.	8x22 in.	12½	7½	6½	18	7 in.	28	332 lbs.	12.78
22P359	7-20	No. 7	19½x16½x12	23x33 in.	9x23 in.	15	8½	7	19	7 in.	30	363 lbs.	14.16
22P360	8-20	No 8	19½x16½x12	23x33 in.	9x23 in.	15	8½	7	19	7 in.	30	363 lbs.	14.43
22P361	9-20	No. 9	19½x16½x12	23x33 in.	9x23 in.	15	8½	7	19	7 in.	30	363 lbs.	14.71
22P362	8-22	No. 8	21½x18½x12½	25x35 in.	9x25 in.	17	8½	8	21	7 in.	31	408 lbs.	16.35
22P363	9-22	No. 9	21½x18½x12½	25x35 in.	9x25 in.	17	8½	8	21	7 in.	31	408 lbs.	16.63

YOUR MONEY WILL BE IMMEDIATELY RETURNED TO YOU FOR ANY GOODS NOT PERFECTLY SATISFACTORY.

$17.95 OUR BIG ACME GRAND SIX-HOLE RANGE

FOR COAL, WOOD, CORN COBS, COKE OR ANY KIND OF FUEL

THIS IS OUR HIGH GRADE, NEW STYLE, UP TO DATE, HANDSOME CAST IRON RANGE. We use nothing but the highest grade stove plate, Birmingham iron; nothing but 72-hour coke for melting; we employ only the most skilled union moulders; our polishing and grinding is all done by automatic machinery (not accomplished by the hand work of other makers); our nickeling is higher grade than you will find on any other stove; the castings we turn out will, by reason of the iron we use and the way it is moulded, stand more strain, is less liable to warp or crack than any other stove plate made.

$17.95 AND UPWARD, ACCORDING TO SIZE. At this special price we furnish this stove, for coal or wood, exactly as illustrated and described, complete with high back and shelf and porcelain lined reservoir, the same delivered on board cars at our foundry at Newark, Ohio, from which point you must pay the freight. The stove, complete as illustrated, weighs from 410 to 450 pounds and the freight will average, for 500 miles, from $1.50 to $2.00 (greater or less distances in proportion); so you see the freight charges will amount to next to nothing compared with what you will save in price.

PLEASE REMEMBER, our special price, $17.95 and upward, according to size, is for the stove exactly as illustrated and does not include pipe or cooking utensils. For prices on stove furniture, pipe and cooking utensils, see pages 419 to 422.

DESCRIPTION

THE OVEN DOOR is tin lined.

THE MAIN TOP, SHELF and HEARTH EDGES are plain black and easily kept clean.

THE FIRE BOX is of correct shape, with large size fire chamber to give wonderful service.

THE DUPLEX GRATE is absolutely the best made, gives free access of air to all parts of the fuel. It is so constructed that the grate will burn coal only or both coal and wood. A half turn of the shaker crank reverses the grate for wood or coal. An extension lengthens the fire box when end coal linings are removed and very long wood can be burned.

BE SURE TO STATE THE KIND OF FUEL USED.

WATER FRONTS for the Acme Grand. Extra, $2.00

Do not mistake water fronts for water reservoirs. Water fronts are used only where there is a water supply furnished with constant pressure through pipes, which can only be obtained in large towns or cities having water works or elevated pressure tanks.

See page 371 about hot water fronts. If desired without high shelf, deduct $1.25

$15.45 TO $17.91

IF WANTED WITHOUT RESERVOIR BUT WITH HIGH SHELF (JUST LIKE THE SMALL PICTURE), DEDUCT $2.50 FROM THE PRICE OF ANY SIZE.

BY OUR FREE TRIAL OFFER you can order this range, enclose our price and we will send it to you with the understanding and agreement that you can give it thirty days' trial in your own home, and if for any reason you become dissatisfied with your purchase, if you do not find, after comparing it with stoves sold by others at double the price we ask for it, a better stove than you could get elsewhere at a saving of $10.00 to $15.00, you can return the stove to us at our expense and we will return your money, together with any freight charges paid by you.

BIG STOCK READY FOR IMMEDIATE SHIPMENT

THIS BIG square oven, high shelf, reservoir range in the very handsome design shown, the latest rococo pattern mounted on a rich rococo base; has a large square oven with deep nickel plated outside oven shelf; large rococo high back shelf with nickel plated teapot holders; six-hole top with one graduated lid and five solid covers; deep porcelain lined reservoir. It is handsomely nickel trimmed.

ABOUT REPAIRS. Understand, we can always furnish you repairs for any stove we sell in any of the years to come, and always at foundry cost.

Prices, with Reservoir and High Shelf, delivered, strongly crated, on the cars at our Newark, Ohio, foundry:

Catalogue Number	Range No.	Size of Lids	Size of Oven, inches	Size of Top, Measuring Reservoir, inches	Size of Fire Box, inches: Length for Coal	Width	Depth	Length for Wood	Capacity of Reservoir in quarts	Height to Main Top, inches	Size of Pipe Collar, ins.	Shipping Weight, pounds	Price
22L357	8-19	No. 8	18x18 x12	43½x27	15	9½	5½	20	17	29½	7	410	$17.95
22L358	8-21	No. 8	20x19¾x12½	46 x28½	17½	9½	5½	21½	17	30½	7	450	20.11
22L359	9-21	No. 9	20x19¾x12½	46 x28½	17½	9½	5½	21½	17	30½	7	450	20.41

$10.95 AND UP With Reservoir NEW IMPROVED HIGH GRADE FOUR HOLE ACME GLOBE COOK STOVE

COMPLETE WITH PORCELAIN LINED RESERVOIR, EXACTLY AS ILLUSTRATED BELOW.

A Reservoir Cook Stove for Coal or Wood, Burns Anything, Hard Coal, Soft Coal, Coke, Wood, or Anything Used for Fuel.

GREAT PRICE REDUCTION

FROM THIS ILLUSTRATION you can get a good idea of the appearance of this handsome new pouch feed coal and wood burning reservoir cook stove which we furnish at from $10.95 to $13.81, according to size.

Our Acme Globe Reservoir Stove, as illustrated is one of our big leaders. It is one of the greatest values that goes out of our foundry, is equal to stoves that sell generally at double our prices, and is sold to you under our thirty days' free trial offer.

IF WANTED WITHOUT RESERVOIR, TAKE OFF $2.00 FROM THE PRICE OF ANY SIZE.

DESCRIPTION.

MAIN TOP is fitted together in a manner to overcome warping; has heavy cut centers, supported by post, with heavy corners.

ASH PIT DOOR is substantially mounted, supplied with check draft to control the fire.

THE HEARTH. Full draw hearth, sufficiently large for the easy removal of the large ash pan.

FIRE BOX has heavy linings, with very heavy sectional coal fire back, is fitted with a convenient and substantial flat dump grate, and with every stove we include, free of all cost, an extra flat dump grate and fire back for wood. Can be easily converted for burning coal or wood.

THE FIRE DOOR is large and opens the full size of the fire box.

THE POUCH FEED mounted to the front of the main top is very convenient for putting in coal, when coal is used as fuel.

THE OVEN will be found unequaled in baking and roasting qualities, is well constructed and well fitted, and finished with handsome oven shelf.

OVEN DOORS—The Acme Globe has two oven doors, tin lined, handsomely nickeled door knobs. The right hand door has foot trip, by the use of which the door may be opened while the hands are full.

THE RESERVOIR—The reservoir casing is made of extra quality stove plate, and the tank is white porcelain lined.

WITHOUT RESERVOIR, but with broad end shelf instead, we furnish this first class cook stove at a reduction of $2.00 from prices quoted below.

We furnish this handsome, new Acme Globe Reservoir Coal and Wood Burning Stove in five sizes, as listed below, securely crated and delivered on the cars at our foundry at Newark, Ohio.

Catalogue Number	Stove Number	Size of Lids	Size of Oven, inches	Size of Top, Including Reservoir	Height, inches	Pipe to Fit Collar, in.	Size of Fire Box, in.: Length for Coal	Width	Depth	Length for Wood	Capacity Reservoir, qts.	Weight, lbs.	PRICE
22L379	7-14	7	13¼x13x9	20½x36	24	6	12	6	4½	15	9½	244	$10.95
22L380	7-16	7	16x14½x10	22x40	26½	6	14	6½	5	17	11½	290	11.81
22L381	8-16	8	16x14½x10	24x44	26½	6	14	6½	5	17	11½	290	12.06
22L382	8-18	8	18x17x11	24x44	28½	7	16	7	5½	19	13½	335	13.56
22L383	9-18	9	18x17x11	22x40	28½	7	16	7	5½	19	13½	335	13.81

Without Reservoir $2.00 less on any size.

OUR 30 DAYS' FREE TRIAL OFFER. All stoves are shipped with the understanding and agreement that they can be given 30 days' trial in your own home, and if you do not find, after using the stove thirty days, that it is better than any stove you could buy from your dealer at home and perfectly satisfactory in every way, you can return the stove to us at our expense and we will immediately return your money, together with any freight charges paid by you.

$10.95 AND UP WITH RESERVOIR AS ILLUSTRATED

WEHRLE MODEL No. 50 FOUR HOLE CAST COOK STOVE

ANOTHER HIGH GRADE STOVE with the name WEHRLE on it. The illustration, engraved by our artist from a photograph, is an exact reproduction of our new Wehrle Model No. 50 Four-Hole Combination Coal and Wood or Exclusive Wood Burning Cast Cook Stove. It is substantially built, reinforced, stayed and braced.

LOWEST PRICE EVER KNOWN.

DESCRIPTION

THE MAIN TOP has a large cooking surface. It is sectional to allow for expansion and contraction without fire cracking. It has four cooking holes; the centers and covers are extra heavy; the long center piece is cut to prevent warping or sagging and is well supported by a center post.

THE FEED OR BROILER DOOR in front of the main top fits flush, is large and so arranged that coal can be fed to the flames or a broiler may be inserted over the bed of red hot coals.

THE ASH PIT DOOR is provided with a check draft to control the fire.

THE HEARTH. The hearth top draws out the full width and exposes to view the full size of the ash pit, making it extremely easy to remove the ash pan and also giving access to the flue stopper behind the ash pan through which to clean soot and dust from under the oven.

THE FIRE BOX has an extra heavy fire back in three sections, which enables the user to replace one section when necessary without purchasing an entire new fire back.

THE WOOD FIRE DOOR is the full size of the fire box.

THE OVEN is full size. All the space therein is available and it will bake the largest loaf of bread to the nicest even brown on both top and bottom.

THE GRATE. We furnish two grates, a wood grate and a coal grate, which may be instantly changed one for the other.

THE OVEN DOORS. This stove is furnished with an oven door on each side of the stove and a handsome oven shelf on the right hand side. The right oven door has an automatic opener, which enables the user to open the door with the foot when the hand is occupied with bread pans to be placed in the oven.

THE RESERVOIR CASING is made of extra quality stove plate.

THE RESERVOIR TANK is of large capacity, white enameled and easy to keep clean.

Prices, with Reservoir, delivered, strongly crated, on cars at our Newark, Ohio, foundry:

Catalogue No.	Stove No.	Size of Lids	Size of Oven, inches	Size of Top, Including Reservoir, inches	Capacity of Reservoir, quarts	Pipe to Fit Collar, ins.	Height to Main Top, inches	Size of Fire Box, inches: Length for Coal	Width	Depth	L'th for Wood	Shipping Weight, lbs.	Price for Coal and Wood	Price for Wood Only
22L367	8-14	8	11x14 x 9	36x20½	9½	6	26½	12½	8½	5½	16	275	$12.41	$12.33
22L368	8-16	8	13x16 x11	38x22½	11½	6	28½	14½	8½	5½	18	295	12.81	12.74
22L369	8-18	8	15x17½x11	40x22½	11½	6	28½	14½	8½	5½	18	325	14.31	14.22
22L370	9-18	9	15x17½x11	40x22½	11½	6	28½	14½	8½	5½	18	325	14.56	14.48
22L371	8-20	8	17x19½x12	42x24½	13	7	29½	16	8½	5½	20	340	15.58	15.47
22L372	9-20	9	17x19½x12	42x24½	13	7	29½	16	8½	5½	20	340	15.98	15.87

WHEN ORDERING this Wehrle Model No. 50 Stove, please be sure to specify in your letter or in your order the kind of fuel you use. Say whether you wish a combination stove for coal and wood, as illustrated, or a stove for wood only. When ordered for wood only, the coal feed door is omitted, as the wood is fed through the end fire door.

$12.41 AND UP ACCORDING TO SIZE

PLEASE REMEMBER, we accept your order for this Wehrle Model No. 50 four-hole combination coal and wood cast cook stove to be shipped with the distinct understanding and agreement that, if it is not perfectly satisfactory after giving it thirty days' trial, you can return it to us at our expense and we will immediately return your money together with any freight charges paid by you.

WITHOUT RESERVOIR. This exact same splendid four-hole cast iron cook stove, of the same high standard of construction but without the reservoir, of which a broad end shelf takes the place, just as shown in the small illustration to the right, furnished at the special prices listed below.

PRICES, WITHOUT RESERVOIR, AS SHOWN IN SMALL ILLUSTRATION, STRONGLY CRATED AND DELIVERED ON THE CARS AT OUR NEWARK, OHIO, FOUNDRY.
Made in six sizes as listed below.

Catalogue No.	Stove No.	Size of Lids	Size of Oven, inches	Size of Top Including End Shelf, inches	Size of End Shelf, inches	Pipe to Fit Collar	Height to Main Top, in.	Size of Fire Box, inches: Length for Coal	Width	Depth	Length for Wood	Shipping Weight, lbs.	Price for Coal and Wood	Price for Wood Only
22L373	8-14	8	11x14 x 9	20½x33	7x20½	6	26½	12½	8½	5½	16	265	$10.43	$10.35
22L374	8-16	8	13x16 x11	22½x35	7x22½	6	28½	14½	8½	5½	18	280	10.80	10.71
22L375	8-18	8	15x17½x11	22½x37	7x22½	6	28½	14½	8½	5½	18	293	12.36	12.24
22L376	9-18	8	15x17½x11	22½x37	7x22½	6	28½	14½	8½	5½	18	293	12.55	12.47
22L377	8-20	9	17x19½x12	24½x38½	7x24½	7	29½	16	8½	5½	20	315	13.57	13.49
22L378	9-20	9	17x19½x12	24½x38½	7x24½	7	29½	16	8½	5½	20	315	14.01	13.89

$10.43 AND UP, ACCORDING TO SIZE

No. 22L373 to No. 22L378

WE HAVE ENORMOUS STOCKS of this our Wehrle Model No. 50, on hand securely crated and ready for immediate shipment.

$8.81 BUYS OUR $10.98 BUYS THE WEHRLE MODEL No. 52 FOUR-HOLE CAST COOK STOVE FOR WOOD ONLY / COMBINATION STOVE FOR COAL AND WOOD EXACTLY AS ILLUSTRATED. A LEADER IN PRICE!

$8.81 is absolutely the lowest price ever made on a four-hole cast cook stove and we know it is a lower price than any other foundry could possibly make and offer a stove that would begin to compare with this in quality of materials, draft control, accurate fitting and general design.

$5.71 AS ILLUSTRATED WITHOUT RESERVOIR

DESCRIPTION.

THE MAIN TOP, COVERS AND CENTERS are heavy and durable; are made of No. 1 pig iron.

When you buy a stove from us you get the best that can be made, in material, construction and design.

THE FIRE BOX is large and exactly the length shown opposite each catalogue number and price. It is fitted with a convenient and substantial flat dump grate. Each stove is equipped with an extra flat grate for burning wood and can be easily converted for burning either coal or wood. To change for wood, remove both end linings and dump grate and put in place of the dump grate the extra flat wood grate.

THE OVEN is commodious and measures exactly as we state but without including the swell of the oven doors, of which there are two—one on each side.

THE ASH PIT DOOR swings to the left and is supplied with slide draft to control the fire.

THIS IS A WONDERFUL VALUE in a splendid four-hole combination coal and wood or exclusive wood burning cook stove, and clearly demonstrates our ability to build the world's best stoves at the lowest prices ever named. In offering this dependable low priced four-hole rococo design combination coal and wood or exclusive wood cook stove, we present an entirely new set of patterns for the use of those who desire to make only a small investment.

$8.81

No. 22L390
Price for wood only......$8.81
Price for coal and wood ..$10.98

WEHRLE MODEL No. 52 COMBINATION COAL AND WOOD OR EXCLUSIVE WOOD BURNING FOUR-HOLE CAST COOK STOVE, WITH RESERVOIR.

Prices, delivered on the cars at our foundry at Newark, Ohio.

Catalogue No.	Stove No.	Size of Lids	Size of Oven, inches	Size of Main Top, Including Reservoir, inches	Height to Main Top, in.	Pipe to fit Collar, in.	Capacity of Reservoir, quarts	Size of Fire Box: Length for Coal, in.	Width, in.	Depth, in.	Length for Wood, in.	Shipping Weight, pounds	Price for Coal and Wood	Price for Wood Only
22L390	8-18	8	18x15x10	22½x37	26	6	11½	17	7	5	19	265	$10.98	$8.81

WEHRLE MODEL No. 52 without reservoir but with same extension shelf, on all sizes with exception of catalogue No. 22L391, size No. 7-14, as shown in small illustration, otherwise the exact size stove as shown in the large illustration, with four-hole top, the highest grade 1909 construction combination coal and wood or exclusive wood burning stove. We furnish your choice in the 14, 16 and 18 sizes at $5.71 to $7.71 for wood only and $6.72 to $8.92 for coal and wood, as listed below, delivered on board the cars at our Newark, Ohio, foundry.

Prices do not include pipe or cooking utensils. For cooking utensils see pages 419 to 422. Oven measurements do not include the swell of oven doors.

$5.71 FOR WOOD ONLY
$6.72 AND UP FOR COAL AND WOOD

A Wonderful Stove Value

Catalogue No.	Stove No.	Size of Lids	Size of Oven, inches	Main Top Without End Shelf, inches	Size of End Shelf	Height, inches	Size of Fire Box, inches: Length for Coal	Width	Depth	Length for Wood	Shipping Wt., pounds	Price for Coal and Wood	Price for Wood Only
22L391	7-14	7	13¾x11½x 9½	19½x23	4x19	24½	14	7	5	16	150	$6.72	$5.71
22L392	8-16	8	15 x13½x10	21½x24½	4x20	25½	16	7	5	18	175	7.82	6.71
22L393	8-18	8	18 x15 x10	22½x26¾	4x21	26	17	7	5	19	195	8.92	7.71

All sizes take 6-inch pipe.

WHEN ORDERING A WEHRLE MODEL No. 52 STOVE be sure to specify in your letter and in your order the kind of fuel you use. Say whether you wish a combination stove for coal and wood, as illustrated, or a stove for wood only. When ordered for wood only the swing front feed door is omitted, as the wood is fed through the end fire door next to the oven.

GAS COOKING STOVES.

GAS HOT PLATES FROM 25c to $2.00. | GAS RANGES ON NEXT PAGE, $11.50 to $21.30. | Gas Cookers from $4.50 to $6.60. Gas Rangettes from $9.00 to $11.40.

IN OFFERING THIS SPLENDID LINE OF GAS COOKING STOVES AND RANGETTES

AT SUCH LOW PRICES, we are endeavoring to give our gas consuming customers the benefit of the cost of material and labor with but our one small percentage of profit added. With gas hot plates at from 25 cents to $2.00, gas cookers with ovens from $4.50 to $6.60, and the little ranges or gas rangettes from $9.00 to $11.40, you will find the assortment second to none in the world. These gas stoves cannot be used with gasoline gas.

ON THE NEXT PAGE IS OUR LINE OF THE WORLD'S BEST GAS RANGES.

Nursery Gas Plate.

No. 22C556 Single Burner Gas Plate. Suitable for nursery use, warming water for shaving or cooking anything in a small vessel. Black iron. Size, 6x3½ inches. Weight, 2 pounds. Price. 25c

Gas Hot Plates.

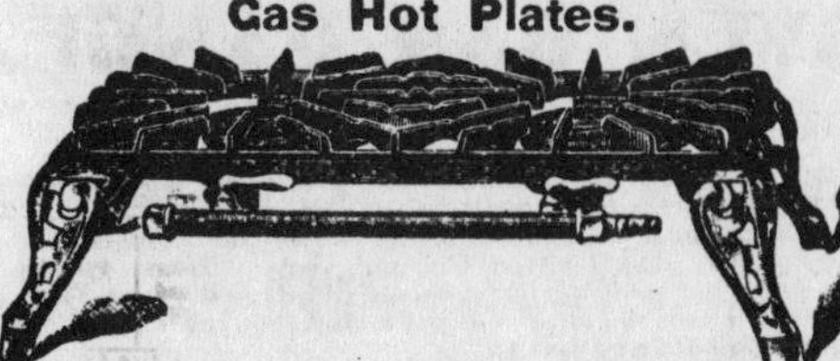

This Gas Hot Plate with two or three burners can be placed on a table or the top of your cooking stove and connected with the gas light fixture by the rubber tube quoted below as No. 22C563. It will cook over each burner just as well as over the burner on the highest priced gas range; the two-burner measures 9x18 inches and weighs 10 pounds and the three-burner measures 9x26¾ inches and weighs 16 pounds. Frame is 5¾ inches high, aluminum finished with nickel legs. A high grade stove. Material and workmanship the best. Will last a lifetime. The burners give a hot flame with two rings of jets, which are directed so as to have the most effect on the cooking utensils above.

No. 22C558 Two burners. Price........... $1.05
No. 22C559 Three burners. Price........... 1.60

Always state whether stoves are intended to be used for natural or artificial gas when writing your order. These gas stoves cannot be used with gasoline gas.

Gas Hot Plates.

This Gas Hot Plate is a handsomer pattern than those shown above and has a larger top. It is made with two or three burners as desired; the two-burner measures 11x20¾ inches and weighs 14 pounds and the three-burner measures 11x30 inches and weighs 18 pounds. Frame is 7 inches high, black japanned, with nickel legs and levers. The top surface is large and so arranged that pots and pans can be slid over it in any direction. The burner has a loose cap and gives two rings of flame.

No. 22C561 Two burners. Price.......... $1.35
No. 22C562 Three burners. Price........... 2.00

Always state whether stoves are intended to be used for natural or artificial gas when writing your order. These gas stoves cannot be used with gasoline gas.

Gas Stove Tubing.

No. 22C563 Flexible Patent End Gas Stove Tubing. Inner tubing made of pure rubber, outside covering is made of braided mohair; will not crack or break. Comes in 4, 5, 6, 8 and 10-foot pieces.

Price, per foot.. 3½c

Saves About Half the Price.

Bradford, Pa.

Sears, Roebuck & Co., Chicago, Ill.

Gentlemen: Some time ago I ordered a gas stove and got it in good order, and am pleased with it. Saved about half on the price. I could not get an inferior stove for twice the price in stores here and near by. I will always be glad to order from you in the future. Yours truly,

THOMAS FISHER.

No Fault to Find.

Youngstown, O.

Sears, Roebuck & Co., Chicago, Ill.

Dear Sirs: The gas stove I purchased from you was received in good condition and is in every way just as you represented it to be. It is a beauty, a grand baker, and takes but little fuel. I have had it almost one year and have no fault to find with it. I think it is the grandest and best stove I ever saw. I could not have purchased a stove like it here for less than double the price. I am well pleased with it. I am,

Yours respectfully,
MRS. MARY SMITH.

$4.50 Gas Cooker.

No. 22C564 With 2 regular cooker burners and burner under oven. The oven in this gas cooker will do as fine work as the most expensive gas range oven, as it is built on practical lines, but being made of sheet steel reduces the cost and enables you to have a two-burner gas range at $4.50. This cooker can be connected with flexible rubber tubing as described under No. 22C563, or it can be connected with gas pipe as desired. First class baking is guaranteed. **STOVE No. 02.** Height, 27½ inches. Top, 24x16½ inches. Oven, 16 inches wide, 12 inches high and 12 inches deep. Oven is a quick and splendid baker. Connect with rubber tubing or gas pipe as desired. Weight, crated, 49 pounds. Rubber tubing extra, see No. 22C563.

No. 22C564 Price, as shown.......................... $4.50

Always state whether stoves are intended to be used for natural or artificial gas when writing your order. These gas stoves cannot be used with gasoline gas.

$5.40 to $6.60 Gas Cookers.

Regular Range Standard Star Burners, same as used in the highest priced gas ranges. The ovens are made with double flues and galvanized tops. This large gas cooker possesses all the first class features of the gas ranges and will do the work done by the best gas range ever produced. It is made with two burners, three burners or four burners on top as desired and one burner under the oven. The main top and the top burners are exactly the same—large powerful burners as those used on our world's best gas ranges. Send us your order and if you are not satisfied you can return the cooker to us at any time within 30 days and your money will be refunded, together with any freight you may have paid.

STOVE No. 2. Height, 30 inches. Top, 24¼x21½ inches. Oven, 18 inches wide, 12 inches high and 12 inches deep. With two burners on top and one burner under oven. Wgt. crated 60 lbs.

No. 22C565 Price.......................... $5.40

STOVE No. 3. As shown in illustration. Height, 30 inches. Top, 24¼x21½ inches. Oven, 18 inches wide, 12 inches high and 12 inches deep. With three burners on top and one burner under oven. Weight, crated, 76 pounds.

No. 22C566 Price.......................... $6.00

STOVE No. 4. Height, 30 inches. Top, 24¼x21½ inches. Oven, 18 inches wide, 12 inches high and 12 inches deep. With four burners on top and one burner under oven. Weight, crated, 83 lbs.

No. 22C567 Price.......................... $6.60

Always state whether stoves are intended to be used for natural or artificial gas when writing your order. These gas stoves cannot be used with gasoline gas.

Gas Rangettes.

For either natural gas or manufactured gas as required. With four burners on top and two-line burner under oven. In offering this gas range at $9.00 and $9.60, according to the kind of gas used, we have met a demand for a lower priced but high class small gas range which has all the good qualities of any gas range made with the defects of none. These low prices are the result of manufacturing large quantities, giving you the benefit of the cost of the material and labor with but our one small percentage of profit added. Try one and your neighbors will want one like it. If not perfectly satisfactory in every respect you can return it to us any time within 30 days and your money will be refunded, together with the freight you have paid.

Our Elegant Low Broiler Rangette.

STOVE No. 16. Has four powerful star burners, one of which is extra large, making it of double power, also simmering burner. Height from floor to main top, 31 inches. Top, 23x23 inches, with two side shelves 6 inches wide. Oven 16x16 inches and 14¼ inches high. Body and oven made of cold rolled steel plate. Has nickeled oven door frame, panel and handle. Furnished with closed top for natural gas, and open grates (as shown) for artificial gas. Weight, crated, 130 pounds.

No. 22C568 For manufactured gas. Price. $9.00
No. 22C569 For natural gas. Price....... 9.60

AT $10.80 AND $11.40. For either natural or manufactured gas as ordered. In offering this little range or rangette, with a low broiler we have enabled our customers to buy a modest priced but handsome small range without being deprived of a broiling oven. The baking oven is 16x16x11 inches and the broiling oven is 16x16x5 inches. This gives ample room for baking and a splendid broiling oven also. Oven door is lined, has cast iron oven bottom and direct action oven. It is fitted with wood handled lever valves and four powerful removable star top burners, the right hand front one extra large, making it of double power, also simmering burner and a perfect broiling and baking burner. Each and every one of these rangettes have our binding guarantee the same as the big gas ranges on the next page. They have all the advantage of the full size ranges excepting in size. See page 14 for our C. O. D. subject to examination offer. If you order one of these rangettes and do not feel perfectly satisfied you can return it any time within thirty days and your money will be refunded, together with any freight you may have paid.

STOVE No. 160. Height from floor to main top, 31 inches. Top 23x23, with two side shelves 6 inches wide. Oven, 16x16 inches and 11 inches high. Broiler, 16x16 inches and 5 inches high. Body and oven made of cold rolled steel plate. Has nickeled oven door frame, panel and handle, nickeled front supply pipe. Furnished with closed top for natural gas and open grates (as shown) for artificial gas. Weight, crated, 135 pounds.

No. 22C570 For manufactured gas.
Price.. $10.80
No. 22C571 For natural gas. Price..... 11.40

SEE NEXT PAGE FOR THE WORLD'S FINEST GAS RANGES.

THE WORLD'S BEST GAS RANGES AT $11.50 TO $21.30

Furnished for either Artificial or Natural Gas and for any Pressure Desired.

THE ACME OF PERFECTION IN GAS SAVING GAS RANGES. Only the best materials are used; the highest grade of polished steel, of beautiful color, not requiring blacking or Japan, the highest finish of smooth, strong stove plate castings, made in a factory noted for the quality of material used. Every range is guaranteed to be perfect in operation and workmanship. The illustrations do not do justice to these elegant goods; they must be seen to be appreciated. We court inspection and comparison with any gas ranges in the market. These ranges are built for economy in fuel. They can be set near an open window or door without being affected by the draft, as the sides are closed all around. Quality in construction is first with us, and the large quantities we produce enables us to sell them at these unheard of prices, $11.50 to $21.30, for the various sizes and styles described; it is the actual cost to us in large quantities with but our one small percentage of profit added.

YOUR GAS COMPANY WILL CONNECT IT FOR YOU at the same small charge they always make when bought from them. Gas companies are always glad to connect our ranges, as they are desirous of selling their product of gas and not anxious to be dealers in gas stoves. They had to go into the gas stove business because the high prices asked by the stove and hardware dealers included so much profit the people did not buy them, thus restricting the consumption of gas, but our prices are so low and we sell so many ranges the gas companies are our friends, encouraging us to sell more and more gas ranges, connecting them for our customers for the same small fee they charge when they sell a gas range, and recommending our ranges everywhere as the most economical, durable and efficient ranges to be found.

The more ranges we sell the more gas they sell, and the consumer is the better pleased on account of the beautiful range at such a low price as $11.50 to $21.30, as described above.

SINGLE OVEN GAS RANGE.

WITH COUNTERBALANCED DROP OVEN DOOR.

AT $11.50 AND $12.98 we offer this famous single oven gas range at prices lower than the lowest, lower than any one can offer them, lower than any gas company cares to sell them, so low that gas companies are buying them from us and are proud to connect them for you at a small fee, and so low that it relieves them of the expense and trouble of trying to sell gas ranges, for we are selling them so fast they are kept busy increasing their facilities and capacity for supplying gas.

They are recommending our gas ranges for economy, good service and low prices. The range is excellence itself, and as handsome as it is good. Has three Standard Star burners, one triple capacity Giant burner with simmering burner in center and lighting separately. Four-line burner for oven, and oven lighter. The illustration shows it ready for manufactured gas. When ordered for natural gas, we furnish it with closed lids or griddle covers.

SEE PAGE 14 FOR OUR LIBERAL $1.00 TO $5.00 C. O. D. SUBJECT TO EXAMINATION OFFER.

PRICE LIST SINGLE OVEN GAS RANGE.
Do not fail to state whether you use manufactured gas or natural gas.

Catalogue Number	Stove No.	Size of Top, Including End Shelves, Inches	Size of Oven, inches	Height from Floor, inches	Shipping Weight, pounds	Price
22C572	416P	35½x22¼	16x16¼x11	29¼	162	$11.50
22C573	418P	37½x22¼	18x16¼x11	29¼	170	12.98

SINGLE OVEN GAS RANGE.

WITH WATER HEATER EXTENSION, CONTAINING WATER COIL TO BE CONNECTED TO A RANGE BOILER HAVING CITY WATER PRESSURE.

AT $16.50 AND $17.98 we offer this famous single oven and Water Heater Gas Range, with three Standard Star Burners and one triple capacity Giant Burner with one small simmering burner. These Standard Star Drilled Burners cannot be surpassed for durability and intense heat for cooking purposes excepting by our Giant burner. Our patent four-line oven burner equally distributes the heat, being the only "Bake Even" Gas Range in use.

The oven sides and bottom are flush with the oven door opening, the oven door is counter balanced and drops on a level with the oven bottom. It is smooth and free from anything to catch the pans when drawn from the oven. The top oven plate is double, forming a circulating flue for the heat, and is the best oven construction in use. The scavenger pan under the top burners catches all the grease and dirt; it is made of galvanized iron and easily removed. When ordered for natural gas, we furnish the range, with closed lids or griddle covers. Gas cocks are nickeled on brass.

SEE PAGE 14 FOR OUR LIBERAL $1.00 TO $5.00 C. O. D. SUBJECT TO EXAMINATION OFFER.

PRICE LIST SINGLE OVEN GAS RANGE.
Do not fail to state whether you use manufactured gas or natural gas.

Catalogue Number	Stove Number	Size of Top, Including Water Heater and End Shelf, Inches	Size of Oven, inches	Height from Floor	Shipping Weight	Price
22C576	416W	39½x22¼	16x16¼x11	29¼ inches	170 pounds	$16.50
22C577	418W	41½x22¼	18x16¼x11	29¼ inches	185 pounds	17.98

THESE RANGES ARE constructed of the best grade of polished steel of beautiful color. The sheet steel is lined with asbestos. The main top, main front and frame of oven doors are of the finest cast stove plate, made from the highest grades of pure pig iron, and must not be confused with the cheap mixtures of scrap iron used in so many other makes of gas ranges. The front supply pipe and cocks are nickeled.

GAS RANGE WITH LOW BROILING OVEN.

AT $14.40 AND $16.30 we offer this Drop Door Gas Range with low Broiler, in competition with the highest priced gas ranges in the world. They are gas savers and customer makers. This is the exact same range as Catalogue Nos. 22C572 and 22C573 at $11.50 and $12.98, with the addition of the low broiling oven, and is 3¼ and 4¼ inches higher. It has the exact same special points of interest to the user, as carefully described above, the same counter balanced oven door, the guarantee of efficiency and economy in the consumption of gas, and is sold at the heretofore unheard of price for such an elegant gas range of $14.40 and $16.30, according to size and attachments.

The four-line oven burner enables you to broil and bake both at the same time. This range costs a little more than the single oven range above but the difference is fully repaid by this saving. The illustration shows it ready for manufactured gas. When ordered for natural gas we furnish this range with closed lids or griddle covers.

SEE PAGE 14 FOR OUR LIBERAL $1.00 TO $5.00 C. O. D. SUBJECT TO EXAMINATION OFFER.

PRICE LIST LOW BROILER GAS RANGE.
Do not fail to state whether you use manufactured gas or natural gas.

Catalogue Number	Stove No.	Size of Top Including End Shelves. Inches	Baking Oven, inches	Broiling Oven, inches	Height from Floor	Shipping Weight	Price
22C574	116P	35½ x 22¼	16x16¼x11	16x16¼ x9¼	32½ in.	181 lbs.	$14.40
22C575	118P	37½ x 22¼	18x16¼x11	18x16¼ x9¼	33½ in.	193 lbs.	16.30

WE CAN ALWAYS FURNISH BURNERS AND REPAIR PARTS FOR GAS RANGES.

GAS RANGE WITH LOW BROILING OVEN.

WITH WATER HEATER EXTENSION CONTAINING WATER COIL TO BE CONNECTED TO A RANGE BOILER HAVING CITY WATER PRESSURE.

AT $19.40 AND $21.30 we offer this Drop Door Gas Range with Low Broiler, in competition with the highest priced gas ranges in the world. They are gas savers and customer makers. This is the exact same range as Catalogue Nos. 22C574 and 22C575 at $14.40 and $16.30, with the addition of the water heater extension, giving six cooking holes. It has the exact same special points of interest to the user, as carefully described above, the same spring balanced oven door, the guarantee of efficiency and economy in the consumption of gas, and is sold at the heretofore unheard of price for such an elegant gas range of $19.40 and $21.30, according to size and attachments. With four-line burner operating the baking and broiling ovens at same time.

The illustration shows it ready for manufactured gas. When ordered for natural gas we furnish this range with closed lids or griddle covers.

See page 14 for our liberal $1.00 to $5.00 C. O. D. subject to examination offer. We can always furnish Burners and Repair Parts for GAS RANGES.

PRICE LIST LOW BROILER GAS RANGE.
Do not fail to state whether you use manufactured gas or natural gas.

Catalogue Number	Stove Number	Size of Top, Including Water Heater and End Shelf, Inches	Baking Oven, inches	Broiling Oven, inches	Height from Floor	Shipping Weight	Price
22C578	116W	39¼x22¼	16x16¼x11	16x16½x9¼	32½ in.	205 lbs.	$19.40
22C579	118W	41½x22¼	18x16¼x11	18x16¼x9¼	33½ in.	225 lbs.	21.30

DETAILED DESCRIPTION OF OUR HARD COAL WEHRLE MODEL No. 100 BASE BURNER

MAIN BODY. The raw materials which enter into the construction of this WEHRLE MODEL are of the very best. The gray iron used in making the castings is of the very highest quality Birmingham iron, than which no better material is obtainable in the world.

EXTRA LARGE FIRE POT.—Special attention is called to our extraordinarily large size fire pot, being nearly the same width at the bottom as it is at the top, each size measuring at least 2 inches more than usually found in base burners of other makes and sold at double our price; in fact, no other manufacturer or dealer makes or offers a stove with an actual 18-inch fire pot. Observe the illustration on this page, showing the ease with which the fire pot may be removed from this base burner through the isinglass doors. It is not necessary to tip up the fire pot on its side and wrestle with it to remove it for repairs or overhauling. It is not necessary to unbolt any part of the stove. It slides straight outward and in this respect it is different from any other hard coal base burner on the market.

Extra Heavy Removable Fire Pot.

THE IMPROVED DUPLEX GRATE WITH SHAKING RING, as shown in illustration is hollow so that it cleans itself when dumped, cuts out the clinkers and dead ashes and has ample space to turn them into the large heavy wire bailed ash pan without crushing the clinkers or necessitating the use of a poker. It is this patent duplex shaker grate, exactly as shown in the picture to the right, which keeps the fire pot free from an accumulation of dead ashes, clinkers and cinders, which gives absolute control of the fire and makes this, our WEHRLE MODEL No. 100 Double Heating Self Feeding Hard Coal Base Burner, the most economical fuel consumer of any base burner in the market.

Famous WEHRLE Duplex Grate With Shaking Ring.

THE ARTISTIC OXIDIZED CAST IRON URN surmounting this handsome WEHRLE MODEL Base Burner is an original pattern with us and by far the most attractive and artistic design ever used on a base burner. By referring to the illustration on the opposite page it will readily be seen what a beautiful finished appearance it gives the stove. The chemical process of producing this oxidized finish is such that the lasting qualities are indestructible. The urn is securely fastened to the highly silver polished mirror finished swing top.

The Artistic Oxidized Cast Iron Urn.

THE SILVER NICKELED SWING TOP is perfectly plain and smooth, is surface ground, making an absolutely airtight joint over the magazine cover, and has a mirror finished silver nickel polish. To each corner is bolted a handsomely carved nickel finished leaf design ornament. It easily swings to the left, automatically lifting the coal magazine cover so that a fresh supply of fuel may be poured into the magazine below.

THE AUTOMATIC INNER MAGAZINE COVER which raises and falls with the swing of the top, forms a tight covering under the nickel top, affording a double protection from escaping gas and also preventing the nickel from tarnishing.

SELF FEEDING MAGAZINE. Special attention is called to the self feeding magazine, which is much larger than usually found in base burners. Its very generous proportions will supply the fire with sufficient coal to operate the stove for many hours without replenishing. It is built with a view to saving fuel and carrying coal enough at one filling to run the heater twenty-four to thirty-six hours.

THE ASH PIT AND ASH PAN are unusually large to provide against the accumulation of a large quantity of ashes and it is only necessary to empty the ash pan once a day when the stove is in ordinary use to prevent the accumulation of ashes against the grate above it. Many base burners are fitted with small ash pans which quickly fill up and there is, therefore, constant danger that the ashes will bank up against the grates and burn them out in a few hours' time unless the ashes are emptied frequently. This is a fault which we have wholly overcome in the WEHRLE MODEL No. 100.

THE ASH PIT DOOR is a handsome rococo pattern, securely mounted to the ash pit with silver nickel tipped hinge pins. In the center is a silver nickeled airtight screw draft register, giving perfect control of the fire, and ornamented with a very artistic contrast silver nickeled and satin finished wreath.

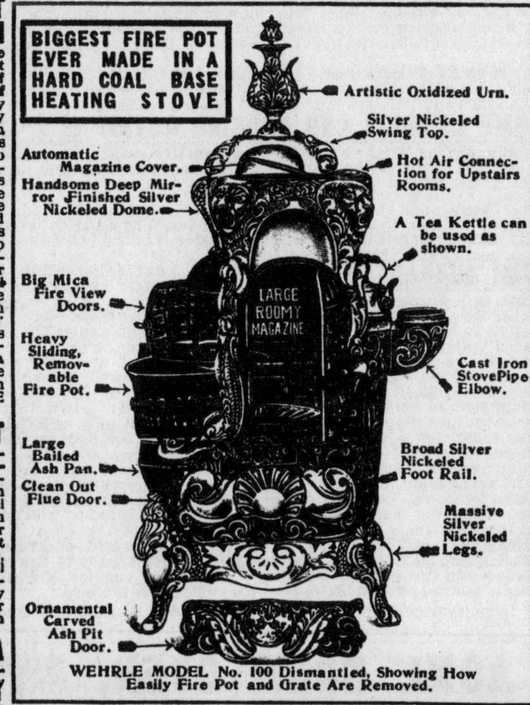

WEHRLE MODEL No. 100 Dismantled, Showing How Easily Fire Pot and Grate Are Removed.

THE MICA DOORS are securely fitted with recessed grooves, making an absolutely airtight joint, and by means of silver nickeled turnbuckles are held firmly in place, fastened to an extra heavy cast iron bar extending from the upper edge of the upper mica doors to the lower edge of the lower mica doors. This bar is securely bolted at both ends to the main front and forms a complete jamb for each door, and with these silver nickeled turnbuckles in the center of both the upper and lower doors, they are drawn up tightly and fit so perfectly that the hottest fire will not expand, warp or spring them out of place.

BRILLIANT MICA ILLUMINATION. The mica or isinglass illumination is full and complete on three sides of the stove. The mica is cut in uniform square pieces, making them easy to put in or replace. They are unobstructed by any iron ornaments, permitting all the light from the bright coals within the fire chamber to pass out into the room, producing absolutely the most cheerful heater in the world.

DOUBLE HEATING CONSTRUCTION. This special feature of our WEHRLE MODEL No. 100 Hard Coal Base Burner means heat for the main floor and living room and surplus heat for upstairs. As shown in the illustration, the hot air flue has a collar at the top, to which a pipe can be connected for carrying the heated air to the upper room. Double the circulation is thus obtained in the hot air flue of the WEHRLE MODEL No. 100, as all three sides of it come in direct contact with the heat from the smoke and flame flue.

THE ELEGANTLY MODELED SILVER NICKELED DOME. The brilliancy of this WEHRLE MODEL No. 100 Hard Coal Base Burner is enhanced by the large mirror finished silver nickeled reflector which surmounts the fire chamber. In designing the massive dome, our artist has given us something entirely new and different from that shown on any other base burner, and the beautiful silver nickeling is by our own patented silver nickeling process, producing an everlasting luster. The broad mirror finished silver nickeled reflectors immediately above the isinglass fire view doors catch the rays of light from the live coals within and give a brilliant illumination and an air of comfort and coziness to the room.

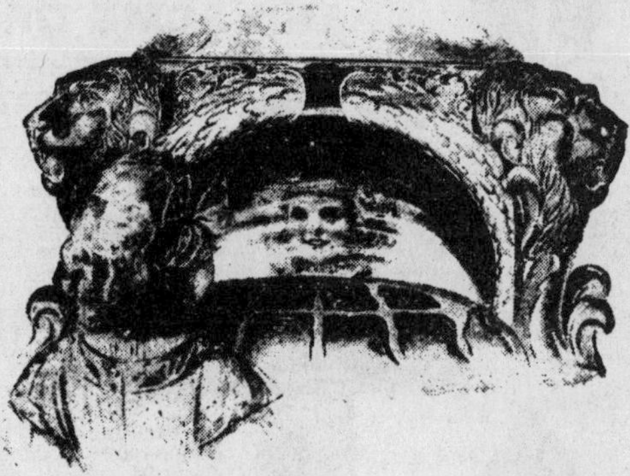

Beautifully Nickeled Mirror Finished Reflector.

THE SILVER NICKELING. Please observe how this magnificent heater sparkles from main top of dome to the base with dazzling nickel trimmings. The nickel plating is done by our own patented process, is so much heavier and finer than can possibly be found on stoves of other makes, and is preserved from tarnishing by an ingenious method which allows the air to circulate behind them, and, with only average care, the nickel parts will retain their brilliancy and luster the full life of the stove itself.

View Showing Fire Travel and Hot Air Flue.

THE WEHRLE SCIENTIFIC FLUE CONSTRUCTION. The base flues are hollowed out in the center, throwing the heat to the outside and increasing the radiating surface near the floor where it is most wanted. To the left may be seen an illustration showing how the heat and flames curl over the flue guards, the long fire travel, how the smoke and flames are forced to travel over 10 feet through the flues before reaching the stove pipe. This scientific flue construction gives us 100 square feet of heat radiating surface in the flues alone, the heat passing down the descending flues, then circling our new specially constructed flue bottom, and diffusing absolutely without loss, the heat product of combustion, ascending the flue at the right hand corner and swerving to the left and back at the smoke collar. This winding and circuitous way, coupled with the constant "staggering" of the heat and vast expanse of radiating surface with which every heat unit is brought into contact, produces unquestionably four times the usual base burner heating capacity. In addition to this we have the hot air circulation furnished by the hot air flue as shown in illustration.

THE HOT AIR FLUE extends from the base to the top of the stove. The cold air is drawn from the floor, circulating upward into the hollow projecting pocket, which forms the bottom flue partition, into the conduit between the ornamental projecting back flue and the always hot inside back that is in contact with the hottest product of the fire, until the superheated air passes out of the hot air collar which, when not used in connection with a pipe to an upper floor, is covered by a handsome openwork silver nickel cap. As a general thing, the heat arising from a hall adjacent to the base burner will be sufficient to heat the upper floor of a large house to a satisfactory temperature, but where it is desirable to centralize a large amount of heat at a given point above, the hot air is conducted from the hot air collar, as shown, by means of a pipe to rooms above and the room above will almost immediately be warmed.

This arrangement means heat for the main lower living rooms, bedrooms, dining room, hall and parlors, and surplus heat for upstairs.

THE DOUBLE REFLECTOR PANELS are made to fit accurately over the mica door section. The pattern is entirely new and was designed by one of the greatest stove artists in the world. The lower portion is perfectly smooth, silver nickel polished and mirror finished and the remaining or upper portion of the panels is artistically carved and with its satin nickel finish harmonizes with the bright silver nickel finish of all the other nickel parts. All four corners are ornamented with a handsome silver nickel casting, carved in a most artistic lion's head design.

THE FRONT SIDE ORNAMENTS OR PILASTERS. Every consideration has been given to the designing and building of this magnificent base burner, and we could go on indefinitely mentioning the points which make our WEHRLE MODEL No. 100 preeminent. In this connection let us call your attention to the unique and original dolphin design pilasters or side wings which ornament the front of the stove and which are tastefully carved, highly polished and in keeping with all the other elaborate nickel parts and ornamentation.

THE LARGE MASSIVE SIDE FOOT RAILS are cast in three parts, fastened together in the center with a cast plate of an artistic shell design, are easily attached to the sides of the stove, highly silver nickel polished, and like other nickeled parts, are noted for their smooth surface and lasting brilliance.

THE SILVER NICKELED BASE. In building this WEHRLE MODEL No. 100 Base Burner, nothing has been left undone, nothing has been omitted to make it THE STRONGEST, MOST DURABLE HEATER EVER MADE, and we cannot give stronger evidence of this fact than by referring you to the substantial high art full nickeled lower base, on which the main body of the stove rests. The front, back and side base strips and legs are elegantly carved, gorgeously silver nickeled.

The Handsome Silver Nickeled Corner Piece.

Made in five sizes, as listed below, securely crated ready for immediate shipment from our foundry at Newark, Ohio, or from a warehouse very near you.

Catalogue Number	Stove No.	Size of FirePot, inches	Height Floor to Urn Base, inches	Floor Space, inches	SizePipe Collar, inches	Shipping Weight, pounds	Size of Hot Air Collar	Price
22L394	12	12	48½	23½x23½	6	265	6 Inches	$26.95
22L395	13	13	51	24½x24½	6	315	6 Inches	28.98
22L396	14	14	53	26½x26½	6	365	6 Inches	30.98
22L397	16	16	55	28½x28½	6	425	7 Inches	33.96
22L398	18	18	58	30½x30½	6	500	7 Inches	36.98

$5.12 FOR OUR ACME LAUNDRY AND COOKING OUTFIT

COMPRISING ONE ACME PRIDE LAUNDRY STOVE, ONE JOINT OF PIPE AND ACME DRUM OVEN, ALL COMPLETE, READY TO USE.

THIS ILLUSTRATION shows our Combination Laundry and Cooking Outfit, an outfit made up of our standard Acme Pride Laundry Stove and our Acme Oven, which will appeal with irresistible force to every housewife. At this special value, $5.12 price, this combination outfit is wonderful value, and as a wash day convenience nothing can begin to compare with it. We have repeatedly had inquiries for just such an outfit as this and the demand was so general we prepared this combination and have been surprised at the general favor with which it has been received.

EVERY WOMAN who undertakes to have the family laundry done at home will appreciate the convenience and saving which this, our Acme Laundry and Cooking Outfit affords; it is a tremendous time saver, it is a great fuel saver and during the warm days of spring and summer and early fall it means more than a saving of time and fuel, because with one fire and that removed from the living section of the house, all the laundry work, as well as the cooking and baking, may be done in comfort.

IF YOU PURCHASE THIS, OUR ACME LAUNDRY AND COOKING OUTFIT, it will no longer be necessary for you to build a hot fire in the kitchen to prepare the noonday meal, it will not be necessary to leave your laundry work an hour or so earlier than you otherwise would to begin the noonday meal, but with this splendid outfit you may do your laundry work and your cooking and your baking with one fire in one room, without loss of time and without heating the living rooms of your home. The hot fire you have prepared to heat water for laundry purposes will at the same time bake bread or roast meat in the Acme Drum Oven above the stove, so that you may make laundry day baking day as well; the same fire will heat the tea kettle, will fry or broil meat or potatoes; it will do the general cooking necessary, and while the preparation of a meal is in course the sadirons may be heated for the ironing immediately after dinner. Every housewife knows what an economy such an arrangement will be, she will understand how many steps this will save her; she knows how much more convenient it will be for her to do her washing and cooking and baking all at once, either in the basement or in some outside building immediately adjoining the home. In most homes the laundry work is done in the basement, in others an open outdoor kitchen or shed is frequently used, and at the wonderfully low price at which we offer this, our Acme Laundry and Cooking Outfit, it will be possible for you to secure just such an outfit as will best serve your purpose at a cost considerably lower than you could purchase a cheap cast range, and when you note the special features of our **Acme Pride Laundry Stove,** which we furnish with this combination outfit, the large pouch feed door, the generous sized top, with its two No. 8 cooking holes, the special sadiron holders around the octagonal firepot of the stove we know that you will decide that this is an ideal laundry and cooking outfit, and one that will not only give you good service, but satisfactory service, and one that we guarantee to be strictly first class in every respect and so well and so thoroughly made of the very highest grade materials that it will last a lifetime.

IF YOU BUY FROM US, WE WILL SEND YOU A FREE PROFIT SHARING CERTIFICATE. SEE PAGES 1 AND 2.

THE LAUNDRY STOVE AND THE OVEN are made in our own stove works at Newark, Ohio, the largest stove foundry in the world, where we manufacture thousands at a time, and as this is only incidental to our other stove manufacturing operations, we are able to produce this combination laundry and cooking outfit at a manufacturing cost very much lower than any other foundry in the world could possibly manufacture them. In fact, at our $5.12 price, this, our Acme Laundry and Cooking Outfit, is offered to you, our customer, at retail, at a price less than other founders could produce this outfit and wholesale in carload lots. When you stop to consider the fact that we consume one thousand tons of pig iron a week, that we manufacture 1,000 finished stoves and ranges every working day in the year, you will readily understand why we are the largest buyers of raw materials, why we are able to secure such wonderfully low prices on every grade of pig iron, sheet steel, rivets, bolts, braces, etc., and why, with our wonderful stove making organization of twenty-six hundred expert stove builders, we are able to outdistance and outclass all other stove founders in the world.

REMEMBER, FURTHERMORE, that not only do we give you the advantage of our wonderful ability to produce the best stoves and ranges at the lowest manufacturing cost possible, but we sell these stoves and ranges to you at the mere cost of materials and labor, with our one small uniform margin of profit added, a profit which is lower than any other stove organization could accept and continue in business; just a few cents on each stove is a satisfactory profit to us, because of our enormous output and because also stoves and ranges are only a portion of the vast line of merchandise which we sell by catalogue. Therefore, this, our Acme Laundry and Cooking Outfit, goes to you at manufacturer's cost, plus a few cents representing a small profit, whereas other dealers at home or elsewhere would be compelled to ask you a much higher price on a combination outfit not nearly so good as this, because their prices represent a higher manufacturing cost, a larger profit to the manufacturer and then additional profits to the wholesaler, the jobber and the retailer, besides the heavy expenses of traveling men, two or three freight charges, etc.

WE OFFER THIS OUTFIT to you at manufacturer's cost, therefore, and it is decidedly to your advantage to place your order with us, as you will agree when we give you such a price advantage as is represented in our $5.12 price for this high grade combination laundry and cooking outfit.

IN OFFERING YOU THIS OUR ACME LAUNDRY AND COOKING OUTFIT at our wonderfully low $5.12 price, an outfit complete with one of the finest laundry stoves that we have in our entire catalogue, a laundry stove that is better than any laundry stove offered by any other founder no matter what its name, make or price, and offering with it our new improved 1907 model Acme Drum Oven with a joint of pipe for connection between the two, we tender you a laundry combination value which cannot be duplicated by any other manufacturing concern and we tender it as an outfit which will be found extremely satisfactory to every housewife for a multitude of purposes, and an outfit which will save untold steps, an outfit which will mean the handling of the laundry and the cooking at one time and assuring greater comfort during the hot summer days, an outfit which we believe will meet with a very large sale and one which we know our customers will appreciate as a combination outfit worthy of a place in any American Home.

IN THESE DAYS OF ADVANCEMENT IN ALL LINES, when the studied effort of manufacturers and dealers has been to anticipate the wants of the people and supply them with labor saving machinery and devices, to offer them greater conveniences than they have had heretofore, we believe that in our Acme Laundry and Cooking Outfit we bring to the housewife an opportunity to greatly lessen the labor, to greatly lessen the inconveniences of wash day and to secure what has come to be known as almost a necessity in every well appointed home. There is no reason why the labor saving appliances of the home, the conveniences for the wife and mother and housekeeper should not be just as up to date, should not be just as modern as the appliances for lessening labor on the farm or in the factory; and with our wonderful organization for the manufacture of this our Acme Laundry and Cooking Outfit, with our great ability to save in manufacturing costs, which advantage we give to you our customer, with our new selling methods which entirely eliminate numerous profits to manufacturers, jobbers and dealers, with our settled policy to bring to the American people opportunity to secure the highest grade merchandise offered in any market at the lowest possible cost, we believe that almost every page in this catalogue brings to you opportunity to live better, to get more out of life than you have ever received before, and as a time saver, as a temper saver, as a health saver our Acme Laundry and Cooking Outfit is confidently offered in the belief that it will meet with a large and gratifying sale.

OUR GUARANTEE OF QUALITY, our satisfaction or your money back proposition stands behind this, our Acme Laundry and Cooking Outfit, just as it stands behind every other stove or range offered in the pages of this book. We guarantee the materials to be the finest that money can buy, we guarantee the workmanship to be strictly high class in every respect, we guarantee the price to be lower than you can secure from any other firm or individual at home or elsewhere, and if you will send us an order for this, our Acme Laundry and Cooking Outfit, and enclose our $5.12 price, we will send the outfit to you with the distinct understanding and agreement that if it is not perfectly satisfactory to you, if at any time within thirty days you feel that you are not fully satisfied, if you feel that you could secure better value from anyone else, you may return the outfit to us at our expense of transportation charges both ways and we will promptly refund your money. Under these liberal terms, on this broad guarantee, on this free trial proposition, under the terms of which the outfit itself must prove all we claim for it, you certainly can well afford to send us an order today and bring to your home the convenience and the saving of time, fuel and money represented in this, our Acme Laundry and Cooking Outfit.

SPECIAL NOTICE. The cooking utensils and sadirons shown in the illustration are not a part of the outfit, and are not included in this price. For pages describing cooking utensils, sadirons, etc., please see the pink index pages in the middle of the book.

No. 22F710 Acme Laundry and Cooking Outfit, consists of our Acme Pride Laundry stove, one length of pipe and our Acme Drum Oven only. Packed complete ready for shipment. Delivered on cars at Newark, Ohio. Price..$5.12

OUR NEW IMPROVED 1907 MODEL ACME DRUM OVEN, NOW ONLY $1.73

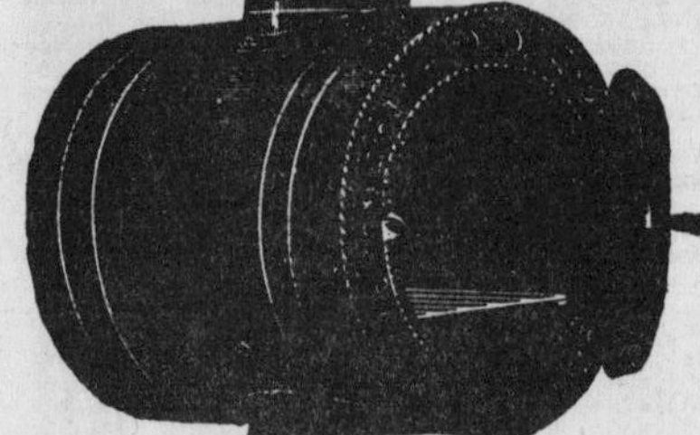

THIS DRUM OVEN will make a good cooking stove out of any heater or laundry stove. Attach this oven to any 6-inch stove pipe and to any laundry stove, or to any heating stove and you have an ideal cooking stove and heater or laundry stove combined in the one. The body is substantially constructed of cold rolled steel, cast front and back, cast collar top and bottom to fit 6-inch pipe. Is fitted with removable steel rack. Oven measures 10 inches wide, will easily accommodate a large 9-inch pie plate or a 9x18-inch baking or roasting pan. It is so constructed to give a circulation of heat that the oven will heat evenly and thoroughly, making it a first class baker. We would especially recommend that in ordering a laundry stove or a small heating stove that you order one of our Acme Drum Ovens. Even though you have a cook stove or range in your kitchen, you will find this the Acme Drum, almost indispensable, attached to your laundry stove or heater, for oftentimes you will find it convenient on wash day to get your lunch or dinner on the laundry stove in connection with the Acme Drum, or in the evenings a quick luncheon or small supper or dinner can be conveniently prepared on one of our heating stoves in combination with this new 1907 Model Acme Drum Oven, which we furnish for only $1.73. The outside measurement of this drum is 20x15 inches. Shipping weight, 40 pounds. It's a wonderfully quick baker, saves the waste of heat passing up the pipe. Tends, in connection with the heating stove, to give more radiation, therefore, more heat, out of a given amount of fuel and is especially efficient when used in connection with a laundry or heating stove.

No. 22F543 Price..$1.73

THE ACME RADIATOR

A WONDERFUL FUEL SAVER.

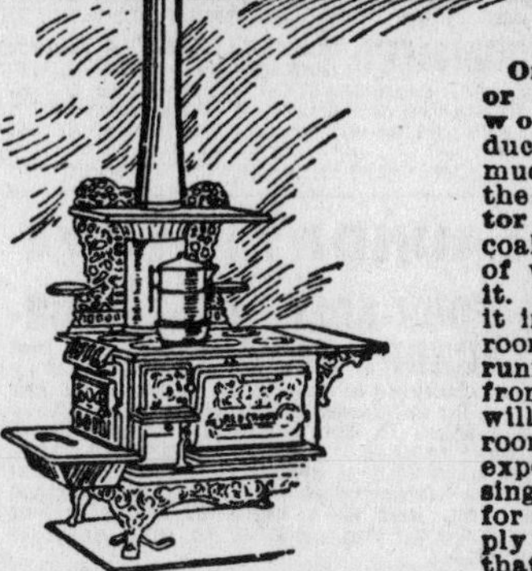

One ton of coal or one cord of wood will produce nearly as much heat with the Acme Radiator as two tons of coal or two cords of wood without it. You can place it in an upstairs room on a pipe running through from below, and it will heat that room without the expenditure of a single extra cent for fuel. It simply uses the heat that is escaping.

AN ACME RADIATOR will pay for itself in one season's use by reason of the waste heat and fuel it will save.

PLAIN SIMPLE FACTS.

Anyone who has a house to heat will want an Acme Hot Air Radiator when he knows the plain, simple facts about it.

An immense proportion of heat made by the fuel burned passes out of the chimney instead of heating your rooms. "Hotter on top of the chimney than down by the stove"; yes, a good deal. The Acme Radiator is a device affixed to a stove pipe or furnace pipe to keep the heat from going up the chimney. It does it. Your fuel bills are nearly twice as large as they would be if you used this waste heat. Don't waste it; stop it before it reaches the chimney with an Acme Radiator. It stops the heat on its way to the chimney and makes it do double duty. You can place an Acme Radiator on the stove pipe in the same room with the stove. It will actually save from one-quarter to one-half the fuel. There is no guess work in this statement. Actual tests have proved it time and time again. It is a stove that throws off heat without requiring any fuel or attention at all. No dust in the room and no ashes to carry out. No gas escapes from them and they cause no obstruction at all to the draft. They can be as easily cleaned and repaired as a stove pipe. An Acme Radiator really costs nothing. It pays for itself in saved fuel in a very short time.

Acme Radiator, Round Pipe Style.

For use on stoves burning anthracite coal or wood.

To meet the demand for a cheaper radiator, this style is added. It is smaller but very efficient either on the back of a stove or to heat small upper rooms. **Cannot be used with soft coal.**

No. 22F460 For 6-inch stove pipe. Made of Woods' refined iron, with aluminum finished cast iron top and base. Diameter, 10 inches; height, 28 inches. Weight, crated, 27 pounds. Price....................**$1.80**

Square Style.

For use with stoves burning anthracite coal or wood. This style is only adapted for floors above the stove. They are very handsome in design, and are bought by many who would not otherwise run a stove pipe through their house. Cannot be used with soft coal.

No. 22F461 For 6-inch stove pipe. Tubes made of Woods' refined iron. Aluminum finished, cast iron top and base. Size of base, 17½x13¾ inches; height, with legs, 37 inches. Weight, crated, 60 pounds. Price....................**$4.09**

No. 22F462 Same as above, except the body is made of Woods' patent planished iron. Price....................**$4.63**

This new style round Acme Radiator can be placed on a stove pipe in the same room with a stove, or it can be placed in an upstairs room on a stove pipe by running through from any kind of a stove below and will heat the upper room without the expenditure of a single extra cent for fuel. When used in the same room with the stove, the feet for the radiator are not required, but when you attach it to the stove pipe in the upper room it has a set of feet to support it at the floor. For use with stoves burning anthracite coal or wood. Weight, crated, 30 pounds.

No. 22F463 For 6-inch stove pipe, made of smooth cold rolled steel. Diameter, 12 inches. Height, with feet, 30½ inches. Price....................**$2.55**

No. 22F464 For 6-inch stove pipe, made of American patent planished iron. Diameter, 12 inches. Height, with feet, 30½ inches. Price....................**$3.20**

The Original Round Style.

HARD OR SOFT COAL.

This style has been successfully sold for many years. They are adapted either for the back of stove or an upper room or hall. Furnished with inner tubes for wood and anthracite coal and without inner tubes for soft coal, for 6-inch stove pipe. Made from Woods' refined iron (sheet steel), with cast iron ends. Aluminum finish. Diameter, 12½ inches; height, with legs, 38 inches. Weight, crated, 50 pounds.

No. 22F465 For soft coal........**$3.68**
No. 22F466 For hard coal or wood. **3.70**

No. 22F467 and No. 22F468 are the same as above, except made of Woods' patent planished iron.

No. 22F467 For hard coal or wood.**$4.25**
No. 22F468 For soft coal........ **4.20**

ACME NEW METHOD GASOLINE VAPOR STOVE AT $11.62 TO $22.31

THE SAFEST, QUICKEST AND MOST ECONOMICAL STOVES FOR GASOLINE.

IT LIGHTS LIKE GAS. A feature that makes it popular, as without heat, smoke or delay the stove can be instantly started into operation, turn the valve wheel and apply the match: the stove is ready for work.

IN OPERATION. By referring to sectional burner cut you will notice that the fluid drips drop by drop (never runs) on the perforated brass evaporator, where it is divided into fine particles, which, passing through the air, evaporate; the vapor thus made being heavier than air, passes down through the evaporator tubes mixing with and carburetting a current of air, which is lighted at the burner, producing a smokeless blue flame of great intensity and heating power.

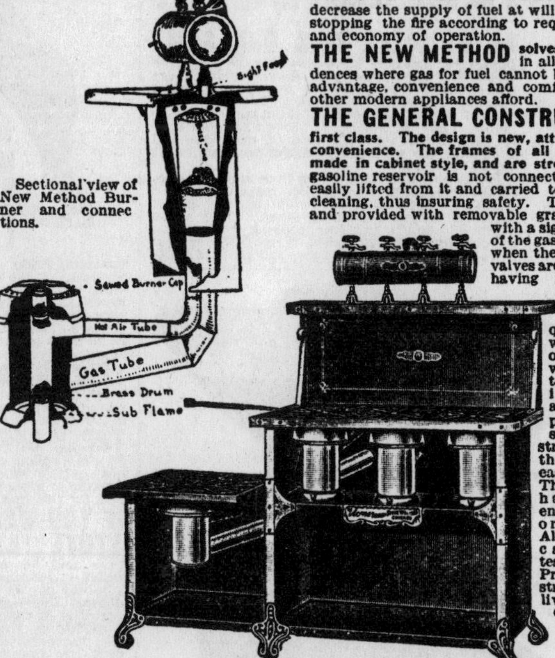

Sectional view of New Method Burner and connections.

THUS IT WILL BE SEEN that the NEW METHOD is a veritable gas machine and gas stove combined, entirely under the control of the user, who can increase or decrease the supply of fuel at will, securing the requisite amount of heat without waste, starting or stopping the fire according to requirement, thereby securing the greatest possible convenience, safety and economy of operation.

THE NEW METHOD solves the problem of economical cooking in all country homes and suburban residences where gas for fuel cannot be obtained, giving to the user every advantage, convenience and comfort which the use of gas stoves and other modern appliances afford.

THE GENERAL CONSTRUCTION of all our stoves is thoroughly first class. The design is new, attractive and well planned for convenience. The frames of all NEW METHOD stoves are made in cabinet style, and are strong and rigid. The tank or gasoline reservoir is not connected to the stove. It can be easily lifted from it and carried to an outer room for filling or cleaning, thus insuring safety. The tops are of ample width and provided with removable grates. The stove is provided with a sight feed, so that the dropping of the gasoline can at all times be seen when the stove is in operation. The valves are provided with needles having non-corrosive points; thus equalizes and regulates the flow of gasoline at all times, consequently the stove works as well with a small amount of gasoline in it as it does when full. Parts exposed to the fire are cast iron and imperishable. All parts are so constructed that they can be easily cleaned. The stoves are handsomely enameled and ornamented. All stoves are carefully tested before shipping. Prices below are for stoves strongly crated and delivered on the cars at our Ohio factory.

No. 22F592 Three-Burner Stove. Size of top 35x19 inches; height to cooking top, 30 inches. Shipping weight, 90 pounds. Price....................**$13.86**

Asbestos Lined Oven, with side door facing front and mounted on casters to roll it back when not in use, extra, $2.50.

No. 22F593 Same style of stove, with two burners. Size of top, 27x19 inches; height to cooking top, 30 inches. Shipping weight, 75 pounds. Price....................**$11.62**

Asbestos Lined Oven, with side door facing front and mounted on casters to roll it back when not in use, extra, $2.50.

If oven is desired, add $2.50 to above prices.

No. 22F594 Three-Burner and Step Stove. Size of main top, 35x19 inches; size of step top, 18x17 inches. Height to cooking top, 30 inches. Shipping weight, 150 pounds. Price....................**$17.59**

Asbestos Lined Oven, with side door facing front and mounted on casters to roll it back when not in use, extra, $2.50.

No. 22F595 Same style stove, with two burners and step. Size of main top, 29x19 inches; size of step top, 18x17 inches; height to cooking top, 30 inches. Shipping weight, 135 pounds. Price....................**$15.35**

Asbestos Lined Oven, with side door facing front and mounted on casters to roll it back when not in use, extra, $2.50.

If oven is desired, add $2.50 to above prices.

No. 22F596 Three-Burner and Step Cabinet Oven Range. Size of main top, 18¼x26¼ inches; size of step top, 12½x16¼ inches; height to cooking top, 35 inches; size of oven, 19¾x13½x11¾ inches. Shipping weight, 150 pounds. Price....................**$22.31**

No. 22F597 Same style stove, without step attachment. Shipping weight, 130 pounds. Price....................**$19.35**

EXTRA LARGE BURNERS ON ALL STEP ATTACHMENTS.

THE STEP ATTACHMENT is a great convenience, as it can be used for heating wash boiler, or for baking with oven, without interfering with the use of the top burners for cooking purposes.

$1.90 BUYS OUR ACME DANDY LAUNDRY STOVE

A WONDERFUL VALUE IN A COAL BURNING LAUNDRY STOVE, THE LOWEST PRICE EVER QUOTED ON A STOVE OF THIS SIZE AND QUALITY.

FOR ONLY $1.90 a very few cents above our actual foundry cost, we offer this, our New Model Acme Dandy Stove, a coal burning laundry stove as our lowest price laundry stove, as our leader in low prices, a good, satisfactory laundry stove, the equal in every way of laundry stoves offered by others at higher prices and sold by others in similar style as a great bargain at $2.25 to $2.75. $1.90 is the lowest price ever attempted by any firm for a guaranteed strictly satisfactory laundry stove, a price made possible only by us, because we make the stove in large quantities in our Newark, Ohio, foundry, and are willing to sell it on the narrowest margin of profit.

WHILE THIS, our New Acme Dandy Laundry Stove at $1.90 is a wonderful value, $1.90 being an astonishingly low price for a good laundry stove, yet it is no greater value than the laundry stoves we show at higher prices. It represents no more value for the money than our Acme Pride represents at $2.90 and up, or our Acme Moose Laundry Stove at $3.72. The Acme Dandy is a satisfactory, reliable laundry stove, a big bargain, much lower in price than you can buy a stove of the same size, weight, style and finish from any other house; yet, in illustrating and describing this, our Acme Dandy Stove at $1.90, we feel compelled to call your attention to the same wonderful bargains you can get in our laundry stoves that we offer at slightly higher prices. We always recommend to our customers the purchase of the better grade of merchandise, for the better goods in every line give so much more satisfaction, and we therefore call your special attention also to our Acme Pride, Acme Pet and Acme Moose Laundry Stoves.

OUR $1.90 ACME DANDY LAUNDRY STOVE is only a fair example of the wonderful values we present throughout our entire stove department. It is a leader price for laundry stoves, the lowest price we or anyone ever quoted for a stove of the same quality, and goes to show our strong position on the stove question. All the wonderful facilities of our immense stove foundry go to make this $1.90 price possible for this laundry stove, and these same facilities are employed to the same degree to make possible our low prices in our larger and finer laundry stoves as well as our entire line of stoves, ranges and heaters.

THIS, OUR ACME DANDY, is an ideal stove for laundry use. It is made with two No. 7½-inch top covers or cooking holes, has front pouch feed for putting in coal. The main top is 15x18 inches, the fire pot is 9 inches and it is made to fit 6-inch stove pipe. The Acme Dandy stands 18 inches high, and the shipping weight is 47½ pounds. You will find it thoroughly well made in every respect, a good job of moulding and fitting, a strong, serviceable, reliable and satisfactory laundry stove; and if you want a small stove of limited size and capacity, we can recommend the Acme Dandy in every way, but if you want a larger stove and one that is large enough for every purpose that is required of a laundry stove, we would refer you to our Acme Moose, Acme Pet and Acme Pride. Remember, the Acme Dandy burns coal only.

WE RECOMMEND that you order a laundry stove large enough to meet your requirements and if you find that the Acme Dandy answers your requirements we gladly accept your order with the understanding and condition that if the stove is not perfectly satisfactory when received, and if you do not find it exactly as illustrated and described and a wonderful value at the price, you can return it to us at our expense of freight charges and we will promptly return your money.

No 22F513 OUR ACME DANDY STOVE. Price...$1.90

$3.72 FOR OUR ACME MOOSE LAUNDRY STOVE

THIS FOUR-HOLE, COAL BURNING LAUNDRY STOVE is the very best coal laundry stove manufactured in any stove foundry in the world. It far outclasses any other laundry stove on the market in every respect, regardless of name, make or price. There is no laundry stove that compares with it either in quality of materials, size, attractiveness of design, special grate features, etc., and as a big, well made, perfect laundry stove we guarantee it to give absolute satisfaction.

AT OUR $3.72 PRICE it is really the most wonderful value; it has a very large top carrying four covers, each fitting in a No. 8 cooking hole, and top measurement over all is 21x22 inches, big enough to accommodate a great big wash boiler and cooking utensils at the same time. It will also take the new style steel or galvanized iron tubs now in common use, and its arrangement of fire pot and construction of main top is such that the heat is evenly distributed and it is a quick heater, economical in the use of fuel and a splendid up to date laundry stove, with all the good features of every laundry stove on the market and the defects of none.

AS WE MAKE THIS OUR ACME MOOSE Laundry Stove ourselves in our own stove foundry at Newark, Ohio, we are able to make it with all its fine features at a much lower manufacturing cost than any other foundry in the world could make it and you pay no profits to any wholesaler, or jobber, or retail dealer, but get it at the mere cost of materials and labor with one small percentage of profit added, at our $3.72 price.

We furnish our Acme Drum Oven at $1.73 extra, as illustrated and described on page 1015, and which, in connection with this laundry stove, makes a complete cooking stove. This stove weighs 92 pounds, has four cooking holes. Top cooking surface, 21x22 inches. Height, 23½ inches.

No. 22F534 Price...................$3.72

$2.90 ACME PRIDE SPECIAL COAL BURNING LAUNDRY STOVE

THIS IS OUR NEW MODEL 1907 IMPROVED SPECIAL COAL BURNING LAUNDRY STOVE our Acme Pride, which we offer at only $2.90 and up, a price representing the mere cost of materials and labor in our own stove foundry at Newark, Ohio, where manufacturing costs are lower than in any other stove foundry in the world, and to this very low manufacturing cost we add only one small margin of profit, so that this stove when sent to you at our $2.90 to $3.29 price represents better value, it is in every way a better laundry stove than you could secure at a much higher price.

THIS OUR ACME PRIDE Improved Laundry Stove, is made with two cooking holes, has a very liberal top and has special eight-faced fire pot equipped with special holders, so that you may heat eight sad-irons at one time.

THESE SPECIAL FEATURES make it an ideal laundry stove and as it is a splendid heater and the irons lie close to the fire they heat quickly while you may be using the top of the stove for cooking or some other purpose. It has large special pouch feed for coal and our special dumping grate.

IF YOU WANT A FIRST CLASS LAUNDRY STOVE with features embodied in its construction not to be found in any other laundry stove, send us our price and we will send the stove to you promptly, safe delivery guaranteed to your nearest railway station and you may use the stove 30 days in your own home, with the distinct understanding and agreement that if you are not perfectly satisfied with it in every respect it may be returned to us, your money will be refunded and we will pay the transportation charges both ways. It will pay you to order one of our very best laundry stoves, either this our Acme Pride at $2.90 to $3.29 or our large Acme Moose at $3.72, stoves which are guaranteed to be the very highest quality laundry stoves produced in any stove foundry in the world.

ACME PRIDE.

Catalogue Number	Stove Number	Size of Covers	Top Surface, Inches	Size of Pipe to fit Cover	Diameter of Fire Pot, Inches	Height, Inches	Weight, Pounds	Price
22F715	7	7 in.	13½x19½	6 in.	11½	25	68	$2.90
22F716	88	8 in.	13½x19½	6 in.	11½	25	68	3.00
22F717	8	8 in.	14 x21	6 in.	12½	25	84½	3.29

ACME PET COAL BURNING LAUNDRY STOVE

$2.77 And up

$2.77

THIS, OUR ACME PET Coal Burning Laundry Stove has every improvement, including our own dumping grate and is made with two No. 8 cooking holes. It has large front pouch feed for putting in coal, has a large size top to take on a big wash boiler and is made to take 6-inch stove pipe.

IF YOU HAVE ANY USE for a laundry stove to burn coal and do not require a stove so large as our Acme Moose at $3.72 you will certainly make no mistake in ordering this our Acme Pet Laundry Stove in any of the three sizes, at $2.77, $2.83 or $3.10, according to size. The freight charges on this laundry stove will amount to practically nothing at all compared with our saving to you in price, as 25 to 75 cents will pay the freight on this stove to any point from 100 to 1000 miles from our foundry at Newark, Ohio.

WE GUARANTEE THE STOVE to be thoroughly well made of high class materials, and we further guarantee it to reach you promptly and safely. You may give it a thorough trial in your own home, and if after using it 30 days you are not perfectly satisfied with your purchase, you may return the stove to us at our expense of transportation charges both ways and we will return your money.

We furnish this stove under our binding guarantee, all complete, delivered on board cars at Newark Ohio, at the different prices, as listed below:

Catalogue Number	Size	Size of Covers	Top Surface, Inches	Diameter of Fire Pot, Inches	Height, Inches	Weight, Pounds	Price
22F540	7	7 in.	14x19½	11 in.	22½	63	$2.77
22F541	88	8 in.	14x19½	11 in.	22½	63	2.83
22F542	8	8 in.	14x21	12½ in.	23½	76	3.10

$2.98 ACME PRIDE SPECIAL HARD OR SOFT COAL BURNING LAUNDRY STOVE.

REDUCED IN PRICE

IMMEDIATE SHIPMENT. We have a large stock stored ready for immediate shipment.

THIS IS OUR NEW MODEL 1909 improved special coal burning Laundry Stove, our Acme Pride, which we offer at only $2.98 and up, a price representing the mere cost of materials and labor in our own stove foundry at Newark, Ohio, where manufacturing costs are lower than in any other stove foundry in the world, and to this very low manufacturing cost we add only one small margin of profit, so that this stove when sent to you at our $2.98 to $3.92 price represents better value, it is in every way a better laundry stove than you could secure at a much higher price.

THIS, OUR ACME PRIDE Improved Laundry Stove, is made with two cooking holes, has a very liberal top and has special eight-faced fire pot equipped with special holders, so that you may heat eight sadirons at one time.

THESE SPECIAL FEATURES make it an ideal laundry stove and as it is a splendid heater and the irons lie close to the fire they heat quickly while you may be using the top of the stove for cooking or some other purpose. It has large special pouch feed for coal and our special dumping grate.

ACME PRIDE, made in three sizes as listed below and delivered on cars at Newark, Ohio.

Catalogue Number	Stove No.	Size of Covers	Top Surface, inches	Size of Pipe to fit Collar	Diameter of Fire Pot, inches	Height, inches	Crated Weight, pounds	Price
22L525	7	7 in.	13½x19½	6 in.	11½	25	80	$2.98
22L526	88	8 in.	13½x19½	6 in.	11½	25	80	3.40
22L527	8	8 in.	14 x21	6 in.	12½	25	90	3.92

$3.98 FOR OUR ACME MOOSE LAUNDRY STOVE

$3.98 A REDUCTION IN PRICE

THIS FOUR-HOLE HARD OR SOFT COAL BURNING LAUNDRY STOVE is the very best coal laundry stove manufactured in any stove foundry in the world. It far outclasses any other laundry stove on the market in every respect, regardless of name, make or price. There is no laundry stove that compares with it either in quality of materials, size, attractiveness of design, special grate features, etc., and as a big, well made, perfect laundry stove we guarantee it to give absolute satisfaction.

AT OUR $3.98 PRICE it is really the most wonderful value; it has a very large top carrying four covers, each fitting in a No. 8 cooking hole, and top measurement over all is 21x22 inches, big enough to accommodate a great big wash boiler and cooking utensils at the same time. It will also take the new style steel or galvanized iron tubs now in common use, and its arrangement of fire pot and construction of main top is such that the heat is evenly distributed and it is a quick heater, economical in the use of fuel and a splendid up to date laundry stove, with all the good features of every laundry stove on the market and the defects of none.

IMMEDIATE SHIPMENT from our factory at Newark, Ohio. We have a large stock stored ready for immediate shipment.

We furnish our Acme Drum Oven at $1.98 extra, as illustrated and described below, and which, in connection with this laundry stove, makes a complete cooking stove. This stove weighs crated 105 pounds, has four cooking holes. Diameter of fire pot, 12½ inches. Top cooking surface, 21x22 inches. Height, 23½ inches.
No. 22L530 Price..............................$3.98

ACME PET

Hard or Soft Coal Burning Laundry Stove

$1.98 TO $3.44

THIS, OUR ACME PET Coal Burning Laundry Stove, has every improvement, including our own dumping grate and is made with two No. 8 cooking holes. It has large front pouch feed for putting in coal, has a large size top to take on a big wash boiler and is made to take 6-inch stove pipe.

IF YOU HAVE ANY USE for a laundry stove to burn coal and do not require a stove so large as our Acme Moose at $3.98, you will certainly make no mistake in ordering this our Acme Pet Laundry Stove in any of the four sizes, at $1.98, $3.11, $3.17 or $3.44, according to size. The freight charges on this laundry stove will amount to practically nothing at all compared with our saving to you in price as 25 to 75 cents will pay the freight on this stove to any point from 100 to 1,000 miles from our foundry at Newark, Ohio.

IMMEDIATE SHIPMENT. We have a large stock stored ready for immediate shipment.

We furnish this stove under our binding guarantee, all complete, delivered on board cars at Newark, Ohio, at the different prices as listed below:

Catalogue Number	Size	Size of Covers	Top Surface, in.	Diameter of Fire Pot	Height, inches	Crated Weight, pounds	Price
22L520	50	7½ in.	15x18	9 in.	18	55	$1.98
22L521	7	7 in.	14x19½	11 in.	22½	75	3.11
22L522	88	8 in.	14x19½	11 in.	22½	75	3.17
22L523	8	8 in.	14x21	12½ in.	23½	85	3.44

OUR NEW IMPROVED 1909 MODEL ACME DRUM OVEN, NOW ONLY $1.98

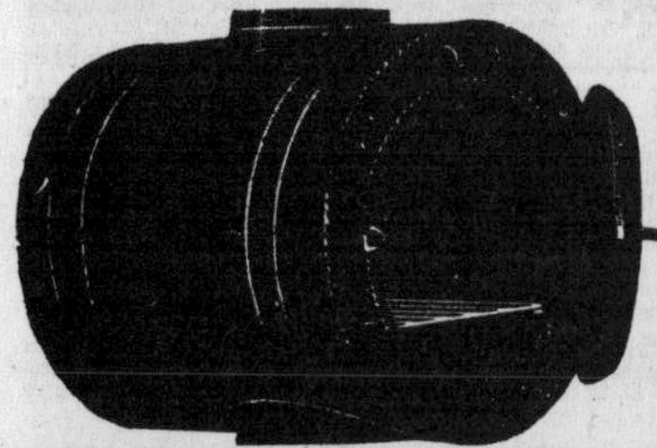

THIS DRUM OVEN will make a good cooking stove out of any heater or laundry stove. Attach this oven to any 6-inch stove pipe and to any laundry stove, or to any heating stove and you have an ideal cooking stove and heater or laundry stove combined in the one. The body is substantially constructed of cold rolled steel, cast front and back, cast collar top and bottom to fit 6-inch pipe. Is fitted with removable steel rack. Oven measures 10 inches wide, will easily accommodate a large 9-inch pie plate or a 9x18-inch baking or roasting pan. It is so constructed as to give a circulation of heat that the oven will heat evenly and thoroughly, making it a first class baker. We would especially recommend that in ordering a laundry stove or a small heating stove you order one of our Acme Drum Ovens. The outside measurement of this drum is 20x15 inches. Shipping weight, 45 pounds. It's a wonderfully quick baker, saves the waste of heat passing up the pipe. Tends, in connection with the heating stove, to give more radiation, therefore, more heat, out of a given amount of fuel and is especially efficient when used in connection with a laundry or heating stove.
No. 22L531 Price..............................$1.98

BEST BOX STOVE MADE, $2.49

THE HIGHEST GRADE BOX STOVE offered or made by any manufacturer in the world is shown below at prices ranging from $2.49 for the smallest size to $7.25 for the big No. 36 Champion Box.

DESIGN AND CASTINGS are up to date in every respect and their construction leaves nothing to be desired.

THE TOP on our box stove swings to one side and the largest chunks of wood may be fed from the top as well as the front. This big top plate swings and is supplied with lids and centers; size 18 has one 6-inch cover, while size 22 has a 7-inch cover; size 25 is supplied with two 7-inch covers; sizes 28 and 30 have 8-inch covers and one short center; sizes 34 and 36 are provided with two 9-inch covers and a short center. The large sized stoves are invaluable as combination big wood heater and cook stoves and are so used by thousands of our customers in the cold winter when breakfast may be gotten on the box stove without firing up the cook stove in the kitchen.

$2.49 TO $7.25 HIGHEST GRADE BOX STOVE FOR WOOD ONLY

FRONT END of the stove has a large swing door with a tight fitting slide damper. Every feature that tends to make an up to date 1909 model box stove enters into the construction of our Champion Box.

We furnish this stove in seven sizes, under our written binding guarantee, all complete, delivered on board cars at Newark, Ohio, at the different prices listed below:

Catalogue Number.	Stove No.	Height, inches	Size of Door Opening	Size Opening in Main Door	Length Inside, inches	Size Pipe to fit Collar	Crated Weight, pounds	Price
22L490	18	19½	5½x 7½	6¾x10	19	5 inches	65	$2.49
22L491	22	21½	7½x 8¾	9 x14	23	6 inches	85	3.40
22L492	25	23	8¾x10	10 x18	25½	6 inches	110	4.20
22L493	28	26	9¾x10	10¾x20¾	28	6 inches	130	5.20
22L494	30	26	9¾x10½	10¾x20¾	30½	6 inches	135	5.40
22L495	34	29½	12½x13½	12¾x25	35	6 inches	185	7.00
22L496	36	29½	12½x13½	12¾x25	37	6 inches	190	7.25

69c

FOR WOOD ONLY

LOWEST PRICE EVER NAMED

BURNS WOOD, COBS, CHIPS, STRAW, ANYTHING EXCEPT COAL

AS A LOW PRICED, wood burning heating stove, this, our DOT Airtight Heater surpasses anything ever produced in any stove foundry. Just think of a perfectly made heating stove, with perfect draft control, constructed of high class material, offered at 69 cents, $1.28 and $1.58, according to size, such prices as no other foundry would attempt to meet and a stove which we know no other foundry in the world could produce. But even at this astonishing price of only 69 cents this, our DOT Wood Burning Sheet Steel Heater is no greater value than any other stove made in our Newark foundry as we have added to the cost of manufacturing this stove the exact same margin of profit, the exact same percentage above the cost of materials and labor that we add to every stove we manufacture, a uniform percentage of profit that is very small, a profit which is less proportionately than any other stove foundry in the world adds to the cost of producing its stoves and ranges, and a profit so low that even the largest foundries in the world could not accept because it would require an enormous volume of business to yield even the most ordinary returns on the investment in buildings, patterns, special machinery, etc.

WE MAINTAIN OUR LEADERSHIP as the world's greatest stove makers because of our unique methods of manufacturing and selling our stoves and ranges. Our prices have been the lowest ever offered on the highest grade stoves and ranges for many years and because of our low prices we have enjoyed a large and steadily increasing patronage until the volume of our business has grown so enormously that a few pennies of profit on a stove yields us a satisfactory return. No matter, therefore, what price you may pay for stoves and ranges manufactured by other dealers you cannot possibly get any more stove for the money than we offer you because with our unequaled manufacturing facilities, because of our reduced expense of marketing our product, no other foundry in the world can approach us in lowness of manufacturing and selling cost on stoves and ranges. When we sell a heating stove or a range we offer it to you at the mere cost of materials and labor with our one small margin of profit added, and selling to you direct from the foundry by means of a catalogue without a single traveling salesman or other middleman intervening between us as manufacturers and you, our customer, you save all these extra profits which all the other middlemen make and which you are compelled to pay other dealers for stoves and ranges when you purchase from them.

ANOTHER REASON that we are able to name prices so much lower than any other manufacturer or dealer lies in the fact that our largest stove foundry in the world is operated to its full capacity every day in the year, and while our sales of stoves and ranges have been increasing for years and we have enlarged the capacity of our works from year to year, we have not been able to fill all the orders we received and we have therefore kept our foundry going day in and day out, in season and out of season, in an endeavor to accumulate sufficient stock to fill every order we receive. Because of this continuous operation of our foundry we are able to buy our materials far in advance, to buy in enormous quantities, taking advantage of falling prices when the market for any reason declines, taking advantage of every price opportunity, every quantity figure named by the smelters and rolling mills and, beyond all this, setting our machinery and placing our molds for thousands of one pattern of stove and manufacturing these stoves day in and day out throughout the year. This process develops a wonderful staff of expert employes, each one doing a certain thing better than it is done in any other stove foundry in the world and not only acquiring skill but speed in production, and you need not be told that it costs much less proportionately to manufacture a thousand stoves than it costs to manufacture one hundred.

WE HAVE STILL FURTHER REDUCED PRICES by developing special machinery to take the place of hand labor and in our largest stove foundry in the world at Newark, Ohio, we have had erected for us many large, powerful and costly special machines for handling steel and stove plates and doing the work better than it has ever been done before and every penny we have been able to save in manufacturing cost we have given to our customers in the form of lower prices and all this special equipment, all this systematizing of labor, all this development, all this enormous stove making plant, the elimination of all middlemen brings to our customers the very highest type of heating stoves, cooking stoves and ranges that it is possible to produce, and explains why we are able to offer at 69 cents and up a perfect heating stove at a price never before equaled by any foundry.

OUR DOT AIRTIGHT HEATER for wood is a very good stove, and suitable for small rooms. It is a direct stove, taking in the draft at the ash opening. It has an oval sheet steel body 18 inches, 20 inches and 24 inches long. It is not lined inside like our better airtights described elsewhere in this catalogue. The small size is built with but three legs, set equal distances apart, while the two larger sizes have four legs or feet as shown in the illustration. If you require a light fire during chilly, damp days, if you have a room upstairs that you would like to heat now and then independent of any other heating plant you may have in your home, or if you desire to make a small bedroom comfortable with light fuel, such as knots, chunks of wood, chips, cobs and other combustible material except coal, this will prove an acceptable stove. But while we offer this our DOT Airtight as worth more than sheet steel heaters offered by other houses at three times our prices, yet we always recommend our hot blast, airtight, double lined heaters as shown on pages 1002 and 1003 because of special features possessed by them and which at the low prices asked for this our DOT Airtight cannot be included in its construction.

ALL OUR AIRTIGHT HEATERS ARE BETTER than any that have ever been offered before, they are skillfully made, they are splendid heaters, and we urge you before you order this our DOT Heater to look at the illustrations and descriptions and printed prices of our full line of airtight heaters as shown on other pages in this catalogue, and we know if you want the very highest type of sheet steel heater, heaters surpassing other airtight stoves offered in competition with them, you will surely send us an order on our liberal 30-day free trial plan and refund proposition, a plan by which you may use the stove 30 days in your own home, during which time you may learn the full value of all these splendid stoves and ranges offered by us, and if after such use in your own home you are not fully satisfied that you have received wonderful value, such a stove as you could not obtain from any other dealer at home or elsewhere, you may return it to us at our expense of transportation charges both ways and we will refund your money.

JUST A FEW YEARS AGO ours was a small stove foundry. Our annual capacity was about one hundred thousand stoves. Our stoves were then no better than the average maker's and they cost us then about the same as it costs other makers today to make stoves. Since then, year by year, we have enlarged our foundry; every year for eight years we have bettered the quality and reduced the cost of manufacture. Formerly we did as most makers do today, namely, bought many of the parts, such as reservoirs, nickel work, trimmings, steel work, etc. Now we make all these parts. We make them better than those that we can buy, better than anything we formerly used, and we make them at a much lower cost than we were formerly compelled to pay for inferior goods, and this you get the benefit of. Formerly our iron, coke and castings, like in other foundries, were handled by hand; now it is done by automatic machinery. Formerly our polishing, grinding, etc., was done by hand; now by automatic machinery. Formerly we were compelled to be contented with ordinary patterns; now nothing but the most extraordinary patterns are acceptable to us. When we would not make more than one or two thousand stoves from a set of patterns we were compelled to consider the cost of the patterns; now where one set of patterns will be used for tens of thousands of stoves we do not need to consider the cost of the patterns, and as a result we produce at a lower cost than any other foundry a higher grade of stove work than goes out of any other foundry in the United States.

IF YOU KNEW WHAT WE KNOW about the quality and price of our stoves we would have to make our stove foundry five times as large as it already is. We make the best stoves made in the world, and, size for size and style for style, we sell them at a little more than one-half the prices that stoves are retailed for everywhere.

EVERY MANUFACTURER OF STOVES IN THE UNITED STATES KNOWS THIS FULL WELL, and they know their only chance for any success is that everyone will not learn all about the kind of stoves we make and the prices we ask. We are being constantly criticised by stove manufacturers everywhere for selling our stoves for so little money. While they are very discreet when they go about their trade trying to sell goods, to us they are very frank in acknowledging that we sell one stove to anyone for less than their stoves actually cost them to build, 25 to 33⅓ per cent less than they are compelled to ask from carload buyers. The only hope of other stove manufacturers is that everyone in the United States will not learn all about the kind of stoves we make and the low prices we ask.

YOU WILL SHARE IN THE PROFITS of our business if you send your order to us. This is fully explained in the first pages of this catalogue. It is the most liberal offer ever made by any maker or seller.

PRICE LIST OF DOT AIRTIGHT SHEET STEEL HEATING STOVES DELIVERED FREE ON BOARD THE CARS AT OUR FOUNDRY, NEWARK, OHIO.

Catalogue Number	Stove Number	Floor to Urn Top, inches	Length, inches	Width, inches	Height, inches	Pipe Collar, inches	Shipping Weight, pounds	Price
22F571	18	28½	17¾	14½	13¾	5	30	$0.69
22F572	21	34	20½	16⅝	19¾	6	36	1.28
22F573	25	38⅝	23¾	17	23¾	6	42	1.58

PROFIT SHARING ARTICLES FREE. SEE PAGES 1 AND 2.

ACME HICKORY AIRTIGHT

$4.22 AND $4.76

HIGHEST GRADE DIRECT DRAFT SHEET STEEL HEATER

OUR ACME HICKORY AT $4.22 AND $4.76 is the same stove as the Acme Glenwood shown on page 1010 excepting it is a direct radiator, instead of a hot air circulator, and is without the nickeled top ring, and is cast in slightly different pattern. It has the same hot blast down draft with screw adjustment, the same ash opening and direct draft screw adjustment, making it airtight when desired to keep fire. The same nickeled urn, foot rails and handsome finish, excepting the nickeled top ring. Not having the double cased hot air circulator, we give 1½ to 2 inches more inside measurement on the Acme Hickory.

YEARS OF EXPERIENCE coupled with facilities afforded us in the largest stove foundry in the world, with the best mechanical skill that can be employed, we pride ourselves that we are turning out in every particular a higher grade airtight hot air circulating wood heater than goes out of any other foundry in America. We guarantee that one of these hot air circulating heaters will heat more cubic feet with less fuel than any other hot air heater of the same size made, regardless of name, make or price. This is accomplished not only in the quality of material used, the heft of the steel and castings, in the careful and accurate fitting, making and finishing, but it is also accomplished through the peculiar construction, which gives free circulation to the hot air, and such as is accomplished in no other hot air circulating heater made

WE CLAIM FURTHER for these hot air heaters that one of our stoves will be found in perfect condition after the ordinary thin, lightly constructed airtight heater has been worn and burnt out. We build these heaters from the best material that money can buy, use only the highest grade of sheet steel, and a thicker steel than is used by other makers. We use stronger, heavier, better fitting and better finished castings, we put on more nickeling and trimming and we guarantee to furnish you a better airtight heater than you could get elsewhere, and that at a little more than one-half the price charged by others. Every stove is put up under our binding guarantee, and after giving it thirty days' thorough trial, if you are not convinced that you have received a better stove in every particular than you could have purchased elsewhere of the same size and style, you can return it to us at our expense, and we will immediately return your money.

WE GUARANTEE this positively the highest grade, best made, most economical in the consumption of fuel and the best distributor of heat of any direct draft, sheet steel airtight stove made, and for the trifling difference in cost between this, our special direct down draft, fancy trimmed airtight, and the more common sheet steel airtight heater as shown on the following page we would especially recommend that you select this stove. This direct draft airtight heater differs from most all other direct draft airtight heaters in that it has a hot blast down draft with the latest screw attachment, making it more economical in the consumption of fuel, more even in the distribution of heat, holding your fire more easily under control. The difference in the cost of the fuel consumed in this stove as against the ordinary direct draft airtight heater will in one winter far more than pay the price we ask for the stove.

OUR SPECIAL PRICE is based on the actual cost of material and labor in our own foundry, the largest stove foundry in the world, with but our one small percentage of profit added. These prices are lower than dealers can buy elsewhere in carload lots. Understand every one of these stoves is put out under our binding guarantee, covering the workmanship and material, and we will accept your order for any one of these stoves to be sent to you with the understanding and agreement that after giving it thirty days' thorough trial if you are not perfectly satisfied and are not convinced that you have received a better stove than you could have obtained elsewhere and at a big saving in cost, you can return it to us at our expense, and we will immediately return your money together with any express charges paid by you.

THIS AIRTIGHT STOVE differs from the airtight stoves made in most foundries and sold by dealers generally in that it is made of the very best Birmingham pig iron and sheet steel. The same care is used in the making and finishing of the castings, in the construction, the mounting fitting, bracing, bolting, reinforcing, staying etc., as is given to the highest priced stoves, and we get clear away from the ordinary sheet steel stove and give you an effect in appearance not approached by any other airtight stove, making this stove especially suitable to homes where wood is to be burnt exclusively. This we effect by a very handsome base neatly shaped foot rails, neatly shaped ornamentation around the top, and with a neat pattern and design effect worked out in the castings. You will find this stove will differ in size and weight, in strength and workmanship, in the control of fire and economical consumption of fuel from almost any other sheet steel stove on the market.

UNLESS YOU ACTUALLY MADE A VISIT TO OUR ENORMOUS STOVE FOUNDRY AT NEWARK, OHIO, and could see the acres of ground this foundry covers, could see the number of stoves going through each separate operation, the army of workmen employed, the tons of castings used, you would be unable to realize the enormous advantages we are offerings our customers in the stove line. If you could actually pay a visit to our Newark, Ohio, foundry, you would realize all of these advantages and if every one of our customers could do this we would be unable to supply one-fourth the number of stoves that would be ordered. There would be no question in the mind of anyone who saw this foundry that we are strictly and undoubtedly headquarters on stoves, that we possess such advantages in manufacturing and price making that make competition with us simply out of the question, and as a fair sample of these wonderful advantages in quality and low price power, we present the Acme Hickory as the best we can offer in the direct draft sheet steel heater and are willing to put it in competition with any similar style stove offered by any dealer at double our price.

WE HAVE PROVEN to our satisfaction time and again that our price to the consumer, one stove at a time, is much lower than the actual cost to other stove manufacturers. A proof of this is that when we have run out of any certain style or kind of stove and we look outside to see if we can buy a similar stove from another manufacturer, we are unable to buy even in thousand lots at within 15 to 20 per cent of our selling price. Another and better proof is in the fact that we have in our employ a great many people who have come from the different stove manufacturing plants of the country familiar with all the details of the cost of these different plants, and every one who has come to us without a single exception, tells us that our selling price to our trade is less than a like stove (size style and weight) could be produced at foundry cost in the foundry from which he came.

WE GUARANTEE the price lower than the same style of stoves can be bought from any other maker, even in carload lots. As a guarantee that you will find this stove even more than we claim for it, and for economy in consumption of fuel, and for comfort, worth a dozen ordinary airtight stoves, we will accept your order and your money with the understanding that, after the stove is received, if it is not found perfectly satisfactory in every way, the best heater you ever used in your home, you can return it to us at our expense of freight charges both ways, and we will immediately return your money.

We take great pains in packing and shipping these stoves, and we guarantee the stove to reach you in the same perfect condition it leaves us.

ABOUT THE FREIGHT CHARGES. These stoves weigh from 95 to 120 pounds, according to the size. The freight on stoves from our Newark, Ohio foundry averages about 40 cents per hundred pounds for each 500 miles. Greater or lesser distances in proportion. So you can see that for from 25 cents to $1.00 the smallest to the largest stoves can be carried to almost any point in the United States, according to distance. The freight charges amount to next to nothing compared with what we save you in price.

OUR OFFER TO STOVE DEALERS. If you are a stove dealer why pay two to ten dollars more for every stove you buy than the price we quote in our catalogue? Mr. Dealer we will guarantee to furnish you handsomer, more stylish and more up to date, better made, better finished, stronger and more lasting stoves than you can buy from any stove jobber or stove maker in America, and we will furnish you these stoves at from 10 to 33⅓ per cent less than you can buy them elsewhere in carload lots. We will furnish them to you as you want them; you can buy one stove or a carload. Every stove is marked "Newark Stove Works, Chicago." They don't bear our name. If you carry this line you will double your sales, you can give your customers much better value for their money and still make the same profit you have been in the habit of making. Our price is the same whether you are a dealer and buy one stove or a carload or a farmer and buy one stove for your own use. Parties sending orders to us are not asked whether they are merchants professional men, mechanics or laborers. Our prices are alike to all, prices much lower than you can buy elsewhere.

WE WILL FURNISH YOU REPAIRS FREE in tho years to come. Remember, on every stove we sell we have a complete set of all parts and repairs, and under our guarantee, if any piece or part gives out by reason of defect in material or workmanship, we will replace it for you free of charge; but if by accident or otherwise, the piece should break and need to be replaced, write us and we will get it to you in just a few days and, different from the retail dealer, who will charge you three or four prices for it, our price for any needed repair or part of any stove you buy from us will be the bare cost of manufacturing, with but our one small manufacturing profit added.

Price List of the Acme Hickory with Hot Blast Draft, Strongly Crated and Delivered on the cars at our Foundry in Newark, Ohio.

Catalogue Number	Stove No.	Length Inside, inches	Width Inside, inches	Top Feed Opening, inches	Shipping Weight, pounds	Price
22F569	21	21	15	9¾	105	$4.22
22F570	24	24	17	11¾	120	4.76

Size of pipe to fit collar is 6-inch on both sizes.

WE SHARE OUR PROFITS WITH YOU

No matter what you may buy that is shown on this page, or in this department, or on any other page or in any other department in this big catalogue, or any of our special catalogues, always remember we share our profits with you by giving you our customers' profit sharing certificates, showing the amount of your purchase in dollars and cents, and when these certificates have been saved by you until you have $50.00 or more, you may exchange them for beautiful, useful and valuable articles which will be given to you free—absolutely without one cent of expense, except transportation charges.

TURN TO THE FIRST TWO PAGES of this big catalogue and read the full particulars of our wonderful and astonishingly liberal profit sharing plan by which our customers may select just the articles they have wanted and get them absolutely free in return for our profit sharing certificates.

NO MATTER WHAT YOU MAY WANT, whether it be a piano, a bookcase, a bicycle, a music cabinet, an easy chair, a rug, a stove, a set of dishes, a camera, a watch, a sewing machine, a clock, wearing apparel or books—REMEMBER, WE GIVE IT TO YOU FREE in exchange for our profit sharing certificates. Not one cent to pay—just a free gift from us in appreciation of the amount of merchandise you buy from us.

YOUR MONEY WILL BE IMMEDIATELY RETURNED TO YOU FOR ANY GOODS NOT PERFECTLY SATISFACTORY.

$2.06

$1.53 if without foot rails.

OUR UNEQUALED ACME AIRTIGHT

AT $2.06 TO $3.62 we offer this our Acme Airtight Heater complete with silver nickel plated foot rails and at $1.53 to $2.91 we offer it complete without silver nickel plated foot rails, as our better grade down draft sheet steel heating stove at a very low price. This our Acme Airtight Down Draft Heater is a better grade stove than our Dot Airtight Heaters quoted on page 1013 as it is equipped with special down draft register and comes in larger sizes. Please note the small illustration shown at the bottom of the page giving an open view of this our Acme Airtight from which you can get an excellent idea of the down draft feature of this stove by which attachment the air becomes heated before it reaches the fuel, thus producing perfect combustion. Another feature of this our Acme Airtight which is not included in the construction of the Dot is the double lining which extends up 12 inches from the bottom of the stove. The cover to ash opening is locked securely to prevent blowing off and the entire stove is honestly constructed of good materials with heavy lining and cannot fail to give perfect satisfaction. The body is made of 26-gauge smooth steel while the lining is 20-gauge steel. It is surmounted with fine nickeled urn and the fuel opening at the top of the stove is from 10½ to 12½ inches in diameter according to size.

THIS SPLENDID HEATING STOVE will burn any sort of fuel except coal. It is especially adapted to burn big tough chunks and knots of wood, straw, cobs, hay or trash, and it is specially well adapted for the plains of the western and northwestern states where many of the settlers use sheet steel heaters for the burning of straw, fodder and other miscellaneous trash and refuse which cannot be burned in any other stove. As the draft register may be fastened airtight the fire may be kept under absolute control and by reason of the down draft special construction of this our Acme Airtight Heater it is quickly responsive to any adjustment of draft and supply of fuel and will be found a perfectly satisfactory sheet steel heating stove and superior to sheet steel stoves offered by other firms and individuals at from two to four times the prices we ask.

WE GUARANTEE ENTIRE SATISFACTION on all the heaters we make, and if after you have received one of these our Acme Airtight Heaters at our special prices ranging from $1.53 to $3.62 and you are not fully satisfied that the stove is up to our representations in every way we shall be glad to have you send it back to us and we will cheerfully refund your money and pay the transportation charges both ways. This guarantee is behind every stove made in our largest stove foundry in the world, and we assure you that you cannot do us a greater favor than to return to us any stove or range ordered from the pages of this catalogue which does not prove satisfactory in every particular. We are striving continually to improve the product of our foundry and develop the very finest stoves and ranges it is possible to manufacture, and we must depend upon our customers who use these stoves and ranges day by day to advise us wherein they are defective in any way or wherein they may be improved in any particular.

LAST YEAR WE MANUFACTURED 3,350 carloads of stoves and ranges; they were all sold by us and we number thousands upon thousands of pleased customers throughout the United States. Our wonderfully low prices and our excellent qualities have given us the largest stove patronage accorded any firm or individual in the world, and we shall strive in the future as in the past to give the greatest value known to the stove making industry.

LET US SEND YOU ONE OF THESE SPLENDID AIRTIGHT HEATERS TODAY if you have any use for a heating stove of this character—let us send it to you under our positive guarantee of quality, under our satisfaction or your money back guarantee, and we will send it to you securely crated and it will reach your nearest railway station in just a few days in the same first class condition in which it leaves our foundry.

THIS ILLUSTRATION SHOWS THE STOVE WITH FOOT RAILS, but we sell this Acme Airtight both with and without foot rails, and in ordering please be very careful to specify whether you want it with or without the foot rails and send us the price for the stove you want as shown in the table below.

WE SHARE OUR PROFITS WITH YOU. No matter what you may buy that is shown in this department, or on any other page or in any other department of this big catalogue or any of our special catalogues, always remember we share our profits with you by giving to our customers profit sharing certificates showing the amount of your purchase in dollars and cents, and when these certificates have been saved by you until you have $50.00 or more you may exchange them for beautiful, useful and valuable articles which will be given to you free—absolutely without one cent of expense, except the transportation charges. See pages 1 and 2 of this catalogue for further particulars.

This illustration shows our hot blast down draft feature in our better grade of sheet steel airtight.

Open View

WE SPENT THOUSANDS OF DOLLARS in our largest stove foundry in the world at Newark, Ohio, in installing specially designed machinery for the handling of sheet steel to construct these our Acme Airtight Heaters and other stoves containing heavy sheet steel, and with all this wealth of machinery we have been enabled to very materially reduce the cost of producing these finest airtight heaters to the lowest possible minimum and we give our customers the advantage of all this price saving as the prices quoted on this page bear positive witness. We use only the very best materials it is possible to secure, carefully bend and fit them; the riveting is done on special machines and we assure you that no sheet steel heater could be better or more carefully constructed than this.

THESE SHEET STEEL HEATERS are specially adapted to climates where coal is seldom if ever used and will be found particularly satisfactory as giving a quick, hot fire, as giving an enormous volume of heat at a very low fuel expense, requiring little care and attention, a stove that is well suited to the requirements of any wood burning section. They are also specially adapted to use in hunting camps and summer homes in the woods; they are desirable for use in bedrooms and sitting rooms in the second story; in short, they may be used in a hundred different ways and places where the high priced hard and soft coal burning stoves are a needless expense.

Price List of the Acme Airtight Smooth Steel Heater without Foot Rails.

Catalogue Number	Stove No.	Floor to Urn Top	Length, inches	Width, inches	Height of Body	Size of Feed Opening	Size of Ash Opening	Shipping Weight	Price, Smooth Steel
22F574	20	34	20½	16½	19¾ in.	10½ in.	6½ in.	40 lbs.	$1.53
22F575	24	38⅝	23¾	17	23¾ in.	12½ in.	6½ in.	45 lbs.	1.85
22F576	30	38⅝	29½	17	23¾ in.	12½ in.	6½ in.	50 lbs.	2.31

Price List of the Acme Airtight Polished Steel Heater without Foot Rails.
Body of this stove is made of polished steel and does not require blacking.

Catalogue Number	Stove No.	Floor to Urn Top	Length, inches	Width, inches	Height of Body	Size of Feed Opening	Size of Ash Opening	Shipping Weight	Price, Polished Steel
22F577	120	34	20½	16½	19¾ in.	10½ in.	6½ in.	40 lbs.	$2.05
22F578	124	38⅝	23¾	17	23¾ in.	12½ in.	6½ in.	45 lbs.	2.37
22F579	130	38⅝	29½	17	23¾ in.	12½ in.	6½ in.	50 lbs.	2.91

Price List of the Acme Airtight Smooth Steel Heater with Foot Rails.

Catalogue Number	Stove No.	Floor to Urn Top	Length, inches	Width, inches	Height of Body	Size of Feed Opening	Size of Ash Opening	Shipping Weight	Price, Smooth Steel
22F580	205	34	20½	16½	19¾ in.	10½ in.	6½ in.	45 lbs.	$2.06
22F581	245	38⅝	23¾	17	23¾ in.	12½ in.	6½ in.	50 lbs.	2.45
22F582	305	38⅝	29½	17	23¾ in.	12½ in.	6½ in.	55 lbs.	3.06

Price List of the Acme Airtight Polished Steel Heater with Foot Rails.
Body of this stove is made of polished steel and does not require blacking.

Catalogue Number	Stove No.	Floor to Urn Top	Length, inches	Width, inches	Height of Body	Size of Feed Opening	Size of Ash Opening	Shipping Weight	Price, Polished Steel
22F583	1205	34	20½	16½	19¾ in.	10½ in.	6½ in.	45 lbs.	$2.59
22F584	1245	38⅝	23¾	17	23¾ in.	12½ in.	6½ in.	50 lbs.	2.98
22F585	1305	38⅝	29½	17	23¾ in.	12½ in.	6½ in.	55 lbs.	3.62

ALL PRICES ARE FOR THESE STOVES STRONGLY CRATED AND DELIVERED ON THE CARS AT OUR FOUNDRY IN NEWARK, OHIO.

$1.99 BEST BOX STOVE EVER MADE

AT FROM $1.99 TO $6.40, according to size, we offer our new improved 1907 Model Acme Champion Wood Burning Box Stove with all its improvements and betterments, under our guarantee as the highest grade exclusive wood burning box heating stove made.

OUR GREAT FREE OFFER. Send us an order for this box stove in any size, state the size wanted, enclose our price, and we will send the stove to you, with the understanding and agreement that you can give the stove thirty days' trial in your own home, during which time you can put it to every test, compare it with any other box stove made, regardless of name, make or price, even though the price may be two or three times the price we ask, and if you are not satisfied that we are furnishing you a better stove, if we don't furnish you heavier castings, better fitting castings, if you don't find our box stove handsomer in design, stronger in interior construction, better bolted, braced, stayed and fitted, if you don't find that you get better control of the drafts and fire in our stove than in any other; in short, if you don't find it the best box heating stove you have ever seen or used, you can return it to us at our expense and we will immediately return your money, together with any freight charges paid by you.

FROM THIS ILLUSTRATION, engraved by our artist direct from a photograph you can get some idea of the general appearance of this, our new improved 1907 Model Acme Champion Wood Burning Box Stove, but it differs so from any of the cheaper box stoves on the market, that it must be seen, examined, and compared with other box stoves for you to appreciate how much more we are giving you for your money than you could buy elsewhere.

WE DO THINGS DIFFERENTLY IN OUR FOUNDRY than the way they are done in most other foundries. Ours being the largest stove foundry in the world, we employ the most skilled mechanics as designers, modelers, pattern makers, etc., and in this, our new improved 1907 Model Acme Champion Stove, we have brought out a set of patterns which for shape, style, fit, general design, while in general appearance very much like the ordinary box stove, yet when compared side by side there really is no comparison between this, our new 1907 model, and the box stoves sold by others.

IT'S A GREAT WOOD BURNER, and suitable for all purposes. The larger sizes are especially suitable for taking in big chunks of wood, big knots, big roots, ends of good sized trees, extra long pieces of wood blocks, etc.

THE LARGER SIZES are suitable in wood burning countries for very large rooms. They will be found in stores, halls, livery stables, hotel offices, factories, churches and schools and other large rooms. They are also used in some of the larger dwellings where one or more rooms upstairs or down are to be heated by one stove, and where in the home you desire to use very large chunks, roots, blocks, etc.

THE SMALLER SIZES are especially suitable for homes in parlors, living rooms, dining rooms and other rooms. While the very smallest sizes are adapted to bedrooms and other small rooms.

WE FURNISH THIS, our new 1907 Model Acme Champion Exclusive Wood Burning Box Stove in a great variety of sizes to meet all possible wants and conditions. If you want a very small stove for a very small room, the first two or three smaller sizes will please you. For a medium or larger size, then one of our stoves at $3.65 to $4.60 will suit you, and these are especially recommended for homes. If it's an extra large room or large house, then our very largest sizes, the 34-inch or 36-inch size at $6.25 to $6.40 is recommended.

OUR VERY LOW PRICE, a price ranging from $1.99 to $6.40, according to size, are prices based on the actual cost of material and labor, with but our one small percentage of profit added, so low in fact, that you can buy one wood burning box stove from us at a lower price than your dealer can buy inferior box stoves from any other maker in carload lots.

SPECIAL FEATURES OF OUR BIG WOOD BURNING BOX STOVE NOT FOUND ON ANY OTHER BOX STOVE MADE.

CASTINGS are made from the best designs that can possibly be procured, brought right up to date. The stoves are beautifully shaped, handsomely ornamented, a new and neat design. The bottom is nicely shaped, full finished castings; back is nicely shaped, full finished and ornamented castings; the interior construction is our own special double bolting, double bracing, double reinforced and stayed construction, a construction not found on any other stove.

THE TOP, peculiar to this wood burning box stove only, and not found on any other stove on the market, is a full swing top, so constructed that the entire top swings to one side, admitting of the largest chunks of wood to be fed from the top as well as from the front. This is a construction that you will especially appreciate, and one that can be had only from us. The tops of these stoves are also fitted with lids and centers, the two smallest stoves having only one lid, the other sizes having two lids, wide cut centers, and comes complete with lifter. The larger sized stoves can be used, and are used by thousands of our customers in the cold winter as a combination big wood heater and cook stove, for with the two big lids and center on the top it takes the place on many a cold morning of a cook stove in the kitchen.

FRONT. The front construction is superior to any other box stove on the market; a handsome, beautifully shaped, full finished, elaborately ornamented swing door; a neat, close fitting sliding damper; a big, full swinging hearth plate; the whole closing airtight, giving you thorough control of the fire, and is the only box stove made in which you can depend upon holding the fire over night.

THIS BIG STOVE stands on a handsomely shaped, full finished and ornamented set of four legs; mitered and carefully fitted. The hearth is extra large, extra deep, extra wide, nicely shaped and fully finished, a special feature of this, our new Acme Champion Wood Burning Stove.

THIS HANDSOME BOX STOVE in the various sizes as listed, you understand, is for wood only, and as a wood stove we guarantee it the highest grade and in every way the best box wood burning heating stove made. We furnish it to you in the various sizes at the specially low prices as listed below.

THIS ILLUSTRATION shows the swing top construction of our box stove, one of the many desirable features that make this in every way the best box wood heating stove on the market. It will take in much larger pieces of wood, it gives you, in a sense, a cook stove and heating stove combined in one, a feature you will appreciate and will not find on other stoves. It's one of the many little features, really important, that go to make this, our box stove, by far the best box stove ever produced; therefore, in comparing ours with others, while you will find our price appreciably low, remember we guarantee you will find the quality even more in our favor.

Sectional view of our Champion Box Stove.

OUR GUARANTEE AND FREE TRIAL OFFER. If you will send us your order for one of these box stoves, we will ship it to you the day we receive your order, we will guarantee it to reach you in just a few days, we will guarantee it to reach you in perfect condition, without break or damage of any kind, you can use it thirty days in your own home, during which time you can put it to every test, compare it with any other box stove you can buy at much higher prices, and if you do not find it the best box stove you have ever used, if you are not perfectly satisfied with it, you can return it to us at our expense, and we will immediately return your money. With every stove we issue a written binding guarantee, under the terms and conditions of which, if any piece or part gives out by reason of defect in material or workmanship, we will replace or repair it free of charge. We bargain in the years to come to be ready at any time to furnish you any needed repair or part on a moment's notice, either free of any cost to you if within our guarantee, otherwise at bare factory cost, a mere fraction of what others charge.

THE FREIGHT CHARGES will amount to next to nothing. As these stoves weigh from 51 to 163 pounds, according to size, and the freight charges per 100 pounds from our Newark, Ohio, foundry, for 500 miles or less average from 25 cents to 40 cents; the freight charges on our biggest box stove will amount to next to nothing as compared to what we will save you in price.

THESE BOX STOVES, the small sizes for small rooms, bedrooms, etc., in the medium sizes for good sized rooms in homes for all purposes, and the big sizes for great big rooms in good sized houses for all purposes, are at our special prices as named herein, furnished all complete, including everything, every new 1907 feature, every up to date improvement, made on our very latest patterns, with our special interior construction and new system of fire control, handsome nickel plated door knob, swing top, top lids, etc. The prices named are for the stove delivered on board the cars at our foundry in Newark, Ohio.

Delivered on the cars at our Newark, Ohio, foundry. The stove number indicates length of wood.

Catalogue Number	Stove No.	Height, inches	Size Pipe to fit Collar	Actual weight, lbs.	Price
22F558	18	19½	5 inches	51	$1.99
22F559	22	21½	6 inches	76	2.90
22F560	25	23	6 inches	92	3.65
22F561	28	26	6 inches	113	4.40
22F562	30	26	6 inches	119	4.60
22F563	34	29½	6 inches	163	6.25
22F564	36	29½	6 inches	163	6.40

$5.40 AND $6.50

ACME GLENWOOD

THE BEST AIRTIGHT HOT AIR CIRCULATOR MADE.

WE CAN ALWAYS FURNISH REPAIRS.

THE LARGE ILLUSTRATION SHOWS OUR NEW 1907 MODEL ACME GLENWOOD WOOD BURNING, AIRTIGHT HEATING STOVE, with hot blast, down draft and hot air circulating system. This is our very highest grade air tight heating stove, and it will burn anything used for fuel with the exception of coal, and we offer it as the very highest type of sheet steel heater, a stove better designed, better made of higher class materials, cast in better pattern, a sheet steel heating stove which far outclasses any other sheet steel heating stove of this type manufactured in any stove foundry in the world. The feed opening is 10½ inches in diameter and the ash opening is 7 inches in diameter. The damper has screw adjustment, while the ash opening is a cast swing door, with a set screw fastening to make it airtight and a screw draft opening in the center to make a straight draft when desired. It is fitted for 6-inch stove pipe, and has our silver nickeled foot rails and silver nickeled band on top.

PLEASE NOTICE the smaller sectional illustration at the bottom of this page, which will give you a very clear idea of the method of constructing this stove with a double jacket open at the bottom and discharging the heated air through the holes in the cast main top. The hot air circulating system with which we have equipped this our Acme Glenwood Airtight Hot Air Circulating Heater is much superior to that used on any other airtight heater. It takes the cold air from the floor and passes it out the top, and as this is a very quick heater, it will warm the largest parlor or sitting room, heating the farthest corner of the room as well as the space near the stove, and as a wood burning airtight heater we guarantee it to give absolute satisfaction.

THE HOT BLAST DOWN DRAFT of this stove is a very cleverly designed attachment which makes this a smoke and gas consuming stove, and it will heat a larger space with less fuel than any other airtight heating stove offered in competition with it. It is particularly well adapted to wood burning sections by reason of its large fire chamber and generous feed top. It will burn the largest chunks of wood which could not be used for fuel in any other type of stove, and in the districts of the west where cobs and other light materials are used for heating purposes, it will be found to be just the stove you have been looking for.

THE MATERIALS USED in manufacturing this Acme Airtight Hot Air Circulator at $5.40 and $6.50 are the very finest grades it is possible to secure. The top is a very ornamental stove plate cast from the best gray pig iron; the base, the legs, the ash front and the down draft opening are likewise cast from the best Birmingham gray iron, and the patterns are new and very attractive. The body is constructed of finest polished steel and heavy sheet steel inner walls, made from No. 20 gauge steel. The height of the stove over all is 45 inches; the height of the body, 26 inches.

IN MANUFACTURING this high grade airtight heater, our ACME GLENWOOD, we not only use the finest materials possible, but this steel is worked over with the largest steel working machinery used in any stove foundry in the world, machinery which we had built expressly for our uses, designed by us, and which handles the heaviest plates of steel as if they were made of paper, and by the use of this steel plate working machinery we have been so enabled to reduce the cost of manufacture that our $5.40 and $6.50 prices represent greater value in an airtight heating stove of this type than is put into any other stove offered by any other founder or dealer at from $10.00 to $13.00. In addition to our special machinery equipment, the men who build these stoves build them exclusively, and we therefore bring to their manufacture a higher grade workmanship and more thorough knowledge of stove making, and as we produce thousands of them every year, we have brought the manufacturing cost to the lowest possible minimum.

OUR $5.40 AND $6.50 PRICES on this our Acme Glenwood Airtight Hot Air Circulator represent the bare cost of materials and labor only with our uniform small margin of profit added, and we assure you that in this our Acme Glenwood we offer you the finest airtight sheet steel heater manufactured, no matter what its name, make or price.

We can always furnish REPAIR CASTINGS FOR ACMES.

HOT AIR CIRCULATOR. HOT BLAST DOWN DRAFT.

Cross section view of hot blast and circulating system in the Acme Glenwood and Acme Buckeye.

OUR BINDING GUARANTEE. Every one of our Airtight Hot Air Circulating Heaters is covered by our binding guarantee, covering every piece and part that enters into the stove. We claim for our airtight stoves, as compared with other airtight stoves on the market, that we use heavier sheet steel, heavier, smoother and better fitting castings, better fittings, better nickel work, and turn out in every way a better heater than you can buy anywhere on the market. As a guarantee that you cannot duplicate this stove in quality of material, workmanship and finish, and that it will produce more heat for a like amount of fuel than any other airtight heater on the market, we are willing to accept your order for one of these stoves, to be sent to you with the understanding and agreement that if after thirty days' trial you are not satisfied with it, and are not convinced that you have received a much better stove than you could have bought elsewhere, you are at liberty to return the stove to us at our expense, and we will immediately return your money, together with any transportation charges you may have paid.

WHY OUR STOVES ARE THE HIGHEST GRADE MADE IN THE WORLD. We use the best patterns that money can buy, we employ only the most skilled mechanics, we use only the highest grade materials that can be produced. No factory in the world maintains the rigid inspection that we do, and as a result we turn out of our foundry such stoves as go out of no other foundry in America, yet our price to our customers is about one-half the prices charged by others, since we only charge you the actual cost of material and labor, with but our one small percentage of profit added.

WE GUARANTEE SAFE DELIVERY.

ABOUT THE FREIGHT CHARGES. The freight charges amount to next to nothing as compared with what you can save in price. The railroad companies will carry this stove from one hundred to a thousand miles from Newark for a mere fraction of what you will save in price.

WIDE AWAKE STOVE DEALERS can make money buying their stoves from us to sell again. While we never particularly solicited the trade of dealers, nevertheless, we know that in this line of merchandise our prices are so far below the prices asked by any other manufacturer, wholesaler or jobber that retail dealers can buy from us to advantage. We would be glad to receive the order of dealers, because the more stoves we sell, the greater is our output, and the larger quantities we can order of raw material. At the same time, we cannot offer any further inducement, and whether you are a customer for one stove or a dealer who is going to order a full line of sizes, the price will be exactly the same, just as plainly printed on this page, and our terms of shipment remain exactly the same and there are no further concessions or reductions that it is possible for us to make. At the same time, we might say that our name and address does not appear on the stoves, but the stoves are simply branded Newark Stove Works, Chicago. You can sell them without anyone knowing that you buy your supplies from us.

Price List of the Acme Glenwood,

With Hot Blast Draft and Hot Air Circulating System Strongly Crated and Delivered on the Cars at our Foundry in Newark, Ohio.

Catalogue Number	Stove No.	Length, inches	Width, inches	Shipping Weight	Price
22F565	26	26	17	126 lbs.	$5.40
22F566	32	32	18	154 lbs.	6.50

THE ACME RADIATOR.

PLAIN SIMPLE FACTS.

Anyone who has a house to heat will want an Acme Hot Air Radiator when he knows the plain, simple facts about it.

An immense proportion of heat made by the fuel burned passes out of the chimney instead of heating our rooms. "Hotter on top of the chimney than down by the stove;" yes, a good deal. The Acme Radiator is a device affixed to a stove pipe or furnace pipe to keep the heat from going up the chimney. **It does it. Your fuel bills are nearly twice as large as they would be if you used this waste heat. Don't waste it; stop it before it reaches the chimney with an Acme Radiator.** It stops the heat on its way to the chimney and makes it do double duty. You can place an **Acme Radiator** on the stove pipe in the same room with the stove. It will actually save from one-quarter to one-half the fuel. There is no guess work in this statement. Actual tests have proved it time and time again. It is a stove that throws off heat without requiring any fuel or attention at all. No dust in the room and no ashes to carry out. No gas escapes from them and they cause no obstruction at all to the draft. They can be as easily cleaned and repaired as a stove pipe. **An Acme Radiator really costs nothing. It pays for itself in saved fuel in a very short time.**

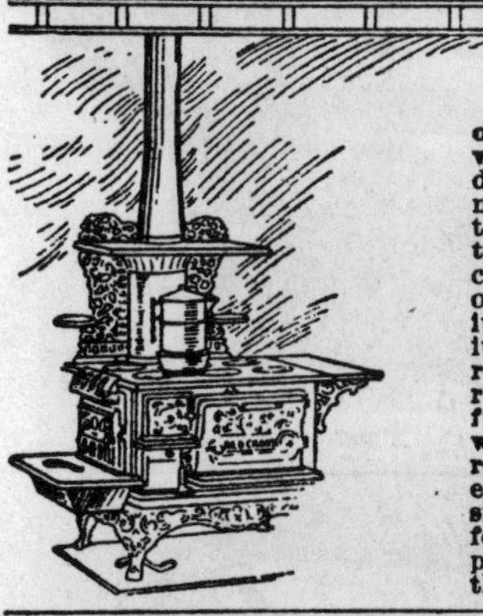

One ton of coal or one cord of wood will produce nearly as much heat with the Acme Radiator as two tons of coal or two cords of wood without it. You can place it in an upstairs room on a pipe running through from below, and it will heat that room without the expenditure of a single extra cent for fuel. It simply uses the heat that is escaping.

OIL HEATING STOVES.

WE OFFER A MOST COMPLETE AND DESIRABLE LINE FOR YOUR SELECTION, STOVES THAT EMBODY ALL THE VERY LATEST IDEAS AND IMPROVEMENTS, AND NOTHING BUT THE BEST MATERIAL AND WORKMANSHIP ENTERS INTO THEIR CONSTRUCTION.

WHY YOU SHOULD USE AN OIL HEATER.

ECONOMY. No waste of fuel, you light it when you are ready for it, and extinguish it as soon as the necessity for its use has passed. A gallon of oil will run it at a cost less than the same amount of heat can be procured with any other fuel.

LABOR SAVING. No kindling to prepare, no coal to carry, no ashes to dispose of.

HEAT WHEREVER YOU WANT IT. All stoves are portable and can be placed where they are needed most. Can be carried from one room to another with absolute safety. No chimney needed.

QUICK HEAT. Light it with a match and you have instant heat. It lights as easily as gas and is ready for use at any hour of the day or night.

CLEANLINESS. Scientific construction insures freedom from smoke or odor. The combustion in these stoves is perfect, and is due to many years of experimenting on the part of the manufacturers, who are the oldest makers of oil heating stoves. All parts can be easily and thoroughly cleaned.

OPERATION. They are simple in construction, there is nothing complicated to get out of order and in reality no directions are necessary. We, however, attach a card of simple directions to each stove before shipping.

FUEL. The fuel used (kerosone-coal oil) can easily be procured; the same oil can that supplies your lamp will also furnish the fuel for heating.

WHERE AN OIL HEATER CAN BE USED TO ADVANTAGE.

In your best room you can use an oil heater without being uneasy, because they make NO SOOT, NO SMOKE, NO ODOR AND ARE ABSOLUTELY SAFE.

WHEN YOUR FURNACE OR BASE BURNER is not in operation and the weather is damp or chilly, an oil heater should be on hand to drive the chill and dampness out of your different rooms, and prevent sickness.

YOUR SUMMER COTTAGE can be made comfortable at all times and you would stay later in the fall if you have an oil heater for the cold evenings,

IF IT IS CHILLY UPSTAIRS, just carry the oil heater up and in a moment your sleeping room will be warm. It makes quick heat.

YOUR BATH ROOM may be cold and unpleasant; here is where an oil heater is a handy thing.

Magic Oil Heater.

Although low priced this stove has good working qualities, is well made and will give excellent satisfaction to the user. Is mica lighted. Top, middle ring, base and legs are finished with aluminum bronze. Steel tank holds 2 quarts and will burn 4 to 5 hours without refilling. Height to top of bail, 23½ inches. Wick circumference, 9½ inches. Diameter of drum, 8 inches. Weight, 8 pounds.

No. 22E599 Price............$2.25

Superb Oil Heater.

Great heat at small expense. We guarantee more heat from the amount of oil consumed than can be derived from any other heater made. Top tips back for lighting.

No. 22E600 Steel tank holds 4 quarts. Has registering oil indicator. Burns 8 to 10 hours with one filling. Height, to top of bail, 31 inches; wick circumference, 11 inches; diameter of drum, 8 inches. Weight, 13 lbs. Price........$2.75

No. 22E602 Extra wicks for either of the above heaters. Price.........................9c

WHITE FLAME OIL HEATERS.

These stoves will be found to meet all requirements of oil stove heating and will keep a large room at a comfortable temperature in cold weather. The drum is made of polished steel and is perforated two-thirds of its length from the top, showing visible flame. Base and reservoir are of heavy aluminum steel, finished in black japan and tastily decorated. Is fitted with powerful central draft burner. Has patent wick raising device and is easily re-wicked. Has convenient bail for carrying stove and top swings back on hinge allowing free access to the burner for lighting and cleaning. Tank can be refilled without removing from stove. Has patent central ventiduct for distributing heat by circulation as well as radiation. Is provided with floor tray which will protect carpets from damage if tank is accidentally overfilled.

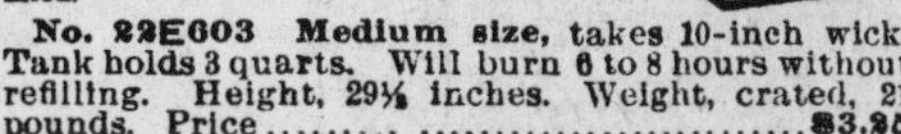

No. 22E603 Medium size, takes 10-inch wick. Tank holds 3 quarts. Will burn 6 to 8 hours without refilling. Height, 29½ inches. Weight, crated, 21 pounds. Price................................$3.25

No. 22E604 Extra wicks for above. Price....10c

No. 22E605 Large size, takes 15-inch wick. Tank holds 5 quarts of oil and will burn 10 to 12 hours without refilling. Height, 32½ inches. Weight, crated, 30 pounds. Price................................$4.35

No. 22E606 Extra Wicks for above..........12c

No. 22E607 This stove has style and dignity and is as practical and durable as any coal stove. Entire stove is cast iron with exception of drum which is of polished steel and oil reservoir which is made of heavy aluminum steel. Has center mica section which reflects a brilliant light when stove is in use. Top swings back to allow access to burners for cleaning purposes. Has swing door in mica section for lighting. Tank holds 5 quarts and stove will burn 10 to 12 hours without refilling, which can be done without removing tank from stove. Has central ventiduct which takes cold air from the floor and circulates it thoroughly heated into the room. Is provided with floor tray which will protect carpets from damage if tank is accidentally overfilled. Wick circumference, 15 inches. Height, 36 inches. Weight, crated, 70 pounds. Price........................$6.95

No. 22E606 Extra wicks for above, each....12c

ACME SMOKELESS - WICKLESS OIL RADIATORS.

This Acme Smokeless-Wickless Blue Flame Oil Radiator Heating Stove is our latest addition to the world's wonder line of Blue Flame Oil Stoves. On another page we fully describe our Wickless Blue Flame Cooking Stoves and we here briefly say the same principle is in the Acme Smokeless Radiators. The world moves and the people reap the benefits. Heat your bath room; heat any room where other heat does not reach; heat all your rooms with the Acme Smokeless-Wickless Oil Radiators and you will find a pleasant comfortable heat. Through the tubular radiators of each stove the heated air continues to pass, taking the cold air from below and passing it out into the room, constantly changing the atmosphere and giving a stronger, larger volume of hot air circulation than can be obtained from any other form of oil heater. The No. 10 will heat a small room or a bath room in the coldest weather. The No. 20 will heat a large room in the most severe weather. Order one and if not found all we claim for it or if it is not satisfactory, you can return it to us within thirty days and we will refund your money including the freight you have paid.

REASONS WHY OUR WICKLESS RADIATORS ARE SUPERIOR TO ORDINARY OIL HEATERS.

1st. **No wick to trim,** or wick raiser to get out of order or bother with.
2nd. **Absolutely smokeless and odorless,** others so called are only so in name.
3rd. **Easily operated.** Intense or slow heat, as may be desired.
4th. **The radiator top is removable,** leaving a most complete and effective cooking stove with a top grate nicely nickeled and finished.
5th. **Have double reservoirs.** Stove keeps on burning while you take upper reservoir away to refill.
6th. **Is economical in consumption of oil and a great labor saver,** one gallon of kerosene will produce a large volume of heat for 8 to 10 hours.

Acme Wickless Radiator, No. 10, $3.80.

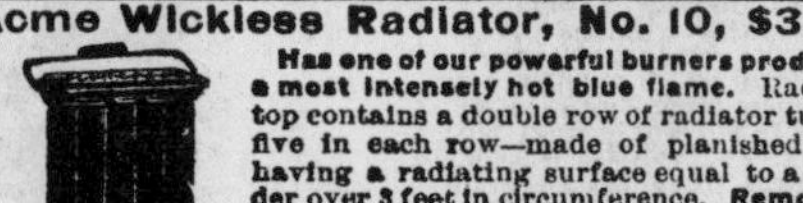

Has one of our powerful burners producing a most intensely hot blue flame. Radiator top contains a double row of radiator tubes—five in each row—made of planished iron, **having a radiating surface equal to a cylinder over 3 feet in circumference. Removable radiator top,** especially designed to leave a leave a lamp stove for cooking purposes. Removable reservoir holds 2½ pints, burning about seven hours. Dimensions: Total height, 25 inches; size of top, 7x12 inches; height of cooking section, 10 inches; height of radiator, 15 inches. Shipping weight, 37 pounds.

No. 22E608 Acme Wickless Radiator, No. 10. Price..........................$3.80

GUARANTEED TO PLEASE OR YOUR MONEY REFUNDED.

Acme Wickless Radiator, No. 20, $6.35.

Contains two powerful Wickless Blue Blue Flame Burners. The radiator top contains the equivalent of 21 radiating tubes. This gives a radiating surface equal to a drum cylinder 34 inches in circumference. **The radiator top is removable,** leaving a most complete and effective cooking stove. Removable reservoir holds over one gallon, permitting both burners to be operated at fair flame nearly 10 hours. Dimensions: Total height, 30 inches; size of radiator, 8x16 inches; size of cooking top, 12x16 inches. Height of cooking stove section, 10 inches; height of radiator section, 20 inches. Shipping weight, 54 pounds.

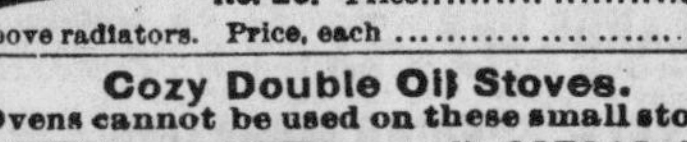

No. 22E609 Acme Wickless Radiator No. 20. Price..............................$6.35

No. 22E610 Extra Asbestos Lighting Rings or Kindlers for the above radiators. Price, each 6c

DUKE LAMP STOVES.

Our 32-Cent Lamp Stove.

Ovens cannot be used on these small stoves.

No. 22E611 One-Burner Lamp Stove. Weight, 3½ pounds. Price..32c

No. 22E612 Two-Burner Lamp Stove. Weight, 5½ pounds. Price..64c

No. 22E613 Three-Burner Lamp Stove. Weight, 8½ pounds. Price...96c

No. 22E614 Wicks for above stoves, 4 inches wide. Price, each............3c

Cash with order prices.

Cozy Single Oil Stoves.

Ovens cannot be used on these small stoves.

The Cozy is a well made stove in every particular, and is the cheapest well made stove on the market.

No. 22E615 No. 102¼, Single. Has two 3½-inch wicks. Weight, 6 pounds. Price...................55c

No. 22E616 No. 102½, Single. Has two 4-inch wicks. Weight, 8 pounds. Price..75c

No. 22E617 No. 103, Single. Has three 4-inch burners. Weight, 9 pounds. Price...........$1.00

Cash with order prices.

Cozy Double Oil Stoves.

Ovens cannot be used on these small stoves.

No. 22E618 No. 102¼ Double. Has four wicks 3½ inches wide. Weight, crated, 18 pounds. Price.$1.15

No. 22E619 No. 102½ Double. Has four wicks 4 inches wide. Weight, crated, 22 pounds. Price.$1.60

No. 22E620 No. 103 Double. Has six wicks 4 inches wide. Weight, crated, 25 pounds. Price..............................$2.10

No. 22E622 4 -inch wicks. Price, each.. .... .03

No. 22E623 3½-inch wicks. Price, each............ .03

Cash with order prices.

ORIGINAL AND SUPERIOR CONSTRUCTION OF THE ACME SUNBURST BASE BURNER

IN PRODUCING THIS, our Acme Sunburst Base Burner, we have striven to make it the very finest stove we build, and it is truly representative of the wonderful value we are able to offer you in the highest and best quality stoves this largest stove foundry in the world produces. The raw materials which enter into its construction are of the very best, the gray iron used in making all the castings is of the very highest quality Birmingham pig iron, than which no better material is obtainable in the world. We employ a skilled chemist whose duty it is to see that the iron we use and the other materials which are used in the smelting and fusing of the molten metal is of a character which will result in the production of the toughest, the most durable castings it is possible to make, and in fitting these castings, in grinding and polishing, in silver nickeling, the parts pass through the hands of the most expert stove builders in the world, and it is for this reason that we are able to offer you this beautiful, highly ornamented stove under a guarantee that it is better made, that it is stronger, that it is easier to operate and more satisfactory in every way than any stove you ever saw or any stove that you can buy at home or elsewhere at any price; and if any of the base burners now on the market were offered you at identically the same prices asked by us for this, our Acme Sunburst, they would not be nearly so economical a stove for you to buy, because in fuel saved and in comfort given you in your home throughout the long cold months of winter, an Acme Sunburst far surpasses any other stove that money can buy.

THE LARGE ILLUSTRATION shown on the opposite page and the smaller illustration shown on this page, though made by our artists direct from the Acme Sunburst Base Burner itself, cannot begin to convey to you the great beauty, the large and massive proportions of this wonderful hard coal, self feeding base burner, our Acme Sunburst. The stove itself should be seen to appreciate the beauty of its design, the elaborate silver nickeling, and it should be very carefully examined to secure an adequate idea of the many superior qualities which go to make this the very best base burner ever produced in any stove foundry. In addition to the sectional views shown on this page we give below a detailed description of the several parts of this our Acme Sunburst base burner, explaining to you just how this wonderful stove is constructed, calling your attention to the special features which make it such a magnificent heater, such an economical fuel consumer, and a stove that will heat a large house and keep it more comfortable under all weather conditions than any other base burner of similar size, though sold at double the prices we ask. We ask you to read this detailed description because if you are in the market for a heater you cannot afford to overlook this wonderful value and we know that if you will note the very careful manner in which it is constructed, the high grade materials used in its manufacture, the new principles embodied in its construction and operation you will immediately decide that this is the stove of all others for you to buy, remembering that we send it to you on our unusually liberal terms of 30 days' free trial and guaranteeing that it is all we represent it to be or your money and the transportation charges will be refunded to you.

ITS GENERAL APPEARANCE. The illustration shown on this and the opposite page will convey to you an idea of the extreme beauty of the design of our Acme Sunburst Hard Coal Self Feeding Base Burner. The pattern is entirely new with us and it was designed by one of the greatest stove artists in the business; its graceful lines appeal to the artistic sense of every stove buyer because it is well balanced, its massive proportions give evidence of its strength and impart a sense of comfort even before the fire is kindled within it. It is elaborately ornamented, and from its handsomely silver nickeled base to the beautiful turned urn on the magazine top, it is without doubt one of the most beautiful and ornamental stoves that was ever placed in any parlor.

THE FRAME. In selecting the materials from which to cast the frame of this large and beautiful heater we use only the choicest Birmingham pig iron, the very best raw material that money will buy. Every casting comprising the frame of this stove is made extra strong; there is no scrimping in the use of material either in the parts which may be seen or the parts unseen, and our chemist so carefully scrutenizes the selection and the combination of the materials that go into our furnaces from which to cast the several parts of the Acme Sunburst Base Burner that we can say that no castings on any stove are better made, are tougher or more durable or will stand harder usage than the castings we use in constructing this heater, and after the parts have been moulded they are carefully inspected, they are severely tested and every piece or part which shows the slightest defect in any way whatsoever, or which does not measure up to our specifications that it shall be the very best and the very highest grade in every respect, is immediately condemned, broken and thrown into the scrap pile.

THE FITTING which follows the making of the several parts, the grinding and adjusting is done on the finest stove working machinery with which any foundry is equipped; each individual part is ground to fit the place it occupies, and all this work is so thoroughly, so carefully done, that the draft and damper control of this base burner is absolute, enabling you to regulate the heat in the room as it cannot be regulated on any other base burner.

REMOVABLE FIRE POT AND GRATE. We direct your special attention to the ease with which the fire pot may be removed from this base burner through the isinglass doors, as shown in the sectional illustration on this page. It isn't necessary to tip up the fire pot on its side and wrestle with it to remove it for repairs or overhauling; it isn't necessary to unbolt any part of the stove, it slides straight outward, and in this respect it is different from any other hard coal base burner on the market. It also indicates to you the unusually large, full sized fire view doors with which this fine base burner is equipped and it indicates also the simplicity of the stove, how easily the parts may be removed and put back or replaced, how easily the stove may be operated and regulated, because it has practically no complicated parts to give trouble or get out of order.

OUR DUPLEX GRATE is another exclusive feature on this finest base burner and it is made with our patent shaking ring and dumping grate, well known wherever our superior stoves have been sold, and acknowledged to be the only perfect hard coal duplex grate. The ashes and clinkers are quickly thrown to the center of the grate by gently shaking from right to left. In this manner the bottom of the fire is quickly freed from all refuse and a slight turn of the shaker handle, dumps the clinkers and cinders through the duplex grate to the ash pan below, without disturbing the fire, permitting free circulation of the air through the grate and fuel. It is this patent duplex shaker grate which keeps the fire pot free from an accumulation of dead ashes, clinkers and cinders, which gives such absolute control of the fire and makes this, our Acme Sunburst, the most economical fuel consumer of any base burner on the market.

THE FLUE CONSTRUCTION of this base burner is entirely new with us and is another exclusive feature which contributes very largely toward the quick, even, satisfactory and economical heating of your home. These flues are made from heavy, fine gray iron, especially designed to withstand intense heat and continual and hard usage. They are so carefully constructed along new lines that the smoke and other products of combustion after leaving the fire chamber, pass downward to the base in the back left hand corner, pass entirely around the sides and front of the base, around the bottom of the hot air flue and up and out of the smoke flue. This scientific arrangement of the hot flues, by which the heat comes in direct contact with both the inside and outside walls of the base, and the designing of the base with open center, through which opening air is drawn up between the back flues, gives us, in this, our Acme Sunburst Base Burner, over double the radiating surface of any other hard coal heating stove. For this reason it does not require the hot fire to heat a given space that would be required in any other base burner, and this flue construction, together with our duplex grate and fire control, places this stove in a class distinctly its own as the most marvelous heater and the most economical fuel consumer ever offered at any price.

THE HOT AIR FLUE extends from the base to the top of the stove and the vent is covered with an ornamented open work cap. A very large proportion of the heated air comes out into the room from this opening immediately behind the swing top. If it is desired to heat the second floor of your home or a room or two above the parlor or sitting room where you have installed the base burner, the ornamental cap may be removed and pipe may be attached and carried up to a register in the floor above and in this manner the entire home may be heated with this one heater. Such an arrangement will prove very economical for you and, in many homes where this stove has gone, it has taken the place of several stoves employed before its purchase to make the house warm and comfortable throughout the long winter months, and it will heat your entire house in this manner without any increase in amount of fuel consumed.

THE LARGE URN surmounting this handsome base burner is most artistic and the highly polished, silver nickeled swing top to which it is attached, easily swings to the left, automatically lifting the coal magazine cover, so that a fresh supply of fuel may be poured into the magazine below.

THE SELF FEEDING MAGAZINE is of very generous proportions and will supply the fire with sufficient coal to operate the stove for many hours without replenishing. It is built with a view to saving fuel and carrying coal enough at one filling to run the heater twelve to sixteen hours.

THE SILVER NICKELED DOME HEAD. In designing the massive dome which surmounts the fire chamber of our Acme Sunburst Base Burner, our artist has given us something entirely different from that shown on any other base burner and it is full silver nickeled by our own patented silver nickeling process, producing an everlasting luster. The broad mirror finished reflectors, immediately above the isinglass fire view doors, catch the rays of light from the live coals within and give a brilliant illumination and an air of comfort and coziness to the room.

THE SILVER NICKELING on other portions of this stove is applied by the same patented process, and with only average care it will retain its brilliancy and luster the full life of the stove itself. The name plate, the full ash pit door with its screw draft register, the foot rails on each side, the massive, elaborate leg frame and legs, the dragon corners, which also display the exquisite taste of our artist who designed this stove, are all silver nickeled by this same patented process, and in wealth of silver nickeling, in striking contrast of reflected color this stove undoubtedly excels in beauty any stove ever attempted by any manufacturer.

THE MICA ILLUMINATION is full and complete on three sides of the stove, from the base to the silver nickeled dome. The mica doors are fitted with recessed grooves, they are absolutely airtight and held firmly in place by silver nickeled turn buckles and the hottest fire will not expand, warp or spring them out of place. The mica sections are all large and unobstructed by any iron ornaments, permitting all the light from the bright coals within the fire chamber to pass out into the room.

THE ASH PIT AND THE ASH PAN are unusually large to provide against the accumulation of a large quantity of ashes and it is only necessary to empty the ash pan once a day when the stove is in ordinary use to prevent the accumulation of ashes against the grate above it. So many base burners are fitted with small ash pans which quickly fill up and there is, therefore, constant danger that the ashes will bank up against the grates and burn them out in a few hours' time unless the ashes are emptied frequently. This is a fault which we have wholly overcome in the Acme Sunburst.

OTHER SPECIAL FEATURES of this base burner are its smoke collar or cast elbow, bolted and fitted to main back so carefully that it is absolutely gastight. The tea kettle attachment on the back of the stove is supplied with removable lid, so that it may be removed for heating water quickly. Please notice in the ash door shown in the sectional view on this page the new perfected type of screw draft register with which this stove is equipped. This register is far superior to the old style sliding register which never could be made airtight unless fitted so closely that it could be opened or closed only with difficulty. With our screw draft register the fire is under absolute control and it is no trouble at all to regulate the heating of the room to the fraction of a degree. This draft may be so set that the stove will run at a uniform heat at all times, burning just an even quantity of fuel without waste.

IN SHORT, EVERY CONSIDERATION has been given to the designing and building of this magnificent base burner, and it has been our endeavor to produce in our Acme Sunburst an absolutely perfect hard coal, self feeding base burner; one that we could offer as a heater excelling in every essential feature the very best base burners offered by any other firm or individual, and if the thousands of Acme Sunburst Base Burners sold and now used in the homes in this country and giving absolute satisfaction are to be accepted as evidence of our success, no stove produced in any foundry even approaches this in heating capacity, in economical consumption of fuel and in lowness of price.

DON'T PAY $50.00 for a hard coal base burner which will not compare with our Acme Sunburst. Send us your order for this, our Acme Sunburst Self Feeding Base Burner, remember our broad guarantee, our 30-day free trial and money back proposition, and surely under these liberal terms, terms which are not offered by any other firm or individual, you can well afford to select one of these fine base burners at our special prices of $22.37, $25.69, and $29.00.

PLEASE NOTE THE ILLUSTRATION HEREWITH showing all the strong features of this, the highest grade base burner offered at any price. Note the large fire view doors, the generous nickeling, the fine grate; note especially the method of removing the fire pot and all the other special features of this high grade base burner. We know that a careful study of this sectional view in connection with the detailed description on this page will convince you that no base burner can be better made, if indeed it can be as well made, as this our Acme Sunburst.

SECTIONAL VIEW SHOWING DETAILED CONSTRUCTION OF THE ACME SUNBURST, THE FINEST HARD COAL BASE BURNER MANUFACTURED IN ANY FOUNDRY IN THE WORLD.

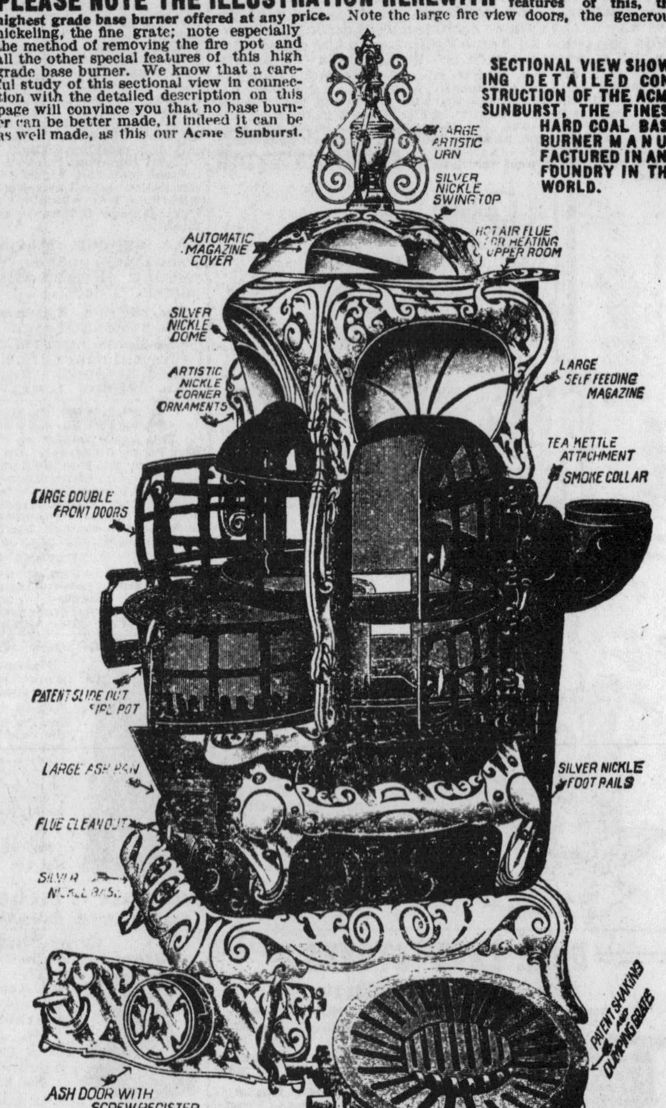

SEE OPPOSITE PAGE FOR SIZES AND PRICES OF ACME SUNBURST.

$19.06

CORONA BASE BURNER

WONDERFUL VALUE OF THE YEAR IN A SELF FEEDING, DOUBLE HEATING, RETURN FLUE, HARD COAL HEATER

AT $19.06, $22.05 AND $25.03, we offer you this, our Acme Corona Automatic, Self Feeding, Double Heating System, Return Flue, Hard Coal Base Burner as the greatest stove value that will be offered this year, a stove which is brought right up to date, carrying all the patented and exclusive features for which our stoves are famous.

WE EXCEL IN THE MANUFACTURE OF BASE BURNERS, and in our Acme Sunburst, described on pages 988 and 989, and in this, our Acme Corona, we offer the finest automatic, self feeding, hard coal base burners that ever have been produced in any stove foundry; stoves that are manufactured from the highest grade Birmingham pig iron; that are more elaborately designed from most beautiful patterns, with more nickeling, with larger isinglass fire view doors, with a finer double heating system than is contained in any other base burner on the market, and offered to you at prices which are about half those charged by others for base burners which are not nearly so well made, which will not heat your home as satisfactorily or as cheaply, and which are, therefore, a great deal more expensive both in purchase price and in cost of operation.

OUR ACME CORONA BASE BURNER, offered at $19.06, $22.05 and $25.03, is made from an entirely new pattern, a pattern designed by our own high class stove artist, and if you will just glance at this illustration you will immediately decide that it is a wonderfully attractive stove and an ornament to any home. It is built along identically the same lines followed by us in manufacturing our Acme Sunburst; it has all the special features which distinguish the Sunburst from all other base burners, the only difference between the two stoves being the amount of silver nickeling with which they are ornamented, and we guarantee it to be in heating power, in simplicity of operation, in quality of materials and workmanship the equal of any hard coal base burner ever produced in any foundry, no matter what its name, make or price, and if you do not feel that you can pay the few dollars extra to secure our beautiful silver nickel plated, handsome Acme Sunburst, as described on pages 988 and 989, then take the next best stove, the exact same stove with less nickeling, this, our Acme Corona at our special prices of $19.06, $22.05 and $25.03, according to size.

DESCRIPTION.

WE HAVE NOT SPARED ANY EXPENSE in designing this handsome stove. The illustration gives you a very good idea of the attractive pattern and delicate tracery of the silver nickeled ornamented parts, and dome, corner ornaments, name plate, draft register, foot rails and leg base are all beautifully nickel plated by our silver nickeling process, polished to the highest degree, and this beautiful finish, with only ordinary care, is practically indestructible. The Reflectors, above the fire view doors with mirror polished surfaces, double and treble the glow of the coals within and flood the room with light.

THE LARGE AND ARTISTIC URN surmounting the stove is finished in brass, trimmed around an ebony globe body. The spearhead and decorated arms are in brass finish, blending harmoniously with the silver nickeled dome shaped swing cover beneath. The Swinging Cover operates the magazine cover automatically, so that when swung to the left the magazine is open for the reception of a new supply of coal. The Magazine itself is of generous proportions and holds a very liberal supply of coal and in the coldest weather it will supply the fire for many hours without replenishing.

THE DOUBLE HEATING FLUE, of the same design identically as that used on our highest grade base burner, our Acme Sunburst, gives this stove its wonderful heating power. The cold air is drawn from the floor at the bottom of the stove, is circulated around the hot surfaces of the stove and discharged through the hot air flue at the top. The air circulates so rapidly and so positively that your home will be free from cold corners, and by actual test this heating process is so rapid and the circulation so perfect that the temperature of the room heated with this our Acme Corona will only vary three or four degrees between the floor and ceiling. No other hard coal base burner, except our Acme Sunburst, will yield such results and it is this exclusive double heating feature with which our base burners are equipped which enables us to heat a great big house so evenly and so satisfactorily at a lower expense for fuel than can be shown by any other hard coal base burner selling for twice the prices we ask.

A PIPE MAY BE ATTACHED to the top of the hot air flue and carried to a register in the floor above, so that a portion of the heat developed by this our Acme Corona will pass to the floors above and heat one or more rooms as comfortably as the floor below with no additional consumption of fuel.

THE SILVER NICKELED DOME TOP surmounting the fire chamber of this handsome base burner is large and handsomely designed; its beautiful, massive outlines are clearly shown in the illustration, which is made direct from a photograph, and we know that if you order this, our Acme Corona at our special prices of $19.06, $22.05 and $25.03, according to size, you will be delighted with your purchase as thousands of our customers have been before you.

THE FIRE POT AND COAL GRATE are of the same type of construction as those used in our Acme Sunburst, our famous shaker ring and duplex dumping grate, and all dead ashes, cinders and clinkers are quickly and easily cut out and dropped to ash pan below without disturbing the fire above. In conjunction with our new screw draft register, which may be regulated to a fraction of a degree, this patented fire pot and grate enables you to so control the fire in this popular, self feeding hard coal base burner that for evenness of heat, economy in the consumption of fuel it is unsurpassed by any stove produced.

THIS STOVE IS WELL ADAPTED to any home and it will heat almost any size room or house. It comes in three sizes, the fire chamber measuring 13, 15 and 17 inches, and it really represents such value as has never before been put in any hard coal base burner on the market. It has the latest tea kettle attachment, it has the latest and best heating flue construction; it has the latest ash pit and pan of large size; it has our highest grade interior construction, and it is altogether one of the very best, longest lived and most satisfactory hard coal, self feeding, base burning stoves on the market.

OUR BINDING GUARANTEE of quality, our thirty day free trial and refund proposition such as we offer on our Acme Sunburst also applies to this our Acme Corona, and we will send it to you with the distinct understanding and agreement that you may use it thirty days in your own home, and if you do not decide that it is in every way all that you could expect or ask for in a high grade, perfectly constructed, hard coal base burner, the very best value that you can secure at home or elsewhere, a stove consuming less fuel than any other base burner, except our Acme Sunburst, and sold to you at a big saving in cost, it may be returned to us at our expense of transportation charges both ways and we will refund your money.

Saved $22.00. Arrived O. K., and Nobody Can Beat It.

Sears, Roebuck & Co., Chicago, Ill. Bloomington, Ill.

Dear Sirs:—

I am very well pleased with our Acme Corona Base Heater. It is a fine stove. It came here O. K. in every respect, and everybody that looks at it says it is a beauty. I will say that I have saved $22.00 on the stove, and have just as good a stove as anybody. There is no doubt but what you will sell more stoves in Bloomington. I know that nobody can beat it for quality. It draws well and heats well in every respect.

Yours truly, J. LE BANDI, 1308 N. Mason Street.

In writing to above party please enclose a 2-cent stamp for reply.

Prices of Acme Corona Base Burner, strongly crated and delivered on the cars at our Newark, Ohio, foundry.

Catalogue Number	Stove Number	Size of Fire Pot	Floor to Base of Urn	Floor Space, inches	Size Pipe Collar, inches	Shipping Weight, pounds	Price
22F473	13	13 inches	52 inches	23½ x 23½	6	331	$19.06
22F474	15	15 inches	54 inches	25½ x 25½	6	375	22.05
22F475	17	17 inches	57 inches	27½ x 27½	6	431	25.03

OUR WONDERFUL QUICK DELIVERY ARRANGEMENT ON THE ACME SUNBURST.

TO MAKE THE FREIGHT CHARGES VERY LOW, we have this our Beautiful Acme Sunburst (the World Wonder Base Burner) in three sizes, at $24.80, $27.95 and $30.98, on hand in warehouses in the cities mentioned, securely crated and ready for immediate shipment and in perfect condition. To insure your having very little freight charges to pay, we have arranged to first ship this beautiful **Acme Sunburst Base Burner** in solid carload lots, direct to the various cities named on page 46, receiving from the railroad company the very lowest carload freight rate, so that you can go to your postmaster, R. F. D. carrier, express agent or banker, and get a money order drawn in our favor, selecting one of these sizes, enclosing the amount in a letter addressed to **Sears, Roebuck & Co., Chicago, Illinois,** and we will immediately send your order by special delivery to our stove warehouse, the one nearest to you, and order the stove shipped to your railroad station on your order at once. We know it leaves the warehouse near you in perfect condition. We know it will reach you from a few hours to a day or two at the most from the time it leaves the warehouse, and when you do get it, you will only have the carload rate to pay from the foundry at Newark, Ohio, to the warehouse nearest you (which is usually half the freight charges that one has to pay when but one stove is shipped by freight). In addition to this very low carload rate from the foundry to the warehouse near you, **you will also have to pay very small freight charges** for the short haul from this warehouse to your nearest railroad station, but the total freight charges you have to pay when you receive the stove will not—as a rule—amount to more than one-half to two-thirds the freight charges you would have to pay if the stove were shipped to you singly as one shipment from the foundry at Newark, Ohio, to your railroad station.

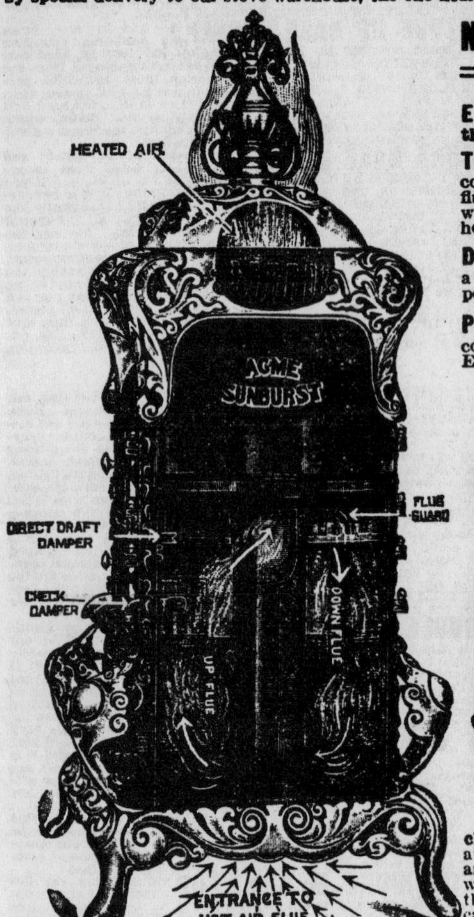

View of Back Flues, Showing Fire Travel and Hot Air Flue.

NEW AND IMPROVED BASE AND FLUE CONSTRUCTION OF THE ACME SUNBURST

EXCLUSIVE AND ORIGINAL SPECIAL FEATURES contained in the Acme Sunburst Burner are indicated in a measure in the pictures on this and preceding page.

TO THE LEFT may be seen an illustration showing how the heat and flames curl over the flue guard at the extreme left, passing down the descending flues, then circling our new specially constructed flue bottom and diffusing, absolutely without loss, the heat product of combustion, ascending the flue at the right hand corner and swerving to the left and back at the smoke collar. This winding, circuitous way, coupled with the constant "staggering" of the heat and vast expanse of radiating surface with which every heat unit is brought into contact, produces unquestionably four times the usual base burner heating capacity.

DESIGN, FINISH AND OPERATION of our perfect base heating flue construction, affording the greatest possible radiation, is completed with such care and with a perfection that the illustrations, which are reproduced from photographs, give but a faint idea of the many points of advantage found in the Acme Sunburst.

PROPORTIONED EXACTLY TO THE QUANTITY of the fire pot's heating product, so that positively no loss of fuel value is entailed, our flue construction results in perfect heat diffusion and not an inch of radiation that can possibly be utilized is lost. Entirely original with us, this perfected example of flue construction contributes largely to the quick, even, satisfactory and economical heating of your home. The flues are made from heavy, fine gray Birmingham pig iron, smoothly finished and specially designed to withstand intense heat and continual hard usage.

SMOKE EXIT

NEWARK STOVE WORKS CHICAGO

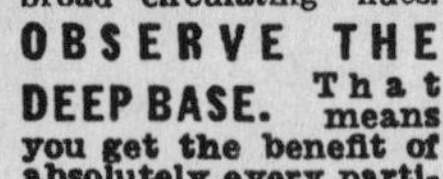

BACK OF STOVE REMOVED

NOT THE USUAL SINGLE FLUE STRIP at the bottom, offered by base burner manufacturers almost universally, but in our base flue construction is supplied a broad, well turned oval flue partition that forces the heat to every recess of our broad and deep bottom flues with vastly augmented heat radiation that insures a floor as "warm as toast" and well and evenly heated surrounding space. The heat is evenly and perfectly distributed over the entire bottom and brought into contact with every inch of our large, broad circulating flues.

OBSERVE THE DEEP BASE. That means you get the benefit of absolutely every particle of heat generated by the fire. See the manifold radiating surfaces brought about by our advanced construction, and by looking at the picture of the fire pot in connection with that of the rear view of the base burner you will see that from the time the flames leave the fire pot, as indicated, until their last remnant passes out at the pipe collar, absolutely each and every heat particle produced is kept continually in contact with some portion of the many radiating surfaces.

CONSCIENTIOUSLY DIRECTED SCIENTIFIC EFFORT earnestly applied has brought to the acme of perfection the inner construction of our Acme Sunburst. It is absolutely without an equal, it is new and original with us, and though imitations have been extensively attempted, no manufacturer has succeeded in applying our perfected flue construction to his product. It is unapproached by any base burner on the market and is in a class distinctly its own as the most marvelous heater and the most economical fuel consumer offered at any price, and with all its expensive improvements and its special characteristic points of excellence and its splendid perfection of construction, we sell it to you at a less price than is charged by manufacturers and dealers generally for an under sized, cheaply constructed, poorly appearing base burner, carrying absolutely none of the various special features of our own highest grade double heating base burner, that is positively the handsomest, simplest and best on the market.

HOT AIR FLUE extends from the base to the top of the stove and is indicated in the sectional view of the stove on this page. It extends from the base where the cold air is drawn by suction into the hollow projecting pocket that forms the bottom flue partition into the conduit between the ornamental projecting back flue and the always hot inside back that is in contact with the hottest product of the fire until the superheated air passes out of the hot air collar, which, when not used in connection with a pipe to an upper floor, is covered by a handsome open work silver nickel cap. As a general thing the heat rising from a hall adjacent to the base burner will be sufficient to heat the upper floor of a large house to a satisfactory temperature, but where it is desirable to centralize a large amount of heat at a given point above, the hot air is conducted from the hot air collar, as shown, by means of a pipe, to rooms above. A register can be added to the pipe in the manner suggested by the accompanying illustration, and the room above will almost immediately be warmed. If you do not wish to convey the heat in this manner, the hot air damper may be opened and the heat will pass out through the ornamental nickel cap into the surrounding air and thereby increase the heat of the first floor of the house.

HOT AIR FLUE

DIRECT DRAFT DAMPER

FLUE GUARD

EXTRA HEAVY REMOVABLE FIREPOT

Sectional View of Fire Pot and Back Flues, Showing Fire Travel.

OBSERVE HOW THE HOT AIR FLUE is kept in constant contact with the heat and also the carefully designed circulating flues for the flame. Compare the Acme Sunburst flue construction with that of absolutely any base burner on the market, irrespective of make, name or price, compare it point by point, and knowing the unquestioned superiority of our base burner we have the strongest personal conviction that we will be favored with your order for one of the world's best heaters, the Acme Sunburst.

How to Heat an Upstairs Room Without Additional Cost.

PRICE LIST OF OUR ACME SUNBURST BASE BURNER.

Catalogue Number	Stove No.	Fire Pot	Floor to Urn Base, inches	Floor Space, inches	Size Pipe Collar	Size Pipe Hot Air Collar	Shipping Weight pounds	Price
22H655	12	12	52	23½x23½	6 inches	7 inches	347	$24.80
22H656	14	14	54	25½x2[illegible]	6 inches	7 inches	403	27.95
22H657	16	16	57	27½x27½	6 inches	7 inches	465	30.98

THE HIGHEST GRADE BASE HEATING WOOD STOVE MADE

OUR ACME SUCCESS

AT $11.52 we offer you this our ACME SUCCESS Parlor Heating Stove under our guarantee that it is the highest grade base heating front diving flue stove made, regardless of name, make or price, a stove which is built on the same lines as those followed in the construction of our Acme Surprise, the exact same stove built with combination coal and wood burning grates.

THIS IS UNQUESTIONABLY the very highest grade wood burning heating stove that has ever been offered by any founder or stove dealer, and we know that it is absolutely impossible for any other founder to begin to equal the value we give you in this stove because it is made by us in the largest stove foundry in the world, where manufacturing costs are lower than in any other stove foundry, where materials cost us less than the same materials cost other founders and where we have developed the largest and most expert corps of trained stove builders to be found in any stove foundry in the world. The low cost of raw materials, our trained employes and hundreds of special machines built under our own supervision and according to our own plans for the handling of stove work have given us such enormous advantages in the manufacture of stoves and ranges that our selling prices as quoted in the pages of this catalogue are lower than the wholesale selling prices in carload lots of any other founder in the business.

THIS BASE HEATING FRONT DIVING FLUE Wood Burning Stove is a splendid example of what we are able to do in this the largest stove foundry in the world in the way of bringing highest quality stoves and ranges to you at the lowest possible cost. No other wood burning heater manufactured in any other foundry equals this stove in size, in massiveness and beauty of design, in rich silver nickel ornamentation, in draft control and in special features of grate and fire pot which give this stove it's wonderful base heating qualities; no other stove manufactured is so carefully and so thoroughly fitted, so thoroughly stayed and braced, no other stove has such superior interior construction as this our Acme Success and when we offer it to you at $11.52, $14.04 and $17.12 special manufacturers' prices we guarantee that it is the greatest value ever offered in a parlor heater designed specially for wood as fuel.

THIS IS ESSENTIALLY A HOME STOVE. It is made in three sizes, will accommodate rooms of a different size or houses of a different size. The largest size stove is amply large to heat any ordinary house, the whole downstairs to be made thoroughly comfortable, the upstairs sleeping rooms to be made comfortable for sleeping, this in the coldest weather with a less amount of fuel than with any other base heating diving flue wood burner made. There is no other stove of this type in which the fire is so thoroughly under control, no other stove of this type that will heat as many cubic feet of air with a like amount of fuel, no other stove of this type that will hold fire as many hours, no other stove of this type that has the graceful lines, the design, trimming, the silver nickeled ornamentation that will permit it to be compared with ours. It is a real ornament to the parlor or living room of any home.

THIS IS A PARLOR STOVE. When we say a parlor stove, we mean that it is in beauty of design, in the silver nickeled mounting and ornamentation effect such an ornament to any parlor in any home as you will find in no other stove of like style made in any other foundry in the country. It is handsomer in that it is richer, newer, more artistic, more up to date, more showy pattern of the rococo design than is being turned out by any other stove foundry in America today. The nickel ornamentation, the urn, the swing top, the base, the medallions excel anything yet produced by any other maker in a stove of this type. The swell front, in which is fitted the transparent mica that brings to view the flame and which flame is reflected through the polished reflector panel above, produces an effect not approached in any other stove made; in short, it is an ideal base heating diving flue, exclusively wood burning stove.

THE ILLUSTRATION, which has been drawn by our artist from a photograph, will give you but a vague idea of the beauty of this stove. It is a stove that must be seen to be appreciated. Beginning with an ornamental urn of bronze and polished copper colors, with a spearhead tip and four arms, as shown in the illustration, we pass to an elegant oval dome swing top which is heavily nickel plated and polished to the highest finish. Underneath it comes a main top with a griddle cover in the center, furnishing a cooking hole when dome is swung aside, and the main top, in which the griddle cover rests, will lift out entirely, leaving the whole main top open to receive irregular chunks of wood which might not go in the large fire door; then follows the elaborate full swell rococo ornamentation in the main top of the stove, where the highest quality of stove plate castings make for it strength, durability and finish unequaled by any other stove maker in the land.

THE UPPER FRONT OF THE STOVE is relieved by a highly finished, silver nickeled, ornamental reflector panel above the mica lights, through which the flame is seen and reflected into the room by the nickel polished reflector panel. Through the mica lights can be seen the flame blazing and curling downward through the diving front flue to the full base flues below, where it travels beneath the ash pit to the back of the stove and starts upward through the smoke pipe. IN THE LOWER FRONT is the screw draft register, highly nickeled and polished, through which the draft supply is obtained, and by which the draft can be cut off air tight. Just below this is the long, elaborate, silver nickeled and highly polished foot rail name plate, a broad, convenient rest for the feet, and an additional ornament to the front of the stove.

THE BASE SKIRTING OR LEG FRAME AND LEGS are all silver nickeled after our own process, incomparable in its finish, and not matched by any other foundry in the world. The right end of the stove contains a large wood fire door, admitting the largest piece of wood cut from any cord stick, and is fitted with a large, silver nickeled handgrip turnkey. At the bottom line of this door is a full silver nickeled ash catch, or small hearth, as shown, and the wood grate, being considerably below this line, combines to make it impossible for ashes to spill on the floor when the door is opened. The ash door has a large silver nickeled turnkey.

THE ASH PAN is large and runs the full length of the bottom grate The draft is toward the front of the stove, down the main front to the base flues, passing back and upward to the pipe collar and into the smoke pipe. There is an automatic damper, the handle of which is shown in contact with a "trip" at the back of the fire door, so that when opening the door the direct draft is also opened automatically, and no smoke creeps out the top line of the door when putting in fuel. When the fuel is put in and the door closed, you can close the direct draft damper, and the heat then passes down the front, as described. THIS WOOD BURNING, BASE HEATING FRONT diving flue stove is made with a view of combining the good points of all high grade base heating stoves of this type made, with the defects of none. If you order this stove you will find it in many ways superior to anything in the same style that is being put out by any other manufacturer; being offered by any other dealer. Understand, every stove bears the name "Newark Stove Works, Chicago," and while the price is the same whether you order one stove or a carload, we especially request the orders of dealers large and small. We guarantee to furnish you better stoves than you can buy elsewhere and at a saving of 25 to 33⅓ per cent in price. If you buy from us you will increase your sales, and at the same profits you are now getting you will be able to give your customers much greater value for their money.

IF YOU BURN COAL SEE OUR ACME SURPRISE FOR COAL ON PAGE 994.

WE FURNISH this handsome stove under our guarantee for quality, under our 30 days' FREE TRIAL OFFER, under our guarantee that it will reach you in perfect condition. We furnish it in the following sizes at the following special prices:

PRICE LIST of the Acme Success Base Heater for burning wood, strongly crated and delivered on the cars at our foundry in Newark, Ohio.

Cat. No.	Stove No.	Lgth. of Fire Box, inches	Size of Door Opening, inches	Height Without Urn, inches	Floor Space, inches	Size of Pipe to Fit Collar	Shipping Weight	Price
22F544	21	21	12 x 9	43	28 x 23	7	267 pounds	$11.52
22F545	23	23	13 x 10	43	30 x 24	7	292 pounds	14.04
22F546	25	25	14 x 12	48½	32 x 25	7	336 pounds	17.12

OUR GUARANTEE AND FREE TRIAL OFFER. Send us your order for this new improved 1907 model wood burning stove, enclose our price, we will send the stove to you, guaranteeing it to reach you in just in a few days, guaranteeing it to reach you in perfect order, without break, crack or damage of any kind; we guarantee it to please you, guarantee that you will find it a much better stove than you can get from your dealer at home at anything like the price. If you do not find it all this and more, you can return it to us at our expense and we will immediately return your money, together with any freight charges paid by you.

OUR LOW PRICED ACME IVY COTTAGE HEATER

FOR WOOD ONLY.

$5.02

FOR WOOD ONLY

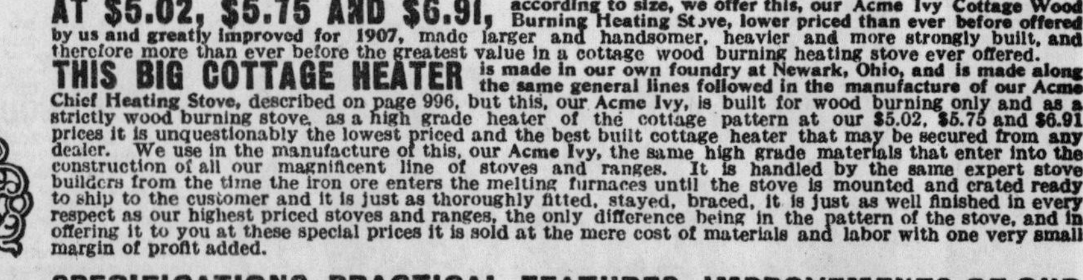

AT $5.02, $5.75 AND $6.91, according to size, we offer this, our Acme Ivy Cottage Wood Burning Heating Stove, lower priced than ever before offered by us and greatly improved for 1907, made larger and handsomer, heavier and more strongly built, and therefore more than ever before the greatest value in a cottage wood burning heating stove ever offered.

THIS BIG COTTAGE HEATER is made in our own foundry at Newark, Ohio, and is made along the same general lines followed in the manufacture of our Acme Chief Heating Stove, described on page 996, but this, our Acme Ivy, is built for wood burning only and as a strictly wood burning stove, as a high grade heater of the cottage pattern at our $5.02, $5.75 and $6.91 prices it is unquestionably the lowest priced and the best built cottage heater that may be secured from any dealer. We use in the manufacture of this, our Acme Ivy, the same high grade materials that enter into the construction of all our magnificent line of stoves and ranges. It is handled by the same expert stove builders from the time the iron ore enters the melting furnaces until the stove is mounted and crated ready to ship to the customer and it is just as thoroughly fitted, stayed, braced, it is just as well finished in every respect as our highest priced stoves and ranges, the only difference being in the pattern of the stove, and in offering it to you at these special prices it is sold at the mere cost of materials and labor with one very small margin of profit added.

SPECIFICATIONS, PRACTICAL FEATURES, IMPROVEMENTS OF OUR 1907 STYLE ACME IVY WOOD BURNING HEATING STOVE.

NICKELED URN. This top ornament, being made by our accessory department within our own foundry, receives the utmost attention and while no more elaborate than is shown in the illustration, is a becoming tasteful ornament.

DOME SWING TOP. This openwork swing top is elaborately carved and very handsome in every particular, but without any nickel plating. When it is swung to the left it exposes to view the cooking holes in the main top which can be utilized for any cooking purposes.

MAIN TOP. With the exception of the smallest size, the main top of the stove is fitted with two griddle covers and a short center, which can be removed, enabling an oval wash boiler to be placed across the length of the main top and will be found quite a convenience when desired to be used in this manner. The smallest size contains but one griddle cover.

MAIN BODY. The main body of the stove is elaborately carved gray iron casting, free from any nickel work, excepting the two nickeled draft registers shown in the illustration. The upper front is mica lighted showing the cheerful flame of the wood fire.

FIRE CHAMBER. The fire chamber is commodious, admitting of large irregular chunks and knots of wood.

NICKEL TRIMMINGS. All knobs are nickeled, the screw draft registers and the foot rail are all nickeled by our improved silver nickeling process.

LEG BASE. The leg frame and feet are massive, completing the most attractive cottage heater yet offered in this class.

On this, our Acme Ivy Cottage Heating Stove for wood only, we do not use any further nickeling than described above, but offer it as a handsome pattern in the natural color of iron.

OUR BINDING GUARANTEE.

EVERY ACME IVY WOOD HEATING STOVE is covered by our binding guarantee as to quality of material, workmanship, etc., and we agree that should any piece or part give out by reason of defective material or workmanship, we will replace or repair it free of charge.

THE ACME IVY is without doubt the greatest value ever offered in the Cottage Style Wood Burning Heating Stove. We are offering it this season at lower prices than any manufacturer or foundry dares to sell such a style stove at wholesale in the largest quantities, in fact, there is no stove foundry in the country that is as large as ours, has the facilities that ours has for producing the best stove at the lowest cost, that embodies so many improvements and labor saving devices which enables us to reduce the cost and, therefore, there is no foundry that would be able to build a high class Cottage Wood Heating Stove for the price at which we offer our Acme Ivy direct to the consumer, which price includes only a very narrow margin of profit.

A BIG OFFER FOR DEALERS.

IN SOME SECTIONS of the country there is a big demand for wood burning heating stoves, and in such sections dealers can make money by buying the Acme Ivy Stoves from us, and selling them again to their customers at a liberal profit.

WE KNOW THAT DEALERS cannot buy this style of stove at as low a price as we offer according to size, and while we have no further inducements to offer than the prices named, regardless of the quantity or the number of stoves ordered at a time, yet the stoves we make do not bear our firm name and, therefore, can be sold again by any dealer as his regular stock.

THE ACME IVY has every practical feature, every improvement of the very best cottage heating stoves made, with the defects of none, and many improvements that we alone use.

THIS LARGE ILLUSTRATION of the stove reproduced direct from a photograph, will give you a good idea of its appearance, yet it must be examined in every feature, the weight and size compared carefully with other stoves, in fact, it must be seen and examined to really appreciate the value we are offering.

THIS STOVE IS IN STYLE, in utility and durability the outgrowth of a stove making organization not approached in any other foundry. With our special artists as designers, with the best wood stove pattern makers, in this country, with moulding facilities unapproached, with a nickeling plant not equalled by any other foundry in the country, with an accessory plant not to be found in any other foundry, with a finishing department that stands alone in its every point of excellence, we produce THE FINEST, HIGHEST GRADE, THE BEST WOOD BURNING STOVES MADE.

TURN TO THE FIRST TWO PAGES of this big catalogue and read the full particulars of our wonderful and astonishingly liberal profit sharing plan by which our customers may select just the articles they have wanted from among the hundreds illustrated there and get them absolutely free in return for our Profit Sharing Certificates. No matter what you may want, whether it be a piano, a bookcase, a bicycle, a music cabinet, an easy chair, a rug, a stove, a set of dishes, a camera, a watch, a sewing machine, a clock, wearing apparel or books—REMEMBER, WE GIVE IT TO YOU FREE in exchange for our Profit Sharing Certificates. Not one cent to pay—just a free gift from us in appreciation of the amount of merchandise you buy from us. It is easy to get these valuable articles free because our prices are lower than ever—but little more than one-half what retailers charge and very much lower than those of any other catalogue house. Therefore, no matter what you need to eat, to wear, or use, you can buy it from us for less money than you would have to pay anywhere else in the world. By purchasing everything of us you will not only save a great deal of money, but you will be surprised how quickly the Profit Sharing Certificates will amount to a total of $50.00, entitling you to an article of great value, usefulness and beauty, absolutely free.

REMEMBER WE GUARANTEE SAFE DELIVERY of every stove we ship and your stove will reach you in the same perfect condition in which it leaves our foundry.

ABOUT REPAIRS.

REMEMBER we carry a complete stock of repairs for all the stoves we make, and in the years to come you can always get any needed parts from us, and we will furnish them to you at actual foundry cost.

THE FREIGHT ON AN ACME IVY COTTAGE HEATER from our foundry in Newark, Ohio, to your railroad station amounts to only a few cents as compared with the big saving in price. Stoves are accepted at third class freight rates and the freight amounts to a small sum. You pay the freight from our foundry at Newark, Ohio, but no matter where you by your stove, you will pay the freight. If you buy it from your home dealer the freight he pays is figured in his selling price. If you buy a stove offered by any other house delivered to you freight prepaid, the cost of the freight will also be figured in the selling price. However, you need not consider the item of freight when you buy the Acme Ivy because it would be a small amount and we guarantee that you will make a big saving even after you pay the freight and add the freight charges to our selling price. In fact, if you don't find that you have still made a big saving after paying the freight, you can return the stove to us and we will return your money and pay the freight charges both ways.

We offer the Acme Ivy Cottage Wood Heating Stoves at the prices listed below, which prices are for the stoves delivered on the cars at our foundry at Newark, Ohio, from which point the customer pays the freight.

Catalogue Number	Stove No.	Length of Fire Box	Height, inches	Floor Space, inches	Actual Weight, pounds	PRICES
22F547	21	22	33	20 x 20	96	$5.02
22F548	23	24	34	20 x 22	105	5.75
22F549	25	26	35	20 x 24	119	6.91

Ornament is not included in measuring height. All sizes take 6-inch stove pipe.

$8.80 FOR A BIG RETURN FLUE TODD STOVE FOR WOOD ONLY.

ACME WILDWOOD

AT $8.80 TO $12.47, ACCORDING TO SIZE, WE OFFER THIS NEWEST, MOST MODERN, UP TO DATE 1907 DESIGN WOOD BURNING HEATING STOVE AS THE VERY HIGHEST GRADE, FINEST QUALITY TODD PATTERN STOVE MADE OR SOLD ANYWHERE. And by far the handsomest stove of this kind that has ever been attempted by anyone, and sold by us at much lower prices than inferior Todd Pattern Stoves are sold generally.

THE VERY SPECIAL PRICES which we make on this, our Acme Wildwood Return Flue Wood Burning Todd Stove represents the actual cost of material and labor, in our largest stove foundry in the world, at Newark, Ohio, with our uniform small percentage of profit added, a narrower margin of profit, by the way than any other foundry in the world is willing to accept for its product, and a narrow margin made possible only because of our enormous output of stoves and ranges, approximating last year over 3,350 carloads. Manufacturing such enormous quantities as this we can well afford to sell on a narrower margin than the manufacturer who produces only a thousand stoves in the course of a year, and, as by our selling method we eliminate every wholesaler, jobber and retailer, putting these fine stoves into your home at manufacturer's special prices, we are in a position to give higher quality, better value in every respect than any other manufacturer or dealer in the world. In this, our Acme Wildwood Todd Pattern Return Flue Heating Stove we have certainly produced the handsomest stove of this pattern ever offered, and with its special features, its screw draft register, its large door and generous fire chamber takes the largest knots and chunks of wood, which will not go into any other wood burning stove. It is in every way a splendid heater and an ornament to any home.

OUR CHALLENGE OFFER. If you want a stove of this pattern, a Todd style return flue stove for burning wood only, send us your order for this, our Acme Wildwood, and if you wish, order such a style stove from any other dealer, set them side by side when they arrive, compare them carefully in every detail, let any of your friends compare them, ask any judge of stoves his opinion, and if you and every one else does not admit that the Acme Wildwood is by far a better stove in every way, the size and quality considered, at least fifty per cent cheaper than the stove from any other dealer, we are perfectly willing that you refuse to accept our stove and return it to us at our expense, and we will return your money and pay freight charges both ways.

OUR BINDING GUARANTEE. Every Acme Wildwood is covered by our binding guarantee for quality, guaranteeing every part of the stove, and should any piece or part give out by reason of defect in material or workmanship, we will replace it or repair it free of charge. Our stoves are built to last and will outwear any stove on the market, because they are better made, more thoroughly and carefully fitted, with a view of making every stove we send out a large advertisement for our house.

DETAIL DESCRIPTION.

THE DIVING RETURN FLUE. The flame and heat pass down the front, around the oval of the bottom and up toward the pipe at the back. This diving return flue and upflue is the full length of the stove and takes advantage of all radiating surface around the oval.

MAIN BODY. The body is made of blue polished steel and the cast ends are of heavy recoco modeling, as shown in the illustration. They are trimmed at the top with massive nickeled end ornaments, nickeled with our unapproachable silver nickel process, and polished to a mirror finish.

ORNAMENTAL URN. The top ornament is a nickeled urn, as shown, and trimmed with two brass arms and a bronze spearhead.

SWING TOP. This openwork but highly polished silver nickeled swing top turns to the left, giving access to one cooking hole in the main top.

MAIN TOP. This heavy rococo model main top extends back to the smoke collar, and this smoke collar is for vertical pipe, as indicated in the illustration, but can be unbolted and reversed to accommodate horizontal pipe entering the chimney directly back of the stove, when so desired.

NICKEL TRIMMINGS. The other nickel finish not described above, consists of the handsome medallion name plate, large and massive foot rail, broad sweeping leg frame and feet, and a nickeled screw draft register in the fire door.

FIRE DOOR. The fire door is large, being 13 inches to 15 inches high and 10 inches to 11 inches wide, according to size. The fire door comes in contact with the rolling damper handle when the door is open, allowing the smoke to go directly up the pipe while placing fuel in the fire chamber. This prevents smoke creeping out the top of the door; and, as an additional protection, we have a drop smoke plate immediately inside the upper front of the fire door.

Sectional View.

LININGS. The inner lining is very heavy cast stove plate, and the oval of the bottom inside is below the hearth line and connecting directly with the ash pit in the hearth.

THE HEARTH. The hearth has a drawout center section with an ash pit in it into which the ashes can be drawn from the fire chamber.

WE OFFER THIS, OUR ACME WILDWOOD DIVING RETURN FLUE TODD STOVE, AT THE FOLLOWING PRICES, DELIVERED ON BOARD CARS AT OUR FOUNDRY IN NEWARK, OHIO

Catalogue Number	Stove No.	Length of Firebox, inches	Size of Door Opening, inches	Floor to Urn Base, inches	Floor Space, inches	Pipe Collar, inches	Shipping Weight, pounds	Price
22F550	26	25	13 x 10	30	26 x 19	6	175	$8.80
22F551	28	27	13 x 10	30	28 x 19	6	181	9.37
22F552	30	29	15 x 11	32	30 x 19	6	202	10.77
22F553	32	31	15 x 11	32	32 x 19	6	212	12.47

SEE INDEX, PINK PAGES 603 TO 610, TO FIND WHAT YOU WANT.

$6.37 AND UP. OUR ACME NUTWOOD

BURNS WOOD ONLY.

THIS MAGNIFICENT DIRECT DRAFT TODD PATTERN WOOD BURNING Heating Stove is fitted and finished in the most elaborate manner and at our manufacturers' prices of $6.37 to $9.49, according to size, as listed below, it is most wonderful value, the greatest value in a heating stove of this pattern that is offered in this or any other catalogue by us or any other dealer, with the single exception of our Acme Wildwood, as described on page 1007, and it presents to those who admire the Todd pattern a low priced direct draft horizontal Oak Stove at unheard of prices. It is made in four sizes full 26 inches, 28 inches, 30 inches and 32 inches inside measurements. It is handsomely designed, very carefully constructed and is a most remarkable value at our special prices.

IN THIS OUR ACME NUTWOOD we offer you a stove which is carefully built and almost as richly ornamented as our Acme Wildwood, as described on the preceding page, but it is without the return flue with which we offer the finest Todd pattern heating stoves that are manufactured in any foundry in the world. We have specially designed machinery for building this type of stove, machinery such as cannot be found in any other stove foundry because it is built for us to perform special work and it is by reason of our great equipment of labor saving machinery which reduces the cost of manufacture as well as our ability to buy raw materials cheaper than any other foundry in the word that we are able to offer this our Acme Nutwood at $6.37 and upward, prices much lower than any other manufacturer or dealer can offer a stove of this pattern that compares in any way whatsoever with the handsome Todd pattern wood burning heater illustrated herewith.

DESCRIPTION. TOP ORNAMENT. The top ornament consists of a modest and handsome nickeled urn, fitted to a full nickel swing top as shown in the illustration.

MAIN TOP. The main top is elaborately carved, as illustrated, and when the swing top is turned to the left one cooking hole is exposed for use as desired. The pipe collar attached to this main top is for fitting on the stove vertically, as shown, but can be unbolted and reversed to accommodate a horizontal stove pipe entering the chimney directly back of the stove if desired.

MAIN BODY. The main body is made of cold rolled sheet steel with elaborate rococo designed cast ends, and the right end is fitted with a capacious wood fire door measuring from 16½ inches high to 18 inches high, and from 10¼ inches wide to 11¼ inches wide, according to size. This door is fitted with a screw draft register, and below the door is a hearth shelf to prevent ashes falling on the floor when being removed.

INSIDE LINING. The inside lining is a heavy cast stove plate shaped to conform to the oval pattern of the sheet body and the body of the fire box is sufficiently below the lower edge of the door to prevent ashes falling out when the door is opened.

NICKEL TRIMMINGS. In addition to the nickeled urn and nickeled swing top is the nickeled name plate on the front, the nickeled foot rail and the nickeled screw draft register in the fire box.

OFFERING THIS, OUR ACME NUTWOOD, as a low priced Todd pattern, we do not offer it in competition with our ACME WILDWOOD on the preceding page, as the Acme Wildwood possesses the additional advantage of being a return flue original Todd pattern, giving additional radiation and getting the best results from the fuel consumed, but this, our ACME NUTWOOD, offers the nicest low priced Todd pattern stove that can be produced by us or any one else.

OUR BINDING GUARANTEE. With each ACME NUTWOOD we issue a written binding guarantee by the terms of which if any piece or part gives out by reason of defect in material or workmanship, we will repair it free of charge, further, that it must be received by you in perfect condition, found exactly as represented and perfectly satisfactory or your money will be returned to you immediately and we will pay the freight charges both ways. We offer the Acme Nutwood at $6.37 to $9.49, according to size, in competition with stoves of this pattern that retail at one-third higher prices. It is a stove made in our own foundry at Newark, Ohio, where we have the largest stove foundry in the world and the prices named represent the actual foundry cost to us with but our one small percentage of profit added. You can buy this stove from us for less money than your home dealer would pay for such a stove in quantities to any other manufacturer, wholesale or jobber.

SPECIAL TO DEALERS. If you are a dealer in stoves it will pay you handsomely to send us an order for one or two of each of the different sizes of the Acme Nutwood, set them on your floor and mark them at a selling price that allows you a fair profit. You can buy the Acme Nutwood Stoves from us, sell them again at a fair profit, and still be furnishing good value to your customers. We invite your attention to these prices and would ask you to compare them with any prices offered by any other house in the world and see if it is not to your advantage to buy your stoves from us. REMEMBER, we operate the largest stove foundery in the world, we buy our materials in the very largest quantities, we have the very smallest selling expense and we accept an extremely low margin of profit, all of which combined, enables us to offer you such advantages that you cannot afford to send your orders elsewhere. DEALERS CAN BUY THIS STOVE TO SELL AGAIN, as every stove bears the name Newark Stove Works, Chicago. We must say, however, that whether you buy the stove from us singly, in lots of ten or in carload lots, the price is exactly the same. It is as low as we can possibly make it regardless of quantity, but you will find that we will give you greater value than you can get from any other stove foundry or stove manufacturer in the country.

ABOUT FREIGHT CHARGES. The freight charges on this stove will amount to a very few cents compared with what you will save in price. By referring to the freight rates on last pages of this catalogue, you can calculate almost exactly what the freight will be to your railroad depot, and you will find that it amounts to very little indeed as compared with the saving in sending your order to us.

REMEMBER, we can always furnish repairs in the years to come for any stove sold by us.

OUR THIRTY DAYS' TRIAL OFFER. As a guarantee we are furnishing in this, our ACME NUTWOOD at $6 37 to $9.49, according to size, the best direct draft Todd pattern stove ever offered, and at a lower price than it can be had from any other source, we will allow you thirty days after purchasing it to compare this stove with any similar stove from any other dealer and during this time you can test it thoroughly, call in any one to examine it, and if you are not thoroughly convinced that you have the best stove of its kind made, that you have saved money by buying from us, you can return the stove to us at our expense and we will return your money including freight charges.

WE OFFER THIS UNEXCELLED, LOW PRICED ACME NUTWOOD at the following prices, delivered on the cars at our foundry in Newark, Ohio.

TO FULLY REALIZE THE VALUE we are offering in the ACME NUTWOOD at our prices, you should get the stove and then compare it with the stove that your dealer will furnish you at the same price. If your dealer has a stove of this kind to offer, at the same price, you will find that our stove would be so much larger, heavier, better constructed, heavier nickeled and in every way a better stove, that there will really be no comparison.

Catalogue Number	Stove No.	Length of Fire Box, inches	Size of Door Opening, inches	Floor to Urn Base, inches	Floor Space, inches	Pipe Collar	Shipping weight, pounds	Price
22F554	26	25	16½ x 10¼	30	22 x 19	6	140	$6.37
22F555	28	27	16½ x 10¼	30	24 x 19	6	145	6.94
22F556	30	29	18 x 11¼	32	26 x 19	6	160	8.10
22F557	32	31	18 x 11¼	32	28 x 19	6	165	9.49

NEW 1907 MODEL COAL BURNING ACME CANNON $1.65

AT $1.65 AND UP we offer this our new 1907 Model Coal Burning Cannon Heating Stove, with all its new features, its new interior construction, bettered in every particular and at these astonishing low prices it is undoubtedly the very best value ever offered in a Cannon stove at a low price. This is the regular old style and original Cannon stove; it is thoroughly well built throughout, cast from the best Birmingham pig iron stove plate, it is thoroughly bolted and reinforced and it has every new and up to date feature known to the construction of a cannon stove. It is an exclusive coal burner, an ideal stove for soft or hard coal and it is built specially for small, medium or large size rooms.

IT IS GREAT VALUE at our $1.65, $2.20, $2.54, $2.94 prices, but of course it will not answer the purpose of our big Acme Giant as a stove for big halls, stores, etc., yet it is a splendid direct draft coal burning Cannon stove for small, medium and large rooms, in private homes, offices, small halls, etc. This, our Acme Cannon, has a swing ash pit door, it has check draft in feed door, our very latest pattern dumping grate, and it is attractively made from new patterns and as a moderate priced cannon stove for use in small rooms it is the very highest grade cannon stove made in any foundry in the world.

THE SPECIAL PRICES which we name on this our Acme Cannon represents the mere cost of materials and labor in our own stove foundry at Newark, Ohio, plus our one uniform small percentage of profit added, a smaller margin of profit than is asked by any other founder in the world, and by our new method of selling, our method of selling by catalogue only, and shipping direct to the customer from the foundry we have eliminated the big profits which go to the founder, the wholesaler, the jobber, the three or four freight charges which the small retail merchant must add to the cost, so that it is not surprising that at these prices we undersell every other cannon stove dealer at home or elsewhere.

BECAUSE OF OUR LOW PRICES this is a great stove dealers' opportunity. The prices at which we offer this our Acme Cannon Heating Stove are lower than the dealer will pay other founders for a cannon stove at wholesale. We have no special inducement to offer, however, and whether you order this stove singly, in dozen lots or carload lots we could not make the price any lower, but as our prices are so much lower than those asked by other founders and wholesalers you can well afford to purchase this stove from us. As our name does not appear on this Acme Cannon you may sell it again at your regular prices and make larger profits than you would make on other cannon stoves purchased from other founders. Many dealers are taking advantage of our low prices on all our heating stoves and ranges and handling our product exclusively. Manufacturing these stoves in such enormous quantities our cost is so low, and our margin of profit so very narrow, that our prices as quoted in the pages of this catalogue are very much lower than the prices asked by any other founder, even in carload lots.

PLEASE REMEMBER, too, that whenever you buy a stove or range from us, if you buy this our Acme Cannon or any other stove or range catalogued in these pages, we send you a Profit Sharing Certificate for the full face value of your purchase and these certificates may be exchanged for many useful and valuable articles, as fully described in our free special Profit Sharing Booklet, which we will be glad to send you free and postpaid upon request, so that in addition to our extremely low prices you share in the profits of every stove we sell and if you purchase other merchandise from us these certificates will quickly amount in volume to a sufficient sum to secure a number of useful and valuable articles with which to furnish your home free; or, if you are a dealer you may sell these profit sharing articles and thus increase your profits on these our high grade stoves and ranges.

WE FURNISH THIS NEW IMPROVED ACME CANNON Coal Burning Heating Stove in four sizes, delivered on the cars at our Newark, Ohio, foundry at the following prices:

Catalogue No.	Stove No.	Diameter of Fire Pot	Height	Size of Pipe to Fit Collar	Actual Weight, pounds	Price
22F536	6	9 in.	23½ in.	5 in.	39	$1.65
22F537	7	10 in.	27½ in.	5 in.	47	2.20
22F538	8	11 in.	29½ in.	6 in.	54	2.54
22F539	9	12 in.	32 in.	6 in.	68	2.94

WEHRLE MODEL No. 110

CLOSED FRONT GAS HEATER

FOR NATURAL OR MANUFACTURED GAS

HANDSOME IN APPEARANCE; PLEASANT, CHEERFUL FIRE.

THIS ENTIRELY NEW PATTERN herewith illustrated, is a decided improvement over all others. The principle of construction is entirely modern, the combination employed original, and we have placed in this, our WEHRLE MODEL No. 110 Gas Heater, every practical convenience that artists experienced in the modern art of gas stove making can suggest, with the result of producing a gas heater that will meet with universal favor. Sold under our BINDING GUARANTEE and 30-DAY FREE TRIAL plan (as fully explained on page 371) and offered to you at actual factory cost, with but our one small margin of profit added. We have combined all the good features essential to the building of a powerful heater, large flue areas, enormous heating surface, powerful heat producing burners which are so arranged in the large fire chamber that the burning gas comes in contact with the incandescent porous fuel in such a manner as to become thoroughly absorbed, thereby producing a red hot flame, which is exposed to view through the mica doors and very much resembles a hard coal fire. The products of combustion all pass into the chimney. The heat units are absorbed and retained.

THE BODY is made of Wellsville polished steel, no blacking or enamel being used. It is ornamented with a handsome silver nickeled drop front panel, forming a convenient warming shelf.

THE MAIN TOP is made of the highest grade cast iron, handsomely designed and carved, ornamented with a genuine silver nickeled reflector which swings to the left, exposing to view a top grate which will be found very convenient for heating cooking vessels.

THE FLUE COLLAR takes 5-inch stove pipe and is cast on the main top.

THE MAIN FRONT is fitted with two large mica swing doors, which are securely fastened with silver nickeled turnkey, and expose to view, when burning, a cheerful fire. Handsome silver nickeled pilasters to the right and left, and silver nickeled foot rail under mica doors add much to the beauty and finish of this magnificent heater.

THE FIRE CHAMBER is substantially constructed and is equipped with a cast iron flame back, protecting the main body from burning out. It is fitted with a basket grate with patent gas fuel, which becomes incandescent when gas is burning, producing a cheerful fire.

THE BURNERS are especially drilled and designed for this stove.

OUR WEHRLE MODEL No. 110 GAS HEATERS have more heating surface than any other gas heater on the market, the outer drum being direct radiating surface. The inner drum, which runs from the floor to the top of stove, forms an immense circulating duct, which takes the cold air from the floor and discharges it at the top, intensely heated.

Made in three sizes, as listed below. Strongly crated and delivered on the cars at our foundry at Newark, Ohio.

No. 22L564 Height, 34½ inches; base, 12x22 inches; drum, 7x18 inches; floor space, 14x24 inches; fuel basket, 5x14 inches; burner producing intensely hot flame from 70 jets; size of pipe, 4-inch. Shipping weight, 100 pounds.
Price for manufactured gas......**$8.23** | Price for natural gas..........**$8.28**

No. 22L565 Height, 37½ inches; base, 13x24 inches; drum, 8x20 inches; floor space, 15x26 inches; fuel basket, 6x16 inches; burner producing intensely hot flame from 80 jets; size of pipe, 5-inch. Shipping weight, 105 pounds.
Price for manufactured gas......**$9.23** | Price for natural gas..........**$9.28**

No. 22L566 Height, 39 inches; base, 13x26 inches; drum, 8x22 inches; floor space, 15x28 inches; fuel basket, 6x18 inches; burner producing intensely hot flame from 85 jets; size of pipe, 5-inch. Shipping weight, 110 pounds.
Price for manufactured gas.....**$10.23** | Price for natural gas..........**$10.28**

Do not fail to state whether you use natural or manufactured gas.

THESE HEATERS are economical in the consumption of gas, absolutely free from any odor and have a capacity more than double that of any other gas heater.

WEHRLE MODEL No. 111

CLOSED FRONT GAS HEATER

FOR NATURAL OR MANUFACTURED GAS

THE PERFECT GAS HEATER HAS COME AT LAST!

THE CLIMAX OF GAS HEATER INVENTION, THE PERFECT, ECONOMICAL EFFICIENT AND ABSOLUTELY SAFE GAS HEATER, FOR WHOSE COMING THE HOUSEKEEPER HAS LONG BEEN WAITING, HAS AT LAST BEEN REACHED IN OUR NEW 1909 WEHRLE MODEL No. 111, WHICH IS HEREWITH FULLY ILLUSTRATED AND DESCRIBED.

A TREMENDOUS SUCCESS.

Perfect in principle. Flawless in construction. Splendidly efficient in operation. THE WORLD WILL NEVER KNOW ITS EQUAL. Please note the careful and accurate construction: the three Wellsville polished steel tubes set directly over the fire, thus bringing a large amount of radiating surface in close contact with the fire, and in this respect, our WEHRLE MODEL No. 111 is different from any other gas heater on the market. By reason of the tubes being massed in the hottest part of the stove, they radiate a veritable blast of hot air, so that it reaches every remote corner of the room, making it warm and cheerful as summer sunshine.

THE MAIN TOP is made of the highest grade cast iron, handsomely designed and carved, ornamented with genuine silver nickeled reflector, which swings to the left, exposing to view a top grate which will be found very convenient for heating cooking utensils.

THE FLUE COLLAR takes 5-inch stove pipe and is cast on the main top.

THE MAIN FRONT is fitted with two large mica swing doors, which are securely fastened with silver nickeled turnkey, and expose to view—when burning—a cheerful fire. Handsome silver nickeled pilasters to the right and left, and silver nickeled foot rail under mica doors add much to the beauty and finish of this magnificent heater.

THE FIRE CHAMBER is substantially constructed and is equipped with a cast iron flame back, protecting the main body from burning out. It is fitted with a basket grate with patent gas fuel, which becomes incandescent when gas is burning, producing a cheerful fire.

THE BURNERS are especially drilled and designed for this heater

THE ADJUSTABLE AIR MIXERS, with needle point silver nickeled valve wheel, the porous clay fuel, and perfect burners make the most perfect combustion it is possible to produce.

SPECIAL FEATURES. **As quick and intense heaters on small gas consumption, there is none better and few as good.**

Do not fail to state whether you use natural or manufactured gas.

Made in three sizes as listed below, strongly crated and delivered on the cars at our foundry at Newark, Ohio.

No. 22L567 Height, 34½ inches; base, 12x22 inches; floor space, 14x24 inches; fuel basket, 5x14 inches; burner producing an intensely hot flame from 70 jets; size of pipe, 4-inch. Sipping weight, 115 pounds.
Price for manufactured gas......**$8.80** | Price for natural gas........**$8.85**

No. 22L568 Height, 37½ inches; base, 13x24 inches; floor space, 15x26 inches; fuel basket, 6x16 inches; burner producing an intensely hot flame from 80 jets; size of pipe, 5-inch. Shipping weight, 120 pounds.
Price for manufactured gas......**$9.80** | Price for natural gas........**$9.85**

No. 22L569 Height, 39 inches; base, 13x26 inches; floor space, 15x28 inches; fuel basket, 6x18 inches; burner producing an intensely hot flame from 85 jets; size of pipe, 5-inch; shipping weight, 130 pounds.
Price for manufactured gas....**$10.80** | Price for natural gas......**$10.85**

WEHRLE MODEL No. 112

NATURAL GAS RADIATORS.

MADE IN THREE SIZES. Are provided with pipe collar for flue connections.

THESE HEATERS, MODELS FOR 1909,

are entirely new and will be found, beyond doubt, the MOST PERFECT, the MOST ECONOMICAL, and by far the MOST ATTRACTIVE radiators made. In their construction we have combined all the good and strong features essential to the building of a powerful heater.

THE TUBES are made of blue polished steel; heat instantly; are ornamented with neat trimmings; mica lights are set in nickel frames.

THE BURNERS are new in principle and exclusively our own. An individual burner is fitted at the bottom of each tube with individual lighter under mica nickel frame, which is operated by an individual "never hot" lever valve so that one or more can be lighted to get the amount of heat required. These burners produce intense heat and the radiator construction gives large heating surface, producing circulation of hot air throughout the room.

THE BASE. The handsomely carved iron base rests on beautifully designed silver nickeled legs and is at just the right height to prevent the possibility of overheating the floor.

THE TOP. The cast top is artistically carved, harmonizing with the large handsome base and is ornamented with an attractive silver nickeled reflector.

Made in three sizes as listed below. Strongly crated and delivered on the cars at our foundry at Newark, Ohio.

No. 22L570 Four-Tube Radiator. Equipped with four burners. Height, 32 inches; length, 25 inches; width, 8 inches; base, 8x25 inches, floor space, 10x27 inches. Shipping weight, 55 pounds. Price....**$4.49**

No. 22L571 Three-Tube Radiator. Equipped with three burners. Height, 31 inches; length, 21 inches; width, 8 inches; base, 8x21 inches; floor space, 10x23 inches. Shipping weight, 45 pounds. Price....**$3.99**

No. 22L572 Two-Tube Radiator. Equipped with two burners. Height, 28 inches; length, 17 inches; width, 8 inches; base, 8x17 inches; floor space, 10x19 inches. Shipping weight, 35 pounds. Price....**$3.49**

THESE RADIATORS are economical in the consumption of gas, absolutely free from any odor, and have a heating capacity more than double that of any steam radiator twice their size.

WEHRLE MODEL No. 113

NATURAL OR ARTIFICIAL GAS RADIATOR.

IN OFFERING OUR CUSTOMERS this entirely new line of natural or artificial gas radiators, we have selected the best and most efficient designs, improvements and economical attachments, and in their construction we have combined all the good and strong features essential to the building of a powerful heater. These radiators will be found **economical in the consumption of gas, absolutely free from any odor,** and have a heating capacity more than double that of any steam radiator twice their size. Each and every one is guaranteed to be perfect in operation and workmanship or your money refunded. We use only the highest grade material in their construction, the highest grade atmospheric burner and the highest class material throughout that it is possible to secure, and we challenge the world with this line of gas radiators. They are handsome in appearance—the radiating tubes being made of blue polished steel with cast top and base finished in gold bronze. **These radiators** have great radiating qualities, with the least possible consumption of gas owing to the improved burners used. **The tubes** are large, each one being provided with two large Scotch tip burners, making the heating capacity greater than in any ordinary radiators.

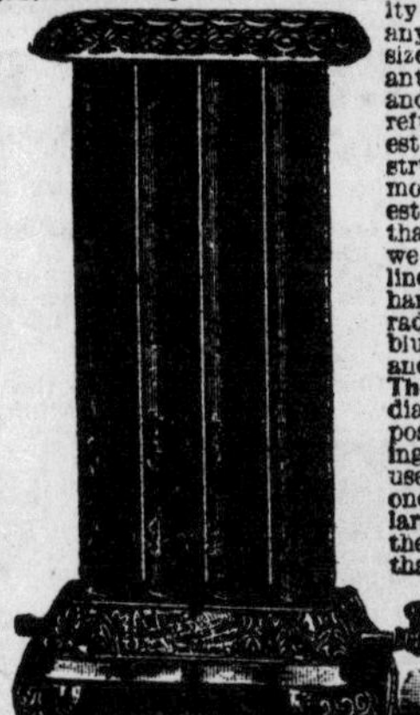

Are also provided with a very large convenient automatic lighting device, so arranged that the flame is carried the entire length of the burner instantaneously when the light is applied. **These radiators are not provided with pipe collar for flue connections. Do not fail to state whether you use natural or manufactured gas. Strongly crated and delivered on the cars at our foundry at Newark, Ohio.**

No. 22L573 Four-Tube Radiator. Equipped with 8 flame jets. Height, 31 inches; length, 15 inches; width, 8 inches. Shipping weight, 35 pounds.
Price for manufactured gas............................**$2.56**
Price for natural gas............................**2.61**

No. 22L574 Six-Tube Radiator. Equipped with 12 flame jets. Height, 31 inches; length, 20 inches; width, 8 inches. Shipping weight, 45 pounds.
Price for manufactured gas............................**$3.84**
Price for natural gas............................**3.89**

No. 22L575 Eight-Tube Radiator. Equipped with 16 flame jets. Height, 31 inches; length, 25 inches; width, 8 inches. Shipping weight, 53 pounds.
Price for manufactured gas............................**$5.13**
Price for natural gas............................**5.18**

WEHRLE MODEL No. 114

OPEN FIREPLACE GAS STOVE, $3.16 AND UP

In bringing out this line of open fireplace gas stoves we have not spared any expense to make them the best in the world. They are supplied with atmospheric blue flame burners, asbestos flame plate in the back and a 3-inch pipe collar for flue connections on the rear. Front is fancy stove plate casting and outer body of blue polished steel. Inner side walls, bottom reflector and front fender are handsome polished copper finish. This style of stove needs no recommendations, as it is too well known and popular. **We guarantee them to please you in every particular, or your money will be refunded.** They are made in three sizes, to heat from the smallest to the largest room in your home. Fitted for either rubber tube or iron pipe connections, as desired. For prices on flexible gas stove tubing see Nos. 22L562 and 22L563 on page 44. **Do not fail to state whether you use natural or manufactured gas. Strongly crated and delivered on the cars at our foundry at Newark, O.**

No. 22L576 Height from floor to top of cast front, 21 inches; width, cast front, 14 inches; depth, 8 inches. Shipping weight, 30 pounds.
Price for manufactured gas..........**$3.16**
Price for natural gas..........**3.21**

No. 22L577 Height from floor to top of cast front, 23 inches; width, cast front, 16 inches; depth, 9 inches. Shipping weight, 35 pounds.
Price for manufactured gas..........**$3.60**
Price for natural gas..........**3.65**

No. 22L578 Height from floor to top of cast front, 26 inches; width, cast front, 18 inches; depth, 10 inches. Shipping weight, 40 pounds.
Price for manufactured gas..........**$4.05**
Price for natural gas..........**4.10**

OIL HEATING STOVES $3.15 TO $7.92

WE OFFER A MOST COMPLETE AND DESIRABLE LINE FOR YOUR SELECTION, STOVES THAT EMBODY ALL THE VERY LATEST IDEAS AND IMPROVEMENTS, AND NOTHING BUT THE BEST MATERIAL AND WORKMANSHIP ENTERS INTO THEIR CONSTRUCTION.

WHY YOU SHOULD USE AN OIL HEATER

ECONOMY. No waste of fuel. You light it when you are ready for it, and extinguish it as soon as the necessity for its use has passed. A gallon of oil will run it at a cost less than the same amount of heat can be procured with any other fuel.

LABOR SAVING. No kindling to prepare, no coal to carry, no ashes to dispose of.

HEAT WHEREVER YOU WANT IT. All stoves are portable and can be placed where they are needed most. Can be carried from one room to another with absolute safety. No chimney needed.

QUICK HEAT. Light it with a match and you have instant heat. It lights as easily as gas and is ready for use at any hour of the day or night.

CLEANLINESS. Scientific construction insures freedom from smoke or odor. The combustion in these stoves is perfect, and is due to many years of experimenting on the part of the manufacturers. All parts can be easily and thoroughly cleaned.

OPERATION. They are simple in construction, there is nothing complicated to get out of order and in reality no directions are necessary. We, however, attach a card of simple directions to each stove before shipping.

FUEL. The fuel used (common kerosene or coal oil) can easily be procured; the same oil can that supplies your lamp will also furnish the fuel for heating.

WHERE AN OIL HEATER CAN BE USED TO ADVANTAGE:

IN YOUR BEST ROOM you can use an oil heater without being uneasy, because it makes NO SOOT, NO SMOKE, NO ODOR AND IS ABSOLUTELY SAFE.

WHEN YOUR FURNACE OR BASE BURNER is not in operation and the weather is damp or chilly, an oil heater should be on hand to drive the chill and dampness out of your different rooms and prevent sickness.

YOUR SUMMER COTTAGE can be made comfortable at all times and you would stay later in the fall if you had an oil heater for the cold evenings.

IF IT IS CHILLY UPSTAIRS, just carry the oil heater up and in a moment your sleeping room will be warm. It makes quick heat.

YOUR BATHROOM may be cold and unpleasant; here is where an oil heater is a handy thing.

BE SURE TO ORDER A STOVE LARGE ENOUGH FOR YOUR REQUIREMENTS.

$3.15 $3.85 $5.35

No. 22L595 No. 22L597 No. 22L599

OUR NEW HANDSOME LINE OF CLOVER SMOKELESS, ODORLESS, SAFE OIL HEATERS

NOTE THE MANY DISTINCTIVE FEATURES.

THESE STOVES will be found to meet all the requirements of oil stove heating and will keep a large room at a comfortable temperature in cold weather. The drums are made of American planished steel and can at all times be easily kept clean. Our SAFETY REMOVABLE FOUNTS AND BURNERS, used on the Clover Heater, are scientifically constructed and two air spaces separate the burning wick from the oil fount. Also a large air chamber passes through the burner, thereby guaranteeing not only perfect combustion but absolute safety. The oil is always kept cold and explosions are impossible. Our perfect wick stop prevents wick from smoking and insures an even flame. There is as much difference between the safety tank and burner used on the Clover Oil Heater and those used on the ordinary oil heaters now offered to the public as there is between day and night. Don't be backward about ordering one on account of the disagreeable features of other oil heaters, which smell and smoke, as you will be pleasantly surprised with one of these stoves. If not found all we claim, the purchase price will be returned upon request. This is the most convincing argument we can offer to impress you that these stoves are all we claim.

THERE IS A DEFLECTOR or partition in the drum which prevents the heat escaping direct to the ceiling the same as in other oil heaters. On the contrary it radiates like a base burner from the bottom and sides as well as the top. The top is handsomely nickeled and is removable, leaving openings in the disc for the purpose of quickly heating anything placed thereon.

THE FLAME SPREADER is made of one solid piece of stamped steel. No complications about the burner whatever, to clog up with oily substances and, therefore, they are always free from smoke and odor. The trimmings are all highly polished nickel and the entire stoves are so simply constructed and so free from complications that any child can operate them. All sizes have center mica section which reflects a brilliant light when stove is in use. They cost less money and produce more heat than any other oil heaters in the market.

No. 22L595 Height, bail down, 23 inches; diameter of steel drum, 7 inches; tank holds 2 quarts; takes 8-inch circular wick. Weight, crated, 11 pounds. This size will heat a small bedroom or bathroom nicely. Price........ $3.15

No. 22L596 Extra wicks for above, each........ .09

No. 22L597 Height, bail down, 25 inches; diameter of steel drum, 7¾ inches; tank holds 3 quarts; takes 10-inch circular wick. Weight, crated, 13 pounds. This size will heat a good size room very comfortably. Price........ $3.85

No. 22L598 Extra wicks for above, each........ .10

No. 22L599 Height, bail down, 28 inches; diameter of steel drum, 9½ inches; tank holds 4 quarts; takes 15-inch circular wick. Weight, crated, 20 pounds. This size will heat a large room or suite of small rooms. Price........ $5.35

No. 22L600 Extra wicks for above, each........ .12

ACME SMOKELESS-WICKLESS OIL RADIATORS

This Acme Smokeless-Wickless Blue Flame Oil Radiator Heating Stove is our latest addition to the world's wonder line of Blue Flame Oil Stoves. On another page we fully describe our Wickless Blue Flame Cooking Stoves, and we here briefly say the same principle is in the Acme Smokeless Radiators. The world moves and the people reap the benefit. Heat your bathroom; heat any room where other heat does not reach; heat all your rooms with the Acme Smokeless-Wickless Oil Radiators and you will find a pleasant, comfortable heat. Through the tubular radiators of each stove the heated air continues to pass, taking the cold air from below and passing it out into the room, constantly changing the atmosphere and giving a stronger, larger volume of hot air circulation than can be obtained from any other form of oil heater. The No. 10 will heat a small room or a bathroom in the coldest weather. The No. 20 will heat a large room in the most severe weather. Order one and if not found all we claim for it, or if it is not satisfactory, you can return it to us within thirty days and we will refund your money, including any transportation charges you have paid. These radiators will not only be found a comfort, but will prove an ornament to any room, as they are handsome and attractive in appearance.

Reasons why our Smokeless-Wickless Radiators are superior to ordinary oil heaters:

1st. No wick to trim, or wick raiser to get out of order or bother with.
2d. Absolutely smokeless and odorless. Others so called are only so in name.
3d. Easily operated. Intense or slow heat, as may be desired.
4th. The radiator top is removable, leaving a most complete and effective cooking stove with a top grate nicely finished.
5th. Have double reservoirs. Stove keeps on burning while you take upper reservoir away to refill.
6th. They are economical in the consumption of oil and are great labor savers. One gallon of kerosene will produce a large volume of heat for eight to ten hours.

No detail of construction, no matter how small, has been overlooked by us to produce the best.

Acme Smokeless-Wickless Radiator, No. 10, $4.69.

Has one of our powerful burners producing a most intensely hot blue flame. Radiator top contains a double row of radiator tubes—five in each row—made of polished iron, having a radiating surface equal to a cylinder over 3 feet in circumference. Removable radiator top, especially designed to leave a lamp stove for cooking purposes. Removable reservoir holds 2½ quarts, burning about seven hours. Dimensions: Total height, 25 inches; size of top, 7x12 inches; height of cooking sections, 10 inches; height of radiator, 15 inches. Shipping weight, 37 pounds.

No. 22L603 Acme Smokeless-Wickless Radiator, No. 10. Price........ $4.69

Guaranteed to please or your money refunded.

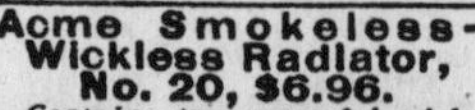

Acme Smokeless-Wickless Radiator, No. 20, $6.96.

Contains two powerful wickless blue flame burners. The radiator top contains the equivalent of 21 radiating tubes and have a radiating surface equal to a drum cylinder 84 inches in circumference. The radiator top is removable, leaving a most complete and effective cooking stove. Removable reservoir holds over one gallon, permitting both burners to be operated at fair flame nearly ten hours. Dimensions: Total height, 30 inches; size of radiator, 8x16 inches; size of cooking top, 12x16 inches. Height of cooking stove section, 10 inches; height of radiator section, 20 inches. Shipping weight, 54 pounds.

No. 22L605 Acme Smokeless-Wickless Radiator, No. 20. Price........ $6.96

No. 22L604 Extra Asbestos Lighting Rings or Kindlers for radiators Nos. 22D603 and 22D605. Price, per dozen........ 72c

Extra Large Size White Flame Oil Heater, $7.92.

No. 22L601 This stove has the style and dignity and is as practical and durable as any coal stove. Entire stove is cast iron with exception of drum which is of polished steel and oil reservoir which is made of heavy aluminum steel. Has center mica section which reflects a brilliant light when stove is in use. Top swings back to allow access to burners for cleaning purposes. Has swing door in mica section for lighting. Tank holds 5 quarts and stove will burn 10 to 12 hours without refilling, which can be done without removing tank from stove. Has central ventiduct which takes cold air from the floor and circulates it thoroughly heated into the room. Is provided with floor tray which will protect carpet from damage if tank is accidentally overfilled. You cannot obtain a better heater at any price. Wick circumference, 15 inches. Height, 36 inches. Diameter of steel drum, 8½ inches. Weight, crated, 70 pounds. Price........ $7.92

No. 22L602 Extra wicks for above, each........ 12c

We accept every stove order to be shipped with the understanding and agreement that if it is not perfectly satisfactory after giving it thirty days' trial, you can return it to us, at our expense, and we will immediately return your money, together with any freight charges paid by you. We have an extra large stock on hand, all ready for immediate shipment and when you decide to send us your order, enclose our price and any one of the stoves illustrated will be sent to you without delay.

OUR $7.08 TO $9.63 ACME HORNET AIRTIGHT SHEET STEEL HEATER.

FOR HARD OR SOFT COAL.

$7.08 AND UP

GUARANTEED the Greatest Value Ever Offered in An Airtight Sheet Steel Heater.

At $7.08 to $9.63 according to size, delivered on the cars at our foundry in Newark, Ohio, we furnish this, the very latest, most improved and best coal burning airtight heater as a practical substitute for the regular $35.00 to $40.00 hard coal burning parlor heater. This is without exception the highest grade, most economical, best finished and most serviceable hot blast draft airtight sheet steel coal burner made. Made to burn hard coal, soft coal, or coke. It possesses all the very latest improvements — everything that can make it the very best stove of the kind on the market. This hot air heater consumes 85 per cent of the smoke. Most economical stove made; it is a very powerful and quick acting heater. It is handsomely ornamented with nickel plated foot rails, highly ornamented with nickel plated ornaments, patent double cover on top. Coal dealers claim that 1¾ tons ordinary grade soft coal will last as long and give as much heat as one ton of the very best hard coal, and that it will hold fire of soft coal over night. From this it will be seen that it is one of the most economical coal burners you can buy. The top of the stove lifts up for feeding in the fuel. The dome swing top swings conveniently aside so the top of the stove can be used for heating a kettle when desired. Has powerful central down draft smoke consumer, mica lighted upper front door. Handsome design and finish. A better stove for the money than ever before put on the market. Has ornamented cast top and cast bottom. It has a nickeled ring around the top of the stove and two air inlets. It is furnished with the draw center shaking grate. Heavy cast fire pot and cast lining above fire pot. Has 18-gauge cold rolled steel body. Patent double cover on top. We accept every stove order to be shipped with the understanding and agreement that if it is not perfectly satisfactory after giving it 30 days' trial, you can return it to us at our expense and we will immediately refund your money, together with any freight charges paid by you.

Prices of our Acme Hornet, strongly crated and delivered on the cars at our foundry in Newark, Ohio.

Catalogue Number	Stove No.	Diameter of Fire Pot, inches	Height from Floor to Urn Base, inches	Size Pipe to Fit Collar	Shipping Weight, pounds	Price
22G520	12	12	39⅛	6-inch	140	$7.08
22G521	14	14	41¾	6-inch	170	8.00
22G522	16	16	45	6-inch	200	8.86
22G523	18	18	45¾	7-inch	235	9.63

OUR $7.86 ACME FIRE KING.

$7.86

Airtight Sheet Steel Heater, coal burning. Our double cased hot air circulating hot blast airtight sheet steel heater for hard or soft coal with its smoke consuming features, has won its recognition during the hard coal famine of the winter 1902-3, and now stands at the head of its class, along with our Acme Hornet as shown above and the Acme Hotspur shown on this page. The scientific construction of the smoke consumer brings heated air on the surface of the coal, and ignites the heavy black smoke which usually goes up the chimney and is wasted. This smoke from soft coal is heavily laden with carbon, and produces as much heat as the coal itself. By burning 85 per cent of the smoke, you obtain the heat desired without the consumption of so much coal, and makes a difference of about half the fuel it would consume without our scientific hot blast construction. The only difference between this, our Acme Fire King at $7.86 to $9.49, and our Acme Hotspur, shown above in next column, consists of a hot air ventilating, circulating flue, all around the jacket of the Acme Fire King. The inner jacket is made of the best cold rolled smooth steel, and is protected on the inside by heavy upper and lower cast iron fire pots to resist the great heat. The outer jacket is made of polished steel plate, leaving an air space between the two jackets, through which a constant circulation of large volume of air is continually passing when there is a fire in the stove. Thousands of this construction have been sold by us, and everywhere give the most universal satisfaction. Has ornamented cast top, cast corrugated bottom, double jacket. It has a nickeled rim around the top of the stove and two air inlets. Is furnished with the **draw center shaking grate and ash pan.** Heavy cast fire pot, cast lining above fire pot to air inlet and 20-gauge steel lining above that. Has polished steel body. Patent double cover on top. **Made to burn hard coal, soft coal, or coke,** it possesses all the very latest improvements—everything that can make it the very best stove of the kind on the market. This hot blast heater consumes 85 per cent of the smoke. Most economical stove made. Is a very powerful and quick acting heater. Strongly crated and delivered on the cars at our foundry in Newark, Ohio.

Catalogue No.	Stove No.	Size of Body, inches	Total Height, inches	Size of Fire Pot, inches	Size Pipe to fit Collar	Shipping Weight	Price
22G524	14	16x30⅛	45⅛	12	6-in.	155 lbs.	$7.86
22G525	16	18x31⅛	46⅛	14	6-in.	185 lbs.	8.60
22G526	18	20x33	48	16	6-in.	205 lbs.	9.49

OUR $5.12 ACME HOTSPUR.

$5.12 TO $7.12

Airtight Sheet Steel Heater for hard or soft coal. Our special $5.12 price is made possible by reason of our producing these at our own foundry; our quantity is so great, we have been able to reduce the cost of material, the cost of labor, and the price we quote you is based on the actual cost of material and the labor, with but our one small percentage of profit added, and, as the result you can own the highest grade airtight coal burning heater for less money than anybody can buy in carloads. They are made from the very best of sheet steel in our own foundry, the best equipped steel stove foundry in America, whose reputation alone is a guarantee of quality. The body is made of smooth steel, has cast ornamented top, cast fire pot, cast lining extending up as far as draft inlet, with 20-gauge steel lining above that. Furnished with the popular **draw center shaking grate and ash pan.** These stoves are claimed, without any contradiction, to consume 85 per cent of the smoke. All sizes use 6-inch stove pipe. We guarantee safe delivery. From this illustration you can form an idea of the appearance of this handsome new model Airtight Hot Blast Heater. It is handsomely ornamented with nickel plated foot rails, nickel plated hot blast dampers, screw adjustment, highly ornamented with nickel plated ornaments, patent double cover on top. Manufacturers claim that 1¾ tons ordinary grade soft coal will last as long and give as much heat as one ton of the very best hard coal, and that it will hold fire of soft coal over night. From this it will be seen that it is one of the most economical coal burners you can buy. **Our special price of $5.12 to $7.12,** according to size, as listed below, is so very much lower in price than these goods have ever been sold, that we believe our customers will appreciate the values we are giving. If you favor us with your order enclosing our price for one of these stoves, we know you will be so well pleased that you will send us your orders for other goods. **We can always furnish repairs for Acmes.** Where we quote prices delivered on the cars at foundry, it is done to save the expense of freight, cartage and handling into and out of our store in Chicago, and all the saving goes to the customer in the low prices we make. It enables us to quote you a price direct from the foundry that barely covers the cost of material and manufacturing, with but our one small percentage of profit added, a price only made possible by eliminating all the handling expenses. Prices, strongly crated, and delivered on the cars at our foundry.

Catalogue No.	Stove No.	Size of Body, in.	Total Height, in.	Size Fire Pot, ins.	Size Pipe to fit Collar	Shipping Weight	Price
22G527	12	14x27	40	12	6-in.	110 lbs.	$5.12
22G528	14	16x29	42	14	6-in.	125 lbs.	6.12
22G529	16	18x31	44	16	6-in.	150 lbs.	7.12

ACME GIANT COAL BURNER.

$5.35 TO $11.45

At from $5.35 for a medium sized stove to $11.45 for one of the great big kind that heats big rooms, stores, halls, etc., about 4½ cents per pound, a price that barely covers the cost of material and labor, with but one small percentage of profit added, we offer you the best stove of its style and kind that ever went out of any stove foundry. **THIS STOVE is made from the highest grade Birmingham pig iron.** It is the latest improved construction in a cannon stove, made extra heavy throughout, has swing feed door, large ash pit, cast foot rails, draw center and shaking grate, nickel plated knobs, made with a special heavy fire pot. The top is so arranged that a drum can be attached at anytime. 25 cents to $2.00 will pay the freight to any point within 100 to 1,000 miles of our Newark, Ohio, foundry, according to distance and size of the stove selected.

Prices, delivered on the cars at our Newark, Ohio, foundry.

Catalogue Number	Stove Number	Diameter of Fire Pot	Height, inches	Size, Pipe	Floor Space, inches	Weight, pounds	Price
22G 530	13	13 ins.	40	6	18 x 20	115	$5.35
22G 531	15	15 ins.	45⅛	6	20½ x 23⅛	155	6.43
22G 532	17	17 ins.	47	7	22 x 25⅛	207	8.62
22G 533	20	20 ins.	56	7	25 x 28	282	11.45

REMEMBER

WHEN YOU HAVE BOUGHT $25.00 WORTH OF GOODS OR MORE FROM US YOU GET YOUR CHOICE OF MANY VALUABLE ARTICLES FREE, AS SHOWN IN OUR FREE PROFIT SHARING BOOK.

OUR $4.20 ACME MOOSE LAUNDRY STOVE.

$4.20

A four-hole, coal burning laundry stove that outclasses any other laundry stove on the market, regardless of make, name or price. Nothing on the market to reach it, and at our special $4.20 price, it is really wonderful value. Made with four No. 8 cooking holes, made with big top, top measuring 21x22 inches. stove stands 23½ inches high.

We furnish our Acme Drum Oven at $2.04 extra as illustrated and described on page 888, and which, in connection with this laundry stove, makes a complete cooking stove. This stove weighs 92 pounds, has four cooking holes. Top cooking surface, 21x22 inches; height, 23½ inches.

No. 22G534 Our special price............$4.20

THE ACME PRIDE FOR $3.25.

$3.25

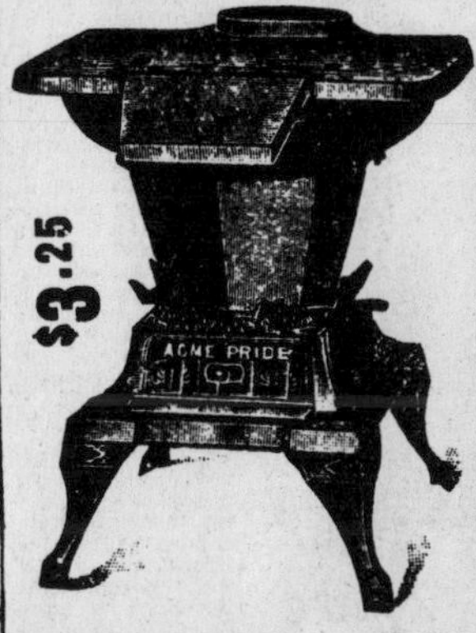

This is our new improved Acme Pride Laundry Stove, made with two cooking holes in the top, a liberal sized surface, will hold eight sad irons around the fire pot and is large enough to take a large boiler on the top at the same time, making it an ideal laundry stove. The irons lay close to the fire and heat very quickly. It is made with a special large pouch feed for feeding in the coal, has our special dumping grate. Top surface is 14x21 inches. The collar takes a 6-inch stove pipe. Diameter of fire pot is 11½ to 12½ inches. Height of stove is 25 inches.

Catalogue No.	Stove No.	Size of Covers	Top Surface inches	Size of Pipe to fit Collar	Diameter of Fire Pot	Height, inches	Weight, pounds	Price
22G715	7	7 in.	13½ x 19½	6-in.	11½	25	68	$3.25
22G716	88	8 in.	13½ x 19½	6-in.	12½	25	68	3.40
22G717	8	8 in.	14 x 21	6-in.	11½	25	84½	3.64

ACME CANNON.

$1.90

This, our Acme Cannon, has a swing ash pit door, register in feed door and dumping grate. Our special prices barely cover the cost of material and labor in our own foundry, with but our one small percentage of profit added, and we offer the stove to you at about 4 cents per pound. Every stove is branded "Newark Stove Works, Chicago." You can buy these stoves for your own use, or you can buy them to sell again at a handsome profit. In buying a stove from us you get every advantage that the largest stove foundry in the world can offer you, with none of the expenses common to other stove makers, with but one small profit to pay.

We furnish this new improved Acme Cannon coal burning stove in four sizes, delivered on the cars at our Newark, Ohio, foundry, at the following special prices:

Catalogue Number	Size	Diameter of Fire Pot	Height, inches	Size of Pipe to Fit Collar	Weight, pounds	Price
22G536	6	9 inches	23⅛	5-inch	39	$1.90
22G537	7	10 inches	27⅛	5-inch	47	2.45
22G538	8	11 inches	29⅛	6-inch	54	2.79
22G539	9	12 inches	32	6-inch	68	3.19

ACME PET LAUNDRY AT $3.11 TO $3.44

$3.11

Has every improvement, including our own dumping grate, made with two top covers or cooking holes, has a large front pouch feed for putting in coal, has a large sized top to take on a large boiler, is made to take 6-inch stovepipe. If you have any use for a laundry stove to burn coal you will make no mistake in ordering this, our Acme Pet Laundry Stove in any of the three sizes at $3.11, $3.17 or $3.44, according to size. 25 to 75 cents will pay the freight on this stove to any point from one hundred to a thousand miles of our stove foundry at Newark, Ohio, according to distance. We guarantee the stove to reach you promptly and safely. You can give it a thorough trial in your own home, and if you are not perfectly satisfied with your purchase, you can return it to us at our expense, and we will immediately return your money.

We furnish this stove under our binding guarantee, all complete, delivered on board cars at Newark, Ohio, at the different prices, as listed below:

Catalogue Number	Size	Size of Covers	Top Surface	Diameter of Fire Pot	Height, Inches	Weight, Pounds	Price
22G540	7	7 in.	14x19½	11 in.	22½	63	$3.11
22G541	88	8 in.	14x19½	11 in.	22½	63	3.17
22G542	8	8 in.	14x21	12½ in.	23½	76	3.44

OUR ACME SUCCESS.

FOR WOOD ONLY.

$12.86 —TO— $18.46

DESCRIPTION. Beginning with an ornamental urn of bronze and polished copper colors, with a spearhead tip and four arms, as shown in illustration, we pass to an elegant oval dome swing top which is heavily nickel plated and polished to the highest finish. Underneath it comes a main top with a griddle cover in the center, furnishing a cooking hole when dome is swung aside, and the main top, in which the griddle cover rests, will lift out entirely, leaving the whole main top open to receive irregular chunks of wood which might not go in the large fire door; then follows the elaborate full swell rococo ornamentation in the main top of the stove, where the highest quality of stove plate castings make for strength, durability and finish unequaled by any other stove maker in the land. The upper front of the stove is relieved by a highly finished, silver nickeled ornamental reflector panel above the mica lights, through which the flame is seen and reflected into the room by the nickel polished reflector panel. In the lower front is the screw draft register, highly nickeled and polished, through which the draft supply is obtained, and by which the draft can be cut off airtight. Just below this is the long, elaborate, silver nickeled and highly polished foot rail name plate, a broad, convenient rest for the feet, and an additional ornament to the front of the stove. The base skirting or leg frame and legs are all silver nickeled after our own process, incomparable in its finish, and not matched by any other foundry in the world. The right end of the stove contains a large wood fire door, admitting the largest piece of wood cut from any cord stick, and is fitted with a large, silver nickeled hand grip turnkey. At the bottom line of this door is a full silver nickeled ash catch, or small hearth, as shown, and the wood grate, being considerably below this line, combines to make it impossible for ashes to spill on the floor when the door is opened. The ash door has a large silver nickeled turnkey. The ash pan is large and runs the full length of the bottom grate. The draft is toward the front of the stove, down the main front to the base flues, passing back and upward to the pipe collar and into the smoke pipe. There is an automatic damper, the handle of which is shown in contact with a "trip" at the back of the fire door, so that when opening the door the direct draft is also opened automatically, and no smoke creeps out the top line of the door when putting in fuel. When the fuel is put in and the door closed, you can close the direct draft damper, and the heat then passes down the front, as described.

Catalogue Number	Stove No.	Lgth. of Fire Box, inches	Size of Door Opening, inches	Heightwithout Urn, inches	Floor Space, inches	Size of Pipe to Fit Collar	Shipping Weight	Price
22G544	21	21	12x 9	43	28x23	7	260	$12.86
22G545	23	23	13x10	43	30x24	7	285	15.38
22G546	25	25	14x12	48½	32x25	7	325	18.46

REMEMBER

WHEN YOU HAVE BOUGHT $[illegible] WORTH OF GOODS OR MORE FROM US YOU GET YOUR CHOICE OF MANY VALUABLE ARTICLES FREE AS SHOWN IN OUR FREE PROFIT SHARING BOOK

ACME IVY COTTAGE WOOD HEATING STOVE

$5.53 AND UP.

ORNAMENTAL AND PRACTICAL FEATURES. Nickeled urn. This top ornament, being made by our accessory department within our own foundry, receives the utmost attention and while no more elaborate than is shown in the illustration, is a becoming, tasteful ornament. DOME SWING TOP. This openwork swing top is elaborately carved and very handsome in every particular, but without any nickel plating. When it is swung to the left it exposes to view the two cooking holes in the main top, which can be utilized for any cooking purposes. MAIN TOP. With the exception of the smallest size, the main top of the stove is fitted with two griddle covers and a short center which can be removed, enabling an oval wash boiler to be placed across the main top and will be found quite a convenience when desired to be used in this manner. The smallest size contains but one griddle cover. MAIN BODY. The main body of the stove is elaborately carved gray iron casting, free from any nickel work, excepting the two nickeled draft registers shown in the illustration. The upper front is mica lighted, showing the cheerful flame of the wood fire. FIRE CHAMBER. The fire chamber is commodious, admitting of large irregular chunks and knots of wood. LEG BASE. The leg frame and feet are massive, completing the most attractive cottage heater yet offered in this class. On this, our Acme Ivy Cottage Heating Stove for wood only, we do not use any further nickeling than described above, but offer it as a handsome pattern in the natural color of the iron.

FOR WOOD ONLY.

Catalogue No.	Stove No.	Length of Fire Box	H'ght, in.	Floor Space, inches	Wght, lbs.	Price
22G547	21	22	33	20x20	94	$5.53
22G548	23	24	34	20x22	105	6.26
22G549	25	26	35	20x24	119	7.42

Ornament is not included in measuring height. All sizes take 6-inch stove pipe.

ACME WILDWOOD RETURN FLUE TODD STOVE.

$9.75 AND UP.

DETAILED DESCRIPTION. The Diving Return Flue. The flame and heat pass down the front, around the oval of the bottom and up toward the pipe at the back. This diving return flue and up flue is the full length of the stove and takes advantage of all radiating surface around the oval. Main Body. The body is made of blue polished steel and the cast ends are of heavy rococo modeling, as shown in the illustration. They are trimmed at the top with massive nickeled end ornaments, nickeled with our unapproachable silver nickel process and polished to a mirror finish. Swing Top. This openwork but highly polished silver nickeled swing top turns to the left, giving access to one cooking hole in the main top. Main Top. This heavy rococo model main top extends back to the smoke collar, and this smoke collar is for vertical pipe, as indicated in the illustration, but can be unbolted and reversed to accommodate horizontal pipe entering the chimney directly back of the stove, when so desired. Nickel Trimmings. The other nickel finish not described above, consists of the handsome medallion name plate, large and massive foot rail, broad, sweeping leg frame and feet, and a nickeled screw draft register in the fire door. The fire door comes in contact with the rolling damper handle when the door is open, allowing the smoke to go directly up the pipe while placing fuel in the fire chamber. This prevents smoke creeping out of the top of the door; and, as an additional protection, we have a drop smoke plate immediately inside the upper front of the fire door. Linings. The inner lining is very heavy cast stove plate and the oval of the bottom inside is below the hearth line and connecting directly with the ash pit in the hearth.

Prices, strongly crated and delivered on board the cars at our foundry in Newark, Ohio.

Catalogue Number	Stove No.	Length Fire Box, inches	Size of Door Opening, inches	Floor to Urn Base, inches	Floor Space, inches	Pipe Collar, inches	Weight, Pounds	Price
22G550	26	25	13 x 10	30	26x19	6	170	$9.75
22G551	28	27	13 x 10	30	28x19	6	175	10.32
22G552	30	29	15 x 11	32	30x19	6	200	11.72
22G553	32	31	15 x 11	32	32x19	6	205	13.42

OUR ACME NUTWOOD.

BURNS WOOD ONLY.

$6.98 AND UP.

$6.98 and upwards. A direct draft Todd pattern, fitted and finished in the most elaborate manner, at the very low cost of $6.98 to $10.16 according to size. While this is not a return flue Todd stove, like the Acme Wildwood, it presents to those who admire the Todd pattern, a low priced direct draft horizontal oak stove at these unheard of prices. It is made in four sizes, full 26 inches, 28 inches, 30 inches and 32 inches, inside measurements. DESCRIPTION. Top Ornament. The top ornament consists of a modest and handsome nickeled urn, fitted to a full nickel swing top as shown in the illustration. Main Top. The main top is elaborately carved, as illustrated, and when the swing top is turned to the left one cooking hole is exposed for use as desired. The pipe collar attached to this main top is for fitting on the stove vertically as shown, but can be unbolted and reversed to accommodate a horizontal stove pipe entering the chimney directly back of the stove if desired. Main Body. The main body is made of cold rolled sheet steel with elaborate rococo design cast ends, and the right end is fitted with a capacious wood fire door measuring from 16½ inches high to 18 inches high, and from 10¼ inches wide to 11¼ inches wide, according to size. This door is fitted with a screw draft register, and below the door is a hearth shelf to prevent ashes falling on the floor when being removed. Inside Lining. The inside lining is a heavy cast stove plate shaped to conform to the oval pattern of the sheet body and the body of the firebox is sufficiently below the lower edge of the door to prevent ashes falling out when the door is opened. Nickel Trimmings. In addition to the nickeled urn and nickeled swing top is the nickeled name plate on the front, the nickeled foot rail and the nickeled screw draft register in the firebox.

Prices, strongly crated and delivered on the cars at our foundry in Newark Ohio.

Catalogue No.	Stove No.	Length of Fire Box, inches	Size of Door Opening, inches	Floor to Urn Base, inches	Floor Space, inches	Pipe Colar	Weight, pounds	Price
22G554	26	25	16½x10¼	30	22 x 19	6	140	$ 6.98
22G555	28	27	16½x10¼	30	24 x 19	6	145	7.5[illegible]
22G556	30	29	18 x11¼	32	26 x 19	6	160	8.71
22G557	32	31	18 x11¼	32	28 x 19	6	165	10.16

ACME GLENWOOD.

WOOD BURNER.

Burns Wood, Straw, Hay, Cobs, Corn, Peat, Trash, or Anything Used for Fuel, Excepting Coal.

$5.97 AND UP.

Our $5.97 and $7.07 Acme Glenwood Airtight Hot Air Circulator, strongly crated and delivered on the cars at our foundry in Newark, Ohio. The illustration shows our Acme Glenwood, with hot blast draft and hot air circulating system. The stove burns everything (excepting coal) that is used for fuel. The feed opening is 10½ inches in diameter. The ash opening is 7 inches in diameter. Damper has screw adjustment. Ash opening is a cast drop door, with a set screw fastening to make it airtight and a screw draft opening in center to make a straight draft when desired. Takes a 6-inch stove pipe. Has nickeled foot rails and a nickeled band around the top. The hot air circulating system takes the cold air from the floor, passes it up between the inner and outer jacket and out at the top, hot. By this system it will warm the farthest corner of the room, as well as the space near the stove. This stove has ornamented cast iron top and corrugated cast iron bottom, polished steel body and heavy sheet steel inner walls, made of 20-gauge steel. Height of stove, 45 inches. Height of body, 26 inches. We can always furnish repair castings for Acmes. Size of pipe to fit collar is 6 inches on both sizes.

Price list of the Acme Glenwood, with Hot Blast Draft and Hot Air Circulating System, strongly crated and delivered on the cars at our foundry in Newark, Ohio.

Catalogue Number	Stove No.	Length, inches	Width, inches	Shipping Weight	Price
22G565	26	26	17	125 lbs.	$5.97
22G566	32	32	18	150 lbs.	7.07

ACME DRUM OVEN NOW ONLY $2.04.

This drum oven will make a good cooking stove out of any heater or laundry stove. Attach this oven to any 6-inch stove pipe and to any one of the laundry stoves, as illustrated and described herein, or to any one of our heating stoves and you have an ideal cooking stove and heater or laundry stove combined in the one. It is so constructed as to give such a circulation of heat that the oven will heat evenly and thoroughly, making it a first class baker. This special oven has been greatly improved for this season, and we would especially recommend that in ordering a laundry stove or a small heating stove you order one of our new 1907 Model Acme Drum Ovens. Even though you have a cook stove or range in your kitchen, you will find this, the Acme Drum, almost indispensable, attached to your laundry stove or heater, for oftentimes you will find it convenient on washday to get your lunch or dinner on the laundry stove in connection with the Acme Drum, or in the evenings a quick luncheon or a small supper or dinner can be conveniently prepared on one of our heating stoves in combination with this new 1907 Model Acme Drum Oven, which we furnish for only $2.04. The outside measurement of this drum is 20x15 inches. Shipping weight, 40 pounds. It's a wonderfully quick baker, saves the waste of heat passing up the pipe. Tends, in connection with the heating stove, to give more radiation, therefore more heat, out of a given amount of fuel, and is especially efficient when used in connection with a laundry or heating stove. We furnish this handsome Drum Oven, exactly as illustrated and described, for only $2.04

No. 22G543 Price...$2.04

$3.76 FOR OUR ACME MOOSE LAUNDRY STOVE.

This Four-Hole Laundry Stove, burning any kind of fuel, with our new and improved dumping grate, is the very best laundry stove manufactured in any stove foundry in the world. It is really the most wonderful value; it has a very large top, carrying four covers, each fitting in a No. 8 cooking hole, and top measurement over all is 21x22 inches—big enough to accommodate a great big wash boiler and cooking utensils at the same time. It will also take the new style steel or galvanized iron tubs now in common use and the arrangement of the fire pot and construction of main top is such that the heat is evenly distributed and it is a quick heater, economical in the use of fuel. Made from the very highest grade of selected Southern pig iron.

We furnish our Neverbreak All Steel Acme Drum Oven at $1.52 extra, as illustrated and described below, and which, in connection with this laundry stove, makes a complete cooking stove. This stove weighs 105 pounds, and has four cooking holes. Diameter of fire pot, 12½ inches. Depth of fire pot 6½ inches. Top cooking surface, 21x22 inches. Height, 23½ inches. 6-inch stove pipe collar.

Immediate Shipment. We have a large stock securely crated ready for immediate shipment from our Newark, Ohio, foundry.

No. 22R530 Price..........................$3.76

$3.06 TO $3.82 ACME PRIDE

SPECIAL HARD OR SOFT COAL OR WOOD BURNING LAUNDRY STOVE.

This is our new model 1910 improved special coal and wood burning laundry stove, our Acme Pride, which we offer at only $3.06 and up, a price representing the mere cost of materials and labor in our own stove foundry at Newark, Ohio, where manufacturing costs are lower than in any other stove foundry in the world, and to this very low manufacturing cost we add only one small margin of profit, so that this stove, when sent to you at our $3.06 to $3.82 price, represents better value and it is in every way a better laundry stove than you could secure at a much higher price.

This, our Acme Pride New Improved Laundry Stove, is made with two cooking holes, has a very liberal top and has special eight-faced fire pot equipped with special holders, so that you may heat eight sadirons at one time. **These special features make it an ideal laundry stove,** and as it is a splendid heater and the irons lie close to the fire they heat quickly while you may be using the top of the stove for cooking or some other purpose. It has large special pouch feed for coal and our special dumping grate.

Immediate Shipment. We have a large stock securely crated ready for immediate shipment.

Acme Pride, made in three sizes as listed below, and delivered on cars at Newark, Ohio.

Catalog No.	Stove No.	Size of Covers	Top Surface, inches	Size of Pipe to Fit Collar	Diameter of Fire Pot, in.	Height, inches	Weight, pounds	Price
22R525	7	7 in.	13½x19½	6 in.	11½	25	80	$3.06
22R526	88	8 in.	13½x19½	6 in.	11½	25	80	3.30
22R527	8	8 in.	14 x21	6 in.	12½	25	90	3.82

$1.87 TO $3.34 ACME PET

LAUNDRY STOVE BURNS ANYTHING USED FOR FUEL.

This, our Acme Pet Coal Burning Laundry Stove, has every improvement, including our own dumping grate and is made with two cooking holes. It has a large front pouch feed for putting in coal, has a large size top to take on a big wash boiler, and is made to take 6-inch stove pipe.

If you have any use for a laundry stove to burn any kind of fuel, and do not require a stove as large as our Acme Moose at $3.76, illustrated on this page, you will certainly make no mistake in ordering this, our **Acme Pet Laundry Stove,** in any of the four sizes, at $1.87, $3.03, $3.07 or $3.34, according to size. The freight charges on this laundry stove will amount to practically nothing at all compared with our saving to you in price, as 25 to 75 cents will pay the freight on this stove to any point from 100 to 1,000 miles from our foundry at Newark, Ohio.

We furnish this stove under our binding guarantee, all complete, securely crated, delivered on board cars at Newark, Ohio, at the different prices as listed below.

Catalog No.	Size	Size of Covers	Top Surface, in.	Diameter of Fire Pot	Height, inches	Weight, pounds	Price
22R520	50	7½ in.	15x18	9 in.	18	55	$1.87
22R521	7	7 in.	14x19½	11 in.	22½	75	3.03
22R522	88	8 in.	14x19½	11 in.	22½	75	3.07
22R523	8	8 in.	14x21	12½ in.	23½	85	3.34

OUR NEW NEVERBREAK DRUM OVEN ALL STEEL $1.52

This all steel drum oven will make a good cooking stove out of any heater or laundry stove. Attach this oven to any 6-inch stove pipe and to any laundry or to any heating stove and you will have an ideal cooking stove and heater or laundry stove combined in one. The entire body is substantially constructed of cold rolled steel, with pipe collar on top and bottom to fit 6-inch pipe. Is fitted with removable steel rack. Oven measures 8⅞ inches wide, will easily accommodate an 8-inch pie plate or an 8x17-inch baking or roasting pan. It is so constructed to get a circulation of heat that the oven will heat evenly and thoroughly, making it a first class baker. We would especially recommend that in ordering a laundry stove or a small heating stove you order one of our Neverbreak All Steel Drum Ovens. Even though you have a cook stove or range in your kitchen, you will find this, our Neverbreak All Steel Drum Oven, almost indispensable, attached to your laundry stove or heater, for oftentimes you will find it convenient on washday to get your lunch or dinner on the laundry stove in connection with the Neverbreak All Steel Drum Oven or, in the evening, a quick luncheon or small supper or dinner can be conveniently prepared on one of our heating stoves in combination with this new 1910 Neverbreak All Steel Drum Oven which we furnish for only $1.52. The outside measurement of the drum is 12x18 inches. Shipping weight, 13½ pounds. It is a wonderfully quick baker, saves the waste of heat passing up the pipe; tends, in connection with the heating stove, to give more radiation, therefore more heat, out of a given amount of fuel, and is especially efficient when used in connection with a laundry or heating stove. Can be shipped from Chicago, Ill., or Newark, Ohio.

No. 22R531 Price..........................$1.52

GAS COOKERS FROM $4.87 TO $5.92
GAS HOT PLATES FROM $1.37 TO $2.38

GAS HOT PLATES.

This Gas Hot Plate with two or three burners can be placed on a table or on the top of your cooking stove and connected with the gas light fixture by the rubber tube quoted below as Nos. 22R562 and 22R563. The two-burner measures 9x18 inches and weighs 10 pounds and the three-burner measures 9x26½ inches and weighs 16 pounds. Frame is 5¾ inches high, aluminum finished with nickel legs. The burners give a hot flame with two rings of jets.

Hot plates and gas tubing shipped from Chicago or Newark, Ohio.		For Manufactured Gas	For Natural Gas
No. 22R558	Two burners. Price....	$1.37	$1.43
No. 22R559	Three burners. Price....	1.97	2.03

This Gas Hot Plate is a handsomer pattern than the one shown above and has a larger top. It is made with two or three burners as desired; the two-burner measures 11x20½ inches and weighs 14 pounds, and the three-burner measures 11x30 inches and weighs 18 pounds. Frame is 7 inches high, black japanned, with nickel legs and levers. The top surface is large and so arranged that pots and pans can be slid over it in any direction. The burner has a loose cap and gives two rings of flame.

Hot plates and gas tubing shipped from Chicago or Newark, Ohio.		For Manufactured Gas	For Natural Gas
No. 22R560	Two burners. Price....	$1.63	$1.70
No. 22R561	Three burners. Price....	2.33	2.38

Always state whether stoves are intended to be used for natural or artificial gas when writing your order. These gas stoves cannot be used with gasoline or acetylene gas.

For ovens to use on hot plates, see page 967.

GAS STOVE TUBING.

No. 22R562 Flexible Patent End Gas Stove Rubber Tubing. Covering is made of braided mohair; will not crack or break. Comes in 4, 5, 6, 8 and 10-foot pieces.

Price, per foot..........................4c

No. 22R563 Pure Rubber Gas Stove Tubing. Guaranteed against leakage for two years. Inner tube is made of pure rubber, outer cover is silk finished webbing. This is the very best tubing made, and will outlast the ordinary kind several years. Comes in 4, 6, 8 and 10-foot lengths. Price, per foot..........................8c

NEW IDEA GAS COOKERS, $4.87 TO $5.92.

THESE STOVES are of a convenient height and we feel sure they will fill a long felt want for an inexpensive stove, will be found very practical, and will do the same work, but on a smaller scale, as our gas ranges.

THE TOP is made of Wellsville blue polished stamped steel, substantially braced, supplied with convenient removable back shelf, and is ornamented with an attractive nickel name plate on the front edge.

THE COOKING HOLES are furnished with open grates.

THE TOP BURNERS are made of the highest grade gray iron, producing an intensely hot flame with two rings of jets.

THE OVEN BURNERS are made of cast iron, cored, in one piece.

THE BURNER VALVES. The top burners are fitted with lever handles.

THE OVEN is thoroughly constructed of polished steel, with drop door, forming an extension or shelf which makes it possible to draw out or turn a roast without having to lift it. It is full flued, bright corrugated tin lined, perfectly ventilated and first class in every particular. The top is protected with a galvanized iron casing. Oven is provided with two racks.

No. 22R555 Stove No. 2, as shown in illustration. Height, 29¾ inches. Top, 14x21 inches. Oven, 18 inches wide, 12 inches high and 12 inches deep. With two burners on top and one one-piece cored cast iron burner under oven. Weight, crated, 55 pounds.

Price, for manufactured gas, **$4.87**; for natural gas.....**$4.92**

No. 22R556 Stove No. 3, same stove as shown in illustration above, but with three top burners instead of two. Height, 29¾ inches. Top, 14x31 inches. Oven, 18 inches wide, 12 inches high and 12 inches deep. With three burners on top and one one-piece cored cast iron burner under oven. Weight, crated, 70 pounds.

Price, for manufactured gas, **$5.87**; for natural gas.....**$5.92**

Strongly crated and delivered on cars at our foundry at Newark, Ohio.

Always state whether stoves are intended to be used for natural or artificial gas when writing your order. These gas stoves cannot be used with gasoline or acetylene gas.

$5.73 FOR OUR ACME LAUNDRY AND COOKING OUTFIT.

Comprising One No. 8 Acme Pride Laundry Stove, One Joint of Pipe and Acme Drum Oven, All Complete, Ready to Use.

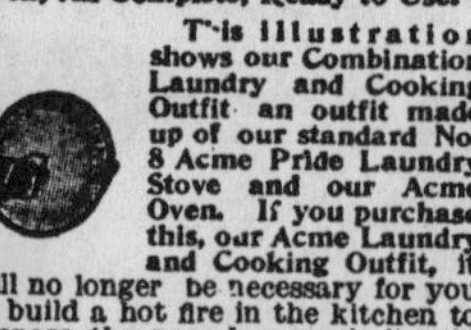

This illustration shows our Combination Laundry and Cooking Outfit, an outfit made up of our standard No. 8 Acme Pride Laundry Stove and our Acme Oven. If you purchase this, our Acme Laundry and Cooking Outfit, it will no longer be necessary for you to build a hot fire in the kitchen to prepare the noonday meal, it will not be necessary to leave your laundry work an hour or so earlier than you otherwise would, to begin the noonday meal, but with this splendid outfit you may do your laundry work and your cooking and baking with one fire in one room, without the loss of time and without heating the living rooms of your home. The hot fire you have prepared to heat water for laundry purposes will at the same time bake bread or roast meat in the Acme Drum Oven above the stove, so that you may make laundry day baking day as well; the same fire will heat the teakettle, will fry or broil meat or potatoes; it will do the general cooking necessary, and, while the preparation of a meal is in course, the sadirons may be heated for the ironing immediately after dinner. Note the special features of our Acme Pride Laundry Stove, which we furnish with this combination outfit, the large pouch feed door, the generous sized top, with its two No. 8 cooking holes, the special sadiron holders around the octagonal firepot of the stove, and we know that you will decide that it is an ideal laundry and cooking outfit, and one that will not only give you good service, but satisfactory service, and one that we guarantee to be strictly first class in every respect, and so well and thoroughly made of the very highest grade materials that it will last a lifetime.

Special Notice.—The cooking utensils and sadirons shown in the illustration are not a part of the outfit, and are not included in this price. For pages describing cooking utensils, sadirons, etc., please see pages 919 to 927.

No. 22G710 Acme Laundry and Cooking Outfit, consisting of our No. 8 Acme Pride Laundry Stove, one length of pipe and our Acme Drum Oven only. Packed complete ready for shipment. Delivered on cars at Newark, Ohio.
Price **$5.73**

$2.12 BUYS OUR DANDY LAUNDRY STOVE.

A Wonderful Value in a Coal Burning Laundry Stove, the Lowest Price on a Stove of this Size and Quality.

For only $2.12, a very few cents above our actual foundry cost, we offer this, our New Model Acme Dandy Stove, the equal in every way of laundry stoves offered and sold by others in similar style as a great bargain at $2.75 to $3.50. While this, our New Acme Dandy Laundry Stove, at $2.12 is a wonderful value, $2.12 being an astonishingly low price for a good laundry stove, yet it is no greater value than the laundry stoves we show at higher prices. It represents no more value for the money than our Acme Pride represents for $3.25 and up, and our Acme Moose Laundry Stove at $4.20. The Acme Dandy is a satisfactory, reliable laundry stove, a big bargain, much lower in price than you can buy a stove of the same size, weight, style and finish from any other house; yet, in illustrating and describing this, our Acme Dandy Stove, at $2.12, we feel compelled to call your attention to the wonderful bargains you can get in our laundry stoves that we offer at slightly higher prices. We always recommend to our customers the purchase of the better grade of merchandise, for the better goods in every line give so much more satisfaction, and we therefore call your special attention to our Acme Pride, Acme Pet and Acme Moose Laundry Stoves, as described on page 888 of this catalogue.

This, Our Acme Dandy, is an ideal stove for laundry use. It is made with two 7½ inch top covers or cooking holes, has front pouch feed for putting in coal. The main top is 15x18 inches, the fire pot is 9 inches and it is made to fit 6 inch stove pipe. The Acme Dandy stands 18 inches high and the shipping weight is 42½ pounds.

No. 22G513 Our Acme Dandy Stove. Price.... **$2.12**

THE ACME CHAMPION.

FOR BURNING WOOD.

At $2.29 to $6.75 this is a handsome and well made box heating stove. Every plate is constructed to avoid cracking. Has swing hearth, swing top and large feed door. The sizes indicate the length wood that the stove will take. Size 18 has one 6-inch cover. Size 22 has one 7-inch cover. Size 25 has two 7-inch covers. Sizes 28 and 30 have two 8-inch covers and short center. Sizes 34 and 36 have two 9-inch covers and short center in swing top.

Price, delivered on the cars at our Newark, Ohio, Foundry. The stove number indicates length of wood.

Catalogue Number	Stove No.	Height, inches	Size Pipe to Fit Collar	Weight, pounds	Price
22G558	18	19½	5 inches	51	$2.29
22G559	22	21½	6 inches	69	3.20
22G560	25	23	6 inches	92	3.95
22G561	28	26	6 inches	113	4.75
22G562	30	26	6 inches	119	4.95
22G563	34	29½	6 inches	161	6.60
22G564	36	29½	6 inches	164	6.75

THE ACME HICKORY AIRTIGHT AT $4.78 AND $5.32.

$4.78

Our Acme Hickory at $4.78 and $5.32 is a direct radiator, instead of a hot air circulator. It has the hot blast down draft with screw adjustment, the large ash opening with direct draft screw adjustment, making it airtight when desired to keep fire. The urn and foot rails are handsomely nickeled. We guarantee this positively the highest grade, best made, most economical in the consumption of fuel and the best distributor of heat of any direct draft, sheet steel airtight stove made, and for the trifling difference in cost between this, our special direct down draft, fancy trimmed airtight, and the more common sheet steel airtight heater, we would especially recommend that you select this stove. This direct draft airtight heater differs from most all other direct draft airtight heaters in that it has a hot blast down draft with the latest screw attachment making it more economical in the consumption of fuel, more even in the distribution of heat, holding your fire more easily under control. The difference in the cost of the fuel consumed in this stove as against the ordinary direct draft airtight heater will in one winter far more than pay the price we ask for the stove. Our special price is based on the actual cost of material and labor in our own foundry, the largest stove foundry in the world, with but our one small percentage of profit added. These prices are lower than dealers can buy elsewhere in carload lots. Size of pipe to fit collar is 6-inch on both sizes. We can always furnish repairs for Acmes if needed in future years.

Price list of the Acme Hickory with hot blast draft, strongly crated and delivered on the cars at our foundry in Newark, Ohio.

Catalogue Number	Stove No.	Length Inside, inches	Width Inside, inches	Top Feed Opening, inches	Shipping Weight, pounds	Price
22G569	21	21	15	9¾	95	$4.78
22G570	24	24	17	11¾	120	5.32

Remember, when you have purchased $25.00 worth of goods or more from us, you get your choice of many valuable articles free, as shown in our Profit Sharing Book.

SHEET STEEL AIRTIGHT HEATING STOVES, 79 CENTS AND UPWARD.

Delivered on the Cars at Our Foundry in Newark, Ohio.

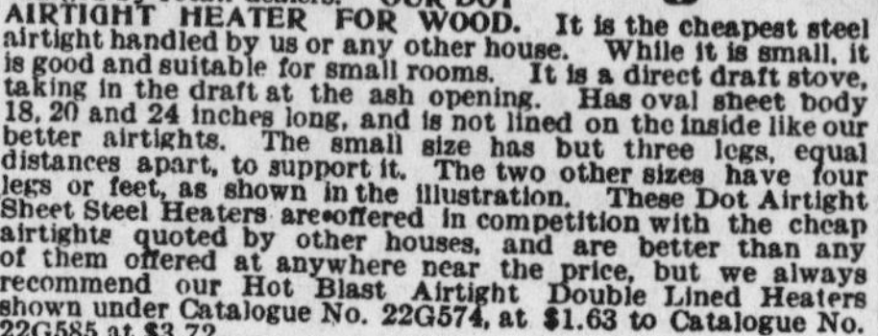

Our line of Sheet Metal Airtight Heaters gives an assortment of styles and sizes not offered by any other makers in the country, and includes the smallest direct draft airtight to the largest down draft hot blast blue polished steel airtight. We sold over ten thousand airtight sheet steel heaters last season, and all the time we were far behind on our orders, and as the indications point to a much larger trade this season, we have made very extensive preparations to not only be able to fill our orders promptly, but with such a line of airtight heaters as will not be offered by any other house, and at prices so low that our customers can order from us, pay the freight, which will add next to nothing to the cost, and own the best airtight heater that can be made, at about half the price charged by retail dealers. **OUR DOT AIRTIGHT HEATER FOR WOOD.** It is the cheapest steel airtight handled by us or any other house. While it is small, it is good and suitable for small rooms. It is a direct draft stove, taking in the draft at the ash opening. Has oval sheet body 18, 20 and 24 inches long, and is not lined on the inside like our better airtights. The small size has but three legs, equal distances apart, to support it. The two other sizes have four legs or feet, as shown in the illustration. These Dot Airtight Sheet Steel Heaters are offered in competition with the cheap airtights quoted by other houses, and are better than any of them offered at anywhere near the price, but we always recommend our Hot Blast Airtight Double Lined Heaters shown under Catalogue No. 22G574, at $1.63 to Catalogue No. 22G585 at $3.72.

Catalogue Number	Stove No.	Floor to Urn Top, inches	Length, inches	Width, inches	Height, inches	Pipe Collar, inches	Shipping Weight, lbs.	Price
22G571	18	28½	17¾	14½	13¾	5	30	$0.79
22G572	21	34	20½	16⅝	19¾	6	35	1.38
22G573	25	38⅝	33¾	17	23¾	6	40	1.68

The Original Round Style Radiator.

HARD OR SOFT COAL.

This style has been successfully sold for many years. They are adapted either for the back of stove or an upper room or hall. Furnished with inner tubes for wood and anthracite coal and without inner tubes for soft coal, for 6-inch stove pipe. Made from Woods' refined iron (sheet steel), with cast iron ends. Aluminum finish. Diameter, 12½ inches; height, with legs, 38 inches. Weight, crated, 50 pounds.

No. 22G465 For soft coal........ **$4.10**
No. 22G466 For hard coal or wood. **4.15**
No. 22G467 and No. 22G468 are the same as above, except made of Woods' patent planished iron.
No. 22G467 For hard coal or wood. **$4.84**
No. 22G468 For soft coal........ **4.80**

REMEMBER, WHEN YOU HAVE BOUGHT $25.00 WORTH OF GOODS OR MORE FROM US YOU GET YOUR CHOICE OF MANY VALUABLE ARTICLES FREE, AS SHOWN IN OUR FREE PROFIT SHARING BOOK.

HOT BLAST SHEET STEEL AIRTIGHTS AT $1.63 TO $3.72.

These illustrations show our better grade with hot blast down draft. A better stove than those quoted under Catalogue Nos. 22G571 to 22G573 for the following reasons: The hot blast draft heats the air before it reaches the fuel, thus producing perfect combustion. The double lining extends up 12 inches from the bottom. The cover to ash opening is locked securely, to prevent blowing off. It is honestly constructed of good material, with heavy lining, and cannot fail to give satisfaction. The body is made of 23-gauge smooth steel, the lining is 20-gauge. Has fine nickel urn. The screw draft can be closed airtight. It will burn chunks, knots, chips, straw, cobs, hay or trash, or anything used for fuel, except coal. The pipe should be provided with a damper. Put two or three inches of ashes in bottom of stove before building fire, and always leave about this quantity when cleaning the stove. Will keep fire over night. In setting up this stove, put the crimped end of stove pipe down. The feed opening is 10½ to 12½ inches in diameter in the different sizes; the ash opening is 6½ inches in diameter; all sizes take 6-inch stove pipe. It has a check draft in the stove top; neat ornament on cover of fuel opening. Delivered on the cars at our foundry in Newark, Ohio.

Price list of the Acme Airtight Smooth Steel Heater without Foot Rails.

Catalogue Number	Stove No.	Floor to Urn Top, in.	Length, inches	Width, inches	Height of Body, in.	Size of Feed Opening, in.	Size of Ash Opening, in.	Shipping Weight, lbs.	Price, Smooth Steel
22G574	220	34	20½	16½	19¾	10½	6½	40	$1.63
22G575	224	38⅝	23¾	17	23¾	12½	6½	45	1.95
22G576	230	38⅝	29½	17	23¾	12½	6½	50	2.41

Price list of the Acme Airtight Polished Steel Heater without Foot Rails.

Catalogue Number	Stove No.	Floor to Urn Top, inches	Length, inches	Width, inches	Height of Body, in.	Size of Feed Opening, in.	Size of Ash Opening, in.	Shipping Weight, lbs.	Price, Polished Steel
22G577	320	34	20½	16½	19¾	10½	6½	40	$2.10
22G578	324	38⅝	33¾	17	23¾	12½	6½	45	2.47
22G579	330	38⅝	29½	17	23¾	12½	6½	50	3.01

Price list of the Acme Airtight Smooth Steel Heater with Foot Rails.

Catalogue Number	Stove No.	Floor to Urn Top, in.	Length, inches	Width, inches	Height of Body, in.	Size of Feed Opening, in.	Size of Ash Opening, in.	Shipping Weight, lbs.	Price, Smooth Steel
22G580	2205	34	20½	16½	19¾	10½	6½	45	$2.16
22G581	2245	38⅝	23¾	17	23¾	12½	6½	50	2.55
22G582	2305	38⅝	29½	17	23¾	12½	6½	55	3.16

Price list of the Acme Airtight Polished Steel Heater with Foot Rails.

Catalogue Number	Stove No.	Floor to Urn Top, in.	Length, inches	Width, inches	Height of Body, in.	Size of Feed Opening, in.	Size of Ash Opening, in.	Shipping Weight, lbs.	Price, Polished Steel
22G583	3205	34	20½	16½	19¾	10½	6½	45	$2.69
22G584	3245	38⅝	23¾	17	23¾	12½	6½	50	3.08
22G585	3305	38⅝	29½	17	23¾	12½	6½	55	3.72

ACME RADIATORS.

Round Pipe Style.

For use on stoves burning anthracite coal or wood.

To meet the demand for a cheaper radiator, this style is added. It is smaller but very efficient either on the back of a stove or to heat small upper rooms. Cannot be used with soft coal.

No. 22G460 For 6-inch stove pipe. Made of Woods' refined iron, with aluminum finished cast iron top and base. Diameter, 10 inches; height, 28 inches. Weight, crated, 27 pounds.
Price........................ **$2.10**

Square Style.

For use with stoves burning anthracite coal or wood. This style is adapted only for floors above the stove. They are very handsome in design, and are bought by many who would not otherwise run a stove pipe through their house. Cannot be used with soft coal.

No. 22G461 For 6-inch stove pipe. Tubes made of Woods' refined iron. Aluminum finished, cast iron top and base. Size of base, 17½x13¾ inches; height, with legs, 37 inches. Weight, crated, 60 pounds.
Price........................ **$4.56**

No. 22G462 Same as above, except the body is made of Woods' patent planished iron. Price................ **$5.22**

This new style round Acme Radiator can be placed on a stove pipe in the same room with a stove, or it can be placed in an upstairs room on a stove pipe by running through from any kind of a stove below and will heat the upper room without the expenditure of a single extra cent for fuel. When used in the same room with the stove, the feet for the radiator are not required, but when you attach it to the stove pipe in the upper room it has a set of feet to support it at the floor. For use with stoves burning anthracite coal or wood. Weight, crated, 30 pounds.

No. 22G463 For 6-inch stove pipe, made of smooth cold rolled steel. Diameter, 12 inches. Height, with feet, 30½ inches.
Price........................ **$2.97**

No. 22G464 For 6-inch stove pipe, made of American patent planished iron. Diameter, 12 inches. Height, with feet, 30½ inches. Price........................ **$3.63**

DETAILED DESCRIPTION OF WEHRLE MODEL No. 20, No. 22 AND No. 30 RANGES, ILLUSTRATED ON PAGES 377, 378 AND 379—CONTINUED.

DROP WOOD FEED DOOR. **Careful examination of many of the steel ranges now offered for sale will show that most manufacturers are careless about fitting doors where they come in contact with the frames.** This is, of course, an exceedingly important point, for a careless fit means a continual flow of cold air to the interior of the stove. If this occurs about the fire box it acts as a check on the fire and makes quick baking almost impossible, owing to the fact that the fire cannot be made to produce the intense heat. From the illustrations of these ranges on pages 377 to 379 you will immediately notice that each door is carefully ground and fitted perfectly tight, touching on every edge, and when closed the doors are held securely in place. They drop down at right angles to the stove when opened, forming a broad ledge, so that no particle of ashes can possibly sift down on the floor. From the illustrations of the ranges you can see that the door is of beautiful design. The nickeled panel on the outside is a separate silver nickeled casting, the process of nickeling being so perfect that discoloring by the action of the fire is impossible.

THE LARGE OVEN. **The oven is the very heart of a range—its most vital part.** The most essential point in an oven is that it must be airtight; otherwise it is impossible to get satisfactory results. The oven in these, our new **Wehrle Model No. 20 and No. 22 Blue Steel Ranges and our Wehrle Model No. 30 Cast Iron Range,** has been constructed with great care and is positively airtight so that it will bake to perfection with the least possible labor and fuel. Our ovens are made of extra heavy steel, hand riveted. No oven ever baked more evenly or quickly. Too much cannot be said in praise and in favor of the oven in these magnificent ranges. All sizes of the **New Wehrle Model Six-Hole Steel Range** and the **Wehrle Model No. 30 Cast Iron Range** are equipped with an oven 21 inches deep and 14 inches high. The width of the oven is 14, 16, 18 or 20 inches, according to the size of the range selected. Your special attention is directed to the liberal space we have allowed in constructing the oven. We have given plenty of room for baking and roasting, and by reason of its modern construction, special arrangement of flues and many other exclusive features, your roast of meat when done is more juicy, and your bread, cakes and pies are lighter and better and more wholesome; in short, our special oven construction represents the highest degree of perfection, making them quick to act and absolutely satisfactory in every particular to the user.

The Big Roomy Oven and Cast Iron Oven Bottom on Wehrle Model No. 20 and No. 22 Steel Ranges and Wehrle Model No. 30 Cast Iron Range.

THE OVEN TOP **is protected with a corrugated cast plate,** which also serves to distribute the heat evenly to all parts of the oven. The oven in these handsome ranges is ventilated so that no dead air is retained in it.

THE OVEN RACK **is made of wrought steel rods and is the full width of the oven** and is so constructed that it easily slips out of the oven and works perfectly free and cannot be broken.

CAST IRON OVEN BOTTOM. **To insure safe, even and quick baking, we call especial attention to the cast iron oven bottom which has proven to be one of the most valuable features ever introduced in steel ranges.** Continued experiments have demonstrated to us, in fact, it is also a well known scientific fact, that steel, after being passed through heavy rollers to bring it to the required gauge or thickness, is by far more dense than cast iron. Cast iron being by far more porous than steel, has about 75 per cent greater radiating efficiency and by using the highest grade cast stove plate for the oven bottom of these **New 1909 Wehrle Model Blue Steel and Cast Iron Ranges,** we get much more heat in the oven with by far less fuel and get it more quickly. We have tested this point thoroughly and find that another advantage a cast iron oven bottom has over the steel is that it will always remain level and will not buckle or warp as a steel oven bottom is almost sure to do unless thoroughly braced. We are introducing this method of cast iron oven bottom construction in the highest grade steel range made in the world and it will be found to combine all the good points of both the steel ranges and cast iron ranges, producing the quickest and most even baker ever made. When put to practical use, we are sure it will surpass your most sanguine expectations, giving an even and uniform heat in all its parts and making it bake evenly over its entire surface, and **IT WILL POSITIVELY NEVER BUCKLE OR WARP.**

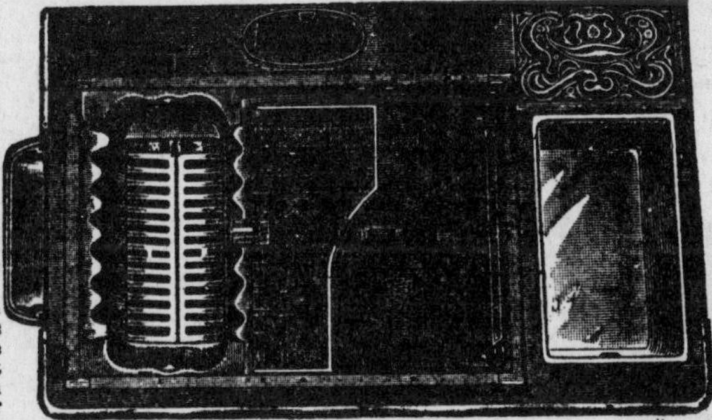

View Showing Heavy Cast Iron Protection Oven Plate and Porcelain Lined Reservoir Tank on Wehrle Model No. 20 and No. 22 Steel Ranges and Wehrle Model No. 30 Cast Iron Range.

THE OVEN DOOR **on our New 1909 Wehrle Model Six-Hole Steel and Wehrle Model No. 30 Cast Iron Ranges represents a decided improvement over all previous designs.** We have employed the very latest style of construction, a drop door with hinges at the bottom, made strong, solid and extra heavy, and so accurately balanced that it cannot shut suddenly. It is handsomely carved, silver nickel plated, and drops flush with the oven bottom, thus forming an extension shelf which makes it possible to draw out and turn a roast without having to lift it—a convenience which will be appreciated. Attention is called to the **oven door handle,** it not only being ornamented and beautifully silver nickeled, but is extra long, making it very convenient in opening and closing the door. It is extra heavy and with our improved catch holds the door firmly to the body of the range and is guaranteed to remain as cold and comfortable to the touch as it is beautiful to the sight.

FOR SLOW BAKING, **the oven door catch is provided with two notches,** so that the door may be partially closed if desired and cold air admitted to the oven. This does away with the necessity of propping the door open to keep the heat of the oven at a low point.

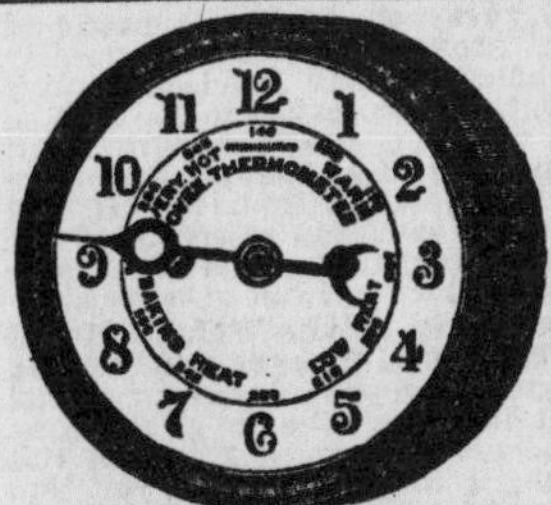

OVEN THERMOMETER. **This is another one of the many exclusive features that can be found only in a range of the Wehrle make.** This dependable oven thermometer is built right in the oven door, thus insuring absolute and even accuracy; a great convenience and an unsurpassed fuel saver. It registers heat by degrees and not by a mere sign telling that the oven may be warm or perhaps hot. The least change of heat can be immediately noticed. This oven thermometer is absolutely the only perfect thermometer in existence. It is susceptible to the least change of the oven temperature and will prove its worth in the preparation of almost every meal. The indicator is in plain sight all the time and indicates not only the progress and rate of baking, but also the condition of the fire and necessity for replenishing the fuel and warns of the cooling of the oven, which is so destructive to good pastry baking. The temperature of the oven and the consequent rate of speed at which the joint or loaf is cooking is accurately shown without opening the oven door and makes the maintenance of an even temperature a very simple matter, insuring cooking of a uniform standard of excellence even to the most inexperienced.

HANDY LEVER FOR DIRECT DRAFT DAMPER. **This feature in our Wehrle Model Steel and Cast Iron Ranges will be greatly appreciated**—a feature to be found in **Wehrle Model Ranges only** and used exclusively by us. The damper rod and silver nickeled handle controlling the direct draft oven damper is located to the right and under the main top in front of the range, as is also the reservoir damper. This special draft damper construction does away altogether with the necessity of the user reaching over the hot stove top to open or close the damper, and being located out of the direct course of the fire, the handle is always cool and will not burn the fingers, as would be the case were the damper located alongside the pipe collar. This novel construction also prevents rust and the possibility of the damper getting out of order.

THE HANDSOME BLUE POLISHED FULL NICKELED STEEL WARMING CLOSET. **This feature of our Wehrle Model No. 20 and No. 22 Six-Hole Blue Steel Ranges and our Wehrle Model Six-Hole Cast Iron Range** is greatly improved over the ordinary warming closets. It extends along the full length of the range body. We have made the high warming closet on the same high grade principles as every other part of the range and it will be found better adapted for the purpose designed than the usual kind furnished on other makes, because we have taken more pains in construction and use a better and heavier grade of material. This equipment has become an almost indispensable attachment to this article of kitchen furniture, and the high warming closet of our **New 1909 Wehrle Model Six-Hole Blue Steel and Cast Iron Ranges** has extra large capacity and is a wonderful convenience. It is just the proper height for the average person to easily reach; has a roll front door which rolls back like the front of a roll top desk, out of the way, taking up no room and permitting the whole of the interior of the closet to be exposed, making a convenient, indispensable receptacle. It is so perfect in construction that it will warm and keep the food wholesome without drying it up. It has a handsome silver nickel trimmed steel guard rail across the full length of the warming closet. Towel rod sockets are provided at each end of the high closet top.

THE WARMING CLOSET DOOR **is so carefully counterbalanced that it works with ease**—the weight of the hand being sufficient to open it. It is held rigidly in shape by silver nickeled stays or bands on either end of the door.

THE WARMING CLOSET NICKEL TRIMMINGS. **Highly polished silver nickel steel bands ornament the front and sides of the warming closet,** as shown in illustrations on page 377 to 379. The upper silver nickeled band is in broad relief to its parallel band at the bottom, while the right and left corner pieces are in keeping with the other nickeled parts.

TO MAINTAIN THE PERFECT HARMONY **of all other parts of the big range, the medallion or panel on the front of the closet,** together with its door handle, is fully silver nickeled on a handsome design.

A CAPACIOUS SMOKE PIPE **connecting with the main top of the stove passes up through the closet, going out through the closet top as shown in illustrations of this range.** This clear joint of smoke pipe passing through the closet is made of Wellsville polished steel plate and on its front, below the closet is a circular cut steel airtight register draft check handsomely silver nickeled, which may be opened to reduce the draft when necessary.

TEAPOT HOLDERS. **Beautifully silver nickeled swinging teapot stands hang on double brackets at either side of the high closet.** They are lifted quickly and easily to attach to either front or back holder at will. An exclusive point.

TOWEL ROD. **A handsome silver nickeled towel rod is mounted on the right side of the main top.** It is both useful and ornamental and protects the cloth from the hot edge of the range. The towel rod is a great improvement over the weak, wabbly rod made from small wire which is generally furnished with higher priced steel ranges. It is easily hooked into the holes provided for it in the main top of the stove or at either end of the top of the high closet.

LARGE ASH PAN. **The size of the ash pan in our 1909 Wehrle Model Steel and Cast Iron Ranges will also be appreciated after the range is in actual use.** Many manufacturers are so anxious to reduce the cost of their materials to the least possible amount that they make the ash pan very small in size, so that it has to be emptied very often—perhaps two or three times a day. The ash pan in these ranges is exceptionally large and will never have to be taken out of the range more than once in twenty-four hours, no matter how much of the time the range is in active operation.

THE ASH PIT DOOR **is perfectly fitted and securely mounted.** It is finished by our silver nickeling process, has never-hot silver nickeled knob, and circular draft register for controlling the fire.

CAST IRON FLUE BACK. **The illustration on page 374 clearly demonstrates one of the greatest improvements embodied in the construction of our steel ranges, viz.:** the large, well constructed cast iron flue back, made in one solid piece and guaranteed not to rust or burn out. Many manufacturers still continue to use sheet steel for their reservoir casing and flue back in spite of the fact well known in the stove trade that a steel casing must necessarily rust out in a comparatively short time. The reason for this continued use is obvious, for a steel construction is considerably less expensive, while the manufacturer receives just as high a price for the range as if he used the better and more expensive material. With our construction, this solid piece of extra heavy cast iron is securely bolted to the back of the range, through which the products of combustion pass to the chimney, and is built to last. Many ranges are made with light sheet iron or sheet steel flue backs, which will not last, for the reason that the creosote and condensation which accumulate in this flue back from the smoke pipe and chimney eat out and perforate sheet steel in a very short time. You will notice that wherever any part of the Wehrle Model No. 20 and No. 22 Steel Range comes in direct contact with the fire we have substituted the best stove plate casting for steel, as it is the best class of material and is more satisfactory and durable. The rivet work on the back of our Wehrle Model No. 20 and No. 22 Steel Ranges is just as perfect as on the front. The illustration on page 374 shows the Wehrle cast iron flue back which will not burn or rust out.

TURN TO NEXT PAGE AND LEARN MORE ABOUT OUR WEHRLE MODEL No. 20, No. 22 AND No. 30 RANGES.

DETAILED DESCRIPTION OF WEHRLE MODEL No. 20, No. 22 AND No. 30 RANGES, ILLUSTRATED ON PAGES 377, 378 AND 379—CONTINUED.

RESERVOIR CASING. **Every part of our reservoir casing is made of the best cast iron stove plate,** is of extremely handsome rococo design, and beautifully ornamented with handsome silver nickeled medallion. It will never rust or burn out. A depression in the bottom of the casing receives and holds all condensation until it is absorbed by the heat. Steel or sheet iron reservoir casings used on ranges by many manufacturers are not found to be practical, for they soon corrode and rust out from creosote and moisture. We call your particular attention to the extension reservoir of the Wehrle Model No. 20 and No. 22 Steel Ranges, made from the finest grade of stove plate and embodying every improvement, and we guarantee it never to rust or burn out.

SPECIAL DAMPER. **A feature in the designing of the Wehrle Model No. 20 and No. 22 Six-Hole Steel Ranges and Wehrle Model No. 30 Cast Iron Range** which will be greatly appreciated is our special damper construction whereby the user has perfect control of the fire at all times. The damper is so constructed that it is easily accessible, and by reason of this scientific construction our big Wehrle Model Ranges will broil, bake, roast and cook perfectly in many chimneys where other ranges have proven complete failures.

GAS ATTACHMENT. **ANOTHER EXCLUSIVE FEATURE TO BE FOUND IN WEHRLE MODEL RANGES ONLY.**

OUR WEHRLE MODEL No. 20 AND No. 22 Six-Hole Steel Ranges and our Wehrle Model No. 30 Cast Iron Range can be equipped with our two-burner gas attachment. This very useful and practical cooking arrangement can be fitted on the right end of the range in place of the reservoir tank, and is equipped with one combination giant simmering and one star burner and a galvanized iron drip pan. It has specially constructed top grates silver nickled supply pipe and air mixers, heat resisting wood handle lever valves, grates and burner tops removable and easily cleaned. Top surface of gas attachment is 12x21 inches. It can be connected to gas supply by rubber tubing or iron pipe. **This is the ideal arrangement** for convenience in quick boiling, heating, frying, etc. This attachment cannot be used with gasoline or acetylene gas. If baking oven is desired, our portable **Drop Door Steel Oven,** illustrated and described on page 417, placed over the burners will be found very effective and economical.

We can furnish our Wehrle Model No. 20, No. 22 and No. 30 Ranges, with gas attachment but without reservoir, in all sizes, at the exact same prices listed on pages 377 to 379. If wanted with gas attachment, BE SURE to say on your order or in your letter, "With Gas Attachment," and state whether you use natural or manufactured gas.

PLEASE REMEMBER **that we cannot fit a gas attachment to a range with reservoir,** as it is connected at the right end where the reservoir is usually placed. Ranges cannot be supplied with both reservoir and gas attachment. Ranges fitted with gas attachment can be shipped only from our Newark, Ohio, foundry. We have in warehouses these ranges and also our Acme Triumph and Acme Charm ranges **but only with reservoir and high closet.**

View Showing Quick Heating and Practical Reservoir with Damper and Flue Construction on Wehrle Model No. 20 and No. 22 Steel Ranges and No. 30 Cast Iron Range.

SCIENTIFIC FLUE CONSTRUCTION. **Every portion of the flue which comes in direct contact with the outside wall of stove has a liberal asbestos protection.** The bottom of flue below the oven is protected on the under side by heavy asbestos, which serves a double purpose—retaining the heat in the flue and protecting the floor from the heat. By reason of our improved scientific flue construction the products of combustion are carried evenly to all six griddles and over oven top; thence down and forward under the entire oven bottom; thence up the back flue of the range to the chimney, making positively the best flue construction ever made; works more quickly and evenly than any other and with much less fuel.

SPECIAL AND IMPROVED RESERVOIR CONSTRUCTION. **We have taken special pains to make the reservoir tank of large capacity,** to make it sanitary, best porcelain lined, easily kept clean and easily lifted out, a feature that we feel sure will be appreciated by every housekeeper. The reservoir capacity of the Wehrle Model Steel and Cast Iron Ranges is from 13½ to 22 quarts, according to size. By turning the reservoir damper, heat is thrown under the reservoir, as shown in illustration above, heating the water boiling hot. **The two reservoir covers** are of the Art Nouveau pattern, beautifully designed to harmonize with the general pattern of the range; they are highly japanned, the japan finish being baked on by our new and original process. No detail of construction, no matter how small, has been overlooked by us in our effort to produce THE BEST.

Large Porcelain Lined Reservoir Tank and Art Nouveau Covers on Wehrle Model No. 20 and No. 22 Steel Ranges and Wehrle Model No. 30 Cast Iron Range.

THE ILLUSTRATIONS HEREWITH **are engraved by our artist and are exact reproductions,** with full descriptions, of our **Duplex Anti-Clinker Grate and our Coal and Wood Fire Box, with Shaking Device,** the best and most satisfactory construction it is possible to build, and used exclusively by us in the highest grade ranges made in the world, our **Wehrle Model No. 20 and No. 22 Steel Ranges** and our magnificent **Wehrle Model No. 30 Cast Iron Range** on legs.

DUPLEX ANTI-CLINKER GRATE. **The highest degree of perfection has been attained in this grate, which is the only one on the market that operates well for either hard coal, coke, wood or corn cobs.** It is almost unnecessary to describe the merits of this grate, because it is the standard construction, too well known to need our praise. Our best mechanics construct this grate and it always operates perfectly and with our poker device and our perfected and easily operating grate lever it is easily and quickly cleaned. We call your special attention to the construction of our improved **Duplex Anti-Clinker Grate.** As shown in illustration, it is made in two parts, so that a slight pull of the shaker cuts out all the dead coal and clinkers, dropping them into the ash pan without in the least disturbing and without loss of a particle of the fire or disturbing the temper of the operator. It is so constructed that it will burn hard or soft coal, coke, wood or corn cobs. **For burning hard coal** with our duplex grate which is furnished with this range, the grate should always have the concave or open side up. This allows the draft to circulate through the opening and gives proper combustion. **For soft coal,** the grate is left in the same way as for burning hard coal. With the large flues we put into this range it is impossible for them to choke up with any kind of fuel, and therefore soft coal can be burned with economy by simply regulating the drafts. **For burning wood,** always be sure to reverse the grate. Simply give it a turn with our perfected and easily operating grate lever. This gives you an entirely new design of grate, made especially for burning wood. Wood requires but one-half the amount of draft that coal requires; therefore, the ribbed side of the grate should be up for burning wood and the slotted side down. When the range is used for burning wood, the two end linings should be removed thus giving a larger fire box, so that a long stick of wood can be used All other fuels can be burned as economically as coal and wood.

Duplex Anti-Clinker Grate.

OUR NEW **improved, perfect, easily operated grate switch or shaking device.** In the construction of these Wehrle Model No. 20, No. 22 and No. 30 Ranges, we have supplied a long felt want by the introduction of our new improved grate switch or shaking device, which entirely does away with the old method and old style troublesome shaker, which invariably slips off when in use, breaks, and frequently cannot be found, thereby making it necessary for the user to rake the fire with a poker. By referring to the illustration below, you will note our entirely new and original grate shaker and switch combined. You will note the big improvement over the old style of grate shaker; that our improved shaking device is bolted to the left end of the range in a convenient position, easily accessible, and is so arranged that one or two movements back and forth will clean the fire of all clinkers and dead ashes, leaving it clear and bright. This device is owned and controlled by us and will be found only in the Wehrle Model Ranges.

Coal Fire Box with Grate Lever and Shaker Combined.

THE FIRE BOX. **This is the most important improvement made in range construction for many years. The Wehrle made fire box insures the greatest possible fuel economy and no heat is wasted in the flues.** The fire boxes in our new Wehrle Model No. 20, No. 22 and No. 30 Ranges have been worked out by designers of long experience in this feature of range construction. The length, width and depth have all been made exactly right for quick baking consistent with the most economical use of fuel. Particular note should be made of the weight of the castings. These are made exceedingly heavy, are corrugated to prevent warping and are constructed to allow ample circulation of air behind them to prevent burning out. We ask you to make comparisons of our fire box castings with those found in the highest priced stoves made. The scientific construction of our fire box is largely responsible for the successful and perfect operation of these Wehrle Model Six-Hole Ranges. It is not only a great saver of fuel but one that gives the best possible results in every way. Our illustration of the fire box will convey to you a clear understanding of the wide adaptability of this range to every sort of fuel. The fire back or back lining in the fire box, which is more directly exposed to the intense heat than any other part of the lining, is made extra heavy and corrugated, and likewise all other linings are made of proper weight to withstand the heat and are well braced and ventilated by air chambers between the oven and lining. The illustration at the left shows the coal fire box with Duplex grate and end linings in proper positions. By a simple device of our own invention you are able to instantly convert this coal fire box into a wood fire box. A simple pull of the grate switch inverts the grate bar, so that you have a solid level grate bottom for wood burning. The end linings are then removed and the fire box then appears as shown in the illustration at right. The wonderful construction of this Duplex grate and grate switch gives us in the Wehrle Model No. 20, No. 22 and No. 30 Ranges the simplest method ever devised for the quick conversion of a perfect coal burning fire box into a perfect wood burning fire box, with an extra space for the reception of long sticks of wood. The length of this wood burning fire box with end linings removed and with extension attached is 26 inches on all sizes of the Wehrle Model No. 20, No. 22 and No. 30 Ranges. We cannot emphasize too strongly the superiority in construction of this fire box over all others, which is among the many exclusive features that stamps the Wehrle method and patent of fire box construction absolutely the most progressive and best in the world.

Wood Fire Box with Grate Lever and Shaker Combined.

REMEMBER, if you order one of our Wehrle Model No. 20 Six-Hole Polished Blue Steel Ranges, complete, as shown on page 377, our Wehrle Model No. 22 Six-Hole Polished Blue Steel Plate Range on legs, complete, as shown on page 378, or our Wehrle Model No. 30 Cast Iron Range, **complete, with reservoir and high closet,** as shown on page 379, we will make **immediate shipment** from a **warehouse very near you** so you will get the stove in **just a day or two** or a few days at most, and with the **very little freight** charges from the warehouse to your town to pay.

INSTRUCTIONS HOW TO ORDER STOVES OR RANGES

No. 7. 7¼ INCHES WIDE

No. 8. 8¼ INCHES WIDE

No. 9. 9¼ INCHES WIDE

Showing relative sizes of stove or griddle covers.

ON THIS PAGE TO THE LEFT YOU WILL FIND ILLUSTRATIONS SHOWING **the relative sizes of griddle covers or lids to fit the cooking holes on stoves and ranges,** likewise to the right illustrations showing the relative sizes of ovens. You will notice the griddle covers or lids are made in three sizes, No. 7, No. 8 and No. 9, noting that they measure 7¼, 8¼ and 9¼ inches, and the ovens are made in four sizes, measuring 14, 16, 18 and 20 inches wide, 14 inches high and 21 inches deep. All cook stoves and ranges are variously numbered "7–14," "7–16," "8–18," "9–20," etc., the first number given indicating the size of the griddle covers or lids and the last two figures the width of the oven in inches. Referring to the illustrations showing the lids and ovens, it will be seen that No. 7–14 is the very smallest size cooking stove or range, having 7¼-inch cooking holes and a 14-inch oven; size 7–16 being the next smallest size, having 7¼-inch cooking holes and a 16-inch oven.

DO NOT BUY THE CHEAPEST STOVE OR THE SMALLEST SIZE STOVE. **Get a stove that is adapted to your purposes and needs and one large enough to do its work right.** That is by far the cheapest in the end, for the difference in price between a small stove or a stove with No. 7 cooking holes and a 14-inch or 16-inch oven and one of the larger sizes with No. 8 or No. 9 cooking holes and an 18-inch or 20-inch oven is so very small and the additional value that you will receive is so great that we know you will find it decidedly to your interest to buy one of our best stoves made in one of the larger sizes. **Therefore let us caution you, before making your selection, to be sure to refer to the illustrations on this page, showing the relative sizes of lids and ovens, also the table of sizes given under each stove illustration, and be sure to observe the stove number, size of lids, size of ovens, and select a stove or range large enough to answer your requirements and to fit your cooking utensils.**

DO NOT ORDER A No. 8 STOVE IF YOUR COOKING UTENSILS ARE No. 9, **as they will not fit.** Measure the oven and top of your old stove or one of your neighbor's stoves if it is about the size you want and then compare it with the measurements given in our catalog.

TO MAKE SURE THAT WE SEND YOU THE RIGHT KIND OF FIRE BOX, **do not fail to state on your order the kind of fuel you use. Say whether you burn hard coal only, or soft coal only, or hard coal and wood, or soft coal and wood, or wood only.** If you order a stove for wood alone, you get a much larger fire box than if you order a combination stove for coal and wood, and one especially suited for wood. **Guard against making the mistake of selecting a stove for soft coal when we offer it as a hard coal burner only. So many stove dealers and manufacturers** are indifferent and careless about the fire boxes they furnish for the different kinds of fuel to be used and we feel that it is very important for us to remind you, when ordering your stove, to tell us exactly the kind of fuel you burn.

WE CAN FURNISH OUR STOVES ONLY **as illustrated and described in catalog.** Do not ask us to send you a range with fire box on the opposite end from that shown in illustration or to leave off or put on more nickel, as we cannot do it. **We do not furnish stove pipe or cooking utensils with our stoves at prices quoted.** Neither does your dealer, unless he charges you enough for the stove to allow him to include them free.

IF AFTER READING THE DESCRIPTIONS CAREFULLY **you still desire information regarding any of our stoves** it will be promptly and cheerfully furnished upon receipt of your inquiry.

AFTER WRITING YOUR ORDER, **check it over closely to see that you have written down correctly** catalog number, fuel used, name and size of stove wanted and correct price.

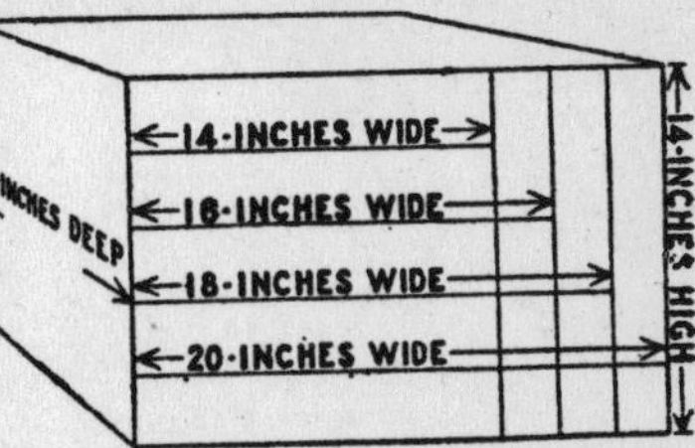

Showing relative sizes of ovens on steel ranges.

FOLLOW THESE INSTRUCTIONS CAREFULLY, THUS AVOIDING ANY POSSIBILITY OF MAKING A MISTAKE IN ORDERING YOUR STOVE.

BE SURE TO ORDER A STOVE BIG ENOUGH, ONE LARGE ENOUGH TO DO ITS WORK RIGHT

No. 18 No. 17 No. 16 No. 15 No. 14 No. 13 No. 12 No. 11 No. 10 No. 9

THE ABOVE ILLUSTRATIONS SHOW THE RELATIVE SIZES OF HEATING STOVES.

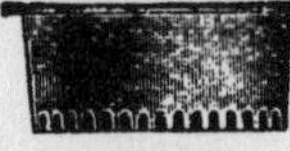
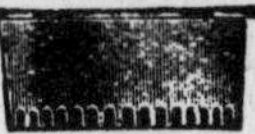
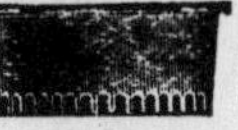
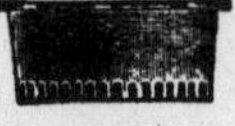
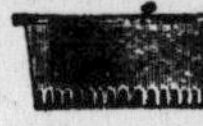
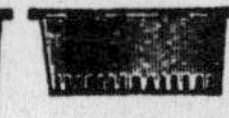

18-inch 17-inch 16-inch 15-inch 14-inch 13-inch 12-inch 11-inch 10-inch 9-inch

THE ABOVE ILLUSTRATIONS SHOW THE RELATIVE SIZES OF FIRE POTS.

WHAT SIZE HEATING STOVE TO ORDER

BE SURE YOU DO NOT ORDER A STOVE TOO SMALL. **It is better to order a heating stove plenty large enough or even too large,** rather than a stove too small. A large heating stove or a heating stove with an extra large fire pot does not necessarily burn up any more fuel than a small heater, because a larger heater can be easily regulated to consume as small an amount of coal as a small heater. Economy in the use of fuel in a heating stove depends largely upon the regulation of the drafts and dampers, and for this reason you need not burn any more coal in a big heater than in one several sizes smaller. In the point of economy in the consumption of fuel, in the use of a minimum amount of fuel, a big heating stove has all the advantages of a small one and, on the other hand, has this great advantage that a smaller one has not, namely, you can get much more heat if you want it. If you have a big space to heat, if you have an exceedingly large space to heat, if you have a very large house with a number of large rooms upstairs as well as downstairs to heat, if you have a large room and adjoining rooms and hall which you wish to heat or a whole house which you wish to heat with one stove, you can make heat enough for the coldest days and nights for the reason that a big heating stove with an extra large fire pot and a large capacious magazine has more radiating surface, so when you need and want more heat you simply adjust the drafts and dampers and you can easily, with one large heating stove, furnish sufficient heat for an area within a large house.

By referring to the above illustrations you can get a very good idea of the relative sizes of heating stoves and fire pots.

HEATING STOVES No. 9, No. 10 AND No. 11 **are very small heaters,** and by reason of their very small sizes are usually known as **"junior"** heaters and are only intended and suitable to heat very small bedrooms, very small dining rooms and other very small rooms.

STOVE No. 12, **with a fire pot measuring 12 inches across,** will be found a desirable medium size heater, suitable and will do for a home with few medium size bedrooms, but really cannot be depended upon to furnish sufficient heat for a number of bedrooms, dining rooms, sitting rooms, parlors, halls, or even large bedrooms.

STOVE No. 14, **with a fire pot measuring 14 inches across, and stove No. 16,** with fire pot measuring 16 inches across, are the popular sizes and are especially suitable for good size houses for all general purposes and are the sizes we recommend; the sizes that never disappoint and the sizes that do all any heating stove can be called on to do. Especially do we recommend No. 16. This is **the ideal size** and the size heating stove to buy. It will heat up all the big rooms in most homes; it will heat all the upstairs as well as downstairs, the entire floor on which it is placed, with the hall and all the adjoining rooms; it does not burn any more coal than a small or medium size heater if you regulate it and give the dampers the proper attention; in short, **it is just the size to do the work right.** It has great radiating surface. It gives you the heat when and where you want it, and when the mercury sneaks way down low in the thermometer, **then** is when your No. 16 heater shines. No temperature can get too low for stove size No. 16. No. 16 does not mind zero or even ten degrees or even twenty degrees below zero weather. Simply open the drafts, fill the magazine if you use hard coal and you will get heat, and all you want of it, because stove No. 16 has the big size fire pot and the greater amount of radiating surface.

STOVE No. 18, **with fire pot measuring 18 inches across, is the wonder size** when you have an exceedingly large space to heat. **It is the biggest size heater made in the world,** and you will find this size most satisfactory in the control of fire and most economical in the consumption of fuel, and it is such a great heater that in the Dakotas, the New England States, Wisconsin, Michigan, up in New York State, in Iowa or wherever the winters are so severe and wherever the dwellings are large with very large rooms, where several large rooms, upstairs and downstairs, are to be heated by one stove, **there is** where stove No. 18 is appreciated. **Wehrle Model No. 100** Base Burner, size No. 18, illustrated and described on pages 968 and 969, is built upon liberal lines with an extra large fire pot and magazine, with a wonderful amount of radiating surface, and is **the greatest heating stove, the most perfect base burner** for driving out the cold and heating up big areas of space ever built, and no other manufacturer or dealer makes a stove with a fire pot measuring actually 18 inches. We are the only concern that offers a heating stove so big. You can get a size No. 18 base burner **from us only** and we make it only in the one model, namely, **Wehrle Model No. 100,** the largest and finest base burner made in the world, illustrated and described on pages 968 and 969.

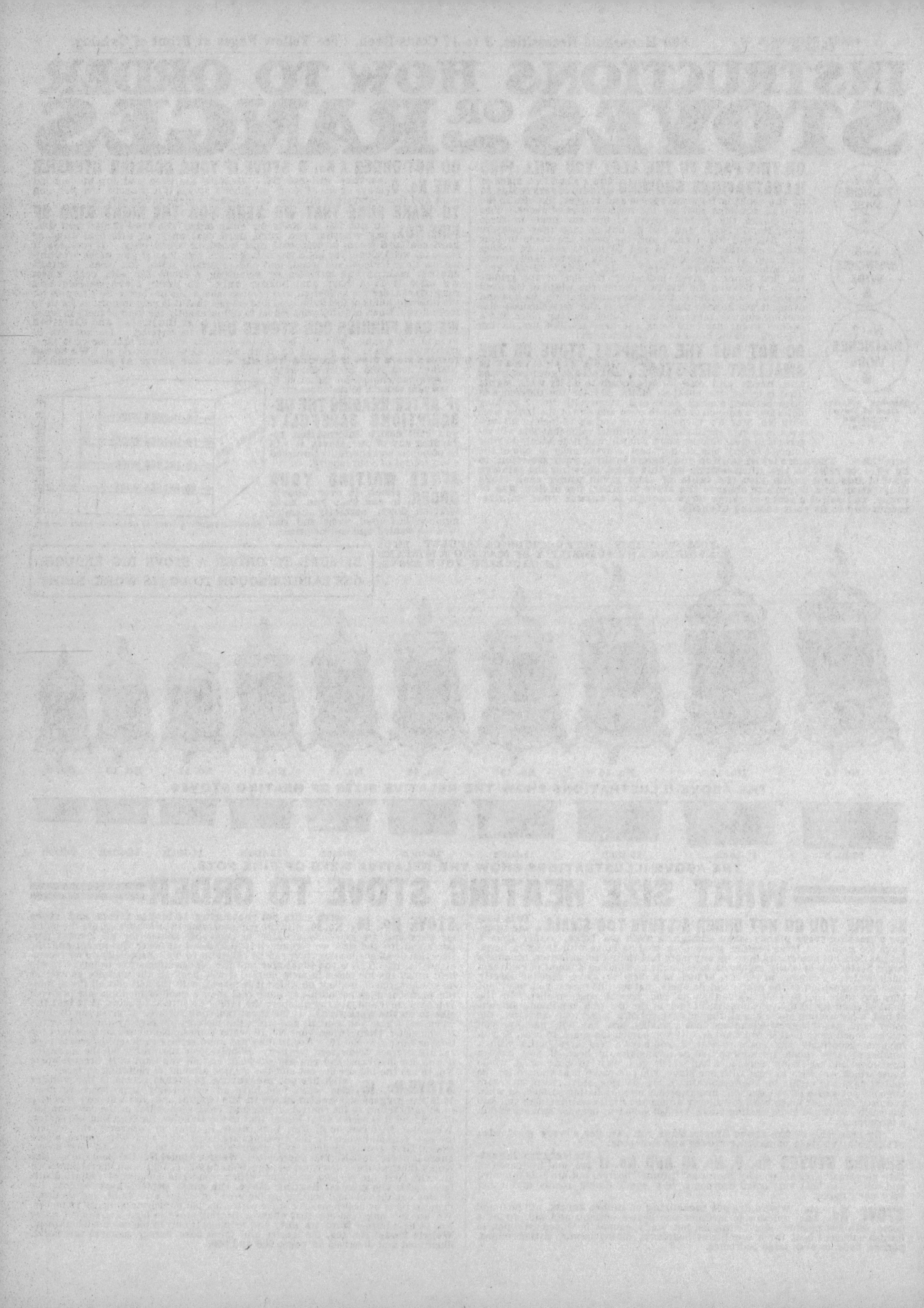

POCKET KNIVES

NEW POCKET KNIVES DIRECT FROM OUR OWN FACTORY.

WE CALL YOUR ATTENTION ESPECIALLY to this line of highest grade American made pocket and penknives, our  brand.

THE BLADES ARE FORGED from S. C. Wardlow's best English special blade steel, the finest and the best that can be procured for knife blades. We also use Wardlow's steel for the springs, which costs nearly double the price at which ordinary spring steel can be bought, but which greatly improves the wearing qualities of the knife and adds greatly to its durability. **Every blade, from the cheapest to the best, which bears our brand, is hammered out by hand.** Instead of using iron for the lining of our cheaper knives, we pay more for steel because it makes a much stronger and better knife. All work is done by skilled mechanics, particular attention being paid to making a keen cutting knife that will carry a lasting edge.

OUR POCKET KNIVES are fully guaranteed in every way. This means we guarantee the blades to be free from flaws, and guarantee them to be neither too hard nor too soft. This does not mean that we guarantee the knives not to break. If we were to do this, we would be obliged to temper them so soft they would be of no practical use for cutting. They are not intended to be used as mortising chisels, tack pullers, can openers, screwdrivers, crowbars, nor for any of the purposes by which pocket knives are frequently misused.

ALL POCKET KNIVES should occasionally be oiled at the joint so the blade will not wear into the spring. Vaseline makes a very good lubricant for this purpose.

No. 28C830 T. T. C. Pocket Knife. Has rosewood handle, steel lining, iron bolster. Length of handle, 3⅜ inches. Length with large blade open, 6 inches. Price....................18c
If by mail, postage extra, 4 cents.

No. 28C833 T. T. C. Pocket Knife, clip point, stag handle, two blades, steel lining, iron bolster. This is a standard size full weight knife; is durable, and will give splendid satisfaction. Length of handle, 3⅜ inches. Length with large blade open, 6⅛ inches. Price....................20c
If by mail, postage extra, 5 cents.

No. 28C838 T. T. C. Stag Handle Chain Knife, clip point, two blades, steel lining, iron bolster and caps, German silver shield, with chain of suitable length to fasten over button. Length of handle, 3⅝ inches. Length with large blade open, 6¼ inches.
Price...(If by mail, postage extra, 6 cents)....35c

No. 28C840 A medium weight, finely finished **T. T. C. Knife, with white bone handle,** brass lining, finished inside and out, German silver bolster, caps and shield. Length of handle, 3⅜ inches. Length with large blade open, 6¼ inches.
Price...(If by mail, postage extra, 5 cents)....39c

No. 28C842 T. T. C. Jack Knife, stag handle, swell butt, steel lining, iron bolsters, German silver shield. Length of handle, 3⅜ inches. Length with large blade open, 6⅛ inches. Price....................35c
If by mail, postage extra, 5 cents.

No. 28C847 T. T. C. Carpenters' Sensible Knife, having two large blades, one with clip point and one sheep's foot or carpenter's marking blade. The blades of this knife are made of 11-gauge steel; has stag handle, steel lining, iron bolsters, German silver shields, finished inside and out. Length of handle, 3½ inches. Length with large blade open, 6⅛ inches.
Price...(If by mail, postage extra, 6 cents)....43c

No. 28C850 T. T. C. Easy Opener Pocket Knife, with stag handle, German silver bolster, caps and shield, brass lining. Finished inside and out. Length of handle, 3½ inches. Length with large blade open, 6½ inches. Price....................47c
If by mail, postage extra, 6 cents.

No. 28C861 T. T. C. Gentlemen's Jack Knife, stag handle, German silver bolster, caps and shield, brass lining, thoroughly finished in every particular inside and out. Length of handle, 3¼ inches. Length with large blade open, 5¾ inches. Price....................42c
If by mail, postage extra, 5 cents.

No. 28C864 T. T. C. Equal End Pocket Knife, has cocoa handle, German silver bolster, caps and shield, brass lined, finished inside and out. Length of handle, 3¼ inches. Length with large blade open, 5¾ inches. Price....................40c
If by mail, postage extra, 5 cents.

No. 28C895 T. T. C. Texas Toothpick, has stag handle, German silver bolsters and shield, brass lining, finely finished inside and out. Clip point saber blade. While the blade is long and slim, the peculiar shape makes it very strong and durable as well as an excellent whittler. Length of handle, 3⅞ inches; length with large blade open, 6⅞ inches. Price....................45c
If by mail, postage extra, 6 cents.

No. 28C875 T. T. C. Balloon Shaped Knife, stag handle, fancy German silver bolster, caps and shield, brass lining, finished inside and out. Length of handle, 3⅝ inches. Length with large blade open, 6½ inches. Price....................53c
If by mail, postage extra, 6 cents.

Pearl Handle Knife.

No. 28C869 T. T. C. Gentlemen's Pearl Handle Jack Knife. Has pearl handle, German silver bolster, caps and shield, German silver lining, satin finish. The blades are full crocus polished. The knife is in every way finished as finely as the best penknife you ever saw. Length of handle, 3¼ inches; length with large blade open, 5¾ inches. Price.........90c
If by mail, postage extra, 5 cents.

No. 28C856 T. T. C. Equal End Jack Knife. Has cocoa handle, brass lining, finished inside and out, German silver bolster, caps and shield. Length of handle, 3½ inches; length with large blade open, 6½ inches. Price....................42c
If by mail, postage extra, 6 cents.

No. 28C857 T. T. C. Equal End Knife, has stag handle, brass lining, German silver bolster, cap and shield. Length of handle, 3½ inches; length with large blade open, 6¼ inches. Price....................45c
If by mail, postage extra, 6 cents.

No. 28C866 T. T. C. Little Giant Equal End Pocket Knife, with saber clip blade, stag handle, German silver bolster, caps and shield, brass lined, finished inside and out. The amount of work which this knife will do is something never before attained in a knife of its size. Length of handle, 3¼ inches; length with large blade open, 5⅝ inches. Price...43c
If by mail, postage extra, 5 cents.

No. 28C908 T. T. C. Missouri Favorite, has clip point saber blade made of full 12-gauge steel. Has ebony handle, long German silver bolsters, caps and shield, brass lined, finished inside and out. Length of handle, 3⅝ inches; length with large blade open, 6 inches. Price....................50c
If by mail, postage extra, 6 cents.

No. 28C845 T. T. C. Solid Worth Jack Knife. Stag handle, brass lining, finished inside and out, iron bolsters and caps, German silver shield. Length of handle, 3⅝ inches; length with large blade open, 6¾ inches. Price....................40c
If by mail, postage extra, 6 cents.

No. 28C886 T. T. C. Jumbo Pocket Knife, with ebony handle 4 inches long; German silver bolster and shield, brass lined, finished inside and out. The blades are made of full size 10-gauge steel. This is a big, strong, heavy, durable knife. Length of handle, 4 inches; length with large blade open, 6⅞ inches. Price....................43c
If by mail, postage extra, 6 cents.

No. 28C896 T. T. C. Austrian Hunter. It has a clip point blade, stag handle, fancy iron bolster and caps, German silver shield, steel lining, finely finished inside and out. Length of handle, 3¾ inches; length with large blade open, 7 inches. Price..75c
If by mail, postage extra, 6 cents.

No. 28C920 T. T. C. Hunter's Pride Knife. It has stag handle, long, heavy German silver bolsters, caps and shield, brass lining, highly finished inside and out. Length of handle, 4½ inches; length with large blade open, 8 inches.
Price..(If by mail, postage extra, 6 cents)..60c

No. 28C945 T. T. C. Arkansas Hunter. A knife in which nearly every cent of the cost is spent in quality, and not looks. It has clip point saber blade, flush lock back so blade cannot shut on the fingers, curved stag handle which just fits the hand nicely, fancy iron bolsters, steel lining. Length of handle, 4⅝ inches; length with blade open, 8½ inches.
Price....................65c
If by mail, postage extra, 7 cents.

No. 28C946 T. T. C. Hudson Bay Hunting Knife A very nicely finished hunting knife. Clip point saber blade, flush lock back, curved stag handle, fancy German silver bolster, caps and lining. Length of handle, 5¼ inches; length with blade open, 9⅝ inches. Price....................$1.00
If by mail, postage extra, 8 cents.

For other Hunting Knives and a full line of Hunters' Goods, see Sporting Goods Department.

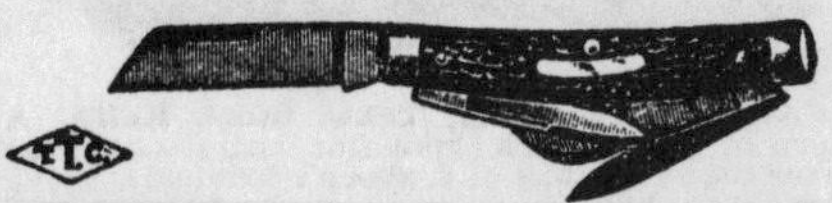

No. 28C884 T. T. C. Sampson Pruning Knife. Blade made of 10-gauge steel. The shape of blade, method of grinding, etc., being according to the ideas of one of the best fruit growers in the country, made just exactly the way he wanted it regardless of expense. Length of handle, 4 inches; length with blade open, 7 inches.
Price..(If by mail, postage extra, 6 cents)...35c

No. 28C980 T. T. C. Large Congress Knife, has two large blades and two pen blades, stag handle, German silver bolsters and shield, brass lined, nicely finished throughout. Length of handle, 3¾ inches; length with large blade open, 6 inches.
Price...(If by mail, postage extra, 5 cents)..74c

No. 28C969 T. T. C. Compact Three-Blade Pocket Knife. The large blade is wide and strong; has two pen blades, stag handle, German silver bolsters and shield, brass lining, finely finished inside and out. Length of handle, 3⅜ inches; length with large blade open, 5⅞ inches. Price....................65c
If by mail, postage extra, 5 cents.

No. 28C982 T. T. C. Jumbo Congress Knife, with two large blades and two pen blades. Stag handle, iron bolsters, German silver shield, steel lined. Finely finished. Those who prefer a congress pattern knife and want something strong and heavy will find this a most desirable pattern. Length of handle, 4⅛ inches; length with large blade open, 6¾ inches. Price 75c
If by mail, postage extra, 5 cents.

No. 28C925 T. T. C. New England Workmen's Knife. A great favorite with carpenters, cabinetmakers and other woodworkers. It has stag handle, German silver bolster and shield, brass lining, finely finished, and polished inside and out. Length of handle, 3¾ inches; length with large blade open, 6 inches. Price ..(If by mail, postage extra, 4 cents).....50c

No. 28C890 T. T. C. Favorite Double Ender, with spear and clip point blades. Stag handle. German silver fancy bolsters and shield, brass lined and finished inside and out. Length of handle, 3¾ inches; length with clip point blade open, 6⅞ inches. Price....(Postage extra, 5 cents).....55c

IF A RAZOR EDGE is put on any of the T. T. C. blades we will guarantee any of them to shave, but a razor edge should never be put on a pocket knife. To get a proper edge on a pocket knife blade, the blade should be held at an angle of about 20 or 25 degrees, and drawn from shoulder to point on each side until a true edge is obtained. This makes a stiff, keen cutting edge, and enables us to furnish a much higher tempered knife blade than we would were the blade to be laid flat and brought down to a razor edge.

No. 28C892 T. T. C. Western Chief. Has clip point saber blade, very heavy, made of full 10-gauge steel; has stag handle, German silver bolsters and shield, brass lining, finished inside and out. The large blade has a flush lock back, which prevents the blade from closing on the hand. Length of handle, 4 inches; length with large blade open, 6¾ inches. Price..(Postage extra, 6 cents).......95c

No. 28C911 T. T. C. Junior Cattle Knife. Has spear, pen and sheep's foot blades. It has stag handle, German silver bolster and shield, brass lining, finished inside and out. Length of handle, 3¼ inches; length with large blade open, 5¾ inches. Price ...(If by mail, postage extra, 5 cents)....60c

No. 28C912 T. T. C. Wild West Cowboys' Knife. Has spear, sheep's foot and pen blades, stag handle, iron bolsters, German silver shield, brass lined; finished inside and out. This is a strong, heavy knife, and is a great favorite with stockmen, hunters, trappers and others who wish a strong, heavy knife in as compact form as possible. Length of handle, 3⅝ inches; length with large blade open, 6¼ inches. Price............ ....65c
If by mail, postage extra, 6 cents.

No. 28C881 T. T. C. Texas Stock Knife. A pattern of knife which is popular with stock raisers all over the world, has clip, sheep's foot and spaying blades, stag handle, German silver bolsters and shield, brass lined, highly finished inside and out. This is our most popular cattle knife, and is made just as good as we know how to make them. Length of handle, 4 inches; length with clip point blade open, 6⅞ inches. Price.........................75c
If by mail, postage extra, 5 cents.

No. 28C899 T. T. C. Ranchero Cattle Knife. Has pearl handle, German silver bolsters and shield, German silver lining, satin finish. The blades are full crocus polished. It cannot fail to give satisfaction to those who want a knife of superior cutting qualities, workmanship and beauty. Length of handle, 3⅝ inches; length with large blade open, 6⅝ inches. Price..(Postage extra, 5 cents)....$1.35

No. 28C901 T. T. C. Montana Beauty Stockmen's Knife. Has clip, sheep's foot and spaying blades, pearl handle, German silver lining, satin finish; the blades are beautifully crocus polished. In our ordinary grades of knives, knives which must sell at popular prices, we pay very much more attention to quality and workmanship than we do to beauty and finish, but in this particular knife we excel all others in finish as well as in quality. Length of handle, 3⅞ inches; length with large blade open, 6¾ inches. Price ...(If by mail, postage extra, 5c)......$1.50

No. 28C954 T. T. C. Popular School or Ladies' Knife. Pearl handle, German silver bolsters and lining, finished inside. Length of handle, 2⅞ inches; length with large blade open, 4⅝ inches. Price...50c
If by mail, postage extra, 3 cents.

No. 28C961 T. T. C. Four-Blade Stag Handle Senator Pattern Penknife, with large blade, two pen blades and nail blade. Stag handle, German silver tips and shield, brass lining, finely finished inside and out, all blades full crocus polished. Length of handle, 3⅛ inches; length with large blade open, 5¼ inches. Price.... ....65c
If by mail, postage extra, 4 cents.

No. 28C962 T. T. C. Small Congress Knife, has one large blade, two pen blades and one nail blade, stag handle, German silver bolsters and shield, brass lined, finely finished throughout. Length of handle, 3⅛ inches; length with large blade open, 5⅝ inches. Price........... .....70c
If by mail, postage extra, 4 cents.

Push Button Knives.

No. 28C1324 Push Button Knife. One blade, clip point, stag handle, single bolster, iron lined. Length of handle, 4¾ inches; length with blade open, 8¾ inches. Price............................66c
If by mail, postage extra, 5 cents.

No. 28C1320 Push Button Knife. One blade, clip point, stag handle, single bolster, iron lined. Length of handle, 3⅝ inches; length with blade open, 6⅞ inches. Price.................................57c
If by mail, postage extra, 5 cents.

No. 28C1326 Push Button Knife. Two blades, stag handle, brass lined. Length of handle, 3⅜ inches; length with large blade open, 5¼ inches. Price.....................55c
If by mail, postage extra, 4 cents.

No. 28C1136 Combination Knife. Has stag handle, German silver bolsters, steel lining, spear blade, reaming awl, hoof cleaver, screwdriver, wire cutter, pliers and wrench. All tools are practical and serviceable. Warranted. Length of handle, 4⅛ inches. Price.......................................98c
If by mail, postage extra, 6 cents.

Genuine Imported Swedish Hunting Knives.

Blade can be removed, folded into its frame, and replaced in the handle. This knife is a popular woodworkers' tool, as well as a hunting knife. Has solid boxwood handle. The blade is best of steel, and cutting qualities and temper are fully guaranteed.

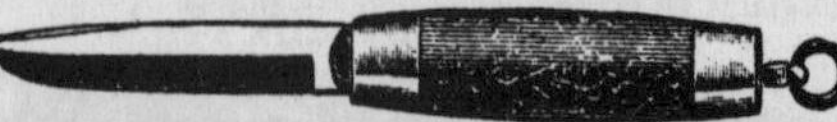

No. 28C1301 Genuine Imported Swedish Hunting Knife, as described above. Length of handle, 2⅞ inches. Price.......................................38c

No. 28C1302 Genuine Imported Swedish Hunting Knife, as described above. Length of handle, 3¼ inches. Price..45c

No. 28C1303 Genuine Imported Swedish Hunting Knife, as described above. Length of handle, 4⅜ inches. Price......................................50c
If by mail, postage extra, 6 cents.

Geo. Wostenholm & Sons' I X L Pocket Knives.

We show some of the most desirable patterns of George Wostenholm & Sons' Celebrated IXL Pocket Knives, which are favorably known all over the world.
If by mail, postage extra, 6 cents.

No. 28C1138 George Wostenholm & Sons' Genuine IXL Pocket Knife; ebony handle, German silver bolster, brass lined. Length of handle, 3⅝ inches. Price.......................................52c

No. 28C1140 George Wostenholm & Sons' IXL Pocket Knife; genuine stag handle, German silver bolster and shield, brass lined. Length of handle, 3⅜ inches. Price...57c

No. 28C1142 George Wostenholm & Sons' IXL Pocket Knife; genuine stag handle, iron bolster, iron lined. Length of handle, 3⅞ inches. Price..66c

No. 28C1144 George Wostenholm & Sons' IXL Pocket Knife; stag handle, German silver bolsters and shield, brass lined. Length of handle, 3¾ inches. Price...75c

No. 28C1146 George Wostenholm & Sons' IXL Pocket Knife; cocobolo handle, German silver bolster and shield, brass lined, finely etched. Length of handle, 3⅞ inches. Price.... ....70c

No. 28C1148 George Wostenholm & Sons' IXL Cattle Knife; genuine stag handle, German silver bolsters and shield, brass lined. Length of handle, 3¾ inches. This knife has spear, sheep's foot and pen blades. Price.............................$1.34

No. 28C1150 George Wostenholm & Sons' IXL Sportsmen's Knife; genuine stag handle, iron bolster, iron lined. Length of handle, 3⅞ inches. This knife has spear and pen blades, hoof cleaner, nut crack, champagne opener, corkscrew and reamer. Price...$1.47

No. 28C1152 George Wostenholm & Sons' IXL Congress Knife; stag handle. This knife has sheep's foot blade, two pen blades and nail blade, iron bolsters, brass lining. Length of handle, 4⅛ inches. Price....................................... ..$1.24

No. 28C1154 George Wostenholm & Sons' IXL Lock Back Hunting Knife; stag handle, iron bolster, iron lining, saber clip point blade. Length of handle, 4⅜ inches. Price..............................70c

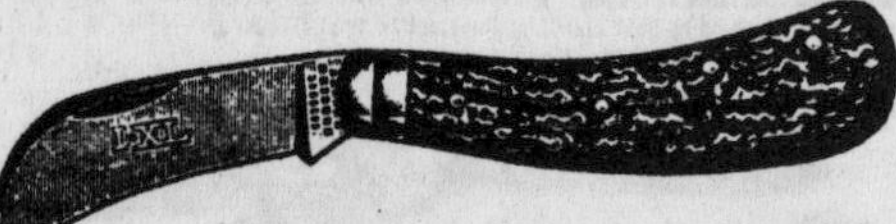

No. 28C1156 George Wostenholm & Sons' IXL Pruning Knife; genuine stag handle, iron bolster, iron lining. Length of handle, 4⅜ inches. Price, 97c

No. 28C1158 George Wostenholm & Sons' IXL Pruning Knife; same as above, except has cocobolo handle. Price.......................................60c

LADIES' SCISSORS

The following patterns represent the highest quality of solid steel Ladies' Imported Scissors. There are numerous grades of scissors on the market, both of American and foreign make, and it is an easy matter for any dealer to sell scissors at lower prices than those we quote, but it is impossible for any dealer to sell the grade of scissors we are handling at prices that will in any way compare with ours. These scissors are fitted, finished and ground in a manner superior to that found in any other line of either American or foreign manufacture. We guarantee every pair of scissors to be perfect in material, cutting qualities, workmanship and finish, or money and transportation charges will be returned.

The Famous Wilbert Scissors.

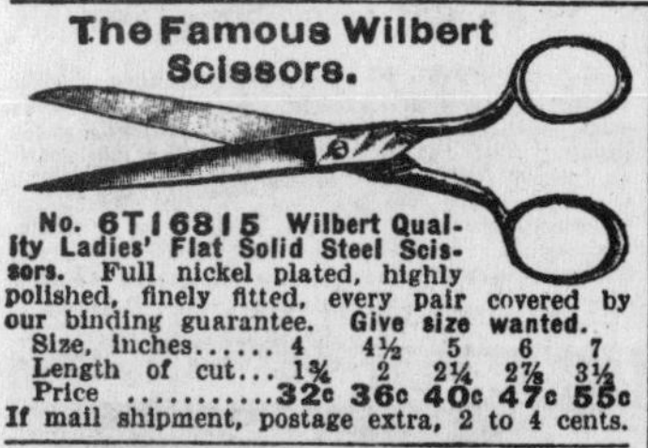

No. 6T16815 Wilbert Quality Ladies' Flat Solid Steel Scissors. Full nickel plated, highly polished, finely fitted, every pair covered by our binding guarantee. **Give size wanted.**

Size, inches	4	4½	5	6	7
Length of cut	1¾	2	2¼	2⅞	3½
Price	32c	36c	40c	47c	55c

If mail shipment, postage extra, 2 to 4 cents.

Wilbert Pocket Scissors.

No. 6T16790 Wilbert Brand, Extra Heavy, Full Gauge Pocket Scissors. These scissors have finely swaged blades. They are made of the best material and guaranteed superior to any pocket scissors on the market. Each pair is guaranteed to give satisfaction or money refunded. **Give size wanted.**

Full length, inches	4	4½	5
Length of cut, inches	1¾	2	2¼
Price	33c	36c	38c

If mail shipment, postage extra, 2 to 3 cents.

AN OCCASIONAL DROP OF OIL AT THE JOINT OF SHEARS, SCISSORS OR POCKET KNIVES TREBLES THEIR USEFULNESS.

The Stork Embroidery Scissors.

No. 6T16817

Body of stork and handles fancy gilt, bill polished steel, making handsome contrast. Best quality tempered steel, finely finished. Length, 3½ inches.
Price.....(Postage extra, 2 cents).....35c

Forged Steel Fancy Scissors.

No. 6T6821 Highest quality Scissors of the latest improved design, stiletto or rib blades, hand forged, highly polished gold plated cross pattern handles, neatly engraved. This is a high grade article; 6-inch length only.
Price 52c
If mail shipment, postage extra, 3 cents.

Buttonhole Scissors.

No. 6T16823 Buttonhole Scissors. Nickel plated with inside set screw to adjust blades for cutting. Length, 4½ inches. Price..........34c
If mail shipment, postage extra, 3 cents.

Ladies' Fancy Solid Steel Scissors.

No. 6T16820 Ladies' Solid Steel Scissors, fancy gilt handle. Every pair guaranteed to give satisfaction. Handles are finely engraved and finished in gold, which makes a handsome contrast to the highly polished oval nickel plated blades. **Give size wanted.**

Size, inches	3½	4½	5½
Price	33c	37c	42c

If mail shipment, postage extra, 2 and 3 cents.

Lace Scissors.

No. 6T6818 Forged Steel Lace Scissors, polished blades; French gray, engraved handles. A very handsome, high grade scissors; 3½ inches long. Price.38c
If mail shipment, postage extra, 2c

Adjustable Buttonhole Scissors.

No. 6T16824 Adjustable Buttonhole Scissors. Solid steel nickel plated and polished, finely fitted, adjusted by means of a small notched brass wheel fitted inside of shank. Six different adjustments, each notch numbered, which guarantees uniformity in cutting the various size buttonholes. Price..........49c
If mail shipment, postage extra, 3 cents.

Four-Piece Scissors Set.

No. 6T16825 This set consists of one pair 8-inch trimmers, one 6-inch scissors, one Stork embroidery scissors, one best quality buttonhole scissors, all highest quality goods. Every article guaranteed to give satisfaction. This set, if the items were bought singly, would cost you double our price. Put up in a neat partitioned flannel bag, as illustrated. Price, per set..........$1.70
If mail shipment, postage extra, 12 cents.

WILBERT QUEEN SEWING BASKET OUTFIT, $3.85.

No. 6T16828 This is the handsomest and best Sewing Basket Outfit ever on the market. The basket is imported from France, and is artistically woven of French willow and rattan. Size, 11 inches long, 7 inches wide, 5¼ inches high. Lined throughout with the finest red satin; the top and bottom of basket are tufted, the sides are laid in folds. The basket alone would sell for almost what we ask for the complete outfit. This basket contains one pair of 8-inch Wilbert quality full nickel plated straight trimmers, one pair of Wilbert quality 6-inch solid steel scissors, one Wilbert solid steel 3½-inch lace or embroidery scissors, one highest quality imported buttonhole scissors, and one sterling silver thimble. When considering this outfit, bear in mind that Wilbert shears and scissors are the highest quality goods made. Weight, 1 pound 12 ounces.
Price, outfit complete, as described..$3.85

POCKET KNIVES

LARGER ASSORTMENT —LOWEST PRICES—

THE POCKET KNIVES WE HANDLE are made specially for us under contract, according to our own specifications, by one of the oldest manufacturers in this country. Our enormous business enables us to control the output of this factory and to give you better value than you could possibly procure elsewhere. Every Wilbert knife is guaranteed. If found unsatisfactory, it may be returned and money will be refunded. **The blades in Wilbert knives are forged from the finest S. C. Wardlow's English steel, tempered by experts, insuring an even temper from heel to point.** The grinding is done by experienced workmen who grind nothing but pocket knives, and are, therefore, able to turn out better work than is usually turned out in a factory whose business is not large enough to confine itself exclusively to pocket cutlery. We guarantee the springs and blades in our knives against breakage through flaws in material or temper. We, of course, do not guarantee them against misuse. We do not recommend the use of pocket knives for purposes where a chisel, screwdriver or hammer would be better adapted. Oil your knife once a month at the joints, so that the blades will not wear into the springs.

The Wilbert Dakota Cowboys' Knife, 60 Cents.

GUARANTEED FOR ONE YEAR.

60c

No. 6T17149 The best Cattlemen's Knife ever made. Appreciating the need that cattlemen have for a good, strong, serviceable knife, a knife with which they can cut leather, wood or rope, and have the edge stand up, we have had this knife made specially and offer it as the best cattlemen's knife ever made. The steel used in these knives is extra heavy gauge and it is the very best English steel suitable for this purpose. The blades are tempered by electricity, insuring uniform temper from heel to point. The grinding, finish and cutler's work in this knife cannot be surpassed. It has three blades; spear point blade, sheep's foot and pen blade; fine stag handle, fitted with German silver shield, heavy German silver polished bolsters, full brass lined and finely finished inside and out. This is an extra strong, heavy knife for the stockman, hunter or trapper, who requires a dependable knife. We guarantee it to give absolute satisfaction or money refunded. It is a knife that would ordinarily sell for $1.25. Length of handle, 3⅝ inches; length with large blade open, 6½ inches.
Our price..........(If mail shipment, postage extra, 6 cents.)..........60c

TWO-BLADE JACK KNIVES WITH COCOBOLO AND EBONY HANDLES.

No. 6T16831 Wilbert Pocket Knife. Has rosewood handle, steel lining, iron bolster. Length of handle, 3½ inches. Length with large blade open, 6 inches. Price..........19c
If mail shipment, postage extra, 4 cents.

No. 6T16835 Wilbert Equal End Pocket Knife. Has cocoa handle, German silver bolsters, caps and shield, brass lined, finished inside and out. Length of handle, 3⅜ inches. Length with large blade open, 5⅝ inches.
Price 39c
If mail shipment, postage extra, 5 cents.

No. 6T16837 Teamster's Knife. Cocoa handle, heavy German silver shield, full brass lined. Length of handle, 3⅝ inches. Length with large blade open, 6¼ inches. One large, heavy, finely tempered and ground spear blade and one punch, or swage blade, with which holes can be bored in leather or wood. Price..........52c
If mail shipment, postage extra, 6 cents.

Wilbert Easy Opener, 48c.

No. 6T16858 Wilbert Hand Fitting High Grade Easy Opener Knife. Ebony handle, German silver bolsters, caps and shield, brass lined. Length of handle, 3⅜ inches. Length with large blade open, 6½ inches.
Price.....(Postage extra, 5 cents).....48c

No. 6T16863 Wilbert Missouri Favorite Has clip point saber blade, made of full 12-gauge steel. Has ebony handle, long German silver bolsters, caps and shield, brass lined, finished inside and out. Length of handle, 3¾ inches. Length with large blade open, 6⅝ inches. Price..........49c
If mail shipment, postage extra, 6 cents.

CHRIS WOLF HAND MADE KNIFE.

46c

No. 6T17199 This knife, as above stated, is made entirely by hand, and for this reason it is probably the ugliest looking knife on the market. No attempt is made to make this knife look attractive, but it contains the very best material and the finest grinding that can possibly be produced. The blade of this knife is hand hammered from a bar of the best crucible steel forged out on an anvil, the same as you have seen your blacksmith forge a bar of steel. The marks of the hammer show plainly on the blade. The handle is made of plain beechwood, not stained or varnished. The linings are of heavy steel. It has but one blade, 3⅜ inches long. Length of knife when open, 7½ inches.
Price 46c
If mail shipment, postage extra, 6 cents.

TWO-BLADE JACK KNIVES WITH STAG HANDLES.

No. 6T16880 Wilbert Pocket Knife. Clip point, stag handle, two blades, steel lining, iron bolster. This is a standard size, full weight knife; is durable, and will give splendid satisfaction. Length of handle, 3½ inches. Length with large blade open, 6⅛ inches. Price..........23c
If mail shipment, postage extra, 5 cents.

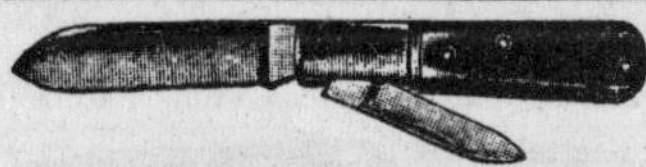

No. 6T16886 Two-Blade Barlow Pattern Jack Knife. Steel lined, 1¼-inch iron bolster, bone handle. This is the original Barlow pattern. Length of knife, 3¼ inches. Length, with spear blade open, 6 inches.
Price 25c
If mail shipment, postage extra, 5 cents.

No. 6T16889 Wilbert Stag Handle Chain Knife. Clip point, two blades, steel lining, iron bolsters and caps, German silver shield, with chain of suitable length to fasten over button. Length of handle, 3⅜ inches. Length with large blade open, 6⅛ inches.
Price 38c
If mail shipment, postage extra, 6 cents.

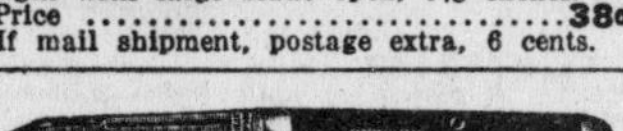

No. 6T16907 Wilbert Gentlemen's Jack Knife. Stag handle, German silver bolsters, caps and shield, brass lining, thoroughly finished in every particular, inside and out. Length of handle, 3⅜ inches. Length with large blade open, 5⅞ inches.
Price.....(Postage extra, 5 cents).....42c

No. 6T16913 Wilbert Little Giant Equal End Pocket Knife. Saber clip blade, stag handle, German silver bolsters, caps and shield, brass lined, finished inside and out. The amount of work which this knife will do is something never before attained in a knife of its size. Length of handle, 3⅜ inches. Length with large blade open, 5¾ inches.
Price 44c
If mail shipment, postage extra, 5 cents.

No. 6T16921 Wilbert Equal End Knife. Has stag handle, brass lining, German silver bolsters, caps and shield. Length of handle, 3⅝ inches. Length with large blade open, 6¼ inches. Price..........46c
If mail shipment, postage extra, 5 cents.

No. 6T16934 Wilbert High Grade Easy Opener Jack Knife. Stag handle, German silver bolsters, caps and shield, brass lined, finely finished throughout. Length of handle, 3⅝ inches. Length with blade open, 6½ inches.
Price.....(Postage extra, 5 cents).....50c

No. 6T16939 Wilbert Texas Toothpick. Has stag handle. German silver bolster and shield, brass lining, finely finished inside and out. Clip point saber blade. While the blade is long and slim, the peculiar shape makes it very strong and durable as well as an excellent whittler. Length of handle, 3⅞ inches. Length with large blade open, 7 inches. Price..........51c
If mail shipment, postage extra, 5 cents.

No. 6T16944 Wilbert Sensible Cattlemen's Knife. Saber clip point blade and spaying blade 3 inches long from bolster. The practical man will readily see the great advantage in the length of spaying blade in this knife. Has stag handle, German silver bolsters and shield, brass lined, highly finished throughout. Length of handle, 4 inches. Length with clip point blade open, 7 inches.
Price.....(Postage extra, 5 cents).....67c

Electricians' Knife.

No. 6T16947 Electricians' Knife. Equ end stag handle, brass lined, and one he blade with screwdriver end and beveled e for scraping insulations. Length of ha 3⅝ inches. Length with large blade open
Price..........
If mail shipment, postage extra, 5 c

OUR HERCULES COMBINATION TOOL KNIFE, $1.26.

THE MOST WONDERFUL VALUE EVER OFFERED IN A POCKET KNIFE.

$1.26

No. 6T17162 The most wonderful value ever offered in a pocket knife. This knife is a complete tool kit in itself. It is very strong; every tool is guaranteed to be as practical and to give the same service that you would derive from the same tool if bought singly. This is a three-spring knife, brass lined, with a large 2¾-inch spear blade, one large sheep's foot blade and one small pen blade. In addition to these three blades, **it has a swaging awl, file, screwdriver and tack puller;** fine stag handle with heavy plated brass bolsters. You could not purchase a regular three-blade knife of like quality from any dealer within 50 cents of our price for this wonderful six-tool knife. The material and workmanship in this knife are absolutely the best. Every knife is guaranteed to give satisfaction or money will be refunded. It is very compact. With large blade open it is 6¾ inches long; with blades closed, 4 inches long. Weight, 4 ounces. Price........(If mail shipment, postage extra, 6 cents)........**$1.26**

PEARL HANDLE JACK KNIVES.

No. 6T17007 Wilbert Pearl Handle Two-Blade Jack Knife. A high class knife fitted with the finest quality pearl scales, heavy German silver bolsters, caps and shield, full German silver lined and polished. One large jack blade for whittling and one small pen blade, full polished. This knife is carefully fitted, highly finished, finely ground and tempered, and is guaranteed to be equal to any knife made, regardless of price. Length of handle, 3⅜ inches. Length with large blade open, 5⅞ inches. Price................**90c**
If mail shipment, postage extra, 5 cents.

$1.40

No. 6T17017 Wilbert Ranchero Cattle Knife. Has pearl handle, German silver bolsters and shield, German silver lining, satin finish. The blades are full crocus polished. It cannot fail to give satisfaction to those who want a knife of superior cutting qualities, workmanship and beauty. Length of handle, 3⅝ inches. Length with large blade open, 6⅜ inches. Price..........................**$1.40**
If mail shipment, postage extra, 5 cents.

No. 6T17025 Wilbert Montana Beauty Stockmen's Knife. Has clip, sheep's foot and spaying blades, pearl handle, German silver lining, satin finish; the blades are beautifully crocus polished. In our ordinary grades of knives, knives which must sell at popular prices, we pay very much more attention to quality and workmanship than we do to beauty and finish, but in this particular knife we excel all others in finish as well as in quality. Length of handle, 3⅞ inches. Length with large blade open, 6¾ inches.

$1.50

Price...............(If mail shipment, postage extra, 5 cents)...............**$1.50**

PRUNING KNIVES.

35c

No. 6T16986 Wilbert Samson Pruning Knife. Blade made of 10-gauge steel. The shape of blade, method of grinding, etc., are in accordance with the ideas of one of the best fruit growers in the country, who had the original made just exactly the way he wanted it regardless of expense. Has cocobolo handle. Length of handle, 4 inches. Length with blade open, 7 inches. Price.............**35c**
If mail shipment, postage extra, 6 cents.

40c

No. 6T17256 George Wostenholm & Sons' IXL Pruning Knife with imitation stag iron handle; iron lined, iron bolsters, 3-inch blade of the best Sheffield steel. Length of knife with blade open, 6⅞ inches.
Price **40c**
If mail shipment, postage extra, 6 cents.

Two-Blade Stag Handle Pruning Knife.

No. 6T16988 An entirely new pattern of our own design. Made with one large 2½-inch hook shaped pruning blade and one 1⅜-inch budding blade with gimped tang to prevent thumb from slipping. The blades are finely tempered and ground especially for the work for which they are intended. Made with heavy back to stand hard service, fine stag handles with nickel shield, polished brass lining with extra heavy tempered spring, and heavy polished bolsters. Length of handle, 4 inches; length with large blade open, 6¼ inches. This is the most practical and serviceable pruning knife on the market. Regular $1.25 value.
Price **76c**
If mail shipment, postage extra, 6 cents.

Two-Blade Art Handle Jack Knife.

No. 6T16914 This is a strong, excellently made knife of the celebrated Wilbert quality, made with one large polished spear blade and one pen blade and fitted with German silver handles of handsome design. The handles are finished in the popular French gray color and depict, in relief or raised design, a cowboy and a grizzly bear on one side and a cowboy on horseback on the reverse side. The handles are very artistic and handsome. The blades are made of the finest Wardlow steel, finely tempered and polished, full brass lined. Length of handle, 3⅜ inches; length with large blade open, 6¼ inches. Price..........**52c**
If mail shipment, postage extra, 5 cents.

Three-Blade Jack Knives With Stag Handles.

No. 6T17136 Wilbert Quality Three-Blade Double End Knife, stag handle, brass lined, German silver bolsters and shield. One large 2⅞-inch clip blade, one small 2-inch clip blade and one pen blade, crocus polished. Blades are made of the best Wardlow steel, every knife guaranteed. Length of knife, 3½ inches; length with large blade open, 6 inches.
Price **70c**
If mail shipment, postage extra, 5 cents.

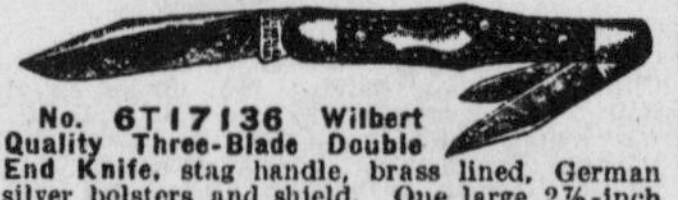

Cattle Knife, 50 Cents.

No. 6T17143 Wilbert Special Offer Cattle Knife. Stag handle, steel lining, iron bolsters, German silver shield. Length of handle, 3⅝ inches. Length with large blade open, 6¼ inches. Has spear point, sheep's foot and pen blades. The cutting qualities of this knife are not excelled by any knife made. It is neatly finished and sold at a price to compete with the cheap imported goods.
Price **50c**
If mail shipment, postage extra, 5 cents.

No. 6T17155 Wilbert Texas Stock Knife. A pattern of knife which is popular with stock raisers all over the world, has clip, sheep's foot and spaying blades, stag handle, German silver bolsters and shield, brass lined, highly finished inside and out. This is our most popular cattle knife. Length of handle, 4 inches; length, with clip point blade open, 7⅛ inches. Price..........**76c**
If mail shipment, postage extra, 5 cents.

HUNTING KNIVES.

58c

No. 6T16965 Wilbert Hunter's Pride Knife. It has stag handle, long, heavy German silver bolsters, caps and shield, brass lining, highly finished inside and out. The blades open and close freely without wearing. The knife blade is always true in the center, and it is these little points, to which we pay so much attention, that cause our knives to give better satisfaction than those you can procure from any other dealer. Length of handle, 4¼ inches. Length with large blade open, 8 inches. Price........................**58c**
If mail shipment, postage extra, 6 cents.

60c

No. 6T16970 Wilbert Daniel Boone Hunting Knife. Cocobolo handle, steel lined, iron bolsters and caps, saber clip point blade. Length of handle, 5¼ inches. Entire length with blade open, 9½ inches. A large, strong, well finished knife, fully warranted.
Price **60c**
If mail shipment, postage extra, 7 cents.

70c

No. 6T16973 Wilbert Arkansas Lock Blade Hunter. A knife in which nearly every cent of the cost is spent in quality and not looks. It has clip point saber blade, flush lock back so blade cannot shut on the fingers, curved stag handle which just fits the hand nicely, fancy iron bolsters, steel lining. Length of handle, 4⅝ inches. Length with blade open, 8⅛ inches. Price..................**70c**
If mail shipment, postage extra, 7 cents.

$1.12

No. 6T16976 Wilbert Hudson Bay Hunting Knife. A very nicely finished hunting knife. Clip point saber blade, flush lock back, curved stag handle, fancy German silver bolsters, caps and linings. Length of handle, 5¼ inches. Length with blade open, 9⅝ inches. Price......................**$1.12**
If mail shipment, postage extra, 7 cents.

Penknives, 45c to $1.00.

No. 6T17033 Wilbert Two-Blade Stag Handle Penknife. German silver bolsters and shield, brass lined; one large pen blade and one nail file blade, nicely polished pocket knife. Length of handle, 3 inches. Length with large blade open, 5 inches. Price..**45c**
If mail shipment, postage extra, 3 cents.

No. 6T17040 Wilbert Physicians' Stag Handle Knife. German silver butt, German silver bolster and brass lining, finely polished and fitted. Length of handle, 3¼ inches. Length with large blade open, 5⅞ inches. Price..............................**54c**
If mail shipment, postage extra, 4 cents.

68c

No. 6T17049 Wilbert Small Congress Knife. Has one large blade, two pen blades and one nail blade, stag handle, German silver bolsters and shield, brass lined, finely finished throughout. Length of handle, 3⅛ inches. Length with large blade open, 5⅜ inches. Price..............................**68c**
If mail shipment, postage extra, 4 cents.

No. 6T17056 Wilbert Popular School or Ladies' Knife. First quality pearl handle, German silver bolsters and German silver lining, finished inside. Length of handle, 2⅞ inches. Length with large blade open, 4⅝ inches. Price..............................**58c**
If mail shipment, postage extra, 3 cents.

No. 6T17059 Wilbert Two-Blade Pearl Handle Penknife. The pearl sides are first quality selected pearl, 2⅝ inches long, tipped with German silver bolsters; one large and one small blade, nicely polished, German silver lined. Length with large blade open, 4⅝ inches. Price....(Postage extra, 3c)....**72c**

No. 6T17074 Wilbert Senator Three-Blade Pearl Handle Penknife. It has a good strong big blade, a pen blade and a nail blade. Fine quality pearl handle, German silver tips, German silver lining, satin finish. The blades are full crocus polished. Length of handle, 3 inches. Length with large blade open, 4⅞ inches. Price..............**$1.00**
If mail shipment, postage extra, 4 cents.

Three-Blade Jack Knives with Ebony Handles.

No. 6T17109 Wilbert Heavy Duty Gentlemen's Knife. Has clip point, large blade, very heavy and strong, spear point pen blade and sheep's foot tobacco blade, ebony handle, German silver bolsters and shield, brass lined and finished throughout. Length of handle, 3¾ inches. Length with large blade open, 6⅝ inches. An unusually strong and heavy knife for its size. Price..(Postage extra, 5c)..**75c**

TWO-BLADE DOUBLE END KNIVES WITH STAG HANDLES.

[...]6T16991 Wilbert New England [...]'s Knife. A great favorite with car[...] cabinet makers, and other woodwork[...] has stag handle, German silver bol[...] shield, brass lining, finely finished [...]d inside and out. Length of [...] inches. Length with large blade [...]ches. Price......................**52c**
[...]ment, postage extra, 4 cents.

No. 6T16993 Wilbert Double End Two-Blade Stag Handle Brass Lined Knife. One large clip blade, one pen blade, polished brass bolsters and shield. Length of handle, 3¼ inches; length with large blade open, 6 inches. This is a well finished and fitted knife, guaranteed to give satisfaction.
Price **49c**
If mail shipment, postage extra, 4 cents.

74c

No. 6T16997 Wilbert Gladiator Double Ender. Has stag handle, German silver bolsters and shield, brass lined and finely finished throughout. Has saber clip and spear point blades. Length of handle, 4¼ inches. Length with spear blade open, 7½ inches. Price **74c**
If mail shipment, postage extra, 5 cents.

No. 6T17117 Wilbert Hercules 4-inch Knife. Ebony handle, German silver bolsters and shield, brass lined, finely finished throughout. The large blade is short and very heavy, being 2¾ inches long from bolster and ⅞ inch wide. Two pen blades. Length of handle, 4 inches. Length with large blade open, 7 inches. Price.......(Postage extra, 6c.).......**89c**

FOR COMPLETE INDEX REFER TO PINK PAGES IN MIDDLE OF BOOK.

No. 28C1160 George Wostenholm & Sons' I X L Pen Knife; stag handle, German silver tips and bolster, brass lined. Length of handle, 3 inches. This knife has spear and pen blades. Price......76c

No. 28C1162 George Wostenholm & Sons' I X L Pen Knife; stag handle, German silver tips and shield, pen blade and fancy nail blade. Length of handle, 2⅞ inches. Price... ... .80c

No. 28C1164 George Wostenholm & Sons Medium Size Congress Knife; stag handle, iron bolster, brass lining. Length of handle, 3½ inches. This knife has sheep's foot, two pen and one nail blade. Price............................$1.07

No. 28C1166 George Wostenholm & Sons' Pen Knife; stag handle, German silver tips, brass lined. Length of handle, 3 inches. This knife has spear, pen and nail blades. Price $1.08

No. 28C1168 George Wostenholm & Sons' Pen Knife; pearl handle, German silver tips, brass lined. Length of handle, 3 inches. This knife has spear and pen blades. Price... ....$1.25

No. 28C1170 George Wostenholm & Sons' IXL Pen Knife; pearl handle, German silver tips and shield, brass lined. Length of handle, 3 inches. This knife has spear, pen and nail blades. Price....$1.60

No. 28C1172 George Wostenholm & Sons' IXL Physicians' Knife; buffalo horn handle, German silver bolster and butt, brass lined. Length of handle, 3¾ inches. This knife has spear and pen blades. Price.............................$1.04

IMPORTED KNIVES.

The following pocket knives are imported from Europe and are not guaranteed. In order that our customers may not be misled, we have described them as good, fair and cheap. The cheap grade is good for the price, but the price is not enough for a good knife. Fair will usually give satisfaction. The good grades are commonly sold as warranted, but we do not warrant them. Any of these goods will be better value than you can secure elsewhere for the same money.

No. 28C1004 Ebony Handle Knife, one blade, iron lined; blade, 2⅝ inches. Cheap grade. Price...5c

If by mail, postage extra, 4 cents.

No. 28C1021 A well finished, fair grade, single blade, Boys' Jack Knife. Length of handle, 3⅛ inches; length with large blade open, 5⅝ inches. Rosewood handle, iron lined. Price..................9c

No. 28C1019 White Bone Handle Jack Knife, two blades, iron lined. Cheap grade knife, 2¾ inches. Price 8c

If by mail, postage extra, 5 cents.

No. 28C1030 Boys' White Bone Handle Knife, with bolster. Two blades, iron lined, 3½ inches. Cheap grade. Price...15c

If by mail, postage extra, 6 cents.

No. 28C1026 A well finished, fair grade, German Jack Knife; length of handle, 3½ inches, dogwood handle, two blades. Price 18c

No. 28C1030 Stag Clip. A fair grade German knife. Stag handle, clip blade. Entire length open, 6¼ inches; length of handle, 3½ inches. Price . 18c

20-Cent Easy Opening Knife.

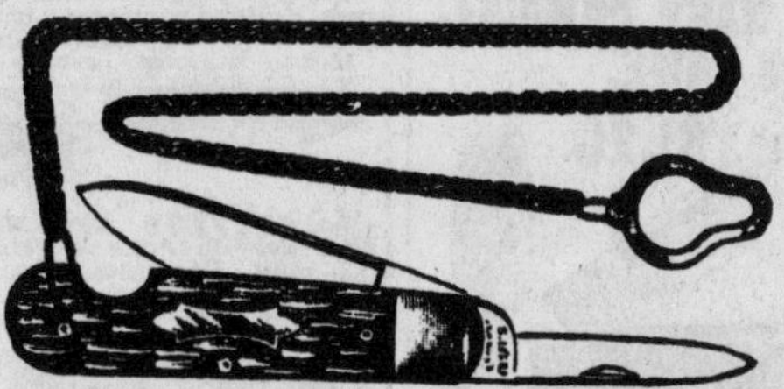

No. 28C1024 This Knife has the easy opening feature, which saves the finger nails, and an 18-inch security chain, which prevents loss. Has two blades, stag handle and is iron lined. Length of handle, 3½ inches; length with large blade open, 6 inches. A fair grade German knife. Price...........................20c

If by mail, postage extra, 6 cents.

No. 28C1025 Another Easy Opening Security Knife, the same as No. 28C1024, but with cocoa handle, which, being smooth, is preferred by many. Length of handle, 3½ inches; length with large blade open, 6 inches. Price...20c

If by mail, postage extra, 6 cents.

No. 28C1032 Stockmen's Knife. Three blades, stag handle, brass lined. Length of handle, 4 inches; length with large blade open, 7 inches. This is a good grade German knife, though we do not warrant it. Price....... ....40c

No. 28C1034 Pearl Handle, Three-Blade Small Cattle Knife. Length of handle, 3¼ inches; length with large blade open, 5⅞ inches. Finely finished and a good grade knife, but not warranted. Price...75c

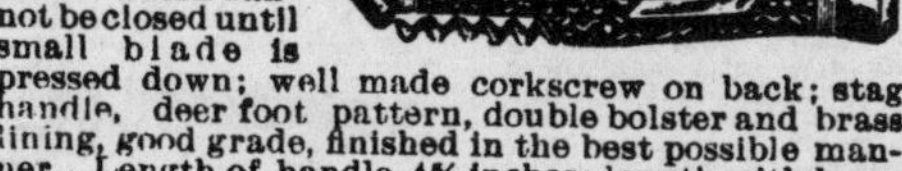

No. 28C1028 Has one small blade and one large clip point blade which cannot be closed until small blade is pressed down; well made corkscrew on back; stag handle, deer foot pattern, double bolster and brass lining, good grade, finished in the best possible manner. Length of handle, 4⅝ inches; length with large blade open, 8⅜ inches. Price 70c

No. 28C1500 Ladies' Two-Blade Pearl Handle Penknife, brass lined. Length of handle, 2⅜ inches; a pretty knife. Price 15c

No. 28C1505 Ladies' Two-Blade Corrugated Pearl Handle Penknife, polished steel blades, and a beauty. Length, 2¾ inches. Price.................20c

No. 28C1510 Ladies' Two-Blade Penknife. Good grade; pearl handle, brass lined, finely finished. Length of handle, 2¾ inches. Price..........................28c

No. 28C1512 Two-Blade Pearl Handle Penknife. Good grade; German make. Length of handle, 3½ inches; length with large blade open, 5 inches. Good value for the money. Price...................40c

No. 28C1515 Three-Blade Pearl Handle Penknife with nail blade. Length of handle, 3⅛ inches; length with large blade open, 5¼ inches. Fair grade; not warranted. Price.......................................50c

No. 28C1519 A Good Grade German Penknife. Pearl handle, three blades with fancy long nail blade. Length of handle, 3 inches; length with large blade open, 4⅞ inches. Price...65c

No. 28C1520 A three-blade with one nail blade, pearl handle, high grade German penknife. Finely finished. Length of handle, 3 inches; length with large blade open, 5⅛ inches. This is an extra good grade German knife, but we do not warrant it. Price...75c

No. 28C1507 A Medium Grade German Penknife, three blades, one nail blade, stag handle, iron lined. Length of handle, 3⅜ inches; length with large blade open, 5¼ inches. Not warranted. Price 25c

No. 28C1508 A Medium Grade German Penknife, four blades, stag handle, Congress pattern. Length of handle, 3¼ inches; length with large blade open, 5⅝ inches. Not warranted. Price.25c

No. 28C1550 Four-Blade Ebony Handle Penknife, elongated shield, brass lined. Length of handle, 3½ inches. A neat knife. Medium grade. Price..........30c

No. 28C1509 A Medium Grade German Penknife, four blades, stag handle. Length of handle, 3¾ inches; length with large blade open, 5⅝ inches. Not warranted. Price.......................28c

No. 28C1513 Stag Handle Corkscrew Knife. Length of handle, 3½ inches; length with large blade open, 6 inches. A good grade knife, but not warranted. Price...... ....45c

No. 28C1517 A Good Grade German Penknife; not warranted. Length of handle, 3⅜ inches; length with large blade open, 5⅞ inches. Three blades. One pen blade. Brass lined. Price......... .38c

Cheap Assorted Knives, $1.25 per Dozen.

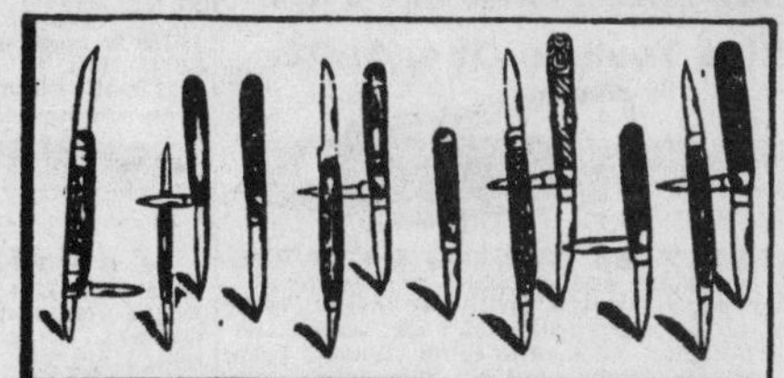

No. 28C1332 Assorted Knives. We have had many calls for cheap knives for knife racks, and we furnish an assortment of twelve styles of knives suitable for this purpose. **We do not sell less than a dozen and do not break dozens.** They are as good or better than the class of goods usually sold for this purpose, but they are not good enough for our customers to use.

Price, per dozen assorted.......................$1.25

We can furnish rack knives at $1.50, $2.00 $2.50, $3.00, $3.50 or $4.00 per dozen, if a better assortment is desired.

No. 28C1334 Wood Rings for Knife Racks. Price, per dozen..10c

Pocket Emery Hone.

No. 28C1676 Pocket Emery Hone. A fine emery knife hone in case. Price...............................9c

Knife Purses.

No. 28C1678 Leather Knife Purse. For knives having handles not longer than 4½ inches. Give length of handle of knife you intend to carry in purse. When ordered with knife, we send purse to fit. Price..

Four-Blade Stockman's Knife, 88 Cents.

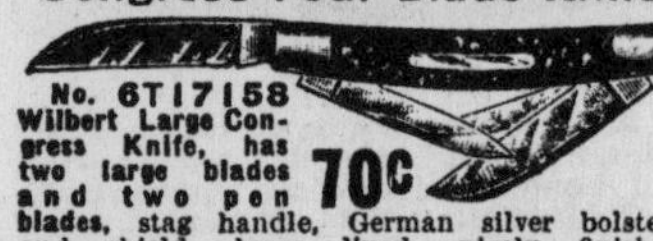

No. 6T17157 Wilbert Four-Blade Stockman's Knife. Stag handle, four heavy blades, clip, pen, sheep's foot and spaying blade, nicely polished, finely tempered and ground. German silver bolsters and shields. A good, strong, serviceable knife. The four blades permit of a great variety of work. Length of handle, 3¾ inches; length with large blade open, 6½ inches. This is a knife that would ordinarily retail for $1.25. Price..........88c
If mail shipment, postage extra, 5 cents.

88c

Congress Four-Blade Knife.

No. 6T17158 Wilbert Large Congress Knife, has two large blades and two pen blades, stag handle, German silver bolsters and shield, brass lined, nicely finished throughout. Length of handle, 3¾ inches; length with large blade open, 6⅛ inches.
Price....(Postage extra, 5 cents)....70c

70c

Push Button Knives.

These knives are fitted with a push button in the bolster. By pressing this button you release a flat spring which opens the blade and locks it so that it cannot be closed accidentally. One-blade knife has one push button; a two-blade knife has push button at each end. The material used in these knives is the best. The push button arrangement is very simple and the knife cannot get out of order.

4¾-inch 67c

No. 6T17181 Push Button Knife. One blade, clip point, stag handle, single bolster, iron lined. Length of handle, 4¾ inches; length, with blade open, 8¾ inches.
Price 67c
If mail shipment, postage extra, 6 cents.

3⅞-inch 59c

No. 6T17182 Push Button Knife. One blade, clip point, stag handle, single bolster, iron lined. Length of handle, 3⅞ inches; length, with blade open, 6⅞ inches.
Price 59c
If mail shipment, postage extra, 5 cents.

3⅜-inch

No. 6T17184 Push Button Penknife. Two blades, stag handle, brass lined. Length of handle, 3⅜ inches; length, with large blade open, 5¼ inches. Price..........56c
If mail shipment, postage extra, 5 cents.

Nine Tools in One, $1.02.

No. 6T17186 This knife will cut wire, wood or leather and embodies a pocket knife, leather punch, swage awl, wire cutter, wire pliers, alligator wrench, hoof hook, screwdriver and screw bit. This knife is no clumsier than the ordinary pocket knife. The pliers and wire cutter are made from drop forged tool steel, the blade is made from the best cutlers' steel, full gauge, tempered and will stand hard usage. All tools are practical and serviceable; one tool does not interfere with the free use of the other. This knife has stag handle, German silver bolsters and shield and is steel lined. Length of handle, 4½ inches.
Price..........$1.02
If mail shipment, postage extra, 6 cents.

Knife Purse.

No. 6T17371 Leather Knife Purse for knives having handles not longer than 4 inches. Give length of handle of knife you intend to carry in purse. When ordered with knife, we send purse to fit.
Price 5c
If mail shipment, postage extra, 1 cent.

Desk Hone.

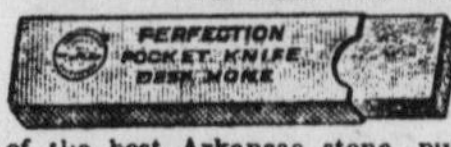

No. 6T17382 Perfection Pocket Knife Hone, made of the best Arkansas stone, put up in a neat case. Will keep a pocket knife or small cutting tool in excellent condition. Regular 25-cent value. Length, 4 inches; width, ⅞ inch.
Price, each..........9c
If mail shipment, postage extra, 4 cents.

Shoot Pointer Loaded Smokeless Shells. Quality the best. Prices one-third less than regular. Send for free Ammunition Price List.

ARMY AND NAVY COMBINATION KNIFE.

$1.20

No. 6T17187 Army and Navy Combination Tool Knife, a high class, well made knife, brass lined, fine stag handle, double bolsters, fitted with corkscrew, swaging awl, can opener, screwdriver, one large spear blade and one medium size pen blade. Six tools in all, and all of them forged of the very best material and guaranteed to give satisfaction. Our price for this knife, with stag handle and double bolsters, is lower than that asked by others for a knife with plain handle and without bolsters. Length of knife when closed, 3½ inches.
Price $1.20
If mail shipment, postage extra, 6 cents.

IMPORTED ENGLISH KNIVES.

Geo. Wostenholm & Sons' IXL Pocket Knives.

We show some of the most desirable patterns of George Wostenholm & Sons' Celebrated IXL Pocket Knives, which are favorably known all over the world.

No. 6T17234 George Wostenholm & Sons' One-Blade Stag Handle Jack Knife. Genuine stag handle, polished steel bolster, steel lined, 2⅜-inch swaged spear blade, finely tempered and ground; length of handle, 3½ inches. An excellent knife, guaranteed to hold its edge. Regular 60-cent value. Price..........34c
If mail shipment, postage extra, 4 cents.

No. 6T17236 George Wostenholm & Sons' IXL Penknife with extra long 3-inch spear point blade and small pen blade, full crocus polished German silver bolsters and shield, brass lined, genuine stag handle. This knife is made of the best Sheffield steel and guaranteed to give satisfaction. Price..72c
If mail shipment, postage extra, 4 cents.

No. 6T17243 George Wostenholm & Sons' IXL Two-Blade Jack Knife. German silver bolsters and shield, brass lined, full crocus polished. Length of blade, 3¼ inches; length, with large blade open, 6 inches. Price..65c
If mail shipment, postage extra, 4 cents.

No. 6T17244 George Wostenholm & Sons' IXL Pocket Knife, stag handle, German silver bolsters and shield, brass lined. Length of handle, 3¾ inches. Price..........72c
If mail shipment, postage extra, 4 cents.

No. 6T17248 George Wostenholm & Sons' IXL Cattle Knife; genuine stag handle; German silver bolsters and shield, brass lined. Length of handle, 3⅝ inches. This knife has spear, sheep's foot and pen blades.
Price $1.20
If mail shipment, postage extra, 4 cents.

No. 6T17254 George Wostenholm & Sons' IXL Lock Back Hunting Knife; blade can't be closed until released by pressing on the spring; stag handle, iron bolsters, iron lining, saber clip point blade. Length of handle, 4⅜ inches. Price..........70c
If mail shipment, postage extra, 5 cents.

IMPORTED GERMAN KNIVES

The following pocket knives are imported from Europe and are not guaranteed. In order that our customers may not be misled, we have described them as good, fair and cheap. The cheap grade is good for the price, but the price is not enough for a good knife. Fair, will usually give satisfaction. The good grades are commonly sold as warranted, but we do not warrant them. Any of these goods will be better value than you can secure elsewhere for the same money.

No. 6T17285 White Bone Handle Jack Knife, two blades, iron lined. Cheap grade knife, 2¾ inches. Price..........9c
If mail shipment, postage extra, 3 cents.

No. 6T17288 Boys' White Bone Handle Knife, with bolster and shield. Two blades, iron lined, 3½ inches. Cheap grade.
Price 15c
If mail shipment, postage extra, 4 cents.

No. 6T17302 Stag, Clip. A fair grade German Knife. Stag handle, clip blade. Entire length open, 6¼ inches; length of handle, 3½ inches. Price..........20c
If mail shipment, postage extra, 6 cents.

No. 6T17305 This knife has the easy opening feature, which saves the finger nails, and an 18-inch security chain, which prevents loss. Has two blades, stag handle and is iron lined. Length of handle, 3½ inches; length with large blade open, 6 inches. A fair grade German knife. Price..........20c
If mail shipment, postage extra, 6 cents.

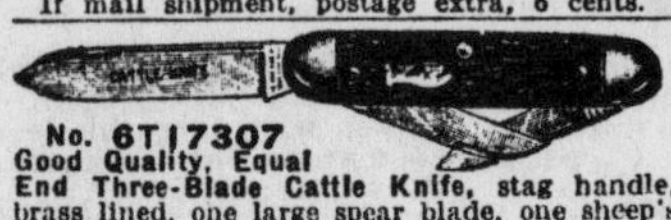

No. 6T17307 Good Quality, Equal End Three-Blade Cattle Knife, stag handle, brass lined, one large spear blade, one sheep's foot and one pen blade. Polished bolsters and shield. Length, 3½ inches; length with large blade open, 6¼ inches. Price....38c
If mail shipment, postage extra, 8 cents.

68c

No. 6T17311 Has one small blade and one large clip point blade which cannot be closed until small blade is pressed down; well made corkscrew on back; stag handle, deer foot pattern, double bolsters and brass lining, good grade, finished in the best possible manner. Length of handle, 4⅝ inches; length with large blade open, 8⅝ inches. Price......68c
If mail shipment, postage extra, 7 cents.

No. 6T17314 Stockman's Knife, three blades, stag handle, brass lined. Length of handle, 4 inches; length with large blade open, 7 inches. This is a good grade German knife. Price..........44c
If mail shipment, postage extra, 7 cents.

No. 6T17318 Good Quality, Pearl Handle Premium Stock Knife. Three blades, one 3-inch clip blade, one sheep's foot and one spaying blade. Brass lined, polished brass bolsters and shield; a well finished, neatly made knife. Full size, 4 inches long. Price....85c
If mail shipment, postage extra, 7 cents.

GENUINE IMPORTED SWEDISH HUNTING KNIVES.

Blade can be removed, folded into its frame, and replaced in the handle. This knife is a popular woodworkers' tool, as well as a hunting knife. Has solid boxwood handle. The blade is best of steel, and cutting qualities and temper are fully guaranteed.

No. 6T17273 Genuine Imported Swedish Hunting Knife, as described above. Length of handle, 2⅞ inches. Price.....47c
If mail shipment, postage extra, 5 cents.

No. 6T17275 Genuine Imported Swedish Hunting Knife, as described above. Length of handle, 4⅜ inches. Price..........59c
If mail shipment, postage extra, 5 cents.

Genuine Imported Swedish Carpenters' Bench Knife. Intended for the tool chest or work bench. Used in manual training schools. Made from the finest quality of Swedish razor steel.

No. 6T17276 Swedish Carpenters' Bench Knife. Length of blade, 3½ inches.
Price 21c
If mail shipment, postage extra, 6 cents.

8c

No. 6T17338 Shoe Pattern Knife, composition handle, one blade. Makes a very pretty knife for the work basket.
Price........(Postage extra, 2c.)........8c

No. 6T17340 Ladies' Two-Blade Pearl Handle Penknife, brass lined. Length of handle, 2⅝ inches. A pretty knife. Fair grade. Price....(Postage extra, 2c)....14c

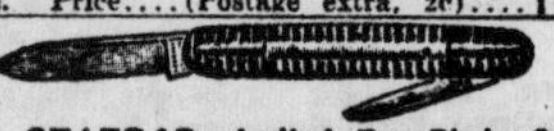

No. 6T17343 Ladies' Two-Blade Corrugated Pearl Handle Penknife, polished steel blades. Length, 2¾ inches. Cheap grade.
Price.......(Postage extra, 2c)........20c

No. 6T17349 Ladies' Two-Blade Penknife. Pearl handle, brass lined, finely finished. Good grade. Length of handle, 2¾ inches. Price..........32c
If mail shipment, postage extra, 2 cents.

No. 6T17361 Two-Blade Pearl Handle Jack Knife, 3 inches long; length with large blade open, 5¼ inches. Good grade. Serviceable, neat looking knife. Price..........48c
If mail shipment, postage extra, 5 cents.

Pearl View or Picture Knife.

No. 6T17364 These knives have miniature pictures of actresses fitted between brass bolsters, which pictures are magnified by a small lens. This knife is 3 inches long, two blades, brass lined, nickel plated brass bolster and shield and neatly finished. Good quality. Price....(Postage extra, 2c)....44c

No. 6T17365 Four-Blade Pearl Handle Penknife. One large blade, two small pen blades and one nail file, brass lined, nickel plated brass bolsters and shield. Length of knife, 3 inches; length with large blade open 5 inches. Good quality. Price..........57c
If mail shipment, postage extra, 3 cents.

No. 6T17368 Four-Blade Ebony Handle German Penknife, elongated shield, brass lined. Length of handle, 3½ inches. A neat knife. Medium grade. Price..........34c
If mail shipment, postage extra, 3 cents.

Hunters' and Campers' Knife.

Separate and Open.

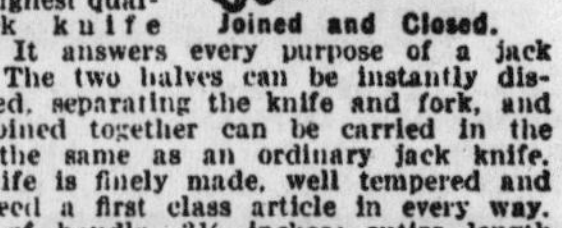

Joined and Closed.

No. 6T17369 A unique and practical combination of knife, fork and corkscrew. Fitted with a spear point highest quality jack knife blade. It answers every purpose of a jack knife. The two halves can be instantly disconnected, separating the knife and fork, and when joined together can be carried in the pocket the same as an ordinary jack knife. This knife is finely made, well tempered and guaranteed a first class article in every way. Length of handle, 3½ inches; entire length with blade open, 6¾ inches. Weight, 4 ounces. Price..........52c
If mail shipment, postage extra, 6 cents.

GUN REPAIRS

We are in a position to supply repair parts for all American made guns, rifles and revolvers, also for most of the foreign made fire arms. The line of repair parts is so extensive that we cannot give it space in this catalog, but we issue a special circular which we would be pleased to mail to you. Write and ask for our Fire Arms Repair List.

We are in a position to do gunsmith work of all kinds, restock, rebore, make new parts by hand and fit sights. We have one of the largest and best equipped shops in the country and would be pleased to send you an estimate on putting your fire arm in first class working order. Send us your gun, rifle or revolver by express or freight, charges prepaid, see that the fire arm is properly tagged with your name and address, and advise us what repairs you want us to make, and we will quote lowest prices.

Heinisch Barbers' Shears.

No. 28G6785 Heinisch Barbers' Shears. Japanned handles, steel laid blades; warranted.

Size, inches	8	8½
Price	44c	47c

No. 28G6786 Heinisch Barbers' Shears. Finely polished and full nickel plated; steel laid blades. Every pair warranted.

Size, inches	8	8½	9
Price	60c	64c	70c

No. 28G6787 Heinisch Left Hand Barbers' Shears. Japanned handles. Laid steel blades; only one size made; length, 9 inches. Price 73c

If by mail, postage extra, 5 cents.

In our Special Barbers' Supply Catalogue (free on request) will be found a complete line of German and American make Barbers' Shears.

Wilbert Pocket Scissors.

No. 28G6790 Wilbert Brand, Extra Heavy, Full Gauge Pocket Scissors. These scissors have finely swedged blades. They are made of the best material and guaranteed superior to any pocket scissors on the market. Each pair is guaranteed to give satisfaction or money refunded. Give size wanted.

Full length, inches	4	4½	5
Length of cut	1¾	2	2¼
Price .... (Postage extra, 2 to 3 cents)	32c	36c	38c

Paperhangers' or Bankers' Shears. Wilbert.

No. 28G6792 Wilbert Paperhangers' or Bankers' Shears. Nickel plated steel laid blades and enameled handles. Highest quality guaranteed. Give size wanted.

Size, inches	10	12	14	16
Length of cut, inches	5¾	7	8½	10
Price	60c	77c	98c	$1.33

If by mail, postage extra, 12 to 18 cents.

REMEMBER, all Wilbert Shears are guaranteed to be absolutely perfect or they can be returned and your money and transportation charges will be refunded. We guarantee Wilbert Shears and Scissors to be the superior of any other line of shears and scissors on the market. **If you do not find them so, return them and your money will be refunded.**

LADIES' SCISSORS.

The following patterns represent the highest quality of solid steel ladies' imported scissors. There are numerous grades of scissors on the market, both of American and foreign make, and it is an easy matter for any dealer to sell scissors at lower prices than those we quote but it is impossible for any dealer to sell the grade of scissors we are handling at the prices that will in any way compare with those we quote. The following scissors, all solid steel goods, are made by the best factory in Germany. These scissors are fitted and finished and ground in a manner superior to that found in any other line of either American or foreign manufacture.

We guarantee every pair of scissors to be perfect in material, cutting qualities, workmanship and finish or money and transportation charges will be refunded

The Famous Wilbert Scissors.

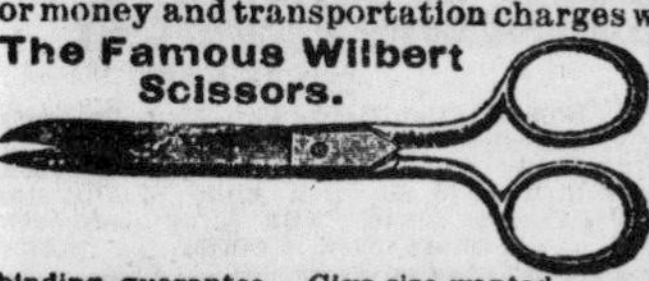

No. 28G6815 Wilbert Quality Ladies' Flat Solid Steel Scissors. Full nickel plated, highly polished, finely fitted, every pair covered by our binding guarantee. Give size wanted.

Size, inches	3½	4	4½	5	6	7
Length of cut	1¼	1¾	2	2¼	2⅔	3½
Price	30c	32c	36c	40c	47c	54c

If by mail, postage extra, 2 to 4 cents.

No. 28G6817 The Stork Embroidery Scissors. Body of stork and handles fancy gilt, bill polished steel, making handsome contrast. Best quality tempered steel, finely finished. Length, 3½ inches. Price .. **34c**

If by mail, postage extra, 2 cents.

Ladies' Fancy Solid Steel Scissors.

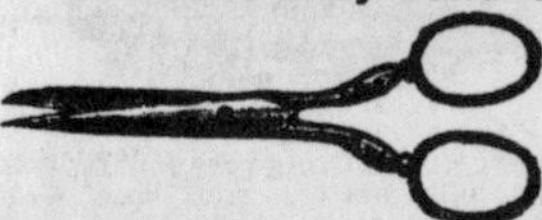

No. 28G6820 Ladies' Solid Steel Scissors, Fancy Gilt Handle. Every pair guaranteed to give satisfaction. Handles are finely engraved and finished in gold, which makes a handsome contrast to the highly polished oval nickel plated blades. Give size wanted.

Size, inches	3½	4½	5½
Price (Postage extra, 2 and 3 cents)	30c	32c	38c

Buttonhole Scissors.

No. 28G6822 Solid Steel Buttonhole Scissors, with adjustable thumbscrew, as illustrated. Length, 4½ inches.

Price **24c**

If by mail, postage extra, 3 cents.

Buttonhole Scissors.

No. 28G6823 Buttonhole Scissors, nickel plated, with inside set screws to adjust blades for cutting. Length, 4½ inches. Price ... **35c**

Postage extra, 3c.

Adjustable Buttonhole Scissors.

No. 28G6824 Adjustable Buttonhole Scissors, solid steel, nickel plated and polished, finely fitted, adjusted by means of a small notched brass wheel fitted inside of shank. Six different adjustments, each notch numbered, which guarantees uniformity in cutting the various sized buttonholes.

Price .. (If by mail, postage extra, 3 cents) **49c**

Three Scissors in Fine Leather Case.

$1.52

No. 28G6827 Ladies' Combination Scissors Set, consisting of a fine black grain leather case lined with silk plush, containing three highest quality fancy handle scissors, one embroidery scissors, one medium scissors, one full size. Length of case, 6 inches. Price, per set **$1.52**

If by mail, postage extra, 8 cents.

OUR POCKET KNIVES ARE MADE IN OUR OWN FACTORY.

WE CALL YOUR ATTENTION ESPECIALLY to this line of highest grade American made pocket and pen knives, our Wilbert brand.

THE BLADES ARE FORGED from S. C. Wardlow's best English special blade steel, the finest and the best that can be procured for knife blades. We also use Wardlow's steel for the springs, which costs nearly double the price at which ordinary spring steel can be bought, but which greatly improves the wearing qualities of the knife and adds greatly to its durability. **Every blade, from the cheapest to the best, which bears our brand, is hammered out by hand.** Instead of using iron for the lining of our cheaper knives, we pay more for steel because it makes a much stronger and better knife. All work is done by skilled mechanics, particular attention being paid to making a keen cutting knife that will carry a lasting edge.

OUR POCKET KNIVES are fully guaranteed in every way. This means we guarantee the blades to be free from flaws, and guarantee them to be neither too hard nor too soft. This does not mean that we guarantee the knives not to break. If we were to do this, we would be obliged to temper them so soft they would be of no practical use for cutting. They are not intended to be used as mortising chisels, tack pullers, can openers, screwdrivers, crowbars, nor for any of the purposes by which pocket knives are frequently misused.

ALL POCKET KNIVES should occasionally be oiled at the joint so the blade will not wear into the spring. Vaseline makes a very good lubricant for this purpose.

Two-Blade Jack Knives with Cocobolo and Ebony Handles.

No. 28G6831 Wilbert Pocket Knife. Has rosewood handle, steel lining, iron bolsters. Length of handle, 3½ inches. Length, with large blade open, 6 inches.

Price ...... (If by mail, postage extra, 4 cents) **23c**

No. 28G6835 Wilbert Equal End Pocket Knife. Has cocoa handle, German silver bolsters, caps and shield, brass lined, finished inside and out. Length of handle, 3⅛ inches. Length, with large blade open, 5⅞ inches.

Price ...... (If by mail, postage extra, 5 cents) **40c**

Wilbert Easy Opener, 49c.

No. 28G6858 Wilbert Hand Fitting High Grade Easy Opener Knife. Ebony handle, German silver bolsters, caps and shield, brass lined. Length of handle 3¼ inches. Length, with large blade open, 6½ inches. Price **49c**

If by mail, postage extra, 5 cents.

No. 28G6863 Wilbert Missouri Favorite, has clip point saber blade made of full 12-gauge steel. Has ebony handle, long German silver bolsters, caps and shield, brass lined, finished inside and out. Length of handle, 3⅜ inches. Length, with large blade open, 6⅜ inches. Price ... (Postage extra, 6 cents) . **48c**

No. 28G6868 Wilbert Jumbo Pocket Knife, with ebony handle 4 inches long; German silver bolsters and shield, brass lined, finished inside and out. The blades are made of full size 10-gauge steel. This is a big, strong, heavy, durable knife. Length of handle, 4 inches. Length, with large blade open, 6⅞ inches. Price .... (Postage extra, 6 cents) **51c**

No. 28G6876 Wilbert Medium Weight Knife, finely finished, with white bone handle, brass lining, finished inside and out, German silver bolsters, caps and shield. Length of handle, 3⅛ inches. Length, with large blade open, 6 inches.

Price .... (If by mail, postage extra, 5 cents) **39c**

Two-Blade Jack Knives with Stag Handles.

No. 28G6880 Wilbert Pocket Knife, clip point, stag handle, two blades, steel lining, iron bolsters. This is a standard size, full weight knife; is durable, and will give splendid satisfaction. Length of handle, 3½ inches. Length, with large blade open, 6⅛ inches. Price **23c**

If by mail, postage extra, 5 cents.

No. 28G6885 Wilbert Razor Blade Jack Knife, stag handle, steel lining, iron bolster. Length of handle, 3¼ inches. Length, with large blade open, 6 inches. Price **27c**

If by mail, postage extra, 5 cents.

No. 28G6886 Two-Blade Barlow Pattern Jack Knife, steel lined, 1⅛-inch iron bolster, bone handle. This is the original Barlow pattern. Length of knife, 3⅛ inches. Length, with spear blade open, 6 inches. Price **27c**

If by mail, postage extra, 5 cents.

No. 28G6889 Wilbert Stag Handle Chain Knife, clip point, two blades, steel lining, iron bolsters and caps, German silver shield, with chain of suitable length to fasten over button. Length of handle, 3⅝ inches. Length, with large blade open, 6⅛ inches. Price **37c**

If by mail, postage extra, 6 cents.

No. 28G6894 Wilbert Jack Knife, stag handle, swell butt, steel lining, iron bolsters, German silver shield. Length of handle, 3⅝ inches. Length with large blade open, 6¼ inches. Price **36c**

If by mail, postage extra, 5 cents.

No. 28G6902 Wilbert Carpenters' Sensible Knife, having two large blades, one with clip point and one sheep's foot or carpenters' marking blade. The blades of this knife are made of 11-gauge steel; has stag handle, steel lining, iron bolsters, German silver shield, finished inside and out. Length of handle, 3½ inches. Length, with large blade open, 6⅛ inches.

Price ...... (If by mail, postage extra, 5 cents) **43c**

No. 28G6907 Wilbert Gentlemen's Jack Knife, stag handle, German silver bolsters, caps and shield, brass lining, thoroughly finished in every particular inside and out. Length of handle, 3⅜ inches. Length with large blade open, 5⅞ inches. Price **42c**

If by mail, postage extra, 5 cents.

de Stag Handle Jack Knives.

No. 28G6913 Wilbert Little Giant Equal End Pocket Knife, with saber clip blade, stag handle, German silver bolsters, caps and shield, brass lined, finished inside and out. The amount of work which this knife will do is something never before attained in a knife of its size. Length of handle, 3⅝ inches. Length with large blade open, 5¾ inches. Price...43c
If by mail, postage extra, 5 cents.

No. 28G6917 Wilbert Easy Opener Pocket Knife, with stag handle, German silver bolsters, caps and shield, brass lining. Finished inside and out. Length of handle, 3½ inches. Length with large blade open, 6¼ inches. Price 45c
If by mail, postage extra, 5 cents.

No. 28G6921 Wilbert Equal End Knife, has stag handle, brass lining, German silver bolsters, cap and shield. Length of handle, 3⅝ inches. Length with large blade open, 6¼ inches. Price................45c
If by mail, postage extra, 5 cents.

No. 28G6924 Wilbert Solid Worth Jack Knife, stag handle, brass lining, finished inside and out, iron bolsters and caps, German silver shield. Length of handle, 3½ inches. Length with large blade open, 6¼ inches. Price.......................................40c
If by mail, postage extra, 5 cents.

No. 28G6929 Wilbert Balloon Shaped Knife, stag handle, fancy German silver bolsters, caps and shield, brass lining, finished inside and out. Length of handle, 3⅝ inches. Length with large blade open, 6⅝ inches. Price......(Postage extra, 5 cents)......52c

No. 28G6934 Wilbert High Grade Easy Opener Jack Knife, stag handle, German silver bolsters, caps, and shield, brass lined, finely finished throughout. Length of handle, 3⅝ inches. Length with blade open, 6⅛ inches. Price 50c
If by mail, postage extra, 5 cents.

No. 28G6939 Wilbert Texas Toothpick, has stag handle, German silver bolsters and shield, brass lining, finely finished inside and out. Clip point saber blade. While the blade is long and slim, the peculiar shape makes it very strong and durable as well as an excellent whittler. Length of handle, 3⅞ inches. Length with large blade open, 7 inches. Price...(If by mail, postage extra, 5 cents)....45c

No. 28G6944 Wilbert Sensible Cattlemen's Knife with saber clip point blade and spaying blade 3 inches long from bolster. The practical man will readily see the great advantage in the length of spaying blade in this knife. Has stag handle, German silver bolsters and shield, brass lined, highly finished throughout. Length of handle, 4 inches. Length, with clip point blade open, 7 inches. Price 60c
If by mail, postage extra, 5 cents.

No. 28G6965 Wilbert Hunters' Pride Knife. It has stag handle, long, heavy German silver bolsters, caps and shield, brass lining, highly finished inside and out. The blades open and close freely without wearing. The knife blade is always true in the center, and it is these little points to which we pay so much attention that cause our knives to give better satisfaction than those you can procure from any other dealer. Length of handle, 4¼ inches. Length with large blade open, 8 inches. Price..................59c
If by mail, postage extra, 6 cents.

REMEMBER, WHEN YOU HAVE BOUGHT $25.00 WORTH OF GOODS OR MORE FROM US YOU GET YOUR CHOICE OF MANY VALUABLE ARTICLES FREE, AS SHOWN IN OUR FREE PROFIT SHARING BOOK.

Hunting Knives.

60c

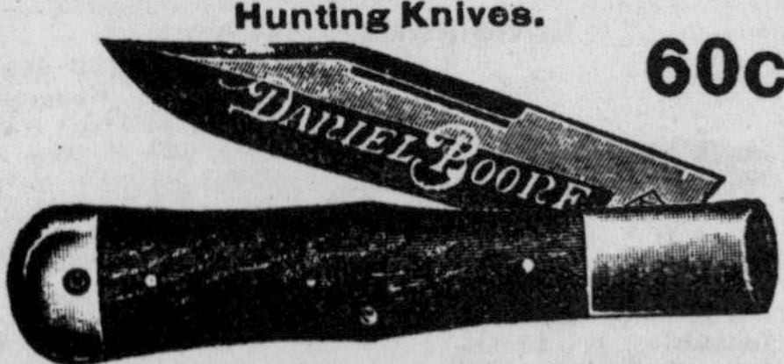

No. 28G6970 Wilbert Daniel Boone Hunting Knife. Cocobolo handle, steel lined, iron bolsters and caps, saber clip point blade. Length of handle, 5¼ inches. Entire length with blade open, 9¼ inches. A large, strong, well finished knife, fully warranted. Price...(If by mail, postage extra, 7 cents) ...60c

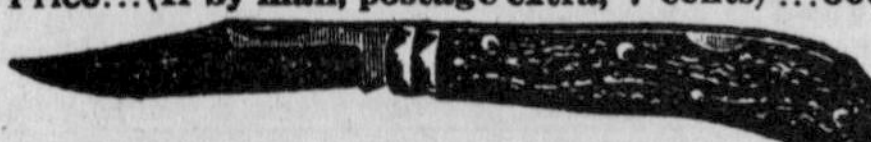

No. 28G6973 Wilbert Arkansas Lock Blade Hunter. A knife in which nearly every cent of the cost is spent in quality and not looks. It has clip point saber blade, flush lock back so blade cannot shut on the fingers, curved stag handle which just fits the hand nicely, fancy iron bolsters, steel lining. Length of handle, 4⅝ inches. Length with blade open, 8⅜ inches. Price...(If by mail, postage extra, 7 cents)....65c

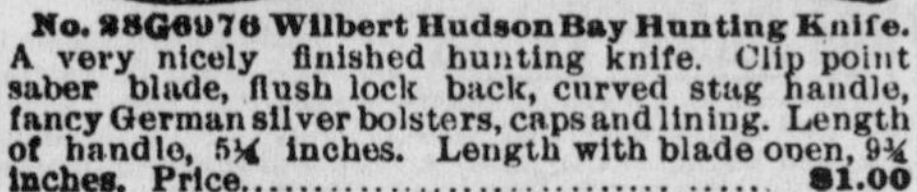

No. 28G6976 Wilbert Hudson Bay Hunting Knife. A very nicely finished hunting knife. Clip point saber blade, flush lock back, curved stag handle, fancy German silver bolsters, caps and lining. Length of handle, 5¼ inches. Length with blade open, 9¾ inches. Price.......................................$1.00
If by mail, postage extra, 7 cents.

For other Hunting Knives and a full line of Hunters' Goods, see Sporting Goods Department.

Pruning Knives.

36c

No. 28G6986 Wilbert Sampson Pruning Knife. Blade made of 10-gauge steel. The shape of blade, method of grinding, etc., being according to the ideas of one of the best fruit growers in the country, who had the original made just exactly the way he wanted it regardless of expense. Length of handle, 4 inches. Length with blade open, 7 inches.
Price, six for $2.05; each......................36c
If by mail, postage extra, 6 cents.

Two-Blade Double End Knives with Stag Handles.

No. 28G6991 Wilbert New England Workmen's Knife. A great favorite with carpenters, cabinet makers and other woodworkers. It has stag handle, German silver bolsters and shield, brass lining, finely finished and polished inside and out. Length of handle, 3¾ inches. Length with large blade open, 6½ ins. Price ..(If by mail, postage extra, 4 cents).....52c

No. 28G6993 Wilbert Double End, Two-Blade, Stag Handle, Brass Lined Knife, one large clip blade, one pen blade, polished brass bolsters and shield. Length, 3¼ inches; length, with large blade open, 6 inches. This is a well finished and fitted knife, guaranteed to give satisfaction. Price... 42c
If by mail, postage extra, 4 cents.

No. 28G6994 Wilbert Favorite Double Ender, with spear and clip point blades. Stag handle, German silver fancy bolsters and shield, brass lined and finished inside and out. Length of handle, 4 inches. Length with clip point blade open, 6⅞ inches. Price....(Postage extra, 5 cents)....62c

No. 28G6997 Wilbert Gladiator Double Ender, has stag handle, German silver bolsters and shield, brass lined and finely finished throughout. Has saber clip and spear point blades. Length with spear blade open, 7¼ inches. Price......................75c
If by mail, postage extra, 5 cents.

Pearl Handle Jack Knives.

No. 28G7007 Wilbert Gentlemen's Pearl Handle Jack Knife. Has pearl handle, German silver bolster, caps and shield, German silver lining, satin finish. The blades are full crocus polished. The knife is in every way finished as finely as the best penknife you ever saw. Length of handle, 3⅝ inches; length with large blade open, 5⅞ inches. Price.......85c
If by mail, postage extra, 5 cents.

No. 28G7017 Wilbert Ranchero Cattle Knife. Has pearl handle, German silver bolsters and shield, German silver lining, satin finish. The blades are full crocus polished. It cannot fail to give satisfaction to those who want a knife of superior cutting qualities, workmanship and beauty. Length of handle, 3⅝ inches; length with large blade open, 6⅝ inches. Price...............................$1.35
If by mail, postage extra, 5 cents.

No. 28G7025 Wilbert Montana Beauty Stockmen's Knife. Has clip, sheep's foot and spaying blades, pearl handle, German silver lining, satin finish; the blades are beautifully crocus polished. In our ordinary grades of knives, knives which must sell at popular prices, we pay very much more attention to quality and workmanship than we do to beauty and finish, but in this particular knife we excel all others in finish as well as in quality. Length of handle, 3⅜ inches; length with large blade open, 6¾ inches.
Price.......(Postage extra, 5 cents).......$1.50

Corn Knife.

No. 28G7028 Wilbert Razor Ground Corn Knife. Is razor ground, razor tempered, and must not be put to any use excepting that for which it is designed. It has stag handle, brass lined; finished in a first class manner inside and out. Length of handle, 3¼ inches; length with blade open, 5⅛ inches. Price....(Postage extra, 3 cents).....29c

Penknives.

No. 28G7031 Wilbert Two-Blade Penknife. Ebony handle, German silver bolsters and shield, brass lined. Highly finished throughout. Length of handle, 3¼ inches; length with large blade open, 5¼ inches Price.....(Postage extra, 3 cents).....39c

No. 28G7033 Wilbert Two-Blade, Stag Handle Penknife. German silver bolsters and shield, brass lined, nicely polished pocket knife. Length of handle, 3 inches; length, with large blade open, 5 inches. Price. 42c
If by mail, postage extra, 3 cents.

No. 28G7037 Wilbert High Grade Two-Blade Penknife, has stag handle, German silver bolsters and shield, brass lined, finely polished throughout. The blades are extra heavy, and are stronger than ordinarily found in a knife of this size. Length of handle, 3¼ inches; length with large blade open, 5⅜ inches. Price.......(Postage extra, 4 cents).........45c

No. 28G7040 Wilbert Physicians' Stag Handle Knife. German silver butt, German silver bolster and brass lining, finely polished and fitted. Length of handle, 3¼ inches; length with large blade open, 5⅝ inches. Price 50c

No. 28G7041 Same knife as above. 3⅝-inch pearl handle. Length with large blade open, 6⅝ inches. Fitted with first quality pearl handles, German silver lined and full polished. Price.........$1.26
If by mail, postage extra, 5 cents.

No. 28G7049 Wilbert Small Congress Knife, has one large blade, two pen blades and one nail blade, stag handle, German silver bolsters and shield, brass lined, finely finished throughout. Length of handle, 3¼ inches; length with large blade open, 5⅜ inches. Price..................69c
If by mail, postage extra, 4 cents.

No. 28G7050 Wilbert Ladies' Penknife. Large blade, just the proper shape for ripping seams, etc. Slender small pen blade, stag handle, brass lining, finished inside. Length of handle, 2⅞ inches; length, with large blade open, 4⅜ inches.
Price ......(Postage extra, 3 cents)........30c

The Wilbert Dakota Cowboys' Knife, 62 Cents.

62c

No. 28G7149 The best cattlemen's knife ever made. Appreciating the need that cattlemen have for a good, strong, serviceable knife, a knife with which they can cut leather, wood or rope, and have the edge stand up, we have had this knife made especially and offer it as the best cattlemen's knife ever made. The steel used in these knives is extra heavy gauge and is the very best English steel suitable for this purpose. The blades are tempered by electricity, insuring uniform temper from heel to point. The grinding, finish and cutler's work in this knife cannot be surpassed. It has three blades spear point blade, sheep's foot, and pen blade; fine stag handle, fitted with German silver shield, heavy polished bolsters, full brass lined and finely finished inside and out. This is an extra strong, heavy knife for the stockman, hunter or trapper, who requires a dependable knife. We guarantee it to give absolute satisfaction or money refunded. It is a knife that would ordinarily sell for $1.25. Length of handle, 3⅝ inches, length, with large blade open, 6½ inches. Price **62c**
If by mail, postage extra, 6 cents.

No. 28G7056 Wilbert Popular School or Ladies' Knife. First quality pearl handle, German silver bolsters and German silver lining, finished inside. Length of handle, 2⅝ inches; length with large blade open, 4⅝ inches. Price **50c**
If by mail, postage extra, 3 cents.

No. 28G7074 Wilbert Senator Three-Blade Pearl Handle Penknife. It has a good, strong, big blade, a pen blade and a nail blade. Fine quality pearl handle, German silver tips, German silver lining, satin finish. The blades are full crocus polished. Length of handle, 3 inches; length with large blade open, 4⅞ inches. Price **$1.00**
If by mail, postage extra, 4 cents.

No. 28G7080 Wilbert Senator Four-Blade Knife. Has pearl handle, German silver tips and shield, German silver lining, satin finish, blades full crocus polished, burnished finish back. Length of handle, 3 inches; length with large blade open, 4⅞ inches. Price **$1.15**
If by mail, postage extra, 4 cents.

Three-Blade Double End Knives.

No. 28G7101 Wilbert The Boss Three-Blade Cattlemen's Knife. This knife has spaying blade 2⅛ inches long, and small blade 2⅝ inches long outside of bolster, with cocobolo handle, German silver bolsters and shield, brass lined, finely finished throughout. Price **85c**
If by mail, postage extra, 6 cents.

No. 28G7109 Wilbert Heavy Duty Gentlemen's Knife. Has clip point, large blade, very heavy and strong, spear point pen blade and sheep's foot tobacco blade, ebony handle, German silver bolsters and shield, brass lined and finished throughout. Length of handle, 3⅜ inches. Length with large blade open, 6⅜ inches. An unusually strong and heavy knife for its size. Price **75c**
If by mail, postage extra, 5 cents.

No. 28G7117 Wilbert Hercules Knife. Ebony handle, German silver bolsters and shield, brass lined, finely finished throughout. The large blade is short and very heavy, being 2¾ inches long from bolster and ⅝-inch wide. Two pen blades. Length of handle, 4 inches. Length with large blade open, 7 inches. Price...(If by mail, postage extra, 6 cents)... **89c**

No. 28G7131 Wilbert Junior Cattle Knife. Has spear, pen and sheep's foot blades. It has stag handle, German silver bolsters and shield, brass lining, finished inside and out. Length of handle, 3⅜ inches; length with large blade open, 5¾ inches. Price.......(If by mail, postage extra, 5 cents) **60c**

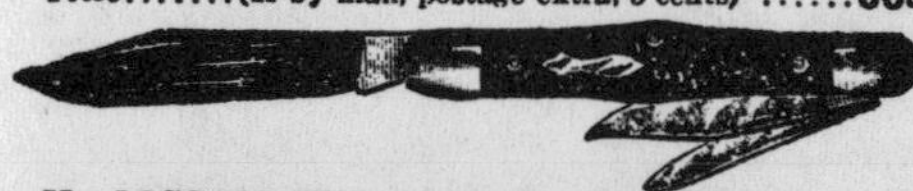

No. 28G7136 Wilbert Quality Three-Blade Double End Knife, stag handle, brass lined, German silver bolsters and shield. One large 2¾-inch clip blade, one small 2-inch clip blade and one pen blade, crocus polished. Blades are made of the best Wardlow steel, every knife guaranteed. Length of knife, 3¾ inches; length with large blade open, 6 inches. Price **64c**
If by mail, postage extra, 5 cents.

No. 28G7140 Wilbert Three-Blade Carpenters' Knife. Stag handle, German silver bolsters and shield, brass lined. Length of handle, 3¾ inches. Length with large blade open, 6¼ inches. Price...(If by mail, postage extra, 5 cents).... **75c**

No. 28G7143 Wilbert Special Offer Cattle Knife. Stag handle, steel lining, iron bolsters, German silver shield. Length of handle, 3⅝ inches. Length with large blade open, 6¼ inches. Has spear point, sheep's foot and pen blades. The cutting qualities of this knife are not excelled by any knife made. It is neatly finished and sold at a price to compete with the cheap imported goods.
Price, per dozen, $5.80; six for $2.93; each.... **50c**
If by mail, postage extra, 5 cents.

No. 28G7146 Wilbert Round Up Cattlemen's Knife. Stag handle, polished steel bolsters, German silver shield, brass lined. Has clip point, large blade, spear point blade and spaying blade. Length of handle, 3¾ inches. Length with large blade open, 6¾ inches. Price **69c**
If by mail, postage extra, 6 cents.

No. 28G7152 Wilbert Western Chief. Has clip point saber blade, very heavy, made of full 10-gauge steel; has stag handle, German silver bolsters and shield, brass lining, finished inside and out. The large blade has a flush lock back, which prevents the blade from closing on the hand. Length of handle, 4 inches; length with large blade open, 6¾ inches. Price..(Postage extra, 6 cents)...... **95c**

No. 28G7155 Wilbert Texas Stock Knife. A pattern of knife which is popular with stock raisers all over the world, has clip, sheep's foot and spaying blades, stag handle, German silver bolsters and shield, brass lined, highly finished inside and out. This is our most popular cattle knife, and is made just as good as we know how to make them. Length of handle, 4 inches; length with clip point blade open, 7¼ inches. Price **75c**
If by mail, postage extra, 5 cents.

Four-Blade Pocket Knives.

No. 28G7158 Wilbert Large Congress Knife, has two large blades and two pen blades, stag handle, German silver bolsters and shield, brass lined, nicely finished throughout. Length of handle, 3⅞ inches; length with large blade open, 6⅛ inches. Price.........(If by mail, postage extra, 5 cents)......... **74c**

No. 28G7161 Wilbert Jumbo Congress Knife, with two large blades and two pen blades. Stag handle, iron bolsters, German silver shield, steel lined, finely finished. Those who prefer a Congress pattern knife and want something strong and heavy will find this a most desirable pattern. Length of handle, 4⅛ inches; length with large blade open, 6¾ inches. Price. **80c**
If by mail, postage extra, 5 cents.

REMEMBER, WHEN YOU HAVE BOUGHT $25.00 WORTH OF GOODS OR MORE FROM US YOU GET YOUR CHOICE OF MANY VALUABLE ARTICLES FREE, AS SHOWN IN OUR FREE PROFIT SHARING BOOK.

Push Button Knives.

These knives are fitted with a push button in the bolster. By pressing this button you release a flat spring which opens the blade and locks it so that it cannot be closed accidentally. One-blade knife has one push button; a two-blade knife has push button at each end. The material used in these knives is the best. The push button arrangement is very simple and the knife cannot get out of order.

61c

No. 28G7181 Push Button Knife. One blade, clip point, stag handle, single bolster, iron lined. Length of handle, 4⅝ inches; length with blade open, 8⅜ inches. Price **61c**
If by mail, postage extra, 6 cents.

No. 28G7182 Push Button Knife. One blade, clip point, stag handle, single bolster, iron lined. Length of handle, 3⅞ inches; length with blade open, 6⅞ inches. Price **55c**
If by mail, postage extra, 5 cents.

No. 28G7184 Push Button Pen Knife. Two blades, stag handle, brass lined. Length of handle, 3⅜ inches; length with large blade open, 5¾ inches. Price **54c**
If by mail, postage extra, 5 cents.

92 Cents. Nine Tools in One. 92 Cents.

No. 28G7186 This knife will cut wire, wood or leather and embodies a pocket knife, leather punch, swedge awl, wire cutter, wire pliers, alligator wrench, hoof hook, screwdriver and screw bit. This knife is no clumsier than the ordinary pocket knife. The pliers and wire cutter are made from drop forge tool steel, the blade is made of the best cutlers' steel, full gauge, tempered and will stand hard usage. All tools are practical and serviceable; one tool does not interfere with the free use of the other. This knife has a stag handle, German silver bolsters and shield and steel lined. Length of handle, 4⅛ inches.
Price........(Postage extra, 6 cents.)........ **92c**

No. 28G7199 Chris. Wolf's Unpolished Hand Made Single Blade Jack Knife. The blade of this knife is hand hammered from a bar of the best crucible steel, correctly tempered and carefully ground, with no attempt to add to its appearance by grinding or polishing. The marks of the hammer show plainly. The handle is plain beechwood, not stained or varnished. The linings are heavy steel. This is the ugliest looking knife you ever saw and will not sell on its appearance. Some people value a knife for its cutting qualities, and to such we offer the Chris. Wolf's knife **as the best cutting knife** they ever saw. It is tempered to cut and hold its edge. Warranted.
Price, per dozen, **$5.40**; six for **$2.75**; each..... **47c**
If by mail, postage extra, each, 6 cents.

IMPORTED ENGLISH KNIVES.

Geo. Wostenholm & Sons' IXL Pocket Knives.

We show some of the most desirable patterns of George Wostenholm & Sons' Celebrated IXL Pocket Knives, which are favorably known all over the world

No. 28G7236 George Wostenholm & Sons' IXL Penknife with extra long, 3-inch spear point blade and small pen blade, full crocus polished. German silver bolsters and shield, brass lined, genuine stag handle. This knife is made of the best Sheffield steel and guaranteed to give satisfaction. Price.. **67c**
If by mail, postage extra, 4 cents.

No. 28G7240 George Wostenholm & Sons' IXL Pocket Knife; genuine stag handle, German silver bolsters and shield, brass lined. Length of handle, 3⅝ inches. Price...(If by mail, postage extra, 4 cents).. **55c**

No. 28G7243 George Wostenholm & Sons' IXL Two-Blade Jack Knife, German silver bolsters and shield, brass lined, full crocus polished. Length of blade, 3¼ inches; length with large blade open, 6 inches. Price **72c**
If by mail, postage extra, 4 cents.

No. 28G7244 George Wostenholm & Sons' IXL Pocket Knife, stag handle, German silver bolsters and shield, brass lined. Length of handle, 3¾ inches. Price **73c**
If by mail, postage extra, 4 cents.

No. 28G7246 George Wostenholm & Sons' IXL Pocket Knife, cocobolo handle, German silver bolsters and shield, brass lined, finely etched. Length of handle, 3⅞ inches. Price.. **68c**
If by mail, postage extra, 5 cents.

A Personal Message

From the President of Sears, Roebuck and Co.

The World's Largest Store is at your service!

Without moving from your own easy chair, you can draw on an almost endless supply of the best of the world's goods. For our buyers go everywhere good merchandise can be bought at prices that insure the biggest savings.

As president of Sears, Roebuck and Co., it is a privilege for me to serve you and the nine million families who buy from us. A privilege, because I feel that we render a genuine service to the country in the form of lower prices; because it was Sears, Roebuck and Co. that first guaranteed merchandise, and that today sells the quality of merchandise that can be honestly guaranteed; because we ship all orders within twenty-four hours.

We have become the World's Largest Store because our customers know that our policy is fair treatment. Through all the years we have been serving this army of thrifty buyers we have taken pride in the fact that we have kept their good will and brought additional members into this great family.

This catalog is the World's Largest Store at its best. It proves the leadership of Sears, Roebuck and Co. It offers 35,000 opportunities to save money. And it is a big factor in the lives of one-fourth of all the families in the United States.

C. M. Kittle

President.

THIS BOOK

WILL BE SENT TO ANY ADDRESS FREE BY MAIL POSTPAID ON APPLICATION

WRITE A LETTER
R A POSTAL CARD
AND SAY
END ME YOUR
IG CATALOGUE
d it will be sent to you im-
mediately free by mail, postpaid.

WRITE A LETTER
OR A POSTAL CARD
AND SAY
SEND ME YOUR
BIG CATALOGUE
and it will be sent to you immediately free by mail, postpaid.

SIMPLE RULES FOR ORDERING.

USE OUR ORDER BLANK IF YOU HAVE ONE. If you haven't one, use any plain paper.

TELL US IN YOUR OWN WAY WHAT YOU WANT, always giving the CATALOGUE NUMBER of each article, d be sure to state size and color where required. Enclose in the letter the amount of money, either a postoffice money order, which you get at the postoffice, an express money order, which you get at the express office, or a draft, which you get at any bank; or put the money in the letter, take it to the postoffice and tell the postmaster you want it registered.

IF YOU LIVE ON A RURAL MAIL ROUTE, just give the letter and the money to the mail carrier and he will get the money order at the postoffice and mail it in the letter for you.

DON'T BE AFRAID YOU WILL MAKE A MISTAKE. We receive hundreds of orders every day from young and old who never before sent away for goods. We are accustomed to handling all kinds of orders.

TELL US WHAT YOU WANT IN YOUR OWN WAY, written in any language, no matter whether good or poor writing, and the goods will be promptly sent to you.

WE HAVE TRANSLATORS TO READ AND WRITE ALL LANGUAGES.

DON'T BE AFRAID OF THE FREIGHT OR EXPRESS CHARGES. You must pay them when you get the goods at the station, but they never amount to much compared with what we save you in cost.

IF YOU FIND IT NECESSARY TO HAVE SOME SPECIAL INFORMATION you can undoubtedly obtain it by ferring to the matter contained within the first twelve pages of this catalogue.

ENKLA REGLER ATT IAKTTAGA VID BESTÄLLNING.

Begagna vår beställningsblankett, om ni har en sådan. Om icke, begagna vanligt rent papper.

Säg oss på edert eget sätt hvad ni önskar, alltid uppgifde katalognumret på hvarje sak. Inneslut beloppet i vet antingen i postoffice money order, hvilken köpes å stkontoret; express money order, hvilken köpes å expressntoret, eller en vexel, hvilken kan köpas å hvilken bank n helst, eller också inneslut kontanta penningar i brefvet, g det till postkontoret och säg postmästaren att ni önskar a det registrerat.

Var icke rädd för att ni gör ett misstag. Vi erhålla huntals beställningar dagligen från unga och gamla hvilka rig förr sändt efter varor. Vi äro vana vid att expediera a slags beställningar.

Säg oss på edert eget sätt hvad ni önskar. Skrif på hvilet språk som helst, bra eller dålig stafning, bra eller dålig andstil, och varorna skola blifva eder prompt tillsända.

Vi ha öfversättare som läsa och skrifva alla språk.

Det är icke nödvändigt för eder att genomläsa de första o sidorna i denna katalog, såvida ni icke önskar någon speell upplysning. Dessa tio sidor innehålla detaljerad uppsning, så att de som i alla delar önska göra sig förtrogna d sättet att beställa och sända varor, fraktkostnader o. s. v., s. v., icke behöfva skrifva till oss, utan helt enkelt kunna a upp dessa sidor och finna den upplysning de önska.

Einfache Regeln zum Bestellen.

Gebraucht unsere Bestellungszettel wenn Sie welche haben, wenn nicht nehmen Sie gewöhnliches Papier.

Im Bestellen erwähnen Sie die Catalog Numero an allen Sachen. Die Bestellung soll das Geld enthalten, entweder eine „Postoffice Money Order," (welche man gewöhnlich an der Post bekommen kann), eine "Expreß Money Order," ein Bank Certificate, das man an jeder Bank bekommen kann, oder legen Sie das Geld in den Brief mit der Bestellung, in welchem Falle Sie den Brief Eingeschrieben schicken sollten. Der Brief wird in der Post Eingeschrieben (Registered.)

Wir erhalten jeden Tag eine große Anzahl von Bestellungen von allen Leuten (Jung und Alt).

Sie brauchen nicht furchtsam zu sein Sachen zu bestellen, wir werden Ihr Bestellung schon verstehen.

Schreiben Sie uns in Ihrer eigener Weise, und in Ihrer eigener Sprache, was Sie wollen, einerlei ob gut oder schlecht geschrieben, und die Waare wird Ihnen sofort zugeschickt.

Wir haben Leute die alle Sprachen schreiben und übersetzen.

Die ersten zehn Seiten in diesem Catalog beziehen sich hauptsächlich an die Frachtbetrage der verschiedenen Waare und hat nur Wichtigkeit für Sie im Falle Sie in diesen Einzelheiten interessiert sind.

O NOT FAIL TO GIVE SIZE, COLOR, WEIGHT, ETC., IF RE[illegible]EN WRITING YOUR ORDER.

ABOUT OUR RELIABILITY.

YOU ARE PERFECTLY SAFE IN SENDING US YOUR ORDERS AND YOUR MONEY. We are one of the largest commercial institutions in the world, and we occupy by far the largest mercantile plant in the world. We own this entire plant, free of indebtedness of any kind, comprising forty acres of ground, in one of the best districts in Chicago; our ground and buildings alone are valued at more than Six Million Dollars. We have nearly nine thousand employes, and our customers now number nearly five million. If you have any doubt, you are at liberty to refer to any bank, business house or resident of Chicago, and we especially refer to our millions of satisfied customers. Ask your neighbor about **Sears, Roebuck & Co.** We have customers in every neighborhood in the United States, and we gladly refer you to any customer.

BE SURE TO READ THE BANK LETTER OF THE FIRST NATIONAL BANK OF CHICAGO, capital and surplus $13,000,000.00, signed by its cashier, F. O. Wetmore; also the Corn Exchange National Bank letter, capital and surplus $6,000,000.00, signed by Frank W. Smith, its cashier; see page 20. Consider our standing everywhere and be convinced it is perfectly safe to send your money to us, we agreeing to return it and pay all transportation charges if the goods do not please you.

HOW WE MAKE EVERY TRANSACTION WITH US STRICTLY CONFIDENTIAL.

Why our name and address do not appear on any box, package, wrapper, tag, envelope or article of merchandise.

As many people, especially merchants, business houses, townspeople and others, do not care to have others know where or from whom they buy their goods, as many people object to having the name of the shipper spread across every box or package, so that when it is unloaded at the station or express office everyone can see what they are getting and where they buy it, to protect all those who care for this protection and make it possible for you to order your goods from us with no fear of anyone learning at the railroad station, express office or elsewhere what you bought or where you bought it, our name and address will not appear on any box, package, tag, envelope or article of merchandise.

For example: If you are a merchant and wish to buy goods to sell again, your customers will be unable to learn from any marks inside or outside where you bought the goods or what you paid for them.

If you are a professional man, or even in the employ of some merchant, who for personal reasons might object to your sending to us for goods, you need have no fear, our name will not appear on any goods or packages you get.

While we would be glad to have our name appear on every article of merchandise and on every box and package, as a valuable means of advertising, we have learned that thousands of our customers need the protection that the omitting of our name affords. This applies especially to townspeople.

NO ORDER WILL BE ACCEPTED FOR LESS THAN 50 CENTS.

PLEASE DO NOT SEND US ANY ORDER AMOUNTING TO LESS THAN 50 CENTS. If you want some article, the price of which is less than 50 cents, please include one or more other needed articles and make your order amount to 50 cents or more.

AS A MATTER OF ECONOMY, BOTH TO OUR CUSTOMERS AND OURSELVES, we do not fill orders for less than 50 cents. The postage or express charges especially make small orders under 50 cents unprofitable to the purchaser, or at least much more expensive than the orders amounting to 50 cents or more.

WE MAKE THIS EXCEPTION: In the case of needed repairs, attachments and supplies, such as needles for our sewing machines, parts of guns, etc., which can be secured only from us, we will fill the order no matter how small it may be.

TO MAKE ORDERING BY MAIL VERY PROFITABLE TO OUR CUSTOMERS we especially urge that you make your order as large as possible. Orders of from $2.00 to $5.00 or more are always very much more profitable to the purchaser than smaller orders, for the express or freight charges are in this way very greatly reduced. It always pays, even if you have to get some friend or neighbor to join with you, to make up an order of from $2.00 to $5.00 or more, and include enough heavy goods to make a profitable freight shipment of fifty to one hundred pounds. In this way you reduce the transportation charges on each item to next to nothing. You then pay the exact same freight charges that your storekeeper must pay on the goods he sells.

ON THE BASIS OF FAR GREATER VALUE FOR YOUR MONEY THAN YOU CAN POSSIBLY GET ELSEWHERE, lower prices than any other house does or can name, the best possible service, every item ordered guaranteed to reach you in perfect condition and give perfect satisfaction or your money to be immediately refunded to you; on our binding guarantee to please you in every way on every dollar sent us, wholly in your own interest we ask you to kindly conform to these terms.

OUR COMPLIMENTS TO THE RETAIL MERCHANT.

IT IS NOT OUR DESIRE TO ANTAGONIZE THE RETAIL MERCHANT (the storekeeper of the country). This is a big, growing country, and there is ample room for us all. Our prices are alike to all. Whether to the largest or the smallest merchant, farmer, mechanic or laborer, our price is exactly the same. Our goods are for sale at the prices plainly printed in this book, and occupation or position restricts no one from buying goods from us at our printed prices.

However, we number thousands of the best merchants of the United States among our valued customers. The prejudice which for a time existed because we would not sell to the dealer and refuse to sell to his customers, is dying out; for the shrewd, careful buying, up to date merchant of today has broader business views. He buys his goods where he can get the best value for his money, and on the basis of more value for the money than is furnished by any other house we especially invite all classes of merchants to carefully compare our prices as printed in this book with the prices you have been in the habit of paying.

As explained on this page, we ship all our goods in plain boxes or packages, and our name appears on no package or article of merchandise. You can buy your goods from us at our selling prices, which are much lower than you can buy elsewhere, you can fix your profit to suit yourself and your customers will not know where you bought the goods or what you paid for them.

We want to correct the impression that may be in the minds of some merchants, that we sell exclusively to the consumer, the party who buys the goods to use. If you have this impression we are anxious to correct it. A goodly percentage of the goods we ship in all lines go direct to merchants, business houses who buy to sell again, and in some lines, especially materials and supplies, a large percentage of our goods go to manufacturers, which they use in the manufacture of their wares, which in turn they sell to dealers. Among our valued customers are the U. S. Government, state and city institutions, railroads and other large corporations, and also jobbers, brokers, retailers and consumers in all parts of the country.

WE ESPECIALLY SOLICIT THE TRADE OF THE SUCCESSFUL, SHREWD BUYING MERCHANT, who wishes to buy his wares where he can get the highest standard of quality at lower prices than he can get elsewhere.

TO THE SHREWD MERCHANT buying for cash to sell again at a profit, to the one who buys where he can get the most for his money.

TO THE PURCHASING AGENT OF RAILROAD COMPANIES and other large corporations, to contractors and builders and to manufacturers of all classes of goods, to all of these who are now dealing with us, we want to thank you for your liberal patronage in the past and again invite you to a careful comparison of our prices in this, our latest, large merchandise catalogue, with the very lowest prices the same goods can be had elsewhere, and on the basis of quality and price we earnestly solicit your future business.

To all this class who have not as yet dealt with us we earnestly solicit a careful study of our catalogue prices, which will point in many directions to a great saving for you.

TO RAILROAD PURCHASING AGENTS we especially direct attention to our incomparably low prices on safes and stoves for station use, also to furniture, hardware, etc., for other uses. We are doing a large business with a number of the large express and railroad companies; therefore, to the purchasing agents of these corporations especially do we direct your attention to the prices quoted in this catalogue and our ability to save you money on the goods we offer.

TO CONTRACTORS, BUILDERS, MANUFACTURERS, ETC., we can save you money on goods you consume and goods that go into your manufactured wares. If you are a builder we can save you money on a large part of all your building material. If you are a manufacturer using any kind of finished parts of iron, wood, leather or cloth, we can save you money on many items that go into your manufactured articles. If you are a contractor, mill operator or the like, you are consuming machinery, tools and supplies of all kinds, and we can save you money on these, and this in competition with any market in the world.

MANY MANUFACTURERS WORKING IN IRON buy all their files, emery wheels and various similar supplies, as well as tools and machinery from us.

MANY MANUFACTURERS WORKING IN WOOD buy their saws and other tools and supplies from us.

MANY MANUFACTURERS WORKING IN LEATHER, such as harness, etc., buy their buckles, trimmings and leather from us.

MANY MANUFACTURERS OF BUGGIES, HARNESS, ETC., buy their wheels, woodwork, leather, cloth, iron, trimmings, etc., from us.

MANY MANUFACTURERS OF FURNITURE buy their hardware, such as locks, hinges, knobs, casters, trimmings, etc., from us.

MANY MANUFACTURERS OF AGRICULTURAL IMPLEMENTS, ETC., buy their paint, various hardware and tools from us.

CONTRACTORS AND BUILDERS OF HOUSES buy their builders' hardware, such as doors, locks, nails, paint, paper, roofing, doors, sash, blinds, millwork, etc., from us.

LUMBERMEN, OPERATORS OF SAW MILLS, LOGGERS, ETC., in all sections of the country, north, south, east and west, buy their general supplies from us, such as saws, files, mechanical tools and supplies, including axes, chains, hooks and all kinds of provisions and supplies.

ALMOST EVERY DEALER IN MERCHANDISE, general store or special store in the United States, sells goods purchased from us, either directly or indirectly, for in the goods you buy from others to sell again, among some of them surely will be found goods that were bought from us, supplies of some kind that entered into the manufacture of the goods you bought. As we are operators, owners or controllers of a great many factories manufacturing finished materials in parts, goods made of iron, wood, leather, cloth, etc., it would be hardly possible for any dealer in hardware, groceries, dry goods, clothing, agricultural implements or other goods to buy the finished goods to sell, from any wholesale dealer anywhere without there would enter into some of the goods which he offers for sale, parts that have come either direct from our store or from one of the many factories in which we are interested.

WE OWN OR CONTROL THE OUTPUT OF FACTORIES MAKING VARIOUS KINDS OF HARDWARE AND HARDWARE SUPPLIES, carriage and wagon material; blacksmiths' materials, materials that enter into clothing, harness, furniture, etc. We also own or control many factories making shoes, stoves, cream separators, organs, musical instruments, plumbing goods of all kinds, paint, wall paper, guns, revolvers, furniture, safes, saws, mechanics' tools, photographic goods, washing machines, household supplies, cameras, clothing, ladies' wearing apparel, electrical goods, tents, canvas goods, gun implements, surgical implements, typewriters, books, jewelry, stereoscopic goods, hardware, special millwork, radiators, agricultural implements, etc. We are either sole owners or controllers of a vast number of these factories. From some we sell the entire output; others, we allow the factory, under our direction, to sell to either wholesale or retail dealers, usually to wholesale dealers, and the wholesale dealers in turn sell to the retail dealer, and the retail dealer to his local trade. So if you could trace the original source of supply of every article in your store or on your shelves, you could trace a liberal percentage of all the goods you are now selling either directly to our store or indirectly to one of our many factories.

Therefore we urge you, if you are a live, up to date merchant, that you buy from first hands.

IF YOU ARE A MERCHANT who buys to sell again you will find thousands of articles in this catalogue on which we can save you money. Remember, every transaction with us is treated in the strictest of confidence. No article you buy from us will bear our name; no box, package or shipment of any kind will bear our name. Our name will not appear on any tag, envelope or any piece of paper that is exposed that will go to you from us. If you buy goods from us no one will know from whom you buy your goods or what you pay for them. You can send your order to us for anything in this catalogue, the goods will go to you with the understanding that they will please you, you will find them lower in price and better in quality than you can buy elsewhere, and you are always at liberty to return any goods you get from us if you are not perfectly satisfied and always at our expense, and we will immediately return your money together with any express or freight charges paid by you.

OUR LIBERAL TERMS OF SHIPMENT.

WE HAVE NO DISCOUNTS, we sell for cash only, and the prices quoted in catalogue are absolutely net, from which there is no discount whatever. prices are alike to one and all, regardless of the amount of the order; the same to merchant, the manufacturer, contractor or corporation as to the farmer, mechanic or laborer. We especially recommend that you send cash in full with your order. Send us either a postoffice money order, express money order, bank draft, your own check or send the money in a registered letter.

If you are a farmer and live on a R. F. D. Route, make up your order, go to the R. F. D. carrier, give him the money you wish to send to us and he will give you a receipt for the money and either issue to you or get for you a postoffice money order for the amount you wish to send.

If you reside in a town, then either go to the postoffice and buy a postoffice money order, to the express office and buy an express money order, or to the bank and buy a draft, or enclose your own check.

WE ESPECIALLY REQUEST THAT YOU SEND THE FULL AMOUNT OF CASH WITH YOUR ORDER, for this is always much more satisfactory than to send part of the money with your order, the balance to be paid C. O. D., and understand, when you send us your order and money we accept your money and your order and ship the goods to you with the understanding and agreement that if they are not perfectly satisfactory in every way, you are at liberty to return any part or all of them to us, at our expense, and we will immediately return your money, together with any freight or express charges paid by you.

YOU CAN FURNISH YOUR HOME FREE

EVERY TIME YOU ORDER FROM US we send you a Profit Sharing Certificate, and in exchange for these Profit Sharing Certificates you can secure **FREE** a wonderful selection of valuable and useful parlor, dining room, bedroom, kitchen and other furniture, rugs, draperies, stoves, organs, pianos and hundreds of other valuable articles **ABSOLUTELY FREE.** Our big **FREE** Profit Sharing Catalogue is being constantly revised and improved. When your Profit Sharing Certificates amount to **$25.00** or more write for the **FREE** Profit Sharing Book. On a postal card, or in a letter to us, simply say, "Send me your latest Profit Sharing Catalogue" and the big **FREE** Profit Sharing Book will go to you by return mail postpaid. In this way you are sure of getting our **LATEST REVISED BOOK WITH ALL THE NEW ARTICLES ADDED.**

SEND YOUR PROFIT SHARING CERTIFICATES TO US AND LET US SEND YOU THIS TOP BUGGY FREE AS EXPLAINED IN OUR FREE PROFIT SHARING BOOK

THIS IS A HIGH GRADE DRESSER AND YOU CAN HAVE IT FREE OF CHARGE IN EXCHANGE FOR PROFIT SHARING CERTIFICATES

YOUR PROFIT SHARING CERTIFICATES BRING YOU THIS HANDSOME IRON BED OR YOUR CHOICE OF MANY OTHERS

IN OUR PROFIT SHARING CATALOGUE WE SHOW A LARGE VARIETY OF LADIES AND GENTS WATCHES FREE IN EXCHANGE FOR PROFIT SHARING CERTIFICATES

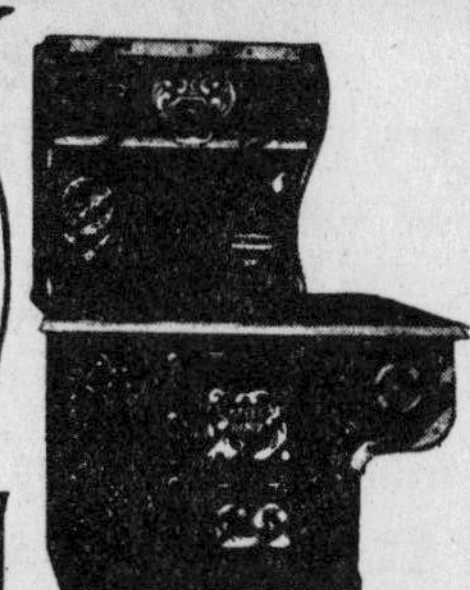

YOUR PROFIT SHARING CERTIFICATES WILL QUICKLY SECURE FOR YOU THIS BIG STEEL RANGE ABSOLUTELY FREE

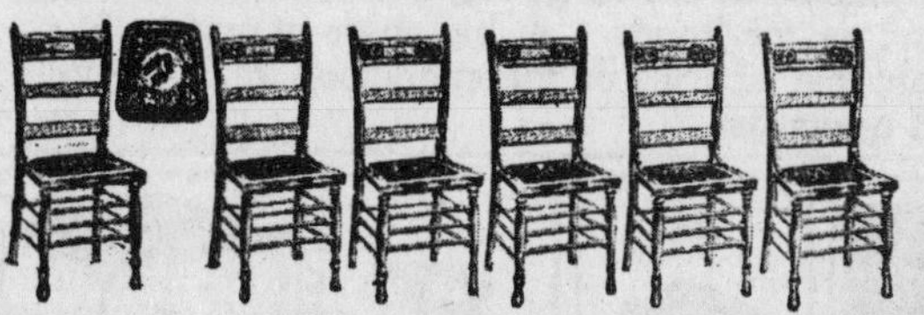

THIS MAGNIFICENT SET OF DINING ROOM CHAIRS IS ONE OF THE MANY ARTICLES OF FURNITURE WHICH WE GIVE FREE FOR YOUR PROFIT SHARING CERTIFICATES

THIS ENTERTAINMENT OUTFIT CONSISTING OF GRAPHOPHONE AND 10 RECORDS FREE FOR YOUR PROFIT SHARING CERTIFICATES

FREE FOR PROFIT SHARING CERTIFICATES THIS 26 PIECE SHELL PATTERN SILVERWARE SET IN NEATLY LINED CASE OUR PROFIT SHARING BOOK SHOWS A FULL LINE OF TABLE SILVERWARE

THESE ORGANS GO TO OUR CUSTOMERS EVERY DAY FREE IN EXCHANGE FOR PROFIT SHARING CERTIFICATES

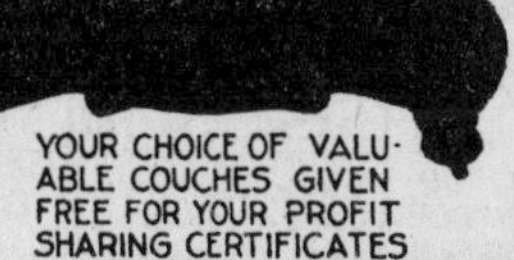

YOUR CHOICE OF VALUABLE COUCHES GIVEN FREE FOR YOUR PROFIT SHARING CERTIFICATES

THIS UPRIGHT PIANO IS YOURS ABSOLUTELY FREE IN EXCHANGE FOR PROFIT SHARING CERTIFICATES

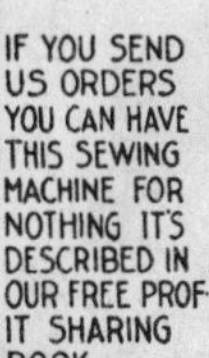

IF YOU SEND US ORDERS YOU CAN HAVE THIS SEWING MACHINE FOR NOTHING IT'S DESCRIBED IN OUR FREE PROFIT SHARING BOOK

YOU CAN HAVE THIS BEDROOM SUITE OR YOUR CHOICE OF MANY OTHER ARTICLES OF FURNITURE FREE FOR YOUR PROFIT SHARING CERTIFICATES

MASSIVE HANDSOMELY CARVED VELOUR UPHOLSTERED MORRIS CHAIR FREE FOR YOUR PROFIT SHARING CERTIFICATES

THIS MASSIVE DINING ROOM TABLE FREE FOR PROFIT SHARING CERTIFICATES. OUR LATEST PROFIT SHARING CATALOGUE SHOWS A NUMBER OF HANDSOME TABLES WHICH ARE SURE TO PLEASE YOU

WE GIVE YOU FREE FOR YOUR PROFIT SHARING CERTIFICATES YOUR CHOICE OF A NUMBER OF HANDSOME GO-CARTS AND BABY BUGGIES

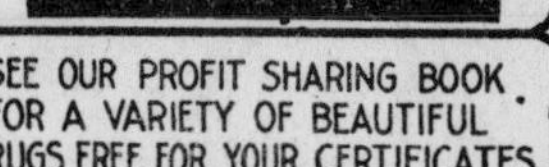

SEE OUR PROFIT SHARING BOOK FOR A VARIETY OF BEAUTIFUL RUGS FREE FOR YOUR CERTIFICATES

ANY ONE OF THESE ARTICLES FREE FOR ONLY $25 IN PROFIT SHARING CERTIFICATES

OUR REVISED, MORE LIBERAL THAN EVER, $25.00 PROFIT SHARING PLAN.

EVERY TIME YOU SEND US AN ORDER OF $1.00 OR MORE

we will send you a Customers' Profit Sharing Certificate for the full amount of money you send us. Keep these Profit Sharing Certificates you get from us until they amount to $25.00 or more and then write for our big free Profit Sharing Book, showing the hundreds of valuable, useful and handsome articles we give to every customer free in exchange for $25.00 or more in Profit Sharing Certificates. Many articles that formerly were given for $100.00 in certificates are now given for only $25.00. Many that more recently were given for from $50.00 to $100.00 in certificates are now given for only $25.00 in certificates.

ALL OUTSTANDING PROFIT SHARING CERTIFICATES ARE GOOD.

If you already hold Profit Sharing Certificates from us, they are good to apply on any article shown in our new free Profit Sharing Book in accordance with our latest plan. Every customer holding certificates is entitled to exchange them according to the latest, best and most liberal terms we have ever made, on our new $25.00 basis, as explained throughout this catalogue, and more fully explained in our new, big, FREE Profit Sharing Book. YOU GET BACK a large part of all the money you send us for goods. A big share of our profit on every purchase you make goes back to you in the shape of valuable articles of merchandise which we give free for your Profit Sharing Certificates amounting to $25.00 and upwards.